THIS VOLUME IS DEDICATED TO
THE MEMORY OF
SPENCER TRACY
AND TO
KATHARINE HEPBURN

THE MOTION PICTURE GUIDE

C - D

1927 - 1983

Jay Robert Nash
Stanley Ralph Ross

CINEBOOKS, INC.

Chicago, 1985

Publishers of THE COMPLETE FILM RESOURCE CENTER

Publishers: Jay Robert Nash, Stanley Ralph Ross; **Editor-in-Chief:** Jay Robert Nash; **Executive Editor:** Stanley Ralph Ross; **Associate Publisher and Director of Development:** Kenneth H. Petchenik; **Senior Editor-in-Charge:** Jim McCormick; **Senior Editors:** David Tardy, Robert B. Connelly; **Production Editor:** William Leahy; **Associate Editors:** Oksana Lydia Dominguez, Jeffrey H. Wallenfeldt, Edie McCormick, Michaela Tuohy, Jeannette Hori, Tom Legge; **Contributing Editors:** James J. Mulay (Chief Contributing Editor), Daniel Curran, Michael Theobald, Arnie Bernstein, Phil Pantone, Brian Brock; **Assistant Editors:** Marla Dorfman, Kim O. Morgan, Susan Doll, Marla Antelis, Debra Schwieder, Susan Fisher, Donna Roth, Marla Kruglik, Kristina Marcy, Sarah von Fremd, Wendy Anderson; **Art Production and Book Design:** Cathy Anetsberger; **Research Staff:** Shelby Payne (Associate Editor and Chief Researcher), William C. Clogston, Tobi Elliott, Carol Pappas, Rosalyn Mathis, Millicent Mathis, Andrea Nash; **Business/Legal:** Judy Anetsberger.

Associate Publishers: Howard Grafman, Lynn Christian, James and Monica Vrettos, Antoinette Mailliard, Brent H. Nettle, Michael Callie, Constance Shea, Barbara Browne Cramer, Alan Watts, Dr. Sir James R. Marks and Shirley R. Marks.

Editorial and Sales Offices: CINEBOOKS, 6135 N. Sheridan Road, Chicago, Illinois 60660.

Library of Congress Catalog Card Number: 85-071145
ISBN: 0-933997-00-0 THE MOTION PICTURE GUIDE (10 Vols.)
0-933997-02-7 THE MOTION PICTURE GUIDE, Vol. II (C–D)

Printed in the United States
First Edition
This volume contains 3,333 entries.

2 3 4 5 6 7 8 9 10

HOW TO USE INFORMATION IN THIS GUIDE

ALPHABETICAL ORDER

All entries have been arranged alphabetically throughout this and all subsequent volumes. In establishing alphabetical order, all articles (A, An, The) appear after the main title (AFFAIR TO REMEMBER, AN). In the case of foreign films the article precedes the main title (LES MISERABLES appears in the letter L) which makes, we feel, for easier access and uniformity. Contractions are grouped together and these will be followed by non-apostrophized words of the same letters. B.F.'s DAUGHTER is at the beginning of the letter B, not under BF.

TITLES

It is important to know what title you are seeking; use the *complete* title of the film. The film ADVENTURES OF ROBIN HOOD, THE, cannot be found under merely ROBIN HOOD. Many films are known under different titles and we have taken great pains to cross-reference these titles. (AKA, also known as) as well as alternate titles used in Great Britain (GB). In addition to the cross-reference title only entries, AKAs and alternate titles in Great Britain can be found in the title line for each entry. An alphabetically arranged comprehensive list of title changes appears in the Index volume (Vol. X).

RATINGS

We have rated each and every film at critical levels that include acting, directing, script, and technical achievement (or the sad lack of it). We have a *five-star* rating, unlike all other rating systems, to signify a film superbly made on every level, in short, a masterpiece. At the lowest end of the scale is *zero* and we mean it. The ratings are as follows: *zero* (not worth a glance), ˚ (poor), ˚˚ (fair), ˚˚˚ (good), ˚˚˚˚ (excellent), ˚˚˚˚˚ (masterpiece, and these are few and far between). Half-marks mean almost there but not quite.

YEAR OF RELEASE

We have used in all applicable instances the year of United States release. This sometimes means that a film released abroad may have a different date elsewhere than in these volumes but this is generally the date released in foreign countries, not in the U.S.

FOREIGN COUNTRY PRODUCTION

When possible, we have listed abbreviated names of the foreign countries originating the production of a film. This information will be found within the parenthesis containing the year of release. If no country is listed in this space, it is a U.S. production.

RUNNING TIME

A hotly debated category, we have opted to list the running time a film ran at the time of its initial U.S. release but we will usually mention in the text if the film was drastically cut and give the reasons why. We have attempted to be as accurate as possible by consulting the most reliable sources.

PRODUCING AND DISTRIBUTING COMPANIES

The producing and/or distributing company of every film is listed in abbreviated entries next to the running time in the title line (see abbreviations; for all those firms not abbreviated, the entire firm's name will be present).

COLOR OR BLACK-AND-WHITE

The use of color or black-and-white availability appears as c or bw following the producing/releasing company entry.

CASTS

Whenever possible, we give *the complete cast and the roles played* for each film and this is the case in 95% of all entries, the only encyclopedia to ever offer such comprehensive information in covering the entire field. The names of actors and actresses are in Roman lettering, the names of the roles each played in Italic inside parentheses.

SYNOPSIS

The in-depth synopsis for each entry (when such applies) offers the plot of each film, critical evaluation, anecdotal information on the production and its personnel, awards won when applicable and additional information dealing with the production's impact upon the public, its success or failure at the box office, its social significance, if any. Acting methods, technical innovations, script originality are detailed. We also cite other productions involving an entry's personnel for critical comparisons and to establish the style or genre of expertise of directors, writers, actors and technical people.

REMAKES AND SEQUELS

Information regarding films that have sequels, sequels themselves or direct remakes of films can be found at the very end of each synopsis.

DUBBING AND SUBTITLES

We will generally point out in the synopsis when a foreign film is dubbed in English, mostly when the dubbing is poor. When voices are dubbed, particularly when singers render vocals on songs mimed by stars, we generally point out these facts either in the cast/role listing or inside the synopsis. If a film is in a foreign language and subtitled, we signify the fact in a parenthetical statement at the end of each entry (In Italian, English subtitles).

CREDITS

The credits for the creative and technical personnel of a film are extensive and they include: p (producer, often executive producer); d (director); w (screenwriter, followed by adaptation, if any, and creator of original story, if any, and other sources such as authors for plays, articles, short stories, novels and non-fiction books); ph (cinematographer, followed by camera system and color process when applicable, i.e., Panavision, Technicolor); m (composer of musical score); ed (film editor); md (music director); art d (art director); set d (set decoration); cos (costumes); spec eff (special effects); ch (choreography); m/l (music and lyrics); stunts, makeup, and other credits when merited. When someone receives two or more credits in a single film the credits may be combined (p&d, John Ford) or the last name repeated in subsequent credits shared with another (d, John Ford; w. Ford, Dudley Nichols).

GENRES/SUBJECT

Each film is categorized for easy identification as to genre and/or subject and themes at the left-hand bottom of each entry. (Western, Prison Drama, Spy Drama, Romance, Musical, Comedy, War, Horror, Science-Fiction, Adventure, Biography, Historical Drama, Children's Film, Animated Feature, etc.) More specific subject and theme breakdowns will be found in the Index (Vol. X).

PR AND MPAA RATINGS

The Parental Recommendation provides parents having no knowledge of the style and content of each film with a guide; if a film has excessive violence, sex, strong language, it is so indicated. Otherwise, films specifically designed for young children are also indicated. The Parental Recommendation (**PR**) is to be found at the right-hand bottom of each entry, followed, when applicable, by the **MPAA** rating. The PR ratings are as follows: **AAA** (must for children); **AA** (good for children); **A** (acceptable for children); **C** (cautionary, some objectionable scenes); **O** (completely objectionable for children).

KEY TO ABBREVIATIONS

Foreign Countries:

Arg.	Argentina
Aus.	Australia
Aust.	Austria
Bel.	Belgium
Braz.	Brazil
Brit.	Great Britain (GB when used for alternate title)
Can.	Canada
Chi.	China
Czech.	Czechoslovakia
Den.	Denmark
E. Ger.	East Germany
Fin.	Finland
Fr.	France
Ger.	Germany (includes W. Germany)
Gr.	Greece
Hung.	Hungary
Ital.	Italy
Jap.	Japan
Mex.	Mexico
Neth.	Netherlands
Phil.	Philippines
Pol.	Poland
Rum.	Rumania
S.K.	South Korea
Span.	Spain
Swed.	Sweden

Key to Abbreviations (continued)

Switz.	Switzerland
Thai.	Thailand
USSR	Union of Soviet Socialist Republics
Yugo.	Yugoslavia

Production Companies, Studios and Distributors (U.S. and British)

AA	ALLIED ARTISTS
ABF	Associated British Films
AE	Avco Embassy
AEX	Associated Exhibitors
AH	Anglo-Hollandia
AIP	American International Pictures
AM	American
ANCH	Anchor Film Distributors
ANE	American National Enterprises
AP	Associated Producers
AP&D	Associated Producers & Distributors
ARC	Associated Releasing Corp.
Argosy	Argosy Productions
Arrow	Arrow Films
ART	Artcraft
Astra	Astra Films
AY	Aywon
BA	British Actors
B&C	British and Colonial Kinematograph Co.
BAN	Banner Films
BI	British Instructional
BIFD	B.I.F.D. Films
BIP	British International Pictures
BJP	Buck Jones Productions
BL	British Lion
Blackpool	Blackpool Productions
BLUE	Bluebird
BN	British National
BNF	British and Foreign Film
Boulting	Boulting Brothers (Brit.)
BP	British Photoplay Production
BPP	B.P. Productions
BRIT	Britannia Films
BRO	Broadwest
Bryanston	Bryantston Films (Brit.)
BS	Blue Streak
BUS	Bushey (Brit.)
BUT	Butchers Film Service
BV	Buena Vista (Walt Disney)
CAP	Capital Films
CC	Christie Comedy
CD	Continental Distributing
CHAD	Chadwick Pictures Corporation
CHES	Chesterfield
Cineguild	Cineguild
CL	Clarendon
CLIN	Clinton
COL	COLUMBIA
Colony	Colony Pictures
COM	Commonwealth
COMM	Commodore Pictures
COS	Cosmopolitan (Hearst)
DE	Dependable Exchange
DGP	Dorothy Gish Productions
Disney	Walt Disney Productions
DIST	Distinctive
DM	DeMille Productions
DOUB	Doubleday
EAL	Ealing Studios (Brit.)
ECF	East Coast Films
ECL	Eclectic
ED	Eldorado
EF	Eagle Films
EFF & EFF	E.F.F. & E.F.F. Comedy
EFI	English Films Inc.
EIFC	Export and Import Film Corp.
EL	Eagle-Lion
EM	Embassy Pictures Corp.

EMI	EMI Productions
EP	Enterprise Pictures
EPC	Equity Pictures Corp.
EQ	Equitable
EXCEL	Excellent
FA	Fine Arts
FC	Film Classics
FD	First Division
FN	First National
FOX	20TH CENTURY FOX (and Fox Productions)
FP	Famous Players (and Famous Players Lasky)
FRP	Frontroom Productions
Gainsborough	Gainsborough Productions
GAU	Gaumont (Brit.)
GEN	General
GFD	General Films Distributors
Goldwyn	Samuel Goldwyn Productions
GN	Grand National
GOTH	Gotham
Grafton	Grafton Films (Brit.)
H	Harma
HAE	Harma Associated Distributors
Hammer	Hammer Films (Brit.)
HD	Hagen and Double
HM	Hi Mark
HR	Hal Roach
IA	International Artists
ID	Ideal
IF	Independent Film Distributors (Brit.)
Imperator	Imperator Films (Brit.)
IP	Independent Pictures Corp.
IN	Invincible Films
INSP	Inspirational Pictures (Richard Barthelmess)
IV	Ivan Film
Javelin	Javelin Film Productions (Brit.)
JUR	Jury
KC	Kinema Club
KCB	Kay C. Booking
Knightsbridge	Knightsbridge Productions (Brit.)
Korda	Alexander Korda Productions (Brit.)
Ladd	Ladd Company Productions
LAS	Lasky Productions (Jesse L. Lasky)
LFP	London Films
LIP	London Independent Producers
Lorimar	Lorimar Productions
LUM	Lumis
Majestic	Majestic Films
Mascot	Mascot Films
Mayflowers	Mayflowers Productions (Brit.)
Metro	Metro
MFC	Mission Film Corporation
MG	Metro-Goldwyn
MGM	METRO-GOLDWYN-MAYER
MON	Monogram
MOR	Morante
MS	Mack Sennett
MUT	Mutual
N	National
NG	National General
NGP	National General Pictures (Alexander Korda, Brit.)
NW	New World
Orion	Orion Productions
Ortus	Ortus Productions (Brit.)
PAR	PARAMOUNT
Pascal	Gabriel Pascal Productions (Brit.)
PDC	Producers Distributors Corp.

Key to Abbreviations (continued)

PEER	Peerless
PWN	Peninsula Studios
PFC	Pacific Film Company
PG	Playgoers
PI	Pacific International
PIO	Pioneer Film Corp.
PM	Pall Mall
PP	Pro Patria
PRC	Producers Releasing Corporation
PRE	Preferred
QDC	Quality Distributing Corp.
RAY	Rayart
RAD	Radio Pictures
RANK	J. Arthur Rank (Brit.)
RBP	Rex Beach Pictures
REA	Real Art
REG	Regional Films
REN	Renown
REP	Republic
RF	Regal Films
RFD	R.F.D. Productions (Brit.)
RKO	RKO RADIO PICTURES
Rogell	Rogell
Romulus	Romulus Films (Brit.)
Royal	Royal
SB	Samuel Bronston
SCHUL	B.P. Schulberg Productions
SEL	Select
SELZ	Selznick International (David O. Selznick)
SF	Selznick Films
SL	Sol Lesser
SONO	Sonofilms
SP	Seven Pines Productions (Brit.)
SRP	St. Regis Pictures
STER	Sterling
STOLL	Stoll
SUN	Sunset
SYN	Syndicate Releasing Co.
SZ	Sam Zimbalist
TC	Two Cities (Brit.)
T/C	Trem-Carr
THI	Thomas H. Ince
TIF	Tiffany
TRA	Transatlantic Pictures
TRU	Truart
TS	Tiffany/Stahl
UA	UNITED ARTISTS
UNIV	UNIVERSAL (AND UNIVERSAL INTERNATIONAL)
Venture	Venture Distributors
VIT	Vitagraph
WAL	Waldorf
WB	WARNER BROTHERS (AND WARNER BROTHERS-SEVEN ARTS)
WEST	Westminster
WF	Woodfall Productions (Brit.)
WI	Wisteria
WORLD	World
WSHP	William S. Hart Productions
ZUKOR	Adolph Zukor Productions

Foreign

ABSF	AB Svensk Film Industries (Swed.)
Action	Action Films (Fr.)
ADP	Agnes Delahaie Productions (Fr.)
Agata	Agata Films (Span.)
Alter	Alter Films (Fr.)
Arch	Archway Film Distributors
Argos	Argos Films (Fr.)
Argui	Argui Films (Fr.)
Ariane	Les Films Ariane (Fr.)
Athos	Athos Films (Fr.)
Belga	Belga Films (Bel.)
Beta	Beta Films (Ger.)
CA	Cine-Alliance (Fr.)
Caddy	Caddy Films (Fr.)
CCFC	Compagnie Commerciale Francais Einematographique (Fr.)
CDD	Cino Del Duca (Ital.)
CEN	Les Films de Centaur (Fr.)
CFD	Czecheslovak Film Productions
CHAM	Champion (Ital.)
Cinegay	Cinegay Films (Ital.)
Cines	Cines Films (Ital.)
Cineriz	Cinerez Films (Ital.)
Citel	Citel Films (Switz.)
Como	Como Films (Fr.)
CON	Concordia (Fr.)
Corona	Corona Films (Fr.)
D	Documento Films (Ital.)
DD	Dino De Laurentiis (Ital.)
Dear	Dear Films (Ital.)
DIF	Discina International Films (Fr.)
DPR	Films du Palais-Royal (Fr.)
EX	Excelsa Films (Ital.)
FDP	Films du Pantheon (Fr.)
Fono	Fono Roma (Ital.)
FS	Filmsonor Productions (Fr.)
Gala	Fala Films (Ital.)
Galatea	Galatea Productions (Ital.)
Gamma	Gamma Films (Fr.)
Gemma	Gemma Cinematografica (Ital.)
GFD	General Film Distributors, Ltd. (Can.)
GP	General Productions (Fr.)
Gray	(Gray Films (Fr.)
IFD	Intercontinental Film Distributors
Janus	Janus Films (Ger.)
JMR	Macques Mage Releasing (Fr.)
LF	Les Louvre Films (Fr.)
LFM	Les Films Moliere (Fr.)
Lux	Lux Productions (Ital.)
Melville	Melville Productions (Fr.)
Midega	Midega Films (Span.)
NEF	N.E.F. La Nouvelle Edition Francaise (Fr.)
NFD	N.F.D. Productions (Ger.)
ONCIC	Office National pour le Commerce et L'Industrie Cinematographique (Fr.)
Ortus	Ortus Films (Can.)
PAC	Production Artistique Cinematographique (Fr.)
Pagnol	Marcel Pagnol Productions (Fr.)
Parc	Parc Films (Fr.)
Paris	Paris Films (Fr.)
Pathe	Pathe Films (Fr.)
PECF	Productions et Editions Cinematographique Francais (Fr.)
PF	Parafrench Releasing Co. (Fr.)
PIC	Produzione International Cinematografica (Ital.)
Ponti	Carlo Ponti Productions (Ital.)
RAC	Realisation d'Art Cinematographique (Fr.)
Regina	Regina Films (Fr.)
Renn	Renn Productions (Fr.)
SDFS	Societe des Films Sonores Tobis (Fr.)
SEDIF	Societe d'Exploitation ed de Distribution de Films (Fr.)
SFP	Societe Francais de Production (Fr.)
Sigma	Sigma Productions (Fr.)
SNE	Societe Nouvelle des Establishments (Fr.)
Titanus	Titanus Productions (Ital.)
TRC	Transcontinental Films (Fr.)
UDIF	U.D.I.F. Productions (Fr.)
UFA	Deutsche Universum-Film AG (Ger.)
UGC	Union Generale Cinematographique (Fr.)
Union	Union Films (Ger.)
Vera	Vera Productions (Fr.)

C

(NOTE: 1984 releases appear in Volume IX)

C. C. AND COMPANY* (1971) 84m Avco Embassy c

Joe Namath (*C.C. Ryder*), Ann-Margret (*Ann McCalley*), William Smith (*Moon*), Jennifer Billingsley (*Pom Pom*), Don Chastain (*Eddie Ellis*), Teda Bracci (*Pig*), Mike Battle (*Rabbit*), Sid Haig (*Crow*), Greg Mullavey (*Lizard*), Bruce Glover (*Capt. Midnight*), Ted King (*Suicide Sam*), Gary Littlejohn (*Sitting Bull*), Frank Noel (*Kraut*), Kiva Kelly (*Eva*), Jackie Rohr (*Zit Zit*), Bob Keyworth (*Charlie Hopkins*), Wayne Cochran and the C. C. Riders.

A truly awful biker film which was the acting debut of its star, N. Y. Jets quarterback Joe Namath. Produced by the wretched team of Carr (who would later go on to produce such turkeys as CAN'T STOP THE MUSIC [1980] and WHERE THE BOYS ARE [1984]), and Smith (Ann-Margret's husband), the story concerns a motorcycle gang that comes across the lovely Margret on the road. Namath, a sensitive type, saves the girl from getting gang-raped by his pack of outlaws. Margret is so grateful she falls for the long-haired biker and has sex with him willingly. Conflict occurs when the powerful Smith (who has starred in dozens of biker movies almost all of which are better than this one) and Namath clash over control of the gang. Smith has the most screen presence of the cast, Ann-Margret seems to be participating in this trash for her producer/writer husband, and Namath is just plain lousy.

p, Allan Carr, Roger Smith; d, Seymour Robbie; w, Smith; ph, Charles Wheeler (DeLuxe color); m, Lenny Stack; ed, Fred Chulack; cos, Jon Shannon.

Adventure (PR:O MPAA:R)

C.O.D.* (1932, Brit.) 64m WEST bw

Garry Marsh (*Peter Cowen*), Hope Davy (*Frances*), Cecil Ramage (*Vyner*), Arthur Stratton (*Mr. Briggs*), Sybil Grove (*Mrs. Briggs*), Bruce Belfrage (*Philip*), Roland Culver (*Edward*), Peter Gawthorne (*Detective*).

Framed for the murder of her stepfather, Davy hires well-bred criminal Marsh to help her hide the body until she can clear her name. Dull British programmer.

p, Jerome Jackson; d, Michael Powell; w, Ralph Smart (based on a story by Philip MacDonald).

Crime (PR:A MPAA:NR)

C.H.O.M.P.S.** (1979) 89m AID c

Wesley Eure (*Brian Foster*), Valerie Bertinelli (*Casey Norton*), Conrad Bain (*Ralph Norton*), Chuck McCann (*Brooks*), Red Buttons (*Bracken*), Larry Bishop (*Ken Sharp*), Hermione Baddeley (*Mrs. Flower*), Jim Backus (*Mr. Gibbs*), Robert Q. Lewis (*Merkle*), Regis Toomey (*Chief Patterson*).

Bain's ailing security systems company is going down the drain and a young electronics genius, Eure, comes up with C.H.O.M.P.S., which is short for Canine Home Protection system. His invention is a robot dog, powerful and vicious when activated, which he hopes will stop a crime wave and help him win Bain's daughter, Bertinelli. The head of a rival company, Backus, hears about the dog and wants it for his firm, so he devises a plan to sabotage Bain's operation. Buttons and McCann do what they can as the saboteurs limned by a bumbling script, but of course Eure wins out in the end. The real hero from beginning to end is the dog, C.H.O.M.P.S.

p, Joseph Barbera; d, Don Chaffey; w, Dick Robbins, Duane Poole, Joseph Barbera (from a story by Barbera); ph, Charles F. Wheeler (Movielab Color); m, Hoyt Curtin; ed, Warner Leighton, Dick Darling; set d, Tony Montenaro.

Juvenile/Comedy (PR:AAA MPAA:G)

C-MAN½ (1949) 76m FC bw

Dean Jagger (*Cliff Holden*), John Carradine (*Doc Spencer*), Lottie Elwen (*Kathe*), Harry Landers (*Owney*), Rene Paul (*Matty Royal*), Walter Vaughan (*Inspector Brandon*), Adelaide Klein (*Mrs. Hoffman*), Edith Atwater (*Lydia Brundage*), Jean Ellyn (*Birdie*), Walter Brooke (*Joe*).

Gritty little programmer shot in a tight, documentary style mostly on the streets of New York. Jagger stars as a U.S. Customs agent on the bloody trail of jewel smugglers from Paris to the Big Apple. Carradine turns in a typically fine performance as a doctor who is the fall guy for the smugglers. The direction is fast-paced, visually interesting, and a surprisingly good score by Kubik make this actioner worth a look.

p&d, Joseph Lerner; w, Berne Giler; ph, Gerald Hirschfield; m, Gail Kubik; ed, Geraldine Lerner.

Crime (PR:A MPAA:NR)

CABARET*** (1972) 124m AA c

Liza Minnelli (*Sally Bowles*), Michael York (*Brian Roberts*), Helmut Griem (*Maximilian von Heune*), Joel Grey (*Master of Ceremonies*), Fritz Wepper (*Fritz Wendel*), Marisa Berenson (*Natalia Landauer*), Elisabeth Neumann-Viertel (*Fraulein Schneider*), Sigrid Von Richthofen (*Fraulein Maur*), Helen Vita (*Fraulein Kost*), Gerd Vespermann (*Bobby*), Ralf Wolter (*Herr Ludwig*), Georg Hartmann (*Willi*), Ricky Renee (*Elke*), Estrongo Nachama (*Cantor*), Kathryn Doby, Inge Jaeger, Angelika Koch, Helen Velkovorska, Gitta Schmidt, Louise Quick (*Kit-Kat Dancers*).

It's difficult to make any movie—the script, the egos, the weather all contribute to submarining a production. The audience never sees any of that and can only concern itself with the result. So when a great movie comes along, it's a miracle. CABARET was one of those rare unique musicals that became even better on the screen. Using the Kit-Kat club, a seedy, smoky boite, as the central location, Fosse and Allen provide a film that throbs with passion. Minelli is an American singer in 1930s Berlin who falls in love with York, a mild-mannered writer who manages to mature in the course of the action. They are both seduced by Helmut Griem, a wealthy playboy suffering from Cole Porter's "old ennui." Marisa Berenson is the Jewish heiress to a department store fortune and she falls in love with Fritz Wepper, who also is Jewish but has been keeping that a secret as the National Socialist party begins to emerge. Minnelli gets pregnant, York confronts his bisexuality, and all five characters interact with the scenes at the Kit-Kat club. Joel Grey (who won a supporting actor Oscar) is the M.C. at the club and the only other major player (besides Minelli) who sings in the movie. This is more a drama with music than your old-fashioned musical. Kander and Ebb wisely tossed out several of their weaker efforts from the score of the play and added much better songs for the film. Fosse has managed to keep an underlying feeling of danger; no matter how happy the songs and dances, you can't help feeling that there's a Nazi lurking in the wings, ready to bring his club down on any one of the characters. Despite the sophistication of the material (every person seems to be as sexually ambiguous as any number of rock stars these days), the movie only garnered a PG rating. Still, it might be wise to keep impressionable children away from it. All secondary roles are perfectly cast, down to the tawdriest transvestite. Technical credits are superb. Although it seems fashionable these days to denigrate CABARET, it was explosive when it burst on the 1972 scene and deservedly won Oscars for Minnelli (Best Actress); Grey ; Fosse (Direction); Unsworth (Cinematography); Zehetbauer, Kiebach, Strabel (Art Direction); Bretherton (Editing); Burns (Music Adaptation); Knudson, Hildyard (Sound).

p, Cy Feuer (ABC Pictures Corp); d, Bob Fosse; w, Jay Presson Allen (based on the stage play by Joe Masteroff, and the stage play "I Am A Camera" by John Van Druten and the writings of Christopher Isherwood); ph, Geoffrey Unsworth (Technicolor); m, Ralph Burns; ed, David Bretherton; m/l, John Kander, Fred Ebb (from the stage play); art d, Jurgen Kiebach, Rolf Zehetbauer; set d, Herbert Strabel; cos, Charlotte Flemming; ch, Fosse.

Musical/Drama Cas. (PR:C MPAA:PG)

CABIN IN THE COTTON** (1932) 79m FN/WB bw

Richard Barthelmess (*Marvin*), Dorothy Jordan (*Betty*), Bette Davis (*Madge*), Henry B. Walthall (*Old Eph*), Berton Churchill (*Lane Norwood*), William LeMaire (*Jake Fisher*), Hardie Albright (*Roland Neal*), Tully Marshall (*Old Slick Harness*), Clarence Muse (*Old Blind Negro*), Edmund Breese (*Holmes Scott*), Dorothy Peterson (*Lilly Blake*).

Barthelmess had just about finished his career when this was made and he teamed with a young woman named Bette Davis. She was perfectly cast as a rich Southern vamp who toyed with the emotions of Barthelmess, an indigent share-cropper's son who works as the night man at the general store owned by Davis's father (Churchill). Barthelmess is promoted to bookkeeper, then learns that Churchill has been cheating his tenant farmers out of much of their profits. But now Barthelmess is almost like a son to Churchill, who hopes to get the younger man to fink on which tenant farmers are planning a rebellion. Barthelmess is in a pickle; he loves Davis but also has a feeling for Dorothy Jordan, his childhood sweetheart. He is also torn between the farmers, who are ripping off the landowner, and the landowner, who is ripping off the farmers. Barthelmess is the only one who knows what's happening on both sides. He brings the two sides together to sign a contract that will be fair to both, and is called a hero. He then decides to continue seeing Jordan. Davis watches them leave and smiles, knowing that he is still smitten and will eventually come back to her. CABIN IN THE COTTON, which sounds like a Gershwin tune for an obscure musical, could have been a powerful screen story but the adaptation from the novel left much on the cutting room floor. This is the movie that contained a famous line of dialog: Davis, ever the sexy and mean coquette, says: "I'd love to kiss you, but I just washed my hair." (Although *she* says it in an accent so thick you could pour it on pancakes.)

p, Jack L. Warner; d, Michael Curtiz; w, Paul Green (based on the novel by Harry Harrison Kroll); ph, Barney McGill; ed, George Amy.

Drama (PR:A-C MPAA:NR)

CABIN IN THE SKY*½ (1943) 98m MGM bw

Ethel Waters (*Petunia Jackson*), Eddie "Rochester" Anderson (*Little Joe*), Lena Horne (*Georgia Brown*), Louis Armstrong (*The Trumpeter*), Rex Ingram (*Lucius, Lucifer, Jr.*), Kenneth Spencer (*Rev. Green, The General*), John "Bubbles" Sublett (*Domino*), Oscar Polk (*The Deacon/Flatfoot*), Mantan Moreland (*First Idea Man*), Willie Best (*Second Idea Man*), Fletcher Rivers (*Third Idea Man, Moke*), Leon James (*Fourth Idea Man, Poke*), Bill Bailey (*Bill*), Ford L. "Buck" Washington (*Messenger Boy*), Butterfly McQueen (*Lily*), Ruby Dandridge (*Mrs. Kelso*), Nicodemus (*Dude*), Ernest Whitman (*Jim Henry*), Duke Ellington and Orchestra, Hall Johnson Choir.

An all-black musical (the first since GREEN PASTURES and HALLELUJAH!) that details the life of ne'er-do-well Little Joe (Anderson) as he parries the sexual wiles of Georgia Brown (Horne) and the devotion of his wife (Waters). He is almost killed in a barroom battle and agents from Heaven (Spencer) and Hades (Ingram) come to fight for his eternal soul. Slim premise that's been seen all too often but it's made palatable by the wonderful score by Duke, LaTouche, Arlen, and Harburg. Songs like: "Happiness Is Just A Thing Called Joe," "Cabin In The Sky," "Taking A Chance On Love," the show-stopping "Life's full of Consequences," and more. Duke Ellington also chimed in with some original music "Going Up." Some fine dance numbers and a general feeling of great sincerity from all parties are what sets this film apart. The script is simplistic and Minnelli's (his first feature film) direction is pedestrian, but the enthusiasm transcends all of it and what's up on the screen is often a delight. Satchmo Armstrong is not used enough, nor is Butterfly McQueen. All carping aside, it's fun and worth watching, if only to see so many black stars at one time.

p, Arthur Freed; d, Vincente Minnelli; w, Joseph Schrank (based on the play by Lynn Root, John Latouche, Vernon Duke); ph, Sidney Wagner; m, Roger Edens; md, Georgie Stoll; ed, Harold F. Kress; m/l, Latouche, Duke, E. Y. Harburg, Harold Arlen.

Musical **(PR:AA MPAA:NR)**

CABINET OF CALIGARI, THE** (1962) 105m FOX bw
Glynis Johns *(Jane)*, Dan O'Herlihy *(Paul and Caligari)*, Dick Davalos *(Mark)*, Lawrence Dobkin *(David)*, Constance Ford *(Christine)*, J. Pat O'Malley *(Martin)*, Vicki Trickett *(Jeanie)*, Estelle Winwood *(Ruth)*, Doreen Lang *(Vivian)*, Charles Fredericks *(Bob)*, Phyllis Teagardin *(Little Girl)*.

This 1962 film written by Robert Bloch has little to do with the classic German expressionist silent of 1919. If one does not expect the newer film to emulate the older model, this effort is respectable enough. Johns stars as a distraught young woman who seeks help at a creepy mansion when her car breaks down. The master of the house, O'Herlihy, invites her in and subjects her to nightmarish torture and humilations, as he does to whomever enters the house. In keeping with the story structure of the original film, Johns wakes up and realizes it's all a dream. The audience sees that she is an inmate in an asylum and the torturer in her dreams is actually her doctor. Interesting sets and cinematography are nowhere near as effective as in the 1919 version, but there is a good, haunting musical score by Fried. This was Bloch's first script after penciling Hitchcock's PSYCHO.

p&d, Roger Kay; w, Robert Bloch; ph, John Russell (CinemaScope); m, Gerald Fried; ed, Archie Marshek.

Horror **Cas.** **(PR:A MPAA:NR)**

CABOBLANCO** (1981) 87m Avco Embassy c
Charles Bronson *(Giff Hoyt)*, Jason Robards, Jr. *(Gunther Beckdorff)*, Dominique Sanda *(Marie Claire Allesandri)*, Fernando Rey *(Tereda)*, Simon MacCorkindale *(Lewis Clarkson)*, Camilla Sparv *(Hira)*, Denny Miller *(Horst)*, Gilbert Roland *(Dr. Ramirez)*.

Lame attempt to remake CASABLANCA by setting it after the war and in Peru where former Nazis on the run are hiding out. Bronson plays an American expatriate who owns and operates the local dive. The small Peruvian village is run by villainous ex-Nazi Robards who has police captain Rey in his pocket. One day, beautiful Frenchwoman Sanda arrives in town to search for her missing lover who went down on a ship that was carrying $22 million worth of gold. A British member of the sunken ship's crew turns up and he attempts to kill Robards but he is shot by the German's native guards and Bronson saves him. Sanda, it turns out, is actually more interested in the gold than her lover, and plays Robards off against Bronson to get what she wants. Eventually, she decides she wants Bronson and the gold. Rey finally assumes a sense of duty and country and decides to kick the Nazi out. Robards capitulates and swallows a cyanide capsule in the glorious Nazi tradition.

p, Lance Hool, Paul A. Joseph; d, J. Lee Thompson; w, Mort Fine, Milton Gelman; ph, Alex Phillips Jr. (Panavision); m, Jerry Goldsmith; ed, Michael F. Anderson.

Drama **Cas.** **(PR:C MPAA:R)**

CABIRIA (SEE: NIGHTS OF CABIRIA, 1957)

CACCIA TRAGICA (SEE: TRAGIC PURSUIT, THE, 1947)

CACTUS FLOWER** (1969) 103m COL c
Walter Matthau *(Julian Winston)*, Ingrid Bergman *(Stephanie Dickinson)*, Goldie Hawn *(Toni Simmons)*, Jack Weston *(Harvey Greenfield)*, Rick Lenz *(Igor Sullivan)*, Vito Scotti *(Senor Sanchez)*, Irene Hervey *(Mrs. Durant)*, Eve Bruce *(Georgia)*, Irwin Charone *(Store Manager)*, Matthew Saks *(Nephew)*.

Bergman is the dowdy assistant to bachelor dentist Matthau, who thinks he is bicuspids over bi-peds in love with Greenwich Village character Hawn (following in the great tradition begun by Carolyn Jones in BACHELOR PARTY). Goldie is being pursued by Rick Lenz, a writer who is much closer to her in age. Matthau asks Bergman to pose as his wife so Hawn won't press for marriage. Bergman sheds her caterpillar skin and emerges a butterfly to snare Matthau. Matthau gets his pal Jack Weston to act as 'wife' Bergman's lover. They all meet at a nightclub where Matthau finally begins to appreciate the sexiness of his assistant. Matthau and Bergman wind up in each other's arms at fadeout and Lenz and Hawn will presumably do the same. The movie was a misfire despite the presence of many of filmdom's best talents. Diamond's script adaptation fails to provide any new wrinkles to the tired plot and Gene Saks' direction is only as good as the material he's been given. In two words, it's "faintly amusing."

p, M. J. Frankovich; d, Gene Saks; w, I.A.L. Diamond (based on the play by Abe Burrows, adapted from the French play by Barillet and Gredy); ph, Charles E. Lang (Technicolor); m, Quincy Jones; ed, Maury Winetrobe; set d, Robert Clatworthy; ch, Miriam Nelson.

Comedy **Cas.** **(PR:C MPAA:M)**

CACTUS IN THE SNOW*½ (1972) 90m General Film Corp c
Richard Thomas *(Harley MacIntosh)*, Mary Layne *(Cissy)*, Lucille Benson *(Mrs. Sawyer)*, Oscar Beregi *(Mr. Albert)*, Jan Burrell *(Woman Pharmacist)*, Ruby Dake *(Dolores)*, Joseph Di Reda *(Mr. Harris)*, Dennis Fimple *(Mr. Murray)*, Corey Fischer *(The Bartender)*, Hugh Fischer *(Drill Instructor)*, Dan Halleck *(Seymour)*, Stan Kamber *(Cal Beamish)*, Maggie King *(Rhoda)*, Tiger Joe Marsh *(Cab Driver)*, Gregory Mead *(Joe)*, Christopher Mitchum *(George)*, Beatriz Monteil *(Valerie)*, Tani Phelps *(Mrs. Harris)*.

Sappy melodrama starring Thomas as a Vietnam era soldier on leave and searching for a woman to lose his virginity to. Shot entirely in Hollywood, the film has no real sense of style or purpose and the only performance worth noting is that of Monteil as a prostitute.

p, Lou Brandt, d&w, Martin Zweiback; ph, Wilbur Grossman (Technicolor); m, Joe Parnello; ed, Robert Swink, William Sands.

Drama **(PR:A MPAA:GP)**

CADDIE½** (1976, Aus.) 107m Atlantic c
Helen Morse *(Caddie)*, Takis Emmanuel *(Peter)*, Jack Thompson *(Ted)*, Jacki Weaver *(Josie)*, Melissa Jaffer *(Leslie)*, Ron Blanchard *(Bil)*, Drew Forsythe *(Sonny)*, Kirrili Nolan *(Esther)*, Lynette Currin *(Maudie)*, Phillip Hinton *(John Marsh)*, Simon Hinton *(Terry Marsh Aged 5)*, Sean Hinton *(Terry Marsh Aged 11)*, Deborah Kounnas *(Ann Marsh Aged 2)*, Marianne Howard *(Aged 9)*, Mary MacKay *(Mater)*, Lucky Grills *(Pawnbroker)*, Robyn Nevin *(Black Eye)*, Pat Evison *(Mrs. Norris)*, June Salter *(Mrs. Marks)*, Joy Hruby *(Mrs. Sweeney)*, Jan Adele *(Daisy)*, Johnny Garfield *(Man at Bar)*, Shirley Cameron *(Alcoholic Woman)*, Frank Lloyd *(Raffle Man)*, Sid Haylan *(Billy)*, Pat Rooney *(Bar Useful)*, Roy Corbett *(Man)*, Norman Erskine *(Man at Counter)*, Ray Marshall *(Tipsy Man)*.

Somewhat dull Australian melodrama starring Morse as a Sydney barmaid whose husband leaves her with two kids to raise in the midst of the Depression. The film is filled with plenty of local flavor of the pubs and townsfolk. One of the regular pub customers, Emmanuel, takes a liking to Morse and gives her a nickname that likens her to his stylish and classy car, a "Caddie". An awkward romance develops between the two. Emmanuel turns in a good performance which outshines Morse who struggles mightily to maintain the air of dignity required of her role.

p, Anthony Buckley; d, Donald Crombie; w, Joan Long; ph, Peter James (Panavision); m, Patrick Flynn; ed, Tim Wellburn; art d, Owen Williams; cos, Judith Dorsman.

Drama **Cas.** **(PR:C MPAA:NR)**

CADDY, THE** (1953) 95m PAR bw
Dean Martin *(Joe Anthony)*, Jerry Lewis *(Harvey)*, Donna Reed *(Kathy Taylor)*, Barbara Bates *(Lisa Anthony)*, Joseph Calleia *(Papa Anthony)*, Fred Clark *(Mr. Baxter)*, Clinton Sundberg *(Charles)*, Howard Smith *(Golf Official)*, Marshall Thompson *(Bruce Reeber)*, Marjorie Gateson *(Mrs. Taylor)*, Frank Puglia *(Mr. Spezzato)*, Lewis Martin *(Mr. Taylor)*, Romo Vincent *(Eddie Lear)*, Argentina Brunetti *(Mama Anthony)*, Houseley Stevenson, Jr. *(Officer)*, John Gallaudet *(Mr. Bell)*, William Edmunds *(Caminello)*, Charles Irwin *(Golf Starter)*, Freeman Lusk *(Official)*, Keith McConnell *(Mr. Benthall)*, Henry Brandon *(Mr. Preen)*, Maurice Marsac *(Mr. Leron)*, Donald Randolph *(Miller, Sr.)*, Stephen Chase *(George Garrison, Sr.)*, Tom Harmon *(Announcer)*, Ben Hogan *(Himself)*, Sam Snead *(Himself)*, Byron Nelson *(Himself)*, Julius Boros *(Himself)*, Jimmy Thomson *(Himself)*, Harry E. Cooper *(Himself)*.

Weak Martin and Lewis vehicle set in the world of professional golf. Martin is the golfer and Lewis his caddy-manager. Numerous professional golfers make cameo appearances during the climactic tournament at Pebble Beach, which degenerates into chaos and leads the boys into a show-biz career. Lewis does his usual juvenile slapstick and sings "What Wouldcha Do Without Me?" and "One Big Love." Martin is typically suave and sings "You're the Right One" and "It's a Whistle-In' Kind of Mornin." The duo do a duet on "That's Amore."

p, Paul Jones: d, Norman Taurog; w, Edmund Hartman, Danny Arnold (added dialog by Ken Englund; based on a story by Arnold); ph, Daniel L. Fapp; md, Joseph J. Lilley; ed, Warren Low; ch, Jack Baker; songs, Harry Warren, Jack Brooks.

Comedy **(PR:A MPAA:NR)**

CADDYSHACK*½** (1980) 99m Orion/WB c
Chevy Chase *(Ty)*, Rodney Dangerfield *(Al)*, Ted Knight *(Judge)*, Michael O'Keefe *(Danny)*, Bill Murray *(Carl)*, Sarah Holcomb *(Maggie)*, Scott Colomby *(Tony)*, Cindy Morgan *(Lacey)*, Dan Resin *(Dr. Beeper)*, Henry Wilcoxon *(Bishop)*, Elaine Aiken *(Mrs. Noonan)*, Albert Salmi *(Noonan)*, Ann Ryerson *(Grace)*, Brian Doyle Murray *(Lou)*, Hamilton Mitchell *(Motormouth)*, Peter Berkrot *(Angie)*, John F. Barmon, Jr. *(Spaulding)*, Lois Kibbee *(Mrs. Smalls)*, Brian McConnachie *(Scott)*, Scott Powell, Ann Crilley, Cordis Heard, Scott Sudden, Jackie Davis, Thomas Carlin, Minerva Scelza, Chuck Rodent.

Slapstick comedy with a host of great clowns, this film revived the sagging fortunes of wonderful Rodney Dangerfield whose opening scenes as he attempts to take over an exclusive, swanky golf club are some of the most hilarious on record. Adorned in garish garb and throwing money right and left as the classic boor, Rodney offends the club's stuffshirts, chiefly Knight, who considers the club his private fiefdom. Chase is the super golfer whose modesty is only exceeded by his roaring ego while O'Keefe is the clean cut kid trying to make good and glean a college scholarship by winning a tournament. Murray is outstanding as a grubby, fantasizing groundskeeper living in a shack and desperately devising explosive ways to rid the course of a pesky gopher who is tunneling through the greens. This was Murray's first big break after MEATBALLS and he makes the most of it; his machinations embrace the moronic but such bumbling is perfectly in keeping with his character. The sight of him being visited in his threadbare, foul-smelling quarter by super rich Chase is properly pathetic. Murray has a wild scene after draining the club pool in frantic search of a particle of human waste which has caused a panic among the snobbish members; it is assumed that the floating Baby Ruth bar is the dropping of an interloping low-class caddy. This scene is so disgusting that it proves a marvel of lowbrow humor. But too much time is spent on the forced romance between O'Keefe and Holcomb, an attractive waitress, and the slapstick gets mindless toward the end (as if the producer typically said, "Okay, it's time for this film to *really* get out of control!"). Yet the laughs are consistent, particularly since the stereotypes are so crushing as to be satiric in and of themselves. There is a marvelous moment when Wilcoxon, a pleasure-loving golf fanatic clergyman, begins to play a perfect game in a raging rainstorm, dropping one hole-in-one after another, laughing hysterically, thanking the Almighty for the greatest game of his life, lifting his club heavenward, and being struck down as lightning courses through the metal putter into his quivering frame as a crescendo claps from the score of THE TEN COMMANDMENTS (in which Wilcoxon played pharoah's general pursuing the Jews into the parted Red Sea only to be consumed by the waters), one of many inside movie jokes permeating the film. Rodney steals the movie when he's present as the man you never want to meet socially and always do.

p, Douglas Kenney; d, Harold Ramis; w, Brian Doyle-Murray, Ramis, Kenney; ph, Stevan Larner (Technicolor); m, Johnny Mandel; ed, William Carruth; prod d, Stan Jolly; art d, George Szeptycki; m/l, Kenny Loggins.

Comedy Cas. (PR:C-O MPAA:R)

CADET GIRL*½ (1941) 69m FOX bw

Carole Landis *(Gene Baxter)*, George Montgomery *(Tex Mallory)*, John Shepperd *(Bob Mallory)* William Tracy *(Runt)*, Janis Carter *(Mary Moore)*, Robert Lowery *(Walton)*, Basil Walker *(Red)*, Charles Tannen *(Jimmy)*, Chick Chandler *(Benny Burns)*.

A harmless little musical boasting nothing more than a pleasant pair as leads. Set against a backdrop of military academies and big bands, brothers Montgomery and Shepperd inconveniently fall for vocalist Landis. As expected from a wartime film about cadets and girls, the brothers choose West Point over Landis. Sugared with a dose of flag-waving songs "Uncle Sam Gets Ahead" and "She's a Good Neighbor" CADET GIRLS is best described by another of its jingoistic jingles, "It Happened, It's Over, Let's Forget."

p, Sol M. Wurtzel; d, Ray McCarey; w, Stanley Rauh, H. W. Hanemann (based on a story by Jack Andrews and Richard English); ph, Charles Clark; ed, Fred Allen; md, Emil Newman; m/l, Leo Robin and Ralph Rainger.

Musical (PR:A MPAA:NR)

CADET-ROUSSELLE** (1954, Fr.) 115m Pathe-Pac c

Francois Perier *(Cadet-Rousselle)*, Dany Robin *(Violetta)*, Bourvil *(Jerome)*, Madeleine Lebeau *(Marguerite)*, Christine Carrere *(Isabelle)*, Noel Rouquevert *(Berton)*, Alfred Adam *(Rovignol)*, Jean Paredes *(General)*, Henri Gremieux *(Mayor)*.

Adaptation of a peasant folk song has Perier in love with the Mayor's daughter, but the class distinction between them makes marriage impossible. He leaves to make his fortune in Paris but falls in with a band of Gypsies who are fronting a counter-revolutionary plot. He unwittingly delivers a message and is arrested and thrown into a cell. He escapes, helps win a battle, is thrown into a cell again, escapes again, turns outlaw, and then is made a general in Napoleon's army. Finally he returns to his village to marry the girl he loves. Fluffy bore somewhat relieved by Bourvil's fine comic performance as Perier's sidekick. This is typical of the French "Tradition of Quality" that the "New Wave" was rejecting at about the same time.

d, Andre Hunnebelle; w, Jean Halain, Jean-Paul Leroix; ph, Marcel Grignon (Eastmancolor); m, Jean Marion, ed, Jean Feyte.

Adventure (PR:A MPAA:NR)

CAESAR AND CLEOPATRA**** (1946, Brit.) 138m Two Cities/EL/VA c

Vivien Leigh *(Cleopatra)*, Claude Rains *(Caesar)*, Stewart Granger *(Apollodorus)*, Flora Robson *(Ftatateeta)*, Francis L. Sullivan *(Pothinus)*, Basil Sydney *(Rufio)*, Cecil Parker *(Britannus)*, Raymond Lovell *(Lucius Septimus)*, Anthony Eustrel *(Achillas)*, Ernest Thesiger *(Theodotus)*, Anthony Harvey *(Ptolemy)*, Renee Asherson *(Iras)*, Olga Edwardes *(Charmian)*, Stanley Holloway *(Belzanor)*, Michael Rennie *(Quayside Centurion)*, James McKechnie *(Wounded Centurion)*, Esme Percy *(Major Domo)*, Leo Genn *(Bel Affris)*, Alan Wheatley *(Persian)*, Anthony Holles *(Vociferous Boatman)*, Charles Victor *(Lazy Porter)*, Ronald Shiner *(2nd Porter)*, John Bryning *(Quayside Sentinel)*, John Laurie, Charles Rolfe, Hamilton Humphries *(Auxiliary Roman Sentinels)*, Felix Aylmer *(Ist Nobleman)*, Ivor Barnard *(2nd Nobleman)*, Valentine Dyall *(Longboat Centurion)*, Charles Deane *(Guardsman)*, Peter Lord *(Special Roman Centurion)*, Shaun Noble *(A.D.C. to Achillas)*, Robert Adams *(Nubian Slave)*, Gerald Case *(Roman Tax Officer)*, Gibb McLaughlin *(High Priest)*, Leonard Llewellyn, Louis de Wohl *(Palace Officials)*, Bernard de Gautier *(Assistant Palace Official)*, Jean Simmons *(Harpist)*, Russell Thorndyke *(Harpist's Master)*, Basil Jayson *(Mithridates)*, Peter Bayliss *(A.D.C. to Mithridates)*, Abdul Wahab *(Cleopatra's Attendant)*, Chick Alexander *(Major Domo's Attendant)*, Gerald Kempinski *(Angry Boatman)*, Harold Franklyn, Charles Minor, Andre Belhomme *(Boatmen)*, Don Kenito *(Singing Boatman)*, Bill Holland, Don Stannard, Ronald Davidson, Peter Lilley, Gordon Gantry *(Special Roman Officers)*, Anne Davis, Ingrid Puxon, Virginia Keiley, Mary Midwinter, Mary Boyle, Daphne Day, Zena Marshall, Agnes Bernelle, Jean Richards *(Ladies-in-Waiting)*, Princess Roshanara, Margaret Fernald, Mary Macklin, Louise Nolan, Rita Lancaster, Dorothy Bramball, Jackie Daniels, Toni Gable, Babette Griffin, Margaret Harvey, Moya Iles, Kay Kendall, Hilda Lawrence, Anne Sassoon, Renee Gilbert, Olwyn Brooks, Anne Moore *(Palace-Steps Ladies and Lady Councillors)*, June Black, Jill Carpenter, Jeanee Williams, Alice Calvert, Lilla Erulkar, Jean Hulley *(Other Ladies-in-Waiting)*, Cathleen Nesbitt, Ena Burrill, Marie Ault *(Egyptian Ladies)*, Cyril Jervis Walter, Roy Ellett, Michael Martin Harvey, Cecil Calvert, Harry Lane, MacKenzie Ward,, Barry Meaton, Paul Croft, Michael Cacoyannis, Roy Russell, Wilfred Walter, Alan Lewis, Charles Paton, George Luck, H. F. Maltby, Hylton Allen *(Councillors)*, Eve Smith, Nantando de Villiers, Roma Miller *(Colored Fan Girls)*, Bernard Bright, B. Q. Alakija *(Ethiopian Princes)*, Bob Cameron *(Bucinator)*.

Extravagant, richly produced and wonderfully enacted, Shaw's acerbic and witty play receives a faithful rendition. Rains is magnificently hammy and imperial as a whimsical Caesar who visits Alexandria with a small military contingent to quell civil war and subdue unruly, mysterious Egypt. He is at first amused then charmed and finally beguiled by Leigh who is an enchanting woman (Cleopatra was twenty-four when Julius Caesar met her in 45 B.C.). Leigh is dominated by a shrewd and manipulating servant, Robson (whose makeup is so dark she appears almost in blackface). Moreover she is in the evil control of the whale-like Sullivan, Leigh's chief minister. Step by step Rains teaches the young queen to take power and responsibility for her actions, while he sets fire to the Egyptian fleet, a blaze that consumes the resplendent Alexandrine Library. Ernest Thesiger, an Egyptian intellectual, at his hysterical best, implores Rains to save the libarary and is permitted to use the Egyptian army to do so. While these troops are thus diverted, Rains and his cohorts under aide Sydney (playing Rufio), seize the real goal of the expedition, the towering Lighthouse of Alexandria, one of the Seven Wonders of the ancient world. Accompanying Rains to the Lighthouse is a dashing Sicilian merchant and adventurer, broadly played by handsome Granger who brings along Leigh wrapped in a rug, ostensibly as a gift for Rains. Through one machination after another, Leigh finally usurps her enemies while Rains leads his men against Harvey (Ptolemy, Cleopatra's conniving brother and, in real life, her husband). Both conquer, Leigh through her servant Robson, who murders Sullivan and, in turn, is killed by Sydney as a precaution of the murderous servant's aim to kill his master, Rains. Leigh assumes the throne, Rains leaves a becalmed Egypt, promising to send his handsome lieutenant, Marc Antony, to visit the queen, before sailing to his native Rome and lethal destiny at the dagger-clutching hands of his assassins. Shaw's witty and erudite dialog, personified in the roles essayed by Raines and Parker, the latter playing the devoted slave Britannus, are delightful. The irascible playwright became so fond of Leigh that he broke precedent and actually wrote an entirely new scene for her, although he adamantly refused to introduce "a little love interest" into the script as politely requested by producer J. Arthur Rank (politely is the only way *anyone* could talk to the truculent Shaw). Rank and director Pascal had been for years determined to film all of Shaw's major works before the playwright died; they had attempted, after producing MAJOR BARBARA, to film "Saint Joan" with Greta Garbo and "Arms and the Man" with Rex Harrison, but neither got off the drawing boards. Pascal went at CAESAR AND CLEOPATRA with a vengeance, intent on proving that the British film industry could rival in scope anything Hollywould could create, particularly in the belt-tightening years of WW II. The result was the most extravagantly expensive film Britain produced up to that time, so opulent that when G.B.S. first viewed it he expressed annoyance at the lavish sets, the hordes of extras and spendthrift feel of the overall production. Pascal and Rank spent about $5.2 million during the overlong shooting schedule and were plagued by recurrent problems. Production had to be shut down repeatedly at the studios in England because of bombing attacks by the Nazis. Then Leigh, whose health had always been fragile (she made only four films in the 1940s, after her smashing success in GONE WITH THE WIND in 1939), suffered a miscarriage which caused another five-week delay. Other postponements arose when scenic materials, costumes for the 2,000 extras, and set equipment became short. Pascal, normally a conservative producer-director, lost his head completely and traveled to Egypt with cast and crew to shoot "atmospheric" background footage, carting along a gigantic paper-mache Sphinx. Cast and crew members bickered constantly and Shaw sent messages repeatedly to Pascal complaining that Bryan's marvelous sets, Messel's colorful costuming, along with the brief battle scenes, interfered with his wonderful dialog. (Here, Pascal could not be faulted in that it was his job to make a movie from a stage play without having the film appear stagy.) American distribution of this film was promoted by Rank and United Artists with an enormous budget that caused U.S. audiences to at first flock to see favorites Leigh and Rains, but disappointment soon set in when viewers realized that this movie was not a lurid reanactment of the Cleopatra tale a la Cecil B. DeMille and box office sales fell drastically. It was a financial bath which all but drowned Pascal's career and brought the Rank organization to the brink of bankruptcy, a then staggering loss of more than $3 million. Yet CAESAR AND CLEOPATRA remains a faithful adaptation of the Shaw masterpiece and its cast members render sterling and memorable performances. Many a future star emerged from the ranks of the film's many bit players, including Michael Rennie, who plays a Centurian, Kay Kendall, a slave girl, and Jean Simmons, a harpist.

p&d, Gabriel Pascal (for J. Arthur Rank); w, George Bernard Shaw, Marjorie Deans (based on Shaw's play); ph, Frederick A. Young, Robert Krasker, Jack Hildyard, Jack Cardiff (Technicolor); m, Georges Auric; ed, Frederick Wilson; set d, John Bryan; cos, Oliver Messel.

Historical Drama/Biography Cas. (PR:A MPAA:NR)

CAESAR THE CONQUEROR*½ (1963, Ital.) 103m Metheus Films/Medallion c

Cameron Mitchell *(Julius Caesar)*, Rick Battaglia *(Vercingetorix)*, Dominique Wilms *(Queen Astrid)*, Ivo Payer *(Claudius Valerian)*, Raffaella Carra *(Publia)*, Nerio Bernardi *(Cicero)*, Carla Calo *(Calpurnia)*, Cesare Fantoni *(Caius Oppio)*, Carlo Tamberlani *(Pompey)*, Lucia Randi *(Clelia)*, Giulio Donnini *(Eporidorige)*, Bruno Tocci *(Mark Anthony)*, Aldo Pini *(Quintus Cicero)*, Fedele Gentile *(Centurion)*, Enzo Petracca *(Titus Azius)*.

Italian costume epic has a bit more to do with hustorical reality than the general run of them (Hercules, Maciste, et al.) but is no better. Mitchell is the Roman emperor and general, attempting to secure more soldiers for his Gallic campaign despite opposition from the Senate. His ward (Carra) and her lover (Payer) are captured by the Gauls under Battaglia, but queen Wilms frees them. The pair warn the Roman camp and Mitchell leads his troops to victory, capturing Battaglia. Only vaguely interesting.

p, Roberto Capitani; d, Amerigo Anton (Tanio Boccia); w, Arpad De Riso, Nino Scolaro (based on *The Gallic Campaign* by Gaius Julius Caesar); ph, Romolo Garroni (Eastmancolor); m, Gian Stellari, Guido Robuschi; ed, Beatrice Felici; art d, Amedeo Mellone; cos, Maria Luisa Panaro.

Historical Drama (PR:C MPAA:NR)

CAFE COLETTE*½ (1937, Brit.) 73m ABF bw (AKA: DANGER IN PARIS)

Paul Cavanagh *(Ryan)*, Greta Nissen *(Vanda Muroff)*, Sally Gray *(Jill Manning)*, Bruce Seton *(Roger Manning)*, Paul Blake *(Ethelred Burke)*, Donald Calthrop *(Nick)*, Dino Galvani *(Josef)*, Fred Duprez *(Burnes)*, Cecil Ramage *(Petrov)*, Denier Warren *(Compere)*.

Safe, calculated tale of an international spy ring which has Cavanagh confronted with enemy spies, a top-secret formula, and a beautiful Russian princess. Even a surprise twist offers barely a gasp as the hero, who is dependent on his good looks, turns out to secretly head an intelligence bureau.

d, Paul L. Stein; w, Val Valentine, Katherine Strueby and Eric Maschwitz (from a story by Maschwitz, Walford Hyden, and Val Gielgud); ph, Ronald L. Neame.

Spy Drama   **(PR:A   MPAA:NR)**

CAFE DE PARIS**   (1938, Fr.) 83m Regina Production bw

Jules Berry, Vera Korene, Pierre Brasseur, Jacques Baumer, Julien Carette, Marcel Carpentier, J. Coquelin, Arthur Devere, Maurice Escande, Roger Gaillard, Jacques Gretillat, Janine Gulse, Florence Marly, Robert Pizani, Marcel Valle, Simone Berriau.

Interesting murder mystery from writer/director Mirande which works equally well as a chronicle of a Parisian cafe. It's characters and plot are easily within convention. A renowned newspaperman and blackmailer is murdered at his table and an array of suspects are rounded up. It is obvious, however, that none are guilty—not his wife, her lover, the arms trafficker, the creditor, or the playboy. They all have their motives, especially the playboy whose interest lies in the dead man's daughter.

d&w, Yves Mirande, ph, Christian Matras; m, Van Parys.

Mystery   **(PR:A   MPAA:NR)**

CAFE EXPRESS**½   (1980, Ital.) 105m Vides Cinematografica c

Nino Manfredi, Adolfo Celi, Vittorio Mezzogiorno, Marzio C. Honorato, Gigi Reder, Luigi Basogaluppi, Marisa Laurito, Vittorio Marsiglia, Vittorio Caprioli.

Manfredi is a vendor illegally peddling coffee aboard Italian express trains. He is hounded by conductors and bureaucrats at every turn but outwits them easily. Decent comedy owes much to BREAD AND CHOCOLATE, which also starred Manfredi, but lacks the earlier film's pointed political aspects. Manfredi's performance carries the film.

p, Franco Cristaldi, Nicola Carraro; d, Nanni Loy; w, Loy, Elvio Porta, Nino Manfredi; ph, Claudio Cirillo (Technoscope Color); m, Giovanna Marini.

Comedy   **Cas.**   **(PR:C   MPAA:NR)**

CAFE HOSTESS*½
                    (1940) 65m COL bw (AKA: STREETS OF MISSING WOMEN)

Preston Foster (Dan Walters), Ann Dvorak (Jo), Douglas Fowley (Eddie Morgan), Wynne Gibson (Annie), Arthur Loft (Steve Mason), Bruce Bennett (Budge), Eddie Acuff (Scotty), Bradley Page (Al), Linda Winters (Tricks), Beatrice Blinn (Daisy), Dick Wessel (Willie); Peggy Shannon (Nellie).

A wall-to-wall assortment of characters fills this weak melodrama about a heroic sailor who braves a gang-run nightspot to steal away the murderous leader's woman. Wandering in and out, the varied cast practically overshadows the cumbersome story. Lacking any spark of spontaneity, it simply struggles through the motions, dragging plot development far behind.

d, Sidney Salkow; w, Harold Shumate (based on a story by Tay Garnett and Howard Higgin); ph, Benjamin Kline; ed, Al Clark; md, Morris Stoloff.

Crime   **(PR:A   MPAA:NR)**

CAFE MASCOT*½   (1936, Brit.) 77m Pascal/PAR-British bw

Geraldine Fitzgerald (Moira O'Flynn), Derrick de Marney (Jerry Wilson), George Mozart (George Juppley), Clifford Heatherley (Dudhope), Richard Norris (Nat Dawson), Paul Neville (Peters), Julian Vedey (Francois), George Turner (Miles), Geoffrey Clark (Benton).

When a man finds 1,000 pounds in a taxi, he uses it to help poor Irish girl Fitzgerald. Typically bleak comedy from the bleak British film industry of the 1930s.

p, Gabriel Pascal; d, Lawrence Huntington; w, Gerald Elliott (based on a story by Cecil Lewis).

Comedy   **(PR:A   MPAA:NR)**

CAFE METROPOLE***   (1937) 84m FOX bw

Adolphe Menjou (Monsieur Victor), Loretta Young (Laura Ridgeway), Tyrone Power (Alexis Penayev, Alexander Brown), Charles Winninger (Joseph Ridgeway), Gregory Ratoff (Paul), Christian Rub (Leroy), Helen Westley (Margaret Ridgeway), Georges Renavent (Maitre d'Hotel), Ferdinand Gottschalk (Monnett), Hal K. Dawson (Thorndyke), Leonid Kinskey (Artist), Louis Mercier (Courtroom Attendant), Jules Raucourt, Albert Pollet, Gino Corrado, and Eugene Borden (Waiters), Rolfe Sedan (Flower Clerk), Albert Morin, Charles De Ravenne (Page Boys), Leonid Snegoff, Octavio J. Giraud (Porters), Fred Cavens (Train Guard), Jean De Briac, Jean Perry (Gendarmes), Andre Cheron (Croupier), Jean Masset, Mario Dominici, George Herbert (Players), George Andre Beranger (Hat Clerk), Paul Porcasi (Police Official), Jacques Lory (Elevator Operator), Fredrik Vogeding (Attendant).

Made in the depths of the Depression, CAFE METROPOLE was a typical lightweight comedy aimed at raising the emotional level of an audience desperately looking for some humor in their dismal existences. Menjou is headwaiter at the Cafe and has been syphoning money from the till. He learns that the auditors are on their way and tries his fortune at the game of Baccarat and defeats Power, who promptly writes a bad check for almost half a million francs. Menjou is livid and orders Power, a young, handsome and penniless Princetonian from a good family, to follow orders and court Loretta Young, a wealthy heiress from the U.S. To do this, Power must pose as Russian royalty. Problems arise when Power really falls for Young (they made three films within a year, and it happened every time). Then the real Russian prince (played by Ratoff, who wrote the story), now a waiter at the restaurant, resents the use of his name and asks that Power cease and desist. Menjou pays Ratoff off. Now Menjou concocts a twisted scheme. He tells Young's father, Winninger, that Power is a fraud and has taken one million francs from Menjou. Winninger pays Menjou for the information and orders

Young to stay away from Power. Spunky as ever, she refuses and marries Power. In the end, Menjou keeps the check to cover the bad one Power wrote in reel one. Young and Power will presumably spend the remainder of their lives spending the money that Winninger has earned in the auto parts industry. It's a pleasant film, with some excellent moments.

p, Nunnally Johnson; d, Edward H. Griffith; w, Jacques Deval (based on a story by Gregory Ratoff); ph, Lucien Andriot; md, Louis Silvers; ed, Irene Morra; cos; Royer; art d, Duncan Crammer, Hans Peters; set d, Thomas Little.

Comedy   **(PR:A-C   MPAA:NR)**

CAFE SOCIETY**   (1939) 83m PAR bw

Madeleine Carroll (Christopher West), Fred MacMurray (Chick O'Bannon), Shirley Ross (Bells Browne), Jessie Ralph (Mrs. De Witt), Claude Gillingwater (Old Christopher West), Allyn Joslyn (Sonny De Witt), Don Alvarado (Prince Vladimir), Mira McKinney (Secretary), Hilda Plowright (Maid), Charles Trowbridge (Mr. Tiller), Paul Hurst (Bartender), Cupid Ainsworth (Bobo), Mary Parker (Southern Girl), Robert Emmett Keane (Random), Frank Dawson (Butler), Dorothy Tree (Lady Photographer), Harlan Briggs (Justice of the Peace), Frances Raymond (Wife of Justice of the Peace), Gloria Williams (Nurse), Gus Glassmire (Doctor), Lillian Yarbo (Mattie Harriett), Johnny Day (Reporter), Eddie Borden (Les), Eddie Dunn (Newsreel Reporter), Ruth Rogers, Gwen Kenyon (Checkroom Girls), Luana Walters (Cigarette Girl), Al Hill (Cab Driver), Helen Lynd (Millie), Max Wagner, Heidy Masbury, Bryant Washburn, Reginald Simpson (Guests), Edward Gargan (Cop), Ethel Clayton (Woman), Dolores Casey, Dorothy Dayton, Harriette Haddon, Judy King, Joyce Mathews, Janet Waldo, Norah Gale (Girls).

Typical screwball comedy starring MacMurray as a shipboard news reporter who meets high-society gal Carroll. Carroll seduces MacMurray by having him take cheesecake photographs of her and soon the couple elope. MacMurray is shocked to find out that the only reason for the hasty marriage is that Carroll wanted to get her name in Joslyn's society column. The comedy then degenerates into the usual "Taming of the Shrew" antics with heavy participation from Gillingwater as the rich girl's uncle. Good cast rescues the trite material.

p, Jeff Lazarus; d, Edward H. Griffith; w, Virginia Van Upp (based on a story by Van Upp); ph, Ted Tetzlaff; ed, Paul Weatherwax; md, Boris Morros; art d, Hans Dreier, Ernst Fegte; m/l, Burton Lane, Frank Loesser.

Comedy   **(PR:A   MPAA:NR)**

CAGE OF EVIL**   (1960) 70m UA bw

Ron Foster (Scott Harper), Pat Blair (Holly Taylor), Harp McGuire (Murray Kearns), John Maxwell (Dan Melrose), Preston Hanson (Tom Colton), Doug Henderson (Barney), Helen Kleeb, (Mrs. Melton), Hugh Sanders (Martin Bender), Robert Shayne (Victor Delmar), Owen Bush (Sgt. Ray Dean), Ted Knight (Ivers), Howard McLeod (Romack), Eva Brent (Lucille Baron), Joe Hamilton (Dewey), Pat Miller (Ozzie Bell), Ralph Sanford (Bar Man), Ralph Neff (Plumber), Jack Kenney (Lewis), Jack Tesler (Francen), Gregg Martell (Mick Borden), Abel Franco (1st Mexican Cop), Henry Delgado (2nd Mexican Cop).

Passed over for promotion to lieutenant for the third time, police detective Foster turns bad. With the help of shady blonde Blair he plots to kill a jewel thief he's investigating and take off to Mexico with the gems and the blonde. Things don't work out that way and the conclusion finds Foster shot dead and Blair in the clink. Not bad Grade-B crime stuff.

p, Robert E. Kent; d, Edward L. Cahn; w, Orville H. Hampton (based on a story by Hampton and Alexander Richard); ph, Maury Gertsman; m, Paul Sawtell; ed, Grant Whytock; art d, Serge Krizman.

Crime   **(PR:A-C   MPAA:NR)**

CAGE OF GOLD**   (1950, Brit.) 83m GFD/Ealing bw

Jean Simmons (Judith Moray), David Farrar (Bill Brennan), James Donald (Alan Keane), Herbert Lom (Rahman), Madeleine Lebeau (Marie), Maria Mauban (Antoinette), Bernard Lee (Inspector Grey), Gregoire Aslan (Dupont), Gladys Henson (Waddy), Harcourt Williams (Dr. Kearns), Leo Ferre (Victor).

Okay crime drama starring Simmons as a young bride whose new husband, Farrar, is "killed" soon after their marriage. The bride recovers and marries Donald. Suddenly the "dead" husband returns and attempts to blackmail his former wife in the old badger game. The blackmailer is killed and eventually Simmons and Donald are cleared of the murder. Cliche-ridden script is helped from a good performance by Simmons. Look for Herbert Lom in a small role as the ringleader of a gang of smugglers.

p, Michael Balcon; d, Basil Dearden; w, Jack Wittingham, Paul Stein (based on a story by Wittingham); ph, Douglas Slocombe; ed, Peter Tanner.

Crime Drama   **(PR:A   MPAA:NR)**

CAGE OF NIGHTINGALES, A***   (1947, Fr.) 78m Gaumont bw

Noel-Noel (Clement Mathieu), Micheline Francey (Martine), George Biscot (Raymond), Rene Genin (Maxence), Rene Blancard (Rachin), Marguerite Ducouret (Mme. Martine), Marcel Praince (The Chairwoman), Marthe Mellot (Old Marie), Georges Paulais (Mr. Langlois), Andre Nicolle (Mon. de la Prade), Richard Francoeur (Mon. de Mezeres), Jean Morel (New Director), Roger Vincent (Academy Member), Michel Francois (Laquerec), Roger Krebs (Laugier) and the Little Singers of the Wooden Cross.

An exhilarating attempt to merge a writer's life with his subject matter. Noel-Noel writes of his life at a reform school in a novel conveniently titled A Cage of Nightingales. The hungry writer takes a job with toy airplane merchant Biscot. Thoughtfully, Biscot has the novel published in the Paris Telegram. Francey, Noel-Noel's girl, reads the story as we see flashbacks of Noel-Noel's brutal reform school days. Overshadowing their delinquency, the boys are shown as members of an angelic choral group. Fatefully, they are saved from death as the school is destroyed by lightning while they are at a wedding. The treatment is both refreshing and starkly realistic, devoting equal energies to the sensitivity and cruelty of youth. (In French; English sub-titles.)

d, Jean Dreville; w, Noel-Noel and Rene Wheeler (dialog by Noel-Noel); ph, Paul Cotteret; m, Paul Cloerec; English titles, Edwin Denby.

Musical Drama (PR:A MPAA:NR)

CAGED*** (1950) 96m WB bw

Eleanor Parker (Marie Allen), Agnes Moorehead (Ruth Benton), Ellen Corby (Emma), Hope Emerson (Evelyn Harper), Betty Garde (Kitty Stark), Jan Sterling (Smoochie), Lee Patrick (Elvira Powell), Olive Deering (June), Jane Darwell (Isolation Matron), Gertrude Michael (Georgia), Sheila Stevens (Helen), Joan Miller (Claire), Marjorie Crossland (Cassie), Gertrude Hoffman (Millie), Lynn Sherman (Ann), Queenie Smith (Mrs. Warren), Naomi Robison (Hattie), Esther Howard (Grace), Marlo Dwyer (Julie), Wanda Tynan (Meta), Peggy Wynne (Lottie), Frances Morris (Mrs. Foley), Edith Evanson (Miss Barker), Yvonne Rob (Elaine), Ann Tyrell (Edna), Eileen Stevens (Infirmary Nurse), June Whipple (Ada), Sandra Gould (Skip), Grace Hayes (Mugging Matron), Taylor Holmes (Sen. Donnolly), Don Beddoe (Commissioner Walker), Charles Meredith (Chairman), George Baxter (Jeffries), Guy Beach (Mr. Cooper), Harlan Warde (Dr. Ashton), Bill Hunter (Guard), Barbara Esback, Marjorie Wood, Evelyn Dockson, Hazel Keener, Jane Crowley (Matrons), Gail Bonney, Doris Kemper, Lovyss Bradley, Ezelle Poule, Margaret Lambert, Eva Nelson, Rosemary O'Neil, Jean Calhoun, Nita Talbot, Marie Melish, Pauline Creasman, Joyce Newhard, Helen Eby-Rock, Sheila Stuart, Claudia Cauldwell, Tina Menard, Carole Shannon, Gladys Roach, Virginia Engels (Inmates), Bill Haade (Laundryman), Ruth Warren (Miss Lyons), Davison Clark (Doctor), Pauline Drake (Doctor's Wife), Gracille LaVinder (Visiting Room Matron), Bill Wayne (Ada's Father), Doris Whitney (Woman Visitor), Grace Hampton, Helen Mowery, Helen Spring, Frances Henderson (Women).

The best, if not the most brutal, woman's prison film ever made was CAGED which offered no relief to its victimized protagonist, Parker, and no quarter to the audience. Parker begins as a sweet, naive, and generous young lady who unwittingly sits in a car while her scheming husband robs a gas station and is killed. She is convicted of being an accomplice and sent to a tough women's prison. Here the innocent 19-year-old is quickly brutalized by the crude inmates and sadistic guards, particularly the Amazonian (6 foot 2 inch) Hope Emerson, a lesbian matron who enjoys mistreating inmates, especially Parker whom she throws into solitary and later shaves her head almost to the bone to instill discipline as well as provide perverse pleasure. Even Jane Darwell, normally a kindly motherly type, is a vicious matron matching Emerson's repugnant sadism. Aside from the timid Corby, frightened of every shadow, none of the inmates has a smidgen of decency. Sterling, Garde, Patrick, Miller, Crossland, and Stevens each work their corrupting wiles on the young girl. To add to her misery she discovers herself pregnant, and later gives birth to a child which she is compelled to give up for adoption. By this time she is at wit's end and Garde attempts to recruit her into a prostitution ring, saying she can get her paroled if she agrees to join a vice ring operated by a state senator, slimy Taylor Holmes (who made a career out of such parts, none more repulsive than in THE KISS OF DEATH). At first she resists, but after Garde murders Emerson and another inmate, Michael, goes stark raving mad, Parker has had enough. She agrees to whore on the streets, anything, to escape the prison. Oily Holmes arranges for her release but the politically helpless warden, Moorehead, the only upstanding person in the entire film, knows her destination. She watches Parker leave the prison, then sadly comments; "She'll be back." CAGED is an utterly ruthless film, grimly directed by Cromwell and based on research gleamed by writer Kellogg who spent some months in female prisons. Even Guthrie's photography is alarmingly contrasting, and saturating the film is an uncomfortable air of claustrophia. Parker gives the performance of her career in a film that realistically portrays the fate of prisoners hardened behind the bars of crude prisons, made into murderous, calculating beasts while society remains unconcerned. The film is a shocker, far surpassing similar films such as LADIES OF THE BIG HOUSE, 1931, in portraying villainous females and a dehumanizing penal system. Not for youngsters or the fainthearted. (Remade as HOUSE OF WOMEN.)

p, Jerry Wald; d, John Cromwell; w, Virginia Kellogg, Bernard C. Schoenfeld; ph, Carl Guthrie; m, Max Steiner; ed, Owen Marks; art d, Charles H. Clarke; set d, G. W. Berntsen; makeup, Perc Westmore, Ed Voight.

Prison Drama (PR:O MPAA:NR)

CAGED FURY** (1948) 60m PAR bw

Richard Denning (Blaney Lewis), Sheila Ryan (Kit Warren), Mary Beth Hughes (Lola Tremaine), Buster Crabbe (Smiley), Frank Wilcox (Dan Corey).

Fair circus thriller features Crabbe as a murderous lion-tamer who engineers a fatal accident for his lady assistant, Hughes, so he can move in on new gal Ryan. No one suspects murder until the jealous animal trainer tries to bump off rival circus performer Denning. Crabbe makes good his escape and returns to the scene of the crime a year later to try to kill Denning again. During his attempt the tents catch fire, the animals are turned loose, and justice triumphs. Entertaining and often exciting programmer.

p, William Pine, William Thomas; d, William Berke; w, David Lange; ph, Ellis W. Carter; ed, Howard Smith.

Drama (PR:A MPAA:NR)

CAGED HEAT (SEE: RENEGADE GIRLS, 1974)

CAGLIOSTRO** (1975, Ital.) 103m FOX c

Bekim Fehmiu (Cagliostro Charlatan), Curt Jurgens (Cardinal Braschi), Rosanna Schiaffino (Lorenza Balsamo), Evelyn Stewart (Serafina Cagliostro), Massimo Girotti (Casanova), Robert Alda (Pope Clement XIII).

Confusing mishmash of ESP, black magic, religion, and history in the first film produced by jewel merchant Puttignani and photographer Pettinari. Story concerns Fehmiu as the title character who founded the Masons in Europe shortly before the French Revolution. Fehmiu combines reincarnation, ESP, and alchemy as a quasi religious-moral response to the omnipotence of existing papal power. Fehmiu is caught, tried,and sentenced to death by the Inquisition, but his sentence is reduced to life imprisonment by a new pope played by Jurgens. The formation of Fehmiu's secret society is interesting, but the script bogs down the premise by introducing an unnecessary subplot involving a lookalike who causes some trouble for Fehmiu and the Jesuits who are trying to capture him. (Orson Wells did it better, if not hammier, in BLACK MAGIC.)

p, Rodolfo Puttignani; d, Daniele Pettinari; w, Pier Carpi, Enrico Bonacorti, Pettinari; ph, Giuseppe Pinori (Eastmancolor); m, Manuel De Sica; ed, Adriano Tagliavia; art d, Giorgio Desideri.

Drama (PR:C MPAA:NR)

CAHILL, UNITED STATES MARSHAL** (1973) 103m WB c

John Wayne (J. D. Cahill), George Kennedy (Fraser), Gary Grimes (Danny Cahill), Neville Brand (Lightfoot), Clay O'Brien (Billy Joe Cahill), Marie Windsor (Mrs. Green), Morgan Paull (Struther), Dan Vadis (Brownie), Royal Dano (MacDonald), Scott Walker (Ben Tildy), Denver Pyle (Denver), Jackie Coogan (Charlie Smith), Rayford Barnes (Pee Wee Simser), Dan Kemp (Joe Meehan), Harry Carey, Jr. (Hank), Walter Barnes (Sheriff Grady), Paul Fix (Old Man), Pepper Martin (Hard Case), Vance Davis (Negro), Ken Wolger (Boy), Hank Worden (Undertaker), James Nusser (Doctor), Murray MacLeod (Deputy Gordine), Hunter von Leer (Deputy Jim Kane).

The Duke in his waning years stars as a busy U. S. Marshal who encounters trouble with his own young sons, Grimes and O'Brien, when they participate in a bank robbery led by the villainous Kennedy. The boys aren't really bad, and the motivation for their participation in the robbery is neglect by their lawman father. Wayne sees the error of his child-rearing ways, makes his peace with his sons, and catches Kennedy to boot. The moral message gets a bit too preachy at times and the performances are somewhat wooden. The final shootout is pretty bloody.

p, Michael Wayne; d, Andrew V. McLaglen; w, Harry Julian Fink, Rita Fink (based on a story by Barney Slater); ph, Joseph Biroc (Panavision, Technicolor); m, Elmer Bernstein; ed, Robert L. Simpson; art d, Walter Simonds.

Western **Cas.** (PR:C MPAA:PG)

CAIN AND MABEL** (1936) 89m COS/WB bw

Marion Davies (Mabel O'Dare), Clark Gable (Larry Cain), Allen Jenkins (Dodo), Roscoe Karns (Reilly), Walter Catlett (Jake Sherman), David Carlyle (Ronny Cauldwell), Hobart Cavanaugh (Milo), Ruth Donnelly (Aunt Mimi), Pert Kelton (Toddy), William Collier, Sr. (Pop Walters), Sammy White (Specialty), E. E. Clive (Charles Fendwick), Allen Pomeroy (Tom Reed), Robert Middlemass (Cafe Proprietor), Joseph Crehan (Reed's Manager), Eily Malyon (The Old Maid).

The music is better than the acting in CAIN AND MABEL. One of the largest disasters of 1936 despite Gable, a raft of superior second bananas, and a handful of some of the best music Harry Warren and Al Dubin ever wrote. Still, none of it could triumph over the inept performance by Marion Davies, whose career was already dim by this time. Publisher William Randolph Hearst, Davies's lover, prevailed on pal Jack Warner to hire Gable away from MGM as Marion's co-star. She's a musical comedy star, he's a heavyweight boxer. Both need something to help their careers. Roscoe Karns concocts a publicity romance but that takes second place to reality when Clark and Marion realize they are really in love. And that's about it. Along the way, there are several spectacular production numbers, singing, dancing, boxing, and yawns. Marion was in her late thirties at this time and a bit long in the tooth to play the naive type. The action off-screen was even more intriguing: Gable was forced to shave off his mustache because director Bacon thought a boxer should be clean-faced; Hearst was angry at MGM for having rejected Marion for two films, Producer Irving Thalberg cast wife Norma Shearer both times (THE BARRETTS OF WIMPOLE STREET and MARIE ANTOINETTE); Hearst was also jealous of Dick Powell's appeal for Marion and nixed the young crooner (Lucky Dick!) for the second lead. In one sequence, Marion, The Ideal Woman, just stands there as hundreds of actors move around her. The entire number revolves around Marion, but she does absolutely nothing. It's hysterical to watch and even funnier if you look closely at the sequence with the enormous white pipe organ. One of the studio workmen wandered across the stage at the height of the number and the boo-boo was only discovered in the editing room. It was impossible to totally cut the nameless grip and the cost of re-takes would have been prohibitive, so the quick shot of the anonymous workman stayed in all prints.

p, Sam Bischoff; d, Lloyd Bacon; w, Laird Doyle (based on a story by H. C. Witwer); ph, George Barnes; ed; William Holmes; md, Leo F. Forbstein; m/l, Harry Warren, Al Dubin; ch, Bobby Connolly.

Musical Comedy (PR:A MPAA:NR)

CAINE MUTINY, THE**** (1954), 123m COL c

Humphrey Bogart (Capt. Queeg), Jose Ferrer (Lt. Barney Greenwald), Van Johnson (Lt. Steve Maryk), Fred MacMurray (Lt. Tom Keefer), Robert Francis (Ensign Willie Keith), May Wynn (May Wynn), Tom Tully (Capt. DeVriess), E. G. Marshall (Lt. Cmdr. Challee), Arthur Franz (Lt. Paynter), Lee Marvin (Meatball), Warner Anderson (Capt. Blakely), Claude Akins (Horrible), Katharine Warren (Mrs. Keith), Jerry Paris (Ensign Harding), Steve Brodie (Chief Budge), Todd Karns (Stilwell), Whit Bissell (Lt. Cmdr. Dickson), James Best (Lt. Jorgenson), Joe Haworth (Ensign Carmody), Guy Anderson (Ensign Rabbit), James Edwards (Whittaker), Don Dubbins (Urban), David Alpert (Engstrand).

First a Pulitzer Prize novel, then a Broadway play, then this film, and in each incarnation it has enough merit to stand on its own. Francis, Johnson, and MacMurray are shipmates aboard the *Caine*, a destroyer-cum-minesweeper. The time is early in WW II, Capt. Tully is replaced by Capt. Philip Francis Queeg (Bogart in one of his greatest performances). Bogart immediately establishes his power over the men and his neurosis about cleanliness. He is so intent on running a spotless ship that he berates a young tar while in the midst of target practice and doesn't pay attention to the *Caine*, which promptly sails in a circle and cuts its own tow line. In a later episode, Bogart pulls the *Caine* away from shore when the ship comes under enemy guns. He signals his departure by tossing a yellow dye marker in the water. When Bogart asks his junior officers for help, he is met with stony stares. A series of incidents follow which indicate that Bogart is under stress. Johnson keeps a log on Bogart's behavior and MacMurray insidiously plants the seed that the captain may be about to go off the deep end. During a storm at sea, Bogart appears to be indecisive and Johnson invokes a Navy rule regarding relief of a captain if an emergency transpires. The ship is saved but Johnson is court-martialed. Ferrer is assigned to defend the young lieutenant against E. G. Marshall for the Navy's prosecution. The trial is a seesaw as evidence mounts against Johnson when his compatriots all back away from assuming any responsibility for his actions, even though they encouraged them at the time. The denouement occurs when Ferrer gets Bogart on the stand and proceeds to destroy the already shaky psyche of the old sailor. It's a masterful piece of writing and performing as the two men square off against each other. In the movie's most famous scene, Bogart reaches for the steel balls that he carries (the way some people carry "worry beads"), and begins to play with them to ease the tension of the moment. The other naval officers now realize that Bogart is cracking up and the charges against Johnson are dismissed. Later, at a celebration, Ferrer arrives and tells off the crew, citing Bogart's long record as a lifetime sailor who was protecting United States shores years before these salt water daffies entered the wartime service. Ferrer finishes his monolog by tossing his champagne in the real perpetrator's face—MacMurray. In a year other than the one in which ON THE WATERFRONT was released, this might have won as Best Picture and Bogart might have garnered the Best Actor Oscar. Technical credits are all excellent, especially the typhoon scene created by Lawrence Butler. The scenes with Bogart disintegrating in the witness chair have become part of the American memory. This is a don't-miss picture, unnecessarily beefed up because of a concocted love story between May Wynn and Robert Francis that goes nowhere but adds to an already-fat script. May Wynn, by the way, uses her own name in the film. As the character did not appear in the play, Wouk couldn't disagree. Bogart was later asked how he managed to totally capture the paranoid personality of Queeg. "Simple," growled Bogie, "everybody knows I'm nuts, anyway."

p, Stanley Kramer; d, Edward Dmytryk; w, Stanley Roberts (based on the play and novel by Herman Wouk); ph, Franz Planer (Technicolor); m, Max Steiner; ed, William Lyon, Henry Batista; art d, Cary Odell; spec eff, Lawrence Butler; m/l, Wouk, Fred Karger, Jimmy McHugh, Clarence Gaskill; cos, Jean Louis.

Drama   **(PR:A   MPAA:NR)**

CAIN'S WAY*   (1969) 93m M.D.A. Associates/Fanfare c
(AKA: CAIN'S CUTTHROATS, THE BLOOD SEEKERS)
John Carradine (*Preacher Sims*), Scott Brady (*Capt. Cain*), Adair Jamison (*Cain's Girl*), Robert Dix (*Gang Chief*), Teresa Thaw, Bruce Kimball, Darwin Joston, Willis Martin, Russ McCubbin, Valda Mansen, Andy Moon.

Slow-moving, pretentious, bloody western set during the Civil War stars Brady as a man whose family has been slaughtered by a gang of Confederate renegades led by Dix (Brady's wife was black). Together with preacher Carradine (who is also a bounty-hunter) Brady tracks down the killers, cuts off their heads, and keeps them as trophies. These moments are intercut with modern-day footage of renegade motorcycle gangs raising hell in a small town. The effect is supposed to be a condemnation/comparison of violence throughout American history. It fails miserably.

p, Kent Osborne, Budd Dell; d, Osborne; w, Wilton Denmark; ph, Ralph Waldo (Eastmancolor).

Western   **(PR:O   MPAA:R)**

CAIRO½   (1942) 101m MGM bw
Jeanette MacDonald (*Marcia Warren*), Robert Young (*Homer Smith*), Ethel Waters (*Cleona Jones*), Reginald Owen (*Philo Cobson*), Grant Mitchell (*O.H.P. Boggs*), Lionel Atwill (*Teutonic Gentleman*), Eduardo Ciannelli (*Ahmed Ben Hassan*), Mitchell Lewis (*Ludwig*), Dooley Wilson (*Hector*), Larry Nunn (*Bernie*), Dennis Hoey (*Col. Woodhue*), Mona Barrie (*Mrs. Morrison*), Rhys Williams (*Strange Man*), Cecil Cunningham (*Mme. Laruga*), Harry Worth (*Bartender*), Frank Richards (*Alfred*).

A disappointing hodge-podge of music and intrigue that marked the end of MacDonald's long-term MGM contract. Young is a war correspondent on his way to Cairo. His ship is torpedoed and he winds up on a raft with Owen. They land in the Libyan desert and have to part when Nazi soldiers approach. But first Owen tells Young to make contact with Barrie in Cairo—she can be recognized by the cocktail she always orders at the same bar every night. Owen claims to be a British spy and the info he wants passed on is classified. Young arrives in Cairo, meets Barrie, and becomes enamored of MacDonald (traveling with her maid, Waters), an American movie queen in Africa to entertain the English troops. Young is informed by Barrie (in reality, a nazi spy) that MacDonald is an enemy agent. Now Young learns that Ciannelli (as an Arab) has invented a device that can drop bombs from a plane via radio control. A chase across the desert leads to one of the most preposterous clues ever. Young has been tossing hundred dollar bills along the sand (like the bread crumbs in the children's tale "Hansel and Gretel") until the trail ceases at a pyramid. MacDonald recognizes the clue as "C-Notes" and so she hits a few high C's and the door to the pyramid swings open! Young is saved and everyone is happy, except he patrons who paid good money to see this turkey. Lots of good music from several famous tunesmiths and a few fine supporting bits, most notabley Hoey as Col. Woodhue. Born Samuel David Hyams, Hoey was always a pleasure to watch, especially in his patented bumbling Scotland Yard man, Inspector Lestrade, in practically all the Sherlock Holmes films.

p, (uncredited but probably Joseph L. Mankiewicz); d, W. S. Van Dyke II; w, John McClain (based on an idea by Ladislas Fodor); ph, Ray June; m, Herbert Stothart; ed, James E. Newcom; md, Georgie Stoll; art d, Cedric Gibbons; set d, Edwin S. Willis; cos, Kalloch; m/l, Leo Delibes, Alfred De Musset, Arthur Schwartz, E. Y. Harburg, L. Wolfe Gilbert, Lewis F. Muir, Harold Arlen.

Musical/Spy Drama   **(PR:A   MPAA:NR)**

CAIRO**   (1963) 92m MGM bw
George Sanders (*Maj. Pickering*), Richard Johnson (*Ali*), Faten Hamama (*Amina*), Eric Pohlmann (*Nicodemus*), Ahmed Mazhar (*Kerim*), Walter Rilla (*Kuchuk*), John Meillon (*Willy*), Kamal El Shennawy (*Ghattas*), Chewikar (*Marie*), Salah Nazmi (*Commandant*), Mona (*Mamba*), Said Abu Bakr (*Osman*), Salah Mansour (*Doctor*), Abdel Khalek Saleh (*Assistant Minister*), Youssef Shaaban (*2nd Officer*), Capt. Mohamed Abdel Rahman (*4th Officer*).

Competent caper film shot on location in Egypt and starring Sanders as a criminal mastermind who arrives in Cairo to steal the Tut-ankh-amen jewels. The plot was hatched while Sanders was in prison and upon his release he forms a gang of thieves and sets the plan in motion. It fails when a series of minor oversights and miscalculations doom the robbers. The suspense is weakened by some glaring plot holes and a museum that is ridiculously easy to rob.

p, Ronald Kinnoch; d, Wolf Rilla; w, Joanne Court (based on the novel *The Asphalt Jungle* by W. R. Burnett); ph, Desmond Dickinson; m, Kenneth V. Jones; ed, Bernard Gribble.

Crime   **(PR:A   MPAA:NR)**

CAIRO ROAD**   (1950, Brit.) 88m AB-Pathe bw
Eric Portman (*Col. Youssef Bey*), Laurence Harvey (*Lt. Mourad*), Maria Mauban (*Marie*), Camelia (*Anna Michelis*), Harold Lang (*Humble*), Coco Aslan (*Lombardi*), Karel Stepanek (*Edouardo Pavlis*), John Bailey (*Doctor*), Martin Boddey (*Maj. Ahmed Mustafa*), John Gregson (*Coastguard*), Marne Maitland (*Gohari*), Abraham Sofaer (*Commandant*).

Good locations (Cairo, Port Said, and the Suez) help this otherwise average crime tale concerning narcotics agent Portman and his bumbling assistant, Harvey, as they battle against a world-wide hashish smuggling operation that has turned the Middle East into a haven for junkies. Uneven and slow-moving.

p, Aubrey Baring, Maxwell Setton; d, David Macdonald; w, Robert Westerby; ph, Oswald Morris; ed, Peter Taylor.

Crime   **(PR:A   MPAA:NR)**

CALABUCH**½   (1956, Span./Ital.) 98m CIFTESA bw
Edmund Gwenn (*Professor George Hamilton*), Valentina Cortese (*TeacherDonna Sophia*), Franco Fabrizi (*Langosta*).

Strange little comedy starring Gwenn as a famous atomic scientist who tries to escape the terrible nuclear world he has helped create by vacationing in a small village on the Spanish seaside. the villagers accept him and make him one of their own. Gwenn relaxes and enjoys his idyllic existence away from the "bomb" until he is discovered and brought back to civilization. Most of the humor is derived from playful criticisms of Spanish institutions, i. e. bullfighting, the police, and the government.

d, Luis G. Berlanga; w, Berlanga, Ennio Flaiano, Leonardo Martin, Florentino Soria, Guerrini; ed, Pepita Orduna.

Comedy   **(PR:A   MPAA:NR)**

CALAMITY JANE**½   (1953) 100m WB c
Doris Day (*Calamity Jane*), Howard Keel (*Wild Bill Hickok*), Allyn McLerie (*Katie Brown*), Philip Carey (*Lt. Gilmartin*), Dick Wesson (*Francis Fryer*), Paul Harvey (*Henry Miller*), Chubby Johnson (*Rattlesnake*), Gale Robbins (*Adelaide Adams*).

A weak imitation of a Betty Hutton picture with Doris doing her best to light a fire under herself and provide the energy the script ignored. Keel is positively statuesque (not his bearing, but his performance) as Wild Bill Hickok, and the whole film fails to be much more than a mild carbon of a much better project called ANNIE GET YOUR GUN. The highlight of the comedy in the pallid script is Howard and Doris cross-dressing. Eleven songs sprinkle the action, the best of which, having Oscared, became a standard, and a million seller for Doris is "Secret Love." If there really weren't such a fabulous character as Calamity Jane (much more realistically played by Jean Arthur in THE PLAINSMAN), this might have been adequate. But truth is not only stranger, it's also a lot more entertaining than fiction—especially in the case of this mild filmbio.

p, William Jacobs; d, David Butler; w, James O'Hanlon; ph, Wilfrid M. Cline (Technicolor); md, Ray Heindorf; ed, Irene Morra; m/l, Sammy Fain, Paul Francis Webster; ch, Jack Donohue.

Musical/Biography   **(PR:AA   MPAA:NR)**

CALAMITY JANE AND SAM BASS**   (1949) 85m UNIV c
Yvonne De Carlo (*Calamity Jane*), Howard Duff (*Sam Bass*), Dorothy Hart (*Katherine Egan*), Willard Parker (*Sheriff Will Egan*), Norman Lloyd (*Jim Murphy*), Lloyd Bridges (*Joel Collins*), Marc Lawrence (*Dean*), Houseley Stevenson (*Dakota*), Milburn Stone (*Abe Jones*), Clifton Young (*Link*), John Rodney (*Morgan*), Roy Roberts (*Marshal Peak*), Ann Doran (*Mrs. Egan*), Charles Cane (*J. Wells*), Walter Baldwin (*Doc Purdy*).

Once again Hollywood plays fast and loose with historical accuracy in this dull oater that glamorizes the life of bloody outlaw Sam Bass. Story concerns Duff as Bass who is thrown into a life of crime after killing a man in self-defense. Romance is worked into the gun-play when good-girl Hart falls for the outlaw, but she loses the battle for his affections to the wicked, more colorful DeCarlo as Calamity Jane. Inevitable conclusion has Duff mortally wounded committing his last robbery while the horrified DeCarlo looks on. (Bass was shot to death by lawmen in 1878 near Bushy Creek, Texas; he died in the arms of Texas Ranger John B. Jones, gasping the last words: "Let me go—the world is bobbing around." He never met Calamity Jane.)

p, Leonard Goldstein; d, George Sherman; w, Maurice Geraghty, Melvin Levy (based on a story by Sherman); ph, Irving Glassberg (Technicolor); md, Milton Schwarzwald; ed, Edward Curtiss; art d, Bernard Herzbrun, Richard Riedel, set d, Russell A. Gausman, Al Fields; cos, Yvonne Wood; makeup, Bud Westmore.

Western **(PR:A MPAA:NR)**

CALAMITY THE COW*½ (1967, Brit.) 59m Island-Shepperton/CFF c
John Moulder-Brown (Rob Grant), Elizabeth Dear (Jo Grant), Stephen Brown (Tim Lucas), Philip Collins (Mike Lucas), Josephine Gillick (Beth Lucas), Grant Taylor (Mr. Grant), Honor Shepherd (Mrs. Grant), Alastair Hunter (Kincaid), Desmond Carrington (Uncle Jim).

A group of children take an ill-treated cow and groom it into a dairy show entrant, saving it from evil rustlers in the bargain. Strictly for the kiddies.

p, Ian Dalrymple; d, David Eastman; w, Eastman, Kerry Eastman.

Children **(PR:AA MPAA:NR)**

CALCULATED RISK*½ (1963, Brit.) 72m McLeod/Bry c
William Lucas (Steve), John Rutland (Kip), Dilys Watling (Julie), Warren Mitchell (Simmie), Shay Gorman (Dodo), Terrence Cooper (Nodge), David Brierly (Ron).

While tunneling from a cellar into a bank vault, a gang of robbers accidentally set off an unexploded bomb from WW II. British crime melodrama has little going for it.

p, William McLeod; d, Norman Harrison; w, Edwin Richfield.

Crime **(PR:A MPAA:NR)**

CALCUTTA*** (1947) 83m PAR bw
Alan Ladd (Neale Gordon), Gail Russell (Virginia Moore), William Bendix (Pedro Blake), June Duprez (Marina Tanev), Lowell Gilmore (Eric Lasser), Edith King (Mrs. Smith), Paul Singh (Mul Raj Malik), Gavin Muir (Inspector Kendricks), John Whitney (Bill Cunningham), Benson Fong (Young Chinese Clerk), Don Beddoe (Jack Collins), Milton Parsons (Desk Clerk), Leslie Fong (Chinese Radio Man at Dinjhan), Jimmy Aubrey (Mac, Mechanic), Lee Tung Foo (Kim), Joey S. Ray (Bodyguard to Lasser), Beal Wong (Native Foreman at Dinjhan), Bruce Wong (Chinese Radio Man at Ed's Place), Eddie Das (Native Boss), Morton Lowry (Scarred Man), Mahmed Tahir (Native Waiter), Robert R. Stephenson, Fred Giermann, Harry Cording (Tea Planters), Marilyn Chow (Chinese Stewardess), Len Hendry (Starter), Eddie Hall (Copilot), Bobby Barber (Taxi Driver), Fred Nurney (Man in Cafe), Peter Cusanelli (Headwaiter), Carmen Beretta (Woman), John Benson (Pilot), Albert Pollet, Julio Bonini (Men), Erno Verebes (Frenchman), George Sorel (Croupier), Charles Stevens (Strangler), Adrienne D'Ambricourt (Croupier's Assistant), Moy Ming (Elderly Chinese Clerk), Shirley Lew (Mrs. Smith's Assistant Hairdresser), Barbara Jean Wong (Mrs. Smith's Manicurist), Leyland Hodgson, Frank Baker, Bruce Carruthers, Colin Kenny (Police Officers), Wong Artarne (Copilot), Madge E. Schofield (Hindu Servant Woman), Anandi Dhalwani (Hindu Woman), Eddie Leo (Jim Wong, Bank Clerk), Hassan Khayyam (Hindu Man), Suran Singh (Doorman), Lal Chand Mehra (Bar Captain), George Kirby (Day Desk Clerk), Bhoghwan Singh (Bar Boy), George Broughton (Hotel Guest), Aminta Dyne (Sleepy Woman), Bill Nind (Police Sergeant), Diane Ervin, Joy Harington (Hotel Guests).

Intrigue abounds in the exotic setting of this film where Ladd and Bendix are cargo plane pilots. When their buddy, Whitney, is found strangled in an alley, Ladd begins to investigate the murder, first questioning the dead man's fiancee, Russell, whom he first suspects of being involved in the killing. When Russell provides an alibi, Ladd softens toward her, although his liaison is not romantic; he has a sometimes girl, Duprez, who sings in the Chalgani Club owned by Gilmore. Still suspicious, Ladd takes a scarab diamond his dead friend had given his fiancee from Russell's hotel room and traces this to a jewelry store run by King, an obese, cigar-smoking woman oozing sinister intentions, and, through her, Singh, a gem smuggler. Ladd's inquiries begin to produce lethal results. After he finds a star sapphire and a bag of jewels hidden on board his transport plane, Ladd realizes that jewel smugglers are using his small airline to smuggle gems out of India and it was for this reason that his friend Whitney had been killed. Singh later confronts Ladd, attempting to kill him with a knife but he is shot to death before injuring Ladd. British inspector Muir first suspects Ladd of being involved in the smuggling ring but Ladd clears himself, then learns from a hotel clerk that Russell's alibi is fabricated. He confronts her, slapping her until she confesses that she was part of his friend's death and involved with the smugglers. Nightclub owner Gilmore (he is the head of the smuggling ring) arrives to threaten Ladd. Ladd struggles with Gilmore and shoots the smuggler with his own gun. He then calls Muir, telling the cop to come and get Russell. The film has a hefty chunk of plot from THE MALTESE FALCON and Ladd's rugged role is unabashedly drawn from Sam Spade. He is fair but tough and relentless, with a glacier attitude toward all women whom he distrusts. After Ladd calls the police, Russell is baffled by him, much the same way Mary Astor reacted to Bogart who turns her over to police in the 1941 FALCON. She draws close to him, purring, "But you said you were crazy about me." Ladd stares back without amour, growling, "Not that much." He next quotes a Gurkha saying, "Man who trust woman walk on duckweed over pond." Russell snarls back in anger, calling Ladd "sadistic and egotistical." He gives her a thin smile and says, "Maybe, but I'm still alive." Russell has killed her pal and she must answer for it, he says. She hasn't fooled him. "You counted on your beauty with guys, even ones you were going to kill." Before she is led away by police, Russell reveals her murderous nature, staring at Ladd and saying, "I would have hated to have killed you." Ladd is a strong lead here, even though his dedication to honor is always manifested by a doubled fist. Supporting player Bendix gives a fascinating performance at his smart-talking sidekick (they had been hard-nosed

buddies in THE BLUE DAHLIA and CHINA). Broadway stage star Edith King is a delight as the den mother to the underworld, side-mouthing her words a la Edward G. Robinson.

p, Seton I. Miller; d, John Farrow; w, Miller; ph, John Seitz; m, Victor Young; ed, Archie Marshek; art d, Hans Dreier, Franz Bachelin, set d, Sam Comer, Jack de Golconda; cos, Dorothy O'Hara; spec eff, Gordon Jennings; ch, Robert Jonay; m/l, "This is Madness" (Bernie Wayne, Ben Raleigh); French Lyrics, Ted Grouya.

Adventure **(PR:A MPAA:NR)**

CALENDAR, THE* (1931, Brit.) 80m Gainsborough/BL bw
Herbert Marshall, Edna Best, Anne Grey, Gordon Harker.

Mystery and deceit at the racetrack starring Best as the gold-digging gal who skips out on race horse owner Marshall after she has spent all of his money. She then marries the brother of the woman who trains her ex-beau's horses. Meanwhile Harker, Marshall's crooked butler, gets his boss drunk and convinces him to throw the next race so that he can get a better price the next time it runs. The butler gets caught, Marshall wins the race, and he marries his horse trainer. Boring melodrama based on an equally dull stage play by Edgar Wallace.

d, T. H. Hunter (based on the stage play by Edgar Wallace).

Drama **(PR:A MPAA:NR)**

CALENDAR, THE* (1948, Brit.) 79m GFD bw
Greta Gynt (Wenda), John McCallum (Garry), Raymond Lovell (Willie), Sonia Holm (Mollie), Leslie Dwyer (Hillcott), Charles Victor (John Dory), Felix Aylmer (Lord Forlingham), Sydney King (Tony), Noel Howlett (Lawyer), Barry Jones (Sir John Garth), Claude Bailey (Inspond), Desmond Roberts (Rainby), Diana Dors (Hawkins).

Uninspired remake of the tepid 1931 British melodrama of the same title. A different cast and crew don't seem to spark into life any of the elements that were lacking in the first version. Plot concerns the efforts of a crooked servant of racehorse owner McCallum to convince his boss to throw a race. No improvement.

p, J. Arthur Rank; d, Arthur Crabtree; w, Geoffrey Kerr (based on the play by Edgar Wallace); ph, Reg Wyer, Cyril J. Knowles.

Drama **(PR:A MPAA:NR)**

CALENDAR GIRL*½ (1947) 88m REP bw
Jane Frazee (Patricia O'Neil), William Marshall (Johnny Bennett), Gail Patrick (Olivia Radford), Kenny Baker (Byron Jones), Victor McLaglen (Matthew O'Neil), Irene Rich (Lulu Varden), James Ellison (Steve Adams), Janet Martin (Tessie), Franklin Pangborn (Dillingsworth/Dilly), Gus Schilling (Ed Gaskin), Charles Arnt (Capt. Olsen), Lou Nova (Clancy), Emory Parnell (The Mayor).

Overly talky turn-of-the-century musical about a group of young hopefuls whose paths cross at the local boarding house run by kind-hearted Miss Rich. Among the boarders seeking fame and fortune in New York are artist Ellison, composer Marshall, and the woman they fight over, Frazee. Ellison pays his bills by painting calendar portraits and he selects Frazee as his next model. This development causes tension in the romance between Marshall and Frazee. The conflicts are resolved through talk, not action, the songs are uninspired, and the direction lackidasical. Songs include: "Have I Told You Lately?" "A Lovely Night To Go Dreaming," "Calendar Girl," "New York's A Nice Place to Visit," and "A Bluebird Is Singing To Me."

p&d, Allan Dwan; w, Mary Loos, Richard Sale, Lee Loeb (based on a story by Loeb); ph, Reggie Lanning; ed, Fred Allen; md, Cy Feuer; orchestrations, Leo Arnaud; m/l, James McHugh, Harold Adamson.

Musical **(PR:A MPAA:NR)**

CALIFORNIA** (1946) 97m PAR c
Ray Milland (Jonathan Trumbo), Barbara Stanwyck (Lily Bishop), Barry Fitzgerald (Michael Fabian), George Coulouris (Pharoah Coffin), Albert Dekker (Mr. Pike), Anthony Quinn (Don Luis), Frank Faylen (Whitey), Gavin Muir (Booth Pennock), James Burke (Pokey), Eduardo Ciannelli (Padre), Roman Bohnen (Col. Stuart), Argentina Brunetti (Elvira), Howard Freeman (Sen. Creel), Julia Faye (Wagon Woman), Minerva Urecal (Emma), Dook McGill (Coffin's Servant), Crane Whitley (Abe Clinton), Gertrude Hoffman (Old Woman), Ethan Laidlaw (Reb), Philip Van Zandt (Mr. Gunce), Lane Chandler, Ralph Dunn, Joe Whitemead, Russ Clark, Jeff Corey, William Hall (Men), Tony Parton, Frederic Santley, George Melford, (Delegates), Dick Wessel (Blacksmith), Will Wright (Chairman).

Average western drama concerning the migration to California in 1848. Milland plays a deserter from the Union Army who drifts to California and tries his luck panning for gold. He becomes embroiled in the struggle for state sovereignty when he, gambler Stanwyck, and tough miner Fitzgerald battle against former slave trader Coulouris who attempts to turn the territory into his personal empire. Good cast and nice color photography help keeps this somewhat overlong effort interesting.

p, Seton I. Miller; d, John Farrow; w, Frank Butler, Theodore Strauss (based on a story by Boris Ingster); ph, Ray Rennahan (Technicolor); m, Victor Young; ed, Eda Warren; art d, Hans Dreier, Roland Anderson; set d, Sam Comer, Ray Moyer; m/l, E. Y. Harburg, Earl Robinson; spec eff, Gordon Jennings; cos, Edith Head, Gile Steele.

Western **(PR:A MPAA:NR)**

CALIFORNIA*   (1963) 86m AIP bw

Jock Mahoney (Don Michael O'Casey), Faith Domergue (Carlotta Torres), Michael Pate (Don Francisco Hernandez), Susan Seaforth (Marianna De La Rosa), Rodolfo Hoyos (Padre Soler), Penny Santon (Dona Ana Sofia Hicenta), Jimmy Murphy (Jacinto), Nestor Paiva (Gen. Micheltorena), Roberto Contreras (Lt. Sanchez), Felix Locher (Don Pablo Hernandez), Charles Horvath (Manuel).

The people of California want to break free of Mexico and join the Union, but the Mexican army is waging a terror campaign. to keep them in line. The soldiers are led by Pate, but Mahoney, his half brother, is helping the revolutionaries. After the Mexican troops are routed, Pate is killed by one of his men and Mahoney ends up with his father's estate and Seaforth, Pate's fiancee. AIP turned its exploitative talents to the western here, and the result is an utterly forgettable programmer. Allegedly based on the 1946 film of the same name, the film bears little resemblance to it.

p&d, Hamil Petroff; w, James West; ph, Ed Fitzgerald; m, Richard La Salle; ed, Bert Honey; art d, Theodore Holsopple.

Western   (PR:A   MPAA:NR)

CALIFORNIA CONQUEST**   (1952) 78m COL c

Cornel Wilde (Don Arturo Bordega), Teresa Wright (Julia Lawrence), Alfonso Bedoya (Jose Martinez), Lisa Ferraday (Helena de Gagarine), Eugene Iglesias (Ernesto Brios), John Dehner (Fredo Brios), Ivan Lebedeff (Alexander Rotcheff), Tito Renaldo (Don Bernardo Mirana), Renzo Cesana (Fray Lindos), Baynes Barron (Ignacio), Rico Alaniz (Pedro), William P. Wilkerson (Fernando), Edward Colmans (Junipero), Alex Montoya (Juan), Hank Patterson (Sam Lawrence), George Eldredge (Capt. John C. Fremont).

The struggle to determine which country would control California (U. S., Mexico, or Russia) in it's early days is chronicled in this not-so-subtly disguised Cold-War western. Wilde plays the leader of a group of Spanish-Californians who would prefer that the U.S. claim the rights to its territory. The villain, Dehner, is a wealthy landowner who has accepted Russia's promise of power and influence if he will ensure its annexation of the California lands. To stage his overthrow, Dehner hires Mexican bandit Bedoya to steal all the weapons from a gun shop owned by Wright and her father. The father is killed and Wright joins Wilde to recover the stolen guns and thwart the Russian takeover. The politics are a little tough to take, but good performances by Wilde, Dehner and Bedoya, combined with some exciting action sequences, carry the material through.

p, Sam Katzman; d, Lew Landers; w, Robert E. Kent; ph, Ellis W. Carter (Technicolor); m, Mischa Bakaleinikoff; ed, Richard Fantl; art d, Paul Palmentola.

Western   (PR:A   MPAA:NR)

CALIFORNIA DOLLS   (SEE: ALL THE MARBLES, 1981)

CALIFORNIA DREAMING**   (1979) 92m AIP c

Glynnis O'Connor (Corky), Seymour Cassel (Duke), Dorothy Tristan (Fay), Dennis Christopher (T.T.), John Calvin (Rick), Tanya Roberts (Stephanie), Jimmy Van Patten (Mike), Todd Susman (Jordy), Alice Playten (Corrine), Ned Wynn (Earl), John Fain (Tenner), Marshall Efron (Ruben).

Silly attempt to update the popular beach movies of the early 1960s starring Christopher (better known for his starring role in BREAKING AWAY) as a Chicago boy who travels to California's beaches in search of the good life. The midwesterner sticks out like a sore thumb among the bikinis and surfers and his attempts to fit into their lifestyle fail until he realizes that their lives are more boring and empty than his. Christopher is somewhat appealing as the "city" boy.

p, Christian Whittaker; d, John Hancock; w, Ned Wynn; ph, Bobby Byrne (Movielab Color); m, Fred Karlin; ed, Sid Leven, Herb Dow, Roy Peterson; art d, Bill Hiney.

Drama   (PR:C   MPAA:R)

CALIFORNIA FIREBRAND*½   (1948) 63m REP c

Monte Hale (Monte Hale), Adrian Booth (Joyce Mason), Paul Hurst (Chuck Waggoner), Alice Tyrrell (Dulcey Waggoner), Tristram Coffin (Jim Requa/Jud Babbit), LeRoy Mason (Luke Hartell), Douglas Evans (Lance Dawson), Sarah Edwards (Granny Mason), Daniel M. Sheridan (Gunsmoke Lowry), Duke York (Zeke Mason), Lanny Reca (Rick), Foy Willing and Riders of Purple Sage.

Routine western actioner starring Hale as a drifter who agrees to defend a gold mining town against a group of baddies led by Coffin. To do this, the hero outwits the outlaws by pretending to be a dangerous gunslinger. Romance surfaces in the guise of local lass Booth, with whom Hale rides off into the sunset. Coffin appears in an inexplicable dual role as the chief crook and as a dumb Indian guide. Hurst, who usually played gangsters, turns up here as Hale's goofy sidekick.

p, Melville Tucker; d, Phillip Ford; w, J. Benton Cheney, John K. Butler (adapted by Royal K. Cole); ph, Reggie Lanning (Trucolor); ed, Tony Martinelli; m/l, Foy Willing, Sid Robin.

Western   (PR:A   MPAA:NR)

CALIFORNIA FRONTIER**   (1938) 54m COL bw

Buck Jones (Buck Pearson), Carmen Bailey (Dolores), Milburn Stone (Mal Halstead), Jose Perez (Juan Cantova), Soledad Jiminez (Mama), Stanley Blystone (Graham), Carlos Villanos (Don Pecho).

Jones stars as a U.S. Army captain sent on a mission to investigate allegations of banditry and racism perpetrated on the native Mexicans in the California territory. Upon his arrival he finds that an old Mexican family has been run off it's land by a band of desperados. Aided by Perez, the hot-tempered, elder son of the family, Jones drives the white trash away and weds the daughter of the Mexican family at the close of the picture. Well done "B" oater with a surprisingly progressive racial attitude for the 1930s.

d, Elmer Clifton; w, Monroe Shaff, Arthur Hoerl; ph, Eddie Linden; ed, Charles Hunt.

Western   (PR:A   MPAA:NR)

CALIFORNIA JOE*   (1944) 55m REP bw

Don "Red" Barry (Lt. Joe Weldon), Wally Vernon (Tumbleweed Smith), Helen Talbot (Judith Cartaret), Twinkle Watts (Twinkle), Brian O'Hara (Delancey Cartaret), Terry Frost (Melbourne Tommy Atkinson), Edward Earle (Col. Burgess), Leroy Mason (Breck Colton), Charles King (Ashley), Pierce Lyden (Harper), Edmund Cobb (Dave), Karl Hackett (Ned Potter), Robert Kortman (Bradshaw), Edward Keane (Gou Glynn).

Barry plays a Union cavalry lieutenant whose mission is to stop a group of Confederate sympathizers during the Civil War. The rebels themselves are being betrayed by their leader who is using them to build his own powerful empire. Romantic interest is provided by Talbot, a southern gal who tries to bring her fellow Dixieites to their senses. Bizarre appearance by child ice-skating star Watts who rides a pony through the movie and never gets a chance (nor would there be a reason) to show off her talent.

p, Eddy White; d, Spencer Bennet; w, Norman S. Hall; ph, Ernest Miller; ed, Harry Keller.

Western   (PR:A   MPAA:NR)

CALIFORNIA MAIL, THE*   (1937) 56m WB bw

Dick Foran (Bill Harkins), Linda Perry (Mary Tolliver), Ed Cobb (Roy Banton), Milton Kibbee (Bard Banton), Tom Brower (Sam Harrison), James Farley (Dan), Edward Keane (Thompson), Bill Hendricks (Pete), Wilfred Lucas (Sheriff), Cliff Saum (Jim), Gene Alsace (Jake), Glenn Strange (Bud), Bob Woodward (Wyatt), Fred Burns (Ferguson).

Sprinting all the way to the bank, Warner Bros. lets Foran loose on another short hour. Called the best of filmdom's singing cowboys in his time, Foran here is a Pony Express rider who, with his horse, Smokey, roughs it out against crooked opposition. But production values are shallow and the plot shallower still.

p, Bryan Foy; d, Noel Smith; w, Harold Buckley, Roy Chanslor; ph, Ted McCord; ed, Doug Gould.

Western   (PR:A   MPAA:NR)

CALIFORNIA PASSAGE**   (1950) 90m REP bw

Forrest Tucker (Mike Prescott), Adele Mara (Beth Martin), Estelita Rodriguez (Maria Sanchez), Jim Davis (Linc Corey), Peter Miles (Tommy Martin), Charles Kemper (Willy), Bill Williams (Bob Martin), Rhys Williams (Norris), Paul Fix (Whalen), Francis McDonald (Kane/Recorder), Eddy Waller (Walter), Charles Stevens (Pedro), Iron Eyes Cody (Indian), Alan Bridge (Conover), Ruth Brennan (Stella).

Fast-paced oater starring Tucker and Davis as uneasy saloon partners who both fall in love with Mara. Davis works on the side stealing gold shipments, and when the authorities begin to close in on him he frames Tucker for the robberies. This predicament sends Tucker fleeing into the hills. Davis grabs Mara and the climax sees Tucker rescuing the heroine and killing his evil partner. Good supporting cast and two decent tunes sung by Rodriguez, "Second-Hand Romance" and "I'm Goin' Round In Circles," help things move along.

p&d, Joseph Kane; w, James Edward Grant; ph, John MacBurnie; ed, Arthur Roberts; m/l, Jack Elliot, Harold Spina.

Western   (PR:A   MPAA:NR)

CALIFORNIA SPLIT**   (1974) 108m COL c

George Segal (Bill Denny), Elliott Gould (Charlie Walters), Ann Prentiss (Barbara Miller), Gwen Welles (Susan Peters), Edward Walsh (Lew), Joseph Walsh (Sparkie), Bert Remsen (Helen Brown), Barbara London (Lady on Bus), Barbara Ruick (Reno Barmaid), Jay Fletcher (Robber), Jeff Goldblum (Lloyd Harris), Barbara Colby (Receptionist), Vince Palmieri (First Bartender), Alyce Passman (Go-Go Girl), Joanne Strauss (Mother), Jack Riley (Second Bartender), Sierra Bandit (Woman at Bar), John Considine (Man at Bar), Eugene Troobnick (Harvey), Richard Kennedy (Used Car Salesman), John Winston (Tenor), Bill Duffy (Kenny), Mike Greene (Reno Dealer), Tom Signotelli (Nugie), Sharon Compton (Nugie's Wife), Arnold Herzstein, Marc Cavell, Alvin Weissman, Mickey Fox, Carolyn Lohmann (California Club Poker Players), "Amarillo Slim" Preston, Winston Lee, Harry Drackett, Thomas Hal Phillips, Ted Say, A. J. Hood (Reno Poker Players).

Robert Altman has almost done the impossible. He's made a gambling story dull. In his constant striving for "loose-ending" a movie, he has strung together a series of vignettes, some funny, some boring, and called it a film. Segal and Gould are both excellent as compulsive gamblers in various situations. Several real gamesmen play themselves in the film (Amarillo Slim, most notably) and the supporting actors all distinguish the craft. The picture crumbles in its overall concept. Altman, to his credit, is always after something elusive—a sense of reality that is often missing with structured films. When it works, it's marvelous. Unfortunately for Altman, it hardly ever works. There have been fifty films where gambling took a front seat. At least forty-nine of them were more entertaining than CALIFORNIA SPLIT (the title of which comes from a form of poker but it might as well refer to the personality of this movie). Writer Walsh gives himself and his father a part. Walsh was a fairly successful young actor at one point who gave it up to sit at the Smith-Corona. This script was not his best effort, but it's not easy to say where the words end and where Altman's improvisational, sketchy technique begins.

p, Robert Altman, Joseph Walsh; d, Altman; w, Walsh; ph, Paul Lohmann (Panavision-Metrocolor); m, Phyllis Shotwell; ed, Louis Lombardo; art d, Leon Ericksen; set d, Sam Jones.

Comedy   (PR:C   MPAA:R)

CALIFORNIA STRAIGHT AHEAD*½
(1937) 57m UNIV bw

John Wayne (Biff Smith), Louise Latimer (Mary Porter), Robert McWade (Corrigan), Theodore Von Eltz (James Gifford), Tully Marshall (Harrison), Emerson Treacy (Charlie Porter), Harry Allen (Fish McCorkle), Leroy Mason (Padula), Grace Goodall (Mrs. Porter), Olaf Hytten (Huggins), Monty Vandergrift (Clancy), Lorin Raker (Secretary).

Early Wayne vehicle has the Duke as partner with Treacy in a small trucking firm that begins to steal business from rival trucker Mason. Meanwhile, Wayne romances Latimer away from the head of the railroad shipping department, Von Eltz. Things go sour when the evil Mason sets events into motion that cause the death of Treacy in a nitro explosion. Wayne, who joins up with big-time truck operator McWade, puts Mason out of business, but the murderer joins forces with Von Eltz leading to a cross-country race between Wayne's trucks and Von Eltz's train to prove which method of shipping is faster. Deceptive title leads most fans to believe the film is a Wayne western.

p, Trem Carr; d, Arthur Lubin; w, Scott Darling (based on a story by Herman Boxer); ph, Harry Neumann; ed, Charles Craft, E. Horsley.

Drama (PR:A MPAA:NR)

CALIFORNIA SUITE***½
(1978) 103m COL c

Alan Alda (Bill Warren), Michael Caine (Sidney Cochran), Bill Cosby (Dr. Willis Panama), Jane Fonda (Hannah Warren), Walter Matthau (Marvin Michaels), Elaine May (Millie Michaels), Richard Pryor (Dr. Chauncy Gump), Maggie Smith (Diana Barrie), Gloria Gifford (Lola Gump), Sheila Frazier (Bettina Panama), Herbert Edelman (Harry Michaels), At Hotel: Denise Galik (Bunny), David Sheehan (Himself), Michael Boyle (Desk Clerk), Len Lawson (Frank), Gino Ardito (Plumber), Jerry Ziman (Man on phone), Clint Young (Doorman), David Matthau (Bellboy), James Espinoza (Busboy), Buddy Douglas (Page), Armand Cerami (Charley), Joseph Morena (Herb), Brian Cummings, William Kux, Zora Margolis (Autograph Seekers), Rita Gomez, Tina Menard (Maids), Lupe Ontiveros, Bert May, Eddie Villery (Waiters). At Academy Awards: Army Archerd (Army Archerd), Judith Hannah Brown (Oscar Winner), Gary Hendrix (Her Date), Jack Scanlan, Bill Steinmetz (P. R. Men), Paolo Frediani (Young Man). At Airport: Dana Plato (Jenny), Nora Boland (Passenger), David Rini (Airline Rep.), John Hawker (Sky Cab), Frank Conn (Bobby), Colleen Drape, Kelly Harmon, Tawny Moyer, Leslie Pagett, Vicki Stephens, Nan Wylder, Linda Ewen (Stewardesses). In Beverly Hills: David Sato (Salesman), Christopher Pennock (Cop).

CALIFORNIA SUITE is the BevHills version of NYC's PLAZA SUITE and it feels as though Simon reached into the trunk and pulled out some old sketches he may have written for Max Liebman's "Show Of Shows," did a fast rewrite, and put them all into one location at the Beverly Hills Hotel. Despite that uncomfortable underlying feeling, this is one of Simon's most interesting efforts. He's renowned as a wordsmith and when in that bailiwick, he shines. It's those moments of slapstick or sentimentality that bring the picture down. Briefly, the quartet of stories are as follows: Alda and Fonda are divorced and are hassling over child custody (serious); Caine and Smith are ambisextrous film stars waiting for the Oscar awards to commence (very funny and inside. Also, Smith actually did win an Oscar [Best Supporting Actress] for playing a woman waiting to win an Oscar); Cosby and Pryor and Frazier and Gifford as two couples whose vacation turns into a slapstick nightmare (much too frenetic and about as believable as Adolph Hitler singing country and western); and Matthau and May shine in the best segment of the bunch—Matthau is at the hotel with a hooker when his wife arrives. The situation is hilarious and Matthau is at his best. So, about half this movie is terrific and the other fifty percent falls flat. Yet, what's good is very, very good and what's bad is still okay.

p, Ray Stark; d, Herbert Ross; w, Neil Simon (based on his play); ph, David M. Walsh (Panavision); m, Claude Bolling; ed, Michael A. Stevenson; cos, Ann Roth, Patricia Norris.

Comedy Cas. (PR:A-C MPAA:PG)

CALIFORNIA TRAIL, THE*
(1933) 65m COL bw

Buck Jones (Santa Fe Stewart), Helen Mack (Dolores), George Humbart (Mayor), Luis Alberni (Commandante), Charles Stevens (Juan), Chris-Pin Martin (Pancho), Carlos Villar (Governor), Bob Steele (Pedro).

Dull Jones outing this time pits the cowpoke against an evil Mexican and his equally vile brother who rule over the local village with iron fists. Humbart is the rotten Mexican mayor of the California town who exploits the farmers and Alberni is his brother, the commandante of the local troops who enforces the will of the mayor. Jones rides into town and kicks the bums out. For die-hard Jones fans only.

d&w, Lambert Hillyer; (based on a story by Jack Natteford); ph, Ben Kline.

Western (PR:A MPAA:NR)

CALIFORNIAN, THE*½
(1937) 59m FOX bw
(AKA: THE GENTLEMAN FROM CALIFORNIA)

Ricardo Cortez (Ramon Escobar), Marjorie Weaver (Rosalia Miller), Katherine DeMille (Chata), Maurice Black (Pancho), Morgan Wallace (Tod Barsto), Nigel de Brulier (Don Francisco Escobar), George Regas (Ruiz), Pierre Watkin (Miller), James Farley (Sheriff Stanton), Edward Keane (Marshal Morse).

Below average Robin Hood/Zorro-type tale starring Cortez as the dashing hero who helps break up a group of unscrupulous tax collectors who have been snatching land from the poor, defenseless peasants. Pretty lame oater all-around and the stilted dialog is not helped by the phony Spanish accents attempted by the cast.

p, Sol Lesser; d, Gus Meins; w, Gilbert Wright (based on a story by Harold Bell Wright, adapted by Gordon Newell); ph, Harry Neumann; ed, Arthur Hilton, Carl Pearson.

Western (PR:A MPAA:NR)

CALL, THE*
(1938, Fr.) 75m Best Films bw

Jean Yonnel (Charles de Foucauld), Pierre de Guigand (Gen. Laperrine), Jacqueline Francell (Mme. Alice Tissot), Jeanne Marie-Laurent (Suzanne Blanchette), Pierre Juvenet (Thomy Bourdelle), Pasquali-Aug. Boverio (Andre Nox-Pierre Nay), Fernand Francell (Alexandra Mihalesco), Jean Kolb (Georges Cahuzac), Maurice Schultz (Henri Defreyn), St.-Ober (Vina), Pierre Darteuil (Maurice de Canonge).

Yonnel plays a titled Frenchman who forsakes his life of decadence and dissipation to become a monk and missionary in the Sahara. Not only does he manage to convert the Bedouins, but he manages to help France tighten its colonial grip on Morocco. The Arabs catch on to him and he becomes a martyr. Released on a limited basis in the U.S. as a fundraising device for Catholic Charities, the film is shoddily done and without interest. Based on a true story.

p,d&w, Leon Poirier; ph, Georges Million.

Biography (PR:A MPAA:NR)

CALL A MESSENGER*½
(1939) 65m UNIV bw

Billy Halop (Jimmy Hogan), Huntz Hall (Pig), Robert Armstrong (Kirk Graham), Mary Carlisle (Marge Hogan), Anne Nagel (Frances O'Neill), Victor Jory (Ed Hogan), Larry Crabbe (Chuck Walsh), El Brendel ("Baldy"), Jimmy Butler (Bob Pritchard), George Offerman, Jr. (Big Lip), Hally Cheater (Murph), William Benedict (Trouble), David Gorcey (Yap), Harris Berger (Sailor).

Dead End Kids Halop and Hall star in this tepid youth/gangster drama. Armstrong is the boss of a messenger service that employs the wayward youths to keep them out of trouble. The boys better themselves through hard work and try to save Halop's older sister Carlisle from taking up with an infamous local gangster. At the same time, Halop's older brother returns from prison and the young messenger boy works overtime to keep his sibling on the straight and narrow. This film came toward the end of the Dead End Kids cycle of socially relevant youth pictures that eventually evolved into the totally ridiculous Bowery Boys series of youth comedies. (See BOWERY BOYS series, Index)

p, Ken Goldsmith; d, Arthur Lubin; w, Arthur T. Horman (based on an original idea by Sally Sandlin and Michel Kraike); ph, Elwood Bredell.

CrimeDrama (PR:A MPAA:NR)

CALL HER SAVAGE**
(1932) 82m FOX bw

Clara Bow (Nasa), Monroe Owsley (Lawrence Crosby), Gilbert Roland (Moonglow), Thelma Todd (Sunny De Lan), Estelle Taylor (Ruth Springer), Willard Robertson (Peter Springer), Weldon Heyburn (Ronasa), Arthur Hoyt (Attorney), Hale Hamilton (Cyrus Randall).

Clara Bow returned to the screen after an absence of over a year in this overblown, melodramatic tale of a feisty half-breed girl (Bow) and her attempts to find happiness in civilized society. The big secret is that Bow doesn't know she's a half-breed, but to demonstrate her instinctual "savageness" the script has her "yipping" quite a bit, running around scantily clothed, and getting into vicious fights. She does not get along with her father, the Indian, Roland, and marries the wrong man just to spite his authority. The marriage ends after a violent quarrel, leaving Bow destitute and with a sick baby to care for. Unable to make ends meet, she walks the streets to earn some cash. Eventually she returns to the country of her heritage, learns of her true identity, and marries a young half-breed boy, finally finding happiness. Maudlin and somewhat racist.

d, John Francis Dillon; w, Edwin Burke (based on the novel by Tiffany Thayer); ph, Lee Garmes; art d, Max Parker.

Drama (PR:A MPAA:NR)

CALL HIM MR. SHATTER*
(1976, Hong Kong) 90m AE/Hammer c
(AKA: SHATTER)

Stuart Whitman (Shatter), Ti Lung (Tai Phah), Lily Li (Mai-Mee), Peter Cushing (Rattwood), Anton Diffring (Hans Leber), Yemi Ajibade, Liu Ka Young, Huang Pei Chi, Liu Ya Ying, Lo Wei, James Ma, Chinag Han, Kao Hsiung.

Rotten, disjointed kung-fu flick that went through three directors (Monte Hellman, Seth Holt, and finally Carreras) and three cinematographers (Probyn, Wilcox, and Ford) before they completed shooting this mess. Whitman wanders through his role as a cynical, world-weary international hit-man who must fight dozens of battles against hordes of arm-flailing Oriental villains. Cushing appears all too briefly as a British undercover agent. Hammer also shot the vastly superior LEGEND OF THE SEVEN GOLDEN VAMPIRES (1973) at the same time starring Cushing. Both films were shot in the early 1970s but neither were released until years later.

p, Michael Carreras, Vee King Shaw; d, Carreras; w, Don Houghton; ph, Brian Probyn, John Wilcox, Roy Ford; m, David Lindup; ed, Eric Boyd-Perkins; art d, Johnson.

Action (PR:O MPAA:R)

CALL IT A DAY*½
(1937) 89m WB bw

Olivia de Havilland (Catherine Hilton), Ian Hunter (Roger Hilton), Anita Louise (Joan Collett), Alice Brady (Muriel West), Roland Young (Frank Haines), Frieda Inescort (Dorothy Hilton), Bonita Granville (Ann Hilton), Peggy Wood (Ethel Francis), Marcia Ralston (Beatrice Gwynn), Walter Woolf King (Paul Francis), Peter Willes (Martin), Una O'Connor (Charwoman), Beryl Mercer (Cook), Elsa Buchanan (Vera), Mary Field (Elsie Lester), Robert Adair (Butler), Jack Richardson (Grocery Store Owner), Sidney Bracy (Flower Shop Owner), Louise Stanley (Girl on Bus), May Beatty (Landlady), Cecil Weston (Beatrice's Maid), Leyland Hodgson (Sir Harold).

Boring sex comedy which takes place entirely on the first day of spring and details the lives of a prosperous British family whose members have been gripped by "spring fever." The husband, Hunter, is almost seduced by a young actress, Ralston. The wife, de Havilland, nearly succumbs to the charms of suave bachelor Young. The daughter,

Inescort, tries to snare handsome artist King, but King's wife Wood puts a stop to it. In the end the fever passes and everybody goes back to normal. Dull, full of cliches, and not particularly funny, notable only in that this was the first film to top bill de Havilland.

p, Hal B. Wallis; d, Archie Mayo; w, Casey Robinson (based on the play by Dodie Smith); ph, Ernest Haller; ed, James Gibbon.

Comedy (PR:A MPAA:NR)

CALL IT LUCK* (1934) 63m FOX bw

"Pat" Paterson *(Pat Laurie)*, Herbert Mundin *(Herbert Biggelwade)*, Charles Starrett *(Stan Russell)*, Gordon Westcott *("Lucky" Luke Bartlett)*, Georgia Caine *(Amy Lark)*, Theodore von Eltz *(Nat Underwood)*, Reginald Mason *(Lord Poindexter)*, Ernest Wood *(Sid Carter)*, Ray Mayer *("Brainwave" Flynn)*, Susan Fleming *(Alice Blue)*.

Lame comedy stars Mundin as a dim London cabbie who wins the sweepstakes and then is conned into buying an old cavalry horse that is being sold as the sibling of a Derby champion. Subplot concerns Mundin's daughter Paterson who ends up in a gangster's nightclub long enough to belt out a few unmemorable tunes and start up a boring romance with Starrett. As it turns out Mundin's candidate for the glue-factory wins the bag race after all the cabbie's friends have laid their money down on the animal.

d, James Tinling; w, Dudley Nichols, Lamar Trotti (based on a story by Nichols and George Marshall, adaptation by Joseph Cunningham, Harry McCoy); ph, Joseph Valentine; m, Richard Whiting; m/l, Sidney Clare.

Comedy (PR:A MPAA:NR)

CALL ME BWANA** (1963, Brit.) 93m Rank/UA c

Bob Hope *(Matt Merriwether)*, Anita Ekberg *(Luba)*, Edie Adams *(Frederica Larsen)*, Lionel Jeffries *(Dr. Ezra Mungo)*, Percy Herbert *(1st Henchman)*, Paul Carpenter *(Col. Spencer)*, Orlando Martins *(Tribal Chief)*, Al Mulock *(2nd Henchman)*, Bari Johnson *(Uta)*, Peter Dyneley *(Williams)*, Robert Nichols *(American Major)*, Robert Arden *(1st CIA Man)*, Kevin Scott *(2nd CIA Man)*, Neville Monroe, Michael Moyer, Richard Burrell *(Reporters)*.

Typical Hope corn, this time set in darkest Africa as ol' ski nose tries to locate a downed American moon-probe that has crash-landed in the jungle. Agent Adams is sent along with the bumbling explorer to keep him out of trouble, but soon enemy agents Ekberg and Jeffries join the expedition posing as medical missionaries. The usual Hope silliness ensues, with our hero battling lions, elephants, and the wily advances of the Amazonian Ekberg. A competent, if somewhat lackluster, Hope comedy.

p, Harry Saltzman, Albert R. Broccoli; d, Gordon Douglas; w, Nate Monaster, Johanna Harwood; ph, Ted Moore (Eastmancolor); m, Muir Mathieson, Monty Norman; ed, Peter Hunt; art d, Syd Cain; set d, Peter Russell; spec eff, John Stears.

Comedy (PR:A MPAA:NR)

CALL ME GENIUS½** (1961, Brit.) 105m ABF bw (GB: THE REBEL)

Tony Hancock *(Anthony Hancock)*, George Sanders *(Sir Charles Brouard)*, Paul Massie *(Paul)*, Margit Saad *(Margot Carreras)*, Gregoire Aslan *(Aristotle Carreras)*, Dennis Price *(Jim Smith)*, Irene Handl *(Mrs. Crevatte)*, Mervyn Johns *(London Art Gallery Manager)*, Peter Bull *(Paris Art Gallery Manager)*, John Le Mesurier *(Office Manager)*, Liz Fraser *(Waitress)*, Nanette Newman *(Josey)*, Marie Burke *(Mme. Laurent)*, Marie Devereux *(Yvette)*, John Wood *(Poet)*, Mario Fabrizi *(Bar Attendant)*, Sandor Eles, Oliver Reed, Gary Lockwood, Neville Becker *(Artists)*.

Hancock leaves his boring office job and goes to London, intending to become an artist. Although his works are devoid of talent, he is adopted by an intellectual clique and becomes the rage. His roommate (Massie), who does show some talent as an artist but receives no recognition, becomes disgusted by Hancock's success and abandons London and his paintings. The paintings are seen by wealthy art connoisseur Sanders who mistakes them for Hancock's work and arranges a show. Hancock's fame increases until finally he is overwhelmed by the magnitude of his deception and confesses that the paintings attributed to him were Massie's. He returns to obscurity and works diligently at his art, confident of his eventual recognition. Frequently amusing.

p, W. A. Whittaker; d, Robert Day; w, Alan Simpson, Ray Galton (based on an original story by Tony Hancock, Simpson, Galton); ph, Gilbert Taylor; m, Frank Cordell; ed, Richard Best; md, Stanley Black; art d, Robert Jones.

Comedy (PR:A MPAA:NR)

CALL ME MADAM*** (1953) 114m FOX c

Ethel Merman *(Mrs. Sally Adams)*, Donald O'Connor *(Kenneth)*, Vera-Ellen *(Princess Maria)*, George Sanders *(Cosmo Constantine)*, Billy De Wolfe *(Pemberton Maxwell)*, Helmut Dantine *(Prince Hugo)*, Walter Slezak *(Tantinnin)*, Steven Geray *(Sebastian)*, Ludwig Stossel *(Grand Duke)*, Lilia Skala *(Grand Duchess)*, Charles Dingle *(Sen. Brockway)*, Emory Parnell *(Sen. Gallagher)*, Percy Helton *(Sen. Wilkins)*, Leon Belasco *(Leader)*, Oscar Beregi *(Chamberlain)*, Nestor Paiva *(Miccoli)*, Sidney Marion *(Proprietor)*, Torben Meyer *(Rudolph)*, Richard Garrick *(Supreme Court Justice)*, Walter Woolf King *(Secretary of State)*, Olan Soule *(Clerk)*, John Wengraf *(Ronchin)*, Fritz Feld *(Hat Clerk)*, Erno Verebes *(Music Clerk)*, Hannelore Axman *(Switchboard Operator)*, Lal Chand Mehra *(Minister from Magrador)*.

Merman repeats her successful Broadway performance in this pleasant musical. She's a Washington hostess who is named ambassador to the tiny European nation of Lichtenburg. She falls in love with foreign minister Sanders while Princess Vera-Ellen dances with and falls for press attache O'Connor. Merman utterly dominates the picture with her boisterous performance, loosely based on the life of former Ambassador to Luxembourg Perle Mesta. Musical numbers (all by Irving Berlin) include "It's A Lovely Day Today" sung by O'Connor and Vera-Ellen (her voice dubbed by Carole Richards), "You're Just In Love," duetted by Merman and O'Connor, "Marrying For Love," soloed by Sanders, and "The Ocarina," performed by Vera-Ellen and a chorus.

p, Sol C. Siegel; d, Walter Lang; w, Arthur Sheekman (based on the Broadway musical comedy by Howard Lindsay and Russel Crouse); ph. Leon Shamroy (Technicolor), m, Irving Berlin; ed, Robert Simpson; md, Alfred Newman; ch, Robert Alton; m/l, Berlin.

Musical/Comedy (PR:A MPAA:NR)

CALL ME MAME*½ (1933, Brit.) 59m WB-FN bw

Ethel Irving *(Mame)*, John Batten *(Gordon Roantree)*, Dorothy Bartlam *(Tess Lennox)*, Winifred Oughton *(Victoria)*, Julian Royce *(Poulton)*, Arthur Maude *(Father)*, Alice O'Day *(Mother)*, Pat Fitzpatrick *(Child)*, Carrol Gibbons and his Savoy Orpheans.

Batten is about to inherit a title but his drunkard mother (Irving) turns up to complicate the succession. Obscure comedy is justifiably so, and was one of the reasons Warner Bros. lost more than $6 million in this Depression year.

p, Irving Asher; d, John Daumery; w, Randall Faye.

Comedy (PR:A MPAA:NR)

CALL ME MISTER*** (1951) 96m FOX c

Betty Grable *(Kay Hudson)*, Dan Dailey *(Shep Dooley)*, Danny Thomas *(Stanley)*, Dale Robertson *(Capt. Johnny Comstock)*, Benay Venuta *(Billie Barton)*, Richard Boone *(Mess Sergeant)*, Jeffrey Hunter *(The Kid)*, Frank Fontaine *(Sergeant)*, Harry Von Zell *(Gen. Steele)*, Dave Willock *(Jones)*, Robert Ellis *(Ackerman)*, Jerry Paris *(Brown)*, Lou Spencer, Art Stanley, Bob Roberts *(Dunhill Dance Team)*, Tommy Bond *(Little Soldier)*, Frank Clark *(Big Soldier)*, Bobby Short *(Specialty Singer)*, Fred Libby *(General's Aide)*, Ken Christy *(Chief of Staff)*, Russ Conway *(Maj. McCall)*, Robert Scott *(Aide to Chief of Staff)*, Dabbs Greer *(Aide to Colonel)*, Mack Williams *(Col. Edwards)*, Maylia *(Kimona Sales Girl)*, Steven Clark *(Lieutenant)*, Robert Easton *(Tennessee)*, John McKee *(Army Clerk)*, Robert Rockwell *(First Sergeant)*, John McGuire.

A Broadway revue redone for the screen, CALL ME MISTER is about Grable, an entertainer working in Japan at the time of the Korean War. She's married to Dailey, who's in the Far East, but they are separated. Dailey forges an official document so he can stay and direct a camp show in which his estranged mate is starring. He does this so he can get close to Grable and win back her hand. Not a terrific idea but the jokes come thick and fast, and just when you think it's sagging, Dailey and Grable dance and/or sing. Busby Berkeley choreographed the large numbers and this marked his reunion with Lloyd Bacon—their first time together since the landmark FORTY-SECOND STREET. Thomas scores as a soldier who can't adjust to military rules and regulations. Songs: "Going Home Train," "Military Life" (Harold Rome, Jerry Seelen), "I Just Can't Do Enough for You Baby," "Japanese Girl Like American Boy," "Love Is Back In Business" (Mack Gordon, Sammy Fain), "Lament to the Pots and Pans" (Seelen, Earl K. Brent), "I'm Gonna Love That Guy" (Frances Ash).

p, Fred Kohlmar; d, Lloyd Bacon; w, Albert E. Lewin, Burt Styler (based on the revue by Harold J. Rome, Arnold M. Auerbach); ph, Arthur E. Arling (Technicolor); m, Leigh Harline; ed, Louis Loeffler; md, Alfred Newman; ch, Busby Berkeley; m/l Rome, Frances Ash, Sammy Fain, Mack Gordon, Earl K. Brent, Jerry Seelin.

Musical (PR:A MPAA:NR)

CALL NORTHSIDE 777**** (1948) 111m FOX bw (AKA: CALLING NORTHSIDE 777)

James Stewart *(McNeal)*, Richard Conte *(Frank Wiecek)*, Lee J. Cobb *(Brian Kelly)*, Helen Walker *(Laura McNeal)*, Betty Garde *(Wanda Skutnik)*, Kasia Orzazewski *(Tillie Wiecek)*, Joanne de Bergh *(Helen Wiecek-Rayska)*, Howard Smith *(Palmer)*, Moroni Olsen *(Parole Board Chairman)*, John McIntire *(Sam Faxon)*, Paul Harvey *(Martin Burns)*, George Tyne *(Tomek Zaleska)*, Richard Bishop *(Warden)*, Otto Waldis *(Boris)*, Michael Chapin *(Frank, Jr.)*, E. G. Marshall *(Rayska)*, Truman Bradley *(Narrator)*, John Bleifer *(Jan Gruska)*, Addison Richards *(John Albertson)*, Richard Rober *(Larson)*, Eddie Dunn *(Patrolman)*, Percy Helton *(Mailman)*, Charles Lane *(Prosecuting Attorney)*, Norman McKay, Walter Greaza *(Detectives)*, William Post, Jr. *(Police Sergeant)*, George Melford, Charles Miller, Joe Forte, Dick Ryan *(Parole Board Members)*, Lionel Stander *(Corrigan)*, Jonathan Hale *(Robert Winston)*, Lew Eckles *(Policeman)*, Freddie Steele, George Turner *(Holdup Men)*, Jane Crowley *(Anna Felczak)*, Robert Karnes *(Spitzer)*, Larry Blake, Robert Williams, Perry Ivins, Lester Sharpe *(Technicians)*, Helen Foster *(Secretary)*, Abe Dinovitch, Jack Mannick *(Polish Men)*, Henry Kulky *(Bartender in Drazynski's Place)*, Cy Kendall *(Bartender in Bill's Place)*, Dollie Caillet *(Secretary)*, Joe Ploski, Peter Seal *(Men)*, George Spaulding *(Man on Parole Board)*, Wanda Perry, Ann Staunton *(Telephone Operators)*, Rex Downing *(Copy Boy)*, Edward Peil, Jr., Buck Harrington *(Bartenders)*, George Cisar, Philip Lord *(Policemen)*, Stanley Gordon *(Prison Clerk)*, Carl Kroenke *(Guard)*, Arthur Peterson *(Keeler's Assistant)*, Duke Watson, George Pembroke *(Policemen)*.

Based on the actual case of Joe Majczek of Chicago, imprisoned for a crime he did not commit, this film is one of the best of the early docu-dramas, shot on location in the Windy City. Stewart is a hardbitten newsman who is handed an assignment by editor Cobb; he is to follow up a small want ad appearing in his newspaper, an ad offering $5,000 reward for information leading to the arrest and conviction of the man responsible for killing a policeman years earlier. Upon investigation, Stewart finds that the person placing the ad is a scrubwoman (Orzazewski) who has worked for almost a decade to save the $5,000. Her son, Conte, has been in prison for eleven years, she tells Stewart, for a crime he did not commit and she is offering her savings to find the real killer. Cynical Stewart believes Conte is guilty but writes a human interest story about the loving mother and the public reaction is overwhelming. Moreover, Cobb thinks there might be something to the woman's claims and he encourages Stewart to back up his original story with some more digging. As he investigates, Stewart unearths evidence that there was some police coverup in the case, that certain evidence is missing, including arrest records which he winds up stealing, and thereby incurring the wrath of the police department. At one point Stewart threatens to look up a retired police captain who was involved in the case and police sergeant Rober snaps: "If you do, you better take a shovel. He's been dead for years." The case is so old that Stewart's only real lead is Garde, who stubbornly clings to her original courtroom testimony that the thief who was robbing her store and killed the cop is Conte. Once he tracks down Garde, she snarls hatred at him for portraying her as a mob woman and a perjurer, telling him that she'll never change her story. By this time Stewart has visited Conte in prison and, after Conte takes a lie detector test, is convinced of his innocence. Then Stewart discovers an old photo showing Garde being taken into a police station with Conte at the time of Conte's arrest to identify him. Just at the time the parole board is meeting to consider Conte's release, Stewart blows up the photo hundreds of times to show the date on a newspaper held by a newsboy in the photo. It is the day before Conte was charged, proving that Garde had seen him first when he was arrested (contradicted by her original testimony) and not at the murder site. Conte is released to have his young son run into his arms as Stewart stands by to witness his own triumph. Stewart brilliantly plays the part of Jim McGuire, the Chicago *Times* reporter who won the Pulitzer Prize for his investigative efforts and the rest of the cast turn in fine, realistic performances. For Stewart, this film was a departure from the genial roles for which he had become famous (IT'S A WONDERFUL LIFE, THE PHILADELPHIA STORY, MAGIC TOWN); his whole persona changed to that of a tough-as-nails street reporter and he managed the transition convincingly. Director Hathaway had recently had a resounding success with the Ben Hecht story, KISS OF DEATH, also shot in grimly realistic terms. MacDonald's on-location photography presented sharp, contrasting scenes and Newman's moody score added depth and feeling to the emotion-charged story.

p, Otto Lang; d, Henry Hathaway; w, Jerome Cady, Jay Dratler (adapted by Leonard Hoffman and Quentin Reynolds from articles by James P. McGuire appearing in the Chicago *Times*); ph, Joe MacDonald; m, Alfred Newman; ed, J. Watson Webb, Jr.; art d, Lyle Wheeler, Mark-Lee Kirk; set d, Thomas Little, Walter M. Scott; cos, Kay Nelson; spec eff, Fred Sersen; makeup, Ben Nye, Dick Smith, Tom Tuttle.

Crime Drama/Biography   **(PR:A   MPAA:NR)**

CALL OF THE BLOOD*   (1948, Brit.) 88m BL bw
Kay Hammond *(Dr. Anne Lester)*, John Clements *(Julius Ikon)*, John Justin *(David Erskine)*, Hilton Edwards *(Dr. Robert Blake)*, Robert Rietty *(Gaspare)*, Carlo Ninchi *(Salvatore)*, Lea Padovani *(Maddelena)*, Jelo Filippo *(Sebastiano)*, H. G. Stoker *(Uncle)*, Keith Pyott *(Dr. Sabatier)*, Marcesa Faciacani *(Lucretia)*.

Rotten British melodrama that takes place during the turn of the century. Pioneer woman doctor Hammond weds Justin and the pair travel to Sicily to stay in the lush villa given to the groom by his mother. While on their honeymoon the couple meet elderly eccentric Clements (who also wrote and directed this trash) who spouts his cynical philosophy of life every chance he gets, grinding what little action there is to a halt. Suddenly the lady doctor gets an emergency call to help combat an epidemic in Tunis. While she is gone the shifty Clements pushes her husband into the arms of the seductive daughter of a local fisherman, which leads the whole mess to a downbeat, tear-jerking conclusion.

p, John Stafford, Steven Pallos; d, John Clements, Ladislas Vajda; w, Clements, Akos Tolnay, Basil Mason (based on the novel by Robert Hichens); ph, Wilkie Cooper; m, Ludovico Lunghi; ed, Carmen Bellaeff.

Drama   **(PR:A   MPAA:NR)**

CALL OF THE CANYON**   (1942) 71m REP bw
Gene Autry *(Gene)*, Smiley Burnette *(Frog)*, Sons of the Pioneers *(Themselves)*, Ruth Terry *(Kit Carson)*, Thurston Hall *(Grantley B. Johnson)*, Joe Strauch, Jr. *(Tadpole)*, Cliff Nazarro *(Pete Murphy)*, Dorothea Kent *(Jane Oakley)*, Edmund MacDonald *(Thomas McCoy)*, Marc Lawrence *(Horace Dunston)*, John Harmon *(The Pigeon)*, John Holland *(Willy Hitchcock)*.

Decent Autry outing sees the singing cowboy as the leader of a group of cattlemen who get short-changed by packing company purchasing agent MacDonald who has gotten himself in debt with the local bookie and is hoping to get some quick cash by pulling a fast one on the ranchers. Outraged, Autry goes into town to see Hall, the head of the packing company, but he can't get past the droves of radio sales agents who want the cattle buyer to sponsor their shows. Terry, a radio saleslady who has her last dollar wrapped up in the show she's trying to sell, discovers the transcript of the show broken when Autry is pushed onto her lap. Stuck without a show to sell, Terry tries to drum up interest by offering to broadcast a show live from her ranch, with her cowboys providing the singing entertainment. Unfortunately the whole thing is a con. Since Terry has no ranch, she rents Autry's spread and drags all the radio equipment into his place for the broadcast. Using the radio gear, the hero manages to trap the dishonest purchasing agent and sing a few songs to boot. Well-paced and believably developed, the songs are worked into the narrative flow naturally through the radio broadcast. Songs include: "Boots and Saddle," "Somebody Else Is Taking My Place," "Montana Skies," the title song sung by Autry, and "When It's Chilly Down in Chile," warbled by Terry.

p, Harry Grey; d, Joseph Santley; w, Olive Cooper (based on a story by Maurice Rapf, Cooper); ph, Reggie Lanning; ed, Edward Mann.

Western   **Cas.**   **(PR:A   MPAA:NR)**

CALL OF THE CIRCUS*½   (1930) 60m Burr Enterprises bw
Francis X. Bushman, Ethel Clayton, Joan Wyndham, William C. Kirby, Dorothy Gay, Sunburnt Jim Wilson.

Overblown early talkie melodrama starring Bushman as an ex-clown who has retired to become a horticulturist. The man is obsessed with his flowers and ignores his wife, a former circus widow whose marriage to Bushman was arranged. The woman has learned to love the grouchy clown but Bushman is not happy with the marriage and targets his stepson to feel his wrath. The boy gets fed up with the abuse and goes back to the circus. Soon after, Busham saves the life of a young woman during a vicious storm. The girl is grateful and Bushman misinterprets her affection for him as love. He falls hard for the younger woman but is soon called away on a trip. In his absence the wife, who sees what is happening to her husband, sends for her son to return and distract the young woman. The scheme works and upon his return Bushman learns of the young couple's intention to marry. The old man makes a last attempt to woo the girl

but he fails and ends up alone among his flowers. Given time to reflect on his actions, the former circus clown realizes his foolishness and seeks to reunite with his loving wife. The subject matter is treated sensitively by the script, but the silent film performers attempting to make the transition to sound pictures tend to overplay their roles.

d, Frank O'Connor; w, Maxine Alton (based on a play by Alton), ph, Louis Physioc; m, Ralph J. Nase.

Drama   **(PR:A   MPAA:NR)**

CALL OF THE FLESH**   (1930) 100m MGM bw/c
                                        (AKA: THE SINGER FROM SEVILLE)
Ramon Novarro *(Juan)*, Dorothy Jordan *(Maria)*, Ernest Torrence *(Esteban)*, Nance O'Neil *(Mother Superior)*, Renee Adoree *(Lola)*, Mathilde Comont *(La Rumbarita)*, Russell Hopton *(Enrique)*.

Romantic musical starring Novarro as a Mexican singing star trying to win the affections of convent girl Jordan. Adoree plays a Spanish dancer in love with the dashing Latin singer from afar. Average, lackluster screenplay is helped somewhat by a standout musical sequence shot in Technicolor. This was to be Adoree's last film; she died in 1933 at the age of 35 after a long battle with tuberculosis. Songs include: "Just For Today," "Not Quite Good Enough For Me" Herbert Stothart, Clifford Grey; "Lonely" Stothart, Grey, Novarro.

d, Charles Brabin (Technicolor); w,, John Colton (based on a story by Dorothy Farnum); ch, Eduardo Cansino.

Musical   **(PR:A   MPAA:NR)**

CALL OF THE JUNGLE*   (1944) 60m MON bw
Ann Corio *(Tana)*, James Bush *(Jim)*, John Davidson *(Harley)*, Claudia Dell *(Gracie)*, Edward Chandler *(Boggs)*, Muni Barwick *(Louie)*, I. Stanford Jolley *(Carlton)*, J. Alex Havier *(Malu)*, Phil Van Zandt *(Dozan)*, Harry Burns *(Kahuna)*.

South Seas drama chronicling the efforts of one-man police force Bush as he hunts down a pair of jewel thieves who are hiding out on his small island. Romance develops between the cop and Corio, who assists him in his search. Way below average.

p, Philip N. Krasne, James S. Burkett; d, Phil Rosen; w, George Callahan; ph, Arthur Martinelli; ed, Marty Cohen.

Adventure/Romance   **(PR:A   MPAA:NR)**

CALL OF THE KLONDIKE*½   (1950) 66m MON bw
Kirby Grant *(Rod)*, Chinook *(Chinook)*, Anne Gwynne *(Nancy)*, Lynne Roberts *(Emily)*, Tom Neal *(Mallory)*, Russell Simpson *(McKay)*, Marc Krah *(Mencheck)*, Paul Bryar *(Fred Foley)*, Pat Gleason *(Billy)*, Duke York *(Luke)*.

Another entry in the Monogram Northwest Mountie series featuring Grant and his faithful pooch Chinook as they investigate a number of murders in the backwoods. While on the trail they discover the lovely Gwynne, whose father has mysteriously disappeared after he struck it rich in a gold mine. The intrepid team conclude, that the murderers are nasty miner Neal and his sister Roberts, who have been stealing gold through a tunnel dug from their dry mine to Gwynne's father's rich one. After some chases, fist-fights, and a lot of barking from Chinook, justice triumphs.

p, Lindsley Parsons; d, Frank McDonald; w, Charles Lang (based on a story by James Oliver Curwood); ph, William Sickner; ed, Ace Herman.

Adventure   **(PR:A   MPAA:NR)**

CALL OF THE PRAIRIE*   (1936) 63m PAR bw
William Boyd *(Hopalong Cassidy)*, Jimmy Ellison *(Johnny Nelson)*, Muriel Evans *(Linda McHenry)*, George Hayes *(Shanghai)*, Chester Conklin *(Sandy McQueen)*, Al Bridge *(Sam Porter)*, Hank Mann *(Tom)*, Willie Fung *(Wong)*, Howard Lang *(Buck Peters)*, Al Hill *(Slade)*, John Merton *(Arizona)*, Jim Mason *(Hoskins)*, Chill Wills and the Avalon Boys.

Mundane Boyd oater with the usual batch of bunkhouse songs and unbelievable shootouts in which our hero walks through a hail of bullets unscathed. Typical plot has Boyd busting up a band of outlaws who are up to no good. (See: HOPALONG CASSIDY series, Index)

p, Harry Sherman; d, Howard Bretherton; w, Doris Schroeder, Vernon Smith (based on *Hopalong Cassidy's Protege* by Clarence E. Mulford); ph, Archie Stout; m, Tot Seymour, Vee Lawnhurst; ed, Edward Schroeder; art d, Lewis Rachmil.

Western   **(PR:A   MPAA:NR)**

CALL OF THE ROCKIES*   (1938) 54m COL bw
Charles Starrett *(Clint Buckley)*, Donald Grayson *(Slim Grayson)*, Iris Meredith *(Ann Bradford)*, Dick Curtis *(Matt Stark)*, Edward LeSaint *(Judge Stockton)*, Edmund Cobb *(Barlow)*, Art Mix *(Trigger)*, John Tyrrell *(Swale)*, George Chesebro *(Monk)*, Glenn Strange *(Kelso)*, and Sons of the Pioneers.

Another Starrett horse opera pitting the cowboy against a villainous banker who is foreclosing the mortgage on heroine Meredith's ranch. Uninteresting storyline and badly placed musical segments weaken the potential for a good time.

p, Harry L. Decker; d, Allan James; w, Ed Earl Repp; ph, Benjamin Kline; ed, William Lyon; md, Morris Stoloff; m/l, Bob Nolan.

Western   **(PR:A   MPAA:NR)**

CALL OF THE SEA, THE*½   (1930, Brit.) 65m Twickenham/WB bw
Henry Edwards *(Lt. Cmdr. Good)*, Chrissie White *(Iris Tares)*, Bernard Nedell *(Ramon Tares)*, Chili Bouchier *(Poquita)*, Clifford McLaglen *(Pedro)*, Alexander Field *(Hooky Walker)*.

Edwards is a British naval officer who visits a remote tropical island searching for a comrade who had disappeared there some time before. Typically tedious programmer.

p, Julius Hagen, Henry Edwards; d, Leslie Hiscott; w, H. Fowler Mear (based on a story by Frank Shaw).
Adventure **(PR:A M:AA:NR)**

CALL OF THE SOUTH SEAS*½ (1944) 50m REP bw
Janet Martin *(Tahia)*, Allan Lane *(Kendall Gaige)*, William Henry *(Russell)*, Roy Barcroft *(Landrau)*, Wally Vernon *(Handsome)*, Adele Mara *(Aritana)*, Duncan Renaldo *(Charcot)*, Frank Jaquet *(Judge Fator)*, Anna Demetrio *(Latona)*, Dick Alexander *(Bailey)*.

Below average romantic drama set on a small island in the Pacific. Martin plays the beautiful native princess who rules the tiny isle. Trouble erupts when a gang of crooks on the run from the FBI invade the island community and start fleecing the locals. Enter FBI agent Lane who goes undercover as a beachcomber and infiltrates the gang in order to catch them in the act. Romance blooms between the princess and the federal agent. The climax involves a none-too-exciting motor boat chase.

p, Walter H. Goetz; d, John English; w, Albert DeMond; ph, William Bradford; m, Thurston Knudson; ed, Richard Van Enger.
Crime/Romance **(PR:A MPAA:NR)**

CALL OF THE WILD*½** (1935) 89m FOX bw
Clark Gable *(Jack Thornton)*, Loretta Young *(Claire Blake)*, Jack Oakie *(Shorty Hoolihan)*, Frank Conroy *(John Blake)*, Reginald Owen *(Smith)*, Sidney Toler *(Groggin)*, Katherine DeMille *(Marie)*, Lalos Encinas *(Kali)*, Charles Stevens *(Francois)*, James Burke *(Ole)*, Duke Green *(Frank)*, Marie Wells *(Hilda)*, Tommy Jackson, Russ Powell, Herman Bing, George McQuarrie.

Prospector Gable loses his stake at the gambling tables, then buys a huge dog, Buck, thought to be too vicious to pull a sled in snow-bound Alaska. He trains the dog with tender care. Owen, a villain through and through, had thought to buy Buck earlier but had almost lost his hand in the dog's mouth. He then wanted to buy the dog merely to kill him. Seeing Gable with the animal incenses Owen and he wagers a hefty sum against Gable that the enormous dog cannot pull a thousand pounds of weight a hundred yards. The destitute Gable takes him on. Buck struggles to drag the back-breaking load to his new master, winning the bet and the approval of the cheering Skagway crowd. Gable and his jocular friend Oakie, the giant St. Bernard heading their dog sled team, then set out to mine a claim but come across Young, who is unconscious, abandoned by her errant prospector husband, Conroy. The trio go to a cabin owned by Conroy who is presumed dead and there mine his claim, filling their sacks with gold. Oakie goes off to file their claim and return with food while Gable and Young stay behind, falling in love. Buck's trace of wolf blood is set to boiling when he hears the plaintive call of a she-wolf in the night and he goes off to seek a mate, answering, of course, the call of the wild. Owen and his cronies next find Conroy and compel him to lead them to his claim. Just as they arrive they club him unconscious, leaving him for dead. After barging into the cabin and holding Gable and Young at gunpoint, Owen and thugs take their gold and leave by canoe, but the small craft overturns in the rapids and the three thieves are drowned, weighted down by the stolen gold. Conroy, who proves to be more durable than the most hearty pioneer, is found still alive by Buck who leads Gable back to the stricken man. Gable carries him to the cabin where Young, shocked, admits that he is her husband. They revive him and Young elects to stay with her husband, going off with him in a canoe but not before telling Gable that she will always love him. Gable is left alone with his dog until Oakie shows up with provisions, a broad grin, and happy jokes about the future. This hearty film was shot on the snowy slopes of Mount Baker in Washington, at five thousand feet where the harsh winter snows caused the cast and crew to use snowplows to get to their daily locations. The below-zero weather caused hardships with everyone, frostbite to a few, and played havoc with the equipment. The company ran out of food several times and had to send expeditions to distant towns for supplies. Director Wellman stylishly helmed this great outdoors adventure with sharp photography from his cinematographer, the talented Rosher. Producer Zanuck diminshed the role of Buck from the original story penned by Jack London to make room for the Gable-Young romance but kept most of the story intact, adding a few touches from London's *White Fang*, a 1903 tale also set in Alaska during the Gold Rush. London's other marvelous outdoors tales were brought to the screen many times, notably in 1941 with Edward G. Robinson in the best version of the oft-filmed SEA WOLF and the following year with THE ADVENTURES OF MARTIN EDEN. Gable was the perfect lead in CALL OF THE WILD since he personified the hero, a great outdoorsman himself who would rather go hunting or fishing than make movies. He reveled in CALL OF THE WILD but got into battles with director Wellman, an unrelenting taskmaster, which, one report had it, culminated in a fistfight behind a cabin (no winner proclaimed). Gable was married at the time of the production but reports also had it that he and Young carried on a brief but torrid affair on the slopes of Mount Baker. Gable's habit of cussing caused Young to criticize him more than once. Typical of his humorous nature, Gable whittled a club for his leading lady and handed it to her between takes. "Here," he said, "if I use those words again hit me over the head with this. That'll teach me a lesson!"

p, Darryl F. Zanuck; d, William Wellman; w, Gene Fowler, Leonard Praskins (based on the novel by Jack London); ph, Charles Rosher; m, Alfred Newman; ed, Hanson Fritch.
Adventure **(PR:AA MPAA:NR)**

CALL OF THE WILD*½ (1972, Ger./ Span./Ital./Fr.) 105m MGM c
Charlton Heston *(John Thornton)*, Michele Mercier *(Calliope Laurent)*, Raimund Harmstorf *(Pete)*, George Eastman *(Black Burton)*, Sancho Garcia, Rik Battaglia, Maria Rohm.

Obscure film version of the Jack London novel starring Heston and bankrolled by a conglomerate of international investors. Unfortunately, outstanding color photography of beautiful Finnish locations does not a movie make and it is hard to maintain interest as Heston plods through the snow in search of adventure. A big, empty picture postcard of a movie.

p, Harry Alan Towers; d, Ken Annakin; w, Peter Welbeck [Harry Alan Towers], Wyn Wells, Peter Yeldman (based on the novel by Jack London); ph, John Cabrera; m, Carlo Rustichelli.
Adventure **Cas.** **(PR:A MPAA:PG)**

CALL OF THE YUKON* (1938) 70m REP bw
Richard Arlen *(Gaston)*, Beverly Roberts *(Jean)*, Lyle Talbot *(Hugo)*, Mala *(Olee John)*, Garry Owen *(Conner)*, Ivan Miller *(O'Malley)*, James Lono *(Topek)*, Emory Parnell *(Swede Trapper)*, Billy Dooley *(Watchman)*, Al St. John *(Joe)*, Anthony Hughes *(Bill)*, Nina Campana *(Knudka)*.

Ridiculous adventure yarn starring Roberts as a spunky woman reporter who is led out of the Arctic wilderness by guide Arlen. Roberts drags along a small menagerie which includes two bear cubs, a talking raven, and a stray collie. While trying to find civilization, the traveling zoo battles snowslides, ice storms, falling trees, rain, and starvation. The tiny group is rescued by another man, Talbot, who takes an immediate liking to Roberts, which causes a violent fight between the new rival and Arlen. A silly sub-plot involves the collie and its boyfriend, a half wolf, who break up and reunite by the end of the pic. Pretty hard to take.

p, Armand Schaefer; d, B. Reeves Eason; w, Gertrude Orr, William Bartlett (based on the novel *Swift Lightning* by James Oliver Curwood); ph, Ernest Miller.
Adventure **(PR:A MPAA:NR)**

CALL OUT THE MARINES** (1942) 66m RKO bw
Victor McLaglen *(McGinnis)*, Edmund Lowe *(Harry Curtis)*, Binnie Barnes *(Vi)*, Paul Kelly *(Jim Blake)*, Robert Smith *(Billy Harrison)*, Dorothy Lovett *(Mitzi)*, Franklin Pangborn *(Wilbur)*, Corinna Mura *(Rita)*, George Cleveland *(Bartender)*, The King's Men, Six Hits and a Miss.

Dull military comedy featuring McLaglen and Lowe as Marine sergeants stationed in San Diego. The pair concentrate most of their time on chasing women and compete against each other physically and mentally to prove who is the better man. Both fall in love with cafe girl Barnes who plays their rivalry to the hilt. Climax sees the boys discovering that their lady love is an enemy spy which requires them to swallow their pride and do their duty. McLaglen and Lowe make a decent team and the songs are better than average, including the catchy title tune, and "The Light Of My Life," "Zana Zaranda," "Beware," and "Hands Across The Border."

p, Howard Benedict; d&w, Frank Ryan, William Hamilton; ph, Nicholas Musuraca, J. Roy Hunt; ed, Theron Warth; spec eff, Vernon L. Walker; m/l, Mort Greene, Harry Revel.
Musical Comedy **Cas.** **(PR:A MPAA:NR)**

CALL THE MESQUITEERS*½ (1938) 55m REP bw
Bob Livingston *(Stony Brooke)*, Ray Corrigan *(Tucson Smith)*, Max Terhune *(Lullaby Joslin)*, Lynn Roberts *(Madge)*, Earle Hodgins *(Dr. Irving)*, Sammy McKim *(Tim)*, Eddy Waller *(Hardy)*, Maston Williams *(Phillips)*, Eddie Hart *(Lefty)*, Pat Gleason *(Joe)*, Roger Williams *(Frank)*, Warren Jackson *(Mac)*, Hal Price *(Sheriff)*, Flash *(Dog)*.

This Mesquiteer outing has our three heroes trying to stop a gang of silk thieves operating in the area. Also in town is Hodkins, a traveling medicine show quack, and his children. Though the medicine man has a beautiful daughter, Roberts, the cowboys are more interested in the information her little brother McKim has concerning the whereabouts of the notorious silk bandits. At one point the authorities suspect the Mesquiteers themselves as the thieves, but after some chases and shootouts the real bandits are caught and our heroes are cleared. One of the last of the Mesquiteers series before Bob Livingston left the gang and John Wayne took over the role of Stony Brooke.

p, William Berke; d, John English; w, Bernard McConville (adaptation by Luci Ward from characters created by William Colt MacDonald); ph, William Nobles; ed, Lester Orlebeck.
Western **(PR:A MPAA:NR)**

CALLAN½** (1975, Brit.) 91m Cinema National c
Edward Woodward *(Callan)*, Eric Porter, Carl Mohner, Catherine Schell, Peter Egan, Russell Hunter.

Woodward is an aging spy losing interest in his work who is demoted for caring too much about the other side, and now assigned to kill a German businessman. Not bad espionage drama based on a British television series, which also starred Woodward.

p, Derek Horne; d, Don Sharpe; w, James Mitchell (based on his novel *A Red File For Callan*); (Eastmancolor).
Spy Drama **(PR:C MPAA:PG)**

CALLAWAY WENT THATAWAY*½**
(1951) 81m MGM bw (GB: THE STAR SAID NO)
Fred MacMurray *(Mike Frye)*, Dorothy McGuire *(Deborah Patterson)*, Howard Keel *("Stretch" Barnes/"Smoky" Callaway)*, Jesse White *(George Markham)*, Fay Roope *(Tom Lorrison)*, Natalie Schafer *(Martha Lorrison)*, Douglas Kennedy *(Drunk)*, Elisabeth Fraser *(Marie)*, Johnny Indrisano *(Johnny Tarranto)*, Stan Freberg *(Marvin)*, Don Haggerty *(Director)*, Clark Gable, Elizabeth Taylor, Esther Williams *(Guest Stars)*, Dorothy Andre *(Girl)*, James Harrison, Carl Sepulveda *(Heavies)*, Hank Weaver *(Announcer)*, Ned Glass *(Mailman)*, Glen Gallagher, Wayne Treadway, Harold Cornsweet *(Salesmen)*, Kay Scott, Margie Liszt *(Phone Girls)*, Emmett Lynn *(Desert Rat)*, Billy Dix, Lynn Farr, Rocky Cameron *(Cowboys)*, Glenn Strange *(Black Norton)*, John Banner *(Headwaiter)*, Ann Robin *(Hatcheck Girl)*, B. G. Norman, Mickey Little *(Two Kids)*, Ben Strobach *(Hotel Clerk)*, Paul Fierro *(Mexican Bartender)*, Burnu Aquanetta *(Native Girl)*, Carlos Conde *(Native)*, Paul "Tiny" Newlan *(Koch)*, Paul Bryar, Douglas Fowley *(Gaffers)*, Helyn Eby-Rock *(Phone Operator)*, Mae Clarke *(Mother)*, Hugh Beaumont *(Mr. Adkins)*, Sam Herrera, Roque Ybarra *(Native Fishermen)*.

Delightful spoof of early TV advertising and promotion executives now stereotyped and captioned in the more ruthless NETWORK. MacMurray and McGuire are TV promoters suddenly handed an assignment from their network: Find "Smoky" Callaway, a yesteryear star of B westerns who has become an overnight smash with millions of youngsters watching his old oaters on TV. They must not only find Callaway but promote him for his new audience as the upstanding, moralistic, and American-way westerner his fans think him to be. But the hero turns out to be a mean-spirited alcoholic who has disappeared. As coincidence would have it (the Hollywood way), the enterprising pair, while visiting a Colorado dude ranch unearth a real-life cowboy, Keel, who is a doppleganger of the missing Callaway. They ask him to impersonate the western star for the benefit of children, and of course, their own paychecks. He is at first disinclined but later agrees, tempted by a $2,000-a week stipend. At first Keel is the model western movie star, gracious, kind, and considerate. But the money and the Hollywood lifestyle begin to corrupt his clean-cut personality. MacMurray and McGuire much to their sorrow, watch him slowly disintegrate into a bragging, swell-headed, money-grubbing, skirt-chasing jerk. They spend most of their time getting him out of trouble and reforming the monster they themselves created. Then the real Callaway, also played by Keel, appears, following the smell of money from his saloon hideaway in South America. He demands to be cut in on the windfall but when he learns that his impersonator, recently reformed, has donated all his earnings to a boy's home, he musters his personal honor and returns to his obscure domicile below the border. MacMurray and McGuire, meanwhile, have fallen in love and are inching toward the altar. The leads all turn in fine and funny performances. Stealing their scenes when present is the marvelous character actor Jesse White, the much-harrassed cowboy star's agent. In one nightclub scene, some top MGM stars—Clark Gable, Elizabeth Taylor and Esther Williams—appear in cameo roles as they are introduced to the phony Callaway. (Taylor appears in this film for the first and only time as herself; she played a cameo part in SCENT OF MYSTERY and, out of caprice, appeared as an extra in QUO VADIS and ANNE OF THE THOUSAND DAYS. Although the Keel character is not that sharply defined, it is undoubtedly drawn from the careers of Gene Autry, Roy Rogers, and chiefly, William Boyd (the latter having shrewdly bought up the rights to most of his "Hopalong Cassidy" movies, reaping a fortune when selling them piecemeal to TV for showing to children.)

p,d&w, Norman Panama, Melvin Frank; ph, Ray June; m, Marlin Skiles; ed, Cotton Warburton; art d, Cedric Gibbons, Eddie Imazu.

Comedy/Western (PR:AA MPAA:NR)

CALLBOX MYSTERY, THE* (1932, Brit.) 73m Samuelson bw
Warwick Ward (Leo Mount), Harold French (Inspector Layton), Wendy Barrie (Iris Banner), Gerald Rawlinson (David Radnor), Harvey Braban (Inspector Brown), Daphne Mowbray (Rose).

Inspector French falls in love with the daughter of an apparent suicide and together they prove that a string of similar suicides are actually murders. Not worth staying up late for.

p, Gordon Craig; d, G. B. Samuelson; w, Joan Wentworth Wood.

Crime (PR:A MPAA:NR)

CALLED BACK*½ (1933, Brit.) 51m REA bw
Franklin Dyall (Dr. Jose Manuel), Lester Matthews (Gilbert Vaughan), Dorothy Boyd (Pauline March), Alexander Sarner (Santos Macari), Anthony Ireland (Anthony March), Francis L. Sullivan (Kaledin), Ian Fleming (Dr. Carter), Margaret Emden (Priscilla), Geoffrey Goodhart (Ivan).

Dyall stars as a revolutionary doctor who plots the overthrow of the oppressive Spanish government. Unfortunately, his efforts are foiled by a blind man and an amnesiac girl.

p, Julius Hagen; d, Reginald Denham, Jack Harris; w, Hugh Conway (based on the novel by Conway).

Drama (PR:A MPAA:NR)

CALLING, THE (SEE: BELLS, 1981)

CALLING ALL CROOKS*½ (1938, Brit.) 85m Mancunian bw
Duggie Wakefield (Duggie), Billy Nelson (Billy), Leslie Perrins (Duvane), Helen Barnes (Joan Bellamy), Chuck O'Neil (Chuck), Jack Butler (Jack), Dan Young, Howard Rogers, Raymond Smith, 7 Royal Hindustanis, Hal Wright and his Circus, 60 Sherman Fisher Girls, 10 Master Singers, 30 Gypsy Revelers.

Imbecilic comedy has Music Hall comedy team Wakefield and Nelson, a pair of bumbling detectives, assuming a variety of disguises and bumbling their way to catching a crooked promoter. Possibly the only chance to see 60 Sherman Fisher Girls and 30 Gypsy Revelers in the same movie.

p, John E. Blakely; d, George Black; w, Arthur Mertz.

Comedy (PR:A MPAA:NR)

CALLING ALL HUSBANDS* (1940) 64m WB bw
George Tobias (Armstrong), Lucille Fairbanks (Betty), Ernest Truex (Trippe), George Reeves (Williams), Florence Bates (Mrs. Trippe), Charles Halton (Weaver), Virginia Sale (Mabel), John Alexander (Sheriff), Clem Bevans (Judge), Sam McDaniel (Nappy).

Bumbling domestic comedy starring Truex as an overworked, underpaid milquetoast who must go home every night to a nagging wife, Bates bemoans the fact that she chose to marry him, a loser, after the many offers from other, better men that passed through her youth, especially Tobias. The only thing that keeps poor Truex going is the love of his daughter, Fairbanks, who supports him emotionally. Fairbanks herself is involved in a romance with a nice, young man, Reeves. Enter Tobias, who arrives at the back door of the home on the lam from the law and begging for handouts. Truex sees his opportunity to rub his wife's nose in her past and saves the small time crook long

enough to present the "better man" to Bates. The nagging wife is shocked into complacency and finally shuts her trap.

p, William Jacobs; d, Noel Smith; w, Robert E. Kent (based on the play "Broken Dishes" by Martin Flavin); ph, Ted McCord; ed, Frank Magee.

Comedy (PR:A MPAA:NR)

CALLING ALL MARINES*½ (1939) 67m REP bw
Donald Barry (Blackie), Helen Mack (Judy), Warren Hymer (Snooker), Robert Kent (Marvin Fox), Cy Kendall (Big Joe), Leon Ames (Murdock), Selmer Jackson (Col. Vincent), Janet McLeay (Pat), Walter McGrail (Capt. Chester), George Chandler (Gordon), Jay Novello (Lefty), James Flavin (Sgt. Smith).

Barry portrays a young mobster who is recruited by an international spy ring to infiltrate the U. S. Marine Corps and steal plans for a new aerial torpedo being developed by engineers. The young hood lifts the entrance papers of a local hayseed because his own records show his arrests and would prevent him from being able to join the service. He then sees an opportunity to grab the secret papers and make good his escape, but the man he is impersonating turns up and blows the whistle on him. The impostor is thrown in the brig, but his gang busts him out against his will to shut him up. Suddenly the hood is overcome by good ol' U. S. patriotism and a newfound love for the Marine Corps and escapes from the gang and assists the military in the capture of the conspirators. Pretty silly stuff, but potentially fun for those not expecting much.

p, Armand Schaefer; d, John H. Auer; w, Earl Felton (based on a story by Harrison Carter); ph, Ernest Miller; m, Cy Feuer; ed, Ernest Nims.

Crime/Espionage (PR:A MPAA:NR)

CALLING ALL MA'S (SEE: BITER BIT, 1937)

CALLING BULLDOG DRUMMOND** (1951, Brit.) 80m MGM bw
Walter Pidgeon (Hugh Drummond), Margaret Leighton (Sgt. Helen Smith), Robert Beatty ("Guns"), David Tomlinson (Algy Longworth), Peggy Evans (Molly), Charles Victor (Inspector McIver), Bernard Lee (Col. Webson), James Hayter (Bill), Patrick Doonan (Alec), Harold Lang (Stan), Michael Allan (Bert).

This was the 22nd "Bulldog Drummond" film and Pidgeon was the twelfth of thirteen portrayers of Hector McNeil's famous character. A desperate gang robs a London store and escapes through the pea-soup fog by using radar equipment. Amateur sleuth Pidgeon comes out of retirement to nail the thieves. Scotland Yard assigns a female officer (Leighton) to him and they go undercover to get close to the brigands. Soon enough, Pidgeon is recognized and put into the basement of a bombed-out building (there still were plenty of those around England after the war). He escapes in time to capture the malfeasants. Saville's direction was better than the slim script and there was a general waste of talent in the casting. Leighton could have phoned in her performance, and Tomlinson, Hayter, and Lee (veterans all) weren't given nearly enough to do. Give it "B" for Bulldog. (See BULLDOG DRUMMOND Series, Index)

p, Hayes Goetz; d, Victor Saville; w, Gerard Fairlie, Howard Emmett Rogers, Arthur Wimperis (based on the novel by Fairlie and characters by Hector McNeil); ph, Graham Kelly; m, Rudolph G. Kopp; ed, Frank Clarke.

Crime (PR:A-C MPAA:NR)

CALLING DR. DEATH* (1943) 62m UNIV bw
Lon Chaney, Jr. (Doctor Steele), Patricia Morison (Stella), J. Carrol Naish (Inspector Gregg), David Bruce (Robert Duval), Ramsay Ames (Maria Steele), Fay Helm (Mrs. Duval), Holmes Herbert (Butler), Alec Craig (Watchman), Fred Gierman (Father), Lisa Golm (Mother), Charles Wagenheim (Coroner), Mary Hale (Marion), George Eldredge (District Attorney), John Elliott (Priest).

The first in a mediocre series of mysteries based on the popular radio program "Inner Sanctum." Chaney stars as a neurologist who hates his beautiful but unfaithful wife. Soon his wife's cut-up corpse is found and the good doctor becomes the main suspect. The only problem is that the doctor himself isn't sure whether he committed the crime while in a fit of self-hypnotic jealousy or if he is indeed innocent. Enter super-sleuth Naish who is determined to get to the bottom of the puzzling mystery. Though the suspense story is nothing special, the cast of competent character actors and good, moody direction helps the film move along at a tight pace. (See INNER SANCTUM series, Index)

p, Ben Pivar; d, Reginald LeBorg; w, Edward Dein; ph, Virgil Miller; ed, Norman A. Cerf; special photography, John P. Fulton.

Mystery (PR:A MPAA:NR)

CALLING DR. GILLESPIE** (1942) 84m MGM bw
Lionel Barrymore (Dr. Gillespie), Philip Dorn (Dr. Gerniede), Donna Reed (Marcia Bradburn), Phil Brown (Roy Todwell), Nat Pendleton (Joe Wayman), Alma Kruger (Molly Byrd), Mary Nash (Emma Hope), Walter Kingsford (Dr. Carew), Nell Craig (Nurse Parker), Ruth Tobey (Susan May Prentiss), Jonathan Hale (Frank Todwell), Charles Dingle (Dr. Kenwood), Robin Raymond ("Bubbles"), Marie Blake (Sally), Nana Bryant (Mrs. Marshall Todwell), Emmett Vogan (Lt. Clifton), Pat McVey (Sgt. Hartwell), Hillary Brooke (Mrs. Brown), Eddie Acuff (Clifford Genet), Ava Gardner (Girl Bit).

Really only notable as the film that Lew Ayres had to stop working on because he had declared conscientious objector status in WW II. The role was rewritten, re-cast, and re-shot using foreign actor Dorn as young doctor Gerniede who was made Dutch to explain his accent. The new casting really doesn't matter because Barrymore, as usual, dominates the film. Plot concerns a homicidal maniac, Brown, and his distraught girl friend, Reed, who call on Barrymore to cure Brown of his illness. Dorn aids the wheelchair-ridden doctor as he follows the maniac's string of murders, searching for a way to end the man's sickness. Look for Ava Gardner in a bit part. (See DR. GILLESPIE series, Index)

d, Harold S. Bucquet; w, Willis Goldbeck, Harry Ruskin (based on a story by Kubec Glasmon from characters created by Max Brand); ph, Ray June; m, Daniele Amfitheatrof; ed, Elmo Veron; art d, Cedric Gibbons.

Medical Drama (PR:A MPAA:NR)

CALLING DR. KILDARE** (1939) 86m MGM bw
Lew Ayres (Dr. James Kildare), Lionel Barrymore (Dr. Leonard Gillespie), Laraine Day (Mary Lamont), Nat Pendleton (Joe Wayman), Lana Turner (Rosalie), Samuel S. Hinds (Dr. Stephen Kildare), Lynne Carver (Alice Raymond), Emma Dunn (Mrs. Martha Kildare), Walter Kingsford (Dr. Walter Carew), Alma Kruger (Molly Byrd), Marie Blake (Sally), Reed Hadley (Tom Crandell), Nell Craig ("Nosey"), Harlan Briggs (John Galt), Henry Hunter (Harry Galt), Ann Todd (Jenny), Aileen Pringle (Mrs. Thatcher), Donald Barry (Collins).

Second in the series of KILDARE medical dramas has the young doctor risking his career by treating the gunshot wounds of a young hoodlum whom Ayres is convinced is innocent. The fact that the wounded punk's sister is Lana Turner further motivates the usually ambitious doc to chance losing his promising future. Barrymore is his usual gruff self and the casting and production values are fine, but it is the terribly inconsistent script which keeps the film from being any better than a "B" melodrama. The Kildare character had been established in the viewer's mind as upright and sensible, therefore it is extremely out of character for him to make an unbelievably risky and stupid decision (to help the wounded hood) just to impress a beautiful blonde. In the end Ayres is vindicated by the actual innocence of the boy and everything turns out fine. (See DR. KILDARE series, Index)

p, Lou Ostrow; d, Harold S. Bucquet; w, Harry Ruskin, Willis Goldbeck (based on the story by Max Brand); ph, Alfred Gilks; ed, Robert J. Kern.

Medical Drama (PR:A MPAA:NR)

CALLING HOMICIDE** (1956) 60m AA bw
Bill Elliott (Lt. Doyle), Don Haggerty (Sgt. Duncan), Kathleen Case (Donna), Myron Healey (Haddix), Jeanne Cooper (Darlene), Thomas B. Henry (Gilmore), Lyle Talbot (Tony Fuller), Almira Sessions (Mrs. Dunsetter), Herb Vigran (Ray Engel), James Best (Arnholt), John Dennis (Benny).

When a young policeman is blown up by dynamite, detective Elliott gets on the case. Soon he finds the strangled corpse of a modeling school operator (Cooper) and this leads him somehow to crack an adoption racket. Well done, considering tiny budget.

p, Ben Schwalb; d&w, Edward Bernds; ph, Harry Neumann; m, Marlin Skiles; ed, William Austin.

Crime (PR:A-C MPAA:NR)

CALLING PAUL TEMPLE*½ (1948, Brit.) 92m Nettlefold bw
John Bentley (Paul Temple), Dinah Sheridan (Steve Temple), Margaretta Scott (Mrs. Trevellyan), Abraham Sofaer (Dr. Kohima), Celia Lipton (Norma Rice), Jack Raine (Sir Graham Forbes), Alan Wheatley (Edward Lathom), Hugh Pryse (Wilfred Davies), Wally Patch (Spider Williams).

Detective Bentley tracks down the mysterious killer who's doing away with the wealthy female patients of a nerve doctor. Nothing special.

p, Ernest G. Roy; d, Maclean Rogers; w, Francis Durbridge, A. R. Rawlinson, Kathleen Butler (based on a radio series "Paul Temple and the Canterbury Case" by Durbridge).

Crime (PR:A MPAA:NR)

CALLING PHILO VANCE*½ (1940) 62m WB bw
James Stephenson (Philo Vance), Margot Stevenson (Hilda Lake), Henry O'Neill (Markham), Edward Brophy (Ryan), Ralph Forbes (Tom McDonald), Donald Douglas (Philip Wrede), Martin Kosleck (Gamble), Sheila Bromley (Doris), James Conlon (Dr. Doremus), Edward Raquello (Grassi), Creighton Hale (Du Bois), Harry Strang (Hennessey), Richard Kipling (Archer Coe), Wedgewood Nowell (Brisbane Coe), Bo Ling (Ling Toy), De Wolfe Hopper (Hotel Clerk), George Reeves (Steamship Clerk), George Irving (Avery).

This lame addition to the Philo Vance saga came close to putting an end to the series of nearly a dozen films. In this reworking of the earlier KENNEL MURDER CASE, attention is paid only to tying together a loose plot, while treating actors merely as meat. An international cast spots this story of a murdered designer of a war plane and Stephenson's calculated efforts to crack the case. A remake that had no right to be remade. (See PHILO VANCE series, Index)

p, Bryan Foy; d, William Clemens; w, Tom Reed (based on the story by S. S. Van Dine); ph, L. William O'Connell; ed, Benjamin Liss.

Spy Drama (PR:A MPAA:NR)

CALLING THE TUNE* (1936, Brit.) 71m Phoenix-IFP bw
Adele Dixon (Julia Harbord), Clifford Evans (Peter Mallory), Sam Livesey (Bob Gordon), Sally Gray (Margaret Gordon), Donald Wolfit (Dick Finlay), Eliot Makeham (Stephen Harbord), Lewis Casson (John Mallory), Ronald Simpson (Bramwell), H. F. Maltby (Stubbins), Cedric Hardwicke, George Robey, Charles Penrose, Reginald Forsyth, Sir Henry Wood and the Queen's Hall Light Orchestra, English Quartette.

The daughter of a record manufacturer falls in love with the son of the man her father cheated years before. A couple of talented actors appear in supporting roles and most of the music is fairly good, but neither help this boring musical.

p, Hugh Perceval; d, Reginald Denham; w, Basil Mason.

Musical (PR:A MPAA:NR)

CALLING WILD BILL ELLIOTT** (1943) 55m REP bw
Bill Elliott, George Hayes, Anne Jeffreys, Herbert Heyes, "Buzzy" Dee Henry, Fred Kohler, Jr., Roy Barcroft, Charles King, Frank Hagney, Bud Geary, Lynton Brent, Fred McCarroll, Eve March, Burr Caruth, Forbes Murray, Ted Mapes, Cliff Parkinson, Herman Hack, Yakima Canutt.

Hayes boasts of his friendship with Wild Bill, but then the hero actually turns up and Hayes helps him put away crooked Gov. Heyes. Above average B western is allegedly the first talkie to incorporate the name of the star into the title.

p, Harry Grey; d, Spencer Bennet; w, Anthony Coldeway (based on a story by Luci Ward); ph, Ernest Miller.

Western (PR:A MPAA:NR)

CALM YOURSELF zero (1935) 70m MGM bw
Robert Young (Pat), Madge Evans (Rosalind), Betty Furness (Mary Elizabeth), Nat Pendleton (Knuckles Benedict), Hardie Albright (Bobby Kent), Ralph Morgan (Mr. Rockwell), Claude Gillingwater (Allenby), Paul Hurst (Roscoe), Shirley Ross (Mrs. Rockwell), Shirley Chambers (Joan Vincent), Hale Hamilton (Mr. Kent), Clyde Cook (Joe), Herman Bing (Bromberg), Richard Tucker (Police Inspector), Charles Trowbridge (Lanselle), Tempe Pigott (Anne), Raymond Hatton (Mike).

Another quickly made programmer by Seitz, one of Hollywood's most prolific directors in his day, and it shows his haste (four films in 1935 within a few weeks of each other). A boresome story of a kidnaping in which adman Young and unsympathetic Furness creak through their roles, with only Evans showing any signs of life. "Calm Yourself" might put you to sleep.

p, Lucien Hubbard; d, George B. Seitz; w, Arthur Kober (based on a story by Edward Hope); ph, Lester White; m, Charles Maxwell.

Comedy (PR:A MPAA:NR)

CALTIKI, THE IMMORTAL MONSTER**½ (1959, Ital.) 76m AA bw (CALTIKI, IL MONSTRO IMMORTALE)
John Merivale, Didi Sullivan [Didi Perego], Gerard Herter, Daniela Rocca, Giacomo Rossi-Stuart, Gay Pearl, Daniele Pitani.

Pretty silly Italian horror outing, but historically interesting because it was one of the first Italian films made to be aimed specifically at an American market (which explains the increasingly ridiculous "American" pseudonyms used by the cast and crew so that their names would be more recognizable to U.S. audiences—a practice that would plague "Spaghetti" westerns). Set in Mexico, a group of scientists led by Merivale discover a radioactive blob (which goes by the name of Caltiki) while excavating a Mayan temple. The adventurers manage to kill the nuclear ooze, but the sample they bring to the lab comes to life and wreaks havoc throughout Mexico by searing the flesh off of it's victims. Eventually our heroes figure out a way to destroy the mobile slime and rid the Earth of it's menace. Shot and co-directed by Mario Bava, who would soon go on to direct scores of effective, scary Italian horror films and become something of a cult figure among European horror aficionados.

p, Samuel Schneider; d, Robert Hampton [Ricardo Freda], (uncredited, Mario Bava); w, Phillip Just [Filippano Sanjust] (based on a Mexican Legend); ph, John Foan [Mario Bava].

Horror (PR:C MPAA:NR)

CALYPSO** (1959, Fr./It.) 95m Enalpa-Fimsonor c
Cy Grant (Peter), Sally Neal (Resy), Louise Bennet (Martha), Carlton Gumbs (Cicero), Paul Savain (Grandpa), Didier Petrus (Washington), W. E. Minto (Rick).

Thin plot about a Caribbean mulatto family trying to marry a daughter to a white to assure a better social standing is mostly an excuse for exotic dances, cockfights, and the title music. Pretty but light.

d, Franco Rossi, Golfiero Colonna, Leonardo Benvenuti; ph, Pierludovico Pavoni (Totalscope, Eastmancolor); m, A. F. Lavagnino; ed, Mario Serandrei.

Musical (PR:A-C MPAA:NR)

CALYPSO HEAT WAVE** (1957) 86m Columbia bw
Johnny Desmond (Johnny Conroy), Merry Anders (Marty Collins), Meg Myles (Mona De Luca), Paul Langton (Mack Adams), Joel Grey (Alex Nash), Michael Granger (Barney Pearl), George E. Stone (Books), The Tarriers, The Hi-Lo's, Maya Angelou (Herself), Dick Whittinghill (Himself), Darla Hood (Girl), Pierce Lyden (Hi Fi Bromley), Gil Perkins (George), William Challee (Andrew), Mac Niles and the Calypsonians, The Treniers.

Silliness about jukebox baron Granger muscling into a record company to profit from the calypso fad. Desmond, as the company's star recording artist, doesn't like the change of management and vanishes. The record company goes into a slide, Granger drops out, Desmond comes back, and everything ends up happily with a calypso carnival. Joel Grey is good as a dancing office boy, but the musical acts are by far the best things here. The Hi-Lo's sing "Swing Low Sweet Chariot" and "My Sugar is so Refined." The Tarriers (Alan Arkin among them) sing "Banana Boat Song," The Treniers do "Day Old Bread and Canned Beans" and "Rock Joe," and Maya Angelou, who went on to literary acclaim, shows her origins singing "Run Joe." Good fun.

p, Sam Katzman; d, Fred F. Sears; w, David Chandler (based on a story by Orville H. Hampton); ph, Benjamin H. Kline; m, Paul Mertz, Ross Di Maggio; ed, Edwin Bryant, Tony DiMarco; ch, Josephine Earl.

Musical (PR:A MPAA:NR)

CALYPSO JOE*½ (1957) 74m AA bw
Herb Jeffries, Angie Dickinson, Edward Kemmer, Stephen Bekassy, Laurie Mitchell, Claudia Drake, Murray Alper, Linda Terrace, Charles R. Keans, Genie Stone, Robert Sherman, Lord Flea and his Calypsonians, The Lester Horton Dancers, Duke of Iron, Herb Jeffries' Calypsomaniacs, The Easy Riders.

The first and the worst of the brief Calypso cycle of films that emerged in 1957, this one was packaged with HOT ROD RUMBLE. Dickinson is an airline stewardess and Kemmer is a TV star. They meet, fall in love, split up, go to South America, and reunite. But mostly there's the music, with Jeffries in the title role singing "There's Only One Love (Between a Man and a Woman)" and six other tunes. The Easy Riders perform their hits "Marianne" and "Sweet Sugar Cane."

p, William F. Broidy; d, Edward Dein; w, Edward and Mildred Dein; ph, Stuart Thompson; m, Richard Hazard; ed, Thor Brooks; songs, Jeffries, Hazard.

Musical   **(PR:A   MPAA:NR)**

CAMELOT***   (1967) 179m WB/7 ARTS c
Richard Harris (King Arthur), Vanessa Redgrave (Guenevere), Franco Nero (Lancelot Du Lac), David Hemmings (Mordred), Lionel Jeffries (King Pellinore), Laurence Naismith (Merlyn), Pierre Olaf (Dap), Estelle Winwood (Lady Clarinda), Gary Marshall (Sir Lionel), Anthony Rogers (Sir Dinaden), Peter Bromilow (Sir Sagramore), Sue Casey (Lady Sybil), Garry Marsh (Tom), Nicolas Beauvy (King Arthur as a boy).

Lovely to look at, pleasant to listen to, interesting to think about — and yet it all added up to a thick and often clumsy $15 million film. CAMELOT as a play went on too long and had many flaws; it was saved by a glorious performance by Richard Burton and the presence of some young singer/actors who did their best work (Robert Goulet-who has never regained that height). The film flags as it retells T. H. White's story of when days were old and knights were bold. Harris is married to Redgrave and planning to re-establish chivalry at The Round Table. Arthur takes in Nero (Lancelot) and treats him as a son. This is rewarded by Nero's taking up with Arthur's wife. She is sent to the stake for her transgressions. From there the film goes downhill. Logan's direction was limpid and his use of color left much to be desired. The score by Lerner and Loewe remains one of their minor efforts. The play was presented when President Kennedy was in the public eye and sentimentalists like to think of that period as the U.S.A.'s "Camelot." The picture remembers better than it actually was. Still, any film with this much production, and certainly this much sincerity attached to it, does merit watching. It was Jack Warner's last project for Warner Brothers.

p, Jack L. Warner; d, Joshua Logan; w, Alan Jay Lerner (based on the play by Lerner and Frederick Loewe and book The Once and Future King by T. H. White); ph, Richard H, Kline (Technicolor); m, Loewe; ed, Folmar Blangsted; md, Alfred Newman; art d, Edward Carrere; m/l, Lerner and Loewe; cos, John Truscott.

Drama   **Cas.**   **(PR:A-C   MPAA:NR)**

CAMELS ARE COMING, THE**   (1934, Brit.) 80m Gainsborough/GAU bw
Jack Hulbert (Jack Campbell), Anna Lee (Anita Rodgers), Hartley Power (Nicholas), Harold Huth (Dr. Zhiga), Allan Jeaves (Sheikh), Peter Gawthorne (Col. Fairley), Norma Whalley (Tourist), Peggy Simpson (Tourist), Percy Parsons (Arab), Tony de Lungo (Servant).

Hulbert is an Officer in the Camel Corps stationed in Egypt. He impersonates a sheikh in order to capture a ring of drug smugglers. Lightweight comedy is slightly above average for British offerings of the period.

p, Michael Balcon; d, Tim Whelan; w, Guy Bolton, Jack Hulbert, W. P. Lipscomb (based on a story by Whelan, Russell Medcraft).

Comedy   **(PR:A   MPAA:NR)**

CAMEO KIRBY*   (1930) 55m FOX bw
J. Harold Murray (Cameo Kirby), Norma Terris (Adele Randall), Douglas Gilmore (Jack Moreau), Robert Edeson (Col. Randall), Charles Morton (Anatole), Stepin Fetchit (Croup), John Hyams (Larkin Bunce), Mme. Daumery (Claire Devezac), Myrna Loy (Lea), Beulah Hall Jones (Poulette).

The third version of this tiresome Cameo Kirby story doesn't get any better this time around. Set in the mid-1800s on the mighty Mississippi, this one has Murray working as a decent riverboat gambler. While up against a gang of delinquents at the New Orleans Mardi Gras, he rescues a pretty lass from their grip. Ungratefully, she slips away without the thank-you he was hoping for. However, after winning the deed to her father's cotton plantation, thet meet again. Murray quickly makes a score of enemies, followed by a lynch mob out for his throat. But the deed is all-powerful, and upon its presentation the townspeople put down their ropes. Based on a play by Booth Tarkington, this slow-mover runs under an hour and is still long. Features Loy in a bit part as a mistress wearing a black wig. Murray, Terris and Gilmore, all silent film stars, quickly faded in the sound era, their voices thought to be unsuited to the new medium.

d, Irving Cummings; w, Marion Orth (based on the play by Booth Tarkington and Harry Leon Wilson); ph, L. William O'Connell, George Eastman; ed, Alex Troffey; m/l, Walter Donaldson and Edgar Leslie, assisted by Ed Brady and Fred Strauss.

Musical Drama   **(PR:A   MPAA:NR)**

CAMERA BUFF***   (1983, Pol.) 112m Cinegate/New Yorker c
Jerzy Stuhr (Filip Mosz), Malgorzata Zabkowska (His Wife), Ewa Pokas (Anna), Stefan Czyzewski (Director), Jerzy Nowak (Osuch), Tadeusz Bradecki (Witek), Marek Litewka (Piotrek), Krysztof Zanussi (Himself), Boguslaw Sobczuk, Andrzej Warchol (TV Directors).

Clever Polish comedy starring Stuhr as a factory worker who changes his life when he purchases a home movie camera. Eventually his creative eye turns from filming family outings to shooting investigative documentaries that get him in trouble with his wife (she leaves him) and his bosses (who attempt to force him into abandoning his hobby). An interesting mix of comedy and sly political criticism. (In Polish, English sub-titles.)

d, Krzysztof Kieslowski; w, Kieslowski, Jerzy Stuhr; ph, Jacek Petrycki; m, Krzysztof

Knittel; ed, Halina Nawrocka; art d, Rafal Waltenberger; cos, Gabriela Star-Tyszkiewicz.

Comedy   **(PR:A   MPAA:NR)**

CAMILLE*****   (1937) 108m MGM bw
Greta Garbo (Marguerite), Robert Taylor (Armand), Lionel Barrymore (Mon. Duval), Elizabeth Allan (Nichette), Jessie Ralph (Nanine), Henry Daniell (Baron de Varville), Lenore Ulric (Olympe), Laura Hope Crews (Prudence), Rex O'Malley (Gaston), Russell Hardie (Gustave), E. E. Clive (Saint Gaudens), Douglas Walton (Henri), Marion Ballou (Corinne), Joan Brodel (Marie Jeanette), June Wilkins (Louise), Fritz Leiber, Jr. (Valentin), Elsie Esmonds (Mme. Duval).

CAMILLE is, simply, one of the best movies ever made. Surely it must rank in the top five love stories. Garbo is radiant as Dumas's Dame aux camelias and Robert Taylor (only 25 at the time and already appearing in his 15th film) does his very best work. To recapitulate the story is to give it short shrift as there is no way to capture on paper what is captured on screen. Garbo is a Parisian woman of no repute who combines coquetry and femininity with cynicism and materialism. And yet, we always have the feeling that under the makeup is a woman who has a backbone of morality. She is being kept by Henry Daniell (absolutely superb as a wealthy Baron) and decides to leave him in favor of young Armand (Robert Taylor), a handsome and passionate swain who doesn't know her history. Her decision is based on her heart, not her head, and the love she feels for Taylor is sincere. Barrymore, as Taylor's father, prevails on the woman to give up the young man. Apparently, Taylor is the only person around who doesn't know her reputation and even if he did, it wouldn't matter to him. The appeal by Barrymore makes sense, as once the word gets out that Taylor and she are together, it might ruin his career. She leaves and tells Taylor a lie. He begins to court her with love, and when that fails, he gets angry. Nothing helps and no one tells Taylor the truth about why she's walked away. But the audience knows that Garbo loves Taylor so much that she could not bear to hurt him, so she returns to a smug Daniell to relive her past (John Barrymore was supposed to play the part but was 'indisposed'). At the conclusion, Garbo is dying of tuberculosis and there is a famous moment where she is overjoyed at seeing Taylor but the secondary texture of the scene is that she knows her death is imminent and it is, in fact, the one way to release them both from the love they feel for each other. No matter how detailed the previous sentences, they could never convey the essence of this incredible movie. Garbo is so convincing that her portrayal has become part of the American fabric (Ernie Kovacs used it in a TV sketch when he walked to a bookcase, took out a copy of CAMILLE, opened it, and we heard a cough!). Every Garbo movement is exquisite. When Daniell orders her to pick up her fan from the floor, she moves sideways with swanlike grace. When she dies in Taylor's arms, her eyes burst wide open, just the reversal of audience expectation, which caused some viewers to later comment that Garbo's soul momentarily left her body. The screenplay is poetic and the production. (Thalberg's last; he died while it was being made and it was completed by Bernard Hyman.) Taylor signed a seven year contract in 1934 for only $35 per week. He was raised to $50 per week in 1936. It is presumed that he got several raises after the release of CAMILLE. It's become de rigueur to knock the overblown love stories of that era and CAMILLE is the first picture to be skewered. Don't believe a word of it. Just sit back, pick up a handful of tissues, and let Greta and Robert and Henry and all the rest take you back to a time when movies were about people, not cyborgs and androids and chrome and steel. (Filmed as silents, 1915, 1917 and 1921)

p, Irving Thalberg [Bernard Hyman]; d, George Cukor; w, Zoe Akins, Frances Marion, James Hilton (based on the novel and play La Dame aux camelias by Alexandre Dumas, fils); ph, William Daniels; m, Herbert Stothart; ed, Margaret Booth.

Romance   **(PR:A-C   MPAA:NR)**

CAMILLE 2000 zero   (1969) 116m Audubon c
Daniele Gaubert (Marguerite Gauthier), Nino Castelnuovo (Armand Duval), Eleanora Rossi-Drago (Prudence), Philippe Forquet (Duke De Varville), Roberto Bisacco (Gaston), Massimo Serato (Armand's Father), Silvana Venturelli (Olympe), Zachary Adams (Gody).

Early "artsy" sex film from the team that brought such fleshy classics as I, A WOMAN, and CARMEN BABY from Sweden to these shores. Shot entirely in Rome with typically lousy post-dubbing, CAMILLE 2000 stars the buxom Gaubert as the title character who sleeps her way into the hearts of the local nobleman, all the while longing for her true love, commoner Castelnuvo, This Camille is not dying from tuberculosis, but of some strange, unexplained disease (one assumes of the venereal variety) and she becomes hooked on the drugs she takes to remedy her ailments. Pretentious, overblown direction and generally awful performances detract from whatever eroticism could possibly develop from this mess.

p&d, Radley Metzger; w, Michael DeForrest (based on "The Lady of the Camellias" by Alexander Dumas fils); ph, Ennio Guarnieri (Panavision, Technicolor); m, Piero Piccioni; ed, Humphrey Hinshelwood, Amedeo Safa; art d, Enrico Sabbatini.

Drama   **Cas.**   **(PR:O   MPAA:R)**

CAMMINACAMMINA**   (1983, Ital.) 165m GAU c
Alberto Fumagalli (Mel, the Priest), Antonio Cuccarre (Rupo, the Boy).

Lengthy religious adventure tale detailing the journey of a rag-tag group of believers who travel to see the baby messiah. Beautifully photographed and lovingly made, the film suffers from it's excessive length and a cast of nonprofessional actors. A four-hour version was slated for release on Italian television.

d,w,ph,ed,set d,&cos, Ermanno Almi; m, Bruno Nicolai.

Adventure   **(PR:AA   MPAA:NR)**

CAMP ON BLOOD ISLAND, THE**½   (1958, Brit.) 82m Hammer bw
Carl Mohner (Piet Van Elst), Andre Morell (Colonel Lambert), Edward Underdown.

Lurid prison camp story from the Hammer studios, where luridness was raised to a fine art. The sadistic commandant has vowed to slaughter all his prisoners should his side lose the war, so when the prisoners learn of the end of the war they keep it a secret until they can stage a revolt. Trash, but decent trash.

p, Anthony Hinds; d, Val Guest; w, Jon Manchip White, Val Guest (based on a story by White); ph, Jack Asher (Megascope); m, Gerard Schurmann; ed, Bill Lenny.

War **(PR:O   MPAA:NR)**

CAMPBELL'S KINGDOM** ½ (1957, Brit.) 100m Rank c
Dirk Bogarde (*Bruce Campbell*), Stanley Baker (*Owen Morgan*), Michael Craig (*Boy Bleden*), Barbara Murray (*Jean Lucas*), James Robertson Justice (*James MacDonald*), Athene Seyler (*Miss Abigail*), Robert Brown (*Creasy*), John Laurie (*Mac*), Sidney James (*Timid Driver*), Mary Merrall (*Miss Ruth*), Roland Brand (*Driver*), George Murcell (*Max*), Finlay Currie (*Old Man*), Peter Illing (*The Doctor*), Stanley Maxted (*Fergus*), Gordon Tanner (*Cliff*), Richard McNamara (*The Stranger*).

Okay adventure yarn starring Bogarde as the grandson of an old eccentric who has left him a valley known as "Campbell's Kingdom" which the old man claimed held a fortune in oil. Bogarde believes in his grandfather's hunch, but conflict arises when unscrupulous contractor Baker attempts to flood the valley to power his new hydro-electric dam. To fight Baker, Bogarde organizes a scruffy army of volunteers who plan an elaborate series of explosions which cause landslides, destroying the dam. Love interest for Bogarde comes in the form of saloon girl Murray who stands by her man as he actually does strike oil on his grandfather's property. Good cast and fairly exciting action sequences help overshadow some of the more predictable elements of the plot line.

p, Betty E. Box; d, Ralph Thomas; w, Robin Estridge (based on the novel by Hammond Innes); ph, Ernest Steward (Eastman Colour; m, Clifton Parker; ed, Frederick Wilson.

Adventure **(PR:A   MPAA:NR)**

CAMPUS CONFESSIONS** (1938) 65m PAR bw
Betty Grable (*Joyce Gilmore*), Eleanore Whitney (*Susie Quinn*), William Henry (*Wayne Atterbury, Jr.*), Fritz Feld ("*Lady MacBeth*"), John Arledge (*Freddy Fry*), Thurston Hall (*Wayne Atterbury, Sr.*), Roy Gordon (*Dean Wilton*), Lane Chandler (*Coach Parker*), Richard Denning (*Buck Hogan*), Matty Kemp (*Ed Riggs*), Sumner Getchell ("*Blimp*" *Garrett*), "Hank" Luisetti (*Himself*).

Typical spirited college rah-rah film, exploiting the name of All-American basketballer Hank Luisetti. William Henry is cast as the son of Middle College dean Thurston Hall. Looker Grable's brushoff makes him determined to conquer academia. He resorts to shooting hoops and palling around with Luisetti, leading to campus popularity. A fine performance from Luisetti helps this one as he does what he does best. Dean Hall, however, in the big game's climactic moment does all he can to keep him on the bench. But, as expected, Hank sinks the winning two. As goofy as it all seems it's still a cheery, fast-paced comedy.

d, George Archainbaud; w, Lloyd Corrigan and Erwin Gelsey; ph, Henry Sharpe; ed, Stuart Gilmore.

Comedy **(PR:A   MPAA:NR)**

CAMPUS HONEYMOON*½ (1948) 61m REP bw
Lyn Wilde (*Skipper Hughes*), Lee Wilde (*Patricia Hughes*), Adele Mara (*Bessie Ormsbee*), Richard Crane (*Robert Watson*), Hal Hackett (*Richard Adams*), Wilson Wood (*Busby Ormsbee*), Stephanie Bachelor (*Dean Carson*), Teddy Infuhr (*Junior Ormsbee*), Edwin Maxwell (*Sen. Hughes*), Boyd Irwin (*Dr. Shumway*), Kay Morley (*Polly Walker*), Charles Smith (*Benjie Briggs*), Edward Gargan (*Motorcycle Cop*), Maxine Semon (*Waitress*), William H. Simon, Jr. (*Messenger*).

Two real-life sisters play sisters in this hokey but inoffensive tale of faked wartime weddings. A couple of war vets return home and plot to marry in order to obtain veteran housing. After the phony matrimony, the boys retire to one home, the girls to the other. You guessed it—they soon fall in love. Marking this one is the not-quite-immortal tune, "Who's Got a Tent for Rent?" Other songs include "How Does It Feel To Fall In Love?" "Are You Happening To Me?" (Sale, Gruskin), "It's So Nice To Have A Man About The House" (Jack Elliot, Harold Spina), "Opalooka Song" (Sale, Nathan Scott), "Rocked In The Cradle Of The Deep" (J. P. Knight, Emma Willard).

d, Richard Sale; w, Sale, Jerry Gruskin (based on a story by Thomas R. St. George); ph, John MacBurnie; m, Sale, J. P. Knight; ed, Arthur Roberts.

Musical/Comedy **(PR:A   MPAA:NR)**

CAMPUS RHYTHM*½ (1943) 61m MON bw
Johnny Downs (*Scoop*), Gale Storm (*Joan*), Robert Lowery (*Buzz*), Candy Candido (*Harold*), Ge-Ge Pearson (*Babs*), Doug Leavitt (*Uncle Willie*), Herbert Heyes (*Hartman*), Marie Blake (*Susie*), Johnny Duncan (*Freshman*), Claudia Drake (*Cynthia*).

The liberating rhythms of Gale Storm overflow as this young radio songbird flees her ad agency and sponsors for a life of education. She assumes an alias, but is eventually caught and returned to her demeaning ad-ditty duties. Songs include: "Walking the Chalk Line" (Jules Lohman, Louis Herscher), "Swing Your Way Through College" (Andy Iona Long, Herscher), "It's Great To Be a College Girl," "College Sweetheart" (Herscher).

p, Lindsley Parsons; d, Arthur Dreifuss; w, Charles R. Marion (based on a story by Ewart Adamson and Jack White, additional dialog by Al Beich and Frank Tarloff); ph, Mack Stengler; m, Edward Cherkose and Edward Kay; ed, Dick Currier.

Musical Comedy **(PR:A   MPAA:NR)**

CAMPUS SLEUTH* (1948) 57m MON bw
Freddie Stewart (*Freddie Trimball*), June Preisser (*Dodie Rogers*), Warren Mills (*Lee

Watson*), Noel Neill (*Betty Rogers*), Donald MacBride (*Inspector Watson*), Monte Collins (*Dean McKinley*), Stan Rose (*Winkler*), Bobby Sherwood (*Bobby Davis*), Billy Snyder (*Ronnie Wallace*), William Norton Bailey (*Coroner*), Charles Campbell (*Dunkel*), Paul Bryar (*Houser*), George Eldredge (*Officer Edwards*), Dottye D. Brown (*Telegraph Girl*), Harry Taylor (*Husband*), Margaret Bert (*Wife*), Lane Chandler (*Police Officer*), Joey Preston (*Joey*), Mildred Jorman (*Little Miss Cornshucks*), Jimmy Grisson (*Boy in Wagon*), George Fields (*Band Boy*), Bobby Sherwood and his Orchestra, Geri Galian.

Formulated campus effort in which a bored group of college kids try to solve the murder of a magazine photographer. The sleuthing kids are soon led to the murderous hand of big band conductor Bobby Sherwood. The lack of musical value is no mystery in this trite whodunit. Tunes include: "What Happened?" "Baby, You Can Count On Me," "Neither Could I," "Sherwood's Forest," "Jungle Rhumba" (Will Jason, Sid Robin).

p&d, Will Jason; w, Hal Collins (based on a story by Collins and Max Wilson); ph, Mack Stengler; m, Freddie Stewart, Jason, Bobby Sherwood, Sid Robin, Tony Beaulieu; ed, William Austin.

Musical Comedy **(PR:A   MPAA:NR)**

CAN-CAN** (1960) 134m Fox c
Frank Sinatra (*Francois Durnais*), Shirley MacLaine (*Simone Pistache*), Maurice Chevalier (*Paul Barriere*), Louis Jourdan (*Philippe Forrestier*), Juliet Prowse (*Claudine*), Marcel Dalio (*Headwaiter*), Leon Belasco (*Orchestra Leader*), Nestor Paiva (*Bailiff*).

During the shooting of CAN-CAN there was a famous incident where Russian chief Nikita Khrushchev came to Fox studios and watched the action. Although he seemed to enjoy the dancing, he was later quoted as saying it was " . . . immoral. The face of humanity is more beautiful than its backside." Nikita may have been more of a critic than he realized because this very expensive and tuneful extravaganza turned out to be a bore. Radically altered from the stage musical, the story tells of an old French law forbidding can-can dancing. Sinatra, as a French lawyer, persuades old pal Chevalier, a judge, to hold back the police who want to shutter girl friend MacLaine's cafe. Jourdan attempts to get the boite raided but on a visit to the spot he falls in love with MacLaine and asks for her hand. MacLaine prefers Sinatra and refuses Jourdan. Then MacLaine utilizes Jourdan's proposal as a wedge to get Sinatra to say "I Do." Sinatra and Chevalier hatch a scheme to get MacLaine to embarrass Jourdan. It works, but Louis is still in love with Shirley and remains undaunted, badgering her to get married. Sinatra finally relents when he realizes he can't live without MacLaine and he proposes. *Naturally*, she accepts. Soon after, the Can-Can is made legal when the girls do a performance before a special court and the innocence of the dance is accepted. At 134 minutes, this was far too long and Sinatra walked through the scenes without his usual verve. Porter's songs were mainly replaced by Porter's songs (tunes from other shows the producers thought were more melodious than those in the CAN-CAN Broadway score). A singularly unfunny screenplay and ordinary performances by almost everyone except Chevalier, who seemed to be the only person having a good time.

p, Jack Cummings; d, Walter Lang; w, Dorothy Kingsley, Charles Lederer (based on the musical by Abe Burrows and Cole Porter);ph, William H. Daniels (Todd-AO, Technicolor); m, Cole Porter; ed, Robert Simpson; md, Nelson Riddle; art d, Lyle Wheeler, Jack Martin Smith; set d, Walter Scott, Paul Fox; cos, Irene Sharaff; ch, Hermes Pan.

Musical **(PR:A-C   MPAA:NR)**

CAN SHE BAKE A CHERRY PIE?**
(1983) 90m International Rainbow/Jagfilm c
Karen Black (*Zee*), Michael Emil (*Eli*), Michael Margotta (*Larry*), Frances Fisher (*Louise*), Martin Harvey Friedberg (*Mort*), Robert Hallak, Anna Raviv (*Young Couple in Cafe*), Paul Williams (*Zee's Husband*), Ariela Nicole (*Eli's Daughter*), Larry David (*Philosopher*), The Lost Wandering Band, Eddie the Pigeon.

Black holds together this slow-moving, talky comedy about a recently-divorced woman who falls into a romance with a confirmed bachelor, Emil (who also happens to be the director's brother). Black portrays the uneasy, nervous woman who is still emotionally tied to her ex-husband with skill she hasn't shown since her famous roles of the early 1970s FIVE EASY PIECES, 1970, NASHVILLE, 1975, and Emil isn't bad as the quirky bachelor who is obsessed with everything from his health to his sex life. Alas, decent performances cannot save a movie which seems almost improvised with some scenes stretching on much longer than they should, making the genuinely-funny moments few and far between.

p, M. H. Simonson; d&w, Henry Jaglom; ph, Bob Fiore; m/l, Karen Black.

Comedy **Cas.** **(PR:C   MPAA:R)**

CAN THIS BE DIXIE? *½ (1936) 68m FOX bw
Jane Withers (*Peg Gurgle*), Slim Summerville (*Robert E. Lee Gurgle*), Helen Wood (*Virginia Peachtree*), Thomas Beck (*Ulysses S. Sherman*), Sara Haden (*Miss Beauregard Peachtree*), Claude Gillingwater (*Col. Robert Peachtree*), Donald Cook (*Longstreet Butler*), James Burke (*Sheriff N. B. F. Rider*), Jed Prouty (*Ed Grant*), Hattie McDaniel (*Lizzie*), Troy Brown (*Jeff Davis Brunch*), Robert Warwick (*Gen. Beauregard Peachtree*), Ferdinand Munier (*Mozart Beethoven von Peachtree*), Billy Bletcher (*John P. Smith Peachtree*), William Worthington (*George Washington Peachtree*), Otis Harlan (*Thomas Jefferson Peachtree*).

An obnoxious satire of the South best described by one of its songs: "Uncle Tom's Cabin is a Cabaret Now." Father and daughter Gurgle lose their medicine show which is on the land of a bankrupt Kentucky colonel. To save it from foreclosure, Miss Gurgle and an enthusiastic bunch of workers put on an amateur show in the old southern home. Dancing girls, the Gurgles, and the Peachtrees can't save this poor specimen of Confederate comedy.

p, Sol M. Wurtzel; d, George Marshall; w, Lamar Trotti (from a story by Trotti and Marshall); ph, Bert Glennon and Ernest Palmer; m, Sidney Clare, Harry Akst; ed, Louis Loeffler; ch, Sammy Lee.

Musical/Comedy   **(PR:A   MPAA:NR)**

CAN YOU HEAR ME MOTHER?**   (1935, Brit.) 77m New Ideal bw
Sandy Powell (Sandy), Mary Lawson (Mary Warner), Paul Thomson (Mike Arnold), Muriel Aked (Mother), Elsie Irving (Mrs. Wilkinson), Katie Kay (Lucy), Norman Pierce (Joe), Raymond Huntley (Dolan), Hal Waters (Taxi Driver), Henry Victor (Father), Cingalee (Himself).

Music Hall comedian Powell uses his radio catch phrase to title this mediocre comedy. He's a rough and tumble Yorkshireman who adopts an abandoned baby while a dancer acquaintance helps him to become a comedian. Pleasant, but no more.

p, Simon Rowson, Geoffrey Rowson; d, Leslie Pearce; w, Sandy Powell, Paul Thomson (based on a story by Powell).

Comedy   **(PR:A   MPAA:NR)**

CANADIAN MOUNTIES VS, ATOMIC INVADERS
                                        (SEE: MISSILE BASE AT TANIAK, 1953)

CANADIAN PACIFIC**   (1949) 94m FOX c
Randolph Scott (Tom Andrews), Jane Wyatt (Dr. Edith Cabot), J. Carrol Naish (Dynamite Dawson), Victor Jory (Dirk Rourke), Nancy Olson (Cecille Gautier), Robert Barrat (Cornelius Van Horne), Walter Sande (Mike Brannigan), Don Haggerty (Cagle), Grandon Rhodes (Dr. Mason), Mary Kent (Mrs. Gautier), John Parrish (Mr. Gautier), John Hamilton (Pere Lacomb), Richard Wessel (Bailey), Howard Negley (Mallis).

Wholly fictitious but nonetheless entertaining saga of the building of the Canadian Pacific Railroad. Shot on location in the Rockies, the story concerns the efforts of a heroic surveyor, Scott, as he makes the way for the train tracks. A romantic triangle develops between tough-gal Olson, who loses Scott to the more feminine lady doc Wyatt. Trouble for the railroad arises when a gang of vicious trappers led by Jory decide that the trains will invade their territory and ruin their livelihood. To halt the railroad's progress Jory stirs up trouble with the local Indians, who then attack the railroaders. In the end, progress triumphs.

p, Nat Holt; d, Edwin L. Marin; w, Jack DeWitt, Kenneth Gamet (based on a story by DeWitt); ph, Fred Jackman, Jr. (Cinecolor); m, Dimitri Tiomkin; ed, Philip Martin.

Western   **(PR:A   MPAA:NR)**

CANADIANS, THE**   (1961, Brit.) 85m FOX c
Robert Ryan (Inspector Gannon), John Dehner (Frank Boone), Torin Thatcher (Master Sgt. McGregor), Burt Metcalfe (Constable Springer), John Sutton (Supt. Walker), Jack Creley (Greer), Scott Peters (Ben), Richard Alden (Billy), Teresa Stratas (White Squaw), Michael Pate (Chief Four Horns).

Disappointing first directorial outing from great western writer Kennedy who wrote such classic Budd Boetticher films as THE TALL T (1957), RIDE LONESOME (1959), and COMANCHE STATION (1960). Story takes place immediately after Gen. Custer and his troops have been massacred at the Little Big Horn. The Indians have fled north and into Canada to avoid capture by the American cavalry. Canadian mountie Ryan and two of his men are sent to meet the Indians and inform them that they may stay in peace. Soon after, the Indians' camp is overrun by vile rancher Dehner and his men who slaughter the red men for stealing their horses. The white men grab a white squaw to prove they were on a "rescue" mission. Ryan agrees to escort the rancher and his men to safety, but the Indians catch up and perform their own brand of summary justice on the killers. Lackluster direction and misused locations (in the Cyprus Hills of Saskatchewan, Canada) detract from what should have been a better western considering the personnel involved.

p, Herman E. Webber; d&w, Burt Kennedy; ph, Arthur Ibbetson (CinemaScope, DeLuxe Color); m, Muir Mathieson; ed, Douglas Robertson; m/l, Ken Darby.

Western   **(PR:A   MPAA:NR)**

CANAL ZONE zero   (1942) 79m COL bw
Chester Morris ("Hardtack" Hamilton), Harriet Hilliard (Susan Merrill), John Hubbard (Harley Ames), Larry Parks (Kincaid), Forrest Tucker (Madigan), Eddie Laughton (Hughes), Lloyd Bridges (Baldwin), George McKay (MacNamara), Stanley Andrews (Commander Merrill), John Tyrrell ("Red" Connors), Stanley Brown (Jones), John Shay (Henshaw).

A blasé, uninspired waste about ferry bombers crossing the Atlantic. Morris is the stubborn boss whose sole interest is high gains and low losses. There's also the foolhardy flyer who later redeems himself, and the jealous gal who doens't understand his convictions. This parasitic film has nothing going for it except the stolen plot of Hawks' ONLY ANGELS HAVE WINGS.

p, Colbert Clark; d, Lew Landers; w, Robert Lee Johnson (based on a story by Blaine Miller and Jean DuPont Miller); ph, Franz F. Planer; ed, James Sweeney.

Drama   **(PR:A   MPAA:NR)**

CANARIES SOMETIMES SING*
                                        (1930, Brit.) 90m W & F Film Service/Gaumont bw
Tom Walls (Geoffrey Lymes), Yvonne Arnaud (Elma Melton), Cathleen Nesbitt (Anne Lymes), Athole Stewart (Ernest Melton).

Static film adaptation of a sex comedy stage play directed by and starring Walls as the dissatisfied husband of a miserable couple who seek a change in their marriage. The change comes when they meet another couple experiencing the same set of circumstances. The couples decide to swap mates and much of the comedy stems from the two husbands who drunkenly boast of their new-found friendship one minute and then are at each other's throats the next to settle a real or imagined insult to their respective spouses. Visually tedious due to the stagey nature of the script and unimaginative camera placement and editing.

d, Tom Walls (adapted from the play "Censor's Certificate" by Frederick Lonsdale); ph, Bernard Knowles.

Comedy   **(PR:A   MPAA:NR)**

CANARIS***   (1955, Ger.) 113m Europa/Fama bw (AKA: CANARIS, MASTER SPY)
O. E. Hasse (Adm. Canaris), Adrian Hovan (Hauptmann Althoff), Barbara Ruetting (Irene von Harbeck), Martin Held (Obergruppenfuehrer Heydrich), Wolfgang Preiss (Oberst Holl), Peter Masbacher (Fernadez), Arthur Schroeder (Herr von Harbeck), Charles Regnier (Baron Trenti), Franz Essel (Beckmann), Herbert Wilk (Oberst Degenhard), Claus Miedel (French Captain), Alice Treff (Fraulein Winter), Ilse Fuerstenberg (Frau Luedike), Oskar Lindner (Gestapo Official), Friedrich Steig (Major Ullmann), Otto Braml (Hauptmann Behrens).

Fascinating post-war film from the Germans chronicling the life of Nazi counter-intelligence head Admiral Canaris, brilliantly played by stage-actor Hasse. Story involves the slow disillusionment of Hasse toward Hitler and his evil empire. As the war drags on, Hasse flirts with participation in anti-Hitler groups, but hesitates to commit himself. Finally, by 1944, he has had enough of watching Germany destroy itself and fails in an attempt to overthrow the Fuerher. For his betrayal he is stripped of his rank and thrown into a concentration camp. Well-made and acted.

d, Alfred Weldenmann; w, Herbert Reinecker (based on a manuscript by Erich Ebermayer); ph, Franz Welhmayr; m, Siegfried Franz.

War Drama   **(PR:C   MPAA:NR)**

CANARY MURDER CASE, THE**½   (1929) 80m PAR bw
William Powell (Philo Vance), Louise Brooks (Margaret O'Dell), James Hall (Jimmy Spotswoode), Jean Arthur (Alice LaFosse), Gustav Von Seyffertitz (Dr. Ambrose Lindquist), Charles Lane (Charles Spotswoode), Eugene Pallette (Ernest Heath), Lawrence Grant (John Cleaver), Ned Sparks (Tony Skeel), Louis John Bartels (Louis Mannix), E. H. Calvert (District Attorney John F. X. Markham), Oscar Smith (Stuttering Hallboy), Tim Adair, George Y. Harvey.

The "Canary" in the title is slang for nightclub singer and the singer is one of the most beautiful women to ever act upon the screen, Louise Brooks. Though sultry and irresistible, Brooks is a vicious and scheming blackmailer who has been padding her bank account with sums from three wealthy playboys; they would rather pay than have their wives drag them into divorce court. When youthful Hall proposes, Brooks notifies her three victims that she expects a large severance pay from each as wedding gifts. Then she is murdered and Hall is arrested for the killing. Enter Powell as the indomitable Philo Vance, a smooth, aristocratic sleuth who adroitly ferrets out the real killer after staging a poker game and drawing out the guilty one. Powell's performance is topflight, as is Brooks' and that of the good girl, Arthur. Oddly enough, Brooks chose, through obstinacy, to end her stellar career with this film. Originally filmed as a silent, this movie was reworked for sound. Paramount executives saw the handwriting (and the wiring) on the wall, realizing that talkies were here to stay. They recalled the entire cast for dubbing, including Brooks, who had gone to Europe to act for G. W. Pabst. When asked to dub her voice, Brooks angrily refused, telling Paramount mogul Adolph Zukor that the talkies were not only a novelty but also decidedly "vulgar." Zukor told her that either she did a voice-over for the film or her lucrative contract with his studio was cancelled. Brooks walked and the contract was torn. Margaret Livingston was brought in to talk for lovely Louise. Brooks did appear in a few films after that, mostly low-budget westerns, but THE CANARY MURDER CASE killed her career. (See PHILO VANCE series, Index)

d, Malcolm St. Clair; w, Florence Ryerson, Albert S. LeVino, Herman J. Mankiewicz, S. S. Van Dine (based on Van Dine's story); ph, Harry Fischbeck; ed, William Shea.

Mystery   **(PR:A   MPAA:NR)**

CANCEL MY RESERVATION*   (1972) 99m WB c
Bob Hope (Dan Bartlett), Eva Marie Saint (Sheila Bartlett), Ralph Bellamy (John Ed), Forrest Tucker (Reese), Anne Archer (Crazy), Keenan Wynn (Sheriff Riley), Henry Darrow (Joe Little Cloud), Doodles Weaver (Cactus), Betty Carr (Mary Little Cloud), Herb Vigran (Snagby), Pat Morita (Yamamoto), Gordon Oliver (Mr. Sparker), Buster Shaefer (Doc Morton), Chief Dan George (Old Bear).

Rotten Hope comedy (his 54th film where the 68-year-old comic plays a 42-year-old Lothario). He is a talk show host who becomes implicated in a murder. To save his marriage to Saint and clear his name, he must set out to solve the crime. The corpse Hope finds in his hotel room is that of a young Indian girl, Carr, and after running into mystic George and the dead girl's father, Darrow, he finally discovers that rich rancher Bellamy is responsible for the murder. Stupid walk-on cameos by Bing Crosby, John Wayne, and Flip Wilson don't make this lousy material any easier to sit through. Somehow this whole mess was based on a novel by Louis L'Amour.

p, Gordon Oliver; d, Paul Bogart; w, Arthur Marx, Robert Fisher (based on the novel "Broken Gun" by Louis L'Amour); ph, Russell L. Metty (Eastmancolor); m, Dominic Frontiere; ed, Michael A. Hoey; art d, Rolland M. Brooks; set d, Anthony Mondell.

Comedy   **(PR:A   MPAA:G)**

CANDIDATE, THE zero   (1964) 84m Atlantic bw
Mamie Van Doren (Samatha Ashley), June Wilkinson (Angela Wallace), Ted Knight

(Frank Carlton), Eric Mason *(Buddy Parker)*, Rachel Romen *(Mona Archer)*, Robin Raymond *(Attorney Rogers)*, William Long, Jr. *(Falon)*, John Matthews *(Sen. Harper)*, Herb Vigran *(Dr. Endicott)*, Art Allessi *(Psychiatrist)*, Phil Arnold *(Plumber)*, Carol Ann Lee, Joyce Nizzari, Beverly St. Lawrence, Susan Kelly, Sharon Rogers, Suzzanne Hiatt *(Party Girls)*.

Really sleazy tale of political corruption stars Knight as a crooked Washington, D. C., senator involved with buxom beauties Van Doren and Wilkinson. When it is discovered that the senator has gotten another girl pregnant at a wild Washington party, Van Doren takes the girl to an abortionist. Inexplicably the scum-bag abortionist rapes her. Meanwhile, Knight decides to marry Wilkinson, but dies of a heart attack when he sees his betrothed in a stag film. Bottom of the barrel.

p, Maurice Duke; d, Robert Angus; w, Joyce Ann Miller, Quentin Vale, Frank Moceri; ph, Stanley Cortez; m, Steve Karmen; ed, William Martin; set d, Lambert Day.

Drama **(PR:C MPAA:NR)**

CANDIDATE, THE*½** (1972) 109m WB c

Robert Redford *(Bill McKay)*, Peter Boyle *(Lucas)*, Don Porter *(Sen. Crocker Jarmon)*, Allen Garfield *(Howard Klein)*, Melvyn Douglas *(John J. McKay)*, Quinn Redeker *(Rich Jenkin)*, Michael Lerner *(Paul Corliss)*, Karen Carlson *(Nancy McKay)*, Morgan Upton *(Henderson)*, Kenneth Tobey *(Starkey)*, Chris Prey *(David)*, Joe Miksak *(Neil Atkinson)*, Jenny Sullivan *(Lynn)*, Tom Dahlgren *(Pilot)*, Gerald Hiken *(Station Master)*, Leslie Allen *(Mabel)*, Susan Demott *(Groupie)*, Jason Goodrow *(Boy in Commercial)*, Robert De Anda *(Jaime)*, Robert Goldsby *(Fleischer)*, Michael Barnicle *(Wilson)*, Lois Fraker *(Large Girl)*, David Moody *(Watts Heckler)*, George Meyer *(Man in Urinal)*, Dudley Knight *(Magazine Editor)*, Natalie Wood, Sen. Hubert H. Humphrey, Sen. George McGovern, Sen. John V. Tunney, Mayor Sam Yorty, Howard K. Smith, Van Amberg, Jesse Birnbaum, Sen. Alan Cranston, Maury Green, Lu Hurley, Assemblyman Walter Krabien, Assemblyman Robert Moretti, Rollin Post, Bill Stout, Dick Whittington, Richard Bergholtz, Assemblyman Ken Cory, Judy Hayward, Cedrick Hardman, Sen. Fred Harris, Ken Jones, Grover Lewis, Terry McGovern, Harvey Orkin, Congressman Jerry Waldie, Jesse M. Unruh *(Themselves)*, Barry Sullivan *(Voice of McKay Narrator)*, Broderick Crawford *(Voice of Jarmon Narrator)*, Pat Harrington, Jr. *(Dinner M. C.)*.

Jeremy Larner won the Academy Award for the screenplay to THE CANDIDATE and yet certain reviewers felt there was no script at all. But *there* was the deception in this movie. Larner and Ritchie collaborated on a documentary-like voyage into the chili-tossed bowels of politics and the result is fascinating, albeit a trifle flawed. Despite those minor glitches, this is about as close to the truth as you will ever see. A modern-day version of ALL THE KING'S MEN it isn't. That's because the nature of the beasts is different. Redford plays an altruistic attorney whose dad had been California's governor. Seeing all the dirt as a young man, Redford has no interest in politics. Porter is the typical big-state senator, bluff, hearty, a man who can shake hands and tug lapels with the best of 'em. There doesn't seem to be anyone who could come close to defeating him in the next election. Redford is asked by Boyle to run for office. After some soul-searching, he agrees, but with the proviso that his father (Douglas) be kept out of the campaign and that he, Redford, be allowed to say what he feels with no political tracts being pushed upon him by the party. His candor appeals to the public and the opinion polls begin to climb. Now the rumors start about his own father's not supporting him. Redford challenges Porter to a debate and it's a brilliant satire of two people speaking but not saying anything. Both men avoid important issues until Redford uses the last few seconds of the televised debate to toss darts at Porter who becomes edgy, then nervous, and finally Queeg-like as he begins to shout at his opponent. This display in front of millions swings public opinion in Redford's direction and he wins the election. At the film's conclusion, Redford admits to Boyle that he has no idea of what to do as a senator, just how to get elected. Harvard-educated Ritchie can be brilliant (this film, DOWNHILL RACER, and even BAD NEWS BEARS) but when he is bad, he's awful (THE ISLAND). Once he gets it all together, he will become one of our best directors. Walter Coblenz comes out of television and his career has also been spotty. After doing this and ALL THE PRESIDENT'S MEN, he went on to produce THE LEGEND OF THE LONE RANGER. There are several real politicans sprinkled through the film and one special irony—Broderick Crawford, dean of filmdom's politicians (Oscared for playing Willie Stark in ALL THE KING'S MEN), does the narration for Don Porter's campaign.

p, Walter Coblenz; d, Michael Ritchie; w, Jeremy Larner; ph, Victor J. Kemper, John Korty (Technicolor); m, John Rubinstein; ed, Richard Harris, Robert Estrin; set d, Patrizia von Brandenstein; cos, Patricia Norris; m/l, Rubenstein, David Colloff; makeup, Gary Lidiard.

Drama **Cas.** **(PR:A-C MPAA:NR)**

CANDIDATE FOR MURDER**

(1966, Brit.) 60m Lester Schoenfield Films bw

Michael Gough *(Donald Edwards)*, Erika Remberg *(Helene Edwards)*, Hans Borsody *(Kersten)*, John Justin *(Robert Vaughan)*, Paul Whitsun-Jones *(Phillips)*, Vanda Godsell *(Betty Conlon)*, Jerold Wells *(Police Inspector)* Annika Wills *(Jacqueline)*, Victor Charrington *(Barman)*, Ray Smith *(Chauffeur)*.

Based on an Edgar Wallace story, this is one of more than fifty short programmers from his works made by producer Greenwood. The fine script by Lukas Heller (who went on to bigger and better things, among them THE DIRTY DOZEN) has Borsody as a German hit man brought to England by Gough to kill Gough's wife, Remberg, because he thinks she is having an affair. Borsody decides she isn't and refuses to kill her. A bloody conclusion follows. As good as Heller's script is, though, it is overwhelmed by bad acting and sloppy direction.

p, Jack Greenwood; d, David Villiers; w, Lukas Heller (based on the story "The Best Laid Plans of a Man in Love" by Edgar Wallace); ph, Bert Mason; m, Charles Blackwell; ed, Bernard Gribble, art d, Peter Proud; set d, Sid Rider; title music, Michael Carr.

Crime **(PR:A MPAA:NR)**

CANDIDE*½ (1962, Fr.) 93m Pathe bw

Jean-Pierre Cassel *(Candide)*, Dahlia Lavi *(Cunegonde)*, Pierre Brasseur *(Pangloss)*, Nadia Gray *(The Ubiquitous Lady)*, Michel Simon *(Nanar)*, Jean Richard *(Black Marketer)*, Louis de Funes *(Gestapo Officer)*, Jean Tissier *(Dr. Jacques)*, Jean Constantin *(Fourak)*, Albert Simonin *(Major Simpson)*, Jacqueline Maillan *(American Mother)*, Don Ziegler *(American Father)*, John William *("Chef")*, Poiret and Serrault *(Policemen)*; Tino Rossi, Luis Mariano, Dario Moreno *(South American Dictators)*; Robert Manuel *(All German Officers)*; Harold Kay, Mathilde Casadesus, Michel Garland, Michele Verez.

A modern updating of Voltaire's classic 18th century satire on optimism follows Cassel as the title character who is taught by his professor, Brasseur, that whatever fate befalls him it is probably for the better. Cassel joins the army, is taken prisoner by the Germans, tortured, and then made to be German because he comes from the German-speaking area of France. Soon he finds himself inspecting concentration camps and then going to Asia and eventually the United States where he finds happiness. Uneven and as talky as Martha Raye without laughs.

p, Clement Duhour; d, Norbert Carbonnaux; w, Carbonnaux, Albert Simonin (adapted from the novel by Voltaire); ph, Robert Lefevbre; m, Hubert Rostaing; ed, Paulette Robert; art d, Jean Douarinou; set d, Jean Bertrand.

Satire **(PR:A MPAA:NR)**

CANDLELIGHT IN ALGERIA½** (1944, Brit.) 85m BL bw

James Mason *(Alan Thurston)*, Carla Lehmann *(Susan Foster)*, Walter Rilla *(Dr. Muller)*, Raymond Lovell *(Von Alven)*, Enid Stamp Taylor *(Maritza)*, Pamela Stirling *(Yvette)*, Lea Seidl *(Sister)*, Leslie Bradley *(Henri de Lange)*, Michael Morel *(Commissioner)*, Albert Whelan *(Kadour)*, Meinhart Maur *(Schultz)*, Harold Berens *(Toni)*, Hella Kurty *(Maid)*, MacDonald Parke *(American)*, Paul Bonifas *(French Proprietor)*, Richard George *(Matthews)*, Bart Norman *(Gen. Mark Clark)*, Berkeley Schultz *(Commando Officer)*, John Slater *(American Officer)*, Jacques Metadier *(Elderly French Officer)*, Richard Mollainas *(French Sergeant)*, Graham Penley *(Pierre)*, Cot d'Ordan *(Hotel Manager)*, Paul Sheridan *(Plainclothes Detective)*, Cecile Chevreau *(Nun)*.

CANDLELIGHT IN ALGERIA is one of the early examples of "faction" (combining fact and fiction) and the real events of the war swept aside the fancifulness of the script and left this movie suffering at the box office. Mark Clark, Ike's right-hand man, and a few other Allied chiefs are due to meet along the coast of Algeria. The exact location is on a piece of film; if it gets into the hands of the Nazis, the whole group could be captured. The film is hidden in the German colony of Algiers, and Mason, a British spy, is sent to recover it. Rilla is a Nazi agent and will trail Mason until the film is uncovered. Lehmann is an American woman in Algiers who pals with Stirling, a French femme. They help Mason recover the film and blast his way out of the Casbah. He then alerts the Allied officers and all are saved. Canadian-born Lehmann had a brief career in British films in the 1940s but retired soon after. Lovell was also a Canadian living in England at the time. When one considers that London and environs were regularly bombed for several years in the early 1940s, it's all the more amazing that they managed to make films while carrying on a war at their gates.

p&d, George King; w, Brock Williams, Katherine Strueby (based on a story by Dorothy Hope); ph, Otto Heller; m, Roy Douglas, James Turner; ed, Terence Fisher, Winifred Cooper; art d, Norman Arnold; m/l, Muriel Watson, Jack Denby, Hans May, Alan Stranks, G. Arbib; md, Jack Beaver.

Spy Drama **(PR:A MPAA:NR)**

CANDLES AT NINE*½ (1944, Brit.) 82m Anglo-American/BN bw

Jessie Matthews *(Dorothea Capper)*, John Stuart *(William Gordon)*, Beatrix Lehmann *(Julia Carberry)*, Winifred Shotter *(Brenda Tempest)*, Reginald Purdell *(Charles Lacey)*, Hugh Dempster *(Hugh Lacey)*, Joss Ambler *(Garth Hope)*, Eliot Makeham *(Everard Hope)*, John Salew *(Griggs)*, Vera Bogetti *(Lucille Hope)*, Andre Van Gyseghem *(Cecil Tempest)*, Ernest Butcher *(Gardener)*, Guy Fielding, Gerry Wilmot.

Tedious mystery concerning young heiress Matthews who is left a small fortune by her recently-deceased uncle. Other, and closer, relatives are outraged that their miserly-relation would dump such a load of cash on a worthless dance-hall girl and they try to grab a piece of the estate from Matthews. A devious bunch, at first they try friendly persuasion. When that fails their thoughts turn to murder. Leave it to evil housekeeper Lehmann to actually attempt such a scheme, but she is stopped and apprehended by clever detective Stuart, who not only saves Matthews' life, but marries her. While fending off greedy relatives Matthews finds time to sing, "I'd Like To Share With You."

p, Wallace Orton; d, John Harlow; w, Basil Mason, Harlow (based on Anthony Gilbert's novel *The Mouse Who Couldn't Play Ball*); ph, James Wilson, Arthur Grant.

Mystery **(PR:A MPAA:NR)**

CANDLESHOE½** (1978) 101m BV c

David Niven *(Priory)*, Helen Hayes *(Lady St. Edmund)*, Jodie Foster *(Casey)*, Leo McKern *(Bundage)*, Vivian Pickles *(Grimsworthy)*, Veronica Quilligan *(Cluny)*, Ian Sharrock *(Peter)*, Sarah Tamakuni *(Anna)*, David Samuels *(Bobby)*, John Alderson *(Jenkins)*, Mildred Shay *(Mrs. McCress)*, Michael Balfour *(Mr. McCress)*, Sydney Bromley *(Mr. Thresher)*, Michael Segal *(Train Guard)*.

Average Disney live actioner starring McKern and Pickles as con artists who pass tomboy Foster off as rich widow Hayes' long-lost granddaughter to bilk her out of some valuable coins hidden on her estate. Little does sweet old lady Hayes know that another, kinder con man, Niven, has talked her into taking in dozens of orphans, not to shelter them, as Hayes is led to believe, but to perform household chores on the widow's financially foundering estate. Niven himself performs as the house's butler, chauffeur, gardener, and cavalry officer. After enough exposure to the kind-hearted Niven, Foster sees the error of her ways and helps save the estate. Fairly lackluster Disney outing saved by a great performance by Niven.

p, Ron Miller; d, Norman Tokar; w, David Swift, Rosemary Anne Sisson (based on the novel *Christmas at Candleshoe* by Michael Innes); ph, Paul Beeson (Technicolor); m, Ron Goodwin; ed, Peter Boita; art d, Albert Witherick; cos, Julie Harris.

Children's Drama   **Cas.**   **(PR:AAA MPAA:G)**

CANDY*   (1968, Ital./Fr.) 123m Cinerama c

Charles Aznavour *(Hunchback)*, Marlon Brando *(Grindl)*, Richard Burton *(McPhisto)*, James Coburn *(Dr. Krankeit)*, John Huston *(Dr. Dunlap)*, Walter Matthau *(Gen. Smight)*, Ringo Starr *(Emmanuel)*, Ewa Aulin *(Candy)*, John Astin *(Daddy, Uncle Jack)*, Elsa Martinelli *(Livia)*, Sugar Ray Robinson *(Zero)*, Anita Pallenberg *(Nurse Bullock)*, Lea Padovani *(Silvia)*, Florinda Bolkani *(Lolita)*, Marilu Tolo *(Conchita)*, Nicoletta Machiavelli *(Marquita)*, Umberto Orsini *(Hood)*, Joey Forman *(Cop)*, Fabian Dean *(Segeant)*, Enrico Maria Salerno *(Jonathan J. John)*, The Byrds and Steppenwolf.

Bombastic, pretentious adaptation of Terry Southern's satirical sex novel boiled down to a series of episodic guest shots by major movie stars. Aulin stars as the incredibly naive and innocent title character who is chased by alcoholic poet Burton, Mexican gardener Starr, right-winged general Matthau, bizarre guru Brando, hunchback Aznavour, and even her own father, Astin. Along the way she also encounters eccentric doctor Coburn, crazed hospital administrator Huston, Sugar Ray Robinson, and Rolling Stones groupie Pallenborg. Filmed on locations in Rome and New York, the movie never really captures the proper satirical angle of Southern's source material. Some of the music is provided by The Byrds and Steppenwolf. Highlights of the film are the opening and closing sequences provided by special effects expert Douglas Trumbull.

p, Robert Haggiag; d, Christian Marquand; w, Buck Henry (based on the novel by Terry Southern, Mason Hoffenberg); ph, Guiseppe Rotunno (Technicolor); m, Dave Grusin; ed, Frank Santillo, Giancarlo Cappelli; art d, Dean Tavoularis; cos, Enrico Sabbatini, Mia Fonssagrives, Vicky Tiel; spec eff, Douglas Trumbull, Augie Lohman; ch, Don Lurio.

Comedy   **(PR:O MPAA:R)**

CANDY MAN, THE zero   (1969) 98m Sagittarius c

George Sanders, Leslie Parrish, Gina Roman, Carlos Cortez, Manolo Fabregas.

Abysmal end-of-career role for Sanders who is a down-and-out drug peddler going destitute in Mexico City (not unlike Bogart/Dobbs in THE TREASURE OF THE SIERRA MADRE). He resorts to kidnapping the child of an American film star to make ends meet. Sanders sadly staggers like a sleepwalker through this uninspired stinkeroo.

p,d&w, Herbert J. Leder.

Crime Drama   **Cas.**   **(PR:O MPAA:NR)**

CANNABIS*½   (1970, Fr.) 85m Oceanic c

Serge Gainsbourg *(Serge)*, Jane Birkin *(Girl)*, Paul Nicholas *(Killer)*, Curt Jurgens *(Emery)*, Gabriele Ferzetti *(Inspector)*.

Fast-paced French drug/crime drama starring Gainsbourg as a Mafioso who is sent to France to find out who is intercepting the heroin trade. With the aide of crazed hippie Nicholas, the pair board a plane bound for Europe. On the flight, Gainsbourg meets the oversexed Miss Birkin who later rescues the hood when he is kidnaped by two deaf-mute French-gangsters. Jurgens plays the French drug kingpin and Ferzetti a police captain. Plenty of gratuitous violence and sex.

d, Pierre Korainik; w, Franz-Andre Burguet, Korainik (based on the novel by F. S. Gilbert); ph, Willy Kurant (Techniscope, Eastmancolor); ed, Francoise Collin.

Crime   **(PR:O MPAA:NR)**

CANNERY ROW***   (1982) 120m UA/MGM c

Nick Nolte *(Doc)*, Debra Winger *(Suzy)*, Audra Lindley *(Fauna)*, Frank McRae *(Hazel)*, M. Emmet Walsh *(Mack)*, Tom Mahoney *(Hughie)*, John Malloy *(Jones)*, James Keane *(Eddie)*, Sunshine Parker *(The Seer)*, Santos Morales *(Joseph and Mary)*, Sharon Ernster *(Agnes)*, Ellen Blake *(Wisteria)*, Mary Margaret Amato *(Lola)*, Kathleen Doyle *(Violet)*, Brenda Hillhouse *(Martha)*, Colleen O'Grady *(Pitcher)*, Mariko Tse *(Blossom)*, Tona Dodd *(Waitress)*, Judy Kerr *(Waitress serving beer milkshake)*, William Bronder *(Suzy's Customer)*, Rosana DiSota *(Ellen Sedgewick)*, Tom Pletts *(Doctor)*, Walter Mathews *(Sonny)*, Joe Terry *(Tucker)*, Joshua Lawrence *(Boy)*, Art LaFleur *(Doorman)*, John Huston *(Narrator)*.

Somewhat mannered but absorbing film of an ex-baseball star living in obscurity among down-and-outers who provide amusing, sometimes hilarious antics. Nolte, as Doc, gives one of his finer performances as the has-been pitcher who cannot forget his one disastrous mistake on the mound nor make up his mind about the young hooker who loves him and is smartly played by Winger. John Huston narrates this Steinbeck pastiche which has moments of sheer poetry on film. (Raquel Welch, originally cast in the Winger part, was fired half way through the film over disputes.)

p, Michael Phillips; d&w, David S. Ward (based on *Cannery Row* and *Sweet Thursday* by John Steinbeck); ph, Sven Nykvist (Metrocolor); m, Jack Nietzche; ed, David Bretherton; art d, William F. O'Brien; cos, Ruth Myers; ch, Lou Wills.

Drama   **Cas.**   **(PR:C-O MPAA:PG)**

CANNIBAL ATTACK*   (1954) 69m COL bw

Johnny Weissmuller *(Johnny Weissmuller)*, Judy Walsh *(Luora)*, David Bruce *(Arnold King)*, Bruce Cowling *(Rovak)*, Charles Evans *(Commissioner)*, Steve Darrell *(John King)*, Joseph A. Allen, Jr. *(Jason)*.

Weissmuller was set to play Jungle Jim in this one, but, at the last minute, the rights to the series were turned over to Screen Gems. Instead, Weissmuller plays himself, battling crocodiles, natives, and a ring selling cobalt to a foreign government. Pretty dumb.

p, Sam Katzman; d, Lee Sholem; w, Carroll Young; ph, Henry Freulich; m, Mischa Bakaleinikoff, ed Edwin Bryant.

Adventure   **(PR:A MPAA:NR)**

CANNIBAL GIRLS*½   (1973) 83m AIP c

Eugene Levy *(Clifford Sturges)*, Andrea Martin *(Gloria Wellaby)*, Ronald Ulrich *(Rev. Alex St. John)*, Randall Carpenter *(Anthea)*, Bonnie Nelson *(Clarissa)*, Mira Prawluk *(Leona)*, Bob McHeady *(Sheriff)*, Alan Gordon *(1st Victim)*, Allan Price *(2nd Victim)*, Earl Pomerrantz *(Third Victim)*, May Jarvis *(Mrs. Wainwright)*.

Pretty lame horror comedy featuring TV stars Levy and Martin as a young couple on a romantic weekend jaunt in a lonely town. Soon they find themselves being pursued by a trio of flesh-eating girls who want to feast on them. Stupid gimmick made prominent in the print ads, "THE PICTURE WITH THE WARNING BELL! When it rings—close your eyes if you're squeamish!" Sounds funnier than it is. Directed by Reitman who would later go on to direct such box office hits as MEATBALLS (1979), STRIPES (1981), and GHOSTBUSTERS (1984).

p, Daniel Goldberg; d, Ivan Reitman; w, Robert Sandler; ph, Robert Saad (Movielab Color); m, Doug Riley; ed, Daniel Goldberg.

Comedy/Horror   **(PR:C MPAA:R)**

CANNIBALS, THE*½   (1970, Ital.) 88m Doria-San Marco c

Britt Ekland *(Antigone)*, Pierre Clementi *(Tiresias)*, Tomas Milian *(Haimon)*, Francesco Leonetti *(Haimon's Father)*, Delia Boccardo *(Ismene)*, Marino Mase *(Ismene's Father)*.

Ekland is a fashionable young thing in Milan, Italy, preoccupied with getting her dead brother's body dragged off the street and hidden in a nearby cave. It's all a modern rendition of Sophocles' "Antigone" with lots of heavy symbolism about youth rebellion, and the characters are so symbolic that they aren't people anymore. It's pretty to look at, but that isn't enough to make this dated item worth watching.

p, Enzo Doria; d, Liliana Cavani; w, Italo Mescati, Cavani (based on an original story by Cavani); ph, Giulio Albonico (Technicolor); m, Ennio Morricone; ed, Giovanni Baragli.

Drama   **(PR:C-O MPAA:NR)**

CANNIBALS IN THE STREETS*   (1982, Ital./Span.) 91m Almi Cinema 5 c
(AKA: SAVAGE APOCALYPSE, THE SLAUGHTERERS, CANNIBALS IN THE CITY, VIRUS, INVASION OF THE FLESH HUNTERS)

John Saxon *(Norman Hopper)*, Elizabeth Turner *(Jane Hopper)*, John Morghen, Cindy Hamilton, Tony King, Wallace Wilkinson, Ray Williams, John Geroson, May Heatherley, Ronnie Sanders, Vic Perkins, Laura Dean.

Very gory horror film shot and released in a hurry to capitalize on the success of George Romero's horror classic DAWN OF THE DEAD (1979). Shot in Atlanta, by an Italian crew, story involves Vietnam vet Saxon and his men who have been infected by a deadly cannibal virus while in Southeast Asia. Soon the soldiers are ripping and chewing their way through the streets of Atlanta until the local law enforcement authorities corner the cannibals in the sewer system and blow them away. Gross special effects done by DeRossi who handled the gore chores on another Romero ripoff, ZOMBIE (1979).

p, Maurizio Amati, Sandro Amati; d, Antonio Margheriti (Anthony Dawson); w, Margheriti, Jimmy Gould (based on a story by Gould); ph, Fernando Arribas (Telecolor); m, Alex Blonksteiner; ed, G. Serralonga; art d, Walter Patriarca; spec eff, Don Shelley; spec makeup eff, Gianetto De Rossi; stunts, Freddy Unger.

Horror   **(PR:O MPAA:R)**

CANNON AND THE NIGHTINGALE, THE**½   (1969, Gr.) 90m Sisyphus bw

THE SECRET WEDDING: Niki Triandafylidou *(Vasiliki)*, George Georgis *(Gregoris Afxendiou)*; THE CLOCK: G. Danis *(Italian Commander)*; ADVERSARIES: Dionysis Papagianopoulos *(Triandafilou)*, George Cambanellis *(German Officer)*, Kostas Papas, Spyros Kostantopoulos, Thanasis, Kedrakas, Athinodoros Fousalis, Eleni Kriti.

Well-made film detailing how the Greeks have dealt with invasion by foreign countries told in three separate episodes. The first is a melancholy love story starring Triandafylidou and Georgis as a young couple betrothed in the traditional manner during the 1957 occupation of Greece by the British, but before the marriage can be consummated the young freedom fighter is forced to flee and is never seen again. The second episode is an amusing story set during the occupation of Greece in 1943 by the bumbling Italians. The Greeks never really took the Italian forces seriously and they take pleasure in making fools of their capturers. The Greeks look at the Italians as minor nuisances and go on with their lives as if nothing has changed. The major frustration of the spit-and-polish Italian commander is the town clock that doesn't work. After many attempts to have it fixed, the Italian gives up, leaving the Greeks to themselves. The final segment concerns a Nazi officer who is stationed in the home of rich Greek Papagianopoulous during the German occupation of 1944. The two are wary of each other at first, but soon they begin to communicate through nonverbal means. Just as the enemies have established a rapport, German soldiers are seen torturing a Greek citizen and the pair realize that there is no possibility of friendship under these circumstances. Unable to face the Greek, the German packs his bags and leaves.

p,d&w, Jacovos and George Cambenellis; ph, S. Danalis, N. Kavoukidis; m, N. Mamangakis.

Drama (PR:A MPAA:NR)

CANNON FOR CORDOBA**

(1970) 104m UA c (AKA: DRAGON MASTER)
George Peppard (Capt. Rod Douglas), Giovanna Ralli (Leonora), Raf Vallone (Cordoba), Pete Duel (Andy Rice), Don Gordon (Sgt. Jackson Harkness), Francine York (Sophia), John Larch (Harry Warner), Nicos Minardos (Peter Andros), John Russell (Brig. Gen. John J. Pershing), Charles Stalnaker (Capt. Riggs), John Clarke (Major Wall), Gabriele Tinti (Lt. Antonio Gutierrez), Hans Meyer (Svedborg), Janis Hansen (Girl), Lionel Murton, Richard Pendry, Takis Emmanuel.

Average western concerning attempts by Gen. John J. Pershing (Russell) to quell a marauding band of Mexican outlaws. The General calls upon intelligence Captain Peppard to stop the bandits led by Vallone. Subplot concerns Ralli as a woman who helps Peppard because she seeks revenge on Vallone for raping her. Nothing special, despite beautiful on-location filming in Spain.

p, Vincent M. Fennelly; d, Paul Wendkos; w, Stephen Kandel; ph, Antonio Macasoli (Panavision, DeLuxe Color); m, Elmer Bernstein; ed, Walter Hanneman; art d, Jose Maria Tapiador; set d, Rafael Salazar; spec eff, Alex Weldon; makeup, Ricardo Vazquez.

Western (PR:C-O MPAA:GP)

CANNONBALL**

(1976, U.S./Hong Kong) 93m New World c (GB: CARQUAKE)
David Carradine ("Cannonball" Buckman), Bill McKinney (Cade Redman), Veronica Hamel (Linda), Gerrit Graham (Perman Waters), Robert Carradine (Jim Crandell), Belinda Balaski (Maryann), Judy Canova (Sharma Capri), Carl Gottlieb (Terry McMillan), Archie Hahn (Zippo Friedman), Martin Scorsese (Mafioso), Mary Woronov (Sandy), Aron Kincaid (David), James Keach (Dick Miller, Louisa Moritz, Allan Arkush, Paul Bartel, Roger Corman, Joe Dante, Jonathan Kaplan, Sylvester Stallone, David Arkin, John Herzfeld, Patrick Wright, Stanley Clay, John Alderman, Deirdre Ardell, Gretchen Ardell, Gary Austin, Wendy Bartel, Linda Vivitello, Jim Connors, Peter Cornberg, Miller Drake, Mike Finnell, Samuel W. Gelfman, Paul Glicker, David Gottlieb, Lea Gould, Diane Lee Hart, Glen Johnson, Saul Krugman, James Lashly, Joe McBride, Todd McCarthy, Keith Michl, Read Morgan, Mary Robin Redd, Glynn Rubin, Donald Simpson, George Wagner, Joe Wong.

Disappointing followup by director Bartel to his classic cult movie DEATH RACE 2000 (1975). This one is set in the present and details a car race that starts in Los Angeles and ends in New York with $100,000 at the finish line. The two main rivals for the prize, Carradine and McKinney, grunt, swear, and "burn rubber" across the country. The story line is incredibly similar to THE GUMBALL RALLY (1976), released the same year. The fun comes, however, from spotting such great Corman talents as directors Martin Scorsese (RAGING BULL [1980]), Joe Dante (THE HOWLING [1981]), (GREMLINS [1984]), Jonathan Kaplan (OVER THE EDGE [1979]), (HEART LIKE A WHEEL [1983]), Allan Arkush (ROCK N' ROLL HIGH SCHOOL [1979]), (GET CRAZY [1983]), Sylvester Stallone (ROCKY II & III), and Corman himself in cameo roles. Far from Bartel's best exploitation work, but worth a look for low-budget cult fanatics.

p, Samuel W. Gelfman; d, Paul Bartel; w, Bartel, Donald C. Simpson; ph, Tak Fujimoto (Metrocolor); m, David A. Axelrod; ed, Morton Tubor; art d, Michel Levesque; stunts, Alan Gibbs.

Comedy/Action Cas. (PR:C MPAA:PG)

CANNONBALL EXPRESS*

(1932) 59m Sono Art bw
Rex Lease, Tom Moore, Lucille Browne, Leon Waycoff, Leon Ames, Ruth Renick.

Meandering domestic drama detailing the story of two brothers, one seemingly good, the other considered the family black sheep by their father, engineer of the railroad train, The Cannonball Express. It appears that the old man's judgment was wrong when the supposedly good offspring gets himself in trouble with some shifty holdup men with whom he was shooting craps. In debt and desperate to pay his IOUs, Jackie the good son steals his dad's money to keep the hoods off his back. The bad brother takes the rap when Pop finds out, but the truth surfaces when the holdup men try to rob the train on which the father is the engineer. Bad dialog, a jumpy structure (the film opens with the birth of the bad son), and very little real action leave this effort in the doldrums.

p, Fanchon Royer; d, Wallace W. Fox; w, Bernard McConville.

Crime/Drama (PR:A MPAA:NR)

CANNONBALL RUN, THE zero

(1981) 95m FOX c
Burt Reynolds (J. J. McClure), Roger Moore (Seymour), Farrah Fawcett (Pamela), Dom DeLuise (Victor), Dean Martin (Jamie Blake), Sammy Davis, Jr. (Fenderbaum), Jack Elam (Doctor), Adrienne Barbeau (Marcie), Terry Bradshaw (Terry), Jackie Chan (Subaru Driver No. 1), Bert Convy (Brad), Jamie Farr (Sheik), Peter Fonda (Chief Biker), George Furth (A. F. Foyt), Michael Hui (Subaru Driver No. 2), Bianca Jagger (Sheik's Sister), Molly Picon (Mom Goldfarb), Jimmy "The Greek" Snyder ("The Greek"), Mel Tillis (Mel), Rick Aviles (Mad Dog), Warren Berlinger (Shakey Finch), Tara Buckman (Jill), John Fiedler (Clerk), Norman Grabowski (Petoski), Joe Klecko (Racing Driver), Grayce Spence, (Chairperson), Bob Tessier (Biker), Alfie Wise (Barman), Johnny Yune (TV Talk Show Host), Ben Rogers (Pennsylvania Cop), Jim Lewis (Missouri Cop), Fred Smith, Bob Stenner, Ken Squier (California Cops), Roy Tatum (Connecticut Cop), Dudley Remus, Hal Carter (New Jersey Cops), Brock Yates (Organizer), Kathleen M. Shea (Starting Girl), Nancy Austin (Phone Booth Lady), Vickie Reigle (Car Hop), Samir Kamoun (Bedouin), John Megna (Arthur), Linda McClure (Dour Lady), Laura Lizer Sommers (Lady in Distress), Richard Losee

(Trans-Am Driver), Richie Burns Wright (Farm Boy), Seymour's Girls: Lois Areno, Simone Burton, Finele Carpenter, Susan McDonald, Janet Woytak.

Unbelievably stupid car-chase movie whose plot was stolen from THE GUMBALL RALLY (1976) and CANNONBALL (1976), is just an excuse for good ol' boy Reynolds to pal around on the set with the largest number of mediocre Hollywood talents ever assembled in one movie. One would at least expect the action scenes to be directed with some flair by former stuntman turned director Needham, but even these scenes are uninspired and lackadaisical compared with the much more creative (and cheaper) stunts found in low-budget Roger Corman movies. If Reynolds would quit appearing in garbage like this, maybe major directors would consider taking him more seriously as a dramatic actor. Completely unfunny and a waste of film and money, but the producers laughed all the way to the bank because the public made this drivel one of the top-grossing movies of 1981. An equally offensive sequel CANNONBALL II (1984) followed this one.

p, Albert S. Ruddy; d, Hal Needham; w, Brock Yates; ph, Michael Butler (Technicolor); m, Al Capps; ed, Donn Cambern, William D. Gordean; art d, Carol Wenger; set d, Rochell Moser.

Action/Comedy Cas. (PR:A MPAA:PG)

CANON CITY**½

(1948) 82m EL bw
Scott Brady (Sherbondy), Jeff Corey (Schwartzmiller), Whit Bissell (Heilman), Stanley Clements (New), Charles Russell (Tolley), DeForest Kelley (Smalley), Ralph Byrd (Officer Gray), Mabel Paige (Mrs. Oliver), Warden Roy Best (Himself), Alfred Linder (La Vergne), Richard Irving (Trujillo), Robert Bice (Turley), Henry Brandon (Freeman), James Magill (Hathaway), Ray Bennett (Klinger), Robert Kellard (W. R. Williams), Raymond Bond (Mr. Oliver), Eve Marsh (Mrs. George Bauer), Bud Wolfe (Officer Clark), Reed Hadley (Narrator), Bob Reeves (Guard), Donald Kerr (Convict Waiter), Victor Cutler (Convict Photographer), Lynn Millan (May), James Ames (Convict Mug), Ruth Warren (Mug's Wife), Brick Sullivan (Guard), Henry Hall (Guard Captain), Cay Forester (Sherbondy's Sister), Bill Walker (Prisoner), Officer McLean (Himself), Paul Scardon (Joe Bondy), Ralph Dunn (Convict Blacksmith), Alvin Hammer (Convict Tailor), Capt. Kenny (Himself), John Shay, Paul Kruger (Officers), Raymond Bond (Mr. Oliver), Esther Summers (Mrs. Higgins), Mack Williams (Mr. Higgins), Capt. Gentry (Himself), Howard Negley (Richard Smith), Virginia Mullens (Mrs. Smith), Bill Clauson (Joel), Shirley Martin (Judith), Elysabeth Goetten (Barbara), Margaret Kerry (Maxine), Eve March (Mrs. Bauer), John Doucette (Mr. Bauer), Phyllis Gallow (Myrna), Anthony Sydes (Jerry), Jack Ellis (Man at Roadblock), John Wald (Radio Commentator).

Good prison escape picture based on an actual jailbreak at the Canon City prison in Colorado in 1947. Brady is fine as the apparently well-behaved, unassuming inmate, who in his spare time makes a home-made pistol. He, along with eleven other inmates, make their escape and then are hunted down, killed, or recaptured. Fine cast of character actors including Bennett as the mastermind of the plan and Corey as one of the co-conspirators. Don't blink or you'll miss "Star Trek's" Dr. McCoy, DeForest Kelley, as one of the prisoners. Strangely, the role of the warden is played by the actual warden of the prison at the time of the escape and some of the prisoners and guards also have roles.

p, Brian Foy; d&w, Crane Wilbur; ph, John Alton; ed, Louis H. Sackin; md, Irving Friedman; art d, Frank Durlauf; set d, Armor Marlow, Clarence Steenson; cos, Frances Ehren; makeup, Ern Westmore, Frank Westmore; hairstyles, Joan St. Oegger, Beth Langston.

Prison Drama (PR:A MPAA:NR)

CAN'T HELP SINGING**½

(1944) 89m UNIV c
Deanna Durbin (Caroline), Robert Paige (Lawlor), Akim Tamiroff (Gregory), David Bruce (Latham), Leonid Kinskey (Koppa), Ray Collins (Sen. Frost), June Vincent (Miss MacLean), Andrew Tombes (Sad Sam), Thomas Gomez (Carstairs), Clara Blandick (Aunt Cissy), Olin Howlin (Bigelow), George Cleveland (Marshal).

Durbin stars in her first color musical, a pleasant production set in 1847, as a feisty daughter of an important senator. She ignores her father's wishes and runs out West to marry a cavalry officer. Outraged, the senator uses his influence to ship the young officer to a remote part of California where Durbin will never find him. It doesn't matter, because Durbin meets up with the handsome and adventurous Paige and falls in love with him by the time she reaches California. Songs by Jerome Kern and E. Y. Harburg include "Can't Help Singing," "More and More," "Cal-i-for-ni-ay," "Elbow Room," "Swing Your Sweatheart," and "Any Moment Now."

p, Felix Jackson; d, Frank Ryan; w, Lewis R. Foster, Ryan (based on the novel Girl of the Overland Trail by Samuel J. and Curtis B. Warshawsky); ph, Woody Bredell, W. Howard Greene (Technicolor); m, Hans J. Salter; ed, Ted J. Kent; m/l, Jerome Kern, E. Y. Harburg.

Musical (PR:A MPAA:NR)

CAN'T STOP THE MUSIC zero

(1980) 118m Associated Film Distribution c
Village People: Ray Simpson (Policeman), David Hodo (Construction Worker), Felipe Rose (Indian), Randy Jones (Cowboy), Glenn Hughes (Leatherman), Alex Briley (GI), Valerie Perrine (Samantha Simpson), Bruce Jenner (Ron White), Steve Guttenberg (Jack Morell), Paul Sand (Steve Waits), Tammy Grimes (Sydney Channing), June Havoc (Helen Morell), Barbara Rush (Norma White), Altovise Davis (Alicia Edwards), Marilyn Sokol (Lulu Brecht), Russell Nype (Richard Montgomery), Jack Weston (Benny Murray), Leigh Taylor-Young (Claudia Walters), Dick Patterson (Record Store Manager), Bobo Lewis (Bread Woman), Paula Trueman (Stickup Lady), Portia Nelson (Law Office Receptionist).

Obnoxious attempt by slapdash producer Allan Carr to ressurrect the "Hey gang, let's put on a show!" musicals of the 1940s. To do this, Carr threw $20 million on the backs of short-lived disco singing group, The Village People (who had strong homosexual undertones), in a gamble that their popularity would pull in the box-office figures. In the end, the film crashed like a lead balloon, losing a bundle for Carr and signaling the end of The Village People's popularity. Plot concerns ex-model Perrine who helps her platonic friend and roommate, struggling pop-composer Guttenberg, by recruiting some friends to sing his songs on a demo tape. The friends, of course, happen to be the members of The Village People. Along the way, Perrine meets uptight tax attorney Jenner (in a role that forever proves his inability to act) and eventually loosens him up. The musical numbers are silly and uninteresting and the whole mess was misdirected by Nancy Walker, who most viewers will remember as Rosy the greasy spoon waitress in an endless TV series of paper towel commercials. Songs include the appropriately titled "Give Me a Break," "The Sound of the City," "Samantha," "I'm A Singing Juggler," "Sophistication," "Liberation," "I Love You to Death," "Magic Night," "Milkshake," and the extremely popular Village People hits "Macho Man" and "Y.M.C.A."

p, Allan Carr, Jacques Morali, Henri Belolo; d, Nancy Walker; w, Bronte Woodward, Carr; ph, Bill Butler (Panavision, Metrocolor); m, Morali; ed, John F. Burnett; art d, Harold Michelson; set d, Richard McKenzie, Eric Orbum; cos, Jane Greenwood, Theoni V. Aldredge; spec eff, Michael Sullivan; ch, Arlene Phillips.

Musical　　　　**Cas.**　　　　**(PR:C　MPAA:PG)**

CANTERBURY TALE, A★★½　　　(1944, Brit.), 124m Archer/EL bw
Eric Portman (*Thomas Colpepper, J. P.*), Sheila Sim (*Joan Webster*), Dennis Price (*Sgt. Peter Gibbs*), Sgt. John Sweet (*Bob Johnson*), Esmond Knight (*Narrator/Soldier/Idiot*), Charles Hawtrey (*Thomas Duckett*), Hay Petrie (*Woodcock*), George Merritt (*Ned Horton*), Edward Rigby (*Jim Horton*), Freda Jackson (*Prudence Honeywood*), Betty Jardine (*Fee Baker*), Eliot Makeham (*Organist*).

A mighty strange movie, one that updates Chaucer's story to wartime Britain. Portman is a rural justice of the peace who takes it upon himself to look out for the GIs stationed near him. To protect his charges from the seductive wiles of the local girls, he takes to sneaking in the girls' rooms during blackouts and pouring glue over their heads. He is found out by London shopgirl-turned-farmer Sim, British tank sergeant Price and GI Sweet (an Ohio schoolteacher discovered by Powell and Pressburger while he was stationed in England with the U.S. Army, who gives a wonderful performance reminiscent of Will Rogers). Together they travel down the road to Canterbury, where each experiences a minor miracle. Wonderfully and meticulously constructed by some of the best people in British films at the time, one memorable shot switches the action from the Dark Ages to the present by showing a falcon set aloft from a medieval pilgrim's wrist, receding into the sky until it is just a speck, then coming back. As it grows larger one realizes that it is not the falcon, but a Spitfire. British officials understandably confused about some elements of the film showed a great deal of reluctance before releasing the picture in the U.S. Not frequently revived, but well worth checking out.

p,d&w, Michael Powell, Emeric Pressburger; ph, Erwin Hillier.

Drama　　　　　　　　　　　**(PR:A　MPAA:NR)**

CANTERVILLE GHOST, THE★★★　　　(1944) 95m MGM bw
Charles Laughton (*Sir Simon de Canterville/The Ghost*), Robert Young (*Cuffy Williams*), Margaret O'Brien (*Lady Jessica de Canterville*), William Gargan (*Sgt. Benson*), Reginald Owen (*Lord Canterville*), Rags Ragland (*Big Harry*), Una O'Connor (*Mrs. Umney*), Donald Stuart (*Sir Valentine Williams*), Elisabeth Risdon (*Mrs. Polverdine*), Frank Faylen (*Lt. Kane*), Lumsden Hare (*Mr. Potts*), Mike Mazurki (*Metropolus*), William Moss (*Hector*), Bobby Readick (*Eddie*), Marc Cramer (*Bugsy McDougle*), William Tannen (*Jordan*), Peter Lawford (*Anthony de Canterville*).

An amusing tale set in an ancient English castle where American soldiers, a crack Ranger group, are billeted during WW II. The lady of the manor is the pert and precocious O'Brien who introduces the Americans to her dead relative, Laughton, a ghost who has haunted the premises for more than 300 years. He had been walled up in the dungeon by his father because he was a coward and must prove his mettle before his spirit is free of his earth-bound chains. Young, one of the Americans, turns out to be a distant relative of O'Brien's, as well as that of the transparent Laughton and, when he learns of the yellow streak runing through his family, he begins to suspect himself of being a coward. O'Brien proves to be the bravest of the lot, inspiring Young to defuse a bomb in the film's finale which saves the lives of the American contingent. Except for the absurd chase-about in a jeep near the end, Laughton is very funny as a ghost afraid of his own footfalls. In one hilarious scene, he is scared witless by the antics of the American soldiers, then comforted and consoled by his understanding relative O'Brien. This was a smash hit for the child star who was box office dynamite during the mid-1940s, one who could turn on a waterfall of tears at a moment's notice (the only other child star who could automatically turn on the tears was Bobs Watson). When producers wanted a tearful tyke in those days they invariably called for O'Brien by shouting, "Hey, get me that little girl who cries a lot!" THE CANTERVILLE GHOST was loosely drawn from the Oscar Wilde tale, so distant in structure that Wilde probably would not have recognized it, but it was a great success with the public, especially younger children, and remains so today.

p, Arthur L. Field; d, Jules Dassin; w, Edwin Harvey Blum (based on the story by Oscar Wilde); ph, Robert Planck; m, George Bassman; ed, Chester W. Schaeffer.

Comedy　　　　　　　　　　　**(PR:AAA　MPAA:NR)**

CANTOR'S SON, THE★½　　　(1937) 90m Eron bw
Moishe Oysher (*Sol*), Florence Weiss (*Helen*), Judith Abarbanel (*Rivke*), Michael Rosenberg (*Yossel*), Isidore Cashier (*Rossevitch*), Judah Bleich (*Zonvel*), Bertha

Guttenberg (*Malke*), Irving Honigman (*Ben*), Rose Wallerstein (*Clara*), Lorraine Abarbanel (*Rivkele*), Vicky Marcus (*Shlomele*).

Technically inept Jewish drama inspired by Al Jolson's THE JAZZ SINGER (1927) and starring Oysher as a runaway child who grows up to be a cafe singer by day and a cantor in the local synagogue by night. When he learns that his now elderly parents are celebrating their golden anniversary back in the old country, the young cantor goes back to his homeland in Europe to participate in the festivities. Once there he reunites with his childhood sweetheart, now a beautiful woman, and falls in love. Complications arrive when his benefactor in the States, a matronly entertainer, follows him to Europe and attempts to win him back. The production values are terrible (the phony beards on some of the actors makes them look like the Smith Brothers of cough drop fame) and the songs have no zing. Oysher is a decent singer, but a bad actor. (In Yiddish: English sub-titles)

p, Arthur Block, Samuel Segal; d, Ilya Motyleff; w, Mark Schweid (story by Louis Freiman); ph, Frank Zucker; m, Alexander Olshanetsky; art d, Robert Van Rosen; English sub-titles, Julian Leigh.

Musical/Drama　　　　　　　**(PR:A　MPAA:NR)**

CANYON AMBUSH★　　　(1952) 53m MON bw
Johnny Mack Brown, Phyllis Coates, Lee Roberts, Denver Pyle, Dennis Moore, Hugh Prosser, Marshall Reed, Pierce Lyden, Frank Ellis, Bill Koontz, Russ Whiteman, Carol Henry, George DeNormand.

Tame oater has fast-gun Brown slinging his pistols to save Coates from gang of baddies, winning her with smile, cunning and horsemanship. More neighs than kicks.

p, Vincent M. Fennelly; d, Lewis Collins; w, Joseph Poland.

Western　　　　　　　　　　　**(PR:A　MPAA:NR)**

CANYON CITY★　　　(1943) 56m REP bw
Don "Red" Barry (*Terry Reynolds/The Nevada Kid*), Wally Vernon (*Beauty Bradshaw*), Helen Talbot (*Edith Gleason*), Twinkle Watts (*Twinkle Hardy*), Morgan Conway (*Craig Morgan*), Emmett Vogan (*Emerson Wheeler*), Stanley Andrews (*Alfred Johnson*), Roy Barcroft (*Jeff Parker*), Leroy Mason (*Webb Hepburn*), Pierce Lyden, Forbes Murray, Edward Piel, Sr., Eddie Gribbon, Tom London, Jack Kirk, Kenne Duncan, Bud Geary, Bud Osborne, Hank Worden.

Yet another Barry oater, this one has our two-fisted cowboy trying to stop a big-city promoter who is attempting to hoodwink the local utility company and some ranchers. Barry suspects the city slicker of murder and with the aid of sidekick Vernon, he pretends to be a dangerous escaped convict in order to get information. The only thing this scheme nets Barry is to be accused of a murder that the promoter had committed. Barry escapes and brings the true killer to justice. Romantic interest is provided by Talbot and, once again, child ice-skating star Twinkle Watts inexplicably rides a pony throughout.

p, Eddy White; d, Spencer Bennet; w, Robert Yost; ph, John MacBurnie; ed, Harry Keller.

Western　　　　　　　　　　　**(PR:A　MPAA:NR)**

CANYON CROSSROADS★★½　　　(1955) 83m UA bw
Richard Basehart (*Larry Kendall*), Phyllis Kirk (*Katherine Rand*), Stephen Elliott (*Larson*), Russell Collins (*Dr. Rand*), Charles Waggenheim (*Pete Barnwell*), Richard Hale (*Joe Rivers*), Alan Wells (*Charlie Rivers*), Tommy Cook (*Mickey Rivers*), William Pullen (*A.E.C. Clerk*)

Strange but fascinating low-budget modern day western starring Basehart as a uranium prospector who agrees to take on geology professor Collins and his daughter Kirk if they will help him locate the mother lode. Conflict arises when sinister mine owner Elliot sends helicopters into the Utah flats to stop the prospectors and Basehart attempts to gun the metal birds down with his six-shooter. Good supporting cast and an outstanding performance by Basehart hold character interest. Unfortunately the film is in black and white and therefore loses some of the impact that some stunning Utah canyons would have had on the viewer had it been in color.

p, William Joyce; d, Alfred Werker; w, Emmett Murphy, Leonard Heideman (based on their original story); ph, Gordon Avile; m, George Bassman; ed, Chester Schaeffer.

Western　　　　　　　　　　　**(PR:A　MPAA:NR)**

CANYON HAWKS★　　　(1930) 57m National Players/Big 4 bw
Wally Wales, Buzz Barton, Rene Borden, Yakima Canutt, Cliff Lyons, Bobby Dunn, Bob Reeves, Robert Walker.

Routine Poverty Row western has Wales twirling his guns and showing remarkable powers of recuperation as he goes from wounded and staggering around in pain to beating the daylights out of the bad guys. For B fans only.

p, F. E. Douglas; d, J. P. McGowan, Alvin J. Neitz [Alan James]; w, Henry Taylor, Neitz.

Western　　　　　　　　　　　**(PR:A　MPAA:NR)**

CANYON OF MISSING MEN, THE★　　　(1930) 64m Syndicate bw
Tom Tyler, Sheila LeGay, Bud Osborne, Tom Forman, Cliff Lyons, Arden Ellis, Bobby Dunn.

Idiotic western sans plot and soggy with "thataway" dialog has Tyler pursued by thieves and then doubling back to snare the bad guys.

d, J. P. McGowan; w, Sally Winters (based on a story by George Williams).

Western　　　　　　　　　　　**(PR:A　MPAA:NR)**

CANYON PASSAGE*** (1946) 91m UNIV c

Dana Andrews (Logan Stuart), Brian Donlevy (George Camrose), Susan Hayward (Lucy Overmire), Patricia Roc (Caroline Marsh), Ward Bond (Honey Bragg), Andy Devine (Ben Dance), Rose Hobart (Marita Lestrade), Halliwell Hobbes (Clenchfield), Lloyd Bridges (Johnny Steele), Stanley Ridges (Jonas Overmire), Dorothy Petersen (Mrs. Dance), Vic Cutler (Vane Blazier), Fay Holden (Mrs. Overmire), Tad Devine (Asa Dance), Dennis Devine (Bushrod Dance), Hoagy Carmichael (Linnet), Onslow Stevens (Lestrade), James Cardwell (Gray Bartlett), Ray Teal (Neil Howison), Virginia Patton (Liza Stone), Francis McDonald (Cobb), Erville Alderson (Judge), Ralph Peters (Stutchell), Jack Rockwell (Teamster), Joseph P. Mack, Gene Stutenroth, Karl Hackett, Jack Clifford, Daral Hudson, Dick Alexander (Miners), Wallace Scott (MacIvar), Chief Yowlachi (Indian Spokesman).

The first foray of famed horror film director Jacques Tourneur, CAT PEOPLE (1942) and I WALKED WITH A ZOMBIE (1943), into the western genre and as usual he comes out with fascinating results. Andrews turns in an outstanding performance as a former scout turned general-store owner in the Oregon Territory of 1854. Also in town is banker Donlevy who has a weakness for spending his depositors' money to cover his gambling debts. Tension between the two arises when Donlevy's fiancee, Hayward, falls in love with Andrews. Soon Donlevy's debts get him into trouble and he becomes involved in the murder of one of his disgruntled depositors. The climax sees an Indian uprising wherein settlers' homes are burned in vivid Technicolor. Carmichael contributes two tunes, "Rogue River Jack" and "Ol' Buttermilk Sky."

p, Walter Wanger; d, Jacques Tourneur; w, Ernest Pascal (based on a story by Ernest Haycox); ph, Edward Cronjager (Technicolor); m, Frank Skinner; ed, Milton Carruth; md, Frank Skinner; art d, John B. Goodman, Richard H. Riedel; set d, Russell A. Gausman, Leigh Smith; cos, Travis Banton; spec eff, D. S. Horsley, m/l, Hoagy Carmichael, Jack Brooks.

Western (PR:A MPAA:NR)

CANYON RAIDERS*½ (1951) 54m MON bw

Whip Wilson, Fuzzy Knight, Jim Bannon, Phyllis Coates, Barbara Woodell, Marshall Reed, I. Stanford Jolley, Riley Hill, Bill Kennedy.

Mildly entertaining sagebrush vehicle where Wilson, Knight, Bannon and Hill as riding pals clean up the range of rustlers and thieves. Coates, one of the reigning queens of B westerns, is given a few more scenes than usual to flirt with the good guys.

p, Vincent M. Fennelly; d, Lewis Collins; w, Jay Gilgore.

Western (PR:A MPAA:NR)

CANYON RIVER** (1956) 79m AA c

George Montgomery (Steve Patrick), Marcia Henderson (Janet Hale), Peter Graves (Bob Andrews), Richard Eyer (Chuck Hale), Walter Sande (Maddox), Robert Wilke (Graycoe), Alan Hale, Jr. (Lynch), John Harmon (Ben), Jack Lambert (Kincaid), William Fawcett (Jergens).

Hackneyed cattle trail movie starring Montgomery as a rancher driving his herd of Herefords from Oregon to Wyoming to crossbreed them and develop a hardier stock. Graves plays the rancher's devious foreman who plots with rival rancher Sande to kill Montgomery and steal his cattle. By the time the herd gets to Wyoming, Graves has developed a respect for his boss and sacrifices his life to thwart the rustlers.

p, Richard Heermance; d, Harmon Jones; w, Daniel B. Ullman; ph, Ellsworth Fredricks (CinemaScope, DeLuxe Color); m, Marlin Skiles; ed, George White.

Western (PR:A MPAA:NR)

CAPE CANAVERAL MONSTERS* (1960) 69m CCM bw

Scott Peters, Linda Connell, Jason Johnson, Katherine Victor, Frank Smith.

Really awful followup by writer/director Tucker to his classic ROBOT MONSTER (considered by many to be the absolute worst sci-fi film of all time). CAPE CANAVERAL MONSTERS details an evil plot by aliens to infiltrate and destroy the U.S. space program by taking over the bodies of good Americans and turning them into mindless zombies. Exciting special effects is actually NASA stock footage of missiles taking off and exploding. Good for some trivial laughs.

p, Richard Greer; d&w, Phil Tucker; ph, Merle Connell.

Science Fiction (PR:A MPAA:NR)

CAPE FEAR***½ (1962) 105m Melville-Talbot/UNIV bw

Gregory Peck (Sam Bowden), Robert Mitchum (Max Cady), Polly Bergen (Peggy Bowden), Lori Martin (Nancy Bowden), Martin Balsam (Mark Dutton), Jack Kruschen (Dave Grafton), Telly Savalas (Charles Sievers), Barrie Chase (Diane Taylor), Paul Comi (Garner), Edward Platt (Judge), John McKee (Marconi), Page Slattery (Deputy Kersek), Ward Ramsey (Officer Brown), Will Wright (Dr. Pearsall), Joan Staley (Waitress), Mack Williams (Dr. Lowney), Thomas Newman (Lt. Gervasi), Bunny Rhea (Pianist), Carol Sydes (Betty), Alan Reynolds (Vernon), Herb Armstrong (Waiter), Paul Levitt (Police Operator), Alan Wells, Allan Ray (Young Men), Norma Yost (Ticket Clerk), Josephine Smith (Librarian), Marion Landers (Cross), Joseph Jenkins (Janitor), Jack Richardson (Deputy), Al Silvani (Man), Bob Noble, Jack Elkins (Pedestrians).

Sex deviate and lethal psychopath, Mitchum is released from prison after serving a six-year term for rape and assault. He is bent on revenge against the man who put him there, one-time prosecutor Peck, now a lawyer with a private practice. At first the family dog is poisoned, then Mitchum takes to the phone, calling Peck's wife, Bergen, plaguing her with obscene remarks. Peck, upon learning Mitchum has returned to the small southern town, has him arrested but Mitchum is freed for having committed no crime. Though he makes no overt threats, Mitchum intimates a dire fate for Peck and family. The police are helpless to jail the lunatic, and watch him closely. The calls and oblique threats continue until Peck decides to handle matters himself. He sends his wife and 12-year-old daughter, Martin, to a house boat on Cape Fear River, later joining them, knowing Mitchum is following. He then pretends to leave the remote spot so that Mitchum will attack his wife and child which Peck actually uses for bait. The maniac does exactly that, catching Bergen, beginning to disrobe her. In this utterly repulsive scene, Mitchum cracks a raw egg and spreads the glutinous, runny contents on Bergen's chest. Just at that moment Peck appears and wildly attacks Mitchum. A battle royal ensues with the incensed lawyer overpowering the madman. Mitchum has killed a deputy, Richardson, who had been guarding the females, and this time goes to prison for life. This film is a chiller all the way, thanks to Mitchum's terrorizing performance, one almost similar to his portrayal of the throat-slitting Harry Powell in NIGHT OF THE HUNTER (a film Mitchum still refuses to discuss). But here Mitchum is not in search of hidden loot, killing to get it. He merely seethes with revenge and lust, oozing evil like a hungry reptile tonguing bugs. Peck is solid and often a powerful match against the nemesis as the righteous family man backed into a corner of violence when Mitchum circumvents the law. Bergen, too, is fine as the frightened wife, and Balsam gives his usual arresting performance as the law-bound police chief. Barrie Chase, as a sexy call girl who is brutalized by Mitchum, and Kruschen his oily lawyer who protects him against the law, are outstanding, as is Savalas, a detective hired by Peck to first bribe, then bully Mitchum out of town, getting killed for his gumshoe efforts. Oddly, the film is superior to the predictable MacDonald novel, again thanks to the bizarre image projected by the talented and formidable Mitchum. Director Thompson maintains a quick pace in the Hitchcockian tradition.

p, Sy Bartlett (Melville-Talbot); d, J. Lee Thompson; w, James R. Webb (based on the novel The Executioners by John D. MacDonald); ph, Samuel Leavitt; m, Bernard Herrmann; ed, George Tomasini; art d, Alexander Golitzen, Robert Boyle; set d, Oliver Emert; cos, Mary Wills; makeup, Frank Prehoda, Thomas Tuttle.

Crime Drama (PR:O MPAA:NR)

CAPE FORLORN (SEE: LOVE STORM, 1931, Brit.)

CAPER OF THE GOLDEN BULLS, THE*½
(1967) 105m Embassy c (GB: CARNIVAL OF THIEVES)

Stephen Boyd (Peter Churchman), Yvette Mimieux (Grace Harvey), Giovanna Ralli (Angela Tresler), Walter Slezak (Antonio Gonzalez), Vito Scotti (Francois Morel), Clifton James (Philippe Lemoins), Lomax Study (Paul Brissard), Tom Toner (Canalli), Henry Beckman (Bendell), Noah Keen (Ryan), Jay Novello (Carlos), Arnold Moss (Mr. Shahari), Leon Askin (Morchek), Leon Charles (Deaf Mute).

Dull, complicated caper film starring Boyd as a retired bank robber who is blackmailed into performing one last job. He is to rob a fortune in jewels from the Pamplona bank during the fiesta for the running of the bulls. Overlong and somewhat tedious, much of the footage seems devoted to being used as a travelog of Spain rather than as a taut thriller.

p, Clarence Greene; d, Russell Rouse; w, Ed Waters, David Moessinger (based on the novel by William McGivern); ph, Hal Stine (Pathe Color); m, Vic Mizzy; ed, Chester Schaeffer; cos, Edith Head; makeup, Wally Westmore; men's wardrobe, Robert Magahay.

Crime/Thriller (PR:A MPAA:NR)

CAPETOWN AFFAIR*½ (1967, U.S./South Afr.) 100m FOX/Killarney c

James Brolin, Jacqueline Bisset, Claire Trevor, Jon Whitely, Bob Courtney.

Pickpocket cops a purse on a South African bus but gets more than expected; the purse contains an envelope holding top secret microfilm. This leads to a communist spy ring and innumerable chases, lamely-photographed and directed. Bisset and Brolin in early roles are not impressive and the only standout is veteran Trevor who reprises the role originally played by Thelma Ritter in PICKUP ON SOUTH STREET upon which this unimaginative remake is based.

p&d, Robert D. Webb; w, Harold Medford, Samuel Fuller; ph, David Millin (DeLuxe Color); m, Bob Adams.

Spy Drama (PR:C MPAA:NR)

CAPONE zero (1975) 101m FOX c

Ben Gazzara (Al Capone), Susan Blakely (Iris Crawford), Harry Guardino (Johnny Torrio), John Cassavetes (Frankie Yale), Sylvester Stallone (Frank Nitti), Peter Maloney (Jake Guzik), Frank Campanella (Big Jim Colosimo), John D. Chandler (Hymie Weiss), John Orchard (Dion O'Banion), Mario Gallo (Aiello), Russ Marin (Stenson), George Chandler (Prosecutor), Royal Dano (Mayor Anton Cermak).

Contrived gangster film has Gazzara portraying the inhuman gorilla Capone who rose through mob ranks in Chicago to dominate a brutal underworld fiefdom in the Roaring Twenties, until his fall through federal conviction of income tax eviction and eventual imprisonment. Gazzara appears to have stuffed ten pounds of cotton into each cheek (replacing the necessary tongue) to get that jowly Capone look or the Godfather image projected by Marlon Brando. No amount of swaggering or overacting by Gazzara is convincing here; he is simply an embarrassment and the scenes showing the gangster going crazy (from paresis of the brain stemming from syphilis) are absurd. Producer Corman geared this cliche-ridden monstrosity simply for violence, his metier, but no new insights nor information on one of America's great monsters are offered. In fact, little new footage is added, most of the mob war scenes culled from other films, chiefly from THE ST. VALENTINE'S DAY MASSACRE which Corman and writer Browne released in 1967, a superior product but no less bloody. The only interesting character is Stallone who gives good support as a Capone turncoat.

p, Roger Corman; d, Steve Carver; w, Howard Browne; ph, Vilis Lapenieks (DeLuxe Color); m, David Grisman; ed, Richard Meyer; art d, Ward Preston; set d, Ned Parsons.

Crime Drama/Biography (PR:O MPAA:R)

CAPPY RICKS RETURNS* (1935) 67m REP bw
Robert McWade (Cappy Ricks), Ray Walker (Bill Peck), Florine McKinney (Barbara), Lucien Littlefield (Skinner), Bradley Page (Winton), Lois Wilson (Florry), Oscar Apfel (Blake), Kenneth Harlan (Peasley).

A none too exciting drama stars McWade as Cappy Ricks, who comes out of retirement to battle a fiendish roofing materials lobby which is pushing legislation to outlaw the use of shingles on roofs. McWade is outraged because such a law would ruin his lumber company. He hires an ambitious young man, Walker, to direct *his* lobbying effort against discriminatory business legislation. Romance erupts when the daughter of the unscrupulous roofing magnate meets Walker, falls in love, and goes to work for him against her father. Soon McWade and Walker discover that there is a spy in their midst when the girl's father learns of the group's plans sooner than they can enact them, which throws suspicion on the girl. Walker can't believe his love would do such a thing and is proved correct when she is eventually cleared. The cast tries hard to make this "shingle wars" plot line interesting, but just can't pull it off. (See CAPPY RICKS series, Index)

p, Trem Carr; d, Mack Wright; w, George Waggner (based on the novel by Peter B. Kyne); ph, Harry Neumann; ed, Carl Pierson.

Drama **(PR:A MPAA:NR)**

CAPRICE* (1967) 97m FOX c
Doris Day (Patricia Fowler), Richard Harris (Christopher White), Ray Walston (Stuart Clancy), Jack Kruschen (Matthew Cutter), Edward Mulhare (Sir Jason Fox), Lilia Skala (Mme. Piasco), Irene Tsu (Su Ling), Larry D. Mann (Inspector Kapinsky), Maurice Marsac (Auber), Michael Romanoff (Butler), Lisa Seagram (Mandy), Michael J. Pollard (Barney).

Dumb Day comedy filmed a few years after Doris should have retired her brand of humor. In this one, she plays an espionage agent employed by a cosmetics firm whose duties include murdering rival agents who may be involved in the narcotics trade. She meets up with charming agent Harris, who saves her from a skiing mishap engineered by an enemy assassin. Harris is rather mysterious himself (he may be an enemy agent) but the couple fall in love and eventually trace their way to the lab of cosmetics genius Walston who is responsible for the murder of Day's secret agent dad. The comedy is predictable and the film tries too hard to be a contemporary 1960s comedy, but it is hopelessly "square." In one ludicrous scene, Day attempts to cut off a lock of hair from the head of one of Walston's mistresses (to discover what kind of cosmetic spray she uses), dangling from the underside of a high-perched sun-deck; she is splashed with water and then staggers backward down a steep Hollywood hill, her mini-dress hiked high to reveal the body of a rather beefy middle-aged woman, not the sleek femme fatale she is supposed to be playing. Day stands in the middle of a dusty mountain road, dripping, unglamourous, unsightly and decidedly ungainly, an awkward portrait that must have shocked the blonde warbler when viewing the rushes and certainly prompted her decision to retire.

p, Aaron Rosenberg, Martin Melcher; d, Frank Tashlin; w, Jay Jayson, Tashlin (story by Martin Hale, Jayson); ph, Leon Shamroy (CinemaScope, DeLuxe Color); m, Frank DeVol; ed, Robert Simpson; cos, Ray Aghayan.

Comedy **(PR:A MPAA:NR)**

CAPRICIOUS SUMMER*** (1968, Czech.) 75m Barrandov Film Studios/Sigma III c
Rudolf Hrusinsky (Dura), Vlastimil Brodsky (Major), Mila Myslikova (Durova), Frantisek Rehak (Abbe), Jana Drchalova (Anna), Jiri Menzel (Tightrope Walker).

Three middle-aged, middle-class Czechs on vacation at a summer resort have their holiday upset by the arrival of a circus tightrope walker and his beautiful daughter. This delightful, gentle comedy isn't for all tastes, but well worth giving a try. Director Menzel is best known outside Czechoslovakia for CLOSELY WATCHED TRAINS, and this is almost as good.

p, Jan Libora; d&w, Jiri Menzel (based on a novel by Vladislav Cancura).

Comedy **(PR:C MPAA:NR)**

CAPRICORN ONE*** (1978) 127m WB c
Elliott Gould (Robert Caulfield), James Brolin (Charles Brubaker), Brenda Vaccaro (Kay Brubaker), Sam Waterston (Peter Willis), O. J. Simpson (John Walker), Hal Holbrook (Dr. James Kelloway), David Huddleston (Hollis Peaker), David Doyle (Walter Loughlin), Denise Nicholas (Betty Walker), Robert Walden (Elliot Whittier), Lee Bryant (Sharon Willis), Alan Fudge (Capsule Communicator), Karen Black (Judy Drinkwater), Telly Savalas (Albain).

Overlong but interesting thriller in which Mission Control commander Holbrook discovers that the ship which is to take the first astronauts to Mars (Brolin, Simpson, and Waterston), is unsafe. Instead of disappointing the public and losing precious government funds due to their failure, Holbrook gets the astronauts to agree to fake the landing on a Hollywood-type soundstage. The deception works, but soon the astronauts realize that their lives are in danger (NASA will have to kill them while in "orbit" to insure their silence) and they escape into the desert. Enter investigative reporter Gould who pieces the conspiracy together. Unfortunately the premise sounds more interesting than it is and the film slowly rambles to its exciting conclusion wherein Gould, in a crop duster piloted by eccentric Savalas, flies into the desert to rescue Brolin. Director Hyams, for some reason, insists on writing his own material and the subsequent films he has directed OUTLAND (1981) and 2010 (1984), have suffered from his mediocre scripting.

p, Paul N. Lazarus III; d&w, Peter Hyams; ph, Bill Butler (Panavision, CFI Color); m, Jerry Goldsmith; ed, James Mitchell; art d, David M. Haber; set d, Rick Simpson; cos, Patricia Norris.

Thriller **Cas.** **(PR:C MPAA:PG)**

CAPTAIN APACHE* (1971, Brit.) 94m Scotia International c
Lee Van Cleef (Capt. Apache), Carroll Baker (Maude), Stuart Whitman (Griffin), Percy Herbert (Moon), Elisa Montes (Rosita), Tony Vogel (Snake), Charles Stalnaker (O'Rourke), Charlie Bravo (Sanchez), Hugh McDermott (Gen. Ryland), Faith Clift (Abigail), Dan Van Husen (Al), D. Pollock (Ben), George Margo (Sheriff), Jose Bodalo (General), Elsa Zabala (Witch), Allen Russell (Maitre D'), Luis Induni (Ezekiel), Vito Salier (Diablo), Fernando Sanchez Pollack (Guitarist).

Stupid American-Spanish western produced by the British stars Van Cleef as an Indian Union army officer assigned to investigate the murder of the Indian Commissioner. During his investigation he discovers that rich landowner Whitman has hatched a plan to start an Indian war by disguising his men as redskins and assassinating President Grant. This in turn would wreak havoc on the Indians because the Union Army would drive the savages off their oil and gold-rich lands, which Whitman would snatch up. Done in a silly tongue-in-cheek style and filled with modern-day humor (one sequence has Van Cleef having drug-induced hallucinations replete with bright colors and psychedelic music) the film comes off as ridiculous and flat.

p, Milton Sperling, Philip Yordan; d, Alexander Singer; w, Sperling, Yordan (based on the novel by S. E. Whitman); ph, John Cabrera (CinemaScope, Technicolor); m, Dolores Claman; ed, Leigh G. Tallas; cos, Tony Pueo.

Western **(PR:C MPAA:GP)**

CAPTAIN APPLEJACK*½ (1931) 76m WB bw
John Halliday, Mary Brian, Kay Strozzi, Louise Closser Hale, Alec B. Francis, Claude Allister, Julia Swayne Gordon, Arthur Edmund Carewe, Otto Hoffman, William Davidson.

Halliday is a meek man whose courage is aroused when robbers come for the treasure hidden in his home. Undistinguished programmer was first filmed in 1923. CAPTAIN APPLEJACK was one of ten films made by popular actor Halliday in 1931, and Brian, of course, was the "nice girl" of early movies.

d, Hobart Henley; w, Maude Fulton (based on the play "Andrew Apple John's Adventures" by Walter Hackett); ph, Ira Morgan.

Crime **(PR:A MPAA:NR)**

CAPTAIN BILL* (1935, Brit.) 81m Leslie Fuller bw
Leslie Fuller (Bill), Judy Kelly (Polly), Hal Gordon (Tim), O. B. Clarence (Sir Anthony Kipps), Georgie Harris (Georgie), D. J. Williams (Cheerful), Tonie Edgar Bruce (Lady Kipps), Ralph Truman (Red).

Fuller is a bargeman who helps schoolmistress Kelly elude a pack of gunrunners who are after her. Fuller was a popular comedian with British audiences of the 1930s, but modern audiences won't find him more than slightly amusing.

p, Joe Rock; d, Ralph Ceder; w, Val Valentine, Syd Courtenay, George Harris; ph, Charles Van Enger.

Comedy **(PR:A MPAA:NR)**

CAPTAIN BLACK JACK* (1952, U.S./Fr.) 90m Classic Pictures bw
George Sanders (Mike Alexander), Patricia Roc (Ingrid Dekker), Agnes Moorehead (Mrs. Birk), Herbert Marshall (Dr. Curtis), Marcel Dalio (Capt. Nikarescu), Jose Nieto (Inspector Carnero).

A talented cast succeeds in embarrassing itself in this piece of trash. Moorehead is a socialite on the Riviera who turns out to be the leader of a gang of drug runners. She is exposed by mild-mannered doctor Marshall, who turns out to be an undercover detective. Sanders maintains his identity as a cad (his usual role) throughout the film, but ends up shot dead. Not worth thirty minutes.

p&d, Julien Duvivier; w, Duvivier, Charles Spaak.

Crime **(PR:A MPAA:NR)**

CAPTAIN BLOOD**** (1935) 119m WB/FN bw
Errol Flynn (Dr. Peter Blood), Olivia de Havilland (Arabella Bishop), Lionel Atwill (Col. Bishop), Basil Rathbone (Capt. Levasseur), Ross Alexander (Jeremy Pitt), Guy Kibbee (Hagthorpe), Henry Stephenson (Lord Willoughby), George Hassell (Gov. Steed), Forrester Harvey (Honesty Nuttall), Frank McGlynn, Sr. (Rev. Ogle), Robert Barrat (Wolverstone), Hobart Cavanaugh (Dr. Bronson), Donald Meek (Dr. Wacker), David Torrence (Andrew Baynes), J. Carrol Naish (Cahusac), Pedro de Cordoba (Don Diego), Leonard Mudie (Lord Jeffries), Jessie Ralph (Mrs. Barlowe), Stuart Casey (Capt. Hobart), Halliwell Hobbes (Lord Sunderland), Colin Kenny (Lord Dyke), E. E. Clive (Court Clerk), Holmes Herbert (Capt. Gardiner), Mary Forbes (Mrs. Steed), Reginald Barlow (Dixon), Ivan F. Simpson (Prosecutor), Denis d'Auburn (Lord Gildoy), Vernon Steele (King James), Georges Renavent (French Captain), Murray Kinnell (Clerk in Gov. Steed's Court), Harry Cording (Kent), Maude Leslie (Baynes' Wife), Chris-Pin Martin (Sentry), Tom Wilson and Henry Otho (Pirates), David Thursby (Lookout), Yola D'Avril, Renee Terres, Lucille Porcett, Tina Minard (Girls in Tavern), Alphonse Martell, Andre Cheron, Frank Puglia (French Officers).

This was the film that made stars of Errol Flynn and Olivia de Havilland. Flynn is a physician, Peter Blood, arrested for doctoring a wounded officer who had been part of the rebellion against tyrannical King James of England in 1685. He and other rebels are sent to Jamaica to be sold as slaves to work the plantations. Wealthy landowner Atwill inspects the human chattel on the dock but after Flynn defies him, the governor intends to leave him to other would-be masters. De Havilland, Atwill's niece, is intrigued and amused by the surly, handsome young man, bidding against cruel masters to buy him. When the beautiful young lady tells Flynn he is lucky to have been purchased by her rather than others, he sneers and says, "I hardly consider it fortunate to be bought by anyone with the name of Bishop." After several run-ins with Atwill, who threatens him with dire punishment for kind treatment of unruly prisoners who have been whipped, Flynn cures the governor's (Hassell) gout and is allowed the freedom of the island. He immediately plans an escape. When he cannot explain his whereabouts, Atwill is about to have him whipped. De Havilland again comes to his rescue, providing an alibi. Flynn thanks her but his brash remarks bring only a slap in the face. Spanish pirates next attack Port Royal but they are overpowered by Flynn and his fellow slaves who capture their ship and sail off as buccaneers who become the most feared pirates of the sea lanes; Flynn leads raids against towns and sinks ships at random after looting them of their precious cargoes. (In one of writer Casey Robinson's more lurid title cards, a silent era device interspersed between the action and dialog, Flynn's reputation and name become synonymous, the title reading: "Blood! Blood! BLOOD!") He encounters another infamous pirate of the sea lanes, Rathbone, the evil Lavasseur, who goads Flynn into a partnership, one he later comes to regret. Rathbone's ship captures an English vessel carrying de Havilland and Stephenson, a royal emissary who holds a commission for Flynn as a captain in the Royal Navy, for he has been pardoned under William III who has taken the throne from James II, the deposed monarch having fled to France. Rathbone takes his hostages to the island stronghold of Virgen Magra where Flynn also makes his headquarters. Here Flynn interrupts Rathbone who is threatening Stephenson after being insulted by the British lord. Rathbone proves his evil-to-the-marrow personality by holding out a knotted rope, sneering at Stephenson: "You know this? It's the rosary of pain. With this it is possible to screw a man's eyes out of his head!" Flynn upbraids his sadistic partner, reminding him that all spoils under their agreement—in this case the hostages—are to be put up to the highest bidder. With that he meets the ransom price and, further insulting Rathbone, tosses priceless pearls to Rathbone's avaricious, grateful French crew. Rathbone draws his blade and the two captains duel to the death at the water's edge, spectacular and energetic swordplay that was to be one of Flynn's hallmarks in many an adventure film to come. The over-confident Rathbone makes a fatal error and is run through. As he dies in the sand Flynn ruefully remarks, "So ends a partnership that should never have begun." De Havilland, incensed that she has been purchased by Flynn, tells him, "I don't wish to be bought by you!" He gives her back her own earlier words to him, "As a lady once said to a slave—you are hardly in a position to have anything to say about it." On their return voyage to Port Royal, de Havilland can only hate her gallant protector for having been a pirate, but Stephenson points out to her that she is nevertheless in love with the buccaneer. Port Royal has been left helpless by Atwill who has taken his ships on a wild goose chase to look for his nemesis Flynn and French frigates are busy shelling the city when Flynn's ships arrive (England and France by then have gone to war). Flynn and his men destroy the enemy ships and enter the harbor victorious. When Atwill returns, Stephenson tells him he is no longer governor of Jamaica; another man sits in his office and he must beg forgiveness from the new governor for leaving Port Royal defenseless. Atwill meekly enters the governor's mansion, imploring mercy from a man seated with his back to him. The chair swivels about to reveal Flynn, the new governor. De Havilland stands beside Flynn, both of them grinning at a sputtering Atwill. "Good morning, Uncle," chuckles Flynn at fadeout. CAPTAIN BLOOD firmly established Flynn as filmdon's leading swashbuckler, inheriting through his dash, athletic prowess, and good looks the mantle from Douglas Fairbanks, Sr. He had appeared in a few programmers before this, his first major film (IN THE WAKE OF THE BOUNTY, a foreign entry, MURDER AT MONTE CARLO, THE CASE OF THE CURIOUS BRIDE and DON'T BET ON BLONDES). With Flynn it was a case of being in the right spot at the right time. Warner Bros. saw the success of MGM's MUTINY ON THE BOUNTY in 1935 and decided to follow suit with one of its own old properties, CAPTAIN BLOOD, which had been filmed as a silent in 1923 by Vitagraph with J. Warren Kerrigan. At first Robert Donat, who had scored heavily in THE COUNT OF MONTE CRISTO in 1934, was selected to play Peter Blood, with Jean Muir as his co-star. But Donat suffered from a chronic asthmatic condition and, after reading a rough draft of the script, decided that the acrobatic role of Blood would be too taxing, so, at the last minute, he turned down the part. Jack Warner then began desperately searching for a leading man. Everywhere he turned, the name of an unknown actor, Flynn, was brought up. Lili Damita, an established star at Warners who had just finished THE FRISCO KID with James Cagney, socialized with Warner's wife and repeatedly pushed Flynn for the part; she had married the handsome Tasmanian in June, 1935. Moreover, Michael Curtiz, the studio's top director, who had seen promise in Flynn when directing him in THE CASE OF THE CURIOUS BRIDE, agreed that he could play Blood well. In an inexplicable move, Warner agreed to give de Havilland the Muir role, banking on two unknowns to carry a major film. (As it turned out, Flynn's health was almost as precarious as that of Donat's; he collapsed on the set during production from recurrent attacks of malaria.) De Havilland had only played a small role in Max Reinhardt's A MIDSUMMER NIGHT'S DREAM, filmed in 1935 by Warners. This spectacle would not go over budget, Warner insisted, especially with two novice leads. Shrewdly, the company decided not to build full-scale sailing ships for the many action scenes. To compensate for the bombardments, navy battles, and sinking of ships, technicians built several miniature ships eighteen feet long with sixteen-foot masts and the battles were fought in a studio tank. Even the town of Port Royal was built in miniature. Clips from silent films (First National's 1924 SEA HAWK and Vitagraph's 1923 CAPTAIN BLOOD) were used to show full-scale ships in battle. The main decks of two ships were constructed on a sound stage for the life-size action and on-location scenes were made along the California shoreline. Flynn's duel with Rathbone was shot at Laguna Beach which had been cleared of bathers for an hour, so Flynn could run a sword through his arch rival. The new film hero, despite his offscreen self-assured ways, was nervous in the first few week's shooting but improved so quickly that this footage was shot over to match the bravura performance throughout. Almost from the day of its release, Flynn was a great Hollywood star, a favorite with a public that would forever see him as the great swashbuckler and he would live up to such expectations in one grand adventure film after another. Immediately after the smash hit of CAPTAIN BLOOD, Warners planned to star Flynn in another sea adventure, CAPTAIN HORATIO HORNBLOWER. This film was repeatedly announced by the studio as a

forthcoming Flynn vehicle until it was finally given to Gregory Peck for a 1951 release. CAPTAIN BLOOD not only served to introduce Flynn as a stellar lead but brought critical acclaim as well to lovely 19-year-old de Havilland who plays her part with great maturity and sophistication. She and the dashing Flynn would appear in eight films altogether. Curtiz, the master of adventure films who shot his scenes like a cavalry charge, would direct a total of nine Flynn epics, and Korngold, whose rich and resonant scores set the musical standard for such spectacular films, would compose seven musical scores for Flynn films. For Errol Flynn, a 26-year-old novice actor from Hobart, Tasmania, CAPTAIN BLOOD served as his rocket to stardom, surprising everyone in the industry and the public-at-large, everyone except Flynn himself. He had been paid $300-a-week to enact the role, taking it on cavalierly, as he did life in general, drinking cognac on the set and spouting lines not in the script. He had been upbraided by Jack Warner and laughed it off. Flynn would look back on this film with wry humor in My Wicked, Wicked Ways, and give Jack Warner his due: "So many people claim discovering me that I get lost getting discovered. Mervyn LeRoy claimed he did. So did Michael Curtiz. But it was Jack Warner who made the decision. He had the guts to take a complete unknown and put me in the lead of a big production. That took real financial foresight."

p, Hal B. Wallis; d, Michael Curtiz; w, Casey Robinson (based on the novel by Rafael Sabatini); ph, Hal Mohr, Ernest Haller; m, Erich Wolfgang Korngold; ed, George Amy; orchestrators, Hugo Friedhofer, Ray Heindorf; art d, Anton Grot; cos, Milo Anderson; spec eff, Fred Jackman; fencing master, Fred Cavens.

Adventure/Historical Drama   **Cas.**   **(PR:A MPAA:NR)**

CAPTAIN BOYCOTT*½   (1947, Brit.) 93m GFD bw

Stewart Granger (Hugh Davin), Kathleen Ryan (Anne Killain), Cecil Parker (Capt. Boycott), Robert Donat (Charles Stewart Parnell), Mervyn Johns (Watty Connell), Alastair Sim (Father McKeogh), Noel Purcell (Daniel McGinty), Niall McGinnis (Mark Killain), Maurice Denham (Lt. Col. Strickland), Maureen Delaney (Mrs. Davin), Eddie Byrne (Sean Kerin), Liam Redmond (Martin Egan), Liam Gaffney (Michael Fagan), Bernadette O'Farrell (Mrs. Fagan), Edward Lexy (Sgt. Demsey), Harry Webster (Robert Hogan), Ian Fleming (Times Correspondent), Reginald Purdell (American Reporter).

Irish historical drama concerning the little-known Captain Boycott whose surname became part of the English language. Action takes place in 1880 and concerns Boycott (Parker) who is in charge of rent—collecting for the Earl of Erne. Parker is brutal to the tenants, and evicts those who can't pay up. The citizens finally become fed up with the rent-collector and decide to unite and banish him. Parker learns of the plan and spends all his money trying to drum up popular support for himself by waging a newspaper campaign extolling his virtues. Desperate to recover his financial losses, Parker spends his last $20 on a race horse and enters it in the big derby. He bets on the horse heavily to win and just as the animal is about to cross the finish line the citizens invade the track (stopping the race) and throw the bum out. Totally demoralized, Parker leaves Ireland as the local priest advises the community to "boycott" whoever else tries to do it harm. Look for famed "James Bond" author Ian Fleming in a bit part as a newspaper reporter.

p, Sidney Gilliat, Frank Launder; d, Launder; w, Launder, Wolfgang Wilhelm (based on the novel by Philip Rooney, additional dialog, Paul Vincent Carroll, Patrick Campbell); ph, Wilkie Cooper, Oswald Morris; m, William Alwyn; ed, Thelma Myers; md, Muir Mathieson; art d, Edward Carrick.

Drama   **(PR:A MPAA:NR)**

CAPTAIN CALAMITY*   (1936) 65m GN bw

George Houston (Capt. Calamity), Marion Nixon (Madge), Vince Barnett (Burp), Juan Torena (Mike), Movita (Annana), Crane Wilbur (Dr. Kelkey), George Lewis (Black Pierre), Roy D'Arcy (Samson), Margaret Irving (Mme. Gruen), Barry Norton (Carr), Louis Natheaux (Joblin), Lloyd Ingraham (Trader Jim).

Dumb South Seas nautical adventure starring Houston as the title character who pretends to have discovered a fortune in Spanish pirate treasure. When word of the phony discovery gets out, every crooked seaman in the islands goes after Houston in an attempt to bump him off and snatch the fictitious loot. This puts the hero's girl Nixon in danger as well, but Houston wipes out his opposition, killing as many as twenty men in one fight. In the end he defeats all his enemies and winds up with Nixon but no loot since it never existed anyway. Flat, contrived, and uninteresting.

p, George A. Hirliman; d, John Reinhardt; w, Crane Wilbur (based on a story by Gordon Young); ph, Mack Stengler; m/l, Jack Stern, Harry Tobias.

Adventure   **(PR:A MPAA:NR)**

CAPTAIN CAREY, U.S.A.**½   (1950) 82m PAR bw (GB: AFTER MIDNIGHT)

Alan Ladd (Webster Carey), Wanda Hendrix (Giula De Cresci), Francis Lederer (Barone Rocco De Greffi), Celia Lovsky (Contessa Francesca De Cresci), Angela Clarke (Serafina), Richard Avonde (Count Carlo De Cresci), Joseph Calleia (Dr. Lunati), Roland Winters (Acuto), Frank Puglia (Luigi), Luis Alberni (Sandro), Jane Nigh (Nancy), Rusty Tamblyn (Pietro), George Lewis (Giovanni), David Leonard (Blind Musician), Virginia Farmer (Angelina), Paul Lees (Frank), Henry Escalante (Brutus).

Another soldier-of-fortune tale for the tough and taciturn Ladd in the vein of his OSS, CALCUTTA, CHINA, and SAIGON. Here Ladd recovers from wounds in the U.S. after WW II. While passing a display window of a NYC art gallery he spots a painting that had once been hidden in an underground hideout in Italy, one where Ladd and his OSS team worked as espionage agents. Realizing that only his team and an Italian girl, Hendrix, had known about the room, he begins to investigate, trying to discover who smuggled out the painting. All of his fellow agents and the girl have been killed and he alone has survived. Now he believes he can unearth the traitor by following the trail of the painting. Once again in a little village near Milan, Italy, Ladd discovers that Hendrix is still alive, married to Lederer. She tells him that she thought him dead and only married Lederer at the insistence of her grandmother, an aristocratic countess. Ladd first suspects Hendrix, then Lederer as the traitor. After several harrowing experiences with village toughs who think *he* is the man who betrayed the village to the Nazis and brought down a bloodbath—Ladd has to use his fists and ingenuity to escape several attackers—the one-time spy learns that Lederer is the man who smuggled out the painting from the underground hideout,thereby having knowledge of the hiding place. Just as he is about to corner him as a spy, he discovers that Lovsky, the doddering countess,is the real traitor, that she told the Nazis about the hideout so they would spare her grandson who was in a concentration camp. Lederer conveniently dies during Ladd's investigation and Hendrix is free to marry him. In a grand gesture Ladd does not turn in the traitorous grandmother but merely leaves her alone with her own devastating memories as he and Hendrix depart for America. Although the dark mood and brooding atmosphere of the film is well sustained, the many twists of the plot confuse the story and muddle the action. This is not one of Ladd's better films but his effort is nevertheless commendable. The film did offer the haunting "Mona Lisa," sung memorably by the great Nat "King" Cole, a tune which won an Academy Award and went on to top the hit parade in 1950.

p, Richard Maibaum; d, Mitchell Leisen; w, Robert Thoeren (based on the novel *After Midnight* by Martha Albrand); ph, John Seitz; ed, Alma Macrorie; m/l, "Mona Lisa," Jay Livingston and Ray Evans.

Spy Drama (PR:A MPAA:NR)

CAPTAIN CAUTION*½ (1940) 84m UA bw

Victor Mature *(Dan Marvin)*, Louise Platt *(Corunna)*, Leo Carrillo *(Argandeau)*, Bruce Cabot *(Slade)*, Robert Barrat *(Capt. Dorman)*, Vivienne Osborne *(Victorine)*, Miles Mander *(Lt. Strope)*, El Brendel *(Slushy)*, Roscoe Ates *(Chips)*, Andrew Tombes *(Sad Eyes)*, Aubrey Mather *(Mr. Potter)*, Alan Ladd *(Newton)*, Pat O'Malley *(Fish Peddler)*, Lloyd Corrigan *(Capt. Stannage)*, Ted Osborn *(Capt. Decatur)*, Ann Codee *(Landlady)*, Romaine Callender *(English Officer)*, Pierre Watkin *(American Consul)*, Clifford Severn, Jr. *(Travers)*, Bud Jamison *(Blinks)*, Olaf Hytten *(Stannage's Aide)*, Frank Lackteen *(Slade's Mate)*, Stanley Blystone *(Sailor)*, George Lloyd *(Sailor)*.

An uneven mix of romance, drama, adventure, and music, CAPTAIN CAUTION details the adventures of an American vessel, the *Olive Branch*, on it's way home carrying a valuable cargo. Suddenly the ship is hijacked by the British who use it as a prison ship. When the captain of the *Olive Branch* dies, young sailor Mature takes command of the ship and of a romance with feisty sailorette Platt. Eventually the Americans are rescued by Osborn and sent on their way. Look hard and fast for Alan Ladd in a minor role.

p, Richard Wallace, Grover Jones; d, Wallace; w, Jones (based on the novel by Kenneth Roberts); ph, Norbert Brodine; m, Phil Ohman; ed, James Newcomb; art d, Nicolai Remisoff, Charles D. Hall; spec eff, Roy Seawright; m/l, Ohman, Foster Carling.

Adventure Cas. (PR:A MPAA:NR)

CAPTAIN CHINA** (1949) 97m PAR bw

John Payne *(Capt. China)*, Gail Russell *(Kim Mitchell)*, Jeffrey Lynn *(Capt. Brendensen)*, Lon Chaney, Jr. *(Red Lynch)*, Edgar Bergen *(Mr. Haasvelt)*, Michael O'Shea *(Trask)*, Ellen Corby *(Miss Endicott)*, Robert Armstrong *(Keegan)*, John Qualen *(Geech)*, Ilka Gruning *(Mrs. Haasvelt)*, Keith Richards *(Alberts)*, John Bagni *(Sparks)*, Ray Hyke *(Michaels)*.

Somewhat silly high-seas melodrama starring Payne as a salty sea captain who loses his command when his ship gets wrecked on a reef while he is drunk over the loss of his girl. It turns out that his crew conspired to ruin the captain so that the first-mate, Lynn, could get his own ship. On Lynn's maiden voyage as captain, Payne climbs on board in an effort to clear himself. After a vicious fight with former crew member Chaney, Payne rescues the ship and its passengers when the incompetent Lynn almost sinks the vessel during a typhoon. Good cast rescues trite material.

p, William H. Pine, William C. Thomas; d, Lewis R. Foster; w, Foster, Gwen Bagni (based on a story by John and Gwen Bagni); ph, John Alton; ed, Howard Smith; m/l, Joseph Marais.

Adventure (PR:A MPAA:NR)

CAPTAIN CLEGG (SEE: NIGHT CREATURES, 1962)

CAPTAIN EDDIE½** (1945) 107m Fox bw

Fred MacMurray *(Edward Rickenbacker)*, Lynn Bari *(Adelaide)*, Charles Bickford *(William Rickenbacker)*, Thomas Mitchell *(Ike Howard)*, Lloyd Nolan *(Lt. Whittaker)*, James Gleason *(Tom Clark)*, Mary Philips *(Elsie Rickenbacker)*, Darryl Hickman *(Eddie Rickenbacker as Boy)*, Spring Byington *(Mrs. Frost)*, Richard Conte *(Pvt. Bartek)*, Charles Russell *(Sgt. Reynolds)*, Richard Crane *(Capt. Cherry)*, Stanley Ridges *(Col. Adamson)*, Clem Bevans *(Jabez)*, Grady Sutton *(Lester Thomas)*, Chick Chandler *(Lacey)*, Dwayne Hickman *(Louis Rickenbacker)*, Mary June Robinson *(Mary Rickenbacker)*, Winifred Glyn *(Emma Rickenbacker)*, Gregory Muradian *(Dewey Rickenbacker)*, David Spencer *(Albert Rickenbacker)*, Elvin Field *(Bill Rickenbacker)*, George Mitchell *(Lt. de Angelis)*, Boyd Davis *(Mr. Frost)*, Don Garner *(Sgt. Alex)*, Mary Gordon *(Mrs. Westrom)*, Joseph J. Greene *(Dinkenspiel)*, Olin Howlin *(Census Taker)*, Robert Malcolm *(Mr. Foley)*, Leila McIntyre *(Mrs. Foley)*,Harry Shannon *(Simmons)*, Virginia Brissac *(Flo Clark)*, Peter Michael *(Charlie)*, Peter Garcy *(Freddie)*, Fred Essler *(Prof. Montagne)*, Lotta Stein *(Mme. Montagne)*, George Chandler *(Heckler)*.

An authentic American hero, Eddie Rickenbacker was properly lionized in this Fox film released between the German and the Japanese surrenders in 1945. By that time, the end of the war in the Pacific was a foregone conclusion and patriotism was rampant, so there couldn't have been a better time to release the movie. MacMurray is believable as the WW I ace who shot down a combined total of 26 balloons and planes. It's all told in flashback as Capt. Eddie and pals sit in a rubber raft in the Pacific having just crash-landed, and where they would spend a harrowing three weeks. It's episodic and bogs down from time to time but it remains an accurate portrayal of a fascinating man. Rickenbacker was always a mechanical type and his early experiments are depicted as well as his marvelous war record, his marriage and his pioneer efforts to make aviation into the force it is today. Rickenbacker went into the auto business after WW I and had a failure with the car named after him. Then, at the age of 48, he began Eastern Airlines with financing from Laurence Rockerfeller. Acting is fine, tech credits are all professional. It's just a nice movie about a nice guy who finished first.

p, Winfield H. Sheehan; d, Lloyd Bacon; w, John Tucker Battle; ph, Joe MacDonald; m, Cyril J. Mockridge; ed, James B. Clark; md, Emil Newman; spec. eff., Fred Sersen.

Biography (PR:AA MPAA:NR)

CAPTAIN FROM CASTILE**** (1947) 140m Fox c

Tyrone Power *(Pedro De Vargas)*, Jean Peters *(Catana Perez)*, Cesar Romero *(Hernando Cortez)*, Lee J. Cobb *(Juan Garcia)*, John Sutton *(Diego De Silva)*, Antonio Moreno *(Don Francisco)*, Thomas Gomez *(Father Bartolome Romero)*, Alan Mowbray *(Prof. Botello)*, Barbara Lawrence *(Luisa De Caravajal)*, George Zucco *(Marquis De Caravajal)*, Roy Roberts *(Capt. Alvarado)*, Marc Lawrence *(Corio)*, Robert Karnes *(Manuel Perez)*, Fred Libby *(Hernando Soler)*, Virginia Brissac *(Dona Maria De Vargas)*, Jay Silverheels *(Coatl)*, John Laurenz *(Cermeno)*, Dolly Arriaga *(Mercedes)*, Reed Hadley *(Escudero)*, Stella Inda *(Donna Marino)*, John Burton *(De Lorn)*, Mimi Aguglia *(Hernandez)*, Vincente Gomez *(Guitarist)*, Edmund Mundy *(Crier)*, Gilberto Gonzales *(Aztec Ambassador)*, Robert Adler *(Reyes)*, Harry Carter *(Capt. Sandoval)*, Bud Wolfe *(Sailor)*, David Cato *(Singer)*, Ramon Sanchez, Willie Calles *(Aztecs)*, Julian Rivero *(Marquis' Servant)*.

A sweeping, majestic spectacle, one of Power's best, which chronicles Cortez's (Cesar Romero) conquest of Mexico. Power is a young 16th century Spanish nobleman who incurs the wrath of Inquisition chief Sutton after helping to free one of Sutton's much-abused slaves. Sutton accuses Power of heresy, imprisons his whole family, and tortures his 12-year-old sister to death. Power's friends, Cobb and a firebrand peasant girl, Peters, who is madly in love with the cavalier, help him and his parents to escape. After Power sees his elderly parents safely out of Spain, he enlists as a mercenary with Romero's contingent going to the New World in search of riches and fame, and biding his time until he can avenge his sister's death on monster Sutton. Yet there is no escape; in the midst of Cortez's march toward Mexico City Sutton arrives with the king's commission to ferret out heretics in the ranks. He accuses Power, who by then has risen to the rank of captain, but Romero refuses to part with such a valiant and trusted aide. When Sutton is murdered, Power is imprisoned and sentenced to be hanged for the crime. Peters, who is going to have his child, stabs him, thinking she has killed Power to save him from disgrace at the end of a rope. His wound is cauterized, however, and Power survives. Then an Aztec prince admits that he has murdered Sutton because his own family has been slaughtered by the Grand Inquisitor. The Indian pays with his life. Power and Romero continue their march upon the last Aztec stronghold, Mexico City, as Peters, the happy camp-follower, walks in the army's wake carrying her child. Though the script for this film is a bit disjointed, the colorful panorama captured by director King is often overwhelming. CAPTAIN FROM CASTILE is a return to the old and glorious pageantry of yesteryear Hollywood, a huge $4.5 million production of grand pomp with one of the most memorable and stirring compositions ever composed by Newman, an eloquent and importnat symphonic score nominated for an Oscar. Power is superb, at his swashbuckling best since THE BLACK SWAN, and Peters is a lusty, sultry utterly-earthy female who scorches the screen. Cobb is a scene-swallowing supporting player who takes attention from all while Mowbray, too, vies with him in histrionics (he wears an eye lens that makes one eye appear milky). Sutton hisses evil and Romero gives a powerful, expansive portrait of conqueror Cortez, one with so wide and toothy a smile that his pearly whites were parodied widely after this film. This was a pet project of Fox boss Zanuck who purchased for $100,000 the unpublished novel by Princeton professor Samuel Shellabarger when it was serialized in *Cosmopolitan* magazine. Henry King, the Fox equivalent to Warner's Curtiz as a top action director, loved to scout locations in his small private plane. He had flown over Morales, a province in southern Mexico, as early as 1933 and selected this remote and rugged area to film CAPTAIN FROM CASTILE. Zanuck had discovered Peters, a 20-year-old coed from Ohio State, and had King test her off-campus. This was her first role, one that made her a Fox star. The trek to deep Mexico was similar to Cortez' own march, except that it was on rails, eight railroad cars packed with dozens of actors and technicians, including a dry cleaning unit for the expensive costumes and a refrigerated car in which the Technicolor film was kept. Power, a pilot himself, flew fifty cast members down in a large chartered plane. Oddly, King attempted to make Power as youthful as the film's protagonist, filming him in positions where he appeared *shorter* than other males in the cast, an oddball technique that didn't cut a second off the actor's real age. A smoldering volcano near the location shooting constantly threatened to erupt, delaying, along with bad weather, the shooting schedule which stretched on for almost four months while the budget doubled and Zanuck fumed. The film lost money but it remains as one of Fox's great epics.

p, Lamar Trotti; d, Henry King; w, Trotti (based on the novel by Samuel Shellabarger); ph, Charles Clarke, Arthur E. Arling (Technicolor); m, Alfred Newman; ed, Barbara McLean; art d, Richard Day, James Basevi; set d, Thomas Little; spec eff, Fred Sersen; cos, Charles LeMaire; second-unit d, Robert D. Webb.

Adventure   (PR:C-O   MPAA:NR)

CAPTAIN FROM KOEPENICK*** (1933, Ger.)

96m American-Rumanian bw (AKA: HAUPTMANN VON KOEPENICK) Max Adalbert (*Wilhelm Voigt*), Willi Schur (*Kallenberg*), Hermann Vallentin (*A. Wormser*), Emil Wabschke (*Wabschke*), Max Guelstorff (*Dr. Obermueller*), Ilse Fuerstenberg (*Marie Hoprecht*), Frederich Kayssler (*Friedrich Hoprecht*), Kaethe Haack (*Mrs. Obermueller*), Hermann Speelmans (*Sgt. Kilian*), Paul Otto (*Colonel*), Alfred Beierle (*Passport Commissioner*), Heinrich Schroth (*President of Police*).

True story of a cobbler (Adalbert) in Kaiser Wilhelm's Germany who acquires an army captain's uniform, orders a troop of soldiers to follow him, marches into a small town, and arrests the mayor and treasurer. After leaving with the town funds, it is realized that the citizens of Koepenick have been the victims of a practical joke and their own fawning toward anyone in uniform. Adalbert confesses to the crime and is imprisoned, but the Kaiser, who seems to enjoy a good joke, pardons him. Slow-moving and surprisingly serious with excellent performances and cinematography. Remade in 1956.

p&d, Richard Oswald; ph, Ewald Daub; set d, Franz Schroeder.

Biography/Drama   (PR:A   MPAA:NR)

CAPTAIN FROM KOEPENICK, THE*** (1956, Ger.) 93m Europa c

(GER: DER HAUPTMANN VON KOEPENICK) Heinz Ruehmann (*Wilhelm Voigt*), Hannelore Schroth (*Mathilde Obermueller*), Martin Held (*Dr. Obermueller*), Erich Schellow (*Capt. Von Schlettow*), Willy A. Kleinau (*Friedrich Hoprecht*), Ilse Fuerstenberg (*Marie Hoprecht*), Leonard Steckel (*Adolph Wormser, Tailor*), Walter Giller (*Willi Wormser, His Son*), Maria Sebaldt (*Auguste Viktoria, His Daughter*), Friedrich Domin (*Prison Director*), Wolfgang Neuss (*Kallenberg*), Reinhard Kolldehoff (*Drunk Soldier*), Willi Rose (*Police Sergeant*).

Good remake of the 1931 Richard Oswald classic condemning Prussian militarism. This version of a fascinating real-life incident stars Ruehmann as the Berlin shoemaker in 1906 who dons a Prussian officer's uniform and wreaks havoc on the system. He captures some soldiers, marches them into the town hall, arrests the Burgomeister, and takes off with the municipal cash box. When the deception is discovered he is made a folk hero in newspapers all over the world. The tale is told with warmth and good humor and Ruehmann's performance is excellent.

d, Helmut Kaeutner; w, Carl Zuckmayer, Kaeutner (based on the play by Zuckmayer); ph, Albert Benitz (Eastmancolor); m, Bernard Eichhorn; ed, Klaus Dudenhoefer; set d, Herbert Kirchoff, Albrecht Becker; cos, Erna Sander.

Biography/Drama   (PR:A   MPAA:NR)

CAPTAIN FURY*** (1939) 91m UA bw

Brian Aherne (*Capt. Fury*), Victor McLaglen (*Blackie*), Paul Lukas (*Francois Dupre*), June Lang (*Jeanette Dupre*), John Carradine (*Coughy*), George Zucco (*Arnold Trist*), Douglas Dumbrille (*Preston*), Virginia Field (*Mabel*), Charles Middleton (*Mergon*), Lawrence Grossmith (*Governor*), Lumsden Hare (*Mr. Bailey*), Mary Gordon (*Mrs. Bailey*), John Warburton (*Bob*), Claude Allister (*Suco*), Will Stanton (*Bertie*), Edgar Norton (*Governor's Aide*), Margaret Roach (*Tess Bailey*), Bill Bevan (*Duffy*), Edwin Brian (*Danny Bailey*).

Decent drama detailing the early days of the Australian bush when it was used as a massive prison for British Empire criminals. Aherne stars as an Irish freedom fighter who is shipped down under and made to work for evil landowner Zucco. Together with new-found ally and fellow prisoner McLaglen, the pair escape and bring four other prisoners with them. The fugitives become an Australian version of Robin Hood and his Merry Men when they defend the rights of small ranchers against the land-grabbing Zucco. After many run-ins with the wicked despot's men, the gang finally brings him to justice and earn pardons for themselves due to their good deeds. Outstanding cast of character actors, good action, and well-balanced comedy sequences make this a winning entertainment. Produced and directed by silent comedy king Hal Roach.

p&d, Hal Roach; w, Grover Jones, Jack Jevne, William De Mille; ph, Norbert Brodine; ed, William Ziegler; spec eff, Roy Seawright.

Adventure   (PR:A   MPAA:NR)

CAPTAIN GRANT'S CHILDREN zero (1939, USSR) 80m Amkino/Mosfilm bw

Y. Yurief (*Capt. Grant*), I. Chuvelef (*Ayerton*), Nikolai Cherkassov (*Pagauel*). M. Strelkova (*Klena*), O. Bazarova (*Mary Grant*), Y. Segal (*Robert Grant*), D. Gutman (*McNabs*), M. Romarov (*Mangels*), A. Adelung (*Talkov*), M. Michurin (*Innkeeper*).

Extremely low-budget Russian adventure tale about two kids who sail the world's oceans searching for their shipwrecked father. On the way, the children have to contend with landslides, erupting volcanos, and sea calamities all photographed in unbelievably inept process shots. Not one of the Soviet cinema's better efforts.

d, V. Weinstock, D. Gutman; w, G. Leonidov (based on the story by Jules Verne); ph, A. Kalsati; m, J. Dunsyevshy.

Adventure   (PR:AA   MPAA:NR)

CAPTAIN HATES THE SEA, THE*** (1934) 80m COL bw

Victor McLaglen (*Schulte*), Helen Vinson (*Janet Grayson*), John Gilbert (*Steve Bramley*), Alison Skipworth (*Mrs. Magruder*), Wynne Gibson (*Mrs. Jeddock*), Walter Connolly (*Capt. Helquist*), Fred Keating (*Danny Checkett*), Tala Birell (*Gerta Klargi*), Leon Errol (*Layton*), Walter Catlett (*Joe Silvers*), Donald Meek, Arthur Treacher, Akim Tamiroff, Claude Gillingwater, Luis Alberni.

Episodic sea soap opera that chronicles the stories of several characters on an ocean cruise. Keating and Vinson play a couple who have stolen bonds and are constantly trying to keep one step ahead of detective McLaglen. Gilbert (in a role uncomfortably close to being autobiographical) plays a chronic alcoholic who takes the cruise to dry out. Unfortunately, he is failing miserably and his drinking becomes even worse. Gibson plays a girl whose past catches up with her, sending her husband into a jealous frenzy which gets him thrown into the brig for the duration of the voyage. Skipworth plays a wealthy widow who takes off with Vinson's husband, Keating. Comedy relief is provided by Errol and Catlett, who pop up whenever needed. The whole ship is steered by Connolly, who hates his job and the people he has to ferry around the ocean. Not bad for a kind of GRAND HOTEL of the sea. This comedic effort, much better than its box office response would indicate, was in the zany tradition of many silent classics. Moreover, the cast was made up of a bevy of ruthless drinkers, especially Gilbert, (born John Pringle, 1895) the great matinee idol of the silent screen who had taken to the bottle when his on-and-off screen lover Garbo refused to marry him. Booze and not Garbo would be his constant companion until his premature death shortly after this, his last film, in 1936. Gilbert's mercurial career had plummeted with the advent of the talkies, not, as is generally believed, because his voice was unsuited to the new medium. As a matter of fact, Gilbert had a fine, resonant voice, and it was MGM mogul Louis B. Mayer who made sure that Gilbert's talkie career was sabotaged in his first talking picture, HIS GLORIOUS NIGHT, by directing sound technicians to accelerate those portions of the sound track carrying Gilbert's voice so that his voice sounded high-pitched, causing the audience to jeer and laugh. This manufactured audience response is what Mayer used to cancel Gilbert's expensive MGM contract which is what he was after all along. THE CAPTAIN HATES THE SEA was loaded with so many heavy drinkers—Gilbert, McLaglen, Connolly, Errol, and Catlett—that director Milestone, also a generous tippler, had difficulty keeping them sober from scene to scene during the on-location shooting which dragged on and on, going way over budget. The cost-conscious head of Columbia, Harry Cohn, took one look at the balance sheet and hit the ceiling, sending a cable to the sea-going director Milestone: "Hurry up! The cost is staggering!" Milestone wired back: "So is the cast!"

d, Lewis Milestone; w, Wallace Smith; ph, Joseph August.

Comedy   (PR:A   MPAA:NR)

CAPTAIN HORATIO HORNBLOWER***½ (1951, Brit.) 116m WB c

(GB: CAPTAIN HORATIO HORNBLOWER, R.N.) Gregory Peck (*Horatio Hornblower*), Virginia Mayo (*Lady Barbara Wellesley*), Robert Beatty (*Lt. William Bush*), James Robertson Justice (*Quist*), Denis O'Dea (*Adm. Leighton*), Terence Morgan (*Lt. Gerard*), Richard Hearne (*Polwheal*), James Kenney (*Midshipman Longley*), Moultrie R. Kelsall (*Lt. Crystal*), Michael Dolan (*Gundarson*), Stanley Baker (*Mr. Harrison*), John Witty (*Capt. Etenza*), Christopher Lee (*Captain*), Kynaston Reeves (*Lord Hood*), Ingeborg Wells (*Hebe*), Ronald Adam (*Adm. Macartney*), Michael Goodliffe (*Caillard*), Amy Veness (*Mrs. McPhee*), Alec Mango (*El Supremo*).

Peck is the jut-jawed young officer of the title (Errol Flynn was originally penciled in but relations with the brothers Warner were strained by this time and Flynn's face was beginning to show the ravages of time). He is assigned to deliver weapons to Alec Mango (El Supremo), a Central American dictator not unlike many of later generations. Mango is fighting the Spanish. Seemingly overnight, the political alliances change and Spain and England are pals and both are fighting El Supremo, who promptly seizes a Spanish galleon. Peck saves the galleon, then rescues Mayo (Lady Barbara, the Duke of Wellington's sister) to take her home to Blighty. But the lass has malaria, contracted at Panama City, and Peck must nurse her through her fevers. Once in England, Peck is given a new command and must now attack the Napoleonic French at La Teste. His ship is damaged and he manages to get it strategically placed so he can sink it and block the harbor, thus keeping the French ships at bay. Peck and his compatriots are taken prisoner and set for a meeting with madame guillotine. Before their necks can be shaved, they escape, commandeer another ship, engage in some further derring-do, and race back to Jolly Olde, there to warm one's heart in the arms of Virginia Mayo, a heart-warmer if there ever was one. CAPTAIN HORATIO HORNBLOWER has a lot of fun with buckles being swashed, lots of dueling, much cannonading, and wall-to-wall heroism. The only problem is that Peck never seems to muster the necessary bravura and bravado, the panache Flynn might have brough to the role. Walsh's direction is breakneck and all the secondary credits top-notch. Particularly notable is Guy Green's camerawork and Farnon's jolly tar score. In the small role as Polwheal is Richard Hearne, who may be remembered as the fellow Ed Sullivan loved—Britain's comic "Mr. Pastry!" a somwhat acrobatic and often hilarious silent comedian.

p, Gerry Mitchell; d, Raoul Walsh; w, Ivan Goff, Ben Roberts, Aeneas MacKenzie (based on the novel by C. S. Forester and adapted by him); ph, Guy Green (Technicolor); m, Robert Farnon; ed, Jack Harris.

Adventure   (PR:A   MPAA:NR)

CAPTAIN HURRICANE zero (1935) 72m RKO bw

James Barton (*Zenas Henry*), Helen Westley (*Abbie*), Helen Mack (*Matie*), Gene

Lockhart (Capt. Jeremiah), Douglas Walton (Jimmy), Henry Travers (Capt. Ben), Otto Hoffman (Silas Coffin), J. Farrell MacDonald, Forrester Harvey, Stanley Fields.

Dull melodrama starring Barton as a crusty sailor who hangs out with his other two sailor buddies Lockhart and Travers. One day, Barton's old flame finally agrees to live with him, but only as a housekeeper. This strains the relationship of the male trio, which is only worsened when a young beauty, Mack, is washed ashore and adopted by Barton. The sailors make a play for her, but she falls for a city slicker and takes off with him. Soon after the city boy returns and financially aids the struggling sailors making everyone happy. Just plain stupid.

d, John Robertson; w, Joseph Lovett (based on the novel The Taming of Zenas Henry by Sara Ware Bassett); ph, Lucien Andriot; ed, George Hively.

Drama (PR:A MPAA:NR)

CAPTAIN IS A LADY, THE * ½ (1940) 63m MGM bw
Charles Coburn (Capt. Abe Peabody), Beulah Bondi (Angie Peabody), Virginia Grey (Mary Peabody), Helen Broderick (Nancy Crocker), Billie Burke (Blossy Storr), Dan Dailey, Jr. (Perth Nickerson), Helen Westley (Abigail Morrow), Marjorie Main (Sarah May Willett), Cecil Cunningham (Mrs. Homans), Clem Bevans (Samuel Darby), Frances Pierlot (Roger Bartlett), Tom Fadden (Pucey Kintner), Robert Middlemass (Peterson), Ralph Byrd (Randy), Harry Tyler (Lem), Earl Hodgins (Man), Helen Dickson, Dorothea Wolbert, Vangie Beilby, Barbara Norton, Helen Bertram (Old Ladies), Joe Bernard, Henry Sylvester, Milton Kibbee (Men in Store), Ed J. Brady, Murdock MacQuarrie, Frank Hammond, Carl Stockdale, George Guhl (Seamen), Robert Homans (Clem).

Coburn is an old sea captain who loses his life's savings in wildcat speculation and is ruined. To prevent his wife from ending up in the poor house, he sells an interest in a ship he doesn't own and uses the money to pay for his mate's stay in an old ladies' home. Unfortunately, he has no place to stay himself and the administration of the home softens and allows him to stay there with his wife, among the ladies. Soon everyone is affectionately calling him "Old Lady 31." All turns out well in the end when the old captain rescues a shipwrecked fishing schooner and earns the salvage rights making him financially sound once again. Uninspired adaptation of a trite stage play by Rachel Crothers.

p, Frederick Stephani; d, Robert H. Sinclair; w, Harry Clork (based on the play "Old Lady 31" by Rachel Crothers, and novel by Louise Forsslund); ph, Leonard Smith; ed, Frank Hull.

Drama (PR:A MPAA:NR)

CAPTAIN JANUARY* (1936) 78m FOX bw
Shirley Temple (Star), Guy Kibbee (Capt. January), Slim Summerville (Capt. Nazro), June Lang (Mary Marshall), Buddy Ebsen (Paul Roberts), Sara Haden (Agatha Morgan), Jane Darwell (Eliza Croft), Jerry Tucker (Cyril Morgan), Nella Walker (Mrs. John Mason), George Irving (John Mason), James Farley (Deputy Sheriff), Si Jenks (Old Sailor).

Good Temple outing sees the ever-cute moppet living with kindly lighthouse keeper Kibbee, who had rescued the youngster when her parents were drowned. Life is good for the pair, joined by Kibbee's crony Summerville, until a truant officer decides that Temple is not being brought up properly. Temple is shipped off to boarding school, but she is rescued by sympathetic relatives who reunite her with Kibbee and employ the lighthouse keeper and his friends as the crew of their boat. Highlight of the film is "At The Codfish Ball" (Sidney Mitchell, Lew Pollack), a delightful song and dance routine by Ebsen and Temple. Other songs include "Early Bird" (Mitchell, Pollack) and "The Right Somebody to Love" (Jack Yellen, Pollack).

p, Darryl F. Zanuck; d, David Butler; w, Sam Hellman, Gladys Lehman, Harry Tugend (based on a story by Laura E. Richards); ph, John Seitz; m/l, Lew Pollack, Sidney D. Mitchell, Jack Yellen; md, Louis Silvers; ch, Jack Donohue.

Musical/Drama (PR:AAA MPAA:NR)

CAPTAIN JOHN SMITH AND POCAHONTAS ** (1953) 75m UA c
Anthony Dexter (Capt. John Smith), Jody Lawrence (Pocahontas), Alan Hale, Jr. (Fleming), Robert Clarke (Rolfe), Stuart Randall (Opechanco), James Seay (Wingfield), Philip Van Zandt (Davis), Shepard Menken (Nantaquas), Douglas Dumbrille (Powhatan), Anthony Eustrel (King James), Henry Rowland (Turnbull), Eric Colmar (Kemp), Joan Nixon (Lacuma), William Cottrell (Macklin), Francesco di Ecaffa (Lacuma).

Average retelling of the founding of Jamestown with Dexter as John Smith and Lawrence as the Indian maiden, Pocahontas. Lawrence saves Dexter from being beheaded by angry redskins, the couple marry, and Dexter must return to England, leaving his bride to marry another. Not bad, just nothing in particular to recommend it.

p, Aubrey Wisberg, Jack Pollexfen; d, Lew Landers; w, Wisberg, Pollexfen; ph, Ellis Carter (Pathecolor);; m, Albert Glasser; ed, Fred Feitshans.

Historical Drama (PR:A MPAA:NR)

CAPTAIN KIDD ** ½ (1945) 89m UA bw
Charles Laughton (Capt. William Kidd), Randolph Scott (Adam Mercy), Barbara Britton (Lady Anne Falconer), Reginald Owen (Cary Shadwell), John Carradine (Orange Povey), Gilbert Roland (William Moore), John Qualen (Bert Blivens), Sheldon Leonard (Boyle), Abner Biberman (Blades), Ian Keith (Lord Albermarle), William Farnum (Ranson), Miles Mander (King William III), Ray Teal (Michael O'Shawn).

Laughton plays the infamous pirate captain in this rather dull swashbuckler. Action takes place on the high seas in the late 1700s and chronicles the adventures of the title pirate as he plunders ships from England to India. One day the King of England foolishly enlists Laughton and his men to safeguard passage of several treasury ships belonging to the crown. Laughton, of course, doublecrosses the King and takes the

loot for himself. The angry King sends Scott to bring the pirate to face the gallows. Good supporting cast including Carradine, Roland, Qualen, and Leonard as Laughton's lackey's, and decent production values can't punch up this mundane script.

p, Benedict Bogeaus; d, Rowland V. Lee; w, Norman Reilly Raine (based on a story by Robert H. Lee); ph, Archie Stout, Lee Zavitz; ed, Joseph Smith.

Adventure Cas. (PR:A MPAA:NR)

CAPTAIN KIDD AND THE SLAVE GIRL * ½ (1954) 82m Reliance/UA c
Anthony Dexter (Capt. Kidd), Eva Gabor (Slave Girl), Alan Hale, Jr., James Seay, Richard Karlan, Noel Cravat, Lyle Talbot, Sonia Sorrell, Mike Ross, Jack Reitzen, Robert Long, Bill Cottrell, Bill Tannen, John Crawford.

Dexter is the pirate chieftain reprieved from the gallows by a greedy nobleman who wants to steal his buried treasure. Gabor is the slave girl who accompanies him around the seven seas. Low-budget swashbuckler has energy going for it, if little else.

p, Aubrey Wisberg, Jack Pollexfen; d, Lew Landers; w, Wisberg, Pollexfen; (CFI Color).

Adventure (PR:A MPAA:NR)

CAPTAIN KRONOS: VAMPIRE HUNTER* (1974, Brit.) 91m PAR/Hammer c
Horst Janson (Kronos), John Carson (Dr. Marcus), Shane Briant (Paul Durward), Caroline Munro (Carla), John Cater (Prof. Grost), Lois Daine (Sara Durward), Wanda Ventham (Lady Durward), Ian Hendry (Kerro).

Good Hammer vampire adventure featuring Janson as the title character who wields a mean sword to dispatch all manner of villains, including the nasty bloodsuckers. With the aid of hunchback professor Carson and the lovely Munro, Janson tackles an elderly vampire woman who must suck blood to maintain her youthful appearance. Written and directed by Brian Clemens, who wrote many of the best episodes of the popular Avengers television series. Fast-paced and with a good sense of humor, this film was unfortunately double-billed upon release with the disastrous FRANKENSTEIN AND THE MONSTER FROM HELL (1974).

p, Albert Fennell, Brian Clemens; d&w, Brian Clemens; ph, Ian Wilson (Humphries Labs); m, Laurie Johnson; ed, James Needs; set d, Robert Jones.

Horror/Comedy Cas. (PR:O MPAA:NR)

CAPTAIN LIGHTFOOT ** (1955) 91m UNIV c
Rock Hudson (Michael Martin), Barbara Rush (Aga Doherty), Jeff Morrow (John Doherty, alias Captain Thunderbolt), Finlay Currie (Callahan), Kathleen Ryan (Lady Anne More), Denis O'Dea (Regis Donnell), Geoffrey Toone (Capt. Hood), Milton Edwards (Lord Glen), Harold Goldblatt (Brady), Charles FitzSimons (Dan Shanley), Louise Studley (Cathy), Christopher Casson (Lord Clonmel), Philip O'Flynn (Trim), Shay Gorman (Tim Keenan), Edward Aylward (Big Tom), James Devlin (Tuer O'Brian), Mike Nolan (Willie the Goat), Kenneth MacDonald (High Steward), Oliver McGauley (Shamus O'Neill), Robert Bernal (Clagett), Nigel Fitzgerald (Sir George Bracey), Paul Farrell (The Magistrate), Austin Meldon (Sir Edward Grant), Sheila Brenna (Waitress), Aiden Grennell (The Umpire), George Blankley (The Dragoon), Lord Mount Charles, Lady Mount Charles (Couple in Coach), Edward Lexy (Army General), Peter Dix (Dragoon Lieutenant), Sean Mooney (Surgeon).

Overly talky and generally disappointing swashbuckler directed by skilled melodrama expert Douglas Sirk. Hudson plays a young Irish patriot who joins up with rebel leader Morrow. Soon Hudson falls for Morrow's daughter Rush between daring fights and heroic deeds. Climax sees Morrow wounded and Hudson assuming command of the rebel army. Shot on location in Ireland, the film looks authentic but problems arise from the dozens of impenetrable Irish accents speaking unnecessarily complex and inane dialog.

p, Ross Hunter; d, Douglas Sirk; w, W. R. Burnett, Oscar Brodney (based on the story by Burnett); ph, Irving Glassberg (CinemaScope/Technicolor); m, Joseph Gershenson; ed, Frank Gross; art d, Alexander Golitzen, Eric Orbom; set d, Russell A. Gausman,,Oliver Emert; cos, Bill Thomas.

Adventure (PR:A MPAA:NR)

CAPTAIN MIDNIGHT
(SEE: ON THE AIR LIVE WITH CAPTAIN MIDNIGHT, 1979)

CAPTAIN MILKSHAKE * ½ (1970) 89m Richmark c
Geoff Gage (Paul), Andrea Cagan (Melissa), David Korn (Thesp), Ron Barca (Anchovy), Evelyn King (Evelyn), Belle Greer (Mrs. Fredericks), Joanne Moore Jordan (Mrs. Randolph), Darlene Conley (Mrs. Hamilton), James Ashton (Uncle Jimson), Stuart Lancaster (Cabby), Bob Reece (Frank), Kip Winsett (Kip), Hal Neilsen, James Hourigan (Border Guards), Wally Starr (Mr. Toliver), Buddy Pantsari (Priest), Barry Leichtling (Lightning), Paul Lagos (Bubber), Edward O'Brien (O.B.) George Driver (Loose George), Richard Morrill (Dr. Haskell), Trans Love Airways.

Badly dated anti-war film starring Gage as a Vietnam-era Marine on emergency leave back home. Unable to relate to the right-wing members of his family, he meets the young and seductive hippie girl Cagan who "turns him on" to sex, drugs, and rock n' roll. Before the viewer has a chance to react the kid is shipped back to 'Nam and ends up in a body bag. This oh-so-tragic drama is punctuated with overly "artsy" switches from color to black and white and also obnoxious psychedelic light shows. Decent musical lineup from several rock bands helps somewhat.

p&d, Richard Crawford; w, Crawford, Barry Leichtling; ph, Robert Sherry (Technicolor); m, Kaleidoscope, Quicksilver Messenger Service, Country Joe and the Fish, Steve Miller Band, Eric Selten; ed, David Korn; spec eff, Joe Purcell, Phra Visuals, Vega Visuals, Cinedepth, Reggie Hager, Harry Woolman.

Drama (PR:O MPAA:R)

CAPTAIN MOONLIGHT* (1940, Brit.) 60m Olympia bw
John Garrick (*Maj. John Peel*), Winifred Shotter (*Lucy Merrall*), Stanley Holloway (*Sam Small*), John Stuart (*Capt. Moonlight*), Leslie Perrins (*Mr. Craven*), Mary Lawson (*Toinette*), Charles Carson (*Francis Merrall*), Morris Harvey (*Glover*).

Sappy melodrama which has little to do with the title character who is seen only incidentally as a masked highwayman who just disappears. The story takes place in 1815 and details the saga of a young country girl who is forced to marry a dishonest gambler because her father owes the man money. The couple live together as man and wife until a young major in the British army, who has loved the girl from afar, discovers that the cardsharp had cheated her father and is already married to a woman in Brussels. Stuck among the histrionics are the dull tunes, "A Soldier's Toast," "The 23rd Regiment," and "Drink To Me Only."

p, Julius Hagen; d, Henry Edwards; w, H. Fowler Mear (based on a story by Charles Cullum); ph, Sydney Blythe; ed, Lister Laurence; m/l, W. L. Trytel.
Drama (PR:A MPAA:NR)

CAPTAIN NEMO AND THE UNDERWATER CITY**½
(1969, Brit.) 106m MGM c
Robert Ryan (*Capt. Nemo*), Chuck Connors (*Fraser*), Nanette Newman (*Helena*), Luciana Paluzzi (*Mala*), Bill Fraser (*Barnaby*), Kenneth Connor (*Swallow*), John Turner (*Joab*), Allan Cuthbertson (*Lomax*), Christopher Hartstone (*Philip*), Vincent Harding (*Mate/Navigator*), Ralph Nossek (*Engineer*), Michael McGovern, Alan Barry, Anthony Bailey (*Sailors*), Ann Patrice, Margot Ley, Patsy Snell (*Barmaids*), Ian Ramsey (*Adam*), John Moore (*Skipper*).

Half a dozen people, Chuck Connors among them, are rescued from a foundering ship by Robert Ryan and his submarine. They are taken to Ryan's utopia, the domed underwater city of Templemer, where everything is made of gold. Their attempts to escape take a backseat to the sets and special effects. Mostly kid stuff, but adults may enjoy it, too.

p, Bertram Ostrer; d, James Hill; w, Pip and Jane Barker, R. Wright Campbell (based on a character created by Jules Verne); ph, Alan Hume (Panavision, Metrocolor); m, Wally Stott; ed, Bill Lewthwaite; art d, Bill Andrews; cos, Olga Lehmann; sp eff, Jack Mills; makeup, Ernest Gasser.
Adventure Cas. (PR:A MPAA:NR)

CAPTAIN NEWMAN, M.D.**½ (1963) 126m UNIV c
Gregory Peck (*Capt. Josiah Newman*), Tony Curtis (*Cpl. Jackson Laibowitz*), Bobby Darin (*Cpl. Jim Tompkins*), Eddie Albert (*Col. Bliss*), Angie Dickinson (*Lt. Francie Corum*), James Gregory (*Col. Pyser*), Bethel Leslie (*Helene Winston*), Jane Withers (*Lt. Grace Blodgett*), Dick Sargent (*Lt. Alderson*), Larry Storch (*Gavoni*), Robert F. Simon (*Lt. Col. Larrabee*), Syl Lamont (*Sgt. Kopp*), Paul Carr (*Werbel*), Vito Scotti (*Maj. Alfredo Fortuno*), Crehan Denton (*Maj. Gen. Snowden*), Gregory Walcott (*Capt. Howard*), Charles Briggs (*Gorkow*), Robert Duvall (*Capt. Paul Cabot Winston*), Penny Santon (*Waitress at Blue Grotto*), Amzie Strickland (*Kathie*), Barry Atwater (*Maj. Dawes*), Ann Doran (*Mrs. Pyser*), Joey Walsh (*Maccarades*), Byron Morrow (*Hollingshead*), David Landfield (*Corporal*), Ron Brogan (*Chaplain* [Priest]), Robert Strong (*Chaplain* [Rabbi]), John Hart (*Officer*), Sammy Reese (*Haskell*), Ted Bessell (*Carrozzo*), Martin West, David Winters, Marc Cavell, Seamon Glass, Jack Grinnage (*Patients*).

Gregory Peck is awesomely wooden as Capt. Josiah Newman, a service psychiatrist in 1944. The action takes place in the waning months of WW II and consists of three integrated stories of Newman's patients, as well as the obligatory romance with a curvaceous nurse (Dickinson). Newman is simultaneously treating Darin, a much-decorated NCO who feels he is a coward for having deserted a pal in a spiraling aircraft; Eddie Albert, the colonel who can't stop torturing himself for sending so many men to their deaths on various Air Force missions; and Robert Duvall, guilt-ridden for having spent one year of the war hidden in a basement in Nazi territory. Tony Curtis is the comic relief of the film and does well in an Ensign Pulver-like role. The strongest acting comes from Darin and Universal put its weight behind getting him an Oscar. He managed a nomination but lost to Melvyn Douglas for HUD. CAPTAIN NEWMAN, M.D. was never quite sure what it was. Funny in spots, mainly due to Curtis, and powerful (Darin, Albert) in others, it eventually attempted to serve too many masters and wound up saccharine-sweet with a nonsensical Christmas party. Twenty minutes could have been cut from the film and Miller's directing at a brisker pace might have helped. But the primary mistake was in the conception, a comedy-drama with no consistent point-of-view.

p, Robert Arthur; d, David Miller; w, Richard Breen, Phoebe and Henry Ephron (based on the novel by Leo Rosten); ph, Russell Metty (Eastmancolor); m, Frank Skinner; ed, Alma Macrorie; art d, Alexander Golitzen, Alfred Sweeney; set d, Howard Bristol; cos, Rosemary Odell; spec eff, Walter Hammond; makeup, Bud Westmore.
Comedy/Drama (PR:C MPAA:NR)

CAPTAIN OF THE GUARD** (1930) 85m UNIV bw
John Boles (*Rouget de Lisle*), Laura La Plante (*Marie Marnay*), Sam De Grasse (*Bazin*), James Marcus (*Marnay*), Harry Cording (*Le Bruin*), Lionel Belmore (*Colonel*), Otis Harlan (*Jacques*), Murdock McQuarrie (*Joseph*), Claude Fleming (*Judge*), Ervin Renard (*Lieutenant*), George Hackathorne (*Robespierre*), Richard Cramer (*Danton*), Stuart Holmes (*Louis XVI*), Evelyn Hall (*Marie Antoinette*).

Early talkie dramatization of the French Revolution told through the eyes of the composer of the French national anthem "La Marseillaise," Rouget de Lisle (Boles). The usual mob scenes with angry peasants flashing scythes, axes, and torches are ever-present and the film is filled with patriotic songs for Boles to warble. Historically inaccurate, the film actually has a pre-credits disclaimer apologizing for the dramatic license. Songs include: "Song Of The Guard," "Maids on Parade," "For You," "Can It Be?" "It's A Sword," "You, You Alone," "La Marseillaise."

d, John S. Robertson (with sequences by Paul Fejos); w, George Manker Watters, Arthur Ripley (based on a story by Houston W. Branch); ph, Gilbert Warrenton; m/l, William Francis Dugan, Heinz Roemheld, scored by Charles Wakefield Cadman.
Historical Drama/Musical (PR:A MPAA:NR)

CAPTAIN PIRATE**½
(1952) 85m COL c (GB: CAPTAIN BLOOD, FUGITIVE)
Louis Hayward (*Peter Blood*), Patricia Medina (*Dona Isabela*), John Sutton (*Hilary Evans*), Charles Irwin (*Angus McVickers*), George Givot (*Tomas Valesquez*), Rex Evans (*Gov. Carlyle*), Ted de Corsia (*Easterling*), Malu Gatica (*Amanda*), Sven Hugo Borg (*Swede*), Robert McNeely (*Manuelito*), Nina Koshetz (*Madame Duval*), Lester Matthews (*Col. Ramsey*), Sandro Giglio (*Don Ramon*), Ian Wolfe (*Viceroy*), Jay Novello (*Egyptian*), Maurice Marsac (*Coulevain*), Genevieve Aumont (*Celeste*), Mario Siletti (*Gen. Chavez*), Robert Bice (*Lieutenant*).

Average adventure yarn detailing the return of famed doctor-turned-pirate, Capt. Blood (Hayward) to the high seas. Opening sees Hayward peacefully retired in the West Indies when he is captured and accused of piracy. Wanting to clear his name, he is freed by his fiancee Medina and his old pirate gang. He steals a ship and tracks down the imposter, Sutton, with whom he has a duel to the death. Justice triumphs, Hayward marries Medina, and he retruns to his idyllic existence. Good action scenes and likable performances by the principals.

p, Harry Joe Brown; d, Ralph Murphy; w, Robert Libbott, Frank Burt, John Meredyth Lucas (based on the novel *Captain Blood Returns* by Rafael Sabatini); ph, Charles Lawton, Jr. (Technicolor); m, George Duning; ed, Gene Havlick.
Adventure/Historical Drama (PR:A MPAA:NR)

CAPTAIN SCARLETT*½ (1953) 75m UA c
Richard Greene (*Capt. Scarlett*), Leonora Amar (*Princess Maria*), Nedrick Young (*Pierre DuCloux*), Manolo Fabregas (*Duke of Corlaine*), Eduardo Norriega (*Count Villiers*), Isobel del Puerto (*Josephine*), Carlos Musquiz (*Etienne Dumas*), George Trevino (*Friar*).

Swashbuckler set in post-Napoleonic France (although shot in Mexico) stars Greene championing justice against the royal tyranny with the help of a runaway Spanish Princess (Amar), and a highwayman (Young). Filled with sword fights, chases, disguises, and the like—in fact one big cliche from start to finish.

p, Howard Dimsdale; d, Thomas Carr; w, Dimsdale; ph, Charles Carbajal (Technicolor); m, Elias Breeskin; ed, Gloria Schoeman.
Adventure (PR:A MPAA:NR)

CAPTAIN SINDBAD*** (1963) 85m MGM c
Guy Williams (*Capt. Sindbad*), Heidi Bruhl (*Princess Jana*), Pedro Armendariz (*El Kerim*), Abraham Sofaer (*Calgo*), Bernie Hamilton (*Quinius*), Helmut Schneider (*Bendar*), Margaret Jahnen (*Lady-in-Waiting*), Rolf Wanka (*The King*), Walter Barnes (*Rolf*), James Dobson (*Iffritch*), Maurice Marsac (*Ahmed*), Henry Brandon (*Col. Kabar*), John Crawford (*Aram*), Geoffrey Toone (*Mohar*), Anna Luise Schubert, John Schapar (*Dancers*), Guy Doleman, Hans Schumm.

Filmed in Germany, CAPTAIN SINDBAD is one of the finest examples of what a Saturday matinee picture should be. This one has everything: huge production values, wit, speed, imagination, and fantastic special effects. Guy Williams (TV star from "Lost In Space" and "Zorro") is Sindbad and his job is to neutralize the villainous El Kerim (Armendariz in his penultimate role, his last before he died was FROM RUSSIA WITH LOVE) by getting into the impossible-to-get-into tower where the man's heart is kept. (He leaves his heart in that building so he can't be killed in combat. Okay, so it's a dumb premise but they do it so well!) In the course of inhuman events he has to face man-eating crocodiles, a multiheaded ogre, an invisible monster; a huge fist with a spiked glove, avalanches, man-eating fish, and more and more. And with all of that, it's not a whit more violent than what the kids see on Saturday morning. Byron "Bunny" Haskin does one helluva job on the usual King Brothers budget.

p, Frank and Herman King; d, Byron Haskin; w, Samuel B. West, Harry Relis; ph, Gunther Senftleben (Technicolor); m, Michel Michelet; ed, Robert Swink; cos, Nathans of London; ch, Gene Reed; spec eff, Tom Howard, Lee Zavitz, Augie Lohman.
Fantasy (PR:A MPAA:NR)

CAPTAIN SIROCCO (SEE: PIRATES OF CAPRI, 1949)

CAPTAIN THUNDER zero (1931) 65m WB bw
Victor Varconi (*Capt. Thunder*), Fay Wray (*Ynez Dominguez*), Charles Judeis (*El Comandante Ruiz*), Robert Elliott (*Pete Morgan*), Don Alvarado (*Juan Sebastian*), Natalie Moorhead (*Bonita Salazar*), Bert Roach (*Pablo*), Frank Campeau (*Hank Riley*), Robert E. Keane (*Don Miguel Salazar*), John Sainpolis (*Pedro Dominquez*).

Ridiculous Robin Hood-type tale starring Varconi as the charming Mexican rogue, Capt. Thunder. Plot concerns his capture of a wedding party where he forces the bride, Wray, to marry a rival cattle rustler instead of the poor groom she was set to marry. The distraught bride expresses her dismay at the situation and so the bandit generously grants her one wish. The bride obviously wants her original groom back, so the obliging Varconi keeps his word and cheerfully guns down the cattle rustler, freeing Wray to marry her real fiancee. A badly-constructed movie, filled with bad performances.

d, Alan Crosland; w, Gordon Rigby, William K. Wells (based on a story by Hal Davitt and Pierre Couderc); ph, James Van Trees; ed, Arthur Hilton.
Comedy/Historical Drama (PR:A MPAA:NR)

CAPTAIN TUGBOAT ANNIE** (1945) 70m REP bw
Jane Darwell *(Tugboat Annie)*, Edgar Kennedy *(Captain Bullwinkle)*, Charles Gordon *(Terry)*, Mantan Moreland *(Pinto)*, Pamela Blake *(Marion)*, Hardie Albright *(Johnny Webb)*, H. B. Warner *(Judge Abbott)*, Saundra Berkova *(Susan)*, Jack Norton *(Shiftless)*, Barton Yarborough *(Missouri)*, Fritz Feld *(Pucci)*, Anthony Warde *(Jake)*, Joe Crehan *(Severn)*, Pierre Watkin *(Dr. Turner)*, Cyril Delevanti *(Fred)*, Guy Wilkerson *(Jenkins)*, Robert Elliot *(Detective Franklin)*, Kernan Cripps *(Cop)*, Harry Lang *(Man)*, Marion McGuire *(First Nurse)*, Betty Sinclair *(Second Nurse)*, Eddie Earle *(Harper)*, Vic Potel *(Swenson)*, Sam Flint *(Fire Chief)*, Ralph Linn *(Cab Driver)*, Eddie Chandler *(Motor Cop)*, Harry Depp *(Mike)*.

Overblown tugboat tale concerning the efforts of rival tug operators Darwell and Kennedy to win a big shipping contract. Along the way romance blooms between tugboat office secretary Blake and ex-convict Gordon, who wants to make good his rehabilitation. Berkova, a child violinist, is worked into the story as Darwell's charge whom she takes under her wing. The rival tugboat operators finally put aside their differences when they must pull together to combat a deadly waterfront fire. Good comedy performances from Kennedy helps maintain this fairly uninteresting meller.

p, James S. Burkett; d, Phil Rosen; w, G. Callahan (based on characters created by Norman Reilly Raine); ph, Harry Neumann; ed, Martin G. Cohen.

Drama **(PR:A MPAA:NR)**

CAPTAINS COURAGEOUS***** (1937) 115m MGM bw
Freddie Bartholomew *(Harvey)*, Spencer Tracy *(Manuel)*, Lionel Barrymore *(Disko)*, Melvyn Douglas *(Mr. Cheyne)*, Charley Grapewin *(Uncle Salters)*, Mickey Rooney *(Dan)*, John Carradine *("Long Jack")*, Oscar O'Shea *(Cushman)*, Jack La Rue *(Priest)*, Walter Kingsford *(Dr. Finley)*, Donald Briggs *(Tyler)*, Sam McDaniel *("Doc")*, Billie Burrud *(Charles)*, Christian Rub *(Old Clement)*, Dave Thursby *(Tom)*, William Stack *(Elliott)*, Leo G. Carroll *(Burns)*, Charles Trowbridge *(Dr. Walsh)*, Richard Powell *(Steward)*, Jay Ward *(Pogey)*, Kenneth Wilson *(Alvin)*, Roger Gray *(Nate Rogers)*, Gladden James *(Secretary Cobb)*, Tommy Bupp, Wally Albright *(Boys)*, Katherine Kenworthy *(Mrs. Disko)*, Philo McCullough, James Kilgannon, Bill Fisher, Dick Howard, Larry Fisher, Gil Perkins, Jack Sterling, Stubby Kreuger *(Crew)*, Dave Wengren *(Lars)*, Murry Kinnell *(Minister)*, Goldie Sloan *(Black Woman)*, Myra McKinney, Lee Van Atta, Gene Reynolds, Sherry Hall, Jr., Henry Hanna, Betty Alden, Reggie Strester, Gertrude Sutton *(Nate's Wife)*, Bobby Watson, Don Brodie, David Kernan, Billy Arnold *(Reporters)*, Frank Sully *(Taxi Driver)*, Billy Gilbert *(Soda Steward)*, Lester Dorr *(Corridor Steward)*, Jimmy Conlin *(Thin Man)*, Lloyd Ingraham *(Skipper of Ship)*, Art Berry, Sr. *(Capt. Anderson)*, Edward Peil, Sr. *(Fisherman)*, Jack Kennedy *(Captain of Flying Swan)*, Monte Vandergrift *(Sailor on Flying Swan)*, Charles Coleman *(Butler)*, Wade Boteler *(Skipper of Blue Gill)*, Norman Ainsley *(Robbins)*, Myra Marsh *(Chester's Wife)*.

Freddie Bartholomew is the spoiled-rotten offspring of Melvyn Douglas, a business tycoon. (Forty years later Douglas played the same role in BEING THERE). Bartholomew believes he can lie and cheat his way through life and when that doesn't work, perhaps a whine may do the trick. On a trip to Europe with his father, the young man falls off the posh ocean liner into the sea while leaning over the rail after downing six ice cream sodas. (The word "posh" stands for the best cabins available when leaving England—p-o means Port-Out and s-h means Starboard-Home. That way you'll always be getting the sun). The boy is picked up by a fishing boat filled with the Portuguese fisherman of the Gloucester area. He wakes with the stink of fish in his nose and learns that he owes his life to Spencer Tracy (Manuel). Bartholomew orders the captain (Barrymore) to take him home. He is then told that the boat will be at sea for three months, until the hold is filled. Mickey Rooney, in a small role as Barrymore's son, offers to give the snooty, snotty brat some clothing. Freddie is adamant; he will do nothing for the duration of the cruise. All the other crewmen wish the kid would jump off *their* ship but Tracy (using a Portuguese accent he worked hard to achieve and which made mockery of the same accent attempted by Edward G. Robinson in TIGER SHARK) befriends the young man, gets into his confidence, and a bond begins. Bartholomew changes his way of thinking and takes an active role in the workings of the ship, starting by working in the galley and later at deck duty. As time passes, Tracy and Bartholomew become closer; he is the father the boy never had. Tracy invites the boy to join him in the dory; a singular honor, as Tracy has not had a dory fishing mate since his father died several years ago. Tracy has fished alone since then (a forerunner to THE OLD MAN AND THE SEA) and when Bartholomew joins him, they achieve another level in the relationship. Finally, the ship's hold is filled and it's time to return to port. Along the way, they are hailed by a rival ship and the two get into a friendly race to see which will arrive at Gloucester first. They break out all their sails and the race is on. Now Tracy's ship is almost capsizing and Tracy goes aloft to furl the topsail. The mast cracks and he falls into the raging sea, trapped between the ropes and the canvas sail. He is almost cut in two by the ropes and shouts, in Portuguese, to be cut loose (he knows he's dying) and allowed to drown. Bartholomew is taken to Tracy for a final farewell, then at Barrymore's orders, Carradine axes the ropes and Tracy goes under. Later, the boy is met by his father but this is a different lad. He wants to remain with the fishermen. From his meager wages he purchases candlesticks for Tracy and Tracy's father, then takes them to the local church. Services are held later at the water's edge and when Tracy's name is spoken, Bartholomew tosses a wreath into the sea. Douglas, finally understanding the nature of his son, also throws a wreath into the water. The two wreaths are entwined, drifting off together. Douglas puts his arm around his son and the two walk off silently, lost in their own thoughts. And if there's a dry eye in the house after that, it has to be owned by someone who wasn't watching. CAPTAINS COURAGEOUS was a huge success at the box office as well as with the critics. Nominated for a few Oscars, it did win for Tracy (he followed it next year with another statuette for BOYS TOWN—the only actor ever to repeat two years in a row and it should have done the same for Victor Fleming, who was one of the finest directors in the medium, with such hits as GONE WITH THE WIND, THE WIZARD OF OZ, TREASURE ISLAND, and many more. Tracy hated the part while he was making it. He didn't like singing, resented having his hair curled, despised his accent, and was convinced that he was doing the worst job of his life. Bartholomew (born Freddie Llewellyn, taking the name of an aunt) was billed above Tracy and Barrymore, but did not manage to survive the terrible teens. He made a few more pictures, tried his hand at being a TV host, and wound up producing soap operas.

p, Louis D. Lighton; d, Victor Fleming; w, John Lee Mahin, Marc Connelly, Dale Van Every (based on the novel by Rudyard Kipling); ph, Harold Rosson; m, Franz Waxman; ed, Elmo Veron; art d, Cedric Gibbons; m/l, Waxman, Gus Kahn.

Adventure **Cas.** **(PR:AAA MPAA:NR)**

CAPTAIN'S KID, THE** (1937) 71m FN/WB bw
May Robson *(Marcia Prentiss)*, Sybil Jason *(Abigail Prentiss)*, Guy Kibbee *(Asa Plunkett)*, Jane Bryan *(Betsy Ann Prentiss)*, Fred Lawrence *(Tom Squires)*, Dick Purcell *(George Cheater)*, Mary Treen *(Libby)*, Gus Shy *(John Shores)*, Maude Allen *(Mabel)*.

Small town drama starring Kibbee as an eccentric but pleasant town drunk who entertains children with outlandish tales of adventure. Robson plays a lonely spinster who forbids her young niece from spending any time with Kibbee. The girl disobeys and becomes one of the drunk's most avid listeners. One day Kibbee discovers a buried treasure and kills a man in self-defense after he is attacked for the loot. The girl is put on the witness stand and her testimony is damaging. After a silly chase scene which sees the kid driving her aunt's Rolls Royce like a maniac, all is sorted out and justice prevails. Two mediocre songs are sung, "I'm The Captain's Kid," and "Drifting Along."

d, Nick Grinde; w, Tom Reed (based on a story by Earl Felton); ph, Ernest Haller; m/l, M. K. Jerome and Jack Scholl; ed, Jack Saper.

Drama **(PR:A MPAA:NR)**

CAPTAINS OF THE CLOUDS½** (1942) 113m WB c
James Cagney *(Brian MacLean)*, Dennis Morgan *(Johnny Dutton)*, Brenda Marshall *(Emily Foster)*, Alan Hale *(Tiny Murphy)*, George Tobias *(Blimp Lebec)*, Reginald Gardiner *(Scrounger Harris)*, Reginald Denny *(Commanding Officer)*, Russell Arms *(Prentiss)*, Paul Cavanagh *(Group Captain)*, Clem Bevans *(Store-Teeth Morrison)*, J. M. Kerrigan *(Foster)*, J. Farrell MacDonald *(Dr. Neville)*, Patrick O'Moore *(Fyffo)*, Morton Lowry *(Carmichael)*, S. L. Cathcart-Jones *(Chief Instructor)*, Frederic Worlock *(President of Court Martial)*, Roland Drew *(Officer)*, Lucia Carroll *(Blonde)*, George Meeker *(Playboy)*, Benny Baker *(Popcorn Kearns)*, Hardie Albright *(Kingsley)*, Ray Walker *(Mason)*, Charles Halton *(Nolan)*, Louis Jean Heydt *(Provost Marshal)*, Bryon Barr [Gig Young], Michael Ames [Tod Andrews] *(Student Pilots)*, Willie Fung *(Willie)*, Carl Harbord *(Blake)*, James Stevens, Bill Wilkerson, Frank Lackteen *(Indians)*, Edward McNamara *(Dog Man)*, Charles Smith *(Bellboy)*, Emmett Vogan *(Clerk)*, Winifred Harris *(Woman)*, Miles Mander *(Churchill's Voice)*, Pat Flaherty *(Drill Sergeant)*, Tom Dugan *(Bartender)*, George Offerman, Jr. *(Mechanic)*, Gavin Muir *(Orderly)*, Larry Williams *(Duty Officer)*.

Cagney's first Technicolor film was a docudrama about a group of Canadians who were in training for the RCAF during WW II. Cagney is one of several bush pilots who is fiercely independent, brash, the kind of guy who swoops in to steal his competition's jobs and women. He is induced into the RCAF and now must fight his normally solo way of thinking and adjust it to a team effort. Naturally, he rankles at the limitations put on him by military discipline. He washes out of the service but eventually proves himself when, as a civilian pilot ferrying a bomber to England, he crashes his plane into an attacking German squadron. Like so many films of the era, this is unabashedly patriotic on the part of the Allies. Making it a Canadian film didn't seem logical, other than that the story emanated from The Great White North. Morgan, Marshall, Hale, and Tobias are featured and all score well. In a small role as Popcorn Kearns, Benny Baker does one of his fine performances. The best part of the movie is the sensational nature photography as well as the air action. It's also the closest thing you'll ever see short of a specially-made film of pilot training. They actually took the time to show us how it's done.

p, Hal B. Wallis; d, Michael Curtiz; w, Arthur T. Horman, Richard Macaulay, Norman Reilly Raine (based on a story by Horman, Roland Gillette); ph, Sol Polito, Wilfred M. Cline (Technicolor); m, Max Steiner; ed, George Amy; cos, Howard Shoup; m/l, Harold Arlen, Johnny Mercer (Title song).

War Drama **(PR:A-C MPAA:NR)**

CAPTAIN'S ORDERS*½ (1937, Brit.) 75m Liberty Films bw
Henry Edwards *(Capt. Trent)*, Jane Carr *(Belle Mandeville)*, Marie Lavarre *(Violet Potts)*, Franklyn Dyall *(Newton)*, Wally Patch *(Johnstone)*, C. Denier Warren *(Lawson)*, Mark Daly *(Scotty)*, Roddy Hughes *(Cookie)*, Basil Radford *(Murdoch)*, Kim Peacock *(Aubrey Chaytor)*, Joss Ambler *(Randolph Potts)*, H. F. Maltby *(Director)*, Rae Collet, Sherman Fisher Girls, Jack Hart and His Band.

Edwards is a merchant captain engaged in a transatlantic race who almost loses the race when he stops to rescue an actress from her foundering yacht. Not very interesting.

d, Ivar Campbell; w, Frank Shaw.

Drama **(PR:A MPAA:NR)**

CAPTAIN'S PARADISE, THE**** (1953, Brit.) 93m London Films/BL bw
Alec Guinness *(Capt. Henry St.James)*, Yvonne De Carlo *(Nita)*, Celia Johnson *(Maud)*, Charles Goldner *(Chief Officer Ricco)*, Miles Malleson *(Lawrence St. James)*, Bill Fraser *(Absalom)*, Tutte Lemkow *(Principal Dancer)*, Nicholas Phipps *(The Major)*, Walter Crisham *(Bob)*, Ferdy Mayne *(Sheikh)*, Sebastian Cabot *(Ali)*, Claudia Gray *(Susan Dailey)*, George Benson *(Salmon)*, Joss Ambler *(Prof. Ebbart)*, Joyce Barbour *(Mrs. Reid)*, Peter Bull *(Kalikan Officer)*, Ann Heffernan Daphne Bligh), Arthur Gomez *(Chief Steward)*, Jacinta Dicks *(Flower Woman)*, Alejandro Martinez *(Guitarist)*, Andrea Malandrinos *(Maitre d'Hotel)*, Amando Guinle *(Chief Engineer)*, Roy Purcell *(Officer of the Watch)*, Paul Armstrong *(Deck Officer)*, Raymond Hoole

(Shop-owner), Henry Longhurst (Prof. Killick), Bernard Rebel (Mr. Wheeler), Catherina Ferraz (Shopowner), Ambrosine Philpotts (Marjorie), Roger Delgado (Kalikan Policeman), Michael Balfour, Robert Adair, Victor Fairley (Customs Officials), Tutte Lemkow (Principal Dancer).

Droll and consistently funny comedy where Guinness, at his conniving best, is the captain of an inter-island steamer sailing between Gibraltar and a North African port with supplies. Instead of having a girl in every port, Guinness has a wife in both ports, each offering him a completely different life style. In Gibraltar it's Johnson, a sedate British housewife, who makes him home-cooked meals and is content to stay at home by the fire. In North Africa, it's De Carlo, a sexy, voluptuous number with whom he does the hot spots, dancing through the exotic nights. This twin life style is told in an almost continuous flashback as Guinness suavely manages both women, enjoying the best of two worlds while his chief officer, Goldner, slavishly admires the grand deception and seeks to emulate his captain. One little device employed by the shifty Guinness is a revolving picture frame which has photos of both wives on either side and one he flips to the appropriate side when entering the ports where Johnson and De Carlo live, just in case one of them happens to come on board. Some harrowing moments arise when Guinness becomes flustered and flips the wrong side of the picture frame. Suspense is sustained since the film shows Guinness about to be shot by a firing squad at the beginning and the viewer does not witness his fate until the very surprise ending. In between, the scheming captain is undone by the women in his life. Everything begins to slip out of order when Johnson becomes emancipated and insists on dining out, seeking adventure and excitement while De Carlo suddenly takes up cooking, tiring of night life and desiring domestic tranquility. When Guinness resists these disturbing transformations both women leave him for their new roles in life. Guinness' role is masterfully enacted while Johnson and De Carlo are superb in their unpredictable parts. The pace is vigorous under Kimmins' direction and he manages to relate the subtle and frivolous story with elan and verve, as smooth in transition from scene to scene as Guinness' own incomparable style. A generous serving of delicious whimsy.

p&d, Anthony Kimmins; w, Alec Coppel, Nicholas Phipps (based on Coppel's original story); ph, Ted Scaife; m, Malcolm Arnold; ed, Gerald Turney-Smith; md, Muir Mathieson; art d, Paul Sheriff; ch, Walter Crisham, Tutte Lemkow.

Comedy   Cas.   (PR:A   MPAA:NR)

CAPTAIN'S TABLE, THE* (1936, Brit.) 55m Fitzpatrick Pictures/MGM bw
Percy Marmont (John Brooke), Marian Spencer (Ruth Manning), Louis Goodrich (Capt. Henderson), Mark Daly (Sanders), Philip Brandon (Eric Manning), Daphne Courtenay (Mary Vaughan), Hugh McDermott (Inspector Mooney).

Marmont (who also directed), with the help of a detective disguised as a steward aboard a luxury liner, finds the murderer of one of the passengers. Typically dull British whodunit of the period.

p, James A. Fitzpatrick; d, Percy Marmont; w, John Paddy Carstairs.

Crime   (PR:A   MPAA:NR)

CAPTAIN'S TABLE, THE**½ (1960, Brit.) 89m FOX/Rank c
John Gregson (Capt. Ebbs), Peggy Cummins (Mrs. Judd), Donald Sinden (Shawe-Wilson), Nadia Gray (Mrs. Porteous), Maurice Denham (Maj. Broster), Richard Wattis (Prittlewell), Reginald Beckwith (Burtweed), Lionel Murton (Bernie Floate), Bill Kerr (Bill Coke), Nicholas Phipps (Reddish), Joan Sims (Maude Pritchett), Miles Malleson (Canon Swingler), John LeMesurier (Sir Angus), James Hayter (Earnshaw), June Jago (Gwenny Coke), Nora Nicholson (Mrs. Lomax), John Warner (Henry Lomax), Harry Locke (Hole), Rosalie Ashley (Annette), Joseph Tomelty (Dalrymple).

Okay shipboard comedy starring Gregson as a former cargo captain suddenly given charge of a luxury yacht. He earns the wrath of his crew and passengers by beefing up the discipline and treating his charges as cargo. The passengers are the usual assortment of eccentrics including a vamp, priest, and swindler. Eventually, Gregson softens up and relaxes his stranglehold on the ship by falling in love with a young widow. Typical material helped by a decent cast.

p, Joseph Janni; d, Jack Lee; w, John Whiting, Bryan Forbes, Nicholas Phipps (based on the novel by Richard Gordon); ph, Christopher Challis (DeLuxe Color); m, Frank Cordell; ed, Frederick Wilson; cos, Joan Ellacott.

Comedy   (PR:A   MPAA:NR)

CAPTIVATION zero (1931, Brit) 76m CAP bw
Conway Tearle (Hugh Somerton), Betty Stockield (Ann Moore), Marilyn Mawn (Lady Froster), A. Bromley Davenport (Col. Jordan), Louise Tinsley (Fluffy), Frederick Volpe (Skipper), George de Warfaz (Clerk), Dorothy Black (Adventuress).

Tedious film concerning a wayward girl, Stockford, who ends up on a yacht in the Mediterranean with a grouchy writer, Tearle, who hates women. When his friends arrive he introduces the girl as his wife. From then on the movie bogs down in a sea of vague and seemingly endless discussions about modern novelists, etc. Pretentious and boring.

p&d,, John Harvel; w, Edgar Middleton (based on a play by Middleton); ph, James Rogers.

Drama   (PR:A   MPAA:NR)

CAPTIVE CITY*** (1952) 91m Aspen Productions/UA bw
John Forsythe (Jim Austin), Joan Camden (Marge Austin), Harold J. Kennedy (Don Carey), Ray Teal (Chief Gillette), Marjorie Crossland (Mrs. Sirak), Victor Sutherland (Murray Sirak), Hal K. Dawson (Clyde Nelson), Geraldine Hall (Mrs. Nelson), Martin Milner (Phil Harding), Gladys Hurlbut (Linda Percy), Ian Wolfe (The Reverend Nash), Jess Kirkpatrick (Anderson), Paul Newlan (Krug), Frances Morris (Mrs. Harding), Charles Waggenheim (Phone Man), Paul Brinegar (Police Sergeant), Vic Romito (Fabretti), Charles Regan (Mobster), Sen. Estes Kefauver.

Designed to capitalize on the 1950 Kefauver Committee's investigation into organized crime, this film splits its attention between drama and a police expose, effectively using a documentary style. Forsythe is the editor of a small-town newspaper who is told by private eye Dawson that the entire city administration and police department of Kennington is in the hands of a crime syndicate headed by gambling czar Sutherland. At first, he disbelieves the tale but when Dawson's license is inexplicably revoked—he has been probing into Sutherland's background while doing spadework on a divorce case—Forsythe begins his own investigation and soon learns that police chief Teal and his minions are all on Sutherland's payroll. When Forsythe and his wife Camden are threatened by Sutherland, the editor flees with his wife, heading for Washington, D.C. to testify before Kefauver, the hoods in hot pursuit. The story is told in flashback beginning with Forsythe's flight, then harkening back to the events leading up to it, ending with syndicate representatives offering the editor a fortune to withhold his testimony from Kefauver. He heroically refuses and goes to the witness stand, knowing he is risking his life and that of his wife. To add authenticity, the producers convinced Kefauver himself to appear before and after the film with strong cautions about organized crime and its encroachment into the everyday life of all Americans. Though the story is weak in spots, Garmes' masterful and moody camerawork and Wise's sharp direction make the overall production taut and suspenseful. Forsythe, originally a stage and early-day TV actor (a medium to which he has returned with resounding success), gives a solid, understated performance. Teal is frighteningly realistic as the corrupt police chief and Sutherland is even more terrifying as the crime boss. Dawson plays the perfect grubbing gumshoe whose honesty exceeds greed.

p, Theron Warth; d, Robert Wise; w, Karl Kamb, Alvin M. Josephy, Jr. (from a story by Josephy, Jr.); ph, Lee Garmes; m, Jerome Moross; ed, Ralph Swink; prod d, Maurice Zuberano; md, Emil Newman.

Crime Drama   (PR:A   MPAA:NR)

CAPTIVE CITY, THE*½ (1963, Ital.) 110m PAR bw (ITAL: LA CITTA' PRIGIONIERA)
David Niven (Maj. Peter Whitfield), Lea Massari (Lelia), Ben Gazzara (Capt. Stubbs), Daniela Rocca (Doushka), Martin Balsam (Feinberg), Michael Craig (Capt. Elliot), Clelia Matania (Climedes), Giulio Bosetti (Narriman), Percy Herbert (Sgt. Reed), Ivo Garrani (Mavroti), Odoardo Spadaro (Janny Mendoris), Roberto Risso (Loveday).

Confused and unfocused suspense thriller starring Niven as a British officer in charge of a group of people holed up in an Athens hotel because of a group of left-wing rebels who are after an arms cache kept in the cellar. Tension arises when it is revealed that one of the besieged is a traitor. The viewer is kept guessing the identity of the turncoat long past the point of caring. Niven is typically fine, but the script and direction don't leave him much room to maneuver.

d, Joseph Anthony; w, Guy Elmes, Eric Bercovici, Marc Brandel (based on the novel by John Appleby); ph, Leonida Barboui; m, Piero Piccioni; ed, Mario Bonitti, Raymond Poulton, Michael Billingsley.

Suspense   (PR:C   MPAA:NR)

CAPTIVE GIRL*½ (1950) 73m COL bw
Johnny Weissmuller (Jungle Jim), Buster Crabbe (Barton), Anita Lhoest (Joan), Rick Vallin (Mahala), John Dehner (Hakim), Rusty Wescoatt (Silva), Nelson Leigh (Missionary).

Another Jungle Jim adventure starring Weissmuller as the intrepid explorer who travels into the heart of darkness to rescue blonde goddess Lhoest who has grown up in the wilds. Trouble arises when crazed medicine man Dehner tries to kill the girl so she won't reveal that he murdered her parents years ago. Sub-plot sees Crabbe as the evil leader of an expedition in search of treasure supposedly sunken in the bottom of Dehner's sacrificial pool. Usual jungle nonsense made somewhat interesting by the presence of Weissmuller and Crabbe, both former Tarzans, in the same movie for the second time in their careers, the first time being SWAMP FIRE in 1946. (See JUNGLE JIM series, Index.)

p, Sam Katzman; d, William Berke; w, Carroll Young (based on "Jungle Jim" comic strip); ph, Ira H. Morgan; md, Mischa Bakaleinikoff; ed, Henry Batista; art d, Paul Palmentola.

Adventure   (PR:A   MPAA:NR)

CAPTIVE HEART, THE*** (1948, Brit.) 108m EL/EAL bw
Michael Redgrave (Capt. Karel Hasek), Rachel Kempson (Celia Mitchell), Frederick Leister (Mr. Mowbray), Mervyn Johns (Private Evans), Rachel Thomas (Mrs. Evans), Jack Warner (Cpl. Horsfall), Gladys Henson (Mrs. Horsfall), Gordon Jackson (Lt. Lennox), Elliot Mason (Mrs. Lennox), Robert Wyndham (Lt. Comdr. Robert Narsden), Basil Radford (Maj. Ossy Dalrymple), Guy Middleton (Capt. Jim Mason), Jimmy Hanley (Pvt. Matthews), Karl Stepanek (Forster), Derek Bond (Lt. Harley), Jane Barrett (Caroline Harley), Margot Fitzsimmons (Elspeth McDougall), David Keir (Mr. McDougall), Meriel Forbes (Beryle Curtiss).

Powerful WWII prisoner-of-war drama starring Redgrave as a Czech captain, educated in England, who takes on the identity of a dead British officer to escape the Gestapo. The ploy works, but he is captured and thrown into a stalag reserved for the British. After many brushes with death, he must convince the British that he is indeed a refugee and not a spy. After he persuades the British and wins his freedom, he then must redeem himself with the widow of the dead soldier he was impersonating. Filled with good performances, with Redgrave a real standout.

p, Michael Balcon; d, Basil Dearden; w, Angus MacPhail, Guy Morgan (based on a story by Patrick Kirwan); ph, Douglas Slocombe, Jack Parker.

War   (PR:C   MPAA:NR)

CAPTIVE OF BILLY THE KID**½ (1952) 64m REP bw
Allan "Rocky" Lane (Himself), Black Jack (His Stallion), Penny Edwards (Nancy McCreary), Grant Withers (Van Stanley), Clem Bevans (Skeeter Davis), Roy Barcroft

(Plute), Clayton Moore *(Paul Howarth)*, Mauritz Hugo *(Randy Brown)*, Garry Goodwin *(Pete)*, Frank McCarroll *(1st Deputy Marshal)*, Richard Emory *(Sam)*.

One of Lane's better westerns which is based on the somewhat ridiculous premise that Billy the Kid buried his accumulation of stolen loot and then ripped the treasure map into five separate pieces and gave these sections to five different friends before he was killed. The buddies were then to meet on a certain date and put the pieces together and claim the treasure. The only hitch, of course, is that one of the friends, Withers, gets greedy and wants the loot all for himself. When one of the five, Bevans, notices that several of the others have died or had their map sections stolen, he calls in sheriff Lane who goes under cover to solve the mystery. Good suspenseful direction by Brannon holds viewer interest.

p, Harry Keller; d, Fred C. Brannon; w, M. Coates Webster, Richard Wormser; ph, John MacBurnie; ed, Robert M. Leeds.

Western (PR:A MPAA:NR)

CAPTIVE WILD WOMAN*** (1943) 61m UNIV bw

Evelyn Ankers *(Beth Colman)*, Acquanetta *(Paula Dupree)*, John Carradine *(Dr. Sigmund Walters)*, Martha MacVicar *(Dorothy Colman)*, Milburn Stone *(Fred Mason)*, Lloyd Corrigan *(John Whippie)*, Vince Barnett *(Curley Barret)*, Fay Helm *(Miss Strand)*, William Edmunds.

Good "B" horror film starring Carradine as a mad scientist who turns a wild ape provided by hunter/trainer Stone into a half-ape, half-woman creature played by Acquanetta. The ape-woman falls in love with Stone and becomes enraged when the hunter spurns her affections for those of his girl friend Ankers. Climax sees the ape-woman putting aside her hostilities and saving the life of Stone when he becomes trapped in a cage of wild cats. Good performances by the entire cast and effectively directed by Dmytryk. Stock footage from THE BIG CAGE, a Clyde Beatty documentary. (Sequels: JUNGLE CAPTIVE, JUNGLE WOMAN)

p, Ben Pivar; d, Edward Dmytryk; w, Henry Sucher, Griffin Jay (original by Ted Fithian and Maurice Pivar); ph, George Robinson; ed, Milton Carruth.

Horror (PR:A MPAA:NR)

CAPTIVE WOMEN*½ (1952) 67m RKO bw (AKA: 1,000 YEARS FROM NOW and 3,000 A.D.)

Robert Clarke *(Rob)*, Margaret Field *(Ruth)*, Gloria Saunders *(Catherine)*, Ron Randell *(Riddon)*, Stuart Randall *(Gordon)*, Paula Dorety *(Captive)*, Robert Bice *(Bram)*, Chili Williams *(Captive)*, William Schallert *(Carver)*, Eric Colmar *(Sabron)*, Douglas Evans *(Jason)*.

Pretty silly post-nuclear sci-fi drama concerning the war between three tribes of survivors inhabiting rubble-strewn and jungle-overgrown Manhattan. The three groups are known as the Norms, who live like cavemen, the Mutes, who are hideously scarred from the blast but peace loving, and the Upriver people, who are brutes. After many inane run-ins with each other, the Uprivers are eliminated by a flood that fills their tunnel under the Hudson River. But hope for mankind glimmers when a Norm woman, Field, and a Mute man, Randell, fall in love. Both tribes soften and look forward to a child born of peace. Halfway decent visual effects help this shaky story by the same producers who brought the public the vastly superior THE MAN FROM PLANET X (1951).

p&w, Aubrey Wisberg, Jack Pollexfen; d, Stuart Gilmore; ph, Paul Ivano; m, Charles Koff; ed, Fred R. Feitshans.

Science Fiction (PR:A MPAA:NR)

CAPTURE, THE*** (1950) 67m RKO bw

Lew Ayres *(Vanner)*, Teresa Wright *(Ellen)*, Victor Jory *(Father Gomez)*, Jacqueline White *(Luana)*, Jimmy Hunt *(Mike)*, Barry Kelley *(Mahoney)*, Duncan Renaldo *(Carlos)*, William Bakewell *(Tobin)*, Milton Parsons *(Thin Man)*, Frank Matts *(Juan)*, Felipe Turich *(Valdez)*, Edwin Rand *(Tevlin)*.

Interesting western written and produced by DUEL IN THE SUN (1946) author Niven Busch. Story concerns a field boss of an American oil company, Ayres, who flees into Mexico on the lam from a murder charge. He hides out in a priest's cabin and tells his tale in flashback. A year earlier he had killed a man he suspected of having stolen the oil company payroll. Obsessed with the belief that the man may have been innocent, Ayres seeks out the dead man's wife, Wright, to find out more about him. Soon Ayres and Wright fall in love and marry. The dead man's possible innocence still bothers Ayres, keeping him from being fully happy. He sets out to find the true robber and discovers that he is now a respectable businessman. The businessman is accidentally killed, causing Ayres' flight to Mexico. In the end, he is captured by the authorities, leaving his and Wright's future in doubt. Great performances by Ayres and Wright with an interesting and powerful use of native Mexican music that haunts the whole film.

p, Niven Busch; d, John Sturges; w, Busch; ph, Edward Cronjager; m, Daniele Amfitheatrof; ed, George Amy.

Western (PR:A MPAA:NR)

CAPTURE THAT CAPSULE zero (1961) 75m Will Zens bw

Richard Miller *(Ed Nowak)*, Dick O'Neill *(Al)*, Richard Jordahl *(Henry)*, Pat Bradley *(Jack Reynolds)*,Carl Rogers *(Hamilton)*, Dorothy Schiller *(Mary)*, Ed Siani *(Borman)*, Doug Hughes *(Joe)*, Wylie Carter *(Mac)*, Michael David *(Boy)*, LaRae Phillips *(Beach Girl)*, Jack Treacy *(Art)*, Ed Gangel *(Webster)*, Richard Twohy *(Persinger)*, Miriam Wilson *(Party Girl)*, Ron Wright, Lee Fortner *(Boat Men)*, Gene Garner, Web Smith *(Game Officers)*.

Bad espionage story has U.S. agent outwitting Communists to recover a data capsule. The Communists come off as stupid, sadistic clowns, and it turns out that the U.S. had the real capsule all the time, and the mindless chasing and killing was over a decoy.

p&d, Will Zens; w, Zens, Jan Elbein; ph, Vilis Lapenieks; m, Arthur Hopkins; ed, Bill Schaefer; art d, Cliff Bertrand.

Spy Drama (PR:C MPAA:NR)

CAPTURED** (1933) 72m WB bw

Leslie Howard *(Allison)*, Douglas Fairbanks, Jr. *(Digby)*, Paul Lukas *(Ehrlich)*, Margaret Lindsay *(Monica)*, Arthur Hohl *(Cocky)*, Robert Barrat *(The Commandant)*, John Bleifer *(Strogin)*, Phillip Faversham *(Haversham)*, Frank Reicher *(The Adjutant)*, Joyce Coad *(Elsa)*, William Le Maire *(Martin)*, J. Carrol Naish *(Guerand)*, Bert Sprotte *(Sgt. Major)*, Reginald Pasch *(Elsa's Lover)*, Harry Cording *(Orderly)*, Hans Joby *(2nd Orderly)*.

They took a first-rate cast and put into it a second-rate movie when they made CAPTURED. Howard and Fairbanks are captured soldiers in a WW I German prison camp. The new commandant of the camp is Lukas, who turns out to have been educated at Oxford with Howard. They become friendly and several concessions are awarded the prisoners, thus removing any tension or animosity between the factions. The men live in the kind of cottages one hates to leave so it's a great surprise when they attempt to escape. Howard gets to the guard's tower and begins to shoot Germans while his fellow prisoners escape in a number of conveniently parked airplanes. How the Germans miss killing Howard, who is exposed from all sides, is a miracle of modern moviemaking. Lindsay is wasted as Howard's cheating wife, and a very youthful Naish is seen as a Frenchman. Naish, an Irishman born in New York, has played just about every ethnic role, with the exception of Irish. And he was good in almost every one of them and particularly memorable for essaying Italians.

p, Hal B. Wallis; d, Roy Del Ruth; w, Edward Chodorov (based on novel *Fellow Prisoners* by Sir Philip Gibbs); ph, Tony Gaudio.

War Drama (PR:A MPAA:NR)

CAR, THE* (1977) 98m UNIV c

James Brolin *(Wade Parent)*, Kathleen Lloyd *(Lauren)*, John Marley *(Everett)*, R. G. Armstrong *(Amos)*, John Rubenstein *(John Morris)*, Elizabeth Thompson *(Margie)*, Roy Jenson *(Ray Mott)*, Kim Richards *(Lynn Marie)*, Kyle Richards *(Debbie)*, Kate Murtagh *(Miss McDonald)*, Robert Phillips *(Metcalf)*, Doris Dowling *(Bertha)*, Henry O'Brien *(Chas)*, Ronny Cox *(Luke)*, Melody Thomas, Bob Woodstock *(Cyclists)*, Eddie Little Sky *(Denson)*, Lee McLaughlin *(Marvin Fats)*, Margaret Wiley *(Navajo Woman)*, Read Morgan *(Mac Gruder)*, Ernie Orsatti *(Dalton)*, Joshua Davis *(Jimmy)*, Geraldine Keams *(Donna)*, Hank Hamilton *(Al)*, John Moio *(Parker)*, Melody Thomas *(Suzie)*, Bob Woodlock *(Pete)*, James Rawley *(Thompson)*, Louis Welch *(Berry)*, Bryan O'Byrne *(Wally)*, Don Keefer *(Dr. Pullbrook)*, Steve Gravers *(Mackey)*, Tony Brande *(Joe)*, Ronny Cox *(Luke)*.

Awful horror film in which a driverless black car terrorizes a small town. Brolin stars as a troubled deputy determined to destroy the Detroit demon. The majority of the movie is dominated by the vehicle overrunning defenseless townsfolk, leaving an inept police department trying to determine what to do. The film is climaxed by an apparent death to the demonic auto as it plunges over a cliff, exploding into a fiery ball. Good score and okay crash sequences are the exception to this poorly-conceived thriller. Take-off on a "Twilight Zone" tale.

p, Elliot Silverstein, Marvin Birdt; d, Silverstein; w, Dennis Shryack, Michael Butler, Lane Slate (based on a story by Shryack); ph, Gerald Hirschfield (Technicolor); m, Leonard Rosenman; ed, Michael McCroskey; art d, Lloyd S. Papez; set d, John McCarthy; stunt coordinator, Everett Creach.

Horror (PR:C MPAA:PG)

CAR 99½** (1935) 60m PAR bw

Fred MacMurray *(Ross Martin)*, Sir Guy Standing *(Professor Anthony)*, Ann Sheridan *(Mary Adams)*, Frank Craven *(Sheriff Pete Arnot)*, William Frawley *(Sgt. Barrel)*, Douglas Blackley *(Recruit Blatsky)*, John Cox *(Recruit Carney)*, Eddy Chandler *(Recruit Haynes)*, Alfred Delcambre *(Recruit Jamison)*, Dean Jagger *(Recruit Burton)*, Nora Cecil *(Granny)*, Marina Schubert *(Nan)*, Joe Sauers *(Whitey)*, Mack Gray *(Smoke)*, Howard Wilson *(Dutch)*, Charles Wilson *(Police Captain)*, Russell Hopton *(Operator Harper)*, John Howard *(Recruit Garney)*, Robert Kent *(Recruit Blatsky)*, Eddie Dunn *(Mac the Servant)*, Peter Hancock *(Eddie)*, Al Hill *(Hawkeye the Hood)*, Hector Sarno *(French Charlie)*, Jack Cheatham *(Sgt. Meyers)*, Ted Oliver *(Sergeant)*, Harry Strang *(Dispatch Sergeant)*, Charles Sullivan *(Green Gang Hood)*, Malcolm McGregor *(Pilot)*.

Fast-paced crime drama starring MacMurray (in an early role) as a Michigan state police officer in pursuit of clever bank robber Standing who has posed as a criminology professor to observe the latest law-enforcement methods that may be used against him. Climax sees MacMurray in charge of a massive manhunt to capture the elusive Standing. Good combination of comedy and thrills.

p, Bayard Veiller; d, Charles Barton; w, Karl Detzer, C. Gardner Sullivan (based on a story by Detzer); ph, William C. Mellor.

Crime (PR:A MPAA:NR)

CAR OF DREAMS** (1935, Brit.) 72m GAU bw

John Mills *(Robert Miller)*, Mark Lester *(Miller, Sr.)*, Norah Howard *(Anne Fisher)*, J. Robertson Hare *(Henry Butterworth)*, Grete Mosheim *(Vera Hart)*, Margaret Withers *(Mrs. Hart)*, Paul Graetz *(Mr. Hart)*, Glennis Lorimer *(Molly)*, Jack Hobbs *(Peters)*, Hay Plumb *(Chauffeur)*.

Average Cinderella tale starring Mosheim as a poor girl who likes to go out window shopping and price extravagant items just for kicks. One day she enters an auto dealership and prices a Rolls Royce. When she is informed that the car has been sold to someone else, she play-acts outrage and demands that she be sold that very car. All of this is observed by young, rich playboy Mills who falls in love with the spunky girl. The girl's frugal, hard-working parents are shocked when the Rolls is delivered to the door of their humble antique shop. Her mother immediately goes to the dealer and insists on knowing who paid for the vehicle. She is told that her daughter won the car in an advertisement give-away. In reality, Mills had bought the car and sent it to her, unbeknownst to Mosheim or her family. The pair finally meet and a romance starts, but

Mills soon discovers that the girl is actually an employee at his father's musical instrument factory. Mills tries to keep his true identity quiet, but eventually the truth comes out, causing a minor scandal at the factory. Soon everything calms down and, in the end, the couple unite. Mills turns in a credible performance as the rich man's son, but the film is damaged by a weak acting job from Mosheim.

d, Graham Cutts, Austin Melford; w, C. Stafford Dickens, R. Benson (based on a story by Melford); ph, M. Greenbaum.

Romance (PR:A MPAA:NR)

CAR WASH*** (1976) 97m UNIV c
Franklyn Ajaye (T.C.), Sully Boyar (Mr. B.), Richard Brestoff (Irwin), George Carlin (Taxi Driver), Prof. Irwin Corey (Mad Bomber), Ivan Dixon (Lonnie), Bill Duke (Duane), Antonio Fargas (Lindy), Michael Fennell (Calvin), Arthur French (Charlie), Lorraine Gary (Hysterical Lady), Darrow Igus (Floyd), Leonard Jackson (Earl), DeWayne Jessie (Lloyd), Lauren Jones (Hooker), Jack Kehoe (Scruggs), Henry Kingi (Goody), Melanie Mayron (Marsha), Garrett Morris (Slide), Clarence Muse (Snapper), Leon Pinkney (Justin), The Pointer Sisters (The Wilson Sisters), Richard Pryor (Daddy Rich), Tracy Reed (Mona), Pepe Serna (Chuco), James Spinks (Hippo), Ray Vitte (Geronimo), Ren Woods (Loretta), Carmine Caridi, Antoine Becker, Erin Blunt, Reginald Farmer, Ricky Fellen, Ben Fromer, Cynthia Hamowy, John Linsom, Ed Metzger, Antar Mubarak, Derek Schultz, Mike Slaney, Al Stellone, Jackie Toles, Janine Williams, Otis Sistrunk, Timothy Thomerson, Jason Bernard, Jay Butler, Rod McGrew, J. J. Jackson, Sarina C. Grant, Billy Bass.

Hilarious, episodic comedy detailing a day in the life of an L.A. car wash featuring an ensemble cast of superb comedic performers. Basically plotless, the film shows the lives, hopes, dreams, ambitions, and foibles of the multiracial employees and customers of Boyar's Car Wash. One of many highlights sees Pryor as a fancy-pants preacher who arrives in his flashy car accompanied by the Pointer Sisters. Great musical score by Norman Whitfield is integrated into the movement of the scenes which gives the film a funky rhythm. Directed by Michael Schultz who also did the interesting inner-city youth film COOLEY HIGH (1975).

p, Art Linson, Gary Stromberg; d, Michael Schultz; w, Joel Schumacher; ph, Frank Stanley (Technicolor); m, Norman Whitfield; ed, Christopher Holmes; art d, Robert Clatworthy; set d, A. C. Montenaro; cos, Daniel Paredes.

Comedy **Cas.** (PR:C MPAA:PG)

CARAVAN** (1934) 102m FOX bw
Charles Boyer (Latzi), Loretta Young (Countess Wilma), Jean Parker (Tinka), Phillips Holmes (Lt. von Tokay), Louise Fazenda (Miss Opitz), Eugene Pallette (Gypsy Chief), C. Aubrey Smith (Baron von Tokay), Charles Grapewin (Notary), Noah Beery (Innkeeper), Dudley Digges (Administrator), Richard Carle (Majordomo), Lionel Belmore (Station Master), Billy Bevan (Police Sergeant).

An early operetta in the European fashion that is well-made technically but ultimately yawnable. Boyer overplays the part of a gypsy as Young arrives in a small Tokay village to claim her inheritance, a huge estate. But she can only get the vast holdings if she marries. Smith, a local Baron, suggests she marry his son, Holmes, but spunky Loretta (supposedly 21 in the film, and, wonder of wonder, actually 21 in real life!) refuses and marries Boyer, leader of a gypsy orchestra that has come to the area to play while the grapes are harvested. Young has never met Smith's son and refused, out of spite. After her marriage to Boyer, she meets the young Lieutenant and falls in love with him. Instead of demonstrating the vaunted gypsy temper, Boyer turns the other cheek, says he understands, and steps aside to allow Young to marry Holmes. It was around this time that the other studios were beginning to put out some modern musicals and CARAVAN suffered by comparison. People were no longer intrigued by operettas, especially ordinary ones, so they spent their movie dollars elsewhere. Songs: "Ha-Cha-Cha," "Wing Song," "Happy, I Am Happy."

p&d, Erik Charell; w, Robert Liebman, Samson Raphaelson (based on the novel Gypsy Melody by Melchior Lengyel); ph, Ernest Palmer, Theodor Sparkuhl; m/l, Werner Richard Heymann, Gus Kahn.

Operetta (PR:A MPAA:NR)

CARAVAN***½ (1946, Brit.) 122m GFD/Gainsborough bw
Stewart Granger (Richard), Anne Crawford (Oriana), Jean Kent (Rosal), Dennis Price (Francis), Robert Helpmann (Wycroft), Gerard Heinz (Don Carlos), Arthur Goullet (Suiza), John Salew (Diego), Julian Somers (Manoel), Peter Murray (Juan), Merie Tottenham (Tweeny), David Horne (Camperdene), Sylvie St. Clair (Marie), Patricia Laffan (Betty), Joseph O'Donohue (Bandit), Mabel Constanduros (Woman), Josef Ramart (Jose), Gypsy Petulengro (Paco).

Granger is perfect as a penniless writer in love with the lady of the manor who, due to an attack of amnesia, falls prey to the wiles of a gypsy vamp. Dennis Price's portrayal of Sir Francis, a cringing coward bent on murder when his daughter is spurned, is brilliant, and Jean Kent as the gypsy displays a degree of ardor in her love scenes with Granger amazing to find in an Englishwoman. Strong direction, brilliant individual performances and production values far above the usual run of British films work beautifully together as one melodramatic situation is piled on another. The British screen has seldom offered in one picture anything more effective than the work of these five principals.

p, Harold Huth; d, Arthur Crabtree; w, Roland Pertwee (based on the novel by Lady Eleanor Smith); art d, John Bryan; ph, Stephen Dade; ed, Charles Knott; md, Louis Levy, Walford Hyden.

Drama (PR:A MPAA:NR)

CARAVAN TO VACCARES** (1974, Brit./Fr.) 98m FOX/Rank c
Charlotte Rampling (Lila), David Birney (Neil Bowman), Michel Lonsdale (Duc de Croytor), Marcel Bozuffi (Henri Czerda), Michael Bryant (Stefan Zuger), Manitas de

Plata (Ricardo), Serge Marquand (Ferenc), Marianne Eggerick (Cecile), Francoise Brion (Stella), Vania Vilers (1st Guardian), Graham Hill (Helicopter Pilot).

Competent but ultimately dull Alistair MacLean thriller starring Birney as a young American hired by rich French Duke Lonsdale to smuggle an Eastern European scientist to the U.S., Sexy British photographer Rampling goes along for the ride as the small group is chased by a rival interest which wants the scientist and his secrets. Stiff dialog and lackluster performances fail to spark much interest or thrills.

p, Geoffrey Reeve, Richard Morris-Adams; d, Reeve; w, Paul Wheeler (based on the novel by Alistair MacLean); ph, John Cabrera, David Bevan, Ted Deason (Panavision/Eastmancolor); m, Stanley Myers; art d, George Petitot.

Adventure (PR:C MPAA:PG)

CARAVAN TRAIL, THE*½ (1946) 53m PRC c
Eddie Dean (Eddie Dean), Al La Rue (Ezra), Emmett Lynn (Cherokee), Jean Carlin (Paula Bristol), Robert Malcolm (Jim Bristol), Charles King (Joe King), Robert Barron (Remo), Forrest Taylor (Silas Black), Bob Duncan (Killer), Jack O'Shea (Poker Face), Terry Frost (Bart Barton), Lloyd Ingraham, Lee Bennett, Wylie Grant, Lee Roberts, Bud Osborne, George Chesebro.

Rare color musical oater for the 1940s stars lackluster cowpoke Dean who accepts a job as a town marshal to get revenge for the murder of his friend by some dishonest bushwhackers who have swiped the land from some hardworking homesteaders. Aided by sidekick La Rue and reformed outlaw Lynn, the lawman shoots and punches the villains into submission. Along the trail are sung the typical horse-opera ballads, "Wagon Wheels," "Crazy Cowboy Song," and "You're Too Pretty To Be Lonesome."

p&d, Robert Emmett; w, Frances Kavanaugh; ph, Marcel LePicard (Cinecolor); ed, Hugh Winn; m, Carl Hoefle; m/l, Billy Hill, Peter DeRose, Eddie Dean, Lewis Hersher, Lew Porter, Johnnie Bond.

Western (PR:A MPAA:NR)

CARAVANS** (1978, U.S./Iranian) 127m UNIV/IBEX c
Anthony Quinn (Zulfigar), Michael Sarrazin (Mark Miller), Jennifer O'Neill (Ellen Jasper), Christopher Lee (Sardar Khan), Joseph Cotten (Crandall), Behrooz Vosoughi (Nazrullah), Barry Sullivan (Richardson), Jeremy Kemp (Dr. Smythe), Duncan Quinn (Moheb), Behrooz Gueramian (Peasant Boy), Mohammad Ali Keshavarz (Shakkur), Parviz Gharib-Afshar (Nur Mohammad), Fahimeh Amouzandeh (Mira), Khosrow Tabatabai (Dancing Boy), Mohammad Kahnemout (Maftoon), Susan Vaziri (Racha), Parviz Jafari (Capt. Majid), Mohammad Poursattar (Mullah 1), Hamid Lighvani (Mullah 2), Djamshid Sadri (Mullah 3), Shahnaz Pakravan (Karima), Parvi Shahinkhoo, Ahmad Kashani, Eskandar Rafu, Firooz Bahjat Mohamadi, Sami Tahasonee, Ali Zandi, Bozorgmeh Rafia.

An Iranian desert epic released in American theaters just before the situation in Iran blew up in the West's face. The film features Sarrazin as a lowly American consular employee who is sent into the desert to find the American wife, O'Neill, of an Iranian colonel, Vosoughi, who has run off with Kochi Chieftain Quinn. Sarrazin finds O'Neill with ridiculous ease and spends the rest of the film trying to convince her to come back to civilization. She won't leave, he won't return without her, and the pair witness a massive amount of intrigue, torture, festivals, executions, and mayhem. There are meaningless walk-ons by Lee, Kemp, and Cotten, and only Quinn shines in his performance. Owes much to John Ford's THE SEARCHERS.

p, Elmo Williams; d, James Fargo; w, Nancy Voyles Crawford, Thomas A. McMahon, Lorraine Williams (based on a book by James Michener); ph, Douglas Slocombe (Technicolor); m, Mike Batt; ed, Richard Marten; art d, Ted Tester, Peter Williams, Peter James; cos, Renie Conley; spec eff, Karli Baumgartner; stunts, John Sullivan.

Adventure (PR:C MPAA:PG)

CARBINE WILLIAMS*** (1952) 90m MGM
James Stewart (Marsh Williams), Jean Hagen (Maggie Williams), Wendell Corey (Capt. H. T. Peoples), Carl Benton Reid (Claude Williams), Paul Stewart ("Dutch" Kruger), Otto Hulett (Mobley), Rhys Williams (Redwick Karson), Herbert Heyes (Lionel Daniels), James Arness (Leon Williams), Porter Hall (Sam Markley), Fay Roope (District Attorney), Ralph Dumke (Andrew White), Leif Erickson (Feder), Henry Corden (Bill Stockton), Howard Petrie (Sheriff), Frank Richards (Truex), Stuart Randall (Tom Vennar), Dan Riss (Jesse Rimmer), Bobby Hyatt (David Williams), Willis Bouchey (Mitchell), Emile Meyer (Head Guard), Bert LeBaron, Duke York, Richard Reeves (Guards), Robert Foulk (Torchy), Harry Cheshire (Judge), Lillian Culver (Mrs. Laura Williams), Marlene Lyden (Mary Eloise Williams), Norma Jean Cramer (Mary Ruth Williams), Robert Van Orden (Bob Williams), Jordan Corenweth (Will Williams),, Harry Macklin (John Williams), Jon Gardner (Mac Williams), Bob Alden (Messenger), Erik Nielsen (Child at Wedding), Sam Flint, Nolan Leary, Marshall Bradford, George Pembroke (Board Members), Fiona O'Shiel (Mrs. Rimmer), James Harrison (Trusty).

Stewart gives a masterful study of a simple but brilliant inventor, Marsh Williams, who is sent to prison for thirty years after his moonshine still is raided and a revenue agent is killed by one of Stewart's associates. In the North Carolina prison farm where Stewart is sent, hardships and brutality abound and Stewart at first bristles against the quiet authority of warden Corey. To occupy his time, Stewart secretly begins to construct a weapon, not one with which to escape, but an entirely new invention. Having a lifelong fascination with firearms, Stewart conceives of a weapon with a short-stroke piston. When Corey discovers the weapon and confiscates it, Stewart goes to him, begging that he be allowed to finish his creation, explaining that the US. military has need of such an invention. Corey realizes Stewart is not intending to use the weapon to escape and allows him to continue his work over much opposition from superiors. The result is the creation of the M-1 carbine. This weapon helped to revolutionize modern warfare and more than eight million carbines were used by American troops during WW II. After serving eight years in prison, and for his achievement, Stewart is released from prison. The uncomplicated story is told exclusively from Stewart's point of view and the star gives a captivating, intense performance, convincingly enacting the real life, hard-as-nails mountain man so that his plight and ambition become thoroughly sympathetic and often overwhelmingly emotional. Thorpe's direction is tight and Mellor's camera never inactive.

p, Armand Deutsch; d, Richard Thorpe; w, Art Cohn; ph, William Mellor; m, Conrad Salinger; ed, Newell P. Kimlin; art d, Cedric Gibbons, Eddie Imazu.

Crime Drama (PR:A MPAA:NR)

CARBON COPY½** (1981) 92m AE c
George Segal *(Walter Whitney)*, Susan St. James *(Vivian Whitney)*, Jack Warden *(Nelson)*, Denzel Washington *(Roger)*, Paul Winfield *(Bob)*, Dick Martin *(Victor)*, Vicky Dawson *(Marie-Ann)*, Tom Poston *(Rev. Hayworth)*, Macon McCalman *(Tubby)*, Parley Baer *(Dr. Bristol)*, Vernon Weddle *(Wardlow)*, Edward Marshall *(Freddie)*, Ed Call *(Basketball Father)*, Angelina Estrada *(Bianca)*.

Uneven morality comedy starring Segal as a Jewish businessman who loses his job, his connections, and his wife, St. James, when it is revealed that he had an illegitimate son from a fling nearly two decades ago and the kid happens to be black. Cut off from his affluent lifestyle, Segal is forced to appreciate his son's existence by taking manual labor jobs in a depressed economy. He is guided into this revelation by his black son, Washington, who is torn between getting lifelong revenge on the man who abandoned him or actually becoming close to his father.

p, Carter DeHaven III, Stanley Shapiro; d, Michael Schultz; w, Shapiro; ph, Fred Koenekamp (Panavision, C); m, Bill Conti; ed, Marion Segal; art d, Ted Howorth.

Comedy Cas. (PR:C MPAA:PG)

CARD, THE (SEE: PROMOTER, THE, 1952)

CARDBOARD CAVALIER, THE** (1949, Brit.) 97m GFD bw
Sid Field *(Sidcup Buttermeadow)*, Margaret Lockwood *(Nell Gwynne)*, Mary Clare *(Milady Doverhouse)*, Jerry Desmonde *(Col Lovelace)*, Claude Hulbert *(Sylvester Clutterbuck)*, Brian Worth *(Tom Pride)*, Anthony Hulme *(Charles II)*, Edmund Willard *(Oliver Cromwell)*, Irene Handl *(Lady Agnes)*, Miles Malleson *(Judge Gorebucket)*, Joan Young *(Maggie)*, Jack McNaughton *(Uriah Croup)*, Alfie Dean *(Murdercasket)*, Michael Brennan *(Barebones)*, Peter Bull *(Mosspot)*, Vincent Holman *(Lord Doverhouse)*, John Salew *(Smug)*.

Silly 17th-century slapstick featuring Field as a bumbling peasant trying to make ends meet who suddenly finds himself involved in a plot to overthrow Cromwell in order to make way for the return of Charles II. Unremarkable farce starring popular British comics.

p&d, Walter Forde; w, Noel Langley; ph, Jack Hildyard, Russel Thomson; m, Lambert Williamson; ed, Alan L. Jaggs.

Comedy (PR:A MPAA:NR)

CARDIAC ARREST zero (1980) 80m Film Ventures International c
Garry Goodron, Mike Chan, Maxwell Gail, Susan O'Connell, Ray Reinhardt.

Another mad slasher is terrorizing San Francisco, and this one's gimmick is that he cuts out the hearts of his victims. Just ignore it and maybe it will go away.

p, Richard Helzberg; d&w, Murray Mintz (DeLuxe Color); m, Andrew Kulberg.

Horror (PR:O MPAA:PG)

CARDINAL, THE zero (1936, Brit.) 70m Pathe bw
Matheson Lang *(Cardinal de Medici)*, Eric Portman *(Giuliano de Medici)*, Robert Atkins *(Gen. Belmont)*, O. E. Clarence *(Monterosa)*, Douglas Jeffries *(Baglioni)*, F. B. J. Sharpe *(Pope Julius II)*, Wilifred Fletcher *(Michaelangelo)*, A. Bromley Davenport *(Bramante)*, Rayner Barton *(Cardinal Orelli)*, K. Edgar Bruce *(Spini)*, David Horne *(English Abbot)*, June Duprez *(Francesca Monterosa)*, Henrietta Watson *(Donna Claricia de Medici)* Dora Barton *(Duenna)*.

Lousy 15th-century Roman drama starring Lang as a Cardinal torn by his vow of silence concerning the confessional because he cannot use the information obtained in confession to clear his own brother of a murder charge. Below-average performances by a cast that forgets they're supposed to be 15th-century Romans and uses too many modern mannerisms to be convincing.

d, Sinclair Hill; w, D. B. Wyndham Lewis (based on a play by Louis N. Parker); ph, Cyril Bristow.

Historical Drama (PR:A MPAA:NR)

CARDINAL, THE*** (1963) 175m COL c
Tom Tryon *(Stephen Fermoyle)*, Carol Lynley *(Mona)*, Dorothy Gish *(Celia)*, Maggie McNamara *(Florrie)*, Bill Hayes *(Frank)*, Cameron Prud'Homme *(Din)*, Cecil Kellaway *(Monsignor Monaghan)*, Loring Smith *(Cornelius J. Deegan)*, John Saxon *(Benny Rampell)*, John Huston *(Cardinal Glennon)*, Jose Duval *(Ramon Gongaro)*, Peter MacLean *(Father Callahan)*, Robert Morse *(Bobby)*, James Hickman *(Father Lyons)*, Berenice Gahm *(Mrs. Rampell)*, Billy Reed *(Master of Ceremonies)*, Pat Henning *(Hercule Menton)*, Burgess Meredith *(Father Ned Halley)*, Jill Haworth *(Lalage Menton)*, Russ Brown *(Dr. Heller)*, Raf Vallone *(Cardinal Quarenghi)*, Tullio Carminati *(Cardinal Giacobbi)*, Ossie Davis *(Father Gillis)*, Don Francesco Mancini *(Ordination Master of Ceremonies)*, Dino Di Luca *(Italian Monsignor)*, Monks of Abbey at Casamari *(Liturgical Chants)*, Carol Lynley *(Regina Fermoyle)*, Donald Hayne *(Father Eberling)*, Chill Wills *(Monsignor Whittle)*, Arthur Hunnicutt *(Sheriff Dubrow)*, Doro Merande *(Woman Picket)*, Patrick O'Neal *(Cecil Turner)*, Murray Hamilton *(Lafe)*, Romy Schneider *(Annemarie)*, Peter Weck *(Kurt Von Hartman)*, Rudolph Forster *(Drinking Man at Ball)*, Josef Meinrad *(Cardinal Innitzer)*, Dagmar Schmedes *(Madame Walter)*, Eric Frey *(Seyss-Inquart)*, Josef Krastel *(Von Hartman Butler)*, Mathias Fuchs *(Father Neidermoser)*, Vilma Degischer *(Sister Wilhelmina)*, Wolfgang Preiss *(S.S. Major)*, Jurgen Wilke *(Army Lieutenant)*, Wilma Lipp *(Soloist)*, The Wiener Jeunesse Choir.

THE CARDINAL is one of Otto Preminger's best films, but that's not saying much as we realize Otto made SKIDDOO!, ROSEBUD, HURRY SUNDOWN, and THE HUMAN FACTOR among his few films. This vast, sprawling epic takes Tom Tryon (who went on to become a very successful novelist) from Monsignor to Cardinal, through so many trials and tests of his spiritual conviction that it's difficult to envision all of this happening to one servant of God. Tryon must face Georgia racists, Nazis in Austria, a sister who sleeps with her Jewish fiancé and refuses to be penitent about it. That's followed by her becoming an unwed mother! Well! The number of sequences in the movie seems endless and it jets across continents with alacrity. It's far better than the disastrous MONSIGNOR of Chris Reeve but nowhere near as good as several other films about the innards of the church. Robert Dozier (producer William Dozier's son) does as good a job as he can in compressing the material to livable length, but working with Preminger is never easy (ask anyone who has ever done it) and he has never been able to edit his own work so THE CARDINAL commits a cardinal sin: it bores. With an hour cut out of it, this might have been a landmark picture. The acting is all first quality, even Tryon and Lynley, neither of whom was ever known for great thespian abilities. Kudos, however for the acting, the music, and Leon Shamroy's photography. None for Preminger's direction.

p&d, Otto Preminger; w, Robert Dozier (based on a novel by Henry Morton Robinson); ph, Leon Shamroy (Panavision/Technicolor); m, Jerome Moross; ed, Louis R. Loeffler; cos, Donald Brooks; ch, Buddy Schwab.

Drama (PR:C MPAA:NR)

CARDINAL RICHELIEU½** (1935) 83m FOX/UA bw
George Arliss *(Cardinal Richelieu)*, Edward Arnold *(King Louis)*, Halliwell Hobbes *(Father Joseph)*, Maureen O'Sullivan *(Lenore)*, Cesar Romero *(Andre de Pons)*, Douglas Dumbrille *(Baradas)*, Violet Kemble-Cooper *(Queen Marie)*, Katherine Alexander *(Queen Anne)*, Francis Lister *(Gaston)*, Robert Harrigan *(Fontailles)*, Herbert Bunston *(Duke of Brittany)*, Murray Kinnell *(Duke of Lorraine)*, Gilbert Emery *(Duke of Normandy)*, Keith Kenneth *(D'Esperron)*, Joseph R. Tozer *(DeBussey)*, Russell Hicks *(Le Moyne)*.

Arliss adds to his collection of historical impersonations here by becoming the shrewd, manipulative prime minister to Louis XIII. Excellent production values and supporting cast make this one worth seeing. Nunnally Johnson collaborated on the screenplay but asked to have his name removed when Arliss made some changes in the script.

p, William Goetz, Raymond Griffith; d, Rowland V. Lee; w, Maude Howell, Cameron Rogers, W. P. Lipscomb (based on a play by Edward Bulwer-Lytton); ph, Peverell Marley; ed, Sherman Todd.

Biography (PR:A MPAA:NR)

CAREER*½ (1939) 79m RKO bw
Anne Shirley *(Sylvia)*, Edward Ellis *(Cruthers)*, Samuel S. Hinds *(Bartholomew)*, Janet Beecher *(Mrs. Cruthers)*, Leon Errol *(Mudcat)*, Alice Eden *(Merta)*, John Archer *(Ray)*, Raymond Hatton *(Deacon)*, Maurice Murphy *(Mel)*, Harrison Greene *(Burnett)*, Charles Drake *(Chaney)*, Hobart Cavanaugh *(Bronson)*.

Strange little movie whose primary purpose was to fulfill a Hollywood screen test competition sponsored by CBS radio and Wrigley's Doublemint gum. The two discovered "talents," Archer and Eden, are of passable skills in this homespun tale. Plot revolves around the long rivalry between two men, Ellis and Hinds, who have lived in the small, midwestern town their whole lives. When younger, they battled for the affection of the same woman. In the end she chose Hinds over Ellis. Hinds becomes the town's banker and Ellis the storekeeper. Both have children, Ellis a son, and Hinds a daughter. Hinds' wife dies, leaving him a widower. The children (Archer and Shirley) grow up and fall in love. Trouble looms when the community begins to distrust Hinds' banking methods and a slight financial panic erupts. Meanwhile, Archer and Shirley's romance hits the skids when the ambitious boy rejects any thought of marriage to pursue a career in medicine. The bank panic only worsens when storekeeper Ellis pulls out his savings of $33,000 which leaves the bank broke. Shirley finally gets fed up with Archer and leaves him for another man. Pretty sappy stuff. (Archer went on to play leads in B pictures and supporting roles in A productions, notably as the chief federal agent who works with undercover agent Edmond O'Brien to trap James Cagney in WHITE HEAT; he is divorced from actress Marjorie Lord. Their daughter, Ann Archer, is a young leading lady in films and on TV. Using her real name, Rowena Cook, Eden made only one more picture, KIT CARSON, in 1940.)

p, Bob Sisk; d, Leigh Jason; w, Dalton Trumbo (based on the story by Phil Stong, adapted by Bert Granet); ph, Frank Redman; ed, Arthur E. Roberts.

Drama (PR:A MPAA:NR)

CAREER½** (1959) 105m PAR bw
Anthony Franciosa *(Sam Lawson)*, Dean Martin *(Maury Novak)*, Shirley MacLaine *(Sharon Kensington)*, Carolyn Jones *(Shirley Drake)*, Joan Blackman *(Barbara)*, Robert Middleton *(Robert Kensington)*, Donna Douglas *(Marjorie Burke)*, Jerry Paris *(Allan Burke)*, Frank McHugh *(Charlie)*, Chuck Wassil *(Eric Peters)*, Mary Treen *(Shirley's Secretary)*, Allan Hewitt *(Matt Helmsley)*, Marjorie Bennett *(Columnist)*.

Franciosa is a young actor looking for his big break on Broadway. He joins a small theater group directed by Martin and marries his home town sweetheart, supporting himself by waiting tables. His wife leaves him and Martin becomes an important director, but he is reluctant to risk his reputation by putting an unknown like Franciosa in a show. Franciosa retaliates by beginning an affair with, and eventually marrying MacLaine, Martin's alcoholic girlfriend. She asks Franciosa for a divorce so she can marry Martin and Franciosa agrees, on the condition that Martin give him the lead in the next show. Martin agrees, but gives the lead to a Hollywood star. Franciosa is drafted, and, upon returning from Korea, he finds that he and Martin have been blacklisted for their involvement in the theatre group. They team up to produce an off-Broadway show and it becomes a hit. Franciosa is finally a star. Originally, MacLaine and Jones had each others' roles, but MacLaine wanted to play the drunken kook, and Jones wanted to play the straight part of Franciosa's agent. They traded parts and MacLaine would spend the next several years trying to escape the "kook" label she was stuck with after this film. Excellent performances by the entire cast keep this grim drama on target.

p, Hal B. Wallis; d, Joseph Anthony; w, James Lee (based on a play by Lee); ph, Joseph La Shelle; (RegalScope); m, Franz Waxman; ed, Warren Low; art d, Hal Pereira; set d, Sam Comer, Arthur Krams; cos, Edith Head; m/l, Sammy Cahn, James Van Heusen.

Drama (PR:C MPAA:NR)

CAREER GIRL*½ (1944) 67m PRC bw
Frances Langford (Joan), Edward Norris (Steve), Iris Adrian (Glenda), Craig Woods (Janice), Linda Brent (Thelma), Alec Craig (Pop), Ariel Heath (Sue), Lorraine Krueger (Ann), Renee White (Polly), Gladys Blake (Janie), Charles Judels (Felix Black), Charles Williams (Louis Horton).

Pointless Broadway drama starring Langford as a Kansas City gal who goes to New York to be a singing star. After a series of predictable setbacks, Langford is signed to be the lead in a new Broadway spectacular that the viewer never sees because the film suddenly ends before the show is out of rehearsals. Bad direction and a trite script don't help Langford, who tries hard to pull it off. Songs: "Blue In Love Again," "Dreams Come True"(Romano, Amsterdam), "That's How the Rhumba Began," "Some Day" (Neuman, Brown).

p, Jack Schwartz; d, Wallace W. Fox; w, Sam Neuman (based on a story by Dave Silverstein and Stanley Rauh); ph, Gustave Peterson; ed., Robert Crandall; m/l, Morey Amsterdam, Tony Romano, Sam Neuman, Michael Breen.

Musical/Drama (PR:A MPAA:NR)

CAREER GIRL zero (1960) 61m Astor c
June Wilkinson, Charles Robert Keane, Lisa Barrie, Joe Sullivan, Cindy Ames, Dave Armstrong, John Redick.

Wilkinson leaves her home and travels to Hollywood to become a star. Super low budget and it shows at every turn, as does the bosomy Ms. Wilkinson. Worthless trash.

p, Marc Frederick; d, Harold Davis; w, H. E. Barrie; (Eastmancolor).

Drama (PR:C MPAA:NR)

CAREER WOMAN** (1936) 75m FOX bw
Claire Trevor (Carroll Aiken), Michael Whalen (Barry Conant), Isabel Jewell (Gracie Clay), Eric Linden (Everett Clark), Virginia Field (Fifi Brown), Gene Lockhart (Uncle Billy Burley), Edward S. Brophy (Doc Curley), El Brendel (Chris Erleson), Guinn Williams (Bede Sanders), Sterling Holloway (George Rogers), Charles Waldron, Sr. (Milt Clark), Paul Stanton (Arthur Henshaw), Kathleen Lockhart (Mrs. Milt Clark), Frank McGlynn, Sr. (Sheriff Duncan), June Storey (Edith Clark), Lynne Berkeley (Helen Clark), Ray Brown (Judge Hite), George Meeker (Mr. Smith), Howard Hickman (Judge Whitman), Spencer Charters (Coroner McInery), Erville Alderson (Dr. Anderson), Eiy Malyon (Miss Brinkerhoff), Otto Hoffman (Frank Jackson), Charles Middleton (Matt Clay).

Trevor stars as a young law school graduate who returns to her small home town to defend a poor girl, Jewell, who is accused of murdering her father. Flamboyant lawyer Waldron arrives on the scene and helps Trevor win the case after a series of great character actors (Holloway, Lockhart, Field, Brophy, and Williams) have a chance to show their stuff on the witness stand. Uneven mix of comedy and serious drama is helped by competent direction and a professional cast.

p, Sol M. Wurtzel; d, Lewis Seiler; w, Lamar Trotti (based on a story by Gene Fowler); ph, James Van Trees and Robert Planck; m, Samuel Kaylin; ed., Louis Loeffler.

Comedy/Drama (PR:A MPAA:NR)

CAREERS*½ (1929) 92m FN bw
Billie Dove (Helene), Antonio Moreno (Victor), Thelma Todd (Hortense), Noah Beery (The President), Holmes Herbert (Carouge), Carmel Meyers (The Woman), Robert Frazer (Lavergne), Sojin (Biwa Player), Marte Faust, Kithnou.

Very early talkie stars Dove as the wife of a French magistrate stationed in French Indochina who is being held back in his career by an unscrupulous boss who only promotes those men whose wives succumb to his amorous advances. Dove refuses to capitulate and storms into the creep's office to demand an explanation regarding the held-up promotion. Realizing that she has made the situation worse by barging in on him, she almost gives in to his sleazy advances. Then a native, who had been hiding in the office closet waiting to steal things, is discovered. In the ensuing struggle the boss is killed. Dove's husband is appointed to investigate the murder, not knowing of his wife's involvement. When he starts to piece the puzzle together, he begins to suspect his wife of infidelity, but she convinces him that the man was killed before anything had happened. Husband and wife reunite and the whole messy affair comes to a merciful close. Carmel Myers sings one song, "I Love You, I Hate You" (Al Bryan, George W. Meyer).

d, John Francis Dillon; w, Forrest Halsey (based on a play by Alfred Schirokauer and Paul Rosenhayn); ph, John Seitz; m/l, George W. Meyer, Al Bryan.

Drama (PR:A MPAA:NR)

CAREFREE** (1938) 83m RKO bw
Fred Astaire (Tony Flagg), Ginger Rogers (Amanda Cooper), Ralph Bellamy (Stephen Arden), Luella Gear (Aunt Cora), Jack Carson (Connors), Clarence Kolb (Judge Travers), Franklin Pangborn (Roland Hunter), Walter Kingsford (Dr. Powers), Kay Sutton (Miss Adams), Tom Tully (Policeman), Hattie McDaniel (Maid), Robert B. Mitchell and his St. Brendan's Boys.

In 1938, just about everyone in Hollywood was seeing a psychiatrist (not much has changed) so the producers thought a lighthearted movie on the subject might be just the ticket. Only four songs to speak of in the Irving Berlin score, so it's more of a comedy with music than the typical Astaire-Rogers musical comedy. Bellamy is a long-faced lawyer who is mad for Rogers, a radio singing star. Rogers must be a Libra because she can't make up her mind about him. Bellamy sends her to pal Astaire who is a psychiatrist. (Astaire has a very strange style of analysis—Carson is a resident anesthetist—huh?—in a white coat and the office is filled with odd-looking ophthalmological tools). Rogers agrees to go but she can't dream and Astaire has nothing to analyze. He makes her eat some weird food so she'll have something to talk about. In her dream she falls in love with Astaire and when she wakes she finds it's true. She admits she loves him and cries when he explains that all patients fall in love with their psychiatrists and it's just a phase. He puts her into a hypnotic trance and implants the idea that she is in love with Bellamy. After some dumb slapstick sequences, Astaire looks deep inside himself and realizes that he loves Rogers (no surprise!) and must get her back. But he may be too late. There's a wedding going on as Astaire breaks in to stop the rite of Spring (with more finesse than Dustin Hoffman in THE GRADUATE). Bellamy swings a roundhouse right, Fred ducks and Rogers gets a shiner. The wedding eventually takes place with Astaire standing in for Bellamy and Rogers nursing a black eye. This was the first of three films Rogers made about women having mental difficulties. In TOM DICK AND HARRY (a much funnier film than this one), she can't decide between her three suitors, and in LADY IN THE DARK the delving into the psyche is deep and dark. CAREFREE tried to combine a Howard Hawks-type wacky comedy with an overlay of music and dancing. It didn't quite work but it's still better than most. The last RKO Astaire-Rogers pairing, CAREFREE was released as the duo slipped out of the exhibitor's top-ten box office draws, a list that they had stood atop just two years earlier. The chief reason for this slide was RKO's constant financial difficulties, and the studio's subsequent inability to produce the kind of big-budget extravaganzas that the audience expected to see the stars in. At the end of 1938, RKO, considering Rogers its top star, launched her on a dramatic career, while Astaire, with his sort of vehicle out of the studio's financial reach, was quietly allowed to run out his contract. Songs include: "I Used To Be Color-Blind," "Since They Turned 'Loch Lomond' Into Swing," "The Yam," "The Night Is Filled With Music," and "Change Partners."

p, Pandro S. Berman; d, Mark Sandrich; w, Allan Scott, Ernest Pagano (story and adaptation by Dudley Nichols, Hagar Wilde, based on an original idea by Marian Ainslee, Guy Endore); ph, Robert de Grasse; m, Victor Baravalle; ed, William Hamilton; art d, Van Nest Polglase, Carroll Clark; set d, Darrell Silvera; cos, Edward Stevenson (Rogers' gowns by Howard Greer); spec eff, Vernon Walker; ch, Fred Astaire, Hermes Pan; m/l, Irving Berlin.

Comedy/Musical **Cas.** (PR:A MPAA:NR)

CAREFUL, SOFT SHOULDERS*½ (1942) 70m FOX bw
Virginia Bruce (Connie Mathers), James Ellison (Thomas Aldrich), Aubrey Mather (Mr. Fortune), Sheila Ryan (Agatha Mathers), Ralph Byrd (Elliot Salmon), Sigurd Tor (Milo), Charles Tannen (Joe), William B. Davidson (Mr. Aldrich), Dale Winter (Mrs. Ipswich).

Monotonous wartime espionage flick that takes place in Washington. Bruce is the daughter of a former senator, and models dresses for a living. One day she is approached by Nazi agent Mather who presents himself as an American counterespionage agent. Playboy son of a naval official Ellison is used to get plans for secret Navy business. When Bruce finally realizes that she is working for the Nazis and not the U.S. it is too late and she and Ellison are kidnapped by Mather. The couple manage to escape, bust up the spy ring, and keep the world safe for democracy.

p, Walter Morosco; d&w, Oliver H. P. Garrett; ph, Charles Clarke; m, Leigh Harline, Emil Newman; ed, Nick DeMaggio.

Spy Drama (PR:A MPAA:NR)

CARELESS AGE* (1929) 65m FN bw
Douglas Fairbanks, Jr. (Wyn), Loretta Young (Muriel), Carmel Myers (Ray), Holmes Herbert (Sir John), Kenneth Thompson (Owen), George Baxter (Le Grande), Wilfred Noy (Lord Durhugh), Doris Lloyd (Mabs), Ilka Chase (Bunty), Raymond Lawrence (Tommy).

Fairbanks plays a dippy British youth in love with a seemingly unattainable musical comedy star, Myers. Dull and uneventful, the story is padded with a few decent musical numbers including "Melody Divine" and the title tune, "Careless Age." Fairbanks handles his role well, Herbert is good as his father, but Myers is saddled with an unsympathetic character which makes it hard for the viewer to warm to her performance.

d, John G. Wray; w, Harrison Macklyn (based on the stage play "Diversion" by John Van Druten); ph, Ben Reynolds; spec eff, Alvin Knechtel.

Drama (PR:A MPAA:NR)

CARELESS LADY* (1932) 74m FOX bw
Joan Bennett (Sally Brown/Mrs. Illington), John Boles (Stephen Illington), Minna Gombell (Yvette Logan), Weldon Heyburn (Jud Carey), Nora Lane (Ardis Delafield), Raul Roulien (Luis Pareda), Fortunio Bonanova (Rodriguez), John Arledge (Hank Oldfield), Josephine Hull (Aunt Cora), Martha Mattox (Aunt Della), Maude Turner Gordon (Mrs. Cartwright), J. M. Kerrigan (Trowbridge), James Kirkwood (Judge), William Pawley (Police Captain), Richard Tucker (Capt. Gerard), James Todd (Peter Towne), Howard Phillips (Jack Merrett).

Vapid tale starring Bennett as an ugly duckling from the country who comes to New York and suddenly transforms herself into a radiant beauty through modeling high fashions. Now a looker and able to attract men, Bennett hits the city's night spots and meets rich charmer Boles in a speakeasy. The joint is busted but all the customers get out of jail. Bennett goes to Paris on a whim and calls herself Mrs. Illington for no apparent reason. Boles pursues her and soon all their friends think they have married.

Upon their return to the States, Bennett makes things worse by trying to end the confusion when she announces that she and her "husband" have broken up. The families are shocked by the news and then an even bigger scandal occurs when the couple finally confess that they were never actually married. Loose plot and hazy, contrived motivations kill whatever interest there could have been in this material.

d, Kenneth MacKenna; w, Guy Bolton (based on a story by Reita Lambert); ph, John Seitz; ed, Alex Troffey; m/l, James F. Hanley, Ralph Freed.

Romance **(PR:A   MPAA:NR)**

CARELESS YEARS, THE½** (1957) 70m UA bw
Dean Stockwell (Jerry Vernon), Natalie Trundy (Emily Meredith), John Larch (Sam Vernon), Barbara Billingsley (Helen Meredith), John Stephenson (Charles Meredith), Maureen Cassidy (Harriet), Alan Dinehart III (Bob Williams), Virginia Christine (Mathilda Vernon), Bobby Hyatt (Biff Vernon), Hugh Sanders (Uncle Harry), Claire Carleton (Aunt Martha), Lizz Slifer (Mrs. Belosi).

Stockwell and Trundy are a teenage couple who meet, fall in love, and want to marry. Their parents demand that they wait, so they decide to elope. An argument breaks out, however, and the two split. The resolution reunites them and they see the wisdom of postponing their wedding. Stockwell is good in his first starring role since his child actor days at MGM. Songs: "The Careless Years" and "Butterfingers Baby" by Joe Lubin.

p, Edward Lewis; d, Arthur Hiller; w, Lewis; ph, Sam Leavitt; m, Leith Stevens; ed, Leon Barsha; art d, McClure Capps.

Drama **(PR:A   MPAA:NR)**

CARETAKER, THE (SEE: GUEST, THE, 1964)

CARETAKERS, THE½** (1963) 97m UA bw (GB: BORDERLINES)
Robert Stack (Dr. Donovan MacLeod), Polly Bergen (Lorna Melford), Joan Crawford (Lucretia Terry), Janis Paige (Marion), Diane McBain (Alison Horne), Van Williams (Dr. Larry Denning), Constance Ford (Nurse Bracken), Sharon Hugueny (Connie), Herbert Marshall (Dr. Jubal Harrington), Ana St. Clair (Anna), Barbara Barrie (Edna), Robert Vaughn (Jim Melford), Susan Oliver (Cathy Clark), Ellen Corby (Irene).

Bergen stars as a young housewife who blames herself for the accidental death of her child and finally has a complete nervous breakdown in the middle of a movie theater while watching a newsreel. She is brought to a mental hospital where progressive doctor Stack seeks to experiment with the patient's therapy (to make it more effective and humane) but his efforts are constantly thwarted by conservative head nurse Crawford. Crawford's methods, of course, cause more harm than good and she even teaches her nurses to use karate on unruly patients. Good performances are marred somewhat by an uneven script which yields some unintentionally funny moments. Great black and white cinematography by Lucien Ballard.

p&d, Hall Bartlett; w, Henry F. Greenberg (from screen story by Bartlett and Jerry Paris, based on the book by Dariel Telfer), ph, Lucien Ballard; m, Elmer Bernstein; ed, William B. Murphy; art d, Rolland M. Brooks, Claudio Guzman; set d, Frank Tuttle.

Drama **(PR:C   MPAA:NR)**

CARETAKER'S DAUGHTER, THE* (1952, Brit.) 89m
Film Studios Manchester/Mancunian bw (GB: LOVE'S A LUXURY)
Hugh Wakefield (Charles Pentwick), Derek Bond (Robert Bentley), Michael Medwin (Dick Pentwick), Helen Shingler (Mrs. Pentwick), Zena Marshall (Fritzi Villiers), Bill Shine (Clarence Mole), Patricia Raine (Molly Harris), Grace Arnold (Mrs. Harris).

Uninspired British comedy has a troupe of actors assuming an array of identities in order to fluster their impresario's jealous wife. Strictly routine.

p, Tom Blakeley; d, Francis Searle; w, Hugh Wakefield, Elwyn Ambrose (based on a play by Guy Paxton and Edward V. Hole).

Comedy **(PR:A   MPAA:NR)**

CAREY TREATMENT, THE* (1972) 101m MGM c
James Coburn (Peter Carey), Jennifer O'Neill (Georgia Hightower), Pat Hingle (Capt. Pearson), Skye Aubrey (Angela Holder), Elizabeth Allen (Evelyn Randall), John Fink (Murphy), Dan O'Herlihy (J.D. Randall), James Hong (David Tao), Alex Dreier (Joshua Randall), Michael Blodgett (Roger Hudson), Regis Toomey (Sanderson), Steve Carlson (Walding), Rosemary Edelman (Janet Tao), Jennifer Edwards (Lydia Barrett), John Hillerman (Jenkins), Robert Mandan (Dr. Barr), Warren Parker (Blaine), Robie Porter (Harvey William Randall), Morgan Sterne (Weston), Melissa Torme-March (Karen Randall).

Essentially boring story of Coburn as a bachelor pathologist (a forerunner of "Quincy") who comes to Boston to join O'Herlihy's staff. Hong is arrested for the alleged abortion-manslaughter death of Torme-March, O'Herlihy's daughter. Coburn meanders through the film, encountering a host of dull characters led by Dreier (the former TV newsman), Hingle, Allen, and Porter. O'Neill is wasted as a girl friend to Coburn and the denouement occurs when Coburn nails the true killer . . . but we won't give that away. Everyone who wasn't related to someone used a nom de guerre on this film. Torme-March is the daughter of Mel Torme, stepdaughter of Hal March. Skye Aubrey is the daughter of Phyllis Thaxter and then-MGM chief Jim Aubrey, Jr. (one-time head of CBS and renowned as "the smiling cobra.") The listed writer doesn't exist, nor does the listed novel author (see credits). Blake Edwards publicly disowned this movie because he felt that MGM (specifically Belasco) aborted it. An oddity in the credits is that the associate producer was Barry Mendelson, owner of the famous Nate 'n' Al's delicatessen on North Beverly Drive in Beverly Hills. It is presumed that his ability with turkey had nothing to do with his part on the team.

p, William Belasco; d, Blake Edwards; w, James P. Bonner (pseudonym for Irving Ravetch, Harriet Frank Jr., John D. F. Black (based on the novel A Case Of Need by Jeffrey Hudson, pseudonym for Michael Crichton); ph, Frank Stanley (Panavision/Metrocolor); m, Roy Budd; ed, Ralph E. Winters; art d, Alfred Sweeney; set d, Raymond Molyneaux.

Mystery **(PR:C   MPAA:PG)**

CARGO TO CAPETOWN½** (1950) 80m COL bw
Broderick Crawford (Johnny Phelan), John Ireland (Steve Conway), Ellen Drew (Kitty Mellar), Edgar Buchanan (Sam Bennett), Ted de Corsia (Rhys), Robert Espinoza (Rik), Leonard Strong (Singh), King Donovan (Sparks), Gregory Gay (Kroll), Peter Mamakos (Gomez), Frank Reicher (Judge Van Meeger), Tom Stevenson (Cariday).

Average shipboard melodrama which was Crawford's first film after winning an Oscar for his performance in Robert Rossen's ALL THE KING'S MEN (1949). Plot involves Ireland, captain of a tired oil tanker, and Crawford, the ship's engineer. The pair soon find themselves at odds over their mutual affection for Drew (who happens to be Crawford's fiancée). Tension turns to violence when Ireland and Crawford get into a knock-down-drag-out fight in which the captain comes out on top. Climax sees a vicious storm which causes a shipboard fire giving Ireland the opportunity to save Crawford's life.

p, Lionel Houser; d, Earl McEvoy; w, Houser; ph, Charles Lawton; m, George Duning; ed, William Lyon; md, Morris Stoloff.

Drama **(PR:A   MPAA:NR)**

CARIBBEAN* (1952) 97m PAR c (GB: CARIBBEAN GOLD)
John Payne (Dick Lindsay), Arlene Dahl (Christine MacAllister), Sir Cedric Hardwicke (Capt. F. Barclay), Francis L. Sullivan (Andrew MacAllister), Willard Parker (Shively), Dennis Hoey (Burford), Clarence Muse (Quashy), William Pullen (Robert MacAllister), Walter Reed (Evans), Ramsey Hill (Townsend), John Hart (Stuart), Zora Donahoo (Elizabeth), Woody Strode (Esau), Ezeret Anderson (Cudjo), Kermit Pruitt (Quarino), Dan Ferniel (Caesar), Rosalind Hayes (Sally).

Overly complex pirate/revenge film starring Hardwicke as a man whose wife and daughter have been kidnapped by evil plantation owner Sullivan who then sells Hardwicke into slavery. Twenty years later, Hardwicke, now an infamous pirate, seeks revenge on Sullivan by using Payne (who bears a remarkable resemblance to the despot's nephew) to infiltrate the villain's private island and whip the native slaves into an armed uprising. Payne also finds the time to fall in love with Hardwicke's now-grown daughter Dahl (who believes she is Sullivan's daughter, her mother having died years ago). A big battle ensues enabling Hardwicke to take over the island.

p, William Pine, William Thomas; d, Edward Ludwig; w, Frank L. Moss, Ludwig (based on the novel by Ellery H. Clark); ph, Lionel Linden (Technicolor); m, Lucien Cailliet; ed, Howard Smith.

Adventure **(PR:A   MPAA:NR)**

CARIBBEAN MYSTERY, THE½** (1945) 65m FOX bw
James Dunn (Mr. Smith), Sheila Ryan (Mrs. Jean Gilbert), Edward Ryan (Gerald McCracken), Jackie Paley (Linda Lane), Reed Hadley (Rene Marcel), Roy Roberts (Capt. Van den Bark), Richard Shaw (Capt. Bowman Hall), Daral Hudson (Hartshorn), William Forrest (Col. Lane), Roy Gordon (McCracken, Sr.), Virginia Walker, Lal Chand Mehra, Katherine Connors, Robert Filmer, Lucien Littlefield.

Okay murder mystery starring Dunn as a former Brooklyn cop who now works as a special investigator for an oil company which hires him to find out what has become of a team of geologists sent to the islands in search of oil deposits. After many setbacks, including frustrating attempts to deal with the local authorities, Dunn tracks down his suspected jungle murderer, who, in cahoots with a corrupt government official, has been killing anyone who strays near the island hideout where they have been hoarding stolen treasure. A short, taut, and well-done thriller.

p, William Girard; d, Robert Webb; w, W. Scott Darling (based on the novel Murder in Trinidad by John W. Vandercook); ph, Clyde De Vinna; ed, John McCafferty.

Mystery **(PR:A   MPAA:NR)**

CARIBOO TRAIL, THE* (1950) 80m FOX c
Randolph Scott (Jim Redfern), George "Gabby" Hayes (Grizzly), Bill Williams (Mike Evans), Karin Booth (Frances), Victor Jory (Frank Walsh), Douglas Kennedy (Murphy), Jim Davis (Miller), Dale Robertson (Will Gray), Mary Stuart (Jane Winters), James Griffith (Higgins), Lee Tung Foo (Ling), Tony Hughes (Dr. Rhodes), Mary Kent (Mrs. Winters), Ray Hyke (Jones), Jerry Root (Jenkins), Cliff Clark (Assayer), Tom Monroe (Bartender), Fred Libby (Chief White Buffalo), "Kansas" Moehring (Stage Driver), Dorothy Adams (Nurse), Michael Barret (Hotel Clerk).

Competent western adventure set in the Cariboo area of British Columbia starring Scott and Williams as partners driving cattle into the territory from Montana. Their herd is stampeded by the powerful boss of the area, Jory, and his men. Williams loses his arm to the spooked cattle and Scott decides to try his luck at gold mining. Meanwhile Jory attempts to thwart his efforts by harrassing Scott with his thugs and stirring up the Indians. Eventually Scott gives up and goes back to cattle. Good color cinematography and decent action sequences. Shot in Colorado which doubles for British Columbia.

p, Nat Holt; d, Edwin L. Marin; w, Frank Gruber (story by John Rhodes Sturdy); ph, Fred Jackman, Jr. (Cinecolor); m, Paul Sawtell; ed, Phillip Martin.

Western/Adventure **(PR:A   MPAA:NR)**

CARLTON-BROWNE OF THE F.O.
(SEE: MAN IN THE COCKED HAT, 1959)

CARMELA* (1949, Ital.) 84m Lopert bw
Doris Durante (Carmela), Pal Javor (Lt. Salvini), Aldo Silvani (Dr. Cavagnetti), Egisto Olivieri (Mayor), Anna Capodaglio (Mayor's Wife), Bella Starace Sainati (Carmela's Mother), Enza Delbi (Teresita).

Overworked Italian melodrama set on a small prison island near Sicily where nothing much ever happens except the changing of the military garrison every three years. Durante stars as a fiery local girl who has fallen in love with a young soldier who leaves the island when his time is up. Durante becomes extremely distraught, and when the new guards arrive, she spots another soldier she thinks is her lover (he just resembles him) and throws herself at him. The soldier eventually realizes that she thinks he is someone else and tries to help the girl regain her sanity by pretending that he is indeed her former lover. This, of course, leads to him falling in love with her. Farfetched and silly. (Italian, English subtitles)

d, Flavio Calzavara; w, Corrado Alvaro, Calzavara, Italo Cremona (based on a story by Edmondo De Amicia); ph, Gabor Pogany; m, Franco Sacavola; English titles, Nat Hoffberg.

Drama **(PR:A MPAA:NR)**

CARMEN*½ (1931, Brit.) 79m BIP/Wardour bw (GB: GIPSY BLOOD)
Marguerite Namara (Carmen), Thomas Burke (Don Jose), Lance Fairfax (Escamillo), Lester Matthews (Zuniga), Mary Clare (Factory Girl), Dennis Wyndham (Doncairo), Lewin Mannering (Innkeeper), D. Hay Petrie (Remenado).

Bizet's classic opera of love and death in old Spain is done scant justice by this primitive British talkie. Only fans of opera will be interested, and they'll probably be disappointed.

d, Cecil Lewis; w, Lewis, Walter C. Mycroft (based on an opera by Georges Bizet, Prosper Mérimee).

Opera **(PR:A MPAA:NR)**

CARMEN**½ (1946, Ital.) 100m Superfilm bw
Viviane Romance (Carmen), Ellie Parvo (Pamela), Margarite Moreno (Dorotea), Jean Marais (Don Jose), Adriano Rimoldi (Lieutenant), Julien Bertau (Lucas Escamillo), Lucien Coedel (Garcia), Bernard Blier (Remendado), Jean Rochard (Lillas Pastia).

An Italian production, featuring French actors working surprisingly well together in this adaptation of Merimee's original novel using some of the music from Bizet's famous opera. Romance spices up the movie as the lusty gypsy has a stormy romance with dragoon Marais. Events lead to the murder of a lowly lieutenant who was the unfortunate victim of Romance's affections. He was killed by Marais, his commanding officer, in a fit of jealous rage. On the run from the murder, Marais is forced to join Romance's band of smugglers but she soon deserts him for a toreador and Marais kills her, too. Good production values and quite a number of decent supporting performances make this version of CARMEN worth a look. (French, English subtitles)

d, Christian Jaque; w, uncredited (adapted from the novel by Prosper Mérimee); ph, Ubaldo Arata; m, Georges Bizet; English titles, Herman G. Weinberg.

Opera/Drama **(PR:A MPAA:NR)**

CARMEN (1949, Span.) 102m Clasa-Mohme/Ariston bw
Imperio Argentina, Rafael Rivelles, Manuel Luna, Alberto Romea, Anselmo Fernandez, Pedro Barreto, Margit Symo, Jose Prada, Pedro F. Cuenca, Julio Roos, Carmen Morando, J. Noe Pena, Juan L. Diaz.

Lackluster adaptation of the Merimee/Bizet classic tale dealing with a Spanish officer who falls in love with a seductive gypsy dancer who ruins his life. The emphasis is on the romance (as opposed to the more sordid aspects of the tale) and many of the more adult themes have been watered down for mass consumption. The highlight of this version is a vicious fight between Carmen and a rival dancer. (Span., English subtitles)

d&w, Florian Rey (based on the novel by Prosper Mérimée); ph, Reimar Kuntze.

Opera/Drama **(PR:A MPAA:NR)**

CARMEN**½ (1983, Span.) 102m Orion c
Antonio Gades (Antonio), Laura del Sol (Carmen), Paco de Lucia (Paco), Cristina Hoyos (Cristina), Juan Antonio Jimenez (Juan), Sebastian Moreno (Escamillo), Jose Yepes (Pepe Giron), Pepa Flores (Pepa Flores).

Another version of the Merimee/Bizet drama, this time using rehearsals for the opera as the setting for a story line similar to the performance piece itself. Del Sol plays the fiery actress/dancer who is slated to play Carmen in a flamenco dance version of the opera. Gades is the choreographer who falls in love with his star. Great dance sequences that become very erotic.

p, Emiliano Piedra; d, Carlos Saura; w, Saura, Antonio Gades; ph, Teo Escamilla (Eastmancolor); m, Paco de Lucia (excerpts from Bizet's "Carmen" performed by Regina Resnik, Mario del Monaco); ed, Pedro Del Rey; set d, Felix Murcia; cos, Teresa Nieto; ch, Saura, Gades.

Opera/Drama **Cas.** **(PR:C MPAA:R)**

CARMEN, BABY* (1967, Yugo./Ger.) 90m Audubon c
Uta Levka (Carmen), Claude Ringer (Policeman), Carl Mohner (Medico), Barbara Valentine (Dolores), Walter Wiltz (Baby Lucas), Christiane Ruecker (Misty), Michael Muenzer (Magistrate), Doris Pistek (Darcy), Doris Arden, Christian Fredersdorf, Arthur Brass.

Another early sexploiter movie from the production team of Metzger and Vogel which is hung on the framework of the classic Merimee/Bizet storyline. Levka stars as a vampish waitress who ruins the lives of policeman Ringer and rock'n' roll star Wiltz. Basically an excuse for extended sensual scenes shot in an irritating, overly artsy manner.

p&d, Radley Metzger; w, Jesse Vogel (based on the novel by Prosper Merimee); ph, Hans Jura (Ultrascope/Eastmancolor); m, Daniel Hart; ed, Humphrey Wood; cos, Milena Kumar; makeup, Katschi Walzel.

Drama **(PR:O MPAA:NR)**

CARMEN JONES* (1954) 105m FOX c
Dorothy Dandridge (Carmen), Harry Belafonte (Joe), Olga James (Cindy Lou), Pearl Bailey (Frankie), Diahann Carroll (Myrt), Roy Glenn (Rum), Nick Stewart (Dink), Joe Adams (Husky), Brock Peters (Sgt. Brown), Sandy Lewis (T-Bone), Mauri Lynn

(Sally), DeForest Covan (Trainer), and the voices of LeVern Hutcherson, Marilynn Horne, Marvin Hayes.

Great music from Bizet's opera combined with new lyrics by Hammerstein II are not enough to gloss over the cardboard characterizations in this update of CARMEN starring an all-black cast. Dandridge and company struggle mightily against racist attitudes and mannerisms forced on them by Kleiner's script and Preminger's direction. Plot update sees Carmen (Dandridge) as a wartime worker in a southern parachute factory who falls in love with handsome soldier Belafonte. After he kills his sergeant in a fight, Belafonte deserts the army and runs off with Dandridge. Soon Dandridge tires of his company and dumps the soldier for prize fighter Escamillo. Belafonte snaps and strangles his love. The singing of the lead players is dubbed by Hutcherson, Horne, and Hayes.

p&d, Otto Preminger; w, Harry Kleiner (based on the book by Oscar Hammerstein II); ph, Sam Leavitt (CinemaScope/DeLuxe Color); m, Georges Bizet; ed, Louis R. Loeffler; m/l, Hammerstein; md, Herschel Burke Gilbert.

Musical **(PR:C MPAA:NR)**

CARNABY, M.D.* (1967, Brit.) 101m RANK c (GB: DOCTOR IN CLOVER)
Leslie Phillips (Dr. Gaston Grimsdyke), James Robertson Justice (Sir Lancelot Spratt), Shirley Ann Field (Nurse Bancroft), John Fraser (Dr. Miles Grimsdyke), Joan Sims (Matron Sweet), Arthur Haynes (Tarquin Wendover), Fennella Fielding (Tatiana Rubikov), Jeremy Lloyd (Lambert Symington), Noel Purcell (O'Malley), Robert Hutton (Rock Stewart), Eric Barker (Prof. Halfback), Terry Scott (Robert), Norman Vaughan (TV Commentator), Elizabeth Ercy (Jeannine), Alfie Bass (Fleming), Anne Cunningham (Women's Ward Sister), Suzan Farmer (Nurse Holiday), Harry Fowler (Grafton), Peter Gilmore (Len), Nicky Henson (Salesman), Bill Kerr (Digger), Justine Lord (New Matron), Roddy Maude-Roxby (Tristam), Lionel Murton (Publicity Man), Anthony Sharp (Dr. Loftus), Dandy Nichols (Fat Woman Patient), Ronnie Stevens (TV Producer), Robin Hunter (Sydney), Barry Justice (Beckwith).

Phillips loses his job as medical officer at a women's prison so he enrolls in a refresher course with his old medical school professor, Robertson Justice. He falls in love with physiotherapist Ercy, but she only has eyes for Lloyd. There are some complications involving a rejuvenation drug which is accidentally injected into Robertson Justice, causing him to wreak havoc at a party and try to sexually assault Matron Sims. A dreary, depressing, unfunny comedy continues the DOCTOR IN THE HOUSE series. They should have stopped before they made this one, though another, DOCTOR IN TROUBLE, followed in 1970 and is even more dreary, depressing, and unfunny. The songs "Doctor In Clover" and "Take A Look At Me" are sung by Kiki Dee.

p, Betty E. Box; d, Ralph Thomas; w, Jack Davies (based on a novel by Richard Gordon); ph, Ernest Steward (Eastmancolor); ed, Alfred Roome; md, Johnny Scott; art d, Alex Vetchinsky; m/l, Rick Jones, Scott.

Comedy **(PR:C MPAA:NR)**

CARNAL KNOWLEDGE* (1971) 97m Avco Embassy c
Jack Nicholson (Jonathan), Candice Bergen (Susan), Arthur Garfunkel (Sandy), Ann-Margret (Bobbie), Rita Moreno (Louise), Cynthia O'Neal (Cindy), Carol Kane (Jennifer).

Seldom interesting, talkative study of Nicholson and Garfunkel from their college days of discovering the joys and pitfalls of sex to their professional years, early and middle, as they go through girl friends and wives, Nicholson dumping neurotic Ann-Margret for hooker Moreno and Garfunkel winding up with flower child Kane. All of the dialogue is predictable 1960s self-examination gibberish emanating from self-indulgent, mindless creatures, none of the inspection of morals and morés of that period being more than sophomoric mutterings that are essentially boring. Nicholson's peculiar self-aggrandizing role is worth watching, if only as a study in Me-ism. Nichols' direction is lazy, often sloppy, offering no action, no character study and no interrelationship between his actors. A disjointed waste of time.

p&d, Mike Nichols (for Joseph E. Levine); w, Jules Feiffer; ph, Giuseppe Rotunno (Panavision, Technicolor); ed, Sam O'Steen; prod d, Richard Sylbert; art d, Robert Luthardt; set d, George R. Nelson; cos, Anthea Sylbert.

Drama **Cas.** **(PR:O MPAA:R)**

CARNATION KID (1929) 76m PAR bw
Douglas MacLean (Clarence Kendall), Frances Lee (Doris Whitely), William B. Davidson (Blythe), Lorraine Eddy (Lucille), Charles Hill Mailes (Crawford Whitely), Francis McDonald (Carnation Kid), Maurice Black (Tony), Bert Swor, Jr. (Blinkey), Carl Stockdale (Deacon).

When the town of Chatham is about to elect an honest district attorney who has pledged to rid the city of vermin like vice king Davidson, the crime kingpin hires out to Chicago for the hitman known only as the "Carnation Kid," a nickname stemming from the white carnation always in his lapel. On the train to Chatham the kid is recognized and a chase ensues on board. The kid corners an unassuming bumpkin, MacLean, and forces him to switch clothes, making good his escape. Unaware of the identity of the man whose clothes he's wearing, MacLean, a typewriter representative, goes about his business in Chatham and spends the rest of the movie being mistaken for the killer by the law and rival crooks alike. Eventually the honest D.A. is elected and he fulfills his campaign promise by ridding the city of evil Davidson, but not before MacLean falls for the D.A.'s daughter, Lee. This comedy begins well enough but the humor begins to fall apart when the viewer is expected to accept the absurd notion that all the cops and crooks are willing to go after a man who bears absolutely no physical resemblance to the man they are out to get, except for a white carnation in his lapel.

p, Al Christie; d, E. Mason Hopper, A. Leslie Pierce; w, Henry McCarty, Arthur Huffsmith (based on a story by Alfred A. Cohn); ph, Alex Phillips, Monte Steadman; ed, Grace Dazey.

Crime/Comedy **(PR:A MPAA:NR)**

CARNEGIE HALL½** (1947) 136m UA bw
Marsha Hunt *(Nora Ryan)*, William Prince *(Tony Salerno, Jr.)* Frank McHugh *(John Donovan)*, Martha O'Driscoll *(Ruth Haines)*, Hans Yaray *(Tony Salerno, Sr.)*, Joseph Buloff *(Anton Tribik)*, Olin Downes *(Himself)*, Emile Boreo *(Henry)*, Alfonso D'Artega *(Tschaikowsky)*, Harold Dyrenforth *(Walter Damrosch)*, Eola Galli *(Katinka)*, Guest Artists: Walter Damrosch, New York Philharmonic Quintette, Bruno Walter, Philharmonic Symphony Orchestra of New York, Lily Pons, Gregor Piatigorsky, Risë Stevens, Artur Rodzinski, Artur Rubinstein, Jan Peerce, Ezio Pinza, Vaughn Monroe Orchestra, Jascha Heifetz, Fritz Reiner, Leopold Stokowski, Harry James.

An outstanding array of musical talent pulls this dim drama out of the doldrums and makes it an entertaining outing. Incidental plot concerns an Irish girl who grows up and works at the title auditorium, eventually living to see her son make his professional debut on its famed stage. Meantime, a wide variety of musical talents and styles cross the boards for the viewers' listening pleasure. Standout performances come mostly from the classical musicians and conductors who include Ezio Pinza, singing an aria from "Simon Di Boccanegra" and the drinking song from "Don Giovanni;" Artur Rubinstein playing "Polonaise in A Flat" and "Ritual Fire Dance;" Jascha Heifetz, "Concerto for Violin and Orchestra in G Major;" Lily Pons singing "Bell Song;" and Jan Peerce singing "O Sole Mio." Also in the mix are conductors Fritz Reiner, Bruno Walter, Artur Rodzinski, Walter Damrosch, and Leopold Stokowski. The only weak spots musically come from an unnecessary capitulation to modern (at the time) popular tastes with performances by Vaughn Monroe and Harry James. Directed by low-budget cult director Edgar G. Ulmer.

p, Boris Morros, William LeBaron; d, Edgar G. Ulmer; w, Karl Kamb (based on a story by Seena Owen); ph, William Miller; ed, Fred R. Feitshans, Jr.; musical advisor, Sigmund Krumgold; orchestration, Russell Bennett; m/l, Sam Coslow, M. and W. Portnoff, Gregory Stone, Frank Ryerson, Wilton Moore, Hal Borne.
Musical (PR:A MPAA:NR)

CARNIVAL*½ (1931, Brit.) 83m GAU bw/c (AKA: VENETIAN NIGHTS)
Matheson Lang *(Silvio Steno)*, Joseph Schildkraut *(Count Andreas Scipio)*, Dorothy Bouchier *(Simonetta Steno)*, Lilian Braithwaite *(Italia)*, Kay Hammond *(Helen)*, Brian Buchel *(Lelio)*, Dickie Edwards *(Nino)*, Brember Wills *(Stage Manager)*, Alfred Rode and his Tzigane Band.

Contrived love triangle melodrama concerning a famed actor and his wife whom he suspects of being unfaithful. Action takes place during a Venetian carnival and the climax sees the actor going mad and almost strangling his wife on stage while playing the closing act of "Othello." After the curtain falls, the actor regains his senses and apologizes to his wife when she insists she did him no wrong. The couple is reconciled and the whole silly thing comes to a close. Unusual use of color during a fireworks sequence at the carnival distracts more than it enhances the film.

p&d, Herbert Wilcox; w, Donald Macardle (based on a play by Matheson Lang, C. M. Hardinge); ph, F. A. Young, Jack Parker.
Drama (PR:A MPAA:NR)

CARNIVAL** (1935) 77m COL bw
Lee Tracy *(Chick Thompson)*, Sally Eilers *(Daisy)*, Jimmy Durante *(Fingers)*, Dickie Walters *(Poochy)*, Thomas Jackson *(Mac)*, Florence Rice *(Miss Holbrook)*, Fred Kelsey *(Detective)*, Lucille Ball *(Nurse)*.

Sappy comedy/melodrama starring Tracy as a puppeteer at a carnival whose wife dies while giving birth to their daughter. Tracy's father-in-law, who disowned his daughter after her marriage to the carny puppet master, sues for custody of the infant, claiming that a carnival is no place for a single man to raise a child. Tracy steals the kid, says goodbye to his female assistant, Eilers, and disappears. Two years later, thinking the coast is clear, he returns to the carnival and Eilers, who introduces him to new-found friend Durante. The homecoming is short-lived, due to the persistence of the child's grandfather who still seeks custody. Tracy, on advice from his lawyer, searches for a woman to marry, which would increase his chances of winning his case. He ignores Ellers, who finally gets fed up with his blindness to her and takes off. Tracy and Durante enter the toddler in a baby contest and then are arrested for trying to fix the results. Ellers returns to care for the child and Tracy realizes that she would make a good mom. He asks her to wait for him until he gets out of a six-month sentence for the contest incident. Maudlin story is helped by the comedy provided by Durante. Look sharp in the hospital scene for Lucille Ball in her first credited film role.

d, Walter Lang, w, Robert Riskin; ph, Al Siegler; ed, Richard H. Cahoon.
Drama/Comedy (PR:A MPAA:NR)

CARNIVAL* (1946, Brit.) 93m GFD bw
Sally Gray *(Jenny)*, Michael Wilding *(Maurice Avery)*, Stanley Holloway *(Charlie Raeburn)*, Bernard Miles *(Trewhella)*,Jean Kent *(Irene Dale)*, Catherine Lacey *(Florrie Raeburn)*, Nancy Price *(Mrs. Trewhella)*, Hazel Court *(May Raeburn)*, Michael Clarke *(Fuzz)*, Brenda Bruce *(Maudie Chapman)*, Anthony Holles *(Coretin)*, Ronald Ward *(Jack Danby)*, Mackenzie Ward *(Arthur Danby)*, Bruce Winston *(Mr. Dutt)*, Dennis Arundell *(Studholme)*, Phyllis Monkman *(Barmaid)*, Amy Veness *(Aunt Fanny)*, Marie Ault *(Mrs. Dale)*, Virginia Kelley *(Elsie Crawford)*, Pamela Foster *(Madge Wilson)*, Aspinosa *(Vergo)*, Bebe De Roland *(Ballerina)*, Carpenter Corps de Ballet.

Grim melodrama set in the 1900s starring Gray as a young London ballerina who leaves her mother and sets out on her own. She meets a sculptor, Wilding, becomes his model, and they fall in love. Despite his protestations she refuses to marry or live with him and he soon becomes bitter and leaves her. Suddenly saddled with having to care for her crippled sister, Gray accepts the marriage proposal of a puritanical Cornish farmer. Her life is made a living hell by the close-minded sod-buster and she refuses to consummate the marriage. One day the sculptor shows up in Cornwall and when the jealous husband spots the two chatting on the beach, he kills his wife, ending her misery and the movie. Overblown script and lousy casting bring this drama precariously close to unintentional comedy. Peter Ustinov had a hand in scripting this sorry mess during his early film days.

p, John Sutro, William Sassoon; d, Stanley Haynes; w, Eric Maschwitz, Haynes, Peter Ustinov, Guy Green (based on a story by Compton Mackenzie); ph, Green; ch, Freddie Carpenter.
Drama (PR:A MPAA:NR)

CARNIVAL½** (1953, Fr.) 100m GAU bw
Fernandel *(Dardamelle)*, Jacqueline Pagnol *(Francine)*, Pauline Carton *(Maid)*, Renee Passeur *(Aunt)*, Arius *(Mayor)*.

Fernandel is in fine form as an architect who learns his wife is cheating on him. He puts a large sign to that effect in front of his house and organizes a syndicate of cuckolded husbands who win first prize for their float in the carnival parade. Finally his wife returns to him and the film ends with a somber speech by Fernandel on what would have happened had he lost her. Essentially a one-joke film, Fernandel squeezes every laugh out of it.

p, Marcel Pagnol; d, Henri Verneuil; w, Pagnol (based on a play by Emile Mazaud); ph, Andre Germain; ed, R. Bianchi.
Comedy (PR:A MPAA:NR)

CARNIVAL BOAT*½ (1932) 61m RKO-Pathe bw
Bill Boyd *(Buck Gannon)*, Ginger Rogers *(Honey)*, Fred Kohler *(Hack)*, Hobart Bosworth *(Jim Gannon)*, Marie Prevost *(Babe)*, Edgar Kennedy *(Baldy)*, Harry Sweet *(Stubby)*, Charles Sellon *(Lane)*, Walter Percival *(De Lacey)*, Jack Carlyle *(Assistant to De Lacey)*, Joe Marba *(Windy)*, Eddie Chandler *(Jordan)*, Bob Perry *(Bartender)*, James Mason, Charles Sullivan *(Loggers)*, Hal Price *(Observer)*, Sam Harris.

Tedious lumber camp drama starring Boyd as a hard-working logger whose head is turned by showgirl Rogers who arrives on the title vessel. His love for the girl causes a falling out between him and his father, Bosworth, who wanted to see his son take over the family logging business. Much footage is devoted to falling trees and buzzing saws and the climactic action sequences see Boyd nearly single-handedly free a log jam, stop a runaway train, and defeat the villain, Kohler. The James Mason in the cast is not the English actor, who did not receive his first screen credit until 1938 in RETURN OF THE SCARLET PIMPERNEL.

d, Albert Rogell; w, James Seymour (based on a story by Marion Jackson, Don Ryan); ph, Ted McCord; ed, John Link; md, Arthur Lange; art d, Carroll Clark; cos, Gwen Wakeling; m/l, Bernie Grossman, Howard Lewis, Max Steiner.
Drama (PR:A MPAA:NR)

CARNIVAL IN COSTA RICA** (1947) 96m FOX c
Dick Haymes *(Jeff Stephens)*, Vera-Ellen *(Luisa Molina)*, Cesar Romero *(Pepe Castro)*, Celeste Holm *(Celeste)*, Anne Revere *(Elsa Molina)*, J. Carrol Naish *(Rico Molina)*, Pedro de Cordoba *(Mr. Castro)*, Barbara Whiting *(Maria)*, Nestor Paiva *(Father Rafael)*, Fritz Feld *(Clerk)*, Tommy Ivo *(Johnny Molina)*, Mimi Aguglia *(Mrs. Castro)*, Lecuona Cuban Boys *(Themselves)*, Anna Demetrio *(Concha)*, Severo Lopez *(Bell Boy)*, William Edmunds *(Waiter)*, Soledad Jiminez *(Maid)*, Alfredo Sabato *(Bartender)*, Martin Garralaga *(Cab Driver)*.

Typical musical plot concerns two Latin youngsters, Romero and Vera-Ellen, whose marriage to each other has been prearranged by their parents. The kids don't love each other and each has a different mate in mind. Romero falls for nightclub singer Holm, and Vera-Ellen goes after coffee buyer Haymes. Comedy relief is provided by the youngsters' fathers, Naish and Cordoba. The excellent Technicolor photography is put to good use during a lively fiesta sequence wherein Holm sings "Qui Pi Pia" (Al Stillman, Sunny Skylar). Other songs: "I'll Know It's Love," "Another Night Like This," "Mi Vida, Costa Rica," "Rhumba Bomba," "Maracas" (Harry Ruby, Ernesto Lecuona).

p, William A. Bacher; d, Gregory Ratoff; w, John Larkin, Samuel Hoffenstein, Elizabeth Reinhardt; ph, Harry Jackson (Technicolor); m, Ernesto Lecuona; ed, William Reynolds; m/l, Harry Ruby, Sunny Skylar, Albert Stillman; ch, Leonide Massine.
Musical (PR:A MPAA:NR)

CARNIVAL IN FLANDERS***
(1936, Fr.) 95m American Tobis bw (LA KERMESSE HEROIQUE)
Francoise Rosay *(Madame Burgomaster)*, Jean Murat *(The Duke)*, Andre Alerme *(Burgomaster)*, Louis Jouvet *(The Priest)*, Lynne Clevers *(The Fishwife)*, Micheline Cheirel *(Siska)*, Maryse Wendling *(The Baker's Wife)*, Ginette Gaubert *(The Innkeeper's Wife)*, Marguerite Ducouret *(The Brewer's Wife)*, Bernard Lancret *(Julien Breughel)*, Alfred Adam *(The Butcher)*, Pierre Labry *(The Innkeeper)*, Arthur Devere *(The Fishmonger)*, Marcel Carpentier *(The Baker)*, Alexander D'Arcy *(The Captain)*, Claude Sainval *(2nd Spanish Lieutenant)*, Delphin *(The Dwarf)*.

Well-done French comedy detailing the occupation of a small Flanders village by Spanish troops. Fearing the brutal treatment received by other towns at the hands of the Spanish, the citizens decide to "play dead." The funniest moments involve the town's burgomaster, who fakes his death, including lying in state at his wake. The burgomaster's wife prepares the village to welcome the invaders and they throw such a good carnival that the town is rewarded by a cancellation of its taxes for one year. Pleasant farce that took the Grand Prix Du Cinema Francais and the gold medal at the Venice International Exposition of Cinematography. (French, English subtitles)

d, Jacques Feyder; w, Bernard Zimmer (based on a story by Charles Spaak); ph, Harry Stradling; m, Louis Beydts; ed, Jacques Brillouin; set d, Lazare Mearson; cos, G. K. Benda.
Drama (PR:A MPAA:NR)

CARNIVAL LADY* (1933) 67m Goldsmith/Hollywood bw
Boots Mallory, Allen Vincent, Jason Robards, Donald Kerr, Rollo Lloyd, Gertrude Astor, Anita Faye, Rich Hayes, Earl McDonald, Kit Guard.

Stupid melodrama concerning rich society boy Vincent who is stood up at the altar when his would-be bride hears that he has lost his fortune in the stock market crash. Broke, Vincent hits the road and hooks up with a carnival where he is befriended by a boxer and pickpocket. The former rich kid lands a job as a high diver after the carnival's current splasher botches a dive. The deposed diver returns to have it out with his replacement, but is accidentally killed when he hits his head on a tree stump during a scuffle. The pickpocket and the boxer attempt to cover up the death and the climax sees Vincent impersonating the dead man by performing his diving act with a black hood over his head.

d, Howard Higgin; w, Harold E. Tarshis (adapted by Wellyn Totman); ph, Edward Kull.

Drama (PR:A MPAA:NR)

CARNIVAL OF BLOOD zero (1976) 87m Kirk/Monarch c
Earle Edgerton, Judith Resnick, Burt Young.

Unwatchable horror/suspense film about a bunch of women getting killed at Coney Island. Lots of dialogue scenes with people sitting on couches yakking away and saying nothing worth listening to. The film was shot in 1971 and not released until 1976. This was character actor Burt Young's first movie. Really dull.

p,d&w, Leonard Kirman.

Horror/Suspense Cas. (PR:C MPAA:PG)

CARNIVAL OF SINNERS* (1947, Fr.) 83m Distinguished Films bw
Pierre Fresnay (Roland), Josseline Gael (Irene), Palau (Small Man), Noel Roquevert (Melisse), Guillaume de Sax (Gibelin), Andre Varennes (Colonel), Antoine Balpetre (Denis), Rexiane (Mme. Denis), Robert Vattier (Perrier), Chamarat (Duval), Jean Coquelin (Le Moine), Jean Davy (Rifleman), Douking (Surgeon), Rene Blancard (Juggler), Garzoni (Painter), Marcel (Boxer), Jean Despeaux (Angel), Pierre Larquey (Diner).

Creepy French film similar to THE DEVIL AND DANIEL WEBSTER (1941) stars Fresnay as a struggling artist who sells his soul to the devil by buying a severed hand that once belonged to a medieval monk. The hand has the power to grant its owner whatever he desires and soon the artist has everything he ever wanted. Fresnay begins to realize his fate when Satan shows up to look over his new merchandise and the artist decides to end his obligation by returning the hand to the grave of its original owner. The artist dies in the process,but saves his soul. Very effective direction by Tourneur, who tells a well-paced, visually interesting and symbolic tale with some genuinely scary sequences. (French, English subtitles)

p&d, Maurice Tourneur; w, Jean-Paul Le Chanois; m, Roger Dumas; English titles, Charles Clement.

Horror (PR:A MPAA:NR)

CARNIVAL OF SOULS* (1962) 80m Herts-Lion bw
Candace Hilligoss (Mary Henry), Herk Harvey (The Man), Frances Feist (Landlady), Sidney Berger (John Linden), Stan Levitt (Doctor), Art Ellison (Minister), Tom McGinnis, Dan Palmquist, Steve Boozer, Pamela Ballard, Larry Sneegas, Cari Conboy, Karen Pyles, Forbes Caldwell, Bill De Jarnette, T. C. Adams, Sharon Scoville, Mary Ann Harris, Peter Schnitzler, Bill Sollner.

Very creepy French film independently produced in Lawrence, Kansas, for less than $100,000. Story opens as Hilligoss and two of her girl friends accidentally drive off a bridge and meet a watery grave in the river below. Hilligoss somehow emerges from the water and drifts into a church where she becomes the new organist. She rents a room from landlady Feist and her fellow boarder across the hall, Berger, tries unsuccessfully to make advances toward the strange woman. Hilligoss finds herself inexplicably drawn to a battered old pavilion in town where she is haunted by the town's dead who can be seen dancing. Eventually the car accident is discovered and when the authorities pull the car out of the river, they find the bodies of all three women, making Hilligoss one of the dead all along. Very atmospheric, with great chilling moments. Director Harvey plays the leader of the dead.

p&d, Herk Harvey; w, John Clifford; ph,Maurice Prather; m, Gene Moore; ed, Dan Palmquist, Bill DeJarnette.

Horror (PR:C MPAA:NR)

CARNIVAL QUEEN*½ (1937) 66m UNIV bw
Robert Wilcox (Art Calhoun), Dorothea Kent (Marion Prescott), Hobart Cavanaugh (Professor Silva), G. Pat Collins (Bert MacGregor), Harry Tyler ("Fingers"), Ernest Cossart (Spaulding), Davis Oliver (Chuck), Billy Wayne (Hanlin), Jonathan Hale (Robert Jacoby), Raymond Brown (Police Chief), Robert Homans (Capt. Charters).

Below-average carny tale starring Kent who inherits the estate of her father, which includes a controlling interest in a floundering carnival. This investment fascinates Kent and she packs up and joins the carnival incognito to see whether there is any way to save it financially. There, she falls into a series of comic adventures, including becoming the assistant of magician Cavanaugh. Dull and uninspired.

p, Robert Presnell; d, Nate Watt; w, James Mulhauser, Harold Buckley (based on a story by Richard Wormser); ph, George Robinson; ed, Maurice Wright.

Drama (PR:A MPAA:NR)

CARNIVAL ROCK (1957) 75m Howco bw
Susan Cabot (Natalie), Brian Hutton (Stanley), David J. Stewart (Christy), Dick Miller (Ben), Iris Adrian (Celia), Jonathan Haze (Max), Ed Nelson (Cannon), Chris Alcaide (Slug), Horace Logan (M. C.) Yvonne Peattie (Mother), Gary Hunley (Boy), Frankie Ray (Billy), Dorothy Neuman (Clara), Clara Andressa (Cleaning Lady No. 1), Terry Blake (Cleaning Lady No. 2), with the music of The Platters, David Houston, Bob Luman, The Shadows, The Blockbusters.

Nightclub owner Stewart loves singer Cabot, who loves gambler Hutton. Hutton wins Stewart's club cutting cards, but Stewart stays on as a clown between rock acts just to be near Cabot. Finale has Hutton and Cabot married and Stewart fired. Only real reason to watch is The Platters.

p, Roger Corman; d, Corman; w, Leo Lieberman; ph, Floyd Crosby; m, Walter Greene, Buck Ram; ed, Charles Gross, Jr.; set d, Robert Kinoshita.

Musical (PR:A MPAA:NR)

CARNIVAL STORY½** (1954) 94m RKO c
Anne Baxter (Willie), Steve Cochran (Joe), Lyle Bettger (Frank), George Nader (Vines), Jay C. Flippen (Charley), Helene Stanley (Peggy), Adi Berber (Groppo).

Baxter is a circus high diver having an affair with seedy advance man Cochran who enacts his bestial role with relish. She leaves him and marries fellow diver Bettger, who soon dies in an accident arranged by Cochran. He seduces her again in order to steal her husband's savings. She falls in love with Nader but soon Cochran turns up again. This time, however, Baxter knows better and he is sent away to die at the hands of halfwitted strong man Berber who has had a crush on Baxter all along. This loose take-off on the silent classic VARIETY is nicely shot on location in Munich. A German version, entitled CARNIVAL OF LOVE, was shot and used a different cast—Eva Bartok, Curt Jurgens, and Bernhard Wicki.

p, Maurice and Frank King; d, Kurt Neumann; w, Hans Jacoby, Neumann (from a story by Marcel Klauber and C. B. Williams); ph, Ernest Haller (Technicolor); m, Willi Schmidt-Gentner; ed, Merrill White, Ludolf Griesbach.

Drama Cas. (PR:A MPAA:NR)

CARNY* (1980) 105m UA c
Gary Busey (Frankie), Jodie Foster (Donna), Robbie Robertson (Patch), Meg Foster (Gerta), Kenneth McMillan (Heavy), Elisha Cook (On-Your-Mark), Theodore Wilson (Nails), John Lehne (Skeet), Tina Andrews (Sugaree), Bert Remsen (Delno), Alan Braunstein (Willie Mae), Bill McKinney (Dill), Woodrow Parfrey (W. C. Hannon), Craig Wasson (Mickey), Tim Thomerson, Jordan Cael, John "Doc" Cassidy, Margaret Jo Lee, William Bartman, Terry Beaver, Jerry Rushing, Dani Dembrosky, Robert Doqui, George Emerson, Bob Hannah, Cathi Harrer, Anita Haynes, Nancy Hazeltine, Robert Kent, Mark Howard Kitchens, Jr., Charles Christian Levy, Sr., Virginia Logan, Jerry Lyles, Randy Patrick, Noelle Massina, Nomi Mitty, Sirl Nyhand, Greg Oliver, Tony C. Petrea, Jeannie Rapp, Mary Siceloff, Albert Smith, Trisha Tiedemann, Janet Thomas, Fred Ward, Janet Wieringa, E. Devan Young, Emmett Bejano, Percilla Bejano, Elaina Doucet, Jimmy Rapp, Johann Peterson, Pete Terhune.

A haunting, moody trip through the world of a carnival trying to hang on in "Disneyland" America. Busey is the carny "Bozo" who sits above the water tank and taunts customers to buy a chance to dunk him by hitting the target with a baseball. His character is filled with rage, a rage that would land him in jail if he weren't allowed to vent his spleen on the public on a daily basis from behind the protection of a cage. Robertson is the carny's peacemaker, the man who handles all disputes. He pays off lawmen and local politicians and settles all tensions between the carnival's acts and employees. Busey and Robertson are pals on the midway. Teenage girl Foster enters the carnival accompanied by her boy friend. She is seduced by the colors and life style of the midway and has run away to join the show. She takes up with Busey at first, then ends up sleeping with Robertson, causing tension between the two. Ultimately, she is independent of both. She belongs to the nomadic, noisy, colorful, and seedy world of the carnival. Begun as a documentary project by nonfiction filmmaker Robert Kaylor (DERBY [1971] about life in the roller derby) who went to different carnivals around the country taping interviews with the acts and employees, he opted for a feature based on some of the characters he met. With financial help from Robertson (one of the driving forces behind the rock music group The Band, whose last concert was beautifully documented by Martin Scorsese in THE LAST WALTZ [1978]), Kaylor was able to make his movie. The result is a creepy, atmospheric little film that uses a great cast to its best advantage. Worth seeing.

p, Robbie Robertson; d, Robert Kaylor; w, Thomas Baum (based on a story by Phoebe Taylor, Kaylor, Robertson); ph, Harry Stradling, Jr. (Technicolor); m, Alex North; ed, Stuart Pappe; art d, Josan F. Russo; set d, Ray Molyneaux, Charles R. Pierce.

Drama Cas. (PR:O MPAA:R)

CAROLINA*½ (1934) 83m FOX bw (GB: HOUSE OF CONNELLY)
Janet Gaynor (Joanna), Lionel Barrymore (Bob Connelly), Robert Young (Will Connelly), Richard Cromwell (Allen), Henrietta Crosman (Mrs. Connelly), Mona Barrie (Virginia), Stepin Fetchit (Scipio), Russell Simpson (Richards), Ronnie Cosbey (Harry), Jackie Cosbey (Jackie), Almeda Fowler (Geraldine), Alden Chase (Jack Hampton), Roy Watson (Jefferson Davis), John Elliott (Gen. Robert E. Lee), John Webb Dillon (Gen. "Stonewall" Jackson), J. C. Fowler (Gen. Leonidas Polk), Andre Cheron (Gen. Beauregard), James Ellison (Dancer), Clinton Rosemund (Black Singer), Shirley Temple (Girl).

Melodrama featuring Gaynor as the daughter of a Pennsylvania farmer who dies while farming in the South on land owned by an anachronistic Dixie family led by Civil War vet Barrymore. Gaynor goes to the plantation to tie up her father's affairs and falls in love with Young, the heir to the fortune. The film becomes mired in scenes depicting the fading South and the efforts of frustrated, alcoholic Barrymore to cling to his past. The end of the film leaps ahead a few years and shows the result of the marriage of North and South (Gaynor and Young), which brings the plantation back to its former glory.

d, Henry King; w, Reginald Berkeley (based on the play "House of Connelly" by Paul Green); ph, Hal Mohr; ed, Robert Bassler.

Drama (PR:A MPAA:NR)

CAROLINA BLUES (1944) 81m COL bw
Kay Kyser (Himself), Ann Miller (Julie Carver), Victor Moore (Phineas J. Carver/Elliot Carver/Hiram Carver/Horatio Carver/Aunt Martha Carver/Aunt Minerva Carver), Jeff Donnell (Charlotte Barton), Howard Freeman (Tom Gordon), Georgia Carroll (Herself), M A. Bogue (Ish Kabibble), Harry Babbitt (Himself), Sully Mason (Himself), Diane Pendleton (Diana), Robert Williams (Roland Frisby), Doodles Weaver (Skinny), Dorothea Kent (Maisie), Frank Orth (Cab Driver), Eddie Acuff (Eddie), Harold Nicholas, The Cristianis, The Layson Brothers, The Four Step Brothers, Kay Kyser's Band.

Average wartime Kay Kyser musical sees the band leader returning from a lengthy USO tour and stopping off at a stateside war plant for a quick show. Enter Moore, a poor relation of the plant's owner, who persuades Kyser to hire his daughter, Miller, to replace his vocalist who has quit the show for matrimony. Kyser falls for Miller while playing a series of musical numbers which include "Thinkin' About the Wabash," "There Goes That Song Again," and the satirical "Mr. Beebe." Moore provides the comedy relief by playing all the roles in a scene involving his wealthy relatives, male and female, through trick photography. Decent little outing.

p, Samuel Bischoff; d, Leigh Jason; w, Joseph Hoffman, Al Martin (based on a story by M. M. Musselman, Kenneth Earl); ph, George Kelley; ed, James Sweeney; md, M. W. Stoloff; m/l, Jule Styne, Sammy Cahn, Dudley Brooks, Walter Bullock; George Duning.

Musical **(PR:A MPAA:NR)**

CAROLINA CANNONBALL* (1955) 73m REP bw
Judy Canova *(Judy)*, Andy Clyde *(Grandpa Canova)*, Ross Elliott *(Don Mack)*, Sig Ruman *(Stefan)*, Leon Askin *(Otto)*, Jack Kruschen *(Hogar)*, Frank Wilcox *(Professor)*.

Inane rural Canova comedy sees Judy and her grandpa Clyde as the only residents of the ghost town known as Roaring Gulch. The pair own and operate a small, steam-powered trolley that runs through the town and connects with the mainline railroad. One day a U.S. guided missile crashes in the area and it is soon followed by incompetent foreign agents Ruman (who played far too many lame roles like this), Askin, and Kruschen, who are out to steal atomic secrets. For fans of dim-witted comedy only.

p, Herbert J. Yates; d, Charles Lamont; w, Barry Shipman (based on a story by Frank Gill, Jr.); ph, Reggie Lanning; m, R. Dale Butts; art d, Frank Hotaling; ed, Tony Martinelli; spec eff, Howard and Theodore Lydecker; m/l, Donald Kahn, Jack Elliot.

Comedy **(PR:A MPAA:NR)**

CAROLINA MOON* (1940) 65m REP bw
Gene Autry *(Gene)*, Smiley Burnette *(Frog)*, June Storey *(Caroline)*, Mary Lee *(Patsy)*, Eddy Waller *(Stanhope)*, Hardie Albright *(Wheeler)*, Frank Dale *(Col. Jefferson)*, Terry Nibert *(Evangeline)*, Robert Fiske *(Barrett)*, Etta McDaniel *(Mammy)*, Paul White *(Billy)*, Fred Ritter *(Thompson)*, Ralph Sanford *(Foreman)*, Jimmie Lewis and his Texas Cowboys.

Routine Autry oater which sees the singing cowboy and his sidekick Burnette in Carolina territory battling nasty con man Albright, who has bilked the old-time plantation owners out of their land. Autry uses his usual fist-fighting, gun-toting skills to vanquish the evildoer and turn over the land to its rightful owner. Seemingly the millionth variation on a wobbly plot line.

p, William Berke; d, Frank McDonald; w, Winston Miller (based on a story by Connie Lee); ph, William Nobles; ed, Tony Martinelli; md, Raoul Kraushaar.

Western **(PR:A MPAA:NR)**

CAROLINE CHERIE½** (1951, Fr.) 135m Cinephonic/GAU bw
Martine Carol *(Caroline)*, Jacques Dacqmine *(Gaston)*, Marie Dea *(Countess)*, Souplex *(Beltemps)*, Pierre Cressoy *(Malenger)*, Yvonne De Bray *(Duchess)*, Jacques Varenne *(Duke)*.

The French Revolution is the backdrop for this romantic costumer. The stunning Martine Carol is in love with a young count but the revolution keeps them apart. After a string of affairs they are reunited.

d, Richard Pottier; w, Jean Anouilh (based on the novel by Cecil St. Laurent); ph, Maurice Barry; m, Georges Auric; ed, Jean Feyte.

Drama **(PR:A MPAA:NR)**

CAROLINE CHERIE** (1968, Fr.) 100m Cineurop/Nordeutsche/Mancori c
France Anglade *(Caroline Cherie)*, Vittorio De Sica *(Father)*, Bernard Blier *(Husband)*, Charles Aznavour *(Coachman)*, Gert Frobe *(Duke)*, Isa Miranda *(Duchess)*, Jean-Claude Brialy *(Count)*, Francoise Christophe *(Madame)*.

Remake of the 1951 film that made Martine Carol a star, this one is more explicit about it's heroine's amorous adventures. This time Anglade is in the title role, sporting low-cut dresses while trying to get to her true love, an officer in Napoleon's army. Along the way she is married off by her father (De Sica) to a lawyer who immediately goes into hiding to avoid the guillotine. Anglade is seduced and raped numerous times until true love triumphs and she is reunited with Brialy.

d, Denys De La Patelliere; w, Cecil Saint-Laurent; ph, Sacha Vierny (Eastmancolor), ed, Claude Durand.

Drama **(PR:C MPAA:NR)**

CAROUSEL**** (1956) 128m FOX c
Gordon MacRae *(Billy)*, Shirley Jones *(Julie)*, Cameron Mitchell *(Jigger)*, Barbara Ruick *(Carrie)*, Claramae Turner *(Cousin Nettie)*, Robert Rounseville *(Mr. Snow)*, Gene Lockhart *(Starkeeper)*, Audrey Christie *(Mrs. Mullin)*, Susan Luckey *(Louise)*, William Le Massena *(Heavenly Friend)*, John Dehner *(Mr. Bascombs)*, Jacques D'Amboise *(Louise's Dancing Partner)*, Frank Tweddell *(Captain Watson)*, Richard Deacon *(Policeman)*, Dee Pollock *(Enoch Snow, Jr.)*, Sylvia Stanton, Mary Orozco, Tor Johnson, Harry "Duke" Johnson, Marion Dempsey, Ed Mundy, Angelo Rossitto.

The musical remake of LILIOM (directed by Fritz Lang in 1935) is one of the most tuneful and haunting musicals any viewer is lucky enough to see. This wonderful and touching fantasy begins with MacRae as a spirit in Heaven who begs the starkeeper for a once-in-an-eternity visit back to earth to help his teenage daughter understand his death and prepare her for high school graduation. Told in flashback from on-high to earth, it is the story of carnival barker MacRae, a brash and boisterous young man living in a New England fishing village changed from Ferenc Molnar's original Budapest setting). He meets and falls in love with a cotton mill worker, Jones, and, after some tempestuous moments, they marry. But MacRae's inability to find a job leads him to the bad company of Mitchell and an attempted robbery in which MacRae is killed by Mitchell after having second thoughts and trying to stop the thief. He is granted leave to return to earth where he sets things right with his daughter before his restless spirit again fades to the Great Beyond. The poignant fantasy features some of the greatest musical numbers ever filmed, all Rodgers and Hammerstein classics: "If I Loved You," sung by MacRae and Jones, "What's The Use Of Wondrin'," sung by Jones, and the stirring "You'll Never Walk Alone," by Jones and Turner. Other memorable numbers include "When I Marry Mister Snow," "When The Children Are Asleep," "A Real Nice Clambake," which provides a wonderful production number and brilliant choreography, and the dance numbers "Carousel Ballet" and "Carousel Waltz." MacRae's "Soliloquy" is spellbinding. Jones is superb as the trusting lover and MacRae radiates in his best musical performance where his fine tenor voice is given a range equalled in OKLAHOMA! Mitchell and other supporting players are excellent in this richly mounted extravaganza that is superb on all technical points and directed with verve and affection by King. Though this film is now a classic musical it was too offbeat for theater audiences when first released and it lost more than $2 million.

p, Henry Ephron; d, Henry King; w, Phoebe and Henry Ephron (based on the musical play by Richard Rodgers and Oscar Hammerstein II, as adapted by Benjamin F. Glazer from *Liliom* by Ferenc Molnar); ph, Charles G. Clarke (CinemaScope, DeLuxe Color); m/l, Richard Rodgers, Oscar Hammerstein II; ed, William Reynolds; ch, Rod Alexander, Louise's Ballet by Agnes de Mille; md, Alfred Newman; cos, Mary Wills.

Musical **(PR:A MPAA:NR)**

CARPETBAGGERS, THE** (1964) 150m Em/PAR c
George Peppard *(Jonas Cord, Jr.)*, Alan Ladd *(Nevada Smith)*, Carroll Baker *(Rina)*, Bob Cummings *(Dan Pierce)*, Martha Hyer *(Jennie Denton)*, Elizabeth Ashley *(Monica Winthrop)*, Lew Ayres *(McAllister)*, Martin Balsam *(Bernard B. Norman)*, Ralph Taeger *(Buzz Dalton)*, Archie Moore *(Jedediah)*, Leif Erickson *(Jonas Cord, Sr.)*, Arthur Franz *(Morrissey)*, Tom Tully *(Amos Winthrop)*, Audrey Totter *(Prostitute)*, Anthony Warde *(Moroni)*, Charles Lane *(Denby)*, Tom Lowell *(David Woolf)*, John Conte *(Ellis)*, Vaughn Taylor *(Doctor)*, Francesca Bellini *(Cynthia Randall)*, Gladys Holland *(French Nurse)*, Lynn Borden *(Starlet)*, Victoria Jean *(Jo-Ann)*, Frankie Darro *(Bellboy)*, Lisa Seagram *(Moroni's Secretary)*, Ann Doran *(Woman Reporter)*, Joseph Turkel *(Reporter)*, Donald Barry *(Sound Man)*, Peter Duryea *(Assistant Director)*.

THE CARPETBAGGERS is first-rate third-rate trash. And trash, when it's terrific trash, is not easy to find. Deny it as much as he wishes, but Harold Robbins has obviously used parts of the life of Howard Hughes as the basis for his major character, Jonas Cord (Peppard). The other roles are not so easily discernible but most of them appear to be melanges of many business and Hollywood types. Alan Ladd is Peppard's avuncular confidante, Nevada Smith, a former outlaw. Peppard inherits his late father's dynamite plant and promptly goes after the old man's widow, Baker. He turns her into a movie sexpot and makes Ladd a Roy Rogers hero when he takes over a movie lot. Baker won't sleep with him so he gets Hyer, a hooker, and dumps Baker, replacing her with Hyer. Then he marries Ashley, the daughter of Tully, then dumps her after a while. Peppard plays a man with absolutely no redeeming graces until he has a fist fight with Ladd that brings him to his senses, whatever they are. Peppard was properly tough and surly in the lead role and the evidence of that is the hatred the audience felt for him all the way through. The universal attitude toward Peppard was indignantly voiced by Baker who seethes at him: "You dirty, filthy, perverted monster! You're the meanest, cruelest, most loathsome thing I've ever met!" Ladd was in his last American film (he did two in Europe before dying in Palm Springs) and was convincing in the part. Had he lived beyond his 51 years, he would have had a fine career as a character man ahead of him, once the stigma of having to be svelte and unlined as a lead player was removed. By today's standards, this is about as mild as the typical ABC Friday Night Movie but it was hot stuff then. Though it is clear that Peppard's role model is Hughes, the Ladd character is one drawn from less obvious sources, chiefly a mysterious Old West character who had been a friend of Hughes' father with some traits of cowboy stars William Boyd ("Hopalong Cassidy") and silent western great William S. Hart. Baker's role of course, is drawn almost wholly from Jean Harlow, Hughes' first discovery and star of his epic WW I film HELL'S ANGELS, with whom he dallied, while Hyer's sensuous character was based upon Jane Russell, Hughes' sexpot star of THE OUTLAW. Note that Cummings uses the first name of "Bob" in the billing. He has the habit of using "Robert Cummings" in dramatic roles (DIAL M FOR MURDER, et al) and "Bob" for comedy parts. He obviously felt that THE CARPETBAGGERS was a comedy.

p, Joseph E. Levine; d, Edward Dmytryk; w, John Michael Hayes (based on the novel by Harold Robbins); ph, Joseph MacDonald (Panavision, Technicolor); m, Elmer Bernstein; ed, Frank Bracht; prod d, Frank Caffey; art d, Hal Pereira, Walter Tyler; set d, Arthur Krams; cos, Edith Head; spec eff, Paul K. Lerpae.

Drama **(PR:C MPAA:NR)**

CARRIE*** (1952) 118m PAR bw
Laurence Olivier *(George Hurstwood)*, Jennifer Jones *(Carrie Meeber)*, Miriam Hopkins *(Julie Hurstwood)*, Eddie Albert *(Charles Drouet)*, Basil Ruysdael *(Mr. Fitzgerald)*, Ray Teal *(Allan)*, Barry Kelley *(Slawson)*, Sara Berner *(Mrs. Oransky)*, William Reynolds *(George Hurstwood, Jr.)* Mary Murphy *(Jessica Hurstwood)*, Harry Hayden *(O'Brien)*, Walter Baldwin *(Carrie's Father)*, Dorothy Adams *(Carrie's Mother)*, Jacqueline de Wit *(Minnie)*, Melinda Plowman *(Little Girl)*, Lester Sharpe *(Blum)*, Don Beddoe *(Goodman)*, Royal Dano *(Captain)*, Albert Astar *(Louis the Headwaiter)*, William Bailey *(Man at Bar)*, James Flavin *(Mike the Bartender)*, Harry Denny *(Elderly Man)*, Harlan Briggs *(Joe Brant)*, Martin Doric *(Maitre D')*, Jack Gargan, Eric Alden, Donald Kerr, Jerry James *(Bartenders)*, Len Hendry *(Frank)*, Jean Debriac *(Wine Steward)*, Margaret Field *(Servant Girl)*, Nolan Leary, F. Patrick Henry *(Cabbies)*, Jerry James *(Boy Friend)*, Jasper D. Weldon *(Porter)*, Mike P. Donovan, Roy Butler *(Conductors)*, Irene Winston *(Anna)*, Anitra Sparrow *(Factory Worker)*, Charles

Halton *(Parson, Factory Foreman)*, Bob Foulk *(Sven)*, Raymond Russell Roe *(Boy)*, Leon Tyler *(Connell)*, Ralph Sanford *(Older Waiter)*, G. Raymond Nye, Bruce Carruthers, James Davies, Ethan Laidlaw *(Waiters)*, George Melford, Al Ferguson *(Patrons at Slawson's)*, John Alvin *(Stage Manager)*, Gail Bonney *(Older Chrous Girl)*, Lois Hall *(Lola)*, Bill Meader, Allen Ray *(Stage Door Johnnies)*, Bill Sheehan *(Assistant Stage Manager)*, Sherry Hall *(Theater Cashier)*, Richard Kipling *(Farmer)*, Howard Mitchell *(Businessman)*, Herman Nowlin *(Hack Driver)*, Charles B. Smith *(Young Man/Job Seeker)*, Jim Hayward *(Hirer)*, Dulce Daye, Jay K. Eaton *(Bride's Parents)*, Kenneth Patterson *(Reporter)*, Mike Mahoney *(Call Boy)*, Judith Adams *(Bride)*, Harry Hines *(Floorman)*, Ralph Moody, Slim Gaut, Kit Guard *(Bums)*, Daria Massey *(Carrie's Sister)*, Edward Clark *(Ticket Agent)*, Gerry Ganzer *(Showgirl)*, Julius Tannen *(John)*, Oliver A. Cross *(Host)*, Jack Roberts *(Bum at Hofer's)* Harper Goff, Chalky Williams, Snub Pollard, Jack Low *(Men)*, Charley McAvoy, Cliff Clark *(Policemen)*, Frank Wilcox *(Maitre D')*, Allen D. Sewall *(Clerk)*, Paul E. Burns *(Coachman)*, Edward J. Marr *(Necktie Salesman)*, Douglas Carter *(Businessman)*, Frances Morris *(Maid)*, Start Holmes, Franklyn Farnum *(Restaurant Patrons)*, James Cornell *(Brakeman)*.

Famous Dreiser tear-jerker about Carrie (Jennifer Jones) who departs a jerkwater town for Chicago. On the train, she meets a traveling salesman (yep, that's what he is!), played by Eddie Albert. After a while, the city of the Big Shoulders offers her no employment so Jones becomes Albert's mistress. They move in together and everything is fine until she meets Olivier, the manager of a swank restaurant, and falls in love with him. Olivier, in his best airy American accent, seduces the young woman, then steals ten thousand dollars of his employer's money, leaves Hopkins, Murphy, and Reynolds (his family) and departs for the Big Apple with Jones. The theft is uncovered and he returns the money, putting the couple on poverty row. Jones leaves Olivier to pursue a career on the stage and he disintegrates, reaching the depths of despair. Several years later, when she is now a huge success, Jones attempts to bring Olivier back from the brink. Critics were mixed in their assessment of Olivier and Jones but almost all agreed that the story was an old-fashioned one and not worthy of all the talents involved. Olivier took the job after Cary Grant nixed it. Not that he was that in love with the script but he needed something to do while his wife, Vivian Leigh, was busy with A STREETCAR NAMED DESIRE. In a small and usually unbilled role as a nameless man, look hard for veteran Snub Pollard, the comedian with the droopy mustache who supported Harold Lloyd in so many one-reelers.

p&d, William Wyler; w, Ruth and Augustus Goetz (based on the novel *Sister Carrie* by Theodore Dreiser); ph, Victor Milner; m, David Raksin; ed, Robert Swink; art d, Hal Pereira, Roland Anderson.

Drama **(PR:C MPAA:NR)**

CARRIE½** (1976) 97m UA c

Sissy Spacek *(Carrie White)*, Piper Laurie *(Margaret White)*, Amy Irving *(Sue Snell)*, William Katt *(Tommy Ross)*, John Travolta *(Billy Nolan)*, Nancy Allen *(Chris Hargenson)*, Betty Buckley *(Miss Collins)*, P. J. Soles *(Norma Watson)*, Sydney Lassick *(Mr. Fromm)*, Stefan Gierash *(Principal Morton)*, Priscilla Pointer *(Mrs. Snell)*, Michael Talbot *(Freddy)*, Cameron De Palma *(Boy On Bicycle)*.

Overrated suspense/horror director Brian De Palma's first big hit, and his best effort to date. Spacek (in a stunning performance that overpowers most of the faults in the movie) stars as a troubled, repressed young high-schooler who slowly realizes that she posesses incredible telekinetic powers. Plagued with problems in school (she feels homely and nobody likes her) and at home (her mother is a religious fanatic who hates men and makes her daughter pray in a closet), she struggles to maintain her dignity and sanity. She is finally driven over the edge when cruel classmates rig it so that she is elected prom queen as an elaborate joke to embarrass her. At the dance, Spacek is in her glory and finally feels accepted, until Soles, Travolta,and Talbot drop a bucket of pig's blood on her head (it was rigged with wires to the ceiling) while accepting her honors. The telekinetic powers (which were only hinted at thus far) go wild and Spacek destroys most of her high school and kills dozens of students and faculty members in an orgy of violence. She then walks home through the rubble, where she puts an end to her and her mother's existence by destroying their home. Cleverly designed to appeal to its target teenage audience, CARRIE finally synthesized all of De Palma's on-and-off real talents for intense, stylish, visual filmmaking. His techniques (elaborate compositions, camera moves, and slow motion) combined with a fairly literate script (due more to King's source material than De Palma's influence) make for an interesting film that successfully deals with the inner rage that every teenager feels, while it remains in the horror genre. Unfortunately, CARRIE also hints at De Palma's penchant for pointless exercises in overblown, style-for-style's sake sequences and his increasingly disturbing portrayal of women as intimidating objects men are driven to destroy (making the audience identify with the killer rather than the victim by using point-of-view shots) that mars much of his later work, making one wonder whether he is a misogynist. While De Palma has his legion of fans, he seems to be a marginal talent (a lack of intellectual insight into his characters hampers taking his stylistic rip-offs of Hitchcock and Hawks seriously) and a sexist, empty stylist. CARRIE marked John Travolta's first screen credit.

p, Paul Monash; d, Brian De Palma; w, Lawrence D. Cohen (based on the novel by Stephen King); ph, Mario Tosi (DeLuxe Color); m, Pino Dinaggio; ed, Paul Hirsch; art d, William Kenny, Jack Fisk; set d, Robert Gould; cos, Rosanna Norton; spec eff, Gregory M. Auer, Kenneth Pepiot; stunt coordinator, Richard Weiker.

Horror **Cas.** **(PR:O MPAA:R)**

CARRINGTON V.C. (SEE: COURT MARTIAL, 1955)

CARRY ON ADMIRAL½**

(1957, Brit.) 85m REN bw (AKA: THE SHIP WAS LOADED)

David Tomlinson *(Tom Baker)*, Peggy Cummins *(Susan Lashwood)*, Brian Reece *(Peter Fraser)*, Eunice Gayson *(Jane Godfrey)*, A. E. Matthews *(Admiral Godfrey)*, Joan Sims *(Mary)*, Lionel Murton *(Psychiatrist)*, Reginald Beckwith *(Receptionist)*, Desmond Walter Ellis *(Willy Oughton-Formby)*, Ronald Shiner *(Salty Simpson)*, Peter Coke *(Lt. Lashwood)*, Derek Blomfield *(Lt. Dodson)*, Tom Gill *(Petty Officer)*, Howard Williams *(Sublieutenant)*, Joan Hickson *(Mother)*, Toke Townley *(Steward)*, Arthur Lovegrove *(Orderly)*, Ronald Adam *(First Sea Lord)*, Sam Kydd *(Attendant)*, Philip Ashley *(First Officer)*, Donald Pickering *(Second Officer)*, Alfie Bass, Everley Gregg.

A drinking bout between two friends (Tomlinson and Reece) leads to their switching clothes and identities. One goes to a job as a press relations executive while the other takes over his friend's job as captain of a RN ship. His ignorance of protocol and accidental torpedoing of the First Sea Lord's launch gets him locked up for psychiatric observation. Finally, thanks to a little blackmail, the pair are restored to their proper positions. Good comedy unrelated to the "Carry On" series.

p, George Minter; d, Val Guest; w, Guest (based on the play "Off the Record" by Ian Hay and Stephen King-Hall); ph, Arthur Grant; m, Philip Green; ed, John Pomeroy.

Comedy **(PR:A MPAA:NR)**

CARRY ON AGAIN, DOCTOR** (1969, Brit.) 89m Rank c

Kenneth Williams *(Frederick Carver)*, Sidney James *(Gladstone Screwer)*, Charles Hawtrey *(Dr. Ernest Stoppidge)*, Joan Sims *(Ellen Moore)*, Hattie Jacques *(Matron)*, Jim Dale *(Dr. James Nookey)*, Barbara Windsor *(Goldie Locks)*, Patsy Rowlands *(Miss Fosdick)*, Lucy Griffiths *(Old Lady)*, Ann Lancaster *(Miss Armitage)*, Faith Kent *(Berkeley Matron)*, Shakira Baksh *(Scrubba)*, Frank Singuineau *(Native Porter)*, Harry Locke *(Porter)*, Georgina Simpson *(Men's Ward Nurse)*, Valerie Shute *(Main Ward Nurse)*, Patricia Hayes *(Mrs. Beasley)*, Valerie Leon *(Clinic Nurse)*.

Dale is a South Seas doctor who discovers a weight control formula, but really this is just an excuse for racy jokes, scantily clad women, and those belly laughs the series is still able to raise. Scripting is flat and jaded in most places,but there still are flashes of wit. (See CARRY ON series, Index.)

p, Peter Rogers; d, Gerald Thomas; w, Talbot Rothwell; ph, Ernest Steward (Eastmancolor); m, Eric Rogers; ed, Alfred Roome; art d, Jack Blezard.

Comedy **(PR:C MPAA:NR)**

CARRY ON CABBIE½**

(1963, Brit.) 91m WB-Pathe bw (GB:CALL ME A CAB)

Sidney James *(Charlie)*, Hattie Jacques *(Peggy)*, Kenneth Conner *(Ted)*, Charles Hawtrey *(Pintpot)*, Esma Cannon *(Flo)*, Liz Fraser *(Sally)*, Bill Owen *(Smiley)*, Milo O'Shea *(Len)*, Judith Furse *("Battleaxe")*, Ambrosine Phillpotts *(Aristocratic Lady)*, Renee Houston *(Molly)*, Jim Dale *(Small Man)*, Amanda Barrie *(Anthea)*, Carole Shelley *(Dumb Girl)*, Cyril Chamberlain *(Sarge)*, Norman Chappell *(Allbright)*, Noel Dyson *(District Nurse)*, Peter Gilmore *(Dancy)*, Michael Ward *(Man in Tweeds)*, Michael Nightingale *(Businessman)*, Ian Wilson *(Clerk)*, Peter Byrne *(Bridegroom)*, Darryl Kavann *(Punch)*, Peter Jesson *(Car Salesman)*, Don McCorkindale *(Tubby)*, Charles Stanley *(Geoff)*, Marion Collins *(Bride)*, Frank Forsyth *(Chauffeur)*.

Better than usual "Carry On" comedy, whose success is probably due to a switch of writers which saw Rothwell replace Norman Hudis. Plot concerns successful entrepreneur James, whose fleet of taxis has made him a prosperous man, much to the dismay of his lonely wife, Jacques,who is sick of her husband spending all his time at work. To teach him a lesson, she secretly invests some of his money in a rival taxi service she develops, with cabs driven by sexy ladies in revealing uniforms. Her venture is a success and James (who doesn't know his wife is behind it) tries to destroy his sudden competition, but is thwarted by the gals. Everything works out in the end. (See CARRY ON Series, Index)

p, Peter Rogers; d, Gerald Thomas; w, Talbot Rothwell (based on a story by Sidney Green, Richard Hills); ph, Alan Hume; m, Eric Rodgers; ed, Archie Ludski; art d, Jack Stephens; set d, Helen Thomas; cos, Joan Ellacott; makeup, Geoffrey Rodway.

Comedy **(PR:C MPAA:NR)**

CARRY ON CAMPING½** (1969, Brit.) 88m Rank c

Sidney James *(Sid Boggle)*, Kenneth Williams *(Dr. Soper)*, Joan Sims *(Joan Fussey)*, Charles Hawtrey *(Charlie Muggins)*, Bernard Bresslaw *(Bernie Lugg)*, Terry Scott *(Peter Potter)*, Barbara Windsor *(Babs)*, Hattie Jacques *(Miss Haggerd)*, Peter Butterworth *(Joshua Fiddler)*, Julian Holloway *(Jim Tanner)*, Betty Marsden *(Harriet Potter)*, Dilys Laye *(Anthea Meeks)*, Trisha Noble *(Sally)*, Sandra Caron *(Fanny)*.

Another "Carry On" with the same cast doing the same things and getting the same laughs. This time James and Bresslaw are trying to get their girl friends to join them on a camping trip to what they believe to be a nudist colony. Once there, they find no nudists but do encounter a gaggle of sex-starved schoolgirls. Somehow this formula just keeps on working. (See CARRY ON series, Index.)

p, Peter Rogers; d, Gerald Thomas; w, Talbot Rothwell; ph, Ernest Steward (Eastmancolor); m, Eric Rogers; ed, Alfred Roome; art d, Lionel Couch; cos, Yvonne Caffin.

Comedy **(PR:C MPAA:NR)**

CARRY ON CLEO*½ (1964, Brit.) 92m WB-Pathe c

Sidney James *(Mark Anthony)*, Kenneth Williams *(Julius Caesar)*, Kenneth Connor *(Hengist)*, Charles Hawtrey *(Seneca)*, Joan Sims *(Calpurnia)*, Amanda Barrie *(Cleo)*, Julie Stevens *(Gloria)*, Victor Maddern *(Sgt. Major)*, Sheila Hancock *(Senna)*, David Davenport *(Bilius)*, Michael Ward *(Archimedes)*, Tanya Billing *(Virginia)*, Francis de Wolff *(Agrippa)*, Tom Clegg *(Sosages)*, Jon Pertwee *(Soothsayer)*, Peter Gilmore *(Galley Master)*, Brian Oulton *(Brutus)*, Warren Mitchell *(Spencius)*, Jim Dale *(Horsa)*, Gertan Klauber *(Marcus)*, Ian Wilson *(Messenger)*, Brian Rawlinson *(Hessian Driver)*, E. V. H. Emmett *(Narrator)*.

The usual cast of British comedians tackles a lame parody of the 1963 big-budget disaster CLEOPATRA. Most of the humor is based on inane puns that sap the film of any life it may have had through the usual slapstick action. Plot concerns slaves saving

Williams (who plays Caesar) from being assassinated by James (Anthony) and Stevens (Cleopatra). (See CARRY ON series, Index.)

p, Peter Rogers; d, Gerald Thomas; w, Talbot Rothwell; ph, Alan Hume (Eastmancolor); m, Eric Rogers; ed, Archie Ludski; art d, Bert Davey.

Comedy   **Cas.**   **(PR:C MPAA:NR)**

CARRY ON CONSTABLE★★½   (1960, Brit.) 86m Anglo-Amalgamated bw
Sidney James (Sgt. Wilkins), Eric Barker (Inspector Mills), Kenneth Connor (Constable Constable), Charles Hawtrey (Constable Gorse), Hattie Jacques (Sgt. Laura Moon), Leslie Phillips (Constable Potter), Joan Sims (Policewoman Passworthy), Kenneth Williams (Constable Benson), Shirley Eaton (Sally Barry), Cyril Chamberlain (Constable Thurston), Joan Hickson (Mrs. May), Irene Handl (Distraught Woman), Terence Longdon (Herbert Hall), Jill Adams (Policewoman Harrison), Freddie Mills (Crook), Brian Oulton (Store Manager), Victor Maddern (Criminal Type), Michael Balfour (Matt), Diane Aubrey (Honoria), Marv Law (Shop Assistant), Dorinda Stevens (Young Woman).

Another broad slapstick in the eternal "Carry On" series. Slim plot concerns a bunch of green recruits brought in to bolster a flu-decimated police station, but mostly it's bawdy humor and every police joke in the book. Barker does a good job as the inept inspector in charge of the station. (See CARRY ON series, Index.)

p, Peter Rogers; d, Gerald Thomas; w, Norman Hudis (based on an idea by Brock Williams); ph, Ted Scaife; m, Bruce Montgomery; ed, John Shirley; art d, Carmen Dillon; set d, Vernon Dixon; cos, Yvonne Caffin; makeup, George Blackler.

Comedy   **(PR:C MPAA:NR)**

CARRY ON COWBOY★★   (1966, Brit.) 94m WB-Pathe c
Sidney James (Rumpo Kid), Kenneth Williams (Judge Burke), Jim Dale (Marshall P. Knutt), Charles Hawtrey (Chief Big Heap), Joan Sims (Belle), Angela Douglas (Annie Oakley), Percy Herbert (Charlie), Bernard Bresslaw (Little Heap), Davy Kaye (Josh), Peter Butterworth (Doc), Sydney Bromley (Sam), Jon Pertwee (Sheriff Earp), Edina Ronay (Dolores), Lionel Murton (Clerk), Peter Gilmore (Curley), Alan Gifford (Fiddler), Brian Rawlinson (Driver), Sally Douglas (Kitikata), Gary Colleano (Slim).

Yet another dim comedy from the "Carry On" players. This one lampoons the old West where Stodge City (funny name, eh?) is taken over by the villainous Rumpo Kid (another funny name), played by James. Judge Williams wants to rid the town of this menace, so he calls for a lawman to clean up his city. The state misunderstands his request and sends sanitary engineer Dale (ha! ha!) to help out. The usual cast does its job with the typical material. (See CARRY ON series, Index.)

p, Peter Rogers; d, Gerald Thomas; w, Talbot Rothwell; ph, Alan Hume (Eastmancolor); m, Eric Rogers; ed, Roderick Kays.

Comedy   **(PR:A MPAA:NR)**

CARRY ON CRUISING★★   (1962, Brit.) 89m Anglo-Amalgamated c
Sidney James (Capt. Crowther), Kenneth Williams (Leonard Marjoribanks), Kenneth Connor (Arthur Binn), Liz Fraser (Gladys Trimble), Dilys Laye (Flo Castle), Lance Percival (Wilfred Haines), Jimmy Thompson (Sam Turner), Cyril Chamberlain (Tom Tree), Esma Cannon (Bridget Madderley), Vincent Ball (Jenkins).

An inexperienced and overeager crew wreak havoc on a Mediterranean cruise. The structure is so simple and the humor so broad that it is nearly impossible for this not to work. Ship's cook, Percival, provides some laughs. (See CARRY ON series, Index.)

p, Peter Rogers; d, Gerald Thomas; w, Norman Hudis (based on a story by Eric Barker); ph, Alan Hume (Eastmancolor); m, Bruce Montgomery; ed, John Shirley.

Comedy   **(PR:C MPAA:NR)**

CARRY ON DOCTOR★★   (1968, Brit.) 95m Rank c
Frankie Howerd (Francis Bigger), Sidney James (Charlie Roper), Kenneth Williams (Doctor Tinkle), Charles Hawtrey (Mr. Barron), Jim Dale (Dr. Kilmore), Barbara Windsor (Sandra May), Hattie Jacques (The Matron), Joan Sims (Chloe Gibson), Anita Harris (Nurse Clarke), Bernard Bresslaw (Ken Biddle), Peter Butterworth (Mr. Smith), June Jago (Sister Hoggett), Dilys Laye (Mavis Winkle), Derek Francis (Sir Edmund Burke), Peter Gilmore (Henry), Dandy Nichols (Mrs. Roper), Valerie Van Ost (Nurse Parkin), Julian Orchard (Fred), Julian Holloway (Simmons), Alexandra Dane (Prenatal Instructor).

The same untiring "Carry On" team does it again, this time in a hospital. Howerd is a medical "mind-over-matter" quack who winds up as a reluctant patient under the care of the incompetent staff. Funnier than some of its predecessors. (See CARRY ON series, Index.)

p, Peter Rogers; d, Gerald Thomas; w, Talbot Rothwell; ph, Alan Hume (Eastmancolor); m, Eric Rogers; ed, Alfred Roome.

Comedy   **(PR:C MPAA:NR)**

CARRY ON EMMANNUELLE★   (1978, Brit.) 88m Hemdale International c
Suzanne Danielle (Emmannuelle), Kenneth Williams (Emile), Kenneth Connor (Leyland), Jack Douglas (Lyons), Joan Sims (Mrs. Dangle), Peter Butterworth (Richmond), Larry Dann (Theodore), Beryl Reid (Mrs. Valentine), Henry McGee (Harold Hump), Howard Nelson (Harry Hernia), Albert Moses (Doctor).

The "Carry On" series in its death throes. This time the gang parodies the successful soft-core EMMANUELLE movies by starring Danielle as the wife of a French ambassador who sleeps with most of London. Rude and raunchy, the humor level is at bottom with its subject matter. (See CARRY ON series, Index.)

p, Peter Rogers; d, Gerald Thomas; w, Lance Peters; ph, Alan Hume (uncredited color); m, Eric Rogers; ed, Peter Boita; art d, Jack Shampan; cos, Courtenay Elliott; m/l, Kenneth Lynch.

Comedy   **(PR:O MPAA:NR)**

CARRY ON ENGLAND★   (1976, Brit.) 89m FOX/Rank c
Kenneth Connor (Capt. S. Melly), Windsor Davies (Sgt. Maj. Bloomer), Patrick Mower (Sgt. Len Able), Judy Geeson (Sgt. Tilly Willing), Jack Douglas (Bombardier Ready), Diane Langton (Pvt. Alice Easy), Melvyn Hayes (Gunner Shorthouse), Joan Sims (Pvt. Ffoulkes Sharpe), Peter Jones (Brigadier), Peter Butterworth (Maj. Carstairs), David Lodge (Capt. Bull), Julian Holloway (Maj. Butcher), Linda Hooks (Army Nurse), Patricia Franklin (Cpl. Cook), Vivienne Johnson (Freda), Barbara Rosenblat (Lil), Johnny Briggs (Melly's Driver), Brian Osborne (Gunner Owen), Larry Dann (Gunner Shaw), Jeremy Conner (Gunner Hiscocks), Barbara Hampshire (Pvt. Carter), Tricia Newby (Pvt. Murray), Jeannie Collings (Pvt. Edwards), Louise Burton (Pvt. Evans), Linda Regan (Pvt. Taylor), Billy J. Mitchell (Gunner Childs), Richard Bartlett (Gunner Drury), Peter Banks (Gunner Thomas), Peter Quince (Gunner Sharpe), Richard Olley (Gunner Parkes), Paul Toothill (Gunner Gale).

Particularly boring "Carry On" series entry which takes place at an anti-aircraft battery at the start of WW II. Bumbling Capt. Conner presides over the usual series of bad puns, pratfalls, and slapstick gags that play with tedious predictability. The series had just about run out of gas at this point. (See CARRY ON series, Index.)

p, Peter Rogers; d, Gerald Thomas; w, Jack Seddon, David Pursall; ph, Ernest Steward (Technicolor); ed, Richard Marden.

Comedy   **(PR:A MPAA:NR)**

CARRY ON HENRY VIII★★
   (1970, Brit.) 89m Adder/RANK/AIP c (GB: CARRY ON HENRY)
Sidney James (Henry VIII), Kenneth Williams (Sir Thomas Cromwell), Joan Sims (Marie of Normandy), Charles Hawtrey (Sir Roger de Loggerley), Terry Scott (Cardinal Wolsey), Barbara Windsor (Bettina), Kenneth Connor (Lord Hampton), Julian Holloway (Sir Thomas), Julian Orchard (Duc de Pinceney), Peter Gilmore (King Francis), Gertan Klauber (Bidet), David Davenport (Major Domo), Margaret Nolan (Lass), William Mervyn (Physician), Norman Chappell (Plotter), Derek Francis (Farmer), Bill Maynard (Fawkes), Douglas Ridley (2nd Plotter), Dave Prowse (Warder), Monica Dietrich (Katherine), Marjie Lawrence (Serving Maid), Patsy Rowlands (Queen), Peter Butterworth (Bristol), Billy Cornelius (Guard), John Bluthal (Tailor), Alan Curtis (Conte Di Pisa).

Yet another of the interminable CARRY ON series. It's the same old jokes (perhaps a little bluer than usual) as James discovers that his queen is pregnant by her lover. For fans of low-brow humor it's not that bad; anyone else will be driven away quickly. (See CARRY ON series, Index.)

p, Peter Rogers; d, Gerald Thomas; w, Talbot Rothwell; ph, Alan Hume (Eastmancolor); m, Eric Rogers; ed, Alfred Roome; art d, Lionel Couch; cos, Courteney Elliott.

Comedy   **(PR:O MPAA:GP)**

CARRY ON JACK★★
   (1963, Brit.) 91m WB-Pathe c (AKA: CARRY ON VENUS)
Bernard Cribbins (Albert), Juliet Mills (Sally), Charles Hawtrey (Walter), Kenneth Williams (Capt. Fearless), Donald Houston (Howett), Percy Herbert (Angel), Peter Gilmore (Patch), Ed Devereaux (Hook), Jim Dale (Carrier), Ian Wilson (Ancient Carrier), Barry Gosney (Coach Driver), George Woodbridge (Ned), Cecil Parker (First Sea Lord), Frank Forsyth (Second Sea Lord), Jimmy Thompson (Nelson), Anton Rodgers (Hardy), Patrick Cargill (Spanish Governor), Jan Muzurus (Captain of the Guard).

The "Carry On" players tackle the high seas in this ocean comedy set in 1805, featuring Williams as Capt. Fearless who hates the sea and violence. Local dim-wit Hawtrey ends up on board and the familiar comedy situations ensue, including parodies of floggings, walking the plank, and battling the Spanish Armada. (See CARRY ON series, Index.)

p, Peter Rogers; d, Gerald Thomas; w, Talbot Rothwell; ph, Alan Hume (Technicolor); m, Eric Rogers; ed, Archie Ludski.

Comedy   **(PR:A MPAA:NR)**

CARRY ON LOVING★½   (1970, Brit.) 90m Rank c
Sidney James (Sydney Bliss), Kenneth Williams (Percy Snooper), Charles Hawtrey (James Bedsop), Joan Sims (Esme Crowfoot), Hattie Jacques (Sophie), Terry Scott (Terence Philpot), Richard O'Callaghan (Bertie Muffet), Bernard Bresslaw (Gripper Burke), Jacki Piper (Sally Martin), Imogen Hassall (Jenny Grubb), Julian Holloway (Adrian), Joan Hickson (Mrs. Grubb), Janet Mahoney (Gay), Bill Maynard (Mr. Dreery), Aelia Bayntun (Corset Lady), Harry Shacklock (Lavatory Attendant), Michael Grady (Boy), Valerie Shute (Girl), Derek Francis (Bishop), Patsy Rowlins (Mrs. Dempsey), Philip Stone (Robinson), Patricia Franklin (Mrs. Dreery), Anthony Sagar (Man In Hospital), Bill Pertwee (Barman), Sonny Farrar (Violinist), Gavin Reed (Window Dresser), Len Lowe (Maitre D'Hotel), Fred Griffiths (Taxi Driver), Kenny Lynch (Conductor), Robert Russell (Policeman), Tom Clegg (Trainer), Joe Cornelius (Second), Lauri Lupino Lane (Husband).

More lame sexual innuendos highlight this "Carry On" entry. Action takes place at a bogus marriage agency run by James and Jacques. Most of the comedic situations arise from the parade of customers who troop through the agency looking for potential mates. If moronic grade school level jokes regarding womens' breasts and buttocks make you laugh, this one's for you. (See CARRY On series, Index.)

p, Peter Rogers; d, Gerald Thomas; w, Talbot Rothwell; ph, Ernest Steward (Eastmancolor); ed, Alfred Roome; art d, Lionel Couch; set d, Peter Howitt; cos, Courtenay Elliott.

Comedy   **(PR:C-O MPAA:NR)**

CARRY ON NURSE * * ½ (1959, Brit.) 86m Anglo-Amalgamated bw
Kenneth Connor (*Bernie Bishop*), Kenneth Williams (*Oliver Reckitt*), Charles Hawtrey (*Hinton*), Terence Longdon (*Ted York*), Bill Owen (*Percy Hickson*), Leslie Phillips (*Jack Bell*), Cyril Chamberlain (*Bert Able*), Brian Oulton (*Henry Bray*), Wilfrid Hyde-White (*Colonel*), Hattie Jacques (*Matron*), Joan Hickson (*Sister*), Shirley Eaton (*Dorothy Denton*), Susan Stephen (*Georgie Axwell*), Joan Sims (*Stella Dawson*), Susan Beaumont (*Frances James*), Ann Firbank (*Helen Lloyd*), Rosalind Knight (*Nightie Nightingale*), Marita Stanton (*Rose Harper*), Harry Locke (*Mick*), Leigh Madison (*Miss Winn*), John Van Eyssen (*Stephens*), John Horsley (*Anaesthetist*), Anthony Sagar (*1st Ambulance Man*), Fred Griffiths (*2nd Ambulance Man*).

The second and perhaps best entry in the "Carry On" series has no real plot, just every cliche and old hospital joke imaginable in this romp through a men's surgical ward. You can see the jokes coming a mile off and still they make you laugh. (See CARRY ON series, Index.)

p, Peter Rogers; d, Gerald Thomas; w, Norman Hudis (based on the play "Ring for Catty" by Patrick Cargill and Jack Beale); ph, Reg Wyler; m, Bruce Montgomery; ed, John Shirley.

Comedy   Cas.   (PR:A   MPAA:NR)

CARRY ON REGARDLESS * * (1961, Brit.) 90m Anglo-Amalgamated bw
Sidney James (*Bert Handy*), Kenneth Connor (*Sam Twist*), Charles Hawtrey (*Gabriel Dimple*), Joan Sims (*Lily Duveen*), Kenneth Williams (*Francis Courtenay*), Bill Owen (*Mike Weston*), Liz Fraser (*Delia King*), Terence Longdon (*Montgomery Infield-Hopping*), Hattie Jacques (*Frosty-Faced Sister*), Stanley Unwin (*Stanley*), Esma Cannon (*Miss Cooling*), Joan Hickson (*Matron*), Sydney Tafler (*Club Manager*), Betty Marsden (*Mata Hari*), Julia Arnall (*Trudi Trelawney*), Fenella Fielding (*Penny Panting*), Terence Alexander (*Trevor Trelawney*), David Lodge (*Wine Connoiseur*), Jerry Desmonde (*Martin Paul*), Eric Pohlmann (*Sinister Man*), June Jago (*1st Sister*), Jimmy Thompson (*Mr. Delling*), Carole Shelley (*Mrs. Delling*), Kynaston Reeves (*Millionaire*), Molly Weir (*Bird Woman*), Michael Ward (*Photographer*), Freddie Mills (*Lefty Vincent*), Ambrosine Phillpotts.

This time the excuse of James running an agency that will take on any job is used to trot out the well-oiled "Carry On" machine. Among the jobs taken on and pumped for every laugh are taking a chimp for a walk, babysitting a married woman, and modeling underwear. Despite its vulgarity it's hard to dislike this titillating story. (See CARRY ON series, Index.)

p, Peter Rogers; d, Gerald Thomas; w, Norman Hudis; ph, Alan Hume; m, Bruce Montgomery; ed, John Shirley; art d, Lionel Couch; set d, Josie MacAvin; cos, Joan Ellacott.

Comedy   (PR:C   MPAA:NR)

CARRY ON SCREAMING * * (1966, Brit.) 97m WB-Pathe (GB) c
Harry H. Corbett (*Detective Sgt. Bung*), Kenneth Williams (*Dr. Watt*), Fenella Fielding (*Valeria*), Joan Sims (*Emily Bung*), Charles Hawtrey (*Dan Dann*), Jim Dale (*Albert Potter*), Angela Douglas (*Doris Mann*), Peter Butterworth (*Detective Col. Slobotham*), Bernard Bresslaw (*Sockett*), Jon Pertwee (*Fettle*), Tom Clegg (*Odbodd*), Billy Cornelius (*Odbodd, Jr.*), Frank Thornton (*Mr. Jones*), Denis Blake (*Rubbatiti*).

Horror and slapstick as bungling detectives try to track down a kidnapping pair of monsters. The trail leads them to the nightmarish castle of Dr. Watt, a reincarnated ghoul, and his femme fatale sister. Together they spend their hours abducting young girls and transforming them into store mannikins. Much of "The Munsters" can be seen here in a sometimes funny film. (See CARRY ON series, Index.)

p, Peter Rogers; d, Gerald Thomas; w, Talbot Rothwell; ph, Alan Hume (Eastmancolor); m, Eric Rogers; ed, Rod Keys.

Comedy   (PR:A   MPAA:NR)

CARRY ON SERGEANT * * ½ (1959, Brit.) 85m Anglo-Amalgamated bw
William Hartnell (*Sgt. Grimshaw*), Bob Monkhouse (*Charlie Sage*), Shirley Eaton (*Mary*), Eric Barker (*Capt. Potts*), Dora Bryan (*Nora*), Bill Owen (*Cpl. Copping*), Kenneth Connor (*Horace Strong*), Charles Hawtrey (*Peter Golightly*), Kenneth Williams (*James Bailey*), Terence Longdon (*Miles Heywood*), Norman Rossington (*Herbert Brown*), Hattie Jacques (*Capt. Clark*), Gerald Campion (*Andy Calloway*), Cyril Chamberlain (*Gun Sgt.*), Gordon Tanner (*1st Specialist*), Frank Forsyth (*2nd Specialist*), Basil Dignam (*3rd Specialist*), John Gatrell (*4th Specialist*), Arnold Diamond (*5th Specialist*), Martin Boddey (*6th Specialist*), Ian Whittaker (*Medical Corporal*), Anthony Sagar (*Stores Sergeant*).

Hartnell is a training sergeant who desperately wants to win the best troop award before retiring. Unfortunately and predictably, he gets the most unlikely bunch of misfits, imaginable only on film. After running through every service joke in the book, they somehow change overnight into a wonder platoon. This is the film that launched the long-lived "Carry On" series. (See CARRY ON series, Index.)

p, Nat Cohen, Stuart Levy; d, Gerald Thomas; w, Norman Hudis (based on the book *The Bull Boys* by R. F. Delderfield); ph, Peter Hennessy; m, Bruce Montgomery; ed, Peter Boita.

Comedy   (PR:A   MPAA:NONE)

CARRY ON SPYING * * ½ (1964, Brit.) 97m WB/Pathe bw
Kenneth Williams (*Desmond Simkins*), Barbara Windsor (*Daphne Honeybutt*), Bernard Cribbins (*Harold Crump*), Charles Hawtrey (*Charlie Bind*), Eric Barker (*Chief*), Dilys Laye (*Lila*), Jim Dale (*Carstairs*), Richard Wattis (*Cobley*), Eric Pohlmann (*The Fat Man*), Victor Maddern (*Milchmann*), Judith Furse (*Dr. Crow*), John Bluthal (*Headwaiter*), Frank Forsyth (*Prof. Clark*), Gertan Klauber (*Code Clerk*), Jill Mai Meredith (*Cigarette Girl*), Nora Gordon (*Elderly Woman*), Angela Ellison (*Cloakroom*

Girl), Norman Mitchell (*Native Policeman*), Hugh Futcher (*Scrawny Native*), Tom Clegg (*Doorman*), Renee Houston (*Madame*), Derek Sydney (*Algerian Agent*), Jack Taylor, Bill Cummings (*Thugs*), Anthony Baird, Patrick Durkin (*Guards*).

A barrage of sleuth-spoofing fills this cheery comedy about a zany quartet of trainee spies. Working for STENCH (The Society for the Total Extinction of Non-Conforming Humans) they attempt to get back Formula "X" from the villainous Dr. Crow. On their travels from Vienna to Algiers via the Orient Express they encounter non-stop nonsense, making this film one of the bright spots in the "Carry On" series. (See CARRY ON series, Index.)

p, Peter Rogers; d, Gerald Thomas; w, Talbot Rothwell, Sid Collins; ph, Alan Hume; m, Eric Rogers; ed, Archie Ludski; art d, Alex Vetchinsky; m/l, Alex Alstone, Geoffrey Parsons, Eric Rogers.

Comedy   (PR:A   MPAA:NR)

CARRY ON TEACHER * * (1962, Brit.) 86m Anglo-Amalgamated bw
Ted Ray (*William Wakefield*), Kenneth Connor (*Gregory Adams*), Leslie Phillips (*Alistair Grigg*), Charles Hawtrey (*Michael Bean*), Joan Sims (*Sarah Allcock*), Kenneth Williams (*Edwin Milton*), Hattie Jacques (*Grace Short*), Rosalind Knight (*Felicity Wheeler*), Cyril Chamberlain (*Alf*), Richard O'Sullivan (*Robin Stevens*), Carol White (*Sheila Dale*), Paul Cole (*Atkins*), Jane White (*Irene*), Larry Dann (*Boy*), Diana Beevers (*Penny Lee*), George Howell (*Billy Haig*), Jacqueline Lewis (*Pat Gordon*), Roy Hines (*Harry Bird*).

The third "Carry On" is set in a school mastered by Ray, who wants another post, but his students want him to stay so they set about sabotaging an inspection from the Ministry of Education. Everyone in the cast and crew does his job, and with such an easy target it's impossible to miss. (See CARRY ON series, Index.)

p, Peter Rogers; d, Gerald Thomas; w, Norman Hudis; ph, Reginald Wyler; m, Bruce Montgomery; ed, John Shirley; art d, Alex Vetchinsky, Lionel Couch; set d, Terence Morgan II; cos, Laurel Staffell.

Comedy   (PR:A   MPAA:NR)

CARRY ON TV (SEE: GET ON WITH IT, 1961, Brit.)

CARRY ON UP THE JUNGLE * * (1970, Brit.) 90m RANK (GB) c
Frankie Howerd (*Prof. Inigo Tinkle*), Sidney James (*Bill Boosey*), Charles Hawtrey (*Tonka*), Joan Sims (*Lady Evelyn Bagley*), Terry Scott (*Jungle Boy*), Kenneth Connor (*Claude Chumley*), Bernard Bresslaw (*Upsidaisi*), Jacki Piper (*June*), Reuben Martin (*Gorilla*), Valerie Leon (*Leda*), Edwina Carroll (*Neuda*).

Shot in the "jungles" of Pinewood Studios, this knee-slapper takes part of the "Carry On" gang on an adventure into the wilds. While seeking a rare bird they encounter head-hunters, a mateless all-girl tribe, and a sex-crazed ape. Stock footage of wildlife and a wide array of plastic plants only add to the charm. (See CARRY ON series, Index.)

p, Peter Rogers; d, Gerald Thomas; w, Talbot Rothwell; ph, Ernest Steward (Eastmancolor); m, Eric Rogers; ed, Alfred Roome; art d, Alex Vetchinsky; cos, Courtenay Elliott.

Comedy   (PR:A   MPAA:NR)

CARRY ON, UP THE KHYBER * * ½ (1968, Brit.) 87m Rank c
Sidney James (*Sir Sidney Ruff-Diamond*), Kenneth Williams (*Khasi of Kalabar*), Charles Hawtrey (*Pvt. James Widdle*), Roy Castle (*Capt. Keene*), Joan Sims (*Lady Ruff-Diamond*), Bernard Bresslaw (*Bungdit Din*), Peter Butterworth (*The Missionary*), Terry Scott (*Sgt. Maj. MacNutt*), Angela Douglas (*Princess Jelhi*), Cardew Robinson (*The Fakir*), Julian Holloway (*Maj. Shorthouse*), Peter Gilmore (*Ginger*), Leon Thau (*Stinghi*), Wanda Ventham (*Wife No. 1*), Michael Mellinger (*Chindi*), Alexandra Dane (*Busti*).

Yet another low comedy by the well-practiced "Carry On" team. This outing finds the gang in colonial India where a native uprising erupts when the natives suspect that the local Highland regiment (the Third Foot and Mouth) actually wear drawers under their kilts. One of the better late series entries spoofing Colonel Blimps, Gunga Dinism, and the ancient notions of the sun never setting on the British empire. (See CARRY ON series, Index.)

p, Peter Rogers; d, Gerald Thomas; w, Talbot Rothwell; ph, Ernest Steward (Eastmancolor); m, Eric Rogers; ed, Alfred Roome; art d, Alex Vetchinsky.

Comedy   (PR:A   MPAA:NR)

CARRY ON VENUS (SEE: CARRY ON JACK, 1963, Brit.)

CARS THAT ATE PARIS, THE * * * ½
(1974, Aus.) 91m Salt-Pan Films (AUS) c (AKA: CARS THAT EAT PEOPLE, THE)
Terry Camilleri (*Arthur*), John Meillon (*Mayor*), Melissa Jaffa (*Beth*), Kevin Miles (*Dr. Midland*), Max Gillies (*Metcalfe*), Peter Armstrong (*Gorman*), Edward Howell (*Tringham*), Bruce Spence (*Charlie*), Derek Barnes (*Al Smedley*), Charlie Metcalfe (*Clive Smedley*), Chris Heywood (*Daryl*), Tim Robertson (*Les*), Max Phipps (*Reu Mowbray*), Frank Saba (*Con Lexux*).

As part of the transformation of Australian cinema, Peter Weir in his directorial debut has created a brilliant black comedy which comes as a precursor to THE ROAD WARRIOR with themes culled from THE WILD ONE and HIGH NOON. Spiked wrecks are driven by adventurous youths through the streets of Paris, Australia, causing an endless string of accidents. These collisions, it turns out, are planned events which serve the vulturous townsfolk in both an economic and medical way. The looters profit by pawning what they can recover, and a town doctor performs questionable medical experiments on the victims. At the center of this fiasco is Camilleri, who is mentally unfit to drive after an earlier homicidal car crash. All order is lost when the arriving vicar is killed. The mayor attempts to restore sanity by scheduling a dance which is attended by the doctor and all his lobotomized patients. The situation is finally reduced to a youth townsfolk blood bath. Bruce Spence, of ROAD WARRIOR fame as the Gyro-Pilot, shines in his role as the town loon who shoots the vicar.

p, Jim and Howard McElroy; d, Peter Weir; w, Weir, Keith Gow, Piers Davies; ph, John McLean (uncredited color); m, Bruce Smeaton; ed, Wayne LeClos.

Adventure   Cas.   **(PR:O   MPAA:NR)**

CARSON CITY**½
(1952) 86m WB c

Randolph Scott (Silent Jeff), Lucille Norman (Susan Mitchell), Don Beddoe (Zeke Mitchell), Raymond Massey ("Big Jack" Davis), Richard Webb (Alan Kincaid), James Millican (Jim Squires), Larry Keating (William Sharon), George Cleveland (Henry Dodson), William Haade (Hardrock Haggerty), Thurston Hall (Charles Crocker), Vince Barnett (Henry).

The title city is hero Scott's destination in this well-crafted western. A Virginia banker tries to stop stagecoach robberies by constructing a railway instead, hiring Scott as foreman. The residents of Carson City, along with a gang of bandits, don't take kindly to this sort of expansion, and attempt to prevent it. After taking blame for the death of a local newsman, Scott falls for the newsman's mourning daughter. Justice prevails, however, when the townsfolk learn that he has been wrongly accused. They come to his aid and the tracks are soon laid. Director De Toth shines with westerns, and this one is no exception in pace and production values, albeit he turned in commendable helmsmanship with MONKEY ON MY BACK and HOUSE OF WAX. CARSON CITY is the first film made in Warner Color, and the hues are not always consistent.

p, David Weisbart; d, Andre De Toth; w, Sloan Nibley, Winston Miller (based on a story by Nibley); ph, John Boyle (Warner Color); m, David Buttolph; ed, Robert Swanson.

Western   **(PR:A   MPAA:NR)**

CARSON CITY CYCLONE**
(1943) 57m REP bw

Don "Red" Barry (Gilbert Phalen), Lynn Merrick (Linda Wade), Noah Beery, Sr. (Judge Phalen), Bryant Washburn (Dr. Andrews), Emmett Lynn (Tombstone), Roy Barcroft (Joe Newman), Stuart Hamblen (Frank Garrett), Bud Osborne (Sheriff Wells), Jack Kirk (Dave), Bud Geary (Walker), Curley Dresden (Tom Barton), Tom London, Reed Howes.

Action-packed western has Red Barry playing a shrewd criminal lawyer. Barry is too smooth and cocky for the tastes of his father, Beery, who is a Carson City judge and banker. The two have a falling out, and Barry is unjustly accused of murdering Beery when the latter is found dead in his office. A series of other killings, bank robberies, lynching parties, posses, several slugfests, and lots of gunplay keep things moving along.

p, Eddy White; d, Howard Bretherton; w, Norman S. Hall; ph, William Bradford; ed, Edward Schroeder.

Western   **(PR:A   MPAA:NR)**

CARSON CITY KID*½
(1940) 68m REP bw

Roy Rogers (Kid), George "Gabby" Hayes (Gabby), Bob Steele (Jessup), Noah Beery, Jr. (Warren), Pauline Moore (Joby), Francis Macdonald (Laramie), Hal Taliaferro (Harmon), Arthur Loft (Kirkie), George Rosener (Tucker), Chester Gan (Wong), Hank Bell, Ted Mapes, Jack Ingram, Jack Kirk, Jack Rockwell, Tom Smith, Art Dillard, Hal Price, Yakima Canutt, Kit Guard, Curley Dresden, Oscar Gahan, Chick Hannon, Al Taylor.

Packed with four greats of the B Westerns, CARSON CITY KID teams Roy Rogers, George "Gabby" Hayes, Bob Steele, and Noah Beery, Jr. proving that the parts are greater than the whole. The story is an old one. Rogers plays a gunslinger chasing Steele, who killed his brother. He finds Steele running a gambling den, under another name. Rogers hires himself out to Steele as a guard, eventually forces him to show his cards, and reaps revenge.

p&d, Joseph Kane; w, Robert Yost, Gerald Geraghty (based on a story by Kane); ph, William Nobles; m, Peter Tinturin; ed, Helene Turner; m/l, Tinturin.

Western   Cas.   **(PR:AA   MPAA:NR)**

CARSON CITY RAIDERS**
(1948) 60m REP bw

Allen "Rocky" Lane (Himself), Black Jack (His Stallion), Eddy Waller (Nugget Clark), Frank Reicher ("Razor" Pool), Beverly Jons (Mildred Drew), Hal Landon (Jimmy Davis), Steve Darrell (Tom Drew), Harold Goodwin (Starkey), Dale Van Sickel (Brennon), Tom Chatterton (John Davis), Edmund Cobb (Sheriff), Holly Bane (Joe), Bob Wilke (Ed Noble).

This fast-paced western packs a lot of action and stunts into a 60-minute film. It tells a lively if standard story. Allan "Rocky" Lane plays an express company agent who goes to Carson City to put a gang of outlaws behind bars. The crooks are trying to grab control of a wagon freight outfit, and blacken the name of a sheriff who at one time had been an outlaw. However, Lane's ready and accurate sixguns, potent fists, and a quick wit keep him on top.

p, Gordon Kay; d, Yakima Canutt; w, Earle Snell; ph, William Bradford; ed, Tony Martinelli.

Western   **(PR:A   MPAA:NR)**

CARTER CASE, THE*
(1947) 67m REP bw

James Ellison (P. Cadwallader Jones), Virginia Gilmore (Terry Parker), Franklin Pangborn (Charley Towne), Paul Harvey (D. A. Winton), Lynne Carver (Joyce Belmont), Spencer Charters (Judge White), Douglas Fowley (Vincent Mackay), John Eldredge (Andrew Belmont), Eddie Acuff (Hypo), John Sheehan (Beanie), Bradley Page (Elliott Carter).

The second film in the MR. DISTRICT ATTORNEY series sees Gilmore as a pert reporter constantly tracking down clues in a homicide case. A publisher of a fashion magazine is murdered, and the finger of blame seems to point at practically everyone. Ellison, as Gilmore's fiance and Assistant D. A., tries to keep her out of the picture for her own protection, but she keeps breaking into the case until it is solved. (See MR. DISTRICT ATTORNEY series, Index)

p, Leonard Fields; d, Bernard Vorhaus; w, Sidney Sheldon, Ben Roberts (Based on Phillips H. Lord radio program MR. DISTRICT ATTORNEY); ph, John Alton; ed, Edward Mann.

Drama   **(PR:A   MPAA:NR)**

CARTHAGE IN FLAMES*½
(1961, Fr./Ital.) 111m COL c

(CARTAGINE IN FIAMME, CARTHAGE EN FLAMMES)

Anne Heywood (Fulvia), Jose Saurez (Hiram), Pierre Brasseur (Sidone), Ilaria Occhini (Ophir), Daniel Gelin (Phegot), Paolo Stoppa (Astarito), Mario Girotti (Tsour), Aldo Silvani (Hermon), Edith Peters (Nurse), Erno Crisa, Ivo Garrani, Cesare Fantoni, Gianrico Tedeschi, Fernand Ledoux.

A wasted spectacle set in 200 b.c. during the Rome-Carthage wars centers around four stubborn lovers—two slave girls in love with the same soldier, and two soldiers in love with the same slave girl. One pair is saved; the other burns in the flaming ruins of Carthage. The awesome sets and costumes aren't enough to keep this poorly-dubbed picture from becoming a cold ember.

p, Guido Luzzato, Carmine Gallone; d, Carmine Gallone; w, Ennio De Concini, Duccio Tessari, Gallone, William De Lane Lea; ph, Piero Portalupi (Technicolor); m, Mario Nascimbene; ed, Nicolo Lazzari; art d, Guido Fiorini, Amedeo Mellone.

Historical Adventure   **(PR:C-O   MPAA:NR)**

CARTOUCHE*
(1957, Ital./US) 85m Venturini/RKO bw

Richard Basehart, Patricia Roc, Massimo Serato, Akim Tamiroff, Isa Barzizza, Nerio Bernardi, Nino Marchetti, Aldo De Franchi.

Basehart swashbuckles through 18th-century France as he tries to clear himself of a charge of murdering a prince during a gambling fracas. He joins a band of wandering players and eludes his enemies (Tamiroff and Serato), as they set a series of traps for him. Totally dull costume epic.

p, John Nasht; d, Steve Sekely; w, Louis Stevens (based on a treatment by Tullio Pinelli).

Adventure   **(PR:A   MPAA:NR)**

CARTOUCHE***
(1962, Fr./Ital.) 125m Ariane/FS/Vides c AKA: SWORDS OF BLOOD)

Jean-Paul Belmondo (Cartouche), Claudia Cardinale (Venus), Odile Versois (Isabelle de Ferrussac), Philippe Lemaire (de Ferrussac), Marcel Dalio (Malichot), Noel Roquevert (Recruiting Sergeant), Jess Hahn (La Douceur), Jean Rochefort (La Taupe), Alain Dekock (Louison), Jacques Charon (Colonel), Lucien Raimbourg (Marshal), Pierre Repp, Jacques Balutin, Rene Marlic, Paul Preboist, Jacques Hilling, Philippe de Broca.

Humorous swashbuckler set in 18th-century France. Belmondo joins the army to evade a rival gang chief, runs off with the regimental payroll, and takes over the gang. He falls for gypsy Cardinale and together they become Robin Hood types, stealing from the rich. Belmondo is captured and Cardinale sacrifices her life to save him. Belmondo dedicates his life to avenging her. Bright colors, fast pacing, good fun.

d, Philippe De Broca; w, Charles Spaak, De Broca, Daniel Boulanger; ph, Christian Matras (Dyaliscope/Eastmancolor); ed, Laurence Mery; m, Georges Delerue; art d, Francois de Lamothe.

Adventure   **(PR:A   MPAA:NR)**

CARVE HER NAME WITH PRIDE***
(1958, Brit.) 119m Rank bw

Virginia McKenna (Violette Szabo), Paul Scofield (Tony Fraser), Jack Warner (Mr. Bushell), Denise Grey (Mrs. Bushell), Alain Saury (Etienne Szabo), Maurice Ronet (Jacques), Anne Leon (Lillian Rolfe), Sydney Tafler (Potter), Avice Landone (Vera Atkins), Nicole Stephane (Denise Bloch), Noel Willman (Interrogator), Bill Owen (N.C.O. Instructor), Billie Whitelaw (Winnie), William Mervyn (Col. Buckmaster), Harold Lang (Commandant Suhren), Michael Goodlife, Michael Caine.

Well-done WW II espionage story based on fact. McKenna plays a London shopgirl whose French officer husband is killed in action. She enlists as a British agent and on her second mission is captured by the Germans. Sent to Ravensbruck concentration camp she is tortured and finally executed, winning a posthumous George Cross for her bravery. Simply told and absorbing, with excellent performances all around.

p, Daniel M. Angel; d, Lewis Gilbert; w, Vernon Harris, Gilbert (based on the book by R. J. Minney); ph, John Wilcox; m, William Alwyn; ed, John Shirley.

Spy Drama   **(PR:A   MPAA:NR)**

CARYL OF THE MOUNTAINS*
(1936) 61m Marcy/Reliable bw

Rin Tin Tin, Jr. (Himself), Francis X. Bushman, Jr. (Brad Sheridan), Lois Wild (Caryl Foray), Earl Dwire (Inspector Bradshaw), Robert Walker (Enos Calvin), Steve Clark (Capt. Edwards), Jack Hendricks (Constable Gary), George Chesebro (Constable O'Brien), Josef Swickard (Foray).

This dog of a film is a vehicle for Rin Tin Tin, Jr., the son of Rin Tin Tin. Set in the North Woods, Rinty helps mounted policeman Francis X. Bushman, Jr. in several disjointed adventures. There is more dog than story in the film, and the dog is not even very good.

p&d, Bernard B. Ray; w, Tom Gibson (based on a story by James Oliver Curwood); ph, Bill Hyer.

Adventure   **(PR:AA   MPAA:NR)**

CASA MANANA zero   (1951) 73m MON bw
Robert Clarke *(Larry)*, Virginia Welles *(Linda)*, Robert Karnes *(Horace)*, Tony Roux *(Pedro)*, Carol Brewster *(Honey)*, Paul Maxey *(Maury)*, Jean Richey *(Marge)*, and featuring Frank Rio, Larry Rio, Jim Rio, Spade Cooley, Yadira Jiminez, Zarco and D'Lores, the Mercer Bros., Armando and Lita, Betty and Beverly, Olga Perez, Davis and Johnson, and the Eddie Le Baron orchestra.

An excuse to film a host of variety acts, this bore about a club owner looking for new talent falls flat. Welles, the star-to-be, is the subject of woo from Clarke and Roux. It's club owner Clarke who ultimately wins her affections. Songs include "Bounce," "People Like You," "I Hear a Rhapsody," "Madame Will Drop Her Shawl," "Cielito Lindo," "Pancho Grande," and the somber "Fifty Games of Solitaire on Saturday Night."

p, Lindsley Parsons; d, Jean Yarbrough; w, Bill Raynor; ph, William Sickner; ed, Ace Herman; m/l, Olsen and Johnson, Ray Evans, Jay Livingston, Otis Bigelow, Harold Cooke, Jack Baker, George Fragos, Dick Gasparre.

Musical   (PR:A MPAA:NR)

CASA RICORDI   (SEE: HOUSE OF RICORDI, 1956, Ital.)

CASABLANCA***   (1942) 102m WB bw
Humphrey Bogart *(Richard "Rick" Blaine)*, Ingrid Bergman *(Ilsa Lund Laszlo)*, Paul Henreid *(Victor Laszlo)*, Claude Rains *(Capt. Louis Renault)*, Conrad Veidt *(Maj. Heinrich Strasser)*, Sydney Greenstreet *(Senor Ferrari)*, Peter Lorre *(Ugarte)*, S. Z. Sakall *(Carl, Headwaiter)*, Madeleine LeBeau *(Yvonne)*, Dooley Wilson *(Sam)*, Joy Page *(Annina Brandel)*, John Qualen *(Berger)*, Leonid Kinskey *(Sascha)*, Helmut Dantine *(Jan Brandel)*, Curt Bois *(Dark European)*, Marcel Dalio *(Emil, The Croupier)*, Corinna Mura *(Singer)*, Ludwig Stossel *(Mr. Leuchtag)*, Ilka Gruning *(Mrs. Leuchtag)*, Charles La Torre *(Senor Martinez)*, Frank Puglia *(Arab Vendor)*, Dan Seymour *(Abdul)*, Oliver Prickett *(Blue Parrot Waiter)*, Gregory Gay *(German Banker)*, George Meeker *(Friend)*, William Edmunds *(Contact)*, Torben Meyer *(Banker)*, Gino Corrado *(Waiter)*, George Dee *(Casselle)*, Norma Varden *(Englishwoman)*, Leo Mostovoy *(Fydor)*, Richard Ryen *(Heinz)*, Martin Garralaga *(Headwaiter)*, Olaf Hytten *(Prosperous Man)*, Monte Blue *(American)*, Michael Mark *(Vendor)*, Leon Belasco *(Dealer)*, Paul Porcasi *(Native)*, Hans von Twardowski *(German Officer)*, Albert Morin *(French Officer)*, Creighton Hale *(Customer)*, Henry Rowland *(German Officer)*, Louis Mercier *(Smuggler)*, Lou Marcelle *(Narrator)*.

America's most popular and beloved movie, and rightly so, CASABLANCA has everything that goes to make up a great film—superlative performances at all levels, an inspired script, and faultless direction and production techniques. Since its November 1942 release, it has been *the* movie, one that perfectly blends a turbulent love story with harrowing intrigue, heroic and evil characters, believable melodrama and the kind of genuine sentiment that makes the heart grow fonder with each viewing. Even at its initial release, the film provided instant nostalgia for the fast-vanishing world between the two great wars, a cafe society that was being crushed by the Prussian heel, a civilized, urbane generation in white linen suits, spectator shoes, and wide-brimmed sunhats desperately clinging to values no longer cherished. The film opens with a narrator describing the German takeover of Europe while the camera depicts, in a March-of-Time-like montage, a stream of endless, desperate refugees fleeing Nazi-dominated Europe, flowing into Casablanca in French Morocco, controlled by an ostensibly neutral Vichy French government. One hapless man without papers is rooted from the crowd by police and chased through the streets to be shot in the back, falling dead beneath a wall poster of the venal Marshal Petain, head of the Vichy government in France, an infamous symbol of traitorous collusion with the Nazis. In his lifeless hand the dead refugee clutches a Free French handbill urging resistance. (In this early scene it is obvious that the local regime is not a sympathetic one.) At the tables in open-air cafes sit the frantic refugees haggling, bargaining, and begging with smugglers and thieves over escape routes and methods, particularly tickets for the Lisbon plane which leaves every day for the neutral port from which passage to America can be arranged. A plane flies overhead and lands at the airport where Veidt, a Nazi major, arrives to be greeted by Rains, the police prefect of Casablanca. Veidt is in search of an escaped underground leader, Victor Laszlo (Henreid), who has recently come to Casablanca. Veidt asks what has been done about two German couriers who have been murdered, important letters of transit taken from them. Rains tells him that the killer will be at Rick's Cafe Americain that night, "everybody comes to Rick's." (This line was a verbal credit to the original title of the unpublished play upon which the film script is based.) It is the first week of December 1941 and the U.S. is at the brink of war, yet the atmosphere inside Rick's Cafe Americain is festive, even jovial; beneath this heady air the sophisticated, wealthy expatriates jamming the tables and bar plot with those who prey upon their plight in arranging escape. Deeper in the cafe, presiding over the gambling tables and playing solitaire chess, is Bogart, the mysterious owner, Rick, cynical, tough, world-weary. He approves checks offered by players, then refuses to allow an executive of a German bank to cash his check, telling him that "you're lucky the bar's open to you." Admiring this insult to the Third Reich is Lorre, a slippery thief who has killed the two German couriers to obtain the priceless letters of transit which he intends to sell for a fortune. Lorre asks Bogart if he despises him for trading in such commodities and the cafe owner replies sarcastically: "I don't mind a parasite; I object to a cut-rate one." Lorre asks Bogart to hide the much-sought-after documents until he can sell them later that night. Bogart agrees, later hiding the papers in the upright piano used by his star attraction and friend, the raspy-voiced singer Wilson (the unforgettable Sam). Greenstreet, head of all the black marketeeting in Casablanca, waddles into the cafe and offers to buy Bogart's place. When he is refused, the smug fat man says: "What do you want for Sam?" Bogart bristles, responding with: "I don't buy or sell human beings." LeBeau, with whom Bogart has had a brief affair, is getting drunk at the bar and he escorts her out of the place to a taxi. Sitting outside at a table is police chief Rains who tells Bogart that he is "extravagant . . . throwing away women like that." They watch the Lisbon plane take off from the nearby airport. Rains playfully

asks Bogart why he hasn't returned to America. "Did you abscond with the church funds or run off with a senator's wife? I'd like to think that you killed a man. It's the romantic in me." Wryly, Bogart tells it was "a combination of all three," and then explains that he came to Casablanca for his health. "I came to Casablanca for the waters." Rains smiles: "What waters? We're in the desert." Bogart shrugs, "I was misinformed." But Bogart is no purposeless nomad; it is later revealed that he has always allied himself with noble causes. Veidt later reads from a dossier on Bogart that he ran guns to Ethopia in 1935 and fought in Spain on the Loyalist side. Bogart minimizes his past by playing the mercenary, saying that he "got well paid for it on both occasions." A short time later, Lorre is arrested at the gambling tables. He tries to elude police and races up to Bogart, begging that he hide him. The police quickly surround Lorre as Bogart backs away from him, saying: "I stick my neck out for nobody." Now, he truly is a mystery, a former patriot it seems, who has became callous and uncaring. Veidt and Rains further seek to unravel Bogart's past but he is noncommital. Veidt asks him his nationality. "I'm a drunkard," replies Bogart. When Veidt tells him they are looking to entrap Henreid, Bogart appears indifferent yet he secretly bets Rains ten thousand francs that Henreid will not be stopped by the Nazis. He excuses himself, telling Veidt and Rains that "Your business is politics, mine is running a saloon." Then, Henreid arrives with Bergman, the beautiful Ilsa Lund. While Henreid meets with another underground agent at the bar (Qualen), Bergman spots Wilson at the piano, instantly recognizing him. Wilson moves his portable piano close to her. She asks that he play "some of the old songs," and he plays "Avalon" for her while she asks about Bogart, her old love. Wilson lies to her, telling her Bogart has a girl friend at Greenstreet's cafe, The Blue Parrot. She sees through him and Wilson, worried, says, "Leave him alone, Miss Ilsa. You're bad luck to him." Bergman asks that he "play it once, Sam, for old time's sake." Wilson pretends he doesn't know what she means. "Play it, Sam . . . play "As Time Goes By." He says he can't remember it. She hums it for him and he begins to play and sing the great love song. Bogart hears the tune and goes to Wilson, angry. "Sam, I thought I told you never to play it!" Then he sees Bergman and they exchange long and telling looks. Rains and Henreid arrive and Bogart breaks a precedent by having a drink with the group, complimenting Henreid for his work as a freedom fighter. After the cafe closes, Bogart sits at a table in his darkened cafe, Wilson begging him to go to sleep. Bogart drinks heavily, telling Wilson that he's "waiting for a lady." Wilson wants him to leave, knowing there will be trouble. Bogart is in agony, remembering her, their past. Painfully, he mutters: "Of all the gin joints in all the towns all over the world, she walks into mine!" Then he asks Wilson to play the piano: "You know what I want to hear . . . You played it for her. You can play it for me . . . If she can stand it, I can. Play it!" (Bogart never says, contrary to the legend, "Play it again, Sam.") As Max Steiner's score mounts in variations of "As Time Goes By" Bogart remembers Bergman and a flashback shows them in Paris, driving down the Champs Elysee, then into the country (director Curtiz makes a quick cut here, audaciously jumping the rear-view projection of the city background to the countryside). The happy couple are on a boat going down the Seine, in her apartment sipping champagne, exchanging tidbits of their pasts, dancing in a Paris nightclub (to "Perfidia", the Warner Brothers standard nightclub tune of the 1940's, used in THE MASK OF DIMITRIOS, DARK PASSAGE, and many other films). As their love affair deepens, the Germans are shown in quick cuts advancing on Paris. Bergman, who has told Bogart that the only other man in her life is dead, worries that the Nazis will imprison him for his anti-fascist activities. As they sip champagne in La Belle Aurore, Wilson plays "As Time Goes By," and Bogart toasts Bergman with the now-classic line: "Here's looking at you, kid," Bogart proposes and agrees to flee Paris with Bergman. He and Wilson are next standing in the rain, at the train station, waiting for her. A note arrives instead of Bergman. Bogart reads the letter as the rain begins to wash away the inky words. It says that she "cannot go with you or ever see you again. You must not ask why. Just believe that I love you. Go, my darling and God bless you. Ilsa." Bogart crumples the letter and is almost dragged onto the departing train by Wilson. In a flash forward, Bogart is back at his cafe and the door opens; Bergman is there. She tries to tell him why she jilted him. He's not interested, but only remembers their "wow finish. A guy standing on a station platform in the rain with a comical look on his face, because his insides had been kicked out." She asks to tell him a story. "Does it have a wow finish?" he sneers. "I don't know the finish yet," she says patiently. (Bergman didn't, neither did the entire cast or director, since the script was almost being written on the spot, according to legend.) She begins to tell him the story of her relationship to Henreid but Bogart is too drunk, and too angry. He likens her to a prostitute when saying: "I've heard a lot of stories in my time. They went along with the sound of a tinny piano, playing in the parlor downstairs. 'Mister, I met a man once when I was a kid,' they'd always begin." She is in tears. He is relentless: "Tell me, who was it you left me for? Was it Laszlo or were there others in between? Or aren't you the kind that tells?" Bergman can bear it no more and leaves as Bogart collapses at the table. In the morning Henreid and Bergman meet with Rains and Veidt. The Nazi attempts to bribe Henreid by telling him that if he gives him the names of underground leaders in Europe he and Bergman will be free to leave Casablanca. Henreid stands up to Veidt, telling him that no amount of threats or even torture will compel him to work with him. Jocularly, Rains tells Henreid that his cooperation will earn him "the honor of having served the Third Reich." Henreid retorts: "I was in a German concentration camp for a year. That's honor enough for a lifetime." Rains next tells them that Lorre, the man Henreid has been searching for, is dead: "We haven't quite decided whether he committed suicide or died trying to escape." Rains allows the couple to go but tells them they must be on call any time. Veidt insists they be kept in Casablanca until Henreid tells him what he wants to know. Henreid next goes to Greenstreet and tries to buy visas but learns that only Bogart can help him. Meanwhile Bogart meets Bergman in the bazaar and apologizes for the previous night. She tells him that she never wishes to see him again but he tells her to visit him at his apartment above the cafe. "Someday you'll lie to Laszlo—you'll be there." She shakes her head and shocks him with the words: "No, Rick, no. You see, Victor Laszlo is my husband. And he was even when I knew you in Paris." Tension mounts that night at the cafe when German and French soldiers begin brawling. A young Bulgarian girl, Page, goes to Bogart, asking his advice. Should she give herself to Rains, the flesh-loving French cop, so she and her husband, Dantine, can receive visas to escape? Since they are penniless, it's her only way to obtain the documents. Bogart is noncommittal but goes to the gambling tables where he asks Dantine: "Have you played 22 tonight?" He repeats the number so that croupier Dalio knows at which number to stop the roulette wheel. The number wins and Bogart tells Dantine to let the chips ride. He wins again with the same number and Bogart tells him to "cash it in and don't come back." Page witnesses this act of magnanimity and kisses Bogart in gratitude. Headwaiter Sakall also sees the generous act, which now allows Page and Dantine to buy their visas, knowing Bogart has saved the girl's honor. He clasps his hands, then whispers the news to bartender Kinskey who kisses Bogart on both cheeks. Henreid arrives and asks Bogart to release the letters of transit so that his wife can escape Casablanca. He refuses and tells Henreid that if he wants to know the reason why he must ask his wife. At that moment German soldiers begin to loudly sing a Nazi war song, having appropriated Wilson's piano. Henreid, defiant, goes to the band and orders the members to "play 'La Marseillaise!' Play it!" Band members look to Bogart who nods agreement. The band strikes up the French national anthem and the crowd begins to sing along with Henreid who conducts the band. The anthem grows louder and louder until the German song is drowned out, ending with heroic cheers from the mostly Free French audience, galvanized into a burst of patriotic fever by Henreid's bold act. (When CASABLANCA is shown in certain revival houses, student audiences habitually get to their feet, cheering, so electric is this scene.) Veidt and his Nazis seethe; Veidt next tells Rains that he must close the cafe for any reason and stomps out. Rains blows his police whistle and announces that the cafe is closed. Bogart angrily confronts him: "How can you close me up? On what grounds?" Rains sidesteps, saying: "I'm shocked, shocked to find that gambling is going on here!" At that moment, croupier Dalio hands Rains a wad of bills, saying, "Your winnings, sir." Rains pockets the money with a curt thank you and proceeds to close up the cafe. Later that night Henreid goes to an underground meeting and Bergman goes to Bogart, begging him for the letters of transit, then threatening to shoot him if he won't give the papers to her. He refuses, walking close to her and the gun in her trembling hand. "Go ahead and shoot," he tells her, "you'll be doing me a favor." She can't shoot, telling him that she still loves him. They remain together as she tells him that she thought Henreid was dead in a concentration camp when they met but, just as she was going to leave Paris with him, she learned he was still alive and it was her wifely duty to remain with him. There is a disturbance downstairs in the empty cafe and Bogart sees Henreid enter with Sakall. They have escaped police who have raided the meeting. Bogart has Sakall take Bergman back to her hotel room through a side door so that her husband will not know she's been there, then he confronts Henreid. The freedom fighter tells him that "if we stop fighting our enemies, the world will die." Bogart tells him that he doesn't care. "Each of us has a destiny," Henreid reminds him, "for good or evil . . . I wonder if you know that you're trying to escape from yourself and you'll never succeed." Then Henreid tells Bogart that he knows all about his relationship with his wife. He asks the saloon keeper to use the letters of transit, to take his wife out of Casablanca so she will be safe. Police burst through the door and arrest Henreid. "It seems that destiny has taken a hand," Bogart says sarcastically as Henreid is led away. Bogart goes to Rains and tells the policeman that he can arrange for Rains to find the proper grounds to hold Henreid. He tells him that if he lets Henreid go, he'll give the underground leader the stolen letters of transit just when Rains arrives at the cafe so that Rains will have a charge that will "chuck him in a concentration camp for years." He then tells Rains that he intends to go off with Bergman. Rains agrees to the plan and orders Henreid's release, remarking: "Ricky, I'm going to miss you. Apparently you're the only one in Casablanca who has even less scruples than I." Bogart makes arrangements with Greenstreet to buy his cafe with the promise that Wilson will get his usual percentage and the help will be kept on. Rains and Bogart then meet in the closed cafe. Bergman arrives while Rains hides. She believes that he is going to give Henreid the letters and that she is to stay behind with him. Henreid arrives, offering money to Bogart for the papers. He turns over the letters, telling Henreid to keep his money. Rains steps from hiding and arrests Henreid "on a charge of accessory to the murder of the couriers from whom these letters were stolen." Henreid and Bergman reel in shock at Bogart's betrayal. Rains flippantly informs them that "Love, it seems, has triumphed over virtue." As the policeman turns he sees a gun in Bogart's hand. Bogart orders Rains to call the airport and inform officials that two more persons will be taking the Lisbon plane. "And remember," Bogart warns Rains, "this gun is pointed right at your heart." Rains grimaces. "That is my least vulnerable spot." Pretending to call the airport, Rains calls Veidt instead, giving instructions and alerting the Nazi to the escape. Veidt calls for his car and races for the airport. Bogart, Henreid, Bergman and Rains arrive at a hanger. Henreid goes off with a guard to get their luggage. Bogart then orders Rains to write the names of "Mr. and Mrs. Victor Laszlo" on the letters of transit. "But, why my name, Richard?" asks Bergman. "Because you're getting on that plane." She doesn't understand. "What about you?" He tells her that he intends to stay behind until the plane is safely on its way. She protests and he tells her that they'd both probably wind up in a concentration camp. "You're saying this only to make me go," Bergman says. He tells her that she must go with Henreid, that she is "the thing that keeps him going," and that if she doesn't go with him she'll regret it. "What about us?" Bergman asks. "We'll always have Paris," he tells her. Then he explains that he's "no good at being noble, but it doesn't take much to see that the problems of three little people don't amount to a hill o' beans in this crazy world . . . Here's looking at you, kid." He touches her cheek with one finger. Henreid returns and Bogart tells him that Bergman had visited him the night before to beg for the letters, pretending to still be in love with him but "that was over long ago. For your sake she pretended it wasn't and I let her pretend." Henreid tells him he understands but what he implies in one look is that he knows that the love between Bergman and Bogart will never end. Bogart hands him the letters. Henreid shakes his hand, telling him: "Welcome back to the fight." The loud whine of the engines of the Lisbon plane is heard and they turn, Bergman and Bogart, in a long last look at each other. "Goodbye, Rick," Bergman says, "God Bless you." He tells them to hurry or they'll miss the plane. He watches Henreid and Bergman walk off into the fog, going to the plane. Rains calls Bogart a sentimentalist, adding: "And that fairy tale you invented to send Ilsa away with him. I know a little about women, my friend. She went but she knew you were lying." Rains tells him that he will, of course, have to arrest him. "As soon as the plane goes, Louis," Bogart says, still holding the gun in his pocket. Veidt arrives and Rains tells him that Henreid and Bergman are in the plane going down the runway. Veidt goes to a phone, attempting to call the control tower and stop the plane. Bogart orders him to put down the phone but Veidt draws a pistol. Both exchange shots and the Nazi is killed. A carload of French police arrive. Rains gives Bogart a studied look, then tells one of his officers: "Major Strasser's been shot. Round up the usual suspects." Rains goes to a table, telling Bogart that "you're not only a sentimentalist, but you've become a patriot." He begins to pour a glass of water as Bogart tells him: "Maybe, but it seemed like a good time to start." Rains looks down at the bottle marked "Vichy Water," symbolizing the regime that sold out his country. He tosses the bottle into a wastebasket, kicking it, saying: "I think, perhaps, you're right." Together they watch the Lisbon plane take flight, climbing into the fog-bound night, taking its passengers to freedom. The two begin to walk across the wet runway, Rains suggesting that he might arrange passes for Bogart to "a Free French garrison over at Brazzaville." Bogart reminds him that he owes him ten thousand francs, the bet he won by virtue of Henreid's successful escape. "And that ten thousand francs should pay our expenses," adds Rains, telling Bogart that he is going with him. They continue walking across the runway, into the enveloping fog as Bogart says: "Louis, I think this is the beginning of a beautiful friendship." And the end of a beautiful film, even though it has some minor distractions. The writers, for instance, could not think of a good French name for Rains so they chose Renault, the name of the popular French auto. Then there are the sacrosanct "letters of transit." Lorre tells Bogart that they are "signed by General de Gaulle. They cannot be rescinded, not even questioned." In truth the Vichy government would never recognize de Gaulle's authority since he represented the exiled French Government in London. Bogart's speech to Bergman at the airport near the end of the film overlaps Robert Jordan's farewell speech to Maria in Hemingway's *For Whom the Bell Tolls*, and Rains' line to Bogart at the very end is odd. He says there is "a Free French garrison *over at* Brazzaville," as if it is nearby and yet this remote African town is more than a thousand miles distant from Casablanca. But all of these little discrepancies are mere spots on the sun. CASABLANCA, despite its haphazard fashioning, was a *lucky* film on all levels. It opened on Thanksgiving Day, 1942 at the Hollywood Theater in New York, three weeks after the Allies had landed at Casablanca and it further enjoyed widespread publicity generated from the Casablanca Conference occurring two months later when the eyes of the free world were focused upon its leaders meeting in the Moroccan city. Yet the beginning of CASABLANCA'S story was inauspicious. NYC high-school teacher and novice playwright Murray Burnett went to Europe in 1938 with his wife to visit relatives. He was present when the Nazis took over Austria and marched into Vienna and witnessed the first flood of refugees pouring out of German-occupied territory. Later, in the south of France, the Burnetts found a small cafe overlooking the Mediterranean which was crammed with well-to-do refugees en route to Casablanca, one of the key way stations to safety. It was in this cafe that Burnett took note of a popular black pianist entertaining an audience incongruously made up of Nazis, French, British, and other nationalities. He then decided to use the setting as a play, which he wrote in 1940 with collaborator Joan Alison. The play, entitled "Everybody Comes to Rick's," was never published nor produced but it was optioned by Martin Gabel and Carly Wharton who wanted to make changes. (They objected to the leading lady—named Lois, later changed to Ilsa—going to bed with Rick to get the visas.) The authors had their agent send out the play to Hollywood studios and Warners bought the script for $20,000 on the recommendation of story analyst Stephen Karnot. Producer Hal Wallis made the script his personal project. Writers Jerry Wald, Aeneas MacKenzie, and Wally Kline all contributed ideas to the script. Then dialogue experts Julius and Philip Epstein, twin brothers known for their bantering wit (FOUR DAUGHTERS, THE MAN WHO CAME TO DINNER, NO TIME FOR COMEDY and, uncredited, YANKEE DOODLE DANDY) were brought in to work over the script. Meanwhile Wallis tried to convince William Wyler, then under contract to Samuel Goldwyn, to direct. When this failed, Wallis tried directors Vincent Sherman and William Keighley. He later opted for the Warner Brothers workhorse, Michael Curtiz. The casting was sketchy and at first the studio announced that the leads would be played by Ronald Reagan, Ann Sheridan, and Dennis Morgan. Then Hedy Lamarr was considered for the role of Ilsa but Louis B. Mayer would not loan her out from MGM. Russian ballerina Tamara Toumanova was tested for the part, mostly at the urging of screenwriter Casey Robinson who later claimed that *he* changed the name of the feminine lead from an American to a European to fit Toumanova's personality (he admitted that he was in love with her at the time and would have done anything to please her). She was discarded by Wallis who decided that the great Swedish actress Ingrid Bergman would be perfect as Ilsa. He went to great lengths to persuade David O. Selznick, to whom she was under personal contract, to release her, even flying to New York and tracking down Selznick to his hotel room. Selznick agreed to exchange Bergman for Olivia de Havilland. Jack Warner asked Wallis what he thought of George Raft in the role of Rick; the producer replied that Raft was not right for the role, that it was being written for Bogart. The third lead was always Henreid's but studio executives felt he would not take a role that was less than that of Bogart's, so several second-leads were discussed, including Ian Hunter, Herbert Marshall, Dean Jagger, and Philip Dorn. Carl Esmond and Jean-Pierre Aumont were tested for the part and found wanting. Even Joseph Cotten was considered. Henreid's RKO contract was bought up by Warners and he was promised co-star billing. He then accepted the role of the heroic Laszlo. The magnificent cast was built player by player. Rains was one of the first actors selected and signed, with Warner players Greenstreet and Lorre added next. The Nazi leader was to be played by Otto Preminger, but Conrad Veidt, who played the evil and conniving Major Strasser to perfection, was later selected. A host of superb character actors were added, S. Z. "Cuddles" Sakall as the delightful headwaiter, Leonid Kinskey, the eccentric Russian bartender, beautiful 19-year-old French actress Madeline LeBeau, Marcel Dalio, the suave croupier, Joy Page and Helmut Dantine, later stars of B-films, as the young Bulgarian couple. The Epstein twins worked excitedly on the script but Howard Koch was also brought in to develop characterization. Everyone contributed to the sparkling script. "Here's looking at you, kid," was provided by the Epsteins, along with the "round up the usual suspects" order by Rains. Wallis himself came up with the last poignant line, "Louis, I think this is the beginning of a beautiful friendship." Much was made up day to day during the 59-day shooting schedule, all on the WB lot, Curtiz actually shaping the scenes, tossing out pages of script he disliked or using that which was in keeping with his own vision. (Curtiz knew what it meant to be a refugee; he had to smuggle his own family out of Hungary before the Nazis swarmed into the country.) The feel of the entire film, its incredible pace and marvelous cross-cutting to inject character roles and bits which gives CASABLANCA its international flavor, emanates from Curtiz. And one of the film's most enduring characters, Dooley Wilson, was almost eliminated from the cast early-on. Wilson, who had appeared in the Broadway production of "Cabin in the Sky" with Ethel Waters, was tested and tentatively accepted by Wallis who later thought veteran black actor Clarence Muse might be better. Even black female singers Lena Horne and Ella Fitzgerald were thought of to play the role of the piano player. Moreover, Wilson didn't play the piano. He had been a singing drummer in New York revues before being discovered. When he was finally chosen for the part, his piano playing was dubbed by studio musician Elliot Carpenter. The theme song selection of "As Time Goes By" (Herman Hupfeld) originated with playwright Burnett; it was a personal favorite from his college days, and a song first sung in the 1931 Broadway musical "Everybody's Welcome" by Frances Williams. Ironically, the song did not catch on until CASABLANCA made it famous. (Later Wilson asked Jack Warner for permission to record the song and was told he could do so, as long as the studio got the lion's share of the profits.) Composer Max Steiner, although he did not initially like the tune, preferring to create his own songs, worked the melody through lyrical and pulsating versions, making it all the more evocative. In his stirring score Steiner mixed, as if in battle, the German and French national anthems, "Deutschland uber Alles," and "La Marseillaise," along with "Die Wacht am Rhein." Moreover, Steiner employed a variation of his score for THE LOST PATROL (1934) in his musical montage in the opening scenes to give the feel of desert-bound Morocco. Sprinkled throughout are songs sung by Wilson, "It Had To Be You," "'Cause," and "Knock on Wood." The performances, by the leads, of course, are stunning. Henreid is quiet and resolute in his role of the underground leader, an understanding man whose tolerance is nobility itself. Bergman is exquisite and never lovelier than as Ilsa Lund, a part to which she brings ultimate sensitivity, a woman who loves two men for two different reasons. When Bergman conferred with writers, the Epsteins told her that she must "play it in between," since they had no idea how the film would end. In one version she was to go with Henreid, in a second ending to be shot she would stay behind with Bogart. Not until the studio saw the first ending did they decide to allow Bogart to lose the girl and win the respect of the world. The second ending was never shot. Bergman had never before acted opposite Bogart and never would again. She was actually fearful of this tough guy whom she had seen in many crime films but she found him a supreme professional who worked hard with every line, labored over every scene then made it seem so terribly easy before the camera. She would later say: "I kissed him [on camera] but I don't know him." Bogart did not stay on the set, telling jokes or passing chatter. He would retreat to his trailer and sit with cronies after his scenes. To acquaint herself with this man of mystery, Bergman watched THE MALTESE FALCON many times, trying to get the feel of Bogart's acting techniques. Their scenes together are charged with adrenaline, a hot chemistry that was magical, as was the case with all the other players. That magic spilled into eight Academy Award nominations. The film won three: Best Picture, Best Screenplay, and Best Director. Curtiz was genuinely surprised to get his Oscar and in his unprepared acceptance speech he sputtered malapropisms: "So many times I have a speech ready, but no dice. Always a bridesmaid, never a mother. Now I win, I have no speech." Wallis received the Irving Thalberg Award for the second time. CASABLANCA shot Bergman's name into superstar status and she quickly followed this film with enormous hits, SPELLBOUND, NOTORIOUS, GASLIGHT, FOR WHOM THE BELL TOLLS. It did even more for Humphrey Bogart who had taken years to shed his second-lead gangster image, emerging only two years before as a sympathetic leading man in HIGH SIERRA and THE MALTESE FALCON. The role of Rick was tailor-made to his chain-smoking, tough-acting personality, a man with a thick hide but a heart that softened for the "wow" finish. Here, for the first time, he was a romantic lead, one in which the real Bogart finally emerged. For the next seven years he would be one of the world's most popular actors and, following the film, with a new WB contract, the highest paid. Despite his many fine performances to follow (THE TREASURE OF THE SIERRA MADRE, THE AFRICAN QUEEN, THE CAINE MUTINY, SAHARA) he would be remembered as Richard Blaine, the outsider, the man who lost his great love and supposedly a better life, but who goes on alone, knowing and accepting his fate, a hero without a name or a future, only a haunted past and magnificent tragedy above and beyond which lingers personal honor, stronger than life itself, his or any other's. His rough but sentimental character is, strangely enough, the envy of most men, his offbeat gallantry a deep attraction to any woman. Enigmatic, unpredictable, fearless in his resignation, here is a man who will risk all for a memory. At the very least he has had priceless moments with Ilsa Lund in Paris before the world slipped into darkness. At the most, he is a man in a frayed trench coat walking into the mist with only a rascal for a friend and the certain knowledge that he is the watch that ends the night.

p, Hal B. Wallis; d, Michael Curtiz; w, Julius J. and Phillip G. Epstein, and Howard Koch (based on the play "Everybody Goes to Rick's" by Murray Burnett and Joan Alison); ph, Arthur Edeson; m, Max Steiner; ed, Owen Marks; art d, Carl Jules Weyl; set d, George James Hopkins; md, Leo Forbstein; orchestrations, Hugo Friedhofer; gowns, Orry-Kelly; makeup, Perc Westmore; spec eff, Lawrence Butler, Willard Van Enger; montages, Don Siegel, James Leicester; tech adv, Robert Aisner; m/l, "Knock on Wood," "That's What Noah Done," "Muse's Call," M.K. Jerome, Jack Scholl, "As Time Goes By," Herman Hupfeld.

Drama **Cas.** **(PR:A MPAA:NR)**

CASANOVA**

(1976, Ital.) 166m Titanus/UNIV c (AKA: FELLINI'S CASANOVA)

Donald Sutherland *(Casanova)*, Tina Aumont *(Enrichetta)*, Cicely Browne *(Madame D'Urfe)*, Olimpia Carlisi *(Isabella)*, Adele Angela Lojodice *(Doll Woman)*.

A destructive film which demystifies the legend of famed bedroom performer Casanova with every frame. Inspired by Fellini's reading of "The History of My Life," Casanova's biography, this film takes place in bedrooms from his native Venice to Paris, Germany, London, Austria, and Rome. Filmed in English, a language foreign to Fellini, Casanova is an exercise in detachment—both of the character from his surroundings, and of the director from the audience. Donald Sutherland is as exceptional as the script will allow, helped along by Nino Rota's ever-present score. The outstanding costumes and art direction were awarded BFA's.

p, Alberto Grimaldi; d, Federico Fellini; w, Fellini, Bernardino Zappone; ph, Giuseppe Rotunno (Eastmancolor); m, Nino Rota; ed, Ruggiero Mastroianni; art d, Danilo Donati; cos, Donati.

Drama **(PR:O MPAA:NR)**

CASANOVA AND COMPANY

(SEE: SOME LIKE IT COOL, 1977, Ger./Fr./Ital.)

CASANOVA BROWN*½** (1944) 93m RKO bw

Gary Cooper *(Casanova Brown)*, Teresa Wright *(Isabel Drury)*, Frank Morgan *(Mr. Ferris)*, Anita Louise *(Madge Ferris)*, Patricia Collinge *(Mrs. Drury)*, Edmond Breon *(Mr. Drury)*, Jill Esmond *(Dr. Zernerke)*, Emory Parnell *(Frank)*, Isobel Elsom *(Mrs. Ferris)*, Mary Treen *(Monica)*, Halliwell Hobbes *(Butler)*, Larry Joe Olsen *(Junior)*, Bryon Foulger *(Fletcher)*, Sara Padden *(Landlady)*, Eloise Hardt *(Doris Ferris)*, Grady Sutton *(Tod)*, Frederick Burton *(Reverend Dean)*, Robert Dudley *(Marriage Clerk)*, Isabel La Mal *(Clerk's Wife)*, Florence Lake *(Nurse Phillips)*, Ann Evers *(Nurse Petherbridge)*, Frances Morris *(Nurse Gillespie)*, Nell Craig *(Nurse)*, Lane Chandler *(Orderly)*, Kay Deslys *(Fat Woman Patient)*, Ottola Nesmith *(Patient's Nurse)*, Lorna Dunn, Kelly Flint, Julia Faye *(X-Ray Nurses)*, Dorothy Tree *(Nurse Clark)*, Isabel Withers *(Nurse Who Helps Casanova)*, Irving Bacon *(Hotel Manager)*, James Burke *(O'Leary)*, Francis Sayles *(Elevator Operator)*, Phil Tead *(License Clerk)*, Snub Pollard *(Father at Baby Window)*, Grace Cunard, Verna Kornman, Anna Luther, Marian Gray, Sada Simmons *(Women at Baby Window)*, Cecile Stewart *(Organist)*, Lelah Tyler *(Switchboard Operator)*, Helen St. Rayner *(Soloist)*, Stewart Garner *(Usher)*, Mary Young *(Mrs. Dean)*, John Brown *(Fire Chief)*, Jack Gargan *(Intern)*.

Sparkling light comedy about a shy English teacher (Cooper) who is about to marry Louise when he learns that he is to be a father by a quickie marriage and divorce a while back to Wright. Cooper visits the maternity hospital and Wright tells him that she will put the baby up for adoption as soon as it is born. The child is a gorgeous girl and Cooper can't bear the thought of anyone else rearing *his* daughter so he kidnaps the infant. Now the fun begins as Cooper attempts to raise his child behind the closed doors of his hotel room. With the help of chambermaid Treen and bellhop Parnell, they turn the hotel room into a nursery. Soon enough, Cooper realizes he can't be mom and dad to the little tyke and he seriously considers marrying Treen so his child can have a mother. Eventually, both wife-to-be and wife-that-was descend upon Cooper and, once he's gone through the rigors of hell, he makes the decision to stick with Wright, mother of his child and the woman he loved all along anyhow. Cooper was never much of a comedian on film and just about as good as the scripts he was given. The ludicrousness of seeing the heroic actor in a room full of diapers was funny enough for many but not enough to make this a memorable comedy. It wasn't a large success, even with Cooper's box office draw and the three Oscar nominations it garnered (Ferguson and Herron, Lange, and Thomas J. Moulton for Sound).

p, Nunnally Johnson; d, Sam Wood; w, Johnson (based on play "The Little Accident" by Floyd Dell and Thomas Mitchell); ph, John Seitz; m, Arthur Lange; ed, Thomas Neff; art d, Perry Ferguson; set d, Julia Heron; cos; Muriel King.

Comedy **(PR:A MPAA:NR)**

CASANOVA IN BURLESQUE½** (1944) 74m REP bw

Joe E. Brown *(Joseph M. Kelly, Jr.)*, June Havoc *(Lillian Colman)*, Dale Evans *(Barbara Compton)*, Marjorie Gateson *(Lucille Compton)*, Lucien Littlefield *(John Alden Compton)*, Ian Keith *(J. Boggs-Robinson)*, Roger Imhof *(Joseph M. Kelly, Sr.)*, Harry Tyler *(Bucky Farrell)*, Patricia Knox *(Peewee Dixon)*, Sugar Geise *(Fannie)*, Jerome Franks, Jr. *(Al Gordon)*, Margia Dean *(Guest)*.

Brown leads a double life, spending his summers as a burlesque comedian and his winters as a professor of Shakespeare at a small-town college. All goes well until stripper Havoc recognizes Brown in his professorial role and blackmails him into giving her the lead in his upcoming production of "The Taming of the Shrew." When the rest of the cast walks out, Brown is forced to call on his burlesque associates to be in the show. Surprisingly good musical comedy with Brown in top form. Songs include: "Who Took Me Home Last Night?" by Harold Adamson and Jule Styne, and "Mess Me Up," "Casanova Joe," "Five-A-Day Fatima," "Willie The Shake," and "Taming Of The Shrew," by Walter Kent and Kim Gannon.

p, Albert J. Cohen; d, Leslie Goodwins; w, Frank Gill, Jr. (based on a story idea by John Wales); ph, Reggie Lafining; ed, Ernest Nims; md, Walter Scharf; ch, Dave Gould; m/l, Harold Adamson, Jule Styne, Walter Kent, Kim Gannon.

Musical/Comedy **(PR:A MPAA:NR)**

CASANOVA '70*** (1965, Ital.) 113m EMB c

Marcello Mastroianni *(Maj. Andrea Rossi-Colombetti)*, Virna Lisi *(Gigliola)*, Michele Mercier *(Noelle)*, Marisa Mell *(Thelma)*, Marco Ferreri *(Count Ferreri)*, Enrico Maria Salerno *(Psychoanalyst)*, Guido Alberti *(Monsignor)*, Margaret Lee *(Dolly Greenwater)*, Rosemarie Dexter *(Chambermaid)*, Yolanda Modio *(Addolarata)*, Seyna Seyn *(Indonesian Airline Hostess)*, Moira Orfei *(Santina)*, Liana Orfei *(Lion Tamer)*, Beba Loncar *(Girl in Museum)*, Frank Gregory *(Gen. Greenwater)*, Luciana Paoli *(Grocer's Wife)*, Augusta Checcotti *(Gigliola's Mother)*, Mario Banchelli *(Gigliola's Father)*, Bernard Blier *(Commissioner)*.

A modern-day version of an old tale pits great lover Casanova against the emancipated woman. Mastroianni is well cast as a NATO officer whose sexual arousal comes only when danger is interwoven with passion. A funny, inspired sex farce which is well-suited to the times. Academy Award nominee for Best Original Screenplay. (In Italian, English subtitles)

p, Carlo Ponti; d, Mario Monicelli; w, Furio Scarpelli, Agenore Incrocci, Monicelli (based on a story by Tonino Guerra); ph, Aldo Tonti; m, Armando Trovajoli; ed, Ruggiero Mastroianni; cos, Giulio Coltellacci, art d, Mario Garbuglia; set d, Georgio Herman.

Comedy **(PR:O MPAA:NR)**

CASANOVA'S BIG NIGHT** (1954) 85m PAR c
Bob Hope *(Pippo Popolino)*, Joan Fontaine *(Francesca Bruni)*, Audrey Dalton *(Elena)*, Basil Rathbone *(Lucio)*, Hugh Marlowe *(Stefano Di Gambetta)*, Vincent Price *(Casanova)*, Arnold Moss *(The Doge of Venice)*, John Carradine *(Minister Foressi)*, John Hoyt *(Maggiorin)*, Hope Emerson *(Duchess of Castelbello)*, Robert Hutton *(Raphael, Duc of Castelbello)*, Lon Chaney Jr. *(Emo)*, Raymond Burr *(Bragadin)*, Frieda Inescort *(Signora Di Gambetta)*, Primo Carnera *(Corfa)*, Frank Puglia *(Carabaccio)*, Paul Cavanagh *(Signor Di Gambetta)*, Romo Vincent *(Giovanni)*, Henry Brandon *(Capt. Rugello)*, Natalie Schafer *(Signora Foressi)*, Lucien Littlefield *(First Prisoner)*, Douglas Fowley *(Second Prisoner)*, Nestor Paiva *(Gnocchi)*, Barbara Freking *(Maria)*, Joan Shawlee *(Beatrice)*, Oliver Blake *(Amadeo)*.

A mildly amusing costume comedy set in the 1700s which casts the wimpy Hope as a mistaken Casanova. He is forced to continue this charade when hired by a duchess to test the faithfulness of her son's fiance. Hope encounters a score of Hollywood villains along the way, including Basil Rathbone, John Carradine, Lon Chaney, Jr., and Raymond Burr. In a cameo, Vincent Price appears as the Casanova Hope is originally mistaken for—the resemblances are uncanny. We are also treated to the tune "Tic-a-Tic-a-Tic" by a couple of gondoliers.

p, Paul Jones; d, Norman Z. McLeod; w, Hal Kanter, Edmund Hartmann (based on a story by Aubrey Wisberg); ph, Lionel Lindon (Technicolor); m, Lyn Murray; ed, Ellsworth Hoagland; spec eff, John P. Fulton; ch, Josephine Earl; m/l, Jay Livingston, Ray Evans.

Musical/Comedy **(PR:A MPAA:NR)**

CASBAH*½** (1948) 94m UNIV bw
Yvonne De Carlo *(Inez)*, Tony Martin *(Pepe le Moko)*, Peter Lorre *(Slimane)*, Marta Toren *(Gaby)*, Hugo Haas *(Omar)*, Thomas Gomez *(Louvain)*, Douglas Dick *(Carlo)*, Katherine Dunham *(Odette)*, Herbert Rudley *(Claude)*, Gene Walker *(Roland)*, Curt Conway *(Maurice)*, Andre Pola *(Willem)*, Barry Bernard *(Max)*, Virginia Gregg *(Madeline)*, Will Lee *(Beggar)*, Harris Brown *(Pierre)*, Houseley Stevenson *(Anton Duval)*, Robert Kendall *(Ahmed)*, Rosita Marstini *(Woman)*, Jody Gilbert, Kathleen Freeman *(American Women)*, John Bagni, Bert Le Baron, Carey Harrison, Tom Tamerez *(Inspectors)*, Antonio Pina, Jerry Pina, Abel Pina, Henry Pina *(Acrobats)*, Paul Fierro *(Policeman)*, Maynard Holmes *(Guide)*, George J. Lewis *(Detective)*, Leander De Cordova *(Doorman)*, Maurice Navarre *(Fire Eater)*, Basil Tellou *(Blind Singer)*, Hassen Khayyan, Samir Rizkallah *(Arabs)*, Major Sam Harris, Kathryn Wilson *(British Tourists)*, Lorraine Gale *(Blonde Girl)*, George Hyland *(American Business Man)*, Jane K. Looffbourrow *(Schoolteacher)*, Carmen Gonzalez, Marie Tavares *(Girls in Inez's Shop)*, Josette Deegan *(Stewardess)*, Barry Norton, Nick Borgani *(Pilots)*, Elsa Walker, Tina Menard *(Women)*, Bob Lugo *(Native Man)*, Phil Friedman *(Native)*, Eddie Randolph, Louise Bates, Robert L. Lorraine *(Tourists)*, Katherine Dunham Dance Troupe with Eartha Kitt *(Performers)*.

CASBAH is a remake of a remake but they added the top spin of music to this one. Let's hope this third version puts an end to the story. Originally lensed in France as PEPE LE MOKO, starring Jean Gabin, it was a trifle too rough for the Hays Office and failed to get that important seal of approval. It was later superbly done with Charles Boyer in the lead in ALGIERS, 1938. The plot in this film remains the same as previously; le Moko (Martin) is hiding out from the police in the Casbah. Inside those walls, Pepe is le Boss but the moment he ventures outside, his name is le mud. Lorre is the policeman who would like to capture Martin but it's next to impossible because everyone in the Casbah protects him. Lorre is willing to wait; he feels there will eventually come a time when Martin must leave his private enclave. De Carlo is a local wench madly in love with Martin but he only has eyes for Toren, a tourist who has just come to the Casbah. Lorre learns that Martin is about to leave Algiers with Toren. He goes to Toren and tells her that Martin has been killed by a knife-wielding enemy. She is understandably distraught and plans to depart at six a.m. the next morning. Lorre had gotten the information about Martin's love for Toren from Dick, who is playing both sides. Dick is trapped by Martin's confederates and confesses to save his own slimy skin. They reward him by execution but it's too late to tell Martin it's a trap. He gets to the airport, sees Toren get aboard the airliner, and is on his way to join her when Lorre puts the pinch on him. The plane begins to taxi, Martin pulls away, runs after the airship, and is shot by one of the accompanying detectives. Martin dies in Lorre's arms as Toren's plane takes off. CASBAH wasn't a very good movie when compared with its two predecessors but on its own it was an interesting musical. Some fine songs by Arlen and Robin including "For Every Man There's A Woman," "What's Good About Goodbye?" and "It Was Written in the Stars." Best performance was by Lorre as the inspector. He underplayed it perfectly and should have had an Oscar nomination. The above-mentioned song garnered one but lost to "Buttons and Bows" from THE PALEFACE.

p, Nat C. Goldstone; d, John Berry; w, L. Bus-Fekete, Arnold Manoff (from a musical story by associate producer Erik Charell; based on novel *Pepe le Moko* by Detective Ashelbe); ph, Irving Glassberg; m, Walter Scharf; ed, Edward Curtiss; m/l, Harold Arlen, Leo Robin; ch, Bernard Pearce; cos, Yvonne Wood; spec eff, David S. Horsley.

Musical/Drama **(PR:C MPAA:NR)**

CASE AGAINST BROOKLYN, THE½** (1958) 82m COL bw
Darren McGavin *(Pete Harris)*, Maggie Hayes *(Lil Polombo)*, Warren Stevens *(Rudi Franklin)*, Peggy McCay *(Jane Harris)*, Tol Avery *(Michael W. Norris)*, Emile Meyer *(Capt. P. T. Wills)*, Nestor Paiva *(Finelli)*, Brian Hutton *(Jess Johnson)*, Robert Osterloh *(Bonney)*, Joseph Turkel *(Monte)*, Thomas B. Henry *(Edmondson)*, Cheerio Meredith *(Mrs. Carney)*, Bobby Helms *(Himself)*, Booth Colman, Michael Garth, Herb Vigran *(Police Sergeant)*.

Darren McGavin is a rookie cop going undercover to expose a gambling ring that's buying off large portions of the police force. He takes up with Hayes, whose husband killed himself over gambling debts, despite the fact that he is married to McCay. Story is further complicated because the superiors he is reporting to are under the influence of the racketeers he's investigating. The film ends with fellow cop and friend Hutton murdered, McCay blown up, and McGavin in the hospital. Based on a true story and not bad at all.

p, Charles H. Schneer; d, Paul Wendkos; w, Raymond T. Marcus (story by Daniel B. Ullman, based on a magazine article by Ed Reid); ph, Fred Jackman; m, Mischa Bakaleinikoff; ed, Edwin Bryant; m/l, Bob Hilliard, Mort Garson.

Crime **(PR:A MPAA:NR)**

CASE AGAINST FERRO, THE** (1980, Fr.) 125m Specialty c
Yves Montand *(Ferro)*, Simone Signoret *(Therese)*, Francois Perier *(Ganay)*, Stefania Sandrelli *(Sylvia)*, Mathieu Carriere *(Menard)*.

Police inspector Montand heads an investigation into a murder and comes to be the chief suspect. He eludes arrest and eventually uncovers the evidence that convicts his boss. Vaguely interesting variation of THE BIG CLOCK, but slow-moving.

d, Alain Corneau; w, Corneau, Daniel Boulanger; ph, Etienne Becker (Eastmancolor); m, Georges Delerue; ed, Marie-Joseph Yoyotte.

Crime **(PR:C MPAA:NR)**

CASE AGAINST MRS. AMES, THE*½ (1936) 85m PAR bw
Madeleine Carroll *(Hope Ames)*, George Brent *(Matt Logan)*, Arthur Treacher *(Griggsby)*, Alan Baxter *(Lou)*, Beulah Bondi *(Mrs. Livingston Ames)*, Alan Mowbray *(Lawrence Waterson)*, Brenda Fowler *(Mrs. Shumway)*, Esther Dale *(Matilda)*, Edward Brophy *(Sid)*, Richard Carle *(Uncle Gordon)*, Scotty Beckett *(Bobbie Ames)*, Mayo Methot *(Cora)*, Guy Bates Post *(Judge Davis)*, June Brewster *(Laurette)*, Elvira Curci *(Jeanette)*, Jonathan Hale *(Judge)*, Margaret Bloodgood *(Police Matron)*, Edward Earle *(Maitland Harris)*, Ed LeSaint *(Dr. Caswell)*, Max Wagner *(Soupy)*, Richard Powell *(Ferryboat Porter)*, Otto Hoffman *(Jury Foreman)*, Tom Ricketts, Bobby Bolder, Phil Dunham, Frank Hammond *(Jurymen)*, Albert Conti *(Headwaiter)*, Bruce Mitchell *(Druggist)*.

Courtroom tedium that has a framed woman, Carroll, on and off the stand, first for the murder of her husband and then for custody of her son. A suspecting assistant D.A., Brent, uncovers another lawyer's rascally plan to frame Carroll, and the lawyer kills himself upon discovery. As expected, Brent finds himself falling for Carroll, allowing for a few scenes outside of the courthouse.

p, Walter Wanger; d, William A. Seiter; w, Gene Towne, Graham Baker (based on the story by Arthur Somers Roche); ph, Lucien Andriot; ed, Dorothy Spencer.

Drama **(PR:A MPAA:NR)**

CASE FOR PC 49, A*½ (1951, Brit.) 80m Hammer bw
Brian Reece *(Archibald Berkeley-Willoughby)*, Joy Shelton *(Joan Carr)*, Christine Norden *(Della Dainton)*, Leslie Bradley *(Victor Palantine)*, Gordon McLeod *(Inspector Wilson)*, Campbell Singer *(Sgt. Wright)*, Jack Stewart *(Cutler)*, Michael Balfour *(Chubby Price)*.

Another lame crime mystery based on a popular radio series, only this time it's British. A detective proves that the murder of a millionaire was committed by a beautiful artist's model.

p, Anthony Hinds; d, Francis Searle; w, Alan Stranks, Vernon Harris (based on a radio series by Stranks and Harris); ph, Walter Harvey.

Mystery **(PR:A MPAA:NR)**

CASE FOR THE CROWN, THE* (1934, Brit.) 70m B&D/Paramount British bw
Miles Mander *(James L. Barton)*, Meriel Forbes *(Shirley Rainsford)*, Whitmore Humphries *(Roy Matherson)*, Lawrence Anderson *(Roxy)*, David Horne *(James Rainsford)*, Gordon McLeod *(Prosecution)*, John Turnbull *(Prof. Lawrence)*.

Another dull British courtroom drama. This time a contractor has made his partner's suicide look like murder to save the man's daughter from the stigma of his end. Nothing sets this one apart from a thousand similar courtroom melodramas.

p&d, George A. Cooper; w, Sherard Powell (based on the story "An Error of Judgment" by Anthony Gittins).

Crime **(PR:A MPAA:NR)**

CASE OF CHARLES PEACE, THE*½ (1949, Brit.) 88m Argyle/Monarch bw
Michael Martin Harvey *(Charles Peace)*, Chili Bouchier *(Katherine Dyson)*, Valentine Dyall *(Storyteller)*, Bruce Belfrage *(Prosecution)*, Ronald Adam *(Defense)*, Roberta Huby *(Sue Thompson)*, Peter Forbes-Robertson *(William Habron)*, Richard Shayne *(Arthur Dyson)*, Peter Gawthorne *(Mr. Justice Lopes)*.

A fictionalized account of one of Victorian England's most celebrated criminals. Harvey is the diminutive picture framer turned burglar and murderer who eventually ends up on the gallows. The real Peace was a singularly ugly man with webbed fingers who had the amazing ability to scale the walls of buildings using an array of tools of his own invention (many of which are in standard usage among burglars today). Despite a fascinating subject, the film is far removed from the facts of the case and pretty boring.

p, John Argyle; d, Norman Lee; w, Doris Davison, Lee; ph, Joseph Amber.

Crime **(PR:A MPAA:NR)**

CASE OF CLARA DEANE, THE*   (1932) 60m PAR bw
(AKA: THE STRANGE CASE OF CLARA DEANE)
Wynne Gibson (Clara Deane), Pat O'Brien (Frank Deane), Frances Dee (Nancy), Dudley Digges (Garrison), George Barbier (Ware), Russell Gleason (Norman), Clara Blandick (Mrs. Lyons), Cora Sue Collins (Nancy as Child).

Gibson gets a long jail term for a crime she did not commit, which forces her to leave daughter Collins an orphan since the father also is in jail. When the child's foster parents find both the real parents have been released from prison and are looking for their daughter, both for different reasons, money becomes a motive, because the daughter, now a grown woman, is engaged to a wealthy young man. A tearjerker all the way and to the production's shame the cheap sentiment is played to the agonizing hilt. O'Brien is wasted as an illiterate thief.

d, Louis Gasnier, Max Marcin; w, Marcin (based on the play by Arthur M. Brilant); ph, Harry Sharp.

Drama   (PR:A   MPAA:NR)

CASE OF DR. LAURENT½   (1958, Fr.) 93m Cocinor bw
Jean Gabin (Dr. Laurent), Nicole Courcel (Francine), Sylvia Monfort (Catherine Loubet), Arius Daxely, Michael Barbey, Serge Davin, Georges Lannes, Orane Demazis, Mag Avril, Balpetre, Josselin.

Gabin is a Paris doctor championing natural childbirth in the countryside in this interesting effort. He faces opposition from the medical establishment and the narrow-minded locals, but when unwed mother Courcel gives birth without difficulty while under his care they are won over and Gabin is triumphant. Actual birth sequences are well handled and the whole film exhibits intelligence in scripting, direction, and acting.

d, Jean-Paul Le Chanois; w, Le Chanois, Rene Barjavel; ph, Henri Alekan; m, Joseph Kosma.

Drama   (PR:C   MPAA:NR)

CASE OF GABRIEL PERRY, THE*   (1935, Brit.) 78m BL bw
Henry Oscar (Gabriel Perry), Olga Lindo (Mrs. Perry), Margaret Lockwood (Mildred Perry), Franklin Dyall (Prosecution), Raymond Lovell (Defense), John Wood (Godfrey Perry), Martita Hunt (Mrs. Read), Rodney Ackland (Tommy Read), Percy Walsh (William Read), Ralph Truman (Inspector White), Mark Lester, Alistair Sim.

Still more British courtroom drama, this time with Lindo, the wife of Justice of the Peace Oscar, discovering that her husband has committed a murder. As tedious as all the others of its ilk.

p, Herbert Smith; d, Albert de Courville; w, L. DuGarde Peach (based on the play "Wild Justice" by James Dale).

Crime   (PR:A   MPAA:NR)

CASE OF MRS. LORING   (SEE: QUESTION OF ADULTERY, A, 1959, Brit.)

CASE OF PATTY SMITH, THE*½   (1962) 93m Leo A. Handel bw
Merry Anders (Mary), J. Edward McKinley (Dr. Miller), Dani Lynn (Patty), Carleton Crane (Allan), Bob Rudelson (Top), Speer Martin (Sidy), Sean Brian (Reep), David McMahon (Father O'Brien), Bruno Ve Sota (Colbert), Jack Haddock (Lt. Powell), Joe Conley (Johnny), Lief Lindstrom (Dr. Neilson), Mary Patton (Myra), Sid Cane (Crawford), Sherwood Keith (Dr. Fridden), Phil Clarke (Pawnbroker), Harrison Lewis (Bartender), Adrienne Hayes (Jean), Mary Benoit (Dr. Miller's Nurse), Sally Hughes (Dr. Fridden's Nurse), Ralph Neff ("Doctor"), Barney Biro (Narrator).

Dani Lynn is a pretty 21-year-old girl who gets pregnant after being raped. Rebuffed by the legitimate medical community, she turns to her priest, but he is unsympathetic. In desperation she goes to an abortionist, but he does a butcher job and she dies. Controversial when released, the film suffers from a preachy story and Lynn's permanently befuddled expression and now it just looks silly.

p,d&w, Leo A. Handel; ph, Howard Schwartz; m, Ingram P. Walters; ed, Stanford Tischler; art d, Ted Holsopple; set d, Ray Bolz.

Drama   (PR:CO   MPAA:NR)

CASE OF SERGEANT GRISCHA, THE*   (1930) 73m RKO bw
Chester Morris (Grischa), Betty Compson (Babka), Jean Hersholt, Alec B. Francis, Gustav von Seyffertitz, Paul McAllister, Leyland Hodgson, Bernard Siegel, Frank McCormack, Jean Hersholt (Posnanski), Alec B. Francis (Gen. von Lychow), Gustav von Seyffertitz (Gen. Schieffenzahn), Paul McAllister (Col. Sacht), Leyland Hodgson (Lt. Winfried), Bernard Siegel (Verressjeff), Frank McCormack (Capt. Spierauge/Kolja).

Morris is a Russian POW in WW I Germany. He manages to escape the compound and is hidden by Compson. After a time he tries to make his way back to Russia but is recaptured by the Germans while wearing the identity tag of a dead Russian spy. Despite evidence of his innocence, Morris is executed as a spy. Adapted from a harrowing novel by Arnold Zweig, the film went out of its way to be serious and weighty but managed to lose dramatic tension, credibility, and audiences.

p, William LeBaron; d, Herbert Brenon; w, Elizabeth Meehan (based on a novel by Arnold Zweig); ph, Roy Hunt; ed, Marie Halvey.

War Drama   (PR:A   MPAA:NR)

CASE OF THE BLACK CAT, THE**   (1936) 65m WB bw
Ricardo Cortez (Perry Mason), June Travis (Della Street), Jane Bryan (Wilma Laxter), Craig Reynolds (Frank Oafley), Carlyle Moore, Jr. (Douglas Keene), Gordon Elliott (Sam Laxter), Nedda Harrigan (Louise DeVoe), Garry Owen (Paul Drake), Harry Davenport (Peter Laxter), George Rosener (Ashton), Gordon Hart (Dr. Jacobs), Clarence Wilson (Shuster), Guy Usher (Burger), Lottie Williams (Mrs. Pixley), Harry Hayden (Rev. Stillwell), Milton Kibbee (Brandon), John Sheehan (Sgt. Holcomb).

Murder whodunit complete with a treasure hunt brands this movie's tense scenes, with a screeching cat creating a foundation for chills and gasps. Suspense and action ample in this fine, completely satisfying technical production. (See PERRY MASON series, Index.)

p, Bryan Foy; d, William McGann; w, F. Hugh Herbert (based on the story, "The Case of the Caretaker's Cat" by Erle Stanley Gardner); ph, Allen G. Siegler; ed, Frank Magee.

Crime Drama   (PR:A   MPAA:NR)

CASE OF THE BLACK PARROT, THE**   (1941) 60m FN/WB bw
William Lundigan (Jim Moore), Maris Wrixon (Sandy Vantine), Eddie Foy, Jr. (Tripod Daniels), Paul Cavanagh (Max Armand), Luli Deste (Mme. de Charriere), Charles D. Waldron (Paul Vantine), Joseph Crehan (Grady), Emory Parnell (Simmonds), Phyllis Barry (Julia), Cyril Thornton (Rogers), Leyland Hodgson (Parks), Ernie Stanton (Col. Piggott), Cliff Baum (Morel).

Newspaperman Lundigan and photographer Foy are on a boat sailing for the U.S. when, during a false submarine warning, a major theft takes place on board. Lundigan thinks it was perpetrated by an international criminal known as the Black Parrot. Two murders and an unconscionable number of false clues later, smart reporter Lundigan comes through with the culprit. Shipboard antics help make it an absorbing sixty minutes, though.

p, William Jacobs; d, Noel M. Smith; w, Robert E. Kent (based on the play "In the next Room" by Eleanor Belmont and Harriet Ford, and the novel Mystery of the Boule Cabinet by Burton E. Stevenson); ph, Ted McCord; ed, Thomas Pratt.

Adventure/Crime   (PR:A   MPAA:NR)

CASE OF THE CURIOUS BRIDE, THE**   (1935) 74m FN bw
Warren William (Perry Mason), Margaret Lindsay (Rhoda Montaine), Claire Dodd (Delila), Donald Woods (Carl), Allen Jenkins (Spudsy), Phillip Reed (Dr. Claude Millsap), Winifred Shaw (Doris Pender), Warren Hymer (Oscar Pender), Olin Howland (Coroner), Henry Kolker (State's Attorney), Charles Richman (Montaine, Sr.), Thomas Jackson (Toots Howard), Errol Flynn (Moxley), Mayo Methot (Florabelle), Barton MacLane (John Lucas), Robert Gleckler (Byrd the Detective), James Donlan (Fritz the Detective), George Humbert (Luigi), Henry Kolker (Stacey), Hector Sarno (Greek Proprietor), Antonio Filauri (Pierre), Mary Green (Girl), Bruce Mitchell and Frank G. Fanning (Detectives), Paul Hurst (Fibo), Milton Kibbee (Reporter), Tom Wilson (Cab Starter), Nick Copeland (Cab Driver), Olive Jones (Telephone Operator), Ky Robinson (Cop), Frank Bull (Broadcaster), George Guhl (Typist).

Supersleuth lawyer William mixes gourmet cooking with humor and his usual breeziness in this early Perry Mason outing. In this case, he is playing around as an amateur chef in a San Francisco restaurant when he encounters a murder, the solution of which he reveals at a ritzy cocktail party. Good entertainment, with an extra dash of spice for the alert—it was Errol Flynn's inauspicious debut in American films. First he is seen as a corpse, then briefly alive in a flashback near the end of the film. (See PERRY MASON series, Index.)

p, Harry Joe Brown; d, Michael Curtiz; w, Tom Reed, Brown Holmes (based on a story by Erle Stanley Gardner); ph, David Abel; m, Bernhard Kaun; ed, Terry Morse; art d, Carl Jules Weyl, Anton Grot; spec eff, Fred Jackman, Fred Jackman, Jr.; cos Orry-Kelly.

Mystery   (PR:A   MPAA:NR)

CASE OF THE 44'S, THE*   (1964 Brit./Den.) 73m D&A Productions bw
Ian Carmichael (Jim Pond), Lotte Tarp (Miss 44), Bent Christensen (Sinister Man), William Rosenberg (English Photographer), Jessie Rindom (Charlady), Carl Stegger (Carl S. Berg), Gunnar Lauring (Laboratory Man), Peter Maalberg (Old Man), Tony Hawes (Narration for Voice of Monty Landis).

An airy British spoof in which the 44's are not a reference to guns, but to female bosoms. Unfunny all the way through this predictable but harmless film photographed in picturesque Copenhagen.

p, Jon Penington, Bent Christensen; d&w, Tom McCowen; ph, Henning Christiansen; m, Bent Fabricius-Bjerre.

Spy Comedy   (PR:C   MPAA:NR)

CASE OF THE FRIGHTENED LADY, THE*
(1940, Brit.) 80m BL bw (AKA: THE FRIGHTENED LADY)
Marius Goring (Lord William Lebanon), Helen Haye (Dowager Lady Lebanon), Penelope Dudley Ward (Isla Crane), Felix Aylmer (Dr. Amersham), Patrick Barr (Richard Ferraby), Ronald Shiner (Detective Sgt. Tatty), George Merritt (Detective Inspector Tanner), Torin Thatcher (Tilling), Mavis Claire (Mrs. Tilling), John Warwick (Stud), Roy Emerton (Gilder).

There is murder in the blood of family heirs Goring and his mother Haye, who is trying to keep Goring's mental deficiency from the world. The family's homicidal tendencies are well developed as the story winds its way through intrigue to a surprise ending. Sparse material sold under the label "entertainment" scarcely manages to break even.

d, George King; w, Edward Dryhurst (based on the play "The Frightened Lady" by Edgar Wallace); ph, Ilone Glendening,

Crime Drama   (PR:C   MPAA:NR)

CASE OF THE HOWLING DOG, THE**   (1934) 75m WB bw
Warren William (Perry Mason), Mary Astor (Bessie Foley), Helen Trenholme (Della Street), Allen Jenkins (Sgt. Holcomb), Grant Mitchell (Claude Drumm), Dorothy Tree (Lucy Benton), Helen Lowell (Elizabeth Walker), Gordon Westcott (Arthur Cartwright), Harry Tyler (Sam Martin), Arthur Aylesworth (Bill Pemberton), Russell Hicks (Clinton Foley), Frank Reicher (Dr. Cooper), Addison Richards (Judge Markham), James Burtis (George Dobbs), Eddie Shubert (Ed Wheeler), Harry Seymour (Donald Clark).

This is the film that introduced Perry Mason to filmgoers, and, at the time, it was thought that the character would be good for only three or four more movies. In this case, Astor is one of three suspects in a murder. William sees through her deceit and reveals her guilt to an unsuspecting jury and audience. Keep an eye on all that happens in the courtroom, or something might slip by. (See PERRY MASON series, Index.)

p, Sam Bischoff; d, Alan Crosland; w, Ben Markson (based on a novel by Erle Stanley Gardner); ph, William Rees; art d, John Hughes.

Mystery **(PR:A MPAA:NR)**

CASE OF THE LUCKY LEGS, THE½ (1935) 76m FN/WB bw
Warren William (Perry Mason), Genevieve Tobin (Della Street), Patricia Ellis (Margie Clune), Lyle Talbot (Dr. Doray), Allen Jenkins (Spudsy), Barton MacLane (Bissonette), Peggy Shannon (Thelma Bell), Porter Hall (Bradbury), Anita Kerry (Eva Lamont), Craig Reynolds (Frank Patton), Henry O'Neill (Manchester), Joseph Crehan (Johnson), Charles Wilson (Ricker), Olin Howland (Doctor), Joseph Downing (Sanborne), Mary Treen (Mrs. Soudsy).

Directing and scripting keep this Perry Mason mystery moving along on a question mark—whodunit? Ellis is the small-town girl with the scent of murder after a "lucky legs" contest promoter is found killed. Sleek William, as usual, sniffs out the secret. Plenty of humor marks this as above-average. (See PERRY MASON series, Index)

p, Henry Blanke; d, Archie L. Mayo; w, Brown Holmes, Ben Markson, Jerome Chodorov (based on a story by Erle Stanley Gardner); ph, Tony Gaudio; ed, James Gibbon; md, Leo F. Forbstein; art d, Hugh Reticker.

Mystery **(PR:A MPAA:NR)**

CASE OF THE MISSING MAN, THE* (1935) 58m COL bw
Roger Pryor (Jimmy), Joan Perry (Peggy), Thurston Hall (Boyle), Arthur Hohl (Steve), George McKay (Frank), Tommy Dugan (Jack), James Burke (Rorty), Arthur Rankin (Hank).

Photojournalist Pryor steps out on his own to make a living as an independent photographer, and accidentally snaps a jewel thief leaving the scene of his crime. Mob then tries to get Pryor's film, which stands as a dangerous record. Some good comedy by street photogs McKay and Dugan help make this story engrossing.

d, D. Ross Lederman; w, Lee Loeb, Harold Buchman; ph, Allen G. Siegler; ed, Al Clark.

Mystery **(PR:A MPAA:NR)**

**CASE OF THE RED MONKEY ***½
(1955, Brit.) 71m AA bw (AKA: LITTLE RED MONKEY)
Richard Conte (Bill Locklin), Rona Anderson (Julia), Russell Napier (Supt. Harrington), Colin Gordon (Martin), Arnold Marle (Dushenko), Sylvia Langova (Hilde), Donald Bisset (Editor), John King-Kelly (Andor), Bernard Rebel (Vinson), Noel Johnson (Sgt. Hawkins), John Horsley (Sgt. Gibson), Colin Tapley (Sir Clive Raglan).

Murderous Russian agents plot to kill a top Soviet scientist who is en route from London to America. Mechanically, and without much intrigue, a U.S. State Department officer is assigned to escort the scientist. After unearthing the clue of a little Commie monkey spotted on the crime scene, the nasty Red gang is toppled.

p, Alec Snowden; d, Ken Hughes; w, Hughes, James Eastwood (based on a story by Eric Maschwitz); ph, Josef Ambor; m, Trevor Duncan; ed, Geoffrey Muller, Inman Hunter.

Spy Drama **(PR:A MPAA:NR)**

CASE OF THE STUTTERING BISHOP, THE*½ (1937) 70m FN/WB bw
Donald Woods (Perry Mason), Ann Dvorak (Della Street), Anne Nagel (Janice Alma Brownley), Linda Perry (Janice Seaton), Craig Reynolds (Gordon Bixter), Gordon Oliver (Phillip Brownley), Joseph Crehan (Paul Drake), Helen MacKellar (Stella Kenwood), Edward McWade (Bishop Mallory), Tom Kennedy (Tim Magooney), Mira McKinney (Ida Gilbert), Frank Faylen (Charles Downs), Douglas Wood (Ronald C. Brownley), George Lloyd (Peter Sacks), Veda Ann Borg (Gladys), Selmer Jackson (Victor Stockton), Gordon Hart (Judge Knox), Charles Wilson (Hamilton Burger), Eddie Chandler (Detective), Jack Richardson (Taxi Driver).

Woods takes over the Perry Mason role from Warren William in this slow-moving entry in the series and does a creditable job. His job is to investigate whether a phony has been substituted for the real heiress to the old man's millions. At the proper juncture, Woods gets the mother of the phony heiress to confess and she wins a pardon in an artificial ending. (See PERRY MASON series, Index.)

p, Bryan Foy; d, William Clemens; w, Don Ryan, Kenneth Gamet (based on the novel by Erle Stanley Gardner); ph, Rex Wimpy; ed, Jack Saper.

Mystery **(PR:A MPAA:NR)**

CASE OF THE VELVET CLAWS, THE** (1936) 60m FN/WB bw
Warren William (Perry Mason), Claire Dodd (Della Street), Winifred Shaw (Eva Belter), Gordon Elliott (Carl Griffin), Joseph King (George C. Belter), Addison Richards (Frank Locke), Eddie Acuff (Spudsy), Olin Howland (Wilbur Stran), Kenneth Harlan (Peter Milnor), Dick Purcell (Crandal), Ruth Robinson (Mrs. Veite), Paula Stone (Norma Veite), Robert Middlemass (Sgt. Hoffman), Carol Hughes (Esther Linton), Stuart Holmes (Digley).

When the publisher of a scandal sheet is murdered, William's honeymoon with his Girl Friday Dodd is interrupted at gunpoint and he is forced to take the case. Pace is so fast throughout that the audience has no time to dwell on the incredibility of all that happens, but that's okay once the spirit of the thing strikes. (See PERRY MASON series, Index.)

p, Bryan Foy; d, William Clemens; w, Tom Reed (based on a story by Erle Stanley Gardner); ph, Sid Hickox; ed, Jack Saper; art d, Esdras Hartley.

Mystery **(PR:A MPAA:NR)**

CASE VAN GELDERN** (1932, Ger.) 85m Ellen Richter Tonfilm/Suedfilm bw
Paul Richter, Ellen Richter, Lucie Hoeflich, Elga Brink, Fritz Kampers, Lizzi Waldmueller, G. Chmara, Hilde Hildebrand, Harry Hardt, Olly Gebauer, Friedrich Kayssler, Walter Steinbeck, Ernst Dumcke, Ernst Busch, Julius Falkenstein, Wladimir Sokoloff, Kurt Lilien, Paul Biensfeldt, Wolfgang Zilzer.

A lawyer falsely accused of murdering his wife depends on the aid of a poor former client, a habitual criminal, who breaks out of prison to uncover the real culprit. Tight script keeps the tension building, adding up to a fine thriller.

p, Ellen Richter; d, Willi Wolff; w, Hans Hyan, W. Solski; ph, Emil Schuenemann; m/l, Joe Hajo.

Crime Drama **(PR:C MPAA:NR)**

CASEY'S SHADOW** (1978) 116m COL c
Walter Matthau (Lloyd Bourdelle), Alexis Smith (Sarah Blue), Robert Webber (Mike Marsh), Murray Hamilton (Tom Patterson), Andrew A. Rubin (Buddy Bourdelle), Stephen Burns (Randy Bourdelle), Susan Myers (Kelly Marsh), Michael Hershewe (Casey Bourdelle), Harry Caesar (Calvin Lebec), Joel Fluellen (Jimmy Judson), Whit Bissell (Dr. Williamson), Jimmy Halty (Donovan), William Pitt (Dr. Pitt), Dean Turpitt (Dean), Sanders Delhomme (Old Cajun), Richard Thompson (Lenny), Galbert Wanoskia (Indian), William Karn (Old Man), Ed Hyman (All American Network Announcer), Thomas Caldwell, Bill Tackett (Auctioneers), Tom Dawson (Starting Gate Announcer), William Thomas (Weight Scales Jockey Room), Robert Dudich (Race Announcer), Warren Richardson (Guard), Ronald L. Schwary (Ticketseller), Justin Buford (Kid), Dean Cormier (Barmaid), Thelma Cormier, Ronald Benoit (Dealers), Norman Faulk (Track Timer), Gene Norman (Head Wrangler), Paul Uccello (Track Timer), W. Patrick Scott, Leonard Blach (Veterinarians), James Hutchinson, Jr. (Bar Man).

Two very urban talents have teamed to bring us a bucolic story in CASEY'S SHADOW. Ritt, a long-time New York actor, then director, and Matthau, also a New York actor and director (THE GANGSTER, 1960) turn their talents to the countryside with mixed results. Matthau is a poor Cajun horse trainer attempting to raise his three sons all alone (Rubin, Burns, and Hershewe). Their horse, Casey's Shadow, named for youngest son Hershewe, is going to run in the rich quarter-horse event at New Mexico's Ruidoso track. Hamilton and Smith would like to buy the animal, Webber would like to have it destroyed. Do we have to tell you what happens in the race? It's slow but steady; the action flags and flees but, in the end, it's a good-natured picture that you could show to your baby or your great-grandmother. Good performances all around plus a general feeling of honesty that is seldom seen in so-called "family pictures."

d, Ray Stark; d, Martin Ritt; w, Carol Sobieski (based on the short story "Ruidoso" by John McPhee); ph, John A. Alonzo (Panavision, Metrocolor); m, Patrick Williams; ed, Sidney Levin; set d, Charles Pierce; cos, Moss Mabry; m/l, Patrick Williams, Will Jennings, Dr. John, Richard Betts.

Family Drama **Cas.** **(PR:A MPAA:PG)**

CASH McCALL** (1960) 102m WB c
James Garner (Cash McCall), Natalie Wood (Lory Austen), Nina Foch (Maude Kennard), Dean Jagger (Grant Austen), E. G. Marshall (Winston Conway), Henry Jones (Gil Clark), Otto Kruger (Will Atherson), Roland Winters (Gen. Danvers), Edward C. Platt (Harrison Glenn), Edgar Stehli (Mr. Pierce), Linda Watkins (Miriam Austen), Parley Baer (Harvey Bannon), Dabs Greer, Olan Soule, Robert Clarke, Walter Coy.

Garner is a corporate raider who finds sick companies, merges them with well ones, takes the ailing firms' losses, and uses them as tax relief for the thriving firms' profits. This was written by Cameron Hawley in his novel and he must know whereof he speaks as he was at one time the advertising boss at Armstrong Cork. One can read the business section and see this tactic used almost daily by several of the more avaricious businessmen. It's ostensibly a love story between Garner and Wood, with Nina Foch as another part of the triangle. The high-diddle-diddling of financial rigmarole punctuates the love story and the film can't quite make up its mind what it is. Some interesting monetary shenanigans are described and Garner is shown as a man who not only makes money for himself but is kind and thoughtful when it comes to the fates of the stockholders in the companies he manipulates. The believability went right out the window with that! This should have been a comedy as much of it borders on the ludicrous, but it just stays within the bounds of credibility and manages to finagle its way into the viewer's good graces.

p, Henry Blanke; d, Joseph Pevney; w, Lenore Coffee, Marion Hargrove (based on a novel by Cameron Hawley); ph, George Folsey (Technicolor); m, Max Steiner; ed, Philip W. Anderson; cos, Howard Shoup.

Romance **(PR:C MPAA:NR)**

CASH ON DELIVERY*½
(1956, Brit.) 79m Welbeck-Gina/RKO bw (GB: TO DOROTHY, A SON)
Shelley Winters (Myrtle La Mar), John Gregson (Tony Rapallo), Peggy Cummins (Dorothy Rapallo), Wilfrid Hyde-White (Mr. Starke), Mona Washbourne (Nurse Appleby), Hal Osmond (Livingstone Potts), Hartley Power (Cy Daniel), M. Kaufman (Elmer the Pianist), John Warren (Waiter), Fred Berger (Furrier), N. Parsons (Clerk), Dorothy Bramhall (Secretary), Ronald Adam (Parsons), Martin Miller (Brodcynsky), Alfie Bass (Cab Driver), Anthony Oliver (Reporter), Joan Sims (Phone Caller), Aubrey Mather (Dr. Cameron), Meredith Edwards (Proprietor), Marjorie Rhodes (Landlady).

Time zone comedy with Winters leading a British cast to give the film U.S. appeal. Winters is an American nightclub singer who is informed that she will inherit a fortune if her ex-husband has not fathered a male heir by a certain date. Zipping over to London to track him down, she finds him remarried and his wife expecting any day. Typical complications ensue, regarding the possible sex of the child, the legitimacy of the marriage and the divorce, and the time difference between New York and London. Twins are born, one of each, just under the wire, but the advent of Daylight Savings Time gets Winters the money, which she generously splits with the Ex. Score includes "Give Me a Man" and "You're the Only One." Not terribly interesting.

p, Peter Rogers, Ben Schrift; d, Muriel Box; w, Rogers (based on the play by Roger MacDougall); ph, Ernest Steward; ed, Alfred Roome; m, Lambert Williamson; m/l, Paddy Roberts, Jacques Abram, Fred G. Moritt, George Thorn.

Comedy **(PR:A MPAA:NR)**

CASH ON DEMAND** (1962, Brit.) 84m Hammer-Woodpecker/COL bw
Peter Cushing *(Fordyce)*, Andre Morell *(Hepburn)*, Richard Vernon *(Pearson)*, Norman Bird *(Sanderson)*, Kevin Stoney *(Detective Inspector Mason)*, Barry Lowe *(Peter Harvill)*, Edith Sharpe *(Miss Pringle)*, Lois Daine *(Sally)*, Alan Haywood *(Kane)*, Charles Morgan *(Collins)*, Vera Cook *(Mrs. Fordyce)*, Gareth Tandy *(Tommy)*, Fred Stone *(Window Cleaner)*.

Morell kidnaps the wife and son of bank manager Cushing and extorts him into aiding him in robbing the bank. An employee of the bank figures out what is going on and Cushing, ever unpopular with his staff, must plead with them not to inform the police. They agree. The police, working independently, capture Morell, and Cushing changes his attitude toward his employees. Decent melodrama and one of Cushing's few non-horror roles.

p, Michael Carreras; d, Quentin Lawrence; w, David T. Chantler, Lewis Greifer (based on a teleplay, "The Gold Inside," by Jacques Gillies); ph, Arthur Grant; m, Wilfred Josephs; ed, Eric Boyd-Perkins; md, John Hollingsworth; art d, Don Mingaye; cos, Molly Arbuthnot.

Crime **(PR:C MPAA:NR)**

CASINO DE PARIS**
(1957, Fr./Ger.) 100m Pathe/Bavaria Filmkunst/Criterion/Elan c
Caterina Valente *(Catherine)*, Gilbert Becaud *(Jacques)*, Vittorio De Sica *(Gordy)*, Gregoire Aslan *(Mario)*, Vera Valmont *(Linda)*, Rudolf Vogel *(Father)*, Grethe Weiser *(Mother)*.

French comedy about aging playwright De Sica turning music hall star Valente into an actress while trying to seduce her. When he takes her to his villa to rehearse, the playwright's ghost writer (Becaud) falls for her. Cast is good, but story is too predictable to hold interest.

d, Andre Hunebelle; w, Hans Wilhelm, Jean Halain; ph, Bruno Mondi (Franscope, Technicolor); m, Paul Durand, Becaud; ed, Jean Feyte; set d & cos, Rene Moulaert.

Comedy **(PR:C MPAA:NR)**

CASINO MURDER CASE, THE*½ (1935) 82m MGM bw
Paul Lukas *(Philo Vance)*, Rosalind Russell *(Doris)*, Alison Skipworth *(Mrs. Llewellyn)*, Donald Cook *(Lynn)*, Arthur Byron *(Kincaid)*, Ted Healy *(Sgt. Heath)*, Eric Blore *(Currie)*, Isabel Jewell *(Amelia)*, Louise Fazenda *(Becky)*, Leslie Fenton *(Dr. Kane)*, Louise Henry *(Virginia)*, Purnell Pratt *(Markham)*, Leo G. Carroll *(Smith)*, Charles Sellon *(Dr. Doremus)*, William Demarest *(Auctioneer)*, Grace Hayle *(Fat Lady)*, Ernie Adams *(Husband of Fat Lady)*, Milton Kibbee, Tom Herbert *(Reporters)*, Keye Luke *(Taki)*, Edna Bennett *(Nurse)*.

After five pictures, Rosalind Russell was just emerging into leading lady status when this Philo Vance mystery came out. The film deals with rich old lady Skipworth playing, to the hilt, a doting mother to an egotistic son. Lukas's accent injures credibility a little as he gumshoes around as an American detective and finally solves a murder. (See PHILO VANCE series, Index)

p, Lucien Hubbard; d, Edwin L. Marin; w, Florence Ryerson, Edgar Allan Woolf (based on a novel by S.S. Van Dine); ph, Charles Clarke; ed, Conrad A. Nervig.

Mystery **(PR:A MPAA:NR)**

CASINO ROYALE** (1967, Brit.) 131m COL c
Peter Sellers *(Evelyn Tremble)*, Ursula Andress *(Vesper Lynd)*, David Niven *(Sir James Bond)*, Orson Welles *(Le Chiffre)*, Joanna Pettet *(Mata Bond)*, Daliah Lavi *(The Detainer)*, Woody Allen *(Jimmy Bond, Dr. Noah)*, Deborah Kerr *(Agent Mimi, Lady Fiona McTarry)*, William Holden *(Ransome)*, Charles Boyer *(Le Grand)*, John Huston *(McTarry)*, Kurt Kasznar *(Smernov)*, George Raft *(Himself)*, Jean-Paul Belmondo *(French Legionnaire)*, Terence Cooper *(Cooper)*, Barbara Bouchet *(Moneypenny)*, Peter O'Toole *(Scotch Piper)*, Angela Scoular *(Buttercup)*, Gabriella Licudi *(Eliza)*, Tracey Crisp *(Heather)*, Anna Quayle *(Frau Hoffner)*, Geoffrey Bayldon *("Q")*, John Wells *("Q's" Assistant)*, Richard Wattis *(British Army Officer)*, Ronnie Corbett *(Polo)*, Bernard Cribbins *(Taxi Driver)*, Colin Gordon *(Casino Director)*, Tracy Reed *(Fang Leader)*, Jacqueline Bisset *(Miss Goodthighs)*, Derek Nimmo *(Hadley)*, Duncan *(1st Piper)*.

CASINO ROYALE is two hours and eleven minutes of non sequitur. It's as though all these talents got together and said, "How can we take a fine spy thriller and turn it into a piece of junk?" They evidently found the solution to that question as the result is as huge a melange of mishmash and mistakes as one could conceive. The plot defies description but here it is: David Niven is Sir James Bond (Author Ian Fleming, a close friend of Niven, always wanted Niven to play *all* the Bond roles.) He's retired, middle-aged, bejowled, and tired. SMERSH is up to no good so Niven is asked to help when John Huston as M is slain. Niven goes north to Scotland to visit Huston's widow, Kerr, who is a SMERSH agent. She attempts to seduce Niven, who firmly rejects her. She reacts by becoming a nun. Now Niven contacts several agents, all of them 007. These include Andress, Sellers, Cooper, and Pettet (who is Niven's daughter, the result of a liaison with Mata Hari). SMERSH is broke and attempting to replenish its exchecquer at the tables of CASINO ROYALE. Sellers, world's greatest baccarat player, is ordered to bring villain Orson Welles to his financial knees. Andress is later kidnaped and Sellers expires in a vain attempt to save her. Then Pettet is kidnaped and taken aboard a flying saucer. Niven soon learns that the real villain behind the scenes is none other than his own nephew, Woody Allen (who has some of the best lines in the script and one wonders if he wrote them himself). Daliah Lavi slips Woody an explosive capsule which the yutz swallows. He detonates and blows up the Casino Royale and all of its customers, except for Niven who beats a hasty retreat. If the foregoing sounds disjointed, you're quite correct. This was such a waste of time and money that it ranked as that year's HEAVEN'S GATE. They have attempted to parodize the other Bondpix (all of which were produced by Harry Saltzman and Albert Broccoli, or Broccoli alone), but satirizing a satire is a mistake and the proof is on this picture. CASINO ROYALE first found life as a one-hour TV show for CBS's "Climax" in 1954, starring Barry Nelson. The film rights were sold in 1955 and eventually acquired by ex-agent Charles Feldman. Almost every actor hammed it up while making this movie and the result is a totally unfocused viewing. But anything with this many stars and this many directors and screenwriters has to rank on anyone's list for sheer volume and chutzpah. This $25-million production lost a lot of money and the only thing anyone may remember is the Oscar-nominated song "The Look of Love" and the title theme played by Herb Alpert.

p, Charles K. Feldman, Jerry Bresler; d, John Huston, Kenneth Hughes, Robert Parrish, Val Guest, Joseph McGrath; w, Wolf Mankowitz, John Law, Michael Sayers [unbilled but also contributing: Billy Wilder, Guest, Joseph Heller, Ben Hecht, Terry Southern] (from the novel by Ian Fleming); ph, John Wilcox, Jack Hildyard, Nicholas Roeg (Panavision, Technicolor); m, Burt Bacharach; ed, Bill Lenny; art d, John Howell, Ivor Beddoes, Lionel Couch; set d, Terence Morgan; m/l, Bacharach, Hal David; ch, Tutte Lemkow.

Adventure/Comedy **(PR:A MPAA:NR)**

CASQUE D'OR****
(1956, Fr.) 96m Speva/Paris bw (AKA: GOLDEN MARIE)
Simone Signoret *(Marie, "Casque D'or")*, Serge Reggiani *(Manda)*, Claude Dauphin *(Felix Leca)*, Raymond Bussieres *(Raymond)*, William Sabatier *(Roland)*, Gaston Modot *(Danard)*, Loleh Bellon *(Leonie Danard)*, Claude Castaing *(Fredo)*, Paul Azais *(Ponsard)*, Emile Genevois *(Billy)*, Jean Clarieux *(Paul)*, Roland Lesaffre *(Anatole)*, Paul Barge *(Inspector Juliani)*, Tony Corteggiani *(Superintendent)*, Dominique Davray *(Julie)*, Odette Barencey *(La Mère Eugénie)*.

One of the great films of French cinema, CASQUE D'OR initially was greeted with less than favorable reviews but met with renewed interest after Lindsay Anderson's praises were read. Set at the turn of the century, it concerns the romance of Signoret and Reggiani. After murdering a childhood friend, Reggiani surrenders to the authorities, though the death was pinned on someone else. Signoret asks a friend to help free her lover, but is forced to compromise herself in return. After she submits, the friend goes back on his word. Reggiani, however, does get out and hunts out the deceitful seducer of Signoret. He spots him in the street and, in front of witnesses, guns him down. His avenging act is met with execution at the guillotine. Most praised is director Becker's fluidity. As Francois Truffaut wrote, "CASQUE D'OR is the only film that Jacques Becker—who is ordinarily very finicky, absorbed by detail, obsessive, restless, and at times uncertain—ever made in one stroke, very quickly, straight through from beginning to end." Critic Jean Couturier took the accolade even further, saying, "Becker employs a language amazing in its simplicity; not an unusual angle, a clever shot, or the self-stylized "aesthetic" pursuit. The camera position and the chosen angle seem to impose themselves . . . which is the height of great art." It is a film which revels in poetic purity, something which Becker surely sharpened in his days as Renoir's assistant. First shown in Paris in 1952.

d, Jacques Becker; w, Becker, Jacques Companeez; ph, Robert Le Febvre; m, George Van Parys; ed, Marguerite Renoir.

Crime/Romance **(PR:C MPAA:NR)**

CASS TIMBERLANE*** (1947) 119m MGM bw
Spencer Tracy *(Cass Timberlane)*, Lana Turner *(Virginia Marshland)*, Zachary Scott *(Brad Criley)*, Tom Drake *(Jamie Wargate)*, Mary Astor *(Queenie Havock)*, Albert Dekker *(Boone Havock)*, Margaret Lindsay *(Chris Grau)*, John Litel *(Webb Wargate)*, Mona Barrie *(Avis Elderman)*, Josephine Hutchinson *(Lillian Drover)*, Rose Hobart *(Diantha Marl)*, Selena Royle *(Louise Wargate)*, Frank Wilcox *(Gregg Marl)*, Richard Gaines *(Dennis Thane)*, John Alexander *(Dr. Roy Drover)*, Cameron Mitchell *(Eino Roskinen)*, Howard Freeman *(Hervey Plint)*, Jessie Grayson *(Mrs. Higbee)*, Griff Barnett *(Herman)*, Guy Beach *(George Hame)*, Cliff Clark *(Humber Bellile)*, Milburn Stone *(Nestor Purdwin)*, Almira Sessions *(Zilda Hatter)*, Tim Ryan *(Charlie Ellis)*, Bess Flowers *(Mary Ann Milligan)*, Lester Dorr *(Salesman)*, Roy Gordon *(Critic)*, Mitchell Kowall *(Doorman)*, Arno Frey *(Waiter)*, Manuel Paris, Albert Pollet *(Frenchmen at Party)*, Buz Buckley *(Newsboy)*, Ed Oliver *(Pianist)*, Emmett Vogan *(Beehouse)*, Walter Pidgeon *(Man at Cocktail Party)*.

Based on Sinclair Lewis's novel, CASS TIMBERLANE is a chronicle of a May-December marriage, intercut with the small-town prejudices that Lewis wrote so well of in ARROWSMITH and MAIN STREET. Spencer Tracy is Cass Timberlane, a fortyish judge in Minnesota who falls for Turner (the advertising campaign read: TNT, Tracy 'n' Turner), a sexpot who is out of his class. Lana never looked better and does a good job as she limns the role of the somewhat confused girl who does her best to fit into Tracy's world. They marry and she is subtly shunned by his snobbish friends, but it doesn't matter to either of them as their love seems solid. Soon enough she begins to show the telltale evidence of ennui and her one enjoyment is the attention showered upon her by local rakehell Zachary Scott. (Scott made a career out of playing ne'er-do-wells and cads, MASK OF DIMITRIOS, MILDRED PIERCE.) When she has a stillborn child,

Turner convinces Tracy to flee the provinces and accept a position at a large Big Apple law firm. She is struck by life in the big city but Tracy longs for the quieter climes of his native state. He wants to leave but she is reluctant and now takes up with Scott again, who has been lurking in the wings ready to pounce on Turner. Then tragedy strikes. Turner is injured and finally finds happiness as Tracy takes her back into his arms for a final fade-out. Fine acting dominates this otherwise predictable film. Lewis has never been the easiest author to adapt for the screen because so much of his genius was in the description of subtleties that cannot be realized without the intrusion of a voice-over description. Excellent supporting cast performances included surprise cameo by Walter Pidgeon as himself in a party scene. Tracy only agreed to do the film after John O'Hara was removed from script chores, because O'Hara had done a version Tracy found unacceptable. It was Donald Ogden Stewart's treatment of the story that intrigued Tracy. Stewart was an actor before turning to writing and played the role of Nick Potter in "The Philadelphia Story" on Broadway in 1928. Twelve years later he won the Oscar for adapting that play for the screen.

p, Arthur Hornblow, Jr.; d, George Sidney; w, Donald Ogden Stewart (adaptation by Sonya Levien and Stewart from the novel by Sinclair Lewis); ph, Robert Planck; m, Roy Webb; ed, John Dunning; md, Constantine Bakaleinikoff; art d, Cedric Gibbons, Daniel Cathcart; set d, Edwin B. Willis, Richard Pefferle; cos, Irene; spec eff, Warren Newcombe, A. Arnold Gillespie.

Romance   **(PR:C MPAA:NR)**

CASSANDRA CROSSING, THE**
(1977), Brit. 125m Associated General Films/AE c

Sophia Loren (Jennifer), Richard Harris (Chamberlain), Ava Gardner (Nicole), Burt Lancaster (Mackenzie), Martin Sheen (Navarro), Ingrid Thulin (Elena), Lee Strasberg (Kaplan), John Phillip Law (Stack), Ann Turkel (Susan), O. J. Simpson (Father Haley), Lionel Stander (Conductor), Raymond Lovelock (Tom), Alida Valli (Mrs. Chadwick), Lou Castell (Swede the Driver), Stefano Patrizi (Attendant), Carlo De Mejo (Patient), Fausta Avelli (Katherine).

A trainload of people are contaminated by terrorists seeking release of prisoners and other sanctions. The bizarre and unbelievable plot is further confused by Lancaster, a military man who purposely tries to send the train across a condemned wooden trestle to certain disaster, putting shock troops on board to kill anyone who attempts to stop a plan wherein all passengers will be killed (not that this will stop the disease; it is designed to besmirch the terrorists). Loren, Harris, Gardner, and others with fast-fading careers contribute little or nothing to this absurd hokum. The forty-three-year-old Loren plays a much younger woman and is not convincing, nor is Gardner, attempting the same kind of role with young lover Sheen who comes down with the plague. Harris, as the doctor who tries to save the passengers, is annoying as he transforms himself into a machinegunner battling hooded guards. The best thing about this forced film is the special effects at the finale.

p, Sir Lew Grade, Carlo Ponti; d, George Pan Cosmatos; w, Tom Mankiewicz, Robert Katz Cosmatos (based on a story by Robert Katz); ph, Ennio Guarnieri (Panavision, Technicolor); m, Jerry Goldsmith; ed, Francois Bonnot, Roberto Silvi; art d, Aurelio Crugnola; cos, Andriana Berselli; spec eff, Tazio Secciaroli.

Adventure   **Cas.**   **(PR:C MPAA:R)**

CASSIDY OF BAR 20**
(1938) 60m PAR bw

William Boyd (Hopalong Cassidy), Russell Hayden (Lucky Jenkins), Frank Darien (Pappy), Nora Lane (Nora Blake), Robert Fiske (Clay Allison), John Elliott (Tom Dillon), Margaret Marquis (Mary Dillon), Gertrude W. Hoffman (Ma Caffrey), Carleton Young (Jeff Caffrey), Gordon Hart (Judge Belcher), Edward Cassidy (Sheriff Hawley), Jim Toney (Cowhand).

Hopalong Cassidy fans will find plenty of hard-riding, fast-shooting intrigue and fist fighting in this, the seventh of the Hopalong series. In the nick of time, Boyd arrives on the scene after Lane, an old sweetheart, sends for him to rid her and Darien's range of rustlers and badmen. Some exceptional photography of mountain backgrounds distinguishes this movie. (See HOPALONG CASSIDY series, Index.)

p, Harry Sherman; d, Lesley Selander; w, Norman Houston (based on a story by Clarence E. Mulford); ph, Russell Harlan; ed, Sherman Rose; art d, Lewis Rachmil.

Western   **(PR:A MPAA:NR)**

CAST A DARK SHADOW***
(1958, Brit.) 85m Eros (GB) bw

Dirk Bogarde (Edward Bare), Mona Washbourne (Monica Bare), Margaret Lockwood (Freda Jeffries), Kay Walsh (Charlotte Young), Kathleen Harrison (Emmie), Robert Flemyng (Phillip Mortimer), Walter Hudd (Coroner), Philip Stainton (Charlie Mann), Myrtle Reed (Waitress), Lita Roza (Singer).

A gripping thriller about a young man who schemes to get the fortunes of elderly women by wedding them and killing them off. He finds his match in the widow of a saloonkeeper who learns of his plans to do her in. He is found out and killed by a widow, an intended booby trap. Unoriginal but effective, with Bogarde turning in one of his finest performances in this well-transformed stage play.

p, Daniel M. Angel; d, Lewis Gilbert; w, John Cresswell (based on Janet Green's play "Murder Mistaken"); ph, Jack Asher; m, Antony Hopkins; ed, Gordon Pilkington.

Drama   **(PR:A MPAA:NR)**

CAST A GIANT SHADOW***½
(1966) 144m Mirisch-Llenroc-Batjac/UA c

Kirk Douglas (Col. David "Mickey" Marcus), Senta Berger (Magda Simon), Angie Dickinson (Emma Marcus), James Donald (Safir), Stathis Giallelis (Ram Oren), Luther Adler (Jacob Zion), Gary Merrill (Pentagon Chief of Staff), Haym Topol (Abou Ibn Kader), Frank Sinatra (Vince), Yul Brynner (Asher Gonen), John Wayne (Gen. Mike Randolph), Ruth White (Mrs. Chaison), Gordon Jackson (James McAfee), Michael Hordern (British Ambassador), Allan Cuthbertson (British Immigration Officer), Jeremy Kemp (Senior British Officer), Sean Barrett (Junior British Officer),

Michael Shillo (Andre), Rina Ganor (Rona), Roland Barthrop (Bert Harrison), Vera Dolen (Mrs. Martinson), Robert Gardett (Gen. Walsh), Michael Balston, Claude Aliotti (Sentries), Samra Dedes (Belly Dancer), Michael Shagrir (Truck Driver), Frank Lattimore, Ken Buckle (U.N. Officers), Rodd Dana (Aide to Gen. Randolph), Robert Ross (Aide to Chief of Staff), Arthur Hansell (Pentagon Officer), Don Sturkie (Parachute Jump Sergeant), Hillel Rave (Yaakov), Shlomo Hermon (Yussuff).

Long but interesting film bio about a man most people never heard of. "So why make this movie?" you might ask. Well, the life of Marcus was fascinating. So was his death. And there were enough heavyweight stars who wanted to see this story told, so it wasn't too much of a chore for Shavelson (p&d&w) to put it together. The time is 1949. The British are on their way out of the newly formed state of Israel and the local Arabs who surround the tiny country are ignoring the nation's sovereignty. Douglas (Marcus) is an American war hero and former advisor to President Roosevelt (he had also graduated from West Point and had been commissioner of Corrections in NYC under Mayor LaGuardia). He's asked by James Donald (Safir) to get the dispirited and undisciplined Isareli army into condition so it can face the Arab hordes when the British depart. Douglas's wife, Angie Dickinson, wishes he'd stay home in the U.S. and forget about war. This is echoed by his superior, John Wayne, who now resides at the Pentagon. Despite their pleading, Douglas resigns from the Army and leaves for Israel to work closely with Luther Adler (playing a fictitious character but obviously modeled after Ben-Gurion, right down to the wispy white hair) and Yul Brynner, who looks like Mosha Dayan without the eyepatch. Douglas is billeted at the home of Senta Berger, a sexy, voluptuous freedom fighter, and they fall in love. The U.S. officially recognizes Israel and a cease-fire is called for between the Arabs and Israelis. Douglas is ordered to get to Jerusalem before the truce goes into effect as boundaries will be drawn based on where the forces were at the time of the cease fire. Ammunition supplies are exhausted and Sinatra, as Vince, the American aviator, keeps on fighting and eventually goes down to his death. The Israelis are victorious and now Douglas realizes that his place is back in America with his wife. He says goodbye to Berger and now takes a walk. He is challenged by an Israeli sentry in Hebrew, a language he, like so many other American Jews, never learned. He continues walking and is shot dead by the confused soldier! Mickey Marcus was never a religious Jew, nor was he a Zionist. It was only after getting to Israel that his fervor was stirred. Much of this film was fanciful and obviously added to fill out the story and provide extra incentive to the customers. In his first American movie, Israeli star Topol (billed as Haym Topol) plays an Arab and marks his presence on the screen. Superb editing by Ruggiero and Bates.

p, Melville Shavelson, Michael Wayne; d&w, Shavelson (based on the book by Ted Berkman); ph, Aldo Tonti (Panavision, De Luxe Color); m, Elmer Bernstein; ed, Bert Bates, Gene Ruggiero; art d, Arrigo Equini; cos, Margaret Furse; spec eff, Sass Bedig.

War   **(PR:A-C MPAA:NR)**

CAST A LONG SHADOW*½
(1959) 82m UA c

Audie Murphy (Matt Brown), Terry Moore (Janet Calvert), John Dehner (Chip Donohue), James Best (Sam Mullen), Rita Lynn (Hortensia), Denver Pyle (Harrison), Ann Doran (Ma Calvert), Stacy B. Harris (Eph Brown), Robert Foulke (Rigdon), Wright King (Noah).

Murphy is a drifter with a shady past who comes into the life of a rancher whose illegitimate son he may be. He tries to start a new life, but old feuds are revived that prevent it. A dull oater with pretentions of psychological insight.

p, Walter Mirisch; d, Thomas Carr; w, Martin G. Goldsmith, John McGreevey (based on a story by Goldsmith and the novel Cast A Long Shadow by Wayne D. Overholser); m, Gerald Fried.

Western   **(PR:C MPAA:NR)**

CASTAWAY COWBOY, THE**
(1974) 91m BV/Disney c

James Garner (Lincoln Costain), Vera Miles (Henrietta MacAvoy), Robert Culp (Bryson), Eric Shea (Booton MacAvoy), Elizabeth Smith (Liliha), Manu Tupou (Kimo), Gregory Sierra (Marrujo), Shug Fisher (Capt. Cary), Nephi Hannermann (Malakoma), Lito Capina (Leleo), Ralph Hanalei (Hopu), Kahana (Oka), Lee Wood (Palani), Luis Delgado (Hatman), Buddy Joe Hooker (Boatman), Patrick Sullivan Burke (Sea Captain).

A formula Disney family adventure set this time in Hawaii. Garner, playing a typical Texan, saves the day for lil' Miss Miles by fending off the vulturous Culp who holds her mortgage. The do-good rancher turns her struggling potato farm into a prosperous cattle ranch while still hoping to return to Texas. Snugly fit into the Disney mold, this pic packaged with ONE LITTLE INDIAN offers a generous helping of upbeat family fare.

p, Ron Miller, Winston Hibler; d, Vincent McEveety; w, Don Tait (based on a story by Tait, Richard Bluel, Hugh Benson); ph, Andrew Jackson (Technicolor); m, Robert F. Brunner; ed, Cotton Warburton; art d, John B. Mansbridge; set d, Robert Clatworthy; cos, Chuck Keehne, Emily Sundby.

Comedy   **Cas.**   **(PR:AAA MPAA:G)**

CASTE*
(1930, Brit.) 70m Harry Rowson/UA bw

Hermione Baddeley (Polly Eccles), Nora Swinburne (Esther Eccles), Alan Napier (Capt. Hawtree), Sebastian Shaw (Hon. George d'Alroy), Ben Field (Albert Eccles), Edward Chapman (Sam Gerridge), Mabel Terry-Lewis (Marquise).

Baddeley is the daughter of a besotted Cockney who marries a marquis's son apparently killed in WW I. Boring comedy of interest only for the chance to see an amazingly young Baddeley.

p, Jerome Jackson; d, Campbell Gullan; w, Michael Powell (based on a play by T.W. Robertson).

Comedy   **(PR:A MPAA:NR)**

CASTILIAN, THE**   (1963, Span./U.S.) 129m Cinemagic/M.D./WB c
(AKA: VALLEY OF THE SWORDS)

Cesar Romero (*Jeronimo*), Frankie Avalon (*Jerifan*), Broderick Crawford (*Don Sancho*), Alida Valli (*Queen Teresa*), Spartaco Santoni (*Fernan Gonzales*), Teresa Velazquez (*Sancha*), Fernando Rey (*Ramiro II, King of Leon*), George Rigaud (*Saint Milan*), German Cobos (*Adberraman*), Julio Pena (*Santiago*), Angel Del Pozo (*Don Sancho's Son*), Linda Darnell, Hugo Pimental, Beny Deus, Tomas Blanco, Rafael Duran, Roberto Rey, Francisco Moran.

Strange cast gathered together for an interesting costume epic. Santoni is a 10th century Spanish nobleman who returns from exile to lead his followers against the Moors and evil king Crawford. He is captured, but escapes with the help of Velazquez, Crawford's daughter. He rejoins his forces and leads them to a total victory over the Moors after Rigaud and Pena, the patron saints of Spain, come to Earth to advise him. He makes peace with the successors of the by-now-dead Crawford, marries Velazquez, and settles down to rule over Castille. Based on a 13th century epic poem, and worth checking out. Songs: "Song of Fernan," "Valley of the Swords," "Song of Love."

p, Sidney W. Pink; d, Javier Seto; w, Pink (based on the Spanish screenplay by Paulino Rodrigo Diaz, Seto, Luis de los Arcos, and on the epic poem "El Poema de Fernan Gonzales"); ph, Mario Pacheco (Panacolor); m, Jose Buenagu; ed, Margarita Ochoa; art d, Jose Antonio de la Guerra; cos, Jose Zamora; m/l, Buenagu, Robert Marcucci, Russell Faith.

Adventure/Historical Drama   (PR:C   MPAA:NR)

CASTLE, THE***   (1969, Ger.) 93m Alfa Film-Glarus-Rudolf Noelte Film produktion/CD c
(DAS SCHLOSS)

Maximilian Schell ("*K*"), Cordula Trantow (*Frieda*), Trudik Daniel (*Innkeeper's Wife*), Helmut Qualtinger (*Burgel*), Franz Misar (*Arthur*), Johann Misar (*Jeremiah*), Hanns Ernst Jager (*Landlord*), Friedrich Maurer (*Mayor*), Else Ehser (*Mizzi*), Iva Janzurova (*Olga*), Martha Wallner (*Amalia*), Georg Lehn (*Barnabas*), Karl Hellmer (*School-master*), Ilse Kunkele (*Schoolmistress*), Benno Hoffmann (*Uniformed Man*), E.O. Fuhrmann (*Momus*), Leo Mally (*Gerstaecker*), Hans Possenbacher (*Innkeeper*), Armand Ozory (*Erlanger*).

Franz Kafka's allegorical, unfinished novel is given fairly good treatment here. Schell is surveyor "K," summoned to a remote village by the unseen occupants of a castle. In the town he finds there is no work for him so he tries to contact the people in the castle. The villagers oppose him at every turn and gradually he becomes obsessed with talking to the authorities in the fortress. At one point he almost meets a visiting secretary from the castle but at the last minute the carriage pulls away heading back for the castle, and Schell is left running behind. The print shown at the 1968 Venice Film Festival ends with Schell's death. Beautifully shot and acted, appropriately abstract study of a man entangled in a faceless bureaucracy that ultimately destroys him. (In German; English subtitles.)

p, Maximilian Schell; d&w, Rudolf Noelte (based on the unfinished novel *The Castle* by Franz Kafka); ph, Wolfgang Treu (Movielab Color); m, Herbert Trantow; ed, Dagmar Hirtz; art d, Otto and Herta Pischinger; cos, Barbara Bilabel.

Drama   (PR:C   MPAA:NR)

CASTLE IN THE DESERT*½   (1942) 51m Fox bw

Sidney Toler (*Charlie Chan*), Arleen Whelan (*Brenda Hartford*), Richard Derr (*Carl Detheridge*), Douglass Dumbrille (*Manderley*), Richard Derr (*Carl Detheridge*), Henry Daniell (*Watson King*), Edmund MacDonald (*Walter Hartford*), Sen Yung (*Jimmy Chan*), Lenita Lane (*Lucretia Manderley*), Ethel Griffies (*Mme. Saturnie*), Milton Parsons (*Fletcher*), Steve Geray (*Dr. Retling*), Lucien Littlefield (*Prof. Gleason*), Paul Kruger (*Bodyguard*), George Chandler (*Bus Driver*), Oliver Prickett (*Wigley, Hotel Manager*).

What was thought to be probably the last of the Charlie Chan whodunits is a mild little murder mystery which seems to have been thrown together in a hurry as though Hollywood was eager to put the poor old gentleman out of work. Chan is called to a medieval castle, home for millionaire Dumbrille and his wife, to unravel strange goings-on among her weekend houseguests who mostly wander about the place dressed in white tie, agonizing over the death of one of the guests. Even efforts to inject slapstick laughs through the antics of Yung (Jimmy Chan) fail to catch fire. (See CHARLIE CHAN series, Index.)

p, Ralph Dietrich; d, Harry Lachman; w, John Larkin (based on the character created by Earl Derr Biggers); ph, Virgil Miller; m, Emil Newman; ed, John Brady.

Mystery   (PR:A   MPAA:NR)

CASTLE KEEP***   (1969) 108m COL c

Burt Lancaster (*Maj. Abraham Falconer*), Peter Falk (*Sgt. Orlando Rossi*), Patrick O'Neal (*Capt. Lionel Beckman*), Jean-Pierre Aumont (*Henri Tixier, Comte de Maldorais*), Astrid Heeren (*Therese, Comtesse de Maldorais*), Scott Wilson (*Cpl. Ralph Clearboy*), Tony Bill (*Lt. Adam Amberjack*), Michael Conrad (*Sgt. Juan de Vaca*), Bruce Dern (*Lt. Billy Byron Bix*), Al Freeman, Jr. (*Pfc. Alistair Benjamin*), James Patterson (*Pvt. Henry Three Ears of an Elk*), Bisera Vukotic (*Baker's Wife*), Ernest Clark (*British Colonel*), Harry Baird (*Dancing Soldier*), Dave Jones (*One-Eared Soldier*), Jean Gimello (*First Puerto Rican*), Caterina Boratto (*The Red Queen*), Karen Blanguernon, Maria Danube, Elizabeth Darius, Merja Allanen, Anne Marie Moscovenko, Elizabeth Teissier, Eya Tuuli (*Red Queen Girls*).

It's 1944. Burt Lancaster, a tired one-eyed major, leads his weary eight-man squad to a castle in the Ardennes Forest. They are going to use the place for R&R, and Burt doesn't realize how much R is intended by Jean-Pierre Aumont, the impotent noble-man who owns Castle Keep. Aumont is married to his niece, Astrid Heeren, and wants a son by her but does not have the necessary wherewithal to do it, so he prevails on Burt, ever an obliging fellow, to be a surrogate sire. Plenty of humor abounds as Falk beds the absent Baker's Wife (Vukotic), the men go to the local brothel, etc. The

dialogue is very salty and the action spotty. It's only when the Germans attack the castle and the squad reacts heroically that the screen is filled with what people come to see war pictures for—blood and guts. It's almost, but not quite, a war comedy. Young Tony Bill later became a very successful film producer (THE STING, HEARTS OF THE WEST, etc.) and restaurateur in Santa Monica.

p, Martin Ransohoff, John Calley; d, Sydney Pollack; w, Daniel Taradash, David Rayfiel (based on the novel by William Eastlake); ph, Henri Decae (Panavision, Technicolor); m, Michel Legrand; ed, Malcolm Cooke; art d, Max Douy Jacques Douy, Mort Rabinowitz; set d, Charles Merangel; ch, Dirk Sanders.

War Drama   (PR:C   MPAA:R)

CASTLE OF BLOOD**½   (1964, Fr./Ital.) 85m Woolner bw
(AKA: DANZA MACABRA, CASTLE OF TERROR, COFFIN OF TERROR)

Barbara Steele (*Elizabeth Blackwood*), Georges Riviere (*Alan Foster*), Margaret Robsahm (*Julia*), Sylvia Sorente (*Eli*), Henry Kruger (*Dr. Carmus*), Montgomery Glenn, Raoul H. Newman, Phil Karson, John Peters, Ben Steffen, Salvo Randone.

Riviere plays a poet who meets writer Edgar Allan Poe and Lord Blackwood at an inn and they bet him he cannot spend the night alone in a certain castle wherein all the inhabitants met their doom on All Soul's Eve. Riviere accepts this challenge and goes to the castle. There he meets Steele and learns that she has no heartbeat. The dead come back to life and re-enact their deaths, most of them horrible murders. Riviere is finally driven from the house and he flees out the door and into a spiked iron fence, where he is impaled and dies. Poe and Blackwood wander by and collect their winnings from the dead man's pocket. One of horror cult queen Steele's best efforts. Director Margheriti remade it as WEB OF THE SPIDER (1970) with Tony Franciosa.

p, Frank Belty, Walter Sarch; d, Antonio Margheriti [Anthony Dawson]; w, Jean Grimaud, Gordon Wilson, Jr.; ph, Richard Kramer; m, Riz Ortolani; ed, Otel Langhel; art d, Warner Scott.

Horror   (PR:O   MPAA:NR)

CASTLE OF CRIMES*½   (1940, Brit.) Mycroft/PRC 68m bw (GB: HOUSE OF THE ARROW)

Kenneth Kent (*Inspector Hanaud*), Diana Churchill (*Betty Harlowe*), Belle Chrystall (*Ann Upcott*), Peter Murray-Hill (*Jim Frobisher*), Clifford Evans (*Maurice Thevenet*), Louise Hampton (*Mme. Harlow*), Catherine Lacey (*Francine Rollard*), Aubrey Dexter (*Giradot*), James Harcourt (*Boris Raviart*), Ivor Barnard (*Jean Cladel*), Athene Seyler.

Wealthy spinster, unable to shake the idea relatives are waiting for her death so they can start spending her money, is murdered. Too bad there's no suspense or intrigue in this stock whodunit obvious from the beginning. Low production values.

p, Walter C. Mycroft; d, Harold French; w, Doreen Montgomery (based on a story by A. E. W. Mason); ph, Walter Harvey; ed, E. B. Jarvis.

Mystery   (PR:A   MPAA:NR)

CASTLE OF EVIL*   (1967) 80m United Pictures/WORLD c

Scott Brady (*Matt Granger*), Virginia Mayo (*Sable*), Lisa Gaye (*Carol Harris*). David Brian (*Robert Hawley*), Hugh Marlowe (*Dr. Corozal*), William Thourlby (*The Robot*), Shelley Morrison (*Lupe Tekal d'Esperanza*), Natividad Vacio (*Machado*), Ernest Sarracino (*Tunki*).

Horrible horror film which only has value in its campiness. A mad scientist, wickedly disfigured by phosphorous salts, dies and leaves a will. A group which is to share in the wealth visits his remote Caribbean castle and learn none of them will receive any of the cash until the one who disfigured him is found. A murderous robot created in the image of its scarred master is programmed to discover and kill the guilty one. The killer, in turn, ingeniously reprograms the robot to kill everyone else instead. This cheapie exploitation film even offered a free funeral if the viewer dropped dead while watching. Does the offer still stand?

p, Earle Lyon; d, Francis D. Lyon; w, Charles A. Wallace; ph, Brick Marquard (Eastmancolor); m, Paul Dunlap; ed, Robert S. Eisen; art d, Paul Sylos; set d, John Bury; spec eff, Roger George.

Horror   (PR:C   MPAA:NR)

CASTLE OF FU MANCHU, THE*   (1968, Ger./Span./Ital./Brit.) 92m International Cinema c
(AKA: ASSIGNMENT: ISTANBUL; DIE FOLTERKAMMER DES DR. FU MANCHU)

Christopher Lee (*Fu Manchu*), Richard Greene (*Nayland Smith*), Howard Marion Crawford (*Dr. Petrie*), Tsai Chin (*Lin Tang*), Gunther Stoll (*Curt*), Rosalba Neri (*Lisa*), Maria Perschy (*Marie*), Jose Manuel Martin (*Omar Pascha*), Werner Aprelat (*Melnik*).

The last and worst installment of the generally spotty Lee/Fu Manchu series has the evil Chinese scientist inventing a machine that freezes water instantly. To help him perfect his insidious device (of course he plans to take over the world with it) he kidnaps a brilliant scientist who suffers from a terminal heart condition and equally brilliant surgeon Stoll to keep him alive by performing a heart transplant. This was so bad that its release was held up for several years and then it was stuck on the lower half of a double bill.

p, Harry Alan Towers; d, Jess [Jesus] Franco; w, Peter Welbeck [Towers]; ph, Manuel Merino (Eastmancolor).

Horror/Science Fiction   Cas.   (PR:C   MPAA:PG)

CASTLE OF PURITY***   (1974, Mex.) 116m Ripstein c

Claudio Brook, Rita Macedo

Brook, alarmed by what he sees around him, locks his entire family within the walls of their house for eighteen years. A haunting drama, well-shot and acted.

d, Arturo Ripstein; w, Ripstein, Jose Emilio Pacheco; ph, Alex Phillips; set d, Manuel Fontanal.

Drama   (PR:C-O   MPAA:NR)

CASTLE OF TERROR   (SEE: CASTLE OF BLOOD, 1964)

CASTLE OF THE LIVING DEAD**   (1964, Ital./Fr.) 90m Malasky bw
                                       (IL CASTELLO DE MORTI VIVI)
Christopher Lee, Donald Sutherland, Gala Germani, Phillippe Leroy, Jacques
Stanislawski.

A group of circus performers travels to the castle of the sinister Count Drago (Lee)
whose hobby is mummifying animals with a drug he has developed. Of course, his
experiments are eventually applied to humans to "preserve their beauty." Lots of
scenes show the circus performers' various talents, and eventually a dwarf emerges as
the story's hero. Donald Sutherland makes his first cinematic appearance in a dual
role, the first as a soldier, and the second in drag as a witch. There is some confusion
over who actually directed, but the end scenes are reported to have been directed by
Michael Reeves.
p, Paul Maslansky; d, Luciano Ricci [Herbert Wise], Michael Reeves; w, Warren Kiefer.
Horror   **(PR:C   MPAA:NR)**

CASTLE OF THE MONSTERS*½   (1958, Mex.) 90m Sotomayor bw
                                       (EL CASTILLO DE LOS MONSTROUS)
Antonio Espino Clavillazo, Evangelina Elizondo, German Robles, Carlos Orellana,
Guillermo Orea.

Mexican haunted house comedy wherein an innocent couple's car breaks down and
they are forced to spend the night in a lonely castle. Eventually every movie monster
known to man terrorizes the couple, including a mummy, a gorilla, a werewolf, a
Frankenstein-type monster, a vampire, and even a Creature From The Black Lagoon-
type thing. For fans of Latin-horror only.
p, Jesus Sotomayor, Alberto Hernandez Curiel; d, Julian Soler; w, Fernando Galiana,
Carlos Orellana; ph, Victor Herrera.
Comedy/Horror   **(PR:C   MPAA:NR)**

CASTLE ON THE HUDSON½**   (1940) 76m WB bw
                                       (GB: YEARS WITHOUT DAYS)
John Garfield (Tommy Gordon), Ann Sheridan (Kay), Pat O'Brien (Warden Long),
Burgess Meredith (Steven Rockford), Henry O'Neill (District Attorney), Jerome Cowan
(Ed Crowley), Guinn "Big Boy" Williams (Mike Cagle), John Litel (Chaplain), Margot
Stevenson (Ann Rockford), Willard Robertson (Ragan), Edward Pawley (Black Jack),
Billy Wayne (Pete), Nedda Harrigan (Mrs. Long), Wade Boteler (Principal Keeper),
Barbara Pepper (Goldie), Robert Strange (Joe Morris), Grant Mitchell (Dr. Ames),
Robert Homans (Clyde Burton), Joseph Downing, Sol Gorss (Gangsters), Charles
Sherlock, Mike Lally, Jack Mower, Frank Mayo, Pat O'Malley, Walter Miller (Guards),
Pat Flaherty (Stretcher Attendant), Ed Kane (Club Manager), Claude Wisberg, Michael
Conroy (Newsboys), Frank Faylen (Guard Who Is Slugged), Nat Carr, William Telark,
Bill Hopper (Reporters), Lee Phelps (Guard in Visitor's Room), James Flavin (Guard
in Death Row).

In a power-packed performance, Garfield does a reprise of Spencer Tracy's role in
20,000 YEARS IN SING SING. He is the wisecracking jewel thief doing 25 to 30 years
with his faithful girl friend, the luscious Ann Sheridan, who attempts to get him
paroled. Shifty lawyer Cowan promises to help but injures Sheridan when she rebuffs
him. A sympathetic warden, O'Brien, allows Garfield to go free on his "honor system"
to visit Sheridan and he walks in on her just as Cowan pays another visit. Sheridan
shoots Cowan but Garfield takes the blame, first fleeing, then returning to prison to
save O'Brien's job and honorably go to the chair. The film lacks the pace of its original
but Garfield's magnetic personality holds it together.
p, Samuel Bischoff; d, Anatole Litvak; w, Seton I. Miller, Brown Holmes, Courteney
Terrett (based on the book 20,000 Years in Sing Sing by Lewis E. Lawes); ph, Arthur
Edeson; m, Leo F. Forbstein; ed, Thomas Richards.
Prison Drama   **(PR:C   MPAA:NR)**

CASTLE SINISTER zero   (1932, Brit.) 50m Delta/Filmophone bw
Haddon Mason (Ronald Kemp), Eric Adeney (Prof. Bandov), Wally Patch (Jorkins),
Ilsa Kilpatrick (Jean), Edmund Kennedy (Father).

Low-budget, utterly forgettable horror film has mad scientist Adeney trying to transplant the brain of a young girl into the skull of his apeman. Totally trashy.
d, Widgey R. Newman.
Horror   **(PR:C   MPAA:NR)**

CASTLE IN THE AIR*   (1952, Brit.) 89m AB-Pathe bw
David Tomlinson (Earl of Locharne), Helen Cherry (Boss Trent), Margaret Rutherford
(Miss Nicholson), Barbara Kelly (Mrs. Clodfelter Dunne), A. E. Matthews (Blair),
Patricia Dainton (Ermyntrude), Ewan Roberts (Menzies), Brian Oulton (Phillips), Clive
Morton (MacFee), Gordon Jackson (Hiker), Pat Sandys (Girl Hiker), Russell Waters
(Moffat), John Harvey (Andrews), Esme Beringer (Mrs. Thompson), Winifred Willard
(Miss Miller), David Hannaford (Small Boy), Helen Christie (Jessie), Archie Duncan
(Constable), Norman Macowan (Pettigrew), Stringer Davis (Hall Porter), Paul Blake
(Hotel Manager).

A stage play which should never have passed the proscenium. A penniless earl, who
must resort to taking in boarders, is about to be bought out by the National Coal Board
which wants to turn his castle into a youth hotel. Also seeing an opportunity is a
millionaire divorcee who wants to buy the castle and hitch the earl. There's still
more—one of the boarders is destined to prove that the earl is actually the heir to the
Scottish throne. Plot, plot, plot, and all of it drab, drab, drab.
p, Edward Dryhurst, Ernest Gartside; d, Henry Cass; w, Dryhurst, Alan Melville (based
on the play by Melville); ph, Erwin Hillier; m, Francis Chagrin; ed, E. B. Jarvis.
Drama   **(PR:A   MPAA:NR)**

CAT, THE**   (1959, Fr.) 108m Essex Universal/Ellis Films bw
Francoise Arnoul (Cora), Bernard Wicki (Bernard), Bernard Blier (Leader), Kurt

Meisel (Capt. Heinz), Roger Hanin (Pierre), Andre Versini (Henri), Louise Roblin
(Bernadette).

Arnoul is a pretty Parisian widow recruited into the Resistance, but things become
complicated when she falls in love with a German soldier. Fairly suspenseful despite
plot holes. Arnoul is quite good.
p, Eugene Tucherer; d, Henri Decoin; w, Decoin, Jacques Remy (based on a novel by
Remy); ph, Pierre Montazel.
War Drama   **(PR:C   MPAA:NR)**

CAT, THE*½   (1966) 87m EMB c
Roger Perry (Pete Kilby), Peggy Ann Garner (Martha Kilby), Barry Coe (Walt Kilby),
Dwayne Redlin (Toby), George "Shug" Fisher (Bill Krim), Ted Darby (Art), John Todd
Roberts (Jesse), Richard Webb (Sheriff Vern), Les Bradley (Deputy Mike).

Too cute and inept survivalist drama about a boy who runs away from home in search
of a neighbor's pet wildcat. He soon meets up with the critter and becomes its friend.
After witnessing a rustler kill someone, the boy is hunted by the villain, only to be saved
by the cat. Too far-fetched to benefit even the youngest and most naive audiences.
p&d, Ellis Kadison; w, William Redlin, Laird Koenig; ph, Monroe Askins (Pathe Color);
m, Stan Worth; ed, Jack Cornall.
Adventure   **(PR:AA   MPAA:NR)**

CAT, THE½**   (1975, Fr.) 88m Joseph Green Pictures (LE CHAT) c
Jean Gabin (Julien), Simone Signoret (Clemence), Annie Cordy (Nelly), Jacques
Rispal (Doctor).

After years of marriage, the love between Gabin and Signoret has evaporated into
hate. They spend their days in a decrepit house on the edge of Paris not speaking and
doing their best to make each other miserable. Gabin and Signoret are superb in their
contempt and director Granier-Deferre makes each gesture and each object speak
volumes. Produced in 1971. (French, English subtitles)
d, Pierre-Granier-Deferre; w, Granier-Deferre, Pascal Jardin (based on a novel by
Georges Simenon); ph, Walter Wottitz (Eastmancolor); m, Philippe Sarde.
Drama   **(PR:C   MPAA:NR)**

CAT AND MOUSE*½   (1958, Brit) 79m Anvil/Eros bw
                                       (AKA: THE DESPERATE MEN)
Lee Patterson (Rod Fenner), Ann Sears (Ann Coltby), Victor Maddern (Supt. Harding),
Hilton Edwards (Mr. Scruby), Roddy McMillan (Mr. Pomeroy), George Rose (Dealer).

Sears is the daughter of a man executed for murder, who is held hostage by GI
deserters who are after the jewels her father had stolen. Historically interesting if dull
melodrama by Rotha, best known for his documentary work.
p,d&w, Paul Rotha (based on a novel by Michael Halliday); ph, Wolfgang Suschitzky.
Crime   **(PR:C   MPAA:NR)**

CAT AND MOUSE   (SEE: MOUSEY, 1974)

CAT AND MOUSE½**   (1978, Fr.) 107m Quartet c
Michele Morgan (Mme. Richard), Serge Reggiani (Inspector Lechat), Philippe
Leotard (His Assistant), Jean-Pierre Aumont (Mon. Richard), Valerie Legrange
(Valerie).

Reggiani is a detective investigating the murder of wealthy philanderer Aumont. A weak
ending mars one of Lelouch's most accessible efforts. (In French; English subtitles.)
p,d&w, Claude Lelouch; ph, Jean Collomb; m, Francis Lai.
Comedy/Mystery   **Cas.**   **(PR:C   MPAA:PG)**

CAT AND THE CANARY, THE***   (1939) 72m PAR bw
Bob Hope (Wallie Campbell), Paulette Goddard (Joyce Norman), John Beal (Fred
Blythe), Douglass Montgomery (Charlie Wilder), Gale Sondergaard (Miss Lu),
Elizabeth Patterson (Aunt Susan), Nydia Westman (Cicily), George Zucco (Lawyer
Crosby), John Wray (Hendricks), George Regas, Chief Thundercloud (Indian Guides),
Milton Kibbee (Photographer), Charles Lane, Frank Melton (Reporters).

Eccentric millionaire dies and lawyer Zucco assembles prospective heirs at the Bayou
mansion. Goddard gets all, setting up Hope as straight man for a top comedic effect.
Hope is terrific as the wise-cracking but spineless character who attempts to protect
Goddard from going insane (if she turns cuckoo she loses the fortune, according to the
bizarre will). Director Nugent, who had guided Hope through NEVER SAY DIE and
GIVE ME A SAILOR, does a great job in presenting some spine-tingling moments as
claw-like hands reach out for the heroine and everyone seems to disappear through
swiveling bookcases, sliding doors, and false panels. Lang's camera work is properly
moody and supporting player Sondergaard gives a high-camp performance as a
spooky, mystic housekeeper, dressed in black with a black cat constantly at her side.
This was Goddard's first starring role; this striking actress with the sultry voice would be
teamed with Hope again in THE GHOST BREAKERS, 1940, following the success of
this film. THE CAT AND THE CANARY was first filmed in 1927 by Universal as a
horror classic, then remade with sound in 1930 and retitled THE CAT CREEPS. The
Hope-Goddard vehicle was remade for the fourth time in 1979 as an oaffish comedy
with less-than-desired results and distantly removed from the original 1922 stage hit.
p, Arthur Hornblow, Jr.; d, Elliott Nugent; w, Walter De Leon and Lynn Starling (based
on the play by John Willard); ph, Charles Lang; m, Dr. Ernest Toch; ed, Archie
Marshek; art d, Hans Dreier, Robert Usher.
Mystery/Comedy   **(PR:A   MPAA:NR)**

CAT AND THE CANARY, THE**   (1979, Brit.) 90m Cinema Shares c
Honor Blackman (Susan Sillsby), Michael Callan (Paul Jones), Edward Fox
(Hendricks), Wendy Hiller (Allison Crosby), Olivia Hussey (Cicily Young), Carol
Lynley (Anabelle West), Peter McEnery (Charlie Wilder), Wilfrid Hyde-White (Cyrus

West), Daniel Massey *(Harry Blythe)*, Beatrix Lehmann *(Mrs. Pleasant)*.

An amusing Christie-esque film which has all the necessary elements of mystery—a mansion, will readings, rainy nights, and an insane killer. Carol Lynley is the sole heir to the fortune in this loose fourth version of the 1922 stage play. The cast plays it for laughs that aren't there.

p, Richard Gordon; d&w, Radley Metzger (based on the play by John Willard); ph, Alex Thompson (Technicolor); m, Steven Cagen; ed, Roger Harrison; set d, Anthony Pratt.

Mystery Cas. (PR:A MPAA:PG)

CAT AND THE FIDDLE*** (1934) 90m MGM bw/c

Ramon Novarro *(Victor)*, Jeanette MacDonald *(Shirley)*, Frank Morgan *(Daudet)*, Charles Butterworth *(Charles)*, Jean Hersholt *(Professor)*, Vivienne Segal *(Odette)*, Frank Conroy *(Theater Owner)*, Henry Armetta *(Taxi Driver)*, Adrienne D'Ambricourt *(Concierge)*, Joseph Cawthorn *(Rudy)*.

In Brussels, failed composer Novarro is running from a restaurateur when he hops into a taxi occupied by MacDonald, who is newly arrived from New York and planning to study with Novarro's music teacher. (That's what they call a "cute-meet" in screen-writer parlance). She asks him to find his own cab but he turns on the charm. They are living next door to each other in matching *pensions*. They grab for her luggage, the valise opens, and her gear is strewn all over the sidewalk. She runs into the little hotel and the cabbie goes after Novarro for the fare. He doesn't have a sou, so the taxi driver takes his sheet music, the only asset he has. Novarro's operetta is opening and the night before the gala event, the husband of Vivienne Segal, the leading lady, withdraws his support when he finds the vampish Segal with her arms about a struggling-to-get-away Novarro. Novarro is desperate, bounces a check to theater-owner Conroy to keep the place open, but it doesn't help as the orchestra and the leading man walks out. Novarro decides to play the lead himself and Butterworth, a harpist who never plays, asks MacDonald if she will step in and do the part as she knows it. She turns him down and concentrates on her upcoming plans to marry the womanizing Morgan. Butterworth arrives at the theater with an ancient singer who promptly drinks herself into a stupor. Novarro is crazed and about to abort the performance and go to jail for writing a rubber check when he hears the glorious MacDonald soprano on stage. The rest of the film is shot in Technicolor as the on-stage musical is running and the off-stage romance is deepening. MacDonald tells Novarro that she is just there to help keep him out of *le clink*. He prevails on her emotions and by the time the curtain is ringing down on the successful premiere of Novarro's show, MacDonald is in his arms and the lovers unite as one. The Kern and Harbach score stood the play in good stead and it ran 395 times on Broadway. On screen, it's not quite so successful. "The Night Was Made For Love" was the only song that survived. Novarro was supposed to be the logical successor to Rudolph Valentino for the "Latin Lover" image but he never caught the public's imagination the way Rudy did. Perhaps fans sensed that he wasn't really into heterosexual romance. Novarro was beaten to death in 1968 by two male hustlers, but when he made this film he was still on top of the world. MacDonald appears in this film version of the 1931 stage musical as her first production for MGM. Mogul Louis B. Mayer intended to have the soprano appear in I MARRIED AN ANGEL but this property was labelled risqué by the Hays Office, Hollywood's censor board. The film was finally made in 1942 as the last film MacDonald made with Nelson Eddy. Adrian designed MacDonald's first costumes for this operetta but she got some hand-me-down treatment when she was dressed for the finale in a gown Joan Crawford had worn a year earlier in DANCING LADY. Other Songs: "The Breeze Kissed Your Hair," "One Moment Alone," "Impressions In A Harlem Flat," "Poor Pierrot." "She Didn't Say Yes," "Don't Tell Us Not To Sing," "I Watch the Love Parade," "A New Love Is Old," "The Crystal Candelabra," "Ha! Cha Cha," "Try To Forget."

p, Bernard Hyman; d, William K. Howard; w, Sam and Bella Spewack (based on stage musical by Jerome Kern and Otto Harbach); ph, Harold Rosson, Charles Clarke (3-color Technicolor); m, Herbert Stothart; ed, Frank Hull; art d, Theodore Toluboff; set d, Edwin B. Willis; cos, Adrian; m/l, Kern, Harbach.

Musical/Romance (PR:A MPAA:NR)

CAT ATE THE PARAKEET, THE zero (1972) 85m KEP Enterprises c

Phillip Pine, Robert Mantell, Madelyn Keen, Dawn Frame, Martin Margules, Sheila Brennán, Paul Appleby, Jane Uhrig, Barbara Bartelme, Jeffery Caron, Arthur Batanides, Barbara James, Scott Campbell, Bert Conway, Victor R. Schulte, Honeycomb.

With possibly the worst plot of 1972, this message film tells us that "drugs are bad." Johnny takes drugs and runs away with "those damned hippies" after his parents show no remorse at the death of the family dog. After a bad trip, man, Johnny sees the evils of drugs and hippies, so he returns home. Johnny's happy, Mom and Dad are happy, everyone's happy, except for Johnny's pet parakeet which was eaten by the family cat. Dad, however, has learned his lesson and tenderly consoles his heartbroken son. Now if only the cat had eaten the script . . .

p, Clark Johnson, Phillip Pine; d&w, Pine; ph, Frank Mills (Eastmancolor); m, Ted Roberts.

Drama (PR:A MPAA:NR)

CAT BALLOU**** (1965) 97m COL c

Jane Fonda *(Cat Ballou)*, Lee Marvin *(Kid Shelleen/Tim Strawn)*, Michael Callan *(Clay Boone)*, Dwayne Hickman *(Jed)*, Tom Nardini *(Jackson Two-Bears)*, John Marley *(Frankie Ballou)*, Reginald Denny *(Sir Harry Percival)*, Jay C. Flippen *(Sheriff Cardigan)*, Arthur Hunnicutt *(Butch Cassidy)*, Bruce Cabot *(Sheriff Maledon)*, Burt Mustin *(Accuser)*, Paul Gilbert *(Train Messenger)*, Nat "King" Cole, Stubby Kaye *(Singers)*, Robert Phillips *(Klem)*, Charles Wagenheim *(James)*, Duke Hobbie *(Homer)*, Ayllene Gibbons *(Hedda)*, Everett L. Rohrer *(Train Engineer)*, Harry Harvey, Sr. *(Train Conductor)*, Hallene Hill *(Honey Girl)*, Gail Bonney *(Mabel Bentley)*, Joseph Hamilton *(Frenchie)*, Dorothy Claire *(Singing Tart)*, Charles Horvath *(Hardcase)*, Chuck Roberson *(Armed Guard)*, Nick Cravat *(Ad-Lib)*, Ted White *(Gunslinger)*, Erik Sorenson *(Valet)*, Ivan L. Middleton *(Train Fireman)*, Carol Veazie *(Mrs. Parker)*.

A rip-roaring and funny spoof on Western pictures that succeeds on just about all counts. Fonda, in the title role, is arriving home after a sojourn to the East. She is accompanied by fledgling bad guys Callan and Hickman. She finds her father, Marley, living in fear. His life has been threatened by a huge conglomerate, the Wolf City Development Corporation, and he will be killed unless he sells his ranch to them. Marley refuses and is killed by Strawn, a professional murderer who has a silver nose that is held in place by a band around his head. (His own nose has been bitten off in a fight.) Fonda realizes she can't face this challenge so she sends for Kid Shelleen, a drunken, woebegone gunfighter who is a double for Strawn. That's because both characters are played by Marvin in this Oscar-winning role. Fonda, a respectable teacher, takes up a life of crime, stages a robbery, then flees to the famous Hole-In-The-Wall to hide. There, she finds a host of ancient outlaws in their dotage who want nothing more than to be left alone to die in their beds. Denny is the villain who rules the town and Fonda shoots him dead. Just as she is about to be hanged for the crime, she is rescued and the picture ends on a high note. Nat "King" Cole (in his last movie) and Stubby Kaye act as a Greek chorus, wandering in and out of scenes to link the action together by singing a lyric about what happened in between. Lots of good jokes; just as many that don't work. Good fun and fine performances by all the supporting actors. Oscar nominations were made for the screenplay, the music, and the title song. This film revived Fonda's drooping career which had taken a nosedive with such bombs as TALL STORY. For Marvin it was the beginning of a whole new career, from a slob brute character actor (BAD DAY AT BLACK ROCK, THE BIG HEAT, THE RAID) to a versatile middle-aged leading man who could handle drama or comedy with alacrity and finesse. Director Silverstein, Yale-educated and later a teacher at Brandeis, came nowhere close to repeating the success of CAT BALLOU and some of his films were soundly trounced by critics and public (THE CAR, THE HAPPENING.) Yet, if he is to be remembered for anything, CAT BALLOU should stand as a good example of comedy at its best.

p, Harold Hecht; d, Elliot Silverstein; w, Frank Pierson, Walter Newman (based on the novel by Roy Chanslor); ph, Jack Marta (Technicolor); m, Frank DeVol; ed, Charles Nelson; cos, Bill Thomas; ch, Miriam Nelson; m/l, Mack David, Jerry Livingston.

Comedy/Western Cas. (PR:A-C MPAA:NR)

CAT BURGLAR, THE*½ (1961) 65m Harvard Film/UA bw

Jack Hogan *(Jack Coley)*, June Kenney *(Nan Baker)*, Gregg Palmer *(Reed Taylor)*, Will J. White *(Leo Joseph)*, Gene Roth *(Pete)*, Bruno Ve Sota *(Muskie)*, Billie Bird *(Mrs. Prattle)*, Tommy Ivo *(Willie Prattle)*, Hal Torey *(Officer Regan)*, John Baer *(Alan Sheridan)*.

Burglar Hogan steals a briefcase containing secret documents stolen by Baer to sell to a foreign power. Baer is ordered to recover the papers but fails, paying for it with his life. The spies track down Hogan but he refuses to hand over the goods, taking two gunmen with him before dying. Baer's girl friend recovers the documents and turns them over to the proper authorities. Routine spy stuff.

p, Gene Corman; d, William Witney; w, Leo Gordon; ph, Taylor Byars; m, Buddy Bregman; ed, Mort Tubor; art d, Daniel Haller.

Spy Drama (PR:C MPAA:NR)

CAT CREEPS, THE*** (1930) 71m UNIV bw

Helen Twelvetrees *(Annabelle West)*, Raymond Hackett *(Paul)*, Neil Hamilton *(Charles Wilder)*, Jean Hersholt *(Dr. Patterson)*, Montagu Love *(Hendricks)*, Lawrence Grant *(Crosby)*, Theodore Von Eltz *(Harry Blythe)*, Blanche Frederici *(Mam' Pleasant)*, Elizabeth Patterson *(Susan)*, Lilyan Tashman *(Clelly)*.

Remake of the 1927 Universal release of THE CAT AND THE CANARY (silent), this is the story of an escaped maniac as told by the insane asylum keeper. Abundant chills with a swift and surprise ending. A few laughs accompany this first-rate production. Remade as a top comedy, THE CAT AND THE CANARY [1939] with Bob Hope.

p, Carl Laemmle, Jr.; d, Rupert Julian; w, Gladys Lehman and William Hurlbut (based on the stage play "The Cat and The Canary" by John Willard); ph, Hal Mohr; ed, Maurice Pivar.

Mystery (PR:AA MPAA:NR)

CAT CREEPS, THE** (1946) 58m UNIV bw

Noah Beery, Jr. *(Flash Laurie)*, Lois Collier *(Gay Elliot)*, Paul Kelly *(Ken Grady)*, Douglass Dumbrille *(Tom McGalvey)*, Fred Brady *(Terry Nichols)*, Rose Hobart *(Connie Palmer)*, Jonathan Hale *(Walter Elliot)*, Vera Lewis *(Cora Williams)*, Iris Clive *(Kyra Goran)*, William Davidson *(Editor)*, Arthur Loft *(Publisher)*, Jerry Jerome *(Polich)*.

Crisp spook chiller has a black cat as the center of attention to aid in solving a number of murders. (The cat possesses the soul of a deceased woman and has extra-sensory abilities.) Brady and Beery team up well as the reporter and photographer who uncover a missing $200,000 for the newspaper while solving a murder in one fell swoop. Gripping drama will provide ghost lovers with enough chills to keep from cat napping. Not a remake of the 1930 film and far afield from THE CAT AND THE CANARY plot.

p, Howard Welsch; d, Erle C. Kenton; w, Edward Dein, Jerry Warner (based on a story by Gerald Geraghty); ph, George Robinson; ed, Russell Schoengarth; md, Paul Sawtell.

Mystery (PR:AA MPAA:NR)

CAT FROM OUTER SPACE, THE*** (1978) 103m BV/DIS c

Ken Berry *(Frank)*, Sandy Duncan *(Liz)*, Harry Morgan *(Gen. Stilton)*, Roddy McDowall *(Stallwood)*, McLean Stevenson *(Link)*, Jesse White *(Ernie)*, Alan Young *(Wenger)*, Hans Conried *(Heffel)*, Ronnie Schell *(Sgt. Duffy)*, James Hampton *(Capt.*

Anderson), Howard T. Platt *(Col. Woodruff)*, William Prince *(Olympus)*, Ralph Manza *(Weasel)*, Tom Pedi *(Honest Harry)*, Hank Jones *(Officer)*, Rick Hurst *(Dydee Guard)*, John Alderson *(Mr. Smith)*, Tiger Joe Marsh *(Omar)*, Arnold Soboloff *(NASA executive)*, Mel Carter, Dallas McKennon, Alice Backes, Henry Slate, Roger Pancake, Roger Price, Jerry Fujikawa, Jim Begg, Pete Renaday, Rich Sorenson, Tom Jackman, Fred L. Whalen, Joe Melalis, Gil Stratton, Jana Milo, Richard Warlock.

An entertaining Disney film which is sort of an E.T. in a litter box. Zunar J5/90 Doric 4-7, a cat more conveniently known as Jake, crash lands on earth and turns to a local physicist for aid. Needed is $120,000 in gold for repairs to Jake's malfunctioning spacecraft. It's soon discovered that this cat has special powers that can foresee outcomes in betting. The cat, however, is inadvertently put into a deep sleep by a bumbling vet. A spaceship can't land on earth without the knowledge of the government, and soon the military is snooping around mistakenly looking for spacemen. A fine sample of a Disney product scripted by cartoonist Ted Key, who is also credited with GUS and THE $1,000,000 DUCK. Rumor has it that Jake was played by two different Abyssinian cats—Rumpler and his sister, Amber.

p, Ron Miller, Norman Tokar; d, Tokar; w, Ted Key; ph, Charles F. Wheeler (Technicolor); m, Lalo Schifrin; ed, Cotton Warburton; art d, John B. Mansbridge, Preston Ames; spec eff, Eustace Lycett, Art Cruickshank, Danny Lee; stunts, Richard Warlock.

Comedy Cas. (PR:AAA MPAA:G)

CAT GANG, THE*½ (1959, Brit.) 50m Realist/CFF bw

Francesca Annis *(Sylvia)*, John Pike *(John)*, Jeremy Bullock *(Bill)*, John Gabriel *(Mason)*, John Stacy *(Dodds)*, Paddy Joyce *(Banks)*.

A group of children helps a customs agent capture a ring of smugglers. Strictly kid stuff.

p, Arthur T. Viliesid; d, Darrell Catling; w, John Eldridge (based on a story by G. Ewart Evans); ph, Leslie Dear.

Children/Crime (PR:AA MPAA:NR)

CAT GIRL** (1957) 67m Malibu/AIP bw

Barbara Shelley *(Leonora)*, Robert Ayres *(Dr. Marlowe)*, Kay Callard *(Dorothy)*, Paddy Webster *(Cathy)*, Ernest Milton *(Edmund)*, Lilly Kahn *(Anna)*, Jack May *(Richard)*, John Lee *(Allan)*, Martin Boddy *(Cafferty)*, John Watson *(Roberts)*, Selma Vaz Dias *(Nurse)*, John Baker *(Male Nurse)*, Frank Atkinson *(Guard)*, Geoffrey Tyrrell *(Caretaker)*.

Minor exploitation film with Shelley as a woman who believes she has inherited a curse which sends her soul into a marauding leopard. Psychiatrist Ayres tries to cure her, but she dies at the same moment the leopard she becomes is killed. Muddy, confusing, and originally packaged with THE AMAZING COLOSSAL MAN.

p, Lou Rusoff, Herbert Smith; d, Alfred Shaughnessy; w, Rusoff; ph, Paddy A-Hearne; ed, Jose Jackson.

Horror (PR:C MPAA:NR)

CAT IN THE SACK, THE*

(1967, Can.) 74m National Film Board of Canada/Pathe Contemporary bw (LE CHAT DANS LE SAC)

Claude Godbout *(Claude)*, Barbara Ulrich *(Barbara)*, Manon Blain *(Manon J'sais-pas-qui)*, Jean-Paul Bernier *(Jean-Paul)*, Veronique Vilbert *(Veronique)*, Andre Leblanc *(Toulouse)*, Paul-Marie Lapointe, Pierre Maheu, Jean-V. Dufresne.

Godbout is a French-Canadian journalist in Montreal alienated from Canadian society but unable to do anything about it. His girl friend, a Jewish drama student, is more interested in her art and sensual pleasures than in changing the world, so Godbout travels to a remote cabin and thinks about it all. Pretentious drama is absolutely stagnant and dull.

p, Jacques Bobet; d&w, Gilles Groulx; ph, Jean-Claude Labrecque; m, John Coltrane, Francois Couperin, Antonio Vivaldi.

Drama (PR:C MPAA:NR)

CAT MURKIL AND THE SILKS zero

(1976) 102m Pine-Thomas/Gamma III c

David Kyle *(Eddie "Cat" Murkil)*, Steve Bond *(Joey)*, Kelly Yaegermann *(Claudine)*, Rhodes Reason *(Detective Harder)*, Meegan King *(Marble)*, Don Carter *(Bumps)*, Derrel Maury *(Punch)*, Joe Reteria *(Carlos Garvanza)*, Ruth Manning *(Mrs. Murkil)*.

Kyle connives and kills his way to the top of his all-white Los Angeles street gang. Amateurish, violent, and not worth a second glance.

p, William C. Thomas; d, John Bushelman; w, Thomas; ph, Bruce Logan; m, Bernie Kaai Lewis; ed, Jeff Bushelman.

Crime (PR:O MPAA:NR)

CAT O'NINE TAILS* (1971, Ital./Ger./Fr.) 112m NG c

Karl Malden *(Franco Arno)*, James Franciscus *(Carlo Giordani)*, Catherine Spaak *(Anna Terzi)*, Cinzia De Carolis *(Lori)*, Carlo Alighiero *(Dr. Calabresi)*, Vittorio Congia *(Righetto)*, Pier Paolo Capponi *(Police Superintendent Spimi)*, Corrado Olmi *(Morsella)*, Tino Carraro *(Prof. Terzi)*, Aldo Reggiani *(Dr. Casoni)*, Horst Frank *(Dr. Braun)*, Emilio Marchesini *(Dr. Mombelli)*, Tom Felleghy *(Dr. Esson)*, Rada Rassimov *(Bianca Merusi)*, Werner Pochat *(Manuel)*.

An excess of murder and sex can't pull this one into respectable ranks. Malden plays a blind puzzle-solver who is teamed with newsman Franciscus to track the killer of a member of a secret research foundation. Morricone's music fits tightly into this sloppily-dubbed suspenser.

p, Salvatore Argento; d&w, Dario Argento (based on a story by Dario Argento, Luigi Collo, Dardano Sacchetti); ph, Erico Menczer (Techniscope, Technicolor); m, Ennio Morricone; ed, Franco Fraticelli; art d, Carlo Leva; spec eff, Luciano Vittori.

Suspense (PR:O MPAA:GP)

CAT ON A HOT TIN ROOF**** (1958) 108m MGM c

Elizabeth Taylor *(Maggie Pollitt)*, Paul Newman *(Brick Pollitt)*, Burl Ives *(Big Daddy Pollitt)*, Jack Carson *(Gooper Pollitt)*, Judith Anderson *(Big Mama Pollitt)*, Madeleine Sherwood *(Mae Pollitt)*, Larry Gates *(Dr. Baugh)*, Vaughn Taylor *(Deacon Davis)*, Patty Ann Gerrity *(Dixie Pollitt)*, Rusty Stevens *(Sonny Pollitt)*, Hugh Corcoran *(Buster Pollitt)*, Deborah Miller *(Trixie Pollitt)*, Brian Corcoran *(Boy Pollitt)*, Vince Townsend, Jr. *(Lacey)*, Zelda Cleaver *(Sookey)*, Tony Merrill, Jeane Wood *(Party Guests)*, Bobby Johnson *(Groom)*.

Censorship reared its prudish head when they adapted Williams's steamy play for the screen. All references to homosexuality were removed and Newman had to play his part as a wimp, rather than as a man struggling with his own sexual identity. To his credit, Newman was able to infuse the character he essayed with enough between-the-lines emotions to get the message across without the keepers of the 1958 Production Code going berserk. Big Daddy Pollitt (Ives in his best role) is dying of cancer but no one's told him. It's his 65th birthday and Big Mama (Anderson), his oldest son, Gooper (Carson), and Gooper's wife, Mae (Sherwood), are there to celebrate what will be the old man's last birthday. Also house-guesting are youngest son, Brick (Paul Newman) and his wife Maggie (Taylor). Newman keeps his passionate wife away from him as he suspects she may have been unfaithful with Newman's best friend, Skip, who is since deceased by his own hand. Despite Newman's rebuffing of Taylor, she does love him and is eagerly attempting to keep Big Daddy and Big Mama from giving a huge $10 million fortune to Carson and Sherwood, both wonderfully obnoxious in their roles. Newman and Taylor have no children and that's one thing Big Daddy wants. He sees right through Carson and Sherwood (she's pregnant again) and their horde of "no-neck monsters" but is wistful that his favorite son hasn't sired a child. Taylor tells the family that she is pregnant but the others know better as they have heard her nightly pleading to be sexually taken by her unresponsive husband. The walls of the house are thin enough to hear desperation. Newman realizes that Taylor does love him after a purging conversation with Big Daddy. He then decides to get her pregnant as he simultaneously lets go of the long obsession about his dead pal, Skip. Six Oscar nominations were awarded for CAT ON A HOT TIN ROOF and no awards were given. Ives, however, did win a supporting Oscar for his work in THE BIG COUNTRY that year. Newman is superb as Brick, although some reviewers felt he was a trifle too strong to play the role. The consensus, however, was that he brought depth to the part that Ben Gazzara had missed on the stage. Taylor was compared with Barbara Bel Geddes's stage version and came up short, although Taylor's passion was always seething under her cool skin and it was most believable. What was truly astounding was that Taylor's husband, Mike Todd, was killed in the crash of his private plane, "The Lucky Liz," while they were shooting this film. She claims that working on the picture was a godsend as she was only able to keep from crying when she was playing Maggie. The rest of the time she was a robot. Critics loved and hated *this* movie but none of them will ever forget what a breakthrough it was.

p, Lawrence Weingarten; d, Richard Brooks; w, Brooks and James Poe (based on the play by Tennessee Williams); ph, William Daniels (Metrocolor); ed, Ferris Webster; art d, William A. Horning, Urie McCleary; set d, Henry Grace, Robert Priestley; cos, Helen Rose; spec eff, Lee LeBlanc; makeup, William Tuttle.

Drama Cas. (PR:C MPAA:NR)

CAT PEOPLE*** (1942) RKO 73m bw

Simone Simon *(Irene Dubrovna)*, Kent Smith *(Oliver Reed)*, Tom Conway *(The Psychiatrist)*, Jane Randolph *(Alice Moore)*, Jack Holt *(Commodore)*, Alan Napier *(Carver)*, Elizabeth Dunne *(Miss Plunkett)*, Elizabeth Russell *(The Cat Woman)*.

Smith is fascinated by New York fashion artist Simon's strange personality and decides to make her his bride. Through a series of weird, keenly exciting surprises, the script shows good style complemented by Tourneur's first full-length film directing effort. Story is based on an old Serbian legend of women from certain tribes who change into panthers or other wild cats when in a jealous rage, killing their rivals, then reverting back to human form. One of the most spellbinding scenes in this film (or any other) depicts Simon stalking her rival Randolph around a swimming pool in the deep night. Viewers were lured by the film's advertising which blared: "Kiss me and I'll claw you to death!" The mood is murky and subtle in what would become the Val Lewton tradition and the film was a great success as a strong B film with unexpectedly large grosses (almost $200,000 its first time out). Lewton economized by using existing RKO sets; the spooky-looking apartment house used in CAT PEOPLE is the gigantic set built for Orson Welles' THE MAGNIFICENT AMBERSONS only a few months earlier in 1942. A loose remake was THE CURSE OF THE CAT PEOPLE.

p, Val Lewton; d, Jacques Tourneur; w, Dewitt Bodeen; ph, Nicholas Musurca; m, Roy Webb; ed, Mark Robson.

Horror Cas. (PR:C MPAA:NR)

CAT PEOPLE½** (1982) 118m UNIV/RKO c

Nastassia Kinski *(Irena Gallier)*, Malcolm McDowell *(Paul Gallier)*, John Heard *(Oliver Yates)*, Annette O'Toole *(Alice Perrin)*, Ruby Dee *(Female)*, Ed Begley, Jr. *(Joe Creigh)*, Scott Paulin *(Bill Searle)*, Frankie Faison *(Detective Brandt)*, Ron Diamond *(Detective Diamond)*, Lynn Lowry *(Ruthie)*, John Larroquette *(Bronte Judson)*, Tessa Richarde *(Billie)*, Patricia Perkins *(Taxi Driver)*, Berry Berenson *(Sandra)*, Fausto Barajas *(Otis)*, John H. Fields *(Massage Parlor Manager)*, Emery Hollier *(Yeatman Brewer)*, Stephen Marshall *(Moonie)*, Robert Pavlovitch *(Ted)*, Julie Denney *(Carol)*, Arione de Winter *(Indian Village Mother)*, Francine Segal *(Churchwoman)*, Don Hood *(Agent)*, David Showacre *(Man in Bar)*, Neva Gage *(Cat-like Woman)*, Marisa Folse, Danelle Hand *(Indian Girls)*, John C. Isbell *(Police Officer)*.

Maybe it's the premise that is the major fault with this overly stylish and gruesome picture—sexual relations bring out the animal in people. Literally, that's the gist of this silly plot. Kinski is a New Orleans virgin who is visited by brother McDowell. He informs her that when she has sex she will subsequently kill her mate, unless he is a relative. But not to worry, love conquers evil and zookeeper Heard (in an underdeveloped role) comes to the rescue, sort of. Director Schrader's Ozu-Bressonian transcendentalism is tossed under chic-bloodiness in his debut at the helm. A jumbled reworking of the 1942 Val Lewton-Jacques Tourneur script by Alan Ormsby (of CHILDREN SHOULDN'T PLAY WITH DEAD THINGS fame) doesn't help Schrader's cause. John Bailey's camera work is at times awesome (most notably in the desert scenes), and treats Kinski's endearing face with all due respect, which, if anything, makes for a terrific poster. Music is effective with David Bowie's title single standing out against Moroder's backdrop of synthetic meanderings.

p, Charles Fries; d, Paul Schrader; w, Alan Ormsby (based on the story by DeWitt Bodeen); ph, John Bailey (Technicolor); m, Giorgio Moroder, title theme by David Bowie; ed, Jacqueline Cambas; art d, Edward Richardson; set d, Bruce Weintraub; cos, Danile Paredes; spec eff, Albert Whitlock; m/l, David Bowie; spec makeup eff, Tom Burman.

Horror/Fantasy   **Cas.**   **(PR:O   MPAA:R)**

CAT WOMEN OF THE MOON*   (1953) 64m Astor Productions bw
(AKA: ROCKET TO THE MOON)

Sonny Tufts (Grainger), Victor Jory (Kip), Marie Windsor (Helen), Bill Phipps (Doug), Doug Fowley (Walter), Carol Brewster (Alpha), Suzanne Alexander (Zeta), Susan Morrow (Lambda), Hollywood Cover Girls: Judy Walsh, Betty Arlen, Ellye Marshall, Roxann Delman.

This one is so bad it's almost good. Tufts as leader of a crew from an American airbase that lands on the moon which is inhabited by a race of telepathic cat women in black tights. The women scheme to hitch a ride to earth, while the men fight giant horned spiders. The cat-women's telepathy gets all crossed when their bickering gets too intense. Shot in 3D, the art direction just begs to be called cheesy. The set of the moon is left over from an old Marco Polo film, and the cat-women control center is an old submarine, complete with periscope. Remade in 1958 as the equally bad MISSILE TO THE MOON.

p, Al Zimbalist, Jack Rabin; d, Arthur Hilton; w, Roy Hamilton (based on an original story by Zimbalist and Rabin); ph, William F. Whitley; m, Elmer Bernstein; ed, John Bushelman.

Science Fiction   **Cas.**   **(PR:A   MPAA:NR)**

CATACOMBS   (SEE: WOMAN WHO WOULDN'T DIE, THE, 1964)

CATALINA CAPER, THE*   (1967) 84m Crown Int. c

Tommy Kirk (Don), Del Moore (Arthur Duval), Peter Duryea (Tad), Robert Donner (Fingers), Ulla Stromstedt (Katrina), Jim Bagg (Larry), Mike Blodgett (Bob Draper), Venita Wolf (Tina), Peter Mamakos (Borman), Sue Casey (Anne Duval), Brian Cutler (Charlie Moss), Lyle Waggoner (Angelo), Lee Deane (Lakopolous), Bonnie Lomann (Redhead), Britt Nilsson (Brunette), Donna Russell (Blonde), Carol Connors, Little Richard, Timothy Carey, The Cascades, Adrian Teen Models.

A couple of wave-catching lads get tired of hanging-ten and turn their attention to being private eyes. While trying to retrieve a rare Chinese scroll from a gang of creepy art thieves, they see lots of sand, teeny-boppers, and beach party rock 'n' roll. Little Richard provides the only highlight with a rave-up rendition of "Scuba Party," Carol Connors sings "Book of Love," and the Cascades croon "There's a New World Opening For Me." Mary Wells sings the title cut over credits.

p, Bond Blackman, Jack Bartlett; d, Lee Sholem; w, Clyde Ware (based on a story by Sam Pierce); ph, Ted Mikels (Eastmancolor); m, Jerry Long; ed, Herman Freedman; ch, Michael Blodgett.

Musical/Mystery   **(PR:A   MPAA:NR)**

CATAMOUNT KILLING, THE**   (1975, Ger.) 93m Hallmark c

Horst Bucholz (Mark), Ann Wedgeworth (Kit), Chip Taylor (Ken), Louise Clark (Iris), Patricia Joyce (Alice), Polly Holliday (Miss Pearson), Stuart Germain (Hardy), Rod Browning (Easton), Peter Brandon (Marthy), Lotti Krekel (Helga), Alexander Bardini (Attendant), Ernest Martin (Rudy), Leon Carter (Trooper).

Two people from a small town try to pull off a bank job and suffer a crisis of conscience. Director Zanussi, known for CAMOUFLAGE and THE STRUCTURE OF CRYSTALS, left his native Poland to direct this film in Vermont for German producers. Interesting rather than exciting.

p, Manfred Durniok; d, Krzysztof Zanussi; w, Julian and Sheila More (based on the story "I'd Rather Stay Poor" by James Hadley Chase); ph, Witold Sobocinski; ed, Ilona Wasgint; prod d, Ruffin Barron Bennett.

Crime   **(PR:C   MPAA:NR)**

CATCH AS CATCH CAN**   (1937, Brit.) 71m Atlantic Episode bw
(AKA: ATLANTIC EPISODE)

James Mason (Robert Leyland), Viki Dobson (Barbara Standish), Eddie Pola (Tony Canzari), Finlay Currie (Al Parsons), John Warwick (Eddie Fallon), Margaret Rutherford (Maggie Carberry), Paul Blake (Cornwallis), Jimmy Mageean (Ben), Paul Sheridan (Fournival), Zoe Wynn (Mrs. Kendal).

Dobson decides to improve her economic situation by smuggling jewels from France to America aboard a luxury ocean liner. She is caught by U.S. customs agent Mason, who, instead of arresting her, talks her into going back to France and returning the jewels. Before she has a chance, three different sets of crooks try to grab the jewels, including a Chicago gangster, Pola, who is murdered. Eventually, after a lengthy gun battle onboard, things are sorted out and justice is served.

p, John Findlay; d, Roy Kellino; w, Richard Llewellyn (from an original story by Alexander George); ph, Stanley Grant.

Crime   **(PR:A   MPAA:NR)**

CATCH AS CATCH CAN**   (1968, Ital.) 95m Embassy/Fair Film c
(LO SCATENATO)

Vittorio Gassman (Bob Chiaramonte), Martha Hyer (Luisa Chiaramonte), Gila Golan

(Emma), Karin Skorreso (Girl Model), Massimo Serato (Agent), Carmelo Bene (Priest), Steffen Zacharias (Police Inspector), Jacques Herlin (Zoology Professor), Claudio Gora (Cabinet Minister), Luigi Proietti, Ivan Scratuglia.

Interesting failure has little plot, just Gassman as a male model constantly harassed by animals of all sorts. Largely an excuse to satirize advertising, politics, and male chauvinism, this film doesn't quite make it despite everyone's best efforts.

p, Mario Cecchi Gori; d, Franco Indovina; w, Indovina, Tonina Guerra, Luigi Malerba; ph, Aldo Toni (Technicolor); m, Luis Bacalov; ed, Marcello Malvestiti.

Comedy   **(PR:C   MPAA:NR)**

CATCH ME A SPY**½   (1971, Brit./Fr.) 94m RANK c

Kirk Douglas (Andrej), Marlene Jobert (Fabienne), Trevor Howard (Sir Trevor), Tom Courtenay (Baxter), Patrick Mower (John), Bernadette Lafont (Simone), Bernard Blier (Webb), Sacha Pitoeff (Stefan), Richard Pearson (Haldane), Garfield Morgan (Jealous Husband), Angharad Rees (Victoria), Isabel Dean (Celia), Robin Parkinson (British Officer), Jonathan Cecil (British Attache), Robert Raglan (Ambassador), Jean Gilpin (Ground Stewardess), Bridget Turner (Woman in Plane), Trevor Peacock (Man in Plane), Clive Gazes (Rumanian in Plane), Ashley Knight (1st Schoolboy), Philip Da Costa (2nd Schoolboy), Robert Gillespie (Man in Elevator), Sheila Steafel (Woman in Elevator), Bunny May (Elevator Attendant), Fiona Moore, Bernice Stegers (Russian Girls), Dinny Powell (1st Heavy), Del Baker (2nd Heavy).

Frenchwoman Jobert is living in London and marries Mower, who she doesn't know is a Soviet agent. They honeymoon in Bucharest and he is arrested by the secret police, but all of that is just a way of getting him into official territory so they can debrief him in comfort. Later that day, a waiter slips into the couple's room and secretes something in her suitcase. Jobert is told that Mower has been taken to Russia so she returns to London to seek advice from her uncle, Howard. The Russians claim that Mower is a spy and they are willing to exchange him for a Russian the British hold (what a ploy!). The deal falls through when the Soviet spy dies accidentally. Jobert now attempts to find some other spy she can barter for her bridegroom. She meets Douglas (he was the waiter in Bucharest) and when she learns he's a spy, she plans to use him in trade for Mower. One night at her flat, they are attacked by they-don't-know-who and taken in a car. When they awake, they leap from the moving automobile and find themselves in Scotland. At a deserted inn, Douglas confesses that he is a British agent who was smuggling Russian documents out of Rumania. His most important piece of data is on microfilm which he puts into her luggage. Jobert is drawn to Douglas (must be his dimples) and is stunned when he is arrested and is to be used as the bartered spy to get her husband back. Jobert can't find the suitcase, which is what provides the proof about Douglas's identity. The prisoner exchange is to be made in mid-river. Two launches approach each other. Mower is on one, Douglas and Jobert on the other. Now Kirk recognizes the suitcase in Mower's hand and asks him to open it. It's filled with cash. Douglas grabs it and races away. Mower runs back to the Soviet side, Jobert tails Douglas until she catches him, and we can only assume they live happily ever after. There's no sex, very little violence, and hardly any believability. It's almost a spoof of THE SPY WHO CAME IN FROM THE COLD but falls short as the humor takes second place to the chicanery. Douglas and Jobert have a good time in their roles, but Courtenay, as the counterespionage officer, is totally wasted.

p, Steven Pallos, Pierre Braunberger; d, Dick Clement; w, Clement, Ian La Frenais (based on the novel by George Marton, Tibor Meray); ph, Christopher Challis (Panavision, Technicolor); m, Claude Bolling; ed, John Bloom; art d, Carmen Dillon.

Spy Drama   **(PR:A-C   MPAA:NR)**

CATCH MY SOUL**½   (1974) 97m Cinerama/Metromedia Producers Corp. c
(AKA: TO CATCH A SPY, SANTA FE SATAN)

Richie Havens (Othello), Lance Le Gault (Iago), Season Hubley (Desdemona), Tony Joe White (Cassio), Susan Tyrrell (Emilia), Bonnie Bramlett, Delaney Bramlett, Raleigh Gardenshire, Wayne Eagle Waterhouse, Family Lotus.

Odd rock adaptation of "Othello" somehow works. Richie Havens is Othello, an itinerant preacher who wanders into Le Gault's desert commune. He marries Hubley and is slowly driven to murder by the jealous Le Gault. Could easily have degenerated into bad camp, but director McGoohan's direction keeps it on line with good performances all around. Songs: "Othello," "Working On A Building" (Tony Joe White), "Wash Us Clean," "Eat the Bread, Drink the Wine," "Book of Prophecy," "Catch My Soul" (White, Jack Good), "That's What God Said," "Chug A Lug," "I Found Jesus" (Delaney Bramlett), "Open Your Eyes" (Leon Lumkins), "Lust of the Blood," "Put Out the Light (Ray Pohlman, Good), "Tickle His Fancy" (Emil Dean Zoughby, Good), "Run Shaker Life" (traditional).

p, Richard Rosenbloom, Jack Good; d, Patrick McGoohan; w, Jack Good (adapted from the play "Othello" by William Shakespeare); ph, Conrad Hall (Cinerama, DeLuxe Color); m, Tony Joe White; ed, Richard Harris; md, Paul Glass, Delaney Bramlett.

Musical   **(PR:C   MPAA:PG)**

CATCH-22***   (1970) 121m PAR/FILMWAYS c

Alan Arkin (Capt. Yossarian), Martin Balsam (Col. Cathcart), Richard Benjamin (Maj. Danby), Art Garfunkel (Capt. Nately), Jack Gilford (Doc Daneeka), Bob Newhart (Maj. Major), Anthony Perkins (Chaplain Tappman), Paula Prentiss (Nurse Duckett), Martin Sheen (Lt. Dobbs), Jon Voight (Milo Minderbinder), Orson Welles (Gen. Dreedle), Seth Allen (Hungry Joe), Robert Balaban (Capt. Orr), Susanne Benton (Gen. Dreedle's WAC), Peter Bonerz (Capt. McWatt), Norman Fell (Sgt. Towser), Chuck Grodin (Aardvark), Buck Henry (Lt. Col. Korn), Austin Pendleton (Col. Moodus), Gina Rovere (Nately's Whore), Olympia Carlisi (Luciana), Marcel Dalio (Old Man), Eva Maltagliati (Old Woman), Elizabeth Wilson (Mother), Liam Dunn (Father), Richard Libertini (Brother), Jonathon Korkes (Snowden), John Brent (Cathcart's Receptionist), Collin Wilcox-Horne (Nurse Cramer), Phil Roth, Bruce Kirby, Jack Riley (Doctors), Wendy D'Olive (Aardvark's Girl), Fernanda Vitobello (Kid Sister), Felice Orlandi (Man in Black).

Bizarre, overproduced, hysterically funny, too long, angry, annoying and, in the end, an ultimately unsatisfying adaptation of Joseph Heller's exquisite antiwar novel that continues to sell, years after its publication. Heller, another graduate of America's most incredible high school, Abraham Lincoln in Coney Island, spent years writing his novel about an Armenian (presumably) captain on the tiny Mediterranean island of Pianosa. Arkin almost recreates the panicky Yossarian as he darts side to side, trying to convince his superiors that he's unfit to fly. The film roams all over the place and there is not one story that can be synopsized, there are several. Balsam is the cliche topkick with Henry as his fawning aide. Perkins is the totally ineffective chaplain and Newhart fumbles in his typical timid role as the squadron commander. Welles is larger than life (as always) as Gen. Dreedle who has one solution for people he thinks are stupid or have disobeyed him. He says: "Take him out and shoot him!" The cameos go on; Benjamin as a sophisticated officer, Gilford as the obsequious medic, Benton as the big-breasted comedy relief, Prentiss as a sex-pot nurse. Voight is featured in what is close to a villain as the picture gets. The real villain here was attempting to make a movie as large as THE LONGEST DAY with a cast of characters that went on forever. The fault must be laid at the feet of director Nichols who was directing his third feature after two enormous successes (THE GRADUATE and WHO'S AFRAID OF VIRGINIA WOOLF?). CATCH-22 is filled with all sorts of in-jokes and touches that must have gone right over the heads of the public. The production credits far outshadow the conceptual credits. Many of Hollywood's best worked on CATCH-22 and it shows in every frame. It wasn't quite a comedy and not quite a real drama. It was right in the middle and consequently not able to define its objectives, other than a general diatribe against war. We all know that war is hell and that it's insane and those who wish it are insane. This picture added nothing to that age-old truth.

p, Martin Ransohoff, John Calley; d, Mike Nichols; w, Buck Henry (based on the novel by Joseph Heller); ph, David Watkin (Panavision, Technicolor); ed, Sam O'Steen; prod d, Richard Sylbert; art d, Harold Michelson; set d, Ray Moyer; cos, Ernest Adler; spec eff, Lee Vasque; helicopter ph, Nelson Tyler; md, Fritz Reiner ("Thus Spake Zarathustra" by Richard Strauss); tech adv, Alexander Gerry; flying seq, Tallmantz Aviation; flying supv., Frank Tallman.

War Drama Cas. (PR:O MPAA:R)

CATCH US IF YOU CAN (SEE: HAVING A WILD WEEKEND, 1965, Brit.)

CATERED AFFAIR, THE**** (1956) 92m MGM bw
(GB: WEDDING BREAKFAST)

Bette Davis *(Mrs. Tom Hurley)*, Ernest Borgnine *(Tom Hurley)*, Debbie Reynolds *(Jane Hurley)*, Barry Fitzgerald *(Uncle Jack Conlon)*, Rod Taylor *(Ralph Halloran)*, Robert Simon *(Mr. Halloran)*, Madge Kennedy *(Mrs. Halloran)*, Dorothy Stickney *(Mrs. Rafferty)*, Carol Veazie *(Mrs. Casey)*, Joan Camden *(Alice)*, Ray Stricklyn *(Eddie Hurley)*, Jay Adler *(Sam Leiter)*, Dan Tobin *(Caterer)*, Paul Denton *(Bill)*, Augusta Merighi *(Mrs. Musso)*, Mae Clarke *(Saleswoman)*, Jimmie Fox *(Tailor)*, Don Devlin, Sammy Shack *(Cabbies)*

The brilliant Chayefsky teleplay almost survives miscasting in this MGM version adapted by Gore Vidal. No matter how hard one tries, it is almost impossible to believe Italian Borgnine as an Irish cab driver or patrician Davis as a slatternly, dumpy Bronx housewife. Borgnine comes home after a night of driving someone else's cab and tells Davis that he is about to realize his dream of owning his own taxi. He works all night and has breakfast before going to sleep for the day. Son Stricklyn can barely conceal his yawns at this news but daughter Reynolds is thrilled, and then announces her own good news; she and fiance Rod Taylor have moved up their wedding date to two weeks so they can combine Taylor's business trip with their honeymoon. All expenses will be paid by Rod's company and, to save further cash, Taylor and Reynolds plan to have a very simple wedding attended only by family members. Fitzgerald, who has been boarding at the Hurleys for twelve years, walks out angrily when he hears he won't be included. Neighbor Merighi tells Davis that it might seem to be a bit too quick to most people. Sudden marriages in that neighborhood can only mean *one* thing. Taylor's wealthy parents, Kennedy and Simon, visit the Bronx apartment and casually speak of the fabulous wedding they provided for their daughters. Davis finally succumbs as she recalls her own tacky wedding. Over Reynolds' and Borgnine's objections, Davis contracts with a local hotel to provide everything for the wedding. The price will exceed two thousand dollars. (Don't laugh! That was a lot of money in 1956.) Borgnine has been planning to use that money to buy his new taxi but Davis prevails as she says that they have never done anything for their daughter and this will be the grandest gift they could bestow. The guest list grows quickly and the cost doubles. Reynolds' best friend, Camden, tells Debbie that she won't be able to attend as she can't afford the price of a gown and her husband can't afford the price of a rented tuxedo. Fitzgerald is livid when he learns that he can't invite his barfly pals and he threatens to move. Now the guest list is so large that a new room must be secured at the hotel but it won't be available for two months. Taylor offers to elope with Reynolds. She refuses, knowing that it would break her mom's heart. After an argument, she agrees and tells her mother to cancel the affair. Now Davis angrily jumps on Borgnine for his inability to bring them a better life. Borgnine tearfully pleads that he did the best he could and that after Reynolds is married and Stricklyn goes into the service, they will still have each other to contend with. They began as a pair and will finish that way. She understands. Reynolds and Taylor return to their prior plans of a small ceremony and reception for the family. On that day, Borgnine arrives at the apartment in his new cab and proudly drives his wife off to the service. Davis's eyes well up with tears; Borgnine loves her and that's all that matters. This could have been one of the best pictures of the 1950s with the right people in the right roles. Brooks' direction was sharp, considering the talkiness of the script. But both Chayefsky and Vidal are known for their dialog and any picture with both their names on the credits would have to have been talky. Ah, but what talk. The nuances, the subtleties, all the undercurrents of Bronxese are here. It will live as an example of the way things were in 1956. Borgnine and Davis made another film together fourteen years later. It was about an ex-con and a widow who team up to ride a motorcycle and dress in hippy clothes. Better you shouldn't know what the title of *that* one was! Just remember these two talented people in THE CATERED AFFAIR and let it go at that.

p, Sam Zimbalist; d, Richard Brooks; w, Gore Vidal (based on the teleplay by Paddy Chayefsky); ph, John Alton; m, Andre Previn; ed, Gene Ruggiero, Frank Santillo; art d, Cedric Gibbons, Paul Groesse.

Drama (PR:A MPAA:NR)

CATHERINE & CO.** (1976, Fr.) 99m WB c

Jane Birkin *(Catherine)*, Patrick Dewaere *(Francois)*, Jean-Claude Brialy *(Guillaume)*, Vittorio Caprioli *(Moretti)*, Jean-Pierre Aumont *(Marquis de Puisargue)*, Mehdi *(Thomas)*, Henri Garcin *(Grandin)*, Nathalie Courval *(Mauve)*, Jacques Marin, Jacques Rosny, Jean Barney, Marion Thebaud, Andre Thorent, Fabienne Arel, Lydia Dalbert, Alexandra Gorski, Madeleine Ganne, Bernard Musson, Dora Doll, Jose Lucioni, Jean Valmence, Carlo Nell, Jean-Pierre Moreux, Gerard Denizot, Catherine Ohotnikoff, Pipo Merisi, Angelina Alias, Pierre Hentz, Gerard Lemaire, Jean-Gabriel Molle.

Birkin is an English girl who finds herself unemployed and hungry in Paris. She drifts into a kind of prostitution that consists of going to bed with wealthy businessmen, but getting them to talk about their business dealings at such length that lust is forgotten. When this operation collapses she sets herself up as a corporation with four stockholders. Mediocre French sex farce has some nice moments, but not many.

p, Leo L. Fuchs; d, Michel Boisrond; w, Fuchs, Catherine Breillat (based on a novel by Edouard DeSegonzac); ph, Richard Suzuki (Technicolor); m, Vladimir Cosma; ed, Jacques Witta; art d, Francois de Lamothe; cos, Simone Baron.

Comedy Cas. (PR:O MPAA:R)

CATHERINE THE GREAT*** (1934, Brit.) 94m LMP/UA bw
(GB: THE RISE OF CATHERINE THE GREAT)

Elisabeth Bergner *(Catherine II)*, Douglas Fairbanks, Jr. *(Grand Duke Peter)*, Flora Robson *(Empress Elizabeth)*, Gerald du Maurier *(Lecocq)*, Irene Vanbrugh *(Princess Anhalt-Zerbst)*, Griffith Jones *(Gregory Orlov)*, Joan Gardner *(Katuschenka)*, Dorothy Hale *(Countess Elizabeth)*, Gibb McLaughlin *(Bestujhev)*, Clifford Heatherley *(Ogarev)*, Lawrence Hanray *(Goudovitch)*, Allan Jeayes *(Col. Karnilov)*, Diana Napier *(Countess Elizabeth)*

The film is all Bergner's in her first English-speaking production. Unlike Marlene Dietrich in THE SCARLET EMPRESS, Bergner plays her auspicious role like a fluttering bird inside a giant Russian cage. She is a frightened girl when brought to the royal court of St. Petersburg as the ignored fiancée of Grand Duke Peter (Fairbanks). She meets her intended only by accident as he runs from his tutors through the palace, a mischievous rake who toys with her before whimsically agreeing to make her his wife. Bergner is suddenly entrapped in one court intrigue after another while Robson, as the shrewd, ugly, and lustful dowager Empress Elizabeth, manipulates her, shaping her destiny. At her death, Robson confides to Bergner that her nephew is mad and she fears for his life and that of Russia. When the old woman dies, Fairbanks becomes even more eccentric, power-crazy, and vindictive toward his czarina. In one memorable scene, at a mad-hatter's banquet, Fairbanks insults his wife royally by having his mistress, Napier, sit in his wife's chair while Bergner becomes the butt of his lunatic jokes. Fairbanks has also insulted the Cossack guards and the army, the leaders of which plot against him, not the least of whom is Jones, playing the dark and mysterious Orlov, the Czarina's lover. He organizes the military overthrow of Peter the Mad. Against his wife's wishes Fairbanks is executed (ostensibly by Orlov, his killer in real life) on the way to a lunatic asylum. Bergner is hailed as the new empress, Catherine the Great and goes gloriously to her throne and legend. This is a grand and extravagant film in the Korda tradition, with thousands of extras on horseback and splendrous sets. (The film was the most expensive ever made in England up to that time, costing about $400,000, the equivalent of a $1 million Hollywood production.) Paul Czinner, who was Bergner's husband, directed the film with complete partiality to its star, showing so much favoritism to his wife that Korda became angry and stepped onto the set to direct many scenes himself, particularly those with Robson This was a serious error in that the producer caused endless friction with his director and allowed Robson to overact. To compensate for her powerful voice, he moved the microphones too far away so that her voice sounds thin and often shrill. Beyond the lush pageantry of this epic and Korda's artistic meddling (which sometimes brought forth better scenes), the film stands as a Bergner tour-de-force and should be seen only to note this exceptional actress' ability, a sensitive saucer-eyed lady with a fascinating voice not much above a whisper. A tiny, sparrow-like woman, Bergner's gamine personality was popular only for a short time. Her thick German accent worked against English-speaking audiences who gave her a short career. Fairbanks is also excellent as the twisted Peter in this manufactured biography. The writers played up Robson's over-sexed role in historical keeping with the bawdy Elizabeth but attempted to maintain Bergner as pure by positing Catherine's numerous affairs (she was a notorious royal slattern) as mere fabrications created by Bergner to make her husband more attentive. American audiences were enticed to see this production on the strength of Korda's recent success, THE PRIVATE LIFE OF HENRY VIII, 1933, but ultimately preferred von Sternberg's more colorful and even more bizarre version of Catherine's life and times as extravagantly portrayed by Dietrich in THE SCARLET EMPRESS, which went head-to-head with the Korda production in 1934.

p, Alexander Korda; d, Paul Czinner; w, Marjorie Deans, Arthur Wimperis (based on the play "The Czarina" by Lajos Biro and Melchior Lengyel); ph, George Perinal; ed, Harold Younger, Stephen Harrison; prod d, Vincent Korda; md, Muir Mathieson; cos, John Armstrong.

Biography/Historical Drama Cas. (PR:C MPAA:NR)

CATHY'S CHILD½** (1979, Aus.) 89m Roadshow c

Michelle Fawdon *(Cathy Baikis)*, Alan Cassell *(Dick Wordley)*, Bryan Brown *(Nicko)*, Harry Michael *(Peter)*, Anna Hruby *(Donna)*, Bob Hughes *(Mike)*, Sophia Haskas

(Angelina), Sarah McKenzie (Young Nun), Judy Stevenson (Lil), Bobbie Ward (Barmaid), Gerry Gallagher (Smedley), Annibale Migliucci (Perilli), Arthur Dignam (Minister), Willie Fennell (Athens Consul).

A surprisingly engrossing low-budget soap about Cathy, a Greek mother living in Sydney, Australia. After her three-year-old is abducted and returned to Greece by her father, Cathy turns to the media for assistance. A tough newspaper editor with a heart devotes his time to her dilemma, printing her story in his daily. An issue film based on a true story which fortunately avoids preachiness.

p, Pom Oliver, Errol Sullivan; d, Donald Crombie; w, Ken Quinnell (based on a book by Dick Wordley); ph, Gary Hansen; ed, Tim Wellburn.

Drama (PR:C MPAA:NR)

CATHY'S CURSE* (1977, Can.) 88m 21st Century c
(AKA: CAUCHEMARES)

Alan Scarfe, Beverley Murray, Randi Allen.

Dull Canadian EXORCIST-inspired horror film starring Allen as a little girl who is possessed by the spirit of her dead aunt who was killed in a car crash when she was the same age as Allen. The aunt's spirit enters the home through Allen's rag doll, which leads to bloody mutilations, cheesy makeup, and inept special effects.

p, N. Mathieu, Nicole Boisvert, Eddy Matalon; d, Matalon; w, Myra Clement, Matalon, A. Sens-Cazenave; (Eastmancolor).

Horror **Cas.** (PR:O MPAA:R)

CATLOW** (1971, Span.) 101m MGM c

Yul Brynner (Catlow), Richard Crenna (Cowan), Leonard Nimoy (Miller), Daliah Lavi (Rosita), Jo Ann Pflug (Christina), Jeff Corey (Merridew), Michael Delano (Rio), Julian Mateos (Recalde), David Ladd (Caxton), Bessie Love (Mrs. Frost).

Tame, innocuous western which has Brynner being hunted by friend and lawman Crenna and killer Nimoy, while trying to heist $2 million of the Fed's money. Standing out are the better-than-average action sequences, credited to Bob Simmons, Lloyd's assistant. Based on the Louis L'Amour novel, it doesn't quite capture the charm of his prose.

p, Euan Lloyd; d, Sam Wanamaker; w, Scot Finch, J. J. Griffith (based on the Louis L'Amour novel); ph, Ted Scaife (Metrocolor); m, Roy Budd; ed, John Glen, Alan Killick; art d, Herbert Smith.

Western (PR:C MPAA:GP)

THE CATMAN OF PARIS**½ (1946) 65m REP bw

Carl Esmond (Charles Regnier), Lenore Aubert (Marie Audet), Adele Mara (Marguerite Duval), Douglass Dumbrille (Henry Borchard), Gerald Mohr (Inspector Severen), Fritz Feld (Prefect of Police), Frances Pierlot (Paul Audet), George Renavent (Guillard), Francis McDonald (Devereaux), Maurice Cass (Paul de Roche), Alphonse Martell (Maurice Cacaignac), Paul Marion (Jules), John Dehner (Georges), Anthony Caruso (Raoul), Carl Neubert (Phillippe), Elaine Lange (Blanche de Clermont), Tanis Chandler (Yvette), George Davis (Concierge).

Amnesia victim Esmond is suspected of murder when crime experts Mohr and Feld bypass clues leading to the real villain. Film is a whodunit with mystical overtones supported by eye-popping makeup and swift direction, all focusing on the homicidal urges of Dumbrille. As a sophisticated devil, Dumbrille is a delight and Feld is a convincing mystic.

p, Marek M. Libkov; d, Lesley Selander; w, Sherman L. Lowe; ph, Reggie Lanning; ed, Harry Keller.

Mystery (PR:A MPAA:NR)

CAT'S PAW, THE*** (1934) 101m Harold Lloyd Corp./FOX bw

Harold Lloyd (Ezekiel Cobb), Una Merkel (Petunia Pratt), George Barbier (Jake Mayo), Nat Pendleton (Strozzi), Grace Bradley (Dolores Dace), Alan Dinehart (Mayor Morgan), Grant Mitchell ("Silk Hat" McGee), Fred Warren (Tien Wang), Warren Hymer (Spike Slattery), J. Farrell MacDonald (Shigley), James Donlan (Red the Reporter), Edwin Maxwell (District Attorney Neal), Frank Sheridan (Police Commissioner Moriarty), David Jack Holt (Ezekiel as a Boy) Vince Barnett (Wilks, a Gangster), Matt McHugh (Taxi Driver), Samuel S. Hinds (Rev. Julian Cobb), Alec B. Francis (Rev. Thatcher), James Burke (Gargan), Nell Craig (Mrs. Cobb), Gertrude W. Hoffmann (Mrs. Noon), Charles Sellon (Rev. Junius P. Withers), John Ince (Burke, a Politician), DeWitt C. Jennings (Pete, Policeman), Richard Cramer (Police Sergeant), Ernie Alexander (1st Man on Street), Tom Dugan (2nd Man on Street), John Wray (3rd Man on Street), Noel Madison, Fuzzy Knight, Herman Bing, Michael Visaroff, Harry Tenbrook, Kit Guard, George Magrill, Paul Panzer, James Mason (Gangsters), Dewey Robinson, Chief Big Tree (Chinese Guards), Arthur Hoyt, Charles Williams, Billy Bletcher (Reporters), Eddie Fetherstone, Eddie Boland (Photographers), Sidney Bracy, Fred Walton, George Davis, Rosa Gore, William Irving, Vangie Bielby (Boarders), Tom London (Murph, Cop), Edward Hearn, Frances Morris (Radio Listeners), Brooks Benedict (Club Patron).

Lloyd returns to his home town after twenty years in the hinterlands of China with his missionary father. He is discovered by corrupt politicians and set up as a mayoral candidate to run against their man. Lloyd unexpectedly wins in a landslide and sets about clearing up the town while expressing himself in cryptic Chinese proverbs. The villains attempt a frameup but Lloyd uses his Oriental wisdom to force confessions out of them before running the lot out of town. Lloyd had been off the screen for two years before this film and it marks a departure from his usual madcap antics (it was only the second film he made with an actual script). The laughs don't come rapid fire as in his other films, but they are more adult and ultimately more satisfying.

p, Harold Lloyd; d&w, Sam Taylor (based on a story by Clarence Buddington Kelland); ph, Walter Lundin; ed, Bernard Burton; md, Alfred Newman; art d, Harry Oliver; ch, Larry Ceballos.

Comedy (PR:A MPAA:NR)

CATSKILL HONEYMOON zero

(1950) 95m Martin Cohen Production (Yiddish-American) bw

Michal Michalesko, Jan Bart, Bas Sheva, Bobby Colt, Henrietta Jacobson, Julius Adler, Mary LaRoche, David and Dorothy Paige, Irving Grossman, Diana Goldberg, Feder Sisters, Gita Stein, Abe Lax, Al Murray, Max and Rose Bozhky, Cookie Bowers, Mike Hammer.

A filmed variety show at Ma Holder Young's Gap Hotel in Parksville, N.Y. Songs and

---

variety acts almost exclusively fill this home movie. The only dramatic story is a couple celebrating their 50th wedding anniversary. Songs: "Scattered Toys," "My Mistake."

p, Martin Cohen; d. Joe Berne; w, Joel Jacobson; ph, Charles Downs; m, Hy Jacobson; m/l Jacobson, Nick and Charles Kenny.

Musical (PR:A MPAA:NR)

CATTLE ANNIE AND LITTLE BRITCHES**½ (1981) 97m UNIV c

Burt Lancaster (Bill Doolin), John Savage (Bittercreek Newcomb), Rod Steiger (Tilghman), Diane Lane (Jenny), Amanda Plummer (Annie), Scott Glenn (Bill Dalton), Redmond Gleason (Red Buck), William Russ (Little Dick Raidler), Ken Call (George Weightman), Buck Taylor (Dynamite Dick), John Quade (Morgan), Perry Lang (Elrod), Steven Ford (Deputy Marshal), Mike Maroff (Deputy), John Hock (Bank Teller), Robert Cudney, Jr. (Fireman), Michael Conrad (Engineer), Chad Hastings (Conductor), Yvette Sweetman (Mrs. Sweetman), Tom Delaney (Ned's Father), Matthew Taylor (Ned), John Sterlini (Corey), Roger Cudney (Capps), Jerry Gatlin (Cop), Russ Hoverson (Guard).

Slow-paced western that describes the last days of the Doolin gang of Oklahoma, joined by two adventure-seeking teenage girls, Plummer and Lane. They become adoptive little sisters who first follow the outlaws, then become members of the gang, aiding its members in escape and robbery. Lancaster is, as always, at his best but has little gritty material to work with and Steiger, his lawman pursuer, plays his role like a child on an Easter Egg hunt, as delighted in capturing Lancaster as an autograph hunter captures the signature of a star. The facts about the real Doolin gang are completely destroyed in the best Hollywood tradition with no real research performed. Oddly, the character of George "Red Buck" Weightman is split into two characters for this film, neither of them capturing the true nature of this most brutal of Old West outlaws. Johnson's direction is shallow and phlegmatic and the script by Eyre and Ward is forced and synthetic. Lensed near Durango, Mexico, Pizer's camerawork is scenic but uninspiring.

p, Rupert Hitzig, Alan King; d, Lamont Johnson; w, David Eyre, Robert Ward (based on a story by Ward from his novel); ph, Larry Pizer (CFI Color); m, Sanh Berti, Tom Slocum; ed, Robbe Roberts, William Haugse; prod d, Stan Jolley; set d, Dick Purdy; cos, Rita Riggs.

Western (PR:C MPAA:PG)

CATTLE DRIVE*** (1951) 77m UNIV c

Joel McCrea (Dan Mathews), Dean Stockwell (Chester Graham, Jr.), Chill Wills (Dallas), Leon Ames (Mr. Graham), Henry Brandon (Jim Currie), Howard Petrie (Cap), Bob Steele (Careless), Griff Barnett (Conductor O'Hara).

A refreshing B-western which avoids the usual stereotypical traps. Photographed in Death Valley, this pic features Stockwell as the snobbish son of a railroad tycoon who is inadvertently left behind in the sun-blistered desert when his father's train pulls away without him. McCrea is perfectly cast as an old trail boss who looks after the lad as McCrea's cattle drive toward civilization. A rare Western lacking any female characters, except for a picture McCrea carries with him of his real-life wife, Frances Dee, who represents an ideal image waiting for him at the end of the trail. A studied exercise in friendship between a respectable man and an impressionable boy.

p, Aaron Rosenberg; d, Kurt Neumann; w, Jack Natteford, Lillie Hayward; ph, Maury Gertsman (Technicolor); ed, Danny B. Landres.

Western (PR:AA MPAA:NR)

CATTLE EMPIRE**½ (1958) 83m FOX c

Joel McCrea (John Cord), Gloria Talbott (Sandy), Don Haggerty (Ralph Hamilton), Phyllis Coates (Janice Hamilton), Bing Russell (Douglas Hamilton), Paul Brinegar (Tom Jeffrey), Hal K. Dawson (George Jeffrey), Duane Grey (Aruzza), Richard Shannon (Garth), Charles Gray (Tom Powis), Patrick O'Moore (Cogswell), William McGraw (Jim Whittaker), Jack Lomas (Sheriff Brewster), Steve Raines (Corbo), Rocky Shahan (Quince), Nesdon Booth (Barkeep), Bill Hale (Grainger), Ronald Foster (Stitch), Howard B. Culver (Preacher), Ted Smile, Edward Jauregui.

Effective oater which has McCrea cast as a trail boss recently released from prison. Hired by a familiar group of townsfolk who can't do without his services, he moves a cattle herd which will bring the town great prosperity, the catch being that these are the same folk his gang shot up years earlier. On the arduous but successful drive McCrea gains the respect of the townsfolk he hired as cowboys to help him on the trail. At times slow-moving, the story is driven along by McCrea's conviction and presence.

p, Robert Stabler; d, Charles Marquis Warren; w, Eric Norden, Endre Bohem (based on a story by Daniel B. Ullman); ph, Brydon Baker (CinemaScope, DeLuxe Color); m, Paul Sawtell, Bert Shefter; ed, Leslie Vidor.

Western (PR:A MPAA:NR)

CATTLE KING*½ (1963) 88m MGM c (GB: GUNS OF WYOMING)

Robert Taylor (Sam Brassfield), Joan Caulfield (Sharleen), Robert Loggia (Johnny Quatro), Robert Middleton (Clay Mathews), Larry Gates (President Chester A. Arthur), Malcolm Atterbury (Clevenger), William Windom (Harry Travers), Virginia Christine (Ruth Winters), Ray Teal (Ed Winters), Richard Devon (Vince Bodine), Robert Ivers (Webb Carter), Maggie Pierce (June Carter), Woodrow Parfrey (Stafford), Richard Tretter (Hobie), John Mitchum (Tex).

An ordinary western with Taylor limning the role of a well-to-do rancher who feels that good fences make good neighbors. The villains of the piece would like to keep barbed wire out of Wyoming in 1883. Caulfield is the femme interest so you can imagine the surprise when she gets drilled about two-thirds into the film. Middleton and his cohorts support something called The National Cattle Trail, which calls for grazing just about anywhere. Middleton is associated with Windom, a wimpy alcoholic who is Caulfield's brother. Taylor enlists the aid of President Chester A. Arthur (Gates in the best characterization in the movie) who agrees to support Taylor's plan. Middleton is enraged when he thinks that Windom has joined up with Taylor. The bullet meant for Windom nails Caulfield, and all concerned realize the need for a speedy conclusion to this range war. The final battle between Middleton and Taylor is swift and the picture fades out with truth and justice on the winning side. This was Taylor's last film for MGM after nearly thirty years. Not a fitting end for the man who co-starred in CAMILLE, BATAAN, A YANK AT OXFORD, and more.

p. Nat Holt; d, Tay Garnett; w, Thomas Thompson; ph, William Snyder (Eastmancolor); m, Paul Sawtell, Bert Shefter; ed, George White; art d, Walter P. Holscher.

Western **(PR:A MPAA:NR)**

CATTLE QUEEN* (1951) 72m UA bw (AKA: QUEEN OF THE WEST)
Maria Hart (Queenie Hart), Drake Smith (Foster), William Fawcett (Alkall), Robert Gardette (Duke), John Carpenter (Tucson Kid), Edward Clark (Doc Hodges), Emile Meyer (Shotgun Thompson), Jim Pierce (Bad Bill Smith), Joe Bailey (Blackie Malone), Douglas Wood (Judge Whipple), Alyn Lockwood (Rosa), I. Stanford Jolley (Scarface), Lane Chandler (Marshal), William N. Bailey (Warden), Frank Marlowe (Driver), Roger Anderson (Lefty), Verne Teters (Trig), Steve Conte (Mac), Robert H. Robinson (Armstrong).

Poorly shot and poorly acted, the only point this one gets is for the novelty of a woman lead. Hart, a whip-cracking rancher, battles a greedy outlaw who's set on taking her land. A male cowhand, Smith, comes to her aid and together they fight evil and fall under love's spell. Unfortunately, Hart's character is too stereotyped to be appreciated.

p. Jack Schwarz [Jack Seeman]; d, Robert Tansey; w, Frances Kavanaugh (based on a story by Robert Emmett); ph, Elmer Dyer; m, Darrell Calker; ed, Richard Currier.

Western **(PR:A MPAA:NR)**

CATTLE QUEEN OF MONTANA** (1954) 92m RKO c
Barbara Stanwyck (Sierra Nevada Jones), Ronald Reagan (Farrell), Gene Evans (Tom McCord), Lance Fuller (Colorados), Anthony Caruso (Nachakos), Jack Elam (Yost), Yvette Dugay (Starfire), Morris Ankrum (J. I. "Pop" Jones), Chubby Johnson (Nat), Myron Healey (Hank), Rodd Redwing (Powhani), Paul Birch (Col. Carrington), Byron Foulger (Land Office Employee), Burt Mustin (Dan), Roy Gordon (Bit), Tom Steele, Dorothy Andre, Danny Fisher, Bob Burrows, Wayne Bursam, John Cason, Bob Woodward, Betty Hanna, Riza Royce, Ralph Sanford.

Shot in Glacier National Park in Montana, this fair western has Stanwyck and her father, Ankrum, driving their huge herd up from Texas so they can find some green grass and space in the Northwest Territory. Indians raid the small party, kill the old man, and run the cattle off in all directions. Stanwyck then finds out that the Indians are working for Evans, a local villain who is planning on building his own cattle empire. Reagan arrives and we find he is an agent sent by the U.S. Army to find out who is behind all this Indian activity. Caruso is the heavy Indian who is taking money from Evans. An internecine squabble erupts inside the tribe with Caruso battling college-educated Lance Fuller. A small love affair develops between Reagan and Stanwyck and the two recover the missing steers and will run the Montana ranch as a duo. Stanwyck did all of her own stunts in this film and was so admired by the local Blackfeet Indians (hired by the hundreds as extras) that they named her with the Indian name of Princess Many Victories and made her a blood sister in the tribe. It may be apochryphal but legend has it that whenever Reagan sees Stanwyck, he always addresses her by her Indian name. Cute, if true.

p. Benedict Bogeaus; d, Allan Dwan; w, Robert Blees, Howard Estabrook (based on a story by Thomas Blackburn); ph, John Alton (Technicolor); m, Louis Forbes; ed, Carl Lodato, Jim Lekester; art d, Van Nest Polglase; set d, John Sturtevant.

Western **Cas.** **(PR:A MPAA:NR)**

CATTLE RAIDERS*½ (1938) 61m COL bw
Charles Starrett (Tom Reynolds), Donald Grayson (Slim Grayson), Iris Meredith (Nancy Grayson), Dick Curtis (Ed Munro), Allen Brook (Steve Reynolds), Edward LeSaint (John Reynolds), Eddie Cobb (Burke), George Chesebro (Brand), Ed Coxen (Doc Connors), Steve Clark (Hank), Art Mix (Keno), Clem Horton (Slash), Alan Sears (Hayes), Ed Peil, Sr. (Sheriff), and the Sons of the Pioneers.

A hackneyed story is helped along by the Sons of the Pioneers, who warble while Starrett seeks to prove his innocence on a murder charge. He clears himself when he uncovers matching bullets fired from the same gun. A fair measure of action keeps the story from sinking entirely.

p. Henry L. Decker; d, Sam Nelson; w, Joseph F. Poland, Ed Earl Repp (based on a story by Folmer Blangsted); ph, John Boyle; ed, Dick Fantl; m/l, Bob Nolan.

Western **(PA:A MPAA:NR)**

CATTLE STAMPEDE* (1943) 58m PRC bw
Buster Crabbe (Billy the Kid), Al St. John (Fuzzy Jones), Frances Gladwin (Mary), Charles King (Coulter), Ed Cassidy (Sam Dawson), Hansel Werner (Ed Dawson), Ray Bennett (Stone), Frank Ellis (Elkins), Steve Clark (Turner), Roy Brent (Slater), John Elliott (Doctor), Budd Buster (Jensen), Hank Bell, Tex Cooper, Ted Adams, George Morrell.

Fast gun play and good fistfights spice up this routine western, which finds Crabbe and St. John battling rustler King, who stampedes herds, then buys what is left at wholesale prices. St. John's comedy spices the action.

p. Sigmund Neufeld; d, Sam Newfield; w, Joe O'Donnell; ph, Robert Cline; ed, Holbrook Todd.

Western **(PR:A MPAA:NR)**

CATTLE THIEF, THE *½ (1936) 58m COL bw
Ken Maynard (Ken Martin), Geneva Mitchell (Alice), Ward Bond (Ranse), Roger Williams (Hutch), Jim Marcus (Cal), Sheldon Lewis (Dolson), Edward Cecil (Doc Brawley), Jack Kirk, Edward Hearn, Glenn Strange, Al Taylor.

Disguised as a traveling peddler by day and "the masked rider" by night, Maynard goes undercover as a cattle detective to lasso corrupt Bond. Maynard does little singing in this one, but engages in two bang-up battles, a lively fistfight, and he stops a runaway horse team. Fancy photography includes some night shots of the mountains.

p. Larry Darmour; d, Spencer Gordon Bennett; w, Nate Gatzert (based on a story by J. A. Duffy); ph, Herbert Kirkpatrick.

Western **(PR:A MPAA:NR)**

CATTLE TOWN ** (1952) 71m WB bw
Dennis Morgan (Mike McGann), Philip Carey (Ben Curran), Amanda Blake (Marian), Rita Moreno (Queli), Paul Picerni (Pepe), Ray Teal (Judd Hastings), Jay Novello (Felipe Rojas), George O'Hanlon (Shiloh), Bob Wilke (Keeno), Sheb Wooley (Miller), Charles Meredith (Governor), Merv Griffin (Joe), A. Guy Teague (Easy), Boyd "Red" Morgan (Bayo), Jack Kenney (Storekeeper).

Hostilities just after the Civil War between a group of small Texas ranchers and Teal, a wealthy Northerner who buys up their land, makes a go-between essential. Morgan plays the peacemaker chosen by the governor to put an end to threats to the ranchers. Through some deceptive moves, he rids the townsfolk of their weapons and order is achieved, but not before the Northerner is killed in a cattle stampede. These land wars are too often interrupted with a number of tunes, such as "Dixie," "Marching Through Georgia," "The Bonnie Blue Flag," and "The Cowboy."

p, Bryan Foy; d, Noel Smith; w, Tom Blackburn; ph, Ted McCord; m, William Lava; ed, Thomas Reilly.

Western **(PR:A MPAA:NR)**

CAUGHT zero (1931) 62m PAR bw
Richard Arlen, Frances Dee, Louise Dresser, Syd Saylor, Edward J. LeSant, Tom Kennedy, Martin Burton, Marcia Manners, Guy Oliver, Charles K. French, Lon Poff, James Mason, Jack Clifford.

Hard-hearted gambling den owner Dresser, who also is a cattle rustler on the side, is about to kill Arlen, a young Army officer sent to clean up the town, when she discovers he is the long-lost son of her no-good husband kidnaped when he was an infant. Arlen lives, and Dresser gets "caught," unlike the audience for this embarrassing quickie.

d, Edward Sloman; w, Agnes Brand Leahy, Keene Thompson; ph, Charles Lang.

Western **(PR:A MPAA:NR)**

CAUGHT** (1949) 88m MGM bw
James Mason (Larry Quinada), Barbara Bel Geddes (Leonora Eames), Robert Ryan (Smith Ohlrig), Ruth Brady (Maxine), Curt Bois (Franzi), Frank Ferguson (Dr. Hoffman), Natalie Schafer (Dorothy Dale), Art Smith (Psychiatrist), Sonia Darrin (Miss Chambers), Bernadene Hayes (Mrs. Rudecki), Ann Morrison (Miss Murray), Wilton Graff (Gentry), Jim Hawkins (Kevin), Vicki Raw Stiener (Lorraine).

Bel Geddes is the shopgirl/model at a department store who has believed since birth that the only way to true and lasting happiness is to marry a rich man. She meets reclusive Ryan (not unlike Howard Hughes in wealth and neuroses) and he marries her just to bug his analyst. Headlines proclaim the story but Bel Geddes is very unhappy as she sits alone every night and faces another of Ryan's paid sycophants, Bois, an Austrian lackey whose only job is to keep the lady occupied. Ryan is not the most wonderful husband in the world and so, despite all the trappings, Bel Geddes leaves, takes a new identity, and gets a job as the receptionist for young, intelligent, and very normal doctor Mason. Ryan finds Bel Geddes and pleads with her to return, saying things will be different. No sooner does she relent than he schedules a trip out of town. She goes back to Mason and is truly happy there. Mason then proposes and she would accept, except that she learns she's pregnant by Ryan. (However did he find the time?) Depressed, she returns to Ryan's mansion, seeking only financial security for her unborn child. Mason finds her and asks that she come away with him. She is torn between love and insecurity. Ryan has a heart attack and dies, then Bel Geddes has a miscarriage. That done, she is now free to marry Mason. Soap bubbled freely in this slow-moving adaptation of a Libbie Block novel. That plus lots of scene-stealing. Bel Geddes from Mason, Ryan from Bel Geddes; no one was safe from depression, least of all the viewer.

p, Wolfgang Reinhardt; d, Max Ophuls; w, Arthur Laurents (based on the novel Wild Calendar by Libbie Block); ph, Lee Garmes; m, Frederick Hollander; ed, Robert Parrish; md, Rudolph Polk; art d, P. Frank Sylos; set d, Edward G. Boyle; cos, Louise Wilson; makeup, Gus Norin.

Drama **(PR:C MPAA:NR)**

CAUGHT CHEATING* (1931) 52m Tiffany bw
Charles Murray (T. McGillicuddy Hungerford), George Sidney (Sam Harris), Nita Martan (Madelynne Cabrond), Robert Ellis (Joe Cabrone), Dorothy Christy (Tessie), Bertha Mann (Lena Harris), Fred Malatesa (Tobey Moran), George Regas (Giuseppe).

When Sidney inadvertently picks up mob chieftain's wife Martan, both are lured to a masquerade ball to be bumped off by the gang boss, Ellis. Sidney meanwhile has won a second gang's admiration through newspaper notoriety, and in the gang's zeal to protect him both rings of hoods are wiped out.

d, Frank Strayer; w, W. Scott Darling, Frances Hyland (based on a story by Darling); ph, Max DuPont.

Crime **(PR:A MPAA:NR)**

CAUGHT IN THE ACT zero (1941) 60m PRC bw
Henry Armetta (Mike), Iris Meredith (Lucy) Robert Baldwin (Jim), Charles Miller (Brandon), Inez Palange (Mary), Dick Terry (Henderson), Joey Ray (Davis), Maxine Leslie (Fay), William Newell (Sgt. Riley).

Armetta, a construction worker promoted to salesman, gets involved with a "protective association" that is preying on construction companies and is innocently jailed. It's all a ruse; he's actually out to get the crooks, and does, in a weakly directed and poorly played hour of mugging and dialect by Armetta.

p, T. H. Richmond; d, Jean Yarborough; w, Al Martin (based on a story by Robert Cosgriff); ph, Mack Stengler.

Crime **(PR:A MPAA:NR)**

CAUGHT IN THE DRAFT* (1941) 82m PAR bw
Bob Hope (Don Gilbert), Dorothy Lamour (Tony Fairbanks), Lynne Overman (Steve), Eddie Bracken (Bert), Clarence Kolb (Col. Peter Fairbanks), Paul Hurst (Sgt. Burns), Ferike Boros (Yetta), Phyllis Ruth (Margie), Irving Bacon (Cogswell), Arthur Loft (Director), Edgar Dearing (Recruiting Sergeant), Murray Alper (Makeup Man), Dave Willock (Colonel's Orderly), Rita Owen (Cleaning Nurse), Frances Morris (Stretcher Nurse), Ella Neal, Eleanor Stewart, Earlene Heath, Gloria Williams, Marie Blake (Nurses), Terry Ray [Ellen Drew], Ed Peil, Jr. (Patients), Jimmy Dodd (Indignant Patient), Archie Twitchell (Stretcher Patient), Jack Chapin, Victor Cutler (Rookies), Jack Luden, Jerry Jerome, Frank Mitchell (Captains), Ray Flynn (Lieutenant Colonel), David Oliver (Cameraman), Frank O'Connor (Major), Frank Marlowe (Twitchell), Heinie Conklin (Sign Hanger), Phyllis Kennedy (Susan), Arch Macnair (Toothless Man), Weldon Heyburn (Sergeant at Examining Depot), George McKay (Quartermaster Sgt.), Andrew Tombes (Justice of the Peace), Len Henry (Corporal).
One of Bob Hope's best and funniest roles has him a Hollywood star trying to evade the draft in WW II. Lamour is the daughter of a colonel in the Army whom Hope plans to marry in a scheme he thinks will keep him out of the service. The plot backfires and Hope is dumped into a training camp, from which every laugh in the book is evoked in eighty-two minutes of sustained zaniness as Hope's rapid-fire delivery touches and makes a burlesque of every subject at hand—the Army, love, Hollywood. Film has the comedian winding up a hero when he saves a company from casualties in a mock battle, winning the training camp war, Lamour's hand, and the respect of her officer father.
p, B. G. DeSylva; d, David Butler; w, Harry Tugend (based on a story by Tugend); ph, Karl Struss; m, Victor Young; ed, Irene Morra; m/l, Frank Loesser, Louis Alter.
Comedy (PR:AA MPAA:NR)

CAUGHT IN THE FOG* (1928) 68m WB bw
May McAvoy (Jane Regan), Conrad Nagel (Bob), Mack Swain (Detective Krausschmidt), Charles Gerrard ("Silk Shirt Harry"), Ruth Cherrington (Mrs. Bolsin), Emil Chautard (Dr. Bolsin), Hugh Herbert (Detective MacDonald).
Valiant part-talkie effort tells the story of two detectives investigating the jewel robbery of a wealthy young heir. Setting on a fogbound boat in Florida provides some interest, but fascination today is to watch the players struggle with the unfamiliar overhead microphones.
d, Howard Bretherton; w, Charles Condon (based on a story by Jerome Kingston); ph, Byron Haskin; ed, Ralph Dawson.
Mystery (PR:A MPAA:NR)

CAUGHT IN THE NET*½ (1960, Brit.) 64m Wallace/CFF bw
Jeremy Bulloch (Bob Ketley), Joanna Horlock (Susan), James Luck (Simon), Anthony Parker (Peter Ketley), Larry Burns (George), Bruce Wightman (Tom), Michael Collins (Arnold).
Bullock, the little brother of fishery researcher Parker, captures a gang using dynamite to poach salmon. Undiscriminating youngsters should like it.
p, A. Frank Bundy; d, John Haggarty; w, Max Anderson (based on the novel The Lazy Salmon Mystery by Sutherland Ross).
Children (PR:AA MPAA:NR)

CAUGHT PLASTERED* (1931) 68m RAD bw
Bert Wheeler (Tommy Tanner), Robert Woolsey (Egbert Higginbotham), Dorothy Lee (Peggy Morton), Lucy Beaumont (Mother Talley), Jason Robards, Sr. (Watters), DeWitt Jennings (Chief Morton), Charles Middleton (Flint), Bill Scott (Clarke).
Wheeler and Woolsey pay off the mortgage on an old woman's failing drugstore and find themselves fighting a bootlegger gang. Cardboard villains and lackluster dialog are saved from utter imbecility by Wheeler and Woolsey's skill in bantering gags.
p, Douglas MacLean; d, William Seiter; w, Ralph Spence (based on a story by MacLean); ph, Jack MacKenzie; m/l, "I'm That Way About You," Victor Schertzinger.
Comedy (PR:A MPAA:NR)

CAUGHT SHORT* (1930) 75m COS/MGM bw
Marie Dressler (Marie Jones), Polly Moran (Polly Smith), Anita Page (Genevieve Jones), Charles Morton (William Smith), Thomas Conlin (Frankie), Douglas Haig (Johnny), Nanci Price (Priscilla), Greta Mann (Sophy), Herbert Pryor (Mr. Frisby), T. Roy Barnes (Mr. Kidd), Edward Dillon (Mr. Thutt), Alice Moe (Miss Ambrose), Gwen Lee (Manicurist), Lee Kohlmar (Peddler), Greta Grandstedt (Fanny Lee).
Dressler and Moran are best friends (but don't tell anybody), but appear to the world as rival boarding-house landladies envious of each other. Moran's son and Dressler's daughter fall in love and the mothers—who have been playing the stock market on the side and winning—try to out-ritz each other at the wedding. In the end the lovers are united and the two old pals have joined hands again. This is considered the apex in the careers of two funny ladies whose humor often approached slapstick but was saved because it was always so endearingly human.
d, Charles F. Riesner; w, Willard Mack, Joseph H. Johnson, Robert Hopkins (based on Eddie Cantor's gag book Caught Short); ph, Leonard Smith; ed, George Hively.
Comedy (PR:A MPAA:NR)

CAULDRON OF BLOOD* (1971, Span.) 101m Cannon c
(AKA: BLIND MAN'S BLUFF; EL COLECCIONISTA DE CADAVERES)
Boris Karloff (Franz Badulescu), Viveca Lindfors (Tania Badulescu), Jean-Pierre Aumont (Claude Marchand), Jacqui Speed (Pilar), Rosenda Monteros (Valerie), Ruven Rojo (Lover), Dianik Zurakowska (Elga), Milo Quesada, Mercedes Rojo, Mary Lou Palermo, Manuyel de Blas, Eduardo Coutelen.
Karloff stars as a blind sculptor living in Spain with his evil wife Lindfors (she had blinded and crippled him previously during a murder attempt that looked like a car

crash). Unknown to Karloff, Lindfors and her lover, Quesada, are committing a series of grisly murders, boiling the corpses in acid, and giving Karloff the bones to use as armatures in a massive sculpture he is working on (he has been using the skeletons of animals and humans as his base, but he doesn't know that the bones are fresh). Soon, a travel reporter (Aumont) who has been interviewing the artist, catches on to the scheme and informs Karloff, who has a violent fight with his wife and he plunges her hand into the acid bath. Screaming in pain, Lindfors goes off to die, Aumont overpowers her lover, and Karloff throws himself off the terrace to the rocks below. The film was shot in 1967 but wasn't released in the U.S. until 1971, three years after Karloff's death. Claude Rains was originally selected to play the role of Badulescu, but illness prevented him from taking the part. The production was shot on-location in and around Madrid which gives it that Old World look and feel.
p, Robert D. Weinbach; d, Santos Alcocer [Edward Mann]; w, John Melson, Jose Luis Bayonas, Alcocer (based on a story by Alcocer), ph, Francisco Sempere (Panoramica, Eastmancolor); m, Jose Luis Navarro, Ray Ellis; ed, J. Antonio Rojo; art d, Gil Parrondo; m/l, Alcocer, Bob Harris.
Horror (PR:C MPAA:GP)

CAULDRON OF DEATH, THE* (1979, Ital.) 78m Film Ventures International c
Chris Mitchum, Arthur Kennedy, Barbara Bouchet, Melisa Longo, Edward Fajardo, Angel Alvarez.
Dull Italian Mafia story with American names to give it box office appeal over here. An offer easily refused.
d, Tulio Demicheli; w, Joe Maesso.
Crime (PR:O MPAA:R)

CAUSE FOR ALARM* (1951) 73m MGM bw
Loretta Young (Ellen Jones), Barry Sullivan (George Z. Jones), Bruce Cowling (Dr. Ranney Grahame), Margalo Gillmore (Mrs. Edwards), Bradley Mora (Hoppy, Billy), Irving Bacon (Mr. Carston, Postman), Georgia Backus (Mrs. Warren), Don Haggerty (Mr. Russell), Art Baker (Superintendent), Richard Anderson (Lonesome Sailor), Kathleen Freeman (Woman), Robert Easton, Carl "Alfalfa" Switzer (Boys), Earl Hodgins (Postman).
Fast-moving thriller about Sullivan, a madly jealous man, who is getting better after some heart problems. Physically he is improving, but mentally he is a wreck as he fantasizes that his wife, Young, is having it away with Cowling, Sullivan's trusted physician. He gets so crazed that he writes a letter accusing Young and Cowling of having killed him. No sooner does she mail it for him when he tells her what he's done. Now he assaults her and the exertion proves too much so he drops dead of a heart attack. Young gets frantic. She knows the letter was sent to the district attorney. She also knows she is totally innocent. So how to get the letter back? Should we tell what happens? Perhaps you might not want to know. If that's the case, don't read another word. If you don't care, read on. The letter never does reach the D.A. because it was a large letter and she only put one stamp on it! The gimmick is sort of given away when we see her mail the letter. This story is based on a radio play and betrays its audio beginnings by that very gimmick. When you hear a letter being written or mailed, there's no way of knowing its size. On screen, the whole thing is evident. Young's then-husband, Tom Lewis, produced the picture and co-wrote the screenplay.
p, Tom Lewis; d, Tay Garnett; w, Lewis, Mel Dinelli (based on an unpublished story by Larry Marcus); ph, Joseph Ruttenberg; m, Andre Previn; ed, James E. Newcom; art d, Cedric Gibbons, Arthur Lonergan; set d, Edwin B. Willis, Alfred E. Spencer.
Thriller/Mystery (PR:C MPAA:NR)

CAVALCADE* (1933) 110m FOX bw
Diana Wynyard (Jane Marryot), Clive Brook (Robert Marryot), Herbert Mundin (Alfred Bridges), Una O'Connor (Ellen Bridges), Ursula Jeans (Fanny Bridges), Beryl Mercer (Cook), Irene Browne (Margaret Harris), Merle Tottenham (Annie), Frank Lawton (Joe Marryot), John Warburton (Edward Marryot), Margaret Lindsay (Edith Harris), Billy Bevan (George Granger), Dick Henderson, Jr. (Edward, Age 12), Douglas Scott (Joey, Age 8), Sheila MacGill (Edith, Age 10), Bonita Granville (Fanny, Age 7), Tempe Pigott (Mrs. Snapper), Desmond Roberts (Ronnie James), Frank Atkinson (Uncle Dick), Ann Shaw (Mirabelle), William Stanton (Tommy Jolly), Stuart Hall (Lt. Edgar), Mary Forbes (Duchess of Churt).
Noel Coward, in one of his serious ventures, traces thirty years of a British family's life from the Boer War through WW I and into the Jazz Age. A big, fine production little shown or remembered today, CAVALCADE was a sensation at the time of its movie release, filled as it is with a wistful look at a couple clinging together through years of love. The epochal scenes start with the Boer War and go on to record the death of Queen Victoria, WW I, the sinking of the Titanic, and the birth of jazz. Though strictly a British film, it was done so well that it won an Oscar for best film of 1933. It also was one of the earliest movies of child movie star Bonita Granville.
p Winfield Sheehan; d, Frank Lloyd; w, Reginald Berkeley (based on the play by Noel Coward); ph, Ernest Palmer; ed, Margaret Clancy; md,, Louis Francesco; spec eff, William Cameron Menzies.
Historical Drama (PR:A MPAA:NR)

CAVALCADE OF THE WEST* (1936) 70m Diversion bw
Hoot Gibson (Clint), Rex Lease (Ace), Marion Shilling (Mary), Adam Goodman (Windy), Nina Gullbert (Martha), Earl Dwire (Chrisman), Phil Dunham (Clemens), Robert McKenzie (Judge Beasley), Steve Clark (John Know), Jerry Tucker (Clint as a Boy), Barry Downing (Ace as a Boy).
While traveling across the western wasteland, a pioneer family is attacked by outlaws who kidnap Lease/Downing, one of two sons. The boys grow up on opposite sides of the law, next meeting before a jury demanding prairie justice. When the brothers discover who they are, Lease is acquitted and the family is reunited. If the hanging in one scene had been staged from a platform as low as some of the lows reached in this film, the culprit would never have left the ground.

p, Walter Futter; d, Harry Fraser; w, Norman Houston; ph, Paul Ivano; ed, Arthur Brooks.

Western **Cas.** **(PR:A MPAA:NR)**

CAVALIER, THE*   (1928) 69m Tiffany-Stahl bw
Richard Talmadge (El Caballero), Barbara Bedford (Lucia D'Arquista), Nora Cecil (Her Aunt), David Torrence (Ramon Torreno), David Mir (Carlos Torreno), Stuart Holmes (Sgt. Juan Dinero), Christian Frank (Pierre Gaston), Oliver Eckhardt (The Padre).

Masked rider Talmadge saves a Spanish girl from a noble but impoverished family from marrying a wealthy man in New Spain, as ordered by her father. The girl then falls for Talmadge and both become the quarry as her father sends out his gang to find them. Almost everything that could go wrong went wrong with this film, from the star not photographing well to his voice being out of sync with the sound track when he tried to sing. The film rarely lives up to the Brand novel.

p, Irvin Willat; w, Victor Irvin (based on the novel The Black Rider by Max Brand); ph, John Stevens, Harrison Cooper; m, Hugo Riesenfeld; ed, Doane.

Western **(PR:A MPAA:NR)**

CAVALIER OF THE STREETS, THE *½   (1937, Brit.) 70m B&D/PAR bw
Margaret Vyner (Fay Avalon), Patrick Barr (The Cavalier), Carl Harbord (Prince Karanov), James Craven (Sir John Avalon), Laura Smithson (Mrs. Rudd), Renee de Vaux (Lady Carnal), Peggy Chester (Daphne Brook), Leo Genn (Attorney General).

Barr is a blackmailer who confesses to murdering his partner to save Vyner, a barrister's wife on trial for the killing. More boring courtroom drama from English directors of the 1930s, who never seemed to tire of this stuff. Genn's brief appearance is the only enlivening factor here.

p, Anthony Havelock-Allan; d, Harold French; w, Ralph Neale, George Barraud (based on a story by Michael Arlen); ph, Francis Carver.

Crime **(PR:A MPAA:NR)**

CAVALIER OF THE WEST**   (1931) 65m Artclass bw
Harry Carey, Carmen LaRoux, Kane Richmond, Paul Panzer, Theodore (Ted) Adams, George Hayes, Maston Williams, Ben Corbett, Christine (Carlotta) Monti.

Light campfire yarn includes singing, guitars, wine, and evening clothes, sheriffs, soldiers, bad men, and Indians, and a murder frame with love triumphant as the sun sets. The movie is considered innovative because it was the first to record the sound of a horse panting, as well as detonating blank cartridges louder than any film since the beginning of sound pictures.

p, Louis Weiss; d, J. P. McCarthy; w, McCarthy, Harry P. Christ; ph, Frank Kessock.

Western **(PR:A MPAA:NR)**

CAVALLERIA RUSTICANA   (SEE: FATAL DESIRE, 1952, Ital.)

CAVALRY*   (1936) 63m REP bw
Bob Steele, Frances Grant, William Welch, Earl Ross, Karl Hackett, Hal Price.

Half-baked western has Steele leading troopers against Indians, rustlers, and assorted bad men to win the respect of Grant. Not much action and less story.

p, A. W. Hackel; d, Robert N. Bradbury; w, George Plympton (based on a story by Bradbury).

Western **(PR:A MPAA:NR)**

CAVALRY COMMAND**   (1963, U.S./Phil.) 80m Parade Pictures c
(AKA: CAVALLERIA COMMANDOS)
John Agar (Sgt. Norcutt), Richard Arlen (Sgt. Heisler), Myron Healey (Lt. Worth), Alicia Vergel (Laura), Pancho Magalona (Capt Magno), William Phipps (Pvt. Haines), Eddie Infante (Priest), Boy Planas (Tibo).

Agar attempts to convince an angry Philippine nationalist to stop his planned rebellion against the U.S. forces during the American occupation in 1902. Rebel changes his mind when he sees the Americans helping his people with food and medicine.

p, Cirio Santiago; d&w, Eddie Romero; ph, Felipe Sacdalan (Technicolor); m, Tito Arevalo, Ariston Avelino; ed, Gervacio Santos, Ted Smith.

War Drama **Cas.** **(PR:A MPAA:NR)**

CAVALRY SCOUT**   (1951) 78m MON c
Rod Cameron (Kirby Frye), Audrey Long (Claire), Jim Davis (Lt. Spaulding), James Millican (Martin Gavin), James Arness (Barth), John Doucette (Varney), William Phillips (Sgt. Wilkins), Stephen Chase (Col. Drumm), Rory Mallinson (Corporal), Eddy Waller (Gen. Sherman), Frank Wilcox (Matson), Cliff Clark (Col. Deering).

An ordinary, well-paced western centering on a conflict between the government and the redskins. Cameron plays an Army scout who tries to break up Millican's gun-smuggling ring to the Indians. A race against time ensues as Cameron rushes to get the needed proof before the Indians get a Gatling gun.

p, Walter Mirisch; d, Lesley Selander; w, Dan Ullman, Thomas Blackburn; ph, Harry Neumann (Cinecolor); m, Marlin Skiles; ed, Richard Heermance.

Western **(PR:A MPAA:NR)**

CAVE OF OUTLAWS**   (1951) 76m UNIV c
Macdonald Carey (Pete Carver), Alexis Smith (Liz Trent), Edgar Buchanan (Dobbs), Victor Jory (Ben Cross), Hugh O'Brian (Garth), Housely Stevenson (Cooley), Charles Horvath (Job Delancey), Jimmy Van Horn (Jed Delancey), Tim Graham (Jones), Clem Fuller (Whitey).

An implausible plot haunts this B-western directed by William Castle, later of horror

fame. Carey, who has just served a robbery term, decides to go back and search for the hidden loot. Along the way he befriends an attractive young widow, Smith, and aids her with her troubled newspaper business. He soon discovers he is being shadowed by a Wells Fargo detective who works for the victims of the heist. The climactic scene occurs in the title cave where the detective gets the cash, and Carey gets the lass. (Shot in the Carlsbad Caverns of New Mexico.)

p, Leonard Goldstein; d, William Castle; w, Elizabeth Wilson; ph, Irving Glassberg (Technicolor); ed, Edward Curtiss.

Western **(PR:A MPA:NR)**

CAVE OF THE LIVING DEAD*   (1966, Yugo./Ger.) 87m bw
(DER FLUCH DER GRUENEN AUGEN)
Adrian Hoven (Inspector Doren), Karin Field (Karin), Erika Remberg (Maria), Wolfgang Preiss (Prof. Adelsberg), Emmerich Schrenk (Thomas), John Kitzmiller (John), Carl Mohner, Vida Juvan, Stane Sever, Danilo Turk, Laci Cigoj, Tito Strozzi.

Dumb horror adventure detailing the efforts of a professor and his secretary to conduct experiments in the bowels of an old castle. Enter Interpol inspector Hovey, who, with the aid of a witch, discovers seven missing girls in the castle. Unfortunately, the girls are zombies and the professor is a vampire.

p&d, Akos Von Rathony; w, C. Von Rock (based on a story by Von Rathony); ph, Hrvoje Saric; m, Herbert Jarczk; ed, Klaus Dudenhofer; art d, Ivan Pengov; set d, Franco Jurjek.

Horror **(PR:A MPAA:NR)**

CAVEMAN**   (1981) 91m UA c
Ringo Starr (Atouk), Dennis Quaid (Lar), Shelly Long (Tala), Jack Gilford (Gog), John Matuszak (Tonda), Barbara Bach (Lana), Cork Hubbert (Ta), Mark King (Ruck), Paco Morayta (Flok), Evan Kim (Nook), Ed Greenberg (Kalta), Carl Lumbly (Bork), Jack Scalici (Folg), Erica Carlson (Folg's Mate), Gigi Vorgan (Folg's Daughter), Sara Lopez Sierra (Folg's Younger Daughter), Esteban Valdez (Folg's Son), Juan Ancona Figueroa (Folg's Youngest Son), Anais de Melo (Meeka), Avery Schreiber (Ock), Miguel Angel Fuentes (Grot), Tere Alvarez (Ock's Mate), Ana de Sade (Grot's Mate), Gerardo Zepeda (Boola), Hector Moreno (Noota), Pamela Gual (Noota's Mate), Richard Moll (Abominable Snowman).

Occasionally funny film set in "One Zillion B.C." with ex-Beatle Ringo Starr playing a cave man. Forming his own tribe from the outcasts of others, Ringo experiences a number of prehistoric adventures. Relying mostly on slapstick visual humor (only 15 words are spoken, the rest are grunts and groans), the action quickly becomes madcap. One of the most memorable and fitting scenes is Ringo's invention of rock 'n' roll, complete with real rocks. The chief object of Ringo's lust is the gorgeous Bach, his real-life love. Film is pushed along by Lalo Shifrin's appropriate score.

p, Lawrence Turman, David Foster; d, Carl Gottlieb; w, Gottlieb, Rudy De Luca; ph, Alan Hume (Technicolor); m, Lalo Shifrin; ed, Gene Fowler, Jr.; art d, Jose Rodriguez Granada; cos, Robert Fletcher; visual and spec eff, David Allen, Roy Arbogast.

Comedy **Cas.** **(PR:C MPAA:PG)**

CAVERN, THE*½**   (1965, Ital./Ger.) 83m FOX bw
John Saxon (Pvt. Joe Kramer), Rosanna Schiaffino (Anna), Larry Hagman (Capt. Wilson), Peter L. Marshall (Lt. Peter Carter), Nino Castelnuovo (Mario), Brian Aherne (Gen. Braithwaite), Hans von Borsody (Hans), Joachim Hansen (German Soldier), Alfredo Varelli, Renato Terra.

In the last days of WW II six soldiers and one woman (Schiaffino) find themstlves trapped deep inside a cave in the Italian mountains. Inside the cave is a cache of ammunition and supplies that are being watched by Italian partisans. Two of the soldiers are killed trying to escape, and the remaining members of the party are slowly getting on each other's nerves. The pressure becomes so great that the British general, Aherne, shoots himself. His gunshot sets off an explosion that enables the other prisoners to escape. Claustrophobic and compelling, this was the last film from great programmer director Edgar G. Ulmer, shot in Italy and Yugoslavia.

p&d, Edgar G. Ulmer; w, Michael Pertwee, Jack Davis; ph, Gabor Pogany; m, Carlo Rustichelli, Gene di Novi; ed, Renato Cinquini; spec eff, Joseph Natanson.

War **(PR:A MPAA:NR)**

CAYMAN TRIANGLE, THE*   (1977) 92m Hefalump Pictures c
Reid Dennis (Dirty Reid), John Morgan (Gen. Smithe), Anderson Humphreys (Richard Nixon), Ed Beheler (Jimmy Carter), Jules Kreitzer (Henry Kissinger), Dale Reeves (Herbo), Dick Barker (Crachit), Mary Gillooly (Virgin), Arek Joseph (Arab), Ryhal Gallagher (Blackbeard), Ron Sinclair (Adm. Gumfault), Bob Ankrom (Gen,. Eastlesslin), Brian Uzzell (Hunchback), Steve Foster (Nazrat), Tian Giri (Scarlett O'Tara), Noel Spencer-Barnes (Maj. Limey), Michael Blackie (Capt. Smedley), Emily Hector (Hot Lips Hector).

A juvenile but enthusiastic independent set in and around the Bermuda triangle region, centering on an investigation of missing ships. Well-shot and well-performed, this farce is full of political impersonations, high school antics, and second-rate laughs.

p/d, Anderson Humphreys; w, Humphreys, Ralph Clemente; ph, Ed Paveitti, Tom Roosester, Egon Stephen.

Satire **(PR:C-O MPAA:NR)**

CEDDO**   (1978, Nigeria) 120m c
Tabara Ndiaye (Princess Dior), Moutapha Yade (Madir Fatim Fall), Ismaila Diagne (The Kidnaper), Makoura Dia (The King), Oumar Gueye (Jaraaf), Mamadou Dioum (Prince Biram), Nar Modou Sene (Saxewar), Ousmane Camara (Diogomay), Ousmane Sembene (A Ceddo Renamed Ibrahima).

Fascinating feature by the Dark Continent's most talented director. In turn-of-the-century Senegal, the local king becomes a convert to Islam and, under the influence of a Moslem advisor, disbands the little Catholic Church in the village of the Ceddo. The people resist this change just as they resisted the Christian missionaries before, going to the length of kidnaping the king's daughter. Most of the film consists of meetings between different factions and groups, all conducted according to ancient tribal customs. The Moslem advisor uses his power to lie and kill until all opposition has been destroyed. This film was banned in Sembene's native Senegal not because of its dim view of that country's conversion to Islam, but because the government insists that "Ceddo" is spelled with only one "d." (In Wolof: English subtitles.)

d&w, Ousmane Sembene; ph, Georges Caristan; m, Manu Dibango; ed, Florence Eymon.

Drama **(PR:C MPAA:NR)**

CEILING ZERO*½** (1935) 95m FN/COS bw

James Cagney *(Dizzy Davis)*, Pat O'Brien *(Jack Lee)*, June Travis *(Tommy Thomas)*, Stuart Erwin *(Texas Clark)*, Henry Wadsworth *(Tay Lawson)*, Isabell Jewell *(Lou Clark)*, Barton MacLane *(Al Stone)*, Martha Tibbetts *(Mary Lee)*, Craig Reynolds *(Joe Allen)*, James H. Bush *(Buzz Gordon)*, Robert Light *(Les Bogan)*, Addison Richards *(Fred Adams)*, Carlyle Moore, Jr. *(Eddie Payson)*, Richard Purcell *(Smiley Johnson)*, Gordon [Bill] Elliott *(Transportation Agent)*, Pat West *(Baldy Wright)*, Edward Gargan *(Doc Wilson)*, Garry Owen *(Mike Owens)*, Mathilde Comont *(Mama Gini)*, Carol Hughes *(Birdie)*, Frank Tomick, Paul Mantz *(Stunt Fliers)*, Jimmy Aye, Howard Allen, Mike Lally, Harold Miller *(Pilots)*, Jerry Jerome *(Mechanic)*, Helene McAdoo, Gay Sheridan, Mary Lou Dix, Louise Seidel, Helen Erickson *(Hostesses)*, Don Wayson, Dick Cherney, Jimmie Barnes, Frank McDonald *(Office Workers)*, J.K. Kane *(Teletype Operator)*, Jayne Manners *(Tall Girl)*, Maryon Curtiz, Margaret Perry *(Girls)*.

The irrepressible, cocky, and dynamic Cagney is a devil-may-care civil aviator who does what he pleases and flies by the legendary seat of his pants. Tolerating his unpredictable-little-boy stunts, his aggravating pranks and general I-don't-give-a-damn attitude is the soft-hearted O'Brien, paired once again with his close friend Cagney, the pal he called "the faraway fella." O'Brien is the ground commander who sends men into the air to test planes, deliver people, goods, and mail, and wet-nurses their families while they are aloft. Cagney, as usual, steals the show with his swaggering and humorous histrionics. He falls in love with aviatrix Travis and begins to shirk his duties. In one scene he goes on a mock crying jag to win sympathy. Next he is chiding and riding fellow flier, dumb-cluck Erwin, joking about Erwin's wife and kids. At first he is encouraged by his fellow fliers and friends, but Cagney's frantic antics begin to wear out his associates. He's too independent to change, telling Travis that he loves lone-wolfing it in the sky. "When you're up there, you're on your own. It's strictly a one-man show." O'Brien reminds him that he's part of a team and should play it that way. "Are you meaning to infer, sir," snaps Cagney sarcastically, "that I am not a cog in the wheel?" Following his independent whims, Cagney dodges a risky assignment, pretending that he has a heart murmur, so he can keep a date with the beautiful Travis. Good old boy Erwin goes up in his place and tragically dies in an accident. Cagney's remorse at losing his good friend is obvious and deep but Jewell, Erwin's wife, confronts him, blaming Cagney for her husband's death, shouting: "You're no good!" The reckless, romantically self-destructive Cagney redeems himself by taking off in a dense fog (ergo the title, CEILING ZERO, meaning fog on the ground) to test a vital de-icing instrument and crashes to his death, finishing as a tragic hero. For O'Brien he remains an unforgettable, flamboyant ace and Travis will always remember him as "sort of goofy and tough and sweet all at the same time." Director Hawks, who had a rich aviation background, gives us a lot of thrills in many action sequences. The pace is so fast at times that it's difficult to keep up with the action and dialog, particularly O'Brien's machine gun-like orders to his pilots, all in flight at the same time. CEILING ZERO was based on a play by Frank "Spig" Wead who wrote the screenplay; Wead had also been a pilot during WW I, but, ironically, returned unscathed by the war, only to fall out of a chair and become paralyzed for life. (John Wayne would later play his life in THE WINGS OF EAGLES). CEILING ZERO capitalized on two earlier civil aviation epics, NIGHT FLIGHT (MGM, 1933), and CHINA CLIPPER, released the same year, in which O'Brien was also the head of a commercial airline opening up trans-Pacific routes and dealing with zany pilots. (Remade as INTERNATIONAL SQUADRON.)

p, Harry Joe Brown; d, Howard Hawks; w, Frank Wead (based on his play); ph, Arthur Edeson; m, Leo F. Forbstein; ed, William Holmes; art d, John Hughes; spec eff, Fred Jackman; tech adv, Paul Mantz; cos, Orry-Kelly; makeup, Perc Westmore.

Adventure/Drama **(PR:A MPAA:NR)**

CELESTE½** (1982, Ger.) 106m Pelemele-Bayerische Rundfunk/New Yorker-Artificial Eye c

Eva Mattes *(Celeste)*, Jurgen Arndt *(Proust)*, Norbert Wartha, Wolf Euba, Joseph Manoth, Leo Bardichewski, Horst Raspe, Andi Stefanescu, Rolf Illig.

The memories of Proust's housekeeper provide the basis for this beautiful film. The author of *A Remembrance of Things Past* is shown as a dying, bedridden crank cared for by the endlessly patient Mattes. Incredibly slow, but beautifully shot and worth the effort. (In German: English subtitles.)

p, Eleanore Adlon; d&w, Percy Adlon (based on the book *Rom Monsieur Proust* by Celeste Albaret); ph, Jurgen Martin, Horst Becker, Helmo Sahliger, Hermann Ramelow (Eastmancolor); m, Cesar Franck; ed, Clara Fabry; art d, Hans Gailing, Marlies Frese, Kurt Diell, Esther Wenger.

Drama **(PR:A MPAA:NR)**

CELIA*½ (1949, Brit.) 67m Exclusive bw

Hy Hazell *(Celia)*, Bruce Lister *(Larry Peters)*, John Bailey *(Lester Martin)*, James Raglan *(Inspector Parker)*, Elsie Wagstaffe *(Aunt Nora)*, Lockwood West *(Dr. Cresswell)*, Joan Hickson, Ferdy Mayne.

Actress Hazell impersonates her aunt to expose her step-uncle as a poisoner. Routine British crime drama.

p, Anthony Hinds; d, Francis Searle; w, Searle, Edward J. Mason, A. R. Rawlinson (based on a radio serial by Mason); ph, Cedric Williams.

Crime **(PR:A MPAA:NR)**

CELINE AND JULIE GO BOATING*** (1974, Fr.) 193m Les Films du Losange/Les Films 7/Renn Productions/SAGA/SIMAR/V. M. Productions/Action Films/Les Films Christian Fachner c (CELINE ET JULIE VONT EN BATEAU)

Juliet Berto *(Celine)*, Dominique Labourier *(Julie)*, Bulle Ogier *(Camille)*, Marie-France Pisier *(Sophie)*, Barbet Schroeder *(Oliver)*, Philippe Clevenot *(Guliou)*.

Berto and Labourier run into each other and become friends. Berto invents a story about a haunted house and while telling Labourier about it she suggests they go there. In the house they view the ghosts playing out their story, and the girls join in at one point. Maddeningly enigmatic and incredibly long, the film becomes hypnotic in its ethereal beauty and strange goings-on. When it finally reaches the end, one is not quite sure what has happened, but it will remain in the mind for a long time afterward. Definitely not for all tastes. Shot in 16mm. (French: English subtitles.)

d, Jacques Rivette; w, Rivette, Eduardo do Gregorio, Juliet Berto, Dominique Labourier, Bulle Ogier, Marie-France Pisier; ph, Jacques Renard, Michel Cenet (Eastmancolor); m, Jean Marie Senia; ed, Nicole Lubtchansky, Chris Tullio-Altan.

Drama **(PR:C MPAA:NR)**

CELL 2455, DEATH ROW** (1955) 77m COL bw

William Campbell *(Whit)*, Robert Campbell *(Whit, as a Teenager)*, Marian Carr *(Doll)*, Kathryn Grant *(Jo-Anne)*, Harvey Stephens *(Warden)*, Vince Edwards *(Hamilton)*, Allen Nourse *(Serl)*, Diane De Laire *(Hallie)*, Bart Bradley *(Whit, as a Young Boy)*, Paul Dubov *(Al)*, Tyler MacDuff *(Nugent)*, Buck Kartalian *(Monk)*, Eleanor Audley *(Blanche)*, Thom Carney *(Hatcheck Charlie)*, Joe Forte *(Lawyer)*, Howard Wright *(Judge)*, Glenn Gordon *(Superior Guard)*, Jimmy Murphy *(Sonny)*, Jerry Mickelsen *(Tom)*, Bruce Sharpe *(Bud)*, Wayne Taylor *(Skipper Adams)*.

A sometimes poignant life story of rapist Caryl Chessman, who was sentenced to San Quentin's Death Row and later executed. He is seen in his teen years (played by lead's younger brother) as a petty thief committing a string of senseless crimes, and through his adult years as a violent man arrogantly defying society's laws. Film tends to fall back on narration as Campbell tells Chessman's thoughts while pacing his cell, instead of Chessman's motivations being worked out through the script and visuals. Lead Campbell later went on to star in Coppola's DEMENTIA 13.

p, Wallace MacDonald; d, Fred F. Sears; w, Jack De Witt (based on the autobiography of Caryl Chessman); ph, Fred Jackson, Jr.; m, Mischa Bakaleinikoff; ed, Henry Batista.

Biography/Crime **(PR:C MPAA:NR)**

CENTENNIAL SUMMER½** (1946) 104m FOX c

Jeanne Crain *(Julia)*, Cornel Wilde *(Philippe Lascalles)*, Linda Darnell *(Edith Rogers)*, William Eythe *(Benjamin Franklin Phelps)*, Walter Brennan *(Jesse Rogers)*, Constance Bennett *(Zenia Lascalles)*, Dorothy Gish *(Harriet Rogers)*, Barbara Whiting *(Susanna Rogers)*, Larry Stevens *(Richard Lewis, Esq.)*, Kathleen Howard *(Deborah)*, Buddy Swan *(Dudley Rogers)*, Charles Dingle *(Snodgrass)*, Avon Long *(Specialty)*, Gavin Gordon *(Trowbridge)*, Eddie Dunn *(Mr. Phelps)*, Lois Austin *(Mrs. Phelps)*, Harry Strang *(Mr. Dorgan)*, Frances Morris *(Mrs. Dorgan)*, Reginald Sheffield *(President Grant)*, William Frambes *(Messenger Boy)*, Paul Everton *(Senator)*, James Metcalfe *(Bartender)*, John Farrell *(Drunk)*, Billy Wayne *(Attendant)*, Robert Malcolm *(Kelly)*, Edna Holland *(Nurse)*, Ferris Taylor *(Governor)*, Winifred Harris *(Governor's Wife)*, Rodney Bell *(Master of Ceremonies)*, Glancy Cooper *(Carpenter)*, Florida Sanders *(Dance Specialty)*, Eddie Dunn *(Mr. Phelps)*, Lois Austin *(Mrs. Phelps)*, Sam McDaniel, Fred "Snowflake" Toones, Napoleon Whiting, Nicodemus Stewart *(Red Caps)*, Hans Moebus *(Subject in Still Life)*, Joe Whitehead *(Railroad Clerk)*.

Otto Preminger directed this essentially lightweight material with his customary heavy hand and the result was a fight between what was on the page and what was on the screen. MGM had made a fortune with MEET ME IN ST. LOUIS, and Fox thought it could do the same with a musical based on the Philadelphia Exposition of 1876. They were mistaken. Brennan and Gish live in Philadelphia with their two lovely daughters, Crain and Darnell. Brennan is sort of an early-day Lorenzo Jones (the radio inventor who, with his wife, Belle, charmed millions every afternoon) who invents clocks and things that he wants to sell to the railroad for which he works. Not much else to report plot-wise but a crackling good score by Jerome Kern (his last before his death) with lyrics by several collaborators. In the hands of another director, and with more attention paid to the dull script, this could have been the rival of the aforementioned MGM movie. With songs like "In Love In Vain" and "All Through The Day" (Oscar-nominated) and "Up With The Lark" it's too bad they didn't sing more and speak less. Other songs: "The Right Romance," Cinderella Sue," "Centennial."

p&d, Otto Preminger; w, Michael Kanin (based on the novel by Albert E. Idell); ph, Ernest Palmer (Technicolor); m, Jerome Kern; ed, Harry Reynolds; md, Alfred Newman; art d, Lyle Wheeler, Lee Fuller; set d, Thomas Little; spec eff, Fred Sersen; ch, Dorothy Fox; m/l, Jerome Kern, Leo Robin, Oscar Hammerstein II, E. Y. "Yip" Harburg.

Musical **(PR:AA MPAA:NR)**

CENTO ANNI D'AMORE** (1954, Ital.) 110m Cines bw

Maurice Chevalier, Alba Arnova, Jacques Sernas, Aldo Fabrizi, Irene Galter, Franco Interlenghi, Carol Ninchi, Vittorio De Sica, Nadia Gray, Luigi Cimara, Carlo Campanini, Eduardo de Filippo, Titina de Filippo, Giulietta Masina, Rina Morelli, Ernesto Almirante, Virgilio Riento, Lea Padovani, Gabriele Ferzetti, Xenia Valderi, Laura Gore.

An Italian anthology film featuring six episodes dealing with love from 1854 to 1954. The first, "Garibaldina," sees an anti-Garibaldi priest who changes his mind about the government and works to have other citizens do likewise. "Pendolin" details an unfaithful wife's affair with a hotel porter who was only trying to return her lost earrings. "Purification" deals with a loyal soldier who cannot bring himself to tell his dying commanding officer's last words to his girl friend because he does not feel she is worthy to hear them. "Golden Wedding" sees an elderly couple becoming disillusioned with each other after they celebrate their golden wedding anniversary. "The Last Ten Minutes" concerns the efforts of a priest and a condemned man who try to spare his wife from the real reason for his execution. "Amore" details the efforts of a father-in-law who tries to convince his daughter's husband not to divorce her. Released in Italy and France, but never released in Britain or the U.S.

p&d, Lionello de Felice; w, Guido Gozzano, Gabriel D'Annunzio, Guilio Rocca, Marino Moretti, de Felice, Oreste Biancoli; ph, Aldo Tonti; m,, Nino Rota, Mario Nascimbene, Ted Usetti; ed, Marion Serandei; art d & set d, Franco Lotti.

Drama **(PR:C MPAA:NR)**

CENTRAL AIRPORT** (1933) 72m FN/WB bw

Richard Barthelmess *(Jim)*, Sally Eilers *(Jill)*, Tom Brown *(Neil)*, Grant Mitchell *(Mr. Blaine)*, James Murray *(Eddie)*, Claire McDowell *(Mrs. Blaine)*, Willard Robertson, John Wayne, Willard Robertson *(Havana Manager)*, Arthur Vinton *(Amarillo Manager)*, Charles Sellon *(Man in Wreck)*.

Eilers marries Brown, the younger brother of the man she loves, to spite sweetheart Barthelmess who says marriage is not for pilots. They are all part of a flying circus. Situations are good but the script is weak. In addition, Eilers is miscast, looking more like Brown's mother than his lover. Barthelmess as the daredevil flier is the main advantage since his scenes are exceptionally well done theatrically and technically. It only flies in the air. The "Duke" appears in one of his early films.

p, Hal B. Wallis; d, William A. Wellman; w, Rian James and James Seymour (based on a story by Jack Moffitt); ph, Sid Hickox; ed, James Morley; spec eff, Frank Jackman.

Adventure **(PR:A MPAA:NR)**

CENTRAL PARK** (1932) 57m FN bw

Joan Blondell *(Dot)*, Wallace Ford *(Rick)*, Guy Kibbee *(Charley)*, Henry B. Walthall *(Eby)*, Patricia Ellis *(Vivian)*, Charles Sellon *(Luke)*, Spencer Charters *(Sgt. Riley)*, John Wray *(Smiley)*, Harold Huber *(Nick)*, Holmes Herbert *(Chairman of Casino Ball)*, DeWitt Jennings *(Police Lieutenant)*, Henry Armetta *(Tony)*, Willard Robertson *(Captain of Detectives)*, Harry Holman *(Police Captain)*, William Pawley *(Hymie)*, Wade Boteler *(Barney)*, Edward LeSaint *(Police Commissioner)*, Irving Bacon *(Oscar)*, George Collins *(Spud)*, Lee Shumway *(Police Lieutenant)*, Ted Oliver *(Joe the Cop)*, Larry Steers *(Headwaiter)*, Dennis O'Keefe *(Casino Diner)*, William Norton Bailey *(Hood)*, Harry Seymour *(Hood Guard)*, Rolfe Sedan *(Casino Parton)*, Morgan Wallace *(Commissioner)*.

A silly but fun look at life in New York's Central Park which involves several different story lines. The most notable episode sees the escape of a lion from the park's zoo, and its subsequent rampage through a casino during a fancy dinner dance. Good cast and two songs, "Young Love" and "Central Park."

p, Ray Griffith; d, John Adolfi; w, Ward Morehouse, Earl Baldwin (based on a story by Morehouse); ph, Sid Hickox; ed, Bert Levy; m/l, Cliff Hess.

Drama **(PR:A MPAA:NR)**

CENTURION, THE*

(1962, Fr./Ital.) 77m Europa Cinematografica-C.F.P.C./PIC c (AKA: CONQUEROR OF CORINTH)

Jacques Sernas *(Caius Vinicius)*, John Drew Barrymore *(Diaeus)*, Genevieve Grad *(Hebe)*, Gianna Maria Canale *(Artemide)*, Gordon Mitchell *(Gen. Metellus)*, Gianni Santuccio *(Critolaus)*, Nando Tamberlani *(Callicrates)*, Ivano Staccioli *(Hippolytus)*, Andrea Fantasia *(Lucius Mummius)*, Gianni Solaro *(Caesar)*, Jose Jaspe *(Traitor)*, Vassili Karamis *(Egeo)*, Dina De Santis *(Chimene)*, Milena Vukotic *(Ancella)*, Adrian Vianello *(Cleo)*.

Sernas is a Roman centurion sent to a Greek city to try to convince the rulers of that city to accept Roman rule. He is wounded in a fight between factions supporting both sides. While recovering, he becomes embroiled in assorted intrigues and falls in love with Grad, the daughter of the leader of the anti-Roman forces (Santuccio). Standard Italian swords-and-sandals epic.

p, Manlio Morelli; d, Mario Costa; w, Nino Stresa; ph, Pier Ludovico Pavoni (Euroscope, Eastmancolor); m, Carlos Innocenzi; ed, Albert Salvadori; cos, Mario Giorsi; spec eff, Antonio Visone.

Historical Drama **(PR:A MPAA:NR)**

CEREBROS DIABOLICOS* (1966, Mex.) 85m Filmica Vergara bw (AKA: ARANAS INFERNALES)

Alejandro Cruz, Blanca Sanchez, Martha Elena Cervantes, Nathanael Leon Frankenstein.

Another in the lengthy series of Mexican adventure/science fiction films featuring popular professional wrestlers as the super-heroes. This one sees the masked Blue Demon go against spider people from outer space who can disguise themselves as humans at will. Unfortunately, the spider-humans' hands have a tendency to revert back to their more spidery-looking form. The highlight sees the Blue Demon wrestle a hulk by the name of Frankenstein. Inexplicably, there is a small cult of fans for these bizarre little adventures.

p, Luis Enrique Vergara; d&w, Federico Curiel; ph, Alfredo Vribe.

Fantasy **(PR:A MPAA:NR)**

CEREBROS INFERNAL

(SEE: BLUE DEMON VERSUS THE INFERNAL BRAINS, 1967, Mex.)

CEREMONY, THE** (1963, U.S./Span.) 106m UA bw (LA CEREMONIA)

Laurence Harvey *(Sean McKenna)*, Sarah Miles *(Catherine)*, Robert Walker *(Dominic)*, John Ireland *(Prison Warden)*, Ross Martin *(LeCoq)*, Lee Patterson *(Nicky)*, Jack McGowran *(O'Brien)*, Murray Melvin *(1st Gendarme)*, Carlos Casarvilla *(Ramades)*, Fernando Rey *(Sanchez)*, Fernando Sanchez *(Shaoush)*, Jose Nieto *(Inspector)*, Noel Purcell *(Finigan)*, Xan Das Bolas *(Arab Peasant)*, Barta Barri *(Death House Guard)*, Edward St. John *(Special Guard)*, Jose Guardiola *(Gate Guard)*, Jose Trinidad *(Police Chauffeur)*, Francisco Montalvo *(1st Guard)*, Jose Riesgo *(Second Guard)*, Eduardo Garcia *(Truck Driver)*, Phil Posner *(Prison Official)*, Jose Manuel Martin, Juan Olaguibel, Juan Garcia Delgado, Julio Tabuyo, James Brown, Rafael Albaicin, Ricardo Rodriquez, Manuel Pena, Carlos Chemenal, Alvaro Varela, Enrique Closas *(Gendarmes)*.

A dark, unmoving film which doesn't quite live up to its interesting premise. Harvey plays a man about to be executed in a Tangiers prison for a crime of which he is innocent. In actuality, he made an attempt to prevent the crime but ended up the scapegoat. A successful scheme devised by his brother allows him to escape from his lockup. Once on the outside, though, he learns that all along his brother has been having an affair with his girl. After a fight and a car crash, the erring brother is captured by the police, mistaken for Harvey, and executed in Harvey's place.

p&d, Laurence Harvey; w, Ben Barzman, Alun Falconer, Harvey; ph, Brian West, Oswald Morris; m, Gerard Schurmann; ed, Ralph Kemplen, cos, Moss Mabry; spec eff, Manolo Vaquero, Arthur Reavis.

Crime **(PR:C MPAA:NR)**

CERTAIN SMILE, A** (1958) 105m FOX c

Rossano Brazzi *(Luc)*, Joan Fontaine *(Francoise Ferrand)*, Bradford Dillman *(Bertrand)*, Christine Carere *(Dominique Vallon)*, Eduard Franz *(Mon. Vallon)*, Kathryn Givney *(Mme. Griot)*, Steven Geray *(Denis)*, Trude Wyler *(Mme. Denis)*, Sandy Livingston *(Catherine)*, Renate Hoy *(Mlle. Minot)*, Muzaffer Tema *(Pierre)*, Katherine Locke *(Mme. Vallon)*.

Beautiful photography, fantastic scenery, very glossy, but still essentially trite in concept and story line, A CERTAIN SMILE tells the story of a young woman who betrays her friend and has an affair with her friend's husband, a much older man. Carere (in her first role) falls out with beau Dillman. His uncle, Brazzi, invites her to stay on the Riviera for a week. Despite the fact that Brazzi's wife, Fontaine, has been very nice to her, she takes up with the aging Casanova and later follows him to his Paris home. Once there, she learns that it was little more than a dalliance for him and that he would just like to forget he ever met her. Fontaine and Carere have one heavy scene followed by Joan's confrontation with her cheating husband. Fadeout happens and the feeling is that Dillman and Carere will eventually unite. The book by Francoise Sagan was much hotter and the 1958 Production Code paled most of the sex so what happens on the screen is mild by any year's standards. The best part of the movie is the photography, which must have sent the tourist business up by five hundred percent.

p, Henry Ephron; d, Jean Negulesco; w, Frances Goodrich, Albert Hackett (based on the novel by Francoise Sagan); ph, Milton Krasner (CinemaScope, DeLuxe Color); m, Alfred Newman; ed, Louis R. Loeffler; m/l, Sammy Fain, Paul Francis Webster (Oscar nominated); cos, Mary Wills; title song sung by Johnny Mathis.

Romance **(PR:C-O MPAA:NR)**

CERTAIN, VERY CERTAIN, AS A MATTER OF FACT . . . PROBABLE**

(1970, Ital.) 110m Clesi-San Marco c

Claudia Cardinale *(Marta)*, Catherine Spaak *(Nanda)*, Robert Hoffman *(Stefano)*, Nino Castelnuovo *(Pietro)*, John Philip Law *(Crispino)*.

Cardinale, a charmer from the country, heads for the city to make it big. Even with her raspy voice she lands the improbable job of switchboard operator, and then sets her sights on a more challenging target. She begins her hunt for a mate, a job which proves to be a snap. She finds out that hanging on to him is a bit tougher. He quickly sets sail on a world cruise, leaving her behind with friend Spaak. Together they soothe the tedium by hooking up with a variety of male catches.

p, Silvio Clementelli; d&w, Marcello Fondato (based on a story by Dacia Maraini), ph, Alfio Contiui (Techniscope, Technicolor); m, Carlo Rustichelli; ed, Sergio Montanari.

Comedy **(PR:O MPAA:NR)**

CERVANTES (SEE: YOUNG REBELS, 1967, Fr./Ital./Span.)

CESAR*½** (1936, Fr.) 117m Pagnol bw

Raimu *(Cesar Olivier)*, Pierre Fresnay *(Marius)*, Orane Demazis *(Fanny)*, Fernand Charpin *(Honore Panisse)*, Andre Fouche *(Cesariot)*, Alida Rouffe *(Honorine Cabinis)*, Milly Mathis *(Aunt Claudine)*, Robert Vattier *(M. Brun)*, Paul Dullac *(Felix Escartefigue)*, Maupi *(Chauffeur)*, Edouard Delmont *(Dr. Felicien Venelle)*, Doumel *(Fernand)*, Thommeray *(The Priest Elzear)*, Robert Brassac *(Pierre Dromard)*.

The third part in Pagnol's Marseilles trilogy completes the story begun in MARIUS and continued in FANNY. Fouche is the eighteen-year-old son of Fresnay and Demazis, but his father disappeared before he was born and he believes aging Charpin, his mother's husband, to be his father. A priest begs Charpin to tell Fouche about his real father but he refuses. When Charpin dies Demazis tells her son about his parentage and he is properly shocked. He learns that Raimu, whom he had always thought to be his godfather, is his grandfather, and the old man tells him about his father and where to find him. Fouche travels to Toulon and meets his father, who is working in a garage, without revealing who he is. The owner of the garage (Doumel) plays a joke on the youth and tells him that Fresnay is an opium smuggler. Fouche believes him and returns home quite upset. Doumel realizes that Fouche is Fresnay's son and tells the man what he has done. Fresnay goes to meet him and the two are reconciled. Fouche takes his father home and a tense series of accusations and attacks follows. Fresnay refuses to marry Demazis since that would mean accepting the money of the dead Charpin. Fouche steals the keys to Fresnay's car to prevent him from leaving and he brings the two long-separated lovers together at last. Magnificent performances, particularly from Raimu, highlight this fine film. The audiences that had made the previous installments of the trilogy such a success did the same for this one, and the fact that the lovers were finally reunited after twenty years didn't hurt the box office, either. While the first two installments had been adapted from the stage, CESAR went the other route, and after being written for the screen was adapted into a play in 1946. In 1948 the trilogy was released in America and became an art house favorite. FANNY, a Broadway musical based on the entire trio followed in 1954, and in 1961 it was filmed with Charles Boyer, Maurice Chevalier, and Leslie Caron. A must-see.

p,d&w, Marcel Pagnol; ph, Willy; m, Vincent Sotto; ed, Suzanne de Troeye, Jeanette Ginestet.

Drama   **Cas.**   **(PR:A   MPAA:NR)**

CESAR AND ROSALIE***
(1972, Fr.) 110m Fildebroc-UPS-Mega Paramount/Orion-Cinema V c
Yves Montand (Cesar), Romy Schneider (Rosalie), Sami Frey (David), Umberto Orsini (Antoine), Eva Marie Meineke (Lucie), Bernard Le Coq (Michel), Gisella Hahn (Carla), Isabelle Huppert (Marite), Henri-Jacques Huet (Marcel), Pippo Merisi (Albert), Carlo Nell (Julien), Herve Sand (Georges).

Schneider carries on a simultaneous affair with both Montand and Frey, but as the years go by the two men become close friends. Pleasant adult comedy. Montand is superb.

d, Claude Sautet; w, Jean-Loup Dabadie, Sautet; ph, Jean Boffety (Eastmancolor); m, Phillipe Sarde; art d, Pierre Guffroy.

Comedy   **(PR:C   MPAA:NR)**

CHA-CHA-CHA BOOM*
(1956) 78m COL bw
Perez Prado (Himself), Mary Kay Trio (Themselves), Helen Grayco (Herself), Luis Arcaraz (Himself), Manny Lopez (Himself), Steve Dunn (Bill Haven), Alix Talton (Debbie Farmer), Jose Gonzales Gonzales (Pablo), Sylvia Lewis (Nita Munay), Dante De Paulo (Elvarez), Charles Evans (George Evans), Howard Wright (Teasdale).

The mambo beat is all that saves this variety showcase from becoming a cha-cha-cha bomb. A trite plot follows a talent scout as he travels to Cuba in search of acts for his record label. He comes back with a suitcase full. One bright spot in the film is the Latin dance team of Lewis and De Paulo, with Lewis also a key character in the story. Songs include: "Get Happy" (Ted Koehler, Harold Arlen), "Lonesome Road" (Gene Austin, Nathaniel Shilkret), "Save Your Sorrow" (Buddy DeSylva, Al Sherman), "Lily's Lament," "Year Round Love," "Cuban Rock and Roll," "Voodoo Suite," Crazy Crazy," "Mambo No. 8."

p, Sam Katzman; d, Fred F. Sears; w, James B. Gordon, Benjamin H. Kline; ed, Jerome Thomas; ch, Earl Barton.

Musical   **(PR:A   MPAA:NR)**

CHAD HANNA***
(1940) 86m Fox C
Henry Fonda (Chad Hanna), Dorothy Lamour (Albany Yates), Linda Darnell (Caroline), Guy Kibbee (Huguenine), Jane Darwell (Mrs. Huguenine), John Carradine (Bisbee), Ted North (Fred Shepley), Roscoe Ates (Ike Wayfish), Ben Carter (Bellboy), Frank Thomas (Burke), Olin Howland (Ciscoe Tridd), Frank Conlan (Mr. Proudfoot), Edward Conrad (Fiero), Edward McWade (Elias), George Davis (Pete Bostock), Paul Burns (Budlong), Sarah Padden (Mrs. Tridd), Tully Marshall (Mr. Mott), Edward Mundy (Joe Duddy), Leonard St. Leo (Mr. Pamplon), Elizabeth Abbott (Mrs. Pamplon), Almira Sessions (Mrs. Mott), Virginia Brissac (Landlady), Si Jenks (Farmer), Victor Kilian (Potato Man), Louis Mason (Constable), Charles Middleton (Sheriff), Rondo Hatton (Canvasman), Nelson McDowell (Bit), Dick Rich, Herbert Ashley, Paul Sutton, Jim Pierce (Men), Clarence Muse (Black Man), Maxine Tucker (Servant Girl).

This was the third picture Fonda starred in which was made from one of the Walter Edmonds stories. Edmonds loved to write about upstate New York (DRUMS ALONG THE MOHAWK and THE FARMER TAKES A WIFE). In this adaptation of "Red Wheels Rolling" Fonda is the gofer in a tavern when he falls for Lamour, the curvaceous bareback rider in a traveling circus which has come to the small New York town. It's 1841 and the tacky circus is one of those tired groups that plays two or three days in each town, then moves on. Fonda is so taken by Lamour that he joins the circus as a roustabout. Also joining the circus is gorgeous Darnell, who is escaping the tiny town of Canastota to get out of the clutches of her overbearing father, Howland. Darnell becomes Lamour's understudy and things go along fairly well until circus owner Kibbee is warned by a rival, North, to keep away from the towns where North's circus performs. North offers Lamour a raise and she takes off with the bounder. There's a physical battle between the two circuses and Kibbee is hurt, so guess who becomes the ringmaster? Fonda falls in love with and marries Darnell, but when the circus's number one star dies (a lion), Kibbee blames Fonda, who reacts by abandoning the circus and his wife to join North's group. Fonda doesn't realize that Darnell is pregnant when he departs in a huff. Once with the rival circus, he almost has an affair with Lamour but stops just short of it when he realizes how much he loves Darnell. Kibbee has now recovered and attempts to put on his circus without the star lion. The result is chaos as a group of thugs get rowdy and are about to tear the place apart (this scene is never fully motivated). The day is saved when Fonda arrives astride a huge elephant. He has promised the behemoth's owner a one-quarter share in the circus in return for said beast. Picture ends with the circus making money and Fonda and Darnell making a life for themselves. If nothing else, CHAD HANNA appears to be an accurate depiction of 19th-century America and had its moments. The picture made little noise at the box office as it seemed to be too mild at a time when the distant sounds of cannon could be heard across the Atlantic.

p, Nunnally Johnson; d, Henry King; w, Johnson (based on the story "Red Wheels Rolling" by Walter D. Edmonds); ph, Ernest Palmer (Technicolor); m, David Buttolph; ed, Barbara McLean; art d, Richard Day.

Drama   **(PR:A-C   MPAA:NR)**

CHAFED ELBOWS**
(1967) 63m Goosedown Production/Filmmakers Distribution Center bw
George Morgan (Walter Dinsmore), Elsie Downey (All Women's Roles), Lawrence Wolfe (Oliver Sinfield), Dan List, Ralph Blasi, Ben Bagley, Ronald Nealy, Lafayette Malatsun, Steve Harris, Jack Harvey, Jack Jobson, Tom O'Horgan, Stan Wardnow.

Writer/producer/director Morgan, in reference to his own film, once wrote, "I wouldn't let anyone over forty years old into the theater unless they're accompanied by a teenager." This New York underground movie made almost entirely of photographed stills, is an accurate and light-hearted look at the oh-so self-consciously hip SoHo scene. Morgan delves into all the topics of 1960s conversation—police, advertising, sex, pop music, and cinema. Morgan makes the observation that in the underground film movement "all the action takes place behind the camera."

p,d&w, Robert Downey; ph, Stan Warnow; m, Tom O'Horgan; ed, Fred Von Bernewitz, Robert Soukis.

Drama   **(PR: C-O   MPAA:NR)**

CHAIN GANG*½
(1950) 70m COL bw
Douglas Kennedy (Cliff Roberts), Marjorie Lord (Rita McKelvey), Emory Parnell (Capt. Duncan), William Phillips (Snead), Thurston Hall (John McKelvey), Harry Cheshire ("Pop" O'Donnell), Don Harvey (Langley), William G. Lechner (Eddie), George Eldredge (Adams), William Tannen (Harry Cleaver), Frank Wilcox (Lloyd Killgallen), Rusty Wescoatt (Yates), George Robotham (Reagan), Dorothy Vaughan (Mrs. Briggs), William Fawcett (Zeke).

Uneventful prison melodrama that follows an undercover reporter as he gathers story material on chain gang brutality. The only excitement comes when his cover is blown and he narrowly escapes a shower of bullets and a pack of guard dogs.

p, Sam Katzman; d, Lew Landers; w, Howard J. Green; ph, Ira H. Morgan; ed, Aaron Stell.

Crime Drama   **(PR:C   MPAA:NR)**

CHAIN LIGHTNING***
(1950) 94m WB bw
Humphry Bogart (Matt Brennan), Eleanor Parker (Jo Holloway), Raymond Massey (Leland Willis), Richard Whorf (Carl Troxall), James Brown (Maj. Hinkle), Roy Roberts (Gen. Hewitt), Morris Ankrum (Bostwick), Fay Baker (Mrs. Willis), Fred Sherman (Jeb Farley).

Bogart is a bomber pilot in 1943. He's in love with Parker, a Red Cross worker in Europe. Their relationship is broken when he's ordered back to the States once he's finished his requisite number of missions. A couple of years later, Bogie is now a free-lance pilot with Brown and they attend a party tossed by Massey, whose secretary is, of course, Parker. The flame of love is rekindled and Bogart is hired as a test pilot by Massey's firm. Whorf has designed a new plane for Massey, who wants to have it tested right away. Whorf is against it until certain safety precautions are refined. Massey offers Bogart thirty thousand dollars if he will pilot the jet in a trip from Alaska to Washington, D.C. in a bold attempt at getting publicity for the plane so a government contract might be secured. The flight is a success. Whorf attempts to rig a better safety device and is killed. Bogart is depressed by Whorf's death and blames himself. He takes up a jet equipped with Whorf's as-yet-untried escape device, ejects himself from the cockpit and lands safely. The plane is a hit, Bogart nabs Parker, and the film ends joyously. Excellent special effects and fine model plane work highlight this fairly fast-paced film. Bogart doesn't get much of a chance to shine, nor does Parker. Whorf is particularly good as the idealistic airplane designer, and Massey is, as ususal, his malevolent self. Baker, Massey's wife in the film, had a brief career in films and TV before settling down to be the wife of screenwriter Arthur Weiss (FLIPPER, etc.). Her father, Dr. Abraham Schwager, was one of America's foremost eye doctors through the first half of the twentieth century.

p, Anthony Veiller; d, Stuart Heisler; w, Liam O'Brien, Vincent Evans (based on a story by J. Redmond Prior); ph, Ernest Haller; ed, Thomas Reilly; art d, Leo K. Kuter; set d, William Wallace; cos, Leah Rhodes; spec eff, William McGann, Harry Barndollar; m/l, "Bless 'Em All," J. Hughes, Frank Lake, Al Stillman.

Drama   **(PR:A   MPAA:NR)**

CHAIN OF CIRCUMSTANCE*
(1951) 68m COL bw
Richard Grayson (Tom Dawson), Margaret Field (Dell Dawson), Marta Mitrovich (Evie Carpenter), Harold J. Kennedy (Marvin), Helen Wallace (Emily Greer), Connie Gilchrist (Mrs. Mullins), Larry Dobkin (Dr. Callen), Sumner Getchell (Fred Martindale), James Griffith (Sid), Oliver Blake (Traeger), Percy Helton (Fogel), Douglas Fowley (Lt. Fenning), Carleton Young (Lt. Sands).

A snappy tearjerker based on a magazine article. In 68 minutes this one manages to squeeze in the loss of a baby, an adoption, a friend's suicide, and an accusation of theft. A last-minute witness turns up to save the lead pair, a young husband and wife.

p, Wallace MacDonald; d, Will Jason; w, David Lang (based on an article in True Story Magazine); ph, Philip Tannura; ed, Aaron Stell.

Drama   **(PR:A   MPAA:NR)**

CHAIN OF EVENTS*½
(1958, Brit.) 62m Beaconsfield/BL bw
Dermot Walsh (Quinn), Susan Shaw (Jill), Lisa Gastoni (Simone), Jack Watling (Freddie), Alan Gifford (Lord Fenchurch), Harold Lang (Jimmy Boy), Kenneth Griffith (Clarke), Ballard Berkeley (Stockman), Freddie Mills (Tiny), Cyril Chamberlain, John Stuart, Martin Boddey, Joan Hickson.

To avoid paying his fare on the bus, a bank clerk tells a lie that snowballs into blackmail and death. Adapted from a radio play written by talented British actor Leo McKern, but that's not sufficient reason to sit through this one.

p, Peter Rogers; d, Gerald Thomas; w, Patrick Brawn (based on a radio play "London Story" by Leo McKern); ph, Peter Hennessy.

Crime   **(PR:A-C   MPAA:NR)**

CHAIN OF EVIDENCE*½ (1957) 62m AA bw

Bill Elliott *(Lt. Doyle)*, James Lydon *(Steve Nordstrom)*, Don Haggerty *(Sgt. Duncan)*, Claudia Barrett *(Harriet Owens)*, Tina Carver *(Claire Ramsey)*, Ross Elliot *(Bob Bradfield)*, Meg Randall *(Polly)*, Timothy Carey *(Fowler)*, John Bleifer *(Jake)*, Dabbs Greer *(Dr. Ainsley)*, John Close *(Deputy)*, Hugh Sanders *(Ramsey)*.

A routine murder film with a substandard script has a paroled amnesiac taking the rap for a wealthy adulteress who murdered her spouse. Her scheme is uncovered by a hard-hitting sheriff's lieutenant and the parolee is cleared.

p, Ben Schwalb; d, Paul Landres; w, Elwood Ullman; ph, Harry Neumann; m, Marlin Skiles; ed, Neil Brunnenkent.

Crime (PR:A MPAA:NR)

CHAIN REACTION***

(1980, Aus.) 87m Palm Beach Pictures/Hoyt Distribution c

Steve Bisley *(Larry)*, Arna-Maria Winchester *(Carmel)*, Ross Thompson *(Heinrich)*, Ralph Cotterill *(Gray)*, Patrick Ward *(Oates)*, Laurie Moran *(Police Sgt. McSweeney)*, Richard Moir *(Junior Constable Piggott)*, Hugh Keays-Byrne *(Eagle)*, Michael Long *(Doctor)*, Lorna Lesley *(Waitress)*.

An ultra-fast-paced editing showcase dealing with the nuclear issue, contamination of a plant, and an employee who tries to get the news out to the public. The employee takes refuge at a friend's house only to learn that plant officials are trying to get to him before he can spread the word. Shades of SILKWOOD.

p, David Elfick; d&w, Ian Barry; ph, Russell Boyd (underwater photography by George Greenough); m, Andrew Thomas Wilson; ed, Tim Tim Wellburn; art d, Graham Walker; stunts, Max Aspin.

Adventure (PR:C MPAA:NR)

CHAINED½** (1934) 73m MGM bw

Joan Crawford *(Diane Lovering)*, Clark Gable *(Mike Bradley)*, Otto Kruger *(Richard Field)*, Stuart Erwin *(Johnny)*, Una O'Connor *(Amy)*, Marjorie Gateson *(Mrs. Field)*, Hooper Atchley, Phillips Smalley, Edward Le Saint, Gordon De Main *(S. S. Officials)*, Theresa Maxwell Conover *(Secretary)*, Lee Phelps *(Bartender)*, Ward Bond *(Sailor)*, Grace Hayle, Nora Cecil *(Spinsters)*, Paul Porcasi *(Hotel Manager)*, Chris-Pin Martin *(Peon)*, Sam Flint *(Clerk)*, Keenan Wynn *(Double for Joan Crawford in speedboat sequence)*, Mickey Rooney *(Boy Swimmer)*, Akim Tamiroff *(Ranch Chef)*, George Humbert *(Cafe Manager)*, Gino Corrado *(Waiter)*, Wade Boteler *(Mechanic)*.

Despite the addition of some very high-potency names, CHAINED failed to be anything more than your typical hanky-rattler of the 1930s. Kruger is a wealthy, middle-aged steamship executive. He's unhappily married to Gateson and she won't grant him a divorce to marry his mistress, Crawford. She goes on a sea journey to South America and meets Gable, a wealthy Argentine rancher. There is immediate electricity but Crawford holds back her flood of feelings in favor of her illicit relationship with Kruger. When Crawford returns to New York she learns that Kruger's wife is suing him for divorce and she will now be free to marry him. The wedding takes place. Gable arrives in New York, still mad for Crawford. When they meet again, bells ring and Gable is determined to face up to Kruger and let him know how he and Crawford feel about each other. The scene is set for a grand confrontation. Up until now, Crawford has remained one hundred percent true blue to her husband. The picture fizzles in the final minutes as Gable explains everything to the hapless Kruger, who is a gentleman, understands the passion of youth, and steps aside to let the lovers unite. Crawford gave this picture her all and got fine notices all around, despite a lightweight script. Gable appeared bored by the whole affair and wishing he could get into another film as soon as possible. He went into another unhappy wife story, FORSAKING ALL OTHERS, almost immediately. Kruger had the best moments as the tired businessman. One cinema oddity was the presence of young Keenan Wynn as Crawford's double in the speedboat sequence. He was eighteen years old and it was another eight years before he officially debuted in MGM's FOR ME AND MY GAL.

p, Hunt Stromberg; d, Clarence Brown; w, John Lee Mahin (based on the story by Edgar Selwyn); ph, George Folsey; m, Herbert Stothart; ed, Robert J. Kern; art d, Cedric Gibbons, Alexander Toluboff; cos, Adrian.

Romance (PR:C MPAA:NR)

CHAINED FOR LIFE*½ (1950) 79m Classic Films bw

Violet and Daisy Hilton, Allen Jenkins.

Pretty sick exploitation drama featuring the Hilton sisters—real Siamese twins who had appeared in Tod Browning's FREAKS in 1932—as a set of inseparable twins, one of whom has been charged with murder. The sisters take time out from their predicament to sing and dance a few numbers. The sisters' real life was much more interesting than this movie. They were born in England in 1908 and exploited by their mother, who dragged them to freak shows across America. From there they appeared in a few movies in the 1930s, and were even named as the third party in a divorce suit in which they were found innocent after a sensational trial. By the 1950s they were the owners of a hotel in Pittsburgh, but they eventually went broke and operated a fruit stand in Florida until they died in 1964.

p, George Moscov; d, Harry L. Fraser; w, Nat Tanchuck.

Drama/Mystery Cas. (PR:C MPAA:NR)

CHAINED HEAT zero (1983 U.S./Ger.) 95m Jensen Farley c

Linda Blair *(Carol)*, John Vernon *(Warden Backman)*, Sybil Danning *(Ericka)*, Tamara Dobson *(Dutchess)*, Stella Stevens *(Capt. Taylor)*, Sharon Hughes *(Val)*, Henry Silva *(Lester)*, Edy Williams, Nina Talbot, Michael Callan, Louisa Moritz.

Gross sexploitation film starring Blair as an innocent girl sentenced to serve time in a women's prison run by a sadistic male warden who has a hot tub in his office. Just another excuse for mindless sex and violence.

p, Billy Fine; d, Paul Nicholas; w, Vincent Mongol, Nicholas; ph, Mac Ahlberg; m, Joseph Conlon; ed, Nino di Marco; art d, Bob Ziembicki.

Drama Cas. (PR:O MPAA:R)

CHAIRMAN, THE*** (1969) 104m Fox c

Gregory Peck *(John Hathaway)*, Anne Heywood *(Kay Hanna)*, Arthur Hill *(Shelby)*, Alan Dobie *(Benson)*, Conrad Yama *(The Chairman)*, Zienia Merton *(Ting Ling)*, Ori Levy *(Shertov)*, Eric Young *(Yin)*, Burt Kwouk *(Chang Shou)*, Alan White *(Gardner)*, Keye Luke *(Prof. Soong Li)*, Francisca Tu *(Soong Chu)*, Mai Ling *(Stewardess)*, Janet Key *(First Girl Student)*, Gordon Sterne *(Air Force Sergeant)*, Robert Lee *(Hotel Night Manager)*, Helen Horton *(Susan Wright)*, Keith Bonnard *(Chinese Officer)*, Cecil Cheng *(Soldier, Baggage)*, Laurence Herder *(Russian Guard)*, Simon Cain *(Signals Captain)*, Anthony Chinn *(Chinese Officer)*, Edward Cast *(Audio Room Technician)*.

Sometimes fascinating thriller that purportedly dealt with Red China but was filmed almost exclusively in Buckinghamshire, England, with a brief sojourn in the Far East. Peck is a U.S. spy who is to have a face-to-face meeting with Chairman Mao. Peck's cover story is that he is a bio-scientist interested in what advances are taking place in the field in China. It seems the Chinese have developed an enzyme (invented by Luke—and it's nice to see him as someone other than "Number One Son") that will hasten the growth of food. Peck would like to get further details on this but the Communists want to keep the discovery for themselves. Nevertheless, the scientific community in China welcomes the visit of so distinguished a colleague. They do not know, or even suspect, that Peck has a tiny transmitter embedded in his head that can monitor all conversations. What Peck does not know is that the device contains enough explosive to blow him and anyone in his immediate vicinity to little bits. The enzyme has to do with molecular botany and when inventor Luke mentions that he feels his country is wrong in keeping it from the rest of a starving world, that costs him his life. Peck is then imprisoned but escapes and gets to the border and crosses the electric-fence area with the help of the Russians. The premise is interesting, but it never caught fire and preferred to stay with the credible rather than the fanciful. Look for Kwouk (Clouseau's valet) in a small role.

p, Mort Abrahams; d, J. Lee Thompson; w, Ben Maddow (based on a novel by Jay Richard Kennedy); ph, John Wilcox (Panavision, DeLuxe Color); m, Jerry Goldsmith; ed, Richard Best; art d, Peter Mullins; cos, Anna Duse.

Spy Drama (PR:A-C MPAA:NR)

CHALK GARDEN, THE½** (1964, Brit.) 106m UNIV c

Deborah Kerr *(Madrigal)*, Hayley Mills *(Laurel)*, John Mills *(Maitland)*, Edith Evans *(Mrs. St. Maugham)*, Felix Aylmer *(Judge McWhirrey)*, Elizabeth Sellars *(Olivia)*, Lally Bowers *(Anna)*, Toke Townley *(Shop Clerk)*, Tonie MacMillan *(Mrs. Williams)*.

Hayley Mills was sixteen when this was made and fairly glowed with good health, perhaps too much excitement for this essentially desiccated story. Mills feels she is an unloved child. Her mother, Sellars, has married again and the child lives with her grandmother, Dame Edith Evans, who spends most of her life tending her garden. Into this comes a mysterious governess, Kerr, whom we later learn is fresh out of the slammer for having knocked off her stepsister. Kerr sees that Mills is on her way to becoming a carbon copy of what she was, so she takes the youngster in tow and straightens her out. And that's about it. Enid Bagnold's long-running play had elements which have been removed from this version. The play seemed to have more tension and one never knew what was going to happen next. In the film, everything is painfully predictable. John Mills plays the house butler with a grand touch of dignity, perhaps a bit too much. Kerr is radiant as the governess who takes great pains to unite the child with the mother, over the objections of the haughty grandmother. When this flim was released, it broke records at The Radio City Music Hall and the studio thought they had a huge hit. What the moguls didn't realize was that it opened during a holiday when all the schoolchildren were out. One of your authors was working at Universal at the time and vividly remembers sitting in a screening room, watching this film. The only other person in the room was producer Ross Hunter. When the lights came up, Hunter was crying. He'd only seen the film countless times since the script, through the shooting and editing. Perhaps it's that kind of passionate involvement that makes a producer successful. The movie is old-fashioned in almost every way, but that is a great deal of its charm.

p, Ross Hunter; d, Ronald Neame; w, John Michael Hayes (based on the play by Enid Bagnold); ph, Arthur Ibbetson (Technicolor); m, Malcolm Arnold; ed, Jack Harris; art d, Carmen Dillon; set d, John Jarvis; cos, Julie Harris; makeup, Ernest Gasser.

Drama (PR:A MPAA:NR)

CHALLENGE, THE **½ (1939, Brit.) 76m Film Alliance bw

Robert Douglas *(Edward Whymper)*, Luis Trenker *(Jean-Antoine Carrel)*, Mary Clare *(Carrel's Mother)*, Fred Groves *(Favre)*, Frank Birch *(Rev. Charles Hudson)*, Joan Gardner *(Felicitas, Favre's Daughter)*, Geoffrey Wardwell *(Lord Francis Douglas)*, Norman Caplat *(Hadow)*, Lyonel Watts *(Morris)*, Lawrence Baskcomb *(The Podesta)*, Ralph Truman *(Giordano)*, Reginald Jarman *(Minister Sella)*, Tony Sympson *(Luc Meynet)*, Cyril Smith *(Customs Officer)*, Lloyd Pearson *(Seiler)*, Violet Howard *(Mrs. Seiler)*, Babita Soren *(Mrs. Croz)*, Luis Gerald *(Croz)*, Max Holsboer *(Elder Guide)*, Emeric Albert *(Younger Guide)*, Howard Douglas *(Ropemaker)*, D. J. Williams, Bernard Miles, Tarva Penna *(Peasants)*.

THE CHALLENGE is a race between British adventurers and an Italian government group to see who first scales a treacherous mountain. Intricacies of script development provide thrilling and chilling sequences expertly produced to delight audiences, and some photographic shots of Alpine scenes are impressive.

p, Gunther Stapenhorst; d, Milton Rosmer, Luis Trenker; w, Patrick Kirwan Milton Rosmer (based on a story by Emeric Pressburger); ph, George Perinal, Albert Benitz; m, Allan Gray; ed, E. B. Jarvis.

Adventure (PR:A MPAA:NR)

CHALLENGE, THE★★ (1948) 68m Reliance/Fox bw
Tom Conway (*Bulldog Drummond*), June Vincent (*Vivian Bailey*), Richard Stapley (*Cliff Sonnenberg*), John Newland (*Algy Longworth*), Eily Malyon (*Kitty*), Terry Kilburn (*Seymour*), Stanley Logan (*Inspector McIver*), Leyland Hodgson (*Sgt. Shubeck*), James Fairfax (*Blinky Henderson*), Pat Aherne (*Jerome Roberts*), Oliver Blake (*Arno*), Housely Stevenson (*Capt. Sonnenberg*).

Decent Bulldog Drummond mystery has Conway investigating the murder of sea captain Stevenson by unscrupulous heirs who are after the casket of gold he has hidden. Conway finds the clue to the treasure's location sewn into the sail of a model clipper. The standard denouement has him gathering all the suspects into one room and exposing the culprits. A nicely scripted and entertaining programmer. (See BULLDOG DRUMMOND series, Index.)

p, Ben Pivar, Bernard Small; d, Jean Yarbrough; w, Frank Gruber, Irving Elman (based on an original story by Sapper); ph, George Robinson; ed, Fred Feitshans, Jr.

Crime/Mystery (PR:A MPAA:NR)

CHALLENGE, THE (SEE: IT TAKES A THIEF, 1960, Brit.)

CHALLENGE zero (1974) 84m Cinemation c
Earl Owensby, William T. Hicks, Katheryn Thompson, Johnny Popwell.

Owensby's family is killed by some bad characters, so he goes about taking vengeance with his shotgun. The opening credits hail this as the return of wholesome entertainment, but it's just as blood-spattered as all the other vengeance films. A film to avoid.

p, Earl Owensby; d, Martin Beck; (Technicolor).

Crime (PR:O MPAA:PG)

CHALLENGE, THE★★ (1982) 110m EM c
Scott Glenn (*Rick*), Toshiro Mifune (*Yoshida*), Donna Kei Benz (*Akiko*), Atsuo Nakamura (*Hideo*), Calvin Jung (*Ando*), Clyde Kusatsu (*Go*), Sab Shimada (*Father of Yoshida*), Yoshio Inaba (*Instructor*), Seiji Miyaguchi (*Old Man*), Miiko Taka (*Yoshida's Wife*), Kiyoako Nagai (*Kubo*), Kenta Fukasaku (*Jiro*).

Disappointing East meets West actioner starring Glenn as an American boxer who accidentally becomes involved in a dispute between Japanese brothers Mifune and Nakamura over the possession of family swords. Unfortunately, the script (co-written by John Sayles, who usually is better than this) mires itself in trite observations on the death of the samurai tradition and the rise of the capitalistic gangster in Japan. Overall, there are enough decent moments to make this one worth a look. Similar material is dealt with more solidly in Sydney Pollack's THE YAKUZA (1975), written by Paul Schrader and Robert Towne.

p, Robert L. Rosen, Ron Beckman; d, John Frankenheimer; w, Richard Maxwell, John Sayles; ph, Kozo Okazaki (DeLuxe Color); m, Jerry Goldsmith; ed, John W. Wheeler; prod d, Yoshiyuki Ishida.

Crime Cas. (PR:C MPAA:R)

CHALLENGE FOR ROBIN HOOD, A★½ (1968, Brit.) 85m Fox c
Barrie Ingham (*Robin*), James Hayter (*Friar Tuck*), Leon Greene (*Little John*), Peter Blythe (*Roger de Courtenay*), Gay Hamilton (*Maid Marian*), Jenny Till ("*Lady Marian*"), John Arnatt (*Sheriff of Nottingham*), Eric Flynn (*Alan-a-Dale*), John Gugolka (*Stephen*), Reg Lye (*Much*), William Squire (*Sir John*), Donald Pickering (*Sir Jamyl de Penitone*), Eric Woolfe (*Henry de Courtenay*), Douglas Mitchell (*Will Scarlet*), John Harvey (*Wallace*), John Graham (*Justin*), Arthur Hewlett (*Edwin*), Alfie Bass (*Pie Merchant*), Norman Mitchell (*Dray Driver*).

Poorly-done film recounting the oft-told tale of Robin and his merry band of outsiders. The only notable difference is a concentration on Robin's hated cousin Roger instead of the usual Robin-sheriff rift.

p, Clifford Parkes; d, C. M. Pennington-Richards; w, Peter Bryan; ph, Arthur Grant (DeLuxe Color); m, Gary Hughes; ed, Chris Barnes.

Adventure (PR:A MPAA:NR)

CHALLENGE OF THE RANGE★★ (1949) 56m COL bw
Charles Starrett (*Steve Roper*), Smiley Burnette (*Himself*), Paula Raymond (*Judy Barton*), William Halop (*Reb Watson*), Steve Darrell (*Cal Matson*), Henry Hall (*Jim Barton*), Robert Filmer (*Grat Largo*), George Chesebro (*Lon Collins*), John McKee (*Cowpuncher*), Frank McCarroll (*Dugan*), John Cason (*Spud Henley*), The Sunshine Boys.

In this Durango Kid episode, the Farmer's Association hires cowpoke Starrett to unearth the mysterious gunmen who are terrorizing a small-ranch owner. It is discovered that these gunners are right under his nose as F.A. workers. Film is the western debut of former "Dead End Kid" Billy Halop.

p, Colbert Clark; d, Ray Nazarro; w, Ed Earl Repp; ph, Rex Wimpy; ed, Paul Borofsky; m/l, Smiley Burnette, Allan Roberts, Doris Fisher.

Western (PR:A MPAA:NR)

CHALLENGE THE WILD★ (1954) 69m UA c
George and Sheila Graham, Zimmie-the-Black-Tail-Fawn, Pat McGeehan (*Narration*).

It's harmless enough, but who needs another wilderness documentary which only feeds the ego of its producer/director/writer/photographer/Graham? Film is long on animal shots, which barely save it.

p,d,w&ph, Frank A. Graham (Ansco Color); m, Marlin Skiles, m/l, Skiles, Les Kaufman, George Fisher.

Adventure (PR:AA MPAA:NR)

CHALLENGE TO BE FREE★★ (1976) 88m Garnett c
(AKA: MAD TRAPPER OF THE YUKON)
Mike Mazurki (*Trapper*), Vic Christy, Jimmy Kane, Fritz Ford, Tay Garnett (*Marshal McGee*).

Mazurki is an Alaska fur trapper who lives at peace with nature, sharing his cabin with a lynx and being kind to wolves. Then one day he accidentally shoots a lawman and is forced to flee across the tundra, his life saved time and again by a wolf he has befriended. Produced in 1972, this dismal film marked the sad end of veteran director Garnett's career.

d, Tay Garnett, Ford Beebe.

Adventure Cas. (PR:A MPAA:NR)

CHALLENGE TO LASSIE★★½ (1949) 76m MGM c
Edmund Gwenn (*John Traill*), Donald Crisp ("*Jock*" *Gray*), Geraldine Brooks (*Susan Brown*), Reginald Owen (*Sgt. Davie*), Alan Webb (*James Brown*), Ross Ford (*William Traill*), Henry Stephenson (*Sir Charles Loring*), Alan Napier (*Lord Provost*), Sara Allgood (*Mrs. MacFarland*), Edmond Breon (*Magistrate*), Arthur Shields (*Dr. Lee*), Lumsden Hare (*MacFarland*), Charles Irwin (*Sergeant Major*), Lassie.

Canine hero Lassie, in one of his noblest roles, watches faithfully over his dead master's grave. Protagonist, this time around, is a policeman who overuses his badge and underuses his heart by ordering the collie out of the cemetery. Townsfolk, however, come to the dog's aid. And rightly so! (See LASSIE series, Index.)

p, Robert Sisk; d, Richard Thorpe; w, William Ludwig (based on Eleanor Atkinson's novel *Greyfriars Bobby*); ph,, Charles Schoenbaum (Technicolor); m, Andre Previn; ed, George White; art d, Cedric Gibbons, Eddie Imazu.

Drama (PR:AAA MPAA:NR)

CHALLENGE TO LIVE★ (1964, Jap.) 99m Toho c
(AI TO HONOHO TO)
Tatsuya Mihashi (*Izaki*), Yoko Tsukasa (*Saeko*), Masayuki Mori (*Sawada*), Yumi Shirakawa (*Keiko*).

Mihashi is a veteran of Japan's WW II Manchurian campaigns who finds himself embittered and haunted by his mercy killing of a friend. He enters a hara-kiri pact with his mistress but fails in his attempt while hers succeeds. He begins to drink heavily and takes up with Tsukasa, the daughter of his boss, whose own lover had entered a hara-kiri pact with another woman (mutually successful). She is just as bitter and bored as he is, so he begins absorbing himself in his business. He ignores a doctor's warning that he has contracted tuberculosis in order to travel to Iraq to close a big oil deal and on the loaded tanker heading back home he suffers a hemorrhage of the lungs and dies. Technically competent and artistically thoughtful, the film suffers the same fate as its protagonist; it's boring for a long time and then it just dies. Strictly for fans of stagnant cinema.

p, Masumi Fujimoto; d, Eizo Sugawa; w, Kenato Shindo; ph, Fukuzo Koizumi (Tohoscope, Eastmancolor); m, Masaru Sato; art d, Iwao Akune.

Drama (PR:O MPAA:NR)

CHAMBER OF HORRORS★★ (1941, Brit.) 85m Rialto-Pathe/MON bw
(GB: THE DOOR WITH SEVEN LOCKS)
Leslie Banks (*Dr. Manetta*), Lilli Palmer (*June Lansdowne*), Romilly Lunge (*Dick Martin*), Gina Malo (*Glenda Blake*), David Horne (*Edward Havelock*), Richard Bird (*Inspector Sneed*), Cathleen Nesbitt (*Ann Cody*), J. H. Roberts (*Luis Silva*), Aubrey Mallalieu (*Lord Selford*), Harry Hutchinson (*Bevan Cody*), Ross Landon (*John Selford*), Phil Ray (*Cawler*), R. Montgomery (*Craig*).

Banks, in a big come-down since his glory days with Hitchcock, plays a mad doctor eliminating the heirs to a fortune through an imaginative series of tortures and experiments. Palmer turns up as an unknown claimant to the estate and Banks menaces her until police inspector Bird puts a stop to his fiendish machinations. Banks seems thoroughly uncomfortable as a mad Spanish scientist, but Palmer does as well as could be expected in a low-budget programmer like this. Remade in German in 1962.

p, John Argyle; d, Norman Lee; w, Lee, Argyle, Gilbert Gunn (based on a novel by Edgar Wallace); ph, Desmond Dickinson.

Science Fiction/Horror Cas. (PR:A MPAA:NR)

CHAMBER OF HORRORS★ (1966) 100m WB c
Cesare Danova (*Anthony Draco*), Wilfrid Hyde-White (*Harold Blount*), Laura Devon (*Marie Champlain*), Patrice Wymore (*Vivian*), Suzy Parker (*Barbara Dixon*), Tun Tun (*Senor Pepe de Reyes*), Philip Bourneuf (*Inspector Strudwick*), Jeanette Nolan (*Mrs. Ewing Perryman*), Marie Windsor (*Mme. Corona*), Wayne Rogers (*Sgt. Albertson*), Patrick O'Neal (*Jason Cravette*), Vinton Hayworth (*Judge Randolph*), Richard O'Brien (*Dr. Cobb*), Inger Stratton (*Gloria*), Berry Kroeger (*Chun Sing*), Charles Seel (*Dr. Hopewell*), Ayllene Gibbons (*Barmaid*), Tony Curtis (*Mr. Julian*).

This HOUSE OF WAX ripoff is so unsure of its frightfulness that it has inserted William Castle-style "Fear Flashes" and "Horror Horns" which clue audience in on the "Supreme Fright Points." Originally intended for TV, this gory thriller follows maniac O'Neal as he terrorizes late 19th-century Baltimore with a weapon-fitted wooden stump for a hand. On his trail are two curators of a local wax museum and their Mexican midget sidekick, Tun Tun. Tony Curtis can be spotted in a brief guest role.

p&d, Hy Averback; w, Stephen Kandel (based on a story by Kandel and Ray Russell); ph, Richard Kline (Technicolor); m, William Lava; ed, David Wages; art d, Art Loel; set d, William H. Kuehl; makeup, Gordon Bau.

Horror (PR:O MPAA:NR)

CHAMELEON zero (1978) 90m Rising Sun Prod. c

Bob Glaudini (Chameleon), Kathleen McKay (Woman), Ellen Blake (Girl), Lee Kissman (Friend).

Made for an incredibly low $35,000, this unimpressive film explores the psyche of a drug pusher by showing his relations with his clients, and by verbalizing his own thoughts. Trash.

p&d, John Jost; w, Jost, Bob Glaudini; ph, Jost.

Drama (PR:C MPAA:NR)

CHAMP, THE*** ½ (1931) 85m MGM bw

Wallace Beery (Champ), Jackie Cooper (Dink), Irene Rich (Linda), Roscoe Ates (Sponge), Edward Brophy (Tim), Hale Hamilton (Tony), Jesse Scott (Jonah), Marcia Mae Jones (Mary Lou).

Until THE CHAMP, Beery had been the invariable heavy in several Paramount pictures. Teaming him with the nine-year-old OUR GANG fugitive Cooper was a stroke of genius on director Vidor's part. Beery and Cooper would make two more films together, both winners, THE BOWERY and TREASURE ISLAND. Beery's onscreen personality was almost childlike which worked well with children. He was able to take the simplest device and turn it into something grand or startling or funny. To calm a tearful Cooper in one scene while sitting in a train station, he asks: "Did you ever spit on a hot stove?" He spits and the sizzle excites the boy. They both begin spitting and laughing at the sizzle, a crude but hilarious boy's game. Yet, Beery was no child at marketing his own career. An assistant director once critized the drab shirt he was wearing in a scene, saying it was nondescript. Beery bear-hugged the lad, lifting him to eye level and roared: "You see this face? This is what I want people to look at, not my shirt!" Beery, who began his show business career in the circus, then moved up to playing a *female* maid named Sweedie in several shorts, won an Oscar for his role as a down-at-the-heels ex-heavyweight boxing champion who is training for a comeback in Tijuana when he's not boozing or gambling. He has his son, Cooper, and the thought of getting back into the ring is a long hope rather than a reality (he was actually 46 years of age when the film was made and his face showed the ravages). He wins some money and buys Cooper a race horse which he promptly loses in a crap game. Rich is Cooper's mother and Hamilton her new husband. They convince Beery that the boy would be better off with them and Beery reluctantly agrees. Later, however, Cooper sneaks back to Beery's side as love is thicker than logic. In the final reel, Beery battles a hostile Mexican and is having the stuffing kicked out of him by the younger man. He is saved by the bell a few times and finally reaches back for his last ounce of strength and sends his opponent rocking onto Queer Street. There is no Rocky-like equivalent of Talia Shire at ringside, just Cooper, his lower lip quivering as he watches his dad (no question about it; Cooper had the best lower lip in the business.) Need we tell you that Beery dies in the dressing room in his child's arms after his Herculean effort? Audiences sobbed audibly at almost every performance of this tailored-to-make-you-cry picture. Writer Marion won her second Oscar for the original story of THE CHAMP. Beery tied with Fredric March for his Oscar as Best Actor. Vidor and the picture were also nominated. There are those cynics who pooh-pooh the emotions of THE CHAMP and say it was mawkish, overly sentimental, etc. They probably didn't cry when Bambi's mother died, either. Avoid these people at all costs and see this film when you can. (Remade as THE CLOWN in 1953 and again in 1979.)

p, Harry Rapf; d, King Vidor; w, Leonard Praskins (based on an original story by Frances Marion); ph, Gordon Avil; ed, Hugh Wynn.

Drama (PR:AA MPAA:NR)

CHAMP, THE ** ½ (1979) 121m UA/MGM c

Jon Voight (Billy), Faye Dunaway (Annie), Ricky Schroder (T. J.), Jack Warden (Jackie), Arthur Hill (Mike), Strother Martin (Riley), Joan Blondell (Dolly Kenyon), Mary Jo Catlett (Josie), Elisha Cook (Georgie), Stefan Gierasch (Charlie Goodman), Allan Miller (Whitey), Joe Tornatore (Hesh), Shirlee Kong (Donna Mae), Jeff Blum (Jeffie), Dana Elcar (Hoffmaster), Randall Cobb (Bowers), Christoff St. John (Sonny), Gina Gallego (Cuban Girl), Jody Wilson (Mrs. Riley), Reginal M. Toussaint (Groom), Bob Gordon (TV Reporter), Gene Picchi (Dolly's Trainer), Anne Logan (Horse Owner), Bill Baldwin (Race Track Announcer), Rita Turner, Dorothy Strelsin, Lionel Dozier, Charles W. Camac, David Peden, William Fuller, Vanna Salviati, Maurice Pete Mitchell, Ernesto Morelli, Robert Ray Sutton, Philip Tuersky, Micki Varro, Geoff Marlowe, George Stidham, Willie White, Curtis Jackson, Wally Rose, Dick Young, Sonny Shields, Larry Duran, Lars Hensen, Jeff Temkin, Eddie "El Animal" Lopez, Ralph Gambina.

The original film took 85 minutes, this one 121. The extra length has not improved the story. This time, Voight (who is a more likely boxer than beefy Wallace Beery was) is a racetrack hanger-on in Florida. He's a drunk, a gambler, and dreaming about an Ali-type comeback as son Schroder keeps an eye on him. Ex-wife Dunaway, now a pillar of society, wants to get Schroder back and a bitter custody battle looms. The rest of the film is an updated and very lush version of the grittiness of the original film. Voight and Schroder look so much alike that it is an extra boon for the audience's eyes and makes their relationship that much more believable. Film eventually falls in love with itself and director Zeffirelli gives it a look it doesn't deserve. It's like Ross Hunter producing TOBACCO ROAD. Once again, this remake did not add anything new to the original. Remakes should only be made if they can improve what came before. Good technical work and an Oscar-nominated score by Dave Grusin.

p, Dyson Lovell; d, Franco Zeffirelli; w, Walter Newman (based on a screenplay by Leonard Praskins and a story by Frances Marion); ph, Fred J. Koenekamp (Metrocolor); m, Dave Grusin; ed, Michael J. Sheridan; prod d, Theoni V. Aldredge; cos, Aldredge.

Drama Cas. (PR:AA MPAA:PG)

CHAMP FOR A DAY** ½ (1953) 90m REP bw

Alex Nicol (George Wilson), Audrey Totter (Miss Gormley), Charles Winninger (Pa Karlsen), Hope Emerson (Ma Karlsen), Joseph Wiseman (Dominic Guido), Barry Kelley (Tom Healy), Henry Morgan (Al Muntz), Jesse White (Willie Foltis), Horace McMahon (Sam Benton), Grant Withers (Scotty Cameron), Eddy Waller (Phil), Richard Wessel (Calhoun), Hal Baylor (Soldier Freeman).

Hard-hitter about a Midwest boxer trying to find out who murdered his manager, while he also tries to fight legitimately in the crooked ring. Together with his lady he blows the whistle on the mobsters before the hoods flee with the gate money.

p, d, William A. Seiter; w, Irving Shulman (based on William Fay's story, "The Disappearance of Dolan"); ph, John L. Russell, Jr.; m, R. Dale Butts; ed, Fred Allen.

Crime (PR:A MPAA:NR)

CHAMPAGNE CHARLIE** (1936) 58m Fox bw

Paul Cavanagh (Charlie Cortland), Helen Wood (Linda Craig), Thomas Beck (Todd Hollingsworth), Minna Gombell (Lillian Wayne), Herbert Mundin (Mr. Fipps), Noel Madison (Pedro Gorini), Montagu Love (Ivan Suchine).

Murder aboard ship told in flashback involves the shenanigans of suave gambler and his high-flying girl friend whose dowry will take care of his gambling debts. Plans to blackmail the woman fail and high-roller is himself killed, with his ex-butler figuring as the prime suspect. Fair technical support with standard performances.

p, Edward T. Lowe; d, James Tinling; w, Allen Rivkin; ph, Daniel Clark; m, Samuel Kaylin; ed, Nick De Maggio.

Mystery (PR:A MPAA:NR)

CHAMPAGNE CHARLIE** ½ (1944, Brit.) 105m EAL bw

Tommy Trinder (George Leybourne), Stanley Holloway (The Great Vance), Betty Warren (Dolly), Jean Kent (Dolly), Austin Trevor (The Duke), Peter de Greeff (Lord Petersfield), Leslie Clarke (Fred Saunders), Eddie Phillips (Tom Sayers), Robert Wyndham (Duckworth), Guy Middleton (Tipsy Swell), Drusilla Wills (Dresser), Frederick Piper (Learoyd), Andrea Malandrinos (Gatti), Paul Fonifas (Targetind), Joan Carol (Cora), Billy Shine (Stage Manager), Eric Boon (Clinker), Hazel Court, James Robertson Justice, Aubrey Mallalieu, Kay Kendall, Richard Harrison.

Trinder plays a young comedian who is given a second chance to make good in the big time. He changes his name to George Leybourne (always a catchy moniker in show biz) and eventually becomes one of the top stars of his day, which just goes to show it is all in a name. Direction and production generally effective and drinking songs add liveliness.

p, Michael Balcon; d, Alberto Cavalcanti; w, Austin Melford, Angus Macphail, John Dighton; ph, Wilkie Cooper; md, Ernest Irving.

Comedy/Drama (PR:A MPAA:NR)

CHAMPAGNE FOR BREAKFAST* (1935) 69m COL bw

Mary Carlisle (Edie Reach), Hardie Albright (Bob Bentley), Joan Marsh (Vivian Morton), Lila Lee (Natalie Morton), Sidney Toler (The Judge), Bradley Page (Osborne), Emerson Tracy (Swifty), Adrian Rosley (Vermicelli), Wallis Clark (Reach), Clarence Wilson (Raeburn), Lucien Prival (Bates), Vince Barnett (Bennie), Tammany Young (Tout), Edward Martindel (Morton).

Always-broke racetrack tout shows his true colors when setting up an apartment for his girl friend. Poor technical effort and just plain bad acting. Flat champagne, no bouquet.

d, Melville Brown; w, George Waggner (based on a story by E. Morton Hough); ph, Gilbert Warrenton; ed, Lou Sackin.

Drama (PR:A MPAA:NR)

CHAMPAGNE FOR CAESAR***** (1950) 99m UA bw

Ronald Colman (Beauregard Bottomley), Celeste Holm (Flame O'Neil), Vincent Price (Burnbridge Waters), Barbara Britton (Gwenn Bottomley), Art Linkletter (Happy Hogan), Gabriel Heatter, George Fisher (Announcers), Byron Foulger (Gerald), Ellye Marshall (Frosty), Vici Raaf (Waters' Secretary), Douglas Evans (Radio Announcer), John Eldredge (Executive No. 1) Lyle Talbot (Executive No. 2), George Leigh (Executive No. 3), John Hart (Executive No. 4), Mel Blanc (Caesar), Peter Brocco (Fortune-teller), Brian O'Hara (Buck), Jack Daly (Scratch), Gordon Nelson (Lecturer), Herbert Lytton (Chuck Johnson), George Meader (Mr. Brown).

CHAMPAGNE FOR CAESAR is one of the funniest movies ever made. It did not get the full benefit of a national run when it was released because of financial dealings on the parts of some of the principals involved. It went almost immediately to television where it has been cut to shreds to fit the time limits of that medium. If you're ever fortunate enough to see the complete 99-minute version, be prepared to howl. Everything about the movie is unlikely; the casting, the director, even the story—and yet it works. Colman is an unemployed Ph.D. genius who reads the encyclopedia for enjoyment and who never forgets a thing he has ever read. He applies for work at a soap company owned by Price and is rebuffed when Price goes into one of his 'trances' (Price is hysterical as a self-proclaimed giant in the soap business.) Colman lives with his piano-teacher sister, Britton, in a small Hollywood bungalow court, very similar to the one in DAY OF THE LOCUST and she enjoys listening to host Linkletter's popular radio show sponsored by the soap company. It's a double-or-nothing-type show and contestants take the chance of losing all if they miss. Colman is so annoyed with the treatment received at Price's hands that he is determined to bankrupt the company. Colman applies for a chance to appear on the show and succeeds in answering the first few questions. Meanwhile, Britton has met and is falling in love with Linkletter, something Colman finds extremely distasteful. As the weeks pass, Colman continues to double his winnings. When the company attempts to cut him off, Colman appeals to the audience in the theater as well as to the radio millions and they agree he should be allowed to continue. Colman suspects Linkletter is a spy for Price but he doesn't suspect Holm, who arrives in a nurse's uniform and has been ostensibly hired by a coterie of Colman's fans. The truth is that Holm is a *femme fatale* hired by Price to find out what Colman's weaknesses may be. His stake is in the millions now and in just a few more weeks Colman will own the entire $40 million company, at which time he intends to fire Price. Colman begins to suspect Holm after Britton makes a few comments. To test her, he casually mentions that he never quite mastered Einstein's theory of relativity. The following show, Linkletter asks Colman about that very theory. By now the show is taking place in a huge theater. The audience holds its breath as Colman answers and is told that he's wrong! Price, in the sponsor's booth, dances with his executives and the audience sighs disappointedly. Then the phone rings in the booth. It's Einstein calling from Princeton; Colman is correct! Price faints. It all comes down to the final show, now at the Hollywood Bowl. Business has been incredible for the soap company as the radio program has been the highest-rated in history. Colman is about to play for $40 million or nothing. By this time, he has confronted Holm and she's admitted being in the employ of the villainous Price but all that's over and she really does love him. Tension mounts as Colman takes center stage to the tumultuous applause of the assembled thousands. Linkletter and Britton have already sealed their affection for each other and Colman is satisfied that Linkletter is neutral. Colman must hand his wallet to Linkletter and the question is asked: what is Colman's Social Security number? Ronald scratches his head, offers three numbers, changes his mind, tries another combination, changes his mind again, and finally offers the nine numbers. And he's wrong! The crowd is devastated. Holm, who thought she was going to be very rich, is also stunned and we wonder, for a moment, if she is going to depart. Later, Holm is at Colman's side and we see that she really cares. The two of them get into a new Cadillac convertible and Holm wonders where it came from. As they are driving off to Las Vegas to get married, Colman admits that he had to know if she wanted him for himself or for the money, and so he made a deal with Price; a lot of cash, a job with the company forever, and a whole bunch of perks—all for conveniently forgetting the Social Security number. She reaches back into the rear seat and tosses out his library of books (he always takes books with him to help him fall asleep!) onto the road, then snuggles next to him as they ride off to Nevada and Nirvana. So where does the title come from? Well, Caesar is a parrot (voiced by Mel Blanc) that they found some time ago and the parrot is always asking for champagne. Later we learn that the bird once belonged to Price and that they are old drinking buddies. Since parrots often live over one hundred years, that makes sense. The bird and Price are left to go on happily drinking together. As of this writing, Henry Winkler's film company is attempting to do a remake of the picture. Let's hope they don't screw it up. This was a strange film for Colman to choose after having won the Oscar for A DOUBLE LIFE two years before. He was disappointed in the public's reaction and vowed to be more discriminating in his script selection and the result was that he didn't lens another movie for six years, finally appearing in a cameo role for Mike Todd in AROUND THE WORLD IN EIGHTY DAYS, followed by a brief bit in THE STORY OF MANKIND, his last movie. Holm, who usually plays the long-suffering wife (ALL ABOUT EVE, etc.), is a bit hard to take at first as the seductive Flame O'Neil but we can eventually see how she would appeal to the intellectuality of Colman's character. Actor-writer-director Whorf had his hands full dealing with the subtle underplaying of Colman against the flamboyance of Price, but he managed to mix apples and oranges and the result is wonderful moviemaking.

p, Harry Popkin, George Moskov; d, Richard Whorf; w, Hans Jacoby, Fred Brady; ph, Paul Ivano; m, Dimitri Tiomkin; ed, Hugh Bennett; art d, George Van Martar; set d, Jacques Mapes.

Comedy   Cas.   (PR:AAA   MPAA:NR)

CHAMPAGNE MURDERS, THE** (1968, Fr.) 98m UNIV c (LE SCANDALE)
Anthony Perkins (*Christopher Balling*), Maurice Ronet (*Paul Wagner*), Stephane Audran (*Jacqueline/Lydia*), Yvonne Furneaux (*Christine Balling*), Suzanne Lloyd (*Evelyn Wharton*), Catherine Sola (*Denise*), Christa Lang (*Paula*), Henry Jones (*Mr. Clarke*), George Skaff (*Mr. Ffeifer*), Marie-Ange Agnes (*Michele*), Annie Vidal (*Blonde*).

Perkins is trying to convince his friend Ronet to sell his interest in a champagne company, but Ronet refuses. The women Ronet sleeps with start turning up dead in the morning and eventually it is revealed that Audran, secretary to Perkins' wife, has been committing the murders so that Perkins can take over his wife's fortune. Alfred Hitchcock's influence on Chabrol is evident in every frame of this film, but THE CHAMPAGNE MURDERS is an infuriatingly elliptical movie, ending in the middle of a struggle for the gun wielded by Audran. Shot simultaneously in French and English.

p, Raymond Eger; d, Claude Chabrol; w, Claude Brule, Derek Prouse, Paul Gegauff (based on a story by William Benjamin); ph, Jean Rabier (Techniscope, Technicolor); m, Pierre Jansen; ed, Jacques Gaillard; art d, Rino Mondellini; cos, Maurice Albray.

Crime   (PR:C   MPAA:NR)

CHAMPAGNE WALTZ**½   (1937) 88m PAR bw
Gladys Swarthout (*Elsa Strauss*), Fred MacMurray (*Buzzy Bellew*), Jack Oakie (*Happy Gallagher*), Frank Forest (*Karl Lieberlich*), Benny Baker (*Flip*), Ernest Cossart (*Waiter*), Fritz Leiber (*Franz Strauss*), James Burke (*Mr. Scribner*), Maude Eburne (*Mrs. Scribner*), Vivienne Osborne (*Countess*), Maurice Cass (*Hugo*), Guy Bates Post (*Lumvedder*), Michael Visaroff (*Ivanovitch*), Ferdinand Munier (*Mayor*), Sam Savitsky (*Chief of Police*), Nora Cecil (*Woman*), Emil Hoch (*Chef*), Henry Roquemore, Russ Powells (*Moustaches*), Ralph Fitzsimmons (*Jiggs*), Lillian Castle (*Maggie*), Stanley Price (*Hohann Strauss*), Rudolph Anders (*Franz Joseph*), Nick Lukats (*Young Man*), Irene Bennett (*Girl*), Arthur Stuart Hall, Ralph Brooks, Harry Stafford, Bernard Suss, Tom Curran (*Men*), Henry Manna (*Heinrich*), Alex Pollard (*Waiter*), Tony Merlo (*Headwaiter*), Raymond Brown (*Commissionaire*), Martha Bamattre, Alex Woloshin (*Peasants*), Harold Nelson (*Driver*), Herman Bing (*Max Snellinek*), Veloz & Yolanda.

Swing meets Strauss when MacMurray and his jazz band invade Vienna and the whole

town goes jazz mad. While the Strauss family fights this unorthodox competition, love interest is planted between the brassy MacMurray and Leiber's darling daughter, Swarthout. The contest is basically 'serious' music versus the popular kind and is climaxed by an elaborate production number featuring both forms, with neither emerging particularly well. Dances staged by LeRoy Prinz add some backbone to a sluggish production whose timing is a little off. Songs: "The Blue Danube" (Johann Strauss), "Champagne Waltz" (Milton Drake, Ben Oakland, Con Conrad), "Could I Be In Love?" (Leo Robin, William Daly), "The Merry-Go-Round" (Ann Ronnell), "Paradise In Waltz Time" (Sam Coslow, Frederick Hollander), "When Is A Kiss Not A Kiss?" (Ralph Freed, Burton Lane).

p, Harlan Thompson; d, A. Edward Sutherland; w, Don Hartman, Frank Butler; ph, William Mellor; ed, Paul Weatherwax; ch, LeRoy Prinz.

Musical   (PR:AAA   MPAA:NR)

CHAMPION*****   (1949) 99m Screen Plays/UA bw
Kirk Douglas (*Midge Kelly*), Marilyn Maxwell (*Grace Diamond*), Arthur Kennedy (*Connie Kelly*), Paul Stewart (*Tommy Haley*), Ruth Roman (*Emma Bryce*), Lola Albright (*Mrs. Harris*), Luis Van Rooten (*Jerome Harris*), John Day (*Johnny Dunne*), Harry Shannon (*Lew Bryce*).

Douglas is positively riveting as Midge Kelly, a product of poverty who has staked his all after WW II to buy, with his crippled brother Kennedy, a small diner on the California coast. To save money, the brothers travel west by boxcar but are jumped by a gang of vicious hoboes who beat them up and throw them from the moving train. Undaunted, they take to the highway, utilizing the power of the thumb, and are picked up by Day, a promising prizefighter who is in the money, driving a new convertible and in the company of a flashy, sexy blonde, Maxwell, who refuses to give the bumming brothers a kind word (the way she flares her nostrils in their direction indicates that she doesn't like the smell of them, either). Kennedy tells Day that his brother is quite an amateur boxer himself and, by the time the brothers are dropped off in Kansas City, Day has encouraged Douglas to go into the ring. He is reluctant but after he and Kennedy realize they don't have the price of another meal, Douglas agrees to go some rounds in a club fight; he is badly beaten but earns a few dollars, most of his pay siphoned off by the local promoter for so-called "expenses." Yet he's happy; he and Kennedy can now get to California. Before they hit the road, savvy manager Stewart offers Douglas a chance to become a professional fighter under his guidance. Douglas laughs at him and tells him he's a businessman and has no time for boxing. But when he and Kennedy arrive at the oceanside cafe they learn they have been hoodwinked by Douglas' Navy pal; the friend owned no interest in the small roadside diner. However, the real owner, Shannon, offers the brothers jobs to cover room and board and walkabout money. Douglas stays mostly because of interest in the owner's sultry, raven-haired daughter, Roman, whom he seduces and then later marries in a shotgun-like ceremony at the hands of the indignant Shannon. In anger, and refusing to listen to Kennedy who urges him to stay with his wife, Douglas leaves for Los Angeles where he looks up Stewart and begins a professional boxing career. He learns every trick in the boxing bag, as well as developing a natural ability, sending one opponent after another to the canvas until he is a ranking middleweight. Finally he is set to fight Day in a much-heralded battle, but crime syndicate members contact Stewart and order him to have his fighter take a dive. It appears that he'll do just that when he gets into the ring. Douglas spots Maxwell at ringside and smiles at her. She turns away, a look of disgust on her face. Rage swells inside Douglas and he attacks Day with a vengeance, beating him unconscious. He pays for this double-cross when he and Stewart are later beaten senseless by a platoon of goons. Yet Douglas is still a power to be reckoned with and Maxwell, sniffing success as always, becomes his mistress, influencing the mob to reinstate the boxer. He becomes the tool of fight manipulator Van Rooten, and also champ, but first dumps Stewart, at the mob's orders, discarding the man who created him as a fighter. Douglas is now thoroughly corrupted and takes what he pleases, including Albright, who is Van Rooten's wife. The promoter shows his wife that Douglas is a rotter through and through by offering him a large amount of money to forget Albright. This he does, right in front of his paramour. Holding the package of money, Douglas shrugs in her direction, smiling wickedly and saying to the shocked woman: "You're his wife." When Douglas learns that Roman is about to divorce him and marry his brother, he entices Kennedy and Roman to help him through a difficult training period. He is going to fight his last match and needs them, he begs. He even persuades Stewart to come back as his manager. The big match arrives with Day the opponent, seeking to regain his reputation from the man he ironically encouraged to become a fighter. Just before the big fight, Kennedy learns that Douglas has seduced Roman and then sent her away. The crippled Kennedy attacks his brother. "You stink with corruption!" he shouts in the dressing room, and brings his cane down on Douglas' head. The champion batters his brother unconscious, then marches into the ring. This time Day begins to carry the fight, beating the sloppily trained Douglas in every round until he is a pulpy, bloody wreck, his face so battered that it is distorted like that of an ugly gargoyle. He is knocked down repeatedly. On the canvas he hears a ring announcer tell radio listeners that the champion is "through, he's finished, all washed up." The berserk rage that has always possessed Douglas through his battles suddenly returns and he makes a Herculean effort to rise and maniacally turn on Day, battering him with inhuman punches until he wins the fight. But in the dressing room later Douglas loses his senses, slams the metal locker, breaks his hand, and holds it out like a small child to manager Stewart. "I can beat 'em," he cries, "the fat bellies with their stinking cigars!" He then collapses, dead. Reporters gather outside the dressing room to learn of his death, beseeching Stewart to give them the real story. Stewart is about to tell all, reveal the true nature of the boxer, but brother Kennedy stops him, preserving the upstanding gladiatorial image by lying: "He was a champion, and he went out like a champion. He was a credit to the fight game to the very end." CHAMPION was a tour de force for Douglas; he played the Ring Lardner anti-hero just as the sports writer had envisioned him—ruthless, merciless, sadistic, and cunning, a man whose inward self was so fierce that he would destroy anything or anyone who stood in the path of his ambition, lust, or whim. It is a shocking and unforgettable portrayal that ranks with

BODY AND SOUL as one of the great boxing (or anti-boxing) films. Kennedy is also superb as the trusting, loving brother, and Stewart is fascinating as a manager who "cannot resist a good middleweight." Roman, in one of her early roles, is captivating and utterly stunning as the victimized wife, while Maxwell and Albright turn in sizzling roles as the ringside and society tramps. Robson's direction is all action and wastes no time in telling this compelling story while Foreman's excellent script captures truly and wholly the idiom and atmosphere of the game, as well as indicting its cruelty and corruption. Planer's sharply contrasting lensing is spellbinding and does visual justice to the classic story. Stanley Kramer, oddly enough, had a hard time making this film. He was just beginning his career in movies and though he had developed a powerful story (told in flashback) with Foreman (they would do many films together), and signed his director, Robson, who had been directing solid films for five years (HOME OF THE BRAVE, BEDLAM, ROUGHSHOD) yet he had no star. He approached Douglas, who was at a turning point in his career. The actor, though promised a meaty role in MGM's THE GREAT SINNER with Gregory Peck and Ava Gardner, wanted to accelerate a lagging Hollywood career. When he read the script and got Kramer's promise of top billing, Douglas took the role of the hateful and unsympathetic boxer. It was a risky undertaking with a relatively unknown independent producer but it proved to be one of Douglas's wisest decisions. CHAMPION made him an overnight sensation, a great movie star, and earned him an Oscar nomination (he lost to Broderick Crawford in ALL THE KING'S MEN).

p, Stanley Kramer; d, Mark Robson; w, Carl Foreman (adapted from the story by Ring Lardner); ph, Franz Planer; m, Dimitri Tiomkin; ed, Harry Gerstad; song, "Never Be It Said," Tiomkin, Goldie Goldmark.

Sports Drama   **Cas.**   **(PR:C MPAA:NR)**

CHAN IS MISSING ★★★   (1982) 80m New Yorker bw
Wood Moy (Jo), Marc Hayashi (Steve), Laureen Chew (Amy), Judi Nihei (Lawyer), Peter Wang (Henry the Cook), Presco Tabios (Presco), Frankie Alarcon (Frankie), Ellen Yeung (Mrs. Chan), Emily Yamasaki (Jenny), George Woo (George), Virginia Cerenio (Jenny's Friend), Roy Chan (Mr. Lee), Leung Pui Chee (Mr. Fong).

Moy and Hayashi are a pair of cab drivers in San Francisco who have their $4,000 savings stolen by the elusive Chan Hung, whom they spend the rest of the film tracking down. A fine, funny independent production filmed in San Francisco's Chinatown on a miniscule budget, it became a major art house success.

p&d, Wayne Wang; w, Wang, Isaac Cronin, Terrel Seltzer; ph, Michael Chin; m, Robert Kikuchi; ed, Wang.

Crime   **(PR:C MPAA:NR)**

CHANCE AT HEAVEN ★★   (1933) 71m RKO bw
Joel McCrea (Blacky Gorman), Ginger Rogers (Marje Harris), Marian Nixon (Glory Franklyn), Andy Devine (Al), Virginia Hammond (Mrs. Franklyn), Lucien Littlefield (Mr. Harris), Ann Shoemaker (Mrs. Harris), George Meeker (Sid Larrick), Herman Bing (Chauffeur), Betty Furness (Betty), Harry Bowen (First Reporter), Helen Freeman, Thelma Hardwick, Alden Chase, Robert McWade.

A rather tedious film that tries hard to be a charmer but instead is too long. Gas station attendant McCrea falls for and weds a rich society girl who one day pulls in for service on her car. Leaving his sweetheart Rogers behind, he drives off with the rich dame to the big city. Through the scheming of the deb's mother, the marriage runs out of gas, sending McCrea back to his faithful puppy of a girl friend.

d, William Seiter; w, Julian Josephson, Sarah Y. Mason (based on a story by Vina Delmar); ph, Nick Musuraca; ed, James B. Morley; md, Max Steiner; art d, Van Nest Polglase, Perry Ferguson.

Drama   **(PR:A MPAA:NR)**

CHANCE MEETING ★★★   (1954, Brit.) 96m Group Films/GFD bw
    (GB: THE YOUNG LOVERS)
Odile Versois (Anna Szobeck), David Knight (Ted Hutchens), Joseph Tomelty (Moffatt), David Kossoff (Geza Szobeck), Paul Carpenter (Gregg Pearson), Theodore Bikel (Joseph), Jill Adams (Judy), John McClaren (Col. Margetson), Betty Marsden (Mrs. Forrester), Peter Illing (Dr. Weissbrod), Peter Dyneley (Regan).

Knight is a State Department employee stationed in London who is accused of being a traitor when he falls in love with Versois, the daughter of an Iron Curtain minister. Good Cold War romance that won the British Film Academy Award for best screenplay in 1954.

p, Anthony Havelock-Allan; d, Anthony Asquith; w, Robin Estridge (based on a story by George Tabori); ph, Jack Asher.

Drama   **(PR:A MPAA:NR)**

CHANCE MEETING ★★½   (1960, Brit.) 95m Sydney Box-Rank-Independent Artists/PAR bw
    (GB: BLIND DATE)
Hardy Kruger (Jan Van Rooyen), Stanley Baker (Inspector Morgan), Micheline Presle (Jacqueline Cousteau), Robert Flemyng (Sir Brian Lewis), Gordon Jackson (Police Sergeant), John Van Eyssen (Westover), Jack MacGowran (Postman), George Roubicek (Police Constable), Redmond Phillips (Police Doctor), Shirley Davien (Girl on Bus), Lee Montague (Sgt. Farrow), Christina Lubicz (The Real Jacqueline Cousteau).

Kruger is a Dutch painter who is framed for the murder of his mistress whose body was found in his cottage in this taut thriller. As the mystery unravels, the insightful detective, Baker, finds that not only was the deceased Kruger's mistress, but she also was the concubine of an important diplomat. Baker becomes convinced of Kruger's innocence, and proves himself correct when he discovers that the diplomat's jealous wife committed the crime. Baker is outstanding as the tough, somewhat eccentric inspector who is determined to catch the killer. The film does suffer somewhat from an overly complicated flashback structure.

p, Davis Deutsch; d, Joseph Losey; w, Ben Barzman, Millard Lampell (based on the

novel by Leigh Howard); ph, Christopher Challis; m, Richard Bennett; ed, Reginald Mills; prod d, Richard MacDonald; art d, Harry Pottle, Edward Carrick; md, Malcolm Arnold; cos, Morris Angel.

Mystery   **(PR:C MPAA:NR)**

CHANCE OF A LIFETIME, THE ★★½   (1943) 66m COL bw
Chester Morris (Boston Blackie), Erik Rolf (Dooley Watson), Jeanne Bates (Mary Watson), Richard Lane (Inspector Farraday), George E. Stone (The Runt), Lloyd Corrigan (Arthur Manleder), Walter Sande (Matthews), Douglas Fowley (Nails Blanton), Cy Kendall (Jumbo Madigan), Larry Joe Olson (Johnny Watson), Sally Cairns (Richie Adair), Trevor Bardette (Manny Vogel), Harry Semels (Egypt Hines), Arthur Hunnicutt (Tex).

Morris does his usual competent job as Boston Blackie, this time sponsoring the parole of a handful of cons so they can go to work in a war plant. One of the cons is Rolf, who served time for a $60,000 stickup in which his two confederates escaped. Action moves swiftly as everyone tries to get their hands on the loot. Everything winds up in fine style and sets the stage for the next adventure of the reformed crook. (See BOSTON BLACKIE series, Index.)

p, Wallace MacDonald; d, William Castle; w, Paul Yawitz; ph, Ernest Miller; ed, Jerome Thoms.

Crime/Mystery   **(PR:A MPAA:NR)**

CHANCE OF A LIFETIME zero   (1950, Brit.) 89m BL/Pilgrim bw
Basil Radford (Dickinson), Niall MacGinnis (Baxter), Bernard Miles (Stevens), Julien Mitchell (Morris), Kenneth More (Adam), Geoffrey Keen (Bolger), Josephine Wilson (Miss Cooper), John Harvey (Bland), Russell Waters (Palmer), Patrick Troughton (Kettle), Hattie Jacques (Alice), Amy Veness (Lady Dysart), Compton Mackenzie (Sir Robert Dysart), Peter Jones (Xenobian), Eric Pohlmann, Gordon McLeod, Alistair Hunter, Nigel Fitzgerald.

This unappealing antiworker story tells about a group of workers who are allowed to take over a plough factory. They soon find that they cannot manage the affairs within the assistance of their bosses. Film was aided by the British government after rejection from a number of major companies, not because of prejudice but obviously because it was poor.

p, Bernard Miles, John Palmer; d, Miles, Alan Osbiston; w, Miles, Walter Greenwood; ph, Eric Cross; ed, Alan Osbiston, Peter Price.

Drama   **(PR:A MPAA:NR)**

CHANCE OF A NIGHT-TIME, THE ★   (1931, Brit.) 70m British and Dominions bw
Ralph Lynn (Henry), Winifred Shotter (Pauline Gay), Kenneth Kove (Swithin), Sunday Wilshin (Stella), Robert English (Gen. Rackham), Dino Galvani (Boris Bolero).

Essentially a one-man picture, with Lynn cast as a sap lawyer unable to go to his girl friend's birthday party because of a professional engagement. Problems arise when the birthday girl later discovers the barrister not so professionally engaged in the arms of another woman. Lynn clowns his way through the picture at a good pace, but there's nothing much here and it's no celebration for the audience.

p, Herbert Wilcox; d, Wilcox, Ralph Lynn; w, W.P. Lipscomb (based on a play "The Dippers" by Ben Travers).

Drama   **(PR:A MPAA:NR)**

CHANCES ★★★   (1931) 72m FN bw
Douglas Fairbanks, Jr. (Jack Ingleside), Anthony Bushell (Tom Ingleside), Mary Forbes (Mrs. Ingleside), Rose Hobart (Molly Prescott), Holmes Herbert (Maj. Bradford), Tyrrell Davis (Archie), Florence Britton (Sylvia), Jeanne Fenwick, Robert Bennett.

This wartime romance has Douglas Fairbanks, Jr. (in one of his finest performances) vying with his brother, Bushell, over the heart and hand of Prescott. Same old story of two boys in love with the same girl but director Dwan has sprinkled it with enough sidelights and some eyefilling war glimpses to make it hold. The acting is excellent throughout and story is enhanced by Young's fine adaptation and Dwan's sensitive direction.

d, Allan Dwan; w, Waldemar Young (based on an A. Hamilton Gibbs story); ph, Ernest Haller; ed, Ray Curtiss.

Drama   **(PR:A MPAA:NR)**

CHANDLER ★½   (1971) 85m MGM c
Warren Oates (Chandler), Leslie Caron (Katherine), Alex Dreier (Carmady), Gloria Grahame (Selma), Lal Baum (Thug), Mitchell Ryan (Chuck), Scatman Crothers (Smoke), Royal Dano (Sal Sachese), Walter Burke (Zeno), Richard Loo (Leo), Marianne McAndrew (Angel Carter), Charles McGraw (Bernie Oakman), Gordon Pinsent (Melchior), John Mitchum (Rudy), James Sikking (Bogardy), Ray Kellog (Captain of Security Guard).

Disappointing crime story with a wonderful lead pairing casts Oates as a private eye shadowing Caron in order to trap a mob boss. Scripting and direction are less than inspiring in this mediocre debut by Magwood. Producer Laughlin was Caron's husband.

p, Michael S. Laughlin; d, Paul Magwood; w, John Sacret Young (based on a story by Magwood) ph, Alan Stensvold (Metrocolor); m, George Romanis; ed, Richard Harris, William B. Gullick; art d, Lawrence G. Paull.

Crime Drama   **(PR:A MPAA:GP)**

CHANDU THE MAGICIAN ★★½   (1932) 72m Fox bw
Edmund Lowe (Chandu), Irene Ware (Princess Nadji), Bela Lugosi (Roxor), Herbert Mundin (Albert Miggles), Henry B. Walthall (Robert Regent), Weldon Heyburn (Abdullah), Virginia Hammond (Dorothy), June Viasek (Betty Lou), Nestor Aber (Bobby).

Wild-eyed, turbaned Lugosi once again holds an inventor captive while he tries to find out the secret of a death ray machine designed to (what else?) wipe out civilization. This is a filmed version of an old radio adventure series and since neither Lowe nor Lugosi is killed off in the end one could safely assume Fox had some hopes of continuing the serial's success on the screen. The film was not warmly received at the time of its release because the acting styles of Lowe in the title role and Lugosi as the villain were so different. Lowe underacted while Lugosi gave one of his celebrated melodramatic performances, leading one critic to comment that that seemed to be in different films. Just the sort of thing that would make the picture high camp now. Sol Lesser, an independent producer, obtained the rights to the character and instituted a serial, THE RETURN OF CHANDU, in 1934, starring Lugosi, which further confused viewers who had fixed him in the villainous Roxor role. (Moreover, Lugosi's evil Roxor image was preserved in a wax replica after this film in the Motion Picture Museum and Hall of Fame in Hollywood.) Ralph Morgan was originally signed to play the role of the death ray inventor but he was replaced by Walthall early in the production. Lowe got the original CHANDU role because he had been effective as the magician in THE SPIDER in 1931, co-directed by Menzies, co-director and art director for CHANDU THE MAGICIAN. (Menzies' career was spectacular; this multi-talented man was not only the art designer for GONE WITH THE WIND in 1939, but he directed the great sci-fi film THINGS TO COME in 1936.

d, Marcel Varnel, William C. Menzies; w, Phillip Klein, Barry Conners (based on a radio series by Harry A. Earnshaw, Vera M. Oldham, and R.R. Morgan); ph, James Wong Howe; ed, Harold Schuster; art d, Max Parker.

Mystery **(PR:A MPAA:NR)**

CHANEL SOLITAIRE*½ (1981) 120m United Film Distribution c
Marie-France Pisier *(Gabrielle Chanel)*, Timothy Dalton *(Boy Capel)*, Rutger Hauer *(Etienne De Balsan)*, Karen Black *(Emilienne D'Alencon)*, Brigitte Fossey *(Adrienne)*, Leila Frechet *(Coco Chanel as a Child)*, Brenda Vaccaro, Catherine Alcover, Albert Augier, Corine Blue, Lyne Chardonnet, Yvonne Dany, Isabelle Duby, Huguette Faget, David Gabison, Louba Guertchikoff, Philippe Mareuil, Nicole Maurey, Jean-Gabriel Nordmann, Lionel Rocheman, Violetta Sanchez, Jimmy Shuman, Jean Valmont, Louise Vincent, Sylvia Zerbib, Philippe Nicaud, Alexandra Stewart, Catherine Allegret, Helene Vallier, Marie-Helene Daste, Jeremy Child, Yves Brainville, Jean-Marie Proslier, Lambert Wilson, Virginie Ogouz, Humbert Balsan.

They tried this story as a musical for the stage and it flopped. The same thing happened with this movie. Perhaps Coco Chanel's life just isn't what the paying customers want to see. Marie-France Pisier, seen in the expensive gobbler THE OTHER SIDE OF MIDNIGHT, is Coco, a hard-driving, talented bisexual designer who uses her talent and seductiveness to build a fashion empire. The picture moves snail-like through a succession of fashion shows (all very delightful to the eye and historically quite correct) and bedroom scenes, with Coco alternating liaisons between the sexes. Despite his knowledge that she occasionally likes her vice versa, Dalton wishes to marry her, after he dumps his current wife. It doesn't work out as he is erased before the final reel. Hauer, as her other suitor, does a good job and is eventually bedded down by Black, in as scene-stealing a role as she's ever had. Black is one of those actresses who always manage to triumph over the material, no matter how ludicrous it might be. That is never more evident than in this biography. The music is much too melodramatic for what happens on screen and the result is almost laughable. With another script, another director, and surely another editor to snip out the dead spots, this might have been an adequate movie.

p, Larry Spangler; d, George Kaczender; w, Julian More (based on the book by Mme. Claude Delay); ph, Ricardo Aronovich; m, Paul Jabara, Jean Musy; ed, Georges Klotz; art d, Jacques Saulnier; cos, Rosine Delamare.

Biography **Cas.** **(PR:C MPAA:R)**

CHANGE FOR A SOVEREIGN*½ (1937, Brit.) 72m WB/FN bw
Seymour Hicks *(King Hugo)*, Chili Bouchier *(Countess Rita)*, Bruce Lister *(Prince William)*, Violet Farebrother *(Queen Agatha)*, Aubrey Mallalieu *(Baron Breit)*, Ralph Truman *(Archduke Paul)*, Wilfrid Hyde-White *(Charles)*, C. Denier Warren *(Mr. Heller)*, Florence Vie *(Mrs. Heller)*, Daphne Raglan *(Katrina Heller)*.

Hicks plays a Ruritanian king on vacation and the inebriated doppelganger who takes his place in a humorous variation of *The Prisoner of Zenda*. Lightweight comedy isn't bad at all. Hicks was a British stage farceur who became a successful writer and producer on stage and screen and was later knighted for his efforts.

p, Irving Asher; d, Maurice Elvey; w, Seymour Hicks; ph, Basil Emmott.

Comedy **(PR:A MPAA:NR)**

CHANGE OF HABIT*½ (1969) 93m UNIV c
Elvis Presley *(Dr. John Carpenter)*, Mary Tyler Moore *(Sister Michelle)*, Barbara McNair *(Sister Irene)*, Jane Elliot *(Sister Barbara)*, Leora Dana *(Mother Joseph)*, Edward Asner *(Lt. Moretti)*, Robert Emhardt *(The Banker)*, Regis Toomey *(Father Gibbons)*, Doro Merande *(Rose)*, Ruth McDevitt *(Lily)*, Richard Carlson *(Bishop Finley)*, Nefti Millet *(Julio Hernandez)*, Laura Figueroa *(Desiree)*, Lorena Kirk *(Amanda)*, Virginia Vincent *(Miss Parker)*, David Renard *(Colom)*, Ji-Tu Cumbuka *(Hawk)*, Bill Elliott *(Robbie)*, Rodolfo Hoyos *(Mr. Hernandez)*.

This was Elvis Presley's 31st movie and, other than two documentaries, his last and, perhaps, his least. Can you believe Elvis as a very hip doctor running a free clinic in a Puerto Rican neighborhood where the rats are the size of motorcycles? If so, you might like this story of three nurses who come to help out at the clinic but who are really nuns in straight clothing. There's the hint of an attraction between Dr. Presley and speech therapist Moore and even at the film's fadeout we're not certain of her decision—does she give up the cloth for the King? There is a very disturbing sequence in which Moore is shown undressing for bed, an unbalanced teenager lurking in her closet and getting an eyeful. He attacks her in a violent rape attempt scene that is traumatic and distasteful, a blatant move by the producers to inject a sex scene in an otherwise dull and plodding film. Very little comedy and even less music, just two songs for Elvis to sing with a ludicrous rock-'n'-roll mass sequence as the wind-up. This film was made a year before the incredibly successful "Mary Tyler Moore Show" went on CBS. Asner plays a small role as an Italian cop. Perhaps this is where they met. Asner played virtually the same role in FORT APACHE, THE BRONX many years later but his New York accent never improved. It always sounded like it was coming from someone who was born in Kansas City in the late twenties, which he was. Songs: "Change Of Habit," "Let Us Pray" (Ben Weisman, Buddy Kaye), "Rubberneckin'" (Bunny Warren).

p, Joe Connelly; d, William Graham; w, James Lee, Eric Bercovici, S. S. "Paddy" Schweitzer (based on a story by John Joseph, Richard Morris); ph, Russell Metty (Technicolor); m, Billy Goldenberg; ed, Douglas Stewart; art d, Alexander Golitzen; set d, John McCarthy; cos, Helen Colvig.

Drama/Musical **Cas.** **(PR:C-O MPAA:G)**

CHANGE OF HEART** (1934) 76m FOX bw
Janet Gaynor *(Catherine Furness)*, Charles Farrell *(Chris Thring)*, James Dunn *(Mack McGowan)*, Ginger Rogers *(Madge Rountree)*, Beryl Mercer *(Harriet Hawkins)*, Shirley Temple *(Shirley, Girl on Airplane)*, Gustav Von Seyffertitz *(Dr. Kurtzman)*, Fiske O'Hara *(T. P. McGowan)*, Irene Franklin *(Greta Hailstrom)*, Kenneth Thomson *(Howard Jackson)*, Theodore Von Eltz *(Gerald Mockby)*, Drue Leyton *(Mrs. Gerald Mockby)*, Nella Walker *(Mrs. Frieda Mockby)*, Barbara Barondess *(Phyllis Carmichael)*, Jane Darwell *(Mrs. McGowan)*, Mary Carr *(Mrs. Rountree)*, Mischa Auer, Jamiel Hassan *(Greenwich Village Sequence)*, Yolanda Patti *(Waitress)*, Ed Mundin *(Barker)*, Nick (Dick) Foran *(Singer)*, Leonid Kinskey *(Guest)*, Frank Moran *(Moving Man)*, Nell Craig *(Adoption Assistant)*, Lillian Harmer *(Landlady)*, Poppy Wilde, Bess Flowers *(Party Guests)*, William Norton Bailey *(Man in Street)*.

The Janet Gaynor-Charles Farrell team had lost its allure by 1934. This is certainly evident in this tired old story of four friends graduating from college and taking off for the Big Apple to seek their fortunes. Each has his heart set on a different career: Gaynor as a newspaper reporter, Farrell as a lawyer, Dunn as a radio crooner, and Rogers as a stage star. Farrell's movie career did not prove to be as lengthy or lucrative as his business enterprises, which included the formation of the Palm Springs Racquet Club with old movie colony pal Ralph Bellamy. (Farrell's career, which began so spectacularly with Gaynor in the silent classic SEVENTH HEAVEN, ended with a dismal Monogram programmer, THE DEADLY GAME, in 1941; Gaynor went on, abandoned by Darryl Zanuck at Fox after LADIES IN LOVE, 1936; she was put under contract by David O. Selznick who put her into his blockbuster, A STAR IS BORN, 1937, which won for her an Oscar nomination and a deserved nose-thumbing for Zanuck, although she lost to Luise Rainer for THE GOOD EARTH. Gaynor officially retired after THE YOUNG IN HEART, 1938, to marry costume designer Gilbert Adrian and have a son, Robin. She returned to Fox to do BERNADINE in 1957.) In CHANGE OF HEART Shirley Temple is simply listed in the credits as Girl on Airplane. Maybe our star-struck kids rubbed her curly top for luck on their flight to New York. At no point is there any real dramatic conflict, gripping situations, or highlights to change your heart about this sluggish production.

p, Winfield Sheehan; d, John G. Blystone; w, Sonya Levien, James Gleason, Samuel Hoffenstein (based on the novel *Manhattan Love Song* by Kathleen Norris); ph, Hal Mohr; m. Louis De Francesco; ed, James B. Morley; set d, Jack Otterson; cos, Rita Kaufman; m/l, "So What?" Harry Akst.

Romance **(PR:A MPAA:NR)**

CHANGE OF HEART** (1938) 65m FOX bw
Gloria Stuart *(Carol Murdock)*, Michael Whalen *(Anthony Murdock)*, Lyle Talbot *(Phillip Reeves)*, Delmar Watson *(Jimmy Milligan)*, Jane Darwell *(Mrs. Thompson)*.

Workaholic husband won't leave the office, which prompts his wife to walk out and go back to professional modeling. With his marriage on the rocks, Whalen takes up golf and learns how to handle his bad temper from a young caddy who teaches him how to relax. Pleasing performances complement the originality and smooth direction of this film.

p, Sol M. Wurtzel; d, James Tinling; w, Frances Hyland, Albert Ray; ph, Daniel B. Clark; ed, Irene Morra; md, Samuel Kaylin.

Drama **(PR:A MPAA:NR)**

CHANGE OF HEART, 1943 (SEE: HIT PARADE OF 1943)

CHANGE OF HEART, A, 1962 (SEE: TWO AND TWO MAKE SIX, 1962, Brit.)

CHANGE OF MIND*½ (1969) 98m Sagittarius/Cinerama c
Raymond St. Jacques *(David Rowe)*, Susan Oliver *(Margaret Rowe)*, Janet MacLachlan *(Elizabeth Dickson)*, Leslie Nielsen *(Sheriff Webb)*, Donnelly Rhodes *(Roger Morrow)*, David Bailey *(Tommy Benson)*, Andre Womble *(Scupper)*, Clarisse Taylor *(Rose Landis)*, Jack Creley *(Bill Chambers)*, Cosette Lee *(Angela Rowe)*, Larry Reynolds *(Judge Forrest)*, Hope Clarke *(Nancy)*, Rudy Challenger *(Howard Culver)*, Henry Ramer *(Chief Enfield)*, Franz Russell *(Mayor Farrell)*, Joseph Shaw *(Gov. LaTourette)*, Sydney Brown *(Attorney Nash)*, Tony Kamreither *(Dr. Bornear)*, Ron Hartmann *(Dr. Kelman)*, Murray Westgate *(Judge Stanton)*, Guy Sanvido, Chuck Samata, Dan MacDonald, Joseph Wynn *(Reporters)*, Charles Elder *(Mako)*, Horace Bailey *(Moorland)*, Buddy Ferens *(Officer)*, Don Crawford *(Callicot)*, Pat Collins *(Mrs. Robinson)*, Sean Sullivan *(Mr. Robinson)* Vivian Reis *(Gloria)*, Ellen Flood *(Mother)*, Danny McIlravey *(Little Boy)*, Keith Williams *(A Guest)*, Clarence Haynes *(Butler)*.

A liberal race-oriented entry which draws interest mainly from its unique, though implausible, plot. A well-respected white district attorney dying of cancer has his brain successfully transplanted into a black man's skull. He now thinks and acts like the DA, but as a black man he is not accepted by both white and black wives and by his fellow workers. As expected, his now inbred lack of prejudice is put to the test when he defends a white sheriff in the murder of his black mistress. One can expect little from this terribly titled gimmick film. Exceptional soundtrack by Duke Ellington.

p, Seeleg Lester, Richard Wesson; d, Robert Stevens; w, Lester, Wesson; ph, Arthur Ornitz (Eastmancolor); m, Duke Ellington; ed, Donald Ginsberg; art d, Harold Maxfield.

Drama   **(PR:C   MPAA:R)**

CHANGE OF SEASONS, A*
(1980) 102m FOX c

Shirley MacLaine (Karen Evans), Anthony Hopkins (Adam Evans), Bo Derek (Lindsey Rutledge), Michael Brandon (Pete Lachapelle), Marybeth Hurt (Kasey Evans), Ed Winter (Steven Rutledge), Paul Regina (Paul DiLisi), K Callan (Alice Bingham), Rod Colbin (Sam Bingham), Steve Eastin (Lance), Christopher Coffey (Fritz), Albert Carriere (Maitre d'), Billy Beck (Older Man), Blake Harris, Karen Philipp (Young Girls), Paul Bryar (Man at Table), Anita Jodelsohn (Woman at Table), Tim Haldeman (Bartender), Paul Young (Disco DJ), James Jeter (Truck Driver), Stan Wright (Bubba Green), Percy Davis (Bobby Mason), Steve Myers (Charlie), John O'Connor (Basketball Player).

Director Paul Mazursky anticipated this by a decade in BOB AND CAROL AND TED AND ALICE and what may have appeared to be a bold subject gets a dull treatment in the hands of the creative team. MacLaine is the wife of Hopkins, a New England college professor. The incidence of divorce among college professors is very high because they philander so often. Such is the case with Hopkins, who is playing with Derek, fresh from her success in "10" and before her subsequent failures. MacLaine takes Brandon as a lover and the foursome go forth on a skiing vacation to see how this menage-a-quartre can sort itself out. (They had to film this Vermont vacation in Colorado because there was no snow in New England, or so the legend goes.) The rest of the film is as predictable as gas after beans, and just about as interesting. Derek, who was so memorable in "10" because she was a dream and not a reality, falls to earth with a thud here and acts about as well as a fourth lead in a high school's dramatic show. Hurt, as MacLaine's and Hopkins's daughter, steals what there is of the picture to steal. This one lost a bundle and deservedly so. Segal was one of the writers. He mined some of this physical territory before with LOVE STORY, but as no one died in this film there was little to offset the dumbness of the script. Even Mancini's score was wrong and that's rare.

p, Martin Ransohoff; d, Richard Lang; w, Erich Segal, Fred Segal, Ronni Kern (based on a story by Ransohoff, E. Segal); ph, Philip Lathrop (DeLuxe Color); m, Henry Mancini; ed, Don Zimmerman; set d, Bill Kenney; m/l, Alan and Marilyn Bergman.

Romance   **Cas.**   **(PR:C-O   MPAA:R)**

CHANGE PARTNERS*½
(1965, Brit.) 63m Merton Park/AA bw

Zena Walker (Anna Arkwright), Kenneth Cope (Joe Trent), Basil Henson (Ricky Gallen), Anthony Dawson (Ben Arkwright), Jane Barrett (Betty Gallen), Pamela Ann Davey (Jean), Peter Bathurst (McIvor), Josephine Pritchard (Sally Morrison).

Walker is the wife of alcoholic Dawson who persuades her husband's partner to kill him and his own wife. Nothing new here and very little suspense in this sorry programmer.

p, Jack Greenwood; d, Robert Lynn; w, Donal Giltinian.

Crime   **(PR:C   MPAA:NR)**

CHANGELING, THE***
(1980, Can.) 107m Pan-Canadian/Associated Film Distributors c

George C. Scott (John Russell), Trish Van Devere (Claire Norman), Melvin Douglas (Sen. Joe Carmichael), John Colicos (DeWitt), Jean Marsh (Joanna Russell), Barry Morse (Dr. Pemberton), James Douglas (Eugene Carmichael), Madeleine Thornton-Sherwood (Mrs. Norman), Roberta Maxwell (Eva Lingstrom), Berrand Behrens (Prof. Robert Lingstrom), Frances Hyland (Elizabeth Grey), Ruth Springford (Minnie Huxley), Helen Burns (Leah Harmon), Eric Christmas (Albert Harmon), Chris Gampel (Tuttle).

A truly frightening haunted house story which has the ghost of a murdered boy doing the terrorizing. Scott, as a widowed music professor, moves into a historic Seattle mansion only to learn that a noisy spirit is the murdered son of a father trying to collect an inheritance. When the father realizes that he cannot collect the cash until his son is twenty-one, he puts a substitute, or changeling, in his place. Years later, this changeling has grown into a wealthy industrialist, Douglas, who thinks Scott is trying to reveal his past and blackmail him. Scott turns to real-life spouse Van Devere of the local historical society for answers to the spirit's existence. They also have to fend off Douglas's thugs who find their match in the young spirit. An eerie atmosphere with genuinely haunting special effects makes this study of an innocent victim a chilling experience.

p, Joel B. Michaels, Garth H. Drabinsky; d, Peter Medak; w, William Grey, Diana Maddox (based on a story by Russell Hunter); ph, John Coquillon (Panavision); m, Rick Wilkins; ed, Lilla Ledersen; art d, Reuben Freed; set d, Trevor Williams; spec eff, Gene Grigg.

Horror   **Cas.**   **(PR:O   MPAA:R)**

CHANGES*½
(1969) 93m Cinerama c

Kent Lane (Kent), Michele Carey (Julie), Manuela Thiess (Bobbi), Jack Albertson (The Father), Marcia Strassman (Kristine), Bill Kelly (Sammy), Tom Fielding (Roommate), Kenneth Washington (Negro), Kim Weston, Sam Chew, Jr., Doug Dowell, Doug Bell, Buddy Hart, Cindy Mitchum, Monica Petersen, Christopher Hayden, Clarice Gillis, Katherine Victory, Sherry Mitchell, Sammy Vaughn, Grant Conroy, Terry Garr, Sammy Tanner, Jesus Alonzo, Jr., John Moio, Vincent George.

A confused youngster decides to leave the security of home and travel down the Big Sur coastline in an attempt to experience life. A heavy-handed try at "youth poetry" in the form of a road movie, which misses the subtleties of the generation. En route, Lane

meets one girl who kills herself over him, a youth specialist who has trouble dealing with his rejection, and a third girl who nearly gets through to the wanderer. Albertson as the concerned, sympathetic father turns in a convincing performance. Tim Buckley, Judy Collins, and Neil Young perform some songs of the period: "Both Sides Now," "Changes," "Expected To Fly."

p&d, Hall Bartlett; w, Bartlett, Bill E. Kelly, Tracy Butler; ph, Richard Moore (Panavision); ed, Peter Zinner; art d, Jack Poplin; spec eff, George Ross; m/l, Joni Mitchell, Neil Young, Kim Weston.

Drama   **(PR:O   MPAA:M)**

CHANNEL CROSSING**
(1934, Brit.) 67m GAU bw

Matheson Lang (Jacob Van Eeden), Constance Cummings (Marion Slade), Anthony Bushell (Peter Bradley), Dorothy Dickson (Vi Guthrie), Nigel Bruce (Nigel Guthrie), Edmund Gwenn (Trotter), Douglas Jeffries (Dr. Walkley), H. G. Stoker (Captain), Viola Lyel (Singer), Ellen Pollock (Actress), Cyril Smith (Beach), Gerald Barry (Passenger), Hay Plumb (Steward), Wally Patch (Sailor), C. Denier Warren (Purser).

Wealthy financier Lang loses all in the stock market. When his secretary's boy friend learns fake bonds are being used to put over a big deal, he threatens to blackmail the banker. Lang panics and throws the man overboard, only to learn later that his secretary was truly in love with him. The captain organizes a search party, the waterlogged little blackmailer is saved, and Lang, realizing the error of his ways, commits suicide. Attention to detail makes this a better-than-average-film.

p, Angus Macphail, Ian Dalrymple; d, Milton Rosmer; w, W. P. Lipscomb, Cyril Campion (based on a story by Lipscomb, Macphail); ph, Phil Tannura; ed, Daniel Burt.

Mystery   **(PR:A   MPAA:NR)**

CHANT OF JIMMIE BLACKSMITH, THE*
(1980, Aus.) 108m Filmhouse,Australia Party Ltd./New Yorker c

Tommy Lewis (Jimmie Blacksmith), Freddy Reynolds (Mort), Angela Punch (Gilda), Ray Barrett (Constable Farrell), Steve Dodds (Tabidgi), Jack Thompson (Rev Neville), Julie Dawson (Mrs. Neville), Tim Robertson (Healy), Jane Harders (Mrs. Healy), Peter Carroll (McCready), Robyn Nevin (Mrs. McCready), Don Crosby (Mr. Newby), Ruth Cracknell (Mrs. Newby), Elizabeth Alexander (Miss Graf), Marshall Crosby (Peter Newby), Matthew Crosby (Young Newby), Rosie Lilley (Jane Newby), Katie Lilley (Vera Newby), Peter Sumner (Dowie Stead), Ray Meagher (Dud Edmonds), Brian Anderson (Hyberry), Rob Steele (Claude Lewis), Thomas Keneally (Cook), Bryan Brown (Kelly).

An offbeat and brutal film featuring non-actor Lewis as a aborigine who is taken in by a Methodist minister, and raised to read and write and to embrace the ethics and morals of Christianity. Yet he leaves to live in the squalor and depravity of his native villages, getting odd jobs and being generally abused by imperialistic whites. After ostensibly getting a white girl pregnant and marrying her, Lewis is allowed to live in a small house and to work on a farmer's estate. The child is born all white but the aborigine accepts it as his own. Then the white family begins to ostracize Lewis, taking in his wife and child and refusing him pay and food for his work. His resentment boils over into hate and massacre. He and an uncle wait for the white males to leave the estate, then they chop up the white women and children with axes and flee to the outback, lawmen and citizens on their trail. After several more killings both aborigines are killed. The attempt here to show the mistreatment of aborigines in Australia misfires completely; Lewis's background is not fully developed nor do his inexplicable decisions show any logical motivation. The slaughtering of the family at his hands is self-indulgent and bloody violence which dwells almost perversely on gore for its own sake. This is a poorly constructed film with erratic direction and a cretinous script, although Baker's lensing is stunning and sharp. Lewis in the early scenes is personable enough but he never rises to a professional acting level and the rest of the cast limps along in home-movie style. Definitely not for children, or thinking adults, for that matter.

p,d&w, Fred Schepisi (based on the novel by Thomas Keneally); ph, Ian Baker (Panavision, Eastmancolor); m, Bruce Smeaton; ed, Brian Kavanaugh; cos, Bruce Finlayson, Daro Gunzberg.

Drama   **(PR:O   MPAA:NR)**

CHAPMAN REPORT, THE zero
(1962) 125m WB c

Efrem Zimbalist, Jr. (Paul), Shelley Winters (Sarah Garnell), Jane Fonda (Kathleen Barclay), Claire Bloom (Naomi), Glynis Johns (Teresa), Ray Danton (Fred Linden), Ty Hardin (Ed Kraski), Andrew Duggan (Dr. Chapman), John Dehner (Geoffrey), Harold J. Stone (Frank Garnell), Corey Allen (Wash Dillon), Jennifer Howard (Grace Waterton), Cloris Leachman (Miss Selby), Chad Everett (Bob Jensen/Waterboy), Henry Daniell (Dr. Stanley Jonas), Hope Cameron (Ruth), Roy Roberts (Alan Roby), Jack Cassidy (Ted Dyson), Evan Thompson (Cass Kelly), John Baer ("Boy" Barclay), Grady Sutton (Simon), Alex Viespi [Alex Cord] (Bardelli), Pamela Austin.

Based on the Irving Wallace fictionalized study of American housewives' sexual behavior, this episodic and star-studded piece is no more than an evening with the latest issue of "Cosmopolitan." Sampling a cross-section of Los Angeles women, Cukor focuses on Bloom, an alcoholic nymphomaniac; Johns, an unsatisfied intellectual; Winters, an adulteress; and a frigid Fonda. All four are "interviewed" by the very manly Zimbalist who, like Cukor, seems to revel in their portrayal as helpless and sexually abnormal females. Sleazy, smug, and simple-minded.

p, Richard D. Zanuck; d, George Cukor; w, Wyatt Cooper, Don M. Mankiewicz (based on the novel by Irving Wallace); ph, Harold Lipstein (Technicolor); m, Leonard Rosenman; ed, Robert Simpson; art d, Gene Allen; cos, Orry-Kelly.

Drama   **(PR:O   MPAA:NR)**

CHAPPAQUA*
(1967) 92km Rooks/Regional c

Conrad Rooks (Russel), Jean-Louis Barrault (Doctor), William S. Burroughs (Opium Jones), Paula Pritchett (Girl), Allen Ginsberg (Messiah), Ravi Shankar (Sun God),

Ornette Coleman *(Peyote Eater)*, Swami Satchidananda *(The Guru)*, Moondog *(The Prophet)*, Jill Lator *(Sacrificed One)*, John Esam *(The Connection)*, The Fugs, Rita Renoir, Penny Brown, Jacques Seiler, Moustique, Sophie Steboun, Elder Wilder, Peter Orlovsky, Pascal Aubier, France Cremieux, Mr. and Mrs. Rene Serisier, Donovan.

A fragmentary film diary of ex-junkie Rooks where scenes are strung together in a meaningless, stream-of-consciousness manner. Alternating between reality and hallucination, Rooks' life in Paris is paralleled with memories of his childhood in Chappaqua, New York. Film is weak effort of drug-influenced free-association which expectedly has aged. It includes a hypnotic score by sitar player Ravi Shankar.

p,d&w, Conrad Rooks; ph, Robert Frank (Eastmancolor) with Etienne Becker; m, Ravi Shankar; ed, Kenout Peltier; art d, Regis Pagniez.

Biography   **(PR:O MPAA:NR)**

CHAPTER TWO*** (1979) 124m COL c
James Caan *(George Schneider)*, Marsha Mason *(Jennie MacLaine)*, Joseph Bologna *(Leo Schneider)*, Valerie Harper *(Faye Medwick)*, Judy Farrell *(Gwen Michaels)*, Alan Fudge *(Lee Michaels)*, Debra Mooney *(Marilyn)*, Isabel Cooley *(Customs Officer)*, Imogene Bliss *(Elderly Lady)*, Larry Michlin *(Maitre d')*, Ray Young *(Gary)*, George Rondo *(Martin)*, Greg Zadikov, Paul Singh, Sumant *(Waiters)*, Elizabeth Farley *(Actress)*, Sunday Brennan *(Tina)*, Danny Gellis *(Bucky)*, Henry Sutton *(Judge)*, E.D. Miller *(Umpire)*, Howard Jeffrey *(Director)*, Marie Reynolds *(Barbara)*.

To anyone who knows the story of Simon's life, it's obvious that this was drawn from reality. Most of his writing is. His older brother, Danny, is a comedy writer-director of some renown and his relationship with Neil has been seen before in COME BLOW YOUR HORN. Danny was also the model for the character of Felix in THE ODD COUPLE. Bologna plays Danny in this film and it is the most difficult and complex role in the picture but he carries it off with aplomb. Caan is an author whose wife has passed away. He meets Marsha Mason (as Simon did in real life) and tries his best to not fall in love with her; the result of his mourning for the late wife he adored. The movie meanders for more than two hours as it details the comedy and drama of a lost love, then a found one. In the end, Caan and Mason do get together, as Simon and Mason did in real life. What was not seen was the result of that marriage—a divorce. Mason is radiant in her real-life role and it's easy to see how and why the playwright fell in love with her. Bologna, as mentioned before, is superb and so is Harper, as Mason's friend. Harper jettisoned her sit-com mannerisms and showed she could play a serious comedy role on the big screen. The picture falls flat in the casting of Caan. He's been quoted as saying he hated the role and the making of the film. This is evident. Further, the man just isn't a comic actor who can deliver well-honed lines. He should stick to the macho roles and leave light comedy to those who can handle it.

p, Ray Stark; d, Robert Moore; w, Neil Simon (based on his play); ph, David M. Walsh (Metrocolor); m, Marvin Hamlisch; ed, Margaret Booth, Michael Stevenson; art d, Pete Smith; set d, Lee Poll; cos, Vicki Sanchez; m/l, Carole Bayer Sager.

Comedy Cas. **(PR:C MPAA:PG)**

CHARADE** (1953) 83m Portland/Monarch bw
James Mason *(The Murderer, Maj. Linden, Jonah Watson)*, Pamela Mason *(The Artist, Pamela, Baroness Tanslan, Lilly)*, Scott Forbes *(Capt. Stamm)*, Paul Cavanagh *(Col. Heisler)*, Bruce Lester *(Capt. van Buren)*, John Dodsworth *(Lt. Meyerdorf)*, Judy Osborne *(Dotty)*, Sean McClory *(Jack Stuydevant)*, Vince Barnett *(Berg)*.

A somewhat vain anthology film featuring Mr. and Mrs. Mason as the producers, writers, and lead players in three separate episodes of love and violence. "Portrait of a Murderer" sees Pamela Mason as a disillusioned young artist who absentmindedly sketches the face of the man next door, Mason. Unknown to her, the man has murdered her girl friend and he returns to the scene of the crime. He seduces the artist, and she falls in love with him, but then his homicidal instincts overtake him and he strangles her. "Duel at Dawn" sees Mason as an Austrian officer in the 1880s who steals Pamela Mason from another officer, Forbes, who then challenges Mason to a duel, and it appears to all that Forbes will win. Mason manages to beat his opponent and barely prevents Pamela Mason from committing suicide because she believes he has lost the duel. "The Midas Touch" concerns Mason as a hard-working, successful man who has amassed a small fortune in New York but is dissatisfied with his life and abandons his wealth and moves to England to start over. There he takes a job as a valet and falls in love with Pamela Mason, a cockney servant girl. Seeing that she wishes (and deserves) a better life, he brings her to New York and once again manages to make another fortune. Mason himself condemned this nepotistic mess; he was quoted as saying: "I had hoped that this curiosity would be lost without a trace."

p, James Mason; d, Roy Kellino; w, James and Pamela Mason.

Drama **(PR:A MPAA:NR)**

CHARADE**** (1963) 113m UNIV c
Cary Grant *(Peter Joshua)*, Audrey Hepburn *(Regina Lambert)*, Walter Matthau *(Hamilton Bartholomew)*, James Coburn *(Tex Panthollow)*, George Kennedy *(Herman Scobie)*, Ned Glass *(Leopold Gideon)*, Jacques Marin *(Inspector Edouard Grandpierre)*, Paul Bonifas *(Felix)*, Dominique Minot *(Sylvie Gaudet)*, Thomas Chelimsky *(Jean-Louis Gaudet)*.

Charming comedy-thriller with an intelligent Peter Stone screenplay and a pseudo-Hitchcock directorial stint by Donen. Pseudo in the sense that it covers much of the same ground Hitch did; high chases, low-life villains, witty dialog, and an enigmatic plot. Hepburn was never more radiant as the heroine who returns to Paris after what appears to be a chance encounter with Grant in an Alpine resort named Megeve. She learns that her husband has been murdered and that four of his wartime buddies think she knows the location of a quarter of a million dollars in gold. She is stalked by the foursome. Grant comes to Paris and offers to be of assistance, but she doesn't know if he's for real or one of the conspirators. Matthau is Hepburn's informant but she also suspects him and doesn't know where to turn. She continues to learn things about Grant. He is obviously living a charade because he's known variously as Carson Dyle, Alexander Dyle, Adam Canfield, Brian Cruikshank and, finally, Peter Joshua. Matthau

is also known as Carson Dyle as well as Hamilton Bartholomew, so it's easy to see that nothing is as it seems. Kennedy is the heaviest of the heavies and he and Grant come to grips on a rooftop in as exciting a denouement as Hitchcock ever filmed. There are so many turns in this amiable nonsense that to reveal them here would be to do a disservice. Just realize that it's all a great charade and enjoy the twists as they come. With more red herrings than a fish store and a host of murders, one cannot take this seriously, and yet there are enough barbed comments in the script to make us realize that the author was attempting just a hint of a message about violence. The theme song by Mancini and Mercer was a big hit, took an Oscar nomination, and, no doubt, helped the box office of CHARADE.

p&d, Stanley Donen; w, Peter Stone (based on the story "The Unsuspecting Wife" by Marc Behm, Stone); ph, Charles Lang Jr. (Technicolor); m, Henry Mancini; ed, James Clark; art d, Jean dEaubonne; cos, Givenchy (Hepburn's clothes only); m/l, Mancini, Johnny Mercer.

Comedy/Thriller Cas. **(PR:A-C MPAA:NR)**

CHARGE AT FEATHER RIVER, THE**½ (1953) 95m WB c
Guy Madison *(Miles Archer)*, Frank Lovejoy *(Sgt. Baker)*, Helen Westcott *(Ann McKeever)*, Vera Miles *(Jennie McKeever)*, Dick Wesson *(Cullen)*, Onslow Stevens *(Grover Johnson)*, Steve Brodie *(Ryan)*, Ron Hagerthy *(Johnny McKeever)*, Fay Roope *(Lt. Col. Kilrain)*, Neville Brand *(Morgan)*, Henry Kulky *(Smiley)*, Lane Chandler *(Poinsett)*, Fred Carson *(Chief Thunder Hawk)*, James Brown *(Connors)*, Ralph Brooke *(Wilhelm)*, Carl Andre *(Hudkins)*, Ben Corbett *(Carver)*, Fred Kennedy *(Leech)*, Dub Taylor *(Danowicz)*, John Damler *(Dabney)*, David Alpert *(Griffin)*, Louis Tomei *(Curry)*, Wayne Taylor, Steve Wayne, Vivian Mason.

In possibly the best of the 3-D westerns, Madison (TV's Wild Bill Hickok) is out to rescue a pair of women from Indian hands, and simultaneously divert the Indians' attention from railroad construction. The twist comes when Madison finds that one of the women has fallen in love with her Indian captor, adopting redskin ways. Everything wraps up with a battle at the title river. Accented by Max Steiner's moving score.

p, David Weisbart; d, Gordon Douglas; w, James R. Webb; ph, Peverell Marley (3-D in Warner Color); m, Max Steiner; ed, Folmar Blangsted.

Western **(PR:C MPAA:NR)**

CHARGE OF THE LANCERS** (1953) 73m COL c
Paulette Goddard *(Tanya)*, Jean-Pierre Aumont *(Capt. Eric Evoir)*, Richard Stapley *(Maj. Bruce Lindsey)*, Karin Booth *(Maria Sand)*, Charles Irwin *(Tim Daugherty)*, Ben Astar *(Gen. Boris Inderman)*, Lester Matthews *(Gen. Stanhope)*, Gregory Gay *(Cpl. Bonikoff)*, Ivan Triesault *(Dr. Manus)*, Lou Merrill *(Col. Zemansky)*, Tony Roux *(Asa)*, Fernanda Eliscu *(Keta)*, Charles Horvath *(Capt. Michael Garetzo)*.

The Crimean War serves as a backdrop as Goddard and Aumont aid the British in capturing the Russian naval base, Sebastopol. Playing a gypsy, the lovely Goddard and Capt. Aumont get themselves taken prisoner by the Russians to better carry on their spy activities. Standard direction, as expected, from William Castle.

p, Sam Katzman; d, William Castle; w, Robert E. Kent; ph, Harry Freulich (Technicolor); ed, Henry Batista; md, Ross Di Maggio; art d, Paul Palmantola.

Spy Drama **(PR:A MPAA:NR)**

CHARGE OF THE LIGHT BRIGADE, THE***** (1936) 115m WB bw
Errol Flynn *(Maj. Geoffrey Vickers)*, Olivia de Havilland *(Elsa Campbell)*, Patric Knowles *(Capt. Perry Vickers)*, Donald Crisp *(Col. Campbell)*, Henry Stephenson *(Sir Charles Macefield)*, Nigel Bruce *(Sir Benjamin Warrenton)*, David Niven *(Capt. James Randall)*, G. P. Huntley, Jr. *(Maj. Jowett)*, Spring Byington *(Lady Octavia Warrenton)*, C. Henry Gordon *(Surat Khan)*, E. E. Clive *(Sir Humphrey Harcourt)*, Lumsden Hare *(Col. Woodward)*, Robert Barrat *(Count Igor Zvolonoff)*, Walter Holbrook *(Cornet Barclay)*, Charles Sedgwick *(Cornet Pearson)*, J. Carrol Naish *(Subahdar Major Puran Singh)*, Scotty Beckett *(Prema Singh)*, Princess Baigum *(Prema's Mother)*, George Regas *(Wazir)*, Helen Sanborn *(Mrs. Jowett)*, George Sorel *(Surwan)*, Dick Botiller *(Native)*, George David *(Suristani)*, Herbert Evans *(Major Domo)*, Carlos San Martin *(Court Interpreter)*, Phillis Coghlan *(Woman at Ball)*, Jon Kristen *(Panjari)*, Carlyle Moore, Jr. *(Junior Officer)*, Charles Croker King *(Lord Cardigan)*, Brandon Hurst *(Lord Raglan)*, Wilfred Lucas *(Captain)*, Reginald Sheffield *(Bentham)*, Georges Renavent *(Gen. Canrobert)*, Crauford Kent *(Capt. Brown)*, Boyd Irwin *(Gen. Dunbar)*, Gordon Hart *(Col. Coventry)*, Holmes Herbert *(Gen. O'Neill)*, Arthur Thalasso, Jack Curtis, Lal Chand Mehra, Stephen Moritz *(Sepoys)*, R. Singh, Jimmy Aubrey, David Thursby, Denis d'Auborn *(Orderlies)*, Martin Garralaga, Frank Lackteen *(Panjaris)*, Yakima Canutt *(Double for Errol Flynn)*.

For the grand swashbuckler Flynn, this film was "the toughest picture I ever made." It was also one of the finest epics ever put on film and features probably the most dynamic and thrilling action sequence in the history of the medium. Though great pains were taken in producing a film that looked like the period of the 1850s, from exact replicas of uniforms down to the last brass button and even postage stamps of the era, Warner Bros. typically discarded the real facts surrounding the magnificent historic blunder known as THE CHARGE OF THE LIGHT BRIGADE, retaining the pomp of the era and Tennyson's stirring lines. The story begins in northwest India, 1850, where Flynn is a dashing British officer who saves the life of a scheming Indian potentate, Gordon, on a hunting expedition. Gordon's subsidy from the British government has been cut off and he quickly allies himself with the Russians, intending to lead a revolt. Flynn is ordered to buy horses in the mountains of India and his company is attacked by Gordon's tribesmen, but he manages to bring his detachment safely back to British lines. He is then sent with Crisp and troops to the remote fortress of Chukoti, all the while believing that his intended, de Havilland, is going to marry him. His brother, Knowles, however, tells him that he and de Havilland are in love and *they* intend to marry. Flynn does not believe him, thinking him only jealous. A bitter resentment between the brothers ends their once loving friendship. At Chukoti, Crisp receives orders to send most of his troops off on maneuvers to show Gordon that the British fear no attack. This leaves the fort undermanned and Flynn objects. Crisp, with typical British discipline, tells him that orders are orders. With the garrison hopelessly depleted of troops, hordes of Gordon's savage tribesmen attack it, quickly reducing the defenders and driving them into a barracks stronghold. Gordon meets with Flynn under a flag of truce, offering him his life in return for saving his earlier. Flynn refuses, taking back a message from Gordon to commandant Crisp, one that he himself disbelieves. Crisp is to surrender, lay down his arms, and his garrison, wives, and children will be allowed safe passage to another British fort. The British accept the terms. When the bedraggled refugees begin boarding small boats at the riverside, the tribesmen open fire on Gordon's orders. It is a massacre. Flynn manages to save de Havilland, swimming downstream with her. Gordon stops his marksmen from shooting so that Flynn remains alive, thus paying his debt. Flynn alerts a nearby garrison commanded by Bruce and rides back to Chukoti in force. They find Crisp and his command wiped out to the last man, woman, and child. The wives of the British officers, their children, the families of the Sepoys, all have been ruthlessly slaughtered by Gordon's merciless tribesmen. Flynn and the remnants of his unit, the 27th Lancers, vow revenge. This comes when the light cavalry unit is transferred to the Crimea where British troops face the well-entrenched Russian forces on Balaclava Heights. Flynn is now adjutant to Stephenson, one of the commanders of the British army, along with King (Lord Cardigan) and Hurst (Lord Raglan). He receives an order to be written for Stephenson's signature which directs the withdrawal of the Light Brigade, of which the 27th Lancers are a part. Consumed by vengeance—Flynn knows that Gordon is with the Russians—he rewrites Stephenson's order and signs the general's name to it, delivering the order to Bruce. The Light Brigade is to attack. In a last Beau Geste, Flynn saves his brother's life by sending him back with a letter to Stephenson, one in which he confesses his gross disobedience, knowing Knowles will be with de Havilland, who loves him. He and Bruce then lead the magnificent charge of the doomed 600 cavalrymen into the "Valley of Death," their ranks decimated by the Russian artillery as they race forward. But nothing can stop this incredibly heroic charge. Not a trooper turns back. The British fall in whole ranks but the remnants keep moving forward as Barrat, the Russian general, and Gordon stand on Balaclava Heights in shock and awe. Even the counter-attacking Russian cavalry cannot stop the lancers who break through the final barricades, Flynn leading the way. He spots Gordon and raises his lance. Gordon shoots him fatally but Flynn manages to hurl his lance into the evil Kahn's heart. Flynn falls from his horse and watches as rider after rider drives a lance into the body of the mass killer. Flynn dies knowing the Chukoti massacre has been avenged. At headquarters, Stephenson takes full responsibility for ordering the suicidal charge. Alone, he reads Flynn's letter of confession, but rather than hold up this dead hero to shame, the general tosses the letter into a fire, murmuring: "For conspicuous gallantry." THE CHARGE OF THE LIGHT BRIGADE is one of the most action-filled movies ever made, its hectic pace maintained by the driving taskmaster Curtiz. The director and his technicians went to any lengths to create realistic battle scenes and the stunts performed were unparalleled. But the toll was heavy; many extras were hospitalized for injuries and dozens of horses in the fatal charge were killed. Trip wires were used to produce realistic falls by the horses which broke their legs and had to be shot. When these scenes were viewed and "The Running W" trip wires were discovered, tens of thousands of animal lovers became incensed. The Society for the Prevention of Cruelty to Animals, a splintered organization up to that time, was galvanized into a powerful force and roared its disapproval, a voice that was immediately heard. Because of the Society's vociferous complaints, hard film production rules were established where no animals would again be subjected to such inhumane treatment. But in this rigorous film, even humans were mistreated. Flynn, always an energetic actor who loved action and did his own stunts whenever possible, found this to be the hardest film he ever made. He later complained bitterly about Curtiz's treatment of the cast and crew, particularly when they were on location. One mountain area was to pass for the high mountains of northern India shot at Lone Pine, California, Hollywood's traditional "India location" (located near America's highest mountain, Mt. McKinley where the final sequence of HIGH SIERRA were filmed). The air was so cold here that the actors, dressed in paper-thin uniforms that conformed to the hot Indian climate, were chilled to the bone. Flynn remembered it as "a cold, piercing wind . . . [that] blew through you—while the illusion was being given that this was blazing Indian heat. Meantime, the hardboiled Curtiz was bundled in about three topcoats, giving orders . . . . He'd keep us waiting hour after hour sitting on the horses, freezing to death." Curtiz was indifferent to any hazard or inconvenience as long as he got the shots he wanted. His thick Hungarian accent and jumbled English didn't help matters. At one point he shouted through a megaphone: "Bring on the empty horses!" On another occasion during the film he bellowed to hundreds of extras: "Stop standing in bundles!" Warner Bros. entrusted this very expensive film, $1,200,000 (then an all-time high), to its top director and he produced the most magnificent cavalry charge ever put onto celluloid, brutal that it was, assisted ably by second-unit horse action expert B. Reeves "Breezy" Eason. Location sites were carefully chosen, at Lone Pine, a leopard hunt near Lake Sherwood, and a complete fort (Chukoti) was built on Lasky Mesa, near Agoura. The actual charge was filmed near Chatsworth in the San Fernando Valley with additional scenes shot outside of Sonora. Max Steiner did the dynamic score for this film, his first for Warners and one that guaranteed his career being rooted at that studio. This "grand old man of movie music" would score fifteen of Flynn's films, all of them having that deeply resonant sound distinctively Steiner's. (Oddly, he preferred scoring love stories in which Bette Davis appeared.) Flynn appreciated Steiner's scores but resented having Curtiz as his perennial director. Complained the actor: "I was to spend five miserable years with him. In each [film] he tried to make all scenes so realistic that my skin didn't seem to matter. Nothing delighted him more than real bloodshed." But Flynn did have his revenge on the rigid Curtiz, much the same way he nailed the hateful Gordon in THE CHARGE OF THE LIGHT BRIGADE. It was Flynn who viewed the slaughter of the horses via the trip wires and then secretly went to the Society for the Prevention of Cruelty to Animals, smuggling pieces of film showing the charge and samples of the "Running W" trip wires to Society members and demanding they protest. The actor reportedly had a hand in bringing his youthful co-star of CAPTAIN BLOOD into the production of THE CHARGE OF THE LIGHT BRIGADE. At first Warners thought to cast Anita Louise as

Flynn's betrothed, but her commitment to another production, plus Flynn's request for the 21-year-old de Havilland, caused Warner to return Olivia to the swashbuckler's arms and from then on they would be a great love team on the screen. Flynn attempted to carry the romance off the set but he only succeeded in frightening the beautiful young woman. A prankster, Flynn thought he would endear himself to de Havilland through caprice. Though married at the time (to Lili Damita), Flynn later wrote in My Wicked, Wicked Ways that "I was sure that I was in love with her." He displayed this emotion by placing a dead snake in her panties. When she went to put them on before a scene she almost fainted, then broke down and cried. "It slowly penetrated my obtuse mind," Flynn admitted, "that such juvenile pranks weren't the way to any girl's heart." Further, during the escape scene fronm Chukoti, Flynn accidentally knocked de Havilland out with a quick movement of his arm. He held her until she regained consciousness, then asked her how she felt. She looked up at him, then pulled away with one word: "Disgusted." The history of THE CHARGE OF THE LIGHT BRIGADE as a film began with the research of a young reporter, Michel Jacoby, who worked for the New York World. He delved into the historic blunder while assigned to a post in China and diligently put together a story outline based on real events, later submitting the manuscript to Warners, where it gathered dust. No one was interested, even though the subject matter had been covered in a 1912 one-reeler and a nonaction British programmer in 1930 (BALACLAVA). Then LIVES OF A BENGAL LANCER with Gary Cooper was produced by Paramount and became an enormous hit. Warner Bros. frantically searched for a competitive Indian epic and came up with Jacoby's treatment, which was promptly tossed out and completely re-written, with a love interest theme inserted and the facts, except for the actual charge, thrown out the window, so that the approach was more in the flavor of Kipling than Tennyson, albeit Tennyson's immortal poem is used, superimposed over the charge scenes at the end. The studio mentors were right in assuming that the public would be unaware of the true facts concerning the Balaclava battle; the "creative" version proved to be enormously popular then as it is now. The facts were set straight in 1968 when Tony Richardson produced a British film CHARGE OF THE LIGHT BRIGADE. In this anemic remake the truth about the military idiocy that led to the senseless slaughter was put forward and no one seemed to care, at least not at the box office.
p, Samuel Bischoff (for Hal B. Willis); d, Michael Curtiz; w, Michel Jacoby, Rowland Leigh (based on a story by Jacoby); ph, Sol Polito; m, Max Steiner; ed, George Amy; art d, John Hughes; cos, Milo Anderson; spec eff, Fred Jackman, H. F. Koenekamp; director of horse action, B. Reeves Eason; tech adv, Capt. E. Rochfort-John, Maj. Sam Harris.

Adventure/WarDrama   Cas.   (PR:A MPAA:NR)

CHARGE OF THE LIGHT BRIGADE, THE***   (1968, Brit.) 145m UA c
Trevor Howard (Lord Cardigan), Vanessa Redgrave (Clarissa), John Gielgud (Lord Raglan), Harry Andrews (Lord Lucan), Jill Bennett (Mrs. Duberly), David Hemmings (Capt. Nolan), Peter Bowles (Paymaster Duberly), Mark Burns (Capt. Morris), Howard Marian-Crawford (Sir George Brown), Mark Dignam (Airey), Alan Dobie (Mogg), Willoughby Goddard (Squire), T.P. McKenna (Russell), Corin Redgrave (Featherstonhaugh), Norman Rossington (Corbett), Ben Aris (Maxse), Leo Britt (Scarlett), Helen Cherry (Lady Scarlett), Peter Woodthorpe (Valet), Rachel Kempson (Mrs. Codrington), Donald Wolfit ("Macbeth"), Valerie Newman (Mrs. Mitchell), Andrew Faulds (Quaker Preacher), Roger Mutton (Codrington), Georges Douking (St. Arnaud), Ambrose Coghill (Douglas), Michael Miller (Sir John Campbell), Chris Cunningham (Farrier), Christopher Chittell, Clive Endersby, Derek Fuke (Troopers), John Hallam (Officer), Barbara Hicks (Mrs. Duberly's Maid), Declan Mulholland (Farrier), Roy Pattison (Sergeant Major), Dino Shafeek (Indian Servant), John Trenaman (Sgt. Smith), Colin Vancao (Capt. Charteris).

Well-researched and thought-provoking film based on the Russian decimation of the English Army at Balaclava. Richardson's always daring direction takes its swipe at the English upper class and its snobbish view of the sport of war. Skillfully, he also brings forth the soldiers' blind acceptance of their belittling supervisors and their required courage. The code of honor, which is so vehemently protested, turns sour in the irony of the humiliating slaughter of England's Light Brigade. Shining performances all around, especially the brilliant Gielgud, and the convincing lovers—Hemmings and Redgrave (previously paired in BLOW UP). A cinematic statement that sums up the feelings of the 1960s generation. Notable animation sequences are rendered by Richard Williams. Don't look for the spectacular war scenes so sweepingly portrayed in Curtiz's 1936 masterpiece; the battle scenes take second place to revisionist satire and political indictment of nineteenth-century imperialistic England. UA producers may have wished that the Curtiz path had been doggedly followed. This was the studio's major release in 1968, one that ate up more than $5 million in production costs and returned only $1 million at the box office. Even the authentic on-location shots filmed in Turkey didn't help. Errol Flynn simply wasn't there to lead the charge and leap the barricades. This was the fifth telling of the famous charge. Two silent shorts were made in 1903 and 1912. The British had a stab at it in an early talkie in 1930 and Warner Bros. produced, of course, the classic (albeit historically inaccurate) charge in 1936.
p, Neil Hartley; d, Tony Richardson; w, Charles Wood; ph, David Watkin (Panavision/DeLuxe Color); m, John Addison; ed, Kevin Brownlow, Hugh Raggett; art d, Edward Marshall; cos, David Walker; spec eff, Robert MacDonald; anim, Richard Williams.

Historical Drama   (PR:C MPAA:NR)

CHARGE OF THE MODEL-T'S*   (1979) 94m Ry-Mac c
Louis Nye, John David Carson, Herb Edelman, Carol Bagdasarian, Arte Johnson, Jim McCullough, Jr., Bill Thurman.

Inane family-oriented comedy about a German spy during WW I driving a specially modified, heavily armed Ford across Texas. Why are family-oriented movies strictly for five-year-olds?
p,d&w, Jim McCullough; ph, Dean Cundey (Panavision), m, Euel Box.

Comedy   Cas.   (PR:AA MPAA:G)

CHARING CROSS ROAD*** (1935, Brit.) 72m BL bw

John Mills (Tony), June Clyde (Pam), Derek Oldham (Jimmy O'Donnell), Belle Baker (Herself), Jean Colin (Cherry), Arthur Sinclair (Mac), Garry Marsh (Berry), C. Denier Warren (Music Salesman), Coral Browne (Lady Ruston), Charles Heslop (Langdon), Alfred Wellesley (Producer), Judy Kelly (Vera).

Provincial vaudeville performers Mills and Clyde decide to add London to their conquests, taking up residence at a theatrical boarding house while they search for work. No-fault production with excellent casting and plenty of individual attention from director De Courville.

p, Herbert Smith; d, Albert De Courville; w, Con West, Clifford Grey (based on a radio play by Gladys and Clay Keyes); ph, Phil Tannura, Harry Rose.

Drama **(PR:A MPAA:NR)**

CHARIOTS OF FIRE**** (1981, Brit.) 123m Enigma/FOX C

Ben Cross (Harold Abrahams), Ian Charleson (Eric Liddell), Nigel Havers (Lord Andrew Lindsay), Nicholas Farrell (Aubrey Montague), Ian Holm (Sam Mussabini), John Gielgud (Master of Trinity), Lindsay Anderson (Master of Caius), Nigel Davenport (Lord Birkenhead), Cheryl Campbell (Jennie Liddell), Alice Krige (Sybil Gordon), Dennis Christopher (Charles Paddock), Brad Davis (Jackson Scholz), Patrick Magee (Lord Cadogan), Peter Egan (Duke of Sutherland), Struan Rodger (Sandy McGrath), David Yelland (Prince of Wales), Yves Beneyton (George Andre), Daniel Gerroll (Henry Stallard), Jeremy Sinden (President, Gilbert and Sullivan Society), Gordon Hammersley (President, Cambridge Athletic Club), Andrew Hawkins (Secretary Gilbert and Sullivan Society), Richard Griffiths (Head Porter, Caius College), John Young (Rev. J.D. Liddell), Benny Young (Rob Liddell), Yvonne Gilan (Mrs. Liddell), Jack Smethurst (Sleeping Car Attendant), Gerry Slevin (Col. Keddie), Peter Cellier (Savoy Head Waiter), Stephen Mallatratt (Watson), Colin Bruce (Taylor), Alan Polonsky (Paxton), Edward Wiley (Fitch), Philip O'Brien (American Coach), Ralph Lawton (Harbormaster), John Rutland (Caius Porter), Alan Dudley (Caius Manservant), Tommy Boyle (Reporter), Kim Clifford (Sybil's Maid), Wallace Campbell (Highland Provost), Pat Doyle (Jimmie), David John (Ernest Liddell), Teresa Dignan (Schoolgirl), Ruby Wax (Bunty), Michael Jeyes (Footman), David Kivlin, Eddie Hughson (Scots Boys), Rosy Clayton (Linda Wallis), Sarah Roache (Doreen Sloane), James Usher (Steven Ambrose), Leonard Mullen (Peter Jones), Dave Turner (Phil Tait), Gayle Grayson, Paul Howard, Garth Jones, Sue Sammon, Alan Lorimer, Graham Brooke, Carol Ashby, Michael Lonsdale, Paul Maho, Linda Boyland.

Winner of four Academy Awards, nominated for four others, and winner also of the BFA for best picture and costume design, CHARIOTS OF FIRE is almost, but not quite, worthy of all the accolades it received. Hugh Hudson came directly from the commercial sound stages to helm this original script by Colin Welland about what it means to win and what one must do to achieve it. Charleson is a serious Scottish Christian who runs for the glory of Jesus and who believes that Christ is his trainer. Cross is an English Jew who is almost paranoid about prejudice and whose main motivation is to be accepted. The movie delineates and crosscuts the lives of both men as they meet and run at the 1924 Olympics in Paris. Cambridge was where both men went to school in real life but that august school refused to allow its site to be used for location shooting, so alternatives had to be found. The scenes at St. Andrew's as the men train along the beach are memorable. Charleson's character, Liddell, became a Christian missionary, went to China, and eventually died in a Japanese prisoner of war camp, true to his faith to the end. Cross's Harold Abrahams eventually was knighted and became the spokesman for English amateur athletics and died in 1978, a venerated and respected elder statesman. The standout performance belongs to Holm as Mussabini, a professional coach whom Cross hires to get him ready for the big race. It's not exactly kosher to utilize the services of a pro and Holm must stay away from the stadium when the race is run. Casting is first-quality down to the smallest roles. Gielgud and director Anderson are wonderfully hateful as two anti-semitic Cambridge officials (Perhaps that's why they weren't allowed to shoot there) and Magee, of A CLOCKWORK ORANGE, provides a wonderfully etched role as a stuffy official of the British track association. Campbell as Jennie Liddell has very little to do, but what she does, she does well. Krige is better shown to advantage as a performer with whom Cross falls in love. The story of their unlikely affair could have been a movie in itself. They married and had a successful union for many decades. CHARIOTS OF FIRE won Oscars for Best Picture, Best Screenplay, Best Costume Design, and Best Musical Score. We would take exception to the latter award as Vangelis's music, while marvelously composed, was synthesized and terribly anachronistic to the era presented. The Oscar nominations went to Holm, Hudson, Terry Rawlings. Holm lost to Gielgud in ARTHUR—a questionable choice.

p, David Puttnam; d, Hugh Hudson; w, Colin Welland; ph, David Watkin; m, Vangelis Papathanassiou; ed, Terry Rawlings; art d, Roger Hall; cos, Milena Canonero.

Historical Biography **Cas.** **(PR:AAA MPAA:PG)**

CHARLATAN, THE* (1929) 60m UNIV bw

Holmes Herbert (Count Merlin/Peter Dwight), Margaret Livingston (Florence), Rockliffe Fellowes (Richard Talbot), Philo McCullough (Doctor Paynter), Anita Garvin (Mrs. Paynter), Crauford Kent (Frank Deering), Rose Tapley (Mrs. Deering), Fred Mackaye (Jerry Starke), Dorothy Gould (Ann Talbot).

Murder mystery eventually unravels in the Agatha Christie mode as a circus clown searches for the aerial performer wife who deserted him 15 years earlier, taking their baby who is brought up by her rich lover. Herbert, the clown, finds his wife, Livingston, just as she is about to leave Fellowes for yet another lover. She doesn't recognize her former spouse who is disguised as a Hindu mystic. Livingston is murdered at a high society party where she is making plans to again run off and Herbert is later accused of the murder. The real killer is later revealed in a muddy ending. Part talkie has all the old conventions, but weak direction ruins an intriguing plot.

d, George Melford; w, Jacques Rollens, Tom Reed, F. G. Hawks (based on a play by Ernest Pascal and Leonard Praskins); ph, George Robinson; ed, Robert Jahns, Maurice Pivar.

Mystery **(PR:A MPAA:NR)**

CHARLES AND LUCIE**½ (1982, Fr.) 97m Avon c

Daniel Ceccaldi, Ginette Garcin, Jean-Marie Proslier,, Samson Fainsilber, Georges Claisse, Guy Grosso, Marcel Gassouk, Albert Konan-Koffi, Henri Tissot, Albert Lerda, Robert Beauvais, Julie Turin, Josy Andrew, Feodor Atkine, Pierre Repp, Jacques Mauny, Pierre Charras, Belen, Sylvain Curtel, Lili Cox, Tania Sourseva, Jean Panisse, Albert Manachi.

A middle-aged hypochondriac junk-seller and his friend—a down-and-out singer—find themselves the victims of a complicated con game and end up stranded and broke in the south of France. There, they are chased by police and sought after by a score of seedy underworld types. A charming but easily forgettable little tale.

p, Claude Makovski; d, Nelly Kaplan; w, Jean Chapot, ph, Gilbert Sanchez; m, Pierre Perret; ed, Kaplan, Chapot.

Drama **(PR:A MPAA:NR)**

CHARLES, DEAD OR ALIVE**½

(1972, Switz.) 93m Le Group 5-Swiss TV/New Yorker c
(CHARLES MORT OU VIE)

Francois Simon (Charles De), Marcel Robert (Paul), Marie-Claire Dufour (Adeline), Andre Schmidt (Pierre De), Maya Simon (Marianne De), Michele Martel (Germaine).

After seeing himself interviewed on television, fifty-year-old Simon chucks his successful watchmaking business and his family and sets out to make a new life. He is taken in by artist Robert and Robert's mistress (Dufour) and lives with them in an urban ghetto. His student revolutionary daughter comes to live with him but Simon continues to retreat from the world. When his son sends an ambulance to take Simon to an asylum, he willingly climbs in. Alain Tanner's first feature was made in 1969, but was not released in the U.S. until his second, LE SALAMANDRE, became a hit here. It shows his preoccupation with leftist political concepts and the roles people play in society, themes that would be further explored in his later (and better) films like JONAH WHO WILL BE 25 IN THE YEAR 2000 and MESSIDOR. An auspicious debut for one of Europe's most consistently intelligent directors. The film won first prize at the 1969 Locarno Film Festival. (In French; English subtitles.)

p,d,&w, Alain Tanner; ph, Renato Berta; ed, Silva Bachmann.

Drama **(PR:C MPAA:NR)**

CHARLESTON zero (1978, Ital.) 77m Analysis Films c

Bud Spencer (Charleston), Herbert Lom (Inspector Watkins), James Coco (Texan).

A confusing film with an unsure plot. What is certain is that it is not about the 1920s dance craze. Spencer is fingered for stealing a Gauguin, and Coco is his chance for freedom. After a faked television benefit, everybody but the imprisoned Coco gets what they want. Too bad it's not about that dance.

p, Elio Scardamaglia; d, Marcello Fondato; w, Scardamaglia, Fondato; m, Guido and Maurizio DeAngelis

Comedy **(PR:A MPAA:PG)**

CHARLEY AND THE ANGEL**½ (1973) 93m Walt Disney/BV c

Fred MacMurray (Charley Appleby), Cloris Leachman (Nettie Appleby), Harry Morgan (The Angel), Kurt Russell (Ray Ferris), Kathleen Cody (Leonora Appleby), Vincent Van Patten (Willie Appleby), Scott Kolden (Rupert Appleby), George Lindsey (Pete), Richard Bakalyan (Buggs), Edward Andrews (Banker), Barbara Nichols (Sadie), Kelly Thordsen (Policeman), Liam Dunn (Dr. Sprague), Larry D. Mann (Felix), George O'Hanlon (Police Chief), Susan Tolsky (Miss Partridge), Mills Watson (Frankie Zuto), Ed Begley, Jr. (Derwood Moseby), Roy Engel (Driver), Christina Anderson (Susie), Pat Delany (Girl in Sadie's Place), Bob Hastings (News Reporter), Jack Griffin (Policeman No. 2).

Disney regular MacMurray (SHAGGY DOG, ABSENT MINDED PROFESSOR), who is too busy with his depression-era business, pays no attention to his rejected family. Visited by an angel, he is told that his time is up. He becomes frantic pleading with the winged messenger, who finally checks up on MacMurray's case. MacMurray shapes up and devotes all his time to his family. Silliness abounds and the film begins to lose focus when a family member gets messed up with the mob, leading to dad's arrest.

p, Bill Anderson; d, Vincent McEveety; w, Roswell Rogers (based on Will Stanton's novel The Golden Evenings of Summer); ph, Charles F. Wheeler (Technicolor); m, Buddy Baker; ed, Ray de Leuw, Bob Bring; art d, John B. Mansbridge, Al Roelofs; cos, Shelby Tatum.

Comedy/Fantasy **(PR:AAA MPAA:G)**

CHARLEY MOON*½ (1956, Brit.) 92m BL c

Max Bygraves (Charley Moon), Dennis Price (Harold Armytage), Michael Medwin (Alf Higgins), Florence Desmond (Mary Minton), Shirley Eaton (Angel Dream), Patricia Driscoll (Rose), Charles Victor (Miller Moon), Reginald Beckwith (Vicar), Cyril Raymond (Bill), Peter Jones (Stewart), Newton Blick (Monty Brass), Vic Wise (Solly Silvers), Lou Jacobi (Theater Manager), Eric Sykes (Brother-In-Law), Bill Fraser (Marber).

A big break takes Bygraves' vaudeville act to the star-studded West End. His career, however, is short-lived and he soon shuffles back to his stereotyped country-girl-in-waiting.

p, Colin Lesslie; d, Guy Hamilton; w, Leslie Bricusse, John Cresswell (based on a novel by Reginald Arkell); ph, Jack Hildyard (Eastmancolor); m, Francis Chagrin; ed, Bertie Rule.

Musical/Drama **(PR:A MPAA:NR)**

CHARLEY-ONE-EYE*½ (1973, Brit.) 107m PAR c

Richard Roundtree (Black Man), Roy Thinnes (Indian), Nigel Davenport (Bounty Hunter), Jill Pearson (Officer's Wife), Aldo Sambrell (Mexican Driver), Luis Aller

(Mexican Youth), Rafael Albaicin *(Mexican Leader)*, Alex Davion *(Tony)*, Johnny Sekka *(Bob)*, Madeline Hinde *(Penelope)*, Patrick Mower *(Richard)*, Imogen Hassall *(Chris)*, Edward Woodward *(Holstrom)*, William Mervyn *(Honeydew)*, David Lodge *(Colonel)*.

Two outcasts, a black Union army deserter and a crippled Indian, hole up in a Mexican church after one of them kills two people. A bounty hunter is soon stalking them and eventually catches up. The ending is overdramatic with the stoning death of the killer. Dull and depressing, though its character treatments are human and well-conceived. The first film from TV personality David Frost's company.

p, James Swann; d, Don Chaffey; w, Keith Leonard; ph, Kenneth Talbot; m, John Cameron; ed, Mike Campbell

Western **(PR:C MPAA:R)**

CHARLEY VARRICK*½** (1973) 111m UNIV c

Walter Matthau *(Charley Varrick)*, Joe Don Baker *(Molly)*, Felicia Farr *(Sybil Fort)*, Andy Robinson *(Harman Sullivan)*, John Vernon *(Maynard Boyle)*, Sheree North *(Jewell Everett)*, Norman Fell *(Mr. Garfinkle)*, Benson Fong *(Honest John)*, Woodrow Parfrey *(Howard Young)*, William Schallert *(Sheriff Bill Horton)*, Jacqueline Scott *(Nadine Varrick)*, Marjorie Bennett *(Mrs. Taff)*, Rudy Diaz *(Rudy Sanchez)*, Colby Chester *(Steele)*, Charlie Briggs *(Highway Deputy)*, Priscilla Garcia *(Miss Ambar)*, Scott Hale *(Mr. Scott)*, Charles Matthau *(Boy)*, Hope Summers *(Miss Vesta)*, Monica Lewis *(Beverly)*, Jim Nolan *(Clerk)*, Tom Tully *(Tom)*, Albert Popwell *(Randolph)*, Kathleen O'Malley *(Jessie)*, Christina Hart *(Jana)*, Craig Baxley *(Van Sickle)*, Al Dunlap *(Taxi Driver)*, Virginia Wing *(Chinese Hostess)*, Donald Siegel *(Murph)*.

Abandoning his considerable bent for comedy, Matthau plays it hard and fast as a small-time thief who robs, with partner Robinson, a tiny New Mexico bank. Instead of the usual loose change, the robbers find $750,000, which turns out to be Mafia money the bank was smoke-screening. It's too much for the pragmatic Matthau but his avaricious punk partner insists that they keep the money. Matthau warns him that if the loot is not returned, the Mafia will start gunning for them, which is exactly what happens. Hit man Baker begins hunting the pair, destroying everyone and everything in his path and enjoying the destruction (he is a sadist to the marrow). Matthau is both shifty and cunning as he evades both the police and the Mafia men, including Vernon, the syndicate front man who tries to mollify the nervous banker, Fell. North, as a money-grubbing photographer preparing Matthau's phony visa, is intriguing, and Farr is properly collusive and sexy as Vernon's secretary. Butler's color lensing is topnotch as is Schifrin's score. The whole film is taut with suspense and is smartly written, thanks to director Siegel and scripters Riesner and Rodman. One of the best action sequences (among many) has Matthau and Baker dueling with a car and a crop-dusting plane as Matthau attempts to take off at film's end.

p&d, Don Siegel; w, Dean Riesner, Howard Rodman (based on the novel *The Looters* by John Reese); ph, Michael Butler (Technicolor); m, Lalo Schifrin; ed, Frank Morriss; art d, Fernando Carrerre; cos, Helen Colvig.

Crime Drama **Cas.** **(PR:C MPAA:NR)**

CHARLEY'S AUNT*½ (1930) 88m COL bw

Charlie Ruggles *(Lord Babberly)*, June Collyer *(Amy Spettigue)*, Hugh Williams *(Charlie Wykeham)*, Doris Lloyd *(Donna D'Alvadores)*, Halliwell Hobbes *(Stephen Spettigue)*, Flora Le Breton *(Ela Delahay)*, Rodney McLennon *(Jack Chesney)*, Flora Sheffield *(Kitty Verdun)*, Phillips Smalley *(Sir Francis Chesney)*, Wilson Benge *(Brassett)*.

Ruggles is an Oxford student called upon by two clasmates to act as a matronly aunt and chaperone them while they entertain two women at tea. Some laughs become howls under Christie's direction. This chestnut was roasted as a silent by Syd Chaplin.

p&d, Al Christie; w, F. M. Willis (based on a story and play by Brandon Thomas); ph, Gus Peterson, Harry Zech, Leslie Rowson.

Comedy **(PR:A MPAA:NR)**

CHARLEY'S AUNT*½** (1941) 80m FOX bw
(GB: CHARLEY'S AMERICAN AUNT)

Jack Benny *(Babbs)*, Kay Francis *(Donna Lucia)*, James Ellison *(Jack Chesney)*, Anne Baxter *(Amy Spettigue)*, Edmund Gwenn *(Stephen Spettigue)*, Reginald Owen *(Redcliff)*, Laird Cregar *(Sir Francis Chesney)*, Arleen Whelan *(Kitty Verdun)*, Richard Haydn *(Charley Wyckham)*, Ernest Cossart *(Brasset)*, Morton Lowry *(Harley Stafford)*, Lionel Pape *(Babberly)*, Claude Allister, William Austin *(Spectators)*, Russell Burroughs, Gilchrist Stuart, John Meredith *(Teammates)*, Bob Conway, Bob Cornell, Basil Walker, Herbert Gunn *(Students)*, Will Stanton *(Messenger)*, C. Montague Shaw *(Elderly Man)*, Maurice Cass *(Octogenarian)*.

This was the third of many CHARLEY'S AUNT films. The first starred Sydney Chaplin in 1925 and the second featured Charlie Ruggles in the lead. The play was written in the last century and still ranks as one of the best good-natured farces ever. Benny is the overage student who masquerades as Haydn's aunt from Brazil who will be the chaperone for Haydn and Ellison as they court Baxter and Whelan. Once Jack is in drag, he's eagerly sought by Cregar, a fortune hunter, and Gwenn. Eventually, Charley's real aunt, played by Francis, shows up and Jack becomes engaged to her. Benny was never better (with the possible exception of his classic TO BE OR NOT TO BE) and totally carries the story with a top-flight performance. This was his first role of any consequence other than tailor-made parts with radio jokes flying thick and fast about his well-known persona. In this movie, Benny had to play a part totally alien to what he'd done before and he proved more than worthy of the task. This was Cregar's fifth role in a brief career that only lasted five years. He died in 1944 at age twenty-eight from a heart attack that resulted from his constant crash dieting. (Cregar got it into his head that he would become a handsome leading man, instead of the fine, whale-like character actor he was, if only he could trim his hulking body by 100 pounds. He did and he died.) Remade as the musical WHERE'S CHARLEY?

p, William Perlberg; d, Archie Mayo; w, George Seaton (based on the play by Brandon Thomas); ph, Peverell Marley; m, Alfred Newman; ed, Robert Bischoff; art d, Nathan Juran, Richard Day; set d, Thomas Little; cos, Travis Banton.

Farce **(PR:AA MPAA:NR)**

CHARLEY'S (BIG-HEARTED) AUNT*½
(1940, Brit.) 76m Gainsborough/GFD bw

Arthur Askey *(Arthur Linden-Jones)*, Richard Murdoch *(Stinker Burton)*, Moore Marriott *(Jerry)*, Graham Moffatt *(Albert Brown)*, Phyllis Calvert *(Betty Forsythe)*, Jeanne de Casalis *(Aunt Lucy)*, J. H. Roberts *(Dean of Bargate)*, Felix Aylmer *(Proctor)*, Wally Patch *(Butler)*.

Brandon Thomas's oft-filmed farce (at least seven times since 1925) has frequently been better, but Askey gives it a good shot, playing the Oxford student who is forced through complicated circumstances to impersonate his maiden aunt from Brazil. When the aunt really does turn up, the circumstances grow even more complicated.

p, Edward Black; d, Walter Forde; w, Marriott Edgar, Val Guest (based on the play "Charley's Aunt" by Brandon Thomas); ph, Arthur Crabtree.

Comedy **(PR:A MPA:NR)**

CHARLIE BUBBLES **½ (1968, Brit.) 89m REG/UNIV c

Albert Finney *(Charlie Bubbles)*, Colin Blakely *(Smokey Pickles)*, Billie Whitelaw *(Lottie Bubbles)*, Liza Minnelli *(Eliza)*, Timothy Garland *(Jack Bubbles)*, Richard Pearson *(Accountant)*, John Ronane *(Gerry)*, Nicholas Phipps *(Agent)*, Peter Sallis *(Solicitor)*, Charles Lamb *(Mr. Noseworthy)*, Margery Mason *(Mrs. Noseworthy)*, Diana Coupland *(Maud)*, Alan Lake *(Airman)*, Yootha Joyce *(Woman in Cafe)*, Peter Carlisle *(Man in Cafe)*, Wendy Padburt *(Girl in Cafe)*, Susan Engles *(Nanny)*, Joe Gladwin *(Hotel Waiter)*, Charles Hill *(Headwaiter)*, Albert Shepherd *(Policeman)*, Ted Norris *(Bill)*, Brian Moseley *(Herbert)*, Rex Boyd *(Receptionist)*, Arthur Pentelow *(Man with Car)*, George Innes *(Garage Attendant)*.

An often tedious look at the life of a tedious man, but a film which is saved by its shining performances. As dull as it sometimes becomes, an insightful look is taken at Bubbles. In his directorial debut, Finney stars as a financially secure and materialistic man who battles his boredom with a drinking buddy and with an affair with his secretary. Billie Whitelaw, as Charlie's estranged wife, won a BFA for her role as Best Supporting Actress.

p, Michael Medwin; d, Albert Finney; w, Shelagh Delaney; ph, Peter Sutchitsky (Technicolor), m, Misha Donat; ed, Fergus McDonell; art d, Edward Marshall; cos, Yvonne Blake.

Drama **(PR:C MPAA:NR)**

CHARLIE CHAN AND THE CURSE OF THE DRAGON QUEEN zero
(1981) 97m American Cinema c

Peter Ustinov *(Charlie Chan)*, Lee Grant *(Mrs. Lupowitz)*, Angie Dickinson *(Dragon Queen)*, Richard Hatch *(Lee Chan, Jr.)*, Brian Keith *(Police Chief)*, Michelle Pfeiffer *(Cordelia Farrington III)*, Roddy McDowall *(Gillespie)*, Rachel Roberts *(Mrs. Dangers)*, Paul Ryan *(Masten)*, Johnny Sekka *(Stefan)*, Bennett Ohta *(Chief of Police)*, David Hirokane *(Lee Chan, Sr.)*, Karlene Crockett *(Brenda Lupowitz)*, Michael Fairman *(Bernard Lupowitz)*, James Ray *(Haynes)*, Momo Yashima *(Dr. Yu Sing)*, Alison Hong *(Maysie Ling)*, Kael Blackwood, Jerry Loo, Laurence Cohen, Robin Hoff, Kathie Kei, James Bacon, Frank Michael, John Hugh, George Chiang, David Chow, Dewi Yee, Joe Bellan, Garrick Huey, Duane Tucker, Don Parker, Kenneth Snell, Nicholas Gunn, Don Murray, Kai Wong, Miya, Gerald Okamura, Lonny Carbajal, Peter Michas, Vic Hunsberger, Larry Duran, Kay Kimler, Jim Winburn, Molly Roden, Pavla Ustinov, Trevor Hook, Paul Sanderson.

Well-deserving of a thesaurus full of synonyms for the word "worthless," this embarrassingly unfunny time-waster has Ustinov in his worst performance. Hatch, in a repulsive profile of Charlie's half-Jewish, half-Chinese grandson, takes up most of this insipid, cliche-ridden film by bumbling through Chinatown, clumsily destroying everything in his path. The host of murders that greet him are on the cute side and the dialog is so inane that a five-year-old will sneer. Donner's mindless direction and stereotypic portrayal of Chinese are good reasons for the picket lines which followed this one's release. (See CHARLIE CHAN series, Index.)

p, Jerry Sherlock; d, Clive Donner; w, Stan Burns, David Axelrod (based on a story by Sherlock); ph, Paul Lohmann (Technicolor); m, Patrick Williams; ed, Walt Hannemann, Phil Tucker.

Comedy **(PR:A MPAA:PG)**

CHARLIE CHAN AT MONTE CARLO** (1937) 71m FOX bw

Warner Oland *(Charlie Chan)*, Keye Luke *(Lee Chan)*, Virginia Field *(Evelyn Gray)*, Sidney Blackmer *(Karnoff)*, Harold Huber *(French Police Inspector)*, Kay Linaker *(Joan Karnoff)*, Robert Kent *(Gordon Chase)*, Edward Raquelo *(Paul Savarin)*, George Lynn *(Al Rogers)*, Louis Mercier *(Cab Driver)*, George Davis *(Pepito)*, John Bleifer *(Ludwig)*, Georges Renavent *(Renault)*, George Sorrel *(Gendarme)*.

This last appearance of Oland as Charlie Chan finds him on a gambling vacation in Monaco. But poor Oland doesn't have a chance of relaxing and is immediately called on to help solve the murders of two men and clear up the mystery of a missing million dollars in bonds. Everyone in the cast is a suspect but the plot is so muddled no one can figure out who the villain is. Since a third of the dialog is in French it's a moot point anyway. (See CHARLIE CHAN series, Index.)

p, John Stone; d, Eugene Forde; w, Charles Belden, Jerry Cady (based on a story by Robert Ellis and Helen Logan, and the character created by Earl Derr Biggers); ph, Daniel C. Clark; m, Samuel Kaylin; ed, Nick De Maggio.

Mystery **(PR:A MPAA:NR)**

CHARLIE CHAN AT THE CIRCUS½** (1936) FOX 72m bw

Warner Oland *(Charlie Chan)*, Keye Luke *(Lee Chan)*, George Brasno *(Tim)*, Francis Ford *(Gaines)*, Olive Brasno *(Tiny)*, Shirley Deane *(Louise Norman)*, John McGuire *(Hal Blake)*, Maxine Reiner *(Marie Norman)*, J. Carroll Naish *(Tom Holt)*, Paul Stanton *(Joe Kinney)*, Boothe Howard *(Dan Farrell)*, Drue Leyton *(Nellie Farrell)*, Wade Boteler *(Lt. Macy)*, Shia Jung *(Su Toy)*, Francis Farnum *(Mike the Ticket Taker)*, John Dilson *(Doctor)*.

Charlie takes his twelve children to the circus where they look on as pop solves a murder committed by a snake charmer in a gorilla suit. Action takes place in a real circus, adding some color to the mystery. Offbeat humor is provided by mixing vaudeville midgets George and Olive Brasno in with the Chan brood. (See CHARLIE CHAN series, Index.)

p, John Stone; d, Harry Lachman; w, Robert Ellis, Helen Logan (based on the character created by Earl Derr Biggers); ph, Daniel C. Clark; ed, Alex Troffey; md, Samuel Kaylin.

Mystery **(PR:A MPAA:NR)**

CHARLIE CHAN AT THE OLYMPICS½** (1937) 71m FOX bw

Warner Oland *(Charlie Chan)*, Katherine De Mille *(Yvonne Roland)*, Pauline Moore *(Betty Adams)*, Allan Lane *(Richard Masters)*, Keye Luke *(Lee Chan)*, C. Henry Gordon *(Arthur Hughes)*, John Eldredge *(Cartwright)*, Morgan Wallace *(Zaraka)*, Jonathan Hale *(Hopkins)*, Layne Tom, Jr. *(Charlie Chan, Jr.)*, Fredrik Vogeding *(Inspector Strasser)*, Andrew Tombes *(Chief Scott)*, Howard Hickman *(Dr. Burton)*, Edward Keane *(Colonel)*, Selmer Jackson *(Navy Commander)*, Don Brodie *(Radio Announcer)*, George Chandler *(Ship's Radio Operator)*, Emmett Vogan *(Ship's Officer)*, Minerval Urecal *(Olympic Matron)*.

Oland outwits international spies with the aid of U.S. Navy officials and No. 1 son Luke, a gold medal-winning member of the American swim team during the infamous 1936 Olympics in Berlin. Quest is for a device allowing remote control flying of aircraft. Newsreel shots of Olympic games are effectively blended into the action. (See CHARLIE CHAN series, Index.)

p, John Stone; d, H. Bruce Humberstone; w, Robert Ellis, Helen Logan (based on a story by Paul Burger and the character created by Earl Derr Biggers); ph, Daniel C. Clark; ed, Fred Allen; md, Samuel Kaylin.

Mystery **(PR:A MPAA:NR)**

CHARLIE CHAN AT THE OPERA*½** (1936) 66m FOX bw

Warner Oland *(Charlie Chan)*, Boris Karloff *(Gravelle)*, Keye Luke *(Lee Chan)*, Charlotte Henry *(Mlle. Kitty)*, Thomas Beck *(Phil Childers)*, Margaret Irving *(Mme. Lilli Rouchelle)*, George Gaye *(Enrico Barelli)*, Nedda Harrigan *(Mme. Lucretia Barelli)*, Frank Conroy *(Mr. Whitely)*, Guy Usher *(Inspector Regan)*, William Demarest *(Sgt. Kelly)*, Maurice Cass *(Mr. Arnold)*, Tom McGuire *(Morris)*, Fred Kelsey *(Cop)*, Selmer Jackson, Emmett Vogan *(Newspaper Wire-Photo Technicians)*, Benson Fong *(Opera Extra)*.

Possibly one of the best of the Charlie Chan series, this one has the added attraction of Karloff in the role of an opera star suffering from amnesia, who is a recent escapee from an insane asylum accused of the murder of his wife and her lover. Karloff plays his role to the hilt and in one scene a fellow performer comments, "Who do you think you are, Frankenstein?" Included in the film is the opera "Carnival," composed especially for the picture by Oscar Levant. So well-made was the movie—and so much fun does it seem today—that its interest ranges far beyond the usual circle of Chan buffs. (See CHARLIE CHAN series, Index.)

p, John Stone; d, H. Bruce Humberstone; w, Scott Darling, Charles S. Belden (based on a story by Bess Meredyth and the character created by Earl Derr Biggers); ph, Lucien Andriot; ed, Alex Troffey; md, Samuel Kaylin; Opera "Carnival," Oscar Levant; libretto, William Kernell.

Mystery **(PR:A MPAA:NR)**

CHARLIE CHAN AT THE RACE TRACK*** (1936) 70m FOX bw

Warner Oland *(Charlie Chan)*, Keye Luke *(Lee Chan)*, Helen Wood *(Alice Fenton)*, Thomas Beck *(Bruce Rogers)*, Alan Dinehart *(George Chester)*, Gavin Muir *(Bagley)*, Gloria Roy *(Catherine Chester)*, Johnathan Hale *(Warren Fenton)*, G. P. Huntley, Jr. *(Denny Barton)*, George Irving *(Maj. Kent)*, Junior Coghlan *(Eddie Brill)*, Frankie Darro *("Tip" Collins)*, John Rogers *(Mooney)*, John H. Allen *("Streamline" Jones)*, Harry Jans *(Al Meers)*, Robert Warwick *(Chief of Police)*, Jack Mulhall *(2nd Purser)*, Paul Fix *(Gangster)*, Charles Williams *(Reporter)*, Sidney Bracey *(Ship's Steward)*.

Oland foils Santa Anita track gangsters after exposing them as murderers and swindlers when they switch horses in an attempt to fix a race. Much of the action takes place on board a steamship from Honolulu (Chan's stomping grounds) to Los Angeles after the owner of a prize horse, and Chan's friend, is found slain and the epigrammatic sleuth goes into action. Luke, as his amateur Sherlock son, provides good situation laughs and the dialog sparkles throughout. Smooth scripting and taut direction keep this picture on the right track. (See CHARLIE CHAN series, Index.)

p, John Stone; d, H. Bruce Humberstone; w, Robert Ellis, Helen Logan, Edward T. Lowe (based on a story by Lou Breslow and Lowe and the character created by Earl Derr Biggers); ph, Harry Jackson; ed, Nick De Maggio; md, Samuel Kaylin.

Mystery **(PR:A MPAA:NR)**

CHARLIE CHAN AT THE WAX MUSEUM*½ (1940) 63m FOX bw

Sidney Toler *(Charlie Chan)*, Sen Yung *(Jimmy Chan)*, C. Henry Gordon *(Dr. Cream)*, Marc Lawrence *(Steve McBirney)*, Joan Valerie *(Lily Latimer)*, Marguerite Chapman *(Mary Bolton)*, Ted Osborn *(Tom Agnew)*, Michael Visaroff *(Dr. Otto Von Brom)*, Hilda Vaughn *(Mrs. Rocke)*, Charles Wagenheim *(Willie Fern)*, Archie Twitchell [Michael Brandon] *(Carter Lane)*, Edward Marr *(Grenock)*, Joe King *(Inspector O'Matthews)*, Harold Goodwin *(Edwards)*, Charles Trowbridge *(Judge)*, Stanley Blystone *(Court Attendant)*, Jimmy Conlin *(Barker)*, Emmett Vogan *(District Attorney)*.

In what was thought to be the last of the Chan series, our master sleuth is found in a wax museum trying to establish the identity of an arch criminal who has taken refuge in the wax chamber of horrors. The demented doctor is also big on facial surgery, making it difficult to tell the humans from the dummies. Among the replicas of Jack the Ripper and Bluebeard is also one of Chan himself, which Number Two son mistakes for dad at one point. In a final scene, by then fed up with the waxworks, Chan's son gives the statue a swift kick in the seat of the pants. Of course it turns out to be the real Charlie. Film is a feeble effort and suffers from lack of amusing dialog originally created by Biggers for the character. (See CHARLIE CHAN series, Index.)

p, Walter Morosco, Ralph Dietrich; d, Lynn Shores; w, John Larkin (based on the character created by Earl Derr Biggers); ph, Virgil Miller; ed, James B. Clark; md, Emil Newman.

Mystery **(PR:A MPAA:NR)**

CHARLIE CHAN AT TREASURE ISLAND** (1939) 72m FOX bw

Sidney Toler *(Charlie Chan)*, Cesar Romero *(Fred Rhadini)*, Pauline Moore *(Eve Cairo)*, Sen Yung *(James Chan)*, Douglas Fowley *(Peter Lewis)*, June Gale *(Myra Rhadini)*, Douglass Dumbrille *(Thomas Gregory)*, Sally Blane *(Stella Essex)*, Billie Seward *(Bessie Sibley)*, Wally Vernon *(Elmer Keiner)*, Charles Halton *(Redley)*, Trevor Bardette *(Abdul the Turk)*, Louis Jean Heydt *(Paul Essex)*, Gerald Mohr *(Dr. Zodiac)*, John Elliott *(Doctor)*, Donald MacBride *(Chief Kilvaine)*.

Charlie gets a hand from Romero in solving the mystery of his novelist friend's supposed suicide. Trail leads them to Zodiac, a racketeering mystic who holds clients in his power through threats of blackmail. Racket is exposed and writer's name is cleared. Picture is slow in spots but will still hold up for Chan fans. (See CHARLIE CHAN series, Index.)

p, Sol M. Wurtzel; d, Norman Foster; w, John Larkin (based on the character created by Earl Derr Biggers); ph, Virgil Miller; ed, Norman Colbert; md, Samuel Kaylin.

Mystery **(PR:A MPAA:NR)**

CHARLIE CHAN CARRIES ON*** (1931) 76m FOX bw

Warner Oland *(Charlie Chan)*, John Garrick *(Mark Kenaway)*, Marguerite Churchill *(Pamela Potter)*, Warren Hymer *(Max Minchin)*, Marjorie White *(Sadie)*, C. Henry Gordon *(John Ross)*, William Holden *(Patrick Tait)*, George Brent *(Capt. Ronald Keane)*, Peter Gawthorne *(Inspector Duff)*, John T. Murray *(Dr. Lofton)*, John Swon *(Elmer Benbow)*, Goodee Montgomery *(Mrs. Benbow)*, Jason Robards, Sr. *(Walter Honeywood)*, Lumsden Hare *(Inspector Hanley)*, Zeffie Tiltbury *(Mrs. Luce)*, Betty Francisco *(Sybil Conway)*, Harry Beresford *(Kent)*, John Rogers *(Martin)*, J.C. Davis *(Eben)*.

This is a wisecrack-packed picture in which Chan solves the murder of a wealthy American found dead in a London hotel. Warren Hymer as a Chicago racketeer provides laughs throughout. When wife White comes trotting down a Hong Kong street carrying a bundle which turns out to be a reading lamp he quips, "I suppose she'll buy a book now." "No," the lady says, "I've already got one." This nicely photographed film has an abundance of foreign backgrounds with various interiors at Nice, San Remo, London, Honolulu, and Hong Kong. Fast paced and snappy. (See CHARLIE CHAN series, Index.)

d, Hamilton MacFadden; w, Philip Klein, Barry Connors (based on the character created by Earl Derr Biggers); ph, George Schneiderman; ed, Al De Gaetano; set d, Joe Wright.

Mystery **(PR:A MPAA:NR)**

CHARLIE CHAN IN BLACK MAGIC*½ (1944) 67m MON bw

Sidney Toler *(Charlie Chan)*, Mantan Moreland *(Birmingham)*, Frances Chan *(Frances Chan)*, Joe Crehan *(Matthews)*, Jacqueline DeWit *(Justine Bonner)*, Ralph Peters *(Rafferty)*, Helen Beverley *(Norma Duncan)*, Frank Jaquet *(Paul Hamlin)*, Dick Gordon *(Bonner)*, Charles Jordan *(Tom Starkey)*, Claudia Dell *(Vera Starkey)*, Geraldine Wall *(Harriet Green)*, Harry Depp *(Charles Edwards)*, Edward Earle *(Dawson)*.

Routine programmer tricksters has Toler meandering through the world of occult fakers in search of a killer. The best part of this tired film is Moreland's extravagant antics, terrified not only by the stalking killer but ghosties and ghoulies conjured by a host of wacky mediums. (See CHARLIE CHAN series, Index.)

p, Philip N. Krasne, James S. Burkett; d, Phil Rosen; w, George Callahan; ph, Arthur Martinelli; ed, John Link.

Mystery **(PR:A MPAA:NR)**

CHARLIE CHAN IN EGYPT*** (1935) 65m FOX bw

Warner Oland *(Charlie Chan)*, Pat Paterson *(Carol Arnold)*, Thomas Beck *(Tom Evans)*, Rita Cansino [Hayworth] *(Nayda)*, Jameson Thomas *(Dr. Anton Racine)*, Frank Conroy *(Prof. John Thurston)*, Nigel De Brulier *(Edfu Ahmad)*, Paul Porcasi *(Soueida)*, Arthur Stone *(Dragoman)*, Stepin Fetchit *(Snowshoes)*, James Eagles *(Barry Arnold)*, Frank Reicher *(Dr. Jaipur)*, George Irving *(Prof. Arnold)*, Anita Brown *(Snowshoes' Friend)*, John Davidson *(Daoud Atrash the Chemist)*, Gloria Roy *(Bit)*, John George *(Dwarf Egyptian Helper)*.

Oland's assignment this time includes horror as he uncovers, with the aid of an X-ray machine, the body of a murdered archaeologist in a sarcophagus. Add to this the antics of hilarious Stepin Fetchit and his eye-rolling reactions to anything connected with the dead. Narrative builds up horror and diverse suspicions as it proceeds to a deftly confected solution. Rita Hayworth appears in her first "series" film during her apprenticeship days. (See CHARLIE CHAN series, Index.)

p, Edward T. Lowe; d, Louis King; w, Robert Ellis, Helen Logan (based on the character created by Earl Derr Biggers); ph, Daniel B. Clark; ed, Al De Gaetano; md, Samuel Kaylin; art d, William Darling.

Mystery **(PR:A MPAA:NR)**

CHARLIE CHAN IN HONOLULU½   (1938) 67m FOX bw
Sidney Toler (Charlie Chan), Phyllis Brooks (Judy Hayes), Sen Yung (Lee Chan),
Eddie Collins (Al Hogan), John King (Randolph), Claire Dodd (Mrs. Carol Wayne),
George Zucco (Dr. Cardigan), Robert Barrat (Capt. Johnson), Marc Lawrence
(Johnnie McCoy), Richard Lane (Detective Arnold), Layne Tom, Jr. (Tommy), Phillip
Ahn (Wing Foo), Paul Harvey (Inspector), Dick Alexander (Sailor), James Flavin
(Police Dispatcher).

Toler, in his first appearance as Chan, uncovers murder aboard a ship anchored at
Honolulu. He orders the boat held until the crime is solved, giving the passengers a few
extra days of intrigue. Measures up to previous technical efforts to complement an
interesting story, but the direction and are script lackluster. (See CHARLIE CHAN
series, Index.)

p, John Stone; d, H. Bruce Humberstone; w, Charles Belden (based on the character
created by Earl Derr Biggers); ph, Charles Clark; ed, Nick De Maggio; md, Samuel
Kaylin.

Mystery   **(PR:A   MPAA:NR)**

CHARLIE CHAN IN LONDON½   (1934) 79m FOX bw
Warner Oland (Charlie Chan), Drue Leyton (Pamela Gray), Douglas Walton (Paul
Gray), Alan Mowbray (Geoffrey Richmond), Mona Barrie (Lady Mary Bristol), Ray
Milland (Neil Howard), George Barraud (Maj. Jardine), Paul England (Bunny
Fothergill), Madge Bellamy (Becky Fothergill), Walter Johnson (Jerry Garton), Murray
Kinnell (Phillips), E. E. Clive (Detective Sgt. Thacker), Elsa Buchanan (Alice Rooney),
Reginald Sheffield (Flight Cmdr. King), Perry Ivins (Kemp), John Rogers (Lake),
Helena Grant (Secretary), Montague Shaw (Doctor), Phyllis Coughlan (Nurse),
Margaret Mann (Housemaid), David Torrence (Sir Lionel Bashford), Claude King
(RAF Commandant).

Charlie Chan rides to the hounds on a wealthy country estate in England to solve a
murder. Well above average mystery sees Oland go after a group of manor-bound
guests, notably a housekeeper, a stableman, and a lawyer, turning up the culprit in the
last reel, of course. Luxurious interior sets add flavor. (See CHARLIE CHAN series,
Index.)

p, John Stone; d, Eugene Forde; w, Philip MacDonald (based on the character created
by Earl Derr Biggers); ph, L.W. O'Connell; md, Samuel Kaylin.

Mystery   **(PR:A   MPAA:NR)**

CHARLIE CHAN IN PANAMA½   (1940) 66m FOX bw
Sidney Toler (Charlie Chan), Jean Rogers (Kathi Lenesch), Lionel Atwill (Cliveden
Compton), Mary Nash (Jennie Finch), Sen Yung (Jimmy Chan), Kane Richmond
(Richard Cabot), Chris-Pin Martin (Lt. Montero), Lionel Royce (Dr. Grosser), Helen
Ericson (Stewardess), Jack La Rue (Manolo), Edwin Stanley (Gov. Webster), Frank
Puglia (Achmed Halide), Don Douglas (Capt. Lewis), Edward Keane (Dr. Fredericks),
Lane Chandler (Officer), Addison Richards (Godley), Eddie Acuff (Suspicious Sailor),
Ed Gargan (Plant Worker), Jimmy Aubrey (Drunken Sailor), Alberto Morin (Desk
Clerk).

Toler continues his career as Chan with this chiller, posing as an employee of the U.S.
government taking on big responsibilities. In this espionage caper he uncovers a plot to
destroy part of the Panama Canal and trap the fleet going through on maneuvers.
Skillfully written with topflight portrayals, particularly from menaces La Rue and
Puglia. (See CHARLIE CHAN series, Index.)

p, Sol M. Wurtzel; d, Norman Foster; w, John Larkin, Lester Ziffren (based on the
character created by Earl Derr Biggers); ph, Virgil Miller; ed, Fred Allen; md, Samuel
Kaylin.

Mystery   **(PR:A   MPAA:NR)**

CHARLIE CHAN IN PARIS   (1935) 70m FOX bw
Warner Oland (Charlie Chan), Mary Brian (Yvette Lamartine), Erik Rhodes (Max
Corday), John Miljan (Dufresno), Ruth Peterson (Renee), Thomas Beck (Victor),
Murray Kinnell (Henri Latouche), Minor Watson (Renaud), Henry Kolker (M.
Lamartine), Keye Luke (Lee Chan), Perry Ivins (Bedell), John M. Qualen (Concierge),
Dorothy Appleby (Nardi), Harry Cording (Gendarme).

A trio of counterfeiters operating their plant out of the sewers of Paris has Chan
scurrying around the city of light to ferret out the rats. Well-sustained suspense and
ingenious plot will please Chan's whodunit fans. (See CHARLIE CHAN series, Index.)

p, Sol M. Wurtzel; d, Lewis Seiler; w, Edward T. Lowe and Stuart Anthony (based on a
story by Philip MacDonald and the character created by Earl Derr Biggers); ph, Ernest
Palmer; md, Samuel Kaylin.

Mystery   **(PR:A   MPAA:NR)**

CHARLIE CHAN IN RENO½   (1939) 70m FOX bw
Sidney Toler (Charlie Chan), Ricardo Cortez (Dr. Ainsley), Phyllis Brooks (Vivian
Wells), Slim Summerville (Sheriff Tombstone Fletcher), Kane Richmond (Curtis
Whitman), Sen Yung (James Chan), Pauline Moore (Mary Whitman), Eddie Collins
(Cab Driver), Kay Linaker (Mrs. Russell), Louise Henry (Jeanne Bently), Robert
Lowery (Wally Burke), Charles D. Brown (Chief of Police), Iris Wong (Choy Wong),
Morgan Conway (George Bently), Hamilton MacFadden (Night Clerk).

Divorce Hawaiian-style finds Toler defending Moore when she is arrested in Reno as a
murder suspect. Pointed direction by Foster, trim scripting by a trio of writers, and
spirited acting that never goes overboard make this whodunit an intriguing yarn. (See
CHARLIE CHAN series, Index.)

p, John Stone; d, Norman Foster; w, Frances Hyland, Albert Ray, Robert E. Kent
(based on a story "Death Makes a Decree" by Philip Wylie and the character created
by Earl Derr Biggers); ph, Virgil Miller; ed, Fred Allen; md, Samuel Kaylin.

Mystery   **(PR:A   MPAA:NR)**

CHARLIE CHAN IN RIO*   (1941) 60m FOX bw
Sidney Toler (Charlie Chan), Mary Beth Hughes (Joan Reynolds), Cobina Wright, Jr.

(Grace Ellis), Ted North (Clark Denton), Victor Jory (Alfredo Marina), Harold Huber
(Chief Souto), Victor Sen Yung (Jimmy Chan), Richard Derr (Ken Reynolds),
Jacqueline Dalya (Lola Dean), Kay Linaker (Helen Ashby), Truman Bradley (Paul
Wagner), Hamilton MacFadden (Bill Kellogg), Leslie Denison (Rice), Iris Wong (Lili),
Eugene Borden (Armando), Ann Codee (Margo).

This Chan saga finds our wily hero in Rio with more music and romance than usual in
the series. Chan's deductive powers are called on by the local police to solve a pair of
murders but the screenplay is childish in plot and dialog and the makeup and camera
work so bad that most of the cast appears to be made up for a carnival instead of a
movie. Even diehard fans will want to get away from this one. (See CHARLIE CHAN
series, Index.)

p, Sol M. Wurtzel; d, Harry Lachman; w, Samuel G. Engel, Lester Ziffren (based on the
character created by Earl Derr Biggers); ph, Joseph P. MacDonald; ed, Alexander
Troffey; md, Emil Newman; m/l, Mack Gordon, Harry Warren.

Mystery   **(PR:A   MPAA:NR)**

CHARLIE CHAN IN SHANGHAI**   (1935) 70m FOX bw
Warner Oland (Charlie Chan), Irene Hervey (Diana Woodland), Charles Locher [Jon
Hall] (Philip Nash), Keye Luke (Lee Chan), Russell Hicks (James Andrews), Halliwell
Hobbes (Chief of Police), Neil Fitzgerald (Dakin), Fredrik Vogeding (Burke), Harry
Strang (Chauffeur), Max Wagner (Taxi Driver), Pat O'Malley (Belden).

Story has Chan on his own turf for the first time, hired by the Chinese government to
break up an international opium ring in Shanghai. Chan's creator Earl Derr Biggers'
death a year before had Fox uneasy about a possible loss of Chan stories as future
screen fodder. Not to worry. Charlie Chan lives on. And on . . . and on . . . (See
CHARLIE CHAN series, Index.)

p, John Stone; d, James Tinling; w, Edward T. Lowe, Gerard Fairlie (based on the
character created by Earl Derr Biggers); ph, Barney McGill; md, Samuel Kaylin.

Mystery   **(PR:A   MPAA:NR)**

CHARLIE CHAN IN THE CITY OF DARKNESS**   (1939) 75m FOX bw
Sidney Toler (Charlie Chan), Lynn Bari (Marie Dubon), Richard Clarke (Tony Madero),
Harold Huber (Marcel), Pedro de Cordoba (Antoine), Dorothy Tree (Charlotte
Rondell), C. Henry Gordon (Romaine), Douglass Dumbrille (Petroff), Noel Madison
(Belescu), Leo G. Carroll (Louis Sentinelli), Lon Chaney, Jr. (Pierre—Assistant to
Sentinelli), Louis Mercier (Max), George Davis (Alex), Barbara Leonard (Lola),
Adrienne d'Ambricourt (Landlady), Fredrik Vogeding (Captain), Alphonse Martell,
Eugene Borden (Gendarmes), Ann Codee (Complainant at Paris Police Station),
Gino Corrado (Cafe Owner), Rolfe Desan (Hotel Manager).

Toler travels to Paris to participate in a reunion with WWI buddies. There he becomes
involved in investigating the murder of munitions manufacturer Dumbrille, who was
supplying arms to the enemy. This Chan mystery was done as a knee-jerk response
to the Munich crisis of 1938 and Toler preaches against the evils of conference table
bargaining at the end of the film. (See CHARLIE CHAN series, Index.)

p, John Stone; d, Herbert I. Leeds; w, Robert Ellis, Helen Logan (based on a play by
Gina Kaus, Ladislaus Fodor and on the character created by Earl Derr Biggers); ph,
Virgil Miller; ed, Harry Reynolds; md, Samuel Kaylin.

Mystery   **(PR:A   MPAA:NR)**

CHARLIE CHAN IN THE SECRET SERVICE*   (1944) 63m MON bw
Sidney Toler (Charlie Chan), Gwen Kenyon (Inez), Manton Moreland (Birmingham),
Arthur Loft (Jones), Marianne Quon (Iris Chan), Lela Tyler (Mrs. Winters), Benson
Fong (Tommie Chan), Gene Stutenroth (Vega), Eddie Chandler (Lewis), George
Lessey (Slade), George Lewis (Paul), Muni Seroff (Peter).

Charlie Chan's move from 20th-Century Fox over to the Monogram lot did not bode
well for the series. Toler tries to carry off his role as a government agent assigned to
solve the mystery surrounding the death of an inventor but is hampered by halting
direction and wordy material. (See CHARLIE CHAN series, Index.)

p, Philip N. Krasne, James S. Burkett; d, Phil Rosen; w, James Callahan (based on the
character created by Earl Derr Biggers); ph, Ira Morgan; ed, Martin G. Cohn; md, Karl
Hajos.

Mystery   **(PR:A   MPAA:NR)**

CHARLIE CHAN ON BROADWAY½   (1937) 68m FOX bw
Warner Oland (Charlie Chan), Keye Luke (Lee Chan), Joan Marsh (Joan Wendall), J.
Edward Bromberg (Murdock), Douglas Fowley (John Burke), Harold Huber (Inspec-
tor Nelson), Donald Woods (Speed Patten), Louise Henry (Billie Bronson), Joan
Woodbury (Marie Collins), Leon Ames (Buzz Moran), Marc Lawrence (Thomas
Mitchell), Toshie Mori (Ling Tse), Charles Williams (Meeker), Eugene Borden (Louis),
Creighton Hale (Reporter), Jack Dougherty (Policeman), Lon Chaney, Jr. (Desk
Man), James Flavin (Cop), Edwin Stanley (Police Lab Technician).

Even busy New York nightlife can't stop our man Chan in his relentless pursuit of
wrongdoers and evil-thinkers. In this caper he thwarts a nightclub singer's plans to
reveal criminals listed in her diary. Of course the diary turns up missing and the canary
turns up dead. New York locale provides some glitz, and swiftly paced dialog in the
modern manner makes this one better than average. (See CHARLIE CHAN series,
Index.)

p, John Stone; d. Eugene Forde; w, Charles Belden, Jerry Cady (based on a story by
Art Arthur, Robert Ellis, and Helen Logan and the character created by Earl Derr
Biggers); ph, Harry Jackson; ed, Al De Gaetano; md, Samuel Kaylin.

Mystery   **(PR:A   MPAA:NR)**

CHARLIE CHAN'S CHANCE**   (1932) 73m FOX bw

Warner Oland (Charlie Chan), Ralph Morgan (Barry Kirk), H.B. Warner (Inspector Fife), Marion Nixon (Shirley Marlowe), Linda Watkins (Gloria Garland), Alexander Kirkland (John Douglas), James Kirkwood (Inspector Flannery), James Todd (Kenneth Dunwood), Charles McNaughton (Paradise), Edward Peil, Jr. (Li Gung), Herbert Bunsten (Garrick Enderly).

Scotland Yard and New York sleuths are no match for Charlie as he outwits mastermind Todd, despite countless false clues. Technical detail is excellent, especially in a studio version of the East River at night which provides brilliance. This time Chan himself is the intended murder victim, avoiding death only by chance while another is killed instead and he must solve this killing through inventive sleuthing. Oland renders the traditional epigrams and sage-like lines such as "Some heads, like nuts, much better if well cracked." (See CHARLIE CHAN series, Index.)

p, Joseph August; d, John Blystone; w, Barry Connors, Phillip Klein (based on a novel by Earl Derr Biggers); ph, Joseph August; ed, Alex Troffey.

Mystery   (PR:A   MPAA:NR)

CHARLIE CHAN'S COURAGE*½   (1934) 70m FOX bw

Warner Oland (Charlie Chan), Drue Leyton (Paula Graham), Donald Woods (Bob Crawford), Murray Kinnell (Martin Thorne), Paul Harvey (J.P. Madden, Jerry Delaney), Jerry Jerome (Maydorf), Harvey Clark (Prof. Gamble), Si Jenks (Will Holley), Jack Carter (Victor Jordan), James Wang (Wong), Reginald Mason (Mr. Crawford), Virginia Hammond (Mrs. Jordan), DeWitt C. Jennings (Constable Brackett), Francis Ford (Hewitt).

Courage mentioned in the title must have been Oland's for making it through this one. Script requires him to assume the disguise of a Chinese servant and largely stand around, looking suspicious and snooping for a murderer. Story revolves around a pearl necklace which is sold for delivery to a millionaire at his ranch. Chan's job is to deliver the necklace, but a murder is committed, prompting the sleuth to don his disguise. Story may please some but it is not deluxe material. (See CHARLIE CHAN series, Index.)

d, George Hadden, Eugene Forde; w, Seton I. Miller (based on a story by Earl Derr Biggers); ph, Hal Mohr; md, Samuel Kaylin.

Mystery   (PR:A   MPAA:NR)

CHARLIE CHAN'S GREATEST CASE**½   (1933) 70m FOX bw

Warner Oland (Charlie Chan), Heather Angel (Carlotta Eagan), Roger Imhof (The Beachcomber), John Warburton (John Quincy Winterslip), Walter Byron (Harry Jennison), Ivan Simpson (Brade), Virginia Cherrill (Barbara Winterslip), Francis Ford (Capt. Hallett), Robert Warwick (Dan Winterslip), Frank McGlynn (Amos Winterslip), Clara Blandick (Minerva Winterslip), Claude King (Capt. Arthur Cope), William Stack (James Egan), Gloria Roy (Arlene Compton), Cornelius Keefe (Steve Letherbee).

Respectable Honolulu bachelor with a side hobby of making half his cash illegally is stabbed to death, which brings in Charlie to solve the mystery. Photographically impressive with desired suspense. (See CHARLIE CHAN series, Index.)

d, Hamilton MacFadden; w, Lester Cole, Marion Orth (based on a novel by Earl Derr Biggers); ph, Ernest Palmer; ed, Alex Troffey; md, Samuel Kaylin.

Mystery   (PR:A   MPAA:NR)

CHARLIE CHAN'S MURDER CRUISE**   (1940) 70m FOX bw

Sidney Toler (Charlie Chan), Marjorie Weaver (Paula Duke), Lionel Atwill (Dr. Suderman), Sen Yung (Jimmy Chan), Robert Lowery (Dick Kenyon), Don Beddoe (James Ross), Leo G. Carroll (Prof. Gordon), Cora Witherspoon (Susie Watson), Kay Linaker (Mrs. Pendleton), Harlan Briggs (Coroner), Charles Middleton (Mr. Walters), Claire DuBrey (Mrs. Walters), Leonard Mudie (Walter Pendleton), James Burke (Wilkie), Richard Keene (Buttons), Layne Tom, Jr. (Willie Chan), Montague Shaw (Inspector Duff), Harry Strang (Guard), Walter Miller (Officer), Wade Boteler (Police Chief), Emmett Vogan (Hotel Manager), Cliff Clark (Lt. Wilson), John Dilson (Police Doctor).

Scotland Yard inspector is murdered in Chan's office as he is about to reveal his plan for trapping a murderer in a world cruise party. Chan joins the cruise, during which passengers are strangled port and starboard. Fair enough mystery with both direction and camera work up to standard. (See CHARLIE CHAN series, Index.)

p, Sol M. Wurtzel; d, Eugene Forde; w, Robertson White, Lester Ziffren (based on a story by Earl Derr Biggers); ph, Virgil Miller; ed, Harry Reynolds; md, Samuel Kaylin.

Mystery   (PR:A   MPAA:NR)

CHARLIE CHAN'S SECRET***   (1936) 72m FOX bw

Warner Oland (Charlie Chan), Rosina Lawrence (Alice Lowell), Charles Quigley (Dick Williams), Henrietta Crosman (Henrietta Lowell), Edward Trevor (Fred Gage), Astrid Allwyn (Janice Gage), Herbert Mundin (Baxter), Jonathan Hale (Warren T. Phelps), Egon Brecher (Ulrich), Gloria Roy (Carlotta), Ivan Miller (Morton), A. Edmund Carew (Prof. Bowman), William Bailey (Harris), Jerry Miley (Allan Coleby), James T. Mack (Fingerprint Man), Francis Ford (Boat Captain), Landers Stevens (Coroner).

Chan sets out to solve the murder of the heir to a vast fortune and protect others from threatening doom. Virtually every member of the cast with the exception of the police and Chan himself is suspect, as usual, in Chan fare. Capable writing injects some logic into this well-directed yarn. (See CHARLIE CHAN series, Index.)

p, John Stone; d, Gordon Wiles; w, Robert Ellis, Helen Logan, Joseph Hoffman (based on the character by Earl Derr Biggers); ph, Rudolph Mate; ed, Nick De Maggio; md, Samuel Kaylin.

Mystery   (PR:A   MPAA:NR)

CHARLIE MC CARTHY, DETECTIVE**   (1939) 78m UNIV bw

Edgar Bergen with Charlie McCarthy and Mortimer Snerd, Robert Cummings (Scotty Hamilton), Constance Moore (Sheila Stuart), John Sutton (Bill Banning), Louis Calhern (Arthur Aldrich), Edgar Kennedy (Inspector Dailey), Samuel S. Hinds (Court Aldrich), Harold Huber (Tony Garcia), Warren Hymer (Dutch), Ray Turner (Harrison "Gravy" Randolph).

Publisher throws a private party at his home and invites Bergen. The host is murdered and Bergen solves the murder with his dummies finding all the clues, leaving their master to tie them together logically. Though the story is a bit wooden, it's good for laughs. Charlie cornballs his lines and sings a tune called "I'm Charlie McCarthy, Detective."

p&d, Frank Tuttle; w, Edward Ediscu, Harold Shumate, Richard Mack (based on a story by Robertson White, Darrell Ware); ph, George Robinson; ed, Bernard Burton; m/l, Sam Lerner, Ben Oakland, Eddie Cherkose, Jacques Press.

Comedy   (PR:AAA   MPAA:NR)

CHARLIE, THE LONESOME COUGAR**½

(1967) 75m Disney/Cangary, Ltd./BV c

Ron Brown (Jess Bradley), Brian Russell (Potlatch), Linda Wallace (Jess's Fiancee), Jim Wilson (Farmer), Clifford Peterson (Mill Manager), Lewis Sample (Chief Engineer), Edward C. Moller (Mill Hand), Rex Allen (Narrator), Charlie the Cougar.

A Disney "True Life Adventure" beautifully photographed in Northwest timber territory. This one follows Charlie the Cougar as it grows into a full-sized cat. While nothing special, as a light piece it is both entertaining and educational.

p, Walt Disney; d, Winston Hibler; w, Jack Speirs (based on a story by Speirs, Hibler); ph, Lloyd Beebe, William W. Bacon III (Technicolor); m, Franklyn Marks; ed, Gregg McLaughlin; m/l, Speirs, Marks.

Adventure   (PR:AAA   MPAA:NR)

CHARLOTTE'S WEB***½   (1973) 94m PAR c

Voice of: Debbie Reynolds (Charlotte), Paul Lynde (Templeton), Henry Gibson (Wilbur), Rex Allen (Narrator), Martha Scott (Mrs. Arable), Dave Madden (Old Sheep), Danny Bonaduce (Avery), Don Messick (Geoffrey), Herb Vigran (Lurvy), Agnes Moorehead (The Goose), Pam Ferdin (Fern Arable), Joan Gerber (Mrs. Zuckerman/Mrs. Fussy), Robert Holt (Homer Zuckerman), John Stephenson (Arable), William B. White (Henry Fussy).

Charming cartoon adaptation of E. B. White's fantasy. Wilbur is a runt pig who has been raised as the pet of a New England farmer. He is then sold to a neighbor where a sheep tells him that he's fated to be what goes with cheese on rye. He is understandably frightened until he meets a spider named Charlotte who devotes her arachnoidal life to saving Wilbur from the fate of most porkers. Charlotte weaves words into her web that convince the superstitious farmer that Wilbur is some sort of miraculous hog. Wilbur is finally assured of a long life and Charlotte dies after having given birth to 514 baby spiders (and do you think any of them would have written to her?). The movie reeks of whimsy and charm. The voices of Reynolds, Gibson, and all the rest are perfectly cast. Songs by the Sherman Brothers were perfect for the film but none of them stepped out to become hits like the ones they wrote for other Disney movies. Listen for Messick (Geoffrey), Gerber (Mrs. Zuckerman/Mrs. Fussy), and Holt (Homer Zuckerman). Although not known to the public, they are three of the best voice people around and their names can be seen on any given Saturday morning on at least five of the cartoon shows. Messick is the voice of "Scooby-Doo" (and that's what it says on his personalized license plate.) He is also on "Smurfs" and barks regularly on several more. The local joke in Hollywood is that if he ever had laryngitis, twenty-six animals would be out of work. The animation for CHARLOTTE'S WEB is far better than what is usually seen these days. A treat for everyone. Songs include: "Charlotte's Web," "A Veritable Smorgasbord," "There Must Be Something More," "I Can Talk," "Mother Earth and Father Time," "We've Got Lots In Common," "Deep In the Dark," "Zuckerman's Famous Pig."

p, Joe Barbera, William Hanna; d, Charles A. Nichols, Iwao Takamoto; w, Earl Hamner, Jr. (based on the book by E.B. White); ph, Roy Wade, Dick Blundell, Dennis Weaver, Ralph Migliori, George Epperson (Movielab Color); m, Richard M. and Robert B. Sherman; ed, Larry Cowan, Pat Foley; md, Irwin Kostal; art d, Bob Singer, Paul Julian, Ray Aragon; m/l, Sherman and Sherman.

Animated Musical   Cas.   (PR:AAA   MPAA:G)

CHARLTON-BROWN OF THE F.O.   (SEE: MAN IN A COCKED HAT, 1959)

CHARLY***   (1968) 103m Selmur/Cinema Releasing Corp. c

Cliff Robertson (Charly Gordon), Claire Bloom (Alice Kinian), Lilia Skala (Dr. Anna Straus), Leon Janney (Dr. Richard Nemur), Dick Van Patten (Bert), William Dwyer (Joey), Ed McNally (Gimpy), Dan Morgan (Paddy), Barney Martin (Hank), Ruth White (Mrs. Apple), Frank Dolan (Eddie).

First a short story, then a novel, this movie, and finally a Broadway musical, CHARLY is a sometimes fascinating, sometimes infuriating story about a man with a 68 I.Q. who becomes a genius almost overnight. Robertson (Charly) is a thirtyish bakery worker who becomes an experiment for Janney (a neurosurgeon) and Skala (a psychiatrist). They have been doing things with mice and a super-mouse named Algernon is able to beat Charly after the mouse has had some sort of vague brain surgery. Charly agrees to the same surgery and is an instant genius (not unlike Ray Bolger in THE WIZARD OF OZ when he got his brain). He is able to fall in love with and totally satisfy his teacher, Bloom. After he allows himself to be observed, analyzed, and used, Charly sees that Algernon is regressing and will soon lose his edge and be just another mouse. In a rush of words, Charly lets the scientists know his feelings on several matters and we see him fall apart and return to his former slack-jawed but earnest self. Robertson earned an Oscar for his role. He was in the Philippines making TOO LATE THE HERO when the Oscars were handed out and director-producer Robert Aldrich refused to allow him to fly back to Los Angeles for the ceremonies. Robertson never forgave Aldrich for that and his performance in TOO LATE THE HERO showed it. Robertson was involved in every aspect of the film and spent hours in Steinkamp's editing room snipping away at Nelson's often overblown direction. In the role of Hank is Martin, a former New York police officer who was Jackie Gleason's understudy during the best TV days of The Great One. Legend has it that Gleason took many of his moves from Martin.

p&d, Ralph Nelson; w, Stirling Silliphant (based on the short story and novel *Flowers For Algernon* by Daniel Keyes); ph, Arthur Ornitz (Techniscope, Technicolor); m, Ravi Shankar; ed, Frederic Steinkamp; art d, Charles Rosen.

Science/Fiction/Drama **Cas.** **(PR:A-C MPAA:NR)**

CHARMING DECEIVER, THE zero

(1933, Brit.) 73m British International/Majestic bw (GB: HEADS WE GO)
Constance Cummings (*Betty Smith/Dorothy Kay*), Frank Lawton (*Toby Tyrrell*), Binnie Barnes (*Lil Pickering*), Gus McNaughton (*Otis Dove*), Iris Ashley (*Singer*), Claude Hulbert (*Reggie*), Emilio Colombo Orchestrak Fred Duprez, Ellen Pollock, Peter Godfrey, Tonie Edgar Bruce, Michael Wilding.

Just a plain bad picture with Cummings as doppelganger for a Hollywood film star with all the ensuing mix-ups. As a down-and-outer, desperate for money, Cummings agrees to pretend to be the film star for snooty newspaper heir, Lawton, just to squelch an uppity hotel clerk at one of the upper-crust resort spas, and that's not enough reason to use up good film. Trite musical comedy shows no signs of relief.

d, Monty Banks; w, Victor Kendall (based on a story by Fred Thompson); m/l Robert Hargreaves, Stanley Damerell, Montague Ewing, Tolchard Evans.

Comedy/Musical **(PR:A MPAA:NR)**

CHARMING SINNERS*½

(1929) 85m PAR bw
Ruth Chatterton (*Kathryn Miles*), Clive Brook (*Robert Miles*), Mary Nolan (*Anne-Marie Whitley*), William Powell (*Karl Kraley*), Laura Hope Crews (*Mrs. Carr*), Florence Eldridge (*Helen Carr*), Montagu Love (*George Whitley*), Juliette Crosby (*Margaret*), Lorraine Eddy (*Alice*), Claude Allister (*Gregson*).

Somerset Maugham's play, "The Constant Wife," does not translate well to the screen and William Powell is wasted in this farce involving marital cat-and-mouse games. Husband falls for wife's girl friend; old flame of wife shows up; everyone ends up in his or her own bed. Production is all talk and no action.

d, Robert Milton; w, Doris Anderson (based on the play "The Constant Wife" by Somerset Maugham); ph, Victor Milner; ed, Verna Willis.

Drama **(PR:A MPAA:NR)**

CHARRO*

(1969) 98m NG c
Elvis Presley (*Jess Wade*), Ina Balin (*Tracy*), Victor French (*Vince*), Lynn Kellogg (*Marcie*), Barbara Werle (*Sara Ramsey*), Solomon Sturges (*Billy Roy*), Paul Brinegar (*Opie Keetch*), James Sikking (*Gunner*), Harry Landers (*Heff*), Tony Young (*Lt. Rivera*), James Almanzar (*Sheriff Ramsey*), Charles H. Gray (*Mody*), Rodd Redwing (*Lige*), Gargy Walberg (*Martin Tilford*), Duane Grey (*Gabe*), J. Edward McKinley (*Henry Carter*), John Pickard (*Jerome Selby*), Robert Luster (*Will Joslyn*), Christa Lang (*Christa*), Robert Karnes (*Harvey*).

Uninspired western with Presley in a rare dramatic appearance which is just too much for him to handle. Presley plays a reformed bandit who is captured by his old gang. Their plot is to frame him for the heist of a jewel-encrusted Mexican cannon. Sturges, cast as the outlaw leader's brother, is the son of director Preston Sturges. Adequate score by Montenegro.

p, Harry Caplan, Charles Marquis Warren; d&w, Warren (from a story by Frederic Louis Fox); ph, Ellsworth Fredericks (Panavision, Technicolor); m, Hugo Montenegro; ed, Al Clark; art d, James Sullivan; set d, Charles Thompson; spec eff, George Thompson, Woodrow Ward, Robert Beck; m/l, Alan and Marilyn Bergman, Billy Strange, Scott Davis.

Western **(PR:A MPAA:G)**

CHARTER PILOT**

(1940) 70m FOX bw
Lloyd Nolan (*King Morgan*), Lynn Bari (*Marge Duncan*), Arleen Whelan (*Raquel Andrews*), George Montgomery (*Charlie Crane*), Hobart Cavanaugh (*Horace Sturgeon*), Etta McDaniel (*Ophie*), Henry Victor (*Faber*), Andrew Tombee (*Brady*), Charles Wilson (*Owen*), Chick Chandler (*Fred Adams*).

Ace pilot Nolan only gets off the ground twice in this slow action movie which doesn't get off the ground at all itself. Nolan marries a radio broadcaster, promising her he will take a desk job, but flying is in his blood and she compromises by using him as the hero of her radio series. Nolan is oddly miscast as the crack pilot and the script is inadequate, but the cast does the best it can.

p, Sol M. Wurtzel; d, Eugene Forde; w, Stanley Rauh, Lester Ziffren (based on story by J. Robert Bren and Norman Houston); ph, Lucien Andriot; ed, Fred Allen; md, Emil Newman.

Drama **(PR:A MPAA:NR)**

CHARTROOSE CABOOSE*½

(1960) 76m UNIV c
Molly Bee (*Doris Warren*), Ben Cooper (*Dub Dawson*), Edgar Buchanan (*Woody Watts*), Mike McGreevey (*Joey James*), O. Z. Whitehead (*J.B. King*), Slim Pickens (*Pete Harmon*), Kay Bartels (*Laura Warren*), Winslow Cuthbert (*Pastor Purdy*), Mack Williams (*Mr. Warren*), Gilbert Reynolds (*Newsboy*).

Simple-minded tale starring Buchanan as a retired railway conductor who owns a fancily furnished, chartreuse-colored caboose which becomes a shelter for lovers Bee and Cooper, a young boy who has left home—McGreevey—and a wacky millionaire-tramp Whitehead. Conflict arises when a thoughtless brakeman, Pickens, sends the caboose to the junkyard, but it is saved by the intervention of Whitehead.

p, Stanley W. Daughtery; d, William "Red" Reynolds; w, Rod Peterson; (Eastmancolor); m, Darryl Calker.

Drama **(PR:A MPAA:NR)**

CHASE, THE***

(1946) 86m UA bw
Robert Cummings (*Chuck*), Michele Morgan (*Lorna*), Peter Lorre (*Gino*), Steve Cochran (*Roman*), Lloyd Corrigan (*Johnson*), Jack Holt (*Cmdr. Davidson*), Don Wilson (*Fats*), Alexis Minotis (*Acosta*), Nina Koshetz (*Mme. Chin*), Yolanda Lacca (*Midnight*), James Westerfield (*Job*), Shirley O'Hara (*Manicurist*), Jimmy Ames (*The Killer*).

Cummings hires on as chauffeur to racketeer Cochran unaware of his boss's seamy life style and total disregard for the lives of others. One of Cochran's favorite little fun things is racing trains to close calls at railroad crossings by operating a second set of controls from the back seat of his limo. Cummings and mobster's wife Morgan decide to escape and make plans to flee to Havana. Some confusion ensues when the easy device of having everything happen in a dream sequence is employed, but then the real chase is on with Cochran and bodyguard Lorre in hot pursuit until the racketeer impatiently takes control of his speeding car in yet another race with a train and loses. Movie has some Hitchcockian flavor and Cummings handles himself well, but he is overshadowed by newcomer Cochran who is suave, confident, and menacing in a manner reminiscent of Humphrey Bogart.

p, Seymour Nebenzal; d, Arthur Ripley; w, Phillip Yordan (based on a novel *The Black Path of Fear* by Cornell Woolrich); ph, Franz; F. Planer; m, Michael Michelet; ed, Ed Mann; md, Heinz Roemheld; art d, Robert Usher; set d, Victor A. Gangelin; cos, Bill Edwards, Peter Tuesday; spec eff, Ray O. Binger.

Mystery **Cas.** **(PR:A MPAA:NR)**

CHASE, THE*

(1966) 135m Horizon/COL c
Marlon Brando (*Sheriff Calder*), Jane Fonda (*Anna Reeves*), Robert Redford (*Bubber Reeves*), E. G. Marshall (*Val Rogers*), Angie Dickinson (*Ruby Calder*), Janice Rule (*Emily Stewart*), Miriam Hopkins (*Mrs. Reeves*),Martha Hyer (*Mary Fuller*), Richard Bradford (*Danon Fuller*), Robert Duvall (*Edwin Stewart*), James Fox (*Jason "Jake" Rogers*), Diana Hyland (*Elizabeth Rogers*), Henry Hull (*Briggs*), Jocelyn Brando (*Mrs. Briggs*), Katherine Walsh (*Verna Dee*), Lori Martin (*Cutie*), Marc Seaton (*Paul*), Paul Williams (*Seymour*), Clifton James (*Lem*), Malcolm Atterbury (*Mr. Reeves*), Nydia Westman (*Mrs. Henderson*), Joel Fluellen (*Lester Johnson*), Steve Ihnat (*Archie*), Maurice Manson (*Moore*), Bruce Cabot (*Sol*), Steve Whittaker (*Slim*), Pamela Curran (*Mrs. Siftifieus*), Ken Renard (*Sam*), Eduardo Ciannelli, Richard Collier (*Guests at Rogers's Party*), Grady Sutton (*Mr. Sifftifieus*), Amy Fonda (*Young Anna in Photograph*), Ralph Moody, George Winters, Howard Wright, Monte Hale, Mel Gallagher, Ray Galvin, Davis Roberts.

This film is completely mistitled in that there is very little chase after escaped con Redford by Brando, the sheriff of a small Texas town whose financial overlord is banker Marshall. Wasted are Fonda, stepdaughter of gin-joint owner Cabot, and Duvall, a cuckolded, meek-mannered vice-president in Marshall's bank. His wife is the slatternly, hip-swinging Rule, who is having affairs with every male in town. Brando appears sporadically in his squad car to quell threats to blacks from the local bully-boy whites, a stupid spinning of wheels for a great talent. Redford is hardly seen at all as he makes his way back to see his woman, Fonda, and to square scores in the home town that railroaded him into prison. Much of the film dwells on a wife-swapping party where Rule just about rapes any available male; she plays a southern trollop with such verve and hokey abandon that her role becomes a grotesque burlesque of the type. Dickinson is Brando's long-suffering spouse, who encourages him to stand up to his sponsor, Marshall. The banker is hosting a party while Redford is running about in the dark and Brando is shooing drunks home. All Brando wants is to make enough money to buy back his father's lost sharecropper's farm, an ambition that makes one doubt his sanity. "I hate this job," he constantly moans to Dickinson, who nags him about having children. "I ain't raisin' no children over a jail," he snarls. Of course, he is the only decent white person in town and one isn't too sure that the unseen Redford isn't better than he is. When Brando bucks Marshall, the banker's goons show up and beat the sheriff to a bloody pulp. Redford finally shows up to meet with Fonda and Fox, the latter being his one-time friend who covets Fonda in a friendly manner and resents his father's (Marshall) power and money. The three are trapped in the town junkyard by Marshall's bullies who shoot into the wrecked cars and hurl Molotov cocktails at the fugitive. Fox is killed and Redford is brought to the local jail by Brando but the fugitive is murdered on the jail steps by a thug whom Brando pulverizes. Brando and Dickinson leave town the next day, utterly disillusioned by the corrupt humanity surrounding them. THE CHASE is a terrible disappointment, a jumbled, disjointed film directed feebly by Penn, whose talents have been overrated as was his so-called masterpiece, BONNIE AND CLYDE. It is a production without purpose or basic interest, since its characters are so stereotyped as to be predictable before each line is spoken or a step taken. It is OUR TOWN gone wrong, but the corrupting elements are so fragmentary and ill-presented that there is no sense of jeopardy or apprehension. Redford was so little used that he had to introduce himself to fellow cast members every time he set foot on the set. He met director Penn only a few times, spending most of his time running through rice fields in Chico, California, with a second unit recording his on-the-run exploits. Penn later denounced the film, complaining that producer Spiegel barred him from participating in the final editing and that Spiegel interfered with the production from beginning to end. He was to say: "I have never made a film under such unspeakable conditions. I was used merely to move the actors around like horses." And it shows, swayback horses and all.

p, Sam Spiegel; d, Arthur Penn; w, Lillian Hellman (based on the novel and play by Horton Foote); ph, Joseph La Shelle and, uncredited, Robert Surtees (Panavision, Technicolor); m, John Barry; ed, Gene Milford; prod d, Richard Day; art d, Robert Luthardt; set d, Frank Tuttle; cos, Donfeld; spec eff, David Koehler.

Drama **(PR:O MPAA:NR)**

CHASE A CROOKED SHADOW***½

(1958, Brit.) 92m Associated British-Pathe/WB bw
Richard Todd (*Ward*), Anne Baxter (*Kimberley*), Herbert Lom (*Vargas*), Alexander Knox (*Chandler Brisson*), Faith Brook (*Mrs. Whitman*), Alan Tilvern (*Carlos*), Thelma d'Aguiar (*Maria*).

An engrossing and superbly crafted thriller about the mysterious arrival of Baxter's presumed-dead brother. His act is convincing enough to fool even the police. She begins to think that it is a plot to drive her mad, then murder her over some diamonds. A fresh approach by Anderson, a remarkably gifted and artistic director, who has long gone unappreciated. Remade for television in 1975 as ONE OF MY WIVES IS MISSING.

p, Douglas Fairbanks, Jr., Thomas Clyde; d, Michael Anderson; w, David D. Osborn, Charles Sinclair; ph, Erwin Hiller; m, Matyas Seiber; ed, Gordon Pilkington; cos, Anthony Mendelson.

Thriller/Drama (PR:A MPAA:NR)

CHASE FOR THE GOLDEN NEEDLES (SEE: GOLDEN NEEDLES, 1974)

CHASER, THE**½ (1938) 73m MGM bw
Dennis O'Keefe (*Thomas Z. Brandon*), Ann Morriss (*Dorothy Mason*), Lewis Stone (*Dr. Prescott*), Nat Pendleton (*Floppy Phil*), Henry O'Neill (*Calhoun*), Ruth Gillette (*Mrs. Olson*), John Qualen (*Lars*), Robert Emmett Keane (*Simon Kelly*), Jack Mulhall (*Joe*), Irving Bacon (*Harvey*), Pierre Watkin (*Mr. Beaumont*), Barbara Pepper (*Mabel*), Lana Turner (*Miss Rutherford in the Office*), Barbara Bedford (*Brandon's Secretary*), Eddie Acuff (*Photographer*), Selmer Jackson (*Judge*).

Ambulance-chasing lawyer falls for the girl planted by his company to get the goods on him. Fairly good plot and capable direction but probably the most interesting note on the film is that it was Turner's second film with MGM. When the picture was released the ads proclaimed, "Watch Out for a Gorgeous Girl!" The lady they meant was the film's leading lady Morriss, making her screen debut, but to film buffs the slogan has taken on a different connotation with the brief appearance of Turner as one of the sleazy lawyer's clients whose big scene ended up on the cutting room floor. Consequently, screen billing was removed, but if one looks quickly she can still be spotted in the lawyer's waiting room, legs crossed provocatively, reading a magazine. Three years and several films later Morriss dropped out of sight. (Remake of THE NUISANCE.)

p, Frank Davis; d, Edwin L. Marin; w, Everett Freeman, Harry Ruskin, Bella and Samuel Spewack (based on a story by Chandler Sprague, Howard Emmett Rogers); ph, Charles Lawton, Jr.; ed, George Boemler; art d, Cedric Gibbons, Randall Duell; set design, Edwin B. Willis.

Drama (PR:A MPAA:NR)

CHASERS, THE (SEE: GIRL HUNTERS, THE, 1960)

CHASING DANGER** (1939) 60m FOX bw
Preston Foster (*Steve Mitchell*), Lynn Bari (*Renee Claire*), Wally Vernon (*Waldo*), Henry Wilcoxon (*Andre Duvac*), Joan Woodbury (*Hazila*), Harold Huber (*Carlos Demitri*), Jody Gilbert (*Teeda*), Pedro de Cordoba (*Gurra Din*), Stanley Fields (*Capt. Fontaine*), Roy D'Arcy (*Corbin*).

Crack photojournalist stationed in Paris is sent to cover an Arab rebellion. Mastermind of desert warfare turns out to be supposedly dead jewel thief. Script is only fair, but director Cortez has allowed Foster-Vernon team plenty of leeway in their roles as a couple of scamps who fast-talk their way out of tight situations.

p, Sol M. Wurtzel; d, Ricardo Cortez; w, Robert Ellis, Helen Logan (based on a story by Leonardo Bercovici); ph, Virgil Miller; ed, Norman Colbert; md, Samuel Kaylin.

Adventure (PR:A MPAA:NR)

CHASING RAINBOWS** (1930) 100m MGM bw/c (AKA: ROAD SHOW)
Bessie Love (*Carlie*), Charles King (*Terry*), Jack Benny (*Eddie*), George K. Arthur (*Lester*), Polly Moran (*Polly*), Gwen Lee (*Peggy*), Nita Martan (*Daphne*), Eddie Phillips (*Cordova*), Marie Dressler (*Bonnie*), Youcca Troubetzkoy (*Lanning*).

Traveling vaudeville team has one half constantly falling in love with leading ladies, causing much consternation to the better half. When King finds his current love interest in the arms of another he sees the light and goes back to his original partner, prompting her to break into "Happy Days Are Here Again," in the song's movie debut. Audiences did not share the sentiment however, weary as they were with musicals, and refused to see the film, though the final segment was shot in technicolor. Benny does a good job in a serious role of a jaundiced stage manager, but the movie did not produce a pot of gold. Songs include: "Happy Days Are Here Again," "Lucky Me, Lovable You," "Do I Know What I'm Doing," "Everybody Tap," (Milton Ager, Jack Yellen), "Love Ain't Nothin' But the Blues" (Joe Goodwin, Louis Alter), "Dynamic Personality" (Fred Fisher, Ed Ward, Reggie Montgomery), "Poor But Honest" (Gus Edwards), "Gotta Feeling For You" (Joe Trent, Alter).

d, Charles F. Reisner; w, Bess Meredyth, Wells Root; ph, Ira Morgan; ed, George Hively.

Musical/Comedy (PR:A MPAA:NR)

CHASING TROUBLE zero (1940) 64m MON bw
Frankie Darro (*Cupid*), Marjorie Reynolds (*Susie*), George Cleveland (*Lester*), Alex Callam (*Morgan*), Lillian Elliott (*Mrs. O'Brien*), Milburn Stone (*Callahan*), Mantan Moreland (*Jefferson*), Tristram Coffin (*Phillips*), I. Stanford Jolley (*Molotoff*), Willy Costell (*Kurt*), Donald Kerr (*Cassidy*), Cheryl Walker (*Phyliss*).

Darro's mania for handwriting analysis is useful in exposing international espionage ring. Picture suffers from the weight of incredible situations and stiff performances.

p, Grant Withers; d, Howard Bretherton; w, Mary McCarthy; ph, Harry Neumann.

Mystery (PR:A MPAA:NR)

CHASING YESTERDAY*½ (1935) 78m RAD bw
Anne Shirley (*Jeanne*), O.P. Heggie (*Sylvestre Bonnard*), Helen Westley (*Therese*), Elizabeth Patterson (*Prefers*), John Qualen (*Coccoz*), Trent Durkin (*Henri*), Etienne Girardot (*Mouche*), Doris Lloyd (*Mme. De Gabry*).

Heggie plays Anatole France's Sylvestre Bonnard, a gentle old archaeologist seeking to find his lost youth through the daughter of the woman he once loved but lost. A sweet but slow-gaited little picture which good direction could not improve.

p, Cliff Reid; d, George Nicholls, Jr.; w, Francis E. Faragoh (based on the novel *The Crime of Sylvestre Bonnard* by Anatole France); ph, Lucien Andriot; ed, Arthur Schmidt; md, Alberto Columbo.

Drama (PR:A MPAA:NR)

CHASTITY** (1969) 81m AIP c
Cher (*Chastity*), Barbara London (*Diana Midnight*), Stephen Whittaker (*Eddie*), Tom Nolan (*Tommy*), Danny Zapien (*Cab Driver*), Elmer Valentine (*1st Truck Driver*), Burke Rhind (*Salesman*), Richard Armstrong (*Husband*), Joe Light (*Master of Ceremonies*), Dolly Hunt (*Church Lady*), Jason Clarke (*2nd Truck Driver*).

Cher takes to the road in this highway drama written and produced by her then-husband Bono. She plays a woman with the title virtue and surprisingly shows some thespian ability while doing so. As expected, the music is by Bono.

p, Sonny Bono; d, Alessio de Paola; ph, Ben Coleman (DeLuxe Color); w&m, Bono; ed, Hugo Grimaldi; cos, Sadie Hayes.

Drama (PR:C MPAA:R)

CHASTITY BELT, THE* (1968, Ital.) 110m Titanus/WB/Seven Arts c
(AKA: ON MY WAY TO THE CRUSADES I MET A GIRL WHO . . .)
Tony Curtis (*Guerrando*), Monica Vitti (*Boccadoro*), Nino Castelnuovo (*Marculfo*), Hugh Griffith (*Ibn-el-Rascid*), John Richardson (*Dragone*), Ivo Garrani (*Duke of Pandolfo*), Francesco Mule, Franco Sportelli, Umberto Raho, Leopoldo Trieste, Gabriella Giorgelli (*Bits*).

Inept comedy set in the Middle Ages which has the gorgeous Vitti locked in a chastity belt. The man holding the key is the over-protective Curtis who, after locking up, leaves for the Crusades. The key changes many hands, but never falls into Vitti's. A rather insulting one-liner which lasts far too long.

p, Francesco Mazzei; d, Pasquale Festa Campanile; w, Luigi Magni, Larry Gelbart (based on the story by Ugo Liberatore); ph, Carlo Di Palma; m, Riz Ortolani; ed, Gabrio Astori, Charles Nelson; md, Ortolani; art d, Piero Poletto; cos, Danilo Donati.

Comedy (PR:C MPAA:NR)

CHATO'S LAND** (1972) 100m UA c
Charles Bronson (*Chato*), Jack Palance (*Quincey Whitmore*), Richard Basehart (*Nye Buell*), James Whitmore (*Joshua Everette*), Simon Oakland (*Jubal Hooker*), Ralph Waite (*Elias Hooker*), Richard Jordan (*Earl Hooker*), Victor French (*Martin Hall*), Willliam Watson (*Harvey Lansing*), Roddy McMillan (*Gavin Malechie*), Paul Young (*Brady Logan*), Lee Patterson (*George Dunn*), Rudy Ugland (*Will Coop*), Raul Castro (*Mexican Scout*), Sonia Rangan (*Chato's Woman*), Clive Endersby (*Jacob Meade*), Rebecca Wilson (*Edna Malechie*), Verna Harvey (*Shelby Hooker*), Sally Adez (*Moira Logan*), Peter Dyneley (*Exra*), Hugh McDermott (*Bartender*).

After killing a white sheriff, embittered Apache Bronson is chased across the West by a posse, led by Palance. A great cast is primarily wasted in this gory, below average, and overlong film. The script could have been written for a silent film to fit in with Bronson's traditional man-of-few-words image (or hardly any words at all, just a few grunts and a lot of squint). Screenwriter Wilson turned in a better scenario for another western, LAWMAN, a Burt Lancaster vehicle. As usual, Bronson must rely upon the belief of those viewers who find silence eloquent. Shot in Spain.

p&d, Michael Winner; w, Gerald Wilson; ph, Robert Paynter (DeLuxe Color); m, Jerry Fielding; ed, Freddie Wilson; art d, Manolo Manpaso.

Western (PR:O MPAA:PG)

CHATTERBOX**½ (1936) 68m RKO bw
Anne Shirley (*Jenny Yates*), Phillips Holmes (*Philip Greene, Jr.*), Edward Ellis (*Uriah Lowell*), Erik Rhodes (*Archie Fisher*), Margaret Hamilton (*Emily Tipton*), Granville Bates (*Philip Greene, Sr.*), Allen Vincent (*Harrison*), Lucille Ball (*Lillian Temple*), George Offerman, Jr. (*Michael Arbuckle*).

Stage-struck Vermont girl wants to follow in her mother's footsteps and become a great stage star, but her first appearance on the great white way turns into a giant fiasco. All is not lost, however, when love enters the picture, quenching the thirst for stardom. Good performances and good comedy save a weak story that takes much of its impetus from MORNING GLORY.

p, Robert Sisk; d, George Nicholls, Jr.; w, Sam Mintz (based on a play by David Carb); ph, Robert De Grasse; ed, Arthur Schmidt.

Drama (PR:A MPAA:NR)

CHATTERBOX* (1943) 77m REP bw
Joe E. Brown (*Rex Vane*), Judy Canova (*Judy Boggs*), John Hubbard (*Sebastian Smart*), Rosemary Lane (*Carol Forest*), Chester Clute (*Wilfred Peckinpaugh*), Emmett Vogan (*Roger Grant*), Gus Schilling (*Gillie*), Anne Jeffreys (*Vivian Gale*), George Byron (*Joe*), Art Whitney (*Assistant Director*), Frank Melton, Gary Bruce, Matty Kemp, Ray Parsons (*Reporters*), Mary Armstrong (*Guest at Dude Ranch*), Mills Brothers (*Specialty*), Roy Barcroft (*Laborer*), Earle Hodgins (*Wrangler*), Nora Lane (*Secretary*), Joe Phillips (*Producer*), Edward Earle, Herbert Heyes, Sam Flint, Gordon DeMain (*Production Assistants*), Spade Cooley (*Singing Musician*), Maris Windsor (*Hostess*), Ruth Robinson (*Wardrobe Woman*), Robert Conway (*Announcer on Train*), Pierce Lyden (*Wrangler*), Billy Bletcher (*Black Jake*), Ben Taggart (*Foreman*), Dickie Dilton (*Indian Boy*).

Mugging broadly and generally overacting, Brown and Canova provide few laughs in this moth-eaten comedy. When broadcaster Brown is signed for a film, he falls off his horse and is rescued by Canova, but adverse publicity surrounding the event makes him appear the fool until a dangerous stint in a mountain cabin about to be dynamited saves his rubber face. Songs: "Mad About Him, Sad About Him, How Can I Be Glad Without Him Blues" (Larry Marks, Dick Charles), "Sweet Lucy Brown" (Leon and Otis Rene).

p, Albert J. Cohen; d, Joseph Santley; w, George Carleton Brown, Frank Gill, Jr.; ph, Ernest Miller; ed, Ernest Nims; md, Walter Scharf; art d, Russell Kimball; spec eff, Howard Lydecker.

Comedy (PR:A MPAA:NR)

CHE!* (1969) 96m FOX c

Omar Sharif *(Che Guevara)*, Jack Palance *(Fidel Castro)*, Cesare Danova *(Ramon Valdez)*, Robert Loggia *(Faustino Morales)*, Woody Strode *(Guillermo)*, Barbara Luna *(Anita Marquez)*, Frank Silvera *(Goatherd)*, Albert Paulsen *(Capt. Vasquez)*, Linda Marsh *(Tania)*, Tom Troupe *(Felipe Munoz)*, Rudy Diaz *(Willy)*, Perry Lopez *(Rolando)*, Abraham Sofaer *(Pablo Rojas)*, Richard Angarola *(Col. Salazar)*, Sarita Vara *(Celia Sanchez)*, Paul Bertoya *(Raul Castro)*, Sid Haig *(Antonio)*, Adolph Caesar *(Juan Almeida)*, Paul Picerni *(Hector)*, Ray Martell *(Camilio Cienfuegos)*.

As a revolutionary Saturday morning cartoon this trite political biography may pass, but it fails when judged at any higher level. A pseudo-documentary approach to the life of Che Guevara, this one gains points only for its attempt to make history entertaining. We see Guevara (Sharif) as a radical youth working for Castro (Palance); taking part in Castro's Batista overthrow; as he becomes disillusioned with Castro; and at his death in a Bolivian revolt. One has not lived until seeing Palance play Cuban dictator Castro.

p, Sy Bartlett; d, Richard Fleischer; w, Michael Wilson, Bartlett (based on a story by Bartlett, David Karp); ph, Charles Wheeler (Panavision, DeLuxe Color); m, Lalo Schifrin; ed, Marion Rothman; art d, Jack Martin Smith, Arthur Lonergan; set d, Walter S. Scott, Stuart A. Reiss.

Political Drama (PR:C MPAA:M)

CHE?** (1973, Ital./Fr./Ger.) 112m PAC c
(AKA: DIARY OF FORBIDDEN DREAMS)

Marcello Mastroianni *(Alex)*, Sydne Rome *(The Girl)*, Romolo Valli *(Administrator)*, Hugh Griffith *(Owner of Villa)*, Guido Alberti *(Priest)*, Giancarlo Piacentini *(Stud)*, Carlo Delle Piane *(The Boy)*, Roman Polanski *(Zanzara)*.

While not a bad film, this is easily Polanski's worst work. Centering on a hitchhiker named Candide, it becomes a diary of her variety of sexual encounters. Mastroianni is cast as an impotent homosexual whose sex life is altered by her arrival. A film in which the brilliant Polish director allows more of his obsessions to be displayed on the screen. Sydne Rome, as Candide, does not have the presence to carry off this part like a Marie Schneider-type.

p, Carlo Ponti; d, Roman Polanski; w, Polanski, Gerard Brach; ph, Marcello Gatti, Giuseppe Ruzzolini (Todd-AO-35-Color); md, Claudio Gizzi; ed, Polanski; art d, Aurelio Crugnola.

Drama (PR:O MPAA:NR)

CHEAP DETECTIVE, THE*** (1978) 92m COL c

Peter Falk *(Lou Peckinpaugh)*, Ann-Margret *(Jezebel Dezire)*, Eileen Brennan *(Betty DeBoop)*, Sid Caesar *(Ezra Dezire)*, Stockard Channing *(Bess)*, James Coco *(Marcel)*, Dom DeLuise *(Pepe Damascus)*, Louise Fletcher *(Marlene DuChard)*, John Houseman *(Jasper Blubber)*, Madeline Kahn *(Mrs. Montenegro)*, Fernando Lamas *(Paul DuChard)*, Marsha Mason *(Georgia Merkle)*, Phil Silvers *(Hoppy)*, Abe Vigoda *(Sgt. Rizzuto)*, Paul Williams *(Boy)*, Nicol Williamson *(Col. Schissel)*, Emory Bass *(Butler)*, Carmine Caridi *(Sgt. Crosseti)*, James Cromwell *(Schnell)*, Scatman Crothers *(Tinker)*, David Ogden Stiers *(Captain)*, Vic Tayback *(Lt. DiMaggio)*, Carole Wells *(Hat Check Girl)*, John Calvin, Barry Michlin, Richard Narita, Jonathan Banks, Lew Gallo, Lee McLaughlin, Zale Kessler, Jerry Ziman, Wally Berns, Bella Bruck, Henry Sutton, Maurice Marks, Joe Ross, Dean Perry, George Rondo, Ronald L. Schwary, Louis H. Kelly, Charles A. Bastin, Armando Gonzalez, Gary L. Dyer, Steven Fisher, Laurie Hagen, Lee Menning, Nancy Warren, Nancy Marlowe Coyne, Lynn Griffis, Paula Friel, Sheila Sisco, Lauren Simon, Cindy Lang, Tina Ritt, David Matthau, Gary Alexander, Michele Bernath, George F. Simmons, Joree Sirianni, Cornell Chulay.

A real romp for Falk playing a wacky Bogart-like gumshoe running around San Francisco and parodying many a Bogie film. Simon's slapstick comedy is a cut below his MURDER BY DEATH but nevertheless consistently funny and often hilarious. Falk's character lurches and scrambles through the plots of THE MALTESE FALCON and CASABLANCA, to name two, with Mason doing a jiggling imitation of his dead partner's wife (she carries his ashes in a jar constantly being spilled, reprising the role of Gladys George). Kahn is a jut-jawed imitation of Astor, Houseman, a blimpish Greenstreet (in a role originally intended to go to overweight black nightclub comedian-impressionist George Kirby, who lost out because of his drug-deal prison sentence), Williams a shrimpish Elisha Cook, Jr., DeLuise an unfunny Lorre type. Fletcher and Lamas do Bergman and Henreid when the theme switches to CASABLANCA and Brennan clutches and claws at Falk in her Lee Patrick /Effie role. Hooligans and Nazis are mixed together in a plot sure to stupify anyone not familiar with those Bogart classics. Ann-Margret's role is sort of Bacall in THE BIG SLEEP and Trevor in MURDER, MY SWEET (combining Hammett and Chandler). Her outfit is so revealing that her ample body does all the acting, bosoms bursting, things flashing. She is married to the real culprit, if one can really pinpoint the villain, millionaire owner of the Golden Gate Bridge, the zany Caesar. The gags run hot and heavy, many of them forced, many genuinely funny. The scene in the cafe where the Germans, led by Williamson, begin singing their war song and are countered by Falk and Brennan bellowing "Deep Purple, " is wonderful, as is the bit where Falk almost breaks Scatman Crothers' fingers for playing *the* song—not "As Time Goes By" but "Jeepers Creepers." It's not vintage Simon but the film has enough lowbrow laughs to keep the viewer interested, and Falk's performance is worth the whole show.

p, Ray Stark; d, Robert Moore; w, Neil Simon; ph, John A. Alonzo (Panavision, Metrocolor); m, Patrick Williams; ed, Sidney Levin, Michael A. Stevenson; prod d, Robert Luthardt; art d, Phillip Bennett; set d, Charles Pierce; cos, Theoni V. Aldredge, John A. Anderson, Agnes G. Henry.

Comedy (PR:C MPAA:PG)

CHEAPER BY THE DOZEN*½** (1950) 85m FOX c

Clifton Webb *(Frank Bunker Gilbreth)*, Jeanne Crain *(Ann Gilbreth)* Myrna Loy *(Mrs. Lillian Gilbreth)*, Betty Lynn *(Libby Lancaster)*, Edgar Buchanan *(Dr. Burton)*, Barbara Bates *(Ernestine)*, Mildred Natwick *(Mrs. Mebane)*, Sara Allgood *(Mrs. Monahan)*, Anthony Sydes *(Fred Gilbreth)*, Roddy McCaskill *(Jack Gilbreth)*, Norman Ollestad *(Frank Gilbreth, Jr.)*, Carole Nugent *(Lillie Gilbreth)*, Jimmy Hunt *(William Gilbreth)*, Teddy Driver *(Dan Gilbreth)*, Betty Barker *(Mary Gilbreth)*, Evelyn Varden *(School Principal)*, Frank Orth *(Higgins)*, Craig Hill *(Tom Black)*, Virginia Brissac *(Mrs. Benson)*, Walter Baldwin *(Jim Bracken)*, Benny Bartlett *(Joe Scales)*, Syd Saylor *(Plumber)*, Ken Christy *(Mailman)*, Mary Field *(Music Teacher)*.

CHEAPER BY THE DOZEN is the predecessor to BELLES ON THEIR TOES and a far superior movie. Clifton Webb is the firm but adoring father of twelve children. He is married to Myrna Loy and the fact that she keeps her sense of humor as well as her figure after a dozen births is enough to make you believe this is a fantasy. Webb is an efficiency expert (though evidently not that efficient in the birth-control department) who is stern, dogmatic, and wants everything his own way. Loy is a psychologist as well as being a mother and she uses much of her knowledge on her husband. The film has no particular driving story but is a host of engaging and heart-warming family incidents that show the closeness of these fourteen people. Webb escorts eldest daughter Crain to the high-school prom and winds up as the hit of the dance; a mass tonsilectomy; twelve cases of whooping cough, etc. In short, the movie is whatever can happen to an only child, times twelve. Webb, who was always epicene, is such a good actor that he manages to convince us he was capable of fathering children, but there is always that prissiness, used to such good advantage in the BELVEDERE pictures, that made Webb a household name. In the 1950s, the filmmakers apparently had a good deal more taste than is evident now, because the death scene (which prompted the Webbless sequel) is so gently handled that it's barely seen. An altogether lovely film, rich with humanity and fine work on all levels.

p, Lamar Trotti; d, Walter Lang; w, Trotti (based on the novel by Frank B. Gilbreth, Jr. and Ernestine Gilbreth Carey); ph, Leon Shamroy (Technicolor); m, Cyril Mockridge; ed, J. Watson Webb, Jr.; md, Lionel Newman.

Comedy (PR:AAA MPAA:NR)

CHEAPER TO KEEP HER zero (1980) 92m American Cinema c

Mac Davis *(Bill Dekkar)*, Tovah Feldshuh *(K. D. Locke)*, Art Metrano *(Tony Turino)*, Ian McShane *(Dr. Alfred Sunshine)*, Priscilla Lopez *(Theresa)*, Rose Marie *(Ida Bracken)*, Jack Gilford *(Stanley Bracken)*, J. Pat O'Malley *(Landlord)*, Gwen Humble *(Laura)*, Shannon Wilcox *(Nora)*, Chuck Hicks *(Abe)*, Bruce Flanders *(Leon)*, Joe Regalbuto *(Chuck)*, Rod McCary *(Brownmiller)*, Steve Gagnon *(Peter)*, Fred Stuthman *(Charlie)*, Jane Strudwick *(Virginia)*, Wallace Shaun *(Mugger)*.

Mac Davis and crew are awful in this sexist and racist example of careless filmmaking. Davis plays an alimony attorney who puts the make on his female clients, and that's about it. Films like this justify the complaints about today's Hollywood.

p, Lenny Isenberg; d, Ken Annakin; w, Timothy Harris, Herschel Weingrod; ph, Roland "Ozzie" Smith (Metrocolor); m, Dick Halligan; ed, Edward Warschilka; set d, Charles Rutherford; m/l Carol Connors.

Comedy Cas. (PR:O MPAA:R)

CHEAT, THE** (1931) 65m PAR bw

Tallulah Bankhead *(Elsa Carlyle)*, Irving Pichel *(Hardy Livingston)*, Harvey Stephens *(Jeffrey Carlyle)*, Jay Fassett *(Terrell)*, Ann Andrews *(Mrs. Albright)*, Willard Dashiell *(Judge)*, Arthur Hohl *(Defense Attorney)*, Robert Strange *(District Attorney)*.

The picture was released at the depths of the Depression and showed that even the Long Island rich can manage to be unhappy. Bankhead is married to Stephens and she loses $10,000 gambling in a club (in 1931, truly a king's ransom). She must keep that from Stephens so she takes some money she'd been harboring for a charity fund and speculates in the market in a vain attempt to win back the earlier money. Naturally, her stock deal sours and she is now in very hot water so she accepts money from a wealthy admirer (Pichel, later a successful B movie director) who has just returned from the Orient. Stephens gives her money to pay Pichel but Pichel would prefer several pounds of her flesh and she fends him off by shooting him to death. The climax in the courtroom features husband Stephens taking the blame for the killing and about to be convicted when Tallu tells all and he is saved. This was originally made as a silent film with Sessue Hayakawa (1915) as the heavy and Fanny Ward as the lady (directed by C. B. de Mille). It had two other incarnations as well: in 1923, and then in France in 1937, but it seldom got any better. Bankhead's father was speaker of the House of Representatives, her uncle was an Alabama senator, and her grandfather was also a senator. They all despaired for Tallu's welfare when she took up with the showbiz crowd. They may have been right for, after a stringent convent education, she let it all hang out and was known far and wide as one of the wildest party women in Hollywood.

d, George Abbott; w, Harry Hervey (based on the original silent film script by Hector Turnbull); ph, George Folren.

Crime Drama (PR:C-O MPAA:NR)

CHEAT, THE** (1950, Fr.) 79m DIF bw

Bernard Blier *(Robert)*, Simone Signoret *(Dora)*, Jacques Baumer *(Louis)*, Jane Marken *(The Mother)*, Frank Villard *(Francois)*, Ozenne *(Eric)*, Laure Diana *(Helen)*, Mona Dol *(Chief Nurse)*, Fernard Rauzena *(Riding Master)*, Jean Gobin *(Emile)*.

Signoret, strong, self-aware, and ripely sensual is married to riding academy owner Blier but with the help of her mother (Marken) she carries on a series of affairs intent on bagging bigger game. Blier is eventually ruined but Signoret, after being jilted by a gigolo she's fallen in love with, suffers a near-fatal accident. Thoroughly competent and typically dull, the film is told in a fractured flashback style that only confuses the story. Signoret (whose real name is Simone Kaminker) is, of course, always worth watching.

p, Emile Natan; d, Yves Allegret; w, Jacques Sigurd.

Drama (PR:C-O MPAA:NR)

CHEATERS** (1934) 65m Liberty/Hollywood bw
Bill Boyd (Steve Morris), June Collyer (Kay Murray), Dorothy Mackaill (Mabel), William Collier, Sr. (K. C. Kelly), Alan Mowbray (Paul Southern), Guinn Williams (Detective Sweeney), Louise Beavers (Lily).

Convoluted story of sweet young thing released on parole, still in love with the cur who put her up to swindling a rich man into marriage. Sweet young thing with mind of melon. Nothing in this movie works in spite of the fact that the technical crew is topnotch.

d, Phil Rosen; w, Adele Buffington (based on the story "The Peacock Screen" by Fanny Heaslip Lea); ph, Harry Neumann, Tom Gallagher.

Drama (PR:A MPAA:NR)

CHEATERS, THE*½ (1945) 87m REP bw (AKA: THE CASTAWAY)
Joseph Schildkraut (Mr. M.) Billie Burke (Mrs. Pidgeon), Eugene Pallette (Mr. Pidgeon), Ona Munson (Florie), Raymond Walburn (Willie), Anne Gillis (Angela), Ruth Terry (Therese), Robert Livingston (Stephen Bates), David Holt (Reggie), Robert Greigs (MacFarland), Norma Varden (Mattie, Mr. Pidgeon's Secretary), Byron Foulger (Process Server), St. Luke's Choristers.

Charming comedy about an upper-crust family about to be dashed on the rocks of poverty because of Burke's featherbrained financial decision. Pallette is Burke's financier husband and he sees the end of his empire unless they can raise some cash. Pallette's rich uncle is about to die and they hope to get some money from him but he leaves his entire fortune to an actress he's never met (Munson), because she once delighted him when he was a boy by her performance as "Little Eva" in a version of "Uncle Tom's Cabin." It's Christmastime and their daughter brings home a charity case—Schildkraut—to spend the holidays. Obviously drawn from the likes of John Barrymore, Schildkraut is an amiable stage star who has fallen from favor. This low station doesn't daunt his ham-on-rye attitudes and he joins the household, thus making it almost, but not quite, as nuts as the family in YOU CAN'T TAKE IT WITH YOU. Schildkraut locates the missing Munson and they take her in, but don't tell her about the inheritance. She is happy to be part of the family and they do their best to convince her that she's an actual blood relative. On Christmas, Schildkraut gets so drunk that he spills the beans to Munson (by this time an attraction has commenced between them) but she is a big girl, takes the news with reality, and agrees to divvy up the $5 million in question with everyone (mind you, this picture was made in 1945, when $5 million was a lot of money; come to think of it, it still is!). The movie owes its derivation to British humorist Jerome K. Jerome's "Passing of the Third Floor Back," with a touch of Charles Dickens tossed in for a heart tug.

p&d, Joseph Kane; w, Frances Hyland (based on a story by Hyland and Albert Ray); ph, Reggie Lanning; m, Walter Scharf; ed, Richard L. Van Enger.

Comedy (PR:A MPAA:NR)

CHEATERS, THE**½ (1961, Fr.) 117m Silver Films-Cinetel-Zebra Film/CD bw
(LES TRICHEURS; PECCATORI IN BLUE JEANS)
Jacques Charrier (Bob Letellier), Pascale Petit (Mic), Andrea Parisy (Clo), Laurent Terzieff (Alain), Roland Lesaffre (Roger), Dany Saval (Nicole), Jacques Portet (Guy), Pierre Brice (Bernard), Alfunso Mathis (Peter), Jean-Paul Belmondo (Lou), Denise Vernac (Mic's Mother), Roland Armontel.

Charrier is a Paris student from a good family who falls in with a group of youths headed by Parisy. They go out their way to defy convention, both moral and social, and after sleeping with Parisy, Charrier falls in love with Petit. She reciprocates, but since love is a bourgeois sentiment rejected by the group they hide their feelings. Petit recruits Charrier into a blackmail scheme she is running in order to buy herself an English sports car. Charrier hesitates, but goes ahead with the plan. When he delivers the money to Petit, he finds her in bed with Terzieff. He throws the money on the bed and walks out. Later they meet at a party at Parisy's and begin to play a truth game. In an attempt to hurt Charrier, Petit tells the players that Terzieff is a much better lover than Charrier. Charrier in turn tells Petit that he never really loved her and that he will marry Parisy. Petit is stunned and runs out to her car. Charrier runs after her shouting that he had cheated at the truth game, but before she can hear him her car smashes into a gasoline truck and she is killed. There are a couple of nice moments in this drama, but overall it's too long and mostly boring. Carne made one great film, CHILDREN OF PARADISE, but everything was downhill from there, including this piece.

p, Robert Dorfmann; d, Marcel Carne; w, Carne, Jacques Sigurd (based on a story by Charles Spaak); ph, Claude Renoir; ed, Albert Jurgenson; art d, Paul Bertrand; cos, Mayo, Christian Dior, Heim, Virginie.

Drama (PR:O MPAA:NR)

CHEATERS AT PLAY** (1932) 58m FOX bw
Thomas Meighan (Michael Lanyard), Charlotte Greenwood (Mrs. Crozier), William Bakewell (Maurice Perry), Ralph Morgan (Freddie Isquith), Barbara Weeks (Fenno Crozier), Linda Watkins (Tess Boyce), William Pawley (Wally), Olin Howland (Secretary), James Kirkwood (Detective Crane), Anders Van Haden (Captain), Dewey Robinson (Strong Arm Algy).

Shipboard caper has reformed jewel thief tracking down $375,000 in stolen pearls while at the same time trying to teach a long-lost son to live the legitimate life. But it's too late for the kid, who made his mind up long ago to go into dad's business. Too many incongruities make this an incoherent film, including one odd scene wherein the crooks are morse-coding each other by tapping on bridge tables or spelling out supposedly subtle messages by tapping a smoking pipe on teeth. Poorly directed. (See THE LONE WOLF series, Index.)

d, Hamilton MacFadden; w, M.S. Boylan (based on a story by Louis Joseph Vance); ph, Ernest Palmer; ed, Irene Morra.

Mystery (PR:A MPAA:NR)

CHEATING BLONDES**½ (1933) 61m EQ bw
Thelma Todd (Anne Merrick/Elaine Manners), Ralf Harolde (Lawson Rolt), Inez

Courtney (Polly), Milton Wallis ("Mike" Goldfish), Mae Busch (Mrs. Jennie Carter), Earl McCarthy (Gilbert Frayle), Dorothy Gulliver (Lita).

Cranky newspaper reporter tries to pin a murder rap on his lady love because she turned down his proposal of marriage. Too many nights on the police beat. Not much plot development and dialog but the story holds some interest in spite of general dragginess.

d, Joseph Levering; w, Lewis B. Foster, Islen Auster (based on a story by Gertie James); ph, James S. Brown; ed, Dwight Caldwell; m, Lee Zahler.

Mystery (PR:A MPAA:NR)

CHEATING CHEATERS** (1934) 67m UNIV bw
Fay Wray (Nan Brockton), Cesar Romero (Tom Palmer), Minna Gombell (Mrs. Brockton), Hugh O'Connell (Steve Wilson), Henry Armetta (Tony Verdi), Francis L. Sullivan (Dr. Brockton), Wallis Clark (Mr. Palmer), Ann Shoemaker (Mrs. Palmer), John T. Murray (Ira Lazarre), Morgan Wallace (Holmes), George Barraud (Phil), Harold Huber (Finelli), Reginald Barlow (Police Captain).

Rival gangs of jewel thieves pose as high-rollers in an effort to rob one another of jewels which they possess. The girl decoy of one gang is actually a detective assigned to get the goods on both gangs. Of course she falls in love with a member of the rival gang. Though produced with care and well-cast, this still remains rather creaky entertainment.

d, Richard Thorpe; w, Gladys Unger, James Mulhauser, Allen Rivkin (based on the play by Max Marcin); ph, George Robinson.

Adventure (PR:A MPAA:NR)

CHECK AND DOUBLE CHECK (SEE: AMOS 'N' ANDY, 1930)

CHECK YOUR GUNS** (1948) 55m EL bw
Eddie Dean (Eddie), Roscoe Ates (Soapy), Nancy Gates (Cathy), George Chesebro (Farrell), I. Stanford Jolley (Brad), Mikel Conrad (Ace), Lane Bradford (Slim), Terry Frost (Sloane), Mason Wynn (Rider No. 1), Dee Cooper (Rider No. 2), Bill Fawcett (Judge Hammond), Ted Adams, Budd Buster, Wally West, Andy Parker and the Plainsmen, "White Cloud."

Bad guys in cahoots with a crooked judge terrorize law-abiding citizens in good old Red Gap, causing headaches for new sheriff Dean and his deputy Ates who've been trying their darndest to outlaw guns in the old home town. There is little originality in the story but plenty of shooting, much to the dismay of the new sheriff.

p, Jerry Thomas; d, Ray Taylor; w, Joseph O'Donnell; ph, Ernie Miller; ed, Joseph Gluck; m/l, Pete Gates, Dean and Hal Blair.

Western (PR:A MPAA:NR)

CHECKERBOARD**½
(1969, Fr.) 105m Zodiaque Productions-Lodice-Globe Films International/AF
(LES TRIPES AU SOLEIL; QUESTIONE DI PELLE)
Jacques Richard (Bob Stanley), Toto Bissainthe (Bessie Vance), Douta Seck (Vance), Gregoire Aslan (Stanley), Roger Blin (Guide), Millie Vitale (Prostitute), Anne Carrere (Tourist), Nico Pepe, Doudou.Babet, Guy Trejan, Alice Sapritch, Samba Ababaka, Lucien Raimbourg, Hubert de Lapparent, Mara Berni, Nicole Dieudonne, Andre Certes, Theo Bipolet, Lud Germain, Paul Bisciglia, J.-P. Drean, Jacques Bezard, Bob Ingarao, Alain Roulleau.

Strange French-made racial melodrama went unreleased in this country for ten years after its Paris premiere. In the desert town of Cicada (apparently in the U.S., though this is never stated), racial segregation is the rule. Richard is a white ex-paratrooper who falls in love with a black girl (Bissainthe). White townspeople beat up Richard and blame it on the blacks. The opposing fathers go out into the desert to fight but they discover a spring which will bring prosperity to the town. Despite their discovery, the men are spurned by the town, so they pack up their respective families and move out to start their own settlement. The French title translates as "Guts in the Sun."

d, Claude Bernard-Aubert; w, Bernard-Aubert, Claude Accursi; ph, Jean Isnard; m, Andre Hodeir; ed, Gabriel Rongier; prod d, Louis Manella; art d, J.-Paul Coutan-Laboureur; cos, Catherine Giboyau.

Drama (PR:O MPAA:NR)

CHECKERED COAT, THE** (1948) 66m FOX bw
Tom Conway (Dr. Michael Madden), Noreen Nash (Betty Madden), Hurd Hatfield (Creepy), James Seay (Capt. Dunhill), Gary Owen (Prince), Marten Lamont (Fred Madden), Rory Mallinson (Perkins), Leonard Mudie (Jerry), Eddie Dunn (Brownlee), John R. Hamilton (Marcus Anson), Lee Tung Foo (Kim), Julian Rivero (Cafe Owner), Fred Browne (Bill Anson), Dorothy Porter (Singer), Sam Hayes (Announcer), Dewey Robinson (Bartender), Lee Bonnell (Dr. Pryor), Russell Arnas (Dr. Stevenson).

Psychiatrist Conway has his hands full with a psychotic patient (Hatfield) who kills, then conveniently conks out. Doctor gives him a letter explaining his condition but which also involves the doctor in the crimes. Good performances in this low-budget film.

p, Sam Baerwitz; d, Edward L. Cahn; w, John C. Higgens (based on a story by Seeleg Lester and Merwin Gerard); ph, Jackson Rose; ed, Paul Landres; md, Edward J. Kay.

Mystery (PR:A MPAA:NR)

CHECKERED FLAG, THE* (1963) 110m Mercury c
Joe Morrison (Bill Garrison), Evelyn King (Bo Rutherford), Charles G. Martin (Rutherford), Peggy Vendig (Ginger).

The stock footage at Sebring overshadows the lame plot about a wealthy playboy auto racer and his alcoholic wife who would like to see him dead. She ends up convincing a rookie driver to perform the dirty work. After a major pile-up which sees her husband killed and the rookie losing his legs, the scheming wife is disfigured by flames as she tries to pull the rookie from his burning car. Script runs out of gas long before the finish line. Songs: "Bikini Baby," "Hip-So Calypso," "(Take Me) Far Away (Alice Simms), "Coconut, Fall on de Head" (Simms, George Symonette).

p, Herb Vendig; d&w, William Grefe; ph, J. R. Remy (Eastmancolor); ed, Edward B. Mulloy; m, Alice Simms; art d, Ken Miller.

Drama (PR:C MPAA:NR)

CHECKERED FLAG OR CRASH*½ (1978) 95m UNIV c
Joe Don Baker, Susan Sarandon, Alan Vint, Larry Hagman, Parnelli Jones, Logan Clark, Dana House.

Just what talented people like Susan Sarandon and Larry Hagman are doing in this dumb Thousand-Mile-Car-Race-Through-the-Jungle movie is a mystery, but it keeps moving at a good enough clip to keep auto fans entertained. Title song is sung by Harlan Sanders.

p, Fred Weintraub, Paul Heller; d, Alan Gibson; w, Michael Allin; m/l, Mel Mandel, Norman Sachs.

Comedy/Adventure (PR:C MPAA:PG)

CHECKERS**½ (1937) 79m FOX bw
Jane Withers (Checkers), Stuart Erwin (Edgar Connell), Una Merkel (Mamie Appleby), Marvin Stephens (Jimmy Somers), Andrew Tombes (Tobias Williams), June Carlson (Sarah Williams), Minor Watson (Dr. Smith), John Harrington (Mr. Green), Spencer Charters (Zeb), Francis Ford (Daniel Snodgrass).

Withers plays the niece of race horse owner Erwin. There's trouble on the farm when Dobbin breaks his leg but a new surgical treatment renders him fit for the big race, much to the delight of Baby Jane, her uncle, the jockey, the banker, and various barnyard animals. Veteran Withers watchers will recall her debut as the nasty little rich girl who broke Shirley Temple's doll in "Bright Eyes." Audiences cheered when a grown-up slapped her face. Swift-paced story with some amusing rural comedy touches.

p, John Stone; d, H. Bruce Humberstone; w, Lynne Root, Frank Fenton, Robert Chapin, Karen De Wolf (based on a play by Rita Johnson Young); ph, Daniel R. Clark; ed, Jack Murray; md, Samuel Kaylin.

Comedy (PR:A MPAA:NR)

CHECKMATE* (1935, Brit.) 68m B&D-PAR British bw
Maurice Evans (Phillip Allen), Felix Aylmer (Henry Nicholls), Evelyn Foster (Mary Nicholls), Sally Gray (Jean Nicholls), Donald Wolfit (Jack Barton), Wilfrid Caithness (Inspector Smith), Percy Walsh (Mr. Curtaill), Ernest Jay (Huntly).

Evans is a detective engaged to Foster who exposes her father as the ringleader of a band of jewel thieves. The British feature of the 1930s seems to consist almost entirely of these crime stories, but a decent cast of supporting players slightly distinguishes this one.

p, Anthony Havelock-Allan; d, George Pearson; w, Basil Mason (based on a novel by Amy Kennedy Gould).

Crime (PR:A MPAA:NR)

CHECKMATE zero (1973) 90m J.E.R. c
Diana Wilson (Pepper Burns), An Tsan Hu (Mme. Chang), Don Draper (Mercer), J. J. Coyle (Mr. Snow), Caren Kaye (Alex), Kurt Mann (Jogger), Reg Roland (Andre Vidal), Ion De Hondol (Boris Petroff).

Every now and then a shot appears in focus in this piece of filmic swill about a woman who seduces government agents to acquire top-secret information. She follows this up by blackmailing them for big bucks, until she is checkmated by Wilson who does her derring-do in hot pants.

p, John Amero; d, Lem Amero; w, LaRue Watts; ph, Roberta Findlay (Movielab Color); ed, Lem Amero

Thriller (PR:O MPAA:R)

CHECKPOINT**½ (1957, Brit.) 84m Rank c
Anthony Steel (Bill Fraser), Odile Versois (Francesca), Stanley Baker (O'Donovan), James Robertson Justice (Warren Ingram), Maurice Denham (Ted Thornhill), Michael Medwin (Ginger), Paul Muller (Petersen), Lee Patterson (Johnny), Anne Heywood (Gabriela), Anthony Oliver (Michael), Philip Gilbert (Eddie), McDonald Hobley (Commentator), Robert Rietty (Frontier Guard), Andrea Malandrinos (Night Watchman), Dino Galvani (Hotel Hall Porter).

Exciting, fast-paced racing story about an auto mogul's plans to lure an Italian auto designer away from his firm and hire him for his company. When negotiations fail, he resorts to stealing blueprints. This snowballs into murder, followed by a fiery crash on the oval at the Grand Prix. Camera and cutting during the intense racing scenes are fantastic.

p, Betty E. Box; d, Ralph Thomas; w, Robin Estridge; ph, Ernest Stewart; m, Bruce Montgomery; ed, Frederick Wilson.

Drama (PR:A MPAA:NR)

CHEECH AND CHONG'S NEXT MOVIE zero (1980) 99m UNIV c
Richard Marin (Cheech), Thomas Chong (Chong), Evelyn Guerrero (Donna), Betty Kennedy (Candy), Sy Kramer (Neatnik), Rikki Marin (Gloria), Bob McClurg (Chicken Charlie), Edie McClurg (Gloria's Mother), Paul Reubens (Pee Wee Herman/Desk Clerk).

Obnoxious and unfunny, the two street comics slide and slur their way around Los Angeles looking for a plot which doesn't exist, bumping into equally boring and mindless types—Reubens as a shabby stand-up idiot of one-liners and Edie McClurg as a rich spinster—until they run out of characters and the film mercifully ends. These two foul-mouths provided a tad of amusement in their sleeper debut, UP IN SMOKE,

but this and subsequent films only go to prove who is responsible for the decline of comedy in the movies. Their humor is forced, incoherent, sophomoric, and scooped from the gutter, slime-talk on every level. Worse, Chong, in his infinite arrogance, undertook to direct this reeking garbage which makes it all the more amateurish. To elevate such talentless and offensive individuals to stardom is unforgivable.

p, Howard Brown; d, Thomas Chong; w, Chong, "Cheech" Marin; ph, King Baggot (Technicolor); m, Mark Davis; ed, Scott Conrad; prod d, Fred Harpman; set d, Bob Benton; spec eff, Albert Whitlock; animation, Paul Power.

Comedy Cas. (PR:O MPAA:R)

CHEECH AND CHONG'S NICE DREAMS zero (1981) 88m COL c
Thomas Chong (Chong), Cheech Marin (Cheech), Stacy Keach (The Sarge), Dr. Timothy Leary (Himself), Evelyn Guerrero (Donna), Paul Reubens (Howie Hamburger), Michael Masters (Willard "Animal" Bad), Jeff Pomerantz (CHP Officer), James Faracci (CHP Officer), Taaffe O'Connell (Nurse), Suzanne Kent (Sidney the Agent), Michael Winslow (Superspade), Shirley Prestio (Singer), Sally K. Marr (Nut No. 5), Robert "Big Buck" Maffei (Goon), Rikki Marin (Blonde in Car), Louis Guss (Herb), Danny Kwan (Lab Technician), Michael Lansing (Nut No. 15), Sab Shimono (Bus Boy), Paul Zegler (Herb, Jr.), Roderick E. Daniels (Janitor), Tim Rossovich (Noodles), Roosevelt Smith (Cop).

More idiocy from the talentless duo who this time practice their moronic routines and gutter talk while dispensing drugs from an ice cream truck, another cretinous concept that will appeal to only drugged-out dropouts. There is no script, other than a million "hey, mans," there is no character development, plot, authentic humor, or basic entertainment, just the usual scum floating in the bird bath. Another ugly product of the Los Angeles sewer system.

p, Howard Brown; d, Thomas Chong; w, Chong, Richard "Cheech" Marin; ph, Charles Correll (Metrocolor); m, Harry Betts; ed, Scott Conrad; prod d, James Newport; set d, Charles Graffeo; cos, Sharon Day.

Comedy Cas. (PR:O MPAA:R)

CHEER BOYS CHEER** (1939, Brit.) 84m ATP/ABF bw
Nova Pilbeam (Margaret Greenleaf), Edmund Gwenn (Edward Ironside), Jimmy O'Dea (Matt Boyle), Moore Marriott (Geordie), Graham Moffatt (Albert), C.V. France (Tom Greenleaf), Peter Coke (John Ironside), Alexander Knox (Saunders), Ivor Barnard (Naseby), Jean Webster Brough (Belle).

The son of a brewery owner gets a job with his father's rival in order to ruin his business, but he falls in love with Pilbeam, his boss's daughter. A predictable plot is nicely done, and the film is a hint of the delightful comedies that would emerge from Ealing Studios after WW II.

p, S. C. Balcon; d, Walter Forde; w, Roger MacDougall, Allan Mackinnon (based on a story by Ian Dalrymple and Donald Bull); ph, Ronald Neame.

Comedy (PR:A MPAA:NR)

CHEER THE BRAVE* (1951, Brit.) 62m SWH-Piccadilly/Apex bw
Elsie Randolph (Doris Wilson), Jack McNaughton (Bill Potter), Geoffrey Keen (Wilson), Marie Ault (Mother-in-Law), Vida Hope, Douglas Ives, Manville Tarrant, Mavis Villiers, Violet Gould, Eileen Wray, David Dunn, Jimmy Bruce, Frank Hawkins, Gordon Mulholland, Sam Kydd, Rose Howlett, Helen Goss, Michael Ward, John Bull, Elizabeth Saunders, Jennifer Duncan, Molly Weir.

When nagging Randolph's first husband returns, her thoroughly henpecked second husband packs his bags and leaves. Lackluster comedy has nothing to recommend it.

p, John Sutro, David Webster; d&w, Kenneth Hume

Comedy (PR:A MPAA:NR)

CHEER UP!*½ (1936, Brit.) 72m ABF bw
Stanley Lupino (Tom Denham), Sally Gray (Sally Gray), Roddy Hughes (Dick Dirk), Gerald Barry (John Harman), Kenneth Kove (Wilfred Harman), Wyn Weaver (Mr. Carter), Marjorie Chard (Mrs. Carter), Ernest Sefton (Tom Page), Syd Crossley (Waiter).

Lupino is a writer mistaken for a millionaire, so he takes advantage of the confusion to finance his new show. Lupino almost singlehandedly represents the prewar British musical, but this isn't one of his better efforts.

p, Stanley Lupino; d, Leo Mittler; w, Michael Barringer (based on a story by Lupino).

Musical (PR:A MPAA:NR)

CHEER UP AND SMILE*½ (1930) 62m FOX bw
Dixie Lee (Margie), Arthur Lake (Eddie Fripp), Olga Baclanova (Yvonne), "Whispering" Jack Smith (Himself), Johnny Arthur (Andy), Charles Judels (Pierre), John Darrow (Tom), Sumner Getchell (Paul), Franklin Pangborn (Professor), Buddy Messinger (Donald), John Wayne.

When forced to sing during a holdup in a broadcasting station, country bumpkin Lake becomes an overnight sensation and sends for his girl with plans for marriage. His boss, however, fears he will lose his singer and sabotages the wedding. This was John Wayne's sixth movie as a bit actor. Frothy and entertaining. Songs: "The Shindig," "Where Can You Be?" "The Scamp of the Campus," "When You Look In My Eyes," "You May Not Like It But It's A Great Idea."

d, Sidney Lanfield; w, Howard J. Green (based on a story by Richard Cornell); ed, Ralph Dietrich; m/l, Jesse Greer, Ray Klages.

Drama/Musical (PR:A MPAA:NR)

CHEERS FOR MISS BISHOP**½ (1941) 91m UA bw
Martha Scott (Ella Bishop), William Gargan (Sam Peters), Edmund Gwenn (President Corcoran), Sterling Holloway (Chris Jensen), Sidney Blackmer (John Stevens), Mary Anderson (Amy Saunders), Dorothy Peterson (Mrs. Bishop), Donald Douglas (Delbert Thompson), Marsha Hunt (Hope Thompson), Ralph Bowman (Richard Clark), Lois

Ranson (*Gretchen Clark*), Rosemary DeCamp (*Minna Fields*), Knox Manning (*Anton Radcheck*), John Arledge (*Snapper MacRae*), Jack Mulhall (*Prof. Carter*), Howard Hickman (*Prof. Lancaster*), Helen MacKeller (*Miss Patton*), William Farnum (*Judge Peters*), Anna Mills (*Mrs. Peters*), John Hamilton (*President Watts*), Pierre Watkin (*President Crowder*), Charles Judels (*Cecco*), Sue Moore (*Stena*), Rand Brooks (*Buzz Wheelwright*), Charles Smith (*Buddy Warner*).

Sort of a lady's version of "Goodbye Mr. Chips" spanning fifty years in the life of a midwestern schoolteacher, Scott, whose two frustrated romances leave her without hope of marriage and concentrating instead on the lives of her students. This is a visual slice of midwestern life and philosophies from the 1880s. Good direction gets the most out of a difficult assignment in spreading an episodic story.

p, Richard A. Rowland; d, Tay Garnett; w, Stephen Vincent Benet, Adelaide Heilbron, Sheridan Gibney (based on the novel *Miss Bishop* by Bess Streeter Aldrich); ph, Hal Mohr; ed, William Claxton; art d, John Du Casse Schultz.

Drama (PR:A MPAA:NR)

CHEERS OF THE CROWD zero (1936) 62m MON bw
Russell Hopton (*Lee Adams*), Irene Ware (*Mary*), Bradley Page (*Walton*), Harry Holman (*Honest John*), Betty Blythe (*Lil Langdon*), Wade Boteler (*O'Reilly*), Roberta Gale (*Betty*), John Qualen (*Eddie*), John H. Dilson (*Barney*).

Public relations expert and newspaper sob sister unravel a mystery surrounding some chain letter murders. Absence of name draw, inexpert direction, and blah plot make this a cheerless venture.

p, Trem Carr; d, Vin Moore; w, George Waggner; ph, Milton Krasner, Harry Neumann; ed, Ernest Leadlay.

Mystery (PR:A MPAA:NR)

CHELSEA GIRLS, THE** (1967) 210m Film-makers' Distribution Center bw/c
THE POPE ONDINE STORY: Ondine (*"Pope"*), Angelina "Pepper" Davis, Ingrid Superstar, Albert Rene Ricard, Mary Might, International Velvet, Ronna; THE DUCHESS: Brigid Polk; THE JOHN: Ed Hood (*Ed*), Patrick Flemming (*Patrick*), Mario Montez (*Transvestite*), Angelina "Pepper" Davis, International Velvet, Mary Might, Gerard Malanga, Albert Rene Ricard, Ingrid Superstar; HANOI HANNA (*QUEEN OF CHINA*), Mary Might (*Hanoi Hanna*), International Velvet, Ingrid Superstar, Angelina "Pepper" Davis; THE GERARD MALANGA STORY: Marie Menken (*Mother*), Gerard Malanga (*Son*), Mary Might (*Girl Friend*); THE TRIP and THEIR TOWN (*TOBY SHORT*): Eric Emerson; AFTERNOON: Edie Sedgwick (*Edie*), Ondine, Arthur Loeb, Donald Lyons, Dorothy Dean; THE CLOSET: Nico, Randy Borscheidt; REEL 1: Nico, Eric Emerson, Ari.

A film which is more important as a cultural and structural statement than as entertainment. Worse than slow-moving, it is practically static. At the same time it holds a place in the 1960s subculture. Produced, directed, written, and photographed by imagist Warhol, who single-handedly began the underground Pop movement, it is an expose on the lifestyles of his New York Factory crowd—an oversexed, drugged-out group of kids who were too hip to be hip. Warhol, in his usual role as a parasitic observer, simply turned on the camera in SoHo's Chelsea Hotel as his crowd ate, slept, talked, and had sex. The film is structureless. There is no narrative, no cutting, no development. Originally presented as a dual-screen event, interesting parallels were drawn, but only by chance. Featured is avant-gard singer Nico of the psychedelic 1960s band, The Velvet Underground.

p&d, Andy Warhol; w, Warhol, Ronald Tavel; ph, Warhol (Eastmancolor); m, The Velvet Underground.

Experimental (PR:O MPAA:NR)

CHELSEA LIFE* (1933, Brit.) 69m B&D/PAR British bw
Louis Hayward (*David Fenner*), Molly Johnson (*Lulu*), Anna Lee (*Hon. Muriel Maxton*), Kathleen Saxon (*Mrs. Bonnington*), Stanley Vilven (*Grillini*), Gordon McLeod (*Lawton Hodge*), Eric Hales (*Harry Gordon*), Patrick Ludlow (*Lancelot Humphrey*), Arthur Chesney (*Ambrose Lincoln*).

Justifiably obscure British romantic drama has Hayward as an artist who steals the paintings of an absent Italian artist (Vilven) and on their strength becomes engaged to a society girl. Hayward's forty-year career began with this film, and he would make only one more movie in Britain before fleeing to the greener pastures of Hollywood.

p&d, Sidney Morgan; w, Joan Wentworth Wood (based on a story by Morgan); ph, Henry Harris.

Drama (PR:A MPAA:NR)

CHELSEA STORY*½ (1951, Brit.) 65m Present Day/Apex bw
Henry Mollison (*Mike Harvey*), Sydney Tafler (*Fletcher Gilchrist*), Ingeborg Wells (*Janice*), Lesley Osmond (*Louise*), Michael Moore (*George*), Wallas Eaton (*Danny*), Laurence Naismith (*Sgt. Matthews*), Michael Ward (*Chris Fawcett*), Andrea Malandrinos, Mercy Haystead, Jonn Bell, Ian Fleming.

Reporter Mollison breaks into a house on a bet, then finds himself framed for the murder of its resident. Routine crime drama.

p, Charles Reynolds; d, Charles Saunders; w, John Gilling; ph, Ted Lloyd.

Crime (PR:A MPAA:NR)

CHEREZ TERNII K SVEZDAM**½ (1981 USSR) 146m Gorki c (AKA: PER ASPERA AD ASTRA)
Elena Metelkina, Nadezhda Sementsova, Vadim Ledogorow, Alexander Lazarev, Alexander Mikhailov, Uldis Liedldidzh, Elena Fadeyeva, Vaclav Dvorzetski, Gleb Strinzhenov, Nikolai Timofeev.

Interesting, though overlong, Soviet science fiction film detailing the arrival of a young and beautiful alien woman (Metelkina) to Earth. She is rescued from her crippled spacecraft by Soviet cosmonauts and allowed to stay as a guest in the chief cosmonaut's home. There she learns the wonders of Earth through a series of charming sequences that have a genuine warmth and humor. Suddenly the idyllic episodes are broken by an urgent plea from Metelkina's home planet Dessa for Earth to help with its severe pollution problem. The cosmonauts travel to the planet only to discover that the evil ruler of Dessa may have led them into a trap. An imaginative movie that has surprising references to the Soviet's involvement in Afghanistan and other Russian preoccupations that somehow passed the censors. (In Russian; English subtitles.)

d, Richard Viktorov; w, Viktorov, Kir Bulychev; ph, Alexander Rybin.

Science Fiction (PR:A MPAA:NR)

CHEROKEE FLASH, THE** (1945) 55m REP bw
Sunset Carson, Linda Stirling, Tom London, Roy Barcroft, John Merton, Bud Geary, Frank Jacquet, Fred Graham, Joe McGuinn, Pierce Lyden, James Lynn, Bud Osborne, Edmund Cobb, Herman Hack, Bill Wolfe, Hank Bell, Chick Hannon, Roy Bucko, Buck Bucko.

Another episode in the short-lived Sunset Carson series of oaters sees Barcroft as an aging gunslinger who goes to his foster son Carson asking for help when members of his old gang try to stop him from retiring. Carson and sidekick London come to the old man's aid, and the three defeat the crooks, allowing Barcroft to go straight. Better than average.

p, Bennett Cohen; d, Thomas Carr; w, Cohen, Betty Burbridge; ph, Reggie Lanning; md, Richard Cherwin; ed, Charles Craft.

Western (PR:A MPAA:NR)

CHEROKEE STRIP*½ (1937) 58m WB/FN bw (AKA: STRANGE LAWS)
Dick Foran (*Dick Hudson*), Jane Bryan (*Janie Walton*), David Carlyle (*Tom Valley*), Helen Valkis (*Molly Valley*), Ed Cobb (*Link Carter*), Joseph Crehan (*Army Officer*), Gordon Hart (*Judge Ben Parkinson*), Frank Faylen (*Joe Brady*), Milton Kibbee (*Blade Simpson*), Jack Mower (*Bill Tidewell*), Tom Brower (*George Walton*), Walter Soderling (*Mink Abbott*), Tommy Bupp (*Barty Walton*), Bud Osborne, Glenn Strange.

Dick Foran is a singing cowboy/attorney in this run-of-the-mill B-western. He pauses twice in his campaign to bring swindler Cobb to justice to sing "My Little Buckaroo" and "Along the Old Frontier."

p, Byron Foy; d, Noel Smith; w, Joseph K. Watson, Luci Ward (based on the story "Cherokee Strip Stampeders" by Earl Repp); ph, L. William O'Connell; ed, Harold McLernon; m/l, M. K. Jerome, Jack Scholl.

Western (PR:A MPAA:NR)

CHEROKEE STRIP** (1940) 84m PAR bw
Richard Dix (*Dave Morrell*), Florence Rice (*Kate Cross*),, Victor Jory (*Coy Barrett*), Andy Clyde (*Tex Crawford*), George E. Stone (*Abe Gabbert*), Morris Ankrum (*Hawk*), Douglas Fowley (*Alf*), Addison Richards (*New Strawn*), Charles Trowbridge (*Sen. Cross*), William Henry (*Tom Cross*), Tom Tyler (*Frank*), William Haade (*Grimes*), Ray Teal (*Smokey*), Hal Taliaferro (*Ben Blivens*), Jack Rockwell (*Ace Eastman*), Robert Winkler (*A Barrett Kid*).

Dix is the forceful new marshall in town, cleaning up the gang headed by Jory, the town banker. Overlong but not bad, with some excellent western backgrounds and plenty of hard riding.

p, Harry Sherman; d, Lesley Selander; w, Norman Houston, Bernard McConville (based on a story by McConville); ph, Russell Harlan; ed, Sherman A. Rose.

Western (PR:A MPAA:NR)

CHEROKEE UPRISING** (1950) 57m MON bw
Whip Wilson (*Bob*), Andy Clyde (*Jake*), Lois Hall (*Mary Lou*), Sam Flint (*Judge*), Forrest Taylor (*Welch*), Marshall Reed (*Sheriff*), Iron Eyes Cody (*Longknife*), Chief Yowlachie (*Gray Eagle*), Lee Roberts (*Kansas*), Stanley Price (*Smokey*), Lyle Talbot (*Marshall*), Edith Mills (*Mrs. Strongbow*).

Routine oater which is part of the Whip Wilson series. This one has Whip on the trail of a corrupt government agent who is supplying booze to Indians in exchange for redskin attacks on wagon trains. Slow stuff, but Whip finally turns the trick.

p, Vincent Fennelly; d, Lewis Collins; w, Dan Ullman; ph, Gil Warrenton; ed, Dick Heermance.

Western (PR:A MPAA:NR)

CHESS PLAYERS, THE** (1978, India) 135m Creative Films c
Richard Attenborough (*Gen. Outram*), Sanjeev Kumar (*Mirza Saljad Ali*), Saeed Jaffrey (*Mir Roshan Ali*), Shabana Azmi (*Mirza's Wife*), Amzad Khan (*Mawah Wajid Ali Shah*), Tom Alter (*Advisor*).

Kumar and Jaffrey are two noblemen in 19th-century India who carry on their endless games of chess oblivious to the efforts of British general Attenborough to annex their province into the Empire. Ponderously allegorical and overlong, a major disappointment from director Ray. (English and Hindi: English subtitles.)

p, Siresh Jinda; d&w, Satyajit Ray; ph, Soumendu Roy (Eastmancolor); m, Ray; ed, Dulal Dutta.

Drama (PR:C MPAA:NR)

CHESTY ANDERSON, U.S. NAVY* (1976) 88m Atlas c (AKA: ANDERSON'S ANGELS)
Shari Eubank (*Chesty*), Dorri Thomson (*Tina*), Rosanne Katon (*Cocoa*), Marcie Barkin (*Pucker*), Timothy Agoglia Carey (*Vincent*), Frank Campanella (*Baron*), Scatman Crothers (*Ben*), Fred Willard (*FBI Agent*).

Exploiter film of female recruits in the U.S. Navy which offers little story but plenty of curves. This one sinks out of sight in the first reel.

p, Paul Pompian; d, Ed Forsyth; w, Pompian, H. F. Green; (Eastmancolor).

Comedy Cas. (PR:O MPAA:R)

CHETNIKS *½   (1943) 73m FOX bw
Philip Dorn *(Gen. Draja Mihailovitch)*, Anna Sten *(Lubitca Mihailovitch)*, John Shepard *(Alexis)*, Virginia Gilmore *(Natalia)*, Martin Kosleck *(Col. Brockner)*, Felix Basch *(Gen. Von Bauer)*, Frank Lackteen *(Maj. Danilov)*, Patricia Prest *(Nada)*, Merrill Rodin *(Mirko)*, Leroy Mason *(Capt. Savo)*.

Brave Yugoslav partisans led by Dorn battle their Nazi occupiers. Gestapo agent Kosleck learns the identity of Dorn's wife (Sten) and uses her as bait to capture Dorn, but he outwits them, capturing their stronghold and freeing her. Largely propaganda, the fact is Mihailovitch's Chetniks spent much of their time collaborating with the Germans to fight Tito's larger and better organized Communist guerrillas.

p, Sol M. Wurtzel; d, Louis King; w, Jack Andrews, E. E. Paramore (based on a story by Andrews); ph, Glen MacWilliams; m, Hugo W. Friedhofer; ed, Alfred Day; md, Emil Newman.

War Drama   **(PR:A   MPAA:NR)**

CHEYENNE **½   (1947) 99m WB bw (AKA: THE WYOMING KID)
Dennis Morgan *(James Wylie)*, Jane Wyman *(Ann Kincaid)*, Janis Paige *(Emily Carson)*, Bruce Bennett *(Ed Landers)*, Alan Hale *(Fred Durkin)*, Arthur Kennedy *(Sundance Kid)*, John Ridgely *(Chalkeye)*, Barton MacLane *(Yancey)*, Tom Tyler *(Pecos)*, Bob Steele *(Lucky)*, John Compton *(Limpy Bill)*, John Alvin *(Single Jack)*, Monte Blue *(Timberline)*, Anne O'Neal *(Miss Kittredge)*, Tom Fadden *(Charlie)*, Britt Wood *(Swamper)*, Norman Willis, Ray Teal, Kenneth MacDonald, Robert Filmer *(Gamblers)*, Lee "Lasses" White *(Charlie, the Hotelkeeper)*, Snub Pollard, Ethan Laidlaw *(Barflies)*, Jack Mower *(Deputy)*.

Raoul Walsh's direction lifts this above the mass of B-westerns. Morgan is a gambler hired to track down dreaded outlaw Bennett. Wyman, as Bennett's wife, tries to stand in his way but ends up falling in love with him. Janis Paige is the sexy saloon singer, performing "Going Back to Old Cheyenne" and "I'm So In Love."

p, Robert Buckner; d, Raoul Walsh; w, Alan LeMay, Thomas Williamson (based on a story by Paul I. Wellman); ph, Sid Hickox; m, Max Steiner; ed, Christian Nyby; m/l, Steiner, Ted Koehler, M. K. Jerome.

Western   **(PR:A   MPAA:NR)**

CHEYENNE AUTUMN ****   (1964) 159m WB c
Richard Widmark *(Capt. Thomas Archer)*, Carroll Baker *(Deborah Wright)*, Karl Malden *(Capt. Oscar Wessels)*, James Stewart *(Wyatt Earp)*, Edward G. Robinson *(Carl Schurz)*, Sal Mineo *(Red Shirt)*, Dolores Del Rio *(Spanish Woman)*, Ricardo Montalban *(Little Wolf)*, Gilbert Roland *(Dull Knife)*, Arthur Kennedy *(Doc Holliday)*, Patrick Wayne *(2nd Lt. Scott)*, Elizabeth Allen *(Miss Guinevere Plantagenet)*, John Carradine *(Maj. Jeff Blair)*, Victor Jory *(Tall Tree)*, Judson Pratt *(Mayor Dog Kelly)*, Mike Mazurki *(1st Sgt. Stanislaus Wichowsky)*, Ken Curtis *(Homer)*, George O'Brien *(Maj. Braden)*, Shug Fisher *(Trail Boss)*, Carmen D'Antonio *(Pawnee Woman)*, Walter Baldwin *(Deborah's Uncle)*, Nancy Hseuh *(Little Bird)*, Chuck Roberson *(Trail Hand)*, Moonbeam *(Running Deer)*, Many Muleson *(Medicine Man)*, John Qualen *(Svenson)*, Sean McClory *(Dr. O'Carberry)*, Walter Reed *(Lt. Peterson)*, James Flavin *(Sergeant of the Guard)*, Stephanie Epper, Mary Statler, Jean Epper, Donna Hall *(Entertainers)*, Ben Johnson *(Trooper Plumtree)*, Harry Carey, Jr. *(Trooper Smith)*, Bing Russell *(Telegrapher)*, Maj. Sam Harris *(Townsman)*, Denver Pyle *(Sen. Henry)*, Carleton Young *(Secretary to Schurz)*, William Henry *(Infantry Captain)*, Louise Montana *(Woman)*, Dan Borzage, Dan Carr, James O'Hara, David Miller, Ted Mapes, John McKee *(Troopers)*, Charles Seel *(Newspaper Publisher)*, Philo McCullough *(Man)*.

This Ford frontier epic opens in 1887 with the disheartened remnants of the Cheyenne Nation waiting for a meeting with government representatives on a wretched Oklahoma reservation, a meeting that never takes place. The Indians have been beseeching the U.S. government for more food and housing. When they are ignored, chiefs Montalban and Roland decide to defy the authorities and migrate the 300 Cheyennes to their old homeland in Wyoming. Thus begins a heroic and terrible trek Northwest with a reluctant cavalry captain, Widmark, and his troops in unenthusiastic pursuit of the Indians, intending to return them to their miserable reservation. Moving with the tribe is Baker, a white schoolteacher who empathizes with the plight of the Indians. Widmark's troops are outfought at every turn by the wily braves under Roland and Montalban. The press portrays the exodus as another Indian war and even civilians Stewart, playing Wyatt Earp in a cameo role, and Kennedy (as Doc Holliday), join half-heartedly in a posse to recapture the Indians. The 1500-mile trek takes its toll on the tribe, with the infirm and elderly dying in a cruel winter. Half the tribe seeks safety at Fort Robinson, surrendering to sadistic commandant Malden who starves and freezes them, keeping them penned up like cattle in an unheated warehouse. They finally break out, killing Malden and some of his troopers, and rejoin the other Indians. Widmark learns of Malden's persecution of the Indians (Malden intended to break their spirit and force them back to the Oklahoma reservation), and goes to Washington, pleading with Robinson (as Carl Schurz U.S. secretary of the interior) to intervene. Robinson and a large contingent of calvary corner the Indians just as they reach their Yellowstone homeland, but instead of ordering a battle, the humanitarian Robinson arranges a truce and allows the Indians to remain in the ancient land of their fathers. Widmark, in love with Baker, remains with the tribe. The acting from all the principals is good, particularly Robinson as the crusty old Schurz, and Widmark as the indignant officer. The Indian leaders are less convincing, Montalban and Roland enacting their competitive chiefs as cigar store statues. Memorable is Dolores Del Rio as Spanish Woman, her perpetual beauty in astonishing evidence. Completely out of character is Mineo as a rebellious brave who sacrifices his life uselessly in a suicide charge against a battery of troopers. Baker, as the Quaker teacher, overacts in her commitment t the Indians, and her devotion to an alien culture is often unbelievable. Yet Ford manages to give such a powerful visual image of the old frontier in his apology to the wronged Indians that the film becomes a great and moving document faithful to its subject's history, the sad chronicle of a doomed but noble tribe that had outlived its place inside advancing civilization and chose annihilation rather than submission and surrender of its old customs. The great director was ill at the time of production but managed to put his indelible stamp upon this tragic tapestry so beautifully photographed by Clothier on location in Monument Valley and Moab, Utah. No single actor stands out in CHEYENNE AUTUMN: it is the director's picture, Ford's perception of a proud people, seen through a white man's eyes, his and his alone, which is as good a portrait as anyone could ever draw.

p, Bernard Smith; d, John Ford; w, James R. Webb (based on the novel by Mari Sandoz); ph, William Clothier (Super Panavision 70, Technicolor); m, Alex North; ed, Otho Lovering; art d, Richard Day; set d, Darrell Silvera; cos, Ann B. Peck, Frank Beetson; spec eff, Ralph Webb; makeup, Norman Pringle.

Western   **(PR:A   MPAA:NR)**

CHEYENNE CYCLONE, THE *   (1932) 57m Kent/FD bw
Lane Chandler, Connie LaMont, Frankie Darro, Yakima Canutt, Edward Hearn, Jay Hunt, Marie Quillan, J. Frank Glendon, Henry Rocquemore, Charles Whitaker, Jack Kirk.

Tame oater has Chandler nailing the bad guys after they terrorize a Western county. Darro is completely out of place with his Brooklyn accent, and Canutt does some fancy stunting.

p, Willis Kent; d, Armand Schaeffer; w, Oliver Drake (based on the story *Sagebrush Romeo* by Drake); ph, William Nobles; ed, Ethel Davey.

Western   **(PR:A   MPAA:NR)**

CHEYENNE KID, THE *   (1930) 63m West Coast Pictures bw
Buffalo Bill, Jr., Joan Jaccard, Yakima Canutt, Jack Mower, Frank Ellis, Fred Burns, Violet McKay, Tom Forman.

Canutt's hair-raising stunts are the best parts of this mediocre oater which is so muddled that it's next to impossible to tell the good from bad characters. Root for Canutt.

d, Jacques Jaccard; w, Jaccard, Yakima Canutt.

Western   **(PR:A   MPAA:NR)**

CHEYENNE KID, THE *½   (1933) 61m RKO bw
Tom Keene, Mary Mason, Roscoe Ates, Al Bridge, Otto Hoffman, Allan Roscoe, Anderson Lawler.

Cowboy Keene is mistaken for outlaw "Denver Ed" and it takes plenty of fist fights, shootouts, and chases to eventually sort everything out, enabling Keene and his lady love, Mason, to ride off into the sunset together. This durable story line was previously filmed as MAN IN THE ROUGH with Bob Steele in 1928 and subsequently filmed as THE FARGO KID in 1940 with Tim Holt.

d, Robert Hill; w, Jack Curtis (based on the story "Sir Peegan Passes" by W. C. Tuttle).

Western   **(PR:A   MPAA:NR)**

CHEYENNE KID, THE *   (1940) 54m MON bw
Jack Randall *(Cheyenne Kid)*, Louise Stanley *(Ruth Adams)*, Kenneth Duncan *(Chet Adams)*, Frank Yaconelli *(Manuel)*, Reed Howes *(Jeff Baker)*, Charles King *(Carson)*, George Chesebro *(Davis)*, Forrest Taylor *(Sheriff)*.

Randall is thrown into jail for a murder he didn't commit, escapes, and captures the guilty parties. Bad acting, bad scripting, and a story lifted from a thousand other B-westerns.

p, Harry S. Webb; d, Raymond K. Johnson; w, Tom Gibson; ph, Edward Kull; ed, Robert Golden.

Western   **(PR:A   MPAA:NR)**

CHEYENNE RIDES AGAIN *½   (1937) 60m Victory bw
Tom Tyler *(Cheyenne)*, Lucille Browne *(Sally)*, Jimmy Fox *(Dopey)*, Creighton Chaney *(Girard)*, Roger Williams *(Mark)*, Ed Cassidy *(Gleason)*, Theodore Lorch *(Rollin)*, Bud Pope *(Shayne)*, Francis Walker *(Joe)*, Carmen La Roux *(Pamela)*.

Tyler is hired by the cattleman's association to infiltrate a gang of outlaws, something he does with little difficulty. Comic relief Fox sings "Storybook Cowboy." Not very good, but it keeps moving as Tyler herds all the outlaws to jail.

p, Sam Katzman; d, Bob Hill; w, Basil Dickey; ph, Bill Hyer; ed, Charles Henkel.

Western   **Cas.**   **(PR:A   MPAA:NR)**

CHEYENNE ROUNDUP *½   (1943) UNIV bw
Johnny Mack Brown *(Gils Brandon/Buck Brandon)*, Tex Ritter *(Steve Rawlins)*, Fuzzy Knight *(Cal Cawkins)*, Jennifer Holt *(Ellen Randall)*, Harry Woods *(Blackie Dawson)*, Roy Barcroft *(Slim Layton)*, Robert Barron *(Judge Hickenbottom)*, Budd Buster *(Bonanza)*, Gil Patric *(Perkins)*, The Jim Wakely Trio.

Brown plays twins, one good, the other a lawbreaker, in this routine western. The bad twin's gang takes over a ghost town until sheriff Ritter kills him. He dies in the arms of his long-lost brother, who then goes on to impersonate his twin to help clean up the rest of the gang.

p, Oliver Drake; d, Ray Taylor; w, Elmer Clifton, Bernard McConville; ph, William Sickner; ed, Otto Ludwig.

Western   **(PR:A   MPAA:NR)**

CHEYENNE SOCIAL CLUB, THE ***   (1970) 103m NG c
James Stewart *(John O'Hanlan)*, Henry Fonda *(Harley Sullivan)*, Shirley Jones *(Jenny)*, Sue Ane Langdon *(Opal Ann)*, Elaine Devry *(Pauline)* Robert Middleton *(Barkeep at Great Plains Saloon)*, Arch Johnson *(Marshal Anderson)*, Dabbs Greer *(Willowby)*, Jackie Russell *(Carrie Virginia)*, Jackie Joseph *(Annie Jo)*, Sharon DeBord *(Sara Jean)*, Richard Collier *(Nathan Potter)*, Charles Tyner *(Charlie Bannister)*, Jean Willes *(Alice)*, Robert J. Wilke *(Corey Bannister)*, Carl Reindel *(Pete Dodge)*, J. Pat

O'Malley *(Dr. Foy)*, Jason Wingreen *(Dr. Carter)*, John Dehner *(Clay Carroll)*, Hal Baylor *(Barkeep at Lady of Egypt)*, Charlotte Stewart *(Mae)*, Alberto Morin *(Ranch Foreman)*, Myron Healey *(Deuter)*, Warren Kemmerling *(Kohler)*, Dick Johnstone *(Yancey)*, Phil Mead *(Cook)*, Hi Roberts *(Scared Man)*, Ed Pennybacker *(Teamster)*, Red Morgan *(Hansen)*, Dean Smith, Bill Hicks, Bill Davis, Walt Davis, John Welty *(Bannister Gang)*.

This is a PG-rated movie about an X-rated subject. THE CHEYENNE SOCIAL CLUB is a brothel, a bordello, a bagnio, in other words, a house of ill repute. Fonda and Stewart are two creaky cowboys, just this side of elderly, who ride up from Texas with Fonda portraying the most boring conversationalist in western history. The opening dialog sets the tone of the film as Fonda runs off at the mouth about his dogs, his family, and such. When he takes a breath, Stewart asks, "Y'know where we are right now, Harley?" Fonda rubs his jaw. "Not exactly." Stewart replies, "We're in the Wyoming territory and you've been talkin' all the way since Texas." Fonda shrugs, "Jes' been keepin you company." Stewart nods, "I appreciate it, Harley, but you say another word the rest of the day and I'm gonna kill ya!" The movie never gets that funny again. Stewart's dead brother has left him the social club and the minute Jimmy learns what it is he wants to close the joint, or at least turn it into a plain saloon. The townspeople are outraged. This is not only a place that serves certain needs of the populace, it also truly is not unlike the one run by the Mmes. Everleigh in Chicago in later years. Jones is the madame and some of her charges are Langdon, Devry, De Bord, Russell, and Joseph, cult star of THE LITTLE SHOP OF HORRORS. After reneging on his original idea to shutter the place or turn it into a legit operation, Stewart gets into a brawl with Wilke and is tossed into the hoosegow. Meanwhile, Wilke (the villain's villain) whacks Jones around. When Stewart gets out of the slammer, he goes after Wilke and guns him down in a shootout. Now Wilke's family seeks to avenge his death and they attack with a horde of hired hands. They are driven back but when Fonda and Stewart learn that there are more onslaughts to come, they decide that discretion is the better part of valor and Stewart signs the house over to Jones and girls. The fadeout takes place as the two men move off into the distance with Fonda bending Stewart's ear once again. Anyone with a mite less patience would have gunned Fonda down immediately. This could have been a classic but Barrett, who wrote SHENANDOAH, BANDOLERO, and FOOL'S PARADE for Stewart, came a cropper with a script that was neither fish nor fowl. Kelly's direction was spongy and the whole thing falls flat. Just the inclusion of the stars and the adorability of the femmes lifts the film above average. That, plus some superb photography by Bill Clothier. Otherwise, a ho-hummer that was too genial to have any bite. Songs; "Rolling Stone," "One Dream."

p&d, Gene Kelly; w, James Lee Barrett; ph, William Clothier (Panavision, Technicolor); m, Walter Scharf; ed, Adrienne Fazan; md, Scharf; art d, Gene Allen; set d, George Hopkins; cos, Yvonne Wood; m/l, Al Kasha, Joel Hirschborn, Scharf.

Western/Comedy **(PR:C MPAA:PG)**

CHEYENNE TAKES OVER*½ (1947) 58m EL bw

Lash LaRue *(Cheyenne)*, Al "Fuzzy" St. John *(Fuzzy)*, Nancy Gates *(Fay)*, George Chesebro *(Dawson)*, Lee Morgan *(Delhaven)*, John Merton *(McCord)*, Steve Clark *(Sheriff)*, Bob Woodward *(Anderson)*, Marshall Reed *(Companion)*, Budd Buster *(Bostwick)*, Carl Matthews *(Messenger)*, Dee Cooper *(Johnson)*, Brad Slaven *(Bailey)*,. Hank Bell.

Villain Chesebro murders the heir to a ranch and witness Gates is too scared to tell the sheriff. Not to fear, though, LaRue sets things right, without once using his lash. Routine western.

p, Jerry Thomas; d, Ray Taylor; w, Arthur E. Orloff; ph, Ernest Miller; ed, Joe Gluck.

Western **(PR:A MPAA:NR)**

CHEYENNE TORNADO* (1935) 61m Kent bw

Reb Russell, Victoria Vinton, Edmund Cobb, Roger Williams, Tina Menard, Dick Botiller, Ed Porter, Winton Perry, Hank Bell, Francis McDonald, Lafe McKee, Bart Carre, Jack Evans, Oscar Gahan, Clyde McClary, "Rebel."

There's no whirlwind in this doldrum of a horse-opera as Russell roams the range looking for rustlers. Poor script, camera, and direction add up to a dead horse.

p, Willis Kent; d, William O'Connor.

Western **(PR:A MPAA:NR)**

CHEYENNE WILDCAT** (1944) 56m REP bw

Bill Elliott, Bobby Blake, Alice Fleming, Peggy Stewart, Francis McDonald, Roy Barcroft, Tom London, Tom Chatterton, Kenne Duncan, Bud Geary, Jack Kirk, Sam Burton, Bud Osborne, Bob Wilke, Rex Lease, Tom Steele, Charles Morton, Forrest Taylor, Franklyn Farnum, Wee Willie Keeler, Universal Jack, Tom Smith, Rudy Bowman, Horace B. Carpenter, Frank Ellis, Steve Clark, Bob Burns, Jack O'Shea.

Fair outing for Elliott in the popular Red Ryder series where the hero is torn between the love of two gals, one good and one not so good, and the baddies who make life miserable for all. Some good writing and stunts raise the level of this production.

p, Louis Gray; d, Lesley Selander; w, Randall Faye; ph, Bud Thackery; ed, Charles Craft.

Western **(PR:A MPAA:NR)**

CHICAGO CALLING*½ (1951) 70m Arrowhead/UA bw

Dan Duryea *(Bill Cannon)*, Mary Anderson *(Mary Cannon)*, Gordon Gebert *(Bobby Kimball)*, Judy Brubaker *(Babs Kimball)*, Ross Elliot *(Jim)*, Marsha Jones *(Peggy)*, Bob Fallon *(Art)*, Melinda Plowman *(Nancy Cannon)*, Grace Loman *(Housewife)*, Carl Vernell *(1st Detective)*, Chuck Flynn *(2nd Detective)*, Roy Engel *(Pete)*, Jean Harvey *(Christine)*, Bud Stark *(Clerk)*, Dick Curtis *(Foreman)*, Mel Pough *(Laborer)*, Eleanor Radcliff *(Relief Agent)*, Bill Lechner *(Finance Clerk)*, Steve Pendleton *(Lt. Ryan)*, Roy Glenn *(Shoe Shine Boy)*, Rudy McKool *(Mr. Blake)*, Gene Roth *(Bank Guard)*, Norman Field *(Railroad Switchman)*, Lorin Raker *(Mr. Cook)*, Smitty *(Dog)*.

A weak soap with an interestingly absurdist approach. Duryea is a down-and-out photographer whose wife and child have skipped out. He learns that they have been involved in a terrible auto wreck, and sits by the phone awaiting news of their condition. The phone becomes the most important thing in his life. His battle gets even tougher when the phone company tries to discontinue service because of an unpaid bill. A novel idea which is treated in an ordinary manner.

p, Peter Berneis; d, John Reinhardt; w, Berneis, Reinhardt; ph, Robert de Grasse; m, Heinz Roemheld; ed, Arthur H. Nadel.

Drama **(PR:A MPAA:NR)**

CHICAGO CONFIDENTIAL½** (1957) 75m UA bw

Brian Keith *(Jim Fremont)*, Beverly Garland *(Laura)*, Dick Foran *(Blane)*, Beverly Tyler *(Sylvia)*, Elisha Cook, Jr. *(Candymouth)*, Paul Langton *(Jake Parker)*, Tony George *(Duncan)*, Douglas Kennedy *(Harrison)*, Gavin Gordon *(Dixon)*, Jack Lambert *(Smitty)*, John Morley *(Partos)*, Benny Burt *(Hallop)*, Mark Scott *(Evans)*, Henry Rowland *(Milt)*, George Cisar *(Tomkins)*, Johnny Indrisano *(Heavy)*, John Pelletti *(Fingerprint Man)*, Joe McGuinn *(Dispatcher)*, Asa Maynor *(Betty)*, Jean Deane *(Marion)*, Sharon Lee *(Chorus Girl)*, Phyllis Coates *(Helen)*, Lynne Storey *("B" Girl)*, Nancy Marlowe *("B" Girl)*, Harlan Warde *(Traynor)*, John Hamilton *(Morgan)*, Jack Kenney *(Martin)*, Joey Ray *(Customer)*, Tom Wade *(Policeman)*, Ralph Volkie *(Mitch)*, Jack Carr *(Waiter)*, Carl Princi *(Narrator)*, Helen Jay *("B" Girl)*, Charles Meredith *(Charing)*, Keith Byron *(TV Announcer)*, Jim Bannon *(Pilot)*, Myron Cook *(Fingerprint Man)*, Dennis Moore *(Jury Foreman)*, Thomas B. Henry *(Judge)*, Frank Marlowe *(Patron)*, Linda Brent *("B" Girl)*, Bud Lewis *(Jordan)*.

An ambitious state's attorney, Keith, innocently uses false evidence to convict union leader Foran of murder, only to discover that the killing was a frame-up and the real criminals are power-hungry mobsters attempting to take over the union. To redeem himself, Keith devotes his time to proving Foran innocent and cleaning up the union. Keith gives a strong performance and one-time western star Foran, though shown only briefly, is solid as the victimized union boss. Garland is believable as the union chief's lady who stands by her man. Good supporting cast, especially Elisha Cook, Jr., as a drunken bindlestiff, makes this *film noir* interesting and sustains the mood and story, which is lifted from the pages of the true crime book by Lait and Mortimer (as part of the "confidential" series these two journalists made popular in the 1950s, although their source material and gossipy style is mostly the stuff of tabloids, not research).

p, Robert E. Kent; d, Sidney Salkow; w, Raymond T. Marcus (based on the book *Chicago Confidential* by Jack Lait and Lee Mortimer); ph, Kenneth Peach, Sr.; m, Emil Newman; ed, Grant Whytock.

Crime **(PR:A MPA:NR)**

CHICAGO DEADLINE*** (1949) 86m PAR bw

Alan Ladd *(Ed Adams)*, Donna Reed *(Rosita Jean D'Ur)*, June Havoc *(Leona)*, Irene Hervey *(Belle Dorset)*, Arthur Kennedy *(Tommy Ditman)*, Berry Kroeger *(Solly Wellman)*, Harold Vermilyea *(Anstruder)*, Shepperd Strudwick [John Shepperd] *(Blacky Franchot)*, John Beal *(Paul Jean D'Ur)*, Gavin Muir *(G. G. Temple)*, Dave Willock *(Pig)*, Paul Lees *(Bat)*, Howard Freeman *(Hotspur Shaner)*, Margaret Field *(Minerva)*, Harry Antrim *(Gribbe)*, Roy Roberts *(Jerry Cavanaugh)*, Marietta Canty *(Hazel)*, Celia Lovsky *(Mrs. Schleffler)*, Ottola Nesmith *(Sister John)*, Jack Overman *(Lou Horan)*, Clarence Straight *(Nelson)*, Dick Keene *(Spingler)*, Leona Roberts *(Maggie)*, Carole Mathews *(Secretary)*, Gordon Carveth *(Marty)*, Laura Elliott *(Marcia)*, Paul Bryar, Jack Gargan *(Bartenders)*, Douglas Carter *(Waiter)*, Phyllis Kennedy *(Maid)*, Donald Wilmot *(Copy Boy)*, Jerry James, Eric Alden, Bill Meader, Charley Cooley, Hal Rand, Ralph Montgomery, Lyle Moraine, Douglas Spencer *(Reporters)*, Frances Sanford *(Telephone Operator)*, Marie Blake *(Operator)*, Joane and Robert Rexer *(Specialty Act)*, Joe Whitehead *(Actor)*, Dulce Day *(Woman)*, Helen Chapman *(Girl)*, Julia Faye *(Nurse)*, Pat Lane *(Assistant Undertaker)*, Harry Cheshire *(Minister)*, Arthur Space *(Peterson)*, Jack Roberts, George Magrill *(Handlers)*, Jim Davies *(Second)*, Ralph Peters *(Taxi Driver)*, Michael Brandon *(Reporter)*.

Ladd is as hardboiled as ever in this minor *film noir* classic. He is a tough reporter in Chicago (never shown working a typewriter) who first appears at a run-down southside rooming house, attempting to talk a runaway girl into returning home. In the next room he finds the emaciated but beautiful body of a girl dead from tuberculosis (Reed). Before police arrive Ladd pockets her address book and then systematically begins to look up the various venal people in her life who tell her story in flashbacks. There is Kroeger, a vicious gangster; Muir, a nervous banker; Freeman, an invalid writer; Lees, a boxer with addled brains; Havoc, a call girl; Hervey, a gangster's moll, and, in a startling performance, Strudwick, as a melancholy mobster. Each tells a tale of Reed as Ladd puzzles her life together, encountering along the way several murders and blackmail victims, finally shooting it out with the culprit Kroeger, killing him and being wounded. He is so enraptured of the dead girl, not unlike Dana Andrews in the classic LAURA, that Ladd leaves his hospital bed to attend her funeral where he burns her address book to protect her memory, a gallant Beau Geste. Seeing this, Kennedy, portraying the dead girl's brother, tells Ladd that he knew her best of all. Based on a roughhouse 1933 novel, it's a sad, sometimes morose film but it's told with great pace and power, most of it steel gray, full of soot and grime and struggle, like Chicago itself, where the exterior shots were made. Ladd is superb as the callous reporter with a soft heart for Reed's memory (this was their second film together after BEYOND GLORY, although they do not appear in any scene as a twosome). CHICAGO DEADLINE is typical of the hard-hitting, well-made crime films hallmarking the late 1940s and Ladd is the epitome of the shadowy hero, the man from the other side of the tracks who didn't give a damn . . . except that he did. (Remade as FAME IS THE NAME OF THE GAME for TV.)

p, Robert Fellows; d, Lewis Allen; w, Warren Duff (based on the novel *One Woman* by Tiffany Thayer); ph, John F. Seitz; m, Victor Young; ed, LeRoy Stone; art d, Hans Dreir, Franz Bachelin; set d, Sam Comer, Ross Dowd; cos, Mary Kay Dodson; makeup, Wally Westmore, Hal Lierley.

Crime Drama **(PR:A MPAA:NR)**

CHICAGO KID, THE** (1945) 68m REP bw
Donald Barry (*Joe Ferrill*), Otto Kruger (*John Mitchell*), Tom Powers (*Mike Thurber*), Lynne Roberts (*Chris Mitchell*), Henry Daniell (*Bill Mitchell*), Chick Chandler (*Squeak*), Joseph Crehan (*Chief Rogers*), Jay Novello (*Pinky*), Paul Harvey (*Carter*), Addison Richards (*The Warden*), Kenne Duncan (*Al*).

Good boy Barry turns bad when his father dies in prison. He becomes a gangster, seeking vengeance on Kruger, whose testimony sent his father up the river. A suspenseful story well-directed and well-performed.

p, Eddy White; d, Frank McDonald; w, Jack Townley (based on a story by Karl Brown); ph, William Bradford; ed, Ralph Dixon.

Crime Drama (PR:A MPAA:NR)

CHICAGO KID, THE, 1969
(SEE: FABULOUS BASTARD FROM CHICAGO, THE, 1969)

CHICAGO 70** (1970) 93m Monitor c
Mel Dixon (*Bobby Seale*), Jim Lawrence (*Mark Lane*), Calvin Butler (*Arlo Guthrie*), Neil Walsh (*Mayor Daley*), George Metesky (*Allen Ginsberg*), Peter Faulkner (*Abbie Hoffman*), Neil Walsh (*Country Joe*), Diane Grant (*Linda Morse*), Francois Klanfer (*DJ*), Ray Whelan, Rick McKenna, Carol Carrington.

This bizarre amalgam of "Alice in Wonderland" and the transcripts of the Chicago 7 Trial makes for an interesting commentary on the American judicial system. Based on a stage play, the 16mm film, while original and topical, still makes little attempt to explore the cinematic possibilities the story has to offer.

p&d, Kerry Feltham (based on the transcripts of the Chicago 7 Trial, and Lewis Carroll's book "Alice in Wonderland" as performed for the stage by the Toronto Workshop); ph, Mogens Gander, Henri Fiks; ed, Italo Costa, Featherstone Fanshaw.

Political Satire (PR:C MPAA:NR)

CHICAGO SYNDICATE** (1955) 84m Clover/COL bw
Dennis O'Keefe (*Barry Amsterdam*), Abbe Lane (*Connie Peters*), Paul Stewart (*Arnie Valent*), Xavier Cugat (*Benny Chico*), Allison Hayes (*Joyce Kern*), Dick Cutting (*David Healey*), Chris Alcaide (*Nate*), William Challee (*Dolan*), John Zaremba (*Robert Fenton*), George Brand (*Jack Roper*), Mark Hanna (*Brad Lacey*), Carroll McComas (*Mrs. Valent*), Hugh Sanders (*Pat Winters*).

O'Keefe plays a justice-conscious accountant out to uncover the mob's secret bookkeeping in a worthy attempt to stop their racketeering. Xavier Cugat and his orchestra provide the picture with its beat, and Abbe Lane sings "One at a Time."

d, Fred F. Sears; w, Joseph Hoffman (based on the story by William Sackheim); ph, Henry Freulich, Fred Jackman, Jr.; ed, Viola Lawrence; md, Ross DiMaggio.

Crime (PR:A MPAA:NR)

CHICK*½ (1936, Brit.) 72m UA bw
Sydney Howard (*Chick Beane*), Betty Ann Davies (*Peggy*), Fred Conyngham (*Sir Anthony Monsard*), Cecil Humphreys (*Sturgis*), Mai Bacon (*Gert*), Wallace Geoffrey (*Latimer*), Aubrey Mather (*The Dean*), Arthur Chesney (*Lord Frensham*), Edmund Dalby (*Rennie*), Robert Nainby (*Mr. Beane*), Merle Tottenham (*Maid*), Aubrey Fitzgerald (*Banks*), Fred Rains (*Warden*).

Howard is a college porter who suddenly finds himself with an inherited earldom. Then he has to defend his estate from con men who pretend to have struck oil on the grounds. Typically bleak and unfunny prewar British comedy.

p, Jack Raymond; d, Michael Hankinson; w, Irving Leroy, Daniel Wheddon, Gerard Fairlie, Cyril Gardner, D. B. Wyndham-Lewis (based on a novel by Edgar Wallace); ph, Francis Carver.

Comedy (PR:A MPAA:NR)

CHICKEN CHRONICLES, THE* (1977) 92m AE c
Phil Silvers (*Max Ober*), Ed Lauter (*Mr. Nastase*), Steve Guttenberg (*David Kessler*), Lisa Reeves (*Margaret*), Meredith Baer (*Tracy*), Branscombe Richmond (*Mark*), Will Seltzer (*Weinstein*), Kutee (*Maddy*), Gino Baffa (*Charlie Kessler*), Robert Resnick (*Stuart*), Joe Medalis (*Phinney*), Robin T. Williams (*Vanessa*).

Working in Silver's greasy spoon, high schooler Guttenberg spends all of his waking hours trying to get Reeves into the sack. A typical juvenile picture which doesn't present a too-promising image of youth.

p, Walter Shenson; d, Francis Simon; w, Paul Diamond (based on his novel); ph, Matthew F. Leonetti (CFI Color); m, Kan Lauber; ed, George Folsey, Jr.; art d, Ray Markham; cos, Richalene Kelsay, Sandra Burke.

Comedy (PR:C MPAA:PG)

CHICKEN EVERY SUNDAY**½ (1948) 91m FOX bw
Dan Dailey (*Jim Hefferen*), Celeste Holm (*Emily Hefferen*), Colleen Townsend (*Rosemary Hefferen*), Alan Young (*Geoffrey Lawson*), Natalie Wood (*Ruth*), William Frawley (*George Kirby*), Connie Gilchrist (*Millie Moon*), William Callahan (*Harold Crandall*), Veda Ann Borg (*Rita Kirby*), Porter Hall (*Sam Howell*), Whit Bissell (*Mr. Robinson*), Katherine Emery (*Mrs. Lawson*), Roy Roberts (*Harry Bowers*), Hal K. Dawson (*Jake Barker*), Percy Helton (*Mr. Sawyer*), Mary Field (*Miss Gilly*), Anthony Sydes (*Oliver*), H. T. Tsiang (*Charley*), Loren Raker (*Mr. Lawson*), Junius Matthews (*Deacon Wilson*), Dick Ryan (*Bartender*), Ruth Rickaby (*Nurse*), Edward Keane (*Joe*), Jack Kirkwood (*Harris*), Francis Pierlot (*Blaine*), Wilson Wood (*Hart*), Eddie Laughton (*Process Server*), Frank Meredith, Jack Daley (*Moving Men*).

Light comedy about a Tucson couple whose marriage falters due to a conflict between the husband's get-rich-quick schemes and his wife's practicality. In his last wild thrust for wealth, Dailey mortgages the homestead to the hilt to buy some worthless mining

stock. Holm has had enough and leaves him, vowing never to make more trips to his lips but loyal friends successfully scheme the couple back together. Amusing, but poorly directed, with a charming backdrop of boarders who support the plot and the family. Based on a play by Julius J. and Philip G. Epstein, writers of ARSENIC AND OLD LACE.

p, William Perlberg; d, George Seaton; w, Seaton, Valentine Davies (based on a play by Julius J. and Philip G. Epstein and from a book by Rosemary Taylor); ph, Harry Jackson; m, Alfred Newman; ed, Robert Simpson.

Comedy (PR:A MPAA:NR)

CHICKEN WAGON FAMILY* (1939) 81m FOX bw
Jane Withers (*Addie Fippany*), Leo Carillo (*J. P. B. Fippany*), Marjorie Weaver (*Cecile*), Spring Byington (*Josephine*), Kane Richmond (*Hibbard*), Hobart Cavanaugh (*Henri*), Hamilton McFadden (*Auctioneer*), Inez Palange (*Mrs. Buzzi*).

Painfully bad comedy about a family of bayou swindlers who come to New York and take up residence in an abandoned fire station—wagon, mules, and all. Withers and Carillo sing a rousing duet on "Daughter of Mademoiselle" (a variation of Gypsy Rose Lee's "BATTLE OF BROADWAY") but it's not enough to sustain interest in the draggy plot.

p, Sol M. Wurtzel; d, Herbert I. Leeds; w, Viola Brothers Shore (based on a novel by Barry Benefield), ph, Edward Cronjager; ed, Fred Allen; md, Samuel Kaylin.

Comedy (PR:A MPAA:NR)

CHIEF, THE* (1933) 80m MGM bw
Ed Wynn (*Henry Summers*), Dorothy Mackaill (*Dixie*), Charles "Chic" Sale (*Uncle Joe*), William Boyd (*O'Rourke*), Effie Ellsler (*Ma Summers*), C. Henry Gordon (*Clayton*), George Givot (*Clothing Merchant*), Mickey Rooney (*Willie*), Bradley Page (*Dapper Dan*), Purnell B. Pratt (*Morgan*), Nat Pendleton (*Mike*).

Dire Ed Wynn vehicle with the comic playing a child (for almost an unbearable hour), a fireman's son, then a dummy candidate for alderman. Wynn's myriad vaudeville routines fall flat in this tedious production, one so poor that the film was never released in England where 1930s audiences were grateful for any Hollywood product.

p,, Harry Rapf; d, Charles F. Reisner; w, Arthur Caesar, Robert Hopkins; ph, Edward Paul; ed, William Gray.

Comedy (PR:A MPAA:NR)

CHIEF CRAZY HORSE**½ (1955) 86m UNIV c (GB: VALLEY OF FURY)
Victor Mature (*Crazy Horse*), Suzan Ball (*Black Shawl*), John Lund (*Maj. Twist*), Ray Danton (*Little Big Man*), Keith Larsen (*Flying Hawk*), Paul Guilfoyle (*Worm*), David Janssen (*Lt. Cartwright*), Robert Warwick (*Spotted Tail*), James Millican (*Gen. Crook*), Morris Ankrum (*Red Cloud/Conquering Bear*), Donald Randolph (*Aaron Cartwright*), Robert F. Simon (*Jeff Mantz*), James Westerfield (*Caleb Mantz*), Stuart Randall (*Old Man Afraid*), Pat Hogan (*Dull Knife*), Dennis Weaver (*Maj. Carlisle*), John Peters (*Sgt. Guthrie*), Henry Wills (*He Dog*), Willie Hunter, Jr. (*Cavalryman*), Charles Horvath (*Hardy*), Robert St. Angelo (*Sergeant*), David Miller (*Lieutenant*).

Exciting and sympathetic look at the life of Chief Crazy Horse and the Indian nations. Living out the prophecy that a great warrior would rise and unite the tribes only to be killed by a fellow redskin, Crazy Horse is nobly portrayed by Mature. Danton is also a standout as the half-caste renegade who murders Mature after he has made peace with the soldiers under Millican's command. Ball, ably portraying Mature's Indian wife, makes her first return appearance on film after having a leg amputated following an illness. Weaver is cast in a small role as Maj. Carlisle.

p, William Alland; d, George Sherman; w, Franklin Coen, Gerald Drayson Adams (based on a story by Adams); ph, Harold Lipstein (CinemaScope, Technicolor); m, Frank Skinner; ed, Al Clark; md, Joseph Gershenson; art d, Alexander Golitzen, Robert Boyle; cos, Rosemary Odell.

Western (PR:A MPAA:NR)

CHILD, THE* (1977) 73m Valiant International c (AKA: KILL AND GO HIDE!)
Laurel Barnett (*Elise*), Rosalie Cole (*Rosalie*), Frank Janson (*Father*), Richard Hanners (*Len*), Ruth Ballen (*Mr. Whitfield*), Slosson Bing Jong (*Gardener*).

Sweet little girl Cole discovers she has demonic powers after her daddy pays the homicidal gardener to bump off mommy. In retaliation, Cole commands the bodies of the dead to rise in a nearby cemetery. New governess Barnett begins to think things are strange when most of the cast is chewed up by things that go bump in the night. The spunky nursemaid sees it will be her turn next, and barricades herself in the pumphouse with an axe waiting for the newly risen dead to find her. When the door opens, she plants the axe in the first thing that wanders in. Unfortunately (or fortunately, depending on how you look at it) it's the little girl who gets her skull split. With their motivational mentor gone, the zombies wander off into the woods and Barnett wanders off in the opposite direction unhinged by the whole gory thing.

p, Robert Dadashian; d, Robert Voskanian; w, Ralph Lucas; ph, Mori Alavi (Eastmancolor); m, Rob Wallace (performed by Michael Quatro).

Horror Cas. (PR:O MPAA:R)

CHILD AND THE KILLER, THE* (1959, Brit.) 65m Danziger/UA bw
Patricia Driscoll (*Peggy Martin*), Robert Arden (*Capt. Joe Marsh*), Richard Williams (*Tommy Martin*), Ryck Rydon (*Mather*), Gorne Sterne (*Sergeant*), John McLaren (*Maj. Finch*), Robert Raglan (*Inspector*).

Arden is a U.S. Army officer on the run from a murder. He forces Williams, the seven-year-old son of widow Driscoll, to lead him to safety in the wilderness. Routine crime melodrama.

p, Edward J. and Harry Lee Danziger; d, Max Varnel; w, Brian Clemens, Eldon Howard.

Crime   (PR:C MPAA:NR)

CHILD IN THE HOUSE½   (1956, Brit.) 90m Eros bw
Phyllis Calvert (*Evelyn Acheson*), Eric Portman (*Henry Acheson*), Stanley Baker (*Stephen Lorimer*), Mandy Miller (*Elizabeth Lorimer*), Dora Bryan (*Cassie*), Joan Hickson (*Cook*), Victor Maddern (*Bert*), Percy Herbert (*Detective Sgt. Taylor*), Joan Benham (*Vera McNally*), Martin Miller (*Prof Topolski*), Christopher Toyne (*Peter McNally*), Alfie Bass (*Ticket Collector*), Molly Urquhart (*Mrs. Parsons*), Bruce Beeby (*P. C. Jennings*), Peter Burton (*Howard Forbes*).

Calculated tearjerker which sees a lonely eleven-year-old enter the home of her inattentive aunt and uncle. With her mother hospitalized and her father a fugitive, she turns to the understanding housemaid for attention. She eventually meets her father, but must promise not to disclose his whereabouts to the snooping police, throwing her into a quandary between truth and loyalty, until the father's final conversion.

p, S. Benjamin Fisz; d, C. Raker Endfield; w, Endfield (based on the novel by Janet McNeill); ph, Otto Heller; m, Mario Nascimbene; ed, Charles Hasse.

Drama   (PR:A MPAA:NR)

CHILD IS A WILD THING, A   (1976) 88m Sudarsky Films c
Marie Antoinette Skinner (*Miette*), Adam (*Himself*), George S. Irving (*Husband's Voice*).

An interesting though heavy-handed look at the behavior of a young boy. Photographed as a pseudo-documentary, it takes a studied and observational approach to childhood. We see the boy and his mother in a home-movie-ish way, as the kin of the 16mm cameraman. An extraordinary semi-incestuous scene provides an example of the unusual depth of this independently financed feature.

p,d,w&ph, Peter Sudarsky [Peter Skinner]; m, Derek Wadsworth; ed, Skinner, Vincent Suprynowicz, Sidney Katz.

Drama   (PR:O MPAA:NR)

CHILD IS BORN, A   (1940) 73m WB bw
Geraldine Fitzgerald (*Grace Sutton*), Jeffrey Lynn (*Jed Sutton*), Gladys George (*Florette*), Gale Page (*Miss Bowers*), Spring Byington (*Mrs. West*), Johnnie Davis (*Ringer Banks*), Henry O'Neill (*Dr. Lee*), John Litel (*Dr. Brett*), Gloria Holden (*Mrs. Kempner*), Johnny Downs (*Johnny Norton*), Eve Arden (*Miss Pinty*), Fay Helm (*The Woman*), Louis Jean Heydt (*Mr. Kempner*), Nanette Fabares [Fabray] (*Gladys Norton*), Jean Sharon (*Mrs. Banks*), Hobart Cavanaugh (*Mr. West*), George Irving (*Dr. Cramm*), Nella Walker (*Mrs. Twitchell*), Esther Dale (*Matron*), Ed Gargan (*Guard*), Edgar Dearing (*Sergeant*), Marie Blake (*Gladys*), Maris Wrixon (*Information Girl*), Sibyl Harris (*Flower Woman*), Creighton Hale (*Elevator Operator*), Buzz Buckley (*Little Tot*), George O'Hanlon (*Young Husband*), John Ridgeley (*William Hopper*), Owen King, Charles Marsh, Carlyle Moore, Jr. (*Interns*), Garry Owen, Sidney Bracy (*Drugstore Clerks*), Frank Mayo (*Policeman*), Winfred Harris (*Mrs. Holt*), Dorothy Adams (*Nurse*), Georgia Caine (*Mrs. Norton's Mother*), Virginia Brissac (*Mr. Norton's Mother*).

Good-hearted but ultimately annoying maternity ward drama has a vaudeville star (George) who resents her pregnancy but has a change of heart, a murderess released from prison to give birth (Fitzgerald), and a woman bearing a stillborn baby for the third time (Holden). In fact, a cliche for everyone. Remake of LIFE BEGINS (1932).

p, Sam Bischoff; d, Lloyd Bacon; w, Robert Rossen (based on the play "Life Begins" by Mary McDougal Axelson); ph, Charles Rosher; ed, Jack Killiter.

Drama   (PR:A MPAA:NR)

CHILD IS WAITING, A*   (1963) 104m UA bw
Burt Lancaster (*Dr. Matthew Clark*), Judy Garland (*Jean Hansen*), Gena Rowlands (*Sophie Widdicombe*), Steven Hill (*Ted Widdicombe*), Bruce Ritchey (*Reuben Widdicombe*), Gloria McGehee (*Mattie*), Paul Stewart (*Goodman*), Lawrence Tierney (*Douglas Benham*), Elizabeth Wilson (*Miss Fogarty*), Barbara Pepper (*Miss Brown*), John Morley (*Holland*), June Walker (*Mrs. McDonald*), Mario Gallo (*Dr. Lombardi*), Frederick Draper (*Dr. Sack*).

Cassavetes has long been successful at mixing his unique blend of documentation and improvisation, and this emotionally draining film is no exception. Set in an institutiton for the mentally retarded, Lancaster plays the objective but sympathetic head of the institution, and Garland the over-attentive teacher. With a large cast of real-life handicapped children, Garland comes to realize that she pays too much attention to one of her students. A fine example of the role that Cassavetes and wife Rowlands play in American cinema. This film takes the social stance of a Stanley Kramer and the institutional approach of a Frederick Wiseman and rises above their judgmental attitudes to produce a wonderfully provocative and sympathetic film.

p, Stanley Kramer; d, John Cassavetes; w, Abby Mann (based on his story); ph, Joseph LaShelle; m, Ernest Gold; ed, Gene Fowler, Jr.; prod d, Rudolph Sternad.

Drama   (PR:A MPA:NR)

CHILD OF DIVORCE½   (1946) 62m RKO bw
Sharyn Moffett (*Bobby*), Regis Toomey (*Ray*), Madge Meredith (*Joan*), Walter Reed (*Michael*), Una O'Connor (*Nora*), Doris Merrick (*Louise*), Harry Cheshire (*Judge*), Selmer Jackson (*Dr. Sterling*), Lillian Randolph (*Carrie*), Pat Prest (*Linda*), Gregory Muradian (*Freddie*), George McDonald (*Donnie*), Patsy Converse (*Betty*), Ann Carter (*Peggy*).

Moffet is the title moppet, watching sadly as her parents divorce, shuffle her from house to house, and finally put her in a boarding school. Depressing but fairly well done thanks to fine acting by Moffet, who was eight years old at the time and would act for five more years before dropping out of sight.

p, Lillie Hayward; d, Richard O. Fleischer; w, Hayward (based on play "Wednesday's Child" by Leopold L. Atlas); ph, Jack MacKenzie; m, Leigh Harline; ed, Samuel E. Beetley.

Drama   (PR:A MPAA:NR)

CHILD OF MANHATTAN   (1933) 70m COL bw
Nancy Carroll (*Madeleine McGonegal*), John Boles (*Paul Vanderkill*), Warburton Gamble (*Eggleston*), Clara Blandick (*Aunt Sophie*), Jane Darwell (*Mrs. McGonegal*), Garry Owen (*Buddy*), Betty Grable (*Lucy*), Luis Alberni (*Bustamente*), Jessie Ralph (*Aunt Minnie*), Charles Jones (*Panama Kelly*), Tyler Brooke (*Dulcey*), Betty Kendall (*Louise*).

Carroll is a dance hall hostess who falls for millionaire Boles, gets pregnant, and then they marry. The baby dies, and Carroll runs away and gets a divorce. On the day she is to marry Jones, Boles turns up and she rushes back to his arms. Wretched melodrama.

d, Eddie Buzzell; w, Gertrude Purcell (based on a play by Preston Sturges); ph, Teddy Tetzlaff.

Drama   (PR:C MPAA:NR)

CHILD UNDER A LEAF   (1975, Can.) 120m Cinema National c
Dyan Cannon (*Domino*), Joseph Campanella (*Her Husband*), Donald Pilon (*Joseph*), Albert S. Waxman, Micheline Lanctot, Bud Knapp, Bess Bloomfield, Julia Bullock.

Sexy Cannon is a married woman torn between lover Pilon and husband Campanella in one of her minor movies. Talented cast can't help static melodrama.

p, Murray Shostak, Robert Baylis; d&w, George Bloomfield; ph, Don Wilder; m, Francis Lai; ed, Bloomfield; art d, Jocelyn Joly.

Drama   (PR:O MPAA:R)

CHILDHOOD OF MAXIM GORKY   (1938, Russ.) 99m Soyezdetfilm bw
Alyosha Lyarsky (*Alexei Peshkov Gorky*), V. O. Massalitinova (*Grandmother*), M. G. Troyanovsky (*Grandfather*), E. Alexeyeva (*Varvara*), V. Novikov (*Uncle Yakov*), A. Zhukov (*Uncle Mikhail*), K. Ziubkov (*Grigori*), D. Sagal (*Gypsy*), S. Tikhonravov (*Lodger*), Igor Smirnov (*Lenka*).

Poor telling of the great writer's humble beginnings. Little orphaned Lyarsky is brought up by a tyrannical grandfather and a crew of conniving uncles. The glory days of Russian cinema gave way under Stalin's "Social Realism" campaign to trash like this. (In Russian; English subtitles.)

d, Mark Donskoi; w, I. Gruzdev; ph, P. Yermolov, I. Malov; m, Lev. Shwartz.

Drama   (PR:A MPAA:NR)

CHILDISH THINGS zero   (1969) 93m Filmworld c
Don Murray (*Tom Harris*), Linda Evans (*Pat*), David Brian (*Jennings*), Angelique Pettyjohn (*Angelique*), Don Joslyn (*Kelly*), Gypsy Boots (*Gypsy*), Rod Lauren (*Rod*), LeRoy Jenkins (*Preacher*), Logan Ramsey (*Mr. Simmons*), Erik Holland (*1st Fighter*), Jack Griffin (*Jack*), Valerie Brooke (*Girl*), Gene LaBelle (*Peanut Man*), Ed Bennett (*Carousel Man*), Seaman Glass (*Ex-Fighter*), George Atkinson (*Last Fighter*), Peter Tenen (*Gene*), Claire Kelly (*Sharon*).

A childish thing indeed about a shallow, hedonistic boxer who divides his time between the ring and the bedroom. Perhaps a faithful rendition of the boxer's life, but the characterization comes off as excessively degenerate with no sign of redemption. Dully scripted by Murray with indulgent and uninspired camera work and direction by Derek. The sexually demeaned Evans is a one-time Derek spouse.

p, Don Murray; d, John Derek; w, Murray; ph, Derek (Eastmancolor); m, Joe Greene; ed, Maurice Wright; art d, John Harris.

Drama   (PR:O MPAA:NR)

CHILDREN, THE½   (1949, Swed.) 101m Scandia bw
Hans Lindgren (*Ante*), Siv Hansson (*Maglena*), Anders Nystrom (*Manke*), Fiffi Honeth (*Anna-Lisa*), Ulf Berggren (*Per-Erik*), Paula Jagaeus (*Britta-Kajsa*), Christina Jagaeus (*Kristina*), John Ericsson (*Shoe-Pelle*), Ragnar Falck (*Gamekeeper Grape*), Britta Brunius (*Mrs. Grape*), Birger Asander (*Big Jon*), Ingrid Luterkort (*His Wife*), Gunnar Sjoberg (*The Minister*), Helge Hagerman (*Oskar Niva*), Solveig Hedengran (*His Wife*).

This heartwarmer about seven orphaned children traveling through the Swedish countryside is a light and pleasant experience. A sugary view cannot be avoided with this charming cast, but you can't help but be affected by their helplessness and bravery. (In Swedish: English subtitles)

p, Sandrew Bauman; d, Rolf Husberg; w, Husberg (based on Laura Fitinghoff's novel *Children of the Moor*); ph. O. Nordemar; m, Sven Skold.

Drama   (PR:AAA MPAA:NR)

CHILDREN, THE zero   (1980) 90m World-Northal c
Martin Shakar (*John Freemont*), Gil Rogers (*Sheriff Billy Hart*), Gale Garnett (*Cathy Freemont*), Jessie Abrams, Tracy Griswold, Joy Glaccum, Suzanne Barnes, Rita Montone, Michelle Le Mothe, Shannon Bolin, Clara Evans, Jeptha Evans, Sarah Albright, Nathanael Albright, Julie Carrier, Edward Terry.

Hands are cut off right and left in this laughable horror film about radioactive kids who, on contact, turn their loving parents into smoldering embers. As a substitute for special effects, the kids get black fingernail polish to show that they indeed are contaminated—a sure sign of radiation. Mother-to-be Garnett is exposed to the leak and gives birth to an infant killer. She and husband Shakar must decide whether to destroy the lad before he hugs someone. Truly bad cinema.

p, Max Kalmanowicz, Carlton J. Albright; d, Kalmanowicz; w, Albright, Edward Terry; ph, Barry Abrams (Panavision); m, Henry Manfredini; ed, Nikki Wessling; makeup, Carla White.

Horror   Cas.   (PR:O MPAA:R)

CHILDREN GALORE*   (1954, Brit.) 60m Grendon/GFD bw
Eddie Byrne (*Zacky Jones*), Marjorie Rhodes (*Ada Jones*), June Thorburn (*Milly Ark*), Richard Leach (*Harry Bunnion*), Betty Ann Davies (*Mrs. Ark*), Jack McNaughton (*Pat Ark*), Peter Evan Thomas (*Lord Redscarfe*), Marjorie Hume (*Lady Redscarfe*), Lucy Griffiths (*Miss Prescott*), Henry Caine (*Bert Bunnion*).

Local squire Thomas offers a free house to the villager with the most grandchildren. Thus, children galore—get it? Byrne and Rhodes were character actors with long years of experience, giving this film whatever reason there might be for seeking it out. Director Fisher would shortly move along into cult status by directing the bulk of Hammer Films' horror efforts for the next 15 years.

p, Henry Passmore; d, Terence Fisher; w, John and Emery Bonnet, Peter Plaskett; ph, Jonah Jones.

Comedy   **(PR:A MPA:NR)**

CHILDREN OF BABYLON zero   (1980, Jamaica) 122m Rainbow c
Tobi (*Penny*), Don Parchment (*Rick*), Bob Andy (*Luke*), Leonie Forbes (*Dorcas*), Elizabeth de Lisser (*Laura*), Keith Wheeler (*Hitchhiker*), Chris Williams, Robin Williams (*Boys on Beach*), Ashton James (*Raftsman*), Thurston Campbell (*Porter*), Cordett Duckie (*Voice of Interviewed Woman*).

Jamaica is a hedonistic pleasure dome in this overlong reggae-charged film with a Marxist message. Tobi, like all the other inhabitants, falls in love with whomever she's with, then bares her breasts for the camera. The political rambling comes across with comparisons of Jamaica to Southern plantations in the U.S.

p,d&w, Lennie Little-White; ph, Franklyn St. Juste; m, Harold Butler; ed, Little-White.

Drama   **(PR:O MPAA:NR)**

CHILDREN OF CHANCE*   (1930, Brit.) 75m British International bw
Elissa Landi (*Binnie/ Lia Monta*), Mabel Poulton (*Molly*), John Stuart (*Gordon*), John Longden (*Jeffrey*), Gus McNaughton (*H. K. Zinkwell*), Wallace Lupino (*O. K. Johnson*), Gus Sharland (*Hugo*), John Deverell (*Harold*), Charles Dormer (*Dude*), Dorothy Minto (*Sally*), Kay Hammond (*Joyce*).

Landi is a doppelganger for a jewel-thief actress. When the actress disappears, Landi takes over her identity, falling in love with one of her admirers. Arrested when the theft is discovered, she proves her true identity and is released in her lover's arms. Best feature of the film is the chance to see Landi in two roles instead of one.

d, Alexander Esway; w, Miles Malleson, Frank Launder; ph, E. H. Palmer, L. Rogers.

Crime   **(PR:A MPAA:NR)**

CHILDREN OF CHANCE*   (1949, Brit.) 99m Ortus/BL bw
Patricia Medina (*Agostina*), Manning Whiley (*Don Andrea*), Yvonne Mitchell (*Australia*), Barbara Everest (*Francesca*), Eliot Makeham (*Vicar*), George Woodbridge (*Butcher*), Frank Tickle (*Mayor*), Eric Pohlmann (*Sergeant*), Edward Lexy (*Doctor*), Carlo Giustini [*Justini*] (*Marco*), Catherine Paul, Richard Molinas, Denis Carey, Peter Iling, Peter Ducrow, Vittoria, Febe.

Medina, a WW II black-marketeer, has sent the profits from her illicit ventures to her friend, the island priest of Ischia. When the collaborative priest is replaced by Whiley, the new pastor finds a better use for the money: to establish a home for the out-of-wedlock foundlings sired by Allied soldiers during the occupation of the island. Medina and her equally avaricious girl friend, Mitchell, arrive at the island to redeem the loot, but undergo a change of heart upon observing the plight of the homeless, parentless waifs, and ultimately concur with Whiley's plans. Overlong and boring; the later Italian version had the added fillip of the ladies earning the dollars in the sack.

p, Ludovico Toeplitz, John Sutro; d, Luigi Zampa; w, Piero Tellini, Michael Medwin (based on a story by Tellini); ph, Carlo Montuori.

Drama   **(PR:A MPAA:NBR)**

CHILDREN OF CHANCE**   (1950, Ital.) 109m Lux Films bw
(CAMPANE A MARTELLO)
Eduardo De Filippo (*Don Andrea*), Gina Lollobrigida (*Agostina*), Yvonne Sanson (*Australia*), Carlo Romano (*Gendarme*), Carlo Giustini (*Marco*), Clelia Matania (*Bianca*), Agostino Salvietti (*Mayor*), Ernesto Almirante (*Landowner*), Luigi Saltamerenda (*Butcher*).

Intelligent treatment of two prostitutes who earn their living by bedding with American GI's in Italy during WW II. The war's end brings about unemployment so the women return to their homeland to spend their profits. Supposedly in the good hands of the local priest, the money is used to set up a home for illegitimate war babies. Great Nino Rota score. A cheaper version of the film was made by a British company.

p, Carlo Ponti; d, Luigi Zampa; w, Piero Tellini; ph, Carlo Montuori; m, Nino Rota; ed, Eraldo De Roma.

Drama   **(PR:A MPAA:NR)**

CHILDREN OF CHAOS**   (1950, Fr.) 91m Victory Films bw
Rene Darcy (*Jean-Victor*), Janine Darcey (*Jenny*), Serge Reggiani (*Jorisse*), Raymond Bussieres ("*Hawk-Nose*"), Jean Meranton (*Droopy*), A. M. Julien (*Lefty*), Robert Demorget (*La "Puce"*).

Drawing on the BOYS' TOWN theme, CHILDREN OF CHAOS attempts to tell the gritty story of a reformatory worker and his boys. Darcy plays a reformer who has been through the process himself. He works on the theory that humane treatment can change a group of cutthroats into good citizens. He encounters many problems along the way, including a group of burglars who try to recruit his boys. Darcy wins his point and most of the boys despite the obstacles. (In French; English subtitles.)

p, Georges Dernier; d, Leon Joannon; w, M. Bessy, Jean-Georges Auriol (based on scenario by Stephane Pizella); ed, Charles Clement.

Drama   **(PR:C MPAA:NR)**

CHILDREN OF DREAMS zero   (1931) 78m WB bw
Margaret Schilling (*Molly Standing*), Paul Gregory (*Tommy Melville*), Tom Patricola (*Gus Schultz*), Bruce Winston (*Hubert Standing*), Charles Winninger (*Dr. Joe Thompson*), Marion Byron (*Gertie*).

Dreadfully dull musical story of country girl Schilling becoming an opera star in New York. The setting is mostly based in a California apple orchard which made this production all the more ludicrous and helped to turn the public sour on musicals which

were being ground out like odorous sausage. Songs: "Fruit Picker's Song," "Oh, Couldn't I Love That Girl," "Her Professor," "Children of Dreams," "Sleeping Beauty," "If I Had A Girl Like You," "Seek Love," "Yes Sir" (Oscar Hammerstein II, Sigmund Romberg). A waste of time.

d, Alan Crosland; w, Oscar Hammerstein II, Sigmund Romberg (based on a story by Hammerstein, Romberg); ph, James Van Trees; ed, Harold McLernon.

Musical   **(PR:A MPAA:NR)**

CHILDREN OF GOD'S EARTH**   (1983, Norwegian) 78m A/S Elan Film c
Anneli Marian Drecker (*Margit*), Torgils Moe (*Baela*), Odd Furoy (*Kristian*), Frode Rasmussen (*Simon*), Randi Koch (*Johanna*), Ernst Rune Huemer (*Arild*), Merete Moen (*Vavva*).

This sparsely written melodrama set on a small Norwegian island is Laila Mikkelsen's first film after the strong and very moving LITTLE IDA, which told about the wartime child of a Norwegian woman and a German soldier. The new story revolves around Drecker, the preteenage ward of an old peasant couple. We see through her wide eyes the slow growth of violence on the island. She witnesses a proposition by a nearby fisherman as he promises a mild-mannered halfwit giant a large sum of money to rip off another man's head. She also takes up with a consumptive teenage boy who dies trying to run after her when he has failed to embrace her beyond a shy allotted kiss. This simple melodrama is made bearable by Mikkelsen's use of frames, landscapes, dialog, and characters in a way to tempt audiences to see something that might not otherwise be apparent. (Norwegian; English subtitles.)

p, Kirsten Bryhni; d&w, Laila Mikkelsen (based on Arvid Hanssen's novel); ph, Rolv Haan (Fuji Color); m, Pete Knudsen; ed, Fred Sassebo; art d & cos, Torunn Mueller.

Drama   **(PR:C MPAA:NR)**

CHILDREN OF HIROSHIMA½**   (1952, Jap.) 97m Kendai Eiga Lyokai/Mingei bw
Nobuko Otowa, Chikako Hoshawa, Niwa Saito.

A-bomb horror at Hiroshima is shown through the eyes of a teacher visiting the ravaged city and her former students. Filmed in semi-documentary style with newsreel footage to emphasize the mindlessness of war, this was one of the first Japanese productions to create American sympathy for a one-time vicious enemy.

p, Gekidan Mingei; d&w, Kaneto Shindo (based on the novel by Arata Osada); ph, Takeo Itch; m, Akira Ifukube.

War Drama   **(PR:C-O MPAA:NR)**

CHILDREN OF PARADISE***
      (1945, Fr.) 195m S.N. Pathe bw (LES ENFANTS DU PARADIS)
Arletty (*Garance*), Jean-Louis Barrault (*Baptiste Debureau*), Pierre Brasseur (*Frederick Lemaitre*), Marcel Herrand (*Lacenaire*), Pierre Renoir (*Jericho*), Maria Casares (*Natalie*), Etienne Decroux (*Anselme Debureau*), Fabien Loris (*Avril*), Leon Larive (*Stage Doorman, "Funambules"*), Pierre Palov (*Stage Manager, "Funambules"*), Marcel Peres (*Director, "Funambules"*), Albert Remy (*Scarpia Barrigni*), Jeanne Marken (*Madame Hermine*), Gaston Modot (*Fil de Soie*), Louis Salou (*Count Edward de Monteray*), Jacques Castelot (*George*), Jean Gold (*Second Dandy*), Guy Faviere (*Debt Collector*), Paul Frankeur (*Police Inspector*), Lucienne Vigier (*First Pretty Girl*), Cynette Quero (*Second Pretty Girl*), Gustave Hamilton (*Stage Doorman, "Grand Theatre"*), Rognoni (*Director, "Grand Theatre"*), Auguste Boverio (*First Author*), Paul Demange (*Second Author*), Jean Diener (*Third Author*), Louis Florencie (*Policeman*), Marcelle Monthil (*Marie*), Robert Dhery (*Celestin*), Lucien Walter (*Ticket Seller*), Jean-Pierre Delmon (*Little Baptiste*), Raphael Patorni (*Another Dandy*), Jean Lanier (*Iago*), Habib Benglia (*Arab Attendant*).

It's been called France's answer to GONE WITH THE WIND and the greatest movie ever made. It's been hailed by most and damned by some. The backset story is almost as intriguing as what's happening on screen because the movie was made at the end of the German occupation and many of the actors were Resistance Fighters who were being sought by the Gestapo. They would hide out, blow up a Nazi building, show up as extras, and then return to wherever it was they slept that night. The original actor who played Jericho, Robert Le Vigan, disappeared when he was suspected of being a Nazi collaborator. He was never seen again and was replaced by Pierre Renoir. It's hard enough to make any movie. To make a classic is near impossible. To make a classic under wartime circumstances and when you are being constantly watched by your captors is a miracle. The story takes place in Paris in the 1820s and '30s. The Children of Paradise are the poor people who inhabit the topmost balconies of the theaters along the Boulevard du Temple (also known as the "Boulevard Of Crime" because the theaters specialized in gory melodramas to satisfy the increasingly blase crowds). A curtain rises and we are in Paris in spring. Arletty, a gorgeous and succulent woman of the area, is accused of pickpocketing a watch. She is innocent and the whole incident has been witnessed by Barrault, who is the son of Decroux, proprietor of the famous Theatre des Funambules. Arletty watches as Barrault gets her off the hook and she rewards him with a tossed rose. When the Barrigni family (led by Remy) quit the Theater, Barrault gets the chance to appear on the stage along with his amie, Brasseur, who wants to be a Shakespearean actor. Barrault is pining for Arletty and he, in turn, is pined for by Casares, the stage manager's daughter. One night, Modot, who works as a blind beggar but who can see perfectly well, takes Barrault to one of the more dangerous bars, Le Rouge-Gorge, for a drink. Barrault is shocked to see Arletty at this bar with Herrand, an acknowledged no-goodnik from Paris's underworld. Barrault attempts to dance with Arletty but Herrand's henchman-thug, Loris, tosses the smitten youth out of the club. Barrault comes back into the club and takes the yegg apart, much to Arletty's delight. Later, they stroll the streets and she tells him of her poor background. Their lips meet as the rains pour down. He secures a room for her at the Grand Relais, where he lives, and then goes to his quarters without making any further romantic moves. Brasseur is also staying at the Grand Relais and when he meets Arletty they fall passionately into lust and become lovers for a short time. Barrault is thunderstruck by this turn and in his despair he creates a mime drama about the triangle. Salou enters the situation. He is a count with untold sums of money and he attempts to intrigue Arletty but she could not care less about the size of his bankbook. Barrault now confesses to Arletty that he loves her more than life but he knows that he can never achieve a response from her. She is drawn to the youth by his ardor and passion. Now Casares enters, says that Barrault is hers alone, and wishes Arletty would get out of the situation. Herrand checks into the Grand Relais to plan a robbery and Arletty is implicated once again, though she is innocent. She is about to go to prison but produces a "courtesy card" which the Count gave her on the off-chance of such a complication. *Dissolve* and we are now in the beginning of Louis Phillipe's reign. Arletty is now the official mistress of Salou but she keeps the love she feels for Barrault deep in her heart where only she can know it exists. Barrault and Casares have now married and have a young son, Delmon. By this time, Barrault has become a famous mime—the Marcel Marceau of his era. Brasseur is also well-known on the stage and leads a rakehell's life with wine, women, song, and more wine. He is keeping his creditors out of his hair with fancy footwork and paying for his excesses with money he earns as a farceur. At present, he is appearing in a dreadful piece and he takes great pleasure in making fun of his role. He does it once too often and the trio of authors challenge him to a duel. He is wounded slightly, but not enough to keep him from Barrault's opening at the Funambules. He's written a new mime drama and all of Paris is eager to see what it is. At the theater, Brasseur meets a disguised Arletty who admits having come to many of Barrault's performances but never having the nerve to re-introduce herself. She tells Brasseur about her life with the count and how happy she is but he, and we, can see right through that. Brasseur goes backstage to tell Barrault that Arletty is in the audience. Casares also learns that Arletty is there and promptly sends her small son out to tell the woman to leave; they are very happy and would appreciate her immediate exit. She does. A moment later, Barrault, who is eager to see what the one love of his life looks like, rushes to her box and finds it unoccupied. He is crushed again. Herrand runs into Arletty and tells her of his successful crime career. Later, he meets the count who snubs him. Herrand is insulted and the count challenges the criminal to a duel but the crook won't bite. Salou realizes that Arletty doesn't really love him but adores another. He doesn't know who that other person is but when they attend Brasseur's opening as "Othello" Salou suspects it's Brasseur and plans to duel him. Barrault is at the same theater to see his friend perform and when he finds Arletty, he takes her to a balcony where they look deeply into each other's hearts and realize that they love only one another. Salou goads Brasseur in a vain attempt to draw him into a confrontation and Brasseur can't understand it. Now Herrand arrives and pulls back the box's curtains to reveal Barrault and Arletty together. Salou is livid and challenges Barrault to a duel the following day. Arletty and Barrault spend what may be their final night together. Salou is at the Turkish baths, getting ready, and Herrand, who is still smarting over the earlier insults, goes to the baths and stabs the count to death! Arletty leaves early in the morning to attempt to convince Salou to forget it and depart with her. She has no idea he's dead. She and Casares have another confrontation as Casares attempts to keep her marriage together. In the final sequence, she leaps into a carriage as Barrault races after her, shouting her name, pushing through a crowd of carnival revelers all dressed in the Pierrot costume he wears on stage. No matter how hard he pushes and how loud he shouts, the carriage carrying his beloved moves faster and eventually out of his sight as the curtain falls. The complex screenplay was by Jacques Prévert, a painter-turned-poet. He and director Marcel Carné had already produced four films and their abilities were internationally recognized. The Nazis had forbidden any film to be longer than 90 minutes so they shot this as *two* films; THE BOULEVARD OF CRIME and THE MAN IN WHITE. Production began on August 16, 1943, and finished in March, 1944. In the meantime, they had to ship their major set back and forth between Paris and Nice to avoid the war. How they managed to complete the film in the midst of air raids, electrical outages, supply limitations, actors disappearing, interference by the Nazi captors, and a thousand other problems is beyond comprehension. Prevert, a Marxist, wrote many subtle references into the script that mirrored what was happening in real life in France at the time. No one knew if the war would be over by the time the film was completed. No doubt the creators would have been jailed if the Germans still held Paris in March, 1945, when the film was premiered. Carne and Prevert ended their collaboration in 1948 and Carne went on to direct more than a dozen more films but none had the power of CHILDREN OF PARADISE. Arletty was in her forties when they made the movie but her beauty transcended the calendar. After the movie opened, she was briefly jailed as a result of an affair with a German officer. Barrault was twelve years younger and a star at the Comedie-Francaise while the movie was being made. The movie has been shown in various cuts; 195 minutes, 188 minutes, and 144 minutes. If you can, see the long version. Better yet, attempt to find a copy of Prevert's script, as it will fill in much of the space that might confuse or addle the viewer.

p, Fred Orain; d, Marcel Carńe; w, Jacques Prévert; ph, Roger Hubert, Marc Fossard; m, Maurice Thiriet, Joseph Kosma, George Mouque; ed, Henri Rust, Madeleine Bonin; art d, A. Barsacq, R. Cabutti, Alexander Trauner.

Historical Drama **(PR:C MPAA:NR)**

CHILDREN OF PLEASURE* (1930) 68m MGM bw
Lawrence Gray *(Danny Regan)*, Benny Rubin *(Andy Little)*, Helen Johnson *(Pat Thayer)*, Wynne Gibson *(Emma Gray)*, Kenneth Thompson *(Rod Peck)*, Lee Kohlmar *(Bernie)*, May Boley *(Fanny Kaye)*.

Tedious musical comedy about Jewish songwriter Gray going after and winning a society blonde. On their wedding day he has a change of heart and runs back to his female partner. Lots of dialect humor. Songs include: "Leave It That Way," "Dust," "Girl Trouble" (Andy Rice, Fred Fisher), "A Couple of Birds With the Same Thought In Mind" (Howard Johnson, Edward Ward, Reggie Montgomery), "The Whole Darned Thing's For You" (Roy Turk, Fred Ahlert).

d, Harry Beaumont; w, Richard Schayer, Crane Wilbur (based on the play "The Songwriter" by Wilbur); ph, Percy Hilburn; ed, Blanche Sewell, George Todd; art d, Cedric Gibbons; ch, Sammy Lee.

Musical/Comedy **(PR:A MPAA:NR)**

CHILDREN OF RAGE* (1975, Brit.-Israeli) 106m Emmessee Productions c
Helmut Griem *(Dr. David Shalom)*, Olga Georges-Picot *(Leyla Saleh)*, Cyril Cusack *(David's Father)*, Simon Ward *(Yaacov)*, Richard Alfieri *(Omar Saleh)*, Simon Andreu *(Ibrahim)*, Robert Salvio *(Abdullah)*, Jacques Sernas *(Dr. Ben-Joseph)*, Gabriele Tinti *(Dr. Russanak)*.

Touching on a sensitive issue, CHILDREN OF RAGE does little to bring out a comprehensive understanding of why the Palestinian terrorist does what he does. This film is very talky and repetitive, beating what little message it gets across with a nine-pound sledge. It follows a series of melodramatic encounters between an Israeli doctor, Griem, and a band of guerillas encamped in a refugee enclave near Israeli-controlled territory. The main action surrounds a Palestinian attempt to blow up an Israeli dance hall crowded with Israeli teenagers. One of the terrorists killed during the attempt is an old friend of Griem. He takes the position that any attempt to open the lines of communication is worth the risk, so he steals off with the terrorist's sister to open a hospital.

p, George R. Nice; d&w, Arthur Allan Seidelman (based on a story by Seidelman, Anan Laura); ph, Ian Wilson (Technicolor); m, Patrick Gowers; ed, Paul Davis.

Drama **(PR:O MPAA:NR)**

CHILDREN OF SANCHEZ, THE* (1978, U.S./Mex.) 126m Bartlett c
Anthony Quinn, Dolores del Rio, Katy Jurado, Lupita Ferrer, Stathis Giallelis.

Quinn plays a sort of Mexican Zorba the Greek but one that evokes neither sympathy nor humor as he tries to keep his phalanx of children together in a slum area. Mere survival is the only grim tale and this mess is both depressing and boring. The only fascinating thing about this waste of time is the ageless beauty of del Rio, a star for fifty years.

p&d, Hall Bartlett; w, Cesare Zavattini, Bartlett (based on the book by Oscar Lewis); ph, Gabriel Figueroa; m, Chuck Mangione.

Drama **Cas.** **(PR:O MPAA:NR)**

CHILDREN OF THE DAMNED** (1963, Brit.) 90m MGM bw
Ian Hendry *(Col. Tom Lewellin)*, Alan Badel *(Dr. David Neville)*, Barbara Ferris *(Susan Eliot)*, Alfred Burke *(Colin Webster)*, Sheila Allen *(Diana Looran)*, Clive Powell *(Paul)*, Frank Summerscales *(Mark)*, Mahdu Mathen *(Rashid)*, Gerald Delsol *(Aga Nagalo)*, Roberta Rex *(Nina)*, Franchesca Lee *(Mi-Ling)*, Harold Goldblatt *(Harib)*, Patrick Whyte *(Mr. Davidson)*, Tom Bowman *(Gen. Miller)*, Martin Miller *(Prof. Gruber)*, Andre Mikhelson *(Russian Official)*, Ralph Michael *(Defence Minister)*.

In this film's predecessor, VILLAGE OF THE DAMNED, all the "Damned" children on Earth were destroyed. So the "Damned" children in this film are different and not directly related to their space-sired cousins. In this loose adaptation of John Wyndham's *The Midwich Cuckoos*, six children are born worldwide with genius IQ's, destructive dispositions, and ray-gun eyes. They are not born as a result of some space rapist, but seem to be premature samplings of man as he will evolve in a million years. The children are brought together by UNESCO investigators Badel and Hendry, and, though highly intelligent, remain as children, to become pawns in a love-hate relationship between the two investigators. While being studied by scientists and threatened by the military, the children escape. They seek refuge in a church, and are blown up accidentally. It seems the children's grim purpose on earth is to be destroyed in a violent manner, enabling the fearful, warlike, and ignorant modern man to learn a valuable lesson about himself.

p, Ben Arbeid; d, Anton M. Leader; w, John Briley (based on the novel *The Midwich Cuckoos* by John Wyndham); ph, David Boulton; ed, Ernie Walter.

Horror **(PR:O MPAA:NR)**

CHILDREN OF THE FOG* (1935, Brit.) 59m Jesba Films/NPFD bw
Barbara Gott *(Mrs. Jenner)*, Ben Soutten *(Butcher)*, Rani Waller *(Alice Crimson)*, Marjorie Corbett *(Joan)*, Kenneth Guthrie *(Butcher)*, Linden Travers *(Polly Mortimer)*, Bert Jenner *(Laurence Hepworth)*, Eric Pavitt *(Syd Butcher)*, Vi Kaley *(Charwoman)*.

Bleak melodrama about the son of a drunken longshoreman marrying the illegitimate daughter of his dead stepmother and emigrating to Australia with his sick brother.

d, Leopold Jessner, John Quin; w, John Cousins, Stephen Clarkson; Eugene Shufftan.

Drama **(PR:A MPAA:NR)**

CHILDREN SHOULDN'T PLAY WITH DEAD THINGS½** (1972) 85m Geneni c
Alan Ormsby, Jane Daly, Anya Ormsby, Jeffrey Gillen, Valerie Mamches, Paul Cronin, Bruce Soloman, Seth Sklarey.

Surprisingly good low-budget (under $100,000) horror film starring screenwriter Ormsby as the leader of a troupe of eccentric actors who travel to a small, lonely island where there is a large cemetery and a small house. Armed with the Book of the Dead, Ormsby digs up a grave site and performs an elaborate ritual to bring the dead to life. Suddenly arms shoot up from the dirt and they claw at the actors. Ormsby bursts into convulsive laughter and the other actors realize the whole thing is an elaborate practical joke staged by their director. The "corpses" are actually other members of the group who have been placed in the ground previously. Now that the jokes are over, Ormsby has the troupe dig up a real corpse whom he calls "Orville." Once again the slightly mad actor performs the ritual to transform the rotting corpse into the living dead. Nothing happens. Disappointed but undaunted, Ormsby brings Orville into the house and the troupe proceeds to have a party with the corpse as the guest of honor. After many (too many) bad cadaver jokes, the spell finally takes hold and the dead in the cemetery begin to pull themselves out of the ground. In a truly terrifying and effective sequence, the decaying bodies slowly lumber off in search of flesh to eat (perhaps a bit too reminiscent of George Romero's NIGHT OF THE LIVING DEAD [1968]). Eventually the dead kill all the performers and wander to the shore and board a boat headed for the mainland. The film is filled with amateurish performances, strained comedy, and zero production values, but there is an undeniable power to the "rising dead" scenes and a genuine mood of unease throughout the film that most big-budget horror outings fail to capture.

p, Benjamin (Bob) Clark, Gary Goch; d, Clark; w, Alan Ormsby, Clark.

Horror **Cas.** **(PR:O MPAA:PG)**

CHILDREN'S GAMES* (1969) 90m Welebit bw

Michael Baseleon *(Peter)*, Margaret Warncke *(Jo)*, Michael Del Medico *(The Man)*, Verna Bloom *(The Girl)*, Scott Yacoby *(The Son)*, Elsie Donald *(Ia Jo)*, Monica Lovett *(Ila Jo)*.

This film is a depressing look at Western society as seen through a young man's eyes. The story centers on the life cycle of Baseleon, from his early manhood to an early grave, as he is taken through disillusionment with political demagoguery into a love affair that ends in a poor marriage and a frustrated suicide attempt. Baseleon's life really begins to come apart; he emerges from psychiatric treatment as a listless victim of a strident, depressive society, and totally incompatible with human communication. War takes him from his wife and child, and he winds up in a hero's grave not knowing how or why. A pointless end to the pointless life of a pointless character in a pointless film.

p, Walter Welebit, Susan Hall; d, Welebit; w, Welebit, Susan Hall, Peter Beach; ph, Bruce Sparks; m, Milan; ed, Jerry Siegel; art d, Philip Rosenberg.

Drama **(PR:C-O MPAA:NR)**

CHILDREN'S HOUR, THE*½** (1961) 107m UA bw (GB: THE LOUDEST WHISPER)

Audrey Hepburn *(Karen Wright)*, Shirley MacLaine *(Martha Dobie)*, James Garner *(Dr. Joe Cardin)*, Miriam Hopkins *(Mrs. Lily Mortar)*, Fay Bainter *(Mrs. Amelia Tilford)*, Karen Balkin *(Mary Tilford)*, Veronica Cartwright *(Rosalie)*, Jered Barclay *(Grocery Boy)*, Mimi Gibson, William Mims, Hope Summers, Florence MacMichael.

A fairly faithful rendition of Lillian Hellman's study of implied lesbianism in an all-girls school. William Wyler directed both versions of this story, the first being THESE THREE, a much milder adaptation of the play. Hepburn and MacLaine are co-headmistresses of a private and chi-chi school for young girls. Balkin is the pre-teen granddaughter of Bainter, the town's leading dowager. The child is ill-tempered, undisciplined, and just this side of Patty McCormack's BAD SEED. Every other word out of Balkin's mouth is a lie and when she is punished for one of her untruths, she runs to Bainter and tells her that MacLaine and Hepburn have an "unnatural relationship." She barely understands what she is talking about, having probably picked it up in hearsay from the other girls or perhaps in some under-the-covers-reading. The effect of this lie is devastating. When she sees how her grandmother responds, Balkin further elaborates and the result is that she is taken out of the school and other parents are told to do the same. MacLaine and Hepburn are against the wall as their income drops to nil. They begin a libel suit against Bainter but lose the case in a shocking turn of events when Hopkins, MacLaine's dotty aunt, succumbs to small-town pressure and refuses to testify on her niece's behalf. Further complications arise when Hepburn's doctor-fiance, Garner, wonders if there might be some truth in the allegations. Garner is given his walking papers and Hepburn thinks that it might be best if the two women pull up stakes and try to make a go of it somewhere else. MacLaine now realizes something deep within her that she had not acknowledged before; she really does love Hepburn in more than just a sisterly fashion. She loves her as a lover! MacLaine cannot bear the guilt she feels and hangs herself. The lie is finally exposed but it is too little and far too late. The film fades as Hepburn leaves MacLaine's funeral and walks past Bainter, Garner, and all the other townspeople who were gulled by the lies of a twelve-year-old. Five Oscar nominations were awarded but none given for THE CHILDREN'S HOUR. It deserved a better fate. The movie broke new ground for 1961 and the performances ranged from adequate (Balkin) to exquisite (MacLaine). These days, it wouldn't have made a difference, but in 1934, when the play was first presented, it dealt with another set of mores.

p&d, William Wyler; w, John Michael Hayes (adaptation by Lillian Hellman from her play); ph, Franz Planer; m, Alex North; ed, Robert Swink; art d, Fernando Carrere; set d, Edward G. Boyle; cos, Dorothy Jeakins.

Drama **(PR:C MPAA:NR)**

CHILD'S PLAY** (1954, Brit.) 68m Group 3/BL bw

Mona Washbourne *(Miss Goslett)*, Peter Martyn *(P. C. Parker)*, Dorothy Alison *(Margery Chappell)*, Ingeborg Wells *(Lea Blotz)*, Carl Jaffe *(Carl Blotz)*, Ballard Berkeley *(Dr. Nightingale)*, Joan Young *(Mrs. Chizzler)*, Robert Raglan *(Superintendent)*, Christopher Beeny *(Horatio Flynn)*, Wendy Westcott *(Mary Huxley)*, Ian Smith *(Tom Chizzler)*, Patrick Wells *(Hans Einstein Blotz)*.

At a center for atomic research, the son of one of the physicists invents atomic popcorn. Decent comedy with some serious moments.

p, Herbert Mason; d, Margaret Thompson; w, Peter Blackmore (based on a story by Don Sharp); ph Denny Densham.

Comedy **(PR:A MPAA:NR)**

CHILD'S PLAY** (1972) 100m PAR c

James Mason *(Jerome Malley)*, Robert Preston *(Joseph Dobbs)*, Beau Bridges *(Paul Reis)*, Ronald Weyand *(Father Mozian)*, Charles White *(Father Griffin)*, David Rounds *(Father Penny)*, Kate Harrington *(Mrs. Carter)*, Jamie Alexander *(Sheppard)*, Brian Chapin *(O'Donnell)*, Bryant Fraser *(Jennings)*, Mark Hall Haefeli *(Wilson)*, Tom Leopold *(Shea)*, Julius Lo Iacono *(McArdle)*, Christopher Man *(Travis)*, Paul O'Keefe *(Banks)*, Robert D. Randall *(Medley)*, Robbie Reed *(Class President)*, Paul Alessi, Anthony Barletta, Kevin Coupe, Christopher Hoag, Stephen McLaughlin *(Students)*.

Plodding adaptation of Marasco's semi-hit play. Bridges returns to St. Charles, a Catholic boys school. He is going to be the sports instructor and Preston welcomes him with open arms. Soon enough, Bridges senses some evil-doings in the school and it seems to be coming from the direction of Mason, who had planned to retire a while ago but who has decided to stay on until God calls him. Mason says that he is innocent of any wrongdoing and that Preston is responsible for inciting the students against him. It was always presumed that Preston would take over the Latin department when Mason left. Now there are some outcroppings of violence here and there in the school. Bridges finds a young man being whacked soundly about the head and shoulders by some other students but when he attempts to get the reasons why from this boy and others, he runs into a wall of silence. Weyand is the cleric-headmaster of the school and says that Mason is suffering from a persecution complex that is heightened by the fact that his aged mother is about to die. Weyand urges Mason to loosen his strict codes. Violence continues and we cannot understand why; a young man almost loses his sight and still it continues. Weyand is certain that it's all Mason's fault and orders him to stop teaching. Mason is stunned, claims total innocence, but it falls on deaf ears. In desperation, Mason gives everyone the ultimate proof of his innocence by leaping to his death from the roof of the school. Bridges uncovers the fact that Preston had been the instigator all along, the person who was needling Mason, and confronts him. Preston makes some lame excuses but the students, who are listening in another room, now understand how they have been used by Preston. Bridges leaves the room in disgust and it is quickly filled by Preston's students; the same ones in whom he instilled the love of violence. They raise their arms and clench them into fists as the picture ends. The stage-bound history of the piece is evident all the way through. Lumet does his best to give it some "air" but the picture remains stuffy and interior. Merrick produced both the play and the picture and made some serious errors. On the stage, Fritz Weaver was a first-rate star and he should have been kept for the film but Merrick, or the studio, evidently felt that this marquee had more value. The play wasn't that great anyhow and reminded one of many others of its ilk; crazed schoolmaster, nut-case students, young hero trying to ferret out the truth. We've seen it all before.

p, David Merrick; d, Sidney Lumet; w, Leon Prochnik (based on the play by Robert Marasco); ph, Gerald Hirschfeld (Movielab Color); m, Michael Small; ed, Joanne Burke, Edward Warschilka.

Drama **(PR:A-C MPAA:PG)**

CHILLY SCENES OF WINTER½** (1982) 92m UA Classics c (AKA: HEAD OVER HEELS)

John Heard *(Charles)*, Mary Beth Hurt *(Laura)*, Peter Riegert *(Sam)*, Kenneth McMillan *(Pete)*, Gloria Grahame *(Clara)*, Nora Heflin *(Betty)*, Jerry Hardin *(Patterson)*, Tarah Nutter *(Susan)*, Mark Metcalf *(Ox)*, Allen Joseph *(Blind Man)*, Frances Bay *(Mrs. Delillo)*, Griffin Dunne *(Dr. Mark)*, Alex Johnson *(Elise)*, Ann Beattie *(Waitress)*, Angela Phillips *(Rebecca)*, Oscar Rowland *(Hardware Man)*, Linda Alper *(Girl Optician)*, Beverly Booth Rowland *(Woman in Park)*.

Heard is a minor functionary in the Utah government who falls in love with Hurt while she is separated from her husband. When she returns to her spouse, Heard is unable to forget her, sitting outside her home in his car watching the lights, and even building a doll-house copy of her home, and stocking it with little figures to represent Hurt, her husband, and her daughter. Full of literary flourishes and interesting at times, the film leaves the viewer vaguely unsatisfied. At the end one realizes that nothing of any significance has happened since the first half hour. In the late 1970s director Silver looked like a woman director who would make the big time, largely due to the success of HESTER STREET (1974), but pretentious, vague efforts like this leave her almost forgotten today. Originally released in 1979 as HEAD OVER HEELS at 99 minutes.

p, Mark Metcalf, Amy Robinson, Griffin Dunne; d&w, Joan Micklin Silver (based on the novel *Head Over Heels* by Ann Beattie); ph, Bobby Byrne (Metrocolor); m, Ken Lauber; ed, Cynthia Scheider; prod d, Peter Jamison.

Drama **(PR:C MPAA:PG)**

CHILTERN HUNDREDS, THE

(SEE: AMAZING MR. BEECHAM, THE, 1949, Brit.)

CHIMES AT MIDNIGHT*½** (1967, Span.,Switz.) 115m Internacional Films Espanola-Alpine Productions/Peppercorn-Wormser-U-M bw (CAMPANADAS A MEDIANOCHE, AKA: FALSTAFF)

Orson Welles *(Sir John "Jack" Falstaff)*, Jeanne Moreau *(Doll Tearsheet)*, Margaret Rutherford *(Hostess Quickly)*, John Gielgud *(King Henry IV)*, Keith Baxter *(Prince Hal, later King Henry V)*, Marina Vlady *(Kate Percy)*, Norman Rodway *(Henry Percy, "Hotspur")*, Alan Webb *(Justice Shallow)*, Walter Chiari *(Mr. Silence)*, Michael Aldridge *(Pistol)*, Tony Beckley *(Poins)*, Fernando Rey *(Worcester)*, Beatrice Welles *(Falstaff's Page)*, Andrew Faulds *(Westmoreland)*, Jose Nieto *(Northumberland)*, Jeremy Rowe *(Prince John)*, Paddy Bedford *(Bardolph)*, Ralph Richardson *(Narrator)*, Julio Pena, Fernando Hilbeck, Andres Meguto, Keith Pyott, Charles Farrell, [British].

The character of Falstaff turns up in no less than five of Shakespeare's plays. Director Welles combined the boisterous character's appearances into one superb performance and an occasionally brilliant film. Welles is the boon companion to Prince Hal (Baxter), heir to the besieged British throne. Rather than come to the defense of his father, Baxter passes his time drinking and carousing with Welles. Finally, though, he does go into battle, slaying the honorable, doomed challenger to the crown, Hotspur (Rodway). After the battle Welles claims to have killed Rodway, when in fact he spent most of the battle feigning death. The old king (Gielgud) dies and Baxter becomes King Henry V. Welles attends the coronation, sure that a high title is forthcoming. Instead, Baxter banishes him. Welles dies, alone and bitter. While much of the film is confusingly edited (evidence of a haphazard and prolonged shooting schedule) and the soundtrack is almost inaudibly murky, the film boasts some of the most stunning visuals since CITIZEN KANE and a host of superb performances, not to mention one of the best battle scenes in cinema—a grim, brutal affair fought on a mud-soaked field. The narration (by Richardson) is taken from Raphael Holinshed's 1577 *The Chronicles of England.* Second-unit director Jesus Franco went on to become one of the mainstays of European exploitation films.

p, Emiliano Piedra; d&w, Orson Welles (based on the plays "Henry IV, Part I," "Henry IV, Part II," "Henry V," "Richard II," "The Merry Wives of Windsor," all by William Shakespeare, and the book *The Chronicles of England* by Raphael Holinshed); ph, Edmond Richard; m, Angelo Francesco Lavagnino; ed, Fritz Muller; prod d, Gustavo Quintana; md, Carlo Franci; art d, Jose Antonio de la Guerra; cos, Cornejo Madrid.

Comedy/Drama **(PR:C MPAA:NR)**

CHINA***   (1943) 78m PAR bw

Loretta Young (Carolyn Grant), Alan Ladd (Mr. Jones), William Bendix (Johnny Sparrow), Philip Ahn (First Brother-Lin Cho), Iris Wong (Kwan Su), Victor Sen Yung (Third Brother-Lin Wei), Marianne Quon (Tan Ying), Jessie Tai Sing (Student), Richard Loo (Lin Yun), Irene Tso ("Donald Duck"), Chingwha Lee (Chang Teh), Soo Yong (Tai Shen), Beal Wong (Capt. Tao-Yuan-Kai), Bruce Wong (Aide to Capt. Tao-Yuan-Kai), Tala Birell (Woman), Barbara Jean Wong (Nan Ti), Chester Gan (Japanese General).

A hard-hitting propaganda war film where Ladd appears as an unscrupulous trader of goods without conscience or national loyalty. Bendix, his buddy, picks a Chinese baby out of the rubble after a Japanese air raid and takes it to Ladd who is just leaving a blonde floozy. Ladd tells him to drop "Donald Duck" (his casual nickname for the baby) and get into their truck; they are to drive to Japanese headquarters to sell the invaders oil. Bendix's blandishments fall on deaf ears; the Japanese "are good business," Ladd answers. During a rainstorm the truck is slowed by the refugees clogging the roadway. Next Chinese guerrillas stop the truck and force Ladd to take a group of schoolgirls with him. The group is led by Young, an American teacher, who pleads with Ladd to take the group to safety, but he intends to drive the girls only a short distance so he can turn off for Shanghai and his business appointment with the Japanese. Adding to his woes, he discovers the baby found by Bendix to be inside the truck, smuggled away by the soft-hearted sidekick. The group stops at a farm to get the child some milk and is left with the kindly farming family. Further up the road, Young discovers that one of the girls has gone back to the farm—the people there are her relatives—and she begs Ladd to return to get her, reminding him what Japanese troops do to women. Returning, Ladd finds that the Chinese family and the baby have been killed and the young schoolgirl beaten and raped. Grabbing a machine gun, Ladd storms into the house to find three enemy soldiers there. He guns them down and later tells Young: "I've got no more feelings about it than if they had been three flies on a pile of manure." When the schoolgirl dies of her injuries, Ladd erupts with a vengeance. He helps guerrillas fight the Japanese while falling in love with Young. To prevent an enemy force from crossing a mountain pass, Ladd and the guerrillas set dynamite next to a narrow passageway but before the charges can be exploded, a column of Japanese transports appears. Ladd goes to the lead car and attempts to stall the troops by double-talking the Japanese general. Then, as a prearranged signal to the guerrillas to set off the dynamite that will take him and the Japanese to doom, Ladd flips a burning cigarette into the general's face. Young and the guerrillas vow to carry on the fight to liberate China. Strong patriotism and a great deal of action permeate this production which was only natural during WW II but Ladd was embarrassed when ads for the film showed him in a drawing bare-chested with muscles he didn't possess and with the words: "Alan Ladd and twenty girls trapped by the rapacious Japs!" Farrow's direction is swift and economical and the lensing by Tover is above-average as is the process photography by Edouart and Jennings' special effects.

p, Richard Blumenthal; d, John Farrow; w, Frank Butler (based on the play by Archibald Forbes); ph, Leo Tover; ed, Eda Warren; spec eff, Gordon Jennings; process photography, Farciot Edouart.

War Drama   **(PR:C   MPAA:NR)**

CHINA CLIPPER**   (1936) 70m WB bw

Pat O'Brien (Dave Logan), Beverly Roberts (Jean Logan), Ross Alexander (Tom Collins), Humphrey Bogart (Hap Stuart), Marie Wilson (Sunny Avery), Henry B. Walthall (Dad Brunn), Joseph Crehan (Jim Horn), Joseph King (Mr. Pierson), Addison Richards (B. C. Hill), Ruth Robinson (Mother Brunn), Lyle Moraine, Dennis Moore (Copilots), Wayne Morris (Navigator), Alexander Cross (Bill Andrews), William Wright (Pilot), Kenneth Harlan (Commerce Inspector), Anne Nagel, Marjorie Weaver (Secretaries), Milburn Stone, Owen King, Carlyle Moore, Jr. (Radio Operators), Shirley Lloyd (Horn's Secretary), Pierre Watkin (Secretary of State), Emmett Vogan, Hal K. Dawson, Edwin Stanley, Harland Tucker, John Marston (Airplane Designers), Frank Faylen, Joseph Cunningham (Weathermen), Walter Miller (Instructor), Milton Kibbee (Mechanic), Irving Bacon (Sam the Janitor), Gordon "Bill" Elliott (Pilot), Ralph Dunn (Plane Announcer at Miami Airport), John Spacey (Australian Broadcaster).

An aviation picture without the usual aviation thrills. In 1936, the first transpacific flight of a commercial airline was recent history, and this film gets so caught up with the technical aspects of the San Franciso-to-China flight that it loses much of its entertainment merits. O'Brien plays a pioneer aviation man obsessed with the establishment of a transpacific airline. His blinding ambition takes its toll on his marriage, friendships, and everyday life in general. We see success after success in his attempt to prepare for the final flight, and by the time he gets around to it there is very little suspense, for we know the outcome will be a success. Bogart puts in a neat little performance in a sympathetic role, quite a departure from the usual gunmen he played at this time in his career. Unfortunately, he is given very little screen time.

p, Sam Bischoff; d, Raymond Enright; w, Frank Wead; ph, Arthur Edeson; m, Bernard Kaun, W. Frank Harling; ed, Owen Marks; art d, Max Parker; cos, Orry-Kelly; spec eff, Fred Jackman.

Drama   **(PR:A   MPAA:NR)**

CHINA CORSAIR*   (1951) 76m COL bw

Jon Hall (McMillen), Lisa Ferraday (Tamara), Ron Randell (Paul Lowell), Douglas Kennedy (Frenchie), Ernest Borgnine (Hu Chang), John Dehner (Pedro), Marya Marco (Lotus), Philip Ahn (Wong San), Peter Mamakos (Juan), Weaver Levy (Kam).

This fast action escapist film concerns itself with a small island off the China coast and the skulduggery that takes place on it. Hall plays an American ship engineer stranded on the island, where he meets an exotic Eurasian girl, Ferraday, and becomes romantically involved. Borgnine plays a double-crossing oriental interested in the antique collection of the girl's uncle. Hall gets a job on a charter boat, but meantime Ferraday is double-crossed by her British lover, Randell, who uses her to get close to the uncle. Randell kills him and runs off with the costly jade on the boat. Ferraday catches up with Randell only to see him killed by Hall, resulting in Hall being taken prisoner. Wounded during the scuffle, Ferraday dies in Hall's arms. There's nothing startling or terribly suspenseful in the film, but the action moves along at a fair pace.

p, Rudolph C. Flothow; d, Ray Nazzaro; w, Harold R. Greene; ph, Philip Tannura; ed, Richard Fantl; md, Mischa Bakaleinikoff.

Adventure   **(PR:C   MPAA:NR)**

CHINA DOLL**½   (1958) 99m UA bw

Victor Mature (Cliff Brandon), Li Li Hua (Shu-Jen), Ward Bond (Father Cairns), Bob Mathias (Phil Gates), Johnny Desmond (Steve Hill), Stu Whitman (Dan O'Neill), Elaine Curtis (Alice Nichols), Ann McCrea (Mona Perkins), Danny Chang (Ellington), Denver Pyle (Col. Wiley), Don Barry (Hal Foster), Tige Andrews (Carlo Menotti), Steve Mitchell (Dave Reisner), Ken Perry (Ernie Fleming), Ann Paige (Sally), Tita Aragon (Shiao-Mee).

A warm and often humorous story of a romance between a burly Air Corps captain and a fragile oriental beauty. The story takes place in China in 1943, at a time in WW II when the Japanese had cut off all U.S. supply lines and American airmen were left with the duty of getting the supplies through. Mature plays the Air Corps captain, a lonely man who has forsaken all but the bottle. In one of his big drunken states, he unknowingly purchases a Chinese girl as a housekeeper. She ends up carrying his child, drawing his love, and marrying him, in that order. Both are killed in an air attack, but the child survives to spend the next thirteen years in Chinese orphanages before being brought to America and her parent's friends.

p&d, Frank Borzage; w, Kitty Buhler (based on a story by James Benson Nablo, Thomas F. Kelly and another story by Buhler); ph, William Clothier; m, Henry Vars; ed, Jack Murray; art d, Howard Richmond; spec eff, David Koehler.

War   **(PR:C   MPAA:NR)**

CHINA GATE**   (1957) 96m FOX bw

Gene Barry (Brock), Angie Dickinson (Lucky Legs), Nat "King" Cole (Goldie), Paul DuBov (Capt. Caumont), Lee Van Cleef (Maj. Cham), George Givot (Cpl. Pigalle), Gerald Milton (Pvt. Andreades), Neyle Morrow (Leung), Marcel Dalio (Father Paul), Maurice Marsac (Col. De Sars), Warren Hsieh (The Boy), Paul Busch (Cpl. Kruger), Sasha Harden (Pvt. Jaszi), James Hong (Charlie), William Soo Hoo (Moi Leader), Walter Soo Hoo (Guard), Weaver Levy (Khuan).

THE GREEN BERETS was not the first film to tell of the Vietnamese fight against communism. CHINA GATE was made ten years before at a time when the French still controlled all of Vietnam and the enemy is portrayed as Chinese instigators, instead of the Vietnamese people themselves. The story concerns an American soldier of fortune, Barry, who joins up with his estranged wife, Dickinson, a Eurasian political activist, to lead a party of guerrillas on an expedition to destroy a Chinese Communist ammunition dump. The guerrillas are composed of a group of French Foreign Legionnaires. Cole renders a good performance as a war-weary American soldier in the legion, as well as singing the title song. The trip is tough and tense, mostly because of the love-hate relationship between Barry and Dickinson. Their relationship is just beginning to mend when Dickinson is killed during the successful sabotage raid. The politics of the film were representative of the beliefs then held by this country towards the Vietnam problem, which wouldn't become a real problem for the U.S. for a few more years. The talented composer Young died during the production. His score was finished by his friend Steiner.

p,d&w, Samuel Fuller; ph, Joseph Biroc (Cinemascope); m, Victor Young, Max Steiner; ed, Gene Fowler, Jr.; m/l, Young, Harold Adamson.

War   **(PR:C   MPAA:NR)**

CHINA GIRL***   (1942) 95m FOX bw

Gene Tierney (Miss Young), George Montgomery (Johnny Williams), Lynn Bari (Capt. Fifi), Victor McLaglen (Maj. Bull Weed), Alan Baxter (Jones), Sig Ruman (Jarubi), Myron McCormick (Shorty), Bobby Blake (Chinese Boy), Ann Pennington (Entertainer), Philip Ahn (Dr. Young), Tom Neal (Haines), Paul Fung (Japanese Colonel), Lal Chand Mehra (Desk Clerk), Kam Tong (Doctor).

Taut, tight tale from a story by Darryl Zanuck (he used the name "Melville Crossman" when scripting in later years). Montgomery is an American in Mandalay just before the Japanese attacked Pearl Harbor. He's a freelance newsreel cameraman who falls in love with Tierney, a Chinese beauty with a stateside education and accent. Bari and McLaglen are in the employ of the Japanese and attempting to get Montgomery into their clutches. Montgomery has a book containing military information, hence the pursuing of him by the villains. We've seen this story before, in various incarnations, but the script by Hecht takes it a cut above the usual and Hathaway's direction adds a certain topspin to what might have been a dead ball. Some excellent action sequences with the final one being Montgomery machine-gunning Japanese planes while Tierney is riddled by their bullets. In a small role as a Chinese boy is Bobby Blake, just after his successful run in the OUR GANG shorts. One wonders how Blake, who has lived in California since the late 1930s (he was born in 1933), has managed to keep his Nutley New Jersey accent.

p, Ben Hecht; d, Henry Hathaway; w, Hecht (from a story by Melville Crossman); ph, Lee Garmes; m, Alfred Newman; ed, James B. Clark.

War Drama   **(PR:A   MPAA:NR)**

CHINA IS NEAR**½   (1968, Ital.) 108m Vides/Royal Films International bw

Glauco Mauri (Vittorio), Elda Tattoli (Elena), Paolo Graziosi (Carlo), Daniela Surina (Giovanna), Pierluigi Apra (Camillo), Alessandro Haber (Rospo), Claudio Trionfo (Giacomo), Laura De Marchi (Clotilde), Claudio Cassinelli (Furio), Renato Jalenti (Don Pino), Mimma Biscardi.

Mauri is a political science professor from a well-to-do family who decides to run for office as a Socialist candidate. Meanwhile, his Maoist brother does everything he can think of to sabotage the campaign. In addition to this slight tale of left-wing Italian politics, the film also features a sex comedy subplot dealing with Surina's attempts to become pregnant in order to marry her upper-class lover. Technically adept and tastefully directed by Bellocchio (best known for FISTS IN THE POCKETS), this is an intelligent comedy well worth watching.

p, Franco Cristaldi; d, Marco Bellocchio; w, Bellocchio, Elda Tattoli (based on a story by Bellocchio); ph, Tonino Delli Colli; m, Ennio Morricone; ed, Roberto Perpignani, art d, Rodolfo Frattaioli, Ugo Novello; set d, Mimmo Scavia; songs; "Poesia," "E la cosa si ripete."

Comedy **(PR:C-O MPAA:NR)**

CHINA 9, LIBERTY 37½** (1978, Ital.) 94m CEA/Titanus c
Fabio Testi *(Shaw)*, Warren Oates *(Sebanek)*, Jenny Agutter *(Catherine)*, Sam Peckinpah *(The Writer)*.

Testi is a gunfighter saved from the gallows by railroad men who want him to kill Oates because the latter's farm is in the way of their line. Testi fails to kill Oates, but he does sleep with Agutter, Oates's wife. He leaves and she follows him, thinking he has killed her husband. The rail barons send out more men to kill Testi, and Oates turns up alive with a couple of his brothers to help him settle the score. They fight together against the railroad men and defeat them. Testi refuses again to kill Oates and rides off alone. An interesting adult western from cult director Hellman. Look for Sam Peckinpah in a small part as a writer of dime novels about the "Old West," a la Nat Buntline.

p, Gianni Bozzacchi, Valerio de Paolis; d, Monte Hellman.

Western **(PR:O MPAA:NR)**

CHINA PASSAGE** (1937) 63m RKO bw
Constance Worth *(Jane Dunn)*, Vinton Haworth *(Tom Baldwin)*, Leslie Fenton *(A. Durand)*, Gordon Jones *(Joe Dugan)*, Alec Craig *(Harvey)*, Dick Elliott *(Philip Burton)*, Frank M. Thomas *(Capt. Williams)*, George Irving *(Dr. Sibley)*, Billy Gilbert *(Bartender)*, Joyce Compton *(Mrs. Collins)*, Eddie Dunn *(Ship's Waiter)*, Alan Curtis, Edgar Dearing *(Ship's Officers)*, Philip Ahn *(Dr. Fang Tu)*, Lotus Long *(Lia Sen)*, Tetsu Komai *(Wong)*, Huntly Gordon.

Soldier-of-fortune Haworth and government agent Worth team up to find a stolen diamond aboard a China-bound steamer. Fenton and Craig are the tame gem thieves who are easily snared through their blatant moves. This one suffers from stodgy direction and a script with ossified arteries. Routine B action stuff.

p, Cliff Reid; d, Edward Killy; w, Edmund L. Hartmann, J. Robert Bren (based on a story by Taylor Caven); ph, Nicholas Musuraca; ed, Desmond Marquette.

Adventure **(PR:A MPAA:NR)**

CHINA SEAS*½** (1935) 87m MGM bw
Clark Gable *(Capt. Alan Gaskell)*, Jean Harlow *(China Doll "Dolly Portland")*, Wallace Beery *(Jamesy MacArdle)*, Lewis Stone *(Tom Davids)*, Rosalind Russell *(Sybil Barclay)*, Dudley Digges *(Dawson)*, C. Aubrey Smith *(Sir Guy Wilmerding)*, Robert Benchley *(Charlie McCaleb)*, William Henry *(Rockwell)*, Live Demaigret *(Mrs. Volberg)*, Lillian Bond *(Mrs. Timmons)*, Edward Brophy *(Wilbur Timmons)*, Soo Yong *(Yu Lan)*, Carol Ann Beery *(Carol Ann)*, Akim Tamiroff *(Romanoff)*, Ivan Lebedeff *(Ngah)*, Hattie McDaniel *(Isabel McCarthy)*, Donald Meek *(Chess Player)*, Emily Fitzroy *(Lady)*, Pat Flaherty *(Second Officer Kingston)*, Forrester Harvey *(Steward)*, Tom Gubbins *(Ship's Officer)*, Charles Irwin *(Bertie, the Purser)*, Willie Fung *(Cabin Boy)*, Ferdinand Munier *(Police Superintendent)*, Chester Gan *(Rickshaw Boy)*, John Ince *(Pilot)*.

This is a rousing actioner where Gable is a rough-and-tumble captain of a tramp steamer who is en route to Singapore from Hong Kong with a load of gold. He has already found pirates secretly coming aboard and fears that he will be attacked en masse at any moment. Further vexing him is his ex-mistress, Harlow, who is heading for Singapore. Also on board is Russell, a one-time Gable lover who left him for another man, married, and was then widowed; she is taking a trip around the world and her cultured bearing angers Harlow who is still crazy about Gable. Harlow commits one social error after another until humiliating herself after openly bragging about her brief relationship with Gable. To drown her sorrows, Harlow gets drunk with Beery, a conniving merchant who is daffy over her. They play cards and she wins, noticing that Chinese symbols appear on some of Beery's currency. She knows that pirates use such identification devices to communicate with their front men and realizes that Beery is in league with the pirates. She goes to Gable who refuses to talk to her. Embittered Harlow agrees to help Beery, stealing the key to the hold where the gold is supposedly stored. The pirates attack but find no gold; the shrewd Gable has moved it elsewhere. During the wild attack, Stone, one of the mates, leaps into the Chinese junk with grenades, blowing himself and the pirates to pieces, thus vindicating himself, as he has been branded a coward for previous misconduct. Rather than face prison, Beery poisons himself and, when the ship reaches Singapore, Harlow is arrested for aiding the culprits. Gable makes a play for his old girl friend Russell who tells him that he would be happier as a skipper sailing the China Seas with Harlow at his side and he agrees. He then goes to Harlow and promises that he will see her through her trial and that they will be married. CHINA SEAS is directed by Garnett with dizzying speed and it is jam-packed with action, particularly the brawling battle scenes between the ship's crew and the pirates. All the principals are appealing in well-rounded roles, even though the plot is somewhat borrowed from RED DUST where Gable and Harlow were at-odds lovers. (This was Harlow's fourth film with Gable.) Gable is superb as the resolute but noble captain, Harlow a delight as the tropical trollop mouthing fractured English, and Beery sinister and humorous so that his ping-pong character fascinates and frightens. Harlow reprises a role she always played to the hilt, the slatternly but moxie dame of the streets with a heart of gold whose jealous-streaked nature makes her fight tooth and nail for her man. At one point she tells Gable that he'll never wind up in the arms of blueblood Russell: "You can't quit me any more than I can quit you, and you can kiss a stack of cookbooks on that!" Beery is again incomparable but this time he's not the lovable oaf, just a rotten-to-the-core brute who knows it, telling Harlow: "Loving you was the only decent thing I ever did in my life and even that was a mistake!" June's photography is splendid and sharp and the script by Furthman and McGuinness is both witty and inventive. MGM's head of production Irving Thalberg personally selected CHINA SEAS for the studio's leading box office stars. He had earlier been involved in high-class literary productions that yielded little income. CHINA SEAS would be different, he vowed: "To hell with art this time. I'm going to produce a picture that will make money." Harlow's role was modeled by Furthman after Shanghai Lily of SHANGHAI EXPRESS, portrayed by Marlene Dietrich, a film which he also wrote. (Some of Furthman's scenes are also heavily dependent upon the sea tales of Joseph Conrad, particularly *Nigger of the "Narcissus"*). Gable's captain is a comic-book hero which he plays to the hilt. At one point he manages to steer his ship through a raging typhoon while still saving a young passenger from being crushed by a sliding piano (the girl was Beery's real-life adopted daughter Carol Ann). When pirates begin to torture Gable so that he will reveal the whereabouts of the gold—they apply the iron boot which causes him to pass out several times—he shows his mettle, refusing to tell them anything. Beery witnesses this bravery and sneers: "There can't be any gold, or he would have talked. Nobody can be that tough!" But the star was that tough. When a two-ton steamroller becomes loose on deck, threatening to crush some coolies, Gable's stand-in was ordered to rush forward and secure the heavy equipment. Gable brushed aside the stunt man and went forward, telling the startled Garnett: "I'm doing this one myself," and he did. (This penchant for doing his own strenuous stunts was to eventually contribute to Gable's death when he insisted on breaking the wild horse in THE MISFITS.) The action in this film was so wild that the doubles for Beery—Chick Collins—and Harlow—Loretta Rush, were almost killed when fifty tons of water accidentally hit them broadside and almost carried them to a concrete soundstage floor twenty feet below the ship's deck. They fortunately fell onto water-soaked cables which broke their fall. Garnett heard Collins quip to Rush: "Hang on, honey, we're just passengers." Thalberg was so anxious for this film to be a hit that he imperiously stepped onto the set and coached the actors for their scenes, going behind Garnett's back. The director was dumfounded in viewing the rushes to see actors doing bits that he had not wanted. When he found out that the boy genius had been interfering, he threatened to quit. Thalberg relented, promising that he would not involve himself further with the production; he appeared a few times later on the set but only for "social reasons," basically to visit and encourage his stars. CHINA SEAS cost more than $1 million, an expensive MGM epic for the time, but the public loved it and the studio more than made its money back.

p, Albert Lewin (for Irving Thalberg); d, Tay Garnett; w, Jules Furthman, James Kevin McGuinness (based on the novel by Crosbie Garstin); ph, Ray June; m, Herbert Stothart; ed, William Levanway; art d, Cedric Gibbons, James Havens, David Townsend; set d, Edwin B. Willis; cos, Adrian.

Adventure **(PR:A MPAA:NR)**

CHINA SKY½** (1945) 78m RKO bw
Randolph Scott *(Thompson)*, Ruth Warrick *(Sara)*, Ellen Drew *(Louise)*, Anthony Quinn *(Chen Ta)*, Carol Thurston *(Siu Mei)*, Richard Loo *(Col. Yasuda)*, Ducky Louie *("Little Goat")*, Philip Ahn *(Dr. Kim)*, Benson Fong *(Chung)*, H. T. Tsiang *(Magistrate)*, Chin Kuang Chow *(Charlie)*, Kermit Maynard, Layne Tom, Jr., Weaver Levy.

Based on the Pearl S. Buck novel of the same name, CHINA SKY is about a love triangle set during WW II in a remote Chinese village under constant pressure from Japanese air raids. Scott and Warrick, as conscientious American doctors, make up two sides of the triangle. Drew, as Scott's selfish and jealous wife, makes up the third. The film lingers on the love triangle too much, and the potential action and intrigue garnered by the surroundings go to waste. Quinn as the guerrilla leader is completely sloughed off, and the film loses what could have been a very interesting side angle. The most interesting aspect of the film is the strange interaction between Ahn and Loo, the former a half-Korean doctor with Japanese bloodlines, the latter a Japanese officer who is taken prisoner after being wounded. Loo, the ever-insidious enemy (he was Hawaiian by birth), works on the secret loyalties of his nurse Ahn to finally free himself and wreak havoc before being killed. These two Orientals dominated WW II films as hateful Japanese oppressors, eager as sunrise to maim, mutilate, and menace.

p, Maurice Geraghty; d, Ray Enright; w, Brenda Weisberg, Joseph Hoffman (based on the novel by Pearl S. Buck); ph, Nicholas Musuraca; m, Roy Webb; ed, Gene Milford, Marvin Coil; md, Constantin Bakaleinikoff; art d, Albert S. D'Agostino, Ralph Berger; spec eff, Vernon L. Walker.

War **(PR:C MPAA:NR)**

CHINA SYNDROME, THE**** (1979) 122m IPC/COL c
Jane Fonda *(Kimberly Wells)*, Jack Lemmon *(Jack Godell)*, Michael Douglas *(Richard Adams)*, Scott Brady *(Herman DeYoung)*, James Hampton *(Bill Gibson)*, Peter Donat *(Don Jacovich)*, Wilford Brimley *(Ted Spindler)*, Richard Herd *(Evan McCormack)*, Daniel Valdez *(Hector Salas)*, Stan Bohrman *(Peter Martin)*, James Karen *(Mac Churchill)*, Michael Alaimo *(Greg Minor)*, Donald Hotton *(Dr. Lowell)*, Khalilah Ali *(Marge)*, Paul Larson *(D. B. Royce)*, Ron Lombard *(Barney)*, Tom Eure *(Tommy)*, Nick Pellegrino *(Borden)*, Daniel Lewk *(Donny)*, Allan Chinn *(Holt)*, Martin Fiscoe *(Control Guard)*, Alan Kaul *(TV Director)*, E. Hampton Beagle *(Mort)*, David Pfeiffer *(David)*, Lewis Arquette *(Hatcher)*, Dennis McMullen *(Robertson)*, Rita Taggart *(Rita Jacovich)*, James Hall *(Harmon)*, Michael Mann, David Eisenbise, Frank Cavestani, Reuben Collins, Carol Helvey, Trudy Lane, Jack Smith, Jr., David Arnsen, Betty Harford, Donald Bishop, Al Baietti, Diandra Morrell, Darrell Larson, Roger Pancake, Joe Lowry, Harry M. Williams, Dennis Barker, Joseph Garcia, James Kline, Alan Beckwith, Clay Hodges, Val Clenard.

THE CHINA SYNDROME was oddly overlooked by the Motion Picture Academy in 1979 but that was a year of blockbusters that included NORMA RAE, KRAMER VERSUS KRAMER, ALL THAT JAZZ, and APOCALYPSE NOW. What began as a fanciful nuclear plant failure premise turned into reality a few weeks after the picture opened as the Three Mile Island nuclear reactor did the same thing in real life. Fonda is a TV reporter who is trying to advance from cutesy stories (like THE ELECTRIC HORSEMAN) to harder news. Her anchorman is honest-to-goodness TV anchorman Bohrman doing a good job of playing himself. Douglas (who doubled as producer) is a freelance cameraman Fonda hires when she attempts to do a feature story on energy.

They are present at the nuclear plant when a crisis arises and a meltdown is avoided by the quick reactions of engineer Lemmon. Douglas has it all on film and rushes it back to the station (KXLA) but management won't put it on the air for fear it might frighten the populace. Late at night, Douglas sneaks into the station and snatches his footage which he plans to show to some nuclear experts who are, at that moment, trying to decide whether to build a larger facility at Point Conception. Lemmon is angry when he learns that the authorities have put a cover on the incident. He begins searching the plant to find the fault and succeeds in locating the problem—inferior welding put there to keep costs down. Lemmon sees there is nothing to keep this from recurring, so he contacts Fonda and Douglas and gives them X-rays of the offending equipment. This information is given to sound man Valdez with instructions to take it to a hearing on the larger nuclear project. He is ambushed and killed along the road and the same two killers are later seen chasing Lemmon, who manages to stay out of their clutches. Lemmon realizes that his life is in danger and it may, in fact, be from those above him in the company. He produces a revolver and takes over the control room, then demands to be interviewed by Fonda, the one newsperson he trusts. Meanwhile, his company heads are beginning the rumor that a madman has taken over the nuclear plant and he must be stopped. Lemmon begins to crumple under pressure and appears unsure of himself and nutty as a fruitcake while Fonda does the interview. He is about to spill the beans when the security police burst in and shoot him dead. If this film had not been so blatantly political and had stuck to a more honest appraisal, it would have been even more effective. Several sidelights prove interesting; there is no music whatsoever in the film because Douglas, to his credit, insisted on stark reality. Gray, a talented writer from Chicago, who wrote the original screenplay, was slated to direct but Columbia officials persuaded Douglas to hire Bridges. Richard Dreyfuss was originally penciled in to play the cameraman but his price rose out of sight after two successes in 1977, so Douglas did it himself. Another oddity is that Bohrman, after completing his role as a newsman covering a nuclear accident, went back to his old news job and covered the nuclear incident at Three Mile Island. Furthermore, Bohrman's son, David, now a senior producer at ABC, *also* covered the TMI problem. Donat is excellent as the TV station's manager. Fine supporting work all around, especially Brimley, Hampton, and Brady.

p, Michael Douglas; d, James Bridges; w, Mike Gray, T. S. Cook, Bridges; ph, James Crabe (Metrocolor); ed, David Rawlins; set d, Arthur Parker; art d, George Jenkins; cos, Donfeld; spec eff, Henry Millar, Jr..

Drama Cas. (PR:A MPAA:PG)

CHINA VENTURE** (1953) 83m COL bw

Edmond O'Brien *(Capt. Matt Reardon)*, Barry Sullivan *(Cmdr. Bert Thompson)*, Jocelyn Brando *(Lt. Ellen Wilkins)*, Leo Gordon *(Sgt. Hank Janowicz)*, Richard Loo *(Chang Sung)*, Dayton Lummis *(Dr. Masterson)*, Leon Askin *(Wu King)*, Dabbs Greer *(Galuppo)*, Alvy Moore *(Carlson)*, Wong Artarne *(Ensign Wong)*, Philip Ahn *(Adm. Amara)*, Guy Way *(Salomon)*, Frank Wilcox *(Capt. Dryden)*, James Anderson *(Corp. Walters)*, Rex Reason *(Lt. Cross)*, Todd Karns *(Lt. March)*.

A U.S. naval Intelligence mission late in WW II is the main plot point for CHINA VENTURE. O'Brien plays a tough marine captain well-versed in jungle warfare. Sullivan plays a tenderfoot naval officer. The two are on a mission to kidnap a Japanese admiral, Ahn, from the China coast for questioning by top intelligence brass. The mission takes them through rainy jungles, and several skirmishes ensue with both Japanese and Chinese guerrillas. Conflicts develop between O'Brien and Sullivan, due to O'Brien's resentment of the younger officer. Sullivan finally sacrifices his life to stave off a Japanese attack.

p, Anson Bond; d, Don Siegel; w, George Worthing Yates, Richard Collins (based on a story by Anson Bond); ph, Sam Leavitt; m, Ross Di Maggio; ed, Jerome Thoms.

War (PR:C MPAA:NR)

CHINA'S LITTLE DEVILS*½ (1945) 74m MON bw

Harry Carey, Paul Kelly, Ducky Louie, Gloria Ann Chew, Hayward Soo Soo, Ralph Lewis, Jimmy Dodd, H. T. Tsiang.

Bloody propaganda film which portrays the Japanese as hideous beasts who oppress the Chinese, this picture concentrates on a group of Chinese children who help Kelly and other downed American pilots escape the enemy dragnets. Most of the movie is carried by Ducky Louie, a talented child star who performs heroic feats in the name of liberty.

p, Grant Withers; d, Monta Bell; w, Sam Ornitz (based on an unpublished story by Richard Davis); ph, Harry Neumann; ed, Dick Currier.

War Drama (PR:C MPAA:NR)

CHINATOWN***** (1974) 131m PAR c

Jack Nicholson *(J. J. Gittes)*, Faye Dunaway *(Evelyn Mulwray)*, John Huston *(Noah Cross)*, Perry Lopez *(Escobar)*, John Hillerman *(Yelburton)*, Darrell Zwerling *(Hollis Mulwray)*, Diane Ladd *(Ida Sessions)*, Roy Jenson *(Mulvihill)*, Roman Polanski *(Man with Knife)*, Dick Bakalyan *(Loach)*, Joe Mantell *(Walsh)*, Bruce Glover *(Duffy)*, Nandu Hinds *(Sophie)*, James O'Reare *(Lawyer)*, James Hong *(Evelyn's Butler)*, Beulah Quo *(Maid)*, Jerry Fujikawa *(Gardener)*, Belinda Palmer *(Katherine)*, Roy Roberts *(Mayor Bagby)*, Noble Willingham, Elliott Montgomery *(Councilmen)*, Rance Howard *(Irate Farmer)*, George Justin *(Barber)*, Doc Erickson *(Customer)*, Fritzi Burr *(Mulwray's Secretary)*, Charles Knapp *(Mortician)*, Claudio Martiniz *(Boy on Horseback)*, Frederico Roberto *(Cross' Butler)*, Allan Warnick *(Clerk)*, Burt Young *(Curly)*, Elizabeth Harding *(Curly's Wife)*, John Rogers *(Mr. Palmer)*, Cecil Elliott *(Emma Dill)*, Paul Jenkins, Lee DeBroux, Bob Golden *(Policemen)*, John Holland, Jesse Vint, Jim Burke, Denny Arnold *(Farmers In the Valley)*.

A wonderfully brooding, suspenseful *film noir* classic, CHINATOWN proves a tour de force for Nicholson. He is a scheming highly self-esteemed private eye who specializes in the most distasteful gumshoe enterprise—divorce. He and his well-paid minions, Mantell and Glover, busy themselves snooping on the sexual promiscuities of rich wayward spouses, snapping photos, noting secret trysts, wallowing happily in the mudholes of disastrous marriages. The film opens routinely enough with Nicholson being hired by Ladd, who passes herself off as Mrs. Mulwray, asking that he investigate her husband's affair with a young girl. Nicholson and fellow snoops take photos of Zwerling with a young girl (Palmer) and these Nicholson turns over to his client. A few days later the photos, much to Nicholson's surprise, are published in a local scandal sheet. The case becomes even more complicated when Zwerling's body is discovered in a remote and empty reservoir outside Los Angeles. Then Dunaway (the real Mrs. Mulwray) sues the detective for smearing the reputation of her dead husband. The befuddled detective investigates Zwerling's past, learning that he had recently blocked the construction of a dam that would have given L.A. more water supplies, and that Zwerling's one-time partner, Huston, would have benefited greatly from the dam since it would have nourished his enormous fruit orchard holdings. Nicholson then convinces Dunaway that he had nothing to do with the publication of the photos and she drops her suit against him. Both are intrigued by each other and a romance develops. Dunaway asks that Nicholson find her husband's murderer and this leads the detective through a series of hazardous adventures. He finds the body of the woman who had impersonated Dunaway (Ladd) and police believe he has something to do with this murder. From a hiding he sees Dunaway arguing with her dead husband's youthful mistress. Then he discovers that land is being purchased by someone using the names of penniless people in retirement homes. In his search for the answers to the murders, Nicholson is beaten by an ex-cop in the employ of gangster Polanski (the director). And Polanski later corners him, slicing his nostril to warn him away from further probing into the mysterious Zwerling death. He visits with Huston, a powerful landowner and egocentric city mover and shaker, later learning that he is the man behind the murders. Moreover, he learns that Dunaway was raped by her father (Houston) at age fifteen and that Zwerling's young mistress is really Dunaway's daughter *and* her sister. Nicholson decides that he will help Dunaway and Palmer escape Huston by sending them to Mexico. They are caught in Chinatown by Huston and his minions, along with unsuspecting police. Nicholson is handcuffed as Dunaway attempts to flee with Palmer after wounding Huston. Police shoot and kill her. The detective watches, powerless, as the events overcome him in an area of the city where he had once worked as a police detective and where his career had been ruined in a case he could never solve. He is led away by his partners, Mantell telling him "forget it . . . it's Chinatown," and therefore inexplicable, a situation he cannot alter, a mystery he could not hope to explain right from the very beginning. CHINATOWN, based on a real event in the late 1930s, was meticulously constructed by writer Towne, and enacted flawlessly by a cast that captured the style of 1937 characters. Goldsmith's score, with its plaintive horn solos, is perfect for the period and as haunting as the strange case filmed so expertly by Polanski. Water is the root of all evil in this film, and it is in actuality the great god that ordains the destiny of desert-bound Los Angeles. The costuming and overall design of the film is a marvel of understatement by Sylbert. Every little touch, down to barber chairs and antique cars, puts the film firmly inside its time frame. There is an overpowering mood of Raymond Chandler's Los Angeles in CHINATOWN and Nicholson's character is certainly drawn on Chandler's unforgettable private eye, Philip Marlowe, although he is a cheaper, more realistic version of that knight errant. The tone and rich flavor of this film evoke strong memories of MURDER, MY SWEET and the original THE BIG SLEEP, yet it is singularly a film that stands on its own merits, chiefly due to Nicholson's superb interpretation and Towne's magnificent script, one that won him an Oscar. Towne had sold the idea to producer Robert Evans in 1973 with a one-line story outline and spent eighteen months writing the screenplay. The writer had scored previously with Nicholson, who enacted his gutter-minded anti-hero of THE LAST DETAIL. Particular kudos go to Alonzo's cinematography which richly blended deep shadings and sun-drenched yellows and browns to give the wonderful feel and look of the period and place. This production more than made back its original $3,200,000 price tag (25 percent of the film being financed by a tax shelter syndicate for about 10 percent of the profits, an avenue of film financing since closed through federal regulation).

p, Robert Evans; d, Roman Polanski; w, Robert Towne; ph, John A. Alonzo (Panavision, Technicolor); m, Jerry Goldsmith; ed, Sam O'Steen; prod d, Richard Sylbert; art d, W. Stewart Campbell; set d, Gabe and Robert Resh; cos, Anthea Sylbert; spec eff, Longan Frazee; makeup, Hank Edds, Lee Harmon. Songs: "I Can't Get Started," Vernon Duke, Ira Gershwin, "Easy Living," Ralph Rainger, Leo Robin, "The Way You Look Tonight," Jerome Kern, Dorothy Fields, "Some Day," "The Vagabond King Waltz," Brian Hooker, Rudolf Friml.

Crime Drama Cas. (PR:O MPAA:NR)

CHINATOWN AFTER DARK zero (1931) 50m Action bw

Rex Lease, Barbara Kent, Edmund Breese, Carmel Myers, Frank Mayo, Billy Gilbert, Lloyd Whitlock, Laska Winter, Michael Viscroff.

Awful melodrama with Kent as a white girl brought up by Chinaman Breese and Myers as a Dragon Lady with a laughable accent. A dagger sought by many plays a role in the film, but it should have been used to rip the script to shreds.

p, Ralph M. Like; d, Stuart Paton; w, Betty Burbridge.

Drama (PR:A MPAA:NR)

CHINATOWN AT MIDNIGHT** (1949) 67m COL bw

Hurd Hatfield *(Clifford Ward)*, Jean Willes *(Alice)*, Tom Powers *(Capt. Howard Brown)*, Ray Walker *(Sam Costa)*, Charles Russell *(Fred Morgan)*, Jacqueline De Wit *(Lisa Marcel)*, Maylia *(Hazel Fong)*, Ross Elliott *(Eddie Marsh)*, Benson Fong *(Joe Wing)*, Barbara Jean Wong *(Betty Chang)*, Victor San Yen *(Proprietor)*, Josephine Whitell *(Mrs. Dryden)*.

This straightforward story of crime and punishment is a neat low-budget film. It has a heightened impact due to a documentary format and a sustained pace. The film takes place in Chinatown, where the police are concentrating their search for a killer, played by Hatfield, of THE PICTURE OF DORIAN GRAY fame. He kills two Chinese men while stealing some antique vases, and knocks off his girl accomplice when she threatens to squeal to the police. Most of the film is taken up with routine detective work, picking up clues, learning of Hatfield's whereabouts, and springing the trap.

p, Sam Katzman; d, Seymour Friedman; w, Robert Libott, Frank Burt; ph, Henry Freulich; m, Mischa Bakaleinikoff; ed, Edwin Bryant.

Crime   **(PR:C   MPAA:NR)**

CHINATOWN NIGHTS**   (1929) 88m PAR bw

Wallace Beery (Chuck Riley), Florence Vidor (Joan Fry), Warner Oland (Boston Charley), Jack McHugh (The Shadow), Jack Oakie (The Reporter), Tetsu Komai (Woo Chung), Frank Chew (The Gambler), Mrs. Wing (The Maid), Peter Morrison (The Bartender), Freeman Wood (Gerald).

A story of Tong wars in San Francisco has Vidor falling for the Irish chief of one gang (Beery) and eventually convincing him to leave the neighborhood. Oland scores as the rival chieftain and Wellman's direction is sharp and fast. Only 60 percent dialog; the rest is titled.

p, David Selznick; d, W. A. Wellman; w, Oliver H. P. Garrett, Ben Grauman Kohn, William B. Jutto (based on the story "Tong Wars" by Samuel Ornitz).

Crime   **(PR:A   MPAA:NR)**

CHINATOWN NIGHTS*½   (1938, Brit.) 70m Victory/COL bw

H. Agar Lyons (Dr. Sin Fang), Anne Grey (Sonia Graham), Robert Hobbs (John Byrne), Nell Emerald (Mrs. Higgins).

Lyons is a Chinese criminal mastermind (ripped off from Sax Rohmer's Fu Manchu) who kidnaps Grey to get her brother's "Silver Ray" into his clutches. Forgotten and deservedly so.

p, Neil Emerald; d, Tony Frenguelli; w, Nigel Byass.

Crime   **(PR:A   MPAA:NR)**

CHINATOWN SQUAD**   (1935) 70m UNIV bw

Lyle Talbot (Ted Lacey), Valerie Hobson (Janet Baker), Hugh O'Connell (Sgt. McLeash), Andy Devine (George Mason), E. Alyn Warren (John Yee), Leslie Fenton (Quong), Clay Clement (Albert Raybold), Bradley Page (Palmer), Arthur Hoyt (William Ward), Wallis Clark (Lt. Norris), Toshia Mori (Wanda), King Baggot, James Flavin, Tom Dugan, Edward Earle, Pat Flaherty, Otis Harlan, Jack Mulhall.

Broken cop-turned-tour bus driver Talbot solves the murder of a Chinese Communist agent, wins back his uniform, and Hobson, too. Not bad, with some good laughs produced by Devine.

p, Stanley Bergman; d, Murray Roth; w, Dore Schary, Ben Ryan (based on a story by L. G. Blochman); ph, George Robinson.

Crime   **(PR:A   MPAA:NR)**

CHINCERO   (SEE: LAST MOVIE, THE, 1971)

CHINESE BUNGALOW, THE*   (1930, Brit.) 73m W. P. Film Co. bw

Matheson Lang (Yuan Sing), Jill Esmond Moore (Jean), Anna Neagle (Charlotte), Ballard Berkeley (Richard Marquess), Derek Williams (Harold Marquess).

Stagy Oriental sinister stuff, THE CHINESE BUNGALOW tells the story of two sisters, one of whom marries a mandarin and then falls in love with an Englishman, prompting a plot by the mandarin to kill his wife's lover. All this while the sinister one delivers sappy lines about cherry blossoms and lotus flowers and the smoke from incense rises to provide some action on the screen. The major fault of the film is that the director seems to be merely photographing a stage play. (Lang repeats his role from 1926 silent.)

p,d&w, J. B. Williams; w, Marion Osmond, James Corbett (based on a play by Osmond, Corbett); ph, Claude McDonnell.

Drama   **(PR:A   MPAA:NR)**

CHINESE CAT, THE*   (1944) 65m MON bw

Sidney Toler (Charlie Chan), Benson Fong (Tommie Chan), Mantan Moreland (Birmingham), Weldon Heyburn (Harvey Dennis), Joan Woodbury (Leah Manning), Ian Keith (Recknick), Sam Flint (Tom Manning), Cy Kendall (Deacon), Anthony Warde (Catlen), John Davidson (Carl/Kurt), Betty Blythe (Mrs. Manning), Dewey Robinson (Salos), George Chandler (Taxi Dispatcher), Jack Norton (Hotel Desk Clerk), I. Stanford Jolley.

Poor Chan programmer has Toler staggering about looking for suspects of multiple murders. Moreland's hijinks and fright scenes are the only appealing aspects of this otherwise forgettable whodunit. (According to technicians who regularly worked on the Charlie Chan series, Oland, Toler and Winters were all notorious imbibers—"all those Chans were drunk on and off camera" remarked one editor—but the miserable scripts undoubtedly contributed to the tippling.) (See CHARLIE CHAN series, Index.)

p, Philip N. Krasne, James S. Burkett; d, Phil Rosen; w, George Callahan; ph, Ira Morgan; ed, Fred Allen; art d, Dave Milton.

Crime   **(PR:A   MPAA:NR)**

CHINESE DEN, THE**   (1940, Brit.) 72m BL bw
(GB: THE CHINESE BUNGALOW)

Paul Lukas (Yuan Sing), Jane Baxter (Charlotte Merivale), Kay Walsh (Sadie Merivale), Robert Douglas (Richard Marquess), Wallace Douglas (Harold Marquess), James Woodburn (Doctor), Mayura (Ayah), Jerry Verno (Stubbins).

Remake of 1930 film THE CHINESE BUNGALOW. Lukas is the Chinese banker married to Englishwoman Walsh. She falls in love with Douglas, a handsome English plantation manager. Lukas avenges himself on him, then decides it's Walsh's sister, Baxter, he really wants, but she wants nothing to do with him. Walsh does a good job singing "There's No Smoke Without Fire." Better than the original.

p&d, George King; w, A. B. Rawlinson, George Wellesley (based on a stage play by Marion Osmond and James Corbett); ph, Hone Glendinning.

Drama   **(PR:A   MPAA:NR)**

CHINESE PUZZLE, THE*½   (1932, Brit.) 81m Twickenham/W&F bw

Leon M. Lion (Marquis Li Chung), Lilian Braithwaite (Lady de la Haye), Elizabeth Allan (Naomi Melsham), Austin Trevor (Paul Markatel), James Raglan (Sir Charles/Sir Roger), Jane Welsh (Victoria), C. M. Hallard (Sir Aylmer Brent), Mabel Sealby (Mrs. Melsham), Francis L. Sullivan (Herman Strumm), Charles Carson (Armand de Coulvais), George Carr (Dr. Fu Yang).

Lion is a Chinese mandarin who confesses to the theft of a secret treaty to save the real thief, the wife of a friend. Not very interesting. (Lion and Braithwaite repeat roles from 1919 silent.)

p, Julius Hagen; d, Guy Newall; w, H. Fowler Mear (based on a play by Leon M. Lion and Frances Barclay).

Crime   **(PR:A   MPAA:NR)**

CHINESE RING, THE*   (1947) 67m MON bw

Roland Winters (Charlie Chan), Warren Douglas (Sgt. Davidson), Victor Sen Young (Tommy), Mantan Moreland (Birmingham), Philip Ahn (Capt. Kong), Louise Currie (Peggy Cartwright), Byron Foulger (Armstrong), Thayer Roberts (Capt. Kelso), Jean Wong (Princess Mei Ling), Chabing (Lilly Mae), George L. Spaulding (Dr. Hickey), Paul Bryar (Sergeant), Charmienne Harker (Stenographer), Thornton Edwards (Hotel Clerk), Lee Tung Foo (Butler), Richard Wang (Hamishin), Spencer Chan (Chinese Officer), Kenneth Chuck (Chinese Boy).

Winters solves the murder of a Chinese princess in America to buy planes. Clues lead to a bank manager trying to steal her funds. Series is nearing its death throes and this is no fun to watch. (See CHARLIE CHAN series, Index.)

p, James S. Burkett; d, William Beaudine; w, W. Scott Darling (based on characters created by Earl Derr Biggers); ph, William Sickner; ed, Ace Herman.

Crime   **(PR:A   MPAA:NR)**

CHINESE ROULETTE***
(1977, Ger.) 96m Films du Losange-Albatross-Multicine/New Yorker c

Margit Carstensen (Ariane), Ulli Lommel (Kolbe), Anna Karina (Irene), Alexander Allerson (Gerhard), Andrea Schober (Angela), Macha Meril (Traunitz), Brigitte Mira (Kast), V. Spengler (Gabriel).

Allerson and Carstensen are a happily married, well-to-do Munich couple with a crippled daughter (Lommel). Allerson tells his wife that he is going to Oslo for a weekend business trip; instead he picks up his French mistress, Karina, and takes her to the castle the family uses as a vacation home. There he finds Carstensen with her lover. They decide that they are all adults and decide to go on with their respective weekends as planned. Son Lommel turns up, manipulating everyone, and Mira appears as a sadistic housekeeper with an androgynous son. Lommel gets everyone to play a truth game and violence results. Excellent Fassbinder film from the director's Douglas Sirk-influenced period. (In German; English subtitles.)

d&w, Rainer Werner Fassbinder; ph, Michael Ballhaus (Eastmancolor); m, Peer Raben; ed, Ila Von Hasperg; subtitles, Fassbinder.

Drama   **(PR:O   MPAA:NR)**

CHINO**   (1976, Ital., Span., Fr.) 97m DD-Coral Film-Universal Production France/Intercontinental Releasing Corp. c (AKA: VALDEZ, THE HALFBREED)

Charles Bronson (Chino Valdez), Jill Ireland (Louise), Vincent Van Patten (Jamie Wagner), Marcel Bozzuffi (Maral), Melissa Chimenti (Indian Girl), Fausto Tozzi (Cruz), Ettore Manni (Sheriff), Adolfo Thous (Cayote), Florencio Amarilla (Little Bear), Corrado Gaida, Diana Lorys (Indians).

Bronson is a halfbreed horse rancher in New Mexico who takes in teenage runaway Van Patten. He clashes with wealthy breeder Bozzuffi and falls in love with Bozzuffi's sister, Ireland. When Bozzuffi sees what is going on, he has Bronson beaten up and jailed. When Bronson returns to his ranch, he sets the horses free, burns down the buildings, and sends Van Patten away. Bronson rides off to start life anew. Bronson packed up wife Ireland, his six children, and three tutors to Almeria, Spain, for filming. Originally Lino Ventura was to play Maral, but when he saw how small the role was, he walked out, and the almost unknown Bozzuffi was hired to replace him. An interesting departure for Bronson; rather than being the vengeance-obsessed killer seen so many times before (and since), he is a sensitive man who wants nothing more than to be left alone. When he is brutalized by the brother of the woman he loves, he doesn't try to save his honor by killing the man and getting the girl; instead he chucks the whole thing, destroying that which his enemies covet before disappearing. Beware of television prints that eliminate the sexual tension between Bronson and Ireland that provides the major concern of the film.

p, Duilio Coletti; d, John Sturges; w, Dino Maiuri, Massimo De Rita, Clair Haffaker (based on the novel The Valdez Horses by Lee Hoffman); ph, Armando Nannuzzi (Eastmancolor); m, Guido De Angelis, Maurizio De Angelis; ed, Vanio Amici, Peter Zinner; art d, Mario Garbuglia; set d, Boris Juraga.

Western   **Cas.**   **(PR:A-C   MPAA:PG)**

CHIP OF THE FLYING U**   (1940) 55m UNIV bw

Johnny Mack Brown (Chip Bennett), Bob Baker (Dusty), Fuzzy Knight (Weary), Doris Weston (Margaret Whitmore), Forrest Taylor (J. G. Whitmore), Anthony Warde (Duncan), Karl Hackett (Hennessey), Henry Hall (Wilson), Claire Whitney (Miss Robinson), Ferris Taylor (Sheriff), Cecil Kellogg (Red), Hank Bell, Harry Tenbrook, Chester Conklin, Vic Potel, Hank Worden, Charles K. French, Frank El lis, Kermit Maynard.

Brown is a ranch foreman suspected of a series of holdups. With the help of sidekick Knight he gets the real desperadoes, who are working for foreign gun smugglers. Above average, considering the tired story line.

d, Ralph Staub; w, Larry Rhine, Andrew Bennison (based on a story by B. M. Bower); ph, William Sickner.

Western   **(PR:A   MPAA:NR)**

CHIP OFF THE OLD BLOCK*** (1944) 76m UNIV bw
Donald O'Connor *(Donald Corrigan)*, Peggy Ryan *(Peggy)*, Ann Blyth *(Glory Marlow III)*, Helen Vinson *(Glory Marlow, Jr.)*, Helen Broderick *(Glory Marlow, Sr.)*, Arthur Treacher *(Quentin)*, Patric Knowles *(Judd Corrigan)*, J. Edward Bromberg *(Blaney Wright)*, Ernest Truex *(Henry McHugh)*, Minna Gombell *(Milly)*, Samuel S. Hinds *(Dean Manning)*, Irving Bacon *(Prof Frost)*, Joel Kupperman *(Quiz Kid)*, Mantan Moreland.

Pleasant musical, with O'Connor, then rising fast as a musical comedy star, heading home from military school and meeting Blyth on the train. Their courtship is interrupted by Ryan, O'Connor's girl, who is waiting for him at the station. The three dance and sing their way through the complications until it's time for O'Connor to get back on the train for school. Blyth is very good in her screen debut. Songs: "Is It Good Or Is It Bad?" (Charles Tobias), "Mighty Nice To Have Met You," "Spelling Prep" (Bill Grage, Grace Shannon), "I Gotta Give My Feet A Break" (Inez James, Sidney Miller), "Love Is Like Music" (Milton Schwarzwald), "My Song" (Lew Brown, Ray Henderson), "Sailor Song" (Eugene Conrad).

p, Bernard W. Burton; d, Charles W. Lamont; w, Eugene Conrad, Leo Townsend (based on a story by Robert Arthur); ph, Charles Van Enger; ed, Charles Maynard; md, Charles Previn; ch d, Louis De Pron.

Musical (PR:A MPAA:NR)

CHIPS** (1938, Brit.) 80m British Fine Arts bw
Tony Wyckham *(Chips)*, Robb Wilton *(P. C. Chester)*, Davy Burnaby *(Alderman)*, Billy Merson *(Harbour Master)*, Peter Dawson *(Salty Sam)*, Joyce Bland *(Lady)*, Bertram Wallis *(Smuggler)*, Terry's Juveniles, Twenty Tiny Tappers.

Wyckham is a young Sea Scout suspended from his troop who redeems himself by capturing a ring of smugglers. Okay musical that will probably appeal to children.

p&d, Edward Godal; w, Vivian Tidmarsh; ph, Desmond Dickinson.

Musical (PR:A MPAA:NR)

CHIQUITO PERO PICOSO*½
(1967, Mex.) 90m Alfa bw (AKA: EL SUPERFLACO)
Evangelina Elizondo, Alfonso Pompin Iglesias, Wolf Ruvinskis, Daniel Chino Herrera, Jose Jasso, Alfredo Varela, Jr., Nacho Contla, Arturo Bigoton Castro, Luis Manuel Pelayo.

Another Mexican wrestler film, this one a parody of the genre. Pompin, playing a Harold Lloyd-type character, receives hormone injections from mad doctor Herrera, making him an invincible wrestler. Unfortunately, the serum wears off just before his big bout with the champion, Ruvinskis. Only for those who like this sort of thing.

p, Fidel Pizarro; d, Miguel M. Delgado; w, Gunther Gerszo, Carlos Orellana; ph, Jose Ortiz Ramos.

Comedy/Action (PR:A MPAA:NR)

CHISUM*** (1970) 110m WB c
John Wayne *(John Chisum)*, Forrest Tucker *(Lawrence Murphy)*, Christopher George *(Dan Nodeen)*, Ben Johnson *(James Pepper)*, Glenn Corbett *(Pat Garrett)*, Bruce Cabot *(Sheriff Brady)*, Andrew Prine *(Alex McSween)*, Patric Knowles *(Tunstall)*, Richard Jaeckel *(Evans)*, Lynda Day *(Sue McSween)*, John Agar *(Patton)*, Lloyd Battista *(Neemo)*, Robert Donner *(Morton)*, Ray Teal *(Justice Wilson)*, Edward Faulkner *(Dolan)*, Ron Soble *(Bowdre)*, John Mitchum *(Baker)*, Glenn Langan *(Dudley)*, Alan Baxter *(Gov. Axtell)*, Alberto Morin *(Delgado)*, William Bryant *(Jeff)*, Pedro Armendariz, Jr. *(Ben)*, Christopher Mitchum *(O'Folliard)*, Abraham Sofaer *(White Buffalo)*, Gregg Palmer *(Riker)*, Geoffrey Deuel *(Billy the Kid)*, Pamela McMyler *(Sally Chisum)*, Chuck Roberson *(A Trail Herder)*, Hank Worden *(Stage Depot Clerk)*, Ralph Volkie *(Blacksmith)*, Pedro Gonzales Gonzales *(Mexican Rancher)*, John Pickard *(Aggressive Sergeant)*.

A traditional action-packed western starring Wayne in the title role, playing the same rugged character he had played in dozens of his other films and that became his trademark. This time he is the largest land-and-cattle owner of the Pecos in New Mexico. He watches his community fall under the villainous yoke of land baron Tucker, and when Wayne feels he has gone far enough, he swings into the saddle with a flair typical of the Duke. Based loosely on the accounts of the Lincoln County wars, which took place in the 1870s, the film attempts to give an accurate feel for the time period. Included in the war was the final gunfight between Pat Garrett and Billy the Kid, which finds itself as an integral part of the plot. The movie is all Wayne, and he sees to it that good triumphs over evil in the end.

p&w, Andrew J. Fenady; d, Andrew V. McLaglen; ph, William H. Clothier (Panavision, Technicolor); m, Dominic Frontiere; ed, Robert Simpson; art d, Carl Anderson; song sung by Merle Haggard.

Western Cas. (PR:A MPAA:G)

CHITTY CHITTY BANG BANG½** (1968, Brit.) 156m Warfield/UA c
Dick Van Dyke *(Caractacus Potts)*, Sally Ann Howes *(Truly Scrumptious)*, Lionel Jeffries *(Grandpa Potts)*, Gert Frobe *(Baron Bomburst)*, Anna Quayle *(Baroness Bomburst)*, Benny Hill *(Toymaker)*, James Robertson Justice *(Lord Scrumptious)*, Robert Helpmann *(Child Catcher)*, Heather Ripley *(Jemima)*, Adrian Hall *(Jeremy)*, Barbara Windsor *(Blonde)*, Davy Kaye *(Admiral)*, Alexander Dore, Bernard Spear *(Spies)*, Stanley Unwin *(Chancellor)*, Peter Arne *(Captain of Guard)*, Desmond Llewelyn *(Coggins)*, Victor Maddern *(Junkman)*, Arthur Mullard *(Big Man)*, Ross Parker *(Chef)*, Gerald Campion, Felix Felton, Monti de Lyle *(Ministers)*, Totti Truman Taylor *(Duchess)*, Larry Taylor *(Lieutenant)*, Max Bacon *(Orchestra Leader)*, Max Wall, John Heawood, Michael Darbyshire, Kenneth Waller, Gerald Taylor, Eddie Davis *(Inve ntors)*, Richard Wattis *(Secretary at Sweet Factory)*, John Baskcomb *(Chef)*.

British-made for American distribution, this big-budget adaptation of Ian Fleming's story could have been a delightful movie but it sort of implodes under its own weight. Many of the staff of MARY POPPINS joined Van Dyke in an attempt to recreate the magic of that earlier Disney film but it came a-cropper under Hughes' leaden direction. Van Dyke is a widower with a penchant for things mechanical. He has this old-fashioned motor car and is about to send it on its way when the auto develops the ability to fly and float. Van Dyke has been wooing Howes, wealthy daughter of candy magnate Justice, but it's not working. Meanwhile, Van Dyke's father, Jeffries, is a wacko who thinks he's still off in Inja fighting the fuzzy-wuzzies. Frobe is monarch of a small but wealthy principality. He is after the car and has it and the inventor kidnaped but winds up with the wrong car and the wrong person, Jeffries. Van Dyke, Howes, and Van Dyke's children, Ripley and Hall, give chase to an OZ-like land where all children are immediately incarcerated (by Helpmann, of RED SHOES fame), a fantastic place where nothing is what it seems. After a predictable and yawning plot twist, we learn that the whole story has been just that, a story told by Van Dyke to his children. They attempted to do a POPPINS-OZ story with every cliche they could borrow from those and many other films like those before them. Absolutely nothing worked. Even the redoubtable Sherman brothers, who have enlivened many films with their excellent work, failed to bring anything to CCBB. This was closer to DOCTOR DOOLITTLE than the aforementioned duo in that they tried too hard to be charming and only succeeded in looking like a very expensive *Bozo The Clown* segment. Ten million dollars or so . . . down the tube. Tsk, tsk, Roald Dahl. Songs: "You Two," "Toots Sweets," "Hushabye Mountain," "Me Ol' Bam-Boo," "Truly Scrumptious," "Chitty Chitty Bang Bang," "Lovely Lonely Man," "Posh," "The Roses of Success," "Chu-Chi Face," "Doll On a Music Box."

p, Albert R. Broccoli; d, Ken Hughes; w, Roald Dahl, Hughes, Richard Maibaum (based on a book by Ian Fleming); ph, Christopher Challis (Super-Panavision, Technicolor), ed, John Shirley; md, Irwin Kostal; art d, Harry Pottle; cos, Elizabeth Haffenden, Joan Bridge; ch, Dee Dee Wood, Marc Breaux; m/l, Richard M. and Robert B. Sherman.

Fantasy/Musical Cas. (PR:AAA MPAA:G)

CHIVATO* (1961) 85m International Film Distributors bw
Bill Fletcher *(Ramon)*, Jake La Motta *(Julio)*, Lon Chaney, Jr. *(Gordo)*, Sonia Marrero *(Sonia Velasco)*, Don Gould *(Eduardo)*, George Rodriguez *(Molito)*, Barbara Lea *(Elena)*.

Strange anti-Castro film about a rebellion on the Isle of Pines that resoundingly defeats the Communist government. With boxer Jake La Motta, later immortalized in Martin Scorcese's RAGING BULL, it was filmed in Cuba and South Miami. The movie also opened in Miami to exploit the large number of Cuban refugees there. An el cheapo production not worth seeking out.

p&d, Albert C. Gannaway; w, Frank Graves (based on a story by Mark Hanna); ph, Ernest Haller.

Drama (PR:A–C MPAA:NR)

CHLOE IN THE AFTERNOON***
(1972, Fr.) 97m Les Films du Losange-Barbet Schroeder/COL c
Bernard Verley *(Frederic)*, Zouzou *(Chloe)*, Francoise Verley *(Helene)*, Daniel Ceccaldi *(Gerard)*, Malvina Penne *(Fabienne)*, Babette Ferrier *(Martine)*, Tina Michelino, Jean-Louis Livi, Pierre Nunzi, Irene Skobline, Frederique Hender, Claude-Jean Philippe, Silvia Badesco, Claude Bertrand, Sylvaine Charlet, Daniele Malat, Suze Randall, Francoise Fabian, Aurora Cornu, Marie-Christine Barrault, Haydee Politoff, Laurence de Monaghan, Beatrice Romand.

The sixth installment in Rohmer's "Six Moral Tales" (others include MY NIGHT AT MAUD'S and CLAIRE'S KNEE), deals with the same thematic material as the other five: Verley is happily married but finds himself sexually attracted to kooky Zouzou. He begins to spend his afternoons with her in conversation, and eventually finds himself wanting to go to bed with her and she does grow more alluring as the film progresses. Like all Rohmer's heroes, he doesn't do it, but he does think about it a lot, and that quandary provides most of the film's content. Rohmer's films are not for all tastes. They are all talk (and being in French, all subtitles), and almost nothing of any import occurs in them. That, of course, is just the point. There is no other director today who has such a clear idea of the preoccupations of adult males in today's world. A very good, significant film. (In French; English subtitles).

p, Pierre Cottrell; d&w, Eric Rohmer; ph, Nestor Almendros; m, Arie Dzierlatka; ed, Cecile Decugis.

Drama (PR:O MPAA:R)

CHOCOLATE SOLDIER, THE*** (1941) 102m MGM bw
Nelson Eddy *(Karl Lang)*, Rise Stevens *(Maria Lanyl)*, Nigel Bruce *(Bernard Fischer)*, Florence Bates *(Mme. Helene)*, Dorothy Gilmore *(Magda)*, Nydia Westman *(Liesel, the Maid)*, Max Barwyn *(Anton)*, Charles Judels *(Klementor)*, Jack Lipson *(Capt. Masakroff)*, Leon Belasco *(Waiter)*, Sig Arno *(Emile)*, Dave Willock *(Messenger Boy)*.

Eddy and Stevens are married and the toast of Vienna. Eddy is jealous of Rise's flirtatious nature and, to test her loyalty, he decides to dress up as a Russian and pass himself off as a visitor from the cold climes. He has himself introduced at a nightclub as a new singer and directs his songs to her. Now, if you can suspend disbelief that Stevens would not recognize her own husband, then this is for you. But of course she does—and that's where the fun comes in. She agrees to have him visit her (knowing full well his jealous streak) and make love. He is extremely ardent and she keeps him at arm's length, telling him that her husband will be out that night and they might get together. She continues to keep him away, then encourages him, and it's making poor Nelson crazy. He is performing in an operetta, "The Chocolate Soldier," and walks on stage dressed in the wrong costume by mistake and singing in his second voice, the one he uses when masquerading as the Russian. Stevens can barely keep from laughing as she sings on stage with him, then tells him that she knew all along what he was up to. Eddy is finally convinced of her fidelity and they leave the stage singing "My Hero." This movie has a strange background. George Bernard Shaw wrote a play called "Arms And The Man." Oscar Straus made it into an operetta called "The Chocolate Soldier" and a few of the tunes are in this movie, but the picture is actually a remake of

Ferenc Molnar's "The Guardsman," which was originally a Lunt-Fontanne vehicle for MGM in 1931. Shaw's play had been committed to Gabriel Pascal (Cecil Lewis directed it in 1932 with Barry Jones starring in the British-made version) and so the MGM story department grafted the musical score onto another plot! Bruce, who was scoring strongly as Dr. Watson, does a neat turn as a family friend, as does Bates. Eddy is at his best in the role, a part that gives him the opportunity to stretch out and overplay as the Russian. He was never this impressive again. Songs: "While My Lady Sleeps" (Gus Kahn, Bronislau Kaper), "Song of the Flea" (Mussorgsky), "Evening Star" (from "Tannhauser"), "Seek the Spy" (Stanislaus Stange, Kahn, Oscar Straus), "My Heart at Thy Sweet Voice" (Saint-Saens), "Mon Coeur" (Bizet), "Ti-Ra-La-La" (Stange, Kahn, Straus), "My Hero," "Thank the Lord the War Is Over," "Sympathy," "The Chocolate Soldier," "Forgive," (Stange, Straus).

p, Victor Saville; d, Roy Del Ruth; w, Keith Winter, Leonard Lee, Ernest Vajda, Claudine West (based on "The Guardsman" by Ferenc Molanr); ph, Karl Freund; m Oscar Straus; ed, James E. Newcom; md, Merrill Pye; art d, Cedric Gibbons; set d, Edwin B. Willis; cos, Adrian; ch, Ernst Matray.

Operetta (PR:A MPAA:NR)

CHOICE OF ARMS**** (1983, Fr.) 135m Parafrance c
Yves Montand (Noel), Gerard Depardieu (Mickey), Catherine Deneuve (Nicole), Michel Galabru (Bonnardot), Gerard Lanvin (Sarlat), Jean-Claude Dauphin (Ricky), Richard Anconina (Dany).

The fifth film made by French action director Alain Corneau sets a generation conflict on a cops-and-robbers theme. The film dramatizes the conflict between a retired underworld figure of the old school, played by Montand, and a homicidal young hood, played by Depardieu. Having broken out of prison and killed a guard, Depardieu takes refuge on Montand's ranch. His fellow escapee is Montand's old crony, who mistakenly believes that Montand has betrayed him and wants revenge. Montand is fearful for his hard-earned tranquility and his mate, Deneuve. He wants to kill Depardieu and his partner, but softens when he learns of the young hood's love for a little girl he has sired. Deneuve is accidentally killed by police bullets in a raid on the ranch, and Depardieu is also killed. Montand finds and adopts Depardieu's little girl, and leaves the country. Under a lot of sloppy sentimentality is a pretty good film about a violent young delinquent doomed by his uncontainable rage. (In French; English subtitles.)

p, Alain Sarde; d, Alain Corneau; w, Corneau, Michel Grisolia; ph, Pierre-William Glenn (Panavision); m, Philippe Sarde; ed, Thierry Derocles; md, Peter Knight; art d & cos, Jean-Pierre Kohut-Svelka.

Crime (PR:C MPAA:NR)

CHOIRBOYS, THE**½** (1977) 119m UNIV c
Charles Durning (Whalen), Louis Gossett, Jr. (Motts), Perry King (Slate), Clyde Kusatu (Tanaguchi), Stephen Macht (Van Moot), Tim McIntyre (Roscoe Rules), Randy Quaid (Proust), Chuck Sacci (Sartino), Don Stroud (Lyles), James Woods (Bloomguard), Burt Young (Scuzzi), Robert Webber (Riggs), Jeanie Bell (Fanny), Blair Brown (Mrs. Lyles), Michele Carey (Ora Lee Tingle), Charles Haid (Yanov), Jack Kapp (Hod Carrier), Barbara Rhodes (Hadley), Jim Davis (Capt. Drobeck), Phyllis Davis (Foxy/Gina), Jack DeLeon (Luther Quigley), George Di Cenzo (Lt. Grimsley), David Spielberg (Lt. Finque), Vic Tayback (Pete Zoony), Michael Wills (Blaney), Susan Batson (Sabrina), Claire Brennon (Carolina Moon).

This film takes a dark, sardonic look at a modern police force. Made up of several vignettes based on Joseph Wambaugh's novel and filled to brimming with weird and crazy characters, THE CHOIRBOYS shows the worst side of the police, in a humorous manner, depending on who is watching the film. Those with a healthy respect for the men in blue will be appalled and disgusted, those who take a lighter view of them will find most of the film generally funny. The film shows that under the public image of callousness that many urban police exude lies something much worse. In this huge cast of characters we find that they all have a weird, kinky hang-up or problem and that not a single one could in any truth be called a choirboy. Choirboys is the ironic term given to the group by police to themselves, when they go out on their wild drunken parties, which they refer to as choir practice. The characters form a cross-section of people in general, from old-style cop Charles Durning, all the way down through minorities, troubled Vietnam vets, naive twerps, and sexually kinky all-American types. The rambling burlesque vignettes all converge when a park-cruising gay teenager is accidentally shot and it is hushed up. The climax comes when Durning is forced to squeal or give up his pension. The cast is made up of many unknowns who would later go on to bigger things.

p, Merv Adelson, Lee Rich; d, Robert Aldrich; w, Christopher Knopf (based on the novel by Joseph Wambaugh); ph, Joseph Biroc (Technicolor); m, Frank DeVol; ed, Maury Winetrobe, William Martin, Irving Rosenblum; art d, Bill Kenney; set d, Raphael Bretton; cos, Tom Dawson, Yvonne Kubis.

Drama/Comedy (PR:O MPAA:R)

CHOPPERS, THE* (1961) 66m Rushmore/Fairway International bw
Arch Hall, Jr. (Cruiser), Marianne Gaba (Liz), Robert Paget (Torch), Tom Brown (Tom Hart), Rex Holman (FLip), Mickey Hoyle (Snooper), Chuck Barnes (Ben), Bruno Ve Sota (Moose McGilh), Britt Woods (Cowboy Boggs), Dee Dee Green (Gypsy), William Shaw (Lt. Fleming), Pat Hawley (Officer Jenks), Richard S. Cowl (Mr. Lester).

Hall is a young hot rodder who steals a set of hub caps for his dragster. Emboldened by his success, he organizes his friends into a car theft ring called "The Choppers." Insurance investigator Brown looks into the sudden rash of thefts, only to have his own car stolen and stripped. Gaba, his secretary (and Playboy's "Miss September," 1959) finds a chicken feather at the scene, leading authorities to the poultry truck the gang uses in its heists. Before police can close in, Hall kills Ve Sota, the junkyard fence. Another piece of bad cinema from Hall, Sr., who made at least six other low-budget

exploitation pieces starring the dubious acting talents and even more dubious singing talents of Hall, Jr. Their most famous (or notorious) effort is EEGAH!, made the following year. Today Hall, Sr. produces documentaries and Hall, Jr. has found his niche as an airline pilot.

p, Arch Hall, Sr.; d, Leigh Jason; w, Hall; ph, Clark Ramsey; m, Al Pellegrini; ed, Jack Ogilvie; m/l, "Konga Joe," "Monkey in My Hatband" (Arch Hall, Jr.).

Crime (PR:C-O MPAA:NR)

CHOSEN, THE*½ (1978, Brit./Ital.) 102m AIP c (AKA: HOLOCAUST 2,000)
Kirk Douglas (Caine), Agostine Belli (Sara), Simon Ward (Angel), Anthony Quayle (Prof. Griffith), Virginia McKenna (Eva), Alexander Knox (Meyer), Romolo Valli (Msgr. Charrier), Massimo Foschi (Assassin).

A stupid thriller starring Douglas as a nuclear power plant designer who discovers that his son, Ward, is the Antichrist and plans to destroy the world by setting off a chain of nuclear explosions. The best thing about this movie is the musical score by Ennio Morricone.

p, Edmundo Amati; d, Alberto de Martino; w, Sergio Donati, Aldo Di Martino, Michael Robson; ph, Enrico Menczer (Technicolor); ed, Vincenzo Tomassi; m, Ennio Morricone; art d, Umberto Batacca.

Horror/Science Fiction (PR:O MPAA:R)

CHOSEN, THE*** (1982) 108m Contemporary c
Maximilian Schell (David Malter), Rod Steiger (Reb Saunders), Robby Benson (Danny Saunders), Barry Miller (Reuven Malter), Hildy Brooks (Mrs. Saunders), Ron Rifkin (Baseball Coach), Val Avery (Teacher).

This film is a first-rate adaptation of the Chaim Potok novel of the same name, depicting the friendship of two young Jewish men of widely different religio-cultural beliefs, during the 1940s. It also explores their individual relationships with their fathers. Benson couldn't have been a worse choice to play the Hassidic Danny Saunders. He does a credible job but cannot hold a candle to Miller who plays his orthodox friend Reuven Malter. Benson and Miller meet as opposing players in a baseball game. Benson deliberately hits a hard ball at Miller's face, breaking his glasses and putting him in the hospital. Benson visits him in order to make up for nearly blinding him and a friendship begins. To Miller, a typical American kid, Benson's Hassidic upbringing, complete with 19th-century attire and long side curls, make him as strange as a creature from space. Benson takes Miller home to meet his father, Steiger, who gives an excellent performance. Steiger is a powerful rabbi, and must approve of all of his son's non-Hassidic friends. Here is where we see that Benson's interest in the outside world makes his relationship with his father very difficult. At the end of WW II the hot issue becomes the birth of the state of Israel. Miller's father is a Zionist, while Benson's is dead set against it. Benson is forbidden to talk to Miller and bows to the wishes of his father. After the issue has ended and Israel has become a state, Benson can talk to Miller again. By this time the two men have had their goals in life reversed and never regain their close friendship.

p, Edie and Ely Landau; d, Jeremy Paul Kagan; w, Edwin Gordon (based on the novel by Chaim Potok); ph, Arthur Ornitz (color); m, Elmer Bernstein; ed, David Garfield; art d, Stuart Wurtzel; cos, Ruth Morley.

Drama Cas. (PR:A MPAA:PG)

CHOSEN SURVIVORS*½ (1974 U.S.-Mex.) 99m COL c
Jackie Cooper (Raymond Couzins), Alex Cord (Steven Mayes), Richard Jaeckel (Gordon Ellis), Bradford Dillman (Peter Macomber), Pedro Armendariz, Jr. (Luis Cabral), Diana Muldaur (Alana Fitzgerald), Lincoln Kilpatrick (Woody Russo), Gwen Mitchell (Carrie Draper), Barbara Babcock (Lenore Chrisman), Christina Moreno (Kristin Lerner), Nancy Rodman (Claire Farraday), Kelly Lange (Mary Louise Borden).

The film involves the fate of eleven people selected by the U.S. government to participate in a below-ground experiment to see how they fare when they are told the rest of the human race has been destroyed by a nuclear holocaust. This strange cross-section of humanity includes a hard drinking businessman, Cooper, a Congresswoman, Muldaur, a novelist, Cord, a black athlete, Kilpatrick, and the crazed government official who thought the whole thing up, Dillman. Not that this wouldn't have been a good enough premise on its own (however it isn't) but to spice things up an electrical vent is accidentally left open, allowing thousands of blood-sucking vampire bats to get into the shelter. The rest of the film is spent in an effort to fight off the bats (which look particularly realistic) and to escape from the shelter. Thanks to Kilpatrick's heroic efforts, those not killed escape from this batty film.

p, Charles Fries, Leon Benson; d, Sutton Roley; w, H. B. Cross, Joe Reb Moffly (based on a story by Cross); ph, Gabriel Torres; m, Fred Karlin; ed, John F. Link II, Dennis Virkler; art d, Jose Rodriguez; set d, Ernesto Carrasco; cos, Alfonso Rubie; spec eff, Dr. G. Clay Mitchell, William Lopez Forment.

Science Fiction (PR:C MPAA:PG)

CHRIST STOPPED AT EBOLI (SEE: EBOLI, 1979)

CHRISTIAN LICORICE STORE, THE*½ (1971) 90m NG c
Beau Bridges (Franklin Cane), Maud Adams (Cynthia Vicstrom), Gilbert Roland (Jonathan Carruthers), Alan Arbus (Monroe), Anne Randall (Texas Girl), Monte Hellman (Joseph), Jaclyn Hellman (Mary), "Butch" Bucholtz (Tennis Opponent), Walter Barnes (P. C. Stayne), McLean Stevenson (Smallwood), Howard Storm (McGhee), Greg Mullavey (Robin Schwartz), Larry Gelman (Assistant Director), Louis De Farra (Mime), Gary Rose (Evans), Billy James, Rusty Durrell (Reporters), Dawn Cleary (Hostess), Barbara Leigh, Joanna Phillips (Starlets), James Jeter (Texas Man), Nina Varela (Parking Lady), Bruce Graziano (Tall Sailor), Harold Keller (Short Sailor), Toni Clayton (Mercedes Girl), Dido and Jean Renoir (Themselves).

Story of a champion tennis player, Bridges, who succumbs to the corrupting influences of Hollywood, public adulation, and commercialism. The film is related through a sparse story line and random dialog, but it is the strong visual images that bring the story across. The golden-boy sports hero, being a native of Hollywood, embodies the morals of that society. He is materially successful but unable to show any true feelings. We see Bridges as he deteriorates from respected champion to the frequenter of decadent parties and the seller of hair tonic. Horatio Alger backsliding on a cliche-riddled story.

p, Michael S. Laughlin, Floyd Mutrux; d, James Frawley; w, Mutrux; ph, David Butler (DeLuxe Color); m, Lalo Schifrin; ed, Richard Harris; art d, Dale Hennessy; m/l, Tim Buckley, Tim McIntire, David Byron.

Drama (PR:C MPAA:GP)

CHRISTIAN THE LION** (1976, Brit.) 89m Scotia American c
Bill Travers, Virginia McKenna, George Adamson, Terence Adamson, Anthony Bourke, John Rendall.

Made 10 years after BORN FREE, CHRISTIAN THE LION has Bill Travers and Virginia McKenna once again involved with the destiny of a lion. This time it is Christian, a young lion born in a London zoo. Travers and McKenna take the lion from its owner and try to return it to the wilds of Africa. The plot line revolves around getting Christian to make the adjustment from humans to other lions. The narration, which Travers and McKenna take turns, is entertaining and often quite witty, but the real star of the show is Christian, a ham who steals the show from his human co-stars. (Sequel to THE LION AT WORLD'S END, 1971.)

p,d&w, Bill Travers, James Hill; ph, Simon Trevor; m, Pentangle; ed, Andrew Borthwick.

Nature/Animal (PR:AAA MPAA:C)

CHRISTINA* (1929) 83m FOX bw
Janet Gaynor (Christina), Charles Morton (Jan), Rudolph Schildkraut (Niklaas), Harry Cording (Dick Torpe), Lucy Dorraine (Mme. Bosman).

Dutch toymaker's daughter Gaynor falls in love with Morton, a shill for a seedy carnival. When the show moves on, Morton lingers with Gaynor but his jealous boss Dorraine has him charged with embezzling carnival funds. Gaynor tries to help but Morton is dragged off to trial in Amsterdam. He manages to return to Gaynor just before she is wed to another and the happy couple reunite. A bad tearjerker; seventeen minutes of dialog were added but it made the film no less tedious.

d, William K. Howard; w, Marion Orth, S. K. Lauren, Katherine Hilliker, H. H. Caldwell (based on a story by Tristram Tupper); ph, Lucien Andriot; ed, Hilliker, Caldwell; song: "Christina" (Con Conrad, Sidney Mitchell, Archie Gottler).

Drama (PRL:A MPAA:NR)

CHRISTINA**
(1974, Can.) 98m New World/International Amusement Corp. c
Barbara Parkins (Christina/Kay), Peter Haskell (Simon Bruce), James McEachin (Donovan), Marlyn Mason (Girl), Barbara Gordon (Mrs. Brice), Audry Kniveton (Mme. Concordia), Wally McSween (Timothy Murphy), Mary Monks (Miss Cooper), Otto Lowy (Otto Wensal), Christine Hauff (Edith Wensal), Sharon Kirk (Eleanor), Scott Maitland (Archie), Jace Van Der Veen (Baldy), Allan Anderson (Employment Clerk), Leo Servo (Tony), Frank Adamson (Queenie's Barman), Susan Wright (Floozie), David G. Jones (Justice of the Peace), Thomas Hauff (Boy), The Fabulous Freaks (Transvestites), Terry Kelly (Passport Officer), Margo Pinvidic (Bank Cashier), Peter Plunkett Norris (Mr. Pierce), Marjorie Knowler (Mrs. Pierce), Terry Mulligan (Policeman), John Thomas (Heavy No. 1), Alex Green (Heavy No. 2).

Luscious Parkins offers unemployed Haskell $25,000 to marry her, but as he begins to fall in love with his in-name-only bride, she disappears. He tries to find her, but finds himself drawn deeper and deeper into a mysterious conspiracy. Some nice visual touches, but the story is hopelessly confused.

p, Trevor Wallace; d, Paul Krasny; w, Wallace; ph, Richard Glouner; m, Cyril Ornadel; ed, Jack McSweeny; prod d, Bob Linnell; art d, Cameron Porteous.

Crime (PR:C MPAA:PG)

CHRISTINE* (1959, Fr.) 100m Cinedis Films c
Romy Schneider (Christine), Alain Delon (Franz), Micheline Presle (Lena), Sophie Grimaldi (Mizzie), Fernand Ledoux (Weiring), Jacques Duby (Binder).

This is a story of a young lieutenant in turn-of-the-century Vienna, who loves an innocent young singer, Schneider. It ends in tragedy when he is killed in a duel over a married woman. A remake of a Max Ophuls film, LIEBELEI, which starred Romy's mother, Magda Schneider, the film is in the large category of remakes that fall far short of the original.

d,w, Pierre-Gaspard-Huit; w, Georges Neveux (based on a play by Arthur Schnitzler); ph, Christian Matras (Eastmancolor); ed, L. Hautecoeur.

Drama (PR:C MPAA:NR)

CHRISTINE* (1983) 116m COL c
Keith Gordon (Arnie Cunningham), John Stockwell (Dennis Guilder), Alexandra Paul (Leigh Cabot), Robert Prosky (Will Darnell), Harry Dean Stanton (Rudolph Junkins), Christine Belford (Regina Cunningham), Roberts Blossom (George LeBay), William Ostrander (Buddy), David Spielberg (Mr. Casey), Malcolm Danare (Moochie), Steven Tash (Rich), Stuart Charno (Vandenberg), Kelly Preston (Roseanne), Marc Poppel (Chuck), Robert Barnell (Michael Cunningham).

Slick, well-made, but strangely uninvolving horror film from John Carpenter about a killer Plymouth Fury car that has a will of its own. The first half of the film is strong and paints an insightful portrait of modern high school life as seen through the eyes of an unpopular nerd, Gordon, that eventually sets up his slow possession by the devil car

which becomes his symbol of status and independence. Unfortunately, the last half of the film degenerates into a tedious and repetitious car chase that sees the driverless(?) car running down all of Gordon's enemies (shades of THE CAR). Prosky is fine as the crotchety garage owner and Stanton is totally wasted in a thankless part that could have been played by an extra. The special effects of the car healing itself are impressive, but much too long. Basically, it just boils down to another frustratingly average adaptation of increasingly weak Stephen King novels that hit Hollywood like a bad rash in 1983.

p, Richard Kobritz; d, John Carpenter; w, Bill Phillips (based on the novel by Stephen King); ph, Donald M. Morgan (Panavision, Metrocolor); m, Carpenter, Alan Howarth; ed, Marion Rothman; art d, William Joseph Durrell; set d, William Joseph Durrell, Jr.; spec eff, Roy Arbogast.

Horror Cas. (PR:C-O MPAA:R)

CHRISTINE JORGENSEN STORY, THE* (1970) 98m UA c
John Hansen (George-Christine Jorgensen), Joan Tompkins (Aunt Thora), Quinn Redeker (Tom Crawford), John W. Himes (George Jorgensen, Sr.), Ellen Clark (Mrs. Florence Jorgensen), Rod McCary (Jess Wanner), Will Kuluva (Prof. Estabrook), Oscar Beregi (Dr. Victor Dahlman), Lynn Harper (Dolly), Trent Lehman (George at 7) Pamelyn Ferdin (Dolly as Child), Bill Erwin (Pastor), Joyce Meadows (Tani), Sondra Scott (Angela), Don Pierce (Jack), Elaine Joyce (Loretta), Eddie Frank (George as Child), Dee Carroll (Mrs. Whalstrom), Peter Bourne (Whalstrom).

This is supposed to be a serious look at the story of the first man to go to Denmark to have a sex change operation. However, the acting tends to lean toward a campiness that draws laughs in the wrong places. Born with three times the normal hormones, we see Hansen (Jorgensen) at seven years of age being picked on by other boys because he would rather play with dolls than footballs. The grown Hansen does a stint in the Army where he cringes at bayoneting dummies. He later has an unsatisfactory encounter with a prostitute. Eventually, as an advertising photographer, Hansen is hit upon by a homosexual account exec. He is so upset that he tries to jump off a bridge but is thwarted. Finally he goes to Denmark for the first sex-change operation. The movie comes in for a lot of laughs after the operation is performed and George becomes Christine, a name he adopted from a dead cousin. Hansen looks like a broad-shouldered queen in drag and nobody could ever buy him as a woman. This provokes a funny and unbelievable sub-plot when Redeker, playing a magazine writer, is supposed to fall in love with and seduces her-him(?).

p, Edward Small; d, Irving Rapper; w, Robert E. Kent, Ellis St. Joseph (based on the autobiography of Christine Jorgensen); ph, Jacques Marquette (DeLuxe-Color); m, Paul Sawtell, Bert Shefter; ed, Grant Whytock; art d, Frank Sylos; cos, Moss Mabry; spec eff, Roger George.

Biography/Drama (PR:O MPAA:R)

CHRISTINE KEELER AFFAIR, THE*½
(1964, Brit.) 90m Topaz Film Corp./JaGold Pictures bw
(AKA: THE KEELER AFFAIR, SCANDAL '64)
Yvonne Buckingham (Christine Keeler), John Drew Barrymore (Dr. Stephen Ward), Alicia Brandet (Mandy Rice-Davies), Mel Welles (Capt. Yevgeni Ivanov), Peter Prowse (Domaren), Mimi Heinrich (Marianne), Christine Keeler (Herself), Jimmy Moore, Gunnar Lemvigh, Carl Ottosen, Ole Ishoj, Bent Thalmay, Lise Henningsen, Anita Rieneck, Knud Hallest.

Opening with an interview with Keeler, herself barely out of prison at the time, the film moves on to show Buckingham coming to London, becoming a model and hostess, and meeting Brandet, who introduces her to Barrymore. Soon she is living with him in a platonic relationship. She leaves him to live with a West Indian musician. At a wild pool party she meets the British minister of war and the Russian naval attache, Welles. She begins sleeping with both, and when the disgruntled musician fires a few shots through her door, Scotland Yard is called in and soon the entire scandal breaks open. In the resulting chaos, the minister is forced to resign, Welles is sent back to the U.S.S.R., and Barrymore commits suicide. Buckingham goes to jail for nine months. A quickie exploitation film capitalizing on the still-fresh scandal, the movie was shot in Denmark and banned in England. Though not very good, the film does have some wild party scenes.

p, John Nasht; d, Robert Spafford; w, Matt White, Ronald Maxwell, Spafford; ph, Michel Rocca; m, Roger Connock, Roger Bourdin.

Biography (PR:O MPAA:NR)

CHRISTMAS CAROL, A*½** (1938) 68m MGM bw
Reginald Owen (Ebenezer Scrooge), Gene Lockhart (Bob Cratchit), Kathleen Lockhart (Mrs. Cratchit), Terry Kilburn (Tiny Tim), Barry Mackay (Fred), Lynne Carver (Bess), Leo G. Carroll (Marley's Ghost), Lionel Braham (Spirit of Christmas Present), Ann Rutherford (Spirit of Christmas Past), D'Arcy Corrigan (Spirit of Christmas Future), Ronald Sinclair (Young Scrooge), Charles Coleman (Charity Canvasser), Halliwell Hobbes (Vicar), Billy Bevan (Watch Officer).

Superb adaptation of the Dickens classic has Owen as the hard-hearted Scrooge in probably the best role of his long and distinguished career. Lockhart is terrific as the much-harassed Cratchit and the rest of the cast do honors to their historic parts. Although this wonderful story has been made many times, the Owen rendition of the skinflint-turned-Maecenas is the best and most believable, including the TV impersonation so wonderfully enacted by George C. Scott. Owens represents the essential Scrooge, never an introspective soul, whose discovery of his own past, his present, and future, is a singular revelation that brings about not a startling transformation of character but an emergence of a kindred soul that was waiting all along to struggle out of ledgerbooks and tally sheets. A great and eternally heart-warming film that can stand an appreciative viewing every year through every decade.

p, Joseph L. Mankiewicz; d, Edwin L. Marin; w, Hugo Butler (based on the story by Charles Dickens); ph, Sidney Wagner; m, Franz Waxman; ed, George Boemler; art d, Cedric Gibbons.

Fantasy (PR:AAA MPAA:NR)

CHRISTMAS CAROL, A** (1951, Brit.) 86m REN/UA bw

Alastair Sim *(Scrooge)*, Kathleen Harrison *(Mrs. Dilber)*, Jack Warner *(Mr. Jorkins)*, Michael Hordern *(Jacob Marley)*, Mervyn Johns *(Bob Cratchit)*, Hermione Baddeley *(Mrs. Cratchit)*, John Charlesworth *(Peter Cratchit)*, Glyn Dearman *(Tiny Tim)*, George Cole *(Scrooge as Young Man)*, Rona Anderson *(Alice)*, Carol Marsh *(Fan, Scrooge's Sister)*, Brian Worth *(Fred, Scrooge's Nephew)*, Olga Edwardes *(Fred's Wife)*, Roddy Hughes *(Mr. Fezziwig)*, Hattie Jacques *(Mrs. Fezziwig)*, Clifford Mollison *(Mr. Wilkins)*, Michael Dolan *(Spirit of the Past)*, Francis De Wolff *(Spirit of Present)*, C. Konarski *(Spirit of the Future)*, Ernest Thesiger *(Undertaker)*, Miles Malleson *(Old Joe)*, Louise Hampton *(Laundress)*, Noel Howlett *(First Collector)*, Fred Johnson *(Second Collector)*, Peter Bull *(First Business Man)*, Douglas Muir *(Second Business Man)*, Eliot Makeham *(Snedrig)*, Henry Hewitt *(Rosehed)*, Hugh Dempster *(Groper)*, Patrick McNee *(Young Marley)*.

A heavy-handed version of Dickens' classic Christmas tale. Little merit to this version of A CHRISTMAS CAROL, as the cast seems to sleepwalk through this story as if it were a children's Christmas pageant done year after year. The familiar story has tight-fisted Scrooge, Alastair Sim, visited by the usual three ghosts on Christmas Eve, causing him to make amends.

p, George Minter; d, Brian Desmond Hurst; w, Noel Langley (based on the story by Charles Dickens); ph, C. Pennington-Richards; m, Richard Addinsell; ed, Clive Donner.

Fantasy Cas. **(PR:AAA MPAA:NR)**

CHRISTMAS EVE**½ (1947, 90m UA bw (AKA: SINNER'S HOLIDAY)

George Raft *(Mario Torio)*, George Brent *(Michael Brooks)*, Randolph Scott *(Jonathan)*, Joan Blondell *(Ann Nelson)*, Virginia Field *(Claire)*, Dolores Moran *(Jean)*, Ann Harding *(Matilda Reid)*, Reginald Denny *(Phillip Hastings)*, Carl Harbord *(Dr. Doremus)*, Clarence Kolb *(Judge Alston)*, John Litel *(FBI Agent)*, Joe Sawyer *(Gimlet)*, Douglass Dumbrille *(Dr. Bunyan)*, Dennis Hoey *(Williams)*, Molly Lamont *(Harriett)*, Walter Sande *(Hood)*, Konstantin Shayne *(Reichman)*, Claire Whitney *(Dr. Bunyan's Wife)*, Andrew Tombes *(Auctioneer)*, Soledad Jimenez *(Rosita)*, Marie Blake *(Girl Reporter)*, Ernest Hilliard *(Assistant Bartender)*, Al Hill *(Bartender)*, John Indrisano *(Gateman)*, Edward Parks *(Drunk)*, Holly Bane *(Page Boy)*.

An omnibus film similar to TALES OF MANHATTAN, this holiday production has Harding as a wealthy spinster whose nephew, the avaricious Denny, is trying to take over her estate. A friendly judge decrees that if Harding can gather to her hearth the three foster children she has raised to help her retain her estate, he will postpone Denny's legal action. The remainder of the film deals with her search for the three missing boys, now grown to manhood and having pursued separate destinies. Scott is an alcoholic cowboy who gets mixed up in a baby racket. Brent is a wastrel who owes Denny a fortune in gambling debts, and Raft is a rich South American cafe owner who is wanted by authorities for a swindle Denny actually committed. After several adventures en route, the three manage to return to Harding on Christmas Eve to save the old homestead and expose the rotter Denny. Though episodic, the offbeat film offers some fine performances, witty dialog, and solid action with Raft emerging as the most sympathetic of the male trio.

p, Benedict Bogeaus; d, Edwin L. Marin; w, Laurence Stallings (based on stories by Stallings, Richard H. Landau, Robert Altman); ph, Gordon Avil; m, Heinz Roemheld; ed, James Smith; md, David Chudnow; art d, Ernst Fegte; set d, Eugene Redd.

Drama **(PR:A MPAA:NR)**

CHRISTMAS HOLIDAY*** (1944) 98m UNIV bw

Deanna Durbin *(Jackie Lamont, Abigail Martin)*, Gene Kelly *(Robert Manette)*, Richard Whorf *(Simon Fenimore)*, Dean Harens *(Charles Mason)*, Gladys George *(Valerie de Merode)*, Gale Sondergaard *(Mrs. Manette)*, David Bruce *(Gerald Tyler)*.

Off-beat casting and a sharp Mankiewicz script take this a cut above many of the *film noir* pieces of the late 1930s and early 1940s. Harens is going home to San Francisco for Christmas but a rainstorm causes the young Army man to stay over in the Crescent City of New Orleans. He meets Durbin, a cynical 22-year-old singer, in a tacky nightclub. They go to church at midnight and she pours her heart out to him. She is married to Kelly who is in jail for having murdered a bookie. Flashback, and we see her meet Kelly at a concert where he is all charm. Kelly and his mother, Sondergaard, are the final members of a well-known and once-wealthy Louisiana clan. Durbin marries him, but soon discovers he is a rat with a temper like a caged mongoose. She senses Kelly and Sondergaard are attempting to conceal something, then learns of the murder. Kelly is quickly dispatched to jail and Sondergaard, who had warned Durbin about her son, tells her off for having married him in the first place! Durbin finishes her tale and returns to the club to find that Kelly has escaped from prison and is holding reporter Whorf hostage. Kelly sees the young Army man and is prepared to kill them both but the New Orleans police arrive before he can do any damage and Kelly is shot and mortally wounded. He dies in Durbin's arms and we can only hope that she wound up with Harens after the fadeout. What a strange movie this was. Durbin was Universal's golden girl and totally out of character for the part of a downtrodden singer, yet she managed to pull it off. Even more out of line was Kelly as the villain. He had done a ne'er-do-well in PAL JOEY but this was much more powerful and he was allowed to act without singing or dancing. Kelly wasn't a huge star at the time and thus was available for loan-out. After the success of COVER GIRL, that would never happen again. Durbin left the screen three years later but said she always felt this was the best acting she ever did. She didn't want to sing at all in the movie but they prevailed on her to do "Always" by Irving Berlin and a tune especially written by 34-year-old Frank Loesser, who was writing songs for his twenty-ninth film. It was called "Spring Will Be A Little Late This Year" and remains a standard. To anyone who read the Maugham novel, this bore little resemblance, as the novel was replete with incest, homosexuality, and prostitution. Because of the Hollywood production code, they were forced to make many compromises, but somehow managed to turn out a fine film.

p, Felix Jackson; d, Robert Siodmak; w, Herman J. Mankiewicz (based on the novel by W. Somerset Maugham); ph, Woody Bredell; m, Hans J. Salter; ed, Ted Kent; art d, John B. Goodman, Robert Clatworthy.

Mystery **(PR:A MPAA:NR)**

CHRISTMAS IN CONNECTICUT***½ (1945) 102m WB/FN bw
(GB: INDISCRETION)

Barbara Stanwyck *(Elisabeth Lane)*, Dennis Morgan *(Jefferson Jones)*, Sydney Greenstreet *(Alexander Yardley)*, Reginald Gardiner *(John Sloan)*, S. Z. Sakall *(Felix Bassenak)*, Robert Shayne *(Dudley Beecham)*, Una O'Connor *(Norah)*, Frank Jenks *(Sinkewicz)*, Joyce Compton *(Mary Lee)*, Dick Elliott *(Judge Crothers)*, Betty Alexander *(Nurse Smith)*, Allen Fox *(Postman)*, Lillian Bronson *(Prim Secretary)*, Charles Sherlock *(Bartender)*, Emmett Smith *(Sam)*, Arthur Aylesworth *(Sleigh Driver)*, Jody Gilbert *(Mrs. Gerseg)*, Charles Arnt *(Mr. Higgenbottom)*, Fred Kelsey *(Harper)*, Walter Baldwin *(Potter)*, Jack Mower *(1st State Trooper)*, John Dehner *(2nd State Trooper)*, Marie Blake *(Mrs. Wright)*, Olaf Hytten *(Elkins)*.

A hilarious farce is made even funnier by scheming Stanwyck, a successful columnist for a housekeeping magazine who pretends to be a happy housewife who knows everything about wifely duties. She is compelled to take in a Navy hero, Morgan, for the holidays, a promotion gimmick concocted by her hoodwinked publisher Greenstreet. There's one thing wrong with the plan: Stanwyck does not have the country home she writes about, nor is she a cook, nor is she married. In desperation, Stanwyck convinces Gardiner to play the role of hubby, rents a rustic house, and brings in "Cuddles" Sakall, a world-famous chef, to teach her kitchen cuisine, all to impress the war hero. To complicate matters, Greenstreet invites himself to view the domestic scene and the machinations Stanwyck goes through for Greenstreet and Morgan are both frantic and often side-splitting. Her attempt to make flapjacks, nearly destroying the kitchen in the process, is a priceless scene. One sham piles upon another until she is exposed as a fraud, but it doesn't matter to Morgan, who by then is in love with her and she with him. Greenstreet also forgives her and keeps her on staff. The action is lively from director Godfrey and Stanwyck proves her considerable flair for comedy. A wonderful holiday romp.

p, William Jacobs; d, Peter Godfrey; w, Lionel Houser, Adele Commandini (based on a story by Aileen Hamilton); ph, Carl Guthrie; m, Frederick Hollander; ed, Frank Magee; md, Leo F. Forbstein; art d, Stanley Fleischer; set d, Casey Roberts; cos, Edith Head.

Comedy **(PR:AAA MPAA:NR)**

CHRISTMAS IN JULY***½ (1940) 66m PAR bw

Dick Powell *(Jimmy MacDonald)*, Ellen Drew *(Betty Casey)*, Raymond Walburn *(Mr. Maxford)*, Alexander Carr *(Mr. Schindel)*, William Demarest *(Mr. Bildocker)*, Ernest Truex *(Mr. Baxter)*, Franklin Pangborn *(Radio Announcer)*, Harry Hayden *(Mr. Waterbury)*, Rod Cameron *(Dick)*, Michael Morris *(Tom)*, Harry Rosenthal *(Harry)*, Georgia Cain *(Mrs. MacDonald)*, Ferike Boros *(Mrs. Schwartz)*, Torben Meyer *(Mr. Schmidt)*, Julius Tannen *(Mr. Zimmerman)*, Alan Bridge *(Mr. Hillbeiner)*, Lucille Ward *(Mrs. Casey)*, Kay Stewart *(Secretary)*, Vic Potel *(Davenola Salesman)*, Byron Foulger *(Mr. Jenkins)*, Arthur Hoyt *(Mild Gentleman)*, Robert Warwick *(Large Gentleman)*, Jimmy Conlin *(Thin, Sour Gentleman)*, Dewey Robinson *(Large, Rough Gentleman)*, Frank Moran *(Patrolman Murphy)*, Georges Renavent *(Sign Painter)*, Preston Sturges *(Man at Shoeshine Stand)*, Snowflake *(Porter)*

Hilarious Sturges film has Powell the victim of an office joke making him the winner of $25,000 in a slogan contest. He goes on a credit spending spree, then learns he hasn't won after all. His dejection is short-lived, however, when he is announced as the actual winner of the contest. Not to be missed. This was director Sturges' second film after his smash hit THE GREAT McGINTY, one of equally zany humor and unpredictable plot twists and turns. Throughout the 1940s Sturges was looked upon as a genius whose common-touch approach made him an overnight stellar director, yet by the following decade he had suddenly gone dry (or was dumped by most of the studios after his constant arguing with production heads) and he became an expatriate in France.

p, Paul Jones; d&w, Preston Sturges; ph, Victor Milner; ed, Ellsworth Hoagland.

Comedy **(PR:A MPAA:NR)**

CHRISTMAS KID, THE**½
(1968, U.S., Span.) 90m Producers Releasing Organization c

Jeffrey Hunter *(Joe Novak)*, Louis Hayward *(Mike Culligan)*, Gustavo Rojo *(Mayor Louis Carrillo)*, Perla Cristal *(Marie Lefleur)*, Luis Prendes *(George Perkins)*, Reginald Gilliam *(Dr. Fred Carter)*, Fernando Hilbeck *(Jud Walters)*, Jack Taylor *(John Novak)*, Eric Chapman *(Percy Martin)*, Dennis Kilbane *(Luke Acker)*, Russ Stoddard *(Pete Prima)*, Carl Rapp *(Sheriff Anderson)*, Guillermo Mendez *(Karl Humber)*, Alvaro De Luna *(Burt Froelich)*, Alejandra Nilo *(Marika Novak)*.

This is one of the best of the string of American-financed westerns made in Spain. Hunter, in the title role, is the mixed-up kid who first becomes a hired gunman for gambler Hayward, who was lured to town by the discovery of copper. He turns to the side of law and order when Hayward begins to take over the town. This film is as much a psychological character study as an action film.

p&d, Sidney W. Pink; w, James Henaghan, R. Rivero; ph, Manolo Hernandez San Juan (Eastmancolor, Movielab); m, Fernando Garcia Morcillo; ed, Anthony Ramirez, John Horvath.

Western **(PR:C MPAA:NR)**

CHRISTMAS STORY, A**** (1983) MGM/UA c

Mellinda Dillon *(Mother)*, Darren McGavin *(Old Man)*, Peter Billingsley *(Ralphie)*, Ian Petrella *(Randy)*, Scott Schwartz *(Flick)*, R. D. Robb *(Schwartz)*, Tedde Moore *(Miss Shields)*, Yano Anaya *(Grover)*, Zack Ward *(Scot)*, Jeff Gillen *(Santa Claus)*, Colin Fox *(Ming)*, Paul Hubbard *(Flash Gordon)*, Les Carlson *(Tree Man)*, Jim Hunter *(Freight Man)*, Patty Johnson *(Head Elf)*, Drew Hocevar *(Male Elf)*, David Svoboda *(Goggles)*, Dwayne McLean *(Black Bart)*, Helen E. Kaider *(Wicked Witch)*, John Wong *(Chinese Father)*, Rocco Bellusci *(Street Kid)*, Tommy Wallace *(Boy in School)*, Johan Sebastian Wong, Fred Lee, Dan Ma *(Waiters)*.

Somehow usually tasteless director Bob Clark, whose specialty was fairly vile exploitation movies (PORKY'S [1981] and the even worse PORKY'S II: THE NEXT DAY [1983]), managed to make a totally charming and lovable Christmas film. Based on the short stories of Midwestern humorist Jean Shepherd (who also narrates in the first person), A CHRISTMAS STORY is an episodic comedy set in the 1940s about the family life of young Billingsley as Christmas approaches. The plot loosely revolves around Billingsley's desire for a Red Ryder BB gun for Christmas that his mother (Dillon) has forbidden because "You'll shoot your eye out, Ralph." Among Shepherd's childhood musings are his narrow escapes from the neighborhood bullies, the old man's (McGavin) battles with the smoke-belching furnace, Mom's attempts to get little brother Petrella to eat, McGavin's infatuation with an obnoxious lamp that looks like a woman's leg, and a nightmarish visit with Santa at the local department store. The cast is wonderful—especially McGavin—the laughs nonstop, and the whole thing deserves to become a Christmastime classic. A must see.

p, Rene Dupont, Bob Clark; d, Clark; w, Jean Shepherd, Leigh Brown, Clark (based on the novel *In God We Trust, All Others Pay Cash* by Shepherd); ph, Reginald H. Morris; m, Carl Ziffrer, Paul Zaza; ed, Stan Cole; art d, Gavin Mitchel; cos, Mary E. McLeod.

Comedy **(PR:A MPAA:PG)**

CHRISTMAS THAT ALMOST WASN'T, THE*
(1966, Ital.) 95m Childhood Production c
(IL NATALE CHE QUASI NON FU)

Rossano Brazzi *(Phineas T. Prune)*, Paul Tripp *(Sam Whipple)*, Alberto Rabagliati *(Santa Claus)*, Lydia Brazzi *(Mrs. Santa Claus)*, Mischa Auer *(Jonathan)*, John Karlsen *(Blossom)*, Sonny Fox *(Department Store Owner)*.

Children's film stars Rossano Brazzi as an old skinflint who tries to evict Santa and Mrs. Claus for not paying rent on the North Pole. Children of the world respond by sending Santa their pennies, and the Clauses are saved. Pretty boring stuff for all but the most undiscriminating kiddies. Songs: "Christmas Is Coming," "The Christmas That Almost Wasn't," "Hustle Bustle," "I'm Bad," "Kids Get All the Breaks," "The Name of the Song Is Prune," "Nothing To Do But Wait," "Santa Claus (Round)," "Time For Christmas," "What Are Children Like When They're Fast Asleep?" "Why Can't Every Day Be Christmas?" (Ray Carter, Paul Tripp).

p, Barry B. Yellen; d, Rossano Brazzi; w, Paul Tripp; ph, Alvaro Mancori (Eastmancolor); m, Bruno Nicolai; ed, Maurizio Lucidi; md, Nicolai; cos, A. Danilo Zanetti.

Juvenile/Musical **(PR:A MPAA:NR)**

CHRISTMAS TREE, THE** (1966, Brit.) 59m Augusta/CFF c

William Burleigh *(Gary)*, Anthony Honour *(Sam)*, Kate Nicholls *(Jane)*, Anthony Baird *(Father)*, Doreen Keogh *(Mother)*, Brian Blessed *(Policeman)*, Sydney Bromley *(Motorist)*, Oliver McGreevy *(Baldy)*.

Burleigh, Honour, and Nicholls are three London children who have a series of adventures as they cross the city bringing a Christmas tree to a hospital. Okay, if undistinguished, children's film.

p, Ed Harper; d, James Clark; w, Clark, Michael Barnes (based on a story by Harper).

Children **(PR:AA MPAA:NR)**

CHRISTMAS TREE, THE**
(1969, Fr.) 110m Walter Reade/Continental c

William Holden *(Laurent)*, Virna Lisi *(Catherine)*, Andre Bourvil *(Verdun)*, Brook Fuller *(Pascal)*, Madeleine Damien *(Marinette)*, Friedrich Ledebur *(Vernet)*, Mario Feliciani *(The Doctor)*.

Terence Young, who's been known to be guilty of screen overindulgence, continues his tradition, as he wrote the screenplay and directed this teary story based on Michel Bataille's novel. Filmed in Paris, Corsica, and Nice, it's the tale of a father, Holden, who watches his son, Fuller, die of radiation poisoning. They're both fishing near a beach when an airplane carrying nuclear weapons explodes. Fuller is poisoned by the radiation and this causes leukemia. Holden, who had been swimming underwater, is spared. He takes his rapidly dying son back to his home in France to be ministered to by his girl friend, Lisi, and his old war pal, Bouvril. The remainder of the film is waiting for Fuller to die. The lad loves wolves so Holden and Bouvril steal some from a Paris zoo. The boy dies on Christmas eve and Holden discovers his body, presents opened and wolves standing guard. Lots of far and near-fetched sequences mar the picture. It was a strange selection for Holden after the success of THE WILD BUNCH. Lisi is the best element of the film; she underplays so well that we can get lost in her performance. The political overtones are such that the heavy-handedness blurs over the basic plot.

p, Robert Dorfmann; d&w, Terence Young (based on the novel *L'Arbre de Noel* by Michel Bataille); ph, Henri Alekan (Movielab Color); m, Georges Auric; ed, Johnny Dwyre; set d, Fernand Bernardi, Robert Turlure; art d, Tony Roman, Eugene Roman, Robert Andre; cos, Tanine Autre, spec eff, Karl Baumgartner.

Drama **Cas.** **(PR:A MPAA:G)**

CHRISTOPHER BEAN* (1933) 90m MGM bw

Marie Dressler *(Abby)*, Lionel Barrymore *(Doctor)*, Beulah Bondi *(Wife)*, Helen Shipman *(Ada)*, Helen Mack *(Susan)*, Jean Hersholt *(Rosen)*, H. B. Warner *(Davenport)*, Russell Hardie *(Warren Creamer)*, George Coulouris *(Tallent)*, Ellen Lowe *(Maid)*.

Mediocre comedy about greed, with slapstick sequences getting in the way of what little story there is. Lionel Barrymore, as usual, is very good. It was one of the few times in her illustrious career that Marie Dressler, who was to die six months after this film's release, received poor notices for her acting.

p, Harry Rapf; d, Sam Wood; w, Sylvia Thalberg, Larry Johnson (based on the play "The Late Christopher Bean" by Sidney Howard, from Rene Fauchois' "Prenez Garde a la Peinture"); ph, William Daniels; ed, Hugh Wynn.

Comedy **(PR:A MPAA:NR)**

CHRISTOPHER COLUMBUS½** (1949, Brit.) 104m Rank/UNIV c

Fredric March *(Christopher Columbus)*, Florence Eldridge *(Queen Isabella)*, Francis L. Sullivan *(Francisco de Bobadilla)*, Kathleen Ryan *(Beatriz)*, Derek Bond *(Diego de Arana)*, Nora Swinburne *(Juana de Torres)*, Abraham Sofaer *(Luis de Santangel)*, Linden Travers *(Beatriz de Peraza)*, James Robertson Justice *(Martin Pinzon)*, Dennis Vance *(Francisco Pinzon)*, Richard Aherne *(Vicente Pinzon)*, Felix Aylmer *(Father Perez)*, Francis Lister *(King Ferdinand)*, Edward Rigby *(Pedro)*, Niall MacGinnis *(Juan de la Cosa)*, Ralph Truman *(Captain)*, Ronald Adam *(Talavera)*, Guy Le Feuvre *(Admiral)*, Lyn Evans *(Lope)*, David Cole *(Columbus' Son)*, Hugh Pryse *(Almoner)*, R. Stuart Lindsell *(Prior)*.

Essentially lifeless story of The Great Navigator starring Mr. and Mrs. Fredric March. Lots of costumes, backstage intrigues at the Spanish court, many extras, and what would appear to be all the elements of a successful movie. But making a film is like baking a cake—if you have all the right ingredients and the wrong recipe, it'll come out flat. And the same thing happens if you have a great recipe and use the wrong chocolate or nonfat milk instead of cream . . . you get the idea. Such was the case with this film. Fully half of it took place in Isabella's court and by the time we get to the good stuff our yawns have superseded our interest. March and son, Cole, want to meet Isabella (Eldridge). They ask Aylmer, a priest, to arrange it. Sullivan has Isabella's ear at court and wants to keep Chris away, so he conspires to keep Columbus at arm's length, claiming that the idea of finding a passage to the new world is foolhardy. Eldridge must be a Libra because she can't make up her mind, so Columbus and son (who is never identified by name) leave and then are called back by the Queen's messenger. The voyage of the Nina, the Pinta, and the Santa Maria looks like a bunch of miniatures and the travails of the sailors are ho-hum. They discover America, have a triumphant return to Spain, then out to sea again, a fall from favor, and eventual obscurity. Which is exactly what happened to this very expensive movie. The dialog is stiff, the actors stiffer, and the whole thing lumbers along like a fat dog after a huge meal.

p, A. Frank Bundy; d, David MacDonald; w, Sydney and Muriel Box, Cyril Roberts; ph, Stephen Dade, David Harcourt (Technicolor); m, Arthur Bliss; ed, V. Sagovsky.

Historical/Biography **(PR:A MPAA:NR)**

CHRISTOPHER STRONG*** (1933) 77m RKO bw

Katharine Hepburn *(Cynthia)*, Colin Clive *(Christopher Strong)*, Billie Burke *(Elaine)*, Helen Chandler *(Monica)*, Ralph Forbes *(Harry Rawlinson)*, Jack La Rue *(Carlo)*, Irene Browne *(Carrie)*, Gwendolyn Logan *(Bradford)*, Desmond Roberts *(Bryce Mercer)* Agostino Borgato *(Fortune Teller)*, Margaret Lindsay *(Girl at Party)*, Donald Stewart *(Mechanic)*, Zena Savina *(Second Maid)*.

After scoring so strongly in BILL OF DIVORCEMENT, Hepburn took it on the chin from many of the critics for her second feature, CHRISTOPHER STRONG. The reviews were equally divided; those who hated her in her debut loved this film and the reverse was also true. Hepburn is Lady Cynthia Darrington, a high-spirited Amelia Earhart aviatrix-type who is so busy piloting that she has no time for men and is still a virgin. In a 1930s "cute-meet" she is introduced to Colin Clive, a happily married man who has never cheated on his wife. His life has been deeply colored by his political career and he has had no time for dallying, not that he'd want to. Then he meets Hepburn and the die is cast. Passion flames across the screen and they are inextricably drawn to each other. They both know it's wrong and that many lives will be affected, but they can't stop their magnetism. Eventually, they realize it would be best if they separated and they do, but later, while she's on a round-the-world flight and he's in New York on business, they meet and the electricity flows once more. They make their commitment to each other and she promises to stay out of the air. Then she learns that she is pregnant. There's no other way out of the situation than suicide, she feels. So she accepts a challenge to break the altitude record, takes the plane up six miles or so, removes her oxygen mask, and deliberately tailspins to her death. Not one of the funniest movies of the year, CHRISTOPHER STRONG was marred by the male lead's casting. Clive never could convince us that vibrant Hepburn would go for such a stick. To sacrifice herself for such a dull stiff was totally unbelievable, as were a few of the other motivations. This was Arzner's eleventh directorial assignment and she was only 33 years of age.

p, David O. Selznick, Pandro S. Berman; d, Dorothy Arzner; w, Zoe Akins (based on the novel by Gilbert Frankau); ph, Bert Glennon; m, Max Steiner; ed, Arthur Roberts; art d, Van Nest Polglase; cos, Howard Greer; spec eff, Vernon Walker.

Romance **(PR:C MPAA:NR)**

CHROME AND HOT LEATHER** (1971) 95m AIP c

William Smith *(T.J.)*, Tony Young *(Mitch)*, Michael Haynes *(Casey)*, Peter Brown *(Al)*, Marvin Gaye *(Jim)*, Michael Stearns *(Hank)*, Kathy Baumann *(Susan)*, Wes Bishop *(Sheriff)*, Herb Jeffries *(Ned)*, Bob Pickett *(Sweet Willy)*, George Carey *(Lt. Reardon)*, Marland Proctor *(Capt. Barnes)*, Cherie Moor *(Kathy)*, Ann Marie *(Helen)*, Robert Ridgely *(Sgt. Mack)*, Lee Parrish *(NCO Bartender)*, Larry Bishop *(Gabe)*.

A film in the classic motorcycle gang genre, but with a tongue-in-cheek attitude about itself and motorcycle films. This film features Gaye in his first dramatic role. Green Beret sergeant Young learns that his beautiful fiancee, Moor, has been killed in an auto accident involving a motorcycle gang. Bent on revenge, he enlists the help of his fellow sergeants, Gaye, Brown, and Stearns to track down the guilty gang whom he knows only as "the Devils." That was the last thing Moor said before she died. The story takes a satiric tone when the four sergeants buy bikes and try to learn to ride them and act as gang members. They don't know a thing about motorcycles and end up flopping and falling all over the place as they learn. However, they get their disguise together, find "the Devils," and corner them in a cavern. They use mortars and tear gas, Green Beret-style, to flush the gang out.

p, Wes Bishop; d, Lee Frost (Movielab Color); w, Michael Haynes, David Neibel, Don Tait (based on a story by Haynes, Neibel); m, Porter Jordan; ed, Alfonso P. La Mastra, Edward Shryver.

Adventure **(PR:O MPAA:GP)**

CHRONICLE OF ANNA MAGDALENA BACH**½

(1968, Ital., Ger.) 93m Franz-Seitz Filmproduktion-Kuratorium Junger Deutscher Film Hessisches Rundfunk-Straub-Huillet-Filmfonds-Telepool-IDI Cinematografica-RAI/New York Films c

Gustav Leonhardt (Johann Sebastian Bach), Christiane Lang (Anna Magdalena Bach), Paolo Carlini (Hoelzel), Ernst Castelli (Steger), Hans-Peter Boye (Born), Joachim Wolf (Rector), Rainer Kirchner (Superintendent), Eckart Bruntjen (Prefect Kittler), Walter Peters (Prefect Krause), Kathrien Leonhardt (Catherina Dorothea Bach), Anja Fahrmann (Regine Susanna Bach), Katja Drewanz (Christine Sophie Henrietta Bach), Bob van Aspern(Johann Elias Bach), Andreas Pangritz (Wilhelm Friedemann Bach), Bernd Weikl (Singer In Cantata No. 205), Wolfgang Schone (Singer In Cantata No. 82), Karl-Heinz Lampe (Singer In Cantata No. 42), Nicholaus Harnoncourt (Prince of Anhalt-Coethen), Karl-Heinz Klein (Bass Voice for Duet In Cantata No. 140), Bernhard Wehle (Soprano Voice In Cantata No. 140), Christa Degler (Voice of Anna Magdalena Bach In Cantata No. 244).

Lang, the impoverished widow of Leonhardt, looks back over her life with the strong-willed composer, a life almost grim. In fact, the only time he speaks to her is when he reads her a letter he has written complaining to some government official. Although there are some sumptuous visuals, the film is largely static, with vast chunks of it devoted to some very good performances of a number of Bach's works. Fans of baroque music should enjoy it, others may be bored. Musical selections: Brandenburg Concerto No. 5; Prelude 6 from the "Little Clavier Book for Wilhelm Friedemann Bach," Minuet 2 of the Suite in D Minor from the "Little Clavier Book for Anna Magdalena Bach," Sonata No. 2 in D Major for Viola and Harpsichord, Partita in E Minor from the "Little Clavier Book for Anna Magdalena Bach," Trio-sonata No. 2 in C Minor, Magnificat in D Major, "St. Mathew Passion," Prelude in B Minor for Organ, Mass in B Minor, Ascension Oratorio, Clavier-Uebung Italian Concerto, "Goldberg Variations," "Musical Offering," "Art of the Fugue," Chorale for Organ, Cantatas No. 205, 198, 244, 42, 215, 140, 82.

p, Gian Vittorio Baldi; d, Jean-Marie Straub; w, Straub, Daniele Huillet; ph, Ugo Piccone; m, Johann Sebastian Bach; ed, Huillet; prod d, Huillet; orch, Concentus Musicus (Vienna); choir, Hanover Boys Choir; choir d, Heinz Hennig.

Biography (PR:A-C MPAA:NR)

CHRONOPOLIS***½

(1982, Fr.) 70m Productions du Cirque-INA-AAA c

Amazing 3-D animation feature tells the story of a city in the far-off future, whose inhabitants, bored beyond belief, begin to manipulate time itself for their own amusement. Polish-born animator Kamler spent five years working almost single-handedly to produce this marvel of design and intelligence out of clay and fabric. The most sophisticated piece of equipment used was a camera dating from 1920. A must-see for fans of science fiction and animation.

p,d,w,ph, animation, prod d, Piotr Kamler; graphics, Diane Chretien, Maria Tatarczuk, Babette Vimenet; voice-over, Michel Lonsdale.

Science Fiction (PR:A-C MPAA:NR)

CHU CHIN CHOW**

(1934, Brit.) 93m GAU bw

George Robey (Ali Baba), Fritz Kortner (Abu Hassan), Anna May Wong (Zahrat), John Garrick (Nur-al-din), Pearl Argyle (Marjanah), Dennis Hoey (Rakham), Sidney Fairbrother (Mahbubah), Lawrence Hanray (Kasim Baba), Frank Cochrane (Mustafa), Thelma Tuson (Alcolom), Kyoshi Takase (Entertainer), Francis L. Sullivan (Caliph), Jetsam (Abdullah).

Musical retelling of Ali Baba and the Forty Thieves is well done if a bit slow. Jetsam, the best singer in the film, is half of the music hall team of Flotsam and Jetsam.

p, Michael Balcon; d, Walter Forde; w, Sidney Gilliat, L. DuGarde Peach, Edward Knoblock (from original musical by Oscar Asche and Frederic Norton); ph, B. Greenbaum; m, Norton; md, Louis Levy; ch, Anton Dolin; m/l, Norton.

Musical (PR:A MPAA:NR)

CHU CHU AND THE PHILLY FLASH**

(1981) 100m FOX c

Alan Arkin (Flash), Carol Burnett (Emily), Jack Warden (Commander), Danny Aiello (Johnson), Adam Arkin (Charlie), Danny Glover (Morgan), Sid Haig (Vince), Vincent Schiavelli (B.J.), Ruth Buzzi (Consuelo), Vito Scotti (Vittorio), Lou Jacobi (Landlord), Barbara Dana (Betty), Scott Beach (Harry), Geoff Hoyle (Clem), Morgan Upton (Butts), Neile McQueen (Car Woman), Tony Arkin (Puppeteer), Francine Lembi (Poet), Dabbs Greer (Wally), John Steadman (Snyder), Jerry Anderson (Mr. Sitro), Arnold Johnson (Bum), Ray Reinhardt (Russian), Sammy Warren, Steven Hirsch (Cat Men), Jennifer Ann Lee (Ticket Lady), Michael Grodenchik (Frankie), Valerie Caplan (Little Girl), Matthew Hautau (Little Boy), Matthew Arkin (Passerby), Jim Haynie, Eugene G. Choy, Ralph Chesse (Hot Dog Men), Jeanne Lauren, Carl Arena, Daniel Forrest (Mimes).

This must have sounded great around the producer's conference table—Arkin as an ex-Phillies relief pitcher who has been drunk for the last twenty years and Burnett as a failed entertainer working the streets with her one-woman band act. Even some of the jokes they tossed around must have played well in the board room. Unfortunately, it all fell flat on the screen. The unlikely duo both spot a briefcase simultaneously and both lay claim to it. This forces them to get together and the rest of the picture has to do with her keeping him from drinking, then returning the goods, then falling in love. It would have made a fair TV movie but as a feature it's inadequate on most levels. The stars do what they can with the material but Arkin's wife, the screenwriter, should have stayed out of it in favor of someone who might have been more objective. Some fine character people are included (Buzzi, Scotti, Jacobi, Warden, et al.) but even they seem uncomfortable with a haphazard script under Rich's overdone direction.

p, Jay Weston; d, David Lowell Rich; w, Barbara Dana (based on a story by Henry Barrow); ph, Victor J. Kemper (DeLuxe Color); m, Pete Rugolo; ed, Argyle Nelson; art d, Daniel Lomino; cos, Ron Talsky; ch, Don Crichton.

Comedy Cas. (PR:A MPAA:PG)

CHUBASCO*½

(1968) 99m WB-Seven Arts c

Richard Egan (Sebastian), Christopher Jones (Chubasco), Susan Strasberg (Bunny), Ann Sothern (Angela), Simon Oakland (Laurindo), Audrey Totter (Theresa), Preston Foster (Nick), Peter Whitney (Matt), Edward Binns (Judge North), Joe De Santis (Benito), Norman Alden (Frenchy), Stuart Moss (Les), Ron Rich (Juno), Milton Frome (Police Sergeant).

A typical story of a wayward youth who tries to go straight is made more intriguing by its setting, the San Diego tuna fishing industry. There is a strong youth-vs.-age conflict between Jones, who joins the tuna fleet rather than be thrown into jail, and Egan, who plays the disapproving father of the Portuguese-American girl he loves. Jones tries to do well and straighten out his life, but there are people who would stop him at every turn. The film was produced by actor William Conrad.

p, William Conrad; d&w, Allen H. Miner; ph, Louis Jennings, Paul Ivano (Panavision, Technicolor); m, William Lava; ed, John W. Holmes; art d, Howard Hollander; m/l, Conrad, Gordon Jenkins.

Drama (PR:A MPAA:NR)

CHUKA**

(1967) 105m PAR c

Rod Taylor (Chuka), Ernest Borgnine (Sgt. Otto Hansbach), John Mills (Col. Stuart Valois), Luciana Paluzzi (Veronica Kleitz), James Whitmore (Trent), Angela Dorian (Helena Chavez), Louis Hayward (Maj. Benson), Michael Cole (Pvt. Spivey), Hugh Reilly (Capt. Carrol), Barry O'Hara (Slim), Joseph Sirola (Baldwin), Marco Antonio (Hanu), Gerald York (Lt. Daly), Herlinda Del Carmen (Indian Girl), Lucky Carson (Stage Driver).

This film is a well-paced western that suffers from the cliches of the genre. The plot surrounds the happenings in a frontier fort the night before it is razed by Indians. Taylor plays the title role, a wandering gunfighter who meanders into the fort on the fateful day. He meets Mills, the block-headed English commandant of the fort, Borgnine, the tough Sergeant, Whitmore, the gruff scout, and Paluzzi, the loved one he's been parted from for so long, only to be reunited in the shadow of death. A stock list of characters, but pulled off well with fine performances. And then there are the Indians who, for once, behave sensibly by attacking at night as they massacre all the inhabitants of the fort.

p, Rod Taylor, Jack Jason; d, Gordon Douglas; w, Richard Jessup (based on a novel by Jessup); ph, Harold Stine (Pathecolor); m, Leith Stevens; ed, Robert Wyman; cos, Edith Head.

Western (PR:C MPAA:NR)

CHUMP AT OXFORD, A**½

(1940) 63m UA bw

Stan Laurel, Oliver Hardy (Themselves), Forrester Harvey (Meredith), Wilfred Lucas (Dean Williams), Forbes Murray (Banker), Frank Baker (Dean's Servant), Eddie Borden (Ghost), Gerald Fielding, Gerald Rogers, Victor Kendall, Charles Hall, Peter Cushing (Students), Rex Lease (Bank Robber), Stanley Blystone (Officer).

Stanley suffers a blow to the head and becomes an aristocratic Englishman, giving the boys a chance to practice their mayhem on the other side of the Atlantic. Not bad, though they're starting to show their ages.

p, Hal Roach; d, Alfred Goulding; w, Charles Rogers, Felix Adler, Harry Langdon; ph, Art Lloyd; m, Marvin Hatley; ed, Bert Jordan.

Comedy Cas. (PR:A MPAA:NR)

CHURCH MOUSE, THE**

(1934, Brit.) 76m WB/FN bw

Laura la Plante (Betty Miller), Ian Hunter (Jonathan Steele), Edward Chapman (Wormwood), Jane Carr (Sylvia James), Clifford Heatherley (Sir Oswald Bottomley), John Batten (Geoffrey Steele), Gibb McLaughlin (Stubbings), Monty Banks (Harry Blump).

Average Cinderella tale featuring La Plante as a dowdy secretary who eventually blossoms into a ravishing beauty after working for big-time banker Hunter.

p, Irving Asher; d, Monty Banks; w, W. Scott Darling, Tom Geraghty (based on the play by Ladislas Fodor and Paul Frank).

Romance (PR:A MPAA:NR)

CHUSHINGURA***½

(1963, Jap.) 115m Toho/Berkeley Cinema Guild c (AKA: 47 SAMURAI, LOYAL 47 RONIN)

Koshiro Matsumoto (Kuranosuke Oishi), Yuzo Kayama (Takuminokami Asano), Chusha Ichikawa (Kouzuke Kira), Toshiro Mifune (Genba Tawaraboshi), Yoko Tsukasa (Yozenin), Setsuko Hara (Riku), Tatsuya Mihashi(Yasubei Horibe), Yosuke Natsuki (Kinemon Okano), Ichiro Arishima (Denpachiro Tamon), Norihei Miki (Gayboy Geisha), Frankie Sakai (Carpenter Goro), Keiju Kobayashi (Lord Awaji), Yuriko Hoshi (Otsuya), Yumi Shirakawa (Ume), Kumi Mizuno (Saho), Akira Takarada (Gunpei Takada), Takashi Shimura (Hyobe Chishaka), Michiyo Aratama.

Kayama is an honest Japanese noble constantly harassed for bribes by his supervisor, Ichikawa. Goaded beyond endurance, Kayama draws his sword and wounds Ichikawa. Kayama is ordered to commit hara kiri, an order he fulfills. His forty-seven samurai retainers swear to avenge their master's death, but, as they are being closely watched, they split up and lead various lives while plotting and waiting for their chance. After twenty-one months, they obtain the layout of Ichikawa's castle, form their final plans, and attack. Ichikawa is decapitated and the people hail the samurai as heroes. They are arrested and tried for the crime and sentenced to death, but because they acted out of loyalty to their dead master, they are allowed to commit hara kiri like true samurai. Adapted from an extraordinarily popular Kabuki play from the eighteenth century, Inagaki's film is probably the best of dozens of film versions of the story going back to 1913. Beautifully designed and shot, it stands with SEVEN SAMURAI and THRONE OF BLOOD as the best of the Japanese samurai genre. (Japanese; English subtitles).

d, Hiroshi Inagaki; w, Toshio Yazumi (based on the Kabuki play-cycle "Kanadehon Chushingura" by Izumo Takeda, Senryu Namiki, Shoraku Miyoshi); ph, Kazuo Yamada (Tohoscope, Eastmancolor); m, Akira Ifukube; art d, Kisaku Ito; ch, Kiyokata Seruwaka; English subtitles, Herman B. Weinberg.

Drama (PR:C MPAA:NR)

CIAO MANHATTAN zero (1973) 90m Maron Films bw/c

Edie Sedgwick *(Susan)*, Wesley Hayes *(Butch)*, Isabel Jewell *(Mummy)*, Paul America *(Paul)*, Viva *(Fashion Editor)*, Roger Vadim *(Dr. Braun)*, Jean Margouleff *(Verdecchio)*, Geoff Briggs *(Geoffrey)*.

Edie Sedgwick had been dead two years when this film came out. Unless you are a student of the Andy Warhol subculture of the 1960s, or a voyeur who has a taste for some grisly bone raking, there is little to be had from this film. Sedgwick, a protege and companion of Warhol, had her 15 minutes of fame in the mid 1960s. CIAO MANHATTAN is the result of piecing together short ends of two Sedgwick vehicles. The first was begun by Chuck Wein in 1967 during the height of Sedgwick's fame. The second was begun three years later in California by John Palmer and David Weisman, who hoped they could make the film rise like the Phoenix from its ashes. The end result looks more like a risen zombie from NIGHT OF THE LIVING DEAD. The film dwells upon Sedgwick residing in the bottom of a tented Santa Barbara pool, narcissistically surrounded by giant blowups of herself. The film dwells on her dope and booze-bloated visage, and her silicone breasts. (For at least half of the film she is topless, so proud is she of her new ornaments.) We get some real and terrible insight into Sedgwicks' mind as we hear her drug-zonked recollections of her glory days, when she was most high, in publicity and drugs. We can see Sedgwick is near the end, and her impending overdose is just around the corner in her real life, but the film leaves us with a "so what?" attitude.

p, Robert Margouleff; d&w, John Palmer, David Weisman; ph, John Palmer, Kiell Rostad; m, John Phillips, Richie Havens, Kim Milford, Skip Battin, Kim Fowley; ed, Robert Farren.

Drama **Cas.** **(PR: MPAA:R**

CIGARETTE GIRL** (1947) 74m REP bw

Leslie Brooks, Jimmy Lloyd, Ludwig Donath, Doris Colleen, Howard Freeman, Joan Barton, Mary Forbes, Francis Pierlot, Eugene Borden, Arthur Loft, Emmett Vogan, David Bond, Russ Morgan and his Orchestra.

Brooks and Lloyd meet and fall in love, each lying to the other about their occupations. Lloyd claims to be an oil baron and Brooks pretends to be a famous nightclub singer. Eventually, he does become a business tycoon and she a Broadway star. Dumb Poverty Row musical has some nice music performed by Russ Morgan and His Orchestra, but little else. Songs: "It's All In The Mind," "The More We Get Together," "How Can You Tell?" "They Won't Let Me Sing," "Honeymoon On A Dime" (Doris Fisher, Allan Roberts).

p, William Bloom; d, Gunther V. Fritsch; w, Henry K. Moritz (based on a story by Edward Huebach); ph, Vincent Farrar; art d, George Brooks; set d, Earl Teass; ed, Jerome Thoms; m/l, Allan Roberts, Doris Fisher.

Musical **(PR:A MPAA:NR)**

CIMARRON**** (1931) 131m RKO bw

Richard Dix *(Yancey Cravat)*, Irene Dunne *(Sabra Cravat)*, Estelle Taylor *(Dixie Lee)*, Nance O'Neil *(Felice Venable)*, William Collier, Jr. *(The Kid)*, Roscoe Ates *(Jess Rickey)*, George E. Stone *(Sol Levy)*, Robert McWade *(Louie Heffner)*, Edna Mae Oliver *(Mrs. Tracy Wyatt)*, Frank Darien *(Mr. Bixby)*, Eugene Jackson *(Isaiah)*, Dolores Brown *(Baby Big Elk "Eldest")*, Gloria Vonic *(Baby Big Elk "Youngster")*, Otto Hoffman *(Murch Rankin)*, William Orlamond *(Grat Gotch)*, Frank Beal *(Louis Venable)*, Nancy Dover *(Donna Cravat "Eldest")*, Helen Parrish *(Donna Cravat "Younger")*, Donald Dilloway *(Cim "Eldest")*, Junior Johnson *(Cim "Younger")*, Douglas Scott *(Cim "Youngest")*, Reginald Streeter *(Yancey Jr)*, Lois Jane Campbell *(Felice, Jr.)*, Ann Lee *(Aunt Cassandra)*, Tyrone Brereton *(Dabney Venable)*, Lillian Lane *(Cousin Bella)*, Henry Rocquemore *(Jonett Goforth)*, Nell Craig *(Arminta Greenwood)*, Robert McKenzie *(Pat Leary)*, Bob Kortman *(Killer)*, Clara Hunt *(Indian Girl)*, William Janney *(Worker)*, Dennis O'Keefe *(Extra)*.

This is a big red-blooded western directed with furious pace by Ruggles, its most overwhelming scene—the Oklahoma Land Rush, with thousands of extras racing pell-mell on horseback, in wagons, on foot, to stake out claims on the two million Cherokee Strip acres opened to settlers on April 22, 1889. The scene is positively awe-inspiring as the landless mass outride and outwit each other in the mad dash for free dirt. Among this frenzied horde are Dix and his young wife Dunne (in her first major role). They manage to stake out a prize piece of territory but scheming Estelle Taylor replaces their marker and takes the land herself. Dix later establishes a newspaper but keeps his own brand of law with a quick gun, conquering his enemies with sword *and* pen. In one dramatic confrontation he shoots the earlobe off a bully and later, at a revival meeting, kills the same ruffian on a showdown. But he is a tough westerner with a big heart. The very same Taylor who robbed him and his wife of their land is later put on trial for prostitution and Dix, much against his wife's wishes, goes to her rescue, defending her in court. He is the knight errant of the Old West wearing a wide white Stetson and big guns on his hips. He is also a man consumed by wanderlust and he often leaves Dunne for long periods of time; she must run the newspaper and be the guiding light of the community. Much of the film rests upon the considerable talents of this lovely lady who begins as a girl-woman and ends as a grand old woman of the West (the film covers forty years, 1889-1929). Periodically, Dix returns to his wife's arms but is soon off again on a new adventure, seeking a new frontier. She becomes, by 1911 a distinguished U.S. Congresswoman, meeting Dix for the last time; he is a penniless oil rigger and is dying. CIMARRON demanded and got a staggering investment from RKO, $1,433,000, the largest budget the studio ever committed to a film up to that time. Though it received across-the-board raves, it lost money, more than a half million. Yet it won Oscars for Best Film, Best Adaptation and Best Set Decoration. (This would be the studio's only Best Picture winner except for Samuel Goldwyn's independently produced THE BEST YEARS OF OUR LIVES.) Dix and Dunne are both superb and won Oscar nominations. The film was considered for decades to be the finest Western ever made until SHANE, RED RIVER, HIGH NOON, and others overshadowed it. But it holds up well today, particularly those emotion-charged Land Rush scenes that certainly equal the same historical event so movingly shown in TUMBLEWEEDS, the 1925 silent classic starring William S. Hart. The 1960 remake fizzles by comparison.

p, William LeBaron; d, Wesley Ruggles; w, Howard Estabrook (based on the novel by Edna Ferber); ph, Edward Cronjager; ed, William Hamilton; art d/cos, Max Ree.

Western **(PR:A MPAA:NR)**

CIMARRON** (1960) 140m MGM c

Glenn Ford *(Yancey Cravet)*, Maria Schell *(Sabra Cravet)*, Anne Baxter *(Dixie)*, Arthur O'Connell *(Tom Wyatt)*, Russ Tamblyn *(The Kid)*, Mercedes McCambridge *(Sarah Wyatt)*, Vic Morrow *(Wes)*, Robert Keith *(Sam Pegler)*, Charles McGraw *(Bob Yountis)*, Henry (Harry) Morgan *(Jesse Rickey)*, David Opatoshu *(Sol Levy)*, Aline MacMahon *(Mrs. Pegler)*, Lili Darvas *(Felicia Venable)*, Edgar Buchanan *(Neal Hefner)*, Mary Wickes *(Mrs. Hefner)*, Royal Dano *(Ike Howes)*, L.Q. Jones *(Millis)*, George Brenlin *(Hoss)*, Vladimir Sokoloff *(Jacob Krubeckoff)*, Ivan Triesault *(Lewis Venable)*, Buzz Martin *(Cim Cravet)*, John Cason *(Suggs)*, Dawn Little Sky *(Arita Red Feather)*, Eddie Little Sky *(Ben Red Feather)*.

This is the second adaptation of Edna Ferber's novel of the first Oklahoma land rush. The first (1931) won the only Academy Award given to the western. One may ask, why would someone remake a film that had already won an Academy Award? This version concentrates almost exclusively on Ford, who plays Yancey, the man with an extreme case of wanderlust. This has an effect of distorting the story told so well the first time. The film starts off with the pell-mell invasion of the Oklahoma territory by the thousands of land seekers. Then it settles down into the familiar story.

p, Edward Granger; d, Anthony Mann; w, Arnold Schulman (based on Edna Ferber's novel); ph, Robert L. Surtees (CinemaScope, Metrocolor); m, Franz Waxman; ed, John Dunning; art d, George W. Davis, Addison Hehr; cos, Walter Plunkett; spec eff, A. Arnold Gillespie, Lee LeBlanc, Robert R. Hoag; m/l, Paul Francis Webster, Waxman.

Western **(PR:A MPAA:NR)**

CIMARRON KID, THE*½ (1951) 84m UNIV c

Audie Murphy *(Cimarron Kid)*, Yvette Dugay *(Rose of Cimarron)*, Beverly Tyler *(Carrie Roberts)*, John Hudson *(Dynamite Dick)*, James Best *(Bitter Creek)*, Leif Erickson *(Marshal Sutton)*, Noah Beery *(Bob Dalton)*, Hugh O'Brian *(Red Buck)*, John Hubbard *(George Weber)*, Palmer Lee *(Grat Dalton)*, Rand Brooks *(Emmett Dalton)*, William Reynolds *(Will Dalton)*, Roy Roberts *(Pat Roberts)*, David Wolfe *(Swanson)*, John Bromfield *(Tulsa Jack)*, Frank Silvera *(Stacey Marshall)*, Richard Garland *(Jim Moore)*, Eugene Baxter *(Tilden)*.

The Dalton boys ride again and in the process get Murphy involved up to his ears in crime, just at the point when he is being paroled from a jail sentence he received for harboring them. He tries to evade the gang, but the train he is riding on is held up, and a brutal sheriff pins the holdup on him. He takes to the hills, joins up with the gang, reorganizes the members after a bloody escapade, and falls in love with the daughter of a rancher on whose spread they have taken refuge. Promising himself only one more job, after which he and his love will run away from the gang, Murphy rides with the Daltons into a trap. He surrenders and faces another jail term, but his love will be waiting when he gets out.

p, Ted Richmond; d, Budd Boetticher; w, Louis Stevens (based on a story by Stevens, Kay Lenard); ph, Charles P. Boyle (Technicolor); ed, Frank Gross.

Western **(PR:A MPAA:NR)**

CINCINNATI KID, THE**** (1965) 102m MGM c

Steve McQueen *(The Cincinnati Kid)*, Edward G. Robinson *(Lancey Howard)*, Ann-Margret *(Melba)*, Karl Malden *(Shooter)*, Tuesday Weld *(Christian)*, Joan Blondell *(Lady Fingers)*, Rip Torn *(Slade)*, Jack Weston *(Pig)*, Cab Calloway *(Yeller)*, Jeff Corey *(Hoban)*, Theo Marcuse *(Felix)*, Milton Selzer *(Sokal)*, Karl Swenson *(Mr. Rudd)*, Emile Genest *(Cajun)*, Ron Soble *(Danny)*, Irene Tedrow *(Mrs. Rudd)*, Midge Ware *(Mrs. Slade)*, Dub Taylor *(Dealer)*, Joyce Perry *(Hoban's Wife)*, Claude Hall *(Gambler)*, Olan Soule *(Desk Clerk)*, Barry O'Hara *(Eddie)*, Bill Zuckert, Pat McCaffrie, John Hart, Sandy Kevin *(Poker Players)*, Robert Do Qui *(Philly)*, Hal Taggert *(Bettor)*, Andy Albin *(Referee)*, Howard Wendell *(Howard, Poker Player)*, Burt Mustin, William Challee, Charles Wagenheim *(Old Men)*, Gregg Martell *(Danny's henchman)*.

An attempt to do for poker what THE HUSTLER did for pool, THE CINCINNATI KID succeeds on its own but might have been a classic with some more attention paid to the script and, perhaps, a little humor sandwiched in to relieve the suspense. McQueen is The Kid, a formidable pokernik who has built a strong reputation among those who know. He's in New Orleans (most stories just look better when shot in that city) hustling small-timers and about to go east to Miami when Robinson rolls into town looking for some action. Robinson is "The Man" and acknowledged to be the king of poker. He's visiting town for a private game but isn't averse to another match against McQueen, as arranged by Malden, another gambler. Torn had earlier been decimated by Robinson and he wants to wreak revenge, so he calls in some old debts and forces Malden, who is dealing the game between Robinson and McQueen, to slip some winning cards to The Kid. Once McQueen realizes that's happening, he eases Malden out of the way, as he is determined to win fair and square. A marathon card game takes place, beautifully directed by Jewison, photographed by Lathrop, and edited by Hal Ashby. Even if you don't understand the game you'll be biting your nails. Naturally, a bit of knowledge about the game will make it even more exciting. If you recall THE HUSTLER, you'll be able to see the parallel between McQueen (Newman) and Robinson (Gleason), and Torn (Scott) and even Malden (McCormick) and Ann-Margret (Laurie). Should we tell you who wins in the end? If you want to know, read on. If not, stop here and go on to the next review or back to whatever it is you were doing before you turned to this page. Okay, that's done. Robinson says that "making the wrong move at the right time" is what gambling is about and when McQueen proudly shows his full house, Robinson lays down his straight flush and the theory that age can always beat youth in a nonathletic event is proven once again. This kind of movie has become a staple: the old expert versus the upstart: THE BALTIMORE BULLET (pool), HARD TIMES (bareknuckle boxing), and others. Excellent supporting work by Joan Blondell as Lady Fingers, a blowsy blonde dealer. In his accustomed role as the desk clerk, look for Olan

Soule, a small elderly man with a young voice. Soule, whom Jack Webb used often in his TV series, was "Mr. First Nighter" during the halcyon days of radio. He also played many other parts and continued to do the voice of "Batman" on Hanna-Barbara's TV series well into his seventies. Then again, the voice of "Robin" was done by Casey Kasem, who was approaching fifty at the time.

p, Martin Ransohoff; d, Norman Jewison; w, Ring Lardner, Jr., Terry Southern (based on the novel by Richard Jessup); ph, Philip Lathrop (Metrocolor); m, Lalo Schifrin; ed, Hal Ashby; art d, George W. Davis, Edward Carfagno; set d, Hugh Hunt, Henry Grace; cos, Donfeld; m/l, Dorcas Cochran.

Drama **Cas.** **(PR:A-C MPAA:NR)**

CINDERELLA* (1937, Fr.) 84m Forrester-Parant bw

Joan Warner *(Evelyne)*, Christiane Delyne *(Dany Rosy)*, Maurice Escande *(Gilbert)*, O'Dett *(Bobecoe)*, Jeanne Fusler *(Mme. Mataplan)*, Suzanne Dehelly *(Virginie)*, Felix Paquet *(Titin)*, Paul Faivre *(Mons. Mataplan)*, Marcel Vallee *(Director)*, Raphael Medina, the bands of Jo Bouillon and Willie Lewis.

This is the childhood tale of the poor little girl who loses a glass slipper and captures the heart of a prince. It is a French attempt to make a musical as Americans were making them in the mid-thirties. Set in France in the 1930s, the film stars Warner, a blonde American fan dancer, who was very popular during this period. The threadbare story revolves around a poor working girl who becomes a nightclub star too quickly, and the eccentric astronomer who falls in love with her. Some good nightclub scenes were shot of Warner leading the band, of Jo Bouillon and Willie Lewis, and Raphael Medina sings some Spanish numbers. (In French)

p, Forrester-Parant; d, Pierre Caron; w, Jean Montazel; ph, Boris Kauffmann; m, Vincent Scotto; ch, Harry Pilcer; m/l, Geo. Koger.

Musical **(PR:A MPAA:NR)**

CINDERELLA**** (1950) 74m Disney/RKO c

Voices: Ilene Woods *(Cinderella)*, William Phipps *(Prince Charming)*, Eleanor Audley *(Stepmother)*, Verna Felton *(Fairy Godmother)*, James MacDonald *(Jacques and Gus-Gus)*, Rhoda Williams *(Anastasia)*, Lucille Bliss *(Drusilla)*, Luis Van Rooten *(King and Grand Duke)*, Don Barclay, Claire DuBrey.

Oliver Wallace and Paul Smith received Oscar nominations for the music as did Mack David, Jerry Livingston, and Al Hoffman for the hit "Bibbidi Bobbidi Boo," but that was just the start of the accolades. CINDERELLA, though not showered with the same kind of praise SNOW WHITE and PINOCCHIO received, stands up just as well after all these years. Disney was the best at full animation and he showed it off to great advantage in his version of CINDERELLA. We say "his version" because the traditional Charles Perrault story was altered to accommodate a number of characters that never appeared in the original. The plot is best summarized as: boy meets girl, girl loses shoe, boy finds shoe and girl. There are little beasties like Jacques and Gus-Gus, two adorable mice who get involved with a flock of bluebirds, and together they form a dress for Cinderella so she can go to the ball. Marvelous color, good voices, lovely music, a delight all the way around. Luis Van Rooten, who vocalized the King and the Grand Duke, was a graduate architect who found acting more rewarding. He was also a well-known horticulturist and demonstrated that knowledge on TV. An off-beat fact about Van Rooten is that he played Nazi Heinrich Himmler twice in his life; in his first film, THE HITLER GANG (1944) and in his last, OPERATION EICHMANN in 1961. He was born in Mexico City, hence the Iberian spelling of his first name. Songs: "Bibbidi Bobbidi Boo," "So This Is Love," "A Dream Is a Wish Your Heart Makes," "Cinderella," "The Work Song," "Oh Sing, Sweet Nightingale" (Mack David, Jerry Livingston, Al Hoffman.)

p, Walt Disney; d, Wilfred Jackson, Hamilton Luske, Clyde Geronomi; w, William Peet, Ted Sears, Homer Brightman, Kenneth Anderson, Erdman Penner, Winston Hibler, Harry Reeves, Joe Rinaldi (based on the original story by Charles Perrault); (Technicolor); m, Oliver Wallace, Paul Smith; ed, Donald Holliday; md, Oliver Wallace, Paul J. Smith; character animators, Marvin Woodward, Hal Ambro, George Nicholas, Hal King, Judge Whitaker, Fred Moore, Hugh Fraser, Phil Duncan, Cliff Nordberg, Ken O'Brien, Harvey Toombs, Don Lusk.

Animated Feature **(PR:AAA MPAA:NR)**

CINDERELLA JONES** (1946) 90m WB bw

Joan Leslie *(Judy Jones)*, Robert Alda *(Tommy Coles)*, S.Z. Sakall *(Gabriel Popik)*, Edward Everett Horton *(Keating)*, Julie Bishop *(Camille)*, William Prince *(Bart Williams)*, Charles Dingle *(Minland)*, Ruth Donnelly *(Cora Elliott)*, Elisha Cook, Jr. *(Oliver S. Patch)*, Hobart Cavanaugh *(George)*, Charles Arnt *(Mahoney)*, Chester Clute *(Krencher)*, Ed Gargan *(Riley)*, Margaret Early *(Bashful Girl)*, Johnny Mitchell *(Soldier)*, Mary Dean *(Singer)*, Monte Blue *(Jailer)*, Marianne O'Brien *(Manicurist)*, Marian Martin *(Burlesque Queen)*.

Originally intended as a small-scale 1944 wartime musical, the release of CINDERELLA JONES was held up for two years so the studio could launch a new male star, Alda, in the more ambitious film RHAPSODY IN BLUE (1945). Unfortunately, neither the film nor Alda became hits and by mistiming the release of CINDERELLA JONES many of its wartime references had to be edited out at the expense of the plot. The plot revolves around a young woman, Leslie, who stands to inherit $10 million if she can marry a man with unusual intelligence by a given date. She figures that an exclusive male technology institute is the proper place to find such a quiz kid, and she attempts to enroll in the school. What she doesn't realize, until the end of the film, is that her boy friend, a bandleader, is quite the quiz kid in his own right. This film was made during a very unhappy period in the personal life of director Berkeley (he had again taken to the bottle over a severed marriage and the death of his mother, a guiding light in his career) and as a result none of the pizzazz usually associated with his name is present. None of the songs in this film has gone on to be a household name. The best is a number called "When the One You Love Simply Won't Love Back." Other songs include: "If You're Waitin' I'm Waitin' Too," "Cinderella Jones," "You Never Know Where You're Goin' Till You Get There," (Sammy Cahn, Jule Styne)

p, Alex Gottlieb; d, Busby Berkeley; w, Charles Hoffman (based on a story by Philip Wylie); ph, Sol Polito; m, Frederick Hollander; ed, George Amy.

Musical/Comedy **(PR:AA MPAA:NR)**

CINDERELLA LIBERTY** (1973) 117m FOX c

James Caan *(John Baggs, Jr.)*, Marsha Mason *(Maggie Paul)*, Kirk Calloway *(Doug)*, Eli Wallach *(Forshay)*, Burt Young *(Master at Arms)*, Bruce Kirby, Jr. *(Alcott)*, Allyn Ann McLerie *(Miss Watkins)*, Dabney Coleman *(Executive Officer)*, Fred Sadoff *(Dr. Osgood)*, Allan Arbus *(Drunken Sailor)*, Jon Korkes *(Dental Corpsman)*, Don Calfa *(Lewis)*, Paul Jackson *(Sam)*, David Proval *(Sailor No. 1)*, Ted D'Arm's *(Cook)*, Sally Kirkland *(Fleet Chick)*, Diane Schenker *(Nurse)*, James Bigham *(Seaman No. 1)*, Wayne Hudgins *(Seaman No. 2)*, Rita Joelson Chidester *(Wave)*, Knight Landesman *(Yeoman)*, Spike Africa *(Hot Dog Beggar)*, Chris F. Prebazac *(Young Sailor)*, David Norfleet *(Messboy)*, Sara Jackson *(Woman)*, James De Closs *(Sailor)*, Niles Brewster *(Paymaster)*, Glen Freeman*(Marine Guard)*, Jonathan Estrin *(Officer)*, John Kauffman *(Sailor)*, Christopher Rydell *(Boy Fishing)*, Joe Locke *(Club Owner)*, Frank O'Neal *(Sailor)*, Catherine M. Balzer *(Examining Nurse)*, Frank H. Griffin, Jr. *(Obstetrician)*, Nella Pugh *(Delivery Nurse)*, Clayton Corzatte *(Doctor)*, Joseph Candiotti *(Officer of the Day)*.

Darryl Ponicsan wrote the screenplay based on his own novel and it might have played better if someone else had adapted it. This was a terrific book and should have been a terrific movie. It's tough to lay the blame for its failure on anyone in particular but if honors had to be awarded they would go to Caan, who is so intent on being macho that he forgets about humanity and just appears to be going through the motions. The title refers to the pass given sailors that requires them to return to quarters by midnight. Caan is a happy-go-lucky sailor who's in Seattle for temporary medical treatment before he gets a new assignment. He meets Mason in a bar where she occasionally picks up tricks. They play a game of pool and he beats her; the reward is her body. She takes him home where he encounters the first of many unexpected twists; Mason has an eleven-year-old mulatto son played very well by Calloway. Caan falls in love with her, much to no one's surprise, and becomes the husband and father to this family. It is then discovered that she is pregnant by some earlier anonymous customer. She gives birth but the baby dies quite soon and she immediately returns to her old ways and means, hooking at the bar. Caan wants to stay with Mason and Calloway so he prevails on an old enemy of his, Wallach. Wallach had once been Caan's crusty drill instructor but has since been dismissed from the service for disobedience. Wallach is currently tending door at a tacky strip joint. Caan prevails on him to switch identities. This delights Wallach who only felt "at home" in the Navy. There's no question that someone would eventually find this duplicity out but it's a nice touch and serves well to end the story. Caan and Calloway find out that Mason has fled and the two seek to catch up to her and show her that someone cares. This was one of Young's first films and he immediately scored with audiences. He also appeared with Caan in THE GAMBLER and they remain pals to this day. Former actor Rydell pulls out all the stops for sentimentality in his direction. There's nothing wrong with a good cry, but when it seems that every frame is geared to extract that reaction, one has a feeling of being manipulated.

p&d, Mark Rydell; w, Darryl Ponicsan (based on a novel by Ponicsan); ph, Vilmos Zsigmond (Panavision, DeLuxe Color); m, John Williams; ed, Donn Cambern, Patrick Kennedy; art d, Leon Ericksen; cos, Rita Riggs; m/l, Paul Williams.

Drama **(PR:C-O MPAA:R)**

CINDERELLA SWINGS IT* (1942) 70m RKO bw

Guy Kibbee *(Scattergood Baines)*, Gloria Warren *(Betty Palmer)*, Helen Parrish *(Sally Burton)*, Dick Hogan *(Tommy Stewart)*, Leonid Kinskey *(Vladimir Smitkin)*, Billy Lenhart, Kenneth Brown *(Butch and Buddy)*, Dink Trout *(Pliny Pickett)*, Willy Best *(Hipp)*, Pierre Watkin *(Brock Harris)*, Lee "Lasses" White *(Ed Potts)*, Fern Emmett *(Clara Potts)*, Ed Waller *(Lem)*,Kay Linaker *(Mme. Dolores)*, Christine McIntyre *(Secetary)*, Grace Costello *(Tap Dancer)*.

This is the last film in the poisonous SCATTERGOOD BAINES series, and RKO brass changed the title from SCATTERGOOD SWINGS IT to CINDERELLA SWINGS IT to get people to see it. No title change could hide that this was a poorly made film in the same Scattergood tradition. This time, Scattergood (Kibbee) is trying to get struggling young singer (Warren) to become noticed. He gets her to change her singing style from classical music to modern swing. He then puts together a USO show in which to unveil her talents. The show turns out to be one of the most agonizing parades of amateur talent ever committed to celluloid. Songs: "I Heard You Cry Last Night" (Ted Grouya, Jerrie Kruger), "The Flag's Still There, Mr. Key" (George Jessel, Ben Oakland).

p, Jerrold T. Brandt; d, Christy Cabanne; w, Michael L. Simmons (based on the "Scattergood Baines" stories by Clarence Buddington Kelland); ph, Arthur Martinelli; ed, Richard Cahoon.

Musical/Comedy **(PR:A MPAA:NR)**

CINDERFELLA** (1960) 88m PAR c

Jerry Lewis *(Fella)*, Ed Wynn *(Fairy Godfather)*, Judith Anderson *(Wicked Stepmother)*, Anna Maria Alberghetti *(Princess Charmein)*, Henry Silva *(Maximilian)*, Count Basie *(Himself)*, Robert Hutton *(Rupert)*.

CINDERFELLA is a satire on the Cinderella story, with a gender change and Jerry Lewis to boot. Produced by Lewis, it tries hard to be funny but suffers from too much of a good thing. In comedy a little is a lot, yet Lewis never comes to realize this as the camera repeatedly lingers on him as he goes through his muggings and rubbery footwork. Ed Wynn is wonderful as the Fairy Godfather. If you like Lewis (you're probably French), you'll like this film. If you don't, this won't be the film to change your mind. Songs: "Somebody," "Princess Waltz," "Let Me Be a People" (Harry Warren, Jack Brooks).

p, Jerry Lewis; d&w, Frank Tashlin; ph, Haskell Boggs (Technicolor); m, Walter Scharf; ed, Artie Schmidt; art d, Hal Pereira, Henry Bumstead; cos, Edith Head; ch, Nick Castle.

Comedy **(PR:A MPAA:NR)**

CIPHER BUREAU*½ (1938) 64m GN bw

Leon Ames *(Philip Waring)*, Charlotte Wynters *(Helen Lane)*, Joan Woodbury *(Therese Brahm)*, Don Dillaway *(Paul Waring)*, Tenen Holtz *(Simon Herrick)*, Gustav Von Seyffertitz *(Albert Grood)*, Walter Bohn *(Anton Decker)*, Si Wills *(Lt. Clarke)*, Peter Lynn *(Lt. Tydall)*, Jason Robards *(Ellsworth)*, Joe Romantini *(Robert Wormer)*, Hooper Atchley *(Cmdr. Nash)*, Tudor Williams *(Norfolk Officer)*, Carl Stockdale *(Judge)*, Robert Frazer *(Paul's Counsel)*, Sidney Miller *(Jimmy)*, John Smart *(Carlson)*, Franklyn Parker *(Announcer)*, Stanley Blystone *(Army Lieutenant)*.

Cipher Bureau stands for the part of the U.S. Intelligence Agency that intercepts secret messages and breaks their codes. Ames plays the bureau officer trying to break a ring of thinly disguised German spies. The film gets bogged down in the technical aspects of how codes are deciphered, how bootleg transmitting stations in the high frequencies are run down, and how even broadcast music can serve as a medium for spies. A clash of wits and gunplay ensues between Ames and the spies, and in the traditional manner the Marines come to the rescue.

p, Franklyn Warner; d, Charles Lamont; w, Arthur Hoerl (based on a story by Monroe Shaff); ph, Arthur Martinelli; ed, Bernard Loftus.

Spy/Drama (PR:A MPAA:NR)

CIRCLE, THE½** (1959, Brit.) 84m BL/Kassler Films bw (AKA: THE VICIOUS CIRCLE)

John Mills *(Dr. Howard Latimer)*, Derek Farr *(Ken Palmer)*, Noele Middleton *(Laura James)*, Wilfrid Hyde-White *(Robert Brady)*, Roland Culver *(Inspector Dane)*, Mervyn Johns *(Dr. George Kimber)*, Rene Ray *(Mrs. Ambler)*, Lionel Jeffries *(Geoffrey Windsor)*, Lisa Daniely *(Frieda Veldon)*, David Williams *(Sgt. Lewis)*, John Gordon *(Surgeon)*, Diana Lambert *(Nurse Kay)*.

Mills is a London doctor who one day finds the body of a German actress on his office floor. Scotland Yard man Culver gets on the case, and though all the clues point to Mills, he eventually uncovers a forgery ring attempting to frame the doctor. Slightly entertaining crime drama adapted from a television serial, with an extremely talented cast seemingly just going through the motions.

p, Peter Rogers; d, Gerald Thomas; w, Francis Durbridge (based on the television serial "The Brass Candlestick" by Durbridge); m, Stanley Black.

Crime (PR:C MPAA:NR)

CIRCLE CANYON* (1934) 68m Superior Talking Pictures bw

Buddy Roosevelt, June Mathews, Clarise Woods, Bob Williamson, Allen Holbrook, Harry Leland, George Hazle, Clyde McClary, Mark Harrison, Ernest Scott, Johnny Tyke.

Routine oater has range rider Roosevelt galloping in circles after the bad guys while falling for Mathews. The film appears sluggish and the script seems to be impromptu. The acting is non-existent.

p&d, Victor Adamson; w, Burl R. Tuttle (based on the story "Gun Glory" by Tuttle).

Western (PR:A MPAA:NR)

CIRCLE OF DANGER** (1951, Brit.) 86m Coronado/EL bw

Ray Milland *(Clay Douglas)*, Patricia Roc *(Elspeth Graham)*, Marius Goring *(Sholto Lewis)*, Hugh Sinclair *(Hamish McArran)*, Naunton Wayne *(Reggie Sinclair)*, Marjorie Fielding *(Mrs. McArran)*, Edward Rigby *(Idwal Llewellyn)*, John Bailey *(Pape Llewellyn)*, Colin Gordon *(Col. Fairbairn)*, Dora Bryan *(Bubbles)*, Michael Brennan *(Bert Oakshott)*, Reginald Beckwith *(Oliver)*, David Hutcheson *(Tony Wrexham)*.

Slow-paced drama about a man's search for the answer to the mysterious death of his brother on a commando raid during WW II. Milland plays the American who travels to England to question the remnants of the commando group about his brother, quizzing a Welsh miner, the Scot officer who led the raid, an English ballet master, and an auto salesman, among others. Each interview gives Milland a little more information which seems to point back to the Scot. The Scot finally admits to killing Milland's brother when the sibling's foolhardy movements endangered the success of the mission. Milland accepts the Scot's answer without question in a contrived scene, and the Scot disavows his love for Roc, so Milland may win her affections.

p, David E. Rose, Joan Harrison; d, Jacques Tourneur; w, Philip MacDonald (based on the novel *White Heather* by MacDonald); ph, Oswald Morris; m, Robert Farnon.

Drama (PR:C MPAA:NR)

CIRCLE OF DEATH*½ (1935) 55m Willis Kent bw

Montie Montana *(Little Buffalo)*, Tove Lindan *(Mary Carr)*, Henry Hall *(J. F. Henry)*, Yakima Canutt *(Yak)*. Ben Corbett, Jack Carson, John Ince, J. Frank Glendon, Dick Botiller, Marin Sais, Olin Francis, George Morrell, Hank Bell, Budd Buster.

Montana is a white baby raised by a tribe of Indians and now grown up. An astute learner and a strong man, he speaks their language and rides horses with the best of them. He befriends a white cattle rancher and helps him thwart a gang of rustlers, meanwhile falling in love with the rancher's daughter. With the rustlers rounded up, Montana deides to return to the white man's life and he rides off with the girl.

p, Willis Kent; d, Frank Glendon; w, Roy Claire; ph, James Diamond.

Western Cas. (PR:A MPAA:NR)

CIRCLE OF DECEIT****

(1982, Fr./Ger.) 108m Bioskop-Artemis-Argos/UA Classics c (AKA: FALSE WITNESS)

Bruno Ganz *(Georg Laschen)*, Hanna Schygulla *(Arianna Nassar)*, Jean Carmet *(Rudnik)*, Jerzy Skolimowski *(Hoffmann)*, Gila von Weitershausen *(Greta Laschen)*, Peter Martin Urtel *(Berger)*, John Munro *(John)*, Fouad Naim *(Excellence Joseph)*, Josette Khalil *(Mrs. Joseph)*, Khaled el Saeid *(Progressive Officer)*, Sarah Salem *(Sister Brigitte)*, Tafic Najem *(Cab Driver)*, Magnia Fakhoury *(Aicha)*, Jack Diagilaitis *(Swedish Journalist)*, Ghassan Mattar *(Ahmed)*, Roger Assaf, Hakmeh Abou Ali, Hassan Husseiny, Isaaf Husseiny, Wasim Soubra, Wally Nachaby, Mohamed Kalach, Isabella, Jeanne, Hans Hackermann, Hans Peter Orff, Joachim Dieter Mues, Wolfgang Karven, Eric Spitella, Bamby Nucho, Peter Kamph, Nich Dobree, Philip Padfield, Rich Panzarella, Toni Maw, Mohamed Chouly, Youssef Raad, Dina Haidar, Sousso Abdel Mafiz, Ghassan Fadallah, Imad Hammoudi, Hussein Kaouk.

German journalist Ganz leaves a troubled marriage and some questions of self-worth behind him and travels to Beirut to write on the obsessive, violent war raging there. Amid a group of disillusioned reporters who see the fighting in the Middle East as just another sign of the times, Ganz vows to get to the heart of the true story and discover the emotional answer to the ever-present question of "why?" He meets and falls in love with the beautiful Schygulla, a wealthy German aristocrat still living in a mansion in the middle of bombed-out rubble. When the fighting becomes more intense and the lives of the journalists become threatened, most of the reporters leave Beirut for safer territory. Ganz remains, determined to understand the violence and report it to the world. Convinced that Schygulla loves him and that she will want him to leave his wife and family for her, Ganz goes to her home on a surprise visit. When approaching the mansion, he sees that Schygulla is with a Lebanese fighter. Realizing that she has never loved him and that he had just been another comfort to her, Ganz wanders the war-torn streets during the night, coming close to death several times. He soon understands that the bloody war in Beirut is indeed another example of man's hatred and brutality and that there is no "reason" for it that he can miraculously discover. Alone but now aware, Ganz returns to Germany. Director Schlondorff, one of the pioneers of the New German Cinema, creates a frightening, effective vision of the nightmarish war in Beirut and the grisly effect it can have on emotions as well as bodies. Ganz is wonderfully powerful as the always observing, curious reporter who realizes that man always has a way of deceiving himself and others into simple answers for complex questions. Schygulla, the mesmerizing star of many of Fassbinder's films, turns in an exquisite performance as the mysterious woman who courts death as well as men. Shot on location in Beirut, the film's recreated on-the-street battle sequences are violently intense and realistic, creating an always-lurking doom over the characters.

p, Eberhard Junkersdorf; d, Volker Schlondorff; w, Schlondorff, Jean-Claude Carriere, Margarethe von Trotta, Kai Hermann; from a novel by Nicolas Born; ph, Igor Luther; (Eastmancolor); m, Maurice Jarre; ed, Suzanne Baron; art d, Alexandre Riachi, Tannous Zougheib; set d, Bernd Lepel, Jacques Bufnoir; cos, Dagmar Niefind; spec eff, Paul and Andre Trielli.

Drama (PR:O MPAA:NR)

CIRCLE OF DECEPTION** (1961, Brit.) 100m FOX bw

Suzy Parker *(Lucy Bowen)*, Bradford Dillman *(Paul Raine)*, Harry Andrews *(Capt. Rawson)*, Paul Rogers *(Maj. Spence)*, John Welsh *(Maj. Taylor)*, Robert Stephens *(Capt. Stein)*, A.J. Brown *(Frank Bowen)*, Martin Boddey *(Henry Crow)*, Charles Lloyd Pack *(Ayres)*, Ronald Allen *(Abelson)*, Jacques Cey *(Cure)*, John Dearth *(Capt. Ormerod)*, Norman Coburn *(Carter)*, Hennie Scott *(Small Boy)*, Richard Marner *(German Colonel)*, Andre Charise *(Lohmann)*, Jean Briant *(His Assistant)*, Richard Shaw *(Liebert)*, Duncan Lamont *(Ballard)*, Meier Tzelniker *(Barman)*, Basil Beale *(Price)*, Jean Harvey *(F.A.N.Y.)*, Mickey Wood *(Instructor)*, Tony Quinn, Frank Forsyth, Stephen Dartnell, Maurice Belfer, Roland Brand, Walter Gotell, George Mikell, Tony Doonan, John Serret, Michael Shaw, Arthur Gross, Theodore Wilhelm, Michael Ripper, Brian Hankins.

Another cold-blooded British espionage film, where "expendables" are written off without the blink of an eye. Andrews, as the British intelligence chief, devises a scheme to plant false information with the Germans during WW II in Normandy, by dropping an agent among them who doesn't realize the real nature of his mission. The idea being that the Germans will believe his story more if they have to beat it out of him. Andrews' assistant, Parker, is told to become friendly with a Canadian officer, Dillman, whom Andrews plans to drop, but her friendliness turns to love. Dillman is parachuted into Normandy and is captured, and then tortured until he gives away the planted information. Later he is rescued by the French resistance and, back in England after the war, filled with self-loathing for having been a coward and cracked to the enemy, he starts drinking himself to death. Parker reappears in his life and convinces him that he was really a hero, "the one man on his own against both sides."

p, Tom Monohan; d, Jack Lee; w, Nigel Balchin, Robert Musel (based on the novel by Alec Waugh); ph, Gordon Dines (CinemaScope); m, Clifton Parker; ed, Gordon Pilkington; cos, Joan Ellacott.

Spy/War (PR:C MPAA:NR)

CIRCLE OF IRON*½ (1979, Brit.) 102m AE c (AKA: THE SILENT FLUTE)

David Carradine *(Chang-Sha, The Blind Man, The Monkey Man, Death)*, Jeff Cooper *(Cord)*, Roddy McDowall *(White Robe)*, Eli Wallach *(Man in Oil)*, Erica Creer *(Tara)*, Christopher Lee *(Zetan)*, Anthony De Longis *(Morthand)*, Earl Maynard *(Black Giant)*, Heinz Bernard *(Gerryman)*, Zipora Peled *(His Wife)*, Jeremy Kaplan *(Monkeyboy)*, Kam Yuen *(Red Band)*, Elizabeth Motzkin *(Japanese Woman)*, Bobby Ne'eman *(Thug Leader)*, Dov Friedman *(Young Monk)*, Ronen Nabah *(Beautiful Boy)*, Michal Nedivi *(Boy's Mother)*, Nissim Zohar *(Boy's Father)*.

Bruce Lee, James Coburn, and Stirling Silliphant originally wrote this martial arts fantasy for Lee, but Carradine ended up as the star due to Lee's tragic early demise. Basically just another chop-chop Kung Fu film, CIRCLE OF IRON lacks the intensity that Lee could have given it. Most of the time Carradine plays Chang-Sha, guide to a knowledge-seeking fighter, Cooper. Carradine leads Cooper through the Zen-packed film (what is the sound of one hand clapping?). The fight scenes in this film are good because almost all the inhabitants of this fantasy world are well-versed in the Oriental arts. Filmed on location in Israel, the settings keep the audience truly mystified as to the time frame and location of this fantasy world.

p, Paul Maslansky, Sandy Howard; d, Richard Moore; w, Stirling Silliphant, Stanley Mann (based on a story by Bruce Lee, James Coburn, Silliphant); ph, Ronnie Taylor (CFI Color); ed, Ernie Walter; set d, Johannes Larsen; cos, Lilly Fenichel.

Adventure   **Cas.**   **(PR:O MPAA:R)**

CIRCLE OF LOVE*   (1965, Fr.) 105m Walter Reade/STER c
Jane Fonda (The Wife), Maurice Ronet (The Husband), Jean Sorel (The Count), Catherine Spaak (The Young Girl), Anna Karina (The Chambermaid), Valerie Lagrange (Her Friend), Jean-Claude Brialy (The Young Gentleman), Francine Berg (The Actress), Bernard Noel (The Author), Marie Dubois (The Prostitute), Claude Giraud (The Soldier), Francoise Dorleac.

Unwanted remake of Max Ophuls' classic 1950 film LA RONDE stars Fonda as one of the cogs in a wheel of romantic affairs that run full circle by the end of the movie. CIRCLE OF LOVE will probably best be remembered for Fonda's threat to sue if a giant Broadway billboard for the film depicting her in the buff was not removed. Fonda married the director, Vadim, which did nothing for her career.

p, Robert and Raymond Hakim; d, Roger Vadim; w, Jean Anouilh (based on the play "La Ronde" by Arthur Schnitzler); ph, Henri Decae (Franscope, Eastmancolor); m, Michel Magne; ed, Victoria Spiri-Mercanton; art d, Francois de Lamothe; cos, Marc Doelnitz.

Romance   **(PR:C-O MPAA:NR)**

CIRCLE OF POWER   (SEE: MYSTIQUE, 1983)

CIRCLE OF TWO**   (1980, Can.) 105m Film Consortium of Canada c
Richard Burton (Ashley St. Clair), Tatum O'Neal (Sarah Norton), Nuala FitzGerald (Claudia Aldrich), Robin Gammell (Mr. Norton), Patricia Collins (Mrs. Norton), Kate Reid (Dr. Emily Reid), Donann Cavin (Smitty), Michael Wincott (Paul), Norma Dell-'Agnese (Raspoli).

A romantic but not sexual affair between a sixty-year-old artist and a sixteen-year-old student is the center of this interesting if superficial film. Burton plays the aged artist who hasn't touched a paint brush in over 10 years, while O'Neal plays the girl. O'Neal first stumbles across Burton at a porno movie after being dared to sit through it by some friends. A careful look will reveal Ryan O'Neal, Tatum's father, and Lee Majors in the porno house. Later, Burton hides her while she is trying to ditch a former boy friend. The romance begins. Burton encourages her to pursue her writing, while she gets him to start painting again. Eventually their secret is uncovered, with Burton facing ridicule and O'Neal being virtually imprisoned by her parents. She follows him to New York, where he decides they have no future. Neither did this pedestrian and often unsavory film.

p, Henk Van der Kolk; d, Jules Dassin; w, Thomas Hedley (based on a story "A Lesson in Love" by Marie Terese Baird); ph, Lazlo George; m, Paul Hoffert; ed, David Nichols; art d, Francois de Lucy; set d, Claude Bonniere.

Drama   **Cas.**   **(PR:O MPAA:NR)**

CIRCUMSTANTIAL EVIDENCE**   (1935) 69m CHES bw
Chick Chandler (Jim Baldwin), Shirley Grey (Adrienne Grey), Arthur Vinton (Fred Stevens), Dorothy Revier (Bernice Winters).

This film is literally about circumstantial evidence and uses a unique angle to get its message across. To prove that circumstantial evidence is not enough to convict anyone, a newspaper reporter, Chandler, fakes evidence to make it look as though he has murdered a fellow employee. He hides his colleague away until he is convicted of murder on circumstantial evidence. The friend is supposed to appear after the guilty verdict but something happens to delay him and Chandler all but hangs as a result.

p, George R. Batcheller; d, Charles Lamont; w, Ewart Adamson (based on a story by Tom Terris); ph, M.A. Andersen; ed, Roland Reed.

Crime   **(PR:A MPAA:NR)**

CIRCUMSTANTIAL EVIDENCE*½   (1945) 67m FOX bw
Michael O'Shea (Joe Reynolds), Lloyd Nolan (Sam Lord), Trudy Marshall (Agnes Hannon), Billy Cummings (Pat), Ruth Ford (Mrs. Simms), Reed Hadley (Prosecutor), Roy Roberts (Marty Hannon), Scotty Beckett (Freddy Hanlon), Byron Foulger (Bolger), Dorothy Adams (Bolger's Wife), John Eldredge (Judge White), Eddie Marr (Mike), Selmer Jackson (Warden), William B. Davidson (Chairman), John Hamilton (Gou Hanlon), Ben Welden (Kenny), Ralph Dunn (Cleary), Ray Teal (Policeman), Thomas Jackson (Detective).

This is a trite film that tries to make a major point: that the fallibility of witnesses to a crime can convict an innocent person. O'Shea is that innocent person, but hot-tempered as well. He gets into a fight with a grocer who is killed during the battle. O'Shea is arrested and charged with the ax murder of the grocer, whose head has been split open. O'Shea claims the grocer fell and struck his head on a stove; three people say they saw O'Shea pick up an ax and strike the grocer. O'Shea is convicted and sentenced to the electric chair. He breaks out of jail but is pursuaded to go back by his son, who thinks he can prove his father innocent in a retrial. He does, and O'Shea is freed.

p, William Girard; d, John Larkin; w, Robert Metzler, Samuel Ornitz (based on a story by Nat Ferber and Sam Duncan); ph, Harry Jackson; m, David Buttolph; ed, Norman Colbert; md, Emil Newman.

Crime   **(PR:C MPAA:NR)**

CIRCUMSTANTIAL EVIDENCE*   (1954, Brit.) 61m ACT Films/Monarch bw
Rona Anderson (Linda Harrison), Patrick Holt (Michael Carteret), John Arnatt (Steve Harrison), John Warwick (Pete Hanken), Frederick Leister (Sir Edward Carteret), Ronald Adam (Sir William Harrison), June Ashley (Rita Hanken), Peter Swanwick (Charley Pott), Lisa Lee (Gladys Vavasour), Ballard Berkeley (Inspector Hall), Ian Fleming.

Holt is a blackmailed doctor standing trial for the murder of the husband of his fiancee (Anderson). Routine courtroom drama.

p, Phil Brandon; d, Dan Birt; w, Allan Mackinnon (based on the story "The Judge Sees The Light" by Mackinnon); ph, Brendan J. Stafford.

Crime   **(PR:C MPAA:NR)**

CIRCUS   (SEE: INVITATION TO THE DANCE, 1956)

CIRCUS BOY**   (1947, Brit.) 50m Merton Park/GFD bw
James Kenney (Michael Scott), Florence Stephenson (Florence), George Stephenson (George), Denver Hall (Bailey), Dennis Gilbert (Borden), Peter Scott (Stewart), Gwen Bacon (Mrs. Scott), Jock Easton (Jeff), Robert Raglan (Trevor), Bertram Mills' Circus.

Kenney is a shy young schoolboy swimmer who overcomes his bashfulness by becoming a circus clown. Okay children's film.

p, Frank Hoare; d, Cecil Musk; w, Musk, Mary Cathcart Borer (based on a story by Patita Nicholson).

Juvenile   **(PR:AA MPAA:NR)**

CIRCUS CLOWN**   (1934) 65m FN/WB bw
Joe E. Brown (Happy Howard), Patricia Ellis (Alice), Dorothy Burgess (Bebe), Donald Dillaway (Jack), Gordon Westcott (Frank), Charles Wilson (Sheldon), Harry Woods (Ajax), Ronnie Cosby (Dickie), John Sheehan (Moxley), Spencer Charters, Earle Hodgins, Bobby Caldwell, Ernest Clark, Poodles Hanneford.

Brown plays a dual role as a circus-struck young man and his father, an ex-circus performer who opposes his son's infatuation with the big top. As the son, Brown falls in love with the female impersonator and joins the circus. Realizing his mistake, he falls in love with Ellis, a trapeze artist, is kicked out of the circus, and returns to save the day when Ellis's brother is too drunk to go on. Not bad, though not one of Brown's better efforts; it borrows heavily from THE CIRCUS KID (1928).

d, Ray Enright; w, Burt Kalmar, Harry Ruby, Paul Gerard Smith; ph, Sid Hickox; ed, Clarence Kolster.

Comedy   **(PR:A MPAA:NR)**

CIRCUS FRIENDS**   (1962, Brit.) 63m Femina Films-London Independent Producers/CD bw
Alan Coleshill (Nicky), Carole White (Nan), David Tilley (Martin), Pat Belcher (Beryl), Meredith Edwards (Farmer Beasley), John Horsley (Bert Marlow), Sam Kydd (George).

Unable to pay the rental fee on a farmer's field, struggling circus owner Horsley gives the farmer the pet pony of Coleshill and White. The children steal the pony back and hide it, and the next day the pony gives such a successful performance that Horsley is able to pay the farmer the money owed him and get the pony back for good. Okay children's film by the team of Rogers and Thomas, who would begin making the "Carry On" series two years later, and continue for another twenty years. Released in England in 1956.

p, Peter Rogers; d, Gerald Thomas; w, Rogers; ph, Otto Heller; m, Bruce Montgomery; ed, Peter Boita.

Children   **(PR:AA MPAA:NR)**

CIRCUS GIRL*½   (1937) 64m REP bw
June Travis (Kay Rogers), Bob Livingston (Bob McAvoy), Donald Cook (Charles Jerome), Betty Compson (Carlotta), Charles Murray (Slippery), Lucille Osborne (Gloria), Donald Kerr (Gabby), Emma Dunn (Molly), John Wray (Roebling), John Holland (Reporter), Kathryn Howard (Nurse).

Routine big top romance with Livingston and Cook competing for the affections of Travis. Trapeze sequences performed by the Escalante family, a famous performing group of the day.

p, Nat Levine; d, John Auer; w, Adele Buffington, Bradford Ropes (based on a story by Frank R. Adams); ph, Jack Marta; ed, Lester Orlebeck.

Drama   **(PR:A MPAA:NR)**

CIRCUS KID, THE**   (1928) 61m Film Booking Office (FBO) bw
Frankie Darro (Buddy), Poodles Hanneford (Poodles), Joe E. Brown (King Kruger), Helene Costello (Trixie), Sam Nelson (Tad), Lionel Belmore (Beezicks), Charles Miller (Cadwallader), Johnny Gough (Skelly Crosley), Sid Crosley (Skelly's Runner), Charles Gemora (Zozo), Frank Hemphill (Officer), Clarence Moorehouse.

Orphan Darro, a natural acrobat, runs away to the circus and joins the troupe which includes rival lion tamer Brown, a once-was, and Nelson, the rising star, who are both competing for bareback rider Costello's affection. A lion escapes and almost kills Nelson but the beast is fought off bare-handed by Brown, who dies a hero but not before blessing the union between Nelson and Costello. Maudlin, mawkish, but a few good animal scenes. This is basically a silent film with a talkie prolog and snippets of conversation throughout.

d, George B. Seitz; w, Melville Baker, Randolph Bartlett (based on a story by James Ashmore Creelman); ph, Philip Tannura; ed, Ann McKnight.

Adventure/Drama   **(PR:A MPAA:NR)**

CIRCUS OF FEAR   (SEE: PSYCHO-CIRCUS, 1967)

CIRCUS OF HORRORS*   (1960, Brit.) 88m AIP c
Anton Diffring (Dr. Schuler), Erika Remberg (Elissa), Yvonne Monlaur (Nicole), Donald Pleasence (Vanet), Jane Hylton (Angela), Kenneth Griffith (Martin), Gonrad Phillips (Inspector Ames), Jack Gwillim (Supt. Andrews), Vanda Hudson (Magda), Yvonne Romain (Melina), Colette Wilde (Evelyn Morley), William Mervyn (Dr. Morley),

John Merivale *(Edward Finsbury)*, Carla Challoner *(Nicole, as Child)*, Peter Swanwick *(Inspector Knopf)*, Walter Gotell *(Von Gruber)*, Chris Christian *(Ringmaster)*, Sasha Coco *(Luis)*, Jack Carson *(Chief Eagle Eye)*, Glyn Houston *(Barker)*, Malcolm Watson *(Elderly Man)*, Kenneth Warren *(1st Roustabout)*, Fred Haggerty *(2nd Roustabout)*.

Sex and sadism are given a strange mix in this big top story of a plastic surgeon, Diffring, who takes over a one-ring circus and staffs it with beautiful women whose faces he has altered. Lest any get out of line or when he tires of one of them, they suffer an "acident" during a performance and are eliminated. A well-made film, comical and horrible both, with a particular grisly ending reserved for the ring-master of the whole thing, Diffring.

p, Julian Wintle, Leslie Parkyn; d, Sidney Hayers; w, George Baxt; ph, Douglas Slocombe (Eastmancolor); m, Franz Reizenstein, Muir Mathieson; ed, Reginald Mills; m/l, Mark Anthony.

Horror **(PR:O MPAA:NR)**

CIRCUS OF LOVE** (1958, Ger.) 93m King Brothers/DCA c (RUMMELPLATZ DER LIEBE)

Eva Bartok *(Lilli)*, Curt Jurgens *(Toni)*, Bernard Wicki *(Franz)*, Robert Freytag *(Richard)*, Willi Rose *(Karl)*, Adi Berber *(Groppo)*, Helene Stanley *(Lore)*.

Bartok is a pretty young high-dive artist married to Wicki. She begins an affair with brutish barker Jurgens, who soon murders Wicki and steals Bartok's savings. She leaves him for photographer Freytag but goes back for more abuse. Finally, while Jurgens is trying to strangle Bartok, not-too-bright strongman Berber crushes him to death and Bartok returns to Freytag. Berber appears in both versions, and the stars of the English language version, CARNIVAL STORY, Anne Baxter and Steve Cochran, can be seen as extras here. Slightly better than CARNIVAL STORY, though not much. (In German; English subtitles)

d, Kurt Neumann; w, Hans Jacobi, Neumann (based on a story by Marcel Klauber and C.B. Williams); (Technicolor); m, Willi Schmidt-Gentner.

Drama **(PR:C MPAA:NR)**

CIRCUS QUEEN MURDER, THE½** (1933) 63m COL bw

Adolphe Menjou *(Thatcher Colt)*, Greta Nissen *(Josie La Tour)*, Ruthelma Stevens *(Kelly)*, Dwight Frye *(Flandrin)*, Donald Cook *(Sebastian)*, Harry Holman *(Dugan)*, George Rosener *(Rainey)*.

Set in a traveling circus performing in a small town, THE CIRCUS QUEEN MURDER is a film about revenge and counter-revenge under the big top. A great portion of the cast is either murdered, planning a murder, or actually murdering their fellow performers in this fast-moving yarn. Menjou in his waxed black mustache and impeccable wardrobe won raves for his role as the police commissioner on vacation.

d, R. W. Neill; w, Jo Swerling (based on a novel by Anthony Abbott); ed, Richard Cahoon.

Mystery **(PR:C MPAA:NR)**

CIRCUS WORLD*** (1964) 135m PAR c (GB: THE MAGNIFICENT SHOWMAN)

John Wayne *(Matt Masters)*, Rita Hayworth *(Lilli Alfredo)*, Claudia Cardinale *(Toni Alfredo)*, Lloyd Nolan *(Cap Carson)*, Richard Conte *(Aldo Alfredo)*, John Smith *(Steve McCabe)*, Henri Dantes *(Emile Schuman)*, Wanda Rotha *(Mrs. Schuman)*, Katharyna *(Giovana)*, Kay Walsh *(Flo Hunt)*, Margaret MacGrath *(Anna)*, Katherine Ellison *(Molly)*, Miles Malleson *(Billy Hennigan)*, Katharine Kath *(Hilda)*, Moustache *(Bartender)*, Robert Cunningham, Francois Calepides *(Ringmasters)*, Acts and Individual Members of the Franz Althoff Circus of Austria.

This big, sprawling film, beautifully filmed in Cinerama, has the Duke starring as the owner/manager of a small-time circus. Wayne is also the foster father of Claudia Cardinale, due to the fact that her mother (an aerialist star) ran out on both of them years before. The circus, one of the Wild West variety so prominent in the late eighteenth and early nineteenth centuries, is in grave financial trouble. Wayne decides that a European tour would give it the boost it needs, since the Wild West act always goes over well there. He also knows in the back of his mind that Cardinale's mother is somewhere in Germany. Disaster hits the circus as its boat capsizes in a European port. Wayne manages to save the tent, performers, and animals, but loses most of the circus. However, the show must go on. They head for Paris, where Wayne performs a stagecoach runaway down the Champs Elysees to the delight of the Parisians who thrill to the glimpse of the American west. The circus is a hit in Europe, and does big business wherever it goes. Meanwhile, Cardinale has been secretly training to become an aerialist, like the mother she cannot remember. Wayne, to keep her as a little girl, discourages her. However, she persists and gets her way. No sooner does this happen than Hayworth starts showing up like a Madam X, watching Cardinale practice. Wayne discovers Hayworth and all is forgiven. She decides to stay with the circus, and she and Cardinale do a mother/daughter aerial act, with Hayworth astounding the crowd by doing one hundred over-the-shoulder one-arm somersaults.

p, Samuel Bronston; d, Henry Hathaway; w, Ben Hecht, Julian Halevy, James Edward Grant (based on a story by Philip Yordan, Nicholas Ray); ph, Jack Hildyard, Claude Renoir (Cinerama, Technicolor); m, Dimitri Tiomkin; ed, Dorothy Spencer; set d, John De Cuir; cos, Renie; spec eff, Alex Weldon; m/l, Tiomkin, Ned Washington.

Adventure/Drama **Cas.** **(PR:A MPAA:NR)**

CISCO KID* (1931) 60m FOX bw

Warner Baxter *(Cisco Kid)*, Edmund Lowe *(Sgt. Mickey Dunn)*, Conchita Montenegro *(Carmencita)*, Nora Lane *(Sally Benton)*, James Bradbury, Jr. *(Dixon, U.S.A.)*, Eddie Dillon *(Bouse, U.S.A.)*, Charles Stevens *(Lopez)*, Chris Martin *(Gordito)*, Douglas Haig *(Billy)*, Marilynn Knowlden *(Annie)*, George Irving, Frederick Burton.

Undistinguished western has Baxter in the title role. The story has three main buoys, around which everything else swirls, Lowe's pursuit of Baxter, Baxter's robbing of a bank to save a widow's ranch, and Baxter's affection for the widow's children. The latter causes Baxter to return after a getaway to confront Lowe, when he thinks he hurt one of the tots during the escape. Lowe, however, explains himself and lets Baxter go free to boot. Baxter had won an Oscar for his portrayal of the happy-go-lucky Mexican bandit in his first sound film two years before, IN OLD ARIZONA, and was to repeat the role once more after this one. (See CISCO KID series, Index.)

d, Irving Cummings; w, Alfred Cohn (based on a story by O. Henry [William Sydney Porter]); ph, Barney McGill; ed, Alex Troffey.

Western **(PR:AA MPAA:NR)**

CISCO KID AND THE LADY, THE½** (1939) 73m FOX bw

Cesar Romero *(Cisco Kid)*, Marjorie Weaver *(Julie Lawson)*, Chris-Pin Martin *(Gordito)*, George Montgomery *(Tommy Bates)*, Robert Barrat *(Jim Harbison)*, Virginia Field *(Billie Graham)*, Harry Green *(Teasdale)*, Gloria Ann White *(Baby)*, John Beach *(Stevens)*, Ward Bond *(Walton)*, J. Anthony Hughes *(Drake)*, James Burke *(Pop Saunders)*, Harry Hayden *(Sheriff)*, James Flavin *(Sergeant)*, Ruth Warren *(Ma Saunders)*.

The "Latin Lover" of Hollywood films takes on the lovable Cisco Kid role in this one, his first of many during the next several years, and reviewers were unanimous in praising him over Warner Baxter, his predecessor. In a made-to-order plot for the Kid, he thwarts the murderer of a prospector whose claim the killer wanted for himself, thereby saving the mine for the prospector's orphaned baby. School teacher Weaver takes in the baby, and Romero, in his suave way, dallies with her. She lets him know that she loves another, so the Mexican border Robin Hood switches his affections to a dance hall girl, who saves him from capture at the end. (See CISCO KID series, Index.)

p, John Stone; d, Herbert I. Leeds; w, Frances Hyland (based on a story by Stanley Rauh, suggested by a character created by O. Henry [William Sydney Porter]); ph, Barney McGill; ed, Nick De Maggio.

Western **(PR:A MPAA:NR)**

CISCO KID RETURNS, THE*½ (1945) 64m MON bw

Duncan Renaldo *(Cisco)*, Martin Garralaga *(Pancho)*, Cecilia Callejo *(Rosita)*, Roger Pryor *(Harris)*, Anthony Warde *(Conway)*, Fritz Leiber *(Padre)*, Vicky Lane *(Mrs. Page)*, Jan Wiley *(Jeanette)*, Sharon Smith *(Nancy)*, Cy Kendall *(Jennings)*, Eva Puig *(Tia)*, Emmett Lynn *(Sheriff)*.

Off to the Navy went Cesar Romero in WW II, and Renaldo steps in as the Cisco Kid. Here, the story has Renaldo attempting to prove that the child in his custody has not been kidnaped, but is with him for "protection" against the man who murdered her father. Romero did not return to films until 1947 in CARNIVAL IN COSTA RICA and never made another Cisco Kid movie beyond the six he did before joining the Navy. (See CISCO KID series, Index.)

p, Philip N. Krasne; d, John P. McCarthy; w, Betty Burbridge (based on a character created by O. Henry [William Sydney Porter]); ph, Harry Neumann; ed, Marty Cohen.

Western **(PR:A MPAA:NR)**

CISCO PIKE** (1971) 94m COL c

Kris Kristofferson *(Cisco Pike)*, Karen Black *(Sue)*, Gene Hackman *(Holland)*, Harry Dean Stanton *(Jesse)*, Viva *(Merna)*, Joy Bang *(Lynn)*, Roscoe Lee Browne *(Music Store Owner)*, Chuy Franco *(Mexican)*, Severn Darden *(Lawyer)*, Herb Weil *(Customer)*, Antonio Fargas *(Buffalo)*, Douglas Sahm *(Rex)*, Don Sturdy *(Recording Engineer)*, Allan Arbus *(Sim)*, Frank Hotchkiss *(Motorcycle Officer)*, Hugh Romney *(Reed)*, James Oliver *(Narc)*, Nawana Davis *(Mouse)*, Timothy Near *(Waitress)*, Lorna Thayer *(Swimmer)*, William Traylor *(Jack R.)*.

CISCO PIKE is Kristofferson's film debut and he does a credible job as the rock star who has vowed to go straight after his release from prison for drug dealing. He is blackmailed by policeman Hackman into selling marijuana. An interesting film, it died at the box office because of the wave of other drug films coming out at the time. This is not a "how to" drug film. In fact, the drugs are used as a prop for Hackman's blackmail of Kristofferson. We find out at the end that Hackman has done this to make extra money, because policemen are underpaid, as much as certain screenwriters are overpaid for scripts like this. Of course, Kristofferson sings.

p, Gerald Ayres; d&w, Bill L. Norton; ph, Vilis Lapenieks (Eastmancolor); m, Kris Kristofferson; ed, Robert C. Jones; md, Bob Johnston; art d, Alfred Sweeney; set d, Ray Malyneaux; m/l, Kristofferson.

Crime **(PR:O MPAA:R)**

CITADEL, THE**** (1938) 110m MGM bw

Robert Donat *(Andrew Manson)*, Rosalind Russell *(Christine Manson)*, Ralph Richardson *(Denny)*, Rex Harrison *(Dr. Lawford)*, Emlyn Williams *(Owen)*, Penelope Dudley Ward *(Toppy Leroy)*, Francis L. Sullivan *(Ben Chenkin)*, Mary Clare *(Mrs. Orlando)*, Cecil Parker *(Charles Every)*, Nora Swinburne *(Mrs. Thornton)*, Edward Chapman *(Joe Morgan)*, Athene Seyler *(Lady Raebank)*, Felix Aylmer *(Mr. Boon)*, Joyce Bland *(Nurse Sharp)*, Percy Parsons *(Mr. Stillman)*, Dilys Davis *(Mrs. Page)*, Basil Gill *(Dr. Page)*, Joss Ambler *(Dr. A. H. Llewellyn)*, Bernard Miles *(Miner)*, Kynaston Reeves *(Doctor)*, Josephine Wilson, Haidee Wright, Charles Quartermaine, Angela Baddeley, Eliot Makeham, Joan Kemp-Welch, Bombardier Billy Wells, Leslie Philips.

Donat is spellbinding as the dedicated doctor who administers to TB-infected Welsh miners and Russell stirring as his devoted and idealistic wife. At first Donat is full of lofty goals as he labors in the slums of a mining town, struggling to save the miserable health of the downtrodden workers, but his noble purpose slowly corrodes to greed and power when he begins to treat aristocratic, wealthy London patients. Donat begins to lead the "good life," at the expense of his beliefs, until his close friend Richardson dies and Russell convinces him that he has lost touch with his true aims in life. He returns to his small-town practice and again takes up his noble pursuit of administering to the impoverished. THE CITADEL was produced by MGM's British production unit in England after the studio had met with success in a similar foreign production, A YANK

AT OXFORD. Director Vidor, who brought only one American star to England, Russell, presents carefully constructed scenes, allowing Donat's consummate acting skills to carry the story forward with sensitivity and his natural charm. Russell is far from the comic zany, awkward and almost unwomanly, she would later project in AUNTIE MAME, or the freakish predator of PICNIC. She plays a beautiful and loving woman, quietly devoted to her husband's search for the holy grail of medicine, the source of his real strength when his spiritual energies are sapped by neurotic wealth. The film is faithful to Cronin's 1937 novel. The book itself was a mirror portrait of the author, a doctor who worked in a backward Scottish mining community and who later moved to London where he established a lucrative and undemanding practice among the rich. Cronin, like his hero, returned to his origins, but not out of traumatic revelations. He grew ill, retired from practice, and lived in the Scottish highlands where he amused himself with writing novels that would hearten the world.

p, Victor Saville; d, King Vidor; w, Ian Dalrymple, Frank Wead, Elizabeth Hill, Emlyn Williams (based on the novel by A. J. Cronin); ph, Harry Stradling; m, Louis Levy; ed, Charles Frend; art d, Lazare Meerson, Alfred Junge.

Drama **(PR:A MPAA:NR)**

CITADEL OF CRIME* (1941) 58m REP bw

Robert Armstrong *(Cal Fullerton)*, Frank Albertson *(Jim Rogers)*, Linda Hayes *(Ellie Jackson)*, Russell Simpson *(Jess Meekins)*, Skeets Gallagher *(Chet)*, William Haade *(Turk)*, Jay Novello *(Vince)*, Paul Fix *(Gerro)*, Bob McKenzie *(Martin Jackson)*, Wade Crosby *(Rufe)*, William Benedict *(Wes Rankins)*.

Anybody who has ever dealt with moonshiners in the hills of Tennessee and Kentucky will quickly note the implausibilities in this script. A mobster gets another hood, Fullerton, a former mountain man, out of prison after exacting a promise from him to go back to the hills (after twenty years of racketeering), and persuade the moonshiners to supply corn liquor to him. Fullerton goes through with his part of the deal, and actually swings it, so that a steady stream of liquor arrives for the syndicate. The law steps in, finally, and Albertson, a U.S. agent, defeats the mob in a wild gun battle, and wins the love of a saloonkeeper's daughter in the bargain.

p&d, George Sherman; w, Don Ryan; ph, Ernest Miller; ed, Les Orlebeck.

Crime Drama **(PR:C MPAA:NR)**

CITIZEN KANE***** (1941) 119m Mercury/RKO bw

Orson Welles *(Charles Foster Kane)*, Joseph Cotten *(Jedediah Leland)*, Dorothy Comingore *(Susan Alexander)*, Everett Sloane *(Mr. Bernstein)*, Ray Collins *(Boss J. W. "Big Jim" Gettys)*, George Coulouris *(Walter Parks Thatcher)*, Agnes Moorehead *(Mrs. Mary Kane)*, Paul Stewart *(Raymond, Head Butler)*, Ruth Warrick *(Mrs. Emily Norton Kane)*, Erskine Sanford *(Herbert Carter)*, William Alland *(Jerry Thompson, Chief Reporter)*, Fortunio Bonanova *(Matisti)*, Gus Schilling *(Head Waiter)*, Philip Van Zandt *(Mr. Rawlston)*, Georgia Backus *(Miss Anderson)*, Harry Shannon *(Jim Kane)*, Sonny Bupp *(Kane III)*, Buddy Swan *(Kane at age 8)*, Alan Ladd *(Reporter)*, Arthur O'Connell *(Reporter)*.

Certainly one of the ten best films of all time, CITIZEN KANE opens in ominous murkiness to show high wrought iron fences filigreed with the initial "K" and beyond which spreads Xanadu, the vast estate of one of the world's wealthiest men. The camera surveys the grounds, empty gondolas swaying on a private lake, the pens of exotic animals in a private zoo, the manicured lawns and shrubbery of another garden of Babylon, all permeated with fog, and towering above the mist of a man-made mountain sits a castle of yore with one light shining. Inside this lit room is a dying man, Kane (Welles), who clutches a crystal ball inside which is a winter scene and make-believe snow. He utters one word: "Rosebud," drops the ball which breaks to tiny shards, and his hand goes limp. He is dead. Thus begins, with a mystery, the story of Charles Foster Kane, newspaper magnate, presidential hopeful, wielder of power and influence. A sudden cut shows a March of Time newsreel recounting the long and colorful career of the publisher and art collector which is stopped. Inside a dark screening room, editor Van Zandt begins to badger a bevy of reporters, asking them to find the real Kane—"It's not enough to tell us what a man did. You've got to tell us who he was. . . . What were the last words he said on earth? Maybe he told us all about himself on his deathbed . . . When Charles Foster Kane died he said but just one word . . . "Rosebud" . . . Now what does that mean?" Alland is assigned to root out Kane/Welles' past and he goes to five people who tell variations of the millionaire's life: Coulouris, his financier guardian; Sloane, his assistant; Cotten, his one-time friend and co-worker; Comingore, his second wife; and Stewart, his shifty eyed butler and head man at Xanadu. Coulouris, a J. P. Morgan character, is long since dead, but Alland visits the Thatcher Memorial Library and is allowed to inspect the financier's memoirs in manuscript. Through Coulouris' words we see Kane as a boy playing with his sled on a snow-swept Colorado farm. He has just inherited, through his mother, a great fortune which was left to her by a recently deceased boarder, a prospector who had discovered one of the world's great silver mines. The boy is to be raised in the East under Coulouris' mentorship. He doesn't like the newcomer, striking him with his sled. Through a series of quick cuts Kane is shown growing up, hating Coulouris and his banker mentality. Coulouris is shown reading a letter from the mature Kane in which he states that of all his holdings a small and struggling old newspaper interests him; "I think it would be *fun* to run a newspaper!" Coulouris reads contemptuously. Welles takes over the newspaper and immediately begins to attack Coulouris' trust and traction interests, infuriating his one-time guardian. Sloane next narrates Welles' early beginnings as a newspaper czar, his takeover of the New York *Enquirer*, his firing of the editor and bringing in a top-notch, expensive staff, making his college friend Cotten the drama critic. Welles is at first a crusader for the downtrodden, opening his first editorial with a Declaration of Principles. He becomes a champion of the little person, hyping his circulation with juicy scandals, crime exposes and, as did newspaper czar William Randolph Hearst, goading the U.S. into the Spanish-American War. Sloane further relates how Welles marries Warrick, the President's niece. The marriage is later shown in quick scenes through several years; first Welles is the devoted husband, then the business-obsessed newsman, and finally the middle-aged crank looking for sexual adventure beyond the breakfast table where all these tense scenes take place. Sloane, by then a corporate executive in flash forward, is pressed by reporter Alland as to the meaning of the word "Rosebud." Sloane doesn't really know: "This 'Rosebud' you're trying to find out about . . . . Maybe that was something he lost. Mr. Kane was a man who lost almost everything he had." Alland next visits Cotten, a senile resident in a Manhattan retirement center who begs him for cigars. Cotten relates his early days in Welles' newspaper empire and the boss' first marriage to Warrick and his second to singer Comingore, along with describing how he created her abortive opera career, even building a $3 million opera house for her in Chicago. Scenes of Welles' disastrous second marriage show the mismatched couple (he met her on a NYC street while she suffered from a toothache) in their cavernous Florida estate, Xanadu. He wanders from chamber to chamber as she sits working enormous puzzles. It is over Comingore that Cotten loses his job, panning her first major operatic performance. It also marks the end of his friendship with the multimillionaire publisher. Comingore then relates her memories of Welles as she sits half-drunk in a nightclub where she is supposedly employed as a singer. Her flashback narration describes her meeting with the married Welles, and their eventual affair, discovered by Warrick who is led to their love-nest by political enemy Collins. Welles explodes, telling Warrick he intends to cling to the relationship with Comingore and threatens to expose Collins and make sure he is imprisoned at "Sing Sing, Gettys . . . . I'm gonna send you to Sing Sing!" Welles does not have to deal with an ugly divorce; his wife and son are killed in an auto accident and he marries Comingore, forcing her into an impossible operatic career, one she unsuccessfully resists. Her first appearance in an opera ends in utter failure with only Welles applauding her from his private box until the audience, packed by Sloane with Welles' cronies, joins in. Comingore attempts suicide and later begs Welles to allow her to stop singing, telling him that audiences "don't like me." He leans close to her and says: "That's when you've got to fight them." She finally convinces him to let her miserable opera career die. Both retire to Xanadu where hordes of servants and friends accompany them on picnics and other outings, but there is no pleasure for them, nor love. Comingore finally decides to leave the media mogul. Welles confronts her with "You can't do this to me." She flares: "I see, it's you this is being done to. It's not me at all. Not what it means to me." With one of the most annoying screeches in film history Comingore lets him have it all: "You don't love me! You want me to love you. Sure. I'm Charles Foster Kane. Whatever you want, just name it and it's yours. But you gotta love me." Welles slaps her and wife number two departs. Welles is left alone in his vast mausoleum of enormous rooms, and his art collection, thousands of statues and paintings still uncrated, never seen nor shown. Shortly thereafter he dies alone, murmuring that word, "Rosebud." Butler Stewart relates the last moments between Welles and Comingore but he, too, is nonplussed about "Rosebud." In the end the reporters gather at Welles' estate, moving through a warehouse that is being cleared of endless piles of curios, stacks of furniture, and countless crates containing Welles' lifetime purchases. They cannot fill in the last piece of the puzzle. As they move off into the dark recesses of the warehouse the camera shows, in a high boom shot, the staggering collection of toys, paintings, statues, then slowly pans the items, coming to a blazing furnace into which workmen throw all items considered junk. One picks up a sled, the very one Welles had as a boy in Colorado, and throws it into the fire. The camera closes in tightly on the top of the sled and as it catches fire the name "Rosebud" is revealed on it before the letters burn off in the consuming flames. The camera shows the outside of the looming castle, going upward to its highest chimney where Welles' youth and past curl upward in smoke into the night sky: then the camera pulls back beyond the iron fence to reveal the sign reading "NO TRESPASSING," the very same sign shown at the film's opening. CITIZEN KANE was a hallmark film for myriad reasons, not the least of which was the incredible techniques employed, quick cuts, imaginative dissolves, even the ancient iris up and down device used in the early silent days. There was nothing of the past that was not used, as well as many innovations, most notable being Gregg Toland's deep-focus photography. Visually this is Toland's film, a cinematic masterpiece of shadow and sharp contrast which reflects the murky moods and occasional moments of gaiety as the camera and Alland search for the meaning of a man's life, the essence of his soul. Welles' direction is awe-inspiring as he chronicles the life in a combination of set dramatic scenes and newsreel-type clips. It is all seen in brief but highly dramatic episodes, a slice here and there forming a patchwork biography. "I don't think any word can explain a man's life," Van Zandt remarks at the end of the film when giving up the quest to solve the "Rosebud" riddle, but his remark is almost a comment on CITIZEN KANE or any other biographical movie, for that matter. Yet this film is so tightly made, so economically shot and written, that every scene counts and every scene fills in a piece of the puzzle, incomplete though it may be at the finish. It is the only way in which anyone's lifetime can be seen on film, concentrating upon the zenith of emotions and events, leaving not a single image but many images all signifying the complexity of a human being. In this case the human being was someone all the world knew in real life—William Randolph Hearst, the most powerful newsman in the U.S. for forty years, a man whose media empire spanned the continent and whose influence was vast, almost as wide as his own political ambitions. Hearst, indeed, did wish to become President. His wife did not die in an accident; he lived apart from her with his paramour, actress Marion Davies, for whom he built San Simeon on the rocky California coast, a stunning palatial estate which is now a state monument. Right from the beginning, Welles denied that Kane was wholly drawn from the newspaper czar: "It is not based upon the life of Mr. Hearst or anyone else. On the other hand, had Mr. Hearst and similar financial barons not lived during the period we discuss, CITIZEN KANE could not have been made." (Welles' portrait of Hearst was drawn accurately enough to bring a 1948 lawsuit against the movie prodigy from Ferdinand Lundberg, author of *Imperial Hearst, A Social Biography*, published in 1936, a suit that was settled out of court.) Welles also took credit for writing most of the superb script, but the bulk of its incisive, witty, and ever-memorable scenes and dialog were no doubt scripted by savant screenwriter Herman Mankiewicz, brother of Joseph Mankiewicz, noted film producer/director/writer. Herman Mankiewicz, a longtime newsman, had intimate knowledge of Hearst, his long affair with Davies, and the strange workings of his empire in that he was Davies's close friend and spent a great deal of time at San Simeon with the Hearsts. His contribution, however, in no way diminished Welles', who wrote many scenes and much dialog, as well as supervised the entire production as director-producer on a shot-by-shot basis, deserving to be credited with the overall masterpiece. This was the first film to introduce this enormous talent, along with the great supporting players Cotten, Moorehead, Collins, Coulouris, Stewart, Sloane, all of whom came out of the distinguished Mercury Players Group in New York City. And by virtue of this extraordinary film, forever linked to Welles' persona, all of the above became permanent fixtures in the best of American films for the next forty years. The story *behind* CITIZEN KANE is almost as fascinating as the film itself. Welles, John Houseman, and others in the Mercury Players produced several successful plays before becoming famous nationwide for the alarming 1938 radio show "War of the Worlds." Many who tuned in on this program late actually thought the U.S. was being invaded by Martians and they panicked, fleeing their homes with hastily grabbed possessions. It was some time before listeners could be convinced that what they were listening to was a dramatic presentation, not a news bulletin. Welles was an overnight sensation and several studios offered him contracts to make his own films, the most attractive coming from the financially shaky RKO, headed by the literate George J. Shaefer, hand-picked by Nelson Rockefeller who had large blocks of stock in the studio (RKO was also infused with lifeblood money at the time by wealthy entrepreneur Floyd Odlum). The Mercury Players were only interested in Hollywood insofar as a contract for a movie would help to finance the group's next Broadway production. Welles at first intended to film Conrad's *Heart of Darkness* as an experimental film where he would narrate with hand-held Eyemo cameras. The budget for this film exceeded $1 million so RKO scratched the project. Welles fielded about for another story. The debate to this day is whether he or Mankiewicz came up with the idea of profiling a multimillionaire which was first called AMERICAN, later JOHN CITIZEN, U.S.A., then finally CITIZEN KANE. Welles studied film at this time night and day and was no doubt inspired by a similar theme encompassed in I LOVED A WOMAN, released in 1933, a story about a millionaire merchant who collects artwork and sponsors a struggling opera singer, one who profits through the Spanish-American War by selling $50 million in spoiled meat to the Army. A MAN TO REMEMBER, 1938, and THE POWER AND THE GLORY, 1933, covered essentially the same ground and were no doubt early influences. Every master filmmaker up to that time came before Welles' darting vision; he spent endless hours watching the films of Vidor, Ford, Lang, Clair, and Capra, being most influenced by the UFA techniques developed by Lang in Germany, dark, brooding camerawork and giant foreboding sets that dwarfed the actors, along with story lines presented in convoluted form. Toland had been experimenting along the UFA lines and was particularly devoted to the deep-focus lensing pioneered by James Wong Howe in TRANSATLANTIC in 1930, and had come into his own with such classics as LES MISERABLES, THE LONG VOYAGE HOME, THE GRAPES OF WRATH, and WUTHERING HEIGHTS, for which he won an Oscar. It was Toland who called the twenty-five-year-old Welles when he heard of the CITIZEN KANE project, requesting the cinematographer slot and getting it instantly. He made good use of dolly, pan, and truck shots in lap dissolves which supplemented direct cuts. The great cameraman explained that his unique deep focus was a simple matter of adjusting lenses. "For example," he stated in a 1941 edition of *The American Cinematographer*, "I discovered that a 24mm lens, stopped down to f:8 or less, becomes almost literally a universal focus objective at a certain point. If it is set to focus on a point 4 feet 6 inches in front of the camera, everything from 18 inches to infinity will be in acceptably sharp focus." Welles not only had a say in every setup shot taken by Toland but was allowed complete control of the film, a rare privilege for any creative artist, especially one so untested and youthful. No one at RKO could interfere with him or anyone in the production, according to his contract. He also retained final editing approval of the film. The budget was another thing. Welles was on a tight financial rein and stayed in harness by masking many of his bigger sets, such as the long exterior shot of the newspaper office and the main hall at Xanadu where a gigantic fireplace and some pillars recede into a darkness where no walls existed. He reversed this image by using floor-to-ceiling shots to enlarge his characters, using muslin set ceilings with rear lighting. Welles kept to his budget which, according to varying reports, was between $686,000 and $842,000. He brought composer Bernard Hermann in to score the film; Hermann had been the composer for the Mercury Players' radio productions, and this gifted man created a chilling haunting score, watching the film unfold reel by reel and composing on the spot, tailoring his music to the scenes as they were freshly made, unlike the usual Hollywood method where the composer comes in to score only after the entire film is completed. "In this way," Hermann was later quoted, "I had a sense of the picture being built and my own music being part of that building." The editing of the film by Wise and Mark Robson (who is uncredited) is as brilliant as every other technical achievement in the film. One of the most startling scenes which convinces the viewer that Toland's camera actually goes through glass from the exterior roof of a nightclub through a skylight and into the club in a single take was achieved with a small trick. As the camera moves over the roof a storm is breaking and, just as the camera zooms down on to a skylight, a flash of lightning causes a few frames to go blank and it is inside these blank frames that the dissolve to the inside of the club takes place. The primary subjects of CITIZEN KANE were undoubtedly the imperialistic William Randolph Hearst, and his evergreen paramour, movie star Marion Davies. Hearst dumped millions into his Cosmopolitan Pictures, the producing unit that made her films (she called Hearst "Old Droopy Drawers"). Many claimed that Welles used munitions magnate Basil Zaharoff or millionaire stock swindler Ivar Kreuger or Kodak's chief Jules Brulatour as the role model for Kane, particularly the latter since he compelled his wife into a failed operatic career. Though Davies' own career was not a failure like the tragic Susan Alexander (Comingore), it is probable that Welles took the Kane-Alexander relationship from *both* Hearst-Davies and the bizarre relationship between Chicago newspaper czar Harold McCormick (of the Chicago *Tribune* family), who left his wife, Edith Rockefeller McCormick, after being vamped by a preposterous Polish prima donna named Ganna Walska. McCormick was the chief sponsor of the Chicago Opera Company and set up Walska to perform in the opera *Zaza*, after hiring Frances Alda, one of the most expensive singing coaches in the world, to help develop her awful voice (Alda being superbly played by Fortunio Bonanova in CITIZEN KANE). The 1920 *Zaza* was a disaster, with Walska walking out and McCormick chasing her to Europe where she convinced him that the only way he could cure his impotence was to have thyroid glands from monkeys transplanted into his own body by a quack Fountain-of-Youth advocate, Dr. Serge Voronoff. After taking Harold for a fortune, Walska waltzed through several other wealthy men and then settled on a vast estate on the California coast. Welles knew well of the McCormick-Walska affair from his boyhood days in the Midwest; in fact, the couple so fascinated him, according to one report, that he kept a notebook on their scandalous activities. But the one person who was utterly convinced that CITIZEN KANE was a scabrous attack on her employer, Hearst, was the powerful gossip columnist Louella Parsons. Her column ran in all the Hearst papers and she was so influential that a bad word from her could mortally wound any film's box office receipts. Hearst himself supposedly received the script of CITIZEN KANE in advance, read it, and said nothing. Parsons, on the other hand, viewed the film with her chauffeur holding her hand and two Hearst lawyers, sitting in the RKO screening room with Welles. She had demanded he show the film to her before its release. After it ended she walked out without saying a word to Welles, and went running to WRH to report that it sullied his good name. Marion Davies called the film "grotesque," after viewing a print shown at San Simeon, but the 79-year-old Hearst strangely enjoyed it, amused by its profile of his empire. To a friend who mentioned the film when visiting his palatial estate, Hearst remarked: "We have it here. I must run it off again sometime." Parsons, however, intended to champion her master and launched a campaign to ban the film or even have it destroyed. Louis B. Mayer, head of MGM, was the first to respond to her pleas. RKO President Schaefer received a call from Nicholas Schenck, a large studio stockholder. According to Bosley Crowther of the New York *Times*, Schenck told Schaefer that "Louis [B. Mayer] has asked me to speak to you about this picture. He is prepared to pay you what it cost, which he understands is $800,000, if you will destroy the negative and all the prints." Schaefer considered, then went to Nelson Rockefeller, who had the lion's share of RKO stock. Rockefeller backed Schaefer, who then got word to Mayer that he would not buckle under, yet when Rockefeller got a phone call from Parsons warning him to disassociate himself from the film, the banker refused to have CITIZEN KANE shown in Radio City Music Hall, his own theater. The Hearst press, with Parsons leading the screaming charge, attacked the film on all sides and it found few bookings outside the RKO theaters. Schaefer finally confronted Warner Bros. executives who had banned it from their far-flung theaters. Bristling with anger, the brave studio chief is quoted as saying to the head of the theatre chain: "You aren't booking it [the film] because Louie Mayer has got together with Joe Schenck and Harry Warner and arranged with them to keep it off the screen. So I'm asking you for the last time—are you going to book it or not? Because if you think this conspiracy is going to keep it off the screen, you are mistaken. I'll sue and expose the conspiracy!" Warner Bros. relented and so did most of the other theater chains. CITIZEN KANE went out to the American public and found critical raves and public acceptance, but it still lost about $160,000, later made up in many successful re-releases (which enriched Welles, who owned 25 percent of its profits). Mayer continued to damn the film but this was to appease the grand harpie, Parsons. His real fear from the first was that Parsons and the Hearst press would publicize the many scandals hidden away in their secret files, especially certain sensational affairs of movie moguls, not the least of whom was Louis B. Mayer. CITIZEN KANE, no matter its role model now, stands as proof that the movies are the most powerful medium in the world. It has influenced important filmmakers and established the taste of discerning audiences. It is the very epitome of filmmaking at its best, its most energetic, most creative. (It is astonishing to see that CITIZEN KANE received only one Oscar, one that was shared by Mankiewicz and Welles for Best Screenplay.) For this incredible achievement Welles will be forever linked with the zenith of the art. It is an unqualified masterpiece and in years to come when Hearst is as wholly forgotten as Parsons is now, Charles Foster Kane will be only Orson Welles, and Welles will be Kane, as it was meant to be at the beginning.

p&d, Orson Welles; w, Herman J. Mankiewicz, Welles; ph, Gregg Toland; m, Bernard Herrmann; ed, Robert Wise and, uncredited, Mark Robson; art d, Van Nest Polglase, Perry Ferguson; cos, Edward Stevenson; spec eff, Vernon L. Walker.

Drama/Biography Cas. (PR:A MPAA:NR)

CITIZEN SAINT** (1947) 73m State-rights bw

Carla Dare *(Mother Cabrini)*, Julie Haydon *(Sister Delphina)*, June Harrison *(Dorine)*, Clark Williams *(The Prisoner)*, Del Cansino *(Perry)*, Robin Morgan *(Cecchina)*, Maurice Cavell *(Anton)*, Lucille Fenton *(Antonia Tordini)*, Joy Bannister *(Sister Grace)*, Ruth Moore *(Sister Chiera)*, William Harrigan *(Father Vail)*, Ralph Simone *(The Peddler)*, William Sharon *(The Prison Guard)*, George Kluge *(Archbishop)*, Lauretta Campeau *(Salesia)*, Jane Dufrayne *(Veronica)*, Kurt Kupfer *(The Baker)*, Alma Du Bus *(Committee Chairman)*, Richard Good *(Dr. Riley)*, Boris Aplon *(Landlord)*.

A story about the life and miracles of Mother Frances Cabrini. The film opens and closes with real clips of Cabrini being canonized by the Pope in Rome. In between we see Cabrini, played by Dare, as she works a few of the sister's best miracles, while showing her devotion to the church and the sense of humor that carried her through trying times. A couple of the miracles have Dare calling a sister, Haydon back from death, and giving the voice back to a singer who has gone mute.

p, Clyde Elliott; d, Harold Young; w, Harold Orlob; ph, Don Malkaunes; m, Orlob; ed, Leonard Anderson; m/l, Orlob, Arthur A. Norris.

Religious Drama (PR:AA MPAA:NR)

CITIZENS BAND* (1977) 98m PAR c (AKA: HANDLE WITH CARE)

Paul LeMat *(Spider, Blaine)*, Candy Clark *(Electra, Pam)*, Ann Wedgeworth *(Joyce Rissley)*, Bruce McGill *(Blood, Dean)*, Marcia Rodd *(Portland Angel, Connie)*, Charles Napier *(Chrome Angel, Harold)*, Alix Elias *(Hot Coffee, Debbie)*, Roberts Blossom *(Papa Thermadyne, Father)*, Richard Bright *(Smilin' Jack, Garage Owner)*, Ed Begley, Jr. *(Priest)*, Michael Rothman *(Cochise)*, Michael Mahler *(Hustler)*, *Harry Northrup (Red Baron)*, Will Seltzer *(Warlock)*.

A philandering truck driver who gets in an accident is a funny angle to this series of vignettes based on the CB radio craze that struck Hollywood several years after the public and truckers discovered the fad. Napier has a lover, Wedgeworth, in Dallas, and another, Rodd, in Portland, and has fathered children by both. In the hospital after his accident, he is recovering at the hands of Elias. Meanwhile, LeMat, a CB junkie, and McGill are romancing Clark in a small town where Napier's two suspicious wives converge to learn the truth. Film was produced by former big-band leader Shep ("Rippling Rhythm") Fields, brother of studio chief Freddie Fields.

p, Shep Fields; d, Jonathan Demme; w, Paul Brickman; ph, Jordan Cronenweth (Movielab Color); m, Bill Conti; ed, John F. Link II; art d, Bill Malley; set d, Ira Bates; cos, Jodie Lynn Tillen.

Comedy **(PR:C MPAA:R)**

CITY ACROSS THE RIVER½** (1949) 90m UNIV bw

Stephen McNally *(Stan Albert)*, Thelma Ritter *(Mrs. Cusack)*, Luis Van Rooten *(Joe Cusack)*, Jeff Corey *(Lt. Macon)*, Sharon McManus *(Alice Cusack)*, Sue England *(Betty)*, Barbara Whiting *(Annie Kane)*, Richard Benedict *(Gaggsy Steens)*, Peter Fernandez *(Frank Cusack)*, Al Ramsen *(Benny Wilks)*, Joshua Shelley *(Crazy Perrin)*, Anthony (Tony) Curtis *(Mitch)*, Mickey Knox *(Larry)*, Richard Jaeckel *(Bull)*, Anabel Shaw *(Jean Albert)*, Robert Osterloh *(Mr. Bannon)*, Al Eben *(Detective Kleiner)*, Sara Berner *(Selma)*, Bert Conway *(Mr. Hayes)*, Frank Cady *(Shirley's Partner)*, Sandra Gould *(Shirley)*, John Pickard *(Detective)*, Judy Ann Nugent *(Little Girl)*, Alfred Croce *(Boy Dancer)*, Joe Draper *(Policeman)*, Joseph Turkel *(Shimmy)*.

Based on Irving Shulman's hot 1940s novel, *The Amboy Dukes*, this was *the* picture for teenagers to see in 1949. It all takes place in the shade of the Brooklyn Bridge and purports to show how crowded tenement life leads to crime. The Amboy Dukes (so named after Amboy Street) are the tough guys in the area and Fernandez, one of their members, goes too far when he and a pal rough up their shop teacher. The result is the man's death and Fernandez becomes a fugitive. The remainder of the film shows the boys hiding out, their ultimate hatred of each other, and a battle between Fernandez and Ramsen on a rooftop. There are several sidebar stories involving the kids and some excellent first-times-out for a few of the young actors. The gang leader is played perfectly by Anthony (Tony) Curtis and especially memorable is Shelley as a somewhat retarded knifer. Much of WEST SIDE STORY comes from the same roots and there are similarities in several of the characters. Benedict (Steens) went on to become a very successful TV director; Shelley is now teaching acting; Jaeckel still works often as an actor and hasn't aged at all—the man must have a direct line to Dorian Gray; Turkel is also often seen and often featured by Stanley Kubrick (THE SHINING, PATHS OF GLORY). Due to the nature of the Production Code, much of the sex was toned down or eliminated altogether. *The Amboy Dukes* was one of those books teenagers passed around in school, for a close perusal of "the good parts" (i.e., sex) by everyone. Because it broke new ground for films like THE BLACKBOARD JUNGLE, CITY ACROSS THE RIVER remembers better than it actually was.

p&d, Maxwell Shane; w, Shane, Dennis Cooper, Irving Shulman (based on Shulman's novel *The Amboy Dukes*); ph, Maury Gertsman; m, Walter Scharf; ed, Ted J. Kent; art d, Bernard Herzbrun, Emrich Nicholson; set d, Russell A. Gausman, John Austin; spec eff, David S. Horsley.

Drama **(PR:C MPAA:NR)**

CITY AFTER MIDNIGHT** (1957, Brit.) 85m Monarch bw (GB:THAT WOMAN OPPOSITE)

Phyllis Kirk *(Eve Atwood)*, Dan O'Herlihy *(Dermot Kinross)*, Wilfrid Hyde-White *(Sir Maurice Lawes)*, Petula Clark *(Janice)*, Jack Watling *(Toby)*, William Franklyn *(Ned)*, Guido Lorraine *(Goron)*, Margaret Withers *(Lady Lawes)*, Balbina *(Prue)*.

Kirk is the ex-wife of a jewel thief accused of the murder of her fiance's father. Enter detective O'Herlihy to clear the innocent girl and apprehend the real killer. No surprises in this routine whodunit.

p, William Gell; d&w, Compton Bennett (based on the novel *The Emperor's Snuffbox* by John Dickson Carr); ph, Lionel Banes; m, Stanley Black.

Crime **(PR:C MPAA:NR)**

CITY BENEATH THE SEA** (1953) 87m UNIV c (GB: ONE HOUR TO DOOM'S DAY)

Robert Ryan *(Brad Carlton)*, Mala Powers *(Terry)*, Anthony Quinn *(Tony Bartlett)*, Suzan Ball *(Venita)*, George Mathews *(Capt. Meade)*, Karel Stepanek *(Dwight Trevor)*, Lalo Rios *(Calypso)*, Hilo Hattie *(Mama Mary)*, Woody Strode *(Djion)*, John Warburton *(Capt. Clive)*, Peter Mamakos *(Mendoza)*, Barbara Morrison *(Mme. Cecile)*, LeRol Antoine *(Calypso Singer)*, Leon Lontoc *(Kip)*, Marya Marco *(Half Caste Woman)*, Bernie Cozier.

Mathews is the only one who knows where the treasure is—in the sunken city of Port Royal, and he persuades Quinn to double-cross Ryan and take the diving job himself. Ryan finds out about this in time and hires out to Stepanek, trying to beat Quinn to the gold. Mathews and Quinn get to the scene just in time to see Ryan go down. The mutual double-cross is forgotten when Quinn rescues Ryan, who becomes trapped underwater by an earthquake.

p, Albert J. Cohen; d, Budd Boetticher; w, Jack Harvey, Ramon Romero (based on the story "Port Royal—Ghost City Beneath The Sea" by Harry E. Riesberg); ph, Charles P. Boyle (Technicolor); m, Frederick Herbert, Arnold Hughes; ed, Edward Curtiss; spec eff, David S. Horsley.

Adventure **(PR:C MPAA:NR)**

CITY FOR CONQUEST*½** (1941) 105m WB/FN bw

James Cagney *(Danny Kenny)*, Ann Sheridan *(Peggy Nash)*, Frank Craven *("Old Timer")*, Donald Crisp *(Scotty McPherson)*, Arthur Kennedy *(Eddie Kenny)*, Frank McHugh *("Mutt")*, George Tobias *(Pinky)*, Blanche Yurka *(Mrs. Nash)*, Elia Kazan *("Googi")*, Anthony Quinn *(Murray Burns)*, Bob Steele *(Callahan)*, George Lloyd *("Goldie")*, Jerome Cowan *(Dutch)*, Lee Patrick *(Gladys)*, Joyce Compton *(Lilly)*, Thurston Hall *(Max Leonard)*, Ben Welden *(Cobb)*, John Arledge *(Salesman)*, Selmer Jackson, Joseph Crehan *(Doctors)*, Billy Wayne *(Henchman)*, Pat Flaherty *(Floor Guard)*, Sidney Miller *(M.C)*, Ethelreda Leopold *(Dressing Room Blonde)*, Lee Phelps, Charles Wilson, Ed Gargan, Howard Hickman, Murray Alper, Dick Wessel, Bernice Pilot, Charles Lane, Dana Dale, Margaret Hayes, Ed Pawley, William Newell, Lucia Carroll.

Cagney is at his dynamic best in this poignant tale about two impoverished youngsters who rise from the ghetto of New York City's Lower East Side, only to slide back down the ladder of success. Truck driver Cagney and Sheridan are engaged to be married but she is discontented and encourages him to make something of himself. She also has the ambition to become a successful dancer. Cagney enters the ring to become a top-ranking boxing contender and Sheridan goes off with Quinn to form a dance act that is the rage of the nightclub circuit. When she returns Cagney will have nothing to do with her; he believes she has been carrying on with smoothie Quinn. He trains furiously for a championship fight but during the match is blinded in the ring when his opponent, his gloves dipped in an acid-like solution, pounds away at his eyes. Cagney's good friend Googi Zucco (Kazan, later one of Hollywood's best directors) attempts to avenge the blinding by killing the hoodlum behind the blinding, but is in turn shot himself. Helpless, Cagney is finally set up by his manager, Crisp, with a newsstand where he sells papers and magazines. All the while Cagney's composer brother Kennedy has been struggling with his symphony, which he manages to complete with Cagney's forceful encouragement. Sheridan then returns, her career a bust and Quinn having deserted her. She visits Cagney at his newsstand in a tear-jerking scene and both of them listen to the radio broadcasting Kennedy's first symphony which is a triumph. The film ends with Cagney and Sheridan merely good friends, their careers smashed but their love for each other intact and it is implied that they will eventually marry. CITY FOR CONQUEST is an often heavy melodrama but it has consistently good dialog and a spritely style. Cagney, of course, emerges with a powerhouse performance that is captivating. Sheridan is a rather wishy-washy prop to Cagney's fiesty persona. Quinn is very good as an oily, thoroughly repugnant lounge lizard whose only talents are quick feet and a bright-lights come-on. Steiner's score is as strong as a right cross and Litvak's direction is never routine, often inspired as he races his cameras along with Cagney's flight to fame and disaster. "It was a very good part," Sheridan said later, when recalling her role in the film, "and of course it was Cagney again. He sold like wildfire. To be in a picture with him was just the greatest." CITY FOR CONQUEST was a hot property that had several directors asking to head it. Raoul Walsh was originally set to helm the film but Litvak took over. Both George Raft and Cesar Romero went after the sleazy dancer role but Quinn won the part. There was a reason for Sheridan to feel lucky in getting her role opposite Cagney. Jack Warner first tried to get Ginger Rogers in her part but she had other commitments. Then he signed Sylvia Sidney to perform the role but Sheridan got the part when Sidney backed out. By this time Sheridan was promoted by the studio as "The Oomph Girl," meaning she had plenty of sex appeal. After completing CITY FOR CONQUEST, Sheridan was stopped by a man at a Hollywood party who asked: "Are you really the Oomph Girl?" She frowned at the thought of it and replied: "That's right. Oomph you!" For Cagney, the film was a tour de force where he brought into play every technique he had learned as an amateur boxer and fight enthusiast. He had been a regular fight-goer, though he argued long and loud against the use of gloves, claiming it was much safer to return to bare knuckles, that gloves caused more injury and the eventual brain damage occurring with many fighters. He was forty-two when he made CITY FOR CONQUEST and carried too much weight on his stocky frame, more than 180 pounds, a result of his food-loving habits. He threw himself into a frenzied training schedule, almost as if he were readying himself for a real championship match, losing thirty pounds and toning his body to hard muscle. His fight scenes are realistically photographed by veteran cameramen Polito and Howe and in many scenes actual hard blows were exchanged between the actor and the fighters opposing him in the ring. One partner sucker-punched him and made his legs go wobbly. Cagney, enraged, let loose his best punch and sent the fighter to the canvas. Litvak, a demanding European-trained director, found the going rough with Cagney. The two argued over just about every scene. The director didn't like the choreography Cagney worked into his footwork (he was also an excellent dancer) and little of this fancy footstepping remains in the film. Most of Cagney's ideas were edited out of the final version. When the actor viewed the film he vowed never again to watch one of his own films. Moreover, he felt the story had been ruined and he sent a note of apology to the author, Aben Kandel. Yet the critics and public alike loved the film and the zesty, dramatic actor whose mere presence on the screen was enough to assure a box-office success.

p&d, Anatole Litvak; w, John Wexley (based on the novel by Aben Kandel); ph, Sol Polito, James Wong Howe; m, Max Steiner; ed, William Holmes; art d, Robert Haas; md, Leo F. Forbstein; cos, Howard Shoup; orches, Hugo Friedhofer, Ray Heindorf; ch, Robert Vreeland; spec eff, Byron Haskin, Rex Wimpy; makeup, Perc Westmore.

Sports Drama **(PR:A MPAA:NR)**

CITY GIRL*½ (1930) 68m FOX bw

Charles Farrell *(Lem Tustine)*, Mary Duncan *(Kate)*, David Torrence *(Tustine)*, Edith Yorke *(Mrs. Tustine)*, Dawn O'Day *(Mary Tustine)*, Tom Maguire *(Matey)*, Dick Alexander *(Mac)*, Pat Rooney *(Butch)*, Ed Brady, Roscoe Ates *(Reapers)*, A.F. "Buddy" Erickson.

This F. W. Murnau film was started as a silent movie. Meant to have been an epic of the wheatfields, it's original title was BREAD, and would account for the film's obsession with wheat. The story takes a long time to unfold. Charles Farrell plays a son of a farmer who goes to town to sell his wheat and find a wife. Though wheat prices are poor, he does find a wife. Back on the farm, his mother is delighted but his father is suspicious of the city girl. A farmhand decides to make a play for the new woman of the farm, and goes into her bedroom during a storm. The father walks in on them and the son promptly beats up the farmhand, exacting a confession.

d, F. W. Murnau; w, Berthold Viertel, Marion Orth (based on the play "The Mud Turtle" by Elliott Lester); ph, Ernest Palmer; m, Arthur Kay; ed, Katherine Hilliker, H. H. Caldwell.

Drama (PR:A MPAA:NR)

CITY GIRL*½ (1938) 60m FOX bw
Phyllis Brooks (*Ellen Ward*), Ricardo Cortez (*Charles Blake*), Robert Wilcox (*Donald Sanford*), Douglas Fowley (*Ritchie*), Chick Chandler (*Mike Harrison*), Esther Muir (*Flo Nichols*), Adrienne Ames (*Vivian Ross*), George Lynn (*Steve*), Charles Lane (*Dr. Abbott*), Paul Stanton (*Ralph Chaney*), Norman Willis (*Leader*), Richard Terry, Lon Chaney, Jr. (*Gangsters*), Lee Phelps (*Sgt. Farrell*), Ralph Dunn (*Mac The Policeman*), Marjorie Main (*Mrs. Ward*), Charles Trowbridge (*Pierson*), Robert Lowery (*Greenleaf*), Heinie Conklin (*Cook*), Gloria Roy (*Girl in Cafe*), Edward Marr (*Gangster, Wearing Derby*), Edgar Dearing (*Detective Lieutenant*), Lee Shumway (*Policeman*), Eddie Hart, Jack Gargan, King Mojave (*Bookies*), Ben Welden (*Blake's Valet*), Lynn Bari (*Waitress*), Harold Goodwin (*Chaney's Aide*), Cyril Ring (*Cigar Stand Proprietor*), George Magrill (*Plainclothesman*), George Reed (*Elevator Operator*), Irving Bacon (*Porter*), Wade Boteler (*Police Radio Announcer*), Emmett Vogan (*Policeman in Phone Booth*), Milton Kibbee (*Doctor's Assistant*), Harry Worth (*Gangster in Phone Booth*), Carroll Nye (*Radio Commentator*), William Newell (*Gas Station Attendant*), Brooks Benedict (*Pete*), Chick Collins (*Customer*).

Meant no doubt to be a tear-jerker, CITY GIRL does nothing more than reiterate the cliche—crime does not pay. A dense waitress, who hopes her way is paved with diamonds and furs when she takes up with a gangster, dumps her boy friend, a district attorney. The gangster's ploy, in turn, is to use her to get information out of the lawman. Before it is over, city girl sacrifices her life for the D.A. she truly loves.

p, Sol M. Wurtzel; d, Alfred Werker; w, Frances Hyland, Robin Harris, Lester Ziffren; ph, Harry Jackson; ed, Norman Colbert; md, Samuel Kaylin.

Crime (PR:C MPAA:NR)

CITY IN DARKNESS
(SEE: CHARLIE CHAN IN THE CITY OF DARKNESS, 1939)

CITY LIMITS*½ (1934) 68m MON bw
Frank Craven (*J. B. Matthews*), Sally Blane (*Helen Matthews*), Ray Walker (*Jimmy Dugan*), Claude Gillingwater (*Oliver*).

Humorous byplay abounds in this story about a railroad president and a reporter on the trail of a good story. The reporter infiltrates the inner council of Craven, the railroad president, who is ill, by pretending to be a doctor's assistant. Craven decides to roll away on his private train to escape the pressures of the office. He meets two hoboes, the reporter meets his daughter, and the old man returns from the train ride in time to hand the reporter a scoop and save the railroad.

p, William T. Lackey; d, William Nigh; w, George Waggner (based on a novel by Jack Woodford); ph, Jerry Ashe; ed, Jack Ogilvie.

Comedy (PR:A MPAA:NR)

CITY LOVERS zero (1982, S. African) 60m TeleCulture Inc./TelePool GmbH c
Joe Stewardson (*Dr. Franz Von Leinsdorff*), Denise Newman (*Yvonne Jacobs*).

Interracial sex in South Africa rears its head in this dull "message" film about a geologist, Stewardson, who falls in love with Newman, a mixed-race woman. Meeting in the supermarket for the first time, Stewardson gives Newman a part-time job as his housekeeper, and before long she is in his bed. Neighbors with their hackles up report the pair to the police, and there follows a search of Stewardson's house and a frightening gynecological exam of the woman by the police. The preachy tone of this film turns it into a bore, and the message vanishes in yawns.

p, Christopher Davies; d&w, Barney Simon (from a story by Nadine Gordimer); ph, Paul Hambides; m, Joan Oakley-Smith; ed, Lionel Selwyn; art d, Anita Berman.

Drama (PR:C MPAA:NR)

CITY NEWS*½ (1983) 65m Cinecom International c
Elliot Crown (*Tom*), Nancy Cohen (*Daphne*), Thomas Trivier (*Frenchy*), Richard Schlesiger (*Lou*), Valerie Felitto (*DeeDee*), Tony Mangis (*Tony*), Gail Gibney (*Gail*), David Fishelson (*Punch*), Zoe Zinman (*Judy*).

A low-budget film that rises to stylishness in its humorous look at the struggles of an underground newspaper to stay afloat. Crown, its publisher-editor, both narrates and acts out his story in flashback as he scribbles his recent life story for the paper. Figuring in the plot twists is a woman he meets in a Greenwich Village bar and who provides the inspiration for his creative escatpe into a "City News" autobiographical cartoon strip his paper publishes. Some chuckles come from deep inside.

p,d,w&ed, David Fishelson, Zoe Zinman; ph, Jonathan Sinaiko (DuArt color); m, Saheb Sarbib, Jules Baptiste, Peter Gordon, Monty Waters, Duke Ellington, The Normal; spec eff, Daniel Nauke, Robert Luttrell.

Comedy/Drama (PR:C MPAA:NR)

CITY OF BAD MEN** (1953) 81m FOX c
Jeanne Crain (*Linda Culligan*), Dale Robertson (*Brett Stanton*), Richard Boone (*Jim Ringo*), Lloyd Bridges (*Gar Stanton*), Carole Mathews (*Cynthia London*), Carl Betz (*Phil Ryan*), Whitfield Connor (*Jim London*), Hugh Sanders (*Sheriff Gifford*), Rodolfo Acosta (*Mendoza*), Pasquel Garcia Pena (*Pig*), Harry Carter (*Jack*), Robert Adler (*Barney*), John Doucette (*Cinch*), Alan Dexter (*Flint*), Don Haggerty (*Thrailkill*), James Best (*Gig*), Leo V. Gordon (*Russell*), Gil Perkins (*Bob Fitzsimmons*), John Day (*James Corbett*), Richard Cutting (*Mr. Davis*), Douglas Evans (*William Brady*), Kit Carson (*Deputy*), Tom McDonough (*Deputy Tex*), Charles B. Smith (*Henry*), Harry Hines (*Stewpot*), Jane Easton (*Singer in Saloon*), Anthony Jochim (*Blister*), Leo Curley (*Harry Wade*), George Melford, George Selk, (*Old Timers*), Charles Tannen (*Cashier*), Gordon Nelson (*Doctor*), Barbara Fuller, Harry Brown.

The Jim Corbett and Bob Fitzsimmons heavyweight championship fight in 1897 in Carson City, Nevada, is recreated in this offbeat western, which finds three outlaws, led by Robertson who is coming home after several years fighting in the Mexican revolution, riding into town hoping to steal the gate receipts of the fight. A smart sheriff, Sanders, swears them in as deputies assigned to protecting the box office cash. This doesn't stop the crooks, however, until Robertson finds his old sweetheart, Crain, in town and changes his mind about stealing the money. In the double-cross of the other two outlaws, he kills them and saves the cash.

p, Leonard Goldstein; d, Harmon Jones; w, George W. George, George F. Slavin; ph, Charles G. Clarke (Technicolor); m, Lionel Newman; ed, George A. Gittens.

Western (PR:A MPAA:NR)

CITY OF BEAUTIFUL NONSENSE, THE** (1935, Brit.) 88m But bw
Emlyn Williams (*Jack Grey*), Sophie Stesart (*Jill Dealtry*), Eve Lister (*Amber*), George Carney (*Chesterton*), Marie Wright (*Dorothy Grey*), Eric Maturin (*Robert Downing*), J. Fisher White (*Thomas Grey*), Daisy Dormer (*Mrs. Deakin*), Hubert Harben (*Mr. Dealtry*), Margaret Damer (*Mrs. Dealtry*), Derek Oldham (*Singer*).

Struggling young composer Williams is in love with Stesart, but she is promised to a rich man. Predictable melodrama first filmed as a silent in 1920.

p, Wilfred Noy; d, Adrian Brunel; w, Donavan Pedelty (based on a novel by E. Temple Thurston); ph, Desmond Dickinson.

Drama (PR:A MPAA:NR)

CITY OF CHANCE*½ (1940) 57m FOX bw
Lynn Bari (*Julie Reynolds*), C. Aubrey Smith (*The Judge*), Donald Woods (*Steve Walker*), Amanda Duff (*Lois Blane*), June Gale (*Molly*), Richard Lane (*Marty Conners*), Robert Lowery (*Ted Blaine*), Alexander D'Arcy (*Baron Joseph*), George Douglas (*Muscles*), Harry Shannon (*Passline*), Edward Marr (*Charlie Nevins*), Robert Allen (*Fred Walcott*), Charlotte Wynters (*Mrs. Walcott*), Nora Lane (*Mrs. Grainger*).

A Texas girl with a mind of her own takes in the New York scene in this amusing tale. Bari gets a job as a newspaper reporter in New York, with the aim of getting her boy friend, Woods, who runs a large gambling operation, to come back to Texas with her. How does she do it? She goes to the casino to gather facts for a story, then tips off the police, who raid the joint, putting her boy friend out of business. Broke, Woods agrees to settle down.

p, Sol M. Wurtzel; d, Ricardo Cortez; w, John Larkin, Barry Trivers; ph, Lucien Andriot; ed, Norma Colbert; md, Samuel Kaylin.

Crime/Drama (PR:C MPAA:NR)

CITY OF FEAR**½ (1959) 75m COL bw
Vince Edwards (*Vince Ryker*), Lyle Talbot (*Chief Jensen*), John Archer (*Lt. Mark Richards*), Steven Ritch (*Dr. Wallace*), Patricia Blair (*Amber*), Joe Mell (*Crown*), Sherwood Price (*Hallon*), Cathy Browne (*Jeanne*), Kelly Thordsen (*Sgt. Johnson*).

What happens to those nuts who think they've stolen something valuable, and find out it's a container filled with radioactive material? CITY OF FEAR attempts an answer as escaped convict Edwards does just that, thinking the container if filled with heroin. The story settles down into a chase, as the authorities try to catch him before he exposes the public to radiation. During the chase, Edwards gets sicker and sicker from the leaking container, and finally the question is answered—they quite possibly die, as Edwards does.

p, Leon Chooluck; d, Irving Lerner; w, Steven Ritch, Robert Dillon; ph, Lucien Ballard; m, Jerry Goldsmith; ed, Robert Lawrence.

Suspense (PR:C MPAA:NR)

CITY OF FEAR*½ (1965, Brit.) 90m Towers of London-Javelin/AA bw
Terry Moore (*Suzan*), Albert Lieven (*Paul*), Marisa Mell (*Ilona*), Paul Maxwell (*Mike Foster*), Pinkas Braun (*Ferenc*), Zsu Zsu Banki (*Magda*), Maria Takacs (*Marika*), Birgit Heiberg (*Zsu Zsu*), Maria Rohm (*Eva*), Helga Lehner (*Eva*).

Maxwell is a Canadian newspaper reporter en route to Hungary who is approached by a man who wants him to carry a package that he says contains medicine into the country for his niece. He gets the package into the country but loses the phone number he is supposed to call. He arranges for a call to be put out on the radio and soon Mell approaches him, claiming to be the recipient. He discovers that the package contains two passports intended to help scientist Lieven escape to Austria, and then learns that Mell is a police spy, as is the man who had given him the package in the first place. He learns that they plan to arrest him as a spy, then trade him to the Americans for one of their own captured agents. Before this nefarious scheme can be put into action, though, Maxwell disarms a border guard and escapes to Austria with Lieven and American fashion expert Moore. Boring, confusing espionage drama shot on location in Austria and Hungary.

p, Sandy Howard, Arthur Steloff, Harry Alan Towers; d, Peter Bezencenet; w, Peter

Welbeck (Harry Alan Towers), Max Bourne; ph, Martin Curtis; m, Johnny Douglas; ed, Peter Boita; art d, Peter Best; set d, Richard Over.

Spy/Drama   **(PR:C   MPAA:NR)**

CITY OF MISSING GIRLS*   (1941) 73m SEL bw
H.B. Warner (Capt. McVeigh), Astrid Allwyn (Nora Page), John Archer (James Horton), Sarah Padden (Mrs. Randolph), Philip Van Zandt (King Peterson), George Rosener (Officer Dugan), Katherine Crawford (Helen Whitney), Patricia Knox (Kate Nelson), Walter Long (Officer Larkin), Gail Storm (Mary Phillips), Boyd Irwin (Joseph Thompson), Danny Webb (William Short).

An awkward murder mystery about a phony art school from which pretty women are booked into a night spot, and some are subsequently murdered. Enter the girl reporter, Allwyn, who slams away at the district attorney for his failure to find the murderer of the women. Turns out that the guilty party is her own father, a theatrical agent, the brains behind the racket.

p, Max Alexander, George M. Merrick; d, Elmer Clifton; w, Oliver Drake, George Rosener; ph, Edward Linden.

Mystery   **PR:A   MPAA:NR**

CITY OF PAIN**   (1951, Ital.) 110m Scalera bw
Luigi Tosi (Berto), Barbara Costanova (Silvana), Gianni Rizzo (Sergio), Elio Steiner (Martini), Constance Dowling (Lubitza).

In 1947 the inhabitants of Pola, Yugoslavia, were given the choice of going to Italy or remaining when the Communists took over. One family that decided to stay, a father who believes in communism, his wife, and their young child, run into difficulties when the child falls sick and needs more medical attention than it can get in Pola. A Yugoslavian official, who has eyes for the wife, manages to get the mother and child to Italy, while the father remains behind. Too late the father realizes his mistake as he is thrown into a concentration camp from which he tries to escape, but is killed. A drab, humorless, political tome.

d, Mario Bonnard; w, A.G. Majano; ph, Tonino Delli Colli.

Docu-drama   **(PR:C   MPAA:NR)**

CITY OF PLAY*½   (1929, Brit.) 80m Gainsborough/WF bw
Chili Bouchier (Ariel), Pat Aherne (Richard Von Rolf), Lawson Butt (Tambourini), James Carew (Gen. Von Rolf), Andrews Englemann (Col. Von Lessing), Leila Dresner (Zelah), Olaf Hytten (Schulz), Harold Huth (Arezzi).

Bouchier is a young Berlin girl who is hypnotized by circus performer Butt and forced to make dangerous parachute jumps. Creaky early British talkie.

p, Michael Balcon; d, Denison Clift; w, Clift, Angus Macphail (based on a story by Clift); ph, Claude MacDonnell.

Drama   **(PR:A   MPAA:NR)**

CITY OF SECRETS**½   (1963, Ger.) 88m Real-Film/Bakros bw
(AKA: DIE STADT IS VOLLER GEHEIMNISSE, SECRETS OF THE CITY)
Annemarie Duringer (Arnie Lauer), Erich Schellow (Engineer), Walther Sussenguth (Boehnke), Margot Trooger (Paula), Paul Horbiger (Herbert Klein), Eva-Ingeborg Scholz (Telephonist), Bruni Lobel (Susi Ecker), Adrian Hoven (Gerhard Scholz), Grethe Weiser (Frida Binder), Carl Ludwig Diehl (Prof. Siebrecht), Lucie Mannheim (Karina), Werner Fuetterer (Dr. Gunther), Karl Heinz Schroth.

Sussenguth is the owner of a factory forced by financial difficulties to close down. The unemployed workers are shown in a series of vignettes as they are reunited with old loves, find new loves, and commit suicide. Though unrelated to the plant closing, the suicide convinces Sussenguth to reopen his factory. Competent, if somewhat predictable, drama directed by actor Kortner, famous for his role in G.W. Pabst's PANDORA'S BOX. He proves here that he can handle actors well, if not especially the camera. Released in Germany in 1955.

d, Fritz Kortner; w, Kortner, Curt Johannes Braun; ph, Albert Benitz, Dieter Bartels; m, Michael Jary; ed, Klaus Dudenhoefer; prod d, Heinz-Gueter Sass; art d, Herbert Kirchhoff.

Drama   **(PR:O   MPAA:NR)**

CITY OF SHADOWS*   (1955) 70m REP bw
Victor McLaglen (Big Tim Channing), John Baer (Dan Mason), Kathleen Crowley (Fern Fellows), Anthony Caruso (Toni Finetti), June Vincent (Linda Fairaday), Richard Reeves (Angelo Di Bruno), Paul Maxey (Davis), Frank Ferguson (District Attorney Hunt), Richard Travis (Phil Jergins), Kay Kuter (Kink), Nicolas Coster (Roy Fellows), Gloria Pall (Waitress), Fern Hall (Miss Hall).

Implausible story of a racketeer who rises to top dog in the underworld. His rise is made possible by a young law student whom he picked up as a boy and sent to law school. The young man finds loopholes in the law to help the gangster on his upward climb. The kid turns honest when he falls in love, much to the dismay of his crooked mentor.

p, Herbert J. Yates; d, William Witney; w, Houston Branch; ph, Reggie Lanning; m, Dale Butts; ed, Tony Martinelli; cos, Adele Palmer.

Crime   **(PR:A   MPAA:NR)**

CITY OF SILENT MEN*   (1942) 64m PRC bw
Frank Albertson (Gil Davis), June Lang (Helen Hendricks), Jan Wiley (Jane Muller), Richard Clarke (Jerry Hendricks), William Gould (Mayor Hendricks), Emmett Lynn (Jeb Parker), Dick Curtis (Frank Muller), Barton Hepburn (Frank), Frank Jacquet (Judge), Frank Ferguson (Fred Bernard), Richard Bailey (Liptine), Jack Baxley (Police Chief), William Kellogg (Captain), Charles Jordon (Gordon), Pat Gleason (Manners).

The peace of a small town with a forward-looking mayor spills over into mob action

in this worthwhile drama about helping ex-convicts get back on their feet. Albertson and Lynn are released from prison and are promptly shunned by society until Gould, the mayor, puts them to work running a cannery that had been closed down due to lack of manpower. Other ex-cons join the venture and all goes well until a mean newspaperman whips up the town against the men. Mob action follows, and an attempt at a lynching, but all is resolved with the cannery getting a war contract, pleasing everybody.

p, Dixon R. Harwin; d, William Nigh; w, Joseph Hoffman (from the original by Robert E. Kent, Hoffman); ph, Gilbert Warrenton; ed, Carl Pierson.

Drama   **(PR:C   MPAA:NR)**

CITY OF SONG   (SEE: FAREWELL TO LOVE, 1931, Brit.)

CITY OF SONGS   (SEE: VIENNA, CITY OF SONGS, 1930)

CITY OF THE DEAD   (SEE: HORROR HOTEL, 1962)

CITY OF THE WALKING DEAD*   (1983, Span./Ital.) 92m 21st Century c
(AKA: NIGHTMARE CITY, NIGHTMARE)
Mel Ferrer, Hugo Stiglitz, Laura Trotter, Francisco Rabal, Maria Rosaria Omaggio.

The dead return to life and terrorize the international cast of this mindless Latin horror movie. Okay if you don't take it too seriously. The film was originally relased in 1980.

d, Umberto Lenzi.

Horror   **Cas.**   **(PR:O   MPAA:NR)**

CITY OF TORMENT***   (1950, Ger.) 84m Films International bw
Hans Albers (Hans Richter), Paul Edwin Roth (Werner Richter), Lotte Koch (Edith Schroeder), Annemarie Hase (Frau Burkhardt), Heidi Scharf (Mizzi Burkhardt), Otto Gebuhr (Heise), Elsa Wagner (Frau Heise), Ursula Barlem (Frau Roland), Ralph Lother (Fritz), Ludwig Linkmann (Georg), Helmut Helisg (Harry).

Focusing on Albers, a middle-aged laborer who returns from WW II to try to get his job back, CITY OF TORMENT shows the ravages Berlin suffered during the war and the herculean job it took to get it back on its feet in peacetime. Albers doesn't get his job back, of course, so he goes into the black market instead, mainly to help the widow of a German soldier and her child. His son learns of Dad's black market dealings and denounces him. Albers then decides to get out of the black market, and does, finding life much better for having done so. Along the way Berlin's devastation is chillingly shown. (In German; English subtitles.)

d, Josef Von Baky; w, Gerhard Grindel; m, Theo Mackenben, Schumann Choirs, Chamber Choir of Berlin Radio.

Drama   **(PR:C   MPAA:NR)**

CITY OF WOMEN***   (1980, Ital./Fr.) 104m GAU c
Marcello Mastroianni (Snaporaz), Ettore Manni (Dr. Xavier Zuberkock), Anna Prucnal (Elena), Bernice Stegers (Woman on Train), Donatella Damiani (Feminist on Roller Skates), Sara Tafuri (Other Dancing Girl), Jole Silvani (Old Woman on Motorcycle), Carla Terlizzi (Dr. Zuberkock's Conquest), Katren Gebelein (Enderbreith Small, with 6 Husbands), Dominique Labourier (Feminist), Alessandra Panelli (Housewife in Skit), Mara Ciukleva (Zuberkock's Elderly Maid), Loredana Solfizi (Feminist in Black), Gabriella Giorgelli (Fishwoman of San Leo), Tatiana and Brigitte Petronio (Blonde Motorcyclists), Armando Parracino, Umberto Zuanelli, Pietro Fumagalli (Troubadours).

Federico Fellini's psychedelic trip into the mysteries of womanhood is another visual tour de force in an elaborate dream framework. Too thin a story line, overlong and overweight, this film is typical of Fellini's efforts in the later part of his career. The film begins with Mastroianni, the threatened male protagonist, trapped in a feminist convention. Manni, as Dr. Zuberkock, later offers Mastroianni refuge in a villa constructed for sexual pleasure. A celebration of Manni's 10,000th conquest ends with an eruption by female militia to tear the big dream apart. This is followed by a brief reunion with Mastroianni's estranged wife, where a fantasy scene evolves. Toward the end of the fantasy Mastroianni is held for trial by a female tribunal and shot down by a sweet young terrorist. The dream ends and he is returned to reality. If you have a difficult time understanding this plot synopsis, you will have an equally difficult time with the film. (In Italian; English subtitles)

p, Renzo Rosselini; d, Federico Fellini; w, Fellini, Bernardino Zapponi, Brunello Rondi; ph, Giuseppe Rotunno (Technovision, Eastmancolor); m, Luis Bacalov; ed, Ruggero Mastroianni; art d, Dante Ferretti; cos, Gabriella Pescucci; ch, Leonetta Bentivoglio.

Fantasy/Drama   **(PR:O   MPAA:NR)**

CITY OF YOUTH**½   (1938, USSR) 86m Amkino/Lenfilm bw
Tamara Makarova (Natasha Solovieva), I. Novoseltsev (Vladmir Soloviev), P. Volkov (Stepan Nikitich), A. Polibin (Organizer of Construction), N. Kriuchkov (Andrei Sazanov), S. Krilov (Subbotin), V. Telegina (Motia), A. Matveyeva (Klavka), E. Golinchik (Cossack Woman), P. Aleinikov (Piotr Aleinikov), G. Zhenov (Maurin), B. Khaidarov (Kilia), Z. Nakhashkiev (Kilia's Father), V. Kulakov (Chekanov), I. Kuznetsov (Butsenko), S. Shinkevich (Silin), N. Litvinov (Technical Superviser).

This Russian-made film chronicles the Soviet's growth in the Far East. Filled with Soviet propaganda, the film is not entirely overrun by it as it shows the transplantation of masses of Soviet youths to Amur River, to build a city and defense base. Intrigue occurs when a Russian school is sabotaged, and the culprit takes the identity of a man he killed in the process. The girl hero of the settlement hunts down the killer, but not before he can destroy the gas supply and kill off witnesses. (In Russian; English subtitles)

d, S. Gerasimov; m, V., Pushkov.

Drama   **(PR:C   MPAA:NR)**

CITY ON A HUNT (SEE: NO ESCAPE, 1953)

CITY ON FIRE* (1979 Can.) 104m Astral/Avco Embassy c
Barry Newman (*Frank Whitman*), Susan Clark (*Diana*), Shelley Winters (*Nurse*), Leslie Nielsen (*Mayor*), James Franciscus (*Jimbo*), Ava Gardner (*Maggie*), Henry Fonda (*Fire Chief*), Mavor Moore (*John*), Jonathon Welsh (*Herman*), Richard Donat (*Captain*), Ken James (*Andrew*), Donald Pilon (*Fox*), Terry Haig (*Terry*), Cec Linder (*Paley*), Hilary LeBow (*Mrs. Adams*), Jeff Mappin (*Beezer*), Earl Pennington (*Clark*), Sonny Forbes (*Tom*), Bronwen Mantel (*Sarah*), Janice Chaikelson (*Debbie*), Steven Chaikelson (*Gerald*), Lee Murray (*Tony*), Jerome Tiberghien (*Fireman*).

An oil refinery explosion in a midwestern town affected by a long hot summer drought is the center of intrigue for this poor excuse for a disaster film. A good cast, but unintentionally funny script, makes this film very difficult to sit through. The plot surrounds itself with the inhabitants of a large hospital threatened by the fire. This is the fifth poorly made disaster film for Fonda whose previous nonhits were ROLLER-COASTER, TENTACLES, SWARM, and METEOR.

p, Claude Heroux; d, Alvin Rakoff; w, Jack Hill, David P. Lewis, Celine La Freniere; ph, Rene Verzier; m, William McCauley, Matthew McCauley; ed, Jean Pol Passet, Jacques Clairoux; art d, Claude Marchand; cos, Yvon Duhaime; spec eff, Cliff Wenger.

Drama (PR:O MPAA:NR)

CITY PARK*½ (1934) 75m CHES bw
Sally Blane (*Rose Wentworth*), Henry B. Walthall (*Col. Ransome*), Matty Kemp (*Raymond Ransome*), Hale Hamilton (*Ransome*), Johnny Harron (*Charlie Hooper*), Claude King (*Bank President*), Gwen Lee (*Maizie*), Judith Vosselli (*Mrs. Ransome*), Wilson Benge (*Andy*), Lafe McKee (*Matt*), Mary Foy (*Landlady Guppy*).

Slow film about a mixed-up young girl played by Blane. Three old men are sitting on a park bench when a starving Blane comes along. She talks to a prostitute who tells her about the good food in jail, and then she tries to get arrested. She is let go and put in the charge of the three old men. Walthall plays an eccentric old colonel whose aim becomes the saving of Blane. Walthall's married son does not like the idea of him carrying on with the young girl, and shuts off the old man's allowance. Walthall scrapes up some money so he and his two bench pals can move into a boarding house. They let Blane earn her keep by entertaining them and cooking their meals.

p, George R. Batcheller; d, Richard Thorpe; w, Karl Brown.

Comedy/Drama (PR:A MPAA:NR)

CITY SENTINEL (SEE: BEAST OF THE CITY, 1932)

CITY STORY* (1954) 78m Davis bw
Ann Doran, June Kenney, Warner Anderson, Herbert Lytton.

A clergyman, concerned about declining attendance in his congregation, visits Doran in jail to get her suggestions for bringing the church closer to the people. Producer Heard was affiliated with the Protestant Film Commission. A weird mixture of teenage exploitation and evangelism directed by one of the most prolific hacks in film history.
p, Paul F. Heard; d, William Beaudine; w, Margaret Fitts.

Drama (PR:C MPAA:NR)

CITY STREETS***½ (1931) 83m PAR bw
Gary Cooper (*The Kid*), Sylvia Sidney (*Nan Cooley*), Paul Lukas (*Big Fellow Maskal*), Guy Kibbee (*Pop Cooley*), William "Stage" Boyd (*McCoy*), Wynne Gibson (*Agnes*), Betty Sinclair (*Pansy*), Stanley Fields (*Blackie*), Terry Carroll (*Esther March*), Edward Le Saint (*Shooting Gallery Patron*), Robert Homans (*Inspector*), Willard Robertson (*Detective*), Hal Price (*Shooting Gallery Patron*), Ethan Laidlaw (*Killer at Prison*), George Regas (*Machine Gunner*), Bob Kortman (*Servant*), Leo Willis (*Henchman*), Bill Elliott (*Dancer*), Allan Cavan (*Cop*), Bert Hanlon (*Baldy*), Matty Kemp (*Man Stabbed with Fork*), Norman Foster (*Extra on Midway*), Kate Drain Lawson, Nick Thompson, Bill O'Brien.

This early-day gangster film is wonderfully stylistic but far removed from reality. Cooper is a westener newly arrived in the big city where he becomes a carnival sharpshooter, impressing Sidney, step daughter of a mobster (Kibbee). She encourages him to join a gang of bootleggers headed by Lukas but he refuses, saying he will make his money for their planned wedding by legitimate means. Lukas, meanwhile, eyes Kibbee's gun moll, Gibson, then has Kibbee killed to get the girl, involving Sidney in the murder. When she refuses to tell police what she knows, Sidney is sent to prison. Now Cooper decides to join the mob to make enough money for Sidney's expensive legal aid. His noble purpose goes to dust as he learns to enjoy the high life and quick bucks. When Sidney is finally released from prison she begs Cooper to quit the rackets but he refuses. His corruption is almost complete but Lukas inadvertently saves him when he dumps Gibson for Sidney. She knows this means he intends to murder Cooper, so she goes to Lukas' mansion and begs for Cooper's life. The discarded Gibson enters and shoots Lukas to death in a jealous rage, then locks Sidney in the room with the body. Cooper arrives to save Sidney but Lukas' vicious bootlegging gang takes them both for a ride, intending to kill them. Cooper is at the wheel of the car and jams down the accelerator until the auto reaches terrific speeds, careening around curves, narrowly missing trees, almost being struck by a speeding train, and inches away from shooting off a mountain road into fatal space. He tells the henchmen that he will kill everyone unless they give up their guns, which they do. Dumping the killers, Cooper and Sidney drive off as a flock of birds shoot upward into the sky, signifying the couple's escape to freedom. CITY STREETS is an offbeat gangster film, nothing like the blood-and-thunder productions in the crime cycle made famous by Warner Bros. Oddly, it lacks violence and not a killing is shown on camera, a fact director Mamoulian pointed out

later with pride: "You know there are ten killings in this film, and you don't actually *see* one of them." The sophisticated director produced an expressionistic view of the gangster world, one that was basically romanticized in the perspective of its leading players, including Sidney, who at one point says to Cooper: "Racketeers are smart, not dumb like some people I know." Mamoulian created a staggering array of innovative camera shots and story techniques for this film, one that branded him a genius director. He had to fight for every creative move. In one scene Sidney's thoughts are heard in prison and Paramount executives believed this would confuse audiences. They tried to cut the scene but Mamoulian fought them tooth and nail and the scene stayed in. Cooper's role was unusual and out of character but he performs with great skill. Sidney, however, steals the film in her first starring role, dominating each scene with her doe-like eyes, pouting lips, and a face that is today a mirror image of the 1930s (she was later aptly dubbed "Depression's Child"). Her career up to CITY STREETS had been sketchy at best; she had small parts in BROADWAY NIGHTS, a 1927 silent, and THRU DIFFERENT EYES in 1929. Hammett's fresh and inventive story heralded the clever clues that would hallmark his future detective tales, such as the length of ash on Kibbee's cigar which proves to be an alibi against a murder charge. The entire film is brush-stroked by master cinematographer Lee Garmes with lengthy shadows and light (signifying hope) is confined to the immediate players. Dialog is ancillary to the techniques Mamoulian brought from the silent era into the talkie world of CITY STREETS.

p, E. Lloyd Sheldon; d, Rouben Mamoulian; w, Max Marcin, Oliver H. P. Garrett (based on a story by Dashiell Hammett); ph, Lee Garmes; m, Sidney Cutner; ed, William Shea.

Crime/Drama (PR:A MPAA:NR)

CITY STREETS*½ (1938) 88m COL bw
Edith Fellows (*Winnie Brady*), Leo Carrillo (*Joe Carmine*), Tommy Bond (*Tommy Devlin*), Mary Gordon (*Mrs. Devlin*), Helen Jerome Eddy (*Miss North*), Joseph King (*Mike Shanahan*), Frank Sheridan (*Father Ryan*), Arthur Loft (*Dr. Goodman*), George Humbert (*Lupo*), Frank Reicher (*Dr. Ferenc Waller*), Grace Goodall (*Mrs. Graham*).

A tear-jerker portraying a crippled orphan, Fellows, who turns to fatherly Carrillo for moral and material sustenance. There is some humor as Carrillo tries to please the kid and buck well-meaning welfare representatives. He sells his store to pay for an operation for the paralyzed Fellows, becomes impoverished, and eventually loses her to the state. Carrillo strives to regain her, accomplishes the feat, but dies of an illness contracted while fighting for her release.

d, Albert S. Rogell; w, Fred Niblo, Jr., Lou Breslow (based on a story by I. Bernstein); ph, Allen S. Siegler; ed, Viola Lawrence.

Drama (PR:A MPAA:NR)

CITY THAT NEVER SLEEPS*** (1953) 90m REP bw
Gig Young (*Johnny Kelly*), Mala Powers (*Sally Connors "Angel Face"*), William Talman (*Hayes Stewart*), Edward Arnold (*Penrod Biddel*), Chill Wills (*Sgt. Joe, the "Voice of Chicago"*), Marie Windsor (*Lydia Biddel*), Paula Raymond (*Kathy Kelly*), Otto Hulett (*Sgt. John Kelly, Sr.*), Wally Cassell (*Gregg Warren*), Ron Hagerthy (*Stubby*), James Andelin (*Lt. Parker*), Thomas Poston (*Detective*), Bunny Kacher (*Agnes*), Philip L. Boddy (*Maitre d'Hotel*), Thomas Jones (*Fancy Dan*), Leonard Diebold (*Cab Driver*), Emmett Vogan (*Doctor*), Tom Irish (*Bellboy*), Walter Woolf King (*Hotel Manager*), Helen Gibson (*Woman*), Gil Herman, Clark Howatt (*Patrolmen*).

A strange and compelling film, this production was aimed at competing with the highly successful THE NAKED CITY, done in the popular 1950s semi-documentary style. Young is a cop resentful at having been talked onto the force by his police sergeant father Hulett. He is in love with Powers, a sultry stripper, but she tells him she intends to run off with ex-lover Cassell unless he leaves the city with her, abandoning his wife, Raymond. Cassell is an entertainer with a bizarre specialty; he is a mechanical man in the show window of the club where Powers works, his face gilded, his arms moving jerkily, his head spasmodically turning back and forth as if powered by tiny motors. Young ponders Powers' offer and then runs into Arnold, a wealthy lawyer, who offers him a great deal of money if he will arrest Talman who is fooling around with his wife, Windsor. Before Young can pinch Talman, his close friend, Arnold, confronts the bounder and is shot to death. Talman also kills Windsor and Hulett, who tries to stop him, and is seen by only one set of eyes, that of mechanical man Cassell whom Talman believes is a robot. Young convinces Cassell to continue his mechanical man act in hopes of identifying Talman again (he doesn't know the killer by name) and report to Young. As he goes through his act, Powers begs Cassell to leave the window and run away with her, promising a new life. Cassell begins to cry at the thought of a clean future and the tears startle the crowd before the window. Cries of "He's real!" bring Talman on the run. He realizes that Cassell has witnessed his triple murder and fires a shot at the mechanical man, but misses. He flees with his one-time pal Young on his heels. The two race up the stairs to the elevated train tracks and struggle. Talman is just about to kill Young when he falls to his death. Young then goes home to his wife where he intends to stay. Wills, as a sentimental cop, narrates the film but injects more bathos than realism; the production was shot on location in Chicago which gives it a realistic feel. The story takes place in one night and there is too much drama crammed into the time period to be believable, but the performances are above-average, particularly by Talman as a dedicated evil-doer. Cassell, normally a lightweight supporting player, gives a surprising portrayal as the mechanical man.

p&d, John J. Auer (for Herbert J. Yates); w, Steve Fisher; ph, John L. Russell, Jr.; m, R. Dale Butts; ed, Fred Allen; art d, James Sullivan; set d, John McCarthy, Jr., Charles Thompson; cos, Adele Palmer; spec eff, Howard and Theodore Lydecker; makeup, Bob Mark.

Crime/Drama (PR:A MPAA:NR)

CITY UNDER THE SEA*½
(1965, Brit.) 83m Bruton/AIP c
(AKA: WAR GODS OF THE DEEP)
Vincent Price, Tab Hunter, David Tomlinson, Susan Hart, John Le Mesurier, Henry Oscar, Derek Newark.

Dull, very loose AIP adaptation of Poe (reportedly inspired by one line in one of his poems) stars Price as the ruler of an undersea kingdom who has one of his gillmen kidnap Hart from the surface because she closely resembles his dead wife. Hunter, Tomlinson, and a pet rooster go underwater in search of her. This was the last film directed by Jacques Tourneur (THE CAT PEOPLE [1942]).

p, Daniel Haller; d, Jacques Tourneur; w, Charles Bennett, Louis M. Heyward; ph, Stephen Dade (Colorscope, Eastmancolor); m, Stanley Black; spec eff, Frank George, Les Bowie.

Science Fiction (PR:A MPAA:NR)

CITY WITHOUT MEN*
(1943) 75m COL bw
Linda Darnell, Michael Duane, Sara Allgood, Edgar Buchanan, Leslie Brooks, Glenda Farrell, Margaret Hamilton, Sheldon Leonard.

Turgid meller dwells inside a boarding house adjacent to a prison where women await the release of their imprisoned menfolk. Little story, suspense or interest adds up to a waste of time in this pooped-out programmer.

p, Samuel Bronston (for B. P. Schulberg); d, Sidney Salkow; w, W.L. River, George Skier, Donald Davis (based on an original story by Budd Schulberg and Martin Berkeley).

Drama (PR:A MPAA:NR)

CLAIR DE FEMME*
(1980,Fr.) 103m Atlantic Releasing Corp. c
Yves Montand (Michel), Romy Schneider (Lydia), Romolo Valli (Senor Galba), Lila Kedrova (Sonia), Heinz Bennent (Georges).

Pretentious, boring, depressing story of Montand and Schneider meeting and confessing their painful pasts to one another in a film loaded with ludicrous dialog and inane situations. Director Costa-Gavras make fine political thrillers, but he's out of his milieu with this romantic drama. (In French; English subtitles)

p, Georges Alain Vuille; d&w, Costa-Gavras (based on a novel by Romain Gary); ph, Ricardo Aranovich; m, Jean Musy; ed, Francoise Bonnot; art d, Mario Chiari, Eric Simon.

Drama (PR:O MPAA:NR)

CLAIRE'S KNEE***½
(1971, Fr.) 103m Films du Losange/COL c
Jean-Claude Brialy (Jerome), Aurora Cornu (Aurora), Beatrice Romand (Laura), Laurence De Monaghan (Claire), Michele Montel (Mme. Walter), Gerard Falconetti (Gilles), Fabrice Luchini (Vincent).

Brialy, a diplomat engaged to a woman in Stockholm, vacations at an isolated resort. There he meets Cornu, an old friend, and De Monaghan, the daughter of the family Cornu is staying with. He soon develops a sexual infatuation with the daughter's knee, unable to think of anything else yet unwilling to consummate it. After a long period of thought and discussion, he actually does put his hand on her knee, an action she takes as one of consolation. The fifth installment in Rohmer's "Six Moral Tales" has the same preoccupations as the others, a man, committed to woman, has a sexual desire for another, but does not act on it. A serious comedy for adults that some may find too talky, but Rohmer is one of the most intelligent, literate directors working today. A classic of contemporary French filmmaking. (In French; English subtitles)

p, Pierre Cottrell; d&w, Eric Rohmer; ph, Nestor Almendros.

Comedy/Drama (PR:C-O MPAA:GP)

CLAIRVOYANT, THE***
(1935, Brit.) 73m Gainsborough/GAU/FOX bw
(AKA: EVIL MIND)
Claude Rains (Maximus), Fay Wray (Rene), Jane Baxter (Christine), Mary Clare (Mother), Ben Field (Simon), Athole Stewart (Lord Southwood), Felix Aylmer (Counsel), Donald Calthrop (Derelict), Jack Raine (Customs Officer), Margaret Davidge (Lodging Housekeeper), C. Denier Warren (Bimeter).

Top-drawer suspense has Rains as a shady mindreader who suddenly and inexplicably develops actual powers to see into the future, a frightening mental transformation in that he is powerless to alter his predictions. His soothsaying is disaster-oriented which he discovers while riding on a train; Rains is seized with the image of the train heading for doom and bolts for the exit at a train stop, yelling for other passengers to get off. No one heeds his warning and the train is derailed and plunges off a cliff. While Rains begins testing his new power he finds time to cheat on his wife, Wray, with Baxter. To satisfy the materialistic whims of his mistress, he picks a derby winner through his powers and becomes rich. But events catch up with him. After predicting a tunnel explosion Rains is put on trial for murder, charged with causing the accident. He is freed when he predicts the miners will escape and they do. The courtroom scenes showing Rains' trial are oddball, even bizarre and worth the whole film as unorthodox legal techniques are employed. This film followed Rains' box office hit THE INVISIBLE MAN and Fox, the U.S. distributor of the British export, touted the film with ad lines like "The Invisible Man makes the future visible." The film's plot was used in THE NIGHT HAS A THOUSAND EYES in 1948 and starring Edward G. Robinson.

p, Michael Balcon; d, Maurice Elvey; w, Charles Bennett, Bryan Edgar Wallace (based on the novel by Ernst Lothar); ph, Errol Hinds.

Drama (PR:A MPAA:NR)

CLAMBAKE**
(1967) 100m UA c
Elvis Presley (Scott Heyward), Shelley Fabares (Dianne Carter), Will Hutchins (Tom Wilson), Bill Bixby (James Jamison III), James Gregory (Duster Heyward), Gary Merrill (Sam Burton), Amanda Harley (Ellie), Suzie Kaye (Sally), Angelique Pettyjohn (Gloria), Olga Kaya (Gigi), Arlene Charles (Olive), Jack Good (Mr. Hathaway), Hal Peary (Doorman), Sam Riddle (Race Announcer), Lisa Slagle (Lisa), Lee Kreiger (Bartender), Melvin Allen (Crewman), Herb Barnett (Waiter), Steve Cory (Bellhop), Robert Lieb (Barasch), Bob "Red" West (Ice Cream Vendor).

One of the assembly line musicals Presley ground out during the 1960s casts him as a rich Texas oil heir. He goes to Miami and switches roles with poor ski instructor, Hutchins, to see whether he can still score with the chicks without the money, fancy clothes, and cars. Presley falls for his first student, Fabares, and Bixby is the playboy raceboat driver who is the rival for her affections. The film comes to a climax during a boat race in which Presley risks both life and limb. Of course he sings several tunes including the title song, "Clambake." Songs: "Clambake" (Sid Wayne, Ben Weisman), "Who Needs Money?" "The Girl I Never Loved" (Randy Starr), "Confidence," "A House That Has Everything" (Sid Tepper, Roy C. Bennett), "Hey, Hey, Hey" (Joy Byers).

p, Jules Levy, Arthur Gardner, Arnold Laven; d, Arthur H. Nadel; w, Arthur Browne, Jr.; ph, William Margulies (Technicolor); m, Jeff Alexander; ed, Tom Rolf; art d, Lloyd S. Papez; set d, James S. Redd; spec eff, Bob Warner; ch, Alex Romero.

Musical (PR:AA MPAA:NR)

CLANCY IN WALL STREET*
(1930) 76m Aristocrat/CAP bw
Charles Murray (Michael Clancy), Lucien Littlefield (Andy MacIntosh), Aggie Herring (Mrs. Clancy), Edward Nugent (Donald MacIntosh), Miriam Seegar (Katie Clancy), Reed Howes (Freddie Saunders).

A watery satire of the 1929 stock market crash with Murray dabbling in stocks. By mistake he gleans a windfall and then dives into stock investment, leaving his partner in a plumbing business and living the life of a ne'er-do-well in a posh apartment. Because of his extravagant and new-found airs, Murray's daughter runs away from home and his problems are compounded when he loses everything in the Crash. All is not lost, however. His partner forgives him and allows him back into the plumbing business and the daughter returns. A creaky antique that bogs down in tickertape.

d, Ted Wilde, Edward Small; w, Ralph Bell, Jack Wagner, William Dugan; ph, Harry Jackson; ed, Phil Cahn; art d, Charles Cadwallader.

Comedy (PR:A MPAA:NR)

CLANCY STREET BOYS**
(1943) 66m MON bw
Leo Gorcey (Muggs), Huntz Hall (Glimpy), Bobby Jordan (Danny), Bennie Bartlett (Bennie), Noah Beery, Sr. (Pete), Amlita Ward (Judy), Rick Vallin (George), Martha Wentworth (Mrs. McGinnis), J. Farrell MacDonald (Flanagan), Dick Chandlee (Stash), Sammy Morrison (Scruno), Eddie Mills (Dave), Billy Benedict (Butch), Jimmy Strand, Johnny Duncan (Cherry Streeters), George DeNormand (Williams), Jan Rubini (Violinist), Bernard Gorcey (Bar Owner), Gino Corrado (Head Waiter), Jack Normand (Goon).

Remnants of the "Dead End Kids" have been grouped under the name "East Side Kids" in this film. The gang, headed by Gorcey and sidekick Hall, are threatened by a rival gang. However, the real story revolves around Gorcey and a rich uncle from Texas. Though Gorcey is an only child, his mother convinces the uncle to think she has seven children. When Gorcey's uncle visits, Gorcey recruits the whole gang to impersonate his siblings. The uncle discovers the deception, but when the gang saves him and his daughter from kidnapers all is forgiven. (See BOWERY BOYS series, Index)

p, Sam Katzman, Jack Dietz; d, William Beaudine; w, Harvey Gates; ph, Mack Stengler; ed, Carl Pierson.

Comedy (PR:A MPAA:NR)

CLANDESTINE*½
(1948, Fr.) 76m J.H. Hoffberg bw (AKA: LES CLANDESTINS)
Suzy Carrier (Yvonne), Andre Reybas (Jean), Samson Fainsilber (Dr. Netter), Georges Rollin (Laurent), Constant Reiny (Priest), Guilluame De Sax (Landlord).

Uninteresting film about French resistance fighters during the Nazi occupation. Rollin is the leader of the group, with Carrier his love interest. The Nazis are little more than cartoon figures here, torturing freedom-loving Frenchmen and Jewish doctors with equal enthusiasm as they try to stamp out an underground newspaper through terror and reprisals. (In French; English subtitles)

p, Paul Pavaux; d, Andre E. Chotin; w, Pierre Le Stringuey; m, Jean Paquet; ed, Walter Klee.

War (PR:C MPAA:NR)

CLARENCE*
(1937) 60m PAR bw
Roscoe Karns (Clarence Smith), Eleanore Whitney (Cora), Eugene Pallette (Mr. Wheeler), Johnny Downs (Bobbie), Inez Courtney (Della), Charlotte Wynters (Violet), Spring Byington (Mrs. Wheeler), Theodore Von Eltz (Tobias), Richard Powell (Dinwiddie).

Karns is a mysterious stranger who drifts into a wealthy, if eccentric, family and puts things right. Daughter Whitney falls in love with him but he ends up marrying the family tutor after saving son Downs from the blackmail scheme of the family servants. Second-rate imitation of MY MAN GODFREY, with Pallette playing virtually the same role again, and not very convincingly. High point is a marvelous drunk scene by the matriarchal Byington.

d, George Archainbaud; w, Seena Owen; Grant Garret (based on Booth Tarkington's play); ph, George Clemens; ed, Arthur Schmidt; md, Boris Morros.

Comedy (PR:A MPAA:NR)

CLARENCE AND ANGEL½** (1981) 75m Gardner c
Darren Brown *(Clarence)*, Mark Cardova *(Angel)*, Cynthia McPherson *(Teacher)*, Louise Mike *(Claree's Mother)*, Lolita Lewis *(Robert's Mother)*, Ellwoodson Williams, Robert Leroy Smith *(Men in Barbershop)*, Janice Jenkins *(Principal)*, Robert Middleton *(Assistant Principal)*.

Cardova is a New York street kid who befriends Brown, a shy, illiterate boy from South Carolina and teaches him to read. Good feature done on a small budget has some excellent performances. Worth checking out.

p,d&w, Robert Gardner; ph, Doug Harris.

Drama **(PR:C MPAA:NR)**

CLARENCE, THE CROSS-EYED LION*** (1965) 92m Ivan Tors/MGM c
Marshall Thompson *(Dr. Marsh Tracy)*, Betsy Drake *(Julie Harper)*, Richard Haydn *(Rupert Rowbotham)*, Cheryl Miller *(Paula)*, Alan Caillou *(Carter)*, Rockne Tarkington *(Juma)*, Maurice Marsac *(Gregory)*, Bob Do Qui *(Sergeant)*, Albert Amos *(Husseini)*, Dinny Powell *(Dinny)*, Mark Allen *(Larson)*, Laurence Conroy *(Tourist)*, Allyson Daniel *(Tourist's Wife)*, Janee Michele *(Girl in Pit)*, Naaman Brown, Napoleon Whiting *(Villagers)*, Chester Jones *(Old Man)*, Clarence *(Himself, A Lion)*, Doris *(Herself, A Chimpanzee)*, Mary *(Herself, A Python)*.

Ivan Tors was expert in bringing this kind of moppet movies to the screen and his CLARENCE, THE CROSS-EYED LION was no exception to his excellent record which included RHINO, FLIPPER, NAMU-THE KILLER WHALE, and many more. Thompson is boss at an Animal Behavior center with daughter Miller providing the gee-whiz point-of-view. He falls in love with Drake who plays a sort of early Jane Goodall as she studies gorilla life. The reason why Clarence is such an adorable beast is that he suffers from cross-eyed condition which did not allow him to grow into a hunter. The villains are led by Marsac who plans to ape-nap Drake's animals and sell them for serious money. The denouement occurs when native troops arrive and foil the plot. They are led by screenwriter Caillou who wrote himself a neat role as a veddy-British officer. Good fun for youngsters and adults who aren't all that discriminating. Some funny sequences but mostly a travelog of Africa. At 92 minutes, it could have lost a reel or so and not suffered one iota. Haydn is the comedy foil as a scared schoolmaster whom Clarence enjoys taunting.

p, Leonard B. Kaufman; d, Andrew Marton; w, Alan Caillou (based on a story by Art Arthur and Marshall Thompson); ph, Lamar Boren (Metrocolor); m, Al Mack ; ed, Warren Adams; art d, George W. Davis, Edward Imazu; set d, Jack Mills, Henry Grace.

Adventure **(PR:AAA MPAA:NR)**

CLARETTA AND BEN½** (1983, Ital., Fr.) 102m Aquarius Film c
(ITAL: PERMETTE SIGNORA CHE AMI VOSTRA FIGLIA)
Ugo Tognazzi *(Gino)*, Bernadette Lafont *(Sandra)*, Franco Fabrizi, Lia Tanzi, Gigi Ballista, Quinto Parmeggiani, Ernesto Colli, Felice Andreasi, Rossana di Lorenzo

A good black comedy starring Tognazzi, riding on the success of his LA CAGE AUX FOLLES. The film has him as a touring actor-playwright. The film's title refers to a play, written by Tognazzi, as a vehicle for himself and his lover-leading lady, the play deals with the life and love of Benito Mussolini and his mistress, Claretta Petracci. When the troupe puts on the play in Italy the local Communists throw rotten tomatoes at the actors and disrupt the performance until Tognazzi finally wins them over by emphasizing the romantic side of the opus.

p, Carlo Ponti; d, Gian Luigi Polidoro; w, Rafael Azcona, Leo Benvenuti, Pero de Bernardi (based on the story by Polidoro); ph, Mario Vulpiani; ed, Carlo Rustichelli.

Comedy **(PR:O MPAA:NR)**

CLASH BY NIGHT**** (1952) 105m RKO bw
Barbara Stanwyck *(Mae Doyle)*, Paul Douglas *(Jerry D'Amato)*, Robert Ryan *(Earl Pfeiffer)*, Marilyn Monroe *(Peggy)*, J. Carroll Naish *(Uncle Vince)*, Keith Andes *(Joe Doyle)*, Silvio Minciotti *(Papa)*, Diane Stewart, Deborah Stewart *(Twin Babies)*, Julius Tannen *(Sad-Eyed Waiter)*, Tony Dante *(Fisherman at Pier)*, Roy D'Amour, Nancy Duke, Sally Yarnell, Irene Crosby, Gilbert Frye, Helen Hansen, Dick Coe, Al Cavens, Dan Bernaducci, William Bailey, Bert Stevans, Mario Siletti, Art Dupuis, Bill Slack

A simple love triangle story is turned into a power-packed, tension-filled tale by the great Lang, one of the world's premier directors. A stunning cast, particularly the three principals, bring stark realism and taut emotions to their parts. Stanwyck is outstanding in one of her most telling roles as a disillusioned woman returning to her seacoast home town of Monterey, California. Life in the big city has embittered her. To add to her dyspepsia, her kid brother Andes gives her a tepid welcome. But Monroe, Andes' girl friend, happily receives Stanwyck. Secretly, the younger woman is consumed with ambition to emulate Stanwyck, leave the small town, and search for adventure in the big city. Andes' friend Douglas, a big-hearted fisherman, is introduced to Stanwyck and he takes her to a movie on their first date. He then introduces her to his friend, Ryan, a sneering, slick hardcase whose own bitterness matches Stanwyck's. She is both repelled and attracted to Ryan but plays it safe, marrying easy-going Douglas. They have a daughter but Stanwyck gradually finds married life humdrum; she begins a secret affair with the cynical Ryan. Outwardly he seems a self-assured mental bully who likes dominating the affair, but inside he's drowning in self-pity, apprehension, and fear. At one point he telephones Stanwyck and almost yells: "Help me . . . I'm dying of loneliness!" Dark menace bubbles to the surface of his character as the affair deepens. "Somebody's throat has to be cut," he utters with chilling frequency. As with all clandestine affairs, the lovers begin to make mistakes. Neighbors and friends see them in compromising situations which makes them all the more furtive, especially Stanwyck, who struggles to maintain two lifestyles, agonizing over her deceit and disservice to Douglas and her compulsive attraction to the acerbic Ryan. Rumors filter down to Douglas, who at first refuses to believe his wife's infidelity but, following a confrontation with Stanwyck, he is convinced of the cuckolding and goes berserk, rushing to the theater and tearing into the projection booth where he and Ryan have a battle royal. The powerful fisherman overcomes Ryan and he begins to choke the life out of him until Stanwyck arrives and her wild screaming brings Douglas to his senses. Douglas goes home, scoops up his child, and takes her to his boat. Stanwyck runs after him, begging forgiveness. Douglas, in the great benevolence of a simple man, takes her back and the film ends with the traumatized family reunited, if not healed. Stanwyck's performance of the erring but contrite wife is superb and Douglas is a tower of generous humanity. Ryan surpasses himself as the essence of brutality, a wholly unsympathetic character that he made so much of in similar roles. He would not again be as hateful a creature until creating his sinister profile in LONELY-HEARTS, where he played the rotten-to-the-core newspaper publisher. CLASH BY NIGHT was based on a failed play by Odets, one in which Ryan played the same role (Stanwyck replaced Tallulah Bankhead and Douglas took Lee J. Cobb's stage role). The original setting of Staten Island was changed to Monterey for the sake of location shooting. Douglas' role name was changed from Wilenski to D'Amato. Marilyn Monroe, in a small part, gave Lang headaches. Her acting ability at this time was limited, even though it was her thirteenth film. Monroe arrived on the set each day visibly nervous, having stage fright at appearing with such professional actors. She botched so many lines that the patient Lang had to retake shots again and again. Douglas became angry at the young amateur but Stanwyck was kind and encouraging to the starlet. So unsure of herself was Monroe that she asked Lang for permission to have her acting coach, Natasha Lytess, on the set with her. He allowed the coach to be present but he sent Lytess away when he saw she was acutally directing Monroe while she was on camera. The flavor of the small fishing community was captured in a documentary prolog shot by Lang and his cameraman, Musuraca, who visited Monterey and shot more than 10,000 feet of film recording the catching of sardines and the processing of the fish through a cannery, a glittering, sun-bathed opening with thousands of seagulls flocking over whitecaps breaking against the rocky shoreline. Lang's direction is a fluid as the ocean itself, tracking and panning, closing in on his actors, then pulling back, the camera seeming to pulsate with the emotional charges flashing from the players, producing a high-voltage film.

p, Harriet Parsons; d, Fritz Lang; w, Alfred Hayes, David Dortort (based on the play by Clifford Odets); ph, Nicholas Musuraca; m, Roy Webb; ed, George J. Amy; md, Constantin Bakaleinikoff; art d, Albert S. D'Agostino, Carroll Clark; set d, Darrell Silvera, Jack Mills; spec eff, Harold Wellman; song: "I Hear A Rhapsody," Joe Gasparre, Jack Baker, George Fragos, sung by Tony Martin.

Drama **Cas.** **(PR:C MPAA:NR)**

CLASH OF THE TITANS½** (1981) 120m MGM/UA c
Laurence Olivier *(Zeus)*, Claire Bloom *(Hera)*, Maggie Smith *(Thetis)*, Ursula Andress *(Aphrodite)*, Jack Gwillim *(Poseidon)*, Susan Fleetwood *(Athena)*, Pat Roach *(Hephaestus)*, Harry Hamlin *(Perseus)*, Judi Bowker *(Andromeda)*, Burgess Meredith *(Ammon)*, Sian Phillips *(Cassiopeia)*, Tim Piggott-Smith *(Thallo)*, Neil McCarthy *(Calibos)*, Donald Houston *(Acrisius)*, Vida Taylor *(Danae)*, Harry Jones *(Huntsman)*, Flora Robson, Anna Manahan, Freda Jackson *(Three Blind Witches)*.

Some incredible special effects are what takes this film out of the usual T&S category (Toga and Sandals). When they are good they are astounding (the flying horse) and when they are bad they are laughable. It's a mythic tale drawn from Greek mythology with Olivier, Smith, and Bloom floating around heaven and wondering what new havoc earthlings are about to wreak. Hamlin is Perseus and spends most of the picture chasing after Bowker, who is Andromeda (we can't resist the opportunity to mention that her performance was strained). Obstacles and dangers pop in and out for what seems to be eons. No one takes anything seriously and if you're able to dial the sound out, the visuals are worth watching. The dialog is stilted and the actors don't appear to have been directed as they all seem to speak in their own ways with no sense of style overlaying the production.

p, Ray Harryhausen, Charles H. Schneer; d, Desmond Davis; w, Beverley Cross; ph, Ted Moore (Metrocolor); m, Laurence Rosenthal; ed, Timothy Gee; art d, Don Picton, Giorgio Desideri, Peter Howitt, Fernando Gonzalez; spec eff, Harryhausen; cos, Emma Porteous.

Fantasy **Cas.** **(PR:AA MPAA:PG)**

CLASS* (1983) 100m Orion c
Jacqueline Bisset *(Ellen)*, Rob Lowe *(Skip)*, Andrew McCarthy *(Jonathan)*, Cliff Robertson *(Burroughs)*, Stuart Margolin *(Balaban)*, John Cusack *(Roscoe)*, Alan Ruck *(Roger)*, Rodney Pearson *(Allen)*, Remak Ramsay *(Kennedy)*, Virginia Madsen *(Lisa)*, Deborah Thalberg *(Susan)*, Fern Persons *(Headmistress)*, Casey Siemaszko *(Doug)*, Aaron Douglas Zuber *(Barry)*, Anna Maria Horsford *(Maggie)*, Hal Frank *(Schneider)*, Dick Cusack *(Chaplain)*, William Visteen *(Dr. Kreiger)*, James O'Reilly *(Bernhardt)*, Caitlin Hart, Virginia Morris, Stewart Figa, Paula Clarendon, Gita Tanner, Joan Cusack, John Kapelos, George Womack, Maria Ricossa, Candace Collins, Marty Britton, Bruce Norris, Kevin Swerdlow, Wayne Kneeland, J. Todd Shaughnessy, Carole Arterbery, Nancy Serlin, Bruno Aclin.

Poorly scripted rites-of-passage youth film starring McCarthy as a naive prep school student who becomes involved in an affair with older woman Bisset. Unknown to him, Bisset is the mother of his roommate, Lowe. Haphazard construction (the film vacillates between low comedy and teenage drama) combined with one-dimensional characters and vague, simpleminded motivations add up to a great waste of talent.

p, Martin Ransohoff; d, Lewis John Carlino; w, Jim Kouf, David Greenwalt; ph, Ric Waite (DeLuxe Color); m, Elmer Bernstein; ed, Dennis Dolan; art d, Jack Poplin; cos, Donfeld.

Comedy/Drama **Cas.** **(PR:O MPAA:R)**

CLASS OF '44** (1973) 95m WB c
Gary Grimes *(Hermie)*, Jerry Houser *(Oscy)*, Oliver Conant *(Benjie)*, William Atherton *(Fraternity President)*, Sam Bottoms *(Marty)*, Deborah Winters *(Julie)*, Joe Ponazecki

(Professor), Murray Westgate *(Principal)*, Marion Waldman *(Grade Advisor)*, Mary Long *(Valedictorian)*, Marcia Diamond *(Mrs. Gilhuly)*, Jeffrey Cohen *(Editor)*, Susan Marcus *(Assistant Editor)*, Lamar Criss *(1st Proctor)*, Michael A. Hoey *(2nd Proctor)*, Dan McDonald *(Father)*, Jan Campbell *(Mother)*.

Sequel to SUMMER OF '42 has Grimes, Houser, and Conant repeating their roles as they graduate from high school. Conant joins the Marines while the other two enroll at a prestigious eastern university, where the film turns into a routine fraternity story as the boys face the hazing of frat president Atherton in a string of episodic gags. At the close, the film veers abruptly back into high melodrama as Grimes' father dies and the boy is forced into manhood.

p,d, Paul Bogart; w, Herman Raucher; ph, Andrew Laszlo (Panavision, Technicolor); m, David Shire; ed, Michael A. Hoey; prod d, Ben Edwards; set d, Brian Beck.

Drama **(PR:C MPAA:PG)**

CLASS OF MISS MAC MICHAEL, THE*½ (1978, Brit./U.S.) 100m Brut c

Glenda Jackson *(Conor MacMichael)*, Oliver Reed *(Terence Sutton)*, Michael Murphy *(Martin)*, Rosalind Cash *(Una Ferrer)*, John Standing *(Fairbrother)*, Riba Akabusi *(Gaylord)*, Phil Daniels *(Stewart)*, Patrick Murray *(Boysie)*, Sylvia O'Donnel *(Marie)*, Sharon Fussey *(Belinda)*, Herbert Norville *(Ronnie)*, Perry Benson *(Timmy)*, Tony London *(Adam)*, Owen Whittaker *(Victor)*, Angela Brogan *(Frieda)*, Victor Evans *(Abel)*, Simon Howe *(Rob)*, Dayton Brown *(John)*, Paul Daly *(Nick)*, Deirdre Forrest *(Deirdre)*, Stephanie Patterson *(Pattie)*, Danielle Corgan *(Tina)*, Peta Bernard *(Mabel)*, Judy Wiles *(Miss Eccles)*, Mavis Pugh *(Mrs. Barnett)*, Patsy Byrne *(Mrs. Green)*, Ian Thompson *(Mr. Bowden)*, Christopher Guinee *(Mr. Drake)*, Constantin de Goguel *(Maj. Brady)*, Sally Nesbitt *(Mrs. Brady)*, Sylvia Marriott *(Mrs. Wickens)*, Marianne Stone *(Mrs. Lee)*, Pamela Manson *(Mrs. Bellrind)*.

Jackson is a dedicated teacher at an English high school whose class is filled with foul-mouthed delinquents one step out of the borstal. She refuses an offer of marriage from Murphy, preferring to remain with her charges and trying to get through to them. Routine variation on THE BLACKBOARD JUNGLE and TO SIR WITH LOVE, with the dubious contribution of promiscuous sex to add interest. No passing grade.

p, Judd Bernard; d, Silvio Narizzano; w, Bernard (based on a novel by Sandy Hutson); ph, Alex Thomson (Technicolor); m, Stanley Myers; ed, Max Benedict; art d, Hazel Peiser.

Comedy/Drama **(PR:O MPAA:NR)**

CLASS OF 1984 zero (1982, Can.) 96m United Film Distribution c

Perry King *(Andy Norris)*, Timothy Van Patten *(Peter Stegman)*, Merrie Lynn Ross *(Diane Norris)*, Roddy McDowall *(Terry Corrigan)*, Al Waxman *(Stawiski)*, Lisa Langlois *(Patsy)*, David Gardner *(Morganthau)*, Stefan Arngrim *(Drugstore)*, Keith Knight *(Barnyard)*, Neil Clifford *(Fallon)*, Erin Flannery *(Deneen Bowden)*, Michael Fox *(Arthur)*.

This volent and bloody update of THE BLACKBOARD JUNGLE is the terrible story of a high school terrorized by a gang of punk rock hoods. Van Patten is the ruthless head of a drug and prostitution ring that terrorizes students and faculty alike. King is the new music teacher who is appalled by the police state tactics used in the school to keep the violent students in check. He quickly makes enemies with Van Patten when he tries to break up a drug deal. King is blocked at every attempt to have the kids arrested by police. For all his troubles, he is rewarded by having his car vandalized and later firebombed. His wife is kidnaped and gang raped by the punks. King is forced to hunt them down one by one and kill them at the school in order to find his wife. Alice Cooper performs "I Am the Future." A sadistic, humiliating production.

p, Arthur Kent; d, Mark Lester; w, John Saxton, Tom Holland, Lester (based on a story by Holland), ph, Albert Dunk (color); m, Lalo Schifrin; ed, Howard Kunin.

Drama **Cas.** **(PR:O MPAA:R)**

CLAUDELLE INGLISH*½ (1961) 99m WB bw (GB: YOUNG AND EAGER)

Diane McBain *(Claudelle Inglish)*, Arthur Kennedy *(Clyde Inglish)*, Will Hutchins *(Dennis Peasley)*, Constance Ford *(Jessie Inglish)*, Claude Akins *(S. T. Crawford)*, Frank Overton *(Harley Peasley)*, Chad Everett *(Linn Varner)*, Robert Colbert *(Rip Guyler)*, Ford Rainey *(Reu Armstrong)*, James Bell *(Josh)*, Robert Logan *(Charles Henry)*, Jan Stine *(Dave Adams)*, Hope Summers *(Ernestine Peasley)*.

McBain is a young farm girl in the rural South who defies her mother's wishes by refusing to marry well-to-do landowner Akins, preferring instead to bestow her favors on dirt-farmer-next-door Everett. When Everett is drafted for a two-year hitch, McBain becomes the town doxy, leading men to fight over her. When one dispute over her charms ends with one of the men running the other over, the father of the dead boy comes to McBain's shack and shoots her dead. Little more than a sleazy exploitation movie, despite a name cast.

p, Leonard Freeman; d, Gordon Douglas; w, Freeman (based on the novel by Erskine Caldwell); ph, Ralph Woolsey; m, Howard Jackson; ed, Folmar Blangsted; art d, Malcolm C. Bert; set d, Alfred E. Kegerris; cos, Howard Shoup.

Drama **(PR:C-O MPAA:NR)**

CLAUDIA*½** (1943) 91m FOX bw

Dorothy McGuire *(Claudia)*, Robert Young *(David Naughton)*, Ina Claire *(Mrs. Brown)*, Reginald Gardiner *(Jerry Seymour)*, Olga Baclanova *(Mme. Daruska)*, Jean Howard *(Julie)*, Frank Tweddell *(Fritz)*, Elsa Janssen *(Bertha)*, John Royce *(Carl)*, Frank Fenton *(Hartley)*, Ferdinand Munier *(Mr. Feiffer)*, Winifred Harris *(Mrs. Feiffer)*, Jessie Grayson *(Maid)*.

Dorothy McGuire makes her film debut in CLAUDIA and repeats the role she created on the stage in Rose Franken's play. Two years before, in 1941, the same material was used in a radio show, "Claudia and David," based on the Redbook stories by Miss Franken. It's little more than the epic of a young bride who is incredibly naive, nervously impulsive, sometimes vague, but always charming. Young is McGuire's very tolerant husband as she goes through the paces of learning to live. Claire scores well as Claudia's mother, a woman doomed to death from the fade-in, and yet that doesn't detract from the essential warm heartedness of the picture. It's funny without being side splitting and sentimental without being mawkish. All-in-all, quite a lovely film with no single "story" to speak of but with enough incidents to fill out 91 minutes under Goulding's deft handling. (Sequel: CLAUDIA AND DAVID).

p, William Perlberg; d, Edmund Goulding; w, Morrie Ryskind (based on the play and the Redbook articles by Rose Franken); ph, Leon Shamroy; m, Alfred Newman; ed, Robert Simpson; m/l, Newman, Charles Henderson.

Comedy/Drama **(PR:A MPAA:NR)**

CLAUDIA AND DAVID*½** (1946) 78m FOX bw

Dorothy McGuire *(Claudia)*, Robert Young *(David)*, Mary Astor *(Elizabeth Van Doren)*, John Sutton *(Phil Dexter)*, Gail Patrick *(Julia Naughton)*, Rose Hobart *(Edith Dexter)*, Harry Davenport *(Dr. Harry)*, Florence Bates *(Nancy Riddle)*, Jerome Cowan *(Brian O'Toole)*, Elsa Janssen *(Bertha)*, Frank Tweddell *(Fritz)*, Anthony Sydes *(Bobby)*, Henry Mowbray *(Mr. Riddle)*, Pierre Watkin *(Hartley Naughton)*, Clara Blandick *(Mrs. Barry)*, Eric Wilton *(Butler)*, Frank Darien *(Charlie)*, Walter Baldwin *(Farmer)*.

Both leads return for this sequel to CLAUDIA that introduced McGuire to the movies. She is still the lovable but air-headed wife who can't make up her mind about anything and might starve to death trying to decide what to have for lunch. They have a young son now (Sydes) and when a bogus seer tells Young he will have an accident if he goes West, problems erupt. Sydes gets sick and McGuire quickly suspects a fatal disease, only to discover it's measles. Astor seeks Young's advice for some building matters but Claudia gets terribly jealous and Sutton, a handsome married man, starts putting a make on McGuire, all of which confuses the already addled woman. There are any number of other incidents and by this time CLAUDIA AND DAVID seems very much like the former film, a string of occurrences held together by the actors. It's light and crammed full of action, pathos, and about every emotion one could shoehorn into 78 minutes. Very good supporting help from Cowan, Bates, Blandick, and all the other regulars on the Fox lot.

p, William Perlberg; d, Walter Lang, w, Rose Franken, William Brown Meloney (based on the story by Franken); ph, Joseph Le Shelle; m, Cyril Mockridge; ed, Robert Simpson; spec eff, Fred Sersen.

Comedy/Drama **(PR:AA MPAA:NR)**

CLAUDINE*** (1974) 92m Fox c

Diahann Carroll *(Claudine)*, James Earl Jones *(Roop)*, Lawrence Hilton-Jacobs *(Charles)*, Tamu *(Charlene)*, David Kruger *(Paul)*, Yvette Curtis *(Patrice)*, Eric Jones *(Francis)*, Socorro Stephens *(Lurlene)*, Adam Wade *(Owen)*, Harrison Avery *(Minister)*, Mordecai Lawner *(Process Server)*, Terry Alexander *(Teddy)*, Carolyn Adams *(Dance Teacher)*, Bob Scarantino, Bill Bressant *(Cops)*, Elisa Loti *(Miss Kabak)*, Roxie Roker *(Mrs. Winston)*, David Blackwell *(Delivery Boy)*, Jay Van Leer *(Bar Woman)*, Judy Mills, Alyce Webb, Lil Henderson, Yvonne Sutherland *(Bus Women)*, Bernie Barrow *(Mr. Winograd)*, Joan Kaye *(Mrs. Winograd)*, Stefan Gierasch *(Sanitation Foreman)*, Tim Pelt *(Cool Cat)*, Charles Cleveland *(Dice Man)*, Sandi Franklin *(Prostitute)*, Rev. Carlton Coleman *(Gospel Leader)*, Lee Dupree, Ralph Wilcox, Arthur Evans *(Young Brothers)*, Alex Steven, Harry Madsen *(Stunt Cops)*.

Very good film takes an unflinching look at black life in America. Carroll is the mother of six, trying to hold her family together in an environment that rewards cheating and promises only disappointment. She falls in love with garbage man Jones, but he runs away when it looks like a long term commitment is in the wings. Her children track him down and convince him to return, leaving the film on an upbeat note. Excellent performances by Carroll and Jones highlight this film, and the soundtrack by Gladys Knight and The Pips is terrific. A welcome change from the black superman movies of the time, and a film that deserved much more recognition than it received.

p, Hannah Weinstein; d, John Berry; w, Tina and Lester Pine; ph, Gayne Rescher (Deluxe-Movielab Color); m, Curtis Mayfield; ed, Luis San Andres; art d, Ben Kasazkow; set d, Ted Haworth; cos, Bernard Johnson.

Drama **(PR:A MPAA:PG)**

CLAY** (1964 Aus.) 85m Giorgio Manglamela Production bw

Janine Lebedew *(Margot)*, George Dixon *(Nick)*, Chris Tsalikis *(Chris)*, Claude Thomas *(Father)*, Robert Clarke *(Charles)*, Sheila Florance *(Deaf and Dumb Woman)*, Lola Russell *(Mary)*, Cole Turnley *(Businessman)*.

The first all-Australian production in nearly a decade, this low-budget film reveals in flashback how Dixon, apparently a fugitive killer, is discovered lying face down in a bank of wet clay. He is taken in by an isolated community of potters and falls in love with Lebedew. A jealous suitor of hers goes to the police and turns Dixon in, but Lebedew avenges him by driving the informant into a tree at high speed.

p,d,w,ph,ed, Giorgio Manglamele.

Drama **(PR:C-O MPAA:NR)**

CLAY PIGEON, THE½** (1949) 63m RKO bw

Bill Williams *(Jim Fletcher)*, Barbara Hale *(Martha Gregory)*, Richard Quine *(Ted Niles)*, Richard Loo *(Tokoyama)*, Frank Fenton *(Lt. Cmdr. Prentice)*, Frank Wilcox *(Hospital Doctor)*, Marya Marco *(Helen Minoto)*, Robert Bray *(Blake)*, Martha Hyer *(Receptionist)*, Harold Landon *(Blind Veteran)*, James Craven *(John Wheeler)*, Grandon Rhodes *(Clark)*.

This was the first RKO film produced with Howard Hughes at the studio helm. Williams is a sailor who regains consciousness in a U. S. Navy hospital after months of being in a coma. Upon coming to, he is informed that he is about to be court-martialed on charges of treason and having caused the death of a friend in a Japanese prison camp. Williams goes to a friend (Quine) for help but Quine is in collaboration with the Japanese guard (Loo) who actually killed Williams's pal. Both are operating a counterfeit ring masterminded by Loo. Hale, the beautiful widow of William's friend, is suspicious of Quine and alerts police who rescue the victimized sailor just before he is pushed off a train to his death. A taut little suspense film that packs plenty of action and thrills.

p, Herman Schlom; d, Richard O. Fleischer; w, Carl Foreman; ph, Robert De Grasse; ed, Samuel E. Beefly.

Crime/Drama (PR:A MPAA:NR)

CLAY PIGEON*½ (1971) 93m Tracon/MGM c

Telly Savalas (Redford), Robert Vaughn (Neilson), John Marley (Police Captain), Burgess Meredith (Sculptor), Ivan Dixon (Simon), Tom Stern (Joe Ryan), Jeff Corey (Clinic Doctor), Marilyn Akin (Angeline), Marlene Clark (Saddle), Belinda Palmer (Tracy), Mario Alcalde (Jason), Peter Lawford (Government Agent).

One of those drug films that came out by the dozens in the early 1970s. Although it professes to be anti-drug, it wallows in the drug environment while providing an education for future abusers. Film centers around Tom Stern, a Vietnam vet, forced to aid narcotics agent Savalas in the latter's hunt for drug king Vaughn. Plot relies heavily on violence as substance instead of a good script.

p,d, Tom Stern, Lane Slate; w, Ronald Buck, Buddy Ruskin, Jack Gross, Jr. (based on a story by Ruskin, Gross, Jr.); ph, Alan Stensvold (Metrocolor); m, Gavin Murrell; ed, Danford Greene; art d, Ned Parsons.

Crime/Drama (PR:O MPAA:R)

CLAYDON TREASURE MYSTERY, THE** (1938, Brit.) 63m Fox British bw

John Stuart (Peter Kerrigan), Garry Marsh (Sir George Ilford), Evelyn Ankers (Rosemary Claydon), Annie Esmond (Lady Caroline), Campbell Gullan (Tollemach), Aubrey Mallalieu (Lord Claydon), Finlay Currie (Rubin), Joss Ambler (Inspector Fleming), Vernon Harris (Rhodes), Ian Fleming, John Laurie.

Stuart is a novelist who unravels a librarian's murder and locates the hidden family treasure. A good supporting cast elevates this one slightly above the mass of British whodunits.

d, Manning Haynes; w, Edward Dryhurst (based on the novel The Shakespeare Murders by Neil Gordon).

Crime (PR:A MPAA:NR)

CLEANING UP** (1933, Brit.) 70m BL bw

George Gee (Tony Pumpford), Betty Astell (Marian Brent), Davy Burnaby (Lord Pumpford), Barbara Gott (Lady Rudd), Alfred Wellesley (Sir Rickaby Rudd), Muriel George (Mrs. Hoggenheim), Joan Matheson (Angela), Dorothy Vernon (Agatha), Rona Ricardo, Max Rivers Girls.

Gee is the son of a lord who forsakes his aristocratic privileges to become a door-to-door salesman and ends up impersonating the husband of dancer Astell. Justifiably obscure comedy.

p, Herbert Smith; d, Leslie Hiscott; w, Michael Barringer; ph, Alex Bryce.

Comedy (PR:A MPAA:NR)

CLEAR ALL WIRES*½ (1933) 78m MGM bw

Lee Tracy (Buckley Joyce Thomas), Benita Hume (Kate), Una Merkel (Dolly), James Gleason (Lefty), Alan Edwards (Pettingwaite), Eugene Sigaloff (Prince Alexander), Ari Kutai (Kostya), C. Henry Gordon (Commissar), Lya Lys (Eugenie), Lawrence Grant (Mackenzie), John Melvin Bleifer (Sozanoff), Guy Usher (J. H. Stevens).

A ho-hum film about a dedicated woman correspondent, Hume, and her conflicts with a double-crossing, slinky Moscow correspondent Tracy. Differences in reportorial styles and ethics are the subject of this film. Hume, a rising British actress, made her American debut in this film.

d, George Hill; w, Bella and Samuel Spewack (based on their play by same name); ph, Percy Hillburn; ed, Hugh Wynn.

Drama (PR:A MPAA:NR)

CLEAR SKIES*** (1963, USSR) 90m Mosfilm/EF c

Nina Drobysheva (Sasha Lvova), Yevgeniy Urbanskiy (Aleksey Astakhov), N. Kuzmina (Lyusya), Vitaliy Konyayev (Petya), G. Kulikov (Mitya), L. Knyazev (Ivan Illich), Oleg Tabakov, Alik Krylov (Sergey), G. Georgiu (Nikolay Avdeyevich), Vitalik Bondarev (Yegorka), A. Aleksandrushkin V. Anisko, K. Bartashevich, A. Dubov, P. Kiryutkin, Tamara Nosova, N. Khryashchikov.

Urbanskiy is a test pilot in WW II Russia who falls in love with Drobysheva. They conceive a child but before it is born Urbanskiy is lost in action. He is made a posthumous hero of the Soviet Union, but after the war he returns from a German POW camp. Suspected of collaborating with the Germans, he is stripped of his decorations and his party membership. Unable to find a job flying, he begins to drink heavily. Only Drobysheva stands by him. Finally Stalin dies and the injustices of that period come to light. Urbanskiy is restored to his former position and honors, and as the film ends he is testing new jet fighters. An interesting Russian film from that slender period of time under Khrushchev when it was all right to show the repression and terror of the Stalinist period in terms of the ruined lives it left behind. Director Chukhray also made the superb BALLAD OF A SOLDIER during this period, but just two years after this film was released in the USSR (1961), Khrushchev was out of power and Leonid Brezhnev again instituted the policy of "Socialist Realism," leaving filmmakers with no choice but to parrot the party line for the greater glorification of the Soviet system.

d, Grigoriy Chukhray; w, Daniil Khrabrovitskiy (based on a story by M. Rooz); ph,

Sergey Poluyanov (Sovcolor); m, Mikhail Ziv; ed, M. Timofeyeva; art d, Boris Nemechek; cos, V. Perelyotov; spec eff, V. Rylach A. Klimenko.

Drama (PR:A-C MPAA:NR)

CLEAR THE DECKS** (1929) 70m UNIV bw

Reginald Denny (Jack Armitage), Olive Hasbrouck (Miss Bronson), Otis Harlan (Pussyfoot), Lucien Littlefield (Plinge), Collette Marten (Blondie), Robert Anderson (Mate), Elinor Leslie (Aunt), Brooks Benedict (Trumbull).

This 1929 film is only part talkie, with three dialog sequences of eight minutes each. The rest is silent, using subtitles that do not work well. The story of mistaken identities centers around Denny, who follows an attractive woman, Hasbrouck, aboard an ocean liner, signing on board in the name of a friend, who was told to take a voyage for his health or be disinherited. A male nurse, Littlefield, mistakes him for his sick friend and confines him to his cabin, putting him on a diet of goat's milk. He escapes his cabin to find the girl and is mistaken by a band of crooks. The crooks want the girl's necklace and think he is a detective. The nurse drags him back to the cabin, telling the ship's crew that he is crazy. It turns out all right, as he unwittingly foils the crooks, makes a hit with the girl, and loses the nurse.

d, Joseph E. Henabery; w, Earl Snell, Gladys Lehman, Albert DeMond, Charles H. Smith (based on the story "When the Devil Was Sick" by E. J. Rath); ph, Arthur Todd; ed, Jack English, B. W. Burton.

Romance/Comedy (PR:A MPAA:NR)

CLEARING THE RANGE* (1931) 64m Allied/Hollywood Pictures bw

Hoot Gibson, Sally Eilers, Hooper Atchley, George Mendoza, Edward Piel, Edward Hearn, Robert Homans, Mme. Eva Grippon, Maston Williams, Jack Byron.

Last film Gibson would make with his wife, Eilers, who after release of her own starring vehicle, BAD GIRL (1931) became for a while a bigger star than her then-husband. In the film, Gibson plays a man who returns to his home town to find the murderer of his brother. He suspects the bank president, but for fear he will get others in trouble, and for lack of evidence, he pretends he is scared. He incurs the wrath of Eilers, who wants nothing to do with a coward. At night he makes his search for evidence and becomes mistaken for a Spanish bandit. He finally brings the murderer to justice and wins the girl, who did not want anything to do with him because she thought he was a coward. Eilers went on to three more marriages after Gibson and finally retired from pictures in 1951.

p, M. H. Hoffman, Jr.; d, Otto Brower; w, Jack Cunningham, John Natteford; ph, Ernest Miller.

Western (PR:A MPAA:NR)

CLEGG** (1969, Brit.) 87m Sutton-Shonteff/Tigon c

Gilbert Wynne (Harry Clegg), Garry Hope (Francis Wildman), Gilly Grant (Suzy the Slag), Norman Claridge (Lord Cruik Shank), A. J. Brown (Joseph Valentine), Michael Nightingale (Col. Sullivan), Noel Davis (Manager), Ronald Leigh Hunt (Inspector Kert), Jenny Robbins (Shirley).

Detective Wynne, investigating a series of murders committed by a crazed prostitute, uncovers the man responsible for the killings. Not very interesting.

p, Herbert Alpert, Lewis Force; d, Lindsay Shonteff; w, Lewis J. Hagleton; (Technicolor).

Crime (PR:O MPAA:NR)

CLEO FROM 5 TO 7** (1961, Fr.) 90m Rome Paris Film bw (AKA: CLEO DE 5 A 7)

Corinne Marchand (Cleo), Antoine Bourseiller (Antoine), Dorothee Blanck (Dorothee), Michel Legrand (Bob, the Pianist), Dominique Davray (Angele), Jose-Luis de Villalonga (The Lover), Jean-Claude Brialy, Anna Karina, Eddie Constantine, Sami Frey, Danielle Delorme, Jean-Luc Godard, Yves Robert, Alan Scott (Actors in Comedy Film), Robert Postee, Lucienne Marchand.

Marchand believes she has cancer as she awaits test results and director Varda dwells on her ever-changing moods. She visits friends, breaks periodically into tears, sings along with an eccentric composer, purchases a hat, is consoled by a model friend, and is finally bolstered to face the test results by a newly met soldier. A lot of self-examination and little movie. (French; English subtitles)

p, George De Beauregard; d,w, Agnes Varda; ph, Jean Rabier; m, Michel Legrand; ed, Janine Verneau; prod d, Edith Tertza, Jean-Francois Adam; art d, Bernard Evein; m, Michel Legrand; cos, Alyette Samazeuilh; m/l, Agnes Varda; subtitles, Rose Sokol.

Drama (PR:C MPAA:NR)

CLEOPATRA***½ (1934) 102m PAR bw

Claudette Colbert (Cleopatra), Warren William (Julius Caesar), Henry Wilcoxon (Marc Antony), Gertrude Michael (Calpurnia), Joseph Schildkraut (Herod), Ian Keith (Octavian), C. Aubrey Smith (Enobarbus), Ian Maclaren (Cassius), Arthur Hohl (Brutus), Leonard Mudie (Pothinos), Irving Pichel (Apollodorus), Claudia Dell (Octavia), Eleanor Phelps (Charmian), John Rutherford (Drussus), Grace Durkin (Iras), Robert Warwick (Achillas), Edwin Maxwell (Casca), Charles Morris (Cicero), Harry Beresford (Soothsayer), Olga Celeste (Slave Girl), Ecki (Leopold), Ferdinand Gottschalk (Glabrio), William Farnum (Senator), Florence Roberts (Flora), Kenneth Gibson, Wedgewood Nowell (Scribes), John Carridine, Jane Regan, Celia Rylan, Robert Manning (Romans), Lionel Belmore (Party Guest), Dick Alexander (Egyptian Messenger), Jack Mulhall, Wilfred Lucas (Romans Greeting Antony), Hal Price (Onlooker at Procession), Edgar Dearing (Murderer).

Lavish in every DeMille detail, CLEOPATRA is a sexy, extravagant tale of that mysterious Egyptian vamp and her two Roman lovers, the sophisticated, middle-aged Julius Caesar, William, and the man of iron and action, Marc Antony, Wilcoxon. William visits Alexandria to quell the internecine war between Colbert and her vying generals, taking the young queen's side after she is delivered to him wrapped in an expensive carpet, ostensibly as a gift. She proceeds to seduce Williams who stands her off but is amused by her machinations, as well as pleased by the eyeful of flesh she offers. (Colbert's costume is a slinky, hip-hugging skirt, slit to the thigh, and her breasts, barely covered by two thin strips of cloth, threaten to jiggle forth at any moment, a costume undoubtedly designed by showman DeMille himself.) This historical vehicle accelerates into high gear when Wilcoxon appears later as Ceasar's surrogate, first battling ; with the obstinate Colbert, who insists that she is the rightful wife of Rome's First Consul. Later she sees in a dream her champion being executed in the Roman Senate and she then allies herself with the truculent Wilcoxon who falls in love with her, throwing away the empire he has inherited from his sponsor, the dead William. He and Colbert form a united front against Octavian (Keith), but both lose their kingdoms and their lives after committing suicide. CLEOPATRA was DeMille at his exaggerated best (or worst, depending on your tastes). Every frame is occupied by his picky set pieces, all heavily laced with sex, from slave dancers to his top star whose every curve is outlined in his lighting and hungrily recorded by his cameras. But DeMille was no historical voyeur. He painstakingly pieced together every scene, insisting that every spear and vase authentically represent the period. In one giant set crammed with hundreds of extras, a great hall that was Ceasar's atrium, his prop people had placed scores of huge tables topped with marble slabs, statuary, dozens of gold goblets. Each of these props the meticulous director insisted upon inspecting. When all was ready he prepared to shoot the scene. Then he stopped everything as his eagle eye spotted a small flagon twenty feet distant. He walked over and picked it up, holding it aloft with disgust. It was silver-plated and represented an era in time much later than the setting of CLEOPATRA. DeMille had an uncanny memory in that he knew almost every prop in the vast Paramount warehouse,often asking for special props he had used twenty years earlier in one of his silent spectacles. Colbert's barge, which takes Marc Antony away in silky seduction, is ornately accurate in every detail, from the ram's heads surrounding the banks of oars to the dais of pillows upon which Colbert rests her long black locks (a wig) next to the curlyheaded Wilcoxon. The wild dance performed by a bevy of half-naked girls before an ox covered with garlands, and the suggested submission of the female slaves to the animal before a thankful fade-out, is pure DeMille, who found it lucrative at the box office to always mix fact with sex. Another scene astounds Wilcoxon as he witnesses a huge net drawn up from the sea; inside of it are dozens of squirming girls, naked except for prudently placed pieces of seaweed which adorn their privates—DeMille's catch of the day. Wriggling like fish out of water, the girls slither to the foot of the dais where Wilcoxon and Colbert recline, offering Wilcoxon giant seashells which spill out priceless gems. With a nod from Colbert a huge veil slowly descends around her and the bedazzled Wilcoxon. DeMille cuts to a shot showing the enormous pleasure barge being rowed by hundreds of slaves into the darkened sea, a cadence drummer beating out not only the demanded strokes of the oarsmen but suggesting the additional rhythm of the unseen seduction. It is DeMille's carnal poetry in action. The director's penchant for realism in sets and props was surmounted always by his insistence upon actual battle conditions when his hordes of extras clashed before the cameras. No warrior ever used a rubber sword in a DeMille film. They were authentic and razor sharp. In one scene Wilcoxon must fight not only the Egyptians but some of his own turncoat men. More than 200 extras assembled to perform the battle. As the soldiers charged each other, the director shook his head, then yelled: "Cut!" He glared at his troops, snarling: "Get in there and fight like you mean it! You're trying to kill each other!" Again the men stumbled about, half-heartedly swinging swords and poking spears at each other. DeMille again stopped the cameras and exploded. "All right! I can see that I made a mistake. One thing I want to know, gentlemen. Are you wearing lace on your panties?" DeMille grabbed a spear and rushed forward, shouting: "This is the way I want you to fight!" He stared straight at his star, Wilcoxon, a strapping British actor appearing for the first time in a DeMille epic. "Henry! Guard yourself," he warned and lunged at the actor with the spear, aiming for his midsection. Wilcoxon was shocked but reacted instantly, defending himself. "DeMille rushed at me like he was going to cut me to pieces," the actor is quoted in *DeMille, The Man and His Pictures* by Gabe Essoe and Raymond Lee. "I had a helluva time keeping him off, and after a few minutes my whole body was wet and I was trying to find a way to end it. I finally succeeded in sidestepping and as he lunged I cut his spear in half, backed up, and threw my weapon on the ground." Wilcoxon at the time was thirty and DeMille fifty-four, the younger man weighing 200 pounds and standing six-foot-three where DeMille was five-ten and no more than 165 pounds, yet the director pushed the actor into frantic exhaustion without seeming a bit tired. After this incredible athletic display, DeMille turned to the extras and boomed: "If you don't want to fight like that, you can leave the set!" Half of the would-be warriors threw down their weapons and left. Wilcoxon and the rest put on a battle royal and during the melee the star took a spear jab that penetrated to the bone and had the tip of a little finger sliced off. But for Wilcoxon, who would later become DeMille's most trusted confidant and associate producer, it was all part of the job. He and the director later watched the battle in a projection room and DeMille happily whispered to Wilcoxon: "It's almost as good as the fight we put on." DeMille was not above putting women to the same kind of test, even his sultry star Colbert, who was always more of a lady than the hip-swinging harlots she impersonated for the illustrious director. When offering her the lead in CLEOPATRA, DeMille blurted: "How would you like to be the wickedest woman in history?" But for all of the bravado and brass she infused in her Egyptian vamp, Colbert maintained her true feminine nature off camera. The director knew that his marvelous star feared and hated snakes of any kind and yet he insisted that at the film's finale she employ a real snake to commit suicide as did Cleopatra by pressing a lethal asp to ber bosom. DeMille waited until the last minute, the last scene, setting up Colbert in her death chamber and letting her believe all along that she would be using a rubber snake. Of course a rubber snake would appear phony (in those days special effects experts had yet to perfect the mechanical snakes so commonly used today). The director walked forward with an enormous boa constrictor (tamed) curling about his neck and shoulders. Colbert's large eyes bulged in fear as he approached. "Oh, please, Mr. DeMille," she begged, "don't come near with that." He kept coming closer and closer and she began screaming. DeMille suddenly stopped and from behind his back he withdrew a tiny harmless garter snake. "Then how about this one?" he smiled. He held it out to her and by comparison with the giant reptile around his body it appeared insignificant. Colbert reacted to the little snake with motherly instinct, taking it and murmuring lowly: "Oh, this poor little thing is scared to death." Moments later she was clutching the snake to her breast in one of the most memorable death scenes in film history as DeMille's camera pulls back into the darkness of the ancient chamber that enshrouds her. CLEOPATRA was a box office smash, but the critics tore at DeMille for interpreting the historical characters as satyrs and nymphomaniacs. "I make pictures for people," the great showman snorted, "not for critics." He added: "Every time I make a picture the critics' estimate of American public taste goes down 10 percent." Some of his severest critics complained about the abundance of British actors dominating the CLEOPATRA cast, speaking in Oxford accents. Some carped about the slangy dialog. At one point Colbert stabs assassin Mudie (Pothinos) hiding behind a drape, explaining that it was his life or Caesar's. William smirks and orders his guards to remove the body. "Take *it* away," he says, referring to the corpse. "The blankest of blank verse would have been better than this 1934 conversation," moaned one reviewer. But DeMille knew what he wanted, always. To the writers of CLEOPATRA, DeMille specified the contemporary approach: "It's just a damned good hot tale, so don't get a lot of thees and thous into the script." They didn't and DeMille kept the film sizzling.

p&d, Cecil B. DeMille; w, Waldemar Young, Vincent Lawrence (based on historical material by Bartlett McCormick, Jeanie MacPherson, Finley Peter Dunne, Jr.); ph, Victor Milner; m, Rudolph Kopp; ed, Anne Bauchens.

Historical Drama (PR:C MPAA:NR)

CLEOPATRA*½** (1963) 243m FOX c

Elizabeth Taylor *(Cleopatra)*, Richard Burton *(Mark Antony)*, Rex Harrison *(Julius Caesar)*, Pamela Brown *(High Priestess)*, George Cole *(Flavius)*, Hume Cronyn *(Sosigenes)*, Cesare Danova *(Apollodorus)*, Kenneth Haigh *(Brutus)*, Andrew Keir *(Agrippa)*, Martin Landau *(Rufio)*, Roddy McDowall *(Octavian)*, Robert Stephens *(Germanicus)*, Francesca Annis *(Eiras)*, Gregoire Aslan *(Pothinos)*, Martin Benson *(Ramos)*, Herbert Berghof *(Theodotus)*, John Cairney *(Phoebus)*, Jacqui Chan *(Lotos)*, Isabelle Cooley *(Charmian)*, John Doucette *(Achillas)*, Andrew Faulds *(Canidius)*, Michael Gwynn *(Cimber)*, Michael Hordern *(Cicero)*, John Hoyt *(Cassius)*, Marne Maitland *(Euphranor)*, Carroll O'Connor *(Casca)*, Richard O'Sullivan *(Ptolemy)*, Gwen Watford *(Calpurnia)*, Douglas Wilmer *(Decimus)*, Marina Berti *(Queen at Tarsus)*, John Karlsen *(High Priest)*, Loris Loddi *(Caesarion Age 4)*, Jean Marsh *(Octavia)*, Gin Mart *(Marcellus)*, Furio Meniconi *(Mithridates)*, Kenneth Nash *(Caesarion Age 12)*, Del Russell *(Caesarion Age 7)*, John Valva *(Valvus)*, Finlay Currie *(Titus)*, John Alderton *(1st Officer)*, Peter Forster *(2nd Officer)*, Laurence Naismith *(Archesilaus)*, Gesa Meiken, Marie Devereux, Michele Bally, Kathy Martin, Maria Badmajev, Maureen Lane, Simon Mizrahi, John Gaylord.

Volumes have already been written about what went on behind the camera while CLEOPATRA was being made. Taylor's near-fatal illness, her passionate affair with Burton, the costly overruns that brought the picture's price to a then-record $40 million replacing Rouben Mamoulian, Peter Finch, and Stephen Boyd with Joe Mankiewicz, Rex Harrison, and Richard Burton, and on and on. CLEOPATRA began shooting the last week in September, 1960. In the third week of November production stopped to accommodate Taylor's recurring cold as well as the rumor that Liz, whose weight has been known to yo-yo, had gone up to porky porportions. Work resumed January 1, 1961, but Liz now wanted the scenes with Finch re-written. With only eleven minutes of usable film in the can (and having already spent $6 million dollars), Mamoulian resigned. Now Taylor became very ill and required the tracheotomy which probably kept her alive. It wasn't until September that the whole thing began again with a new group. The finished film was more than six hours long and Fox thought it might make a few extra bucks by dividing it into two films. The idea was scrapped and the 243-minute version was issued. It was later trimmed to 222 minutes but that hardly mattered. By then, the word was out that this was a debacle and it never did the box office it needed to keep it from being a flop. Looking at the picture years later, one realizes that it's not nearly so bad as one thought. Physically exquisite with some smart dialog for all involved, all it needed was a lot less to have been worth a lot more. The plot, in case you were wondering, is as follows: Rex Harrison (Caesar), the Consul of Rome, arrives in Egypt after beating the togas off Pompey at Pharsalia. It's 48 B.C. and Cleopatra (Taylor) is forced from the throne she shares with O'Sullivan, her brother. She joins forces with Harrison, becomes his lover, and gives him a son. He, in turn, helps her retake Egypt. Later, he sends for her and she arrives in Rome in as triumphant a procession as any Pope ever encountered. Her happiness at being with Harrison is short-lived when he is assassinated by Haigh and a group of others in the Roman Senate (see Marlon Brando in JULIUS CAESAR for a closer look at that). Before returning to Egypt, the sorrowful Cleo is noticed by Antony (Burton) but it's almost three years later when they meet again on her royal barge at Tarsus. She uses her wiles to nab Burton (it was happening on and off the screen at the same moment) and they return to Rome as lovers. However, to keep his political base, Burton must wed Jean Marsh (the same one from "Upstairs, Downstairs"), the sister of MacDowall. Together, all three will rule Rome. But lust is thicker than politics and Burton eventually returns to Taylor's arms. He is so in love with her that he gives Taylor all of Rome's eastern provinces as a gift and then marries her, thus becoming the world's first well-known bigamist. MacDowall is irked by this insult to his family and so attacks Burton's forces at Actium. A battle royal ensues and Taylor is informed that Burton has been killed in the fighting. She leaves the area and takes her powerful fleet, thus hastening the actual defeat of Burton's forces. She seeks peace in a mausoleum and when Burton arrives, Danova, who adores her and has been jealous of Burton, tells Burton that Taylor is dead. Burton is disconsolate, stabs himself, and is later taken to Taylor to die in her arms. She cannot bear life without him and puts the famous asp to her breast for the poisonous bite of death. Reading the reviews more than twenty years later, we must take note that Bosley Crowther of the New York *Times* called it "One of the great epic films of our day." The smart-alecs who were lying in wait (John Simon, Judith Crist, et al.) were less kind. Four Oscars awarded; cinematography, art direction, costume design and special effects. Time has not been kind to many films but it has been to CLEOPATRA. Forget the machinations off-screen and just enjoy this very enjoyable film. With sixty minutes out (as has been the case on some TV runs), it's a helluva entertainment.

p, Walter Wanger; d, Joseph L. Mankiewicz; w, Mankiewicz, Ranald MacDougall, Sidney Buchman (based on works by Plutarch, Appian, Suetonius and *The Life And Times Of Cleopatra*, a novel by Carlo Mario Franzero); ph, Leon Shamroy (Todd A-O, DeLuxe Color); m, Alex North; ed, Dorothy Spencer; prod d, John De Cuir; art d, Jack Martin Smith, Hilyard Brown, Herman Blumenthal, Elven Webb, Maurice Pelling, Boris Juraga; set d, Walter M. Scott, Paul S. Fox, Ray Moyer; cos, Irene Sharaff, Vittorio Nino Novarese; spec eff, L. B. Abbott, Emil Kosa, Jr.; ch, Hermes Pan; makeup, Alberto De Rossi.

Historical Drama **Cas.** **(PR:A-C MPAA:NR)**

CLEOPATRA JONES* (1973) 89m WB c

Tamara Dobson *(Cleopatra Jones)*, Bernie Casey *(Reuben)*, Brenda Sykes *(Tiffany)*, Antonio Fargas *(Doodlebug)*, Bill McKinney *(Officer Purdy)*, Dan Frazer *(Detective Crawford)*, Stafford Morgan *(Sgt. Kert)*, Mike Warren *(Andy)*, Albert Popwell, Caro Kenyatta *(The Johnson Boys)*, Esther Rolle *(Mrs. Johnson)*, Shelley Winters *(Mommy)*, Paul Koslo, Joseph A. Tornatore *(Mommy's Hoods)*, Hedley Mattingly *(Chauffeur)*, George Reynolds, Theodore Wilson *(Doodlebug's Hoods)*, Christopher Joy *(Snake)*, Keith Hamilton *(Maxwell Woodman)*, Angela Gibbs *(Annie)*, John Garwood *(Lt. Thompkins)*, John Alderman *(Mommy's Assistant)*.

CLEOPATRA JONES is at the tail end of the black exploitation films that pockmarked the 1960s, presenting a story of an Amazonian secret agent, Dobson, and her improbable experiences. She drives a heavily armed sports car and busies herself looking for poppy fields before they are harvested and distributed by pushers. She appears in Watts, the Los Angeles black ghetto, to investigate a phony raid on a halfway house run by her lover. The raid is a ruse to lure Dobson to L. A., concocted by Winters, an obnoxious lesbian gang leader and drug queen (endearingly called "Mommy") so that she can murder the agent. Rolle and her karate-trained sons aid Dobson in foiling Winters and gang. The violence is near-incessant in this miserably scripted waste of time.

p, William Tennant; d, Jack Starrett; w, Max Julien, Sheldon Keller (based on the story by Max Julien); ph, David Walsh (Panavision, Technicolor); m, Carl Brandt, J. J. Johnson, Brad Shapiro (Title theme Joe Simon); ed, Allan Jacobs; art d, Peter Wooley; set d, Cheryal Kearney.

Exploitation **(PR:O MPAA:PG)**

CLEOPATRA JONES AND THE CASINO OF GOLD*
(1975 U. S. Hong Kong) 94m WB c

Tamara Dobson *(Cleopatra Jones)*, Stella Stevens *(Dragon Lady)*, Tanny *(Mi Ling)*, Norman Fell *(Stanley Nagel)*, Albert Popwell *(Matthew Johnson)*, Caro Kenyatta *(Melvin Johnson)*, Chan Sen *(Soo)*, Christopher Hunt *(Mendez)*, Lin Chen Chi *(Madalyna)*, Liu Loke Hua *(Tony)*, Eddy Donno *(Morgan)*, Bobby Canavarro *(Lin Ma Chen)*, Mui Kwok Sing *(Benny)*, John Cheng *(David)*.

In Hollywood the credo is that if something even comes close to making decent money, make a sequel. The predecessor to this film, CLEOPATRA JONES, made some good money, so the sequel wasn't far behind. As in most sequels, the second film usually has none of the qualities that made the first box office gold but in this case it didn't matter; both are terrible. Dobson is the six-foot two black Amazon fighting woman, still trying to stamp out the drug trade. This time it brings her to Hong Kong to fight multiracial villains, including Stevens, the leader of an international narcotics operation, and search for two agents who vanished while trying to detect a drug operation.

p, William Tennant; d, Chuck Bail; w, Tennant (based on characters created by Max Julien); ph, Alan Hume (Panavision, Technicolor); m, Dominic Frontiere; ed, Willy Kemplen; art d, Johnson Tsao.

Spy Drama **(PR:O MPAA:NR)**

CLEOPATRA'S DAUGHTER**
(1963, Fr., Ital.) 93m Explorer Film-C.F.P.C./Medallion c
(AKA: DAUGHTER OF CLEOPATRA; FR. LA VALLEE DES PHARAONS; ITAL: IL SEPOLCRO DEI RE)

Debra Paget *(Shila)*, Ettore Manni *(Resi)*, Erno Crisa *(Kefren)*, Robert Alda *(Inuni)*, Corrado Pani *(Nemorat)*, Yvette Lebon *(Queen Tegi)*, Andreina Rossi *(Kefren's Mistress)*, Ivano Staccioli, Renato Mambor, Betsy Bell.

After the Syrians are defeated by the Egyptians, Paget, the Syrian daughter of Cleopatra, is carried back to Egypt and forced to marry Pani. Before their marriage is consummated, though, Pani is poisoned by his uncle (Crisa). Paget is accused of the crime and sentenced to be buried alive with her husband in a pyramid. Court physician Manni gives her a drug which simulates death, and during the night he and a group of tomb robbers break into the burial chamber and free her. Manni and Paget escape through the desert with a caravan. More swords-and-sandals stuff with the usual second-rate American stars to give it box office appeal.

d, Fernando Cerchio (dubbed version Richard McNamara); w, Cerchio, Damiano Damiani; ph, Anchise Brizzi (Ultrascope, Technicolor); m, Antonio Fusco; ed, Antonietta Zita; art d, Arrigo Equini; cos, Giancarlo Bartolini Salimbeni.

Adventure **(PR:C MPAA:NR)**

CLIMAX, THE* (1930) 62m UNIV bw

Jean Hersholt *(Luigi Golfanti)*, Kathryn Crawford *(Adella Donatelli)*, LeRoy Mason *(Dr. Gardoni)*, John Reinhardt *(Pietro Golfanti)*, Henry Armetta *(Anton Donatelli)*.

A slow film based on a 1909 play of the same name. Story revolves around a young opera star, Crawford, who is taken under the wing of a singing maestro (Hersholt), who taught her mother. Crawford falls in love with the son of the maestro. A handsome doctor falls in love with the girl, complicating matters. Later the girl goes in for an operation to improve her voice. The young doctor is the surgeon's assistant. He spoils the operation and the girl is left voiceless. The girl decides to marry the doctor to rid the maestro of his responsibility, but just before the wedding she recovers her voice and runs off with the maestro's son.

d, Renaud Hoffman; w, Julian Josephson, Clarence Thompson, Lesley Mason (based on a play of the same name by Edward Locke); ph, Jerry Ash; ed, Bernard Burton.

Musical **(PR:A MPAA:NR)**

CLIMAX, THE½** (1944) 86m UNIV c

Susanna Foster *(Angela)*, Boris Karloff *(Dr. Hohner)*, Turhan Bey *(Franz)*, Gale Sondeergaard *(Luise)*, Thomas Gomez *(Count Seebruck)*, June Vincent *(Marcellina)*, George Dolenz *(Amato)*, Ludwig Stossel *(Carl Bauman)*, Jane Farrar *(Jarmilla Vadek)*, Erno Verebes *(Brunn)*, Lotte Stein *(Mama Hinzl)*, Scotty Beckett *(King)*, William Edmunds *(Leon)*, Maxwell Hayes *(Aide)*, Dorothy Lawrence *(Miss Metzger)*.

This near relative to THE PHANTOM OF THE OPERA was made one year after the successful 1943 remake and by the same director, George Waggner. THE CLIMAX stars Karloff in one of his stronger performances. He is the resident doctor of a European opera house, who labors under a chronic disability—madness. Many years before, he had been in love with a beautiful soprano who did not love him in return. He strangled her in the cellar of the opera house, embalmed her, and built a shrine around her. Twenty years later a young music student, Foster, auditions, and Karloff is struck by the similarities in their voices. When Foster is cast in the same role as his lost love, Karloff goes mad. He puts her under his influence through hypnotism, and tries to make her drop out of the show. Her fiance won't allow it, and Karloff realizes he must kill her. His housekeeper tips off the police, who chase Karloff to the opera house. He meets his death, next to the shrine of his dead love, when an overturned lamp engulfs him in flame. Ostensibly a remake of THE CLIMAX of 1930, this version appears lavish in rich Technicolor and because the ever cost-conscious Universal shot the film on the sets of THE PHANTOM OF THE OPERA, and that film employed the original Paris Opera House used in the 1925 silent classic with Lon Chaney, Sr.

p&d, George Waggner; w, Curt Siodmak, Lyn Starling (from a play by Edward Locke); ph, Hal Mohr, W. Howard Greene (Technicolor); m, Edward Ward; ed, Russell Schoengarth; art d, John B. Goodman, Howard Golitzen; set d, Russell A. Gausman, Ira S. Webb; md, Don George; spec eff, John P. Fulton; m/l, Waggner; makeup, Jake P. Pierce.

Horror **(PR:A MPAA:NR)**

CLIMAX, THE½** (1967, Fr., Ital.) 97m Produzioni Associate Delphos-Les Productions Artistes Associes-R.P.A.-Compagnia Cinematagrafica Montoro-Dear Film/Lopert Pictures c
(AKA: TOO MUCH FOR ONE MAN; ITAL: L'IMMORALE; FR: BEAUCOUP TROP POUR UN SEUL HOMME)

Ugo Tognazzi *(Sergio Masini)*, Stefania Sandrelli *(Marisa Malagugini)*, Renee Longarini *(Giulia Masini)*, Maria Grazia Carmassi *(Adela Baistrocchi)*, Gigi Ballista *(Don Michele)*, Sergio Fincato *(Colasanti)*, Marco Della Giovanna *(Riccardo Masini)*, Ildebrando Santafe *(Caputo)*, Riccardo Billi *(Filiberto Malagugini)*, Carlo Bagno *(Mr. Malagugini)*, Lina Lagalla *(Mrs. Malagugini)*, Stefano Chierchie *(Bruno)*, Costantino Bramini *(Nini)*, Cinzia Sperapani *(Luisa)*, Mimosa Gregoretti *(Mita)*, Giorgio Bianchi *(Head Doctor)*, Giovanna Lenzi *(Nurse)*.

Tognazzi is a concert violinist who maintains a family and two mistresses, phoning them all constantly to assure them of their place in his heart. While waiting for the birth of a baby by his newest mistress (Sandrelli) he goes to a church and confesses his arrangement. The priest recommends a divorce but Tognazzi is unwilling to do that because all his women need him. Finally, it all proves too much for him and he suffers a fatal heart attack while trying to phone his wife. From heaven he watches his funeral and wonders if his wife knew his secret. Fairly good comedy from director Germi, who made at least two fine comedies, DIVORCE, ITALIAN STYLE and SEDUCED AND ABANDONED.

p&d, Pietro Germi; w, Germi, Alfredo Giannetti, Tullio Pinelli, Carlo Bernari; ph, Aiace Parolin; m, Carlo Rustichelli; ed, Sergio Montanari; prod d, Carlo Egidi; set d, Andrea Fantacci; cos, Angela Sammaciccia.

Comedy **(PR:C-O MPAA:NR)**

CLIMBING HIGH½** (1938, Brit.) 79m GAU/MG bw

Jessie Matthews *(Diana)*, Michael Redgrave *(Nicky)*, Noel Madison *(Gibson)*, Alastair Sim *(Max)*, Margaret Vyner *(Lady Constance)*, Mary Clare *(Lady Emily)*, Francis L. Sullivan *(Madman)*, Enid Stamp-Taylor *(Winnie)*, Torin Thatcher *(Jim)*, Tucker McGuire *(Patsy)*, Basil Radford *(Reggie)*, Athole Stewart *(Uncle)*.

Funny film about a poor model, Matthews, who is run down in the road by young millionaire, Redgrave. Pretending poverty, Redgrave tries to court her. He wins her heart, but when she discovers his true identity she refuses to see him. He almost ends up getting engaged to snooty Vyner, but it is Matthews who winds up with him. One hilarious scene portrays an escaped lunatic in the Swiss Alps who interrupts a mountain-climbing party when he suddenly believes himself a bird capable of flying from peak to peak; he takes off and lands safely in soft snow up to his eyeballs.

p, Michael Balcon; d, Carol Reed; w, Stephen Clarkson (based on a story by Lesser Samuels, Marion Dix); ph, Mutz Greenbaum.

Comedy **(PR:A MPAA:NR)**

CLINIC, THE** (1983, Aus.) 92m Film House Generation/Eagle c

Chris Haywood, Simon Burke, Rona McLeod, Gerda Nicolson, Suzanne Roylance, Veronica Lang, Pat Evison, Max Bruch, Gabrielle Hartley, Jane Clifton, Ned Lander, Martin Sharman, Tom Travers, Tony Rickards, Mark Little, Betty Bobbitt, Marilyn O'Donnell, Geoff Parry, Laurence Mah, Paul Kuek, Danny Nash, Alan Pentland, Jesse

Mogensen, Terrie Sinclair, Evelyn Krape, Simon Thorpe, Alkex Menglet, Nicky Zakariah, Andrew Thompson, Mark Minchinton, Karl Bendix Hansen, Tracey Harvey, Rod Richardson, Richard Healey, Tracey Kelly, Liddy Holloway, Johnny Quinn, Daryl Pellizzer, Doug Tremlett, Gerry Murtagh.

Australian comedy about a day in the life of a VD clinic run by gay doctor Haywood. The film has some fresh sensibilities and honesty that helps overcome some of the more obvious "liberal" messages regarding sexuality being pounded home.

p, Robert Le Tet, Bob Weis; d, David Stephens; w, Greg Millin; ph, Ian Baker; ed, Edward McQueen-Mason; prod d, Tracy Watt; md, Redmond Symons.

Comedy (PR:O MPAA:NR)

CLIPPED WINGS* (1938) 62m N/Ace bw
Lloyd Hughes *(Capt. Lofton)*, Rosalind Keith *(Molly)*, William Janney *(Mickey)*, George Regas *(Fernando)*, Henry Otho *(Sgt. Phalen)*, Richard Cramer *(Moran)*, Jason Robards *(Raoul)*, Joseph Girard *(Dr. Clayton)*, Glen Boles *(Cecil)*, Delmar Watson *(Mickey As a Boy)*.

When his half-brother disappears during an air battle in WW I, Janney decides to follow in his footsteps. Turned down by the armed forces because he fears storms, Janney is about to give up all hope in life until he learns that his brother is still alive and working as a G-man. The two join forces and track down a gang of oil thieves. Ineptly made action tale about family loyalty and personal bravery.

d, Stuart Paton; w, Harry Forbes; ph, Elmer Dyar.

Crime Drama (PR:A MPAA:NR)

CLIPPED WINGS*½ (1953) 62m AA bw
Leo Gorcey *(Slip)*, Huntz Hall *(Sach)*, Bernard Gorcey *(Louie)*, David Condon *(Chuck)*, Bennie Bartlett *(Butch)*, Renie Riano *(W. A. F. Sgt. Anderson)*, Todd Karns *(Lt. Dave Moreno)*, June Vincent *(Dorene)*, Mary Treen *(Mildred)*, Philip Van Zandt *(Eckler)*, Frank Richards *(Dupre)*, Michael Ross *(Anders)*, Elaine Riley *(Sgt. White)*, Jeanne Dean *(Hilda)*, Anne Kimbell *(Allison)*, Fay Roope *(Col. Davenport)*, Henry Kulky *(Sgt. Broski)*, Lyle Talbot *(Col. Blair)*, Ray Walker *(Federal Officer)*, Arthur Space, Conrad Brooks, Lou Nova.

When Bowery Boys Gorcey, Hall, and chums visit pal Karns at the army base he is stationed at, they unknowingly enlist when they believe they are simply signing a guest register. Unaware that Karns is aiding the FBI in a search for Nazi spies, the boys not only manage to irritate officers, infiltrate a woman's barracks, and create general havoc, they nab the espionage ring as well. Typical outing from that ever-entertaining bunch of jobless street punks. (See BOWERY BOYS series, Index.)

p, Ben Schwalb; d, Edward Bernds; w, Charles R. Marion, Elwood Ullman (based on the story by Marion); ph, Harry Neumann; ed, Lester A. Sanson, Bruce B. Pierce; art d, David Milton.

Comedy (PR:A MPAA:NR)

CLIVE OF INDIA*** (1935) 92m FOX/UA bw
Ronald Colman *(Robert Clive)*, Loretta Young *(Margaret Maskelyne Clive)*, Colin Clive *(Capt. Johnstone)*, Francis Lister *(Edmund Maskelyne)*, Vernon Downing *(Stringer)*, Peter Shaw *(Miller)*, Neville Clark *(Vincent)*, Ian Wolfe *(Kent)*, Robert Greig *(Pemberton)*, Montagu Love *(Gou Pigot)*, Leo G. Carroll *(Manning)*, Etienne Girardot *(Warburton)*, Lumsden Hare *(Sgt. Clark)*, Wyndham Standing *(Col. Townsend)*, Douglas Gerrard *(Lt. Walsh)*, Connie Leon *(Ayah)*, Ann Shaw *(Lady Lindley)*, Doris Lloyd *(Mrs. Nixon)*, Mischa Auer *(Suraj Ud Dowlah)*, Cesar Romero *(Mir Jaffar)*, Ferdinand Munier *(Adm. Watson)*, Gilbert Emery *(Sullivan)*, C. Aubrey Smith *(Prime Minister)*, Ferdinand Gottschalk *(Old Member)*, John Carradine *(Drunken-Faced Clerk)*, Emmett O. King *(Merchant)*, Pat Somerset *(Lt. Walsh)*, Olaf Hytten *(Parson at Hasting)*, Don Ameche *(Black Hole of Calcutta Prisoner)*, Herbert Bunston *(1st Director)*, Edward Cooper *(Clive's Butler)*, Eily Malyon *(Mrs. Clifford)*, Keith Kenneth *(2nd Director)*, Desmond Roberts *(3rd Director)*, Joseph Tozer *(Sir Frith)*, Phyllis Clare *(Margaret's Friend)*, Phillip Dare *(Capt. George)*, Leonard Mudie *(Gen. Burgoyne)*, Lila Lance *(Mango Seller)*, Charles Evans *(Surveyor)*, Vesey O'Davern *(2nd Surveyor)*.

An absorbing biopic, CLIVE OF INDIA chronicles the career of Robert Clive, England's man of destiny in India which he felt was best ruled as a British colony. Colman is a sensitive but ambitious Clive, beginning as a clerk with the manipulative East India Company and becoming the courageous warrior, tirelessly campaigning to unite the vast tribal country under the Union Jack. There are many stirring scenes such as the incredible monsoons and a battle between cavalry mounted on elephants draped with barbed armor (in a recreation of the battle of Plassey) as well as a brief but telling scene of the infamous Black Hole of Calcutta where prisoners of cruel Indian warlords suffocated on poisonous gasses (one of the victims in a brief but moving part is Don Ameche). Young, as Colman's tolerant and much-abandoned wife, is effective but too briefly seen on camera. Auer, usually known for his comedic roles,is surprisingly chilly as the vicious native tyrant,and Romero counterpoints this ruthless portrait with an idealized role of an Indian leader sympathetic to Clive's purposes. All the great actors from Hollywood's then populous British colony are present and are pleasing to watch (as well as listen to,their voices being mellifluous on the sound track)—Smith, Love, Hare. Director Boleslawski packs enormous detail into this film which is more of a historian's delight than a viewer's entertainment. Producer Zanuck personally bought this vehicle, a popular London play called "Clive," for his favorite star, Colman. So enthusiastic was the actor for the role that he shaved off his famous mustache to the dismay of his ardent female following. Colman spent months studying Clive's life and his devotion to his subject shows in every frame. At the time the actor was considered by female moviegoers to be the most handsome man in films. History, however, was considerably altered in the film. Colman is tried for treason in the House of Commons but instead of committing suicide as did the real Clive in 1757, he survives to be reunited with his wife, Young, in an ending that was mandatory for Depression audiences.

p, William Goetz, Raymond Griffith (for Darryl F. Zanuck); d, Richard Boleslawski; w, W. P. Lipscomb, R. J. Minney (based on their play, "Clive"); ph, Peverell Marley; m, Alfred Newman; ed, Barbara McLean; cos, Omar Kiam.

Biography (PR:A MPAA:NR)

CLOAK AND DAGGER*** (1946) 106m United States Pictures/WB bw
Gary Cooper *(Prof. Alvah Jasper)*, Lilli Palmer *(Gina)*, Robert Alda *(Pinkie)*, Vladimir Sokoloff *(Dr. Polda)*, J. Edward Bromberg *(Trenk)*, Marjorie Hoshelle *(Ann Dawson)*, Ludwig Stossel *(German)*, Helene Thimig *(Katerin Loder)*, Dan Seymour *(Marsoli)*, Marc Lawrence *(Luigi)*, James Flavin *(Col. Walsh)*, Pat O'Moore *(Englishman)*, Charles Marsh *(Erich)*, Don Turner *(Lingg)*, Clifton Young *(American Commmander)*, Ross Ford *(Paratrooper)*, Robert Coote *(Cronin)*, Hans Schumm, Peter Michael *(German Agents)*, Yola D'Avril, Claire Du Brey, Lottie Stein *(Nurses)*, Lynn Lyons *(Woman in Bank, Double)*, Rory Mallinson *(Paul)*, Ed Parker, Gil Perkins *(Gestapo)*, Bruce Lester *(British Officer)*, Leon Lenoir *(Italian Soldier)*, Otto Reichow, Arno Frey *(German Soldiers)*, Maria Monteil, Lillian Nicholson *(Nuns)*, Bobby Santon *(Italian Boy)*, Elvira Curci *(Woman in Street)*, Hella Crosley *(Rachele)*, Douglas Walton *(British Pilot)*, Vernon Downing *(British Sergeant)*, Holmes Herbert *(British Officer)*, Frank Wilcox *(American Officer)*, Michael Burke *(OSS Agent)*, Eddie Dunn *(Radio Operator)*.

An improbable but exciting story has Cooper as a physics professor recruited by the OSS (Office of Strategic Services). He is asked to go to Italy at the end of WW II to locate Sokoloff, an atomic scientist being held by the Nazis. He first meets with a female scientist, Thimig, in Switzerland but she is killed and Cooper is followed to Italy by Hoshelle, a Nazi agent. He evades her. Once in Italy, Palmer and Alda, Italian partisans, contact Cooper and help him find Sokoloff—Palmer and Cooper developing a romance. Sokoloff is found living in fear for his life but Cooper manages to smuggle him to a secret airfield. While Alda, Palmer, and their partisans hold off approaching Nazis, Cooper and Sokoloff escape in a plane. Cooper promises to return for Palmer after the war is over. CLOAK AND DAGGER marked Palmer's American debut after her smashing performance in RAKE'S PROGRESS/NOTORIOUS GENTLEMAN with Rex Harrison, her real-life husband. She is stunning as the devoted Italian girl sacrificing all for the Allies and Cooper. But the role of a sophisticated scientist made Cooper uneasy and he is somewhat miscast as a plain American attempting to pass himself off as a foreigner. The action is brisk under Lang's expert direction, but the film is nowhere near what he envisioned. In fact, Warner Brothers cut most of the fourth reel, which was an attack on nuclear weapons. At one point Cooper states: "This is the first time I am sorry that I am a scientist. Society is not ready for atomic energy. I'm scared stiff." Of course, Cooper's mission is to prevent the Nazis from developing the bomb, which viewers knew in advance never happened. Lang at least was able to realistically present the dirty side of espionage and total war. When Cooper attempts to embrace Palmer, the beautiful but hardened resistance fighter pulls away, flaring: "Don't make love to me! Don't be someone I like . . . In my work I kiss without feeling . . . When you fight scum you become scum." But she later softens: "I want you to like me. I want you to think I'm nineteen, with a white dress, a girl who has never been kissed before." Lang had provided a shuddering ending to the film, one never seen. Sokoloff dies on the plane but manages to pinpoint the Nazi factory where the A-bomb is being manufactured. A massive raid on the secret mountain plant is made but the cavernous area is deserted. Cooper emerges from the cave entrance pondering the whereabouts of the secret bomb center. Is it now in Spain or Argentina? States Cooper: "God have mercy on us if we ever thought we could really keep science a secret—or even wanted to. God have mercy on us if we think we can wage other wars without destroying ourselves . . . And God have mercy on us if we haven't the sense to keep the world in peace." All of this was eliminated from the released version and the footage is completely lost. Warner Brothers feared that such hortatory anti-nuclear speeches, particularly mouthed by such homespun heroes as Cooper, would unnerve audiences still in shock over Hiroshima and Nagasaki. The story was based on an actual experience by producer Sperling and technical advisor Burke. Both men had smuggled an Italian admiral out of Italy, one who had developed an electronic torpedo mechanism which the Nazis were prevented from using.

p, Milton Sperling; d, Fritz Lang; w, Albert Maltz,Ring Lardner,Jr. (based on a story by Boris Ingster and John Larkin, suggested by the book by Corey Ford and Alastair MacBain); ph, Sol Polito; m, Max Steiner; ed, Christian Nyby; md, Leo F. Forbstein; art d, Max Parker; set d, Walter Tilford; cos, Leah Rhodes; spec eff, Harry Barndollar, Edwin B. DuPar; tech adv, Michael Burke; makeup, Perc Westmore.

Spy Drama (PR:A MPAA:NR)

CLOAK WITHOUT DAGGER (SEE: OPERATION CONSPIRACY, 1957, Brit.)

CLOCK, THE***½** (1945) 90m MGM bw (GB: UNDER THE CLOCK)
Judy Garland *(Alice Mayberry)*, Robert Walker *(Cpl. Joe Allen)*, James Gleason *(Al Henry)*, Keenan Wynn *(The Drunk)*, Marshall Thompson *(Bill)*, Lucile Gleason *(Mrs. Al Henry)*, Ruth Brady *(Helen)*, Chester Clute *(Michael Henry)*, Dick Elliott *(Friendly Man)*.

A first-rate sleeper of a picture featuring Garland in a rare non-singing role, directed by her eventual husband. The story is deceptively simple because it is in the touches that the genius of this film lies. Garland and Walker meet under the big clock at Pennsylvania Station in New York. They fall in love and marry within 48 hours. This kind of thing happened often in real life and Gallico's story smacks of authenticity. So does the incredible rear screen projection work and the huge sets that would cause any New Yorker to bet serious money that the film was done on location in the Big Apple. Not so. It was a back-lot job and a tribute to the talents of those technicians. Every single bit player is perfectly cast and special plaudits to Wynn, who plays a drunken patriot. This was Minnelli's first straight directing job and he went on to distinguish himself away from musicals with such giants as THE BAD AND THE BEAUTIFUL, FATHER OF THE BRIDE, and many others. Looking at the two young, well-scrubbed stars, it's hard to believe that both their lives would end tragically. Walker was only 33 at the time of his death and had been married to Jennifer Jones and John Ford's daughter, Barbara. He'd been institutionalized for alcohol abuse almost a year before returning to work in Alfred Hitchcock's STRANGERS ON A TRAIN. While filming MY SON JOHN in 1951, he died from too many sedatives doctors had prescribed to calm his emotional instability. p, Arthur Freed; d, Vincente Minnelli; w, Robert Nathan, Joseph Schrank (based on a story by Paul and Pauline Gallico); ph, George Folsey; m, George Bassman; ed, George White; art d, Cedric Gibbons, William Ferrari; set d, Edwin B. Willis, Mac Alper; cos, Irene; spec eff, A. Arnold Gillespie.

Romance   **(PR:A MPAA:NR)**

CLOCKMAKER, THE***

(1976, Fr.) 105m Lira Films/Joseph Green Pictures c
Phillippe Noiret *(Michel Descombes)*, Jean Rochefort *(Commissioner Guiboud)*, Jacques Denis *(Antoine)*, William Sabatier *(Lawyer)*, Andree Tainsy *(Madeleine)*, Sylvain Rougerie *(Bernard Descombes)*, Christine Pascal *(Lilliane)*, Cecile Vassort *(Martine)*.

Noiret is a Lyons clockmaker who suffers an abrupt shock when his son (Rougerie) kills a factory foreman, burns his car, and runs off with Pascal. Finally caught, the son gives as the reason for the killing only that the victim "was a pig" and "I'm sick of the same ones always winning." Good, thoughtful drama is former critic Tavernier's first film. He would go on to direct such fine films as DEATH WATCH and COUP DE TORCHON. Well worth seeing. (French; English subtitles)

d, Bertrand Tavernier; w, Jean Aurenche, Pierre Bost (based on the novel *The Clockmaker of Everton* by Georges Simenon); ph, Pierre William Glenn.

Drama   **(PR:O MPAA:NR)**

CLOCKWORK ORANGE, A*

(1971, Brit.) 137m WB c
Malcolm McDowell *(Alex)*, Patrick Magee *(Mr. Alexander)*, Michael Bates *(Chief Guard)*, Warren Clarke *(Dim)*, John Clive *(Stage Actor)*, Adrienne Corri *(Mrs. Alexander)*, Carl Duering *(Dr. Brodsky)*, Paul Farrell *(Hobo)*, Clive Francis *(Lodger)*, Michael Gover *(Prison Warden)*, Miriam Karlin *(Cat Lady)*, James Marcus *(Georgie)*, Aubrey Morris *(Deltoid)*, Godfrey Quigley *(Prison Chaplain)*, Sheila Raynor *(Mum)*, Madge Ryan *(Dr. Branom)*, John Savident *(Conspirator Dolin)*, Anthony Sharp *(Minister of Interior)*, Philip Stone *(Dad)*, Pauline Taylor *(Psychiatrist)*, Margaret Tyzack *(Conspirator Rubinstein)*, Steven Berkoff *(Constable)*, Lindsay Campbell *(Inspector)*, Michael Tarn *(Pete)*, David Prowse *(Julian)*, Jan Adair, Prudence Drage, Vivenne Chandler *(Handmaidens)*, John J. Carney *(C.I.D. Official)*, Richard Connaught *(Billyboy)*, Carol Drinkwater *(Nurse Feeley)*, George O'Gorman *(Bootick Clerk)*, Cheryl Grunwald *(Rape Victim)*, Gillian Hills *(Sonietta)*, Craig Hunter *(Dr. Friendly)*, Barbara Scott *(Marty)*, Virginia Wetherell *(Stage Actress)*, Katya Wyeth *(Girl in Fantasy)*, Gaye Brown, Peter Burton, Barrie Cookson, Lee Fox, Neil Wilson, Shirley Jaffe.

In this brutal, self-indulgent exercise in ulta-violence, Kubrick portrays a sadistic British youth, McDowell (in his most odious role), as he wreaks mayhem upon society and, in turn, is brutalized by the system he attacks. McDowell, Clarke, Marcus, and Tarn begin their day by beating and robbing helpless victims. They beat a hobo half to death for fun, then attack a gang in a deserted theater just as they are about to rape a girl. McDowell and the others pleasure themselves with the girl. Wearing disguises, the foursome roar into the countryside on motorcycles, invading the home of prominent writer Magee, beating him senseless, and brutally gang-raping his attractive wife Corri. (Magee later becomes manic and his wife dies as a result of the attack.) McDowell skips school while his parents trudge off to factory jobs. He listens to Beethoven, his favorite composer,and brings girls to his room for quick copulation. Later, he and his goon friends invade another home of a walthy, cat-loving eccentric, beating and raping her. McDowell is knocked senseless by one of his own gang, before police arrive, in reprisal for disciplining him earlier. Arrested, McDowell is sent to prison and later agrees to undergo experiments in order to shorten his term. He is strapped to a chair and made to watch gory war films and all manner of violence on the screen with his eyes taped open and drops regularly administered to his eyes to fend off sleep, while Beethoven is loudly played into his ears. He becomes nauseated at the mere sight of violence and is pronounced cured. Released, McDowell is frightened of even a gnat sting but will not react to violence. He is recognized by the hobo he once attacked and is beaten by the man and his tramp friends; later he is attacked by policemen who turn out to be his one-time henchmen Clarke and Marcus. Thrown out of his home, McDowell wanders into the country and is taken in by Magee who does not recognize him, thinking him only a victim of cruel science. When McDowell unwittingly sings "Singin' In the Rain,"—the song he had sung while raping Magee's wife—the writer recognizes him and goes berserk, locking McDowell in a room and turning on Beethoven's Ninth full blast which sends McDowell into raving hysteria. Taken back to prison, McDowell recovers and is later relased to live with his welcoming parents. But he once more has evil thoughts and it is understood that he will take up his old criminal ways. This film stems from a novel by British author Anthony Burgess who based the story on his own awful experiences, a cathartic work which helped to dissipate his own rage. Burgess's wife, pregnant at the time, was raped, beaten, and robbed during a blackout in WW II London by three AWOL American soldiers. She lost her baby and later died of internal bleeding caused by the attack. Yet Kubrick's rendition of the book, which Burgess later praised, goes far beyond a grim portrayal of violence.It gratuitously paddles around in a cesspool of brutality, dwelling upon every punch, kick, and violation of human dignity. In a perverted way, McDowell becomes a disgusting hero as anti-hero, his street savvy and chic sadistic humor passing for sophistication. There isn't one noble scene in this paean to destruction, both of body and mind. It is an utterly pessimistic view of humanity which condemn's all as brutal and savage. Kubrick, a brilliant director (THE KILLING, PATHS OF GLORY, 2001), gave himself completely to this deranged tale and misused the medium in his zeal to show a vile story too well. This is future shock for its own sake that neither instructs nor entertains. The film is intellectual waste put to film instead of being flushed. Universally condemned by critics, the film originally received an X rating but minor editing brought an R listing. The real rating is BT—bad taste.

p,d&w, Stanley Kubrick (based on the novel by Anthony Burgess); ph, John Alcott; m, Walter Carlos; ed, Bill Butler; prod d, John Barry; art d, Russell Hagg, Peter Shields; cos, Milena Canonero; makeup, Fred Williamson, George Parleton, Barbara Daly; stunts, Roy Scammel.

Drama   **Cas.**   **(PR:O MPAA:R)**

CLONES, THE*½

(1973) 94m Film Makers International c (AKA: CLONES)
Michael Greene, Gregory Sierra, Otis Young, Susan Hunt, Stanley Adams, Barbara Burgdorph, John Barrymore, Jr., Alex Nicol, Bruce Bennett, Angelo Rossito.

Routine thriller starring Greene as a research scientist who discovers that he's been cloned by Adams (as have many other top brains) as part of a plot to control the world. Sierra spends most of the picture chasing the clones around. There are a few decent moments (when Greene meets his clone and the clone doesn't like being a duplicate) but the overall effect is tedium.

p, Paul Hunt; d, Hunt, Lamar Card; w, Steve Fisher; ph, Gary Graver (Eastmancolor).

Science Fiction/Thriller   **(PR:A MPAA:PG)**

CLONUS HORROR, THE**

(1979) 90m Group I c
(AKA: PARTS: THE CLONUS HORROR)
Tim Donnelly *(Richard)*, Dick Sargent *(Dr. Jameson)*, Peter Graves *(Jeff)*, Paulette Breen *(Lena)*, David Hooks *(Richard)*, Keenan Wynn *(Jake)*, James Mantell *(Ricky)*, Zale Kessler *(Nelson)*, Frank Ashmore *(George)*, Lurene Tuttle *(Anna)*, Boyd Hollister *(Senator)*.

At a secret labratory, scientists are engaged in a nefarious scheme to create a perfect race in test tubes. One of their ideal offspring escapes, though, to warn the world. Shot on a tiny budget of less than $350,000, the film boasts a decent cast and a few nice moments.

p, Myrl A. Schreibman, Robert S. Fiveson; d, Fiveson; w, Schreibman, Fiveson; ph, Max Beaufort; m, Hod David Schudson; ed, Robert Gordon; art d, Steve Nelson; cos, Dorinda Rice Wood.

Horror   **(PR:O MPAA:R)**

CLOPORTES***

(1966, Fr., Ital.) 102m
Les Films du Siecle-Produzioni Artistiche Internazionali/International Classics bw
(AKA: LA METAMORPHOSE DES CLOPORTES)
Lino Ventura *(Alphonse)*, Charles Aznavour *(Edmond)*, Irina Demick *(Catherine)*, Maurice Biraud *(Arthur)*, Georges Geret *(Rouquemoute)*, Pierre Brasseur *(Tonton)*, Francoise Rosay *(Gertrude)*, Annie Fratellini *(Leone)*, Georges Blaness *(Omar)*, Francois Mirante *(1st Inspector)*, Francois Dalou *(2nd Inspector)*, Patricia Scott *(Elizabeth)*, Marie-Helene Daste *(Mme. Clancul)*, Daniel Ceccaldi *(Lescure)*, Georges Chamarat *(Clancul)*, Norman Bart, Dorothee Blank, J. P. Caussade, Marcel Charvey, Michel Dacquin, Carlos Da Silva, Michel Duplaix, Michel Garland, Donald O'Brien, Renee Passeur, Andre Thorent, Francois Valorbe.

Ventura is a stolen art dealer recruited into a plan to rob a moneylending establishment by thieves Aznavour, Biraud, and Geret. When the heist fails, the other men speed off in the getaway car, leaving Ventura behind to be captured by the police. Rather than betray his cohorts, he serves a five-year jail term. Upon his release he finds that his former comrades have been stealing his property, so he sets out to avenge himself by murdering the thieves. After the killing of the last one, Ventura is framed for another killing by the girl friend of Geret, with whom he has fallen in love (Demick). Ventura is sent to prison and Demick reaps all the profit. Good, funny caper comedy with a marvelous cast.

p, Bertrand Javal; d,Pierre Granier-Deferre; w, Michel Audiard, Albert Simonin (based on the novel *La Metamorphose des Cloportes* by Alphonse Boudard); ph, Nicolas Hayer (Cinemascope); m, Jimmy Smith; ed, Jean Ravel; set d, Jacques Saulnier; cos, Charles Merangel.

Crime/Comedy   **(PR:C-O MPAA:NR)**

CLOSE CALL FOR BOSTON BLACKIE, A**½

(1946) 68m COL bw
Chester Morris *(Boston Blackie)*, Lynn Merrick *(Gerry Peyton)*, Richard Lane *(Inspector Farraday)*, Frank Sully *(Sgt. Matthews)*, George E. Stone *(The Runt)*, Claire Carleton *(Mamie Kirwin)*, Erik Rolf *(Smiley Slade)*, Charles Lane *(Hack Hagen)*, Robert Scott *(John Peyton)*, Emmett Vogan *(Coroner)*, Russell Hicks *(Harcourt)*, Doris Houck *(Josie)*, Ruth Warren *(Milk Woman)*, Jack Gordon *(Cab Driver)*.

Morris is framed for murder and he and pal Stone evade Lane long enough to expose the evil Merrick as the culprit. Although it is a rather disappointing series, this is an entertaining Boston Blackie vehicle made appealing by Morris's charm. (See BOSTON BLACKIE series, Index.)

p, John Stone; d, Lew Landers; w, Ben Markson, Paul Yawitz (based on a story by Yawitz); ph, Bernet Guffey; ed, Jerome Thoms; md, Mischa Bakaleinikoff; art d, Carl Anderson.

Mystery   **(PR:A MPAA:NR)**

CLOSE CALL FOR ELLERY QUEEN, A**

(1942) 65m COL bw
William Gargan *(Ellery Queen)*, Margaret Lindsay *(Nikki Porter)*, Charley Grapewin *(Inspector Queen)*, Ralph Morgan *(Alan Rogers)*, Kay Linaker *(Margo Rogers)*, Edward Norris *(Stewart Cole)*, James Burke *(Sgt. Velie)*, Addison Richards *(Lester Younger)*, Charles Judels *(Corday)*, Andrew Tombes *(Bates)*, Claire DuBrey *(Housekeeper)*, Michael Cheirel *(Marie Dubois)*, Ben Weldon *(Fisherman)*, Milton Parsons *(Butler)*.

When an aging businessman begins to search for his two long-lost daughters, two old partners connected to the man's shady past climb out of the woodwork and hire a girl to act as one of the missing heirs. Gargan stumbles onto the scene and with the help of Lindsay exposes the impostor and discovers the truth about the missing girls. Replacing

Ralph Bellamy as one of the most popular fictional detectives of all time, Gargan does a nice job in bringing the amateur sleuth's intelligence and wit to a mediocre script. (See ELLERY QUEEN series, Index)

p, Larry Darmour; d, James Hogan; w, Eric Taylor (based on a story by Ellery Queen); ph, James S. Brown, Jr.; ed, Dwight Caldwell.

Mystery   **(PR:A   MPAA:NR)**

CLOSE ENCOUNTERS OF THE THIRD KIND** (1977) 135m COL c
Richard Dreyfuss (Roy Neary), Francois Truffaut (Claude Lacombe), Teri Garr (Ronnie Neary), Melinda Dillon (Jillian Guiler), Cary Guffey (Barry Guiler), Bob Balaban (Interpreter Laughlin), J. Patrick McNamara (Project Leader), Warren Kemmerling (Wild Bill), Roberts Blossom (Farmer), Philip Dodds (Jean Claude), Shawn Bishop, Adrienne Campbell, Justin Dreyfuss (Neary Children), Lance Hendricksen (Robert), Merrill Connally (Team Leader), George Dicenzo (Maj. Benchley), Carl Weathers (M.P.), Roger Ernest (Highway Patrolman), Josef Sommer (Larry Butler), Gene Dynarski (Ike), Gene Rader (Hawker), Phil Dodds (ARP Musician), F. J. O'Neil (ARP Project Member).

A feast for the eyes, this opulent special effects story begins in rural Indiana during a blackout. Lineman Dreyfuss, investigating the power shortage, encounters a UFO when his truck comes to a halt and the spacecraft hovers about it, bathing it in blinding light. Signposts and postal boxes jiggle and wave, his car instruments go haywire, and he is burned beet red when looking up into the light which vanishes in seconds. Speeding into the hills, Dreyfuss meets two others, Dillon and her son Guffey, who have undergone similar "close encounters." They sit atop a large hill and their vigilance is rewarded when a squadron of small UFOs suddenly appears, darting about and sailing over them. Dreyfuss returns home obsessed with what he has seen. He cannot work, sleeps to excess, and disrupts his married life with Garr. Dillon's farmhouse is later surrounded by UFOs searching for her child Guffey, who playfully invites the aliens inside. Dillon locks up the house but alien power intrudes through electrical outlets, appliances, vents. Her son is finally dragged by unseen hands into a UFO and whisked away. Dreyfusss, meanwhile, has been sculpting with his childrens' clay, attempting to build a strange-looking mountain. Others having seen the UFOs frantically consume their time by sketching the same mountain. Scientists from around the world gather under the leadership of Truffaut and begin to uncover missing ships and planes in unlikely spots. In the middle of a desert they find a huge cargo vessel and later a squadron of U.S. fighter planes which disappeared in the Bermuda Triangle decades earlier. They also begin to piece together a musical code from tribesmen all over the world who have heard certain notes played by the visiting aliens. Dreyfuss, Dillon, and others who have encountered the aliens inexplicably make their way to Devil's Tower in Wyoming: this is the rendezvous arranged between the aliens and world scientists. Although quarantined—the area has been put off limits under the guise of protecting residents from poisonous gases—Dreyfuss, Dillon, and others manage to get into the district. They are captured and ordered home but they escape from a helicopter and run into the mountain area, climbing to the other side of Devil's Tower by nightfall to witness a secretly prepared landing strip where scientific crews await the aliens' visit. First a group of smaller UFOs appear, then an enormous spaceship. It is so gigantic that it dwarfs the Devil's Tower, hovering above the landing strip. The scientists communicate with the mother ship through musical codes they have learned and the ship answers. Then a cargo door opens and hundreds of people missing for decades are released, along with Dillon's small son. Oddly, the long missing people have not aged a day. A slender alien, shaped like a human embryo, appears and communicates with Truffaut via sign language, gesturing peace and love. Dreyfuss has by this time joined the team chosen to go with the aliens on a space expedition. The humans are led aboard the huge spacecraft by childlike aliens and the craft roars upward into darkness and unknown adventure. (In the special edition of this film, outtakes were put back into the film to show Dreyfuss entering the craft and beholding a blinding inner universe of marvelous lights and machines, more of a fantastic light show than an explanation of how and why the aliens visited tired old Earth.) Of all the UFO films ever made this is the most edifying, a wonder of superb special effects, from the cleverly designed spaceships to the manipulation of elements, weird cloud formations, winds, lightning, all heralding the approach of the UFOs. What sets this film apart in its popular genre is that the aliens are loving and benificent, not the raging creatures lusting for human lives as found in THE THING or WAR OF THE WORLDS. CLOSE ENCOUNTERS OF THE THIRD KIND is space turned good and godlike, ending on a wonderful optimistic note instead of fatalistic gloom and doom. Writer-director Spielberg had long envisioned this film, even before making JAWS, and he originally thought to have the lead be a middle-aged man. He wanted Jack Nicholson for the part, but Dreyfuss, who had appeared in JAWS, pleaded for the role and got it, proving himself to be a major talent. Spielberg drew his material from Dr. J. Allen Hynek's book, The UFO Experience, published in 1972, and Hynek himself served as a technical advisor and appears in the movie during the final landing strip encounter (smoking a pipe and looking on knowingly). French director Truffaut plays a role based on French UFO expert Jacques Vallee, who had worked with Hynek. The appeal of this film was enormous and still is. Spielberg took a simplistic attitude toward UFOs and approached the subject as would a naive and accepting child, as did the millions of viewers who look to the skies in sanguine awe and wonder. His magnificent vision, expanded upon in a more prosaic manner in E.T. (1982), resulted in staggering box office returns. The original version grossed more than $77 million and another $6 million was added in 1980 when Spielberg inserted more footage and used film cut out of the original production, releasing the expanded version under the title CLOSE ENCOUNTERS OF THE THIRD KIND—THE SPECIAL EDITION (sort of a THAT'S ENTERTAINMENT of sci-fi films).

p, Julia and Michael Phillips; d&w, Steven Spielberg; ph, Vilmos Zsigmond, with additional sequences by John A. Alonzo, William A. Fraker, Laszlo Kovacs, Douglas Slocombe, Dave Stewart, Robert Hall, Don Jarel, Dennis Muren, Richard Yuricich (Metrocolor); m, John Williams; ed, Michael Kahn; prod d, Joe Alves; art d, Dan

Lomino; set d, Phil Abramson; cos, Jim Linn; spec eff, Roy Arbogast, Gregory Jein, Douglas Trumbull, Matthew and Richard Yuricich.

Science Fiction   **Cas.**   **(PR:A   MPAA:PG)**

CLOSE HARMONY½**   (1929) 66m PAR bw
Charles "Buddy" Rogers (Al West), Nancy Carroll (Marjorie), Harry Green (Max Mindel), Jack Oakie (Ben Barney), Skeets Gallagher (Johnny Bray), Ricca Allen (Mrs. Proesser), Baby Mack (Sybil), Matty Roubert, Wade Boteler, Oscar Smith, Greta Granstedt, Gus Partos, Jesse Stafford and His Orchestra.

With the constant prodding of his girl friend, Carroll, timid warehouse clerk Rogers finally shows the show business world what he can do when he whips his rag-tag band into shape by showing each one of them how much spunk they should be putting into the playing of their instruments. Designed as a vehicle to enrich the sagging post-WINGS career of Rogers, he does a little of everything to prove how talented he is. Too bad the run-of-the-mill material does not match the effervescent display of Rogers. Songs: "She's So I Dunno," "I Want To Go Places and Do Things," "I'm All A-Twitter, I'm All A-Twirl" (Richard A. Whiting, Leo Robin), "Twelfth Street Rag" (Euday L. Bowman, Spencer Williams).

d, John Cromwell, Edward Sutherland; w, Percy Heath, J. V. A. Weaver (based on a story by Elsie Janis and Gene Markey); ph, J. Roy Hunt; ed, Tay Malarkey.

Musical   **(PR:A   MPAA:NR)**

CLOSE TO MY HEART½**   (1951) 90m WB bw
Ray Milland (Brad Sheridan), Gene Tierney (Midge Sheridan), Fay Bainter (Mrs. Morrow), Howard St. John (E. O. Frost), Mary Beth Hughes (Arlene), Ann Morrison (Mrs. Barker), James Seay (Evarts Heilner), Baby John Winslow (Himself), Eddie Marr (Taxi Driver Dunne), Nan Boardman (Woman Patient), Elizabeth Flournoy (Receptionist), John Alvin (Haggard Man), Louis Jean Heydt (Mr. Duncan), Ralph Byrd (Charlie), Kathleen Stendal (Woman Doctor), Lois Hall, Rodney Bell (Young Parents), George LaMond (Hotel Clerk), Fred Graham (Guard), Lee Prather (Farmer).

Unable to have children of their own, Milland and Tierney explore the possibilities of adopting one, but become frustrated and impatient when they learn that they may have to wait two years before they can adopt. When newspaperman Milland learns of a foundling being held at police headquarters, he informs Tierney about the situation and the two seek to adopt the child. The legal agency appears to be fairly optimistic about the situation and Tierney's love for the lost child grows and grows. Milland, however, begins an obsessive search to learn who the baby's parents were, a search that convinces the adoption agency that Milland's unstable behavior is characteristic of an unfit parent. Milland makes an impassioned plea to the agency, even after learning the the baby's father was a murderer, and the couple is granted custody of the child. Well-meaning melodrama focusing on the importance of a loving environment in the upbringing of a child. Although the premise borrows heavily from PENNY SERE-NADE, Tierney and Milland are touching as the couple who know that their tenderness will help soften the baby's cruel past.

p, William Jacobs; d, William Keighley; w, James R. Webb (based on the story "A Baby for Midge" by Webb); ph, Robert Burks; m, Max Steiner; ed, Clarence Kolster; art d, Leo K. Kuter.

Drama   **(PR:A   MPAA:NR)**

CLOSE-UP* *   (1948) 72m Marathon/EL bw
Alan Baxter (Phil Sparr), Virginia Gilmore (Peggy), Richard Kollmar (Beaumont), Loring Smith (Avery), Phil Huston (Gibbons), Russell Collins (Beck), Wendell Phillips (Harold), Joey Faye (Roger), Marcia Walter (Rita), Michael Wyler (Fredericks), Sid Melton (Cabby), Jimmy Sheridan (Jimmy), Maurice Manson (Inspector Lonigan), Lauren Gilbert (Miller), Erin O'Kelly (Receptionist).

Ex-Nazi Kollmar vows to stop at nothing to retrieve some film newsreel cameraman Baxter has shot that will prove that the German is alive and well and living in New York City. Kollmar captures Baxter and the negative print, but a positive delivered to the police spurs a city-wide manhunt and the Nazi is killed in a three-way shoot-out between Baxter, Kollmar, and a former henchman of the Nazi who has been double-crossed. Famous during its time for being one of a small group of features shot entirely in New York, this espionage/action drama could have been shot in the most glamorous spots around the world but its tiresome plotting, mundane acting, and unsuspenseful action sequences would have still made it a pedestrian effort.

p, Frank Satenstein; d, Jack Donohue; w, John Bright, Max Wilk, Donahue (based on a story by James Poe); ph, William Miller; m, Jerome Moross; ed, Robert Klager.

Spy Drama   **(PR:A   MPAA:NR)**

CLOSELY WATCHED TRAINS*½**   (1967, Czech.) 89m Sigma III bw
Vaclav Neckar (Trainee Milos), Jitka Bendova (Conductor Masa), Josef Somr (Train Dispatcher Hubicka), Vladimir Valenta (Station Master), Vlastimil Brodsky (Counselor Zednick), Jiri Menzel (Doctor).

The first feature film by Czech filmmaker Jiri Menzel (he had previously directed an episode called "The Death of Mr. Baltazar" in an anthology film called PEARLS AT THE BOTTOM [1965]) stars Neckar as a tragi-comic hero during the German occupation of Czechoslovakia. During the course of the film Neckar, a railroad worker turned underground freedom fighter, experiences a variety of incidents including sexual initiation, suicide, and heroism. In the end, realizing the absurdity of his existence, Neckar sacrifices his life to blow up an enemy train. Charming and powerful, CLOSELY WATCHED TRAINS won the Academy Award as Best Foreign Film. (Czechoslovakian; English subtitles)

p, Zdenek Oves; d, Jiri Menzel; w, Menzel, Bohumil Hrabal; ph, Jaromir Sofr; m, Jiri Sust; ed, Jirina Lukesova; art d, Oldrich Bosak; set d, Jiri Cvrcek; cos, Ruzena Bulickova; subtitles, M. A. Gebert.

Comedy/Drama   **Cas.**   **(PR:A   MPAA:NR)**

CLOTHES AND THE WOMAN**

(1937, Brit.) 70m JH Productions/ABPC bw
Rod La Rocque (Eric Thrale), Tucker McGuire (Joan Moore), Constance Collier (Eugenia), George E. Stone (Count Bernhardt), Dorothy Dare (Carol Dixon), Alastair Sim (Francois), Mona Goya (Cecilie), Mary Cole (Marie Thrale), Jim Gerald (Enrico Castigliani), Renee Gadd (Schoolmistress).

McGuire is a schoolgirl who runs away and pretends to be svelte society woman in order to capture the attentions of R.A.F. pilot La Rocque. Lightweight romance is pleasant and nothing more.

p, Julius Hagen; d, Albert de Courville; w, F. McGrew Willis (based on a story by Franz Schulz).

Drama (PR:A MPAA:NR)

CLOUD DANCER**

(1980) 108m Melvin Simon/Blossom c
David Carradine (Bradley Randolph), Jennifer O'Neill (Helen St. Clair), Joseph Bottoms (Tom Loomis), Colleen Camp (Cindy), Albert Salmi (Ozzie Randolph), Salome Jens (Jean Randolph), Arnette Jens Zerbe (Edith Randolph), Norman Alden (Dr. Putnam), Nina Van Pallandt (Caroline Sheldon).

Throwback to the pilot-as-romantic-hero films of the 1930s and 1940s featuring Carradine as a brooding flyboy whose daring airborne antics in a flying circus thrill the crowd but worry his friends and family. Photograher O'Neill, an old flame of Carradine's, visits the flying circus but is unable to tell Carradine about her child, one he had unknowingly fathered. Only feeling comfortable in the sky, Carradine's humanity finally becomes apparent when he straightens out drug-dealing flier Bottoms and accepts the love of O'Neill and their baby. Although Carradine's quiet anti-heroics are intriguing, the filmmakers' primary interest seems to lie in the never-ending photography of the aerial sequences that are indeed beautiful to watch but fail to advance the plot or embellish the emotional tension with metaphorical meaning. Owes a nod to THE TARNISHED ANGELS.

p&d, Barry Brown; w, William Goodhart (based on a story by Brown, Goodhart, Daniel Tamkus); ph, (MGM Color), Travers Hill; m, Fred Karlin; ed, Marshall Borden.

Drama Cas. (PR:A MPAA:PG)

CLOUDBURST**½

(1952, Brit.) 83m UA bw
Robert Preston (John), Elizabeth Sellars (Carol), Colin Tapley (Inspector Davis), Sheila Burrell (Lorna), Harold Lang (Mickie), Mary Germaine (Peggy), Thomas Heathcote (Jackie), George Woodbridge (Sgt. Ritchie), Lyn Evans (Chuck Peters), Edith Sharpe (Mrs. Reece), James Mills (Thompson), Daphne Anderson (Kate), Edward Lexy (Cardew), Noel Howlett (Supervisor), Robert Brown (Carter), Charles Saynor (Constable), Gerald Case (Doctor), Fredric Steger (Porter), Stanley Baker (Milkman), Martin Boddey (Desk Sergeant).

Preston and Sellars,both working for British intelligence during WW II, marry and plan for a happy life in London. Their plans, however, are shattered when a hit-and-run car kills Sellars. His world shattered, Preston's mind becomes twisted and he sets out to get back at every occupant of the car that destroyed his beloved. Utilizing techniques he perfected in cryptography and commando units in the army, Preston methodically begins to murder the guilty people. Scotland Yard Inspector Tapley comes on the case and traps Preston by breaking the code of the cryptographic clues he has left at the killing scenes. Well-written, disturbing story that analyzes the power to kill inherent in everyone. Preston's normal, likable demeanor nicely contrasts with the obsessive behavior of his character and Tapley is wonderfully smart as the keen detective.

p, Anthony Hinds, Alexander Paal; d, Francis Searle; w, Searle, Leo Marks (based on the play by Marks); ph, Jimmy Harvey; m, Frank Spencer; ed, John Ferris.

Mystery (PR:A MPAA:NR)

CLOUDED CRYSTAL, THE**

(1948, Brit.) 57m Grossman-Cullimore-Arbeid/But bw
Patrick Waddington (Jack), Lind Joyce (Cathy Butler), Dorothy Bramhall (Paula), Frank Muir (Frank Butler), Dino Galvani (Manzetti), Ethel Coleridge (Mme. Zamba).

Unfunny comedy about what happens to a couple when a fortune teller predicts the husband's death within a month. Not terribly interesting.

p, Ben Arbeid, A. Grossman; d&w, Alan J. Cullimore.

Comedy (PR:A MPAA:NR)

CLOUDED YELLOW, THE***

(1950, Brit.) 95m Carillon/GFD bw
Jean Simmons (Sophie Malraux), Trevor Howard (David Somers), Sonia Dresdel (Jess Fenton), Barry Jones (Nicholas Fenton), Maxwell Reed (Nick), Kenneth More (Willy), Andre Morell (Chubb), Gerald Heinz (Karl), Lily Kann (Minna), Geoffrey Keen (Police Inspector), Michael Brennan (Superintendent), Sandra Dorne (Kyra), Gabrielle Blunt (Addie), Eric Pohlmann, Richard Wattis, Sam Kydd.

When shy and somewhat unstable Simmons is accused of murdering the handyman who worked for her guardians (Jones and Dresdel), Howard, having been fired from his job in the British Secret Service, comes to her aid. Convinced that Simmons is innocent, he helps her escape from jail and the two flee to Liverpool where they plan to stow away on a ship bound for Mexico. Aware of the plans, the police follow them, hoping to nab the real killer, for they, too, are convinced of Simmons's innocence. When Simmons's father-like guardian Jones approaches them in Liverpool, Howard and the girl become aware of his homicidal psychosis and realize that he and his equally demented wife killed the worker and convinced poor Simmons that she was the guilty one. The police arrive in the nick of time and capture Jones before he can do any more harm. Suspenseful, exciting drama rich with character and given an imposing, dark, yet hauntingly romantic look by master cinematographer Geoffrey Unsworth. An interestingly cast romantic couple, Simmons and Howard weave a passionate but restrained spell as the young couple whose fate is in question.

p, Betty E. Box; d, Ralph Thomas; w, Eric Ambler (from a story by Janet Green); ph, Geoffrey Unsworth; ed, Gordon Hales.

Drama (PR:A MPAA:NR)

CLOUDS OVER EUROPE***

(1939, Brit.) 93m Harefield-London/COL bw (GB: Q PLANES)
Laurence Olivier (Tony McVane), Valerie Hobson (Kay Hammond), Ralph Richardson (Charles Hammond), George Curzon (Jenkins), George Merritt (Barrett), Gus McNaughton (Blenkinsop), David Tree (Mackenzie), Sandra Storme (Daphne), Hay Petrie (Stage Doorman), Frank Fox (Karl), Gordon McLeod (Baron), John Longden (John Peters), Reginald Purdell (Pilot), George Butler (Air Marshall Gosport), John Laurie (Editor), Pat Aherne (Officer), Ronald Adam, Derek Farr.

Made before the U.S. got into the war, there's no doubt who the villains are in this story of a German ship anchored in mid-ocean to intercept Allied flights. The ship is outfitted with a wall full of sci-fi equipment including a special radio beam that can knock out an airplane's motors so it will come down at sea to be taken away by the nefarious Nazis. Hobson is a newspaperwoman on to this scheme but her brother (Richardson), a dotty Scotland Yard man, gets most of the good lines. Olivier is top-featured but has little to do except look like a matinee idol. The title belies the picture's content as this is almost Bond-like in its spoofery. Matter of fact, it is just this side of satire and angered some of the early audiences before they realized that their legs were not being pulled, they were being yanked!

p, Irving Asher, Alexander Korda; d, Tim Whelan; w, Ian Dalrymple (based on a story by Jack Whittingham, Brock Williams, Arthur Wimperis); ph, Harry Stradling, Sr.; ed, Hugh Stewart; md, Muir Mathieson; art d, Frederick Pusey.

Spy Comedy (PR:A MPAA:NR)

CLOUDS OVER ISRAEL**½

(1966, Israel) 85m Israel Co-Production Films-Harold Cornsweet Productions-Du-Or Films/Hemisphere Pictures bw (AKA: SINAIA)
Yiftah Spector (Dan), Ehud Banai (Bedouin Boy), Dina Doronne (Bedouin Woman), Hadara Azulai (Sinaia), Shaika Levi (Enemy Pilot), Itzhak Benyamini (Enemy Scout), Itzhak Barzilai (Enemy Soldier), Ygal Alon (Enemy Jeep Soldier), Shimon Israeli (Uri), Sinaia Hamdan.

Spector is an Israeli jet pilot forced to bail out over the Sinai. Upon landing he discovers that the crash of his plane wiped out an entire Bedouin encampment, leaving only a woman, her five-year-old son, and her infant daughter. The woman is badly burned and the pilot cares for her and her children. Later, another Israeli officer (Israeli) turns up and wants to kill the Bedouins. Spector stops him and the group begins to work together as Israeli changes from an embittered soldier to a compassionate man. They capture a small Egyptian reconnaissance plane and work to repair it. When it is ready to take off, Israeli stays behind and watches as the plane lifts off,then crashes. The infant girl is the only survivor, and Israeli picks her up and carries her into the desert as the film ends. Very nice war story with a human touch. The development of Israeli's character is logical and inevitable and it really pulls on the heartstrings. (In Hebrew and Arabic; English subtitles)

p, Mati Raz, Harold Cornsweet; d, Ivan Lengyel; w, Moshe Hadar; ph, Marko Yakovlevich; m, Naom Sheriff; ed, Dani Schick.

War Drama (PR:C-O MPAA:NR)

CLOWN, THE***

(1953) 91m MGM bw
Red Skelton (Dodo Delwyn), Tim Considine (Dink Delwyn), Jane Greer (Paula Henderson), Loring Smith (Goldie), Philip Ober (Ralph Z. Henderson), Lou Lubin (Little Julie), Fay Roope (Dr. Strauss), Walter Reed (Joe Hoagley), Edward Marr (Television Director), Jonathan Cott (Floor Director), Don Beddoe (Gallagher), Steve Forrest (Young Man), Ned Glass (Danny Dayler), Steve Carruthers (Maitre D'Hotel), Billy Barty (Midget), Lucille Knoch (Girl), David Saber (Silvio), Sandra Gould (Bunny), Gil Perkins (Dundee), Danny Richards, Jr. (Herman), Mickey Little (Lefty), Charles Calvert (Jackson), Karen Steele (Blonde), Jack Heasley, Bob Heasley (Twins), Helene Millard (Miss Batson), Forrest Lewis (Pawnbroker), Charles Buchinsky [Charles Bronson] (Eddie), Robert Ford (Al Zerney), John McKee (Counterman), Jan Wayne, Vici Raaf (Women), Jesse Kirkpatrick (Sergeant), Martha Wentworth (Neighbor), Inge Jolles (Secretary), Harry Staton (Hogarth), Linda Bennett (Judy), Wilson Wood (Wardrobe Man), Frank Nelson (Charlie), Thomas Dillon (Clancy), Paul Raymond (Young Man), James Horan, Al Freeman (Men), Tom Urray (Vendor), Mary Foran (Heavy Girl), Sharon Saunders (Girl), David Blair (TV Pageboy), Brick Sullivan (Stagehand), Cy Stevens (Makeup Man), G. Pat Collins (Mr. Christenson), Shirley Mitchell (Mrs. Blotto), Robert R. Stephenson (Counterman), Jimmie Thompson, Allen O'Locklin, Tony Merill (Ad-Libbers), Al Hill, Jerry Schumacher, Barry Regan (Dice Players), Lennie Bremen (George), Lee Phelps (Sergeant), Joe Evans, Walter Ridge, George Boyce, Donald Kerr, Mickey Golden (Attendants), Roger Moore (Man with Hogarth), Jules Brock, Eve Martell, Neva Martell (Dancers).

Former vaudeville great Skelton, now a has-been alcoholic, loses job after job because of drinking and gambling but remains somewhat stable through the love of his ever-caring son, Considine. Miraculously offered his own television show, Skelton makes Considine proud by doing the first show sober and turning in a brilliant performance. Knowing that the show will again make his father a star, Considine rushes to congratulate his dad, but is horribly saddened when he learns Skelton has died moments after the show's close. Show-business remake of THE CHAMP nicely displays Skelton's mastery of comedy and pathos, but cannot help but fall victim to the script's almost laughable melodramatics. Look for the future superhero James Bond, Roger Moore, in one of his early bit parts.

p, William H. Wright; d, Robert Z. Leonard; w, Martin Rackin (based on the 1931 movie THE CHAMP written by Leonard Praskins, Frances Marion); ph, Paul Vogel; m, David Rose; ed, Gene Ruggiero; art d, Cedric Gibbons, Wade B. Rubottom.

Drama Cas. (PR:A MPAA:NR)

CLOWN AND THE KID, THE*

(1961) 65m Harvard Film/UA bw

John Lupton (*Peter Stanton*), Mike McGreevey (*Shawn*), Don Keefer (*Moko*), Mary Webster (*Robin*), Mary Adams (*Mother Superior*), Peggy Stewart (*Sister Grace*), Barry Kelley (*Detective Barker*), Ken Mayer (*Trooper*), Charles G. Martin (*Daly*), Victor French (*1st Patrolman*), James Parnell (*2nd Patrolman*), Edith Evanson.

Dying clown Keefer is taking son McGreevey to a convent school in Texas when he dies. The boy takes up with an escaped convict, Stanton, who eludes the police by wearing the makeup of the boy's late father. McGreevey learns Stanton's identity and rides his horse out into a raging tornado. The police show up to arrest Stanton, but he escapes and goes out to look for the boy. He finds him unconscious and brings him back, turning himself in to the cops. Trashy sentiment with a no-name cast. Pass it by.

p, Robert E. Kent; d, Edward L. Cahn; w, Herbert Abbott Spiro, Jerry Sackheim; ph, Gilbert Warrenton; ed, Irving Berlin; set d, Don Webb; cos, Bill Edwards, Barbara Maxwell; spec eff, Barney Wolff.

Drama   (PR:A   MPAA:NR)

CLOWN AND THE KIDS,THE*½

(1968, U.S./Bulgaria) 75m
Brown-Fox Film Productions-Bulgarian State Films/Childhood Productions c
(AKA: SVIRACHUT)

Emmett Kelly (*The Piper*), Burt Stratford (*Mark, His Son*), Katie Dunn (*Freny, His Daughter*), Mikhail Mikhailov (*Mr. Scrag*), Leo Conforti (*Mayor*), Bogomil Simeonov (*Scrag's Lieutenant*), Oleg Kovachev (*Billy*), Naicho Petrov.

Strange U.S.-Bulgarian coproduction has the legendary circus clown Kelly the leader of a family circus traveling through the Balkans. They arrive in the town of Scragsville, ruled over by the evil miller Mikhailov, who forbids the children to have fun. Kelly teaches the children to feign crying so the miller will allow them to go to the circus. Kelly teaches the children a number of important lessons as well as a song, but when it comes time to move on, Mikhailov won't permit it. Kelly pulls out his flute and summons the children, who destroy Mikhailov and live happily ever after. Kelly is always worth watching, and some of the camera work is superb, but it's really just another Pied Piper film that will bore adults. Songs: "Good Friends, Good-Bye," "Happiness Will Be Your Reward," "I Hate Kids," "I Mean He's Mean," "I Used To Be A Griper," "I've Got A Brother (I've Got A Sister)," "Love and Be Loved," "My House Is Empty," "The Piper's Song," "What Is a Circus?" (Tony Velona).

p, Silas Fox; d&w, Mende Brown (based on a story by Wilhelm Hauff); ph, Dimo Kolarov (Eastmancolor).

Children/Musical   (PR:AA   MPAA:NR)

CLOWN MURDERS, THE**

(1976, Can.) 94m Magnum/Astral c

Stephen Young (*Charlie*), Susan Keller (*Alison*), Lawrence Dane (*Philip*), John Candy (*Ollie*), Gary Reineke (*Rosie*), John Bayliss (*Peter*), Al Waxman (*Police Officer*), Michael Magee (*Compton*), Cec Linder (*The Promoter*).

A group of well-educated professional men decide to live dangerously and kidnap an ex-girlfriend of one of them who is now married to a wealthy man. The "fun" crime turns disturbingly tragic when two of them are killed as tension mounts at their hideout. Effective, well-acted drama that suffers from a television director's sense of pacing and visualization. Candy, later to become famous on television's "Second City Television" is good in a minor role, but the true scene stealer is Reineke, whose brooding, drunken, violent behavior gives the film its unsettling quality.

p, Christopher Dalton; d&w, Martyn Burke.

Crime   (PR:C   MPAA:NR)

CLOWN MUST LAUGH, A*½

(1936, Brit.) 92m Trafalgar/UA bw/c
(GB: PAGLIACCI)

Richard Tauber (*Canio Tonini*), Steffi Duna (*Nedda Tonini*), Diana Napier (*Trina*), Arthur Margetson (*Tonio*), Esmond Knight (*Silvio*), Jerry Verno (*Beppo*), Gordon James (*Leone*), Harry Milton (*Officer*).

Tauber is a famous clown who kills his wife and her soldier lover in a fit of jealousy. The film did quite well in England when it came out thanks to the novelty of its color sequences at the beginning and end. Mostly a curiosity today.

p, Max Schach; d, Karl Grune; w, Monckton Hoffe, John Drinkwater, Roger Burford, Ernest Betts (based on the opera "I Pagliacci" by Ruggiero Leoncavallo); ph, Otto Kanturek (Chemicolour, 2 sequences); md, Hans Eisler; m/l, Drinkwater.

Musical   (PR:A   MPAA:NR)

CLUB, THE**½

(1980, Aus.) 99m South Australian—New South Wales/Roadshow c

Jack Thompson (*Laurie*), Graham Kennedy (*Ted*), Frank Wilson (*Jock*), Harold Hopkins (*Danny*), John Howard (*Geoff*), Alan Cassell (*Gerry*), Maggie Doyle (*Susy*).

Thompson, a former soccer star and now a fading coach, becomes increasingly angry as he sees big business enter into the management and training of the club. Made soon after his powerful BREAKER MORANT, its director Beresford adapted another work by Australian playwright David Williamson, the first being the irritating DON'S PARTY. A talented director, Beresford again falls victim to his faithfulness to Williamson's usual conglomeration of screaming, complaining, and annoying people. The ins and outs of contemporary sports management is excellent subject matter, as displayed by the superior NORTH DALLAS FORTY, but Beresford's film loses its intensity and insight to a group of characters whose sympathetic plight is overshadowed by their exasperating behavior.

p, Matt Carroll; d, Bruce Beresford; w, David Williamson (based on his play); ph, Don McAlpine (Panavision); m, Mike Brady; ed, William Anderson; art d, David Copping.

Drama   (PR:C   MPAA:M)

CLUB HAVANA*

(1946) 62m PRC bw

Tom Neal (*Bill Porter*), Margaret Lindsay (*Rosalind*), Don Douglas (*Johnny Norton*), Isabelita (*Isabelita*), Dorothy Morris (*Lucy*), Ernest Truex (*Willy Kingston*), Renie Riano

(*Mrs. Cavendish*), Gertrude Michael (*Hetty*), Eric Sinclair (*Jimmy*), Paul Cavanagh (*Rogers*), Marc Lawrence (*Joe Reed*), Pedro De Cordoba (*Charles*), Sonia Sorel (*Myrtle*), Carlos Molina Orchestra; Iris and Pierre (*Themselves*).

When a young nightclub singer attempts suicide because of her lover's departure, doctor Neal heals the girl's wounds and reunites her with her estranged boy friend. Routine nightclub-based melodrama featuring Neal as a god-like figure who teaches night-life lovers the benefits of kindness and understanding. Sappy, but very stylized, thanks to director Ulmer. Ulmer improvised this ridiculously cheap version of GRAND HOTEL from a one-page outline and shot it on a single set. Songs include "Tico Tico" and "Besame Mucho."

p, Leon Fromkess; d, Edgar G. Ulmer; w, Raymond L. Schrock (based on a story by Fred Jackson); ph, Benjamin H. Kline; m, Howard Jackson; ed, Carl Pierson.

Musical/drama   (PR:A   MPAA:NR)

CLUE OF THE MISSING APE, THE**

(1953, Brit.) 58m GAU/CD bw
(GB: GIBRALTAR ADVENTURE)

Nati Banda (*Pilar Ellis*), Roy Savage (*Jimmy Sutton*), George Cole (*Gobo*), Patrick Boxill (*Mr. Palmer*), William Patrick (*Lt.-Cmdr. Collier*), Marcus Simpson (*Petty Officer Ellis*), Bill Shine (*Henchman in Opening Sequence*), John Ocello, Peter Copley, Evelyn Roberts, Harold Siddons, John Welsh, Julian Somers, Wilfrid Walter, Luis Ellul, Carla Challoner.

As a reward for rescuing a pilot from a burning plane, sea cadet Savage is sent to Gibraltar. There he meets Banda, the daughter of an officer stationed on "The Rock." They discover a plot by foreign saboteurs to destroy the ape population, whose presence has long been a symbol of British dominion. The saboteurs also plan to destroy part of the fleet moored there by using frogmen to attach explosives to the hulls of the ships. The children report their discovery but are not believed. Finally, they manage to steal the plans from the saboteurs and show them to the authorities. The bombs are found, the bad guys caught, and the apes saved. Fair adventure film for children.

p, Frank Wells; d&w, James Hill (based on a story Frank Wells, Donald Carter, Cmdr. Hackforth-Jones); ph, James Allen; m Jack Beaver; ed, Arthur Stevens; art d, Jack Stephens.

Children   (PR:AA   MPAA:NR)

CLUE OF THE NEW PIN, THE **

(1929, Brit.) 81m BL/PDC bw

Benita Hume (*Ursula Ardfern*), Kim Peacock (*Tab Holland*), Donald Calthrop (*Yeh Ling*(, John Gielgud (*Rex Trasmere*), H. Saxon-Snell (*Walters*), Johnny Butt (*Wellington Briggs*), Colin Kenney (*Inspector Carver*), Fred Rains, Caleb Porter, The Hippodrome Chorus.

When a wealthy recluse is found dead in a sealed room with the key next to him, police are baffled. His will leaves everything to his ward, Hume, so suspicion falls on her. A reporter investigating the case is almost set afire, and the nephew who found the body is revealed as the killer. Britain's first talkie is, inevitably, an Edgar Wallace thriller, and the sound was on the soon-to-be-abandoned disc, rather than on the film. Gielgud's second film appearance.

p, S. W. Smith; d, Arthur Maude; w, Kathleen Hayden (based on a novel by Edgar Wallace); ph, Horace Wheddon.

Mystery   (PR:A   MPAA:NR)

CLUE OF THE NEW PIN, THE**½

(1961, Brit.) 58m Merton Park/AA bw

Paul Daneman (*Rex Lander*), Bernard Archard (*Supt. Carver*), James Villiers (*Tab Holland*), Catherine Woodville (*Jane Ardfern*), Clive Morton (*Ramsey Brown*), Wolfe Morris (*Yeh Ling*), David Horne (*John Trasmere*), Leslie Sands (*Sgt. Harris*), Ruth Kettlewell (*Mrs. Rushby*).

Villiers is a television interviewer who gets involved in a complicated string of killings, saving Woodville from a similar fate. Slightly better than the bulk of the 47 Edgar Wallace second features producer Greenwood put out between 1960-63.

p, Jack Greenwood; d, Allan Davis; w, Philo Mackie (based on a novel by Edgar Wallace).

Crime   (PR:A-C   MPAA:NR)

CLUE OF THE SILVER KEY, THE**½

(1961, Brit.) 59m Merton Park/AA bw

Bernard Lee (*Supt. Meredith*), Lyndon Brook (*Gerry Dornford*), Finlay Currie (*Harvey Lane*), Jennifer Daniel (*Mary Lane*), Patrick Cargill (*Binny*), Derrick Sherwin (*Quigley*), Anthony Sharp (*Mike Hennessey*), Stanley Morgan (*Sgt. Anson*), Sam Kydd (*Tickler*).

Scotland Yard man Lee uncovers the killer of a stingy moneylender, thanks to the title evidence. Lee gives a very good peformance and a few decent names populate the supporting cast.

p, Jack Greenwood; d, Gerard Glaister; w, Philip Mackie (based on a novel by Edgar Wallace).

Crime   (PR:A-C   MPAA:NR)

CLUE OF THE TWISTED CANDLE**

(1968, Brit.) 61m Merton Park/Lester Schoenfeld Films bw

Bernard Lee (*Supt. Meredith*), David Knight (*John Lexman, Dr. Griswold*), Francis DeWolff (*Ramon Karadis*), Colette Wilde (*Grace Neilson*), Christine Shaw (*Linda Holland*), Stanley Morgan (*Sgt. Anson*), A. J. Brown (*Com. of Police*), Richard Caldicott (*Pike Fisher*), Edmond Bennett (*Manservant*), Simon Lack (*Jock*), Gladys Henson (*Landlady*), Roy Purcell (*Brennan*), Alfred Maron (*Finch*), Richard Vernon (*Viney*), Kenneth Fortescue (*Secretary, C.I.D.*), Hazel Hughes (*Miss Cunningham*), Harry Locke (*Amis*).

When the rivals of financial wizard Knight are murdered one by one, Lee investigates the paranoid, reclusive businessman and discovers how the fellow could have left his locked room to perpetrate the crimes. Predictable murder mystery based on a book by Edgar Wallace, an author whose familiar plots were always rich with eccentric characters and grisly killings. Those interesting elements are dealt with rather lightly here, making the entire affair much too simplistic.

p, Jack Greenwood; d, Allan Davis; w, Philip Mackie (based on a novel by Edgar Wallace); ph, Brian Rhodes; m, Francis Chagrin; ed, Bernard Gribble; art d, Wolf Arnold.

Mystery (PR:A MPAA:NR)

CLUNY BROWN**** (1946) 100m FOX bw

Charles Boyer *(Adam Belinski)*, Jennifer Jones *(Cluny Brown)*, Peter Lawford *(Andrew Carmel)*, Helen Walker *(Betty Cream)*, Reginald Gardiner *(Hilary Ames)*, Reginald Owen *(Sir Henry Carmel)*, Sir C. Aubrey Smith *(Colonel Duff-Graham)*, Richard Haydn *(Wilson)*, Margaret Bannerman *(Lady Alice Carmel)*, Sara Allgood *(Mrs. Maile)*, Ernest Cossart *(Syrett)*, Florence Bates *(Dowager)*, Una O'Connor *(Mrs. Wilson)*, Queenie Leonard *(Weller)*, Billy Bevan *(Uncle Arn)*, Michael Dyne *(John Frewen)*, Christopher Severn *(Master Snaffle)*, Rex Evans *(Guest Pianist)*, Ottola Nesmith *(Mrs. Tupham)*, Harold DeBecker *(Mr. Snaffle)*, Jean Prescott *(Mrs. Snaffle)*, Al Winters *(Rollins)*, Clive Morgan *(Waiter)*, Charles Coleman *(Constable Birkins)*, George Kirby *(Latham)*, Whitner Bissell *(Dowager's Son)*, Bette Rae Brown *(Girl at Party)*, Philip Morris *(New York Policeman)*, Betty Fairfax *(Woman in Chemist's Shop)*, Norman Ainsley *(Mr. Tupham)*, Brad Slaven *(English Boy on Bike)*, Billy Gray *(Boy in Shop)*, Mira McKinney *(Author's Wife)*.

Somebody once asked a Lubitsch alumnus "What exactly is the 'Lubitsch Touch' that everyone keeps talking about?" The answer came back from the smiling German writer: "Zer Lubitsch Touch is dot he beleafs he shoot get zer best zcript he ken, make zer actors mamorize it, turn on zer kemeras, zen get zer hell out of zer vay!" And that about sizes up all of Ernest Lubitsch's greatest works. One never gets the feeling there's a director standing next to the camera. It all seems so natural—no fancy angles,no rack dissolves, no clever cuts, just people saying interesting things in an interesting setting. Boyer is a Czech author who has fled the wrath of the Nazis before the war and is now in residence at a country home of a very rich and snobbish family. The maid at said manor is Jones, who is also a plumber with the ability to fix anything. This unlikely duo meets and falls in love and that's the plot. There are, however, moments of satire that raise this movie to classic status as Lubitsch and Hoffenstein and Reinhardt take shots at upper-class England with such aim that the gentry may not have yet recovered. Owen is the lord of the manor and Margaret Bannerman is his wife,with young Lawford as the son. They know vaguely that something is happening in Europe and it concerns some Austrian but that's as far as their immediate knowledge goes. Theirs is a life of gardening, garden parties, tea, and weed-killers until Jones and Boyer upset the apple cart and bring some spirit into the household. The mores and manners of uppercrust British society have been a target for satirical barbs since before Oscar Wilde wrote THE IMPORTANCE OF BEING EARNEST. If one were to visit England even today, the intelligence and insight of CLUNY BROWN'S barbs would still be in evidence. Jones, who was always more of a looker than an actress, gives her best performance under Lubitsch's thumb—light as it is. Some wonderful bits by the British colonials who occupied much of Brentwood during and after the war; notably Smith and the two Reginalds, Gardiner and Owen. All that was missing was Reginald Denny. The "Lubitsch Touch" can probably be seen in the final frames of this, the great director's last film. It is all done in the reflectionof a shopwindow where Jones faints on the street and Boyer kneels beside her. A crowd gathers and a policeman begins to bend forward but Boyer stops him with a smile. No words are spoken as smiles cross the faces in the crowd and Jones comes to, and it is universally realized that the mild fainting is the result of her being pregnant. Lubitsch, ever the energetic craftsman, began another film almost immediately, THAT LADY IN ERMINE, but he lasted only eight days, suffering a relapse. (Otto Preminger took over the direction.) Lubitsch had had five heart attacks but refused to give up his cigars which he inhaled. He joked about the illness at a party with Jeanette MacDonald but died four days later, on November 30, 1947, of his sixth heart attack.

p&d, Ernst Lubitsch; w, Samuel Hoffenstein, Elizabeth Reinhardt (based on the novel by Margery Sharp); ph, Joseph La Shelle; m, Cyril Mockridge; ed, Dorothy Spencer; md, Emil Newman; art d, Lyle Wheeler, J. Russell Spencer; set d, Thomas Little, Paul Fox; spec eff, Fred Sersen.

Comedy/Drama (PR:A MPAA:NR)

C'MON, LET'S LIVE A LITTLE*½ (1967) 84m PAR c

Bobby Vee *(Jesse Crawford)*, Jackie DeShannon *(Judy Grant)*, Eddie Hodges *(Eddie Stewart)*, Suzie Kaye *(Bee Bee Vendemeer)*, Patsy Kelly *(Mrs. Fitts)*, John Ireland, Jr. *(Rego)*, Mark Evans *(Tim Grant)*, Russ Conway *(John W. Grant)*, Jill Banner *(Wendy)*, Kim Carnes *(Melinda)*, Joy Tobin *(Joy)*, Frank Alesia *(Balta)*, Ken Osmond *(The Beard)*, Don Crawford *(Jeb Crawford)*, Tiger Joe Marsh *(Spuko)*, Ben Frommer *(Jake)*, Ethel Smith *(An' Effel)*, Bo Belinsky *(Bo-Bo)*, The Pair Extraordinaire.

Silly 1960s campus drama has pop singer Vee portraying a backwoods folksinger who wins a scholarship to a small college after saving dean's daughter DeShannon from a car accident. When the local radical, Ireland, Jr., uses him as a way to get the students to attend his "free speech" rally, Vee punches the troublemaker in the nose and lets the kindly dean tell the student body that everything's all right and they don't need any of those silly ideas about freedom. The low-grade pop tunes can't help this bargain basement look at youthful ideals. Songs: "C'mon, Let's Live A Little," "Instant Girl," "Baker Man," "What Fool This Mortal Be," "Tonight's the Night," "For Granted," "Back-Talk," "Over and Over," "Let's Go Go," "Way Back Home" (Don Crawford).

p, June Starr, John Hertelandy; d, David Butler; w, Starr; ph, Carl Berger (Techniscope, Technicolor); m, Don Ralke; ed, Eve Newman; art d, Frank Sylos.

Teenage Drama (PR:A MPAA:NR)

COACH*½ (1978) 100m Crown International c

Cathy Lee Crosby *(Randy)*, Michael Biehn *(Jack)*, Keenan Wynn *(Fenton)*, Steve Nevil *(Ralph)*, Channing Clarkson *(Bradley)*, Jack David Walker *(Ned)*, Meredith Baer *(Janet)*, Myron McGill *(Danny)*, Robyn Pohle *(Candy)*, Kristine Greco *(Darlene)*, Brent Huff *(Keith)*, Rosanne Kayon *(Sue)*, Lenka Novak *(Marilyn)*, Otto Felix *(Tom)*, Milt Oberman *(Coach)*, Ron Wright *(Gorman)*, Cindy Daly *(Wanda)*, Derek Barton *(Jack's Stunt Double)*, Bill McLean *(Harold)*, Ted Dawson *(Marvin)*, Tom Mahoney *(Janitor)*.

Upset with the high school basketball team's record, Wynn, the local bigwig, has the coach fired. Using a computer to analyze possible replacements, he decides to hire a "Randy Rawlings" (Crosby), unaware that *he* is a she. Crosby arrives in the town and her attractive physique catches quite a few glances from the team players and hostility from the local female prudes. Surprising Wynn, Crosby whips the team into shape and instructs basketball star Biehn in some private forms of physical exercise as well. Idiotic drive-in entry with just enough peek-a-boo nudity and "sexy" situations to titillate young viewers.

p, Mark Tenser; d, Bud Townsend; w, Stephen Bruce Rose, Nancy Larson (based on an idea by Tenser); ph, Mike Murphy (Metrocolor); m, Anthony Harris; ed, Bob Gordon; art d, Ken Hergenroeder.

Drama Cas. (PR:C-O MPAA:PG)

COAL MINER'S DAUGHTER**** (1980) 125m UNIV c

Sissy Spacek *(Loretta)*, Tommy Lee Jones *(Doolittle "Mooney" Lynn)*, Levon Helm *(Ted Webb)*, Phyllis Boyens *(Clara Webb)*, Bill Anderson, Jr., Foister Dickerson, Malla McCown, Pamela McCown, Kevin Salvilla *(Webb Children)*, William Sanderson *(Junior Webb at 16)*, Sissy Lucas, Pat Paterson, Brian Warf, Elizabeth Watson, *(Loretta and Mooney's Children)*, Beverly D'Angelo *(Patsy Cline)*, Robert Elkins *(Bobby Day)*, Bob Hannah *(Charlie Dick)*, Ernest Tubb *(Himself)*, Jennifer Beasley *(Patsy Lynn)*, Jessica Easley *(Peggy Lynn)*, Michael Baish *(Storekeeper)*, Susan Kingsley *(Girl at Fairgrounds)*, David Gray *(Doc Turner)*, Royce Clark *(Hugh Cherry)*, Gary Parker *(Radio Station Manager)*, Billy Strange *(Speedy West)*, Bruce Newman *(Opry Stage Manager)*, Grant Turner *(Opry Announcer)*, Frank Mitchell, Merle Kilgore, Jackie Lynn Wright, Rhonda Rhoton, Vernon Oxford, Ron Hensley, Doug Bledsoe, Aubrey Wells, Russell Varner, Tommie O'Donnell, Lou Headley, Ruby Caudill, Charles Kahlenberg, Alice McGeachy, Ken Riley, Jim Webb.

Spacek won the Oscar and the film, Rickman, Bode, Schmidt, Corso, and Dwyer all received Academy Award nominations. A musical biography of Nashville's reigning queen, Loretta Lynn, COAL MINER'S DAUGHTER might have won all the above awards had it not been over two hours long. That aside, this is a fascinating look at a country singer's life through the eyes of a British director. It's not always honest and it is, in fact, somewhat romanticized but remains close enough to the truth that we can warrant it as a real biography rather than a fanciful one. Spacek lives with her parents and five siblings in a tumbledown shack in Butcher Holler (Hollow), the worst part of town. She's just into her teens as the film begins and already tired because she shoulders much of the responsibility of raising her brothers and sisters as her parents, Boyens and Helm, seem to be having a tough time of it. Jones comes back from the Army and an immediate attraction occurs. She is little more than still a child when she and Jones leave town as husband and wife. Fade out, then fade in again as Spacek is now nineteen years old and already a mother several times. She sings at home and Jones thinks she might be able to do it for a living. Hell, they could use any extra money they could get, right? He buys her a guitar and before you could say "Ernest Tubbs" she's working at a local sleazebar. From there on, it's straight up in as cliche a rags-to-riches story as anyone could conceive. But in this case, it's all true! Any screenwriter walking into a producer's office with this story would be hustled out the door double-quick and yet cliches become cliches because they *do* happen. The one jarring note to anyone who is a Lynn fan is that the authors of the film have conveniently glossed over the other side of success; the drugs, marital discord,nervous breakdowns, and the death of Loretta's best friend, Patsy Cline (beautifully portrayed and sung by D'Angelo). Spacek sings all of Lynn's songs and could have a career as a singer if she had the right material. Lots of laughs, tears, and a pretty good look at what it means to be a star and what one has to do to get to that lofty position. Songs: "I'm a Honky Tonk Girl," "You Ain't Woman Enough To Take My Man," "You're Lookin' at Country," "Coal Miner's Daughter," (Loretta Lynn), "One's On The Way," (Shel Silverstein), "Back in My Baby's Arms" (Bob Montgomery).

p, Bernard Schwartz; d, Michael Apted; w, Tom Rickman (based on autobiography by Loretta Lynn with George Vescey); ph, Ralf D. Bode (Technicolor); m, Owen Bradley; ed, Arthur Schmidt; prod d, John Corso; set d, John M. Dwyer; cos, Joe I. Tompkins; m/l, Lynn, Shel Silverstein, Bob Montgomery.

Musical Biography Cas. (PR:A-C MPAA:PG)

COAST GUARD** (1939) 72m COL bw

Randolph Scott *(Speed Bradshaw)*, Frances Dee *(Nancy Bliss)*, Ralph Bellamy *(Lt. Raymond Dower)*, Walter Connolly *(Tobias Bliss)*, Warren Hymer *(O'Hara)*, Robert Middlemass *(Capt. Lyons)*, Stanley Andrews *(Cmdr. Hooker)*, Edmund MacDonald *(Lt. Thompson)*.

Coast Guard pals Scott and Bellamy both fall for the attractive Dee, who finally settles for the quiet but tough Scott. When her husband's macho characteristics become irritating, Dee leaves Scott who in turn cracks up one of the Navy's planes trying to impress his estranged sweetheart. Losing his wings as a result of the incident, Scott begs to get them back in order to lead a rescue mission to find Bellamy who is lost in the Arctic. Scott rescues his old chum and wins back Dee through his display of devotion and friendship. Cliche-ridden drama is given an appealing flavor by its stars.

p, Fred Kohlmar; d, Edward Ludwig; w, Richard Malbaum, Albert Duffy, Harry Segall; ph, Lucien Ballard; m, M.W. Stoloff; ed, Gene Milford.

Drama (PR:A MPAA:NR)

COAST OF SKELETONS** (1965, Brit.) 90m Seven Arts c

Richard Todd *(Harry Sanders)*, Dale Robertson *(A. J. Magnus)*, Heinz Drache *(Janny von Koltze)*, Marianne Koch *(Helga)*, Elga Andersen *(Elizabeth von Koltze)*, Derek Nimmo *(Tom Hamilton)*, Gabriel Bayman *(Charlie Singer)*, George Leech *(Carlo*

Seton), Gordon Mulholland *(Mr. Spyker)*, Josh DuToit *(Hajo Petersen)*, Dietmar Schoenherr *(Piet van Houten)*.

Insurance investigator Todd uncovers a plot by unscrupulous American Robertson to pillage diamonds and gold from sunken ships whose contents belong to Todd's employers. Occasionally exciting adventure film that fails to generate any interest in the plight of its protagonist. Todd reprises a role from DEATH DRUMS ALONG THE RIVER.

p, Oliver A. Unger, Harry Alan Towers; d, Robert Lynn; w, Anthony Scott Veitch (based on the story by Peter Welbeck, inspired by "Sanders of the River" by Edgar Wallace); ph Stephen Dade; m, Christopher Whelen; ed, John Trumper; cos, Louis Feraud.

Adventure (PR:A MPAA:NR)

COAST TO COAST*½ (1980) 95m PAR c

Dyan Cannon *(Madie Levrington)*, Robert Blake *(Charlie Callahan)*, Quinn Redeker *(Benjamin Levrington)*, Michael Lerner *(Dr. Froll)*, Maxine Stuart *(Sam Klinger)*, Bill Lucking *(Jules)*, Ellen Gerstein *(Nurse No. 1)*, Patricia Conklin *(Nurse No. 2)*, David Moody *(Chester)*, Rozelle Gayle *(Orderly)*, Martin Beck *(Albert)*, Karen Rushmore *(Callahan's Wife)*, Mae Williams *(Waitress)*, George P. Wilbur *(Billy Ray)*, Tom Pletts *(Attendant)*, Henry Wills *(Chef)*, Hap Lawrence *(Mechanic)*, Tom J. Delaney, Darwin Joston *(Drunken Truckers)*, Dick Durock *(Greg)*, Grace Spence, Dorothy Frazier *(Salesladies)*, Joe Finnegan, Jerry Gatlin, Leonard P. Geer, Casandra Peterson, Karen Montgomery, Arsenio Trinidad, Vicki Frederick, John Roselius, Al Robertson, Clarke Gordon, Cynthia Gable.

Fleeing from a husband who is trying to convince everyone she is crazy (to avoid a costly divorce), Cannon joins up with trucker Blake in New York and finagles a ride out of town from him. Unable to tolerate his companion's constant chatter, Blake tries to get rid of Cannon, but she constantly finds some way to convince him to let her tag along. In dire economic straits, Blake contemplates turning Cannon in when he learns that her husband is offering a reward for her return, but does not when he realizes that he truly loves the nutty New Yorker. The loving couple continue on to Los Angeles with a divorce from Cannon's husband in the distance. Dim-witted, loud comedy, the film conveys its "jokes" with the force of a sledge hammer. Unbelievably, Blake manages to give a typically fine performance as the world-weary, penniless trucker. It's a shame his blabbermouth co-star and the film's director could not understand Blake's insight into human nature and the humor that can arise out of people simply being people.

p, Steve Tisch, Jon Avnet; d, Joseph Sargent; w, Stanley Weiser; ph Mario Tosi (Movielab Color); m, Charles Bernstein; ed, George Jay Nicholson; art d, Hilyard Brown; cos, Sandra Davidson.

Comedy Cas. (PR:A MPAA:PG)

COBRA, THE* (1968) 93m Roma Dollar/Productores Exhibidores/AIP c (ITAL.: IL COBRA: SPAN.: EL COBRA)

Dana Andrews *(Kelly)*, Peter Martell *(Mike Rand)*, Anita Ekberg *(Lou)*, Elisa Montes *(Corianne)*, Jesus Puente *(Stiarkos)*, Peter Dane *(Hullinger)*, Luciana Vincenzi *(Ulla)*, George Histman *(Crane)*, Omar Zoulficar *(Sadek)*, Giovanni Petrucci *(King)*, Chang'e *(Li Fang)*, Ehshane Sadek *(Gamel)*, Lidia Biondi.

Treasury agents Andrews and Martell, with the aid of the top-heavy Ekberg, uncover a plot by the Red Chinese to control the minds of world youth by regulating global heroin trade. Ludicrous multinational production roaming from Turkey to the Middle East that would make most comic books look brilliant in comparison.

p, Fulvio Lucisano; d, Mario Sequi; w, Cumersindo Mollo (based on a story by Adriano Bolzoni); ph, Claudio Racca (Techniscope, Technicolor); m, Jose Antonio Abril.

Spy Drama/Adventure Cas. (PR:A MPAA:NR)

COBRA STRIKES, THE* (1948) 61m EL bw

Sheila Ryan *(Dale)*, Richard Fraser *(Mike Kent)*, Leslie Brooks *(Olga Kaminoff)*, Herbert Heyes *(Dr. Damon Cameron/Ted Cameron)*, James Seay *(Capt. Monohan)*, Richard Loo *(Hyder Ali)*, Lyle Latell *(Sgt. Harris)*, Pat Flaherty *(Atlas Kilroy)*, Phillip Ahn *(Kasim)*, Fred Nurney *(Franz Lang)*, George Sorel *(Victor Devereaux)*.

Newspaperman Fraser uncovers the makings of a jewel heist after a prominent scientist is killed. Terribly inane "mystery" that falls short of creating even the mildest form of suspense.

p, David I. Stephenson; d, Charles F. Reisner; w, Eugene Conrad; ph, Guy Roe; ed, Louis Sackin.

Crime Drama (PR:A MPAA:NR)

COBRA WOMAN** (1944) 70m UNIV c

Maria Montez *(Tollea/Naja)*, Jon Hall *(Ramu)*, Sabu *(Kado)*, Edgar Barrier *(Martok)*, Mary Nash *(Queen)*, Lois Collier *(Veeda)*, Samuel S. Hinds *(Father Paul)*, Moroni Olsen *(MacDonald)*, Lon Chaney, Jr. *(Hava)*, Robert Barron *(Chief Guard)*, Vivian Austin, Beth Dean, Paulita Arvizu *(Handmaidens)*, Fritz Leiber *(Venreau)*; Belle Mitchell *(Native Woman)*, John Bagni *(Native)*, Dale Van Sickel, Eddie Parker, George Magrill *(Guards)*.

Montez stars in a dual role as the rightful queen of a cobra-worshipping cult and her evil sister who tries to steal away the throne. Montez's previous film teammates, Sabu and Hall, lend their usual support in saving the good queen. Laughable jungle superstition plot is given a highly stylized, colorful visual representation by talented director Siodmak who created some of the best films noir of the 1940s and 1950s before returning to Germany where he directed until his death in 1973.

p, George Waggner; d, Robert Siodmak; w, Gene Lewis, Richard Brooks; (based on a story by W. Scott Darling); ph, George Robinson, W. Howard Greene (Technicolor); m, Edward Ward; ed, Charles Maynard; art d, John B. Goodman, Alexander Golitzen; spec eff, John Fulton.

Fantasy/Drama (PR:A MPAA:NR)

COBWEB, THE½** (1955) 122m MGM c

Richard Widmark *(Dr. Stewart McIver)*, Lauren Bacall *(Meg Faversen Rinehart)*, Charles Boyer *(Dr. Douglas N. Devanal)*, Gloria Grahame *(Karen McIver)*, Lillian Gish *(Victoria Inch)*, John Kerr *(Steven W. Holte)*, Susan Strasberg *(Sue Brett)*, Oscar Levant *(Mr. Capp)*, Tommy Rettig *(Mark)*, Paul Stewart *(Dr. Otto Wolff)*, Jarma Lewis *(Lois DeMuth)*, Adele Jergens *(Miss Cobb)*, Edgar Stehli *(Mr. Holcomb)*, Sandra Descher *(Rosemary)*, Bert Freed *(Abe Irwin)*, Mabel Albertson *(Regina Mitchell-Smythe)*, Fay Wray *(Edna Devanal)*, Oliver Blake *(Curly)*, Olive Carey *(Mrs. O'Brien)*, Eve McVeagh *(Shirley)*, Virginia Christine *(Sally)*, Jan Arvan *(Mr. Appleton)*, Ruth Clifford *(Mrs. Jenkins)*, Myra Marsh *(Miss Gavney)*, James Westerfield *(James Petlee)*, Marjorie Bennett *(Sadie)*, Stuart Holmes *(Mr. Wictz)*.

An all-star cast, a brilliant director, an eminent producer, and a script from a fascinating book all contribute to making this a very dull movie. It's a segmented look at the ins-and-outs of a large psychiatric clinic with the notion that the stuff may be more neurotic than the patients. There is a new set of drapes to be chosen for the institute's library and Grahame, the often overlooked wife of clinic topper Widmark, wants the honor of making the selection. Gish, making her first MGM movie in 22 years, is the spinster business affairs director who insists on muslin drapes so they can save money. Widmark is asking Kerr, a new patient with a suicidal tendency, to design said drapes. (Kerr has one of the only good scenes in the film as he escorts Strasberg, another patient, to the movies; it was the movie debut of both.) The rest of the plot is various romantic angles with Boyer as a satyr with a male nymphomaniac complex; Bacall as the activities director and a lonely woman who only lives for her work, and a host of interesting patients. The picture was verbose and decidedly low-key with none of THE SNAKE PIT's sensationalism—and that was to its credit. Levant, who spent a lot of time on psychiatric couches, is excellent, as is Albertson and Wray. It's nice to see Wray in other roles than the one she made famous atop the Empire State Building in Kong's clutches.

p, John Houseman; d, Vincente Minnelli; w, John Paxton, William Gibson (based on the novel by Gibson); ph, George Folsey (CinemaScope, Eastmancolor); m, Leonard Rosenman; ed, Harold F. Kress.

Drama (PR:A MPAA:NR)

COCAINE COWBOYS* (1979) 87m International Harmony c

Jack Palance *(Raf)*, Tom Sullivan *(Destn)*, Andy Warhol *(Himself)*, Susanna Love *(Lucy)*, Pete Huckabee *(Dean)*, Tony Manufo *(Phil)*, Richard Young *(Terry)*, Richard Basset *(Herman)*, Esther Oldham-Farfan, The Cowboy Island Band.

Members of a rock group sit around Andy Warhol's summer home on Montauk and wait for their album to hit big, supporting themselves in the meantime by smuggling cocaine. Warhol stalks around with a Polaroid, and Palance, the only professional in the cast, looks embarrassed. Largely improvised and obviously so, directed by Lommel, who appeared in a number of Fassbinder's films. Presumably his acting talent is superior to his directorial ability. Simply dreadful.

p, Christopher Francis Giercke; d, Ulli Lommel; w, Lommel, S. Compton, Tom Sullivan, V. Bockris; ph, Jochen Breitenstein; m, Elliot Goldenthal.

Drama Cas. (PR:O MPAA:R)

COCK O' THE NORTH*½ (1935, Brit.) 84m Mitchell Films-Panther/But bw

George Carney *(George Barton)*, Marie Lohr *(Mary Barton)*, Ronnie Hepworth *(Danny Barton)*, Horace Kenney *(Alf Coggins)*, Frederick Peisley *(Fred Coggins)*, Eve Lister *(Edna Barton)*, Peggy Novak *(Maggie Harris)*, Johnnie Schofield *(Bert Harris)*, Roddy Hughes *(Taffy)*, Leslie "Hutch" Hutchinson, Naughton & Gold, Robert Chisholm, Simone Rogers.

Carney is a fire engine driver forced into retirement after a crash. His son (Hepworth) consoles him and a number of decent songs fill out the time. Forgotten British musical with little to recommend it.

p, Oswald Mitchell; d, Mitchell, Challis Sanderson; w, Mitchell; ph, William Luff.

Musical (PR:A MPAA:NR)

COCK O' THE WALK½** (1930) 50m Sono-Art-World Wide bw

Joseph Schildkraut *(Carlos)*, Myrna Loy *(Narita)*, Phillip Sleeman *(Jose)*, Edward Peil *(Ortego)*, John Beck *(Cafe Manager)*, Olive Tell *(Rosa Vallejo)*, Wilfred Lucas *(Senor Vallejo)*, Frank Jonasson *(Pedro)*, Sally Long *(Paulina Castra)*, Natalie Joyce *(Maria)*.

After years of preying on lonely wives of rich husbands, gigolo Schildkraut falls for suicidal waif Loy. Romantic tear-jerker that nicely displays the awakening of love in the cold, cynical Schildkraut. Loy, giving a typically perfect performance, shines as the distraught girl who brings a touch of humanity to a lout.

p, James Cruze; d, R. William Neill, Walter Lang; w, Nagene Searle, Francis Guihan, Brian Marlow, Ralph Bell (based on the play "Happiness Insurance" by Arturo S. Mom); ph, R.W. McNeill; m/l, "Play Me a Tango Tune" (Paul Titsworth).

Romantic Drama (PR:A MPAA:NR)

COCK OF THE AIR** (1932) 72m Hughes/UA bs

Chester Morris *(Lt. Roger Craig)*, Billie Dove *(Lilli de Rousseau)*, Matt Moore *(Terry)*, Walter Catlett *(Col. Wallace)*, Luis Alberni *(Capt. Tonnino)*, Katya Sergeiva *(1st Italian Girl)*, Yola D'Avril *(2nd Italian Girl)*, Vivian Oakland *(Irate Woman)*, Emile Chautard *(French Ambassador)*, Ethel Sutherland *(Lilli's Companion)*, Peggy Watts *(Lilli's Maid)*.

When temperamental French actress Dove declares that she is not receiving enough adoration from the WW I Allies, the powers that be arrange a meeting in Italy between the flamboyant Dove and Army charmer Morris. At first angered by their manipulated encounter, the couple slowly but surely fall in love. Pleasant romantic comedy that uses its nationality-bonding thematics in a heartfelt way. Dove, who had had a brief affair with millionaire producer Hughes—he had even paid for her divorce from director

Irving Willat on 1931—was rewarded for her affections with a lead in this film and another, THE AGE OF LOVE.

p, Howard Hughes; d, Tom Buckingham; w, Charles Lederer (based on a story by Lederer and Robert E. Sherwood); ph, Lucien Andriot; m, Alfred Newman; ed, W. Duncan Mansfield.

Comedy (PR:A MPAA:NR)

COCKEYED CAVALIERS** *(1934) 72m RKO bw*

Bert Wheeler *(Bert)*, Robert Woolsey *(Bob)*, Thelma Todd *(Lady Genevieve)*, Dorothy Lee *(Mary Ann)*, Noah Beery, Sr. *(Baron)*, Robert Greig *(Duke of Weskit)*, Henry Sedley *(Baron's Friend)*, Franklyn Pangborn *(Town Crier)*, Alf P. James *(Mary Ann's Father)*, Jack Norton, Snub Pollard *(King's Physicians)*, Billy Gilbert.

Witty duo of Wheeler and Woolsey don 16th-century garb in this funny comedy in which the pair are mistaken for king's doctors and taken to the palace to help an ailing emperor, giving Wheeler ample opportunity to exhibit his kleptomania tendencies. Noah Beery, Sr., provides some exuberant comic support. A hilarious highlight spoofs a scene from Greta Garbo's QUEEN CHRISTINA where she discards her disguise as a boy to a startled John Gilbert.

d, Mark Sandrich; w, Edward Kaufman, Ben Holmes; ed, Jack kitchen; md, Roy Webb; m/l, "Dilly Dally," "I Went Hunting and the Big Bad Wolf Was Dead" (Will Jason, Val Burton).

Comedy **Cas.** (PR:A MPAA:NR)

COCKEYED COWBOYS OF CALICO COUNTY, THE**

(1970) 100m UNIV c

Dan Blocker *(Charley)*, Nanette Fabray *(Sadie)*, Jim Backus *(Staunch)*, Wally Cox *(Mr. Bester)*, Jack Elam *(Kittrick)*, Henry Jones *(Hanson)*, Stubby Kaye *(Bartender)*, Mickey Rooney *(Indian Tom)*, Noah Beery, Jr. *(Eddie)*, Marge Champion *(Mrs. Bester)*, Donald Barry *(Rusty)*, Hamilton Camp *(Mr. Fowler)*, Tom Basham *(Traveler)*, Iron Eyes Cody *(Crazy Foot)*, James McCallion *(Dr. Henry)*, Byron Foulger *(Rev. Marshall)*, Ray Ballard *(Carson)*, Jack Cassidy *(Roger Hand)*.

When his mail-order bride fails to show up at the train station on her designated arrival date, blacksmith Blocker threatens to pack up and leave town to escape the humiliation. When the townspeople realize that they could be losing their *only* blacksmith, they hire dancehall girl Fabray to portray the tardy bride. Blocker eventually discovers the ruse, but since he has fallen in love with the substitute decides to marry the equally loving Fabray. Riding high on his success in television's *Bonanza*, star Blocker tries to do what he can with this uninspired western comedy.

p, Ranald MacDougall; d, Tony Leader; w, MacDougall; ph, Richard L. Rawlings (Technicolor); m, Lyn Murray; ed, Richard G. Wray; art d, Alexander Golitzen, George Patrick; cos, Helen Colvig.

Western Comedy (PR:AA MPAA:G)

COCKEYED MIRACLE, THE**½ *(1946) 81m MGM bw*

Frank Morgan *(Sam Griggs)*, Keenan Wynn *(Ben Griggs)*, Cecil Kellaway *(Tom Carter)*, Audrey Totter *(Jennifer Griggs)*, Richard Quine *(Howard Bankson)*, Gladys Cooper *(Amy Griggs)*, Marshall Thompson *(Jim Griggs)*, Leon Ames *(Ralph Humphrey)*, Jane Green *(Mrs. Lynne)*, Morris Ankrum *(Dr. Wilson)*, Arthur Space *(Amos Spellman)*, Naomi Childers, Howard Mitchell *(Visitors)*, Guy deWolf, Robert Anderson, Billy Chapin *(Boys)*, Susan Simon, Grete deWolf *(Girls)*.

Happy ghost stories were all the rage at the time (the TOPPER series, HERE COMES MR. JORDAN), so they decided to take a not-very-successful George Seaton play and transfer it to the screen and hope that the audience's taste for other-world humor would include this story. It didn't. It's the early 1900s and Frank Morgan a 63-year-old New England shipbuilder, is called to his reward by his own father, a thirty-six-year-old wastrel played by Wynn. He'd been dispatched by a whiskey bottle over the head or, as he puts it, "I was launched." Since Morgan's family had lots of troubles when he passed away, the two men have to stay on to straighten out the problems. Naturally, no one can see them at all or hear them, so much of the visual and verbal humor stems from that hoary trick. Totter, Morgan's daughter, is in love with Quine (the same one who became a director years later), a bumbling and dotty rockhound who is too intent on everything else to propose to Totter. Wynn creates a rainstorm while Trotter and Quine ride in an open shay and they have to go into a barn. Once inside, the magnetic attraction erupts and Quine is a gone goose. Thompson, Morgan's son, wants to quit his job with dogmatic uncle Ames. He'd like to build ships again, like his Daddy did, but all of Morgan's money was sunk into a real estate deal with former partner Kellaway and the property they purchased was not turning over. Meanwhile, Kellaway, knowing full well that Morgan's family doesn't know a thing about the real estate, sells the piece in question to Space and is preparing to run off with all the lucre when Kellaway is struck by lightning and a check for Morgan's share of the sale is found on Kellaway's body and turned over to Morgan's widow, Cooper. Naturally, that lightning was in a Wynn-created storm. Now that the family is straight, Wynn and Morgan go to their rest, still arguing. Morgan: "All you left ma and me was a fifteen dollar saloon bill." Wynn: "I'll thank you to treat your father with somewhat more respect." Morgan: "Respect? Why I'm twice as old as you are!" Now that joke coming from the gray-haired man to the dark-haired youth can only play once, but the screenplay does it too many times and it soons wears thin.

p, Irving Starr; d, S. Sylvan Simon; w, Karen deWolf (based on the play "But Not Goodbye" by George Seaton); ph, Ray June; m, David Snell; ed, Ben Lewis.

Comedy/Fantasy (PR:AA MPAA:NR)

COCK-EYED WORLD, THE** *(1929) 115m FOX bw*

Victor McLaglen *(Top Sgt. Flagg)*, Edmund Lowe *(Sgt. Harry Quirt)*, Lily Damita *(Elenita)*, Lelia Karnelly *(Olga)*, El Brendel *(Olson)*, Bobby Burns *(Connors)*, Jean Bary *(Fanny)*, Joe Brown *(Brownie)*, Stuart Erwin *(Buckley)*, Ivan Linow *(Sanovich)*, Solidad Jiminez *(Innkeeper)*, Albert Dresden *(O'Sullivan)*, Joe Rochay *(Jacobs)*, Jeanette Dagna *(Katinka)*, Warren Hymer *(Scout)*.

Repeating their roles from WHAT PRICE GLORY? McLaglen and Lowe continue their hard-drinking, profane, two-fisted, girl-chasing ways as a couple of Marines traveling from Vladivostock to Nicaragua via Coney Island. Criticized during its time for being excessively bawdy, this Raoul Walsh macho comedy is, of course, tame by today's standards, but its tough-minded, warm-hearted soul is still appealing. It was one of six motion pictures made in 1929 by Lila Damita, who six years later would embark on a tempestuous marriage with Errol Flynn. Songs: "Semper Fidelis" (John Philip Sousa), "Over There" (George M. Cohan), "Rose of No Man's Land" (James Caddigan, James Brennan), "Ka-Ka-Katy" (Geoffrey O'Hara), "What Has Become of Hinky Dinky Parlay Voo" (Al Dubin, Irving Mills, Jimmy McHugh, Irwin Dash), "You're the Cream In My Coffee" (Buddy DeSylva, Les Brown, Ray Henderson), "Gloriana" (Sidney Clare, Lew Pollack), "So Long," "So Dear To Me" (Con Conrad, Sidney Mitchell, Archie Gottler).

d, Raoul Walsh; w, Walsh, William K. Wells; (based on an unpublished play by Laurence Stallings and Maxwell Anderson; ph, Arthur Edeson.

Comedy/Musical (PR:C MPAA:NR)

COCKFIGHTER (SEE: BORN TO KILL, 1975)

COCKLESHELL HEROES, THE*** *(1955) 97m Warwick/COL c*

Jose Ferrer *(Maj. Stringer)*, Trevor Howard *(Capt. Thompson)*, Victor Maddern *(Sgt. Craig)*, Anthony Newley *(Clarke)*, David Lodge *(Ruddock)*, Peter Arne *(Stevens)*, Percy Herbert *(Loman)*, Graham Stewart *(Booth)*, John Fabian *(Cooney)*, John Van Eyssen *(Bradley)*, Robert Desmond *(Todd)*, William Fitzgerald *(Gestapo Commandant)*, Karel Stepanek *(Gestapo Officer)*, Dora Bryan *(Myrtle)*, Beatrice Campbell *(Mrs. Ruddock)*, Sydney Tafler *(Policeman)*, Gladys Henson *(Barmaid)*, Jacques Brunius, Andrea Malendrinas *(French Fishermen)*, Christopher Lee *(Submarine Commander)*, Judith Furse, Yana.

Ferrer leads a small group of Royal Marines on a secret raid in which they travel by canoe to the docks of Bordeaux to plant mines on Nazi vessels. During the assault, five men are killed, two escape, and the rest men are taken to Gestapo headquarters where they refuse to answer questions and are shot as saboteurs. Intense, exciting war drama that has a tragic feeling at its center. Ferrer and Howard are superb as the feuding mission leaders whose mutual respect forms a deep bond.

p, Irving Allen, Albert R. Broccoli; d, Jose Ferrer; w, Bryan Forbes, Richard Maibaum; story, George Kent; ph, John Wilcox (CinemaScope, Technicolor), Ted Moore; m, John Addison; ed, Alan Osbiston; m/l, George Posford, Harold Purcell.

War Drama (PR:A MPAA:NR)

COCKTAIL HOUR*½ *(1933) 73m COL bw*

Bebe Daniels *(Cynthia Warren)*, Randolph Scott *(Randolph Morgan)*, Muriel Kirkland *(Olga)*, Jessie Ralph *(Princess)*, Sidney Blackmer *(Lawton)*, Barry Norton *(Philippe)*, Marjorie Gateson *(Mrs. Lawton)*, George Nardelli *(Alvarez)*.

Convincing herself that she needs to "experience life" to be a true artist, young painter Daniels compromises her virtue with a near-stranger, jeopardizing her relationship with kind-hearted Scott. Ridiculous tear-jerker that fails to truly explore the nature of its naive, confused heroine. Scott, in an early performance, displays the beauty of calm, restrained screen acting.

d, Victor Schertzinger; w, Gertrude Purcell, Richard Schayer (based on a story by James K. McGuiness); ph, Joseph August; ed, Jack Dennis; m/l, "Listen, Heart of Mine" (Schertzinger).

Drama (PR:C MPAA:NR)

COCKTAIL MOLOTOV***

(1980, Fr.) 100m Antenne 2-Alexandre Films/AMLF c

Elise Caron *(Anne)*, Philippe Lebas *(Frederic)*, Francois Cluzet *(Bruno)*, Genevieve Fontanei *(Anne's Mother)*, Henri Garcin *(Todd)*, Michel Puterfiam *(Her Father)*, Jenny Cleve *(Frederic's Mother)*, Armando Brancia *(His Father)*, Malene Sveinbjornsson *(Little Sister)*, Stefania Cassini *(Anna-Maria)*, Frederique Meininger *(Doctor)*, Patrick Chesnais *(Rucker)*.

Feeling pressure from her mother to become a conformist, Caron leaves Paris for Venice, hoping to lead a more spontaneous, carefree life there. Her boy friend, Lebas, and his pal, Cluzet, follow Caron, intent on convincing her to return to France. The boys' car and Caron's belongings are stolen in Italy and when they hear that a worker-student series of riots have been occurring in Paris, they decide to return home and join in the political struggle, whatever its motives are. Having made a very fine film about the problems of adolescence (PEPPERMINT SODA), talented director Kurys returned to similar subject matter with this youth-oriented road movie. Though not as successful as her previous work, the film still manages to convey the troubling, questioning, yet vital feelings of becoming an adult while still maintaining the hope of youth.

d, Diane Kurys; w, Kurys, Philippe Adrien, Alain LeHenry; ph, Philippe Rousselet; m, Yves Simon; ed, Joelle Van Effentree; art d, Hilton McConnico, Tony Egry; songs performed by Murray Head.

Drama (PR:A MPAA:NR)

COCOANUT GROVE**½ *(1938) 90m PAR bw*

Fred MacMurray *(Johnny Prentice)*, Harriet Hilliard *(Linda Rogers)*, The Yacht Club Boys *(Turk, Eli, Pete, Windy)*, Ben Blue *(Joe DeLemma)*, Rufe Davis *(Bibb Tucker)*, Billy Lee *(Half-Pint)*, Eve Arden *(Sophie DeLemma)*, Harry Owens *(Hula Harry)*, George Walcott *(Tony)*, Dorothy Howe *(Hazel DeVore)*, Red Stanley *(Dixie)*, Gloria Williams *(Woman)*, Charles Lane *(Weaver)*, Roy Gordon *(Grayson)*, Ronnie Rondell *(Headwaiter)*, Stanley Andrews *(Truant Officer)*, William Davidson *(Hawty)*, Egon Brecher *(Pawnbroker)*, Jack Pennick *(Bus Driver)*, Ethel Clayton *(Woman)*, Virginia Vale *(Hazel DeVore)*, Jimmy Conlin *(Motel Proprietor)*, Harry Owens and His Royal Hawaiian Orchestra *(Themselves)*, Paul Newlan *(Tourist in Trailer Camp)*, Dorothy

Dayton (Dancing Coach), Frances Morris (Receptionist), Max Wagner (Brakeman), Archie Twitchell, Phillip Warren (Radio Station Technicians), Jack Hubbard (Radio Station Attendant), Ellen Drew (Radio Station Receptionist), Cliff Clark (Auctioneer), Jack Gardner (Father), Larry Harris (Boy with Father), Murray Alper (Concessionaire), Ruth Rogers, Janet Waldo, Mary Parker, Joyce Mathews, Barbara Jackson, Norah Gale, Gwen Kenyon, Carol Parker, Cheryl Walker, Sheila Darcy, Louise Seidel, Barbara Salisbury (Girls).

MacMurray and his band leave their Chicago-based stint on a Lake Michigan showboat for California, where MacMurray has been promised an audition at the title nightclub. MacMurray, a sax player in a band before he went into movies, gets a chance to toot in this entertaining film and also vocalizes in a serenade to Hilliard. Songs: "You Leave Me Breathless" (Ralph Freed, Frederick Hollander), "Says My Heart" (Frank Loesser, Burton Lane), "Dreamy Hawaiian Moon," "Cocoanut Grove" (Harry Owens), "Ten Easy Lessons" (Loesser, Lane, "Jock"), "Swami Song" (Alfred Santell, Lane), "The Musketeers Song" (Bert Kalmar, Harry Ruby, The Yacht Club Boys), "The Four of Us Went to Sea" (Yacht Club Boys).

p, George Arthur; d, Alfred Santell; w, Sy Bartlett and Oliver Cooper; ph, Leo Tover; ed, Hugh Bennett.

Musical (PR:AA MPAA:NR)

COCOANUTS, THE**** (1929) 90m PAR bw
Groucho Marx (Hammer), Harpo Marx (Harpo), Chico Marx (Chico), Zeppo Marx (Jamison), Mary Eaton (Polly), Oscar Shaw (Bob), Katherine Francis (Penelope), Margaret Dumont (Mrs. Potter), Cyril Ring (Yates), Basil Ruysdael (Hennessey), Sylvan Lee (Bell Captain), Alan K. Foster Girls, Gamby-Hale Girls (Dancing Bellhops), Barton MacLane (Bather).

The greatest zanies of film perform with dizzying speed in this farcical and nearly plotless romp through a Florida hotel, ostensibly dealing with the arrival and departure of would-be millionaires getting richer or poorer during the Florida land boom of the late 1920s. Groucho is the hotel manager—or mismanager—who never misses insulting or abusing the guests with the help of brothers Chico and Harpo. The mayhem is often side-splitting in this "pure" Marx vehicle with the love story only incidental. The boys were given their usual freedom to ad lib as they went along, but kept basically to the routines audiences had enjoyed from the original play by Kaufman and Berlin, but these were constantly changing, even during the shooting of the film. Groucho attempts to bamboozle the amazingly tolerant Dumont into a phony investment while Harpo arrives with a bag containing phone directories. While bored, the magnificent silent one begins tearing up the hotel mail and later attempts to interrupt Groucho's impromptu monologs by chasing blondes across the screen. Harpo originally did this as a gag in the play to distract his quipster brother but it didn't work. When Harpo first ran across the stage after the bribed blonde, Groucho merely shrugged, arched his heavy eyebrows, and remarked: "First time I ever saw a taxi hail a passenger." Harpo's ploy almost backfired offstage. He had chosen a chorus girl who was at the time the girl friend of New York City gangster Jack "Legs" Diamond. The gangster warned the girl thereafter to stay in the background and away "from them loony actors." There are many memorable lines in this antic-filled film. When a guest calls down for some ice water, Groucho tells him on the phone: "I'll send up an onion. That'll make your ice water!" But few of the original Kaufmann-Ryskind lines remained since the boys were notorious for discarding scripts and cues. The playwrights didn't even recognize their work when they first viewed the film and Berlin's music is not memorable, particularly since he had cut many tunes that were never sung as the brothers cavalierly changed the play each night and the movie scenes filmed later. One tune Berlin cut was his famous "Always," a classic ballad. When the play was being shaped, the great composer saw one song after another chopped. "My God," he finally exclaimed, "any more cuts and this will be a musical without music!" To calm him, Kaufman responded: "Tell you what, Irving, you waive the songs and I'll waive the story." This was a crude talkie, a technically bad film where the sound is static and the camera immobile with the comedians leaping into the set scenes. Yet the boys are there in all their frenetic glory and Harpo honks his horn for the first time, chasing but never catching the scantily clad cutie. He would pursue her in vain for decades to come while his brothers chewed up the sets and spat out laughter. This was officially the debut of the madcap brothers although they had appeared in an obscure silent production, HUMOR RISK, which is now an apparently lost film. Also debuting in this shapeless slapsticker is Kay Francis, then using the name Katherine; she would rise to stardom during the 1930s. Songs include: "Florida by the Sea," "Monkey-Doodle-Doo," "When My Dreams Come True" (written for the film), and "The Tale of A Shirt" (deleted from the final version, all by Berlin).

p, Monta Bell, James R. Cowan (for Walter Wanger); d, Robert Florey, Joseph Santley; w, Morris Ryskind (based on the play by George S. Kaufman and Irving Berlin); ph, George Folsey; ch, Joseph Santley, Robert Florey.

Comedy (PR:A MPAA:NR)

CODE NAME, RED ROSES
(SEE: RED ROSES FOR THE FUEHRER, 1969, Ital.)

CODE NAME: TRIXIE (SEE: THE CRAZIES, 1973)

CODE OF HONOR* (1930) 59m Syndicate Production bw
Mahlon Hamilton, Doris Hill, Robert Graves, Jr., William Dyer, Lafe McKee, Stanley Taylor, Jimmy Aubrey, Harry Holden.

This creaking oater deals with the ancient tale of cheating the rancher out of his homestead deed, but hero Hamilton makes it all right in the end.

d, J. P. McGowan; w, G. A. Durlam; ph, Otto Himm; ed, Arthur Brooks.

Western (PR:A MPAA:NR)

CODE OF SCOTLAND YARD½** (1948) 92m REP bw
Oscar Homolka (Descius Heiss), Derek Farr (Robert Graham), Muriel Pavlow (Margaret Heiss), Kenneth Griffith (Archie Fellowes), Manning Whiley (Corder Morris), Kathleen Harrison (Mrs. Catt), Garry Marsh (Maj. Elliot), Jan Van Loewen (Prof. Vanetti), Irene Handl (Ruby Towser), Johnnie Schofield (Inspector Robson).

When a bookkeeper for an antique dealer discovers that his employer, Homolka, is an escaped convict from Devil's Island and a former jewel thief's fence, the wormy character threatens to expose him unless he pays blackmail money. Fearing that exposure would ruin the career of his concert violinist daughter, and unable to pay the exorbitant ransom, Homolka kills the clerk. When he comes under suspicion by Scotland Yard, Homolka saves his daughter from scandal by committing suicide. Interesting melodrama rich with character, thanks to the excellent performance by Homolka and a uniformly fine British cast.

p&d, George King; w, Katherine Strueby (based on a play by Edward Percy); ph, Hone Glendinning; m, George Melachrino; ed, Manuel Del Campo.

Drama (PR:C-O MPAA:NR)

CODE OF SILENCE** (1960) 75m STER bw (AKA: KILLER'S CAGE)
Terry Becker, Elisa Loti, Ed Nelson, Bruno Ve Sota.

A retired gangster writing novels in Mexico is hunted by FBI men who want him to testify before a Senate committee and by mob hit men who want him dead because he is dropping names in his fiction. Low-budget crime drama of little interest.

p, Berj Hagopian; d, Mel Welles; w, Norman Toback, Allan Adrian.

Crime (PR:C MPAA:NR)

CODE OF THE CACTUS* (1939) 56m Victory bw
Tim McCoy, Dorothy Short, Ben Corbett, Dave O'Brien, Alden Chase, Ted Adams, Forrest Taylor, Bob Terry, Slim Whitaker, Frank Wayne, Kermit Maynard, Art Davis, Carl Sepulveda, Carl Mathews, Lee Burns, Clyde McClary, Jack King, Rube Dalroy.

Mindless horse-opera which offers the great McCoy little script or purpose of action as he ferrets out the baddies. Even the little buckeroos will turn off this one.

p, Sam Katzman; d, Sam Newfield; w, Edward Halperin.

Western (PR:A MPAA:NR)

CODE OF THE FEARLESS* (1939) 56m Spectrum bw
Fred Scott, Claire Rochelle, John Merton, Harry Harvey, Walter McGrail, Roger Williams, Carl Mathews, Frank LaRue, George Sherwood, William Woods, Gene Howard, Don Gallagher, James "Buddy" Kelly.

Routine oater has range rider Scott winning the heart of ranch girl Rochelle while subduing her evil oppressors. Tepid script and direction and merry-go-round chases add up to a poor effort.

p, C. C. Burr; d, Raymond K. Johnson; w, Fred Myton.

Western (PR:A MPAA:NR)

CODE OF THE LAWLESS½** (1945) 60m UNIV bw
Kirby Grant (Grant Carter), Poni Adams [Jane Adams] (Julie Randall), Fuzzy Knight (Bonanza), Hugh Prosser (Lester Ward), Barbara Sears (Ruth), Edward Howard (Bart Rogan), Rune Hultman (Chad Hilton, Jr.), Pierce Lyden (Pete), Roy Brent (Sam), Edmund Cobb (Nelson), Budd Buster (Rufe), Rex Lease (Crenshaw), Carey Harrison (Reb), Bob McKenzie (Amos Judd), Pietro Sosso (Perkins), Stanley Andrews (Chad Hilton, Sr.).

Grant pretends to be the son of a rancher fighting a crooked combine that has been forcing landowners to pay phony taxes; while battling the baddies, Grant wins the hand of a pretty postmistress. Not a very distinguished effort.

p&d, Wallace Fox; w, Patricia Harper; ph, Maury Gertsman; ed, Saul A. Goodkind.

Western (PR:A MPAA:NR)

CODE OF THE MOUNTED* (1935) 60m Ambassador bw
Kermit Maynard, Robert Warwick, Lillian Miles, Jim Thorpe, Syd Saylor, Wheeler Oakman, Dick Curtis, Stanley Blystone, Roger Williams, "Rocky".

A wasted western has Maynard battling Indians and bad guys who gang up on defenseless settlers. A poor production noted only for the inclusion of the great athlete Jim Thorpe who, by this time, was given small parts by charitable producers knowing his down-and-out status.

p, Maurice Conn, Sigmund Neufeld; d, Sam Newfield; w, George Sayre (based on the novel Wheels of Fate by James Oliver Curwood); ed, Jack English.

Western (PR:A MPAA:NR)

CODE OF THE OUTLAW½** (1942) 55m REP bw
Bob Steele, Tom Tyler, Rufe Davis, Weldon Heyburn, Ronnie Bartlett, Melinda Leighton, Donald Curtis, John Ince, Kenne Duncan, Phil Dunham, Max Waldman, Chuck Morrison, Carleton Young, Al Taylor, Robert Frazer, Forrest Taylor, Dick Alexander, Jack Ingram, Wally West, Edward Piel, Sr., Bud Osborne, Hank Worden, Cactus Mack.

A little boy, afraid to break a promise made to his father to never be a snitch, fails to inform his pals, the Three Mesquiteers (Steele, Tyler, and Davis), of a killer's identity. Boring plot in the usually adventurous series, that has Steele and Tyler giving clone-like performances, but Davis is funny as always.

p, Louis Gray; d, John English; w, Barry Shipman (based on characters created by William Colt MacDonald); ph, Reggie Lanning; ed, Charles Croft.

Western (PR:A MPAA:NR)

CODE OF THE PRAIRIE**

(1944) 56m REP bw

Sunset Carson (Himself), Smiley Burnette (Frog Millhouse), Peggy Stewart (Helen Matson), Weldon Heyburn (Jess Thorpe), Tom Chatterton (Bat Matson), Roy Barcroft ("Professor" David Larson Graham), Bud Geary (Lem), Tom London (Loomis), Jack Kirk (Boggs), Tom Steele (Burley), Bob Wilke, Frank Ellis (Outlaws in Office), Rex Lease, Henry Wills (Outlaws on Trail), Ken Terrell (Outlaw in Brawl), Charles King (Election Informer), Nolan Leary (Rancher), Hank Bell (Stage Driver Jim), Karl Hackett (Deputy Sheriff), Jack O'Shea (Townsman), Horace B. Carpenter (Townsman Jim).

Carson and sidekick Burnette ride into town to find their old friend, one-armed lawman Chatterton, being accosted by outlaws. They come to the rescue and learn that the town is being corrupted by the slimy heavy Barcroft. Barcroft is running his own candidate for sheriff, so Carson runs against him. Barcroft's man strongarms his way into office and appoints a number of his henchmen as deputies. Carson and Burnette come across these deputies robbing a stagecoach, and when the sheriff arrives shortly after, the bad guys finger Carson and Burnette as the robbers. He arrests them but suffers a crisis of conscience and confronts Barcroft with the crime. Barcroft decides to get rid of his man by framing him for the murder of Chatterton. Carson breaks jail, figures the whole thing out, and brings the lot to justice after a huge gunfight. Exciting, above average B Western.

d, Spencer Bennet; w, Albert DeMond, Anthony Coldeway (based on a story by DeMond); ph, Bud Thackery; ed, Harry Keller; md, Joseph Dubin.

Western   **(PR:A   MPAA:NR)**

CODE OF THE RANGE*½

(1937) 58m COL bw

Charles Starrett (Lee Jamison), Mary Blake (Janet Parker), Edward Coxen (Angus McLeod), Allan Caven (Parker), Albert J. Smith (Barney Ross), Ed Peil, Sr. (Sheriff), Edmund Cobb (Ed Randall), Edward Le Saint (Adams), Ralph McCullough (Quigley).

Starret stars as a kindly rancher who is willing to alter his property deed to accommodate a group of sheepmen. When the local cattle baron hears of this, he swipes Starrett's deed from a timid bank clerk whom he quickly kills in order to frame Starrett. When Starrett is given a chance to prove his innocence at a barroom trial, he collects enough evidence to prove the treachery and murderous tendencies of the cattle baron. Familiar western but one that helped Starrett, as a newcomer to westerns, slowly build a following in the genre that lasted through the early 1950s.

d, C. C. Coleman; w, Ford Beebe; story, Peter B. Kyne; ph, George Meehan; ed, William Lyon.

Western   **(PR:A   MPAA:NR)**

CODE OF THE RANGERS*½

(1938) 56m Concord/MON bw

Tim McCoy (Tim Strong), Rex Lease (Jack Strong), Judith Ford (Ann Sage), Frank La Rue (Dave Sage), Wheeler Oakman (Miller), Roger Williams (Lawson), Kit Guard (Red), Zeke Clemens (Singer).

When his no-good brother robs a bank, kind-hearted cowpoke McCoy takes the blame. Unable to deal with the guilt, brother Lease turns himself in and exposes the other members of the gang. Tame McCoy western that comes complete with just about every Western cliche imaginable.

d, Sam Newfield; w, Stanley Roberts; ph, Jack Creenhalgh.

Western   **(PR:A   MPAA:NR)**

CODE OF THE SADDLE*½

(1947) 53m MON bw

Johnny Mack Brown, Raymond Hatton, Riley Hill, Kay Morley, William Norton Bailey, Zon Murray, Ted Adams, Bud Osborne, Kenne Duncan, Jr., Gary Garrett, Curley Gibson, Jack Hendricks, Boyd Stockman, Bob McElroy, Ray Jones, Chick Hannon.

Brown provides the fisticuffs and gunplay and Hatton the chuckles in this horsey programmer which has more gunmen than Johnny has bullets.

p, Barney Sarecky; d, Thomas Carr; w, Eliot Biggons (based on a story by Albert DeMond).

Western   **(PR:A   MPAA:NR)**

CODE OF THE SECRET SERVICE*½

(1939) 58m WB bw

Ronald Reagan (Lt. "Brass" Bancroft), Rosella Towne (Elaine), Eddie Foy, Jr. (Gabby), Moroni Olsen (Friar Parker), Edgar Edwards (Ross), Jack Mower (Decker), John Gallaudet (Crackett), Joseph King (Saxby), Stevan Darrell (Butch), Sol Gorss (Dutch), George Regas (Officer), Frank Puglia (Conductor), Rafael Corio (1st Detective), Antonio Filauri (2nd Detective), Maris Wrixon (Secretary), George Offerman (Messenger), John Harron (Player), Jack Wise, Al Lloyd, Tom Wilson, Leo White, Jack Richardson (Men), Stuart Holmes (Croupier), Dick Botiller (Police Chief), Glen Cavender, Cliff Saum (Policemen), Frank Mayo (Manager) June Gittelson (Fat Girl), Pedro Regas (Diego), Martin Garralaga, Theodore Rand (Soldiers), Julian Rivero (Jailkeeper), Jose Luis Tortosa, Demetris Emanuel (Border Officers), Chris-Pin Martin (Pottery Proprietor), Wally West (Croupier).

When the engraving plates to some U.S. Treasury bank notes are stolen, T-men Reagan and Foy trail the counterfeiters to Mexico where they run into trouble with the locals. Drama succeeds in creating only the most absurd forms of suspense, a la Pearl White. For kids only. (Sequel to SECRET SERVICE OF THE AIR.)

p, Bryan Foy; d, Noel Smith; w, Lee Katz and Dean Franklin (based on their story "Smashing the Money Ring"); ph, Ted McCord; ed, Frederick Richards.

Crime   **(PR:A   MPAA:NR)**

CODE OF THE SILVER SAGE*½

(1950) 60m REP bw

Allan "Rocky" Lane (Himself), Black Jack (His Stallion), Eddy Waller (Nugget Clark),

Roy Barcroft (Hulon Champion), Kay Christopher (Ann Gately), Lane Bradford (Curt Watson), William Ruhl (Maj. Duncan), Richard Emory (Lt. John Case), Kenne Duncan (Dick Cantwell), Rex Lease (Capt. Matthews), Hank Patterson (Sgt. Woods), John Butler (Charlie Speed), Forrest Taylor (Sandy Wheeler).

When the law-abiding citizens of the Arizona territory write the President and ask him to make a public appearance that will warn off a group of killers, Secret Service agent Lane travels West to make sure that the area is safe for a presidential visit. Uncovering an assassination plot masterminded by cattle baron Barcroft, who dreams of being president himself, Lane captures the evil-doers before they can harm his employer. Mildly interesting oater whose plot could have been a pilot episode for television's Wild, Wild West series.

p, Gordon Kay; d, Fred C. Brannon; w, Arthur E. Orloff; ph, John MacBurnie; ed, Irving M. Schoenberg.

Western   **(PR:A   MPAA:NR)**

CODE OF THE STREETS*½

(1939) 73m UNIV bw

Harry Carey (Lt. Lewis), Frankie Thomas (Bob Lewis), James McCallion (Danny Shay), Leon Ames ("Chick" Foster), Juanita Quigley (Cynthia), Paul Fix (Tommy Shay), El Brendel (Merchant), Marc Lawrence (Halstead), Dorothy Arnold (Mildred), Stanley Hughes (Young Man), Harris Berger ("Sailor"), Hally Chester ("Murph"), Charles Duncan ("Monk"), William Benedict ("Trouble"), David Gorcey ("Yap").

When a teenager he believes is innocent is sent to prison for a killing, demoted cop Carey enlists the aid of street punks Berger, Chester, Duncan, Benedict, and Gorcey in tracking down the murderer. Unspectacular entry in the "Little Tough Guy" series that's given its only charm through Carey's simple acting style. (See BOWERY BOYS series, Index.)

p, Burt Kelly; d, Harold Young; w, Arthur T. Horman; ph, Elwood Brendel.

Drama   **(PR:A   MPAA:NR)**

CODE OF THE WEST**

(1947) 57m RKO bw

James Warren (Bob Wade), Debra Alden (Ruth), John Laurenz (Chito), Steve Brodie (Saunders), Rita Lynn (Pepita), Robert Clarke (Harry), Carol Forman (Milly), Harry Woods (Hatfield), Raymond Burr (Carter), Harry Harvey (Stockton), Phil Warren (Wescott), Emmett Lynn (Doc Quinn).

Warren leads a group of aspiring settlers in battle against outlaws who are inhibiting their rights to land and free enterprise. Routine but enjoyable western given a delightfully evil edge by magnetic-voiced Burr in his role as the leader of the desperadoes. In films for only a year, Burr won raves in CODE OF THE WEST for his playing of a smooth and sinister heavy.

p, Herman Schlom; d, William Berke; w, Norman Houston (based on a novel by Zane Grey); ph, Jack Mackenzie; m, Paul Sawtell; ed, Ernie Leadlay; m/l, "Rainbow Valley" (Lew Pollack, Harry Harris).

Western   **(PR:A   MPAA:NR)**

CODE 7, VICTIM 5*½

(1964, Brit.) 88m Towers of London/COL c (GB: VICTIM FIVE)

Lex Barker (Steve Martin), Ronald Fraser (Inspector Lean), Ann Smyrner (Helga Swenson), Veronique Vendell (Gina), Walter Rilla (Wexler), Dietmar Schoenherr (Paul), Percy Sieff (Anderson), Gustel Gundelach (Kramer), Gert Van den Bergh (Vanberger), Howard Davis (Rawlings), Sophia Spentzos (Leila).

When the beloved valet of a millionaire is murdered, American private detective Barker is hired by the old businessman to uncover the murderer. Barker travels to South Africa where he discovers that the murder was linked to a group of Nazi prisoners of war who never returned to Germany. Stupid James Bond ripoff given a clean, lush look by cinematographer Roeg who later became one of the most complex, disturbing directors of the 1970s and 1980s, his films including DON'T LOOK NOW and THE MAN WHO FELL TO EARTH.

p, Harry Alan Towers, Skip Steloff; d, Robert Lynn; w, Peter Yeldham (based on a story by Peter Welbeck [Towers]); ph, Nicholas Roeg (Techniscope, Technicolor); m, Johnny Douglas; ed, John Trumper; prod d, John Comfort.

Action Drama   **(PR:A   MPAA:NR)**

CODE TWO**½

(1953) 69m MGM bw

Ralph Meeker (Chuck O'Flair), Sally Forrest (Mary Hardley), Keenan Wynn (Jumbo), Robert Horton (Russ Hardley), James Craig (Lt. Redman), Elaine Stewart (Jane), Jeff Richards (Harry Whenlon), Jonathan Cott (Truck Driver), Robert Burton (Capt. Williams), William Campbell (Companion), Fred Graham (Sgt. Payne).

More than thirty years after this film was made the comedy version, POLICE ACADEMY, was a huge success. This was not, and probably because it could have used some humor to lighten the ordinary tale it told. Meeker, Richards and Horton are three aspiring policemen taking the three-months motorcycle course at the police academy. Meeker is a confident Jimmy Cagney type without the elan to carry it off. The three buddies are like the Geste brothers until Richards is killed when two hijackers run him down. The rest of the film is a chase that culminates when Meeker nails the gang at the finale. Most of the actors were bit players before getting their big chances in this second-biller. It didn't enhance their careers much. Craig, who had already been a star (THE DEVIL AND DANIEL WEBSTER, THE HUMAN COMEDY, KISMET, etc.), was on his way down. Craig was educated at Rice Institute and had intended being a doctor until sidetracked by the acting bug. There was a rumor to the effect that Craig, born James Meador, had taken his name from a role he played in CRAIG'S WIFE in the same way that Gig Young and L. Q. Jones took their screen names from roles in films. His first film was THUNDER TRAIL. Producer Grady was son of the MGM chief of talent at that time. Nepotism will out.

p, William Grady, Jr.; d, Fred M. Wilcox; w, Marcel Klauber; ph, Ray June; m, Alberto Colombo; ed, Frederick Y. Smith.

Crime Drama (PR:A MPAA:NR)

COFFY* (1973) 91m AIP c

Pam Grier (Coffy), Booker Bradshaw (Brunswick), Robert DoQui (King George), William Elliott (Carter), Allan Arbus (Vitroni), Sid Haig (Omar), Barry Cahill (McHenry), Morris Buchanan (Sugar-Man), Lee de Broux (Nick), Bob Minor (Studs), John Perak (Aleva), Ruben Moreno (Ramos), Carol Lawson (Priscilla), Linda Haynes (Meg), Lisa Farringer (Jeri).

When her adolescent sister becomes permanently spaced-out because of heroin addiction, tough street mama Grier packs up her shotgun and goes on a one-woman killing spree, wiping out the vermin who forced her sister's habit upon her. Intense, edgy, extremely violent black exploitation thriller that made a star out of the incredibly attractive Grier. Many may consider the film's bloodletting morally reprehensible.

p, Robert A. Papazian; d, Jack Hill; w, Hill; ph, Paul Lohmann (Movielab Color); m, Roy Ayers; ed, Charles McClelland; art d, Perry Ferguson.

Drama (PR:O MPAA:R)

COGNASSE** (1932, Fr.) 95m Joinville-PAR/PAR bw

Tramel (Cognasse), Therese Doray (Mme. Cognasse), Marguerite Moreno (The Nurse), Andre Roanne (Paul Fargeot).

When laborer Tramel is given complete control of his worker-conscious employer's factory, his socialist tendencies dissipate quickly when he begins to appreciate being part of the elite. (In French; English subtitles.)

d, Louis Mercanton; based on the play by Rip; m, Raoul Moretti; m/l, Rip.

Comedy (PR:A MPAA:NR)

COHENS AND KELLYS IN AFRICA, THE*½ (1930) 70m UNIV bw

George Sidney (Mr. Cohen), Charlie Murray (Mr. Kelly), Vera Gordon (Mrs. Cohen), Kate Price (Mrs. Kelly), Frank Davis (Windjammer Thorn), Lloyd Whitlock (Sheik), Nick Cogley (Guide), Ed Kane (Chief).

Poor entry in the long-running "The Cohens and Kellys" series starring Sidney and Murray as the always feuding Jewish and Irish business rivals. This time, Sidney and Murray are piano manufacturers who travel to Africa to replenish their ivory supply, with less than hysterical results. (See COHENS AND KELLYS series, Index.)

d, Vin Moore; w, W. K. Wells (based on a story by Moore and Edward Luddy); ph, Hal Mohr.

Comedy (PR:A MPAA:NR)

COHENS AND KELLYS IN ATLANTIC CITY, THE** (1929) 70m UNIV bw

George Sidney (Mr. Cohen), Mack Swain (Mr. Kelly), Kate Price (Mrs. Kelly), Vera Gordon (Mrs. Cohen), Nora Lane, Tom Kennedy, Cornelius Keefe.

When the son and daughter of conservative bathing suit manufacturing rivals Sidney and Swain surprise their parents by introducing a new line of risque swim attire in Atlantic City, their respective moms and dads fume over the immorality of the attire but delight in its economic profitability. Fair entry with synchronized score and incidental dialog. Moderately appealing. (See COHENS AND KELLYS series, Index.)

d, William J. Craft; w, Jack Townley (based on the play "Two Blocks Away" by Aaron Hoffman).

Comedy (PR:A MPAA:NR)

COHENS AND KELLYS IN HOLLYWOOD, THE** (1932) 75m UNIV bw

George Sidney (Mr. Cohen), Charlie Murray (Mr. Kelly), June Clyde (Kitty Kelly), Norman Foster (Melville Cohen), Emma Dunn (Mrs. Cohen), Esther Howard (Mrs. Kelly), Eileen Percy (Writer), Edwin Maxwell (Chauncey Chadwick), Dorothy Christy (Mrs. Chadwick), Luis Alberna (Solarsky), Joh Roche (Gregory Gordan) Robert Greig (Chester Field) Harris Barris.

The usual Sidney/Murray Jewish/Irish business rivalry is downplayed in this Cohens and Kellys entry, the filmmakers paying more attention to Foster's devotion to aspiring actress Clyde. With father Sidney owning a movie house, son Foster finagles a screen test for his beloved and soon Clyde is a popular screen star. She forgets her former beau when faced with affluent living and socialite friends, but returns to Foster when her popularity fades with the advent of sound in cinema. Boris Karloff, Tom Mix, Lew Ayres, Sidney Fox, and Genevieve Tobin appear in cameo roles in the Cocoanut Grove restaurant, where the film-struck families visit to gawk at celebrities. (See COHENS AND KELLYS series, Index.)

p, Carl Laemmle, Jr.; d, John Francis Dillon; w, Howard J. Green, James Mulhouser (based on characters created by Aaron Hoffman); ph, Jerome Ash; ed, Harry Webb.

Comedy (PR:A MPAA:NR)

COHENS AND KELLYS IN SCOTLAND, THE½** (1930) 84m UNIV bw

George Sidney (Nathan Cohen), Charlie Murray (Patrick Kelly), Vera Gordon (Mrs. Cohen), Kate Price (Mrs. Kelly), E. J. Ratcliffe (McPherson), William Colvin (McDonald), Lloyd Whitlock (Prince), John McDermott.

When they both predict that Scottish tartan will be the next big thing in fashion, clothing business rivals Murray and Sidney travel to bonnie Scotland to monopolize the plaid trade. Perhaps the best in the Cohens and Kellys cycle, the film contains a truly hilarious golf match between the two protagonists. (See Cohens and Kellys series, Index.)

d, William James Craft; w, Albert DeMond (based on a story by John McDermott from characters created by Aaron Hoffman).

Comedy (PR:A MPAA:NR)

COHENS AND KELLYS IN TROUBLE, THE** (1933) 69m UNIV bw

George Sidney (Nathan Cohen), Charles Murray (Patrick Kelly), Maureen O'Sullivan (Mollie Kelly), Andy Devine (Andy Anderson), Jobyna Howland (Queenie Truelove), Maude Fulton (Miss Fern), Frank Albertson (Bob Graham), Henry Armetta (Captain Silva).

This time around, Sidney and Murray are rival tugboat captains whose ownership of the waterways is hilariously contested. Another outstanding feature in the Cohens and Kellys series. (See Cohens and Kellys series, Index.)

d, George Stevens; w, Homer Croy and Vernon Smith (based on characters created by Aaron Hoffman).

Comedy (PR:A MPAA:NR)

COLD JOURNEY*½ (1975, Can.) 75m National Film Board of Canada c

Johnny Yesno, Buckley Petawabano, Chief Dan George.

Yesno is a Canadian Indian raised in the white man's world who finds himself out of place in either world. Should have been much better, but unfortunately isn't, largely due to incompetent and uninspired direction.

p, George Pearson; d, Martin Defalco; w, David Jones; ph, Tony Ianzelo (Eastmancolor); m, Eldon Rathburn; art d, Denis Boucher; m/l, Willie Dunn.

Drama (PR:C MPAA:NR)

COLD RIVER*½ (1982) 94m Cold River Pictures/PI c

Suzanne Weber (Lizzy Allison), Pat Petersen (Tim Hood), Richard Jaeckel (Mike Allison), Robert Earl Jones (The Trapper), Brad Sullivan (Reuben Knat), Elizabeth Hubbard (Pauline Hood Allison), Augusta Dabney (Elizabeth Allison), Adam Petroski (Seth Bishop), David Thomas (Senate Chairman), Wade Barnes (Pompous Senator), Deborah Beck (Reporter), Trent Gough (Minister), Robert Donley (Pete the Guide), Thomas Kubiak (Storekeeper), Mary Ellen Badger (Receptionist), Muriel Mason (Lady in Wheelchair), Margo Lacy (Lady's Daughter), Theodore C. Sweeney, Linda Videtti, Chris Curran, Ken Briell, Jan Naud.

Ridiculous look at the rough but kind people who inhabit the harsh Adirondack region in New York state and those who wishto destroy its rugged beauty. Poorly made low-budget "wilderness" picture where the scenery is supposed to be the only thing the audience is interested in.

p,d&w, Fred G. Sullivan (based on a novel by William Judson); ph, Bill Godsey (Technicolor); m, Michael Gibson; ed, John Carter; m/l, "Winter Nights" (Michael Gibson, Jim Wann).

Adventure Cas. (PR:A MPAA:PG)

COLD SWEAT** (1974, Ital., Fr.) 94m Emerson c
(L'UOMO DALLE DUE OMBRE; DE LA PART DES COPAINS)

Charles Bronson (Joe), Liv Ullman (Fabienne), James Mason (Ross), Jill Ireland (Moira), Jean Topart (Katanga), Yannick Delulle (Michele), Luigi Pistilli (Fausto), Michael Constantin (Whitey).

Typical Bronson blood 'n' guts fare in which the whipcord-muscled hero plays an American expatriate operating a small fishing boat on France's Cote d'Azur. There he lives an idyllic existence with his wife, Ullman, and their daughter, Delulle. But Bronson has kept his past secret and soon drug smugglers (former comrades) led by Mason (attempting an American Southern accent) try to force him into more illegal activities by kidnapping his family. Bronson retaliates by kidnapping Mason's mistress, Ireland, who has the money necessary for the crooks to pull their caper. After many bloody gun battles and dangerous auto chases, Mason and his hoods are killed and Bronson and family go off to enjoy the Bastille Day celebration.

p, Robert Dorfmann; d, Terence Young; w, Shimon Wincelberg, Albert Simonin (based on the novel Ride The Nightmare by Richard Matheson); ph, Jean Rabier (Eastmancolor); m, Michael Magne; ed, Johnny Dwyre; art d, Tony Roman.

Crime Cas. (PR:O MPAA:PG)

COLD TURKEY** (1971) 99m UA c

Dick Van Dyke (Rev. Clayton Brooks), Pippa Scott (Natalie Brooks), Tom Poston (Mr. Stopworth), Edward Everett Horton (Hiram C. Grayson), Bob Elliott, Ray Goulding (TV Personalities Bob and Ray), Bob Newhart (Merwin Wren), Vincent Gardenia (Mayor Wrappler), Barnard Hughes (Dr. Procter), Graham Jarvis (Amos Bush), Jean Stapleton (Mrs. Wrappler), Barbara Cason (Letitia), Judith Lowry (Odie), Sudie Bond (Cissy), Helen Page Camp (Mrs. Watson), Paul Benedict (Zen Buddhist), Simon Scott (Mr. Kandiss), Raymond Kark (Homer Watson), Peggy Rea (Mrs. Proctor), George Mann (Bishop Manley), Charles Pinney (Col. Galloway), M. Emmet Walsh (Art), Gloria LeRoy (The Hooker), Eric Boles (Dennis), Jack Grimes (TV Stage Manager), Walter Sande, Woodrow Parfrey (Tobacco Executives), Harvey Jason (Hypnotist).

Horton is a tobacco king who offers $25 million to any town that can quit smoking. It's all a fraud perpetrated by public relations flack Newhart to get the company a billion dollars worth of publicity. Van Dyke is a hick-town parson who sees that he can put himself and the town on the map by winning this challenge. His motivations are strictly selfish but the secondary benefits will be worth it, he feels. Lots of finely etched characterizations from Stapleton, as the wife of mayor Gardenia, who begins eating furiously and gains weight as we watch; super-patriots Jarvis and Lowry (she's a little old lady out hunting commie rats with a pistol); Poston as the town's cad; Hughes as the doctor; Bond as the banker, and Scott, one of the sanest people in the film, as Van Dyke's wife. The ending is a cop-out as Lear writes himself into a box that he cannot escape from. Until then there's enough solid laughter from the excellent cast to keep you going for a long while. Lear wears too many hats in this production and drops the ball more than once as he over indulges us with jokes rather than more human character humor. This was before he became CBS's savior with "All In The Family" and several other comedy hits. Lear is definitely more at home on the small screen where flaws are not so easily spotted and where a story need run only twenty-four minutes and twenty-five seconds to fill out the commercial half-hour. When he attempts to work on the big screen (NEVER TOO LATE; DIVORCE, AMERICAN STYLE, etc.), his shortcomings are evident. This was his best film to date. Horton gave his last performance in COLD TURKEY and didn't say a word. His eloquence was appreciated. Stapleton had a small role and was cast for "All In The Family" after working with Lear on this film. The best thing about the movie was the appearance of Bob and Ray as TV personality newscasters (Walter Chronic, etc.).

p&d, Norman Lear; w, Lear (based on a story by Lear and William Price Fox, Jr. Based on unpublished novel *I'm Giving Them Up For Good* by Margaret and Neil Rau); ph, Charles F. Wheeler (DeLuxe Color); m, Randy Newman; ed, John C. Horger; art d, Arch Bacon; cos, Rita Riggs.

Comedy   **(PR:A   MPAA:PG)**

COLD WIND IN AUGUST**
(1961) 79m Aidart Pictures bw
Lola Albright *(Iris Hartford)*, Scott Marlowe *(Vito Perugino)*, Herschel Bernardi *(Juley Franz)*, Joe De Santis *(Papa Perugino)*, Clark Gordon *(Harry)*, Janet Brandt *(Shirley)*, Skip Young *(Al)*, Ann Atmar *(Carol)*, Jana Taylor *(Alice)*, Dee Gee Green *(Mary)*.

After his sexy, kind upstairs neighbor Albright introduces 17-year-old Marlowe to the pleasures of the flesh, he, of course, falls in love with the older woman, but is heartbroken when he learns that she is a body goddess on the burlesque circuit. Mildly interesting tale of adolescent attitudes towards morality and love.

p, Phillip Hazelton; d, Alexander Singer; w, Burton Wohl (based on his novel); ph, Floyd Crosby;m, Gerald Fried; ed, Jerry Young.

Drama   **(PR:O   MPAA:NR)**

COLDITZ STORY, THE***
(1955, Brit.) 97m BL bw
John Mills *(Pat Reid)*, Eric Portman *(Col. Richmond)*, Christopher Rhodes *(Mac)*, Lionel Jeffries *(Harry)*, Bryan Forbes *(Jimmy)*, Ian Carmichael *(Robin)*, Richard Wattis *(Richard)*, David Yates *(Dick)*, Frederick Valk *(Kommandant)*, Denis Shaw *(Priem)*, Anton Diffring *(Fischer)*, Ludwig Lawinski *(Franz Josef)*, Carl Duering *(German Officer)*, Keith Pyott *(French Colonel)*, Eugene Deckers *(La Tour)*, Rudolf Offenbach *(Dutch Colonel)*, Theodore Bikel *(Vandy)*, Arthur Butcher *(Polish Colonel)*.

At Colditz castle, the Nazis' escape-proof war prison, Mills and other "problem" POWs from the British, Dutch, French, and Polish armies, try to figure out various ways of escape. After a tunnel is discovered through the cooperation of a Polish spy planted by the Germans and several men are machine-gunned to death trying to bridge the sea of barbed wire that surrounds the fortress, Mills and three others successfully escape when they don German uniforms and casually walk through the officers' mess and out of the main gate of Colditz. Suspenseful, often humorous war drama that portrays the compelling drive to escape that was inherent in many British POWs. The imposing, frightening qualities of Colditz are well-presented, lending credence to "impossible task" qualities of the script. The cast, especially Mills, is uniformly excellent. The story was based on the personal experiences of the author and conscientiously adapted for the screen.

p, Ivan Foxwell; d, Guy Hamilton; w, Hamilton, Foxwell (based on book by P. R. Reid); ph, Gordon Dines; m, Francis Chagrin; ed, Peter Mayhew.

War Drama   **Cas.**   **(PR:A   MPAA:NR)**

COLE YOUNGER, GUNFIGHTER**
(1958) 78m AA c
Frank Lovejoy *(Younger)*, James Best *(Kit)*, Abby Dalton *(Lucy)*, Jan Merlin *(Frank)*, Douglas Spencer *(Woodruff)*, Ainslie Pryor *(Follyard)*, Frank Ferguson *(Wittrock)*, Myron Healey *(Bennett Twins)*, George Keymas *(Price)*, Dan Sheridan *(Phelps)*, John Mitchum *(Bartender)*.

After protesting the dishonesty of local government, cowpoke Best is forced out of town, leaving his sweetheart, Dalton, open to the advances of Merlin. Best befriends kind-hearted outlaw Lovejoy and when Best is accused of murders Merlin committed, Lovejoy bursts into the courtroom and "sticks up" the proceedings. Merlin is exposed as the actual killer, Best is reunited with Dalton, and Lovejoy returns to the secret life of a frontier fugitive. Romanticized view of Cole Younger that uses the ruthless desperado as a kind of savior in terms of resolving the familiar drama. A lightweight effort from scriptwriter Mainwaring, who did much better with tougher pictures like OUT OF THE PAST and BABY FACE NELSON. It was the last film for Lovejoy, whose career was in decline; he was to die four years later.

p, Ben Schwalb; d, R. G. Springsteen; w, Daniel Mainwaring (based on a story by Clifton Adams); ph, Harry Neumann (CinemaScope, DeLuxe Color); m, Marlin Skiles; ed, William Austin.

Western   **(PR:A   MPAA:NR)**

COLLECTOR, THE**
(1965) 117m William Wyler/COL c
Terence Stamp *(Freddie Clegg)*, Samantha Eggar *(Miranda Grey)*, Mona Washbourne *(Aunt Annie)*, Maurice Dallimore *(The Neighbor)*, William Beckley *(Crutchley)*, Gordon Barclay, David Haviland *(Clerks)*.

Four Oscar nominations were awarded (Mann, Kohn, Wyler, Eggar) but no statuettes were given to this thriller that could have been one of the best were it not for sluggish direction from one of the best helmsmen around. The story concerns Stamp, a wimpy bank clerk with a dull life that is only relieved by his collection of butterflies. He falls in love with Eggar, a lovely art student, and wishes she could return the feelings, but she is frankly repulsed by his attentions. When Stamp wins $200,000 in the football pools he is able to quit his job and indulge any whim he wishes, so he purchases a farmhouse a good distance out of town where no one will bother him. This house has a most comfortable cellar, which is the reason why he bought the house in the first place. He kidnaps Eggar and forces her into the basement, which has been comfortably furnished

with anything she might need and several accoutrements that indicate a loving nature; clothes in her size, art books, records of fine classical pieces—everything one might ask for in prison. And that's just what he's built—a plush cell for the woman of his dreams. At no time does he lay a hand on her but the tension keeps building; unfortunately it doesn't build fast enough. This might have made a better play than a film as it suffers from constriction in much the same way SLEUTH did. There are only two other actors with speaking roles and they do the best with what they have, which isn't much. Eggar was first seen in this country in a bit part in THE WILD AND THE WILLING, an interesting collegiate drama that also served to acquaint American audiences with the talents of John Hurt, Ian McShane, Jeremy Brett, and Virginia Maskell. Her role in THE COLLECTOR won her the Best Actress award at the Cannes Film Festival.

p, Jud Kinberg; d, William Wyler; w, Stanley Mann, John Kohn (based on the novel by John Fowles); ph, Robert L Surtees (Hollywood), Robert Krasker (England) (Technicolor); m, Maurice Jarre; ed, Robert Swink; art d, John Stoll.

Drama   **Cas.**   **(PR:C   MPAA:NR)**

COLLEEN***
(1936) 89m WB bw
Dick Powell *(Donald Ames III)*, Ruby Keeler *(Colleen Reiley)*, Jack Oakie *(Joe Cork)*, Joan Blondell *(Minnie Mawkins)*, Hugh Herbert *(Cedric Ames)*, Louise Fazenda *(Alicia Ames)*, Paul Draper *(Paul)*, Luis Alberni *(Carlo)*, Marie Wilson *(Mabel)*, Mary Treen *(Miss Hively)*, Hobart Cavanaugh *(Noggin)*, Berton Churchill *(Logan)*, J. M. Kerrigan *(Pop Reiley)*, Spencer Charters *(Dr. Frothingham)*, Addison Richards *(Schuyler)*, Charles Coleman *(Butler)*, Colleen Colman *(Lois)*, Herbert Evans *(Footman)*, Viola Lowry *(Receptionist)*, Emmett Vogan *(Official)*, Cyril Ring *(Client)*, Harry Depp *(Assistant)*, Shirley Lloyd *(Girl)*, Bob Murphy, Ward Bond *(Cops)*, Alma Lloyd *(Nurse)*, Sarah Edwards, Laura Pierpont *(Society Women)*, John Albright *(Page Boy)*, Alphonse Martel *(Head Waiter)*, Andre Cheron *(Waiter)*, Iris March *(Miss Graham)*, Edward Keane *(Edwards)*, George Andre Beranger *(Jeweler)*, Pauline Caron *(Maid)*, Antonio Filauri *(Bartender)*, Charles E. Delaney *(Ship's Radio Operator)*, Joan Barclay *(Cafe Guest)*.

Powell and Keeler had starred together five times before this and it's a shame they had to go out with one of the studio's weaker efforts. Herbert is a nutty millionaire who falls in love with blowsy Blondell, factory worker. He puts her in charge of a fancy-shmancy dress salon he buys for her. Meanwhile, Blondell's real boyfriend, Oakie, promises to marry her as soon as Herbert adopts the blonde as his daughter. Herbert has other ideas on his mind. Powell enters (he's Herbert's nephew) and sees that the dotty old fella is being taken but good by Joan and Jack. Powell convinces Herbert to close the shop, despite the good work being done by Keeler who is running the millinery operations. Herbert pays off Oakie and Blondell, then offers money to Keeler to quit the store. By this time, Keeler is head over tap shoes in love with Powell (for the sixth movie) and she doesn't know that Dick had no part of that offer. She takes the ten grand check, opens a dress shop on a cruise ship, not knowing that Powell and Herbert are on the same vessel going to Europe. Dick and Ruby meet, fall in love again, and wind up holding hands and singing to each other. Harry Warren and Al Dubin didn't turn out any hits for this film but the songs were pleasant enough and Ruby did get a chance to do two dance routines with Paul Draper, who was sort of a Triple-A Fred Astaire. This really was the typical 1930s musical; pleasant, inoffensive, toe-tapping, and funny at times. Songs "I Don't Have To Dream Again," "You've Gotta Know How To Dance," "An Evening With You," "A Boulevardier From the Bronx" (Al Dubin, Harry Warren).

d, Alfred E. Green; w, Peter Milne, F. Hugh Herbert, Sig Herzig (based on a story by Robert Lord); ph, George Barnes; ed, Byron Haskin; md, Leo Forbstein; art d, Max Parker; cos, Orry-Kelly; ch, Bobby Connolly.

Musical Comedy   **(PR:A   MPAA:NR)**

COLLEGE COACH**
(1933) 75m WB bw (GB: FOOTBALL COACH)
Dick Powell *(Phil Sargent)*, Ann Dvorak *(Claire Gore)*, Pat O'Brien *(Coach Gore)*, Arthur Byron *(Dr. Phillip Sargent)*, Lyle Talbot *(Buck Weaver)*, Hugh Herbert *(Barnett)*, Guinn "Big Boy" Williams *(Matthews)*, Donald Meek *(Spencer Trask)*, Harry Beresford *(Professor)*, Herman Bing, Joe Sauers.

Cynical, unsympathetic, often amusing look at college football and the big-headed coaches who make the amateur sport entertaining. Powell is woefully miscast as a crooning football star who needs to be whipped into shape, but O'Brien is a delight as the tyrannical coach who does the whipping. Songs: "Lonely Lane," "Men of Calvert" (Irving Kahal, Sammy Fain), "Just One More Chance" (Sam Coslow, Arthur Johnson), "Meet Me In the Gloaming" (Arthur Freed, Al Hoffman, Al Goodhart), "What Will I Do Without You?" (Johnny Mercer, Hilda Gottlieb).

p, Robert Lord; d, William Wellman; w, Niven Busch, Manuel Seff; ph, Arthur Todd; ed, Thomas Pratt; art d, Jack Okey.

Sports Drama   **(PR:A   MPAA:NR)**

COLLEGE CONFIDENTIAL**
(1960) 91m UNIV bw
Steve Allen *(Steve Macinter)*, Jayne Meadows *(Betty Duquesne)*, Mamie Van Doren *(Sally Blake)*, Rocky Marciano *(Deputy Sheriff)*, Mickey Shaughnessey *(Sam Grover)*, Cathy Crosby *(Fay Grover)*, Herbert Marshall *(Henry Addison)*, Conway Twitty *(Marvin)*, Randy Sparks *(Phil)*, Pamela Mason *(Edna Blake)*, Elisha Cook *(Ted Blake)*, Theona Bryant *(Lois Addison)*, Norman Grabowski *(Skippy)*, Ziva Rodann *(Gogo Lazlo)*, Robert Montgomery, Jr. *(2nd Boy)*, William Wellman, Jr. *(Bob)*, Nancy Root *(Sweet Young Thing)*, Walter Winchell, Sheilah Graham, Earl Wilson, Louis Sobol, and the Hollywood press corps *(Themselves)*.

Ridiculous expose on campus sex from the man who brought out another ridiculous expose on teenage drug abuse, HIGH SCHOOL CONFIDENTIAL (1958), Albert Zugsmith. Allen stars as a college professor taking a scientific survey on the sexual habits of modern-day college students. Before he knows it he's brought up on indecency charges, much to the dismay of Meadows (Mrs. Allen in real life). The climax sees Allen on trial (in a grocery) with such real-life journalists as Winchell and Graham in attendance. Bizarre cast includes boxer Marciano as a deputy sheriff and Conway Twitty who sings. Strange.

p&d, Albert Zugsmith; w, Irvin Shulman; m/l, Randy Sparks, Conway Twitty.

Drama (PR:C MPAA:NR)

COLLEGE COQUETTE, THE zero (1929) 68m COL bw
Ruth Taylor (*Betty Forrester*), William Collier, Jr. (*Tom Marion*), Jobyna Ralston (*Doris Marlowe*), John Holland (*Harvey Porter*), Adda Gleason (*Ethel Forrester*), Gretchen Hartman (*Mrs. Marlowe*), Frances Lyons (*Edna*), Edward Piel, Jr. (*Slim*), Edward Clayton (*Ted*), Morris Murphy (*Jimmy Doolittle*).

Anxious to be socially accepted by the college crowd, shy freshman Ralston becomes friends with campus tramp Taylor who fixes the innocent girl up with local cad Collier. After falling in love with the dapper Collier and compromising her virtue for him, Ralston is heartbroken when she learns that he was simply having some fun with her. Terribly upset and in tears, Ralston dies a tragic accidental death when she falls down an elevator shaft. Absurd melodrama about the perils of popularity and peer pressure that is unintentionally laughable.

d, George Archinbaund; w, Ralph Graves.

Drama (PR:A MPAA:NR)

COLLEGE HOLIDAY**½ (1936) 87m PAR bw
Jack Benny (*J. Davis Bowster*), George Burns (*George Hymen*), Gracie Allen (*Calliope Dove*), Mary Boland (*Carola Gaye*), Martha Raye (*Daisy Schloggenheimer*), Etienne Girardot (*Prof. Hercules Dove*), Marsha Hunt (*Sylvia Smith*), Leif Erikson (*Dick Winters*), Eleanore Whitney (*Eleanor Wayne*), Johnny Downs (*Johnny Jones*), Olympe Bradna (*Felice L'Hommedieu*), Louis DaPron (*Barry Taylor*), Ben Blue (*Stage Hand*), Jed Prouty (*Sheriff*), Richard Carle (*Judge Bent*), Margaret Beddon (*Mrs. Schloggenheimer*), Nick Lukats (*Wisconsin*), Spec O'Donnell (*Lafayette*),Jack Chapin (*Colgate*), California Collegians (*Themselves*), Nora Cecil (*Miss Elkins*), Ellen Drew (*Student*), Snowflake Toones (*Porter*), Charlie Arnt (*Clerk*), Harry Hayden (*Mr. Smith*), Howard Mitchell (*Deputy*), Buddy Messinger (*Minstrel*), Joseph Franz, Earl Pingree (*Policemen*), Ray Hansford (*Deputy Sheriff*), Marjorie Reynolds, Eddie Foy (*Dancers*).

A truly silly spoof that is like the little girl with the little curl right in the middle of her forehead. When it's good, it's very good and when it is bad it is horrid. Allen is an ancient Greece buff (hence the name Calliope Dove) who holds the mortgage on a failing resort hotel. She wants to convert the place into a gigantic sexual laboratory for the express purpose of mating perfect specimens of both sexes. (While this movie was satirizing eugenics, the practice was actually taking place in Nazi Germany where a master race of perfect Aryans was being attempted.) Benny's job is to recruit prospects but he gets a bunch of college students instead, all of whom happen to be terrific performers. They put on a minstrel show, make a lot of money, and the hotel is saved. The whole thing is never taken seriously and, in case you happened to mistake the intent, Benny comes on screen at the tail end to explain that none of this was for real and he hopes you enjoyed it. This movie was in the genre of the BIG BROADCAST films of the era in that they all had paper-thin storylines with a chance to string together a raft of specialty numbers. In the case of COLLEGE HOLIDAY, the specialities were Ben Blue's wonderful mime work, Martha Raye's singing, comedy duets by Burns and Allen, and some neat dancing by Whitney and Downs. Not much else to recommend here as the dialog is hokey (even for that day) and the theme is mindless. All of that aside, you'll laugh a little and marvel at some of the dancing. Songs include: "I Adore You," "A Rhyme For Love," "So What?" "Love In Bloom" (Ralph Rainger, Leo Robin), "Who's That Knocking At My Heart?" "The Sweetheart Waltz" (Burton Lane, Ralph Freed).

p, Harlan Thompson; d, Frank Tuttle; w, J. P. McEvoy, Jay Gorney, Harlan Ware, Henry Myers; ph, Theodore Sparkuhl, William C. Meller; md, Boris Morros; ch, LeRoy Prinz.

Musical Comedy (PR:A MPAA:NR)

COLLEGE HUMOR** (1933) 68m PAR bw
Bing Crosby (*Frederick Danvers*), Jack Oakie (*Barney Shirrel*), Richard Arlen (*Mondrake*), Mary Carlisle (*Barbara Shirrel*), Mary Kornman (*Amber*), George Burns (*Himself*), Gracie Allen (*Herself*), Joseph Sauers (*Tex Roust*), Lona Andre (*Ginger*).

When campus queen Carlisle falls for singing professor Crosby, her football star admirer Arlen becomes jealous and his interest in his sport diminishes, jeopardizing the team's standings. Sloppily made early vehicle for Crosby who would soon enter the most important stage of his career. Songs: "Down the Old Ox Road," "Learn To Croon," "Moon Struck," "Play Ball," "Alma Mater," "Colleen Of Killarney," "I'm A Bachelor Of the Art Of Ha-Cha-Cha" (Arthur Johnston, Sam Coslow).

d, Wesley Ruggles; w, Claude Binyon and Frank Butler (based on a story by Dean Fales); ph, Leo Tover; m/l, Sam Coslow and Arthur Johnston.

Musical (PR:A MPAA:NR)

COLLEGE LOVE*½ (1929) 80m UNIV bw
George Lewis, Dorothy Gulliver, Eddie Phillips, Churchill Ross, Hayden Stevenson, Sumner Getchell.

When his football pal, Phillips, is suspected of having been drunk on the day of a game, Lewis takes the blame for his pal's indiscretion and is sacked from the team. On the day of the big game, when the entire team knows that they need Lewis for a key play, Phillips tells the truth about the drinking incident and Lewis is brought onto the field in time to save the day. Hokey, part-talkie football picture that has the unmistakeable Carl Laemmle, Jr. assembly-line signature on it.

p, Carl Laemmle, Jr.; d, Nat Ross; w, Leonard Fields, John B. Clymer, Pierre Couderc, Albert De Mond; ph, George Robinson.

Sports Drama (PR:A MPAA:NR)

COLLEGE LOVERS*½ (1930) 61m FN bw
Jack Whiting (*Frank Taylor*), Frank McHugh (*"Speed" Haskins*), Guinn Williams (*Al "Tiny" Courtlay*), Russell Hopton (*Eddie Smith*), Wade Boteler (*Coach Donovan*), Marion Nixon (*Mary Hutton*), Phyllis Crane (*Josephine*), Richard Tucker (*Gene Hutton*), Charles Judels.

College football mates Whiting and McHugh try to out-do each other on the gridiron to win the affections of campus cutie Nixon, who unknown to them, is in love with a bookworm. Comedy contains a few humorous scenes that detail the stupid masculine deeds. Songs: "Up And At' Em," "One Minute Of Heaven."

d, John Adolfi; w, Douglas Doty (based on a story by Earl Baldwin); ph, Frank Kesson; ed, Fred Smith.

Sports Comedy (PR:A MPAA:NR)

COLLEGE RHYTHM** (1934) 75m PAR bw
Joe Penner (*Joe*), Lanny Ross (*Larry Stacey*), Jack Oakie (*Finnegan*), Helen Mack (*June Cort*), Lyda Roberti (*Mimi*), Mary Brian (*Gloria Van Dayham*), George Barbier (*J. P. Stacey*), Franklin Pangborn (*Peabody*), Mary Wallace (*Peggy Small*), Dean Jagger (*Coach*), Joseph Sauers (*Spud Miller*), Julian Madison (*Jimmy Pool*), Robert McWade (*Whimple*).

Two rival department stores serve as the backdrop for a group of young singing and dancing college kids who choose a football match as a way to prove one store's superiority over the other. When the owners of the two shops decide to merge,the outcome of the game becomes a moot point, but everybody is happy at the climax. Odd combination of the "Hey kids, let's put on a show!" formula and the standard college football drama that comes across as a lifeless mixed bag. Penner makes an easy transition from radio to the screen and provides the film with a central humorous character. (Penner is best remembered for his tag-line: "Wanna buy a duck?") Songs: "College Rhythm," "Stay As Sweet As You Are," "Goo-Goo I'm Ga-Ga Over You," "Let's Give Three Cheers For Love," "Take A Number From One To Ten" (Mack Gordon, Harry Revel).

d, Norman Taurog; w, Walter DeLeon, John McDermott, Frances Martin (based on a story by George Marion, Jr.); ph, Leo Tover, Ted Tetzlaff; ch, LeRoy Prinz.

Musical Comedy (PR:A MPAA:NR)

COLLEGE SCANDAL** (1935) 75m PAR bw
Arline Judge (*Sally Dunlap*), Kent Taylor (*Seth Dunlap*), Wendy Barrie (*Julie Fresnel*), William Frawley (*Chief of Police Magoun*), Benny Baker (*Cuffie Lewis*), William Benedict (*Penny Parker*), Mary Nash (*Mrs. Fresnel*), Edward Nugent (*Jake Lansing*), William Stack (*Prof. Henri Fresnel*), Johnny Downs (*Paul Gedney*), Douglas Blackley (*Dan Courtridge*), Joyce Compton (*Toby Carpenter*), Samuel S. Hinds (*Mr. Cummings*), Douglas Wood (*Dean Traynor*), Edith Arnold (*Posey*), Helena Phillips Evans (*Melinda*), Mary Ellen Brown (*Marjorie*), Stanley Andrews (*Jim*), Sam Godfrey (*Doctor*).

Unusual entry in the "college" series has a student being murdered on campus and the majority of the student body turning away from their studies to investigate the crime. Entertaining mystery that overcomes its "campus drama" limitations and provides some genuine suspense.

p, Albert Lewis; d, Elliott Nugent; w, Frank Partos, Charles Brackett, Marguerite Roberts (based on a story by Beulah Marie Dix and Bertram Millhauser); ph, Theodor Sparkuhl; m/l, "In The Middle Of A Kiss" (Sam Coslow).

Mystery (PR:A MPAA:NR)

COLLEGE SWEETHEARTS* (1942) 60m MON bw
Grace Hayes (*Grace*), Peter Lind Hayes (*Peter Hendricks*), Mary Healy (*Mary*), Huntz Hall (*Skeets Skillborn*), Jan Wiley (*Annabella*), Skeets Gallagher (*Prof. Warren*), Benny Rubin (*Nick*), Frank Elliott (*Mr. Hendricks*), Eddie Kane (*James J. Kane*), Roland Dupree (*Dancer*), Leonard Seus (*Leonard*).

Hayes stars as a nightclub singer who is secretly financing her never-seen son's college education. When she goes to the lad's school to observe his studies, she is shocked to learn that he is a notorious party-goer and womanizer. When the university comes under financial pressure, Hayes opens a club nearby and uses the profits to get the school back on its feet again. Her son realizes the importance of hard work and changes his wasteful ways. Unstructured drama fails to bring life to any of its characters or interest in the routine methods.

p, Sam Katzman; d, William Nigh; w, Harvey Gates, Jack Henley (based on a story by Gates and Connie Lee); ph, Marcel Le Picard; ed, Robert Golden; m/l, Johnny Lange and Lew Porter, Neville Fleeson, Joan Baldwin and Charles R. Callender, Earl Hammond and Lee Eilon; songs include: "Annabella," "Put Your Trust In the Moon."

Drama (PR:A MPAA:NR)

COLLEGE SWING* (1938) 82m PAR bw (GB: SWING, TEACHER, SWING)
George Burns (*George Jonas*), Gracie Allen (*Gracie Alden*), Martha Raye (*Mabel*), Bob Hope (*Bud Brady*), Edward Everett Horton (*Hubert Dash*), Florence George (*Ginna Ashburn*), Ben Blue (*Ben Volt*), Betty Grable (*Betty*), Jackie Coogan (*Jackie*), John Payne (*Martin Bates*), Cecil Cunningham (*Dean Sleet*), Robert Cummings (*Radio Announcer*), E. C. "Skinny" Ennis (*Skinnay*), The Slate Brothers (*Themselves*), The Playboys (*Themselves*), Bob Mitchell and the St. Brendan's Choristers (*Themselves*), Jerry Colonna (*Prof. Yascha Koloski*), Charles Trowbridge (*Dr. Ashburn*), Jerry Bergen (*Prof. Jasper Chinn*), Tully Marshall (*Grandpa Alden*), Edward J. LeSaint

(Dr. Storm), Barlowe Borland *(Dean)*, Alphonse Martel *(Headwaiter)*, Richard Denning, John Hubbard *(Students)*.

When Allen inherits a small town college, she turns the stuffy, respectable institution into a haven for her vaudeville pals. Typical Burns and Allen feature whose familiar routines get tedious, though Hope and Horton do their best to inject some cynical wit to the lightweight plotting. Songs: "I Fall In Love With You Every Day" (Frank Loesser, Manning Sherwin, Arthur Altman); "What A Rumba Does To Romance," "You're A Natural," "The Old School Bell" (Loesser, Sherwin), "Moments Like This," "How 'Dja Like To Love Me?" "What Did Romeo Say To Juliet?" (Loesser, Burton Lane), "College Swing" (Loesser, Hoagy Carmichael).

p,Lewis Gensler; d, Raoul Walsh; w, Walter DeLeon, Francis Martin (based on an adaptation by Frederick Hazlitt Brennan from a story by Ted Lesser); ph, Victor Milner; ed, LeRoy Stone; md, Boris Morros; songs, Frank Loesser, Burton Lane, Manning Sherwin, Hoagy Carmichael; ch, LeRoy Prinz.

Musical Comedy   **(PR:A   MPAA:NR)**

COLLEGIATE*   (1936) 80m PAR bw (GB: THE CHARM SCHOOL)
Joe Penner *(Joe)*, Jack Oakie *(Jerry Craig)*, Ned Sparks *("Scoop" Oakland)*, Frances Langford *(Miss Hay)*, Betty Grable *(Dorothy)*, Lynne Overman *(Sour Puss)*, Betty Jane Cooper *(Dance Instructress)*, Mack Gordon *(Himself)* Harry Revel *(Himself)*, Henry Kolker *(Mr. MacGregor)*, Donald Gallagher *(Thomas J. Bloodgood)*, Albert Conti *(Headwaiter)*, Julius Tannen *(Detective Browning)*.

When his aunt wills him the deed to a girl's college, Oakie leaves Broadway to introduce some classes in crooning and hoofing into the school curriculum. When funding becomes a problem, the eccentric and wealthy Penner decides to become the "show-biz" school's principal backer. Lightweight romp through academia lacking in spirit and charm. Songs: "I Feel Like A Feather In the Breeze," "You Hit the Spot," "Rhythmatic," "My Grandfather's Clock in the Hallway," "Who Am I?" "Guess Again," "Will I Ever Know?" "Learn To Be Lovely" (Mack Gordon, Harry Revel).

p, Louis D. Lighton; d, Ralph Murphy; w, Walter DeLeon, Francis Martin (based on a story, "The Charm School," by Alice Duer Miller); ph, William Mellor.

Musical Comedy   **(PR:A   MPAA:NR)**

COLLISION*   (1932, Brit.) 79m Samuelson/UA bw
Sunday Wilshin *(Mrs. Oliver)*, Gerald Rawlinson *(Jack Carruthers)*, Wendy Barrie *(Joyce Maynard)*, Henrietta Watson *(Mrs. Carruthers)*, A. G. Poulton *(Mr. Maynard)*, Irene Rooke *(Mrs. Maynard)*, Peter Coleman *(Brabazon)*.

Yet another of the talky drawing room mysteries that compose the bulk of British filmmaking in the thirties. Widow Wilshin frames young bridegroom Rawlinson for a jewel heist. Wendy Barrie's first motion picture showed its stage origins in its static movement. Producer Craig was the first member of the British film industry to be knighted.

p, E. Gordon Craig; d, G. B. Samuelson; (based on a play by E. C. Pollard).

Crime   **(PR:A   MPAA:NR)**

COLLISION COURSE   (SEE: BAMBOO SAUCER, THE, 1968)

COLONEL BLIMP***   (1945, Brit.) 163m The Archers/GFD c
(GB: THE LIFE AND DEATH OF COLONEL BLIMP)
Roger Livesey *(Clive Candy)*, Deborah Kerr *(Edith Hunter/Barbara Wynne/Johnny Cannon)*, Anton Walbrook *(Theo Kretschmar-Schuldorff)*, Roland Culver *(Col. Betteridge)*, James McKechnie *(Spud Wilson)*, Albert Lieven *(Von Ritter)*, Arthur Wontner *(Embassy Counsellor)*, David Hutcheson *(Hoppy)*, Ursula Jeans *(Frau von Kalteneck)*, John Laurie *(Murdoch)*, Harry Welchman *(Maj. Davis)*, Reginald Tate *(Van Zijl)*, A. E. Matthews *(President of Tribunal)*, Carl Jaffe *(Van Reumann)*, Valentine Dyall *(Von Schonborn)*, Muriel Aked *(Aunt Margaret)*, Felix Aylmer *(Bishop)*, Frith Banbury *(Babyface Fitzroy)*, Neville Mapp *(Stuffy Graves)*, Vincent Holman *(Club Porter, 1942)*, Spencer Trevor *(Period Blimp)*, James Knight *(Club Porter, 1902)*, Dennis Arundell *(Cafe Orchestra Leader)*, David Ward *(Kaunitz)*, Jan van Loewen *(Indignant Citizen)*, Eric Maturin *(Col. Goodhead)*, Robert Harris *(Embassy Secretary)*, Count Zichy *(Col. Berg)*, Jane Millican *(Nurse Erna)*, Phyllis Morris *(Pebble)*, Diana Marshall *(Sibyl)*, Capt. W. Barrett, U.S. Army *(Texan)*, Corp. Thomas Palmer *(Sgt.)*, Yvonne Andree *(Nun)*, Marjorie Gresley *(Matron)*, Helen Debroy *(Mrs. Wynne)*, Norman Pierce *(Mr. Wynne)*, Edward Cooper *(B.B.C. Official)*, Joan Swinstead *(Secretary)*.

Livesey is superb as the old colonel, a fat-necked reactionary and decidedly stuffy British soldier whose life is shown in episodes ranging from his dashing career as a young officer in the Boer War of 1902, to 1943 where he creaks crankily about in the London blitz, looking for his youth and lost loves. Kerr plays three different roles from separate eras; Walbrook is a charming Prussian officer whose sensitivity and understanding far exceeds Livesey's. Livesey loses Kerr to Walbrook during the Boer War. He later marries a nurse during WW I (again Kerr) because she reminds him of his lost love, and she returns as his youthful driver during WW II when Livesey has turned into an out-of-touch brigadier on the brink of retirement, representing everything archaic in the changing British Empire. Livesey is magnificent in the best role of his career, showing amazing versatility in his ages-of-man profiles. Walbrook, a consummate performer, counterpoints the strutting martinet with a role packed with mystique, displaying sympathetic friendship for a man who cannot break out of his rigid mold. Kerr's versatility is shown in her three-part role about which she was later to comment: "It was an amazing acting opportunity—but rather frightening. The only way I could tackle it was to think of the characters as being in completely different films. While playing one, I had to forget about the other two." This was the first production of The Archers, sponsored by J. Arthur Rank and headed by Powell and Pressburger, who had produced ONE OF OUR AIRCRAFT IS MISSING and THE INVADERS, a superb episodic portrait of Nazi submariners in Canada. Another hallmark of COLO

NEL BLIMP was that it offered one of the few color productions made during WW II when such film stock was scarce. Moreover, the movie's scathing portrait of a stuffy British officer was condemned by the British press, "disastrously bad propaganda," according to one reviewer, who thought the film undermined British confidence during wartime. Prime Minister Winston Churchill viewed the film and became enraged, personally banning it from exportation. Because of this, the film, completed in 1943, was not shown until 1945 in the U.S. and even then the movie had been heavily edited to give a more favorable view to the British. The character stems from a cartoon strip appearing in The London *Evening Standard*, acidly drawn by David Low who specialized in exposing the pomposity of the British upper class.

p, Michael Powell, Emeric Pressburger; d, Powell; w, Powell, Pressburger; ph, Jack Cardiff, Georges Perinal (Technicolor); m, Allan Gray; ed, John Seabourne; military advisor, Lt. Gen. Sir Douglas Brownrigg.

Historical Drama   **(PR:A   MPAA:NR)**

COLONEL BLOOD**   (1934, Brit.) 98m Sound City/MGM bw
Frank Cellier *(Col. Blood)*, Anne Grey *(Lady Castlemaine)*, Mary Lawson *(Susie)*, Allan Jeayes *(Charles II)*, Hay Petrie *(Mr. Edwards)*, Hilda Trevelyan *(Mrs. Edwards)*, Arthur Chesney *(Samuel Pepys)*, Stella Arbenina *(Mrs. Pepys)*, Desmond Jeans *(Parrot)*, Robert Nainby *(Desborough)*, Arthur Goullet *(Tim)*, Percy Standing *(Duke of Ormonde)*, Ena Grossmith *(Jane)*.

Cellier is the celebrated Irish patriot and outlaw whose attempt to steal the Crown Jewels from the Tower of London is foiled. Brought before monarch Jeayes, he so charms him that he is pardoned. Based on fact, though the real reason Charles II spared Blood's life was so the renegade officer could inform on a number of his sympathizers. Okay costume drama with a decent cast.

p, Norman Loudon; d&w, W. P. Lipscomb.

Drama   **(PR:A   MPAA:NR)**

COLONEL BOGEY**   (1948, Brit.) 51m Production Facilities/GFD bw
Jack Train *(Voice of Uncle James)*, Mary Jerrold *(Aunt Mabel)*, Jane Barrett *(Alice Graham)*, John Stone *(Wilfred Barriteau)*, Ethel Coleridge *(Emily)*, Hedli Anderson *(Millicent)*.

Train's ghost refuses to leave his home, causing much concern among his survivors. Pleasant little fantasy movie. Director Fisher went on to cult fame by directing the bulk of the Hammer horror films of the 1950s and 1960s.

p,John Croydon; d, Terence Fisher; w, William Fairchild, John Baines (based on a story by Fairchild).

Fantasy   **(PR:A   MPAA:NR)**

COLONEL CHABERT*½   (1947, Fr.) 90m Siritsky bw
Raimu *(Colonel Chabert)*, Marie Bell *(Countess Faraud)*, Aime Clariond *(Derville)*, Fernand Fabre *(Count Ferraud)*,, Jacques Baumer, Jacques Charon, Roger Blin, Andre Varonne, Rene Stern.

Though reported killed in the Napoleonic Wars, Raimu, an aristocrat, returns to his palatial home and discovers that his wife, thinking him dead, has remarried. Never having loved Raimu, and happier with her wealthier present husband, she accuses Raimu of being an impostor and has him committed to an asylum. Raimu escapes and begins to wander the streets, befriending penniless people who sleep in the local poor houses. When evidence is uncovered that proves his true identity, Raimu nonetheless renounces his past and stays with his poverty-stricken comrades. Slow-moving social drama that, despite an excellent performance from its star, fails to generate any sympathy for its protagonist's tragedy. (In French: English sub-titles.)

d, Rene Le Henaff; w, Pierre Benoit (based on a novel by Honore de Balzac); ph, Robert Le Febvre; m, Louis Beydts.

Drama   **(PR:A   MPAA:NR)**

COLONEL EFFINGHAM'S RAID**   (1945) 70m FOX bw (GB: MAN OF THE HOUR)
Charles Coburn *(Col. Effingham)*, Joan Bennett *(Ella Sue Dozier)*, William Eythe *(Al)*, Allyn Joslyn *(Earl Hoats)*, Elizabeth Patterson *(Emma)*, Donald Meek *(Doc Buden)*, Frank Craven *(Dewey)*, Thurston Hall *(Mayor)*, Cora Witherspoon *(Clara Meigh)*, Emory Parnell *(Alsobrook)*, Henry Armetta *(Jimmy Economy)*, Michael Dunne *(Ed Bland)*, Roy Roberts *(Capt. Rampey)*, Boyd Davis *(Bibbs)*, Charles Trowbridge *(Tignor)*, Frank Orth *(Wild Man)*, Nicodemus Stewart *(Ninety-Eight)*, Robert Dudley *(Pete)*, Ferris Taylor *(Wishum)*, Oliver Blake *(Bill Silk)*, Frank Mitchell *(Maj. Hickock)*, Clyde Fillmore *(Engineer)*, Carol Andrews *(Sadie)*, George Melford *(Park Commissioner)*, Harry Hayden *(Box Smith)*, Charles Wagenheim *(Young Man)*, Olin Howlin *(Painter)*, Edward Fielding *(Monadue)*, Mildred Gover *(Esther)*, Minerva Urecal, Hallene Hill *(Women)*, Walter Baldwin *(Bus Driver)*, George O'Hara *(Telegrapher)*, Edward Keane *(Doctor)*, David Vallard *(Reporter)*, Sam McDaniel *(Janitor)*, George Chandler *(Drummer)*, Ed Allen, James Adamson *(Black Cab Drivers)*, Charles Moore *(White Cab Driver)*, Gus Glassmire, Herbert Heywood, Jim Toney, Harry Humphrey *(Men)*, Guy Beach, Ken Christy *(Motor Cops)*, George Read *(Janitor)*, Paul Burns *(Man in Restaurant)*, Paul Kruger *(Cop)*, Clinton Rosemond *(Servant)*, Cecil Weston *(Teacher)*, Phil Tead *(Advertising Manager)*, Henry Hastings *(Courthouse Janitor)*, Abe Dinovitch *(Electrician)*, Marshall Ruth *(Painter)*, Ralph Dunn *(Commissioner of Streets)*, Alma Kruger *(Mrs. Monadue)*, Elizabeth Williams *(Guest at Tea)*.

Aging army colonel Coburn retires from the service and moves back to his small home town in Georgia. Unhappy to find that the townspeople have lost their civic pride and that the local government is trying to modernize the area, Coburn starts writing an editorial column in the town paper criticizing the apathetic people and the corrupt politicians who've taken over the town. When public opinion starts to sway in favor of Coburn's ideas, the town council tries to cool the old man's fire, but cub reporter Eythe keeps his spirits up and they triumph over the crooked politicos. Charming little comedy that generates some good-natured patriotism and pride in small-town values.

p, Lamar Trotti; d, Irving Pichel; w, Kathryn Scola (based on a novel by Barry Fleming); ph, Edward Cronjager; m, Cyril J. Mockridge; ed, Harmon Jones; md, Emil Newman; art d, Lyle Wheeler, Albert Hogsett; set d, Thomas Little, Ernest Lansing.

Comedy   (PR:A   MPAA:NR)

COLONEL MARCH INVESTIGATES**   (1952, Brit.) 70m Criterion bw
Boris Karloff (Col. March), Ewan Roberts (Inspector Ames), Richard Wattis (Cabot), Sheila Burrell (Joan Forsythe), Anthony Forwood (Jim Hartley), John Hewer (John Parrish), Joan Sims (Marjorie Dawson), Ronald Leigh Hunt (Ireton Bowlder), Roger Maxwell (Maj. Rodman), Patricia Owens (Betty Hartley), Dagmar Wynter (Francine Rapport), Sonya Hana (Paula), Bernard Rebel (The Count).

Episodic feature, with three pilot episodes of the British television series "Colonel March of Scotland Yard" put together and released in the theaters. Karloff stars (with a distinguished-looking black eye patch and cloak) as the head of the Department of Queer Complaints at Scotland Yard. It is his job to investigate any unusual cases that fall beyond the realm of routine criminal activities. During the course of the film he solves a bank robbery (in which an innocent man was framed), and two murders involving elaborate tricks and disguises utilized by the perpetrators. The scripts are nothing special, but Karloff is a joy to watch, as usual.

p, Donald Ginsberg; d, Cyril Endfield; w, Leo Davis (based on stories by Carter Dickson); ph, Jonah Jones; m, John Lanchberry; ed, Stan Willis; md, Eric Robinson; art d, George Paterson.

Mystery/Crime   (PR:A   MPAA:NR)

COLOR ME BLOOD RED zero
                             (1965) 74m Box Office Spectaculars/Jacqueline Kay, Inc. c
Don Joseph (Adam Sorg), Candi Conder (April), Elyn Warner (Gigi), Scott H. Hall (Farnsworth), Jerome Eden (Rolf), Patricia Lee (Sydney), James Jackel (Jack), Iris Marshall (Mrs. Carter), William Harris (Gregorovich), Cathy Collins (Mitzi).

Another blood-spattered offering from gore king Herschell Gordon Lewis, this one concerning an artist, Joseph, who gains fame when he begins to use his own blood on the canvas. Later he turns to killing his models for their blood, using a number of grisly methods to dispatch them. Fans of this film should seek professional help.

p, David F. Friedman; d,w&ph, Herschell Gordon Lewis; ed, Robert Sinise.

Horror   Cas.   (PR:O   MPAA:NR)

COLOR ME DEAD*½   (1969, Aus.) 97m Goldsworthy/COM c
Tom Tryon (Frank Bigelow), Carolyn Jones (Paula Gibson), Rick Jason (Bradley Taylor), Patricia Connolly (Marla Rukubian), Tony Ward (Halliday), Penny Sugg (Miss Foster), Reg Gilliam (Eugene Phillips), Margot Reid (Mrs. Phillips), Peter Sumner (Stanley Phillips), Michael Lawrence (George Reynolds), Sandy Harbott (Chester).

After supervising some business dealings for a shady uranium company, accountant Tryon discovers that he has been given a slow-acting posion. Desperate to find out if there is an antidote, he attempts to track down the poisoner and uncovers a trail of poisoned bodies that leads to the uranium company. Dull remake of the 1949 low budget film noir classic D.O.A. that fails to recreate the edgy, gritty, intriguing quality of its predecessor. The film earns its "R" rating because of some bare breasts shown on two strippers in a night club scene, a wholly unnecessary sequence as it turns out. The movie was shot in Sidney, Australia.

p&d, Eddie Davis; w, Russell Rouse, Clarence Greene (based on their 1949 film script D.O.A.); ph, Mick Borneman (Eastmancolor); m, Bob Young; ed, Warren Adams; prod d, Eddie Davis; art d, Sid Fort.

Crime   (PR:C   MPAA:R)

COLOR OF POMEGRANATES, THE***
                                       (1980, Armenian) 75m c (AKA: SAYAT NOVA)
Sophico Tchiaourelli (Young Poet, Poet's Love, Nun With White Lace, Angel Who Has Risen From The Dead, Mime), M. Alekian (Poet as a Child), V. Galestian (Poet in the Cloister), G. Gueguetchkori (Poet as an Old Man), O. Minassian (The Prince).

Surreal, symbolic film about the life of the 18th-century Armenian poet Sayat Nova. Filled with imagery of church and animals, and almost totally undecipherable. Director Paradjanov made the film in 1969, and was subsequently exiled to Siberia. Well worth seeing, if only as a visual treat. (In Armenian.)

d, Sergei Paradjanov; ph, A. Samvellian.

Biography   (PR:C-O   MPAA:NR)

COLORADO*½   (1940) 57m REP bw
Roy Rogers (Jerry Burke), George "Gabby" Hayes (Gabby), Paulina Moore (Lylah Sanford), Milburn Stone (Capt. Stone), Maude Eburne (Etta Mae), Arthur Left (Jim Macklin), Hal Taliaferro (Weaver), Vester Pegg (Sam), Fred Burns (Sheriff Harkins), Lloyd Ingraham (Sanford).

Good-hearted Rogers tracks down his brother who failed to join the Union forces during the Civil War in this cliche-ridden western. It was the second relase within a matter of weeks by Republic of stories dealing with the same theme, the other being WAGONS WESTWARD starring Chester Morris.

p&d, Joseph Kane; w, Louis Stevens and Harrison Jacobs; ph, Jack Marta; ed, Edward Mann; md, Cy Feuer; m/l, Peter Tinturin.

Western   Cas.   (PR:A   MPAA:NR)

COLORADO AMBUSH*½   (1951) 52m MON bw
Johnny Mack Brown (Johnny), Myron Healey (Chet Murdock), Lois Hall (Janet

Williams), Tommy Farrell (Terry Williams), Christine McIntyre (Mae Star), Lee Roberts (Gus), Marshall Bradford (B. Williams), Lyle Talbot (Sheriff Ed Lowery).

When a series of payroll transports are robbed, undercover federal agent Brown tracks down the wonderfully nasty Healey and his outlaw gang. Entertaining yet unspectacular Johnny Mack Brown adventure penned by costar Healey, who appropriated the best role for himself.

p, Vincent M. Fennelly; d, Lewis Collins; w, Myron Healey; ph, Gilbert Warrenton; ed, Fred Maguire.

Western   (PR:A   MPAA:NR)

COLORADO KID zero   (1938) 56m REP bw
Bob Steele (Colorado Kid), Marian Weldon (Iram Toles), Karl Hackett (Wolf Hines), Ernie Adams (Pibben Tucker), Ted Adams (Sheriff Hennon), Frank La Rue (Toles), Horace Murphy (Col. Gifford), Kenne Duncan, Budd Busier, Frank Ball, John Merton, Horace B. Carpenter, Wally West.

Wanderer Steele is unjustly accused of murder and tossed in jail. When a pal helps him break out, Steele is given the opportunity to find the real killer. Familiar story, poorly executed.

p, A. W. Hackel; d, Sam Newfield; w, Charles Francis Royal (based on a story by Harry F. Olmsted); ph, Robert Cline; ed, S. Roy Luby.

Western   (PR:A   MPAA:NR)

COLORADO PIONEERS**   (1945) 57m REP bw
Bill Elliott, Bobby Blake, Alice Fleming, Roy Barcroft, Bud Geary, Billy Cummings, Freddie Chapman, Frank Jacquet, Tom London, Monte Hale, Buckwheat Thomas, George Chesebro, Emmett Vogan, Tom Chatterton, Edward Cassidy, Fred Graham, Cliff Parkinson, Horace B. Carpenter, Bill Wolfe, Jess Cavin, Howard Mitchell, Jack Rockwell, George Morrell, Jack Kirk, Gary Armstrong, Bobby Anderson, Roger Williams, Richard Lydon, Robert Goldschmidt, Romey Foley.

Good outing for Elliott in the exciting Red Ryder series; here he not only rounds up the bad guys with some snappy shooting but battles a bevy of villains on several occasions without scuffing his kid gloves and winds up with Fleming in his long arms. Blake is cute as his little Indian sidekick, a role the actor desperately attempts to live down to this day.

d, R. G. Springsteen; w, Earle Snell (based on a story by Peter Whitehead).

Western   (PR:A   MPAA:NR)

COLORADO RANGER*   (1950) 55m Lippert bw
Jimmy Ellison (Shamrock), Russ Hayden (Lucky), Raymond Hatton (Colonel), Fuzzy Knight (Deacon), Betty Adams (Ann), Tom Tyler (Pete), George Lewis (Tony), John Cason (Loco Joe), Stanley Price (Sheriff), Stephen Carr (Morgan), Dennis Moore (Juan), George Chesebro (Jenkins), Bud Osborne (Regan), Jimmy Martin (Sandy), Gene Roth (Barber), I. Stanford Jolley (Bartender), Joseph Richards (Baby).

Undercover Colorado rangers Ellison, Hayden, and Hatton stop a swindler from driving homesteaders off their land. Sloppy, boring entry in the Ellison-Hayden series of westerns and quite a comedown for Ellison, who played Buffalo Bill in Cecil B. DeMille's THE PLAINSMAN in 1937. He retired from films two years later and began a career in real estate.

p, Ron Ormond; d, Thomas Carr; w, Ormond, Maurice Tombragel; ph, Ernest Miller; ed, Hugh Winn.

Western   (PR:A   MPAA:NR)

COLORADO SERENADE**   (1946) 68m PRC c
Eddie Dean (Eddie), David Sharpe (Nevada), Roscoe Ates (Soapy), Mary Kenyon (Sherry), Forrest Taylor (Judge Hilton), Dennis Moore (Duke), Abigail Adams (Lola), Warner Richmond (Dad Dillon), Lee Bennett (Mr. Trimble), Robert McKenzie (Col. Blake), Bob Duncan (Ringo), Charles King.

Dean, Sharpe, and the stuttering Ates stop a young punk outlaw from terrorizing a small town. Routine oater highlighted by some exuberant athleticism from the appealing Sharpe and a good comic performance by King. Songs: "Home On the Range," "Western Lullaby," "Riding Down To Rawhide," "Riding To the Top Of the Mountain."

p&d, Robert Emmett Tansey; w, Frances Kavanaugh; ph, Robert Shackelford (Cinecolor); ed, Hugh Winn; songs, Eddie Dean, H. L. Canova, Sam Armstrong, Carl Hoefle.

Western   (PR:A   MPAA:NR)

COLORADO SUNDOWN**   (1952) 67m REP bw
Rex Allen (Himself), Koko (The Miracle Horse of the Movies), Mary Ellen Kay (Jackie Reynolds), Slim Pickens (Slim), June Vincent (Carrie Hurley), Fred Graham (Dan Hurley), John Daheim (Dusty Hurley), Louise Beavers (Mattie), Chester Clute (Law-yer Davis), Clarence Straight (Postman), The Republic Rhythm Riders.

Allen and his miracle steed Koko accompany a friend to the Colorado Territory where the pal is supposed to inherit a large area of ranch land. When they arrive, they find that the ownership of the land is being contested by a conniving brother-and-sister team and Kay, a pretty girl from the city who thought she was the only heir. When a couple of corpses spring up around them, Allen and Koko discover that the brother and sister are murdering everyone who stands in their way. Extremely low-budget Allen vehicle that relies heavily on stock footage to push its bare-bones story along. Songs: "Down By the Riverside," "Pine Valley Stage," "Under Colorado Stars."

p, Edward J. White; d, William Witney; w, Eric Taylor, William Lively (based on a story by Taylor); ph, John MacBurnie; m, R. Dale Butts; ed, Tony Martinelli.

Western   (PR:A   MPAA:NR)

COLORADO SUNSET**½ (1939) 58m REP bw
Gene Autry (Gene), Smiley Burnette (Frog), June Storey (Carol), Barbara Pepper (Ginger), Larry "Buster" Crabbe (Haines), Robert Barrat (Doc Blair), Patsy Montana (Herself), The CBS-KMBC Texas Rangers (Themselves), Purnell Pratt (Mr. Hall), William Farnum (Sheriff), Kermit Maynard (Drake), Jack Ingram (Clanton), Elmo Lincoln (Burns), Frankie Marvin (Frankie), Ethan Laidlaw, Fred Burns, Jack Kirk, Budd Buster, Ed Cassidy, Slim Whitaker, Murdock McQuarrie, Ralph Peters, "Champion."

When Autry and a few of his hard-as-nails cowhand friends (Burnette and the Texas Rangers) decide to buy a ranch, they send Burnette to Colorado to pick out a spot and purchase some livestock. When the gang joins up with Burnette, they are astonished to learn that he has acquired a dairy not a cattle ranch. Deciding to make a go of the sissified operation, Autry and his cohorts find themselves in the midst of a war between the local milk cow ranchers and a "protection" outfit that threatens the safety of the dairy goods reaching market. Silly Autry vehicle complete with crooning cowpokes and mooing cows.

p, William Berke; d, George Sherman; w, Betty Burbridge and Stanley Roberts (based on a story by Luci Ward and Jack Natteford); ph, William Nobles; m, Raoul Kranshaar.

Western (PR:A MPAA:NR)

COLORADO TERRITORY*** (1949) 94m WB bw
Joel McCrea (Wes McQueen), Virginia Mayo (Colorado Carson), Dorothy Malone (Julie Ann), Henry Hull (Winslow), John Archer (Reno Blake), James Mitchell (Duke Harris), Morris Ankrum (U.S. Marshall), Basil Ruysdael (Dave Rickard), Frank Puglia (Brother Thomas), Ian Wolfe (Wallace), Harry Woods, (Pluthner), Houseley Stevenson (Prospector), Victor Kilian (Sheriff), Oliver Blake (Station Agent).

Excellent western reworking of Walsh's own HIGH SIERRA has kind-hearted outlaw McCrea deciding that he and his gang must pull one more robbery before disappearing forever. Inevitably, a posse tracks down the gang and McCrea and his half-breed lover Mayo are killed in a romantic, yet horrifying, blaze of gunfire at the film's climax. Just as HIGH SIERRA was primarily a character study of Bogart, COLORADO TERRITORY analyzes the tragedy of the good McCrea who sadly chose a life of crime. Hauntingly photographed in richly contrasting black and white tones, the film is truly a film noir western, not only in its look, but in its themes of despair, the inability to love, and the inevitability of doom. (Remade as I DIED A THOUSAND TIMES.)

p, Anthony Veiller; d, Raoul Walsh; w, John Twist and Edmund H. North; ph, Sid Hickox; m, David Buttolph; ed, Owen Marks.

Western (PR:A MPAA:NR)

COLORADO TRAIL** (1938) 54m COL bw
Charles Starrett (Grant Bradley), Iris Meredith (Joan Randall), Edward LeSaint (Jeff Randall), Al Bridge (Mark Sheldon), Robert Fiske (Deacon Webster), Dick Curtis (Slash Driscoll), Bob Nolan (Bob), Hank Bell (Tombstone Terry), Edward Peil, Sr. (Hobbs), Edmund Cobb (Cameron), Jack Clifford (Judge Bennett), Sons of the Pioneers.

Wandering gunfighter Starrett stumbles into a small Colorado town and saves the life of a prominent local rancher. As a gesture of thanks, the rancher offers Starrett a job protecting his stock and land against a rival, more violent ranch owner. When it is learned that Starrett is the son of this dastardly honcho, he is fired from his position as hired gun and tossed into the middle of the range war. When his father takes control of the only route to market, Starrett goes up against the old man and makes the passage accessible to everyone. Ho-hum western is made mildly palatable by Starrett's enthusiasm and the mellifluous crooning of the Sons of the Pioneers.

p, Harry Decker; d, Sam Nelson; w, Charles Francis Royal; ph, Ben Kline; md, Morris Stoloff; m/l, Bob Nolan.

Western (PR:A MPAA:NR)

COLOSSUS OF NEW YORK, THE*½ (1958) 70m PAR bw
Ross Martin (Dr. Jeremy Spensser), Mala Powers (Anne Spensser), Charles Herbert (Billy Spensser), John Baragrey (Dr. Henry Spensser), Otto Kruger (Dr. William Spensser), Robert Hutton (Prof. John Carrington), Ed Wolff (The Colossus).

When brilliant scientist Martin dies, his demented brother Kruger transplants Martin's brain into the body of a twelve-foot tall robot (Wolff). Though the initial days after the transplant point to a successful transferral, Wolff begins to show monstrous homicidal tendencies, emotional factors that eventually lead him on a rampage within the United Nations. In a moment of surprisingly real sadness, Martin's little son calms the monster down and halts the violent attack. Attempting to create a Frankenstein-like emotional tragedy, director Lourie makes the mistake of offering a ridiculous-looking creature that generates more laughs than sympathy.

p, William Alland; d, Eugene Lourie; w, Thelma Schnee (based on a story by Willis Goldbeck); ph, John F. Warren; m, Van Cleave; ed, Floyd Knudston.

Horror/Science fiction (PR:A MPAA:NR)

COLOSSUS OF RHODES, THE** (1961, Ital., Fr., Span.) 128m Procusa-Cineproduzioni/MGM c
Rory Calhoun (Dario), Lea Massari (Diala), Georges Marchal (Peliocles), Conrado Sanmartin (Thar), Angel Aranda (Koros), Mabel Karr (Mirte), Jorge Rigaud (Lissipo), Roberto Camardiel (Serse), Mimmo Palmara (Ares), Felix Fernandez (Carete), Carlo Tamberlani (Xenon), Alfio Caltaviano (Creonte), Jose McVilches (Eros), Antonio Casas (Phoenician Ambassador), Yann Larvor (Mahor), Fernando Calzado (Sirione), Ignazio Dolce, Arturo Cabre.

Calhoun leads an army of slaves in revolt against a group of oppressors who use the title edifice as a secret torture chamber and battle fortress. Ludicrous costume epic complete with hambone acting that is of interest to film buffs because it is an early directorial effort from the king of the spaghetti Westerns, Sergio Leone. Although Leone himself has labeled the film an impersonal project, his keen, formalistic compositional eye and exciting handling of action sequences is evident. The unmistakable use of remarkable structuralized images that is a great part of THE GOOD, THE BAD, AND THE UGLY and ONCE UPON A TIME IN THE WEST is being experimented with and analyzed in THE COLOSSUS OF RHODES. This is an important work for those obsessed with Leone's style of storytelling. Leone has allowed the Colossus itself, straddling the harbor of Rhodes, to dominate much of the film and in one scene Calhoun gives a measure of its enormity by emerging from its ear to fight several soldiers on its horizontal upper arm, while the center of the screen is filled with the sightless face, heedless of the tiny figures hacking away at each other beneath.

p, Michele Scaglione; d, Sergio Leone; w, Ennio De Concini, Leone, Cesare Seccia, Luciano Martino, Duccio Tessari, Age Gavioli, Carlo Gualtieri, Luciano Chittarini; ph, Antonio Ballesteros (SupertotalScope, Eastmancolor); m, Angelo Francesco Lavagnino; ed, Eraldo Da Roma; prod d, Cesare Ceccia; cos, Vittorio Rossi.

Historical Drama (PR:A MPAA:NR)

COLOSSUS: THE FORBIN PROJECT***½ (1969) 100m UNIV c
(AKA: THE FORBIN PROJECT and COLOSSUS 1980)
Eric Brandon (Dr. Charles Forbin), Susan Clark (Dr. Cleo Markham), Gordon Pinsent (The President), William Schallert (Grauber), Leonid Rostoff (1st Chairman), Georg Stanford Brown (Fisher), Willard Sage (Blake), Alex Rodine (Dr. Kurpin), Martin Brooks (Johnson), Marion Ross (Angela), Dolph Sweet (Missile Commander), Byron Morrow (Secretary of State), Lew Brown (Peterson), Sid McCoy (Secretary Of Defense), Tom Basham (Harrison), Sergei Tschernisch (Russian Translator), Robert Cornthwaite, James Hong (Other Scientists).

Taut, well made sci-fi thriller about a massive computer, Colossus, which is designed by Brandon to control the entire American missile defense system. Once put into service, however, it takes over and develops a plan of its own to safeguard mankind from nuclear disaster. It hooks up with its Russian counterpart, Guardian, and together the two computers hold the world hostage—threatening to destroy the earth. Brandon is forced to attempt to destroy his creation, but the computer thwarts him at every turn. Colossus could easily kill its creator, but it seems to have a respect for the man and allows him to live despite his efforts to reprogram it. All attempts fail and at the end it appears that forced nuclear disarmament will continue under the watchful eyes of the computer.

p, Stanley Chase; d, Joseph Sargent; w, James Bridges; ph, Gene Polito; m, Michel Columbier; ed, Folmar Blangsted; art d, John J. Lloyd, Alexander Golitzen; set d, John McCarthy, Ruby Levitt; spec eff, Whitey McMahon.

Science Fiction (PR:A MPAA:NR)

COLT COMRADES* (1943) 67m UA bw
William Boyd (Hopalong Cassidy), Andy Clyde (California Carlson), Jay Kirby (Johnny Nelson), George Reeves (Lin Whitlock), Gayle Lord (Lucy Whitlock), Earl Hodgins (Wildcat Willy), Victor Jory (Jebb Hardin), Douglas Fowley (Joe Brass), Herb Rawlinson (Varney), Bob [Robert] Mitchum.

While drilling for oil, Boyd and Clyde discover an underground well which threatens the villainous Jory's monopolization of water distribution in the territory. Unspectacular Hopalong Cassidy adventure has the then-unknown Mitchum playing a henchman of Jory's. Film also served as testing ground for Reeves, who, beginning with COLT COMRADES, played minor hero-villain roles in the series. (See HOPALONG CASSIDY series, Index.)

p, Harry Sherman; d, Lesley Selander; w, Michael Wilson; ph, Russell Harlan; ed, Sherman A. Rose; art d, Ralph Berger.

Western (PR:A MPAA:NR)

COLT .45**½ (1950) 74m WB c (AKA: THUNDERCLOUD)
Randolph Scott (Steve Farrell), Ruth Roman (Beth Donovan), Zachary Scott (Jason Brett), Lloyd Bridges (Paul Donovan), Alan Hale (Sheriff Harris), Ian MacDonald (Miller), Chief Thundercloud (Walking Bear), Lute Crockett (Judge Tucker), Walter Coy (Carl), Charles Evans (Redrock Sheriff), Buddy Roosevelt, Hal Taliaferro, Art Miles, Barry Reagan, Howard Negley, Aurora Navarro, Paul Newland, Franklyn Farnum, Ed Piet, Sr., Jack Watt, Carl Andre, Royden Clark, Clyde Hudkins, Jr., Leroy Johnson, Ben Corbett, Kansas Moehring, Warren Fisk, Forrest R. Colee, Artie Ortego, Richard Brehm, Dick Hudkins, Leo McMahon, Bob Burrows, William Steele.

When Colt firearms representative Randolph Scott goes on a promotional tour out west touting the new rapid-fire .45, Zachary Scott steals a pair of the guns and begins a deadly bank-robbing spree. Feeling responsible, Randolph swears to stop the crimes and catch the culprit. Exciting western adventure released the same year as Anthony Mann's similarly plotted but far superior WINCHESTER '73.

p, Saul Elkins; d, Edwin L. Marin; w, Thomas Blackburn (based on a story by Blackburn); ph, Wilfrid M. Cline (Technicolor); ed, Frank Magee; m, William Lava.

Western (PR:A MPAA:NR)

COLUMN SOUTH** (1953) 84m UNIV c
Audie Murphy (Lt. Jed Sayre), Joan Evans (March Whitlock), Robert Sterling (Capt. Lee Whitlock), Ray Collins (Brig. Gen. Storey), Dennis Weaver (Menguito), Palmer Lee (Chalmers), Russell Johnson (Corp. Biddle), Jack Kelly (Trooper Vaness), Johnny Downs (Lt. Posick), Bob Steele (Sgt. McAfee), James Best (Primrose), Ralph Moody (Joe Copper Face), Rico Alanix (Trooper Chavez), Raymond Montgomery (Keit), Richard Garland (Lt. Fry), Ed Rand (Sabbath).

Idealistic cavalry officer Murphy is transferred to a New Mexico fort where he shows the hard-nosed Sterling how to live peacefully with Weaver and his Navajo tribe. When

Murphy discovers that powerful general Sterling is planning to turn over his troops to the Confederate forces at the outbreak of the Civil War, Murphy must again butt heads with Sterling who refuses to believe the plot. Murphy and Sterling eventually halt Collins' treacherous ways and Murphy, of course, wins the heart of Sterling's daughter, Evans. Familiar cavalry drama that owes its charm to the difficult-to-explain appeal of Murphy.

p, Ted Richmond; d, Frederick de Cordova; w, William Sackheim; ph Charles P. Boyle (Technicolor); ed, Milton Carruth.

Western (PR:A MPAA:NR)

COMA** (1978) 113m UA c

Genevieve Bujold *(Dr. Susan Wheeler)*, Michael Douglas *(Dr. Mark Bellows)*, Elizabeth Ashley *(Mrs. Emerson)*, Rip Torn *(Dr. George)*, Richard Widmark *(Dr. Harris)*, Lois Chiles *(Nancy Greenly)*, Harry Rhodes *(Dr. Morelind)*, Gary Barton *(Computer Technician)*, Frank Downing *(Kelly)*, Richard Doyle *(Jim)*, Alan Haufrect *(Dr. Marcus)*, Lance Le Gault *(Vince)*, Michael MacRae *(Chief Resident)*, Betty McGuire *(Nurse)*, Tom Selleck *(Murphy)*, Charles Siebert *(Dr. Goodman)*, William Wintersole *(Lab Technician)*, Ernest Anderson *(1st Doctor)*, Harry Basch *(2nd Doctor)*, Maury Cooper *(3rd Doctor)*, Joni Palmer *(Dance Instructor)*, Joanna Kerns *(Diane)*, Kay Cole *(Sally)*, Sarina C. Grant *(Woman in Elevator)*.

When inquisitive hospital physician Bujold discovers that the unsrupulous higher-ups on the staff are selecting healthy patients, drugging them into comatose states, killing them, and selling their organs to rich patients in desperate need of a transplant, she confronts doctor Douglas, her lover, with the information, but he refuses to believe her. When Widmark, one of the devilish doctors involved in the business, hears of Bujold's action, he hires a hit man to get rid of the pesky woman. Bujold evades the killer, but Widmark captures her and prepares to "operate" on her. In an exciting closing scene, Douglas saves Bujold from Widmark's scalpel. Adapted from the best-selling book by Robin Cook, the film is the second feature to be directed by novelist-turned-filmmaker Michael Crichton, the first being the popular WESTWORLD. Though he can create some Hitchcock-like suspense, Crichton's themes of conspiracy and the dangers of modern technology lack the personal feelings and style that would make him an outstanding director. In COMA, he wastes a superb performance by Bujold on a simplistic, never-challenging series of cliche suspense scenes and last-minute moralizing on contemporary medicine.

p, Martin Erlichman; d&w, Michael Crichton (based on the novel by Robin Cook); ph, Victor J. Kemper, Gerald Hirschfeld (Metrocolor); m, Jerry Goldsmith; ed, David Bretherton; prod d, Albert Brenner; set d, Rick Simpson; cos, Eddie Marks, Yvonne Kubis; spec eff, Joe Day, Ernie Smith.

Suspense Drama Cas. (PR:A MPAA:PG)

COMANCHE½** (1956) 87m UA c

Dana Andrews *(Read)*, Kent Smith *(Quanah Parker)*, Linda Cristal *(Margarita)*, Lowell Gilmore *(Ward)*, Nestor Paiva *(Puffer)*, Stacy Harris *(Downey)*, Mike Mazurki *(Flat Mouth)*, Henry Brandon *(Black Cloud)*, Reed Sherman *(French)*, John Litel *(Gen. Miles)*.

As racial tension builds between white settlers and Comanche tribes, Andrews does his best to calm the violent attacks by Smith and his tomahawk warriors who are feeling pressure from the Indian-hating Gilmore and Harris. Exciting western adventure relies heavily on the scenic beauty of the Mexican landscape, making it long on pictorial beauty as well. The film introduced Mexican actress Linda Cristal to American audiences.

p, Carl Krueger; d, George Sherman; w, Krueger; ph, George Stahl, Jr. (CinemaScope, DeLuxe Color); m, Herschel Burke Gilbert; ed, Charles L. Kimball; m/l "A Man Is As Good As His Word" (Gilbert, Alfred Perry).

Western (PR:A MPAA:NR)

COMANCHE STATION**** (1960) 74m Renown/COL c

Randolph Scott *(Jefferson Cody)*, Nancy Gates *(Mrs. Lowe)*, Claude Akins *(Ben Lane)*, Skip Homeier *(Frank)*, Richard Rust *(Dobie)*, Rand Brooks *(Station Man)*, Dyke Johnson *(Mr. Lowe)*, Foster Hood *(Comanche Lance Bearer)*, Joe Molina *(Comanche Chief)*, Vince St. Cyr *(Warrior)*, P. Holland *(Boy)*.

Postponing a futile ten-year search for a wife kidnapped by Indians, Scott agrees to track down a settler's wife, Gates, who has been raped and captured by Comanche Indians. On their way back to the husband, Scott and Gates are met by outlaw Akins and his two adolescent proteges, Homeier and Rust, who inform the couple that they are being trailed by Comanche braves. Akins and the boys, offering to accompany Scott and Gates on their journey, create an uneasiness in the group, with Akins frequently commenting on the cowardice of Gates' husband in sending another man to do his work. Scott avoids retorting but the verbal abuse affects Gates and she begins to question the virility of her husband. When it becomes apparent that Akins is planning to kill Scott and return Gates for a reward, Scott steals away from the gang, taking Gates with him. In the final confrontation, after the two idealistic boys are killed, Scott offers Akins, whom he has always respected, the chance to escape. Needing to prove *his* masculinity, Akins goes for his gun, but is promptly cut down by Scott. Scott and Gates continue their journey. When they reach the husband's homestead, Gates sees that her husband is now blind, and could never have aided in the search for her. His mission of mercy over, Scott leaves the reunited couple and continues his never-ending search for his wife. This fine, haunting western, the last of the Scott/Boetticher collaborations—its predecessors were SEVEN MEN FROM NOW (1956), THE TALL T, (1957), and DECISION AT SUNDOWN (1957), BUCHANAN RIDES ALONE (1958), RIDE LONESOME (1959), and WESTBOUND (1959)—encapsulates the themes that made the films some of the most striking, intelligent, and complex westerns ever made. Boetticher,an often unrecognized talent, created films that dealt with the sadness of independence, the need to search, the overpowering qualities of the land and nature, and the importance of past events influencing present deeds. In COMANCHE STATION, Boetticher stresses the impossibility of his hero to give up, to lose faith, in his hopes and ideals, or to feel it necessary to prove one's importance through useless violence. Scott is truly a loner in the film, as he is in many of the Renown westerns, a man whose personal code limits his ability to coexist with others. Adhering to the mythic structure of the western hero, Scott remains true to the ideals of honesty, courage, and the need to aid those who need help, positions that are not held by his antagonist, Akins. Akins is an honorable man who sees faith in the Code as useless and sissified, a way of life that holds none of the excitement and financial payoff of the life of an outlaw. There is a mutual respect between the two men, but it is Boetticher *and* Scott who extinguish his life, suggesting that the honorable way of life may be a lonely one, but a more spiritually satisfying one. Boetticher's films are not happy, light-hearted westerns where evil is destroyed before the final credits roll by. They are sad westerns that focus on isolated men and the harsh world they exist in, men who strive for things that they will probably never attain.

p, Harry Joe Brown, Budd Boetticher, Randolph Scott; d, Boetticher; w, Burt Kennedy; ph, Charles Lawton (CinemaScope, Eastmancolor); m, Mischa Bakaleinikoff; ed, Edwin Bryant.

Western (PR:A MPAA:NR)

COMANCHE TERRITORY** (1950) 76m UNIV c

Maureen O'Hara *(Katie)*, Macdonald Carey *(James Bowie)*, Will Geer *(Dan'l Seeger)*, Charles Drake *(Stacey Howard)*, Pedro de Cordoba *(Quisima)*, Ian MacDonald *(Walsh)*, Rick Vallin *(Pakanah)*, Parley Baer *(Boozer)*, James Best *(Sam)*, Edmund Cobb *(Ed)*, Glenn Strange *(Big Joe)*.

Carey, frontiersman and designer of the Bowie knife, travels to Comanche country where he meets government man Geer, who informs him that the local politicos have decided that the surrounding mountains, rich with silver, have been designated as land belonging to the Comanche. Always a friend to the Indian, Carey accompanies Geer to the nearest town where bar owner O'Hara and her evil brother Drake steal from Geer the document that proves the Comanche ownership. At first as unscrupulous as her brother, O'Hara soon falls for Carey and agrees to help him get the deed back from Drake. As silver-hungry Drake prepares to massacre innocent Indians for "trespassing," O'Hara and the 7th Cavalry furiously drive a wagonload of rifles to the Comanche, allowing them to defend themselves against the unprovoked attack. Drake is stopped, Geer arrives with a new document, the Indians have their land, and O'Hara and Carey decide to settle down. Although Geer tries to inject it with some crotchety humor, the film is a routine western with pretty technicolor pictures.

p, Leonard Goldstein; d, George Sherman; w, Oscar Brodney, Lewis Meltzer, (based on a story by Meltzer); ph, Maury Gertsman (Technicolor); ed, Frank Gross; spec eff, David S. Horsley.

Western (PR:A MPAA:NR)

COMANCHEROS, THE½** (1961) 107m FOX c

John Wayne *(Cutter)*, Stuart Whitman *(Regret)*, Ina Balin *(Pilar)*, Nehemiah Persoff *(Graile)*, Lee Marvin *(Crow)*, Michael Ansara *(Amflung)*, Pat Wayne *(Tobe)*, Bruce Cabot *(Maj. Henry)*, Joan O'Brien *(Melinda)*, Jack Elam *(Horseface)*, Edgar Buchanan *(Judge Bean)*, Henry Daniell *(Gireaux)*, Richard Devon *(Estevan)*, Steve Baylor *(Comanchero)*, John Dierkes *(Bill)*, Roger Mobley *(Bub Schofield)*, Bob Steele *(Pa Schofield)*, Luisa Triana *(Spanish Dancer)*, Iphigenie Castiglioni *(Josefina)*, Aiessa Wayne *(Bessie)*, George Lewis *(Iron Shirt)*, Tom Hennessy *(Graile's Bodyguard)*, Jackie Cubat, Leigh Snowden *(Hotel Girls)*, Guinn "Big Boy" Williams *(Ed McBain)*.

Texas Ranger Wayne enlists the aid of gambler Whitman in the apprehension of a group of sleazy white outlaws, led by Persoff, who help the Comanche run guns and whiskey. When it is learned that ex-Confederate officer Persoff plans to build an empire in Mexico and use his Indian pals as armies to attack the Union, Wayne's job becomes more pressing. The last film to be directed by classic Hollywood filmmaker Michael Curtiz (he died the next year), sadly has none of the style and adventure of his great films of the 1930s and 1940s. A part of the blame should be placed on Wayne who was entering into his self-parody stage, a period that seemed to make fun of the great screen persona he had created and developed over the years, a style of acting still misunderstood by most critics today. THE COMANCHEROS is not a terrible film, in fact much of it is entertaining, but it *is* obviously the effort of two talented men who were far from their peak powers.

p, George Sherman; d, Michael Curtiz; w, James Edward Grant,, Clair Huffaker (based on the novel by Paul I. Wellman); ph, William H. Clothier (CinemaScope, DeLuxe Color); m, Elmer Bernstein; ed, Louis Loeffler; art d, Jack Martin Smith, Alfred Ybarra; set d, Walter M. Scott, Robert Priestley; cos, Marjorie Best; ch, Hal Belfer.

Western Cas. (PR:A MPAA:NR)

COMBAT SQUAD*½ (1953) 72m COL bw

John Ireland *(Sgt. Fletcher)*, Lon McCallister *(Martin)*, Hal March *(Gordon)*, George E. Stone *(Brown)*, Norman Leavitt *(Jonas)*, Myron Healey *(Marley)*, Don Haggerty *(Sgt. Wiley)*, Tris Coffin *(Capt. Johnson)*, David Holt *(Garvin)*, Dick Fortune *(Kenson)*, Robert Easton *(Lewis)*, Jill Hollingsworth *(Yvonne)*, Linda Danson *(Anne)*, Neva Gilbert *(Virginia)*, Eilean Howe *(Patricia)*, Paul Keast *(Colonel)*, Dirk Evans *(GI Hero)*, Bob Peoples *(Wounded GI)*.

Grizzled combat vet Ireland helps battle-shy GI replacement McCallister cope with being smack-dab in the middle of the Korean War. When Ireland and his unit come under attack, McCallister finds that being brave can be quite easy. Uninspiring but well-intentioned war drama.

p, Jerry Thomas; d, Cy Roth; w, Wyatt Ordung; ph, Charles Van Enger; m, Paul Dunlap; ed, Harry Gerstad.

War Drama (PR:A MPAA:NR)

COME ACROSS* (1929) 60m UNIV bw
Lina Basquette, Reed Howes, Flora Finch, Crauford Kent.

Six minutes of dialog at the end of this otherwise silent comedy help conclude the story of society girl who falls in love with a "crook," not knowing that he is an eccentric playwright who is gathering research for a new work on the underworld. Basquette dances in the film, showing the talent that made her the premiere danseuse of the 1923 edition of the ZIEGFELD FOLLIES. The six minutes of sound in COME ACROSS did little to advance the career of Harvard graduate Howes, who in the early twenties became famous as the "Arrow Collar Man." With the advent of all-sound movies the handsome hero of silent films was reduced to playing supporting roles.

d, Roy Taylor; w, Peter Milne (based on the story "The Stolen Lady" by William Dudley Pelley).

Comedy **(PR:A MPAA:NR)**

COME AND GET IT*** (1936) 99m Samuel Goldwyn/UA bw
(AKA: ROARING TIMBERS)
Edward Arnold *(Barney Glasgow)*, Joel McCrea *(Richard Glasgow)*, Frances Farmer *(Lotta Morgan/Lotta Bostrom)*, Walter Brennan *(Swan Bostrom)*, Andrea Leeds *(Evvie Glasgow)*, Frank Shields *(Tony Schwerke)*, Mady Christians *(Karie)*, Mary Nash*(Emma Louise Glasgow)*, Clem Bevans *(Gunner Gallagher)*, Edwin Maxwell *(Sid Le Maire)*, Cecil Cunningham *(Josie)*, Harry Bradley *(Gubbins)*, Rollo Lloyd *(Steward)*, Charles Halton *(Hewitt)*, Phillip Cooper *(Chore Boy)*, Al K. Hall *(Goodnow)*.

Arnold gives a powerhouse performance as the brawling, ambitious, money-hungry lumber tycoon in Wisconsin who rejects Farmer's love to pursue his earthbound goals. He later meets the daughter of the woman he abandoned, also played by Farmer, and tries to win her heart, losing it to his own son, McCrea. To glue this sprawling story together Brennan acts as a coalescing force, close friend to Arnold and husband to the woman Arnold leaves in the lurch. (He would win an Oscar for his sentimentally crude supporting role.) There are several great scenes in this movie, one where Arnold, Farmer, and Brennan get into a saloon brawl, hurling trays at their antagonists, and the scenes of the lumber areas where Arnold carves out his empire. The dialog is often snappy. When tough saloon girl Farmer (playing the mother) meets Arnold she says: "Do you think money grows on trees?" Timber magnate Arnold retorts: "Mine did." Arnold does a great job with an unwieldy role, a villain who has a bit of heart, one who realizes his misspent life and makes some restitution at the end. Farmer appears in her best role, a tragic person in real life playing *two* star-crossed women. As the mother she is rough and low-voiced, moving her big-boned body about awkwardly, her wide shoulders almost bumping into Toland's camera. As the daughter she is more feminine, soft-spoken (purposely talking in a higher pitch to differentiate the roles). She is fascinating to watch in her dual parts, even singing "Aura Lee" for the enraptured Arnold as the mother,and later singing it again as the daughter. Farmer was later to state in *Will There Really Be a Morning?*: "I never devoted greater effort to any motion picture than COME AND GET IT." She honored director Hawks as "one of the finest and most sensitive directors in the business, and there was nothing routine or cut-and-dried in his approach. He gave every scene a minute examination, both psychological and visual, and under his direction I was secure and full of anticipation." Hawks himself once stated that if a film had "one great scene" it was a good film. This movie has many, although it is overlong and often bogs down in a story uncertain of destination, a tale far removed from the generation-to-generation Ferber novel. McCrea, as Arnold's son who eventually winds up with daughter Farmer, is miscast in a role that is painfully brief and unrewarding. Hawks was not alone in directing this film. William Wyler also directed some scenes before Hawks took over and Rosson is credited by most sources as helming the logging scenes which are shot in semi-documentary style, much the same way the tuna fishing scenes are captured in TIGER SHARK, also directed by Hawks and Rosson. COME AND GET IT is a simple disjointed story that doesn't stick together as well as the scene where Farmer and McCrea become momentarily joined while pulling taffy.

p, Samuel Goldwyn; d, Howard Hawks, William Wyler (Richard Rosson, logging scenes); w, Jules Furthman, Jane Murfin (based on the novel by Edna Ferber); ph, Gregg Toland, Rudolph Mate; m, Alfred Newman; ed, Edward Curtiss; art d, Richard Day; set d, Julia Heron; cos, Omar Kiam; spec eff, Ray Binger.

Historical Drama/Romance **(PR:A MPAA:NR)**

COME BACK BABY zero (1968) 100m Film-Makers bw
John Terry Riebling *(Cal Thacker)*, Barbara Theitelbaum *(Carrie Da Silva)*, Mark Wieshaus *(Mike Rubel)*, Crag Bovia *(Richard "Stoney" Morgan)*, Barbara Rubel *(Stoney's Sister)*, Mary Anne Seibert *(Silvia)*, Colette Bablon *(Stoney's Victim)*, Jaqueline Uytenbogaart *(Girl in Bed)*, Henry Gribbin, Dave Stegstra, Len Wanetik *(Policemen)*, Jane Hornick *(Girl at Party)*, Steve Steinhauer *(Boy at Party)*, Barbara Riebling *(Prostitute)*, George Gerdes *(Thief)*, John McDonald *(Mugging Victim)*, Felicia Waynesbro *(Streetwalker)*.

Irritating, self-indulgent, independently made drug drama about a self-described artist, Riebling, his dope-peddling pal, Bovia, and their always out-of-work cohort, Weishaus. When his girl friend catches him in bed with another girl, Riebling sinks even deeper into his "Oh, pity me" state and mopes around his filthy apartment. When the old girl friend calls the police and informs them of Bovia's shady marijuana dealing, a fight breaks out between Bovia and Riebling that leaves Bovia dead. Desperate and on the run, the pudgy and unappealing Riebling is gunned down by the police at the film's climax. Occasionally, trigger-happy cops are a blessing. Written, directed, photographed, and edited by David Allen Greene, COME BACK BABY has to rank with the worst of the pretentious slice-of-life "art" films made by people who feel that they have something extremely important to say but have no idea what "it" is and have no dramatic talent at all. Lacking in humor, understanding, and compassion, the film is a complete waste of time.

p,d,w,ph&ed, David Allen Greene; m, Musicues; additional music, Greene, J. T. Riebling, Lightnin' Hopkins, Lonnie Mack.

Drama **(PR:O MPAA:NR)**

COME BACK CHARLESTON BLUE** (1972) 100m WB c
Godfrey Cambridge *(Gravedigger Jones)*, Raymond St. Jacques *(Coffin Ed Johnson)*, Peter De Anda *(Joe)*, Jonelle Allen *(Carol)*, Maxwell Glanville *(Caspar)*,Minnie Gentry *(Her Majesty)*, Dick Sabol *(Jarema)*, Leonardo Cimino *(Frank Mago)*, Percy Rodrigues *(Bryce)*, Toney Brealond *(Drag Queen)*, Tim Pelt *(Earl J)*, Darryl Knibb *(Douglas)*, Marcia McBroom *(Girl Barber)*, Adam Wade *(Benjy)*, Joseph Ray *(Bubba)*, Theodore Wilson *(Cemetery Guard)*, Dorothi Fox *(Streetwalker)*.

When prominent New York photographer De Anda proclaims that he wants to rid Harlem of drugs, no one, except reigning drug king Glanville, realizes that he is merely scouting out the territory for himself. When De Anda blames a series of murders on the ghost of Charleston Blue, a depression-era gangster, the local drug dealers, being a superstitious lot, become frightened and avoid any illegal activity, giving De Anda a clear path. Onto the scene come black New York detectives Cambridge and St. Jacques who use their super cool ways to stop both De Anda and Glanville. Though not as fun and light-hearted as its predecessor, this sequel to COTTON COMES TO HARLEM is still enjoyable, thanks to the engaging banter between Cambridge and St. Jacques. Mark Warren, for a long time director of the "Rowan and Martin Laugh-In" TV revues of the 1960s and early 1970s, made his feature directorial bow in COME BACK CHARLESTON.

p, Samuel Goldwyn, Jr.; d, Mark Warren; w, Bontche Schweig (Ernest Kinoy), Peggy Elliott (based on the novel "The Heat's On" by Chester Himes); ph, Dick Kratina (Technicolor); m, Donny Hathaway, Quincy Jones; ed, Gerald Greenburg, George Bowers; prod d, Robert Gundlach; art d, Perry Watkins; set, George De Titta; Cos, Anna Hill Johnstone; m/l, Jones.

Comedy **(PR:O MPAA:PG)**

COME BACK, LITTLE SHEBA**** (1952) 95m PAR bw
Burt Lancaster *(Doc Delaney)*, Shirley Booth *(Lola Delaney)*, Terry Moore *(Marie Buckholder)*, Richard Jaeckel *(Turk Fisher)*, Philip Ober *(Ed Anderson)*, Liza Golm *(Mrs. Goffman)*, Walter Kelley *(Bruce)*.
COME BACK, LITTLE SHEBA opened Christmas week of 1952 in order to qualify for an Academy Award—the rules state that a film must play one week in either Los Angeles or New York City to be considered. The strategy was excellent as Shirley Booth won out over Joan Crawford (SUDDEN FEAR), Julie Haris (THE MEMBER OF THE WEDDING), Bette Davis (THE STAR), and Susan Hayward (WITH A SONG IN MY HEART). Moore, in her finest performance, lost out as Best Supporting Actress to Gloria Grahame in THE BAD AND THE BEAUTIFUL. Lancaster is Doc Delaney, an alcoholic who has been dry for a year. Booth is his frumpy wife, a woman who never shuts up and who lives for the day when little Sheba (her lost dog) will return to the house. Theirs is a life of Eliot's "quiet desperation" until vibrant Moore comes to their home to rent a room. Moore is attending a local school and her presence is the frying pan into which the fat flies. Moore is seeing perennial youth Jaeckel and Lancaster doesn't like the young man or what he has in mind for Moore (something that must also be lurking at the back of Lancaster's head). Booth and Lancaster married young, the result of pre-marital love-making, and that memory bubbles under the surface. Lancaster has a violent outburst and, once again, reaches for the whiskey to slake his great thirst. While under the influence, he berates Booth for her slatternly appearance, the slovenliness of the house, her living in the past. After sleep heals his hangover, Lancaster returns to the docile, sweet man he was before and Booth comes to a realization of what their lives have become and resolves to make changes for the better. And that's about that. But Booth's work is so brilliant that it remains etched forever in the memory of anyone who saw it. True, she had several hundred opportunities to hone that performance as she played the role on Broadway, but many other stage actresses came to the screen and were never able to repeat their successes on celluloid (Lynn Fontanne, Katherine Cornell, et al.). Booth was forty-five years old when she made the film, just about the same age as she portrayed in the role. Lancaster was thirty-nine and his elan and vitality showed through the makeup so he was an odd choice to play the downtrodden ex-medical student. No doubt his inclusion was to bolster a film that had no major names without him. Old-timers love to talk about certain stage performances that were never captured on film, roles that live only in some aged stage manager's memory. We must be thankful that Booth's work in COME BACK, LITTLE SHEBA will remain frozen in time for countless years to come.

p, Hal B. Wallis; d, Daniel Mann; w, Ketti Frings (based on the play by William Inge); ph, James Wong Howe; m, Franz Waxman; ed, Warren Low.

Domestic Drama **(PR:A-C MPAA:NR)**

COME BACK PETER* (1952, Brit.) 80m Present Day/Apex bw
Patrick Holt *(John Neilson)*, Peter Hammond *(George Harris)*, Humphrey Lestocq *(Arthur Hapgood)*, Kathleen Boutall *(Mrs. Hapgood)*, Charles Lamb *(Mr. Hapgood)*, Pamela Bygrave *(Myrna Hapgood)*, Aud Johansen *(Virginia)*, Dorothy Primrose *(Phyllis Hapgood)*, Doris Groves *(Dandy)*, John Singer *(Ted)*.

Unmemorable comedy concerning the married children of an aging couple who come to live with their parents in their new, but tiny house. A pedestrian cast in a stumbling movie.

p, Charles Reynolds; d&w, Charles Saunders (based on a play by A. P. Dearsley).

Comedy **(PR:A MPAA:NR)**

COME BACK PETER* (1971, Brit.) 65m Donwin/RSE c
Christopher Matthews *(Peter)*, Erika Bergmann *("Au Pair")*, Penny Riley *(Model)*, Yolanda Turner *(Socialite)*, Valerie St. Helene *(Black Girl)*, Maddy Smith *(Socialite's Daughter)*, Annabel Leventon *(Hippie)*, Nicola Pagett *(Jenny)*, Mary and Madeleine Collinson.

Butcher's helper Matthews, out to prove himself a young stud, succeeds in bedding a German girl, a snobby model, a holier-than-thou socialite, a black singer, a hippie girl, and a timid Salvation Army worker, whom he thinks he may have fallen in love with. Silly attempt to analyze the morals of youth in "swinging London" during the late 1960s and early 1970s lacks any understanding of its characters' emotions.

p,d,w&ed, Donovan Winter; ph, Gus Corna, Ian D. Struthers (Eastmancolor); m/l, Gloria Stewart.

Drama **(PR:C MPAA:NR)**

COME BACK TO THE 5 & DIME, JIMMY DEAN, JIMMY DEAN**½ (1982) 109m Sandcastle 5/Viacom c

Sandy Dennis *(Mona)*, Cher *(Sissy)*, Karen Black *(Joanne)*, Sudie Bond *(Juanita)*, Marta Heflin *(Edna Louise)*, Kathy Bates *(Stella May)*, Mark Patton *(Joe Qualley)*, Caroline Aaron *(Martha)*, Ruth Miller *(Clarissa)*, Gena Ramsel *(Sue Ellen)*, Ann Risley *(Phyllis Marie)*, Dianne Turley Travis *(Alice Ann)*.

Five women who had grown up together in a small Texas town idolizing James Dean reunite in their teenage hangout, the town's 5 & Dime Store, to discuss their past, their failures, their loves, their lives. The most touching moment comes when Dennis shatters her self-generated illusion that Dean was the father of her child. Originally producer of the play on Broadway with the same cast, director Altman's screen treatment recaptures the vitality of a live theater performance from every one of his cast members, but it cannot overcome the visual limitations of the story. The film is not cinematic at all, but the emotional intensity of Black, and particularly Dennis, make the character-study approach intriguing and challenging. The constant technical invention, the taste, sensitivity, and scrupulous attention to detail in evidence throughout the movie rate bravos, considering that it was shot in only nineteen days.

p, Scott Bushnell; d, Robert Altman; w, Ed Graczyck (based on his play of the same title); ph, Pierre Mignot; ed, Jason Rosenfield; prod d, David Gropman.

Drama **Cas.** **(PR:O MPAA:NR)**

COME BLOW YOUR HORN*** (1963) 112m PAR c

Frank Sinatra *(Alan)*, Lee J. Cobb *(Mr. Baker)*, Molly Picon *(Mrs. Baker)*, Barbara Rush *(Connie)*, Jill St. John *(Peggy)*, Tony Bill *(Buddy)*, Dan Blocker *(Mr. Eckman)*, Phyllis McGuire *(Mrs. Eckman)*, Carole Wells *(Eunice)*, Herbie Fay *(Waiter)*, Romo Vincent *(Barber)*, Charlotte Fletcher *(Manicurist)*, Greta Randall *(Tall Girl)*, Dean Martin *(The Bum)*, Joyce Nizzari *(Snow)*.

Affable adaptation of Simon's first big stage hit, Lear's screenplay almost, but not quite, deadens Simon's wit. This was back in the days before Simon could write his own ticket (and screenplay). Simon, as always, was writing about himself and his family. His relationship with older brother Danny (himself a successful writer-director who was one of the early TV comedy mavens) is explored, with Sinatra playing Danny and Tony Bill as Neil. Bill leaves his parents, Cobb and Picon, to move in with swinger brother, Sinatra. Frank works for the family wax-fruit business but his pleasure-chasing far outstrips his order-taking. Sinatra lives in a high-rise ring-a-ding-ding pad with hot and cold running women, and is thrilled that his conservative sibling has tossed off the family yoke and is reaching out to see what life is like in the real world. He buys Bill a new set of threads and begins teaching the boy the ins and outs of being a wastrel. Bill learns quickly and soon appropriates Sinatra's booze, women, and even his manner of speech. Soon enough Frank is jilted by St. John (his upstairs sweetie, who falls for Bill), he's jilted by Rush (his favorite date) and he's whacked soundly about the head and shoulders by Blocker, husband of McGuire—another girl friend. Meantime, Cobb and Picon arrive at the bachelor pad and attempt to convince their younger son not to go the way of the older one. Cobb feels that anyone over thirty who isn't married is a bum! Sinatra attempts to get Bill to settle down but Bill is feeling his own sense of independence and tells his brother to cool it and leave him be. Sinatra proposes to Rush and she accepts. Next he unites his arguing parents and finally cedes the pad, the whiskey, and the rolodex filled with numbers to Bill. Bud Yorkin does well enough with what his partner handed him to shoot and the editing keeps things at a fairly quick clip. The best lines go to Cobb and Picon and they do quite well with the solid Simon jokes. St. John is ageless and appears to be in the 1980s what she was in the 1960s—a very sexy, well-built woman. Bill became a successful film producer (THE STING) and director (MY BODYGUARD) and restaurateur (72 Market in Venice, California). Veteran burlesquers Vincent and Fay do neat turns in their bits and the hit theme song is still a standard. Funny unbilled bum bit by Dean Martin.

p, Bud Yorkin, Norman Lear; d, Yorkin; w, Lear (based on the play by Neil Simon); ph, William H. Daniels (Panavision, Technicolor); m, Nelson Riddle; ed, Frank P. Keller; art d, Hal Pereira, Roland Anderson; set d, Sam Comer, James Payne; cos, Edith Head; spec eff, Paul K. Lerpae; m/l, Sammy Cahn, James Van Heusen; makeup, Wally Westmore.

Comedy **(PR:A-C MPAA:NR)**

COME CLOSER, FOLKS* (1936) 61m COL bw

James Dunn *(Jim Keene)*, Marian Marsh *(Peggy Woods)*, Wynne Gibson *(Mae)*, Herman Bing *(Herman)*, George McKay *(Rudolph)*, Gene Lockhart *(Elmer Woods)*, John Gallaudet *(Pitchman)*, Gene Morgan *(Pitchman)*, Wallis Clark *(Mr. Houston)*.

Street hawker Dunn worms his way into a minor position at a prominent department store and slowly works his way to become assistant manager of the company. Horatio Alger-ish story still has some mildly appealing features, most notably Herman Bing as the merchant through whom the pitchmen buy their wares.

d, D. Ross Lederman; w, Lee Loeb, Harold Buchman (based on a story by Aben Kandel); ph, Henry Freulich; ed, Byron Robinson.

Comedy **(PR:A MPAA:NR)**

COME DANCE WITH ME** (1950, Brit.) 58m Anglofilm/COL bw

Max Wall *(Manager)*, Gordon Humphris *(Boy)*, Yvonne Marsh *(Girl)*, Barbara Hamilton *(Stage Girl)*, Vincent Ball *(Secretary)*, Anne Shelton, Derek Roy, Anton Karas, Marquis Trio, Aida Foster Girls.

Humphris is a valet impersonating a baronet who falls in love with Marsh, a maid impersonating a Lady. All of it happens in Wall's nightclub. Okay for a light diversion.

p&d, Mario Zampi; w, Cyril Roberts.

Musical **(PR:A MPAA:NR)**

COME DANCE WITH ME!*½ (1960, Fr.) 91m Kingsley International c (AKA: VOULEZ-VOUS DANSER AVEC MOI)

Brigitte Bardot *(Virginia)*, Henri Vidal *(Harvey)*, Dawn Addams *(Anita)*, Noel Roquevert *(Albert)*, Dario Moreno *(Flores)*, Philippe Nicaud *(Daniel)*, Paul Frankeur *(Inspector)*, Serge Gainsbourg *(Leon)*.

Bardot goes undercover as a dance hall girl to find the real culprit in a murder her husband (Vidal) is accused of. Sloppily constructed, the film is only an excuse to watch Bardot in living color. (In French: English sub-titles; some prints dubbed).

p, Francis Cosne; d, Michel Boisrond; w, Annette Wademant (based on the novel *The Blonde Died Dancing* by Kelley Roos); ph, Robert LeFebvre (Eastmancolor); m, Henri Crolla, Andre Hodeir.

Crime **(PR:C-O MPAA:NR)**

COME FILL THE CUP***½ (1951) 112m WB/FN bw

James Cagney *(Lew Marsh)*, Phyllis Thaxter *(Paula Copeland)*, Raymond Massey *(John Ives)*, James Gleason *(Charley Dolan)*, Gig Young *(Boyd Copeland)*, Selena Royle *(Dolly Copeland)*, Larry Keating *(Julian Cuscaden)*, Charlita *(Maria Diego)*, Shedon Leonard *(Lennie Garr)*, Douglas Spencer *(Ike Bashaw)*, John Kellogg *(Don Bell)*, William Bakewell *(Hal Ortman)*, John Alvin *(Travis Ashbourne III)*, King Donavan *(Kip Zunches)*, Torben Meyer *(Welder)*, James Flavin *(Police Captain)*, Norma Jean Macias *(Ora)*, Henry Blair *(Bobby)*, Elizabeth Flournoy *(Lila)*.

In the role of a talented newsman/dipsomaniac Cagney gives one of his most startling bravura performances. His inability to resist booze causes Cagney to lose his job and also the love of a girl who wants to marry him. He goes on a spectacular bender and, with legs turned to jelly, eyelids closed to slits, mouth quivering, Cagney collapses into the gutter to almost be run over by a truck. He is later thrown into a drunk tank to undergo the horrors of withdrawal and to share the nightmares of those around him. With grim resolve, Cagney vows never to drink again and joins an AA-type group, with Gleason's help. He regains his job and rises to the position of city editor but is always "one drink away" from destruction. He lives with Gleason, who keeps an unopened bottle of booze in the kitchen cabinet as a reminder, and to let Cagney know that if he takes a drink from it, the long slide to the bottom will begin all over again. Cagney's publisher, Massey, comes to him, asking that he help reform his alcoholic nephew, Young who, ironically, is involved with Cagney's old girl friend, Thaxter. Cagney undertakes the difficult job, which proves almost impossible, and during the course of the wet-to-dry conversion, drunkard Young unwittingly causes the death of Gleason through his mobster contacts. One of the most powerful scenes occurs near the end when sadistic mobster Leonard (did he ever play anything else?), knowing Cagney and Young are reformed drunks, pours booze all over them, then gives Cagney a large drink and orders him to gulp it down. Cagney throws the booze in Leonard's face, instead of swallowing what he evidently craves. Cagney's performance is absolutely spellbinding. He easily convinces the viewer that he is stone drunk in some scenes, even though the great actor was never a tippler. When he is sober, his agonizing over the waiting booze in the cupboard makes the viewer's throat feel parched. The realistic drunk scenes by Cagney were pulled from his own boyhood experiences; his father suffered from alcoholism. The actor also studied the mannerisms of drunks, how an alcoholic forces himself to stagger stiff-legged to compensate for wobbly legs, incorporating these movements into his role. Cagney's part was actually based upon the life of one of his close friends, Jimmy Richardson, the famous city editor of the Los Angeles *Examiner* whom the actor interviewed at great length. The role of the publisher was originally set for the suave Adolph Menjou, Cagney's choice, but he had commitments elsewhere, so Massey was chosen. Young's role was tragically close to his own life; the handsome actor, later an Oscar winner for THEY SHOOT HORSES, DON'T THEY? (1969), ruined his career and life with booze, which led to suicide. As usual, Cagney went out of his way for the actors in the production. When Young read for his role, Cagney arrived on the set to go through the test with him so that he would be at ease. "It was unheard of for a star to do that," Young later remarked. But not for Cagney, a superstar, and a super human being. COME FILL THE CUP just misses approaching the excellence of THE LOST WEEKEND but Cagney's unforgettable performance makes the production superior.

p, Henry Blanke; d, Gordon Douglas; w, Ivan Goff, Ben Roberts (based on the novel by Harlan Ware); ph, Robert Burks, William Scheerr; ed, Alan Crosland, Jr.; md, Ray Heindorf; art d, Leo F. Kuter; set d, William L. Kuehl; cos, Leah Rhodes; makeup, Gordon Bau.

Drama **(PR:C MPAA:NR)**

COME FLY WITH ME** (1963) 107m MGM c

Dolores Hart *(Donna Stuart)*, Hugh O'Brian *(1st Officer Ray Winsley)*, Karl Boehm *(Baron Franz Von Elzingen)*, Pamela Tiffin *(Carol Brewster)*, Karl Malden *(Walter Lucas)*, Lois Nettleton *(Hilda Bergstrom)*, Dawn Addams *(Katie)*, Richard Wattis *(Oliver Garson)*, Andrew Cruickshank *(Cardwell)*, James Dobson *(Flight Engineer Teddy Shepherd)*, Lois Maxwell *(Gwen)*, John Crawford *(Captain)*, Robert Easton *(Navigator)*, Guilo Wieland *(Armand)*, Maurice Marsac *(M. Rinard)*, Bibi Morat *(French Urchin)*.

Three flight attendants, Hart, Nettleton, and Tiffin each fall in love during a flight from New York to Paris. Hart falls for wealthy aristocrat Boehm, but is saddened to learn that he has only paid attention to her to use her in his diamond-smuggling plans.

Nettleton doesn't have to try much at all to land over-attentive millionaire Malden, and Tiffin discovers that her heart belongs to flyboy O'Brian. Sappy but cute airborne romance picture that contains a wonderfully perky performance from Tiffin.

p, Anatole De Grunwald; d, Henry Levin; w, William Roberts (based on the novel *Girl On A Wing* by Bernard Glemser); ph, Oswald Morris (Panavision, Technicolor); m, Lyn Murray; ed, Frank Clarke; prod d, Albert Becket; art d, William Kellner; cos, Pierre Balmain; m/l, "La chansonnette" (Phillippe Gerard, Jean Drejac), "Come Fly With Me"(Sammy Cahn, James Van Heusen), "In einem kleinem Cafe in Hernals" (Hermann Leopoldi).

Comedy **(PR:A MPAA:NR)**

COME LIVE WITH ME*½ (1941) 85m MGM bw
James Stewart *(Bill Smith)*, Hedy Lamarr *(Johnny Jones)*, Ian Hunter *(Barton Kendrick)*, Verree Teasdale *(Diana Kendrick)*, Donald Meek *(Joe Darsie)*, Barton MacLane *(Barney Grogan)*, Edward Ashley *(Arnold Stafford)*, Ann Codee *(Yvonne)*, King Baggott *(Doorman)*, Adeline de Walt Reynolds *(Grandma)*, Si Jenks *(Farmhand)*, Fritz Feld *(Headwaiter)*, Dewey Robinson *(Chef)*, Joe Yule *(Sleeping Neighbor)*, Tom Fadden *(Hired Hand)*, Horace McMahon *(Taxi Driver)*, Greta Meyer *(Frieda)*, Frank Orth *(Jerry)*, George Watts *(Waiter)*.

A charming film as relevant today as it was in 1941. Lamarr is a gorgeous refugee named Johanna Janns (she takes the name Johnny Jones) who is having it away with wealthy publisher Hunter. Hunter and wife Teasdale live a "modern" marriage with each free to do as they please, no questions asked. Lamarr is about to be deported and finds Stewart, a broke writer (aren't they all?), and arranges to marry him for money. She'll pay him something weekly but he is not to follow her or know where she lives. Stewart is understandably in love with Lamarr and with her story, so he uses it for a plot, writes a novel, and sends it to a publisher. Guess which publisher? Right! Hunter buys the book, sends Stewart a check, and the young writer is elated. His mood is dashed when Lamarr serves him divorce papers in preparation for her marriage to Hunter. Stewart notes Lamarr's address on the documents and decides to give her a visit. He tells her that she must spend one weekend with him and then and only then will he agree to the divorce. Lamarr calls Hunter, explains what's happening, and asks that Hunter follow them to the house of Stewart's grandmother. As time passes, Lamarr comes to look at Stewart in quite another way and realizes that she is falling in love with him. Hunter arrives and Stewart thinks he's come to discuss the novel but shortly realizes that Hunter is, in fact, the other man. Stewart stomps out of the house in anger. Hunter and Lamarr have a talk in the comfortable farmhouse surroundings and he makes a vain but valiant attempt to win her back but it's to no avail as her heart now belongs to Jimmy. Hunter departs and Stewart returns to find the radiant Hedy awaiting him. It's a flimsy yet winning film that never won the audiences it should have. Lamarr was luminous and Stewart ingenuous and the sparks they made could light up an air raid brown-out.

p&d, Clarence Brown; w, Patterson McNutt (based on a story by Virginia Van Upp); ph, George Folsey; m, Herbert Stothart; ed, Frank E. Hull; art d, Cedric Gibbons; set d, Edwin B. Willis; cos, Adrian.

Comedy **(PR:A MPAA:NR)**

COME 'N' GET IT (SEE: LUNCH WAGON, 1980)

COME NEXT SPRING*½ (1956) 98m REP c
Ann Sheridan *(Bess Ballot)*, Steve Cochran *(Matt Ballot)*, Walter Brennan *(Jeff Storys)*, Sherry Jackson *(Annie)*, Richard Eyer *(Abraham)*, Edgar Buchanan *(Mr. Canary)*, Sonny Tufts *(Leroy Hytower)*, Harry Shannon *(Mr. Totter)*, Rad Fulton *(Bob Storys)*, Mae Clarke *(Myrtle)*, Roscoe Ates *(Shorty Wilkins)*, Wade Ruby *(Delbert Meaner)*, James Best *(Bill Jackson)*.

Having left his family years earlier because of drinking and wild living, a much calmer Cochran returns to his wife Sheridan and their Arkansas farm. Anxious to prove himself not only to Sheridan but to his mute daughter and never-seen baby boy as well, Cochran commits himself to putting the delapidated farm in order. In an emotional climax, Cochran saves his daughter from an old mine pit after hearing her screams, the first sounds she has made in years. Genuinely appealing film depicting the simple, yet thoughtful lives of small farm-belt families.

p, Herbert J. Yates; d, R. G. "Bud" Springsteen; w, Montgomery Pittman; ph, Jack Marta (Trucolor); m, Max Steiner; ed, Tony Martinelli; cos, Adele Palmer; m/l, "Come Next Spring" (Lenny Adelson, Steiner) sung by Tony Bennett.

Drama **(PR:AA MPAA:NR)**

COME ON, THE*½ (1956) 82m AA bw
Anne Baxter *(Rita Kendrick)*, Sterling Hayden *(Dave Arnold)*, John Hoyt *(Harley Kendrick)*, Jesse White *(J. J. McConigle)*, Walter Cassell *(Tony Margoli)*, Lee Turnbull *(Joe Tinney)*, Alex Gerry *(Chalmers)*, Paul Picerni *(Jerry Jannings)*, Karolee Kelly *(Tony's Girl)*, Theodore Newton *(Capt. Getz)*, Tyler McVey *(Hogan)*.

While fishing in Mexico, down-on-his-luck wanderer Hayden falls for the shapely Baxter after spying her on a beach. When she tries to convince Hayden to aid her in killing her overbearing husband, Hoyt, Hayden refuses, but remains attracted. After discovering his wife's infidelity, Hoyt pretends to blow himself up, hoping the police will think it the work of Baxter and her lover. When shifty private eye White clears Baxter with the officials, he turns quickly around and tries to blackmail Baxter, threatening to expose her affair with Hayden. Baxter neatly kills White, but is surprised to learn that Hoyt has reappeared. At the film's climax, Baxter, Hoyt, and Hayden meet on the beach where the lovers had first met. Baxter quickly shoots her husband, but Hoyt musters up enough energy to fire back at his treacherous wife. With Hoyt dead, Baxter perishes in Hayden's arms. Vaguely reminiscent of Orson Welles' THE LADY FROM SHANGHAI, this tale of deception and murder doesn't contain the edgy suspense that makes such a thriller interesting. Baxter and Hayden do their best with their lightweight roles, but cannot help the sub standard direction and plotting.

p, Lindsley Parsons; d, Russell Birdwell; w, Warren Douglas, Whitman Chambers (based on the novel by Chambers); ph, Ernest Haller; m, Paul Dunlap; ed, Maurice Wright.

Drama **(PR:A MPAA:NR)**

COME ON, COWBOYS*½ (1937) 53m REP bw
Robert Livingston *(Stoney Brooke)*, Ray Corrigan *(Tucson Smith)*, Max Terhune *(Lullaby Joslin)*, Maxine Doyle *(Mary)*, Willie Fung *(Charlie)*, Horace Murphy *(Harris)*, Edward Cassidy *(Rigby)*, Roger Williams *(Lou)*, Fern Emmett, Yakima Canutt, George Burton, Merrill McCormack, Loren Riebe, Victor Allen, Al Taylor, George Plues, Milburn Morante, Carleton Young, George Morrell, Ernie Adams, Jim Corey, Jack Kirk.

Livingston, Corrigan, and Terhune, good-natured and honest cowpokes that they are, help unmask a counterfeit ring that uses a carnival for a front. Routine entry in the "Three Mesquiteers" series.

p, Sol C. Siegel; d, Joseph Kane; w, Betty Burbridge; ph, Ernest Miller; ed, Lester Orlebeck.

Western **(PR:A MPAA:NR)**

COME ON DANGER!*½ (1932) 60m RKO bw
Tom Keene, Julie Haydon, Rosco Ates, Robert Ellis, Wade Boteler, William Scott, Harry Tenbrook, Bud Osborne, Roy Stewart, Frank Lackteen, Nell Craig, Monte Montague, Flash the Horse.

The first oater Keene made for RKO and it's not half bad. Haydon plays a woman forced to become an outlaw to save her ranch from villain Ellis and his band of thieves. Texas Ranger Keene thinks Haydon murdered his brother when he attempted to bring her in (Ellis really pulled the trigger) and the ranger vows to bring the outlaw gal to justice. Eventually Keene figures out the situation and gets his revenge on Ellis, freeing Haydon from a life of crime. Good performances by Haydon and Keene rise above the trite and labored scripting by Cohen.

d, Robert Hill; w, Bennett Cohen; ph, Nick Musuraca.

Western **(PR:A MPAA:NR)**

COME ON DANGER* (1942) 56m RKO bw
Tim Holt *(Johnny)*, Frances Neal *(Ann)*, Ray Whitley *(Smokey)*, Lee "Lasses" White *(Whopper)*, Karl Hackett *(Ramsey)*, Malcolm "Bud" McTaggart *(Russ)*, Glenn Strange *(Sloan)*, Evellyn Dockson *(Aunt Fanny)*, Davison Clark *(Blake)*, John Elliott *(Saunders)*, "Slim" Whitaker *(Sheriff)*, Kate Harrington *(Maggie)*, Henry Rocquemore *(Jed)*.

When a Robin Hood-like woman outlaw, Neal, is accused of murder, Holt sets out to capture her, but discovers she is innocent. Figuring out that the ruthless businessmen who took her property away from her years ago now are trying to frame her, Holt uncovers the fact that they are the killers. Made twice before as COME ON DANGER! in 1932 and THE RENEGADE RANGER in 1938 with George O'Brien and Rita (Cansino) Hayworth, this third version holds nothing new or exciting, although Holt is, as always, appealing.

p, Bert Gilroy; d, Edward Killy; w, Norton S. Parker (based on a story by Bennett Cohen); ph, Harry Wild; ed, Frederic Knudston.

Western **(PR:A MPAA:NR)**

COME ON GEORGE* (1939, Brit.) 88m ATP/ABFD bw
George Formby *(George)*, Pat Kirkwood *(Ann Johnson)*, Joss Ambler *(Sir Charles Bailey)*, Meriel Forbes *(Monica Bailey)*, Cyril Raymond *(Jimmy Taylor)*, George Hayes *(Bannerman)*, George Carney *(Sgt. Johnson)*, Ronald Shiner *(Nat)*, Gibb McLaughlin *(Dr. MacGregor)*, Hal Gordon *(Stableboy)*, Davy Burnaby *(Col. Bollinger)*, C. Denier Warren *(Barker)*, James Hayter *(Banker)*, Syd Crossley *(Police Constable)*.

Formby is a nervous stableboy who tames a skittish horse and rides him to victory in the big race. Formby was a major comedic star in the late thirties, but this is one of his lesser efforts.

p, Jack Kitchin; d, Anthony Kimmins; w, Kimmins, Leslie Arliss, Val Valentine.

Comedy **(PR:A MPAA:NR)**

COME ON, LEATHERNECKS*½ (1938) 65m REP bw
Richard Cromwell *(Jimmy)*, Marsha Hunt *(Valerie)*, Leon Ames *(Baroni)*, Edward Brophy *(Max Maxwell)*, Bruce MacFarlane *(Hy)*, Robert Warwick *(Col. Butler)*, Howard Hickman *(Cmdr. Felton)*, James Bush *(Dick Taylor)*, Walter Miller *(Coach Welles)*, Anthony Warde *(Nick)*, Ralph Dunn *(Capt. Niles)*, Harry Strang *(Slats)*, Alan Ladd.

After graduating from Annapolis, football star and new second lieutenant Cromwell must decide on joining the Marines as his father, a colonel, wants him to, or accepting Brophy's offer to join his pro football team. When he uncovers a gun-smuggling ring, the lieutenant realizes that he receives more satisfaction from helping Uncle Sam than scoring touchdowns and he joins the Leathernecks. Mildly entertaining patriotic story hampered by a wooden performance from Cromwell. Alan Ladd has an uncredited bit role as a club waiter.

p, Herman Schlom; d, James Cruze; w, Sidney Salkow, Dorrell and Stuart McGowan (based on an original story by Salkow); ph, Ernest Miller; ed, Edward Mann.

Drama **(PR:A MPAA:NR):**

COME ON, MARINES*½ (1934) 64m PAR bw
Richard Arlen *(Lucky Davis)*, Ida Lupino *(Esther Cabot)*, Roscoe Karns *(Spud McGurke)*, Grace Bradley *(JoJo La Verne)*, Virginia Hammond *(Susie Raybourne)*, Gwenilian Gill *(Katherine)*, Clara Lou Sheridan *(Shirley)*, Toby Wing *(Dolly)*, Lona Andre *(Loretta)*, Leo Chalzel *(Bumpy)*, Pat Flaherty *(Peewee)*, Fuzzy Knight *(Wimpy)*, Julian Madison *(Brick)*, Edmund Breese *(General)*, Monte Blue *(Lieutenant)*, Jean

Chatburn (*1st Girl*), Jenifer Gray (*2nd Girl*), Kay McCoy (*3rd Girl*), Mary Blackwood (*4th Girl*).

Womanizing leatherneck Arlen finds himself assigned the task of leading a small group of Marines to rescue Lupino and her finishing-school companions who have become stranded on an island after their world-touring cruise ship sank in the Pacific. Hopelessly implausible comedy that must have been quite risque in its day. It was skilled craftsman director Hathaway's second credited directorial job.

p, Albert Lewis; d, Henry Hathaway; w, Byron Morgan and Joel Sayre (based on a story by Philip Wylie); ph, Ben Reynolds; m, Ralph Rainger; ed, James Smith; art d, Earl Hedrick.

Comedy/Drama   **(PR:A   MPAA:NR)**

COME ON RANGERS**   (1939) 57m REP bw

Roy Rogers (*Roy*), Mary Hart (*Janice*), Raymond Hatton (*Jeff*), J. Farrell MacDonald (*Col. Forbes*), Purnell Pratt (*Harvey*), Harry Woods (*Burke*), Bruce MacFarlane (*Nelson*), Lane Chandler (*Ken*), Chester Gunnels (*Smith*), Lee Powell (*Earp*), Frank McCarroll, Chick Hannon, Jack Kirk, Al Taylor, Horace B. Carpenter, Bob Wilke, Al Ferguson, Allan Cavan, Ben Corbett, Burr Caruth, "Trigger."

Although replaced by regular cavalry, a group of Texas Rangers are brought out of retirement by Rogers after he learns that one of their former members has been murdered. Finding that the present policing forces cannot cope with the guerrilla tactics of Texas bandits and the corrupt local governments, the old Rangers whip Texas back into shape and capture the ruthless businessmen who killed their comrade. Mildly enjoyable Roy Rogers western.

p, Charles E. Ford; d, Joseph Kane; w, Gerald Geraghty, Jack Natteford; ph, Al Wilson; ed, Edward Mann; md, Cy Feuer.

Western   **Cas.**   **(PR:A   MPAA:NR)**

COME ON TARZAN**   (1933) 61m KBS/World Wide bw

Ken Maynard, Myrna Kennedy, Kate Campbell, Roy Stewart, Bob Kortman, Niles Welch, Ben Corbett, Jack Rockwell, Nelson McDowell, Jack Mower, Edmund Cobb, Robert Walker, Hank Bell, Jim Corey, Slim Whitaker, Al Taylor, Jack Ward, Bud McClure, "Tarzan."

Early release western in which ranch foreman Maynard fights off bid by bad guys to hunt down wild horses for use as dog food. There's also romance as Maynard first scorns, then falls in love with Kennedy.

p, Burt Kelly, Sam Bischoff, William Saal; d&w, Alan James.

Western   **Cas.**   **(PR:A   NPAA:NR)**

COME OUT FIGHTING**   (1945) 62m MON bw

Leo Gorcey (*Muggs*), Huntz Hall (*Glimpy*), Billy Benedict (*Skinny*), Gabriel Dell (*Pete*), June Carlson (*Jane*), Amelia Ward (*Rita*), Addison Richards (*Mr. Mitchell*), George Meeker (*Henley*), Johnny Duncan (*Gilbert*), Fred Kelsey (*Mr. McGinnis, Sr.*), Douglas Wood (*Mayor*), Milton Kibbee (*Police Chief*), Pat Gleason (*Little Pete*), Robert Homans (*Riley*), Patsy Moran (*Mrs. McGinnis*), Alan Foster (*Whitey*), Davidson Clark (*Officer McGowan*), Meyer Grace (*Jake*), Mende Koenig (*Danny Moore*), Bud Gorman (*Sammy*).

Entertaining East Side Kids comedy deals with the gang trying to repay the police commissioner for saving their clubhouse by helping his son, who gets involved with gamblers. Fifteenth picture in the series allows a girl to join the club for the first time. (See BOWERY BOYS series, Index.)

p, Sam Katzman, Jack Dietz; d, William Beaudine; w, Earl Snell; ph, Ira Morgan; ed, William Austin; prod d, Mel Delay; md, Edward Kay; art d, David Milton.

Comedy   **(PR:A   MPAA:NR)**

COME OUT OF THE PANTRY**½

(1935, Brit.) 73m British & Dominions/UA bw

Jack Buchanan (*Lord Robert Brent*), Fay Wray (*Hilda*), James Carew (*Mr. Beach-Howard*), Olive Blakeney (*Mrs. Beach-Howard*), Fred Emney (*Lord Axminster*), Kate Cutler (*Lady Axminster*), Ronald Squire (*Eccles*), Maire O'Neill (*Mrs. Gore*), Ethel Stewart (*Rosie*), Ben Welden (*Tramp*), W. T. Ellwanger (*Porteous*).

Buchanan stars in this entertaining musical as a down on his luck English lord who ends up working as a footman for a New York millionaire. He meets and falls in love with the millionaire's niece, played by Wray.

p, Herbert Wilcox; d, Jack Raymond; w, Austin Parker; Douglas Furber (based on the play "Come Out of the Kitchen" by Alice Duer Miller); ph, Fred Young.

Comedy/Musical   **(PR:AA   MPAA:NR)**

COME SEPTEMBER**½

(1961) 112m UNIV c

Rock Hudson (*Robert Talbot*), Gina Lollobrigida (*Lisa Fellini*), Sandra Dee (*Sandy Stevens*), Bobby Darin (*Tony*), Walter Slezak (*Maurice Clavell*), Brenda De Banzie (*Margaret Allison*), Rosanna Rory (*Anna*), Ronald Howard (*Spencer*), Joel Grey (*Beagle*), Ronnie Haran (*Sparrow*), Chris Seitz (*Larry*), Cindy Conroy (*Julia*), Joan Freeman (*Linda*), Nancy Anderson (*Patricia*), Michael Eden (*Ron*), Claudia Brack (*Carol*), Charles Fawcett (*Warren*), John Stacy (*Douglas*), Katherine Guildford (*Claire*), Betty Foa (*Elena*), Helen Stirling (*Katherine*), Del Balzo (*Mother Superior*), Anna Maestri, Stella Vitelleschi, Milena Vukotic, Edy Nogara (*Lisa's Maids*), Francesco Tensi (*Robert's Secretary*), Liliana Celli (*Seamstress*); Robert De Bernardis (*Bus Driver*).

Wealthy American businessman Hudson arrives at his Italian villa in July rather than September and surprises his caretaker, who runs the villa as a hotel eleven months of the year. Guest Lollobrigida becomes his love interest while Dee and Darin play and are real-life newlyweds. Gina sizzles every frame she enters.

p, Robert Arthur; d, Robert Mulligan; w, Stanley Shapiro, Maurice Richlin; ph, William

Daniels (CinemaScope, Technicolor); m, Hans J. Salter; ed, Russell F. Schoengarth; prod d, Ernest B. Wehmeyer; art d, Henry Bumstead; set d, John P. Austin; cos, Mortan Haack; m/l, "Come September," "Multiplication" (Bobby Darin).

Comedy   **(PR:A   MPAA:NR)**

COME SPY WITH ME*

(1967) 85m MPO-Futurama Entertainment-ABC Films/FOX c

Troy Donahue (*Pete Barker*), Andrea Dromm (*Jill Parsons*), Albert Dekker (*Walter Ludeker*), Mart Hulswit (*Larry Claymore*), Valerie Allen (*Samantha*), Dan Ferrone (*Augie*), Howard Schell (*Corbett*), Chance Gentry (*Chance*), Louis Edmonds (*Gunther Stiller*), Kate Aldrich (*Chris*), Pam Colbert (*Pam*), Gil Pratley (*Kieswetter*), Georges Shoucair (*Pantin*), Alston Bair (*Keefer*), Tim Moxon (*Morgan*), Eric Coverly (*Karl*), Jack Lewis (*Brooks*), Lucienne Bridou (*Linda*).

Weak spy thriller set in lush Jamaica and Bermuda deals with an underworld villain trying to sabotage a scheme for world peace. Scuba diving expert Donahue foils the plan. Amateurish entry in the genre.

p, Paul Heller; d, Marshall Stone; w, Cherney Berg (based on a story by Stuart James); ph, Zoli Vidor; m, Bob Bowers; ed, Hy Goldman; prod d, Eva Monley; art d, Howard Barker; cos, Georganne Aldrich; m/l, "Come Spy With Me" (William "Smokey" Robinson), "The Shark" (Jerry Butler).

Comedy/Thriller   **(PR:A   MPAA:NR)**

COME TO THE STABLE***½

(1949) 94m FOX bw

Loretta Young (*Sister Margaret*), Celeste Holm (*Sister Scolastica*), Hugh Marlowe (*Robert Mason*), Elsa Lanchester (*Miss Potts*), Thomas Gomez (*Luigi Rossi*), Dorothy Patrick (*Kitty*), Basil Ruysdael (*Bishop*), Dooley Wilson (*Anthony James*), Regis Toomey (*Monsignor*), Mike Mazurki (*Heavy Man*), Henri Letondal (*Father Barraud*), Walter Baldwin (*Jarman*), Tim Huntley (*Mr. Thompson*), Virginia Kelley (*Mrs. Thompson*), Louis Jean Heydt (*Mr. Newman*), Pati Behrs, Nan Boardman, Louise Colembet, Georgette Duane, Yvette Reynard, Loulette Sablon (*Nuns*), Ian MacDonald (*Mr. Matthews*), Jean Prescott (*Mrs. Matthews*), Gordon Gebert (*Willie*), Gary Pagett (*Johnnie*), Nolan Leary (*Station Master*), Wallace Brown (*Sheldon*), Danny Jackson (*George*), Edwin Max (*Whitey*), Russ Clark, Robert Falk (*Policemen*), Marion Martin (*Manicurist*).

Delightful and gentle story about two French nuns, Young and Holm, who leave their abbey in Europe and arrive in a New England town called Bethlehem, where they intend to establish a children's hospital. Clare Booth Luce, a serious Catholic convert, wrote this story of faith and her beliefs show through every frame. Holm and Young are determined to build the hospital and there is no way they can be talked out of it. (This was obviously Fox's response to Paramount's GOING MY WAY and THE BELLS OF SAINT MARY'S.) No one can resist the nuns' charm as they cajole their way into getting what they want. Lanchester is a painter who specializes in religious works and she allows them to use her studio, a stable she's converted and furnished, as a home base (hence the decidedly non-commercial title of the film). Holm and Young go out and hustle everyone in the area and finally achieve their goal. Although very Catholic in intent, it's a movie that celebrates tenacity and demonstrates that faith can move molehills, if not mountains. As the local Monsignor, Toomey does a neat job and reminds us that he is one of the rare human beings who ever had a parody of a song written about him. In the 1960s, Alan Sherman sang in his act . . . "I'll be gloomy, but send that Regis Toomey" and no one knew who he was talking about! The song "Through A Long and Sleepless Night" became a hit.

p, Samuel G. Engel; d, Henry Koster; w, Oscar Millard, Sally Benson (based on a story by Clare Boothe Luce); ph, Joseph La Chelle; m, Cyril Mockridge; ed, William Reynolds; md, Lionel Newman; spec eff, Fred Sersen; m/l, Mack Gordon, Alfred Newman.

Comedy/Drama   **(PR:AA   MPAA:NR)**

COMEBACK, THE**

(1982, Brit.) 100m Lone Star c
(AKA: THE DAY THE SCREAMING STOPPED)

Jack Jones (*Nick Cooper*), Pamela Stephenson (*Linda Everett*), David Doyle (*Webster Jones*), Bill Owen (*Mr. B*), Sheila Keith (*Mrs. B*), Holly Palance (*Gail Cooper*), Peter Turner (*Harry*), Richard Johnson (*Dr. Macauley*).

Jones stars as an American singer who returns to England after a six-year layoff to make a comeback, but while he's at a spooky country mansion his estranged wife is murdered at their London penthouse. This stodgy horror story deals with Jones' problems with his wife's ghost, the murderer, and a growing love for his manager's secretary, Stephenson.

p&d, Pete Walker; w, Murray Smith; ph, Peter Jessop (Eastmancolor); m, Stanley Myers; ed, Alan Brett; prod d, Denis Johnson; m/l, Jamie Anderson.

Horror   **Cas.**   **(PR:C   MPAA:R)**

COMEBACK TRAIL, THE*½

(1982) 76m Dynamite Entertainment-Rearguard c

Chuck McCann (*Enrico Kodac*), Buster Crabbe (*Duke Montana*), Robert Staats (*E. Eddie Eastman*), Ina Balin (*Julie Thomas*), Jara Kahout (*German Producer*), Henny Youngman, Irwin Corey, Hugh Hefner, Joe Franklin, Monti Rock III, Lenny Schultz, Mike Gentry.

Incohesive, largely improvised comedy stars McCann and Staats as a pair of shady producers (of films like BULL DYKE BABY) who come up with a scheme to hire a washed-up star and have him die on the set, allowing them to collect enough insurance money to keep their operation going. They hire Crabbe, but he turns out to be in much better health than anticipated, so the pair start trying to murder him. Some of it works quite well, but much of the film is painful to watch. A number of celebrities turn up in cameos as stars of the producers' previous efforts. The film sat on the shelf for ten years before being given a minor release, whereupon it immediately vanished again.

p,d&w, Harry Hurwitz (based on a story by Roy Frumkes, Robert J. Winston, Hurwitz); ph, Victor Petrashevitz (Deluxe Color); m, Igo Kantor; ed, Hurwitz; stunts, Ted White.
Comedy **(PR:O MPAA:NR)**

COMEDIANS, THE½** (1967) 156m MGM c
Elizabeth Taylor *(Martha Pineda)*, Richard Burton *(Brown)*, Alec Guinness *(Jones)*, Peter Ustinov *(Ambassador Pinada)*, Paul Ford *(Smith)*, Lillian Gish *(Mrs. Smith)*, Raymond St. Jacques *(Cancasseur)*, Zaeks Mokae *(Michel)*, Roscoe Lee Browne *(Petit Pierre)*, Douta Seck *(Joseph)*, Aliba Peters *(Cesar)*, Gloria Foster *(Mrs. Philipot)*, Robin Langford *(Angelito)*, Georg Stanford Brown *(Henri Philipot)*, James Earl Jones *(Dr. Magiot)*, Cicely Tyson *(Marie-Therese)*.

Filmed in Dahomey, Africa, this Graham Greene story of Haiti had to be shot away from the original locations or none of the cast or crew might have survived. Francois Duvalier, known as "Papa Doc," was still in power and his dictatorial and allegedly murderous attitudes were rampant over a poor and ill-educated populace. Surely a terrific backdrop for an intriguing film, yes? Unfortunately, Greene adapted his own novel and didn't know what to cut out so he left it all in and the 156-minute length seems interminable. Tourists are hard to come by in Haiti ever since Duvalier and his secret police have taken to disappearing people off the streets and Burton is having a hard time finding a buyer for his resort hotel. He comes back from an unsuccessful scouting expedition where he searched for a prospective buyer. Arriving simultaneously are Ford and Gish, a pair of Americans who desire to open a vegetarian center in Haiti. Another guest is Alex Guinness, who is jailed by the police almost upon arriving. Burton looks the other way at Guinness's incarceration but Ford and Gish, almost acting as the story's conscience, convince him to aid in freeing Guinness. Before too long, Ford and Gish are exposed to the full panoply of Haiti's corruption and brutality and they depart, totally devastated by frustration. Ustinov is a South American ambassador married to pneumatic Liz Taylor,whom Burton is diddling behind the former's back. We now learn that Guinness, who's been faking a military background, is, in reality, an arms dealer. He makes a deal for some weapons with the government and is released. When that deal comes a-cropper,the Haitians want him in jail again and he turns to Burton for assistance. Ustinov's embassy gives Guinness a place to stay and, while there, he becomes closer to Taylor (whose name is Martha, same as the character in WHO'S AFRAID OF VIRGINIA WOOLF?). Burton is annoyed at Guinness's relationship with Taylor and provokes him into boasting that he could overthrow the country with a small group of rebels. Burton arranges for Guinness to head such a group and Guinness finally admits that he isn't an ex-soldier at all but would never dream of running away from such a challenge. Before Guinness can lead the group, he is murdered by Duvalier's Tonton Macoute—the most dreaded secret service since the Gestapo. Burton now feels contrite at Guinness's death and thus takes over the ill-equipped and untrained band of rebels, presumably to go into the mountains and fight until Duvalier is overthrown. Well, he never was and his son, "Baby Doc," occupies the throne in the 1980s. The best character in the picture was Ustinov who did his customary scene-stealing every time he could. The steamy love scenes between Taylor and Burton were usually boring and just a lot of groping around in the back seat of a car. They missed the whole point by a mile with this picture, preferring to take the safe way (Taylor and Burton's love story) than a carving up of the worst dictatorship in the western hemisphere.

p&d, Peter Glenville; w, Graham Greene (based on his novel); ph, Henri Decae (Panavision, Metrocolor); m, Laurence Rosenthal; ed, Francoise Javet; md, Rosenthal; art d, Francois de Lamothe; set d, Robert Christides; cos, Tiziani of Rome.
Drama **(PR:C MPAA:NR)**

COMEDY MAN, THE½** (1964) 92m BL bw
Kenneth More *(Chick Byrd)*, Cecil Parker *(Rutherford)*, Dennis Price *(Tommy Morris)*, Billie Whitelaw *(Judy)*, Norman Rossington *(Theodore)*, Angela Douglas *(Fay)*, Frank Finlay *(Prout)*, Edmund Purdom *(Julian)*, J. C. Devlin *(Sloppitt)*, Valerie and Leila Croft *(Twins)*, Freddie Mills *(Indian Chief)*, Jill Adams *(Jan Kennedy)*, Alan Dobie *(Jack Lavery)*, Gerald Campion *(Gerry)*.

Middle-aged stock actor goes to London to try the big time. After much frustration, he lands a job doing TV commercials, gaining wealth and recognition. But he eventually gives it all up to return to stage work and keep his pride. Good cast and solid story is sometimes slowed by mediocre direction.

p, Jon Pennington; d, Alvin Rakoff; w, Peter Yeldham (based on a novel by Douglas Hayes); ph, Ken Hedges; m, Bill McGuffie.
Drama **(PR:A MPAA:NR)**

COMEDY OF TERRORS, THE** (1964) 88m AIP c
Vincent Price *(W. Trumbull)*, Peter Lorre *(Felix Gillie)*, Boris Karloff *(Amos Hinchley)*, Basil Rathbone *(John F. Black)*, Joe E. Brown *(Cemetery Keeper)*, Joyce Jameson *(Amaryllis Trumbull)*, Beverly Hills *(Mrs. Phipps)*, Paul Barsolow *(Riggs)*, Linda Rogers *(Phipps' Maid)*, Luree Nicholson *(Black's Servant)*, Buddy Mason*(Mr. Phipps)*, Rhubarb *(Cleopatra)*.

Mortician (Price) helps his business along by "creating" his own customers. He is foiled by Lorre, Karloff, Rathbone, and Jameson. Film is neither funny nor terrifying, and shows the fact that it was shot in twenty days on a twelve-hour-a-day shooting schedule.

p, Anthony Carras, Richard Matheson; d, Jacques Tourneur; w, Matheson; ph, Floyd Crosby (Panavision); ed, Anthony Carras; art d, Daniel Haller; m, Les Baxter; set d, Harry Reif; cos, Marjorie Corso.
Horror Comedy **(PR:A MPAA:NR)**

COMES A HORSEMAN*½ (1978) 118m UA c
James Caan *(Frank)*, Jane Fonda *(Ella)*, Jason Robards *(Ewing)*, George Grizzard *(Neil Atkinson)*, Richard Farnsworth *(Dodger)*, Jim Davis *(Julie Blocker)*, Mark Harmon *(Billy Joe Meynert)*, Macon McCalman *(Hoverton)*, Basil Hoffman *(George Bascomb)*, James Kline *(Ralph Cole)*, James Keach *(Kroegh)*, Clifford A. Pellow *(Cattle Buyer)*.

COMES A HORSEMAN comes to naught despite some of the most beautiful photography of the West that anyone has ever seen. The major trouble is that the mammoth mountains dwarf the midget talents of Caan in the top-billed role. Fonda is a rancher who won't give in to local mogul Robards who is attempting to carve out an empire in this post-WW II world out west. Fonda and Robards had slept together when she was a slip of a thing and she hates him for that and a host of other reasons. Caan is also an independent who is newly returned from the service and he teams with Fonda when his partner is killed (probably on Robards' mandate). While Fonda and Caan are resisting Robards, he is resisting the pleas of an oil company that wants to come in and drill. Robards is a throwback to the old days, when the men who ran the ranches were almost kings and he yearns for those times. Fonda wishes Robards would leave her alone so she could run her ranch and take some time to fall in love with Caan, who is trying to forget the horrors of war. It's an old premise, seen in countless Rocky Lane and Roy Rogers films; villain wants little guys out so he can (a) build a railroad on the property, (b) run his cattle,(c) run his sheep, (d) mine for gold, (e) drill for oil. Guy and gal fight him until truth and justice prevail. The wonderful photography by Gordon Willis is almost *too* wonderful in that all the interior scenes are so perfectly balanced that they appear a trifle stagey. Willis, who lives in the East and usually specializes in urban films (lots of Woody Allen pictures including ANNIE HALL, MANHATTAN), shows his versatility with his lensing of the exteriors. Would that everyone else concerned with this turkey did the same.

p, Gene Kirkwood, Dan Paulson; d, Alan Pakula; w, Dennis Lynton Clark; ph, Gordon Willis (Panavision, Technicolor); m, Michael Small; ed, Marion Rothman; prod d, George Jenkins; set d, Arthur J. Parker; cos. Luster Bayless; stunts, Walter Scott.
Western **Cas.** **(PR:A-C MPAA:PG)**

COMET OVER BROADWAY** (1938) 65m WB bw
Kay Francis *(Eve Appleton)*, Ian Hunter *(Bert Ballin)*, John Litel *(Bill Appleton)*, Donald Crisp *(Grant)*, Minna Gombel *(Tim Adams)*, Sybil Jason *(Jackie)*, Melville Cooper *(Emerson)*, Ian Keith *(Wilton Banks)*, Leona Marical *(Janet Eaton)*, Ray Meyer *(Brogan)*, Vera Lewis *(Mrs. Appleton)*, Nat Carr *(Haines)*, Chester Clute *(Willis)*, Edward McWade *(Harvey)*, Clem Bevans *(Benson)*, Linda Winters *(Miss McDermott)*, Jack Mower *(Hotel Manager)*, Jack Wise *(Stage Manager)*, Edgar Edwards *(Waiter)*, Lester Dorr *(Performer)*, Alice Connor, Fern Barry, Susan Hayward *(Amateur Actors)*, Owen King *(Actor)*, Janet Shaw *(Woman)*, Kay Gordon, Jessie Jackson *(Chorus Girls)*, Frank O'Connor *(Officer)*, Henry Otho *(Baggage Man)*, Frank Orth *(Cab Driver)*, Sidney Bracy *(English Porter)*, Jimmy Conlin *(Comic)*, Charles Seel *(Jury Foreman)*, Mitchell Ingraham *(Court Clerk)*, Raymond Brown *(Judge)*, Emmett Vogan *(Prosecutor)*, Ed Stanley *(Doctor)*, Howard Mitchell *(Court Officer)*, Dorothy Comingore *(Miss McDermott)*, Jack Mower *(Hotel Manager)*.

Francis stars as a woman with a devouring ambition to be a successful actress and raise enough money to free her husband (Litel) from jail (he had been hounded into committing murder). Movie covers the seven years it takes her to become a star and its effect on her life. It was the second movie that year for screen newcomer Hayward.

d, Busby Berkeley; w, Mark Hellinger, Robert Bucker (based on a story by Faith Baldwin); m, Heinz Roemheld; ph, James Wong Howe; ed, James Gibbons; md, Leo F. Forbstein; art d, Charles Novi; cos, Orry-Kelly.
Drama **(PR:A MPAA:NR)**

COMETOGETHER zero (1971) 90m ABKCO/AA c
Tony Anthony *(Tony)*, Luciana Paluzzi *(Lisa)*, Rosemary Dexter *(Ann)*.

Anthony, an American actor living in Italy, plays an American actor living in Italy in this unfortunate production that he also co-produced and co-wrote. He meets a pair of American girls (played by Italian Paluzzi and Briton Dexter) and they have a three-way affair, intercut randomly with scenes of a car crash, a body being pulled out of a Venice canal, and a massacre of American POWs in Vietnam. Without any redeeming value.

p, Tony Anthony, Saul Swimmer; d, Swimmer; w, Swimmer, Anthony; ph, Tonino Delli Colli; m, Stelvio Cipriani.
Drama **(PR:O MPAA:R)**

COMIC, THE* (1969) 95m COL c
Dick Van Dyke *(Billy Bright)*, Michele Lee *(Mary Gibson)*, Mickey Rooney *(Cockeye)*, Cornel Wilde *(Frank Powers)*, Nina Wayne *(Sybil)*, Pert Kelton *(Mama)*, Steve Allen *(Himself)*, Barbara Heller *(Ginger)*, Ed Peck *(Edwin C. Englehardt)*, Jeannine Riley *(Lorraine)*, Gavin MacLeod *(1st Director)*, Jay Novello *(Miguel)*, Craig Huebing *(Doctor)*, Paulene Myers *(Phoebe)*, Fritz Feld *(Armand)*, Jerome Cowan *(Lawrence)*, Isabell Sanford *(Woman)*, Jeff Donnell *(Nurse)*, Carl Reiner *(Al Schilling)*.

In a half-hearted attempt to capture the flavor of the silent era, Van Dyke does a poor and unconvincing take-off on an egocentric movie comic who is made up of Harry Langdon, Buster Keaton and Stan Laurel, one whose early success leads to his carousing, drinking, and eventual self-ruination. He abuses his friend Rooney (who wears a contact over one eye to make it appear that he is cross-eyed), he cheats on his wife, and he becomes a miserable, dangerous drunk, contending until the end that he has been unfairly treated by the industry. He makes a brief comeback after Allen rediscovers him, meets a gold-digging floozie, and dies while marrying her in his hospital bed. His life is seen in flashback with Van Dyke narrating. The production is turgid and the dialog is cliche-ridden. No one really makes an effort to be funny and the laughs are woefully few. Van Dyke's bits are looted from the silent era routines of Keaton and Chaplin and he mercilessly mugs Laurel's mannerisms. Lee is cute but gives an uninspired performance. Technically, the film is professional but the chronicle of a silent film comic's rise and fall is wholly disappointing. The shorts such as "Love, Honor, and Oh-Boy" and "Dr. Jerk and Mr. Hyde," lack the imagination of the actual short comedies of Laurel and Keaton. THE COMIC was a good idea spoiled by an anemic script, lethargic acting, and directed so lamely by Reiner that each frame becomes predictable. This film marks the real decline of Reiner as a comedic force in films.

p, Carl Reiner, Aaron Ruben; d, Reiner; w, Reiner, Ruben; ph, W. Wallace Kelley (Berkey Pathe Color); m, Jack Elliott; ed, Adrienne Fazan; prod d, Walter Simonds; set d, Morris Hoffman; cos, Guy Verhille; makeup, Ben Lane; spec eff, Butler-Glouner.

Comedy (PR:A MPAA:NR)

COMIN' AT YA!* (1981) 91m Filmways c

Tony Anthony (H. H. Hart), Gene Quintana (Pike), Victoria Abril (Abilene), Ricardo Palacios (Polk), Lewis Gordon (Old Man).

First 3-D movie in nearly 20 years stars Anthony as an avenging hero out to retrieve his kidnapped fiancee. Quintana is the slave trader who is holding her hostage. This extremely brutal film hawks gratuitous sex and violence.

p, Tony Anthony; d, Ferdinando Baldi; w, Lloyd Battista, Wolf Lowenthal, Gene Quintana (based on a story by Tony Petitto); ph, Fernando Arribas (Dimensionscope, Technicolor); m, Carlo Savina; e, Franco Fraticelli; art d, Luciano Spadoni; spec eff, Fredy Unger; cos, Spadoni.

Western (PR:O MPAA:R)

COMIN' ROUND THE MOUNTAIN** (1936) 60m REP bw

Gene Autry (Gene), Ann Rutherford (Dolores), Smiley Burnette (Frog), Roy Mason (Matt Ford), Champion (The Horse), Raymond Brown (Caldwell), Ken Cooper (Slim), Tracy Lane (Butch), Robert McKenzie (Marshall), John Ince, Frank Lackteen.

Autry is upstaged by his horse Champion in this mixed-up western centering on a horse race and a burlesque bull fight. Burnette relieves his badly scripted lines through improvisation and outstanding comedic timing. Ranch owner Rutherford gives an acceptable performance, though her part is not demanding. Noble's good camerawork picks up action and outdoor scenery with a flair mainly responsible for the movie's limited success.

p, Nat Levine; d, Mack V. Wright; w, Oliver Drake, Dorrell and Stuart McGowan (based on a story by Drake); ph, William Nobles.

Western (PR:AA MPAA:NR)

COMIN' ROUND THE MOUNTAIN½** (1940) 62m PAR bw

Bob Burns (Jed Blower), Una Merkel (Belina Walters), Jerry Colonna (Argyle Phifft), Don Wilson (Mr. Wilson), Pat Barrett (Uncle Ezra Walters), Harold Peary (Mayor Gildersleeve), Bill Thompson (Barney Smoot), Olin Howland (Pa Blower), Brenda Fowler (Ma Blower), Richard Carle (Lester Smoot), Leona Roberts (Aunt Polly Walters), Zeffie Tilbury (Granny Stokes), Cliff Arquette (Droopy Beagle), William Demarest (Gusty Mann), Marandy (Mrs. Beagle), Walter Catlett (W.P.A. Clerk).

Following a brief adventure in the big city, Burns returns to his hillbilly Tennessee family and becomes mayor of the town with some help from his mountaineer friends. What was intended to be a musical comedy assembles a smattering of radio personalities, then gives them shoddy material to work with. Tunes are presented as authentic music from the Tennessee hill country but the novelty wears off after the first few songs.

p, William C. Thomas; d, George Archainbaud; w, Lewis R. Foster, Maxwell Shane, Duke Attebury (based on the story by Foster); ph, William C. Mellor; ed, Stuart Gilmore.

Musical/Comedy (PR:AA MPAA:NR)

COMIN' ROUND THE MOUNTAIN** (1951) 76m UNIV bw

Bud Abbott (Al Stewart), Lou Costello (Wilbert), Dorothy Shay (Dorothy McCoy), Kirby Grant (Clark Winfield), Joe Sawyer (Kalem McCoy), Glenn Strange (Devil Dan Winfield), Ida Moore (Granny McCoy), Guy Wilkerson (Uncle Clem McCoy), Bob Easton (Luke McCoy), Margaret Hamilton (Aunt Huddy), Russell Simpson (Judge), Shaye Cogan (Matt), Virgil "Slats" Taylor (Jasper Winfield), O. Z. Whitehead (Zeke), Norman Leavitt (Zeb), Jack Kruschen, Peter Mamakos, Barry Brooks (Gangsters in Nightclub), Joe Kirk (Man), William Fawcett (Old Mountain Man), Herold Goodwin (Second Mountain Man).

Director Lamont hangs Abbott and Costello out to dry by snipping their routines which could usually save a flimsy caper like this. Backwoods Kentucky town finds McCoy cousins—Shay, a cafe singer, and Costello, a magician—seeking the fortune left to Costello by a dead uncle. The performing cousins are unaware that their families have been feuding for years over a love potion. Shay's singing is the only bright spot in this one. Songs: "You Broke Your Promise" (George Wyle, Irving Taylor, Eddie Pola), "Agnes Clung" (Hessie Smith, Dorothy Shay), "Why Don't Someone Marry Mary Ann?" (Wilbur Beatty, Britt Wood), "Sagebrush Sadie" (Wood). (See ABBOTT AND COSTELLO series, Index.)

p, Howard Christie; d, Charles Lamont; w, Robert Lees, Frederic I. Rinaldo, John Grant; ph, George Robinson; ed, Edward Curtiss; md, Joseph Gershenson.

Comedy (PR:AAA MPAA:NR)

COMIN' THRO' THE RYE* (1947, Brit.) 55m Advance Films bw

Terrence Alexander (Robert Burns), Patricia Burleigh (Highland Mary), Beryl Bowen (Clarinda), Olivia Barley (Jean Armour), Sylvia Abbott (Handsome Nell), Trefor Jones, Sylvia Welling, Walter Saull's Scotia Singers.

Still-life biography of poet Robert Burns has Alexander illustrating his romances and experiences using the slide projector-and-lecture-with-commentary technique to cover ground. Amateur production plays more like a tedious college play. Unoriginal in concept.

p, Arthur Dent; d, Walter C. Mycroft; w, Gilbert McAllister; ph, Cedric Williams; ed, Robert Hill.

Biography (PR:A MPAA:NR)

COMING ATTRACTIONS (SEE: LOOSE SHOES, 1980)

COMING HOME** (1978) 126m UA c

Jane Fonda (Sally Hyde), Jon Voight (Luke Martin), Bruce Dern (Capt. Bob Hyde), Robert Ginty (Sgt. Dink Mobley), Penelope Milford (Viola Munson), Robert Carradine (Bill Munson), Charles Cyphers (Pee Wee), Mary Jackson (Fleta Wilson), Ken Augustine (Ken), Tresa Hughes (Nurse De Groot), Willie Tyler (Virgil), David Glennon (Tim), Olivia Cole (Corrine), Ron Amador (Beany), Cornelius H. Austin, Jr. (Corny), Richard Blanchard (Rick).

Of all the raft of Vietnam veteran pictures made, this is the one that best tells the story. It competed with THE DEER HUNTER for the Academy's favor and lost out as Best Picture and Best Direction but Fonda, Voight, and the screenplay won in their respective categories. It's too long and too preachy and the final scenes aren't the best, but the moments between Fonda and Voight and Dern are a joy to watch and recall. The time is 1968 and Dern, a gung-ho Marine captain, is going off to Nam on active duty. Wife Fonda wants to do her share so she begins volunteer work at a local veterans' hospital where she meets Voight, an angry paraplegic, as well as Milford and brother, Carradine, who is being treated for severe depression. In the next month, Fonda and Voight learn that they went to the same high school, had many of the same friends, and have much more in common than most people at the hospital. Voight begins to ease up on his anger and accepts an invitation to Fonda's for dinner. He asks, "This isn't just have-a-gimp-for-dinner-night, is it?" and she glares, answering that it isn't. Relaxed, Voight admits that "I spend much of my time thinking about making love to you." Fonda is tempted to confess her feelings about Voight but remains faithful to Dern. A few weeks later, she flies to Hong Kong and spends some time with Dern who is on furlough. He's a changed man. Gone is the patriotic flag-waver; now he's quiet, taciturn, and obviously shaken by his experiences in Vietnam. Fonda returns home and learns that Carradine has committed suicide and that Voight has been released from the hospital. The following evening, Voight chains his wheelchair to the gates of a Marine corps recruiting post to protest the war. The media flock to the story and Fonda sees it happening on TV. She contacts him and helps him through the ordeal he faces, then takes him home. Later that night they make a form of love. Voight is not able to sustain any intercourse due to his injury, but that doesn't stop him from exploring Fonda in other ways and bringing her to the climax her husband was never able to accomplish. It's a highly erotic scene and gives the picture it's R rating. A relationship begins and they are happy for quite some time, watched all the while by the FBI who are gathering a dossier on their activities, both political and sexual. Dern comes home and is totally changed. He has no interest in Fonda and prefers to sit with "the guys" and drink and tell stories. He is already unbalanced but goes over the edge when the G-men tells him about Fonda and Voight's affair. He grabs his rifle and threatens Fonda but Voight arrives and calms him down. Later, we learn that Dern has walked into the sea and drowned himself. With husband out of the way, Voight and Fonda are free to pursue happiness, but that's only implied and not shown, as the final scenes are Fonda shopping with a girl friend and Voight lecturing a group of young high-schoolers who are considering going into the service. The shame of the Academy Awards was overlooking Dern, who had the most difficult role of all as the flag-waving soldier who was shot down by what he saw in actual combat. The film was tasteful, often funny, well-shot, and remains the definitive post-Vietnam war picture.

p, Jerome Hellman; d, Hal Ashby; w, Waldo Salt, Robert C. Jones (based on a story by Nancy Dowd); ph, Haskell Wexler (Deluxe Color); m, various artists of the era; ed, Don Zimmerman; prod d, Mike Haller; set d, George Gaines; cos, Ann Roth, Mike Hoffman, Silvio Scarano, Jennifer Parson.

War Drama **Cas.** (PR:C-O MPAA:R)

COMING OF AGE** (1938, Brit.) 68m GS Enterprises/COL bw

Eliot Makeham (Henry Strudwick) Joyce Bland (Isobel Strudwick), Jack Melford (Roger Squire), Ruby Miller (Julia Knight), Jimmy Hanley (Arthur Strudwick), Evelyn Ankers (Christine Squire), Annie Esmond (Mrs. Crowther), Aubrey Mallalieu (Mr. Myers).

Okay comedy has Makeham having an affair with singer Ankers, while wife Bland dallys with Ankers' husband (Melford). Some good character actors save this one from obscurity.

p, George Smith; d, Manning Haynes; w, Paul White, Rowan Kennedy.

Comedy (PR:A MPAA:NR)

COMING OUT PARTY* (1934) 80m FOX bw

Frances Dee (Joy Stanhope), Gene Raymond (Chris Hansen), Alison Skipworth (Miss Vanderdoe), Nigel Bruce (Troon), Harry Green (Harry Gold), Gilbert Emery (Mr. Stanhope), Marjorie Gateson (Mrs. Stanhope), Clifford Jones (Jimmy Wolverton), Jessie Ralph (Nora), Germaine De Nec (Louise).

Lovely leading lady Dee plays a debutante whose mother, naturally, wants her to marry wealth, but she is in love with a violinist in a jazz band, Raymond. On the night of her debut into society her social adviser sees to it that she is swamped with dancing partners, incurring the wrath of Hansen. Both get angry with each other and out of pique Dee marries money, in the form of a suitor, Green, who is noted for his bouts with drunkenness. All works out in the end, when Green agrees to an annulment and handsome Raymond wins her hand again. The film is the American screen debut for Bruce, who plays a Scotch butler.

p, Jesse Lasky; d, John Blystone; w, Jesse Lasky, Jr., and Gladys Unger (based on an original story by Becky Gardiner Unger); ph, John Seitz.

Drama (PR:A MPAA:NR)

COMING-OUT PARTY, A½** (1962, Brit.) 98m Independent Artists/Union Film Distributors bw (GB: A VERY IMPORTANT PERSON)

James Robertson Justice (Sir Ernest Pease), Leslie Phillips (Jimmy Cooper), Stanley

Baxter *(Everett/Maj. Stampfel)*, Eric Sykes *(Willoughby)*, Richard Wattis *(Woodcock)*, Godfrey Winn *(Himself, an Interviewer)*, Colin Gordon *(Briggs)*, Joan Haythorne *(Miss Rogers)*, John Forrest *(Grassy Green)*, Jeremy Loyd *("Bonzo" Baines)*, Peter Myers *(Shaw)*, Ronald Leigh Hunt *(Clynes)*, John Ringham *(Plum Pouding)*, John Le Mesurier *(Piggott)*, Norman Bird *(Travers)*, Ronnie Stevens *(Hankley)*, Vincent Ball *(Higgins)*, Ed Deveraux *(Webber)*, Brian Oulton *(Scientist)*, Nancy Nevinson, Heidi Erich *(German Fraus)*.

Justice is a radar scientist during World War II on a reconnaissance mission over Germany when he is shot down. Placed in a POW camp, the other prisoners first think him a spy, but then orders filter to the men telling them that Justice has top priority to escape. After a few failed attempts, Justice devises a scheme in which he hides in the camp while the other men say that he has escaped. While the Germans go crazy trying to find him, he puts on a Swedish Red Cross uniform and walks out through the main gate. One of the best of the Justice vehicles of the 1960s.

p, Julian Wintle, Leslie Parkyn; d, Kenn Annakin; w, Jack Davies, Henry Blyth; ph, Ernest Steward; m, Reg Owen; ed, Ralph Sheldon; art d, Harry Pottle; set d, Alan Maley; cos, Vi Murray.

Comedy **(PR:A-C MPAA:NR)**

COMMAND, THE*** (1954) 94m WB c

Guy Madison *(Capt. MacClaw)*, Joan Weldon *(Martha)*, James Whitmore *(Sgt. Elliott)*, Carl Benton Reid *(Col. Janeway)*, Harvey Lembeck *(Gottschalk)*, Ray Teal *(Dr. Trent)*, Bob Nichols *(O'Hirons)*, Don Shelton *(Maj. Gibbs)*, Gregg Barton *(Capt. Forsythe)*, Boyd "Red" Morgan *(Cpl. Fleming)*, Zachary Yaconelli *(Mr. Pellegrini)*, Renata Vanni *(Mrs. Pellegrini)*, Tom Monroe *(Nikirk)*.

This was Warner Bros.' first film in CinemaScope, and in the final eleven-minute running fight between Indians and a wagon train, action spreads across the wide screen, virtually making participants of the audience, equalling the stagecoach-Indians brawl in STAGECOACH. Story concerns Army medical officer, Madison, assuming command over cavalry troop when its major is killed in action. Pressed into escorting a wagon train through hostile Indian territory, Madison, who is used to healing, finds he must take lives to preserve his command and must learn the realities of war from tough sergeant Whitmore. Direction is taut, especially when the film takes on more movement, with an excellent climax.

p, David Weisbart; d, David Butler; w, Russell Hughes, Samuel Fuller (based on the novel *Rear Guard* by James Warner Bellah); ph, Wilfrid M. Cline (CinemaScope, Warner Color); m, Dimitri Tiomkin; ed, Irene Morra; md, Ray Heindorf.

Western **(PR:A MPAA:NR)**

COMMAND DECISION*½** (1948) 111m MGM bw

Clark Gable *(Brig. Gen. K. C. "Casey" Dennis)*, Walter Pidgeon *(Maj. Gen. Roland G. Kane)*, Van Johnson *(Tech. Sgt. Immanuel T. Evans)*, Brian Donlevy *(Brig. Gen. Clifton L. Garnet)*, Charles Bickford *(Elmer Brockhurst)*, John Hodiak *(Col. Edward R. Martin)*, Edward Arnold *(Congressman Arthur Malcolm)*, Marshall Thompson *(Capt. George W. B. Le)*, Richard Quine *(Maj. George Rockton)*, Cameron Mitchell *(Lt. Ansel Goldberg)*, Clinton Sundberg *(Maj. Homer V. Prescott)*, Ray Collins *(Maj. Desmond Lansing)*, Warner Anderson *(Col. Earnest Haley)*, John McIntire *(Maj. Belding Davis)*, Moroni Olsen *(Congressman Stone)*, John Ridgely *(James Carwood)*, Michael Steele *(Capt. Lucius M. Jenks)*, Edward Earle *(Congressman Watson)*, Mack Williams *(Lt. Col. Virgil Jackson)*, James Millican *(Maj. Garrett Davenport)*.

In one of his best postwar roles, Gable is a rugged brigadier general given a tough Air Force command. He must send his bomber squadrons deep into Germany to knock out secret airplane plants where the Nazis are frantically assembling jet fighters. It's a race against time; if Gable's bombers don't destroy the jet factories, the jets will destroy the Allied air forces. There is a break in the weather for several days and Gable orders his entire command to attack Schweinhafen. The losses are staggering, with 48 Flying Fortresses being shot down, Pidgeon, Gable's superior, is shocked and asks Gable if the sacrifice is worth it. Gable insists that it is and struggles with his own conscience, arguing that daylight precision bombing must be abandoned if the jet factories are not obliterated. When the second mission to the German city returns, the losses are equally devastating. One plane comes in for a landing with the pilots dead, Gable talking down the navigator who is at the controls. (This scene is truly harrowing and one of the film's most suspenseful sequences.) Hodiak, leader of the group, reports to Gable that the second mission is a complete failure, that the squadrons bombed a city that appeared identical to the target and that the real target was completely missed. Gable agonizes over his command decision to lose even more men, but orders the group to make another attack. The target is hit and half destroyed but the cost is high, half of the command, including Hodiak, whose plane is blown out of the sky. Pidgeon is pressured by visiting U.S. congressmen to replace Gable; they label him a butcher but Pidgeon knows Gable is taking the responsibility for the entire high command. He replaces Gable with another tough commander, Donlevy. Before Gable leaves the airfield, he watches Donlevy address the pilots, announcing that the target for the day is Schweinhafen; Donlevy is convinced that Gable has made the right decision and intends to carry out the operation to save future lives. Based on a successful stage drama, COMMAND DECISION offers powerful performances from Gable, Pidgeon, Hodiak, and Donlevy. Mitchell as the navigator attempting to land the Flying Fortress, is superb, as is Bickford, the sympathetic but hardnosed newsman. Johnson is also great as the cynical, conniving sergeant-aide to Gable. Director Wood helms a tight film and keeps a pace equal to the taut life-and-death story. The Rozsa score is stirring and poignant.

p, Sidney Franklin; d, Sam Wood; w, William R. Laidlaw, George Froeschel (based on the play by William Wister Haines); ph, Harold Rosson; m, Miklos Rozsa; ed, Harold F. Kress; art d, Cedric Gibbons, Urie McLeary.

War Drama **(PR:A MPAA:NR)**

COMMAND PERFORMANCE** (1931) 72m James Cruze/TIF bw

Neil Hamilton *(Prince Alexis/Peter Fedor)*, Una Merkel *(Princess Katerina)*, Helen Ware *(Queen Elinor of Serblandt)*, Albert Gran *(King Nicholas of Kordovia)*, Lawrence Grant *(Vellenburg)*, Thelma Todd *(Lydia)*, Vera Lewis *(Queen Elizabeth of Kordovia)*, Mischa Auer *(Duke Charles)*, Burr McIntosh *(Masoch)*, William Von Brincken *(Boyer)*, Murdock MacQuarrie *(Blondel)*.

When an actor (Hamilton) slugs it out with a prince (also Hamilton, in a dual role), he is summoned by the Queen mother who wants to get a gander at the person who gave her boy such a bad beating. As luck would have it, he's a dead ringer for the prince and mom dispatches him to another little Balkan country where he is instructed to woo and win the little spitfire enthroned there, Merkel. Good subject that he is, he does the queen's bidding, falls in love with the girl, and brings her home, only to have the prince stamp his feet and toss his pretty curls and even go so far as to denounce the throne rather than marry the hoydenish princess. This is just fine for the actor, who is then accepted by the Queen mother as her son and is cast in his finest role as prince of the kingdom, leaving the real prince to go off pouting, presumably in search of his own Wally Simpson. Adapted from a stage play, this little fairy tale does not make it on the screen.

p, Samuel Ziegler; d, Walter Lang; w, Maude Fulton, Gordon Rigby (based on the play by C. Stafford Dickens); ph, Charles Schoenbaum.

Drama **(PR:A MPAA:NR)**

COMMAND PERFORMANCE*½

(1937, Brit.) 84m Grosvenor Sound Film/GFD bw

Arthur Tracy *(Street Singer)*, Lilli Palmer *(Susan)*, Mark Daly *(Joe)*, Rae Collett *(Betty)*, Finlay Currie *(Manager)*, Jack Melford *(Reporter)*, Stafford Hilliard *(Sam)*, Julien Vedey *(Toni)*, Phyllis Stanley *(Olga)*.

When popular stage idol Tracy's voice breaks down due to nerves, he does the natural thing and runs away to a gypsy camp to become a tramp street singer. There he falls in love with gentle, elegant Palmer, who has no idea who he is. Dialog is clumsy, but the story succeeds in spite of itself. Picture was one of many made in England by Palmer, before she came to the U.S. in 1945 with her then husband, Rex Harrison.

p, Harcourt Templeman; d, Sinclair Hill; w, George Pearson, Michael Hankinson, Hill (based on the play by C. Stafford Dickens); ph, Cyril Bristow.

Drama **(PR:A MPAA:NR)**

COMMANDO½** (1962, Ital., Span., Bel., Ger.) 98m Tempo Film-Galatea-Fl. C. IT.-Midega Film-Monachia-Zeyn-Filmproduktion/AIP bw (AKA: MARCIA O CREPA)

Stewart Granger *(Capt. LeBlanc)*, Dorian Gray *(Nora)*, Maurizio Arena *(Dolce Vita)*, Ivo Garrani *(Col. Dionne)*, Fausto Tozzi *(Brascia)*, Riccardo Garrone *(Paolo)*, Carlos Casaravilla *(Ben Bled)*, Peter Carsten *(Barbarossa)*, Hans von Borsody *(Fritz)*, Rafael Luis Calvo *(Kappa-kappa)*, Dietmar Schonherr *(Petit Prince)*, Leo Anchoriz *(Garcia)*, Alfredo Mayo, Guillermo Carmona, Pablito Alonso, Jaime de Pedro, Francisco Cornet.

During the 1961 Algerian War, Foreign Legion captain Granger is ordered to lead a small force into the desert and capture rebel leader Casaravilla. The mission succeeds, but the helicopter assigned to pick up the men is shot down and they must make their way overland through fierce opposition. They take heavy losses but finally reach their own forces. There they learn that the political situation has changed and that Casaravilla is now an important figure who will help negotiate the French withdrawal. Granger is furious and thinks to kill his prisoner, but he does not, remembering instead the vain sacrifice his men made. Not bad as an action film, and with a modicum of intelligence not usually found in this sort of film.

d, Frank Wisbar; w, Giuseppe Mangione, Mino Guerrini, William Demby, Milton Krims, Wisbar, Eric Bercovici; (based on a story by Arturo Tofanelli); ph, Cecilio Paniagua; m, Angelo Francesco Lavagnino; ed, Mario Serandrei; art d, Enrique Alarcon.

War Drama **(PR:C MPAA:NR)**

COMMANDOS STRIKE AT DAWN, THE*½** (1942) 100m COL bw

Paul Muni *(Erik Toresen)*, Anna Lee *(Judith Bowen)*, Lillian Gish *(Mrs. Bergesen)*, Sir Cedric Hardwicke *(Adm. Bowen)*, Robert Coote *(Robert Bowen)*, Ray Collins *(Bergesen)*, Rosemary DeCamp *(Hilma Arnesen)*, Richard Derr *(Gunner Korstad)*, Alexander Knox *(German Captain)*, Rod Cameron *(Pastor)*, Louis Jean Heydt *(Lars Arnesen)*, Elizabeth Fraser *(Anna Korstad)*, Erville Alderson *(Johan Garmo)*, George Macready *(Schoolteacher)*, Barbara Everest *(Mrs. Olav)*, Arthur Margetson *(German Colonel)*, Ann Carter *(Solveig Toresen)*, Elsa Janssen *(Mrs. Korstad)*, Ferdinand Munier *(Mr. Korstad)*, John Arthur Stockton *(Alfred Korstad)*, Lloyd Bridges *(Young Soldier)*, Walter Sande *(Otto)*, Philip Van Zandt *(Thirsty Soldier)*.

Muni is dynamic and compelling as the simple fisherman living on the coast of Norway. A widower, he falls in love with Lee whose father, Hardwicke, is a British admiral. Shortly after Lee and her father return to England the Nazis invade Norway, occupying the small village where Muni lives with his daughter, Carter. The German captain, Knox, immediately orders harsh measures taken against anyone caught with radios or sabotaging the fishing quota. When the situation worsens, Muni and others escape in a small boat and sail to England. Here Muni agrees to lead British troops in a commando raid against the village to knock out a German airfield, on the promise that the British will help rescue his daughter who, along with others, is being held hostage. The airfield is destroyed and Muni leads the troops into the village where a desperate battle ensues; he is killed but Carter is rescued and taken to England to live with Lee. The film is a sensitive portrait of occupied people, not a wild and woolly war action film, although the final battle for the airfield and village is spectacular and exciting, staged by veteran action director Farrow who did such a splendid job with WAKE ISLAND. Muni performs his chores with intense restraint and carries the film with the private majesty he always personified. The rugged Norwegian coast was duplicated for this film by utilizing the coastal area outside of Vancouver Island in British Columbia, Canada, where the film was shot on location. The Royal Canadian Navy and Air Force, as well as candidates from the Norwegian Flying School (all of whom had fled from Nazi-occupied Norway) gave enormous help to the production.

p, Lester Cowan; d, John Farrow; w, Irwin Shaw (based on a story by C. S. Forester); ph, William C. Mellor; m, Louise Gruenberg; ed, Anne Bauchens; md, M. W. Stoloff; art d, Edward Jewell.

War Drama   **(PR:A   MPAA:NR)**

COMMISSIONAIRE*½   (1933, Brit.) 72m Granville/MGM bw
Sam Livesey (*Sgt. George Brown*), Barrie Livesey (*Tom Brown*), George Carney (*Sgt. Ted Seymour*), Betty Huntley-Wright (*Betty Seymour*), Julie Suedo (*Thelma Monsell*), Robert English (*Col. Gretton*), Hannah Jones (*Mrs. Brown*), Granville Ferrier (*Desborough*), Georgie Harris (*Briggs*), Humberston Wright (*Quartermaster*).

Sam Livesey is a pensioned-off sergeant doing odd jobs who is blamed when his son, Barrie Livesey, is accused of robbing an office. So-so melodrama. Sam Livesey is the father of British actors Jack and Roger Livesey, as well as Barrie, though Barrie had the least distinguished career.

p, Edward G. Whiting; d, Edward Dryhurst; w, Herbert Ayres.

Crime   **(PR:A   MPAA:NR)**

COMMITMENT, THE*   (1976) 88m Commitment/Borden c
Richard Grand (*Steve*), Barbara Graham (*Amie*), Joseph Turkel (*Jules*), Diane Vincent (*Terri*), Jon Ian Jacobs (*Bill North*), Tom Bower (*Abe*), Bruce Kirby (*Simon Benson*), Richard Adams, Frank Arata, Mimi Davis, Cal Haynes, Esther Sutherland, Jeremiah Gorwitz, Syl Words, Peg Shirley, John Kirby, Joe Valino, Carol McGinnis, Allen Garfield.

A grim, low-budget film cloning the John Cassavetes school of semi-improvisatory filmmaking on ho-hum subjects. But while the makers avoid their mentor's self-indulgence, they lack his flair with actors, and the product has a veneer of honesty without being interesting. Story is indulgence in bleak locations where neurotic characters rant at each other.

p, Elliott Brandes; d, Richard Grand, Louis A. Shaffner; w, Andrew Laskos, Shaffner, Grand (based on a story by Barbara Grand); ph, Shaffner; m, Dobie Gray, John D'Andrea; ed, Elen Orson; art d, Karen Shaffner, Janice Orson; m/l, Gray, Troy Seals, Eddie Setser, Max D. Barns, Will Jennings, Barry Goldberg.

Drama   **(PR:C   MPAA:PG)**

COMMITTEE, THE*   (1968, Brit.) 58m Craytic/Planet c
(AKA: SESSION WITH THE COMMITTEE)
Paul Jones (*Central Figure*), Tom Kempinski (*Victim*), Robert Lloyd (*Director*), Pauline Munro (*Girl*), Jimmy Gardner (*Boss*), The Crazy World of Arthur Brown.

Pop singer Paul Jones is Central Figure in this strange, allegorical curio of the late 1960s. He is a hitch-hiker who murders his drivers and is finally called to face a strange committee. The Crazy World of Arthur Brown is remembered today—if at all—for their wild, scream-filled hit, "Fire."

p, Max Steuer; d, Peter Sykes; w, Steuer, Sykes (based on a story by Steuer).

Fantasy   **Cas.**   **(PR:C   MPAA:NR)**

COMMON CLAY*½   (1930) 88m FOX bw
Constance Bennett (*Ellen Neal*), Lew Ayres (*Hugh Fullerton*), Tully Marshall (*W. H. Yates*), Matty Kemp (*Bud Coakley*), Beryl Mercer (*Mrs. Neal*), Hale Hamilton (*Judge Filson*), Purnell B. Pratt (*Richard Fullerton*), Ada Williams (*Anne Fullerton*), Charles McNaughton (*Edwards*), Genevieve Blinn (*Mrs. Fullerton*).

This story of a speakeasy hostess sullied by men, who pulls herself out of the gutter and emerges as a defiant heroine, was touted at the time as being a lady's magazine story foisted on a tabloid generation. Tully Marshall, in an inconspicuous part as a fire-eating old lawyer, breathes some life into a well-done but overly long production. Ayres' third picture, it appeared four months after the great ALL QUIET ON THE WESTERN FRONT. Remake of the 1919 silent film.

d, Victor Fleming; w, Jules Furthman (based on the play by Cleves Kinkead); ph, Glen MacWilliams.

Drama   **(PR:A   MPAA:NR)**

COMMON LAW, THE*½   (1931) 72m RKO-Pathe bw
Constance Bennett (*Valerie*), Joel McCrea (*Neville*), Lew Cody (*Cardemon*), Robert Williams (*Sam*), Hedda Hopper (*Mrs. Clare Collis*), Marion Shilling (*Stephanie*), Walter Walker, Paul Ellis, Yola D'Avril.

Bennett of the sophisticated manner and voice is living with sugar daddy Cody in Paris when she agrees to model for impoverished artist, McCrea. They fall in love and she abandons money for art by moving in with the painter. The story is comprised of stormy breakups and reconciliations, with abortive attempts by Cody to sabotage the affair. Bennett is happy with the arrangement and refuses to consider marrying McCrea until he is called home to Tarrytown, New York, proving he has been a closet conservative all along. The family exerts pressure on them to give up their decadent European lifestyles and tie the knot. There was some titillation over the scene wherein Bennett peels off her clothes for the artist, and the suggestion of Bennett, naked and posing, is well carried through. Mainly though, one is left wondering why she left the sugar daddy in the first place. The lively and literate piece became an RKO money-maker in a very lean Depression year. Remake of silent versions in 1916 and 1923.

p, Charles R. Rogers; d, Paul L. Stein; w, John Farrow, Horace Jackson (based on the novel by Robert W. Chambers); ph, Hal Mohr.

Drama   **(PR:C   MPAA:NR)**

COMMON LAW WIFE*
(1963) 81m Texas Film Producers/Cinema Distributors of America bw
Lacy Kelly (*Jonelle "Baby Doll"*), Shugfoot Rainey (*Uncle Chug*), Annabelle Lee (*Linda*), Jody Works (*Sheriff Jody*), Bull Connors (*Bull*), Emma Lou Watkins (*Brenda*), Anne MacAdams, George Edgley.

Rainey's common-law marriage to Lee is threatened by the arrival of Rainey's niece, Kelly. Kelly is after Rainey's money, so she conspires with local moonshiner Connors to poison the old man's whiskey. Rainey dies and Lee suspects Kelly of foul play. She lures the girl into a car, then throws her out at high speed, stopping to shoot her. Lee then commits suicide by drinking the poisoned liquor. Low budget redneck exploitation designed for the drive in trade.

p, Fred Kadane; d, Eric Sayers; w, Grace Knowland.

Drama   **(PR:O   MPAA:NR)**

COMMON TOUCH, THE½**   (1941, Brit.) 104m BN/Anglo bw
Greta Gynt (*Sylvia Meadows*), Geoffrey Hibbert (*Peter Henderson*), Joyce Howard (*Mary Weatherby*), Harry Welchman (*Lincoln's Inn*), Edward Rigby (*Tich*), George Carney (*Charlie*), Bransby Williams (*Old Ben*), Wally Patch (*Nobby*), Eliot Makeham (*Inky*), John Longden (*Stuart Gordon*), Raymond Lovell (*Cartwright*), Percy Walsh (*McFarlane*), Bernard Miles (*Perkins*), Charles Carson (*Haywood*), Bill Fraser (*Harris*), Arthur Maude (*Martin*), Jerry Verno (*Messenger*), Mark Hambourg, Carroll Gibbons, Sandy Macpherson, Scott Sanders.

Hibbert is a rich young man who poses as a tramp to save a flophouse from demolition. An attempt at social consciousness. Remade from the 1932 DOSS HOUSE.

p&d, John Baxter; w, Barbara K. Emary, Geoffrey Orme (based on a novel by Herbert Ayres); ph, James Wilson.

Drama   **(PR:A   MPAA:NR)**

COMMUNION   (SEE: ALICE, SWEET ALICE, 1977)

COMPANEROS**   (1970 Ital./Span./Ger.) 118m GSF c
Tritone Filmindustria/Atlantida Film/TerraFilmkunst
(AKA: VAMOS A MATAR, COMPANEROS!)
Franco Nero (*Yod*), Tomas Milian (*Vasco*), Jack Palance (*Xantos*), Iris Berben (*Lola*), Francisco Badalo (*Gen. Mongo*), Karin Schubert (*Zaira*).

Another political spaghetti western from director Sergio Corbucci who developed the "Zapata-Spaghetti" form which infused the narrative with populist sentiments—seeing the bad guys on the Right and the good guys on the Left. In this sequel to A PROFESSIONAL GUN (1968), Nero plays a mercenary who signs up with revolutionary Milian (costumed to resemble Che Guevara) to help free pacifist professor Rey and his students who are being held by the Americans in Texas. Nero's true motivation is a search for gold, the key to which Rey possesses. Along the way they meet Palance, an eccentric, pot-smoking gunslinger with a wooden hand and a pet falcon who has an old score to settle with Nero. He lost his hand when he had been nailed to a cross and his falcon chewed off his hand to free him. Eventually the capitalist urges of the mercenary wear on Milian's nerves and the revolutionary leader challenges Nero to a duel. Before the showdown can be played, however, there is an attack by counter-revolutionaries and Nero opts to help fight them off against impossible odds. Over-direction by Corbucci and typically extreme over-acting by Palance spoil any chance the material has.

p, Alberto Grimaldi; d, Sergio Corbucci; w, Corbucci, Dino Maiuri, Massimo De Rita, Fritz Ebert; ph, Alejandro Ulloa (Techniscope/Technicolor); m, Ennio Morricone, Bruno Nicolai.

Western   **(PR:C   MPAA:R)**

COMPANIONS IN CRIME*½   (1954, Brit.) 70m REP bw
Clifford Evans (*Inspector Stryker*), George Woodbridge, Kenneth Haigh, Maurice Kaufmann, Christine Silver, Billie Whitelaw, Gaylord Cavallaro, Ian Fleming, Cyril Chamberlain, Jack Lambert, Fred Griffiths, Russell Napier, Patrick Jordan, Gillian Lutyens, Eliot Makeham, Dorothy Alison, Tim Turner, David Perrin, Guy Deghy, Philo Hauser.

Two episodes from the Inspector Stryker series are linked together for this mediocre filler feature. In the first story, Evans clears a man convicted of murder with the help of the man's fiancee. In the second, he gets a tip that a yachtsman is smuggling jewels on the side, but it turns out that the tipster is the boss of the smuggling gang.

p, William N. Boyle; d, John Krish; w, Kenneth Hayles, Patricia Latham, Lester Powell; ph, Basil Emmott.

Crime   **(PR:A   MPAA:NR)**

COMPANY OF COWARDS   (SEE: ADVANCE TO THE REAR, 1964)

COMPANY OF KILLERS**   (1970) 90m UNIV c
Van Johnson (*Sam Cahill*), Ray Milland (*Georges DeSalles*), John Saxon (*Dave Poohler*), Clu Gulager (*Frank Quinn*), Brian Kelly (*Tich*), Fritz Weaver (*John Shankalien*), Susan Oliver (*Thelma Dwyer*), Diana Lynn (*Edwina DeSalles*), Robert Middleton (*Owen Brady*), Terry Carter (*Max Jaffie*), Ahna Capri (*Maryjane Smythe*), Anthony James (*Jimmy Konic*), Marian Collier (*Sylvia Xavier*), Nate Esformes (*Peterson*), Mercer Harris (*Luke*), Joyce Jameson (*Marnie*), Gerald Hiken (*Chick*), Vince Howard (*Dale Christian*), Larry Thor (*Clarington*), Donna Michelle (*Gloria*), Jeanne Bal (*Patricia Cahill*).

Saxon is an underworld assassin for Murder, Inc., on the run from his bosses and the police department. In a confused plot, the police are busy tracking down a bevy of hit men under Middleton's control before they can kill a multimillionaire. Lots of conspiracy and a final fiery auto crash.

p, E. Jack Neuman, Jerry Thorpe; d, Thorpe; w, Neuman; ph, Jack Marta (Technicolor); m, Richard Hazard; ed, John Elias; art d, Alexander Golitzen, Joseph Alves; set d, John McCarthy; cos, Burton Miller.

Crime   **(PR:A   MPAA:G)**

COMPANY SHE KEEPS, THE½   (1950) 82m RKO bw
Lizabeth Scott (*Joan*), Jane Greer (*Diane*), Dennis O'Keefe (*Larry*), Fay Baker (*Tilly*), John Hoyt (*Judge Kendall*), James Bell (*Mr. Nelley*), Don Beddoe (*Jamieson*), Bert Freed (*Smitty*), Irene Tedrow (*Mrs. Seeley*), Marjorie Wood (*Mrs. Haley*), Marjorie Crossland (*Mrs. Griggs*), Virginia Farmer (*Mrs. Harris*).

From the title one would think this was a light comedy. It's anything but. Greer is a parolee who has just done two years of a five-year term for passing a bad check. Scott is her parole officer, a sweetie who is dating O'Keefe, a newspaper columnist. Greer is understandably itchy after having been in the company of other women for so long and makes a play for O'Keefe. Next, Greer attempts to help a fellow parolee, Baker, who has gotten into some trouble. That little beneficence puts Greer in danger of going back inside until Scott does a sacrificial thing and gets Greer off the hook with the authorities. By doing that, Scott loses the love of O'Keefe, who is now smitten with Greer. Before we fade out, O'Keefe is made to realize that he is giving up a helluva woman for Greer. It's basically a woman's movie (not that men won't be interested) in that it concerns feminine problems best understood by distaff viewers.

p, John Houseman; d, John Cromwell; w, Ketti Frings; ph, Nicholas Musuraca; m, Leigh Harline; ed, Robert Swink.

Drama   (PR:C   MPAA:NR)

COMPELLED**   (1960, Brit.) 56m Danziger/UA bw
Ronald Howard (*Paul Adams*), Beth Rogan (*Carol*), John Gabriel (*Fenton*), Richard Shaw (*Jug*), Jack Melford (*Grimes*), Mark Singleton (*Derek*), Colin Tapley (*Inspector*).

Howard is an ex-con turned engineer blackmailed into complicity with a jewel heist. Nothing special about this British programmer.

p, Brian Taylor; d, Ramsey Herrington; w, Mark Grantham.

Crime   (PR:A-C   MPAA:NR)

COMPETITION, THE*½   (1980) 129m COL c
Richard Dreyfuss (*Paul Dietrich*), Amy Irving (*Heidi Schoonover*), Lee Remick (*Greta Vandemann*), Sam Wanamaker (*Erskine*), Joseph Cali (*Jerry DiSalvo*), Ty Henderson (*Michael Humphries*), Vickie Kriegler (*Tatiana Baronov*), Adam Stern (*Mark Landau*), Bea Silvern (*Mme. Gorshev*), Philip Sterling (*Mr. Dietrich*), Gloria Stroock (*Mrs. Dietrich*), Delia Salvi (*Mrs. DiSalvo*), Priscilla Pointer (*Mrs. Donellan*), James B. Sikking (*Brudnell*), Elaine Welton Hill (*Mitzi*), Ben Hammer (*Nichols*), Rhio H. Blair (*Karnow*), Ross Evans (*Judge Heimling*), Sterling Swanson (*Rudko*), Jimmy Sturtevant (*Vinnie DiSalvo*), Kathy Talbot (*Denise DiSalvo*).

A dreary portrait of the classical music world made even more so by Dreyfuss's uninspired performance and the turgid script and direction by Joel Oliansky, a man who did some excellent writing for a TV series called "The Law" and won several awards. Dreyfuss plays an aging piano competitor who is making one final attempt at international recognition in one of those piano contests. If he muffs this one, he'll retire to a life of teaching more talented players than he. Sometime before, Dreyfuss had met Irving, a more talented but less driven pianist. They meet again at this competition and a spark is rekindled, at least at her end. But Dreyfuss is too tunnel-visioned to recognize this at first and concentrates on his preparations for the upcoming evening. Eventually he notices Irving but this is complicated by her thrashing him at the competition. Dreyfuss really does love Irving but he is so crushed by her victory that he rejects her. In what appears to be a coda to the scene where he kisses her off, Irving and Dreyfuss are reunited in a scene that makes no sense and they end the film dancing to some heavy disco music. Most of the movie made no sense or was totally predictable. Dreyfuss wanted to win for his dying father, Sterling, and Irving did what she could to please her mother, a terribly written role for Lee Remick. Some even dumber sub-plots with a defecting Russian and a gay black pianist and a family of Italian hams. Irving is one of the few bright spots in this otherwise dim picture. The dialog is often gross, seldom witty, and far too long. Furthermore, there is an appalling lack of taste in the presentation of the music. Here is a movie that claims to be an accurate portrayal of the classical music world and yet has the gall to excise the famous pieces and condense others so they can fit into the time frame. Word on the street was that the scenes of piano-playing were cut down after trade sceeenings proved disastrous. Even the small character roles suffer and usually reliable Wanamaker is left with little to do. In the role of Dreyfuss' mother is Stroock, sister of Geraldine Brooks, and member of the Brooks Costume family, long one of the leading costumers on Broadway.

p, William Sackheim; d&w, Joel Oliansky (based on a story by Oliansky and Sackheim); ph, Richard H. Kline (Metrocolor); m, Lalo Schifrin; ed, David Blewitt; prod d, Dale Hennesy; cos, Ruth Myers; set d, James Payne; m/l, "People Alone" (Schifrin); classical music by Brahms, Chopin, Prokofiev, Beethoven played by Eduardo Delgado, Ralph Grierson, Daniel Pollack, Chester B. Swiatowski, Lincoln Mayorga, and the Los Angeles Philharmonic Orchestra.

Musical Drama   Cas.   (PR:C   MPAA:PR)

COMPLIMENTS OF MR. FLOW*½   (1941, Fr.) 80m Hoffberg bw
Fernand Gravet (*Antonin Rose*), Edwige Feuillere (*Lady Helena Scarlett*), Louis Jouvet (*Durin/Mr. Flow*), Tsjundo Maki (*Maki*), Vladimir Sokoloff (*Merlow*).

Slick safecracker inside prison keeps his cash flowing with the aid of criminals on the outside. When their schemes are foiled by a penniless lawyer, who has also won the heart of the gangster's girl friend, love and justice triumph. Pleasant enough French farce in spite of some haphazard camera work.

d, Robert Slodmak; w, Henri Jeanson (based on a novel by Gaston Leroux); ph, Gaveau, Bachelet, Thomas; md, Michel Levine.

Drama   (PR:A   MPAA:NR)

COMPROMISED*½   (1931) 65m FN bw (GB: WE THREE)
Ben Lyon (*Sidney Brock*), Rose Hobart (*Ann*), Juliette Compton (*Connie Holt*),

Claude Gillingwater (*John Brock*), Delmar Watson (*Sandy*), Bert Roach, Emma Dunn.

When the son of a wealthy industrialist is lured back to his factory home town to learn the family business, he ends up marrying the boarding house servant who nursed him through a hangover and incurs the wrath of his family. Rest of the film deals with his father's machinations to undermine the new bride at every opportunity. The dialog is uninteresting, the situations flat, and it's mainly a matter of waiting and hoping something will happen. It doesn't.

d, John Adolfi; w, Florence Ryerson, Waldemar Young (based on the play by Edith Fitzgerald).

Drama   (PR:A   MPAA:NR)

COMPROMISED! zero   (1931, Brit.) 55m British International bw
                                          (GB: COMPROMISING DAPHNE)
Jean Colin (*Daphne Ponsonby*), Phillis Konstam (*Sadie Bannister*), C. M. Hallard (*Mr. Ponsonby*), Viola Compton (*Mrs. Ponsonby*), Charles Hickman (*George*), Leo Sheffield (*Mr. Bannister*), Frank Perfitt (*Hicks*), Barbare Gott (*Martha*), Margot Grahame (*Muriel*).

This is a 100 percent bad movie. In what is supposed to be a comedy, a sweet young thing is compromised by a cad in an effort to force her father to consent to marriage. Movie is as shaky as the marriage premise.

p, John Maxwell; d, Thomas Bentley; w, Val Valentine (based on the play by Edith Fitzgerald); ph, John F. Fox.

Drama   (PR:A   MPAA:NR)

COMPROMISING DAPHNE   (SEE: COMPROMISED! 1931, Brit.)

COMPULSION***   (1959) 103m FOX bw
Orson Welles (*Jonathan Wilk*), Diane Varsi (*Ruth Evans*), Dean Stockwell (*Judd Steiner*), Bradford Dillman (*Artie Straus*), E. G. Marshall (*Horn*), Martin Milner (*Sid*), Richard Anderson (*Max*), Robert Simon (*Lt. Johnson*), Edward Binns (*Tom Daly*), Robert Burton (*Mr. Straus*), Louise Lorimer (*Mrs. Straus*), Wilton Graff (*Mr. Steiner*), Gavin MacLeod (*Padua*), Terry Becker (*Benson*), Russ Bender (*Edgar Llewellyn*), Gerry Lock (*Emma*), Harry Carter, Simon Scott (*Detectives*), Voltaire Perkins (*Judge*).

Only the names have been changed in the film; the story is straight out of fact, the notorious Loeb and Leopold murder of Bobby Franks in 1924 in Chicago. Dillman is superb as the mother-dominated, sadistic, superior Loeb, here called Artie Straus, and Stockwell plays out his role of the submissive, introverted Leopold (Judd Steiner) to perfection in what is undoubtedly his finest adult role, far surpassing his stumbling performance of LONG DAY'S JOURNEY INTO NIGHT. Of course, Welles commands all the attention once on the screen to defend the two arrogant killers who methodically plot their crime as if acting out roles and then have the effrontery to offer the police aid in solving the killing (which is exactly what Loeb did, which led to his arrest and that of Leopold). Raised by wealthy families and spoiled to black corruption, both Dillman and Stockwell have no sense of common decency in that they felt themselves wholly uncommon masterminds. This is no less evident than in the terrifying scene where they try to run down a drunk on their way to court. Further, the cold-blooded murder they plan and execute is done without remorse or conscience. The clients inherited by Welles offer him no defense so, like Clarence Darrow, the man who so brilliantly defended the real killers, Welles defends by attacking the system and the wealthy Establishment which created the perverted pair. Both were homosexual but this is glossed over, obliquely exposed when Varsi, Stockwell's occasional girl friend, explains his distant, aloof air and inexplicable dependence upon Dillman. The courtroom scenes are electrifying as Welles struggles to save the bodies if not the minds of the defendants, raging against the philosophy of an eye-for-an-eye, condemning capital punishment. Welles looks strange in this film in that he used heavy amounts of gum arabic to distort his nose which he has never liked and always altered in his many varied parts. COMPULSION is a shocker and full of suspense, even though the informed viewer knows its outcome. Taut direction is rendered by Fleischer and a terse and telling script from Murphy who almost took the story word-for-word from the best-selling Meyer Levin novel. Dillman takes scenes away from Welles in his courtroom appearances with a stupefying performance. Up to this film he was considered lightweight material, appearing in such frothy productions as A CERTAIN SMILE and IN LOVE AND WAR. With his intense portrayal of the psychotic killer, Dillman came of age and emerged as a major actor. Welles' cunning, flamboyant lawyer is met well by the opposing state's attorney, Marshall, who gives an understated, excruciatingly patient performance of a man who knows his quarry is mortally wounded and behind which bush it hides.

p, Richard D. Zanuck; d, Richard Fleischer; w, Richard Murphy (based on the novel by Meyer Levin); ph, William C. Mellor (CinemaScope); m, Lionel Newman; ed, William Reynolds; cos, Charles LeMaire.

Crime Drama   (PR:C-O   MPAA:NR)

COMPULSORY HUSBAND, THE**   (1930, Brit.) 100m British International bw
Monty Banks (*Monty*), Lillian Manton (*Joy*), Clifford Heatherley (*Mr. Pilluski*), Gladys Frazin (*Mrs. Pilluski*), Trilby Clark (*Gilda*), Reginald Fox (*Father*), Janet Alexander (*Mother*), Michael Powell (*Man*).

When bride-to-be Manton takes her parents to meet fiance Banks, they find he is hiding another woman in the closet. Nice ski chase in the French Alps complete with a cliff-hanging automobile. Fast action and plenty of laughs but picture needs tighter editing.

p, John Maxwell; d, Harry Lachman, Monty Banks; w, John Glyder, Val Valentine (based on the novel by Glyder); ph, T. Sparkhull, James Rogers, Rene Guissart.

Comedy   (PR:A   MPAA:NR)

COMPULSORY WIFE, THE** (1937, Brit.) 57m WB/FN bw

Henry Kendall *(Rupert Sinclair)*, Joyce Kirby *(Bobby Carr)*, Margaret Yarde *(Mrs. Thackery)*, Robert Hale *(Col. Craven)*, Agnes Laughlan *(Mrs. Craven)*, George Merritt *(Mr. Thackery)*, Anthony Shaw *(George Bittleston)*, Mercia Swinburne *(Mrs. Bittleston)*.

Kendall and Kirby are forced to spend the night together in a remote cottage when a burglar steals their clothes. Okay comedy for the nondiscriminating.

p, Irving Asher; d, Arthur Woods; w, Reginald Purdell, John Dighton (based on a play by John Glyder); ph, Basil Emmott.

Comedy **(PR:A MPAA:NR)**

COMPUTER FREE-FOR-ALL** (1969, Jap.) 84m Toho c (BUCHAMUKURE DAIHAKKEN)

Hajime Hana *(Hanakawado)*, Hitoshi Ueki *(Uemura)*, Kei Tani *(Tanii)*, Hiroshi Inuzuka, Senri Sakurai, Eitaro Ishibashi, Shin Yasuda.

Hana is a computer salesman who, expecting a big deal to go through, uses company funds to pay his bar tab. When he learns that a computer foul-up has paid out far more money than owed on the tab, he goes to the apartment of the bar girl the money was paid to. He finds her murdered and uses his computer to restore her to life. The money is recovered, the girl becomes a sweet thing, and Hana is cleared of embezzling charges. Dumb Japanese comedy from Oriental funnyman Hana.

d, Kengo Furusawa; w, Yasuo Tanami; ph, Senchiki Nagai; m, Naozumi Yamamoto; art d, Kazuo Ogawa.

Comedy **(PR:C MPAA:NR)**

COMPUTER WORE TENNIS SHOES, THE*** (1970) 90m BV c

Cesar Romero *(A. J. Arno)*, Kurt Russell *(Dexter)*, Joe Flynn *(Dean Higgins)*, William Schallert *(Prof. Quigley)*, Alan Hewitt *(Dean Collingsgood)*, Richard Bakalyan *(Chillie Walsh)*, Debbie Paine *(Annie)*, Frank Webb *(Pete)*, Michael McGreevey *(Schuyler)*, Jon Provost *(Bradley)*, Frank Welker *(Henry)*, Alexander Clarke *(Myles)*, Bing Russell *(Angelo)*, Pat Harrington *(Moderator)*, Fabian Dean *(Little Mac)*, Fritz Feld *(Sigmund Van Dyke)*, Pete Renoudet *(Lt. Hannah)*, Hillyard Anderson *(J. Reedy)*.

Walt Disney does it again in this delightful comedy. College non-student Russell acquires the entire contents of a computer's memory bank when an electrical accident causes it to be transferred into his brain. Unfortunately, along with other data he now possesses information on the nefarious activities of the computer's original owner, gangster Romero. When he becomes a contestant on a quiz show to raise money for the college, the word "applejack" triggers an enumeration of Romero's illegal activities. The chase is on, and an exciting one it is. The success of this film led to two follow-ups, also starring Russell, NOW YOU SEE HIM, NOW YOU DON'T, where he discovers a formula to make himself invisible, and THE STRONGEST MAN IN THE WORLD, where he discovers a formula which gives him great strength. These films may be repetitious, but they are among Disney's better comedies.

p, Bill Anderson; d, Robert Butler; w, Joseph L. McEveety; ph, Frank Phillips (Technicolor); ed, Cotton Warburton; m, Robert F. Brunner; art d, John R. Mansbridge; set d, Emile Kuri, Hal Gausman; cos, Chuck Keehne, Emily Sundby; m/l, "The Computer Wore Tennis Shoes" (Robert F. Brunner).

Comedy **(PR:AAA MPAA:G)**

COMRADE X*** (1940) 87m MGM bw

Clark Gable *(McKinley B. Thompson)*, Hedy Lamarr *(Theodora)*, Oscar Homolka *(Vasiliev)*, Felix Bressart *(Vanya)*, Eve Arden *(Jane Wilson)*, Sig Rumann *(Emil Von Hofer)*, Natasha Lytess *(Olga)*, Vladimir Sokoloff *(Michael Bastakoff)*, Edgar Barrier *(Rubick)*, John Piccori *(Laszlo)*, Mikhail Rasumny *(Russian Officer)*.

Louis B. Mayer of MGM pushed along the production of COMRADE X, believing it would have great box office appeal since it was a spinoff of NINOTCHKA, but the amusing farce just missed, even though Gable and the sultry Lamarr gave it their all. Gable is an American newsman in Moscow who has been smuggling out stories embarrassing the regime. Bressart, a porter at Gable's hotel, discovers the newsman's ploy and blackmails him into smuggling his daughter, Lamarr, out of Russia. Bresssart tells him that Lamarr is being investigated because she is a pure Communist and that is suspect in Russia. Gable agrees but finds his hands full when Lamarr, a streetcar driver, refuses to leave the country; he must pretend to be a Communist and convince her to spread communism in the U.S. Lamarr consults with her political mentor, Homolka, who insists that before Lamarr embarks on her propagnada mission Gable marry her. In a wild mood, Gable agrees but police apprehend the couple. Homolka has informed Sokoloff, head of the secret police, about their plans. Gable, Bressart, and Lamarr, along with Homolka's counterrevolutionary followers, are condemned to death, but Gable gets them off after blackmailing Homolka with a photo showing him in a compromising position with a secretary. Gable, Lamarr, and Bressart then flee the country in a stolen tank, escaping through Russian war games, a wild chase, as improbable as the entire story, which nevertheless delights. The Hecht-Lederer script is tension-packed and full of satirical barbs and lowbrow slapstick which saved COMRADE X from being just another predictable melodrama. The screenplay was based on a story by Reisch, who was nominated for an Oscar; Reisch had co-scripted NINOTCHKA the year before. (This story received yet another twist when Hecht, never one to let a tale go fallow, came up with another version of the beautiful Communist lady being converted to capitalistic ways in THE IRON PETTICOAT, 1956.) Gable and Lamarr were teamed in this film instantly after their success in BOOM TOWN but failed to spark as a love duo. The actor felt that Lamarr (who was making $25,000 a film then) was too cool on screen (and off), while she once caustically remarked that he had no sex appeal, which befuddled every woman in America. Carole Lombard, Gable's wife at the time, was extremely jealous of her man and visited the COMRADE X set regularly to make sure no hanky-panky took place. It was during this film that Gable developed a superstition; Burberry made a special trenchcoat for him, one of his own design, which he wore in COMRADE X. He considered this his "lucky coat" and wore it for 20 years in almost every film he made. When MGM held its 1969 public auction, the coat was put up for sale and Burberry's flew a representative from London to purchase the coat but the mission failed. An anonymous buyer outbid everyone, buying Gable's "lucky coat" for $1,250.

p, Gottfired Reinhardt; d, King Vidor; w, Ben Hecht, Cherles Lederer (based on a story by Walter Reisch); ph, Joseph Ruttenberg; m, Bronislau Kaper; ed, Harold F. Kress; art d, Cedric Gibbons; set d, Edwin B. Willis; spec eff, Arnold Gillespie.

Comedy **(PR:A MPA:NR)**

CON ARTISTS, THE* (1981, Ital.) 93m S.J. International Pictures c (AKA: THE CON MAN)

Anthony Quinn *(Bang)*, Adriano Celentano *(Felix)*, Corinne Clery *(Charlotte)*, Capucine *(Belle)*.

Quinn is a con man recently released from jail who teams with youngster Celentano to cheat crime boss Capucine. One can't help but wonder why a talented actor like Quinn continues to hurt his career by doing garbage like this.

p, Mario C. Gori; d, Serge Corbucci.

Crime **Cas.** **(PR:O MPAA:PG)**

CON MEN, THE*

(1973, Ital.,Span.) 99m F. P. Cinematografica Canaria/Tecisa c (TE DEUM)

Jack Palance, Timothy Brent, Lionel Stander, F. Romana Coluzzi, Renzo Palmer, Maria Vico Villardo.

Spaghetti western farce starring Palance and Stander as a pair of con artisits looking for a sucker to buy what they believe to be a useless gold mine. Soon they realize that the mine is actually a mother-lode and they have to plow through a growing number of people to get it back. Comedy is often strained.

p, Franco Palaggi, Virgilio De Blasi; d, Enzo G. Castellari; w, Castellari, Gianni Simonelli, Tito Carpi, J. Maesso; ph, Manolo Rojas.

Comedy/Western **(PR:A MPAA:NR)**

CONAN THE BARBARIAN** (1982) 115m UNIV c

Arnold Schwarzenegger *(Conan)*, James Earl Jones *(Thulsa Doom)*, Max Von Sydow *(King Osric)*, Sandahl Bergman *(Valeria)*, Ben Davidson *(Rexor)*, Cassandra Gaviola *(The Witch)*, Gerry Lopez *(Subotai)*, Mako *(The Wizard)*, Valerie Quinnessen *(The Princess)*, William Smith *(Conan's Father)*, Luis Barboo *(Red Hair)*, Franco Columbo *(Pictish Scout)*, Leslie Foldvary *(Snake Girl)*, Gary Herman *(Guard)*, Erick Holmey *(Officer)*, Akio Mitamura *(General)*, Nadiuska *(Conan's Mother)*, Jorge Sanz *(Young Conan)*, Jack Taylor *(Priest)*, Sven Ole Thorsen *(Thorgrim)*, Kiyoshi Yamasaki *(Sword Master)*.

At an early age Schwarzenegger's Conan becomes a slave to the bad guys after they have brutally murdered his mother and father. But it's the baddies' fatal flaw that they shove Conan into an arena to fight chosen competitors to the death, where the kid realizes he's a little stronger than the average guy. Not so dumb, this Conan. Off he goes on his own and with the help of some colorful friends sets out to avenge his parents. The picture is tiresome and never goes anywhere, just a series of meaningless adentures with the final expected confrontation. Schwarzenegger will be remembered mostly for punching out a camel. Sequel: CONAN THE DESTROYER.

p, Buzz Feitshans, Raffaella De Laurentiis; d, John Milius; w, Milius, Oliver Stone (based on the character created by Robert E. Howard); ph, Duke Callaghan (Todd-AO, Technicolor), John Cabrera; m, Basil Poledouris; ed, C. Timothy O'Meara, Fred Stafford; prod d, Ronn Cobb; art d, Pierluigi Basile, Benjamin Fernandez; set d, Giorgio Postiglione; cos, John Bloomfield.

Adventure/Fantasy **Cas.** **(PR:C-O MPAA:R)**

CONCENTRATIN' KID, THE*½ (1930) 57m Gibson/UNIV bw

Hoot Gibson, Kathryn Crawford, Duke Lee, Robert Homans, James Mason.

In Gibson's final film for Universal he falls in love with a radio songstress and vows to marry her. But upon arriving in town dandied up for courtship he learns the cattle have been rustled and the girl kidnaped, taken to the range, and forced to serenade the cowboys. Old Hoot doesn't want his canary warbling in just anybody's ear, nor does he want his cows grazing on some stranger's lawn, so off he goes to capture the rustlers and rescue the cows and the girl. There isn't one shooting in this picture. Not even a good fist fight. Shucks.

p, Hoot Gibson; d, Arthur Rosson; w, Harold Tarshis, Charles Saxton; ph, Harry Neumann.

Western **(PR:A MPAA:NR)**

CONCENTRATION CAMP*** (1939, USSR) 60m Amkino bw

O. Jakov *(Paul)*, S. Shirokova *(Mary)*, S. Mezhinsky *(The Pharmicist)*, I. Kudriatsev *(Tideman)*, V. Vanin *(Camp Commander)*, A. Konsovsky *(Frantz)*, I. Doromin *(Robert)*, A. Gribov *(Schultz)*, I. Koval-Samborsky *(Walter)*, S. Muratov *(Oswald)*.

Russian propaganda film takes a realistic and grim look at Hitler's regime and its effect on communism and the Worker's Party. Focus is on the underground system of secret meetings whereby the laboring group manages to escape much of the Nazi terrorism. In the final scenes the workers revolt against the military regimentation in a German airplane factory and go on strike, with the red front comrades ganging up on the Nazi military and a last-minute plug for the Soviet Union. The picture is well-directed and the message effective. (Russian; English subtitles.)

d, A. Macharet; w, I. Olesha, Macharet; ph, E. Andrikanis; m, Lev Schwartz.

Drama **(PR:A MPAA:NR)**

CONCERNING MR. MARTIN½** (1937, Brit.) 59m FOX British bw

Wilson Barrett *(Leo Martin)*, William Devlin *(Martell)*, Marjorie Peacock *(Gloria)*, Derek Williams *(Robin)*, Lionel Montgomery *(Foo)*, Herbert Cameron *(Detective)*, Billy Wells *(Commisionaire)*, Madge Somers, Dominick Sterlini.

When a sleazy nightclub owner cheats an innocent girl, a dapper thief frames him to see justice done. A clever thriller, some tense moments between good thief Barrett and the crooked nightclub owner Devlin make for exciting scenes in director Kellino's first directorial production.

p, John Findley; d, Roy Kellino; w, Ernest Dudley; ph, Stanley Grant.

Crime Drama **(PR:A MPAA:NR)**

CONCORDE, THE—AIRPORT '79** (1979) 123m UNIV c (AKA: AIRPORT '79) (GB:AIRPORT '80: THE CONCORDE)

Alain Delon *(Metrand)*, Susan Blakely *(Maggie)*, Robert Wagner *(Kevin Harrison)*, Sylvia Kristel *(Isabelle)*, George Kennedy *(Patroni)*, Eddie Albert *(Eli)*, Bibi Anderson *(Francine)*, Charo *(Margarita)*, John Davidson *(Robert Palmer)*, Andrea Marcovicci *(Alicia)*, Martha Raye *(Loretta)*, Cicely Tyson *(Elaine)*, Jimmie Walker *(Boise)*, David Warner *(O'Neill)*, Mercedes McCambridge *(Nelli)*, Avery Schreiber *(Coach Markov)*,

Sybil Danning *(Amy)*, Monica Lewis *(Gretchen)*, Nicholas Coster *(Dr. Stone)*, Robin Grammell *(William Halpern)*, Jon Cedar *(Froelich)*, Ed Begley, Jr., Sheila DeWindt, Pierre Jalbert, Kathleen Maguire, Macon McCalman, Stacy Heather Tolkin, Selma Archerd, Brian Cutler, Michele Lesser, Conrad Palmisano, Jerry M. Prell, Dick McGarvin, George Sawaya, Leonora Wolpe, David Matthau, Frank Parker, Mario Machado.

This time out, pilots Kennedy, Delon, and flight engineer Warner save half of Hollywood from an attack of electronic missiles, a near run-in with a French fighter jet, the loss of a cargo door, a crash landing in an Alpine snowbank, a runway landing with no brakes, and an explosion which occurs only seconds after tinsel-towners disembark. Meantime, back in the cabin, newshen Blakely is sitting on incriminating evidence against Wagner who is behind all the hijinks. But this time the supersonic jet takes center stage, sparing audiences from most of the babbling of the two-dimensional characters. The picture's one distinction is that there are more bedroom scenes and suicides than in any other airport movie. But after all, it is the Concorde. (This one grossed almost $9 million on first take-off.)

p, Jennings Lang; d, David Lowell Rich; w, Erich Roth, Lang (inspired by the film AIRPORT, based on the novel by Arthur Hailey); ph, Philip Lathrop (Technicolor); m, Lalo Schifrin; ed, Dorothy Spencer; prod d, Henry Bumstead; set d, Mary Ann Biddle, Mickey S. Michaels; spec eff, Universal Hartland, Abe Milrad; stunts, George Sawaya.

Disaster Drama **(PR:A-C MPAA:PG)**

CONCRETE JUNGLE, THE*** (1962, Brit.) 97m Anglo/Amalgamated bw (GB: THE CRIMINAL)

Stanley Baker *(Johnny Bannion)*, Sam Wanamaker *(Mike Carter)*, Gregoire Aslan *(Frank Saffron)*, Margit Saad *(Suzanne)*, Jill Bennett *(Maggie)*, Rupert Davies *(Mr. Edwards)*, Laurence Naismith *(Mr. Town)*, John Van Eyssen *(Formby)*, Noel Willman *(Prison Governor)*, Derek Francis *(Priest)*, Redmond Phillips *(Prison Doctor)*, Kenneth J. Warren *(Clobber)*, Patrick Magee *(Chief Warder, Barrows)*, Kenneth Cope *(Kelly)*, Patrick Wymark *(Sol)*, Jack Rodney *(Scout)*, John Molloy *(Snipe)*, Brian Phelan *(Pauly Larkin)*, Paul Stassino *(Alfredo Fanucci)*, Jerold Wells *(Warder Brown)*, Tom Ball *(Flynn)*, Neil McCarthy *(O'Hara)*, Keith Smith *(Hanson)*, Nigel Green *(Ted)*, Tom Gerard *(Quantock)*, Larry Taylor *(Chas)*, Murray Melvin *(Antlers)*, Sydney Bromley *(Frightened Prisoner)*, Luigi Tiano *(Italian-speaking Prisoner)*, Edward Judd *(Young Warder)*, Richard Shaw *(Warder in Van)*, Charles Lamb *(Mr. Able)*, Maxwell Shaw *(1st Man at Party)*, Victor Beaumont *(2nd Man at Party)*, Dorothy Bromiley *(Angela)*, Ronald Brittain *(Kitchen Warder)*, Tommy Eytle *(West Indian Prisoner)*, Dickie Owen *(1st Man in Prison)*, Roy Dotrice *(Nicholls)*, Bobby R. Naidoo *(Serang)*, Maitland Williams *(West Indian Prisoner)*.

Hard-hitting and noncompromising, this Alun Owen screenplay shows the criminal's life the way it seldom was seen before—all the sleazy characters, all the dark recesses of existence in a jail. Baker is inside for three years and, like cream, he rises to the top of the con population. While twiddling his thumbs and cooling his heels, he has planned a large robbery of a racetrack. After pulling the job, his money-washer indicates that the promised percentage for laundering the cash has now gone up. Rather than pay a usurious figure, Baker hides the money by interring it in a desolate spot, but not before taking a nice hunk to buy a bauble for new girl friend, Saad. Old girl friend Bennett is annoyed at that, so she blows the whistle and Baker goes up for a 15-year stretch. They offer him a reduced sentence if he'll tell the authorities where the money is but he's determined to do his time and come out of the jail a rich man. His outside gang uses their inside pals to attempt to put pressure on Baker but it's not working, so they decide to utilize Saad as the hook. A prison riot is arranged. That occasions a break and Baker leads the other crooks to the money. They get rid of Baker and are left digging for the moolah as the pic ends. There was something missing from this otherwise crackling film. Baker was the star and the person we were supposed to root for. True, he was a crook and capable of many crimes, but he was a man of principles, low though they were. Still, he was not enough for us to hang our hopes upon. American Sam Wanamaker was an admitted liberal who feared the McCarthy investigations in the late 1940s so he moved to England and carved out a career for himself in British drama. As it turned out, he was never mentioned by any committee. Wanamaker's portrayal of Baker's double-dealing aide is a study in seething anger. This was Magee's first film in an all-too-brief career that was highlighted by his work in CHARIOTS OF FIRE, THE BIRTHDAY PARTY, and A CLOCKWORK ORANGE. Best information indicates writer/director Jimmy Sangster did some uncredited writing on the script.

p, Jack Greenwood; d, Joseph Losey; w, Alun Owen (based on a story by Jimmy Sangster); ph, Robert Krasker; m, Johnny Dankworth; ed, Reginald Mills; prod d, Richard MacDonald; art d, Scott Macgregor; cos, Ron Beck.

Prison Drama **(PR:C MPAA:NR)**

CONCRETE JUNGLE, THE** (1982) 99m Pentagon c

Jill St. John *(Warden Fletcher)*, Tracy Bregman *(Elizabeth Demming)*, Barbara Luna *(Cat)*, June Barrett *(Icy)*, Peter Brown *(Danny)*, Aimee Eccles *(Spider)*, Sondra Currie *(Katherine)*, Susan Mechsner *(Breaker)*, Nita Talbot *(Shelly Meyers)*, Niki Dantine *(Margo)*.

Innocent girlfriend of a drug smuggler is caught at the airport with a load of cocaine and sent up the river where she is at the mercy of warden St. John and leader of the pack, Luna, a murderess and apparent lesbian. This is a usual women-in-prison movie, though Bregman makes a convincing transition from sweet young thing to hardened survivor. Highlight of the film is a prison-yard melee toward the end which turns into a mud-wrestling free-for-all.

p, Billy Fine; d, Tom DeSimone; w, Alan J. Adler; ph, Andrew W. Friend (CFI Color); m, Joe Conlan; ed, Nina Di Marco.

Drama **Cas.** **(PR:O MPAA:R)**

CONDEMNED½** (1929) 93m Goldwyn/UA bw

Ronald Colman *(Michel Oban)*, Ann Harding *(Mme. Vidal)*, Dudley Digges *(Warden Jean Vidal)*, Louis Wolheim *(Jacques Duval)*, William Elmer *(Pierre)*, William Vaughn *(Vidal's Orderly)*, Albert Kingsley *(Felix)*, Henry Ginsberg, Bud Somers, Stephen Selznick, Baldy Biddle, John George, Arthuro Kobe, Emil and John Schwartz *(Inmates)*, Constantine Romanoff *(Brute Convict)*.

The normally discerning Sidney Howard couldn't do much with the screenplay of the predictable novel by Blair Niles. Colman, in his second sound film (BULLDOG DRUMMOND being the first) plays a suave thief condemned to Devil's Island. His good manners have gotten him a job inside the warden's house (Digges, who also doubled as dialog director). Digges' wife, Ann Harding, is as tasty a bit of fluff as you ever did see and it isn't long before she and Colman fall in love. He is sent to solitary confinement but an escape is planned to coincide with Harding's return to France. They get away together, have a series of hair-raising and totally unbelievable adventures in the swamps, and are caught in her stateroom aboard the ship going to France. Colman utters a memorable line before being apprehended, one that mirrored the viewer's perception of this improbable film: "I thought this was going to be an escape and it turns into a yacht race." Colman is returned to finish out his sentence and the picture ends when the lovers are united in Paris. Colman is excellent and proves his worth in every frame while Ann Harding just doesn't quite come up to snuff. (Colman got an Oscar nomination just for this performance and for BULLDOG DRUMMOND.) Many other pictures were made in later years with Devil's Island as the base (PAPILLON, DEVIL'S ISLAND, I ESCAPED FROM DEVIL'S ISLAND) and they were essentially alike.

p, Samuel Goldwyn; d, Wesley Ruggles; w, Sidney Howard (suggested by the book *Condemned To Devil's Island* by Blair Niles); ph, George Barnes, Gregg Toland; ed, Stuart Heisler; set d, William Cameron Menzies.

Prison Romance **(PR:C MPAA:NR)**

CONDEMNED OF ALTONA, THE** (1963) 112m FOX bw

Sophia Loren *(Johanna)*, Maximilian Schell *(Franz)*, Fredric March *(Gerlach)*, Robert Wagner *(Werner)*, Francoise Prevost *(Leni)*, Alfredo Franchi *(Grounds Keeper)*, Lucia Pelella *(His Wife)*, Roberto Massa *(Driver)*, Antonio Cianci *(Maid)*, Carlo Antonini *(Police Official)*, Armando Sifo *(Policeman)*, Aldo Pecchioli *(Cook)*, Ekkehard Schall.

A many-starred muddle that tried to tell too much at one time and failed. But the actors were so intent on doing their best that they all deserve a pat on the back. March is a Krupp-like character who owns a titanic industrial complex in Germany. He calls his son, Wagner, and Wagner's actress wife, Loren, to the family estate, Altona. Wagner is offered the family holdings but refuses. He is a lawyer with a sense of justice and knows how many lives have been lost through his dying father's efforts. Wagner is the second son and his late brother would have controlled the family holdings had it not been for the fact that he was cited at the Nuremberg war-crimes trials and executed. Late at night, Loren hears screams in the huge house and decides to investigate, then learns Altona's secret: Wagner's brother is alive. Schell is insane and being tended to by sister Prevost, who tells Schell lies about how Germany has never recovered and poverty reigns over the land. Loren then tells him the truth and the confused Schell races to close-by Hamburg to find out which of the women is lying to him. Before he leaves, he tells Loren that the house was used as a concentration camp during the war. She is disturbed by that and confronts Wagner, who has now changed his mind and will take over the company. Schell is arrested in Hamburg and brought back to Altona where he asks Loren for her forgiveness for all he has done. He tells her how he led his own troops into a trap rather than allow them to torture some Russian farmers. Loren believes him and attempts to comfort Schell, but sister Prevost worms the truth out of him; he was a killer and torturer several times over. Faced by his deep guilt, Schell commits suicide by leaping from scaffolding and drags March with him. Sartre's original monologs are mostly retained by Mann and Zavattini and the movie's stage origins are betrayed by lots and lots of talk. The major problem here was that nobody, least of all the audience, cares about the guilt of some Germans. Here we have a family that has recovered from the war and is now richer than ever. This family was responsible for many deaths and we are expected to care about such human scum? Never. A host of brilliant creators was behind this mess, many of whom had won recognition and awards for other works. In the case of THE CONDEMNED OF ALTONA, nothing went right and reputations could have been shattered but for the fact that the movie business gives someone at least five at-bats for strikeouts after they have hit one home run. Mann and Schell worked over some of the same material in JUDGMENT AT NUREMBERG in 1961. They should have left hell enough alone.

p, Carlo Ponti; d, Vittorio DeSica; w, Abby Mann, Cesare Zavattini (based on the play "Les Sequestres d'Altona" by Jean-Paul Sartre); ph, Roberto Gerardi (CinemaScope); m, Dmitri Shostakovich; ed, Manuel Del Campo, Adriana Novelli; art d, Ezio Frigerio; cos, Pier Luigi Pizzi.

Drama **(PR:O MPAA:NR)**

CONDEMNED TO DEATH** (1932, Brit.) 76m Twickenham/ED bw

Arthur Wontner *(Sir Charles Wallington)*, Edmund Gwenn *(Banting)*, Gordon Harker *(Sam Knudge)*, Jane Welsh *(Sonia Wallington)*, Cyril Raymond *(Jim Wrench)*, Norah Howard *(Gwen Banting)*, Griffith Humphreys *(Prof. Michaels)*, Bernard Brunel *(Tobias Lantern)*, H. St. Barbe West *(Sir Rudolph Cantler)*, Gillian Lind, James Cunningham, Gilbert Davies.

Brunel plays a condemned murderer who projects his criminal mind through hypnosis into Wontner, the judge passing sentence. This results in a dual personality for his honor, and a great deal of confusion for the audience. Forde directed as best he could, given the muddled but sometimes interesting script.

p, Julius Hagen; d, Walter Forde; w, H. Fowler Mear, Brock Williams, Bernard Merrivale (based on the play "Jack O'Lantern" by George Goodchild); ph, Sydney Blythe, William Luff; art d, James Carter.

Mystery **(PR:A MPAA:NR)**

CONDEMNED TO LIFE (SEE: WALK IN THE SHADOW, 1962, Brit.)

CONDEMNED TO LIVE** (1935) 67m IN bw
Ralph Morgan *(Prof. Paul Kristan)*, Maxine Doyle *(Marguerite Mane)*, Russell Gleason *(David)*, Pedro De Corboda *(Dr. Anders Bizet)*, Mischa Auer *(Zan)*, Lucy Beaumont *(Mother Molly)*, Carl Stockade *(John Mane)*.

Man, wife, and friend escape from African savages to New England in the Puritan days. Shortly before their journey pregnant mom was bitten by a vampire bat. Later, on American soil, several women are murdered by Morgan who attacks his victims at the throat, draining their blood. It is never made clear whether he is Doyle's son, fogging up the story quite a bit. No need for garlic or wooden stakes in this one.

p, Maury M. Cohen; d, Frank Strayer; w, Karen DeWolf; ph, M.A. Anderson; ed, Roland D. Reed.

Horror **Cas.** **(PR:A MPAA:NR)**

CONDEMNED WOMEN* (1938) 77m RKO bw
Sally Eilers *(Linda Wilson)*, Louis Hayward *(Phillip Duncan)*, Anne Shirley *(Millie Anson)*, Esther Dale *(Matron Glover)*, Lee Patrick *(Big Annie)*, Leona Roberts *(Kate)*, George Irving *(Warden Miller)*, Richard Bond *(David)*, Netta Packer *(Sarah)*, Rita La Roy *(Cora)*, Florence Lake.

Inmate Eilers taking the blame for her boy friend so he can finish law school, falls in love with the prison psychologist who befriends her and works to free her. (Their trysting is confined to the prison furnace room.) In the meantime she must put up with abuse from the obligatory tough matron who believes in old-school methods of rehabilitation. There is a prison break where the girls do their level best to kill each other off but the movie suffers from a glut of plots. Patrick as the hardboiled prison hen is funny, not frightening. Many scenes in CAGED (1950) were inspired by this film.

p, Robert F. Sisk; d, Lew Landers; w, Lionel Houser; ph, Nicholas Musuraca.

Drama **(PR:A MPAA:NR)**

CONDORMAN½** (1981) 90m Disney/BV c
Michael Crawford *(Woody)*, Oliver Reed *(Krokov)*, Barbara Carrera *(Natalia)*, James Hampton *(Harry)*, Jean-Pierre Kalfon *(Morovich)*, Dana Elcar *(Russ)*, Vernon Dobtcheff *(Russian Agent)*, Robert Arden *(CIA Chief)*.

Cartoonist Crawford gets a chance to live out his comic strip hero fantasies when CIA chum Hampton enlists his help in exchanging some papers with Russian civilian Carrera. The mission is supposed to be a safe and simple one but turns out otherwise, allowing Crawford to cavort around in a superman suit testing his hero's exploits in real life. He of course falls in love with the beautiful Russian girl Carrera, who turns out to be a KGB agent wanting to defect. A pleasant movie but too hackneyed and heavy-handed to work well.

p, Jan Williams; d, Charles Jarrot; w, Marc Stirdivant, Glen Caron, Mickey Rose (based on the novel *The Game of X* by Robert Sheckley); ph, Charles F. Wheeler (Panavision, Technicolor); m, Henry Mancini; ed, Gordon D. Brenner; prod d, Albert Witherick; art d, Marc Frederix; spec eff, Colin Chilvers.

Comedy **Cas.** **(PR:AAA MPAA:PG)**

CONDUCT UNBECOMING*** (1975, Brit.) 107m AA c
Michael York *(2nd Lt. Arthur Drake)*, Richard Attenborough *(Maj. Lionel Roach)*, Trevor Howard *(Col. Benjamin Strang)*, Stacy Keach *(Capt. Rupert Harper)*, Christopher Plummer *(Maj. Alastair Wimbourne)*, Susannah York *(Mrs. Marjorie Scarlett)*, James Faulkner *(2nd Lt. Edward Millington)*, Michael Culver *(2nd Lt. Richard Fothergill)*, James Donald *(Regimental Doctor)*, Rafiq Anwar *(Pradah Singh)*, Helen Cherry *(Mem Strang)*, Michael Fleming *(Lt. Frank Hart)*, David Robb *(2nd Lt. Winters)*, David Purcell *(2nd Lt. Boulton)*, Andrew Lodge *(2nd Lt. Hutton)*, David Neville *(2nd Lt. Truly)*, Persis Khambatta *(Mrs. Bandanai)*, Michael Byrne *(2nd Lt. Toby Strang)*.

Based on a play that opened in London, CONDUCT UNBECOMING is a fair adaptation but essentially a tempest in a teapot. Like A PASSAGE TO INDIA it concerns the question of whether or not a woman was molested and the drama turns into a contrived mystery. Faulkner is the accused and he is defended by M. York in the secret trial run by the officers at a remote Indian outpost in the last century. S. York is the woman in question who accuses Faulkner of the deed. Essentially a courtroom piece, it is the forerunner of BREAKER MORANT in feeling but not as electric as that Aussie effort. Acting is uniformly good and the script by Enders clearly delineates all that need be said. The major problem is that it remains a one-set work and somewhat claustrophobic despite yeoman efforts by Enders and Anderson to give it some air. Keach is the soldier acting as judge and his is the juiciest role as it requires him to visibly alter his strong feelings to convict as new evidence is given. The ending is a great disappointment and a cop-out, but until then the picture sails along and involves the audience. Jeremy Clyde, of the singing group of Chad and Jeremy, starred in the play. But, as it usually happens, studios prefer having insurance for their investments so they employ what they believe are stars. It made no difference in the box office receipts of this movie, which were sparse.

p, Michael Deeley, Barry Spikings, Andrew Donally; d, Michael Anderson; w, Robert Enders (based on a play by Barry England); ph, Bob Huke (Technicolor); m, Stanley Myers; ed, John Glen; art d, Ted Tester; cos, Joan Bridge, Elizabeth Haffenden.

Drama **(PR:A-C MPAA:PG)**

CONDUCTOR, THE*** (1981, Pol.) 101m PRF/Zespol/Cinegate c (DYRYGENT)
John Gielgud, Krystyna Janda, Andrzej Seweryn, Marysia Seweryn, Anna Lopatowska, Mavis Waler, Jan Ciecierski, Jozef Fryzlewicz, Janusz Gajos, Mary Ann Krasiniski, Tadeusz Czechowski, Marek Dabrowski, Stanislaw Gorka, Jerzy Kleyn, Elzbieta Stralkowska, Jerzy Szmidt, Wojciech Wysocki, Stanislaw Zatloka.

John Gielgud is fantastic as a New York orchestra conductor who returns to his native Poland as a guest conductor, one of the principal violinists being the daughter of a dead lover, who happens to be married to the resident conductor. Gielgud carries the film forward (even though he is obnoxiously dubbed into Polish) through Wajda's occasionally heavy directorial hand. (Polish; English subtitles.)

d, Andrzej Wajda; w, Andrzej Kijowski (from conversations with Andrzej Markowski); ph, Slawomir Idziak (Orwocolor); m, Beethoven; ed, Halina Prugar; prod d, Allan Starski.

Drama **(PR:A-C MPAA:NR)**

CONE OF SILENCE (SEE: TROUBLE IN THE SKY, 1960)

CONEY ISLAND*½** (1943) 93m FOX c
Betty Grable *(Kate Farley)*, George Montgomery *(Eddie Johnson)*, Cesar Romero *(Joe Rocco)*, Charles Winninger *(Finnigan)*, Phil Silvers *(Frankie)*, Matt Briggs *(William Hammerstein)*, Paul Hurst *(Louie)*, Frank Orth *(Bartender)*, Phyllis Kennedy *(Dolly)*, Carmen D'Antonio *(Dancer)*, Hal K. Dawson *(Cashier)*, Andrew Tombes *(Carter)*, Harry Seymour *(Piano Player)*, Byron Foulger *(Organist)*.

This film had little to do with Coney Island in the flesh and it was, in fact, just a long look at Grable's luscious gams. Still and all, that wasn't bad in the dark days of 1943 when the world was at war and the home front needed some enjoyment to take its mind off the news from the front. Romero and Montgomery (talking in much the same voice as Clark Gable) are rivals in turn-of-the century Coney Island (so named, by the way, because when it was discovered by the Spaniards; it was overrun by rabbits; they called it Isla de los conejos) and they are given to staging overwrought schemes on each other to put the other out of business. They are both in love with and responsible for the success of Grable. Romero owns the honky-tonk and Montgomery figures Cesar owes him a half interest in repayment of an earlier favor. Romero balks and there's the plot. The rest of the story is little more than a song-and-danceathon with the ending taking place at the Victoria theater in Manhattan with Grable starring in a William Hammerstein (Briggs) musical. Somebody in research goofed because the Victoria was a vaudehouse and Hammerstein never produced musicals, but no matter, the fun was there. Silvers and Winninger dominate the screen whenever they are allowed to, and Silvers is exceptionally on the nose as a sideshow owner. Lots and lots of music and huge production numbers. The Technicolor photography was of the highest quality and all tech credits are top-notch. Coney Island, known as "Sodom By The Sea" in an early book, was never as plush as depicted on screen here but it was far more interesting. Performers like Jimmy Durante and Eddie Cantor and even Irving Berlin got their starts in the less-than-one-mile-long entertainment area that included several amusement parks such as Steeplechase, Dreamland, Luna Park, and countless saloons like The Atlantis, The Blue Bird Casino, The Seven Seas, and many more. To make the point about how little this actually had to do with Coney Island, consider the fact that the movie was remade in 1950 under the name of WABASH AVENUE. Songs: "Cuddle Up A Little Closer" (Karl Hoschna, Otto Harbach), "Pretty Baby" (Gus Kahn, Tony Jackson, Egbert Van Alstyne), "Put Your Arms Around Me Honey" (Albert Von Tilzer, Junie McCree), "Take It From Here," "Lulu From Louisville," "There's Danger In Dance," "Get the Money," "Old Demon Rum," "Beautiful Coney Island" (Ralph Rainger, Leo Robin), "Who Threw the Overalls In Mrs. Murphy's Chowder?" (George L. Giefer), "Darktown Strutters Ball" (Sheldon Brooks), medley: "Deep River," "Oh Susanna," "The Old Folks at Home" (Stephen Foster), "Let Me Call You Sweetheart" (Beth Slater Whitson, Leo Friedman), "Dengozo [Maxixe]" (Ernesto Nazareth).

p, William Perlberg; d, Walter Lang; w, George Seaton; ph, Ernest Palmer (Technicolor); ed, Robert Simpson; md, Alfred Newman; ch, Hermes Pan.

Musical Comedy **(PR:A MPAA:NR)**

CONFESS DR. CORDA½** (1960, Ger.) 101m Film-Artur Brauner/President bw
Hardy Kruger *(Dr. Fred Corda)*, Elizabeth Mueller *(Beate Corda)*, Lucie Mannheim *(Mrs. Bieringer)*, Hans Nielsen *(Dr. Nagel)*, Fritz Tillman *(Police Commissioner Pohlhammer)*, Eva Pflug *(Gabriele)*, Rudolf Fernau *(Prof. Schliessman)*, Siegfried Lowitz *(Inspector Guggitz)*, Hans Binner *(The Cyclist)*, Maria Krasna *(Carmen)*, Emmy Burg, Lore Hartling, Paul Edwin Roth, Ernst Sattler, Roma Bahn, Werner Butler, Heinhard Kolldehoff, Georg Gutlich, Siegrid Hackenberg, Barbara Wieczik, Maria Krasna.

Kruger is a respected doctor who finds his lover murdered at their rendezvous site. He is immediately under suspicion and as the media pick up on the case, the police become less interested in finding the real killer, and more interested in bending the evidence to convict Kruger. It is finally another murder that clears Kruger, though not before the community has turned against him and his wife has attempted suicide. Occasionally interesting drama, though Kruger is totally miscast.

p, Artur Brauner; d, Josef Von Baky; w, R.A. Stemmle; m, George Haentzchel.

Crime **(PR:C MPAA:NR)**

CONFESSION½** (1937) 85m WB/FN bw
Kay Francis *(Vera)*, Ian Hunter *(Leonide Kilrow)*, Basil Rathbone *(Michael Michailow)*, Jane Bryan *(Lisa)*, Donald Crisp *(Presiding Judge)*, Mary Maguire *(Hildegard)*, Dorothy Peterson *(Mrs. Koslov)*, Laura Hope Crews *(Stella)*, Robert Barrat *(Prosecuting Attorney)*, Ben Welden *(Defense Attorney)*, Veda Ann Borg *(Xenia)*, Helen Valkis *(Wanda)*, Anderson Lawlor *(Reporter)*, Lawrence Grant *(Doctor)*, Michael Mark *(Russian Interpreter)*, Sam Rice, Albert Lloyd, Perc Teeple, Jack Richardson *(Men at Station)*, Lyle Moraine *(Usher at Theatre)*, Ferdinand Munier *(Bald Man at Theatre)*, Peggy Keys, Jewel Jordan *(Autograph Fans)*, Sam Ash *(Waiter)*, Edward Keane *(Cabaret Manager)*, Pierre Watkin *(Lawyer)*, Dawn Bender *(Lisa as a Baby)*, Lawrence Grant *(Doctor)*, Janet Shaw, Jody Gilbert, Evelyn Mulhall, Symona Boniface, Elsa Peterson *(Actress Friends)*, Edward Price, Jeffrey Sayre, John Mather, Lane Chandler, Jack Davidson, Maurice Brierre *(Actor Friends)*.

It may take a whole box of Kleenex to get through this heart-rending drama of a cabaret singer who kills a philandering concert pianist when she learns he's been performing with her own daughter. Story is told in flashback from the courtroom where mom is on trial but remaining mum on why she killed the man who years before had been responsible for separating her from her husband and little girl. The entire cast is excellent and the production is a fine vehicle for Francis. Other important contributions include the special attention paid to the music, and the decision that the actors speak English without a trace of accent though the locale is Warsaw. Song: "One Hour Of Romance" (Jack Scholl, Peter Kleuder).

p, Hal Wallis; d, Joe May; w, Julius J. Epstein, Margaret LaVino, Stanley Logan (based on the screenplay "Mazurka" by Hans Hameau); ph, Sid Hickox; m, Peter Kreunder, Jack Scholl; ed, James Gibbon; md, Leo F. Forbstein; art d, Anton Grot; cos, Orry-Kelly.

Drama (PR:A MPAA:NR)

CONFESSION, 1955 (SEE: THE DEADLIEST SIN, 1955)

CONFESSION, THE****

(1970, Fr.) 135m Films Corona/Pomereu/VALORIA c (L'AVEU)
Yves Montand (Gerard), Simone Signoret (Lise), Gabriele Ferzetti (Kohoutek), Michel Vitold (Smola), Jean Bouise (Boss), Laszlo Szabo (Secret Policeman), Monique Chaumette, Guy Mairesse, Marc Eyraud, Gérard Darrieu, Gilles Ségal, Charles Moulin, Nicole Vervil. Georges Aubert, André Cellier, Pierre Delaval, William Jacques, Henri Marteau, Michel Robin, Antoine Vitez, Michel Beaune, Marc Bonseignour, Thierry Bosc, Jean-Paul Cisife, Marcel Cuvelier, Pierre Decazes, Basile Diaman-topoulos, Jacques Emin, Jean-Francois Gobbi, Maurice Jacquemont, Jean-Pierre Janic, Patrick Lancelot, Jean Lescot, Francois Marthouret, Pierre Moncorber, Umberto Raho, Jacques Rispal, Paul Savatier, Claude Vernier, Pierre Vielhescazes.

"Z" was the film that brought Costa-Gavras to the public's eye and THE CONFESSION was an excellent follow-up to what has become a career of politically aware movies such as STATE OF SIEGE, SPECIAL SECTION, and MISSING. It's 1951 and Montand is an East European Communist official who notices that he's being followed. During the Spanish Civil War Montand was a Loyalist and he mentions his fears to some friends who served that cause. They admit that they think they are also being watched. He is arrested and taken to a building that will temporarily serve as a jail. Signoret, his wife in real and reel life, is not told the whereabouts of his incarceration but she is falsely reassured that it will all be over shortly. Montand has no idea why he is being held but is forced to endure some painful treatment. His captors put him in prison garb and make him walk endlessly with little food or drink. As he becomes weaker and thinner, they quiz him unmercifully and begin dredging up old memories. They tell him that all his friends have already confessed, they talk about his days in the Loyalist movement, his years with the Resistance, and they keep asking how and why he, a Jew, managed to avoid the gas chambers at the concentration camps. Montand is a dedicated Communist and takes solace in the fact that these men are also Communists and only doing what they feel is right. With that knowledge, he is able to sustain himself at their cruel hands. Finally, in tiredness, he starts signing documnts and is rewarded by food, medical treatment, and some hours under a sunlamp so his pallor is tanned away. Montand is being readied for a nationally covered trial and he hopes his side will be heard, but then he learns that it's being covered by the government-controlled radio and he will be cut off the instant he utters a word. Montand is one of many on trial and the other defendants are rehearsed until they know their roles perfectly. The trial takes place and several of the men are sentenced to death. Montand gets life imprisonment but is later released. It is not all clear what causes the jailing, trial, and eventual release. Montand and Signoret are reunited, go to Prague just in time to see the Russians roll in, and the film ends when Yves and Simone get ready to leave for France. Costa-Gavras likes to present his films in a grainy, fragmented fashion so that by the time one's over you've gotten the whole of it, if not in a linear fashion. Ironies abound in all of his work and the picture of interrogator Ferzetti, meeting Montand in jail and wondering how they all got there, is indicative of the director's sense of humor. In the U.S., where political intrigues are far subtler and the results are seldom publicly seen, it may be difficult to fathom what Costa-Gavras has in mind sometimes, but it's never dull. Born in Greece, Costa-Gavras (Konstantin Gavras) is now a naturalized Frenchman and married to daring journalist Michele Ray, who excited the world with her dipatches from Vietnam and her account of being held captive by the Viet Cong.

p, Robert Dorfmann, Bertrand Javal; d, Costa-Gavras; w, Jorge Semprun (based on a book by Lise and Arthur London); ph, Rapul Coutard (Eastmancolor); ed, Francoise Bonnot; prod d, Claude Hauser; art d, Bernard Evein.

Drama (PR:C MPAA:NR)

CONFESSIONAL, THE zero

(1977, Brit.) 104m Atlas c
(AKA: HOUSE OF MORTAL SIN)
Anthony Sharp (Meldrum), Susan Penhaligan (Jenny), Stephanie Beacham (Vanessa), Norman Eshley (Bernard), Sheila Keith (Miss Brabazon), Hilda Barry (Mrs. Meldrum), Stewart Beven (Terry), Julia McCarthy (Mrs. Davey), Jon Yule (Robert), Mervyn Johns (Father Duggan), Victor Winding (Dr. Gaudio), Kim Butcher (Valerie), Bill Kerr (Davey), Ivor Salter (Gravedigger), Jack Allen, Jane Hayward, Andrew Sachs, Austin King, Melinda Clancy.

Trashy anti-Catholic horror from director Peter Walker who was also responsible for such slimy classics as SCHOOL FOR SEX and HOT GIRLS FOR MEN ONLY. In THE CONFESSIONAL, Sharp plays a demented priest who tape-records the confessions of young women to be used as blackmail against them. When a few unfortunate parishioners stumble upon the priest's activities, he kills them too, using a variety of religious icons. One victim is strangled with a rosary, another is given a poisoned host, and yet another's skull is bashed in with an incense burner. Really vile stuff.

p&d, Peter Walker; w, David McGillivray; ph, Peter Jessop; m, Stanley Myers.

Horror (PR:O MPAA:R)

CONFESSIONS FROM A HOLIDAY CAMP* (1977, Brit.) 88m COL c
Robin Askwith (Timothy Lea), Anthony Booth (Sidney Noggett), Doris Hare (Mom), Bill Maynard (Dad), Sheila White (Rosie), Colin Crompton (Roughage), Liz Frazer (Mrs. Whitemonk), Linda Hayden (Brigitte), John Junkens (Mr. Whitemonk), Lance Percival (Lionel), Nicholas Owen (Kevin), Janet Ede (Kevin's Mom), Mike Savage (Kevin's Dad).

A window cleaner, pop performer, and driving instructor turn into bad actors when scheduled as entertainment at a British Holiday Camp. Another in the "Confessions" series serves up the usual numbing dosage of slapstick, vulgarity, and innuendo peppered with scenes of Hayden stripping at every opportunity. Basic American ignorance of the British Holiday Camp system makes it hard to understand.

p, Greg Smith; d, Norman Cohen; w, Christopher Wood (based on a novel by Timothy Lea); ph, K. Hodges; ed, Geoffrey Foot; art d, Harry Pottle.

Comedy (PR:A MPAA:NR)

CONFESSIONS OF A CO-ED** (1931) 74m PAR bw
Philips Holmes (Dan), Sylvia Sidney (Patricia), Norman Foster (Hal), Claudia Dell (Peggy), Florence Britton (Adelaide), Martha Sleeper (Lucille), Dorothy Libaire (Mildred), Marguerite Warner (Sally), George Irving (President), Winter Hall (Dean Winslow), Eulalie Jensen (Dean Marbridge), Bruce Coleman (Mark), Bing Crosby (Band Vocalist Bing).

In this college drama dealing with four capricious university students who become involved in a series of campus scandals, the principals look as though they would be more comfortable in adult-education classes. Action unfolds slowly and possibly the only point of interest is that it marked the end of Bing Crosby's bit parts in the movies.

d, Dudley Murphy, David Burton; ph, Lee Garmes; art d, Hans Dreier.

Comedy (PR:A MPAA:NR)

CONFESSIONS OF A NAZI SPY**** (1939) 110m WB/FN bw
Edward G. Robinson (Ed Renard), Francis Lederer (Schneider), George Sanders (Schlager), Paul Lukas (Dr. Kassel), Henry O'Neill (D.A. Kellogg), Lya Lys (Erika Wolff), Grace Stafford (Mrs. Schneider), James Stephenson (Scotland Yard Official), Sig Rumann (Krogman), Fred Tozere (Phillips), Dorothy Tree (Hilda), Celia Sibelius (Mrs. Kassel), Joe Sawyer (Renz), Lionel Royce (Hintze), Hans Von Twardowsky (Wildebrandt), Henry Victor (Helldorf), Frederick Vogeding (Capt. Richter), George Rosener (Klauber), Robert Davis (Straubel), John Voight (Wesphal), Willy Kaufman (Gruetzwald), William Vaughn [Von Brincken] (Capt. Von Eichen), Jack Mower (McDonald), Robert Emmett Keane (Harrison), Eily Malyon (Mrs. MacLaughlin), Frank Mayo (Staunton), Alec Craig (Postman), Jean Brooks (Kassel's Nurse), Lucien Prival (Kranz), Frederick Burton (U.S. District Court Judge), Ward Bond (American Legionnaire), Charles Trowbridge (U.S. Intelligence Official), John Ridgely (Army Hospital Clerk), Emmett Vogan (Hotel Clerk), Edward Keane (FBI Agent), Martin Kosleck (Josef Goebbels), Selmer Jackson (Customs Agent), Egon Brecher (Nazi Spy), Niccolai Yoshkin (Man), Bodil Rosing (Anna), Charles Sherlock (Young), John Deering (Narrator).

This was Hollywood's opening propaganda salvo against Hitler's Third Reich, and it was a shot heard around the world. The film begins in rural Scotland where a reclusive woman suddenly begins receiving mail from all points of the globe. When a resident philatelist asks if she will give him the foreign stamps for his collection, the woman explodes, refusing and slamming her door in his face. He reports this strange behavior to Scotland Yard. British Intelligence agents soon discover that she is part of a Nazi spy ring. One of her letters from Lederer is intercepted; it tells of the Nazi spy network in America and its plans to kidnap an American Air Force general. British Intelligence contacts the U.S. Government and FBI man Robinson enters the investigation, probing into the Nazi underground in America. Systematically, Robinson pinpoints key spies, concentrating on Lederer, the weak link to the Nazi network. He is finally taken into custody and slowly interrogated by Robinson, admitting that he was recruited by the Nazis to obtain secret government information. He explains that he is a reluctant spy, nagged into his espionage activities by a wife wanting the "good life," and ridiculed for not being "a big shot." He admits impersonating a medical official and calling hospitals for military personnel figures in order to figure out the strength of garrisons in the New York area. Sanders is his superior and has paid him miserably, about $50 per report. Lederer also names Lukas, head of a Nazi Bund, who is recruiting American youth into Hitler Jugend legions, and who is in league with Sanders. Tripped up by Robinson, Lukas next agrees to inform on the ruthless Sanders but he is kidnaped by German agents before surrendering to the FBI and is smuggled out of the country on a German ocean liner where Lys, posing as a hairdresser, orders him beaten senseless and held prisoner until he can be turned over to the Gestapo in Germany. But Robinson has enough information and rounds up the key Nazis before they can do further harm. CONFESSIONS OF A NAZI SPY frightened audiences with the real threat of Nazi tyranny which was the courageous aim of Warner Bros. This film established the studio as the leading film company of socially oriented productions. Robinson is terrific as the FBI man, subduing his normally extravagant gestures and speaking quietly in almost every scene, underplaying a dynamic part with wonderful agility and cold-blooded effectiveness in keeping with Litvak's semi-documentary style. The spy ring activities are shown in newsreel fashion, and some actual clips are employed from the 1937 spy trials of four Nazis convicted of espionage, the case on which the film is based (profiled in a series of articles written by former FBI agent Leon G. Turrou). Much of the film parades Nazi brutality. There is a great deal of beating, gouging, kicking in the groin, and Hitler, Goebbels, and company are openly vilified. Warners knew there would be a strong reaction and it came almost immediately from heads of the various Nazi Bundist groups in the U.S., as well as from Germany which banned the film. Eighteen other countries followed suit, fearful of offending Hitler. But in the U.S. audiences cheered for Robinson and hissed the Nazi goons. Distributors had been warned that Nazi sympathizers might start riots in the first-run theaters showing the film so squads of detectives patrolled the theaters to arrest would-be agitators. Litvak's direction is unbashedly biased, and rightly so; his hatred for the Nazis seethes throughout the film and audiences supported that prejudice. At one point a Nazi spy protests to Robinson about the mass arrests of his fellow agents. When he is told: "After all, New York harbor is still within the jurisdiction of the United States," viewers applauded and cheered.

p, Robert Lord; d, Anatole Litvak; w, Milton Krims, John Wexley (based on an original story by Krims and Wexley and Leon Turrou's articles "Storm Over America"); ph, Sol Polito; ed, Owen Marks; tech adv, Leon G. Turrou.

Spy Drama **(PR:C MPAA:NR)**

CONFESSIONS OF A NEWLYWED**½ (1941, Fr.) 80m World bw

Raimu *(The Professor)*, Sylvia Bataille *(Daughter)*, Pierre Brasseur *(Son-in-Law)*, Pauline Carton *(Wife)*, Alerme *(Her Boyfriend)*, Germaine Aussey *(Showgirl)*.

Raimu is an entomologist whose assistant is engaged to his daughter. That both father and son-in-law are more familiar with the mating habits of bugs than brides is evident when the couple return from their week-long honeymoon with the marriage still unconsummated. The new bridegroom beseeches his wife's father to help him with a solution to his problem and Raimu goes off to seek advice, all of which is handled with great delicacy in a situation that could easily become objectionable. A clever parallel is drawn between the difficulties of the bridegroom and a pair of rare bugs in the professor's laboratory. The comedy has been modestly produced but the cast, story and direction are all good. (French; English subtitles.)

p&d, Leo Joannon; w, Jean Aurenche, Yves Allegret (based on the stage comedy "Have You Nothing to Declare?" by d'Hennequin and Veber); m, d'Oberfeld.

Comedy **(PR:A MPAA:NR)**

CONFESSIONS OF A POLICE CAPTAIN*** (1971, Ital.) 101m Euro International c

Martin Balsam *(Comm. Bonavia)*, Franco Nero *(D. A. Traini)*, Marilu Tolo *(Serena Li Puma)*, Claudio Gora *(Chief Magistrate)*, Luciano Lorcas *(Lomunno)*, Arturo Dominici *(Lomunno's Lawyer)*, Adolfo Lastretti *(Michele Li Puma)*, Michele Gammino *(Himself)*, Giancarlo Prete *(Rizzo)*.

This film is a part of the growing trend of political action pictures coming out of Italy by film directors raised on neo-realism. Damiani, a political action pioneer, was already probing the political sore spots of a Mafia-infested social structure with his Sicilian-localed DAY OF THE OWL. CONFESSIONS is in the same locale. It concerns the story of Balsam as a police commissioner frustrated for years in his attempts to bring to justice a local lawbreaker who continues to rise to power in politics, society, and speculative real estate. Thwarted at every turn, he finally makes the decision to mete out his own kind of justice. Intelligently directed, this suspenseful drama gets an exciting performance from Balsam.

p, Mario Montanari, Bruno Turchetto; d, Damiano Damiani; w, Damiani, Salvatore Laurani; ph, Claudio Ragona (Eastmancolor); m, Riz Ortolani; ed, Antonio Siciliano; art d/cos, Umberto Turco.

Drama **(PR:A MPAA:NR)**

CONFESSIONS OF A POP PERFORMER* (1975, Brit.) 91m COL c

Robin Askwith *(Timothy Lea)*, Anthony Booth *(Sidney Noggett)*, Bill Maynard *(Mr. Lea)*, Doris Hare *(Mrs. Lea)*, Sheila White *(Rosie)*, Bob Todd *(Mr. Barnwell)*, Jill Gascoine *(Mrs. Barnwell)*, Peter Cleall *(Nutter Normington)*, Peter Jones *(Maxy Naus)*, Carol Hawkins *(Jill Brown)*, Richard Warwick, Maynard Williams, Mike King, David Auker, Diane Langton, Linda Regan, Robert Dorning, Margaret Heald, Ian Lavender, Irene Gorst, Andee Cromarty, Rita Webb, Anita Kay, Bill Pertwee, Maggie Wright, Suzette St. Clair, David Hamilton, Helli Louise, Sally Harrison, Lynda Westover, John Francois Landry, Vicki Woolf, Rula Lenska, Jackie Blackmore, David Belcher, Robert Nicholson, Jane Hayden, Bobby Sparrow, David Prowse, Emma Booth, Eric Francis.

Simple-minded soft core sex comedy has Askwith once again playing the accident-prone city bumpkin (as he did in CONFESSIONS OF A WINDOW CLEANER). This time the plot has Askwith and his brother-in-law promoting a fifth-rate pop group. They succeed briefly in getting the group into the big time but then disaster plagues them and they are left with nothing to do but cavort around with a bevy of big-breasted girls. U.S. TV-commercial aficionados will note the brief appearance of the redoubtable Rula Lenska.

p, Greg Smith; d, Norman Cohen; w, Christopher Wood (based on "Confessions" novels by Timothy Lea); ph, Alan Hume (Eastmancolor); ed, Geoffrey Foot; art d, Bernard Sarron.

Comedy **(PR:O MPAA:NR)**

CONFESSIONS OF A ROGUE*** (1948, Fr.) 84m Constellation Films/Distinguished Films bw

Louis Jouvet *(Ismora)*, Suzy Delair *(Caroline)*, Annette Poivre *(Charlotte)*, Jane Marken *(Concierge)*, Madeleine Suffel *(Mme. Charles)*, Jean Jacques Delbo *(Oscar)*, Leon Lapara *(Andre)*, Jean Carmet *(An Accomplice)*, Pally *(Laprune)*, Henri Charrett *(M. Charles)*, Fernand Rauzena *(Peroni)*, George Cusin *(Pauzat)*, Robert Seller *(Judge)*.

Jouvet is a one-man show in this French comedy of a double identity mixup. He plays a super swindler, assuming half a dozen roles in his efforts to sell museums to the gullible. When one of his doubles is picked up by the police and charged with his crimes, the other doubles team up to confound the cops, and the suspect ends up with the loot and the girl. Jouvet is excellent in this role of the ever-changing con man, able to suggest a new personality through an eyebrow flick or a slight resetting of his chin. Good performances in a movie brimming with Gallic wit. (French; English subtitles.)

d, Constantin Geftman; w, Henri Jeanson (based on a scenario by Jacques Companeez); ph, Jean Feyte; subtitles, Walter Klee.

Comedy **(PR:A MPAA:NR)**

CONFESSIONS OF A WINDOW CLEANER* (1974, Brit.) 90m COL c

Robin Askwith *(Timothy Lea)*, Anthony Booth *(Sidney)*, Sheila White *(Rosie)*, Dandy Nichols *(Mrs. Lea)*, Bill Maynard *(Lea)*, Linda Hayden *(Elizabeth)*, John LeMesurier *(Inspector)*, Joan Hickson *(Mrs. Radlett)*, Katya Wyeth *(Carol)*, Richard Wattis *(Carol's Father)*, Melissa Stribling *(Mrs. Villiers)*, Anita Graham *(Ingrid)*, Sam Kydd, Brian Hall *(Removal Men)*, Christine Donna *(Lil)*, Sue Longhurst *(Jacqui)*, Olivia Munday *(Brenda)*, Judy Matheson *(Elvie)*, Elaine Baillie *(Ronnie)*, Christopher Owen *(Vicar)*, Peter Dennis *(Waiter)*, Marianne Stone *(Woman in Cinema)*, Andee Cromarty *(Window Dresser)*, David Rose *(Store Manager)*, Totti Truman Taylor *(Elderly Lady)*, Frank Sieman *(Driver)*, Anika Pavel *(Dolly)*, Hugo DeVernier *(Reception Manager)*, Bruce Wightman *(Cafe Owner)*, Carole Augustine *(Sunlamp Girl)*, Lionel Murton *(Landlord)*, Peter Fontaine *(Returning Husband)*, Porjai Nicholas *(Stripper)*, Derek Lord *(Policeman)*, Robert Longdon *(Apprentice)*, Jenny Westbrook *(Girl in Street)*, Jeannie Collings, Claire Russell, Jo Peters, Monika Ringwald *(Baby Dolls)*.

First in the "Confessions" series has Askwith an apprentice window washer peeking in the windows of a French maid, a nymphomaniac, a frustrated schoolteacher, a stripper, and a lesbian. Laughs are gotten through double entendre, pseudo-slapstick, and obvious wisecracks. The girls, of course, are all gorgeous and there is full nudity and simulated sex. But good talent is wasted in a picture that basically exploits women.

p, Greg Smith; d, Val Guest; w, Christopher Wood, Guest (based on a book by Timothy Lea); ph, Norman Warwick; m, Sam Sklair; ed, Bill Lenny; prod d, Frank Revis; art d, Robert Jones.

Comedy **(PR:O MPAA:R)**

CONFESSIONS OF AMANS, THE*** (1977) 90m Bauer International c

William Bryan *(Amans)*, Michael St. John *(Absalom)*, Susannah MacMillan *(Anne)*, Richard Gardener *(Petrus)*, Leon Liberman *(Arnolfo)*, Feliciano Ituero Bravo *(Nicholas)*, Stephen Bateman *(Landlord)*, Robert Case *(Steward)*, Maria Rodriguez *(Maidservant)*, Jeanne Graham *(Nurse)*, Delfina Bayon *(Cook)*, Mari Carmen Moza *(Child)*.

Bryan is a wandering philosophy student who falls in love with the wife of a lord he is hired to tutor. A painstaking, beautiful film shot on a budget of just $20,000 in locations in Spain using costumes left over from EL CID.

p&d, Gregory Nava; w, Nava, Anna Thomas; ph&ed, Nava; cos, Cornejo.

Drama **(PR:C-O MPAA:NR)**

CONFESSIONS OF AN OPIUM EATER** (1962) 85m AA bw
(AKA: SOULS FOR SALE or SECRETS OF A SOUL)
(GB: EVILS OF CHINATOWN)

Vincent Price *(DeQuincey)*, Linda Ho *(Ruby Low)*, Richard Loo *(George Wah)*, June Kim *(Lotus)*, Philip Ahn *(Ching Foon)*, Yvonne Moray *(Child)*, Caroline Kido *(Lo Tsen)*, Terence DeMarney *(Scrawny Man)*, Gerald Jann *(Fat Chinese)*, Vivianne Manku *(Catatonic Girl)*, Miel Saan *(Look Gow)*, John Mamo *(Auctioneer)*, Victor Sen Yung *(Wing Young)*, Ralph Ahn *(Wah Chan)*, Arthur Wong *(Kwai Tong)*, Alicia Li *(Ping Toy)*, Jo Anne Miya *(1st Dancing Girl)*, Geri Hoo *(2nd Dancing Girl)*, Keiko *(3rd Dancing Girl)*, Carol Russell *(Slave Girl)*, Vincent Barbi *(Captain)*, Richard Fong.

Bizarre little drug adventure (producer/director Zugsmith seemed somewhat obsessed by this subject matter) starring Price as an early 1800s thrill seeker who becomes embroiled in San Francisco's Tong wars. He soon finds himself helping runaway slave girls escape the violence in the streets. Strange, drug-induced interlude involving a violent, slow-motion fight a real standout for 1962. Zugsmith soon graduated to "adults only" fare by producing Russ Meyer's FANNY HILL (1964).

p&d, Albert Zugsmith; w, Robert Hill, Seton I. Miller (based on the memoir by Thomas DeQuincey); ph, Joseph Biroc; m, Albert Glasser; ed, Roy Livingston, Robert S. Eisen, Edward Curtiss; prod d, Edward Morey, Jr.; art d, Eugene Lourie; set d, Joe Kish; spec eff, Milt Olsen; ch, Jon Gregory.

Drama **(PR:C MPAA:NR)**

CONFESSIONS OF BOSTON BLACKIE*** (1941) 60m COL bw

Chester Morris *(Boston Blackie)*, Harriet Hilliard *(Diane Parrish)*, Richard Lane *(Insp. John Farraday)*, George E. Stone *(The Runt)*, Lloyd Corrigan *(Arthur Manleder)*, Joan Woodbury *(Mona)*, Walter Sande *(Sgt. Mathews)*, Ralph Theadore *(Joe Buchanan)*, Walter Soderling *(Joseph Allison)*, Billy Benedict *(Ice Cream Man)*, Mike Pat Donovan *(Cop)*, Jack Clifford *(Motorcycle Cop)*, Eddie Laughton *(Express Man)*, Jack O'Malley *(Taxi Driver)*, Al Hill *(Police Desk Sgt.)*, Ralph Dunn *(Officer McCarthy)*, Harry Hollingsworth *(Plainclothesman)*, Budd Fine *(Express Man's Helper)*, Martin Spellman *(Jimmy Parrish)*, Harry Bailey, Betty Mack, Dorothy Curtis *(Bidders)*, Bill Lally *(Sgt. Dennis)*, Julius Tannen *(Dr. Crane)*, Eddie Kane *(Auctioneer)*, Herbert Clifton *(Albert the Butler)*, Jessie Arnold *(First Nurse)*, Lorna Dunn *(Second Nurse)*, Gwen Kenyon *(Third Nurse)*, Harry Depp *(Mr. Bigsby)*, Stanley Brown *(Intern)*, Eddie Fetherstone *(Taxi Driver)*.

This was the second in the Boston Blackie series and it moves at such a fast pace you don't have time to wonder where the "confessions" come in. Morris is on the trail of a valuable sculpture of Augustus Caesar stolen from Hilliard (Harriet of Ozzie and Harriet fame) who wants to sell the statue to raise funds for her tubercular brother's hospitalization. There are the usual brushes with the law, with Morris being suspected of every crime. Great fun is provided by Morris's constant sparring with bumbling Inspector Farraday. In one scene, Morris is disguised as a doctor. Lane complains to him that he has these pains in his fingers occasionally. "Soak them five times a day in boiling water and mustard. And go heavy on the mustard," Dr. Morris advises. Later when some one asks Lane what happened to his hand he mumbles, "Oh, a little mustard burn." Action-packed and well acted. This may not be art but its pace and sense of its own ridiculousness could give some of today's filmmakers a lesson. (See BOSTON BLACKIE series, Index.)

p, William Berke; d, Edward Dmytryk; w, Paul Yawitz, Jay Dratler (based on the character created by Jack Boyle); ph, Philip Tannura; ed, Gene Milford; md, M. W. Stoloff.

Mystery   **(PR:A   MPAA:NR)**

CONFESSIONS OF FELIX KRULL, THE**½

(1957, Ger.) 107m Filmaufbau/Distributors Corporation of America bw
Horst Bucholz *(Felix Krull)*, Lisa Pulver *(Zaza)*, Ingrid Andree *(Zouzou)*, Susi Nicoletti *(Mme. Houpfle)*, Paul Dahlke *(Prof. Cuckoo)*, Ilse Steppat *(Maria Pia)*, Walter Rilla *(Lord Killmarnock)*, Peer Schmidt *(Marquis de Venosta)*, Paul Henckels *(Schimmelpreester)*.

Good adaptation of Thomas Mann's last novel (in turn based on one of his early short stories) has Bucholz a young man who avoids being drafted into the German army and makes his way to Paris, where he takes a job as elevator operator in a hotel. A number of women (and at least one man) take a romantic interest in the young lad, who seems to be more interested in discussing anthropology. It gets a little dull toward the second half, but well worth checking out.

d, Kurt Hoffmann; w, Robert Thoeren, Erika Mann (based on the novel by Thomas Mann); m, Hans-Martin Majewski.

Drama   **(PR:C-O   MPAA:NR)**

CONFESSOR**½

(1973) 83m Ancris bw, c
Robert Waterhouse *(Confessor)*, Helen Dream *(Woman)*.

The Vietnam war was not over yet when this fragmented film delving into the fading of the American myth was released. But despite its theme, wry humor and hope keep it from being despairing. There is the titled confessor who seems to have a bug on lines that bring him mainly stories of woe, but also conjure up the various episodes. And there is the girl who dreams of the white knight, who does come but bears sterility. Some things have changed since this provocative film (started in 1968) was made, but not its intrinsic theme of a groping moralism in a questioning society.

p,d,ph&ed, Edward Bergman, Alan Soffin; m, Chico Hamilton.

Drama   **(PR:A   MPAA:NR)**

CONFIDENCE**½   (1980, Hung.) 105m Mafilm/Cinegate c (BIZALEM)
Ildiko Bansagi *(Kata)*, Peter Andorai *(Janos Biro)* O. Gombik, Karoly Csaki, Ildiko Kishonti, Lajos Balazsovits, Tamas Dunai, Zoltan Bezeredi, Eva Bartis, Danielle du Tombe, Gyorgyi Dorogi, Bela Eles, Gyula Gazdag, Dr. Laszlo Littmann.

During WWII, Bansagi discovers that her husband has gone underground and that she also must go into hiding. She is told to go to Andorai and the two must pretend to be man and wife. Andorai constantly tests Bansagi, seeing if she will betray him. Eventually the two become lovers, then drift apart into distrust again. Beautifully directed and shot, by the director of the superb MEPHISTO, winner of the Academy Award for Best Foreign Language Film in 1981. (Hungarian; English subtitles.)

d&w, Istvan Szabo (based on a story by Szabo and Erika Szanto); ph, Lajos Koltai (Eastmancolor); ed, Zsuzsa Csakany; art d, Jozsef Romvary.

Drama   **(PR:C-O   MPAA:NR)**

CONFIDENCE GIRL*½   (1952) 81m UA bw
Tom Conway *(Roger Kingsley)*, Hillary Brooke *(Mary Webb)*, Eddie Marr *(Johnny Gregg)*, Dan Riss *(Lt. Fenton)*, Jack Kruschen *(Sgt. Quinn)*, John Gallaudet *(Chief Brownell)*, Paul Livermore *(Hal Speel)*, Aline Towne *(Peggy Speel)*, Hellen Van Tuyl *(Maggie)*, Walter Kingsford *(Markwell)*, Charlie Colins *(Charlie)*, Bruce Edwards *(1st Detective)*, Tyler McVey *(2nd Detective)*, Paul Guilfoyle *(John Pope)*, Edmund Cobb *(Brownell's Assistant)*, Pamela Duncan *(Braddock's Nurse)*, Barbara Woodell *(Miss Seabury)*, Madge Crane *(Mrs. Markwell)*, Roy Engle *(Det. Walsh)*, Margo Karen *(Hilda)*, Yvonne Peattie *(Gertrude Palmer)*, Joel Allen *(Mr. Palmer)*, John Phillips *(Allen Ridgeway)*, Helen Chapman *(Mrs. Ridgeway)*, Leo Cleary *(Insurance Broker)*, Carmen Clothier *(Saleslady)*, Gilbert Frye *(1st Con Operator)*, Duke York *(2nd Con Operator)*, Michael Vallon *(Downs)*.

Brooke and Conway are conartists who swindle a Los Angeles department store out of a mink, cheat a pawn broker out of $8,000, and leave the police confounded. The fun ends when Brooke decides to go straight. Tedious and overlong, story tends to neglect action and suspense in favor of dialog.

p,d&w, Andrew L. Stone; ph, William Clothier; ed, Virginia Stone; m, Lucien Calliet.

Crime   **(PR:A   MPAA:NR)**

CONFIDENTIAL**   (1935) 68m Mascot/REP bw
Donald Cook *(Dave Elliot)*, Evalyn Knapp *(Maxine)*, Warren Hymer *(Midget)*, J. Carroll Naish *(Lefty)*, Herbert Rawlinson *(J. W. Keaton)*, Theodore Von Eltz *(Walsh)*, Morgan Wallace *(Van Cleve)*.

G-man detective Cook chases public enemy No. 1 Rawlinson by plane and on land, by hook or by crook, fulfilling his vow to finish the murdering bandit. Well-made film is an expose of gangsters in business garb.

d, Edward L. Cahn; w, Weilyn Totman, Olive Cooper (based on a story by John Rathmell and Scott Darling); ph, Ernest Miller, Jack Marts.

Crime   **(PR:A   MPAA:NR)**

CONFIDENTIAL AGENT**½   (1945) 113m WB/FN bw
Charles Boyer *(Denard)*, Lauren Bacall *(Rose Cullen)*, Victor Francen *(Licata)*, Wanda Hendrix *(Else)*, George Coulouris *(Capt. Currie)*, Peter Lorre *(Contreras)*, Katine Paxinou *(Mrs. Melandey)*, John Warburton *(Neil Forbes)*, Holmes Herbert *(Lord Benditch)*, Dan Seymour *(Mr. Muckerji)*, Art Foster *(Chauffeur)*, Miles Mander

(Brigstock), Lawrence Grant *(Lord Fetting)*, Ian Wolfe *(Dr. Bellows)*, George Zucco *(Detective Geddes)*.

Boyer is a once-famous concert pianist who travels secretly from Spain to England in 1937 to purchase coal for the Loyalist cause and to keep the fuel from falling into Fascist hands. He meets Bacall before arriving in London and is almost killed by Francen, Nazi spymaster. Boyer goes to a small London hotel operated by Paxinou, a dedicated Fascist who practices her sadism on a helpless hotel employee, Hendrix. She later pushes the girl out a window to her death while fellow agent Lorre looks on, smirking. Boyer is hounded and hunted by Fascist goons while trying to prevent Francen from making a deal with Fascist-leaning coal king Herbert, but he is too late. He addresses the workers with an impassioned speech, telling them that the fuel they have dug out of the earth will be used to eventually kill women and children in blockaded free Spain, but he is shouted down. Before returning in defeat to Spain, Boyer confronts Paxinou, telling her that she will answer for Hendrix's death. She takes poison before police arrive. Boyer then holds a gun on Lorre. Slowly he pulls the trigger but the automatic misfires. It's too much for Lorre who dies of a heart attack. Later, Boyer reads in a newspaper that his speech has caused the cancellation of the coal contract. Bacall, who has aided him all along, joins him in his political cause. It is assumed that they will be together. She remarks: "I can't be faithful to people I can't see, so I came along." This was Bacall's second film after her electrifying debut in TO HAVE AND HAVE NOT with Humphrey Bogart, but CONFIDENTIAL AGENT did not serve her career well. It is a plodding film under Shumlin's unimaginative direction (he had directed only one other film, WATCH ON THE RHINE). The dialog rings false in a pat story. Bacall's lines are forced and she delivers them in an unsure, near monotone. Her lack of enthusiasm may be due to the fact that she thought she might again be acting opposite Bogart in this film and wound up with Boyer. Bogart was originally announced to play the Boyer role, with Eleanor Parker in Bacall's slot. Both were scratched for Boyer and Bacall in a love team that didn't jell. There are some powerful scenes in this film nonetheless—Paxinou's harassment of Hendrix, and Boyer's magnificent address to the miners. Bacall had actually completed THE BIG SLEEP before CONFIDENTIAL AGENT but the latter was released first in a hurry-up attempt to cash in on her popularity. She was unhappy about Jack Warner rushing her into this contrived film and later remarked in *Lauren Bacall, By Myself*: . . . to cast me as an aristocratic English girl was more than a stretch. It was dementia." Boyer carries the film with wonderful sensitivity, but even this marvelous actor is finally drowned in the murk and gloom of a muddled story, swarmed over by an army of grotesque creatures who steal the film away into an unsatisfying conclusion.

p&w, Robert Buckner; d, Herman Shumlin; (based on the novel by Graham Greene); ph, James Wong Howe; m, Franz Waxman; ed, George Amy; art d, Leo Kuter.

Spy Drama   **(PR:C   MPAA:NR)**

CONFIDENTIAL LADY**   (1939, Brit.) 75m WB/FN bw
Ben Lyon *(Jim Brent)*, Jane Baxter *(Jill Trevor)*, Athole Stewart *(Sir Joshua Morple)*, Ronald Ward *(John Carter)*, Jean Cadell *(Amy Boswell)*, Frederick Burtwell *(Phillips)*, Gibb McLaughlin *(Sheriff)*, Vera Bogetti *(Rose)*, Gordon McLeod *(Somers)*, Stewart Rome *(Alfred Trevor)*.

Angry reporter helps jilted girl in her fight to ruin the press lord who destroyed her father. Film was typical of escapist fare turned out in England before WW II broke out.

p, Sam Sax; d, Arthur Woods; w, Brock Williams, Derek Twist; ph, Basil Emmett..

Romance   **(PR:A   MPAA:NR)**

CONFIDENTIAL REPORT   (SEE: MR. ARKADIN, 1955)

CONFIDENTIALLY CONNIE**½   (1953) 71m MGM bw
Van Johnson *(Joe Bedloe)*, Janet Leigh *(Connie Bedloe)*, Louis Calhern *(Opie Bedloe)*, Walter Slezak *(Emil Spangenberg)*, Gene Lockhart *(Dean Magruder)*, Hayden Rorke *(Simmons)*, Robert Burton *(Dr. Willis Shoop)*, Marilyn Erskine *(Phyllis Archibald)*, Katheleen Lockhart *(Mrs. Magruder)*, Arthur Space *(Archibald)*, Barbara Ruick *(Barbara)*, June Whitley *(Betty Simmons)*, Dick Sands *(Moska)*, Phil Tead, Byron Foulger *(Professors)*.

Writer Max Shulman's influence is evident in this zany comedy about a newly married couple too poor to afford meat. Johnson is a professor at a small Maine college who has had a falling out with his father, Calhern, a big Texas rancher, over his choice of profession and wants no help from home. When dad comes to visit and learns he is to be a grandfather he takes the bull by the horns and cuts a deal with the local butcher to give the kids their beef at half price. When word leaks out, it starts a meat price war and Calhern has to cover the losses. Calhern is wonderful as the flamboyant, scheming cattle baron who ends up providing yearly pay raises for all the college profs because he feels sorry for them and their families. Not for health food faddists.

p, Stephen Ames; d, Edward Buzzell; w, Max Shulman (based on a story by Shulman and Herman Wouk); ph, Harold Lipstein; m, David Rose; ed, Fredrick Y. Smith.

Comedy   **(PR:A   MPAA:NR)**

CONFIDENTIALLY YOURS***
(1983, Fr.) 111m Les Films du Carosse-Films A2-Soprofilms/Artificial Eye bw
(VIVEMENT DIMANCHE! AKA: FINALLY, SUNDAY)
Fanny Ardant, Jean-Louis Trintignant, Philippe Laudenbach, Caroline Sihol, Philippe Morier-Genoud, Xavier Saint-Macary, Jean-Pierre Kalfon, Anik Belaubre, Jean-Louis Richard, Yann Dedet, Nicole Felix, Georges Koulouris, Roland Thenot, Pierre Gare, Jean-Pierre Kohut-Svelko, Pascale Pellegrin, Castel Casti, Michel Aubossu, Paulina Aubret, Isabelle Binet, Dany Castaing, Alain Gambin, Michel Grisoni, Marie-Noelle Guilliot, Pierrette Monticelli, Adrien Silvio.

Trintignant is a businessman in hiding from the police because of a murder charge, while secretary Ardant plays detective to look for the real killer. Francois Truffaut's last film before a brain tumor took his life is certainly not the film his historical reputation will rest on, but it is a pleasant comic thriller in the Hitchcockian style. Truffaut keeps it all very light, letting Ardant's amateur sleuthing turn up a number of funny scenes and an ominous conspiracy underneath. The performances are nice, particularly Ardant's, the last love of the director's life. Toward the end of Truffaut's career, he was no longer interested in redefining the nature of narrative film, as he had in JULES AND JIM or THE 400 BLOWS, but rather in making well-crafted, intelligent entertainments like DAY FOR NIGHT and THE LAST METRO. CONFIDENTIALLY YOURS, an adaptation of a pulp novel from 1962, is Truffaut's chance to show all he has learned, and the film is filled with quotations from other films. Shot in stunning black and white, the film ends in the most classical of ways—Ardant and Trintignant are married and presumably live happily ever after. Truffaut died a little more than a year later.

p, Armand Barbault; d, Francois Truffaut; w, Truffaut, Suzanne Schiffman, Jean Aurel (based on the novel *The Long Saturday Night* by Charles Williams); ph, Nestor Almendros; m, Georges Delerue; ed, Martine Barraque; prod d. Hilton McConnico.

Drama **(PR:A-C MPAA:NR)**

CONFIRM OR DENY** (1941) 73m FOX bw

Don Ameche *(Mitch)*, Joan Bennett *(Jennifer Carson)*, Roddy McDowall *(Albert Perkins)*, John Loder *(Capt. Channing)*, Raymond Walburn *(H. Cyrus Sturtevant)*, Arthur Shields *(Jeff)*, Eric Blore *(Mr. Hobbs)*, Helene Reynolds *(Dorothy)*, Claude Allister *(Williams)*, Roseanne Murray *(M. I. Girl)*, Stuart Robertson *(Johnny Dunne)*, Queenie Leonard *(Daisy)*, Jean Prescott *(Elizabeth Harding)*, Billy Bevan *(Mr. Bindle)*, Alan Napier *(Updyke)*, Lumsden Hare *(Sir Titus Scott)*, Dennis Hoey *(Duffield)*, Leonard Carey *(Floorman)*.

Weak story involving Ameche as a foreign correspondent who will do anything to get his story, and Bennett as the teletype operator in the Ministry of Information in London who wishes Ameche were more prudent but falls for him anyway while he dodges bombs during the London blitz. There are realistic scenes of ruins caused by bombings, but ten minutes of this picture could have been trimmed without losing anything of importance.

p, Len Hammond; d, Archie Mayo; w, Jo Swerling (based on the story by Henry Wales and Samuel Fuller); ph, Leon Shamroy; ed, Robert Bischoff.

War Drama **(PR:A MPAA:NR)**

CONFLAGRATION (SEE: ENJO, 1958, Jap.)

CONFLICT*½ (1937) 60m UNIV bw

John Wayne *(Pat)*, Jean Rogers *(Maude)*, Tommy Bupp *(Tommy)*, Eddie Borden *(Spider)*, Frank Sheridan *(Sam)*, Ward Bond *(Carrigan)*, Margaret Mann *(Ma Blake)*, Harry Wood *(Kelly)*, Bryant Washburn *(City Editor)*, Frank Hagney *(Malone)*.

John Wayne plays a crooked fighter who slugs it out with Ward Bond in some pretty convincing scenes before he sees the light and trades it all in for the love of a beautiful blonde and an orphan. Wayne's performance is best when he's slugging.

p, Trem Carr; d, David Howard; w, Charles A. Logue, Walter Weems (based on the story "The Abysmal Brute" by Jack London); ph, A. J. Stout; ed, Jack Ogilvie.

Drama **(PR:A MPAA:NR)**

CONFLICT½** (1939, Fr.) 94m Cipra-Arnold Pressburger/DIF bw

Corinne Luchaire, Annie Ducaux, Raymond Rouleau, Roger Duchesne, Claude Dauphin, Armand Bernard, Jacques Copeau, Marcel Dallo, Pauline Carton, Leon Beileres, Marguerite Pierry, Arvel, Philippe Richard, Lamontier, Madeline Suffel.

Moguy has taken great pains in this film to show us why people behave as they do. Story concerns two sisters, one married and desperately wanting a child although barren, the other single and pregnant, abandoned by the father of her child. In this case the married sister convinces her sibling to let her raise the child as her own in an effort to save her marriage and keep her husband from leaving her. The younger sister then falls in love and is faced with the dilemma of how to tell her soon-to-be husband when the natural father shows up and threatens to reveal all unless he is paid off. The suspense is maintained well throughout in this sensitive and disturbing movie.

d, Leonide Moguy; w, Hans Wilhelm, Ch. Gombault (based on a story by Gina Kaus); ph, Ted Pahle.

Drama **(PR:O MPAA:NR)**

CONFLICT*½** (1945) 86m WB/FN bw

Humphrey Bogart *(Richard Mason)*, Alexis Smith *(Evelyn Turner)*, Sydney Greenstreet *(Dr. Mark Hamilton)*, Rose Hobart *(Katherine Mason)*, Charles Drake *(Prof. Norman Holdsworth)*, Grant Mitchell *(Dr. Grant)*, Patrick O'Moore *(Detective Lt. Egan)*, Ann Shoemaker *(Nora Grant)*, Frank Wilcox *(Robert Freston)*, James Flavin *(Detective Lt. Workman)*, Edwin Stanley *(Phillips)*, Mary Servoss *(Mrs. Allman)*, Doria Caron *(Nurse)*, Ray Hanson, Billy Wayne *(Cab Drivers)*, Ralph Dunn *(Highway Patrolman)*, John Harmon *(Hobo)*, Bruce Bilson *(Bellboy)*, Marjorie Hoshelle *(Telephone Operator)*, Frances Morris *(Receptionist)*, George Carleton *(Harris)*, Oliver Prickett, Harlan Briggs *(Pawnbrokers)*, Wallis Clark *(Prof. Berens)*, Jack Mower *(Desk Clerk)*, Emmett Vogan *(Luggage Salesman)*.

This solid psychological thriller is heightened by Bogart's subtle portrayal of a calculating wife-killer. A successful architect, Bogie falls in love with Smith, sister of wife Hobart. He asks his wife for a divorce but she refuses. Then he crashes his car and is invalided with a leg injury that prevents him from walking. He heals sooner than the doctors expect and uses this to cover his murderous plans. His wife goes off to a mountain retreat, leaving Bogie at home alone to work. He follows her, meeets her car on a mountain road, then strangles her and puts her into her car, which he pushes over a cliff. It roars downward into freshly cut timber and the logs cover her car in a strange configuration, similar to that of a giant tepee. Scurrying home, Bogie awaits the news of his wife's death but it does not come. He reports his wife missing and then weird incidents take place. Although he pursues Smith, she rebuffs him for younger man Drake. Everywhere Bogie turns he meets Hobart's ghost. He smells her perfume, finds her handkerchiefs, and other small effects. He traces a brooch to a pawn shop where he checks a ledger which ostensibly shows his wife's signature; when he returns with a policeman, the clerk is gone, another is in his place, and the ledger shows no trace of the signature. Bogie begins to follow women dressed in his wife's clothes, women he sees only from behind. He begins to doubt his sanity and returns to the scene of the crime, climbing down the cliff to examine Hobart's car beneath the timber. It is there but her body is gone. Then flashlights flick on and he is bathed in light. Behind the lights are police and Greenstreet, psychologist and family friend who had suspected Bogart all along. Bogie had given himself away to Greenstreet after his wife's disappearance. The pyschologist asked Bogart to describe what his wife was wearing when she disappeared and he had mentioned that she was wearing a rose. He could not have known about the flower since it had been given to Hobart by Greenstreet after she had left her husband on her way to the mountain retreat. Of course she was wearing the rose when he murdered her. Bogart is led away by police, undone by his own clever machinations. The direction by Bernhardt is first-rate and the suspense is maintained throughout in a vehicle tailor-made for the magical Bogart.

p, William Jacobs; d, Curtis Bernhardt; w, Arthur T. Horman, Dwight Taylor (based on story by Robert Siodmak and Alfred Neumann); ph, Merritt Gerstad; m, Frederick Hollander; ed, David Weisbart; md, Leo F. Forbstein; art d, Ted Smith; set d, Clarence I. Steensen; cos, Milo Anderson; makeup, Perc Westmore; song: "Tango of Love."

Mystery **(PR:A MPAA:NR)**

CONFLICT OVER WINGS (SEE: FUSS OVER FEATHERS, 1954, Brit.)

CONFORMIST, THE*** (1971, Ital., Fr.) 110m Mars-Marianne/PAR c (IL CONFORMIST)

Jean-Louise Trintignant *(Marcello)*, Stefania Sandrelli *(Giulia)*, Dominique Sanda *(Anna Quadri)*, Pierre Clementi *(Nino Seminara)*, Gastone Moschin *(Manganiello)*, Enzo Tarascio *(Prof. Quadri)*, Jose Quaglio *(Italo)*, Milly *(Marcello's Mother)*, Giuseppe Addobbati *(Marcello's Father)*, Yvonne Sanson *(Giulia's Mother)*, Fosco Giachetti *(Colonel)*, Benedetto Benedetti *(Minister)*, Gio Vagni Luca *(Secretary)*, Christian Alegny *(Raoul)*, Antonio Maestri *(Priest)*, Christian Belegue *(Gypsy)*, Pasquale Fortunato *(Marcello as a Child)*, Marta Lado *(Marcello's Daughter)*, Pierangelo Givera *(Male Nurse)*, Carlo Gaddi, Franco Pellerani, Claudio Cappelli, Umberto Silvestri *(Hired Killers)*.

This is the story of a coward, Trintignant, who compromises on everything just to get along, including his marriage to Sandrelli. He is sent to Paris by a Fascist espionage organization he has joined and ordered to murder a leftist political refugee he studied under in college. His mind riddled with doubts and fears, he botches the job which is then violently carried out by hard-core Fascist henchmen as he once again watches, totally uncommitted. Glimmering and refined performances shine down to the smallest role. A satisfying and powerful film.

p, Maurizio Lodi-Fe; d&w, Bernardo Bertolucci (based on the novel by Alberto Moravia); ph, Vittorio Storaro (Technicolor); m, Georges Delerue; art d, Nedo Azzini; cos, Gitt Magrini.

Drama **Cas.** **(PR:C MPAA:R)**

CONGO CROSSING** (1956) 85m UNIV c

Virginia Mayo *(Louise Whitman)*, George Nader *(David Carr)*, Peter Lorre *(Col. Arragas)*, Michael Pate *(Bart O'Connell)*, Rex Ingram *(Dr. Gorman)*, Tonio Selwart *(Carl Rittner)*, Kathryn Givney *(Amelia Abbott)*, Raymond Bailey *(Peter Mannering)*, George Ramsey *(Miguel Diniz)*, Tudor Owen *(Emile Zorfus)*, Bernard Hamilton *(Pompala)*, Harold Dyrenforth *(Steiner)*, Maurice Doner *(Marquette)*.

Playgirl Mayo, suspected of murder, hies to Congotanga, a piece of West Africa where fugitives gather because of a lack of extradition laws. There she meets Nader who is surveying the land for the Belgian Congo government to prove it falls within that country's boundaries. Lorre is the law official who keeps all the crooks in line. Much of the plot hinges on the outcome of the survey, especially for Lorre who stands to lose his job if the Belgians gain jurisdiction, and Selwart, the local drug runner and town honcho. There is an ambush at the airstrip as Mayo and Nader try to leave town but Lorre comes to their rescue at the last minute, wryly explaining as only Lorre could do, "It just occurred to me—the Belgians, they need a chief of police, too!" Other than Lorre, the picture has little to recommend it, the plot drawing from CASBAH and CASABLANCA.

p, Howard Christie; d, Joseph Pevney; w, Richard Alan Simmons (based on a story by Houston Branch); ph, Russell Metty (Technicolor); m, Joseph Gershenson; ed, Sherman Todd; art d, Alexander Golitzen, Robert Boyle.

Crime Drama **(PR:A MPAA:NR)**

CONGO MAISIE*½ (1940) 70m MGM bw

Ann Sothern *(Maisie Ravier)*, John Carroll *(Dr. Michael Shane)*, Rita Johnson *(Kay McWade)*, Shepperd Strudwick *(Dr. John McWade)*, J. M. Kerrigan *(Capt. Finch)*, E. E. Clive *(Horace Snell)*, Everett Brown *(Jallah)*, Tom Fadden *(Nelson)*, Lionel Pape *(British Consul)*, Nathan Curry *(Luemba)*, Leonard Mudie *(Farley)*, Martin Wilkins *(Zia)*, Ernest Whitman *(Varnai)*.

This was the second of the MAISIE series with Ann Sothern as the glib-talking, fast-thinking showgirl. This time she finds herself in the interior of West Africa after stowing away on a steamer to escape paying her hotel bill. Settling at last in a rubber plantation hospital, the spitfire with a heart of gold prevents Carroll from breaking up a doctor's marriage and saves everybody from an attack by the natives. The picture has sagging sequences depending entirely on the antics of Sothern to lift it above the swampy script which leans heavily on TORRID ZONE.

p, J. Walter Ruben; d, Henry Potter; w, Mary C. McCall, Jr. (based on the book *Congo*

Landing by Wilson Collison); ph, Charles Lawton; m, Edward Ward; ed, Frederick Y. Smith; art d, Cedric Gibbons.

Comedy **(PR:A MPAA:NR)**

CONGO SWING (SEE: BLONDIE GOES LATIN, 1941)

CONGRESS DANCES½** (1932, Ger.) 92m UFA/UA bw (DER KONGRESS TANZT)

Lillian Harvey *(Christel Weinzinger)*, Conrad Veidt *(Prince Metternich)*, Lil Dagover *(The Countess)*, Henri Graat *(Czar Alexander of Russia/Uralsky)*, Gibb McLaughlin *(Bibikoff, the Czar's Adjutant)*, Reginald Purdell *(Pepi, his Secretary)*, Eugen Rex *(Ambassador of Saxony)*, Jean Dax *(Ambassador of France)*, Helen Haye *(The Princess)*, Olga Engel *(The Duchess)*, Spencer Trevor *(The Finance Minister)*, Thomas Weguelin *(The Mayor of Vienna)*, Tarquini d'Or *(The Cafe Singer)*.

During the 1814 Congress of Vienna, Veidt conspires to keep Czar Graat away from the negotiating table by putting a number of pretty women in his way. What he doesn't know is that the czar has a double, and thus can be two places at once. There are a lot of people falling in love, sneaking about at night, and secret identities, all to wonderful effect. One of the best of the early European musicals that came with sound, though today it seems dated. A German language version was also released. Remade in 1957.

p, Erich Pommer; d, Eric Charell; w, Norman Falk, Robert Liebmann; ph, Carl Hoffmann; m, Werner Heymann.

Musical **(PR:A MPAA:NR)**

CONGRESS DANCES** (1957, Ger.) 79m Cosmos-Neusser/REP c

Johanna Matz *(Christl Weinzinger)*, Rudolf Prack *(Alexander I/Uralsky)*, Hannelore Bollmann *(Babette)*, Marte Harell *(Countess Ballansky)*, Jester Naefe *(Lydia)*, Hans Moser *(Schoberl)*, Josef Meinrad *(Franzl Eder)*, Gunther Philipp *(Pepi Gallinger)*, Karl Schonbock *(Count Metternich)*, Oscar Sima *(Bibikoff)*, Paul Westermeier *(Franz)*.

Lackluster remake of the 1932 musical. Prack plays the double role of the Czar and his unhappy double, romancing and negotiating in 1814 Vienna.

w, Kurt Nachmann (CinemaScope, Trucolor); m, Werner Richard Heymann; cos, Gerdago; ch, Willy Schulte Vogelheim.

Musical **(PR:A MPAA:NR)**

CONJUGAL BED, THE½** (1963, Ital.) 90m Sancro Film-Fair Film-Les Films Marceau/EM bw (UNA STORIA MODERNA [L'APE REGINA])

Ugo Tognazzi *(Alfonso)*, Marina Vlady *(Regina)*, Walter Giller *(Father Mariano)*, Linda Sini *(Mother Superior)*, Riccardo Fellini *(Riccardo)*, Achille Maieroni *(Aunt Mafalda)*, Pietro Tattanelli *(Uncle Don Giuseppe)*, Jusupoff Ragazzi *(Aunt Jolanda)*, Igi Polidoro *(Igi)*, Melissa Drake *(Maria Costanza)*, Sandrino Pinelli *(Maria Costanza's Fiance)*, Mario Giussani *(Count Ribulsi)*, Polidor *(Brother Lorenzo)*, Jacqueline Perrier, Nino Vingelli.

Tognazzi is a middle-aged car dealer who marries a young, beautiful girl (Vlady) and finds himself unable to keep up with her sexual demands on him. She wants to become pregnant as quickly as possible and Tognazzi endures a series of hormone shots to help him out. Finally he goes to the seashore for a rest, but she comes after him. They make love violently and he suffers a heart attack. In the hospital he learns that she has finally become pregnant. Now she wants nothing to do with him and he is placed in a maid's room where he enjoys his solitude before dying. Very funny sex comedy, well worth seeing. The Italian subtitle translates as "The Queen Bee." (Italian; English subtitles.)

p, Henryk Chroscicki, Alfonso Sansone; d, Marco Ferreri; w, Ferreri, Geoffredo Parise, Massimo Franciosa, Diego Fabbri, Rafael Azcona, Pasquale Festa Campanile (based on a story by Parise); ph, Ennio Guarnieri; m, Teo Usuelli; ed, Lionello Massobrio; art d, Massimiliano Capriccioli; set d, Rosa Sansone; cos, Luciana Marinucci.

Comedy **(PR:O MPAA:NR)**

CONNECTICUT YANKEE, A**** (1931) 95m FOX bw

Will Rogers *(Hank)*, William Farnum *(King Arthur)*, Myrna Loy *(Queen Morgan Le Fay)*, Maureen O'Sullivan *(Alisande)*, Crank Albertson *(Clarence)*, Mitchell Harris *(Merlin)*, Brandon Hurst *(Sagramor)*.

This was the second of three versions of Mark Twain's classic. Harry Myers starred in the first 1920 version after Doug Fairbanks turned it down. Bing Crosby did the musical version, A CONNECTICUT YANKEE IN KING ARTHUR'S COURT, and it was a pleasant, colorful romp. This picture combined Rogers' charm with an excellent adaptation of the book. Rogers runs a small-town radio shop and is requested to visit a mysterious old house to install a battery. The nut who owns the house thinks he can contact King Arthur if he has a powerful enough radio. Rogers is felled by an accidental blow on the head and dreams his way back to days when knights were bold. The locals think he's a warlock and he manages to save his skin by predicting a solar eclipse. Since the picture was made at the depths of the Depression, Rogers does a lot of timely jokes which may be lost on today's audiences, but the visual gags (Rogers lassoes a Knight of the Round Table in the midst of one of their jousts) stay just as funny as ever. Loy supplies the distaff villainess and O'Sullivan is the femme love interest. Some very funny bits and a frantic conclusion with Rogers saved from the noose by an armada of twentieth-century inventions: planes, tanks, cars, and even an autogyro, to save his life. A lot of money was spent on this production and it's all up there on screen for everyone to see. Fun for everyone.

d, David Butler; w, William Conselman, Owen Davis (based on the novel by Mark Twain); ph, Ernest Palmer; ed, Irene Morra.

Comedy **(PR:AAA MPAA:NR)**

CONNECTICUT YANKEE IN KING ARTHUR'S COURT, A**** (1949) 106m PAR c (GB: YANKEE IN KING ARTHUR'S COURT, A)

Bing Crosby *(Hank Martin)*, William Bendix *(Sir Sagramore)*, Sir Cedric Hardwicke *(King Arthur)*, Rhonda Fleming *(Alisande La Carteloise)*, Murvyn Vye *(Merlin)*, Virginia Field *(Morgan Le Fay)*, Henry Wilcoxon *(Sir Lancelot)*, Richard Webb *(Sir Galahad)*, Joseph Vitale *(Sir Logris)*, Alan Napier *(High Executioner)*, Julia Faye *(Lady Penelope)*, Mary Field *(Peasant Woman)*, Ann Carter *(Peasant Girl)*.

Twain's grand fantasy is pleasing from every angle in this lavishly mounted production, rich in color and songs. Crosby, at the height of his immense popularity, is the Connecticut blacksmith knocked unconscious in a wild rainstorm and sent into another world, waking up in King Arthur's Camelot. In his modern garb he is instantly mistaken for a dragon by dim-witted but affable Bendix, playing Sagramore, one of Arthur's knights. Bendix befriends Crosby and takes him to the court of Arthur (Hardwicke). He is still regarded as a weird monster and many clamor for his death, including the ever-suspicious Vye, playing the role of Merlin the Magician. Crosby amazes the folks of Camelot with simple modern-day devices which they perceive as magical powers—a compass, a photographic lens, and kitchen matches which he lights in a way where the fire appears to leap from his fingertips. He is rewarded for his wizardy by Hardwicke who allows him to become a blacksmith in the kingdom. Crosby is attracted to Fleming, Hardwicke's ravishing niece, but she is betrothed to Lancelot (Wilcoxen); he nevertheless visits her secretly. She too is taken with Crosby but fears Wilcoxen's wrath. When the two are discovered together, Wilcoxen demands a jousting match to the death. Crosby fights him cowboy style, using his lariat to entangle him and render him helpless. After the joust, Hardwicke seeks Crosby's counsel and is convinced that he must move among his overtaxed subjects to discover how really unhappy they are. Incognito, Hardwicke sets out with Crosby and Bendix, disguised as beggars of the road. In his absence, Vye and cronies try to take over the kingdom, taking Fleming hostage and holding her prisoner. Crosby, Hardwicke, and Bendix are waylaid and sentenced to death as thieves. No matter how much Hardwicke insists that he is King Arthur, he is jeered. Before all three are burned at the stake, Crosby produces his trusty *Farmer's Almanac* which tells him that a total eclipse of the sun took place at this very hour in Arthur's time. He pretends to blot out the sun to prove he is the renowned "Sir Boss," the great wizard. The sun goes black and Crosby and friends go free, returning to rescue Fleming and depose Vye. Crosby, however, is struck unconscious and returns to modern times. He visits England, going to a castle owned by one of Arthur's descendants, also played by Hardwicke, telling him about his trip through time. As he is leaving he meets Hardwicke's grandniece, Fleming, who is the spitting image of the girl he loved centuries ago. This film is a pure delight, certainly the most enjoyable of the many versions of the Twain story brought to the screen. (Fox made the first movie in 1920 with Harry C. Meyers in the silent role; the same studio remade the tale in 1931 starring Will Rogers in an exceptional production listed by the New York *Times* as one of the Ten Best Films of that year.) The quality of the Crosby version far outstrips its predecessors, with wonderful sets, softly-focused color lensing by Rennahan, and memorable music. Famed art director Dreier created a spectacular and authentic medieval castle for the Crosby film with an enormous dining hall for Hardwicke's round table knights, a huge ballroom, verdant gardens, courtyards, and jousting grounds. Rhonda Fleming's titian-haired beauty is stunning in the rich Technicolor process and Garnett's direction is smooth and well-paced. Most pleasing are the Van Heusen and Burke tunes: "Once And For Always" (sung by Crosby and Fleming), "If You Stub Your Toe On The Moon" (Crosby), "When Is Sometime?" (Fleming), Twixt Myself And Me" (Hardwicke), and the memorable "Busy Doing Nothing" (Crosby, Bendix and Hardwicke). The film was a tremendous hit and Paramount was so pleased with Garnett that they offered the director a nonexclusive contract to direct a film each year for three years at $100,000 a film. But Garnett was fiercely independent and he found even this dream deal too constricting. He packed his bags and went off to Paris, a decision he would later regret. (Remade in 1979 as UNIDENTIFIED FLYING ODDBALL.)

p, Robert Fellows; d, Tay Garnett; w, Edmund Beloin (based on the novel by Mark Twain); ph, Ray Rennahan (Technicolor); m, Victor Young; ed, Archie Marshek; art d, Hans Dreier, Roland Anderson; set d, Sam Comer, Bertrand Granger; cos, Edith Head; makeup, Wally Westmore; m/l, James Van Heusen, Johnny Burke; spec eff, Farciot Edouart.

Fantasy/Musical **(PR:AAA MPAA:NR)**

CONNECTING ROOMS** (1971, Brit.) 102m Telstar-Three Capitols-DeGrunwald/London Screen c

Bette Davis *(Wanda Fleming)*, Michael Redgrave *(James Wallraven)*, Alexis Kanner *(Mickey Hollister)*, Kay Walsh *(Mrs. Brent)*, Gabrielle Drake *(Jean)*, Olga Georges-Picot *(Claudia Fouchet)*, Leo Genn *(Dr. Norman)*, Richard Wyler *(Dick Grayson)*, Brian Wilde *(Ellerman)*, John Woodnutt *(Doctor)*, Tony Hughes *(Lew)*, Mark Jones *(Johnny)*, James Maxwell *(Principal of Art College)*, Eyes of Blue & The Lady-birds *(Themselves)*.

Dull, sappy melodrama that takes place in a boarding house. Davis plays a street musician, and Redgrave is a recently fired schoolmaster who is in love with a young cellist. Unfortunately, the cellist is involved with rebellious pop-song writer Kanner who becomes the bane of Redgrave's existence.

p, Harry Field, Jack Smith, Arthur S. Cooper; d&w, Franklin Gollings (based on the play "The Cellist" by Marion Hart); ph, John Wilcox (Technicolor); m, Joan Shakespeare; ed, Jack Slade; md, Shakespeare; art d, Herbert Smith, Morley Smith; set d, Jill Oxley; m/l, Shakespeare, Derek Warne.

Romance **(PR:A MPAA:NR)**

CONNECTION, THE½** (1962) 110m Allen-Clarke bw

William Redfield *(Jim Dunn)*, Warren Finnerty *(Leach)*, Garry Goodrow *(Ernie)*, Jerome Raphel *(Solly)*, James Anderson *(Sam)*, Carl Lee *(Cowboy)*, Barbara Winchester *(Sister Salvation)*, Roscoe Lee Browne *(J. J. Burden)*, Henry Poach

(Harry), Freddie Redd *(Piano)*, Jackie McLean *(Alto Sax)*, Michael Mattos *(Bass)*, Larry Ritchie *(Drums)*.

Eight drug addicts gather in a Manhattan loft to wait for their connection. To pay for their drugs, they have agreed to allow Dunn, a would-be documentary filmmaker, to photograph them. Film within a film records their conversation, reflections, and an impromptu jam session among four of the junkies who are musicians. The "connection" arrives with a soldier from the Salvation Army who suspects the addicts are drinking and beats a hasty retreat. Dunn is then persuaded to try some heroin so he will have a deeper understanding of the subject of his film and he becomes violently ill. This film was considered a tour-de-force for director Clarke who heretofore had specialized in prize-winning shorts. It is a jolting look at the drug crowd. The characters get laughs with their crisp lingo and wry wit, showing them to be acceptable types one can empathize with. There are no phony dramatics here.

p, Lewis Allen, Shirley Clarke; d, Clarke; w, Jack Gelber (based on his play); ph, Arthur J. Ornitz; m, Freddie Redd; ed, Clarke; prod d, Richard Sylbert; art d, Albert Brenner; set d, Gene Callahan; cos, Ruth Morley.

Drama   **(PR:O   MPAA:NR)**

CONQUERED CITY**½   (1966, Ital.) 91m Maxima Film-Lux-Galatea/AIP bw
(LA CITTA PRIGIONIERA) (AKA: THE CAPTIVE CITY)
David Niven *(Maj. Peter Whitfield)*, Lea Massari *(Lelia)*, Ben Gazzara *(Capt. George Stubbs)*, Daniela Rocca *(Doushka)*, Martin Balsam *(Feinberg)*, Michael Craig *(Capt. Elliot)*, Clelia Matania *(Miss Climedes)*, Giulio Bosetti *(Narriman)*, Percy Herbert *(Sgt. Reed)*, Ivo Garrani *(Mabroti)*, Odoardo Spadaro *(Mendoris)*, Roberto Risso *(Cpl. Loveday)*, Venantino Venantini *(Gen. Ferolou)*, Carlo Hintermann *(Sergeant)*, Adelmo Di Fraia *(Andrea)*, Massimo Righi *(Pollit)*, Francesco Tensi *(Gen. Bennet)*, Renato Moretti *(The "Saint")*, Lamberto Antinori.

While the Germans pull out of Athens in the closing days of WW II, various factions fight for control of the city. Niven is a British officer who finds himself commanding the defense of a hotel where arms desperately needed by the rebel forces are stored. With the help of American officer Gazzara they withstand a number of attacks, but Gazzara is captured and tortured and Niven discovers that there is a spy in the hotel. He figures out that Craig is the traitor and they shoot it out. Niven wins and while evacuating the hotel under a flag of truce, he blows up the arms hidden there. An interesting war programmer, above average for this sort of thing.

d, Joseph Anthony; w, Guy Elmes, Eric Bercovici, Marc Brandel (based on the novel *The Captive City* by John Appleby); ph, Leonida Barboni; m, Piero Piccioni; ed, Marion Bonitti, Raymond Poulton, Michael Billingsley; art d, Mario Chiari.

War Drama   **(PR:C   MPAA:NR)**

CONQUERING HORDE, THE**½   (1931) 73m PAR bw
Richard Arlen *(Dan McMasters)*, Fay Wray *(Taisie Lockhart)*, Claude Gillingwater *(Jim Nabore)*, Ian MacLaren *(Marvin Fletcher)*, Frank Rice *(Spud Grogan)*, Arthur Stone *(Lumpy Lorrigan)*, George Mendoza *(Cinco Centavos)*, James Durkin *(Mr. Corley)*, Charles Stevens *(John)*, Edwin J. Brady *(Splint Goggin)*, Robert Kortman *(Digger Hale)*, Harry Cording *(Butch Daggett)*, Chief Standing Bear *(White Cloud)*, John Elliott *(Capt. Wilkins)*, Kathrin Clare Ward *(Mrs. Corley)*.

Texan turned Yank, Arlen becomes the President's diplomat when the state resists efforts to let railroads cut into the land after the Civil War. This leads to bad times as the ranchers are unable to get their cattle to the nearest market in Abilene, Kansas. Lots of comedy throughout, including Gillingwater, who hates hero Arlen and can't understand women.

d, Edward Sloman; w, Grover Jones, William Slavens McNutt (based on a story by Emerson Hough); ph, A. J. Stout; ed, Otho Lovering.

Western   **(PR:A   MPAA:NR)**

CONQUEROR, THE*½   (1956) 111m Hughes/RKO c
John Wayne *(Temujin)*, Susan Hayward *(Bortai)*, Pedro Armendariz *(Jamuga)*, Agnes Moorehead *(Hunlun)*, Thomas Gomez *(Wang Kahn)*, John Hoyt *(Shaman)*, William Conrad *(Kasar)*, Ted DeCorsia *(Kumlek)*, Leslie Bradley *(Targutai)*, Lee Van Cleef *(Chepei)*, Peter Mamakos *(Bogurchi)*, Leo Gordon *(Tartar Captain)*, Richard Loo *(Captain of Wang's Guard)*, Billy Curtis *(Midget Tumbler)*.

For a turkey, more has been written about this movie than any other. That was due to several reasons, not the least of which was the terrible toll taken on the cast and crew because they shot the film in Utah, only 136 miles from a huge atomic test site. There were 220 people who worked on the film and more than 90 contracted cancer, with half of those dead from the disease. The deaths included director Powell, stars Wayne, Hayward, Armendariz, and Moorehead. Howard Hughes had 60 tons of Utah earth shipped back to a Hollywood sound stage for retakes and that probably caused a few deaths as well. Many people have died making movies—Ty Power among them—but never before has such a swath been cut through the community. And, worst of all, it was a dreadful picture, miscast from the start with Wayne as Kahn and redheaded Hayward as an Asian beauty. Hughes had a feeling this would be his last film and he wanted to go out in style. Well, he did—bad style. Screenwriter Millard admitted he had trouble spelling the name of Khan and had to spend days in the library finding out about the Mongol. It didn't matter. The story was as follows: Wayne and Armendariz are Mongols who love nothing better than raping and pillaging. They attack a caravan and capture Hayward, daughter of DeCorsia, the Tartar ruler. Moorehead, Wayne's mother, and Armendariz try to talk the headstrong Wayne out of keeping Hayward but he likes the lass and says things like "For good or ill, she is my destiny." And when Hayward tells him off in no uncertain terms, glib Wayne retorts "You're beautiful in your wrath!" Troops sent by Hayward's father storm Wayne's enclave to rescue her. They are beaten back but she escapes. Wayne goes after her and captures the perky Tartar. Now Wayne enlists the aid of Gomez, leader of the Chinese. Together they will wipe out the Tartars. Hoyt is Gomez's aide and helps Wayne convince the wily

Gomez. Just before the onslaught is to take place, Wayne is wounded and Hayward is rescued. Armendariz inadvertently leads the Tartars to Wayne's hiding place and the Duke is captured and sentenced to death by DeCorsia. By this time Hayward loves Wayne and she has him released but she knows that this is far from over and both men have nothing but hatred for each other. Hoyt tells Wayne that Gomez is planning to take over the Mongol's hordes so Wayne attacks, captures Gomez's city, and becomes ruler. The next battle has Wayne against DeCorsia with the Duke as the victor. Hayward has watched her father die but she so loves Wayne that she marries him and they plan to live happily ever after. They shot much of this movie in the little town of St. George, Utah, with temperatures hovering in the 120-degree bracket. Almost half the residents of the town of St. George developed cancer in the years since the Yucca Flat A-tests. That Gordon and Van Cleef and Conrad were spared remains a mystery. The only thing about this film that was never a mystery was Wayne's love of the script. He happened to read it by mistake while visiting Powell's office and committed to it overnight. Everyone knew it was a wrong choice but how do you say "no thank you" to the No. 1 star of the year? You can't and they didn't and the result was the eleventh highest grossing movie of the year. Sounds good, huh? Well, it still hasn't made its money back and here's hoping it never will. (An RKO Radioactive picture.)

p&d, Dick Powell; w, Oscar Millard; ph, Joseph LaShelle, Leo Tover, Harry J. Wild, William Snyder (CinemaScope, Technicolor); m, Victor Young; ed, Robert Ford, Kenneth Marstella; md, C. Bakaleinikoff; ed sup, Stuart Gilmore; cos, Michael Woulfe, Yvonne Wood; ch, Robert Sidney.

Adventure   **Cas.**   **(PR:C-A   MPAA:NR)**

CONQUEROR OF CORINTH   (SEE: CENTURION, THE, 1962, Fr./Ital.)

CONQUEROR WORM, THE***   (1968, Brit.) 87m Tigon British/AIP c
(AKA: EDGAR ALLAN POE'S CONQUEROR WORM;
GB: WITCHFINDER GENERAL)
Vincent Price *(Matthew Hopkins)*, Ian Ogilvy *(Richard Marshall)*, Rupert Davies *(John Lowes)*, Hilary Dwyer *(Sara)*, Robert Russell *(John Stearne)*, Patrick Wymark *(Oliver Cromwell)*, Wilfrid Brambell *(Master Loach)*, Nicky Henson *(Trooper Swallow)*, Tony Selby *(Salter)*, Bernard Kay *(Fisherman)*, Godfrey James *(Webb)*, Michael Beint *(Capt. Gordon)*, John Trenaman *(Trooper Harcourt)*, Bill Maxwell *(Trooper Gifford)*, Morris Jar *(Paul)*, Maggie Kimberley *(Elizabeth Clark)*, Peter Haigh *(Lavenham Magistrate)*, John Kidd *(Magistrate)*, Hira Talfrey *(Hanged Woman)*, Ann Tirard *(Old Woman)*, Peter Thomas *(Farrier)*, Edward Palmer *(Shepherd)*, David Webb *(Jailer)*, Paul Dawkins *(Farmer)*, Lee Peters *(Infantry Sergeant)*, David Lyell *(Foot Soldier)*, Alf Joint *(Sentry)*, Martin Terry *(Hoxne Innkeeper)*, Jack Lynn *(Brandeston Innkeeper)*, Beaufoy Milton *(Priest)*, Dennis Thorne, Michael Segal *(Villagers)*, Toby Lennon *(Old Man)*, Gillian Aldham *(Young Woman in Cell)*, Paul Ferris *(Young Husband)*, Margaret Nolan, Sally Douglas, Donna Reading, Tasma Brereton, Sandy Seager *(Wenches at Inn)*, Philip Waddilove, Derek Ware, Susi Field.

During the English Civil War, Price is appointed "Witchfinder General" by the Puritans under Cromwell. He is empowered to travel the countryside with henchman Russell and collect a fee for each witch from whom he extracts a confession. They ride into one town where village priest Davies is accused and proceed to torture him by driving steel spikes into his flesh, looking for "The Devil's Mark." Dwyer, Russell's niece, offers herself to the pair, but Russell just rapes her and hangs her uncle anyway. Ogilvy, her fiance, is a soldier with the Royalists who has sworn to protect her, and when he learns what has happened he leaves his army to hunt down Price and Russell. The pair soon realize that Ogilvy is after them, particularly when Russell barely escapes him after a vicious fight. They go to the village where Dwyer is hiding and use her to set a trap for Ogilvy that ends with both of them chained to a dungeon wall. Price begins searching for the "Devil's Mark" on Dwyer, hoping that Ogilvy will confess to witchcraft so he can be legally executed. Instead, the vengeance-obsessed young man only reaffirms his vow to kill Price. Ogilvy manages to escape, blinding Russell with a well-placed boot heel in the process, and, grabbing an axe, begins hacking at Price. One of Ogilvy's comrades comes into the dungeon and finishes Price off with his pistol. Totally unhinged now, Ogilvy screams at the man, "You've taken him from me!" while Dwyer, still chained to the wall, screams and screams. A masterful study in terror by director Reeves, who made just three films before killing himself in 1969 at age 25 (variously, reported as by an overdose of pills, a car crash, and a fall from a window). The films, THE SHE-BEAST, THE SORCERERS, and THE CONQUEROR WORM, the best of the lot, all show a thoroughly depressing world where evil runs rampant and heroes become evil while fighting it. The performances are all quite good, with Price giving one of his finest portrayals as an intelligent, civilized madman in a place and time that encourages him to act out his darkest impulses. There was a real Matthew Hopkins, Cromwell's Witchfinder General, who, with his assistant Stearne, killed some two hundred alleged witches in 1645 and 1646. He retired in 1646 to write his memoirs and died in bed the following year. A profoundly disturbing film that was played off on the American market as just another entry in AIP's Vincent Price/Edgar Allan Poe series like THE RAVEN or THE PIT AND THE PENDULUM, with Price reading Poe's poem "The Conqueror Worm" over the opening and closing titles. Not for the faint of heart, but not to be missed by horror fans.

p, Arnold Louis Miller; d, Michael Reeves; w, Reeves, Tom Baker, Louis M. Heyward (based on the novel *Witchfinder General* by Ronald Bassett); ph, John Coquillon (Eastmancolor); m, Paul Ferris; ed, Howard Lanning; art d, Jim Morahan; set d, Jimmy James, Andrew Low; cos, Jill Thomson.

Horror   **(PR:O   MPAA:NR)**

CONQUERORS, THE**   (1932) 84m RKO bw
(AKA: PIONEER BUILDERS)
Richard Dix *(Roger Standish)*, Ann Harding *(Caroline Ogden Standish)*, Edna May Oliver *(Matilda Blake)*, Guy Kibbee *(Dr. Daniel Blake)*, Julie Haydon *(Frances Standish)*, Donald Cook *(Warren Lennox)*, Harry Holman *(Stubby)*, Skeets Gallagher

(Benson), Walter Walker (Mr. Ogden), Wally Albright (One of the Twins), Marilyn Knowlden (One of the Twins), Jason Robards, Sr.

A Depression movie made to inspire audiences at a time when all the economic news was dire. Dix and Harding head a family that we trace from the 1870s to the present (1931 or so). The family is beset by hard times but always manages to survive and become stronger and, most importantly at the time, richer, as they build a banking dynasty. Harding and Dix leave New York after the financial collapse of 1873. Their river boat is assaulted by criminals and Dix is wounded but then nursed to health by kindly Oliver, a hotel owner in Nebraska. Dix starts a bank (it must have been easier to do then—just hang out a shingle and people bring you money) and overcomes three panicky periods. The segments are short and interesting and we watch Dix and Harding age, win some, lose some, and, in the end, prove that love and fortitude will conquer all. Well, it didn't conquer the audience apathy as this picture wound up losing money despite the stars and the presence of top-flight director Wellman. (Dix doubles as his own grandson, joining the Lafayette Escadrille during WW I; this was undoubtedly a pleasurable sequence for Wellman to film since he served in that distinguished French flying squadron.) The best person in the film is Kibbee as Oliver's drunken doctor husband. Kibbee was a truly funny man and knew how to wring every last smile out of his lines. He actually began his career as a performer on Mississippi river boats so the river boat sequence in this film was like old home week. This was his thirteenth film after just two years of working in Hollywood. He was fifty at the time. Poor take-off of CIMARRON.

p, David O. Selznick; d, William Wellman; w, Robert Lord (based on a story by Howard Estabrook); ph, Edward Cronajer; m, Max Steiner; ed, William Hamilton; art d, Carroll Clark.

Historical Drama   **(PR:A   MPAA:NR)**

CONQUEST*   (1929) 63m WB bw
Monte Blue (Donald Overton), H. B. Warner (James Farnham), Lois Wilson (Diane Holden), Tully Marshall (Doctor Gerry), Edmund Breese (Mr. Holden).

An early talkie, this film is poorly made with static direction and scratchy sound. The best thing about it is Warner's sleazy portrayal of a thoroughly rotten scoundrel. He deserts a wounded friend, accepts honors not his, and steal's his friend's girl. Warner caps his nefarious career by using a hammer to kill a rival.

d, Roy Del Ruth; w, C. Graham Baker, Eve Unsell (based on the story "Candle in the Wind" by Mary Imlay Taylor); ph, Barney McGill; ed, Jack Killifer.

Drama   **(PR:C   MPAA:NR)**

CONQUEST***   : (1937) 115m MGM bw (GB: MARIE WALEWSKA)
Greta Garbo (Marie Walewska), Charles Boyer (Napoleon), Reginald Owen (Talleyrand), Alan Marshall (Capt. D'Ornano), Henry Stephenson (Count Walewska), Leif Erikson (Paul Lachinski), Dame May Whitty (Laetitia Bonaparte), C. Henry Gordon (Prince Poniatowski), Maria Ouspenskaya (Countess Pelagia), Claude Gillingwater (Stephan), George Houston (Marshal Duroc), George Zucco (Senator Malachowski), Noble Johnson (Roustan), Scotty Beckett (Alexandre), Henry Kolker (Senator Wybitcki), Ivan Lebedeff (Cossack Captain), Bodil Rosing (Anna), Lois Meredith (Countess Potocka), Oscar Apfel (Count Potocka), Betty Blythe (Princess Mirska), George Davis (Grenadier), Dr. Farid (Persian Ambassador), Pasha Khan (Persian Interpreter), Carlos de Valdez (Turkish Ambassador), Roland Varno (Staos), Robert Warwick (Capt. Laroux), Ien Wul (Prince Metternich), Jean Fenwick (Maria Louisa), Rosina Galli (Bianca), Ralph Harolde (Lejeune), Vladimir Sokoloff (Dying Soldier).

This spendidly mounted period film opens in 1807 when Boyer as Bonaparte visits Poland and becomes enamored of Garbo, playing the beautiful Countess Marie Walewska. She is asked by the country's leaders to go to Napoleon and persuade the conqueror to help Poland become independent. Even her aging husband, Stephenson, urges her to go, an assignment which is tantamount to throne-room prostitution. Garbo goes reluctantly and has an affair with Boyer which causes her husband to divorce her. She becomes Boyer's mistress, has a child by him, and is later discarded when Owen, playing the scheming Talleyrand, arranges a marriage between "Nappy" and Marie Louise, a Hapsburg princess. Though abandoned, Garbo remains loyal to Boyer and, following his horrendous defeat at Waterloo, takes their son, Beckett, to see his father just before Boyer's permanent exile at St. Helena. CONQUEST was Garbo's twenty-fifth film and it lacked the verve and majesty of CAMILLE. Moreover, Boyer stole the movie from his co-star, even though he appeared only occasionally. This would be the only movie in which the two would appear together. The production was lavish and director Brown, Garbo's favorite, was sluggish at the helm; the film drags on and on. Much of the lethargy had to do with the script, which was worked on by no less than seventeen writers, including Donald Ogden Stewart, who received no credit. (After the film's release many writers filed complaints against MGM, saying that they had submitted scripts which were wholly taken for the screenplay.) The dialog is stilted and sometimes ridiculous. At one point Boyer says to Garbo: "Are you real, or born of a snowdrift?" Adding to the confusion were a bevy of busybody MGM executives agonizing over the title of the movie. Originally the film was entitled MARIE WALEWSKA and it was released in Europe as such, but studio heads felt that this title would be too much for American audiences to digest, let alone pronounce. For months titles poured in from MGM executives, dozens of them, including: THE WOMAN BEFORE WATERLOO, LESS THAN THE DUST, FLAME OF THE CENTURY, BEFORE WATERLOO, THE GREAT SURRENDER, SYMPHONY WITHOUT MUSIC, SANDS OF GLORY, STAR-CROSSED, THE ROAD TO WATERLOO, WHERE IS THE GLORY? THE NIGHT BEFORE WATERLOO, GLORY, THE IMMORTAL SIN, A WORLD IS BORN, THE CAPTAINS AND THE KING. Finally, in exasperation, F. L. Hendrickson chose CONQUEST, which Warner Bros. held as a title. MGM exchanged its title MAN WITHOUT A COUNTRY for CONQUEST and this was the final U.S. release title. The production was a costly, time-consuming affair, where the budget exploded to almost $3 million (only the 1926 silent epic BEN HUR

had cost MGM more up to that time). Even the cast and crew grew weary in the five-month-long production, jocularly forming the "Walewska-Must-End Association." Mercifully it did, and, even though audiences in Europe flocked to see Garbo and Boyer, CONQUEST was a box office failure in the U.S.

p, Bernard H. Hyman; d, Clarence Brown; w, Samuel Hoffenstein, Salka Viertel, S. N. Behrman (based on a dramatization by Helen Jerome and the novel Pani Walewska by Waclaw Gasiorowski); ph, Karl Freund; m, Herbert Stothart; ed, Tom Held.

Historical Drama/Romance   **(PR:C   MPAA:NR)**

CONQUEST OF CHEYENNE**   (1946) 55m REP bw
Bill Elliott (Red Ryder), Bobby Blake (Little Beaver), Alice Fleming (The Duchess), Peggy Stewart, Kay Kirby, Emmett Lynn, Milton Kibbee, Tom London, Kenne Duncan, George Sherwood, Frank McCarroll, Jack Kirk, Tom Chatterton, Ted Mapes, Jack Rockwell.

The 16th entry in the Red Ryder series has Elliott and faithful sidekick Blake chasing a stock cast of B-western heavies. Elliott's last Red Ryder film, though Blake would continue on in seven more with Allan "Rocky" Lane.

d, R. G. Springsteen; w, Earle Snell (based on a story by Bert Horswell, Joseph Poland); ph, William Bradford; ed, Charles Craft; md, Richard Cherwin.

Western   **(PR:A   MPAA:NR)**

CONQUEST OF COCHISE*½   (1953) 70m COL c
John Hodiak (Cochise), Robert Stack (Maj. Burke), Joy Page (Consuelo de Cordova), Rico Alaniz (Felipe), Fortunio Bonanova (Mexican Minister), Edward Colmans (Don Francisco de Cordova), Alex Montoya (Garcia), Steven Ritch (Tukiwah), Carol Thurston (Terua), Rodd Redwing (Red Knife), Robert E. Griffin (Sam Maddock), Poppy del Vando (Senora de Cordova), John Crawford (Bill Lawson), Joseph Waring (Running Cougar), Guy Edward Hearn (General Gadsden).

Apaches and Comanches gang up on the Mexicans in this routine Indian Western. But Stack as commander of American troops brings the mayhem to detente. Hodiak is an unconvincing Cochise (Jeff Chandler really owned this role, made famous in BROKEN ARROW) and the whole story of the Gadsden Purchase of territory from Mexico is distorted.

p, Sam Katzman; d, William Castle; w, Arthur Lewis, DeVallon Scott (based on a story by Scott); ph, Henry Freulich (Technicolor); m, Mischa Bakaleinikoff; ed, Al Clark.

Western   **(PR:A   MPAA:NR)**

CONQUEST OF MYCENE*½
                                (1965, Ital., Fr.) 102m Explorer Film '58-C.F.P.C./EM c
                                                    (ERCOLE CONTRO MOLOCK)
Gordon Scott (Glauco/Hercules), Rosalba Neri (Pasifae), Alessandra Panaro (Medea), Michel Lemoine (Oinco), Arturo Dominici, Jany Clair, Nerio Bernardi.

Scott adopts the name of Hercules and does battle with evil queen Neri and her son. Routine Italian muscleman epic.

p, Bruno Turchetto; d, Giorgio Ferroni; w, Remigio Del Grosso, Ferroni; ph, Augusto Tiezzi (Eastmancolor); m, Carlo Rustichelli; art d, Arrigo Equini.

Drama   **(PR:A-C   MPAA:NR)**

CONQUEST OF SPACE*½   (1955) 81m PAR c
Walter Brooke (Samuel Merritt), Eric Fleming (Barney Merritt), Mickey Shaughnessy (Mahoney), Phil Foster (Siegle), William Redfield (Cooper), William Hopper (Fenton), Benson Fong (Imoto), Ross Martin (Fodor), Vito Scotti (Sanella), John Dennis (Donkersgoed), Michael Fox (Elsbach), John Shawlee (Rosie), Iphigenie Catiglioni (Mrs. Fodor).

George Pal never forgave Paramount for cutting the budget and adding a love story subplot to his planned follow-up to DESTINATION MOON. The film was a financial disaster and ended Pal's uneasy relationship with the studio as well as marking the end of the cycle of "realist" space films until the spectacular success of 2001—A SPACE ODYSSEY. Plot involves a spaceship taking off for Mars from a floating space station in spite of protests from the captain (Brooke), who considers the flight a blasphemous attempt to reach God and sets out to sabotage the voyage. He is proven wrong when the crew lands on Christmas day, about to die from thirst, and fate, thumbing its nose at the sanctimonious captain, makes it snow. Real stars are the props, lensing, and astronomical art.

p, George Pal; d, Byron Haskin; w, Philip Yordan, Barre Lyndon, George Worthington Yates (based on the book The Mars Project by Chesley Bonestell and Willy Ley); ph, Lionel Lindon (Technicolor); m, Van Cleave; art d, Chesley Bonestell; ed, Everett Douglas; spec eff, John P. Fulton, Irmin Roberts, Paul Lerpae, Ivyl Burks, Jan Domels.

Science Fiction   **(PR:A   MPAA:NR)**

CONQUEST OF THE AIR*½   (1940) 71m London Film Productions/UA bw
Frederick Culley (Roger Bacon), Franklin Dyall (Jerome de Ascoli), Alan Wheatley (Borelli), Hay Petrie (Tiberius Cavallo), John Abbott (DeRozier), Laurence Olivier (Vincent Lunardi), Byran Powley (Sir George Cayley), Henry Victor (Otto Lilienthal), John Trumbull (Von Zeppelin), Charles Lefaux (Louis Bleriot), Charles Hickman (Orville Wright), Percy Marmont (Wilbur Wright), Ben Webster (Leonardo da Vinci), Dick Vernon (Simon the Magician), Denville Bond (Oliver the Monk), Margaretta Scott (Isobella d'Este), David Horne, Michael Rennie.

Early docu-drama detailing the history of flight from cave-man days through the Wright brothers and into pre-WW II days. Olivier plays an early-day balloonist. H. G. Wells worked on an early draft of the screenplay. Produced in 1935, financial difficulties shelved the picture for five years. Finally released in 1940, it was then cut several minutes with a warning to exhibitors not to bill it as a vehicle for its stars, as they make only minor appearances.

p, Alexander Korda; d, Alexander Shaw, John Monk Saunders, Alexander Esway, Zoltan Korda; w, Hugh Gray, Peter Bezencenet (based on stories by Saunders and Antoine de St. Exupery); ph, Wilkie Cooper, Hans Schneeberger, George Noble; m, Muir Mathieson; ed, Bezencenet, Charles Frend.

Historical Drama   **(PR:A   MPAA:NR)**

CONQUEST OF THE EARTH*½   (1980) 99m Glen A. Larson c
Kent McCord, Barry Van Dyke, Robyn Douglass, Lorne Greene, Patrick Stuart, Robbie Rist, Robert Reed, John Colicos.

The third film spliced together from various episodes of the television series "Battlestar Galactica" (the other two being BATTLESTAR GALACTICA [1978] and MISSION GALACTICA: THE CYCLON ATTACK [1979]) for theatrical release overseas. Plot sees Greene and his caravan finally reaching Earth in time to warn scientist Reed of the immninent attack of the Cyclons. Superior special effects or not, it's still bad TV.

p, Jeff Freilich, Frank Lupo, Gary B. Winters; d, Sidney Hayers, Sigmund Nuefeld, Jr., Barry Crane; w, Glen A. Larson; ph, Frank P. Beascoechea, Mario DiLeo, Ben Colman; spec eff, David M. Garber, Wayne Smith.

Science Fiction   **Cas.**   **(PR:A   MPAA:NR)**

CONQUEST OF THE PLANET OF THE APES½**   (1972) 87m FOX c
Roddy McDowall (Caesar), Don Murray (Breck), Ricardo Montalban (Armando), Natalie Trundy (Lisa), Hari Rhodes (MacDonald), Severn Darden (Kolp), Lou Wagner (Busboy), John Randolph (Commission Chairman), Asa Maynor (Mrs. Riley), H. M. Wynant (Hoskyns), David Chow (Aldo), Buck Kartalian (Frank), John Dennis (Policeman), Gordon Jump (Auctioneer), Dick Spangler (Announcer), Joyce Haber (Zelda), Hector Soucy (Ape with Chain), Paul Comi (2nd Policeman).

When dogs and cats are wiped out by a mysterious disease, apes take their place as pets. But unlike dogs and cats, the apes can perform household chores as well. Their human masters become more and more oppressive so Roddy McDowall finds it necessary to put on his chimpanzee head once more and organize a bloody revolt which occupies the last third of the movie. This was the fourth of the ape series and a fine entry, but the ape makeup could use a little touching up the fourth time around. Sequel: BATTLE FOR THE PLANET OF THE APES.

p, Arthur P. Jacobs; d, J. Lee Thompson; w, Paul Dehn (based on characters created by Pierre Boulle); ph, Bruce Surtees (DeLuxe Color); ed, Marjorie Fowler, Alan Jaggs; m, Tom Scott; art d, Philip Jeffries; set d, Norman Rockett.

Science Fiction   **(PR:A   MPAA:PG)**

CONRACK*½**   (1974) 107m FOX c
Jon Voight (Pat Conroy), Paul Winfield (Mad Billy), Hume Cronyn (Skeffington), Madge Sinclair (Mrs. Scott), Tina Andrews (Mary), Antonio Fargas (Quickfellow), Ruth Attaway (Edna), James O'Reare (Little Man), MacArthur Nelson (Mac), William Hunter III (William), Kathy Turner (Kathy), LaCrisia Hardee (LaCrisia), Freida Williams (Freida), Johnny Bell (Jonny), Margaret Perry (Margaret), Cathy Wilson (Cathy), Rosemary Miller (Rosemary), Ronnie Leggett (Ronnie), Veola Clements (Veola), Ronny Harris (Ronny), Rickey Walker (Rickey), Rebecca Cobbs (Rebecca), Anthony Demery (Anthony), Dennis Williams (Dennis), Kevin Perry (Kevin), Ellis Lamar Cash (Top Cat), Deborah Jones (Deborah), Carlos Chambliss (Carlos), John Kennedy (John).

This is the true story of Pat Conroy (he wrote the book the film is based on), a teacher who went to a small island off the coast of South Carolina where the black children were deprived of education. Their inability to pronounce his name resulted in the title. Voight is most sympathetic to the young people as he arrives on the island of St. Simon's, Georgia, in 1969 (used to duplicate the Carolina island where they could not shoot, for various reasons). Many of the children are illiterate or retarded and he is a latter-day Mr. Chips in that he opens their eyes to the wonders of the Great Out There; a life that includes classical music, other religions, baseball, and several other things they never dreamed existed in their insular world. At first, the kids and their parents are against Voight's methods but they are gradually taken into his camp by his sweetness and dedication. There has to be a villain and it's Cronyn, an educational official of the state, who is a strict 3 R's man. Cronyn arranges to have Voight removed and he must leave, but the influence left behind is powerful and, one hopes, lasting. Winfield is excellent as an island resident whom everyone thinks is mad. Ritt was the ultimate New York actor as a young man but in later years he fell in love with the south and has spent many happy films working below the Mason-Dixon line (SOUNDER, NORMA RAE, HOMBRE, and HUD). As a former Group Theatre actor, he understands the problems of emoters and has been able to elicit fabulous performances from some people one would not expect to have those depths. CONRACK did not do the kind of box office business the studio had expected. Surely, it had nothing to do with the quality of the work and the consensus was that the paying customers didn't much care for a film that might have been made in 1950.

p, Martin Ritt, Harriet Frank, Jr.; d, Ritt; w, Irving Ravetch, Frank (based on the book The Water Is Wide by Pat Conroy); ph, John Alonzo (Panavision, DeLuxe Color); m, John Williams; ed, Frank Bracht; prod d, Walter Scott Herndon.

Drama   **(PR:A   MPAA:PG)**

CONSCIENCE BAY*½   (1960, Brit.) 60m Rickra/Cross S Channel bw
John Brown (Ben), Rosemary Anderson (Nelly), Mark Dignam (Caleb), Catherine Wilmer (Aunt Boo), Marc Sheldon (Fred).

Anderson, the adopted daughter of a preacher, falls in love with the preacher's hunchbacked son who steals lobsters along the Nova Scotia coast. Grade B melodrama.

p, Norman Thaddeus Vane, Henry Passmore; d&w, Vane.

Drama   **(PR:C   MPAA:NR)**

CONSOLATION MARRIAGE½**
                             (1931) 82m RKO bw (GB: MARRIED IN HASTE)
Irene Dunne (Mary), Pat O'Brien (Steve), John Halliday (Jeff), Matt Moore (The Colonel), Leslie Vail (Aubrey), Myrna Loy (Elaine), Pauline Stevens (Baby).

This film is about a couple who are drowning their sorrows at a bar, meet, and decide to get married as they have both been jilted by their respective lovers. O'Brien is a sports reporter with the right combination of brashness and sentiment, and Dunne, in her first starring role, is properly vulnerable. Loy is O'Brien's former lady and when the blonde comes back from having traveled the world and wants the relative comfort of being married to O'Brien, Irene and Pat's vows take on a new significance. Vail is Dunne's former boy friend but he is dispensed with easily. The problem arises when Loy returns. She's a madcap type who goes around the globe with speed and a toss of the head. She soon learns that life on the run can be trying. Dunne has to wonder if the glamorous Loy will manage to snag O'Brien. Not to worry. Pleasant enough pastiche. Loy and O'Brien had to wait nearly half a century before they worked together again as Burt Reynolds' parents in THE END. This was one of O'Brien's favorite films which he later enjoyed watching on the late show on TV because he envied his younger self, particularly "his head of hair and his speed running upstairs." Depression or not, this was the era of extravagant Hollywood; the entire cast and crew of the film rode in private cars 500 miles north to San Francisco to shoot one scene in the S.F. Aquarium because an episode involved two sea-horse fish available only in that city. So new a star was O'Brien that during the L.A. premiere at the old Cathay Theatre master of ceremonies Ken Murray, when introducing the stars to the audience, forgot O'Brien's name. The fast-talking Warner Bros. player (he had been loaned to RKO for this film) brashly grabbed the microphone from Murray's hands and blurted: "I may never get this chance again. I'm going to talk." With that he thanked each and every crew member of the film by name.

d, Paul Sloane; w, Humphrey Pearson (based on a story by William Cunningham),; ph, J. Roy Hunt; m, Max Steiner, Myles Connolly.

Comedy   **(PR:A   MPAA:NR)**

CONSPIRACY Zero   (1930) 69m RKO bw
Bessie Love, Ned Sparks, Hugh Trevor, Rita La Roy, Ivan Lebedeff, Gertrude Howard, Otto Matiesen, Walter Long, Donald Mackenzie.

Love and her brother attempt to expose the drug ring responsible for their father's death. This overly long mystery suffers from no intrigue or suspense. The characters are introduced, a murder is committed, a romance blooms, and a full confession is made, and all in the first fifteen minutes. Then the story repeats itself over and over. A revamped remake of a Famous Players silent production. Audiences were scarce for this programmer which gleaned only $135,000 at the box office.

p, Bertram Millhauser; d, Christy Cabanne; Beulah M. Dix (based on the play by Robert Baker and John Emerson).

Mystery   **(PR:A   MPAA:NR)**

CONSPIRACY**   (1939) 58m RKO bw
Allan Lane (Steve), Linda Hayes (Nedra), Robert Barrat (Tio), Charley Foy (Studs), Lionel Royce (Lieutenant), J. Farrell MacDonald (Captain), Lester Matthews (Gair), Henry Brandon (Carlson), William Von Brincken (Wilson).

The problem with this movie, which capitalizes on anti-fascist sentiments and abounds with wild chases, heroics, assassinations, heavy firing between speedboats, secret police lurking everywhere, and cranky dictators, is that a locale is never established and the characters speak in so many bewildering accents it appears to have been cast in the tower of Babel. Tale concerns a shipment of poison gas being delivered for use in a mythical Central American country.

p, Cliff Reid; d, Lew Landers; w, Jerome Chodorov (based on a story by John McCarthy, Faith Thomas); ph, Frank Redman; m, Frank Tours; ed, George Hively; m/l, "Take the World Off Your Shoulders" (Lew Brown, Sammy Fain).

Spy Drama   **(PR:A   MPAA:NR)**

CONSPIRACY IN TEHERAN*   (1948, Brit.) 83m Selected Films/UA bw
                                           (AKA: THE PLOT TO KILL ROOSEVELT)
Derek Farr (Pemberton Grant), Marta Labarr (Natalie Trubetzin), Manning Whiley (Paul Sherek).

Farr is a British journalist in Iran during WW II who discovers that a group of international arms dealers led by Whiley is plotting to blow up President Roosevelt during his visit to the city. Whiley alone gives the closest appearance to acting, and the technical end is almost totally incompetent.

d, William Freshman.

Spy Drama   **(PR:A   MPAA:NR)**

CONSPIRACY OF HEARTS½**   (1960, Brit.) 113m Rank/RFD bw
Lilli Palmer (Mother Katherine), Sylvia Syms (Sister Mitya), Yvonne Mitchell (Sister Gerta), Ronald Lewis (Maj. Spoletti), Albert Lieven (Col. Horsten), Peter Arne (Lt. Schmidt), Nora Swinburne (Sister Tia), Michael Goodliffe (Father Desmaines), Megs Jenkins (Sister Constance), David Kossoff (Rabbi), Jenny Laird (Sister Honoria), George Coulouris (Petrelli), Phyllis Neilson-Terry (Sister Elisaveta), Rebecca Dignam (Anna), Joseph Cuby (Joseph).

A convent in Italy in 1943 is the locale for this movie about the plight of young Jewish children whose parents have been killed by the Nazis. Palmer and her nuns help the children escape to the safety and comfort of foster parents, but their efforts are thwarted when a Nazi colonel and his sadistic lieutenant take over the transit camp, discovering the nun's activities and ordering three of them to be executed. The kids, of course, are the scene-stealers and it is to Syms' credit that she is able to hold her own with them on several occasions.

p, Betty E. Box, Ralph Thomas; d, Thomas; w, Robert Presnell, Jr., (based on material by Dale Pitt); ph, Ernest Steward; m, Angelo Lavagnino; ed, Alfred Roome; cos, Yvonne Caffin.

War Drama **(PR:AAA MPAA:NR)**

CONSPIRATOR** (1949, Brit.) 87m MGM bw

Robert Taylor *(Maj. Michael Curragh)*, Elizabeth Taylor *(Melinda Greyton)*, Robert Flemyng *(Capt. Hugh Ladholme)*, Harold Warrender *(Col. Hammerbrook)*, Honor Blackman *(Joyce)*, Marjorie Fielding *(Aunt Jessica)*, Thora Hird *(Broaders)*, Marie Ney *(Lady Pennistone)*, Wilfrid Hyde-White *(Lord Pennistone)*, Jack Allen *(Raglan)*, Cicely Paget-Bowman *(Mrs. Hammerbrook)*, Helen Haye *(Lady Witheringham)*, Karel Stepanek *(Radek)*, Cyril Smith *(Inspector)*, Nicholas Bruce *(Alek)*.

Thirty-eight-year-old Taylor and seventeen-year-old Taylor are strange bedfellows as CONSPIRATOR tells the story of Taylor, a British army officer in the employ of the USSR. Liz is his young naive American wife. Taylor's Soviet contacts do not like the fact that he is newly wed but he is seriously in love with his wife and listens closely when she pleads with him to give up his spy chores. The Russkies inform Robert that, like the Mafia, one does not resign from the spy service of the USSR. He is ordered to kill her before any further time goes by. How does one kill one's wife? Particularly one as beautiful as teenage Liz T? Robert T goes to meet his contacts at their rendezvous and they are not there. When Robert T calls the Russian embassy and gives his name, he is told that he is dead! The picture disintegrates and winds up with Robert T putting a gun to himself. A depressing film that might have made more sense with a screenplay by someone like Graham Greene. Benson stuck fairly close to the Slater novel and would have been wise to alter it. Shot in Britain, it could have easily been done on MGM's London street. Taylor (Liz) was excellent and sexy in all the love scenes with husband, Robert. She was still going to high school and her tutor dutifully sat on the set to give her lessons in between some of the steamier scenes.

p, Arthur Hornblow, Jr.; d, Victor Saville; w, Sally Benson, Gerard Fairlie (based on the novel by Humphrey Slater); ph, Freddie Young; m, John Wooldridge; ed, Frank Clarke; art d, Alfred Junge; spec eff, Tom Howard.

Spy Drama **(PR:A-C MPAA:NR)**

CONSPIRATORS, THE½** (1944) 100m WB/FN bw

Hedy Lamarr *(Irene)*, Paul Henreid *(Vincent)*, Sydney Greenstreet *(Quintanilla)*, Peter Lorre *(Bernazsky)*, Victor Francen *(Von Mohr)*, Joseph Calleia *(Capt. Pereira)*, Carol Thurston *(Rosa)*, Vladimir Sokoloff *(Miguel)*, Eduardo Ciannelli *(Almeida)*, Steven Geray *(Dr. Schmitt)*, Kurt Katch *(Lutzke)*, Gregory Gay *(Wynat)*, Marcel Dalio *(Croupier)*, George Macready *(The Con Man)*, Doris Lloyd *(Mrs. Benson)*, Louis Mercier *(Leiris)*, Monte Blue *(Jennings)*, Billy Roy *(Page Boy)*, David Hoffman *(Antonio)*, Otto Reichow *(The Slugger)*, Leon Belasco *(Waiter)*, Frank Reicher *(Casino Attendant)*.

In flavor and storyline this film attempts to cash in on the success of CASABLANCA, but still maintains its own melodramatic appeal, mostly due to its fine cast. Henreid is a resistance leader escaped from Holland and known as "The Flying Dutchman." He meets Lamarr in Lisbon, along with Lorre, Greenstreet, and other anti-Nazi underground workers. Greenstreet warns Henreid that Lamarr might be a traitor; she is married to Francen, a high-ranking official at the German legation. When one of the group's agents, Blue, is killed before leaving for occupied territory on a top secret mission, Henreid is arrested and charged with murdering Blue in an obvious frame-up. Henreid manages to escape and is hidden by Greenstreet after proving his innocence in the death of Blue. Greenstreet then tells him that Francen is no Nazi but one of their best agents. Skeptical of Francen's loyalties, Henreid suggests a plan where Blue's real killer can be detected. He and Greenstreet inform the conspirators that another man will take Blue's place on the secret mission and they will all meet him in a hotel, room 865. The traitor is later discovered to be double-agent Francen who tries to inform the Nazis by playing that number at roulette. Confronted by the underground workers, Francen flees but Henreid shoots him to death, then takes on the secret mission, leaving in a little fishing boat to sail to occupied France. It is clear that Lamarr will be waiting for him if he survives the hazardous job. THE CONSPIRATORS, despite its lavish settings and perfect mood camerawork by Edeson, failed to generate inner sparks in a superb cast. Director Negulesco, who had pumped so much spirit into the recent THE MASK OF DIMITRIOS, constructed a film where all the important moves appear false. Many of the scenes are preposterous and the relationship between Henreid and Lamarr is so forced that at the end they seem like strangers pretending affection for each other. Lamarr is lovely to look at in stunning Leah Rhodes gowns and Grot's marvelous sets are impressive, particularly the Cafe Imperium, the Estoril gaming casino, and the twisting, cobblestone streets of Lisbon, but the whole thing is empty and meaningless, except for the scenes in which Greenstreet and Lorre appear. Even Frederic Prokosch, the author of the novel upon which the film is based, took exception to the production, voicing his critical opinion in the *New Republic* in the form of a letter to the editor (which did not endear him to Jack Warner). Wrote Prokosch: "I have just been to see my first film after a year and a half abroad . . . It was called THE CONSPIRATORS . . . All I felt when I rose to go was weariness, intense boredom, and a certain amazement. Weariness and boredom after the preposterous rubbish I had been observing; amazement at the mentality which can concoct such nonsense with a straight face; amazement also at the mentality which is willing to pay to see such tedious stuff." However, Lamarr, on loan from MGM to Warners, thought THE CONSPIRATORS was a good property and personally chose her role. Her laconic, almost indifferent posturing in the film undoubtedly had much to do with the fact that she discovered she was pregnant during the early stages of production. Critically, few reviewers agreed with Lamarr, but the public made the film a success so her commerical instincts were correct.

p, Jack Chertok; d, Jean Negulesco; w, Vladimir Pozner, Leo Rosten (based on the novel by Frederic Prokosch); ph, Arthur Edeson; m, Max Steiner; ed, Rudi Fehr; art d, Anton Grot; set d, Walter Tilford; gowns, Leah Rhodes; md, Leo Forbstein; spec eff, Willard Van Enger, William McGann, James Leicester.

Spy Drama **(PR:A MPAA:NR)**

CONSTANT FACTOR, THE½**

(1980, Pol.) 96m Polish Corporation for Film Production c (CONSTANS)

Tadeusz Bradecki *(Witold)*, Zofia Mrozowska *(Witold's Mother)*, Malgorzata Zajaczkowska *(Grazyna)*, Cezary Morawski *(Stefan)*, Witold Myrkosz *(Marlusz)*, Ewa Lejczak *(Stefan's Wife)*, Jan Jurewicz *(Zenek)*, Juliusz Machulski *(Wladek)*, Marek Litewka *(Wlodzimierz)*, Jacek Strzemzalski *(Mate)*, Edward Zebrowski *(Scientist)*.

Bradecki is an innocent abroad in Communist Poland. He is an amateur mathematician who believes that everything can be explained by working out the math involved, but he comes to learn that it doesn't work that way. After his mother dies because he fouled up the bribe to the doctor who could have her moved out of a draft in the hospital, he loses his good job and ends up as a window washer. Shot at the same time as the slightly better THE CONTRACT. (In Polish; English subtitles)

d&w, Krzysztof Zanussi; ph, Slawomir Idziak; m, Wojciech Kilar; ed, Urszula Silwinska.

Drama **(PR:C-O MPAA:NR)**

CONSTANT HUSBAND, THE*½** (1955, Brit.) 88m LFP/BL c

Rex Harrison *(Charles Hathaway)*, Margaret Leighton *(Miss Chesterman)*, Kay Kendall *(Monica)*, Cecil Parker *(Llewellyn)*, Nicole Maurey *(Lola)*, George Cole *(Luigi Sopranelli)*, Raymond Huntley *(J.F. Hassett)*, Michael Hordern *(Judge)*, Robert Coote *(Jack Carter)*, Eric Pohlmann *(Papa Sopranelli)*, Marie Burke *(Mama Sopranelli)*, Valerie French *(Bridget)*, Jill Adams *(Miss Brent)*, Muriel Young *(Clara)*, John Robinson *(Secretary)*, Eric Berry *(Prosecuting Counsel)*, Arthur Howard *(Clerk of the Court)*, Charles Lloyd Pack *(Solicitor)*, Derek Synney *(Giorgio Sopranelli)*, Guy Deghy *(Stromboli)*, Ursula Howells *(Miss Pargiter)*, Roma Dunville *(6th Wife)*, Stephen Vecoe *(Dr. Thompson)*, Sally Lahee *(Nurse)*, Nora Gordon *(Housekeeper)*, Noel Hood *(Gladys)*, Pat Kenyon, Doreen Dawn *(Models)*, Myrette Morven *(Miss Prosser)*, Sam Kydd *(Adelphi Barman)*, Paul Connell *(Cardiff Barman)*, Nicholas Tannar *(Usher)*, Graham Stuart *(Government Messenger)*, Jill Melford *(Monica's Golf Partner)*, Enid McCall *(Welsh Chambermaid)*, Janette Richer *(Typist)*, Michael Ripper *(Left Luggage Attendant)*, Alfred Burke *(Porter)*, David Yates, Robert Sydney *(Detectives)*, Monica Stevenson *(Olwen)*, Stuart Saunders *(Policeman)*, Joe Clark, George Woodbridge, Frank Webster *(Old Bailey Warders)*), Arthur Cortez *(Luigi's Driver)*, Peter Edwards, Evie Lloyd *(Fishermen)*, Paul Whitsun Jones *(Welsh Farmer)*, Arnold Diamond *(Car Loan Manager)*, Olive Kirby *(Car Loan Assistant)*, Geoffrey Lovat *(Commissionaire)*, Leslie Weston *(Prison Jailer)*, George Thorne *(Horrocks)*.

Frothy souffle about Harrison, an amnesiac, who wakes up to find that he is the husband of several women. He finds himself in an obscure town in Wales one a.m. and has no idea who he is. As he talks to Parker, his psychiatrist, things begin to come back to him and he realizes that he has seven mates! Leighton enters a plea of not guilty on Harrison's behalf but he chooses jail to facing the wrath of several women scorned. Kendall is exceptional as the last wife in Harrison's string and Hordern does a fine job as the judge in the case. Harrison was married to actress Palmer at the time this movie was made and just two years later he married Kay Kendall and they were ecstatically happy until her death of lukemia in 1959. Leighton was married to publisher Max Reinhardt, actor Laurence Harvey, and actor Michael Wilding and was nominated for an Oscar for THE GO-BETWEEN.

p, Frank Launder, Sidney Gilliat; d, Gilliat; w, Gilliat, Val Valentine; ph, Ted Scaife (Technicolor); m, Malcolm Arnold; ed, G. Turney-Smith; md, Muir Mathieson.

Comedy **(PR:A-C MPAA:NR)**

CONSTANT NYMPH, THE½** (1933, Brit.) 85m GAU/FOX bw

Victoria Hopper *(Tess Sanger)*, Brian Aherne *(Lewis Dodd)*, Leonora Corbett *(Florence)*, Lyn Harding *(Albert Sanger)*, Mary Claire *(Linda Sanger)*, Jane Baxter *(Antonio Sanger)*, Fritz Schultz *(Jacob Birnbaum)*, Tony de Lungo *(Roberto)*, Jane Cornell *(Kate Sanger)*, Peggy Blythe *(Lena Sanger)*, Athole Stewart *(Charles Churchill)*, Beryl Laverick *(Susan Sanger)*, Jim Gerald *(Trigorin)*.

British-made adaptation of the Margaret Kennedy novel (1924) concerns an impoverished composer living in the Tyrol with his musician mentor and the mentor's hoydenish daughters, one of whom falls in love with him. Aherne is subsequently distracted by a visiting relative, socially prominent and sophisticated, and marries her, hoping to improve his station and achieve success. Before long he realizes it is his mentor's carefree daughter he loves and who has been the inspiration in his work. Soft, delicate, meandering picture, beautifully directed to its tragic conclusion, in which his new love dies from a leaky heart valve.

p, Michael Balcon; d, Basil Dean; w, Margaret Kennedy, Dean, Dorothy Farnum (based on the novel and play by Kennedy); ph, Mutz Greenbaum.

Drama **(PR:A MPAA:NR)**

CONSTANT NYMPH, THE*** (1943) 106m WB bw

Charles Boyer *(Lewis Dodd)*, Joan Fontaine *(Tessa Sanger)*, Alexis Smith *(Florence Creighton)*, Charles Coburn *(Charles Creighton)*, Brenda Marshall *(Toni Sanger)*, Dame May Whitty *(Lady Longborough)*, Peter Lorre *(Fritz Bercovy)*, Joyce Reynolds *(Paula Sanger)*, Jean Muir *(Kate Sanger)*, Montagu Love *(Albert Sanger)*, Eduardo Ciannelli *(Roberto)*, Jeanine Crispin *(Marie)*, Doris Lloyd *(Miss Hamilton)*, Joan Blair *(Lina)*, André Charlot *(Dr. Renée)*, Richard Ryan *(Firil Trigorin)*, Crauford Kent *(Thorpe)*, Marcel Dalio *(Georges)*, Clemence Groves *(Concert Soloist)*.

Boyer is a talented but impoverished musician living in the home of his slightly mad mentor and four wild daughters in the Austrian Alps. Fontaine is one of the daughters and she develops a crush on Boyer of which he is not aware. When Coburn, an uncle, turns up with his socially prominent daughter, Smith, a romance emerges between her and the musician and they eventually marry and return to England. Fontaine pops up in England just in time to give Boyer the inspiration he needs to continue his work. He soon realizes it is really Fontaine he loves but during the presentation of his successful symphonic poem his young love is so elated she has a heart attack and dies. Fontaine is brilliant. (Remade from the 1933 production; a silent version in 1928 starred Ivor

Novello and Mabel Poulton.) The musical tone poem "Tomorrow" evolved from Korngold's powerful score. The film was originally set for Errol Flynn and Joan Leslie to star.

p, Henry Blanke; d, Edmund Goulding; w, Katheryn Scola (based on the novel and play by Margaret Kennedy); ph, Tony Gaudio; m, Erich Wolfgang Korngold; ed, David Weisbert; md, Leo F. Forbstein; art d, Carl Jules Weyl.

Drama (PR:A MPAA:NR)

CONSTANTINE AND THE CROSS**½ (1962, Ital.) 120m Embassy c
Cornel Wilde (Constantine), Christine Kaufmann (Livia), Belinda Lee (Fausta), Elisa Cegani (Helena), Massimo Serato (Maxientius), Fausto Tozzi (Hadrian), Tina Carraro (Maximianus), Carlo Nichi (Constantius Cloro), Vittorio Sanipoli (Apuleius).

Blood-letting, political intrigue, and romance as warrior Constantine rises to emperor status and finally gets the Romans and the lions off the backs of the outlawed Christians in this dubbed film of old Roman sword play. The battle scenes are well staged—but a few of the sequences of torture and Christian-eating lions do get a bit graphic. A child actress in German films in the 1950s, Kaufmann developed into an attractive leading lady in international productions in the 1960s and married Tony Curtis in 1963. After their divorce in 1967 she returned to Germany.

p, Ferdinando Felicioni; d, Lionello de Felice; w, Ennio de Concini, de Felice, Ernesto Guida, Franco Rossetti, Guglielmo Santangelo, Diego Fabri, Fulvio Palmieri; ph, Massimo Dallamano (Totalscope, Eastmancolor); ed, Mario Serandrei, Gabriele Varriale; m, Mario Nascimbene; art d, Franco Lolli; cos, Giancarlo Bartolini-Salimbene.

Drama (PR:C-O MPAA:NR)

CONTACT MAN, THE (SEE: ALIAS NICK BEAL, 1949)

CONTEMPT** (1963, Fr./Ital.) 100m
Films Concordia/Compagnia Cinematographica Champion-Marceau-Cocinor/EM c
(LE MEPRIS; IL DISPREZZO)
Brigitte Bardot (Camille Javal), Michel Piccoli (Paul Javal), Jack Palance (Jeremy Prokosh), Fritz Lang (Himself), Giorgia Moll (Francesca Vanini), Jean-Luc Godard (Lang's Assistant Director), Linda Veras (Siren).

Piccoli is a screenwriter who longs to write for the stage, but his extravagant wife, Bardot, expects more financially than the theater can offer. He is approached by Palance, an American producer, to write a screenplay for his version of Homer's Odyssey , to be directed by the great German director Fritz Lang (playing himself). When Piccoli accepts the job, Bardot is angry at his lack of conviction and begins to mistrust him (her reaction is a more accurate, but less cinematic, translation of the French title LE MEPRIS), even though he accepted the job to benefit her. Bardot turns to Palance in what is apparently an affair. They take off together for a ride in Palance's sports car and meet a violent death under the wheels of a large truck. An adaptation of Alberto Moravia's novel A Ghost At Noon, the film is essentially concerned with the art of adapting novels for the screen. This idea is transferred to Palance and Lang's adaptation of The Odyssey. Godard specifically relates the characters in his film to those in Homer's and Moravia's books: Odysseus, Penelope, and Poseidon, who in real life can represent Godard, his wife Anna Karina, and distributor Joseph E. Levine. At the film's conception, Italian producer Ponti approached Godard about making a film. Godard in turn suggested the Moravia novel with Kim Novak and Frank Sinatra in the lead roles. Not surprisingly, they disagreed. Next, Ponti suggested Sophia Loren and Marcello Mastroianni, an idea greeted unfavorably by Godard. Eventually Bardot was stumbled upon, a decision welcomed enthusiastically by all involved because of the potential financial rewards her flesh would bring. Ponti personally guaranteed Levine that the film would be commercial, the most accessible Godard yet. He was foolish in saying so, the Americans finding it too "artsy," and lacking a naked Bardot. An opening scene was tacked on (by Godard, not Levine), which showed a nude, bedded Bardot. Not especially racy but enough to put a grin on the male viewer's face. Godard himself is cast as Lang's assistant director, clearly putting his philosophy in Lang's mouth. Godard has said that he chose Lang because "he represents cinema, for which he is both the director and the voice of its conscience. From a more symbolic point of view, however, particularly since he is shooting a film on The Odyssey, he is also the voice of the gods, the man who looks at men." This statement describing Lang can easily be used in reference to Godard, something which he is no doubt aware of. CONTEMPT is a brilliant film which is a difficult but rewarding experience and perhaps the definitive statement on the art of adaptation for the screen. Watching Lang in the movie is a fantastic and exciting experience for any film devotee, which ranks with Nicholas Ray's appearance in Wenders' AN AMERICAN FRIEND and Francois Truffaut's in Spielberg's CLOSE ENCOUNTERS. The rest of the casting is equally perfect. Palance is in his best role since the evil gunfighter in SHANE, the moist-lipped Bardot displays more eroticism fully clothed than most actresses in the buff, and Piccoli can don a hat with perfect cinematic elegance.

p, Georges de Beauregard, Carlo Ponti, Joseph E. Levine; d&w, Jean-Luc Godard (from the novel A Ghost At Noon/Il Disprezzo by Albert Moravia); ph, Raoul Coutard (Cinemascope); m, Georges Delerue; ed, Agnes Guillemot; prod d, Phillipe Dussart, Lila Lakshmanan.

Drama Cas. (PR:C-O MPAA:NR)

CONTENDER, THE** (1944) 63m PRC bw
Buster Crabbe (Gary), Arline Judge (Linda), Julie Gibson (Rita), Donald Maye (Mickey), Glenn Strange (Biff), Milton Kibbee (Pop), Roland Drew (Kip), Sam Flint (Commandant), Duke York (Bomber), George Turner (Sparky).

Crabbe is a truck driver who turns to prizefighting to keep his kid in an expensive military academy, but he ends up on the skids due to hooch and a money-grabbing blonde. Eventually, his old friends come to his rescue in the nick of time. He makes up with his old girl friend and has a happy reunion with his son, who it turns out didn't

want to go to the swanky school anyway because what he really wants to be is a newspaperman, and everyone knows you don't need an education for that! Movie doesn't have much punch.

p, Bert Sternbach; d, Sam Newfield; w, George Sayre, Jay Dolen, Raymand Schruck (based on a story by Sayre); ph, Robert Cline; ed, Holbrook N. Todd.

Drama (PR:A MPAA:NR)

CONTEST GIRL (SEE: BEAUTY JUNGLE, THE, 1966)

CONTINENTAL DIVIDE** (1981) 103m Amblin/UNIV c
John Belushi (Souchak), Blair Brown (Nell), Allen Goorwitz (Howard), Carlin Glynn (Sylvia), Tony Ganios (Possum), Val Avery (Yablonowitz), Liam Russell (Deke), Everett Smith (Fiddle), Bill Henderson (Train Conductor), Bruce Jarchow (Hellinger), Eddie Schwartz (Jimmy), Harold Holmes (Mr. Feeney), Elizabeth Young (Mrs. Feeney).

Belushi is a Chicago newspaper columnist (a young overweight Royko) who enjoys all the goings-on around City Hall. A true city creature, Belushi consumes cigarets and coffee and whiskey with abandon and no regard for his health (this was an obvious portent). When a series of stories about a crooked politician backfires, Belushi is sent to the Rockies to interview a wacky ornithologist (Brown), but mostly to get him out of town. He gets to her aerie atop a mountain and she tosses him out but he is stranded and so they get together and fall in love. When Belushi returns to the Windy City, the politician has been routed and one thinks he will return to his old ways, but the love for Brown is strong and he must return to her. This is as unlikely a love story as one could hope for but one could hope it works. It doesn't. Kasdan is in over his head when he tries to write reality. Even THE BIG CHILL had a bit of exaggeration in it and his scripts for the Lucas films are self-evident. Apted does a good job in trying to keep things going. He is one of the rare British directors who can capture Americana (COAL MINER'S DAUGHTER). The co-exec producer was Bernie Brillstein, Belushi's manager. All too often that credit is given to the people who guide the careers of the stars of the film but who have very little to do with movies. Brillstein was also an exec on the awful BLUES BROTHERS.

p, Bob Larson; d, Michael Apted; w, Lawrence Kasdan; ph, John Bailey (Technicolor); m, Michael Small; ed, Dennis Virkler; prod d, Peter Jamison; set d, Linda Spheeris; cos, Moss Mabry, m/l, "Never Say Goodbye" (Michael Small, Carol Bayer Sager).

Comedy/Romance Cas. (PR:A-C MPAA:PG)

CONTINENTAL EXPRESS** (1939, Brit.) 84m Pinebrook/MON bw
(GB: THE SILENT BATTLE)
Rex Harrison (Sauvin), Valerie Hobson (Draguisha), John Loder (Bordier), Muriel Aked (Mme. Duvivier), George Devine (Sonneman), John Salew (Ernest), Kay Seeley (Bostoff), Carl Jaffee (Rykoff), Megs Jenkins (Louise), Arthur Maude (Editor).

On board the Oriental Express bound for Istanbul, French agent Harrison foils a plot by revolutionaries to blow up a politician aboard the train. Competent prewar spy drama with a fairly talented cast, but it doesn't pack the action or suspense of the great espionage drama NIGHT TRAIN (1940), also starring Harrison.

p, Anthony Havelock-Allan; d, Herbert Mason; w, Wolfgang Wilhelm, Rodney Ackland (based on the novel Le Poisson Chinois by Jean Bommart); ph, Bernard Browne; m, Francis Chagrin; ed, Philip Charlot.

Spy Drama (PR:A MPAA:NR)

CONTINENTAL TWIST (SEE: TWIST ALL NIGHT, 1961)

CONTRABAND (SEE: BLACKOUT, 1940)

CONTRABAND LOVE½ (1931, Brit.) 67m British Screenplays/PAR bw
C. Aubrey Smith (Paul Machin, J.P.), Janice Adair (Janice Machin), Haddon Mason (Roger), Rosalinde Fuller (Belle Sterling), Sydney Seaward (Sampson), Jude Sterling (Charles Paton), Marie Ault (Sarah Sterling).

A detective pretends to be an escaped convict in order to infiltrate a gang of smugglers along the Cornish coast. Obscure British programmer.

p&d, Sidney Morgan; w, Joan Wentworth Wood (based on a story by Morgan).

Crime (PR:A MPAA:NR)

CONTRABAND SPAIN** (1955, Brit.) 82m Diadem/British Pathe c
Richard Greene (Lee Scott), Anouk Aimee (Elena Vargas), Michael Denison (Ricky Metcalfe), Jose Nieto (Pierre), John Warwick (Bryan), Philip Saville (Martin Scott), Alfonso Estella (Marcos), G. H. Mulcaster (Col. Ingleby), Robert Ayres (Official), Olive Milbourne (Mrs. Ingleby), Arnold Bell (Preventive Officer), Conrado San Martin (Juan), Antonio Almoros (Lucien).

Enlisting the aid of his "chantoosie" girl friend, Aimee, and a British customs officer, Denison, American agent Greene rounds up a pack of smugglers and counterfeiters on the French-Spanish border after his brother, himself one of the smugglers, is murdered. Lots of action against beautiful continental backgrounds makes up for weaknesses in plot structure.

p, Philip Gartside; d&w, Lawrence Huntington; ph, Harry Waxman (Eastmancolor); ed, Tom Simpson.

Mystery (PR:A MPAA:NR)

CONTRACT, THE** (1982, Pol.) 111m PRF-Zespol/Cinegate c
Maja Komorowska, Tadeusz Lomnicki, Magda Jaroszowna, Krzystof Kolberger, Nina Andrycz, Zofia Mrozowska, Beata Tysziewicz, Janusz Gajos, Edward Lubaszenko, Ignacy Machowski, Christine Paul, Peter Bonke, Leslie Caron, Irena Byrska, Jolanta Kozak, Maciej Robakiewica, Jerzy Swiech, Bozena Dykiel, Lilianna Glabczynska, Krystyna Szner, Laura Lacz, Eugeniusz Priwiezencew, Jan Jurewicz.

Satirical look at Polish life surrounds the wedding reception of a marriage that did not take place. The couple are pushed into an arranged marriage, and when the bride backs out at the last minute the groom's father decides to have the reception anyway. The end result is a celebration of nothing that is filled with drunken altercations, sexual liaisons, and flaring of tempers between the rival families. Caron is a standout as a kleptomaniac rich woman symbolizing Western decadence. Filmed at the same time as THE CONSTANT FACTOR.

d&w, Krzysztof Zanussi; ph, Slawomir Idziak; m, Wojciech Kilar; ed, Urszula Sliwinska, Ewa Smal; art d, Tadeusz Wybult, Maciej Putowski, Teresa Gruber, Gabriela Allina, Joanna Lelanow.

Comedy **(PR:A MPAA:NR)**

CONVENTION CITY*** (1933) 65m WB bw

Joan Blondell *(Nancy Lorraine)*, Adolphe Menjou *(T. R. Kent)*, Dick Powell *(Jerry Ford)*, Mary Astor *(Arlene Dale)*, Guy Kibbee *(George Ellerbe)*, Frank McHugh *(Will Goodwin)*, Patricia Ellis *(Claire Honeywell)*, Ruth Donnelly *(Mrs. Ellerbe)*, Hugh Herbert *(Hotstetter)*, Hobart Cavanaugh *(Orchard)*, Grant Mitchell *(J.B. Honeywell)*, Gordon Westcott *(Phil Lorraine)*, Johnny Arthur *(Travis)*, Huey White *(Bootlegger)*.

Slap-happy comedy about the antics of salesmen when they get together for their annual anything-goes conventions. Blondell is great as a good-hearted golddigger cavorting around with Kibbee, who is doing his best to avoid his wife. Picture moves quickly and is chock full of laughs. McHugh and Herbert are hilarious as drunken conventioneers.

p, Henry Blanke; d, Archie Mayo; w, Robert Lord (based on a story by Peter Milne); ph, William Reese; ed, Owen Marks; art d, Esdras Hartley.

Comedy **(PR:A MPAA:NR)**

CONVENTION GIRL* (1935) 66m Flacon/FD bw

Rose Hobart *(Babe Laval)*, Weldon Heyburn *(Bill Bradley)*, Sally O'Neil *(Gracie)*, Herbert Rawlinson *(Ward Hollister)*, Shemp Howard *(Dan)*, Lucila Mendez *(Peg)*, James Spottswood *(Cupid)*, Nancy Kelly *(Betty)*, Alan Brooks *(Ernest)*, Neil O'Day *(Daley)*, Toni Reed *(Tommy)*, Ruth Gillette *(Helen)*, William H. White *(Penrod)*, Isham Jones and His Orchestra.

Cabaret hostess with a heart of gold gets herself in trouble when she lends a hand to a traveling salesman from Philadelphia, much to the chagrin of her boy friend, gangster Heyburn, whom she refuses to marry because of his profession. Script is trite and inept. Song: "I've Got Sand in My Shoes."

p, David M. Thomas; d, Luther Reed; w, George Boyle, Max Lief (based on a novel by Boyle); ph, Nicholas Rogelli.

Drama **(PR:A MPAA:PR)**

CONVERSATION, THE**** (1974) 113m PAR c

Gene Hackman *(Harry Caul)*, John Cazale *(Stan)*, Allen Garfield *(Bernie Moran)*, Frederick Forrest *(Mark)*, Cindy Williams *(Ann)*, Michael Higgins *(Paul)*, Elizabeth MacRae *(Meredith)*, Teri Garr *(Amy)*, Harrison Ford *(Martin Stett)*, Mark Wheeler *(Receptionist)*, Robert Shields *(The Mime)*, Phoebe Alexander *(Lurleen)*, Robert Duvall *(The Director)*.

A gripping crime picture that served as Coppola's follow-up to his landmark THE GODFATHER. Coppola can always be depended upon to do whatever you least expect and he wisely did not attempt to top his prior success with another blockbuster. Instead, he chose to tell the story of Harry Caul (Gene Hackman), a professional surveillance expert who is a wire-tapper and industrial spy for hire—by anyone—for the right price. The twisting tale begins with Hackman, Cazale, and Higgins using the highest order of technical expertise to track Williams and Forrest and deliver the tapes (culled from high-powered shotgun mikes) and photographs to a character no one quite knows, played by Duvall (in a cameo). After listening to the tapes repeatedly, it seems that this young couple are the prospective victims of a murder plot, due to what appears to be a case of marital infidelity. Hackman is a fierce independent who protects his own privacy with all the knowledge that he uses to invade that of others. Girl friend Garr doesn't even know how to locate him or what he actually does for a living. Ford wants the tapes Hackman has made. He's acting as Duvall's assistant. But Hackman will only deliver to the man who hired him. MacRae uses her wiles to seduce Hackman to get the tapes and she is obviously one of Ford's people. The murder does happen but it's not what anyone expects. Listening to the tapes again, one realizes that Forrest and Williams are not the victims, they are the killers! Like an onion, the story keeps unpeeling, with Garfield in an outstanding characterization as a rival bugger who is at once friendly and envious. Watching this film and then seeing DePalma's BLOW-OUT, one realizes what a genius we have in Coppola. There is hardly any violence, virtually no sex, and the story whips along like a throroughbred heading for the wire. The dialog is real and points are made without belaboring them. In the end, Hackman realizes that *he* is now being bugged and his apartment is no longer safe. He sits there in the torn-apart room and plays his saxophone to jazz records as a hidden camera watches him mockingly. THE CONVERSATION was released just after the Watergate break-in and was that much more intriguing to audiences than it might have been, but the truth is the film was written many years before Watergate and was already shooting when the famous Republican downfall took place. Coppola kept a firm hand on all the proceedings in his triple job of writing, producing, and directing. It is a rare talent who can handle all of those tasks without losing ground on one of them. A special citation to Walter Murch, who handled the all-important sound department. Murch, a USC pal of George Lucas and one of the San Francisco group, also did Coppola's THE RAIN PEOPLE, Lucas's AMERICAN GRAFFITI, and the aforementioned THE GODFATHER. THE CONVERSATION was not a well-publicized or promoted movie and received only two Oscar nominations—best picture and best screenplay. It deserved many more.

p,d&w, Francis Ford Coppola; ph, Bill Butler (Technicolor); m, David Shire; ed, Walter Murch, Richard Chew; prod d, Dean Tavoularis; set d, Doug von Koss.

Crime Drama **Cas.** **(PR:A-C MPAA:PG)**

CONVERSATION PIECE** (1976, Ital., Fr.) 120m Rusconi/GAU c (VIOLENCE ET PASSION; GRUPPO DI FAMIGLIA IN UN INTERNO)

Burt Lancaster *(Professor)*, Silvana Mangano *(Bianca)*, Helmut Berger *(Konrad)*, Claudia Marsani *(Lietta)*, Stefano Patrizi *(Stefano)*, Elvira Cortese *(Erminia)*, Dominique Sanda *(Mother)*, Claudia Cardinale *(Wife)*.

Lancaster is an American professor who lives alone in an ornate Roman house filled with 18th-century British paintings of families which are called Conversation Pieces. Into this well-ordered life comes Mangano, a decadent matriarch, her nubile teenage daughter, her husband, and, sometimes, her lover, Berger. They rent the upstairs apartment and thus begins a series of intrigues, sexual involvements, and, eventually, the death of Berger. Flashbacks of Lancaster's life indicate his relationship with wife Cardinale, and his mother, Sanda. It's an interior film, with the main sets being Lancaster's and Mangano's apartments and little else. The language is as ornate as the furniture and the central theme of corruption may be just a tad esoteric for most viewers. Unlike many Italian films of the period, all of the dialog is in English with synchronized sound and none of the Leone-like looping of voices. This was directed by Visconti after his stroke and so the usual camera movement that distinguished THE DAMNED and even THE LEOPARD (which was truly one of the most boring movies ever made) is absent.

d, Luchino Visconti; w, Suso Checchi D'Amico, Visconti (based on a story by Enrico Medioli); ph, Pasqualino De Santis (Todd-AO, Technicolor); m, Franco Manno; ed, Ruggero Mastroianni; art d, Mario Garbuglia.

Drama **(PR:C MPAA:NR)**

CONVICT 99½** (1938, Brit.) 91m Gainsborough/GFD bw

Will Hay *(Benjamin Twist)*; Moore Marriott *(Jerry The Mole)*, Graham Moffatt *(Albert)*, Googie Withers *(Lottie)*, Garry Marsh *(Johnson)*, Peter Gawthorne *(Sir Cyril Wagstaffe)*, Basil Radford *(Governor)*, Denis Wyndham *(Warder)*, Wilfrid Walter *(Max Slessor)*, Alf Goddard *(Sykes)*, Teddy Brown *(Slim Charlie)*, Kathleen Harrison *(Mabel)*, Roy Emerton *(Charles Benjamin)*.

Hay is a seedy schoooteacher mistakenly named to become the new warden of a prison. He turns the place into a corporation and lets the convicts run it. Not one of Hay's better efforts, and surprisingly serious in spots, but well worth seeing.

p, Edward Black; d, Marcel Varnel; w, Marriott Edgar, Val Guest, Jack Davies, Ralph Smart (based on a story by Cyril Campion); ph, Arthur Crabtree; md, Louis Levy.

Comedy **(PR:A MPAA:NR)**

CONVICT STAGE*½ (1965) 71m FOX bw

Harry Lauter *(Ben Lattimore)*, Donald Barry *(Marshal Karnin)*, Jodi Mitchell *(Sally)*, Hanna Landy *(Ma Simes)*, Joseph Patridge, Walter Reed, Michael Carr, Fred Krone, George Sawaya, Karl MacDonald.

Routine oater where angry cowboy Lauter sets out to revenge the killing of his sister by a gang of cutthroats led by a woman, Landy. Before he can vent his bloodlust, veteran lawman Barry brings the gang to justice, while lecturing Lauter on the dangers of taking the law into one's own hands.

p, Hal Klein; d, Leslie Selander; w, Daniel Mainwaring (based on a story by Donald Barry); ph, Gordon Avil; m, Richard LaSalle; ed, John F. Schreyer; cos, Patrick Cummings; spec eff, Robert George.

Western **(PR:A MPAA:NR)**

CONVICTED½** (1931) 63m Supreme Features/Artclass Pictures bw

Richard Tucker, Wilfred Lucas, Niles Welch, John Vosburg, Aileen Pringle, Jameson Thomas, Harry Meyers, Dorothy Christy.

Producer Tucker, in love with Pringle who had starred in his show, steals thousands of dollars belonging to his company and boards a ship on which the actress has booked passage. When he is murdered, evidence points to Pringle, but she is eventually cleared by a newspaper investigator. Nicely developed murder mystery with all the action taking place on an ocean liner.

d, Christy Cabanne; w, Jo Van Ronkel (based on a story by Ed Barry); ph, Sidney Hickox; ed, Thomas Persons.

Mystery **(PR:A MPAA:NR)**

CONVICTED*½ (1938) 50m COL bw

Charles Quigley *(Burns)*, Rita Hayworth *(Jerry Wheeler)*, Marc Lawrence *(Milton Miltis)*, George McKay *(Kane)*, Doreen MacGregor *(Mary Allen)*, Bill Irving *(Cobble-Puss Coley)*, Eddie Laughton *(Berger)*, Edgar Edwards *(Chick Wheeler)*, Phyllis Clare *(Ruby Rose)*, Bob Rideout *(Rocco)*, Michael Heppell *(Pal)*, Noel Cusack *(Aggie)*, Grant MacDonald *(Frankie)*, Don Douglas *(District Attorney)*.

One of Hayworth's earliest efforts at Columbia, her eighth film under the name of Hayworth. Prior to that she was known as Rita Cansino. Mild little programmer featuring the torrid redhead as a nightclub dancer, Quigley (and whatever happened to *him?*) as a detective who convicts Rita's brother, Edwards, of a murder he didn't commit, and Lawrence as the gangster behind it all. Edwards is cleared as Hayworth and Quigley uncover the plot. Not much to recommend this film other than the curiosity value. Lawrence was in more than 115 movies and almost always played the villain. He was only 28 years old when this picture was made and was already a seasoned and vicious movie killer. There are huge holes in the story that couldn't be plugged with a ton of caulking. Cornell Woolrich wrote many excellent stories that were turned into films (REAR WINDOW, etc.). This was not one of them.

p, Kenneth J. Bishop; d, Leon Barsha; w, Edgar Edwards (based on the story "Face Work" by Cornell Woolrich); ph, George Meehan; ed, William Austin; md, Morris Stoloff.

Crime **(PR:A MPAA:NR)**

CONVICTED*** (1950) 91m COL bw (AKA: ONE WAY OUT)

Glenn Ford *(Joe Hufford)*, Broderick Crawford *(George Knowland)*, Millard Mitchell *(Malloby)*, Dorothy Malone *(Kay Knowland)*, Carl Benton Reid *(Capt. Douglas)*, Frank Faylen *(Ponti)*, Will Geer *(Mapes)*, Martha Stewart *(Bertie Williams)*, Henry O'Neill *(Detective Dorn)*, Douglas Kennedy *(Detective Baley)*, Ronald Winters *(Vernon Bradley)*, Ed Begley *(Mackay)*, Frank Cady *(Eddie)*, John Doucette *(Tex)*, Ilka Gruning *(Martha Lorry)*, John A. Butler *(Curly)*, Peter Virgo *(Luigi)*, Whit Bissell *(Owens)*, Fred Sears *(Fingerprint Man)*, Fred Graham, Eddie Parker, James Millican, Ray Teal, Robert Malcolm, James Bush, Bill Tannen, Clancy Cooper *(Guards)*, William E. Green *(Dr. Masterson)*, Charles Cane *(Sergeant)*, Wilton Graff *(Dr. Agar)*, Vincent Renno *(Freddie)*, Harry Cording *(Brick, 3rd Convict)*, Griff Barnett *(Mr. Hufford)*,

Richard Hale *(Judge)*, William Vedder *(Whitey, 2nd Convict)*, Alphonse Martell *(Melreau)*, Harry Harvey, Marshall Bradford, Bradford Hatten *(Patrolmen)*, Jimmie Dodd *(Grant)*, Benny Burt *(Blackie)*, Thomas Kingston *(Conductor)*, Jay Barney *(Nick)*, Chuck Hamilton, Charles Sherlock *(Policemen)*.

When a wealthy man is murdered, family member Ford is wrongly accused of the killing. The evidence against him is so slim that even district attorney Crawford is convinced of Ford's innocence and tries to help him during the trial. But Ford's lawyer, hired by a family believing Ford guilty, mismanages the entire case and, more than the flimsy circumstantial evidence, causes Ford to be convicted. He is given a minimum sentence and while in prison Crawford works to prove him innocent, along with his daughter, Malone, who has fallen for the framed man. Well scripted and tautly directed, there are some good twists and turns in this wrong man story where Ford excels as the victim, a role he worked to perfection in THE BIG HEAT, FRAMED, and UNDERCOVER MAN.

p, Jerry Bresler; d, Henry Levin; w, William Bowers, Fred Niblo, Jr., Seton I. Miller (based on the play "Criminal Code" by Martin Flavin); ph, Burnett Guffey; m, George Duning; ed, Al Clark; art d, Carl Anderson; set d, James Crowe; md, Morris Stoloff; makeup, Newt Jones.

Prison Drama (PR:A MPAA:NR)

CONVICTED WOMAN** (1940) 65m COL bw
Rochelle Hudson *(Betty Andrews)*, Frieda Inescort *(Mary Ellis)*, June Lang *(Duchess)*, Lola Lane *(Hazel)*, Glenn Ford *(Jim Brent)*, Iris Meridith *(Nita)*, Lorna Gray *(Frankie)*, Esther Dale *(Miss Brackett)*, William Farnum *(Comm. McNeil)*, Mary Field *(Gracie)*, Beatrice Blinn *(May)*, June Gittleson *(Tubby)*, Dorothy Appleby *(Daisy)*.

This women-behind-bars picture takes on a different look in that the confined women are given a stab at establishing their own form of self-government. Cast includes the obligatory reforming lady lawyer Inescort, railroaded inmate Hudson, newspaper reporter Ford, tough-talking lifer Lane, and sniveling spy Lang. Snappy, sometimes sappy dialog.

p, Ralph Cohn; d, Nick Grinde; w, Joseph Carole (based on a story by Martin Mooney and Alex Gottlieb); ph, Benjamin Kline; ed, James Sweeney; m, M. W. Stoloff.

Drama (PR:A MPAA:NR)

CONVICTS AT LARGE zero (1938) 57m Selig Productions/Principal bw
Ralph Forbes *(David)*, Paula Stone *(Ruth)*, William Boyle *(Steve)*, John Kelly *(Huggsie)*, George Traveil *(Gus)*, Charles Brokaw *(Squire)*, Florence Lake *(Hattie)*.

An escaped convict steals the clothes of a dimwit architect, leaving him with no recourse but to wear the prison threads. The architect then blunders into the drinking hangout of gun-toting jewel thieves waiting for the convict. There, he falls for a song-and-dance girl and gets involved in the mob. Scripting is neither plausible nor interesting, with faulty technical details putting the performers in their worst light.

d, Scott E. Beal, David Friedman; w, Walter James, Beal (based on a story by Ambrose Barker).

Mystery (PR:A MPAA:NR)

CONVICT'S CODE*½ (1930) 65m W. Ray Johnston/Syndicate Pictures bw
Cullen Landis *(Kenneth Avery)*, Eloise Taylor *(Nan Perry)*, William Morris *(Theodore Perry)*, Robert Cummings *(Gov. Johnson)*, Lyle Evans *(Robert Shannon)*, Mabel Z. Carroll *(Maisie Lawrence)*, John Irwin *(A Lifer)*, John Burkell *(Trustee)*.

Landis is about to go to the chair for murdering Carroll but his lover Taylor begs Cummings, the governor, to stay the execution. She recounts Landis' story, told in flashback, how he is inveigled by Carroll to her apartment where she foists herself upon him but he will have none of her. She is shot and killed after Taylor and Evans enter the apartment and Landis is blamed for the killing. After hearing the story, Cummings still isn't convinced of Landis' innocence and orders the execution to continue. As fate and Hollywood would have it there is a prison break just before the juice is thrown and Shannon, one of the escapees, is mortally wounded and confesses to murdering Carroll, which vindicates the condemned Landis for a happy reunion with Taylor.

d, Harry Revier; w, Mabel Z. Carroll, Vincent Valentini; ph, George Peters, Al Harsten.

Prison Drama (PR:A MPAA:NR)

CONVICT'S CODE* (1939) 83m MON bw
Robert Kent, Anne Nagel, Sidney Blackmer, Victor Kilian, Norman Willie, Maude Eburne, Ben Alexander, Pat Flaherty, Carleton Young, Howard Hickman, Joan Barclay, Harry Strang.

Football player Kent is framed by gamblers into taking the rap for a bank holdup to keep him out of a crucial game. After serving three years, he is paroled as a chauffeur to Blackmer, the gambler who framed him, now posing as an investment broker. Complications arise when Kent falls in love with the hood's beautiful sister. Draggy film, with the only speed in evidence being how fast it must have been put together.

p, E. B. Derr; d, Lambert Hillyer; w, John W. Krafft; ph, Arthur Martinelli; ed, Russell Schoengarth.

Drama (PR:A MPAA:NR)

CONVICTS FOUR*** (1962) 105m AA bw (AKA: REPRIEVE)
Ben Gazzara *(John Resko)*, Stuart Whitman *(Principal Keeper)*, Ray Walston *(Iggy)*, Vincent Price *(Carl Carmer)*, Rod Steiger *(Tiptoes)*, Broderick Crawford *(Warden)*, Dodie Stevens *(Resko's Sister)*, Jack Kruschen *(Resko's Father)*, Sammy Davis, Jr. *(Wino)*, Naomi Stevens *(Resko's Mother)*, Carmen Phillips *(Resko's Wife)*, Susan Silo *(Resko's Daughter)*, Timothy Carey *(Nick)*, Tom Gilson *(Lefty)*, Arthur Malet *(Storekeeper)*, Lee Kreiger *(Stanley)*, Myron Healey *(Gunther)*, Josip Elic *(Barber)*, Jack Albertson *(Art Teacher)*, Robert Harris *(Commissioner)*, Andy Albin *(Con)*, Burt Lange *(Gallery Man)*, John Kellogg, Adam Williams, Robert Christopher, Warren

Kemmerling, Kreg Martin, John Close, Billy Varga *(Guards)*, Reggie Nalder *(Greer)*, John Dennis *(Cell Block Guard)*.

Unusual prison drama featuring Gazzara (aided by a bizarre supporting cast) as an unruly convict serving a life sentence whose life is suddenly changed when his artistic abilities are discovered. The authorities encourage his interest, and, eventually, with the help of art-critic Price, he is paroled and becomes a sensation in the art world. Based on the true story of John Resko.

p, A. Ronald Lubin; d&w, Millard Kaufman (based on the book *Reprieve* by John Resko); ph, Joseph Biroc; m, Leonard Rosenman; ed, George White; art d, Howard Richmond; set d, Joseph Kish; spec eff, Milt Olsen.

Prison Drama (PR:A MPAA:NR)

CONVOY**½ (1940) 95m ABF bw
Clive Brook *(Capt. Armitage)*, John Clements *(Lt. Crawford)*, Edward Chapman *(Capt. Eckersley)*, Judy Campbell *(Lucy Armitage)*, Edward Rigby *(Mr. Mathews)*, Charles Williams *(Shorty Howard)*, Allan Jeayes *(Cmdr. Blount)*, David Hutchenson *(Capt. Sandeman)*, George Carney *(Bates)*, Al Millen *(Knowles)*, Charles Farrell *(Walker)*, John Laurie *(Gates)*, Hay Petrie *(Minesweeper Skipper)*, Stewart Granger *(Sutton)*, Edward Lexy *(Skipper)*, John Glyn Jones, Mervyn Jones *(Mates)*, Penelope Dudley Ward *(Mabel)*, Albert Lieven *(Commander of U-37)*, Michael Wilding *(Dot)*, Harold Warrender *(Lt. Cmdr. Martin)*, Hans Wangraf *(Cmdr. Deutschland)*, George Benson *(Parker)*.

German battleship picks on a small English cruiser in this story of life aboard a boat doing convoy duty in the North Sea. A friendly battle squadron comes upon the fighting and chases the intruder away. Picture noted as the first from Britain in WW II to depict a war subject on screen with realism and a plausible plot. Director Tennyson tries for comic relief at times but fails with overzealous treatment. Technical efforts secure a spot for finesse in production archives.

p, Michael Balcon; d, Pen Tennyson; w, Tennyson, Patrick Kirwan; ph, Roy Kelline, Gunther Krampf.

Drama (PR:A MPAA:NR)

CONVOY* (1978) 110m UA c
Kris Kristofferson *(Rubber Duck)*, Ali MacGraw *(Melissa)*, Ernest Borgnine *(Lyle Wallace)*, Burt Young *(Pig Pen)*, Madge Sinclair *(Widow Woman)*, Franklyn Ajaye *(Spider Mike)*, Brian Davies *(Chuck Arnoldi)*, Seymour Cassel *(Gov. Haskins)*, Cassie Yates *(Violet)*, Walter Kelley *(Hamilton)*.

Truck driver Kristofferson butts heads with corrupt sheriff Borgnine in this excuse for a series of chases and crashes. Kristofferson's performance is as monotone as his singing, showing few changes in dramatic emphasis. Unmotivated story riddled with confusion and disarray. Production staff does the job with little imagination.

p, Robert M. Sherman; d, Sam Peckinpah; w, B. W. L. Norton (based on the song by C. W. McCall); ph, Harry Strading (Panavision, DeLuxe Color); m, Chip Davis; ed, Graeme Clifford, John Wright, Garth Craven; prod d, Fernando Carrere; art d, J. Dennis Washington, Francis Lombardo; cos, Carol James; m/l, Bill Fries.

Comedy (PR:C MPAA:PG)

COOGAN'S BLUFF***½ (1968) 93m UNIV c
Clint Eastwood *(Coogan)*, Lee J. Cobb *(Sheriff McElroy)*, Susan Clark *(Julie)*, Tisha Sterling *(Linny Raven)*, Don Stroud *(Ringerman)*, Betty Field *(Mrs. Ringerman)*, Tom Tully *(Sheriff McCrea)*, Melodie Johnson *(Millie)*, James Edwards *(Jackson)*, Rudy Diaz *(Running Bear)*, David F. Doyle *(Pushie)*, Louis Zorich *(Taxi Driver)*, Meg Myles *(Big Red)*, Marjorie Bennett *(Mrs. Fowler)*, Seymour Cassel *(Young Hood)*, John Coe *(Bellboy)*, Skip Battyn *(Omega)*, Albert Popwell *(Wonderful Digby)*, Conrad Bain *(Madison Avenue Man)*, James Gavin *(Ferguson)*, Albert Henderson *(Desk Sergeant)*, Syl Lamont *(Room Clerk)*, Jess Osuna *(Prison Hospital Guard)*, Jerry Summers *(Good Eyes)*, Antonia Rey *(Mrs. Amador)*, Marya Henriques *(Go-Go Dancer)*, James McCallion *(Room Clerk)*.

COOGAN'S BLUFF was the first joint effort by Eastwood and Siegel and raised the hackles of many a moralist with what was considered needless violence and too much sex. By the standards of the 1980s, it's a mild effort. Eastwood is an Arizona deputy who has been sent to New York to bring back Stroud, a criminal. The moment he sets boot in the Big Apple, he feels out of place and soon comes to grips with tough detective Cobb. Stroud managed to get some LSD and has overdosed on the stuff so Eastwood will have to cool his heels while the villain recovers. He finds a use for some of his time by making passes at Clark, a social worker/probation officer. Time passes slowly for Eastwood and he finally pushes the hospital staff into releasing Stroud in his custody, but not before he notices Stroud whisper something to sweetheart Sterling. At the heliport, Eastwood is whacked senseless by Stroud's gang. Stroud escapes and Eastwood is hospitalized. Even worse, he is ordered off the case. His pride is bruised more than his body and Clark attempts to give him some balm and solace at her apartment. Once there, Eastwood notices that one of Clark's parole charges is none other than Sterling! He gets her address and makes his way to Sterling's apartment, puts a heavy make on her, and gets her to promise to lead him to Stroud, who, unexplainably, is still hanging around Manhattan. Eastwood is led to a run-down billiards parlor and ambushed by Stroud's gang. One of the best fight scenes ever follows as Eastwood uses pool cues and billiard balls and a lot of fancy athletic ability to extricate himself from being totally outmanned. He beats the tar out of most of them before being hurt badly himself. The police arrive a few seconds after he's escaped and gone to Sterling's apartment. Now he raps her around a bit until she agrees to *really* take him to Stroud's hideout. He's holed up at The Cloisters, New York's famous monastery along the Hudson River. The denouement is a motorcycle chase around the concrete canyons and the final scene is taking Stroud back to Arizona and saying farewell to Cobb and Clark. As Eastwood leaves, Cobb begrudgingly admits his admiration for the Arizona deputy although he can never accept the unique methodology of the man. No matter what anyone claimed, this really was the pilot film for the "McCloud" TV series. All they did was change his home base from Arizona to New Mexico. One hopes the originators got their royalties. Cassel, who plays a small role as a hood, did a slightly larger role in 1968. He was so good in that that he was nominated for an Oscar as Best Supporting Actor in FACES. It would have been lovely to say he won but truth is crueler than fiction and he lost to Jack Albertson in THE SUBJECT WAS ROSES. Cobb, who played the kind of part in so many movies, gave the standout performance. Eastwood was just beginning to develop his screen persona and this was a transitional movie in that metamorphosis from the unnamed cowboy in the Italian westerns to Dirty Harry Callaghan.

p&d, Donald Siegel; w, Herman Miller, Dean Reisner, Howard Rodman (based on a story by Miller); ph, Bud Thackery (Technicolor); m, Lalo Schifrin; ed, Sam E. Waxman; art d, Alexander Golitzen, Robert MacKiehan; set d, John McCarthy, John Austin; cos, Helen Colvig; m/l, "Pigeon-Toed Orange Peels," "Everbody" (Wally Holmes, Schifrin); stunts, Paul Baxley.

Police Drama **Cas.** **(PR:C-O MPAA:NR)**

COOL AND THE CRAZY, THE** (1958) 78m AIP bw

Scott Marlowe *(Bennie Saul)*, Gigi Perreau *(Amy)*, Dick Bakalyan *(Jackie Barzan)*, Dick Jones *(Stu Summerville)*, Shelby Storck *(Lt. Sloan)*, Marvin J. Rosen *(Eddie)*, Caroline von Mayrhauser *(Mrs. Ryan)*, Robert Hadden *(Cookie)*, Anthony Pawley *(Mr. Saul)*, James Newman *(Sgt. Myers)*, Joe Adelman *(Police Sergeant)*, Kenneth Plumb *(Marty)*, Jackie Storck *(Amy's Mother)*, Leonard Belove *(Amy's Father)*, Jim Bysol *(Blue Note Proprietor)*, John Hannahan *(Drunk)*, John Quihas, Paul Culp, Bob Hall, Frank Tebeck, Bill Stevens, Jeanne Gallagher, Dona Baldwin, Ruth Marquez, Gaul Greenwell, Dorothy Haefling.

Fabled version of what happens when high school student and reform school veteran Marlowe begins pushing marijuana on his classmates. All but one gets hooked on the weed, which drives the teenagers to killings and service station holdups to support their habits. Photography from Birch has good journalistic quality, with Kraushaar's music bringing out the bizarre story. Kansas City location tends to give a strong feel of reality to the production. Fifties version of REEFER MADNESS.

p, E. C. Rhoden, Jr.; d, William Witney; w, Richard C. Sarafian; ph, Harry Birch; m, Raoul Kraushaar; ed, Helene Turner; m/l, Bill Nolan, Ronnie Norman.

Drama **(PR:C-O MPAA:NR)**

COOL BREEZE** (1972) 101m MGM c

Thalmus Rasulala *(Sidney Lord Jones)*, Judy Pace *(Obalese Eaton)*, Jim Watkins *(Travis Battle)*, Lincoln Kilpatrick *(Lt. Brian Knowles)*, Sam Laws *(Finian)*, Margaret Avery *(Lark)*, Wally Taylor *(John Battle)*, Raymond St. Jacques *(Bill Mercer)*, Rudy Challenger *(Roy Harris)*, Royce Wallace *(Emma)*, Paula Kelly *(Mrs. Harris)*, Margaret Avery *(Mercer's Mistress)*, Stewart Bradley *(Police Captain)*, John Lupton *(Detective)*.

A remake of THE ASPHALT JUNGLE with an all-black cast. Well-done but totally unnecessary, COOL BREEZE was made to pander to the black audiences that had been flocking to see the SHAFT films. Rasulala is a cool dude crook out on parole. His plan is to steal three million in baubles, sell the stuff, and use the proceeds to start a bank that will aid black businesses. Watkins and Pace are his compatriots in the plan, along with Taylor as Watkins's half-brother and Challenger as a preacher who doubles as a thief. The man behind the whole deal is St. Jacques (in the Calhern role). His wheelchair-ridden wife, Wallace, is the reason why he's taken up with mistress Avery, looking absolutely scrumptious and doing a very convincing job as a black Marilyn Monroe (same role in the original). The local cops are scrutinized by director-writer Pollack and shown off to good advantage and the picture would have made some sense were it not for the fact that it was a remake. To the production's credit, nothing was made of the fact that everyone was black and there were absolutely no racial over- or undertones. Some fine music by Solomon Burke helps the feeling of the film and all technical credits are good.

p, Gene Corman; d&w, Barry Pollack (based on a novel by W. R. Burnett); ph, Andy David (Metrocolor); m, Solomon Burke; ed, Morton Tubor; art d, Jack Fisk.

Crime Caper **(PR:C MPAA:R)**

COOL HAND LUKE**** (1967) 126m WB c

Paul Newman *(Luke)*, George Kennedy *(Dragline)*, J. D. Cannon *(Society Red)*, Lou Antonio *(Koko)*, Robert Drivas *(Loudmouth Steve)*, Strother Martin *(Captain)*, Jo Van Fleet *(Arletta)*, Clifton James *(Carr)*, Morgan Woodward *(Boss Godfrey)*, Luke Askew *(Boss Paul)*, Marc Cavell *(Rabbitt)*, Richard Davalos *(Blind Dick)*, Robert Donner *(Boss Shorty)*, Warren Finnerty *(Tattoo)*, Dennis Hopper *(Babalugats)*, John McLiam *(Boss Kean)*, Wayne Rogers *(Gambler)*, Dean Stanton *(Tramp)*, Charles Tyner *(Boss Higgins)*, Ralph Waite *(Alibi)*, Anthony Zerbe *(Dog Boy)*, Buck Kartalian *(Dynamite)*, Joy Harmon *(The Girl)*, James Gammon *(Sleepy)*, Joe Don Baker *(Fixer)*, Donn Pearce *(Sailor)*, Norman Goodwins *(Stupid Blondie)*, Chuck Hicks *(Chief)*, John Pearce *(John, Sr.)*, Eddie Rosson *(John, Jr.)* Rush Williams *(Patrolman)*, James Jeter *(Wickerman)*, Robert Luster *(Jabo)*, Rance Howard *(Sheriff)*, James Bradley, Jr., Cyril "Chips" Robinson *(Black Boys)*.

Under the helm of first-time feature director Stuart Rosenberg, COOL HAND LUKE nabbed four Oscar nominations (screenplay, music, star, and supporting actor) and won the gold statuette for Kennedy. Produced by Jack Lemmon's company for Warner Bros., the movie purports to take place in the south but was actually shot near Stockton, California, where so many other films have been made over the years. Newman is Luke, a loner who's been sent to a chain gang camp for drunkenly destroying parking meters. (See I AM A FUGITIVE FROM A CHAIN GANG, SULLIVAN'S TRAVELS, BLACKMAIL, 1939 for other depicitions of this.) It's a cruel sentence in a cruel place. Luke is a tough nut and refuses to crack under the pressure applied. He does the roughest jobs, under the hottest sun, and never loses his cool. The convict boss of the chain gang is Kennedy and he takes an instant dislike to Newman which results in a memorable fist fight in which Kennedy whales the daylights out of Newman but cannot get him to roll over. From that moment, a grudging respect is accorded Newman, especially when he lashes back against the maltreatment by the guards at the camp. Now Newman demonstrates his abilitites at poker and that wins further nods from the inmates. But it is his huge appetite that wins a pile of money for him and his backers when he manages to eat fifty (gulp) hard-boiled eggs. Newman's mother, Van Fleet, comes to visit but she can't leave her bed in the back of the truck as she is too ill. Newman then learns she's died and he goes temporarily insane and must be disciplined. Now he begins to think of escaping. He saws a hole in the wooden floor, gets away, and is recaptured and put in leg chains. He escapes again and is captured again. The camp authorities, led by Martin, begin a systematic campaign to break his spirit. Every possible variation of prison cruelty is attempted and still he won't bend. The officials feel that they must get Newman to cease being independent as that sort of behavior might just inspire the other inmates, who have heretofore been sheep, to rise up. Finally, Newman pleads with the guards to leave him be, have some mercy, have some pity. This kind of behavior loses whatever image he had in the eyes of the other convicts. But it's all a sham. What Newman really wants is the chance to escape again. He gets away with Kennedy and they take refuge in a church. Then Kennedy leaves and returns with the guards and we're not sure if it's for Newman's own good or it just might be to win some time off for Kennedy. No matter as, in the end, Newman is killed by the guards when he refuses to live like an animal any longer. He perishes with a smile on his lips and the knowledge that they never did break him. Almost every major star has made his "prison" movie. Muni in I AM A FUGITIVE FROM A CHAIN GANG; Redford in BRUBAKER: McQueen in PAPILLON, Cagney and Robinson in countless slammer epics and even a host of women like Susan Hayward in I WANT TO LIVE. It's definitely a star status genre and Newman knew it when he took the job. The fact that they made such a good movie out of somewhat cliched material is a tribute to all concerned. The original novel had more than a ring of truth to it as Pearce was a reformed safecracker and had served time in such a camp. He does a bit role as "Sailor," one of the cons. Also in small roles are Baker (WALKING TALL), Rogers (ONCE IN PARIS) and Hopper (EASY RIDER). Only one other female besides Fleet, Harmon, and she does a silent bit as a sexual tease washing a car. Without a word, she steamed the screen. Two famous bits came out of COOL HAND LUKE: Martin standing over the defiant Newman saying: "What we got here is a failure to communicate," and Newman singing the irreverent "I don't care if it rains or freezes long as I got my plastic Jesus/sittin' on the dashboard of my car." If Newman was ever to win an Oscar, it should have been for this.

p, Gordon Carroll; d, Stuart Rosenberg; w, Donn Pearce, Frank R. Pierson (based on a novel by Pearce); ph, Conrad Hall (Panavision, Technicolor); m, Lalo Schifrin; ed, Sam O'Steen; art d, Cary Odell; set d, Fred Price; cos, Howard Shoup; makeup, Gordon Bau.

Prison Drama **Cas.** **(PR:C MPAA:NR)**

COOL IT, CAROL!*½ (1970, Brit.) 110m Miracle Films c

Janet Lynn *(Carol Thatcher)*, Robin Askwith *(Joe Sickles)*, Peter Elliot *(Philip Stanton)*, Jess Conrad *(Jonathan)*, Stubby Kaye *(Rod Strangeways)*, Pearl Hackney *(Mother)*, Martin Wyldeck *(Father)*, Chris Sandford *(David Thing)*, Derek Aylward *(Tommy Sanders)*, Peter Murray *(Himself)*, Eric Barker *(Signalman)*.

Backwoods Britons Lynn and Askwith decide to journey to London for fame and fortune. On the way, she persuades him to have sex with her at a stopover hotel where they are swindled out of their traveling money. Askwith puts her on the street to make money and works as her pimp. They get to London where Lynn becomes an overnight success as a model but continues her call girl duties. Askwith parlays them both into blue movies. They get bored and return to the respectability of village life. West End London is graphically portrayed.

p&d, Peter Walker; w, Murray Smith; ph, Peter Jessopi (Eastmancolor); m, Cyril Ornandel; ed, Tristan Cones.

Drama **(PR:O MPAA:NR)**

COOL MIKADO, THE**

(1963, Brit.) 81m Film Productions of Gilbert and Sullivan Operas/UA c

Frankie Howerd *(Ko-Ko)*, Stubby Kaye *(Judge Mikado/Charlie)*, Tommy Cooper *(Detective)*, Dennis Price *(Ronald Fortescue)*, Mike and Bernie Winters *(Mike and Bernie)*, Lionel Blair *(Nanki)*, Kevin Scott *(Hank Mikado)*, Glenn Mason *(Harry)*, Pete Murray *(Man in Boudoir)*, Jacqueline Jones *(Katie Shaw)*, Dermot Walsh *(Elmer)*, Jill Mai Meredith *(Yum-Yum)*, Yvonne Shima *(Peep-Bo)*, Tsai Chin *(Pitti-Sing)*, The John Barry Seven.

Silly updating of the Gilbert and Sullivan opera laid in post-war Japan, where the soldier son of an American judge is in love with a Japanese girl, but finds himself kidnaped by her jealous gangster fiance. Veteran farceur Howerd leads a competent cast, but a more authentic staging of the opera would probably have been better.

p, Harold Baim; d, Michael Winner; w, Winner, Maurice Browning, Lew Schwartz (based on the opera "The Miado" by W. S. Gilbert and Arthur Sullivan); ph, (Eastmancolor).

Musical **(PR:A MPAA:NR)**

THE COOL ONES* (1967) 98m WB c

Roddy McDowall *(Tony)*, Debbie Watson *(Hallie)*, Gil Peterson *(Cliff)*, Phil Harris *(MacElwaine)*, Robert Coote *(Stan)*, Nita Talbot *(Dee Dee)*, George Furth *(Howie)*, Mrs. Elvira Miller *(Mrs. Miller)*, Jim Begg *(Charles Forbes)*, James Milhollin *(Manager)*, Phil Arnold *(Uncle Steve)*, Melanie Alexander *(Sandy)*, the Bantams, Glen Campbell, The Leaves, T. J. and the Fourmations.

In a spoof of the music business, matchmaker McDowall joins pop singer Watson on her way up and Peterson on his way down in a romantic linkup for a publicity stunt. Few surprises as action carries the two to stardom as a team anyway. Light no-brainer competently handled by production team. Songs: "The Cool Ones," "A Bad Woman's Love," "Whiz Bam Opener," "This Town," "High," "Up Your Totem Pole with Love," "Tantrum," "It's Your World," "Hands," "Baby, Baby, Your Love Is All I Need" (Lee

Hazlewood), "Where Did I Go Wrong?" (Billy Strange, Jack Lloyd), "It's Magic" (Sammy Cahn, Jule Styne).

p, William Conrad; d, Gene Nelson; w, Nelson, Robert Kaufman (based on a story by Joyce Geller); ph, Floyd D. Crosby (Panavision, Technicolor); m, Ernie Freeman; ed, James Heckart; art d, LeRoy Deane; set d, Ralph S. Hurst; cos, Howard Shoup; ch, Toni Basil.

Comedy/Musical   **(PR:A   MPAA:NR)**

COOL WORLD, THE½**   (1963) 125m Wiseman/Cinema 5 bw
Hampton Clayton (Duke), Yolanda Rodriguez (Luanee), Bostic Felton (Rod), Gary Bolling (Littleman), Carl Lee (Priest), Gloria Foster (Mrs. Custis), Georgia Burke (Grandma), Charles Richardson (Beep Bop), Bruce Edwards (Warrior), Teddy McCain (Saint), Ronald Perry (Savage), Lloyd Edwards (Foxy), Ken Sutherland (Big Jeff), Billy Taylor (Mission), Jay Brooks (Littleman's Father), Clarence Williams III (Blood), Claude Cave (Hardy), Marilyn Cox (Miss Dewpoint), Gloria Foster (Mrs. Custis), Jerome Raphel (Mr. Shapiro), Joe Oliver (Angel), J. C. Lee (Coolie), John Marriott (Hurst), Bert Donaldson (45), Joseph Dennis (Douglas Thurston), Maurice Sneed (Rocky), William Ford (Ace), Alfred Callymore (China), Ted Butler (Mr. Osborne), Pheta Canegata (Pheta), Nettie Avery (Big Daddy), Riley Mac (Mac), Sandra McPherson (Coney Island Girl), Wilbur Green (Priest's Buddy), Val Bisoglio, Vic Romano (Gangsters), Dean Cohen, Peter De Anda, Alan Mercer, William Canegata (Cops), George W. Goodman (Newscaster), Richard Ward (Street Speaker), Esther Bodie, Irma Williams (Ladies), Milton Williams, Evadney Canegata.

Film focuses on Clayton's efforts to rise to authority in his Harlem street gang after hearing a Black Muslim evangelist spouting words of hate against whites and claiming black supremacy. Effective look at the mind-set of bored youths who see violence as a way out of the ghetto. Jazz background music adds texture to camera work, emphasizing Harlem rhythms and a sense of desperation. Characters are well-etched, making a clear statement about tenement life and how federal laws fail to better conditions.

p, Frederick Wiseman; d, Shirley Clarke; w, Clarke (based on the novel by Warren Miller and the play by Miller and Robert Rossen); ph, Baird Bryant; m, Mal Waldron; ed, Clarke; set d, Roger Furman.

Drama   **Cas.**   **(PR:C-O   MPAA:NR)**

COOLEY HIGH*   (1975) 107m AIP c
Glynn Turman (Preach), Lawrence-Hilton Jacobs (Cochise), Garrett Morris (Mr. Mason), Cynthia Davis (Brenda), Corin Rogers (Pooter), Maurice Leon Havis (Willie), Joseph Carter Wilson (Tyrone), Shermann Smith (Stone), Norman Gibson (Robert), Maurice Marshall (Damon), Steven Williams (Jimmy Lee), Christine Jones (Sandra), Jackie Taylor (Johnny Mae), Lynn Caridine (Dorothy).

Film follows Chicago high school students Turman and Jacobs through girl trouble, school trouble, and law trouble and ranges from mass appeal comedy to deathly serious. Film has heart and warmth in the AMERICAN GRAFFITI vein. Everything carried out top notch in this sociological study of black youths with a touch of fun added.

p, Steve Krantz; d, Michael Schultz; w, Eric Monte; ph, Paul Von Brack (Movielab Color); m, Freddie Perren; ed, Christopher Holmes; art d, William B. Fosser.

Comedy/Drama   **(PR:C   MPAA:PG)**

COONSKIN½**   (1975) Bryanston 82m c
Barry White (Samson/Brother Bear), Charles Grodone (Preacher/Brother Fox), Scatman Crothers (Pappy/Old Man Bone), Phillip Thomas (Randy/Brother Rabbit).

Animated story of three rural black guys seeking a way out of the ghetto life of crime and vice. One becomes a manipulated sports hero, one seizes control of black crime in the area, and the other sells him out to the mafia. Plenty of gallows humor in this cynical and yet human story.

p, Albert S. Ruddy; d&w, Ralph Bakshi; ph, William A. Fraker (Technicolor); m, Chico Hamilton; ed, Donald Ernst; animation ph, Ted C. Bemiller.

Drama   **(PR:C   MPAA:R)**

COP, A   (1973, Fr.) 100m Corona-Oceania-Euro Film c (UN FILE)
Alain Delon (Coleman), Catherine Deneuve (Cathy), Richard Crenna (Simon), Riccardo Cucciolla (Paul), Michael Conrad (Costa), Andre Pousse (Albouis), Paul Crauchet (Morand), Simone Valere (Wife), Jean Desailly (Man).

Police inspector Delon, who achieves results by brutal treatment of suspects, abuses a penniless transvestite informer, the victim of a courageous act rather than false information, during an intercut of a bank holdup. The leader of the thieves is curiously a friend of Delon's, a sort of mirror image of crook and cop. They finally have it out, with the cop winning, while fragile beauty Deneuve gets little more than a walk-on as the woman carrying on with both of them.

p, Robert Dorfman; d, Jean-Pierre Melville; w, Melville; ph, Walter Wottitz (Eastmancolor); m, Michel Comobler; ed, Patricia Renaut; art d, Theo Meurisse.

Crime Drama   **(PR:O   MPAA:NR)**

COP HATER*   (1958) 75m UA bw
Robert Loggia (Steve Carelli), Gerald O'Loughlin (Mike Maguire), Ellen Parker (Teddy), Shirley Ballard (Alice), Russell Hardie (Lt. Byrne), Hal Riddle (Mercer), William Neff (Kling), Gene Miller (Killer), Miriam Goldina (Mama Lucy), Lincoln Kilpatrick (Dave Foster), Ralph Stanley (Willis), Ted Gunther (Havilland), John Seven, Glenn Cannon, Jerry Orbach, Vince Gardenia, Thomas Nello, Kate Harkin, Alan Manson, Sandra Stevens, Alan Bergnan, Joan Kalionzes, Lulu King, John Gerstad.

Murder mystery has a band of police searching the summer city streets of Manhattan for a cop-killer. Acting shows finesse without excess dramatics. Technical effort above par, making film almost poetic. Imaginative and interesting.

p&d, William Burke; w, Henry Kane (based on the novel by Ed McBain); ph, Burdi Contner; ed, Ed Sutherland.

Mystery   **(PR:C   MPAA:NR)**

COP-OUT*   (1967, Brit.) 95m Selmur/Cinerama c (GB: STRANGER IN THE HOUSE)
James Mason (John Sawyer), Geraldine Chaplin (Angela Sawyer), Bobby Darrin (Barney Teale), Paul Bertoya (Jo Christophorides), Ian Ogilvy (Desmond Flower), Bryan Stanyon (Peter Hawkins), Pippa Steel (Sue Phillips), Clive Morton (Col. Flower), James Hayter (Harley Hawkins), Megs Jenkins (Mrs. Christophorides), Lisa Daniely (Diana), Moira Lister (Mrs. Flower), Yootha Joyce (Girl at Shooting Range), John Menderson (Old Clerk), Rita Webb (Mrs. Plaskett), Danvers Walker (Chetham), Julian Orchard (Policeman), Ivor Dean (Inspector Colder), Marjie Lawrence (Brenda), Lindy Aaron (Angela as a Child), Lucy Griffiths (Library Cleaner), Charlotte Selwyn (Salesgirl), Melinda May (Librarian), Tom Kempinski (Shop Assistant), Sheila White (Hazel), Toni Palmer (Doorwoman), Michael Standing (Fashion Photographer), Anne Hart (Barmaid).

Mason is an alcoholic lawyer who has lived in seclusion since his wife left him fifteen years earlier. His daughter, Chaplin, runs around with a swinging crowd, and when one of them is found dead, evidence points to Bertoya, another member of the group. Mason comes out of retirement to defend the boy, and he finally pieces the puzzle together and exposes Ogilvy as the real killer. Mason's professionalism and talent redeem the scenes he's in, but the rest of the film is hopeless. Georges Simenon's novel was previously filmed in France in 1942 and released in the U.S. as STRANGER IN THE HOUSE in 1949.

p, Dimitri De Grunwald; d&w, Pierre Rouve (based on the novel Les Inconnus dans La Maison by Georges Simenon); ph, Ken Higgins (Eastmancolor); m, Patrick John Scott; ed, Ernest Walter; art d, Tony Woolard; cos, Felix Evans; m/l, Scott, Vic Briggs "Ain't That So."

Crime Drama   **(PR:C-O   MPAA:NR)**

COPACABANA*   (1947) 90m UA bw
Groucho Marx (Lionel Devereaux), Carmen Miranda (Carmen Novarro), Steve Cochran (Steve Hunt), Gloria Jean (Anne), Ralph Sanford (Liggeti), Andy Russell (Himself).

Groucho, without his brothers, doesn't quite make it in this silly farce about the famous New York nightclub that Barry Manilow re-introduced with his hit song. Marx is a fast-talking small-time manager (not unlike BROADWAY DANNY ROSE) with only one client, Miranda. He gets her an audition at the Copa where she dons her usual Souse American accent and fruited hat. The owner (Cochran) likes her but he also needs a French chanteuse for the smaller room. Groucho, ever resourceful, puts Miranda in a wig and different outfit. She auditions for the other singing job and gets both of them. Further, Cochran won't take one without the other as he wants a package deal. This forces Miranda to do both gigs, managing a quick-change between the big floor show and the lounge. She is rapidly running down and something must be done so Groucho concocts a fight between the two women behind closed doors. Cochran is making eyes at the French half of Carmen, so the story goes that the Brazilian whacked the Frenchwoman and sent her scampering. The police are called in by a distraught Cochran, who was really beginning to fall hard for the Gallic gal. Just when the cops are about to arrest Groucho for the murder of said woman, all is explained and the picture ends happily. A piece of fluff without too many good jokes. Chili Williams, the 1940s sexpot, does a brief bit and three well-known Broadway columnists (Louis Sobol, Abel Green, and Earl Wilson) play themselves. Producer Coslow wrote several songs, none of which was memorable. The only tune anyone can recall from the picture is "Tico, Tico." Songs: "Je Vous Amie," "Stranger Things Have Happened," "My Heart Was Doing a Bolero," "Let's Do the Copacabana," "I Haven't Got a Thing To Sell," "We've Come to Copa" (Coslow), "Tico Tico" (Ervin Drake, Aloysio Oliveira, Zequinha Abreu).

p, Sam Coslow; d, Alfred E. Green; w, Laslo Vadnay, Alan Boretz, Howard Harris (based on a story by Vadnay); ph, Bert Glennon; ed, Philip Cahn; ch, Larry Ceballos.

Musical Comedy   **Cas.**   **(PR:A   MPAA:NR)**

COPPER, THE*   (1930, Brit.) 82m British International-Suedfilm bw (DER GREIFER)
Charlotte Susa, Hans Albers, Margot Walter, Herman Blass, Karl Ludwig Diehl, Harry Hardt, Hugh Fischer-Koeppe.

Lively detective yarn by one of Germany's most successful prewar directors puts Albers and Susa through their paces in a genuine action interest film. An early all talkie, Susa's fine voice comes across with an exaggeration in tone, and Albers, for a German, looks like a true Scotland Yard copper as everybody imagines them.

p&d, Richard Eichberg; w, Rudolp Katscher, Egon Els; ph, Heinrich Gartner.

Drama   **(PR:A   MPAA:NR)**

COPPER CANYON*   (1950) 83m PAR bw
Ray Milland (Johnny Carter), Hedy Lamarr (Lisa Roselle), Macdonald Carey (Lane Travis), Mona Freeman (Caroline Desmond), Harry Carey, Jr. (Lt. Ord), Frank Faylen (Mullins), Hope Emerson (Ma Tarbet), Taylor Holmes (Theodosius Roberts), Peggy Knudsen (Cora), James Burke (Jeb Bassett), Percy Helton (Scamper), Phillip Van Zandt (Sheriff Wattling), Francis Pierlot (Moss Balfour), Erno Verebes (Professor), Paul Lees (Bat Laverne), Robert Watson (Bixby), Georgia Backus (Martha Bassett), Ian Wolfe (Mr. Henderson), Bob Kortman (Bill Newton), Nina Mae McKinney (Theresa), Len Hendry (Bartender), Earl Hodgins, Robert Stephenson (Miners), Buddy Roosevelt (Lew Partridge), Julie Faye (Proprietor's Wife), Joe Whitehead (Proprietor), Hank Bell (Man), Ethan Laidlaw, Russell Kaplan (Deputies), Alan Dinehart III (Youngest Bassett Boy), Rex Lease (Southerner), Stanley Andrews (Bartender), Kit

Guard *(Storekeeper/Miner)*, Stuart Holmes *(Barber/Townsman)*.

Debonair vaudeville marksman Milland hides his identity as a Confederate army officer wanted by the Union army on a theft charge. Though the Civil War is over, southerners asked him to aid them in their fight, but he declines. Undercover, he schemes to trick the guys who are after him and ends up wooing Lamarr. The two are responsible for the film's better action moments, which get a beautiful display of physical values through Lang's lenses.

p, Mel Epstein; d, John Farrow; w, Jonathan Latimer (based on a story by Richard English); ph, Charles B. Lang, Jr. (Technicolor); ed, Eda Warren; art d, Hans Dreier, Franz Bachelin; m/l, Jay Livingston.

Drama **(PR:A MPAA:NR)**

COPPER SKY* (1957) 76m FOX bw

Jeff Morrow *(Hack Williams)*, Coleen Gray *(Nora)*, Paul Brinegar *(Charlie Martin)*, William R. Hamel *(Trumble)*, Jack M. Lomas *(Lawson)*, Strother Martin *(Pokey)*, John Pickard *(Trooper Hadley)*, Patrick O'Moore *(Col. Thurston)*, Rocky Shahan *(Stunt Man)*, Bill McGraw *(Man No. 1)*, Jerry Oddo *(Juror)*, Rush Williams *(Corporal)*, Rod Redwing *(Indian)*.

This is sort of a sleazy, western AFRICAN QUEEN with Morrow and Gray as the sole survivors of an Indian massacre. He's the town drunk, she's a schoolteacher. They set off together for the nearest white settlement and safety; Gray, blathering and moralizing the whole time while Morrow stares morosely off into space and wishes he had another drink. May set a record high for lack of action.

p, Robert Stabler; d, Charles Marquis Warren; w, Eric Nordon (based on a story by Stabler); ph, Brydon Baker (RegalScope Color); ed, Fred W. Berger; m, Raoul Kraushaar; m/l, Kraushaar, Joe and Marilyn Hooven.

Western **(PR:A MPAA:NR)**

COPS AND ROBBERS½** (1973) 89m UA c

Cliff Gorman *(Tom)*, Joe Bologna *(Joe)*, Dick Ward *(Paul Jones)*, Sheppard Strudwick *(Eastpoole)*, John Ryan *(Patsy)*, Ellen Holly *(Secretary)*, Nino Ruggeri *(Bandell)*, Gayle Gorman *(Mary)*, Lee Steel *(Hardware Store Owner)*, Frances Foster *(Black Lady)*, Arthur Pierce, Martin Cove *(Attendants)*, Jim Ferguson *(Clerk)*, Walter Gorney *(Wino)*, Frank Gio *(Rocco)*, Jeff Ossuno *(Ed)*, Joseph Spinell *(Marty)*, George Harris II *(Harry)*, Lucy Martin *(Grace)*, Jacob Weiner *(Thief)*.

Two cops turned crooks devise a plan to steal $10 million in pay-to-bearer certificates from a Manhattan investment company, timing their caper to coincide with a parade of visiting astronauts, figuring everyone will be so busy watching the parade they will forget to mind the store. They get through an intricate security system and then they hear over a closed-circuit system that cops are closing in for a holdup in the building, and rather than be caught with the goods in their effort to escape, they put the certificates through a paper shredder after which the shreds are tossed down on the astronauts along with the ticker tape. A fair amount of suspense and some laughs, with good performances by Gorman and Bologna.

p, Elliott Kastner; d, Aram Avakian; w, Donald E. Westlake; ph, David Quaid (DeLuxe Color); m, Michel Legrand; ed, Barry Malkin; art d, Gene Rudolph; cos. John Boyt.

Crime Drama **(PR:A MPAA:PG)**

COQUETTE½** (1929) 75m UA bw

Mary Pickford *(Norma Besant)*, Johnny Mack Brown *(Michael Jeffery)*, Matt Moore *(Stanley Wentworth)*, John Sainpolis *(Dr. John Besant)*, William Janney *(Jimmy Besant)*, Henry Kolker *(Jasper Carter)*, George Irving *(Robert Wentworth)*, Louise Beavers *(Julia)*.

Based on an original play by George Abbott and Ann Preston, which they wrote for Helen Hayes, COQUETTE is a creaky drama that served to introduce the previously silent Pickford to the talkies. Surprisingly, she beat out Jeanne Eagels for the Best Actress Oscar in this role and it was a wonderment. She had a lovely voice (something in short supply among many of the silent stars who could not make the transition) and she looked marvelous, but the minute movies began to speak, Mary began to fade, and no one could understand why. She made KIKI in 1931 and SECRETS in 1933 and, of course, her one appearance with husband, Doug Fairbanks, in THE TAMING OF THE SHREW, but this was the start of the end for Pickford. She is a flapper down south with a flirtatious nature. She falls hard for Brown (before he became the cowboy star) who is hated by her father, Sainpolis. Her dad despises the young man so much he shoots him and Brown and Pickford do a death scene that's the highlight of the picture. Next, daddy commits suicide and leaves Mary to face the world on her own. Not a lot of laughs, is it? The stage version had the heroine killing herself but movie audiences would have risen in revolt if America's Sweetheart had done that. She changed her hair style for this film and went far astray from the goody-goody girls she'd played for so long. Perhaps she shouldn't have. COQUETTE was made when Pickford was in her late thirties and still able to convince audiences of her relative innocence; a tribute to her acting ability.

d, Sam Taylor; w, John Grey, Allen McNeil, Taylor (based on a play by George Abbott, Anne Preston); ph, Karl Struss.

Drama **(PR:C MPAA:NR)**

CORDELIA½** (1980, Fr., Can.) 118m National Film Board of Canada c

Louise Portal *(Cordelia Viau)*, Gaston Lepage *(Samuel Parslow)*, Pierre Gobeil *(Isidore Poirier)*, Gilbert Sicotte *(M. Leduc)*, Raymond Cloutier *(Joseph Fortier)*, Jean-Louis Roux *(Judge Taschereau)*, James Blendick *(Hangman Radcliff)*, Rolland Bedard *(Jailer Grouix)*.

This is a beautifully photographed film recreating the 1899 story of the only murder conviction in Canada based solely on circumstantial evidence. Cordelia Viau, a nonconforming, vampish housewife, was accused, along with her handyman Parstow, of murdering her husband who was found in bed with his throat cut. Both had strong alibis for the night of the murder but the crown's case hung on flimsy conflicting testimony of two witnesses on whether a lamp in the window was on or off that fateful night. One witness, an old friend of the deceased, denied the lamp was lit and his testimony condemned the couple to death. That they were railroaded to their deaths by the puritanical attitudes of the townspeople and sensationalist press coverage is clear both in the movie and in real life. The double hanging was enthusiastically attended by crowds from all over Canada, the U.S., and even France. The story fails however, making the same mistake Cordelia's lawyer made during the trial, insisting on the couple's innocence, painting them as victims of society but not explaining the fact of the murdered man. It is unfortunate that this fascinating tale of murder comes across as weakly as it does, but the photography is exquisite and worth the trip.

p, Jean-Marc Garand; d, Jean Beaudin; w, Beaudin, Marcel Sabourin (based on the novel *La Lampe dans La Fenetre* by Pauline Cadieux); ph, Pierre Mignot; m, Maurice Blackburn; ed, Beaudin; art d, Denis Boucher, Vianney Gauthier.

Crime Drama **(PR:C-O MPAA:NR)**

CORKY** (1972) 88m MGM c (AKA: LOOKIN' GOOD)

Robert Blake *(Corky)*, Charlotte Rampling *(His Wife)*, Patrick O'Neal *(Randy)*, Christopher Connelly *(Billy)*, Pamela Payton-Wright *(Rhonda)*, Ben Johnson *(Boland)*, Laurence Luckinbill *(Wayne)*, Paul Stevens *(Tobin)*.

Blake is a loser from the deep south. Rampling, doing her best to disguise her British accent with a cornpone overlay, is his wife. He's selfish, arrogant, biased, and annoying. She is long-suffering. Together, they make for as unattractive a couple as one could ever hope to find on any screen. Producer Geller so hated the treatment accorded this movie by James Aubrey, MGMogul in charge, that he removed his name from the screenplay and attempted to take it off as producer but could not, due to contractual obligations. Blake has this cherry car that he loves and spends more time with than he does with his wife. She takes a job working for Johnson and Blake gets jealous and accuses the two of infidelity. A fight ensues and soon enough Blake is wanted by the police. A chase and, little by little, Blake's gorgeous car is dinged and whacked and he winds up driving it in a Demolition Derby and destroying it altogether. Nobody wanted to take credit or blame for this movie. Eugene Price, solo writer credit, claims that very little of what he wrote remains and the connecting material that explained why Blake's character was the way he was was edited out. Director Horn did not have much of an opportunity to put the sort of humor he was so good at into this film. Horn's best job, before his early death, was directing the TV pilot of "Wonder Woman" with Linda Carter. Geller also died young, in a plane crash with ABC-TV executive Steve Gentry. They were practicing takeoffs and landings in the Santa Barbara area and evidently misinterpreted a radio signal, turning the plane in the wrong direction and slamming into the side of a mountain. Price went on to become a successful soap opera writer and was once part of "The Texas Trio"—three well-known Lone Star state writers who all had offices in the same small building in Beverly Hills; Price, Jack Sowards (STAR TREK, TWO), and David Westheimer (MY SWEET CHARLIE, VON RYAN'S EXPRESS). In that building at the same time were well-known TV writers Budd Grossman, Martin Ragaway, actress-novelist Joanna Barnes, novelist John Sherlock, screenwriter Karen Raskind, playwright Ben Starr, and five others who came and went. Price was one of the many writers who would be called in for summit meetings when one of the other writers was stuck on a story and needed a few more brains to help unstick the problems. That was before he wrote the screenplay of CORKY. Had it been concurrently, many of the problems might have been solved.

p, Bruce Geller; d, Leonard Horn; w, Eugene Price; ph, David Walsh (Metrocolor); m, Jerry Styner, John Parker; ed, Hugh S. Fowler, Albert P. Wilson; art d, George W. Davie, Walter Scott Herndon; m/l, Jeff Barry, Larry Murray, James Hendricks.

Drama **(PR:A-C MPAA:PG)**

CORKY OF GASOLINE ALLEY** (1951) 80m COL bw

Scotty Beckett *(Corky)*, JImmy Lydon *(Skeezix)*, Don Beddoe *(Walt Wallet)*, Gordon Jones *(Elwood Martin)*, Patti Brady *(Judy)*, Susan Morrow *(Hope)*, Kay Christopher *(Nina)*, Madelon Mitchel *(Phyllis)*, Dick Wessel *(Pudge McKay)*, Harry Tyler *(Avery)*, Ralph Votrian *(Larry)*, John Doucette *(Rocky)*, Charles Williams *(Morde)*, Lester Matthews *(Ellis)*, Jack Rice *(Ames)*, Ludwig Stossel *(Dr. Hammerschlag)*, John Dehner *(Jefferson Jay)*, Lewis Russel *(Hull)*.

All the folks who ever peopled Gasoline Alley unite to deal with the problems caused by the black sheep cousin of Corky's wife, a drifter who has moved in to sponge off the Wallets. He raids the fridge, spoils the kid's games, blows up the stove in Corky's diner, wrecks Skeezix's Fixit-Shop with chemical pills he hopes will triple the octane rating of ordinary gasoline, and then feigns a back injury so he can continue his mooching. A few bright moments but basically overlong and heavy-handed. (See GASOLINE ALLEY series, Index.)

p, Wallace MacDonald; d&w, Edward Bernds (based on the comic strip by Frank O. King); ph, Henry Freulich; ed, Jerome Thomas; md, Mischa Bakaleinikoff.

Comedy **(PR:AA MPAA:NR)**

CORN IS GREEN, THE*½** (1945) 114m WB bw

Bette Davis *(Miss Lilly Moffat)*, John Dall *(Morgan Evans)*, Joan Lorring *(Bessie Watty)*, Nigel Bruce *(The Squire)*, Rhys Williams *(Mr. Jones)*, Rosalind Ivan *(Mrs. Watty)*, Mildred Dunnock *(Miss Ronberry)*, Gwyneth Hughes *(Sarah Pugh)*, Billy Roy *(Idwal Morris)*, Thomas Louden *(Old Tom)*, Arthur Shields *(William Davis)*, Leslie Vincent *(John Owen)*, Robert Regent *(Rhys Norman)*, Tony Ellis *(Will Hughes)*, Elliott Dare *(Glyn Thomas)*, Robert Cherry *(Dai Evans)*, Gene Ross *(Gwilym Jones)*, George Mathews *(Trap Driver)*, Brandon Hurst *(Lewellyn Powell)*, Herbert Evans, Billy Evans, David Hughes, Robert Cory *(Miners in Bar)*, Rhoda Williams *(Wylodine)*, Stub Mussellman, Bert Speiser *(Bits)*.

The year is 1895 and schoolmistress Davis has come to a small mining town in Wales, Glensarno, to live in a home she has recently been willed. She is shocked to find many of the miners illiterate and living in abject poverty. She opens a school with her own money and teaches basic skills to any of the poor villagers who wish to avail themselves of it. Her housekeeper, an ex-shoplifter (Ivan) who has now become born again, and her trollop daughter (Lorring), both think the whole idea is dreadful and will never catch on. Davis encourages Dunnock and Williams to join her as assistant teachers. Bruce is a rich landowner who is against the school. If the young children get an education they'll see what life can be, they'll leave the mines, they'll rebel, etc. Davis finds a building in the heart of town that would be perfect but Bruce will not lease it to her, so she converts her home into the school and opens for business. Dall is an aggressive, rude, and angry young man who soon demonstrates that he also has a touch of brilliance. Davis had been ready to toss it all in but when she sees how Dall is responding she spends the next two years working with him. The scenes with the two of them, as student learns from teacher, are a joy and highlight the middle of the film and the original Emlyn Williams play. Davis pushes Dall to enter Oxford and the pressure is too much for the young man. He walks out, gets drunk, and winds up seducing (or, more to the point, being seduced by) Lorring. Soon enough, Dall resumes his studies and then, a short time later, Lorring happily announces that she is carrying Dall's child. Davis doesn't want to let Dall know that so she bribes Lorring to leave Glensarno. Many months later Dall is leaving to study at Oxford when Lorring arrives with their baby. Dall is torn between his desire to get an education and his guilt about the child. He decides to stay in the village, marry Lorring, and give the child a decent life. Davis sees another solution and offers to adopt the baby to give Dall the chance to make something of himself. Lorring doesn't love Dall and actually got pregnant in a fit of pique after an argument with Davis, so she agrees. Dall leaves and the baby is safe in Davis's care. Sybil Thorndike did the role on Broadway for well over a year but the studio wanted to lead with a heavyweight so they padded out the svelte Davis to simulate the thickness of middle age. She was actually 37 when the film was made. The film team was respectful of the stage play, perhaps a bit too much so. In today's more sophisticated eyes, we can see it's an obvious back-lot set that serves as the village, but it doesn't matter as the acting is uniformly good and the script is presented intelligently. Dall and Lorring were both nominated by the Academy for their work in THE CORN IS GREEN. Neither ever realized much success after this film other than Dall's devilish work in Hitchcock's ROPE. Producer Chertok later presented "My Favorite Martian" to America.

p, Jack Chertok; d, Irving Rapper; w, Casey Robinson, Frank Cavett (based on the play by Emlyn Williams); ph, Sol Polito; m, Max Steiner; ed, Frederick Richards; art d, Carl Jules Weyl; set d, Fred M. MacLean; cos, Orry-Kelly.

Drama   **(PR:A   MPAA:NR)**

CORNBREAD, EARL AND ME**½   (1975) 94m AIP c
Moses Gunn (Blackwell), Rosalind Cash (Sarah), Bernie Casey (Atkins), Madge Sinclair (Leona), Keith Wilkes (Cornbread), Tierre Turner (Earl), Antonio Fargas (One Eye), Vincent Martorano (Golich), Charles Lampkin (Jenkins), Stack Pierce (Sam), Logan Ramsey (Deputy Coroner), Thalmus Rasulala (Charlie), Bill Henderson (Watkins), Sarina C. Grant (Mrs. Parsons), Stefan Gierasch (Sgt. Danaher), Larry Fishburne III (Wilford), The Blackbyrds (Themselves).

A young black basketball star, raised in the ghetto, the hope of his community, is mistakenly slain by a police officer. While this script is uneven, a good job is done of portraying ghetto life in an affectionate and moving way without reverting to stereotypes. Keith Wilkes (former UCLA All-American, later playing with the NBA's Golden State Warriors) plays the title role with charm and conviction and the picture goes to great lengths to portray the sensitive situation in three-dimensional terms. Unfortunately the courtroom scenes bog it down.

p&d, Joe Manduke; w, Leonard Lamensdorf (based on the novel Hog Butcher by Ronald Fair); ph, Jules Brenner (Movielab Color); ed, Aaron Stell; m, Donald Byrd; art d, David Haber; cos, Ann McCarthy.

Drama   **(PR:C   MPAA:NR)**

CORNERED*½   (1932) 58m COL bw
Tim McCoy, Shirley Grey, Niles Welch, Raymond Hatton, Lloyd Ingraham, Claire McDowell, Charles King, John Eberts, John Elliott, Walter Long, Bob Kortman, Art Mix, Merrill McCormack, Noah Beery, Sr., Artie Ortego, Jim Corey, Edward Piel, Ray Jones, Jack Evans, Blackie Whiteford.

Not one of McCoy's better efforts; he spends his time riding in circles after the bad guy while pretending not to see Grey batting her cow girl eyes in his whooping direction.

d, B. Reeves Eason; w, Wallace MacDonald (based on a story by Ruth Todd); ph, John Stumar; ed, Otto Meyer.

Western   **(PR:A   MPAA:NR)**

CORNERED***½   (1945) 102m RKO bw
Dick Powell (Gerard), Walter Slezak (Incza), Micheline Cheirel (Mme. Jarnac), Nina Vale (Senora Camargo), Morris Carnovsky (Santana), Edgar Barrier (DuBois), Steven Geray (Senor Camargo), Jack La Rue (Diego), Luther Adler (Marcel Jarnac), Gregory Gay (Perchon), Jean Del Val (1st Prefect), Igor Dolgoruki (Swiss Hotel Clerk), Ellen Corby (French Maid), Louis Mercier (Rougon), Jacques Lory (French Clerk), Martin Cichy (Jopo), George Renevant (2nd Prefect), Nelson Leigh (Dominion Official), Leslie Dennison (Finance Officer), Tanis Chandler (Airline Hostess), Egon Brecher (Insurance Man), Gloria De Guarda, Beverly Bushe (Girls), Hans Moebus, Joaquin Elizondo, Warren Jackson (Men), Byron Foulger (Night Clerk), Michael Mark (Elevator Operator), Ken McDonald (Businessman), Al Murphy (Bartender), Al Walton, Milton Wallace (Waiters), Cy Kendall (Detective), Belle Mitchell (Hotel Maid), Simone La Brousse (Maria), Carlos Barbe (Regules), Hugh Prosser (Police Assistant), Jerry de Castro (Taxi Driver), Stanley Price (Hotel Clerk), Nestor Paiva (Police Official), Frank Mills (Stumblebum), Carl De Lora (Mean-faced Man), Richard Clark (Cab Driver), Paul Bradley (Policeman), Rod De Medici (Bellboy).

A provocative and powerful film noir entry, CORNERED has Powell as an ex-Canadian officer having survived a POW camp seeking a mysterious Vichy official and Nazi collaborator, Adler, who caused the death of his French wife. Although all reports have Adler dead (like Martin Bormann and the insidious Josef Mengele), Powell refuses to believe the war criminal is under the sod. He pursues leads through Switzerland and then to Buenos Aires where he encounters an underground group of Nazi-hunters, Carnovsky, Barrier, and La Rue. The hunter's quest is further complicated when he finds himself drawn to attractive Cheirel, who had married the vicious Adler, especially after he is convinced that she has never even met Adler, that she married him by proxy so she and her invalid sister, daughters of a collaborator, could safely immigrate. Powell then learns that Geray and his wife are in league with pro-Nazi forces and may be the links to Adler. Following Slezak, a notorious double-dealer and aide to Geray, he finds Adler in a nightclub but not before Slezak is killed by Geray on Adler's orders. Adler attacks Powell with a knife and at that moment Powell goes blank, suffering one of his recurrent spells from wartime shock. He regains his senses and discovers that he has strangled the Nazi. Carnovsky and Barrier help him out of the club and arrange for his passage back to Canada. CORNERED is a superb suspense film, tightly directed by the talented Dmytryk. Powell is at his tough-talking, hardboiled best as a man seeking vengeance with cold-blooded determination but one who convincingly agonizes over the image of his murdered wife, showing his humanity in that subdued, clipped technique uniquely Powell's. The story for CORNERED, or at least the film's title, came from a loose story written by Ben Hecht. It was flimsy, announced Dmytryk, who felt Hecht had merely put his name to a tale written by one of his many collaborators and collected the lion's share of the $50,000 payment, as he was wont to do on occasion. Several writers were brought into the project, including John Wexley, author of THE LAST MILE and a pal of producer Scott, both avowed Communists, according to Dmytryk, who packed a great deal of far left credo into a script without much action. John Paxton was next brought in and toned down the rhetoric, adding pace and intense scenes with crackling dialog. Dmytryk had problems when arriving to set up location shooting in Buenos Aires. Evita Peron, wife of Argentina's military dictator, had appropriated most of the available raw film for use in films depicting her own bad melodramas, leaving the director to scratch around for negative. The director nevertheless finished the film on time and inside his budget, although he later stated that Wexley summoned him and Scott to a Communist cell meeting where he upbraided them for removing party philosophy from the film and then demanded that they be kicked out of the party for doing so. This led, according to Dmytryk, to his quitting the Communist Party in Hollywood. Powell's performance in CORNERED came quickly on the heels of MURDER, MY SWEET, his first tough-guy film and it made even more money than that great crime classic.

p, Adrian Scott; d, Edward Dmytryk; w, John Paxton (based on a story by John Wexley and a title by Ben Hecht); ph, Harry J. Wild; m, Roy Webb; ed, Joseph Noriega; md, Constantin Bakaleinikoff; art d, Albert S. D'Agostino, Carroll Clark; set d, Darrell Silvera; cos, Renie.

Thriller/Crime Drama   **(PR:C   MPAA:NR)**

CORONADO**   (1935) 77m PAR bw
Jack Haley (Chuck Hornbostel), Andy Devine (Pinky Falls), Leon Errol (Otto Wray), Alice White (Violet Wray Hornbostel), Johnny Downs (Johnny Marvin), Betty Burgess (June Wray), Jameson Thomas (Carlton), Berton Churchill (Walter Marvin), Nella Walker (Mrs. Gloria Marvin), James Burke (Slug Moran), Jacqueline Wells (Barbara Forrest), Eddie Duchin Orchestra.

Flat little musical about a wealthy young man and the poor, seaside resort singer he falls in love with. Film suffered a painful and humiliating demise at the box office in spite of fairly good songs and the Eddie Duchin Orchestra. Songs: "All's Well In Coronado By The Sea," "You Took My Breath Away," "How Do I Rate With You?" "Keep Your Fingers Crossed," "Midsummer Madness," "Down On The Beach At Oomph," "Mashed Potatoes" (Sam Coslow, Richard A. Whiting), "I've Got Some New Shoes" (Coslow, Walter Bullock, Whiting), "Which Is Which?" (Sidney Clare, Troy Sanders).

p, William LeBaron; d, Norman McLeod; w, Don Hartman, Frank Butler (based on a story by Brian Hooker and Hartman); ph, Gilbert Warrenton; ed, Hugh Bennett; ch, LeRoy Prinz.

Musical   **(PR:A   MPAA:NR)**

CORONER CREEK***   (1948) 89m Producers-Actors/COL c
Randolph Scott (Chris Danning), Marguerite Chapman (Kate Hardison), George Macready (Younger Miles), Sally Eilers (Della Harms), Edgar Buchanan (Sheriff O'Hea), Barbara Reed (Abbie Miles), Wallace Ford (Andy West), Forrest Tucker (Ernie Combs), William Bishop (Leach Conover), Joe Sawyer (Frank Yordy), Russell Simpson (Walt Hardison), Douglas Fowley (Stew Shallis), Lee Bennett (Tip Henry), Forrest Taylor (McCune), Phil Schumacher (Bill Arnold), Warren Jackson (Ray Flanders).

The first western from Scott and Brown's Producers-Actor's production company (later to produce the brilliant Bud Boetticher films that would make Scott a western icon). The film opens with an Indian attack on a stagecoach and the suicide of Scott's bride-to-be. Scott tracks the money stolen from the stage to the town of Coroner Creek where villain Macready has used the money to make himself a respected citizen. A long brutal fight with henchman Tucker, during which each stomps on the gun hand of the other, leaves Scott unable to shoot for the rest of the film. Just as he is about to take his revenge on Macready, the villain falls on the very knife Scott's fiancee used to kill herself. An important western; one that marks the transition from the simple-minded horse operas of the 1930s and 1940s to later adult themes and sensibilities of the genre.

p, Harry Joe Brown; d, Ray Enright; w, Kenneth Gamet (based on a novel by Luke Short); ph, Fred H. Jackman (Cinecolor); m, Rudy Schrager; ed, Harvey Manger.

Western   **PR:C   MPAA:NR)**

CORPSE CAME C.O.D., THE½   (1947) 86m COL bw
George Brent *(Joe Medford)*, Joan Blondell *(Rosemary Durant)*, Adele Jergens *(Mona Harrison)*, Jim Bannon *(Detective Mark Wilson)*, Leslie Brooks *(Peggy Holmes)*, John Berkes *(Larry Massey)*, Fred Sears *(Detective Dave Short)*, William Trenk *(Fields)*, Grant Mitchell *(Mitchell Edwards)*, Una O'Connor *(Nora)*, Marvin Miller *(Rudy Frasso)*, William Forrest *(Lance Fowler)*, Mary Field *(Felice)*, Cliff Clark *(Emmett Willard)*, Wilton Graff *(Maxwell Kenyon)*, Cosmo Sardo *(Hector Rose)*, Judy Stevens *(Specialty Singer)*, Lane Chandler *(Prison Guard)*, Robert Kellard, Myron Healy, Paul Bryar, Michael Towne *(Reporters)*, Martha West *(Cigarette Girl)*, Leon Lenoir *(Waiter)*.

When a corpse turns up in a box of dresses sent to whistle-bait movie star Jergens, Hollywood reporter Brent and rival reporter Blondell get on the case. They trace it back to a ring of jewel thieves led by crooked detective Bannon. Lightweight comedy is okay, but no more.

p, Samuel Bischoff; d, Henry Levin; w, George Bricker, Dwight Babcock (based on the novel by Jimmy Starr); ph, Lucien Andriot; m, George Duning; ed, Jerome Thoms; md, Morris Stoloff; art d, Stephen Goosson, George Brooks; set d, Wilbur Menefee, James Crowe; m/l, "He's Got A Warm Kiss" (Allan Roberts, Doris Fisher).
Comedy   (PR:A   MPAA:NR)

CORPSE GRINDERS, THE zero   (1972) 72m Geneni c
Sean Kenney *(Dr. Howard Glass)*, Monika Kelly *(Angie Robinson)*, Sanford Mitchell *(Landau)*, J. Byron Foster *(Maltby)*, Warren Ball *(Caleb)*, Ann Noble *(Cleo)*, Vince Barbi *(Monk)*, Harry Lovejoy *(The Neighbor)*, Earl Burnam *(De Sisto)*, Zenna Foster *(Mrs. Babcock)*, Ray Dannis *(Babcock)*, Charles Fox *(Willie)*, Stephen Lester *(Mortician)*, William Kirschner *(B.K.)*, George Bowden *(David)*, Don Ellis *(Factory Workman)*, Mike Garrison *(Assistant to De Sisto)*, Andy Collings *(De Sisto's Secretary)*, Mary Ellen Burke *(Annie)*, Curt Matson *(Paul, The Stranger)*, Drucilla Hoy *(Tessie)*.

Sick horror comedy about a doctor and his nurse (Kenney and Kelly) investigating why harmless housecats are turning bloodthirsty and attacking their masters. They come to find out that grave robbers Mitchell and Foster are selling their wares to a cat food company. Bad in every sense, yet a minor cult classic.

p&d, Ted V. Mikels; w, Arch Hall, Joseph L. Cranston; ph, Bill Anneman (Eastmancolor); prod d, John Robinson, Laura Young; ed, Mikels.
Horror/Comedy   (PR:O   MPAA:NR)

CORPSE OF BEVERLY HILLS, THE**
                        (1965, Ger.) 85m Modern Art Film/Medallion Pictures bw/c
                                        (DIE TOTE VON BEVERLY HILLS;
                                        AKA: THAT GIRL FROM BEVERLY HILLS)
Heidelinde Weis *(Lu Sostlov)*, Klausjurgen Wussow *(C. G.)*, Horst Frank *(Manning/Dr. Steininger)*, Wolfgang Neuss *(Ben)*, Ernst Fritz Furbringer *(Prof. Sostlov)*, Peter Schutte *(Swendka)*, Bruno Dietrich *(Peter de Lorm)*, Alice Kessler, Ellen Kessler *(The Tiddy Sisters)*, Herbert Weissbach *(Priest)*, Walter Giller.

When Weis's naked corpse is found in a small woods in Beverly Hills, Detective Neuss goes through her diary and discovers a long series of affairs, though she is married to a Czech scientist. Following a lead that takes him to Las Vegas, Neuss finds the killer. Not terribly interesting. The flashback sequences are in color.

p, Hansjurgen Pohland; d, Michael Pfleghar; w, Peter Laregh, Pohland, Pfleghar (based on the novel *Die Tote von Beverly Hills* by Kurt Gotz); ph, Ernst Wild (Franscope, Eastmancolor); m, Heinz Kiessling; ed, Margot von Schlieffen; cos, Helmut Holger.
Crime   (PR:O   MPAA:NR)

CORPSE VANISHES, THE*½   (1942) 64m MON bw
Bela Lugosi *(Dr. Lorenz)*, Luana Walters *(Pat Hunter)*, Tristam Coffin *(Dr. Foster)*, Elizabeth Russell *(Countess)*, Minerva Urecal *(Fagah)*, Kenneth Harlan *(Keenan)*, Vince Barnett *(Sandy)*, Joan Barclay *(Alice)*, Frank Moran *(Angel)*, Angelo Rossitto *(Toby)*, Gwen Kenyon *(Peggy)*, George Eldridge *(Mike)*.

Lugosi's career was well on the skids by 1942, as this programmer testifies. He plays a mad botanist kidnaping brides from the altar to provide glandular injections needed to keep his 80-year-old wife (Russell) fresh and young. Assisting Lugosi are an old woman and her halfwit son (Urecal and Moran, respectively), and dwarf Rossitto. Walters is the girl reporter who cracks the case. Working a hint of Lugosi's vampire image into the film by having him and Russell sleep in matching coffins created a problem during the twenty days of shooting this quickie. When the time came for the couple to retire for the night, Russell was afraid to step into the coffin and refused to do the scene. A double was used instead.

p, Sam Katzman, Jack Dietz; d, Wallace Fox; w, Harvey Gates, Sam Robins, Gerald Schnitzer; ph, Art Reed; ed, Robert Golden.
Horror   **Cas.**   (PR:C   MPAA:NR)

CORPUS CHRISTI BANDITS**   (1945) 55m REP bw
Allan Lane *(Capt. James Christie/Corpus Christi Jim)*, Helen Talbot *(Dorothy)*, Twinkle Watts *(Nancy)*, Tom London *(Rocky)*, Francis McDonald *(Dad Christie)*, Jack Kirk *(Alonzo Adams)*, Roy Barcroft *(Wade Larkin)*, Kenne Duncan *(Spade)*, Bob Wilke *(Steve)*, Ruth Lee *(Mom Christie)*, Edward Cassidy *(Dan Adams)*, Emmett Vogan *(Governor)*, Dickie Dillon *(Brush)*, Freddie Chapman *(Stinky)*, Shelby Bacon *(Moonlight)*, Neal Hart, Horace B. Carpenter, Hal Price, Frank Ellis, Frank McCarroll, Henry Wills.

Lane plays a dual role as a veteran of WW II returning home, and a veteran of the Civil War returning home. The Civil War vet finds his home burned down and is unable to land a job. Desperate, he robs a stage to raise money to start again, but is tormented by guilt, leading him to try to redeem himself. Slightly above average series western with a serious theme.

d, Wallace A. Grissell; w, Norman S. Hall; ph, Bud Thackery; ed, Charles Craft; md, Richard Cherwin.
Western   (PR:A   MPAA:NR)

CORREGIDOR**   (1943) 74m PRC bw
Otto Kruger *(Jan Stockman)*, Elissa Landi *(Dr. Royce Lee)*, Donald Woods *(Michael)*, Frank Jenks *(Sgt. Mahoney)*, Rick Vallin *(Pinky)*, Wanda McKay *(Hey Dutch)*, Ian Keith *(Captain)*, Ruby Dandridge *(Hyacinth)*, Eddie Hall *(Brooklyn)*, Charles Jordan *(Bronx)*, Ted Hecht *(Filipino Lieutenant)*, Frank Hagney *(Lieutenant No. 2)*, Frank Jaquet *(Priest)*, Jack Rutherford *(General)*, John Grant *(Soldier No. 1)*, Stan Jolley *(Soldier No. 2)*, Jimmy Vilan *(No. 1 Boy)*, Gordon Hayes *(Marine)*.

Badly produced routine WW II propaganda film presents little action, using the heroic stand on "The Rock" in spring 1942 as a weak backdrop for an even weaker love triangle. Two doctors, Kruger and Woods, compete for the love of a third physician, Landi, when they are not operating on the endless lines of wounded soldiers inside an underground tunnel. Corregidor was honeycombed with such tunnels which allowed the poverty row PRC studio to confine its scenes to such claustrophobic quarters and use only stock footage of Japanese troops in their conquest of China a decade earlier. Only Kruger gives a palatable performance in a crudely directed vehicle. The beautiful Landi, an Italian actress of limited talent, had appeared in only a few significant films, including DeMille's SIGN OF THE CROSS, before she was shunted into cheap productions such as this. She was first given a hefty contract by William Fox in the early 1930s when he believed the story that her mother, Countess Zenardi Landi, was the illegitimate offspring of Empress Elizabeth of Austria. Hollywood, then nobility-struck, offered contracts right and left to anyone claiming a lofty title.

p, Dixon R. Harwin, Edward Finney; d, William Nigh; w, Doris Malley, Edgar Ulmer; ph, Ira L. Morgan; m, Leo Erdody; ed, Charles Henkel; md, David Chudnow.
War Drama   (PR:C   MPAA:NR)

CORRIDOR OF MIRRORS**½   (1948, Brit.) 105m GFD/Apollo bw
Eric Portman *(Paul Mangin)*, Edana Romney *(Mifanwy Conway)*, Barbara Mullen *(Veronica)*, Hugh Sinclair *(Owen Rhys)*, Bruce Belfrage *(Sir David Conway)*, Joan Maude *(Caroline Hart)*, Alan Wheatley *(Edgar Orsen)*, Leslie Weston *(Mortimer)*, Lois Maxwell *(Imogene)*, Valentine Dyall *(Defense)*, Christopher Lee *(Charles)*, John Penrose *(Brand)*, Leslie Weston *(Mortimer)*, Hugh Latimer *(Bing)*, Mavin Villiers *(Babs)*, Noel Howlett *(Psychiatrist)*, Gordon McLeod *(Prosecutor)*, Thora Hird *(Old Woman)*.

Artist Portman becomes obsessed with 400-year-old portrait of a young woman. He comes to believe himself the reincarnation of the girl's lover and sets out to find the reincarnation of the girl. He finds her in Romney, whom he takes back to his home and dresses in period clothing. Mullen is Portman's housekeeper, driven by jealousy to first try to scare away Romney, and finally to murder her, a crime for which Portman takes the blame. Christopher Lee makes his film debut in a minor part in this interesting melodrama. Two people involved in CORRIDOR OF MIRRORS expanded their artistic roles in the making of the film. Screenwriter Terence Young was making his directorial debut, which would carry him to DR. NO and a couple of other James Bond spectaculars, with their dazzling visual effects and dynamic pacing, and actress Romney helped write the screenplay.

p, Rudolph Cartier; d, Terence Young; w, Cartier, Edana Romney (based on a novel by Chris Massie); ph, Andre Thomas; m, Georges Auric; ed, Douglas Myers.
Drama   (PR:A   MPAA:NR)

CORRIDORS OF BLOOD***
                        (1962, Brit.) 85m Producers Associates/MGM bw
                                        (AKA: THE DOCTOR FROM SEVEN DIALS)
Boris Karloff *(Dr. Thomas Bolton)*, Betta St. John *(Susan)*, Finley Currie *(Dr. Matheson)*, Christopher Lee *(Resurrection Joe)*, Francis Matthews *(Dr. Jonathan Bolton)*, Adrienne Corri *(Rachel)*, Francis De Wolff *(Black Ben)*, Basil Dignam *(Chairman)*, Frank Pettingell *(Dr. Blount)*, Marian Spencer *(Mrs. Matheson)*, Carl Bernard *(Ned The Cow)*, Yvonne Warren *(Rosa)*, Charles Lloyd Pack *(Hardcastle)*, Robert Raglan *(Wilkes)*, John Gabriel *(Dispenser)*, Nigel Green *(Inspector Donovan)*, Howard Lang *(Chief Inspector)*, Julian D'Albie *(Bald Man)*, Roddy Hughes *(Man With Watch)*.

Karloff stars as a humanitarian London doctor attempting to develop a workable anesthetic that will end the pain and suffering involved in surgery in the days when hospitals were like torture chambers. Unfortunately, he performs the experiments on himself and slowly becomes addicted to drugs. Thinking he has found a proper anesthetic, he performs a demonstration of his pain-killing gas for an audience of physicians and students. Unexpectedly, the gas wears off too soon and Karloff's patient awakens during the operation and bolts from the table, attempting to attack the audience. Karloff is fired from his position and begins to become desperate for drugs (his access to them now cut off). In a seedy tavern he meets shady gravediggers De Wolff and Lee who sell cadavers to hospitals. They lure Karloff into their scheme by offering to supply him with drugs if he will sign phony death certificates for them. The doctor reluctantly agrees, but when the gravediggers kill a hospital guard, the police raid their hideout and Karloff is killed during a struggle. Eventually Karloff's son Matthews carries on his father's work and perfects an anesthetic. CORRIDORS OF BLOOD was produced in England in 1958, but wasn't released in the U.S. until 1962, after bit-player Lee had become a horror film star in his own right. Surprisingly, he had scarcely any contact with Karloff on the set of their first film together. The film has some early examples of British erotica, expanded, of course, for the continental versions, with whippings and a show of nipples in a disorderly house.

p, John Croydon, Charles Vetter; d, Robert Day; w, Jean Scott Rogers; ph, Geoffrey Faithfull; m, Buxton Orr; ed, Peter Mayhew; md, Frederick Lewis; art d, Anthony Masters.
Drama   (PR:C-O   MPAA:NR)

CORRUPT ONES, THE**   (1967, Ger.) 92m WB c
                (IL SIGILLO DE PECHINO; DIE HOLLE VON MACAO; LES CORROMPUS;
                                AKA:THE PEKING MEDALLION and HELL TO MACAO)
Robert Stack *(Cliff Wilder)*, Elke Sommer *(Lily)*, Nancy Kwan *(Tina)*, Christian

Marquand (Brandon), Werner Peters (Pinto), Maurizio Arena (Danny), Richard Haler (Kua-Song), Dean Heyde (Hugo), Ah-Yue-Lou (Chow), Marisa Merlini (Mme. Vulcano), Heide Bohlen (Jasmine).

Trashy adventure flick has Stack as a photographer pursued by Kwan from a Tong and Marquand from a crime syndicate. Both are after the key to an ancient Chinese emperor's tomb and Stack unwittingly has it. Originally titled HELL TO MACAO, it was retitled to capitalize on "The Untouchables," then in European syndication and very popular.

p, Arthur Brauner; d, James Hill; w, Brian Clemens (based on a story by Ladislas Fodor); ph, Heinz Pehlke (Techniscope, Technicolor); m, Georges Garvarentz; ed, Fred Srp; art d, Hans-Juergen Kiebach, Ernst Schomer; cos, Paul Seltenhammer; m/l, "The Corrupt Ones" (Buddy Kaye, Garvarentz).

Crime (PR:C MPAA:NR)

CORRUPTION* (1933) 67m Imperial bw
Evalyn Knapp (Ellen Manning), Preston Foster (Tim Butler), Charles Delaney (Charlie Jasper), Tully Marshall (Gorman), Natalie Moorhead (Sylvia Gorman), Warner Richmond (Regan), Huntley Gordon (D.A.), Lane Chandler (Assistant D.A.), Mischa Auer (Volkov), Jason Roberts (Police Commissioner), Gwen Lee (Mae).

Political leaders are being killed, the mayor has been framed, and no one can find the bullets. Finally it turns out that they were made of ice. Laughable crime picture, with Foster the wrongfully jailed mayor.

p, William Berke; d, Edward Roberts; w, Roberts, Charles Berner; ph, Robert Cline; ed, H. W. de Bouille, Finn Ulback.

Crime (PR:A MPAA:NR)

CORRUPTION** (1968, Brit.) 90m Titan/COL c
Peter Cushing (Sir John Rowan), Sue Lloyd (Lynn Nolan), Noel Trevarthen (Steve Harris), Kate O'Mara (Val Nolan), David Lodge (Groper), Anthony Booth (Mike Orme), Wendy Varnals (Terry), Billy Murray (Rik), Vanessa Howard (Kate), Jan Waters (Girl In Flat), Phillip Manikum (Georgie), Alexandra Dane (Sandy), Valerie Van Ost (Girl in Train), Victor Baring (Mortuary Attendant), Diana Ashley (Claire), Shirley Stelfox (Girl At the Party).

Brilliant surgeon Cushing, during a fight with a photographer, accidentally knocks a hot lamp onto the face of his wife (Lloyd), putting an abrupt end to her modeling career. He manages to restore her beauty with the help of fresh glands and his laser beam, but the restoration is short-lived, and Cushing is forced to kill prostitutes for their glands, storing their heads in his refrigerator. Finally a band of crazed hippies, enraged that one of their number has been killed by the doctor and his now completely flipped-out wife, besiege their country home. Lloyd turns on the laser beam, zapping everyone and everything. Cushing wakes up and realizes it was all a dream and he takes his beautiful wife to a party. Comically trashy.

p, Peter Newbrook; d, Robert Hartford-Davis; w, Donald and Derek Ford; ph, Newbrook (Perfect Color); m, Bill McGuffie; prod d, Bruce Grimes; ed, Don Deacon; spec eff, Michael Albrechtsen.

Horror (PR:O MPAA:R)

CORRUPTION OF CHRIS MILLER, THE** (1979, Span.) 107m Analysis Films c (AKA: BEHIND THE SHUTTERS)
Jean Seberg (Ruth), Marisol (Chris), Barry Stokes (Barney).

Pretentious, dull melodrama has Seberg (in her last film) as the stepmother of Marisol, with whom she may or may not be having an incestuous relationship. Into their tense existence comes Stokes, who goes about bedding both of them. Meanwhile, a series of hatchet murders are occurring over the countryside. Could one of these be involved? An annoying film, made palatable only by Seberg's presence. Filmed in 1972, but unreleased here until Seberg's death made her a box office attraction.

p, Xavier Armet; d, Juan Antonia Bardem; w, Santiago Moncada; ph, Juan Gelpi; m, Waldo de los Rios; ed, Emilio Rodriguez.

Drama (PR:O MPAA:NR)

CORSAIR*** (1931) 75m UA bw
Chester Morris (John Hawks), Alison Loyd [Thelma Todd] (Alison Corning), William Austin (Richard Bentinck), Frank McHugh ("Chub" Hopping), Emmett Corrigan (Stephen Corning), Fred Kohler (Big John), Fred Rice (Fish Face), Ned Sparks (Slim), Mayo Methot (Sophie).

Offbeat gangster film has Morris rejected by Loyd (Thelma Todd) because he fails to excite her. The one-time college football star then goes to work for her father Corrigan, a Wall Street swindler who is financing an enormous and lucrative bootlegging operation. Morris becomes his chief rum-runner who quits the racket in disgust. Next he forms his own sea-going gang and hijacks his former boss's shipments, selling them back to Corrigan. In their oddball philosophy, Loyd and Corrigan suddenly show deep respect for Morris' thievery. He manages to convince them of their errant ways and they reform but utterly escape retribution, a rare ending in an era when censors had their way. Morris is tough and quick to action while heavy Kohler as a derbie-wearing smuggler is truly scary. McHugh provides some chuckles as the tipsy playboy. West's direction is full of pep, even though the script is sometimes dizzy. Location shooting included New York and Miami, a crisp approach by top lenser June.

p&d, Roland West; Josephine Lovett (based on the novel by Walton Green); ph, Ray June, ed, Hal Kern.

Crime Drama (PR:C MPAA:NR)

CORSICAN BROTHERS, THE**** (1941) 111m UA bw
Douglas Fairbanks, Jr. (Mario/Lucien), Ruth Warrick (Isabelle), Akim Tamiroff (Colonna), J. Carrol Naish (Lorenzo), H. B. Warner (Dr. Paoli), John Emery (Tomasso),

Henry Wilcoxon (Count Franchi), Gloria Holden (Countess Franchi), Walter Kingsford (M. Dupre), Nana Bryant (Mme. Dupre), Pedro de Cordoba (Gravini), Veda Ann Borg (Maria), William Farnum (Priest), Sarah Padden (Nurse), Manart Kippen (Martelli), Ruth Robinson (Angela).

This incredible Dumas tale, which has some basis in fact, is brought to the screen with great gusto on the part of Fairbanks whose dashing feats rival in many scenes the acrobatic antics of his illustrious father. It is the tale of Siamese-type twin boys born in Corsica and separated by brilliant doctor Warner just before their parents and relatives are destroyed by Tamiroff's henchmen in a blood feud. One child is sent to Paris to be raised, the other into the mountains with family retainer Naish. When both grow to manhood they are introduced, Fairbanks playing both roles of Mario and Lucien with great skill, using his posture, facial workings, and voice modulations to make slight identity separations. He excels in showing how the emotional/intellectual telepathy works on each twin, particularly the agony one feels whenever the other is emotionally upset or physically wounded, and the jealousy he feels when the other falls in love with Warrick. The twins launch a military hit-and-run campaign against the island's tyrannical ruler Tamiroff, confusing him and his villainous lieutenant Emery until the final confrontation when one twin dies coming to the rescue of the other. Ratoff's direction is as eccentric as his poker-playing personality but he provides great pace and the script is excellent. Tamiroff plays his evil role with the usual gutteral relish, almost as if practicing for his superb bad guy, Pablo, in FOR WHOM THE BELL TOLLS. Always a delight to watch as he went through his hysterical antics, Tamiroff was almost a non compos mentis offscreen but had an inexplicable knack of being able to learn his lines instantly and know exactly what pose to strike before the cameras. The special effects are outstanding.

p, Edward Small; d, Gregory Ratoff; w, George Bruce (based on an adaptation of the Dumas novel by Bruce and Howard Estabrook); ph, Harry Stradling; ed, Grant Whytock, William Claxton; spec eff, Howard Anderson.

Adventure **Cas.** (PR:A MPAA:NR)

CORVETTE K-225**** (1943) 99m UNIV bw (GB: THE NELSON TOUCH)
Randolph Scott (Lt. Comdr. MacClain), James Brown (Paul Cartwright), Ella Raines (Joyce Cartwright), Barry Fitzgerald (Stooky O'Meara), Andy Devine (Walsh), Fuzzy Knight (Cricket), Noah Beery, Jr. (Stone), Richard Lane (Admiral), Thomas Gomez (Smithy), David Bruce (Rawlins), Murray Alper (Jones), James Flavin (Gardner), Walter Sande (Evans), Holmes Herbert (Convoy Commander), John Frederick (1st Officer), Oscar O'Shea (Merchant Ship Captain), Robert Mitchum (Shepard), Gene O'Donnell (Wardrobe Steward), John Diggs (Bailey), Edmund MacDonald (Lieutenant LeBlanc), Lester Matthews, Milburn Stone, Peter Lawford, Addison Richards, Oliver Prickett, George O'Hanlon.

Scott is superb as a skipper of a Canadian warship (the corvette being a bit smaller than a U.S. destroyer, a sleek, fast 200-foot-long craft packed with depth charges and guns) in this semi-documentary account of Atlantic convoys going to Russia. After having lost a ship to U-boats, Scott returns to Canada where he meets Raines who reluctantly falls in love with him; her older brother has been lost at sea and she's wary of becoming involved with a sailor. Scott is given command of a brand new ship, Corvette K-225, and takes Raines' younger brother, Brown, on board to make a seaman of him. The convoy to Russia, which occupies most of the film—the romance being ancillary—is fraught with dangers and loaded with action, many scenes taken from actual combat footage. Rosson's direction pops with lively scenes and the realistic script does much to make clear Canada's deep involvement in WW II, something that had been generally ignored by Hollywood in its fever to promote U.S. war films. Rosson and Guadio, his veteran cameraman, went to sea for three months, hazarding the U-boats in the Atlantic, to get background footage, along with using combat lensing by Harry Perry, who had gone on several corvette convoys to capture astounding battle shots. The result was an excellent production that still stands up today, unlike many of the propaganda films the studios churned out in the 1940s. John Rhodes Sturdy, an officer in the Royal Canadian Navy, was employed by Rosson as a technical advisor. He was so expert in his advice to the director that Rosson had him write the screenplay.

p, Howard Hawks; d, Richard Rosson; w, John Rhodes Sturdy; ph, Tony Gaudio (convoy cinematography Harry Perry); m, David Buttolph; ed, Edward Curtiss; spec eff, John Fultes.

War Drama (PR:A MPAA:NR)

CORVETTE SUMMER*** (1978) 105m UA c (GB: THE HOT ONE)
Mark Hamill (Kent Dantley), Annie Potts (Vanessa), Eugene Roche (Ed McGrath), Kim Milford (Wayne Lowry), Richard McKenzie (Principal), William Bryant (Police P.R.), Philip Bruns (Gil), Danny Bonaduce (Kootz), Jane A. Johnston (Mrs. Dantley), Albert Insinnia (Ricci), Isaac Ruiz, Jr. (Tico), Stanley Kamel (Con Man), Jason Ronard (Tony), Brion James (Jeff).

An unfortunate title makes this sound like just another California blonde movie, and it hurt at the box office. Creative team of Barwood and Robbins have fashioned a sweet comedrama about a teenager, ably played by Hamill, who goes after a car that's been stolen. Roche (the Ajax Man in the TV commercials) is the shop teacher at a high school and the class has lovingly restored a Corvette, only to have it stolen. Hamill is picked up by adorable Potts who is a fledgling hooker attempting to learn her trade in the rear of a van equipped with a water bed. The writer and director manage to integrate several plot lines into the movie; Gene Roche is squeezed between a teacher's salary and a family man's obligations and he gets involved with a hot car ring in order to support his clan; Milford runs the warm auto business and attempts to enlist Hamill into the field; Potts tries to make a go of being a prostitute but it just doesn't work as she and Hamill fall in love, and more and more. All in all, a very funny movie with enough solid underfooting of believable story to take it out of the realm of teenage summer fare.

p,Hal Barwood; d, Matthew Robbins; w, Robbins, Barwood; ph, Frank Stanley

(Panavision, Metrocolor); m, Craig Safan; ed, Amy Jones; art d, James Schoppe; set d, Richard Spero; cos, Aggie Guerard Rodgers; stunts, Bobby Bass.

Comedy/Drama   **Cas.**   **(PR:C-O   MPAA:PG)**

COSH BOY   (SEE: SLASHER,THE, 1953, Brit.)

COSMIC MAN, THE**½   (1959) 72m AA bw
Bruce Bennett (*Dr. Karl Sorenson*), John Carradine (*Cosmic Man*), Angela Greene (*Kathy Grant*), Paul Langton (*Col. Mathews*), Scotty Morrow (*Ken Grant*), Lyn Osborn (*Sgt. Gray*), Walter Maslow (*Dr. Richie*), Robert Lytton (*Gen. Knowland*).

Interesting low budget science fiction film inspired by THE DAY THE EARTH STOOD STILL and the general fear of nuclear war in the 1950s. John Carradine arrives from space in a large sphere. He has black skin and casts a white shadow (the film's only special effect), and brings a message of peace and nuclear sanity. Almost everyone on Earth is suspicious and hostile, even after he heals a crippled boy. Could have been a classic with a larger budget and more thought, but an intriguing failure as is.

p, Robert A. Terry; d, Herbert Greene; w, Arthur C. Pierce; ph, John F. Warren; m, Paul Sawtell, Bert Shefter; ed, Richard C. Currier, Helene Turner.

Science Fiction   **(PR:A   MPAA:NR)**

COSMIC MONSTERS*½
          (1958, Brit.) 75m Eros/Distributors Corporation of America bw
Forrest Tucker (*Gil Graham*), Gaby Andre (*Michele Dupont*), Martin Benson (*Smith*), Wyndham Goldie (*Brig. Cartwright*), Alec Mango (*Dr. Laird*), Hugh Latimer (*Jimmy Murray*), Geoffrey Chater (*Gerald Wilson*), Patricia Sinclair (*Helen Forsyth*), Catherine Lancaster (*Gillian Betts*).

Scientist Tucker causes trouble for Earth when his experiments accidentally blow a hole in the ionosphere. Big, mean bugs from another dimension invade the planet and wreak havoc on the populace until alien Benson arrives in his saucer and saves the day. Pretty silly stuff based on the BBC-TV series "The Strange World Of Planet X."

p, George Maynard; d, Gilbert Gunn; w, Paul Ryder, Joe Ambor (story by Rene Ray).

Science Fiction   **(PR:A   MPAA:NR)**

COSSACKS, THE*½   (1960, It.) 114m Vanguard/UNIV c (I COSSACCHI)
Edmund Purdom (*Shamil*),John Drew Barrymore (*Giamal*), Georgia Moll (*Tatiana*), Pierre Brice (*Boris*), Elena Zareschi (*Patimat*), Erno Crisa (*Casi*), Grazia Maria Spina (*Alina*), Massimo Girotti (*Alexander II*), Mario Pisu (*Voronzov*), Laura Carli (*Ferguson*).

Barrymore is the son of a rebellious Cossack chief sent to St. Petersburg as a hostage to the Russians. He attends military school and becomes an officer. When his father (Purdom) rises up against the Russians once again, Barrymore tries to talk him out of it. The old man is unmoved and Barrymore reluctantly joins him to fight against his former comrades. Costume spectacle poorly dubbed and mediocre in all respects.

p, W. Tourjansky; d, Giorgio Rivalta; ph, Massimo Dallamano (Totalscope, Eastmancolor); m, Giovanni Fusco; cos, Giancarlo Bartolini Salimbeni.

War   **(PR:A   MPAA:NR)**

COSSACKS IN EXILE*
          (1939, Ukrainian) 82m Avramenko bw (ZAPOROZHETZ ZA DUNAYEM)
Maria Sokil (*Odarka*), Michael Shvetz (*Ivan Karas*), Nicholas Karlash (*Sultan*), Alexis Tcherkassky (*Andrey*), Helen Orlenko (*Oksana*), D. Creona (*Kobzar*[bard]), Vladimir Zelitsky (*Selih-Agha*), Gen. Vladimir Sikevitch (*Kalnyshewsky*).

Ukrainian-made operetta about a poor Cossack family driven out of its homeland by the Czar's soldiers and into exile in Turkey. Lots of galloping horses, lots of stirring songs, lots of boredom. (Ukrainian; English subtitles.)

p, V. Avramenko; d, E. G. Ulmer; w, (based on operetta "Zaporozhetz Za Dunayem" by S. Artemowsky); m, Anthony Rudnicky; Ukrainian advisor, Prof. L. Biberavich.

Musical   **(PR:A   MPAA:NR)**

COSSACKS OF THE DON zero   (1932, USSR) 75m Soyuzkino/Amkino bw
Emma Cessarskaya (*Aksinya*), M. Abrikosov (*Grisha*), R. Puzhnoya (*Natalie*), M. Stepanov (*Stephen*), N. Churakovska (*Evgeni*).

Bad Russian romance has lovely Cessarskaya in love with Abrikosov, though each is married to someone else. He goes off to war and returns to find her dallying with the rich landowner's son. He beats up the interloper, kicks his love in the face, and sadly walks off into the sunset. Curiously, another film of the same title was the first Russian-made movie, in 1908, and consisted entirely of trick-riding and scenes from camp life.

d, Olga Preobrajenskaya; ph, D. Feldman.

Drama   **(PR:A   MPAA:NR)**

COSTELLO CASE, THE*   (1930) 65m Educational bw
Tom Moore (*Irish Cop*), Lola Lane (*Mystery Girl*), Wheeler Oakman (*Gangster*), Roscoe Karns (*Reporter*).

Urban crime drama, with Moore the big-hearted Irish cop, Karns the wisecracking reporter, a mystery girl, a burglar, and an incomprehensible story line.

p, James Cruze; d, Walter Lang; w, F. McGrew Willis; ph, Harry Jackson.

Mystery   **(PR:A   MPAA:NR)**

COTTAGE ON DARTMOOR
          (SEE: ESCAPED FROM DARTMOOR, 1929, Brit.)

COTTAGE TO LET   (SEE: BOMBSIGHT STOLEN, 1941, Brit.)

COTTON COMES TO HARLEM***   (1970) 97m UA c
Raymond St. Jacques (*Coffin Ed Johnson*), Godfrey Cambridge (*Grave Digger Jones*), Calvin Lockhart (*Rev. Deke O'Malley*), Judy Pace (*Iris*), Redd Foxx (*Uncle Bud*), John Anderson (*Bryce*), Emily Yancy (*Mabel*), J. D. Cannon (*Calhoun*), Mabel Robinson (*Billie*), Dick Sabol (*Jerema*), Theodore Wilson (*Barry*), Eugene Roche (*Anderson*), Frederick O'Neal (*Casper*), Vinnette Carrol (*Reba*), Gene Lindsey (*Luddy*), Van Kirksey (*Early Riser*), Cleavon Little (*Lo Boy*), Helen Martin (*Church Sister*), Turk Turpin (*Dum Dum*), Tom Lane (*44*), Arnold Williams (*Hi Jenks*), Lou Jacobi (*Goodman*), Leonardo Cimino (*Tom*).

Ossie Davis made his directorial debut in this excellent blaxploitation crime comedy, filmed on location in Harlem. St. Jacques and Cambridge are, respectively, Coffin Ed Johnson and Grave Digger Jones, a pair of Harlem plainclothesmen investigating a "Back-to-Africa" campaign run by shady preacher Lockhart. A huge success, it inspired an inferior sequel (COME BACK, CHARLESTON BLUE) as well as a new genre of the 1970s. Songs: "Cotton Comes To Harlem," "Goin' Home" (Galt MacDermot, Joseph S. Lewis), "Ain't Now But It's Going To Be" (MacDermot, Ossie Davis), "Down In My Soul" (MacDermot, William Dumaresq), "My Salvation" (MacDermot, Paul Laurence Dunbar).

p, Samuel Goldwyn, Jr.; d, Ossie Davis; w, Davis, Arnold Perl (based on a novel by Chester Himes); ph, Gerald Hirschfield (DeLuxe Color); m, Galt MacDermot; ed, John Carter, Robert Q. Lovet; art d, Manny Gerard; cos, Anna Hill Johnstone; set d, Bob Drumbeller; spec eff, Sol Stern; m/l, MacDermot, Davis; stunts, Max Kleven.

Crime/Comedy   **(PR:O   MPAA:R)**

COTTON QUEEN*½   (1937, Brit.) 80m Rock Studios/BIED bw
          (AKA: CRYING OUT LOUD)
Will Fyffe (*Bob Todcastle*), Stanley Holloway (*Sam Owen*), Mary Lawson (*Joan*), Helen Haye (*Margaret Owen*), Marcelle Rogez (*Zita de la Rue*), Jimmy Hanley (*Johnny Owen*), C. Denier Warren (*Joseph Cotter*), Syd Courtenay (*Mayor*), Gibson Gowland (*Jailer*).

Lawson is the daughter of a textile mill owner who goes undercover in the mill of one of her father's rivals. Lightweight comedy with a few good names in the cast.

p, Joe Rock; d, Bernard Vorhaus; w, Louis Golding, Scott Pembroke (based on a story by Syd Courtenay and Barry Peake); ph, Horace Wheddon, Cyril Bristow.

Comedy   **(PR:A   MPAA:NR)**

COTTONPICKIN' CHICKENPICKERS zero
          (1967) 92m Southeastern Pictures-Southern Musical Productions c
Del Reeves (*Darby Clyde Fenster*), Hugh X. Lewis (*Jerry Martin*), Sonny Tufts (*Cousin Urie*), David Houston (*Deputy Burke*), Greta Thyssen (*Greta*), Slapsy Maxie Rosenbloom (*Mailman*), Lila Lee (*Viola Zickafoose*), Tommy Noonan (*Bird-Dog Berrigan*), Hank Mills (*Deputy Will*), Philip Hunter (*Judge Beale*), Margie Bowes (*Susie Zickafoose*), David Wilkins (*David*), J. D. Marshall (*Dreama Sue*), Birgitta Andersson (*Brigit*), Ted Lehmann (*Uncle Ned*), Christian Anderson (*Cousin Elwood*), Mel Tillis (*Hound-Dog Berrigan*), Jack Morey (*Sheriff Mathis*), Buck Bayliss (*Liquid Louie Tallfeathers*).

Reeves and Lewis are riding a freight they think is bound for Hollywood, California, but is really bound for Hollywood, Florida. Hunger drives them to jump off the train somewhere in the rural south, and they try to steal a chicken. They are detected by the Zickafoose family and a prolonged, silly chase ensues. Moonshiners get involved and the whole thing degenerates into a string of dumb hick jokes and lousy songs. Some fairly talented people manage to embarrass themselves in this redneck musical. The last film in Sonny Tufts' bleak career. Songs include: "Cottonpickin' Chickenpickers" (Hanks Mills), "This Must Be The Bottom" (Del Reeves), "Almost Persuaded," "Where Could I Go (But To Her)" (Glenn Sutton, Billy Sherrill), "Comin' On Strong" (Lyn Parker), "Dirty Ole Egg Suckin' Dog," "Not Me," "Messed Up."

p&d, Larry E. Jackson; w, Bob Baron, Jackson; ph, Gerhard Maser (Eastmancolor); ed, Signpost, Inc.; art d, Peter Rotondo; set d, James Williams; cos, Wanda Mack.

Musical Comedy   **(PR:C   MPAA:NR)**

COUCH, THE*   (1962) 100m WB bw
Grant Williams (*Charles Campbell*), Shirley Knight (*Terry*), Onslow Stevens (*Dr. Janz*), William Leslie (*Lindsay*), Anne Helm (*Jean*), Simon Scott (*Lt. Kritzman*), Michael Bachus (*Sgt. Bonner*), John Alvin (*Sloan*), Harry Holcombe (*D.A.*), Hope Summers (*Mrs. Quimby*).

There is nothing here that has not been seen before in this homicidal-maniac-on-the-loose picture. Williams is the weirdo, recently released from prison and undergoing analysis, but committing a string of murders after calling up the cops to tell them about it.

p&d, Owen Crump; w, Robert Bloch (based on a story by Blake Edwards and Crump); ph, Harold Stine; m, Frank Perkins; ed, Leo H. Shreve; art d, Jack Poplin; set d, William L. Kuehl.

Crime   **(PR:C-O   MPAA:NR)**

COUNSEL FOR CRIME**   (1937) 61m COL bw
Otto Kruger (*William Mellon*), Douglass Montgomery (*Paul Maddox*), Jacqueline Wells (*Ann McIntyre*), Thurston Hall (*Sen. Maddox*), Nana Bryant (*Mrs. Maddox*), Gene Morgan (*Friday*), Marc Lawrence (*Edwin Mitchell*), Robert Warwick (*Asa Stewart*), Stanley Fields (*George Evans*).

Suave, polished Kruger is a shady lawyer, specializing in providing alibis for gangsters. Montgomery is his son, although he doesn't know it, who grows up to convict his father of murder in this routine courtroom melodrama. Kruger, fifty two years old at the time and long a matinee idol, was given some added glamor for his role by the makeup department, which handed him gray hair.

d, John Brahm; w, Fred Niblo, Jr., Grace Neville, Lee Loeb, Harold Buchman (based on a story by Harold Shumate); ph, Henry Freulich; ed, Otto Meyer.

Drama (PR:A MPAA:NR)

COUNSEL FOR ROMANCE** (1938, Fr.) 90m Regal bw (AVOCATE D'AMOUR)

Danielle Darrieux *(Jacqueline Serval)*, Henry Garat *(Pierre Meynard)*, Alerme *(Mon. Serval)*, Marguerite Templey *(Mme. Serval)*, Suffel *(Marie)*, Pasquall *(Little Louie)*, R. Casa *(President of the Bar)*, Emile Prud' Hommee *(Accordionist)*, Jean Hebey *(Slim)*.

Lightweight star vehicle for Darrieux, one of the last films she made in France before coming to Hollywood and starring in THE RAGE OF PARIS. Here she is a young woman intent on becoming a lawyer. Her father would rather see her married, but he agrees to support her efforts for eighteen months, and if she hasn't passed the bar by then she agrees to marry. Her father brings her a client (Garat), an accused burglar who turns out to be a good guy, in time for the lovestruck Darrieux to drop her career plans and marry him. Darrieux sings three songs, one of them while playing cards and smoking a cigarette, and it is her extremely energetic and likable performance, along with very skilled direction by Ploquin, that lift this one slightly above the bland ranks of French comedies of the time. (In French; English subtitles.)

d, Raoul Ploquin; w, Jean Boyer; m, George Van Parys; English titles, Mark A. Brum, Charles Jahrblum.

Musical Comedy (PR:A MPAA:NR)

COUNSELLOR-AT-LAW**** (1933) 80m UNIV bw

John Barrymore *(George Simon)*, Bebe Daniels *(Regina Gordon)*, Doris Kenyon *(Cora Simon)*, Onslow Stevens *(John P. Tedesco)*, Isabel Jewell *(Bessie Green)*, Melvyn Douglas *(Roy Darwin)*, Thelma Todd *(Lillian La Rue)*, Marvin Kline *(Weinberg)*, Conroy Washburn *(Sandler)*, John Qualen *(Breitstein)*, J. Hammond Dailey *(McFadden)*, Malka Kornstein *(Sarah Becker)*, Angela Jacobs *(Goldie Rindskopf)*, Clara Langsner *(Lena Simon)*, T. H. Manning *(Peter J. Malone)*, Elmer Brown *(F. C. Baird)*, Vincent Sherman *(Harry Becker)*, Bobby Gordon *(Henry Susskind)*, Barbara Perry *(Dorothy)*, Richard Quine *(Richard)*, Victor Adams *(David Simon)*, Mayo Methot *(Zedorah Chapman)*, Frederick Burton *(Crayfield)*.

Barrymore gives one of his finest performances as a Jewish lawyer who works his way to the top of his profession only to have his gentile wife (Kenyon) leave him. Barrymore was the second choice to play the role after Paul Muni, who had played the role on stage but who feared being typecast as a Jew on film, a decision that brought Barrymore $25,000 a week for what was to have been two weeks, but the film ran into overruns. An excellent movie, superbly directed by pantheon helmsman Wyler who discarded a musical score, having music only at the opening and closing credits, so that the dramatic weight fell upon the crisp; dialog and Barrymore's spellbinding deliveries. Wyler was just beginning his directorial career at the time and was nervous about handling the temperamental Barrymore. "The Great Profile" took him aside at their first meeting and smilingly told Wyler: "You and I are going to get along fine, you know. Don't worry about all the temperamental stuff you've heard about the Barrymores. It all comes from my sister and she's full of it." Barrymore tried to insert what he thought were "Jewish gestures" into his scenes but the young Wyler would not be intimidated, quietly correcting him. The film was made at breakneck speed and the dialog was delivered in rapid-fire manner, then popular in the new talkies. Barrymore, who churned out five films that year and made almost $400,000 to supply his expensive ways, was letter perfect except for one scene with Qualen which he was called back to reshoot after the film was ostensibly finished. Barrymore appeared tired, some on the set said drunk, and he flubbed one line again and again, causing Wyler to order more than twenty takes, but even he lost count as they labored into the night and one tally had it at fifty-two takes. But they finally had it and the film opened to critical and public raves. Wyler offered a new brand of filmic realism where he kept his cameras inside the lawyer's offices through almost the first reel, jump cutting from one office to another, but centering on Barrymore and his nerve-center desk, providing urgency and high drama at an electrifying pace. Today the lightning still crackles through this masterful film.

p, Carl Laemmle, Jr.; d, William Wyler; w, Elmer Rice (based on his play); ph, Norbert Brodine; ed, Daniel Mandell.

Drama (PR:A MPAA:NR)

COUNSEL'S OPINION** (1933, Brit.) 76m LFP/PAR bw

Henry Kendall *(Logan)*, Binnie Barnes *(Leslie)*, Cyril Maude *(Willock)*, Lawrence Grossmith *(Lord Rockburn)*, Harry Tate *(Taxi Driver)*, Francis Lister *(James Govan)*, Mary Charles *(Stella Marston)*, Margaret Baird *(Saunders)*, J. Fisher White *(Judge)*, C. Denier Warren *(Manager)*, Stanley Lathbury *(George)*.

Barnes is a widow who impersonates the cheating wife of Lord Grossmith in order to win the affections of lawyer Kendall. Okay comedy directed by one of the most prolific directors in film history. (Remade as THE DIVORCE OF LADY X in 1938.)

p, Alexander Korda; d, Allan Dwan; w, Arthur Wimperis, Dorothy Greenhill (based on a play by Gilbert Wakefield); ph, Phil Tannura; ed, Harold Young; prod d, Holmes-Paul.

Comedy (PR:A MPAA:NR)

COUNT DRACULA** (1971, Sp., Ital., Ger., Brit.) 100m Filmer Compagnia Cinematografica (Rome)-Phoenix Film (Madrid)-Korona Film Produktion (Munich) c

Christopher Lee *(Dracula)*, Herbert Lom *(Van Helsing)*, Klaus Kinski *(Renfield)*, Soledad Miranda, Maria Rohm, Fred Williams, Jack Taylor, Paul Muller.

Lee wanted to play Dracula according to the novel, and despite a few laughable discrepancies, he does a fairly good job. His count is a respectable-looking, aging man, with white hair and mustache, who is rejuvenated after his sanguineous meal. Kinski steals the show as Renfield, raving incoherently and munching insects in his padded cell. Sure it's trash, but it's fun trash.

p, Harry Alan Towers; d, Jesus Franco; w, Franco, August Finochi, Towers, Carlo Fadda, Milo G. Cuccia, Dietmar Behnke (based on the novel by Bram Stoker); ph, Manuel Marion (Panavision, Eastmancolor); m, Bruno Nicolai.

Horror (PR:C-O MPAA:NR)

COUNT DRACULA AND HIS VAMPIRE BRIDE** (1978, Brit.) Hammer/Dynamic Entertainment c (AKA: SATANIC RITES OF DRACULA)

Christopher Lee *(Count Dracula)*, Peter Cushing *(Van Helsing)*, Michael Coles *(Murray)*, William Franklyn *(Torrence)*, Freddie Jones *(Prof. Keeley)*, Joanna Lumley *(Jessica)*, Richard Vernon *(Mathews)*, Patrick Barr *(Lord Carradine)*, Barbara Yu Ling *(Chin Yang)*, Richard Mathews *(Porter)*, Lockwood West *(Freeborne)*, Maurice O'Connell *(Hanson)*, Valerie Van Ost *(Jane)*,

Another incarnation of Christopher Lee finds him in modern London developing a new strain of bubonic plague with which to annihilate life on Earth. Peter Cushing, who has Ph.D. in evil, sets about stopping him. Dull, humorless, and thankfully, the last of the Dracula films produced by Hammer.

p, Alan Gibson; d, Gibson; w, Don Houghton (based on the character created by Bram Stoker); ph, Brian Probyn; m, John Cacavas; ed, Chris Barnes; art d, Lionel Couch.

Horror (PR:C-O MPAA:R)

COUNT FIVE AND DIE½** (1958, Brit.) 92m FOX bw

Jeffrey Hunter *(Ranson)*, Nigel Patrick *(Howard)*, Annemarie Duringer *(Rolande)*, David Kossoff *(Mulder)*, Claude Kingston *(Willem)*, Philip Bond *(Piet)*, Rolf Lefebvre *(Faber)*, Larry Burns *(Martins)*, Arthur Gross *(Jan)*, Robert Raglan *(Miller)*, Peter Prowse *(Parrish)*.

WW II espionage thriller has Hunter as an American officer attached to a British counter-espionage unit. Working alongside commander Patrick and a group of Dutch resistance fighters, they attempt to mislead the Germans as to where the invasion will take place. Into the unit comes Duringer, supposedly a Dutch agent, but in reality a German spy. Patrick suspects her and warns Hunter, who has fallen in love with her. Eventually she is exposed and kills Hunter, being killed in turn by her own side to prevent her from talking. Title refers to cyanide capsules agents conceal in their mouths. Fairly interesting, and based on OSS files.

p, Ernest Gartside; d, Victor Vicas; w, Jack Seddon, David Pursall; ph, Arthur Grant (Cinemascope); m, John Wooldridge; ed, Russell Lloyd.

War (PR:A MPAA:NR)

COUNT OF BRAGELONNE, THE

(SEE: LAST MUSKETEER, THE, 1954, Fr.)

COUNT OF MONTE CRISTO, THE**** (1934) 113m Reliance/UA bw

Robert Donat *(Edmond Dantes)*, Elissa Landi *(Mercedes)*, Louis Calhern *(De Villefort, Jr.)*, Sidney Blackmer *(Mondego)*, Raymond Walburn *(Danglars)*, O. P. Heggie *(Abbe Foria)*, William Farnum *(Capt. Leclere)*, Georgia Caine *(Mme. De Rosas)*, Walter Walker *(Morrel)*, Lawrence Grant *(De Villefort, Sr.)*, Luis Alberni *(Jacopo)*, Irene Hervey *(Valentine)*, Douglas Walton *(Albert)*, Juliette Compton *(Clothilde)*, Clarence Wilson *(Fouquet)*, Eleanor Phelps *(HayJee)*, Ferdinand Munier *(Louis XVII)*, Holmes Herbert *(Judge)*, Paul Irving *(Napoleon)*, Mitchell Lewis *(Yampa)*, Clarence Muse *(Ali)*, Lionel Belmore *(Prison Governor)*.

Dumas' oft-told tale was never better served than in this Edward Small production with Donat giving one of his finest performances. He is the wronged man, sailor Edmond Dantes, who has just received a promotion and is about to marry the beautiful Mercedes (Landi). Calhern, Blackmer and Walburn, all secret supporters of the deposed Napoleon, make Donat the scapegoat in a Bonaparte-involved plot which is exposed. The innocent man is arrested, tried and speedily convicted, sent to life imprisonment in the terrible sea-locked Chateau d'If where he languishes for years, clinging to life and hope but aging rapidly on his meager supply of food. He knows in his miserable solitary confinement that Calhern turned him in, claiming no knowledge of the secret message from Napoleon's spy, that Blackmer stole his girl and married her, and that Walburn helped to convict him so he could advance his own naval career. One day Donat hears a tapping on the wall of his cell and he begins to dig with hands and a spoon, finally removing a rock to discover another prisoner, Heggie, a saintly abbe. Heggie has been digging for years only to work himself into Donat's cell. The two begin to dig together, working their way to freedom. Through the years, the abbe imparts to Donat his vast knowledge in the sciences and humanities, also describing where a great pirate treasure is hidden on the island of Monte Cristo. When the abbe dies, Donat buries his body in the tunnel and then takes his place, sewing himself up in the canvas bag reserved for Heggie's body. It is thrown into the ocean and Donat struggles free, and is later picked up by pirates whom he befriends. They take him to Monte Cristo where he discovers the fabulous treasure hidden in a cave. He becomes the wealthiest man alive, dubbing himself the Count of Monte Cristo. His bearing and intellectual prowess, learned from Heggie, help to establish his new identity. Only vengeance burns in Donat's ambitions. He uses his great wealth to bring about the downfall of Blackmer, Walburn and Calhern, revealing himself finally as Dantes to Landi who renews her romance with him. Donat is captivating as the good-hearted victim and the cool seeker of justice, measuring his vengeance with subtle moves and the kind of slow deliberation that has the viewer rooting for him; anyone ever victimized by his fellow man can identify with Donat's perfect performance. He is at the beginning sensitive, carefree, full of hope and even during his darkest hours his faith and strength of character preserve his sanity. When rich and powerful, Donat does not flaunt his wealth nor offend any man but those who stole his youth and love. Producer Small spared no expense in this lavish and technically top notch production, the only Hollywood-backed film in which Donat ever appeared. The great British star was sought by Hollywood studios after the enormous success of this film.

Warner Brothers offered him the lead role in its epic adventure film, CAPTAIN BLOOD and he was thought to be perfect for ANTHONY ADVERSE and THE ADVENTURES OF ROBIN HOOD. But after reading the CAPTAIN BLOOD script, the asthmatic Donat shook his head and told Warners that he could not perform the acrobatic role of the swashbuckling doctor-turned-pirate. An unknown named Errol Flynn finally got the part. The always frail Donat confined himself to gentler parts, winning an Oscar for his role of an elderly, kind teacher in GOODBYE, MR. CHIPS. He would die at age fifty-three in 1958, a victim of the asthma that plagued him all his life. THE COUNT OF MONTE CRISTO has been produced many times, in many variations, since the earliest silent film era. Even James O'Neill, father of America's greatest playwright, Eugene O'Neill, played the role in the 1913 Famous Players production. (O'Neill actually played this role more times on American stages than any other actor. A Shakespearean actor, O'Neill longed for any other part but audiences so identified with him as Edmond Dantes that he stayed with this role for most of his career.) Created by Alexandre Dumas the elder,the story of Dantes and his transformation to the fabulous count was researched well by the successful, pleasure-seeking writer. In 1844 while visiting Marseilles, Dumas hired a boatman to guide him about the nearby islands. He inspected Elba, once the exile island of Napoleon, and the bleak, craggy isle of Monte Cristo which was so thickly infested with malaria-carrying mosquitoes that everyone gave it a wide birth and legends about it abounded, particularly that pirates had secreted great treasures in its caves decades earlier. Dumas used this thought-provoking legend as a setting for THE COUNT OF MONTE CRISTO which was published in 1845 and came on the heels of his enormously popular THE THREE MUSKETEERS. He would author more than 300 novels (or take credit for them, often signing his name to the works of others in later life) but few would be as successful as the tale of Edmond Dantes. One canard has it that when the old man was wasted away with drink and excessive living, his playwright son came to his deathbed to read his novels to him; Dumas' memory had fled and he died while his son read from THE COUNT OF MONTE CRISTO, his last longing words being: "I have only one regret. I wish I knew how it all comes out." It didn't come out in the film exactly the way Dumas had written it. Hollywood tacked on a happy ending where Dantes and Mercedes are reunited. No one seemed to mind. This was one classic that couldn't be destroyed. (See COUNT OF MONTE CRISTO, Index.)

p, Edward Small; d, Rowland V. Lee; w, Philip Dunne, Dan Totheroh, Lee (based on the novel by Alexandre Dumas); ph, Peverell J. Marley; m, Alfred Newman; ed, Grant Whytock.

Adventure/Historical Drama Cas. (PR:AAA MPAA:NR)

COUNT OF MONTE-CRISTO** (1955, Fr., Ital.) 86m Sirius c (ITAL: COMTE DE MONTE-CRISTO)

Jean Marais, Lia Amanda, Folco Lulli, Daniel Ivernal, Jacques Castelot, Roger Pigaut, Daniel Cauchy.

Part two of a mediocre adaptation of the Dumas costume novel concentrates on the vengeance wreaked by Marais after his escape from the Chateau D'If.

p, Jacques Roitfield; d, Robert Vernay; w, Georges Neveux, Vernay (based on the novel by Alexandre Dumas); ph, Robert Juillard (Gevacolor); ed, Monique Kirsonoff.

Adventure (PR:A MPAA:NR)

COUNT OF MONTE CRISTO*** (1976, Brit.) 103m ITC c

Richard Chamberlain *(Edmond Dantes)*, Tony Curtis *(Mondego)*, Trevor Howard *(Abbe Faria)*, Louis Jourdan *(De Villefort)*, Donald Pleasence *(Danglars)*, Kate Nelligan *(Mercedes)*, Angelo Infante *(Jacopo)*, Taryn Power *(Valentine De Villefort)*, Harold Bromley *(M. Morrell)*, Carlo Puri *(Andrea Bendetto)*, Alessio Orano *(Caderousse)*, Domenic Guard *(Albert Mondego)*, Isabelle De Valvert *(Hayde)*, Ralph Michael *(M. Dantes)*, Dominic Barto *(Bertuccio)*, Harry Baird *(Ali)*, George Willing *(Andre Morrell)*, David Mills *(Guard)*, Anthony Dawson *(Noirtier De Villefort)*.

Well-mounted retelling of the Dumas classic with Chamberlain quite good as the wrongly imprisoned and vengeance-obsessed Dantes, but it's Howard who steals the show, playing the wise old prisoner who helps him escape. Debuted on U.S. television, released theatrically in Europe.

p, Norman Rosemont; d, David Greene; w, Sidney Carroll (based on the novel by Alexandre Dumas); ph, Aldo Tonti (Eastmancolor); m, Allyn Ferguson; ed, Gene Milford.

Adventure Cas. (PR:A MPAA:NR)

COUNT OF THE MONK'S BRIDGE, THE** (1934, Swed.) 84m Svenskifilmindustri bw (MUNKBROGREVEN)

Valdemar Dahlquist, Sigurd Wallen, Eric Abrahamson, Weyler Hildebrand, Artur Cederborg, Edvin Adolphson, Ingrid Bergman, Tollie Zellman, Julia Caesar, Arthur Fisher, Emil Fjellstrom, Viktor "Kulorten" Andersson.

Swedish drinking comedy that was Bergman's first film. Loose plot sees a group of pals drinking their way from one bar to the next, keeping one step ahead of the police who are trying to break up the party. The whole thing is basically a travelog of Stockholm in 1934. Bergman plays a maid in a cheap hotel who is the love interest for Adolphson. An undistinguished debut to say the least, but she caught the attention of Swedish critics who called her "sunny of spirit, self assured," but hefty and a little overweight.

d, Edvin Adolphson, Sigurd Wallen; w, Gosta Stevens (based on the play "Greven fran Gamla Sta'n" by Arthur and Sigfried Fischer); ph, Ake Dahlquist; m, Jules Sylvain; ed, Rolf Husberg.

Comedy (PR:A MPAA:NR)

COUNT OF TWELVE* (1955, Brit.) 51m Danzigers/AB-Pathe bw

Ron Randell, John Longden, Genine Graham, Jill Adams, Garrard Green, Mona Washbourne, Enid Lorrimer, John Bentley, Eunice Gayson, Leonard Sachs, Patrick Holt.

Unimaginative anthology film with two stories. in the first, a man is convinced that his maid will poison him at midnight. As the hour approaches, he has a heart attack and dies, exactly as the maid had planned. In the second story a prominent doctor runs away with the wife of a friend, but both are killed when their car crashes.

p, Edward J. Danziger, harry Lee Danziger; d, Paul Gerrard; w, Rex Rienits, Paul Tabori; ph, Jimmy Wilson.

Drama (PR:A MPAA:NR)

COUNT THE HOURS** (1953) 74m RKO bw (GB: EVERY MINUTE COUNTS)

Teresa Wright *(Ellen Braden)*, MacDonald Carey *(Doug Madison)*, Dolores Moran *(Paula Mitchener)*, Adele Mara *(Gracie)*, Edgar Barrier *(Gillespie)*, John Craven *(George Braden)*, Jack Elam *(Max Verne)*, Ralph Sanford *(Alvin Taylor)*.

Migrant farm worker Craven is accused of two murders, but court-appointed lawyer Carey thinks he's innocent. The night before Craven is executed Carey comes up with the real killer. Sloppily scripted and performed, but Siegel's direction keeps it moving.

p, Benedict Bogeaus; d, Don Siegel; w, Doane R. Hoag, Karen De Wolf (based on a story by Hoag); ph, John Alton; m, Louis Forbes; ed, James Leicester.

Crime (PR:A MPAA:NR)

COUNT THREE AND PRAY½** (1955) 102m Copa/COL c

Van Heflin *(Luke Fargo)*, Joanne Woodward *(Lissy)*, Phil Carey *(Albert Loomis)*, Raymond Burr *(Yancey Huggins)*, Allison Hayes *(Georgina Decrais)*, Myron Healey *(Floyd Miller)*, Nancy Kulp *(Matty)*, James Griffith *(Swallow)*, Richard Webb *(Big)*, Kathryn Givney *(Mrs. Decrais)*, Robert Burton *(Bishop)*, Vince Townsend *(Colossus)*, John Cason *(Charlie Vancouver)*, Jean Willes *(Selma)*, Adrienne Marden *(Mrs. Swallow)*, Steven Raines *(Jake)*, Jimmy Hawkins *(Corey)*, Juney Ellis *(Lilly Mae)*.

Rambling post-Civil War saga of a young girl (Woodward), who survived the horrors of 1860-65 by taking to the mountains and living the way Truffaut's THE WILD CHILD did. Once found and cleaned up, the tattered girl, thought to be pre-pubescent, turns out to be 18 years old and nubile. Parson Heflin, a one-time hell-raiser,has come back to town completely reformed and determined to rebuild the local church and preach love to the defeated Southerners. Heflin is not above using his fists to pound a point across. Lots of small bits rate mentioning: Willes makes the cliche prostitute come to life and Burr provides the villainous character with his usual hissable intelligence. In the end, Heflin and Woodward get married and will, presumably, oversee peace in the valley. This was Woodward's first movie and she was 25 years of age and fresh off the "live" TV screen. She later won an Oscar for THE THREE FACES OF EVE and an Emmy for the TV movie "See How She Runs." Woodward has been married since 1958 to Paul Newman with whom she occasionally appeared in several box office disappointments (A NEW KIND OF LOVE, THE SECRET WAR OF HARRY FRIGG, WINNING, and others). The unbilled producer for this film was Tyrone Power.

p, Ted Richmond; d, George Sherman; w, Herb Meadow; ph, Burnett Guffey (CinemaScope, Technicolor); m, George Duning; ed, William A. Lyon; cos, Jean Louis.

Drama (PR:A MPAA:NR)

COUNT YORGA, VAMPIRE** (1970) 90m AIP c

Robert Quarry *(Count Yorga)*, Roger Perry *(Hayes)*, Michael Murphy *(Paul)*, Michael Macready *(Michael)*, Donna Anders *(Donna)*, Judith Lang *(Erica)*, Edward Walsh *(Brudah)*, Julie Conners *(Cleo)*, Paul Hansen *(Peter)*, Sybil Scotford *(Judy)*, Marsha Jordan *(Mother)*, Deborah Darnell *(Vampire)*, Erica Macready *(Nurse)*, George Macready *(Narrator)*.

Pretty good vampire stuff set in Los Angeles. Moves at a good clip from the opening scene of a coffin being driven through the streets on a flatbed truck, through a slew of victims and sexy vampiresses, to Quarry's howling death scene. Judith Lang eating a cat is reason alone to check this out. Conceived as a sex film, COUNT YORGA, VAMPIRE, was wisely turned into a vampire film but still used some of the veterans of countless soft-core sex movies of the 1960s, including Marsha Jordan. Sequel: THE RETURN OF COUNT YORGA.

p, Michael Macready; d&w, Bob Kelljan; ph, Arch Archambault (Movielab Color); m, William Marx; ed, Tony De Zarraga; art d, Bob Wilder; spec eff, James Tanenbaum.

Horror (PR:O MPAA:GP)

COUNT YOUR BLESSINGS* (1959) 102m MGM c

Deborah Kerr *(Grace Allingham)*, Rossano Brazzi *(Charles-Edouard de Valhubert)*, Maurice Chevalier *(Duc de St. Cloud)*, Martin Stephens *(Sigismond)*, Tom Helmore *(Hugh Palgrave)*, Ronald Squire *(Sir Conrad Allingham)*, Patricia Medina *(Albertine)*, Mona Washbourne *(Nanny)*, Steven Geray *(Guide)*, Lumsden Hare *(John)*, Kim Parker *(Secretary)*, Frank Kreig *(Tourist)*.

Filmed in France and England, this lightweight attempt at sophisticated comedy falls flat as a flapjack under Negulesco's lifeless direction and Tunberg's turgid adaptation of the novel by Nancy Mitford. Kerr and Brazzi have been married quite some time and even have a son, Stephens, age nine, but they've not lived together for a long time, nor have they had the opportunity for a proper honeymoon. Why, you ask? Well, it all happened during WW II when Brazzi met and wed and impregnated Kerr on a whirlwind three-day pass. Since then, he's been flying off to various trouble spots and fighting wars in Indochina, Lebanon, and Algeria for France. He finally comes home but trouble erupts immediately when Kerr discovers that Brazzi has a number of lady friends as well as one official mistress, Medina, and they are all waiting for Kerr to toss Brazzi out so they can move in and take over his care and feeding. Kerr can't fathom this kind of life but Chevalier, Brazzi's uncle, explains that this is the way a Frenchman must live. It's nothing personal toward her, only a Gallic tradition. Now Kerr discovers that Stephens has been keeping his parents apart deliberately because, the moment the two get together, they only have eyes for each other and he feels neglected. When they separately take him, he is indulged to his heart's content. Stephens runs away and his by-now separated parents unite in an attempt to find him. On this journey, they rediscover their love for each other. They find their son and unite as a happy family. Mitford had written a somewhat spicier story than what was seen in this film. Brazzi's amours are glossed over so quickly that they hardly seem worth a mention in this squeaky-clean script. A waste of Chevalier's time and ours.

p, Karl Tunberg; d,Jean Negulesco; w, Tunberg (based on novel *The Blessing* by Nancy Mitford); ph, Milton Krasner, George Folsey (CinemaScope, Metrocolor); m, Franz Waxman; ed, Harold F. Kress; art d, William A. Horning, Randell Duell, Don Ashton; set d, Henry Grace, Keogh Gleason; cos, Helen Rose.

Comedy (PR:A-C MPAA:NR)

COUNT YOUR BULLETS***

(1972) 92m Brut c

(AKA: CRY FOR ME BILLY; FACE TO THE WIND; NAKED REVENGE)

Cliff Potts (Billy), Oaxchitl (Indian Girl), Harry Dean Stanton (Luke Todd), Don Wilbanks (Sergeant), Woodrow Chambliss (Prospector), Roy Jensen (Blacksmith), Richard Breeding (Fat Man).

Intriguing western has young gunfighter Potts trying to get out of his profession before it kills him. He runs across a group of Indian prisoners being escorted by a cavalry troop under the command of sadistic Sgt. Wilbanks. Later he encounters the Indians again, all massacred by the troopers except for a few survivors, Oaxchitl among them. Potts tries to lead the Indians to safety and a romance develops between him and Oaxchitl. An intelligent western well worth seeking out.

p, Elliot Kastner; d, William A. Graham; w, David Markson; ph, Jordan Cronenweth; m, Richard Markwitz; ed, Jim Benson.

Western (PR:O MPAA:R)

COUNTDOWN***½

(1968) 101m WB c

James Caan (Lee), Joanna Moore (Mickey), Robert Duvall (Chiz), Barbara Baxley (Jean), Charles Aidman (Gus), Steve Ihnat (Ross), Michael Murphy (Rick), Ted Knight (Larson), Stephen Coit (Ehrman), John Rayner (Dunc), Charles Irving (Seidel), Bobby Riha, Jr. (Stevie).

Made before Robert Altman fell in love with technique and forgot about people, this sci-fi suspenser top-lined James Caan in his seventh movie, when he was able to put an honest emotion on screen without being supermacho. Good script by Loring Mandel depicts Caan as a civilian scientist who has been chosen to replace Duvall in a space capsule that will land on the moon. Moore is Caan's wife and suffers from being in the fishbowl of publicity and has difficulty with her newfound celebrity status. Duvall's wife, Baxley, reaches for the booze when Duvall's dedication to his work takes him away from home for long stretches of time. The idea is to get a man on the moon before the Russians, but project manager Ihnat and flight medico Aidman carry on a running battle over safety precautions versus the need to be first on Earth's satellite. Caan gets to the moon in a well-photographed sequence with lots of suspense and finds . . . should we tell you? If you don't want to know, stop here. If yes, keep reading. Well, once he gets there he finds a crew of dead Russians! The movie was made just about the time the real things were happening and it was a race to see which came first; Life or Art. This was a precursor to THE RIGHT STUFF and, in it's own small way, a very good film. The lives of astronauts and the support team are explored quickly but with enough depth to give us more than a passing glance at their existence. Altman carped that the film was edited without his okay. He should have thanked them instead.

p, William Conrad; d, Robert Altman; w, Loring Mandel (based on a novel by Hank Searls); ph, William W. Spencer (Panavision, Technicolor); m, Leonard Rosenman; ed, Gene Milford; art d, Jack Poplin; set d, Ralph S. Hurst.

Adventure/Science Fiction (PR:A MPAA:NR)

COUNTDOWN AT KUSINI**½

(1976, Nigerian) 99m Tan International Ltd. of Nigeria-Glipp Productions/COL c

Ruby Dee (Leah Matanzima), Ossie Davis (Ernest Motapo), Greg Morris (Red Salter), Tom Aldredge (Ben Amed). Michael Ebert (Charles Henderson), Thomas Baptiste (John Okello), Jab Adu (Juma Bakari), Elsie Olusola (Mamouda), Funso Adeolu (Marni).

Okay story of African revolutionary leader Davis being stalked by mercenary Aldredge, who has been hired by a large corporation because Davis' policies are interfering with their profits. Film tends to ramble all over the place, but its intentions are good. The film was financed by DST Communications, a subsidiary of Delta Sigma Theta, the world's largest black sorority. Soundtrack by African musician Dibango is outstanding.

p, Ladi Ladebo; d, Ossie Davis; w, Davis, Ladebo, Al Freeman, Jr. (based on a story by John Storm Roberts); ph, Andrew Laszlo (Metrocolor); m, Manu Dibango.

Drama (PR:C MPAA:PG)

COUNTDOWN TO DANGER*½

(1967, Brit.) 63m Wallace/CFF c

David Macalister (Mike), Paul Martin (Tony), Angela Lee (Sandie), Penny Spencer (Sue), Richard Coleman (Capt. Wright), Lane Meddick (Sgt. Thompson), Frank Williams (Harry).

While on vacation, young Macalister becomes trapped in a warehouse full of old German mines. Knowing that they won't let the boy blow up ruins any chance at suspense the film might have had. Just for the kids.

p, A. Frank Bundy; d&w, Peter Seabourne; ph, (Eastmancolor).

Children (PR:AA MPAA:NR)

COUNTER-ATTACK***

(1945) 90m COL bw

(GB: ONE AGAINST SEVEN)

Paul Muni (Alexei Kulkov), Marguerite Chapman (Lisa Elenko), Larry Parks (Kirichenko), Philip Van Zandt (Galkronye), George Macready (Col. Semenov), Roman Bohnen (Kostyuk), Harro Meller (Ernemann), Erik Rolf (Vassilev), Rudolph Anders (Stillman), Ian Wolfe (Ostrouski), Frederick Giermann (Weiler), Paul Andor (Krafft), Ivan Triesault (Grillparzer), Ludwig Donath (Mueller), Louis Adlon (Huebsch), Trevor Bardette (Petrov), Richard Hale (Gen. Kalinev).

It was just a few years after this film was released that Muni, Parks, Lawson, and supervisor Sidney Buchman were named by the House Un-American Activities Committee as having had Communist affiliations. Lawson refused to testify and was branded as one of the "Unfriendly Ten" while the other three were blackballed from the industry for most of the rest of their lives. At the time COUNTER-ATTACK was made, the Russians and the U.S. were allies but in the cold light of several years after, witch-hunters read things into the script that were never intended. Based on a Russian play ("Pobyeda"), it was brought to Broadway where Morris Carnovsky played the part to fair success. Muni was chosen for the film, the title of which was also ONE AGAINST

SEVEN before they changed it to what eventually reached the screen. The film betrayed its stage origination as it was essentially a one-set picture with Muni as a Russian soldier trapped in a bombed-out building's basement. The small town is held by the Nazis and Muni and Chapman, a Russian woman trapped with him, hold off a septet of German soldiers while they await rescue in the destroyed factory's cellar. Muni learns that Meller, one of the Germans, is an officer and a mental war begins between the two men, each eager to learn information from the other so that they can pass it on to their own army, depending on who digs them out. Muni tells Meller that the Russians are building an underwater bridge in order to cross a river. Chapman is shocked by the admission but Muni lets her know he can kill Meller before the man can tell anyone, if they are rescued by Germans. Time passes slowly and Muni and Chapman begin to nod off. The Germans get the weapon Muni has been using, and in the melee Chapman is wounded. Rudolph Anders, another German, owns up to the fact that he did not agree with Hitler and he is in the army under duress. He tells Muni that he will keep the other Germans covered with a rifle in order to let Muni close his eyes. Muni gives him an unloaded rifle (without telling him of the lack of ammunition) and nods off. True to his word, Anders does keep the men covered with the rifle. Now the sounds of digging are heard, followed by some words in German from the diggers. Meller begins shouting the information about the bridge and Muni shoots him dead, then prepares to shoot everyone else in the basement. The German language is just a ruse and the rescuers are, in fact, Russians who have just taken the town. The Germans are taken away and Muni is removed on a stretcher, sound asleep. The picture was not a success and no one could figure why. Muni was a major star for many years and the play was a proven commodity on Broadway. Or was it just that people were tired of the war by 1945 and were not at all interested in the plight of an obscure Russian? Larry Parks's career was shattered by the communist accusations and, although never officially blacklisted, frightened producers did not avail themselves of Parks and he only did three roles in the last fifteen years of his life. Faced with the lack of screenwriting work, Lawson took up books and had several successful how-to tomes on drama and film. Billy Wilder, commenting on the "Unfriendly Ten" said: "Only three of them had any real talent. The other seven were just unfriendly."

p&d, Zoltan Korda; w, John Howard Lawson (adapted from the play by Janet and Philip Stevenson, based on the play "Pobyeda" by Ilya Vershinin, Mikhail Ruderman); ph, James Wong Howe; m, Louis Gruenberg; ed, Charles Nelson, Al Clark; md, Morris Stoloff; art d, Stephen Goosson, Edward Jewell.

War Drama (PR:A MPAA:NR)

COUNTER-ESPIONAGE**

(1942) 71m COL bw

Warren William (Michael Lanyard), Eric Blore (Jameson), Hillary Brooke (Pamela), Thurston Hall (Inspector Crane), Fred Kelsey (Dickens), Forrest Tucker (Anton Schugg), Matthew Boulton (Inspector Stephens), Kurt Katch (Gustave Sossel), Morton Lowry (Kent Wells), Leslie Denison (Harvey Leeds), Billy Bevan (George Barrow), Stanley Logan (Sir Stafford Hart), Tom Stevenson (Police Constable Hopkins).

One of the short-lived Lone Wolf series with William as the supersleuth and Blore his faithful servant. This time he's in London, protecting secret plans from Nazi spies. Above average series entry. (See LONE WOLF series, Index.)

p, Wallace MacDonald; d, Edward Dmytryk; w, Aubrey Wisbrook (based on a story by Louis Joseph Vanca), ph, Philip Tannura; ed, Gene Havlick.

Espionage (PR:A MPAA:NR)

COUNTER TENORS, THE

(SEE: WHITE VOICES, THE, 1965, Ital.)

COUNTERBLAST**

(1948, Brit.) 99m BN/Pathe bw

Robert Beatty (Dr. Rankin), Mervyn Johns (Dr. Bruckner),Nova Pilbeam (Tracy Shaw), Margaretta Scott (Sister Johnson), Sybilla Binder (Martha), Marie Lohr (Mrs. Coles), Karel Stepanek (Prof. Inman), Alan Wheatley (Kennedy), Gladys Henson(Mrs. Plum), John Salew (Padre), Anthony Eustrel (Dr. Forrester), Karl Jaffe (Heinz), Ronald Adam (Col. Ingram), Martin Miller (Seaman), Aubrey Mallalieu (Maj. Walsh), Horace Kenney (Cab Driver).

Johns kills a British scientist and assumes his identity, carrying on his bacteriological experiments for the benefit of his Nazi masters. When Binder, his German undeground superior, orders him to murder Pilbeam, an assistant who is learning too much about their covert operation, Johns refuses, then kills Binder. He flees back to Germany, stowing away in the hold of a Dutch ship where escaping poisonous fumes kill him. A rather twisted plot is overcome by some good performances by Johns and Pilbeam.

p, Louis H. Jackson; d, Paul Stein; w, Jack Whitingham (based on a story by Guy Morgan); ph, James Wilson.

Spy Drama (PR:A MPAA:NR)

COUNTERFEIT**

(1936) 73m COL bw

Chester Morris (John Joseph Madden), Margot Grahame (Aimee Maxwell), Lloyd Nolan (Capper Stevens), Marian Marsh (Verna Maxwell), Claude Gillingwater (Tom Perkins), Geroge McKay (Angel White), John Gallaudet (Pete Dailey), Gene Morgan (Gus), Pierre Watkins (Matt McDonald), Marc Lawrence (Dint Coleman).

Hoodlums led by Nolan kidnap a Treasury Department engraver and force him to make them a set of plates to print money from. Enter Morris as an undercover T-man saving the day, and just in the nick of time, too. Hardly a classic, but for unpretentious entertainment, not bad.

p, B.P. Schulberg; d, Erle C. Kenton; w, William Rankin, Bruce Manning (based on a story by Rankin); ph, John Stumar, E. Roy Davidson; ed, Richard Cahoon.

Crime (PR:A MPAA:NR)

COUNTERFEIT COMMANDOS**

(1981, Ital.) 99m Aquarius c (AKA: INGLORIOUS BASTARDS)

Bo Svenson (Lt. Yeager), Fred Williamson (Fred), Peter Hooten (Tony), Michael

Pergolami (*Nick*), Jackie Basehart (*Berle*), Raymund Harmstorf (*Otto*), Michel Constantin (*Veronique*), Debra Berger (*Nicole*), Ian Bannen (*Col. Buckner*).

Inane war movie with five soldiers facing courts-martial in France escaping and trying to make their way to the Swiss border. Some decent action scenes, but all in all the kind of movie they stopped making in the early 1960s with good reason.

d, Enzo G. Castellari; w, Sergio Grieco; ph, Gianfranco Bergamini; m, Francesci do Masi; ed, Gianfranco Amicucci.

War (PR:O MPAA:R)

COUNTERFEIT CONSTABLE, THE*½ (1966, Fr.) 87m
Le Film d'Art-Les Films Arthur Lesser-C.I.C.C.-Films Borderie/Seven Arts c
(ALLEZ FRANCE)

Robert Dhery (*Henri*), Colette Brosset (*Yvette, Lady Brisbane*), Ronald Fraser (*Yvette's Husband*), Diana Dors (*Herself*), Pierre Olaf (*Police Telephone Operator*), Arthur Mullard (*Bank Robber*), Bernard Cribbins (*Police Sergeant*), Catherine Sola (*Sister*), Robert Rollis (*Desk Sergeant*), Henri Genes (*Friend*), Ferdy Mayne (*Diana Dors' Agent*), Richard Vernon, Jean Richard, Raymond Bussieres, Jean Carmet, Pierre Doris, Godfrey Quigley, Pierre Dac, Bernard Lajarrige, Robert Burnier, Pierre Tchernia, Billy Kearns, Robert Destain, Jacques Legras, Colin Blakely, Tim Brinton, Margaret Whiting, Colin Gordon, Georgina Cookson, Jean Lefebvre.

Frenchman Dhery goes to London with a group of his friends to see a soccer match. While waiting to see a dentist there, he playfully dons the uniform of a British policeman and scares away some thugs about to rob Dors. He's afraid to open his mouth to explain because his two front teeth have been knocked out earlier, so a long, silly chase follows until he takes off the uniform. Feeble at best. (In French; English subtitles.)

p, Henri Diamant-Berger; d, Robert Dhery; w, Dhery, Pierre Tchernia, Jean Lhote, Colette Brosset; ph, Jean Tournier, Henri Tiquet (Eastmancolor); m, Gerard Calvi; ed, Albert Jurgenson; art d, Jean Mandaroux; English subtitles, Noelle Gillmor.

Comedy (PR:A-C MPAA:NR)

COUNTERFEIT KILLER, THE** (1968) 95m UNIV c
Jack Lord (*Don Owens*), Shirley Knight (*Angie Peterson*), Jack Weston (*Randolph Riker*), Charles Drake (*Dolan*), Joseph Wiseman (*Rajeski*), Don Hanmer (*O'Hara*), Robert Pine (*Ed*), George Tyne (*George*), Cal Bartlett (*Reggie*), Dean Heyde (*Keyser*), L.Q. Jones (*Hotel Clerk*), David Renard (*Ambulance Attendant*), Nicholas Colasanto (*Plainclothes Policeman*), Mercedes McCambridge (*Frances*).

Secret Service Agent Jack Lord pretends to be a hit man in order to infiltrate a counterfeiting run by Wiseman. Most of the action takes place in a waterfront bar run by McCambridge. Nothing special. Based on the TV film THE FACELESS MAN.

p, Harry Tatelman; d, Josef Leytes; w, Harold Clements, Steven Bochco (based on TV production THE FACELESS MAN); ph, Benjamin H. Kline, John F. Warren; m, Quincy Jones; ed, Tony Martinelli; art d, John J. Floyd, Henry Larrecq; set d, John McCarthy, Robert C. Bradfield.

Crime (PR:A MPAA:NR)

COUNTERFEIT LADY*½ (1937) 56m COL bw
Ralph Bellamy (*Johnny*), Joan Perry (*Phyllis*), Douglass Dumbrille (*Marino*), George McKay (*Pinky*), Gene Morgan (*Clancy*), Henry Mollison (*Bemis*), John Tyrell (*Mike*), Max Hoffmann, Jr. (*Kit*), Edward Le Saint (*Girard*), John Harrington (*Swanson*).

Uninteresting crime drama has Perry a diamond thief pursued by private eye Bellamy, the cops, and a pair of gangster friends of the ripped-off jeweler. Some nice performances, but little more. New York model Perry, at that time still a relative newcomer to pictures, won rave reviews for her role as the implausible gem thief but she was to drop completely out of sight a mere six years later.

d, D. Ross Lederman; w, Tom Van Dycke (based on a story by Harold Shumate); ph, Allen G. Siegler; ed, James Sweeney.

Crime (PR:A MPAA:NR)

COUNTERFEIT PLAN, THE**½ (1957, Brit.) 79m Anglo Amalgamated/WB bw
Zachary Scott (*Max Brandt*), Peggie Castle (*Carol*), Mervyn Johns (*Louis*), Sydney Tafler (*Flint*), Lee Patterson (*Duke*), Chili Bouchier (*Housekeeper*), Eric Pohlmann (*Wandermann*), Robert Arden (*Bob*), John Welsh (*Inspector Grant*), David Lodge (*Watson*), Alvar Lidell (*Newsreader*), Aubrey Dexter (*Lepton*), Horace Lindrum, Mark Bellamy.

Escaped murderer Scott forces reformed forger Johns to counterfeit British five pound notes. All goes well until Castle, Johns's daughter, enters the picture to set off a string of events that will bring about Scott's downfall. Well made if not especially interesting.

p, Alec. C. Snowden; d, Montgomery Tully; w, James Eastwood; ph, Philip Grinwood; m, Richard Taylor; ed, Geoffrey Muller.

Crime (PR:A MPAA:NR)

COUNTERFEIT TRAITOR, THE***½ (1962) 140m PAR c
William Holden (*Eric Erickson*), Lilli Palmer (*Marianne Mollendorf*), Hugh Griffith (*Collins*), Ernst Schroder (*Baron Von Oldenbourg*), Eva Dahlbeck (*Ingrid Erickson*), Eulf Palme (*Max Gumpel*), Carl Raddatz (*Otto Holtz*), Helo Gutschwager (*Hans Holtz*), Erica Beer (*Klara Holtz*), Charles Regnier (*Wilhelm Kortner*), Werner Peters (*Bruno Ulrich*), Wolfgang Preiss (*Col. Nordoff*), Jochen Blume (*Dr. Jacob Karp*), Dirk Hansen (*Lt. Nagler*), Ludwig Naybert (*Stationmaster*), Klaus Kinski (*Kindler*), Erik Schumann (*Nazi Gunboat Officer*), Gunter Meissner (*Priest*), Stefan Schnabel (*Jaeger*), Martin Berliner (*Porter*), Phil Brown (*Harold Murray*), Peter Capell (*Unger*), Max Bucksbaum (*Fischer*), Egner Federspiel (*Prof. Christiansen*), Eva Fiebig (*Frau Hecker*), Holger Hagen (*Carl Bradley*), Kai Holm (*Gunnar*), Reinhard "Rene"

Kolldehoff (*Col. Erdmann*), Louis Miehe-Renard (*Poul*), Jens Osterholm (*Lars*), Paul Reichardt (*Fishing Boat Skipper*); Bendt Rothe (*Mogens*), Albert Rueprecht (*Capt. Barlach*), Ted Taylor (*Monitor Man*), Werner Van Deeg (*Oil Refinery Manager*), Georg Voelmmer (*Lt. Bretz*), John Wittig (*Sven*).

A fascinating true story of an American-born Swede (Holden) who is an oil trader doing business with the Nazis during WW II. This business gets the neutral businessman on the Allied enemies list and he is eager to change that status when British intelligence officer Griffith makes him an offer he can't refuse; they will clear his name at war's end if he agrees to spy on the Nazis for them. Holden agrees, although this fawning to the German forces causes him no end of aggravation with his family and friends. Wife Dahlbeck wants nothing to do with him and he is shunned by everyone as a traitor. On a trip to Berlin, he encounters fellow spy Palmer. They go into the espionage business together and, as fate would have it, fall in love. Holden convinces the Nazi officials that he is eager to erect an oil refinery in Sweden and is thus allowed to visit all the German refineries for ideas on how to do what he plans. In actuality, he is making notes on the plants' locations, capacities, and various other facts so he can pass them on to his Allied contacts. The Gestapo discover that Palmer is an agent and she is captured and executed, in full view of Holden, who can barely contain his fear, anger, and frustration. Despite his terrible mental strain, Holden is wise enough to gull the Nazis into believing that he knew nothing of Palmer's duplicity. Holden is eventually freed but placed in jeopardy again by Helo Gutschwager (his real name, honest!), a twelve-year-old Hitler Youth who would and did betray his own father (not unlike Skippy Homeier in TOMORROW THE WORLD). Holden manages to escape into the underground and is spirited to Denmark and thence home to Sweden where he sits out the rest of the war. After the hostilities ended, Holden is lauded by his government for his courageous spying and welcomed back into the fold. The picture was half an hour too long but Seaton's script was quite witty and showed his stage origins. Too bad his director didn't cut some of the dialog, but since his director was also Seaton, it's not easy. Filmed in West Berlin, Hamburg, Copenhagen, Stockholm, and various places in Holland, it is a delight to watch, if only for the backgrounds. Palmer (born Lillie Marie Peiser) is from Posen, Germany. Her father was a physician and her mother and sister were both actresses. Married to Rex Harrison for years, she is now wed to Carlos Thompson and happily writing best-sellers like *The Red Raven* and *Change Lobsters And Dance*.

p, William Perlberg; d&w, George Seaton (based on the book by Alexander Klein); ph, Jean Bourgoin (Technicolor); m, Alfred Newman; ed, Hans Ebel, Alma Macrorie: cos, Edith Head.

Spy Drama (PR:A-C MPAA:NR)

COUNTERFEITERS, THE** (1948) 73m FOX bw
John Sutton (*Jeff MacAllister*), Doris Merrick (*Margo*), Hugh Beaumont (*Philip Drake*), Lon Chaney (*Louie*), George O'Hanlon (*Frankie*), Douglas Blackley (*Tony*), Herbert Rawlinson (*Norman Talbott*), Pierre Watkins (*Carter*), Don Harvey (*Dan Taggart*), Fred Coby (*Piper*), Joyce Lansing (*Art Model*), Gerard Gilbert (*Jerry McGee*).

Decent crime tale of Scotland Yard detective Sutton teaming up with U.S. Secret Service agents to break up an international counterfeiting ring run by Beaumont. Merrick is Beaumont's daughter, in love with Sutton and trying to destroy the evidence that will convict her father.

p, Maurice H. Conn; d, Peter Stewart; w, Fred Myton, Barbara Worth (based on a story by Conn); ph, James B. Brown, Jr.; m, Irving Gertz; ed, Martin G. Conn.

Crime (PR:A MPAA:NR)

COUNTERFEITERS, THE*½ (1953, Ital.) 90m IFE/Gallo bw
Fosco Giachetti (*Moroni*), Doris Duranti (*Teresa*), Erno Crisa (*Pietro*), Lianella Carell (*Lucia*), Saro Urzi (*Commissioner*), Mario Angelotti (*Nicola*), Gabriele Ferzetti (*Dario*), Nerio Bernardi (*Maggiori*), Roberto Murolo (*Singer*).

Giachetti is an Italian detective breaking up a counterfeiting ring based in Naples. Starts out well, but bogs down in the second half. (In Italian; English subtitles.)

d, Franco Rossi; w, Edoardo Anton, Nazareno Gallo, Ugo Guerra, Leopold Trieste; ph, Domenico Scala; m, Carlo Rustichelli.

Crime (PR:A MPAA:NR)

COUNTERFEITERS OF PARIS, THE**½ (1962, Fr., Ital.) 99m Cite Films-CCM MGM bw
(LE CAVE SE REBIFFE IL RE DEI FAISARI; AKA: MONEY, MONEY, MONEY)
Jean Gabin (*The Boss*), Bernard Blier (*Charles*), Martine Carol (*Solange*), Francoise Rosay (*Pauline*), Ginette Leclerc (*Lea*), Antoine Balpetre (*Lucas*), Maurice Biraud (*Robert*), Frank Villard (*Eric*), Clara Gansard (*Georgette*), Heinrich Gretler (*Tauchmann*), Albert Dinan, Gerard Buhr, Lisa Jouvet, Gabriel Gobin, Robert Dalban, Jacques Marin, Paul Faivre, Helene Dieudonne, Claude Ivry, Rene Hell, Max Doria, Charles Bouillaud, Albert Michel, Marcel Charvey, Jean Moulart, Antonio Ramirez.

Blier and Villard decide to get out of the prostitution business and begin a counterfeiting ring. They recruit old timer Gabin to supervise the operation, planning to cheat him out of his 50 percent cut. Gabin proves too cagey for the pair and along with engraver Biraud he steals all the profits and goes to South America. Okay crime drama.

p, Jacques Bar; d, Gilles Grangier; w, Albert Simonin, Michel Audiard, Grangier, Michel Audiard (based on the novel *Le Cave Se Rebiffe* by Simonin); ph, Louis Page; m, Francis Lemarque, Michel Legrand; ed, Jacqueline Thiedot; set d, Jacques Colombier.

Crime Drama (PR:C MPAA:NR)

COUNTERPLOT* (1959) 76m UA bw
Forrest Tucker (*Brock*), Allison Hayes (*Connie*), Gerald Milton (*Bergmann*), Edmundo

Rivera Alvarez *(Alfred)*, Jackie Wayne *(Manuel)*, Miguel Angel Alvarez *(Spargo)*, Rita Tanno *(Girl)*, Charles Gibbs *(McGregor)*, Richard Vernie *(Murdock)*, Art Bedard *(Dugan)*, Ulises Brenes *(Nibley)*, Guardo Albani *(Police Chief)*, Raul Davila *(Messenger)*, Ted Smith *(Bartender)*, Yvonne Peck *(Maid)*.

Tucker is on the lam in Puerto Rico from a murder in New York he didn't commit. Wayne is the native boy who helps him until he can clear his name in this dull melodrama where Hayes plays the romance side as the girl who sticks with Tucker through it all.

p&d, Kurt Neumann; w, Richard Blake.

Crime **(PR:A MPAA:NR)**

COUNTERPOINT**½** (1967) 105m UNIV c

Charlton Heston *(Evans)*, Maximillian Schell *(Schiller)*, Kathryn Hays *(Annabelle)*, Leslie Nielsen *(Victor)*, Anton Diffring *(Arndt)*, Linden Chiles *(Long)*, Pete Masterson *(Calloway)*, Curt Lowens *(Klingerman)*, Neva Patterson *(Dorothy)*, Cyril Delevanti *(Tartzoff)*, Gregory Morton *(Jordon)*, Parley Baer *(Hook)*, Dan Frazer *(Chaminant)*, Ed Peck *(Prescott)*, Ralph Nelson *(Belgian Officer)*.

One of those rare films in which Heston is not in a toga, doublet and hose, or a western costume. Jut-jawed Charlton is the conductor of a large orchestra giving a concert in a small European town in the winter of 1944. The town is bombed and the orchestra scurries for cover. Heston boards them on a bus but not before announcing that none will board until all are ready: "It will be the first time in this tour that the orchestra will finish together." (And that gives you some idea of Heston's character; rude, cold, and arrogant. We are supposed to root for him against the German who is equally vicious. Leaves us precious little to care about, si?) The bus is stopped by German soldiers, led by Diffring, who must have played this part a hundred times in his career. Diffring takes the musicians to a castle where he plans to kill them all (no doubt a very strict critic). Their lives are saved by Schell, playing a Nazi for the umpteenth time in *his* career, who says that a concert by Heston and his crew will be helpful to the German war effort by relieving boredom. Heston refuses and Schell sits at the piano and plays a classical piece with no style whatsoever. Heston can't bear it. He plays the piece correctly. Later, Heston announces that the group will play for the German as "we've all toured with corrupt concert managements, so this should be a familiar experience." Heston consults with Hays, wife of concertmaster Nielsen and one-time lover of Charlton's. She is to dine with Schell later that night and Heston informs her that Max is an "arrogant, egotistical martinet with a God complex." Hays, smiles, repeats Heston's words . . . "that should be a familiar experience." The seduction doesn't work and Schell presses Heston to perform, but Charlton realizes that could spell their end as once the concert takes place the game is over and Schell just might agree to Diffring's suggestion that they all be machine-gunned. Two American soldiers are part of the orchestra, but not really. They are in hiding and masquerading as part of the band. They attempt to get away and are killed by the Nazis in a sidebar story that just takes up time. Schell must now leave the castle and realizes that he can't take the orchestra with him. Unknown to the musicians, a mass grave is dug and they are going to be killed after their final concert for Schell. In the midst of the concert, the musicians fight back and a battle takes place. A few are killed and the others rush for the bus that brought them and a getaway. Heston has the last scene with Diffring who is about to shoot the conductor when Schell shoots Diffring with no emotion. Turns out he likes Charlton better than Anton. The picture ends with Heston having won the battle of wills and Schell philosophically looking forward to the end of the war. Surely the best thing about the movie was the classical music played by the Los Angeles Philharmonic Orchestra. Selections from Schubert, Brahms, Beethoven, Wagner, Tchaikovsky with mood music by Bronsilaw Kaper are what will be most remembered about this film.The music, plus the fact that Heston smiled in one scene! Oliansky, who co-scripted, must love the world of classical music because, many years later, he wrote and directed the numbing THE COMPETITION. Producer Dick Berg has always been known as a man who worked hard for the projects in which he believed. His television credits are legendary but his films are not. There *is* a difference.

p, Dick Berg; d, Ralph Nelson; w, Joel Oliansky, James Lee (based on *The General* by Alan Sillitoe); ph, Russell Metty (Techniscope, Technicolor); m, Bronislaw Kaper; ed, Howard G. Epstein; art d, Alexander Golitzen, Carl Anderson; set d, John McCarthy, George Milo; cos, Burton Miller; music: Selections from "Unfinished Symphony" (Franz Peter Schubert), "Swan Lake" (Peter Ilich Tchaikovsky), "Tannhauser Overture" (Richard Wagner), *Symphony No. 1* (Johannes Brahms), *Symphony No. 5* (Ludwig von Beethoven).

War/Musical **(PR:A-C MPAA:NR)**

COUNTERSPY MEETS SCOTLAND YARD**** (1950) 67m COL bw

Howard St. John *(David Harding)*, Amanda Blake *(Karen Michele)*, Ron Randell *(Simon Langton)*, June Vincent *(Barbara Taylor)*, Fred Sears *(Peters)*, John Dehner *(Robert Reynolds)*, Lewis Martin *(Dr. Victor Gilbert)*, Rick Vallin *(McCullough)*, Jimmy Lloyd *(Burton)*, Ted Jordan *(Brown)*, Gregory Gay *(Prof. Schuman)*, Douglas Evans *(Col. Kilgore)*, Paul Marton *(Paul)*, Don Brodie *(Jimmy)*, Everett Glass *(Doc Ritter)*, Charles Meredith *(Miller)*, Robert Rice *(Fields)*, John Doucette *(Larry)*.

Based on "Counterspy" radio series, St. John plays the supersleuth, tracking down the killer of one of his agents at a guided missile base. Randell is a Scotland Yard detective who helps out by taking the dead man's place. Cast seems to be having fun, and audiences should, too.

p, Wallace MacDonald; d, Seymour Friedman; w, Harold R. Greene (based on "Counterspy" radio series created by Phillips H. Lord); ph, Philip Tannura; ed, Aaron Stell; md, Mischa Bakaleinikoff.

Spy Drama **(PR:A MPAA:NR)**

COUNTESS DRACULA***** (1972, Brit.) 94m Hammer/FOX c

Ingrid Pitt *(Countess Elizabeth Nadasdy)*, Nigel Green *(Capt. Dobi)*, Sandor Eles *(Imre Toth)*, Maurice Denham *(Master Fabio)*, Patience Collier *(Julia)*, Peter Jeffrey *(Capt. Balogh)*, Lesley-Anne Down *(Ilona)*, Leon Lissek *(Sergeant)*, Jessie Evans *(Rosa)*, Andrea Lawrence *(Zizi)*, Nike Arrighi *(Gypsy)*, Charles Farrell *(Seller)*, Hulya Babus *(Belly Dancer)*.

Superior Hammer horror film starring Pitt as an elderly countess who finds she can regain her youth and beauty by bathing in the blood of virgins. With the help of her loyal servant Green, Pitt keeps herself supplied with the blood of young beauties whose corpses are being discovered by the locals scattered about the countryside. For sexual interest, Pitt latches onto young stud Eles by passing herself off as her own daughter. Unfortunately, as the bloodbaths increase so does Pitt's madness, until finally . . . Based upon the real-life mass murderess, Countess Elizabeth Bathory, a mad Hungarian harridan who was found guilty of murdering virgins and bathing in their blood to preserve her youthful appearance. She is credited with 610 murders. The blood-letting countess was walled up in her rooms where she died in 1614.

p, Alexander Paal; d, Peter Sasdy; w, Jeremy Paul (based on a story by Paal, Sasdy, Gabriel Ronay); ph, Ken Talbot (Eastmancolor); art d, Philip Harrison.

Horror **(PR:O MPAA:PG)**

COUNTESS FROM HONG KONG, A*** (1967, Brit.) 120 Chaplin/Rank UNIV c

Marlon Brando *(Ogden Mears)*, Sophia Loren *(Natasha)*, Sydney Chaplin *(Harvey Crothers)*, Tippi Hedren *(Martha)*, Patrick Cargill *(Hudson)*, Michael Medwin *(John Felix)*, Oliver Johnston *(Clark)*, John Paul *(Captain)*, Angela Scoular *(Society Girl)*, Margaret Rutherford *(Miss Gaulswallow)*, Peter Bartlett *(Steward)*, Bill Nagy *(Crawford)*, Dilys Laye *(Saleswoman)*, Angela Pringle *(Baroness)*, Jenny Bridges *(Countess)*, Arthur Gross *(Immigration Officer)*, Balbina *(French Maid)*, Burnell Tucker *(Hotel Receptionist)*, Leonard Trolley *(Purser)*, Len Lowe *(Electrician)*, Francis Dux *(Head Waiter)*, Cecil Cheng *(Cab Driver)*, Kevin Manser *(Photographer)*, Carol Cleveland *(Nurse)*, Charles Chaplin *(Old Steward)*, Anthony Chin, Jose Sukhum Boonive *(Hawaiians)*, Geraldine Chaplin, Janine Hill *(Girls at Dance)*, Michael Spice, Ronald Rubin, Ray Marlow *(American Sailors)*, Josephine Chaplin, Victoria Chaplin *(Young Girls)*.

Chaplin's final return to the screen after a 10-year hiatus (THE KING IN NEW YORK, 1957), is a dismal, uninviting comedy. Brando is a stuffy American diplomat whose coffers bulge with millions. He sails from Hong Kong on a luxury liner, heading for Honolulu where his estranged wife, Hedren, is to join him. Complicating his life is a white Russian countess, Loren, utterly penniless, who seeks a new life in the U.S. and stows away in Brando's suite. She met him in a nightclub after explaining that since age thirteen she had been earning a living as a dance-hall floozie. She begs him, once he discovers her hiding in his suite, to allow her to go to America. When he refuses, she threatens to charge him with abduction and ruin his good name. Brando allows her to stay while he attempts to figure out a way to explain her presence. This leads to innumerable comic situations, few of them funny, while the ship sails closer and closer to Hedren and more dilemma. When Loren is discovered, Brando saves the day and marries her, giving her U.S. citizenship. She believes he hates her and when the ship nears Hawaii, Loren dons a revealing native costume and leaps overboard, swimming to shore. Hedren arrives and Brando realizes he does not love her at all. He races off the docked boat to find Loren and make their marriage a happy reality. This kind of bedroom farce, so dear to Chaplin's heart, died at a box office long tired of such archaic plots. Brando's great talent is entirely wasted. He accepted the acting assignment without ever having glanced at the script, assuming that any film Chaplin would make would be a masterpiece, a decision he lived to regret. Chaplin's story and script employed moth-eaten dialog and static scenes which none of the actors could enliven. He also directed with eyes closed in memory of another age and his leaden hand fondles situations that died decades earlier on the Sennett lot. Loren spends most of her time teasing Brando and the audience while wearing his silk pajamas, running in and out of closets and toilets to hide, a peek-a-boo performance that is embarrassing. She is used purely as a sex object which Chaplin was not wrong in employing since Loren's entire career is based upon that kind of appeal. In once scene, clothes Brando has bought for her arrive and she holds up an enormous bra that would fit Mrs. King Kong. Her lines are delivered phlegmatically and are almost unintelligible through her thick Italian accent. Loren gives merely another breast-jutting performance incongruous with the role of a petite, ultra feminine lady. She is earthy and peasant-like where the role calls for sophistication and culture. Her unbelievability is matched by Brando who struts about mouthing diplomatic ambiguities and anxieties over what Loren's sexy presence will do to his image and career. Hedren's appearance is thankfully brief as a pretty prop who speaks her lines as if they are being ground out of a mechanical toy. (Both Loren and Hedren, of course, were manufactured stars, the Italian actress wholly constructed into an Amazonian glamour queen by her husband-producer Carlo Ponti, and one-time model Hedren being a creation of Alfred Hitchcock.) Chaplin's return to the movies is a sad failure and was universally shunned. The only redeeming feature of A COUNTESS FROM HONG KONG were the brief scenes dominated by the always charming Rutherford who plays an eccentric old lady confined to her stateroom because of illness. But her magic presence is not enough to turn this fiasco around. Further leaving a bad taste is the rampant nepotism practiced by Chaplin; he gave roles to his son Sydney, his daughter Geraldine and a bevy of other Chaplin offspring. He himself couldn't resist the limelight, appearing as an elderly crew member. Chaplin fought back against critics who condemned the film, sending out a release which he had penned. The film, he explained, "resulted from a visit I made to Shanghai in 1931 where I came across a number of titled aristocrats who had escaped the Russian Revolution. They were destitute and without a country, their status was of the lowest grade. The men ran rickshaws and the women worked in ten cent dance halls. When the second World War broke out many of the old aristocrats had died and the younger generation migrated to Hong Kong where their plight was even worse for Hong Kong was overcrowded with refugees. This is the background to A COUNTESS FROM HONG KONG. I have tried to achieve a simplicity of direction which should lend realism to the situation, and which should create a compelling belief in the comedy." Despite Chaplin's plea, no one was compelled to see this film. It would probably have been better if he had filmed the 1931 story of deprivation in Shanghai instead of the glossed over tale surrounded in luxury liner comforts decades later. Brando started with nothing but praise for Chaplin but by the end of the film he hardly spoke to the director. It was a film he wanted to forget instantly after final shooting. Chaplin did not take the critical attacks he received gracefully. "If they [the critics] don't like it," he roared, "they're bloody fools!" When some critics called the film "old fashioned," the producer-director-writer exploded, saying: "*They* are old fashioned! I still think it's a great film, and I think audiences will agree with me rather than the critics." No one agreed with him except Sophia Loren who later carped: "I don't think the film's reception was fair at all." She commented that when A COUNTESS FROM HONG KONG was released on Italian TV it got good reviews. Songs: "This Is My Song," "My Star" (Chaplin).

p, Jerome Epstein, Charles Chaplin; d, w&m, Chaplin; ph, Arthur Ibbetson (Technicolor); ed, Gordon Hales; prod d, Don Ashton; md, Lambert Williamson; art d, Bob Cartwright; set d, Vernon Dixon; cos, Rosemary Burrows.

Comedy/Romance   **(PR:C MPAA:NR)**

COUNTESS OF MONTE CRISTO, THE**   (1934) 74m UNIV bw
Fay Wray (*Janet*), Paul Lukas (*Rumowski*), Reginald Owen (*The Baron*), Patsy Kelly (*Mimi*), Paul Page (*Stefan*), Carmel Myers (*Flower Girl*), Robert McWade (*Hotel Manager*), Richard Tucker (*Director*), Bobby Watson (*Hotel Valet*), Frank Reicher (*Police Commissioner*), John Sheehan.

Fay Wray is a disenchanted extra from a Viennese movie who runs off with her costume to a posh resort and impersonates a countess. Owen and Lukas are a pair of dashing jewel thieves who help her (and themselves). Patsy Kelly gets all the laughs as Wray's maid in this slim comedy remade from a German film of some years earlier. (Remade in 1948.)

d, Karl Freund; w, Karen De Wolf, Gene Lewis, Gladys Unger (based on a story by Walter Fleischer from a German film of the same name); ph, Charles Stumar.

Comedy   **(PR:A MPAA:NR)**

COUNTESS OF MONTE CRISTO, THE*   (1948) 76m UNIV bw
Sonja Henie (*Karen*), Olga San Juan (*Jenny*), Dorothy Hart (*Peg Manning*), Michael Kirby (*Paul von Cram*), Arthur Treacher (*Managing Director*), Hugh French (*Count Holgar*), Ransom Sherman (*Mr. Hansen*), Freddie Trenkler (*Skating Specialty*), John James (*Freddie*), Arthur O'Connell (*Assistant Director*), Joseph Crehan (*Joe*), Ray Teal (*Charlie*), Jim Nolan (*Lieutenant*), Lester Dorr (*Clerk*), John Elliott (*Innkeeper*), Pierce Lydeon (*2nd Officer*), Phil Sherard (*Bell Hop*), Bess Flowers (*Woman*), Robert Rich (*Man*).

Sonja Henie's last film, and her worst, is a musical version of the story of the costumed film extras who pass themselves off as aristocrats. This time Henie runs out of an Oslo studio with her friend San Juan in tow and they set themselves up in Treacher's resort. Henie skates her way through six numbers and San Juan sings three: "The Friendly Polka," "Count Your Blessings," and "Who Believes in Santa Claus," (Jack Brooks, Saul Chaplin). (Remake of the 1934 film.)

p, John Beck; d, Frederick De Cordova; wm William Bowers (based on the story by Walter Reisch from a German film of the same name); ph, Edward Cronjager; m, Walter Scharf; ed, Edward Curtiss.

Musical   **(PR:A MPAA:NR)**

COUNTRY BEYOND, THE*   (1936) 67m FOX bw
Rochelle Hudson (*Jean Alison*), Paul Kelly (*Sgt. Cassidy*), Robert Kent (*Corp. Robert King*), Alan Hale (*Jim Alison*), Alan Dinehart (*Ray Jennings*), Andrew Toombes (*Sen. Rawlings*), Claudia Coleman (*Mrs. Rawlings*), Matt McHugh (*Constable Weller*), Paul McVey (*Fred Donaldson*), Holmes Herbert (*Inspector Reed*), Buck (*Himself*), Prince (*Wolf*).

Inspired by the success of comedy-mystery as seen in THE THIN MAN, Fox decided to try it in a Mountie film, where it flopped utterly. Kent is the Royal Canadian Mountie in love with Hudson, Hale's daughter. Kent suspects Hale of theft and murder, but finally Dinehart is revealed as the real culprit. Buck, the St. Bernard, had previously starred opposite Clark Gable in CALL OF THE WILD, 1935.

p, Sol M. Wurzel; d, Eugene Forde; w, Lamar Trotti, Adele Commandini (based on a story by James Oliver Curwood); ph, Barney McGill; ed, Fred Allen.

Western   **(PR:A MPAA:NR)**

COUNTRY BOY zero   (1966) 84m Ambassador Films/Howco International c
                         (AKA: HERE COMES THAT NASHVILLE SOUND)
Randy Boone (*Link Byrd, Jr.*), Sheb Wooley (*Himself*), Paul Brinegar (*Mr. Byrd*), Paul Crabtree (*Fats Jackson*), Majel Barrett (*Miss Wynn*), James Dobson (*George Washington Byrd*), Sondra Rodgers (*Mrs. Byrd*), John Pickard (*Claude Springer*), Maurice Dembsky (*Dave Rupp*), Chuck Doughty (*Thomas Jefferson Byrd*), Ed Livingston (*John Adams Byrd*), Paulette Leeman (*Lucinda May*), Bob Stewart (*Ernie*), Ivan Purser (*Mr. Bean*), R.N. Pelot (*Mr. Potts*), Dick Brackett (*Reporter*), C.B. Anderson (*Angry Man*), Bob Jennings (*Television Announcer*), Ruth Charron (*Angry Woman*), Joe Kane (*The President*), Skeeter Davis, Grandpa Jones, Lonzo & Oscar, Glaser Brothers, Ray Pillow, Lois Johnson, Stoney Mountain Cloggers, Hillous Butrum, Bobby Dyson, James Steward, Jane Colvard, Walter Haynes, Beegie Cruser.

Wretched country-western musical has Boone a gas station attendant discovered by Wooley. He goes to Nashville but is stricken with stage fright. He is picked up by an agent who dresses him as Abraham Lincoln and makes him a rock singer. Audiences are furious at this sacrilege and the President calls Boone's father to the White House to try to convince him to talk his son out of his act. The father travels to New York, where Boone is going to be on television. He comes out on stage and begins tongue-lashing his son. Boone sings a patriotic song, gets a standing ovation, and

returns home with his father. A number of C&W stars make cameos. Just plain bad. Songs: "Country Boy," "Cry, Cry Lily," "A Little Hunk Of America," "Somewhere," "First Kiss," "She Passed My Way," "Would You Believe," "Wanted Dead Or Alive" (Paul Crabtree), "Draggin' The River," (Sheb Wooley), "Tomorrow," "Baby, They're Playing Our Song," "Fifteen Cents Worth Of Pinto Beans," "The Grass Grows Greener," "Cindy."

p, E. Stanley Williamson; d, Joe Kane; w, Paul Crabtree; ph, Akan Stensvold; ed, Verna Fields; md, Hillous Butrum; art d, J. Don Fields.

Comedy/Musical   **(PR:A MPAA:NR)**

COUNTRY BRIDE zero   (1938, USSR) 85m Ukrainfilm/Amkino bw
                                (AKA: THE RICH BRIDE)
F. N. Kuirkhin (*Naum*), Maria Ladynina (*Marinka*), Boris Bezgin (*Pavlo Zgara*), Ivan Diubeznov (*Alexei Kovinko*), Anna Dinokhovskaya (*Palaga Fedorovna*), Ivan Matveyev (*Senka*), Liubov Sveshnikova (*Frosska*).

More musical propaganda from the Social Realism folks in the USSR. Story deals with a romantic triangle between a pretty blonde collective farmhand, the handsome tractor driver, and the guitar-playing warehouse checker. The girl, of course, opts for the heroic man of the soil. Unbearable, except for a few character portrayals and a little tuneful music. Director Piriov, who was associated with avante garde theater in the 1920s, originally became famous for his musicals but later did some fine screen adaptations of Dostoyevsky's work.

d, Ivan Piriov; w, Yvegeni Pomeschikov; ph, Vladimir Okulich; m, Isaac O. Dunayevsky; m/l, V. J. Lebedev-Kumach.

Musical   **(PR:A MPAA:NR)**

COUNTRY DANCE   (SEE: BROTHERLY LOVE, 1970, Brit.)

COUNTRY DOCTOR, THE**½   (1936) 93m FOX bw
Jean Hersholt (*Dr. John Luke*), June Lang (*Mary MacKenzie*), Slim Summerville (*Constable Jim Ogden*), Michael Whalen (*Tony Luke*), Dorothy Peterson (*Nurse Katherine Kennedy*), Robert Barrat (*MacKenzie*), Jane Darwell (*Mrs. Graham*), John Qualen (*Asa Wyatt*), Frank Reicher (*Dr. Paul Luke*), Montagu Love (*Sir Basil Crawford*), David Torrence (*Governor General*), George Chandler (*Greasy*), Helen Jerome Eddy (*Mrs. Ogden*), Aileen Carlyle (*Mrs. Wyatt*), George Meeker (*Dr. Wilson*), J. Anthony Hughes (*Mike*), William Benedict (*The Gawker*), The Dionne Quintuplets.

Fictionalized telling of the birth of the Dionne quints and the backwoods doctor who pulled it off and a worldwide bull's-eye at the box office at the time. Hersholt plays Dr. Dafoe (here called Dr. Luke) who battles against small-town narrow-mindedness to get a hospital built. Finally it is erected, but the backers pick someone else to head it. Then Qualen rushes in to fetch Hersholt to help his wife deliver and the quintuplets make their appearance, stealing the last quarter of the film. Nazi Germany's Minister of Propaganda Josef Goebbels banned this film because of Hersholt being Jewish. In desperation of getting a foreign buck and to their everlasting shame some Fox officials actually corresponded with the Nazis to get them to relent, pointing out that Hersholt was only a little bit Jewish, and that his nearest Jewish relative had been dead for three generations. Goebbels read the correspondence and sneered a definite no; the film was not shown in the Third Reich. Almost all the Hollywood studios of the era buckled under to anti-Semetic pressure from Hitler's regime, all except the feisty Jack Warner. His distribution official in Germany, Joseph Kaufmann, was dragged out of his office one day by Jew-baiting Brownshirt thugs and beaten so badly in the street in front of scores of passersby that he died of his wounds. Warner immediately closed down all his offices in Germany and told the Nazis to go to hell. From that moment on Warner Brothers films attacked the Nazis at every turn, losing money and winning the respect of the free world.

p, Darryl F. Zanuck; d, Henry King; w, Sonya Levien (based on a story by Charles E. Blake); ph, John Seitz, Daniel B. Clark; ed, Barbara McLean; md, Louis Silver; technical supervision, Dr. Allan Dafoe.

Drama   **(PR:A MPAA:NR)**

COUNTRY DOCTOR, THE zero   (1963, Portuguese) 93m Filipe de Solms bw
Jorge Sousa Costa (*Doctor*), Joao Guedes (*Dr. Valenca*), Emilio Gulmaraes (*Pharmacist*), Irene Cruz (*Luisa*).

Dull story of young doctor Costa taking over a rural practice and meeting the opposition of the locals, not to mention getting little help from the retiring doctor or from Portugal's inexperience in making films.

p, Filipe de Solms; d, Jorge Brum do Canto; w, Fernando Namora, do Canto; ph, Mario Moreira; m, Shegundo Calarza.

Drama   **(PR:A MPAA:NR)**

COUNTRY FAIR*½   (1941) 74m REP bw
Eddie Foy, Jr. (*Johnny Campbell*), June Clyde (*Pepper Wilson*), Guinn "Big Boy" Williams (*Gunther Potts*), William Demarest (*Stogie McPhee*), Harold Huber (*Cash Nichols*), Ferris Taylor (*Cornelius Simpson*), Maurice Cass (*Sneezy*), Lulubelle Wiseman (*Lulubelle*), Scotty Wiseman (*Scotty*), Harold Peary (*Gildersleeve*), Whitey Ford (*Whitey*), The Vass Family, The Simp Phonies.

A number of old-time radio personalities enliven this otherwise dull comedy. Fast-talking campaign manager Foy talks Clyde into marrying him should his candidate for governor (Demarest) win. She immediately sets about helping the opponent (Peary aka: The Great Gildersleeve on the Fibber McGee radio show). Musical interludes are sprinkled at random throughout the show, including "Mornin' on the Farm" (Jack Elliott).

p, Armand Schaefer; d, Frank McDonald; w, Dorrell and Stuart McGowan (based on an original idea by Jack Townley); ph, Ernest Miller; m, Cy Feuer; ed, Ernest Nims.

Comedy   **(PR:A MPAA:NR)**

COUNTRY GENTLEMEN** (1937) 66m REP bw
Ole Olsen *(Hamilton)*, Chic Johnson *(Williams)*, Joyce Compton *(Gertie)*, Lila Lee *(Mrs. Heath)*, Pierre Watkin *(Grayson)*, Donald Kirke *(Martin)*, Ray Corrigan *(Briggs)*, Sammy McKim *(Billy Heath)*, Wade Boteler *(1st Deputy)*, Ivan Miller *(2nd Deputy)*, Olin Howland *(Lawyer)*, Frank Sheridan *(Chief of Police)*, Harry Harvey *(Shorty)*, Joe Cunningham *(Chuck)*, Prince *(Dog)*.

The old vaudeville team of Olsen and Johnson play a pair of con men in this pleasant comedy. They sell phony stocks, get locked up on kidnaping charges, and get released to sell oil wells shares at a veterans home. When the well turns up dry the boys are chased down by the enraged vets, but just as they are about to get theirs, the well comes up a gusher.

p, Nat Levine; d, Ralph Staub; w, Joseph Hoffman, James P. Medbury, Gertrude Orr (based on a story by Milton Raison, Jack Harvey, Jo Graham); ph, Ernest Miller.

Comedy **Cas.** **(PR:A MPAA:NR)**

COUNTRY GIRL, THE**** (1954) 104m PAR bw
Bing Crosby *(Frank Elgin)*, Grace Kelly *(Georgie Elgin)*, William Holden *(Bernie Dodd)*, Anthony Ross *(Phil Cook)*, Gene Reynolds *(Larry)*, Jacqueline Fontaine *(Singer-Actress)*, Eddie Ryder *(Ed)*, Robert Kent *(Paul Unger)*, John W. Reynolds *(Henry Johnson)*, Frank Scanell *(Bartender)*, Ida Moore, Ruth Ricksby *(Women)*, Hal K. Dawson, Howard Joslin, Richard Keene, Jack Kenney, Les Clark *(Actors)*, Charles Tannen, John Florio *(Photographers)*, Jonathan Provost *(Jimmie)*, Don Dunning, Max Wagner *(Expressmen)*, Bob Alden *(Bellboy)*, Allan Douglas, Jack Roberts *(Men)*.

Cool, collected Kelly won the Oscar for playing the wife of alcoholic Crosby, a has-been stage actor with a fondness for Mssrs. Haig and Haig. George Seaton's adaptation of Clifford Odets's play also captured the Oscar while Crosby, Warren's camerawork, and the film itself lost out in the Academy Awards to Marlon Brando and Boris Kaufman for best picture, ON THE WATERFRONT. That aside, in any other year this movie might have swept. Crosby is auditioning for a part in a new play for martinet director Holden who had been a great fan of Crosby's years before and now wants to fulfill a dream by casting his idol as the lead. Holden feels certain he can keep Crosby off the sauce but Bing is not quite so confident. He's never been the same since he let go of his little son's hand to pose for a picture and the lad was killed by an auto. Since then, Crosby has spent much of his time drowning that sorrow in various libations. Holden visits Bing's house and meets the wife, Kelly. He suspects she may be the reason why Crosby is always in such a state of turmoil, so he insists that she doe not attend rehearsals. Crosby pleads with Holden to allow Kelly to be there as she is, he claims, very unstable and might commit suicide if shunted aside. Holden can't see anything shaky about the seemingly strong woman and they start having some pitched verbal wars which peak when Holden informs Kelly that she is the reason why Crosby may never get back to his old level in show business. Kelly tells Holden that he has no idea of what he's talking about and that he must mind his own business and stick to Crosby's life on the stage, nothing more. Just before opening night, Crosby goes off on a toot and is located at the police station, drying out in the drunk tank with the dregs of the city for his partners. The cops turn him over to Holden and Kelly who, by this time, have learned that all of their angry talk was just postponing the fact that they were magnetically attracted to each other. Holden has now realized that Kelly is what she seems, solid and bright with no neurosis, and Crosby is the weaker of the two and using Kelly as an excuse for his own frailties. Holden goes to work on Crosby to get him into condition for the play. Countless hours of direction are given to Crosby and the payoff is that he opens to brilliant notices and universal approval from the audience. At a party after the opening, Crosby's sensitivity is high and he sees that Holden and Kelly are closer than one's director and one's wife usually are. Before any confrontation is made, Kelly sees that her husband is no longer the pitiful alcoholic he was in reel one and she vows to stay with him. He has his confidence back and is, once again, the man she married. Kelly only made eleven pictures in her brief career. THE COUNTRY GIRL was her sixth and also garnered her the New York Film Critics award as Best Actress. Crosby never had much of an opportunity to play serious roles, as audiences demanded he sing, and who could blame them? This is just one of few films where the baritone wasn't much heard (MAN OF FIRE, STAGECOACH). It was the audience's loss because Crosby was a far better actor than most of his roles allowed. In this movie he was able to totally rid himself of the screen persona that was so well known and allow another person to emerge; a fully-rounded character as conceived by Odets and realized by Seaton. Had Brando not been eligible that year, the statuette would have been Crosby's. As the third character in this three-character piece, it's possible to be washed away by the waves of drama from the other two. Not so with Holden. He more than held his own and added another dimension to the role that became uniquely his. They added a song for Bing to do with nightery performer Fontaine. That, plus the other tunes were not needed and only served to remind us that Crosby was Crosby and not Frank Elgin, the drunken actor. Insuring the production with some Crosby tunes was a poor decision but, luckily, the value of the material and the quality of the performance ably overcame any front office interference.

p, William Perlberg, George Seaton; d&w, Seaton (based on the play by Clifford Odets); ph, John F. Warren; m, Victor Young; ed, Ellsworth Hoagland; art d, Hal Pereira, Roland Anderson; set d, Sam Comer, Grace Gregory; cos, Edith Head; spec eff, John P. Fulton; ch, Robert Alton; m/l, "The Pitchman," "Live and Learn," "The Search Is Through" (Ira Gershwin, Harold Arlen).

Drama **Cas.** **(PR:A-C MPAA:NR)**

COUNTRY MUSIC HOLIDAY* (1958) 80m Aurora/PAR bw
Ferlin Husky *(Verne Brand)*, Zsa Zsa Gabor *(Zsa Zsa)*, Rocky Graziano *(Rocky)*, Faron Young *(Clyde Woods)*, Al Fisher *(Himself)*, Lou Marks *(Lou Marks)*, June Carter *(Marietta)*, Jesse White *(Sonny Moon)*, Cliff Norton *(Morty Chapman)*, Rod Brasfield *(Pappy)*, Hope Sansberry *(Ma)*, Patty Duke *(Sis)*, Art Ford *(Donovan)*, Lew Parker *(Lew Parker)*, The Jordanaires, Drifting Johnny Miller, Lonzo and Oscar, the LaDell Sisters, Bernie Nee.

Cornball comedy has hick Husky a singer, half owned by Jesse White and half by Gabor. But his slim plot is secondary as most of the running time is taken up with musical numbers including: "Somewhere There's Sunshine," "Terrific Together," "Don't Walk Away From Me," "Wide Wide World," "My Home Town," "Just One More Chance," "The Face of Love," and "When It Rains It Pours." Most of the specialty acts that appear in the film are long gone from public attention.

p, Ralph Serpe, Howard B. Kreitsek; d, Alvin Ganzer; w, H.B.Cross; ph, William B. Kelly; ed, Ralph Rosenbloom; md, Dave Dryer.

Musical **(PR:A MPAA:NR)**

COUNTRYMAN*** (1982, Jamaica) 102m Island c
Countryman, Hiram Keller, Kristina St. Clair, Carl Bradshaw, Basil Keane, Ronnie McKay, Ronald Gossop. Oliver Sammuels, Chin, Jahman, Buster Jameson, Freshey Richardson, Bobby Russell, Lucien Tai Ten Quee, Claudia Robinson, Papa Threecards, Monair Zacca, Peter Packer, Dee Anthony, Jim Newman, Kingsley Rose, Honey Fernandez, Duncan Booth.

Enjoyable film that recaptures the magic of reggae cult-classic THE HARDER THEY COME (1973). Countryman stars as a native fisherman with mystical powers who rescues an American couple whose plane has crashed nearby. The kindly Rastaman protects the Americans from a group of local politicians who want to use the couple as a political symbol to aid them in the upcoming elections. The usual political messages, ganja smoking, and Rasta-preachiness surface, but there is also plenty of great music from Bob Marley and the Wailers, The Gladiators and others.

p, Chris Blackwell; d, Dickie Jobson; w, Jobson, Michael Thomas; ph, Dominique Chapuis (Technicolor); m, Wally Badarou; ed, John Victor Smith, Peter Boyle; art d, Bernard Leonard.

Drama/Musical **Cas.** **(PR:C MPAA:NR)**

COUNTY CHAIRMAN, THE*** (1935) 85m FOX bw
Will Rogers *(Jim Hackler)*, Evelyn Venable *(Lucy Rigby)*, Kent Taylor *(Ben Jarvey)*, Louise Dresser *(Mrs. Mary Rigby)*, Mickey Rooney *(Freckles)*, Frank Melton *(Henry Cleaver)*, Berton Churchill *(Elias Rigby)*, Robert McWade *(Tom Cruden)*, Russell Simpson *(Vance Jimmison)*, William V. Mong *(Uncle Eck)*, Jan Duggan *(Abigail Teksbury)*, Gay Seabrook *(Lorna Cruden)*, Charles Middleton *(Riley Cleaver)*, Stepin Fetchit *(Sassafras)*.

A story of small time politics in 1880s Wyoming has Rogers as the attorney who promotes his adopted son (Taylor) in a race for public prosecutor against corrupt incumbent Churchill. Starts out slow but not bad once it gets going, and for an appearance that suits the personality, talents, and voice of the legendary Rogers this should not be missed.

p, Edward W. Butcher; d, John Blystone; w, Sam Hellman, Gladys Lehman (based on a play by George Ade); ph, Hal Mohr.

Comedy **(PR:A MPAA:NR)**

COUNTY FAIR, THE* (1932) 67m MON bw
Hobert Bosworth *(Col. Ainsworth)*, Marion Shilling *(Alice Ainsworth)*, Ralph Ince *(Diamond Barnett)*, William Collier, Jr. *(Jimmie Dolan)*, Snowflake *(Curfew)*, Kit Guard *(Lefty)*, Otto Hoffman *(Matthews)*, Arthur Millet *(Bradley)*, Thomas R. Quinn *(Tout)*, Edward Kane *(Fisher)*, George Chesebrough.

Racketeers dope a horse in this poor programmer. Collier is the heroic ex-jockey, Bosworth the Kentucky colonel, Ince the villain, and Snowflake the horse. Highlight is an utterly extraneous scene of a black revival meeting.

p, I. E. Chadwick; d, Louis King; w, Harvey Harris Gates (based on a story by Roy Fitzroy); ph, Archie Stout.

Crime/Sports Drama **(PR:A MPAA:NR)**

COUNTY FAIR½**
(1933, Brit.) 68m Sound City/MGM bw (GB: SONG OF THE PLOUGH)
Stewart Rome *(Farmer Freeland)*, Rosalinde Fuller *(Miss Freeland)*, Allan Jeayes *(Joe Saxby)*, Hay Petrie *(Farmhand)*, Kenneth Kove *(Archie)*, Jack Livesey *(Squire's Son)*, Edgar Driver *(Barber)*, James Harcourt *(Doctor)*, Freddie Watts *(Bandsman)*, Albert Richardson *(Singer)*.

Rome is a farmer who saves his land by entering and winning a sheepdog competition. Well directed by one of the most influential British filmmakers of the 1930s.

p, Ivar Campbell; d, John Baxter; w, Reginald Pound.

Drama **(PR:A MPAA:NR)**

COUNTY FAIR*½ (1937) 71m MON bw
John Arledge *(John Hope)*, Mary Lou Lender *(Julie Williams)*, J. Farrell MacDonald *(Calvin Williams)*, Fuzzy Knight *(Whitey)*, Jimmy Butler *(Buddy Williams)*, Harry Worth *(Turner)*, Matty Roubert *(Snipe)*, William Hunter *(Dutch)*, Henry Hall, Edwin Mordant, Horace Murphy, Charles Murray.

Mediocre racetrack story has Arledge a jockey banned from racing after his horse is doped by a racetrack gang. He and sidekick Knight take jobs as hands on MacDonald's farm. Arledge takes up with Lender, MacDonald's daughter, and enters his horse in a race, both against the old man's opposition. The gang from the beginning try their tricks again, but are foiled, and MacDonald accepts both the romance and the racing.

p, E.R. Derr; d, Howard Bretherton; w, John T. Neville; ph, Arthur Martinelli; ed, Donald Barratt; md, Abe Meyer.

Drama **(PR:A MPAA:NR)**

COUNTY FAIR*½ (1950) 76m MON c
Rory Calhoun *(Peter Brennan)*, Jane Nigh *(Lorry Ryan)*, Florence Bates *(Ma Ryan)*,

Warren Douglas (*Tommy Blake*), Raymond Hatton (*Sad Sam*), Emory Parnell (*Tim Brennan*), Rory Mallinson (*Grattan*), Harry Cheshire (*Auctioneer*), Milton Kibbee (*Racing Secretary*), Joan Vohs, Clarence Muse, George L. Spaulding, Leary Nolan, Sam Flint, Bob Carson, Heinie Conklin, Roy Mallinson, Benny Corbett, Jasper Weldon, Jack Mower, Frank O'Connor, Stanley Blystone, Joe Forte, Renny McEvoy.

Rory Calhoun is a trainer who fixes a race with the help of track stewards and owners so that the old nag owned by Bates can win. His reasons for this action have to do with his romantic interests in Nigh, Bates' daughter. Nothing special.

p, Walter Mirisch; d, William Beaudine; w, W. Scott Darling; ph, Gilbert Warrenton (Cinecolor); m, Ozzie Caswell; ed, Richard Heermance.

Drama   **(PR:A   MPAA:NR)**

COUP DE FOUDRE   (SEE: ENTRE NOUS, 1983, Fr.)

COUP DE GRACE½   (1978, Ger./Fr.) 96m Argos/Cinema V bw
Margarethe von Trotta (*Sophie*), Matthias Habich (*Erich*), Rudiger Kirschstein (*Konrad*), Matthieu Carriere (*Volkmar*), Valeska Gert (*Tante Praskovia*), Marc Eyraud (*Dr. Paul Rugen*), Frederik Zichy (*Franz von Aland*), Bruno Thost (*Chopin*), Henry van Lyck (*Borschikoff*).

This offbeat political film takes place during the Latvian 1919-1920 Civil War between anti- and pro-Communist forces. Trotta is the aristocratic wife of a Prussian commander, Habich. She supports the Reds as a liberal but does not foresee the pillage and killing in and around her vast country estate near Riga as Habich's cause evaporates. In an ambiguous way this film attempts to give reason why Hitler later found so much support in his anti-Communist campaign by showing the feeble effort made by the Allies against Bolshevik encroachment. Yet the tale dwells too much on the vagaries of the wealthy and such filips as a crazy aunt giving formal teas in her carefully appointed dining room while bombs explode in the garden outside. An aesthetic effort that cannot decide on the history it presumes to record.

p, Eberhard Junkersdorf; d, Volker Schiondorff; w, Genevieve Dormann, von Trotta; Jutta Bruckner (based on the novel by Marguerite Yourcenar); ph, Igor, Luther; m, Stanley Myers.

Historical Drama   **Cas.**   **(PR:C   MPAA:NR)**

COUP DE TETE   (SEE: HOTHEAD, 1979, Fr.)

COUP DE TORCHON*
                (1981, Fr.) 128m Film de la Tour-Films A2-Little Bear/Par-Afrance c
                                        (GB:CLEAN SLATE)
Philippe Noiret (*Lucien Cordier*), Isabelle Huppert (*Rose*), Jean-Pierre Marielle (*Le Peron/His Brother*), Stephane Audran (*Hughuette Cordier*), Eddy Mitchell (*Nono*), Guy Marchand (*Chavasson*), Irene Skobline (*Anne*), Michel Beaune (*Vanderbrouck*), Jean Champion (*Priest*), Victor Garrivier (*Mercaillou*), Gerard Hernandez (*Leonelli*), Abdoulaye Dico (*Fete Nat*), Daniel Langlet (*Paulo*), Francois Perrot (*Colonel*), Raymond Hermantier (*Blind Man*), Mamadou Dioum (*Actor*), Samba Mane (*Friday*).

Interesting drama based on an obscure American novel with a cult following in France. Tavernier has transposed the setting from the 1910s American South to 1938 French Colonial Africa, and the main character has been changed from a sheriff to the police chief, played by Noiret, but the story of the man taking on a messianic mission to murder everyone who makes his life difficult remains the same. Among his victims are his wife and her lover, his mistress's husband, and a troublesome pimp (whose brother shows up later and is treated like a ghost). Well done all around, but it tends to bog down in its own metaphysics.

p, Adolphe Viezzi, Henri Lassa; d, Bertrand Tavernier; w, Tavernier, Jean Aurenche (based on the novel *Pop. 1280* by Jim Thompson); ph, Pierre William Glenn; m, Philippe Sarde; ed, Armand Psenny; prod d, Alexandre Trauner; cos, Jacqueline Laurent.

Drama   **(PR:O   MPAA:NR)**

COURAGE**   (1930) 65m WB bw
Belle Bennett (*Mary Colbrook*), Marian Nixon (*Muriel Colbrook*), Rex Bell (*Lynn Willard*), Richard Tucker (*James Rudlin*), Leon Janney (*Bill Colbrook*), Carter De Haven, Jr. (*Reginald Colbrook*), Dorothy Ward (*Gladys Colbrook*), Byron Sage (*Richard Colbrook*), Don Marion (*Vincent Colbrook*).

Poor beset Bennett is a widow raising seven children. Six are dedicated to making her life miserable and only the youngest (Janney) sides with his mother. He saves them all, though, by befriending a miserly old lady who leaves him $50,000 when she dies. Sentimental, but not intolerably so. Remade in 1938 as MY BILL. DeHaven, who played Reginald Colbrook, is the brother of actress Gloria DeHaven.

d, Archie Mayo; w, Walter Anthony (based on a play by Tom Barry).

Drama   **(PR:A   MPAA:NR)**

COURAGE OF BLACK BEAUTY**   (1957) 78m FOX c
John Crawford (*Bobby Adams*), Mimi Gibson (*Lily Rowden*), John Bryant (*Sam Adams*), Diane Brewster (*Ann Rowden*), J. Pat O'Malley (*Mike Green*), Russell Johnson (*Ben Farraday*), Ziva Rodann (*Janet Corday*).

Children's film about Crawford, alienated from his widower father (Bryant), raising a foal into a fine horse. Boy and horse survive a number of minor crises, then Bryant's carelessness seriously injures the horse and it looks as if it will have to be destroyed. A miraculous recovery followed by a reconciliation between father and son concludes this simplistic film.

p, Edward L. Alperson; d, Harold Shuster; w, Steve Fisher; ph, John Snyder (Pathe Color); m, Edward L. Alperson, Jr.; ed, John Ehrin; song, "Black Beauty" (Alperson

and Paul Herrick), "The Donkey Game Song" (Alperson, Dick Hughes, Richard Stapley).

Animal   **(PR:AA   MPAA:NR)**

COURAGE OF LASSIE**   (1946) 93m MGM c (AKA: BLUE SIERRA)
Elizabeth Taylor (*Kathie Merrick*), Frank Morgan (*Harry McBain*), Tom Drake (*Sgt. Smith*), Selena Royle (*Mrs. Merrick*), Harry Davenport (*Judge Payson*), George Cleveland (*Old Man*), Catherine McLeod (*Alice Merrick*), Morris Ankrum (*Farmer Crews*), Arthur Walsh (*Freddie Crews*), Mitchell Lewis (*Farmer Elson*), Jane Green (*Mrs. Ellison*), David Holt (*Peter Merrick*), William Lewin (*Sergeant*), Minor Watson (*Sheriff Grayson*), Windy Cook (*Youth*), Donald Curtis (*Charlie*), Clancy Cooper (*Casey*), Byron Foulger (*Dr. Coleman*), James Flavin (*Lt. Arnold*), Charles Sullivan (*Officer Instructor*), Addison Richards, Arthur Space (*Officers*), Robert Emmett O'Conner (*Deputy*), William "Bill" Phillips (*Sgt. Tyler*), Douglas Cowan (*Sgt. Lewis*), Lyle Mulhall (*Corporal*).

A Lassie picture wherein the loyal collie plays a pooch named Bill not Lassie, indicating a last-minute title change, obviously for box office purposes. As a pup, Lassie is found by sweet teenager Taylor who nurses him back to health after he has been accidentally shot by two boys out bird hunting. Soon Lassie becomes a healthy and useful dog and even helps out by rounding up stray sheep on kindly rancher Morgan's land. Tragedy strikes one day when Lassie is hit by a car and through a complicated series of events, ends up in the Army chewing up Japs in WW II. After the war Lassie comes back shell-shocked and vicious. It takes all the kindness Taylor can muster to rehabilitate the canine veteran. Eventually she succeeds and all ends up well. Taylor received top-billing in COURAGE OF LASSIE after her popularity in NATIONAL VELVET (1944).

p, Robert Sisk; d, Fred M. Wilcox; w, Lionel Houser; ph, Leonard Smith (Technicolor); m, Scott Bradley; ed, Conrad Nervig; art d, Cedric Gibbons, Paul Youngblood; set d, Edwin B. Willis, Paul Huldschinsky; co-director of animal sequences, Basil Wrangell.

Drama   **(PR:AAA   MPAA:NR)**

COURAGE OF THE WEST½   (1937) 56m UNIV bw
Bob Baker (*Jack Saunders*), Lois January (*Beth Andrews*), J. Farrell MacDonald (*Buck Saunders*), Fuzzy Knight (*Hank Givens*), Carl Stockdale (*Rufe Lambert*), Harry Woods (*Al Wilkins*), Albert Russell (*Abraham Lincoln*), Charles French (*Secretary Stanton*), Thomas Monk (*Secretary Seward*), Oscar Gahen (*George Wilkins*), Buddy Cox (*Jackie Saunders*), Richard Cramer (*Murphy*), Jack Montgomery (*U.S. Marshall*).

Bob Baker's first in a series of musical westerns for Universal, for which he beat out Dick Weston—soon to be known as Roy Rogers—for the spot to replace Buck Jones when Jones quit the studio in 1937. The series died quite quickly, and this is the best one of them, thanks to Lewis' inspired direction. Baker is the adopted son of Ranger MacDonald, who grows into a Ranger himself, only to learn that his real father (Woods) is the outlaw leader he has been tracking.

p, Paul Malvern; d, Joseph H. Lewis; w, Norton S. Parker; ph, Virgil Miller; ed, Charles Craft.

Western   **(PR:A   MPAA:NR)**

COURAGEOUS AVENGER, THE*   (1935) 58m Supreme/William Steiner bw
Johnny Mack Brown, Helen Erikson, Warner Richmond, Edward Cassidy, Edward Parker, Frank Ball, Earl Dwire, Forrest Taylor, Robert Burns.

Poor programmer for Brown who rides after rustlers without too much enthusiasm for the plot or romance-sparking Erikson.

p, A. W. Hackel; d, Robert N. Bradbury; w, Charles Francis Royal; ph, E. M. MacManigal; ed, S. Roy Luby.

Western   **(PR:A   MPAA:NR)**

COURAGEOUS DR. CHRISTIAN, THE*½   (1940) 67m RKO bw
Jean Hersholt (*Dr. Paul Christian*), Dorothy Lovett (*Judy Price*), Robert Baldwin (*Roy Davis*), Tom Neal (*Dave Williams*), Maude Eburne (*Mrs. Hastings*), Vera Lewis (*Mrs. Stewart*), George Meader (*Harry Johnson*), Bobby Larson (*Jack Williams*), Babette Bentley (*Ruth Williams*), Reginald Barlow (*Sam*), Jacqueline DeRiver (*Martha*), Edmund Glove (*Tommy Wood*), Mary Davenport (*Jane Wood*), Earle Ross (*Grandpa*), Sylvia Andrews (*Mrs. Sam*), Catherine Courtney (*Mrs. Morris*), Ann Bridge (*Sheriff*), James C. Morton (*Bailey*), Fred Holmes (*Wilson*), Frank LaRue (*Stanley*), Broderick O'Farrell (*Harris*), Budd Buster (*Jones*), Heinie Conklin (*Pinball Addict*).

Jean Hersholt plays the saintly Dr. Christian in the second film of the six-film series. This time he's fighting a spinal meningitis epidemic, crusading for a slum cleanup, and fighting off the advances of an amorous old maid. Saccharin and dull today, when few of us can picture a really "saintly" doctor, people flocked to the movie theaters to see the pipe-smoking, chuckling Hersholt in each of his Dr. Christian pictures. (See DR. CHRISTIAN series, Index.)

p, William Stephens; d, Bernard Vorhaus; w, Ring Lardner, Jr., Ian McLellan Hunter; ph, John Alton; ed, Edward Mann; md, Constantin Bakaleinikoff; art d, Bernard Herstrum; cos, Bridgehouse.

Drama   **Cas.**   **(PR:A   MPAA:NR)**

COURAGEOUS MR. PENN, THE*½   (1941, Brit.) 78m Hoffberg/BN bw
                                        (AKA: PENN OF PENNSYLVANIA)
Clifford Evans (*William Penn*), Deborah Kerr (*Gugliema*), Dennis Arundell (*Charles II*), Aubrey Mallalieu (*Chaplain*), D. J. Williams (*Lord Arlington*), O. B. Clarence (*Lord Cecil*), James Harcourt (*Fox*), Charles Carson (*Adm. Penn*), Henry Oscar (*Samuel Pepys*), Max Adrian (*Elton*), John Stuart (*Bindle*), Maire O'Neill (*Cook*), Edward Rigby (*Bushell*), Joss Ambler (*Lord Mayor*), J. H. Roberts (*Ford*), Edmund Willard

(Captain), Percy Marmont *(Holme)*, Gibb McLaughlin *(Indian Chief)*, Herbert Lomas *(Cockle)*, Gus McNaughton *(Mate)*.

Tedious, inaccurate biography of London-born William Penn, founder of the Quaker movement, crusader for religious freedom, and finally leader of his ardent followers to the settlement of Pennsylvania.

p, Richard Vernon; d, Lance Comfort; w, Anatole de Grunwald (based on the book *William Penn* by C. E. Vulliamy).

Biography   **(PR:A   MPAA:NR)**

COURIER OF LYONS✶✶   (1938, Fr.) 92m Eclair/Pax bw
Pierre Blanchar *(Lesurques/Dubosc)*, Dita Parlo *(Mina Lesurques)*, Jacques Copeau *(Daubenton)*, Alcover *(Durochat)*, Jean Tissier *(Courriol)*, Charles Dullin *(L'Aveugle)*, Dorville *(Choppart)*, Sylvia Bataille *(Madeleine Breban)*, Andre Noel *(Excoffon)*.

Interesting though depressing period story of Blanchar being arrested for a robbery and murder he did not commit. He is identified as the highwayman whom he resembles (also played by Blanchar), and because of an interlude with a prostitute on the night of the crime he cannot provide an alibi. Finally he is convicted and guillotined. Based on a factual incident. (In French; English subtitles)

p, Albert N. Chaperau; d, Maurice Lehmann; w, Jean Auteche; ph, Michel Belber; m, Louis Beydts, Herman Weinberg, Ted Laurence. (English subtitles)

Drama   **(PR:A   MPAA:NR)**

COURRIER SUD✶✶   (1937, Fr.) 90m Pan-Cine/Pathe Consortium bw
Pierre Richard-Willm *(Jacques Bernis)*, Charles Vanel *(Ambassador Herlin)*, Jany Holt *(Genevieve)*, Baron Fils *(Genevieve's Father)*, Gabrielle Dorziat *(Genevieve's Mother)*, Marguerite Pierry *(Genevieve's Aunt)*, Raymond Aimos *(Sergeant of Post)*, Alexandre Rignault *(Hubert)*, Roger Legris *(Radio Operator)*.

Muddled tale of trans-Saharan airlines and a romantic triangle between pilot Richard-Willm, ambassador Vanel, and Vanel's wife, Holt. Flight sequences and a Bedouin attack are highlights. Of literary interest for screenplay by novelist Antoine de Saint-Exupery.

d, Pierre Billon; w, Antoine de Saint-Exupery, Lustig and Bresson; ph, Robert Lafevre.

Drama   **(PR:A   MPAA:NR)**

COURT CONCERT, THE✶✶✶   (1936, Ger.) 85m UFA bw
(DAS HOFKONZERT)
Martha Eggerth *(Christine Holm)*, Johannes Heesters *(Walter von Arnegg)*, Kurt Meisel *(Florian Schwalbe)*, Herbert Hubner *(State Minister)*, Ernst Waldow *(Traveling Corset Salesman)*, Alfred Abel *(Knips the Poet)*, Hans H. Schaufuss *(Bookworm)*, Otto Tressler, Rudolf Klein-Rogge, Flockina von Platen, Hans Richter, Ingeborg von Kusserow, Rudolf Platte, Edwin Jurgensen, Oscar Sabe, Iwa Wanja, Willi Schur, Werner Stock, Toni Tetzlaff, Gunther Bellier, Johannes Bergfeld, Fritz Berghof, Jac Diehl, Rudolf Essek, Hans Halden, Carl Merznicht, Arnim Sussenguth, Max Vierlinger.

Eggerth is a young singer in 19th-century Vienna who learns that her father is the king. Douglas Sirk directed under his real name and he has described the film as "a piece of Viennese pastry." Extremely well-done, one of the best of the pre-war German musicals. Remade as DAS KONZERT in 1944.

p, Bruno Duday; d, Detlef Sierck (Douglas Sirk); w, Franz Wallner-Baste, Sierck (based on the play "Das Kleine Hofkonzert" by Paul Verhoeven and Toni Impekoven); ph, Franz Weihmayr; m, Edmund Nick, Ferenc Vecsey, Robert Schumann; set d, Fritz Maurischat.

Musical/Romance   **(PR:A   MPAA:NR)**

COURT JESTER, THE✶✶✶½   (1956) 101m PAR c
Danny Kaye *(Hawkins)*, Glynis Johns *(Maid Jean)*, Basil Rathbone *(Sir Ravenhurst)*, Angela Lansbury *(Princess Gwendolyn)*, Cecil Parker *(King Roderick)*, Mildred Natwick *(Griselda)*, Robert Middleton *(Sir Griswold)*, Michael Pate *(Sir Locksley)*, Herbert Rudley *(Captain of The Guard)*, Noel Drayton *(Fergus)*, Edward Ashley *(Black Fox)*, John Carradine *(Giacomo)*, Alan Napier *(Sir Brockhurst)*, Lewis Martin *(Sir Finsdale)*, Patrick Aherne *(Sir Pertwee)*, Richard Kean *(Archbishop)*, Larry Pennell *(Novice Knight)*, Hermine's Midgets, The American Legion Zouaves, Tudor Owen, Charles Irwin, Leo Britt, Russell Gaige, Ray Kellog, Eric Alden, William Pullen, Joel Smith, Robin Hughes, Robert E. Smith, Nels Nelson, Edward Gibbons, Thomas J. Cotton, Billy Curtis, A.J. Buster Resmondo, Irving Fulton, Frank Delfino, Little Billy Rhodes, Henry Lewis Stone, George Louis Spotts, Irving Douglas, Harry Monty, James B. Jordan, Floyd Hugh Dixon, Robert Smith, Robert Hart, Burnell Dietch, Chad Dee Block, Leo Wheeler, John P. O'Malley, Leslie Dennison, Paul "Tiny" Newlan, Trevor Ward, Michael Mahoney, Phyllis Coughlan, William Cartledge, Len Hendry, Claud Wuhrman, Harry Lloyd Nelson, John O'Malley.

Outstanding entertainment starring Kaye (quite possibly his best film) as a lowly valet who rises to become the leader of a peasant rebellion to restore the rightful heir to the throne of England. He disguises himself as a court jester to gain access to the evil baron, played by Rathbone (the real power behind the throne), and overthrow his oppressive rule. A great cast handles the laughs with dash and aplomb, but the real standout is Rathbone, whose charmingly villainous manner and comedic timing provide the perfect foil for Kaye's antics. One of Kaye's classic routines is confusing a secret message beginning with the alliterative line (whispered to him by Natwick): "I've put a pellet of poison in the vessel with the pestle." A stylish, well done, genre parody. Songs: "Life Could Not Better Be," "Outfox the Fox," "I'll Take You Dreaming," "My Heart Knows A Love Song" (Sylvia Fine, Sammy Cahn), "Maladjusted Jester" (Fine).

p,d&w, Norman Panama, Melvin Frank; ph, Ray June, Tom McAdoo (VistaVision/Technicolor); m, Victor Schoen; cos, Edith Head, Yvonne Wood; ch, James Starbuck.

Comedy/Adventure   **Cas.**   **(PR:AAA   MPAA:NR)**

COURT MARTIAL✶✶✶½   (1954, Brit.) 105m IF/BL bw
(GB: CARRINGTON V.C)
David Niven *(Maj. Carrington V.C.)*, Margaret Leighton *(Valerie Carrington)*, Noelle Middleton *(Capt. Alison Graham)*, Laurence Naismith *(Maj. Panton)*, Clive Morton *(Lt. Col. Huxford)*, Mark Dignam *(Prosecutor)*, Allan Cuthbertson *(Lt. Col. Henniker)*, Victor Maddern *(Sgt. Owen)*, John Glyn-Jones *(Evans)*, Raymond Francis *(Maj. Mitchell)*, Newton Blick *(Judge Advocate)*, John Chandos *(Adjutant Rawlinson)*, Geoffrey Keen *(President)*, Maurice Denham *(Lt. Col. Reeve)*, Michael Bates *(Maj. Broke-Smith)*, Robert Bishop *(Capt. Foljambe)*, Stuart Saunders *(Sgt. Crane)*, R.S.M. Brittain *(Sgt. Major)*, Johnnie Schofield, Basil Dignam, Deryck Barnes, Vivienne Martin, Ann Heffernan, Elizabeth Digby-Smith.

Niven is superb as the title character, an officer accused of stealing military funds, in this taut courtroom drama. Plot sees Niven, a celebrated war hero, shoved into a nowhere position in peacetime. Plagued by financial troubles and a nagging wife who always harasses him about money, he is pushed into taking what is rightfully his (his commanding officer had been holding up reimbursement of a large amount of cash Niven had spent out of his own pocket that should have been covered by his expense account) without official permission. His C.O. is outraged and orders a court martial. During the trial it is revealed that Niven has had an affair with a young female officer, Middleton, who tried to cover up her lover's theft. When this is disclosed, Niven's shrewish wife, Leighton, gets her revenge by falsifying her testimony and sealing her husband's fate. Eventually, the tribunal puts in a guilty verdict, but Niven's future happiness appears hopeful. Powerful portrayals help diffuse the somewhat static visuals that usually accompany long courtrooms dramas. Based on a successful stage play by Dorothy and Campbell Christie.

d, Anthony Asquith; w, John Hunter (based on a play by Dorothy and Campbell Christie); ph, Desmond Dickinson; ed, Ralph Kemplen.

Drama   **(PR:A   MPAA:NR)**

COURT MARTIAL✶✶   (1962, Ger.) 82m Arca-Film/UA bw (KREIGSGERICHT)
Karlheinz Bohm *(Lt. Duren)*, Christian Wolff *(Stahmer)*, Klaus Kammer *(Hinze)*, Werner Peters *(Brenner)*, Sabina Sesselmann *(Frau Duren)*, Hans Nielsen, Carl Wery, Berta Drews, Robert Meyn, Charles Regnier, Herbert Tiede, Edith Hancke, Albert Heyn, Carola von Kayser.

After the Nazi battleship *Pommern* is sunk, three survivors are rescued. They are given a heroes' welcome, but an investigation reveals that the battle went on for three hours after the men claimed to have abandoned ship. They are arrested for desertion, tried, and sentenced to death. Interesting war drama.

p, Helmut Volmer; d, Kurt Meisel; w, Will Berthold, Heinz Oskar Wuttig (based on the novel *Kreigsgericht* by Berthold); ph, Georg Krause; m, Werner Eisbrenner.

Drama   **(PR:A-C   MPAA:NR)**

COURT-MARTIAL OF BILLY MITCHELL, THE✶✶✶✶
(1955) 100m United States/WB c (GB: ONE-MAN MUTINY)
Gary Cooper *(Gen. Billy Mitchell)*, Charles Bickford *(Gen. Guthrie)*, Ralph Bellamy *(Cong. Frank Reid)*, Rod Steiger *(Maj. Allan Guillion)*, Elizabeth Montgomery *(Margaret Lansdowne)*, Fred Clark *(Col. Moreland)*, James Daly *(Col. Herbert White)*, Jack Lord *(Cmdr. Zachary Lansdowne)*, Peter Graves *(Capt. Elliott)*, Darren McGavin *(Russ Peters)*, Robert Simon *(Admiral Gage)*, Charles Dingle *(Senator Fullerton)*, Dayton Lummis *(Gen. Douglas MacArthur)*, Tom McKee *(Capt. Eddie Rickenbacker)*, Steve Roberts *(Maj. Carl Spaatz)*, Herbert Heyes *(Gen. John J. Pershing)*, Robert Brubaker *(Maj. H.H. Arnold)*, Ian Wolfe *(President Calvin Coolidge)*, Phil Arnold *(Fiorella LaGuardia)*, Will Wright *(Adm. William S. Sims)*, Steve Holland *(Stu Stewart)*, Adam Kennedy *(Yip Ryan)*, Manning Ross *(Ted Adams)*, Carleton Young *(Gen. Pershing's Aide)*, Griff Barnett *(Civilian Steno)*, Edward Keane, Anthony Hughes, John Maxwell, Ewing Mitchell *(Court Judges)*, Max Wagner *(Sgt.-Major)*, Jack Perrin *(Court Reporter)*, Gregory Walcott *(Reporter Millikan)*, Robert Williams *(Reporter Tuttle)*, Edna Holland *(Woman Secretary)*, William Forrest *(Commandant F.S.H.)*, Frank Wilcox *(Officer Tom)*, William Henry, Peter Adams *(Officers)*, Charles Chaplin, Jr., Joel Smith, Jordan Shelley, Fred Perce, Al Page, George Mayon, Michael Lally, Cy Malis *(Reporters)*.

Fine courtroom drama with Gary Cooper as the visionary and much-maligned Billy Mitchell who was placed in 1925 on secret military trial for bucking the Army and fighting for a separate Air Force, not to mention his predictions that the U.S. would some day have to fight Japan. Cooper, as Assistant Chief of the Army Air Service following WW I, unsuccessfully tries to convince superiors of the necessity of a strong air force. When he persists in annoying the high brass he is demoted from general to colonel, relieved of his post and sent to a remote Texas command. The dogged Cooper launches a letter-writing campaign to convince superiors and politicians that air power must be America's first line of defense but he fails to gain support. After several air disasters, including the crash of an unsafe Navy dirigible, *Shenandoah*, Cooper goes public with his complaints, condemning the War and Navy Departments as being guilty of "incompetence and criminal negligence." The top brass retaliates by putting him on trial in a Washington, D.C. warehouse, intending to railroad him as soon as possible, but Bellamy, a congressman who agrees with Cooper, rallies to his side and defends him before a military tribunal. Prosecutor Clark is obnoxious and insulting as he vilifies Cooper's prestigious background but when he appears to fail in making the Military's case against Cooper, Steiger, a truly hateful prosecutor, is brought in to destroy the upstart general. Even though appearing late in the film, Steiger's ruthless portrayal makes a powerful impact as he does just about everything to denigrate Cooper, except kick him in the face, a role not unlike the unsavory Dancer enacted by George C. Scott in AN ANATOMY OF A MURDER. Cooper is ultimately convicted, suspended for five years, but is later vindicated in a brief epilog. Preminger's direction is inexplicably lethargic but the script is wonderfully literate, even though there's not much action outside the courtroom antics, with only Steiger's magnetic personality enlivening the legal circus. The many real life profiles—MacArthur,

LaGuardia, Sims, Spaatz, Coolidge, Arnold, Pershing—are portrayed rather woodenly as if these movers and shakers were marble statues. The only female lead, Montgomery, plays the wife of a Navy commander killed in a crash (her film debut), but even she is subdued in her anger and grief. (The 22-year-old daughter of actor-director Robert Montgomery, she would go on to a sterling TV career on "Betwitched"). Tiomkin's score is excellent and Leavitt's lensing is lively, despite Preminger's penchant for dwelling on details that bear little significance to the story. The Sperling-Lavery story and screenplay were unexpectedly nominated for an Oscar.

p, Milton Sperling; d, Otto Preminger; w, Sperling, Emmet Lavery (based on their story); ph, Sam Leavitt (CinemaScope, WarnerColor); m, Dimitri Tiomkin; ed, Folmar Blangsted; art d, Malcolm Bert; set d, William Kuehl; cos, Howard Shoup; makeup, Gordon Bau; spec eff, H.F. Koenekamp; tech adv, Maj.-Gen. Keeney, USAF, Res. (Ret.).

Military-Courtroom Drama/Biography   (PR:A   MPAA:NR)

COURT MARTIAL OF MAJOR KELLER, THE½**
                              (1961, Brit.) 69m Danziger/WPD bw
Laurence Payne (*Maj. Keller*), Susan Stephen (*Laura Winch*), Ralph Michael (*Col. Winch*), Richard Caldicott (*Harrison*), Basil Dignam (*Morrell*), Austin Trevor (*Power*), Simon Lack (*Wilson*), Jack McNaughton (*Miller*), Hugh Cross (*Capt. Cuby*), Peter Sinclair (*Sergeant*), Humphrey Lestocq (*Lt. Cameron*).

Payne is on trial for killing his commanding officer, but he proves that the man was deserting to the enemy when he shot him. Occasionally interesting courtroom drama.

p, Brian Taylor; d, Ernest Morris; w, Brian Clemens.

Drama   (PR:A-C   MPAA:NR)

COURTIN' TROUBLE½**   (1948) 56m MON bw
Jimmy Walker (*Jimmy*), Dub "Cannonball" Taylor (*"Cannonball"*), Virginia Belmont (*Carol*), Leonard Penn (*Dawson*), Marshall Reed (*Cody*), Steve Clark (*Reed*), House Peters, Jr. (*Larsen*), Frank LaRue (*Judge*), William N. Bailey (*Curtis*), Bud Osborne (*Sheriff*), Bill Hale (*Stewart*), Bob Woodward (*Gill*), Carol Henry (*Bartender*), Bill Potter (*Graves*).

Routine B western features Wakely cleaning up the outlaw gang headed by saloon-keeper Penn; he manages to sing three songs along the way.

p, Louis Gray; d, Ford Beebe; w, Ronald Davidson; ph, Harry Neumann; ed, Carl Pierson; md, Edward Kay; m/l, Jimmy Wakely, Oliver Drake, Tommy Dilbeck.

Western   (PR:A   MPAA:NR)

COURTIN' WILDCATS½**   (1929) 56m UNIV bw
Hoot Gibson, Eugenia Gilbert, Harry Todd, Joseph Girard, Monty Montague, John Oscar, Jim Corey, James Farley, Pete Morrison, Joe Bonomo, Joe Farley.

Hoot Gibson's last part-talking film. He plays a bookish eastern college boy sent west by his father to toughen him up. He meets Gilbert, the pistol-packin' wildcat accused of murdering her father's enemy, clears her name, and winds up marrying her. Usual tenderfoot-to-toughguy tedium.

p, Hoot Gibson; d, Jerome Storm; w, Dudley McKenna; ph, Harry Neumann; m/l, "Courtin' Calamity" (William Dudley Pelley).

Western   (PR:A   MPAA:NR)

COURTNEY AFFAIR, THE½**   (1947, Brit.) 120m BL bw
(GB: THE COURTNEYS OF CURZON STREET)
Anna Neagle (*Catherine O'Hallaron*), Michael Wilding (*Sir Edward Courtney*), Gladys Young (*Lady Courtney*), Michael Medwin (*Edward Courtney*), Coral Browne (*Valerie*), Daphne Slater (*Cynthia*), Jack Watling (*Teddy Courtney*), Helen Cherry (*Mary Courtney*), Bernard Lee (*Col. Gascoyne*), Percy Walsh (*Sir Frank Murchison*), Thora Hird (*Kate*), Max Kirby (*Algie Longworth*).

Sentimental film of aristocrat Wilding marrying Neagle, his mother's Irish maid, despite social ostracism. After being horribly insulted at a society function she goes back to Ireland to have their child, only to reappear years later as an entertainer during WW I. Wilding sees her, they are reconciled and live happily ever after. Final scene is set in 1945, when their soldier-grandson brings home a girl of humble origins who hopes her family won't object to her marrying into aristocracy. The top British moneymaker in 1947.

p&d, Herbert Wilcox; w, Nicholas Phipps (based on a story by Florence Tranter); ph, Max Greene.

Drama   (PR:A   MPAA:NR)

COURTSHIP OF ANDY HARDY, THE½**   (1942) 94m MGM bw
Mickey Rooney (*Andy Hardy*), Lewis Stone (*Judge Hardy*), Fay Holden (*Mrs. Emily Hardy*), Cecilia Parker (*Marian Hardy*), Ann Rutherford (*Polly Benedict*), Sara Haden (*Aunt Milly*), Donna Reed (*Melodie Nesbit*), William Lundigan (*Jeff Willis*), Frieda Inescort (*Janet Nesbit*), Harvey Stephens (*Clarence O. Nesbit*), George Breakston (*Beezy*), Todd Karns (*Harry Land*), Frank Coghlan, Jr. (*Red*).

Judge Hardy (Stone) orders Andy (Rooney) to date Reed in an attempt to break her of the haughtiness that stands in the way of a reconciliation with her parents. Trite and predictable, but better than average for the series. (See ANDY HARDY series, Index.)

d, George B. Seitz; w, Agnes Christine Johnson (based on characters created by Aurania Rouverol); ph, Lester White; ed, Elmo Vernon.

Comedy   (PR:A   MPAA:NR)

COURTSHIP OF EDDIE'S FATHER, THE½**   (1963) 118m MGM c
Glenn Ford (*Tom Corbett*), Shirley Jones (*Elizabeth Marten*), Stella Stevens (*Dollye*

Daly), Dina Merrill (*Rita Behrens*), Roberta Sherwood (*Mrs. Livingston*), Ronny Howard (*Eddie*), Jerry Van Dyke (*Norman Jones*), John LaSalle Jazz Combo.

Charming if somewhat slow story of a widower (Ford) who is raising his 6-year-old son (Howard, already stealing scenes). Women are attracted to the handsome widower and all must pass muster through little Howard who has some very definite ideas on what kind of woman he might want his daddy to marry. Sherwood is the housekeeper and quite funny as she studies her Spanish, unaware that her trip to Brazil will be to a country where Portuguese is the language. Howard judges women by their eyes and busts and doesn't much like Ford's beloved, Merrill, who he thinks has "skinny eyes" and would much prefer dad getting together with next-door-neighbor Jones, rather than Merrill or Stevens or anyone else. Do you want three guesses as to who dad winds up with? Some early scenes tend to lose you because they are serious to a fault and there are also some lines attributed to young Howard that could have only come from a grown screenwriter like John Gay, but it all winds up to be pleasant fare. Minnelli, Ford, and Gay had just come away from THE FOUR HORSEMEN OF THE APOCALYPSE fiasco and needed something to stay in the studio's good graces. This proved just the ticket. Howard was 9 years old when this was made and on his fourth film, having already impressed everyone with his work in THE MUSIC MAN. His career has been a marvel, with success in whatever he touches. Now, as a director, he is using his many years of experience to great advantage.

p, Joe Pasternak; d, Vincente Minnelli; John Gay (based on the novel by Mark Toby); ph, Milton Krasner (Metrocolor); m, George Stoll; ed, Adrienne Fazan; art d, George W. Davis, Urie McCleary; set d, Henry Grace, Keogh Gleason; cos, Helen Rose; spec eff, Robert R. Hoag; m/l, "The Rose and the Butterfly" (Victor Young, Stella Unger).

Comedy/Drama   (PR:AA   MPAA:NR)

COUSIN, COUSINE*   (1976, Fr.) 95m Les Films Pomereu-GAU c
Marie-Christine Barrault (*Marthe*), Victor Lanoux (*Ludovic*), Marie-France Pisier (*Karine*), Guy Marchand (*Pascal*), Ginette Garcin (*Biju*), Sybil Maas (*Diane*), Jean Herbert (*Sacy*), Pierre Plessis (*Gobert*), Catherine Verlor (*Nelsa*), Hubert Gignoux (*Thomas*).

Good-natured comedy has cousins by marriage, Barrault and Lanoux, meeting and falling in love—although both are already married. A surprise success in the U.S., winning three Oscar nominations in 1976: Marie-Christine Barrault for Best Actress, Jean-Charles Tacchella and Daniele Thompson for Writing (Screenplay Written Directly for the Screen, and Best Foreign Language Film. (In French; English subtitles.)

p, Bertrand Javal; d, Jean-Charles Tacchella; w, Tacchella, Daniele Thompson; ph, Georges Lendi (Eastmancolor); m, Gerard Anfosso; ed, Agnes Guillemot.

Comedy   Cas.   (PR:O   MPAA:R)

COUSINS, THE*   (1959, Fr.) 112m AJYM/Films-Around-the-World bw
(FR: LES COUSINS)
Gerard Blain (*Charles*), Jean-Claude Brialy (*Paul*), Juliette Mayniel (*Florence*), Claude Cerval (*Clovis*), Genevieve Cluny (*Genevieve*), Michele Meritz (*Yvonne*), Corrado Guarducci (*Italian Count*), Guy Decombie (*Librarian*).

Claude Chabrol's second feature deals with the contrast between two cousins studying law in Paris. Blain is the country bumpkin at odds with the decadent, city-bred Brialy. They compete for the same girl, and in the end Blain destroys Brialy. A major film of the French "new wave" and a grim, clear-eyed look at the cynicism of youth, this is not to be missed.

p&d, Claude Chabrol; w, Chabrol, Paul Gegauff; ph, Henri Decae; m, Paul Misraki.

Drama   (PR:C-O   MPAA:NR)

COUSINS IN LOVE*   (1982) 91m Stephan-Filmedis-TV-13/Alpha c
Thierry Tevini, Jean Rougerie, Catherine Rouvel, Anja Shute, Valerie Dumas, Laure Dechasnel, Hannes Kaetner, Evelyne Dandry, Elisa Cervier, Gaelle Legrand, Anne Fontaine, Carmen Weber, Fanny Meunier, Jean-Louis Fortuit, Pierre Chantepie, Jean-Pierre Vernier, Macha Meril, Jean-Yves Chatelais, Silke Rein, Ester Weber.

Photographer and sometime filmmaker Hamilton again adds life to his dreamy compositions of naively incestuous young girls. An alarming sensuality is achieved, but it is only enjoyable if one is a voyeur.

p, Linda Gutenberg, Georg M. Reuther; d, David Hamilton; w, Pascal Laine (based on his own novel); ph, Bernard Daillencourt; m, Jean-Marie Senia, Karinne Trow; ed, Jean-Bernard Bonis; art d, Eric Simon.

Drama   (PR:O   MPAA:NR)

COVENANT WITH DEATH, A**   (1966) 97m WB c
George Maharis (*Ben Lewis*), Laura Devon (*Rosemary*), Katy Jurado (*Eulalia*), Earl Holliman (*Bryan Talbot*), Arthur O'Connell (*Judge Hockstadter*), Sidney Blackmer (*Col. Oates*), Gene Hackman (*Harmsworth*), John Anderson (*Dietrich*), Wende Wagner (*Rafaela*), Emilio Fernandez (*Ignacio*), Kent Smith (*Parmalee*), Lonny Chapman (*Musgrave*), Jose De Vega (*Digby*), Larry D. Mann (*Chillingworth*), Whit Bissel (*Bruce Donnelly*), Russell Thorson (*Dr. Shilling*), Paul Birch (*Governor*), Erwin Neal (*Willie Wayte*), Robert Dunlap (*Policeman*), Jadine Vaighn (*Louise Talbot*), Albuquerque Polo Club, Santa Fe Country Sheriff's Posse (*Polo Players*).

So-so courtroom drama stars Maharis as a Mexican-American judge in a small New Mexico town deciding the case of Earl Holliman, town good-for-nothing accused of the murder of his wife. Holliman scuffles on the scaffold and accidentally kills the hangman just as Whit Bissel confesses to the crime. A nice concept gone boringly astray.

p, William Conrad; d, Lamont Johnson; w, Larry B. Marcus, Saul Levitt (based on a novel by Stephen Becker); ph, Robert Burks (Technicolor); m, Leonard Rosenman; ed, William Ziegler; art d, Howard Hollander; set d, Ralph S. Hurst.

Drama   (PR:C   MPAA:NR)

COVER GIRL**** (1944) 105m COL c
Rita Hayworth (Rusty Parker/Maribelle Hicks), Gene Kelly (Danny McGuire), Lee Bowman (Noel Wheaton), Phil Silvers (Genius), Jinx Falkenburg (Jinx), Leslie Brooks (Maurine Martin), Eve Arden (Cornelia Jackson), Otto Krueger (John Coudair), Jess Barker (Coudair as a Young Man), Anita Colby (Anita), Curt Bois (Chem), Ed Brophy (Joe), Thurston Hall (Tony Pastor), Jean Colleran, Francine Counihan, Helen Mueller, Cecilia Meagher, Betty Jane Hess, Dustry Anderson, Eileen McClory, Cornelia B. von Hessert, Karen X. Gaylord, Cheryl Archibald, Peggy Lloyd, Betty Jane Graham, Martha Outlaw, Susann Shaw, Rose May Robson (Cover Girls), Jack Norton (Harry the Drunk), Robert Homans (Pop the Doorman), Eddie Dunn (Mac the Cop), Sam Flint (Butler), Shelley Winters (Girl), Kathleen O'Malley (Cigarette Girl), William Kline (Chauffeur), Victor Travers (Bartender), Robert F. Hill (Headwaiter), John Tyrrell (Electrician), Frank O'Connor (Cook), Eugene Anderson, Jr. (Bus Boy), Sam Ash (Assistant Cook), Vin Moore (Waiter), Ralph Sanford, Ralph Peters (Truckmen), Barbara Pepper, Grace Leonard (Chorus Girls), Gwen Seager, Sally Cairns, Eloise Hart, Diane Griffith, Wesley Brent, Lucille Allen, Virginia Gardner, Helene Garron, Muriel Morris, Patti Sacks, Marion Graham (Cover Girl Contestants), Frances Morris (Coudair's Secretary), Billy Benedict (Florist Boy), William Sloan (Naval Officer), Grace Hayle, Fern Emmett (Women Columnists), Rudy Wissler, Glenn Charles, Jackie Brown (Boys), Ilene "Betty" Brewer (Autograph Hound), Warren Ashe (Rusty's Interviewer), John Dilson (Rusty's Photographer), Jack Rice (Reporter), Sam Flint (Coudair's Butler), Ed Allen (Best Man), George Lessey (Minister), Miriam Lavelle, Miriam Franklin, Ronald Wyckoff (Specialty Dancers), Grace Gillern, Eddie Cutler, Randolph Hughes, Jack Bernett, George Dobbs, Al Norman, Larry Rio, Jack Boyle, Virginia Wilson, Betty Brodel (Dancers), Johnny Mitchell (Pianist-Maribelle's Love), Patti Sheldon (Girl).

COVER GIRL is one of those rare instances where style triumphs over substance. But in this case the substance referred to is the skimpy story concocted by four writers and surely not the score by Kern and Gershwin, which includes some of their best work, notably "Long Ago and Far Away" which couldn't even be destroyed by Gene Kelly's reed-thin voice. Hayworth works in Brooklyn at a nightclub owned by Kelly. He also happens to love her madly and looks at her as though she were the Statue of Liberty and he an immigrant standing at the rail of a steamer. Silvers is the house comic and the three of them are closer than close. Kruger is an editor who spots Hayworth when his magazine is conducting a search for cover girls. The old man is enthralled by Hayworth, especially in view of the fact that he had a fling with her grandmother years before and lost out. Her picture on the cover results in Rita getting an audition with a Broadway show. Hayworth and Kelly have a huge argument and she goes uptown to Manhattan with producer Bowman, who is also in love with her, so in love that he proposes marriage. The film ends happily when Rita wises up and leaves the mustached Bowman at the altar to return to Brooklyn and Kelly. And if you can believe that, you'll believe anything. You can see by the above that the story was not what packed 'em into the theaters when COVER GIRL opened. This was a tuneful romp that was released three months before D-Day, when the weather was still cold and the news from the front had not yet turned around in the Allies' favor. Flashback sequences feature Rita as her own grandmother and give us a chance to see some beautiful costumes and hats by Travis Banton, Gwen Wakeling, Muriel King, and Kenneth Hopkins. The film was nominated for a host of Oscars but only won for musical direction (Carmen Dragon, Father of Darryl Dragon of "The Captain and Tenille," and Morris Stoloff). GOING MY WAY and WILSON ran off with most of the awards and Columbia boss Harry Cohn quipped, "It took two priests and a President to beat us." Martha Mears looped Rita's voice but no one could substitute for her legs in those years. She and Kelly made a marvelous duo and even a marvelous trio when Phil Silvers joined them for "Make Way For Tomorrow"—as acrobatic and roughhouse a dance number as Kelly ever created. The most famous dance in the film, the one that changed Kelly forever from dancer to a Dancer, was the "alter ego" sequence, whereby he confronts his mirror image in a store window and does a serious terpsichorean piece as he examines how he feels on the surface versus what he's thinking deep in his heart. Two dances had to be invented, then synchronized and perfectly filmed or it wouldn't have worked. Kelly claims he spent over a month just planning the dance and four days to shoot it with co-choreographer Stanley Donen, with whom he was to work many more times, standing by to cue the cameras. Kelly had been a regular player at MGM but Mayer was loath to allow him the kind of leeway he got with Cohn on this loan-out to Columbia. It was after the success of COVER GIRL that Kelly could do no wrong and thus began a string of musical hits for Metro that will never be equaled. Songs: "Make Way for Tomorrow" (Jerome Kern, Ira Gershwin, E.Y. "Yip" Harburg), "Long Ago and Far Away," "Put Me To the Test," "Sure Thing," "That's the Best of All," "The Show Must Go On," "Who's Complaining?" "Poor John" (Kern, Gershwin).

p, Arthur Schwartz; d, Charles Vidor; w, Virginia Van Upp, Marion Parsonnet, Paul Gangelin (based on a story by Erwin Gelsey); ph, Rudolph Mate, Allen M. Davey (Technicolor); m, Carmen Dragon; ed, Viola Lawrence; md, M.W. Stoloff; art d, Lionel Banks, Cary Odell; set d, Fay Babcock; cos, ch, Val Raset, Seymour Felix, Gene Kelly, Stanley Donen.

Musical Comedy Cas. (PR:AA MPAA:NR)

COVER GIRL KILLER*½** (1960, Brit.) 61m But-Parroch/Eros bw
Harry H. Corbett (The Man), Felicity Young (June Rawson), Spencer Teakle (John Mason), Victor Brooks (Inspector Brunner), Tony Doonan (Sergeant), Bernardette Milne (Gloria), Christina Gregg (Joy), Charles Lloyd Pack (Capt. Adams).

A mad killer is on the loose, killing off models. The publisher of a pinup magazine and his model help the police set a trap to catch the psychopath. Effective, above-average British crime drama.

p, C. Jack Parsons; d&w, Terry Bishop.

Crime (PR:C-O MPAA:NR)

COVER ME BABE zero (1970) 88m FOX c
Robert Forster (Tony Hall), Sondra Locke (Melisse), Suzanne Benton (Sybil), Robert S. Fields (Will Ames), Ken Kercheval (Jerry), Sam Waterston (Cameraman), Michael Margotta (Steve), Mike Kellin (Derelict), Floyd Mutrux (Ronnie), Meggie Thrett (Prostitute), Jeff Corey (Paul), Regis Toomey (Michael), Mitzi Hoag (Mother), Franklin Townsend (Transvestite), Mello Alexandria (Male Puppet), Linda Howe (Female Puppet), Michael Payne, Carmen Argenziano (Students).

Pretentious story of film student Forster running around filming things in search of reality. After alienating everyone around him, his professor (Fields) points out that reality is subjective and just because something is on film doesn't make it true. Last shot has Forster running along a beach, thinking about it. Director Black made one great film, PRETTY POISON, but he should be sent back to film school with Forster for foisting self-indulgent nonsense like this on the public.

p, Lester Linsk; d, Noel Black; w, George Wells; ph, Michel Hugo (DeLuxe Color); m, Fred Karlin; ed, Harry Gerstad; art d, Jack Martin Smith, Dale Hennesy; set d, Walter M. Scott, Robert De Vestel.

Drama (PR:O MPAA:NR)

COVERED TRAILER, THE*½ (1939) 66m REP bw
James Gleason (Joe Higgins), Lucille Gleason (Lil Higgins), Russel Gleason (Sidney Higgins), Harry Davenport (Grandpa), Mary Beth Hughes (Betty Higgins), Tommy Ryan (Tommy Higgins), Maurice Murphy (Bill), Maude Eburne (Widow Jones), Spencer Charters (Sheriff), Tom Kennedy (Otto), Hobart Cavanaugh (Beamish), Pierre Watkin (Cartwright), Frank Dee (Police Chief), Richard Tucker (Doctor), Willie Best (Baltimore), Walter Fenner (Wells).

A "Higgins Family" series entry with nothing to recommend it. The family has to give up its planned trip to South America when an expected check fails to arrive. Rather than humble themselves in front of their neighbors by cancelling their trip, the family members go on a fishing trip in the wilderness. It turns out they were lucky not to have gone south because the ship on which they had booked passage sinks, and everyone back home thinks they've drowned. Predictable situations and predictable jokes abound in this program filler. (See HIGGINS FAMILY series, Index.)

d, Gus Meins; w, Jack Townley (based on a story by Townley and M. Coates Webster); ph, Arthur Martinelli; ed, Ray Snyder; md, Cy Feuer.

Comedy (PR:AA MPAA:NR)

COVERED WAGON DAYS*½ (1940) 56m REP bw
Robert Livingston (Stony Brooke), Raymond Hatton (Rusty Joslin), Duncan Renaldo (Rico), Kay Griffith (Maria), George Douglas (Ransome), Ruth Robinson (Mama Rinaldo), Paul Marion (Carlos), John Merton (Gregg), Tom Chatterton (Maj. Norton), Guy D'Ennery (Diego), Tom Loudon (Martin), Reed Howes (Stevens).

Another Three Mesquiteers film, one of seven with Renaldo. The trio gallop to the rescue of Renaldo's brother, framed for the murder of his uncle when he discovers the silver smuggling operation of villains Merton and Howes. (See THREE MESQUITEERS series, Index.)

p, Harry Gray; d, George Sherman; w, Earle Snell (based on characters created by William Colt MacDonald); ph, William Nobles; m, Cy Feuer; ed, Bernard Loftus.

Western (PR:A MPAA:NR)

COVERED WAGON RAID*½ (1950) 60m REP bw
Allan "Rocky" Lane (Himself), Eddy Waller (Nugget Clark), Alex Gerry (Harvey Grimes), Lyn Thomas (Gail Warren), Byron Barr (Roy Chandler), Dick Curtis (Grif), Pierce Lyden (Brag), Sherry Jackson (Susie), Rex Lease (Bob Davis), Lester Dorr (Pete), Lee Roberts (Steve).

Pioneers trying to settle a rich valley are continuously being robbed and murdered. Insurance investigator Lane goes to investigate and discovers a gang headed by the town postmaster, who reads peoples' mail to learn who is worth robbing. Nothing special.

p, Gordon Kay; d, R. G. Springsteen; w, M. Coates Webster; ph, John MacBurnie; ed, Harry Keller.

Western (PR:A MPAA:NR)

COVERED WAGON TRAILS* (1930) 51m SYN bw
Bob Custer, Phyllis Bainbridge, J. P. McGowan, Charles Brinley, Martin Cichy, Perry Murdock.

A pioneer film without a bit of epic and only a few prairie schooners harrassed by Indians, rustlers, bad weather and worse acting.

d, J. P. McGowan; w, Sally Winters.

Western (PR:A MPAA:NR)

COVERED WAGON TRAILS* (1940) 52m MON bw
Jack Randall (Jack), Sally Cairns (Carol), David Sharpe (Ed Cameron), Lafe McKea (John Bradford), Budd Buster (Manny), Glenn Strange (Fletcher).

The cattleman's association has hired Strange to chase off the farmers who are settling the range, but Randall uses his fists and six gun to make the West safe for decent hardworking citizens. Substandard.

p, Harry S. Webb; d, Raymond K. Johnson; w, Tom Gibson; ph, Edward Kull; ed, Robert Golden; m/l, "Under Western Skies" (Johnny Lange, Lew Porter).

Western (PR:A MPAA:NR)

COVERT ACTION*
(1980, Ital.) 80m 21st Century c

David Janssen, Corinne Clery, Maurizio Merli, Arthur Kennedy, Philippe Leroy.

Dull espionage drama has Janssen a former CIA agent hunted by killers because of a book he has written about his experiences in the agency. Shot on location in Greece.

d, Romolo Guerrieri.

Spy Drama   (PR:O   MPAA:R)

COVER-UP**
(1949) 82m UA bw

William Bendix (Larry Best), Dennis O'Keefe (Sam Donovan), Barbara Britton (Anita Weatherby), Art Baker (Stu Weatherby), Helen Spring (Bessie Weatherby), Ann E. Todd (Cathie Weatherby), Doro Merande (Hilda), Virginia Christine (Margaret Baker), Russell Armes (Frank Baker), Dan White (Gabe), Paul E. Burns (Mr. Abbey), Ruth Lee (Mrs. Abbey), Emmet Vogan (Blakely), Jamesson Shade (Editor), Henry Hall (Mayor), Jack Lee (Addison).

Dennis O'Keefe is an insurance investigator who has come to a small town to look into the death of one of its citizens. The deeper he digs, the harder it gets as it seems the town is covering up and doesn't want the truth known. The man who was killed was a rat and a bully and the report said it was suicide, but O'Keefe doesn't believe it. We finally realize why the town is keeping things under wraps when we learn that the dead man was killed by a local hero. The killer himself, a doctor of the highest quality, is now also dead of a heart attack and the town would like to keep the story that way. O'Keefe falls in love with local Britton while he's investigating, and Bendix, who appears to be a lazy sheriff, wishes the Irishman would just get the hell out of there. This might have been a dandy story in the manner of BAD DAY AT BLACK ROCK which also has to do with the investigation of a death in a small town. But they missed the boat with languid direction and a script that threw light jabs when it should have gone for a knockout punch.

p, Ted Nasser; d, Alfred E. Green; w, Jerome Odlum, Jonathan Rix, Francis Swann, Lawrence Kimble; ph, Ernest Laszlo; m, Hans J. Salter; ed, Fred W. Berger.

Mystery   (PR:A   MPAA:NR)

COW AND I, THE***
(1961, Fr., Ital., Ger.) 98m Les Films du Cyclope-Omnia Film-Da. Ma. Film/Zenith International bw

(LA VACHE ET LE PRISONNIER; LA VACCA E IL PRIGIONIERO)

Fernandel (Charles Bailly), Rene Havard (Bussiere), Albert Remy (Colinet), Bernard Musson (Pommier), Maurice Nasil (Bertoux), Pierre-Louis, Richard Winckler (Officers), Ingeborg Schoner (Helga), Franciska Kinz (Helga's Mother), Ellen Schwiers (Josephine), Benno Hoffmann (Camp Guard), Marguerite (Herself, A Cow).

Fernandel is a French farmer forced to work in Germany during WW II. He decides to escape back to France and, borrowing a cow (Marguerite), he sets out to walk across Germany. The strange pair have a number of odd adventures, and when Fernandel has to leave the cow at the bank of a river while he rows across, the cow finds a pontoon bridge and rejoins him. Finally Fernandel reaches France, but is spotted by collaborationist police. He jumps on another train, but it is headed back to Germany. One of Fernandel's lesser films, but still funny and charming. (In French; English subtitles.)

d, Henri Verneuil; w, Verneuil, Jean Manse, Henri Jeanson (based on a story by Jacques Antoine); ph, Roger Hubert; m, Paul Durand; ed, James Cuenet, Gabriel Rongier; art d, Franz Bi, Jacques Chalvet, Max Seefelder; English subtitles, Rose Sokol.

Comedy   (PR:A   MPAA:NR)

COW COUNTRY*½
(1953) 82m AA bw

Edmond O'Brien (Ben Anthony), Helen Westcott (Linda Garnet), Bob Lowry (Harry Odell), Barton MacLane (Parker), Peggie Castle (Melba Sykes), Robert H. Barrat (Walt Garnet), James Millican (Fritz Warner), Don Beddoe (Joe), Robert Wilke (Sledge), Raymond Hatton (Smokey), Charles Courney (Tom), Steve Clark (Skeeter), Rory Mallinson (Tim Sykes), Marshall Reed (Riley), Brett Houston (Stubby), Tom Tyler (Pete), Sam Flint (Maitland), Jack Ingram (Terrell), George Lewis (Sanchez).

Tedious, talky oater has O'Brien saving rancher Barrat from banker MacLane and rustler Lowry, both in cahoots in a plan to bankrupt him. Westcott is a nice girl engaged to Lowry, even though he is having an affair with saloon singer Castle.

p, Scott R. Dunlap; d, Leslay Selander; w, Adele Buffington (from the novel Shadow Range by Curtis Bishop); ph, Harry Neumann; m, Edward J. Kay; ed, John C. Fuller.

Western   (PR:A   MPAA:NR)

COW TOWN*½
(1950) 70m COL bw

Gene Autry (Himself), Gail Davis (Ginger Kirby), Harry Shannon (Sandy Reeves), Jock O'Mahoney (Tod Jeffreys), Clark "Buddy" Burroughs (Duke Kirby), Harry Harvey (Sheriff Steve Calhoun), Steve Darrel (Chet Hilliard), Sandy Danders ("Stormy" Jones), Ralph Sanford (Martin Dalrymple), Bud Osborne (George Copeland), Robert Hilton (Miller), Ted Mapes (Ed Loomis), Charles Roberson (Mike Grady), House Peters, Jr. (Gill Saunders), Walt LaRue, Herman Hack, Ken Cooper, Victor Cox, Holly Bane, Felice Raymnd, Frank McCarroll, Pat O'Malley, Blackie Whiteford, Frankie Marvin, "Champion, Jr."

Done in mock documentary style, complete with grave narration, COW TOWN stars Autry as a rancher who fights a wave of rustling by putting barbed wire around his range. The rustlers stir up opposition to this measure until a range war breaks out. Autry, of course, restores order to things.

p, Armand Schaefer; d, John English; w, Gerald Geraghty; ph, William Bradford; ed, Henry Batista; md, Mischa Bakaleinikoff.

Western   (PR:A   MPAA:NR)

COWARDS zero
(1970) 88m Jaylo c

John Rose (Philip Haller), Susan Sparling (Joan Boyd), Will Patent (Peter Yates), Thomas Murphy (Howard Yates), Philip B. Hall (Father Reis), Alexander Gellman (Gregory Haller), Edith Briden (Nancy Haller), Stephen Snow (Terry), George Linjeris (Jim), Spalding Gray (Radical), Kelly Houser (Man at Physical), Larry Hunter (Detective).

Inept anti-draft picture stars Rose wandering about trying to decide whether he should run off to Canada or stay at home and fight the draft. Final scene has priest Hall leading Rose and some others in a Carrie Nation-type assault on a draft board office. A film best forgotten.

p,d&w, Simon Nutchern; ph, Robert T. Megginson (Eastmancolor); m, Stephen Lerner; ed, Megginson.

Drama   (PR:C-O   MPAA:NR)

COWBOY***½
(1958) 92m COL c

Glenn Ford (Tom Reece), Jack Lemmon (Frank Harris), Anna Kashfi (Maria Vidal), Brian Donlevy (Doc Bender), Dick York (Charlie), Victor Manuel Mendoza (Mendoza), Richard Jaeckel (Paul Curtis), King Donavan (Joe Capper), Vaughn Taylor (Mr. Fowler), Donald Randolph (Senor Vidal), James Westerfield (Mike Adams), Eugene Iglesias (Manuel Arriega), Frank de Kova (Alcalde), Buzz Henry (Slim Barrett), Amapola Del Vando (Aunt), Bek Nelson (Charlie's Girl), William Leslie (Tucker), Guy Wilkerson (Peggy).

A refreshing look at what it meant to be a cowboy, without villains, Indian raiders, cigar-chewing town bullies, or even desperadoes. From a book by Frank Harris, that man who did it all, then told it all, COWBOY is the story of Lemmon as the tenderest foot ever, sitting in Chicago as a hotel clerk and dreaming about the west. Ford is in the Windy City to do some business and meets Lemmon who hangs around Ford like a puppy. When Ford, a cattle rancher, needs a few bucks to cover a poker bet, Lemmon lends it to him and the die is cast. Ford doesn't really want Lemmon tagging along so he makes the trip even more difficult than it is. There are many funny moments in Ed North's adaptation of Harris' book. Ford has one speech regarding the fact that cattle are stupid and not adorable, horses are ornery cusses and can't be trusted, and cowboy songs about how wonderful it is out there on the trail are just romanticized ballads of a life most of those songwriters never knew. The trek takes them into Mexico where Lemmon falls in love with Anna Kashfi, daughter of some rich Mexicans. Romance blooms but never interferes with the essential core of the story: Lemmon's maturation from a weak city boy to a hardened trail boss. Along the way, Donlevy does a short, but telling, cameo as a gun-slinger with no place to sling. The days of the Old West are gone now and Donlevy knows it and eventually commits suicide. This situation was handled, in an updated fashion, in LONELY ARE THE BRAVE. Without a strong story to guide it, COWBOY did not capture the pocketbooks of the American moviegoer but it remains a fine film. Kashfi was born in India and was married to Marlon Brando, whom she destroyed in her autobiography, Breakfast With Brando. DeKova (Alcalde) made a fine living playing gangsters on TV as well as Indians. His mean face belied his very gentle personality and the fact that he was able to project such evil is a tribute to his acting ability.

p, Julian Blaustein; d, Delmer Daves; w, Edmund H. North (from the book My Reminiscences As A Cowboy by Frank Harris); ph, Charles Lawton, Jr. (Technicolor); m, George Duning; ed, Al Clark, William A. Lyon; md, Morris Stoloff, Arthur Morton; art d, Cary Odell; set d, William Kiernan, James M. Crowe.

Western   (PR:A   MPAA:NR)

COWBOY AND THE BANDIT, THE*
(1935) 57m International/Superior bw

Rex Lease, Bobby Nelson, Janet Morgan, Dick Alexander, Ada Belle Driver, Bill Patton, Wally Wales, William Desmond, Franklyn Farnum, Art Mix, Lafe McKee, Ben Corbett, Vic Potel, George Chesebro, Alphonse Martel, Jack Kirk, Fred Parker.

Mixed-up oater about a good guy and bad guy trading places and then reversing the roles while forming a bond of friendship. Get off at the next stagestop.

p, Louis Weiss; d, Al Herman; w, Jack Jevne.

Western   (PR:A   MPAA:NR)

COWBOY AND THE BLONDE, THE**
(1941) 68m FOX bw

Mary Beth Hughes(Crystal Wayne), George Montgomery (Lank Garrett), Alan Mowbray (Phineas Johnson), Robert Conway (Don Courtney), John Miljan (Bob Roycroft), Richard Lane (Gilbert), Robert Emmett Keane (Mr. Gregory), Minerva Urecal (Murphy), Fuzzy Knight (Skeeter), George O'Hara (Melvyn), Monica Bannister (Maybelle), William Halligan (Franklyn).

Rodeo champ Montgomery is discovered by a talent scout and taken to Hollywood to appear in B westerns. All goes well until he runs up against Hughes, a tantrum-throwing actress, and a "Taming of the Shrew" type comedy ensues. Montgomery eventually decides he has had enough and heads back to his ranch, only to have Hughes realize she loves him and follow him. Okay series entry, with a few funny Hollywood jokes.

p, Ralph Dietrich, Walter Morosco; d, Ray McCarey; w, Walter Bullock (based on a story by Bullock and William Brent); ph, Charles Clark; ed, Harry Reynolds; md, Cyril J. Mockridge.

Western   (PR:A   MPAA:NR)

COWBOY AND THE INDIANS, THE**
(1949) 68m COL bw

Gene Autry (Himself), Sheila Ryan (Nan Palmer), Frank Richards ("Smiley" Martin), Hank Patterson (Tom Garber), Jay Silverheels (Lakohna), Claudia Drake (Lucky Broken Arm), George Nokes (Rona), Charles S. Evens (Broken Army), Alex Frazer (Fred Bradley), Clayton Moore (Luke), Frank Lackteen (Blue Eagle), Chief Yowlachie

(*Chief Long Arrow*), Lee Roberts (*Joe*), Nolan Leary (*Sheriff Don Payne*), Maudie Prickett (*Miss Summers*), Harry Mackin (*Bob Collins*), Charles Quigley (*Henderson*).

Indians have been stealing food from around the reservation so Gene investigates. He finds that corrupt Indian agent Richards is systematically cheating the Indians into starvation and their raids for self-preservation. Gene, with the help of Dr. Sheila Ryan, saves the Indians, sees that Richards gets his just desserts, and also sees romance spring between Ryan and educated Chief Silverheels. Average oater of interest for its advanced attitudes toward Indians. Songs: "One Little Indian Boy," "America," "Silent Night," "Here Comes Santa Claus."

p, Armand Schaefer; d, John English; w, Dwight Cummins, Dorothy Yost; ph, William Bradford; ed, Henry Batista.

Western (PR:A MPAA:NR)

COWBOY AND THE KID, THE*
(1936) 58m UNIV bw

Buck Jones (*Steve Davis*), Dorothy Revier (*June Caldwell*), Billy Burrud (*Jimmy Thomas*), Harry Worth (*Jess Watson*), Charles LeMoyne (*Sheriff Stanton*), Dick Rush (*Sheriff Morton*), Lefe McKee (*Sheriff Bailey*), Bob McKenzie (*Hank Simmons*), Burr Caruth (*Judge Talbot*), Eddie Lee (*Chinese Laundryman*), Kernan Cripps (*Jim Thomas*), Oliver Eckhart (*Dr. Wilson*), Mary Merach (*Mrs. Wilson*), Mildred Gober (*Mammy*), Silver (*Himself*).

Buck Jones wrote and starred in this sticky, sentimental oater. He raises little Burrud, whose father is shot dead in the opening reel, and falls for Revier, who overacts as the village schoolmarm.

p, Buck Jones; d, Ray Taylor; w, Frances Guihan (based on a story by Jones); ph, Allen Thompson, Herbert Kirkpatrick.

Western (PR:A MPAA:NR)

COWBOY AND THE LADY, THE***
(1938) 91, Goldwyn/UA bw

Gary Cooper (*Stretch*), Merle Oberon (*Mary Smith*), Patsy Kelly (*Katie Callahan*), Walter Brennan (*Sugar*), Fuzzy Knight (*Buzz*), Mabel Todd (*Elly*), Henry Kolker (*Mr. Smith*), Harry Davenport (*Uncle Hannibal Smith*), Emma Dunn (*Ma Hawkins*), Walter Walker (*Ames*), Berton Churchill (*Henderson*), Charles Richman (*Dillon*), Frederick Vogeding (*Captain*), Arthur Hoyt (*Valet*), Mabel Colcord (*Old Woman*), Billy Wayne, Ernie Admas, Russ Powell, Jack Baxley, Johnny Judd (*Rodeo Riders*).

This unfunny comedy had very little to distinguish it and yet was nominated for three Oscars and did win one for Thomas Moulton, head of Goldwyn's sound department. The Newman score and the title song by Newman, Alfred Quenzer, and L. Wolfe Gilbert were the other citations by the Academy. Oberon and her uncle, Davenport, are picked up when the nightclub they are attending is raided. Kolker, Merle's dad, is running for President and wants to keep his madcap daughter out of the papers so he deposits her on his palatial Florida estate. Merle can't take the quiet so she goes off with Patsy Kelly and Mabel Todd (the house maid and cook) and they have blind dates with three cowboys who are at a local rodeo. Oberon is paired with Cooper and tells him that she is a poor working girl who is struggling to support an alcoholic father and four younger sisters. Cooper believes her and they all go back to the big house for a party which they hold in the kitchen, in much the same way the "Downstairs" group in "Upstairs, Downstairs" might have. Cooper falls in love with Oberon and returns the following day to propose marriage but she is so nervous at what he's attempting that a failure to communicate ensues, and Cooper stalks out and gets aboard a ship sailing for the port city of Galveston. Oberon realizes that she does love the galoot so she joins him on the boat and they are married by Vogeding, captain of the vessel. After a while, Oberon gets mentally saddle sore and wants out of rodeo existence so Cooper tells her to take a rest back in Florida and join him later at his Montana spread. The marriage is discovered by Kolker's aides and they would like to keep it quiet as Kolker is getting closer to the nomination for President. Cooper receives word that Oberon can't go to Montana right now and he responds by rushing to Florida where he walks in on a huge fete tossed for the prospective president. While the others are in dinner clothes, Cooper dresses as a cowboy (why not, that's what he is) and the party guests look at him as though he were from another planet, not another state. Oberon tries to avoid him and he eventually gets the picture, turns to the snobs, and makes one of his famous speeches extolling the virtues of Americanism, manliness, and solid citizenry. With a few alterations, the words could have come right from the mouth of MR. DEEDS, GOOD SAM, or JOHN DOE. Cooper turns on his boot heels and exits. No sooner has he left when Kolker's assistant suggests an annulment. Oberon faints and Kolker is stunned. Davenport, ever the avuncular actor, then explains that Kolker's political ambitions are destroying his beloved daughter's opportunity for lifelong happiness. The light having been seen, Kolker withdraws from the political arena and Oberon and Cooper will be able to achieve happiness forever. Walter Brennan won an Oscar this year but it wasn't for this picture. He got his second statuette as Best Supporting Actor in KENTUCKY after having received his first two years before in COME AND GET IT. He was to win again in 1940 for supporting Gary Cooper again, in THE WESTERNER.

p, Samuel Goldwyn; d, H.C. Potter; w, S.N. Behrman, Sonya Levien (based on a story by Leo McCarey, Frank R. Adams); ph, Gregg Toland; m, Alfred Newman; ed, Sherman Todd; art d, Richard Day, James Basevi; set d, Julie Heron; cos, Omar Kiam; songs, "Er-ru-ti-tu-ti," "The Cowboy and the Lady" (Lionel Newman, Arthur Quenzer, L. Wolfe Gilbert).

Comedy (PR:A MPAA:NR)

COWBOY AND THE PRIZEFIGHTER**
(1950) 60m EL/EPC c

Jim Bannon (*Red Ryder*), Little Brown Jug (*Little Beaver*), Emmett Lynn (*Buckskin*), Don Haggerty (*Steve*), Karen Randle (*Sue*), John Hart (*Palmer*), Marshall Reed (*Osborne*), Forrest Taylor (*Stevenson*), Lou Nova (*Bull*).

Haggerty saves Bannon's life and the pair (along with sidekick Little Beaver, of course) put an end to the nefarious schemes of fight-promoter Hart and big boxer Nova. Haggerty has a vested interest in capturing the crooks in this Red Ryder series entry,

because he believes Hart is responsible for the murder of his father. (See RED RYDER series, Index.)

p, Jerry Thomas; d, Lewis D. Collins; w, Thomas (based on the "Red Ryder" comic strip by Fred Harman); ph, Gilbert Warrenton (Cinecolor); m, Ralph Kraushaar.

Western (PR:A MPAA:NR)

COWBOY AND THE SENORITA**
(1944) 77m REP bw

Roy Rogers (*Roy*), Mary Lee (*Chip Williams*), Dale Evans (*Ysobel Martinez*), John Hubbard (*Craig Allen*), Guinn "Big Boy" Williams (*Teddy Bear*), Fuzzy Knight (*Fuzzy*), Dorothy Christy (*Lulubelle*), Lucien Littlefield (*Judge Loomis*), Hal Taliaferro (*Ferguson*), Jack Kirk (*Sheriff*), Specialty Dancers: Cappella and Patricia, Jane Beebe and Ben Rochelle, Tito and Corinne Valdez, Bob Nolan and the Sons Of The Pioneers.

The first teaming of Rogers and Evans who would go on to make twenty films in a row together until they finally married in 1947. Evans plays the cousin of youngster Lee who has been left a gold mine that will be turned over to her on her sixteenth birthday. Villainous gambler Hubbard tries to weasel the mining rights away from the teenager, but Rogers and Williams come to the rescue. Songs: "The Cowboy and the Senorita," "What'll I Use For Money," "The Enchilada Man," "Round Her Neck She Wore A Yellow Ribbon," and "Bunk House Bugle Boy" (Ned Washington, Phil Ohman).

p, Harry Grey; d, Joseph Kane; w, Gordon Kahn (based on a story by Bradford Ropes); ph, Reggie Lanning; ed, Tony Martinelli; md, Walter Scharf; ch, Larry Ceballos.

Western **Cas.** (PR:A MPAA:NR)

COWBOY BLUES*
(1946) 62m COL bw

Ken Curtis, Jeff Donnell, Guy Kibbee, The Hoosier Hotshots, Guinn "Big Boy" Williams, Peg LaCentra, Robert Scott, The Town Criers, Deuce Spriggins and his Band, Carolina Cotton, The Plainsmen, Alan Bridges, Jack Rockwell, Forbes Murray, Vernon Dent, Coulter Irwin.

Modern-day oater is just an excuse to parade some range songs that are as instantly forgettable as the muddled plot and the Curtis-Donnell romance.

p, Colbert Clark; d, Ray Nazzaro; w, J. Benton Cheney; ph, George F. Kelley; ed, Jerome Thomas; md, Paul Mertz; art d, Charles Clague.

Western (PR:A MPAA:NR)

COWBOY CANTEEN**½
(1944) 72m COL bw

Charles Starrett, Jane Frazee, Vera Vague [Barbara Jo Allen], Tex Ritter, Guinn "Big Boy" Williams, The Mills Brothers, Jimmy Wakely and his Saddle Pals, Chickie and Buck, Roy Acuff and his Smoky Mountain Boys and Girls, The Tailor Maids, Dub Taylor, Max Terhune, Emmett Lynn, Edythe Elliott, Jeff Donnell, Dick Curtis.

Entertaining western twist on HOLLYWOOD CANTEEN stars Starrett as a rancher who turns his property into an entertainment mecca for GI's after he is drafted into the armed services. Instead of the usual fistfights and showdowns, there are musical numbers by Tex Ritter, Roy Acuff (one of his few screen appearances), and the Mills Brothers. Songs: "Spot In Arizona," "You Man You" (Walter G. Samuels, Saul Chaplin), "Wait For The Light To Shine" (Fred Rose) "Walking Down The Lane With You" (Jimmy Wakely), "Lazy River" (Sidney Arodin, Hoagy Carmichael).

p, Jack Fier; d, Lew Landers; w, Paul Gangelin, Felix Adler; ph, George Meehan; ed, Aaron Still.

Western (PR:A MPAA:NR)

COWBOY CAVALIER*
(1948) 57m MON bw

Jimmy Wakely, Dub "Cannonball" Taylor, Jan Bryant, Douglas Evans, Claire Whitney, William Ruhl, Steve Clark, Milburn Morante, Bud Osborne, Carol Henry, Bob Woodward, Louis Armstrong, Don Weston.

Weak western with the usual bad guys rounded up by Wakely who manages to croon a few prairie ballads. Taylor is the best part of the film with his oddball clowning.

p, Louis Gray; d, Derwin Abrahams; w, J. Benton Cheney, Ronald Davidson.

Western (PR:A MPAA:NR)

COWBOY COMMANDOS*½
(1943) 53 MON bw

Ray Corrigan (*Crash*), Dennis Moore (*Denny*), Max Terhune (*Alibi*), Evelyn Finney (*Joan*), Johnny Bond (*Slim*), Budd Buster (*Werner*), John Merton (*Fraser*), Edna Bennett (*Katie*), Steve Clark (*Bartlett*), Bud Osborne (*Hans*).

"I'll Get The Fuhrer, Sure As Shootin'," as sung by cowboy Bond, just about sums up this wartime oater which was one of the last of the Range Buster series of westerns. Corrigan, Moore, and Terhune set out to stop Nazi spies who are after "a valuable secret ore" called magnesite. Merton and Buster are the Huns who play their evil roles very well. (See RANGE BUSTER series, Index.)

p, George W. Weeks; d, S. Roy Luby; w, Elizabeth Beecher (based on a story by Clark Paylow); ph, Edward Kull; ed, Ray Claire.

Western **Cas.** (PR:A MPAA:NR)

COWBOY COUNSELOR**
(1933) 63m AA bw

Hoot Gibson, Sheila Mannors, Skeeter Bill Robbins, Bobby Nelson, Fred Gilman, Jack Rutherford, William Humphreys, Gordon DeMain, William M. McCormack, Samm Allen, Al Bridge, Frank Ellis.

Gibson stars as a fast-talking law book salesman who clears accused stagecoach robber Gilman's name as a favor to his lovely sister Mannors. The comedy comes off somewhat stilted and the plot resolution is fairly ludicrous, even for a programmer.

p, M.H. Hoffman, Jr.; d, George Melford; w, Jack Natteford; ph, Tom Galligan, Harry Neumann; ed, Mildred Johnson; art d, Gene Hornbostel.

Western (PR:A MPAA:NR)

COWBOY FROM BROOKLYN**½
(1938) 80m WB bw

Dick Powell (Elly Jordan), Pat O'Brien (Roy Chadwick), Priscilla Lane (Jane Hardy), Dick Foran (Sam Thorne), Ann Sheridan (Maxine Chadwick), Johnnie Davis (Jeff Hardy), Ronald Reagan (Pat Dunn), Emma Dunn (Ma Hardy), Granville Bates (Pop Hardy), James Stephenson (Prof. Landis), Hobart Cavanaugh (Mr. Jordan), Elisabeth Risdon (Mrs. Jordan), Dennie Moore (Abby Pitts), Rosella Towne (Panthea), May Boley (Mrs. Krinkenheim), Harry Barris (Louie), Candy Candido (Spec.), Donald Briggs (Star Reporter), Jeffrey Lynn (Chronicle Reporter), John Ridgely (Beacon Reporter), William B. Davidson (Mr. Alvey), Mary Field (Myrtle Semple), Monte Vandergrift, Eddy Chandler (Brakemen), Cliff Saum (Conductor), Sam Hayes (New Commentator), Jack Wise, Eddie Graham (Reporters), Don Marion (Bellboy), Jack Mower (Station Manager), John Harron (Technician), Wen Niles (Announcer), John T. Murray (Col. Rose), George Hickman (Newsboy), Dorothy Vaughan (Fat Woman), Jimmy Fox (Photographer), Stuart Holmes (Doorman), Mary Gordon (Chambermaid), Emmett Vogan (Loudspeaker Announcer).

So-so satire of the singing cowboys of the era, notably Gene Autry. Powell is a Brooklyn-born crooner who arrives at a Dude Ranch and scores with the way he warbles sagebrush songs. As a New Yorker, he has farmophobia, which is an unlikely fear of any animal larger than a cockroach. This causes him to be very nervous around little critters like chickens and a donkey almost sends him off the deep end. O'Brien is a fast-talking talent scout who signs up Powell and sends him to the big town masquerading as a real range rider. Powell hits the nation's ears on the radio and is an overnight sensation but now he has to appear at Madison Square Garden and prove to his fans that he is what he is: a true cowboy. To facilitate that, Powell is hypnotized with the help of pretty Priscilla Lane and all ends with a clinch and a chorus. Reagan played O'Brien's con-man pal and had a bit of trouble at first because he chose to be a drawling, slow-talker as a contrast to O'Brien's rat-a-tat manner of speech. That decision threw the pacing off and Reagan's lines kept being cut until O'Brien explained what the problem was and Ronnie was able to pick it up immediately. It was a brief two years later that Reagan gave his all for O'Brien who pleaded for the team to "win one for the Gipper" in KNUTE, ROCKNE, ALL-AMERICAN. Songs: "I've Got A Heartful of Music," "I'll Dream Tonight," "Ride, Tenderfoot, Ride," (Johnny Mercer, Richard A. Whiting), "Cowboy From Brooklyn" (Mercer, Harry Warren). Film was remade as TWO GUYS FROM TEXAS.

p, Hal B. Wallis; d, Lloyd Bacon; w, Earl Baldwin (based on the play "Howdy, Stranger" by Robert Sloane, Jr., Robert Sloane); ph, Arthur Edeson; ed, James Gibbons; md, Leo F. Forbstein; art d, Esdras Hartley.

Musical Comedy (PR:A MPAA:NR)

COWBOY FROM LONESOME RIVER*½
(1944) 55, COL bw

Charles Starrett, Vi Athens, Dub Taylor, Jimmy Wakely, Kenneth MacDonald, Ozie Waters, Arthur Wenzel, Shelby Atkinson, Foy Willing, Al Sloey, Craig Woods, Ian Keith, John Tyrell, Bud Geary, Steve Clark, Jack Rockwell.

A horse opera with some catchy cowpoke jingles sung by Wakely while Starrett bests vicious range boss MacDonald. Taylor's moronic clowning adds a few good belly laughs.

p, Jack Fier; d, Benjamin Kline; w, Luci Ward; ph, David Ragin; ed, Aaron Stell; art d, Lionel Banks.

Western (PR:A MPAA:NR)

COWBOY FROM SUNDOWN*
(1940) 57m MON bw

Tex Ritter (Tex Rokett), Pauline Haddon (Bec Davis), Rose Ates (Gloomy), Carleton Young (Nick Cuttler), George Pembroke (Cylus Cuttler), Dave O'Brien (Steve Davis), Patsy Morgan (Prunella Wallaby), James Farrar (Varco), Chick Hannon (Pete), Slim Andrews (Judge Pritchard), Bud Osborne (Pronto), Glen Strange (Bret Stockton).

Dull and technically inept Ritter vehicle has the singing cowboy rescuing heroine Haddon from a band of crooks trying to foreclose the mortgage on her ranch. Even the songs the singing cowboy warbles fail to impress.

p, Edward Finney; d, Spencer G. Bennet; w, Roland Lynch, Robert Emmett [Tansey] (based on an original story by Lynch); ph, Marcel LePicard; md, Frank Sanucci; m/l, Tex Ritter, Frank Harford, Johnny Lange, Lew Porter.

Western (PR:A MPAA:NR)

COWBOY HOLIDAY*½
(1934) 56m Beacon bw

Guinn "Big Boy" Williams, Janet Chandler, Julian Rivero, Dick Alexander, John Elliott, Alma Chester, Julia Bejarano, Frank Ellis.

Williams uses his brawn to undo the bad guys while mooning about Chandler, the ranch lady, in this weak western grinder.

p, Max Alexander, Arthur Alexander; d, Bob Hill; w, Rock Hawley; ph, Gilbert Warrenton; ed, Holbrook Todd.

Western (PR:A MPAA:NR)

COWBOY IN AFRICA
(SEE: AFRICA—TEXAS STYLE! 1967)

COWBOY IN MANHATTAN*½
(1943) 56m UNIV bw

Robert Paige (Bob), Frances Langford (Babs), Leon Errol (Hank), Walter Catlett (Ace), Joe Sawyer (Louie), Jennifer Holt (Mitzi), George Cleveland (Wild Bill), Will Wright (Higgins), Dorothy Granger (Tommy), Lorin Raker (Potter), Marek Windheim (Count Kardos) Matt McHugh (Cab Driver), Jack Mulhall (Headwaiter), Tommy Mack (Mac), Billy Nelson (Bill).

Tired tale of a Texas hotel musical group discovered by Catlett and brought to Broadway to start rehearsals for his new show. Cowpoke songwriter Paige pretends to be a millionaire to win the love of singing lead Langford. It's all basically a remake of YOU'RE A SWEETHEART (1937). Songs: "A Cowboy Is Happy," "Whistle Your Blues

To A Bluebird," "Mr. Moon," "Private Cowboy Jones," "Need I Say More," "Dancing On Air," "Got Love" (Everett Carter, Milton Rosen).

p, Paul Malvern; d, Frank Woodruff; w, Warren Wilson (based on an original by William Thomas, Maxwell Shane, Wilson); ph, Woody Bredell; ed, Fred R. Feitshans, Jr.; md, H.J. Salter; ch, Aida Broadbent.

Western/Musical (PR:A MPAA:NR)

COWBOY IN THE CLOUDS**
(1943) 54m COL bw

Charles Starrett (Steve Kendall), Dub Taylor (Cannonball), Julie Duncan (Dorrie Bishop), Jimmy Wakely (Glen Avery), Davidson Clark (Amos Fowler), Hal Taliaferro (Hadley), Dick Curtis (Roy Madison), Edward Cassidy (Sheriff Page). Paul Zaremba (Dean), Charles King, Jr. (Thripp), John Tyrrell (Mack Judd), The Jesters (Themselves).

Starrett stars as a cowboy rancher who defends the newly established Civil Air Patrol from rich cattlemen who think it useless. He proves them wrong when he uses a CAP plane to fly into a raging forest fire and rescue a cattle baron's daughter. He also finds time to catch a murderer while buzzing around above the range. First directorial effort from Starrett series cameraman Kline for Columbia emphasizes action, a talent that would grow in his future outings.

p, Jack Fier; d, Benjamin Kline; w, Elizabeth Beecher; ph, George Meehan; ed, Aaron Stell.

Western (PR:A MPAA:NR)

COWBOY MILLIONAIRE**
(1935) 65m Atherton/FOX bw

George O'Brien (Bob Walker), Evalyn Bostock (Pamela Barclay), Edgar Kennedy (Persimmon), Alden Chase (Hadley Thornton), Maude Allen (Henrietta Barclay), Dan Jarrett (Doyle), Lloyd Ingraham, Dean Benton, Thomas Curran.

Bostock plays a young Englishwoman who finds herself on an American dude ranch run by O'Brien. Soon the couple fall in love, but there is the predictable misunderstanding that sends her back to merry ol' England. Not being one to let a little disagreement stand in the way of future happiness, O'Brien ventures overseas and wins her back.

p, Sol Lesser; d, Edward F. Cline; w, George Waggner, Dan Jarrett; ph, Frank B. Good; m, Abe Meyer; ed, Donn Hayes.

Western (PR:A MPAA:NR)

COWBOY QUARTERBACK*½
(1939) 54m WB bw

Bert Wheeler (Harry Lynn), Marie Wilson (Maizie Williams), Gloria Dickson (Evelyn Corey), De Wolf Hopper (Handsome Sam), William Demarest (Rusty Walker), Eddie Foy, Jr. (Steve Adams), William Gould (Col. Moffett), Charles Wilson (Hap Farrell), Fredric Tozere (Mr. Slater), John Harron (Mr. Gray), John Ridgely (Mr. Walters), Eddie Acuff (Airplane Pilot), Clem Bevans (Lem), Sol Gross (Cozy Walsh), Don Turner (Joe Wade), Max Hoffman, Jr. (Lon Ring), Dick Wessell (Gyp Galbraith), Dutch Hendrian (Berries O'Leary).

Dull-witted comedy about football scout Demarest who discovers dumb hick Wheeler heaving sacks of potatoes around Wilson's general store and signs him up to be the Packer's quarterback. Of course the kid falls in with some gamblers and makes the inevitable last-minute push to extricate himself from their clutches in just enough time (40 seconds to be exact) to win the big game. Story is a poor remake of Ring Lardner and George M. Cohan's play "Elmer the Great," about a baseball player played by Joe E. Brown.

d, Noel Smith; w, Fred Nibio, Jr. (based on a story by Ring Lardner and a play by Lardner, George M. Cohan); ph, Ted McCord; m, Howard Jackson; ed, Doug Gould.

Comedy (PR:A MPAA:NR)

COWBOY SERENADE**
(1942) 66m REP bw

Gene Autry, Smiley Burnette, Fay McKenzie, Cecil Cunningham, Randy Brooks, Addison Richards, Tris Coffin, Slim Andrews, Melinda Leighton, Johnny Berkes, Forrest Taylor, Hank Worden, Si Jenks, Ethan Laidlaw, Hal Price, Otto Ham, Loren Raker, Bud Wolfe, Forbes Murray, Bud Geary, Frankie Marvin, Tom London, Ken Terrell, Ralph Kirby, Ken Cooper, Rick Anderson, "Champion."

On par with Autry's best, the singing cowboy sets out to break up a gambling ring. Things get messy when he learns it is headed by the father of McKenzie, in one of her many films with Autry. Featured is the title tune, "Cowboy Serenade."

p, Harry Grey; d, William Morgan; w, Olive Cooper; ph, Jack Marta; ed, Lester Orleback; md, Raoul Kraushaar.

Musical/Western (PR:A MPAA:NR)

COWBOY STAR, THE**
(1936) 56m COL bw

Charles Starrett (Spencer Yorke), Iris Meredith (May Baker), Si Jenks (Buckshot), Marc Lawrence (Johnny Sampson), Ed Peil, Jr. (Clem Baker), Wally Albright (Jimmy), Ralph McCullough (Pretty Boy Hogan), Dick Terry (Midget), Landers Stevens (Kinswell), Winifred Hari, Nick Copeland, Lew Meehan.

Fed up with his life as a movie cowboy, Starrett and sidekick Jenks leave Hollywood and travel to Arizona. He denies that he is a movie star, though young Albright recognizes him. He buys a ranch and begins a romance with Meredith (who would go on to play opposite Starrett twenty more times). Albright is kidnaped by bandits hiding out in a ghost town, and Starrett teams up with Sheriff Peil to rout the bad guys after a fight with machine guns and fists. Decent B western is one of Starrett's earlier efforts. He would go on playing western heroes for another sixteen years, including the Durango Kid series.

d, David Selman; w, Frances Guihan (based on a story by Frank Melford and Cornelius Reece); ph, Allen G. Siegler; ed, William Lyon.

Western (PR:A MPAA:NR)

COWBOYS, THE*** (1972) 128m WB c

John Wayne *(Will Anderson)*, Roscoe Lee Browne *(Jebediah Nightlinger)*, Bruce Dern *(Long Hair)*, Colleen Dewhurst *(Kate)*, Slim Pickens *(Anse)*, Lonny Chapman *(Preacher)*, Charles Tyner *(Jenkins)*, A. Martinez *(Cimarron)*, Alfred Barker, Jr. *(Singing Fats)*, Nicolas Beauvy *(Four Eyes)*, Steve Benedict *(Steve)*, Robert Carradine *(Slim Honeycutt)*, Norman Howell, Jr. *(Weedy)*, Stephen Hudis *(Charlie Schwartz)*, Sean Kelly *(Stuttering Bob)*, Clay O'Brien *(Hardy Fimps)*, Sam O'Brien *(Jimmy Phillips)*, Mike Pyeatt *(Homer Weems)*, Sarah Cunningham *(Annie Andersen)*, Allyn Ann McLerie *(Ellen Price)*, Matt Clark *(Smiley)*, Wallace Brooks, Jim Burk, Larry Finley, Maggie Costain, Jerry Gatlin, Walter Scott, Dick Farnsworth, Charise Cullin, Collette Poeppel, Margaret Kelly, Larry Randles, Norman Hiwell, Joe Yrigoyen, Tap Canutt, Chuck Courtney.

Mark Rydell shows some fine touches in his third feature but the final result is an overlong and often dull movie that had the rare distinction of being one of the few John Wayne westerns that gasped at the box office. Eleven youths, from age nine through fifteen, are hired by rancher Wayne when his regular hands desert him in search of gold that's been discovered nearby. They drive a herd of cattle 400 miles and then Wayne is shot by nutty Dern, who is angry that he wasn't hired. The young boys become a revenge-minded gang under the eye of Browne, a wagon train cook. They go out and nail Dern and his gang. All of this takes more than two hours to tell and that's twenty minutes too long. Ravetch and Frank have written many memorable films (CONRACK, HUD, HOMBRE, NORMA RAE, and more) but this is not one of them. Colleen Dewhurst has a nice moment as the madam of a bordello and it's Slim Pickens who gives Wayne the idea to use kids in lieu of adults, but other than those two, the bit roles aren't much.

p&d, Mark Rydell; w, Irving Ravetch, Harriett Frank, Jr., William Dale Jennings (based on a novel by Jennings); ph, Robert Surtees (Panavision, Technicolor); m, John Williams; ed, Robert Swink, Neil Travis; prod d, Philip Jeffries; set d, William Kiernan; cos, Anthea Sylbert.

Western **Cas.** **(PR:A-C MPAA:PG)**

COWBOYS FROM TEXAS* (1939) 57m REP bw

Robert Livingston *(Stony Brooke)*, Raymond Hatton *(Rusty Joslin)*, Duncan Renaldo *(Renaldo)*, Carole Landis *(June)*, Charles Middleton *(Kansas Jones)*, Ivan Miller *(Allison)*, Betty Compson *(Belle Starkey)*, Ethan Laidlaw *(Plummer)*, Yakima Canutt *(Dawson)*, Walter Wills *(Morgan)*, Edward Cassidy *(Jed Taylor)*, Forbes Murray, Bud Osborne, Charles King, Horace Murphy, Harry Strang, Jack Kirk, David Sharpe, Lew Meehan, Jack O'Shea.

A less than exciting horse opera set in 1906 which is part of the Three Mesquiteers series. Livingstone and his love, Landis, are a couple of homesteaders taking advantage of Teddy Roosevelt's Reclamation Act. Trying to ruin their hopeful future out west is a nasty group interested in deflating the government's plan. For twenty-year-old Landis, who would go on to win acclaim for "the best legs in town," it was her second screen credit. (See THREE MESQUITEERS series, Index.)

p, Harry Grey; d, George Sherman; w, Oliver Drake (based on characters created by William Colt MacDonald); ph, Ernest Miller; ed, Tony Martinelli; md, William Lava.

Western **(PR:A MPAA:NR)**

COYOTE TRAILS* (1935) 68m Reliable/William Steiner bw

Tom Tyler, Helen Dahl, Ben Corbett, Lafe McKee, Dick Alexander, Robert Walker, Roger Williams, George Chesebro, Slim Whitaker, Jack Evans.

Routine sagebrush saga has Tyler trying to save Dahl's homestead from the heavies. Inept production and less-than-average plot reduces this one to a sick nag.

p&d, Bernard B. Ray; w, Carl Krusada, Rose Gordon.

Western **(PR:A MPAA:NR)**

CRACK IN THE MIRROR*** (1960) 97m FOX bw

Orson Welles *(Hagolin/Lamoriciere)*, Juliette Greco *(Exponine/Florence)*, Bradford Dillman *(Larnier/Claude)*, Alexander Knox *(President)*, Catherine Lacy *(Mother Superior)*, William Lucas *(Kerstner)*, Maurice Teynac *(Doctor)*, Austin Willis *(Hurtelaut)*, Cec Linder *(Murzeau)*, Eugene Deckers *(Magre)*, Yves Brainville *(Prosecutor)*, Vivian Matalon *(Young Man at Buvette)*, Jacques Marin *(Watchman)*, Martine Alexis *(Doctor's Wife)*.

Often intriguing film done in Paris that might have been better accepted as a French film, rather than an American movie made in France. Two parallel stories are told with the three stars playing dual roles—for no other reason than to show their versatility and also for the fact that the parts wouldn't have been large enough to attract six people of any magnitude. Both stories are of love triangles and eventually they cross. In the first, Welles is a crude, boorish construction worker married to Juliette Greco, who is having an affair with laborer Bradford Dillman. The couple have two children but that doesn't stop Greco from her passionate fling with Dillman as the kids are asleep in the same room. Their passion gets so strong that they agree to kill Welles, who is asleep in the kitchen. In the second story, Dillman is a hot-shot lawyer who is again sleeping with Greco but now she is the wife of very successful attorney Welles. Dillman-the-lawyer is hired to defend Dillman-the-laborer and Greco-the-wife while he is sleeping with the other Greco-the-wife. Welles-the-lawyer eventually dies of a heart attack when he learns that his protege and his spouse have been closer than he suspected. The poor killers are sent away and the wealthy ones are set free. Fleischer and Zanuck must have been attempting to make a point about justice, French or otherwise, but much of it was lost. The technique is more important and certainly more noticeable than the story and once that happens the audience is usually lost. Zanuck wrote the screenplay under his nom de plume. He was a fascinating character with many odd habits. He loved the number thirteen and had it on his license plates. He considered thirteen his lucky number and his full name (with the F in the middle) had thirteen letters. It is rumored that he changed the name of the movie 13 RUE MADELINE from the original address which was 32 Rue Madeline. He was also renowned as being one of the great swordsmen of his day, and we are not referring to rapiers, epees, or sabres.

p, Darryl F. Zanuck; d, Richard Fleischer; w, Mark Canfield (Zanuck) (based on the novel *Drama In The Mirror* by Marcel Haedrich); ph, William C. Mellor (CinemaScope); m, Maurice Jarre; ed, Roger Dwyre; art d, Jean d'Eaubonne; cos, Givenchy.

Crime Drame **(PR:C MPAA:NR)**

CRACK IN THE WORLD*½ (1965) 96m PAR c

Dana Andrews *(Dr. Stephen Sorensen)*, Janette Scott *(Mrs. Maggie Sorensen)*, Kieron Moore *(Ted Rampion)*, Alexander Knox *(Sir Charles Eggerston)*, Peter Damon *(Masefield)*, Gary Lasdun *(Markov)*, Mike Steen *(Steele)*, Todd Martin *(Simpson)*, Jim Gillen *(Rand)*, Alfred Brown, Emilio Carrere, Sydna Scott, John Karlsen, Ben Tatar.

Dana Andrews is a scientist who wants to drill through the Earth's crust to get at the molten rock below, hoping to use it as an energy source for mankind. He is warned by his young assistant, Moore, that such an attempt will cause the earth to crack, but Andrews goes ahead. At first all goes as planned, until a crack appears, causing disasters around the globe. The scientists in all their wisdom decide to explode a nuclear bomb in the path of the ever-growing crack, but it only alters its direction and doubles its speed, causing a large chunk on the Earth to fly off, creating a second moon. Andrews, dying of cancer and with nothing to lose, lowers a second bomb into the crack, sacrificing his life. The bomb finally stops the crack and the end of the film sees the nearly decimated world beginning over again.

p, Bernard Glasser, Lester A. Sansom; d, Andrew Marton; w, Jon Manchip White, Julian Halevy (based on a story by White); ph, Manuel Berenguer; m, John Douglas; ed, Derek Parsons; art d, Eugene Lourie; cos, Laure de Zarate; spec eff, Alex Weldon.

Science Fiction **(PR:A MPAA:NR)**

CRACK-UP, THE*** (1937) 70m FOX bw

Peter Lorre *(Col. Gimpy)*, Brian Donlevy *(Ace Martin)*, Helen Wood *(Ruth Franklin)*, Ralph Morgan *(John Fleming)*, Thomas Beck *(Joe Randall)*, Kay Linaker *(Mrs. Fleming)*, Lester Matthews *(Sidney Grant)*, Earl A. Foxe *(Operative No. 30)*, J. Carrol Naish *(Operative No. 77)*, Gloria Roy *(Operative No. 16)*, Oscar Apfel *(Alfred Kruxton)*, Paul Stanton *(Daniel D. Harrington)*, Howard C. Hickman *(Maj. White)*.

An offbeat, even weird film where Donlevy is a crackerjack test pilot who receives a bribe from an airport worker to steal the plans of the experimental DOX plane, but he works against the spy ring by escaping in another experimental transcontinental plane, the Wild Goose, an enormous craft not unlike the legendary "Spruce Goose," later designed and barely flown by Howard Hughes. On board is Morgan, the plane's designer, a copilot, Beck, and the airport's cretinous mascot, Lorre, who has spent much of the first reel running around like a wide-eyed idiot, blowing a bugle. A fierce storm forces the plane down into the sea and as it begins to sink Lorre suddenly reveals himself as Baron Rudolf Maximilian Taggart, a notorious master spy. He has been feigning his nitwit role, and now tries to steal the plans of the DOX craft from Donlevy. The four men realize that there is only one life preserver and, observing the kind of chivalry only found in story books, give it to the youngest, Beck, who has had no part in his machinations. Beck survives and the rest go down with the ship. As a final gesture, Lorre slips the plans for the DOX plane into Beck's pocket. Donlevy is solid in his role as the double-crossing pilot but Lorre steals the show as the apparently feeble-minded spy who is constantly reciting "The Walrus and the Carpenter." The special effects employed in staging the air crash are spectacular and not to be missed.

p, Samuel G. Engel; d, Malcolm St. Clair; w, Charles Kenyon, Sam Mintz (based on a story by John Goodrich); ph, Barney McGill; m, Samuel Kaylin; ed, Fred Allen; art d, Duncan Cramer, Lewis Creber; spec eff, Aaron Rosenberg; m/l, "Top Gallant," Sidney Clare, Harry Akst.

Spy Drama **(PR:A MPAA:NR)**

CRACK-UP*½** (1946) RKO bw

Pat O'Brien *(George Steele)*, Claire Trevor *(Terry Cordeau)*, Herbert Marshall *(Traybin)*, Ray Collins *(Dr. Lowell)*, Wallace Ford *(Cochrane)*, Dean Harens *(Reynolds)*, Damian O'Flynn *(Stevenson)*, Erskine Sanford *(Mr. Barton)*, Mary Ware *(Mary)*, Harry Harvey *(Moran)*, Robert Bray *(Man with Drunk)*, Tom Noonan *(Vendor)*, Bob White, Eddie Parks *(Drunks)*, Chef Milani *(Joe)*, Al Hill, Carl Hansen, Roger Creed, Gloria Jetter *(Gamblers)*, Horace Murphy *(Conductor)*, Alvin Hammer *(Milquetoast)*, Tiny Jones, Dorothea Wolbert *(Old Ladies)*, Sam Lufkin, Carl Faulkner *(Detectives)*, Ed Gargan, Harry Shannon, Tex Swan, Cap Somers, George Bruggerman, Philip Morris *(Cops)*, Joe Kamaryt *(Waiter)*, Harry Monty *(Midget)*, Bob Pepper *(Intern)*, Frank Moran *(Bartender)*, Kernan Cripps *(Ticket Clerk)*, Rose Plummer *(Impatient Woman)*, Frank Shannon *(Gateman)*, Sam McDaniels *(Porter)*, Lee Elson *(Man)*, Shemen Ruskin *(Wide-Eyed Man)*, Bonnie Blair *(Dorothy)*, Dick Rush *(Ship's Captain)*, Delmar Costello *(Deck Hand)*, Jimmy O'Gatty *(Mate)*, Guy Beach *(Station)*, Johnny Indrisano *(Detective)*, Richard Ryen *(Butler)*, Ellen Corby *(Maid)*, Jack Cheatham *(Attendant)*, Belle Green *(Woman in Audience)*, Alf Haugan *(Man in Audience)*, John Ince, Fred Hueston, Alex Akimoff, J. C. Fowler, John Ardell *(Men)*.

O'Brien is an art expert who had served in the Army exposing Nazi forgeries and is now one of the officials of a New York museum. Just before he is to give a lecture using his X-ray device to demonstrate how to spot a bogus piece of art, he loses consciousness. O'Brien is first shown crashing through a museum door and the furious pace of this story never quits. He is suspended for his erratic behavior which he claims is the result of a train wreck. He cannot, however, explain what has happened between the time of the wreck and his outburst in the museum. Trevor, his girl friend and a reporter, along with Marshall, a secret official for Scotland Yard investigating art forgeries, help O'Brien piece the missing moments together. He is the victim of a plot, it turns out, masterminded by elitist art collector Collins, who realized that O'Brien could have inadvertently discovered one of the forgeries he had placed in the museum. Collins and others have been systematically looting the museum, replacing the great masterworks with clever forgeries, compelling the museum director, Sanford, to go along with the scheme. O'Brien's blackout was engineered by the devious Collins who had administered sodium pentothal to create in his mind a train wreck that never existed and blank out his witnessing a murder. In retracing his steps, O'Brien runs into lurking danger everywhere, but he survives, and exposes the evil Collins who spits out his hatred for "democratic art" at film's end: "Did you ever want to possess something that was unattainable? These masters became everything in life to me . . . Unfortunately museums have a habit of wasting good art on dolts who can't distinguish between it and trash." CRACK-UP, the first film directed by Reis after leaving the Army, is a tight, suspenseful film with eerie lensing that puts it solidly in the realm of classic film noir. O'Brien is terrific as the groping victim, and Collins is wry and hatefully shrewd as the manipulating gobbler of art. Although way above standard in every detail, this film, with its flashbacks and flash forwards, and a script with a few holes in it, did not do as well at the box office as RKO production chief Charles Koerner expected. He died of leukemia during the filming. When Koerner's close friend, mogul David O. Selznick, heard of his condition, he spent a great deal of money trying to get opinions on treatment from world medical experts but to no avail. Koerner's death was also a great blow to O'Brien who considered him the reason for the studio's financial well-being. "With his passing," O'Brien later stated, "the great days of RKO were over. It did little more than limp along until my Cuban friend, Desi Arnaz, gobbled it up for TV."

p, Jack J. Gross; d, Irving Reis; w, John Paxton, Ben Bengal, Ray Spencer (based on the short story "Madman's Holiday" by Fredric Brown); ph, Robert de Grasse; m, Leigh Harline; ed, Frederick Knudtson; md, Constantin Bakaleinikoff; art d, Albert S. D'Agostino, Jack Okey; set d, Darrell Silvera, Michael Orenbach; cos, Renie.

Mystery/Crime Drama	**(PR:A	MPAA:NR)**

## CRACKED NUTS*½	(1931) 65m RKO bw

Bert Wheeler (Wendell Graham), Robert Woolsey (Zander U. Parkhurst), Edna May Oliver (Aunt Van Varden), Dorothy Lee (Betty Harrington), Leni Stengel (Carlotta), Stanley Fields (Gen. Bogardus), Harvey Clark, Boris Karloff, Ben Turpin, Frank Thornton, Frank Lackteen, Wilfred Lucas.

One of the few features done by Woolsey and Wheeler, the Abbot and Costello of their day. They were usually relegated to the twenty-minute "two reeler," and this film suffers from the excess padding required to make it full length. The story concerns Wheeler, who, in an attempt to make good and please his fiancee's aunt, buys a revolution to become the king of El Dorania. He arrives in the kingdom to find that his friend Woolsey has won the crown from the previous king in a crap game. There cannot be two kings in one kingdom, so Wheeler is ordered to kill Woolsey. The bombs intended to kill Woolsey expose an oil gusher, and all is well as the country is drenched in prosperity. Karloff also appears in this film, which was written and produced by Douglas MacLean, a big comedy star during the silent era.

p, Douglas MacLean; d, Edward F. Cline; w, Ralph Spence Boasberg (based on a story by MacLean, Boasberg); ph, Nick Musuraca.

Comedy	**(PR:AA	MPAA:NR)**

## CRACKED NUTS*	(1941) 61m UNIV bw

Stuart Erwin (Lawrence Trent), Una Merkel (Sharon), Mischa Auer (Kabikoff), William Frawley (Mitchell), Ernie Stanton (Ivan), Mantan Moreland (Burgess), Hattie Noel (Chloe), Astrid Allwyn (Ethel), Francis Pierlot (Mayor Wilfred Smun), Will Wright (Mr. Sylvanus Boogle), Elaine Morley (Blonde), Dorothy Darrell (Maid), Pierre Watkin (Benson), Hal K. Dawson (Saw Horse Man), Tom Hanlon (Radio Announcer), Emmett Vogan (McAneny), Billy Bletcher (Parachute Man), Milton Parsons (Olson), Marion Martin (Blonde), Pat O'Malley (1st Officer), Lyle Clement (2nd Officer), Dave Willock (Radio Technician), Marin Sais (Woman), Bobby Barker (Waiter), Shemp Howard (Robot).

Feeble comedy has Erwin a backwoods hick who wins a $5,000 prize by coming up with the winning entry in a refrigerator slogan competition. Along come some confidence tricksters from the city with a phony robot to take the bumpkin's cash. A big chase winds this one up, though it doesn't make it any better.

p, Joseph G. Sanford; d, Edward E. Cline; w, Erna Lazarus, W. Scott Darling; ph, Charles van Enger; ed, Milton Carruth; md, Charles Previn; art d, Jack Otterson.

Comedy	**(PR:A	MPAA:NR)**

## CRACKERJACK	(SEE: MAN WITH 100 FACES, 1938, Brit.)

## CRACKING UP*	(1977) 69m Comedy Jam/AIP c

Phil Proctor (Walter Concrete), Peter Bergman (Barbara Halters), Michael Mislove, Fred Willard, Paul Zegler, Steve Bluestein, The Credibility Gap, Harry Shearer, Michael McCane, David Lander, The Graduates, Jim Fisher, Jim Staahl, Gino Insana, "Kansas City" Bob McClurg, Leslie Ackerman, Rowby Goren, Neil Israel, Rick Murray, C.D. Taylor, Edie McClurg, Mary McCusker, Cris Pray, Ron Prince, Lynn Marie Stuart, Steven Stucker, Kurt Taylor, Paul Willson, Fee Waybill.

The title of this poor attempt at humor refers to California as it has finally suffered the big Earthquake, causing it to slide into the ocean. Filled with members of the Ace Trucking Company, Fire Sign Theater, and Second City comedy troops, the cast attempts to enact the events as viewed by a TV news crew. Proctor, as TV reporter Walter Concrete, interviews victims and loots on the side, and Bergman, in drag, plays the role of newscaster Barbara Halters. A bright point is music by The Tubes.

p, C. D. Taylor, Rick Murray; d, Rowby Goren, Chuck Staley; w, cast written; m, Ward Jewel, The Tubes; ed, Roger Parker; art d, C. D. Taylor; title animation, Linda Taylor.

Comedy	**(PR:O	MPAA:R)**

## CRACKING UP	(SEE: SMORGASBORD, 1983)

## CRACKSMAN, THE**	(1963, Brit.) 112m WB-Pathe c

Charlie Drake (Ernest Wright), George Sanders (The Guv'nor), Dennis Price (Grantley), Nyree Dawn Porter (Muriel), Eddie Byrne (Domino), Finlay Currie (Feathers), Percy Herbert (Nosher), Geoffrey Keen (Magistrate), George A. Cooper (Fred), Christopher Rhodes (Mr. King), Norman Bird (Policeman), Wanda Ventham (Sandra), Richard Shaw (Moke), Tutte Lemkow (Choreographer), Sheila Holt, Tom Gillis (Apache Dancers).

Charlie Drake, a crack locksmith called to open the toughest of locks, like the one to the Tower of London, when it became stuck, is persuaded by a con man into opening a locked car and safe. He winds up in jail for a year. When he gets out, he is tricked into opening some more locks, and gets three years. Drake winds up with a reputation as the top safe-cracker around. He wants to get out of the business when he is released again, but finds himself a pawn between two rival gangs. The gangs get together to do one job—steal the Stamford Collection of Fine Gems. Drake and undercover policewoman Porter trip up the crooks and bring them to justice.

p, W.A. Whittaker; d, Peter Graham Scott; w, Lew Schwarz, Charlie Drake, Mike Watts (based on a story by Schwartz); ph, Harry Waxman; m, Ron Goodwin; ed, Richard Best.

Comedy	**(PR:A	MPAA:NR)**

## CRADLE SONG*	(1933) 78m PAR bw

Dorothea Wieck (Joanna), Evelyn Venable (Teresa), Sir Guy Standing (The Doctor), Louise Dresser (Prioress), Kent Taylor (Antonio), Gertrude Michael (Marcella), Georgia Caine (Vicaress), Nydia Westman (Sagrario), Marion Ballou (Ines), Eleanor Wesselhoeft (Mistress of Novices), Diane Sinclair (Christina).

This film was supposed to be the successful American debut of Dorothea Wieck, one of the many fine German performers who fled their country when Hitler came to power. However, her accent was too strong for American tastes, and she would never find the success that Marlene Dietrich did. The story has Wieck as a nun in a Spanish cloister. A baby is left on the steps of the nunnery, and Wieck unofficially adopts and raises it. Ironically, the film featured another Hollywood newcomer, Venable, who went on to star in several quality productions before retiring in the early forties.

p, E. Lloyd Sheldon; d, Mitchell Leisen; w, Marc Connelly, Franke Partos, Martinez Sierra (based on a play by Sierra); ph, Charles Lang; m, W. Franke Harling.

Drama	**(PR:A	MPAA:NR)**

## CRAIG'S WIFE****	(1936) 73m COL bw

Rosalind Russell (Harriet Craig), John Boles (Walter Craig), Billie Burke (Mrs. Frazier), Jane Darwell (Mrs. Harold), Dorothy Wilson (Ethel Landreth), Alma Kruger (Miss Austen), Thomas Mitchell (Fergus Passmore), Raymond Walburn (Billy Birkmire), Robert Allen (Gene Fredericks), Elisabeth Risdon (Mrs. Landreth), Nydia Westman (Mazie), Kathleen Burke (Adelaide Passmore), Frankie Vann (Cabdriver).

George Kelly's play won a Pulitzer Prize and was made first as a silent in 1928 with Warner Baxter as Craig and Irene Rich as the shrew. Joan Crawford did it third as Harriet Craig fourteen years after this one. Harry Cohn wisely handed over the adaptation chores to McCall and the directing job to Arzner. If ever a film screamed to be put on celluloid by women, this was it. Russell was only twenty-eight when she starred opposite John Boles, but she had such bearing and such an imperious manner that she was able to convince audiences that she *could* be that frozen bitch. Harriett Craig is the ultimate Virgo (if you believe in astrology: If not, forget this interjection) in that she is far more interested in keeping a spotless, gleaming house than in the welfare of any member of her household, least of all, her husband. This compulsive behavior causes her to lose contact with any humanity, character by character, until she is finally alone. Her husband is gone, her sister has died, and even the servants have fled. Though Boles make a fine foil for Russell and there is excellent work on the part of Burke as a neighbor who can't understand Harriett Craig's iciness, Darwell as the housekeeper, and Westman as another member of the household staff, the picture is definitely Roz Russell's from start to finish. Arzner and McCall did take some liberties with the original play. Some of the dialog, of course, couldn't be used in the film as the Production Code was still stringent. Kelly also took exception to Boles's portrayal as a man with a slight Oedipus complex. He thought it was enough that Harriett and he had found each other out of some sort of need and that was sufficient. Kelly's working arrangement with MGM typified the confusion then rampant among personnel. Production chief Irving Thalberg brought the playwright in from NYC to work on the script with McCall, then forgot all about him. For two months the playwright languished in a silent office then got fed up and went back to New York without telling anyone. Returning to Los Angeles on another matter, Kelly went to his old MGM office and found a pile of weekly paychecks made out in his name. Just as he turned to leave, Thalberg burst through the door, smiling and pumping his hand, saying: "I'm so sorry not to have had time to see you. Let's get together next week for sure." Someone at the studio, perhaps, thought that the sadist-masochist relationship may have been a trifle subtle for the filmgoing crowd and that they might have required some sort of easily recognized motivation in order to accept Boles as a wimp. In real life, Boles was anything but, having served as a spy in WW I in Germany, Turkey, and Bulgaria. A good-looking man, he also had a deep, resonant voice and was an excellent singer. Despite all that, his career never really ascended into the stratosphere, but he made a fine living as the handsome foil for women like Russell, Irene Dunne (BACK STREET), and Barbara Stanwyck (often). CRAIG'S WIFE was a character study more suited for the stage than film but McCall, Arzner, and the actors managed to infuse it with enough movement to cause audiences to flock to the theater for what was, essentially, a very distasteful portrait of a woman that not even her own mother could love.

p, Edward Chodorov; d, Dorothy Arzner; w, Mary C. McCall, Jr. (based on a play by George Kelly); ph, Lucien Ballard; ed, Viola Lawrence; md, Morris Stoloff.

Drama	**(PR:A-C	MPAA:NR)**

CRANES ARE FLYING, THE***** (1960, USSR) Mosfilm/WB bw (LETYAT ZHURAVIT)

Tatyana Samoilova *(Veronica)*, Alexei Batalov *(Boris)*, Vasily Merkuryev *(Byodor Ivanovich)*, A. Shvorin *(Mark)*, S. Kharitonova *(Irina)*, K. Nikitin *(Volodya)*, V. Zubkov *(Stepan)*, A. Bogdanova *(Grandmother)*.

Winner of the Cannes Film Festival's Palme D'or, this right-wing, hence non propaganda, Soviet love story set during WW II is one of that country's most visually stimulating films in years. Samoilova is left behind by the man she loves when he goes off to war, and soon afterwards she becomes a widow. She resigns herself to marry his brother, whom she has no feelings of affection toward, presumedly because she sees him as a surrogate. A beautiful performance is given by the gorgeous Samoilova, the great niece of Stanislavsky and daughter of an actor father, Yevgeni Samoilova. Her electrifying performance in THE CRANES ARE FLYING won her international attention. Among the others involved in this great film were Batalov, who later in the decade was to turn to directing, and cameraman Urussevsky, who was a front line photographer in the violent days of WW II.

p&d, Mikhail Kalatozov; w, V. Rozov (based on a play by Rosov); ph, Sergei Urussevsky; m, M. Vainberg; set d, Y. Svidetelev.

Romance **(PR:A MPAA:NR)**

THE CRASH* (1932) 59m FN bw

Ruth Chatterton *(Linda Gault)*, George Brent *(Geoffrey Gault)*, Paul Cavanagh *(Ronald Sanderson)*, Barbara Leonard *(Celeste)*, Henry Kolker *(John Fair)*, Lois Wilson *(Marcia Peterson)*, Ivan Simpson *(Hodge)*, Helen Vinson *(Esther Parish)*, Hardie Albright *(Arthur)*, Edith Kingdom *(Landlady)*, Richard Tucker *(Frank Parrish)*, Virginia Hammond *(Nadine)*.

A boring film about a stupid woman, with Ruth Chatterton as the dolt of a female. The story has her, at the beginning of the film, a wife supported in luxury by her doting husband, Brent, who plays the market on tips she gets from her rich lover. She tires of the lover and makes up a false stock market tip, in which her husband invests heavily. The market crashes, Chatterton takes the remainder of her husband's money, and heads for Bermuda. There she meets a rich Australian who wants to marry her. Her husband in the meantime has made back most of his wealth by blackmailing Chatterton's rich ex-lover. She leaves the Australian, goes back to her husband, and tears up the blackmail check, for reasons that are vague. This film was made on the tail of Chatterton's divorce from one husband and her marriage to Brent.

d, William Dieterle; w, Earl Baldwin, Larry Barretto (based on the novel *Children of Pleasure* by Barretto); ph, Ernest Haller.

Drama **(PR:A MPAA:NR)**

CRASH* (1977) 78m Group I c

Jose Ferrer *(Mark)*, Sue Lyon *(Kim)*, John Ericson *(Greg)*, Leslie Parrish *(Kathy)*, John Carradine *(Dr. Edwards)*, Jerome Guardino *(Lt. Pegler)*.

Weird horror movie has Ferrer trying to kill wife Lyons by sending a satanically possessed antique car after her. She retaliates with a few bits of her own black magic. Steer clear.

p&d, Charles Band; w, Marc Marais; ph, (Panavision, DeLuxe Color); m, Andrew Belling.

Horror **(PR:C-O MPAA:PG)**

CRASH DIVE**** (1943) 105m FOX c

Tyrone Power *(Lt. Ward Stewart)*, Anne Baxter *(Jean Hewlett)*, Dana Andrews *(Lt. Cmdr. Dewey Connors)*, James Gleason *(McDonnell)*, Dame May Whitty *(Grandmother)*, Henry Morgan *(Brownie)*, Ben Carter *(Oliver Cromwell Jones)*, Charles Tannen *(Hammond)*, Frank Conroy *(Capt. Bryson)*, Florence Lake *(Doris)*, John Archer *(Curly)*, George Holmes *(Crew Member)*, Minor Watson *(Butler)*, Kathleen Howard *(Miss Bromley)*, David Bacon *(Lieutenant)*, Stanley Andrews *(Captain)*, Paul Burns *(Clerk)*, Gene Rizzi *(Sailor)*, Frank Dawson *(Henry the Butler)*, Edward McWade *(Crony)*, Thurston Hall *(Senator from Texas)*, Trudy Marshall *(Telephone Operator)*, Leila McIntyre *(Senator's Wife)*, Betty McKinney, Ruth Jordan, Sally Harper, Ruth Thomas, Sue Jolley *(Schoolgirls)*, Cecil Weston *(Woman)*, Lionel Royce *(German Q-Boat Commander)*, Hans Moebus *(German Officer)*, Chester Gan *(Lee Wong)*, Bruce Wong *(Waiter)*, David Bacon *(Lieutenant)*.

Fast-moving, slam-bang paean of praise to the United States submarine service starring Power in his swan song screen appearance before going into the Marines. Matter of fact, Fox proudly billed him as "Tyrone Power, U.S.M.C.," and if that wasn't enough to get you to support the film, consider the plot: Power is the commander of a PT boat with several successful missions on his record. He is summoned to the sub base at New London, Connecticut, and reassigned to a sub as exec officer by his uncle, admiral Minor Watson. Power will be serving under Andrews and any time you have two good-looking guys in a 1940s picture, the die is cast for some rivalry. The competition comes in the shapely form of Baxter, teacher in a local girls' school. Power meets her as he is on his way to Washington and she is taking some of her charges on a field trip to the Capitol. He puts a move on her and there's a bit of comedy aboard the sleeper train as well as some humor at the hotel where they both check in. Power hounds Baxter until she agrees to have dinner with him. Understandably enthralled by Power (he was handsome and Jo Swerling wrote him some charming dialog), she becomes frightened by the attraction and rushes back to New London to ask her fianc e, Andrews, to speed up their wedding plans; the girl obviously does not want to be tempted. The sub leaves and Power and Andrews work closely with each other and have a great deal of mutual respect, but with all their rapping about various things, they conveniently do not speak of the girl they've left behind. The Nazis are laying mines in the North Atlantic and the sub's job is to seek and destroy the U-Boat responsible. There's a joust between the two and the submarine eventually sinks the enemy ship. (Director Mayo does a splendid job in finely detailing much of the technical aspects of running a sub without letting the hardware overtake the people). At New London, Power returns to his assault on Baxter while Andrews is off (again conveniently) in Washington, making his official statements to the Navy about their just-concluded mission. Power convinces Baxter that she is the one woman in his life and that she is just as smitten by him. This agreed to, Power takes Baxter to meet his imperious grandmother, Whitty, who turns in a splendid job as the persnickety matriarch. Andrews returns and gets their next orders; they are to find a secret Nazi base. Upon their return, Andrews is planning to marry Baxter. Power hears this and turns pale; he had no idea that Baxter and Andrews were affianced. He takes Baxter to the officer's club for cocktails and asks for the truth. After some serious soul-searching, Baxter admits what has happened and says that she will break off the engagement with Andrews who is, again conveniently, near enough to hear the conversation. On the sub the next day, Andrews becomes Captains Ahab/Queeg/Bligh. Gone is the sweet demeanor and, in its place, is the hard-bitten, all-business sub commander. Power attempts to explain the situation but Andrews is hurt and refuses to listen. They spot a tanker with odd markings and trail it surreptitiously through a heavily mined area to eventually discover their goal: the secret base. Power leads a group of men onto the island where they detonate the Nazis and their supplies. Gleason, who was fifty-seven at the time, is the only casualty as he keeps the Germans at bay while Power organizes the troops and arranges their escape. Andrews is wounded when the sub twists through the dangerous waters, forcing Power to take command. Naturally, they return safely and Andrews gallantly gives up any claim on Baxter as she waits for them on the dock. The love story seemed tacked on to this very exciting action piece. It was trite stuff, having been done as far back as the Greeks and more recently by Edmond Rostand in CYRANO. That aside, the action sequences were as rousing as anything ever done and this was a prime example of an early Technicolor flag-waver and a modern-day swashbuckler. Fred Sersen and Roger Heman received Oscar nominations for special effects and sound and more might have been awarded, but this was the year of CASABLANCA, WATCH ON THE RHINE, and SONG OF BERNADETTE, and there was barely any room for anything else in such stellar company. Screenwriter Jo Swerling was to later achieve fame on the Broadway stage by co-authoring the book for "Guys And Dolls." His son, Joe Swerling, Jr., is one of television's busiest producers.

p, Milton Sperling; d, Archie Mayo; w, Jo Swerling (based on a story by W.R. Burnett); ph, Leon Shamroy (Technicolor); m, David Buttolph; ed, Walter Thompson, Ray Curtiss; md, Emil Newman; art d, Richard Day, Wiard Ihnen; set d, Thomas Little, Paul Fox; cos, Earl Luick; spec eff, Fred Sersen.

War Adventure **(PR:A MPAA:NR)**

CRASH DONOVAN** (1936) 55m UNIV bw

Jack Holt *("Crash" Donovan)*, John King *(Johnny Allen)*, Nan Gray *(Doris Tennyson)*, Eddie Acuff *(Alabam)*, Hugh Buckler *(Capt. Tennyson)*, Ward Bond *(The Drill Master)*, James Donlan *(Smokey)*, Douglas Fowley *(Harris)*, William Tannen *(Tony)*, Huey White *(Fizz)*, Al Hill *(Mike)*, Gardner James *(Pete)*, Paul Porcasi *(Cafe Owner)*, George Stinson *(The Singing Cop)*.

Jack Holt plays the title role, an ex-carnival stunt rider turned California motorcycle highway patrolman. The film shows the life and lifestyle of motorcycle cops, how they are trained and what is expected of them. Holt is followed as he has run-ins with reckless drivers, a road house cabaret gang, and a gang of smugglers. There is the usual assortment of daring motorcycle stunts.

p, Julian Bernheim; d, William Nigh; w, Eugene Solow, Charles Grayson, Karl Detzer (based on the story by Harold Shumate); ph, Milton R. Krasner.

Crime/Adventure **(PR:A MPAA:NR)**

CRASH DRIVE* (1959, Brit.) 65m Danziger/UA bw

Dermot Walsh *(Paul Dixon)*, Wendy Williams *(Ann Dixon)*, Ian Fleming *(Dr. Marshall)*, Anton Rodgers *(Tomson)*, Grace Arnois *(Mrs. Dixon)*, Ann Sears *(Nurse Phillips)*, George Roderick *(Manotti)*, Rolf Harris *(Bart)*, Geoffrey Hibbert *(Henry)*.

Walsh is a race-car driver wallowing in self-pity after he is paralyzed in a crash. Wife Williams returns to him in the wake of the accident and cures him of his depression. Mostly boring, but it offers another glimpse of versatile author-actor Fleming before he soared to fame as creator of James Bond.

p, Edward J. & Harry Lee Danziger; d, Max Varnel; w, Brian Clemens, Eldon Howard; ph, Jimmy Wilson.

Drama **(PR:A-C MPAA:NR)**

CRASH LANDING* (1958) 76m Clover/COL bw

Gary Merrill *(Steve Williams)*, Nancy Davis *(Helen Williams)*, Irene Hervey *(Bernice Willouby)*, Roger Smith *(John Smithback)*, Bek Nelson *(Nancy Arthur)*, Jewell Lain *(Ann Thatcher)*, Sheridan Comerate *(Howard Whitney)*, Richard Keith *(Arthur White)*, Celia Lovsky *(Mrs. Ortega)*, Lewis Martin *(Maurice Stanley)*, Hal Torey *(Calvin Havelick)*, John McNamara *(Phil Burton)*, Dayle Rodney *(Adele Burton)*, Rodolfo Hoyos *(Carlos Ortego)*, Kim Charney *(Barrie Williams)*, Robin Warga *(Teddy Burton)*, Robert Whiteside *(Red)*, Ronald Green *(Mel)*, Richard Newton *(Jed Sutton)*.

This grandfather to the AIRPORT pictures stars the future Nancy Reagan—Davis, as the wife of the pilot whose plane is doomed. Story concerns the passengers of the plane, and the changes they go through when they discover the plane is going to crash in the Atlantic. As in the AIRPORT films, the passengers are made up of a random assortment of people; a retired businessman, a pretty school teacher, a rugged self-made business tycoon and his drunken associate, an elderly Portuguese grandmother on her first flight, priests, chorus girls, and many more. None die, however, as the plane ditches near a U.S. destroyer. The cliches in this film are uproarious, probably making this the First Lady's funniest film.

p, Sam Katzman; d, Fred F. Sears; w, Fred Freiberger; ph, Benjamin H. Kline; m, Mischa Bakaleinikoff; ed, Jerome Thomas.

Disaster **(PR:A MPAA:NR)**

CRASH OF SILENCE**½   (1952, Brit.) 92m EAL/GFD bw (GB: MANDY)
Phyllis Calvert (*Christine*), Jack Hawkins (*Searle*), Terence Morgan (*Harry*), Godfrey
Tearle (*Mr. Garland*), Mandy Miller (*Mandy*), Marjorie Fielding (*Mrs. Garland*), Nancy
Price (*Jane Ellis*), Edward Chapman (*Ackland*), Patricia Plunkett (*Mrs. Crocker*),
Eleanor Summerfield (*Lily Tabor*), Colin Gordon (*Woolard, Jr.*), W.E. Holloway
(*Woolard, Sr.*), Dorothy Alison (*Miss Stockton*), Julian Aymes (*Jimmy Tabor*), Gabrielle
Brune (*Secretary*), John Cazabon (*Davey*), Gwen Bacon (*Mrs. Paul*), Phyllis Morris
(*Miss Tucker*), Gabrielle Blunt (*Miss Larner*), Jane Asher (*Nina*).

A touching mix of documentary and narrative, about a child, Miller, born deaf and
dumb, and the trials she must go through in trying to adapt to life in an unsympathetic
world. Miller's realistic portrayal is marred by the performance on the part of the
adults.

p, Michael Balcon; d, Alexander Mackendrick; w, Nigel Balchin, Jack Whittingham
(based on the novel *The Day Is Ours* by Hilda Lewis); ph, Douglas Slocombe; m,
William Alwyn; ed, Seth Holt.

Drama   (PR:A   MPAA:NR)

CRASHIN' THRU DANGER*   (1938) 61m Excelsior bw
Ray Walker (*Torchy*), Sally Blane (*Ann*), Guinn Williams (*Slim*), James Bush (*Eddie*),
Guy Usher (*Superintendent*), Robert Homans (*Pop*), Syd Saylor (*Tom*), Dick Curtis
(*Foreman*), Margaret O'Connell (*The Nurse*), Alexander Schoenberg (*Dr. Michaels*).

Story about three telephone linemen who adopt their dead supervisor's daughter as a
housekeeper, and then, one by one, try to win her affections. Two of the linemen are
taken out of action by those things linemen fear most—fire, flood, and storms—and
the hero wins the girl without stepping on toes.

p, Sig Neufeld, Leslie Simmonds; d, Sam Newfield; w, Norman Houston.

Drama   (PR:A   MPAA:NR)

CRASHING BROADWAY*   (1933) 55m MON bw
Rex Bell, Doris Hill, Harry Bowen, George Hayes, Charles King, Louis Sargent,
G. D. Wood, Ann Howard, Blackie Whiteford, Perry Murdock, Henry Rocquemore,
Max Asher, Allan Lee, George Morell, Archie Ricks, Tex Palmer.

Modern-day oater has cowboy Bell hitting Gotham with trail songs and charming Hill
in a weak cowboy-makes-the-big-time script.

p, Paul Malvern; d, John P. McCarthy; w, Wellyn Totman.

Western   Cas.   (PR:A   MPAA:NR)

CRASHING HOLLYWOOD**½   (1937) 60m RKO bw
Lee Tracy (*Michael*), Joan Woodbury (*Barbara*), Paul Guilfoyle (*Horman*), Lee Patrick
(*Goldie*), Richard Lane (*Wells*), Bradley Page (*Darey-Hawk*), Tom Kennedy (*Al*),
George Irving (*Peyton*), Frank M. Thomas (*Decker*), Jack Carson (*Dickson*), Alec
Craig (*Receptionist*), James Conlin (*Crisby*).

A good little comedy that satirizes the movie studio system of the 1930s. Lee Tracy is a
screenwriter who collaborates with an ex-convict on a screenplay. The ex-con writes
about a bank robbery he took part in, and was framed for. The film comes out and gives
the police new leads on the ex-con's partners who were never convicted. The gangsters
come to Hollywood to prevent the writing of other exposes, and run amok in a film
studio. CRASHING HOLLYWOOD is a remake of a 1923 film called LIGHTS OUT,
which was also the name of the original play. There is a double irony in this film; one of
the extras in a crowd scene, Harry "Big Harry" Greenberg, a former member of the
Bugsy Siegel-Meyer Lansky mob in New York, was spotted by Abe "Kid Twist" Reles, a
top killer for Murder Inc when Reles was watching the film in a Brooklyn theater.
Greenberg had deserted the mob and disappeared; he was being sought by his former
gangster pals who thought he might turn informer. Reles reported seeing Greenberg in
CRASHING HOLLYWOOD and in this way Greenberg was later located and
murdered by Siegel and others, bringing to a violent end Big Harry's brief hour before
the cameras.

p, Cliff Reid; d, Lew Landers; w, Paul Yawitz, Gladys Atwater (based on the play "Lights
Out" by Paul Dickey and Mann Page); ph, Nicholas Musuraca, Frank Redman; ed,
Harry Marker; spec eff, Vernon L. Walker.

Comedy/Crime   (PR:A   MPAA:NR)

CRASHING LAS VEGAS*½   (1956) 62m AA bw
Leo Gorcey (*Terrence Aloysius "Slip" Mahoney*), Huntz Hall (*Horace Debussy "Sach"
Jones*), David Condon (*Chuck*), Jimmy Murphy (*Myron*), Mary Castle (*Carol LaRue*),
Nicky Blair (*Sam*), Mort Mills (*Oggy*), Don Haggerty (*Tony Murlock*), Doris Kemper
(*Mrs. Kelly*), Jack Rice (*Wiley*), Bob Hopkins ("*Live Like A King*" Host), John Bleifer
(*Joe Crumb*), Emil Sitka (*Man in Seat 87*), Dick Foote (*1st Policeman*), Don Marlowe
(*2nd Policeman*), Jack Grinnage (*Bellboy*), Terry Frost (*Police Sergeant*), Minerva
Urecal (*Woman*), Frank Scannell (*Croupier*), Joey Ray (*Floor Manager*), Jack Chefe
(*Waiter*), Frank Hagney (*Guard*), Speer Martin (*Elevator Operator*), Jimmy Brandt
(*Usher*), Cosmo Sardo (*Waiter*), Alfred Tonkel.

After an electrical shock, Hall discovers that he can predict numbers. He goes on a TV
game show and wins a trip to Las Vegas. When he starts winning big at roulette,
gangsters take interest and after convincing Hall that he
has killed a man, blackmail him into turning over all his winnings. The rest of the boys,
of course, come to the rescue. The boys make their forty-first appearance since their
debut as "The Dead End Kids" in DEAD END, and they are definitely showing their
ages. When CRASHING LAS VEGAS was released, Hall was 36 years old Gorcey 38.
In addition, Gorcey had started drinking heavily after the death of his father in a car
crash, and is visibly drunk in a number of scenes in this film. It was to be his last
"Bowery Boys" film, though the series would limp along for seven more films over the
next two years, when it would finally die a long-overdue death.

p, Ben Schwalb; d, Jean Yarbrough; w, Jack Townley; ph, Harry Neumann; ed, George

White; md, Marlin Skiles; art d, David Milton; set d, Joseph Kish; cos, Bert Henrikson;
spec eff, Ray Mercer.

Comedy   (PR:A   MPAA:NR)

CRASHING THRU*   (1939) Am 61m MON bw
James Newill (*Sgt. Renfrew*), Warren Hull (*Corn Kelly*), Jean Carmen (*Ann*), Milburn
Stone (*Herrington*), Walter Byron (*McClusky*), Stanley Blystone (*LaMonte*), Robert
Frazer (*Dr. Smith*), Joseph Girard (*Captain*), David O'Brien (*Fred*), Earl Douglas
(*Slant Eyes*), Ted Adams (*Eskimo Pete*), Roy Barcroft (*Green*), Iron Eyes Cody (*Indian
Joe*).

Last of the "Renfrew of the Mounties" series (due to the fact that Grand National
Studios went bankrupt) has the singing Mountie stopping crime in the north woods.
Renfrew, played by Newill, is trying to stop an American gangster and his sister from
hijacking a shipment of gold going to a mining company, which had already had it
stolen once. Lots of action with fistfigths and gun play, and Newill sings two songs,
"You're Easy On the Eyes," "Crimson Sunset" (Jack Brooks, Jules Loman).

p, Philip N. Krasna; d, Elmer Clifton; w, Sherman Lowe (based on the novel *Renfrew
Rides the Range* by Laurie York Erskine); ph, Edward Linden; ed, Roy Luby; m/l, Jack
Brooks, Jules Loman.

Crime   (PR:A   MPAA:NR)

CRASHING THRU*   (1949) 58m MON bw
Whip Wilson, Andy Clyde, Christine Larson, Kenne Duncan, Tristam Coffin, Steve
Darrell, George Lewis, Jan Bryant, Virginia Carroll, Boyd Stockman, Dee Cooper,
Jack Richardson, Tom Quinn, Bob Woodward.

Routine oater has the whip-cracking Wilson and his wise-cracking sidekick Clyde
coming to Larson's rescue and rout the bad guys rustling her cattle. Only a mediocre
outing for old Whip.

p, Barney Sarecky; d, Ray Taylor; w, Adele Buffington.

Western   (PR:A   MPAA:NR)

CRASHOUT**   (1955) 88m Filmakers bw
William Bendix (*Van Duff*), Arthur Kennedy (*Joe Quinn*), Luther Adler (*Pete
Mendoza*), William Talman (*Swanee Remsen*), Gene Evans (*Monk Collins*), Marshall
Thompson (*Billy Lang*), Beverly Michaels (*Alice Mosher*), Gloria Talbot (*Girl on
Train*), Adam Williams (*Fred*), Percy Helton (*Dr. Barnes*), Melinda Markey (*Girl in Bar*),
Chris Olsen (*Timmy*), Adele St. Maur (*Mrs. Mosher*), Edward Clark (*Conductor*), Tom
Dugan (*Bartender*), Morris Ankrum (*Head Guard*).

The story of six convicts who break out of prison to get to a fortune in gold coins,
stashed away by their leader. Bendix, the leader, promises to cut the other cons in on
the loot he has hidden in the mountains if they get him to a doctor to treat a wound
suffered during the break. They get him to a doctor and then help him to the cache.
One by one the six become fewer until only Bendix and Kennedy are left to uncover the
coins. Bendix attempts to kill his partner, but ends falling off the mountain himself. A
good cast keeps the story believable and moving along.

p, Hal E. Chester; d, Lewis R. Foster; w, Chester, Foster; ph, Russell Metty; m, Leith
Stevens; ed, Robert Swink; art d, Wiard Ihnen.

Crime   (PR:C   MPAA:NR)

CRATER LAKE MONSTER, THE*   (1977) 85m Crown International c
Richard Cardella, Glenn Roberts, Mark Siegel, Kacey Cobb, Richard Garrison,
Michael Hoover, Bob Hyman, Suzanne Lewis.

An animated dinosaur is shaken back to life after a crashing meteor awakens him. The
animation is done by David Allen who also gave life to Mrs. Butterworth, as well as
animating EQUINOX and FLASH GORDON.

p&d, William R. Stromberg; w, Stromberg, Richard Cardella; ph, Paul Gentry; animation, David Allen (in "Fantamation").

Fantasy   Cas.   (PR:A   MPAA:PG)

CRAWLING EYE, THE*   (1958, Brit.) 84m Tempean/Eros bw
(GB: THE TROLLENBERG TERROR)
Forrest Tucker (*Alan Brooks*), Laurence Payne (*Philip Truscott*), Janet Munro (*Anne
Pilgrim*), Jennifer Jayne (*Sarah Pilgrim*), Warren Mitchell (*Prof. Crevett*), Andrew
Fauls (*Brett*), Stuart Sanders (*Dewhurst*), Frederick Schiller (*Klein*), Colin Douglas,
Derek Sydney, Richard Golding, George Herbert, Anne Sharp, Caroline Glazer,
Garard Green, Jeremy Longhurst, Anthony Parker, Leslie Heritage, Theodore
Wilhelm.

Headless Swiss mountaineers are being found scattered around the Alps, and extrater-
restrial eyes with deadly tentacles are blamed. ESP gal Munro, with Tucker's aid,
contacts the retinal terrors in a cloud hanging overhead and they join to save humanity
from the alien invasion. A near-sighted mess.

p, Robert Baker, Monty Berman; d, Quentin Lawrence; w, Jimmy Sangster (from a TV
series by Peter Key).

Horror   Cas.   (PR:C   MPAA:NR)

CRAWLING HAND, THE*   (1963) 64m AIP bw
Peter Breck (*Steve Curan*), Kent Taylor (*Doc Weitzberg*), Rod Lauren (*Paul Lawrence*),
Sirry Steffen (*Marta Farnstrom*), Arline Judge (*Mrs. Hotchkiss*), Alan Hale (*Sheriff*),
Richard Arlen, Ross Elliott, Allison Hayes, Ed Wermer, Tris Coffin, Syd Saylor, G.
Stanley Jones, Ashley Cowan, Jock Putnam, Beverly Lunsford, Andy Andrews.

A mediocre take-off on THE BEAST WITH FIVE FINGERS, this has a spacecraft
exploding while returning to Earth's atmosphere. Breck and Taylor play scientist trying
to track down the spacecraft. The astronaut is blown to pieces in the crash but his hand

survives. Lauren, a young medical student,picks up the hand and takes it home, not realizing that it is infected with an alien force. The hand kills his landlady, and then starts to exert influence over Lauren himself. It makes him want to kill (and the makeup darkens under his eyes). In the end, a cat eats the hand and Lauren becomes himself again.

p, Joseph F. Robertson; d, Herbert L. Strock; w, Strock, William Edelson (based on a story by Robert Young, Joseph Granston); ph, William Van Der Leer; ed, Strock; m/l, "Papa Oom Mow Mow" (The Rivingtons).

Horror   **Cas.**   **(PR:A   MPAA:NR)**

CRAWLING MONSTER, THE   (SEE: CREEPING TERROR, THE, 1964)

CRAZE zero   (1974, Brit.) 96m WB c (AKA: THE INFERNAL IDOL)
Jack Palance (*Neal Mottram*), Diana Dors (*Dolly Newman*), Julie Ege (*Helena*), Edith Evans (*Aunt Louise*), Hugh Griffith (*Solicitor*), Trevor Howard (*Supt. Bellamy*), Michael Jayston (*Detective Sgt. Wall*), Suzy Kendall (*Sally*), Martin Potter (*Ronnie*), Percy Herbert (*Detective Russet*), David Warbeck (*Detective Wilson*), Kathleen Byron (*Muriel*), Venecia Day (*Dancer*), Marianne Stone (*Barmaid*), Dean Harris (*Ronnie's Friend*).

Poor excuse for a horror film has a fine cast placed in the worst roles. Palance plays an antique shop owner who prays to the African idol of Chuku, which he keeps in his basement. He believes the god will reward him with riches if he makes live sacrifices. Palance begins luring prostitutes to his shop and sacrificing them in his basement. Palance's assistant knows what he is doing, but is too scared to do anything about it, even when the police get suspicious.

p, Herman Cohen; d, Freddie Francis: w, Aben Kandel, Herman Cohen (based on the novel *Infernal Idol* by Henry Seymour); ph, John Wilcox (Technicolor); m, John Scott; ed, Henry Richardson; art d, George Provis.

Horror   **Cas.**   **(PR:C   MPAA:R)**

THE CRAZIES★★★   (1973) 103m Cambist c (AKA: CODE NAME: TRIXIE)
Lane Carroll (*Judy*), W.G. McMillan (*David*), Harold Wayne Jones (*Clank*), Lloyd Hollar (*Col. Pockem*), Richard Liberty (*Artie*), Lynn Lowry (*Kathie*), Richard France (*Dr. Watts*), Edith Bell (*Woman Lab Technician*), Harry Spillman (*Maj. Ryder*), Will Disney (*Dr. Brookmyre*), W.L. Thunhurst, Jr. (*Brubaker*), Leland Starnes (*Shelby*), A.C. MacDonald (*Gen. Bowden*), Robert J. McCully (*Hawks*), Robert Karlowsky (*Sheriff*).

This is one of George Romero's lesser-known films, but a classic in the horror, sci-fi genre. The story centers around an Army cargo plane that crashes near the small town of Evans City, Pennsylvania, where the film was made. The plane is carrying a strain of bacteria for which there is no cure. The population of Evans City is infected, and the Army moves in to quarantine it. The soldiers are dressed in white bacteria-proof suits, scaring the inhabitants, who they are trying to herd into the local high school. The effects of the bacteria either causes death or transforms the person into a lunatic killer, hence the title. A group of people not yet affected are trying to escape from the military and get out of town, while scientists work around the clock to find a cure. The military who hunt down the group are shown to be as crazy as the CRAZIES. The film comes to an end as the soldiers botch the whole thing. They accidentally kill the scientist who discovers the cure before he can tell anyone about it, ignore the man from the group who has the antibodies in his blood, and let the epidemic spread throughout the U.S. The film's jumbled feel and confused approach give it a true feeling of the craziness occurring on the screen.

p, Alvin C. Croft; d,w,ed, George A. Romero (based on original script by Paul McCollough); ph, S. William Hinzman; m, Bruce Roberts; ed, Romero; song, "Heaven Help Us."

Horror/Science Fiction   **(PR:O   MPAA:NR)**

CRAZY DESIRE★★½   (1964, Ital.) 108m DD/EM bw
                    (LA VOGLIA MATTA)
Ugo Tognazzi (*Antonio Berlinghieri*), Catherine Spaak (*Francesca*), Gianni Garko (*Piero*), Beatrice Altariba (*Silvana*), Jimmy Fontana (*Boy Friend*), Franco Giacobini (*Alberghetti*), Fabrizio Capucci, Margherita Girelli, Oliviero Prunas, Diletta D'Andrea, Stelvio Rosi, Lylia Neyung (*Francesca's Friends*), Luciano Salce.

Lightweight Italian comedy has respectable electrical engineer Tognazzi becoming infatuated with young Spaak, who travels with her friends to the beach with Tognazzi in tow to pick up the tab. She taunts him as he tries to prove himself the equal to the young men. Finally, he fights with Spaak's boy friend and takes a beating. He triumphs, however, with a lucky swing. and is hailed as the new leader of the group. He falls asleep in Spaak' s arms and awakens to find himself alone on the beach, the others gone. Entertaining without the ponderousness this sort of film generally exhibits.

p, Isidoro Broggi, Renato Libassi; d, Luciano Salce; w, Salce, Franco Castellano, Pipolo [Guiseppe Moccia] (based on the short story "A Girl Named Francesca" by Enrico Stella); ph, Erico Menczer; (Totalscope); m, Ennio Morricone; ed, Roberto Cinquini; art d, Nedo Azzini.

Comedy/Drama   **(PR:C   MPAA:NR)**

CRAZY FOR LOVE★   (1960, Fr.) 80m Cite-Films bw
Brigitte Bardot (*Javotte Lemoine*), Bourvil (*Hippolyte*), Jane Marken (*Augustine Lemoine*), Jeanne Fusier Gir (*Maria*), Georges Baconnet (*Pichet*), Nadine Basile (*Madelene*), Noel Roquevert (*Mayor*).

In the wake of the sensation caused by Brigitte Bardot in AND GOD CREATED WOMAN, a number of her earlier films found their way to our shores. This is certainly one of the lesser films of that group. A feeble plot has village idiot Bourvil inheriting an inn on the condition that he get his grammar school diploma. It's a chance for him to

do a number of slapstick scenes while foiling greedy cousin Bardot and winning Marken.

p, Walter Rupp; d, Jean Boyer; w, D'Arlette De Pitray; m, Paul Misraki.
Comedy   **(PR:C-O   MPAA:NR)**

CRAZY HOUSE★★   (1943) 78m UNIV bw
Ole Olsen and Chic Johnson (*Themselves*), Cass Daley (*Sadie*), Patric Knowles (*Mac*), Martha O'Driscoll (*Margie*), Leighton Noble (*Johnny*), Thomas Gomez (*Wagstaff*), Percy Kilbride (*Col. Merriweather*), Hans Conried (*Roco*), Richard Lane (*Hanley*), Andrew Tombes (*Gregory*), Billy Gilbert (*Stone*), Chester Clute (*Fud*), Edgar Kennedy (*Judge*), Franklin Pangborn (*Hotel Clerk*), Shemp Howard (*Mumbo*), Fred Sanborn (*Jumbo*), Tony and Sally DeMarco, Count Basie Orchestra, Marion Hutton, Glenn Miller Singers, Chandra Kaly Dancers, Delta Rhythm Boys, Leighton Noble Orchestra, Allan Jones, Leo Carrillo, Andy Devine, Robert Paige, Alan Curtis, Lon Chaney, Jr., Basil Rathbone, Nigel Bruce, Fiorello La Guardia, The Five Hertzogs.

Fast-paced musical comedy has the team of Olsen and Johnson on the loose in Hollywood. They're a couple of filmmakers none of the studios want to see. When they can't get backing for a film from Universal, they rent a movie lot and do it on their own. The film has a loose plot which is an excuse for Olsen and Johnson's wackiness, and to showcase quite a few musical numbers and specialty acts. Cameos are made by the dozens, and it is like a who's who of the people under contract to Universal in 1943. Songs: "Pocketful of Pennies," (Eddie Cherkose, Franz Steininger), "Tropicana," "Get on Board, Little Children" (Don Raye, Gene DePaul); "Crazy House" (Cherkose, Milton Rosen), "Lament of a Laundry Girl" (Gerry Seelen, Lester Lee, Ted Shapiro), "Donkey Serenade" (Rudolf Friml, Bob Wright, Chet Forrest), "I Ought To Dance" (Sammy Cahn, Saul Chaplin), "My Rainbow Song" (Mitchell Parish, Matt Malneck, Frank Signorelli), "My Song Without Words" (John Latouche, Vernon Duke).

p, Eric C. Kenton; d, Edward F. Kline; w, Robert Lees, Frederic L. Rinaldo; ph, Charles Van Enger; ed, Arthur Hilton; md, Charles Previn; spec eff, John P. Fulton; ch, George Hale.

Musical/Comedy   **(PR:A   MPAA:NR)**

CRAZY HOUSE, 1975 (SEE: NIGHT OF THE LAUGHING DEAD, 1975, Brit.)

CRAZY KNIGHTS★   (1944) 73m MON bw (AKA: GHOST CRAZY)
Shemp Howard, Billy Gilbert, "Slapsie" Maxie Rosenbloom, Minerva Urecal, Tim Ryan, Jayne Hazard, Bernie Sell, Tay Dunn, Buster Brodie, Art Miles, Dan White, John Hamilton, Betty Sinclair.

Dumb slapstick comedy with second-string stooges Howard, Gilbert, and Rosenbloom in a haunted house facing fake ghosts and a giant gorilla. Prolific director Beaudine made no less than eleven films in 1944, well-deserving his nickname "One-Shot." Viewers will swear they've seen this one before.

p, Sam Katzman; d, William Beaudine; w, Tim Ryan; ph, Marcel LePicard; ed, Dick Durrier.

Comedy   **(PR:A   MPAA:NR)**

CRAZY JACK AND THE BOY   (SEE: SILENCE, 1974)

CRAZY JOE★★   (1974) 100m COL c
Peter Boyle (*Crazy Joey*), Paula Prentiss (*Anne*), Fred Williamson (*Willy*), Charles Cioffi (*Coletti*), Rip Torn (*Richie*), Luther Adler (*Falco*), Fausto Tozzi (*Frank*), Franco Lantieri (*Nunzio*), Eli Wallach (*Don Vittorio*), Louis Guss (*Magliocco*), Carmine Caridi (*Jelly*), Henry Winkler (*Mannie*), Gabrielle Torrei (*Cheech*), Guido Leontini (*Angelo*), Sam Coppola (*Chick*), Mario Erpichini (*Danny*), Adam Wade (*J.D.*), Timothy Holley (*Lou*), Ralph Wilcox (*Sam*), Peter Savage (*DeMarco*), Herve Villechaize (*Samson*), Robert Riesel, Dan Resin, (*FBI Agents*), Nella Dina (*Mrs. Falco*).

Another GODFATHER inspired film lavishes violence on the screen and the berserk ambitions of one of Brooklyn's toughest hoodlums, Joey Gallo, a Sartre-reading thug who strutted "class" and brass. Boyle and his brother Torn pull off a routine caper and Boyle is sent to Attica where he forms alliances with NYC black gangs which he later uses to buck the Manhattan Mafia when released from prison. At first Adler, the shifty Mafia don, tells Boyle "take all you can hold," believing the young Turk doesn't have the "soldiers" to launch a full-scale war. When he realizes that black criminals in great numbers are in league with Boyle he panics and orders Boyle killed. Just as he is about to take control of the Mafia organization, Boyle is gunned down in a restaurant (designed identically to Umberto's Clam House in Little Italy where the real Crazy Joe was shot to death in 1972). Boyle gives a fascinating performance but the excessive violence is jarring, even disturbing to adults. This is not one for the children. Torn renders a solid performance as Boyle's brother who commits suicide when he realizes that he and his brother are doomed in a bloody crusade to dominate a system that will eventually gobble them up. To avoid problems with the Gallo family, Boyle is never referred to by his last name which is only suggested when the camera lingers on a case of Gallo Wine in a scene showing a liquor store robbery. The story is based upon a poor profile done by Gage which offers little or no background information on Gallo other than to stereotype him as a trigger-happy lout with intellectual pretensions. Distracting is the ill-fitting rug adorning Boyle's famous bald pate. Tonti's camera is swift and sharp but the story lags in spots where an absence of plot is taken up with bursts of explosive anger on Boyle's part. This is shown early so viewers know what to expect. He is hailed by street children as a hero, buying them gum out of a gumball machine which moments later he smashes to pieces when the sweetshop owner refuses to pay weekly extortion money.

p, Nino E. Krisman (for Dina De Laurentiis); d, Carlo Lizzani; w, Lewis John Carlino (based on the book by Nicholas Gage); ph, Aldo Tonti; m, Gian Carlo Caramello; ed, Peter Zinner; art d, Robert Gundlach.

Crime Drama   **(PR:O   MPAA:R)**

CRAZY MAMA zero
(1975) 82m New World c

Cloris Leachman (*Melba*), Stuart Whitman (*Jim Bob*), Ann Sothern (*Sheba*), Jim Backus (*Albertson*), Donny Most (*Shawn*), Linda Purl (*Cheryl*), Bryan Englund (*Snake*), Merle Earle (*Bertha*), Sally Kirkland (*Ella Mae*), Clinet Kimbrough (*Daniel*), Dick Miller (*Wilbur Janeway*), Carmen Argenziano (*Supermarket Manager*), Harry Northup (*FBI Man*), Ralph James (*Sheriff-1932*), Dinah Englund (*Melba-1932*), Robert Reece (*Mover*), Mickey Fox (*Mrs. Morgan*), John Aprea (*Marvin*), Cynthia Songey (*Lucinda*), Hal Marshall (*Bartender*), Beach Dickerson (*Desk Clerk*), Barbara Ann Walters (*Lady Teller*), Bill McLean (*Bank Manager*), William Luckey (*Newsman*), Warren Miller (*Justice of the Peace*), Saul Krugman (*Col. Snodgrass*), Vince Barnett (*Homer*), Trish Sterling (*Sheba-1932*).

This mindless, thoroughly tasteless violence film begins in 1932 when police shoot Leachman's criminal father to death and drive her and her mother off their sharecropping farm in Jerusalem, Arkansas. A flash forward finds the two females being kicked out of their sleazy beauty parlor in Long Beach, California for failing to pay rent. Leachman collects mother Sothern and daughter Purl and they embark on a nation-wide crime spree, shooting and looting at will, picking up Whitman, a bigamist sheriff who aids them in their crimes and later sets up a phony kidnapping that goes awry. Lawmen shoot Whitman, and Earle, an 82-year-old woman who has been cleaned out by Las Vegas slot machines and joins up with the weird lot. There is not one scene worth viewing in this odious garbage bag. The dialog is written for cretins and it seeps foul language with every other word. The characters to the last, including Sterling, Leachman's real life daughter who plays her mother as a girl, act like a pack of savages, practicing sadism and loveless sex at every opportunity. Leachman, Sothern and Whitman should have changed their names for this monstrosity which will not fail to offend anyone human. It's amazing that director Demme could turn out this misshappen abortion and later helm such an affecting film as MELVIN AND HOWARD.

p, Julie Corman; d, Jonathan Demme; w, Robert Thom (based on a story by Francis Doel); ph, Bruce Logan (Metrocolor); ed, Allan Holzman, Lewis Teague; art d, Peter Jamison; set d, Linda Spheeris; cos, Jac McAnelly; stunts, Alan Gibbs.

Crime   Cas.   **(PR:O MPAA:PG)**

CRAZY OVER HORSES**
(1951) 65m MON bw
(GB: WIN, PLACE AND SHOW)

Leo Gorcey (*Slip*), Huntz Hall (*Sach*), William Benedict (*Whitey*), Bernard Gorcey (*Louie*), David Gorcey (*Chuck*), Bennie Bartlett (*Butch*), Ted de Corsia (*Duke*), Allen Jenkins (*Weepin' Willie*), Mike Ross (*Swifty*), Tim Ryan (*Flynn*), Gloria Saunders (*Terry*), Peggy Wynne (*Mazie*), Bob Peoples (*Uniformed Guard*), Pere Launders (*Charlie*), Leo "Ukie" Sherin (*Groom*), Robert Whitfield (*Crap-shooting Stable Attendant*), Sam Balter (*Announcer*), Ray Page (*Evans*), Darr Smith (*Pinkerton Man*), Wilbur Mack (*Elderly Man*), Gertrude Astor (*Elderly Woman*), Bill Cartledge, Whitey Hughes, Delmar Thomas, Bernard Pludow (*Jockeys*), Ben Frommer (*Silent Man*).

This film has Gorcey and some other former "Dead End Kids," now called the "Bowery Boys," given a race horse in payment of a food bill. The gang members think they can make money off the horse, and comedy occurs as they try to take care of the animal. Trouble crops up when racketeers try to steal the mount, but the gang keeps the horse in the race. Hall ends up riding it in the big race, and wins despite himself, and the gang catches the crooks to boot.

p, Jan Grippo; d, William Beaudine; w, Tim Ryan, Max Adams; ph, Marcel LePicard; ed, William Austin; md, Edward Kay; art d, David Milton; set d, Robert Priestley; cos, Sidney Mintz.

Comedy   **(PR:A MPAA:NR)**

CRAZY PARADISE*
(1965, Den.) 95m Palladium/Sherpix c
(DET TOSSEDE PARADIS)

Dirch Passer (*Angelus Goat*), Hans W. Petersen (*Thor Goat*), Ove Sprogøe (*Simon*), Ghita Nørby (*Edith Paste*), Paul Hagen (*Vicar Paul Paste*), Bodil Steen (*Foreign Minister Bertha Virginius*), Karl Stegger (*Per Mortensen*), Lone Hertz (*Greta*), Lily Broberg (*Anne*), Judy Gringer (*Ursula*), Kjeld Petersen (*Ove Bierman, Reporter*), Kai Holm (*Prime Minister*), Jørgen Ryg (*Von Adel, His Secretary*), Axel Strøbye (*Hjalmar, The Blacksmith*), Gunnar Lemvigh (*Trommesen*), Poul Muller (*Thomas Asmussen, Editor*), Valsø Holm (*Janus*), Keld Markuslund (*Casper Cash, Grocer*), Arthur Jensen (*Tripledick*), Hugo Herrestrup (*Frederik*), Gunnar Strømvad (*Laurids*), Helge Scheuer (*Jens*), Lotte Tarp (*Karen*), Erik Paaske (*Borge*), Elsebeth Larsen (*Betsy Buttock*), Henning Moritzen (*Narrator*), Jørgen Beck.

Danish sex comedy has Passer an old man on a Danish island who sucks on aphrodisiac eggs to maintain his virility and drive the local women to amorous frenzy. When the island declares itself independent of Denmark, Steen is sent to investigate, and she falls under the randy old man's influence. He leaves the island with her, while son Petersen learns the secret of the eggs and takes his father's place in the affections of the island females. Clumsily plotted, though occasionally funny. (In Danish; English subtitles.)

d, Gabriel Axel; w, Axel, Bob Ramsing (based on a novel by Ole Juul); ph, Henning Bendtsen (Eastmancolor); m, Ib Glindemann; ed, Lars Brydesen; prod d, Willy Berg Hansen; art d, Kai Rasch; cos, Edith Sørensen, Bente Riber.

Comedy   **(PR:O MPAA:NR)**

CRAZY PEOPLE**
(1934, Brit.) 67m BK/MGM bw

Henry Kendall (*Hippo Rayne*), Nancy O'Neil (*Nanda Macdonald*), Kenneth Kove (*Birdie Nightingale*), Helen Haye (*Aunt Caroline*), Vera Bogetti, Wally Patch, Hal Walters, Hugh E. Wright, Herschel Henlere, Al Oakes and his Three Stooges.

Kendall has his friends act like lunatics to fool rich aunt Haye. The plot, such as it is, has Kendall losing his aunt's (Haye) prize ring, suspecting that Bogetti has stolen it until Haye's secretary, O'Neil, finds it. Occasionally funny second feature at a time when second features were required add-ons in film houses.

d, Leslie Hiscott; w, Michael Barringer (based on the novel *Safety First* by Margot Neville).

Comedy   **(PR:A MPAA:NR)**

CRAZY QUILT, THE**
(1966) 72m Farallon bw

Tom Rosqui (*Henry*), Ina Mela (*Lorabella*), Ellen Frye (*Noel*), Harry Hunt (*Cyrus the Actor*), Calvin Kentfield (*Jim the Fisherman*), Robert Marquis (*Dr. Milton Tugwell*), Doug Korty (*Falbuck Wheeling*), Pavel Wald (*Big Game Hunter*), Jerry Mander (*Voice Teacher*), Sonia Berman (*Fortuneteller*), Vicki Miller (*Noel, as Child*), Burgess Meredith (*Narrator*).

This low-budget independent film is based on a novel which could easily have justified a longer picture. Rosqui, a carpenter, a man without illusions about life, and Mela, a good-natured girl who believes in the beauty of life, fall in love and marry. A miscarriage leads to a separation. He does not want a divorce, but she leaves him anyway. She hops from one romance to another, each ending in disillusion, and finally returns to Rosqui, who has become sick, and takes care of him. They have a daughter together and a fairly normal family life.

p,d,w&ph, John Korty (based on the novel *The Illusionless Man and the Visionary Maid* by Allen Wheelis); m, Peter Schickele; ed, Korty, commentary, Burgess Meredith.

Drama   **(PR:A MPAA:NR)**

CRAZY THAT WAY***
(1930) 64m FOX c/bw

Kenneth MacKenna (*Jack Gardner*), Joan Bennett (*Ann Jordan*), Regis Toomey (*Robert Metcalf*), Jason Robards (*Frank Oakes*), Sharon Lynn (*Marion Sears*), Lumsden Hare (*Mr. Jordan*), Baby Mack (*Julia*).

A superior little comedy finds young girl Bennett keeping two suitors on hold. She can't seem to make up her mind, and neither suitor wants to step down. In walks MacKenna, a young engineer, to sweep Bennett off her feet and make her come to a decision.

p, George Middleton; d&w, Hamilton MacFadden, Marion Orth (based on the play "In Love With Love" by Vincent Lawrence); ph, Joseph Valentine; ed, Ralph Dietrich; art d, Duncan Cramer; cos, Sophie Wachner.

Comedy   **(PR:A MPAA:NR)**

CRAZY WORLD OF JULIUS VROODER, THE*
(1974) 98m FOX c
(AKA: VROODER'S HOOCH)

Timothy Bottoms (*Julius Vrooder*), Barbara Seagull (*Zanni*), Lawrence Pressman (*Dr. Passki*), Albert Salmi (*Splint*), Richard A. Dysart (*Father*), Dena Dietrich (*Mother*), Debralee Scott (*Sister*), Lou Frizzell (*Fowler*), Jack Murdock (*Millard*), Michael Ivan Cristofer (*Allessini*), DeWayne Jessie (*Rodali*), Ron Glass (*Quintus*), Barbara Douglas (*Roberta*), Andrew Duncan (*Chaplain*), Jack Colvin (*Sergeant*), Jarion Monroe (*Mosby*), George Marshall (*Corky*).

In yet another film about a Vietnam vet who has gone crazy, Bottoms plays the title character, who is in the psycho ward of a veterans' hospital. He will not come to grips with his problems, and withdraws from the world, building himself a booby-trapped hideaway under a nearby highway ramp. He also falls in love with a sympathetic nurse, Seagull, with whom he hopes to run away to Canada. Bottoms, however, is discovered in his hideaway by the telephone company because he's been tapping emergency lines to make calls. One consolation—at least it has crazy vets from WW I and WW II, and doesn't blame the whole phenomenon on Vietnam.

p, Edward Rissien, Arthur Hiller; d, Hiller; w, Daryl Henry; ph, David M. Walsh (Panavision, DeLuxe Color); m, Bob Alcivar; ed, Robert C. Jones; art d, Hilyard Brown; set d, Frank Lombardo.

Drama/Comedy   **(PR:C-O MPAA:PG)**

CRAZYLEGS, ALL-AMERICAN**½
(1953) 87m REP bw

Elroy "Crazylegs" Hirsch (*Himself*), Lloyd Nolan (*Win Brockmeyer*), Joan Vohs (*Ruth*), James Millican (*Rams' Coach*), Bob Waterfield (*Himself*), Bob Kelley (*Himself*), James Brown (*Bill*), John Brown (*Keller*), Norman Field (*Mr. Hirsch*), Louise Lorimer (*Mrs. Hirsch*), Joseph Crehan (*Hank Hatch*), Joel Marston (*Joey*), Bill Brundige (*Himself*), Win Hirsch (*Himself*), Melvyn Arnold (*Himself*), The Los Angeles Rams (*Themselves*).

The story spans Elroy "Crazylegs" Hirsch's career from high school through All-American fame at Wisconsin, where he won letters in four major sports. We then see his pro football career begin with the Chicago Rockets after service in the Marines. Hirsch is forced to make a comeback with the Rams after doctors tell him the injuries he received while with the Rockets would end his career. He goes on, changes the position he plays from fullback to end, and becomes one of the greats of all time. Footage of football games in which Hirsch appeared is effectively used in the film.

p, Hall Bartlett; d, Francis D. Lyon; w, Bartlett; ph, Virgil E. Miller; m, Leith Stevens; ed, Cotton Warburton; m/l, "Rams Fight Song" (Bartlett, Stevens).

Sports Drama/Biography   **(PR:AAA MPAA:NR)**

CREATION OF THE HUMANOIDS*
(1962) 75m Genie/Emerson c

Don Megowan (*Craigus*), Frances McCann, Erica Elliott, Don Dolittle, Dudley Manlove, David Cross, George Milan, Reid Hamilton, Richard Vath, Malcolm Smith.

It is post-WW III and man has created an advanced race of work robots, looking very much like humans (economizing on makeup, no doubt). With most of the surviving Human population sterile, the robots soon become the majority. Scientist Megowan tries to inject emotions into the heartless creatures by filling them with human blood. Complications arise when Megowan discovers he himself is an extremely advanced android capable of procreation. Pop artist Andy Warhol called this his favorite film, which is not surprising, given the similarities between the emotionless robots and Warhol's Factory crowd.

p, Wesley E. Barry, Edward J. Kay; d, Barry; w, Jay Simms; ph, Hal Mohr; ed, Leonard W. Herman; art d, Ted Rich.

Science Fiction   **(PR:C MPAA:NR)**

CREATURE CALLED MAN, THE** (1970, Jap.) 93m Toho c
(JAGA WA HASHITTA)

Yuzo Kayama *(Toda)*, Jiro Tamiya *(Kujo)*, Mariko Kaga *(Toda's Assistant)*, Nancy Sommers *(Kujo's Girl Friend)*, Nobuo Nakamura *(Head of N-Bussan)*, Shigeru Koyama.

When a revolution in a Southeast Asian country ousts the president, he seeks asylum in Japan. He is welcomed by a corporation, N-Bussan, which had supplied arms to his regime, but the executives accept a deal with the new rulers of the country to sell them arms if they can kill the fugitive ruler. They hire a professional assassin, Tamiya, and the police, learning of the plot, assign top detective and Olympic marksman Kayama to protect him. Kayama kills Sommers, Tamiya's American girl friend, and Tamiya retaliates by killing Kaga, Kayama's assistant. The two men then face off on a deserted beach to duel it out. Routine Japanese spy melodrama.

d, Kiyoshi Nishimura; w, Hiroshi Nagano, Yoshihiro Ishimatsu; ph, Kazutami Hara (Panavision, Eastmancolor); m, Mitsuhiko Sato; art d, Shinobu Muraki.

Drama **(PR:C MPAA:NR)**

CREATURE FROM BLACK LAKE, THE*½
(1976) 95m Howco International c

Jack Elam, Dub Taylor, Dennis Fimple, John David Carson, Bill Thurman.

Entertaining performances by Jack Elam (ONCE UPON A TIME IN THE WEST) and Dub Taylor (BONNIE AND CLYDE) save this loser Bigfoot picture from sinking to the bottom of its Louisiana lake, where two college students are trying to document the sighting of a mythical creature.

p, Jim McCullough; d, Joy Houck, Jr.; w, Jim McCullough, Jr.; ph, (Todd-AO, Eastmancolor); m, Jaime Mendoza-Nava.

Horror **(PR:C MPAA:PG)**

CREATURE FROM THE BLACK LAGOON*** (1954) 79m UNIV bw

Richard Carlson *(David Reed)*, Julia Adams *(Kay Lawrence)*, Richard Denning *(Mark Williams)*, Antonio Moreno *(Carl Maia)*, Nestor Paiva *(Lucas)*, Whit Bissell *(Edwin Thompson)*, Ben Chapman *(Gill-Man)*, Harry Escalante *(Chico)*, Bernie Gozier *(Zee)*, Sydney Mason *(Dr. Matos)*, Julio Lopez *(Tomas)*, Rodd Redwing *(Louis)*.

Classic horror film made at the capital of the modern horror film, Universal Studios, THE CREATURE FROM THE BLACK LAGOON, practically saved Universal from bankruptcy in the 1950s. A scientific expedition heads into the tropic backwaters to hunt for fossils. The scientists, however, are surprised to discover a live, very human-acting, and amorous creature (the creation of Bud Westmore and Jack Kevan, and played on land by Ben Chapman, with then swimming champ Ricou Browning playing the creature in underwater sequences. Browning had to hold his breath for four minutes at a time because the tight-fitting suit did not permit the use of an aqua lung). The scientists drug and capture the creature, who later escapes, and ends up killing half the expedition crew. The lonely creature kidnaps Adams, whom he has seen parading around in a one-piece white bathing suit. The head scientist, Carlson, must track the creature through his underwater lairs. Carlson and other members of the expedition find the creature and Adams, and shoot the creature, who slinks off into the depths of the Black Lagoon. The film achieves a certain amount of pathos for the creature, reminiscent of the feel one had for the unfortunate title character in KING KONG. Filmed in 3-D, the movie is a delight to see in its originally intended form. Two sequels followed: REVENGE OF THE CREATURE and THE CREATURE WALKS AMONG US.

p, William Alland: d, Jack Arnold; w, Harry Essex, Arthur Ross (based on a story by Maurice Zimm); ph, William E. Snyder (in 3-D); ed, Ted J. Kent; md, Joseph Gershonson; spec eff, Charles S. Welbourne; makeup, Bud Westmore; ph underwater sequences, James C. Havens.

Horror **Cas.** **(PR:A MPAA:NR)**

CREATURE FROM THE HAUNTED SEA**½ (1961) 63m Filmgroup bw

Antony Carbone *(Renzo Capeto)*, Betsey Jones-Moreland *(Mary-Belle)*, Edward Wain *(Sparks Moran)*, Edmundo Rivera Alvarez *(Col Tostada)*, Robert Bean *(Jack)*, Sonya Noemi *(Mango)*, Beach Dickerson, Roger Corman.

An entertaining quickie from Roger Corman which could have been called "The Boy Who Cried Sea Monster." Bogart-esque criminal Carbone helps some loyalists escape from a revolution-torn Caribbean island with a hefty cargo of cash. Blinded by greed, he kills the men and blames their deaths on a legendary sea monster. Nobody buys it until a real sea monster starts chomping up everyone in sight. Done in the Corman tradition—quick, cheap, and using the same cast and crew as two previous island films, THE BATTLE OF BLOOD ISLAND and LAST WOMAN ON EARTH.

p&d, Roger Corman; w, Charles Griffith; ph, Jacques Marquette; m, Fred Katz; ed, Angela Scellars.

Horror/Comedy **Cas.** **(PR:C MPAA:NR)**

CREATURE OF THE WALKING DEAD*½
(1960, Mex.) Alameda Films/A.D.P. Productions bw
(LA MARCA DEL MUERTO)

Rock Madison, Katherine Victor, Bruno Ve Sota, Ann Wells, George Todd, Willard Gross.

A Mexican horror pic about a scientist who revives his dead grandfather which was recut in 1965 with added American footage edited in. The Frankenstein-ish grandpa goes on the usual blood-thirsty rampage. The film suffers from its spliced-in American footage.

p, Jerry Warren (U.S.); d, Warren (U.S.), Fernando Cortes (Mex.); w, Alfredo Varela, Jr., Fernando Cortes (based on a story by Jose Maria Fernandez Unsain); ph, Jose

Oritz Ramons, Richard Wallace; ed, Alfredo Rosas Priego; prod d, Luis de Leon; spec eff, Nicolas Reye.

Horror **(PR:C MPAA:NR)**

CREATURE WALKS AMONG US, THE* (1956) 78M UNIV bw

Jeff Morrow *(Dr. William Barton)*, Rex Reason *(Dr. Thomas Morgan)*, Leigh Snowden *(Marcia Barton)*, Gregg Palmer *(Jed Grant)*, Maurice Manson *(Dr. Borg)*, James Rawley *(Dr. Johnson)*, David McMahon *(Capt. Stanley)*, Paul Fierro *(Morteno)*, Lillian Molieri *(Mrs. Morteno)*, Larry Hudson *(State Trooper)*, Frank Chase *(Steward)*, Don Megowan, Ricou Browning *(Creature)*.

This is the sequel to REVENGE OF THE CREATURE and the third time around, with little of the magic of the original picture present. Also done in 3-D, the film has the creature—again played by then-swimming champ Browning in the underwater sequences—captured and brought to the U.S. to be studied. Through an accidental lab fire, the creature's gills are burned off, but scientist Morrow discovers it has air-breathing lungs. He performs a tracheotomy and the creature is able to live out of water. Things are going along well until Morrow becomes jealous of fellow scientist Palmer's attentions toward his wife and kills him in a fight, in the process wounding the creature. The creature escapes and walks off into the ocean either to make another sequel or drown, its destiny obviously being the latter.

p, William Alland; d, John Sherwood; w, Arthur Ross; ph, Maury Gertsman; m, Joseph Gershenson; ed, Edward Curtiss; cos, Jay A. Morley, Jr.; special photography, Clifford Stine.

Horror **(PR:A MPAA:NR)**

THE CREATURE WASN'T NICE* (1981) 88m Creature Features c
(AKA: SPACESHIP)

Cindy Williams *(McHugh)*, Bruce Kimmel *(John)*, Leslie Nielsen *(Jameson)*, Gerrit Graham *(Rodzinski)*, Patrick MacNee *(Stark)*, Ron Kurowski *(Creature)*, Kenneth Toby.

Film centers on a lone spaceship and its small crew. Stopping at an unknown planet, the ship takes on a small clump of matter, which quickly grows into a monster. Mad scientist MacNee seeks to protect it from the frightened crew. Highlight of the film comes when the monster is hooked up to a communication computer, and does a funny dance and song routine called, "I Want to Eat Your Face." Kimmel, director of this misguided attempt at horror comedy, also directed Cindy Williams in THE FIRST NUDIE MUSICAL.

p, Mark Haggard; d&w, Bruce Kimmel; ph, Denny Lavil (Metrocolor); m, David Spear; ed, David Blangsted; prod d, Lee Cole; art d, Cole; cos, Katherine Dover; makeup, Hud Bannon; spec eff, William J. Hedge, Bob Greenberg, Anthony Doublin, Thomas H. Payne; miniatures, Jene Omens, Carl Bostrom, Will Guest.

Comedy **(PR:A MPAA:PG)**

CREATURE WITH THE ATOM BRAIN* (1955) 69m Clover/COL bw

Richard Denning *(Dr. Chet Walker)*, Angela Stevens *(Joyce Walker)*, S. John Launer *(Capt. Dave Harris)*, Michael Granger *(Frank Buchanan)*, Gregory Gay *(Prof. Steigg)*, Linda Bennett *(Penny Walker)*, Tristram Coffin *(District Attorney MacGraw)*, Harry Lauter, Larry Blake *(Reporters)*, Charles Evans *(Chief Camden)*, Pierre Watkin *(Mayor Bremer)*, Lane R. Chandler *(Gen. Saunders)*, Nelson Leigh *(Dr. Kenneth Norton)*, Don C. Harvey *(Lester Banning)*, Paul Hoffman *(Dunn)*, Edward Coch *(Jason-Franchot)*, Karl Davis.

A film so bad its got to be liked. Mad ex-Nazi scientist Gay devises a method of removing people's brains and replacing them with atomic energy, making them into nuclear-powered zombies. Gay teams up with mobster Granger, who uses the zombies to take care of his rivals and nosey public officials. Dennings heads an investigation that discovers the origin of the zombies and the person behind them. When Granger is cornered and has nothing to lose, he unleashes an army of zombies, who go on a rampage and terrorize the city. The zombies are taken care of in gruesome style by the police and Granger gets his just desserts.

p, Sam Katzman; d, Edward L. Cahn; w, Curt Siodmak; ph, Fred Jackman, Jr.; ed, Aaron Stell; md, Mischa Bakaleinikoff.

Horror **(PR:O MPAA:NR)**

CREATURE WITH THE BLUE HAND** (1971, Ger.) 78m New World c

Klaus Kinski, Diana Korner, Harold Lepnvitz.

Kinski plays twins in this muddled Edgar Wallace thriller. The title creature is stalking about the castle grounds committing murders. This was the fifteenth Edgar Wallace film in which the impressive character actor in German and international films performed, and one of the few German Wallace thrillers released in the U.S. Not bad, though no more.

p, Horst Wendlandt, Preben Philipsen; d, Alfred Vohrer; w, Alex Berg (based on a story by Edgar Wallace).

Horror **(PR:O MPAA:NR)**

CREATURES (SEE: FROM BEYOND THE GRAVE, 1973, Brit.)

CREATURES OF THE PREHISTORIC PLANET (SEE: HORROR OF THE BLOOD MONSTERS, 1970)

CREATURE'S REVENGE, THE (SEE: BRAIN OF BLOOD, 1971)

CREATURES THE WORLD FORGOT*½
(1971, Brit.) 95m Hammer/COL c

Julie Ege *(Girl)*, Tony Bonner *(Fair Boy)*, Robert John *(Dark Boy)*, Brian

O'Shaughnessy *(Father)*, Sue Wilson *(Mother)*, Rosalie Crutchley *(Old Crone)*, Marcia Fox *(Dumb Girl)*, Gerard Bonthuys *(Young Fair Boy)*, Hans Kiesouw *(Young Dark Boy)*, Josje Kiesouw *(Young Dumb Girl)*, Beverly Blake, Doon Baide *(Young Lovers)*, Don Leonard *(Old Leader)*, Frank Hayden *(Murderer)*, Rosita Moulan *(Dancer)*, Fred Swart *(Marauder Leader)*, Ken Hare *(Fair Tribe Leader)*.

This stone-age horror production stars Ege, a former Miss Norway, as a sexy cavewoman. The film has almost no dialog. The people speak in grunts and "ughs," which is fortunate since Ege's English is not very good. The story centers around a tribe of cavemen. When the leader dies there is a rivalry between twin brothers, who want the top spot and the sexy Ege. Ege has a tough time of it, too, with everyone in sight trying to rape her, and a witch's apprentice is out to get her, too. Lots of good fight sequences for action-lovers, and a well done earthquake scene highlight this film.

p&w, Michael Carreras; d, Don Chaffey; ph, Vincent Cox (Technicolor); m, Mario Nascimbene; ed, Charles Barnes; prod d, John Stoll; spec eff, Sid Pearson; stunts, Frank Hayden; animal handler, Uwe Schultz.

Horror   **(PR:O   MPAA:GP)**

CREEPER, THE**   (1948) 63m FOX bw
Eduardo Ciannelli *(Dr. Van Glock)*, Onslow Stevens *(Dr. Bordon)*, June Vincent *(Gwen)*, Ralph Morgan *(Dr. Cavigny)*, Janis Wilson *(Nora)*, John Baragrey *(Dr. John Reade)*, Richard Lane *(Inspector Fenwick)*, Philip Ahn *(Wong)*, Lotte Stein *(Nurse)*, Ralph Peters *(Porter)*, David Hoffman *(Andre)*.

A contrived spook film shows two scientists experimenting with phosphorus, aimed at illuminating internal organs as an aid in operations. The experiment gets mixed up, and a serum from the West Indies, developed from cats, gets injected into one of the scientists, turning him into a killer with cat paws. The other scientist believes the experiments must stop, but the scientist injected with the serum does not, and kills the other. Several people are clawed to death before the cat-killer scientist is stopped.

p, Bernard Small; d, Jean Yarbrough; w, Maurice Tombragel (based on a story by Don Martin); ph, George Robinson; m, Milton Rosen; ed, Saul A. Goodkind.

Horror   **(PR:O   MPAA:NR)**

CREEPER, THE*   (1980, Can.) 100m Coast c (AKA: RITUALS)
Hal Holbrook, Lawrence Dane, Robin Gammell, Ken James, Gary Reineke, Peter Carter.

Holbrook and four fellow doctors take a vacation in the woods and are terrorized by baddies. Cheap ripoff of DELIVERANCE from north of the border.

p, Lawrence Dane; d, Peter Carter; w, Ian Sutherland.

Crime   **(PR:O   MPAA:R)**

THE CREEPING FLESH**
                    (1973, Brit.) 91m Tigon British World Film/COL c
Christopher Lee *(James)*, Peter Cushing *(Emmanuel)*, Lorna Heilbron *(Penelope)*, George Benson *(Waterlow)*, Kenneth J. Warren *(Lenny)*.

This gothic science fiction horror film has an excellent cast which carries out its campy script in believable fashion. The story has two plot lines. One revolves around scientist Cushing, who tries to develop a serum to kill evil in the bloodstream, from an antediluvian skeleton that grows flesh when it come into contact with water. Cushing gives the serum to his daughter, but instead of turning into a saint she turns into a murderer. The other part of the plot centers on Cushing's brother and the head of an insane asylum, Lee, who is trying to get the skeleton and the secret of evil. Lee ends up putting the flesh-growing skeleton out into the rain and produces an instant monster. Meanwhile, a killer escapes from the asylum. The two plots converge, resulting in Cushing and his daughter both residing in the brother's bobby hatch.

p, Michael Redbourn; d, Freddie Francis; w, Peter Spenceley, Jonathon Rumbold; ph, Norman Warwick; m, Paul Ferris; ed, Oswald Hafenrichter.

Horror   **Cas.**   **(PR:O   MPAA:PG)**

CREEPING TERROR, THE*
                    (1964) 75m Metropolitan International/Teledyn bw
            (AKA: THE CRAWLING MONSTER; DANGEROUS CHARTER)
Vic Savage [Art J. Nelson], Shannon O'Neill, William Thourlby.

Call it what you will, after all is there that much difference between a crawling monster and a creeping terror? No. Especially when a budget only allows the special effects crew enough money to buy a big hunk of foam, and then expect it to look like a "terror." Supposedly, the film is about an alien being who crash-lands in the desert and devours innocent people. Actually, a few crew members crawl under the hunk of foam (we can see their feet) in dusty Lake Tahoe. To add to the legend of perhaps the worst horror movie of all time (second only to PLAN 9 FROM OUTER SPACE) is the fact that the entire sound track was lost. Not to be defeated, the producers (more aptly, reducers?) simply added a hysterically bad and matter-of-fact narrator. Pure camp trash, one of the best.

p&d, Art J. Nelson; w, Robert Silliphant, Alan Silliphant; ph, Irving Phillips; ed, Argyle Nelson, Jr.; art d, John Lackey; spec eff, Clifford Stine, Lackey.

Horror   **Cas.**   **(PR:C   MPAA:NR)**

THE CREEPING UNKNOWN**   (1956, Brit.) 78m Hammer/UA bw
            (AKA: THE QUATERMASS XPERIMENT)
Brian Donlevy *(Prof. Bernard Quatermass)*, Jack Warner *(Inspector Lomax)*, Margia Dean *(Judith Carroon)*, Richard Wordsworth *(Victor Carroon)*, David King Wood *(Dr. Gordon Briscoe)*, Thora Hird *(Rosie)*, Gordon Jackson *(TV Producer)*, Harold Lang *(Christie)*, Lionel Jeffries *(Blake)*, Maurice Kaufmann *(Marsh)*, Frank Phillips *(BBC Announcer)*, Gron Davies *(Green)*, Stanley Van Beers *(Reichenheim)*.

Based on a successful British television series, this film features the super scientist Quatermass and was Hammer's first international hit, and moved the studio to do films in the sci-fi and horror genres. The plot surrounds the sole survivor of a rocketship crash, Wordsworth, who comes back to Earth with a strange fungus on his hand. Put into isolation at a hospital in London, the fungus begins to consume him. He breaks out of the hospital and the fungus totally consumes him. The creature goes on a reign of terror, killing everything in sight and growing larger all the time. The monster becomes a national menace, and the army, police, and civil defense are called out, but it is a BBC television crew, shooting a documentary, that finds the creature in Westminster Abbey. Quatermass corners the monster in the abbey and kills it with a huge electric shock that puts the city of London in a blackout. Sequel: ENEMY FROM SPACE.

p, Anthony Hinds; d, Val Guest; w, Richard Landau, Guest (based on a TV BBC serial by Nigel Kneale); ph, Walter Harvey, J. Elder Willis; ed, James Needs.

Horror/Science Fiction   **(PR:C   MPAA:NR)**

CREEPSHOW***   (1982) 129m Alpha/Laurel WB c
Hal Holbrook *(Henry)*, Adrienne Barbeau *(Wilma)*, Fritz Weaver *(Dexter)*, Leslie Nielsen *(Richard)*, Carrie Nye *(Sylvia)*, E.G. Marshall *(Upson)*, Viveca Lindfors *(Aunt Bedelia)*, Ed Harris *(Hank)*, Ted Danson *(Harry)*, Stephen King *(Jordy)*, Warner Shook *(Richard)*, Robert Harper *(Charlie)*, Elizabeth Regan *(Cass)*, Gaylen Ross *(Becky)*, Jon Lorner *(Nathan)*, Don Keefer *(Janitor)*, Bingo O'Malley *(Jordy's Dad)*, John Amplas *(Corpse)*, David Early *(White)*, Nann Mogg *(Mrs. Danvers)*, Iva Jean Saraceni *(Billy's Mother)*, Joe King *(Billy)*, Christine Forrest *(Tabitha)*, Chuck Aber *(Richard Raymond)*, Katie Karlovitz *(Maid)*, Peter Messer *(Yarbro)*, Marty Schiff, Tom Savini *(Garbage Men)*, Ted Atkins *(Stan)*.

This film is the result of the collaboration of America's greatest horror director and the horror novelist of the 1970s, Romero and King. CREEPSHOW is their effort to reproduce on film the horror and style of an E.C. comic book of the 1950s. The film starts off on a stormy night when an angry father discovers that his son has been reading an E.C. comic book. He throws it into the street and the wind blows it open to the first of five vignettes. Skillfully Romero combines thrills and a sense of fun in linking the tales with animated bridges in the style of comics. Stylistically, he pulls it off but the whole isn't as good as the pieces. The film has scares in all the right places, but it leaves a "so what" attitude at the end. A great cast is assembled in every vignette, including King in "The Lonesome Death of Jordy Verrill." Horror makeup man Tom Savini has a cameo appearance as one of the garbage men.

p,, Richard P. Rubinstein; d, George A. Romero; w, Stephen King; ph, Michael Gornick (Technicolor); m, John Harrison; ed, Michael Spolan, Pasquale Buba, Romero, Paul Hirsch; prod d, Cletus Anderson; cos, Barbara Anderson; makeup, Tom Savini.

Horror   **Cas.**   **(PR:O   MPAA:R)**

CREMATOR, THE***   (1973, Czech.) 90m Herz c
Rudolf Hrusinsky *(Mr. Kopfrkingl)*, Vlasta Chramostova.

Hrusinsky is the proprietor of a Czech crematorium who takes great pride in his work, if not in his half-Jewish wife and children. When the Nazis invade the country, Hrusinsky's drop of German blood serves him in good stead as he is put in charge of the crematorium at a death camp. Hrusinsky's scary performance highlights this morbid, darkly funny work.

d, Juraj Herz.

Drama   **(PR:O   MPAA:NR)**

CREMATORS, THE**½   (1972) 75m New World c
Maria Di Aragon, Marvin C. Howard, Eric Alison, Mason Caulfield.

A sphere falls from outer space and rolls across beaches, absorbing people who get in its way. An absorbing low-budget ($40,000) science fiction thrill directed by Harry Essex, unpretentious action and sci-fi writer now working mostly in TV.

p&d, Harry Essex; (based on the novelette *The Dune Rollers* by Judy Kitky).

Science Fiction   **(PR:C   MPAA:NR)**

CRESCENDO*   (1972, Brit.) 83m Hammer/WB c
Stefanie Powers *(Susan)*, James Olson *(Georges/Jacques)*, Margaretta Scott *(Danielle)*, Jane Lapotaire *(Lillianne)*, Joss Ackland *(Carter)*, Kirsten Betts *(Catherine)*.

Not one of Hammer's better efforts, this film has Powers going to the south of France to do research for her thesis on a recently deceased composer. She stays with the composer's widow and crippled dope-addict son, and becomes involved in a family situation when she discovers the composer's mad twin locked in the attic. Powers barely escapes with her life.

p, Michael Carreras; d, Alan Gibson; w, Jimmy Sangster, Alfred Shaughnessy; ph, Paul Beeson (Technicolor); m, Malcom Williamson; ed, Chris Barnes; art d, Scott MacGregor.

Horror   **(PR:A   MPAA:PG)**

CREST OF THE WAVE**½   (1954, Brit.) 92m MGM bw
                (AKA: SEAGULLS OVER SORRENTO)
Gene Kelly *(Lt. Bradville, USN)*, John Justin *(Lt. Wharton)*, Bernard Lee *(Lofty Turner)*, Jeff Richards *(Butch Clelland, USN)*, Sidney James *(Charlie Badger)*, Patric Doonan *(P. O. Herbert)*, Ray Jackson *(Sprog Sims)*, Fredd Wayne *(Shorty Kaminsky, USN)*, Patrick Barr *(Lt. Cmdr. Sinclair)*, David Orr *(Haggis Mackintosh)*.

Based on the play "Seagulls Over Sorrento" by Hugh Hasting, which ran three years in London but only a few weeks on Broadway, the film gives Kelly a chance to act without singing and dancing. The story is about a group of naval men stationed off the northeast coast of Britain who are engaged in highly dangerous research work on a new torpedo. Kelly plays a U.S. scientist called in when the British scientists are killed in a test. Bringing in two more Americans causes some feuding between the British and Americans. Both drama and comedy are drawn from these situations. The film is much more interesting than the research being done on the island.

p&d, John and Roy Boulting; w, Frank Harvey, Roy Boulting (based on the play by Hugh Hastings); ph, Gilbert Taylor; m, Miklos Rozsa; ed, Max Benedict.

War **(PR:A MPAA:NR)**

CRIES AND WHISPERS**** (1972, Swed.) 95m New World c (SWED: VISKINGAR OCH ROP)

Ingrid Thulin *(Karin)*, Liv Ullmann *(Maria)*, Harriet Andersson *(Agnes)*, Kari Sylwan *(Anna)*, Erland Josephsen *(Doctor)*, George Arlin *(Karin's Husband)*, Henning Moritzen *(Joakin)*.

A relentlessly depressing tale of a young woman who is dying of cancer and being comforted by her two sisters. Ingrid Thulin and Liv Ullmann return to the family home to be with sister Harret Andersson who has been cared for by Kari Sylwan, a long-time family retainer. Bergman uses his four women metaphorically, as a representation of humanity, to see how they respond to anxiety, death, and to what appears to be a wrathful, rather than a benevolent God. Thulin is on the brink of suicide and we learn that she is so anti-love that she once mutilated her own genitalia, rather than have to visit the marriage bed with her husband. Ullman is far earthier and once had an affair which caused her husband to attempt to do away with himself. Housekeeper Sylwan is the glue that holds these Checkovian sisters together. She can accept God's will and imparts the fatalistic theory to Andersson. Sylwan had lost a child early in life and understands what death is; neither hard nor bad, just a new voyage. But Andersson is in terrible pain and cannot fully accept that. Still, she is much closer to the housekeeper than she is to her sisters and the Death Watch is what occupies most of the movie. There are many times when no words are spoken and the silence is more eloquent than anything that might have been said. Bergman and Nykvist range the camera in and out with remarkable fluidity and the beauty of the photography is in odd opposition to the starkness of the subject matter. Nykvist's work took the Oscar and Bergman was nominated as Best Writer and Best Director, with the movie also securing a nomination but they all lost in THE STING sweep that year. Distributed by Roger Corman's New World Pictures, CRIES AND WHISPERS managed to do more business than Swedish imports usually do, but it was tough emotional going for most Americans and although one could marvel at the technical brilliance of the piece (and the actresses), it was not easy to identify with any of them. Sound takes a huge step in the movie as Bergman uses ticking clocks rustling dresses, sighs, cries, and whispers to make his point. He is always trying something different and we must be thankful that he is not dictated to by studio chiefs in a mad rush to show profits. Bergman works for the state-controlled film industry and does what he wishes. Would that might happen in a few more places.

p,d&w, Ingmar Bergman; ph, Sven Nykvist (Eastmancolor); m, Frederic Chopin, J. S. Bach.

Drama **(PR:C MPAA:NR)**

CRIES IN THE NIGHT, 1964 (SEE: AWFUL DR. ORLOFF, THE, 1964)

CRIES IN THE NIGHT, 1982 (SEE: FUNERAL HOME, 1982, Can.)

CRIME AFLOAT* (1937) 67m Fanchon Royer bw

William Bakewell *(Bob)*, Arletta Duncan *(Wynne)*, Duncan Renaldo *(Count Ribalto)*, Vivien Oakland *(Marie)*, Wilfred Lucas *(Drexel)*, Earle Douglas *(Strauss)*, Etta McDaniels *(Eunice)*.

This poorly constructed melodrama was written by Duncan Renaldo, who is also featured. The plot revolves around the world of motorboat racing. Renaldo plays the bad guy, a false count, who is trying to swindle the hero's boss. The hero is Bakewell, a young inventor of a new boat, who is in love with the boss's daughter. Bakewell saves the day by exposing Renaldo, and wins the boss's blessing to marry his daughter.

d, Elmer Clifton; w, Edwin Anthony (based on a story by Duncan Renaldo); ph, Arthur Martinelli.

Drama **(PR:A MPAA:NR)**

CRIME AGAINST JOE½** (1956) 69m UA bw

John Bromfield *(Joe Manning)*, Julie London *(Slacks)*, Henry Calvin *(Red Waller)*, Patricia Blake *(Christy Rowen)*, Joel Ashley *(Philip Rowen)*, Robert Keyes *(Detective Hollander)*, Alika Louis *(Irene Crescent)*, John Pickard *(Harry Dorn)*, Frances Morris *(Nora Manning)*, Rhodes Reason *(George Niles)*, Mauritz Hugo *(Dr. Tatreau)*, Joyce Jameson *(Gloria Wayne)*, Morgan Jones *(Luther Wood)*, James Parnell *(Ralph Corey)*.

Holding its secret to the end, this well-done mystery finds Bromfield accused of a murder he did not commit. After a night of drunken reveling, he is arrested and charged with the murder of a night club singer who is found clutching a 1945 high school pin in her hand, which happens to be Bromfield's class. London comes to his aid with a phony alibi after several others have in their turn lied about him. He is released, and, knowing the cops do not believe his story, starts his own investigation of others in the class of '45, coming up with the answer after almost being killed himself.

p, Howard W. Koch; d, Lee Sholem; w, Robert C. Dennis; ph, William Margulies; m, Paul Dunlap; ed, Mike Pozen; cos, Wesley V. Jefferies.

Comedy/Drama **(PR:C MPAA:R)**

CRIME AND PASSION*½ (1976, U.S., Ger.) 92m Gloria Films/AIP c

Omar Sharif *(Andre)*, Karen Black *(Susan)*, Joseph Bottoms *(Larry)*, Bernhard Wicki *(Rolf)*, Heinz Ehrenfreund *(Henkel)*, Elma Karlowa *(Masseuse)*, Volker Prechtel *(Innkeeper)*, Erich Padalewski *(Car Salesman)*, Robert Abrams *(Mr. Blatt)*, Franz Muxeneder *(Priest)*, Margarete Soper *(Sylvia)*.

A poor comedy/drama starring Sharif as an investment counselor who gets into trouble with his bad investments. Black plays his girl friend/tranquilizer. Sharif also gets in trouble with a vengeful tycoon, Wicki, who wants to murder him and most of the cast. Black marries Wicki to keep Sharif out of trouble, but it is to no avail. Extremely weak plot, but Sharif gives a surprisingly good account of himself.

p, Robert L. Abrams; d, Ivan Passer; w, Jesse Lasky, Jr., Pat Silver (based on the novel *An Ace Up Your Sleeve* by James Hadley Chase); ph, Denis C. Lewiston (Technicolor); m, Van Gelis Papathanassiou; ed, Bernard Gribble, John Jympson; art d, Herta Pischinger; cos, Yvonne Blake.

Comedy/Drama **(PR:C-O MPAA:R)**

CRIME AND PUNISHMENT*½** (1935, Fr.) 110m Lenauer/GP bw (CRIME ET CHATIMENT)

Harry Baur *(Porphyre)*, Pierre Blanchar *(Raskolnikov)*, Madeleine Ozeray *(Sonia)*, Marcelle Geniat *(Mme. Raskolnikov)*, Lucienne Lemarchand *(Dounia)*, Alexandre Rignault *(Raxoumikhine)*, Magdelaine Berubet *(Aliona)*, Alme Clariond *(Loujine)*, Sylvie *(Catherine Ivanovna)*, Delaitre *(Marmeladov)*, Paulette Elambert *(Polia)*, Catherine Hessling *(Elisabeth)*, Georges Douking *(Nicolas)*, Claire Gerard *(Nastassia)*.

The first and probably the best adaptation of the famous Dostoyevsky novel, this French production of CRIME AND PUNISHMENT keeps everything from the book that works on film, and discards the nondramatic material, at the same time avoiding distortion. The film works equally well as a detective story or as the psychological study for which the novel is famous. It centers around a murderer, his crime, and his punishment, and is set in Russia. We follow the student murderer, Blanchar, through the planning of his crime and its execution to his confession to Baur, who plays the examining magistrate who engages Blanchar in a series of stirring verbal battles. (In French.)

d, Pierre Chenal; w, Marcel Ayme, Chenal, Christian Stengel, Wladimir Strijewski (based on the novel by Feodor Dostoyevsky); ph, Rene Colas, Joseph-Louis Mundviller; m, Arthur Honegger; ed, Andre Galitzine.

Crime/Drama **(PR:A MPAA:NR)**

CRIME AND PUNISHMENT*½** (1935) 88m COL bw

Edward Arnold *(Inspector Porfiry)*, Peter Lorre *(Raskolnikov)*, Marian Marsh *(Sonya)*, Tala Birell *(Antonya)*, Elizabeth Risdon *(Mrs. Raskolnikov)*, Robert Allen *(Dmitri)*, Douglas Dumbrille *(Grilov)*, Gene Lockhart *(Lushin)*, Charles Waldron *(University President)*, Thurston Hall *(Editor)*, Johnny Arthur *(Clerk)*, Mrs. Patrick Campbell *(Pawnbroker)*, Rafaelo Ottiano *(Landlady)*, Michael Mark *(Painter/Prisoner)*.

The American versionof the great Dostoyevsky novel had to comp ete with the French production which had been released one week earlier in 1935 but in many ways this film provides a greater insight into the Russian classic, even though one of the originial two plot murders was eliminated for the sake of time. Lorre, as the guilt-laden Russian student, is superb. His murder of the pawnbroker, Campbell, is ostensibly committed to aid his sister and mother (Birell and Risdom) and his guilt is affixed by his own arrogance and conscience. He becomes apprehensive when first called into police headquarters, but learns with relief that he is there to answer charges of not paying his rent. His confidence inflated, he then foolishly accepts an invitation by police sleuth Arnold to observe the investigation into Campbell's murder since he has written an academic but critical article on police methods. Lorre's ego exults in being able to follow his own spotty trail with the pursuer, but his vanity gets the better of him and he begins to volunteer small clues to the identity of the killer, himself, just as Arnold knew he would do when he set this intellectual trap. (Oddly, the very same procedure in real life occurred in 1924 when Chicagoan Richard Loeb, who had killed the Bobby Franks child with Nathan Leopold, volunteered his investigative services to police and aided them in tracking down the killers, himself and Leopold, trapping himself out of vanity. It is ironic that he had read the Dostoyevsky novel religiously but was nevertheless snared in the same situation.) Lorre and Arnold play cat-and-mouse with each other but Arnold's case is thin and he knows it. Lorre, alternating between manic depressive and superman optimist, is persecuted by his own inner feelings, further confused by the love he feels for prostitute Marsh who stops him from committing suicide when his sense of guilt becomes overwhelming. He confesses all to her and she convinces him to turn himself into Arnold. The pair enter the suave detective's office and he greets them with a knowing: "I've been waiting for you." Lorre does a magnificent job of condensing his impossible role, displaying the intellectual confidence of an arrogant killer on one hand and then being overcome by nagging guilt. Von Sternberg's direction is masterful, quickly paced and economically shot, with Ballard's moody, murky lensing adding just the right somber quality to the film. Much was made of converting CRIME AND PUNISHMENT into a popular vehicle and Von Sternberg took most of the criticism. The director, however, did not actually want to make this film, inheriting the assignment from Columbia where he had a two-film iron-clad contract to fulfill. The French version has always been more acceptable to critics but it is showier, with Chenal's actors offering histrionic melodrama as opposed to Von Sternberg's more subdued approach which is really in keeping with Dostoyevsky's reflective novel. The director also had his hands full with the temperamental cast. Lorre, then addicted to morphine, was often high on the drug and Von Sternberg had to wait until the volatile, diminutive actor was in "the proper mood to play this despicable killer." Even harder to handle was the notorious eccentric, Mrs. Patrick Campbell, who played the pawnbroker victim. Stella Campbell had been a stellar name in the legitimate theater for decades; she migrated to Hollywood in 1930 where she found almost everything and everyone tasteless and repugnant. She proceeded to insult the community at large. She would regally sweep into Hollywood galas with her white Pekinese, Moonbeam, tucked under her arm (the very image recreated by Marie Dressler in DINNER AT EIGHT which was a parody on the fabulous Mrs. Campbell). Once at the party, Mrs. Campbell would pretend not to know the famous people around her, suggesting to already established stars such as Marion Davies, Norma Shearer, and Constance Bennett that they try for screen tests. She once approached a sharply profiled actor and told him: "You're a beautiful young man. Why don't you make a film?" Startled, the famous actor retorted: "My dear Mrs. Campbell, my name is Joseph Schildkraut!" She clucked her tongue and replied: "You had better change that name first." Appearing on the set of CRIME AND PUNISHMENT, an executive spotted her dog and asked its name. Her reply is quoted in Alan Dent's *Mrs. Patrick Campbell*: "Not wishing to be outdone in cheerfulness and humor . . . I answered with dignity 'Tittiebottles.' From that moment I was dubbed a nut." But since she had an illustrious stage past and was still an ardent correspondent with the great George Bernard Shaw—she had played leads in all the American productions of his plays—she was treated with great deference. When she arrived on the CRIME AND PUNISHMENT set, she told a disgruntled Von Sternberg that she hadn't had time to read either the Dostoyevsky classic or even the screenplay with her part. He had her sit down while he coached Marian Marsh in her role of the prostitute, telling Marsh to shed a few tears which she worked hard to deliver. Mrs. Campbell frowned at this thespian exertion, thinking Von Sternberg too demanding. "You're a nasty man," she called out to him, asking that he stop hounding Marsh. Von Sternberg patiently explained to the grande dame that Marsh had to "shed a few tears" to be convincing. The confrontation heated up, Von Sternberg later remembered in his memoirs, *Fun In a Chinese Laundry*. "What does this manuscript of yours require me to shed?" asked the imperial actress. "Only your impudence, Stella," snapped the director. "I'm not impudent," said Mrs. Campbell. "I only want to know what I am to portray." Von Sternberg held up her unread script. "Your part calls for a pawnbroker." Mrs. Campbell rolled her eyes in disgust, stating: "I cannot possibly become a *tradesperson!*" But she did play the small role and to perfection. She would receive a few more parts in Hollywood, and then, thoroughly rejected by the community, go to France, dying in poverty at Pau, in 1940, still writing angry letters to Shaw about Hollywood moguls who refused her parts because she was "too celebrated for small parts and too English to star."

p, B. P. Schulberg; d, Josef Von Sternberg; w, S. K. Lauren, Joseph Anthony (based on the novel by Feodor Dostoyevsky); ph, Lucian Ballard,; m, Louis Silvers; ed, Richard Calhoon; set d, Stephen Gooson.

Crime Drama (PR:C MPAA:NR)

CRIME AND PUNISHMENT*
(1948, Swed.) 100m Terrafilm/Film Rights International bw
Hampe Faustman (*Raskolnikov*), Gann Wallgren (*Sonia*), Sigurd Wallen (*Samlotov*), Elsie Alblin (*Dunia*), George Funkquist (*Lusjin*), Tekia Sjoblom (*Modern*), Tolvo Pawlo (*Rasumikin*), Elsa Widborg (*Aliona*), Hugo Bjorne (*Marmeladov*), Lisskulla Jobs (*Katarina*), Harriet Philipson (*Nataschka*).

This is a slow, talky version of the Dostoyevsky novel, with the added defect of the scriptwriter trying to improve on the novel by creating some original story details. The story, about a conscience-stricken murderer who is finally driven to confessing his crime, does offer an authentic look at old Russia, but the film as a whole doesn't work. (In Swedish; English subtitles.)

d, Hampe Faustman; w, Bertil Malmberg, Sven Stolpe (based on the novel by Feodor Dostoyevsky); ph, Goram Strindberg.

Crime/Drama (PR:A MPAA:NR)

CRIME AND PUNISHMENT** (1975, USSR) 200m c
Georgi Taratorkin (*Raskolnikov*), Victoria Fyodorova (*Dunia*), Innokenti Smoktunovsky (*Porfiry*).

Immensely long, painfully faithful adaptation of Dostoyevsky's classic novel of murder and guilt, this is probably the most ponderous of all the filmings of the book. Uninspired direction by the strongly realist director Kulijanov makes it seem even longer than its three-hour-and-twenty-minute running time. Fyodorova achieved some fame in the early 1970s when she visited her father, a retired U.S. Navy admiral, in this country.

d&w, Lev Kulijanov (based on the novel *Crime and Punishment* by Feodor Dostoyevsky).

Drama (PR:A MPAA:NR)

CRIME AND PUNISHMENT, U.S.A.½** (1959) 96m AA bw
George Hamilton (*Robert*), Mary Murphy (*Sally*), Frank Silvera (*Porter*), Marian Seldes (*Debbie*), John Harding (*Swanson*), Wayne Heffley (*Rafe*), Toni Merrill (*Mrs. Cole*), Lew Brown (*Samuels*), Sid Clute (*Doctor*), Ken Drake (*Hendricks*), Jim Hyland (*Man in Coffee Shop*), Len Lesser (*Desk Officer*), Eve McVeagh.

An update of the Dostoyevsky novel from 19th-century czarist St. Petersburg to 1959 Santa Monica. Raskolnikov has been changed to Robert Cole (played by George Hamilton in his first screen credit), a law student. His nemesis is a Lt. Porter of the Santa Monica Police Department, played by Silvera. Hamilton murders a pawnbroker because he fears that his school tuition is driving his sister, Seldes, to marry a man she does not love for his money. Silvera suspects Hamilton even after someone else has confessed to the crime, his instincts telling him Hamilton will eventually confess the crime. The film seems to work in a way that Dostoyevsky would have approved.

p, Terry Sanders; d, Denis Sanders; w, Walter Newman (based on the novel by Feodor Dostoyevsky); ph, Floyd Crosby; m, Herschel Burke Gilbert; ed, Merrill G. White.

Crime/Drama (PR:A MPAA:NR)

CRIME AT BLOSSOMS, THE** (1933, Brit.) 77m B&D PAR bw
Hugh Wakefield (*Chris Merryman*), Joyce Bland (*Valerie Merryman*), Eileen Munro (*Mrs. Woodman*), Ivor Barnard (*A Late Visitor*), Frederick Lloyd (*George Merryman*), Iris Baker (*Lena Denny*), Arthur Stratton (*Mr. Woodman*), Maud Gill (*Mrs. Merryman*), Wally Patch (*Palmer*), Barbara Gott (*Fat Lady*), Moore Marriott (*Driver*), George Ridgwell (*Process-Server*).

Wakefield and Bland move into a country cottage and Bland becomes obsessed with the mysterious death of the previous occupant. Bland gets the bright idea of charging admission to curious and morbid sightseers, then becomes outlandish by reenacting the murder with startling results. Okay crime melodrama. Remade as DARK SECRET in 1949.

p&d, Maclean Rogers; (based on a play by Mordaunt Shairp).

Crime/Drama (PR:A MPAA:NR)

CRIME AT PORTA ROMANA** (1980, Ital.) 94m Titanus c
(DELITTO A PORTA ROMANA)
Tomas Milian (*Inspector Giraldi*), Olimpia Di Nardo (*His Wife*), Nerina Montagnani (*Grandma*), Bombolo (*Thief*).

A SERPICO-type character is the protagonist of this Italian film. Hippie police inspector Milian is called on a murder case to Milan because he grew up in the same ghetto as the suspect, who was hiding under the bed when the victim was strangled. The trail leads through a sports events and a strip joint for a lot of local color before Milian can bring the murderer to justice.

p, Giovanni Di Clemente; d, Bruno Corbucci; w, Mario Amendola, Corbucci; ph, Giovanni Ciarlo (Technicolor); m, Franco Miccolizzi; ed, Daniele Alabiso; art d, Claudio Cinini.

Crime/Drama (PR:O MPAA:NR)

CRIME BOSS*½ (1976, Ital.) 93m Cinema Shares International c
Telly Savalas, Lee Van Cleef, Antonio Sabato, Paola Tedesco.

Mob chief Savalas takes on an apprentice who double-crosses him. Uninteresting spaghetti gangster film. Versatile talent Savalas, a Peabody Award winner in journalism when he was with ABC as a news director, made a slew of films overseas during the 1970s, chiefly on the strength of the international fame he garnered as the star of TV's "Kojack" series.

p, Gino Mordini; d, Alberto DeMartino.

Crime (PR:C MPAA:PG)

CRIME BY NIGHT** (1944) 72m WB bw
Jane Wyman (*Robbie Vance*), Jerome Cowan (*Sam Campbell*), Faye Emerson (*Ann Marlow*), Charles Lang (*Paul Goff*), Eleanor Parker (*Irene Carr*), Stuart Crawford (*Larry Borden*), Cy Kendall (*Sheriff Ambers*), Charles C. Wilson (*District Attorney Hyatt*), Juanita Stark (*Telephone Operator*), Creighton Hale (*Grayson*), George Guhl (*Dick Blake*), Hank Mann (*Desk Clerk*), Bill Kennedy (*Hospital Attendant*), Dick Rich (*Chauffeur*), Fred Kelsey (*Dad Martin*), Bud Messinger (*Bellboy*), Jack Cheatham, Eddie Parker, Jack Stoney, Frank Mayo (*Deputies*), Jack Mower (*Tenant*), Roy Brant (*Roy the Waiter*).

Slow-moving low-budget mystery has Cowan as a slick private eye who, while on vacation with his secretary, Wyman, stumbles onto a murder case. The mystery in the plot is mostly in how they could call it one, since the identity of the murderer is revealed early in the film. This was the last starring role for veteran actor Cowan, who, for the rest of his career until his death in 1972, played diversified character roles, most often as the typically intelligent and urbane character wearing a pencil-thin-mustache.

p, William Jacobs; d, William Clemens; w, Richard Weil, Joel Malone (based on the novel *Forty Whacks* by Geoffrey Homes); ph, Henry Sharpe; ed, Doug Gould.

Mystery (PR:A MPAA:NR)

CRIME DOCTOR, THE** (1934) 75m RAD bw
Otto Kruger (*Dan Gifford*), Karen Morley (*Andra*), Nils Asther (*Eric Anderson*), Judith Wood (*Blanche Flynn*), William Frawley (*Fraser*), D:nald Crisp (*District Attorney*), Frank Conroy (*Martin Crowder*), J. Farrell MacDonald (*Kemp*), Fred Kelsey (*Bloodgood*), G. Pat Collins (*Walters*), Willie Fung, Pat O'Malley, Wallis Clark, Samuel S. Hinds, Ethel Wales.

An imperfect film about the perfect crime. Mastermind detective Kruger is the title character who plots the perfect crime. Believing his wife unfaithful, he kills a woman who has been blackmailing the suspected lover, and pins the crime on him. After the trial and conviction of the lover, Kruger's wife still wants nothing to do with him. Kruger commits suicide, and sends a sealed letter to his confederates who believe they had convicted the right man. To pacify the censors of the time, the film destroys a good ending by sticking on an epilog: it was really the fictional writings of a criminologist for publication. This film was a remake of a 1928 part-talkie of the same name.

d, John Robertson; w, Jane Murfin (based on a story by Israel Zangwill); ph, Lucien Androit; ed, William Hamilton.

Crime/Drama (PR:A MPAA:NR)

CRIME DOCTOR½** (1943) 66m COL bw
Warner Baxter (*Dr. Robert Ordway*), Margaret Lindsay (*Grace Fielding*), John Litel (*Three Fingers*), Ray Collins (*Dr. Carey*), Harold Huber (*Joe*), Don Costello (*Nick*), Leon Ames (*Capt. Wheeler*), Constance Worth (*Betty*), Dorothy Tree (*Pearl*), Vi Athens (*Myrtle*).

First film in the CRIME DOCTOR series, based on a popular radio program of the time, has Warner Baxter in the title role. He plays the former brains of a burglary gang who loses his memory due to a hit on the head by one of his suspicious comrades in crime. Suffering amnesia, he starts again from scratch and becomes a psychiatrist, while all the time he is trying to regain his memory. He becomes the head of the state parole board and gets mixed up with some of the old gang, who hit him on the head again. He regains his memory, and remembering his criminal past, turns himself in. Luckily, he receives a suspended sentence. (See CRIME DOCTOR series, Index)

p, Ralph Cohen; d, Michael Gordon; w, Graham Baker, Louise Lantz, Jerome Odlum

(based on a radio program, "Crime Doctor," by Max Marcin); ph, James S. Brown, Jr.; m, Lee Zahler; ed, Dwight Caldwell.
Crime/Mystery **(PR:A MPAA:NR)**

CRIME DOCTOR'S COURAGE, THE*½ (1945) 70m COL bw
Warner Baxter *(Dr. Robert Ordway)*, Hillary Brooke *(Kathleen Carson)*, Jerome Cowan *(Jeffers Jerome)*, Robert Scott *(Bob Rencoret)*, Lloyd Corrigan *(John Massey)*, Emory Parnell *(Capt. Birch)*, Stephen Crane *(Gordon Carson)*, Charles Arnt *(Butler)*, Anthony Caruso *(Miguel Bragga)*, Lupila Tovar *(Dolores Bragga)*, Dennis Moore *(David Lee)*, King Kong Kashay *(Luga)*, Jack Carrington *(Detective Fanning)*.

A poorer entry in the CRIME DOCTOR series. Baxter solves a murder with a detective story writer, a fortune hunter, two Spanish dancers, and a young student as suspects. The plot is poor as it puts the suspicion on all but one person, whom it conveniently overlooks. (See CRIME DOCTOR series, Index.)

p, Rudolph C. Flothow; d, George Sherman; w, Eric Taylor (based on a radio program, "Crime Doctor," by Max Marcin); ph, L. W. O'Connell; ed, Dwight Caldwell; art d, John Dala.
Crime/Mystery **(PR:A MPAA:NR)**

CRIME DOCTOR'S DIARY, THE** (1949) 61m COL bw
Warner Baxter *(Dr. Robert Ordway)*, Stephen Dunne *(Steve Carter)*, Lois Maxwell *(Jane Darrin)*, Adele Jergens *(Inez Grey)*, Robert Armstrong *("Goldie" Harrigan)*, Don Beddoe *(Philip Bellem)*, Whit Bissell *(Pete Bellem)*, Cliff Clark *(Inspector Manning)*, Lois Fields *(Roma)*, George Meeker *(Anson)*, Crane Whitley *(Mac)*, Claire Carleton *(Louise)*, Selmer Jackson *(Warden)*, Sid Tomack *(Blane)*.

A standard mystery but one of the better films in the series. Baxter helps framed arsonist Dunne get paroled from jail. While attempting to discover who was responsible for his framing, Dunne becomes the chief suspect in the murder of the man who got his old job when Dunne went to prison. It's up to Baxter to unravel the mess, and he comes up with a pretty good surprise ending when he discovers the identity of the killer. (See CRIME DOCTOR Series, Index.)

p, Rudolph C. Flothow; d, Seymour Friedman; w, Edward Anhalt (based on a story by David Dressler from the radio program "Crime Doctor" by Max Marcin); ph, Vincent Farrar; ed, Jerome Thoms; md, Mischa Bakaleinikoff; art d, Harold MacArthur; set d, George Montgomery.
Crime/Mystery **(PR:A MPAA:NR)**

CRIME DOCTOR'S GAMBLE** (1947) 65m COL bw
Warner Baxter *(Dr. Robert Ordway)*, Micheline Cheirel *(Mignon)*, Roger Dann *(Henri Jardin)*, Steven Geray *(Jules Daudet)*, Marcel Journet *(Jacques Morrell)*, Eduardo Ciannelli *(Maurice Duval)*, Henri Letondal *(Louis Chabonet)*, Jean Delval *(Theodore)*, Leon Lenoir *(Auctioneer)*, Wheaton Chambers *(Brown)*, Emory Parnell *(Otheilly)*, George Davis *(Paul Romaine)*.

CRIME DOCTOR series star Baxter is in Paris when he becomes involved in a murder case. A young Frenchman is charged with killing his father, but Baxter steps in and proves the old man was killed because a famous painting he owned was stolen and a substitute put in its place. In the final clash, Baxter discovers the murderer, and is nearly done in by him. (See CRIME DOCTOR series, Index.)

p, Rudolph C. Flothow; d, William Castle; w, Edward Boch (based on a story by Raymond L. Schrock from a radio program, "Crime Doctor," by Max Marcin); ph, Philip Tannura; ed, Dwight Caldwell; md, Mischa Bakaleinikoff; art d, George Brooks; set d, Louis Diage.
Crime/Mystery **(PR:A MPAA:NR)**

CRIME DOCTOR'S MAN HUNT*½ (1946) 64m COL bw
Warner Baxter *(Dr. Robert Ordway)*, Ellen Drew *(Irene Cotter)*, William Frawley *(Inspector Manning)*, Frank Sully *(Bigger)*, Claire Carleton *(Ruby Farrell)*, Bernard Nedell *(Waldo)*, Jack Lee *(Sgt. Bradley)*, Francis Pierlot *(Gerald Cotter)*,Myron Healy *(Philip Armstrong)*, Olin Howlin *(Marcus Leblanc)*, Ivan Triesault *(Alfredi)*, Paul E. Burns *(Tom)*, Mary Newton *(Martha)*, Leon Lenoir *(Herrera)*.

Psychiatric symptom forms the basis for the plot of this film in the CRIME DOCTOR series. A jumbled plot with a lot of unexplained twists concerns a WW II vet who comes to Baxter suffering from amnesia. The vet is murdered by two hoods, who in turn are killed by a mysterious woman, thought to be the sister of the vet's fiancee. Baxter finds out that it was the fiancee herself, suffering from a split personality, who became the killer sister and murdered the two hoods. (See CRIME DOCTOR series, Index.)

p, Rudolph C. Flothow; d, William Castle; w, Leigh Brackett (based on a story by Eric Taylor from a radio program, "Crime Doctor," by Max Marcin); ph, Philip Tannura; ed,Dwight Caldwell; md, Mischa Bakaleinikoff; art d, Hans Radon; set d, George Montgomery.
Crime/Mystery **(PR:A MPAA:NR)**

CRIME DOCTOR'S STRANGEST CASE*½ (1943) 68m COL bw
Warner Baxter *(Dr. Robert Ordway)*, Lynn Merrick *(Mrs. Trotter)*, Lloyd Bridges *(Jimmy Trotter)*, Rose Hobart *(Mrs. Burns)*, Barton MacLane *(Rief)*, Virginia Brissac *(Patricia Cornwell)*, Gloria Dickson *(Mrs. Keppler)*, Reginald Denny *(Paul Ashley)*, Sam Flint *(Addison Burns)*, Jerome Cowan *(Malory)*, Constance Worth *(Betty Watson)*, Thomas Jackson *(Yarnell)*, George Lynn *(Walter Burns)*.

Nothing really strange about this film in the CRIME DOCTOR series where Baxter plays the famous psychiatrist who has given up his position on the parole board to practice psychiatry and solve mysteries part time. The story concerns the poisoning of a retired realty operator, who at one time shared in a cafe venture with a man who supposedly vanished with $50,000, but really had been killed. Baxter learns that the nephew of the slain man did the poisoning to get his money. (See CRIME DOCTOR series, Index.)

p, Rudolph C. Flothow; d, Eugene J. Forde; w, Eric Taylor (based on a radio program, "Crime Doctor," by Max Marcin); ph, James S. Brown; ed, Dwight Caldwell; art d, George Van Marten.
Crime/Mystery **(PR:A MPAA:NR)**

CRIME DOCTOR'S WARNING** (1945) 69m COL bw
Warner Baxter *(Dr. Robert Ordway)*, John Litel *(Inspector Dawes)*, Dusty Anderson *(Connie Mace)*, Coulter Irwin *(Clive Lake)*, Miles Mander *(Frederick Malone)*,John Abbott *(Jimmy Gordon)*, Eduardo Ciannelli *(Nick Petroni)*, Alma Kruger *(Mrs. Wellington)*, J. M. Kerrigan *(Robert MacPherson)*, Franco Corsaro *(Joseph Duval)*.

Another good film in the CRIME DOCTOR series finds an artist from New York's Latin Quarter coming to Baxter with complaints of blackout periods during which he cannot be held responsible for his actions. A few models are murdered, and the artist's own model girl friend is found strangled. Baxter goes on the case, faces a few tough situations and finally gets to the bottom of the mystery. (See CRIME DOCTOR series, Index.)

p, Rudolph C. Flothow; d, William Castle; w, Eric Taylor (based on a radio program, "Crime Doctor," by Max Marcin); ph, L. W. O'Connell; ed, Dwight Caldwell; md, Paul Sawtell.
Crime/Mystery **(PR:A MPAA:NR)**

CRIME DOES NOT PAY½**
(1962, Fr.) 159m Transworld Production-G.E.F.-Teledis Films/EM bw
(AKA: THE GENTLE ART OF MURDER)
"The Mask": Edwige Feuillere *(Dona Lucrezia)*, Gabriele Ferzetti *(Giraldi)*, Rosanna Schiaffino *(Francesca)*, Laura Efrikian *(Antonella)*, Gino Cervi, Rina Morelli, Serge Lifar; "The Hugues Case"' Michele Morgan *(Jeanne Hugues)*, Lucienne Bogaert *(Mme. Lenormand)*, Jean Servais *(Vaughan)*, Renaud Mary *(Mon. Lenormand)*, Philippe Noiret *(Mon. Hugues)*, Marie Daems, Claude Cerval; "The Fenayrou Case": Annie Girardot *(Gabrielle Fenayrou)*, Pierre Brasseur *(Martin Fenayrou)*, Christian Marquand *(Louis Aubert)*, Paul Guers *(The Doctor)*; "The Man On The Avenue": Richard Todd *(Col. Roberts)*, Danielle Darrieux *(Mme. Marsais)*, Perrette Pradier *(Helene)*, Louis de Funes *(Bartender)*, Raymond Loyer *(Pierre Marsais)*, Frank Villard, Yves Brainville.

Loyer goes to the cinema and sees a film that depicts three historical murder cases. In the first, Lucrezia Borgia (Feuillere) poisons her lover (Ferzetti), but a maid who secretly loved him avenges his death by coating the inside of Feuillere's nightime beauty mask with acid. In the second story, set in 19th-century Paris, Morgan is wrongly accused of adultery. She sues for libel, but the accuser, a private detective hired by the wife of the man she is alleged to be having an affair with, bribes the jury to acquit him. Morgan kills him, and a sympathetic jury frees her. In the third episode, Girardot maneuvers her husband into killing her unfaithful lover, then turns him into the police, freeing her to take up with a new lover. The two toast each other with a bottle of wine the husband poisoned to kill the lover. The film over, Loyer leaves the theater and is run over by American Army officer Todd. An investigation reveals that Loyer was planning to kill his wife. Overlong,though talented performers keep it interesting. The third episode is the best,the framing story only mediocre.

p, Gilbert Bokanowski; d, Gerard Oury; w, Jean-Charles Tacchella, Paul Gordeuax, Oury; Jean Aurenche, Pierre Bost ("The Mask"); Henri Jeanson, Rene Wheeler ("The Hugues Case"); Jacques Sigurd, Pierre Boileau, Thomas Narcejac ("The Fenayrou Case"); Frederic Dard ("The Man On The Avenue"); ph, Christian Matras; m, Georges Delerue; ed, Roger Dwyre, Raymond Lamy; set d & cos, Georges Wakhevitch.
Crime **(PR:C-O MPAA:NR)**

CRIME IN THE STREETS½** (1956) 91m AA bw
James Whitmore *(Ben Wagner)*, John Cassavetes *(Frankie Dane)*, Sal Mineo *(Baby Gioia)*, Mark Rydell *(Lou Macklin)*, Denise Alexander *(Maria Gioia)*, Malcolm Atterbury *(Mr. McAllister)*, Peter Votrian *(Richie Dane)*, Virginia Gregg *(Mrs. Dane)*, Ray Stricklyn *(Benny)*, Daniel Terranova *(Blockbuster)*, Will Kuluva *(Mr. Gioia)*, Peter Miller *(The Fighter)*, Steve Rowland *(Glasses)*, James Ogg *(Lenny)*, Robert Alexander *(Phil)*, Duke Mitchell *(Herky)*, Richard Curtis *(Redtop)*, Doyle Baker *(Chuck)*.

Siegel followed INVASION OF THE BODY SNATCHERS with low-budget street realism and juvenile delinquency. CRIME IN THE STREETS was originally performed on television on the Elgin Playhouse. Adapted for the screen, the cast still retains Cassavetes, Mineo, and Rydell. Whitmore is the social worker who observes the troubled kids and offers unheeded advice. Cassavetes is the leader of the gang who plots to murder a man who slapped him publicly. Only Mineo, who had just completed REBEL WITHOUT A CAUSE, and Rydell, who later directed THE ROSE and ON GOLDEN POND, go along with his plans. They practice murder on a wino, then go for their real target. They corner the man in an alley, but Cassavetes' younger brother intervenes and keeps him from killing.

p, Vincent M. Fennelly; d, Don Siegel; w, Reginald Rose (based on a television play by Rose); ph, Sam Leavitt; m, Franz Waxman; ed, Richard C. Meyer; art d, Serge Krizman.
Crime **(PR:C-O MPAA:NR)**

CRIME, INC.* (1945) 82m PRC bw
Leo Carrillo *(Tony Marlow)*, Tom Neal *(Jim Riley)*, Martha Tilton *(Betty Van Cleve)*, Lionel Atwill *(Pat Coyle)*,Grant Mitchell *(Wayne Clark)*, Sheldon Leonard *(Capt. Ferrone)*, Harry Shannon *(Commissioner Collins)*, Danny Morton *(Bugs Kelly)*, Virginia Vale *(Trixie Waters)*, Don Beddoe *(Dixon)*, George Meeker *(Parry North)*, Rod Rogers *(Lucas)*, Ed Cronley *(Sgt. Hayes)*, Jack Gordon *(Stecker)*, Monk Friedman *(Convict)*.

An unimpressive gangster film dealing with prohibition-age hoods. The story is built around a respected citizen who also is chairman of the crime syndicate and foreman of the grand jury! A newshound reporter, Neal, exposes them all as the clock ticks mercilessly on.

p, Martin Mooney; d, Lew Landers; w, Ray Shrock (based on a book *Crime Incorporated* by Mooney); ph, James Brown; ed, Roy Livingston; m/l, "I'm Guilty," "Lonely Little Camera Girl" (Jay Livingston, Ray Evans).

Crime (PR:A MPAA:NR)

CRIME NOBODY SAW, THE* (1937) 60m PAR bw
Lew Ayres (*Nicholas Carter*), Ruth Coleman (*Kay Mallory*), Benny Baker (*Horace Smith*), Eugene Pallette (*Babe*), Colin Tapley (*Dr. Brooks*), Howard C. Hickman (*Robert Mallory*), Vivienne Osborne (*Suzanne Duval*), Robert Emmett O'Connor (*Burke*), Jed Prouty (*William Underhill*), Hattie McDaniel (*Ambrosia*), Ferdinand Gottschalk (*John Atherton*).

A comic murder mystery based on a play by Ellery Queen and Lowell Brentano. The film has three playwrights who, just having collected $500 in advance for a mystery play, gather in an apartment to write. A drunk from across the hall enters the apartment and passes out. The three writers pretend he has been murdered, and summon the men he has blackmailed. While interrogating the suspects, someone actually does kill the drunk. The playwrights solve the mystery, find the murderer, and have something to write a play about, they wish.

d, Charles Barton; w, Bertram Millhauser (based on the play "Danger, Men Working" by Ellery Queen and Lowell Brentano); ph, Harry Fischbeck; ed, James Smith.

Comedy/Mystery (PR:A MPAA:NR)

CRIME OF DR. CRESPI, THE** (1936) 64m REP bw
Eric von Stroheim (*Dr. Crespi*), Dwight Frye (*Dr. Thomas*), Paul Guilfoyle (*Dr. Arnold*), Harriet Russell (*Mrs. Ross*), John Bohn (*The Dead Man*), Geraldine Kay (*Miss Rexford*), Jeanne Kelly (*Miss Gordon*), Patsy Berlin (*Jeanne*), Joe Verdi (*Di Angelo*), Dean Raymond (*Minister*).

A bastardization of Edgar Allen Poe's "The Premature Burial" stars von Stroheim in one of his most outrageous roles. Stroheim injects his rival with a drug that induces suspended animation. He then has the rival buried so that he can gloat over the imagined response of the awakened man's reaction to finding himself in a coffin. Von Stroheim is so campy in his portrayal that the film's entertainment comes from its unintentional laughs.

p&d, John H. Auer; w, Lewis Graham, Edward Olmstead (based on a story by Auer from Edgar Allen Poe's "The Premature Burial"); ph, Larry Williams; ed, Leonard Wheeler.

Horror (PR:C MPAA:NR)

CRIME OF DR. FORBES*½ (1936) 75m FOX bw
Gloria Stuart (*Ellen Godfrey*), Robert Kent (*Dr. Michael Forbes*), Henry Armetta (*Luigi*), J. Edward Bromberg (*Dr. Eric Godfrey*), Sara Haden (*Dr. Anna Burkhart*), Alan Dinehart (*Prosecuting Attorney*), Charles Lane (*Defense Attorney*), DeWitt Jennings (*Judge Benson*), Taylor Holmes (*Dr. Robert Empey*), Paul Stanton (*Dr. John Creighton*), Russell Simpson (*Sheriff Neil*), Paul McVey, Charles Crocker-King.

A medical crime tale dealing with mercy killing, this story revolves around a doctor, Bromberg, who suffers a life-debilitating accident. He begs his young protege, Kent, to give him an overdose of an opiate to end his suffering. Kent falls in love with Bromberg's wife, and Bromberg soon after dies of an overdose. Kent is accused of murder and a suspenseful trial ensues. A surprise finish proves that Bromberg killed himself by secretly gathering bits of lethal drugs together until he had enough to ingest fatally.

p, Sol M. Wurtzel; d, George Marshall; w, Frances Hyland, Saul Elkins (based on a story by Elkins and Hyland); ph, Ernest Palmer; m, Gene Rose, Sidney Claire; ed, Alex Troffey; md, Samuel Kaylin.

Crime/Drama (PR:A MPAA:NR)

CRIME OF DR. HALLET* (1938) 65m UNIV bw
Ralph Bellamy (*Dr. Paul Hallet*), William Gargan (*Dr. Jack Murray*), Josephine Hutchinson (*Dr. Mary Reynolds*), Barbara Read (*Claire Saunders*), Nella Walker (*Mrs. Carpenter*), John King (*Dr. Philip Saunders*), Charles Stevens (*Talamu*), Honorable Wu (*Molugi*), Elenor Hansen (*Anna*), Constance Moore (*Susan*).

A far-fetched story of bacteria research in the mosquito-infested jungles of Sumatra has King as a young Park Avenue doctor with a lucrative practice, leaving it to find a cure for the dreaded red fever. King arrives and is given the cold shoulder by the doctors, led by Bellamy, already doing research. Assigned menial tasks, King researches on his own in a jungle clearing. Though he discovers a cure for the fever, he infects himself and accepts the other doctors' cure, proving it is of no value, and he dies as a result. When King's notes are found, the other doctors feel guilty about having treated him shabbily and decide to carry on his research. They finance it by forging $4,000 worth of his travelers checks enabling them to hire a new assistant, Hutchinson, who falls in love with Bellamy. King's wife shows up and charges the doctors with fraud and murder. She succumbs to the fever, and a cure results from her late husband's efforts. Bellamy and Hutchinson proceed as a team and another obstacle is conquered in modern medicine. Remade in 1946 as STRANGE CONQUEST.

d, S. Sylvan Simon; w, Lester Cole, Brown Holmes (based on a story by Cole, Carl Dreher); ph, Milton Krasner; md, Charles Previn.

Drama (PR:A MPAA:NR)

CRIME OF HELEN STANLEY* (1934) 58m COL bw
Ralph Bellamy, Shirley Grey, Gail Patrick, Kane Richmond, Bradley Page, Vincent Sherman, Clifford Jones, Arthur Rankin, Lucien Prival, Ward Bond, Helen Eby-Rock.

Poor murder mystery set in a film studio has Bellamy as the detective trying to solve the murder of an actress. He does the usual finger-pointing until he finds that a movie camera was rigged with a gun that would shoot after a certain number of turns. The killer must have done some enormous camera footage mathematics before he could be sure that the camera would be aiming at that point at the actress, but what formula he used is never explained.

d, D. Ross Lederman; w, Harold Shumate (based on a story by Chas. R. Condon); ph, Al Siegler.

Mystery (PR:A MPAA:NR)

CRIME OF MONSIEUR LANGE, THE**** (1936, Fr.) 90m Oberon/Brandon bw (LE CRIME DE MONSIEUR LANGE)
Rene Lefevre (*Mon. Amedee Lange*), Florelle (*Valentine*), Henri Guisol (*Meunier*), Marcel Levesque (*Bessard, the Concierge*), Odette Talazac (*Mme. Bessard*), Maurice Baquet (*Charles*), Nadia Sibirskaia (*Estelle*), Jules Berry (*Batala*), Sylvia Bataille (*Edith*), Marcel Duhamel, Guy Decomble, Jean Daste, Paul Grimault (*Printers*), Jacques Brunius, Sylvain Itkine (*Retired Police Inspector*), Edmond Beauchamp (*Priest on Train*), Rene Genin (*Customer in Cafe*), Paul Demange (*Creditor*), Claire Gerard (*Prostitute*), Henri Saint-Isles, Max Morise, Fabien Loris, Yves Deniaud, Pierre Huchet, Marcel Lupovici, Jean Bremaud, Janine Loris, Charbonnier.

Lefevre is a meek author of French novels about the American West whose avaricious boss, Berry, cheats him out of his earnings. Berry embezzles the company funds and flees, and is later reported dead in a train wreck. The employees of the publishing house are overjoyed and form a cooperative which is a great success publishing Lefevre's "Arizona Jim" series of novels. Lefevre falls in love with a woman from a neighboring laundry, but then Berry returns (he survived the wreck and took the clothes of a priest). He demands a share in the company's new-found prosperity, but Lefevre decides to kill the villain. Fleeing the murder, Lefevre and his fiancee stop at a cafe where they are recognized by some workers. He tells them the story and they happily help him escape the country. One of Renoir's best films, charming and technically flawless. (In French; English subtitles.)

d, Jean Renoir; w, Jean Castanier, Renoir, Jacques Prevert (based on a story by Castanier); ph, Jean Bachelet; m, Jean Wiener; ed, Marguerite Renoir; set d, Castanier, Robert Gys; m/l, Joseph Kosma.

Comedy/Drama (PR:C-O PAA:NR)

CRIME OF PASSION* (1957) 85m UA bw
Barbara Stanwyck (*Kathy*), Sterling Hayden (*Doyle*), Raymond Burr (*Inspector Pope*), Fay Wray (*Alice Pope*), Royal Dano (*Alidos*), Virginia Grey (*Sara*), Dennis Cross (*Detective Jules*), Robert Griffin (*Detective James*), Jay Adler (*Nalence*), Malcolm Atterbury (*Officer Spitz*), John S. Launer (*Chief of Police*), Brad Trumbull (*Detective Johns*), Skipper McNally (*Detective Jones*), Robert Quarry (*Reporter*), Jean Howell (*Mrs. Jules*), Peg La Centra (*Mrs. James*), Nancy Reynolds (*Mrs. Johns*), Marjorie Owens (*Mrs. Jones*), John Conley (*Delivery Boy*), Stuart Whitman (*Lab Technician*), Eddie Kafafian, Geraldine Wall, Helen Jay, Madelon Erin, Sally Yarnell, Nan Dolan.

Stanwyck is at it again as a ruthlessly ambitious femme fatale and plays this one with all the gusto of an attacking Valkerie. She begins as a tough sob sister columnist for a San Francisco newspaper, managing a terrific scoop by talking a murderess into surrendering to police. Working with her is police lieutenant Hayden whom she visits in Los Angeles before going on to a better media spot in New York City. She becomes involved with Hayden and marries him but bungalow life as a cop's wife proves mundane, and she finds his friends boring. To liven things up, Stanwyck avidly pushes hubby Hayden toward promotion; there's no reason why he shouldn't eventually become chief of police. To help his cause and relieve her own ennui, buttressing Barbara trysts with Burr, Hayden's superior, while firing off countless poison-pen letters that cause Dano, Hayden's friend and rival for a lofty post, to be transferred to a remote position. Burr fails to come through for Stanwyck, double-crossing her by reneging on his promise to promote Hayden and appointing another cop to the top slot. In a rage, Babs steals a gun from the police station and shoots the ignoble Burr dead. Hayden then investigates, tracks down the stolen gun, and arrests his shrike wife, taking her into custody with a sad shake of the head. Strong performances from Stanwyck, Hayden, and Burr cause this outlandish melodrama to rise above its own methodical doom. Stanwyck provides moments of sheer fascination in her cynical portrait of a hardboiled newswoman sneering at middle-class dilemmas, then enacting a part so preposterous as to make her former letter-writers anemic by comparison.

p, Herman Cohen; d, Gerd Oswald; w, Jo Eisinger; ph, Joseph LaShelle; m, Paul Dunlap; ed, Marjorie Fowler; art d, Leslie Thomas; set d, Morrie Hoffman; cos, Grace Houston.

Crime/Drama (PR:C MPAA:NR)

CRIME OF PETER FRAME, THE* (1938, Brit.) 61m Fox British bw (GB: SECOND THOUGHTS)
Frank Fox (*Tony Gordon*), Evelyn Ankers (*Molly Frame*), Frank Allenby (*Peter Frame*), A. Bromley Davenport (*George Gaunt*), Marjorie Fielding (*Mrs. Gaunt*), Joan Hickson (*Ellen*).

Allenby, a chemist disfigured in a lab accident, is driven to drastic measures when he suspects his wife (Ankers) of having an affair with playwright Fox. Undistinguished second feature in spite of all the spent rage.

d, Albert Parker; w, David Evans; ph, Ronald Neame.

Drama (PR:A MPAA:NR)

CRIME OF THE CENTURY, THE* (1933) 72m PAR bw
Jean Hersholt (*Dr. Emil Brandt*), Wynne Gibson (*Mrs. Freda Brandt*), Stuart Erwin (*Dan McKee*), Frances Dee (*Doris Brandt*), David Landau (*Lt. Frank Martin*), Gordon

Westcott (Gilbert Reid), Robert Elliott (Capt. Tim Riley), Torben Meyer (Eric Ericson), Bodil Rosing (Hilda Ericson), Samuel S. Hinds (Philip Ames), William Janney (James Brandt).

A physician is driven to distraction by the demands of a younger second wife. He hypnotizes a bank official and commands him to take $100,000 from the bank, while planning to rob and murder him. He breaks down from revulsion and confesses his intentions to the police. The doctor promises the police he will compel the bank official to return the money, but the official is killed and robbed while the doctor is rendered unconscious by chloroform. A unique scene in the film has an intermission during which a speaker says that crime movies move too fast to be properly solved, and announces a one-minute time-out for reflection and reconstruction. A clock is shown ticking off the seconds, while characters and clues are flashed over the swinging pendulum of the clock. However, the film still holds back the key clue until the very end.

d, William Beaudine; w, Florence Ryerson, Brian Marlow (based on the play "The Grootman Case" by Walter Maria Espe.); ph, David Abel.

Crime/Mystery (PR:A MPAA:NR)

CRIME OF THE CENTURY* (1946) 56m REP bw
Stephanie Bachelor (Audrey Brandon), Michael Browne (Hank Rogers), Martin Kosleck (Paul), Betty Shaw (Margaret Waldham), Paul Stanton (Andrew Madison), Mary Currier (Agatha Waldham), Ray Walker (Jim Rogers), Tom London (Dr. Jackson).

This couldn't even make the crime of the month club. An industrial tycoon attempts to suppress the news of his associate's death for a few days in order to fix a board of directors' election. A newshound gets on the trail of the corpse, and when he gets close to solving the crime he is kidnaped. His brother gets on the trail but is duped by a woman he falls in love with, who works for the tycoon. The dead man's daughter gets on the scene, really making this a family affair, and leads the brother to her dead father, who is lying in a bathtub up to his neck in ice cubes.

p, Walter H. Goetz; d, Philip Ford; w, O'Leta Rhinehart, William Hagens, Gertrude Walker (based on a story by Rhinehart, Hagens); ph, Reggie Lanning; ed, William P. Thompson.

Crime/Drama (PR:A MPAA:NR)

CRIME ON THE HILL* (1933, Brit.) 69m BIP/Wardour bw
Sally Blane (Sylvia Kennett), Nigel Playfair (Dr. Moody), Lewis Casson (Rev. Michael Gray), Anthony Bushell (Tony Fields), Phyllis Dare (Claire Winslow), Judy Kelly (Alice Green), George Merritt (Inspector Wolf), Reginald Purdell (Reporter), Gus McNaughton (Collins), Hal Gordon (Sgt. Granger), Jimmy Godden (Landlord), Hay Petrie (Jevons), Kenneth Kove (Tourist).

Vicar Casson investigates the murder of a rich man and discovers that the man imprisoned for the crime, the fiance of the victim's niece, is innocent. Okay second feature mystery.

d, Bernard Vorhaus; w, Michael Hankinson, Vera Allinson, E. M. Delafield, Bernard Vorhaus (based on a play by Jack de Leon and Jack Celestin).

Crime (PR:A MPAA:NR)

CRIME OVER LONDON* (1936, Brit.) 84m Criterion Film/UA bw
Margot Grahame (Pearl Dupres), Paul Cavanagh (Inspector Gary), Joseph Cawthorn (Sherwood Riley), Basil Sydney (Joker Finnegan), Rene Ray (Joan Vane), Bruce Lister (Ronald Martin), David Burns (Sniffy), Edmon Ryan (Spider), John Darrow (Jim), Danny Green (Klemm), Googie Withers (Miss Dupres).

A British attempt to make the type of gangster picture being made by the dozens in America in the mid-1930s. The story tells of a group of Chicago gangsters who find things too hot on their native soil, and migrate to London. The gang wants to take over the entire town, but the leader keeps them in line until he can find the right job. The leader coerces an aide of a millionaire department store owner to help the gangsters rob the store for everything it's got. Of course, it doesn't work out and the crooks meet with the local bobbies and disaster.

p, Marcel Hellman, Douglas Fairbanks; d, Alfred Zeisler; w, Norman Alexander, Harold French (based on a novel House of a Thousand Windows by Louis de Wohl); ph, Victor Armenise.

Crime (PR:A MPAA:NR)

CRIME PATROL, THE* (1936) 58m Empire bw
Ray Walker (Bob Neal), Geneva Mitchell (Mary Prentiss), Herbert Corthell (Commissioner Cullen), Hooper Atchley (Dr. Simmons), Wilbur Mack (Vic Santell), Russ Clark (Patrolman Davis), Max Wagner (Bennie), Virginia True Boardman (Mrs. Neal), Henry Roquemore (Fight Promoter), Snub Pollard (Gyp).

A so-so crime film has young prize fighter Walker joining the police department so he can take advantage of the police gym facilities and boxing instruction. However, law and order gets into his blood as he goes through training and falls in love. At the end of the film he outwits a holdup mob from his own neighborhood, rescues a couple of cops who were being held hostage, and gets the girl.

p, Harry S. Knight; d, Eugene Cummings; w, Betty Burbridge (based on a story by Arthur T. Horman); ph, Bert Longenecker.

Crime (PR:A MPAA:NR)

CRIME RING* (1938) 69m RKO bw
Allan Lane (Joe), Frances Mercer (Judy Allen), Clara Blandick (Phoebe Sawyer), Inez Courtney (Kitty), Bradley Page (Whitmore), Ben Welden (Nate), Walter Miller (Jenner), Frank M. Thomas (Redwine), Jack Arnold (Buzzell), Morgan Conway (Taylor), George Irving (Clifton), Leona Roberts (Mrs. Wharton), Charles Trowbridge (Marvin), Tom Kennedy (Dummy), Paul Fix (Slim), Jack Mulhall (Brady).

An unexciting film about a fledgling reporter's fight against phony clairvoyants. A ring of bogus fortune tellers works with a group of stock swindlers who lead their clients to believe they are guided by the spirits when making investments which prove unsound. Reporter Lane and an out-of-work actress, Mercer, go undercover with an elaborate plan and succeed in smashing the ring.

p, Cliff Reid; d, Leslie Goodwins; w, J. Robert Bren, Gladys Atwater (based on a story by Reginald Taviner); ph, Jack MacKenzie; md, Roy Webb.

Crime (PR:A MPAA:NR)

CRIME SCHOOL** (1938) 90m FN/WB bw
Billy Halop (Frankie Warren), Bobby Jordan (Squirt), Huntz Hall (Goofy), Leo Gorcey (Spike), Bernard Punsly (Fats), Gabriel Dell (Bungs), Humphrey Bogart (Mark Braden), Gale Page (Sue Warren), George Offerman. Jr. (Red), Weldon Heyburn (Cooper), Cy Kendall (Morgan), Charles Trowbridge (Judge Clinton), Milburn Stone (Joe Delaney), Harry Cording (Guard), Spencer Charters (Old Doctor), Donald Briggs (New Doctor), Frank Jaquet (Commissioner), Helen MacKellar (Mrs. Burke), Al Bridge (Mr. Burke), Sybil Harris (Mrs. Hawkins), Paul Porcasi (Nick Papadopolo), Jack Mower (John Brower), Frank Otto (Junkie), Ed Gargan (Officer Hogan), James B. Carson (Schwartz), John Ridgely (Reporter), Harry Cording (Official), Hally Chester (Boy).

A follow up to the movie DEAD END has the "Dead End Kids" in another adventure. This time they are in a film which attempts to make a commentary on reform schools, and how they teach the youngsters criminal behavior instead of reforming them. The gang is thrown into the Gatesville Reformatory, which teaches discipline at the end of a cat-o'-nine-tails. The boys are in a bad situation, and settle down to make the best of the bad bargain handed them by the juvenile court. Bogart, who is machine gunned at the end of DEAD END, plays the deputy commissioner of corrections who comes to Gatesville on a surprise inspection. He fires the cruel and corrupt warden and introduces humane methods of dealing with the boys. They in turn save Bogart from a political double-cross. The boys are paroled for good behavior and the reformatory is truly reformed. Remade in 1939 as HELLS KITCHEN. Based on the MAYOR OF HELL.

d, Lewis Seiler; w, Wilbur and Vincent Sherman (based on a story by Crane Wilbur); ph, Arthur Todd; m, Max Steiner; ed, Terry Morse; md, Hugo Friedhoffer, George Parish; art d, Charles Novi; cos, N'Was McKenzie.

Comedy/Drama (PR:AA MPAA:NR)

CRIME TAKES A HOLIDAY** (1938) 59m COL bw
Jack Holt (Walter Forbes), Marcia Ralston (Peggy Stone), Russell Hopton (Jerry Clayton), Douglass Dumbrille (J. J. Grant), Arthur Hohl (Joe), Thomas Jackson (Brennan), John Wray (Howell), William Pawley (Spike), Paul Fix (Louie), Harry Woods (Stoddard), Joe Crehan (Gou Allen).

Less than shining crime picture which coincided with the Thomas Dewey-Herbert Lehman New York race for governor. The resemblances were then timely, but now long forgotten. Holt, a tough-as-can-be district attorney who rarely loses a case, is urged into the political arena. In the process, courtroom drama has him knowingly pin a rap on an innocent man to pry out a mobster's guilt. Holt's performance is outstanding, though technically the film isn't up to his level.

d, Lewis D. Collins; w, Jefferson Parker, Henry Altimus, Charles Logue; ph, James S. Brown, Jr.

Crime (PR:A MPAA:NR)

CRIME UNLIMITED* (1935, Brit.) 72m FN/WB bw
Esmond Knight (Pete Borden), Lilli Palmer (Natasha), Cecil Parker (Assistant Commissioner), George Merritt (Inspector Cardby), Raymond Lovell (Delaney), Wyndham Goldie (Conway Addison), Peter Gawthorne (Newall), Jane Millican (Lady Sybil), Stella Arbenina (Lady Mead).

Pedestrian picture which has a private eye disguised as a jewel thief to crack a crime ring. The film marked the screen debut of Lilli Palmer, the love interest in this otherwise totally undistinguished film.

p, Irving Asher; d, Ralph Ince; w, Brock Williams, Ralph Smart (based on the novel by David Hume); ph, Basil Emmott.

Crime (PR:A MPAA:NR)

CRIME WAVE½** (1954) 73m WB bw (GB: THE CITY IS DARK)
Sterling Hayden (Detective Sgt. Sims), Gene Nelson (Steve Lacey), Phyllis Kirk (Ellen), Ted de Corsia ("Doc" Penny), Charles Buchinsky [Bronson] (Hastings), Jay Novello (Dr. Otto Hessler), James Bell (Daniel O'Keefe), Dub Taylor (Gus Snider), Gayle Kellogg (Kelly), Mack Chandler (Sully), Timothy Carey (Johnny), Richard Benjamin (Mark), Sandy Sanders, Harry Lauter, Dennis Dengate, Joe Bassett, Fred Boby (Officers), Diane Fortier, Mary Alan Hokanson, Ruth Lee, Eileen Elliott (Police Announcers), Fritz Feld, Bill Schroff (Men), Shirley O'Hara, Shirley Whitney (Girls), Charles Cane, Don Gibson, Bert Moorhouse, Jack Kenney (Detectives), Harry Wilson (Parolee), Jack Woody (Stoolie), Hank Worden (Sweeney), Ted Ryan (Janitor), Tommy Jackson (Guard), Iris Adrian (Hasting's Girl Friend), Mary Newton (Mrs. O'Keefe), Faith Kruger, Tom Clarke (Salvation Army Singers), Guy Wilkerson, Lyle Latell (Hoodlums).

Low-budget story where the title tells all. Nelson, forsaking his dancing shoes, is an ex-convict now on parole and trying to make a success out of the straight life with wife Kirk. Hayden is a tough cop in the mold of Kirk Douglas's character in DETECTIVE STORY. He hates criminals with a burning passion and trusts no one who has ever been "inside." Charles Buchinsky (Bronson), De Corsia, and Carey are three escapees from San Quentin who come to Nelson's home to hide out. Nelson, to save his life and keep Kirk away from crazy Carey, agrees to help them. Meanwhile, Hayden is keeping an eye on Nelson. He comes to Nelson's home on information from fink Novello who is promptly killed by Buchinsky. Carey is also killed and Buchinsky and De Corsia take Nelson and Kirk to Chinatown where they will stay under cover for a while as they plan their big score, a bank robbery. Nelson leaves a clue behind in his house and Hayden tracks the crooks down. The final sequence at the bank has the cops lying in wait for the crooks, a big shootout, and a happy ending. Nelson is most believable in a nonhoofing role. He continued that side of his career, and then into directing, with some success. The same was true for a young bit player (Mark), named Richard Benjamin. This was his second film at age 15. His first was THUNDER OVER THE PLAINS. CRIME WAVE was a good example of the *film noir* genre; anti-heros alienated from society, emotionally-uninvolved protagonists, etc. Director DeToth was not particularly known for this type of film (his only other was PITFALL). Actually, the movie made by this same producer/director/writer team just prior to CRIME WAVE was HOUSE OF WAX, which was Bronson's tenth picture and the one that brought him to national prominence as Vincent Price's personal Igor-like assistant.

p, Bryan Foy; d, Andre DeToth; w, Crane Wilbur, Bernard Gordon, Richard Wormser (based on a story by John and Ward Hawkins); ph, Bert Glennon; m, David Buttolph; ed, Thomas Reilly; art d, Stanley Fleischer.

Crime Drama (PR:A-C MPAA:NR)

CRIME WITHOUT PASSION***   (1934) 70m PAR bw

Claude Rains (*Lee Gentry*), Margo (*Carmen Brown*), Whitney Bourne (*Katy Costello*), Stanley Ridges (*Eddie White*), Paula Trueman (*Buster Malloy*), Leslie Adams (*O'Brien*), Greta Granstedt (*Della*), Esther Dale (*Miss Keeley*), Charles Kennedy (*Lt. Norton*), Fuller Mellish (*Judge*), Ben Hecht, Charles MacArthur (*Reporters*), Helen Hayes (*Woman in Hotel Lobby*), Fanny Brice (*Woman Sitting in Lobby*), Marjorie Main (*Woman*).

A lightning film loosely based on New York City criminal lawyer William J. Fallon, the great "mouthpiece" for criminals during the 1920s. This superb drama is an all-Hecht-and-MacArthur production, with Rains playing the suave, ever-confident legal wizard. The film opens with Rains defending a killer who is obviously guilty; the lawyer gets him off with a startling trick, snatching up and drinking "Exhibit A," a vial supposedly containing poison used by the murderer. (He then has his stomach pumped during a recess.) But where the lawyer shines in his profession, he barely flickers in his love life, trapped by vixen Margo, a honky tonk singer who is insanely jealous of him. Though he is attempting to dump her for the affections of Bourne, a hot blonde, Margo inveigles him into shooting her. Thinking her dead, he prepares an elaborate alibi which involves the killing of another man. Margo survives to haunt him in court and the real killing is finally laid at his door in a surprise ending where Rains tries to shoot himself. Hecht and MacArthur directed this minor masterpiece and used imaginative techniques in almost every frame. (They even appear before the cameras as newsmen interviewing Rains after a legal victory; Helen Hayes, MacArthur's wife, can be seen in a hotel lobby, sitting in a chair and looking almost directly at the camera which substitutes for Rains moving quickly through the lobby, hurrying to establish an alibi.) The opening and closing credits for this film show three female "Furies" darting through the canyons of New York, selecting their victims at random, those whom they will make mad and upon whom they will visit their evil ways—a marvelous bit of special effects constructed by Stavko Vorkapich. Garmes' camerawork is fluid and his scenes beautifully lit. Hecht unselfishly gave credit to Garmes for the overall quality of this film, as well as others where he collaborated with the talented cameraman (THE SCOUNDREL, SPECTER OF THE ROSE, ACTORS AND SIN): "Standing on a set, Lee saw a hundred more things than I did," he would later write in *A Child of the Century.* "He saw shadows around mouths and eyes invisible to me, high lights on desk tops, ink stands, and trouser legs. He spotted wrong reflections and mysterious obstructions—shoulders that blocked faces in the backgrounds, hands that masked distant and vital objects. These were all hazards that no look of mine could detect. He corrected them with a constant murmur of instructions . . . . As the director of the movie being shot, I was the final word on all matters. But I would sit by silent and full of admiration as Lee and his overalled magicians prepared the set for my 'direction.'" This one should not be missed by any film noir fan.

p,d&w, Ben Hecht, Charles MacArthur; ph, Lee Garmes; spec eff, Stavko Vorkapich.

Crime/Drama (PR:A MPAA:NR)

CRIMES AT THE DARK HOUSE½**   (1940, Brit.) 69m Pennant/BL bw

Tod Slaughter (*Sir Percival Glyde*), Hilary Eaves (*Marian Fairlie*), Sylvia Marriott (*Laura Fairlie*), Hay Petrie (*Dr. Fosco*), Geoffrey Wardwell (*Paul Hartwright*), David Horne (*Mr. Fairlie*), Margaret Yarde (*Mrs. Bullen*).

Slaughter was a singular institution in British theater, touring the country in lurid melodramas camped up into absurdity like SWEENEY TODD and SEXTON BLAKE AND THE HOODED TERROR. Most of these were filmed and CRIMES AT THE DARK HOUSE is one of the best, adapted from Wilkie Collins' 1860 novel. Slaughter kills his rich wife and replaces her with a double, an escaped lunatic from the local asylum. Pretty entertaining if you don't take it seriously. Warner Bros. remade the story as THE WOMAN IN WHITE in 1948 with Alexis Smith and Sidney Greenstreet, but it was a dud.

p&d, George King; w, Edward Dryhurst, Frederick Hayward, H. F. Maltby (based on the novel *The Woman In White* by Wilkie Collins); Hone Glendinning.

Crime (PR:A-C MPAA:NR)

CRIMES OF STEPHEN HAWKE, THE**   (1936, Brit.) MGM bw

Tod Slaughter (*Stephen Hawke*), Marjorie Taylor (*Julia Hawke*), Eric Portman (*Matthew Trimble*), Gerald Barry (*Miles Archer*), Ben Soutten (*Nathaniel*), D. J. Williams (*Joshua Trimble*), Charles Penrose (*Sir Franklyn*), Norman Pierce (*Landlord*), Mr. Flotsam and Mr. Jetsam.

Another of Slaughter's Grand Guignol horror stories is brought from the stage to the screen with Slaughter a royal moneylender who spends his spare time breaking the spines of strangers. Light, lurid entertainment.

p&d, George King; w, H. F. Maltby (based on a story by Jack Celestin); ph, Ronald Neame.

Crime (PR:A-C MPAA:NR)

CRIMES OF THE FUTURE*½   (1969, Can.) 65m CRONENBERG bw

Ronald Mlodzik, Jon Lidolt, Tania Zolty, Jack Messinger, Paul Mulholland, William Haslem, Willem Poolman.

Canadian horror king Cronenberg's extremely low-budget follow up to his equally cheap film STEREO (1969) sees a society in the near future where most of the women have died off due to an airborne contaminant triggered by additives in cosmetics. The disease causes the victims to bleed various colored fluids from the nose and mouth which is eventually followed by death. A cult springs up of men who have become pedophiliacs who want to mate with children because all the women of child-bearing age have expired. The plot revolves around the kidnaping of a five-year-old girl by these men and the subsequent efforts of Owen, an agent for the Institute of Skin (who is trying to find a cure for the disease), to find the missing child. Unfortunately, the execution of this interesting premise turns the film into a slow (extremely long, static takes), dull thriller with no soul. Cronenberg's subsequent work (THEY CAME FROM WITHIN, RABID, THE BROOD, SCANNERS, the completely incomprehensible VIDEODROME, and the *only* successful adaptation of Stephen King, THE DEAD ZONE) all expand upon the director's favorite "adult" themes of irresponsible science, repression, and sick sexuality, with wildly uneven degrees of success. Cronenberg has a legion of followers but he is a sporadically interesting filmmaker at best whose intellectual ramblings tend to confuse his narratives.

p,d,w&ph, David Cronenberg.

Science Fiction/Horror (PR:O MPAA:NR)

CRIMINAL, THE   (SEE: CONCRETE JUNGLE, THE, 1962)

CRIMINAL AT LARGE*   (1932, Brit.) 87m Gainsborough/BL bw
                              (AKA: THE FRIGHTENED LADY)

Emlyn Williams (*Lord Lebanon*), Cathleen Nesbitt (*Lady Lebanon*), Norman McKinnel (*Chief Inspector Tanner*), Gordon Harker (*Sgt. Toddy*), Cyril Raymond (*Sgt. Ferraby*), Belle Chrystall (*Aisla Crane*), D. A. Clarke-Smith (*Dr. Amersham*), Percy Parsons (*Gilder*), Finlay Currie (*Brooks*), Julian Royce (*Kelver*), Eric Roland (*Stedd*).

This stodgy British mystery, though cleverly scripted, can't rise up from under its stiff, calculated performances. Shadowing a mad killer, McKinnel gives the only tolerable performance as a police inspector fine-toothing a dark and dreary castle.

p, Michael Balcon; d, T. Hayes Hunter; w, Edgar Wallace, Angus Macphail (based on Wallace's story and stageplay "The Frightened Lady").

Mystery (PR:A MPAA:NR)

CRIMINAL CODE**   (1931) 96m COL bw

Walter Huston (*Warden Brady*), Philliis Holmes (*Robert Graham*), Constance Cummings (*Mary Brady*), Mary Doran (*Gertrude Williams*), DeWitt Jennings (*Gleason*), John Sheehan (*McManus*), Boris Karloff (*Ned Galloway*), Otto Hoffman (*Fales*), Clark Marshall (*Runch*), Arthur Hoyt (*Nettleford*), Ethel Wales (*Katie*), Nicholas Soussanin (*Dr. Rinewulf*), Paul Porcasi (*Spelvin*), James Guilfoyle (*Doran*), Lee Phelps (*Doherty*), Hugh Walker (*Lew*), Jack Vance (*Reporter*), John St. Polis, Andy Devine.

This Howard Hawks prison opus is a melodramatic bust, creaking with silent film techniques and dialog best described as inane. Holmes kills a man while defending the honor of his date after a night on the town. Huston, the D.A., convicts the youth quickly and is later put in charge of the very prison where Holmes resides. He attempts to befriend Holmes, whom he believes to be a decent person, but the new convict has nothing but contempt for the new warden. Huston gives Holmes a job as a chauffeur; he must drive his daughter Cummings about and the two fall in love. When a ruthless killer murders squealer Marshall, Holmes refuses to tell Huston who did it, maintaining the so-called criminal code. The killer is Karloff, who gives chilling performance as the trusty killer. Holmes is sent to solitary confinement where he languishes until Karloff confesses. Based on a successful Broadway play, the script offered little sparkle other than innumerable "yeahs." Huston is terrific and keeps the film from sinking altogether, but many of his scenes are stolen by Karloff in a striking role of a tough convict. This role was later enacted by Marc Lawrence in the remake of this film, PENITENTIARY, 1938, and by Millard Mitchell in a third version, CONVICTED, 1950. A segment from THE CRIMINAL CODE was used in TARGETS, 1967. Huston appeared in the film STAR WITNESS which is almost identical in plot in the same year, 1931.

p, Harry Cohn; d, Howard Hawks; w, Fred Niblo, Jr., Seton I. Miller (based on the play by Martin Flavin); ph, James Wong Howe; ed, Edward Curtis.

Prison Drama (PR:A MPAA:NR)

CRIMINAL CONVERSATION½**   (1980, Ireland) 61m BAC Films c

Emmet Bergin (*Frank*), Deirdre Donnelly (*Margaret*), Peter Caffrey (*Charlie*), Leslie Lalor (*Bernadette*), Kate Thompson (*Susan*), Garrett Keogh (*Student*).

An intelligent low-budgeter from Ireland which chiefly suffers from it's ethnicity. The title comes from the Irish legal term for which a husband victimized by his wife's adultery can sue the other man for damages. After a Christmas Eve with too much Irish coffee, one of the men decides to tell all present that he has been bedding the other's wife. Pulling between comic and dramatic bounds, this picture is a fine example of the future of filmmaking in the Irish Free State.

d, Kieran Hickey; w, Hickey, Philip Davison; ph, Sean Corcoran; ed, J. Patrick Duffner.

Drama (PR:C MPAA:NR)

CRIMINAL COURT* (1946) 63m RKO bw
Tom Conway (*Steve Barnes*), Martha O'Driscoll (*Georgia Gale*), June Clayworth (*Joan Mason*), Robert Armstrong (*Vic Wright*), Addison Richards (*District Attorney*), Pat Gleason (*Joe West*), Steve Brodie (*Frankie*), Robert Warwick (*Marquette*), Phil Warren (*Bill Brannegan*), Joe Devlin (*Brownie*), Lee Bonnell (*Gil Lambert*), Robert Clarke (*Dance Director*).

A fine display of criminal investigation for the big screen. Produced by ex-crime reporter Martin Mooney, this one packs the wallop of a tough newspaper piece. Conway plays the bright young lawyer with well-known courtroom antics who accidentally kills a disliked barkeep. His unassuming dame is unlucky enough to stumble upon his body, taking the rap for his death. Through his outlandish courtroom technique, Conway tries to prove that it was he who murdered the man. Eventually the jury swallows the story, acquitting both Conway and the girl. Well-directed with due credit going to director Wise for his extraordinary pacing.

p, Martin Mooney; d, Robert Wise; w, Lawrence Kimble (based on a story by Earl Felton); ph, Frank Redman; m, Paul Sawtell; ed, Robert Swink; md, C. Bakaleinikoff; spec eff, Russell A. Cully.

Crime (PR:A MPAA:NR)

CRIMINAL LAWYER (1937) 72m RKO bw
Lee Tracy (*Brandon*), Margot Grahame (*Madge Carter*), Eduardo Ciannelli (*Larkin*), Erik Rhodes (*Bandini*), Betty Lawford (*Molly Walker*), Frank M. Thomas (*William Walker*), Wilfred Lucas (*Brandon's Assistant*), William Stack (*District Attorney Hopkins*).

A familiar story about a district attorney, Tracy, promoted with the help of a mob kingpin. While being primed for the job of governor, Tracy must defend the mobster who relies on the testimony of Tracy's girl friend, Grahame, for his freedom. To protect him, Grahame passes a phony story off to the jury which doesn't gel with Tracy who has a change of heart because of his love for Grahame. He gets to the bottom of the scam, ruining the mobster's career but also exposing his own spotted connections. He, however, gains the respect of the girl who eyes him lovingly. Adding some lighter moments is the comic delivery of the tune, "Tonight, Lover, Tonight" (Jack Stern, Harry Tobias). A remake of the successful 1932 film STATE'S ATTORNEY.

p, Cliff Reid; d, Christy Cabanne; w, G. V. Atwater, Thomas Lennon (based on the story by Louis Stevens); ph, David Abel; m, Jack Stern, Harry Tobias; ed, Jack Hively.

Crime/Drama (PR:A MPAA:NR)

CRIMINAL LAWYER½ (1951) 73m COL bw
Pat O'Brien (*James Regan*), Jane Wyatt (*Maggie Powell*), Carl Benton Reid (*Tucker Bourne*), Mary Castle (*Gloria Lydendecker*), Robert Shayne (*Clark Sommers*), Mike Mazurki ("*Moose*" *Hendricks*), Jerome Cowan (*Walter Medford*), Marvin Kaplan (*Sam Kutler*), Douglas Fowley (*Harry Cheney*), Mickey Knox (*Vincent Cheney*), Louis Jean Heydt (*Frank Burnett*), Harlan Warde (*Byron Claymore*), Wallis Clark (*Melville Webber*), Mary Alan Hokanson (*Mrs. Johnson*), Lewis Martin (*Judge Selders*), Charles Lane (*Frederick Waterman*), Guy Beach (*Edward Cranston*), Grandon Rhodes (*Judge Larrabee*), Darryl Hickman (*Bill Webber*).

A courtroom drama which boasts O'Brien in an effortless role as a top-notch attorney capable of buying off both judges and jury. When the bar association holds back its endorsement, the disgruntled lawyer takes to the bottle. However, he is soon working his way back to his usual prowess. Praiseworthy for its fresh and thoughtful character study.

p, Rudolph C. Flothow; d, Seymour Friedman; w, Harold R. Greene; ph, Philip Tannura; ed, Charles Nelson.

Drama (PR:A MPAA:NR)

CRIMINAL LIFE OF ARCHIBALDO DE LA CRUZ, THE*½
(1962, Mex.) 91m Alianza Cinematografica/Dan Talbot bw
(ENSAYO DE UN CRIMEN; AKA: REHEARSAL FOR A CRIME)
Ernesto Alonso (*Archibaldo de la Cruz*), Miroslava (*Lavinia*), Rita Macedo (*Patricia*), Ariadne Welter (*Carlota*), Rodolfo Landa (*Alejandro*), Andrea Palma (*Cervantes*), Carlos Riquelme (*Chief of Police*), Jose Maria Linares Rivas (*Willy*), Leonor Llausas (*Governess*), Eva Calvo (*Mother*), Carlos Martinez Baena, Roberto Meyer.

As a child, Alonso wishes death on a governess using a music box he believes is magic. Later the woman is killed by a stray bullet, and, in a strangely erotic sequence, dies in front of the boy with her dress hiked up and displaying her beautiful legs. He grows up associating sexual desire with killing, and as a man he finds the long-lost music box in a junk store. Taking it home, he formulates plans for the murder of pretty women. Before he can act, though, the women always die sudden deaths, either accidental or criminal. Tormented by guilt from these deaths, Alonso confesses to the police but they laugh him out of the station. One woman he plans to kill, a model, tells him that he can find her at a certain department store. There, he finds only a mannequin in the girl's image, and taking it he places it in an oven and burns it. Finally unable to live with his guilt, Alonso takes his music box and throws it off a bridge. Just then the model walks by whose effigy he burned. They smile at one another and walk off hand in hand. The twelfth film Bunuel made in five years after the release of LOS OLVIDADOS put him back on the world film scene. It is a mysterious, subtly erotic film about intellectualized passion. Alonso is not driven by a desire to kill women so much as a desire to recreate the feeling of power and sex and sudden freedom that the sight of blood slowly trickling down the shapely stockinged leg of his governess gave him. When he finds the music box in the shop, it brings that sensation to the forefront of his memories. It is beautifully photographed and full of the surreal touches Bunuel is famous for. The scene where the mannequin is burned—coming to horrible melting life in the oven—is comparable to the famous scene of the razor slicing the eyeball UN CHIEN ANDALOU. Definitely not for everyone, but a fascinating, haunting film by one of the cinema's most important figures. (In Spanish; English subtitles.)

p, Alfonso Patino Gomez; d, Luis Bunuel; w, Bunuel, Eduardo Ugarte Pages (based on

a story by Rodolfo Usigli); ph, Agustin Jimenez; m, Jorge Perez; ed, Jorge Bustos; art d, Jesus Bracho.

Comedy/Drama (PR:O MPAA:NR)

CRIMINALS OF THE AIR (1937) 61m COL bw
Rosalind Keith (*Nancy Rawlings*) Charles Quigley (*Mark Owens*), Rita Hayworth (*Rita*), John Gallaudet (*Ray Patterson*), Marc Lawrence (*Blast Reardon*), Patricia Farr (*Mamie*), John Hamilton (*Capt. Wallace*), Ralph Byrd (*Williamson*), Walter Soderling (*Camera-Eye Condon*), Russell Hicks (*Kurt Feldon*), Johnny Tyrrell (*Bill Morris*), Lester Dorr (*Trigger*), Frank Sully (*Contact*), Herbert Heywood (*Hot-Cake Joe*), Lucille Lund (*Ruby*), Crawford Weaver (*Ronnie*), Ruth Hilliard (*Ronnie's Wife*), Matty Kemp (*Arnold*), Robert Fiske (*Groom*), Martha Tibbetts (*Bride*), Howard C. Hickman (*Harrison*), Sam Flint (*Chafin*), Eddie Fetherston (*Simmons*), Jay Eaton (*Harry the Actor*), Jane Weir (*Actor's Wife*), Norman Pabst (*Field Porter*), Sammy Blum (*Bartender*), Richard Botiller (*Mike*).

The criminals referred to in the title are smugglers who are using quickie border marriages as their cover. Quigley is on their trail as a hired cop, while Keith is also digging up facts for the press. Quigley meets up with the energetic Hayworth south of the border as she performs an eye-opening dance number. A stock drama which isn't short of thrills.

d, C. C. Coleman, Jr.; w, Owen Francis (based on a story by Jack Cooper); ph, George Meehan; ed, Dick Fantl.

Crime/Drama (PR:A MPAA:NR)

CRIMINALS WITHIN zero (1941) 67m PRC bw
Eric Linden (*Greg*), Ann Doran (*Linda*), Constance Worth (*Alma*), Donald Curtis (*Lt. Harmon*), Weldon Heyburn (*Sgt. Blake*), Ben Alexander (*Sgt. Paul*), Dudley Dickerson (*Sam Dillingham*), Bernie Pilot (*Mamie*), Ray Erlenborn (*Private Norton*), I. Stanford Jolley (*Cobbler*), Emmett Vogan (*Harold*), Robert Frazer (*Capt. Bryant*), Boyd Irwin (*Col. Longstreet*), William Ruhl (*Capt. Grey*).

A confused search for the killer of a chemist is the subject of this poorly executed script. Slowed with useless baggage, the hero tries to uncover the leader of a spy ring in order to save the lives of the dead man's colleagues and save a secret formula. Oddly, the well-cast women's roles are cut short: the delectable Worth's part expires at the half-way point, at which time reporter Doran is first seen.

p, E. B. Derr; d, Joseph Lewis; w, Arthur Hoerl; ph, Arthur Martinelli; ed, Howard Dillinger.

Crime (PR:A MPAA:NR)

CRIMSON ALTAR, THE (SEE: CRIMSON CULT, THE, 1968, Brit.)

CRIMSON BLADE, THE (1964, Brit.) 83m COL c
(AKA: THE SCARLET BLADE)
Lionel Jeffries (*Col. Judd*), Oliver Reed (*Sylvester*), Jack Hedley (*Edward*), June Thorburn (*Clare*), Michael Ripper (*Pablo*), Harold Goldblatt (*Jacob*), Duncan Lamont (*Maj. Bell*), Clifford Elkin (*Philip*), Suzan Farmer (*Constance*), John Harvey (*Sgt. Grey*), Charles Houston (*Drury*), Michael Byrne (*Lt. Hawke*), John Stewart (*Beverley*), Harry Towb (*Cobb*), Robert Rietty (*King Charles I*), John H. Watson (*Fitzroy*), Douglas Blackwell (*Blake*), Leslie Glazer (*Gonzales*), John Woodnutt (*Lt. Wyatt*), Eric Corrie (*Duncannon*), Denis Holmes (*Chaplain*).

Seventeenth-century England is the backdrop for this historical drama centered around King Charles' Royalists and Oliver Cromwell's underground resistance, and a romance between two young people on opposite sides in the struggle. The technically skilled Jeffries is tugged back and forth between his daughter's loyalty to the throne and his loyalty to Cromwell. Reed is commendable as Jeffries' aide and the lover of his daughter.

p, Anthony Nelson Keys; d&w, John Gilling; ph, Jack Asher (MegaScope, Eastmancolor); m, Gary Hughes; ed, John Dunsford; prod d, Bernard Robinson; md, John Hollingsworth; art d, Don Mingaye; spec eff, Les Bowie.

Historical Drama (PR:A MPAA:NR)

CRIMSON CANARY* (1945) 64m UNIV bw
Noah Beery, Jr. (*Danny*), Lois Collier (*Jean*), Danny Morton (*Johnny*), John Litel (*Quinn*), Claudia Drake (*Anita*), Steven Geray (*Vic*), James Dodd (*Chuck*), Steve Brodie (*Hillary*), John Kellogg (*Pete*), Arthur Space (*Carlisle*), Christine MacIntyre (*Anita's Roommate*), Josh White (*Singing Specialty*), Esquire All-American Band Winners Coleman Hawkins, Oscar Pettiford.

Accusations swing back and forth between two suspect members of a jazz band on the brink of success as their female lead singer is found dead. On the night before they are to leave a small town for San Francisco, their plans are tragically affected. Equal attention is paid to both suspects and their motives—Morton is found drunk the morning after in the dead lady's room suffering from a blackout, while trumpet blower Beery, Jr., is spotted leaving her place with a dented horn in hand. The beat picks up near the coda when it is discovered that the night spot owner is the guilty one, killing the singer because he didn't want her to leave town with the jazz-makers—though that's certainly not the best way to do it. Cool tunes color this one as hot—"The Walls of Jericho," "One Meatball (and No Spaghetti)," "I Never Knew I Could Love Anybody," and "China Boy."

p, Bob Faber; d, John Hoffman; w, Henry Blankfort, Peggy Phillips, (based on a story by Phillips); ph, Jerome Ash; m, Edgar Fairchild; ed, Paul Landres.

Thriller (PR:A MPAA:NR)

CRIMSON CANDLE, THE*½ (1934, Brit.) 67m MGM bw
Derek Williams (*Leonard Duberley*), Kynaston Reeves (*Inspector Blunt*), Eliot

Makeham *(Dr. Gaunt)*, Eve Gray, Arthur Goullet, Kenneth Kove, Eugene Leahy, Audrey Cameron.

Williams is convinced that a family curse will claim his life before the night is over, but inspector Reeves suspects Williams' stepmother and her son of trying to get him out of the way by frightening him to death. In the morning Williams is dead, but doctor Makeham proves that the jilted maid (Cameron) killed her employer/lover. Won't light up your life.

p,d&w, Bernard Mainwaring.

Crime **(PR:A-C MPAA:NR)**

CRIMSON CIRCLE, THE* (1930, Brit.) 70m British International/International Photoplay bw

Stewart Rome, Lya Mara, Hans Marlow, Louis Lerch, John Castle, Albert Steinrueck, Otto Walldurg.

Troubled by its challenging structure, this partially silent picture has a hidden plot which is eventually revealed through flashbacks. A corrupt youth blackmails prominent men with threatening messages bordered by a crimson circle. Eventually leading to a trio of deaths, he becomes feared and hunted. His love for the daughter of the police inspector, who is a policewoman, leads to his demise. This film is the sound remake of the 1915 Cinema Club movie of the same name, but a confusing recreation of the novel's suspense technique.

d, Friedrich Zelnik (dialogue sequences directed by Sinclair Hill); w, Howard Caye (based on the novel by Edgar Wallace); ph, Karl Puth; m, Edmund Meisel.

Mystery **(PR:A MPAA:NR)**

CRIMSON CIRCLE,THE** (1936, Brit.) 75m/60m DuWorld/UNIV bw

Hugh Wakefield *(Derek Yale)*, Alfred Drayton *(Inspector Parr)*, Niall McGinnis *(Jack Beardmore)*, June Duprez *(Sylvia Hammond)*, Paul Blake *(Sgt. Webster)*, Noah Beery *(Felix Marl)*, Basil Gill *(James Beardmore)*, Gordon McLeod *(Inspector Brabazon)*, Renee Gadd *(Millie Macroy)*, Ralph Truman *(Lawrence Fuller)*, Robert Rendell *(Commissioner)*.

Sloppily edited film, again based on Edgar Wallace's blackmail novel, was tightened by fifteen minutes shortly after its release. The movie concerns the head of an extortion ring and his attempts to outwit Scotland Yard by becoming an amateur private eye and mingling with the big boys. Equal attention is devoted to the criminal's scheming as to the Yard's thwarted attempts to catch him. Most of the situations, though, are highly implausible, unusual in a Wallace story. The longer version is considerably less suspenseful, gaining nothing by extra film stock. (Remake of the 1930 version.)

p, Richard Wainwright; d, Reginald Denham; w, Howard Irving Young (based on the novel by Edgar Wallace); ph, Phil Tannura.

Mystery **(PR:A MPAA:NR)**

CRIMSON CULT, THE zero
(1970, Brit.) 87m British-American International/AIP c
(AKA: CURSE OF THE CRIMSON ALTAR; THE CRIMSON ALTAR)

Boris Karloff *(Prof. Marshe)*, Christopher Lee *(J. D. Morley)*, Mark Eden *(Robert Manning)*, Barbara Steele *(Lavinia)*, Virginia Wetherell *(Eve)*, Michael Gough *(Elder)*, Rupert Davis *(Dr. Radford)*, Rosemarie Reede *(Esther)*, Derek Tansley *(Judge)*, Denys Peek *(Peter Manning)*, Millicent Scott *(Stripper)*, Ron Pomber *(Attendant)*, Michael Warren *(Basil)*, Nita Loraine *(Woman with Whip)*, Carol Anne *(1st Virgin)*, Jenny Shaw *(2nd Virgin)*, Vivienne Carlton *(Sacrifice Victim)*, Roger Avon *(Sgt. Tyson)*, Paul McNeil *(Guest)*, Vicky Richards *(Belly Dancer)*, Tasma Bereton *(Girl who Is Painted)*, Kevin Smith *(Drunk)*, Lita Scott *(Girl with Cockerel)*, Terry Raven *(Driver)*, Nova St. Claire *(Girl in Car Chase)*, Douglas Mitchell *(Driver)*.

An 80-year-old Karloff in wheelchair is pathetically cast as an expert on the supernatural with a wide array of torture devices he has collected over the years. Evil Christopher Lee propels the plot as the owner of Greymarsh Lodge, to which he invites Eden, a descendant of the bloke who burned Lee's descendant at the stake. Lee's tortured relative is a green-faced witch played all-too-unconvincingly by Steele, who is reincarnated in an attempt to terrorize Eden. The tongue-in-cheek humor is at its peak when early on Eden notes the similarity that Greymarsh has to "one of those houses in the horror films." His lady Wetherell answers, "I know, it's like Boris Karloff is going to pop up at any moment." And sure enough Karloff pops up — as well as one can pop up in a wheelchair — and scolds them, "It's not nice to joke of such things." The loathesome marketing of this one tried to capitalize on Boris' subsequent death by billing this as his last film. It wasn't, thankfully. He made four more in Mexico. A semi-faithful, though uncredited, adaptation of H. P. Lovecraft's "The Dream in the Witch House."

p, Louis M. Heyward; d, Vernon Sewell; w, Mervyn Haisman, Henry Lincoln; ph, Johnny Coquillon (Movielab Color); m, Peter Knight; ed, Howard Lanning; art d, Derek Barrington.

Horror **(PR:O MPAA:GP)**

CRIMSON EXECUTIONER, THE
(SEE: BLOODY PIT OF HORROR,THE, 1965)

CRIMSON GHOST,THE (SEE: CYCLOTRODE X, 1946)

CRIMSON KEY, THE½** (1947) 76m FOX bw

Kent Taylor *(Larry Morgan)*, Doris Dowling *(Mrs. Loring)*, Dennis Hoey *(Steven Loring)*, Louise Currie *(Heidi)*, Ivan Triesault *(Peter Vandaman)*, Arthur Space *(Fitzroy)*, Vera Marshe *(Dizzy)*, Edwin Rand *(Jeffrey Regan)*, Bernadene Hayes *(Mrs. Swann)*, Victoria Horne *(Miss Phillips)*, Doug Evans *(Dr. Swann)*, Ann Doran *(Parris Wood)*, Victor Sen Young *(Wing)*, Chester Clute *(Hotel Clerk)*, Ralf Harolde *(Gunman)*, Milton Parsons *(Dr. Harlow)*, JImmy Magill *(Detective Sergeant)*, Marietta Canty *(Petunia)*, Stanley Mann *(Night Clerk)*.

A well-trodden whodunit which puts Taylor on the trail of a wealthy and jealous wife's night-owl doctor husband. He endlessly beats the pavement when both husband and client are murdered. Getting knocked about many times on the way, his path leads to the door of Dowling, an exotic-looking miss who steams the screen and is a patient of the dead doctor. Nosing around with the expected aptitude, Taylor finally exposes the guilty party. Could have been much better if the plotty script had allowed for some breathing room.

p, Sol M. Wurtzel; d, Eugene Forde; w, Irving Elman; ph, Benjamin Kline; ed, Frank Baldridge; md, Morton Scott.

Mystery **(PR:A MPAA:NR)**

CRIMSON KIMONO, THE*** (1959) 81m COL bw

Victoria Shaw *(Christine Downs)*, Glenn Corbett *(Detective Sgt. Charlie Bancroft)*, James Shigeta *(Detective Joe Kojaku)*, Anna Lee *(Mac)*, Paul Dubov *(Casale)*, Jaclynne Greene *(Roma)*, Neyle Morrow *(Hansel)*, Gloria Pall *(Sugar Torch)*, Barbara Hayden *(Mother)*, George Yoshinaga *(Willy Hidaka)*, Kaye Elhardt *(Nun)*, Aya Oyama *(Sister Gertrude)*, George Okamura *(Karate)*, Rev. Ryosho S. Sogabe *(Priest)*, Robert Okazaki *(Yoshinaga)*, Fuji *(Shuto)*, Robert Kino *(Announcer)*, Rollin Moriyama, Jack Carol *(Men)*, Brian O'Hara *(Police Captain)*, Carol Nugent *(Girl)*, David McMahon *(Police Officer)*, Harrison Lewis *(Waiter)*, Walter Burke *(Ziggy)*, Torau Mori *(Kendo Referee)*, Edo Mita *(Gardener)*, Chiyo Toto *(Woman)*, Katie Sweet *(Child)*, Stafford Repp *(City Librarian)*, Nina Roman *(College Girl)*, Allen Pinson, Stacey Morgan *(Stunt Doubles)*.

Sam Fuller likes to make movies that startle and surprise moviegoers. Nothing ever is what it seems in a Fuller movie and when it is, you're still not certain that's what he meant. Corbett and Shigeta are pals who work on the Los Angeles homicide squad of the police department. Friends since the Korean War, they joined the force together and are inseparable, until Gloria Pall, a stripper, is murdered and both are told to work on the case. In doing so, they meet beauteous Victoria Shaw. Corbett falls hard for her and is soon followed by Shigeta, who is, by nature, a quieter and more conservative man. Shaw responds to Shigeta's gentleness and is soon enamored of him. Corbett is jealous and Shigeta thinks it's racism, but it isn't. Corbett's feelings are solely motivated by having his best friend in love with the woman he loves. The two battle it out in a Kendo match where Shigeta goes too far and almost destroys his friend. They continue their investigation which pits them against a Korean behemoth in the twisting streets of Los Angeles' Little Tokyo area as they chase the killer in and out of the bemasked and colorfully costumed celebrants of the Japanese New Year. The killer is eventually cornered and killed and it is, surprise, a woman, Green, who confesses that she killed Pall because she mistakenly thought her boy friend, Morrow, was in love with Pall. This serves as a lesson for Shigeta and he and Shaw wind up the picture in a super-charged kiss. Fuller had an ordinary little murder mystery here that he added an interracial overlay to and attempted to meld the two. It doesn't work, though Fuller's camera is always interesting and his cross-cutting techniques almost bring off the two themes. In a tiny role as the librarian, look hard for Stafford Repp, who went on to become a cult figure as Chief O'Hara in TV's "Batman."

p,d&w, Samuel Fuller; ph, Sam Leavitt; m, Harry Sukman; ed, Jerome Thoms; md, Leo Shuken, Jack Hayes; art d, William E. Flannery, Robert Boyle; set d, James A. Crowe; cos, Bernice Pontrelli.

Crime **(PR:A-C MPAA:NR)**

CRIMSON PIRATE, THE**** (1952) 104m WB c

Burt Lancaster *(Vallo)*, Nick Cravat *(Ojo)*, Eva Bartok *(Consuelo)*, Torin Thatcher *(Humble Bellows)*, James Hayter *(Prudence)*, Leslie Bradley *(Baron Gruda)*, Margot Graham *(Bianca)*, Noel Purcell *(Pablo Murphy)*, Frederick Leicester *(El Libre)*, Eliot Makeham *(Governor)*, Frank Pettingill *(Colonel)*, Dagmar Wynter *(La Signorita)*, Christopher Lee *(Attache)*.

Unbuckle your swash, plant your tongue firmly in your cheek, reach for a large grain of salt, then sit back and watch just about the best pirate send-up ever made. To appreciate how good this one is, look at YELLOWBEARD or SWASHBUCKLER to see how easily they can go wrong. Lancaster is the leader of a tacky band of pirates, none of whom can be trusted as far as you can throw a whale. Cravat, an old-time pal of Lancaster's who often appeared with him, is the deaf-mute aide and the only person who can be relied upon aboard the scurvy ship. They raid a merchant vessel and learn Leslie Bradley is an emissary to the King of Spain and is planning to counteract the revolution of a small but tough band on a Caribbean island. Lancaster sails for the island with plans to get El Libre (Frederick Leicester) to buy the hijacked cannons he's just ripped from the ship. His secondary plan is to inform the king's men where Leicester is and take home a large gold reward. Those plans go awry when Lancaster falls hard for Bartok, Leicester's daughter. Under her Hungarian spell, she converts Lancaster to the revolutionary point of view. Meanwhile, Hayter (so good in so many British films, notably Maugham's TRIO) is an early-day Thomas Edison with a penchant for inventing dangerous weapons, including a black powder that almost destroys friend and foe alike. Once Lancaster is on the side of the rebels, can there be any doubt that the small island will achieve independence? There's very little else to the story, just a great deal of derring-do, leaping from yardarms, swordplay and acrobatics, many flashing smiles from Lancaster's famous teeth, and the feeling that everyone, from the director to the best boy, was having a wonderful time when they filmed THE CRIMSON PIRATE. Writer Roland Kibbee stayed with Lancaster and wrote two other films of some note for the actor: VERA CRUZ (with two other writers) and THE DEVIL'S DISCIPLE (cowritten with John Dighton). Before his death, Kibbee worked for many seasons on TV's "Barney Miller," where he put his sense of humor to good use. Filmed in England and Spain, the picture feels as though it may have begun with the idea of doing a straight seafaring movie, but somewhere along the way everyone started to enjoy themselves so much that they altered their course a few degrees and came up with what is now a cult movie.

p, Harold Hecht; d, Robert Siodmak; w, Roland Kibbee; ph, Otto Heller (Technicolor); m, William Alwyn; ed, Jack Harris.

Adventure/Satire (PR:A MPAA:NR)

CRIMSON ROMANCE*** (1934) 70m Mascot bw
Ben Lyon (Bob Wilson), Sari Maritza (Alida Hoffman), Erich von Stroheim (Wolters), Hardie Albright (Hugo), James Bush (Fred von Bergen), William Bakewell (Adolph), Herman Bing (Himmelbaum), Bodil Rosing (Mama von Bergen), Vincent Barnett (The Courier), Arthur Clayton (Baron von Eisenlohr), Oscar Apfel (John Fleming), Purnell Pratt (Franklyn Pierce), Jason Robards (Pierre), William von Brincken (Von Gering), Eric Arnold (Von Muller), Fred Vogeding (German Colonel), Harry Schultz (Drill Sergeant).

This interesting 1934 film about the German army unfortunately suffers from preachiness and poor timing with rising anti-Nazi sentiments. The film, primarily an opus of loyalty and pacifism, has no real winners or heroes. Two enthusiastic American lads join the German air force only to learn that they will soon be battling against the boys from their homeland. Lyon decides to remain loyal to America and fight on its side. Bush's loyalty, however, is to his German ancestry and he continues flying with the Luftwaffe. Before long he is shot down and killed, leaving Lyon to move in on his fraulein, Maritza. A marriage follows. It is back in the States where the two friends are reunited, though one is six feet under in a pine overcoat. His mom, at the film's preachiest, delivers an anti-war eulogy that still rings true today. Eric von Stroheim is awesome in the granite-hard role of a sadistic captain.

p, Nat Levine; d, David Howard; w, Mildred Krims, Doris Schroeder (based on a story by Al Martin, Sherman Lowe); ph, Ernest Miller; ed, Doris Drought.

War (PR:C MPAA:NR)

CRIMSON TRAIL, THE**½ (1935) 58m UNIV bw
Buck Jones (Billy Carter), Polly Ann Young (Kitty Bellaire), Carl Stockdale (Jim Bellaire), Charles French (Frank Carter), Ward Bond (Luke Long), John Bleifer (Loco), Bob Kortman, Bud Osborne, Charles Brinley, Hank Pott, George Sowards, Paul Fix, Robert Walker, "Silver."

Proof that an endless flow of action with only a touch of plot can be an effective piece of entertainment is this Buck Jones oater which has two ranch owners each mistakenly believing the other is a rustler. Eventually they solve their differences, but not before one's daughter finds herself in the arms of the other's nephew. One of the better westerns, with an exceptionally photographed midnight raid on one of the ranches.

p, Buck Jones; d, Al Raboch; w, Jack Natteford (based on a story by Wilton West); ph, John Hickson.

Western (PR:AA MPAA:NR)

CRIPPLE CREEK**½ (1952) 78m COL c
George Montgomery (Bret Ivers), Karin Booth (Julie Hanson), Jerome Courtland (Larry Galland), William Bishop (Silver Kirby), Richard Egan (Strap Galland), Don Porter (Denver Jones), John Dehner (Emil Cabeau), Roy Roberts (Marshall Tetheroe), George Cleveland ("Hardrock" Hanson), Byran Foulger (Hawkins), Robert Bice (James Sullivan), Grandon Rhodes (Drummond), Zon Murray (Lefty), Peter Brocco (Cashier), Cliff Clark (Winfield Hatton), Robert G. Anderson (Muldoon), Harry Cording (Hibbs), Cris Alcaide (Jeff).

This frequently seen plot is given some guts with Montgomery's portrayal of a leathery federal agent and Nazarro's skillful hand at the reins. To land a death blow on a smuggling operation during the gold rush days, a pair of undercover agents join the bandit gang. Teetering constantly on the brink of discovery, they work with the gang as heisted gold is shipped out of the country. After unmasking, the agents, with the needed proof, send the crooked bunch up the creek. Booth, in an underdeveloped role, convincingly plays a gambling hall lovely.

p, Edward Small; d, Ray Nazarro; w, Richard Schayer; ph, William V. Skal (Technicolor); m, Mischa Bakaleinikoff; ed, Richard Fantl.

Western (PR:A MPAA:NR)

CRISIS*** (1950) 95m MGM bw
Cary Grant (Dr. Eugene Norland Ferguson), Jose Ferrer (Raoul Farrago), Paula Raymond (Helen Ferguson), Signe Hasso (Senora Isabel Farrago), Ramon Novarro (Col. Adragon), Gilbert Roland (Gonzales), Leon Ames (Sam Proctor), Antonio Moreno (Dr. Emilio Nierra), Teresa Celli (Rosa), Pedro de Cordoba (Father Del Puento), Vincente Gomez (Cariago), Martin Garralaga (Senor Magano), Soledad Jimenez (Senora Farrago), Jose Dominguez (Rubio), Robert Tafur (Marco Aldana), Maurice Jara (Louis), Rodolfo Hoyos, Jr. (Chauffeur), Rita Conde (Pretty Girl), Roque Ybarra (Man in Car), Felipe Turich (Man with Valise), Charles Rivero, Mickey Contreras (Ad Libs), Capt. Garcia (Miguel Farrago), Carlos Condi (Man), George Lewis (Desk Clerk), Carlo Tricoli (Nervous Man in Lobby), Kenneth Garcia, Harry Vejar, Trina Varela, Bridget Carr (Guests), Audrey Betz (Servant), Robert Lugo, Myron Marks (Soldiers), Alex Montoya (Robust Indian), Margaret Martin (Indian Woman), Juan Duval (Proud Little Man), Al Haskell, Rafael Gomez, Z. Yacconelli (Soldiers), Fernando Del Valle (Bull Routine Man), A. Carillo, Robert Polo, Jerry Riggio (Men at Table), Melba Meredith (Woman in Cafe), Lillian Israel, Carlotta Monti, Connie Montoya (Nurses), George Novarro (Dr. Gracian), Orlando Beltran, Eddie Gomez (Doctor's Assistants), Pepe Hern, David Cota, George Brady, Joaquin Garay, Neyle Morrow, Larry Crane (Students), Felipe Turich (Voice on Loudspeaker), Danilo Valenti (Eduardo), Sam Herrera (Man at Door), William M. MacCormack (Man with Scar), Carlos Figueroa (Old Man), Robert Cabal (Very Young Man), Manuel Paris (Julio), Carlos Barbee, Amapola Del Vando (Farrago's Friends).

Foolishly vacationing in a revolution-torn South American country, brain surgeon

Grant and wife Raymond are kidnaped by dictator Ferrer's thugs. This melodrama, while overlong, is nonetheless intriguing as a comparison between a dictatorial regime and democracy. Forced to operate on the waning Ferrer, Grant tediously explains the steps of the surgery while demonstrating on a dummy's head. The rebel forces try to get Grant to make a slip of the knife, but they are unsuccessful. Before the operation begins Grant's wife is abducted by the revolutionaries, but he is unaware of her disappearance. Grant successfully performs the operation, but in a touch of irony the recovering Ferrer collapses in an attempt to put down a revolt. His successor is felled by a sniper's bullet, and the democratic forces come to power. Slow-moving script is well-executed by cerebral director Brooks, and given vitality by Rozsa's atmospheric sound-tracking.

p, Arthur Freed; d&w, Richard Brooks (based on a story "The Doubters" by George Tabori); ph, Ray June; m, Miklos Rozsa; ed, Robert J. Kern; art d, Cedric Gibbons, Preston Ames; set d, Edwin B. Wallis, Hugh Hurd; spec eff, A. Arnold Gillespie, Warren Newcombe; makeup, Jack Dawn.

Drama (PR:A MPAA:NR)

CRISS CROSS***½ (1949) 87m UNIV bw
Burt Lancaster (Steve Thompson), Yvonne De Carlo (Anna), Dan Duryea (Slim), Stephen McNally (Ramirez), Richard Long (Slade Thompson), Esy Morales (Orchestra Leader), Tom Pedi (Vincent), Percy Helton (Frank), Alan Napier (Finchley), Griff Barnett (Pop), Meg Randall (Helen), Joan Miller (The Lush), Edna M. Holland (Mrs. Thompson), John Doucette (Walt), Marc Krah (Mort), James O'Rear (Waxie), John "Skins" Miller (Midget), Robert Osterloh (Mr. Nelson), Vincent Renno (Headwaiter), Charles Wagenheim (Waiter), James [Tony] Curtis (Gigolo), Beatrice Roberts, Isabel Randolph (Nurses), Robert Winkler (Clark), Vitto Scotti (Track Usher), John Roy (Bartender), Timmy Hawkins (Boy), Tung Foo (Chinese Cook), Ann Staunton, Dolores Castle, Jeraldine Jordan, Kippee Valez (Girl Friends), Diane Stewart, Jean Bane (Girls), Stephen Roberts (Doctor), Garry Owen (Johnny), Kenneth Paterson, Gene Evans (Guards), George Lynn (Andy), Michael Cisney (Chester).

A bleak but compelling film noir tale has forceful Lancaster as an honest armored-car guard who takes up with his ex-wife De Carlo, who is now married to sleazy gangster Duryea. When the mobster finds Lancaster with his wife he is told by Lancaster that the rendezvous was strictly business, that they had merely been planning the robbery of the armored car he drives. His lie leads him into a bizarre robbery plan where he must work with Duryea and his henchman while dodging suspicious cop McNally. De Carlo complicates matters by promising Lancaster to run off with him after he completes the robbery and double-crossing Duryea's gang. He kills two thieves during the robbery but is also wounded. Hospitalized, his leg in a cast, Lancaster asks a stranger to help him get to a hideout where De Carlo is waiting with the money. The stranger, Osterloh, is really abducting Lancaster for Duryea, but Lancaster bribes him to take him to De Carlo. She sees the helpless Lancaster, then realizes that Duryea will hunt them both down and kill them. She prepares to run out on her lover but Duryea arrives and kills them both before police on his tail shoot him to death. A somber, utterly grim film, the suspense is maintained throughout by Siodmak's taut direction, his handling of flashbacks, and a clever staging of the robbery. Lancaster is powerful as the love-torn guard, and De Carlo smokes up the screen with her earthy portrayal of a money-hungry vamp, a role almost twin to Ava Gardner's slippery portrayal opposite Lancaster in THE KILLERS. The violence in this film is excessive.

p, Michel Kraike; d, Robert Siodmak; w, Daniel Fuchs (based on the novel by Don Tracy); ph, Franz Planer; m, Miklos Rozsa; ed, Ted J. Kent; art d, Bernard Herzbrun, Boris Leven; set d, Russel A. Gausman, Oliver Emert; cos, Yvonne Wood; makeup, Bud Westmore; spec eff, David S. Horsley.

Crime/Drama (PR:C MPAA:NR)

CRITIC'S CHOICE** (1963) 100m WB c
Bob Hope (Parker Ballantine), Lucille Ball (Angela Ballantine), Marilyn Maxwell (Ivy London), Rip Torn (Dion Kapakos), Jessie Royce Landis (Charlotte Orr), John Dehner (S. P. Champlain), Jim Backus (Dr. von Hagedorn), Ricky Kelman (John Ballantine), Dorothy Green (Mrs. Champlain), Marie Windsor (Sally Orr), Evan McCord (Phil Yardley), Richard Deacon (Harvey Rittenhouse), Joan Shawlee (Marge Orr), Jerome Cowan (Joe Rosenfield), Donald Losby (Godfrey), Laurene Tuttle (Mother), Ernestine Wade (Thelma), Stanley Adams (Bartender).

A successful Broadway play that poorly makes the transition to celluloid. The comic talents of Hope and Ball can't save its implausibility. Hope is cast as the usual one-dimensional character—this time as a theater critic who must review his wife's new play. With the outcome being potential marital ruin, he laboriously decides to pen a review, but not before booze, analysis, and the comfort of first wife, Maxwell. Arriving drunk at the opening, Hope becomes the center of attention immediately. Ball takes the expected measures, which lead to a comically routine wrap-up. Edith Head's costumes are above par.

p, Frank P. Rosenberg; d, Don Weis; w, Jack Sher (based on the play by Ira Levin); ph, Charles Lang (Technicolor); m, George Duning; ed, William Ziegler; md, Arthur Morton; art d, Edward Carrere; set d, William L. Kuehl; cos, Edith Head.

Comedy (PR:A MPAA:NR)

CROCODILE zero (1979, Thai./Hong Kong) 91m Cobra Media c
Nat Puvanai, Tany Tim, Angela Wells, Kirk Warren.

A wasted meritless film shows how an atomic test produces a giant crocodile and it eats the people of Bangkok and makes big waves with its tail when it swims. The picture has childish miniatures, excessive blood, and inept rear-screen projection of the title killer. No campy value, either. Almost no credits are given and who can blame them?

p, Dick Randall, Robert Chan; d, Sompote Sands.

Horror Cas. (PR:O MPAA:R)

CROISIERES SIDERALES* (1941, Fr.) 80m bw
Madeleine Sologne, Jean Marchat, Julien Carette, Suzanne Dehelly, Jean Daste, Maupi.

A space-age love story which has Sologne leave on a two-week celestial voyage only to find, upon her arrival home, that everything and everyone has aged by twenty-five years. Her lover Marchat decides that he, too, will take the voyage in order to come back in twenty-five years and be the same age as Sologne. Fairly idiotic.

p, Pierre Guerlais; d, Andre Zwoboda; w, Guerlais, Pierre Bost; ph, Isnard.

Science Fiction **(PR:A MPAA:NR)**

CROMWELL** (1970, Brit.) 139m COL c
Richard Harris *(Oliver Cromwell)*, Alec Guinness *(King Charles I)*, Robert Morley *(Earl of Manchester)*, Dorothy Tutin *(Queen Henrietta Maria)*, Frank Finlay *(John Carter)*, Timothy Dalton *(Prince Rupert)*, Patrick Wymark *(Earl of Stafford)*, Patrick Magee *(Hugh Peters)*, Nigel Stock *(Sir Edward Hyde)*, Charles Gray *(Lord Essex)*, Michael Jayston *(Henry Ireton)*, Richard Cornish *(Oliver Cromwell II)*, Anna Cropper *(Ruth Carter)*, Michael Goodliffe *(Solicitor General)*, Jack Gwillim *(Gen. Byron)*, Basil Henson *(Hacker)*, Patrick Holt *(Capt. Lunsford)*, Stratford Johns *(Pres. Bradshaw)*, Geoffrey Keen *(John Pym)*, Anthony May *(Richard Cromwell)*, Ian McCulloch *(John Hampden)*, Patrick O'Connell *(John Lilburne)*, John Paul *(Gen. Digby)*, Bryan Pringle *(Trooper Hawkins)*, Llewelyn Rees *(The Speaker)*, Robin Stewart *(Prince of Wales)*, Adreevan Gysegham *(Archbishop Rinucinni)*, Zena Walker *(Mrs. Cromwell)*, John Welsh *(Bishop Juxon)*, Douglas Wilmer *(Thomas Fairfax)*, Anthony Kemp *(Henry Cromwell)*, Stacy Dorning *(Mary Cromwell)*, Melinda Churcher *(Bridget Cromwell)*, George Merritt *(Old Man William)*, Gerald Rowland *(Drummer Boy)*, Josephine Gillick *(Elizabeth Cromwell)*.

Long and tedious costume epic that never made half the production money back and anyone who sees the movie can easily understand why. It did win the Oscar for Best Costume Design but when that is all one notices, we know we are in for a yawning evening. Cromwell (Harris) was a religious fanatic who considered God as his only ally and anything done in His name would be all right. He was an Anglican puritan who had two missions: to clean up the corruption he felt was rampant and to keep England from again slipping under Catholic influence. Alec Guinness is Charles I, weak ruler with a Catholic Queen (Tutin), who duels with Cromwell. The English are persecuting the Irish Catholics while the Scots are advancing on England with an army. The King's treasury is light, due to repeated plunderings by the entire court. Cromwell rallies Parliament and a battle 'twixt the Cavaliers and the Roundheads results in Cromwell having a solid base of supporters. Guinness tries an end-around on Cromwell but his two-timing is spotted and he pays for it with a trial and execution. But this is not a history lesson, this is a report on a movie, And, as a movie, CROMWELL has little to recommend it other than the aforementioned costumes, a fine acting job by Guinness (and when was he ever not good?) and a lot of money spent on visuals but not enough care and feeding of the script. Ken Hughes gets credit for the screenplay with Ronald Harwood as his "script consultant" but not getting a full writing credit. They would have been wise to have brought someone else in to cut the daylights out of the script. A lot of words but very little flesh.

p, Irving Allen; d, Ken Hughes; w, Hughes, Ronald Harwood; ph, Geoffrey Unsworth (Panavision, Technicolor); m, Frank Cordell; ed, Bill Lenny; prod d, John Stoll; art d, Herbert Westbrook; set d, Arthur Taksen; cos, Vittorio Nino Novarese; spec eff, Bill Warrington; stunts, Gerry Crampton.

Historical Drama **(PR:A MPAA:NR)**

CROOK, THE*** (1971, Fr.) 120m UA c (AKA: LE VOYOU)
Jean-Louis Trintignant *(Simon)*, Daniele Deforme *(Janine)*, Charles Denner *(Mon. Gallois)*, Christine Lelouch *(Martine)*, Amidou *(Bill)*, Pierre Zimmer *(Martine's Husband)*, Charles Gerard *(Charles)*, Judith Magre *(Mme. Gallois)*, Vincent Roziere *(Daniel Gallois)*, Yves Robert *(Inspector)*, Sacha Distel.

Trintignant, his moll Lelouch, and his sidekick Gerard kidnap little Roziere and force the bank his father works for to pay a million-dollar ransom. All goes well, and even the bank comes out ahead because sentimental Parisian savers open new accounts at the bank, but a slight complication develops. Excellent entertainment without the heavy-handedness that marred many of the director's later works.

p, Alexandre Mnouchkine; d, Claude Ledlouch; w, Lelouch, Pierre Uytterhoeven, Claude Pinoteau; ph, Jean Collomb (DeLuxe Color); m, Francis Lai.

Crime **(PR:A MPAA:GP)**

CROOKED BILLET, THE** (1930, Brit.) 82m Gainsborough/W&F bw
Carlyle Blackwell *(Dietrich Hebburn)*, Madeleine Carroll *(Joan Easton)*, Miles Mander *(Guy Morrow)*, Gordon Harker *(Slick)*, Kim Peacock *(Philip Easton)*, Danny Green *(Rogers)*, Frank Goldsmith *(Sir William Easton)*, Alexander Field *(Alf)*.

International spy Blackwell, along with assorted spies and detectives, descends on a remote inn searching for secret documents hidden there. Released as a silent in 1929, a bad soundtrack was added a year later. Dated, but with a first-class cast still worth seeing. Beautiful, ladylike Carroll had only been in British films for two years, but already was a popular star locally.

p, Michael Balcon; d, Adrian Brunel; w, Angus MacPhail (based on a play by Dion Titherage); ph, Claude MacDonnell.

Spy Drama **(PR:A MPAA:NR)**

CROOKED CIRCLE*½ (1932) 68m World-Wide bw
Ben Lyon *(Brand Osborne)*, ZaSu Pitts *(Nora)*, James Gleason *(Crimmer)*, Irene Purcell *(Thelma)*, C. Henry Gordon *(Yoganda)*, Raymond Hatton *(Harmon)*, Roscoe Karns *(Harry)*, Berton Churchill *(Col. Wolters)*, Spencer Charters *(Kinny)*, Robert Frazer *(The Stranger)*, Ethel Clayton, Frank Reicher, Christian Rub.

A comic mystery that has more laughs than suspense. Essentially held together by slapstick policeman Gleason, the thin plot concerns a secret agent who goes undercover as a swami. A tame script and troubled photography don't help this meager picture.

p, William Sistrom; d, H. Bruce Humberstone; w, Ralph Spence, Tim Whelan; ph, Robert Kurrie.

Comedy **(PR:A MPAA:NR)**

CROOKED CIRCLE, THE** (1958) 72m REP bw
John Smith *(Tommy Kelly)*, Fay Spain *(Carol Smith)*, Steve Brodie *(Ken Cooper)*, Don Kelly *(Joe Kelly)*, Robert Armstrong *(Al Taylor)*, John Doucette *(Larry Ellis)*, Philip Van Zandt *(Max Maxwell)*, Richard Karlan *(Sam Lattimer)*, Bob Swan *(Carl)*, Don Haggerty *(Adams)*, Peter Mamakos *(Nick)*.

Fair boxing story has Smith the younger brother of an ex-fighter who leaves his Maine fishing camp to go to New York with sports reporter Brodie and become a fighter himself. He falls in with gangsters who have him throw fights, and when his brother (Kelly) sees what is happening, he comes to New York with Spain to confront Smith. They decide that Smith will win the next fight he is supposed to throw, though the gangsters will amost certainly try to kill him. Kelly is recognized by corrupt manager Doucette as the fighter who had vanished years before after winning a fight he was supposed to throw, so Doucette decides to tell Smith to win the fight so the mobsters will get rid of him. Smith wins in a K.O. and immediately after, the fight mob goons take him for a ride. Brodie learns what has happened and forces one criminal to tell him where they have taken Smith. Police arrive in the nick of time, and the conclusion has Smith and Spain married.

p, Rudy Ralston; d, Joe Kane; w, Jack Townley; ph, Jack Marta (Naturama); ed, Frederic Knudtson; md, Gerald Roberts; art d, Ralph Oberg; set d, John McCarthy, Jr.; cos, Alexis Davidoff; makeup, Bob Mark.

Sports Drama **(PR:A-C MPAA:NR)**

CROOKED LADY, THE** (1932, Brit.) 75m Real Art/MGM bw
George Graves *(Sir Charles Murdoch)*, Isobel Elsom *(Miriam Sinclair)*, Ursula Jeans *(Joan Collinson)*, Austin Trevor *(Capt. James Kent)*, Alexander Field *(Slim Barrett)*, Edmund Willard *(Joseph Garstin)*, S. J. Warmington *(Inspector Hilton)*, Frank Pettingell *(Hugh Weldon)*, Moore Marriott *(Crabby)*, H. B. Longhurst *(John Morland)*, Paddy Browne *(Susie)*.

Unemployed former police officer Trevor steals a string of pearls from a famous actress, then falls in love with the woman detective investigating the case, and there goes the perfect crime. Routine early British second feature.

p, Julius Hagen; d, Leslie Hiscott; w, H. Fowler Mear (based on a novel by William C. Stone).

Crime **(PR:A MPAA:NR)**

CROOKED RIVER* (1950) 58m Lippert bw
Jimmy Ellison *(Shamrock)*, Russ Hayden *(Lucky)*, Raymond Hatton *(Colonel)*, Fuzzy Knight *(Deacon)*, Betty Adams *(Ann)*, Tom Tyler *(Weston)*, George Lewis *(Gentry)*, John Cason *(Kent)*, Stanley Price *(Sheriff)*, Stephen Carr *(Butch)*, Dennis Moore *(Bob)*, George Chesebro *(Dad Ellison)*, Bud Osborne *(Stage Driver)*, Jimmy Martin *(Dick)*, Cliff Taylor *(Doctor)*, Helen Gibson *(Mother)*, Carl Matthews *(Cherokee)*, George Sowards, Scoop Martin, Joe Phillips *(Ranchers)*.

This low-budget quickie with the five others in the Ellison-Hayden series were all shot in a one-month period. It shows. Back-to-back cliches leave not an imaginative frame in this assembly-line oater. Ellison is on the trail of the bandits who murdered his parents. He hooks up with amiable outlaw Hayden and together they track down the baddies. The clue which gives outlaws away is the ring stolen from Ellison's dead dad. The film's only distinguishing feature is a narrator who describes the meritorious achievements of the West's pioneers.

p, Ron Ormand; d, Thomas Carr; w, Ormond, Maurice Tombragel; ph, Ernest Miller; m, Walter Greene; ed, Hugh Winn.

Western **(PR:A MPAA:NR)**

CROOKED ROAD, THE*½ (1940) 69m REP bw
Edmund Lowe *(John Vincent)*, Irene Hervey *(Louise)*, Henry Wilcoxon *(Bob Trent)*, Paul Fix *(Nick Romero)*, Arthur Loft *(Gobel)*, Claire Carleton *(Virgie)*, Charles Lane *(Phil)*.

An ordinary melodrama about the affluent Lowe whose past begins to threaten his position. A fellow jailbird blackmails the long-ago prison escapee. After a series of incidents, Lowe gets a murder pinned on him, only to be let off the hook by some fancy sleuthing. However, in the process Lowe's self-shortened prison term is revealed and he is sent back to jail.

p, Robert North; d, Phil Rosen; w, Garnett Weston, Joseph Krumgold (based on a story by E. E. Paramore, Jr., Richard Blake); ph, Ernest Miller; ed, Ernest Nims.

Drama **(PR:A MPAA:NR)**

CROOKED ROAD, THE**
(1965, Brit., Yugo.) 90m Argos Triglav Film-Trident Films/Seven Arts bw
Robert Ryan *(Richard Ashley)*, Stewart Granger *(Duke of Orgagna)*, Nadia Gray *(Cosima)*, Marius Goring *(Harlequin)*, George Coulouris *(Carlos)*, Catherine Woodville *(Elena)*, Robert Rietty *(Police Chief)*, Milan Micic, Demeter Bitenc, Murray Kash.

Ryan is a journalist collecting information on despotic Balkan dictator Granger. When a contact he was to buy some incriminating documents from is found dead, Ryan is arrested and put in the custody of Granger, who begs him not to publish what he knows. Ryan refuses, and after getting the documents from Granger's mistress, the mistress's father stabs Granger to death. Crudely directed and acted, the film does have a few effective moments.

p, David Henley; d, Don Chaffey, w, Jay Garrison, Chaffey (based on the novel *The Big Story* by Morris L. West); ph, Stephen Dade; m, Bojan Adamic; ed, Peter Tanner.

Drama **(PR:C MPAA:NR)**

CROOKED SKY, THE** (1957, Brit.) 77m Luckwin/RFD bw
Wayne Morris *(Mike Conklin)*, Karin Booth *(Sandra Hastings)*, Anton Diffring *(Fraser)*, Bruce Seton *(Mac)*, Sheldon Lawrence *(Bill)*, Collette Barthrop *(Penny)*, Frank Hawkins *(Robson)*, Murray Kash *(Lewis)*, Wally Peterson *(Wilson)*, Seymour Green, Richard Shaw, Bill Brandon, Guy Kingsley Pointer.

Morris, an American detective in Britain, investigates a counterfeiting operation and discovers that a prosperous gambler is running the caper. Interesting British attempt to put an American-style hard-boiled detective in their own yard, even going so far as to name the hero "Mike" instead of the usual "Geoffrey" or "Ronnie."

p, Bill Luckwell, Derek Winn; d, Henry Cass; w, Norman Hudis (based on a story by Lance Z. Hargreaves and Maclean Rogers); ph, Phil Grindrod.

Crime **(PR:A MPAA:NR)**

CROOKED TRAIL, THE* (1936) 60m Supreme/William Steiner bw
Johnny Mack Brown, Lucile Brown, John Merton, Ted Adams, Charles King, Dick Curtis, John Van Pelt, Edward Cassidy, Horace Murphy, Earl Dwire, Artie Ortego, Hal Price.

Unexciting oater where J. M. Brown faces down bad guy Merton and gang and wins the heart of L. Brown, saving her honor and ranch to boot. An uncluttered script would have made this sloppily produced horse opera much better.

p, A. W. Hackel; d, S. Roy Luby; w, George Plympton.

Western **(PR:A MPAA:NR)**

CROOKED WAY, THE** (1949) 80m UA bw
John Payne *(Eddie Rice)*, Sonny Tufts *(Vince Alexander)*, Ellen Drew *(Nina)*, Rhys Williams *(Lt. Williams)*, Percy Helton *(Petey)*, John Doucette *(Sgt. Barrett)*, Charles Evans *(Capt. Anderson)*, Greta Granstedt *(Hazel)*, Harry Bronson *(Danny)*, Hal Fieberling *(Coke)*, Crane Whitley *(Dr. Kemble)*, John Harmon *(Kelly)*, Snub Pollard *(News Vendor)*.

John Payne is mustered out of the Army. He's been a patient at a vet hospital where he is suffering from amnesia and he has no idea who he was or where he came from. All he knows is that he's from Los Angeles. Upon arrival at L.A.'s Union Station, he is greeted by Rhys Williams, a local police lieutenant. Williams is with a few other cops and they all identify Payne as a gangster who had a successful illegal operation going in partnership with Tufts. This is all a shock to Payne. The next surprise comes when he meets his ex-wife, Drew, and she escorts him to his former residence, a local hotel. When he meets Tufts, he is promptly rewarded by a whacking around because Tufts doesn't believe Payne's story and thinks that Payne left L.A. and joined the service under a phony name to let Tufts get the blame for an earlier crime. Payne is truly an amnesiac but still finds Drew exciting. She's told by Tufts to take Payne to bed and keep an eye on him. Williams gets to Tufts and wants to know about a particular murder that he suspects Sonny for. Tufts guns the officer down, then frames Payne for it. Payne gets away and Drew now believes that he has no memory of the rat he used to be. She is wounded by one of Tuft's henchmen but manages to give Payne some information: find Helton, an old pal, who is under cover at a local warehouse. Helton tells Tufts that Payne is on his way and there's a gun battle between the two men. Cops arrive and Tufts uses Payne as a shield but Helton manages to get Payne free. The cops fire at Tufts and the film ends as Drew and Payne get back together and can only hope that he stays unaware of his former life. Nice photography of Los Angeles and a fine acting job by Helton as an authentic L.A. weirdo who lives with scores of cats. Small, chubby Helton began in silent films in 1922 and continued until his death in 1971. He could always be counted upon to give a director exactly the job for which he was hired: the high-voiced, sometimes maniacal, sometimes silly, but always fun-to-watch little man. Helton was one of the many character people who made movies memorable—he, Donald Meek, Percy Kilbride, Franklin Pangborn, and even Fritz Feld, professionals all.

p, Benedict Bogeaus; d, Robert Florey; w, Richard H. Landau (based on the radio play "No Blade Too Sharp" by Robert Monroe); ph, John Alton; m, Louis Forbes; ed, Frank Sullivan; prod d, Van Nest Polglase; set d, Joseph Kish.

Crime **(PR:A-C MPAA:NR)**

CROOKED WEB, THE** (1955) 77m Clover/COL bw
Frank Lovejoy *(Stan Fabian)*, Mari Blanchard *(Joanie Daniel)*, Richard Denning *(Frank Daniel)*, John Mylong *(Herr Koenig)*, Harry Lauter *(Jancoweizc)*, Steven Ritch *(Ray Torres)*, Louis Merrill *(Herr Schmitt)*, Roy Gordon *(Richard Atherton)*, Van Des Autels *(Tom Jackson)*, George Cezar *(Don Gillen)*, John Hart *(Charlie Holt)*, Richard Emory *(Doc Mason)*, Harold Dyrenforth *(German Guard)*, Judy Clark *(Singer)*.

Suffering chiefly from a far-fetched plot, this melodrama sets its sights on an American GI, Lovejoy, who wrongly killed a German eight years earlier in Berlin. The rich father of the dead German hires a pair of private eyes to hunt down the guilty party and return him to Germany for prosecution. Agent Blanchard gets herself hired to work in a drive-in owned by Lovejoy. She eventually squeezes a marriage proposal out of him, when fellow agent Denning comes on the scene posing as her long-lost brother. He tells the two of a scheme to earn $200,000 in Berlin. The killer bites and they are soon on their way to Germany where justice is done. A slow mover with barely adequate direction.

d, Hathan Hertz; w, Lou Breslow; ph, Henry Freulich; m, Mischa Bakaleinikoff; ed, Edwin Bryant; art d, Paul Palmentola.

Drama **(PR:A MPAA:NR)**

CROOKS AND CORONETS (SEE: SOPHIE'S PLACE, 1970)

CROOKS ANONYMOUS **½ (1963, Brit.) 87m Independent Artists/Janus Films bw
Leslie Phillips *(Dandy Forsdyke)*, Stanley Baxter *(R.S. Widdowes)*, Wilfrid Hyde-White *(Montague)*, Julie Christie *(Babette)*. James Robertson Justice *(Sir Harvey Russelrod)*, Michael Medwin *(Ronnie)*, Pauline Jameson *(Prunella)*, Robertson Hare *(Grimsdale)*, Charles Lloyd Pack *(Fletcher)*, Bryan Coleman *(Holding)*, Harry Fowler *(Woods)*, Raymond Huntley *(Wagstaffe)*, John Bennett *(Thomas)*, Arthur Mullard *(Grogan)*, Arthur Lovegrove *(Jones)*, Joyce Blair *(Carol)*, Colin Gordon *(Drunk)*, Dick Emery *(Cundall)*, Norma Foster, Dandy Nichols, David Drummond, Alfred Burke, Timothy Bateson.

Phillips is a thief trying to break himself of the habit and settle down with his fiancee, stripper Christie. At her suggestion, he joins "Crooks Anonymous," an organization headed by Hyde-White and dedicated to reforming criminals. After some weeks he is pronounced cured of criminal thoughts and is given a job as a Santa Claus in despotic manager Robertson Justice's department store. All goes well until he is accidentally locked in the store overnight with all the Christmas shopping proceeds. Unable to control his urge to steal the loot, he calls his friends from Crooks Anonymous to lend him support. They rush over to the store, and the temptation proves too much for the lot. They steal the money, but Christie threatens to turn them in unless it is returned. After some difficulty, the money is replaced, and Phillips marries Christie. Nice crime comedy with a marvelous cast.

p, Julian Wintle, Leslie Parkyn; d, Ken Annakin; w, Jack Davies, Henry Blyth; ph, Ernest Steward; m, Muir Mathieson; ed, John Trumper, Henry Martin; md, Mathieson; art d, Harry Pottle.

Comedy **(PR:A-C MPAA:NR)**

CROOKS IN CLOISTERS*** (1964, Brit.) 97m WB-Pathe/ABF c
Ronald Fraser *(Walt)*, Barbara Windsor *(Bikini)*, Gregoire Aslan *(Lorenzo)*, Bernard Cribbins *(Squirts)*, Davy Kaye *(Specs)*, Melvyn Hayes *(Willy)*, Wilfrid Brambell *(Phineas)*, Joseph O'Connor *(Father Septimus)*, Corin Redgrave *(Brother Lucius)*, Francesca Annis *(June)*, Patricia Laffan *(Lady Florence)*, Alister Williamson *(Mungo)*, Russell Waters *(Ship's Chandler)*, Howard Douglas *(Publican)*, Arnold Ridley *(News Agent)*, Max Bacon *(Bookmaker)*, Barbara Riscoe *(Kate)*, Karen Kaufman *(Strip Girl)*.

The success of this British comedy comes from its potentially brilliant premise of an amiable gang of crooks who hole up in a deserted island monastery. Fraser plays the gang boss who, with his fellow thieves, dons the look of a monk. They become accustomed to life on the quiet island, struggling through monastic chores of minding the animals and crops, though it takes some practice. Two of the funniest scenes occur when there are visits to the island: first from tourists, and then from authentic monks. One of the crooks blows their cover when his gambling habits are noticed by local bobbies. A good effort somewhat weighed down by an underdeveloped script and restrained direction.

p, Gordon L.T. Scott; d, Jeremy Summers; w, T.J. Morrison, Mike Watts (based on a story by Watts); ph, Harry Waxman (Technicolor); m, Don Banks; ed, Ann Chegwidden.

Comedy **(PR:A MPAA:NR)**

CROOKS TOUR* (1940, Brit.) 80m BN/Anglo American bw
Basil Radford *(Charters)*, Naunton Wayne *(Caldicott)*, Greta Gynt *(La Palermo)*, Charles Oliver *(Sheik)*, Gordon McLeod *(Rossenger)*, Abraham Sofaer *(Ali)*, Bernard Rebel *(Klacken)*, Cyril Gardiner *(K7)*, Noel Hood *(Edith Charters)*, Morris Harvey *(Waiter)*, Leo de Pokorny, Billy Shine, Peter Gawthorne, Andrea Malandrinos.

The incorporation of newsreel footage is the only inventive portion of this lackluster picture which falls short of its comic goal. Radford and Wayne play a pair of tourists who get mixed up in amateur sleuthing. Soon they connect with a Nazi fraulein who is blessed with a Union Jack heart. It's slow going with characters too corny to be adequately portrayed.

p, John Corfield; d, John Baxter; w, John Watt, Max Kester; ph, James Wilson.

Spy Drama **(PR:A MPAA:NR)**

CROONER*** (1932) 64m FN bw
David Manners *(Teddy)*, Ann Dvorak *(Judy)*, Ken Murray *(Peter)*, Sheila Terry *(Hat Check Girl)*, William Janney *(Pat)*, Eddie Nugent *(Henry)*, J. Carrol Naish *(Meyers)*, Betty Gillette *(His Secretary)*, Guy Kibbee *(The Drunk)*, William Halligan *(Theater Manager)*, Teddy Joyce *(Mack)*, Sumner Getchel *(Boy)*, Clarence Norstrum *(Tom)*, Allen Vincent *(Ralph)*, William Ricciardi *(Head Waiter)*, Claire Dodd *(Constance)*.

A nasty swipe at success which in turn was panned viciously in one review. "Totally ungracious" and "a general slap" is how the clearly offended writer responded to this hard-hitting polished satire. Loosely paralleling Rudy Vallee's rise, it stars Manners as Teddy, a college saxman who is instantly boosted to stardom when his manager makes him a vocalist. His overblown ego gets the better of him and sends him into a tailspin back to the cellar. A slick script and well-honed direction gives this one its sting. It predates Schulberg's similar A FACE IN THE CROWD by 25 years. Songs: "I Send My Love With the Roses" (Al Dubin, Joe Burke), "Three's A Crowd" (Dubin, Irving Kahal, Harry Warren), "Sweethearts Forever" (Cliff Friend, Irving Caesar), "Now You've Got Me Worrying For You" (Kahal, Sammy Fain), "Banking On the Weather" (Joe Young, Fain), "In A Shanty In Old Shanty Town" (Young, John Siras).

p, Lucien Hubbard; d, Lloyd Bacon; w, Charles Kenyon (based on a story by Rian James); ph, Robert Kurrle; ed, B. Bretherton; art d, Robert Haas.

Musical/Satire **(PR:A MPAA:NR)**

CROSBY CASE, THE*
(1934) 62m UNIV bw

Wynne Gibson (Lynn Ashton), Onslow Stevens (Scotty Graham), Alan Dinehart (Inspector Thomas), William Collier Sr. (Sgt. Melody), Richard "Skeets" Gallagher (Miller), Warren Hymer (Sam Collins), Edward Van Sloan (Lubeck), John Wray (Willie), J. Farrell MacDonald (Costello), Harold Huber (Rogers), Harry Seymour (Weems), Leon Waycoff [Ames] (Cliff), Mischa Auer (DeCobra), Doris Canfield (Sam's Wife), Wade Boteler (Gerard), Harry Woods (Logan), James Flavin (O'Shea), Arthur Hoyt (Wilson).

A murder mystery that comes together like a jigsaw puzzle with a lot of pieces missing. A quack doctor staggers out of his apartment with a bullet in his body. Who did it? Five suspects offer a 20 percent chance of making a correct guess.

d, Edwin L. Marin; w, Warren Duff, Gordon Kahn (based on a story by Duff and Kahn); ph, Norbert Brodine; ed, Robert Carlisle.

Crime/Mystery   (PR:A   MPAA:NR)

CROSS AND THE SWITCHBLADE, THE**
(1970) 106m Dick Ross Associates c

Pat Boone (David Wilkerson), Erik Estrada (Nicky), Jackie Giroux (Rosa), Jo-Ann Robinson (Little Bo), Dino DeFilippi (Israel), Don Blakely (Abdullah), Gil Frazier (Big Cat), Don Lamond (Sgt. Delano), Sam Capuano (Mr. Gomez), Alex Colon (Mingo), Hector Mercado (Moonlight), Stew Silver (Augie), Dorothy James (Mrs. Gomez), David Connell (Pusher), Michelle Galjour (Angela), Jackie Cronin (Norma), Virginia Alonso (Mary), Darryl Speer (Bottlecap), Thomas Mooney (Chance), Vincent O'Brien (Judge), Jay Devlin (District Attorney), Paul Haney (Lawyer), Darrel Adleman (Pawnbroker), Victor Bumbalo (Hugo), Stanley Finesmith (Trial Defendant), Sal Christi (Court Policeman), Andrew T. Murphy (Reporter), Kleg Seth (Photographer), Laura Figueroa (Mau Mau Deb), Jonelle Allen (Bishop Deb), Mark Dawson (Policeman), Dolores Raskin (Ederly Woman), Norman Bly (Heckler), Tim Pelt (Bishop).

Pat Boone is cleanly cast in a well-suited role as a minister on a mission to rid the streets of delinquents. A young Erik Estrada (of TV's C.H.I.P.S. fame) is Nicky, the streetwise gang leader, who acts as receptacle for Boone's moralistic backwash. Geared for a church-going audience which, in all fairness, is a true attempt to better people's attitudes. Unfortunately for the filmmakers this simply comes off as a bit preachy. It is unrealistic and sugary in its portrayal of street people, and succeeds only on a soap-box level. The movie was filmed on location in New York City.

p, Dick Ross; d, Don Murray; w, Murray, James Bonnet (based on a book by David Wilkerson, John and Elizabeth Sherrill); ph, Julian C. Townsend (Eastmancolor); m, Ralph Carmichael; ed, Angelo Ross; art d, Charles Bailey; cos, Pearl Somner.

Drama   **Cas.**   (PR:A   MPAA:GP)

CROSS CHANNEL*½
(1955, Brit.) 61m REP bw

Wayne Morris (Tex Parker), Yvonne Furneaux (Jacqueline Moreau), Arnold Marle (Papa Moreau), Patrick Allen (Hugo Platt), Carl Jaffe (Otto Dagoff), Peter Sinclair (Soapy), Charles Laurence (Jean-Pierre), Michael Golden (Carrick), June Ashley, Jack Lambert, Jacques Cey.

Charter boat captain Morris is framed on a murder charge by a gang of jewel smugglers. Morris gets tossed overboard, spends perilous time at sea, and finally lands in a French fishing village where he falls in love with Furneaux. He is ultimately exonerated but not before some shoot-outs and a lot of plot-twisting without suspense. Weak British actioner, one of four directed in England in 1955 by low-budget veteran Bud Springsteen.

p, William N. Boyle; d, R.G. Springsteen; w, Rex Rienits; ph, Basil Emmott; m, Lambert Williamson; ed, John Seabourne; art d, John Stoll.

Crime   (PR:A-C   MPAA:NR)

CROSS COUNTRY**½
(1983, Can.) 95m Filmline-Ronald Cohen/MGM-UA c

Richard Beymer (Evan Bley), Nina Axelrod (Lois Hayes), Michael Ironside (Detective Sgt. Ed Roersch), Brent Carver (John Forrest), Michael Kane (Harry Burns), August Schellenberg (Glen Cosgrove), Paul Bradley (Nick Overland), Roberta Weiss (Alma Jean), George Sperkados (Welles), David Conner (Rico), Anna Vitre (Judith).

When a call girl is savagely murdered, suspicion falls on TV ad man Beymer. While he flees across Canada, detective Ironside, a lawman with questionable ethics, pursues him doggedly. The plot twists and turns confusingly, and in the end sputters out. Decent production values and performances can't help this miserable script. A poor man's NORTH BY NORTHWEST.

p, Pieter Kroonenburg, David J.Patterson; d, Paul Lynch; w, Logan N. Danforth, William Gray (based on a novel by Herbert Kastle); ph, Rene Verzier; m, Chris Rea; ed, Nick Rotundo; prod d, Michel Proulx.

Crime   **Cas.**   (PR:O   MPAA:R)

CROSS COUNTRY CRUISE*
(1934) 75m UNIV bw

Lew Ayres (Norman), June Knight (Sue), Alice White (May), Alan Dinehart (Steve), Minna Gombell (Nita), Eugene Pallette (Bronson), Arthur Vinton (Murphy), Robert McWade (The Grouch), Henry Armetta (The Italian).

This is almost a seventy-five minute Greyhound commercial. A sort of GRAND HOTEL via bus with lots of footage of Americana, Chicago, the Mormon Tabernacle, a carnival, and lots of other picturesque goodies. The slim plot has a two-timing husband who plans to do away with his wife. He succeeds in what is perhaps the greatest middle-class murder in cinema. In the middle of a department store, husband grabs a bow and arrow and sends the latter into the torso of his wife. A wise hero, though, doesn't buy the common belief that the jealous mistress did the deed, and is able to pin the rap on the marksman murderer. Seemingly unintentional, this picture becomes a black comedy about America's middle-class killers—the kind who use a bus as a getaway car!

d, Edward Buzzell; w, Elmer Harris (based on the story by Stanley Rauh); ph, George Robinson; ed, Philip Cahn.

Drama   (PR:A-C   MPAA:NR)

CROSS COUNTRY ROMANCE***
(1940) 67m RKO bw

Gene Raymond (Larry), Wendy Barrie (Diane), Hedda Hopper (Mrs. North), Billy Gilbert (Orestes), George P. Huntley (Walter Corbett), Berton Churchill (Conway), Tom Dugan (Pete), Edgar Dearling (1st Cop), Frank Sully (2nd Cop), Cliff Clark (Capt. Burke), Dorothea Kent (Millie).

Ending a two-year hiatus which began after his marriage to Jeanette MacDonald, Raymond returns to the screen in this pleasantly whimsical picture which offers just what the title promises. Doctor Raymond meets up with the soon-to-be-wed Barrie and they do the continental hop. Working their way west, they encounter garden variety situations which lead to their eventual spell of love. What he doesn't know about her is that she's traveling under a false banner. When he learns the truth, he quickly takes a walk. The obligatory reunion follows. When people today exclaim that "they don't make 'em like they used to" this is the type of crowd-pleaser they're referring to. A well-crafted script from Browne's novel seems to be the key, a lesser version of Capra's IT HAPPENED ONE NIGHT with less charismatic performances and trailer provided for the leads.

p, Cliff Reid (for Lee Marcus); d, Frank Woodruff; w, Jerry Cady, Bert Granet (based on the novel Highway to Romance by Eleanor Browne); ph, J. Roy Hunt; ed, Harry Marker; md, Roy Webb.

Romance   (PR:A   MPAA:NR)

CROSS CREEK**
(1983) 127m UNIV c

Mary Steenburgen (Marjorie Kinnan Rawlings), Rip Torn (Marsh Turner), Peter Coyote (Norton Baskin), Dana Hill (Ellie Turner), Alfre Woddard (Geechee), Joanna Miles (Mrs. Turner), Ike Eisenmann (Paul), Gary Guffey (Floyd Turner), Toni Hudson (Tim's Wife), Bo Rucker (Leroy), Jay O. Sanders (Charles Rawlings), John Hammond (Tim), Tommy Alford (Postal Clerk), Keith Michel (Preston Turner), Terrence Gehr (Store Keeper), Nora Rogers (Mary Turner), Kenneth Vickery (Minister), C.T. Wakefield (Sheriff), Malcolm McDowell (Max Perkins).

Marjorie Kinnan Rawlings' memoirs of a stay in the backwoods of Florida during the 1930s provide the loose basis of this film. Steenburgen plays the author of The Yearling isolating herself in the wilderness to observe the locals and "find herself." It's all very pretty and pasteurized, though Torn does a decent job on chewing up the scenery as a redneck. Steenburgen's real-life husband, McDowell, plays famed book editor Maxwell Perkins in a brief part. Steenburgen, with her weird marquee name, is one of the most overrated actresses now employed. Ungainly and with a voice that would annoy the sensitivities of a hod-carrier, she unfailingly delivers her lines as if coming out of a coma. Her highest emotional projection is on a par with kelp and she has not given a performance that does not beg for the hook or, at least, instant resuscitation.

p, Robert B. Radnitz; d, Martin Ritt; w, Dalene Young (based on the book Cross Creek by Marjorie Kinnan Rawlings); ph, John A. Alonzo (Panavision, Technicolor); m, Leonard Rosenman; ed, Sidney Levin; prod d, Walter Scott Herndon; cos, Joe I. Tompkins.

Drama   (PR:C   MPAA:PG)

CROSS CURRENTS**
(1935, Brit.) 66m B&D-PAR British bw

Ian Colin (Tony Brocklehurst), Marjorie Hume (Mrs. Stepping-Drayton), Evelyn Foster (Margery Weston), Frank Birch (Rev. Eustace Hickling), Aubrey Mallalieu (Gen. Trumpington), Kate Saxon (Miss Cruickshank), Aubrey Dexter (Col. Bagge-Grant), Bryan Powley (Cmdr. Mannering), Sally Gray (Sally Croker).

Local vicar Birch is accused of murder after his rival for a local widow turns up dead. Competent crime melodrama doesn't hold much interest today.

p, Anthony Havelock-Allan; d, Adrian Brunel; w, Brunel, Pelham Leigh Amann (based on the novel Nine Days Blunder by Gerald Elliott); ph, Francis Carver.

Crime   (PR:A   MPAA:NR)

CROSS MY HEART**
(1937, Brit.) 65m B&D-PAR British bw (AKA: LOADED DICE)

Kathleen Gibson (Sally Nichols), Kenneth Duncan (Steve King), Tully Comber (Chesty Barlow), Aubrey Fitzgerald (The Major), Robert Field (Mabardi), Muriel Johnson (Miss Bly), Eric Hales (Mr. Bland), Sylvia Coleridge (Alice).

Gibson inherits a boardinghouse and turns it into a swanky nightclub. Simultaneously she is romanced by a musician and a gambler. Lightweight romantic fluff.

p, Anthony Havelock-Allan; d, Bernard Mainwaring; w, Basil N, Keyes (based on a story by Robert Skinner); ph, Frances Carver.

Drama   (PR:A   MPAA:NR)

CROSS MY HEART**
(1946) 85m PAR bw

Betty Hutton (Peggy Harper), Sonny Tufts (Oliver Clarke), Rhys Williams (Prosecutor), Ruth Donnelly (Eve Harper), Alan Bridge (Detective Flynn), Iris Adrian (Mrs. Baggart), Howard Freeman (Wallace Brent), Lewis L. Russell (Judge), Michael Chekhov (Peter), Milton Kibbee, Nolan Leary, Shimen Ruskin, John Kelly, Ethel Mae Halls, Chester Morrison,Besse Wade, Mae Busch, Wilbur Mack, William Meader (Jurors), Ida Moore (Little Lady Juror), Jimmy Conlin (Jury Foreman), Lou Lubin (Tony Krouch), Tom Dugan, Tom Fadden (Truck Drivers), Almira Sessions (Old Hag), Dorothy Vaughan (Matron), Larry Thompson (Mr. Dennis), Arthur Loft (Deputy), Walter Baldwin (Coroner), Syd Saylor, Frank Ferguson, Harry Harvey (Reporters), Frank Faylen (Fingerprint Expert), Jody Gilbert (Miss Stewart), Kathleen Howard (Mrs. Klute), Bobby Larson (Newsboy).

Screwball comedy has Hutton taking the rap for a murder she did not commit, in order to showcase the talents of her fiance, lawyer Tufts, in defending her. He does, but even wacky Hutton's antics can't take the minds of the audience off of the criminal job the scriptwriters pulled in calling this entertainment. Remake of TRUE CONFESSION.

Songs: "Love Is the Darndest Thing," "That Little Dream Got Nowhere," "How Do You Do It?" "Does Baby Feel Alright?" "It Hasn't Been Chilly in Chile" (Johnny Burke, Jimmy Van Heusen), "Cross My Heart" (Robert Emmett Dolan, Larry Neill).

p, Harry Tugend; d, John Berry; w, Tugend, Claude Binyon, Charles Schnee (based on a play by Louis Verneiul, George Berr); ph, Charles Lang, Jr., Stuart Thompson; m, Robert Emmett Dolan; ed, Ellsworth Hoaglund; md, Joseph L. Lilley.

Musical Comedy **(PR:A MPAA:NR)**

CROSS OF IRON*** (1977, Brit., Ger.) 133m AE c

James Coburn *(Steiner)*, Maximilian Schell *(Stransky)*, James Mason *(Brandt)*, David Warner *(Kiesel)*, Klaus Lowitsch *(Kruger)*, Vadim Glowna *(Kern)*, Roger Fritz *(Triebig)*, Dieter Schidor *(Anselm)*, Burkhardt Driest *(Maag)*, Fred Stillkraut *(Schnurrbart)*, Michael Nowka *(Dietz)*, Veronique Vendell *(Marga)*, Arthur Brauss *(Zoll)*, Senta Berger *(Eva)*, Slavco Stimac *(Mikael)*.

A war story similar to THE BLUE MAX told from the point of view of the Germans as they see the myth of their invincibility being shattered on the Russian front in 1943. Coburn is a sergeant who is tired of the war, tired of a government he doesn't support, and angry at the world. Schell is a Prussian officer who has but one goal in life, to win an Iron Cross (the highest medal Germany could award) and he will do anything to achieve that. Mason is a colonel and Warner is his staff captain. Both men can sense which way the war is going and both look forward to an end of hostilities and a peace with honor. Roger Fritz is a gay lieutenant whom Schell uses to do his bidding, and Peckinpah examines "male camaraderie" with a razor's edge. So does a Russian female soldier when her post is overrun by the Germans and she is forced to submit to a rape by one of the Nazis. She takes the opportunity to castrate the German. Yet Peckinpah keeps gratuitous violence to a reasonable level as he strives to show us that war is hell. Coquillon's cinematography is spectacular and Yugoslavia looks wonderful, even under the shelling and gunfire. Very few female roles in the movie, with the standout being awarded to Senta Berger as a hospital nurse who offers Coburn balm and solace beyond what Blue Cross might proffer. Peckinpah uses his by-now-trademarked slow-motion technique, with bodies flying all over the landscape. Enough is enough! This was obviously a co-production designed to get many international stars into it so the picture could make money in theater guarantees before it ever opened. But it was too late by 1977. WW II was, by that time, a subject for satire. Lenny Bruce had it right when he said that "Satire is tragedy, plus time." The film was presented by Alex Winitsky and Arlene Sellers with several other production companies coming in to lend a hand. Co-writer Julius Epstein is the same Julius Epstein who co-wrote CASABLANCA with his brother and Howard Koch, and who is responsible for many very funny films. There is not a shred of that sense of humor in this screenplay. Sequel: BREAKTHROUGH.

p, Wolf C. Hartwig; d, Sam Peckinpah; w, Herbert Asmodi, Julius J. Epstein (based on the book *Cross of Iron* by Willi Heinrich); ph, John Coquillon (Technicolor); m, Ernest Gold; ed, Mike Ellis, Tony Lawson, Herbert Taschner; spec eff, Richard Richtsfeld.

War Drama **Cas.** **(PR:O MPAA:R)**

CROSS OF LORRAINE, THE*** (1943) 89m MGM bw

Jean Pierre Aumont *(Paul)*, Gene Kelly *(Victor)*, Sir Cedric Hardwicke *(Father Sebastian)*, Richard Whorf *(Francois)*, Joseph Calleia *(Rodriguez)*, Peter Lorre *(Sgt. Berger)*, Hume Cronyn *(Duval)*, Billy Roy *(Louis)*, Tonio Selwart *(Maj. Bruhl)*, Jack Lambert *(Jacques)*, Wallace Ford *(Pierre)*, Donald Curtis *(Marcel)*, Jack Edwards, Jr. *(Rene)*, Richard Ryen *(Lt. Schmidt)*, Frederick Giermann *(Corp. Daxer)*.

An uncompromising and often brutal war film. Kelly and Aumont star as French soldiers who surrender to the Germans at the fall of France in 1940 after being promised that they will be returned to their homes and loved ones if they lay down their arms. Of course, these are lies and the soldiers are quickly herded into boxcars and shipped to a concentration camp where they are sadistically treated and starved to death. Lorre is at his most vicious as the demented Nazi sergeant, tossing a loaf of bread from a full basket onto the dirty floor of a barracks to see the starving prisoners tear at each other for a morsel. Kelly refuses to buckle under and is tortured, yet he won't break, even when Lorre kicks him in the face and opens up his skull. Aumont, on the other hand, meekly submits to the Nazi tyranny, serving his new masters with a groveling smile but biding his time. Hardwicke, a priest interned with the soldiers, offers a mass and Lorre attends. He listens for a moment, a weak smile crossing his face. Then he takes out his gun and shoots the priest dead with a single shot. Kelly goes berserk and attacks Lorre and he is beaten senseless by guards. He is sent to the infirmary where Aumont works. Meanwhile, Cronyn, another Frenchman who speaks fluent German, decides to work for the Nazis, becoming their pawn and spy. He is exposed and then tossed out into the camp yard in the middle of the night to be shot by guards. (This scene was almost duplicated frame for frame in STALAG 17.) Aumont next switches the sick Kelly for an ailing German soldier and both manage to leave the camp and escape. They make their way to a small village with the help of underground workers. A German detachment arrives a short time later to take all males into a labor battalion. Aumont pretends to volunteer but, once in front of the villagers, excitedly denounces the Germans and encourages everyone to resist. He is summarily shot to death by a German officer, and Kelly, who up to this time has been in a semi-comatose state, suddenly leads the villagers in a wholesale attack on the Germans, wiping out the Nazis to the last man in a wild battle. The villagers then burn their town to the ground in a "scorched earth" tactic, similar to that being practiced against the Germans in Russia, and the entire town migrates into unoccupied territory to continue the fight against the Nazi regime. The propaganda in this WW II film is thick and "La Marseillaise" is sung at the drop of helmet. The overacting is rampant, even with Kelly, who usually practices restraint in his serious dramatic roles. Garnett directs with his usual gusto but his story is overcome with senseless brutality which deadens the viewer by the end of the first reel. Harry Truman, then a senator and on a political errand in Los Angeles, visited the set of CROSS OF LORRAINE and met Lorre just after he had been practicing torture on the French prisoners. With Truman was MGM boss Louis B. Mayer who approached the small, eccentric actor, saying: "Well, Peter, you look fit—almost as if being a storm trooper agreed with you." Lorre, who was as Jewish as Mayer, smirked and startled Mayer and Truman by wryly remarking: "Oh yes, sir, it does. I eat a Jew every morning for breakfast." With that Mayer beat a hasty retreat with Truman in tow. Cedric Harwicke, a titled British "Sir," stopped with director Garnett on a lunch break from the production one day to listen to some swing played by Tommy Dorsey's band. He suddenly began dancing crazily about with uncharacteristic abandon, bumping into Greer Garson hurrying to the set of MRS. MINIVER. She thought she had almost knocked over a real priest and lowered her eyes, saying: "I'm *so* sorry, Father." With that he blessed her and then went into a burlesque bump and grind that first shocked her, then sent her into gales of laughter when she recognized her famous countryman. Ever after Hardwicke, when meeting the actress, greeted her with the words: "Bless you, my daughter."

p, Edwin Knopf; d, Tay Garnett; w, Michael Kanin, Ring Lardner, Jr., Alexander Esway, Robert D. Andrews (based on a story by Lilo Damert and Robert Aisner, taken from the book *A Thousand Shall Fall* by Hans Habe); ph, Sidney Wagner; m, Bronislau Kaper; ed, Dan Milner; art d, Cedric Gibbons.

War Drama **(PR:C-O MPAA:NR)**

CROSS OF THE LIVING*½

(1963, Fr.) 90m Christina Films/Cari Releasing Corp. bw (LA CROIX DES VIVANTS)

Pascale Petit *(Marie)*, Karlheinz Bohm *(Gus)*, Giani Esposito *(Yan)*, Gabriele Ferzetti *(Abbe)*, Christine Darvel *(Nell)*, Roger Dumas *(Sylvain)*, Jacques Richard *(Franz)*, Max de Rieux *(Karl)*, Alain Cuny *(Count)*, Madeleine Robinson *(Mme. Dorneck)*, Marika Green.

Returning to his village after being acquitted of his stepfather's murder, Esposito finds most of the villagers against him. Only his best friend, Bohm, remains loyal. Esposito finds himself increasingly drawn to Petit, Bohm's mistress. The two begin an affair, and when Bohm finds out he determines to kill his friend. He is unable to carry out his plan, though, and Esposito realizes that he can't hurt his only friend this way. He tells Petit that he cannot take her away, so she runs off into the night and is struck by a car driven by Bohm's mother. Inept, wooden melodrama enlivened only by the lovely Petit.

p, Christine, Jean-Claude Dumoutier; d, Yvan Govar; w, Christine, Jean-Claude Dumoutier, Alain Cavalier, Maurice Clavel; ph, Andre Bac; ed, Paul Cayatte; art d, Leon Barsacq.

Drama **(PR:C-O MPAA:NR)**

CROSS ROADS*½ (1930, Brit.) 58m British Projects/PAR bw

Percy Marmont *(Jim Wyndham)*, Anne Grey *(Mary Wyndham)*, Betty Faire *(The Other Woman)*, Langhorne Burton *(The Lawyer)*, Wilfred Shine *(The Father)*.

A mother thwarts her daughter's elopement by telling her the story of a wife (Grey) who shot her husband (Marmont) when she learned he was seeing another woman. Creaky early talkie.

p&d, Reginald Fogwell; w, Fogwell, A.E. Bundy.

Drama **PR:A MPAA:NR)**

CROSS STREETS* (1934) 65m IN/CHES bw

Claire Windsor *(Anne Clement)*, Johnny Mack Brown *(Adam Blythe)*, Anita Louise *(Clara Grattan)*, Kenneth Thomson *(Mort Talbot)*, Matty Kemp *(Ken Barclay)*, Josef Swickard *(Dean Todd)*, Niles Welch *(Jerry Clement)*.

A doctor on the skids is given the chance at a big operation, but is too honest to do it. Later he is killed for his part in a love rectangle by a man who is angry that he has been dallying with both his daughter and his wife. The dying doctor nobly makes his end look like suicide. Nothing sane going on here.

d, Frank Strayer; w, Anthony Coldeway (based on a story by Gordon Morris); ph, M.A. Anderson.

Drama **(PR:A MPAA:NR)**

CROSSED SWORDS** (1954) 83m UA c (IL MAESTRO DI DON GIOVANNI)

Errol Flynn *(Renzo)*, Gina Lollobrigida *(Francesca)*, Cesare Danova *(Raniero)*, Nadia Gray *(Fulvia)*, Paola Mori *(Tomasina)*, Roldano Lupi *(Pavoncello)*, Alberto Rabagliati *(Gennarelli)*, Silvio Bagolini *(Buio)*, Renata Chiantioni *(Spiga)*, Mimo Billi *(Miele)*, Pietro Tordi *(The Duke)*, Ricardo Rioli *(Lenzi)*.

Fun-loving Flynn jousts about in this swashbuckler which hinges on an archaic Italian law. The choice given to young bachelors is to get married or face a prison sentence. Not surprisingly, Flynn and his royal friend, the Duke's son, aren't leaping over this judiciary mess. Taking a back seat to the dreaded wedding is a plot to overthrow the Duke. Lollobrigida convinces Flynn that tying the knot doesn't mean putting an end to his swashbuckling nights, and they agree to marry. A well-behaved directorial approach simply doesn't do justice to the exuberance of Flynn.

p, J. Barrett Mahon, Vittorio Vassarotti; d&w, Milton Krims; ph, Jack Cardiff (PatheColor); art d, Arrigo Equini; cos, Nino Novarese; makeup, C. Gambarelli.

Adventure **(PR:A MPAA:NR)**

CROSSED SWORDS½** (1978) 113m WB c (GB: THE PRINCE AND THE PAUPER)

Oliver Reed *(Miles Hendon)*, Raquel Welch *(Lady Edith)*, Mark Lester *(Edward/Tom)*, Ernest Borgnine *(John Canty)*, George C. Scott *(Ruffler)*, Rex Harrison *(Duke of Norfolk)*, David Hemmings *(Hugh Hendon)*, Harry Andrews *(Hertford)*, Julian Orchard *(St. John)*, Murray Melvin *(The Prince's Dresser)*, Graham Stark *(Jester)*, Sybil Danning *(Mother Canty)*, Lalla Ward *(Princess Elizabeth)*, Felicity Dean *(Lady Jane)*, Charlton Heston *(Henry VIII)*.

A standard remake of Mark Twain's classic tale about two identical twins—one a prince, the other a pauper, both played with fine comic timing by Lester. A star-studded cast helps elevate the tame direction, with the most memorable performances coming from Scott and Borgnine. Welch's beauty is enhanced by some excellent photography, but Ward, in a bit, shines the most.

p, Pierre Spengler; d, Richard Fleischer; w, George MacDonald Fraser, Berta Dominquez, Spengler (based on Mark Twain's novel *The Prince And The Pauper)*; ph, Jack Cardiff (Panavision, Technicolor); m, Maurice Jarre; ed, Ernest Walter; prod d, Tony Pratt; cos, Judy Moorcroft; ch, Sally Gilpin.

Adventure **(PR:A MPAA:PG)**

CROSSED TRAILS*** (1948) 57m MON bw

Johnny Mack Brown *(Johnny)*, Raymond Hatton *(Bodie)*, Lynne Carver *(Maggie)*, Douglas Evans *(Hudson)*, Kathy Frye *(Melissa)*, Zon Murray *(Curtin)*, Mary MacLaren *(Mrs. Laswell)*, Ted Adams *(Laswell)*, Steve Clark *(Blake)*, Frank LaRue *(Judge)*, Milburn Morante *(Anderson)*, Robert D. Woodward *(Wright)*, Pierce Lyden *(Whitfield)*, Henry Hall *(Stoddard)*, Hugh Murray *(Jury Foreman)*, Bud Osborne *(Sheriff Cook)*, Artie Ortego, Boyd Stockman.

Punching and shooting his way through this oater, Johnny Mack Brown packs enough wallop to carry it on his own. Brown has an easy time of defending Carver's ranch from a duo of blackhats with a plan to control area water rights. The evil pair try to frame ranchman Hatton for murder, but Brown's brain and brawn trip them up.

p, Louis Gray; d, Lambert Hillyer; w, Colt Remington; ph, Harry Neumann; m, Edward J. Kay; ed, Fred Maguire.

Western **(PR:A MPAA:NR)**

CROSS-EXAMINATION*

(1932) 60m Supreme Features/Weiss Bros-Artclass bw

H.B. Warner *(Gerald Waring)*, Sally Blaine *(Grace Varney)*, Natalie Moorhead *(Inez Wells)*, Edmund Breese *(Dwight Simpson)*, William V. Mong *(Emory Wells)*, Donald Dillaway *(David Wells)*, Sarah Padden *(Mary Stevens)*, Wilfred Lucas *(Judge Hollister)*, Niles Welch *(Warren Slade)*, Nita Cavalier *(Etta Billings)*, Margaret Fealy, Alexander Pollard, B. Wayne LaMont, Frank Clark, John Webb Dillon, Lee Phelps.

A tedious recreation of a courtroom scene which seems to believe that story is secondary. Dillaway is on the stand for the murder of his father. After the testimony of the dead man's former maid, it is learned that she is really Dillaway's mother. Warner and Breese battle back and forth to win their case in this turgid exercise in early synchronization.

d, Richard Thorpe; w, Arthur Hoerl; ph, A. Anderson.

Drama **(PR:A MPAA:NR)**

CROSSFIRE** (1933) 44m RKO bw

Tom Keene *(Tom Allen)*, Betty Furness *(Patricia Plummer)*, Edgar Kennedy *(Ed Wimpy)*, Edward Phillips *(Bert King)*, Lafe McKee *(Daniel Plummer)*, Nick Cogley *(Doc Stiles)*, Jules Cowan, Tom Brown, Murdock McQuarrie, Stanley Blystone.

A detail-ridden mix of the old West and Chicago gangsters that has Keene returning from WW I duty in France only to find trouble in his home town. One friend is murdered and another is wrongly accused of the crime. The son of a mine owner is the actual culprit, who, together with some Chicago thugs, fights against justice-bound Keene. Our hero's ways of the West prevail and the gangsters are sent back to the Windy City, leaving him with the delightful Furness in his arms,

p, David O. Selznick; d, Otto Brower; w, Harold Shumate, Tom McNamara; ph, Nick Musuraca; ed, Frederick Knudtsen.

Western/Crime **(PR:A MPAA:NR)**

CROSSFIRE**** (1947) 86m RKO bw

Robert Young *(Finlay)*, Robert Mitchum *(Keeley)*, Robert Ryan *(Montgomery)*, Gloria Grahame *(Ginny)*, Paul Kelly *(The Man)*, Sam Levene *(Joseph Samuels)*, Jacqueline White *(Mary Mitchell)*, Steve Brodie *(Floyd)*, George Cooper *(Mitchell)*, Richard Benedict *(Bill)*, Richard Powers *(Detective)*, William Phipps *(Leroy)*, Lex Barker *(Harry)*, Marlo Dwyer *(Miss Lewis/Miss White)*, Harry Harvey *(Man)*, Carl Faulkner *(Deputy)*, Jay Norris, Robert Bray, George Turner, Don Cadell *(Military Police)*, Philip Morris *(Police Sergeant)*, Kenneth McDonald *(Major)*, Allen Ray *(Soldier)*, Bill Nind *(Waiter)*, George Meader *(Police Surgeon)*.

Anti-Semitism had been a bugbear in Hollywood for decades; no studio really wanted to take on this social evil until Fox decided to film GENTLEMAN'S AGREEMENT, but RKO beat Fox to the punch by releasing CROSSFIRE first and the impact was tremendous. It is a simple and chilling story centering about sadistic bully Ryan who is about to be mustered out of the service with three Army buddies, Brodie, Cooper, and Phipps. All of them get drunk after meeting Levene and his girl friend Grahame in a nightclub. They go to Levene's apartment where they drink themselves into near collapse. In a drunken rage Ryan, who seethes with hatred for foreigners and religious creeds, particularly Jews, beats Levene to death. His friends vaguely recall the incident but vanish so they can't be questioned by authorities. Young, a pipe-smoking, introspective detective, begins to investigate, aided by Mitchum, another GI who knows the soldiers involved and is stationed at the same mustering out center with them. He profiles the four suspects and eventually helps to lay a trap for Ryan, who has so far smoothly sidestepped Young's probing. To silence Brodie, who appears about to crack and tell all, Ryan beats him to death. Mitchum tracks down Phipps and Cooper, with Grahame's help, and then manages to get a message to Ryan that Brodie wants to see him. Thinking Brodie is still alive, Ryan shows up at the rendezvous to make sure he is dead this time and is arrested by Young and the police who are waiting for him. All of the performances are fine, particularly Ryan's, who is electric and terrifying as the brutish xenophobic killer. This was a part he wanted immediately after reading Brooks' novel; both of them were in the Marine Corps together and Ryan told Brooks that if the book was filmed he wanted to play the part of Montgomery. In the novel the issue is not race nor religion but sex. The victim is a homosexual who is beaten to death by other Marines, but this theme in 1947 was still taboo. Producer Scott,, who convinced RKO to buy the book, did so on the proviso that anti-Semitism would replace the homosexual theme and Brooks agreed. Young renders a restrained, beautifully timed performance with a powerhouse monolog at film's end. Mitchum, a pivotal character, acts almost like an avenging angel, putting all the pieces together for the police and bringing the disturbed soldiers together. Grahame is generally wasted as a prop. Levene, as the victim, is simply magnificent in one of his most memorable roles. Kelly is the oddball in the cast, first a strong suspect, then merely a man adrift who can't make up his mind whether or not he loves Grahame. This Dore Schary thriller gleaned $1,270,000 at the box office the first time around, then a whopping amount. This was the last film director Dmytryk and producer Scott, long a duo, would jointly create and their last at RKO: after this film's completion, both men were brought before HUAC and became enmeshed in the Communist witchhunt. This was Schary's first production for RKO which he had recently taken over. Dmytryk's direction is first rate, tight, and well-paced. He took only twenty days to complete the film, using only 140 setups in the entire film, about seven per day, aided tremendously by RKO's wizard cinematographer, Hunt, who invented dozens of machines to help facilitate shooting. For this film, Hunt, in one night inside the studio's machine shop, invented an involved extension to a crab dolly so that Dmytryk could get one difficult shot. The film bolstered RKO's lagging prestige and made Dmytryk the momentary king of the studio lot. The public responded well to the film. The Audience Research Institute conducted polls of those going into the theaters to see the film and after they left, later reporting that the film reduced anti-Semitism by 14 percent among viewers. Yet there were those upon whom the film made no impact whatsoever. One of Dmytryk's own production members approached the director after the film's completion, saying: "It's such a fine suspense story. Why did you have to bring in that stuff about anti-Semitism? . . . There is no anti-Semitism in the United States. If there were, why is all the money in America controlled by Jewish bankers?" Dmytryk could only shake his head and murmur: "That's why we made the film." For Ryan, the image of the Jew-hating bigot was to stay with him all his life, typecasting him as a vicious, meanminded character, particularly after he spat out such lines as: "Jew-boys who lived on easy street during the war while the white people fought in the front-line trenches." He regretted forever the villain he created, never talking about the part again, actually hating it, although he was acclaimed world-wide for the performance. Instead, when CROSSFIRE was brought up, Ryan would shift the conversation to his favorite film, THE SET-UP, a 1949 film about a has-been boxer which Ryan played to perfection. A great actor, he was capable of any difficult role, and was always, lamentably, underrated by critics who came to hiss him.

p, Adrian Scott (for Dore Schary); d, Edward Dmytryk; w, John Paxton (based on the novel *The Brick Foxhole* by Richard Brooks); ph, J. Roy Hunt; m, Roy Webb; ed, Harry Gerstad; md, Constantin Bakaleinikoff; art d, Albert S. D'Agostino, Afred Herman; set d, Darrell Silvera, John Sturtevant; makeup, Gordon Bau; spec eff, Russell A. Cully.

Crime Drama **Cas.** **(PR:C MPAA:NR)**

CROSSPLOT** (1969, Brit.) 97m Tribune/UA (GB) c

Roger Moore *(Gary Fenn)*, Martha Hyer *(Jo Grinling)*, Claudie Lange *(Maria Kogash)*, Alexis Kanner *(Tarquin)*, Francis Matthews *(Ruddock)*, Bernard Lee *(Chilmore)*, Derek Francis *(Sir Charles Moberley)*, Ursula Howells *(Maggie Thwaites)*, Veronica Carlson *(Dinah)*, Dudley Sutton *(Warren)*, Tim Preece *(Sebastian)*, Mona Bruce *(Myrna)*, Norman Eshley *(Athol)*, Michael Culver *(Jim)*, Gabrielle Drake *(Celia)*, John Lee *(Blake)*.

Spy thriller writers seem to think that they have license to be politically profound—and in most cases they are hurt by their gross oversimplification. This Moore showcase is no exception. Playing his patented "Saint"-ly role, he pursues a mysterious girl with only one clue—a portrait which bears her name. The chase takes him to a rally in celebration of the birthday of an African statesman. An assassination attempt by a crazed group of anarchists is foiled by the alert Moore. Lots of lookers, comedy, and action, but all of it heartless.

p, Robert S. Baker; d, Alvin Rakoff; w, Leigh Vance, John Kruse (based on a story by Vance); ph, Brendan J. Stafford (Eastmancolor); m, Stanley Black with songs by Lois Lane, Les Reed; ed, Bert Rule; art d, Ivan King.

Spy Drama **(PR:C MPAA:NR)**

CROSSROADS*½**

(1938, Fr.) 73m B.U.P. Francaise/Eclair-Journal bw (CARREFOUR)

Charles Vanel, Jules Berry, Suzy Prim, Tania Fedor, Marcelle Geniat, Jean Caludio, J. Tissler, Argentin, Otto Walburg, Paul Amiot, Clary, Palau, P. de Ramey, Auguste Boverlo.

A plotty French drama involving a shell-shocked war veteran with a split personality. Wealthy manufacturer Vanel, who was under attack in the war, is the subject of a blackmail scheme which accuses him of having a criminal record. He brings the blackmailer to court and wins his case, thanks to the efforts of Berry, a surprise witness. Berry, however, turns out to be a blackmailer also who insists Vanel really was a criminal. An old song that Berry whistles clicks in the vet's mind, causing him to think he actually is guilty of the crimes. Confused, he decides to sell his business and turn himself in. His decision is made tough by his unconvinced family, and his son who, aggravated by his friend's accusations, tries suicide. Fate is sealed when Prim—the former lover of Vanel and present mate of Berry—shoots her blackmailing mate and then herself. Interestingly, the character and the audience never are really sure of his innocence or guilt. A provocative film in which the question holds more importance than the answer. (In French; English subtitles.) Remade with equal success in the U.S. in 1942.

p, Eugene Tuscherer; d, Kurt Bernhardt (based on a story by Hans Kafka); ph, L.H. Buret; m, Michael Emer; subtitles: Clement Douenias, Larry Schneider.

Drama **(PR:A MPAA:NR)**

CROSSROADS***½

(1942) 82m MGM bw
(AKA: THE MAN WHO LOST HIS WAY)

William Powell (David Talbot), Hedy Lamarr (Lucienne Talbot), Claire Trevor (Michelle Allaine), Basil Rathbone (Henri Sarrow), Felix Bressart (Dr. Andre Tessier), Margaret Wycherly (Mme. Pelletier), Reginald Owen (Concierge), Philip Merivale (Commissionaire of Police), Sig Ruman (Dr. Alex Benoit), Vladimir Sokoloff (Le Duc), H.B. Warner (Prosecuting Attorney), Guy Bates Post (President of Court), Fritz Leiber (Deval), John Mylong (Baron de Lorraine), Frank Conroy (Defense Attorney), James Rennie (Martin), Bertram Marburgh (Landers), Harry Fleischmann (Assistant Defense Attorney), Louis Montez, Octavio Giraud, Enrique Acosta, Adolph Faylauer (Associate Judges), Jean Del Val (Court Clerk), Paul Weigel, Torgen Meyer (Old Men), John St. Polis (Professor), Jack Zoller (Student), Francis X. Bushman, Jr. (Giant Policeman), Christian J. Frank (Guard), Alex Davidoff (Detective), Theodore Rand (Orchestra Leader), Anna Q. Nilsson (Mme. Deval), Alphonse Martell (Headwaiter), Hector Sarno (Organ Grinder), William Edmunds (Driver), Armand Cortes (Clerk), Lester Sharpe, George Davis (Clerks), Marek Windheim (Clerk at Airport), John Picorri (Waiter), Billy Roy, Frank Morales, Jo Jo LaSavio, Adrian Kerbrat (Boys), Ferdinand Munier (Fat Man), Guy D'Ennery, Shirley McDonald, Gibson Gowland, Jack Chefe, Louis Natheaux, Edith Penn, Sandra Morgan (Reporters), Irene Shirley (Maid), Alice Ward (Nurse Receptionist), Grace Hayle (Patient), Lester Sharpe, Budd Fine (Paris Policemen).

Following their marriage, Powell and Lamarr are suddenly harassed by an extortionist who sends a note to Powell demanding a payment of a million francs. A nightmare then begins as Powell is openly accused by Sokoloff, the blackmailer, as being another man, a wanted criminal. In court, the confused Powell, believing he is a victim of amnesia, is confronted by Trevor who claims he is indeed the wanted criminal, now using another name, that she had been his lover. Her testimony and that of Sokoloff is destroyed in one lightning appearance by Rathbone who testifies for Powell's defense, stating that he knew the real criminal Powell is accused of being and that that man died in his arms some time earlier. Powell is vindicated, Sokoloff sent to jail for bringing a false suit, and Trevor's reputation is ruined. Then, in another surprise twist, Rathbone visits the grateful Powell, telling him that he lied at the trial, that Powell is truly the wanted criminal, and that he, Rathbone, is the man behind the blackmailing scheme. According to Rathbone, Powell received a blow on the head during a robbery-murder they both committed and has lost his memory. He shows him a photo where Trevor is posing intimately with Powell, to convince him that he is the wanted criminal. Powell is about to pay the blackmail to Rathbone but Lamarr finds a doctor, Bressart, who treated him for his head injury. Bressart explains that Powell has been injured on the right side of his head, which is the side he once used to part his hair, but now parts it on the left side to cover the scar. Since the photo with Trevor shows his hair parted on the left side, Powell realizes that it is a current photo of him and not taken when he supposedly lived under another name. Further investigation proves the photo a fake and Rathbone's entire scheme is an elaborate fraud to convince Powell that he is someone he isn't. Powell sets up a clever trap with police help and snares Rathbone, who is later sent to prison. A clever, witty, and suspenseful "victim" film in the Hitchcockian tradition. Director Conway moves the story along briskly while Powell, as the bewildered diplomat (a member of France's Foreign Office living in Paris, circa 1935), is marvelous. Lamarr turns in a good performance as the beautiful wife desperate to help her husband. Rathbone as the supreme rascal steals the film. Bressart as the neurologist is convincing. The double-dealing Trevor gives another sterling performance and sings one song as a nightclub chanteuse. Her voice is pleasing and the nightclub setting for her appearance under "a baby spot," is almost a precursor to the scene she describes as the fallen entertainer six years later in KEY LARGO. The entire production received top MGM attention and budget. Studio bosses went so far as to offer Trevor's role to Marlene Dietrich, who bristled when she learned that she would only be a supporting player under Lamarr. Snapped Dietrich when refusing the role: "I share my glamour with nobody!" This was Lamarr's film, even though Powell was the central figure. MGM touted the Hungarian beauty for many new major films on the drawing boards, including something called SCORCHED EARTH where she would play a Russian guerrilla, a film never made. She was also announced to play opposite Robert Taylor in a film entitled THE LAST TIME I SAW PARIS. This never happened but the title was used later for a film starring Van Johnson and Elizabeth Taylor, based on F. Scott Fitzgerald's story, "Babylon Revisited."

p, Edwin Knopf; d, Jack Conway; w, Gus Trosper (based on a story by John Kafka and Howard Emmett Rogers); ph, Joseph Ruttenberg; m, Bronislau Kaper; ed, George Boemler; art d, Cedric Gibbons, John S. Detlie; set d, Edwin B. Willis; gowns, Kalloch; m/l, "Till You Remember," Arthur Schwartz, Howard Dietz.

Mystery **(PR:A MPAA:NR)**

CROSSROADS OF PASSION**½

(1951, Fr.) 90m Films International of America bw

Viviane Romance (Irene Dumesnil), Valentina Cortese (Maria Pilar), Clement Duhour (Mario da Falla), Fosco Giachetti (Torriani), Gina Falkenberg (Hilde van Baldur), Giovanni Hinrich (Fischer), Olinto Cristina (Dr. Slaceck), Job Van Huelsen (Schmidt), Sembt (Von Baldur), Jean Wall (Jean Claes).

Mediocre spy story about a group of resistance fighters in Lisbon, and Romance's attempt to avenge a lover's death which they are responsible for. The primary aim is to explore the motivations of the characters, as opposed to exhibiting methods of resistance. This interesting angle is pulled off chiefly because of skillful scripting and well-defined stage settings. (In French; English subtitles.)

p, Ettore Giannini; d, Jacques Companeez (based on a story by Companeez, Claude Heymann); m, Joseph Kosma; subtitles, Sidney H. Mayers.

Spy Drama **(PR:A MPAA:NR)**

CROSSROADS TO CRIME**

(1960, Brit.) 57m AP Films/AA bw

Anthony Oliver (Don Ross), Patricia Heneghan (Joan Ross), Miriam Karlin (Connie Williams), George Murcell (Diamond), Ferdy Mayne (Miles), David Graham (Johnny), Arthur Rigby (Sgt. Pearson), Victor Maddern (Len).

Policeman Oliver pretends to take a bribe in order to expose a gang of truck hijackers. Interesting crime yarn.

p, Gerry Anderson, John Read; d, Anderson; w, Alun Falconer.

Crime Drama **(PR:C MPAA:NR)**

CROSSTALK**½

(1982, Aus.) 82m Wall to Wall c

Gary Day, Penny Downie, Brian McDermott, Peter Collingwood, Kim Deacon.

A thinking computer challenges the morality and intelligence of its inventor and his wife in a logical, nonfearing manner. It (he? she?) begins to play such a large part in the inventor's life that his wife gets extremely jealous. After it witnesses a murder and makes a time-consuming, deductive decision on how to handle the situation, the pair shower the computer with praise and gratitude. An interesting, uniquely photographed film which is hurt by its excessive talkiness/preachiness. A commendable debut from director Egerton.

p, Errol Sullivan; d, Mark Egerton; w, Egerton, Linda Lane, Denis Whitburn; ph, Vincent Monton.

Science Fiction/Drama **(PR:A MPAA:NR)**

CROSSTRAP*½

(1962, Brit.) 61m Newbery Clyne Avon/Unifilms bw

Laurence Payne (Duke), Jill Adams (Sally), Gary Cockrell (Geoff), Zena Marshall (Rina), Bill Nagy (Gaunt), Robert Cawdron (Joe), Larry Taylor (Peron).

A writer and his wife travel to their holiday cottage and find it occupied by a gang of thieves, with another gang outside besieging them. Silly crime drama of little importance.

p, Michael Deeley, George Mills; d, Robert Hartford-Davis; w, Philip Wrestler (based on a novel by John Newton Chance).

Crime **(PR:C MPAA:NR)**

CROSS-UP*½

(1958) 83m UA bw (AKA: TIGER BY THE TAIL)

Larry Parks (John Desmond), Constance Smith (Jane Claymore), Lisa Daniely (Anna Ray), Cyril Chamberlain (Foster), Donald Stewart (MacAuley), Thora Hird (Mary), Joan Heal (Annabelle), Alexander Gauge (Fitzgerald), Ronan O'Casey (Mick), Marie Bryant (Melodie).

The matter-of-fact direction of this uninspired script leaves one cold while trudging through the thick plot. Parks, an American newsman in London, befriends Daniely, who turns out to be a secret agent. Carrying a valuable list of enemy agents which looks like a diary, she accidentally drops it. Parks picks it up, only to have a gun drawn on him. A struggle ensues and the woman accidentally is shot and killed. With the book in his hands, the enemy tries to track him down before he can expose them. Calculated and tired.

p, Robert S. Baker, Monty Berman; d, John Gilling; w, Gilling, Willis Goldbeck (based on the novel I'll Never Come Back by John Mair); ph, Eric Cross; m, Stanley Black; m/l, Black, Sid Colin.

Spy Drama **(PR:A MPAA:NR)**

CROSSWINDS**½

(1951) 93m PAR c (AKA: JUNGLE ATTACK)

John Payne (Steve Singleton), Rhonda Fleming (Katherine Shelley), Forrest Tucker (Jumbo Johnson), Robert Lowery (Nick Brandon), Alan Mowbray (Sir Cecil Daubrey), John Abbott (Sykes), Frank Kumagai (Bumidal).

High adventure in the low jungles of New Guinea (much of it was actually shot in Florida). Payne is the muscular, sea-faring master of a good-sized ship that works the South Seas in search of things to do. Tucker and Lowery have a good use for that ship and arrange to have Payne framed so they can get the boat. They want it to transport a shipment of gold aboard a plane they arrange to have crash-land in some shallow waters. There's a passenger on the plane and it's curvaceous Fleming, who is rapidly becoming an alcoholic due to bitterness at her husband's death in the war. Payne joins forces with Mowbray and Abbott, two funny conmen, to find the gold, his boat, and Rhonda. In the course of inhuman events, they must face the standard adventure fare that Steven Spielberg and George Lucas used to such financial gain many years later: mad natives, big jungle cats, alligators, etc. They eventually locate the girl and the gold and must then race through another native gamut before returning to safety. It's a fun picture but as memorable as last July 22nd's weather report. Fleming is luscious, Payne is strong and not silent enough, and Tucker is just too amiable to take seriously as a villain.

p, William Pine, William Thomas; d, Lewis R. Foster; w, Foster (based on the novel New Guinea Gold by Thomson Burtis); ph, Loyal Griggs (Technicolor); m, Lucien Cailliet; ed, Howard Smith; m/l, "Crosswinds" (Jay Livingston, Ray Evans).

Adventure **(PR:A MPAA:NR)**

CROUCHING BEAST, THE*

(1936, U.S./Brit.) 68m RKO bw

Fritz Kortner (Ahmed Bey), Wynne Gibson (Gail Dunbar), Richard Bird (Nigel Druce), Andrews Engelmann (Prince Dmitri), Isabel Jeans (The Pellegrini), Fred Conyngham (Rudi Von Linz), Peter Gawthorne (Kadir Pasha), Ian Fleming (Maj. Abbott), Marjorie Mars (Ottillie), Gus McNaughton, A. Bromley Davenport, Margaret Yarde.

Even cutting twelve minutes from the original British version released one year earlier can't rid this one of its molasses pace. Gibson as an American newswoman is detailed to Turkey to cover WW I items. While working there she gets mixed up in the usual spy ring. For most of the picture, she tries to avoid Kortner, a club-footed Turkish agent. Her cohort in crime and love, a German lieutenant, is discovered in his role as her aide, and forced to commit suicide. She soon forgets his noble act and hooks up with Bird. Kortner's wooden performance as Gibson's pursuer makes one wonder whether the club belongs on his leg or in his mouth. The inept direction fails to support any of the characters, and the script is uncredited.

p, John Stafford; d, W. Victor Handbury (based on the novel *Clubfoot* by Valentine Williams); ph, James Wilson.

Spy Drama (PR:A MPAA:NR)

CROW HOLLOW** (1952, Brit.) 69m Merton Park-Bruton/AA bw
Donald Houston *(Robert)*, Natasha Parry *(Ann)*, Nora Nicholson*(Opal)*, Esma Cannon *(Judith)*, Susan Richmond *(Hester)*, Pat Owens *(Willow)*, Melissa Stribling *(Diana)*.

Nicholson attempts to secure a large inheritance for herself by poisoning nephew Houston's bride (Parry) in a gloomy mansion called "Crow Hollow," peopled by three mad sisters. When a maid is stabbed, Parry launches her own investigation. Occasionally decent melodrama.

p, William Williams; d, Michael McCarthy; w, Vivian Milroy; ph, Bob Lapresle.

Crime (PR:A-C MPAA:NR)

CROWD INSIDE, THE* (1971, Can.) 102m January One/NG c
Genevieve Deloir *(Christine)*, Alan Dean *(David)*, Patricia Collins *(Barbara)*, Larry Perkins *(Vyvian)*, Ken James *(Alex)*, Albert S. Waxman *(Director)*.

Dated Canadian drama which tells the story of four folks living together in a dumpy old house. Two inhabitants are Deloir, a peaceful nature girl, and Collins, a cold and distant one. Joining them are two young men, each affecting their lives in a different way. Deloir's man is a pathetic drug pusher who parasitically lives off her cash. Collins' mate is a sensitive artist who helps her to come out of her shell. Most important is the men's ability to alter the gals' lives—one in a positive manner, the other in a negative one. Of less concern is a plot to blackmail a lustful member of parliament. Poorly conceived and amateurishly executed.

p,d&w, Albert S. Waxman; ph, Harry Makin; m, Herbie Helbig; ed, Havelock Gradidge; art d, Lillian Sarafinchan.

Drama (PR:C MPAA:NR)

CROWD ROARS, THE***½ (1932) 84m WB bw
James Cagney *(Joe Greer)*, Joan Blondell *(Anne)*, Ann Dvorak *(Lee)*, Eric Linden *(Eddie Greer)*, Guy Kibbee *(Dad Greer)*, Frank McHugh *(Spud Connors)*, William Arnold *(Bill Arnold)*, Leo Nomis *(Jim)*, Charlotte Merriam *(Mrs. Spud Connors)*, Regis Toomey *(Dick Wilbur)*, Harry Hartz, Ralph Hepburn, Fred Guisso, Fred Frame, Phil Pardee, Spider Matlock, Jack Brisko, Lou Schneider, Bryan Salspaugh, Stubby Stubblefield, Shorty Cantlon, Mel Keneally, Wilbur Shaw *(Drivers)*, James Burtis *(Mechanic)*, Sam Hayes *(Ascot Announcer)*, Ralph Dunn *(Official)*, John Conte *(Announcer)*, John Harron *(Red—Eddie's Pitman)*, Robert McWade *(Tom the Counterman)*.

Is there a car racing movie worth its while that doesn't wind up at the Indy 500? Yes, a few, but most aim for that Memorial Day weekend and this one is no exception. Cagney is a successful car racer who is living with Dvorak. (In 1932, that was okay. In the 1938 remake, it had to be altered.) His kid brother, Linden, idolizes him the way only kid brothers can. Cagney wants to keep Linden away from the tracks and away from the kind of dames Cagney likes. But blood tells and Linden winds up with Blondell, of whom Cagney absolutely disapproves. The two brothers are at odds and when they race against each other it looks like one or both could get killed. Frank McHugh is Cagney's mechanic and is driving in the race and attempting to keep the two brothers apart. Cagney does a reckless move and McHugh is sent over a fence to flaming death. Cagney is destroyed and distraught by what happened. He quits racing and takes up drinking. He descends to the depths in a fast montage and stays there until Linden is racing in the Indy 500, hurts his arm, and Cagney jumps into the car, takes over, and wins the race. Filmed at Indy, Ventura, and Ascot, THE CROWD ROARS was not too far from the truth. Billy Arnold, winner of the 500 in 1930, worked in the film and gave the script his nod. Cagney was on the way to developing his ultimate screen personality: aggressive, cocky, supercilious. It was a character the people wanted to see him play and he played it to the hilt in countless movies, with countless variations, but always managing to come up with some sort of difference that made the character unique. Hawks could make comedies and he could make action pictures and it was a toss-up which were better. In THE CROWD ROARS there is very little comedy and the movie suffers some from it. Cagney takes his role a bit too seriously, whereas a slightly cock-eyed look at the driver might have been called for. In 1932, Cagney was on the brink of stardom and still too new to dictate to the studio, so we can assume his performance was as a direct result of Hawks' direction. The race footage is excellent and was used in the remake, INDIANAPOLIS SPEEDWAY.

d, Howard Hawks; w, John Bright, Niven Busch, Kubec Glasmon (based on the story "The Roar of the Crowd" by Seaton I. Miller, Hawks); ph, Sid Hickox; ed, Thomas Pratt; md, Leo F. Forbstein; art d, Jack Okey.

Racing Drama (PR:A-C MPAA:NR)

CROWD ROARS, THE*** (1938) 87m MGM bw
Robert Taylor *(Tommy McCoy)*, Edward Arnold *(Jim Cain)*, Frank Morgan *(Brian McCoy)*, Maureen O'Sullivan *(Sheila Carson)*, William Gargan *(Johnny Martin)*, Lionel Stander *("Happy" Lane)*, Jane Wyman *(Vivian)*, Nat Pendleton *("Pug" Walsh)*, Charles D. Brown *(Bill Thorne)*, Gene Reynolds *(Tommy McCoy as a Boy)*, Donald Barry *(Pete Mariola)*, Donald Douglas *(Murray)*, Isabel Jewel *(Mrs. Martin)*, J. Farrell MacDonald *(Father Ryan)*.

Typical 1930s fight film but distinguished by a good script and sharp direction from Thorpe. Taylor, trying desperately to outgrow his "pretty boy" image, stars as a young boxer from the poor neighborhood who gets to the top of the fight game due, in great

part, to the efforts of his father, Morgan, a man with a bad habit of nipping at the bottle. Taylor gets the nickname of "Killer" McCoy but it proves to be an omen when he inadvertently kills his boxing teacher. He is depressed and turns off the fight business after he is acquitted of a manslaughter charge. Arnold is a bookmaker, manager, and general no-goodnick, but he does have one saving grace—his daughter O'Sullivan, who is so naive that she thinks her father sells stocks. Plot complications arise, a kidnaping is to take place, Arnold is in jeopardy, the fight game is shown to be a rotten business filled with crooks and criminals, and what else is new? Taylor was one of the best movie fighters on the screen, probably due to the serious training he took in order to make this movie and not embarrass himself. One of his best friends was boxer-actor Max Baer, senior, and they trained together for the film. Taylor, who had been working out for several years when starting at MGM, had added six inches to his chest, almost three inches to his biceps and inches to his thigh and calf muscles (according to studio publicity at the time). He and Baer trained so furiously for the role that the professional boxer broke two fingers and Taylor one while using light-weight gloves. Taylor's mother went to see this film and found it "disgusting," walking out before it was over. She later upbraided her son, warning him that he might get hurt. He told her he preferred to do his own stunts, explaining to her that he was tired of the delicate male star image created in CAMILLE. "Anyway, Mother," he told her, "people better get used to the idea that I am not going to trip daintily into a room, kiss a lady's fingertips, hand her a rose and speak softly into her ear." It's odd that two U.S. movies of the era had the same name but they are as different as the two studios could make and yet both deal with the celebration of an individual in a sport where life is cheap. Remade in 1947 as KILLER MCCOY.

p, Sam Zimbalist; d, Richard Thorpe; w, Thomas Lennon, George Bruce, George Oppenheimer (based on a story by Bruce); ph, John Seitz; m, Edward Ward; montage, Stavko Vorkapich.

Boxing Drama (PR:A MPAA:NR)

CROWDED DAY, THE**½ (1954, Brit.) 82m Advance/Adelphi bw
John Gregson *(Leslie)*, Joan Rice *(Peggy)*, Freda Jackson *(Mrs. Morgan)*, Patricia Marmont *(Eve)*, Josephine Griffin *(Yvonne)*, Sonia Holm *(Moira)*, Patricia Plunkett *(Alice)*, Rachel Roberts *(Maggie)*, Vera Day *(Suzy)*, Thora Hird *(Woman)*, Dora Bryan *(Marge)*, Sydney Tafler *(Alex)*, Edward Chapman *(Mr. Bunting)*, Cyril Raymond *(Philip Stanton)*, Sidney James *(Watchman)*, Richard Wattis *(Mr. Christopher)*, Kynaston Reeves *(Mr. Ronson)*.

Episodic story of the trials and tribulations of five salesgirls in a London department store during the Christmas shopping season, Pleasant, though no more.

p, David Dent; d, John Guillermin; w, Talbot Rothwell (based on a story by John Paddy Carstairs, Moie Charles); ph, Gordon Dines.

Drama (PR:A MPAA:NR)

CROWDED PARADISE**½ (1956) 94m Tudor bw
Hume Cronyn *(George Heath)*, Nancy Kelly *(Louise Heath)*, Frank Silvera *(Papa Diaz)*, Enid Rudd *(Felicia Diaz)*, Mario Alcalde *(Juan Figueroa)*, Stefan Schnabel *(Big Man)*, David Opatoshu, Ralph Dunn, Carlos Montalban, Santos Ortega, Miriam Colon, Marita Reid, Henry Silva.

A realistic portrayal of a young Puerto Rican battling the odds in gritty New York City. Lead Alcalde arrives in the Big Apple and is determined to find a wife and a job. In a ray of optimism shone against the backdrop of the dark metropolis, Alcalde succeeds at both. The dark side is seen when his crazy, bigoted landlord threatens to bomb his wedding ceremony. A convincing cast treats the audience to a thespian delight in this picture photographed by Kaufman, Oscar-winning cameraman of ON THE WATERFRONT.

p, Ben Gradus; d, Fred Pressburger; w, Arthur Forrest, Marc Connelly; ph, Boris Kaufman; m, David Brockman (special numbers by Broekman, Terry Stern, William Gonzalez, Rafael Alers); ed, Rita Roland.

Drama Cas. (PR:C MPAA:NR)

CROWDED SKY, THE**½ (1960) 105m WB c
Dana Andrews *(Dick Barnett)*, Rhonda Fleming *(Cheryl Heath)*, Efrem Zimbalist, Jr. *(Dale Heath)*, John Kerr *(Mike Rule)*, Anne Francis *(Kitty Foster)*, Keenan Wynn *(Nick Hyland)*, Troy Donahue *(McVey)*, Joe Mantell *(Louis Capelli)*, Patsy Kelly *(Gertrude Ross)*, Donald May *(Norm Coster)*, Louis Quinn *(Sidney Schreiber)*, Edward Kemmer *(Caesar)*, Tom Gilson *(Rob Fermi)*, Hollis Irving *(Beatrice Wiley)*, Paul Genge *(Samuel N. Poole)*, Jean Willis *(Gloria Panawek)*, Frieda Inescourt *(Mrs. Mitchell)*, Nan Leslie *(Bev)*.

This is a typical soap-opera-in-a-doomed-plane picture which has come to dull our sensibilities. Andrews and Zimbalist, Jr., are the pilots of a commercial jet and a Navy plane on a collision course. While trying to fly the commercial plane, Andrews is dealing with his hooligan child in flashbacks; in the Navy jet, which is blown out of the sky at the last moment, averting a crash, Zimbalist is trying to cope with his flirty wife. No wonder their signals get mixed up. Donahue and Wynn turn in stock but entertaining performances as passengers. The common fault with this film, like most disaster stories, is the necessity to cram into two hours the lives of a dozen or more passengers. A HIGH AND MIGHTY it isn't!

p, Michael Garrison; d, Joseph Pevney; w, Charles Schnee (based on the novel by Hank Searls); ph, Harry Stradling, Sr. (Technicolor); m, Leonard Rosenman; ed, Tom McAdoo; art d, Eddie Imazu.

Disaster Drama (PR:A MPAA:NR)

CROWN VS STEVENS** (1936) 66m WB/FN bw
Beatrix Thomson *(Doris Stevens)*, Patric Knowles *(Chris Jensen)*, Reginald Purdell *(Alf)*, Glennis Lorimer *(Molly)*, Allan Jeayes *(Inspector Carter)*, Frederick Piper

(Arthur Stevens), Googie Withers *(Ella)*, Mabel Poulton *(Mamie)*, Morris Harvey *(Julius Bayleck)*, Billy Watts, Davina Craig.

One-time dancer Thomson marries wealthy Piper but cannot get him to part with a penny, and she winds up killing a loan shark who has her on the hook. Before she can gas her husband to death in a locked garage to collect insurance monies, Piper's employee Knowles prevents the murder and then compels Thomson to tell the police the truth. Occasionally suspenseful but the plot is soggy and the actors all wet. Patric Knowles, of the patrician good looks and the cultivated personality, would come to the U.S. the same year and make the great THE CHARGE OF THE LIGHT BRIGADE, in which he wins Olivia de Havilland's heart away from the dashing Errol Flynn, thus beginning a busy U.S. screen career.

p, Irving Asher; d, Michael Powell; w, Brock Williams (based on the novel *Third Time Unlucky* by Laurence Maynell); ph, Basil Emmott.

Crime Drama   **(PR:A   MPAA:NR)**

CROWNING EXPERIENCE, THE   (1960) 102m Moral Re-Armament c
Muriel Smith *(Emma Tremaine)*, Ann Buckles *(Sarah Miller Spriggs)*, Louis Byles *(Charlie as a Man)*, George McCurdy *(Charlie as a Boy)*, William Pawley, Jr. *(Mr. Spriggs)*, Phyllis Konstan Austin *(Mrs. Spriggs)*, Anna Marie McCurdy *(Julie)*, Robert Anderson *(Blaney)*, Cecil Broadhurst *(Editor)*.

Based in part on the life of black educator Mary McLeod Bethune, this message film sponsored by Moral Re-Armament never quite delivers. It's all right in spots but fails to bring across the teacher's emotional and societal struggles. Instead of drama, Smith's talents are pushed toward singing by this weak script. The tunes are fine, but character insight is much more valuable. Bethune's career is traced from her days as a tough news gal to her activity in MRA. It is presented in candied manner which reflects the decade's uneasiness about the subject—a treatment which drains the emotional punch.

d, Marion Clayton Anderson; w, Alan Thornhill; ph, Richard Tegstrom (Technicolor); md, Paul Dunlap; m/l, Will Reed, George Fraser.

Musical Drama   **(PR:A   MPAA:NR)**

CROWNING GIFT, THE*½   (1967, Brit.) 50m Religious Films/RFD c
Michael Gwynn *(Jesus Christ)*.

An English businessman remembers the sacrifice made by a sergeant in a prisoner-of-war camp during WW II. Minor oddity harks back to the 1930s, when producer Rank went broke making documentaries promoting Methodism.

p, Lord Rank, R.N.F. Evans; d, Norman Walker; w, Lawrence Barratt; ph (Eastmancolor).

Religious Drama   **(PR:A   MPAA:NR)**

CROWNING TOUCH, THE**   (1959, Brit.) 75m Crescent/But bw
Ted Ray *(Bert)*, Greta Gynt *(Rosie)*, Griffith Jones *(Mark)*, Sydney Tafler *(Joe)*, Dermot Walsh *(Aubrey Drake)*, Maureen Connell *(Julia)*, Colin Gordon *(Stacey)*, Irene Handl *(Bebe)*, Allan Cuthbertson *(Philip)*, Diane Hart *(Tess)*.

Okay English comedy in which three people make up stories to explain why a certain hat was sold to a young lady but never picked up. A number of distinguished performers lift this one above the average.

p, Charles Leeds, Jon Pennington; d, David Eady; w, Margot Bennett (based on a story by Cecily Finn and Joan O'Connor); ph, Ernest Palmer.

Comedy   **(PR:A   MPAA:NR)**

CRUCIBLE OF HORROR*½   (1971, Brit.) 91m Cannon-Abacus/GN c
(AKA: VELVET HOUSE; GB: THE CORPSE)
Michael Gough *(Eastwood)*, Yvonne Mitchell *(Edith)*, Sharon Gurney *(Jane)*, Simon Gough *(Rupert)*, Olaf Pooley *(Reid)*, David Butler *(Gregson)*, Nicholas Jones *(Benjy)*, Mary Hignett *(Sevant)*, Howard Goorney *(Gas Attendant)*.

Mitchell and Gurney play a mother and daughter who kill the sadistic Gough who returns from the dead to haunt them. Same old back-from-the-dead script stuff that does not come close to plausibility.

p, Gabrielle Beaumont; d, Viktor Ritelis; w, Olaf Pooley; m, John Hotchkis.

Horror   **Cas.**   **(PR:C   MPAA:GP)**

CRUCIBLE OF TERROR*   (1971, Brit.) 79m Scotia/Barber c
Mike Raven, Mary Maude, Melissa Stribling, James Bolam.

Yet another sculptor is driven to coating the bodies of models in bronze. This time it's one-time BBC disc jockey Raven doing the coating, all because he has been possessed by the ghost of a dead woman. No redeeming value here, just exploitation.

p, Tom Parkinson; d, Ted Hooker; w, Hooker, Parkinson.

Horror   **Cas.**   **(PR:O   MPAA:NR)**

CRUCIFIX, THE*½   (1934, Brit.) 70m New Era/UNIV bw
Nancy Price, Sydney Fairbrother, Farren Soutar, Brenda Harvey, Audrey Cameron, Pollie Emery, Minnie Taylor.

Price is a wealthy woman not far from death who hires a companion (Fairbrother). When Fairbrother accidentally smashes a valuable vase, her mean employer stops paying her until the item is paid for. As Price lies dying, Fairbrother steals a valuable crucifix. Soon captured by the police, they tell her that Price left her entire estate to her. Very good performances highlight this otherwise routine melodrama.

p, Gordon Craig; d, G.B. Samuelson; w, Samuelson, Roland Pertwee.

Drama   **(PR:A   MPAA:NR)**

CRUEL SEA, THE**   (1953) 120m Ealing/Balcon/GFD bw
Jack Hawkins *(Ericson)*, Donald Sinden *(Lockhart)*, John Stratton *(Ferraby)*, Denholm Elliott *(Morrell)*, Stanley Baker *(Bennett)*, John Warner *(Baker)*, Bruce Seton *(Tallow)*, Liam Redmond *(Watts)*, Virginia McKenna *(Julie Hallam)*, Moira Lister *(Elaine Morell)*, June Thorburn *(Doris Ferraby)*, Megs Jenkins *(Tallow's Sister)*, Meredith Edwards *(Yeoman Wells)*, Glyn Houston *(Phillips)*, Alec McCowan *(Tonbridge)*, Leo Phillips, Dafydd Havard, Fred Griffiths, Laurence Hardy, Sam Kydd, John Singer, Barry Steele, Gerard Heinz, Gerik Schjelderup, Gaston Richer, Andrew Cruickshank, Barry Letts, Kenn Kennedy, Harold Goodwin, George Curzon, Anthony Snell, Ronald Simpson, Don Sharp, Herbert C. Walton, Jack Howard, Russell Waters, Harold Jamieson, Warwick Ashton.

Tough, often gruesome account of British corvette life on the war-torn Atlantic during WW II as seen through the tormented view of skipper Hawkins. He loses one ship to a U-boat while protecting a convoy and he and a handful of men barely survive on a raft to be picked up many days later. Given a new command, Hawkins anguishes over once again risking the lives of his men, and is also obsessed with taking revenge on the Germans by sinking a submarine—which he and his crew finally manage to do, no little feat. The film is shot in documentary style with harsh black and white lensing by Dines which works well in realistically portraying war at sea. Baker, Sinden, Elliott, Warner, and others are shown in cameo style as members of the crew and the females in the cast are seen in brief flashback and furlough sequences. Ambler's script, though necessarily telescoping the lengthy Monsarrat novel, is admirably taut with telling dialog and poignant scenes. A top-notch film on all levels, with Hawkins turning in an intense, fascinating performance.

p, Leslie Norman (for Michael Balcon); d, Charles Frend; w, Eric Ambler (based on the novel by Nicholas Monsarrat); ph, Gordon Dines; m, Alan Rawsthorne; ed, Peter Tanner.

War Drama   **Cas.**   **(PR:A   MPAA:NR)**

CRUEL SWAMP   (SEE: SWAMP WOMEN, 1955)

CRUEL TOWER, THE*   (1956) 79m AA bw
John Ericson *(Tom)*, Mari Blanchard *(Mary Thompson)*, Charles McGraw *(Stretch)*, Steve Brodie *(Casey)*, Peter Whitney *(Joss)*, Alan Hale *(Rocky)*, Diana Darrin *(Kit)*, Carol Kelly *(Waitress)*, Barbara Bel Wright *(Rev. Claver)*.

A dizzying story which focuses on the sky-high conflicts of two steeple-jacks in love with the same woman. McGraw is the crew boss who gives the acrophobic Ericson a chance to work in high rigs. Blanchard is the indecisive woman below torn between McGraw's security and Ericson's love. The two rivals' dislike for one another comes to a chilling aerial climax as they settle their differences atop the tower. A well-paced and beautifully photographed melodrama.

p, Lindsley Parsons; d, Lew Landers; w, Warren Douglas (based on a novel by William B. Hartley); ph, Ernest Haller; m, Paul Dunlap; ed, Maurice Wright; m/l, Dick Herman.

Drama   **(PR:A   MPAA:NR)**

CRUISER EMDEN*   (1932, Ger.) 85m Emelka/World Trade bw
Louis Ralph *(Capt. von Mueller)*, Renee Stobrawa *(Grete)*, Hans Schlenok *(Adjutant)*, Frau Forster-Larrinaga *(Anluschka)*, Werner Fuetterer *(Petzold)*, Fritz Greiner *(Mertens)*, Will Dohn *(Russian Captain)*, Kaiser Heyl *(Australian Captain)*.

Written, directed, and starring Louis Ralph, this film makes no real attempt at stirring audience sympathy. Based on the real life story of the German warship *Emden*, it is a hard-hitting look at the naval men who terrorized the seas, indiscriminately sinking anything in their path. But, as with all bullies, someone comes along and hits a little harder—this someone being an Australian cruiser. After a long game of underwater cat-and-mouse, the *Emden* takes it in the guts and goes on an unscheduled voyage to the bottom of the sea. An often powerful study of aggression. Not to be confused with the unrelated silent, RAIDER EMDEN.

d, Louis Ralph; w, Alfred Halm, Ralph; m, Friedrich Jung.

War   **(PR:A   MPAA:NR)**

CRUISIN' DOWN THE RIVER*½   (1953) 79m COL c
Dick Haymes *(Beauregard Clemment)*, Audrey Totter *(Sally Jane)*, Billy Daniels *(William)*, Cecil Kellaway *(Thadius Jackson)*, Connie Russell *(Melissa Curry)*, Douglas Fowley *(Humphrey Hepburn)*, Larry Blake *(Dave Singer)*, Johnny Downs *(Young Thad)*, Benny Payne *(Benny)*, Bell Sisters *(Themselves)*, Dick Crockett *(Sheriff)*, Byron Foulger *(Ben Fisher)*, Erze Ivan *(Specialty Dancer)*.

A river boat musical which casts Haymes as a nightclub crooner from New York City whose grandfather has willed him a boat with a past. Told in flashbacks, with Haymes doubling as the granddad, is an old feud over the *Chattahoochee Queen*. It seems this boat was won from old man Kellaway in a gambling bet with his granddaughter as part of the purse. Totter, as the young filly, helps the younger Haymes and her grandpappy reach an amiable agreement. Before too long, the boat is a floating nightclub. Mildly amusing screenplay co-penned by Blake Edwards. "Cruisin' Down the River" (Eily Beadell, Nell Tollerton), "There Goes That Song Again" (Sammy Cahn, Jule Styne), "Pennies From Heaven" (Johnny Burke, Arthur Johnson), "Sing You Sinners" (Sam Coslow, W. Frank Harling), "Swing Low Sweet Chariot" (traditional), "Father Dear" (Emmet G. Coleman).

p, Jonie Taps; d, Richard Quine; w, Blake Edwards; Quine; ph, Charles Lawton, Jr. (Technicolor); ed, Jerome Thoms; md, George Dunning; ch, Lee Scott.

Musical   **(PR:A   MPAA:NR)**

CRUISING zero   (1980) 106m Lorimar/UA c
Al Pacino *(Steve Burns)*, Paul Sorvino *(Capt. Edelson)*, Karen Allen *(Nancy)*, Richard Cox *(Stuart Richards)*, Don Scardino *(Ted Bailey)*, Joe Spinell *(Patrolman DiSimone)*, Jay Acovone *(Skip Lee)*, Randy Jurgensen *(Detective Lefransky)*, Barton Heyman

(Dr. Rifkin), Gene Davis *(Da Vinci)*, Sonny Grosso *(Detective Blasio)*, Larry Atlas *(Eric Rossman)*, Allan Miller *(Chief of Detectives)*, Edward O'Neil *(Detective Schreiber)*, Michael Aronin *(Detective Davis)*, James Remar *(Gregory)*, William Russ *(Paul Gaines)*, Mike Starr *(Patrolman Desher)*, Steve Inwood *(Martino)*, Keith Prentice *(Joey)*, Leland Starnes *(Jack Richards)*, Robert Pope, Leo Burmester, Bruce Levine, Charles Dunlap, Powers Boothe, James Sutorius, Richard Jamieson, James Ray Weeks, David Winnie Hayes, Carmine Stipo, James Hyden, Todd Winters, Sylvia Gassell.

A disgusting film on all levels, Pacino is a New York City cop assigned by superior Sorvino to go undercover into the slimy S&M gay world to find a homosexual killer. Purportedly a study in the psychological degradation of a "straight," this production is just an excuse to parade every known form of sexual perversion. The language is foul from beginning to end and the portrayal of street humanity is equally filthy as Pacino undergoes one brutality after another and the cops are shown to be sadistic brutes, beating to a bloody pulp one gay suspected of being the killer. The viewer is spared nothing here. One *minor* example is shot showing a man greasing his fist and a cut to another man in apparent ecstatic pain. The only frames missing to make this an X-rated film are the ones between. Nothing and no one in this film provides anything other than a repulsive view of society. CRUISING undoubtedly caused Friedkin's quick decline as a film prodigy. This cesspool of human waste put on film is not fit for viewing by man, woman, child or beast.

p, Jerry Weintraub; d&w, William Friedkin (based on the novel by Gerald Walker); ph, James Contner; m, Jack Nitzsche; ed, Bud Smith; prod d, Bruce Weintraub; art d, Edward Pisoni; cos, Robert deMora.

Crime **Cas.** **(PR:O MPAA:R)**

CRUSADE AGAINST RACKETS½** (1937) 53m Principal bw

Lona Andre *(Dona)*, Donald Reed *(Phillip Miller)*, Wheeler Oakman *(Jim Murray)*, John Merton *(Nick)*, Richard Cramer *(Dutch)*, William Royale *(City Editor)*, Edward Piele, Sr. *(Detective Captain)*, Louise Small *(Mary Lou)*, Matty Roubert *("Good Looking Freddy")*, Suzanna Kim *(Fan Dancer)*.

A lame quickie about a crusade against a crime racket, hence the title. The lack of imagination in the choice of the title is even more apparent in it's fifty-three familiar minutes. Police are sniffing out a white slave racket which snags unaware gal who answer a phony ad for a manicurist's shop. A melodrama which is just as harmless as it is hopeless. The only bright spot is a fan dance by Suzanna Kim which is completely unrelated to the plot.

p, J.D. Kendis; d, Elmer Clifton; w, Robert A. Dillon; ph, Eddie Linden; ed, Earl Turner.

Crime **(PR:A MPAA:NR)**

CRUSADER, THE* (1932) 65m Majestic bw

Evelyn Brent *(Tess Brandon)*, H.B. Warner *(Phillip Brandon)*, Lew Cody *(Jimmie Dale)*, Ned Sparks *(Eddie Crane)*, Walter Byron *(Joe Carson)*, Marceline Day *(Marcia Brandon)*, John St. Polis *(Robert Henley)*, Arthur Hoyt *(Oscar Shane)*, Ara Haswell, Joseph Girard, Syd Saylor, Lloyd Ingraham.

Cliche-ridden news reporters and managing editors fill up space in this story about district attorney Warner's attempt to get his innocent sister acquitted of a shooting charge. It's harmless but no doubt there are countless better versions of the same plot. Warner is the bright spot struggling through his underdeveloped character.

d, Frank Strayer; w, Edward T. Lowe (based on a play by Wilson Collison); ed, Otis Garrett.

Drama **(PR:A MPAA:NR)**

CRUSADES, THE*½** (1935) 123m PAR bw

Loretta Young *(Berengaria)*, Henry Wilcoxon *(Richard)*, Ian Keith *(Saladin)*, Katherine De Mille *(Alice)*, C. Aubrey Smith *(The Hermit)*, Joseph Schildkraut *(Conrad of Montferrat)*, Alan Hale *(Blondel)*, C. Henry Gordon *(Philip of France)*, George Barbier *(Sancho)*, Montagu Love *(Blacksmith)*, Hobart Bosworth *(Frederick of Germany)*, William Farnum *(Hugo of Burgundy)*, Lumsden Hare *(Earl Robert of Leicester)*, Ramsey Hill *(John Lackland)*, Pedro de Cordoba *(Karakush)*, Paul Satoff *(Michael, Prince of Russia)*, Mischa Auer *(Monk)*, Maurice Murphy *(Alan, Richard's Squire)*, Jason Robards, Sr. *(Amir)*, J. Carroll Naish *(Arab Slave Seller)*, Oscar Rudolph *(Philip's Squire)*, Albert Conti *(Leopold, Duke of Austria)*, Sven-Hugo Borg *(Sverre, the Norse King)*, Paul Satoff *(Michael, Prince of Russia)*, Fred Malatesta *(William, King of Sicily)*, Hans Von Twardowski *(Nicholas, Count of Hungary)*, Anna Demetrio *(Duenna)*, Perry Askam *(Soldier)*, Edwin Maxwell *(Ship's Master)*, Winter Hall *(Archibishop)*, Emma Dunn *(Mother of Alan)*, Georgia Caine *(Nun)*, Robert Adair *(English Chamberlain)*, Pat Moore *(Leicester's Squire)*, Ann Sheridan *(Christian Girl)*, Josef Swickard *(Buyer)*, Jean Fenwick *(Christian Girl)*, Edgar Dearing *(Cart Man)*, Alphonse Ethier *(Priest)*, Gilda Oliva *(1st Lady-in-Waiting to Alice)*, Mildred Van Buren *(2nd Lady-in-Waiting to Alice)*, John Rutherford *(Knight)*, Colin Tapley *(Stranger*/Messenger), Harry Cording *(Amir)*, Stanley Andrews *(Amir)*, Addison Richards *(Sentry)*, Maurice Black *(Amir)*, William B. Davidson *(Amir)*, Guy Usher *(Grey Beard)*, Boyd Irwin *(Templar)*; Kenneth Gibson *(Capt. of English Men-at-Arms)*, Gordon Griffith *(Templar)*, Guy Usher *(Templar)*, Vallejo Gantner *(Chanting Monk)*, George MacQuarrie *(Capt. of Templars)*, Sam Flint *(Capt. of Hospitalers)*, Harold Goodwin *(Wounded Man)*.

The master of spectacle, DeMille, produces a superb filmic pageantry in this fanciful version of the bloody Third Crusade. Wilcoxon, as King Richard the Lion-Hearted of England, is bold, brave, but sometimes boring. His ignored and beautiful queen, Young, seems hopelessly miscast. But the film is still utterly captivating as a glamorous interpretation of an ancient era of iron men and wily infidels. This opus opens with Saladin, Keith, sacking the city of Jerusalem, slaughtering the resident Christians with alacrity. He is confronted by the venerable C. Aubrey Smith, a zealot holy man known as The Hermit. Smith defies him, telling him that if he is spared he will travel throughout Europe and raise a mighty host of crusaders who will return to the Holy Land and destroy Saladin and his infidel followers. Keith, supremely confident of his power, haughtily spares Smith. The Hermit goes to King Philip of France, Gordon, and inspires him to lead the crusade. Smith then accompanies Gordon and his sister, Katherine DeMille, to England where Wilcoxon is to marry DeMille as both were betrothed when children. Wilcoxon puts Gordon off, which worries the French King who believes that unless this royal union is cemented Wilcoxon will later invade France. The Hermit solves Wilcoxon's dilemma when he tells him that anyone taking the Cross in a pledge to the holy crusade is automatically free of any other promises. Wilcoxon leaps at the opportunity, vowing to lead the great crusade and enlisting every able-bodied man in England. He assumes complete command, much to Gordon's chagrin, and the armies depart for France. Short of supplies in Marseille, Richard obtains great quantities of food from Barbier, the King of Navarre, agreeing cavalierly to wed his daughter Berengaria, Young, in return for the goods. To show his unconcern for this arrangement, Wilcoxon sends one of his aides, Hale, to Young's tent, carrying his broadsword. The sword being the symbol of the king, it is substituted for Wilcoxon who is too busy elsewhere to go through the ceremony. Young marries the sword in an elaborate ceremony and thus Richard. When Wilcoxon actually sets eyes on Young he is stupified by her beauty and begs her forgiveness for humilating her. She has nothing but contempt for this unchivalrous monarch and insults him. In a rage he orders her to accompany him on his march to the Holy Land. A series of battles follow as Palestine is wrested from infidel control. A magnificent attack on Acre is followed by victory but at a high cost. The enemy troops are equal to the men of iron. The European kings become divided on how best to conquer Jerusalem, with Schildkraut, Bosworth, and Gordon disagreeing with Wilcoxon's plan to attack. Meanwhile, Young is kidnapped by Keith's men and held hostage. A wild cavalry attack then ensues as Wilcoxon goes after his wife. (The clashing of two massive mounted armies is one of the many highlights of this spectacular film.) Dismounted and surrounded, Wilcoxon fights like a madman, killing his enemies by the score. After the battle he surveys his countless dead and then meets with Keith's representatives who take him under a flag of truce to the mighty Saladin. Keith, who has not violated Young, proves to be a refined, cultured man of great sensitivity. He tells the vanquished Wilcoxon that he will return his wife to him and that the crusaders will be allowed into the Holy City to worship at their beloved shrines but he, and he alone, cannot enter Jerusalem. Wilcoxon accepts the humiliating terms. Young joins her husband on a hilltop as they watch the grateful crusaders enter the city. Love for each other has replaced Wilcoxon's vainglorious ambitions as a conqueror. Of course, much of THE CRUSADE is fabrication, particularly the romance scenes and even history itself is turned about and around by DeMille to suit his action-packed story line. He brought author Lamb to Hollywood to work on the script after buying the writer's book, *The Crusade: Iron Men and Saints.* Lamb soon learned that the facts meant nothing to the director, only those elements of history that lent themselves to his interpretation of history. Smith's role of The Hermit was filched from another period, 1095, when this zealot inspired The First Crusade, while Richard's Third Crusade began in 1190. Also, in all fairness to the courageous Richard, he achieved more in his war against Saladin than DeMille presented, winning in a treaty from Saladin, access to the Holy City for any Christian wanting to visit its shrines. The 30-year-old Wilcoxon does an admirable job portraying the dedicated warrior, earning his leading role after appearing in CLEOPATRA as Marc Antony a year earlier. But his wooden personality failed to ignite viewership interest and this was his last starring role. He later became a strong supporting player and a DeMille stalwart, acting as a co-producer on many of the great showman's films and completing the 1958 version of THE BUCCANEER when DeMille grew ill. As with all his historical epics, THE CRUSADES contains that stilted, often leaden DeMille feel, as if the director were moving props about instead of people, yet the sets and action prove astounding, along with wonderful costuming and with unparalleled crowd scenes, which was DeMille's meat. History to DeMille was largely a matter of human masses moving toward a single goal. About this film he commented: "THE CRUSADES is a good example of what I call telescoping history. Actually there were several Crusades extending over two centuries. It would be impossible to tell the story of them all in two hours of film. Audiences are not interested in dates, but in events and their significance. And they do not want to be educated, but entertained." Here, of course, he was right about his 1930s audience, something that could not be said of today's more enlightened viewer, contrary to what some present day studio bosses archaically and contemptuously believe (that "the public will buy what it gets"). Yet DeMille was ever conscious of using the right props and the correct costuming. He personally staged every massive crowd scene, demanding of his extras absolute obedience to his direction. In one crowd shot he assembled hundreds of extras on the back lot of Paramount (he used most of this enormous property as a set for THE CRUSADES). The director made his intentions perfectly clear. He announced over a microphone hookup to the assembled crusaders and their women crowded in streets and on rooftops that represented old Marseille: "Ladies and gentlemen, I want absolute quiet during this scene . . . .The cost of this single scene is already over eighteen thousand dollars. So take off your dark glasses, put your wrist watches into your pockets, and spit out your chewing gum. We can't afford to shoot this scene twice. Remember—absolute quiet from the moment I say go—Lights! Cameras! Action!" Three cameras began to record the scene before the director screamed "Cut!" Livid, DeMille stared with his eagle eyes to a distant rooftop where an attractive extra with flaming red hair stood. "You there," he pointed and shouted, "the woman with the green dress and red hair. Come down here. You were talking." A tech crew had to wheel out a ladder and remove the nervous extra who was brought to the great director. She was lifted to the high scaffold where he was directing so that all could see her. Then, with microphone still blaring his words, he scolded her: "Since it was so important for you to talk, even though I requested silence, since you felt it necessary to break into a carefully rehearsed crowd scene, I would like everyone here to know what was so important that it could not wait. I would like for you to tell us all. All!" He stuck the microphone in her face. "I'd rather not, Mr. DeMille," the frightened extra almost whispered. "You're not grasping my point, young lady," roared the irate DeMille. "I demand that you tell us all what you said. And if you don't, I promise you'll never work in a picture of mine again! Now out with it!" Blurted the terrified extra: "Well, I was just telling a friend of mine out there on the roof, I turned and said 'I wonder when the old bald-headed son-of-a-bitch is going to call lunch.' " For a moment there was stunned silence. Then DeMille grinned, turned to his army of extras and said: "All right. Lunch!" The director respected honesty and kept the extra on, using her in many of his films to come. THE CRUSADES, despite its wonderful pageantry, cost Paramount a fortune which was not initially returned at the box office. Studio boss Adolph Zukor was aghast to see that the film lost more than $700,000 its first time around. Shown the figures, he buried his head in his hands in front of executives and moaned: "The king is dead!" Yet DeMille's prestige was quickly strengthened when he shifted his films to more contemporary themes, particularly THE PLAINSMAN in 1937, THE BUC-CANEER in 1938, and UNION PACIFIC in 1939.

p&d, Cecil B. DeMille; w, Harold Lamb, Walemar Young, Dudley Nichols (based on Lamb's book, *The Crusade: Iron Men and Saints*); ph, Victor Milner; m, Rudolph Kopp; ed, Anne Bauchens; cos, Travis Banton; spec eff, Gordon Jennings.

Historical Drama/Biography (PR:A MPAA:NR)

CRY BABY KILLER, THE* (1958) 62m AA bw

Jack Nicholson (*Jimmy*), Harry Lauter (*Porter*), Carolyn Mitchell (*Carole*), Brett Halsey (*Manny*), Lynn Cartwright (*Julie*), Ralph Reed (*Joey*), John Shay (*Gannon*), Barbara Knudson (*Mrs. Maxton*), Jordan Whitfield (*Sam*), Claude Stroud (*Werner*), Ruth Swanson (*Mrs. Wallace*), William A. Forester (*Mr. Maxton*), John Weed (*Reed*), Frank Richards (*Gambelli*), Bill Erwin (*Mr. Wallace*), James Fillmore (*Al*), Ed Nelson (*Rick*), Mitzi McCall (*Evelyn*).

The importance of executive producer Roger Corman is once again displayed in this picture which casts a twenty-one-year-old Jack Nicholson in his first movie role. While his character of Jimmy is thinly conceived, it is brought to life by the skillful Nicholson. Confronted by two brass-knuckled toughs, a gun-wielding Jimmy lays the pair out and then flees to a nearby drive-in. He barricades himself in a storeroom, taking three hostages—a janitor, a woman, and her child. Police and friends try to talk Jimmy into surrendering while the crowded drive-in becomes a profitable carnival. As the number of spectators increase, a television news team arrives, providing a morbid look at American voyeurism, as well as its consumerism. Jimmy's ordeal has become "an entertainment" more satisfying than the drive-in screen to the popcorn-eating crowd —a lift from the basic theme of THE BIG CARNIVAL. The bloodless end may be a let-down but it is in keeping with the film's style. Corman can be spotted as a news cameraman on top of a van, and Mitzi McCall also plays a bit. "Cry Baby Cry" is dutifully crooned by Dick Kallman. Overall, a fine example of Corman's no-cost production, and a must-see for Nicholson devotees.

p, David Kramarsky, David March (for Roger Corman); d, Jus Addiss; w, Leo Gordon, Melvin Levy (based on a story by Gordon); ph, Floyd Crosby; m, Gerald Fried; ed, Irene Morra; m/l, "Cry Baby Cry" (Dick Kallman).

Drama (PR:C MPAA:NR)

CRY BLOOD, APACHE½** (1970) 82m Golden Eagle/Goldstone c

Jody McCrea (*Pitcalin*), Dan Kemp (*Vittorio*), Marie Gahva (*Jemme*), Don Henley (*Benji*), Rick Nervick (*Billy*), Robert Tessier (*Two Card*), Jack Starrett (*Deacon*), Carolyn Stellar (*Cochalla*), Carroll Kemp (*Old Indian*), Barbara Sanford (*Mother*), Dawn Stellar (*Child*), Andy Anza (*Crippled Indian*), Joel McCrea (*Older Pitcalin*).

Hidden underneath its exploitative facade is an intriguing little western starring Jody McCrea and his dad, Joel. Told in flashback, Joel reminisces about his days as a young Indian killer,played by Jody. He tells the story of a Redskin massacre in which all but one of the Indians were killed. Gahva, the survivor, is spared after striking a deal with McCrea to lead the gang to a gold mine. Her avenging brother, however, begins killing them off one by one. In a final showdown, Gahva kills her own flesh and blood in the defense of the man who saved her life. Starrett co-stars as one of the outlaws.

p, Jody McCrea, Harold Roberts; d, Jack Starrett; w, Sean MacGregor (based on a story by Harold Roberts); ph, Bruce Scott (Eastmancolor); m, Elliot Kaplan; ed, T. Robinson.

Western (PR:O MPAA:NR)

CRY DANGER* (1951) 79m Olympic/RKO bw

Dick Powell (*Rocky*), Rhonda Fleming (*Nancy*), Richard Erdman (*Delong*), William Conrad (*Castro*), Regis Toomey (*Cobb*), Jean Porter (*Darlene*), Jay Adler (*Williams*), Joan Banks (*Alice Fletcher*), Gloria Saunders (*Cigarette Girl*), Hy Averbach (*Bookie*), Renny McEvoy (*Taxi Driver*), Lou Lubin (*Hank*), Benny Burt (*Bartender*).

A taut and clever mystery, CRY DANGER has hard-talking Powell released from the pen after serving five years for a robbery he didn't commit. To exonerate a friend still in prison for the same crime, he begins to investigate, aided by a crippled U.S. marine, Erdman, who has some of the snappiest bits of dialog in the film. The pair move into a trailer camp to be near sexy Fleming, who lives there. She is the wife of the pal in the pen and had once been Powell's girl. He links her up with gangster Conrad who almost frames him in a neat ploy where Powell appears to be caught with some of the $100,000 he purportedly stole five years earlier. Along the way to the truth, Powell is beaten by heavies and shot at by an army of unknown assassins, doing some beating of his own. He not only survives the onslaught but manages to pin the crime on Conrad and Fleming, the real culprits. A good script and economical direction from Parrish (his debut as a director after having been a film editor) make this one solid and entertaining.

p, Sam Wiesenthal; W.R. Frank; d, Robert Parrish; w, William Bowers (based on an unpublished story by Jerome Cady); ph, Joseph F. Biroc; m, Emil Newman, Paul Dunlap; ed, Bernard W. Burton; art d, Richard Day; set d, Joseph Kish; cos, Elois Jenssen, Jack E. Miller; makeup, Kiva Hoffman; m/l, "Cry Danger," Hugo Friehofer, Leon Pober.

Crime/Mystery (PR:A MPAA:NR)

CRY DR. CHICAGO zero (1971) 98m Leahy c

Alvin Lucier (*Dr. Chicago*), Mary Ashley (*Sheila Marie*), Steve Paxton (*Steve*), Claude Kipnis (*Clo Clo*), Viera Collaro (*Viera/Lily*), Joseph Wehrer, William Finneran, Alan Schreiber, Michael Frost, Betty Wong, Shirley Wong, Lincoln Scott, Pat Oleszko, Roberts Bloom, Ruth Reichl, Liz Hall, Kathy Schuetz, Carol Kladder, Nick Bertoni, Jack Starkweather.

A self-indulgent comedy, of sorts, which features the title character and a cast of weirdos in a cryptic mansion. The doctor hangs out for a while, recites Poe's "The Raven," and wears his sunglasses indoors. Amateurish slapstick effort which has no pluses.

p, Margaret Leahy, Robert Halper; d&w&ph, George Manupelli (Eastmancolor); ed, Tom Berman; md, George Burt.

Comedy (PR:C MPAA:NR)

CRY DOUBLE CROSS (SEE: BOOMERANG, 1960, Ger.)

CRY FOR HAPPY*½ (1961) 110m COL c

Glenn Ford (*Andy Cyphers*), Donald O'Connor (*Murray Prince*), Miiko Taka (*Chiyoko*), James Shigeta (*Suzuki*), Miyoshi Umeki (*Harue*), Michi Kobi (*Hanakichi*), Howard St. John (*Adm. Bennett*), Joe Flynn (*MacIntosh*), Chet Douglas (*Lank*), Tsuruko Kobayashi (*Koyuki*), Harriet E. MacGibbon (*Mrs. Bennett*), Robert Kino (*Endo*), Bob Okazaki (*Izumi*), Harlan Warde (*Chaplain*), Nancy Kovack (*Miss Cameron*), Ted Knight (*Lt. Glick*), Bob Quinn (*Lyman*), Ciyo Nakasone (*Keiko*).

A pleasant flick about four Navy men who unknowingly hole up in a geisha establishment. Enjoying the good life with the gals, they have to disguise the joint as an orphanage for the nosey upper crust. Lots of funny bits with Ford and O'Connor holding up well. Unfortunately, the gorgeous geishas seem to have been cast on the basis of their authentic looks and names. They don't falter, but it seems that no effort was put into developing anything but a stereotyped character. Ted Knight can be spotted in a bit. Remake of 1956 TEAHOUSE OF THE AUGUST MOON, also with Glenn Ford.

p, William Goetz; d, George Marshall; w, Irving Brecher (based on the novel by George Campbell); ph, Burnett Guffey (CinemaScope, Eastmancolor); m, George Duning; ed, Chester W. Schaeffer; md, Arthur Morton; art d, Walter Holscher; set d, William Kiernan; cos, Norma Koch.

Romance/Comedy (PR:C MPAA:NR)

CRY FOR ME, BILLY (SEE: COUNT YOUR BULLETS, 1972)

CRY FREEDOM* (1961, Phil.) 93m Parallel bw

Pancho Magalona (*Marking*), Rosa Rosal (*Yay*), Johnny Reyes (*Cabalhim*), Jack Forster (*Sid*), Charles Kelly (*Lt. Stoddard*), Tony Santos (*Juanito*).

The liberation of two lovers is set against the Filipino liberation from Japan in this simple, yet well constructed, drama. Magalona leads a group of resistance fighters and falls in love with one of the members—the exotic Rosal. She, however, is much more intelligent than he and he fears that he will lose her when the American troops arrive on the islands. In the nature of true love, nothing can destroy the bond created between then, and they remain lovers. One must look beyond the crudities of the production to find the story's beauty. Winner of six major Philippine awards.

p, Edith Perez De Tagle; d, Lamberto V. Avellana; w, Rolf Bayer; ph, Mike Accion; m, Restie Umali.

Romance/War (PR:A MPAA:NR)

CRY FROM THE STREET, A*½ (1959, Brit.) 100m Eros bw

Max Bygraves (*Bill Lowther*), Barbara Murray (*Ann Fairlie*), Colin Petersen (*Georgie*), Dana Wilson (*Barbie*), Kathleen Harrison (*Mrs. Farrer*), Sean Barrett (*Don Farrer*), Eleanor Summerfield (*Gloria*), Mona Washbourne (*Mrs. Daniels*), Toke Townley (*Mr. Daniels*), Charles McShane (*Derek*), David Bushell (*Alex*), Tony Baker (*Tony*), Glyn Houston (*Police Sergeant*), Dandy Nicholls (*Mrs. Jenks*), Basil Dignam (*Police Inspector*), Avice Landone (*Rachael Seymour*), Vi Stevens (*Mr. Robbins*), Fred Griffiths (*Mr. Hodges*).

A film featuring wide-eyed orphans simply cannot miss, and sure enough this one doesn't. Welfare worker Murray grows fond of a group of homeless tots and with the help of the equally enraptured Bygraves tries to bring them some happiness. Delightfully sensitive performances and fresh direction makes this a thoroughly pleasurable film and likely to bring tearful smiles. Bygraves sings "Gotta Have Rain" with the kids, a tune he also composed.

p, Ian Dalrymple; d, Lewis Gilbert; w, Vernon Harris (based on a novel *The Friend In Need* by Elizabeth Coxhead); ph, Harry Gilliam; m, Larry Adler; ed, Peter Hunt.

Drama (PR:AAA MPAA:NR)

CRY HAVOC*½ (1943) 96m MGM bw

Margaret Sullavan (*Lt. Smith*), Ann Sothern (*Pat*), Joan Blondell (*Grace*), Fay Bainter (*Capt. Marsh*), Marsha Hunt (*Flo Norris*), Ella Raines (*Connie*), Frances Gifford (*Helen*), Diana Lewis (*Nydia*), Heather Angel (*Andra*), Dorothy Morris (*Sue*), Connie Gilchrist (*Sadie*), Gloria Grafton (*Steve*), Fely Franquelli (*Luisita*).

During WW II there were any number of all-male pictures, but this is one of the rare all-female pictures ever made. There are a couple of men in and out but it's the women who have all the lines. Nine nurses are gathered from the Manila evacuation and put to work at a field hospital. As it is with most stage dramas (and make no mistake, this was a play and it shows in almost every frame), the members of the cast are from different backgrounds. Joan Blondell is a former burlesque queen who gave up the G-string in favor of the stethoscope, Ann Sothern was a waitress, etc. They wind up together in a bomb shelter on Bataan, discussing life, men and war while awaiting the advance of Japanese soldiers who are about to take over. Just about the same time, MGM was making BATAAN with Robert Taylor, George Murphy, and several others. One can only presume that these may have been the same sets used for both films. The play was not very good and the picture was not much better.

p, Edwin Knopf; d, Richard Thorpe; w, Paul Osborne (based on the play "Proof Thro' The Night" by Allen R. Kenward); ph, Karl Freund; m, Daniele Amphitheatrof; ed, Ralph E. Winters; art d, Cedric Gibbons, Stephen Goosson; set d, Edwin B. Willis, Glen Barner.

War Drama (PR:A MPAA:NR)

CRY IN THE NIGHT, A**½ (1956) 75m Jaguar/WB bw
Edmond O'Brien (Taggart), Brian Donlevy (Bates), Natalie Wood (Liz), Raymond Burr (Loftus), Richard Anderson (Owen), Irene Hervey (Helen), Carol Veazie (Mrs. Loftus), Mary Lawrence (Madge), Anthony Caruso (Chavez), George J. Lewis (Gerrity), Peter Hanson (Dr. Frazee), Tina Carver (Marie Holzapple), Herb Vigran (Jensen).

A dark melodrama about a psychotic mama's boy who abducts the young Wood. Burr, in his perfected killer role as the kidnaper, spies on Wood as she steams the windows with her beau. He knocks the boy friend out and pulls Wood away from their Lover's Loop car. Holed up in an abandoned brickyard, Wood becomes increasingly distraught when she discovers a dead puppy under Burr's bed. O'Brien, as her father and the tough police captain, teams up with Donlevy to track the captor. When they finally discover his hiding place, they slap him around until he pitifully begs for his mama. Weak and occasionally implausible script is overlooked in light of tight performances and intriguing characterizations.

p, George C. Bertholen; d, Frank Tuttle; w, David Dortort (based on the novel All Through the Night by Whit Masterson); ph, John Seitz; m, David Buttolph; ed, Folmar Blangsted; cos, Moss Mabry.

Drama (PR:C MPAA:NR)

CRY MURDER* (1936) 63m FC bw
Carole Mathews (Norman Alden), Jack Lord (Tommy Warren), Howard Smith (Sen. Alden), Hope Miller (Rosa Santorre), Tom Pedi (Santorre), Eugene Smith (Michael Alden), Harry Clark (Joe, the Bartender), Tom Aherne (Phillips), William Gibberson (Blair), Bill Dwyer (Patrolman), Lionel MacLyn (Sergeant).

Unimpressive blackmail scheme has Mathews scared about some relatively harmless letters found by a sinister New York artist. Cast as an ex-movie star who hitches up with a rising politician, she is haunted by the implausibilities of the script. In the standard finale the criminal is exposed and Mathews' reputation is saved.

p, Edward Leven; d, Jack Glenn; w, James Carhardt (from a play by A.B. Shiffrin); ph, Don Malkames; ed, Carl Lerner.

Mystery (PR:A MPAA:NR)

CRY OF BATTLE** (1963) 99m AA bw (AKA: TO BE A MAN)
Van Heflin (Joe Trent), Rita Moreno (Sisa), James MacArthur (David McVey), Leopoldo Salcedo (Manuel Careo), Sidney Clute (Col. Ryker), Marilou Munoz (Pinang), Oscar Roncal (Atong), Liza Moreno (Vera), Michael Parsons (Capt. Davis), Claude Wilson (Matchek), Vic Solyin (Capt. Garcia), Oscar Keesee.

WW II actioner which rides the whole journey with its brakes on, never shifting into high gear. MacArthur is the green son of a wealthy businessman who joins the cause and ends up in Pearl Harbor. Under the wing of seasoned Heflin he learns a thing or two about the war and women. Moreno is typically cast in a one-dimensional role which leaves her no room to develop.

p, Joe Steinberg; d, Irving Lerner; w, Bernard Gordon (based on Benjamin Appel's novel Fortress in the Rice); ph, Felipe Sacdalan; m, Richard Markowitz; ed, Verna Fields; cos, Felisa Salcedo; art d, Benjamin Rosella; spec eff, Hilario Brothers.

War (PR:A MPAA:NR)

CRY OF THE BANSHEE*½ (1970, Brit.) 87m AIP c
Vincent Price (Lord Edward Whitman), Elisabeth Bergner (Oona), Essy Persson (Lady Patricia), Hugh Griffith (Mickey), Patrick Mower (Roderick), Hilary Dwyer (Maureen), Carl Rigg (Harry), Stephen Chase (Sean), Marshall Jones (Father Tom), Andrew McCullough (Bully Boy), Michael Elphick (Burke), Robert Hutton (Guest), Godfrey James (Rider), Terry Martin (Brander), Richard Everett (Timothy), Quinn O'Hara (Witch Girl), Jan Rossini (Wench), Gertan Klauber (Landlord), Peter Forest (Party Man), Joyce Mandre (Party Woman), Pamela Farbrother (Margaret), Pamela Moiseiwitsch (Maid), Guy Deghy (Party Guest), Jean Deady (Naked Girl), Sally Geeson (Sarah), Peter Benson (Brander), Louis Selwyn (Apprentice), Mickey Baker (Rider), Carol Desmond (Girl), Ann Barrass, Nancy Meckler, Hugh Portnow, Stephen Rea, Maurice Colbourne, Dinah Stabb, Tony Sibbald, Neil Johnston, Rowan Wylie, Tim Thomas, Ron Sahewk, Maya Roth, Philly Howell, Guy Pierce.

A standard tale of an avenging witch who brings wrath down upon Price. As witch hunter Lord Whitman, Price and family are terrorized by witch Bergner and werewolf Mower in a Vermeeresque Dark Ages setting. Slow-moving and distractingly plotty, with unnecessary gore and nudity.

p&d, Gordon Hessler; w, Tim Kelly, Christopher Wicking (based on a story by Kelly); ph, John Coquillon (Movielab Color); m, Les Baxter; ed, Oswald Hafenrichter; md, Al Simms; art d, George Provis; set d, Scott Slimon; makeup, Tom Smith.

Horror (PR:O MPAA:GP)

CRY OF THE BEWITCHED (SEE: YOUNG AND EVIL, 1957, Mex.)

CRY OF THE CITY***½ (1948) 96m FOX bw
Victor Mature (Lt. Candella), Richard Conte (Martin Rome), Fred Clark (Lt. Collins), Shelley Winters (Brenda), Betty Garde (Mrs. Pruett), Berry Kroeger (Niles), Tommy Cook (Tony), Debra Paget (Teena Riconti), Hope Emerson (Rose Given), Roland Winters (Ledbetter), Walter Baldwin (Orvy), June Storey (Miss Boone), Tito Vuolo (Papa Roma), Mima Aguglia (Mama Roma), Dolores Castle (Rosa), Claudette Ross (Rosa's Daughter), Tiny Francone (Perdita), Elena Savonarola (Francesca), Thomas Ingersoll (Priest), Vito Scotti (Julio), Konstantin Shayne (Dr. Veroff), Howard Freeman (Sullivan), Robert Karnes, Charles Tannen (Interns), Oliver Blake (Caputo), Antonio Filauri (Vaselli), Joan Miller (Vera), Ken Christy (Loomis), Eddie Parks (Mike), Charles Wagenheim (Counterman), Kathleen Howard (Mrs. Pruett's Mother), Jane Nigh (Nurse), Martin Begley (Bartender), Michael Sheridan (Detective), Emil Raneau (Dr. Niklas), John Cortay (Policeman), George Melford (Barber), Harry Carter (Elevator Operator), Robert Adler, Harry Seymour (Men), Ruth Clifford (Nurse), Tom Moore (Doctor), George Beranger (Barber), Michael Stark (Cop), Davison Clark (Mounted Policeman), Helen Troya (Girl), Tommy Nello (Julio).

A complex, grim crime drama set in New York City, CRY OF THE CITY becomes more than routine under Siodmak's excellent direction, fluid camera, and quick cutting that adds to the suspense. Conte gives a blood-chilling performance as a conniving, unrepentant murderer who kills a cop during a jewelry holdup and is held in a prison hospital awaiting trial. Police lieutenant Mature visits him in a vain effort to get Conte to reveal the identity of a young girl, Paget, who may be a confederate and involved in an unsolved jewelry theft. Flattering Garde, the nurse attending him, Conte convinces her to take Paget into her home to protect her from police "harassment." As he is being transferred from the hospital to prison, Conte escapes, going to crooked lawyer Kroeger and killing him when he refuses to lend him escape funds. He finds the gems from the jewelry heist in Kroeger's safe and takes these to pay for his way out of the country. Mature is hot on his trail, tracking Conte to his parents' home, but the elusive criminal again escapes, this time hiding out with former girl friend Winters before being taken in by Emerson, an Amazon masseuse as vicious as he is. Conte offers Emerson a deal: She must give him $5,000 and a steamship ticket to South America and he will give her the jewels which are stored in a subway locker. Conte has also been working on his kid brother, Cook, to steal money from their parents to finance his escape. Wary, Emerson agrees to exchange the jewels for the cash but she insists that Conte accompany her to the locker before she pays him. Once in the subway she sees Mature, and believes Conte has set her up. She fires at the fleeing Conte but wounds Mature. The cop pursues the killer, both wounded, to a church where Conte meets with Paget. Mature confronts both of them, telling the girl that Conte, his boyhood pal, is evil through and through and to leave him. Conte's true nature emerges as he threatens to kill the wounded Mature, and Paget is persuaded to depart. Conte pulls a gun on Mature, who says that he will pull out his own and kill the murderer even though he pays for it with his own life. He has no weapon but his bluff works and Conte turns over his gun. Once outside, Mature collapses from his wound and Conte makes a run for it. The cop shouts for him to stop but Conte keeps going and Mature kills him with a single shot. Cook then arrives at the scene, weeping over the fallen body of his dead brother, telling Mature that he couldn't bring himself to steal from his parents, even for the bad brother he loved. Splendid on-location lensing from Sersen and top performances from Mature, Conte, and the wicked Emerson make this a film noir must, one on the top level of KISS OF DEATH, THE STREET WITH NO NAME, and NAKED CITY. Remake of MANHATTAN MELODRAMA.

p, Sol Siegel; d, Robert Siodmak; w, Richard Murphy (based on the novel The Chair for Martin Rome by Henry Edward Helseth); ph, Fred Sersen; m, Alfred Newman; ed, Harmon Jones; md, Lionel Newman; art d, Lyle Wheeler, Albert Hogsett; set d, Thomas Little, Ernest Lansing; cos, Bonnie Cashin; makeup, Ben Nye, Harry Maret, Pat McNally; spec eff, Sersen.

Crime Drama (PR:C MPAA:NR)

CRY OF THE HUNTED*** (1953) 78m MGM bw
Vittorio Gassman (Jory), Barry Sullivan (Lt. Tunner), Polly Bergen (Janet Tunner), William Conrad (Goodwin), Mary Zavian (Ella), Robert Burton (Warden Keeley), Harry Shannon (Sheriff Brown), Jonathan Cott (Deputy Davis).

Stylishly directed chase film from Lewis who had previously shown his talent in GUN CRAZY. Gassman plays a reed-hopping fugitive who is closely trailed by Sullivan through Louisiana's swamplands. The location, which is strikingly lensed, adds to the gritty sweatiness of the pursuit. While being transported to a courthouse to play informer, Gassman makes his move and escapes. At one point he is caught but again breaks free, only to be captured again at the finale. Interesting subplot has Conrad waiting for Sullivan to make a wrong move so he can grab his job.

p, William Grady, Jr.; d, Joseph H. Lewis; w, Jack Leonard (from a story by Leonard, Marion Wolfe); ph, Harry Lipstein; m, Rudolph G. Kopp; ed, Conrad A. Nervig.

Drama (PR:A MPAA:NR)

CRY OF THE PENGUINS** (1972, Brit.) 101m P.G.I. Production/BL c
(AKA: MR. FORBUSH AND THE PENGUINS)
John Hurt (Forbush), Hayley Mills (Tara), Dudley Sutton (Starshot), Tony Britton (George Dewport), Thorley Walters (Forbush, Sr.), Judy Campbell (Mrs. Forbush), Joss Ackland (Head of Board), Nicholas Pennell (Julian), Avril Angers (Fanny), Cyril Luckham (Prof. Tringham), Sally Geeson (Jackie), Brian Oulton (Food Store Clerk), Salmaan Peer (Ahaz Khan), Hugh Moxey (Lord Cheddar), Norman Claridge (Principal), John Comer (Police Sergeant), Geraldine Sherman (Penny), Jumoke Debayo (Traffic Warden), Lew Luton (1st Pilot), Burnell Tucker (2nd Pilot), Richard Bond (3rd Pilot), Margaret Lacey (Auntie), Marianne Stone (Policewoman), Andy Robins (Barry), Amanda Steer (Wendy).

Corny story has Hurt as a young scientist who has no problems making it with the ladies. So when Mills turns him down, he decides to redeem himself through an expedition to the Antarctic to study penguins. His growing fondness for the birds, and how they manage to adapt to their rugged environment, sparks a transformation in Hurt. Shallow story is given some life by the beautiful Antarctic photography by Sucksdorff. Remade as NEVER CRY WOLF.

p, Henry Tretttin; d, Al Viola; w, Anthony Shaffer (based on the novel *Mr. Forbush and the Penguins* by Graham Billing); ph, Edward Scaife, Harry Waxman, Arne Sucksdorff (Technicolor); m, John Addison; ed, Bernard Gribble; art d, Tony Masters; cos, John Furniss.

Adventure/Drama **(PR:A MPAA:NR)**

CRY OF THE WEREWOLF** (1944) 63m COL bw

Nina Foch *(Celeste)*, Stephen Crane *(Bob Morris)*, Osa Massen *(Elsa Chauvet)*, Blanche Yurka *(Bianca)*, Barton MacLane *(Lt. Barry Lane)*, Ivan Triesault *(Yan Spavero)*, John Abbott *(Peter Althius)*, Fred Graff *(Pinkie)*, John Tyrrell *(Mac)*, Robert Williams *(Max)*, Fritz Leiber *(Dr. Charles Morris)*, Milton Parsons *(Adamson)*.

The striking vampiric Foch carries her role as Queen Celeste, the gypsie queen, as well as can be expected in this average horror picture. As the daughter of a missing New Orleans belle, she keeps secret her dead mother's grave, now stored in a museum. She keeps watch over her mummified mom's remains, turning into a wolf and ripping apart anyone who poses a threat.

p, Wallace MacDonald; d, Henry Levin; w, Griffin Jay, Charles O'Neal; ph, L.W. O'Connell; ed, Reg Browne.

Horror **(PR:C-O MPAA:NR)**

CRY TERROR*** (1958) 96m MGM bw

James Mason *(Jim Molner)*, Rod Steiger *(Paul Hoplin)*, Inger Stevens *(Joan Molner)*, Neville Brand *(Steve)*, Angie Dickinson *(Kelly)*, Kenneth Tobey *(Frank Cole)*, Jack Klugman *(Vince)*, Jack Kruschen *(Charles Pope)*, Carleton Young *(Robert Adams)*, Barney Phillips *(Pringle)*, Harlan Warde, Ed Hinton *(Operatives)*, Chet Huntley, Roy Neal *(Themselves)*, Jonathan Hole *(Executive)*, William Schallert *(Henderson)*, Portland Mason *(Pat's School Friend)*, Mae Marsh *(Woman in Elevator)*, Terry Ann Ross *(Pat Molner)*.

Unfortunately, this fanciful premise came to pass a few times in real life, not unlike Rod Serling's TV show about skyjacking that happened with terrible regularity for the next few decades. A bomb has been placed aboard one of the airplanes of a large airline. The company is informed and when the authorities locate and detonate the bomb, TV repairman James Mason is watching on TV and recognizes the device as one he built years ago for his pal, Rod Steiger, when they were trying to land a contract from the government for some armed forces work. Mason is stunned but not half as amazed as when Steiger arrives and whisks Mason, wife Inger Stevens, and daughter, Terry Ann Ross, to his aerie, high atop a building. Steiger's plan is simple. He's proven that he can put a bomb on a plane so now he wants to threaten the airlines with another weapon but he won't give them a warning unless a ransom is paid. The company is forced to acquiesce. Stevens is sent to get the money while Steiger keeps Mason and Ross as hostages to insure Stevens' return with the money. The FBI has been nosing around and already is aware that Dickinson, Steiger's girl, placed the first bomb. Stevens gets the money and returns to the penthouse while being tailed by FBI agents. Brand and Klugman are Steiger's aides and Brand is especially menacing. A battle ensues and Mason escapes when Stevens kills one of the crooks. Steiger chases Stevens into the New York subway system. The feds are following close behind but not quite close enough. The final action sequence is in the darkness of the subway as a terrified Stevens attempts to get away from Steiger. He is trapped between the electric "third rail," an onrushing train, and the trailing agents. The result is foregone. This is a very fast moving picture that never allows you to sit back and realize the holes in the story, but it doesn't much matter as Andrew and Virginia Stone take us across New York and into the back alleys of the city for a speedy glimpse of story-telling at its quickest. News correspondents Roy Neal and Chet Huntley play themselves in the film and Mason's daughter, Portland, plays the best friend of Mason's daughter in the movie.

p, Virginia and Andrew Stone; d&w, Andrew Stone; ph, Walter Strenge; m, Howard Jackson; ed, Virginia Stone; cos, Bernard.

Crime Drama **(PR:A-C MPAA:NR)**

CRY, THE BELOVED COUNTRY*½** (1952, Brit.) 105m LFP/Lopert bw (AKA: AFRICAN FURY)

Canada Lee *(Stephen Kumalo)*, Charles Carson *(James Jarvis)*, Sidney Poitier *(Reu Maimangu)*, Joyce Carey *(Margaret Jarvis)*, Edric Connor *(John Kumalo)*, Geoffrey Keen *(Father Vincent)*, Vivien Clinton *(Mary)*, Michael Goodliffe *(Martens)*, Albertina Temba *(Mrs. Kumalo)*, Lionel Ngakane *(Absalom)*, Charles MacRae *(Kumalo's Friend)*, Henry Blumenthal *(Arthur Jarvis)*, Ribbon Dhlamini *(Gertrude Kumalo)*, Cyril Kwaza *(Matthew Kumalo)*, Max Dhlamini *(Father Thomas)*, Shayiaw Riba *(Father Tisa)*, Evelyn Nayati *(Mrs. Lithebe)*, Jsepo Gugusha *(Gertrude's Child)*, Reginald Ngcobo *(Taxi Driver)*, Emily Pooe *(Mrs. Ndela)*, Bruce Meredith Smith *(Capt. Jaarsveldt)*, Bruce Anderson *(Farmer Smith)*, Berdine Grunewald *(Mary Jarvis)*, Cecil Cartwright *(Harrison, Sr.)*, Andrew Kay *(Harrison, Jr.)*, Danie Adrewmah *(Young Man)*, Clement McCallin *(1st Reporter)*, Michael Golden *(2nd Reporter)*, Stanley Van Beers *(Judge)*, John Arnatt *(Prison Warden)*, Scott Harrold *(Police Superintendent)*.

Made in South Africa and London, this film version of Paton's bestseller is the dramatic version and it followed the stage version, "Lost In The Stars," by two years. Canada Lee is a decent man of the cloth who comes from the hinterlands to Johannesberg to find his son and his sister, both of whom have fled the sweet-smelling country and now live in the dank, rat-infested slum of the city. Ngakane is Lee's son and already contaminated enough by the city to have killed a white man in a robbery. Ironically, that man was kind to the blacks and was the son of a rich farmer, Carson, who has his ranch in the area where Lee preaches the gospel. Carson and Lee have both lost their sons; Carson's to Lee's son's weapon and Lee's to prison. Ribbon Dhlamini is the girl that's pregnant by Ngakane and standing by the young man through his trial and subsequent tribulations. The movie takes us through the trial and we meet all of the parties involved; Carey is the dead boy's mother; Connor as Lee's devious brother; Keen as the white head of the church mission and a very young Poitier as a young black preacher. The details of the movie are what make it so good. It's poignant and sentimental but never overly so. The simplicity of the story and the sincerity of the people make it a movie one cannot relegate to a pile of memories. To look at it in the 1980s, one must realize that things have not changed much in South Africa. Lee, born Lionel Canegata, only made four movies and died at the age of 45. Korda, one of the three Korda brothers (Alexander and Vincent), also helmed SAHARA, THE MACOMBER AFFAIR, THE FOUR FEATHERS, and many more. His films could always be counted upon to have a secondary meaning and to give an audience something to mull over when leaving the theater.

p, Alan Paton, Zoltan Korda; d, Korda; w, Paton (based on his novel); ph, Robert Krasker; m, R. Gallois-Montbrun; ed, David Eady; cos, Maisie Kelly; md, Dr. Hubert Clifford.

Drama **(PR:A MPAA:NR)**

CRY TOUGH½** (1959) 84m UA bw

John Saxon *(Miguel Estrada)*, Linda Cristal *(Sarita)*, Joseph Calleia *(Senor Estrada)*, Arthur Batanides *(Alvears)*, Paul Clarke *(Emilio)*, Joe DeSantis *(Cortez)*, Don Gordon *(Incho)*, Perry Lopez *(Toro)*, Barbara Luna *(Tina)*, Frank Puglia *(Lavandero)*, Penny Stanton *(Senora Estrada)*, Harry Townes *(Carlos)*, John Sebastian *(Alberto)*.

Spanish Harlem is the environ for this melodrama about a Puerto Rican street kid's response to social and racial prejudice. After doing a year in the slammer, Saxon is released and decides to live a clean life, instead of renewing a policy of thievery. A well-acted piece in which the characters meld into their seedy surroundings. Active editing job by Knudtson accelerates the pace.

p, Harry Kleiner; d, Paul Stanley; w, Kleiner (based on the novel *Children of the Dark* by Irving Shulman); ph, Philip Lathrop, Irving Glassberg; m, Laurindo Almeida; ed, Frederic Knudtson.

Drama **(PR:A MPAA:NR)**

CRY VENGEANCE*** (1954) 81m AA bw

Mark Stevens *(Vic Barron)*, Martha Hyer *(Peggy Harding)*, Skip Homeier *(Roxey)*, Joan Vohs *(Lily Arnold)*, Douglas Kennedy *(Tino Morelli)*, Don Haggerty *(Lt. Ryan)*, Cheryl Callaway *(Marie Morelli)*, Warren Douglas *(Mike Walters)*, Mort Mills *(Johnny Blue-Eyes)*, John Doucette *(Red Miller)*, Lewis Martin *(Nick Buda)*, Dorothy Kennedy *(Emily Miller)*.

Gripping crime caper which has Stevens on the hunt for Kennedy, who supposedly framed him and killed his wife and kid. After spending three years in San Quentin, Stevens, disfigured from the auto explosion that killed his family, follows his subject's trail to Alaska. Kennedy, now a respected business man, turns out to be innocent. The real baddie again tries to frame Stevens by hiring Homeier to kill Kennedy. Thanks to a tipoff from Vohs, Stevens is saved from a second frameup. Slick score from Dunlap which matches the frenetic pace set by director Stevens and editor Veron.

p, Lindsley Parsons; d, Mark Stevens; w, Warren Douglas, George Bricker; ph, William Sickner; m, Paul Dunlap; ed, Elmo Veron.

Drama **(PR:A MPAA:NR)**

CRY WOLF½** (1947) 83m WB bw

Errol Flynn *(Mark Caldwell)*, Barbara Stanwyck *(Sandra Marshall)*, Richard Basehart *(James Demarest)*, Geraldine Brooks *(Julie Demarest)*, Jerome Cowan *(Sen. Caldwell)*, John Ridgely *(Jackson Laidell)*, Patricia White *(Angela)*, Rory Mallinson *(Becket)*, Helene Thimig *(Marta)*, Paul Stanton *(Davenport)*, Barry Bernard *(Roberts the Groom)*, John Elliott *(Clergyman)*, Lisa Golm *(Mrs. Laidell)*, Jack Mower *(Watkins)*, Paul Panzer *(Gatekeeper)*, Creighton Hale *(Dr. Reynolds)*.

Barbara Stanwyck is a grieving widow who arrives at the family house and surprises the other members of the clan who had no idea that the deceased was married. Stanwyck admits the truth; it was a marriage in name only and only done so that the dead man would be able to inherit a large fortune that was being held by his uncle, Errol Flynn. A divorce was to follow in short order and Miss Stanwyck would get a fee for the use of her being. Flynn is suspicious of Stanwyck and she returns the raised eyebrows. Flynn maintains a secret lab in a section of the huge house that is off-limits to everyone. She begins her own reconnoitering and finds out why that section is cloistered. Her husband, Basehart, is not dead at all. He's quite alive and quite nuts and wanders around the estate. (Isn't this beginning to sound a bit like THE CONDEMNED OF ALTONA, but without the Nazi angle?) Basehart attempts to kill Flynn and dies accidentally. Now Stanwyck knows the secret; there's an insanity streak as wide as the Mississippi running through the family. Flynn has been trying to keep it mum because Cowan is running for office and it wouldn't do for the world to know that the senator had some bats in the family's belfry. And that's it, the mystery is revealed and everyone can go home. Geraldine Brooks is introduced in this film as an hysterical niece who commits suicide and her acting is a touch overblown for the film. Most of the other thesps are wooden and Flynn is totally miscast and as stiff as a board—which just might have been the problem.

p, Henry Blanke; d, Peter Godfrey; w, Catherine Turney (based on the novel by Marjorie Carleton); ph, Carl Guthrie; m, Franz Waxman; ed, Folmar Blangsted; md, Leonid Raab; art d, Carl Jules Weyl; set d, Jack McConaghy; cos, Travilla, Edith Head; spec eff, William McGann, Robert Burks.

Mystery **(PR:A MPAA:NR)**

CRY WOLF** (1968, Brit.) 58m Damor Leaderfilm/CFF c

Antony Kemp *(Tony)*, Mary Burleigh *(Mary)*, Martin Beaumont *(Martin)*, Judy Cornwell *(Stella)*, Eileen Moore *(Muriel Walker)*, Maurice Kaufmann *(Jim Walker)*, John Trenaman *(Ben)*, Alfred Bell *(Inspector Blake)*, Pat Coombs *(Mrs. Blades)*, Wilfrid Brambell *(Delivery Man)*, Adrienne Corri *(Woman)*, Ian Hendry, Janet Munro.

Little Kemp, who has tended to show a vivid imagination, is not believed by grownups when he stumbles across a plot to kidnap the British prime minister. The oldest story in children's literature gets an okay treatment here, but it's strictly kid stuff.

p, Michael Truman; d, John Davis; w, Derry Quinn (based on a story by Davis), ph, (Eastmancolor).

Children (PR:AA MPAA:NR)

CRYPT OF THE LIVING DEAD zero (1973) 75m Coast Industries c
Andrew Prince, Mark Damon, Teresa Gimpera, Patty Sheppard, Francisco Brana.

"She's 700 years old and still going strong" says the ad about this cheap picture directed by actor Ray Danton (THE CHAPMAN REPORT). Vampire Island is the setting for some routine terrorizing by an undead gal from the 13th century. Anyone going to a place called Vampire Island deserves to suffer.

p, Lou Shaw; d, Ray Danton; w, Shaw (based on a story by Lois Gibson); ph, (Metrocolor).

Horror **Cas.** (PR:C MPAA:PG)

CRYSTAL BALL, THE½** (1943) 80m UA bw
Ray Milland (Brad Cavanaugh), Paulette Goddard (Toni Gerard), Gladys George (Mme. Zenobia), Virginia Field (Jo Ainsley), Cecil Kellaway (Pop Tibbets), William Bendix (Biff Carter), Mary Fields (Foster), Frank Conlan (Dusty), Ernest Truex (Mr. Martin), Mabel Paige (Lady with Pekinese), Regina Wallace (Mrs. Smythe), Peter Jamieson (Brad's Secretary), Donald Douglas (Mr. Bowman), Nestor Paiva (Stukov), Sig Arno (Waiter at Stukov's), Hillary Brooke (Friend of Jo's), Tom Dugan (Plumber), Iris Adrian (Mrs. Martin), Babe London, June Evans (Tandem Riders), Reginald Sheffield (Dad in Shooting Gallery), Maude Eburne ("Apple Annie" Character), Yvonne De Carlo, Maxine Ardell (Secretaries), Christopher King, Alice Kirby, Marcella Phillips, Lorraine Miller, Lynda Grey, Donivee Lee (Garter Girls—Bazaar Sequence), Eric Alden, Donald Gallaher (Ambulance Drivers), Marjorie Deanne (Cigarette Girl), May Beatty (Dowager), Charles Irwin (Spieler).

Mild comedy starring Milland as a rich attorney who is engaged to an even richer widow, Field, until perky, sassy Goddard comes into the plot to upset the best-laid plans. Goddard, a one-time beauty contestant, takes a job as a phony fortune teller and tells Milland to buy some property. Paulette plays two roles and Milland and the others involved don't know that she is the fraudulent fortune teller. The big comedy sequence is a pie-throwing flight at the end and that was 30 years old by the time this movie was done. There are so many characters in the picture and so little time that one doesn't have the opportunity to really get to know anyone. Bendix does his tough chauffeur act and Truex and Adrian are cute as a Bickersons-type couple. Yvonne DeCarlo (born Peggy Middleton in Canada) does one of the many bits she played (secretary) before Walter Wanger cast her as SALOME, WHERE SHE DANCED in 1945. South African-born Cecil Kellaway was always an elf of an actor and won two Oscar nominations for THE LUCK OF THE IRISH and GUESS WHO'S COMING TO DINNER. He was also the victim of one of the strangest bits of casting in Hollywood history as Lana Turner's Greek husband in THE POSTMAN ALWAYS RINGS TWICE.

p, Richard Blumenthal; d, Elliott Nugent; w, Virginia Van Upp (from a story by Steven Vas); ph, Leo Tover; m, Victor Young; ed, Doane Harrison; art d, Hans Dreier, Roland Anderson; set d, George Sawley.

Comedy (PR:A MPAA:NR)

CUBA* (1979) 122m UA c
Brooke Adams (Alexandra Pulido), Sean Connery (Robert Dapes), Jack Weston (Gutman), Hector Elizondo (Ramirez), Denholm Elliott (Skinner), Martin Balsam (Gen. Bello), Chris Sarandon (Juan Pulido), Alejandro Rey (Faustino), Lonette McKee (Therese), Danny De La Paz (Julio), Louisa Moritz (Miss Wonderly), Dave King (Press Agent), Walter Gotell (Don Pulido), Earl Cameron (Col. Rosell Y Leyva), Pauline Peart (Dolores), Anna Nicholas (Maria), David Rappaport (Jesus), Tony Matthews (Carillo), Leticia Gerrado (Cecilia), John Morton (Gary), Anthony Pullen Shaw (Spencer), Stefan Kalipha (Ramon).

The successful writer/director team of Wood and Lester score again in this satirical comedy set during the fall of the Batista regime. But opening to scathing reviews, this Sean Connery vehicle hardly got a chance to move. The story centers around Dapes, a British mercenary who is sent to Cuba in 1959. His mission is to train the Batistas who are under attack from Castro's revolutionary forces. Once on the island he rekindles old flame Adams, who is torn between Connery and husband Sarandon. A strong parallel is drawn between the revolutions of Batista and Castro, which is mistakenly viewed as pro-Socialist. Most important to this satire is the observation that situations don't always change when governments do—officials still get drunk, policemen still take bribes, and the people, as usual, come last. Well-honed cynicism which fires on target and often produces sincere laughter.

p, Arlene Sellers, Alex Winitsky; d, Richard Lester; w, Charles Wood; ph, David Watkin (Technicolor); m, Patrick Williams; ed, John Victor Smith; prod d, Gil Parrondo; art d, Denis Gordon Orr; set d, Gil Parrondo; cos, Shirley Russell.

Adventure/Satire (PR:C MPAA:R)

CUBA CROSSING zero (1980) 90m Key West c
(AKA: KILL CASTRO; ASSIGNMENT: KILL CASTRO)
Stuart Whitman (Capt. Tony Terracino), Robert Vaughn (Hudd), Raymond St. Jacques (Bell), Caren Kaye (Tracy), Woody Strode (Titi), Sybil Danning (Veronica), Mary Lou Gassen (Maria), Albert Salmi (Delgato), Michael Gazzo (Rosselini), Monty Rock III (Bar Gay).

Call it what you will, it is still vile and worthless from all vantage points. A fine cast is entirely wasted in this low-budgeter shot in Key West, Florida. Stock footage of Castro and the Bay of Pigs tries to authenticize the outlandish plot, but only makes one laugh harder. Whitman as Capt. Terracino is a bartending soldier-of-fortune who gets

involved in a plot to kill Castro. Well, better people than the captain have tried, and maybe they should have made a movie about them instead.

p, Peter J. Barton; d/w, Chuck Workman.

Spy Drama (PR:O MPAA:NR)

CUBAN FIREBALL** (1951) 78m REP bw
Estelita Rodriguez (Herself), Warren Douglas (Tommy Pomeroy), Mimi Aguglia (Senora Martinez), Leon Belasco (Hunyabi), Donald MacBride (Capt. Brown), Rosa Turich (Maria), John Litel (Pomeroy, Sr.), Tim Ryan (Bacon), Russ Vincent (Ramon), Edward Gargan (Ritter), Victoria Horne (Maid), Jack Kruschen (Lefty), Pedro de Cordoba (Don Perez), Olan Soule (Jimmy), Tony Barr (Estaban Martinez), Luther Crockett (Rafferty).

Uninspired mambo film which has Rodriguez on her way to sunny Los Angeles to collect a whopping twenty million dollar inheritance. Expecting a horde of money hounds to harass her, she disguises her tiny, perfect-figure little body in old woman's garb, leading predictably to a series of comic situations, none of which are very funny. She was easily the most luscious young woman ever snared by Republic, and the studio was attempting in this film to recreate the old Lupe Velez features and hoped to launch a series of comedies with it, but, though the formula was right, the feeling was not there. CUBAN FIREBALL featured such Latin tunes as "Lost and Found," "A Slave" (Jack Elliott, Aaron Gonzalez), and "Un Poquito De Tu Amor" (Julio Gutierres).

p, Sidney Picker; d, William Beaudine; w, Charles E. Roberts, Jack Townley (based on a story by Roberts); ph, Reggie Lanning; ed, Tony Martinelli.

Musical (PR:A MPAA:NR)

CUBAN LOVE SONG, THE* (1931) 80m MGM bw
Lawrence Tibbett (Terry), Lupe Velez (Nenita), Ernest Torrence (Romance), Jimmy "Schnozzola" Durante (O. O. Jones), Karen Morly (Crystal), Hale Hamilton (Elvira), Mathilda Comont (Aunt Rosa), Phillip Cooper (Terry, Jr.), Louise Fazenda.

Metropolitan Opera star Tibbett is cast in this ditty-filled tale centered around the then-popular tune "The Peanut Vendor." Tibbett joins the Marines and leaves his deb girl behind in the States. He and pal Durante are sent to Cuba where they meet the vivacious Velez, a peanut vendor. The hungry Tibbett has a time with the senorita, but returns to his gal when the war ends. Time goes by and Tibbett's mind wanders towards Velez. By chance, he meets up with the Schnozzola and the duo take off in search of the vendor. They soon learn that she died, leaving a small remembrance behind—a son. Being a good father and lousy husband he returns to the States with the babe in his arms. Obediently his deb wife accepts the little one into her home. Tibbett is good, but better off at the Met, though he is well supported by Velez and Durante in one of the best films of this genre. Songs: "The Cuban Love Song," "Peanut Vendor" (Marion Sunshine, I. Wolfe Gilbert, Moises Simons), "The Marine Hymn," "Tramps At Sea," "You're In the Army Now" (Dorothy Fields, Jimmy McHugh), "Nobody's Sweetheart" (Gus Kahn, Ernie Erdman, Billy Meyers, Elmer Schoebel.)

d, W.S. Van Dyke; w, John Lynch, John Colton, Gilbert Emery, Robert E. Hopkins, Paul Hervey Fox (based on original story by C. Gardner Sullivan, Bess Meredyth); ph, Harold Rossen; m, Herbert Stothart; ed, Margaret Booth.

Musical (PR:A MPAA:NR)

CUBAN PETE½** (1946) 61m UNIV bw (GB:DOWN CUBAN WAY)
Desi Arnaz (Himself), Beverly Simmons (Brownie), Don Porter (Roberts), Jacqueline de Wit (Lindsay), The King Sisters (Themselves), Ethel Smith (Herself), Pedro de Cordoba (Perez), Igor de Navrotzki, Yvette von Koris (Specialty Dancers), Joan Fulton (Shawlee/Ann), Del Sharbutt (Radio Announcer), Eddie Parks (Doctor), Ruth Lee (Woman on the Table), Charles Jordan (Police Sergeant), Roseanne Murray (Receptionist), Shirley O'Hara (Girl), Rico De Montez (Cuban Driver) Ellen Corby, Ann Lawrence, Peggy Leon, Diane Carroll (Screaming Patients), Robert O'Connor (Cuban Servant), Chick Bedell (Barker), Cleo Morgan (Nurse), Samuel Schultz (Boy), Peter Seal (Cossack).

Harmless mambo-jumbo which has Arnaz conveniently cast as a Cuban bandleader. Sappy plot has Fulton trying to lure Arnaz away from his native Havana and bring him to the Big Apple to play on a radio spot. If he doesn't play, the show's sponsor is going to withdraw. Fulton has a tough time of it until she is helped out by Arnaz's favorite niece. Songs: "The Breeze and I" (Al Stillman, Ernesto Lecuona), "El Cumbanchero" (Rachel Hernandez), "Lullaby" (adapted by Bill Driggs from the Mexican folk song "Cielito Lindo"), "After Tonight" (Jack Brooks, Milton Schwartzwald), "Rhumba Matumba" (Bobby Collaza).

p, Howard Welsch, Will Cowen; d, Jean Yarbrough; w, Robert Presnell, Sr., M. Coates Webster (based on a story by Bernard Feins); ph, Maury Gertsman; ed, Otto Ludwig; md, Milton Rosen.

Musical (PR:A MPAA:NR)

CUBAN REBEL GIRLS zero (1960) 68m Exploit/Brenner bw
(AKA: ASSAULT OF THE REBEL GIRLS)
Errol Flynn (Himself/Narrator), Beverly Aadland (Beverly), John MacKay (Johnny), Jackie Jackler (Jacqueline), Marie Edmund (Maria), Ben Ostrovsky (Raoul), Regnier Sanchez, Esther Oliva, Todd Brody, Al Brown, Clelle Mahon.

The withering Flynn tried desperately to repaint a portrait of himself as heroic modern-day swashbuckler, but instead revealed his dissipation in this sad semidocumentary tribute to Fidel Castro. Set in Cuba during Castro's overthrow of the Batistas, the film boasts "actual footage shot during the star's real-life adventure's with the Castro rebels." It is actually nothing more than a pitiful exit for a once-great film star. Flynn also chose to cast Beverly Aadland, the sixteen-year-old girl friend who submitted to his wicked, wicked ways, perhaps to liberate himself, once and for all, of his negative aura. Interesting only as an autobiographical footnote to his sordid later years and ironically released a year after his death of a heart attack at the age of 50. p&d, Barry Mahon; w, Errol Flynn.

Adventure (PR:A MPAA:NR)

CUCKOO CLOCK, THE** (1938, Ital.) 90m Era/MGM bw
Vittorio De Sica (Capt. Ducc), Guglielmo Sinaz (Rosen), Oretta Flume (Paolina), Lamberto Picasso (Count Scarabelli), Ugo Ceseri (Bami), Laura Solari (Elvira), Francesco Rissone (The Admiral).

An ultra-plotty mystery which nearly sinks in its complexities. An old English count who doubles as a spy meets up with a businessman who wants to smuggle gold into England in a giant cuckoo clock. The count agrees to help only if he can marry the smuggler's niece. The problem is that she is in love with a sea captain who happened to bring the clock over on his ship. Everything is set to go, but in the morning the count is found dead inside the clock. The innocent captain is nearly convicted when the real culprit steps forward. The murderer, one of Napoleon's ex-soldiers, tells the jury that the count uncovered a plot to get Napoleon out of his exile in Elba. In an attempt at realism, all of this takes place within a twenty-four-hour period, but too much talk and not enough mystery mars its chances.

d, Camillio Mastrocinque; w, Mario Soldati, Renato Castellani (based on a story by Alebtor Domini), ph, J. Stevens; m, Vittorio Rieti; ed, Ernesto Lucente.

Mystery (PR:A MPAA:NR)

CUCKOO IN THE NEST, THE** (1933, Brit.) 85m GAU/W&F bw
Tom Walls (Maj. Bone), Ralph Lynn (Peter Wyckham), Yvonne Arnaud (Marguerite Hickett), Robertson Hare (Reu Sioley-Jones), Mary Brough (Mrs. Spoker), Veronica Rose (Barbara Wyckham), Gordon James (Noony), Grace Edwin (Mrs. Bone), Mark Daly (Pinhorn), Cecil Parker (Claude Hickett), Roger Livesey (Alfred), Frank Pettingell (Landlord), Joan Brierley (Maid).

Lynn and Arnaud, once engaged to each other and now married to others, are forced by circumstances to spend a night together in the only room at an inn. A number of talented players distinguish this one slightly. Remade as FAST AND LOOSE in 1954.

p, Angus Macphail, Ian Dalrymple; d, Tom Walls; w, Ben Travers, A. R. Rawlinson (based on a play by Travers); ph, Glen MacWilliams.

Comedy (PR:A-C MPAA:NR)

CUCKOO PATROL zero (1965, Brit.) 76m Grand National bw
Freddie and the Dreamers (Themselves), Kenneth Connor (Willoughby Wick), Victor Maddern (Dicko), John Le Mesurier (Gibbs), Arther Mullard (Yossie), Ernest Clark (Marshall), Basil Dignam (Snodgrass), Michael Brennan (Superman), Peggy Ann Clifford (Scout Mistress), Jack Lambert (Inspector), Vic Wise (Moley).

Somebody decided that Freddie and the Dreamers were going to be the next big band during the mid 1960s British invasion of the U.S. They were wrong. They were a flash-in-the-pan band that made a forgettable film. Freddie and the boys dress up as Boy Scouts and do a whole bunch of silly things with wrestlers and robbers. What can be expected from a film with this one's title—high art maybe?

p, Maurice J. Wilson; d, Duncan Wood; w, Lew Schwarz.

Comedy (PR:A MPAA:NR)

CUCKOOS, THE***½ (1930) 90m RAD bw/c
Bert Wheeler (Sparrow), Robert Woolsey (Prof. Bird), June Clyde (Ruth), Hugh Trevor (Billy), Dorothy Lee (Anita), Ivan Lebedeff (The Baron), Marguerita Padula (Gypsy Queen), Mitchell Lewis (Julius), Jobyna Howland (Fanny Furst).

THE CUCKOOS is one of the funniest silly movies of the 1930s and, if we were to judge it by the comedies made fifty years later, this must rank as one of the funniest silly movies ever. Wheeler and Woolsey went on to make many wonderfully whacky films until Woolsey died in 1938 at the early age of forty-nine. Bert and Bob are a pair of bogus fortune tellers who are hot on the trail of a kidnaped heiress. Meanwhile, Mitchell Lewis, a mad gypsy, is chasing them because Wheeler has been paying too much attention to Dorothy Lee, who was living with the Romanies. The young lovers in the piece are June Clyde and Hugh Trevor, but all they do is take up screen time while the face is relaxing from all the laughter provided by Wheeler and Woolsey. No more plot than what's listed above but the jokes come like waves on a Hawaiian shore, one after another and each bigger than the one before. Sight gags galore as well as well-turned verbal humor, mostly from Woolsey. Based on a broadway play that starred Clark and McCullough, THE CUCKOOS is musical anarchy in a slightly different fashion than what Laurel and Hardy were doing at the same time. Wheeler and Woolsey are both comedians but they could also sing, dance, and act in high or low style. It's too bad their years together were so short, but there are many films one might watch to see their versatility and charm. Songs: "I Love You So Much," "Knock Knees," "Looking for the Limelight In Your Eyes," "All Alone Monday" (Bert Kalmar, Harry Ruby), "Dancing the Devil Away" (Kalmar, Otto Harbach, Ruby), "Wherever You Are" (Charles Tobias, Cliff Friend), "If I Were A Traveling Salesman" (Al Dubin, Joe Burke).

d, Paul Sloane, Louis Sarecky; w, Cy Woods (based on the play "The Ramblers" by Guy Bolton, Harry Ruby, Bert Kalmar); ch, Pearl Eaton.

Comedy (PR:AA MPAA:NR)

CUJO** (1983) 91m WB c
Dee Wallace (Donna), Danny Pintauro (Tad), Daniel Hugh-Kelly (Vic), Christopher Stone (Steve), Ed Lauter (Joe), Kaiulani Lee (Charity), Billy Jacoby (Brett), Mills Watson (Gary), Sandy Ward (Bannerman), Jerry Hardin (Masen), Merritt Olsen, Arthur Rosenberg, Terry Donovan-Smith, Robert Elross, Robert Behling, Claire Nono, Daniel H. Blatt.

A disappointing horror film from director Lewis Teague whose homage to "B" monster movies, ALLIGATOR (1980), was a surprisingly effective (and funny) film. This time the "monster" is a rabid St. Bernard dog (it was bitten by bats) that goes on a rampage, slobbering spit and goo all over its big snout, until he finally corners Wallace and her son in a stranded Pinto station wagon in 100-degree heat for what seems like weeks. The characters are all unsympathetic and the dog is just not scary enough to maintain any interest. In fact, the dog is the most sympathetic because he is basically a good pup turned vicious against his will, therefore the viewer could really care less about the humans involved. In addition to these weaknesses, there is none of the sly sense of humor (Teague really misses a great opportunity to make the ultimate in dog-bites-mailman jokes when a letter carrier ventures to the farmhouse where Wallace is trapped) that made ALLIGATOR so appealing. Most of the weaknesses arise from the lameness of the Stephen King source material, but the film is an unfortunate waste of potential.

p, Daniel H. Blatt, Robert Singer; d, Lewis Teague; w, Don Carlos Dunaway, Lauren Currier (based on the novel by Stephen King); ph, Jan DeBont (CFI Color); m, Charles Bernstein; ed, Neil Travis.

Horror Cas. (PR:O MPAA:NR)

CUL-DE-SAC*** (1966, Brit.) 111m Sigma/FILMWAYS bw
Donald Pleasence (George), Francoise Dorleac (Teresa), Lionel Stander (Richard), Jack MacGowran (Albert), Iain Quarrier (Christopher), Geoffrey Sumner (His Father), Renee Houston (His Mother), William Franklyn (Cecil), Trevor Delaney (Nicholas), Marie Kean (Mrs. Fairweather), Robert Dorning (Mr. Fairweather), Jackie Bissett (Jacqueline).

Neat little chiller with Polanski honing his abilities as a director and stand-out performances from Pleasence, Stander, and Dorleac. Pleasence is a hermit who lives with his succulent wife, Dorleac, in a large, dank, and dark castle on a small island off the northeast coast of Britain. Dorleac is a nymphomaniac in training and always looking for someone new to take her mind off the fact that she's living with this shaved-head nut. Lionel Stander and Jack MacGowran are escaped criminals who make their way to this remote outpost and what we get is Polanski's version of THE DESPERATE HOURS. Both men are wounded and MacGowran soon dies of his wounds, leaving nosey and noisy Stander to terrorize Pleasence and spouse. Tension builds as Stander and Pleasence get into a psychological battle that ends when Pleasence shoots Stander, quite accidentally, and Stander dies in the longest and hammiest death scene in modern history. This is a very macabre picture and there are those who would deem it black comedy due to the overplaying of Pleasence and Stander. It isn't funny enough in any way to be called comedy, no matter what color. But Polanski exhibits such style in his writing and direction that one can forgive the excesses. In a tiny role, Jacqueline Bissett is seen for the second time in her career and in the first role that wasn't a bit part (THE KNACK). CUL-DE-SAC is exaggerated, sinister, bleak, and spine-tingling. It is also somewhat thick in the middle and could have used a serious editor to whack away at it. Still, it's well worth seeing for the radiance of the late Dorleac who died the following year in an automobile crash.

p, Gene Gutowski, Sam Waynberg; d, Roman Polanski; w, Gerard Brach, Polanski; ph, Gil Taylor; m, Komeda; ed, Alistair MacIntyre; ex p, Michael Klinger, Tony Tensor.

Drama (PR:C-O MPAA:NR)

CULPEPPER CATTLE COMPANY, THE*** (1972) 92m FOX c
Gary Grimes (Ben Mockridge), Billy "Green" Bush (Frank Culpepper), Luke Askew (Luke), Bo Hopkins (Dixie Brick), Geoffrey Lewis (Russ), Wayne Sutherlin (Missoula), John McLiam (Pierce), Matt Clark (Pete), Raymond Guth (Cook), Anthony James (Nathaniel), Charlie Martin Smith (Tim Slater), Larry Finley (Mr. Slater), Bob Morgan (Old John), Jan Burrell (Mrs. Mockridge), Hal Needham (Burgess), Jerry Gatlin (Wallop), Bob Orrison (Rutter), Walter Scott (Print), Royal Dano (Rustler), Paul Harper (Trapper), Jose Chavez (Cantina Bartender), Gregory Sierra (One-eyed Thief), John Pearce (Spectator), Dennis Fimple (Wounded Man in Bar), William O'Connell (Piercetown Bartender), Arthur Malet (Doctor), Ted Gehring (Tascosa Bartender), Lu Shoemaker (Prostitute), Patrick Campbell (Br. Ephraim).

A "rite-of-passage" film which takes a young boy, Grimes, and places him against the murderous ways of the West. After convincing hard-edged trail boss Bush to bring him along on a cattle drive from Texas to Colorado, the soft-skinned Grimes is exposed to the leathering effects of the post-Civil War era. Great efforts are made to establish historic authenticity and detail in Richards' first film. Unfortunately, not enough time was spent on the script, leaving an occasional feeling of unsatisfaction. An interesting film which is a must for western buffs.

p, Paul H. Helmick; d, Dick Richards; w, Eric Bercovici, Gregory Prentiss (based on a story by Richards); ph, Lawrence Edward Williams, Ralph Woolsey (DeLuxe Color); m, Tom Scott, Jerry Goldsmith; ed, John F. Burnett; art d, Jack Martin Smith, Carl Anderson; set d, Walter M. Scott; cos, Ted Parvin.

Western (PR:C MPAA:PG)

CULT OF THE COBRA** (1955) 75 UNIV bw
Faith Domergue (Lisa), Richard Long (Paul Able), Marshall Thompson (Tom Markel), Kathleen Hughes (Julia), Jack Kelly (Carl Turner), Myrna Hansen (Marian), David Janssen (Rico Nardi), William Reynolds (Pete Norton), Leonard Strong (Daru), James Dobson (Nick Hommel), Walter Coy (Inspector), The Carlsons (Dance Team), Olan Soule (Maj. Martin Fielding), Helen Wallace (Mrs. Weber), Mary Alan Hokanson (Army Nurse), John Halloran (High Priest), Alan Reynolds (Capt. Williams).

A mysterious horror film about six GIs who photograph a secret ritual in which members of a cult transform themselves into snakes. Cult leader Domergue changes back into her human shape in time to put a curse on the voyeuristic group. Back in the States the murders begin, and GI Long tells his story to the police. They are suspicious at first, but after finding venom in the corpses they believe his tale. Meantime, snake-lady Domergue has fallen in love with Long's roommate, though he isn't aware of her slithery other half. The roommate sees a snake about to attack Long's fiance and pushes the creepy creature out an open window. As it lands on the pavement below it makes its final transformation—into Domergue. A gimmicky attempt at creating the snake's point-of-view as it is about to attack is interesting but laughable. A cheesy flick which can be fun.

p, Howard Pine; d, Francis D. Lyon; w, Jerry Davis, Cecil Maiden, Richard Collins (based on a story by Davis); ph, Russell Metty; ed, Milton Carruth.

Horror (PR:A-C MPAA:NR)

CULT OF THE DAMNED (SEE: ANGEL, ANGEL, DOWN WE GO, 1969)

CUP FEVER*½ (1965, Brit.) 53m Century/CFF bw
Bernard Cribbins (Policeman), David S. Lodge (Mr. Bates), Dermot Kelly (Bodger), Norman Rossington (Driver), Sonia Graham (Mrs. Davis), Johnny Wade (Milkman), Denis Gilmore (Skipper), Susan George (Vicky), Jim Morgan (Rocket), Raymond Davis (Denis), Matt Busby, Manchester United Football Team.

The police and the local soccer team join with a children's team to foil the nefarious schemes of a shifty local politician. Not very interesting, though kids will enjoy it.

p, Roy Simpson; d&w, David Bracknell.

Children (PR:AA MPAA:NR)

CUP OF KINDNESS, A*½ (1934, Brit.) 81m GAU bw
Tom Walls (Fred Tutt), Ralph Lynn (Charlie Tutt), Robertson Hare (Ernest Ramsbottom), Dorothy Hyson (Betty Ramsbottom), Claude Hulbert (Stanley Tutt), Marie Wright (Mrs. Ramsbottom), Eva Moore (Mrs. Tutt), Veronica Rose (Tilly Wynn), Gordon James (Nicholas Ramsbottom), D. A. Clarke-Smith (Mr. Finch), J. Fisher White (Vicar).

Despite a long-standing feud between their parents, young couple marry and are promptly accused of fraud. Routine romantic comedy.

p, Michael Balcon; d, Tom Walls; w, Ben Travers (based on a play by Travers).

Comedy (PR:A MPAA:NR)

CUP-TIE HONEYMOON*½ (1948, Brit.) 93m Film Studios Manchester/Mancunian bw
Sandy Powell (Joe Butler), Dan Young (Cecil Alistair), Betty Jumel (Betty), Pat McGrath (Eric Chambers), Violet Farebrother (Mary Chambers), Frank Groves (Jimmy Owen), Joyanne Bracewell (Pauline May), Vic Arnley (Granddad), Harold Walden (Himself).

Powell, the son of the company chairman, wins the affections of his secretary by playing in the championship soccer match. Bleak comedy from bleak Manchester.

p&d, John E. Blakeley; w, Anthony Toner, Harry Jackson; ph, Geoffrey Faithfull.

Comedy (PR:A MPAA:NR)

CUPS OF SAN SEBASTIAN, THE (SEE: FICKLE FINGER OF FATE, THE, 1967)

CURE FOR LOVE, THE**½ (1950, Brit.) 98m BL bw
Robert Donat (Jack), Renee Asherson (Milly), Marjorie Rhodes (Mrs. Hardacre), Charles Victor (Harry), Thora Hird (Mrs. Dorbell), Dora Bryan (Jenny), Gladys Henson (Mrs. Jenkins), John Stratton (Sam), Francis Wignall (Claude), Norman Partridge (Vicar), Edna Morris (Mrs. Harrison), Michael Dear (Albert), Tonie MacMillan (Mrs. Donald), Lilian Stanley (Mrs. Small), Margot Bryant (Mrs. Hooley), Lucille Gray (Tough Girl), Jack Howarth (Hunter), Sam Kydd (Charlie Fox), Jack Rodney (Eddie), Reginald Green (Douglas), Johnnie Catcher (Canadian Soldier), Jim Conrad (Polish Soldier).

A fair output from Donat, who almost single-handedly made this film. Story concerns a GI on leave who visits his fiance of three years in the hopes that she'll want to break it off. He has no such luck. In fact, she is even more determined than ever to hitch him. What he hasn't told her is that he has amorous feelings for another lass. He finds that he left his bravery on the front line, and can't get up the nerve to tell her the news. But, as expected, his bravery eventually catches up with him. An energetic attempt from Donat which probably suffers more from his lack of objectivity than anything else.

p&d, Robert Donat; w, Donat, Alexander Shaw, Albert Fennell (based on a play by Walter Greenwood); ph, Jack Cox; m, William Alwyn; ed, Bert Bates; md, Muir Mathieson; set d, Wilfred Shingleton.

Drama (PR:A MPAA:NR)

CURFEW BREAKERS*½ (1957) 78m Screen Guild bw
Regis Toomey, Paul Kelly, Cathy Downs, Marilyn Madison, Sheila Urban.

Toomey and Kelly are a pair of community leaders investigating the murder of a gas station attendant by a drug-crazed youth. They uncover a number of teenagers on a rampage and an Elvis look-alike who sings "Baby Baby Blues" and "Jump For George." Laughable exploitation film.

p, Charles E. King; d, Alex Wells.

Crime (PR:C MPAA:NR)

CURIOUS DR. HUMPP* (1967, Arg.) 85m Productores Argentinos/Unicorn bw
(LA VENGANZA DEL SEXO)
Richard Bauleo, Gloria Prat, Aldo Barbero, Susan Beltran, Justin Martin, Michel Angel, Mary Albano, Al Bugatti, Alex Klapp, Hector Biuchet, Greta Williams, Norbert Nelson.

A heavy medical entry which casts Bauleo as a reporter investigating mad scientist, Barbero. After an outbreak of murders, the guilty Barbero is traced to a purchase of large amounts of aphrodisiacs. Bauleo discovers the killer's laboratory full of living experiments. Morbid.

p, Orestes Trucco; d&w, Emilio Vieyra; w, Raul Zorrilla; ph, Canibal Gonzalez; ed, Jacinto Cascales; m, Victor Buchino.

Horror (PR:O MPAA:NR)

CURIOUS FEMALE, THE zero (1969) 75m Fanfare c
Angelique Pettyjohn (Susan), Charlene Jones (Pearl), Bunny Allister (Joan), David

Westberg (Paul), Julie Conners (Andre), Michael Greer (Bixby), Elaine Edwards (Mrs. Wilde), Carol Jean Thompson (Gloria), Sebastian Brook (Mr. Burton), Ron Gans (Jerome Bruce, David Pritchard (Guy Ryan), Slim Gaillard (Mr. Lushcomb), Harry Sodoni (Harry), Lincoln Kilpatrick (Uncle Charlie), Mildred Harrison (Mrs. Lushcomb), Randee Jensen (Joy), David Buchanan (Young Man), Mary Virginia Pittman (Scarlet), Junero Jennings (Roy), Betty Gumn (Girl), Mike Castle (Everet), Christopher Riordan (Troy), Ron Graham (Bouncer), Josh Bryant (Mr. Tower), David Osterhout (Hinkley), Al Quick (Weeny).

It is the year 2117 and sex runs rampant in a society without romance, where a group of movie-goers are arrested for illegally viewing a film. The one they flock to see is called "The Three Virgins," about three students who refuse to have sex without love. Only the 1960s could have produced this sort of ridiculous film—a condemning view on society's sexuality, or was it an honest portrayal of campus life?

p&d, Paul Rapp; w, Winston R. Paul; ph, Don Birnkrant (Eastmancolor); m, Stu Phillips; ed, Reg Browne; set d, Ray Boltz.

Science Fiction (PR:O MPAA:NR)

CURLY TOP**** (1935) 75m FOX bw
Shirley Temple (Elizabeth Blair), John Boles (Edward Morgan), Rochelle Hudson (Mary Blair), Jane Darwell (Mrs. Denham), Rafaela Ottiano (Mrs. Higgins), Esther Dale (Aunt Genevieve Graham), Etienne Girardo (Mr. Wyckoff), Maurice Murphy (Jimmie Rogers), Arthur Treacher (Butler).

As one of the strongest Shirley Temple showcases, a nifty argument for the idea of the actor as auteur can be made here. What is most remembered and most significant about this film is little Miss Temple herself. The nearly unimportant plot has Shirley and big sis Hudson discovered in an orphanage by millionaire Boles. He shows them Park Avenue and the life of luxury, and naturally falls for the post-pube sis. Shirley doesn't forget where she came from though, and returns to the orphanage to sing a few ditties with her moppet friends. CURLY TOP was a masked remake of DADDY LONG LEGS (1919), starring Mary Pickford, and was remade again in 1955 with Fred Astaire and Leslie Caron. Songs: "Animal Crackers In My Soup," "It's All So New To Me" (Ted Koehler, Irving Caesar, Ray Henderson), "Curly Top" (Koehler, Henderson), "The Simple Things In Life," "When I Grow Up" (Edward Heyman, Henderson).

p, Winfield Sheehan; d, Irving Cummings; w, Patterson McNutt, Arthur Beckhard (based on a story by Jean Webster); ph, John Seitz; m, Ray Henderson, Ted Koehler, Edward Heyman; md, Oscar Bradley; ch, Jack Donohue.

Musical (PR:AAA MPAA:NR)

CURSE OF BIGFOOT, THE* (1972) 87m Universal Entertainment c
William Simonsen, Robert Clymire.

A low-budget monster movie from the early 1960s is spliced into a framing episode where a teacher talks to his class about the unknown, then flashes back to his recollections of disturbing an old Indian burial ground and facing the big, hairy monster that guards the spot. Utterly dumb.

d, John Fields; w, J. T. Fields.

Horror (PR:C MPAA:NR)

CURSE OF DRACULA, THE (SEE: RETURN OF DRACULA, THE, 1958)

CURSE OF FRANKENSTEIN, THE*** (1957, Brit.) 82m Hammer/WB c
Peter Cushing (Baron Victor Frankenstein), Christopher Lee (The Creature), Hazel Court (Elizabeth), Robert Urquhart (Paul Krempe), Valerie Gaunt (Justine), Noel Hood (Aunt Sophia), Marjorie Hume (Mother), Melvyn Hayes (Young Victor), Sally Walsh (Young Elizabeth), Paul Hardtmuth (Prof. Bernstein), Fred Johnson (Grandfather), Claude Kingston (Small Boy), Henry Caine (Schoolmaster), Michael Mulcaster (Werner), Patrick Troughton (Kurt), Joseph Behrman (Fritz), Hugh Dempster (Burgomaster), Anne Blake (Burgomaster's Wife), Raymond Rollett (Father Felix), Alex Gallier (Priest), Ernest Jay (Undertaker), J. Trevor Davis (Uncle), Bartlett Mullins (Tramp), Eugene Leahy (Second Priest).

Cushing and Lee team up to retell Mary Shelley's classic tale in the first of the gruesome and bloody Hammer horror series. A ground-breaking film which almost single-handedly revived the interest in gothic horror when sci-fi was taking over. Confronted with Universal's copyrighted squarehead, makeup man Jack Pierce came up with a more realistic monster for Lee to portray. In a style uncommon to horror films the tale is told through flashbacks—a manner which distances the audience instead of drawing it into the picture—as Cushing awaits execution for the murder of his wife, who died in an acid battle between himself and the monster. As the young Victor Frankenstein, we see his early experiments with the creation of a monster, as well as his more advanced discoveries in his later years. Shot for $250,000 and grossing millions, a successful formula was found by Hammer. Cushing stayed on for five less successful sequels.

p, Anthony Hinds; d, Terence Fisher; w, Jimmy Sangster (based on the novel Frankenstein by Mary Shelley); ph, Jack Asher; m, Leonard Salzedo; ed, James Needs; makeup, Jack Pierce.

Horror (PR:O MPAA:NR)

CURSE OF THE AZTEC MUMMY, THE* (1965, Mex.) 65m
Cinematografica Calderon-AIP-TV/K. Gordon Murray Productions bw
(LA MALDICION DE LA MOMIA AZTECA)
Ramon Gay, Rosita Arenas, Crox Alvarado, Luis Aceves Castaneda, Angel d'Esteffani, Jesus Velazquez, Alejandro Cruz, Enrique Yanez, Alberto Yanez, Francisco Segura, Jaime Gonzalez Quinones, Arturo Martinez, Guillermo Hernandez, Julian de Meriche.

An evil scientist escapes from prison and unleashes a fiendish plot to steal the treasure hidden in an Aztec pyramid. Just when he has captured all the good guys and his plan is on the verge of success, the Aztec mummy comes out of its tomb and subdues the villain. Laughable sequel to the laughable THE ROBOT VS. THE AZTEC MUMMY, though the most outrageous installment in the series would come a few years later with WRESTLING WOMEN VS. THE AZTEC MUMMY.

p, William Calderon Stell [Guillermo Calderon]; d, Rafael Portillo; w, Alfredo Salazar (based on a story by Stell, Salazar); ph, Enrique Wallace; m, Antonio Diaz Conde; ed, Jorge Bustos; art d, Javier Torres Torija.

Horror (PR:A-C MPAA:NR)

CURSE OF THE BLOOD GHOULS zero

(1969, Ital.) 72m Mercury Film International/Pacemaker Pictures c
(AKA: THE SLAUGHTER OF THE VAMPIRES; CURSES OF THE GHOULS)
Dieter Eppler (The Blood Ghoul Vampire), Walter Brandi, Graziella Granata, Paolo Solvay, Gena Gimmy, Alfredo Rizzo, Edda Ferronao, Carla Foscari, Marietta Procaccini.

After moving into a castle outside Vienna, a young couple experience strange feelings. During the night a male vampire kills the woman. A doctor diagnoses her cause of death, and then she reappears and attacks her husband. The husband and the doctor uncover the place where she and another female vampire hide, and the doctor destroys them. The husband finds the resting place of his wife's vampire lover and drives an iron spike through his heart (a measure useful only on Italian vampires). Silly dubbed horror film.

p, Dino Sant'Ambrogio; d&w, Roberto Mauri; ph, Ugo Brunelli; m, Aldo Piga; ed, Jenner Menghi; art d, Giuseppe Ranieri.

Horror (PR:O MPAA:G)

CURSE OF THE CAT PEOPLE, THE***½

(1944) 70m RKO bw
Simone Simon (Irena), Kent Smith (Oliver Reed), Jane Randolph (Alice Reed), Ann Carter (Amy), Elizabeth Russell (Barbara), Eve March (Miss Callahan), Julia Dean (Julia Farren), Erford Gage (State Trooper Captain), Sir Lancelot (Edward), Joel Davis (Donal), Juanita Alvarez (Lois).

"Its disturbingly Disney-esque fairy tale qualities have perplexed horror fans for decades," is how director Joe Dante, a Val Lewton fan, describes this Lewton-produced film. It is not so much a horror film as the title implies, but a look at a child's lonely fantasies. Nor is it really a sequel to the Lewton-Jacques Tourneur classic CAT PEOPLE. It is the story of a six-year old girl whose playtime includes her father's dead wife, Simon. Ghostly images of Simone appear, haunting everyone except the child. The blame is supposedly placed on the supernatural powers the mother once had. Wise took over the direction from Fritsch early on in the production. A chilling film if only for its apparent simplicity and child-like innocence.

p, Val Lewton; d, Robert Wise, Gunther V. Fritsch; w, DeWitt Bodeen; ph, Nicholas Musuraca; ed, J. R. Whittredge.

Horror/Fantasy Cas. (PR:C-O MPAA:NR)

CURSE OF THE CRIMSON ALTAR (SEE: CRIMSON CULT, THE, 1968)

CURSE OF THE CRYING WOMAN, THE zero

(1969, Mex.) 74m
Cinematografica A.B.S.A./Trans-International Films-AIP-TV bw
(LA MALDICION DE A LLORONA; AKA: LA CASA EMBRUJADA)
Rosita Arenas, Abel Salazar, Rita Macedo, Carlos Lopez Moctezuma, Mario Sevilla, Enrique Lucero, Domingo Soler.

A young woman, descended from the "Crying Woman" of Mexican folklore, inherits a house and finds it infested with ghosts and witches. Released in Mexico in 1961 and as worthless as they come.

p, Abel Salazar; d, Rafael Baledon; w, Baledon, Fernando Galiana; ph, Jose Ortiz Ramos; m, Gustavo Cesar Carrion; ed, Alfredo Rosas Priego; art d, Roberto Silva.

Horror Cas. (PR:C MPAA:NR)

CURSE OF THE DEMON***½

(1958) 82m COL bw
(AKA: NIGHT OF THE DEMON)
Dana Andrews (John Holden), Peggy Cummins (Joanna Harrington), Niall MacGinnis (Dr. Karswell), Maurice Denham (Prof. Harrington), Athene Seyler (Mrs. Karswell), Liam Redmond (Mark O'Brien), Reginald Beckwith (Mr. Meek), Ewan Roberts (Lloyd Williamson), Peter Elliott (Kumar), Rosamond Greenwood (Mrs. Meek), Brian Wilde (Rand Hobart), Richard Leech (Inspector Mottram), Lloyd Lamble (Detective Simmons), Peter Hobbes (Superintendent), Charles Lloyd-Pack (Chemist), John Salew (Librarian), Janet Barrow (Mrs. Hobart), Percy Herbert (Farmer), Lynn Tracy (Air Hostess).

Trying to expose a devil cult, Andrews helps Denham investigate a sect-related murder. In spite of warnings from Denham's lovely niece Cummins, the skeptical Andrews finally becomes a believer in the occult. MacGinnis, the secret leader of the cult, manages to slip a cursed parchment into Andrews' files. He discovers the papers and, believing they are going to kill him, rushes to return them before it's too late. Luckily the parchment passes back into the hands of MacGinnis, and the ghoulish demon devours him instead. An exceedingly eerie and suspenseful film from director Tourneur who is desperately in need of producer and former collaborator Val Lewton here. The insensitivity of producer Chester shows in this film which is less successful than it should have been. However, its intelligent ideas and graceful approach still manage to surface, even under the weight of Chester's heavy hand. One of this picture's most overlooked aspects is its similarity to Hitchcock's themes. It is no accident, seeing that scripter Charles Bennett also penned THE 39 STEPS, THE SECRET AGENT, SABOTAGE, and YOUNG AND INNOCENT. It has Andrews in a familiar Hitchcockian role of a man who loses rationality and is no longer in charge of his own life. Unfortunately, Chester took a number of liberties, including rewriting a well-crafted script, for greater commercial appeal. Another cretinous Chester decision was overriding Tourneur and Bennett's idea of not showing the monster. They believed that what lies in one's imagination is more frightening than what is on the screen. Originally released in England at 95 minutes.

p, Hal E. Chester; d, Jacques Tourneur; w, Charles Bennett, Chester (based on a story, "Casting the Ruins," by Montague R. James); ph, Ted Sciafe; m, Clifton Parker; ed, Michael Gordon; set d, Ken Adam.

Horror (PR:O MPAA:NR)

CURSE OF THE DEVIL*

(1973, Span./Mex.) 73m Goldstone c
(EL RETORNO DE LA WALPURGIS)
Paul Naschy, Maria Silva.

Female gypsy witches curse Naschy, the descendant of the executioner who put many of their coven to death 400 years before, by turning him into a werewolf. Blood-spattered horror from the Iberian peninsula follows up the success of FRANKEN-

STEIN'S BLOODY TERROR. It was heavily excised of blood and sex to get an "R" rating in the U.S.

p, Luis Gomez; d, Charles Avred; w, Jacinto Molina.

Horror (PR:O MPAA:R)

CURSE OF THE DOLL PEOPLE, THE**

(1968, Mex.) 83m Cinematografica Calderon/Trans-International Films-AIP-TV bw
(MUNECOS INFERNALES)
Elvira Quintana, Ramon Gay, Roberto G. Rivera, Quintin Bulnes, Alfonso Arnold, Jorge Mondragon, Javier Loya, Nora Veyran, Luis Aragon.

Four Mexican tourists in Haiti witness a forbidden voodoo rite and are cursed by the witch doctor. When they return home, mysterious boxes are delivered to thir homes. During the night, masked midgets emerge from the boxes and fulfill the curse. Laughably dubbed, though a few scenes with the midgets stalking about are eerily effective.

p, William Calderon Stell [Guillermo Calderon]; d, Benito Alazraki; w, Alfredo Salazar; ph, Enrique Wallace; m, Antonio Diaz Conde; ed, Alfredo Rosas Priego; art d, Manuel Fontanals.

Horror (PR:C-O MPAA:NR)

CURSE OF THE FACELESS MAN*

(1958) 67m UA bw
Richard Anderson (Dr. Paul Mallon), Elaine Edwards (Tina Enright), Adele Mara (Maria Fiorillo), Luis Van Rooten (Dr. Fiorillo), Gar Moore (Dr. Enricco Ricci), Felix Locher (Dr. Emanuel), Jan Arvan (Inspector Renaldi), Bob Bryant (Quintillus).

Idiotic yarn which has a mummified gladiator, who has been buried under the volcanic ash from Vesuvius, returning to life. He escapes in the back of a truck and, obsessed with a reincarnated lover from his past, sets out to kidnap her from her apartment. The man isn't faceless, he just has a kind of a lava-encrusted mug.

p, Robert E. Kent; d, Edward L. Cahn; w, Jerome Bixby, ph, Kenneth Peach; ed, Grant Whytlock.

Horror (PR:C MPAA:NR)

CURSE OF THE FLY*½

(1965, Brit.) 86m Lippert/FOX bw
Brian Donlevy (Henri Delambre), George Baker (Martin Delambre), Carole Gray (Patricia Stanley), Yvette Rees (Wan), Michael Graham (Albert Delambre), Rachel Kempson (Mme. Fournier), Bert Kwouk (Tai), Jeremy Wilkins (Inspector Ranet), Charles Carson (Inspector Charas), Stan Simmons (Creature), Mary Manson (Judith), Warren Stanhope (Hotel Manager), Arnold Bell (Porter), Mia Anderson (Nurse), Stan Simmons.

So where's the fly? The only connection between this picture and its predecessors, THE FLY and THE RETURN OF THE FLY, is the employment of a teleportation device to transport humans electronically from one place to another. Scientist Donlevy spends all his free time experimenting with the machine, while his son Baker weds the loony Gray. She gets even goofier when she finds a closet full of mutants—all failed experiments from Donlevy's work. The police are informed and when they arrive Donlevy uses his faulty machine to make his getaway. While transmitting, the machine goes on the fritz, leaving the scientist a molecular mess.

p, Robert Lippert, Jack Parsons; d, Don Sharp; w, Harry Spalding (based on characters created by George Langelaan); ph, Basil Emmott (CinemaScope); m, Bert Shefter; ed, Robert White; art d, Harry White; spec eff, Harold Fletcher, makeup, Eleanor Jones.

Horror (PR:C MPAA:NR)

CURSE OF THE GOLEM (SEE: IT!, 1967)

CURSE OF THE LIVING CORPSE, THE**

(1964) 84m FOX bw
Helen Warren (Abigail Sinclair), Roy Scheider (Philip Sinclair), Margot Hartman (Vivian Sinclair), Robert Milli (Bruce Sinclair), Hugh Franklin (James Benson), Candace Hilligoss (Deborah Benson), Dino Narizzano (Robert Harrington), Linda Donovan (Letty Crews), J. Frank Lucas (Seth Lucas), Jane Bruce (Cook), Paul Haney (Constable Barnes), George Cotton (Constable Winters), William Blood (Minister).

A dying man who has a history of seizures which make him appear to be dead actually gets buried alive. At the reading of his will, his family learns that he will haunt them from beyond if he is ever prematurely buried. Before long, heads start to roll. Laughable at times, but still creepy. Roy Scheider (JAWS) makes his film debut.

p,d&w, Del Tenney; ph, Richard L. Hilliard; m, Bill Holmes; ed, Gary Youngman; art d, Robert Verberkmoss.

Horror (PR:O MPAA:NR)

CURSE OF THE MUMMY'S TOMB, THE**

(1965, Brit.) 80m Hammer/COL c
Terence Morgan (Adam Beauchamp), Fred Clark (Alexander King), Ronald Howard (John Bray), Jeanne Roland (Annette DuBois), George Pastell (Hashmi Bey), John Paul (Inspector MacKenzie), Jack Gwillim (Sir Giles Dalrymple), Bernard Rebel (Prof. DuBois), Dickie Owen (The Mummy), Michael McStay (Ra), Jill Mai Meredith (Jenny), Vernon Smythe (Jessop), Harold Goodwin (Fred), Michael Ripper (Achmed), Marianne Stone (Landlady), Jimmy Gardner.

When are scientists going to learn not to stick their shovels just any old place in Egypt? An expedition foolishly opens a tomb with the complimentary death curse. The leader of the excavation crew decides to give the ruins to a museum, but a fast-talking American grabs the tomb for a sideshow attraction. Blood-red murders exploiting the use of color are typical of this indistinguishable low-budgeter. THE MUMMY—1959 was the follow-up.

p&d, Michael Carreras; w, Henry Younger; ph, Otto Heller (Technicolor); m, Carlo Martelli; ed, Eric Boyd Perkins; prod d, Bernard Robinson; md, Philip Martell.

Horror (PR:C MPAA:NR)

CURSE OF THE MUSHROOM PEOPLE

(SEE: ATTACK OF THE MUSHROOM PEOPLE, 1964)

CURSE OF THE PINK PANTHER zero (1983) 110m MGM/UA c
David Niven (*Sir Charles Litton*), Ted Wass (*Clifton Sleigh*), Robert Wagner (*George Litton*), Herbert Lom (*Dreyfus*), Joanna Lumley (*Chandra*), Capucine (*Lady Litton*), Robert Loggia (*Bruno*), Harvey Korman (*Prof. Balls*), Leslie Ash (*Juleta Shane*), Graham Stark (*Bored Waiter*), Andre Maranne (*Francois*), Peter Arne (*Col. Bufoni*), Patricia Davis (*Michelle Chauvin*), Michael Elphick (*Valencia Police Chief*), Steve Franken (*Drunk*), Ed Parker (*Chong*), Denise Crosby (*Bruno's Moll*), Emma Walton (*Angry Hooker*), Sidi Bin Tanney (*Lugash Secret Policeman*), Liz Smith, Danny Schiller, Lawrence Davidson, Roger Moore, Pat Corley, Donald Sumpter, Harold Kasket, William Hootkins, Mollie Maureen, David Schiller, Arthur Howard, William Abney, Hugh Fraser, Maurcie O'Connell, Tim Wylton, Geoffrey Beevers, Patrick Murray.

Blake Edwards scrapes the bottom of the barrel in an attempt to make a final buck from the late Peter Sellers' character in this unfunny and unethical picture. His tastelessness doesn't stop there. After Niven's untimely death, Edwards proceeded to have Rich Little dub in the actor's voice for the remaining scenes. This film is primarily a collage of previous Panther outtakes and guest stars, which pad the boring adventures of the new bumbling detective, Wass. Unforgivable and shameful. Many of the co-stars stepped in for their cameos and also had cameos in TRAIL OF THE PINK PANTHER.

p, Blake Edwards, Tony Adams; d, Edwards; w, Edwards, Geoffrey Edwards; ph, Dick Bush (Panavision, Technicolor); m, Henry Mancini; ed, Ralph E. Winters, Bob Hathaway; prod d, Peter Mullins; art d, Tim Hutchinson, Alan Tomkins, John Siddall; set d, Peter Mullins; cos, Patricia Edwards.

Comedy **Cas.** **(PR:A MPAA:PG)**

CURSE OF THE STONE HAND zero
(1965, Mex./Chile) 72m Associated Distributors Pictures bw
John Carradine (*Hypnotist*), Ernest Walch, Sheila Bon, Katherine Victor, Lloyd Nelson.

Enterprising producer Warren bought up (probably cheaply) a Mexican horror film from 1959 and a Chilean shocker from 1946, added some footage shot with the apparently immortal John Carradine, and released it on the unsuspecting public. A sculpture of a pair of hands inspires various occupants of a house to murder. Worth seeing if only to get a look at a Chilean horror film.

p, Jerry Warren; d, Warren, Carl Schleipper, Carlos Hugo Christensen; w, Amos Powell, Marie Laurent; ph, Ricardo Younis.

Horror **(PR:C MPAA:NR)**

CURSE OF THE SWAMP CREATURE* (1966) 80m AIP-TV c
John Agar, Francine York, Shirley McLine, Bill Thurman, Jeff Alexander.

A geological expedition in the Everglades takes a turn for the worse when it runs across a mad scientist creating half alligator-half man monsters. Agar comes off worse than usual in this silly movie.

p&d, Larry Buchanan; w, Tony Huston.

Horror **(PR:C MPAA:NR)**

CURSE OF THE UNDEAD*½ (1959) 79m UNIV bw
Eric Fleming (*Preacher Dan*), Michael Pate (*Drake Robey*), Kathleen Crowley (*Dolores Carter*), John Hoyt (*Dr. Carter*), Bruce Gordon (*Buffer*), Edward Binns (*Sheriff*), Jimmy Murphy (*Tim Carter*), Helen Kleeb (*Dora*), Jay Adler (*Bartender*), Edwin Parker, John Truax, Frankie Van, Rush Williams (*Henchmen*).

The novel combination of mixing a mediocre western with a mediocre vampire picture produces a mediocre vampire western. Fleming, who became the star of TV's "Rawhide," is cast as a cattletown preacher who takes it upon himself to defang the vampiric Pate. After a trough full of murders, the gunslinging Dracula goes after Crowley, the woman rancher who originally hired Pate. Dismissing the messy notion of a wooden stake through the heart, Fleming shoots the blood-sucker with a cross-engraved bullet. As usual, the dying vampire shrivels into sunlit nothingness.

p, Joseph Gershenson; d, Edward Dein; w, Edward, Mildred Dein; ph, Ellis W. Carter; m, Irving Gertz; ed, George Gittens; art d, Alexander Golitzen, Robert Clatworthy; cos, Bill Thomas.

Horror/Western **(PR:C MPAA:NR)**

CURSE OF THE VAMPIRE
(SEE: PLAYGIRLS AND THE VAMPIRE, THE, 1963, Ital.)

CURSE OF THE VAMPIRES**
(1970, Phil., U.S.) 90m Sceptre Industries/Hemisphere Pictures c
(AKA: CREATURES OF EVIL)
Amalia Fuentes (*Leonora*), Eddie Garcia (*Eduardo*), Romeo Vasquez (*Daniel*), Mary Walter (*Mother*), Johnny Monteiro, Rosario del Pilar, Francisco Cruz, Paquito Salcedo, Quiel Mendoza, Andres Benitez, Luz Angeles, Tessie Hernandez, Linda Rivera.

Fascinating Filipino vampire film has Garcia returning to the family estate after many years. There he finds that his father has imprisoned his mother in the basement because she is a vampire. Garcia goes to the cellar to visit her and she bites him, turning him into a vampire. He then goes to his fiancee and vampirizes her. The father, learning what has happened, kills his wife. He in turn is killed by Garcia. Meanwhile, the fiance of Garcia's sister (Fuentes) is killed in an accident and shortly afterward Fuentes is turned into a vampire by her brother. Villagers descend on the mansion, and while watching Fuentes change into a vampire they see the ghost of her lover appear and pray beside her bed. A crucifix appears floating above the bed, then it turns and plunges through her heart. The villagers set the house on fire while the ghost of Fuentes and the ghost of her lover walk through the fields of Heaven. One of the best of the usually wretched Filipino horrors, this film is an incredible amalgam of Hollywood mythology, native superstition, and Catholic dogma. A fascinating variation on an old theme.

p, Amalia Muhlach; d, Gerardo de Leon; w, Ben Feleo, Pierre L. Salas (based on a

story by Feleo); ph, Mike Accion (Eastmancolor); m, Tito Arevalo; ed, Ben Barcelon; set d, Ben Otico; cos, F. P. Bautista; spec eff, Tony Gosalves.

Horror **(PR:O MPAA:GP)**

CURSE OF THE VOODOO*½
(1965, Brit.) 77m Galaworld Film-Gordon/AA bw (AKA: CURSE OF SIMBA)
Bryant Halliday (*Mike Stacy*), Dennis Price (*Maj. Thomas*), Lisa Danielly (*Janet Stacey*), Mary Kerridge (*Janet's Mother*), Ronald Leigh Hunt (*Doctor*), Jean Lodge (*Mrs. Lomas*), Dennis Alaba Peters (*Saidi*), Tony Thawnton (*Radlett*), Michael Nightingale (*Second Hunter*), Andy Meyers (*Tommy Stacey*), Louis Majoney (*African Expert*), Jimmy Feldgate (*Barman*), Nigel Feyistan (*Simbasa in London*), Beryl Cunningham (*Nightclub Dancer*), Bobby Breen Quintet (*Nightclub Band*).

While on a lion-hunting expedition in deep Africa, Halliday bags himself a "king of the jungle," only to be cursed by Chief M'Gobo, the leader of a lion-worshipping cult. While on the hunt, he gets clawed in a scuffle with one of the cats, and returns to London for some R&R. There he is haunted by hallucinations of natives chasing him through Endland, and plagued by a rising fever. In the meantime, M'Gobo is playing with a Halliday voodoo doll. Wife Danielly learns that the only way he'll recover is by returning to the dark continent and killing his tormentor. Halliday does this, but runs out of the necessary ammunition. Some quick thinking tells the Brit to run M'Gobo over with his Jeep, ending the vile curse. Lots of stock footage of lion hunts, and a shoestring budget cheapen any value this may have had.

p, Kenneth Rive; d, Lindsay Shontoff; w, Tony O'Grady, Leigh Vance; ph, Gerald Gibbs; m, Brian Fahey; ed, Barry Vince; art d, Tony Inglis.

Horror **(PR:O MPAA:NR)**

CURSE OF THE WEREWOLF, THE**** (1961) 91m Hammer/UNIV c
Clifford Evans (*Alfredo*), Oliver Reed (*Leon*), Yvonne Romain (*Servant Girl*), Catherine Feller (*Christina*), Anthony Dawson (*Marques Siniestro*), Josephine Llewellyn (*Marquesa*), Richard Wordsworth (*Beggar*), Hira Talfrey (*Teresa*), John Gabriel (*Priest*), Warren Mitchell (*Pepe Valiente*), Anne Blake (*Rosa Valiente*), George Woodbridge (*Dominique*), Michael Ripper (*Old Soaker*), Ewen Solon (*Don Fernando*), Peter Sallis (*Don Enrique*), Martin Matthews (*Jose*), David Conville (*Rico Gomez*), Denis Shaw (*Gaoler*), Charles Lamb (*Chef*), Serafina Di Leo (*Senora Zumara*), Sheila Brennan (*Vera*), Joy Webster (*Isabel*), Renny Lister (*Yvonne*), Justin Walters (*Leon, as a Young Child*).

Save for 1941's THE WEREWOLF, this Hammer picture is the most interesting and effective look at the myth of werewolves. Spending nearly the entire first half on the origins of the monster, it is not so much a horror film as an attempt at understanding folklore. The tale, set in 18th-century Spain, opens on an imprisoned beggar in a musty jail. Left there to waste away, he is joined by a mute servant girl, Romain, whom he rapes. She escapes from the primitive madman, and is later found nearly dead by a kind-hearted professor. She discovers that she is pregnant by the prisoner, and allows the professor and his wife to adopt the child. Years later the young Leon, Reed, is sent to a monastery which he escapes from to be with his sweetheart. As he ages, he becomes progressively more animalistic and enraged, until he meets the standard silver bullet end. Reed is mesmerizing as the creature. His role is made even more chilling by Roy Ashton's ingenius makeup work. A gruesome horror picture of the sort that Hammer has become identified with. The portrayal of Spain caused this film to be banned for 15 years in that country.

p, Anthony Hinds; exec p, Michael Carreras; d, Terence Fisher; w, John Elder (Hinds) (based on the novel *The Werewolf of Paris* by Guy Endore); ph, Arthur Grant (Eastmancolor); m, Benjamin Frankel; ed, Alfred Cox; prod d, Bernard Robinson; art d, Thomas Goswell; spec eff, Les Bowie; makeup, Roy Ashton.

Horror **(PR:O MPAA:NR)**

CURSE OF THE WRAYDONS, THE*½
(1946, Brit.) 94m Bushey/Ambassador bw
Tod Slaughter (*Philip Wraydon*), Bruce Seton (*Capt. Jack Clayton*), Gabriel Toyne (*Lt. Payne*), Andrew Laurence (*George Heeningham*), Lorraine Clewes (*Helen Sedgefield*), Pearl Cameron (*Rose Wraydon*), Ben Williams (*John Rickers*), Barry O'Neill (*George Wraydon*).

Yet another one of Tod Slaughter's old-fashioned melodramas. This time he is a crazed inventor—his career as a spy ended by the defeat of Napoleon—adopting the identity of "Springheeled Jack" and seeking revenge on the family of his brother. Slaughter had put on quite a bit of weight by this time, so an already lightweight horror story becomes an out-and-out comedy. Fairly entertaining.

p, Gilbert Church; d, Victor M. Gover; w, Michael Barringer (Based on the play "Springheeled Jack The Terror of London" by Maurice Sandoz); ph, S. D. Onions.

Crime **(PR:A-C MPAA:NR)**

CURSES OF THE GHOULS
(SEE: CURSE OF THE BLOOD-GHOULS, 1969, Ital.)

CURTAIN AT EIGHT*½ (1934) 66m Majestic bw
(AKA: BACKSTAGE MYSTERY)
Dorothy Mackaill (*Lola Cresmer*), C. Aubrey Smith (*Jim Hanvey*), Paul Cavanaugh (*Wylie Thornton*), Sam Hardy (*Marty Gallagher*), Marion Shilling (*Anice*), Russell Hopton (*Terry Mooney*), Natalie Moorhead (*Alma Jenkins/Thornton*), Hale Hamilton (*Maj. Manning*), Ruthelma Stevens (*Doris Manning*), Jack Mulhall (*Carey Weldon*).

A lethargic mystery which drones around behind the scenes of a theater production. An actor is murdered without explanation, though it is obvious that the leading lady, who is also his unhappy lover, did the deed. The only other suspect seems to be a mischievous monkey seen toying around with a pistol in the prop shop. A lame picture which probably would have been improved if the simian had done the killing.

d, E. Mason Hopper; w, Edward T. Lowe (based on a story by Octavus Roy Cohen); ph, Ira Morgan; ed, Earl Crain.

Mystery **(PR:A MPAA:NR)**

CURTAIN CALL*½

(1940) 61m RKO bw

Barbara Read (*Helen Middleton*), Alan Mowbray (*Donald Avery*), Helen Vinson (*Charlotte Morley*), Donald MacBride (*Jeff Crandall*), John Archer (*Ted Palmer*), Leona Maricle (*Miss Smith*), Frank Faylen (*Spike Malone*), Tom Kennedy (*Attendent*), Ralph Forbes (*Leslie Barrixale*), J. M. Kerrigan (*Mr. Middleton*), Ann Shoemaker (*Mrs. Middleton*), Tommy Kelly (*Fred Middleton*).

A misfire better targeted for the stage than for the silver screen. Centering on Broadway, the picture makes no attempt to employ any cinematic devices. The static camera and tediously long shots also typify the statue-like thespian delivery. The story concerns a stage producer, Mowbray, and his pal director, MacBride, as they try to ruin the career of one of their contracted actresses, Vinson. With her contract about to expire and no chance of her renewing, they decide to make her final production with them a disaster with a twist later employed uproariously in THE PRODUCERS. To do so they scout around for the worst script they can find and decide on a work by neophyte lady playwright, Read. Vinson falls in love with the script, keenly entitled, "The End of Everything," and can't do it fast enough. The tables are turned when the play becomes the smash hit of the season. The same success was not to be had here.

p, Howard Benedict; d, Frank Woodruff; w, Dalton Trumbo (based on a story by Howard J. Green); ph, Russell Metty; ed, Harry Marker.

Drama (PR:A MPAA:NR)

CURTAIN CALL AT CACTUS CREEK**

(1950) 86m UNIV c
(GB: TAKE THE STAGE)

Donald O'Connor (*Edward Timmons*), Gale Storm (*Julie Martin*), Walter Brennan (*Rimrock*), Vincent Price (*Tracy Holland*), Eve Arden (*Lily Martin*), Chick Chandler (*Ralph*), Joe Sawyer (*Jake*), Harry Shannon (*Clay*), Rex Lease (*Yellowstone*), I. Stanford Jolley (*Pecos*), Edward Waller.

Donald O'Connor chewed up the scenery as the stage hand for a poor group of players who are touring the west along the edge of civilization. They all yearn to be thespians and none more avidly than O'Connor. He manages to capture bank robber Brennan (a familiar face in post offices across the west) and becomes a hero. Price hams it up as the Barrymore type who has seen better days and whose words are a mixed bag of play dialog; Arden is Storm's mother, a one-time actress, and Storm is Donald's amour. It's a barely passable programmer that is only distinguished by the sprightliness of the cast as they read their lines and sing a few old-time songs. Eve Arden was only ten years Gale Storm's senior but she always played characters much older. Like Angela Lansbury, Arden is one of the most durable young "old" woman in movies.

p, Robert Arthur; d, Charles Lamont; w, Howard Dimsdale (based on a story by Stanley Roberts, Dimsdale); ph, Russell Metty (Technicolor); m, Walter Scharf; ed, Frank Gross; m/l, Stanley Murphy, Henry Marshall, Fred Leigh, Henry Pether, Jack Yellen, George Cobb, Fred Arndt; m/l, "Be My Little Bumble Bee" (Stanley Murphy, Henry I. Marshall), "Waiting At the Church" (Henry Pether, Fred Leigh), "Are You from Dixie?"

Comedy/Western (PR:AA MPAA:NR)

CURTAIN FALLS, THE**

(1935) 68m CHES. bw

Henrietta Crosman (*Sarah Crabtree*), Dorothy Lee (*Dot Scorsby*), Holmes Herbert (*John Scorsby*), Natalie Moorhead (*Katherine Scorsby*), John Darrow (*Allan Scorsby*), William Bakewell (*Barry Graham*), Jameson Thomas (*Martin Deveridge*), Dorothy Revier (*Helene Deveridge*), Edward Kane (*Taggart*), Aggie Herring (*Mrs. McGillicuddy*), Tom Ricketts (*Hotel Manager*).

A speech-heavy drama which ploddingly tells the tale of an aging actress who plays one final role. Close to suicide, the pauperish Crosman learns that a wealthy old actress friend has disappeared. To help the missing dame's family out of numerous problems, she decides to impersonate the old woman. After the difficult ends are tied up, she admits her deception.

p, George R. Batcheller; d, Charles Lamont; w, Karl Brown; ph, M. A. Anderson.

Drama (PR:A MPAA:NR)

CURTAIN RISES, THE**

(1939, Fr.) 90m Regina/Kassler bw

Louis Jouvet (*Prof. Lambertin*), Claude Dauphin (*Francois Polti*), Janine Darcey (*Isabelle*), Odette Joyeux (*Cecilia*), Andre Brunot (*Grenaison, the Uncle*), Madeleine Geoffroy (*Mme. Grenaison*), Mady Made (*Denise*), Roger Blin (*Dominick*), Carette (*Reporter*), Dalio (*District Attorney*).

Girl students at a Paris acting school compete for the affections of school Lothario Dauphin. Somber drama differs from the run of aspiring-actor films by leaving its characters a long way from fame and fortune at the end. Jouvet does all right, but the rest of the cast members look as though they were taken from the dropouts of an acting school. (In French; English subtitles.)

d, Marc Allegret; w, Henri Jeanson; subtitles: Martin Lewis, Harold Neuberger.

Drama (PR:A MPAA:NR)

CURTAIN UP*½

(1952, Brit.) 82m Constellation/GFD bw

Robert Morley (*Harry*), Margaret Rutherford (*Catherine*), Olive Sloane (*Maud*), Joan Rice (*Avis*), Charlotte Mitchell (*Daphne*), Kay Kendall (*Sandra*), Liam Gaffney (*Norwood*), Margaret Avery (*Mary*), Lloyd Lamble (*Jackson*), Michael Medwin (*Jerry*), Charles Lamb (*George*), Diana Calderwood (*Scenic Artist*), Stringer Davis (*Vicar*), Joan Hickson (*Landlady*), Constance Lorne (*Sarah Stebbings*), John Cazabon (*Mr. Stebbings*).

Another example of the cinema being stuck in the groove of theatricality. After a successful British stage run, this script fails in its attempt to capture a film audience. The problem is inherent in its material. It is the story of a small theater group that must stage an inept play penned by the owner's aunt. The climax is a confrontation between the aunt and the play's director. An underdeveloped idea which loses the depth it may have had on the stage.

p, Robert Garrett; d, Ralph Smart; w, Michael Pertwee, Jack Davies (based on the play "On Monday Next" by Philip King); ph, Stanley Pavey; m, Malcolm Arnold; ed, Douglas Robertson.

Comedy (PR:A MPAA:NR)

CURTAINS zero

(1983, Can.) 90m Simcon/Jensen Farley c

John Vernon (*Jonathon*), Samantha Eggar (*Samantha*), Linda Thorson (*Brooke*), Anne Ditchburn (*Laurian*), Lynne Griffin (*Patti O'Connor*), Sandra Warren (*Tara*), Leslie Donaldson (*Christie*), Deborah Burgess (*Amanda*), Michael Wincott (*Matthew*), Maury Chaykin (*Monty*), Joann McIntyre (*Secretary*), Calvin Butler (*Dr. Pendleton*), Kate Lynch (*Receptionist*), Booth Savage, William Marshall, James Kidnie, Jeremy Jenson, Donald Adams, Diane Godwin, Janelle Hutchison, Virginia Laight, Kay Griffin, Bunty Webb, Daisy White, Vivian Reis, Sheila Currie, Frances Gunn, Suzanne Russell, Jenna Louise, Anna Migliarese, Elaine Crosley, Mary Durkin, Angela Carrol, Julie Massie, Pat Carroll Brown, Teresa Tova, Janie Nicholson, Alison Lawrence, Jo-Anne Hannah.

Worthless slasher movie has producer Vernon married to actress Eggar. When she goes into an asylum to research her next part, he makes sure she isn't let back out. He then invites six promising starlets to his house, subjecting them to various forms of sexual harassment as he tries to pick one to replace his strait-jacketed wife. Then a mad killer wearing a mask starts killing off the nubile ingenues. Viewers should be able to figure out who the killer is before the film is one-third over. They would do well to leave the movie at that point.

p, Peter R. Simpson; d, Jonathan Stryker; w, Robert Guza, Jr.; ph, Robert Paynter, Fred Guthe; m, Paul Zaza; ed, Michael MacLaverty; prod d, Roy Forge Smith.

Horror Cas. (PR:O MPAA:R)

CURUCU, BEAST OF THE AMAZON*

(1956) 75m UNIV bw

John Bromfield (*Rock Dean*), Beverly Garland (*Dr. Andrea Romar*), Tom Payne (*Tupanico*), Harvey Chalk (*Fr. Flaviano*), Sergio De Oliviera (*Capt. Caceres*), Wilson Viana (*Tico*), Larri Thomas (*Dancer*).

A moderately amusing jungle adventure which places Bromfield in dangerous Amazon territory alongside the courageous Garland. Bromfield plays a plantation owner who wants to find out why his workers are leaving the fields and returning to the jungles. Garland is trudging through the marshes on a mission to find a cure for cancer in a native's head-shrinking formula. They face the usual creepy jungle obstacles—spiders and snakes and piranhas—but none of them stop Bromfield from getting some answers. Payne, poorly suited as a giant bird, is trying to frighten the peasants away from the exploitative plant owners. Garland's conquest for a cancer cure goes ignored as the two travelers fall under the spell of Eros.

p, Richard Kay, Harry Rybnick; d&w, Curt Siodmak; ph, Rudolf Icsey (Eastmancolor); m, Raoul Kraushaar; ed, Terry Morse; cos, Oscar Nelson.

Adventure (PR:C MPAA:NR)

CUSTER MASSACRE, THE (SEE: GREAT SIOUX MASSACRE, THE, 1965)

CUSTER OF THE WEST**

(1968, U.S., Span.) 143m Security/Cinerama c

Robert Shaw (*Gen. George Custer*), Mary Ure (*Elizabeth Custer*), Jeffrey Hunter (*Lt. Benteen*), Ty Hardin (*Maj. Marcus Reno*), Charles Stalnaker (*Lt. Howells*), Robert Hall (*Sgt. Buckley*), Lawrence Tierney (*Gen. Philip Sheridan*), Kieron Moore (*Cheyenne Chief*), Marc Lawrence (*Goldminer*), Robert Ryan (*Mulligan*).

This film hints at being a successful epic, but is reduced instead to a modest biography of Civil War general George Custer. Originally to have been directed by Japanese director Akira Kurosawa (THE SEVEN SAMURAI), it was unfortunately helmed in a cheap, bloodless manner in Spain. Shaw coarsely portrays the fork-tongued legend who pushed the Cheyenne Indians to the breaking point. (In reality, it was the Sioux.) Nothing new is learned this time around, but we are treated to a fine performance by Shaw and by Robert Ryan in a cameo as a gold-obsessed deserter. The Cinerama technique is exploited in an otherwise standard arrow barrage which highlights the general's last stand. The Spanish landscape is picturesque, but it's not quite the Remington West.

p, Philip Yordan, Louis Dolivet; exec p, Irving Lerner; d, Robert Siodmak (Civil War sequences by Irving Lerner); w, Bernard Gordon, Julian Halevy; ph, Cecilio Paniagua (Cinerama, Technicolor); m, Bernardo Segall; ed, Maurice Rootes; art d, Jean d' Eaubonne, Eugene Lourie, Julio Molina; set d, Antonio Mateos; cos, De Zarate; m/l, "Marching Song," "Maxwell House," "Heroes Die" (Bernardo Segall, Will Holt), "Follow Custer" (Segall, Robert Shaw).

Western (PR:C MPAA:NR)

CUSTOMS AGENT**

(1950) 71m COL bw

William Eythe (*Bert Stewart*), Marjorie Reynolds (*Lucille Gerrard*), Griff Barnett (*McGraw*), Howard St. John (*Charles Johnson*), Jim Backus (*Thomas Jacoby*), Robert Shayne (*J. G. Goff*), Denver Pyle (*Al*), John Doucette (*Hank*), Harlan Warde (*Perry*), James Fairfax (*Pettygill*), Clark Howat (*Phillips*), Marya Marco (*Miss Kung*), Guy Kingsford (*Watkins*), William Phillips (*Barton*).

There's nothing special to watch for in this substandard yarn about an undercover customs agent who sides with a group of smugglers. Once on the inside, he learns that they are importing drugs from China and selling them on the U.S. black market. He blows the whistle and a fight to the finish takes place on the California coast. A documentary tone is attempted by the inclusion of an urgent, social-minded narrator who colors the scenes. Wonderfully shot by craftsman Tannura.

p, Rudolph C. Flothow; d, Seymour Friedman; w, Russell S. Hughes, Malcolm Stuart Boylan (based on a story by Hal Smith); ph, Philip Tannura; ed, Aaron Stell.

Crime (PR:A MPAA:NR)

CUTTER AND BONE**** (1981) 105m UA c (GB: CUTTER'S WAY)
Jeff Bridges *(Richard Bone)*, John Heard *(Alex Cutter)*, Lisa Eichhorn *(Mo Cutter)*, Ann Dusenberry *(Valerie Duran)*, Stephen Elliott *(J. J. Cord)*, Arthur Rosenberg *(George Swanson)*, Nina Van Pallandt *(Woman in Hotel)*, Patricia Donahue *(Mrs. Cord)*, Geralding Baron *(Susie Swanson)*, Katherine Pass *(Toyota Woman)*, Frank McCarthy *(Toyota Man)*, George Planco *(Toyota Cop)*, Jay Fletcher *(Security Guard)*, George Dickerson *(Mortician)*, Jack Murdock *(Concession Owner)*, Essex Smith, Rod Gist, Leonard Lighfoot *(Blacks)*, Julia Duffy *(Young Girl)*, Randy Shephard *(Young Man)*, Roy Hollis *(Working Stiff)*, Billy Drago *(Garbage Man)*, Caesar Cordova *(Garbage Truck Driver)*, Jon Terry *(Police Captain)*, William Pelt, Ron Marcroft *(Detectives)*, Ted White, Tony Epper, Andy Epper, Chris Howell, H. P. Evetts, Ron Burke.

A fiercely powerful film about heroes, romanticism, and friendship among three initially unlikable characters. Heard is Alex Cutter, a vulgar, crippled Vietnam vet who is an outlaw in a society without commitment, without heroes. At the opposite end is Bridges as Bone, a pretty boy with no convictions at all. The simultaneously strong and tender Mo is Eichhorn as the fulcrum that keeps Cutter and Bone together. While she is the wife of the former, she has a repressed desire for the latter. After nearly taking the rap for a girl's murder, Bridges thinks he spots the real killer at a parade. The man he points out is Elliott, a powerful oil tycoon. Heard lets his imagination run free and comes up with elaborate details about the night of the murder. Convinced that Elliott must be the killer, he comes up with a plan for blackmail. With Bridges and the dead girl's sister they agree to turn Elliott in if he pays. While Heard is spending his time gathering the evidence needed to prove Bridges' innocence, Bridges and Eichhorn are extending their relationship into the bedroom. Late in the night he leaves, only to learn that early the next morning the house was torched in an apparent attempt to get Bridges. Now having a personal stake in the matter, Heard sets out to kill the oil tycoon. With an uneasy Bridges, he sneaks into the estate and rides a white stallion into Cord's office window. Violently crashing to the ground, Heard struggles to shoot the fearless powermonger. Exposed to his dying friend's commitment, Bridges puts his hand on the gun which is still in Heard's hand and together they kill Cord. Raped by the critics on its initial release, it was almost instantly pulled from exhibition. Slowly rave reviews praising its stark reality began to surface. With a new, less medical-oriented title, CUTTER'S WAY, it was re-released. It went on to practically sweep the Houston Film Fest taking Best Picture, Best Director (Ivan Passer), Best Screenplay (Jeffrey Alan Fiskin), and Best Actor (John Heard). An inspiring film which may require multiple viewings to fully appreciate. The Jack Nitzsche score is hauntingly effective.

p, Paul R. Gurian; d, Ivan Passer; w, Jeffrey Alan Fiskin (based on the novel *Cutter and Bone* by Newton Thornburg); ph, Jordan Cronenweth (Technicolor); m, Jack Nitzsche; ed, Caroline Ferriol; art d, Josan Russo.

Drama **Cas.** **(PR:O MPAA:R)**

CYBORG 2087*½ (1966) 86m Features bw
Michael Rennie *(Garth)*, Karen Steele *(Sharon)*, Wendell Corey *(Sheriff)*, Warren Stevens *(Dr. Zeller)*, Eduard Franz *(Prof. Marx)*, Harry Carey, Jr., *(Jay C.)*, Adam Roarke, Chubby Johnson, Tyler MacDuff, Dale Van Sickel, Troy Melton, Jimmy Hibbard, Sherry Alberoni, Betty Jane Royale, John Beck, George Fisher.

It is the time of Earth 2087 AD, and the world is controlled by Cyborgs, a race of humans whose minds are surgically altered to prevent free thought. Rennie plays Cyborg Garth, a rebellious member who steals a time-machine and returns to the year 1965. It is here that he meets the scientist who developed Cyborg technology, and in an attempt to change the future tries to prevent any further advancements. His noble efforts, of course, save mankind from a totalitarian future. Far from subtle in its anti-Communist message (the scientist is named Marx), it is an honest attempt to make a statement, but poorly executed.

p, Earle Lyon; d, Franklin Andreon; w, Arthur C. Pierce; ph, (Eastmancolor); m, Paul Dunlap, ed, Frank P. Keller; art d, Paul Sylos, Jr.

Science Fiction **(PR:A MPAA:NR)**

CYCLE, THE*** (1979, Iran) 95m Telefilm c (DAYEREH MINA)
Ezat Entezami, Fourouzan, Ali Nassirian, Said Kangarani, Bahman Forsi.

Fascinating Iranian comedy was banned under the Shah, then banned under Khomeini. But when the Shah's power was on the wane he allowed it to be released in the U.S. to show the freedom art enjoyed under his regime. The story deals with a young man from the country who comes to the big city with his ailing father and falls into the netherworld between the rich and privileged and the abject poor. At every turn the film exposes the inherent corruption of Iranian society and the Iranian people. An intriguing artifact from a brief flowering of filmmaking in the middle of a string of restrictive dictatorships. Well worth seeing. (In Farsi; English subtitles.)

d, Darius Mehrjui; w, Golam H. Saedi, Mehrjui (based on the story "Garbage Dump" by Saedi); ph, Houshang Bahariou; ed, Talat Mirfenderski.

Comedy **(PR:A-C MPAA:NR)**

CYCLE SAVAGES*½ (1969) 82m AIP c
Bruce Dern *(Keeg)*, Chris Robinson *(Romko)*, Melody Patterson *(Lea)*, Maray Ayres *(Sandy)*, Karen Ciral *(Janie)*, Virginia Hawkins *(Woman)*, Danny Ghaffouri *(Marvin)*, Lee Chandler *(Doug)*, Tom Daly *(Docky)*, Walt Robles *(Walter)*, Casey Kasem *(Keeg's Brother)*, Mick Mehas *(Bob)*, Jack Konzal *(Bartender)*, Anna Sugano *(Motorcycle Girl)*, Gary Littlejohn *(Motorcycle Boy)*, Ron Godwin *(Walter)*, Marjorie Dayne *(Motorcycle Girl)*, Randee Lee *(One of the Girls)*, Jerry Taylor *(Storekeeper)*, Denise Gilbert *(Little Girl)*, Peter Fain, Steve Brodie *(Police Detectives)*, Scott Brady *(Vice Squad Detective)*, Joe McManus, Linda Banks.

Total cycle sleaze which is barely saved from the gutter by a strong performance from Dern (SILENT RUNNING) as a crazed leader of a motorcycle gang. Up against the bikers is artist Robinson, who is not afraid to let his drawing hands throw a few punches. When Dern's gal poses in the buff for Robinson, the gang leader goes on a rampage. After a drunken orgy, Dern and his gang track down their man, and in an excruciatingly brutal torture scene crush the artist's hands in a vice. Casey Kasem, of American Top Forty, and one-time California Lt. Gov., Mike Curb are the film's exec. producers. Actors Scott Brady and Steve Brodie both appear uncredited as cops.

p, Maurice Smith, Ray Dorn; d&w, Bill Brame; ph, Frank Ruttencutter (Movielab Color); m, Jerry Styner; ed, Herman Freedman; art d, Ray Robles; stunts, Chuck Bail; makeup, Louis Lane; cos, Sally Jordan, spec eff, Modern Film Effects.

Adventure **(PR:O MPAA:R)**

CYCLONE FURY** (1951) 53m COL bw
Charles Starrett *(The Durango Kid/Steve Reynolds)*, Smiley Burnette *(Himself)*, Fred F. Sears *(Capt. Barham)*, Clayton Moore *(Grat Hanlon)*, Bob Wilke *(Bunco)*, Louis Lettieri *(Johnny)*, George Chesebro *(Bret Fuller)*, Frank O'Connor *(Doc)*, Merle Travis and His Bronco Busters.

An interesting oater from the Durango Kid series which has Starrett turning in a dual role. Helping out an Indian kid, Starrett tries to round up a herd of horses so the Redskin can get a government contract. Masked man Moore plays the black hat who wants the contract for himself, making things tough for Starrett and the youngster. But the singing Durango Kid can't be stopped,and he completes the roundup on schedule.

p, Colbert Clark; d, Ray Nazarro; w, Barry Shipman; ph, Henry Freulich, Edward Earl Repp; ed, Paul Borofsky.

Western **(PR:A MPAA:NR)**

CYCLONE KID*½ (1931) 60m Big Four bw
Buzz Barton *(Buddy Comstock)*, Caryl Lincoln *(Rose Comstock)*, Francis X. Bushman, Jr. *(Steve Andrews)*, Lafe McKee *(Harvey Comstock)*, Ted Adams *(Joe Clark)*, Silver Harr *(Pepita)*, Blackie Whiteford *(Pete)*.

A thin, padded script greatly mars this early horse opera. Barton and Lincoln get involved in some incredibly dull situations, which only serve to make their love bond more solid as they narrowly escape the baddies. Lincoln's part was small and she stayed as silent as possible.

d, J. P. McGowan; w, George Morgan; ph, Edward Kull; ed, Fred Bain.

Western **(PR:A MPAA:NR)**

CYCLONE KID, THE*½ (1942) 55m REP bw
Don "Red" Barry *(Johnny Dawson)*, John James *(Dr. Dawson)*, Lynn Merrick *(Mary Phillips)*, Alex Callam *(Big Jim Johnson)*, Joel Friedkin *(Judge Phillips)*, Lloyd "Slim" Andrews *(Pop Smith)*, Rex Lease *(Rankin)*, Joe McGuinn *(Ames)*, Monte Montague *(Sheriff)*, Frank La Rue *(Marshall)*.

A tamely treated story about a battle between homesteaders and a cattleman who wants to get their land. Barry is cast as a gunslinging outlaw pitted against a younger brother who he sent through medical school. The peacemaking doctor finally convinces his older kin to straighten out his life. Barry decides to live lawfully, saving himself from a nearly inevitable lynching.

p&d, George Sherman; w, Richard Murphy; ph, Bud Thackery; m, Cy Fever;ed, Edward Schroeder; art d, Russell Kimball.

Western **(PR:A MPAA:NR)**

CYCLONE OF THE SADDLE* (1935) 71m Argosy/Superior bw
Rex Lease, Janet Chandler, Bobby Nelson, William Desmond, Yakima Canutt, Art Mix, Chief Thunder Cloud, Helen Gibson, Milburn Morante, Chick Davis, George Chesebro, Chief Standing Bear, The Range Ranglers.

Tepid tale of a range war with Lease and Chandler pitching noncommital woo at each other. A B picture typical of the many westerns made by Lease as he switched from romantic leads in dramas and comedies in the 1920s and 1930s to oaters. He would make one more type switch later in the 1930s, to supporting roles, mostly villainous.

p, Louis Weis; d, Elmer Clifton; w, Clifton, George Merrick.

Western **(PR:A MPAA:NR)**

CYCLONE ON HORSEBACK* (1941) 58m RKO bw
Tim Holt, Marjorie Reynolds, Ray Whitley, Lee "Lasses" White, Harry Worth, Dennis Moore, Eddie Dew, Monte Montague, Slim Whitaker, Max Wagner, John Dilson, Lew Kelly, Terry Frost.

A stiff, calculated western which breaks one of the genre's commandments of trying too hard to be respectable. Holt plays a horse rancher who can sell his herd to a young phone line contractor, Moore, or to veteran franchise owner, Worth. Sabotage is the prime feature in this tired oater which can at least boast some picturesque lensing of the old West. Songs: "Bangtail," "Tumbleweed Cowboy," and "Blue Nighfall" (Fred Rose, Ray Whitley).

p, Bert Gilroy; d, Edward Killy; w, Norton S. Parker (based on a story by Tom Gibson); ph, Harry Wild; m, Fred Rose, Ray Whitley; ed, Frederick Knudtson.

Western/Musical **(PR:A MPAA:NR)**

CYCLONE PRAIRIE RANGERS** (1944) 56m COL bw
Charles Starrett, Dub Taylor, Constance Worth, Jimmy Davis, Jimmy Wakely and his Saddle Pals, Foy Willing, Clancy Cooper, Bob Fiske, Ray Bennett, I. Stanford Jolley, Edmund Cobb, Forrest Taylor, Paul Zaremba, Eddie Phillips, John Tyrell, Ted Mapes.

Fair horse opera with Starrett and sidekick Taylor coming to Worth's rescue as villains threaten to rustle her father's cows. Plenty of action, stunts, and some cowboy tunes by Wakely and his Saddle Pals.

p, Jack Fier; d, Ben Kline; w, Elizabeth Beecher; ph, Fayte M. Brown; ed, Aaron Stell; art d, Lionel Banks.

Western **(PR:A MPAA:NR)**

CYCLONE RANGER★★   (1935) 65m Spectrum bw

Bill Cody (*Pecos Kid*), Nena Quartaro (*Nita Garcia*), Eddie Gribbon (*Duke*), Soledad Jiminez (*Donna Castelar*), Earl Hodgins (*Pancho Gonzales*), Zara Tazil (*Martha*), Donald Reed (*Juan Castelar*), Colin Chase (*Luke Saunders*), Budd Buster (*Clem Rankin*).

A straightforward western conveying the essential morals and ideology of the genre. Cody is a rustler who turns good in the hope of bringing joy to an old blind woman by emulating her murdered son. Turning one good deed after another, Cody also lends a hand to the sheriff in capturing a gang of rustlers. Too much talk detracts from the action-oriented performance of Cody.

p, Ray Kirkwood; d, Bob Hill; w, Oliver Drake; ph, Donald Keyes.

Western   (PR:A   MPAA:NR)

CYCLOPS★½   (1957) 75m AA bw

James Craig (*Russ Bradford*), Gloria Talbott (*Susan Winter*), Lon Chaney, Jr. (*Martin Melville*), Tom Drake (*Lee Brand*), Duncan Parkin (*Cyclops*).

Prosaic sci-fi pic which focuses on a schmaltzy 50-foot mutated monster. Craig helps out Talbot in her search for her missing fiance, Parkin. They don't have much trouble finding the big fellow who was accidentally enlarged through a radiation experiment. Some feeble special effects of over-sized rodents also confront the expedition. The strained relationship is terminated when a giant flaming spear is hurled into the monster's mammoth eye. This picture's trash value, however, cannot be overlooked.

p,d&w, Bert I. Gordon; ph, Ira Morgan; m, Albert Glasser; ed, Carlo Lodato; spec eff, Bert Gordon.

Science Fiction   (PR:C-O   MPAA:NR)

CYCLOTRODE X★★   (1946) 100m REP bw
                                                        (AKA: THE CRIMSON GHOST)

Charles Quigley, Linda Stirling, Clayton Moore, Keene Duncan, Joe Forte, Rex Lease, I. Stafford Jolley, Bud Geary.

A 12-chapter serial originally entitled THE CRIMSON GHOST re-released in 1966 in a condensed version as CYCLOTRODE X. Masked villain the Crimson Ghost spends his time trying to gain use of Cyclotrode X, a machine which can short-circuit electricity. With this handy invention, he can rule the planet. To achieve his goal he kidnaps the machine's inventor, but a sharp criminal investigator follows his trail and saves the day. TV's Lone Ranger, Clayton Moore, then playing both baddies and goodies, is effective as the baddie's thug. Interestingly, Geary played the masked villain, making it easy to dub in someone else's voice. The voice chosen was that of I. Stafford Jolley, who also appears in the film. Difficulty then arose in the scenes where they appear together, forcing the producers to dub in another voice for Jolley. It seems it could have all been avoided by getting a villain who could use his own voice.

p, Ronald Davidson; d, William Witney, Fred C. Brannon; w, Alfred DeMond, Basil Dickey, Jesse Duffy, Sol Shor; ph, Bud Thackery.

Crime   (PR:A   MPAA:NR)

CYNARA★★★½   (1932) 78m Goldwyn/UA bw
                                                        (AKA: I WAS FAITHLESS)

Ronald Colman (*Jim Warlock*), Kay Francis (*Clemency Warlock*), Phyllis Barry (*Doris Lea*), Henry Stephenson (*John Tring*), Viva Tattersall (*Milly Miles*), Florine McKinney (*Garla*), Clarissa Selwyn (*Onslow*), Paul Porcasi (*Joseph*), George Kirby (*Mr. Boots*), Donald Stewart (*Henry*), Wilson Benge (*Merton*), C. Montague Shaw (*Constable*), Charlie Hall (*Court Spectator*).

Colman is a solid citizen and London lawyer who is conservative in every way; his business, his marriage and his personal ethics. He is happily, if sleepily married to Kay Francis and has been for seven years. Then the itch settles in and Colman finds himself attracted to a shopgirl, Barry, and has an affair with her while his wife is away on a trip. It begins casually enough but gets much more passionate. When Colman tells Barry that he must cut it short as he wants to make the marriage work, Barry commits suicide. A scandal erupts and Colman must testify in court, an action that ruins his good name. He will not sully the late girl's image even though she had been known to be free with her favors. Rather than face the shame of being in London, he chooses exile in South Africa. Francis realizes that he is a good man, a man of integrity, and rushes to the ship as it's leaving and they will begin a new life together. Based on a novel and a play, CYNARA is taken from poetic phrase "I have always been faithful to thee, Cynara, in my fashion." The odd title and the image of Colman as a philanderer, where he'd always been perceived as a gentleman and a scholar—he was unhappy with this part—may have been what served to make the film a flop at the turnstiles.

p, Samuel Goldwyn; d, King Vidor; w, Francis Marion, Lynn Starling (from the play by H. M. Harwood, Robert Gore-Brown and based upon *An Imperfect Lover*, a novel by Gore-Brown); ph, Ray June; ed, Hugh Bennett.

Drama   (PR:A-C   MPAA:NR)

CYNTHIA★★½   (1947) 97m MGM bw (GB: THE RICH, FULL LIFE)

Elizabeth Taylor (*Cynthia Bishop*), George Murphy (*Larry Bishop*), S. Z. Sakall (*Prof. Rosenkrantz*), Mary Astor (*Louise Bishop*), Gene Lockhart (*Dr. Fred I. Jannings*), Spring Byington (*Carrie Jannings*), James Lydon (*Ricky Latham*), Scotty Beckett (*Will Parker*), Carol Brannan (*Fredonia Jannings*), Anna Q. Nilsson (*Miss Brady*), Morris Ankrum (*Mr. Phillips*), Kathleen Howard (*McQuillan*), Shirley Johns (*Stella Regan*),

Barbara Challis (*Alice*), Harlan Briggs (*J. M. Dingle*), Will Wright (*Gus Wood*).

Murphy and Astor are Taylor's parents. She's been a sheltered young woman who has never been on a date. The simple plot, based on Vina Delmar's flop play, has to do with the maturation of Taylor, her first date, kiss, and just about everything teenage with the possible exception of pregnancy and acne. Lydon (Henry Aldrich on radio and in film) gives Liz the first of many, many screen kisses and for that alone he will always be a trivia question. It's such a mild comedy that offends absolutely no one that it's a shame to say it is also a somewhat dull picture. Nice comedy bits from Sakall, Lockhart, and Byington in the roles they always seemed to have played. Liz also sings but it's hardly worth mentioning.

p, Edwin H. Knopf; d, Robert Z. Leonard; w, Charles Kaufman, Harold Buchman (from Vina Delmar's play "The Rich, Full Life"); ph, Charles Schoenbaum; m, Bronislau Kaper; ed, Irvine Warburton; md, Johnny Green; art d, Cedric Gibbons; set d, Edwin Willis, Paul G. Chamberlain; cos, Irene; m/l, Johnny Green.

Comedy   (PR:AA   MPAA:NR)

CYRANO DE BERGERAC★★★★   (1950) 112m UA bw

Jose Ferrer (*Cyrano*), Mala Powers (*Roxane*), William Prince (*Christian*), Morris Carnovsky (*Le Bret*), Ralph Clanton (*De Guiche*), Lloyd Corrigan (*Ragueneau*), Virginia Farmer (*Duenna*), Edgar Barrier (*Cardinal*), Elena Verdugo (*Orange Girl*), Albert Cavens (*Valvert*), Arthur Blake (*Montfleury*), Don Beddoe (*The Meddler*), Percy Helton (*Bellerose*), Virginia Christine (*Sister Marthe*), Gil Warren (*Doctor*), Philip Van Zandt (*Man with Gazette*), Eric Sinclair (*Guardsman*), Ricard Avonde (*Marquis*), Paul Dubov, John Crawford, Jerry Paris, Robin Hughes (*Cadets*).

If ever an actor was born to play a role it was Ferrer as Cyrano. Brian Hooker's translation of Rostand serves as the basis for Foreman's screenplay and it is the best translation of the many available. What a shame that this was such an obvious backlot picture with a black and white camera instead of one in color. Ferrer won the Academy Award for his perfect portrayal of one of the greatest characters in literature. Cyrano was a poet, a romantic, a beautiful man in a beast's body. His long nose pained him to such a degree that he would kill anyone who spoke of it in his presence. And yet he was only too happy to discourse on his proboscis but it was usually when he was composing a poem as he was planning to run someone through. Cyrano is in love with his cousin, Powers, and she is in love with Prince, a handsome but tongue-tied youth. Cyrano feeds Prince the right words in letters and then in a scene where Prince stands beneath her window as Cyrano whispers the right words to say. When Prince dies, Powers goes into mourning. Then Cyrano is waylaid by detractors and he is dying. She recognizes some of the words he speaks as the same words Prince had spoken and she realizes that it was Cyrano all along. Even the meanest person's eyes will well up as she says, "I have loved one man, and he died twice." Cyrano, bleeding from a head wound caused by his killers, sits with her in a garden and eventually death takes him but not before he jousts with the grimmest of all reapers. Cyrano reckons they can kill him, but they can never take away his panache. The picture is stagey in many ways and looks like it didn't have that large a budget, but the play is surely the thing and Gordon's direction keeps this play moving with alacrity. Peter Donat did a different version of the character for ACT in San Francisco in the 1970s. His was an old and tired Cyrano and it was, in its way, brilliant. But Ferrer, who had the good fortune to also play Toulouse Lautrec and the lawyer in THE CAINE MUTINY, will always be recalled for this role. Every actor should be forced to watch it.

p, Stanley Kramer; d, Michael Gordon; w, Carl Foreman (based on Brian Hooke's translation of the play by Edmond Rostand); ph, Frank Planer; m, Dimitri Tiomkin; ed, Harry Gerstad.

Drama   **Cas.**   (PR:AA   MPAA:NR)

CZAR OF BROADWAY, THE★★   (1930) 79m UNIV bw

John Wray (*Morton Bradley*), Betty Compson (*Connie Colton*), John Harron (*Jay Grant*), Claud Allister (*Francis*), Wilbur Mack (*Harry Foster*), King Baggot (*Dane Harper*), Edmund Breese (*McNab*).

Matter-of-fact treatment of news reporter Harron, who is keeping an eye on gambler Wray in a seedy night spot. In the process he falls in love with singer Compson, who aptly delivers the tune "Homestead Steady of Mine." Harmless but poorly paced early talkie, which has a nifty title, but a bad soundtrack.

d, William James Craft; w, Gene Towne (based on a story by Towne).

Crime/Romance   (PR:A   MPAA:NR)

CZAR WANTS TO SLEEP★★

                              (1934, U.S., USSR) 69m Amkino/Belgaskino bw

B. Goringorianinov, M. Yanshin, M. Shaternikova, S. Magarill, E. Garin, V. Lepke, M. Rostovtsev.

A poorly constructed film held together by a humorous anecdote from the crazed Czar Paul I. A cry from inside the palace is heard, waking up the sleepy czar. It turns out that the noise was blurted out by a pinched emissary who was playfully grabbed by a palace servant girl. The czar demands a list of everyone in the palace. On the list appears the name of a non-existent soldier, whom the czar promptly banishes to Siberia. A sometimes funny and poignant satire of czarist Russia, which suffers from a padded script. Outstanding score from prominent Russian composer, Prokofiev.

d, Alexander Feinzimmer; m, Sergei Prokofiev.

Satire   (PR:A   MPAA:NR)

D.C. CAB** (1983) 104m UNIV c

Adam Baldwin *(Albert)*, Charlie Barnett *(Tyrone)*, Irene Cara *(Herself)*, Anne DeSalvo *(Myrna)*, Max Gail *(Harold)*, Gloria Gifford *(Miss Floyd)*, DeWayne Jessie *(Bongo)*, Bill Maher *(Baba)*, Whitman Mayo *(Mr. Rhythm)*, Mr. T *(Samson)*, Jose Perez *(Bravo)*, Paul Rodriquez *(Xavier)*, David Barbarian *(Buzzy)*, Peter Barbarian *(Buddy)*, Marsha Warfield *(Ophelia)*, Gary Busey *(Dell)*, Bob Zmuda *(Cubby)*, Jim Moody *(Arnie)*, Denise Gordy *(Denise)*, Alfredine P. Brown *(Matty)*, Scott Nemes, Senta Moses *(Ambassador's Son and Daughter)*, Jill Schoelen *(Claudette)*, Diana Bellamy *(Maudie)*, John Diehl, Bonnie Keith, J.W. Smith *(Kidnapers)*, Moriah Shannon *(Waitress)*, Newton D. Arnold *(FBI Chief)*, Michael Elliott Hill, Dennis Stewart, Paula Earlette Davis, Jacki Clark, Don Jacob, Ann Guilford-Grey, Timothy Rice, Patricia Duff, Martha Jane Urann, Michael DeSanto, Dale Stephenson, Esther Lee, Scott Perry, Marti Soyoa, Anthony Thompkins.

Mindless but likeable comedy about a failing Washington, D.C., cab company which is revitalized when the eccentric group of cabbies pull together to save the company. A good cast pulls the uninspired material along with them.

p, Topper Carew, Cassius Vernon Weathersby; d&w, Joel Schumacher (based on a story by Carew, Schumacher); ph, Dean Cundey (Technicolor); m, Giorgio Moroder; ed, David Blewitt; prod d, John J. Lloyd; art d, Bernie Cutler; set d, Lloyd; cos, Roberta Weiner; ch, Jeffrey Hornaday.

Comedy **Cas.** **(PR:C MPAA:R)**

D-DAY, THE SIXTH OF JUNE*** (1956) 106m FOX c (AKA: THE SIXTH OF JUNE)

Robert Taylor *(Brad Parker)*, Richard Todd *(John Wynter)*, Dana Wynter *(Valerie)*, Edmond O'Brien *(Colonel Timmer)*, John Williams *(Brigadier Russell)*, Jerry Paris *(Raymond Boyce)*, Robert Gist *(Dan Stenick)*, Richard Stapley *(David Archer)*, Ross Elliott *(Major Mills)*, Alex Finlayson *(Colonel Harkens)*, Marie Brown *(Georgina)*, Rama Bai *(Mala)*, Dabbs Greer *(Arkinson)*, Boyd "Red" Morgan *(Sergeant Brooks)*, Queenie Leonard *(Corporal)*, Geoffrey Steel *(Maj. McEwen)*, George Pelling *(Capt. Waller)*, Cyril Delevanti *(Coat Room Attendant)*, Conrad Feia *(Lieutenant at Party)*, Richard Aherne *(Grainger)*, Victoria Ward *(Mrs. Hamilton)*, Patricia McMahon *(Suzette)*, John Damier *(Lt. Col. Cantrell)*, Thomas B. Henry *(Gen. Bolthouse)*, Damien O'Flynn *(Gen. Pike)*, Ben Wright *(Gen. Millensbeck)*, Howard Price *(American War Correspondent)*, Reggie Dvorak *(Taxi Driver)*, Chet Marshall *(Lt. Clayford Binns)*, Parley Baer *(Sgt. Gerbert)*, Ashley Cowan *(Lance Corp. Bailey)*, June Mitchell *(Waitress)*.

A solid cast and excellent production values give this love triangle story amidst the havoc of WW II poignancy and many memorable scenes. Taylor is a London-assigned officer working for ego-eccentric O'Brien (in a revealing, often grating performance) who longs to make a name for himself in combat. Taylor's story is told in flashback as he awaits the sailing of the invasion armada to Normandy. He thinks back to first meeting Wynter whose sheer beauty steals most of her scenes; she is an English enlisted woman whose fiance, Todd, is fighting in Africa, and she tries unsuccessfully to resist falling in love with Taylor, who has a wife in the states. Their trysting is interrupted when Todd is furloughed seriously wounded and Wynter returns to him. Both men later participate in the D-Day landings, Todd knowing about Taylor's affair with Wynter and gallantly ignoring it. During the beachhead battle Taylor is wounded and Todd sees him off to a waiting boat which will return him to England. Then Todd walks into a mine area and is blown up. Wynter visits Taylor in the hospital and leads him to believe that she is staying with Todd, even though she knows he is dead, she too being noble in sending Taylor back to his wife, making for a bittersweet finale. Koster's direction is swift and is aided by Garmes' sharp photography and Murray's moving score. The story bogs down in spots, but is enlivened by O'Brien's unmilitary, often bizarre conduct. When Taylor first read the script he thought this film would match his favorite film, WATERLOO BRIDGE. It didn't and he cooled about its prospects after production even though it did well at the box office.

p, Charles Brackett; d, Henry Koster; w, Ivan Moffat, Harry Brown (based on the novel by Lionel Shapiro); ph, Lee Garmes (CinemaScope, DeLuxe Color); m, Lyn Murray; ed, William Mace; md, Lionel Newman; art d, Lyle R. Wheeler, Lewis H. Creber; cos, Charles LeMaire; spec eff, Ray Kellogg.

War Drama/Romance **(PR:A MPAA:NR)**

D.I., THE*** (1957) 104m WB bw

Jack Webb *(T/Sgt. Jim Moore)*, Don Dubbins *(Pvt. Owens)*, Jackie Loughery *(Anne)*, Lin McCarthy *(Capt. Anderson)*, Monica Lewis *(Burt)*, Virginia Gregg *(Mrs. Owens)*, Jeannie Beacham *(Hostess)*, Lu Tobin *(Bartender)*, Earle Hodgins *(Guard)*, Jeanne Baird *(Mother)*, Barbara Pepper *(Customer)*, Melody Gale *(Little Girl)*, and Men of the U.S. Marine Corps.

A tough, uncompromising portrait of Marine training on Parris Island where Webb is a tough drill instructor (i.e., D.I.), a hard-nosed sergeant with creases to his eyebrows who puts recruits through night-and-day rigors that make many think they've turned into robots. Webb runs the would-be shock troops through one shock after another, from night hikes to barracks scrub downs. Aside from a minor romance with an off-base cutie, Webb spends most of his time trying to make a man out of sniveling, whining Dubbins who has only joined up to appease his mother, upholding a family tradition, since his father and two brothers had been Marines (all killed during WW II). Instead of coddling or reasoning with the youth, Webb lays on the double-duty, almost breaking his spirit. But Dubbins' courage seeps out of sweating pores and he finally earns his place in the Corps. Webb is the whole show, producing and directing the taut film with furious pace and articulating his orders like a battleship firing salvos.

p&d, Jack Webb; w, James Lee Barrett (based on his teleplay "Murder of A Sandflea"); ph, Edward Colman; m, David Buttolph; ed, Robert M. Leeds; art d, Field Gray, Gibson Holley; cos, Maxwell Shieff, Alex Velcoff; m/l, "Somebody Else Will," Ray Coniff, Fred Weismantel.

Military Drama **(PR:A MPAA:NR)**

D.O.A.*½** (1950) 83m UA bw

Edmond O'Brien *(Frank Bigelow)*, Pamela Britton *(Paula Gibson)*, Luther Adler *(Majak)*, Beverly Campbell *(Miss Foster)*, Lynn Baggett *(Mrs. Philips)*, William Ching *(Halliday)*, Henry Hart *(Stanley Philips)*, Neville Brand *(Chester)*, Laurette Luez *(Marla Rakubian)*, Jess Kirkpatrick *(Sam)*, Cay Forrester *(Sue)*, Virginia Lee *(Jeanie)*, Michael Ross *(Dave)*.

In a clever twist a murder victim, O'Brien, discovers he has been poisoned and begins tracking down his own killer. CPA O'Brien arrives in San Francisco on vacation but after a night on the town he grows ill and consults a doctor who tells him he has been dosed with radiation poison and his days are numbered to only a few. Hospitalized, O'Brien realizes that his murderer will escape punishment unless he himself hunts him down. He begins to investigate after fleeing the hospital, calling his home office in Banning, California. His secretary/fiancee Britton tells him that he notarized a shipment of deadly iridium and he later discovers criminals have obtained the shipment and used it to murder the head of the company shipping the poison. He has been dosed because he notarized the shipment and might lead a trail to the killers. Before he can locate the killer, the murderer finds him and a wild chase through Los Angeles ensues with O'Brien killing his pursuer, then going to a police station. He has been telling the tale from the beginning and all the harrowing events are revealed in flashback. When he finishes his frightening story O'Brien collapses dead on the police officer's desk. He is removed, his body marked "D.O.A." (Dead on Arrival). O'Brien is great as the victimized businessman, harassed by psychopath Brand and an even more sinister Ching. Mate's direction suitably increases his pace as the story unravels and the chase becomes more hectic, particularly when Brand is stalking O'Brien and then, laughing maniacally, chases him in a car at devastating speeds. Tiomkin's score is both chilling and humorously offbeat. The film takes much of its basic story line from Robert Siodmak's 1931, German-made DER MAN, DER SEINEN MORDER SUCHT where a dying man tries to find out the reason for his untimely death. Laszlo's superb contrasting lensing provides the proper *film noir* mood for this memorable production. Remade as COLOR ME DEAD.

p, Leo C. Popkin; d, Rudolph Mate; w, Russell Rouse, Clarence Green; ph, Ernest Laszlo; m, Dmitri Tiomkin; ed, Arthur H. Nadel; art d, Duncan Cramer; set d, Al Orenbach; cos, Maria Donovan; makeup, Irving Berns.

Crime Drama **Cas.** **(PR:A MPAA:NR)**

DAD AND DAVE COME TO TOWN½** (1938, Aus.) 90m Cinesound/British Empire Films bw

Bert Bailey *(Dad Rudd)*, Shirley Ann Richards *(Jill)*, Dave McDonald *(Dave)*, Billy Rayes *(Jim Bradley)*, Alec Kellaway *(Entwistle)*, Sydney Wheeler *(Pierre)*, Connie Mertyn *(Mum)*, Ossie Wenban *(Joe)*, Valarie Scanlan *(Sarah)*, Leila Steppe *(Sonia)*, Marshall Crosby *(Ryan, Sr.)* Peter Finch *(Bill Ryan)*, Cecil Perry *(Rawlings)*.

A good comedy for its time, this was made in Australia by Australians and starred Australians. The story concerns an outback farmer who inherits a city fashion salon. He moves his wife and son into town to run the shop. He is dubbed "the farmer dressmaker," and goes to outrageous lengths to attract business, one example of which is an embarrassingly funny radio commercial father and son duo. Australian films at this time were rare.

d, Ken G. Hall; w, Bert Hailey, Frank Harvey; ph, George Heath, m, Hamilton Webber, Maurie Gillman.

Comedy **(PR:A MPAA:NR)**

DADDY LONG LEGS**** (1931) 80m FOX bw

Janet Gaynor *(Judy Abbott)*, Warner Baxter *(Jervis Pendleton)*, Una Merkel *(Sally McBride)*, John Arledge *(Jimmy McBride)*, Claude Gillingwater, Sr. *(Riggs)*, Kathlyn Williams *(Mrs. Pendleton)*, Louise Closser Hale *(Miss Pritchard)*, Elizabeth Patterson *(Mrs. Lippett)*, Kendall MacComak *(Freddie Perkins)*, Sheila Mannors *(Gloria Pendleton)*, Edwin Maxwell *(Wykoff)*, Effie Ellsler *(Mrs. Semple)*, Martha Lee Sparks *(Katie)*.

DADDY LONG LEGS is one of those stories that always works. Made in 1919 with Mary Pickford, then in 1935 as CURLY TOP with Shirley Temple, then again in 1955 with Leslie Caron, this 1931 version features Gaynor and Baxter as protagonists in a May-December relationship. It's another variant on the CINDERELLA theme with perky Gaynor living in a Little Annie Orphanage and bridling under the harsh treatment of matron Patterson. The place is filled with the most adorable kids that, in real life, would have had no problem finding adoptive parents because each is cuter than the next. Gaynor is sent to college by a mystery man who is a trustee of the orphanage. This, of course, is Baxter. Matters get a bit complex when her roommate (Una Merkel) has a brother (John Arledge) who falls in love with Gaynor. But it all ends well when she discovers that the man she loves is also the man who has been her benefactor for all those years. Baxter is a wealthy bachelor who is besieged by people for his money, power, and influence, but in Gaynor he finds a person who loves him for *who* he is, not *what* he is or what he can do. The movie has a lot of laughs, plenty of romance, enough pathos for two hankies, and just about everything a first-rate picture should have. The story was already a cliche by this lensing but the good spirits of the cast and crew kept it from falling into bathos. Gaynor was 25 and Baxter was 40, not quite a May-December romance, more like a June-October, but why quibble? Patterson was the perfect crotchety old lady. She didn't get into movies until she was in her fifties but she made more than fifty features including excellent roles in such famous films as SING YOU SINNERS, THE STORY OF ALEXANDER GRAHAM BELL, TOBACCO ROAD, THE CAT AND THE CANARY, and LADY ON A TRAIN. Directors loved her because she always "brought something" to every role. There are actors who learn the lines, speak the lines, collect the money, and go home. Patterson always had a little extra to give.

d, Alfred Santell; w, Sonya Levien, S.N. Behrman (based on the novel and play by Jean Webster); ph, Lucien Andriot; ed, Ralph Dietrich.

Comedy/Drama   **(PR:AAA MPAA:NR)**

DADDY LONG LEGS****   (1955) 126m FOX c

Fred Astaire (Jervis Pendleton), Leslie Caron (Julie), Terry Moore (Linda), Thelma Ritter (Miss Pritchard), Fred Clark (Griggs), Charlotte Austin (Sally), Larry Keating (Alexander Williamson), Kathryn Givney (Gertrude), Kelly Brown (Jimmy McBride), Sara Shane (Pat), Numa Lapeyre (Jean), Ann Codee (Mme. Sevanne), Steven Geray (Emile), Percival Vivian (Professor), Helen Van Tuyl (College Dean), Damian O'Flynn (Larry Hamilton), Joseph Kearns (Guide), Larry Kent (Butler), Charles Anthony Hughes (Hotel Manager), Ralph Dumke (Mr. Bronson), Kathryn Card (Mrs. Carrington), Tim Johnson (Bellhop), Harry Seymour (Cab Driver), Olan Soule (Assistant Hotel Manager), J. Anthony Hughes (Delivery Man), George Dunn (Chauffeur), Ray Anthony Orchestra.

Musical version of three-times-filmed Jean Webster story about a love affair that has everything going against it but eventually works. Caron is a waif in an orphanage. Astaire is a playboy who occasionally does something or other for the U.S. government. One such mission takes him to France where he is enthralled by Caron and begins to support her from afar. Time passes and Caron falls in love with Astaire without knowing who he is or what he's done. She writes long letters of thanks to Astaire that his secretary, Ritter, gets teary-eyed over and Astaire is prevailed upon to get to know her better. That's when friendship turns to love. The story always was a thin one and the 1931 film only took 80 minutes or so. This is fully 46 minutes longer and all of the time is accounted for musically. Johnny Mercer, writing music and lyrics for one of the few times in his life, received an Oscar nomination for "Something's Gotta Give," which remains a standard. The other tunes are not so strong but serve as wonderful backdrops to Caron and Astaire as they dance their ways into our hearts. There are several dream sequences (one could always get away with a great deal under the guise of dreams), an Astaire drum ballet, and another ballet by Caron. The weakest element of the film was Petit's choreography for the dream ballets. They were overdone and showed little of the brilliance he'd demonstrated in ANYTHING GOES. Fred Clark, Ritter, and Terry Moore were just right in their supporting roles and Terry looked absolutely scrumptious. It was about this time she caught the eye of noted talent scout Howard Robard Hughes. She was 26 and in her 17th movie, having already garnered an Oscar nomination for her work in COME BACK, LITTLE SHEBA. Songs: "History of the Beat," "C-A-T Spells Cat," "Daddy Long Legs," "Welcome Egghead," "Dream," "Something's Got to Give," "Sluefoot" (Johnny Mercer). Dances: "Hong Kong" (Caron), "Texas Millionaire," "International Playboy" (Astaire), "Guardian Angel" (Caron, Astaire), "The Daydream Sequence," "Dancing Through Life" (ballet ensemble), "Something's Gotta Give," "Sluefoot" (Astaire, Caron).

p, Samuel G. Engel; d, Jean Negulesco; w, Phoebe and Henry Ephron (based on the novel and play by Jean Webster); ph, Leon Shamroy (CinemaScope, Technicolor); m, Alfred Newman, Alex North; ed, William Reynolds; ch, Roland Petit, David Robel, Fred Astaire.

Musical/Romance   **Cas.**   **(PR:AAA MPAA:NR)**

DADDY-O*   (1959) 74m Imperial AIP bw (AKA:OUT ON PROBATION)

Dick Contino (Phil Sandifer), Sandra Giles (Jana Ryan), Bruno VeSota (Sidney Chillas), Gloria Victor (Marcia), Ron McNeil (Duke), Jack McClure (Bruce Green), Sonia Torgeson (Peg), Kelly Gordon (Ken), Joseph Donte (Frank Wooster), Bab Banas (Sonny DiMarco), Hank Mann (Barney), Joseph Martin (Kerm).

Dumb teen exploitation has singer Contino forced by hoodlums to drive the getaway car in a heist. Good for a laugh.

p, Elmar C. Rhoden, Jr.; d, Lou Place; w, David Moessinger; m, John Williams.

Crime   **(PR:C MPAA:NR)**

DADDY'S GONE A-HUNTING**   (1969) 108m NG c

Carol White (Cathy Palmer), Scott Hylands (Kenneth Daly), Paul Burke (Jack Byrnes), Mala Powers (Meg Stone), Rachel Ames (Dr. Parkington's Nurse), Barry Cahill (FBI Agent Crosley), Matilda Calnan (Ilsa), Andrea King (Brenda Frazier), Gene Lyons (Dr. Blanker), Ron Masak (Paul Fanning), Dennis Patrick (Dr. Parkington), James Sikking (FBI Agent Menchell).

This film was directed by Mark Robson the year after his huge success with VALLEY OF THE DOLLS. It is the story of a British woman living in San Francisco. She discovers she is pregnant by her photographer boy friend, who is a violent man not playing with a full deck. He wants to marry her, but she decides that would be a mistake and has an abortion. Years later, she marries a lawyer, has a baby, and is a happy fulfilled woman. However, her happy life is turned upside down when her crazed ex-boy friend shows up, demanding that she kill her baby to rectify the wrong done to him. Co-writer Cohen later directed his own babies in peril movies, IT'S ALIVE, and its sequel.

p&d, Mark Robson; w, Larry Cohen, Lorenzo Semple Jr.; ph, Ernest Laszlo (Panavision/Technicolor); m, John Williams; ed, Dorothy Spencer; art d, James Sullivan; set d, Charles Thompson; cos, Travilla; m/l, Dory Previn.

Suspense/Drama   **(PR:C MPAA:M)**

DAD'S ARMY**½   (1971, Brit.) 95m COL c

Arthur Lowe (Capt. Mainwaring), John Le Mesurier (Sgt. Wilson), Clive Dunn (Cpl. Jones), John Laurie (Pvt. Frazer), Arnold Ridley (Pvt. Godfrey), Ian Lavender (Pvt. Pike), Liz Fraser (Mrs. Pike), Bernard Archerd (Gen. Fuller), Derek Newark (R.S.M.), Bill Pertwee (Hodges), Frank Williams (Vicar), Edward Sinclair (Verger).

Based on a British television series of the same name, the story is set in 1940, depicting Britons who weren't in the armed forces and their rallying to the crisis of the expected Nazi invasion. Local defense volunteers were formed as the Home Guard, recruits not having weapons or uniforms but having a lot of enthusiasm. The film focuses in on a particular group of the guard, the Walsingham-on-sea contingent. Led by a bank official and consisting of a bunch of misfits who wade through a series of humorous misadventures, the climax being the capture of three German aviators who parachute into Britain.

p, John R. Sloan; d, Norman Cohen; w, Jimmy Perry, David Croft (based on a television series); ph, Terry Maher (Technicolor); m, Wilfred Burns; ed, Willy Kemplen; art d, Terry Knight; m/l, "Dad's Army" (Jimmy Perry, David Taverner).

Comedy   **(PR:A MPAA:NR)**

DAFFODIL KILLER   (SEE: DEVIL'S DAFFODIL, THE, 1967, Brit./Ger.)

DAFFY   (SEE: WILD SEED, 1965)

DAFFY DUCK'S MOVIE: FANTASTIC ISLAND**½
                                                              (1983) 78m WB c

Voices of: Mel Blanc, June R. Foray, Les Tremayne.

A number of old Warner Bros. cartoons are trotted out and re-edited into a lame parody of television's "Fantasy Island." The old cartoons are always worth seeing, but a better selection of them would have helped this film immensely. Kids will love it.

p&d, Friz Freleng; w, John Dunn, David Detiege, Freleng; ed, Jim Champin; prod d, Bob Givens, Michael Mitchell.

Animation   **Cas.**   **(PR:AAA MPAA:G)**

DAGGERS OF BLOOD (SEE: INVASION SEVENTEEN HUNDRED, 1965)

DAGORA THE SPACE MONSTER*   (1964, Jap.) 83m Toho c
          (UCHUDAI DOGORA; AKA: DAGORA; SPACE MONSTER DOGORA)

Yosuke Natsuki, Yoko Fujiyama, Akiko Wakabayashi, Hiroshi Koizumi.

Dagora is a large octopus-like creature that, like all mutated monsters from Toho studios, terrorizes Japan. A scientist discovers that wasp venom will destroy the creature as Dagora flies around Tokyo eating everything in sight.

p, Tomoyuki Tanaka; d, Inoshiro Honda; w, Shinichi Sekizawa; ph, Hajime Koizumi; ed, Eiji Tsuburaya.

Horror/Monster   **Cas.**   **(PR:A MPAA:NR)**

DAISIES*½   (1967, Czech.) 74m Barrandov Studio of Prague/Sigma III c
                                       (SEDMIKRASKY; AKA: DAISIES, THE)

Jitka Crhova (Marie I), Ivana Karbanova (Marie II), Julius Albert (Man About Town).

Incoherent film has two young women (Crhova and Karbanova) living off various men and generally being antisocial as they wander from the beach, to a nightclub, to a pop-art-filled apartment, and so on. Eventually they end up back at the beach, where they started. Interesting chiefly as an example of the freedom allowed Czech filmmakers before the Russian tanks rolled into Prague.

d, Vera Chytilova; w, Chytilova, Ester Krumbachova; Pavel Juracek; ph, Jaroslav Kucera (Eastmancolor/Wo Color); m, Jiri Sust, Jiri Slitr; ed, Miroslav Hajek.

Comedy/Drama   **(PR:C-O MPAA:NR)**

DAISY KENYON***½   (1947) 100m FOX bw

Joan Crawford (Daisy Kenyon), Dana Andrews (Dan O'Mara), Henry Fonda (Peter), Ruth Warrick (Lucile O'Mara), Martha Stewart (Mary Angelus), Peggy Ann Garner (Rosamund), Connie Marshall (Marie), Nicholas Joy (Coverly), Art Baker (Lucile's Attorney), Robert Karnes (Attorney), John Davidson (Mervyn), Victoria Horne (Marsha), Charles Meredith (Judge), Roy Roberts (Dan's Attorney), Griff Barnett (Thompson), Tito Vuolo (Dino), Marion Marshall (Telephone Operator), George E. Stone (Waiter), John Butler, Jimmy Ames (Cab Drivers), John Garfield (Man in Restaurant), Monya Andre (Mrs. Ames), Mauritz Hugo (Mr. Ames), Walter Winchell (Himself), Leonard Lyons (Himself).

A patently obvious soap opera but done with such chic, such style, such panache, that it doesn't make a difference. This was Fonda's final film on what he felt was a terribly restrictive contract so he was only too happy to accept whatever the studio offered in order to fulfill the terms of the agreement. Crawford is Daisy Kenyon, a fashion artist living in a walk-up in New York's Greenwich Village. Her relationship with powerful attorney Andrews is behind the scenes because Andrews's wife, Ruth Warrick, means too much to him and he is loathe to leave her and the children, Garner and Marshall. Crawford applies as much pressure as she can but Andrews is adamant about keeping things the way they are. Though Warrick is somewhat of a shrew, Andrews has a sense of loyalty and will not change his situation, so Crawford must accept those stolen moments they can have with each other. Fonda is an army sergeant just home from WW II and looking forward to returning to his pre-war occupation as a ship architect. He meets Crawford and she sees that he is a sweet, kind, and gentle man, almost too nice for us to believe because Crawford has been thriving under the mean thumb of Andrews. Fonda falls in love with Crawford and offers her marriage, a home, affection—all the things she wants but cannot have from Andrews. They marry and move to his cottage on Cape Cod. Andrews can't keep away from Crawford and after he loses a civil rights case he took to please her, he calls Crawford at her home. Warrick overhears the conversation and breaks in to tell him that she wants a divorce as well as the children. If she doesn't get custody, she intends to name Crawford as co-respondent. A divorce trial is planned but matters get complicated when the children claim they would rather live with their father. Warrick relents, takes a payoff, Andrews gets the divorce, and then goes after Crawford and asks her to give up life with dull Fonda and to come away with him to Nassau and such places and start a new life. Fonda realizes she is wavering and decides to fight for her by not fighting for her; he'll sit back in an attitude of watchful waiting. Andrews and Fonda meet, discuss the situation, and then, when Crawford returns home, they put it to her: which of them will she choose? Several emotions race across that memorable face before her decision is made; she realizes that she has stopped loving Andrews and started loving Fonda, and he is the man with whom she will spend the rest of her life. Was there any doubt? Fonda was passive in this film, too passive to be attractive to a woman like Daisy, but that's the way writers Hertz and Janeway saw it. Perhaps it was the emphasis larded on by Preminger that throws the emotions out of whack. It's Crawford's picture from frame one, and the other two roles could have been played by anyone. Andrews is strong but not strong enough, and Fonda is as bland as a mayonnaise sandwich on supermarket white.

p&d, Otto Preminger; w, David Hertz (based on the novel by Elizabeth Janeway); ph, Leon Shamroy; m, David Raksin; ed, Louis Loeffler; md, Alfred Newman; art d, Lyle Wheeler, George Davis; set d, Thomas Little, Walter Scott; spec eff, Fred Sersen.

Drama **(PR:A-C MPAA:NR)**

DAISY MILLER* (1974) 90m PAR c

Cybill Shepherd *(Annie P. "Daisy" Miller)*, Barry Brown *(Frederick Winterbourne)*, Cloris Leachman *(Mrs. Ezra B. Miller)*, Mildred Natwick *(Mrs. Costello)*, Eileen Brennan *(Mrs. Walker)*, Dulio Del Prete *(Giovanelli)*, James McMurtry *(Randolph C. Miller)*, Nicholas Jones *(Charles)*, George Morfogen *(Eugenio)*, Jean Pascal Bongard *(Hotel Receptionist in Vevey)*, Albert Messmer *(Tutor)*, Jacques Guhl, Hubert Goldin *(Polish Boys)*, David Bush *(Man at Chillon)*, Henry Hubinet *(Chillon Guide)*, Maurizio Lucci *(Miniaturist)*, Tom Felleghy *(Mrs. Walker's Butler)*, Luigi Gabellone *(Punch and Judy)*, John Bartha, Salamon Amedeo *(Hotel Receptionist in Rome)*, Renato Talvacchia *(Pianist)*, Salvatore Lisitano *(Opera Singer)*, Bondi Esterhazy *(Doctor)*, Rodolfo Lodi, Elaine Olcott, Cesare Rotondi *(Mrs. Walker's Guests)*.

Daisy Miller as a book is a good read, but the filmization by Peter Bogdanovich is truly a dud in spite of handsome sets and an intelligent writing job. Henry James is, to say the least, hard to adapt for the screen, but this job becomes hopeless because of Shepherd's shallow performance as a woman who flirts all over Europe in the late 19th century and finally dies of malaria. The 23-year-old actor Brown (Winterbourne) also wrote on film. Four years after the release of DAISY MILLER, he was dead, a suicide.

p&d, Peter Bogdanovich; w, Frederic Raphael (based on the novel by Henry James); ph, Albert Spagnoli (Eastmancolor); ed, Verna Fields; art d, Ferdinando Scarfiotti; set d, Gianni Silvestri; cos, John Furness.

Drama **(PR:C-O MPAA:G)**

DAKOTA½** (1945) 82m REP bw

John Wayne *(John Devlin)*, Vera Hruba Ralston *(Sandy)*, Walter Brennan *(Capt. Bounce)*, Ward Bond *(Jim Bender)*, Mike Mazurki *(Bigtree Collins)*, Ona Munson *("Jersey" Thomas)*, Olive Blakeney *(Mrs. Stowe)*, Hugo Haas *(Marko Poli)*, Nicodemus Stewart *(Nicodemus)*, Paul Fix *(Carp)*, Grant Withers *(Slagin)*, Robert Livingston *(Lieutenant)*, Olin Howlin *(Devlin's Driver)*, Pierre Watkin *(Wexton Geary)*, Robert H. Barrat *(Mr. Stowe)*, Jonathan Hale *(Col. Wordin)*, Bobby Blake *(Little Boy)*, Paul Hurst *(Capt. Spotts)*, Eddy Waller *(Stagecoach Driver)*, Sarah Padden *(Mrs. Plummer)*, Jack LaRue *(Slade)*, George Cleveland *(Mr. Plummer)*, Selmer Jackson *(Dr. Judson)*, Claire DuBrey *(Wahtonka)*, Roy Barcroft *(Poli's Driver)*, Larry Thompson *(Poli's Footman)*, Jack Roper, Fred Graham, Russ Kaplan, Cliff Lyons *(Bouncers)*, Al Murphy *(Trainman)*, Houseley Stevenson *(Railroad Clerk)*, William Haade, Dick Wessel *(Roughnecks)*, Rex Lease *(Railroad Conductor)*, Betty Shaw, Martha Carroll, Adrian Booth, Linda Stirling, Virginia Wave, Cay Forester *(Entertainers)*, Eugene Borden, Peter Cusanelli, Hector Sarno *(Italians)*, Michael Visaroff *(Russian)*, Victor Varconi *(Frenchman)*, Paul E. Burns *(Swede)*, Arthur K. Miles *(Ciano)*, Dorothy Christy *(Nora)*.

Wayne and Ralston are a young couple setting out into the Dakota territory to find their fortune. They come across a gang of crooks who are buying up land cheaply from unsuspecting farmers, who don't know that the land is worth three times as much because a railroad is to be built through it. When the crooks try to swindle Wayne out of land he covets, they get more trouble than they bargained for as Wayne takes care of them in his usual manner. Behind the scenes, DAKOTA was almost never made because Wayne refused to work with Ralston, who was the wife of Republic's owner Herbert J. Yates. He finally relented, but that may be a good reason for a below-average performance on his part.

p&d, Joseph Kane; w, Lawrence Hazard, Howard Estabrook (based on a story by Carl Foreman); ph, Jack Marta; ed, Fred Allen; md, Walter Scharf; art d, Russell Kimball, Gano Chittenden; set d, John McCarthy, Jr., James Redd; spec eff, Howard and Theodore Lydecker; ch, Larry Ceballos; m/l, Andrew Sterling, Harry Von Tilzer.

Western **Cas.** **(PR:A MPAA:NR)**

DAKOTA INCIDENT½** (1956) 88m REP c

Linda Darnell *(Amy Clarke)* Dale Robertson *(John Banner)*, John Lund *(Carter Hamilton)*, Ward Bond *(Sen. Blakely)*, Regis Toomey *(Minstrel)*, Skip Homeier *(Brank Banner)*, Irving Bacon *(Tully Morgan)*, John Doucette *(Rick Largo)*, Whit Bissell *(Mark Chester)*, William Fawcett *(Mathew Barnes)*, Malcolm Atterbury *(Bartender-Desk Clerk)*, Diane Du Bois *(Giselle)*, Charles Horvath *(Indian Leader)*.

A group of strangers are thrown together in a struggle for survival when they are attacked by Indians. In the group are Robertson, a bank robber, Darnell, a loose lady of the West, and Lund, a bank clerk, all fleeing the law for a crime Robertson committed; Bond, a loud-mouthed politician, Toomey, a drunken minstrel man, and Bissell, the easterner who thinks he's found gold. One by one they get killed off by the Indians or by thirst, until only Robertson and Darnell are left. Cinematographer Haller won an Oscar for his lighting in GONE WITH THE WIND.

p, Michael Baird; d, Lewis R. Foster; w, Frederic Louis Fox; ph, Ernest Haller (Trucolor); m, R. Dale Butts; ed, Howard Smith.

Western **Cas.** **(PR:A MPAA:NR)**

DAKOTA KID, THE* (1951) 70m REP bw

Michael Chapin *(Red)*, Eilene Janssen *(Judy)*, James Bell *(Sheriff Tom White)*, Dean Morton *(Dakota Kid)*, Margaret Field *(Mary Lewis)*, Robert Shayne *(Ace Crandall)*, Roy Barcroft *(Turk)*, Mauritz Hugo *(Squire Mason)*, House Peters, Jr. *(Sam Dawson)*, Lee Bennett *(Cole White)*, Michael Ragan *(Marker)*.

This is the second film starring Chapin and Janssen as the two venturesome children who always come to someone's rescue in the west. This time they help out the sheriff, Bell, whom the evil saloonkeeper wants to get rid of so he can control the county for his own immoral purposes. The bad guy brings in the title outlaw, Morton, to pose as the long absent nephew of Bell, so he may dispose of him easily. Fortunately, the kids discover the real identity of Morton and tip off Bell, allowing Bell to bring the outlaw and the saloonkeeper to justice.

p, Rudy Ralston; d, Philip Ford; w, William Lively; ph, John MacBurnie; ed, Harry Keller; m/l, "What Are Cowboys Made Of?," Eddie Cherkose, Jule Styne.

Western **(PR:AAA MPAA:NR)**

DAKOTA LIL** (1950) 87m FOX c

George Montgomery *(Tom Horn)*, Rod Cameron *(Harve Logan)*, Marie Windsor *(Lil)*, John Emery *(Vincent)*, Wallace Ford *(Carter)*, Jack Lambert *(Dummy)*, Larry Johns *(Sheriff)*, Marion Martin *(Blonde)*, Walter Sande *(Butch)*, Kenneth MacDonald *(Sentry)*, Bill Perrott *(Cashier)*, James Flavin *(Chief)*, Lillian Bronson *(Sheriff's Wife)*, Clancy Cooper *(Bartender)*, Albert Morin *(Rurales)*, J. Farrell MacDonald *(Expert)*, Frank Lackteen, Joel Friedkin, Saul Gorss, Bob Morgan, Leo McMahon, Jamesson Shade, Ben Harris, Alvin Hammer, John Dako, Tom Greenway, Nacho Galindo, Soledad Jiminez, Daniel Estrada, Rosa Turich, Bryan Hightower, Arne Hjorth.

A group of counterfeiters in the old West, headed by Cameron, has stolen a bundle of unsigned bank notes. Secret service agent Montgomery is sent out to retrieve the notes and break up the gang. Montgomery uses Windsor, the title chorus girl and forger fleeing from the law, as bait. She gets into the gang, as they were in need of a forger, and brings Montgomery, whom she does not know is an agent, with her. The two fall in love and by the time Windsor discovers that Montgomery is an agent she is more than happy to help him bring the gang to justice.

p, Edward L. Alperson; d, Lesley Selander; w, Maurice Gehaghty (based on a story by Frank Gruber); ph, Jack Greenhalgh (Cinecolor); m, Dmitri Tiomkin; ed, Francis Lyon; Song: "Ecstasy."

Western **(PR:A MPAA:NR)**

DALEKS—INVASION EARTH 2150 A.D.** (1966, Brit.) 84m BL c (AKA: INVASION EARTH 2150 A.D.)

Peter Cushing *(Dr. Who)*, Bernard Cribbins *(Tom Campbell)*, Ray Brooks *(David)*, Jill Curzon *(Louise)*, Roberta Tovey *(Susan)*, Andrew Keir *(Wyler)*, Godfrey Quigley *(Dortmun)*, Roger Avon *(Wells)*, Keith Marsh *(Conway)*, Geoffrey Cheshire *(Roboman)*, Steve Peters *(Leader Roboman)*, Robert Jewell *(Leader Dalek)*.

This is the sequel to DR. WHO AND THE DALEKS which also starred Cushing as Dr. Who. The character is based on a long-running BBC television series of the same name. This adventure starts when a London bobby mistakes the doctor's time machine, called the T.A.R.D.I.S., for a police emergency call box. The doctor and his niece and granddaughter are all in it, and because the bobby touches something he shouldn't have, all are thrown into the future—2150 A.D. to be exact. There they find that London has been ravaged by the Daleks, mutated aliens sitting in metal mobile transporters, and the doctor's worst enemies. The Daleks have razed the world, turned most of mankind into living zombies called robomen, and made the rest do forced labor in a huge mine. They are planning to rip out the metallic core of the Earth and use the hollowed-out planet as a space ship. There is a small band of free resistance fighters in London, and the doctor and his entourage join with them to defeat the aliens. The doctor accomplishes the feat by creating a huge and powerful magnetic field inside the deep mine, which sucks all the Daleks into the Earth's core.

p, Max J. Rosenberg, Milton Subotsky; d, Gordon Flemyng; w, Subotsky (based on a television serial by Terry Nation), ph, John Wilcox (Techniscope, Technicolor); m, Bill McCuffie; ed, Ann Chegwidden; art d, George Provis; set d, Maurice Pelling; spec eff, Ted Samuels.

Science Fiction **(PR:A MPAA:NR)**

DALLAS*** (1950) 94m WB c

Gary Cooper *(Blayde "Reb" Hollister)*, Ruth Roman *(Tonia Robles)*, Steve Cochran *(Brant Marlow)*, Raymond Massey *(Will Marlow)*, Barbara Payton *(Flo)*, Leif Erickson *(Martin Weatherby)*, Antonio Moreno *(Felipe)*, Jerome Cowan *(Matt Coulter)*, Reed Hadley *(Wild Bill Hickok)*, Gil Donaldson *(Luis)*, Zon Murray *(Cullen Marlow)*, Will Wright *(Judge Harper)*, Monte Blue *(The Sheriff)*, Byron Keith *(Jason Trask)*, Steve Dunhill *(Dink)*, Charles Watts *(Bill Walters)*, Jose Dominguez *(Carlos)*, Gene

Evans (Drunk), Jay "Slim" Talbot (Stage Driver), Billie Bird (School Teacher), Frank Kreig (Politician), Tom Fadden (Mountaineer), Hal K. Dawson (Drummer), Buddy Roosevelt (Northerner), Alex Montoya (Vaquero), Dolores Corvall (Mexican Servant), Fred Graham (Lou), Charles Horvath, Winn Wright, Carl Andre (Cowpunchers), Ann Lawrence (Mrs. Walters), O. Z. Whitehead (Settler), Mike Donovan (Citizen), Glenn Thompson (Guard), Frank McCarroll, Larry McGrath, Al Ferguson (Citizens), Dewey Robinson, Roy Bucko, Buddy Shaw, Dave Dunbar, Oscar Williams (Prisoners), Fred Kelsey (Carter), Benny Corbett (Bystander).

Strong silent Cooper is a gunslinging ex-Confederate officer whom we first see in the middle of a sun-baked street facing Wild Bill Hickok (Hadley), and is ostensibly killed by the frontier marshal. It's all an act to allow the notorious Cooper to later pose as a newly appointed U.S. Marshal in wide-open Dallas, switching identities with namby-pamby Erickson. In Dallas, Cooper goes after the evil Marlow brothers—Massey, the brains, and Cochran and Murray, the brawn of the gang that runs Dallas. This is also the same terrible trio that burned down Cooper's ancestral home during the Civil War, he later learns. Coupled to these sins, Massey hatches a scheme to steal the vast lands owned by Moreno, whose sultry daughter Roman has captured Coop's heart. After gunning down Murray and Cochran, Cooper rides to the rescue of Moreno's family. Massey and thugs are holding Roman for ransom until Moreno returns to the hacienda with all the funds he can draw from the bank. But the serape-clad man entering the hacienda estate is Cooper in disguise. He kills several henchmen before dueling it out with Massey in the darkened Spanish mansion, saving his girl and gleaning vengeance for past wrongs with one fatal shot. DALLAS is an above-average western with a strong score by Steiner, who never created a bad one, and brisk direction by Heisler, but the story is an old one and despite Cooper's commanding presence the plot is fairly predictable.

p, Anthony Veiller; d, Stuart Heisler; w, John Twist (based on his story); ph, Ernest Haller (Technicolor); m, Max Steiner; ed, Clarence Kolster; art d, Douglas Bacon; set d, George James Hopkins; cos, Marjorie Best.

Western (PR:A MPAA:NR)

DALTON GANG, THE*½ (1949) 62m Lippert bw

Don Barry (Larry West), Robert Lowery (Blackie Mullet), James Millican (Sheriff Jeb Marvin), Betty Adams (Polly), Byron Foulger (Amos Boling), J. Farrell MacDonald (Judge Price), Greg McClure (Missouri Ganz), George Lewis (Chief Irahu), Marshall Reed (Joe), Ray Bennett (Gorman), Lee Roberts (Mac), Cliff Taylor (Doctor), Cactus Mack (Stage Driver).

Barry, with the help of a tribe of friendly Indians, tracks down the notorious Dalton boys and brings them to justice, while at the same time romancing, in his rugged way, Adams, but in no way that will offend the juvenile trade. A fair western for its time.

p, Ron Ormond; d&w, Ford Beebe; ph, Archie Dalzell; m, Walter Greene; ed, Hugh Winn.

Western (PR:A MPAA:NR)

DALTON GIRLS, THE** (1957) 71m UA bw

Merry Anders (Holly Dalton), Lisa Davis (Rose Dalton), Penny Edwards (Columbine Dalton), Sue George (Marigold Dalton), John Russell (W. T. "Illinois" Grey), Ed Hinton (Detective Hiram Parsh), Glenn Dixon (Mr. Slidell, The Mortician), Johnny Western (Joe), Malcolm Atterbury (Mr. Sewell the Bank Manager), Douglas Henderson (Bank Cashier), Kevin Enright (George the Bartender), Al Wyatt (Sheriff St. Ives), H. E. Willmering (Marshal), Red Morgan (Stage Driver), K.C. MacGregor (Way Station Hostler), David Swapp (Way Station Helper).

Four daughters of one of the famous outlaw Daltons turn to banditry after their father is killed. Using their womanly wiles, they pull off several successful robberies. Two of the sisters want out of the bandit business, while the other two have grown to like it. Intertwined through the story is a gambler who romances one of the girls. The film ends in a tragic manner as the girls try to gun their way to freedom after being cornered in a town. Only one survives, and she marries the gambler. None of this rather witless fare is based on fact.

p, Howard W. Koch; d, Reginald Le Borg; w, Maurice Tombragel, Herbert Purdom; ph, Carl E. Guthrie; m, Les Jim Baxter; ed, John F. Schreyer.

Western (PR:A MPAA:NR)

DALTON THAT GOT AWAY* (1960) 69m Dalton Film Co. bw

Michael Connors, Elsie Cardenas, Carlos Rivas, Felix Moreno, Zachary Milton, Stilman Segar, George Russell, Reed Howes, Francisco Reynolds, Quintin Bulnes, Sam Murphy, Arlene King.

Routine, rather dull oater dealing with Emmett Dalton, the one brother who survived the disastrous Coffeyville, Kansas raid in 1892. (Another brother, Bill, was not with Bob, Grat, and Emmett at Coffeyville but was later shot to death by peace officers while sitting on his front porch.)

p, Henry H. Lube; d, Jimmy Salvador; w, E. L. Erwin.

Western (PR:A MPAA:NR)

DALTONS RIDE AGAIN, THE** (1945) 72m UNIV bw

Alan Curtis (Emmett Dalton), Kent Taylor (Bob Dalton), Lon Chaney, Jr. (Grat Dalton), Noah Beery, Jr. (Ben Dalton), Martha O'Driscoll (Mary), Jess Barker (Jeff), Thomas Gomez (McKenna), Milburn Stone (Graham), John Litel (Bohannon), Walter Sande (Wilkins), Douglas Dumbrille (Sheriff), Virginia Brissac (Mrs. Walters), Stanley Andrews (Walters), Fern Emmett (Miss Crain), Charles Miller (Haines), Cyril Delevanti (Jennings), Frank Dae (Judge), Ruth Lee (Mrs. Bohannon), Ed Cassidy (Sproules), Ethan Laidlaw (Trailer), Henry Hall (Marshal).

This action-packed western sees the title brothers trying to go straight, but being forced back into a life of crime. The boys in the beginning of the film are about to

give up their life of crime and migrate to Argentina. However, they get sidetracked when they help a friend who is about to be the victim of a land grab plot. The friend gets murdered by a land company's hired killer. The boys save his widow but are forced to hide out in the hills, and are accused of assorted crimes which have really been perpetrated by the land company's thugs. So, as the title so aptly says, "the Daltons ride again," but this time they are committing their own crimes. O'Driscoll plays the daughter of a newspaper publisher who falls in love with brother Curtis. Three of the boys end up getting killed in an attempted bank robbery, with Curtis being very badly wounded and facing a life prison sentence. O'Driscoll, faithful to him despite his wrongdoings, says she'll wait for him.

p, Howard Welsch; d, Ray Taylor; w, Roy Chanslor, Paul Gangelin, Henry Blankfort; ph, Charles Van Enger; ed, Paul Landres; md, Frank Skinner; art d, John B. Goodman, Harold H. MacArthur; set d, Russell A. Gausman, Arthur D. Leddy.

Western (PR:A MPAA:NR)

DALTON'S WOMEN, THE* (1950) 80m Western Adventure/Howco bw

Lash LaRue, Al St. John, Jack Holt, Tom Neal, Pamela Blake, Jacqueline Fontaine, Raymond Hatton, Lyle Talbot, Tom Tyler, J. Farrell MacDonald, Terry Frost, Stanley Price, Bud Osborne, Cliff Taylor, Buff Brown, Clarke Stevens, Lee Bennett, Jimmie Martin, Archie Twitchell.

Mindless mess about the female followers and wives of the Dalton gang destroyed in Kansas in 1892. LaRue, all in black as usual, tries to bring the female felons to justice with a sneer and a whip.

p, Ron Ormond; d, Thomas Carr; w, Ormond, Maurice Tombragel.

Western (PR:A MPAA:NR)

DAM BUSTERS, THE***½ (1955, Brit.) 125m ABF/WB bw

Richard Todd (Wing Cmdr. Guy Gibson), Michael Redgrave (Dr. Barnes N. Wallis), Ursula Jeans (Mrs. Wallis), Basil Sydney (Sir Arthur Harris), Derek Farr (Group Capt. J. N. H. Whitworth), Patrick Barr (Capt. Joseph Summers), Charles Carson (Doctor), Stanley Van Beers (Sir David Pye), Colin Tapley (Dr. W. H. Glanville), Raymond Huntley (Laboratory Official), Ernest Clark (AVM Ralph Cochrane), John Fraser (Flt. Lt. Hopgood), Nigel Stock (Flt. Lt. Spofford), Bill Kerr (Flt. Lt. Martin), George Baker (Flt. Lt. Maltby), Robert Shaw (Flt. Sgt. Pulford), Anthony Doonan (Flt. Lt. Hutchinson), Harold Goodwin (Crosby), Laurence Naismith (Farmer), Frank Phillips (BBC Announcer), Ewen Solon, Patrick McGoohan.

Exciting war story based on two books about the RAF's destruction of the Ruhr dams that supplied industrial Germany with the power needed to run the huge factories. Redgrave is a scientist with an idea about how to demolish the Nazi war machine. The dams are built in such a fashion that they could not be done in by the bombs of 1943. He conceives of what might be called a "bouncing baby bomb" which would be delivered low, skip along the water like a flat stone thrown sidearm, and hit the dam in the middle. Redgrave tries his theory with golf balls and ping pong balls but they can never be certain it'll work in practice unless they attempt it. The bomb must be dropped from a height of 60 feet by a plane traveling exactly 240 miles per hour precisely 1,800 feet from the target. The job of educating the crew is taken on by Richard Todd and much of this absorbing film has to do with that training. Since this is based on history, we know that it did work and marked an important turning point in the war effort. The final sequences are a combination of the real newsreel footage and some fine special effects work by Gilbert Taylor. Although the film has many other actors, the honors belong to Todd and Redgrave as the men who were actually responsible. There was no love interest, no phony bravado, just an honest depiction of the way it was, understated and quietly heroic. It was well made but 20 minutes too long. Director Michael Anderson followed this with 1984 and AROUND THE WORLD IN EIGHTY DAYS.

p, Robert Clark, W.A. Whittaker; d, Michael Anderson, Sr.; w, R.C. Sherriff (based on Enemy Coast Ahead by Wing Cmdr. Guy Gibson and The Dam Busters by Paul Brickhill); ph, Edwin Hillier; m, Louis Levy (also attributed to Eric Coates, Leighton Lucas); ed, Richard Best; prod d, Robert Jones; spec eff, Gilbert Taylor.

Historical Drama/War **Cas.** (PR:A MPAA:NR)

DAMAGED GOODS* (1937) 56m GN bw

Pedro de Cordoba (Dr. Walker), Phyllis Barry (Margie), Douglas Walton (George), Arletta Duncan (Henrietta), Ferdinand Munier (Mr. Allen), Esther Dale (Mrs. Dupont), Clarence Wilson (Dr. Shryer), Greta Meyer (Bertha), Frank Melton (Jack), Gretchen Thomas (The Victim).

Venereal disease was the hot topic of 1937, and several films came out on the subject. The story here concerns a young married man who contracts syphilis, and infects his wife and child. The villain of the story isn't the disease itself but the public ignorance of it. The film is based on a French play by Eugene Brieux and is a remake of the 1914 film of the same name. Upton Sinclair adapted this film and set the story in America. DAMAGED LIVES, another film dealing with the same subject, was released a week before this one.

p, Phil Goldstone; d, Phil Stone; w, Joseph Hoffman (adapted by Upton Sinclair from the play by Eugene Brieux); ph, Ira Morgan; ed, Holbrook Todd.

Drama (PR:C MPAA:NR)

DAMAGED LIVES* (1937) 61m Weldon bw

Diane Sinclair (Joan), Lyman Williams (Donald Bradley), Cecelia Parker (Rosie), George Irving (Mr. Bradley, Sr.), Almeda Fowler (Mrs. Bradley), Jason Robards (Dr. Hall), Marceline Day (Mrs. Hall), Charlotte Merriam (Clyce), Murray Kinnell (Dr. Leonard), Harry Meyers (Nat).

Another film dealing with 1937's hot topic, venereal disease. It tells the story of a young married couple and of a mistake of the husband's that nearly ruins their lives. The film went through a tough struggle with censors when it opened, but by today's standards it is understandably sophomoric in its handling of the subject. At the end of the sixty-one-minute narrative, the actor playing the doctor gives a twenty-nine-minute lecture on venereal disease. This film was released one week before the opening of another film on the subject, DAMAGED GOODS.

d, Edgar C. Ulmer; w, Donald Davis, Ulmer (based on a story by Davis and Ulmer); ph, Al Sieglar.

Drama **(PR:C MPAA:NR)**

DAMAGED LOVE*

(1931) 65m Superior Talking Pictures/Worldwide Sonoart bw

Charles Starrett *(Jim Powell)*, Eloise Taylor *(Rose Powell)*, Betty Garde *(Madge Sloan)*, Charles Trowbridge *(Ned Indicott)*, June Collyer *(Nita Meredith)*.

This far-below-par love story/triangle has Collyer as a free-love exponent determined to get her already married man. She starts down the road to motherhood to trap him in marriage, but he goes back to his wife, leaving Collyer out in the cold.

d, Irvin Willat; w, Frederic and Fanny Hatton (based on the stage play "Pleasant Sins" by Thomas W. Broadhurst); song, "As Long As We Are In Each Other's Arms."

Drama **(PR:C MPAA:NR)**

DAMES***½

(1934) 90m WB bw

Joan Blondell *(Mabel Anderson)*, Dick Powell *(Jimmy Higgens)*, Ruby Keeler *(Barbara Hemingway)*, ZaSu Pitts *(Mathilda Hemingway)*, Hugh Herbert *(Ezra Ounce)*, Guy Kibbee *(Horace)*, Arthur Vinton *(Bulger)*, Sammy Fain *(Buttercup Baumer)*, Phil Regan *(Johnny Harris)*, Arthur Aylesworth *(Conductor)*, Leila Bennett *(Laura the Maid)*, Berton Churchill *(H. Elsworthy Todd)*, Patricia Harper, Ruth Eddings, De Don Blunier, Gloria Faythe, Diana Douglas *(Chorus Girls)*, Lester Dorr *(Elevator Starter)*, Eddy Chandler *(Guard)*, Harry Holman *(Spanish War Veteran)*, Fred "Snowflake" Toones *(Porter)*, Frank Darien *(Druggist)*, Eddie Kane *(Harry, the Stage Manager)*, Charlie Williams *(Dance Director)*, Phil Tead *(Reporter)*, Johnny Arthur *(Billings the Secretary)*.

A mindless story is punctuated by mind-boggling choreography from Berkeley and a sprightly score by Warren, Dubin, Wrubel, Dixon, Fain, and Kahal. The see-through plot is that Hugh "Woo Woo" Herbert is a rich nut who tells his cousin, Kibbee, that he is going to get ten million dollars because he is such a moral man. Herbert is an eccentric reformer who has but one goal in life: the eradication of anything that's "fun." Herbert is starting a new Reformers Society and Kibbee is to help him. The main thing they must do is keep distant cousin Powell away as Powell is associated with the theater which makes him morally reprehensible. While Herbert sucks on his cure-all libation, "Dr. Silver's Golden Elixir," he and Kibbee are aboard a train where stranded chorus girl Blondell is found in Kibbee's compartment. He gives her a few bucks to keep mum and asks her not to tell anyone about being in his compartment because if there were the slightest impropriety, cousin Herbert would withdraw the money. In New York, Powell and Blondell meet and he tells her that he's having a problem finding enough money to produce his new musical (it's always the case in real life, why not in movies?). Blondell thinks she can wangle it out of Kibbee and she does. Meanwhile Kibbee's daughter, Keeler, has fallen hard for Powell (they were to play these roles in many movies) and is jealous of his friendship with Blondell. (In real life, Dick Powell's friendship with Joan Blondell blossomed into love and they were wed two years later, 1936, and remained married until 1945). Keeler is given a role in the musical and rehearsals continue. Kibbee and Herbert are going to this scandalous show and Herbert is going to hire thugs to wreck the show if other kinds of persuasions fail. But the "Golden Elixir"—which is little more than alcohol with some flavoring—has taken its toll and the hoodlums are erroneously signaled. They begin pelting the stage with eggs, tomatoes, and other debris, and a riot ensues. Everyone, including Kibbee and Herbert, is tossed in the slammer. While incarcerated, Herbert finds that chorus girls are people, too, and a lot more fun than some of those bluenoses he's been palling around with. He revises his thinking; Powell and Keeler (who are thirteenth cousins, lest you fear that the specter of, gasp, incest arise) reconcile a trumped-up disagreement, and everyone is happy. Now, plot aside, watch this film to see Berkeley's inventive staging of what lesser minds might have ruined. Intricate geometry mixed with succulent pulchritude and creative photography are seen in spectacular order as several knockout women, each with a jigsaw piece on her back, bend over to make a full face of Keeler which then becomes real. Blondell is at an ironing board and the pile of pajamas and underwear comes to life, and more and more. There is surely enough of Berkeley's material to make a movie on its own. He was one of a kind. Songs: "The Girl At the Ironing Board," "Dames," "I Only Have Eyes For You" (Al Dubin, Harry Warren), "When You Where A Smile On Your Mother's Lips and A Twinkle In Your Father's Eye" (Irving Kahal, Sammy Fain), "Try To See It My Way" (Mort Dixon, Allie Wrubel).

p, Darryl F. Zanuck; d, Ray Enright; w, Delmer Daves (based on a story by Robert Lord, Daves); ph, Sid Hickox; ed, Harold McLernon; md, Leo F. Forbstein; art d, Robert Haas, Willie Pogany; cos, Orry-Kelly; ch, Busby Berkeley.

Musical Comedy **Cas.** **(PR:AA MPAA:NR)**

DAMES AHOY*

(1930) 63m UNIV bw

Glenn Tryon *(Jimmy Chase)*, Eddie Gribbon *(Mac Dougal)*, Otis Harlan *(Bill Jones)*, Helen Wright *(Mabel McGuire)*, Gertrude Astor *(The Blonde)*.

A comedy about three sailors looking for a blonde woman who tricked one of them out of his pay. Old sea dog Harlan was in a drunken stupor when he married the golddigger. All he can remember is that she had a strawberry birthmark above her knee. A large portion of the film has Harlan and his two buddies looking up the skirts of all the blondes they come across. In the end, one of the other sailors finds the girl, falls in love with her, and, with Harlan's blessing, marries her. Song: "Barnacle Bill The Sailor."

d, William James Craft; w, Matt Taylor, Albert De Mond (based on a story by Sherman Lowe); ph, C. Allen Jones; ed, Harry Lieb.

Comedy **(PR:AAA MPAA:NR)**

DAMIEN—OMEN II*

(1978) 109m FOX c

William Holden *(Richard Thorn)*, Lee Grant *(Ann Thorn)*, Jonathan Scott-Taylor *(Damien Thorn)*, Robert Foxworth *(Paul Buher)*, Nicholas Pryor *(Charles Warren)*, Lew Ayres *(Bill Atherton)*, Sylvia Sidney *(Aunt Marion)*, Lance Henriksen *(Sgt. Neff)*, Lucas Donat *(Mark Thorn)*, Alan Arbus *(Pasarian)*, Meshach Taylor *(Dr. Kane)*, John J. Newcombe *(Teddy)*, John Charles Burns *(Butler)*, Paul Cook *(Colonel)*, Robert Ingham *(Teacher)*, William B. Fosser *(Minister)*, Corney Morgan *(Greenhouse Technician)*, Russell P. Delia *(Truck Driver)*, Judith Dowd *(Maid)*, Thomas O. Erhart, Jr. *(Sergeant)*, Anthony Hawkins *(Pasarian's Assistant)*, Robert J. Jones, Jr. *(Guide)*, Rusdi Lane *(Jim)*, Charles Mountain *(Priest)*, Cornelia Sanders *(Girl)*, Felix Shuman *(Dr. Fiedler)*, James Spinks *(Technician)*, Owen Sullivan *(Byron)*, William J. Whelehan *(Guard)*, Elizabeth Shepherd *(Joan Hart)*, Fritz Ford *(Murray)*.

The sequel to the chilling and disturbing THE OMEN, this film would have been better left unmade. However, a sequel is the price a film must pay for success, and this fits the pattern of all sequels, as it is lousy. At the end of THE OMEN, little Damien was six years old, already one hell of an Antichrist, and responsible for the deaths of his mother and father and a slew of other people. At the end of the first film, he is holding hands with the President of the U.S. Some years later Damien is now thirteen years old and has a double-edged problem. Besides being the Antichrist, he is a spoiled and obnoxious teenager. He lives with his aunt and uncle, Grant and Holden, who suspect nothing as Damien has been on good behavior for the last seven years. Suddenly his old cranky aunt Sidney becomes suspicious of him, and a raven, Damien's protector, scares her to death. The raven kills a few more people for Damien, until Damien reads the Book of Revelations at military school and finds out what he is all about. Now Damien does all his own killing. He quickly gets rid of his second set of relatives, and becomes the heir of an industrial empire, leaving the door open for an even worse sequel, THE FINAL CONFLICT.

p, Harvey Bernhard; d, Don Taylor; w, Stanley Mann, Michael Hodges; ph, Bill Butler (Panavision, DeLuxe Color); m, Jerry Goldsmith; ed, Robert Brown; prod d, Philip M. Jeffries, Fred Harpman.

Horror **Cas.** **(PR:O MPAA:R)**

DAMN CITIZEN**

(1958) 88m UNIV bw

Keith Andes *(Col. Francis C. Grevemberg)*, Maggie Hayes *(Dorothy Grevemberg)*, Gene Evans *(Maj. Al Arthur)*, Lynn Bari *(Pat Noble)*, Jeffrey Stone *(Paul Musso)*, Edward C. Platt *(Joseph Kosta)*, Ann Robinson *(Cleo)*, Sam Buffington *(DeButts)*, Clegg Hoyt *(Sheriff Lloyd)*, Rusty Lane *(Inspector Sweeney)*, Kendall Clark *(Col. Thomas Hastings)*, Charles Horvath *(Lt. Palmer)*, Carolyn Kearney *(Nancy)*, Aaron M. Kohn *(Himself)*, Rev. J.D. Grey *(Himself)*, Richard R. Foster *(Himself)*, Pershing Gervais *(Big Jim)*, Aaron A. Edgecombe *(Maj. Sterling)*, Rev. Robert H. Jamieson *(Capt. Desmond)*, Paul S. Hostetler *(Father Masters)*, Nathaniel F. Oddo *(Thomas Gleason)*, Dudley C. Foley, Jr. *(Fowler)*, Charles A. Murphy *(Judge)*, George M. Trussell *(Harry)*, Jack Dempsey *(Reporter)*, Frank Hay *(Reporter)*, Tiger Flowers *(News Commentator)*, John Schowest *(Satchel Man)*.

This film is based on the true-to-life exploits of Col. Francis C. Grevemberg, a WW II hero who single-handedly won a war against crime and corruption in his native Louisiana. Grevemberg, played by Andes, is invited by the new governor to serve as the superintendent of state police and to wage an all-out, no-holds-barred battle on the crime and corruption that had flourished in the state for years. He finds himself opposed at every turn, but with the aid of his staff he cleans up. The screenplay was written by Stirling Silliphant, who would go on to win an Oscar for his screenplay of IN THE HEAT OF THE NIGHT.

p, Herman Webber; d, Robert Gordon; w, Stirling Silliphant; ph, Ellis W. Carter; m, Henry Mancini; ed, Patrick McCormack; md, Joseph Gershenson.

Crime Drama **(PR:A MPAA:NR)**

DAMN THE DEFIANT!***

(1962, Brit.) 101m G.W. Films/COL c (GB: HMS DEFIANT)

Alec Guinness *(Capt. Crawford)*, Dirk Bogarde *(Lt. Scott-Padget)*, Maurice Denham *(Surgeon Goss)*, Nigel Stock *(Senior Midshipman Kilpatrick)*, Richard Carpenter *(Lt. Ponsonby)*, Peter Gill *(Lt. D'Arblay)*, David Robinson *(Harvey Crawford)*, Robin Stewart *(Pardoe)*, Ray Brooks *(Hayes)*, Peter Greenspan *(Johnson)*, Anthony Quayle *(Vizard)*, Tom Bell *(Evans)*, Murray Melvin *(Wagstaffe)*, Victor Maddern *(Dawlish)*, Bryan Pringle *(Sgt. Kneebone)*, Johnny Briggs *(Wheatley)*, Brian Phelan *(Grimshaw)*, Toke Townley *("Silly Billy" Whiting)*, Declan Mulholland *(Morrison)*, Walter Fitzgerald *(Adm. Jackson)*, Joy Shelton *(Mrs. Crawford)*, Anthony Oliver *(Tavern Leader)*, Russell Napier *(Flag Captain)*, Michael Coles *(Flag Lieutenant)*, André Maranne *(Col. Giraud)*, Ann Lynn *(Young Wife)*.

British sea adventure set in the late 1700s during the Napoleonic wars sees Guinness as the captain of the *HMS Defiant* and Bogarde as his brutal lieutenant, whose cruel treatment of the sailors has added fuel to the fire among the crew who have planned to participate in a fleet-wide mutiny against the British Navy. Guinness is unaware of Bogarde's behavior, but when the lieutenant inflicts a vicious punishment upon Guinness' son (who serves as a midshipman on the vessel) he begins to see the light. A confrontation between the two is delayed when the ship comes across a French frigate and a battle ensues for its capture. The *Defiant* wins the contest, but it costs Guinness an arm. A captured French officer reveals that his country plans to invade England when the massive mutiny is put into action (because the fleet will be useless). Eventually, the mutiny is done under the leadership of Quayle, but Guinness convinces the mutineer to head the ship back to England to warn the military of the planned invasion by the French. When the king hears of the mutiny, he agrees to meet the demands of the men and the ship returns to an uneasy state of normality. The truce is shattered, however, when an angry crew member knifes Bogarde and once again Quayle heads the ship out to sea. There it meets up with a French fireship and a massive battle ensues wherein Quayle redeems himself by leading his men into action.

p, John Brabourne; d, Lewis Gilbert; w, Nigel Kneale, Edmund H. North (based on the novel *Mutiny* by Frank Tilsley); ph, Christopher Challis (CinemaScope/Eastmancolor); m, Clifton Parker; ed, Peter Hunt; art d, Arthur Lawson; set d, Terence Morgan II; spec eff, Howard Lydecker, Ernie Sullivan.

War/Adventure **(PR:A MPAA:NR)**

DAMN YANKEES**** (1958) 110m WB c (GB: WHAT LOLA WANTS)

Tab Hunter *(Joe Hardy)*, Gwen Verdon *(Lola)*, Ray Walston *(Applegate)*, Russ Brown *(Van Buren)*, Shannon Bolin *(Meg)*, Nathaniel Frey *(Smokey)*, Jimmie Komack *(Rocky)*, Rae Allen *(Gloria)*, Robert Shafer *(Joe Boyd)*, Jean Stapleton *(Sister)*, Albert Linville *(Vernon)*, Bob Fosse *(Mambo Dancer)*, Elizabeth Howell *(Doris)*.

So many movies have used the Faust legend that they are too numerous to recall. The ones that immediately come to mind are ALL THAT MONEY CAN BUY, THE BAND WAGON, and ALIAS NICK BEAL. The stage version of DAMN YANKEES ran more than one thousand performances and can still be found on stages everywhere where baseball is loved and the Yankees are despised. Rooting for the Yankees was like rooting for General Motors and the most lowly team of the era was the Washington Senators, about whom it was said: "First In War, First In Peace, and Last In The American League." Shafer is a middle-aged Senators fan who knows that summer means depression. It's muggy, rainy, and the team is due for what may be the worst season ever, a painful prospect for someone who has followed the team since the glory days when Bucky Harris, age twenty-four, managed the 1924 team to the pennant. Shafer says aloud that he would sell his soul to the devil for a long ball hitter and the chance to beat the hated Yankees. That's heard by Walston, the devil, and a deal is struck. Shafer disappears and in his place is tall, handsome, blond Hunter. Neighbors wonder what happened to Shafer but his wife knows in her heart that he will return. Hunter tries out for the Senators and knocks the cover off the ball. The manager, Brown, says they'll sign him up but he has to spend a year in the minors before having a crack at the big leagues. Hunter explains that he doesn't have the time and manages to convince the team that he's ready. A female reporter, Allen, wants to learn more about this young man so she begins to investigate and Hunter's stories about his youth, his town of birth, just don't jibe. Meanwhile, he is whacking the old horsehide around the diamond and the lowly Senators are making a run for it. Hunter takes a room in his former house, just so he can look at the woman who has been his wife for so many wonderful years, Bolin. As the season comes near the conclusion, there's a bit of waffling on the part of Hunter regarding his soul-for-sale deal with Walston. Serious reinforcements are called for and it's Gwen Verdon, a 172-year old witch, who is the devil's sexiest seductress. Verdon had been the ugliest woman in New England and made the same deal with the devil. Now she looks wonderful but must do his evil bidding for eternity. Verdon uses all of her wiles. The contract with the devil comes due on the last day of the season and the Senators must win this game to get into the series. The last play is a long, long drive out to Hunter who races after it and turns into an old man as he catches the ball and falls. Pandemonium. The Senators have vanquished the Yanks and in the melee that follows Hunter/Shafer leaves the field and is never seen again by anyone except the wife he loves so much, and the devil is foiled by Shafer's love for Bolin. This picture had absolutely everything—except the right male lead. Hunter was out of his element singing and dancing with such consummate pros as Verdon and Walston. There were several hit songs from the show and they became even more popular once the film was released, and the superb dancing matches the music. There were touches of reality in the story as several of the players mimicked real-life big-leaguers. The manager was like Casey Stengel and one of the Senators looked and sounded like Yogi Berra. The buck-toothed kid, Rocky, was the man who later wrote, produced, and directed many television series, including "The Courtship of Eddie's Father," "Welcome Back, Kotter," and "Chico And The Man." Jimmie Komack, has since moved into features with PORKY'S REVENGE. Tunesmiths Adler and Ross had a short career together as Ross died at an early age after the success of this show and their prior hit, PAJAMA GAME. Other than Hunter, just about everyone else was brought from New York to appear in the film. Evidently, one of the brothers Warner thought Hunter would be the proper insurance for their investment as he had already appeared in ten films and was one of the leading fan-mail recipients on the Warner Bros. lot. In later years, as he matured, Hunter actually got much better and began to spoof himself in several films as well as on the stage in various productions. In a small role as Bolin's sister is a little-known Broadway actress who also appeared in the New York version of "Bells Are Ringing" and was able to reprise her role in the film. Born Jeanne Murray and married for many years to producer Bill Putch, it is Jean Stapleton, who was already getting her characterization of Edith in gear, long before Norman Lear wrote it. Look hard at her performance and you'll see what we mean. The character of Joe Hardy was loosely based on some of baseball's "phenoms" that were coming up after the war. The best-remembered of them was the Giant's Clint Hartung who was to be the new messiah for the men of Coogan's Bluff. He wasn't. That role was reserved for a young man whom Leo Durocher called "The Say Hey Kid" and if you don't know who he is, you should not be bothered with reading a review about a baseball movie in the first place. Songs: "Heart," "Whatever Lola Wants," "Who's Got the Pain?" "Shoeless Joe From Hannibal Mo," "There's Something about an Empty Chair," "Two Lost Souls," "A Little Brains, a Little Talent," "Those Were the Good Old Days," "Goodbye, Old Girl," "Six Months out of Every Year," "Game" (Richard Adler, Jerry Ross).

p&d, George Abbott, Stanley Donen; w, Abbott (based on the play by Abbott and Douglas Wallop, from Wallop's novel *The Year The Yankees Lost The Pennant*); ph, Harold Lipstein (Technicolor); ed, Frank Bracht; prod d, cos, William and Jean Eckart; art d, Stanley Fleischer; ch, Bob Fosse, Pat Ferrier.

Musical/Comedy **Cas.** **(PR:A MPAA:NR)**

DAMNATION ALLEY* (1977) 95m FOX c

Jan-Michael Vincent *(Tanner)*, George Peppard *(Denton)*, Dominique Sanda *(Janice)*, Paul Winfield *(Keegan)*, Jackie Earle Haley *(Billy)*, Kip Niven *(Perry)*, Robert Donner, Seamon Glass, Trent Dolan, Mark L. Taylor, Bob Hackman.

A poor adaptation of Roger Zelazny's post-nuclear holocaust novel of the same name, the film has Peppard, Vincent, and Winfield as the only survivors of an underground military complex blast after the holocaust. They set out across the country in two tank-like landmobiles to get to Albany, New York, which for some unexplained reason is the only place not destroyed by the bombs, and which has normal people still alive there. Along the way they encounter giant scorpions, flesh-eating cockroaches (which devour Winfield), weird electrical storms, and bands of marauding hillbillies. They also pick up Sanda, a lone woman, and Haley, a rock-throwing teen. Though Sanda is the first woman the men have seen since before the war, there is no romance or sex introduced into the film. The convoy rides through weird weather and a freak tidal-wave flood, and surfaces about two miles from Albany, where it is welcomed by the population. The film lacks any suspense or drama, and the special effects are not that special.

p, Jerome M. Zeitman, Paul Maslansky; d, Jack Smight; w, Alan Sharp, Lukas Heller (based on the novel by Roger Zelazny); ph, Harry Stradling, Jr. (DeLuxe Color); m, Jerry Goldsmith; ed, Frank J. Urioste; prod d, Preston Ames; art d, William Cruse; spec eff, Milt Rice; stunts, Dean Jeffries.

Science Fiction **(PR:C MPAA:PG)**

DAMNED, THE*** (1948, Fr.) 105m DIF bw (LES MAUDITS)

Henri Vidal *(The Physician)*, Florence Marly *(Hilde Garosi)*, Kurt Kronefeld *(Gen. Von Hauser)*, Anne Campion *(Ingrid)*, Jo Dest *(Forster)*, Michel Auclair *(Willy Morus)*, Fosco Giachetti *(Garosi)*, Paul Bernard *(Coutourier)*, Jean Didier *(The Captain)*, Dalio *(Larga)*.

In the closing days of World War II, a number of Nazi officials and various hangers-on flee Oslo in a U-boat, trying to make their way to South America. Along the way they are attacked by a destroyer and depth-charged. Marly, the wife of Count Giachetti and the mistress of German general Kronefeld, is wounded in the attack so the submarine lands along the French coast and they kidnap doctor Vidal. He realizes the danger he is in and so begins sowing the seeds of defeatism and despair among the passengers. Quite an interesting drama confined almost totally to one set, with very good performances by the entire cast. (In French, English, German, and Italian; English subtitles).

p, Andre Paulve; d, Rene Clement; w, Clement, Jacques Remy (based on a story by Jacques Companeez and Victor Alexandroff); ph, Henri Alekan; m, Yvies Baudirier; ed, Roger Dwyre; prod d, Paul Bertrand.

Drama **(PR:C MPAA:NR)**

DAMNED, THE (SEE: THESE ARE THE DAMNED, 1965, Brit.)

DAMNED DON'T CRY, THE*** (1950) 103m WB bw

Joan Crawford *(Ethel Whitehead [Lorna Hansen Forbes])*, David Brian *(George Castleman)*, Steve Cochran *(Nick Prenta)*, Kent Smith *(Martin Blackford)*, Hugh Sanders *(Grady)*, Selena Royle *(Patricia Longworth)*, Jacqueline de Wit *(Sandra)*, Morris Ankrum *(Mr. Whitehead)*, Eddie Marr *(Walter Talbot)*, Allan Smith *(Surveyor)*, Tris Coffin *(Maitre d'Hotel)*, Ned Glass *(Taxi Driver)*, Dabbs Greer, Paul McGuire *(Reporters)*, Rory Mallinson *(Johnny Enders)*, John Maxwell *(Doctor)*, Lyle Latell *(Trooper)*, Edith Evanson *(Mrs. Castleman)*, Richard Egan *(Roy)*, Sara Perry *(Mrs. Whitehead)*, Jimmy Moss *(Tommy)*.

Crawford arrives at her poverty-stricken homestead on the lam from gangsters and a long flashback then relates why she turned to a life of crime. A frustrated housewife living with her parents and married to laborer Egan, she leaves the factory town after her child is killed in an accident, becoming a cigar-store girl and meeting brilliant but boring Smith, an accounting wizard she latches onto and pushes into an association with crime czar Brian, promising Smith marriage but then becoming Brian's mistress, even though the underworld boss has an invalid wife. To smooth out Crawford's rough edges, Brian hires a down-and-out socialite, Royle, who brings culture and polish to the ruthlessly ambitious housewife. But Brian is just as ruthless and uses Crawford, passing her off as a Texas heiress, to worm information from a west coast rival, Cochran. Both men shoot it out after double-dealing and wheeling with Crawford. Cochran is killed and Brian is about to shoot Crawford but faithful Kent talks him out of it. Crawford flees into the night, driving her fur-wrapped body back to the shabby home where she began. At dawn, the story has come full circle and she sees Brian outside, waiting. She swallows her fear, steps outside and is shot down. But loyal Kent then shoots Brian to death. He clutches Crawford in his arms and at the fade-out it is not clear whether she will live or die but by then her character is so doubtful that any moralizing viewer would opt for curtains. The acting here is excellent, though Crawford infects her male leads with that melodramatic flair uniquely hers. (You either like Joan Crawford or you don't; no one was ever undecided about this actress.) The story is fine *film noir* and though it seems patched together in spots bears a strong resemblance to the life and times of mob girl Virginia Hill, with Cochran doing a convincing Bugsy Siegel.

p, Jerry Wald; d, Vincent Sherman; w, Harold Medford, Jerome Weidman (based on a story by Gertrude Walker); ph, Ted McCord; m, Daniele Amfitheatrof; ed, Rudi Fehr; md, Ray Heindorf; art d, Robert Haas; set d, William L. Kuehl; cos, Sheila O'Brien; makeup, Perc Westmore, Otis Malcolm.

Crime Drama **(PR:A-C MPAA:NR)**

DAMON AND PYTHIAS**

(1962) 99m MGM c (AKA: THE TYRANT OF SYRACUSE)

Don Burnett (Pythias), Guy Williams (Damon), Ilaria Occhini (Nerissa), Liana Orfei (Adrianna), Arnoldo Foa (Dionysius), Carlo Giustino (Cariso), Andrea Bosic (Arcanos), Carla Bonavera (Mereka), Osvaldo Ruggeri (Demetrius), Maurizio Baldoni (Dionysius the Younger), Franco Fantasia (Fencing Master), Marina Berti (Mereka), Lawrence Montaigne (Flutist), Carlo Rizzo (Libia), Gianni Bonagura (Philemon), Aldo Silvani (Digenis), Carolyn Fonseca (Chloe), Giovanna Maculani (Hermione), Enrico Salvatore, Tiberio Murgia, Enrico Glori, Luigi Bonos, Vittorio Bonos, Franco Ressel, Tiberio Mitri.

This spear and sandal epic was shot on location in Italy, and stars Don Burnett and Guy Williams, who would later go on to fame in the TV series "Lost in Space" as the title characters. The story is based on the Damon and Pythias legend of two friends who have their friendship put to the test. Williams is a rascally Bohemian in ancient Syracuse, while Burnett is the Athenian proponent of the Pythagorean, pre-Christ, love thy neighbor philosophy.

p, Sam Jaffe; d, Curtis Bernhardt; w, Bridget Boland, Barry Oringer (based on a story by Sam Marx, Oringer, Franco Riganti); ph, Aldo Toni (Eastmancolor); m, Angelo Francesco Lavagnino; ed, Nicolo Lazzari; md, Franco Ferrara; cos, Adriana Berselli.

Drama (PR:A MPAA:NR)

DAMSEL IN DISTRESS, A***

(1937) 100m RKO bw

Fred Astaire (Jerry), George Burns (George), Gracie Allen (Gracie), Joan Fontaine (Lady Alyce Marshmorton), Reginald Gardiner (Keggs), Ray Noble (Reggie), Constance Collier (Lady Caroline Marshmorton), Montagu Love (Lord John Marshmorton), Harry Watson (Albert), Jan Duggan (Miss Ruggles), Mario Berini (Singing Voice of Gardiner), Pearl Amatore, Betty Rone, Mary Dean, Jac George (Madrigal Singers), Joe Niemeyer (Halliday Impersonator), Bill O'Brien (Chauffeur), Mary Gordon (Cook), Ralph Brooks, Fred Kelsey (Sightseers), Maj. Sam Harris (Dance Extra).

Take Astaire to sing and dance, take the Gershwins to write the score, take Burns and Allen to provide the comedy and what do you get? The first box-office loser for Astaire ever! But why? It was a remake of a 1920 film and seemed to have everything on its side, including a very witty screenplay by Wodehouse, Lauren, and Pagano about an American dancer who was visiting Blighty and fell in love with a royal bit of fluff, Fontaine, who was virtually a prisoner in her own castle. After the usual complications, love conquers and there is a happy "hands across the Atlantic" marriage. With tunes like "A Foggy Day In London Town" and "Nice Work If You Can Get It" and with Oscar-winning choreography from Hermes Pan, the only answer to the film's lack of success was in the casting of Joan Fontaine to be one half of the dancing team. The trouble was, Joan Fontaine was *not* a musical performer. Legend states that Astaire had been wanting to do a musical without Ginger Rogers (to see if he could make it on his own?) and other gossip counters that Rogers wanted a break from dancing so she could make HAVING A WONDERFUL TIME and VIVACIOUS LADY, two nontuners. Burns and Allen were funny as usual and display more than a passing acquaintanceship with Terpsichore. Love and Gardiner are properly stiff-upper-lipped in their Jolly Olde roles. The choreography is particularly inventive, especially the "Fun House" sequence with all stops pulled out; treadmills, slides, rollers, distorted mirrors, tunnels, revolving barrels, and more. Despite all this, the picture fizzled because audiences felt that Fred without Ginger was like corned beef without cabbage; edible, but only if you're very, very hungry. Some wag was quoted as citing the Astaire-Rogers charm by saying: "She gave him sex, and he gave her class." Other songs: "The Jolly Tar and Milkmaid," "Stiff Upper Lip," "I Can't Be Bothered Now," "Put Me To The Test" (instrumental only), "Sing of Spring," "Things Are Looking Up," "Ah Che A Voi Perdoni Iddio" (from Flotow's "Marta").

p, Pandro S. Berman; d, George Stevens; w, P.G. Wodehouse, S.K. Lauren, Ernest Pagano (based on a play by Wodehouse and Ian Hay and a novel by Wodehouse); ph, Joseph H. August; ed, Henry Berman; md, Victor Baravelle; m/l, George and Ira Gershwin; art d, Van Nest Polglase; spec eff, Vernon L. Walker; ch, Hermes Pan and (uncredited) Astaire.

Musical/Comedy Cas. (PR:A MPAA:NR)

DAN CANDY'S LAW

(SEE: ALIEN THUNDER, 1975)

DAN MATTHEWS*

(1936) 66m COL bw (AKA: THE CALLING OF DAN MATTHEWS)

Richard Arlen (Dan Matthews), Charlotte Wynters (Hope Strong), Douglass Dumbrille (Hardy), Mary Kornman (Kitty Marley), Donald Cook (Blair), Frederick Burton (J.B. Strong), Lee Moran (Hypo), Tommy Dugan (Herman), Edward McWade (Partington), Carlyle Blackwell, Jr. (Tommy).

This film is a mediocre adaptation of the Harold Bell Wright novel of the same name. The story has the title character, a militant minister, trying to clean up the gambling, dancing, and similarly "decadent" activities in a section of his community called "Old Town," where youth is running rampantly to hell. Pretty creaky film fare today.

p, Sol Lesser; d, Phil Rosen; w, Dan Jarrett, Don Swift, Karl Brown, (based on the novel by Harold Bell Wright); ph, Allen G. Siegler.

Drama (PR:A MPAA:NR)

DANCE BAND*½

(1935, Brit.) 75m BIP bw

Charles Buddy Rogers (Buddy Morgan), June Clyde (Pat Shelley), Steven Geray (Steve Sarel), Magda Kun (Anny Ginger), Fred Duprez (Lewes), Leon Sherkot (Jim), Richard Hearne (Drunk), Hal Gordon (Spike), Albert Whelan (Bourne), Fred Groves (Mason), Jack Holland, June Hart (Dancers).

A light piece of musical fluff has Buddy Rogers as the leader of a dance band. He falls in love with the leader of an all-girl orchestra, Clyde, when the two compete in a band contest. Not much plot, but Rogers gets to strut his stuff as he croons, dances, and plays about a dozen instruments.

p, Walter C. Mycroft; d, Marcel Varnel; w, Roger Burford, Jack Davies, Jr., Denis Waldock; ph, Brian Langley; ed, S. Cole; md, Harry Acres; art d, David Rawnsley; m/l, Mabel Wayne, Desmond Carter, Arthur Young, Sonny Miller, Jack Shirley; songs: "Valparaiso," "Turtle-Dovey."

Musical (PR:A MPAA:NR)

DANCE, CHARLIE, DANCE**

(1937) 65m WB bw

Stuart Erwin (Andy Tucker), Jean Muir (Mary Mathews), Glenda Farrell (Fanny Morgan), Allen Jenkins (Alf Morgan), Addison Richards (Gordon Fox), Charles Foy (MacArthur), Chester Clute (Alvin Gussett), Mary Treen (Jennie Wolfe), Collette Lyons (Bobbie Benson), Tommy Wonder (Charlie), Frank Faylen (Ted Parks), Robert Homans (Tim), Harvey Clark (Richard Milton), Olive Olson (Jane Arden).

Based on George S. Kaufman's play "The Butter and Egg Man," the story has a gullible chump from the sticks, Erwin, who has twenty thousand dollars and a yen for show business. He is cornered into sinking all his money into a flop of a play by some shady promoters. Erwin turns the tables on them when he doctors the show's books and makes it a success in New York. Then he sells it back to the original promoters in time for them to be zapped with a plagiarism suit. The title for Kaufman's play came out of the raucous mouth of NYC nightclub hostess of the 1920s, Texas Guinan, who once asked a patron how he came by his money. He replied that he owned a large farm with many cows and chickens. "Oh, a butter and egg man, eh?" quipped the quick-witted Guinan. This film was made as a silent in 1928 for First National.

p, Bryan Foy; d, Frank McDonald; w, Crane Wilbur, William Jacobs (based on the play "The Butter and Egg Man" by George S. Kaufman); ph, Warren Lynch; ed, Frank Magee; m/l, "Dance, Charley, Dance," "Ballet De Bunk" (M.K. Jerome, Jack Scholl).

Comedy (PR:A MPAA:NR)

DANCE, FOOLS, DANCE***

(1931) 80m MGM bw

Joan Crawford (Bonnie Jordan), Lester Vail (Bob Townsend), Cliff Edwards (Bert Scranton), William Bakewell (Rodney Jordan), William Holden (Stanley Jordan), Clark Gable (Jake Luva), Earle Foxe (Wally Baxter), Purnell B. Pratt (Parker), Hale Hamilton (Selby), Natalie Moorhead (Della), Joan Marsh (Sylvia), Russell Hopton (Whitey), James Donlan (Police Reporter), Mortimer Snow, Sherry Hall (Reporters), Robert Livingston (Jack, a Hood), Tommy Shugrue (Photographer), Harry Semels (Dance Extra).

Based loosely on the St. Valentine's Day Massacre and the Jake Lingle murder case in Chicago, this fast-moving vehicle features Crawford, who came out of silent movies unscathed, and a very young Gable who was new to the MGM lot and just feeling his way around when he was sixth-billed here. Crawford and Bakewell have been spoiled terribly by their doting stockbroker father, Holden (no relation to the one you know about, whose name was William Beedle, Jr.), but when the stock market takes a nosedive, their lives are radically altered. Crawford has been having an affair with Vail and he'd like to make her an honest woman but she refuses, as honesty is not her best policy. Bakewell signs on with Gable, a local hooch-maker, but tells Crawford that he is going into the stock market as a customer's man. Crawford gets a job with a local newspaper. Gable arranges the murder of seven of his rivals and the whole town is certain he's the man behind the bloody assassinations but no one has a shred of evidence. Edwards (the same one who was a musical star as "Ukulele Ike" and who became famous for dubbing the voice of Jiminy Cricket in PINOCCHIO) is a reporter who gets the goods on Gable but Bakewell, under threat of death, must rub the scribe out before the news is spread. Crawford wants to know who killed Edwards so she changes her profession and goes undercover as an entertainer and joins the gang at Gable's club. Soon enough, Gable wiggles his ears at her and starts moving in. It's then that she finds out her brother was the trigger man on the Edwards snuff. Gable learns that Crawford isn't as jake as he thought she was and orders a ride for her. Bakewell can't bear the thought of losing his sister so a fight breaks out twixt him and Gable and both men are killed. Crawford escapes, gets the news of the Gable gang to the paper, and it's published. The crooks are gathered and then and only then does she agree to become housewifely to Vail. One scene had a bit of trouble clearing the censors; Crawford and some pals strip to their underwear to dive off a yacht. These days it would be totally nude and yawnable. In 1931, that was hot stuff.

d, Harry Beaumont; w, Aurania Rouverol, Richard Schayer (based on a story by Rouverol); ph, Charles Rosher; ed, George Hively; m/l, Frank Crumit, Lou Klein, Dale Winbrow, L. Cornell, Roy Turk, Fred Ahlert, Dorothy Fields, Jimmy McHugh.

Crime Drama (PR:A-C MPAA:NR)

DANCE, GIRL, DANCE*

(1933) 74m Invincible/Chesterfield bw

Alan Dinehart (Wade Valentine), Evalyn Knapp (Sally), Edward Nugent (Joe), Gloria Shea (Cleo), Ada May (Claudette), Theodore von Eltz (Laddie Norton), George Grandee (Mozart), Mae Busch (Lou Kenton).

A backstage story about a vaudeville actor, Nugent, who introduces Knapp to show business. They split soon after they marry. Tough trooper Busch helps Knapp by introducing her to cabaret owner, Dinehart, who helps her financially through motherhood, and Nugent shows up after the birth of their child for a happy ending. Songs: "It Takes a Lot of Jack," J. Keirn Brennan, George Grandee, "Seeing Is Believing," James Morley, Lee Zahler, "Peanut Vendor's Little Missus," Eugene Conrad, Harry Carroll.

d, Frank Strayer; w, Robert Ellis; ph, M.A. Anderson; ch, Pearl Eaton.

Musical/Comedy (PR:A MPAA:NR)

DANCE, GIRL, DANCE***½   (1940) 88m RKO bw

Maureen O'Hara (Judy), Louis Hayward (Jimmy Harris), Lucille Ball (Bubbles), Virginia Field (Elinor Harris), Ralph Bellamy (Steve Adams), Maria Ouspenskaya (Madame Lydia Basilova), Mary Carlisle (Sally), Katherine Alexander (Miss Olmstead), Edward Brophy (Dwarfie), Walter Abel (Judge), Harold Huber (Hoboken Gent), Ernest Truex (Bailey No. 1), Chester Clute (Bailey No. 2), Lorraine Krueger (Dolly), Lola Jensen (Daisy), Emma Dunn (Mrs. Simpson), Sidney Blackmer (Puss in Boots), Vivian Fay (The Ballerina), Ludwig Stossel (Caesar), Erno Verebes (Fitch), Ruth Seeley (Dimples), Thelma Woodruff (Mary), Marjorie Woodworth (Jane), Lasses White (Stage Manager), Philip Morris, Wade Boteler, Lee Shumway (Policemen), Robert Emmett O'Connor, Lee Phelps (Plainclothesmen), Paul Rensy (Headwaiter), Clyde Cook (Claude), Leo Cleary (Clerk), Kernan Cripps (Bailiff), Bob McKenzie (Fat Man), Harry Tyler (Barker), Jean La Fayette (Nanette), Paul Fung (Chinese Waiter), Dewey Robinson (Nightclub Manager), Ralph Sanford (Taxi Driver), Tony Martelli, Gino Corrado (Waiters), Milton Kibbee, Lew Harvey, Paul Burns, Paul Phillips (Reporters).

An unusual backstage musical where O'Hara, a budding ballerina, is forced to find work in burlesque houses where she becomes a stooge for stripper Ball while both compete for the affections of playboy Hayward. Ball plays it crassy and brassy all the way, hip-grinding to stardom on the back of O'Hara who is the butt of on-stage jokes as she attempts to perform ballet for lowbrow audiences jeering and taunting her artistic efforts until she stops mid-way during an act and reads the riot act to the mostly males present, a hortatory tirade that seems out-of-place in this otherwise humdrum and hokey programmer. Today the film is a feminist cult product, especially because it was directed by Arzner, Hollywood's lone female director for decades, but the production was never her brainchild. Roy Del Ruth began directing DANCE, GIRL, DANCE, but quit in two weeks of shooting because the script was so miserable he thought it beyond repair. Arzner scrapped his footage and started over again but she too sank deep into the boggy story where Ball stole almost every scene as the man-eating exploiteer and O'Hara came off as a rather simpy and decidedly stupid victim who twirls through her degradations with almost endless abandon. Everyone else in the cast appears lethargic and unenthusiastic in delivering their lines which were banal at best. Condemned as bad filmmaking when released, RKO lost more than $400,000 on this oddball creation. Songs include: "Jitterbug Bite," "Morning Star" (Edward Ward, Chet Forrest, Bob Wright), "Mother, What Do I Do Now?" (Forrest, Wright).

p, Harry E. Edington, Erich Pommer; d, Dorothy Arzner; w, Tess Slesinger, Frank Davis (based on a story by Vicky Baum); ph, Russell Metty; m, Edward Ward, Chester Forrest, Robert Wright; ed, Robert Wise; art d, Van Nest Polglase; ch, Ernst Matray; spec eff, Vernon L. Walker.

Musical   (PR:A   MPAA:NR)

DANCE HALL**   (1929) 65m RKO bw

Olive Borden (Gracie Nolan), Arthur Lake (Tommy Flynn), Margaret Seddon (Mrs. Flynn), Ralph Emerson (Ted Smith), Joseph Cawthorn (Bremmer), Helen Kaiser (Bee), Lee Moran (Ernie), Tom O'Brien (Truck Driver).

Shipping clerk Lake tries to dance his way into taxi dancer Borden's heart. She, however, has eyes for aviator Emerson. Emerson crashes in a cross-country record attempt, and Borden goes into a swoon. Lake takes her to his place to take care of her, and hides the fact that Emerson has recovered and is living with another woman. Borden discovers this piece of news and blows up at Lake. She goes to Emerson, who proves to be a rat and throws her aside. She returns to Lake, and the two dance off into the sunset. The film's sequences of a "taxi dance" ballroom are especially noteworthy.

d, Melville Brown; w, Jane Murfin, J. Walter Ruben (based on a story by Vina Delmar); ph, Jack Mackenzie; ed, Ann McKnight.

Drama   (PR:A   MPAA:NR)

DANCE HALL**   (1941) 73m FOX bw

Carole Landis (Lily Brown), Cesar Romero (Duke McKay), William Henry (Joe Brooks), June Storey (Ada), J. Edward Bromberg (Max Brandon), Charles Halton (Mr. Newmeyer), Shimen Ruskin (Moon), William Haade (Moon), Trudi Marsdon (Vivian), Russ Clark (Cook), Frank Fanning (Turnkey).

Some nice singing by Landis graces this slim comedy romance in which one-time ballroom and nightclub manager Romero (before he reached films) gets some barbs for a very dull performance. He is a lothario, of course, chasing Landis with the object of acquiring one more notch in his belt. When she discovers this (what every woman should have known), she cools on him, he grows suddenly serious, but in the end decides to put in a good word for his protege, Henry, assuring their marriage and his continued bachelorhood.

p, Sol M. Wurtzel; d, Irving Pichel; w, Stanley Rauh, Ethel Hill (based on a novel by W.R. Burnett); ph, Lucien Andriot; ed, Louis Loeffler; md, Emil Newman; m/l, "There's a Lull in My Life," Mack Gordon, Harry Revel, "There's Something in the Air," Jimmy McHugh, Harold Adamson.

Musical Comedy   (PR:AA   MPAA:NR)

DANCE HALL*   (1950, Brit.) 80m EAL/GFD

Donald Houston (Phil), Bonar Colleano (Alec), Petula Clark (Georgie Wilson), Natasha Parry (Eve), Jane Hylton (Mary), Diana Dors (Carol), Gladys Henson (Mrs. Wilson), Sydney Tafler (Manager), Douglas Barr (Peter), Fred Johnson (Mr. Wilson), James Carney (Mike), Kay Kendall (Doreen), Eunice Gayson (Mona), Dandy Nichols (Mrs. Crabtree), Geraldo and Orchestra, Ted Heath and His Music, Hy Hazell, Wally Fryer, Margaret Barnes, Harold Goodwin, Michael Trubshawe.

This film is about four British women who work in a factory and spend all their leisure time in the local dance hall. The conflict comes about when one of them wants to enter a dance contest with another man, because her husband isn't a

good dancer. This decision endangers the new marriage and results in a good battle between the two men. Best of the four women is Dors, whose training at the London Academy of Dramatic Arts hardly prepared her for the slight role she plays.

p, Michael Balcon; d, Charles Crichton; w, E. V. H. Emmett, Diana Morgan, Alexander Mackendrick; ph, Douglas Slocombe; ed, Seth Holt.

Drama   (PR:A   MPAA:NR)

DANCE HALL HOSTESS*   (1933) 73m Mayfair bw

Helen Chandler, Jason Robards, Sr., Edward Nugent, Natalie Moorhead, Alberta Vaughn, Jake Kickley, Ronnie Crowbey, Clarence Geldert.

Tame and uninteresting little story about Chandler's escapades as a Texas Guinan type hostess in a cheap dance hall. Director Eason later became known as a second-unit helmsman and worked with Michael Curtiz in THE CHARGE OF THE LIGHT BRIGADE (1938); it was he who was responsible for the special trip wires that spilled dozens of horses in the charge, maiming them and causing them to be shot.

d, Reeves Eason; Betty Burbridge (based on a story by Tom Gibson); ph, Jules Cronjager; ed, Byron Robinson.

Drama   (PR:A   MPAA:NR)

DANCE LITTLE LADY*½   (1954, Brit.) 87m REN c

Terence Morgan (Mack Gordon), Mai Zetterling (Nina Gordon), Guy Rolfe (Dr. John Ransome), Mandy Miller (Jill Gordon), Eunice Gayson (Adele), Reginald Beckwith (Poldi), Ina de la Haye (Mme. Bayanova), Harold Lang (Mr. Bridson), Richard O'Sullivan (Peter), Jane Aird (Mary), William Kendall (Mr. Matthews), Alexander Gauge (Joseph Miller), Lisa Gastoni (Amaryllis), David Poole, Maryon Lane, Joan Hickson, Marianne Stone, Vera Day.

A trite film about a worthless opportunist who pushes his wife to become a prima ballerina. On the night of her triumphant performance, she finds that he has been cheating on her with another dancer. Enraged, she drives off and gets into a near fatal accident. The doctors tell her that she will never dance again, and the husband leaves her and their child to do a Continental European and American tour with his new meal-ticket lover. A sympathetic doctor helps the ex-ballerina to recovery, while the infant daughter is quite a dance prodigy. The child wishes to follow in Mom's steps and Mom teaches the child all she knows. However, the husband returns to the scene as a Hollywood talent scout. He wants to take the kid away from the mother, bring her to Hollywood, and make her a star. His plans go awry, and he ends up sacrificing his life for the toddler.

p, George Minter; d&w, Val Guest; w, Guest, Doreen Montgomery (based on story by R. Howard Alexander and Alfred Dunning); ph, Wilkie Cooper (Eastmancolor); m, Ronald Binge; ed, John Pomeroy; md, Muir Mathieson.

Drama   (PR:A   MPAA:NR)

DANCE OF DEATH, THE*½   (1938, Brit.) 64m Glenrose/Fidelity bw

Vesta Victoria (Lady Lander), Stewart Rome (Armand Chabrier), Julie Suedo (Mara Gessner), Elizabeth Kent, Jimmy Godden, Betty Norton, Billy Merrin and His Commanders, Dino Galvani, Basil Broadbent, Iris Terry, Ralph Dowson, John Rowal.

Ex-convict Rome steals an allegedly cursed gem from a nobleman and is driven by it to kill dancer Suedo. Veddy awful English crime yarn.

p&d, Gerald Blake; w, Ralph Dawson.

Crime   (PR:A   MPAA:NR)

DANCE OF DEATH, THE**½

(1971, Brit.) 148m British Home Entertainment-National Theatre/PAR c

Laurence Olivier (Edgar), Geraldine McEwan (Alice), Robert Lang (Kurt), Janina Faye (Judith), Malcolm Reynolds (Allan), Jeanne Watts (Old Woman), Peter Penry-Jones (Lieutenant), Maggie Riley (Kristin), Carolyn Jones (Jenny), Frederyne Pyne, Barry James, David Ryall (Sentries).

The great Larry overstepped quite a bit in this role. Olivier is Edgar, an artillery captain. He and wife McEwan live hermetically on a small island that is almost a fortress. It's one of those tiny landfalls off the coast of Sweden. Olivier is angry at everything—at never making the grade as major, at his wife, at the world. McEwan and Olivier, the Scandinavian version of George and Martha, argue and bicker and yell long and loud. Olivier is very ill but will not admit it to his wife or even to himself. Lang, McEwan's cousin, arrives on the island as quarantine officer for the encampment and Olivier systematically seeks to ruin him financially, professionally and socially. Lang's son then falls in love with Olivier's daughter and the two youngsters see how sick the relationship is between their fathers. She berates Olivier and he suffers a stroke, falls to the floor foaming at the mouth, and ultimately dies. This will not make a wonderful musical remake. Everyone hams it up under Giles's direction but guiltiest of all is Sir Laurence. The essence of Strindberg's power is people speaking at the bottom of their voices, not the top. This is gloomy, complex and, in the end, not a pleasure to see.

p, John Brabourne; d, David Giles; w, C. D. Locock (based on the play by August Strindberg); ph, Geoffrey Unsworth (Technicolor); ed, Reginald Mills; art d, Herbert Smith; set d, Helen Thomas; cos, Amy C. Binney.

Drama   (PR:C   MPAA:NR)

DANCE OF THE DWARFS**   (1983, U.S., Phil.) 93m Dove & Panache c

Deborah Raffin, Peter Fonda, John Amos, Carlos Palomino, "Turko" Cervantes, Cherron Hoye, Gil Arceo.

Anthropologist Raffin hires drunken chopper pilot Fonda to fly her deep into the Philippine jungle in search of a lost race of dwarfs with rudimentary wings.

AFRICAN QUEEN ripoff goes on much too long until the little creatures turn up, and then they only look like some short guys in costumes.

p, Michael Viner; d, Gus Trikonis; w, Viner, G.W. King, Larry Johnson (based on the novel by Geoffrey Household); ph, Michael Butler, David Butler; m, Perry Botkin; makeup, Craig Reardon; spec eff, Teofilo Hilario, Jun Santiago, Narciso Tolentino, Andy Aturba; m/l, Snuff.

Science Fiction   **(PR:C MPAA:NR)**

DANCE OF THE VAMPIRES (SEE: FEARLESS VAMPIRE KILLERS: OR PARDON ME BUT YOUR TEETH ARE IN MY NECK, THE, 1967, U.S./Brit.)

DANCE OF LIFE, THE***½**   (1929) 115m PAR c/bw
Nancy Carroll (Bonny Lee King/Bonny Kaye), Hal Skelly (Ralph "Skid" Johnson), Ralph Theadore (Harvey Howell), Charles D. Brown (Lefty), Dorothy Revier (Sylvia Marco), Al St. John (Bozo), May Boley (Gussie), Oscar Levant (Jerry), Gladys Du Bois (Miss Sherman), James T. Quinn (Jimmy), James Farley (Champ Melvin), George Irving (Minister), Thelma McNeal ("Lady of India"), Gordona Bennett, Miss La Reno, Cora Beach Shumway, Charlotte Ogden, Kay Deslys, Magda Blom (Amazon Chorus Girls), John Cromwell (Doorkeeper), A. Edward Sutherland (Theater Attendant), Al St. John, James Farley.

This gritty backstage story deals with the petty jealousies, hates, loyalty, and loves of a third-rate burlesque troupe. Skelly is the prat-falling entertainer who takes to drinking when success on Broadway goes to his head. His wife, Carroll, divorces him after he resumes an affair with a former flame. Carroll remarries a rich man, but when she sees the poor shape Skelly is in, she returns to him, figuring he needs her more. Two-color Technicolor is used in a scene inside the Ziegfeld Follies. This film was remade twice, as SWING HIGH, SWING LOW (1937), and as WHEN MY BABY SMILES AT ME (1948). Carroll, incidentally, replaced the stage Bonny, who had no "name" recognition. She was Barbara Stanwyck. Besides being the first credited film role for self-declared genius Levant, the film is best remembered for its graphic scenes of backstage life at the time, and a withering look at a performer on the skids. Songs: "True Blue Lou," "King of Jazzmania," "Cuddlesome Baby," "Flippity Flop," "Ladies of the Dance," "The Mightiest Matador," "Sweet Rosie O'Grady," "In the Gloaming," "Sam, The Accordion Man" (Sam Coslow, Richard A. Whiting, Leo Robin).

p, David O. Selznick; d, John Cromwell, A. Edward Sutherland; w, Benjamin Glazer, George Manker Watters (based on the play "Burlesque" by Watters and Arthur Hopkins); ph, J. Roy Hunt (Technicolor sequences); ed, George Nichols, Jr.

Musical/Drama   **(PR:A MPAA:NR)**

DANCE PRETTY LADY***½**   (1932, Brit.) 64m BI/Wardour bw
Ann Casson (Jenny Pearl), Carl Harbord (Maurice Avery), Michael Hogan (Castleton), Moore Marriott (Mr. Raeburn), Flora Robson (Mrs. Raeburn), Leonard Brett (Alf), Norman Claridge (Jack Danby), Sunday Wilshin (Irene), Rene Ray (Elsie), Eva Llewellyn (Aunt Mabel), Alban Conway, Hermione Gingold, Marie Rambert's Corps de Ballet.

Despite her love for an artistic nobleman, Cockney ballerina Casson refuses to become his mistress. Soppy romantic drama. Flora Robson's first film.

p, H. Bruce Woolfe; d&w, Anthony Asquith (based on the novel Carnival by Compton Mackenzie); ph, Jack Parker; art d, Ian Campbell-Gray; ch and tech adv on ballet sequences, Frederick Ashton.

Drama   **(PR:A MPAA:NR)**

DANCE TEAM**   (1932) 83m FOX bw
James Dunn (Jimmy Mulligan), Sally Eilers (Poppy Kirk), Minna Gombell (Cora Stuart), Edward Crandall (Fred Penworthy), Ralph Morgan (Alec Prentice), Harry Beresford (Herbert Wilson), Charles Williams (Benny Weber).

A couple of would-be ballroom dancers meet by chance but soon decide to team up and try to make it as a team. They start dancing in some lesser clubs, but get a big break and make it into a hot joint. The two are a hit, but are torn apart by his groundless jealousy of a rich man's attention toward her. However, there is a happy reunion after he has hit bottom trying to go it alone. The Dunn-Eilers love team began in 1931 with BAD GIRL, which was based on a best-seller of the era and won Oscars for that film's director, Frank Borzage, and its writer, Edwin Burke, who went on to script DANCE TEAM. Both Dunn and Eilers were colorful Hollywood characters, alcoholics whose drinking habits gave them wobbly reputations. Eilers was particularly acid-tongued when in her cups and given to notorious foul language. A visitor to the MGM lot once mentioned to its studio head Louis B. Mayer that Carole Lombard had the filthiest mouth in movieland. Mayer snorted and said: "I guess you never heard of Sally Eilers!"

d, Sidney Lanfield; w, Edwin Burke (based on the novel by Sarah Addington); ph, J. Wong Howe; ed, Margaret Clancy.

Musical/Comedy   **(PR:AA MPAA:NR)**

DANCE WITH ME, HENRY**   (1956) 80m UA bw
Bud Abbott (Bud Flick), Lou Costello (Lou Henry), Gigi Perreau (Shelley), Rusty Hamer (Duffer), Mary Wickes (Miss Mayberry), Ted de Corsia (Big Frank), Ron Hargrave (Ernie), Sherry Alberoni (Bootsie) Frank Wilcox (Father Mullahy), Richard Reeves (Mushie), Paul Sorenson (Dutch), Robert Shayne (Proctor), John Cliff (Knucks), Phil Garris (Mickey), Walter Reed (Drake), Eddie Marr (Garvey), David McMahon (Savoldi), Gil Rankin (McKay), Rod Williams (Porter).

Abbott and Costello's last film together sees Lou running a kiddie carnival and Bud as his gambling, debt-ridden buddy. Costello also has two adopted moppets whom the state consistently tries to seize from him due to his lifestyle. When the noble carny owner tries to help bail his buddy out of his illegal financial troubles he soon finds himself the chief suspect in an investigation into the gang slaying of the local

district attorney and in trouble with the mob. The jokes are labored and even director Barton, who had directed some of the team's finest work, can't hide the fact that it was obvious that Bud and Lou no longer wished to work together. Costello made one more film before he died at age 53 in 1959; Abbott made a weak attempt to continue in comedy with another partner, but was unsuccessful. Although their work has not held up well over the years, their brilliant routine, "Who's On First?" made it to baseball's Hall of Fame, where it is enshrined on a plaque.

p, Bob Goldstein; d, Charles Barton; w, Devery Freeman (based on a story by William Kozlenko, Leslie Kardos); ph, George Robinson; m, Paul Dunlap; ed, Robert Golden.

Comedy   **(PR:A MPAA:NR)**

DANCERS, THE*   (1930) 70m FOX bw
Lois Moran (Diana), Walter Byron (Berwin), Phillips Holmes (Tony), Mae Clarke (Maxine), Mrs. Patrick Campbell (Aunt Emily), Tyrell Davis.

This syrupy love story has an English younger son, Holmes, going to the Canadian north woods to make his fortune. He is surrounded by a polite group of lumberjacks who act like jolly good Britishers and who spend most of their time in a frontier dance hall. Holmes meets a dancer, Clarke, and falls in love. They go back to England when the present earl and his nearest relative are killed in an accident. Holmes becomes the new earl, and the couple live happily ever after. Mrs. Patrick Campbell was the darling of the British stage in the early 1900s and the original Liza Doolittle in Pygmalion, written for her by her close friend, George Bernard Shaw.

d, Chandler Sprague; w, Edwin Burke (based on the play by Gerald Du Maurier, Viola Tree); ph, Arthur L. Todd; ed, Alexander Troffey.

Drama   **(PR:A MPAA:NR)**

DANCERS IN THE DARK*   (1932) 70m PAR bw
Miriam Hopkins (Gloria Bishop), Jack Oakie (Duke Taylor), William Collier, Jr. (Floyd Stevens), Eugene Pallette (Gus), Lyda Roberti (Fanny Zabowolski), George Raft (Louie Brooks), Maurice Black (Max), Frances Moffett (Ruby), DeWitt Jennings (Sgt. McGroody), Alberta Vaughn (Marie), Walter Hiers (Ollie), Paul Fix (Benny), Paul Gibbons, Steve Grajeda, Alberto Mateu, Eduardo Aguilar (Eduardo Duran's Orchestra), Kent Taylor (Saxophone Player), James Bradbury, Jr. (Happy, Trombonist), William Halligan (Terry, Trumpet Player), Fred Warren (Al, Pianist), All Hill (Smitty, Bouncer), Mary Gordon (Cleaning Lady), George Bickel (Spiegel), Claire Dodd (Girl at Bar).

Set in a taxi dance hall, the story has bandleader Oakie trying to save his kid pal from the clutches of one of the dancers he thinks is a shady lady, Hopkins. Oakie dates her when his pal is lured away, and falls in love with her himself. He becomes the target of gangster George Raft, who also loves the girl. In a melee at the end, Raft is killed, Oakie is shot, and the two young lovers are reunited. Among the film's three songs is "St. Louis Blues," by W.C. Handy, sung by Hopkins.

d, David Burton; w, Herman J. Mankiewicz, Brian Marlow, Howard Emmett Rogers (based on the play "Jazz King" by James Ashmore Creelman; adaptation, Brian Marlow); ph, Karl Struss.

Musical/Drama   **(PR:A MPAA:NR)**

DANCING CO-ED***
                        (1939) 80m MGM bw (GB: EVERY OTHER INCH A LADY)
Lana Turner (Patty Marlow), Richard Carlson (Pug Braddock), Artie Shaw (Himself), Ann Rutherford (Eve), Lee Bowman (Freddie Tobin), Leon Errol (Pop Sam Marlow), Roscoe Karns (Joe Drews), Monty Woolley (Prof. Lange), Thurston Hall (H.W. Workman), Walter Kingsford (President Cavendish), Mary Field (Miss May), Chester Clute (Braddock), Edythe Elliott (Housemother), Benny Baker (Evans), Bert Moorhouse, Lee Phelps (Stooges), Mary Beth Hughes (Toddy), Johnny Day (Assistant Stage Director), June Preisser (Ticky James), Wayne "Tiny" Whitt (Fat Student), Hal Le Seuer (Steve), Maxine Marx (Girl), Laura Treadwell (Dean of Women), Constance Keane [Veronica Lake], Dick Winslow (Couple on Motorcycle), Robert Walker (Boy), Edward Arnold, Jr. (Student), Ethelreda Leopold (Flapjack Waitress), Barbara Bedford (Secretary's Voice), Minerva Urecal (Woman's Voice on Radio).

Lightweight but amusing and tuneful, DANCING CO-ED was 19-year-old Turner's first starring role for MGM and showed off her legs (and the legs of several other attractive young women) to great advantage. Karns is a high-powered press agent (and when did anyone ever meet a low-powered press agent?) who launches a national contest to find the star for a new movie. Turner is planted in a college in the Midwest to be chosen in the fraudulent function. There is no way they'll take a chance and get a non-pro so they insure their bet by sending Lana to the educational institution. Accompanied by lovely Ann Rutherford (who made GONE WITH THE WIND right after this job. It was like going from the ridiculous to the sublime), who is Karns's secretary, Lana enrolls in school while Karns is going across America conducting phony screen tests at various colleges. Carlson is the college newspaper editor and suspects that the whole thing is a fake and threatens to expose it to everyone via his newspaper. But by that time, he and Lana are in love and he need go no further: she confesses the truth to him. Carlson doesn't want her to appear at the contest so he has some pals kidnap her and keep her out of the way. In her place, Rutherford enters the contest and wins the chance for stardom in Hollywood. Lana decides to stay in the Midwest and marry Carlson. Very thin premise that was stretched even thinner by the treatment accorded it. But the secondary players were uniformly excellent and Shaw, the most popular bandleader of the year, conducted his group in fine fashion. Shaw married Turner about two years later, the first of seven for her. Shaw was also married many times. In a tiny bit as one of the students, you'll spy a young man in his third small part before he moved on to become very successful, Robert Walker. Another tiny bit was Constance Keane, before she changed her name and became the "Peek-a-boo" girl, Veronica Lake. Artie Shaw instrumentals: "Back Bay Shuffle," "At Sundown," "I'm Yours," "Nightmare," "Stealin' Apples," "Racket Rhythm"; song: "Jungle Drums" (Ernesto Lecuona, Carmen Lombardo, Charles O'Flynn).

p, Edgar Selwyn; d, S. Sylvan Simon; w, Albert Manheimer (based on a story by Albert Treynor); ph, Alfred Gilks; m, Edward Ward, David Snell; ed, W. Donn Hayes; art d, Cedric Gibbons, Harry McAfee; set d, Edwin Willis; cos, Dolly Tree; ch, George King.

Musical Comedy   **(PR:A   MPAA:NR)**

DANCING DYNAMITE*   (1931) 63m Talmadge bw

Richard Talmadge (Dick Barton), Blanche Mehaffey (Helen Van Lane), Robert Ellis (Lucas), Richard Cramer (Kelsey), Harvey Clark (Murray Van Lane), Dot Farley (Effie), Jack Ackroyd (Shorty), Stanley Blystone (Bull Evans).

Poor screen entertainment filmed in an engaging locale involves a poor fisherman, a rich woman, and gangsters who try to kidnap her. Talmadge is the fisherman off beautiful Catalina Island who makes a bet with another angler that he can get into high society, and be photographed with them. He gets caught up in a kidnap plot and ends up saving the day and winning his bet.

p, Richard Talmadge; d, Noel Mason.

Comedy   **(PR:A   MPAA:NR)**

DANCING FEET*   (1936) 70m REP bw

Ben Lyon (Peyton), Joan Marsh (Judy), Eddie Nugent (Jimmy), Isabel Jewell (Mabel), James Burke (Phil), Purnell Pratt (Silas), Vince Barnett (Willoughby), Nick Condos (Specialty Dancer), Herbert Rawlinson (Groves), Lillian Harmer (Aggie), Herbert Corthell (Jenkins), Jimmy Burtis (Stupe).

This is a ridiculous semimusical, semidance film that has rich society girl Marsh become a taxi dancer to show her nasty grandfather, Pratt, that she can make a living on her own. Lyon is the rejected lover who is replaced by Nugent, the bellhop who aspires to be a hoofer in vaudeville. The dancing is not good in this one. Songs: "Every Time I Look At You," "Dancing Feet," "In and Out," "Land of Dreams," "And Then," "Get In Step," "Here I Am Again," "Here Comes Love," "Water Wheel," "I'm Glad It's Me," "Dreaming of You," "Never Give Up," "Recollections of Love" (Sidney Mitchell, Sammy Stept).

p, Colbert Clark; d, Joseph Santley; w, Jerry Chodorov, Olive Cooper, Wellyn Totman (based on a story by David Silverstein from a novel by Rob Eden); ph, Ernest Miller, Jack Marta; m, Sammy Stept, Sidney Mitchell; ed, Ralph Dixon.

Musical   **(PR:A   MPAA:NR)**

DANCING HEART, THE*½
(1959, Ger.) 91m Capital-Film/Sam Baker c (DAS TANZENDE HERZ)

Gertrud Kueckelmann (Susanne), Gunnar Moeller (Viktor, The Duke), Paul Hoerbiger (The Sovereign), Herta Staal (Annchen), Paul Henckels (Haberling), Wilfried Seyferth (Leopold), Maria Fris (The Doll), Harald Johnke (Julius), Heinz Rosen (Robert), Charlotte Ander (Therese), Herbert Kiper (Innkeeper), Erwin Biegel (Applinger), Toni Lander, Michel Rayne, Maria Fris, Rainer Koechermann, Genia Ugrinsky (The Dancers).

Vapid musical stars Kueckelmann as the daughter of a puppet maker threatened by foreclosure by banker Seyferth. The banker wants Kueckelmann in exchange for leaving her father alone, but he is duped with a life-size puppet while Kueckelmann marries her true love, a forester in the service of the Duke. Some nice color photography almost makes this one watchable, though in the end it just sinks in its own sticky sentiment.

d&w, Wolfgang Liebeneiner (based on a story by W.F. Fichelscher); ph (Agfa Color); m, Norbert Schultze.

Musical   **(PR:A   MPAA:NR)**

DANCING IN MANHATTAN*   (1945) COL bw

Fred Brady (Eddie Martin), Jeff Donnell (Julie Connors), William Wright (Steve Crawford), Ann Savage (Valerie Crawford), Cy Kendall (Inspector Kirby), Howard Freeman (George Hartley), Eddie Kane (Andre), Sally Bliss (Billie), Adelle Roberts (Sally), Jean Stevens (Rita), George McKay (Joe), Dorothy Vaughan (Mrs. Bundy), Cy Kindall.

This unmemorable film was the debut of a radio comedian, Brady, trying to make a transition to film. Needless to say, he was unsuccessful. The story concerns a truck driver, Brady, who finds $5,000, and rather than trying to trace the owner decides to blow it on a good time. He and his gal help capture the blackmailer of the money's rightful owner. The man being blackmailed is so grateful to Brady that he gives him the found money as a thank you.

p, Wallace MacDonald; d, Henry Levin; w, Erna Lazarus; ph, L. W. O'Connell; ed, Richard Fantl; art d, George Brooks.

Comedy/Musical   **(PR:A   MPAA:NR)**

DANCING IN THE DARK***   (1949) 92m FOX c

William Powell (Emery Slide), Mark Stevens (Bill Davis), Betsy Drake (Julie), Adolphe Menjou (Grossman), Randy Stuart (Rosalie), Lloyd Corrigan (Barker), Hope Emerson (Mrs. Schlaghammer), Walter Catlett (Joe Brooks), Don Beddoe (Barney Basset), Jean Hersholt (Himself), Sid Grauman (Himself), Louis Bacigalupi (Rubber), Syd Saylor (Projectionist), Milton Parsons (Butler), Bob Adler (Officer), Ann Corcoran, Phyllis Planchard, Claire Richards (Women), George MacDonald (Boy), Joe Bautista (Filipino), Fred Fisher, Sammy Finn, Cosmo Sardo, Harry Seymour (Men), Elaine Edwards (Girl), Walter Clinton, George Beranger (Waiters), Frank Ferguson (Sharkey), Charles Tannen (Jack), Harry Crocker (Master of Ceremonies), Edward Clark (Costumer), Max Willenz (Sommelier), Gregory Gay

(Headwaiter), Helen Brown (Esther), Sherry Hall (Cameraman), Dick Cogan (Wes), Jean "Babe" London (Hula Girl), Sally Forrest (Secretary), Erville Alderson (Neighbor), Grandon Rhodes (Producer), Belle Daube, Larry Keating, Claire Whitney, John Davidson, Joseph Crehan (Board Members), George E. Stone (Cutter), Helen Westcott (June), Johnny Berke (Marshall), Byron Foulger (Stefan), Marion Marshall (Myrna).

Screenwriter Mary C. McCall Jr. (et al.) takes what might have been a tired premise and dresses it up with some heart-tugging scenes that integrate well with the comedy. It's a souffle that never falls flat as washed-up movie star Powell is given a mission by studio boss Menjou. The task is to convince a Broadway star to come out west and topline the Dietz-Schwartz revue THE BANDWAGON (which actually was made by MGM four years later!). He gets the job because he knows the star's father. But Powell double-crosses the studio and, instead, contacts Drake, a nobody, and signs her. This results in the loss of his job as well as Stevens losing his job as press agent. It all works out well when Drake is discovered to have talent and she grabs off a ton of publicity by having her screen test slipped into the newsreel at Grauman's Chinese Theatre. It's then discovered that Powell is the errant father who sired Drake and then disappeared. She is livid at that but eventually calms down and accepts Powell as daddy. Music dominates the movie and what music it is. This could have been a very minor entry in the musical panoply but the witty screenplay distinguishes it. Good credit for Jessel who was seguing from performing to producing at the time. Much of the production for the film was set inside the actual Fox Studio at the time, and includes a reproduction of Darryl F. Zanuck's office, and Menjou's role is obviously Zanuck-inspired. Also appearing in the film is Sid Grauman, in a sequence shot in front of his Chinese Theatre, and Mike Romanoff, who is seen presiding over his once-popular restaurant. Songs: "Dancing in the Dark," "I Love Louisa," "New Sun in the Sky," "Something to Remember You by" (Howard Dietz, Arthur Schwartz).

p, George Jessel; d, Irving Reis; w, Mary C. McCall, Jr., Marion Turk, Jay Dratler (based on the musical "Bandwagon" by George S. Kaufman, Howard Dietz, Arthur Schwartz); ph, Harry Jackson (Technicolor); ed, Louis Loeffler; md, Alfred Newman; art d, Lyle Wheeler, George W. Davis; set d, Thomas Little, Paul S. Fox; cos, William Travilla; spec eff, Fred Sersen; ch, Seymour Felix.

Musical Comedy   **(PR:A   MPAA:NR)**

DANCING LADY***   (1933) 90m MGM bw

Joan Crawford (Janie Barlow), Clark Gable (Patch Gallagher), Franchot Tone (Tod Newton), Fred Astaire (Himself), Nelson Eddy (Himself), May Robson (Dolly Todhunter), Winnie Lightner (Rosette Henrietta La Rue), Robert Benchley (Ward King), Ted Healy (Steve), Moe Howard, Jerry Howard, Larry Fine (Three Stooges), Gloria Foy (Vivian Warner), Maynard Holmes (Jasper Bradley, Jr.), Sterling Holloway (Pinky, The Author), Florine McKinney (Grace Newton), Bonita Barker, Dale Dean, Shirley Aranson, Katharine Barnes, Lynn Bari (Chorus Girls), Jack Baxley (Barker), Frank Hagney (Cop), Pat Somerset (Tod's Friend), Charles Williams (Man Arrested in Burlesque House), Ferdinand Gottschalk (Judge), Eve Arden (Marcia, the "Southern" Actress), Matt McHugh (Marcia's Agent), Charlie Sullivan (Cabby), Harry Bradley, John Sheehan (Author's Pals), Stanley Blystone (Traffic Cop), Charles C. Wilson (Club Manager), Bill Elliott (Cafe Extra), Larry Steers, C. Montague Shaw (First Nighters), Art Jarrett (Art), Grant Mitchell (Bradley, Sr.).

The previous outing for Crawford and Gable had Clark sixth-billed in DANCE, FOOLS, DANCE. It's now two years later and they are equal stars in the MGM heaven. Crawford is a poor but honest hoofer who is forced to tap her toes at a local burlesque house in downtown Manhattan. Tone is a rich wastrel out for a night on the town with some equally snobby friends and they wander into said theater to slum a while. The place is raided by the police for indecency and the uptowners follow the cast to the police court where Crawford twits the judge and gets fined fifty bucks. She doesn't have it and will go to jail, but Tone bails her out and that begins their relationship. (They were seeing each other off-screen and married from 1935 through 1939.) Tone takes her back to his place and tries to put a move on her but she rejects it and says that she will repay him every penny as soon as she gets work. Well, it just happens that Tone is the cash behind a new musical for Broadway that Gable is directing for producer Mitchell. He pushes his weight around so she can get a job with the show and this is heavily resented by Gable who doesn't want anyone telling him who to hire. Crawford realizes this and works her rear end off. Gable reluctantly admits to himself that the kid has spunk and decides to feature her in the show. Tone wants to marry Crawford and she promises that she will, if the show flops. With this in the back of his mind, Tone tries to sabotage the show and eventually buys out Mitchell to close the production. Crawford is livid at his underhandedness and she and Gable manage to open the show, with his savings. The play is a hit and Crawford is the toast of the town. Gable and Crawford decide they are in love and Tone leaves with his money belt between his legs. This was a landmark film in a few different ways: Fred Astaire and Lynn Bari made their debuts; Eve Arden acted under the name of Eunice Quedens—her real monicker; it was the first film in which Moe, Jerry and Larry were billed as "The Three Stooges" (prior to this, they had made one film as "The Racketeers"); Nelson Eddy played himself; and eight of America's best song-writers contributed their talents. And it still wasn't a great picture. Songs: "My Dancing Lady," (Dorothy Fields, Jimmy McHugh), "Everything I Have Is Yours," "Let's Go Bavarian," "Heigh-Ho the Gang's All Here" (Harold Adamson, Burton Lane), "Rhythm of the Day," (Richard Rodgers, Lorenz Hart), "Hold Your Man" (Arthur Freed, Nacio Herb Brown).

p, David O. Selznick; d, Robert Z. Leonard; w, Allen Rivkin, P.J.Wolfson (based on the novel by James Warner Bellah); ph, Oliver T. Marsh; m&md, Lou Silvers; ed, Margaret Booth; art d & set d, Cedric Gibbons, Harry Oliver; cos, Adrian; ch, Sammy Lee, Edward Prinz; spec eff, Slavko Vorkapich.

Musical   **(PR:A   MPAA:NR)**

DANCING MAN*
(1934) 64m Pyramid bw

Judith Allen (*Diane Trevor*), Reginald Denny (*Paul Drexel*), Edmund Breese (*J.C.Trevor*), Natalie Moorhead (*Tamara Trevor*), Edwin Maxwell (*Reynolds*), Douglas Cosgrove (*Donovan*), Robert Ellis (*Cavendish*), Charlotte Merriam (*Celestine Castle*), Huntley Gordon (*Mason*), Maude Truax, Donald Stuart.

Gigolo Denny gets mixed up in too many situations for his own good. First he romances a married woman as well as her daughter. The one resents the other while the daughter resents Denny for being a gigolo. The mother is found murdered, and Denny is implicated. The daughter hires a detective to get to the bottom of the matter, and before he can prove that it was the father who committed the murder, the daughter and Denny have reconciled.

p, Rose Judell Reisman; d, Albert Ray; w, Ray (based on the novel by Beulah Poynter); ph, James S. Brown, Jr.; ed, Dan Milner.

Drama/Mystery   **(PR:A   MPAA:NR)**

DANCING MASTERS, THE**
(1943) 63m Fox bw

Laurel and Hardy (*Themselves*), Trudy Marshall (*Mary Harlan*), Robert Bailey (*Grant Lawrence*), Matt Briggs (*Wentworth Harlan*), Margaret Dumont (*Mrs. Harlan*), Allan Lane (*George Worthing*), Nestor Paiva (*Silvio*), George Lloyd (*Jasper*), Bob Mitchum (*Mickey*), Edward Earle (*Clerk*), Charles Rogers (*Butler*), Sherry Hall (*Dentist*), Sam Ash (*Pianist*), William Haade (*Truck Driver*), Arthur Space (*Director*), Daphne Pollard (*Mother*), Hank Mann (*Vegetable Man*), Emory Parnell (*Featherstone*), Robert Emmett Keane (*Auctioneer*), Chick Collins (*Bus Driver*), Florence Shirley (*Dowager*), Harry Tyler (*Man on Crutches*), George Tyne (*Gangster*), Hallam Cooley (*Barker*), Jay Wilsey [Buffalo Bill, Jr.] (*Stage Driver*).

A below-par Laurel and Hardy comedy has the boys being evicted from their dancing school for nonpayment of rent. The two are trying to raise money for an inventor friend working on a new type of gun. They decide to get money from an insurance company by signing up Stan for an accident policy, and inflicting an injury on him. Hardy ends up in the hospital after a roller-coaster ride on a bus that crashes.

p, Lee Marcus; d, Malcolm St. Clair; w, W. Scott Darling (based on a story by George Bricker); ph, Norbert Brodine; m, Arthur Lange; ed, Norman Colbert; md, Emil Newman; art d, James Basevi, Chester Gore.

Comedy   **(PR:A   MPAA:NR)**

DANCING ON A DIME*
(1940) 73m PAR bw

Robert Paige (*Ted Brooks*), Grace McDonald (*Lorie Fenton*), Peter Hayes (*Dandy Joslyn*), Eddie Quillan (*Jack Norcross*), Frank Jenks (*Phil Miller*), Virginia Dale (*Dolly Stewart*), Carol Adams (*Polly Adams*), Lillian Cornell (*Doris Marlowe*), William Frawley (*Mac*), Phillip Terry (*Brent Martin*), Tom Collins (*Sammy Brook*), George Meader (*L.L. Bancroft*), Charles Lane (*Freeman Taylor*), Arthur Aylesworth (*Joe Phillips*), Wanda McKay (*Lulu*), Fay Helm (*Miss Greenfield*).

A routine backstage story about a theatrical troupe that gets stranded when its federal WPA funds are cut off. Discovery of a wad of counterfeit bills enables the troupe to put up the deposit for a theater rental. The phony money backfires on opening night, but smart maneuvering saves the day and the show. Songs: "I Hear Music," "Manana," "Dancing on a Dime" (Frank Loesser, Burton Lane), "Lovable Sort of Person" (Loesser, Victor Young).

p, A. M. Botsford; d, Joseph Stan Santley; w, Maurice Rapf, Anne Morrison Chapin, Allen Rivkin (based on a story by Jean Lustig and Max Kolpe); ph, Charles Lang, Jr.; ed, Doane Harrison.

Musical   **(PR:A   MPAA:NR)**

DANCING PIRATE**
(1936) 83m RKO c

Charles Collins (*Jonathan Pride*), Frank Morgan (*Alcalde*), Steffi Duna (*Serafina*), Luis Alberni (*Pamfilo*), Victor Varconi (*Don Baltazar*), Jack LaRue (*Chago*), Alma Real (*Blanca*), William V. Mong (*Tecolote*), Mitchell Lewis (*Pirate Chief*), Cy Kendall (*Pirate Cook*), Julian Rivero (*Shepherd*), Harold Waldridge (*Orville*), Vera Lewis (*Orville's Mother*), Nora Cecil (*Landlady*), Ellen Lowe (*Miss Ponsonby*), John Eberts (*Mozo*), Max Wagner (*Pirate Mate*), James Farley (*Sailor*), the Royal Cansinos.

The novelty of this early Technicolor film drew audiences to it, but the plot, acting, and songs all caused it to walk the plank. The story is about a Boston dance teacher, Collins, who gets shanghaied by pirates. While on the voyage from Boston to Los Angeles by way of Cape Horn, Collins jumps ship in Mexico, meets the local mayor, Frank Morgan, and wins the heart of his daughter. Even songs written by Rodgers and Hart were of little help in this film, which only wanted to exploit the new technology of Technicolor by parading every color under the rainbow in front of the camera. The Royal Cansinos featured in one of the sequences was Rita Hayworth's family, Spanish-born dancer Eduardo Cansino and his "Ziefield Follies" partner Volga Haworth. Songs: "Are You My Love?" "When You're Dancing the Waltz" (Richard Rodgers, Lorenz Hart).

p, John Speaks; d, Lloyd Corrigan; w, Ray Harris, Jack Wagner, Boris Ingster, Francis Faragoh (based on a story by Emma-Lindsay Squier); ph, William Skall (Technicolor) ed, Archie Marshek; md, Alfred Newman; art d, Willian Ihnen; ch, Russell Lewis.

Musical   **(PR:A   MPAA:NR)**

DANCING SWEETIES*
(1930) 70m WB bw

Grant Withers (*Bill Cleaver*), Sue Carol (*Molly O'Neill*), Edna Murphy (*Jazzbo Gans*), Eddie Phillips (*Needles*), Kate Price (*Mrs. O'Neal*), Tully Marshall (*Mr. Cleaver*), Sid Silvers (*Jerry Browne*), Margaret Seddon (*Mrs. Cleaver*), Vincent Barnett (*Ted Hoffman*), Eddie Clayton (*Onions*), Billy Bletcher (*Bud*).

Withers and Carol meet during a dance contest, fall in love, and get married. Withers is an ambitious dancer and separates from Carol when she is unable to

learn complicated dance routines. They get reunited by the end of the film, and settle down to married life. One song written for the film, "Dancing With Tears in My Eyes" (Al Dubin, Joe Burke), deleted from the final print, later became an enduring hit after it was introduced by Rudy Vallee on radio. Songs: "Wishing and Waiting For Love" (Grant Clarke, Harry Akes), "Hullabaloo" (Bobby Dolan, Walter O'Keefe), "I Love You, I Hate You" (Al Bryan, Joseph Meyer), "The Kiss Waltz" (Dubin, Burke).

d, Ray Enright; w, Gordon Rigby, Joseph Jackson; ph, Robert Kurrie.

Musical Drama   **(PR:A   MPAA:NR)**

DANCING WITH CRIME*
(1947, Brit.) 81m Coronet/PAR bw

Richard Attenborough (*Ted Peters*), Barry K. Barnes (*Paul Baker*), Sheila Sim (*Joy Goodlan*), Garry Marsh (*Sgt. Murray*), John Warwick (*Inspector Carter*), Judy Kelly (*Toni*), Barry Jones (*Gregory*), Bill Rowbotham (*Dave Robinson*), Cyril Chamberlain (*Sniffy*), John Salew (*Pogson*), Peter Croft (*Johnny*), Diana Dors, Norman Shelley, Patricia Dainton, Dirk Bogarde, Denis Wyndham (*Sam*), Hamish Menzies (*Orchestra Leader*).

A below-par gangster film has Attenborough and Rowbotham as old Army buddies. The former drives a taxi; the latter is a gangster. Rowbotham is killed when he asks a gangster chief for a bigger part of the cut, and dies in Attenborough's taxi. Attenborough and his girl keep one step ahead of Scotland Yard and bring the murderers to justice.

p, James A. Carter; d, John Paddy Carstairs; w, Brock Williams (based on a story by Peter Fraser); ph, Reginald Wyer; m, Benjamin Frankel; ed, Eily Boland; art d, Harry Moore; m/l, Frankel, Harold Purcell.

Crime   **(PR:A   MPAA:NR)**

DANCING YEARS, THE*
(1950, Brit.) 98m ABPC/A-B Pathe c

Dennis Price (*Rudi Kleiber*), Giselle Preville (*Maria Zeitler*), Patricia Dainton (*Grete*), Anthony Nicholls (*Prince Reinaldt*), Olive Gilbert (*Frau Kurt*), Grey Blake (*Franzl*), Muriel George (*Hatti*), Jeremy Spenser (*Maria's Son*), Gerald Case (*Rudi's Secretary*), Carl Jaffe (*Headwaiter*), Moyra Frazer, Pamela Foster, Igo Barcinszki, Barry Ashton, Martin Ross (*Tenor*).

This ho-hum British musical is set in 1910 Vienna. A love story triangle, it has Price as a composer who rises from obscurity to fame. He is in love with Dainton, who marries the Prince of Austria but is really in love with Price's son. Not much here to compete with the string of Hollywood musicals of the time.

p&w, Warwick Ward; d, Harold French; w, Jack Whittingham, Ward (based on a play by Ivor Novello); ph, Stephen Dade (Technicolor); m, Novello; ed, Richard Best.

Musical/Drama   **(PR:AA   MPAA:NR)**

DANDY, THE ALL AMERICAN GIRL**
(1976) 89m MGM/UA (GB:SWEET REVENGE)

Stockard Channing (*Dandy*), Sam Waterston (*Le Clerq*), Richard Doughty (*Andy*), Norman Matlock (*John T.*), Franklyn Ajaye (*Edmund*), Ed. E. Villa (*Greg*), Evan Lottman (*Bailiff*).

Channing gives a good performance in this film which suffers from poor writing. The story has Channing, donning a series of disguises, as a compulsive car thief whose sole ambition is to one day buy an expensive foreign car. She spends the time on film either ducking the law or stealing vehicles.

p&d, Jerry Schatzberg; w, B. J. Perla, Marilyn Goldin (based on a story by Perla); ph, Vilmos Zeigmond (Panavision, Metrocolor); m, Paul Chihara; ed, Evan Lottman, Richard Fetterman; art d, Bill Kenney; set d, Rick T. Gentz; stunts, Ted Duncan.

Comedy/Crime   **(PR:A   MPAA:PG)**

DANDY DICK*½
(1935, Brit.) 75m BIP/Wardour bw

Will Hay (*Rev. Richard Jedd*), Nancy Burne (*Pamela Jedd*), Esmond Knight (*Tony Mardon*), Davy Burnaby (*Sir William Mardon*), Mignon O'Doherty (*Georgiana Jedd*), Syd Crossley (*Wilkins*), Robert Nainby (*Bale*), Hal Gordon (*Mullins*), Jimmy Godden (*Creecher*), John Singer (*Freddie*), Wally Patch (*Police Constable Topping*), Moore Marriott (*Stableboy*).

This mediocre British comedy centers on a country vicar and his attempt to raise funds for a steeple by betting on a horse. His sister is half-owner of the thoroughbred and enters it in the local race. The vicar bets everything he has on the horse, then is arrested by the town's new constable and accused of doping the horse. He clears himself in time to get to the race and see his horse come in. Weak stuff from a classic playwright who usually served stronger social commentary.

p, Walter C. Mycroft; d&w, William Beaudine; w, Frank Miller, Beaudine; Clifford Grey, Will Hay (based on the play by Arthur Wing Pinero); ph, Jack Parker.

Comedy   **(PR:A   MPAA:NR)**

DANDY IN ASPIC, A*½
(1968, Brit.) 107m COL c

Laurence Harvey (*Alexander Eberlin*), Tom Courtenay (*Gatiss*), Mia Farrow (*Caroline*), Lionel Stander (*Sobakevich*), Harry Andrews (*Intelligence Chief Fraser*), Peter Cook (*Prentiss*), Per Oscarsson (*Pavel*), Barbara Murray (*Heather Vogler*), Norman Bird (*Copperfield*), Michael Trubshawe (*Flowers*), Richard O'Sullivan (*Nevil*), Geoffrey Denton (*Pond*), Geoffrey Lumsden (*Ridley*), James Cossins (*Heston-Stevas*), Calvin Lockhart (*Brogue*), Geoffrey Bayldon (*Lake*), John Bird (*Henderson*), Michael Pratt (*Greff*), Monika Dietrich (*Hedwig*), Lockwood West (*Quince*), Arthur Hewlett (*Moon*), Vernon Dobtcheff (*Stein*), Paulene Stone (*Red Bird*).

This poor spy thriller stars Harvey as a Russian agent posing as a British agent, and everybody seems to know it but his boss. Conflict arrives when British agent

Harvey is ordered to kill his Russian counterpart. Mia Farrow is in the cast just after her marriage to Frank Sinatra, and just before the film that would make her famous, ROSEMARY'S BABY. Director Mann died during the production of DANDY IN ASPIC, and the star, Harvey, completed direction of the film.

p&d, Anthony Mann; w, Derek Marlowe (based on a novel by Marlowe); ph, Christopher Challis (Panavision, Technicolor); m, Quincy Jones; ed, Thelma Connell; md, Jones; art d, Carmen Dillon, Patrick McLoughlin; cos, Pierre Cardin; m/l, "If You Want Love," Ernie Sheldon, Jones; dubbing, Christopher Greenham.

Drama   (PR:A   MPAA:NR)

DANGER AHEAD*   (1935) 65m Victory bw

Lawrence Gray, Sheila Mannors, J. Farrell MacDonald, Fuzzy Knight, Bryant Washburn, Fred Kelsey, John Elliott, Eddie Phillips, Gordon Griffith, Arthur Loft, J. Hershel Mayall, Dick Cramer, George Chesebro.

Routine programmer with Gray saving Mannors from all manner of hazards. Knight tries to provide a few laughs but they fall flat. The directing is anemic and the writing awful, a typical Katzman mess.

p, Sam Katzman; d, Albert Heyman; w, Al Martin (based on a story by Peter B. Kyne); ph, William Hyer; ed, Dan Milner.

Drama   (PR:A   MPAA:NR)

DANGER AHEAD*   (1940) 57m Criterion/MON bw

James Newill (Renfrew), Dorothea Kent (Genevieve), Guy Usher (Inspector), Dave O'Brien (Kelly), Maude Allen (Mrs. Hill), John Dilson (Hatch), Al Shaw (Yergerson), Dick Rich (Maxwell), Harry Depp (James), Bob Terry (Gimpy), Lester Dorr, Earl Douglas.

Another film in the RENFREW OF THE MOUNTIES series stars Newill as the man in red. Newill does his usual thing, protecting the north woods and the people who live there from the unscrupulous gang that would run things themselves. Of course, Newill gets to sing a couple of songs along the way in this slipshod outing.

d, Ralph Staub; w, Edward Halperin (based on the novel Renfrew's Long Trail by Laurlee Yorke Erskine); ph, Mack Stengler; ed, Martin Cohn; m/l, Johnny Lange, Lew Porter.

Adventure   (PR:A   MPAA:NR)

DANGER BY MY SIDE**   (1962, Brit.) 63m But bw

Anthony Oliver (Inspector Willoughby), Maureen Connell (Lynne), Alan Tilvern (Venning), Bill Nagy (Sam Warren), Sonya Cordeau (Francine Dumont), Tom Naylor (Sgt. Roberts).

Connell takes a job in Tilvern's strip club to prove that Tilvern killed her detective brother. Okay program filler.

p, John I. Phillips; d, Charles Saunders; w, Ronald C. Liles, Aubrey Cash.

Crime   (PR:A-C   MPAA:NR)

DANGER: DIABOLIK**
          (1968, Ital./Fr.) 98m PAR c (AKA: DIABOLIK; DANGER DIABOLIK)

John Phillip Law (Diabolik), Marisa Mell (Eva Kant), Michel Piccoli (Inspector Ginko), Adolfo Celi (Ralph Valmont), Terry-Thomas (Minister of Finance), Mario Donen (Sergeant Danek), Claudio Gora (Police Chief), Edward Febo Kelleng (Sir Harold Clark), Caterina Boratto (Lady Clark), Giulio Donnini (Dr. Vernier), Annie Gorassini (Rose), Renzo Palmer (Minister's Assistant), Andrea Bosic (Bank Manager), Lucia Modugno (Prostitute), Giorgio Gennari (Rudy), Giorgio Sciolette (Morgue Doctor), Carlo Croccolo (Lorry Driver), Giuseppe Fazio (Tony), Lidia Biondi (Policewoman), Isarco Ravaioli, Federico Boito, Tiberio Mitri, Wolfgang Hillinger (Valmont's Henchmen).

Law delights the populace by destroying Italy's tax records, and then he steals a twenty-ton radioactive gold ingot. In a bizarre ending, he melts down the ingot in his hideout and it explodes and showers him with molten gold, turning him into a golden statue. If slight in content, the sets and set pieces introduced by one-time cinematographer Bava show his visual panache and are quite memorable.

p, Dino De Laurentiis; d, Mario Bava; w, Bava, Dino Maiuri, Brian Degas, Tudor Gates (based on a story by Angela and Luciana Giussani, Maiuri, Adriano Baracco); ph, Antonio Rinaldi (Technicolor); m, Ennio Morricone; ed, Romana Fortini; art d, Flavio Mogherini; cos, Luciana Marinucci, Piero Gherardi.

Crime/Spy Drama   (PR:A   MPAA:NR)

DANGER FLIGHT**½   (1939) 61m MON bw

John Trent (Tailspin Tommy), Marjorie Reynolds (Betty Lou), Milburn Stone (Skeeter), Jason Robards (Paul Smith), Tommy Baker (Whitey), Dennis Moore (Duke), Julius Tannen (Dawson), Edwin Parker (Williams), Joe Bernard (Brown), Harry Harvey, Jr. (Johnny), Walter Wills (Cap).

This film about flying and building model airplanes is based on a popular comic strip of the time, "Tailspin Tommy." Tommy, played by Trent, tries to help some juvenile delinquents by getting them interested in model airplane building. Baker works out a way that kids can give distress signals by having model planes do miniature skywriting. This comes in handy when Trent's plane crashes, and Baker finds him because of the special model plane. The publicity that arises from the rescue causes the formerly delinquent Baker to re-evaluate his outlook on life.

p, Paul Malvern; d, Howard Bretherton; w, Byron Morgan, Edwin C. Parsons (based on a story by Hal Forrest): ph, Fred Jackman, Jr.; ed, Edward Schroeder.

Adventure   (PR:AAA   MPAA:NR)

DANGER IN THE PACIFIC**   (1942) 60m UNIV bw

Leo Carrillo (Leo Marzell), Andy Devine (Andy Parker), Don Terry (David Lynd), Louise Allbritton (Jane Claymore), Edgar Barrier (Zambesi), Turhan Bey (Tagani), Holmes Herbert (Commissioner), David Hoffman (Storekeeper), Paul Dubov (Manolo), Neyle Marx (Lobo).

Carrillo is a British intelligence agent searching for a hidden arsenal on a small Pacific island during WW II. Carrillo talks Terry, the scientist-explorer, into postponing his marriage to wealthy sportswoman Allbritton, and going to the Pacific island in search of the weapons. Accompanying them is Terry's photographer pal, Devine. Turhan Bey is the evil owner of the arsenal, keeping it for Axis use, who tries to sabotage the expedition. His men are hired by Terry as guides, but as soon as they are into the jungle, the guides split. The three are left on their own to fight off pythons, a jaguar, crocodiles, and bales of feathers which are supposed to be headhunters, who capture them. The boys escape, are captured by Bey, and get rescued by the RAF.

p, Ben Pivar; d, Lewis D. Collins; w, Walter Doniger, Maurice Tombragel (based on a story by Neil P. Varnick, Doniger); ph, William Sickner; ed, Maurice Wright; md, H. J. Salter; art d, Jack Otterson.

Adventure/Spy Drama   (PR:A   MPAA:NR)

DANGER IS A WOMAN**
                  (1952, Fr.) 100m DIF bw (AKA: QUAI DE GRENELLE)

Henri Vidal (Jean-Louis), Maria Mauban (Mado), Francoise Arnoul (Simone), Jean Tissier (Vance), Micheline Francey (Janine), Pierre Louis (The Inspector), Dalbon (Cafe Owner).

A trite story of a man who goes in two easy steps from jaywalking to murder. Vidal, a husky Tarzan type, hunts snakes for a living. He is in love with a shopgirl, Arnoul. He gets into a heated argument with a gendarme who tries to ticket them for jaywalking and accidentally kills the policeman. He becomes a hunted man, spending most of his time hiding from the police and having liaisons with an eccentric maker of women's shoes, a prostitute, and the mistress of the newspaper reporter who sensationalized his crime. Vidal deliberately kills a man in his further attempts to elude the police, but is wounded and then slain in a chase. (In French; English subtitles.)

p, Robert Woog; d&w, E. E. Reinert; w, Jacques Laurent (based on the novel La Mort a Boire by Laurent); ph, Marcel Gringon; m, Joe Hajos; English subtitles, Jean Lenauer.

Drama   (PR:C-O   MPAA:NR)

DANGER ISLAND   (SEE: MR. MOTO ON DANGER ISLAND, 1939)

DANGER LIGHTS*   (1930) 87m RKO bw

Louis Wolheim (Dan Thorn), Robert Armstrong (Larry Doyle), Jean Arthur (Mary Ryan), Hugh Herbert (Professor), Frank Sheridan (Ed Ryan), Robert Edeson (Engineer), Alan Roscoe (General Manager), William P. Burt (Chief Dispatcher), James Farley (Joe Geraghty).

The only significant feature of this routine railroad story is that it was the first showing of a new wide-screen system called Spoor-Bergen Natural Vision, which added punch and depth to action sequences. But the film needed a projector which cost $22,000 and required a three-man crew to run. Thought to be an important technical achievement at the time, it died due to the Depression and the new expenses involved in the industry's switch to talkies. The story is slight, centering around some wholesome, healthy people and their railroad and how they run it.

p, William LeBaron; d, George B. Seitz; s, James Ashmore Creelman, Hugh Herbert; ph, Karl Struss, John Boyle; ed, Archie Marshek.

Comedy/Drama   Cas.   (PR:AA   MPAA:NR)

DANGER—LOVE AT WORK**½   (1937) 81m FOX bw

Ann Sothern (Toni Pemberton), Jack Haley (Henry MacMorrow), Mary Boland (Mrs. Alice Pemberton), Edward Everett Horton (Howard Rogers), John Carradine (Herbert Pemberton), Walter Catlett (Uncle Alan), Bennie Bartlett (Junior Pemberton), Maurice Cass (Uncle Goliath), Alan Dinehart (Allan Duncan), Etienne Girardot (Albert Pemberton), E.E.Clive (Wilbur), Margaret McWade (Aunt Patty), Margaret Seddon (Aunt Pitty), Elisha Cook, Jr. (Chemist), Hilda Vaughn (Pemberton's Maid), Charles Coleman (Henry's Butler), George Chandler (Attendant), Spencer Charters (Hick), Hal K. Dawson (Chauffeur), Stanley Fields (Thug), Paul Hurst (Police Officer), Claude Allister (Salesman), Jonathan Hale (Parsons), Charles Lane (Gilroy), Paul Stanton (Hilton).

A funny screwball comedy, made under the firm hand of director Preminger. Haley, a young lawyer from New York, is sent to a small town to buy up a piece of property. He is invited to stay for dinner, and the night, by the eccentric family from whom he is buying. He has a hard time trying to get signatures on the contract, and the daughter falls in love with him. Haley escapes from the crazy family without the signature, but the daughter follows him to New York City, brings her family so they can sign the papers, and makes sure he won't lose his job. Haley ends up marrying the daughter, of course.

p, Harold Wilson; d, Otto Preminger; w, James Edward Grant, Ben Markson (based on a story by Grant); ph, Virgil Miller; ed, Jack Murray; md, David Buttolph; art d, Duncan Cramer; m/l, Mack Gordon, Harry Revel.

Comedy   (PR:A   MPAA:NR)

DANGER ON THE AIR**   (1938) 70m UNIV bw

Donald Woods (Butts), Nan Grey (Reenie), Berton Churchill (Kluck), Jed Prouty (Jones), William Lundigan (Chapman), Skeets Gallagher (Fish), Edward Van Sloan

(Sylvester), George Meeker *(Tuttle)*, Lee J. Cobb *(Tony)*, Johnny Arthur *(Oren)*, Lind Hayes *(Lake)*, Louise Stanley *(Marian)*.

This film is a behind-the-microphone murder mystery at a radio station. The hero isn't a detective or a policeman. In fact, there aren't any to be found in the entire picture. Instead, he is a quick-thinking radio engineer, and the mystery arises when a womanizing sponsor, who is hated by all, is found murdered during the climax of a live radio show. The engineer, Woods, quickly gets down to solving the case, and finds that it is the radio announcer who is the killer. It seems that the sponsor was responsible for the suicide of the announcer's father.

p, Irving Starr; d, Otis Garrett; w, Betty Laidlow, Robert Lively (based on the novel *Death Catches Up With Mr. Kluck*, by Xantippe); ph, Stanley Cortez; ed, Maurice Wright; md, Charles Previn; art d, Jack Otterson.

Mystery   **(PR:A   MPAA:NR)**

DANGER ON WHEELS∗∗   (1940) 61m UNIV bw

Richard Arlen *(Larry Taylor)*, Andy Devine *("Guppy" Wexel)*, Peggy Moran *(Pat O'Shea)*, Herbert Corthell *(Pop O'Shea)*, Harry C. Bradley *(Jones)*, Sandra King *(June Allen)*, Landers Stevens *(Lloyd B. Allen)*, John Holmes *(Danny Winkler)*, Jack Arnold *(Bruce Crowley)*, Jack Rice *(Parker)*, Mary Treen *(Esme)*, Eddie Chandler *(Police Officer)*, Fred Santley *(Official)*, Eddie Fetherston *(Pete)*, Harry Strang *(First Mechanic)*, Jimmie Lucas *(Second Mechanic)*, Joe King *(Race Commissioner)*, James Morton *(Police Sergeant)*, Frank Mitchell *(Truck Driver)*, Tony Paton *(Race Driver)*, Jack Gardner *(Joe)*, Arthur Roberts *(Official)*, Harold Daniels *(Male Secretary)*.

An average race car stunt car thriller has Arlen as the testing grounds chief for Atlas Motors. Devine is his sidekick mechanic. Rivalry arises between Arlen and Arnold, the top driver. It reaches the point where Arnold is fired just before the big race, and Arlen has to drive the car himself. He gets into an accident, kills the brother of the girl he loves, and nearly destroys her father's oil-burning engine. He tries to put things right by placing her father's engine in the body of his car, winning the race and the girl.

p, Ben Pivar; d, Christy Cabanne; w, Maurice Tombragel (based on a story by Pivar); ph, Elwood Bredell.

Action   **Cas.**   **(PR:A   MPAA:NR)**

DANGER PATROL∗∗½   (1937) 59m RKO bw

Sally Eilers *(Cathie Street)*, John Beal *(Dan Loring)*, Harry Carey *("Easy" Street)*, Frank M. Thomas *(Rocky Sanders)*, Crawford Weaver *(Eric Trumble)*, Lee Patrick *(Nancy Donovan)*, Edward Gargan *(Gabby Donovan)*, Paul Guilfoyle *(Tim)*, Solly Ward *(Julius)*, Ann Hovey *(Ada)*, Richard Lane *(Pilot)*, Walter Miller *(Smokey Nelson)*, George Shelley *(Tommy Hayes)*, Jack Arnold [Vinton Haworth] *(Ed Novak)*, Herman Brix [Bruce Bennett] *(Joe)*.

This exciting story about nitroglycerine handlers is told in a pedestrian manner. Film centers on Carey, a veteran transporter of nitro, which is used to squelch oil field blazes. He doesn't approve of his daughter's desire to marry Beal, the would-be medical student, because Beal is also involved in the suicidal profession. Carey finally sees that the couple's love is inevitable, and substitutes for Beal on a very dangerous mission. Carey is killed in mid-flight when the nitro explodes, leaving Beal and his daughter to carry on.

d, Lew Landers; w, Sy Bartlett (based on a story by Helen Vreeland, Hilda Vincent); ph, Nick Musuraca; ed, Ted Cheesman.

Drama   **(PR:A   MPAA:NR)**

DANGER ROUTE∗∗   (1968, Brit.) 92m UA c

Richard Johnson *(Jonas Wilde)*, Carol Lynley *(Jocelyn)*, Barbara Bouchet *(Mari)*, Sylvia Syms *(Barbara Canning)*, Gordon Jackson *(Stern)*, Diana Dors *(Rhoda Gooderich)*, Maurice Denham *(Peter Ravenspur)*, Sam Wanamaker *(Lucinda)*, David Bauer *(Bennett)*, Robin Bailey *(Parsons)*, Harry Andrews *(Canning)*, Julian Chagrin *(Matsys)*, Reg Lye *(Balin)*, Leslie Sands *(Man in Cinema)*, Timothy Bateson *(Halliwell)*.

Johnson is a secret agent, and his mission is a strange one. The British government wants him to kill a Soviet scientist who has defected to the West, before he can give any information to the Americans, who have him in custody so they can question him. After having done away with the scientist, the British see to it that Johnson himself is eliminated, and we are never really sure why. Johnson is surrounded by a bevy of beauties, including Lynley, his double-crossing girl friend, whom he kills at the end of the film because she was aiding the enemy against him.

p, Max J. Rosenberg, Milton Subotsky; d, Seth Holt; w, Meade Roberts (based on the novel *The Eliminator*, by Andrew York); ph, Harry Waxman (DeLuxe Color); m, John Mayer; ed, Oswald Hafenrichter; prod d, Bill Constable; md, Philip Martell; art d, Don Mingaye; m/l, "Danger Route" (sung by Anita Harris), Lionel Bart.

Spy Drama   **(PR:A   MPAA:NR)**

DANGER SIGNAL∗∗∗   (1945) 78m WB bw

Faye Emerson *(Hilda Fenchurch)*, Zachary Scott *(Ronnie Mason/Marsh)*, Dick Erdman *(Bunkie Taylor)*, Rosemary DeCamp *(Dr. Silla)*, Bruce Bennett *(Dr. Andrew Lang)*, Mona Freeman *(Anne Fenchurch)*, John Ridgely *(Thomas Turner)*, Mary Servoss *(Mrs. Fenchurch)*, Joyce Compton *(Katie)*, Virginia Sale *(Mrs. Crockett)*, Addison Richards *(Inspector)*, Clancy Cooper *(Captain)*, Robert Arthur *(Young Boy)*, Monte Blue, James Notaro *(Policemen)*.

Scott is superb as a despicable cad who preys on women and doesn't have a decent bone in his lounge-lizard body. The film opens with Scott hastily departing a hotel room in the East, stealing money and a wedding ring from a dead woman on the floor. He appears in Los Angeles under an assumed name and proceeds to use Emerson and Freeman, two gullible sisters, to build a fortune. Scott, pretending to

be an injured war veteran, first pursues Emerson but then goes after her younger sister Freeman when he learns she is about to inherit a fortune. Emerson reveals Scott's insidious personality to Freeman but she refuses to see him in a bad light. Sis then decides she will kill Scott but she can't go through with it. The scoundrel meets his doom, however, when the husband of the woman left dead in the East shows up and confronts Scott. In terror, Scott flees and accidentally falls off a cliff, a fate that had the audiences cheering. The script of DANGER SIGNAL is weak and Flory's direction is slightly above average. It's Scott's incredibly hateful performance, almost equaling his role in THE MASK OF DIMITRIOS, that makes this one a little gem.

p, William Jacobs; d, Robert Florey; w, Adele Commandini, Graham Baker (based on the novel by Phyllis Bottome); ph, James Wong Howe; m, Adolph Deutsch; ed, Frank Magee; md, Leo F. Forbstein; art d, Stanley Fleischer; set d, Jack McConaghty; cos, Milo Anderson; spec eff, Harry Barndollar, Edwin DuPar.

Crime Drama   **(PR:A   MPAA:NR)**

DANGER STREET∗   (1947) 68m PAR bw

Jane Withers *(Pat Marvin)*, Robert Lowery *(Larry Burke)*, Bill Edwards *(Sandy Evans)*, Elaine Riley *(Cynthia Van Loan)*, Audrey Young *(Dolores Johnson)*, Lyle Talbot *(Charles Johnson)*, Charles Quigley *(Carl Pauling)*, Lucia Carroll *(Smitty)*, Nina Mae McKinney *(Veronica)*, Paul Harvey *(Turlock)*.

A murder mystery without police or detectives, having instead the two heads of a magazine as the sleuths. Withers and Lowery buy up the magazine they work for when it is sold. To raise money, they sell a compromising photo of a rich girl's fiance to a rival magazine for a high price. The purchaser of the photo is murdered, and the two turn detectives to catch the killer. Another killing allows Withers to trick the killer into a confession and she solves the case.

p, William Pine, William Thomas; d, Lew Landers; w, Maxwell Shane, Winston Miller, Kae Salkow (based on a story by Miller and Salkow); ph, Benjamin H. Kline; ed, Howard Smith; art d, F. Paul Sylow.

Mystery   **(PR:A   MPAA:NR)**

DANGER TOMORROW∗∗   (1960, Brit.) 61m Parroch/AA bw

Zena Walker *(Ginny Murray)*, Robert Urquhart *(Bob Murray)*, Rupert Davies *(Dr. Robert Campbell)*, Annabel Maule *(Helen)*, Russell Waters *(Steve)*, Lisa Daniely *(Marie)*.

Walker, the wife of a doctor and the possessor of extrasensory powers, has her sanity threatened when she has visions of murder in an attic. Occasionally effective thriller.

p, C. Jack Parsons; d, Terry Bishop; w, Guy Deghy (based on a story by Frank Charles).

Crime   **(PR:A-C   MPAA:NR)**

DANGER TRAILS∗   (1935) 55m Beacon/FD bw

Guinn "Big Boy" Williams, Marjorie Gordon, Wally Wales, John Elliott, Ace Cain, Edmund Cobb, Steve Clark, George Chesebro.

Tired programmer has Williams saving Gordon's honor and ranch while battling the bad hombres with fists and guns. Don't bother saddling up.

p, Max and Arthur Alexander; d, Bob Hill; w, Roch Hawley [Bob Hill] (based on a story by Guinn "Big Boy" Williams).

Western   **(PR:A   MPAA:NR)**

DANGER VALLEY∗   (1938) 52m MON bw

Jack Randall *(Jack)*, Lois Wilde *(Mickey)*, Hal Price *(Lucky)*, Charles King *(Dana)*, Frank LaRue *(Pappy)*, Earl Dwire, Chick Hannon, Ernie Adams *(Old Timers)*, Jimmy Aubrey, Glenn Strange, Bud Osborne, Tex Palmer, Merrill McCormack, Oscar Gahan, Denver Dixon.

Randall is the singing cowboy in this story which involves a gold strike in the hills. When the news leaks out, it lures promoters with forged papers who claim-jump everything in sight. The deserted ghost town suddenly becomes repopulated with hoodlums and bad guys of all kinds. Randall, being the good guy, tries to clean things up between singing "On The Wide Open Plains" and "Little Tenderfoot."

p&d, R.N. Bradbury; w, Robert Emmett; ph, Bert Longenecker; m/l, Johnny Lange, Fred Stryker.

Western   **(PR:AA   MPAA:NR)**

DANGER WITHIN   (SEE: BREAKOUT, 1960, Brit.)

DANGER WOMAN∗   (1946) 59m UNIV bw

Don Porter *(Claude Ruppert)*, Brenda Joyce *(June)*, Patricia Morison *(Eve Ruppert)*, Milburn Stone *(Gerald King)*, Samuel S. Hinds *(Sears)*, Kathleen Howard *(Eddie)*, Ted Hecht *(Lane)*, Leonard East *(Howard)*, Charles D. Brown *(Inspector Pepper)*, Griff Barnett *(Dr. Carey)*, Howard Negley *(Maxwell)*, Keith Richards *(Reporter No. 1)*, Eddie Acuff *(Reporter No. 2)*, Ronnie Gilbert, Doug Carter, Chuck Hamilton *(Other Reporters)*.

Uninspired story has Porter as a young scientist working on a formula for commercial use of the atom. He is assisted by girl friend Joyce, but their romance is complicated by the sudden appearance of Porter's wife, Morison, who has been missing for three years. Reentering his life, she becomes involved with some crooks who want her to steal the formula. A few murders occur, but the bad guys are held accountable for them, so Porter and Joyce can live happily ever after.

p, Morgan B. Cox; d, Lewis D. Collins; w, Josef Mischel; ph, Maury Gertsman; ed, Russell Schoengarth; md, Paul Sawtelle; art d, Jack Otterson, Harold MacArthur.

Crime   **(PR:A   MPAA:NR)**

DANGER! WOMEN AT WORK** (1943) 62m PRC bw

Patsy Kelly, Mary Brian, Isabel Jewell, Wanda McKay, Betty Compson, Cobina Wright, Jr., Allan Byron, Warren Hymer, Vince Barnett, Michael Kirk, Charles King, Jack Ingram.

Kelly inherits a trucking company from her uncle and enlists two of her friends to help her run it. They get involved in transporting gambling equipment to Las Vegas but are arrested and thrown into jail. Their boy friends come to the rescue and there is a triple Las Vegas wedding. So-so second feature comedy directed by the prolific Sam Newfield on one of his infrequent excursions from the B-western and co-written by cult director Edgar G. Ulmer.

p, Jack Schwarz; d, Sam Newfield; w, Martin Mooney (based on a story by Gertrude Walker, Edgar G. Ulmer); ph, Ira Morgan; ed, Robert G. Crandall; art d, Frank Sylos.

Comedy (PR:A MPAA:NR)

DANGER ZONE* (1951) 55m Lippert bw

Hugh Beaumont (Dennis O'Brien), Edward Brophy (Professor Shicker), Richard Travis (Lt. Bruger), Tom Neal (Edgar Spadely), Pamela Blake (Vicki Jason), Virginia Dale (Claire Underwood), Ralph Sanford (Larry Dunlap), Paula Drew (Sheila Jason), Jack Reitzen (Cole), Edward Clark (Elderly Man), Richard Monahan (Henry, The Bartender), Don Garner (Bud Becker).

A lightweight action whodunit with the best part being the title. There are two stories in this film. The first is Beaumont, who would later go on to be the father in TV's "Leave It To Beaver," as a happy-go-lucky guy who gets hired by Dale to make a bid for a saxophone at an auction. With the sax in his possession, Beaumont is knocked out and relieved of it by the man he bid against. Beaumont discovers that the instrument contains valuable jewelry, for which the original owner was murdered. He solves the case and captures the crooks at the airport. In the second part, Beaumont is hired by the beautiful Blake to escort her to a yacht party. The party turns out to be for the two alone. Blake seduces Beaumont and they are photographed by a private eye, Neal, working for Blake's husband. The husband is found murdered, and Beaumont is the prime suspect. He, however, proves to the police that Blake and Neal were working together and killed the husband for his money.

p&d, William Berke; w, Julian Harmon (based on stories by Lewis Morheim, Herbert Margolis); ph, Jack Greenhalgh; m, Bert Shefter; ed, Carl Pierson, Harry Reynolds; art d, F. Paul Sylos.

Mystery (PR:C MPAA:NR)

DANGEROUS*** (1936) 78m WB bw

Bette Davis (Joyce Heath), Franchot Tone (Don Bellows), Margaret Lindsay (Gail Armitage), Alison Skipworth (Mrs. Williams), John Eldredge (Gordon Heath), Dick Foran (Teddy), Pierre Watkin (George Sheffield), Walter Walker (Roger Farnsworth), George Irving (Charles Melton), William Davidson (Reed Walsh), Douglas Wood (Elmont), Richard Carle (Pitt Hanly), Milton Kibbee (Williams, Roger's Chauffeur), George Andre Beranger, Larry McGrath (Waiters), Frank O'Connor (Bartender), Miki Morita (Cato), Gordon "Bill" Elliott (Male Lead in Play), Libby Taylor (Beulah), Craig Reynolds (Reporter), Eddie Foster (Passerby), Billy Wayne (Teddy's Chauffeur), Mary Treen (Nurse), Edward Keane (Doctor).

Academy Award voters are an odd lot. They gave Liz Taylor an Oscar for nearly losing her life, not for her work in the unsatisfying BUTTERFIELD EIGHT. They gave one to a Cambodian doctor for living the role, rather than acting it, in THE KILLING FIELDS. The same went for Harold Russell in THE BEST YEARS OF OUR LIVES. In the case of DANGEROUS, Davis got an award and she did a pretty good job, but this was more sentiment than judgment as she'd missed the Oscar the year before for OF HUMAN BONDAGE when IT HAPPENED ONE NIGHT swept everything. Bette is an alcoholic former star of stage and screen. She is reeling down the street one night when slumming architect Tone (he was also slumming in DANCING LADY when he met Joan Crawford. That boy sure got around to all the sleazy places) spots her and follows Bette into a rundown dive where everyone greets her warmly. Tone recognizes her, buys her a libation, and comments about how much he enjoyed her early acting successes. She has feelings of low self-esteem and a vague sense that everything she touches will turn to dross. This is the nadir of her life and she is broke and, other than the people in this bar, friendless. Tone takes Davis to his Connecticut home where housekeeper Skipworth tsk-tsks as Davis gets demanding and asks for booze. She eventually gets looped and is in that condition when Tone returns from New York. He tells her to shape up or ship out. She sees that he is falling in love with her and now uses all of her feminine wiles to cause him to leave his fiancee, Lindsay. He holds off making that decision but does offer to sponsor Davis in a play of her choosing. He'll angel the production (something he also did in DANCING LADY). Davis hasn't told Tone but she is still wed to Eldredge, although they haven't seen each other for quite some time. It just didn't seem worth it to arrange for a divorce as neither of them had anyone else waiting in the wings. Tone tells Lindsay that he is in love with Davis and wants to marry her. When he pops the question to Davis, she hems and haws and suggests they wait until after the play opens. Now she contacts Eldredge and asks for the divorce, but he refuses. She is stuck and decides that she must take matters into her own hands. She takes a drive with Eldredge and pulls a POSTMAN ALWAYS RINGS TWICE trick as she crashes the car deliberately, thinking that she can kill Eldredge and escape unscathed. Backfire! Both escape, but Eldredge is paralyzed for life. Tone finds out the truth about the accident and Eldredge but is willing to toss it aside as he is madly in love with Davis. She realizes that she has been a dreadful woman and suggests he give her up and go back to Lindsay. Davis now opens the play, enthralls cast and audiences alike and makes a triumphant return to the stage. But the fact that Eldredge lies in the hospital gnaws at her. She visits him while he's recuperating, asks his forgiveness, and suggests that they make an attempt to keep the marriage together. Davis was

wonderful in the role but Elizabeth Bergner, Katherine Hepburn, Miriam Hopkins, Merle Oberon, and Claudette Colbert were all better that year and they lost. This picture was remade as SINGAPORE WOMAN in 1941 with Brenda Marshall. It wasn't very good.

p, Harry Joe Brown; d, Alfred E. Green; w, Laird Doyle; ph, Ernest Haller; m, Leo Forbstein, Bernhard Kaun; ed, Tommy Richards; art d, Hugh Reticker; cos, Orry-Kelly.

Drama (PR:A-C MPAA: NR)

DANGEROUS ADVENTURE, A** (1937) 58m COL bw

Don Terry (Tim Sawyer), Rosalind Keith (Linda Gale), Nana Bryant (Marie), John Gallaudet (Hadley), Frank C. Wilson (Depan), Marc Lawrence (Calkins), Russell Hicks (Allen), Joseph Sawyer (Dutch).

This film is set in the steel industry of the 1930s but ignores the social questions of the day. It is merely a drama with a steel setting. The story deals with a know-nothing rich girl who, previously only bothered with society matters, suddenly inherits a steel mill. Keith is the heiress who tries to make a go of it, teaming with tough guy Terry. Hicks and Gallaudet conspire to run the mill down so they can take it away from her at a cheap price and deliver it to the competition, and they almost succeed.

d, D. Ross Lederman; w, John Rathmell, Owen Francis (based on a story by Francis); ph, Benjamin Kline; ed, Gene Havlick.

Drama (PR:A MPAA: NR)

DANGEROUS AFFAIR, A* (1931) 75m COL bw

Jack Holt (Lt. McHenry), Ralph Graves (Wally Cook), Sally Blane (Marjory Randolph), Susan Fleming (Florence), Blanche Friderici (Letty), Edward Brophy (Nelson), De Witt Jennings (City Editor), Tyler Brooke (Harvey), William V. Mong (Lionel), Fredric Stanley (Tom), Sidney Bracy (Plunkett), Charles Middleton (Tupper), Esther Muir (Peggy).

A plodding story set in an outlying suburban police precinct where nothing much happens. Holt is a police lieutenant, and Graves is a district reporter. The two have a relationship of friendly animosity. Mystery arises when a lawyer is murdered after he has read a will to a group of relatives. The two set off in search of the murderer, but it is a long slow walk to a solution.

d, Edward Sedgwick; w, Howard J. Green; ph, Teddy Tetzlaff.

Mystery/Comedy (PR:A MPAA: NR)

DANGEROUS AFTERNOON*½ (1961, Brit.) 62m Theatrecraft/Bryantston bw

Ruth Dunning (Miss Frost), Nora Nicholson (Mrs. Sprule), Joanna Dunham (Freda), Howard Pays (Jack Loring), May Hallatt (Miss Burge), Gwenda Wilson (Miss Berry), Ian Colin (Rev. Everard Porson), Gladys Henson (Miss Cassell), Barbara Everest (Mrs. Judson).

Escaped convict Dunning runs a halfway house for female ex-cons. When her cover is threatened by a blackmailer, she poisons him. Occasionally interesting, but mostly dull.

p, Guido Coen; d, Charles Saunders; w, Brandon Fleming (based on a play by Gerald Anstruther).

Crime (PR:A-C MPAA: NR)

DANGEROUS AGE, A*½ (1960, Can.) 70m Modern Film Distributors bw

Ben Piazza, Anne Pearson, Lloyd Jones, Claude Rae, Aileen Seaton, Kate Reid, Shane Rimmer, Reed Willis, John Sullivan, Austin Willis, Barbara Hamilton, Bea Fair, Jacob Reinglass.

Routine melodrama has Piazza and Pearson as a young couple facing the problems that usually plague young couples. Interesting chiefly as director Furie's debut feature. He would go on to make some very good films (THE IPCRESS FILE, THE BOYS IN COMPANY C) as well as some real stinkers (GABLE AND LOMBARD).

p,d&w, Sidney J. Furie.

Drama (PR:A MPAA: NR)

DANGEROUS ASSIGNMENT** (1950, Brit.) 58m Target/Apex bw

Lionel Murton (Joe Wilson), Pamela Deeming (Laura), Ivan Craig (Frank Mayer), Macdonald Parke (B. G. Bradley), Michael Hogarth, Bill Hodge.

An American reporter in England (Murton) is aided by local girl, insurance investigator Deeming, in breaking up a ring of car thieves. Barely decent crime drama.

p, Miriam Crowdy; d&ph, Ben R. Hart; w, Chick Messina.

Crime (PR:A-C MPAA:NR)

DANGEROUS BLONDES*½ (1943) 81m COL bw

Allyn Joslyn (Barry Craig), Evelyn Keyes (Jane Craig), Edmund Lowe (Ralph McCormick), John Hubbard (Kirk Fenley), Anita Louise (Julie Taylor), Frank Craven (Inspector Clinton), Michael Duane (Harry Duerr), Ann Savage (Erika McCormick), William Demarest (Detective Gatling), Hobart Cavanaugh (Pop), Frank Sully (Detective Henderson), Robert Stanford (Jim Snyder), Lynn Merrick (May Ralston), Stanley Brown (Lee Kenyon), Bess Flowers (Madge Lawrence), Mary Forbes (Mrs. Fleming), John Abbott (Roland Smith).

A husband-and-wife-sleuth team, the Craigs, go on the trail of a murderer. Joslyn is a detective-story writer who solves real mysteries on the side, while being constantly accompanied by his wife, Keyes. He has a policeman nemesis who resents his constant interference, but still comes to the rescue when the Craigs get into trouble. Joslyn makes the police look bad on a fictional detective writers vs. real detectives radio quiz contest, and shows them up again when involved in a real murder committed against the background of a high-fashion studio. The mystery arises when the owner of the studio is unjustly accused of murdering his wife, and the sleuth twosome get down to the bottom of it.

p, Samuel Bischoff; d, Leigh Jason; w, Richard Flournoy, Jack Henley (based on a story by Kelley Roos); ph, Philip Tannura; ed, Jerome Thomas; md, M. W. Stoloff; art d, Lionel Banks.

Comedy   (PR:A   MPAA:NR)

DANGEROUS BUSINESS**   (1946) 59m COL bw

Forrest Tucker, Lynn Merrick, Gerald Mohr, Gus Schilling, Shemp Howard, Frank Sully, Cora Witherspoon, Thurston Hall, William Forrest, Matt Willis, Ben Welden.

Tucker and Mohr are a pair of young attorneys who save the president of a utility company facing a false embezzlement charge. Marginally interesting second feature material.

p, Ted Richmond; d, D. Ross Lederman; w, Hal Smith (based on the play *Corpus Delicti* by Harry J. Essex); ph, George B. Meehan, Jr.; ed, Richard Fantl; md, Mischa Bakaleinikoff; art d, Robert Peterson.

Crime   (PR:A   MPAA:NR)

DANGEROUS CARGO**   (1939, Brit.) 79 ABF bw
                                      (GB: HELL'S CARGO)

Walter Rilla (*Commandant Lestailleur*), Kim Peacock (*Cmdr. Falcon*), Robert Newton (*Cmdr. Tomasov*), Penelope Dudley Ward (*Annette Lestailleur*), Geoffrey Atkins (*Pierre Lestailleur*), Ronald Adam (*Capt. Dukes*) Charles Victor (*Mr. Martin*), Martin Walker (*Dr. Laurence*), Henry Oscar (*Liner Captain*), Henry Morell (*Father Blanc*), Louis Hampton (*Civil Defense Warden*).

An English, a French, and a Russian sailor are accused of murder of a ship's doctor. They clear themselves and discover that the owner of the ship's cargo killed the doctor, and that the killer's cargo is a mysterious aniline dye that, mixed with water, creates a poison gas. The owner dumps the cargo into the ocean when the sailors and the three men must travel through the gas to save a nearby passenger liner.

p, Walter C. Mycroft; d, Harold Huth; w, Dudley Leslie (based on the story "Alerte en Mediteranee" by Leo Joannon); ph, Philip Tannura.

Action/Adventure   (PR:A   MPAA:NR)

DANGEROUS CARGO*½   (1954, Brit.) 61m ACT Films/Monarch bw

Susan Stephen (*Janie Matthews*), Jack Watling (*Tom Matthews*), Karel Stepanek (*Pliny*), Richard Pearson (*Noel*), Terence Alexander (*Harry*), John Le Mesurier (*Luigi*), Ballard Berkeley (*Findley*), Genine Graham (*Diana*), John Longden (*Worthington*), Trevor Reid, Arthur Rigby, John H. Watson.

Watling, a security man in a London airport, is blackmailed into helping robbers pull off a gold heist. Mostly dull second feature.

p, Stanley Haynes; d, John Harlow; w, Haynes (based on a story by Percy Hoskins).

Crime   (PR:C   MPAA:NR)

DANGEROUS CHARTER*   (1962 76m Crown International c

Chris Warfield (*Marty*), Sally Fraser (*June*), Richard Foote (*Dick*), Peter Forster (*Manet*), Chick Chandler (*Kick*), Wright King (*Joe*), Carl Milletaire, Steve Conte, John Zaremba, John Pickard, Alex Montoya.

Three broke fishermen come across an abandoned yacht containing the body of a corpse. The Coast Guard strikes a deal with the three—Warfield, Chandler, and King—awarding them the yacht to use as a charter boat if they will help solve the mystery of its ownership. Soon, the men who own the boat show up, and they are drug smugglers. They force the fishermen to sail the boat and half a million dollars worth of heroin hidden on it to Santa Catalina Island, where the fishermen finally outwit them.

p, Robert Gottschalk, John R. Moore; d, Gottschalk; w, Paul Strait (based on a story by Gottschalk); ph, Meredith M. Nicholson (Panavision, Technicolor); m, Ted Dale; ed, George White; m/l, "The Sea Is My Woman," "Lonely Guitar," Rod Sherwood.

Action/Mystery   (PR:A   MPAA:NR)

DANGEROUS CORNER*½   (1935) 65m RKO bw

Melvyn Douglas (*Charles*), Conrad Nagel (*Robert*), Virginia Bruce (*Olwen*), Erin O'Brien Moore (*Freda*), Ian Keith (*Martin*), Betty Furness (*Betty*), Henry Wadsworth (*Gordon*), Doris Lloyd (*Miss Mockridge*).

The theft of some government bonds and the supposed suicide of the chief suspect provide the pivotal acts on which the theme of truth-telling is built. In determining the circumstances of the suicide and the whereabouts of the bonds, the people close to the dead man are drawn into a seance where everyone is compelled to tell the truth. The devastating consequences of total candor are felt as each person delivers a damaging confession, revealing suppressed passions and guilty secrets, mostly about illicit loves.

p, Arthur Sibcom; d, Phil Rosen; w, Anne Morrison Chapin, Madeleine Ruthven (based on a play by J. B. Priestley); ph, J. Roy Hunt; ed, Archie Marshek.

Mystery   (PR:A   MPAA:NR)

DANGEROUS CROSSING**½   (1953) 75m FOX bw

Jeanne Crain (*Ruth Bowman*), Michael Rennie (*Dr. Paul Manning*), Casey Adams (*Jim Logan*), Carl Betz (*John Bowman*), Mary Anderson (*Anna Quinn*), Marjorie Hoshelle (*Kay Prentiss*), Willis Bouchey (*Capt. Peters*), Yvonne Peattie (*Miss*

Bridges), Karl Ludwig Lindt (*Foreign Man*), Gayne Whitman (*Purser*), Anthony Jochim, Charles Tannen (*Stewards*), Stanley Andrews (*Ship Pilot*), William Tannen (*Ship Officer*), Adrienne Marden (*Operator*), Harry Carter (*Attendant*), Harry Seymour (*Bar Steward*), Madge Blake (*Large Woman*).

So-so suspense piece that borrows from SO LONG AT THE FAIR. Lovely Crain is married to handsome Betz and they will take their honeymoon on a cruise ship going east across the Atlantic. Suddenly, Betz disappears and no one will believe that he even got on board. As Crain investigates, she learns that she's listed under her maiden name and that only one ticket, hers, was purchased. Furthermore, she can't find anyone aboard the ship who saw them together. Rennie, who was suavity personified, is the ship's physician and he thinks the poor lass is seeing things. As the film continues, he understands that this is not an hysterical young woman and he begins to believe her. What's happening is that Betz is in hiding and trying to drive Crain over the edge so that when he tosses her over the rail, everyone will think it was the suicide of a deranged young woman rather than an intricate plot to get at her money. The treatment of the plot, the photography, etc., are better than the script by Leo Townsend, who later went on to write many of the BEACH PARTY pictures.

p, Robert Bassler; d, Joseph M. Newman; w, Leo Townsend (based on a story by John Dickson Carr); ph, Joseph La Shelle; m, Lionel Newman; ed, William H. Reynolds; art d, Lyle Wheeler, Maurice Ramsford.

Mystery   (PR:A   MPAA:NR)

DANGEROUS CURVES**½   (1929) 73m PAR bw

Clara Bow (*Pat Delaney*), Richard Arlen (*Larry Lee*), Kay Francis (*Zara Flynn*), David Newell (*Tony Barretti*), Anders Randolf (*Col. P.P. Brock*), May Boley (*Ma Spinelli*), T. Roy Barnes (*Pa Spinelli*), Joyce Compton (*Jennie Silver*), Charles D. Brown (*Spider*), Stuart Erwin, Jack Luden (*Rotarians*), Oscar Smith (*Black Porter*), Ethan Laidlaw (*Roustabout*), Russ Powell (*Counterman*).

Clara Bow playing a circus waif is quite a departure from her usual flapper role. This early talkie is set in a circus, with Bow as the high-wire apprentice. She wants to be the star and worships the young man who performs the high-wire act. He is going to pieces due to the faithlessness of the woman he loves, the partner in his act. She deserts him and he falls completely apart and takes to drinking. Bow coaxes him back on the right path but one night walks in on him before the show and finds him passed out, drunk. Bow puts on his clown makeup and performs for him, ruining her chances to be a star in her own act. But the high-wire star realizes that she saved him and he makes up for it. After four years of seeing Bow in her flapper roles, the public was beginning to tire of the bobbed hair, the cupid-bow lips, and the bright eyes, and DANGEROUS CURVES represented a change of style by which her studio bosses hoped to regain her popularity. It was not to be, however.

d, Lothar Mendes; w, Donald Davis, Florence Ryerson, Viola Brothers Shore, George Marion, Jr. (based on a story by Lester Cohen); ph, Harry Fischbeck; ed, Eda Warren.

Comedy Drama   (PR:AA   MPAA:NR)

DANGEROUS DAVIES—THE LAST DETECTIVE**
                (1981, Brit.) 111m ITC/Inner Circle Films/Maidenhead c

Bernard Cribbens (*Dangerous Davies*), Bill Maynard (*Mod Lewis*), Joss Ackland (*Chief Inspector Yardbird*), Bernard Lee (*Sgt. Ben*), Frank Windsor (*Fred Fennell*), John Leyton (*Dave Boot*), Maureen Lipman (*Ena Lind*), Lucy Aston (*Celia*).

Cribbens is a bumbling detective whose methods have been out of date for decades. The story's intrigue occurs when he inadvertently stumbles across a long-unsolved murder of a teenage girl and relentlessly tracks down the murderer, encountering the dregs of human civilization before finding what he's looking for under his nose.

p, Greg Smith; d, Val Guest; w, Guest, Leslie Thomas (based on a novel by Thomas); ph, Frank Watts; m, Ed Welch; ed, Bill Lenny; art d, Geoffrey Tozer; set d, Denise Exshaw.

Mystery/Comedy   (PR:A   MPAA:NR)

DANGEROUS EXILE**½   (1958, Brit.) 100m RANK c

Louis Jourdan (*Duc de Beauvais*), Belinda Lee (*Virginia Traill*), Keith Michell (*Col. St. Gerard*), Richard O'Sullivan (*Louis XVII*), Martita Hunt (*Aunt Fell*), Finlay Currie (*Mr. Patient*), Anne Heywood (*Glynis*), Jean Mercure (*Chief of Police*), Jean Claudio (*De Castres*), Terence Longdon (*Sir Frederick Venner*), Frederick Leister (*Ogden*), Laurence Payne (*Lautrec*), Austin Trevor (*Petival*), Jacques Brunius (*De Chassagne*), Brian Rawlinson (*Dylan Evans*), Derek Oldham (*William*), John Dearth, Lisa Lee, Andre Mikhelson, Sam Kydd, Richard Clarke.

British period cloak-and-dagger film is set during the French Revolution. Jourdan plays a French nobleman who saves the ten-year-old son of Louis XVI and Marie Antoinette after his royal parents have been beheaded. Jourdan substitutes the prince, O'Sullivan, for his own son in prison, and then takes the royal child to a small Welsh island where he is protected by Lee. Jourdan feels that it is his duty to return O'Sullivan to France and have him retake the throne, but the boy wants none of that. Meanwhile, a local newspaper editor on the island discovers the boy's true identity and acts as a spy for the French Republicans. There is a romantic sideline as Jourdan falls in love with the young O'Sullivan's benefactor, Lee. Lee's maid has been a spy for the news editor, and soon a zealous Republican soldier is ordered to go to the island and kill the boy. Jourdan discovers his own son has been killed in prison, and dispatches the soldier in a free-for-all sword fight. The end of the film sees Jourdan, Lee, and O'Sullivan setting up domestic life on the island.

p, George H. Brown; d, Brian Desmond Hurst; w, Robin Estridge, Patrick Kirwan (based on the novel *A King Reluctant* by Vaughan Wilkins); ph, Geoffrey Unsworth

(Eastmancolor, Vista Vision); m, Georges Auric; ed, Peter Bezencenet; md, Muir Mathieson; art d, Jack Maxsted; cos, Eleanor Abbey.

Adventure/Spy Drama (PR:A MPAA:NR)

DANGEROUS FEMALE (SEE: MALTESE FALCON, THE, 1931)

DANGEROUS FINGERS
(SEE: WANTED BY SCOTLAND YARD, 1937, Brit.)

DANGEROUS FRIEND (SEE: TODD KILLINGS, THE, 1971)

DANGEROUS GAME, A* (1941) 61m UNIV bw
Richard Arlen (Dick), Andy Devine (Andy), Jeanne Kelly, [Jean Brooks] (Anne), Edward Brophy (Bugs), Marc Lawrence (Joe), Robert O. Davis (Fleming), Richard Carle (Agatha), Andrew Toombes (Silas), Tom Dugan (Clem), Vince Barnett (Ephraim), Mira McKinney (Mrs. Hubbard).

A comedy-thriller that justly belongs in the loony bin. A DANGEROUS GAME takes place in an insane asylum and throws together a bizarre assortment of crooks, detectives, phony doctors, doped-up patients, who all rush around looking for something that seems to be an awful lot of money. The pace, frantic, finally leads nowhere.

p, Ben Pivar; d, John Rawlins; w, Larry Rhine, Ben Chapman, Maxwell Shane (based on a story by Rhine and Chapman); ph, Stanley Cortez; md, Charles Previn.

Comedy/Mystery (PR:A MPAA:NR)

DANGEROUS GROUND*½ (1934, Brit.) 68m B&D-PAR British bw
Malcolm Keen (Mark Lyndon), Jack Raine (Philip Tarry), Joyce Kennedy (Claire Breedon), Martin Lewis (John Breedon), Kathleen Kelly (Joan Breedon), Gordon Begg (Holford), Henry Longhurst (Inspector Hurley).

When her fiance, a detective, is killed by a mysterious fence, a woman exposes a socialite as the culprit. Lame British mystery, not as good as a thousand films just like it.

d, Norman Walker; w, Dion Titheradge, Dorothy Rowan (based on a story by Titheradge); ph, Cyril Bristow.

Crime (PR:A MPAA:NR)

DANGEROUS HOLIDAY* (1937) 58m REP bw
Ra Hould (Ronnie Kimball), Hedda Hopper (Lottie), Guinn Williams (Duke), Jack La Rue (Gollenger), Jed Prouty (Gifford), Lynne Roberts (Jean), William Bakewell (Tom), Fern Emmett (Aunt Elsie), Virginia Sale (Aunt Augusta), Franklin Pangborn (Doffie), Grady Sutton (Max), William Newell (Solitaire), Thomas E. Jackson (Marty), Olaf Hytten (Popcorn), Jack Mulhall (Sergeant), Michael Jeffrey (Jerry Courtney), Harvey Clark (Robbins), Wade Boteler (Police Captain), Carleton Young (Tango).

A many-times-told story about a poor little violin prodigy, Hould, who runs away from home so he can play like the other kids. While the search for him is on, poor darling is wandering about and soon stumbles on a gangster's hideout. He is instrumental in the hoods' capture, and can look forward to understanding treatment from his parents upon his return home.

p, William Berke; d&w, Nicholas Barrows (based on a story by Karen deWolf, Barry Shipman); ph, William Nobles; m, Alberto Colombo; ed, Roy Livingston; m/l, Sam Stept, Ted Koehler.

Drama Cas. (PR:AA MPAA:NR)

DANGEROUS INTRIGUE** (1936) 59m COL bw
Ralph Bellamy (Tony), Gloria Shea (Greta), Joan Perry (Carol), Fred Kohler (Brant), Fredrik Vogeding (Joe Kosovic), Edward Le Saint (Dr. Miller), George Billings (Danny), Boyd Irwin, Sr. (Dr. Wagner), Gene Morgan (Taxi Driver), Stanley Andrews (Mrs. Mitchell).

Not much danger or intrigue in this one. Bellamy plays a famous surgeon who is belittled by his society-minded fiancee. He falls victim to amnesia and finds himself transported to Scranton, Pennsylvania. He still remembers his medical skills, however, and gets a job aiding injured workers in a steel mill. Kohler is the bad guy, out to wreck the steel mill and kill Bellamy. However, the villain has a change of heart when Bellamy saves his son's life in a tricky operation.

d, David Selman; w, Grace Neville (based on a story by Harold Shumate); ph, George Meehan; ed, Al Clark.

Drama (PR:A MPAA:NR)

DANGEROUS INTRUDER** (1945) 58m PRC bw
Charles Arnt (Max Ducane), Veda Ann Borg (Jenny), Richard Powers (Curtis), Fay Helm (Millicent), John Rogers (Foster), JoAnn Marlowe (Jackie), Helena P. Evans (Mrs. Swenson), Roberta Smith (Freckles), George Sorel (Holt), Forrest Taylor (Dr. Bascom), Eddie Rocco (Chauffeur).

A suspenseful little story about a showgirl, good-looking Borg, who is knocked down by a car while hitchhiking to New York, and convalescing at the home of the man who hit her, Arnt, a wealthy art dealer. During the night, Borg hears screams ring out in the house, and naturally gets scared. However, she is told by Arnt's stepdaughter, Marlowe, that the screams were made by her ill mother. Thickening the plot a little comes the realization by Borg that Arnt is unnaturally obsessed by his art masterpieces, and finally that the family got its wealth from a spinster aunt. Let down? That's how the film ends. Borg, originally a model and then chiefly a supporting player in scores of films, was the victim of a terrible auto crash in 1939, after which she had to endure a complete reconstruction of her face by plastic

surgery. She returned to films the next year and acted for twenty more years before retiring.

p, Martin Mooney; d, Vernon Keays; w, Martin M. Goldsmith (based on a story by Philip MacDonald and F. Ruth Howard); ph, James Brown; m, Karl Hajos; ed, Carl Pierson.

Mystery (PR:A MPAA:NR)

DANGEROUS KISS, THE* (1961, Jap.) 78m Toho c
Akira Takarada, Michiyo Aratama, Reiko Dan, Mitsuko Kusabue, Akemi Kita, Ichiro Nakatani, Seizaburo Kawazu, Haruko Togo, Takao Zushi, Kichijiro Ueda, Shintaro Ishihara, Sachio Sakai, Ichiro Arishima, Yuriko Hoshi, Sadako Sawamura.

Forgettable Japanese comedy stars Takarada as a prizefighter harassed by a bevy of attractive oriental vixens. Properly neglected today.

d, Yuzo Kawashima; ph, (Tohoscope, Eastmancolor).

Comedy (PR:A MPAA:NR)

DANGEROUS LADY* (1941) 63m PRC bw
June Storey (Phyllis Martindel), Neil Hamilton (Duke Martindel), Douglas Fowley (Brent), John Holland (Guy Kisling), Emmett Vogan (Dr. Grayson), Evelyn Brent (Hester Engel), Greta Granstedt (Leila Bostwick), Carl Stockdale (Judge Harding), Jack Mulhall (Clerk Jones), Kenneth Harlan (Dunlap), John Suce (Capt. Newton), Terry Walker (Annie), Ward McTaggart (Joe Link), James Aubrey (Manager).

This film has a plot so mysterious that one can scarcely follow it. Beginning with a flashback, it is about the murder of a judge and the framing of his secretary, who goes to prison only to escape to try to find the killer. Which brings us to the present and the real hero of the film, private detective Martindel, played by Hamilton. With his attorney-wife Storey, who tags along to keep him out of jail, Hamilton goes in search of the killer. It is Storey, however, who accidentally stumbles across the answers to the questions.

p&d, Bernard B. Ray; w, Jack Natteford, Sidney Sheldon (based on a story by Leslie T. White); ph, Jack Greenhalgh; ed, Carl Himm; md, Clarence Wheeler.

Mystery (PR:A MPAA:NR)

DANGEROUS LOVE AFFAIR
(SEE: LES LIASONS DANGEREUSES, 1961, Fr./Ital.)

DANGEROUS MEDICINE**½ (1938, Brit.) 72m WB bw
Elizabeth Allan (Victoria Ainswell), Cyril Ritchard (Dr. Noel Penwood), Edmond Breon (Totsie Mainwaring), Antony Holles (Alistair Hoard), Aubrey Mallalieu (Judge), Basil Gill (Sir Francis), Leo Genn (Murdoch), Gordon McLeod (Mr. Buller), Allan Jeayes (Supt. Fox), Quinton McPherson (Dr. Macomber), Frederick Burtwell (Mr. George), Patch (Boy), Dick Francis.

A wealthy old man marries his secretary and makes a will leaving everything to his young wife. The girl is accused of murder when the old man is found dead. She is found guilty, and on the way from court the car in which she and the police are traveling has an accident. She suffers a concussion and a piece of glass enters her heart. A young doctor makes medical history removing the splinter, but when she recovers she has suffered a memory loss and can't remember that she has been sentenced to death. The young doctor is angry when he realizes he saved the girl only to have her executed. He smuggles her out of the hospital and they go through the usual hide-and-seek with the police. While they are fugitives, the real killer is found, and the doctor and the girl get married. A well-directed and photographed film, with competent acting.

p, Jerome Jackson; d, Arthur Woods; w, Paul Gangelin, Connery Chappell (based on a novel by Edmond Deland); ph, Basil Emmott.

Mystery (PR:A MPAA:NR)

DANGEROUS MILLIONS** (1946) 69m FOX bw
Kent Taylor (Jack Clark), Dona Drake (Elena Valdez), Tala Birell (Sonia Bardos), Leonard Strong (Bandit Chieftain), Rex Evans (Lance Warburton), Robert Barrat (Hendrick Van Boyden), Konstantin Shayne (Jan Schuyler), Otto Reichow (Nils Otter), Rudolph Anders (Rudolph Busch), Franco Corsaro (Alfredo Charles), Henry Rowland, Victor Sen Yung.

A millionaire shipping magnate sends out word that eight of his relatives should gather at his mountain retreat in China after his death to split his wealth equally. Once there, two of the relatives are murdered, and several more murder attempts are made before the millionaire steps out alive. He faked his death to test his relatives' worthiness, and finally that none of them fits the bill.

p, Sol M. Wurtzel; d, James Tinling; w, Irving Cummings, Jr., Robert G. North (based on a story by Cummings and North); ph, Benjamin Kline; ed, William F. Claxton.

Mystery (PR:A MPAA:NR)

DANGEROUS MISSION*½ (1954) 75m RKO c
Victor Mature (Matt Hallett), Piper Laurie (Louise Graham), William Bendix (Joe Parker), Vincent Price (Paul Adams), Betta St. John (Mary Tiller), Steve Darrell (Katoonai), Marlo Dwyer (Mrs. Elster), Walter Reed (Dobson), Dennis Weaver (Pruitt), Harry Cheshire (Elster), George Sherwood (Mr. Jones), Maureen Stephenson (Mrs. Jones), Fritz Apking (Hawthorne), Kem Dibbs (Johnny Yonkers/Killer), John Carlyle (Bellhop), Frank Griffin (Tedd), Trevor Bardette (Kicking Bear), Roy Engel (Hume), Grace Hayle (Mrs. Alvord), Jim Potter (Cobb), Mike Lally (Fletcher), Sam Shack, Craig Moreland, Ralph Volkie (Firefighters), Bert Moorehouse (Piano Player), Virginia Linden (Mrs. Brown), Chet Marshall (Bellhop), Helen Brown (Miss Thorndyke), Chester Jones (Porter), Richard Newton (Young Man Boone), Bill White, Jr. (Hotel Clerk), Charles Cane (Barrett), Jack Chefe (Headwaiter), Steve

Rowland *(Parking Lot Attendant)*, Russ Thorson *(Radio Man)*, Robert Carraher *(Praskins)*.

A very early Irwin Allen film in 3-d and it is heartening to see that some things don't change. Allen makes dumb pictures these days and he made dumb pictures in the 1950s. Consistency is everything in the movie business. This way, studio chiefs know exactly what to expect. Allen makes dumb movies, Altman makes dumber movies, and DePalma makes the dumbest movies. In this case, the story is as follows: Laurie witnesses a gangland slaying one night after hours at a nightclub. She knows the killer and the cops are both after her for different reasons. She flees to Glacier National Park in Montana (don't all fleeing people also wind up in a place like that?) where the vistas are incredible and do wonders for the 3-D photography, but nothing at all for the story. The cops and the killer each send someone after her. The good guy is to bring her back safely where she can testify. The bad guy is there to arrange a fatal accident. One of the men is Price and the other is Mature and if you can't tell which of them is the criminal, you should take up another hobby besides movies. Once the true villain is revealed, there's a forest fire, an avalanche, and a chase across a glacier to the not-so-thrilling conclusion. Bill Bendix chimes in as a forest ranger but has little to do and can't save this terribly edited, cheap imitation of a Hitchcock film.

p, Irwin Allen; d, Louis King; w, Horace McCoy, W.R. Burnett, Charles Bennett (based on a story by McCoy, James Edmiston); ph, William Snyder (Technicolor, 3 -D); m, Roy Webb; ed, Gene Palmer; art d, Albert S. D'Agostino, Walter Keller.

Crime Drama   **Cas.**   **(PR:A-C MPAA:NR)**

DANGEROUS MONEY**   (1946) 66m MON bw

Sidney Toler *(Charlie Chan)*, Victor Sen Yung *(Jimmy Chan)*, Willie Best *(Chattanooga)*, Joseph Crehan *(Capt. Black)*, Dick Elliott *(P.T. Burke)*, Elaine Lange *(Cynthia Martin)*, Amira Moustafa *(Laura Erickson)*, Gloria Warren *(Rona Simmonds)*, Joe Allen, Jr. *(George Brace)*, Rick Vallin *(Tao Erickson)*, Bruce Edwards *(Harold Mayfair)*, Emmett Vogan *(Professor Martin)*, John Harmon *(Freddie Kirk)*, Alan Douglas *(Mrs. Whipple)*, Leslie Denison *(Rev. Whipple)*, Dudley Dickerson *(Big Ben)*, Tristam Coffin *(Scott Pearson)*, Rito Punay *(Pete)*, Selmer Jackson *(Ship's Doctor)*.

On a ship bound from Samoa to Pago Pago, a federal agent is murdered. Fortunately Toler and Number Two Son Yung are aboard to expose a gang that looted the Philippines just before the Japanese occupation. Mediocre but enjoyable second feature. (See CHARLIE CHAN series, Index.)

p, James S. Burkett; d, Terry Morse; w, Miriam Kissinger (based on a character created by Earl Derr Biggers); ph, William Sickner; ed, William Austin; md, Edward J. Kay.

Crime   **(PR:A MPAA:NR)**

DANGEROUS MOONLIGHT   (SEE: SUICIDE SQUADRON, 1941)

DANGEROUS NAN McGREW**   (1930) 71m PAR-Publix bw

Helen Kane *(Dangerous Nan McGrew)*, Victor Moore *(Doc Foster)*, James Hall *(Bob Dawes)*, Stuart Erwin *(Eustace Macy)*, Frank Morgan *(Muldoon)*, Roberta Robinson *(Clara Benson)*, Louise Closser Hale *(Mrs. Benson)*, Allen Forrest *(Godfrey Crofton)*, John Hamilton *(Grant)*, Bob Milash *(Sheriff)*.

Feeble musical comedy stars Helen Kane, the original "boop-boop-a-doop" girl. Kane and Moore are owners and stars of a flea-bitten medicine show which is heading for the poorhouse. They get a $10,000 reward for the accidental capture of an escaped murderer. Film is played mostly for laughs and gets plenty of them. Kane won brief fame for her squeaky "boop-boop-a-doop" rendition of the song "I Wanna Be Loved by You" in the musical "Good Boy" in 1928. After DANGEROUS NAN McGREW, however, she made only one more movie, HEADS UP (1930). Songs: "Dangerous Nan McGrew," "I Owe You" (Don Hartman, Al Goodheart), "Aw! C'mon, Whatta Ya Got To Lose?" (Richard A. Whiting, Leo Robin), "Once a Gypsy Told Me [You Were Mine]" (Irving Kahal, Sammy Fain, Pierre Norman).

d, Malcolm St. Clair; w, Paul Gerard Smith, Pierre Collings (based on a story by Charles Beahan, Garrett Fort); ph, George Folsey; ed, Helene Turner.

Musical Comedy   **(PR:A MPAA:NR)**

DANGEROUS NUMBER**   (1937) MGM bw

Robert Young *(Hank)*, Ann Sothern *(Elinor)*, Reginald Owen *(Cousin William)*, Cora Witherspoon *(Gypsy)*, Dean Jagger *(Dillman)*, Marla Shelton *(Vera)*, Barnett Parker *(Minehardi)*, Charles Trowbridge *(Hotel Manager)*, Franklyn Pangborn, Spencer Charters.

A marginally humorous film has a conservative rich guy, Young, who falls in love with a crazy showgirl. They are an improbable couple and don't comprehend each other, but get married anyway, which leads to some gaiety. It was Sothern's first picture for MGM, preceding a long contract with the studio.

d, Richard Thorps; w, Carey Wilson (based on a story by Leona Dalrymple); ph, Leonard Smith; ed, Blanche Sewall.

Comedy   **(PR:A MPAA:NR)**

DANGEROUS PARADISE*½   (1930) 58m PAR bw

Nancy Carroll *(Alma)*, Richard Arlen *(Heyst)*, Warner Oland *(Schomberg)*, Gustav von Seyffertitz *(Mr. Jones)*, Francis McDonald *(Ricardo)*, George Kotsonaros *(Pedro)*, Dorothea Wolbert *(Mrs. Schomberg)*, Clarence H. Wilson *(Zangiacomo)*, Evelyn Selbie *(His Wife)*, Willie Fung *(Wang)*, Wong Wing *(His Wife)*, Lillian Worth *(Myrtle)*.

Set on a South Sea island, the story concerns the adventures of a hermit-hero, Arlen, and girl violinist, Carroll. She has been hired to play at a resort on the island, but is pushed into entertaining the male guests. She does not like this kind of work and stows away on Arlen's skiff to get away from it all. There are five bad guys in the film. Three are after the gold Arlen allegedly has hidden away, and two are after Carroll. By the end of the film, all the baddies are either dead or in jail and it turns out that Arlen had no gold after all. The film's strictly a snicker nowadays.

d, William A. Wellman; w, William Slavens McNutt, Grover Jones (based on incidents from the novel *Victory* by Joseph Conrad); ph, A. J. Stout; m/l, "Smiling Skies," Leo Robin, Richard Whiting.

Adventure   **(PR:A MPAA:NR)**

DANGEROUS PARTNERS zero   (1945) 74m MGM bw

James Craig *(Jeff Caighn)*, Signe Hasso *(Carola Ballister)*, Edmund Gwenn *(Albert Richard Kingby)*, Audrey Totter *(Lili Roegan)*, Mabel Paige *(Marie Drumman)*, John Warburton *(Clyde Ballister)*, Henry O'Neill *(Duffy)*, Grant Withers *(Jonathan)*, Felix Bressart *(Prof. Budlow)*, Warner Anderson *(Miles Kempen)*, Horace [Stephen] McNally *(Co-Pilot)*, John Eldredge *(Farrel)*, Sondra Rogers *(Woman)*, Harry Hayden *(Doctor)*, Edward Gargan *(Sergeant)*, Katharine Booth *(Miss Day)*, George H. Reed *(Porter)*, Wally Cassell *(Youngest Brother)*, John Carlyle *(4th Brother)*, Chester Clute *(Stranger)*, Eddie Dunn *(Counterman)*, Charles Wagenheim *(Small Man)*, Clancy Cooper *(Ben Albee)*, Teddy Infuhr *(Boy)*, Douglas Madore *(Violin Boy)*, Jack Luden *(Clerk)*, Sam Finn *(2nd Clerk)*, Tom Dillon *(Captain of Police)*, Robert Malcolm *(Detective)*, John Valentine *(Police Doctor)*, Thomas Louden *(Charles, the Valet)*, George Davis *(Waiter)*.

A terrible spy mystery involving a Nazi spy and some money-grubbing people. A briefcase belonging to Gwenn, who has been knocked unconscious, is found at the scene of a plane crash. In it are four wills indicating where large sums of money willed to Gwenn are kept. Hasso's husband is killed while trying to get the money, and she teams up with Craig to finish the work. Just when they are about to succeed, they are confronted by Gwenn, who reveals that he is a top Nazi agent trying to get the money and escape to Germany. The two end up capturing Gwenn and they unrealistically turn the money over to the government.

p, Arthur J. Field; d, Edward L. Cahn; w, Marion Parsonnet, Edmund L. Hartmann (based on the story "Paper Chase" by Oliver Weld Bayer); ph, Karl Freund; m, David Snell; ed, Ferris Webster; art d, Cedric Gibbons, Hubert Hobson.

Spy Mystery   **(PR:A MPAA:NR)**

DANGEROUS PASSAGE**   (1944) 61m Pine-Thomas/PAR bw

Robert Lowery *(Joe Beck)*, Phyllis Brooks *(Nita Paxton)*, Charles Arnt *(Daniel Bergstrom)*, Jack LaRue *(Mike Zomano)*, Victor Kilian *(Buck Harris)*, William Edmunds *(Captain Saul)*, Alec Craig *(Dawson)*, John Eldredge *(Vaughn)*.

A fast-paced but uninspired film has Lowery trying to make it from South America to Galveston, Texas, to pick up his inheritance. He grabs a slow boat from a Central American port after an attorney locates him (Lowery has been unable to be reached for quite a while, because he was in the jungles.) On the boat are the lawyer, Brooks, and others, for what turns out to be a mysterious voyage. Strange events and attempts on his life occur. He falls in love with Brooks, and the two remain on the boat when it docks at a Mexican port. The boat is deliberately wrecked for insurance purposes by the owners, but Lowery and Brooks hang on to the wreckage to be picked up by a scout plane for safe arrival in Galveston.

d, William Berke; w, Geoffrey Homes; ph, Fred Jackman, Jr.; ed, Henry Adams.

Mystery   **(PR:A MPAA:NR)**

DANGEROUS PROFESSION, A**   (1949) 79m RKO bw

George Raft *(Kane)*, Ella Raines *(Lucy)*, Pat O'Brien *(Farley)*, Bill Williams *(Brackett)*, James Backus *(Ferrone)*, Roland Winters *(McKay)*, Betty Underwood *(Elaine)*, Robert Gist *(Collins)*, David Wolfe *(Dawson)*, Mack Gray *(Fred, Taxi Driver)*, Lynne Roberts *(Miss Wilson)*, Jonathan Hale *(Lennert)*, Paul Maxey *(Judge Thompson)*, Charmienne Harker *(Helen)*, Steven Flagg *(Roberts)*, Gloria Gabriel *(Kane's Secretary)*, Dick Dickenson *(Thin Man)*, Barry Brooks *(Detective)*, Don Dillaway *(Young Drunk)*, Ralph Volkie *(Men)*, Terry Wilson, Ken Terrell *(Men)*, Frank Shannon *(Barman)*.

Somewhat anachronistic film that would have been more suited for 1939 than 1949. Raft passes his usual criminal mantle onto others and checks in as an ex-cop, now a bail bondsman. Before the movie ever started, he'd trifled with Raines and fallen in love with her. Now she confesses that she's married to Williams and the guy has been jailed for embezzlement. Can Raft provide the necessary bond money to get him out? She and Williams had been separated when she waltzed with Raft but now she wants to make her marriage work and appeals to Raft as a friend. Raft's partner, O'Brien, thinks it's a dumb deal but Raft insists that they put up the money. Williams wakes up dead and Raft is livid. Now he seeks out the killers and in so doing crosses paths with Backus as a tough local detective hard on the case. They attempted to make this a semi-documentary about a business that most people don't know about or ever want to know about. Even the kind-hearted and generally tolerant O'Brien thought this, his last film for RKO, "a dog." He went on to quote his agent who saw the film and carped: "Everyone connected with it should have been locked up without benefit of bail before it ever went into production." It failed to excite interest at the box office. Winters also played Charlie Chan in a few films but is acknowledged as the least effective of all the Chan portrayers, with the possible exception of Ross Martin in a TV film.

p, Robert Sparks; d, Ted Tetzlaff; w, Martin Rackin, Warren Duff; ph, Robert De Grasse; m, Frederick Hollander; ed, Frederic Knudtson; md, C. Bakaleinikoff; art d, Albert S. D'Agostino, Al Herman; set d, Darrell Silvera, Harley Miller.

Crime   **(PR:A MPAA:NR)**

DANGEROUS SEAS**

(1931, Brit.) 53m Edward G. Whiting/Filmophone bw

Julie Suedo (Nan Penwardine), Sandy Irving (Capt. Muddle), Charles Garrey (Penwardine), Gerald Rawlinson (Standford), Wally Bosco (Sunny Bantick), Gladys Dunham (Polly).

Royal Excise officer Irving falls in love with Suedo, the daughter of innkeeper Garrey, unaware that Garrey is the smuggler he is seeking. Vaguely interesting early British talkie.

p, Edward G. Whiting; d&w, Edward Dryhurst.

Crime   **(PR:A MPAA:NR)**

DANGEROUS SECRETS**½

(1938, Brit.) 59m GN bw

Paul Lukas (Prof. Paul Bernardy), Linden Travers (Helen Bernardy), Hugh Williams (Jim Wyndham), Marie Ney (Martha Russell), Renee Gadd (Girl Friend), Fred Withers (Gardner), Howard Douglas (Mr. Coleman).

Travers and Williams meet in a London restaurant, then end up spending the night together. They realize that they love one another but must return to their respective duties. Williams goes to India to take care of some business, while Travers returns to her scientific research. Once in India, Williams realizes that he can't live without her, and cables from India proposing marriage, but she never receives the message. Five years later he returns to London and finds her happily married to her kindly professor. Williams and Travers are once again thrown into each others' arms and realize that they still are in love. The professor is jealous. The couple are on the verge of running away when they hear the husband's defense of his wife against a servant who accuses her of infidelity. This brings the two lovers' consciences into play. Williams decides to fade out of the picture, while Travers and her husband resume life together with a new understanding. A sensible, adult picture, dignified and worthwhile.

p, Hugh Perceval; d, Edmond Greville; w, Basil Mason; ph, Ronald Neame; ed, Ray Pitt; md, George Walter.

Drama   **(PR:A MPAA:NR)**

DANGEROUS TO KNOW*

(1938) 68m PAR bw

Anna May Wong (Mme. Lan Ying), Akim Tamiroff (Stephen Recka), Gail Patrick (Margaret Van Kase), Lloyd Nolan (Inspector Brandon), Harvey Stephens (Phillip Easton), Anthony Quinn (Nicholas Kusnoff), Roscoe Karns (Duncan), Porter Hall (Mayor Bradley), Barlowe Borland (Butler), Hedda Hopper (Mrs. Carson), Hugh Sothern (Harvey Greggson), Edward Pawley (John Rance), Eddie Marr (Crouch), Harry Worth (Hanley), Robert Brister (Councilman Murkil), Pierre Watkin (Sen. Carson), Garry Owen (Mike Tookey), John Hart (Man), Donald Brian (Judge Parker), Stanley Blystone (Motorcycle Cop), Terry Ray [Ellen Drew] (Secretary), Rita La Roy (Mrs. Barnett), Harvey Clark (Mr. Barnett), Jack Knoche (Messenger), Gino Corrado (Headwaiter).

This appears to be an attempt to tailor material to the strong screen presence of Tamiroff, who was having a fairly successful career at Paramount as an unsavory, mysterious foreigner with a heavy accent. The film has Tamiroff as the hero-gangster who will stop at nothing to get what he wants. The Moscow Art Theater-trained Tamiroff eventually became equally effective in broad comedy roles.

d, Robert Florey; w, William R. Lipman, Horace McCoy (based on the play "On The Spot" by Edgar Wallace); ph, Theodor Sparkuhl; ed, Arthur Schmidt; art d, Hans Dreier, John Goodman.

Crime   **(PR:A MPAA:NR)**

DANGEROUS VENTURE**

(1947) 59m UA bw

William Boyd (Hopalong Cassidy), Andy Clyde (California Carlson), Rand Brooks (Lucky Jenkins), Fritz Leiber (Xeoli), Douglas Evans (Dr. Atwood), Harry Cording (Morgan), Betty Alexander (Sue Harmon), Francis McDonald (Kane), Neyle Morrow (Jose), Patricia Tate (Talu), Bob Faust (Stark), Elaine Riley.

The third Hopalong Cassidy movie under the aegis of Boyd, who took over the series when producer Harry Sherman dropped the episodes in 1943, stars Boyd as the hero cowboy searching for a tribe of American Indians who claim to be descendants of the Aztecs. An archeological expedition is sent, headed by a lovely woman archeologist, to verify the Indians' lineage. Meanwhile, a gang of crooks tries to discredit the tribe by committing crimes dressed as Indians. The assistant archeologist discovers gold relics buried with the Indians' dead. He hooks up with the bad guys so he can loot the burial grounds. Through all of this ride Boyd and his sidekicks, who end up coming to the rescue of the archeologist, and who save the Indian burial ground from the bad guys. (See HOPALONG CASSIDY series, Index.)

p, Lewis J. Rachmil; d, George Archainbaud; w, Doris Schroeder; ph, Mack Stengler; M, David Chudnow; ed, Fred W. Berger; art d, Harvey T. Gillett.

Western   **(PR:A MPAA:NR)**

DANGEROUS VOYAGE

(SEE: TERROR SHIP, 1954)

DANGEROUS WATERS*½

(1936) 62m UNIV bw

Jack Holt (Jim Marlowe), Robert Armstrong (Dusty Johnson), Grace Bradley (Joan), Diana Gibson (Ruth Denning), Charlie Murray (McDuffy), Willard Robertson (Bill McKeechie), Dewey Robinson (Chips), Ed Gargan (Bosun), Guy Usher (Capt. Denning), Richard Alexander (Hayes), Billy Gilbert, Edwin Maxwell.

Holt is a tough-and-ready captain of an old wreck of a boat, who must deliver it to port. He is thwarted by racketeers who plant their henchmen in the crew to sink the boat and collect more insurance money than the tub is worth. The bad guys blow a hole in the hold of the boat and, with water rushing in, Holt goes down to

stem the flow. His wife, a two-timing harlot, meanwhile makes a play for the second mate, who is also Holt's best friend. After saving the ship, Holt comes up on top to find his wife and best friend in an embrace. She lies, claiming the friend attacked her. Holt promptly floors his friend. Later he discovers the truth about his wife's two-timing ways, and makes up with his friend. When Holt finally brings the boat into port, he is rewarded with $10,000 from Lloyd's of London, and given a new commission.

p, Fred S. Meyer; d, Lambert Hillyer; w, Richard Schayer, Hazel Jamieson, Malcolm Stuart Boylan (based on a story by Theodore Reeves); ph, Harry Forbes; ed, Murray Seldeen.

Adventure   **(PR:A MPAA:NR)**

DANGEROUS WHEN WET**½

(1953) 95m MGM c

Esther Williams (Katy), Fernando Lamas (Andre Lanet), Jack Carson (Windy Webbe), Charlotte Greenwood (Ma Higgins), Denise Darcel (Gigi Mignon), William Demarest (Pa Higgins), Donna Corcoran (Junior Higgins), Barbara Whiting (Suzie Higgins), Bunny Waters (Greta), Henri Letondal (Joubert), Paul Bryar (Pierre), Jack Raine (Stuart Frye), Richard Alexander (Egyptian Channel Swimmer), Tudor Owen (Old Salt), Ann Codee (Mrs. Lanet), Michael Dugan (Ad Lib), Roger Moore, Reginald Simpson (Reporters), John McKee (Photographer), Arthur Gould-Porter (English Steward), Eugene Borden (French Mayor), Aminta Dyne (English Woman Guest), James Fairfax (English Cab Driver), Molly Glessing (English Waitress), Pat O'Moore (Bob Gerrard), Jimmy Aubrey (Bartender).

Esther Williams and Fernando Lamas were both married to other people when they met and made this movie. It took many years but they eventually shed their mates, married each other, and had one of Hollywood's most enduring relationships until Lamas passed away. This movie was not as memorable as their marriage. Williams, Greenwood, Corcoran, and Whiting are a swimming family that decides to go across the English Channel en masse when smooth salesman Jack Carson convinces them they can make some serious money doing it. Carson hustles liquid vitamins and figures that he can utilize their names in the sale of his merchandise. The family needs the money to buy a bull for their farm in Arkansas. Lamas is a champagne salesman who has made many francs at his work. He has an eye for gams as well as grapes and rescues Williams at sea when she's become disoriented in the fog. A few mild complications muddle the middle but it's all aimed at the finale, the solo swimming of the channel by Williams when the local muckety-mucks forbid the entire family from doing it. Williams almost gives up near the end of the swim but Lamas leaps in and inspires her to finish. And that's about that. The highlight of the picture is a live action/animated sequence that features Williams and Tom and Jerry. It was directed by Fred Quimby, William Hanna, and Joe Barbera, the latter two eventually leaving MGM to establish their own cartoon dynasty. A few pleasant songs by Mercer and Schwartz but nothing that anyone can hum these days. Bill Demarest, as the father of the swimming clan, does his usual on-the-nose job as a foil. Songs: "I Got Out Of Bed On the Right Side," "Ain't Nature Grand?", "I Like Men," "Fifi," "In My Wildest Dreams" (Arthur Schwartz, Johnny Mercer).

p, George Wells; d, Charles Walters; w, Dorothy Kingsley; ph, Harold Rosson (Technicolor); m, Arthur Schwartz, Johnny Mercer; ed, John McSweeney, Jr.; md, Georgie Stoll; ch, Billy Daniel, Walters; cartoon sequence, Fred Quimby, William Hanna, Joe Barbera.

Musical Comedy   **(PR:A MPAA:NR)**

DANGEROUS WOMAN*½

(1929) 80m PAR bw

Baclanova (Tania Gregory), Clive Brook (Frank Gregory), Neil Hamilton (Bobby Gregory), Clyde Cook (Tubbs), Leslie Fenton (Peter Allerton), Snitz Edwards (Chief Macheria).

Baclanova, as Tania, is the Russian-born wife of Brook, the commissioner of a land deep in the African jungles. She is an evil woman who uses jungle magic to seduce young men, and then disposes of them when she is finished. The first to fall for her magic is Brook's assistant, Fenton. She has her way with him, tires of the boy, and causes him to kill himself by a self-inflicted gunshot wound to the head. Brook's kid brother, Hamilton, comes to the jungle to replace Fenton. Baclanova tries to do the same to him. He is stronger than his predecessor, but succumbs none the less. Learning that his brother has fallen prey to his wicked wife, Brook puts poison in her orange juice, killing her. He is protected from the truth of his successful murder by his good friend, Cook, who places a dead snake next to her bed and refills the orange juice glass, making it look as though the poisonous snake did the killing.

p, Louis D. Lighton; d, Rowland V. Lee; w, John Farrow, Edward Paramore, Jr. (based on a story by Margery Lawrence); ph, Harry Fischbeck.

Horror   **(PR:A MPAA:NR)**

DANGEROUS YEARS*

(1947) 60m FOX bw

William Halop (Danny Jones), Ann E. Todd (Doris Martin), Jerome Cowan (Weston), Anabel Shaw (Connie Burns), Richard Gaines (Edgar Burns), Scotty Beckett (Willy Miller), Darryl Hickman (Leo Emmerson), Harry Shannon (Judge Raymond), Dickie Moore (Gene Spooner), Donald Curtis (Jeff Carter), Harry Harvey, Jr. (Phil Kenny), Gil Stratton, Jr. (Tammy McDonald), Joseph Vitale (August Miller), Marilyn Monroe (Evie), Nana Bryant (Miss Templeton), Tom Kennedy (Adamson), Lee Shumway (Alec), Mimi Doyle (Reporter), Claire Whitney (Woman).

The title refers to the years in which juvenile delinquency is most prevalent. The story concerns a young hoodlum, Halop, who recruits students into his gang. On a warehouse raid he kills the most popular teacher in the school. At the trial Gaines' adopted daughter, Todd, rises to Halop's defense as he did for her when they were both in an orphanage. District attorney Gaines throws the book at Halop, but the defense lawyer, Cowan, lays the blame at the feet of the parents of delinquents. Halop is sentenced to life imprisonment, but what Gaines doesn't realize is that the boy he just condemned is his own son. The William Halop who is the star of this film is former "Dead End Kid" Billy Halop. Marilyn Monroe's role was a bit part to be sure, but it did not end up on the cutting room floor as did shots of her in her debut film, SCUDDA-HOO! SCUDDA-HAY! the year before (except for a long shot of her rowing a boat in a distant background). Nonetheless, Fox, which had signed her to a year's contract, dropped the contract before anything more substantial came about.

p, Sol M. Wurtzel; d, Arthur Pierson; w, Arnold Belgard; ph, Benjamin Kline; m, Rudy Schrager; ed, Frank Baldridge, William Claxton.

Crime   **(PR:A MPAA:NR)**

DANGEROUS YOUTH**

(1958, Brit.) 97m WB bw (GB: THESE DANGEROUS YEARS)

George Baker (Padre), Frankie Vaughan (Dave Wyman), Carole Lesley (Dinah Brown), Jackie Lane (Maureen), Katherine Kath (Mrs. Wyman), Thora Hird (Mrs. Larkin), Eddie Byrne (Danny), Kenneth Cope (Juggler), Robert Desmond (Cream O'Casey), John Le Mesurier (Commanding Officer), David Lodge (Sgt. Lockwood), Reginald Beckwith (Hairdresser), Ray Jackson (Smiler Larkin), Richard Leech (Capt. Brewster), Michael Ripper (Pvt. Simpson), Ralph Reader, Eric Morley, David Lodge, Reginald Beckwith, Lloyd Lamble, Martin Boddey, John Breslin, Victor Brooks, David Gregory.

From the slum area of Liverpool, Vaughan, a would-be rock singer and full-time leader of a street gang, is drafted into the army, and the film follows him through basic training. The army makes a man of the street punk. His best friend in boot camp is killed by a troublemaker, and Vaughan deserts after wounding the bully in retaliation. He later straightens the mess out, settles down, and marries his singing partner, Lesley. Anna Neagle, one of Britain's leading actresses at the time, made her producing debut in this one. Songs: "Isn't It A Lovely Evening?" "These Dangerous Years," "Cold Cold Shower" (Richard Mullen, Peter Moreton, Bert Waller).

p, Anna Neagle; d, Herbert Wilcox; w, Jack Trevor Story; ph, Gordon Dines; m, Stanley Black; ed, Basil Warren.

Crime/Musical Comedy   **(PR:A MPAA:NR)**

DANGEROUSLY THEY LIVE***½

(1942) 77m WB bw

John Garfield (Dr. Michael Lewis), Nancy Coleman (Jane), Raymond Massey (Dr. Ingersoll), Moroni Olsen (Mr. Goodwin), Esther Dale (Dawson), Lee Patrick (Nurse Johnson), John Ridgely (John), Christian Rub (Steiner), Frank Reicher (Jarvis), Ben Welden (Eddie), Cliff Clark (John Dill), Roland Drew (Dr. Murdock), Arthur Aylsworth (Gate Keeper), John Harmon (George, Taxi Driver), Matthew Boulton (Capt. Hunter), Gavin Muir (Capt. Strong), Ilka Gruning (Mrs. Steiner), Frank M. Thomas (Ralph Bryan), James Seay (Carl), Ben Cavender (Tobacconist), Adolph Milar (Storekeeper), Charles Drake (Joe), Joan Winfield, Audra Lindley (Nurses), Jack Mower (Mailman), Leah Baird (Telephone Operator), Dick Wessel (Grant), Tod Andrews (Craig), Murray Alper (Miller), Henry Victor (Capt. Horst), Henry Rowland (Telegraph Operator), Leslie Denison (Flt. Lt. Tyler), Sven Hugo Borg (Under-Officer), Spec O'Donnell (Usher), Lon McCallister (Newsboy).

A fairly ordinary spy story that would have been laughed off the screen at any other time than when it was released. Garfield had been complaining about the pictures he was given to do and went on suspension. Eventually, his money ran out and he had to do something to make a living so he took this job. Coleman is second-billed as an Allied spy who is carrying top-secret information when she is kidnaped by the Nazis, led by Olsen. She tries to escape and is hurt in a cab crash, then taken to a hospital where Garfield is interning. He's assigned to watch over her and she takes a liking to him and explains what she's up to. She'd had the fastest case of amnesia on record and it quickly cleared once she took a look at Garfield. Olsen arrives at the hospital and pretends to be Coleman's father. As it happens in so many films of this genre, the co-star never believes the star's story until it's too late. That's what happens here as Garfield allows Olsen and his "psychiatrist" associate to sign Coleman out of the hospital on the pretext that she is suffering from delusions of paranoia. In a quietly understated role, the real leader of the spies is Massey (he doubles as the shrink). Garfield is beginning to raise an eyebrow at what's happening so he is invited to join them at the family estate. Once there, he realizes that he and Coleman are prisoners. Garfield flies the coop, is caught and tossed into jail when Massey testifies against him. Coleman is removed from the mansion and brought to a Nazi hideout. She has valuable shipping information and they intend to torture it out until they get it. They will then send that via shortwave to Nazi subs that wait offshore. Garfield does his second escape, this time from jail, gets to the hideout, and saves Coleman. The German subs' location is radioed to some allied bombers and the U-boats are bombed to bits. The nation was in an uproar about the Germans in Europe and the Japanese in the Pacific and any film that was anti-Axis would get people cheering in the theaters. This was filled with holes, wasn't terribly exciting, and Garfield walked through his part. You could almost tell he was only doing it for the money. Olsen's unique first name came from the fact that he was born in Utah, probably a Mormon, and named after the angel Moroni whom the Mormons revere.

p, Ben Stoloff; d, Robert Florey; w, Marion Parsonnet (from the story "Remember Tomorrow" by Parsonnet); ph, L. William O'Connell; ed, Harold McLernon; art d, Hugh Reticher.

Spy Drama   **(PR:A MPAA:NR)**

DANGEROUSLY YOURS**

(1933) 74m FOX bw

Warner Baxter (Andrew Burke), Miriam Jordan (Claire Roberts), Herbert Mundin (Grove), Florence Eldridge (Jo Horton), Florence Roberts (Mrs. Lathem), William Davidson (George Carr), Arthur Hoyt (Dr. Ryder), Mischa Auer (Kassim), Nella

Walker (Lady Gregory), Tyrell Davis (Theodore Brill), Edmund Burns (Tony), Robert Greig (White).

Warner Baxter is the gentleman thief, and Jordan a woman detective for an insurance company. They meet socially, and end up on the opposite sides of the law but on the same side of the sheets. Dignified in manner and carriage, and a fabulous looker, Jordan only had a three-year career in Hollywood before she retired from the screen because of public apathy.

d, Frank Tuttle; w, Horace Jackson (based on a story by Paul Hervey Fox); ph, John Seitz; ed, Harold Schuster.

Crime   **(PR:A MPAA:NR)**

DANGEROUSLY YOURS*½

(1937) 60m FOX bw

Cesar Romero (Victor Morell), Phyllis Brooks (Valerie Barton), Jane Darwell (Aunt Cynthia), Alan Dinehart (Julien Stevens), Natalie Garson (Flo Davis), Douglas Wood (Walter Chandler), Earle Foxe (Eddie), Leon Ames (Phil), Albert Conti (Monet), Leonid Snegoff (Boris), John Harrington (Louis Davis).

Romero, a detective posing as a jewel thief, sails from Europe to New York in the company of a band of jewel thieves who are after a famous diamond. Romero is sent on the voyage by the insurance company to stop the crooks from stealing the diamond, which is as large as a doorknob. He falls in love with the woman in the gang, Brooks, making it necessary for him to clear her when the gang is captured. The film's triteness shows when Brooks, as much a jewel thief as the others, decides to go straight and the court gives her a suspended sentence, putting her on parole, with orders to report to Romero as her parole officer.

p, Sol M. Wurtzel; d, Malcolm St. Clair; w, Lou Breslow, John Patrick; ph, Harry Davis; ed, Al De Gaetano; md, Samuel Kaylin.

Crime   **(PR:A MPAA:NR)**

DANIEL**

(1983) 13m PAR c

Timothy Hutton (Daniel Isaacson), Edward Asner (Jacob Ascher), Mandy Patinkin (Paul Isaacson), Lindsay Crouse (Rochelle), Joseph Leon (Selig Mindish), Amanda Plummer (Susan Isaacson), Ellen Barkin (Phyllis Isaacson), Tovah Feldshuh (Linda Mindish), John Rubinstein (Robert Lewin), Maria Tucci (Lise Lewin), Julie Bovasso (Frieda Stein), Carmen Matthews, Norman Parker, Lee Richardson, Colin Stinton, Rita Zohar, Ilan M. Mitchell-Smith, Will Lee, David Margulies, Jena Greco, Dael Cohen, Peter Friedman, George Axler, Lori Berhon, Alexander Bernstein, Leo Burmeister, Burton Collins, Luis Garzon, Joe Dabenigno, Rachael Goldman, Martha Greenhouse, Leon Gross, Burtt Harris, Joe Kopmar.

Overlong, overblown adaptation of E.L. Doctorow's fictionalized account of the famous case against the Rosenbergs (who were accused of passing atomic secrets to the Russians and executed). Hutton, who plays the son of the "Isaacsons" (Rosenbergs), spends the majority of the film soulfully staring into space, musing over whether or not his parents were guilty. These scenes are intercut with sepia-toned flashbacks to his childhood which detail his parents' trial and execution. Eventually, Hutton decides he can live with it and triumphantly marches off to a protest rally with his wife and kid. While the material has ample ground for insight into the Rosenberg case, family heritage, and the contrast between the America of the early 1950s and late 1960s (witch-hunts in the 1950s and massive, organized dissension in the 1960s), the film meanders along at a snail's pace which is only highlighted by overly labored performances (or in the case of Hutton, nearly catatonic) that lend no compassion or understanding to the characters.

p, Burtt Harris; d, Sidney Lumet; w, E.L. Doctorow (based on his novel The Book Of Daniel); ph, Andrzej Bartkowiak (shot in Technicolor, released in Metrocolor); m, Bob James; ed, Peter Frank; prod d, Philip Rosenberg; cos, Anna Hill Johnstone.

Drama   **Cas.**   **(PR:C MPAA:R)**

DANIEL BOONE**

(1936) 75m RKO bw

George O'Brien (Daniel Boone), Heather Angel (Virginia), John Carradine (Simon Girty), Ralph Forbes (Stephen Marlowe), Clarence Muse (Pompey), George Regas (Black Eagle), Dickie Jones (Jerry), Huntley Gordon (Sir John Randolph), Harry Cording (Joe Burch), Aggie Herring (Mrs. Burch), Crauford Kent (Attorney General), Keith Kenneth (Commissioner).

O'Brien, as Daniel Boone, leads the settlers from North Carolina to the wilds of Kentucky. They have a few hostile encounters with some Indians, but stave off their attacks. Then they have to fight for their lives when renegade Carradine, decked out in a skunk-skin cap, unites five tribes, and incites them to attack the new town the settlers have built. The attack lasts nine days, and with the settlers' water and ammunition running low, it looks like curtains for O'Brien and company. Suddenly it begins to rain and the Indians scatter. All of this goes for naught, as a group of treacherous Virginian aristocrats usurp their land after it has been cleared and made livable.

p, George A. Hirliman; d, David Howard; w, Daniel Jarrett (based on a story by Edgecumb Pinchon); ph, Frank Good; ed, Ralph Dixon; md, Hugo Riesenfeld, Arthur Kay.

Adventure   **Cas.**   **(PR:AAA MPAA:NR)**

DANIEL BOONE, TRAIL BLAZER*½

(1957) 76m REP c

Bruce Bennett (Daniel Boone), Lon Chaney, Jr. (Blackfish), Faron Young (Faron Callaway), Kem Dibbs (Girty), Damian O'Flynn (Andy Callaway), Jacqueline Evans (Rebecca Boone), Nancy Rodman (Susannah Boone), Freddy Fernandez (Israel Boone), Carol Kelly (Jemima Boone), Eduardo Noriega (Squire Boone), Fred Kohler, Jr. (Kenton), Gordon Mills (John Holder), Claude Brook (James Boone), Joe Ainley (Gen. Hamilton), Lee Morgan (Smitty).

Filmed in Mexico, the story has Bennett and his band of settlers traveling from Yakin Valley, North Carolina, to Boonesborough, Kentucky. The bad guys are the

Shawnee Indians who are incited to fight the settlers by a French renegade and some British redcoats. Bennett saves the day by convincing Shawnee chief Chaney, Jr., that the settlers want nothing but peace.

p, Albert C. Gannaway; d, Gannaway, Ismael Rodriguez; w, Tom Hubbard, John Patrick; ph, Jack Draper (Trucolor); m, Raul Lavista; ed, Fernando Martinez; m/l, Gannaway, Hal Levy.

Adventure (PR:AA MPAA:NR)

DANIELLA BY NIGHT** (1962, Fr/Ger.) 83m Contact Organisation-Paris Inter Productions-Cinelux-Film-Pandora-Film/Cambist Films-Audobon Films bw
(DE QUOI TU TE MELES, DANIELA!; ZARTE HAUT IN SCHWARZER SEIDE)

Elke Sommer (Daniella), Ivan Desny (Count Castellani), Danik Patisson (Claudine), Claire Maurier (Esmeralda), Helmut Schmid (Karl Bauer), Rene Dary (Lanzac), Sandrine (Mannequin), Kathe Haack, Romana Rombach, France Lonbard, Brigitte Banz, Rudy Lenoir, Albert Dinan.

Sommer is a French model working in Rome who gets involved with spies when some secret microfilm is hidden in her lipstick case. Boring espionage drama, though Sommer is nice to look at.

p, Leopold Branover, Rene Thevent; d, Max Pecas; w, Wolfgang Steinhardt, Grisha M. Dabat, Pecas, Jean Clouzot; ph, Andre Germain; m, Charles Aznavour, Georges Garvarentz; ed, Paul Cayatte; set d, Sidney Bettex, Bob Luchaire.

Spy Drama (PR:C MPAA:NR)

DANNY BOY** (1934, Brit.) 83m Panther/But bw

Frank Forbes-Robinson (Pat Clare), Dorothy Dickson (Jane Kaye), Archie Pitt (Silver Sam), Ronnie Hepworth (Danny), Denis O'Neil (Mike), Cyril Ritchard (John Martin), Fred Duprez (Leo Newman), Paul Neville (Maloney), Herbert Cameron, Sydney Thornton, Bobbie Slater, Henry de Bray, Marcel de Haes and His Band.

Sentimental musical has singer Dickson searching all England for her husband and son, who have left her to pursue a career singing on the streets. Remade in 1941 with Ann Todd in the lead.

p&d, Oswald Mitchell, Challis Sanderson; w, Mitchell, H. Barr-Carson, Archie Pitt; ph, Desmond Dickinson.

Musical (PR:A MPAA:NR)

DANNY BOY*½ (1941, Brit.) 80m But bw

David Farrar (Martin), Wilfred Lawson (Newton), Ann Todd (Jane), Grant Tyler (Danny), John Warwick (Carter), Wylie Watson (Fiddlesticks), Tony Quinn (Maloney), Norah Gordon (Mrs. Maloney), Pat Lennox (Manager), Albert Whelan (Scotty), Harry Herbert (Skinny), Percy Manchester.

Todd plays a successful Britisher who leaves Broadway to return to England to help the war effort. Once she returns, she searches for the child and husband she left behind when she went off to pursue her career. Eventually, a rich admirer of Todd's helps her find her estranged family and they are reunited. Schmaltzy melodrama.

p, Hugh Perceval; d, Oswald Mitchell; w, Mitchell, A. Barr-Carson, Vera Allinson; ph, Stephan Dade.

Drama (PR:A MPAA:NR)

DANNY BOY** (1946) 53m PRC bw

Robert "Buzz" Henry (Jimmy Bailey), Ralph Lewis (Joe Cameron), Helen Brown (Mrs. Bailey), Sybil Merritt (Margie Bailey), Eve March (Mrs. Johnson), Tay Dunn (Mr. Johnson), Joseph Granby (Lafe Dunkell), Walter Soderling (Grumpy Andrews), Richard Kipling (Judge Carter), Michael McGuire (Pudgie), Myron Wilton (Hal), Charles Bates (Louis), Bobby Valentine (Rinky), Larry Dixon (Tuffy), Eric Younger (Jackie), Ace, the Dog (Danny Boy).

The title character is a dog that had been a Marine mascot during WW II and has recently returned to the States. A group of kids clamor over the famous dog, who is owned by Henry. The dog is kidnaped by a couple of crooks, but escapes. Later it attacks the two men when it sees them on the street. The dogknapers press charges against the pooch, and the ensuing court battle results in the dog being sentenced to the gas chamber. Lewis, a veteran, and Henry fight to change the canine's sentence to death by firing squad, since the dog was a Marine. The dog is saved in the nick of time, when Henry obtains incriminating evidence against the dogknapers, proving that they had caused the dog to attack them. The dog's lack of cooperation on the set is often apparent throughout this film. Cornball film but kids will like it.

p, Martin Mooney; d, Terry Morse; w, Raymond L. Schrock (based on a story by Taylor Caven); ph, Jack Greenhalgh; ed, George McGuire; md, Walter Green; art d, Edward C. Jewell.

Children (PR:AAA MPAA:NR)

DAN'S MOTEL* (1982) 78m Barrish Film c

George Berg, Jim Rudolph, Mary Catherine Wright, Evan Davis, Tallie Cochrane, Michael King, Patrick Wright, Jim Bowyer, Francesca Knittel-Bowyer, Sam David.

Jerry R. Barrish did about everything but act out all the roles in this low-budget independent production. The film contains three stories that happen inside the title motel. The first story, entitled "Conduit," is a pretentious film noir sketch of a man retreating into himself. He is holed up in his motel room, serviced by a prostitute, and linked to the outside world by his crippled, handless sidekick. The second part is the best and is titled "Kathleen." This segment is about a lonely would-be suicide who is cheered by her standup comic motel neighbor. The third is titled "The Advantage," and is an indulgent showcase for Cochrane, who sings

several songs, suffers an attempted rape, and seduces a young boy, while philosophizing on life the whole time. The film was shot on a shoestring budget in eight days.

p,d,w&ph, Jerry R. Barrish (Monaco Labs Color); m, Rick Burnley; ed, Barrish; m/l, Tallie Cochrane, Barrish.

Drama (PR:O MPAA:NR)

DANS LES GRIFFES DU MANIAQUE
(SEE: DIABOLICAL DR. Z, THE, 1967)

DANSE MACABRE (SEE: CASTLE OF BLOOD, 1964)

DANTE'S INFERNO*** (1935) 88m FOX bw

Spencer Tracy (Jim Carter), Claire Trevor (Betty McWade), Henry B. Walthall (Pop McWade), Scotty Beckett (Sonny), Alan Dinehart (Jonesy), Astrid Allwyn, Ruthelma Stevens (Girls in Stoke-Hold), Joe Brown (Baseball Concessionaire), George Humbert (Tony, The Hamburger-Stand Proprietor), Robert Gleckler (Dean), Maidel Turner (Mme. Zucchini), Nella Walker (Mrs. Hamilton), Lita Chevret (Mrs. Martin), Richard Tucker (Mr. Hamilton), Edward Pawley (Clinton, the Ship's Officer), Morgan Wallace (Captain Morgan), Harry Woods (2nd Officer Reynolds), Gary Leon, Rita [Hayworth] Cansino (Specialty Dancers), Ruth Clifford (Mrs. Gray), Dorothy Dix (Ticket Seller), Hal Boyer, J. Lloyd (College Boys), Jayne Regan (College Girl), Gardner James (Radio Operator), Jerry Gamble (Spieler), Edward McWade (Professor of Anatomy), Patricia Caron (Sailor's Girl), John Spacey (Andrew, The Hunchback Spieler), Ronald Rondell (Ticket Buyer), Harry Schultz, John Carpenter, George Chan (Concessionaires), Gertrude Astor, Tiny Jones (Concessionaires' Wives), Frank Austin (Photographer), Frank Moran (Mike, The Stoker), Kenneth Gibson (Assistant Purser), Harold A. Miller, Barrett Whitelaw, Jean Fenwick (Group in Boiler Room), Warren Hymer (Bozo, The Stoker), Ray Corrigan, Paul Schwegeler, Noble Johnson (The Devils), Lorna Lowe (Cleopatra), Elinor Johnson (Sappho), Andre Johnsen (Salome), Constantine Romanoff, Harry Wilson (Stokers), Paul McVey (Assistant), Charlie Sullivan (Drunken Sailor), Leona Lane (Borgia), Joana Sutton (Catherine de Medici), Marion Strickland (Eve), Gale Goodson (Little Bo Peep), Eve Kimberly (Oriental Maid), Margaret McCrystal, Dorothy Stockmar (Trumpeters), Jay Eaton, Reginald Sheffield (Bidders), Maude Truax (Fat Dowager), Oscar Apfel (Williams), Willard Robertson (Inspector Harris), Aloha Porter (Devil), Charles C. Wilson (Police Inspector), John H. McGuire (Wireless Operator), Bob Reel McKee (Wireless Operator's Assistant), Hale Hamilton (Wallace), George Meeker, Barbara Pepper, Lloyd Pantages (Drunks at Ship's Cafe), Eddie Tamblyn (Page Boy), Jack Norton, Robert Graves (Drunks in Cabin), Harry Holman (Jolly Fat Man), Harry Strang, George Magrill, Paul Palmer (Ship's Officers), Bud Geary (Park Attendant), Billie Huber, Paddy O'Flynn (Married Couple), Andrea Leeds (Anna, Maid to Betty), Mary Ashcraft, Paul Power, Marion Ladd (Bits—New Inferno), Robert Ross (Court Clerk), Russell Hicks (Prosecuting Attorney), Frank Conroy (Defense Attorney), George Irving (Judge), Cliff Lyons, Yakima Canutt (Stokers on the Paradise), Dennis O'Keefe (Extra—Ship's Fire).

Ambitious to the point of ruthlessness, Tracy is a ship's stoker who is fired for insulting a drunken female passenger making fun of him (not unlike O'Neill's "Hairy Ape") and gets a job as a carnival barker, touting a sideshow owned by Walthall, who had played The Little Colonel in Griffith's classic silent film THE BIRTH OF A NATION. The sideshow depicts scenes of Hell as originally envisioned by Dante in his Inferno, a shuddering panorama for the morally righteous. Through huckstering methods Tracy puts the show on a paying basis, marrying Walthall's daughter, Trevor. They have a son but Tracy ignores his family and goes pell-mell after wealth, packing an unsafe amusement pier with customers, bribing an inspector to look the other way. The pier collapses and scores are killed and injured, including Walthall who lectures Tracy about the lower depths of fire awaiting evil-doers. His lecture is accompanied with a truly frightening 10-minute insertion which depicts a roaring, terrible Hell (this was taken from Fox's 1924 DANTE'S INFERNO, dressed up with some added frames to work into the talkie version, a little masterpiece of special effects). Tracy is not moved, despite the gruesome fact that the inspector commits suicide when learning of the disaster he could have prevented. Tracy is brought to trial but lies his way to freedom with the help of his wife's testimony. The sham is too much for Trevor and she leaves Tracy, taking her son with her. Tracy next invests his money in a gambling ship, hiring an inexperienced crew which leads to a fire while the packed ship is at sea. Following his compassion instead of his mercenary streak, Tracy beaches the boat to save lives and loses his fortune. At the end, however, Trevor and son rejoin him in seeking an honest future. The story is overlong and most of the cast move about like zombies, except for the magnificent Tracy who brings the kind of intensity to his performance that typified his memorable career; the actor was simply incapable of turning in a bad performance. Walthall is intriguing as the sideshow owner but he is a tired old man as he was in real life, dying a year after this film's completion. The fire scene on board Tracy's gambling ship was almost as spectacular as the borrowed segment of Hell, and was started by a pair of twirling dancers entertaining shipboard guests in a lavish dining room. One of the dancers, Leon, sprained his ankle severely during a wild dance that did little for an obscure film career. His partner, however, appearing in her first feature-length film under the name Rita Cansino, later became one of Hollywood's great sex symbols and stars, Rita Hayworth. Even though she appeared only briefly in DANTE'S INFERNO, Fox reissued this film in the mid-1940s, giving her star billing. Tracy never liked the film, despite his terrific portrayal of a ne'er-do-well, undoubtedly disliking the uncharacteristic role itself. He stated in the late 1940s that "Rita Hayworth's first film was DANTE'S INFERNO, the last one I made at Fox under my old contract and one of the worst pictures ever made anywhere, anytime. The fact that she survived in films *after that* screen debut is testament enough that she deserves all the recognition she's getting right now."

p, Sol M. Wurtzel; d, Harry Lachman; w, Philip Klein, Robert Yost (based on a story by Cyrus Wood, adapted by Edmund Goulding); ph, Rudolph Mate; m, Hugo Friehofer, Sammy Kaylin, R.H. Bassett, Peter Brunelli; ed, Alfred DeGaetano; md, Kaylin; art d, William Darling; allegorical sets, Willy Pogany; ch, Eduardo Cansino; makeup, Ernest Westmore.

Drama **(PR:A MPAA:NR)**

DANTON* ** (1931, Ger.) 88m CAP bw

Fritz Kortner *(Danton)*, Gustaf Grundgens *(Robespierre)*, Lucie Mannheim *(Louise Gely)*, Alexander Granach *(Marat)*, Ernst Stahl-Nachbaur *(Louis XVI)*, Gustav von Wangenheim *(Desmoulins)*, Herman Speelmans *(Legendre)*, Walter Werner *(Malesherbes)*, G.H. Schnell *(Duke of Koburg)*, Georg John, Till Klockow, Frederick Gnass.

A fine example of the high standards German filmmaking achieved before the Nazis came to power. This film is the German's view of the French Revolution, and Kortner is masterly in the role of the revolutionist, Danton. The story suffers a little due to the lack of clarity on the comparative values of Danton, Robespierre, and Marat. We see the three involved in the revolution, carrying out their historic duties, but not sure why. Louis XVI is portrayed in a different way. Instead of the weak-willed, humorless person that he was, he is portrayed as a proud man, willing to bow to circumstances, but not allowed to by the mandates of the bloodthirsty crowd. Director Behrendt uses some very effective shadow and light, instead of movement, to get the action across. Kortner is excellent as Danton, physically resembling the crafty politician. This fine German actor, who gave a sterling performance in WARNING SHADOWS, fled Germany in 1933 since he was on the Nazi blacklist and only hours after he was told that fellow actors in a Brecht play in which he was appearing were arrested in their dressing rooms. Upon his arrival in England Kortner spent endless days studying English, carrying an English dictionary through the lobby of his hotel and occasionally shouting happily to strangers: "I am now knowing so many thousand words of English!" (In German.)

d, Hans Behrendt; (based on the book by Hans Rehfisch; ph, Nikolaus Farkas; m, Arthur Guttmann.

Historical Drama **(PR:A MPAA:NR)**

DANTON½** (1983) 136m Gaumont/Triumph (Fr./Pol.) c

Gerard Depardieu *(Georges Danton)*, Wojciech Pszoniak *(Maximillian Robespierre)*, Patrice Chereau *(Camille Desmoulins)*, Angela Winkler *(Lucile Desmoulins)*, Boguslaw Linda *(Saint-Just)*, Roland Blanche *(Lacroix)*, Anne Alvaro *(Eleonore Duplay)*, Roger Planchon *(Fouquier Tinville)*, Serge Merlin *(Philippeaux)*, Lucien Melki *(Fabre d'Eglantine)*, Andrzej Seweryn *(Bourdon)*, Franciszek Starowieyski *(David)*, Emmanuelle Debever *(Louison Danton)*, Jerzy Trella *(Billaud-Varenne)*, Tadeusz Huk *(Couthon)*, Jacques Villeret *(Westermann)*, Krzysztof Globisz *(Amar)*, Ronald Guttman *(Herman)*, Gerard Hardy *(Tallien)*, Stephane Jobert *(Panis)*, Marian Kociniak *(Lindet)*, Marek Kondrat *(Barere De Vieuzad)*, Alain Mace *(Heron)*, Bernard Maitre *(Legendre)*, Erwin Nowiaszack *(Collot d'Herbois)*, Leonard Pietraszak *(Carnot)*, Angel Sedgwick *(Frere d'Eleonore)*, Anne-Marie Vennel *(Chanteuse Boulangerie)*, Jean-Loup Wolff *(Herault de Sechelles)*, Czeslaw Wollejko *(Vadier)*, Wladimir Yordanoff *(Chef des Gardes)*, Matgorzata Zajaczkowska *(Servante des Duplay)*, Szymon Zaleski *(Lebas)*.

Another disappointing film from Wajda, who is considered to be the best Polish filmmaker, is this heavy-handed attempt to illustrate the rivalry between Danton and Robespierre during the French Revolution. Set in 1793 during the last two months of Danton's life, it ends with his public execution. French matinee idol Depardieu convincingly portrays the spirited title character who is thought to be the heart and soul of the revolution. When he learns that Robespierre is urging the Committee of Public Safety to execute citizens en masse, Danton returns to Paris from the French countryside. It is this period, known as the Terror, and those who fought against it, that interests Wajda. One would think that after Poland's military takeover and the oppression of Solidarity, Wajda would be able to deliver a film with a strong, heartfelt sentiment. The opposite is actually more true. It is a cold and safe historical drama, which can possibly be blamed on the fact that it was filmed in a language foreign to the director. More a disappointing film than a bad one, it does contain some fine performances. Depardieu is well cast as the feisty lead, and Pszoniak is physically convincing, though his voice is dubbed. Based on a play which Wajda staged on numerous occasions in Poland. (In French; English subtitles.)

p, Margaret Menegoz; d, Andrzej Wajda; w, Jean-Claude Carriere, Wajda, Agnieszka Holland, Boleslaw Michalek, Jacek Gasiorowski (based on the play "The Danton Affair" by Stanislawa Przybyszewska); ph, Igor Luther; m, Jean Prodromides; ed, Halina Prugar-Ketling; art d, Allan Starski, Gilles Vaster; set d, Allan Starski; cos, Yvonne Sassinot de Nesle.

Historical Drama **Cas.** **(PR:O MPAA:PG)**

DAPHNE, THE* (1967) 106m Toho c (JINCHOGE)

Machiko Kyo *(1st Daughter)*, Haruko Sugimura *(Daphne)*, Reiko Dan *(3rd Daughter)*, Yuriko Hoshi *(4th Daughter)*, Yoko Tsukasa *(2nd Daughter)*, Yosuke Natsuki *(4th Daughter's Husband)*, Daisuke Kato, Akira Takarada, Makoto Sato, Tadao Takshima, Hiroshi Koizumi, Keiju Kobayashi, Tatsuya Nakadai.

A popular Japanese soap opera is expanded out to almost three hours and pumped up with an all-star cast to produce this exercise in tedium. Sugimura is the widowed mother of four daughters, two of them married and two of them still living at home. Dull script and lousy performances will put most viewers to sleep in no time.

p, Masumi Fujimoto; d, Yasuke Chiba; w, Zenzo Masuyama; ph, Choichi Nakai (Tohoscope, Eastmancolor); m, Toshiro Maiyuzumi.

Drama **(PR:A-C MPAA:NR)**

DARBY AND JOAN*½ (1937, Brit.) 75m Rock Studios/MGM bw

Peggy Simpson *(Joan Templeton)*, Ian Fleming *(Sir Ralph Ferris)*, Mickey Brantford *(Yorke Ferris)*, Tod Slaughter *(Mr. Templeton)*, Audrene Brier *(Connie)*, Pamela Bevan *(Darby Templeton)*, Ella Retford *(Nurse)*, Harvey Braban *(Coroner)*, Charles Sewell.

Silly romantic melodrama has Simpson marrying wealthy aristocrat Fleming so that her blind sister (Bevan) will be taken care of. Then her rejected fiance turns up to complicate the arrangement. Based on a novel by the pseudonymous "Rita."

p, Nat Ross; d&w, Syd Courtenay (based on a novel by "Rita"); ph, John Silver.

Drama **(PR:A MPAA:NR)**

DARBY O'GILL AND THE LITTLE PEOPLE***** (1959) 93m Disney/BV c

Albert Sharpe *(Darby O'Gill)*, Janet Munro *(Katie)*, Sean Connery *(Michael McBride)*, Jimmy O'Dea *(King Brian)*, Kieron Moore *(Pony Sugrue)*, Estelle Winwood *(Sheelah)*, Walter Fitzgerald *(Lord Fitzpatrick)*, Dennis O'Dea *(Fr. Murphy)*, J.G. Devlin *(Tom Kerrigan)*, Jack MacGowran *(Phadrig Oge)*, Farrell Pelly *(Paddy Scanlon)*, Nora O'Mahony *(Molly Malloy)*.

This excellent fantasy is a romp through the Leprechaun world of Ireland, with Sharpe as an aging caretaker of a large estate who is to be replaced by Connery. The old man is further vexed by the fact that Connery is making a play for his daughter, Munro, competing for his job and the affections of his only relative. While chasing a horse Sharpe falls into a well and lands in the cavernous realm of the Little People, ruled by King Brian (O'Dea). He is asked to play his fiddle, which he does. At the end of a wild Leprechaun celebration the rock walls open and O'Dea leads his men out on miniature horses to frolic in the countryside. Sharpe escapes but O'Dea finds him at home. The two have a drinking contest and Sharpe gets the little king so drunk that he consents to granting Sharpe three wishes. O'Dea hoodwinks Sharpe into wasting two wishes but agrees that the third will be to assure a happy marriage between Munro and upstart Connery. Munro, however, is seriously injured in an accident and Sharpe begs to change his third wish, asking O'Dea to have the fearful Costa Bower (Death) come for him instead of his daughter. O'Dea sadly agrees and the sinister Death Coach arrives to take Sharpe away, but at the last minute O'Dea wheedles another wish out of Sharpe and that *fourth* wish, in the tradition of Leprechaunism, cancels the other three and thus the tragic events coming to pass. O'Dea kicks Sharpe out of the Death Coach and rides off laughing. Munro miraculously recovers and winds up in Connery's arms while Sharpe swears he is through with meddling with the Little People for a happy ending. This wonderful tale is told in a brisk, imaginative pace and the Leprechauns are marvelously reduced to miniature, with great special effects magic (careful and detailed matte shots) by Ellenshaw, Lycett, and Meador. The sharp lensing by Hoch is enhanced with brilliant colors and music by Wallace and Watkin is delightfully and capriciously Irish. (Connery himself croons a ditty in the film that predates his superstar James Bond image.) Sharpe and O'Dea capture the film with their canny, devious, laughable charm. Sharpe was pinpointed as the lead role ten years earlier by Disney after the animator viewed Sharpe's Broadway performance in "Finian's Rainbow." Disney had long planned this gem of a film, visiting Ireland as early as 1947 to get the feel of the land, having hired scriptwriter Watkin a year earlier to develop the story line. This was the first major film directed by Stevenson and he would go on to helm many a future Disney production. As usual, the overall production reflects Disney's perfectionist detail, so well conceived and executed on every level that the viewer, after only a few minutes into this wonderful film, will be convinced that O'Dea and his Little People are really a mere 20 inches in height! The dialect is a bit thick but any child who hasn't seen DARBY O'GILL AND THE LITTLE PEOPLE has missed an important bit of fancy, and that goes for adults too. Songs include: "Pretty Irish Girl" and "The Wishing Well" (Oliver Wallace, Lawrence E. Watkin).

p, Walt Disney; d, Robert Stevenson; w, Lawrence E. Watkin (suggested by Darby O'Gill stories by H.T. Kavanagh); ph, Winton C. Hoch (Technicolor); m, Oliver Wallace; ed, Stanley Johnson; art d, Carroll Clark; set d, Emile Kuri, Fred MacLean; cos, Chuck Keehne, Gertrude Casey; spec eff, Peter Ellenshaw, Eustace Lycett; animation eff, Joshua Meador; makeup, Pat McNalley; hairstyles, Ruth Sandifer.

Fantasy **Cas.** **(PR:AAA MPAA:NR)**

DARBY'S RANGERS½** (1958) 120m WB bw (GB: YOUNG INVADERS)

James Garner *(Maj. William Darby)*, Etchika Choureau *(Angelina De Lotta)*, Jack Warden *(Master Sgt. Saul Rosen)*, Edward Byrnes *(Lt. Arnold Dittman)*, Venetia Stevenson *(Peggy McTavish)*, Torin Thatcher *(Sgt. McTavish)*, Peter Brown *(Rollo Burns)*, Joan Elan *(Wendy Hollister)*, Corey Allen *(Tony Sutherland)*, Stuart Whitman *(Hank Bishop)*, Murray Hamilton *(Sims Delancey)*, Bill Wellman, Jr. *(Eli Clatworthy)*, Andrea King *(Sheilah Andrews)*, Adam Williams *(Heavy Hall)*, Frieda Inescort *(Lady Hollister)*, Reginald Owen *(Sir Arthur)*, Philip Tonge *(John Andrews)*, Edward Ashley *(Lt. Manson)*, Raymond Bailey *(Maj. Gen. Wise)*, Willis Bouchey *(Brig. Gen. Truscott)*.

Here is the saga of Major William Darby, who organized a group of American rangers into a spearhead landing and covert operations group for use in North Africa and Italy during WW II. Darby is played by Garner, who was making a hit on television with his role in "Maverick." The first half of the film shows the origin and commando training of the rangers. The second half shows the enormous success they had as they seized coastal defenses, established beachheads, raided behind enemy lines, and made fierce lightning attacks. The film is equally interested in the men's social activities. Chasing of women rather than the enemy puts the brakes on the action and slows the pace but the battle sequences are outstanding.

p, Martin Rackin; d, William Wellman; w, Guy Trosper (based on a book by Maj. James Altieri); ph, William Clothier; m, Max Steiner; ed, Owen Marks; art d, William Campbell; cos, Marjorie Best.

War   **(PR:A   MPAA:NR)**

DAREDEVIL, THE*   (1971) 70m Stringer c

George Montgomery, Terry Moore, Gay Perkins, Cyril Poitier, Bill Kelly.

Montgomery stars as a stock-car racer who becomes a driver for a drug ring headed by Poitier, after his career is ruined because of a death he caused on the race track. Lots of action and some touches of voodoo as Montgomery tries to wriggle out of this one.

d, Robert W. Stringer; m, The Brooklyn Bridge.

Crime   **(PR: C   MPAA:NR)**

DAREDEVIL DRIVERS*   (1938) 60m FN/WB bw

Beverly Roberts (Jerry Neeley), Dick Purcell (Bill Foster), Gloria Blondell (Lucy Mack), Gordon Oliver (Mark Banning), Charley Foy (Stud Wilson), Donald Briggs (Tommy Burnell), Eric Stanley (Mr. Lane), Max Hoffman, Jr. (Joe Bailey), Ferris Taylor (Councilman Baker), Cliff Clark (Mr. McAullife), Earl Dwire (Mr. Perkins), William Hopper (Neeley Bus Driver), Fred Lawrence (Burnell Bus Driver), Anderson Lawlor (Mr. Bounty), John Harron (Mr. Mayfield).

Purcell is an auto racer under suspension. Roberts is the owner of a bus company. Purcell rolls into Roberts' town and out of spite for her goes to work for a rival bus company. He makes it all up to her when he ends up destroying the rival company for the benefit of Roberts. In between, we see a lot of racing footage and a lot of crashes, and get another look at Gloria Blondell, sister of Joan, in her second picture for Warner Bros.

p, Bryan Foy; d, B. Reeves Eason; w, Sherman Lowe (based on the short story "Midnight Cargo" by Charles R. Condon); ph, Ted McCord; ed, Harold McLernon, Everett Dodd.

Romance/Action   **(PR:A   MPAA:NR)**

DAREDEVIL IN THE CASTLE***   (1969, Jap.) 97m Frank Lee/Toho c
(OSAKA MONOGATARI; AKA: DEVIL IN THE CASTLE)

Toshiro Mifune (Mohei), Kyoko Kagawa (Ai), Isuzu Yamada (Yodogimi), Yuriko Hoshi (Senhime), Yoshiko Kuga (Kobue), Akihiko Hirata (Hayato), Takashi Shimura, Hanshiro Iwai, Seizaburo Kawazu, Yu Fujiki, Jun Tazaki, Danko Ichikawa, Yosuke Natsuki, Susumu Fujita.

An above-average samurai action film, starring Mifune as a wandering lone samurai. The story has two rival families at war with one another. The 17th-century setting features the use of imported Portuguese guns and cannons during a siege. Mifune steps in and saves both families from mutual annihilation. The camera work by Yamada is excellent, making feudal Japan look well worth fighting and dying for. The western music used and the machinegun-paced editing make this film less traditional than those of Kurosawa and Ozu.

d, Hiroshi Inagaki; w, Takeshi Kimura Inagaki (based on a story by Genzo Murakami); ph, Kazuo Yamada (Tohoscope, Eastmancolor); m, Yoshio Nishikawa; spec eff, Eiji Tsuburaya.

Drama   **(PR:A   MPAA:NR)**

DAREDEVILS OF EARTH*   (1936, Brit.) 57m Hallmark bw

Ida Lupino, Cyril McLaglen, John Loder, Marie Ault, Moore Mariott, George Merritt, Sam Wilkinson, Ginger Lees.

A poor film about dirt track motorcycle racing. Ida Lupino stars as a female racer. McLaglen plays Big Bill Summers, a dirt track champ and ladies' man. Loder, another racer, jams Lupino on the track. McLaglen gets mad and cracks up Loder in a race. As a result, McLaglen is barred from racing. Lots of scratchy newsreel footage.

d, Bernard Vorhaus.

Action   **(PR:A   MPAA:NR)**

DAREDEVILS OF THE CLOUDS*½   (1948) 60m REP bw

Robert Livingston (Terry O'Rourke), Mae Clark (Kay Cameron), James Cardwell (Johnny Martin), Grant Withers (Matt Conroy), Edward Gargan (Tapit Bowers), Ray Teal (Mitchell), Jimmie Dodd (Eddy Clark), Pierre Watkin (Douglas Harrison), Jayne Hazard (Mollie), Bob Wilke (Joe), Frank Melton (Frank), Russell Arms (Jimmy), Hugh Prosser (Sergeant), Charles Sullivan (Bartender).

Polar Airways is a small airline headed by Livingston, who is hard-pressed to keep his pilots on a paying basis. A big airline, Trans-Global, wants to absorb his company and, unknown to him, plants Cardwell on his payroll to do some dirty work. After being on the brink of disaster, everything straightens itself out at the end.

p, Stephen Auer; d, George Blair; w, Norman S. Hall (based on a story by Ronald Davidson); ph, John MacBurnie; ed, Richard L. Van Enger; md, Morton Scott; art d, Frank Hotaling.

Drama   **(PR:A   MPAA:NR)**

DARING CABALLERO, THE*   (1949) 60m UA bw

Duncan Renaldo (Cisco), Leo Carrillo (Pancho), Kippee Valez (Herself), Charles Halton (Hodges), Pedro de Cordoba (Padre), Stephen Chase (Brady), David Leonard (Del Rio), Edmund Cobb (Marshal Scott), Frank Jaquet (Judge Perkins), Mickey Little (Bobby Del Rio).

This is the third picture in the Renaldo CISCO KID series. Renaldo and sidekick Carrillo rescue a frontier town's outstanding citizen from jail after he is framed for

murder and embezzlement. The pair hide the fugitive in the wine cellar of a mission while they track down the real criminals. They go through many adventures and scrapes before they come up with the answers to tie the crimes to a mayor, banker, and marshal conspiracy. Renaldo also was associate producer of the film. (See CISCO KID series, Index.)

p, Philip N. Krasne; d, Wallace Fox; w, Betty Burbridge (based on a story by Frances Kavanaugh from the Cisco Kid Character created by O. Henry); ph, Lester White; m, Albert Glasser; ed, Marty Cohn; art d, Edward Jewell.

Western   **(PR:A   MPAA:NR)**

DARING DANGER*   (1932) 58m COL bw

Tim McCoy, Alberta Vaughn, Wallace McDonald, Murdock McQuarrie, Edward Le Saint, Bobby Nelson, Max Davidson, Vernon Dent, Robert Ellis, Richard Alexander, Edmund Cobb.

Tim McCoy is nearly killed in a fight with Alexander. He recovers and goes after the bad man, catching up to him and finding that he has taken up with a rustler. So, of course, McCoy has to go after the rustler, too. He gets caught holding the rustler's trick iron used to alter brands, and gets into a fight with bad guy Ellis, while his horse runs for help. Pretty laughable ending as the film cuts back and forth between the overblown fight and McCoy's horse that runs about two hundred miles in search of help. The film is based on a story by William Colt MacDonald, whose later stories would give birth to the THREE MESQUITEERS series, the first and most significant of all the trio series westerns.

p, Irving Briskin; d, D. Ross Lederman; w, Michael Trevelyan (based on a story by Colt McDonald); ph, Benjamin Kline; ed, Otto Meyer.

Western   **(PR:A   MPAA:NR)**

DARING DAUGHTERS   (1933) 63m Tower bw

Kenneth Thomson (Alan Preston), Marian Marsh (Terry Cummings), Joan Marsh (Betty Cummings), Bert Roach (Joby Johnson), Allen Vincent (Edgar Barrett), Lita Chevret (Gwen Moore), Richard Tucker (Lawton), Arthur Hoyt (Hubbard), Florence Roberts (Grandmother), Bryant Washburn, Jr. (Roy Andrews).

The actresses who portray this story of two sisters have the same last name of Marsh, but are unrelated. Marian is the older sister, a hard-hearted golddigger. Joan is the younger sister, a fresh kid just up from the country. Marian protects little sister from the fast-moving city men, but gets herself into a jam when the man she loves steals a thousand dollars to help her. Everything works out at the end.

d, Christy Cabanne; w, Barry Barringer, F. Hugh Herbert (based on a story by Sam Mintz); ph, Harry Forbes; ed, Irving Birnbaum.

Drama   **(PR:A   MPAA:NR)**

DARING DOBERMANS, THE**   (1973) 90m Dimension c

Charles Knox Robinson, Tim Considine, David Moses, Claudio Martinez, Joan Caulfield.

Sequel to THE DOBERMAN GANG has a gang of bank robbers again avoiding security cameras by training a bunch of dogs to stick the place up. Children and other dogs should enjoy it.

p, David Chudnow; d, Byron Ross Chudnow; ph, (Metrocolor).

Crime   **(PR:AA   MPAA:G)**

DARING GAME*   (1968) 101m PAR c

Lloyd Bridges (Vic Powers), Nico Minardos (Ricardo Balboa), Michael Ansara (President Eduardo Delgado), Joan Blackman (Kathryn Carlyle), Shepperd Strudwick (Dr. Carlyle), Alex Montoya (Gen. Tovrea), Irene Dailey (Mrs. Carlyle), Brock Peters (Jonah Hunt), Barry Bartle (Larry Sedgewick), Michael Walker (Bink Binkenshpilder), Perry Lopez (Reuben), Marie Gomez (Maria), Oren Stevens (Miguel).

Bridges is the leader of a group known as the Flying Fish, tough individuals who are proficient in commando-type operations in the air, in water, and on land. They are enlisted by the wife of an economics professor who has been kidnaped, along with his daughter, by the dictator of a small Latin American country. The crew goes down to the little country on a rescue mission, and, using all the skills at their command, brings the raid off without a hitch. The underwater sequences were directed by Ricou Browning, who was the underwater actor inside THE CREATURE FROM THE BLACK LAGOON costume.

p, Gene Levitt; exec p, Ivan Tors; d, Laslo Benedek; w, Andy White (based on a story by Art Arthur, White); ph, Edmund Gibson (Eastmancolor); m, George Bruns; ed, Jack Woelz.

Action   **(PR:A   MPAA:NR)**

DARING YOUNG MAN, THE*   (1935) 76m FOX bw

James Dunn (Don McLane), Mae Clarke (Martha Allen), Neil Hamilton (Gerald Raeburn), Sidney Toler (Warden Palmer), Warren Hymer (Pete Hogan), Stanley Fields (Rafferty), Madge Bellamy (Sally), Frank Melton (Cub Reporter), Raymond Hatton (Flaherty), Jack LaRue (Cubby), Arthur Treacher (Col. Baggott), Dorothy Christy (Helen Kay), Robert Gleckler (Editor Hooley), William Pawley (Muggs), James Donlan (Asst. Warden), Phil Tead (Star Reporter), James Donlan, DeWitt Jennings, Del Henderson.

Dunn and Clarke are reporters for rival newspapers. Though they seem not to like each other at first, it is not too long before they fall in love. They are about to be married when Dunn gets shipped off to do an undercover story in a prison, leaving Clarke standing at the altar. Perhaps the real story would have been to tell how a society writer like Dunn suddenly gets sent to do a hard crime story in a prison.

p, Robert T. Kane; d, William A. Seiter; w, William Hurlbut, Sam Hellman, Glenn Tryon (based on a story by Bla Claude Binyoh, Sidney Skolsky; ph, Meritt Gerstad.

Crime **(PR:A MPAA:NR)**

DARING YOUNG MAN, THE** (1942) 73m COL bw (AKA: BROWNIE)

Joe E. Brown, Marguerite Chapman, William Wright, Claire Dodd, Lloyd Bridges, Don Douglas, R.E. Keane, Robert Middlemass, Arthur Lake, Minerva Urecal, Irving Bacon, Philip Van Zandt, Danny Mummert, Carl Stockdale.

Rejected by the draft, Brown becomes a war hero anyway by capturing a Nazi spy ring in New York. Fans of Brown's broad humor should enjoy it, others should stay clear.

p, Robert Sparks; d, Frank Strayer; w, Karen De Wolf, Connie Lee; ph, Franz Planer; m, John Leipold.

Comedy **(PR:A MPAA:NR)**

DARK, THE, (SEE:HORROR HOUSE, 1970, Brit.)

DARK, THE* (1979) 92m Film Ventures International c

William DeVane *(Roy)*, Cathy Lee Crosby *(Zoe)*, Richard Jaeckel *(Mooney)*, Keenan Wynn *(Moss)*, Warren Kemmerling *(Capt. Speer)*, Biff Elliott *(Bresler)*, Jacquelyn Hyde *(DeRenzey)*, Casey Kasem *(Pathologist)*, Vivian Blaine *(Courtney)*, John Bloom *(Killer)*, William Derringer *(Herman)*, Jay Lawrence *(Jim)*, Russ Marin *(Dr. Baranowski)*, Vernon Washington *(Henry)*, Mel Anderson, John Dresden, Horton Willis *(Policemen)*, Roberto Contreras *(Bartender)*, Paul Crist, Joann Kirk *(Stewardesses)*, Erik Howell *(Antwine)*, Ron Iglesias *(Rudy)*, William Lampley *(Young Man)*, Sandra Walker McCulley *(Carhop)*, Valla Rae McDade *(Camille)*, Ken Menyard *(Sportscaster)*, Monica Peterson *(Mrs. Lydell)*, Penny Ann Phillips *(Zelza)*, Jeffrey Reese *(Randy)*, Kathie Richards *(Shelly)*.

Science fiction-horror film has an alien that looks like a werewolf in blue jeans running around Los Angeles murdering people, either ripping the heads off its victims, or burning them to a crisp with its laser vision. Thrown into this nightmare is a good cast headed by author Devane, television newscaster Crosby, and frustrated policeman Jaeckel. The three are all trying to solve the mystery of the murders. The answer, which tells us what, but not how or why, comes when Devane and Crosby are trapped by the creature in a deserted house. The cops ineffectually shoot at it with their conventional weapons, until suddenly the alien self-destructs into thin air, leaving the film open for a sequel. John (Bud) Cardos took over the direction from Tobe Hooper of TEXAS CHAINSAW MASSACRE fame just before the beginning of shooting. Lucky Hooper.

p, Dick Clark, Edward L. Montoro; d, John "Bud" Cardos; w, Stanford Whitmore; ph, John Morrill (Panavision, DeLuxe Color); m, Roger Kellaway; ed, Martin Dreffke; art d, Rusty Rosene.

Science Fiction/Horror **Cas.** **(PR:O MPAA:R)**

DARK ALIBI*½ (1946) 61m MON bw

Sidney Toler *(Charlie Chan)*, Mantan Moreland *(Birmingham Brown)*, Ben Carter *(Carter)*, Benson Fong *(Tommy Chan)*, Russell Hicks *(Warden Cameron)*, Joyce Compton *(Emily Evans)*, Edward Earle *(Thomas Harley)*, Teala Loring *(June Harley)*, George Holmes *(Hugh Kenzie)*, Janet Shaw *(Miss Petrie)*, Edna Holland *(Mrs. Foss)*, John Eldredge *(Morgan)*, William Ruhl *(Thompson)*, Milton Parsons *(Johnson)*, Ray Walker *(Danvers)*, Anthony Warde *(Slade)*, Tim Ryan *(Foggy)*, Frank Marlowe *(Barker)*, George Eldredge *(Brand)*.

The 38th Chan film has Toler as the oriental sleuth discovering that forged fingerprints have put several innocent people in prison. The series had about run out of steam by this time, though it would continue to suffer through nine more films and one more Chan (Roland Winters). (See CHARLIE CHAN Series, Index.)

p, James S. Burkett; d, Phil Karlson; w, George Callahan (based on the character created by Earl Derr Biggers); ph, William A. Sickner; art d, Dave Milton; ed, Ace Herman.

Crime **(PR:A MPAA:NR)**

DARK ANGEL, THE*½** (1935) 105m Goldwyn/UA bw

Fredric March *(Alan Trent)*, Merle Oberon *(Kitty Vane)*, Herbert Marshall *(Gerald Shannon)*, Janet Beecher *(Mrs. Shannon)*, John Halliday *(Sir George Barton)*, Henrietta Crosman *(Granny Vane)*, Frieda Inescort *(Ann West)*, Claud Allister *(Lawrence Bidley)*, George Breakston *(Joe)*, Fay Chaldecott *(Betty)*, Dennis Chaldecott *(Ginger)*, Douglas Walton *(Roulston)*, Sarah Edwards *(Mrs. Bidley)*, John Miltern *(Mr. Vane)*, Olaf Hytten *(Mills)*, Lawrence Grant *(Mr. Tanner)*, Helena Byrne-Grant *(Hannah)*, Ann Fielder *(Mrs. Gallop)*, David Torrence *(Mr. Shannon)*, Cora Sue Collins *(Kitty as a Child)*, Jimmy Butler *(Gerald as a Child)*, Jimmy Baxter *(Alan as a Child)*, Randolph Connolly *(Lawrence as a Child)*, Edward Cooper *(Martin, the Butler)*, Andy Arbuckle *(Mr. Gallop)*, Colin Campbell *(Vicar)*, Silvia Vaughan *(Landlady at Inn)*, Murdock MacQuarrie *(Waiter at Inn)*, Holmes Herbert *(Major in Dugout)*, Robert Hale *(Orderly in Dugout)*, Douglas Gordon *(Porter at Station)*, Gunnis Davis *(News Vendor at Station)*, Harold Howard *(Jarvis, The Station Attendant)*, Bud Geary, Jack Deery, Roy Darmour, Walt Voegeler, Carol Voss, Colin Kenny *(Officers at Station)*, Montague Shaw *(Train Passenger)*, Clare Verdera, Vesey O'Davoren *(Voices at Station)*, Albert Russell *(Innkeeper)*, Vernon P. Downing, Charles Tannen, Frederick Sewall, Robert Carlton, Philip Dare *(Men in Dormitory)*, Claude King *(Sir Mordaunt)*, Phillis Coghlan *(Shannon Maide)*, Francis Palmer Tilton *(Chauffeur)*, Tom Moore, Major Sam Harris, Doris Stone, Louise Bates, Audrey Scott *(Hunt Guests)*.

A ten-handkerchief movie, this tasteful, sentimental Goldwyn production is one mighty film for the ladies. March and Oberon are childhood sweethearts whose impending marriage is interrupted by WW I. March is thought to be dead and Oberon turns to another old friend, gallant Marshall, accepting his proposal after a long courtship. It was Marshall, as March's commanding officer, who had sent March on a dangerous mission from which he did not return. March, however, is very much alive, but he has been permanently blinded. Feeling he will be a burden to Oberon, he asks old friend Halliday to conceal him in England under a different name when he is released from the military hospital. March becomes a world-famous writer of children's stories. When Halliday reads about the upcoming nuptials of Marshall and Oberon, he goes to the future bride and tells her that the man he believes she truly loves is still alive. Then March learns of his friend's disclosure and before Oberon arrives with Marshall he memorizes every detail of his drawing room so they will not learn of his blindness. His ruse works but only for a while. Oberon discovers his affliction and goes to him; the lovers are bound together in a happy ending. Though heavily melodramatic, the film holds together today through the restrained and genteel performances of the three fine leads. This grand weeper was personally selected by Goldwyn, who originally hired his favorite writer, Thornton Wilder, to script the screenplay, but he later brought in the bright and unpredictable Hellman and Mordaunt Shairp to adapt the script from Bolton's successful stage play. Franklin's direction is well-paced and Toland's lensing sharp and innovative. This was another attempt by Goldwyn to create an overnight star of his leading lady. He had failed with Anna Sten but the Tasmanian-born Oberon (the same little island that gave the world Errol Flynn) became a sensation with this film, her second American production; she had completed ten films in England before answering Hollywood's plaintive call. This was a remake of Goldwyn's 1925 silent, starring Ronald Colman in the touching tearjerker, and the remake proved much superior, winning an Academy Award nomination for Oberon (losing to Bette Davis for DANGEROUS) and boosting the careers of March and Marshall. March, who at the time was America's favorite leading man after Colman, gave one of his best performances of the decade. Goldwyn's coffers bulged with the success of the talking DARK ANGEL and encouraged him to remake his silent films RAFFLES and STELLA DALLAS, thinking they, too, would be profitable in sound versions. They were.

p, Samuel Goldwyn; d, Sidney Franklin; w, Lillian Hellman, Mordaunt Shairp (based on a play by Guy Bolton, nee R.B.Trevelyan); ph, Gregg Toland; m, Alfred Newman; ed, Sherman Todd; art d, Richard Day; cos, Omar Kiam.

Drama **(PR:A MPAA:NR)**

DARK AT THE TOP OF THE STAIRS, THE*½** (1960) 123m WB c

Robert Preston *(Rubin)*, Dorothy McGuire *(Cora)*, Eve Arden *(Lottie)*, Angela Lansbury *(Mavis)*, Shirley Knight *(Reenie)*, Lee Kinsolving *(Sammy)*, Frank Overton *(Morris)*, Robert Eyer *(Sonny)*, Penney Parker *(Flirt)*, Ken Lynch *(Harry Ralston)*, Dennis Whitcomb *(Punky Givens)*, Nelson Leigh *(Ed Peabody)*, Emerson Treacy *(George Williams)*, Ben Erway *(Joseph Moody)*, Helen Brown *(Mrs. Haycox)*, Jean Paul King, John Elman, Mike Chain, Bobby Beakman, Butch Hengen *(Boys)*, Helen Wallace *(Lydia Harper)*, Peg LaCentra *(Edna Harper)*, Paul Birch *(Jonah Mills)*, Mary Patton *(Mrs. Ralston)*, Paul Comi *(Jenkins)*, Addison Richards *(Harris)*, Robin Warga *(Harold)*, Charles Seel *(Percy Weems)*, Stoddard Kirby *(Cadet)*.

The play won the Pulitzer Prize but it never really captured a large audience. The Ravetch-Frank screen adaptation did as well as it could with the stage-bound material. Preston is again a larger-than-life character the way he was as THE MUSIC MAN. His performance jars the screen because everyone else underplays filmically under director Mann's hand. It's the saga of an Oklahoma family with several problems; father temporarily leaves mother, Dorothy McGuire, for mistress Angela Lansbury; Shirley Knight is in love with a Jewish boy, Lee Kinsolving, who eventually commits suicide because he can't take the anti-Semitism; McGuire's sister, Eve Arden, is married to a weak wimp, Frank Overton, and the son, Robert Eyer, is afraid of The Dark At The Top Of The Stairs. Each story is played out and intertwined with the others and when it's all over not that much has happened. It must have been about Inge's life while he was growing up in the 1920s. The title refers to life and that we must not be afraid of it. Shirley Knight got an Oscar nomination as Best Supporting Actress for her small but effective role. She lost out that year to Shirley Jones in ELMER GANTRY. This was difficult subject matter for a 1960s audience to sit through. It never achieved the kind of success the studio had anticipated (movies seldom do).

p, Michael Garrison; d, Delbert Mann; w, Irving Ravetch, Harriet Frank, Jr. (based on the play by William Inge); ph, Harry Stradling, Sr. (Technicolor); m, Max Steiner; ed, Folmar Blangsted; art d, Leo K. Kuter; cos, Marjorie Best.

Drama **(PR:C MPAA:NR)**

DARK AVENGER, THE (SEE: WARRIORS, THE, 1955, Brit.)

DARK CITY*** (1950) 97m PAR bw

Charlton Heston *(Danny Haley)*, Lizabeth Scott *(Fran)*, Viveca Lindfors *(Victoria Winant)*, Dean Jagger *(Capt. Garvey)*, Don DeFore *(Arthur Winant)*, Jack Webb *(Augie)*, Ed Begley *(Barney)*, Henry Morgan *(Soldier)*, Walter Sande *(Swede)*, Mark Keuning *(Billy Winant)*, Mike Mazurki *(Sidney Winant)*, Stanley Prager *(Sammy)*, Walter Burke *(Bartender)*, Byron Foulger *(Motel Manager)*, Ralph Peters *(Proprietor)*, Greta Granstedt *(Margie)*, Stan Johnson *(Room Clerk)*, Otto Waldis *(Benowski)*, John Bishop *(Fielding)*, Sally Corner *(Woman)*, Mike Mahoney *(Cashier)*, James Dundee *(Detective)*, Dewey Robinson, Jeffrey Sayre, Bill Sheehan *(Gamblers)*, Robin Camp *(Boy)*, Jack Carroll *(Pianist)*, William J. Cartledge *(Bellhop)*, Edward Rose *(Shoeshine Boy)*, Fred Aldrich *(Civilian Detective)*, Owen Tyree *(Desk Clerk)*, Franz J. Roehn *(Photographer)*, Jay Morley *(MacDonald)*, Mike P. Donovan *(Sergeant)*.

Heston's first film after Hal Wallis saw him on TV and signed him to a contract. Heston leads a group of con men who fleece businessman Don DeFore in a rigged poker game. DeFore loses money that isn't his and pays for his guilt by hanging himself. His psychotic brother, Mazurki, begins to hound the four gamblers, intent on killing them for what they did to DeFore. Heston's girl friend is Lizabeth Scott, as a nightclub singer, in one of her better roles. Heston doesn't have any idea of who the killer is so he goes to Los Angeles to visit DeFore's widow and get some sort of line on Mazurki, who is rapidly knocking off Heston's compatriots, ably played by Ed Begley, Jack Webb, and Harry Morgan (who were to make TV history on the other side of the law with "Dragnet"). Jagger is a dogged cop who is on the trail of Mazurki and it's a tossup who will get to whom first. Heston, despite his predicament, is not a very lovable guy, nor are his confederates. The only innocents in the piece are Lindfors and Keuning, surely not enough for us to get emotionally involved. And yet DARK CITY is a well-done film with enough suspense to keep us on the edge. Five songs are included to break up the criminality and they manage to keep toes tapping, despite Scott's raspy singing voice. Songs: "If I Didn't Have You" (Jack Elliott, Harold Spina), "That Old Black Magic" (Harold Arlen, Johnny Mercer), "I Wish I Didn't Love You So" (Frank Loesser), "I'm In The Mood For Love" (Jimmy McHugh, Dorothy Fields), "Letter From A Lady In Love."

p, Hal B. Wallis; d, William Dieterle; w, Larry Marcus, John Meredyth Lucas (based on a story by Marcus); ph, Victor Milner; m, Franz Waxman; ed, Warren Low; art d, Hans Dreier, Franz Bachelin; set d, Sam Comer, Emile Kuri; cos, Edith Head.

Mystery (PR:A MPAA:NR)

DARK COMMAND, THE***½ (1940) 91m REP bw

John Wayne (Bob Seton), Claire Trevor (Mary McCloud), Walter Pidgeon (William Cantrell), Roy Rogers (Fletch McCloud), George "Gabby" Hayes (Doc Grunch), Porter Hall (Angus McCloud), Marjorie Main (Mrs. Cantrell), Raymond Walburn (Buckner), Joseph Sawyer (Bushropp), Helen MacKellar (Mrs. Hale), J. Farrell MacDonald (Dave), Trevor Bardette (Hale), Alan Bridge (Bandit Leader), Ferris Taylor (Banker), Ernie S. Adams (Wiry Man), Harry Cording (Killer), Edward Hearn, Edmund Cobb (Jurymen), Glenn Strange (Tough), Mildred Gover (Ellie, The Maid), Tom London (Messenger), Dick Alexander (Sentry), Yakima Canutt (Townsman/Stunts), Hal Taliaferro (Townsman), Jack Rockwell (Assassin), Harry Woods (Dental Patient), Dick Rich, John Merton (Cantrell Men), Frank Hagney, John Dilson, Clinton Rosemund, Budd Buster, Howard Hickman, Al Taylor, Jack Low, Edward Earle, Joe McGuinn, Harry Strang, Tex Cooper, Jack Montgomery, Ben Alexander, Cliff Lyons.

This film, with a budget of three-quarters of a million dollars, was the most expensive and successful film of Republic's early years. It was also Wayne's second film after his career breakthrough in STAGECOACH, and his first successful one. The story is set in Kansas in 1859 where the political tensions were rising due to the slave state-free state issue. Wayne is the two-fisted cowhand from Texas who is elected the marshal of Lawrence. Pidgeon is the scholarly teacher who becomes the guerrilla leader making the raids on Lawrence, supposedly on behalf of the Confederacy. It is Wayne's job to track down Pidgeon and his bunch, but he only gets them after they have burned the town to the ground in a spectacular scene. Trevor is the Dixie belle, caught in the middle of a love triangle with Wayne and Pidgeon, who ends up with Wayne. Rogers is Trevor's trigger-happy younger brother, while most of the humor is provided by Hayes as Wayne's dentist sidekick. The film is well directed by Walsh, one of the westerns' most unappreciated directors. Stunt man Canutt pulls off one of his most famous stunts by having four men and a team of horses slung off a bluff into a lake. This action sequence and many inferior imitations brought down the wrath of the Society for the Prevention of Cruelty to Animals, an intense storm of protest almost equalling the outcry produced by THE CHARGE OF THE LIGHT BRIGADE (1936).

p, Sol C. Siegel; d, Raoul Walsh; w, Grover Jones, Lionel Hauser, F. Hugh Herbert, Jan Fortune (based on the novel by W.R. Burnett); ph, Jack Marta; ed, Murray Seldeen, William Morgan; art d, John Victor MacKay.

Western **Cas.** (PR:A MPAA:NR)

DARK CORNER, THE***½ (1946) 99m FOX bw

Mark Stevens (Bradford Galt), Lucille Ball (Kathleen), Clifton Webb (Hardy Cathcart), William Bendix (White Suit), Kurt Kreuger (Tony Jardine), Cathy Downs (Mari Cathcart), Reed Hadley (Lt. Frank Reeves), Constance Collier (Mrs. Kingsley), Molly Lamont (Lucy Wilding), Forbes Murray (Mr. Bryson), Regina Wallace (Mrs. Bryson), John Goldsworthy (Butler), Charles Wagenheim (Foss), Minerva Urecal (Mother), Raisa (Daughter), Matt McHugh (Milk Man), Hope Landin (Scrubwoman), Gisela Verbisek (Mrs. Schwartz), Vincent Graeff (Newsboy), Frieda Stoll (Frau Keller), Thomas Martin (Major Domo), Mary Field (Cashier), Ellen Corby (Maid), Eloise Hardt (Saleswoman), Steve Olsen (Barker), Thomas Louden (Elderly Man), Eugene Goncz (Practical Sign Painter), Lee Phelps, Charles Tannes (Cabbie), Colleen Alpaugh (Little Girl), Alice Fleming, Isabel Randolph (Women), John Elliott, Pietro Sosso, Peter Cusanelli (Men), Lynn Whitney (Stenographer), Charles Cane, John Russell, Ralph Dunn, John Kelly, Donald MacBride, Tommy Monroe (Policemen), Eddie Heywood & Orchestra (Themselves).

A tough as nails private eye yarn begins with seething anger in Stevens, a gumshoe framed for a crime he didn't commit. He rightly suspects his one-time partner Kreuger as the culprit but can't prove it. Moreover, police harass him as he attempts to reestablish himself in a profession that is at best unrealistic, unsavory and dangerous. Added to his woes is a man in a white suit, Bendix, who dogs the private eye's trail. He and Stevens battle but Stevens can't determine why the man is dogging him. Only his faithful secretary Ball is supportive as well as deeply in love with him. At one point Stevens sums up his puzzling predicament, telling Ball: "I feel all dead inside. I'm backed up in a dark corner and I don't know who's hitting me." The man hitting Stevens from afar is the calculating, sinister Webb, a wealthy art dealer with a Machiavellian plan. Insanely jealous of his beautiful wife, Downs, Webb decides to get rid of her lover, Kreuger. He assigns Bendix to make life miserable for Stevens, insinuating that Kreuger is paying him to foul up his life and career so that Stevens will kill his former partner. The plan fizzles when Stevens doesn't rise to the bait. Next, Webb orders Bendix to kill Kreuger and

place his body beneath Stevens' bed, blaming the detective for the murder. But Stevens who has been knocked out by Bendix before the body is planted, wakes up before police arrive, finds the body, and hides it, then launches into an impossible investigation. Just before he tracks down Bendix and is to receive information about the killing—Bendix is at odds with Webb for not paying him off—Webb meets with his hired killer on the top floor of a skyscraper and pushes him out of the window with his walking stick. Stevens, however, manages to identify Webb through a series of hard-established little clues and confronts him in his gallery. The arrogant Webb admits the killings and then pulls a gun, planning to do away with Stevens as a common criminal who broke into his gallery. But Downs, who overhears Webb's confession of killing her lover, shoots her husband dead, saving Stevens and allowing him to return to his office and Ball's waiting arms. THE DARK CORNER is captivating film noir surely directed by Hathaway and well-acted by all the players. MacDonald's sharp lensing and contrasting lighting, along with the moody score from Mockridge, adds to the overall suspense of this fine production. Stevens was being groomed by Fox for leading man status and for a few years he maintained that image, giving terse, sullen performances popular in the late 1940s. Ball is a beautiful prop here but Webb is amazing as the cool mastermind and jut-jawed Bendix again gives a stellar supporting performance.

p, Fred Kohlmar; d, Henry Hathaway; w, Jay Dratler, Bernard Schoenfeld (based on a short story by Leo Rosten); ph, Joe MacDonald; m, Cyril Mockridge; ed, J. Watson Webb; md, Emil Newman; art d, James Basevi, Leland Fuller; set d, Thomas Little, Paul S. Fox; cos, Kay Nelson; makeup, Bill Nye; spec eff, Fred Sersen.

Crime Drama (PR:C MPAA:NR)

DARK CRYSTAL, THE*** (1982, Brit.) 94m UNIV
-Associated Film/ITC Entertainment c

Puppet Operators/Character Voices: Jim Henson/Stephen Garlick (Jen), Kathryn Mullen/Lisa Maxwell (Kira), Frank Oz/Billie Whitelaw (Aughra), Dave Goelz/Percy Edwards (Fizzgig), Frank Oz/Barry Dennen (Chamberlain), Dave Goelz/Michael Kilgarriff (General), Jim Henson/Jerry Nelson (High Priest), Steve Whitmire (Scientist), Louise Gold/Thick Wilson (Gourmand), Brian Muehl (Ornamentalist), Bob Payne/John Baddeley (Historian), Mike Quinn/David Buck (Slave Master), Tim Rose/Charles Collingwood (Treasurer), Brian Muehl/Sean Barrett (Urzah), Brian Muehl (Dying Master), Jean Pierre Amiel (Weaver), Hugh Spight (Cook), Robbie Barnett (Numerologist), Swee Lim (Hunter), Simon Williamson (Chanter), Hus Levant (Scribe), Toby Philpott (Alchemist), Dave Greenaway/Richard Slaughter (Healer), Joseph O'Conor (Urskeks/Narrator).

Muppet inventor Jim Henson creates a brilliantly detailed universe with a fairy tale adventure story. The characters in the film are all muppets but there is little evidence of Kermit or Miss Piggy here. The tale is set in the world ruled by the monstrous flesh-eating Skeksis. The Mystics are their counterparts. The Skeksis rule because the Dark Crystal has been broken. Prophesy predicts that their rule will come to an end when a Gelfling heals the crystal. The Skeksis kill all the Gelflings but two. One was saved by the Mystics and raised by them, while the other was hidden in the swamps and raised by the Podlings. The Mystics give their Gelfling, Jen, the shard from the broken crystal with cryptic instructions on how to heal it. The evil Skeksis, of course, don't want this to happen and try to stop him. He is aided by Kira, the last female Gelfling, whom he bumps into in a swamp, and Aughra, a sorceress who helps him understand the Mystics' instructions. Though Jen overcomes many obstacles by finding his hidden strengths, he remains basically a wimp, and nearly botches the healing of the crystal. The day is saved by Kira, who sacrifices her life to save Jen. With the crystal healed, the Skeksis and the Mystics are shown to be in reality the same entities, who had split apart. Now that they are whole again, they restore Kira to life and restore the crystal palace. Jen and Kira ride off together so that they can repopulate the Gelfling population. A note of caution to children under the age of ten: Like those great children classics such as SNOW WHITE AND THE SEVEN DWARFS and SLEEPING BEAUTY, this film has some very graphic and possibly distressing scenes which could be the cause of nightmares.

p, Jim Henson, Gary Kurtz; d, Henson, Frank Oz; w, David Odell (based on a story by Henson) ph, Oswald Morris (Panavision, Technicolor); m, Trevor Jones; ed, Ralph Kemplen; prod d, Harry Lange; md, Marcus Dods; art d, Terry Ackland-Snow, Malcolm Stone, Brian Ackland-Snow; set d, Peter Young; ch and mime, Jean Pierre Amiel; spec eff, Roy Field, Brian Smithies.

Children **Cas.** (PR:A MPAA:PG)

DARK DELUSION** (1947) 90m MGM bw (AKA: CYNTHIA'S SECRET)

Lionel Barrymore (Dr. Leonard Gillespie), James Craig (Dr. Tommy Coalt), Lucille Bremer (Cynthia Grace), Jayne Meadows (Mrs. Selkirk), Warner Anderson (Teddy Selkirk), Henry Stephenson (Dr. Evans Biddle), Alma Kruger (Molly Byrd), Keye Luke (Dr. Lee Wong How), Art Baker (Dr. Sanford Burson), Lester Matthews (Wyndham Grace), Marie Blake (Sally), Ben Lessy (Napoleon), Geraldine Wall (Miss Rowland), Nell Craig (Nurse Parker), George Reed (Conover), Mary Currier (Nurse Workman), Clarke Hardwicke (Interne), Eddie Parks (Mild Little Man), John Burton (Minister).

This is the 15th film in which Barrymore portrayed Dr. Gillespie, who had taken over the main character responsibilities from Dr. Kildare. The series retains most of the same cast, minus Lew Ayres, who played Kildare many times. In this film Craig is Barrymore's foil. The young doctor is farmed out from the hospital to take over a rich private practice temporarily. While there, he is called on to co-sign an order sending Bremer to an insane asylum. Craig pleads with her rich father to give the girl another chance, but when she goes through an insane fit, the father says no. Craig steals her away and finds out what is wrong with her through narcosynthesis (treating a patient while he or she is under the influence of a narcotic). He operates on a blood clot, and restores the girl's sanity. The day, if not the movie, is saved.

p, Carey Wilson; d, Willis Goldbeck; w, Jack Andrews, Harry Ruskin; ph, Charles Rosher; ed, Gene Ruggiero; md, David Snell; art d, Cedric Gibbons, Stan Rogers.

Drama　　　　　　　　　　　　　　　　　**(PR:A MPAA:NR)**

DARK END OF THE STREET, THE*½ (1981) 89m First Run Features c
Laura Harrington (Donna), Henry Tomaszewski (Billy), Michelle Green (Marlene), Lance Henriksen (Jimmy), Pamela Payton-Wright (Mary Ann), Terence Grey (Ethan), Al Eaton (Brian), Gustave Johnson (Reynolds), George Martin (Salvucci), Flash Wiley (Mr. Thomas), Bennie Wiley (Mrs. Thomas).

This urban drama captures some convincing street characters in authentic locations. Set and shot in Cambridge, Massachusetts, the story concerns a young couple, Harrington and Tomaszewski, who, after working all day, hang out with the crowd at a nearby housing project at night. The two are on the roof of the project one night when a black friend accidentally falls. They cover up the incident, feeling that Tomaszewski might be blamed. Harrington's black girl friend, Green, is arrested as a suspect in the murder of the boy who dies of his injuries. Here, the director veers from Tomaszewski and concentrates on Harrington and her home life. Most of the story lines in general are dropped, leaving the viewer up in the air. Harrington finally admits her knowledge of the incident, getting Green off the hook, and regaining her friendship. All the other characters are left in limbo, where they belong.

p, Dian K. Miller; d&w, Jan Egelson; ph, D'Arcy Marsh (color-16m); m, Marion Gillon, Tyrone Johnson; ed, Jerry Bloedow.

Drama　　　　　　　　　　　　　　　　　**(PR:O MPAA:NR)**

DARK EYES** (1938, Fr.) 80m Milo Films/Frank Kassler bw
(OTCHI TCHORNIA)
Harry Baur (Ivan Petrov), Simone Simon (Tania), Jean-Pierre Aumont (Karpof), Jean Max (Roudine), Dubosc, Jeanne Brindeau, Viviane Romance, Claude Lehman, Maxudian and Paulais.

Simple boy-loses-girl story is set in Moscow. Aumont is the boy and Simone the girl with the roving as well as dark eyes, who gets enmeshed with a middle-aged banker out to seduce her. To meet him, she waits until her governess is asleep, and then joins him in a posh restaurant. He takes her into a private salon where he wines and dines her and all but gets her clothes off. Simone is rescued by her father who, unknown to her, is the head waiter at the restaurant. Deception is countered by deception, but all is explained and the whole experience is chalked up to growing pains. The boy steps back into the picture and gets a wiser but sadder girl. (In French; English subtitles.)

d, V. Tourjansky; w, Tourjansky, Jacques Natanson, Jean Feyday; ph, Thirard; m, Michel Levine; set d, Pimenoff.

Drama　　　　　　　　　　　　　　　　　**(PR:O MPAA:NR)**

DARK EYES OF LONDON (SEE: HUMAN MONSTER, THE, 1939, Brit.)

DARK EYES OF LONDON**½ (1961, Ger.) 95m Rialto Film bw (DIE TOTEN AUGEN VON LONDON; AKA: THE DEAD EYES OF LONDON)
Joachim Fuchsberger, Karin Baal (Blauermel), Dieter Borsche, Ady Berber, Klaus Kinski, Eddi Arent, Wolfgang Lukschy.

A re-make of the 1939 British horror classic THE HUMAN MONSTER stars Fuchsberger as a Scotland Yard investigator embroiled in an investigation into the mysterious deaths of heavily insured old men in Germany. A gang of blind men, led by an evil reverend, turn out to be responsible for the killings. This version of the story is much more faithful to the Edgar Wallace source material and is one of the best of the Wallace mysteries filmed in Germany in the 1960s. Look for Klaus Kinski (great German actor and father of Nastassia) in an early villainous performance.

p, Herbert Sennewald; d, Alfred Vohrer; w, Trygve Larsen; (based on the novel The Testament of Gordon Stuart by Edgar Wallace); ph, Karl Loeb.

Crime　　　　　　　　　　　　　　　　　**(PR:A MPAA:NR)**

DARK HAZARD*** (1934) 72m WB/FN bw
Edward G. Robinson (Jim Turner), Genevieve Tobin (Marge Mayhew), Glenda Farrell (Valerie), Robert Barrat (Tex), Gordon Westcott (Joe), Hobart Cavanaugh (George Mayhew), George Meeker (Pres. Barrow), Henry B. Walthall (Schultz), Sidney Toler (Bright), Emma Dunn (Mrs. Mayhew), Willard Robertson (Fallen), Barbara Rogers (Miss Dolby), William V. Mong (Plummer).

A rare picture that has Robinson as a weakling who is motivated by a compulsion to gamble. In this film, he is manipulated by others and it's a refreshing role as, until then, Robinson had been the pusher rather than the pushee. Robinson is one of those gamblers who can win or lose thousands and appear the same. He goes to work as a cashier at a small Ohio track and moves into a boarding house run by Dunn. Dunn's daughter, Tobin, falls for him despite Dunn's attempt to match her up with Meeker, one of the town's bigwigs. Tobin and Robinson get married after he swears off gambling. They leave Ohio and move to Chicago where Robinson takes a temporary job in a cheap hotel. That ends when he accepts an offer to run a small dog track in California. He is soon gambling again, just small sums, but Tobin knows where that can lead and she lets him know how she hates that side of his personality. Farrell, a one-time flame of Robinson's, shows up at the track and they are glad to see each other. Later, Farrell arrives at the Robinson house under the influence. Tobin is riled, locks her husband out, and she retaliates by taking Farrell to a local gambling house where he wins twenty thousand dollars! Later, he returns home and apologizes to Tobin and swears he'll never do it again. After he falls asleep, Tobin takes the fresh cash and leaves him a note saying that she's gone back to Ohio and will be waiting for him once he quits gambling. Robinson

drifts around for a while, then goes back to Tobin but learns that she's now in love with Meeker. At the local track, Robinson recognizes a dog named Dark Hazard. The dog is about to be destroyed after being injured, but Robinson intervenes and buys the animal. Later, he finds Tobin in Meeker's arms and realizes the truth about the situation. He gets drunk, starts a fight with Meeker, but eventually gives up when he sees that Tobin is genuinely concerned about his rival. Robinson leaves with the dog, helps the animal recover, and begins winning lots of money. The two of them go to Australia where Robinson makes a bundle at the track, then promptly goes broke at roulette. Fade to black. More of a character study than a plotted film. Robinson shows his acting versatility and gets our sympathy with his portrayal of a man who just can't help himself. James Caan made a film many decades later called THE GAMBLER that also touched upon the subject but it fell short by comparison with Robinson's effortless work which made it all the more realistic. Remade in 1937 as WINE, WOMEN AND HORSES with Barton MacLane and Ann Sheridan.

d, Alfred E. Green; w, Ralph Block, Brown Holmes (based on the novel by W.R. Burnett); ph, Sol Polito; ed, Herbert Levy; art d, Robert Haas.

Drama　　　　　　　　　　　　　　　　　**(PR:A MPAA:NR)**

DARK HORSE, THE** (1932) 73m FN/WB bw
Warren William (Hal S. Blake), Bette Davis (Kay Russell), Guy Kibbee (Zachary Hicks), Frank McHugh (Joe), Vivienne Osborne (Maybelle), Sam Hardy (Black), Robert Warwick (Clark), Harry Holman (Jones), Charles Sellon (Green), Robert Emmett O'Connor (Sheriff), Berton Churchill (William A. Underwood).

The title refers to Guy Kibbee, a dumb gubernatorial candidate who is bullied by his political party. With the benefit of demon promoter and publicist Williams, the party is trying to put over "Hicks From the Sticks" on the voters. Williams, while manipulating Kibbee, is manipulated by the two female interests in the film. The first is Davis, his working girl friend who helps him pay off his alimony-grabbing wife, and Osborne, who holds an arrest order over Williams' head throughout the film. Climax of the film comes when Kibbee is set up. He is invited up to a mountain cabin retreat by Osborne, and during a game of strip poker he must escape in his long underwear. Breezy but threadbare.

p, Samuel Bischoff; d, Alfred E. Green; w, Joseph Jackson, Wilson Mizner (based on a story by Melville Crossman, [Darryl Zanuck] Jackson, Courtney Terrett); ph, Sol Polito; ed, George Marks; art d, Jack Okey.

Comedy　　　　　　　　　　　　　　　　　**(PR:A MPAA:NR)**

DARK HORSE, THE*½ (1946) 59m UNIV bw
Phillip Terry (George Kelly), Ann Savage (Mary Burton), Allen Jenkins (Willis Trimble), Jane Darwell (Aunt Hattie), Donald MacBride (John Rooney), Edward Gargan (Eustace Kelly), Raymond Largay (Mr. Aldrich), Ruth Lee (Mrs. Aldrich), Mary Gordon (Mrs. Mahoney), Si Jenks (Old Man), Arthur Q. Bryan (Mr. Hodges), Henri De Soto (Maitre de), Maxine Gates (Fat Lady), Mauritz Hugo (J.B. Norton), Dick Elliott (Ben Martin), Roseanne Murray (Sally), Jack Overman (2nd Ambulance Attendant), Sammy Stein (1st Ambulance Attendant), Alice Fleming (Mrs. Garfield), Eddie Dunn (1st Policeman), Robin Short (Lem), Len Hendry (Eustace's Friend), Dick Crockett (Milkman), Lane Chandler (2nd Policeman), Bill O'Brien (Waiter), Buz Buckley (Small Boy), Jerome Root (Scotty), Ronnie Ralph (Newsboy), Jerry Wissler (Child), Ethyl May Halls (Woman), Jean Van (Emily), John Roche (Man), Gwen Stith, Betty Lee, Sally Loomis, Mary Bezemes (Drum Majorettes).

An honest politician emerges in this screen fare about a WW II vet, Terry, who after the war is persuaded by the powers in town to run for alderman. Reluctantly he agrees, but then, his hackles up because of the pressure put on him, he rebels and exposes a crooked political setup in town. The grateful voters elect him to office and hope for the best.

p, Howard Welsch; d, Will Jason; w, Charles R. Marion, Leo Solomon (based on a story by Sam Hellman); ph, Paul Ivano; ed, Paul Landres; md, Hans J. Salter; art d, Jack Otterson, Harold MacArthur; m/l, Will Jason.

Drama　　　　　　　　　　　　　　　　　**(PR:A MPAA:NR)**

DARK HOUR, THE* (1936) 72m CHES bw
Ray Walker (Jim Landis), Irene Ware (Elsa Carson), Berton Churchill (Paul Bernard), Hedda Hopper (Mrs. Tallman), Hobart Bosworth (Charles Carson), E.E. Clive (Foot), William V. Mong (Henry Carson), Harold Goodwin (Blake), Aggie Herring (Mrs. Dubbin), Katherine Sheldon (Helen Smith), Rose Allen (Mrs. Murphy), Miki Morita (Choong), John St. Polis (Dr. Munro), Fred Kelsey (Watson), Lloyd Whitlock (Dr. Bruce), Harry Strang (Policeman).

A killer attempts to slay an already dead man and there is a triple solution when four of the least suspected persons are revealed as actual murderers, only to have the guilt fastened onto another person, until the final culprit is discovered. The search is carried out by two detectives, one from the old school, the other from the new. The two spend the whole picture discussing their theories, or cross-examining suspects. But they still don't discover the murderer until the last minute. This was another of the scores of films in which Hollywood gossip columnist Hedda Hopper appeared over a period of fifty years, her last being THE OSCAR, in 1966.

p, George R. Batcheller; d, Charles Lamont; w, Ewart Adamson (based on the novel The Last Trap by Sinclair Gluck); ph, M.A. Anderson; ed, Roland D. Reed; art d, Edward C. Jewell.

Crime　　　　　　　　　　　　　　　　　**(PR:A MPAA:NR)**

DARK INTERVAL* (1950, Brit.) 60m Present Day/Apex bw
Zena Marshall (Sonia Jordan), Andrew Osborn (Walter Jordan), John Barry (Trevor), John le Mesurier (Cedric, Butler), Mona Washbourne, Wallas Eaton, Charmian Innes.

Marshall's honeymoon turns sour when she learns that new husband Osborn is insane with jealousy. Dull crime drama.

p, Arthur Reynolds; d, Charles Saunders; w, John Gilling; ph, E. Lloyd.

Crime (PR:C MPAA:NR)

DARK INTRUDER** (1965) 59m UNIV bw

Leslie Nielsen (*Brett Kingsford*), Gilbert Green (*Harvey Misbach*), Charles Bolender (*Nikola*), Mark Richman (*Robert Vandenburg*), Judi Meredith (*Evelyn Lang*), Werner Klemperer (*Prof. Malaki*), Peter Brocco (*Chi Zang*), Vaughn Taylor (*Dr. Burdett*), Harriet Vine (*Hannah*), Bill Quinn (*Neighbor*), Ken Hooker (*1st Sergeant*), Richard Venture (*1st Man*), Mike Ragan (*Plainclothesman*), Ingvard Nielsen (*2nd Man*), Claudia Donelly (*Woman*), Anthony Lettier (*2nd Sergeant*), Chester Jones (*Doorman*).

This is a Victorian horror film set in San Francisco. Nielsen is a criminologist who often ends up playing second fiddle to his dwarf valet, Bolender, and a hypersensitive mandrake plant. Nielsen has a run-in with a horrible looking demon from hell, made to look very scary. The monster has been called up to transfer ugly and deformed sorcerer Richman into the body of his good-looking socialite twin brother, but Nielsen manages to thwart it. This originally was made as a pilot for a projected "Black Cloak" TV series.

p, Jack Laird; d, Harvey Hart; w, Barre Lyndon; ph, John F. Warren; m, Lalo Schifrin; ed, Edward W. Williams; md, Stanley Wilson; art d, Lloyd S. Papez; set d, John McCarthy, Julia Heron; cos, Vincent Dee; makeup, Bud Westmore.

Horror (PR:C MPAA:NR)

DARK IS THE NIGHT*** (1946, USSR) 70m Erevan Studios/Artkino bw

Irina Radchenko (*Varya*), Ivan Kuznetsov (*Artankin, Viatkin*), Boris Andreyev (*Christophorov*), Vladimir Leonov (*The Grandfather*), Alexei Yudin (*The School Principal, The German Sergeant*), Boris Barnet (*The German Commandant*), Nikolai Viazemsky (*The Doctor*), Olga Goreva (*The Old Woman*).

After recovering from the shock of Germans invading her homeland, schoolgirl Radchenko becomes a partisan, hiding two wounded Soviet fliers in the rubble of Stalingrad. Tense drama with good performances all around, particularly Kuznetsov in a dual role. One memorable scene has Russian civilians rounded up to hear a speech given by school principal Yudin supporting the Germans. When he begins verbally attacking the Nazis, the crowd begins to cheer and the Germans machine gun them all. Shot on location in the bombed-out remains of Stalingrad, with director Barnet doing a turn as the German commander. (In Russian; English subtitles).

d, Boris Barnet; w, Fedor Knorre; ph, Sergei Gevorkian; m, David Blok; English Titles, Charles Clement.

War Drama (PR:C-O MPAA:NR)

DARK JOURNEY***½
(1937, Brit.) 77m Korda/LF/UA bw (AKA: THE ANXIOUS YEARS)

Conrad Veidt (*Baron Karl von Marwitz*), Vivien Leigh (*Madeleine Godard*), Joan Gardner (*Lupita*), Anthony Bushell (*Bob Carter*), Ursula Jeans (*Gertrude*), Eliot Makeham (*Anatole*), Margery Pickard (*Colette*), Austin Trevor (*Dr. Muller*), Sam Livesey (*Major Schaffer*), Cecil Parker (*Captain*), Edmund Willard (*German Intelligence Officer*), Charles Carson (*Fifth Bureau Man*), William Dewhurst (*Killer*), Henry Oscar (*Magistrate*), Reginald Tate (*Mate*), Robert Newton (*Officer of U-Boat*), Philip Ray (*Faber*), Lawrence Hanray (*Cottin*), Percy Walsh (*Captain of the Swedish Packet*), Laidman Browne (*Rugge*), Martin Harvey (*Bohlan*), Anthony Holles (*Dutch Man*).

Clever espionage drama has Leigh as a double agent whose loyalties are really with the French and the Allies. She runs a smart dress shop in neutral Stockholm and travels extensively during WW I by boat to France to pick up new designs. Veidt, new head of the German Secret Service in Sweden, arrives in that country with the reputation of an ex-officer whose extravagances have gotten him cashiered. He and Leigh play cat-and-mouse in some fine underplayed scenes, then fall in love. When Leigh finally leaves for France on one last desperate mission Veidt follows her in a German submarine, stopping the ship and boarding it with German officers. He conducts a search for Leigh, threatening to sink the liner unless she is turned over to him. Just before he becomes his prisoner a British warship sinks the U-Boat and, with the tables turned, it is Veidt who becomes the prisoner. The plot is clever, the acting superb, and the production top-notch in this sophisticated film.

p, Alexander Korda; d, Victor Saville; w, Arthur Wimperis (based on a story by Lajos Biro); ph, Georges Perinal, Harry Stradling; m, Richard Addinsell; ed, William Hornbeck, Hugh Stewart, Lionel Hoare; md, Muir Mathieson; prod d, Andre Andrejew, Ferdinand Bellan; cos, Rene Hubert; spec eff, Ned Mann, Lawrence Butler, Edward Cohen; tech adv, L. Stackell.

Spy Drama (PR:A MPAA:NR)

DARK LIGHT, THE*½ (1951, Brit.) 66m Hammer/Exclusive Films bw

Albert Lieven (*Mark*), David Greene (*Johnny*), Norman MacOwan (*Rigby*), Martin Benson (*Luigi*), Catherine Blake (*Linda*), Jack Stewart (*Matt*), John Harvey (*Roger*), John Longden (*Stephen*), Joan Carol.

A pair of lighthouse keepers rescue bank robbers from the sea, then are almost convinced to help them escape. One of producer Carreras' earliest efforts, before he became managing director of Hammer, the studio his father co-founded.

p, Michael Carreras; d&w, Vernon Sewell; ph, Walter Harvey.

Crime (PR:C MPAA:NR)

DARK MAN, THE* (1951, Brit.) 91m Independent Artists/GFD bw

Edward Underdown (*Inspector Jack Viner*), Maxwell Reed (*The Dark Man*), Natasha Parry (*Molly Lester*), William Hartnell (*Superintendent*), Barbara Murray

---

(*Carol Burns*), Cyril Smith (*Samuel Denny*), Leonard White (*Detective Evans*), John Singer (*Adjutant*), Geoffrey Sumner (*Major*), Sam Kydd, Geoffrey Bond, Gerald Anderson, Betty Cooper, Robert Lang, Grace Denbigh Russell, Norman Claridge, John Hewer.

This thriller bereft of thrills opens with a double murder. The killer then pursues a young actress whom he thinks may be able to identify him. He attempts to strangle her in her home but fails. He is later cornered by the police and the army on a practice shooting range. Flabby direction lets this one fall flat.

p, Julian Wintle; d&w, Jeffrey Dell; ph, Eric Cross; ed, Geoffrey Muller.

Crime (PR:A MPAA:NR)

DARK MANHATTAN* (1937) 77m Renaldo Films bw

Ralph Cooper (*Curley Thorpe*), Cleo Herndon (*Cleo*), Clarence Brooks (*Larry Lee*), Jeff Lee Brooks (*Lt. Allen*), Sam McDaniel (*Jack Jackson*), Corny Anderson (*Attorney Brown*), Rubeline Glover (*Miss Hall*), James Adamson (*Lem*), Nicodemus (*Pete*), Jack Lincy (*Butch Williams*).

The only notable feature of this film is that it has an all black cast. Made in the 1930s specifically for black audiences, it concerns a lad who rises to control the rackets in Harlem. He meets a sweet nightclub singer and falls in love. Before he can change his ways and marry the beautiful singer, a rival gang tries to muscle into his territory and shotguns our hero to death.

p, George Randol, Ralph Cooper; d, Harry Fraser; w, Randol; ph, Arthur Reed.

Crime (PR:C MPAA:NR)

DARK MIRROR, THE***½ (1946) 85m UNIV bw

Olivia de Havilland (*Terry Collins/Ruth Collins*), Lew Ayres (*Dr. Scott Elliott*), Thomas Mitchell (*Detective Stevenson*), Dick Long (*Rusty*), Charles Evans (*District Attorney Girard*), Garry Owen (*Franklin*), Lester Allen (*George Benson*), Lela Bliss (*Mrs. Didriksen*), Marta Mitrovich (*Miss Beade*), Amelita Ward (*Photo Double*), William Halligan (*Sgt. Halligan*), Ida Moore (*Mrs. O'Brien*), Charles McAvoy (*O'Brien, Janitor*), Jack Cheatham (*Policeman*), Barbara Powers (*Girl*), Ralph Peters (*Dumb Policeman*), Rodney Bell (*Fingerprint Man*), Lane Watson (*Mike, Assistant*), Ben Erway (*Police Lieutenant*), Jean Andren (*District Attorney's Secretary*), Jack Gargan (*Waiter*), Lane Chandler (*Intern*).

This dual-personality film, one of the first to enter the realm with a psychological approach, proves to be a tour de force for de Havilland, the consummate actress. After a society physician is found dead, police detective Mitchell uncovers witnesses who pin the blame on de Havilland's good twin, although she has a concrete alibi. When Mitchell discovers the twin, the evil one, he cannot get witnesses to tell one from another and the good twin sides with the evil one, not believing her capable of murder. Psychologist Ayres is brought into the case to analyze the two women, administering lie detector tests and Rorschach blot examinations. The good twin falls in love with Ayres as does the evil one until Ayres realizes that the bad sister plans to kill the good one out of sibling rivalry for his affections. Nothing, however, can shake the good twin's belief in her sister's innocence and the entire film is doubly mystifying in that the evil sister often duplicates the good sister's exact behavior. Through a clever ruse which almost gets him murdered, Ayres exposes the vicious and murderous personality of the evil twin to the good sister and the murder is solved, the evil one sent to an asylum and the good one into Ayres' arms for a smiling finale, or one hopes that's the way it ends. De Havilland is absolutely riveting in her spellbinding roles. Special effects wizards Jennings and Lerpae created intimate scenes where the actress plays opposite herself so effectively that she actually appears to be two people, touching herself repeatedly in a marvel of camera magic. Director Siodmak shows a sure hand at his specialty, *film noir*, with fast cuts and sharp angles that quicken pace and heighten suspense. (In 1945 Siodmak directed the engrossing THE SUSPECT and the following year provided such dark masterpieces as THE SPIRAL STAIRCASE and THE KILLERS.) The film was not without shuddering memories for its star. De Havilland was later to say: "The technical problems involved in playing a dual role were extremely difficult to solve, and that horrible Terry I had to play in that picture haunts me to this day." The good-and-evil twin theme was not new to the screen, first profiled in the 1913 German production DER STUDENT VON PRAG, directed by Stellan Rye, but it has seldom been so effective as in THE DARK MIRROR.

p, Nunnally Johnson; d, Robert Siodmak; w, Johnson (based on the novel by Vladimir Pozner); ph, Milton Krasner; m, Dmitri Tiomkin; ed, Ernest Nims; prod d, Duncan Cramer; set d, Hugh Hunt; cos, Irene Sharaff; makeup, Norbert Miles; spec eff, J. Devereaux Jennings, Paul Lerpae.

Crime Drama (PR:C MPAA:NR)

DARK MOUNTAIN*½ (1944) 56m Pine-Thomas/PAR bw

Robert Lowery (*Don Bradley*), Ellen Drew (*Kay Downey*), Regis Toomey (*Steve Downey*), Eddie Quillan (*Willie*), Elisha Cook, Jr. (*Whitey*), Ralph Dunn (*Sanford*), Walter Baldwin (*Uncle Sam*), Rose Plumber (*Aunt Pattie*), Virginia Sale (*Aletha*), Byron Foulger (*Harvey Bates*), Johnny Fisher (*Hunk*), Alex Callam (*Dave Lewis*), Eddie Kane (*Waiter*), Angelos Desfia (*Bookkeeper*).

Lowery is a hard-working forest ranger trying to get a promotion to supervisor so he can marry his childhood sweetheart, Drew. He gets the promotion, but comes out of the woods too late—Drew has married Toomey, a suave racketeer. After committing a crime, Toomey tells Drew to find a hideout on Dark Mountain, and he will meet her later. Lowery takes her there and sets her up in a mountain cabin. Toomey shows up and hides out for a month. Drew keeps trying to escape, and

Lowery finally realizes that Toomey is with her. The climax is a wild mountain road chase, with Toomey killed in a car crash, and Lowery and Drew finally together.

p, William Pine, William Thomas; d, William Berke; w, Maxwell Shane (based on a story by Paul Franklin and Charles Royal); ph, Fred Jackman, Jr.; ed, Henry Adams; art d, F. Paul Sylos.

Crime **(PR:A MPAA:NR)**

DARK ODYSSEY** (1961) 85m Era bw (AKA: PASSIONATE SUNDAY)

Athan Karras *(Yianni Martakis)*, Jeanne Jerrems *(Niki Vassos)*, David Hooks *(George Andros)*, Rosemary Torri *(Helen Vassos)*, Edward Brazier *(Jack Fields)*, Ariadne Zapnoukayas *(Mrs. Vassos)*, Nicholas Zapnoukayas *(Mr. Vassos)*, Warren Houston *(Bartender)*, Chris Marx *(Freighter Captain)*, Maggie Owens *(Cleaning Woman)*.

Karras plays a young Greek sailor who jumps ship in New York City to avenge the seduction, rape, and suicide of his sister which was caused by a fellow Greek who has fled to the U.S. Karras meets Jerrems, a Greek-American girl, whom he befriends, and she tries to dissuade him from his vendetta. Her efforts fail and eventually Karras finds the man and kills him. Wanted by the police, Karras flees back to his ship and is nearly persuaded to give himself up by Jerrems, but in the struggle for the gun it discharges, killing him.

p&d, William Kyriakys, Radley Metzger; w, Kyriakys, Metzger, James Vlamos; ph, Peter Erik Winkler; m, Laurence Rosenthal; ed, Metzger, Kyriakys; set d, David Jones.

Drama **(PR:C MPAA:NR)**

DARK OF THE SUN**

(1968, Brit.) 100m MGM c (GB: THE MERCENARIES)

Rod Taylor *(Capt. Bruce Curry, Yvette Mimieux (Claire)*, Jim Brown *(Ruffo)*, Kenneth More *(Dr. Reid)*, Peter Carsten *(Henlein)*, Olivier Despax *(Surrier)*, Andre Morrell *(Bussier)*, Guy Deghy *(Delage)*, Calvin Lockhart *(President Ubi)*, Bloke Modisane *(Cpl. Kataki)*, Monique Lucas *(Mme. Bussier)*, Louise Bennett *(Mrs. Ubi)*, Paul Jantzen *(Capt. Hansen)*, David Bauer *(Adams)*, Murray Kash *(Cochrane)*, Alan Gifford *(Jansen)*, Danny Daniels *(General Moses)*, John Serret *(Father Dominic)*, Emery J. Ujvari *(Functionary)*, Alex Gradussov *(Belgian Refugee)*.

In the Congo uprising in the late 1950s, Taylor is a tough mercenary who doesn't care what side he is on so long as the side pays well. He is hired by Congo's president to take a train through rebel-held territory and bring back fugitives and a load of uncut diamonds hidden in a beleaguered town, with only three days to complete the mission. He is accompanied by Brown, a native of the Congo, who works for more patriotic purposes, Carsten, an ex-Nazi officer, More, a drunken doctor, and forty Congolese troops. Mimieux is the sole female interest as a French refugee taken aboard the train. The perilous journey makes up the story.

p, George Englund; d, Jack Cardiff; w, Quentin Werty, Adrian Spies (based on a novel by Wilbur A. Smith); ph, Edward Scaife (Panavision, Metrocolor); m, Jacques Loussier; ed, Ernest Walter.

Drama **(PR:A MPAA:NR)**

DARK PASSAGE*½** (1947) 106m WB bw

Humphrey Bogart *(Vincent Parry)*, Lauren Bacall *(Irene Jansen)*, Bruce Bennett *(Bob)*, Agnes Moorehead *(Madge Rapf)*, Tom D'Andrea *(Sam, Taxi Driver)*, Clifton Young *(Baker)*, Douglas Kennedy *(Detective)*, Rory Mallinson *(George Fellsinger)*, Houseley Stevenson *(Dr. Walter Coley)*, Bob Farber, Richard Walsh *(Policemen)*, Clancy Cooper *(Man on Street)*, Pat McVey *(Taxi Driver)*, Dude Maschemeyer *(Man on Street)*, Tom Fadden *(Waiter in Cafe)*, Shimen Ruskin *(Driver-Watchman)*, Tom Reynolds *(Hotel Clerk)*, Lennie Bremen *(Ticket Clerk)*, Mary Field *(Mary the Lonely Woman)*, Michael Daves, Deborah Daves *(Children)*, John Arledge *(Lonely Man)*, Ross Ford *(Ross, the Bus Driver)*, Ian MacDonald *(Policeman)*, Ramon Ros *(Waiter)*, Craig Lawrence *(Bartender)*.

An offbeat but fascinating story has Bogart escaping from San Quentin, where he has been imprisoned for murdering his wife. He is picked up by Young, a small-time crook who suspects he is a lamming convict. Bogart knocks him out and is later picked up by Bacall who has been looking for him ever since news of his break has been announced. Bacall doesn't believe he's guilty of murder and hides him in her lavish San Francisco apartment. When she goes out to get him some clothes someone comes to her door, Moorehead, a friend of Bacall's. He tells her through the door to go away and she does, thinking he is Bennett, her on-and-off boy friend who is attracted to Bacall. Oddly, Bogart recognizes her voice, realizing she was a woman he knew years earlier, one who had tried to win his affections and caused havoc between him and his wife. Bacall returns with the clothes and Bogart decides to get out of her life. After finding an old clipping which tells how Bacall's father was sent to the gas chamber for murdering her stepmother he realizes that she identifies with his plight. She believes her father was innocent and he, like Bogart, was a victim of injustice. After leaving Bacall, Bogart meets a friendly cab driver, D'Andrea, who takes him to an underworld plastic surgeon who arranges to change his features. He visits a close friend, Mallinson, the only person other than Bacall who believes him innocent, arranging to stay with him after the surgery is performed. Bogart then undergoes the painful operation and, bandaged completely about the head, returns to Mallinson's place to find his friend dead. With nowhere to turn, Bogart goes back to Bacall but he is followed by the punk Young, who stands vigil outside Bacall's apartment. Bogart is nursed by Bacall as his face heals. When his bandages come off he is a different man. By then Moorehead has been turned away by Bacall, along with Bennett. Moorehead thinks she is still seeing Bennett on the sly and makes nasty accusations. To protect her, Bogart again leaves, this time planning to escape to South America. Young, however, confronts him and Bogart kills him in self-defense. Then he learns that it was Moorehead who really murdered his wife and he tricks her into meeting him in a hotel room. There she admits killing his wife and his friend Mallinson, saying she did it so *they* could be together. Startled, Bogart moves toward her and, frightened, Moorehead backs suddenly away, lurching out an open window and falling downward to her death. With Moorehead dead, Bogart realizes there is no chance of clearing his name so he leaves for South America. Before going he calls Bacall and asks her to join him "if you can see your way clear." She does; the film ends with the great love team dancing in a South American nightclub. It's an involved plot, really a mystery, which is made more complex in the first forty minutes since Bogart's face is not shown, only his voice heard as the camera shows only his viewpoint, a very effective device employed with equal success a year earlier in LADY IN THE LAKE when the camera took on Robert Montgomery's persona as the legendary Philip Marlowe. Bacall is stunning and Bogie is sympathetic, commanding and full of his usual intrigue, playing with his lines and the supporting cast with cynical humor. His banter with suspicious plainclothesman Kennedy in a S.F. diner is a delight. D'Andrea is great as the helpful but talkative cabby but Moorehead overacts with a vengeance, her lines delivered in a permanent shriek. Her hideous character becomes a grotesque caricature inside her nervously twitching performance, a too-convenient catchall culprit. The Bogart-Bacall scenes are less torrid than in TO HAVE AND HAVE NOT, less tempestuous than in THE BIG SLEEP, most of them underplayed where sentiment is carried by the tune "Too Marvelous For Words" as they dine alone and exchange looks instead of conversation. Shot on location in San Francisco, the apartment building where Bogie hid out is still standing and serves as an insider's tourist site. At the time of this movie, Bogart was Hollywood's highest paid actor, making more than $450,000 a year.

p, Jerry Wald; d&w, Delmar Daves (based on the novel by David Goodis); ph, Sid Hickox; m, Franz Waxman; ed, David Weisbart; md, Leo F. Forbstein; art d, Charles H. Clarke; set d, William Kuehl; cos, Bernard Newman; spec eff, H.F. Koenekamp.

Mystery **Cas.** **(PR:A MPAA:NR)**

DARK PAST, THE*** (1948) 75m COL bw

William Holden *(Al Walker)*, Nina Foch *(Betty)*, Lee J. Cobb *(Dr. Andrew Collins)*, Adele Jergens *(Laura Stevens)*, Stephen Dunne *(Owen Talbot)*, Lois Maxwell *(Ruth Collins)*, Berry Kroeger *(Mike)*, Steven Geray *(Prof. Fred Linder)*, Wilton Graff *(Frank Stevens)*, Robert Osterloh *(Pete)*, Kathryn Card *(Nora)*, Bobby Hyatt *(Bobby)*, Ellen Corby *(Agnes)*, Charles Cane *(Sheriff)*, Robert B. Williams *(Williams)*, Phil Tully *(Cop)*, Harry Harvey, Jr. *(John Larrapoe)*, Edward Earle *(McCoy)*, Pat McGeehan *(Commentator)*.

Based on 1939's BLIND ALLEY (play and film), this fast psychological drama is just a little too slick for its own good in that it offers audiences sort of a Reader's Digest lesson in how the criminal mind functions. Not unlike THE DESPERATE HOURS in theme, THE DARK PAST is the story of pipe-smoking Cobb, a psychiatrist, and Holden, an escaped criminal, and how one conquers the other. Cobb, Maxwell, Hyatt, Graff, and Jergens are at Cobb's cabin near a beautiful lake, waiting for the arrival of fellow professor Geray, when the radio announces that a killer has escaped from a nearby prison. Almost immediately, said killer, Holden, breaks into the cabin with his amour, Foch, and two pals Kroeger and Osterloh. They are going to hold these innocents as hostages while transportation for their escape is arranged. Cobb spots Holden's mental weakness and begins to work on him in a cool fashion. Cobb's calm attitude contrasts greatly with Holden's hyper-active mien and the picture settles into a battle of psyches. In the end, Cobb successfully analyzes Holden's antisocial behavior and it turns out to be your standard, everyday Oedipus complex. Once Holden sees what's been troubling him, the angry veneer disappears and he is an easy mark for the authorities to nab. The film asks for psychoanalysis of juvenile offenders and how that might lead to a lowering of the crime rate. Results of this kind of treatment have proved otherwise. The movie was guilty of attacking a very complicated subject in an overly straightforward fashion. There was never any doubt as to who would win, just how long it would take. Holden was excellent as we watched him shrivel from fast-talking, gun-toting killer to little boy lost.

p, Buddy Adler; d, Rudolph Mate; w, Philip MacDonald, Michael Blankfort, Albert Duffy, Malvin Wald, Oscar Saul (based on the play "Blind Alley" by James Warwick); ph, Joseph Walker; m, George Duning; ed, Viola Lawrence; md, Maurice W. Stoloff; art d, Cary Odell; set d, Frank Tuttle; cos, Jean Louis.

Crime **(PR:A MPAA:NR)**

DARK PLACES* (1974, Brit.) 91m Cinerama c

Christopher Lee *(Dr. Mandeville)*, Joan Collins *(Sarah)*, Robert Hardy *(Edward/Andrew)*, Herbert Lom *(Prescott)*, Jane Birkin *(Alta)*, Carleton Hobbs *(Old Marr)*, Jennifer Thanisch *(Jessica)*, Michael McVey *(Francis)*, Jean Marsh *(Victoria)*, Martin Boddey *(Police Sergeant)*, Roy Evans *(Baxter)*, John Glyn Jones *(Bank Manager)*, John Levene *(Doctor)*, Barry Linehan *(Gatekeeper)*, Linda Gray *(Woman on Hill)*, Lysandre de-la-Haye, Earl Rhodes *(Children on Hill)*.

Hardy is a mental hospital administrator who is willed an estate in which a large sum of money is hidden. The dead man's doctor, Lee, the doctor's sister, Collins, and the estate's lawyer, Lom, all are hot on his trail as he tries to locate the money. Hardy is possessed by the spirit of the original owner, who had murdered his wife and children after they killed his mistress. In all respects this is very mediocre stuff.

p, James Hannah, Jr.; d, Don Sharp; w, Ed Brennan, Joseph Van Winkle; ph, Ernest Steward (Eastmancolor); m, Wilfred Josephs; ed, Teddy Darvas; art d, Geoffrey Tozer.

Horror **Cas.** **(PR:A MPAA:PG)**

DARK PURPOSE* (1964) 97m UNIV c (L'INTRIGO)

Shirley Jones *(Karen Williams)*, George Sanders *(Raymond T. Fontaine)*, Rossano Brazzi *(Count Paolo Barbarelli)*, Micheline Presle *(Monique Bouvier)*, Georgia Moll *(Cora Barbarelli)*.

Brazzi is an Italian count who invites Jones and Sanders to his villa to appraise his art treasures. He seeks to seduce Jones, who wants little to do with him. Brazzi tries to pass off his mentally ill wife as his daughter, so that he may wed the protesting Jones. There is murder but not much intrigue as the action plods along to its inevitable conclusion. The Italian Riviera landscapes provide the picture its only pleasing moments.

p, Steve Barclay; d, George Marshall; w, David Harmon, Barclay (based on a novel by Doris Hume Kilburn); ph, Gabor Pogany (Technicolor); m, Angelo F. Lavagnino; ed, Giancarlo Cappelli; art d, Massimo Tavazzi.

Mystery   **(PR:C   MPAA:NR)**

DARK RED ROSES**   (1930, Brit.) 63m New Era Films bw

Stewart Rome (David), Frances Doble (His Wife), Hugh Eden (Anton), Kate Cutler (The Mother), Jack Clayton (Jack), Jill Clayton (Jill), Sydney Morgan (Tim), Una O'Connor (Mrs. Weeks), Anton Dolin, Lydia Lopokova, George Balanchine

A love triangle set in English suburbia of the 1920s finds a mutual interest and admiration between Doble and cellist Eden, misinterpreted by Doble's sculptor husband, Rome. Rome lures Eden to his studio under the guise of making a cast of his hands. While Eden's hands are confined in hardened plaster, Rome tells of his suspicions about him and his wife, and pretends that he is going to cut the musician's hands off as a lesson. Rome slashes down with a knife that is a fake, but succeeds in scaring the cellist to near death. A long Russian ballet sequence foreshadows the action with the story it tells. The film has become a singular event in the history of dance. The ballet sequence was choreographed and danced by the great George Balanchine, then twenty-six years old and in the process of forming the Ballets Russe de Monte Carlo, and who was to migrate from England to America three years later to found Ballet Theater.

d, Sinclair Hill; w, Leslie Howard Gordon, Harcourt Templeman (based on a story by Stacy Aumonier); ph, A. Virago; ch, George Ballanchine.

Drama   **(PR:A   MPAA:NR)**

DARK RIVER*   (1956, Arg.) 88m Times Film bw

Hugo del Carril (Santos Peralta), Pedro Laxalt (Rufino Peralta), Gloria Ferrandez (Paraguaya), Raul del Valle (Barreito), Adriana Benetti (Amelia), Pedro Laxaet, Elroy Alvarez, Herminia Franco, Joaquin Petrosino.

This import tells the story of a motley group of laborers who travel up an Argentine river to work on a Paraguayan tea plantation. Here the workers, both men and women, are put to slave labor and are beaten at the bidding of one man who claims, "I am the boss." Of course, these people can only take so much, so after Benetti is raped, Laxalt is savagely lashed, and several other workers are killed for minor infractions of discipline, the workers, led by Carril, form a union and rise up against their oppressors. Carril, who is also the producer of the film, ends up escaping with Benetti downriver where they start a new life for themselves. (In Spanish; English subtitles.)

p&d, Hugo del Carril; w, Eduardo Borras; ph, Jose Maria Beltran; m, Tito Ribero; md, Prudencio Giminez; English subtitles, Herman Weinberg.

Drama   **(PR:O   MPAA:NR)**

DARK ROAD, THE*   (1948, Brit.) 72m Marylebone/Exclusive bw

Charles Stuart (Sidney Robertson), Joyce Linden (Ann), Antony Holles, Roddy Hughes, Patricia Hicks, Mackenzie Ward, Veronica Rose, Maxine Taylor, Michael Ripper, Cyril Chamberlain, Rory McDermott, Sefton Yates, Joanna Carter, Gale Douglas, Peter Reynolds, Sydney Bromley.

Stuart, just out of reform school, persuades Linden to help him in a life of crime. He climbs the ladder to power in the underworld, and then fate topples him. Too much high moral tone to be entertaining.

p, Henry Halstead; d, Alfred Goulding; ph, Stanley Clinton.

DARK SANDS**½   (1938, Brit.) 66m Buckingham/GFD bw
                                                                  (AKA: JERICHO)

Henry Wilcoxon (Captain Mack), Wallace Ford (Mike Clancy), Paul Robeson (Jericho Jackson), Princess Kouka (Gara), John Lauri (Hassan), James Carew (Maj. Barnes), Laurence Brown (Pvt. Face), Rufus Fennell (Sgt. Gamey), Ike Hatch (Tag), Frank Cram (Col. Lake), Frank Cochrane (Agouba), George Barraud, Frederick Cooper, Henry Aubin (Explorers).

Famed black singer/actor Robeson once again struggles mightily with fairly routine material and almost wins. Here he plays a black American corporal in WW I who is court-martialed for a murder he didn't commit and is sentenced to die. A kindly white captain, Wilcoxon, takes pity on Robeson and lets him out under his recognizance so that he may spend a final New Year's Eve with his buddies. Being no dummy, Robeson escapes, causing Wilcoxon to be drummed out of the military and imprisoned as well. Feeling betrayed (though Robeson never knew that Wilcoxon's neck was on the line), Wilcoxon vows to follow Robeson to the ends of the earth seeking revenge. Robeson, meanwhile, has gone to Africa and set himself up as the leader of a powerful tribe and started a family. Eventually, Wilcoxon tracks Robeson down and intends to kill him, but he has a change of heart at the last minute and decides to go back. Robeson offers to go back with him in an effort to clear his name, but knowing that Robeson's return to civilization would mean certain death, Wilcoxon overpowers the black man and leaves him behind. Unfortunately, some of Robeson's native followers misinterpret the white man's intentions and they shoot him dead. Probably considered fairly progressive in its attitudes toward race in 1938, today it seems almost entirely racist (black man's place is in Africa, white man must save him, etc.).

p, Walter Futter; d, Thornton Freeland; w, Robert N. Lee, Peter Rurie, George Barraud (based on a story by Futter); ph, John W.W. Boyle; ed, E.B. Jarvis.

Drama/Musical   **(PR:AA   MPAA:NR)**

DARK SECRET*½   (1949, Brit.) 85m Nettleford/But bw

Dinah Sheridan (Valerie Merryman), Emrys Jones (Chris Merryman), Irene Handl ("Woody" Woodman), Hugh Pryse (A Very Late Visitor), Barbara Couper (Mrs. Barrington), Percy Marmont (Vicar), Geoffrey Sumner (Jack Farrell), Mackenzie Ward (Artist), Charles Hawtrey (Arthur Figson), John Salew (Mr. Barrington), George Merritt (Mr. Lumley), Stanley Vilven (Mr. Woodman), Grace Arnold, Edgar Driver, Laurence Naismith, Esme Beringer, Molly Hamley-Clifford, Terry Randall, Johnnie Schofield.

Ex-pilot Jones and wife Sheridan move into a cottage whose previous occupant was murdered. Soon Sheridan finds herself becoming more and more obsessed with the crime. A remake of CRIME AT BLOSSOMS (1933).

p, Ernest G. Roy; d, Maclean Rogers; w, A.R. Rawlinson, Moie Charles (based on the play "Crime At Blossoms" by Mordaunt Shairp); ph, W.J. Harvey.

Crime   **(PR:A   MPAA:NR)**

DARK SHADOWS   (SEE: HOUSE OF DARK SHADOWS, 1970)

DARK SIDE OF TOMORROW, THE*   (1970) 84m Able c

Elizabeth Plumb (Denise), Alisa Courtney (Adria), John Aprea (Jim), Wayne Want (David), Marland Proctor (Casey), Luanne Roberts (Producer's Wife), Jamie Cooper, Sally Fedem, Linda Hendelman, Vince Romano, Laura Patton, Geretta Taylor, Russ Milburn.

A sensitive portrayal of loneliness and lesbianism, the story involves two suburban housewives, Plumb and Courtney. Their husbands are constantly away on aerospace business, leaving the two alone. The women are lunching at a Sunset Strip cafe when they spy a lesbian couple at the next table. The two are fascinated by their behavior. Courtney is intrigued but scared, while Plumb is upset by her attraction to her friend. Courtney initiates the affair and the two behave like two teenage lovers until Courtney switches her attention to a young actor, Aprea. Plumb is deeply hurt and tries to go gay all the way with a dykie fashion designer who seduces her on a pool table in the middle of a party. The film is often heavy-handed and gets bogged down in long philosophical dissertations.

p, David Novik; d&w, Barbara Peeters, Jacque Deerson (based on a story by Deerson); ph, Deerson (Eastmancolor); m, Jerry Wright, The Friends, London Dri, Queen Mary Dancers; ed, Richard Weber.

Drama   **(PR:O   MPAA:R)**

DARK SKIES   (SEE: DARKENED SKIES, 1930)

DARK STAIRWAY, THE**   (1938, Brit.) 72m WB/FN bw

Hugh Williams (Dr. Thurlow), Chili Bouchier (Betty Trimmer), Garry Marsh (Dr. Mortimer), Reginald Purdell (Askew), James Stephenson (Inspector Clarke), Glen Alyn (Isabel Simmonds), John Carol (Merridew), Lesley Brook (Mary Cresswell), Robert Rendel (Dr. Fletcher), Aubrey Pollok (Dr. Cresswell), Ross Landon, Elsa Buchanan, Ivy Tresmand, Muriel Pope, Katie Johnson.

British-made crime drama which sees a hospital doctor murdered in a quarrel over a new anaesthetic. One of American mystery writer Mignon G. Eberhart's fifty-two thrillers, it is, as usual, a well-plotted, interesting story.

p, Irving Asher; d, Arthur Woods; w, Brock Williams, Basil Dillon (based on the novel From What Dark Stairway by Mignon G. Eberhart); ph, Basil Emmott.

Crime   **(PR:A   MPAA:NR)**

DARK STAR**½   (1975) 83m Jack H. Harris c

Brian Narelle (Doolittle), Andreijah Pahich (Talby), Carl Kuniholm (Boiler), Dan O'Bannon (Pinback), Joe Sanders (Powell).

John (HALLOWEEN) Carpenter's first directorial effort is a funny satire on the phenomenally successful 2001—A SPACE ODYSSEY. Carpenter's spaceship is piloted by four goofy astronauts who live like slobs and are bored out of their skulls by their long and uneventful mission. The crew is leaderless because, during the voyage, their commander has died and is kept in a freezer but is still able (somehow) to grudgingly give his men advice when need be. Also in the ship are two talking computers and a pet alien which looks like a red beachball with claws (one of the consistently funny things in the film). The film is a series of vignettes which detail how the men deal with their boredom, and it eventually sees one of the crew, Narelle, surfing through space on a board-shaped piece of debris. Half the film was shot on 16mm by Carpenter (Dan O'Bannon, who would later go on to write ALIEN, co-wrote the screenplay and was in charge of the set design and special effects) as his thesis project for the University of Southern California film school. Hoping to get major financing from a studio to expand the film (as George Lucas did with his thesis THX 1138), he dropped out of school and went hunting for investors. Eventually, a Canadian investor gave him enough money to blow up the 16mm footage to 35mm, which led to exploitation distributor Jack Harris financing the rest of the film (which allowed for a modicum of special effects). Unfortunately, Harris' company went broke and the rights to the film went to Bryanston, who had distributed THE TEXAS CHAINSAW MASSACRE. The film eventually got some bookings but it never really caught on until it hit the midnight show circuit where it has found considerable popularity. DARK STAR is an interesting, if flawed film (it is overlong and occasionally very flat), and is worth a look from those interested in the career genesis of John Carpenter and Dan O'Bannon.

p&d, John Carpenter; w, Carpenter, Dan O'Bannon; ph, Douglas Knapp (Metrocolor); m, Carpenter; ed, O'Bannon; prod d, O'Bannon; set d, O'Bannon; spec eff, O'Bannon, Bill Taylor.

Science Fiction   **Cas.**   **(PR:C   MPAA:G)**

DARK STREETS*½ (1929) 55m FN bw

Jack Mulhall (*Pat McGlone/Danny McGlone*), Lila Lee (*Katie Dean*), Aggie Herring (*Mrs. Dean*), Earl Pingree (*Cuneo*), Will Walling (*Police Captain*), E. H. Calvert (*Police Lieutenant*), Maurice Black (*Beefy Barker*), Lucien Littlefield (*Census Taker*), Pat Harmon.

Here is the first talking film to feature an actor in a dual role as Mulhall plays twin brothers, one a cop, the other a crook. They both love the same girl, Lee. The bad brother belongs to a gang of garment district robbers the good brother is out to get. The police captain has given all police orders to shoot first and ask questions later. The good brother tips off the bad that this rule is in effect and warns him to stay out of the garment district. Bad brother warns good to do the same, but both are too stubborn to get out. Bad brother kidnaps good, puts on his uniform, and gets killed in an effort to save good brother who is left to marry Lee.

p, Ned Marin; d, Frank Lloyd; w, Bradley King (based on a story by Richard Connell); ph, Ernest Haller; m, Vitaphone Orchestra; ed, Edward Schroeder.

Crime (PR:A MPAA:NR)

DARK STREETS OF CAIRO* (1940) UNIV bw

Sigrid Gurie (*Ellen*), Ralph Byrd (*Dennis*), Eddie Quillan (*Jerry Jones*), George Zucco (*Abadi*), Katherine DeMille (*Shari*), Rod LaRocque (*Inspector Joachim*), Sig Arno (*Khattab*), Yollande Mollot (*Margo*), Lloyd Corrigan (*Baron*), Henry Brandon (*Hessien*), Nestor Paiva (*Ahmend*), Dick Botiller (*Nardo*), Steve Geray (*Bellboy*), Wright Kramer (*Prof. Wynham*).

Well-knit story follows a group of Cairo jewel thieves in their efforts to steal the "seven jewels" uncovered by a scientific expedition. Zucco, the lead cutthroat, has perfect copies of the jewels made and kills the gem cutter who made them. Zucco is thwarted by LaRocque, who captures the bandits and returns the jewels.

p, Joseph G. Sanford; d, Leslie Kardos; w, Alex Gottlieb; ph, Elwood Bredell; ed, Paul Landers; m, Charles Previn; md, H.J. Salter.

Crime (PR:A MPAA:NR)

DARK TOWER, THE* (1943, Brit.) 90m WB bw

Ben Lyon (*Phil Danton*), Anne Crawford (*Mary*), David Farrar (*Tom Danton*), Herbert Lom (*Torg*), Frederick Burtwell (*Willie*), Bill Hartnell (*Towers*), Josephine Wilson (*Mme. Shogun*), Elsie Wagstaffe (*Eve*), J.H. Roberts (*Dr. Wilson*).

Lom, a hypnotist, is hired by the same circus in which the owner's brother is a trapeze artist. Lom falls in love with the brother's partner, Crawford, and tries to break up the two by hypnotizing her into dropping her partner during their act. Lom meets his end at the hands of another circus member. This is Herbert Lom's first film, and he would later go on to major character parts in many first-rate films.

p, Max Milder; d, John Harlow; w, Brock Williams, Reginald Purdell (based on a play by George S. Kaufman and Alexander Woolcott); ph, Otto Heller.

Crime (PR:A MPAA:NR)

DARK VENTURE zero (1956) 81m FN bw

John Trevlac [Calvert], John Carradine, Ann Cornell.

Bargain-basement adventure starring Trevlac [Calvert] as an explorer out to get the slightly deranged Carradine, who is guarding an elephant's graveyard in darkest Africa.

d&w, John Calvert.

Adventure (PR:A MPAA:NR)

DARK VICTORY**** (1939) 105m WB/FN bw

Bette Davis (*Judith Traherne*), George Brent (*Dr. Frederick Steele*), Humphrey Bogart (*Michael O'Leary*), Geraldine Fitzgerald (*Ann King*), Ronald Reagan (*Alec Hamin*), Henry Travers (*Dr. Parsons*), Cora Witherspoon (*Carrie Spottswood*), Virginia Brissac (*Martha*), Dorothy Peterson (*Miss Wainwright*), Charles Richman (*Colonel Mantle*), Herbert Rawlinson (*Dr. Carter*), Leonard Mudie (*Dr. Driscoll*), Fay Helm (*Miss Dodd*), Diane Bernard (*Agatha*), Jack Mower (*Veterinarian*), William Worthington, Alexander Leftwitch (*Specialists*), Ila Rhodes (*Secretary*), Frank Darien (*Anxious Little Man*), Stuart Holmes (*Doctor*), John Harron, John Ridgely (*Men*), Rosella Towne (*Girl in Box*), Edgar Edwards (*Trainer*), Lottie Williams (*Lucy*), Jeffrey Sayre, Will Morgan, Wedgwood Nowell, Stuart Holmes, Nat Carr, Ed Graham, Jack Goodrich (*Doctors*), Maris Wrixon, Richard Bond, Wilda Bennett, Leyland Hodgson, Mary Currier, David Newell, Marian Alden, Paulette Evans, Frank Mayo (*Judith's Friends*), Sidney Bracy (*Bartender*), Speirs Buskell (*Dr. Steele's Assistant*).

Would that 1939 could happen again and again in the picture business. It was the year for GONE WITH THE WIND; THE WIZARD OF OZ; GOODBYE, MR. CHIPS; STAGECOACH; MR. SMITH GOES TO WASHINGTON; WUTHERING HEIGHTS; BABES IN ARMS; LOVE AFFAIR; NINOTCHKA; GUNGA DIN; OF MICE AND MEN and the film we are about to discuss, DARK VICTORY, which was nominated as best movie, for best actress, and for music and didn't win a single Academy Award. Based on a short-lived play that starred the great Tallulah Bankhead, DARK VICTORY was first acquired by David O. Selznick but he gave up on it shortly before production. Warner Bros. took it over and the result is a memorable soap opera that goes right for the tear ducts and doesn't stop for 105 minutes. Bette Davis is a high-living Long Island heiress who is the darling of the horsey set. Her life revolves around her thoroughbreds who are overseen by her rough Irish stableman, Bogart. Bette is hip-deep in hedonism, drinks too much, smokes too much, but won't slow down. She begins to have headaches which cause her friends more concern than she has for her own welfare. When the headaches become dizzy spells, she is prevailed upon to see a specialist. She reluctantly consults Brent, who determines that she has a brain tumor and an immediate operation is ordered. The surgery is successful, or so it seems, and Davis has fallen hard for Brent. Fitzgerald, in her first picture, is Davis' secretary and she learns that Bette has but ten months left to live. All of her pals learn what is about to happen and conspire to keep it from her; Bogart, her long-time friend, Reagan, et al. Eventually, Davis learns the truth and she rejects Brent, thinking that he is going to marry her out of pity, knowing full well that she will not exist one more year. She sets out on a whirlwind dash of cocktail parties and faster living than she's ever imagined. Late one night, she's in the stable talking to her favorite horse, Challenger, where she is overheard by Bogart, who has always loved her from afar but realized they were of different castes. He tells her to swallow her pride and understand that Brent loves her for herself. Life is short and one must take one's happiness where one can. She understands full well, better than anyone, what that means and rushes to Brent, asking that they be married immediately before any more precious time is wasted. The wedding takes place and they move to his farm in Vermont. Life is simple and Davis begins finding deep pleasures in the most basic functions. The sun shines, the flowers grow, the birds sing . . . and she appreciates all of it with a passion one can feel from the screen. In a stirring scene, she plants flowers with Fitzgerald just as she is going blind. She knows she'll never see the hyacinths bloom but the knowledge that they will is enough to make her smile. As her eyesight fails, it's clear that life is also waning. She sends Brent off to a medical conference and Fitzgerald helps her into bed. The sunlight begins to fade in her eyes but she is contented and knows that she has crammed a lifetime of joy into a few months. The light continues to diminish and she smiles as she awaits the end. This is her victory over death; she has *lived*. The End. This movie sold more Kleenex than any other film of the era, for good reason. It was a prime example of how to manipulate the emotions of the audience but it was done so well that we didn't care at all. Bogart was barely visible, as was Reagan, who was more epicene than macho. Matter of fact, almost everyone else pales as it is Davis' picture from start to finish. Davis made two other movies in 1939, THE OLD MAID and THE PRIVATE LIVES OF ELIZABETH AND ESSEX. There are actresses today who haven't made that many good films in a lifetime. Jack Warner never thought the picture would do a thing and was quoted as saying, "Who wants to see a dame go blind?" The profits from this picture allowed him to build several new stages as well as indulge himself in several new cars. Remade as STOLEN HOURS.

p, Hal B. Wallis, David Lewis; d, Edmund Goulding; w, Casey Robinson (based on the play by George Emerson Brewer, Jr., and Bertram Bloch); ph, Ernest Haller; m, Max Steiner; ed, William Holmes; md, Leo F. Forbstein; art d, Robert Haas; cos, Orry-Kelly; m/l, Goulding, Elsie Janis.

Drama Cas. (PR:A MPAA:NR)

DARK WATERS**½ (1944) 90m UA bw

Merle Oberon (*Leslie Calvin*), Franchot Tone (*Dr. George Grover*), Thomas Mitchell (*Mr. Sydney*), Fay Bainter (*Aunt Emily*), John Qualen (*Uncle Norbert*), Elisha Cook, Jr. (*Cleeve*), Rex Ingram (*Pearson Jackson*), Odette Myrtil (*Mama Boudreaux*), Eugene Borden (*Papa Boudreaux*), Eileen Coghlan (*Jeanette*), Nina Mae McKinney (*Florella*), Alan Napier (*The Doctor*), Rita Beery (*The Nurse*), Gigi Perreau (*Girl*).

Oberon stars as a young woman whose parents drowned when the ship they were traveling on sank, while she survived. The deaths have made her emotionally unstable, and evil conniver Mitchell attempts to drive her into the asylum to grab her inheritance, but Tone frustrates him. A first-class cast holds up a second-class story in which there are some chilling moments.

p, Benedict Bogeaus; d, Andre De Toth; w, Joan Harrison, Marian Cockrell, Arthur Horman (based on the novel by Frank Cockrell, Marian Cockrell); ph, Archie Stout, John Mescall; m, Miklos Rozsa; ed, James Smith; md, Rozsa; art d, Charles Odds; set d, Maurice Yates; spec eff, Harry Redmond; ch, Jack Crosby.

Suspense/Drama (PR:A MPAA:NR)

DARK WORLD*½ (1935, Brit.) 73m FOX British bw

Tamara Desni (*Brigitta*), Leon Quartermaine (*Stephen*), Hugh Brooke (*Philip*), Olga Lindo (*Eleanor*), Morton Selten (*Colonel*), Fred Duprez (*Schwartz*), Viola Compton (*Auntie*), Googie Withers (*Annie*), Kynaston Reeves (*John*), Betty Shale.

Driven by jealousy, a man attempts to kill his brother by electrocution, but accidentally kills the wrong man. Routine British crime drama.

p, Leslie Landau; d, Bernard Vorhaus; w, Hugh Brooke (based on a story by Landau and Selwyn Jepson.)

Crime (PR:A MPAA:NR)

DARKENED ROOMS*½ (1929) 63m PAR bw

Evelyn Brent (*Ellen*), Neil Hamilton (*Emory Jago*), Doris Hill (*Joyce Clayton*), David Newell (*Billy*), Gale Henry (*Mme. Silvara*), Wallace MacDonald (*Bert Nelson*), Blanche Craig (*Mrs. Fogarty*), E.H. Calvert (*Mr. Clayton*), Sammy Bricker (*Sailor*).

An expose of phony seances and spiritualists. Brent plays a medium partnered with Hamilton, as a clairvoyant. The film reveals the tricks of the trade used by so-called spiritualists, who were the rage during the 1920s.

d, Louis Gasnier; w, Patrick Konesky, Melville Baker, Patrick Kearney (based on the story by Philip Gibbs); ph, Archie Stout; ed, Frances Marsh.

Mystery (PR:A MPAA:NR)

DARKENED SKIES*½ (1930) 67m Biltmore/CAP bw
(AKA: DARK SKIES)

Wallace MacDonald (*Capt. Pedro Real*), Evelyn Brent (*Juanita Morgan*), William V. Mong (*Mr. Morgan*), Tom O'Brien (*Pete*), Josef Swickard (*Senor Moreno*), Larry Steele (*Capt. Nelson*), Tom Wilson (*Mike*).

Early talker has Brent falling in love with rumrunner MacDonald, who agrees to quit smuggling and marry her after one more run. She is supposed to warn him of danger with a light from the coast, but is prevented from doing so by government agent Steele, who then catches MacDonald red-handed. Fairly entertaining, though completely forgotten today.

d, Harry O. Hoyt; w, John Francis Natteford; ph, Ray Reis, Harry Fowler.

Crime Drama (PR:A MPAA:NR)

DARKER THAN AMBER*½ (1970) 96m Cinema Center/NG c

Rod Taylor *(Travis McGee)*, Suzy Kendall *(Vangie/Merrimay)*, Theodore Bikel *(Meyer)*, Jane Russell *(Alabama Tiger)*, James Booth *(Burk)*, Janet MacLachlan *(Noreen)*, William Smith *(Terry)*, Ahna Capri *(Del)*, Robert Phillips *(Griff)*, Chris Robinson *(Roy)*, Jack Nagle *(Farnsworth)*, Sherry Faber *(Nina)*, James H. Frysinger *(Dewey Powell)*, Oswaldo Calvo *(Manuel)*, Jeff Gillen *(Morgue Attendant)*, Michael DeBeausset *(Dr. Fairbanks)*, Judy Wallace *(Ginny)*, Harry Wood *(Ed Judson)*, Marcy Knight *(Landlady)*, Don Schoff *(Steward)*, Warren Bauer, Wayne Bauer *(Roy's Companions)*.

A gory private eye film that is overlong and confusing. Taylor plays the gumshoe, with Bikel as his sidekick. The two rescue Kendall from drowning at the hands of psychotic sadists Smith and Phillips, her former partners in a shakedown racket. Later Kendall is killed by the two crooks. Taylor uses Kendall, playing a dual-role look-alike for her dead character, as bait to trap Smith and Phillips. The story is of little importance in this film as the extreme violence seems to be the main interest.

p, Walter Seltzer, Jack Reeves; d, Robert Clouse; w, Ed Waters (based on the novel by John D. MacDonald); ph, Frank Phillips (Technicolor); m, John Parker; ed, Fred Chulack; art d, Jack Collis; set d, Don Ivey.

Mystery (PR:O MPAA:R)

DARKEST AFRICA*½
(1936) 100m REP bw (AKA: BATMEN OF AFRICA or KING OF THE JUNGLELAND)

Clyde Beatty *(Clyde Beatty)*, Manuel King *(Baru Tremaine)*, Elaine Shepard *(Valerie Tremaine)*, Lucien Prival *(Dagna)*, Ray Benard *(Bonga)*, Wheeler Oakman *(Durkin)*, Edward McWade *(Gorn)*, Edmund Cobb *(Craddock)*, Ray Turner *(Hambone)*.

Famed animal trainer Beatty stars as himself in an adventure that takes him to a hidden jungle city where he meets with cute-but-brave jungle boy King. Together they fight their way through the evil, flying batmen to reach King's sister who has been captured and held hostage in the hidden city. Republic's first serial which was re-cut and turned into a 100-minute feature.

p, Barney Sarecky; d, Breeves Easton, Joseph Kane; w, John Rathmell, Sarecky, Ted Parsons (based on a story by Rathmell, Tracy Knight); ed, Dick Fantl.

Adventure (PR:A MPAA:NR)

DARKTOWN STRUTTERS zero
(1975) 93m New World c (AKA: GET DOWN AND BOOGIE)

Trina Parks *(Syreena)*, Edna Richardson *(Carmen)*, Bettye Sweet *(Miranda)*, Shirley Washington *(Theda)*, Roger E. Mosley *(Mellow)*, Christopher Joy *(Wired)*, Stan Shaw *(Raunchy)*, Dewayne Jesse *(V.D.)*, Charles Knapp *(Tubbins)*, Edward Marshall *(Emmo)*, Dick Miller *(Hugo)*, Milt Kogan *(Babel)*, Norman Bartold *(Cross)*, Gene Simms *(Flash)*, Sam Laws *(Philo)*, Frankie Crocker *(Stuff)*, Della Thomas *(Lixie)*, Ed Bakey *(Rev. Tilly)*, Fuddle Bagley *(Casabah)*, Frances Nealy *(Cinderella)*, Barbara Morrison *(Mrs. Parasol)* Raymond Allen *(Six Bits)*, Charles Woolf *(Fallow)*, Alvin Childress *(Bo)*, Zara Cully *(Lorelai)*, The Dramatics, John Gary Williams and the Newcomers, Oaky Miller and Company, The Minstrels.

An amateurish comedy about a motorcycle-travelling, black female singing group. The film makes a bad attempt at being a contemporary social satire as it follows the group through various encounters in roadside fast-food places. Whites are characterized in the film either as incredibly stupid buffoons, like the police, or as rabid racists like the Ku Klux Klan.

d, William N. Witney; w, George Armitage; ph, Joao Fernandes (Metrocolor); ed, Morton Tubor; art d, Peter Jamison; set d, Jack Fisk; cos, Michael Nicola.

Comedy (PR:C MPAA:PG)

DARLING**** (1965, Brit.) 128m Vic-Appia/EM bw

Laurence Harvey *(Miles Brand)*, Dirk Bogarde *(Robert Gold)* Julie Christie *(Diana Scott)*, Roland Curram *(Malcolm)*, José Luis De Villalonga *(Cesare)*, Alex Scott *(Sean Martin)*, Basil Henson *(Alec Prosser-Jones)*, Helen Lindsay *(Felicity Prosser-Jones)*, Pauline Yates *(Estette Gold)*, Tyler Butterworth *(William Prosser-Jones)*, Peter Bayliss *(Lord Grant)*, Ernst Walder *(Kurt)*, Lucille Soong *(Allie)*, Sidonie Bond *(Gillian)*, John G. Heller *(Gerhard)*, James Cossins *(Basildon)*, Lydia Sherwood *(Lady Brentwood)*, Georgina Cookson *(Carlotta Hale)*, Brian Wilde *(Willett)*, David Harrison *(Charles Glass)*, Irene Richmond *(Mrs. Glass)*, Ann Firbank *(Sybil)*, Richard Bidlake *(Rupert Crabtree)*, Annette Carroll *(Billie Castiglione)*, Jean Claudio *(Raoul Maxim)*, Trevor Bowen *(Tony Bridges)*, Helen Stirling *(Governess to Cesare)*, Hugo Dyson *(Matthew Southgate)*, Angus MacKay *(Ivor Dawlish)*, Margaret Gordon *(Helen Dawlish)*, Jane Downes *(Julie)*, Carlo Palmucci *(Curzio)*, Dante Posani *(Gino)*, Umberto Raho *(Palucci)*.

Joseph Janni, John Schlesinger, and Frederic Raphael combined to write the story, the screenplay, provide the production and direction, and totally oversee the making of the definitive 1960s movie, DARLING. Christie won an Oscar for her portrayal of a totally amoral woman of the period who jumped in and out of men's beds the way some people jump in and out of showers. She is a beautiful English model who has but one enemy, ennui, and her frantic attempts to overcome boredom are the basis for the plot. One decade earlier, the censorship standards would have been so stringent that this film would have been truncated to the point where it might not have made sense. As it is, when shown on commercial (rather than cable) TV, it appears jumpy with many unmotivated sequences. The film begins with an unfashionable flashback; Christie is now the wife of millionaire Villalonga, a widower with several children and a huge mansion in the country. We learn that she began her hegira with an ill-advised teenage marriage that soon disintegrated. Christie then drifts into the world of modeling and acting in commercials. She meets and falls for Bogarde, a TV newsman, who leaves his wife and brood for her. She departs her young mate and they move in together. Soon enough, Christie reckons Bogarde is small potatoes compared to Harvey, the ultimate sleaze, a public relations man with a multinational organization. She leaps into the sack, then goes off to Paris with Harvey and tells Bogarde that she is testing for a film. She does get a part in the small horror epic but it's hardly memorable. After the opening, she tells Bogarde that she is enceinte. They look forward to it for a while, then she secures an abortion and tells Bogarde that she could not stand the alteration to her life style, and, besides, she never liked sex anyhow (which may or may not have been a clue to what appeared to be nymphomania), or so she claims. She goes to her sister's home to recuperate but soon drifts back into Bogarde's life. Just as that is seeming to click, she leaves Bogarde and returns to Harvey. He takes her to Paris where they embark on a whirlwind voyage to all of the decadence of France's version of LA DOLCE VITA. There is an orgy sequence that was supposedly snipped a bit by the British censors but still steams. Christie returns to Bogarde in London but he is disgusted by her and strolls. She takes up with a gay photographer, Curram, who accompanies her to Italy where she does a chocolate commercial. While there, she meets Villalonga and he is immediately smitten and practically proposes on the spot. She rejects him but he continues his onslaught. She returns to England and is again rejected by Bogarde so she returns to Villalonga, marries him, and settles down to a life of wealthy boredom. There is only one person we can care about in the film and that's Bogarde's long-suffering wife, Pauline Yates, who is totally innocent. Christie is the proverbial bitch on wheels who goes from "bed to worse" (Bosley Crowther, *New York Times*) and we can admire her cool beauty and her calculating charm, but we cannot ever feel she doesn't get what she deserves, the tedium-filled life she so desperately sought to avoid. There are many quotable lines from Raphael's screenplay. Bogarde tells Christie, "Your idea of fidelity is not having more than one man in your bed at one time!" Many awards were given to DARLING. Raphael's screenplay won both the American and British Academy Awards. The same went for Christie, who also garnered the New York Film Critics' Award as did Schlesinger. Harris took the Oscar for best costumes and Simm won the British award for art direction. Schlesinger and the film were also nominated by the Academy but lost to THE SOUND OF MUSIC and Robert Wise. Nineteen Hundred Sixty-Five was a banner year for excellence and featured DARLING, THE SOUND OF MUSIC, CAT BALLOU, SHIP OF FOOLS, A THOUSAND CLOWNS, A PATCH OF BLUE, DOCTOR ZHIVAGO, THE GREAT RACE, THUNDERBALL, THE SHOP ON MAIN STREET, and several others. They don't hardly make years like that anymore. DARLING was a startling movie for its time but does pale in retrospect. Nevertheless, filmmakers do make movies for the time, not the ages, and in that it totally reflected that slim segment of the international jet set who call each other "darling."

p, Joseph Janni; d, John Schlesinger; w, Frederic Raphael (based on a story by Raphael, Schlesinger, Janni); ph, Ken Higgins; m, John Dankworth; ed, James Clark; set d, Ray Simm; cos, Julie Harris.

Drama (PR:O MPAA:NR)

DARLING, HOW COULD YOU! *½ (1951) 95m PAR bw

Joan Fontaine *(Alice Grey)*, John Lund *(Dr. Robert Grey)*, Mona Freeman *(Amy)*, Peter Hanson *(Dr. Steve Clark)*, David Stollery *(Cosmo)*, Virginia Farmer *(Fanny)*, Angela Clarke *(Nurse)*, Lowell Gilmore *(Aubrey Quayne)*, Robert Barrat *(Mr. Rossiter)*, Gertrude Michael *(Mrs. Rossiter)*, Mary Murphy *(Sylvia)*, Frank Elliott *(Simms)*, Billie Burke *(Rosie)*, Willard Waterman *(Theater Manager)*, Gordon Arnold *(Man)*, John Bryant *(Lieutenant)*, Robin Hughes *(Neville)*, Allan Douglas *(Steward)*, Dave Willock *(Usher)*, Maureen Lynn Reimer *(Molly)*, Patsy O'Byrne *(Mrs. Jones)*, Gloria Winters *(Girl)*, Maria J. Tavares *(Pretty Nurse)*, Fred Zendar *(Rugged Sailor)*, William Meader *(Ship's Officer)*, Houseley Stevenson *(Old Man)*, Jimmie Dundee *(Girl's Father)*, Allan Douglaus *(Customs Officer)*, Charles Sherlock *(Customs Inspector)*, Mickey Little, Rudy Lee *(Boys)*, Kathryn Towne *(Mother)*, Dolores Hall *(Daughter)*, Percy Helton, Robert E. Burns *(Cabbies)*.

Based on the James M. Barrie play, "Alice-Sit-By-The-Fire," this film is a very uninspired adaptation. It has Fontaine and Lund returning from five years digging in Central America, getting reacquainted with their three children. A side plot has oldest child, Freeman, who sees a wicked play about straying mothers, mistaking her own mother's friendly attentions toward young doctor Hanson as indiscreet and wanting to break it up. The film tries to be touching, but ends up forced and overlong.

p, Harry Tugend; d, Mitchell Leisen; w, Dodie Smith, Lesser Samuels (based on the play "Alice-Sit-By-The-Fire," by James M. Barrie); ph, Daniel L. Fapp; m, Frederick Hollander; ed, Alma Macrorie, Eda Warren; art d, Hal Pereira, Roland Anderson.

Comedy (PR:A MPAA:NR)

DARLING LILI* (1970) 136m Geoffrey Prod/PAR c

Julie Andrews *(Lili Smith)*, Rock Hudson *(Maj. William Larrabee)*, Jeremy Kemp *(Kurt von Ruger)*, Lance Percival *(Lt. Carstairs, T.C. [Twombley-Crouch])*, Jacques Marin *(Maj. Duvalle)*, Michael Witney *(Lt. George Youngblood Carson)*, Andre Maranne *(Lt. Liggett)*, Bernard Kay *(Bedford)*, Doreen Keogh *(Emma)*, Gloria Paul *(Suzette)*, Carl Duering *(Kessler)*, Vernon Dobtcheff *(Kraus)*, A.E. Gould-Porter *(Sgt. Wells)*, Louis Mercier, Laurie Main *(French Generals)*, Ingo Mogendorf *(Baron von Richthofen, The Red Baron)*, Niall MacGinnis *(von Hindenberg)*, Mimi Monti *(Chanteuse)*.

This big-budget WW I espionage melodrama is a hollow shell production where Andrews is a Mata Hari-type German spy using her wiles to milk information out of Allied officers. She is a music hall favorite singing old-fashioned ditties until she is taken to a nightclub to hear Paul strip and sing. She is at first shocked, but then adapts the striptease to her normally mundane act. In between this drastic transformation Andrews proves not to be the hard-hearted spy but a vulnerable woman who falls deeply in love with Hudson, a flyer, and cannot bring herself to betray him, thus reforming and giving up the espionage business. For all its pretentious pomp and expensive production look, DARLING LILI is an overlong, often boring film prop for Andrews and her husband, producer-director Edwards, the entire effort seemingly designed for the exclusive purpose of having the once prim-and-proper Julie strip to slender nakedness, something she had wanted to do for years to rid herself of the do-gooder Maria von Trapp and Mary Poppins images. Oddly, Andrews does not have the figure to appear alluring or voluptuous, being on the skinny side and slightly bowlegged. Always the entrepreneur, Edwards undoubtedly thought Andrews' leap to sex goddess would shock the money out of moviegoers. It didn't. The film, not Julie, was an enormous bust. Andrews received from nervous Paramount executives a towering contract that gave her $1,100,000 plus 10 percent of the profits for this inconsequential musical extravaganza where Julie vamped a number of men and also took a steamy shower, another scene Edwards insisted upon. The songs she sang were at the studio's insistence and composers Mancini and Mercer produced seven new but instantly forgettable tunes just for her. This team had successfully produced "Moon River" for BREAKFAST AT TIFFANY'S and the title tune for DAYS OF WINE AND ROSES, both Edwards productions, yet their efforts here are lifeless and without the slightest novelty. Hudson and Andrews were mismatched, their love scenes decidedly tepid and uninteresting which may have been due to their reportedly strained relationship during filming. Edwards and Andrews, according to some sources, constantly teased Hudson about his masculinity and one columnist wrote that Andrews, on several occasions, told Hudson jocularly: "Remember, *I'm* the leading lady!" The arrogant air of the pair spilled over to the press. So involved with DARLING LILI was Andrews that she told Paramount bosses that she couldn't attend the premiere of STAR!, the musical film celebrating the life of Gertrude Lawrence which Andrews had just finished shooting. The press destroyed that movie which all but lost its entire investment of $12 million. And when Edwards, in retaliation to bad reviews on STAR! barred the press from the DARLING LILI sets, the critics went after the haughty producer and his actress-bride. The studio also insisted that the dogfights, that were to be the highlights of the film, be shot in Ireland where surplus antique WW I planes were stored and which Paramount had used for the brilliant WW I film THE BLUE MAX in 1966. Bad weather forced delays and enormous waste ($70,000 a day for rental equipment alone). Edwards decided finally to shoot against a clouded sky but then the weather cleared up and the sun shone for weeks, preventing new takes until the sky again clouded over. All of this drove Paramount and Gulf and Western (its holding firm) executives into tirades. On-location shooting in Belgium was also enormously expensive. Edwards and Andrews lived high during this fast-developing disaster, residing in an Irish castle at one point with servants galore in attendance. Outside of Paris, the couple leased with Paramount funds the former home of the Duke of Windsor, and also a one-time residence of Napoleon III. The production turned in by Edwards caused Paramount brass to explode. Said one: "It was $15 million worth of unusable film—and no picture." Studio chief Robert Evans went even further, raging that the production was "the most flagrant misappropriation and waste of funds I've ever seen in my career. The primary reason the film went over budget was Edwards' drive to protect 'his lady'. Queen Elizabeth was never treated half as well! The extravagance was unbelievable. He was writing a love letter to his lady and Paramount paid for it!" The total budget soared beyond $25 million, which was four times the budget given the film, earning back only $5 million when released, a devastating flop, the worst financial drubbing Paramount ever took on a musical to that date. For a while the couple were believed to be box office poison, until Edwards put together the huge smash hit, 10, and later VICTOR/VICTORIA. Most of Edwards' productions since then have been opulent but empty films done on a Hollywood reputation that has come to signify vacuous, turgid, and unrewarding films where the paying public also gets 5¢ on the dollar. Songs include: "Whistling Away the Dark," "The Girl In No Man's Land," "Smile Away Each Raining Day," "I'll Give You Three Guesses" (Mancini, Mercer, all sung by Andrews); "Your Good Will Ambassador" (Mancini, Mercer, sung by Paul).

p&d, Blake Edwards; w, Edwards, William Peter Blatty; ph, Russell Harlan (Panavision, Technicolor); m, Henry Mancini, Johnny Mercer; ed, Peter Zinner; prod d, Fernando Carrere; set d, Reg Allen, Jack Stevens; cos, Jack Bear, Donald Brooks; makeup, Allan Snyder, Willard Buell, Lynn Reynolds; ch, Hermes Pan; special ph eff, Anthony Squire, Guy Tabary; spec eff, Rex Wimpy, Linwood Dunn, Van Der Veer Photo Co, Bob Peterson.

Musical/Spy Drama **(PR:C MPAA:G)**

DARTS ARE TRUMPS**½

(1938, Brit.) 72m George Smith Productions/RKO bw

Eliot Makeham *(Joe Stone)*, Nancy O'Neil *(Mary Drake)*, Ian Colin *(Harry)*, Muriel George *(Mrs. Drake)*, H.F. Maltby *(Stephen Sims)*, Paul Blake *(Hon. Bernard Jaye)*, Johnny Singer *(Jimmy)*, Michael Ripper, George Pembroke, Bryan Powley.

A clerk uses his skill at dart playing to capture a clever jewel thief. Plenty of comic touches hit the bull's-eye.

p, George Smith; d, Maclean Rogers; w, Kathleen Butler, H.F. Maltby (based on a story by Gordon Bushell); ph, Geoffrey Faithfull.

Comedy **(PR:A MPAA:NR)**

DARWIN ADVENTURE, THE**

(1972, Brit.) 91m Palomar/FOX c

Nicholas Clay *(Charles Darwin)*, Susan Macready *(Emma Wedgewood)*, Ian Richardson *(Capt. Fitzroy)*, Robert Flemyng *(Prof. Henslow)*, Christopher Martin *(Lt. Sullivan)*, Philip Brack *(Huxley)*, Michael Malnick *(Hooker)*, Aubrey Woods *(Bishop Wilberforce)*, Hugh Morton *(Josiah Wedgewood)*, David Davenport *(Robert Darwin)*, Carl Bernard *(Moreno)*, Richard Ireson *(Wickman)*, John Baskomb *(Professor Draper)*, Tony Robinson *(Man in Crowd)*, Luke Batchelor, Rachel Brennock, Denise Gyngell, Michael Gyngell, Paul Gyngell *(The Darwin Children)*, Joy Stewart *(Lady Gilroy)*, Rollo Gamble *(Master of Hounds)*, Geoffrey Russell *(Journalist)*, Charles Simon *(Lay Preacher)*, Philip Newman *(Member of Parliament)*, Faith Kent, Susan Travers *(Ladies)*, Brian Anthony *(Undergraduate)*, Gentle Roy Denton *(Gentleman with Cold)*, Archies Wilson *(Lecturer)*, Michael Shearg, Derek Deadman *(Men)*.

Unexciting film about the famed naturalist who shocked Victorian England with his theories that man evolved from apes, and was not created by the hand of God as set down in the Bible. Darwin is played by Clay, who portrays him from youth to old age. There is a good amount of nature footage, and the story presents Darwin's gradual success against great religious prejudice.

p, Joseph Strick; d, Jack Couffer; w, William Fairchild (based on a story by Couffer, Max Bella); ph, Couffer, Robert Crandall, Ken Middleman, Denys Coop (DeLuxe Color); m, Mark Wilkinson; ed, Robert Dearberg; art d, Jack Stoll; cos, Verena Coleman.

Biography **(PR:A MPAA:G)**

DAS BOOT****

(1982) 150m Bavaria Atelier/COL c (AKA: THE BOAT)

Jurgen Prochnow *(The Captain)*, Herbert Gronemeyer *(Lt. Werner/Correspondent)*, Klaus Wennemann *(Chief Engineer)*, Hubertus Bengsch *(1st Lt./Number One)*, Martin Semmelrogge *(2nd Lt.)*, Bernd Tauber *(Chief Quartermaster)*, Erwin Leder *(Johann)*, Martin May *(Ullmann)*, Heinz Honig *(Hinrich)*, U.A. Ochsen *(Chief Bosun)*, Claude-Oliver Rudolph *(Ario)*, Jan Fedder *(Pilgrim)*, Ralph Richter *(Frenssen)*, Joachim Bernhard *(Preacher)*, Oliver Stritzel *(Schwalle)*, Konrad Becker *(Bockstiegel)*, Lutz Schnell *(Dufte)*, Martin Hemme *(Bruckenwilli)*, Roger Barth *(Thomas Boxhammer)*, Christian Bendomir *(Gunther Franke)*, Albert Kraml *(Norbert Fronwald)*, Peter Pathenis *(Jean-Claude Hoffmann)*, Christian Seipolt *(Arno Kral)*, Ferdinand Schaal *(Helmut Neumeier)*, Rolf Weber *(Wilhelm Pietsch)*, Lothar Zajicek *(Dirk Salomon)*, Rita Cadillac *(Monique)*, Otto Sander *(Thomsen)*, Gunter Lamprecht *(Captain of the* Weser*)*, Edwige Pierre *(Nadine)*, Uwe Ochenknecht *(Boatman)*.

A superbly filmed action movie, this was the most expensive film produced by what was touted as an "all German" company, actors, crew and investors alike, an almost $12 million production that shows its painstaking expense in every frame. Based on the actual experiences of WW II photographer Lothar-Guenther Buchheim, the film shows in detail the single cruise of a U-boat in 1941, replete with every known horror above and below the waves, as well as the mundane, boring hours spent at sea. Although most of the footage is spent on Prochnow (the intense, noble captain, members of the crew receive cameo attention), the only fully developed character in the film is the boat itself as it undergoes battle and attack to survive and return to port only to be destroyed in an air attack upon the subpens of La Rochelle in occupied France. The chief attraction of this film is the incredible camerawork, performed for the most part with handheld cameras that zoom through the boat as it rises and submerges in and out of attack, going through tiny openings. Photographer Jost Vacano practiced running from compartment to compartment for days through an actual submarine used in the production until he could race along without stumbling or smashing his camera. The result is a spectacular, life-like recreation of sea battle on the Atlantic. The sweaty, claustrophobic atmosphere of the submarine is fully and frighteningly captured here, although the lack of dialog and the quickly-flashed subtitles distract occasionally. Oddly, this film closely follows in story line a 1933 UFA production, MORGENROT (DAWN), which Nazi leaders Hitler and Goebbels admired and promoted as good military propaganda. The film is understandably and decidedly anti-Hitler and his Nazi regime, the submariners profiled as individual warriors upholding their own brand of honor and sneering in the direction of the Third Reich. That attitude, however, like the end of the film is anti-climactic. As a technical achievement this film is a marvel to behold, a breathtaking and powerful portrait of war and death.

p, Gunter Rohrbach, Michael Bittins; d&w, Wolfgang Petersen (based on the novel by Lothar-Guenther Buchheim); ph, Jost Vacano (Fujicolor); m, Klaus Doldinger; ed, Hannes Nikel; prod d, Rolf Zehetbauer; art d, Gotz Weidner; cos, Monika Bauert; spec eff, Karl Baumgartner.

War Drama **Cas.** **(PR:CO MPAA:R)**

DAS LETZTE GEHEIMNIS*

(1959, Ger.) 95m Divina Film
(ARZT OHNE GEWISSEN; PRIVATKLINIK PROF. LUND)

Wolfgang Preiss, Karin Baal (Blauermel), Ewald Balser, Barbara Ruetting, Cornell Borchers, Wolfgang Kieling, Erica Beer, Walter Jacob, Emmerich Schrenk, Agnes Windeck.

Sick little German "medical horror" film starring Preiss as a mad doctor performing horrible experiments on "worthless" prostitutes and nightclub singers. Preiss later went on to play Dr. Mabuse in Fritz Lang's last film, THE THOUSAND EYES OF DR. MABUSE (1960).

p, Ilse Kubaschewski; d, Falk Harnack; w, Werner Zibaso; ph, Helmut Ashley.

Horror **(PR:C MPAA:NR)**

DATE AT MIDNIGHT**

(1960, Brit.) 57m Danziger/PAR bw

Paul Carpenter *(Bob Dillon)*, Jean Aubrey *(Paula Burroughs)*, Harriette Johns *(Lady Leyton)*, Ralph Michael *(Sir Edward Leyton)*, John Charlesworth *(Tommy)*, Philip Ray *(Jenkins)*, Howard Lang *(Inspector)*, Robert Ayres *(Gordon Baines)*, Vernon Smythe, Carole Lorimer, Totti Truman Taylor, Janet Rowell, Paddy Webster.

American reporter in England Carpenter clears the nephew of a prominent lawyer accused of murdering a girl. Competent, though no more.

p, Edward J. and Harry Lee Danziger; d, Godfrey Grayson; w, Mark Grantham; ph, Jimmy Wilson.

Crime   (PR:A-C   MPAA:NR)

DATE BAIT*   (1960) 71m Filmgroup bw

Gary Clarke, Marlo Ryan, Richard Gering, Danny Logan, Brad Martinelli, Sue Randall.

Clarke (of HONDO and THE VIRGINIAN) and Ryan star as two rebellious teenagers determined to get married despite the opposition of their parents, Ryan's former boy friend (who is aided by his psychopath dope-taking brother), and some gangsters. Originally played on a double-bill with HIGH SCHOOL CAESAR.

p&d, O'Dale Ireland; w, Robert Slaven, Ethel Mae Page.

Drama   (PR:O   MPAA:NR)

DATE WITH A DREAM, A**   (1948, Brit.) 55m Tempean/GN bw

Terry-Thomas (Terry), Jean Carson (Jean), Len Lowe (Len), Bill Lowe (Bill), Wally Patch (Uncle), Norman Wisdom, Elton Hayes.

Four entertainers, a group which staged concert parties during the war, have a reunion and wind up finding success as a nightclub act. One of Terry-Thomas's first films and one at least partly based on his own experiences.

p, Robert S. Baker, Monty Berman; d, Dicky Leeman; w, Leeman, Baker, Berman (based on a story by Carl Nystrom); ph, Berman.

Comedy   (PR:A   MPAA:NR)

DATE WITH DEATH, A zero   (1959) 81m PI

Liz Renay (Paula Warren), Gerald Mohr (Mike Mason), Harry Lauter (George Caddell), Robert Clarke (Joe Emanuel), Stephanie Farnay (Edith Dale), Ed Erwin (Art Joslin), Red Morgan (Urbano), Lew Markman (Potter), Tony Redman (Mayor Langlie), Frank Bellew (Weylin), William Purdy (Huber), Ray Dearholt (Sam), Melford Lehrman (Bender), Ken Duncan (Andrews).

Mohr plays a vagabond who takes on the identity of a murdered cop and decides to solve the crime and avenge his namesake by busting up the local gangster's rackets. The movie was shot in "Psychorama" (which threw some ineffective subliminal messages at the audience, a process borrowed from Daniels' earlier effort, TERROR IN THE HAUNTED HOUSE. Renay was up for a contract at Warner Bros., when funny business with gangster Mickey Cohen put her off limits in the film colony. Her screen test was shelved and she landed in Arizona to make this picture.

p, William S. Edwards; d, Harold Daniels; w, Robert C. Dennis.

Crime   (PR:A   MPAA:NR)

DATE WITH DISASTER*½   (1957, Brit.) 61m Fortress/Eros bw

Tom Drake (Miles), William Hartnell (Tracy), Shirley Eaton (Sue), Maurice Kaufmann (Don), Michael Golden (Inspector Matthews), Richard Shaw (Ken), Charles Brodie (Charles), Deirdre Mayne (Judy), Peter Fontaine (Sgt. Brace), Robert Robinson (Young Man), John Drake (Constable Wilson), Robert Mooney (Sergeant), Van Boolen (Night Watchman).

Drake, a car salesman, saves fiancee Eaton from kidnapers even though he is a suspected safecracker. Yet another undistinguished (and almost indistinguishable) crime melodrama from Britain.

p, Guido Coen; d, Charles Saunders; w, Brock Williams; ph, Brendan Stafford.

Crime   (PR:C   MPAA:NR)

DATE WITH JUDY, A***½   (1948) 113m MGM c

Wallace Beery (Melvin R. Foster), Jane Powell (Judy Foster), Elizabeth Taylor (Carol Pringle), Carmen Miranda (Rosita Conchellas), Xavier Cugat (Cugat), Robert Stack (Stephen Andrews), Selena Royle (Mrs. Foster), Scotty Beckett (Ogden "Oogie" Pringle), Leon Ames (Lucien T. Pringle), George Cleveland (Gramps), Lloyd Corrigan (Pop Scully), Clinton Sundberg (Jameson), Jean McLaren (Mitzie), Jerry Hunter (Randolph Foster), Buddy Howard (Jo-Jo Hoffenpepper), Lillian Yarbo (Nightingale), Eula Guy (Miss Clarke), Francis Pierlot (Professor Green), Rena Lenart (Olga), Sheila Stein (Little Girl in Drug Store), Paul Bradley (Headwaiter), Polly Bailey (Elderly Woman), Alice Kelley (Girl), Fern Eggen (Miss Sampson).

Cheerful and amiable musical that began as a radio series, became a movie, and wound up as a TV series. The town is Santa Barbara and Powell is seeing Beckett but soon falls for older man Stack. Taylor is Powell's best friend and they both misconstrue father Beery's relationship with Miranda as an affair when, in reality, the Brazilian Bombshell has been teaching Beery how to dance so he can surprise his wife, Royale. In the end, Powell loses Stack to Taylor and returns to Beckett. Taylor was breathtakingly beautiful and most of the reviewers made mention of that, but the film's best performance was by Miranda, who purloined every scene. Her famous malapropisms were delivered straight-faced and she may well be the idol upon whom Charo based her career. It's as shallow as a soap dish but done with such good humor that it makes no never mind. The music and the dancing more than compensate for any lack of story involvement. Stanley Donen handled the choreography chores and the songs, by a raft of composers, including, Miranda's specialty "Cuanto La Gusta." Cugat plays himself and must have been reminded of Miranda when he met and married Charo. Miranda died at the age of 46 after performing a particularly strenuous number on Jimmy Durante's TV show in 1955. She was so popular both in the U.S. and in her native Brazil that there was national mourning "souse of zee border" when the happy-go-lucky

Miranda passed away. A screen original, she only made fourteen films in the U.S. but anyone who saw her "live" on stage remembers her brilliant abilities to this day. Miranda made her American stage debut in the Broadway musical "Streets Of Paris" when she was 30 and then performed at New York's Waldorf-Astoria where she was eventually discovered for the movies. Songs and musical numbers: "Cuanto La Gusta" (Ray Gilbert, Gabriel Ruiz), "Strictly On The Corny Side" (Stella Unger, Alec Templeton), "It's A Most Unusual Day" (Harold Adamson, Jimmy McHugh), "Judaline" (Don Raye, Gene De Paul), "I've Got A Date With Judy," "I'm Gonna Meet My Mary" (Bill Katz, Calvin Jackson), "Temptation" (Arthur Freed, Nacio Herb Brown), "Mulligatawny."

p, Joe Pasternak; d, Richard Thorpe; w, Dorothy Cooper, Dorothy Kingsley (based on the radio series by Aleen Leslie); ph, Robert Surtees (Technicolor); ed, Harold F. Kress; md, Georgie Stoll; art d, Cedric Gibbons, Paul Groesse; set d, Edwin B. Willis, Richard A. Pefferle; cos, Helen Rose; spec eff, Warren Newcombe; ch, Stanley Donen.

Musical Comedy   (PR:AA   MPAA:NR)

DATE WITH THE FALCON, A**   (1941) 63m RKO bw

George Sanders (Falcon), Wendy Barrie (Helen Reed), James Gleason (O'Hara), Allen Jenkins (Goldy), Mona Maris (Rita Mara), Victor Kilian (Max), Frank Moran (Dutch), Russ Clark (Needles), Ed Gargan (Bates), Alec Craig (Waldo Sampson/H. Sampson), Eddie Dunn (Grimes), Frank Martinelli (Louie), Hans Conried (Hotel Clerk), Elizabeth Russell (Girl on Plane).

The second in the "Falcon" amateur series, with Sanders in the title role, has Sanders standing up his fiancee, Barrie, in order to investigate the kidnaping of a brilliant scientist for his formula for producing synthetic diamonds, which are badly needed in defense manufacturing. Sanders, always keeping out an eye on the girls, of course, allows himself to be captured so that he may come up with a plan to rescue himself and the scientist, while at the same time capturing the crooks. Light comedy as Sanders continually stands up Barrie, who wants to take an air trip west, and plenty of mugging by the cast keeps the whole thing going at a cheerful pace. (See FALCON series, Index).

p, Howard Benedict; d, Irving Reis; w, Lynn Root, Frank Fenton (based on a character created by Michael Arlen); ph, Robert DeGrasse; ed, Harry Marker; art d, Alberto D' Agostino, Al Herman.

Crime   (PR:A   MPAA:NR)

DATELINE DIAMONDS*   (1966, Brit.) 70m Viscount Films/Rank bw

William Lucas (Maj. Fairclough), Kenneth Cope (Lester Benson), George Mikell (Paul Verlekt), Conrad Phillips (Tom Jenkins), Patsy Rowlands (Mrs. Edgecombe), Burnell Tucker (Dale Meredith), Anna Cartaret (Gay Jenkins), Vanda Godsell (Mrs. Jenkins), Gertan Klauber (Meverhof), Doel Luscombe (Assistant Commissioner), Peter Sander (Spankharen), Geoffrey Lumsden (Army Officer), Ronald Bridges (Garage Attendant), David Kirk (Dock Policeman), Small Faces, Kiki Dee, The Chantelles, Mark Richardson, Kenny Everett.

Cashiered explosive officer Lucas masterminds a series of daring diamond robberies, blackmailing reformed criminal, but successful pop group manager Cope into smuggling the gems. Using a ship, they take the diamonds to Holland. Two patient cops, Mikell and Conrad, build up clues until they spring their trap at a teenage pop dance. Musical cameos are made by many British pop groups popular in the mid-1960s. The film was made for $90,000 and put in the can in six weeks, which speaks well for the talent involved.

p, Harry Benn; d, Jeremy Summers; w, Tudor Gates (based on an idea by Shampan); ph, Stephen Dade; m, Johnny Douglas; ed, Sidney Stone.

Crime   (PR:A   MPAA:NR)

DAUGHTER OF CLEOPATRA
(SEE: CLEOPATRA'S DAUGHTER, 1960, Ital.)

DAUGHTER OF DARKNESS**½   (1948, Brit.) 91m PAR bw

Anne Crawford (Bess Stanforth), Maxwell Reed (Dan), Siobhan McKenna (Emily Beaudine), George Thorpe (Mr. Tallent), Barry Morse (Robert Stanforth), Liam Redmond (Father Cocoran), Honor Blackman (Julie Tallent), Grant Tyler (Larry Tallent), David Greene (David Price), Denis Gordon (Saul Trevethick), Arthur Hambling (Jacob), George Merritt (Constable), Norah O'Mahony (Miss Hegarty), Ann Clery (Miss Foley), Alexis Milne.

Bizarre crime drama dealing with the activities of homicidal nymphomaniac McKenna, who happens to work for a priest in a small Irish village. She proceeds to seduce and kill quite a few of the local men-folk until irate townswoman Crawford traps her. McKenna gives a disturbing performance as the seductive psychotic killer. Strong stuff for 1948. Honor Blackman, the future Pussy Galore in GOLDFINGER, who was 22 years-old at the time, had been in films for only a year but won rave reviews for her small part.

p, Victor Hanbury; d, Lance Comfort; w, Max Catto (based on his play "They Walk Alone"); ph, Stan Pavey; m, Clifton Parker; ed, Lito Carruthers; art d, Ivan King.

Crime   (PR:O   MPAA:NR)

DAUGHTER OF DECEIT**½   (1977, Mex.) 80m Ultramar/Bauer International bw
(LA HIJA DEL ENGANO; DON QUINTIN EL AMARGAO)

Fernando Soler (Don Quintin), Alicia Caro (Marta), Ruben Rojo (Paco), Nacho Contra (Jonron), Fernando Soto (Angel), Lily Aclemar (Jovita).

Soler, convinced that his daughter is not his, leaves the infant on the doorstep of the town drunkard. Years later, tormented by guilt, he searches for her, finally finding her happily married and pregnant. A rarely seen Bunuel film from his

Mexican period, the film was produced in 1951 and was a remake of DON QUINTIN EL AMARGAO, a film on which Bunuel had acted as executive producer in Spain in 1935.

p, Oscar Dancigers; d, Luis Bunuel; w, Raquel Rojas, Luis Alcoriza (based on the play "Don Quintin el Amargao" by Carlos Arniches); ph, Jose Ortiz Ramos; m, Manuel Esperon; ed, Carlos Savage; set d, Edward Fitzgerald.

Drama   **(PR:A-C MPAA:NR)**

DAUGHTER OF DR. JEKYLL**   (1957) 67m AA bw

John Agar (George Hastings), Gloria Talbot (Janet Smith), Arthur Shields (Dr. Lomas), John Dierkes (Jacob), Martha Wentworth (Mrs. Merchant), Mollie McCart (Maggie).

Talbot learns from her old guardian, Shields, that her deceased father was the infamous Dr. Jekyll (though the character in Robert Louis Stevenson's novel was never married). Soon after, many townsfolk wind up murdered and the populace grabs the torches and heads for Talbot. All turns out well when Talbot's fiance, Agar (who's a little strange himself), discovers that the killings are actually being committed by Shields, who turns out to be a werewolf doctor. Disappointing effort by excellent low-budget director Edgar G. Ulmer.

p, Jack Pollexfen; d, Edgar G. Ulmer; w, Pollexfen; ph, John F. Warren; ed, Holbrook N. Todd; md, Melvyn Lenard; art d, Theobold Holsopple.

Horror   **(PR:A MPAA:NR)**

DAUGHTER OF EVIL**   (1930, Ger.) 103m UFA bw (ALRAUNE)

Brigitte Helm, Albert Bassermann, Agnes Straub, Kaethe Haack, Bernhard Goetzke, Martin Kosleck, Paul Westermeier, Liselott Schaak, Harald Paulsen, Henry Bender, E.A. Lichs, Ivan Koval-Samborski.

Bassermann plays a scientist experimenting with genetic splicing who artificially inseminates a prostitute with the semen of a hanged murderer. This union produces a beautiful, but cold and morally corrupt daughter, Helm. Lackluster direction by Oswald fails to charge the material with any of the sensuality or atmosphere needed to make it successful. This was the fourth version of this material (two in 1918, one in 1928) and it would be made again in 1952.

p, Erich Pommer; d, Richard Oswald; w, Charlie Roellinghoff, Richard Weisbach (based on the novel by Hanns Heinz Ewers); ph, Guenther Krampf; m, Bronislaw Kaper; art d, Otto Erdmann, Hans Sohnie.

Horror/Science Fiction   **(PR:O MPAA:NR)**

DAUGHTER OF MATA HARI
                              (SEE: MATA HARI'S DAUGHTER, 1954, Ital.)

DAUGHTER OF ROSIE O'GRADY, THE**½   (1950) 104m WB c

June Haver (Patricia O'Grady), Gordon MacRae (Tony Pastor), James Barton (Dennis O'Grady), Debbie Reynolds (Maureen O'Grady), S. Z. "Cuddles" Sakall (Miklos Teretzky), Gene Nelson (Doug Martin), Sean McClory (James Moore), Marsha Jones (Katie O'Grady), Jane Darwell (Mrs. Murphy), Irene Seidner (Mama Teretzky), Oscar O'Shea (Mr. Flannigan), Jack Lomas (Sergeant), Kendall Kapps (Actor), Virginia Lee.

Haver, Jones, and youngster Reynolds, in her second film, are the three Irish daughters of horsecar trolley driver Barton, a man with a great thirst for "the divil's" own brew. He has but one definite conviction; none of his daughters will go into show business. His late wife had been drawn to the footlights and makeup and he is determined to keep the colleens out of it. So, guess what happens? Haver falls for Tony Pastor, played by Gordon MacRae, and leaves home to join him in his highly successful five-a-day review. Then we have a few of the usual complications and it all winds up in smiles and hugs as Haver and Barton reconcile just in time for the conclusion. If that seems like a slim story, you're correct because thirteen songs and eight dances are wrapped around the dialog and there's barely enough time to get interested in anyone's plight as the musical numbers far outweigh everything else. Warner Bros. hadn't been known for this type of musical for many years and made an attempt to get back into what had been the Twentieth Century-Fox field for many years. This was mildly successful and the studio began to think musicals again until they took a bath many years later with CAMELOT. The dancing wasn't much except for Gene Nelson, a great barroom sand-dance by Barton, and two roughhouse comedy pieces by the Lees. Song and dance numbers include: "My Own True Love And I" (M.K. Jerome, Jack Scholl), "As We Are Today" (Ernesto Lecuona, Charles Tobias), "Ma Blushin' Rosie" (Edgar Smith, John Stromberg), "The Rose of Tralee" (Charles Glover), "A Farm Off Old Broadway," "A Picture Turned To the Wall," "Winter, Winter" (A. Bryan-Gumble), "Winter Serenade," "The Daughter of Rosie O'Grady" (Monty C. Brice, Walter Donaldson).

p, William Jacobs; d, David Butler; w, Jack Rose, Melville Shavelson, Peter Milne (based on a story by Rose and Shavelson); ph, Wilfrid M. Cline (Technicolor); ed, Irene Morris; art d, Douglas Bacon; ch, LeRoy Prinz.

Musical Comedy   **(PR:AA MPAA:NR)**

DAUGHTER OF SHANGHAI**½   (1937) 60m PAR bw

Anna May Wong (Lan Ying Lin), Phillip Ahn (Kim Lee), Charles Bickford (Otto Hartman), Larry Crabbe (Andrew Sleete), Cecil Cunningham (Mrs. Mary Hunt), J. Carrol Naish (Frank Barden), Evelyn Brent (Olga Derey), Anthony Quinn (Harry Morgan), Gino Corrado (Interpreter), John Patterson (James Lang), Fred Kohler (Capt. Gulner), Frank Sully (Jake Kelly), Ching Wah Lee (Quan Lin), Maurice Liu (Ah Fong), Pierre Watkin (Mr. Yorkland), Archie Twitchell (Secretary), Mrs. Wong Wing (Amah), Ernest Whitman (Sam Blike), Mae Busch (Lil), Guy Bates Post (Lloyd Burkett), Paul Fix (Miles), Layne Tom, Jr. (Chinese Candy Vendor), Gwen Kenyon (Phone Girl), Charles Wilson (Schwartz), Virginia Dabney (American Dancer), John

Hart (Sailor), Alex Woloshin (Gypsy), Agostino Borgato (Gypsy), Bruce Wong (Chinese), Andre P. Marsaudon (South American), Lee Shumway (Ship's Officer), Marie Burton, Paula Di Cardo, Alma Ross, Blanca Vischer (Girls), Carmen Bailey, Paulita Arvizu, Carmen LaRue, Tina Menard (Dancers).

Good "B" actioner starring Wong as the American-Chinese daughter of a man who was slain by a powerful group of smugglers who specialize in the illegal alien trade. The crooks, led by a powerful San Francisco society matron, had Wong's father murdered when he threatened to expose them. Wong vows vengeance and trails the hoods to their island stronghold where she goes undercover as a dance hall girl. There she seduces one of the gang and obtains the necessary evidence to bust up their racket. Well made and fast-paced. Hollywood's penchant for reading the newspapers and attempting to commercialize on what has become topical therein is demonstrated in the title of this palatable trifle. The story has nothing to do with Shanghai, but at the time China and Japan were at war and America was intensely interested in the outcome. Thus Wong became a "Daughter of Shanghai."

p, Harold Hurley; d, Robert Florey; w, Gladys Unger, Garnett Weston (based on a story by Weston); ph, Charles Schoenbaum; ed, Ellsworth Hoagland; md, Boris Morros; art d, Hans Dreier, Robert Odell.

Crime Drama   **(PR:A MPAA:NR)**

DAUGHTER OF THE DRAGON**   (1931) 70m PAR bw

Anna May Wong (Ling Moy), Warner Oland (Fu Manchu), Sessue Hayakawa (Ah Kee), Bramwell Fletcher (Ronald Petrie), Frances Dade (Joan Marshall), Holmes Herbert (Sir John Petrie), Nella Walker (Lady Petrie), Nicholas Soussanin (Morloff), Lawrence Grant (Sir Basil), Harold Minjir (Rogers), E. Alyn Warren (Lu Chow), Harrington Reynolds (Hobbs), Tetsu Komai (Lao), Ole Chan (The Amah) Olaf Hytten (Butler).

A continuation of the Fu Manchu saga starring Oland as the evil Chinese villain. Oland seeks revenge on his arch nemesis Fletcher for the death of his wife and son during the Boxer rebellion in China. (See FU MANCHU Series, Index.)

d, Lloyd Corrigan; w, Corrigan, Monte Katterjohn, Sidney Buchman (based on a story by Sax Rohmer); ph, Victor Milner.

Crime   **(PR:A MPAA:NR)**

DAUGHTER OF THE JUNGLE*½   (1949) 69m REP bw

Lois Hall (Ticoora), James Cardwell (Paul Cooper), William Wright (Carl Easton), Sheldon Leonard (Dalton Kraik), Jim Nolan (Lamser), Frank Lackteen (Mahorib), George Carleton (Vincent Walker), Francis McDonald (Montu), Jim Bannon (Kenneth Richards), Charles Soldani (Liongo), Alex Montoya (Tongo), Al Kikume (Native), Leo C. Richmond, George Piltz (Porters).

Jungle adventure which sees a small plane piloted by Cardwell go down in the wilds of Africa. The pilot and the passengers, who include a Chicago hood and his pal being transported back to the U.S. by the cops, survive to hack their way through brush until they discover missing millionaire Carleton and his Tarzan-like daughter, Hall. Hall helps the troop of survivors get back to civilization, battling gorillas and hostile natives every step of the way. The plot is preposterous and the African natives are obviously white men wearing a few bones around their necks and sporting finger-paint stripes on their noses, but 1949 was the year for jungle pictures, and Republic tried to cash in on the craze. Leonard, the Chicago mobster in the film, went on to become one of the top producers in television, with shows like "I Spy," "The Young Girl," "The Dick Van Dyke Show," and "Gomer Pyle," to his credit. As a gangster in films, though, he made quite a mark. Los Angeles Times reporter Don Page once characterized him as "so realistic that legitimate (?) gangsters started emulating him. He became the pin-up boy of the Mafia."

p, Franklin Adreon; d, George Blair; w, William Lively (based on the story by Sol Shor); ph, John MacBurnie; m, Harold Wilson; ed, Harold Minter.

Adventure   **(PR:A MPAA:NR)**

DAUGHTER OF THE SANDS***   (1952, Fr.) 68m Studio
                         Maghreb/Discina International bw (LES NOCES DE SABLE)

Denise Cardi (The Young Girl), Larbi Tounsi (The Prince), Itto Bent Lahsen (The Mad Woman), Himmoud Brahimi (The Buffoon), narrated by Duncan Elliott.

A strange, poetic tragedy written by Jean Cocteau and shot on location in the Atlas Mountains and the Sahara. Story concerns Cardi, the unwanted daughter of a tribal chief, who falls in love with the unattainable son of a sheik. When the elder sheik dies he leaves his son the throne. Saddened by the fact that her romance can never be, Cardi throws herself off a mountain. Lahsen, the girl's guardian, unites the lovers in death by murdering the young sheik. The two are buried together and water appears from their graves as the sheik's jester dances before them. Lyrical and very French in its symbolism, but editing and translations leave something to be desired.

d, Andre Zwobada; w, Jean Cocteau (based on a story by Zwobada); ph, Andre Bac; m, Georges Auric.

Drama   **(PR:C-O MPAA:NR)**

DAUGHTER OF THE SUN GOD**
                      (1962) 75m Condor/Herts-Lion International c

William Holmes (Kent), Lisa Montell (Christine), Harry Knapp (Dr. Howard Knapp), Juanita Llosa (Daughter of the Sun God), Al Bello, Emilio Meiners, Juan Caycho.

Holmes is a writer and explorer vacationing in Peru, and Montell is the niece of an archeologist who has disappeared with a map of a legendary lost Inca city. She persuades Holmes to set up an expedition to find the city, with Knapp, another American archeologist, as their guide. Knapp, who had stolen the map, splits from the group and forms a bandit gang to steal the gold from the lost city. Holmes and Montell make it to the city first and warn the natives, and the Incas take care of

Knapp and the mountain bandits. Lots of snakes, crocodiles, jaguars, and even quicksand help keep the tension going.

p, Edward A. Biery; d&w, Kenneth Herts; ph (Eastmancolor); m, Les Baxter.

Adventure (PR:A MPAA:NR)

DAUGHTER OF THE TONG*

(1939) 56m Metropolitan bw

Evelyn Brent (The Illustrious One), Grant Withers (Ralph Dickson), Dorothy Short (Marion), Dave O'Brien (Jerry), Dirk Thane (Slade), James Coleman (Hardy), Harry Harvey (Mugsy), Budd Buster (Lefty), Richard Loo (Wong), Hal Taliaferro (Lawson), Robert Frazer (Williams).

Technically inept (bad photography seemed the norm at Metropolitan at the time) crime melodrama starring Withers as an FBI agent sent out to bust femme fatale Brent's ring of smugglers. Saddled with long, dull fights and a silly opening narration explaining the activities of the FBI, the film seems more like a commercial for then-FBI Director J. Edgar Hoover than a crime drama. Acting throughout is far superior to the merits of the story, and even the bad photography may not be the cameraman's fault, but the quality of stock used.

p, Lester F. Scott, Jr.; d, Raymond K. Johnson; w, Alan Merritt (based on a story by George H. Plympton); ph, Elmer Dyer; ed, Charles Diltz.

Crime (PR:A MPAA:NR)

DAUGHTER OF THE WEST**½

(1949) 76m Film Classics c

Martha Vickers (Lolita Moreno), Philip Reed (Navo), Donald Woods (Ralph Connors), Marion Carney (Okeema), William Farnum (Father Vallejo), James Griffith (Jed Morgan), Luz Alba (Wateeka), Tony Barr (Yuba), Pedro de Cordova (Indian Chief), Tommy Cook (Ponca), Willow Bird (Medicine' Man), Milton Kibbee, Helen Servis.

Vickers plays a convent-raised half-breed who doesn't know she is part Indian until she meets and falls in love with educated Navajo Reed. The two then defeat nasty Indian agent Woods, who is trying to bilk the tribe out of its rich mineral deposits by getting the Indians liquored up and having them sign away the rights to their land. The plot's not much, but Vickers' journey of self-discovery is handled thoughtfully. Native music and Indian dances lend a piquant touch to the proceedings, and an interesting sequence is Reed's trial by fire.

p, Martin Mooney; d, Harold Daniels; w, Raymond L. Schrock, Irwin Franklyn (based on the novel by Robert E. Callahan); ph, Henry Sharpe (Cinecolor); m, Victor Granadas, Juan Duval; ed, Doug Bagier; art d, George Van Marter; song: "Autumn Harvest."

Western (PR:A MPAA:NR)

DAUGHTERS COURAGEOUS***

(1939) 107m WB bw

John Garfield (Gabriel Lopez), Claude Rains (Jim Masters), Jeffrey Lynn (Johnny Heming), Fay Bainter (Nan Masters), Donald Crisp (Sam Sloane), May Robson (Penny), Frank McHugh (George), Dick Foran (Eddie Moore), George Humbert (Manuel Lopez), Berton Churchill (Judge Hornsby), Priscilla Lane (Buff Masters), Rosemary Lane (Tinka Masters), Lola Lane (Linda Masters), Gale Page (Cora Masters).

DAUGHTERS COURAGEOUS is sort of, but not quite, a sequel to Warner Bros. very successful FOUR DAUGHTERS, which had the same cast but was about a different family because the Garfield character had been killed off in the earlier film. So they found another piece of source material, hired most of the same people behind and in front of the camera, and hoped that lightning would strike twice. It almost did. Later, the studio did two honest sequels without Garfield; FOUR WIVES and FOUR MOTHERS, and the film was eventually done again with Doris Day and Frank Sinatra as YOUNG AT HEART, with the same screenwriters doing the script. In DAUGHTERS COURAGEOUS, Rains is an Enoch Arden who returns home after twenty years of roaming the world with no true reason why he left other than the inability to stay in one place. Now he's back and wife Bainter is about to marry local solid-as-cement Crisp. Rains is charming but his daughters, Page and the Lanes, want nothing to do with him and who can blame them? They try to make his life uncomfortable in the little seaside town of Carmel, California, but Rains perseveres and soon they are in his spell. Garfield is about to marry P. Lane but Rains sees in Garfield a younger version of himself, destined for the nomad's life. Bainter is in a tizzy about what to do. Crisp is respectable and conservative and loves her but Rains is the father of her children and a man with considerable charisma. She must make a decision because the date for the marriage is close; Rains has been declared dead and even though he is alive, she is now free to re-marry. Rains and Garfield recognize each other for what they are; two men who must see what lies over the next hill, and the next, and the next. They join forces and leave Carmel before their presence causes any further rifts in the family. With the success of CAPTAINS COURAGEOUS just two years before, perhaps the studio thought it would help box office to include that word in the title. It was wrong. There was nothing particularly courageous about any female in the film and the most courageous action was on the part of Rains and Garfield as they left town to seek other vistas. All performances were excellent and the script had many funny lines which set it far apart from the melodrama of the previous FOUR DAUGHTERS. Garfield gives his usual standout performance, wise-guying his way to Lane's heart and hard-boiled about his attraction to her. When they meet he looks her up and down and then invites her affection with the terse question: "Wanna buy me a beer?"

p, Hal B. Wallis; d, Michael Curtiz; w, Julius J. and Philip C. Epstein (based on the play "Fly Away Home" by Irving White and Dorothy Bennett); ph, James Wong Howe; m, Max Steiner; ed, Ralph Dawson.

Drama (PR:A MPAA:NR)

DAUGHTERS OF DARKNESS***

(1971, Bel./ Fr./ Ger./ Ital.) 87m Roxy-Mediterranea/Gemini c (LE ROUGE AUX LEVRES)

Delphine Seyrig (Countess Elisabeth Bathory), Daniele Ouimet (Valerie Tardieu), John Karlen (Stefan Chiltern), Andrea Rau (Ilona Harczy), Paul Esser (Porter), Georges Jamin (The Man), Joris Collet (Butler), Fons Rademakers (Mother).

Fascinating erotic vampire film with stylish direction by Harry Kumel. Honeymooning couple Karlen and Ouimet meet up with mysterious lesbian couple (who may or may not be vampires), Seyrig and Rau. Ouimet is strangely drawn to Seyrig, evoking jealousy from their respective mates. Karlen proves to be a brutal, chauvinistic husband (and it appears he may be a homosexual) who beats Ouimet and then has sex with her. Seyrig senses Ouimet's dissatisfaction with her husband (Seyrig herself is having problems with Rau, who no longer wants to be among the undead) and arranges for Rau to seduce him. Rau corners Karlen in the shower, but she panics, slips and falls, impaling herself on his straight razor. That night Seyrig seduces Ouimet and the pair sleep together. Ouimet feels free with her new lover and tells her husband so. He is repulsed and becomes enraged, which leads to a struggle with the women, where he is killed. The pair flee by car into Hungary, but the sun gets into Ouimet's eyes, blinding her, and she wrecks the car, killing Seyrig. The film ends much as it begins, as we see Ouimet meeting a young honeymoon couple at a resort. A strange and disturbing film, tastefully done, with some truly haunting imagery.

p, Paul Coilet, Alain C. Guilleaume; d, Harry Kumel; w, Pierre Drouot, Kumel, J.J. Amiel; ph, Edward Van Der Enden; m, Francois De Roubaix; ed, Gust Verschueren, Denis Bonan; art d, Francoise Hardy; cos, Bernard Perris.

Horror (PR:O MPAA:R)

DAUGHTERS OF DESTINY***

(1954, Fr./Ital.) 105m Cinedis/Franco-London bw (DESTINEES)

Claudette Colbert (Elisabeth), Eleanora Rossi-Drago (Angela), Michele Morgan (Jeanne), Martine Carol (Lysistrata), Raf Vallone (Cassias), Daniel Ivernel (Barata), Paola Stoppa (Senator), Mirko Ellis, Andre Clement, Robert Dalban.

Three episodes dealing with the theme of women and war. In the first, Colbert is an American WW II widow who goes on an almost holy mission to retrieve her husband's body in Italy. There she finds he had lived with an Italian family whose daughter had a child by him. In the second story, Morgan is Joan of Arc, shown at the moment she has been abandoned by her king and her soldiers. The third episode is a humorous version of the Greek play "Lysistrata," with the wives of Athens withholding their favors until their men call off their war. The three episodes are very well done, with the final story the best, all put together by three of the finest commercial film directors of their time.

d, Marcel Pagliero, Jean Delannoy, Christian Jaque; w, Jean Aurenche, Vladimir Pozner, Sergio Amidei, Pierre Bost, Jean Ferry, Henri Jeanson, Carlo Rim, Andre Tabot; ph, Robert Lefevbre, Christian Matras; ed, James Cuenet.

Drama/Comedy (PR:C MPAA:NR)

DAUGHTERS OF SATAN*

(1972) 90m UA c

Tom Selleck (James Robertson), Barra Grant (Chris Robertson), Tani Phelps Guthrie (Kitty Duarte), Paraluman (Juana Rios), Vick Silayan (Dr. Dangal), Vic Diaz (Carlos Ching), Gina Laforteza (Andrea), Ben Rubio (Tommy Tantunico), Paquito Salcedo (Mortician), Chito Reyes (Guerrilla), Bobby Greenwood (Mrs. Postelwaite).

Selleck is an American art collector living in the Philippines with his young wife, Grant. He buys an old painting that depicts three witches being burned at the stake because one of the witches resembles Grant. As it turns out, there seems to be more of a connection between Grant and the witch in the painting than Selleck thought, because she soon begins acting strangely and eventually tries to kill him. At the end we see another old painting by the same artist that depicts the same three women being convicted as witches and the judge in the painting looks just like Selleck. The whole thing plays like an extremely lame episode of "The Twilight Zone" and Selleck doesn't play at all.

p, Aubrey Schenck; d, Hollingsworth Morse; w, John C. Higgins (based on a story by John Bushelman); ph, Nonong Rasca (DeLuxe Color); m, Richard LaSalle; ed, Tony DiMarco; md, LaSalle; art d, Hernando Balon; set d, Mario Carmona.

Horror (PR:C MPAA:R)

DAUGHTERS OF TODAY*

(1933, Brit.) 74m FWK Productions/UA bw

George Barraud (Forbes), Betty Amman (Joan), Marguerite Allan (Mavis), Gerald Rawlinson (Lionel Pendayre), Hay Petrie (Sharpe), Herbert Lomas (Lincoln), Marie Ault (Mrs. Tring).

Sisters Amman and Allan leave their strait-laced father on the farm and come to London. They get jobs working for a financier and their father soon turns up in London looking for the duo. He is nearly cheated out of his money in a phony mine scheme, but the financier comes to the rescue, saving the old man's life savings, then getting the hand of one of the girls in marriage. Boring.

p&d, F. W. Kraemer; w, Michael Barringer; ph, Desmond Dickinson.

Drama (PR:A MPAA:NR)

DAVID***

(1979, Ger.) 125m Kino International c

Walter Taub (Rabbi Singer), Irena Vrkljan (Wife), Eva Mattes (Toni), Mario Fische (David), Dominique Horwitz (Leo), Torsten Henties (David as Child), Rudolph Sellner (Krell).

Germany's answer to the success of American television's mini-series "Holocaust" stars Fische as a teenage Jewish boy whose family is caught in Nazi Germany. His rabbi father, Taub, sees his synagog burned down by the Nazis, who also carve a swastika on the top of his bald head. The family is forced to pay a shoemaker to hide the daughter, Mattes, in his shop. Fische separates from his family, hides out, makes money from odd jobs, and eventually is able to get to Israel with the help of a sympathetic German official. A powerful if overlong film, which is a minor addition to the awesome and often more penetrating film literature on the subject. (In German; English subtitles.)

p, Joachim von Vietinghoff; d, Peter Lilienthal; w, Lilienthal, Jurek Becker, Ulla Zieman (based on the novel by Joel Konig); ph, Al Ruban (Eastmancolor); m, Wojciech Kilar; ed, Sieg un Jager.

Drama **(PR:C MPAA:NR)**

DAVID AND BATHSHEBA*½** (1951) 116m FOX c

Gregory Peck *(David)*, Susan Hayward *(Bathsheba)*, Raymond Massey *(Nathan)*, Kieron Moore *(Uriah)*, James Robertson Justice *(Abishai)*, Jayne Meadows *(Michal)*, John Sutton *(Ira)*, Dennis Hoey *(Joab)*, Walter Talun *(Goliath)*, Paula Morgan *(Adulteress)*, Francis X. Bushman *(King Saul)*, Teddy Infuhr *(Jonathan)*, Leo Pessin *(David as Boy)*, Gwyneth Verdon *(Specialty Dancer)*, Gilbert Barnett *(Absalom)*, John Burton *(Priest)*, Lumsden Hare *(Old Shepherd)*, George Zucco *(Egyptian Ambassador)*, Allan Stone *(Amnon)*, Paul Newlan *(Samuel)*, Holmes Herbert *(Jesse)*, Robert Stephenson, Harry Carter *(Executioners)*, Richard Michelson *(Jesse's 1st Son)*, Dick Winters *(Jesse's 2nd Son)*, John Duncan *(Jesse's 3rd Son)*, James Craven *(Court Announcer)*.

DAVID AND BATHSHEBA, though much too long, is definitely one of the better GBEs (Good Book Epics). It was made in and around the time of QUO VADIS, THE TEN COMMANDMENTS, SAMSON AND DELILAH, THE ROBE, and other, smaller episodes out of the Bible. Gregory Peck is David. He's attacked Rabgah, saved the life of Moore, and is now returning to Jerusalem to recover from a small wound and have a bit of rest. Once home, Massey, his personal prophet, applauds Peck's idea to bring the sacred Ark of The Covenant back from the clutches of the Philistines. Meanwhile, Meadows, his shrewish wife, is giving him a hard time because she doesn't think he compares with her father, Bushman (Saul). Meadows and Peck can't agree on anything and are in dire need of a change or, at least, some serious marital counseling. Standing on his balcony, Peck sees Hayward taking a bath in the next house and learns that she is Bathsheba, wife of Moore. Peck arranges to meet Hayward; they soon fall crown over sandals in love with each other, and an adulterous affair commences. Meanwhile, the Ark of The Covenant has been captured and now arrives at the gates of the city. Peck goes to meet it and sees a soldier fall dead when he attempts to touch the Ark to keep it from falling off the animal. Peck decrees that it must be a sign from on high and that a tabernacle be built at this very spot to house this most holy of all holy items. Now the rains cease and the land becomes dry. Starvation is imminent and Peck believes he is being punished by God for his transgressions. Hayward now tells Peck that she is pregnant with his child and they both know that if it's found out she will be stoned to death as an adulteress, according to the customs of the time. Peck has a way out of it and sends Moore off to war, in the hope that the man will be killed. And that's what happens. The moment they learn of Moore's death, Peck marries Hayward with all the royal accompaniment of the era. She has the baby just a little too soon after the wedding and tongues wag. The baby dies and the couple are now convinced that the Lord is wreaking havoc on them. So is Massey. He leads a group of dissidents to the palace where they demand Hayward pay for her sin. The people are starving and the only reason they can fathom is that God is frowning on all of them. Peck says that it is *he* who is guilty and should be chastised, not Hayward. He prays at the Ark and the vision of Bushman appears. Now he sees his famous bout with Goliath and how that victory saved the Jews. Lots of special effects as the Ark is bathed in various colors and David now improvises the 23rd Psalm. When he finishes the words, a pitter-patter of rain is heard on the roof. Soon enough, the rain begins to fall heartily. The drought is over. Peck returns to Hayward and they pledge the remainder of their lives to the Lord's work. A fine script by Dunne and ecclesiastical advising by Dr. C.C. McCown are what distinguish this film from the usual Biblical epics. Peck was excellent as David but, in later years, he never seemed to get off that stentorian pattern of speech and it didn't wear well in roles without togas. Massey is properly wildeyed as Nathan, the Prophet, and most of the smaller roles are well cast. In a tiny part as a specialty dancer is the 25-year-old Gwyneth Verdon, who later changed her name to Gwen and starred on Broadway in so many shows. The wardrobe is spectacular and all technical credits are superior. The color consultant on this Fox film, as well as many, many others, was Leonard Doss, who moonlighted as an interior decorator in and around Beverly Hills. DAVID AND BATHSHEBA was Oscar-nominated for music, art and sets, photography, script, costumes.

p, Darryl F. Zanuck; d, Henry King; w, Philip Dunne (based on the second book of Samuel); ph, Leon Shamroy (Technicolor); m, Alfred Newman; ed, Barbara McLean; art d, Lyle Wheeler, George Davis; set d, Thomas Little, Paul S. Fox; cos, Edward Stevenson, spec eff, Fred Sersen; ch, Jack Cole; makeup, Ben Nye.

Biblical/Religious **(PR:C MPAA:NR)**

DAVID AND GOLIATH*½

(1961, Ital.) 95m Ansa Cinematografica/AA c (DAVID E GOLIA)

Orson Welles *(King Saul)*, Ivo Payer *(David)*, Edward Hilton *(Prophet Samuel)*, Massimo Serato *(Abner)*, Eleonora Rossi Drago *(Merab)*, Giulia Rubini *(Michal)*, Pierre Cressoy *(Jonathan)*, Furio Meniconi *(Asrod)*, Kronos *(Goliath)*, Dante Maggio *(Cret)*, Luigi Tosi *(Benjamin Di Gaba)*, Umberto Fiz *(Lazar)*, Ugo Sasso *(Huro)*, Carlo D'Angelo, Gabriele Tinti, Ileana Danelli, Carla Foscari, Fabrizio Capucci, Roberto Miali, Renato Terra, Emma Baron.

Terrible Italian Bible epic featuring Welles as King Saul. Many liberties are taken with the Old Testament as the plot plods inevitably to its climax, where David (Payer) slays Goliath (some badly made up wrestler-type who goes by the name of Kronos). The highlight of this post-dubbed story is a laughably "erotic" dance number which sees dozens of undulating beauties surround the giant Kronos and taunt him with their bodies. Another in an unfortunately long series of bad guest appearances in inferior movies by Welles.

p, Emimmo Salvi; d, Richard Pottier, Ferdinando Baldi; w, Umberto Scarpeli, Gino Mangini, Ambrogio Molteni, Salvi; ph, Carlo Fiore, Adalberto Albertini (Totalscope, Eastmancolor); m, Carlo Innocenzi; ed, Franco Fraticelli; art d, Oscar D'Amico; cos, Ditta Peruzzi; ch, Carla Renalli.

Biblical/Religious **Cas.** **(PR:A MPAA:NR)**

DAVID AND LISA**** (1962) 95m CONTINENTAL bw

Keir Dullea *(David)*, Janet Margolin *(Lisa)*, Howard Da Silva *(Dr. Swinford)*, Neva Patterson *(Mrs. Clemens)*, Clifton James *(John)*, Richard McMurray *(Mr. Clemens)*, Nancy Nutter *(Maureen)*, Matthew Anden *(Simon)*, Coni Hudak *(Kate)*, Jaime Sanchez *(Carlos)*, Janet Lee Parker *(Sandra)*, Karen Gorney *(Josette)*.

A "little" film that made it big was DAVID AND LISA. Prior to this, there had been many films like THE SNAKE PIT and THE THREE FACES OF EVE, but the understated charm of DAVID AND LISA is what set the movie apart from so many other attempts at depicting the problems of the mentally ill. Dullea is a bright young man who cannot bear to be touched by anyone. His overly protective mother and father, Patterson and McMurray, leave him at the private school with Da Silva, the intelligent doctor who runs the institution which caters to children with mental problems. Margolin is a very troubled schizophrenic who talks in rhyme and is deeply ensconced in her shell. The two meet and the gradual falling-in-love-story is what forms the basis for the film. As they begin to trust each other, Dullea is able to be touched and Margolin begins to reveal her emotions without burrowing into silence. The story was based on a real case history by Dr. T.I. Rubin, and Eleanor Perry handled the screenplay with taste, tact, and tenderness without falling into mawkishness. This is a thoughtful, poignant film with just enough comic moments; the absence of psychiatric argot in favor of English as spoken by human beings. It's almost a documentary in feeling and technique and therein lies much of the believability. Frank Perry directs with a sure hand and won the Best New Director award at the Venice Film Festival in 1962. Both Perrys were also nominated by the Academy for their work and Margolin and Dullea were honored as best actress and actor at the San Francisco Film Festival.

p, Paul M. Heller; d, Frank Perry; w, Eleanor Perry (based on the book by Dr. Theodore Isaac Rubin); ph, Leonard Hirschfield; m, Mark Lawrence; ed, Irving Oshman; art d, Heller; set d, Gene Callahan; cos, Anna Hill Johnstone.

Drama **(PR:A-C MPAA:NR)**

DAVID COPPERFIELD***** (1935) 133m MGM bw

W.C. Fields *(Micawber)*, Lionel Barrymore *(Dan Peggotty)*, Maureen O'Sullivan *(Dora)*, Madge Evans *(Agnes)*, Edna May Oliver *(Aunt Betsey)*, Lewis Stone *(Mr. Wickfield)*, Frank Lawton *(David as Man)*, Freddie Bartholomew *(David as Child)*, Elizabeth Allan *(Mrs. Copperfield)*, Roland Young *(Uriah Heep)*, Basil Rathbone *(Mr. Murdstone)*, Elsa Lanchester *(Clickett)*, Jean Cadell *(Mrs. Micawber)*, Jessie Ralph *(Nurse Peggotty)*, Lennox Pawle *(Mr. Dick)*, Violet Kemble-Cooper *(Jane Murdstone)*, Una O'Connor *(Mrs. Gummidge)*, John Buckler *(Ham)*, Hugh Williams *(Steerforth)*, Ivan Simpson *(Limmiter)*, Herbert Mundin *(Barkis)*, Fay Chaldecott *(Little Emily as Child)*, Marilyn Knowlden *(Agnes as Child)*, Florine McKinney *(Little Emily as Woman)*, Harry Beresford *(Dr. Chillip)*, Mabel Colcord *(Mary Ann)*, Hugh Walpole *(Vicar)*, Renee Gad *(Janet)*, Arthur Treacher *(Dishonest Coachman)*, Margaret Seddon *(Bit)*.

Charles Dickens never dreamed that his work would have been made into so many movies. His novels were first serialized in the newspapers and he was paid by the word. Consequently, as interesting as they are to read, Dickens often overwrote to a degree that could cause numbed eyes. To condense DAVID COPPERFIELD to a manageable 133 minutes and not lose one whit of the charm or Dickens's sheer story-telling ability was a marvel of the screenwriter's art. When one thinks that OLIVER TWIST, A TALE OF TWO CITIES, THE PICKWICK PAPERS, GREAT EXPECTATIONS, and so many more all came from one fertile brain, it makes us understand why he was a legend in his own time. Selznick and Cukor cast this version with an eye toward the offbeat. To use Fields as Micawber was a shock to those audiences who only thought of W.C. in one fashion. And mild-mannered Roland Young as Heep was another case of unique and original thought. Bartholomew was discovered when Selznick and Cukor were location-hunting in England. As it turned out, they shot the entire film on the lot and the only benefit of their trip was the discovery of young Freddie who went on to delight millions in CAPTAINS COURAGEOUS and nineteen other films. If you're one of the very few people who've not had the pleasure of reading the book or of seeing the film (not to be confused with the magician), the plot is as follows: Allan gives birth to young David six months after her husband has died. She is a young widow and mother and, to help pull herself up out of the mire, she marries Rathbone, who is as mean a stepfather as any young lad ever encountered. Bartholomew (David) is terribly mistreated by Rathbone and eventually sent to boarding school so he is out of Rathbone's hair. Soon enough, Allan dies and Rathbone pulls the plucky youth out of school and puts him to work in the dank export warehouse he owns. Bartholomew meets Fields (Micawber), a compleat pauper but with a regal bearing that belies his low financial station. The unlikely duo lodge together until Fields is hauled off to debtors' prison. Bartholomew races to Dover to live with Edna May Oliver. He is found by Rathbone and his sister, Violet Kemble-Cooper, who attempt to get him back. Their efforts are foiled by Oliver and Pawle. Eventually, Bartholomew grows up to become Frank Lawton and returns to school. He meets Evans (whom he knew when they were smaller) and learns that her father, Stone, is being manipulated in business by Young (Uriah Heep) and Williams, two of the most heinous types Dickens ever invented. Lawton uses his intelligence to overcome Young and Williams and then leaves Evans to marry Maureen O'Sullivan. She is definitely not the right woman, one who becomes ill, and eventually dies. Lawton meets Evans again and they unite once more. Barrymore was excellent as Dan Peggoty and Elsa Lanchester charming as Clickett. Matter of fact, the film is acknowledged as being one of the best casting jobs ever! Co-author Hugh Walpole did a small bit as the Vicar and Una O'Connor chimed in well as

Mrs. Gummidge. But it was Fields all the way when it comes to the plum role. His Micawber will never be forgotten. Some say it was old Bill playing old Bill but any student of Fields will see how far he had to stretch to get the nuances Dickens intended. This was a huge smash at the box office, yet only received one nomination as Best Picture despite all the critical and financial acclaim. But that was the year of THE INFORMER, LES MISERABLES, CAPTAIN BLOOD, A MIDSUMMER NIGHT'S DREAM, RUGGLES OF RED GAP, THE LIVES OF A BENGAL LANCER, and the movie that took the big prize, MUTINY ON THE BOUNTY. These days the Academy seems to have trouble finding five movies good enough to nominate. Producer Selznick was lavish with budget right from the beginning, much to studio mogul Mayer's twitching rage. Selznick called London early on, waking up British writer Hugh Walpole in the middle of the night and asking him to spend "a few weeks" working on the DAVID COPPERFIELD script. Walpole wound up spending most of his life in Hollywood thereafter. Initially, Charles Laughton was contracted to play Micawber. He worked for a week, agonizing over his role. He spent countless hours working on elaborate makeup drawn from old Cruickshank sketches and put equal research time in pinpointing his own costumes which he paid for, yet he felt inadequate in the part. He begged director Cukor for more time to perfect his lines and the delays caused arguments between them. Laughton kept fluffing lines and became so involved with interpreting his part that he was near collapse. At the end of the week the great actor broke down and begged to be released from the role. He knew that Fields had been considered for the Micawber role and strongly suggested he take it over. Fields proved a strain on Cukor's nerves too, once he assumed the job, insisting room be found for his juggling and pool playing bits. Fields had relied on ad-libbing and bolstered a weak memory by having cue-cards with large print held behind the cameras. He labored even harder than had Laughton and the result was a magnificent portrayal, rendered in only two weeks of work. "He was born to play the part," Cukor was later quoted, ". . . he realized he was working with something that was a classic and he behaved that way." Cukor himself slaved to get top work from all the cast members. In Dora's deathbed scene, O'Sullivan, normally a fine actress who could produce whatever the script called for, could not provide a single tear and she had to cry buckets for the tragic sequence. Cukor made her cry all right, finally sitting at the end of the bed, just beyond camera range, twisting her feet until the pain produced a flood of tears. Rathbone, on the other hand, took little time in perfectly adjusting to the hateful Murdstone character, a role that bothered him, albeit this fine British actor was to become one of the arch screen villains of all time. He particularly found one scene repugnant, one where he had to beat helpless Bartholomew within an inch of his life. "It was a most unpleasant experience," he later commented in his memoirs, *In and Out of Character*. "I had a vicious cane with much whip to it, but fortunately for Freddie Bartholomew and myself, under his britches and completely covering his little rump, he was protected by a sheet of foam rubber. Nevertheless, Freddie howled with pain (mostly anticipatory I presume) and in his 'closeups' his face was distorted and he cried real tears most pitifully . . . . When it was over I rushed over to Freddie and took him in my arms and kissed him. We had become great friends, and he was often over to our house for a swim in the pool and dinner. This made the playing of Mr. Murdstone all the harder for me." Selznick's internecine wars with Mayer over this film were long and loud. Mayer harassed Selznick to cut the time down after its premiere and Barrymore's role was cut but a storm of protest crackled from a bevy of schoolteachers objecting to Peggotty's disappearance and these scenes were restored when the original 133-minute version was released. The great success of this film, critically and at the box office, angered Louis B. Mayer who had tried to prevent its production from the first day in 1934 when his son-in-law, Selznick, proposed to film the classic. Mayer insisted that classics could not be brought off well on the screen, that attempting to convert immortal literary works to film always ended in box office disaster, that the public wouldn't pay to see DAVID COPPERFIELD. Selznick was adamant, doggedly hounding Mayer for approval almost every day for a year until Mayer reluctantly agreed. The project was all-consuming with Selznick and for a personal reason. His immigrant father used the novel to teach himself English and read to his children from it for years, teaching them the language of their adopted country with the precise and marvelous prose of Charles Dickens. Mayer wanted Jackie Cooper for the boy lead. Selznick didn't. Selznick's search for young David was almost as frantic as his hunt for Scarlett O'Hara four years later, but director Cukor solved that by bringing Bartholomew from England to Hollywood, ushering the sweet-faced boy into Selznick's office. Cukor had Bartholomew costumed in the role he wanted him to play, right up to a tall beaver hat. "Mr. Selznick," Bartholomew announced, tipping his lid, "I am David Copperfield, sir," The producer took one look at him and replied: "Right you are." Dickens died in 1870 at the age of 58 leaving his final work THE MYSTERY OF EDWIN DROOD unfinished, which didn't stop Universal from making it into a movie this same year of 1935. He would have been thrilled at DAVID COPPERFIELD and bored with the latter.

p, David O. Selznick; d, George Cukor; w, Howard Estabrook, Hugh Walpole (based on the novel by Charles Dickens); ph, Oliver T. Marsh; m, Herbert Stothart; ed, Robert J. Kern; art d, Cedric Gibbons; spec eff, Slavko Vorkapich; cos, Dolly Tree.

Drama **(PR:A MPAA:NR)**

DAVID COPPERFIELD** (1970, Brit.) 118m Omnibus/FOX c

Richard Attenborough *(Mr. Tungay)*, Cyril Cusack *(Barkis)*, Edith Evans *(Betsey Trotwood)*, Pamela Franklin *(Dora Spenlow)*, Susan Hampshire *(Agnes Wickfield)*, Wendy Hiller *(Mrs. Micawber)*, Ron Moody *(Uriah Heep)*, Laurence Olivier *(Mr. Creakle)*, Robin Phillips *(David Copperfield)*, Michael Redgrave *(Mr. Peggotty)*, Ralph Richardson *(Mr. Micawber)*, Emlyn Williams *(Mr. Dick)*, Isobel Black *(Clara Copperfield)*, Sinead Cusack *(Emily)*, James Donald *(Mr. Murdstone)*, James Hayter *(Porter)*, Megs Jenkins *(Clara Peggotty)*, Anna Massey *(Jane Murdstone)*, Nicholas Pennell *(Traddles)*, Corin Redgrave *(Steerforth)*, Liam Redmond *(Quinion)*, Alastair Mackenzie *(Little David)*, Andrew McCulloch *(Ham)*, Donald Layne-Smith *(Mr. Wickfield)*, Helen Cotterill *(Mary Ann)*, Kim Craik *(Child Emily)*, Christopher Moran *(Boy Steerforth)*, Jeffrey Chandler *(Boy Traddles)*, Brian Tipping *(Boy)*, Alison Blair *(Girl)*, Gordon Rollings *(Milkman)*, George Woodbridge *(Vicar)*, William Lyon-Brown *(Doctor)*, Christine Ozanne *(Midwife)*, Phoebe Shaw *(Prostitute)*, Robert Lankesheer *(Mr. Sharp)*, Anne Stallybrass *(Martha)*.

You'd have to see this version of DAVID COPPERFIELD next to Cukor's 1935 classic to realize how two separate teams could take the same material and go so far afield. Phillips is the twenty-eight-year-old Copperfield telling the story in flashback. He recalls his schoolmasters (funnily played by Olivier and Attenborough) and the rest of his life but it is so jerkily put together that the flashbacks jar the eyes and brain. Characters appear in this version that were omitted from the 1935 version (Traddles and Quinion) but the addition means less time for Micawber and Peggoty and many of the others. Screenwriter Pulman, who wrote so well for BBC's "I, Claudius" was led astray in his adaptation of Dickens' novel. Too much was attempted and not enough was accomplished. The plot is detailed in the other review (1935) and doesn't vary much here. It is in the "touches" that this version falls apart. Moody is much too obvious as Heep and so is James Donald as Murdstone. This picture was essentially made for television and released in the theaters in other countries than the U.S. It is presumed that producer Brogger and the network that financed it felt that the story had to be simplified and laid out so the "unwashed" watching TV would understand. When will they learn?

p, Frederick H. Brogger; d, Delbert Mann; w, Jack Pulman (based on the novel by Charles Dickens); ph, Ken Hodges (Technicolor); m, Malcolm Arnold; ed, Peter Boita; art d, Alex Vetchinsky; cos, Anthony Mendleson.

Drama **Cas.** **(PR:A MPAA:NR)**

DAVID GOLDER** (1932, Fr.) 83m Vandal & Delac/Protex bw

David Golder *(Harry Baur)*, Gretillat Franceschi *(Marcus)*, Paule Andral *(Gloria)*, Jackie Monnier *(Joyce)*, Jean Coquelin *(Fischl)*, Jean Bradin *(Alec)*, Gaston Jacquet *(Hoyor)*, Camille Bert *(Tubingen)*.

Baur is a Jew who emigrates from Poland and comes to New York. After years of hard work, he is rich, but his wife is systematically spending all his money. When he confronts her, she tells him that she has been cheating on him for years and that their daughter (Monnier) is not his. He retaliates by retiring and letting his empire collapse. When the money is all gone, Monnier comes to Baur and tells him that her mother is forcing her into a marriage with a wealthy young man, though she loves another. Baur goes back to work, closing a big oil deal with the Russians, giving the money to his daughter after making sure that his wife will get no part of it. Then he dies. Occasionally interesting drama dragged under by muddy sound, bad photography, and thin acting. (In French; English subtitles.)

d&w, Julien Duvivier (based on a novel by Irene Nemirovsky); ph, George Perinal, Armand Thirard.

Drama **(PR:A MPAA:NR)**

DAVID HARDING, COUNTERSPY** (1950) 70m COL bw

Willard Parker *(Jerry Baldwin)*, Audrey Long *(Betty Iverson)*, Howard St. John *(David Harding)*, Raymond Greenleaf *(Dr. George Vickers)*, Harlan Warde *(Hopkins)*, Alex Gerry *(Charles Kingston)*, Fred Sears *(Peters)*, John Dehner *(Frank Reynolds)*, Anthony Jochim *(Robert Barrington)*, Jock O'Mahoney *(Brown)*, John Pickard *(McCullough)*, Steve Darrell *(Edwards)*, Jimmy Lloyd *(Burton)*, Charles Quigley *(Grady)*, Allen Mathews *(Baker)*.

First in a series of spy dramas inspired by Phillips H. Lord's then popular radio series. While the title character played by St. John does appear, the majority of the action belongs to naval officer Parker who is assigned to investigate the murder of the head of a torpedo plant. Parker suspects the dead man's wife, Long, to be involved with spies and so he romances her to get some clues. Unfortunately, he falls in love with her and begins to doubt her complicity in the espionage. The rest of the ring is caught eventually, but not before they (the spies) kill Long because of her love for Parker. A fast-paced programmer.

p, Milton Feldman; d, Ray Nazarro; w, Clint Johnson, Tom Reed (based on a radio program created by Phillips H. Lord); ph, George E. Diskant; ed, Henry Batista; art d, Harold MacArthur.

Spy Drama **(PR:A MPAA:NR)**

DAVID HARUM½** (1934) 82m FOX bw

Will Rogers *(David Harum)*, Louise Dresser *(Polly)*, Evelyn Venable *(Ann)*, Kent Taylor *(John)*, Stepin Fetchit *(Sylvester)*, Noah Beery *(Gen. Woolsey)*, Roger Imhof *(Edwards)*, Frank Melton *(Elwin)*, Charles Middleton *(Deacon)*, Sarah Padden *(Widow)*, Lillian Stuart *(Sairy)*.

Rogers once again spreads his earthy brand of comedy and philosophy as the title character who is a small town banker in the 1890s. He is a confirmed bachelor and horse trader whose main rival is the stingy and hard-boiled town deacon, with whom Rogers makes a number of trades in horse flesh. Sub-plot concerns city-boy bank teller Taylor who is in love with Venable, the daughter of a wealthy man. Taylor feels he cannot propose marriage due to his low income, so he places a $4,500 bet on a 10-to-1 shot in a trotting race that pays off, making him a partner in Rogers' bank and wealthy enough to marry his sweetheart. Usual Rogers hokum, this time easier to take than usual, and a good look at ye olden times in pre-many-wars America.

d, James Cruze; w, Walter Woods (based on a novel by Edward Royes Westcott); ph, Hal Mohr; md, Louis DeFrancesco; ed, Jack Murray.

Comedy **(PR:A MPAA:NR)**

DAVID HOLZMAN'S DIARY***　　　(1968) 74m Paradigm Films bw

L. M. Kit Carson (David Holzman), Eileen Dietz (Penny Wohl), Louise Levine (Sandra), Lorenzo Mans (Pepe), Fern McBride (Girl on the Subway), Mike Levine (Sandra's Boyfriend), Bob Lesser (Max, Penny's Agent), Jack Baran (Cop).

Excellent satire on Cinema Verite shot in just five days on a $2500 budget. Carson is a young filmmaker in New York who determines to get a handle on his life by putting it all down on film. Things don't go as he plans; his girl friend (Dietz) leaves him in annoyance with his constantly filming her, his artist friend Mans tells him that his concept is invalid, and the police punch him for harassing people with his camera. Gradually he grows more desperate as it becomes obvious that his life is only getting more confusing on film. One day he announces to the camera that he has to go to his uncle's funeral in New Jersey. In the next scene we see photographs of Carson of the type taken by coin-operated booths. His voice on a scratchy record tells that he is recording the record in another coin-operated booth and that when he returned from New Jersey that day, he found his apartment broken into and all his equipment stolen. He tries to come to some conclusion about his life and this project, but is unable to. Audiences who don't know that this is a fictional piece are almost invariably fooled by this film, today regarded as one of the best independent films of the 1960s.

p,d,w&ed, Jim McBride; ph, Michael Wadleigh, Paul Glickman, Paul Goldsmith.

Drama　　　　　　　　　　　　　(PR:C-O MPAA:NR)

DAVID LIVINGSTONE*　　　(1936, Brit.) 71m Fitzpatrick Pictures/MGM bw

Percy Marmont (David Livingstone), Marian Spencer (Mary Moffatt), James Carew (Gordon Bennett), Pamela Stanley (Queen Victoria), Hugh McDermott (Henry Morton Stanley).

Bleak biopic has Marmont as the famed missionary and explorer. He leaves his little English village for the dark continent, gets mauled by a lion, has his mission burned down by slavers, and eventually is discovered by American reporter McDermott. Episodic structure only succeeds in making this one more confusing.

p&d, James A. Fitzpatrick; w, W.K. Williamson.

Biography　　　　　　　　　　　(PR:A MPAA:NR)

DAVY**　　　(1958, Brit.) 82m Ealing/MGM c

Harry Secombe (Davy), Ron Randell (George), George Relph (Uncle Pat), Susan Shaw (Gwen), Bill Owen (Eric), Peter Frampton (Tim), Alexander Knox (Sir Giles), Adele Leigh (Joanna), Isabel Dean (Miss Carstairs), Kenneth Connor (Herbie), Clarkson Rose (Mrs. Magillicuddy), George Moon (Jerry), Campbell Singer (Stage Doorkeeper), Joan Sims, Gladys Henson (Waitresses), Bernard Cribbins, Rachel Roberts, Principals and Chorus of The Royal Opera House.

Secombe, a top British comedian of the time, stars in his movie debut as a member of a family of vaudeville performers known as "The Mad Morgans" who tour the small-time circuit waiting for their big break. When Secombe gets a chance to audition his singing voice at the opera, and is subsequently offered a lucrative contract, he is torn between abandoning his family (thus destroying their act and a chance for stardom) and making it on his own. Eventually, he opts to stick it out with the act, keeping the family together. Pleasant if unimpressive drama.

p, Michael Balcon, Basil Dearden; d, Michael Relph; w, William Rose; ph, Douglas Slocombe (Technirama, Technicolor); ed, Peter Tanner.

Comedy/Drama　　　　　　　　　(PR:A MPAA:NR)

DAVY CROCKETT AND THE RIVER PIRATES**½
(1956) 81m Disney/BV c

Fess Parker (Davy Crockett), Buddy Ebsen (George Russel), Jeff York (Mike Fink), Kenneth Tobey (Jocko), Clem Bevans (Cap'n Cobb), Irvin Ashkenazy (Moose), Mort Mills (Sam Mason), Paul Newlan (Big Harpe), Frank Richards (Little Harpe), Walter Catlett (Col. Plug), Douglas Dumbrille (Saloon Owner), George Lewis (Black Eagle), Troy Melton, Dick Crockett, Hank Worden.

The second time Disney cut together a couple of the popular "Davy Crockett" television adventures and released them in the theaters after they had already appeared on free TV. The result is a two-part kiddie show starring Parker and his sidekick, Ebsen, as they put the villainous river-rat York in his place by beating him in a river race to New Orleans. The second segment has the intrepid backwoods duo, with the help of their new ally York, battling a gang of pirates that has been pulling raids disguised as Indians. Songs: "Ballad of Davy Crockett," "King of the River," "Yaller, Yaller Gold" (George Bruns, Tom Blackburn).

p, Bill Walsh; d, Norman Foster; w, Tom Blackburn, Foster; ph, Bert Glennon (Technicolor); m, George Bruns; ed, Stanley Johnson; art d, Feild Grey; set d, Emile Kuri, Bertram Granger; cos, Carl Walker.

Adventure　　Cas.　　　　　(PR:AAA MPAA:NR)

DAVY CROCKETT, INDIAN SCOUT***　　　(1950) 71m UA bw

George Montgomery (Davy Crockett), Ellen Drew (Frances), Philip Reed (Red Hawk), Noah Beery, Jr. (Tex), Paul Guilfoyle (Ben), Addison Richards (Capt. Weightman), Robert Barrat (Lone Eagle), Erik Rolf (Mr. Simms), William Wilkerson (High Tree), John Hamilton (Col. Pollard), Vera Marshe (Mrs. Simms), Jimmy Moss (Jimmy Simms), Chief Thundercloud (Sleeping Fox), Kenneth Duncan (Sgt. Gordon), Ray Teal (Capt. McHale).

Montgomery is a U.S. military scout named after his famous uncle (making this a somewhat bogus Davy Crockett adventure). He is assigned to stop Indian attacks on a defenseless group of wagon trains making their way west. Soon he realizes that someone in his outfit has been tipping the redskins off, because they seem to know what his next move will be before he does it. Suspicion falls on his loyal redskin sidekick Reed, but he is vindicated when it is revealed that half-breed Drew is the traitor. Drew repents and assists Montgomery in saving a group of

soldiers who are pinned down by hostile savages. Montgomery then allows Drew and Reed to ride off together to freedom.

p, Edward Small; d, Lew Landers; w, Richard Schayer (based on the story by Ford Beebe); ph, George Diskant, John Mescall; m, Paul Sawtell; ed, Stuart Frye, Kenneth Crane; art d, Rudolph Sternad, Martin Obzina.

Western　　　　　　　　　　　(PR:AAA MPAA:NR)

DAVY CROCKETT, KING OF THE WILD FRONTIER***
(1955) 90m Disney/BV c

Fess Parker (Davy Crockett), Buddy Ebsen (George Russel), Basil Ruysdael (Andrew Jackson), Hans Conried (Thimblerig), William Bakewell (Tobias Norton), Kenneth Tobey (Col. Jim Bowie), Pat Hogan (Chief Red Stick), Helene Stanley (Polly Crockett), Nick Cravat (Bustedluck), Don Megowan (Col. Billy Travis), Mike Mazurki (Bigfoot Mason), Jeff Thompson (Charlie Two Shirts), Henry Joyner (Swaney), Benjamin Hornbuckle (Henderson), Hal Youngblood (Opponent Political Speaker), Jim Maddux (1st Congressman), Robert Booth (2nd Congressman), Eugene Brindel (Billy), Ray Whitetree (Johnny), Campbell Brown (Bruno).

Disney spliced together three episodes of the successful "Davy Crockett" television series and came up with an unbelievably lucrative box office hit that also ushered in the coonskin cap craze of the 1950s. Basic plot shows the rise of Crockett (pleasantly played by Parker) from an Indian fighter, through his days in Congress, and concluding with his heroic death at the Alamo. At least the audiences weren't gypped by the visuals, because the film was presented in widescreen technicolor which was all but lost when originally shown on television. The theme song, "The Ballad of Davy Crockett" became a minor popular hit. Evidence that the Disney people did not expect Davy Crockett to become a national hero all over again abounds in the film. For example, Davy is seen bayoneting redskins and also venting his ego by announcing at one point, "We'll give 'em the old Crockett charge." Writers Tom Blackburn and Norman Foster were more careful after Davy became the idol of millions to make him a fault-free character.

p, Bill Walsh; d, Norman Foster; w, Tom Blackburn (based on the Disneyland TV shows); ph, Charles Boyle (Technicolor), m, George Bruns; ed, Chester Schaeffer; m/l, "The Ballad of Davy Crockett," Blackburn, Bruns, "Farewell, Davy Crockett," Bruns.

Western　　Cas.　　　　　(PR:AAA MPAA:NR)

DAWN, THE　　　(SEE: DAWN OVER IRELAND, 1936, Brit.)

DAWN*½　　　(1979, Aus.) 111m Aquataurus/Hoyts c

Bronwyn Mackay-Payne (Dawn), Tom Richards (Harry), John Diedrich (Gary), Bunney Brooke (Mum), Ron Haddrick (Pop), Gabrielle Hartley (Kate), Ivar Kantz (Len), David Cameron (Joe), Kevin Wilson (Bippy), Lyndall Barbour (Edie), John Clayton (Syd), Margaret Gerard (Louise), Don Barkham (Doctor), Joan Evatt (Vivian), Go Mikami (Japanese Police Inspector), Carmelina Caterina (Dawn, Age 6).

Flat movie biography of controversial Australian Olympic gold medal swimmer Dawn Fraser. The action takes place during the span between the Melbourne games of '56, the Rome games of '60, and the Tokyo games of '64, where the young swimmer created headlines with her unruly and adolescent behavior. The mischief climaxed at the Tokyo games when she stole a flag and was banned from the games for 10 years. The technical and acting credits are competent enough, but the life of Fraser just doesn't have the right combination of elements to hold together a feature-length film.

p, Joy Cavill; d, Ken Hannam; w, Cavill; ph, Russell Boyd; ed, Max Lemon; art d, Ross Major.

Drama　　　　　　　　　　　(PR:C MPAA:NR)

DAWN AT SOCORRO***　　　(1954) 80m UNIV c

Rory Calhoun (Brett Wade), Piper Laurie (Rannah Hayes), David Brian (Dick Braden), Kathleen Hughes (Clare), Alex Nicol (Jimmy Rapp), Edgar Buchanan (Sheriff Cauthen) Mara Corday (Lotty Diamond), Roy Roberts (Doc Jameson), Skip Homeier (Buddy Ferris), James Millican (Harry McNair), Lee Van Cleef (Earl Ferris), Stanley Andrews (Old Man Ferris), Richard Garland (Tom Ferris), Scott Lee (Vince McNair), Paul Brinegar (Desk Clerk), Philo McCollough (Rancher), Forrest Taylor (Jebb Hayes).

Calhoun plays a gunfighter who got his reputation (shown in flashback) by gunning down the evil Ferris family (Homeier, Van Cleef, Andrews, and Garland) of New Mexico singlehandedly. After the gunfight, Calhoun hangs up his guns and meets young beauty Laurie, who has been kicked out of her home by her stern and repressive father. Eventually, she drifts into becoming a dance hall girl in a saloon run by the sleazy crook Brian. Calhoun decides she deserves better, so he tries to win the girl and the saloon in a card game, but loses. Thinking Calhoun a danger to his authority, Brian and his hired gun Nicol attempt to murder the outlaw in the streets of Socorro, but he kills them instead. Decent, fast-paced western with a strong supporting cast.

p, William Alland; d, George Sherman; w, George Zuckerman; ph, Carl Guthrie (Technicolor); ed, Edward Curtiss; md, Joseph Gershenson.

Western　　　　　　　　　　　(PR:A MPAA:NR)

DAWN EXPRESS, THE*½
(1942) 63m PRC bw (AKA: NAZI SPY RING)

Michael Whalen (Robert Norton), Anne Nagel (Nancy Fielding), William Bakewell (Tom Fielding), Constance Worth (Linda Pavlo), Hans von Twardowski (Captain Gemmler), Jack Mulhall (James Curtis), George Pembroke (Karl Schmidt), Kenneth

Harlan (Detective Brown), Robert Fraser (John Oliver), Hans von Morhart (Heinrich), Michael Vallin (Argus), William Costello (Otto).

All the decent writers and directors must have been helping with the war effort when this one was made. A handful of Nazi spies hit the United States in an effort to get a secret formula from a pair of young scientists. The formula is for doubling the power of gasoline. Instead of telling some U.S. people, one of the young idiots gives up his life to blow up the whole ring of Nazis. Makes sense, doesn't it?

p, George M. Merrick, Max Alexander; d, Albert Herman; w, Arthur St. Claire; ph, Eddie Linden; m, Lee Zahler; set d, James Altwell.

Spy Drama   **(PR:A   MPAA:NR)**

DAWN OF THE DEAD***   (1979) 125m United Film c

David Emge (Stephen), Ken Foree (Peter), Scott Reiniger (Roger), Gaylen Ross (Francine), David Crawford (Dr. Foster), David Early (Mr. Berman), George A. Romero (TV Director), The Zombies.

Low-budget horror genius George Romero's brilliant sequel to his midnight-show shocker, NIGHT OF THE LIVING DEAD (1968), DAWN OF THE DEAD begins where the first film left off, with the country in the throes of a ghastly epidemic which sees the recently dead returning to life and eating the flesh of the living. The film opens at a panicked local television station trying to stay on the air despite the masses of flesh-eating dead that have invaded the community. Dozens of the station's employees have fled, leaving only a skeleton crew to broadcast emergency information. Ross, a female employee of the station, is outraged that they are continuing to broadcast out-of-date and inaccurate emergency information that may lead to the deaths of thousands of viewers who would travel to empty relief stations. Her program director refuses to stop broadcasting the incorrect information, because people will tune in to another station and the ratings will fall. Seeing that the station is gripped by madness, Ross finally agrees to leave with her boy friend, Emge (who is the station's traffic copter pilot), in his helicopter. Meanwhile, the city's SWAT team is attempting to evacuate the residents of a low-income, minority housing complex who refuse to leave despite the threat of zombies. The police storm the building and in a long (and extremely bloody and intense) siege clean out the building which had been infested with zombies (the minorities, having no money, had been dumping the bodies of their recently dead in the basement, where they returned to life and fed on the living in the building). Revolted by the total insanity of the operation, which killed more living than dead, SWAT team member Reiniger decides to escape in the helicopter with his friend Emge, and he brings along fellow cop Foree (who is black), to the slight dismay of his hosts. (Their reaction is not racial, but motivated purely by survival instincts.) The four escape, not knowing where to go or how far the living-dead epidemic has spread. Needing fuel, they land in a small airport in the country to gas up. Nearby, a group of rednecks have organized themselves into a hunting party and make an outing of shooting down the zombies, while swigging beer and cooking hot dogs on portable grills. At the airport, the group barely escape with their lives after several zombies appear and attack. Flying over Pennsylvania, they venture to a large, empty suburban shopping mall where they land to collect supplies. Leaving the helicopter on the roof, they watch hundreds of zombies wandering the empty acres of a parking lot that surrounds the mall. Entering the mall through the roof, they discover a fairly secure set of rooms that may have been empty office space. They make this area their home base and the two SWAT members enter the shopping area of the mall. They find that the place is infested with zombies who wander around as though window shopping. Since the zombies are spread out in the mall and lumber so slowly and haphazardly, Foree and Reiniger decide to venture among them, easily outmaneuvering their lame attempts to grab at them. Seeing that the mall would be easy to secure, and the answer to all their needs, the group decides to stay and set up house. Emge finds the electricity plans to the mall and they turn all the power on, including the moving window displays and innocuous Muzak that permeates every shop, lending a bizarre sense of humor to the proceedings. To secure the area the men decide to block all the entrances to the mall (so no more zombies can enter) with semi-trailers stored in a nearby truck depot. After the doors are blocked, the group plans to kill all the zombies inside the mall, ridding themselves of the menace. While they move the trucks, Reiniger (who has slowly been demonstrating a slight bit of madness by exhibiting a disturbing amount of foolhardiness) is bitten several times by the zombies who wander about the entrances to the mall. This turn of events (they all know that soon Reiniger will die and come back a zombie) coupled with the announcement by Ross that she is pregnant with Emge's child, brings an uneasy tension to the group that is translated into the vicious slaughter of the zombies in the mall. Fearing that they may not all survive, Ross demands to be taught how to fly the helicopter in the event that Emge is injured or killed. The rest of the group agrees, and soon the comrades arm themselves (with weapons from the mall's gun shop) and proceed to slay the remaining zombies. Having finished their bloody work (and stacked all the bodies in a meat locker) the group relaxes and enjoys the splendor of free access to the best of America's consumer-happy achievements, the shopping mall. They indulge in every shopping fantasy they have ever had. They hoard clothes, food, and merchandise until it all begins to become a bore. Their idyllic existence comes to an abrupt end when Reiniger begins to die from his bites. As the disease spreads, his face turns gray and he begs Foree to kill him if he should return to life. He dies soon after and in moments his body begins to sit up. Foree shoots him down. Tension builds between the remaining friends. The news on television and radio has stopped. The group begins to feel isolated and claustrophobic at the same time. Suddenly their isolation is shattered when a nomadic, well-armed motorcycle gang invades the mall, allowing zombies to pour through the entrances. Outraged that their palace has been violated, Emge (despite the protests of Foree and Ross to just lie low until the bikers take what they want and leave), shoots at the gang and starts a three-way war between the group, the bikers, and the zombies. During the battle Emge is shot by a biker, and then partly eaten by zombies in a terrifying sequence in an elevator. Foree and Ross decide to leave the mall, as do the bikers, who have lost too many members to the zombies. Before they have a chance to

gather their belongings, Emge, who has returned to life as a zombie, leads the rest of his brood to their stronghold. Having had enough of the madness, Foree stays and tells Ross he will hold off the zombies as long as he can while she and her unborn child escape in the helicopter. Ross protests, but when the zombies begin to shuffle into their apartment, she reluctantly leaves him to his fate. After killing his former friend/zombie Emge, Foree puts a gun to his own head to end the insanity of this existence. He suddenly changes his mind and battles his way to the helicopter where Ross has been waiting as long as possible. The chopper leaves the mall to the zombies and Ross and Foree fly off to an uncertain future. Brought in at a budget somewhere in the area of $2 million (incredibly cheap for a film of this size) Romero made every dollar count. The film looks as if ten times the amount of money (it has grossed over $55,000,000 to date) were spent on it. Shot in a Pennsylvania shopping mall after hours, Romero and his crew worked diligently through the night and had the place cleaned up every morning when the mall was ready to do business. Special makeup effects were done by the masterful Tom Savini (who also plays one of the bikers), who did them on a shoestring budget and very little planning, having to improvise his bloody effects on a daily basis. Romero and producer Richard Rubenstein opted to release their film without an MPAA rating because the association surely would have given it an X for violence. The film is incredibly violent (quite possibly the most violent film ever made), but it uses its bloodiness not to shock (the shocks are over by the time the siege on the housing project is over), but to numb. To translate the horror of existing in a societal structure that requires shooting down the risen corpses of loved ones, friends, neighbors, strangers, Romero barrages the viewer with image upon image of quick, violent, almost cartoon-like death. His visual style is the antithesis of the current trend in horror films (started by John Carpenter in HALLOWEEN, 1978) which uses long, floating, hand-held camera moves that invite us into the point of view of the killers. Romero's visual style is all based on well-composed static shots and editing which gives the film an internal kinetic energy that translates the powerful madness that has gripped his society. But he also does something else. While we sympathize with the protagonists of the film (Ross, Emge, Reiniger, and Foree) we actually feel for the zombies themselves. Romero does this by injecting heavy doses of broad comedy and farce to the zombies who are condemned to wander around slowly, helplessly, staring into store windows, battling with moving escalators, and being totally humiliated by the bikers who throw pies in their faces. But there is also compassion for the undead because they never asked to be brought back to life (there is a moment where a zombie boy, dressed in a baseball uniform, stares longingly at Ross which perfectly illustrates this point). Which leads to a deeper, more complex, and more disturbing theme of DAWN OF THE DEAD. The zombies represent humanity in general (and American consumers in particular) by being the most logical and extreme example of greedy, selfish human behavior. We, in our lesser moments, wish to consume everything. There is a moment when Ross wonders why the zombies are hanging around the mall. The answer is simple, "It's instinct. This is the place they always wanted to be." In DAWN OF THE DEAD, Romero has created the ultimate American nightmare. We are feeding on ourselves. Some consider this one of the most important American films of the last decade and it should be seen, though it is most definitely not for children. Followed by DAY OF THE DEAD (1985).

p, Richard Rubinstein; d&w, George Romero; ph, Michael Gornick (Technicolor); m, Dario Argento; ed, Romero, Kenneth Davidow; makeup & spec eff, Tom Savini; cos, Josie Caruso.

Horror   **Cas.**   **(PR:O   MPAA:NR)**

DAWN ON THE GREAT DIVIDE**½   (1942) 63m MON bw

Buck Jones (Buck Roberts), Rex Bell (Jack Carson), Raymond Hatton (Sandy Hopkins), Mona Barrie (Sadie Rand), Robert Lowery (Terry), Harry Woods (Jim Corkle), Christine MacIntyre (Mary), Betty Blythe (Elmira Corkle), Robert Frazer (Judge Corkle), Tristram Coffin (Rand), Jan Wiley (Martha), Dennis Moore (Tony Corkle), Roy Barcroft (Loder), Silver (Silver), Steve Clark, Reed Howes, Bud Osborne, I. Stanford Jolley, Artie Ortego, George Morrell, Milburn Morante, Ray Jones.

Jones' last movie, released just after his tragic death in the Coconut Grove fire in Boston. After the third member of the Rough Riders, McCoy, was drafted into the service in WW II, the producers replaced him with cowboy actor Bell, who was really no replacement. Plot sees Jones as a scout guiding a wagon train of settlers and railroad supplies through Indian territory. With the help of Bell and Hatton, Jones discovers that the hostile redskins are not redskins at all but renegade whites posing as Indians to stop the railroad settlement. Unusually good production values stand out due to a larger than normal budget for this oater.

p, Scott R. Dunlap; d, Howard Bretherton; w, Jess Bowers (based on a story "Wheels Of Fate" by James Oliver Curwood); ph, Harry Newman; ed, Carl Pierson.

Western   **Cas.**   **(PR:A   MPAA:NR)**

DAWN OVER IRELAND**
           (1938, Irish) 89m International Productions/Hibernia bw (GB: THE DAWN)

Tom Cooper (Dan O'Donovan), Brian O'Sullivan (Brian Malone), Eileen Davis (Eileen O'Donovan), Herbert Martin (Brassie), Marian O'Connell (Mrs. Malone), Donal O'Cahill (Billy Malone), James Gleeson (John Malone), Johnny McCarthy (Johnny), Jerry O'Mahoney (Officer in Charge), Bill Murphy (Sgt. Geary).

Slow, confused Irish melodrama detailing the saga of a family wrongly accused of being traitors to Ireland during the Fenian uprising of 1866. Three generations later, at the end of WW I, the grandsons, O'Sullivan and O'Cahill, get fed up with the treatment their family has received at the hands of the Irish. O'Sullivan joins the ranks of the British police, and O'Cahill appears to drop out of political activity and keeps to himself. O'Sullivan can't tolerate the British, either, and when troops arrive in his village to quash another Irish rebellion, he deserts and proves his bravery to the IRA in a fight against the royal soldiers. The family's honor is finally restored and soon after it is discovered, after his death, that the other brother, O'Cahill, was actually the IRA's most valuable spy. Pretty lame performances by most of the cast make one concentrate on the beautiful Irish scenery to help the time pass.

p&d, Thomas Cooper; w, Cooper, Donal O'Cahill, D.A. Moriarty; ph, James Lawler.

Drama (PR:A MPAA:NR)

DAWN PATROL, THE*** (1930) 105m FN bw

Richard Barthelmess (Dick Courtney), Douglas Fairbanks, Jr. (Douglas Scott), Neil Hamilton (Major Brand), William Janney (Gordon Scott), James Finlayson (Field Sergeant), Clyde Cook (Bott), Gardner James (Ralph Hollister), Edmund Breon (Lt. Bathurst), Frank McHugh (Flaherty), Jack Ackroyd, Harry Allen (Mechanics).

Director Howard Hawks' first foray into sound cinema shows his typically interesting and exciting visuals, but there is little evidence of his future skill with dialog in the stilted and overly talky screenplay penned by Totheroh, Miller, and Hawks himself. Action takes place during WW I where Barthelmess and Fairbanks, Jr., are hot-dog aces of the British air corps who consistently disobey orders to settle disputes of "honor" with the Germans. After German fliers taunt the pair regarding their flying prowess, Barthelmess and Fairbanks jump into their planes and ruthlessly strafe a helpless German air squadron, killing many pilots before they can get off the ground. On their return, outraged commanding officer Hamilton vents his fury on the boyish pilots only to be suddenly handed a message telling him that he has been transferred to another unit. Hamilton delights in informing Barthelmess that he is now in command and perhaps now he will develop a sense of responsibility when he must deal with a group of unruly fliers like himself. The duty proves rough as many of the fliers under Barthelmess' command are killed during increasingly dangerous and foolhardy missions, causing his former comrades to despise him for sending them out. When Fairbanks is slated to fly a particularly dangerous mission, Barthelmess gets him drunk and flies in his place. He destroys an entire German supply depot before he goes down in flames. Hawks' film is a strong antiwar statement which illustrates the futility of heroics that only end in death on both sides. The dogfight footage is some of the best aerial fighting photography ever filmed, but the movie suffers from the stagey, stiff dialog sequences that obviously frustrated Hawks. DAWN PATROL was re-made in 1938 by Edmund Goulding starring Basil Rathbone, Errol Flynn and David Niven, and it is this version that modern-day audiences find easier to sit through due to the more polished handling of the dialog sequences. A must-see for Hawks devotees.

p, Robert North; d, Howard Hawks; w, Hawks, Dan Totheroh, Seton I. Miller (based on the story "The Flight Commander" by John Monk Saunders); ph, Ernest Haller; m, Leo F. Forbstein; ed, Ray Curtiss; spec eff, Fred Jackman.

War Drama (PR:A MPAA:NR)

DAWN PATROL, THE**** (1938) 103m WB bw

Errol Flynn (Courtney), David Niven (Scott), Basil Rathbone (Major Brand), Donald Crisp (Phills), Melville Cooper (Watkins), Barry Fitzgerald (Bott), Carl Esmond (Von Mueller), Peter Willes (Hollister), Morton Lowater (Ronny Scott), Michael Brooke (Squires), James Burke (Flaherty, the Motorcycle Driver), Stuart Hall (Bentham, the Singer), Herbert Evans (Scott's Mechanic), Sidney Bracy (Ransom, Brand's Orderly), John Sutton (Adjutant), George Kirby (Kirby, the Orderly), Tyrone Brereton, Tim Henning, Douglas Gordon (Orderlies), John Rodion (Russell, the Replacement), Norman Willis (German Aviator), Gordon Thorpe (Smythe), Wally Reardon (Cleaver), Gilbert Wilson (Moorehead), Anthony Marsh (Rutherford), Hal Brazeale (Gregory), Tom Seidel (Jones).

A top-drawer remake of the 1930 DAWN PATROL, this version actually has a better cast and superior performances by its principals. Flynn, in one of his best enactments, is the dashing, conscience-haunted flight commander who, at first, is superficially carefree, bantering cynical humor with his men, all members of the British Royal Flying Corps. They fly the most impossible aircraft, rickety crates that almost fall apart before they are off the ground, another source of Flynn's seething anger. This creates unsafe odds for the fliers and contributes to their untimely deaths, fatalities that mount so drastically that raw recruits with little flying experience are sent into the skies to battle without much chance of survival. Between dawn patrols each day that decimate the command, the fliers face death with stiff upper lips and scotch and sodas at the club bar where a battered gramophone continuously grinds out the plaintive "Poor Butterfly". The melancholy talk soon leads to bolstering bravado when Flynn and other veterans lead the novices in a fatalistic ditty, singing: "So stand by your glasses steady/This world is a world of lies./Here's to the dead already—/Hurrah for the next man who dies!" In another room sits Rathbone, the desk-bound commander whose job it is to assign fliers to each dawn patrol, mechanically writing their names on a blackboard and methodically erasing those killed each day. Flynn, in a rage at the mounting deaths of the innocents, explodes at Rathbone, calling him a butcher. Rathbone bursts back with words that become the heart of this pacifistic classic: "It's a slaughterhouse, that's what it is, and I'm the executioner. You send men in rotten ships up to die . . . They don't argue or revolt . . . They just say 'Righto' and go out and do it!" He gestures toward the bar and singing fliers: "Listen to them. Bluffing themselves, pretending death doesn't mean anything to them, trying to live just for the minute, the hour, pretending they don't care if they go up tomorrow and never come back." Flynn is responsible for leading these doomed fliers and when he sends up Niven's untrained kid brother and later learns of his death he takes to the bottle, his nerve shot, his belief shattered. Then a perilous mission is assigned to his best friend, Niven, who is told to bomb a behind-the-lines ammunition dump. Flynn cannot bear to see his noble buddy die so he gets him drunk and then takes his place. After bombing the dump, Flynn engages the feared and deadly Esmond (playing the German ace, Von Mueller, based, of course on von Richthofen, the legendary Red Baron). Following a spectacular air duel Flynn is shot down and

dies. Niven, realizing his friend's sacrifice, then takes over command of the squadron, assuming the same dedicated but guarded attitude typified by Flynn, sending more men on the dawn patrol at film's end. Though many of Hawks' fine aerial dogfights from the 1930 film are intercut with the remake action, Warner Brothers shot much new footage for this version, using its Calabasas Ranch for the airfield site and gathering vintage planes actually used in WW I such as Thomas-Morse Scouts and the most-used Allied planes, the Nieuports, dozens of them. Though the original story was retained, the dialog was re-written and polished to great improvement. Flynn and Niven are far superior and more believable than the relationship between Richard Barthelmess and Douglas Fairbanks, Jr., in the original film, giving more gusto and comaraderie to their roles, which was not hard since they were pals offscreen. All the supporting players—Crisp, Cooper, Fitzgerald—are standouts and give further dimension to the film. Goulding's direction is not as expansive as Hawks' but is economical and creative. Gaudio's photography is sensational. Unlike most remakes, this version is decidedly a notch above the original.

p, Hal B. Wallis, Robert Lord; d, Edmund Goulding; w, Seton I. Miller, Dan Totheroh (based on the story "The Flight Commander" by John Monk Saunders); ph, Tony Gaudio; m, Max Steiner; ed, Ralph Dawson; art d, John Hughes; spec eff, Edwin A. DuPar; tech adv, Captain L.G.S. Scott.

War Drama (PR:C MPAA:NR)

DAWN RIDER** (1935) 53m Lone Star bw

John Wayne (John Mason), Marion Burns (Alice), Yakima Canutt (Barkeep), Reed Howes (Ben), Denny Meadows [Dennis Moore] (Rudd), Bert Dillard (Buck), Jack Jones (Black), Nelson McDowell, Archie Ricks, Tex Phelps, James Sheridan.

Wayne stars as a cowboy obsessed with getting revenge on the gang that killed his father. He finds their trail and picks them off one by one until he corners their leader, Meadows, and sets a time for a showdown. As the time approaches, Wayne's friend Howe, who suspects Wayne of seeing his girl on the sly, empties the Duke's gun so that he will be sure to be killed. At the last minute, Howe repents and guns down Meadows himself, only to be killed by a surviving gang member. A bit confused and far-fetched, but a decent entry in Wayne's Lone Star series of westerns.

p, Paul Malvern; d&w, R.N. Bradbury (based on a story by Lloyd Nosler); ph, Archie Stout; ed, Carl Pierson.

Western (PR:A MPAA:NR)

DAWN TRAIL, THE** (1931) 60m COL bw

Buck Jones (Larry), Miriam Seegar (June), Charles Morton (Mart), Erville Alderson (Denton), Edward Le Saint (Amos), Charles L. King (Skeets), Hank Mann (Cock Eye), Vester Pegg (Mac), Slim Whittaker (Steve), Charles Brinley (Nestor), Inez Gomez (Maria), Bob Burns (Settler), Robert Fleming (Henchman), Violet Axzelle (Molly), Buck Connors (Jim Anderson), Jack Curtis (Hank).

Early Jones oater sees our hero as the sheriff of Osage county, which happens to be in the middle of a vicious range war between cattlemen and the sheepherders who are fighting over access to the one decent watering hole in the valley. Jones almost engineers a truce, but the brother of his girl friend kills a sheepherder, which renews the hostilities and destroys Jones' credibility. Things calm down when Jones wins back the ranchers' confidence after justice is done, with the killer's father mistakenly shooting his son, whom he thought to be a sheepherder. Contrived, but the cast and technical crew perform their duties well.

p, Harry Cohn; d, Christy Cabanne; w, J.T. Neville (based on a story by Forrest Sheldon); ph, T.D. McCord; ed, James Sweeney.

Western (PR:A MPAA:NR)

DAY AFTER, THE (SEE: UP FROM THE BEACH, 1965)

DAY AFTER HALLOWEEN, THE zero (1981, Aus.) 90m Group 1 c (AKA: SNAPSHOT)

Chantal Contouri (Madeline), Sigrid Thornton (Angela), Robert Bruning (Elmer), Hugh Keays-Byrne (Linsey), Vincent Gil (Daryl), Denise Drysdale (Lilly), Jacqui Gordon, Peter Stratford, Lulu Pinkus, Stewart Faichney, Julia Blake, Jon Sidney, Christine Amor, Chris Milne, Peter Flemingham, Bob Brown.

A poor and obscure Australian crime film passed off as a sequel to John Carpenter's low-budget box-office smash HALLOWEEN (1978) by an unscrupulous distributor. The plot, which has nothing whatsoever to do with the Carpenter film, concerns a young model, Contouri, who is menaced by her ex-boy friend, shrewish mother, bratty sister, and a variety of lecherous rich old men. The resulting film is awful. An outrageous attempt to fleece the movie-going public.

p, Anthony I. Ginnane; d, Simon Wincer; w, Chris and Everett DeRoche; ph, Vincent Monton (Eastmancolor); m, Brian May; ed, Philip Reid; art d, Jon Dowding, Jill Eden.

Crime (PR:O MPAA:R)

DAY AFTER THE DIVORCE, THE*½ (1940, Ger.) 90m Tobis bw (DER TAG NACH DER SCHEIDUNG)

Johannes Riemann, Hilde Hildebrand, Hans Sohnker, Luise Ullrich, Kathe Haack.

Uninteresting German comedy has Riemann leaving wife Ullrich and taking up with singer Hildebrand, but he regrets it when Sohnker begins wooing his ex-wife. Occasionally amusing and with some good performances, but not a surprise to be found anywhere. (In German; English subtitles.)

d, Paul Verhoven.

Comedy (PR:A MPAA:NR)

DAY AND THE HOUR, THE**½** (1963, Fr./ Ital.) 115m
Cipra-Terra-Societe Nouvelle des Films Cormoran-CCM.-Monica/MGM bw (LE JOUR ET L'HEURE; IL GIORNO E L' ORA; VIVIAMO OGGI; AKA: TODAY WE LIVE)

Simone Signoret *(Thérese Dutheil)*, Stuart Whitman *(Capt. Allan Morley)*, Genevieve Page *(Agathe)*, Michel Piccoli *(Antoine)*, Reggie Nalder *(German Policeman)*, Pierre Dux *(Inspector Marboz)*, Billy Kearns *(Pat Riley)*, Mark Burns, Roger Kemp *(English Pilots)*, Henri Virlogeux *(Pharmacist)*, Colette Castel *(Lucie)*, Edward Meeks *(3rd English Pilot)*, Marcel Bozzufi *(Inspector Lerat)*, Jean Gras *("Gorilla" Richebois)*, Hubert de Lapparent *(Prosecutor)*, Georges Staquet *(Innkeeper)*, Maurice Garrel *(Head Militiaman)*, Guy Dakar *(Militiaman)*, Robert Bazil, Marcel Gassouk *(Peasants)*, Etienne Dirand *(Informer)*, Fred Fisher *(German Officer)*, Henia Suchar *(Girl in Blue)*, Marie Mergey *(Innkeeper's Wife)*, Anthony Stuart *(Wing Commander)*, Carl Studer *(Maj. Gordon)*, Clara Gansard *(Member of the Maquis)*, Yvette Etievant *(Cashier)*, Hugues Wanner *(Retired Army Officer)*, Gessie Azoulai *(Michou)*, Catherine Azoulai *(Charlotte)*.

Signoret stars as a bored aristocratic Frenchwoman who is oblivious to the sufferings of WW II until she is forced to become involved in the Resistance. One day, while returning home from a country farm to obtain food, she discovers three Allied soldiers stowed away in her vehicle. She takes them to Resistance headquarters but is angered when she is told to take one of the soldiers, Whitman, and hide him in her home because there is not enough room at the hideout. Getting more deeply involved with the soldier, Signoret accompanies Whitman on his escape route to the Spanish border. They fall in love and Whitman attempts to bring her with him to Spain, but he is forced to leave her in France. Her patriotism revitalized by the encounter, Signoret stays at the border to help other Allied soldiers escape the Nazis.

p, Jacques Bar; d, Rene Clement; w, Clement, Roger Vailland, Clement Biddle Wood (based on a story by Andre Barret); ph, Henri Decae (Franscope); m, Claude Bolling; ed, Fedora Zincone; set d, Bernard Evein; song, "La Romance de Paris."

War/Romance (PR:A MPAA:NR)

DAY AT THE BEACH, A*½** (1970) 93m PAR c

Mark Burns, Beatrice Edney, Peter Sellers.

Director Polanski wrote the screenplay to this mess "for want of anything better to do" (as he states in his 1984 autobiography). The result is a tedious drama wherein a young, alcoholic drifter, Burns, and a crippled little girl, Edney (actress Sylvia Sims' daughter), bounce around the picture getting into trouble until the drunken sot collapses in the street with the crying tot tugging at his sleeve. What little compassion there is for Polanski's main character is lost by an incredibly inept performance by Burns (it was his first film and Polanski felt he was "miscast") and some weak direction by Hesera. In fairness, Polanski states that the studio saddled the production with a small budget and haphazard support, but perhaps the executives saw what was happening before the filmmakers did. Sellers makes an unpaid cameo as a homosexual kiosk-keeper at the beach.

p, Roman Polanski, Gene Gutowski; d, Simon Hesera; w, Polanski; ph, Gil Taylor (Eastmancolor); m, Mortimer Shuman; ed, Alistair McIntire.

Drama (PR:O MPAA:NR)

DAY AT THE RACES, A***½** (1937) 109m MGM bw/c

Groucho Marx *(Dr. Hugo Z. Hackenbush)*, Chico Marx *(Tony)*, Harpo Marx *(Stuffy)*, Allan Jones *(Gil)*, Maureen O'Sullivan *(Judy)*, Margaret Dumont *(Mrs. Upjohn)*, Leonard Ceeley *(Whitmore)*, Douglas Dumbrille *(Morgan)*, Esther Muir *("Flo")*, Sig Rumann *(Dr. Steinberg)*, Robert Middlemass *(Sheriff)*, Vivien Fay *(Solo Dancer)*, Charles Trowbridge *(Dr. Wilmerding)*, Frank Dawson, Max Lucke *(Doctors)*, Frankie Darro *(Morgan's Jockey)*, Pat Flaherty *(Detective)*, Si Jenks *(Messenger)*, Hooper Atchley *(Race Judge)*, John Hyams, Wilbur Mack *(Judges)*, Mary MacLaren *(Nurse)*, Edward LeSaint *(Doctor)*, Jack Norton *(Drunk)*, Ivie Anderson, Crinoline Choir.

There are those who think this was the best example of "Marxism" in movies. We disagree. It surely was opulent with huge sets, semi-colored (the ballet sequence) and a huge cast. Further, the brothers Marx went out into the boondocks and tested their routines for more than one hundred "live" performances until they believed they had all of the gags in the right places and could do no wrong. Yes, it was funny, but not as funny as *they* must have thought it was. Groucho is a horse doctor who takes over a large sanitarium at the behest of Dumont, who is in love with the mustached one. The sanitarium is owned by O'Sullivan, but she's having trouble paying off the mortgage. O'Sullivan and Allan Jones provide the romantic angles with Ceeley and Dumbrille as the heavies. For some reason, they ring in a whole host of black singers and dancers in a Harlem tribute that makes no sense. Several songs, a water carnival, a horse race, and a very funny paper-hanging scene are what stand out, but it is so disjointed that no amount of sight gags can rank it any higher. There are three Marxmen in this film but there were five when they started. Zeppo (Herbert) did several films, then dropped out after DUCK SOUP. Gummo (Milton) was with the act in vaudeville but departed before the Marx Brothers made it to Broadway, then Hollywood. The other three's real names were Leonard (Chico), Julius (Groucho) and Adolph, also known as Arthur (Harpo). Songs "All God's Chillun Got Rhythm," "Tomorrow Is Another Day," "A Message From the Man in the Moon" (Gus Kahn, Walter Jurmann, Bronislau Kaper); dance sequence: "Blue Venetian Waters."

p, Lawrence Weingarten; d, Sam Wood; w, Robert Pirosh, George Seaton, George Oppenheimer (based on a story by Pirosh and Seaton); ph, Joseph Ruttenberg; m, Bronislaw Kaper, Walter Jurmann, Gus Kahn; ed, Frank Hull; md, Franz Waxman; art d, Cedric Gibbons; ch, Dave Gould.

Comedy/Musical Cas. (PR:AA MPAA:NR)

DAY FOR NIGHT******* (1973, Fr.) 120m
Les Films Du Carrosse-PECF-PIC/WB-COL c (LA NUIT AMERICAINE)

Francois Truffaut *(Ferrand)*, Jacqueline Bisset *(Julie)*, Jean-Pierre Leaud *(Alphonse)*, Valentina Cortese *(Severine)*, Jean-Pierre Aumont *(Alexandre)*, Dani *(Lilianna)*, Alexandra Stewart *(Stacey)*, Jean Champion *(Bertrand)*, Nathalie Baye *(Assistant)*, Bernard Menez *(Bernard the Prop Man)*, Jean-Francois Stevenin *(1st Assistant Director)*, Nike Arrighi *(Odile the Makeup Girl)*, Gaston Joly *(Gaston Lajoie, Production Manager)*, Zenaide Rossi *(Mme. Lajoie)*, David Markham *(Julie's Husband)*, Maurice Seveno *(Television Announcer)*, Christophe Vesque *(Boy With Cane in Dream Sequences)*, Henry Graham [British author Graham Greene in guest appearance] *(English Insurance Broker)*, Marcel Berbert [the film's executive producer] *(French Insurance Broker)*.

From the moment filmmakers began making films, they began making films about making films. In some cases, it was satire (THE PURPLE ROSE OF CAIRO), in others, it was with anger (THE BIG KNIFE, THE BAD AND THE BEAUTIFUL, and a hundred more). DAY FOR NIGHT is not about "the movies"—it is about the making of *a* movie, and not even a very good movie. But it is simply the best movie ever made about how it is to make a movie. Now, that is a bold statement but anyone who has ever worked on a set, particularly an on-location set, will quickly recognize the truths of the script. Truffaut draws often from his own life but never more specifically than in this picture. He plays himself, a director helming a film, and his acting is effortless and believable; everything he might ask from one of his actors. Leaud, star of Truffaut's first feature, THE 400 BLOWS, is perfect as a confused young actor who leaves the unit because of a problem d'amour. As it is in so many synopses, the black and white plot falls far short of the colorful conclusions but here it is: the movie takes place during the seven-week shooting schedule of a film known as "Meet Pamela," which has to do with Leaud bringing his bilingual British bride, Bisset, home to meet *pere* Aumont *et mere* Cortese. Aumont and Bisset fall for each other and elope. Bisset dies in a car accident and Leaud shoots his father as they run across a Parisian square. Now, that's the plot of "Meet Pamela" but what is happening behind the scenes is the actual plot of DAY FOR NIGHT. Bisset is a skittish young woman with a pushy theatrical mother and a history of being a star at a very young age, all of which have caused her to be just now recovering from a nervous breakdown. Cortese is drinking heavily, forgetting lines, walking into closets, but we soon learn that this is a temporary madness brought on by the fact that her son is, at that moment, dying of a blood disease. Leaud is acting like an ass over script girl Dani who insists on flirting with everyone. Leaud is madly in love with her and can't tolerate her attitude. In charge of what's happening on and off screen is Truffaut, a patient but authoritative man who must oversee the filming as well as the personal lives of his charges. Dani leaves with the stunt man and Leaud goes into a complete blackout. His heart is aching and he wants to leave the film, leave the area, and probably put his head in an oven. Bisset attempts to reason with him and has a Tea and Sympathy night in bed with him. Emotional Leaud is now certain that Bisset loves him and he loves her so he long distances Bissett's physician husband, David Markham, and demands that the doctor give his wife a divorce! Markham phones Bissett, wants to know what the hell is going on at the location. She responds by locking herself in her room and swearing never to emerge. Truffaut steps in and calms the nervous actress until Markham arrives. He's been a Hollywood husband long enough to realize that these things *do* happen when people are tossed into such close quarters a long way from hearth and home. Bisset is put back on an even keel, then tragedy strikes when Aumont is killed in a car accident while joyriding with his young male lover. They are close to the conclusion of the film and a double is used for the final scenes. "Meet Pamela" ends and the cast and crew bid each other farewell, then move on to their next jobs and DAY FOR NIGHT is over. The unusual title refers to those scenes which are shot during the day but with a special camera filter so they might look as though they were shot at night. Due to budgets and overtime costs, this was done often in early western films where price was a great consideration. Since the technique was developed in the U.S., it's called "The American Night" in France, hence the French title. Truffaut had run into the very problem faced by Aumont's death in the picture. While making one of his few disasters, THE SOFT SKIN, beauteous actress Francois Dorleac was killed in an automobile accident in 1967 at Nice. Truffaut was determined to show only true incidents that took place during the filming of his previous works and people familiar with Truffaut will recognize the occurrences as well as the people. It was made with no point of view. There was no false sentiment, no melodrama, some humor, some passion, lots of madness—in other words, exactly what happens on location while making a movie. The remarkable part of it to American moviemakers was that this very French film could have been easily made anywhere in the U.S. DAY FOR NIGHT understandably won many awards; the Oscar for Best Foreign Film (nominations for Truffaut, Cortese, and the screenplay); the New York Film Critics Awards for Best Motion Picture, Best Direction, and Best Supporting Actress (Cortese), The British Society for Film and Television Awards for Best Film, Best Direction, and Cortese once more for Best Supporting Actress. Truffaut had some fun with the audience in casting author Graham Greene as a British insurance broker and executive producer Berbert as the French insurance broker. The movie they were making, "Meet Pamela," was of no consequence and probably would not have grossed enough to cover advertising costs. But DAY FOR NIGHT was, and remains, the definitive movie about moviemaking. As in so many European productions, this was a co-venture between Les Films Du Carosse-PECF-PIC but too many cooks did not spoil the broth in the case of DAY FOR NIGHT. For reasons known only to Truffaut, the movie was dedicated to Lillian and Dorothy Gish.

p, Marcel Berbert; d, Francois Truffaut; w, Truffaut, Suzanne Schiffman, Jean-Louis Richard; ph, Pierre-William Glenn (Eastmancolor); m, Georges Delerue; ed, Yann Dedet, Martine Barraque; art d, Damien Lanfranchi; cos, Monique Dury.

Drama Cas. (PR:A-C MPAA:PG)

DAY IN COURT, A* (1965, Ital.) 70m Excelsa-Documento-Bellotti/Ultra bw (UN GIORNO IN PRETURA)

Peppino De Filippo *(Judge Del Russo)*, Silvana Pampanini *(Gloriana)*, Alberto Sordi *(Meniconi)*, Tania Weber *(Elena)*, Walter Chiari *(Don Michele)*, Sophia Loren *(Anna)*, Leopoldo Trieste, Virgilio Riento.

Inane Italian courtroom comedy told in four parts. The first, "Adultery in 16mm," details a woman's efforts to sue her husband for abandonment. Her husband counters with a charge of adultery and claims he can prove it with movies taken with his home-movie camera. Despite the objections from both attorneys the judge allows the evidence, and the courtroom is shocked to see the woman indeed committing adultery, with her *husband's* lawyer. The second tale, "The Priest and the Prostitute," stars Loren as a hooker who stole a priest's wallet. The enraged pastor follows the girl to a pool hall where she gives the cash to her pimp. A fight ensues between the priest and the pimp and soon the police arrive and take the whole lot of them to jail. In court, the priest nobly states that he gave the money to Loren to start a new life and the judge lets him off with a suspended sentence. The third chapter, "Indecent Exposure," details the efforts of a health nut (who swims in the buff at a big, water-filled ditch in Rome) to retrieve his clothes that have been stolen. The fourth tale, "The Lustful Lieutenant," sees an aging prostitute up before a judge on a charge of soliciting. The woman reminds the judge of a woman he was in love with during the war, and though he's not positive she is the same woman, he lets her go free.

p, Carlo Ponti, Dino De Laurentiis; d, Steno [Stefano Vanzina]; w, Lucio Fulci, Alberto Sordi, Alessandro Continenza (based on an idea by Fulci); ph, Marco Scarpelli; m, Armando Trovajoli; art d, Piero Filippone.

Comedy/Drama (PR:O MPAA:NR)

DAY IN THE DEATH OF JOE EGG, A** (1972, Brit.) 106m Domino/COL c

Alan Bates *(Bri)*, Janet Suzman *(Sheila)*, Peter Bowles *(Freddie)*, Sheila Gish *(Pam)*, Joan Hickson *(Grace)*, Elizabeth Robillard *(Jo)*, Murray Melvin *(Doctor)*, Fanny Carby *(Nun)*, Constance Chapman *(Moonrocket Lady)*, Elizabeth Tyrell *(Midwife)*.

Disturbing, black-humored comedy concerning an English couple, Bates and Suzman, who are trying to raise spastic daughter Robillard. As is to be expected from the director of THE RULING CLASS (1972), Medak fills his film with bizarre character twitches and weird turns which lead to the parents' decision to perform a "mercy killing" on their daughter. In the end, filled with the Christmas spirit, the couple decide to let their child live and have her institutionalized. Good performances all around save the material from becoming totally tasteless.

p, David Deutsch; d, Peter Medak; w, Peter Nichols (based on his play); ph, Ken Hodges (Eastmancolor); m, Marcus Dods; ed, Ray Lovejoy; art d, Ted Tester; set d, Dimity Collins.

Comedy (PR:O MPAA:R)

DAY MARS INVADED EARTH, THE** (1963) 70m AP&D bw

Kent Taylor *(Dr. David Fielding)*, Marie Windsor *(Claire Fielding)*, William Mims *(Dr. Web Spencer)*, Betty Beall *(Judi Fielding)*, Lowell Brown *(Frank)*, Gregg Shank *(Rocky Fielding)*, Henrietta Moore, Troy Melton, George Riley.

INVASION OF THE BODY SNATCHERS inspired this sci-fi tale starring Taylor as a Cape Canaveral scientist who has successfully landed a probe on Mars, but is puzzled as to why it exploded shortly after landing. He travels to California to visit his estranged wife, Windsor, and his two children to try to save his marriage and mull over the scientific puzzle. While there, he meets up with people he has known, but they all seem to be behaving strangely. Suddenly he is confronted with exact duplicates of himself and his family. It is soon discovered that Martians have landed on Earth and are slowly killing off humans and taking over their bodies until they can control the planet. Though he tries, Taylor is unable to stop the Martians and their plan succeeds. Surprisingly grim ending is weakened by a mediocre cast and script.

p&d, Maury Dexter; w, Harry Spalding; ph, John Nickolaus Jr.; m, Richard La Salle; ed, Jodie Copelan; set d, Harry Reif.

Science Fiction (PR:C MPAA:NR)

DAY OF ANGER* (1970, Ital./Ger.) 109m Sancrosiap-Corona-K.G. Divina/NG c (I GIORNI DELL'IRA; DER TOD RITT DIENSTAGS)

Giuliano Gemma *(Scott Mary)*, Lee Van Cleef *(Frank Talby)*, Walter Rilla *(Murphallan)*, Andrea Bosic *(Murray Abel)*, Ennio Balbo *(Turner)*, Lukas Ammann *(Judge Cutchel)*, Christa Linder *(Judge's Daughter)*, Pepe Calvo *(Blind Bill)*, Yvonne Sanson *(Vivien Skill)*, Giorgio Gargiullo, Virgilio Gazzolo, Franco Balducci, Eleonora Morana, Giorgio Di Segni, Anna Maria Orso, Karl Otto Alberty, Benito Stefanelli, Nino Nini.

Lackluster spaghetti western directed by Valerii, who was once Sergio Leone's assistant and who would later go on to direct the wonderful MY NAME IS NOBODY (1973). Van Cleef stars as a master gunman who decides to allow drifter Gemma to apprentice under him. Soon the two take over a town and Van Cleef goes mad, killing everyone in town, until Gemma stands up and shoots his teacher down. A western with no sense of style and just another blood-dripping oater.

p, Alfonso Sansone, Enrico Chroscicki; d, Tonino Valerii; w, Ernesto Gastaldi, Renzo Genta, Valerii; (based on a novel by Ron Barker); ph, Enzo Serafin (Techniscope/Technicolor); m, Riz Ortolani; ed, Franco Fraticelli; art d, Piero Filippone; cos, Carlo Simi.

Western (PR:O MPAA:GP)

DAY OF FURY, A** (1956) 78m UNIV c

Dale Robertson *(Jagade)*, Mara Corday *(Sharman Fulton)*, Jock Mahoney *(Marshal Allan Burnett)*, Carl Benton Reid *(Judge John J. McLean)*, Jan Merlin *(Billy Brand)*, John Dehner *(Preacher Jason)*, Dee Carroll *(Miss Timmons)*, Sheila Bromley *(Marie)*, James Bell *(Doc Logan)*, Dani Crayne *(Claire)*, Howard Wendell *(Vanryzin)*, Charles Cane *(Duggen)*, Phil Chambers *(Burson)*, Sydney Mason *(Beemans)*, Helen Kleeb *(Mrs. McLean)*, Dayton Lummis, Harry Tyler.

Strange little oater starring Robertson as an aging gunfighter resisting the old West's efforts to become civilized. The film opens as the gunslinger saves the life of town marshal Mahoney. Mahoney, who was to marry his sweetheart that day (former dance hall girl Corday), thanks the stranger and heads off to his wedding. The marriage is interrupted when Robertson rides into town, shoots the lock off the saloon door (it's Sunday), and sends for the dance hall girls who were sent packing to another county after the town decided to reform. Because he owes the gunslinger his life, Mahoney refrains from doing anything about the ruckus and even ignores the fact that Robertson has killed a man (apparently in self-defense). The townsfolk have just about had enough, when Mahoney repays his debt by saving Robertson from receiving a bullet shot at him by Corday. Having settled all accounts, Mahoney then shoots it out with the outlaw, ridding the town of the menace.

p, Robert Arthur; d, Harmon Jones; w, James Edmiston, Oscar Brodney (based on a story by Edmiston); ph, Ellis W. Carter (Technicolor); ed, Sherman Todd; md, Joseph Gershenson; art d, Alexander Golitzen, Robert Boyle; cos, Rosemary Odell.

Western (PR:A MPAA:NR)

DAY OF RECKONING** (1933) 65m MGM bw

Richard Dix *(John Day)*, Madge Evans *(Dorothy Day)*, Conway Tearle *(Hollins)*, Una Merkel *(Mamie)*, Stuart Erwin *(Jerry)*, Spanky McFarlane *(Johnny)*, Isabel Jewell *(Kate Lovett)*, James Bell *(Slim)*, Raymond Hatton *(Hart)*, Paul Hurst *(Harry)*, Wilfred Lucas *(Guard)*, Samuel Hinds *(O'Farrell)*, John Larkin.

Grim prison picture featuring Dix as a man sent to a sky-scraping Los Angeles hoosegow for embezzling his employer's profits. Dix was driven to the act by his venal and shrewish wife, Evans, who immediately takes up with big shot businessman Tearle. Unfortunately, Tearle's former mistress goes into a jealous rage, kills Evans, and Tearle takes the rap and ends up in the same jail as Dix. Dix catches up to the man he believes killed his wife and before you know it, Tearle takes a nosedive off the roof of the prison and is killed. A surprisingly vicious programmer churned out at Culver City in two weeks to help keep release schedules filled.

d, Charles Brabin; w, Zelda Sears, Eve Green (based on a story by Morris Lavine); ph, Ted Tetzlaff; ed, Adrienne Fazan.

Crime (PR:O MPAA:NR)

DAY OF THE ANIMALS zero (1977) 95m Film Ventures c (AKA: SOMETHING IS OUT THERE)

Christopher George *(Steve Buckner)*, Leslie Nielsen *(Mr. Jenson)*, Lynda Day George *(Terry Marsh)*, Richard Jaeckel *(Prof. MacGregor)*, Michael Ansara *(Santee)*, Ruth Roman *(Mrs. Shirley Goodwin)*, Jon Cedar *(Frank Young)*, Paul Mantee *(Roy Moore)*, Walter Barnes *(Ranger Tucker)*, Susan Backlinie *(Mrs. Young)*, Andrew Stevens *(Bob Denning)* Kathleen Bracken *(Beth Hughes)*, Bobby Porter *(Jon Goodwyn)*, Michelle Stacy *(Little Girl)*, Garrison True *(Newscaster)*, Michael Rougas *(Military Officer)*, Gil Lamb *(Old Man in Restaurant)*, Michael Andreas *(Sheriff)*, Jan Andrew Scott *(Helicopter Pilot)*, Gertrude Lee *(Ranger's Wife)*.

Laughable horror film from director Girdler who had previously aped such horror classics as THE EXORCIST (1973) by making his own version, ABBY (1974), and JAWS (1975), by making the shark a bear and calling it GRIZZLY (1976). This time "creative genius" was inspired by Hitchcock's classic, THE BIRDS (1963), and he brought the public this trash which has the animals of the world going wacko and attacking humans because of mankind's destruction of the ozone layer due to the irresponsible use of aerosol cans! Bad casting (Roman and Jaeckel as scientists?) and inept special effects make this Girdler outing an unintentional comedy for those masochistic enough to sit through it. See the similar FROGS (1972).

p, Edward E. Montoro; d, William Girdler; w, William Norton, Eleanor E. Norton (based on a story by Montoro); ph, Bob Sorrentino (Todd-AO 35, DeLuxe Color); m, Lalo Schifrin; ed, Bub Asman, James Mitchell; cos, Michael R. Faeth, Nancy Sales.

Horror Cas. (PR:C MPAA:PG)

DAY OF THE BAD MAN** (1958) 81m UNIV c

Fred MacMurray *(Judge Jim Scott)*, Joan Weldon *(Myra Owens)*, John Ericson *(Sheriff Barney Wiley)*, Robert Middleton *(Charlie Hayes)*, Marie Windsor *(Cora Johnson)*, Edgar Buchanan *(Sam Wyckoff)*, Eduard Franz *(Andrew Owens)*, Skip Homeier *(Howard Hayes)*, Peggy Converse *(Mrs. Quary)*, Robert Foulk *(Silas Mordigan)*, Ann Doran *(Mrs. Mordigan)*, Lee Van Cleef *(Jake Hayes)*, Eddy Waller *(Mr. Slocum)*, Christopher Dark *(Rudy Hayes)*, Don Haggerty *(Floyd)*, Chris Alcaide *(Monte Hayes)*.

Competent western sees MacMurray as a small-town judge who is about to sentence a vicious outlaw to death when four members of the killer's gang show up to free him. The gang, led by Middleton and Homeier, spook the town (including the spineless sheriff) into pleading for the release of the killer. MacMurray refuses to yield, and seeing that he'll get no help from the weak townsfolk, puts on his guns and with the help of his close friend Buchanan, kills off all four members of the gang, keeping the murderer's date with the hangman. Interesting and effective variation on the HIGH NOON (1952) theme, which, with the mimicking that goes on in Hollywood, by 1958 had made a cliche out of the sight of townspeople cowed into submission by gun-toting badmen.

p, Gordon Kay; d, Harry Keller; w, Lawrence Roman (based on a story by John M. Cunningham); ph, Irving Glassberg (CinemaScope, Eastmancolor); m, Hans J. Salter; ed, Sherman Todd; art d, Alexander Golitzen, Al Sweeney.

Western   **(PR:A   MPAA:NR)**

DAY OF THE DOLPHIN, THE**   (1973) 104m AE c

George C. Scott (*Dr. Jake Terrell*), Trish Van Devere (*Maggie Terrell*), Paul Sorvino (*Mahoney*), Fritz Weaver (*Harold DeMilo*), Jon Korkes (*David*), Edward Herrmann (*Mike*), Leslie Charleson (*Maryanne*), John David Carson (*Larry*), Victoria Racimo (*Lana*), John Dehner (*Wallingford*), Severn Darden (*Schwinn*), William Roerick (*Dunhill*), Elizabeth Wilson (*Mrs. Rome*), Pat Englund, Julie Follansbee, Brooke Hayward, Florence Stanley (*Women at Club*), Willie Meyers (*Stone*), Phyllis Davis (*Secretary*).

Henry and Nichols, who collaborated so well on THE GRADUATE, then not quite so well on CATCH-22, totally missed the boat with their pseudo-sci-fi-adventure-comedy about trained dolphins who are mammal-naped by a right-wing terrorist group which intends to use them to blow up the presidential yacht. Scott and Van Devere are researchers dealing with the intelligence of dolphins. Their sponsor is Weaver, who heads a large foundation. Sorvino is a writer who is really a government agent doing some undercover investigation of Weaver's group. The truth is that Weaver and his villainous cohorts Darden, Dehner, and Roerick, are planning to use the dolphins to further their own political ambitions. The plot soon disintegrates into dumbness, despite Scott's believable portrayal of an aquatic Dr. Dolittle. The screenplay chooses some poor times to relieve tension and the jokes fall flat. Hitchcock often used a touch of humor in his most suspenseful scenes but he laid it on with a tweezer, not a trowel. Henry did the unconvincing voice of the dolphins, which seemed like Saturday Morning TV cartoon sounds. The photography, both over and underwater, is the highlight of the movie. Delerue, who did the music for many superior French films, garnered an oscar nomination for his music but lost that year to Marvin Hamlisch for "The Way We Were." The movie cost over $8 million and never got close to recovering it theatrically, which should give the lie to the theory of "bankable stars and writers and directors." The play is, and always will be, the thing. In this case, it wasn't, and so the picture sank.

p, Robert Relyea; d, Mike Nichols; w, Buck Henry (based on a novel by Robert Merle); ph, William A. Fraker (Panavision, Technicolor); m, Georges Delerue; ed, Sam O'Steen; prod d, Richard Sylbert; art d, Angelo Graham; set d, George Nelson; cos, Anthea Sylbert; spec eff, Albert Whitlock, Jim White.

Drama   **Cas.**   **(PR:A   MPAA:PG)**

DAY OF THE EVIL GUN**   (1968) 93m MGM c

Glenn Ford (*Warfield*), Arthur Kennedy (*Forbes*), Dean Jagger (*Jimmy Noble*), John Anderson (*Capt. Addis*), Paul Fix (*Sheriff*), Nico Minardos (*DeLeon*), Harry Dean Stanton (*Sgt. Parker*), Pilar Pellicer (*Lydia*), Parley Baer (*Willford*), Royal Dano (*Dr. Prather*), Ross Elliott (*Rev. Yearby*), Barbara Babcock (*Angie*), James Griffith (*Storekeeper*).

Tedious, unnecessary reworking of John Ford's masterpiece, THE SEARCHERS, sees peaceful neighbor Kennedy joining forces with cold-blooded ex-gunslinger Ford in a search for his wife and children who have been kidnaped by Apaches. Accompanied by eccentric trader and scout Jagger, the men encounter Indian raids, bandits, and torture until slowly (and predictably) Kennedy becomes the cold-blooded killer and Ford the "voice-of-reason." Eventually they find Ford's wife and kids and return home, until Kennedy challenges Ford to a deadly gunfight. Originally made for ABC-TV but the studio opted for the theaters instead.

p&d, Jerry Thorpe; w, Charles Marquis Warren, Eric Bercovici (based on a story by Warren); ph, W. Wallace Kelly (Panavision/Metrocolor); m, Jeff Alexander; ed, Alex Beaton; art d, George W. Davis.

Western   **(PR:A   MPAA:NR)**

DAY OF THE HANGING, THE   (SEE: LAW OF THE LAWLESS, 1964)

DAY OF THE JACKAL, THE****   (1973, Brit./Fr.) Warwick/UNIV c

Edward Fox ("*The Jackal*"), Terence Alexander (*Lloyd*), Michel Auclair (*Colonel Rolland*), Alan Badel (*The Minister*), Tony Britton (*Inspector Thomas*), Denis Carey (*Casson*), Adrien Cayla-Legrand (*The President*), Cyril Cusack (*Gunsmith*), Maurice Denham (*General Colbert*), Vernon Dobtcheff (*Interrogator*), Jacques Francois (*Pascal*), Olga Georges-Picot (*Denise*), Raymond Gerome (*Flavigny*), Barrie Ingham (*St. Clair*), Derek Jacobi (*Caron*), Michel Lonsdale (*Lebel*), Jean Martin (*Wolenski*), Ronald Pickup (*Forger*), Eric Porter (*Colonel Rodin*), Anton Rodgers (*Bernard*), Delphine Seyrig (*Colette*), Donald Sinden (*Mallinson*), Jean Sorel (*Bastien-Thiry*), David Swift (*Montclair*), Timothy West (*Berthier*), Jacques Alric, Colette Berge, Edmond Barnard, Gerard Buhr, Philippe Leotard, Maurice Teynac, Van Doude, Nicolas Vobel.

A secret military organization in France believes that DeGaulle has betrayed the country by giving Algeria independence; in retaliation the organization, OAS, backs an abortive assassination on July 22, 1962. The head of OAS, an officer in the army, is caught and executed for his role in the assassination attempt. The new OAS leader, Porter, takes refuge in Austria and from there plans another assassination of President DeGaulle, this time hiring, for $500,000, one of the world's most feared professional killers, a man known only as "The Jackal," reportedly responsible for the murders of Trujillo and Lumumba. Top French police investigator Lonsdale learns the name "Jackal" from an informer in the plotter's ranks and then pieces the identity of the killer-for-hire together, learning that the name constitutes the first three letters of the assassin's first and last names, *Chacal* in French, Jackal in English, full name Charles Calthrop (Fox). Meanwhile, Fox, using a forged French passport, I.D., and driver's license, has an underground gunsmith,

Cusack, fashion a portable single-shot rifle using explosive ammunition. When the passport forger attempts to blackmail Fox, the assassin murders him. Fox is aided by Georges-Picot, the beautiful mistress of one of the high-ranking conspirators; she provides Fox with day-to-day activities of DeGaulle, all provided by her lover, a member of the President's staff. Then, using a series of disguises, Fox next slips past the roadblocks at the French border and hides out in a chateau with a wealthy blueblood, Seyrig, making love to her, then murdering her when she is of no more use to him. Once in Paris, Fox goes to a bathhouse and befriends Rodgers, pretending to respond to his homosexual advances. Once inside Rodgers' apartment, Fox kills him and uses the place to plan his final attack on Liberation Day, knowing DeGaulle will be in attendance at the festivities. Lonsdale by then also learns that Fox is in Paris and has chosen that day to murder the President of France. He saturates the ceremonial area with police on target day, August 25, 1963, but Fox, using the guise of a legless war veteran penetrates the area, getting into an apartment where he can easily shoot DeGaulle. Lonsdale and his men, however, track him down and burst into the apartment just as he has DeGaulle in his sights, shooting the fanatical assassin to death. A short time later the real Calthrop returns to his London apartment from a vacation to be seized and arrested by police. The stunned man is soon proved innocent and the identity of the real killer is never learned. This film faithfully follows the Forsyth best seller, registering frame by frame, as is director Zinnemann's style, a precise, almost painful reconstruction of the story. Fox is superb as the coldly impassionate killer and Lonsdale is properly plodding and magnificently analytical as the detective tracking him down. Although no one in the film is empathic as a human character the suspense is terrific, as the movements of the methodical killer are recorded. The lensing by Tournier is sharp and often breathtaking. The semi-documentary approach and Cayla-Legrand, an amazing doppelganger for DeGaulle enacting the role of the French president, give further suspense to an already exciting story. Zinnemann had not made a film for seven years until DAY OF THE JACKAL, his last being his Oscar-winning A MAN FOR ALL SEASONS. The director had spent more than four years and $4 million of MGM money to produce MAN'S FATE, based on the Andre Malraux novel, but the project was scrapped by new studio boss James Aubrey who felt the additional $6 million needed to finish MAN'S FATE was excessive. Cusack is outstanding as the bloodless gun-maker, asking Fox at one point: "Will you be trying for a head or chest shot?"

p, John Woolf, David Deutsch, Julien Derode; d, Fred Zinnemann; w, Kenneth Ross (based on the novel by Frederick Forsyth); ph, Jean Tournier (Technicolor); m, Georges Delerue; ed, Ralph Kemplen; art d, Willy Holt, Ernest Archer; set d, Pierre Charron, Robert Cartwright; cos, Elizabeth Haffenden, Joan Bridge, Rosine Delamare, Jean Zay, Chanel; makeup, Pierre Berroyer; spec eff, Georges Iaconelli, Cliff John Richardson.

Spy Drama   **Cas.**   **(PR:C   MPAA:PG)**

DAY OF THE LANDGRABBERS   (SEE: LAND RAIDERS, 1970)

DAY OF THE LOCUST, THE*****   (1975) 144m PAR c

Donald Sutherland (*Homer*), Karen Black (*Faye*), Burgess Meredith (*Harry*), William Atherton (*Tod*), Geraldine Page (*Big Sister*), Richard A. Dysart (*Claude Estee*), Bo Hopkins (*Earle Shoop*), Pepe Serna (*Miguel*), Lelia Goldoni (*Mary Dove*), Billy Barty (*Abe*), Jackie Haley (*Adore*), Gloria LeRoy (*Mrs. Loomis*), Jane Hoffman (*Mrs. Odlesh*), Norm Leavitt (*Mr. Odlesh*), Madge Kennedy (*Mrs. Johnson*), Ina Gould, Florence Lake (*Lee Sisters*), Margaret Willey, John War Eagle (*The Gingos*), Natalie Schafer (*Audrey Jennings*), Gloria Stroock (*Alice Estee*), Nita Talbot (*Joan*), Nicholas Cortland (*Projectionist*), Alvin Childress (*Butler*), Ann Coleman, Gyl Roland (*Girls*), Byron Paul, Virginia Baker, Roger Price, Angela Greene, Robert Oliver Ragland (*Guests at Audrey Jennings*), Paul Stewart (*Helverston*), John Hillerman (*Ned Grote*), William C. Castle (*Director*), Fred Scheiwiller (*First Assistant Director*), Wally Rose (*Second Assistant Director*), Grainger Hines (*French Lieutenant*), DeForest Covan (*Shoeshine Boy*), Michael Quinn (*Major Domo*), Robert Pine, Jerry Fogel, Dennis Dugan, David Ladd (*Apprentices*), Bob Holt (*Tour Guide*), Paul Jabara (*Nightclub Entertainer*), Queeny Smith (*Palsied Lady*), Margaret Jenkins (*Choral Director*), Jonathan Kidd (*Undertaker*), Kenny Solms (*Boy in Chapel*), Wally Berns (*Theatre Manager*), Dick Powell, Jr. (*Dick Powell*), Bill Baldwin (*Announcer at Premiere*).

Where almost all other films on Hollywood tout the glamour, the success, and the fame of that legendary Nirvana, DAY OF THE LOCUST, like West's incisive and powerful novel, focuses upon the seamy side of the street, portraying with brutal accuracy the losers, the misfits, the neurotic fringe society that hovered about the unreal core that was Hollywood in the 1930s. Black is a voluptuous aspiring actress with little talent who lives with her father, Meredith, a one-time vaudevillian who hit the skids long ago and is still sliding downward. Black realizes that her talent is limited to walk-ons and to obtain bit parts she joins a group of women who make themselves available sexually to producers, yet she continues to see herself as a legitimate actress. She is a mannequin, her gestures and demeanor nothing more than exaggerations of reigning movie queens, her conversation lifted wholly from cheap gossip columnists. Despite her transparency, Atherton, an altruistic art director, falls in love with her. She responds to his affection with typical ice-blonde remarks, such as: "I could never love a man who wasn't criminally handsome." He is simply too nice for her sluttish nature. Black not only toys with him, showering their relationship with inane platitudes, but taunts him by establishing a competitive *manage a trois* with two crude, cretinous stunt men, Serna and Hopkins. When Meredith, who has been squeezing out a living as a door-to-door salesman, dies raving about theatrical successes never his, Black is left destitute. She moves in with a sensitive but oafish accountant, Sutherland, who loves her from afar. She and all about him use and ridicule him as he lumbers through life; Sutherland is particularly vexed by an evil neighborhood child, Haley, who taunts the bumbling, large accountant at every turn. The Iowa-bred bookkeeper is finally devastated when he stumbles upon Black and Serna having sex, later weeping out his sorrow to friend Atherton: "People just won't understand that people need love." The sordid end of the film is traumatic. Attending a premiere of C.B. DeMille's THE BUCCANEER, Sutherland is cornered by Haley; he is by then in a state of shock over Black's whoring and an easy mark. The child taunts and jeers at him, causing him to explode maniacally, stomping Haley to death. Members in the crowd spot the action, one screaming hysterically "Some big creep just killed a kid!" The movie-goers suddenly turn into a mob bent on vengeance and dozens swarm, like locusts, about Sutherland, tearing him limb from limb in a gruesome execution. Atherton attempts to prevent the killing but is knocked aside, stomped on, has his leg broken. He pulls himself up to rest on the hood of car, watching helplessly as his friend is slaughtered. Atherton then hallucinates an apocalypse where the mob runs amuck, smashing windows, looting stores, overturning cars, torching the block. All about Atherton is black destruction, flames roaring and rising upward until the theater, the very essence of Hollywood society, is destroyed by fire, purged, cleansed as it were. This grim finale, along with the stark and unsavory story and characters, brought audiences to shudders and undoubtedly caused this excellent film to fail at the box office. It remains, nevertheless, one of the most brilliant productions of the 1970s, capturing precisely the mood and intent of West's masterpiece novel. Black is the perfect slattern with movie ambition—cheap, shallow, conniving, and utterly reprehensible. Sutherland gives one of his best performances ever as the doltish but sensitive outsider whose concern for films is marginal at best. The film is peopled with excellent supporting players, not the least of whom is Atherton as the ethereal art director. He is savvy to Hollywood and gives it back the banal glibness that is the hallmark of its society. At one point a successful but jaded art director, Dysart, remarks to Atherton: "You're a little too facile for your own good, but that can be an advantage out here." One character not in the novel but played to devastating accuracy is Page's "Big Sister," a duplication of the influential West Coast evangelist Aimee Semple McPherson. Another real life inspiration in West's novel is Hollywood's most infamous and successful madam, Lee Francis, one-time actress down to peddling flesh and enacted sharply by Schafer. It is to Schafer's swanky Hollywood Hills brothel that Black, Atherton and others are taken by Dysart to watch a "stag film" early on in the movie. Barty, the colorful, nasty-mouthed dwarf selling newspapers, is patterned upon a tough little character West recorded in his Hollywood Boulevard wanderings. William Castle, a real-life director of crime and horror films, renders a marvelous stereotype Hollywood director in the movie, puffing on a cigar as he oversees an epic entitled "The Battle of Waterloo," one which is lavishly and impressively mounted. Everything about THE DAY OF THE LOCUST exudes authenticity, from the costuming to the cars, from the exotic clothes to the marcelled hair styles, particularly Black's sharp finger-waves indenting her platinum blond tresses, a style painfully close to that of Jean Harlow; in fact Black is doing a cheap Harlow throughout. (She studied films of the early 1930s to learn how to mimic the mannerisms of brassy blonde bombshells.) The legend and lore of Hollywood's past is everywhere in the film but Black and company treat with it as incidental memorabilia. In one scene two characters, Greener and Hackett, go on a Hollywood tour but are so caught up in their own lives that they completely ignore a tour guide pointing out the famous "Hollywood" sign overlooking the movie Mecca (the real sign was erected in 1923 as a real estate promotion and originally read "Hollywoodland"). Nothing can intrude upon their petty conversation, not even the bizarre true-to-life tale of how a failed actress, Peg Entwistle, emotionally crushed at losing a bit part, climbed to the top of the letter H on the sign and jumped to her death in 1932. Some filmic trickery lends deeper credence to the lensing of the movie when Black, acting as if she were Garbo at the premiere of CAMILLE, takes Hopkins and Atherton to a Glendale showing of ALI BABA GOES TO TOWN, starring Eddie Cantor, a film in which Black has a walk-through part and can be seen only for a moment. This was achieved by filming new black-and-white shots of Black in an identical background to the actual 1937 Cantor film and intercutting these new shots with the original frames of the old film. Some celebrities of that Depression-haunted era are represented by doppelgangers. Dick Powell, Jr., a ringer for his father, plays Powell senior at the premiere of THE BUCCANEER. More important, the attitudes of Hollywood at that time are marvelously and chillingly put onto celluloid. In the filming-within-the film scenes of Castle directing "The Battle of Waterloo," Atherton finds that "Danger" signs have been removed from the set which is uncompleted so that production schedules can be met, the hordes of extras not told that they are risking their lives. The scaffolding collapses near the completion of the film and hundreds of extras crash through to the concrete floor of the sound stage, many seriously injured. One stretcher-laden extra, however, typifies the mass mania that gripped all who worked in the movies then when he cries out: "A broken leg is worth at least five hundred bucks!" (Paul Stewart, one of the finest character actors ever to grace the screen, portrays the studio head, disgustingly cool and impersonal to the devastating disaster on the "Battle of Waterloo" set. He sits in a chair in the studio barber shop getting a trim and ordering underlings to look into the massive accident with no more concern over the fate of his employees than a man annoyed at having to order garbage removed from the premises.) The hysterical craving for big money and fame is carried into the sub-human ending of THE DAY OF THE LOCUST, a Gotterdamerung image that seared the memory of Budd Schulberg, close friend of novelist West, whom he called "Pep." Schulberg, later a screenwriter and Hollywood chronicler, was to write in his book *The Four Seasons of Success*: "Reacting to the mass hysteria of Pep's climax. I remembered as a young teenager driving to just such a World Premiere at Grauman's Chinese Theatre as Pep described...Suddenly a fat girl who looked about sixteen broke from the crowd, ducked under the rope and jumped onto our running board. 'Who are you? Who are you?' she screamed into my face. 'I'm nobody,' I said, 'nobody.' Clinging to the running board, in a paroxysm of self-abasement, she turned her head to the crowd and shouted, 'He's nobody! Nobody! Just like us!' "

p, Jerome Hellman; d, John Schlesinger; w, Waldo Salt (based on the novel by Nathanael West); ph, Conrad Hall (Panavision, Technicolor); m, John Barry; ed, Jim Clark; prod d, Richard MacDonald; art d, John Lloyd; set d, George Hopkins; cos, Ann Roth.

Drama **Cas.** **(PR:C-O MPAA:R)**

DAY OF THE NIGHTMARE* (1965) 89m Screen Group/Herts-Lion bw

John Ireland, Elena Verdugo, John Hart, Jimmy Cross, Maralou Gray, Michael Kray, Bette Treadville, Liz Renay, Beverly Bain, Cliff Fields.

This retread of PSYCHO details the murderous impulses of a commercial artist who is suspected of killing a woman. The cops can't find the body, therefore tying their legal hands, but the man's wife is suspicious of him and attempts to find out the truth. After visiting her father-in-law, who happens to be a psychiatrist, she is confronted with the missing woman, who attempts to kill her. The mad woman's attempt fails, but the woman travels to the father-in-law's home and kills him. Just before he dies, the old man recognizes that the "woman" is his son dressed in drag. After another attempt to kill the wife, the police arrive and chase the "woman" down a dock, but the crazed artist falls into the water in front of an on-coming yacht, which kills him.

p, Leon Bleiberg; exec p, Michael Kraike; d, John Bushelman; w, Leonard Goldstein; ph, Ted V. Mikels; m, Andre Brummer.

Mystery **(PR:C MPAA:NR)**

DAY OF THE OUTLAW*** (1959) 91m Security Pictures/UA bw

Robert Ryan *(Blaise Starrett)*, Burl Ives *(Jack Bruhn)*, Tina Louise *(Helen Crane)*, Alan Marshal *(Hal Crane)*, Nehemiah Persoff *(Dan)*, Venetia Stevenson *(Ernine)*, Donald Elson *(Vic)*, Helen Wescott *(Vivian)*, Robert Cornthwaite *(Tommy)*, Jack Lambert *(Tex)*, Lance Fuller *(Pace)*, Frank DeKova *(Denver)*, Paul Wexler *(Vause)*, Jack Woody *(Shorty)*, David Nelson *(Gene)*, Arthur Space *(Clay)*, William Schallert *(Preston)*, Michael McGreevey *(Bobby)*, Dabbs Greer *(Doc Langer)*, Betty Jones Moreland *(Mrs. Preston)*, Elisha Cook *(Larry)*, Dan Sheridan *(Lewis)*, George Ross *(Clagett)*.

A stark, cold-looking western starring Ives as the savage leader of a group of Army renegades who take over a lonely town. The settlement is doomed to having its women raped and its men killed unless someone takes a stand against the outlaws. Finally, no-nonsense rancher Ryan, seeing that the townsfolk would rather let themselves be overrun than fight, reluctantly takes on Ives and his marauders, which leads to a final gunbattle between the rancher and the outlaw leader in the middle of a raging snowstorm. Ryan and Ives turn in brilliant performances and the film has an unusually powerful look in which the black-and-white photography by Russell Harlan really conveys the bleakness and isolation that is essential to the mood of the story. Worth seeing.

p, Sidney Harmon; d, Andre De Toth; w, Philip Yordan; ph, Russell Harlan; ed, Robert Lawrence.

Western **(PR:A MPAA:NR)**

DAY OF THE OWL, THE***

(1968, Ital./Fr.) 113m Euro International c (IL GIORNO DELLA CIVETTA)

Claudia Cardinale *(Rosa Nicolosi)*, Franco Nero *(Capt. Bellodi)*, Lee J. Cobb *(Don Mariano Arena)*, Gaetano Cimarosa *(Zecchinetta)*, Nehemiah Persoff *(Pizzuco)*, Serge Reggiani *(Parrinieddu)*.

Surprisingly good crime tale set in a Mafia-dominated village in Sicily. Nero plays a northern Italian police captain who is sent into the heart of mob territory to investigate the murder of a construction supplier who refused to give "The Friends" their due. Nero's efforts are constantly frustrated by the citizens' unwillingness to talk and face the wrath of the local Don, Cobb. Nero finally finds a witness willing to testify, but he soon winds up dead, leaving the man's widow, Cardinale, torn between aiding the detective or keeping her mouth shut. Nero eventually finds the assassins and has them incarcerated, but his prisoners are turned loose and he finds himself being transferred to a remote part of Italy. Cobb is great as the powerful Mafia leader, and Nero turns in a credible performance as the tireless police investigator.

p, Ermanno Donati, Luigi Carpentieri; d, Damiano Damiani; w, Damiani, Ugo Pirro (based on the novel by Leonardo Sciascia); ph, Tonino Delli Colli; m, Giovanni Fusco; ed, Nino Baragli; art d, Sergio Canevari.

Crime Drama **(PR:C MPAA:NR)**

DAY OF THE TRIFFIDS, THE*** (1963) 93m AA c

Howard Keel *(Bill Masen)*, Nicole Maurey *(Christine Durrant)*, Janette Scott *(Karen Goodwin)*, Kieron Moore *(Tom Goodwin)*, Mervyn Johns *(Prof. Coker)*, Janina Faye *(Susan)*, Alison Leggatt *(Miss Coker)*, Ewan Roberts *(Dr. Soames)*, Colette Wilde *(Nurse Jamieson)*, Carole Ann Ford *(Bettina)*, Geoffrey Matthews *(Luis)*, Gilgi Hauser *(Teresa)*, Katya Douglas *(Mary)*, Victor Brooks *(Poiret)*, Thomas Gallagher *(Burly Man)*, Sidney Vivian *(Ticket Agent)*, Gary Hope *(Pilot)*, John Simpson *(Blind Man)*.

Decent, albeit uneven, British sci-fi/horror film. Keel stars as an American sailor who has escaped being blinded by a sudden meteor shower that has robbed most of the Earth's population of its sight. The mysterious meteor storm has also brought with it alien plant spores which grow into large, carnivorous plants that multiply and threaten to overrun the planet. The man-eating plants are known as "Triffids" and resemble rampaging stalks of broccoli that have an easy time feeding off of the blind humans who can't protect themselves. Keel becomes the leader of a small band of people who have somehow escaped being blinded, and the troop travels to Spain to make a final stand against the vicious plants. Meanwhile, marine biologist Moore and his wife, Scott (who have been trapped in a lighthouse by the Triffids), discover that the vegetables are attracted by sound and can be killed by saltwater. Keel uses this information and sort of pied-pipers the nasty botanic monsters to their doom by sending them over a cliff and into the drink. Mankind has been saved, but the vast majority of the population remains blind, making one wonder what new abuses of power (by those who can see) will rise from this disaster. Always interesting but bogged down by lengthy romantic interludes, the film is thought-provoking and scary at times (the Triffids are more effective than they have any right to be). This is the third adaptation from the works of John Wyndham, the first two yielding the superb VILLAGE OF THE DAMNED (1960) and CHILDREN OF THE DAMNED (1963). For fans of the once great untrained baritone voice of Keel, it is interesting that in THE DAY OF THE TRIFFIDS he rewrote his own dialog (to give himself more range?), because he was so displeased by screenwriter Yordan's efforts.

p, George Pitcher; d, Steve Sekely, (uncredited) Freddie Francis; w, Philip Yordan (based on the novel by John Wyndham); ph, Ted Moore (Cinemascope/ Eastmancolor); m, Ron Goodwin; ed, Spencer Reeve; art d, Cedric Dawe; spec eff, Wally Veevers.

Science Fiction/Horror   Cas.   (PR:C   MPAA:NR)

DAY OF THE WOLVES   (1973) 95m Gold Key Entertainment c

Richard Egan, Rick Jason, Martha Hyer, Jan Murray.

Seven mysterious bearded men appear in an isolated town and proceed to cut off all communication with the outside while they sack the place. Egan, as the ex-sheriff of the town, comes to the rescue. Sporadically interesting heist film, but nothing audiences haven't seen before.

d, Ferde Grofe, Jr.

Crime   (PR:A-C   MPAA:NR)

DAY OF TRIUMPH*   (1954) 110m Century Films c

Lee J. Cobb (Zadok), Robert Wilson (The Christ), Ralph Freud (Caiaphas), Tyler McVey (Peter), Touch (Michael) Connors (Andrew), Toni Gerry (Cloas), Joanne Dru (Mary Magdalene), James Griffith (Judas), Everett Glass (Annas), Lowell Gilmore (Pilate), Anthony Warde (Barabbas), Peter Whitney (Nikator), John Stevenson.

The first film detailing the crucifixion and resurrection of Christ since Cecil B. DeMille's KING OF KINGS (1927). The resulting production is handsomely mounted with decent sets and costumes complemented by fine color camerawork by Ray June. Cobb is good as the leader of the Zealots, and Dru is fine as Mary Magdalene. Wilson (as do all actors playing Christ) does a good job at looking saintly and noble in this production that abounds in dignity, restraint, and distinction.

p, James K. Friedrich; d, Irving Pichel, John T. Coyle; w, Arthur T. Horman; ph, Ray June (Eastmancolor); m, Daniele Amfitheatrof; ed, Thomas Neff.

Biblical Drama/Religious   (PR:A   MPAA:NR)

DAY OF WRATH**   (1948, Den.) 97m Brandon Films bw (VREDENS DAG)

Thirkild Roose (Absalon Pedersson), Lisbeth Movin (Anne, His Wife), Sigrid Neiiendam (Meret, His Mother), Preben Lerdorff (Martin, Son by His First Marriage), Albert Hoeberg (The Bishop), Olaf Ussing (Laurentius), Anna Svierkier (Herlofs Marte).

The first feature film directed by great Danish director Carl Dreyer since his masterwork VAMPYR (1932). In DAY OF WRATH Dreyer returned to familiar territory, that of the witches, religion, and spiritualism that marked his earlier, silent masterpiece, THE PASSION OF JOAN OF ARC (1928). Set in the 17th century, the film centers around a young woman, Movin, who is married to a much older, puritanical man whom she hates. She falls in love with his son, with whom she spends idyllic afternoons in the woods. The pressure begins to build and she is heard to whisper aloud how she hungers for the death of her husband. Soon after, the husband dies, and she is accused of being a witch. She is put before an inquisition and tortured until she begins to believe that she is indeed a witch. She resigns herself to her fate and allows herself to be burned at the stake without protest. While the plot is deceptively simple, Dreyer's films are not. His pacing is slow and deliberate. He allows the camera to linger on images, waiting for the "right" look on a face, the correct movement of a hand. Uninitiated audiences find his films dull and boring, but his slowness of style is not to be misinterpreted as such. There is a power that builds in Dreyer's work and the viewer must allow himself to be drawn in to the spiritual, transcendental experience the characters are undergoing. A stark, austere masterpiece. (In Danish; English subtitles.)

p&d, Carl Dreyer; w, Dreyer, Poul Knudsen, Mogens Skot-Hansen (based on the novel by Wiers Jenssens); ph, Carl Anderson; m, Poul Schierbeck; ed, Edith Schlussel, Anne Marie Petersen.

Drama   Cas.   (PR:C   MPAA:NR)

DAY THAT SHOOK THE WORLD, THE*½
(1977, Yugo./Czech.) 111m Mundo/AIP c

Christopher Plummer (Archduke Ferdinand), Florinda Bolkan (Duchess Sophie), Maximilian Schell (Djuro Sarac), Irfan Mensur (Gavrilo Princip), Rados Bajic (Nedeljko Carbrinovic), Jan Hrusinsky, Branko Duric, Libuse Safrankova, Iana Jvandova, Otomar Korbelar, Henjo Haase.

Tedious, overlong historical drama about the assassination of the heir to the Austro-Hungarian throne and Europe's subsequent plunge into the carnage of World War I. Not terribly interesting.

d, Veljko Bulajic; w, Paul Jarrico (based on a story by Stephan Bulajic, Vladimir Bor); ph, Jan Curik (Movielab Color); m, Juan Carlos Calderon, Libus Fiser; ed, Roger Dwyre; md, Ulpio Minucci; cos, Jan Kropacedk, Branko Hundic.

Historical Drama   (PR:A-C   MPAA:PG)

DAY THE BOOKIES WEPT, THE½**   (1939) 53m RKO bw

Joe Penner (Ernest Ambrose), Betty Grable (Ina Firpo), Richard Lane (Ramsey Firpo), Tom Kennedy (Pinky Brophy), Thurston Hall (Col. March), Bernadene Hayes (Margie), Carol Hughes (Patsy March), William Wright (Harry), Prince Alert (The Horse), Emory Parnell (Cop), Vinton Haworth (Taxi Custodian), William "Billy" Newell (Maxie T. Bookmaker), Lloyd Ingraham (Race Track Patron), Paul E. Burns (Race Track Taxi Patron), Eddie Dunn, Jack Arnold.

A silly but fun programmer starring Penner as the sap chosen out of a group of taxi drivers to purchase a race horse as their collective ticket to easy street. Penner buys an alcoholic nag that runs like the wind when a few gallons of beer are poured into her. Penner proved that he could handle a lighter brand of comedy than the usual goofy slapstick roles he played, and Grable made an early appearance as his girl friend.

p, Robert Sisk; d, Leslie Goodwins; w, Bert Granet, George Jeske (based on a story by Daniel Fuchs); ph, Jack MacKenzie; ed, Desmond Marquette.

Comedy   Cas.   (PR:A   MPAA:NR)

DAY THE EARTH CAUGHT FIRE, THE*
(1961, Brit.) 99m UNIV/Pax bw

Janet Munro (Jeannie), Leo McKern (Bill Maguire), Edward Judd (Peter Stenning), Michael Goodliffe (Night Editor), Bernard Braden (News Editor), Reginald Beckwith (Harry), Gene Anderson (May), Arthur Christiansen (Editor), Austin Trevor (Sir John Kelly), Renee Asherson (Angela), Peter Butterworth (2nd Sub Editor), Charles Morgan (Foreign Editor), Edward Underdown (Sanderson), John Barron (1st Sub Editor), Geoffrey Chater (Holroyd), Ian Ellis (Michael), Jane Aird (Nanny), Robin Hawdon (Ronnie).

Fascinating Armageddon film in which a reporter, McKern, discovers that the Earth has been knocked off its axis by simultaneous nuclear bomb tests conducted on the same day by the Americans and Russians on opposite poles of the planet. Because of the different orbit, the Earth is now moving toward the sun, and it will eventually burn up (hence, the title). Most of the action takes place in the newspaper offices of the London Daily Express which lends a documentary-like quality to the proceedings as the world gets warmer and scientists sweat it out until they decide to try exploding four strategically placed nuclear bombs at the same time to restore the Earth's proper orbit. Silly premise is pulled off beautifully by Guest and Mankowitz's literate script, and Guest's fast-paced and exciting direction.

p&d, Val Guest; w, Guest, Wolf Mankowitz; ph, Harry Waxman; m, Stanley Black; ed, Bill Lenny; art d, Tony Masters; set d, Scott Slimon; cos, Beatrice Dawson; spec eff, Les Bowie.

Science Fiction   Cas.   (PR:A   MPAA:NR)

DAY THE EARTH FROZE, THE**
(1959, Fin./USSR) 67m Mosfilm-Suomi-Filmi/AIP bw (SAMPO)

U.S. Version: Nina Anderson (Anniky), Jon Powers (Lemminkainen), Ingrid Elhardt (Loukhy the Witch), Peter Sorenson (Ilmarinen), Marvin Miller (Narrator); Original Cast: Urho Somersalmi (Vainamoinen), A. Orochko (Louhi), I. Voronov (Ilmarinen), Andris Oshin (Lemminkainen), Ada Voytsik (His Mother), Eve Kivi (Annikki), Georgiy Millyar (Sorcerer), Mark Troyanovskiy (Soothsayer), L. Laurmaa, T. Rompainen, E. Hippelainen, N. Kollen, A. Barantsev, V. Uralskiy, V. Boriskin, P. Modnikov, Valentin Bryleyev, A. Macheret, A. Lenskaya.

A fantasy film based on the Finnish epic poem which details a mystical land complete with a magical mill that produces grain, salt, and gold; a witch queen who seeks to capture the mill for herself; and a dashing hero who foils the witch's plan. When the witch is denied her mill, she steals the sun, an act which covers the land with snow and ice, freezing everything. Luckily, the playing of sacred harps turns the witch to stone, thus freeing the land again. AIP took this Finnish fantasy, re-shot the dialog scenes with American actors, and tossed in narration so that no one would get too confused. Faithful presentation of the Kalevala.

U.S. Production Credits: p, Julius Strandberg; d, Gregg Sebelious; ph, Sid Roth (VistaScope); m, Otto Strode; art d, Bart Donner; cos, Ingrid Mannson; spec eff, Gerome Langstrome; Original Production Credits: d, Aleksandr Ptushko, Holger Harrivirta; w, Viktor Vitkovich, Grigoriy Yagdfeld; ph, G. Tsekaviy, V. Yakushev (Sovcolor); m, Igor Morozov; art d, L. Milchin; set d, A. Makarov; spec eff, A. Renkov, L. Dovgvillo.

Fantasy   (PR:AA   MPAA:NR)

DAY THE EARTH STOOD STILL, THE**   (1951) 92m FOX bw

Michael Rennie (Klaatu), Patricia Neal (Helen Benson), Hugh Marlowe (Tom Stevens), Sam Jaffe (Dr. Barnhardt), Billy Gray (Bobby Benson), Frances Bavier (Mrs. Barley), Lock Martin (Gort), Drew Pearson (Himself), Frank Conroy (Harley), Carleton Young (Colonel), Fay Roope (Major General), Edith Evanson (Mrs. Crockett), Robert Osterloh (Maj. White), Tyler McVey (Brady), James Seay (Government Man), John Brown (Mr. Barley), Marjorie Grossland (Hilda), Glenn Hardy (Interviewer), House Peters, Jr. (M.P. Captain), H.V. Kaltenborn (Himself), Elmer Davis (Himself), Carlton Young (Colonel), Rush Williams (M.P. Sergeant), Olan Soule (Mr. Krull), Gil Herman (Government Agent), James Craven (Businessman), Harry Lauter (Platoon Leader), Wheaton Chambers (Jeweler), Dorothy Neumann (Barnhardt's Secretary), George Lynn (Col. Ryder), Freeman Lusk (Gen. Cutler), John Burton (British Radio M.C.), George Reeves (Newscaster), Harry Harvey (Taxi Driver).

Robert Wise's science-fiction classic based on Harry Bates' story, "Farewell to the Master," adapted in a beautiful, literate script by Edmund H. North. Plot sees Rennie, a Christ-like figure, descending into Washington, D.C., in his spaceship, accompanied by his massive robot, Gort. He was sent by a federation of planets to warn Earth to stop its foolish nuclear testing or it will be destroyed. American soldiers stupidly shoot the intruder from another planet, and Gort destroys them. Rennie, wounded, stops the robot from destroying the planet by uttering the now-classic phrase "Klaatu barada nikto." Rennie is taken to a military hospital where he escapes, disguised as a normal human, and seeks shelter in Neal's boarding house to examine what earthlings are really like. Since he can make no formal contact with the governments of Earth, Rennie arranges a demonstration of his power through sympathetic scientist Jaffe, who organizes a worldwide array of scientists to watch the display. Rennie returns to his spaceship and proves his power by shutting off all electrically powered machinery, worldwide, for one hour. After finally getting the world's attention, Rennie gives a powerful, eloquent warning to the peoples of Earth to curb their war-like ways or suffer the consequences. Upon saying his piece, he re-enters his spaceship, leaving Gort on Earth to watch over Earth's behavior, and disappears into space. Superb performances by all involved, restrained direction by Wise, and a magnificent score by Bernard Herrmann help keep this 35-year-old film just as relevant today as it was the day it was released.

p, Julian Blaustein; d, Robert Wise; w, Edmund H. North (based on a story by Harry Bates); ph, Leo Tover; m, Bernard Herrmann; ed, William Reynolds; art d, Lyle Wheeler, Addison Hehr; spec eff, Fred Sersen.

Science Fiction				**Cas.**			**(PR:A MPAA:NR)**

DAY THE FISH CAME OUT, THE*
(1967, Brit./Gr.) 109m International Classics c

Tom Courtenay (Navigator), Sam Wanamaker (Elias), Colin Blakely (Pilot), Candice Bergen (Electra), Ian Ogilvy (Peter), Dimitris Nicolaidis (Dentist), Nikos Alexiou (Goatherd), Patrick Burke (Mrs. Mauroyannis), Paris Alexander (Fred), Arthur Mitchell (Frank), Marlena Carrere (Goatherd's Wife), Tom Klunis (Mr. French), William Berger (Man in Bed), Kostas Papakonstantinou (Manolios), Dora Stratou (Travel Agent), Alexander Lykourezos (Director of Tourism), Tom Whitehead (Mike), Walter Granecki (Base Commander), Demetris Loakimides (Policeman), Lynn Bryant, James Connolly, Assaf Dayan, Robert Killian, Derek Kulai, Alexis Mantheakis, Raymond McWilliams, Michael Radford, Peter Robinson, Grigoris Stefanides, James Smith, Peter Stratful, Kosta Timvios, Herbert Zeichner (Tourists).

Silly and pretentious nuclear disaster drama from the director of ZORBA THE GREEK (1964), Cacoyannis. Two NATO airmen, Blakely and Courtenay, accidentally drop their payload of H-bombs *and* a doomsday-type device into the sea near a small Greek island. The pilots ditch their plane in the sea and swim to shore to call their superiors. They arrive on the beach clad only in their underwear, which makes it difficult for them to find a phone. It doesn't matter because the government knows of the accident anyway and has dispatched an agent, Wanamaker, and his men to the island posing as hotel experts looking to expand their operations in the area. While this cover provides Wanamaker with mobility, it also causes a mad rush of interest in the island and hundreds of tourists stampede the place, making his mission more difficult. Among the visitors is an archeological assistant, Bergen, who promptly has an affair with one of the agents, Ogilvy. It becomes apparent that something is wrong on the island when thousands of dead fish float to the surface of the steadily blackening sea. The tourists, realizing they are all going to die, suddenly begin dancing with abandon on the beach (Bergen being the standout in this sequence), all of them wearing stupid-looking, futuristic swimwear designed by the director. In the end, the island blows up. The film is an uneasy mess of farce, allegory, drama, and surrealism that becomes laughable due to lousy dialog and bad performances by a cast which doesn't seem to know *what* is going on.

p,d&w, Michael Cacoyannis; ph, Walter Lassally (DeLuxe Color); m, Mikis Theodorakis; ed Vassilis Syropoulos; art d, Spyros Vassiliou; ch, Arthur Mitchell.

Drama							**(PR:C MPAA:NR)**

DAY THE HOTLINE GOT HOT, THE*½ (1968, Fr./Span.) 102m Commonwealth United/AIP c (LE ROUBLE A DEUX FACES; EL RUBLO DE LAS DOS CARAS; AKA: THE HOT LINE)

Charles Boyer (Vostov, Head of Russian Secret Police), Robert Taylor (Anderson, Chief of American CIA), George Chakiris (Eric Ericson, Computer Expert with IBM), Marie Dubois (Natasha), Gerard Tichy (Truman), Marta Grau, Irene D'Astrea, Josefina Tapias (The Three Old Ladies), Maurice de Canonge (Director of the Hotel), Gustavo Rey (Police Chief), Oscar Pellicer, Frank Oliveras.

Taylor and Boyer star in this espionage comedy pitting them against each other as rival agents (American and Russian) who are double-crossed by double-agent Tichy whom they both employ. Embroiled in this mess is an innocent IBM computer operator, Chakiris, and Dubois, the telephone operator at the hot-line center in Stockholm. A poor film and a sad ending to the career of Taylor, who was stricken with lung cancer soon after filming was completed and died the next year.

p, Francisco Balcasar; d, Etienne Perier; w, Paul Jarrico, Dominique Fabre, Guerdon Trueblood; ph, Manuel Berenguer (Eastmancolor); m, Paul Misraki; ed, Teresa Alcocer, Renee Lichtig; art d, Juan Alberto Soler.

Spy Drama/Comedy					**(PR:A MPAA:NR)**

DAY THE SCREAMING STOPPED, THE
(SEE: COMEBACK, THE, 1982, Brit.)

DAY THE SKY EXPLODED, THE*½ (1958, Fr./Ital.) 85m Lux-CCF Lux-Royal Film/Excelsior bw (LA MORTE VIENE DALLA SPAZIO; LE DANGER VIENT DE L'ESCAPE; AKA: DEATH FROM OUTER SPACE)

Paul Hubschmid (John MacLaren), Madeleine Fischer (Katy Dandridge), Fiorella Mari (Mary MacLaren), Ivo Garrani (Herbert Weisser), Dario Michaelis (Pierre Leducq), Sam Galter (Randowsky), Jean-Jacques Delbo (Sergei Boetnikov), Peter Meersman (Gen. Wandorf), Massimo Zeppieri (Dennis MacLaren), Giacomo Rossi Stuart, Annie Berval, Gerard Landry.

Ineffective sci-fi outing starring Hubschmid as an astronaut sent on a joint U.S., USSR, and British rocket launch from Australia. In space, something goes wrong,

forcing Hubschmid to abandon ship and return to Earth. Unfortunately, the rocket continues on its path and smashes into the Sun, sending asteroids spinning toward the Earth and causing the face of the planet to shift. While the populace tries to contend with tidal waves, heat waves, and earthquakes, scientists try to figure out a way to prevent the asteroids from slamming into an already chaotic planet. They eventually talk all the world governments into making a combined effort to send atomic missiles into space to destroy the incoming asteroids.

p, Guido Giambartolomei; d, Paolo Heusch; w, Marcello Coscia, Alessandro Continenza (story by Virgilio Sabel); ph, Mario Bava; m, Carlo Rustichelli; ed, Otello Colangeli; art d, Beni Montresor.

Science Fiction					**(PR:A MPAA:NR)**

DAY THE SUN ROSE, THE**½ (1969, Jap.) 81m Nihon Eiga Fukko Kyokai/Shochiku Films of America c (GION MATSURI)

Kinnosuke Nakamura (Shinkichi), Toshiro Mifune (Kuma), Shima Iwashita (Ayame), Yunosuke Ito (Akamatsu), Takahiro Tamura (Sukematsu), Takashi Shimura (Tsuneemon), Eitaro Ozawa (Kadokura), Kamatari Fujiwara.

The action takes place in 16th-century Japan in the town of Kyoto, which has been split politically by a large tax on food, with the farmers pitted against the wealthy townspeople. Mifune organizes a group of peasants to help the farmers, and the townspeople have hired samurai. The farmers defeat the townspeople and the samurai flee. Nakamura organizes the farmers and townspeople to work together to fight the high tax. The tax is raised even higher and Nakamura gets Mifune to have his peasants bring food into the town. A festival is organized to illustrate the farmers' and townspeoples' desire for peace.

d, Tetsuya Yamanouchi; w, Hisayuki Suzuki, Kunio Shimizu.

Action Drama					**(PR:A MPAA:NR)**

DAY THE WAR ENDED, THE**½ (1961, USSR) 90m Gorky Film Studio/Artkino bw (PERVYY DEN MIRA; AKA: THE FIRST DAY OF PEACE)

Valeriy Vinogradov (Mikhail Platonov), Lyudmila Butenina (Olya), Pyotr Shcherbakov (Capt. Nefyodov), A. Vovsi (Surgeon), G. Dunts (Colonel), Lyudmila Ovchinnikova (Natasha), I. Pushkaryov (Petya Kovalyov), A. Fayt (Old German), N. Menshikova (Frau Fisher), Kh. Braun (SS Officer), A. Temerin (Priest), V. Zakharchenko (Fisher), Yu. Fomichyov (Semyonych, the Orderly), E. Knausmyuller (Kuntse), Galya Karakulova, A. Danilova, S. Yurtaykin, Ye. Kudryashov, V. Korneyev, A. Vasilyev, A. Sezemann, V. Chumak, R. Daglish.

Vinogradov is an interpreter with the Russian army in the closing days of WW II. Assigned to secure the surrender of a group of Germans holed up in a church, he approaches the building with a white flag, while inside three SS men decide to go on fighting. A flashback shows Vinogradov earlier that day meeting and falling in love with Butenina, a field nurse. They plan to be married after the war, but the SS men shoot him down. Competent, but strangely static, filled with long periods where the actors just stand around looking noble.

d, Yakov Segel; w, Iosif Olshanskiy, Nina Rudneva; ph, Boris Monastyrskiy; m, M. Fradkin; ed, L. Rodionova; art d, Boris Dulenkov; cos, Ye. Aleksandrova; lyrics, Yu. Kamenetskiy, V. Lazarev.

War Drama					**(PR:A-C MPAA:NR)**

DAY THE WORLD CHANGED HANDS, THE
(SEE: COLOSSUS: THE FORBIN PROJECT, THE, 1970)

DAY THE WORLD ENDED, THE** (1956) 78m AIP bw

Richard Denning (Rick), Lori Nelson (Louise), Adele Jergens (Ruby), Touch (Mike) Connors (Tony), Paul Birch (Maddison), Raymond Hatton (Pete), Paul Dubov (Radek), Jonathan Haze (Contaminated Man), Paul Blaisdell (Mutant).

Roger Corman's first sci-fi film launched American International to exploitation success. Brought in at a cost of $65,000, the movie concerned itself with the aftermath of "T.D. Day" (Total Destruction), the day of a complete nuclear holocaust. Seven survivors—Birch, his daughter Nelson, geologist Denning, gangster Connors, and his moll, Jergens, scientist Hatton, and terminal radiation case Dubov—form an uneasy alliance as they make their way to a mountain retreat. Along the way they notice how the forest and animals have mutated due to the radiation. The obvious tension between the parties is overshadowed by the larger threat that looms outside the shelter when it is invaded by cannibalistic, three-eyed, four-armed, telepathic mutants with horns, led by Blaisdell. Silly but fun.

p&d, Roger Corman; w, Lou Russoff (based on a story by Russoff); ph, Jock Feindel; m, Ronald Stein; ed, Ronald Sinclair; spec eff, Paul Blaisdell.

Science Fiction					**(PR:A MPAA:NR)**

DAY THEY ROBBED THE BANK OF ENGLAND, THE**½
(1960, Brit.) 85m MGM bw

Aldo Ray (Norgate), Elizabeth Sellars (Iris Muldoon), Hugh Griffith (O'Shea), Peter O'Toole (Fitch), Kieron Moore (Walsh), Albert Sharpe (Tosher), John Le Mesurier (Green), Joseph Tomelty (Cohoun), Wolf Frees (Dr. Hagen), Miles Malleson (Assistant Curator), Michael Golden (Gamekeeper), Peter Myers (Piers), Andrew Keir (Sergeant of the Guard), Michael Brennan (Walters), Colin Gordon (Benge), Erik Chitty (Gudgeon), Frederick Piper, Charles Lloyd-Pack.

Disappointing caper film set in 1901 stars Ray as the leader of a faction of the IRA that plans to rob the Bank of England. The plan requires that the gang renovate a sewer that runs under the stronghold and use it as a tunnel into the vault. The plan almost works, but the gang is captured by young bank guard O'Toole (in an early role). Good idea for a robbery movie, but Ray is badly miscast.

p, Jules Buck; d, John Guillermin; w, Howard Clewes, Richard Maibaum (based on the novel by John Brophy); ph, Georges Perinal (Metroscope); m, Edwin Astley; ed, Frank Clarke.

Crime					**(PR:A MPAA:NR)**

DAY TIME ENDED, THE*½ (1980, Span.) 80m Compass International/Manson International/Vortex (AKA: VORTEX)

Jim Davis *(Grant)*, Chris Mitchum *(Richard)*, Dorothy Malone *(Ana)*, Marcy Lafferty *(Beth)*, Natasha Ryan *(Jenny)*, Scott Kolden *(Steve)*.

Overly ambitious low-budget sci-fi film starring Davis as the head of a family who has just moved into a modern, solar-powered home. At the same time, Earth experiences the effects of a trinary super-nova (three stars exploding simultaneously), which cause strange things to happen in the Davis home. Tiny aliens appear to daughter Ryan, and then a small spaceship arrives. Soon it is discovered that the house has entered a time-space warp, which probably explains the dinosaurs fighting in the back yard. The Davis family is treated to a Close Encounterish light show and the family wanders over the hill into the "City of Light." The effects are poor, especially the stop-motion animation which obviously needed more time and money spent on it. The whole movie is entirely derivative of other films, from THE WIZARD OF OZ (1939) to CLOSE ENCOUNTERS OF THE THIRD KIND (1977). Filmed once before in 1978 as TIME WARP.

p, Wayne Schmidt, Steve Neill, Paul W. Gentry; d, John "Bud" Cardos; w, Schmidt, J. Larry Carroll, David Schmoeller (based on a story by Neill); ph, John A. Morrill (Panavision, Metrocolor); m, Richard Band; ed, Ted Nicolaou; art d, Rusty Rosene; spec eff; Gentry, David Allen, Randy Cook, Peter Kuran, Rich Bennette.

Science Fiction Cas. (PR:A MPAA:PG)

DAY-TIME WIFE*** (1939) 71m FOX bw

Tyrone Power *(Ken Norton)*, Linda Darnell *(Jane)*, Warren William *(Dexter)*, Binnie Barnes *(Blanche)*, Wendy Barrie *(Kitty)*, Joan Davis *(Miss Applegate)*, Joan Valerie *(Mrs. Dexter)*, Leonid Kinskey *(Coco)*, Mildred Gover *(Melbourne)*, Renie Riano *(Mrs. Briggs)*, Robert Lowery, David Newell *(Bits)*, Otto Han *(House Boy)*, Marie Blake *(Western Union Girl)*, Mary Gordon *(Scrubwoman)*, Alex Pollard *(Waiter)*, Frank Coghlan, Jr. *(Office Boy)*.

According to her published date of birth, gorgeous Linda Darnell was only eighteen when she made this film and played Power's wife of two years. This was Power's fifth film of 1939 and a step in the right direction as he'd been so associated with heroic-type films, so it was quite right for him to expand into comedy. Power is a roofing executive who calls wife Darnell and tells her that he'll be home late that night (their second anniversary) as he has to toil late at the office. Some lipstick is present on his collar so Darnell consults pal Barnes, who's been married three times, and Binnie tells Darnell to give the cad a dose of his own medicine. Darnell takes a job with Warren William, an architect with a good eye for structures, both concrete and flesh. Davis, the receptionist, warns Darnell about William's roaming hands with some funny lines. No one at the office knows Darnell is married or that William is one of Power's clients. One night, Darnell goes out to dinner with William (to make Power jealous), and they run into Power and secretary Barrie. It all becomes veddy Noel Coward as they go to William's penthouse. Then William's wife, Valerie, arrives and the party breaks up. Darnell invites Power and Barrie to spend the night at their apartment but Barrie leaves, and the marriage is saved when Power sees the folly of his ways. Pretty strong stuff for the 1939 era when Gable couldn't even say "I don't give a damn" in GONE WITH THE WIND without starting a controversy. Perhaps the censors were looking the other way when Zanuck slipped this picture past them. It is a funny script with very tight direction by Power's pal, Gregory Ratoff, who will also be recalled for his excellent acting jobs in such films as ALL ABOUT EVE, EXODUS, and scores more. He also directed INTERMEZZO—A LOVE STORY and THE CORSICAN BROTHERS. Four years after this, Darnell married the cameraman, Marley.

p, Darryl F. Zanuck; d, Gregory Ratoff; w, Art Arthur, Robert Harari (based on a story by Rex Taylor); ph, Peverell Marley; ed, Francis Lyons; md, Cyril Mockridge; art d, Richard Day, Joseph Wright; set d, Thomas Little; cos, Royer.

Comedy (PR:A-C MPAA:NR)

DAY TO REMEMBER, A*** (1953, Brit.) 92m GFD bw

Stanley Holloway *(Charley Porter)*, Donald Sinden *(Jim Carver)*, Joan Rice *(Vera Mitchell)*, Odile Versois *(Martine Berthier)*, James Hayter *(Fred Collins)*, Harry Fowler *(Stan Harvey)*, Edward Chapman *(Mr. Robinson)*, Peter Jones *(Percy Goodall)*, Bill Owen *(Shorty Sharpe)*, Meredith Edwards *(Bert Tripp)*, George Coulouris *(The Captain)*, Vernon Gray *(Marvin)*, Thora Hird *(Mrs. Trott)*, Theodore Bikel *(Henri Dubot)*, Brenda de Banzie *(Mrs. Collins)*, Lilly Kahn *(Grandmere)*, Arthur Hill *(Al)*, Patricia Raine *(May)*, Marianne Stone *(Shorty's Girl)*, Harold Lang, Germaine Delbat, Robert Le Beal, Georgette Anys, Marcel Poncin, Jacques Cey, Jacqueline Robert, Richard Molinas.

Gentle tale detailing the road trip of a British dart team to an area of France where many of the players had served in the war. In the most sentimental segment, one dart player meets the little girl who had taught him French songs during the war, and now she has grown into a beautiful young woman. Touching and pleasant drama.

p, Betty E. Box; d, Ralph Thomas; w, Robin Estridge (based on the novel *The Hand and Flower* by Jerrard Tickell); ph, Ernest Steward; m, Clifton Parker; ed, Gerald Thomas; art d, Maurice Carter; cos, Yvonne Caffin.

Drama (PR:A MPAA:NR)

DAY WILL COME, A** (1960, Ger.) 91m Casino bw (ES KOMMT EIN TAG)

Dieter Borsche *(Friedrich)*, Maria Schell *(Madeline)*, Lil Dagover *(Mme. Mombour)*, Herbert Huebner, Gustav Knuth, Renate Mannhardt, Gerd Martienzen, Ernst Legal, Else Ehser, Alfred Schieske, Wilhelm Meyer-Ottens, Hans Mahnke, Norbert Zeuner.

During the Franco-Prussian War of 1870, Borsche is a German soldier who kills a French officer. Stricken with guilt, he goes through the man's pockets and learns his name. Later while going through a French village, he sees the man's name on a door. Knocking, he finds Dagover and daughter Schell awaiting the return of the dead soldier. Dagover thinks that Borsche looks like her son so she asks him to stay. Schell and Borsche fall in love and he tells her that he killed her brother. Schell begs him not to to tell the now-dying Dagover and later she convinces him to put on her dead brother's uniform and go to Dagover's bedside. Minutes later he goes out on the street still in the French uniform and is shot dead by Prussian troops. Interesting, occasionally successful drama has some good performances.

p, Rolf Tbiele, Hans Abich; d, Rudolph Jugert; w (based on the novel *Corporal Mombour* by Ernest Penzoldt).

Drama (PR:A MPAA:NR)

DAY WILL DAWN, THE (SEE: AVENGERS, THE, 1942)

DAYBREAK*½ (1931) 73m MGM bw

Ramon Novarro *(Willi)*, Helen Chandler *(Laura)*, Jean Hersholt *(Herr Schnabel)*, C. Aubrey Smith *(Gen. von Hartz)*, William Bakewell *(Otto)*, Karen Morley *(Emily Kessner)*, Kent Douglass *(Von Lear)*, Glenn Tryon *(Franz)*, Clyde Cook *(Josef)*, Sumner Getchell *(Emil)*, Clara Blandick *(Frau Hoffman)*, Edwin Maxwell *(Herr Hoffman)*, Jackie Searle *(August)*.

Overwrought, complicated melodrama starring Novarro as a pre-war Austrian lieutenant who gets himself in debt (where the honorable solution is to repay it in cash or put a bullet in your head) to Hersholt. Novarro also feels responsible for the fate of Hersholt's mistress, Chandler, an innocent piano teacher until she met Novarro one night at a bar and he got her drunk. After their breakup she took up with Hersholt. Finding no other honorable way out, Novarro is about to put a bullet in his brain when his uncle coughs up the money and bails him out. Novarro pays his debt, quits the service, and runs off with Chandler to make a new life. The great Austrian playwright stylist Arthur Schnitzler, from whose play DAYBREAK was made, died the year the film came out at the age of 69. Subsequently, four more of his witty, lightly amoral plays would be made into movies.

d, Jacques Feyder; w, Ruth Cummings, Cyril Hume, Zelda Sears (based on a play by Arthur Schnitzler); ph, Merritt B. Gerstad; ed, Tom Held.

Drama (PR:A MPAA:NR)

DAYBREAK***** (1940, Fr.) 88m Productions Sigma/A.F.E. bw (LE JOUR SE LEVE)

Jean Gabin *(Francois)*, Jules Berry *(M. Valentin)*, Jacqueline Laurent *(Francoise)*, Arletty *(Clara)*, Rene Genin *(Concierge)*, Mady Berry *(Concierge's Wife)*, Bernard Blier *(Gaston)*, Marcel Peres *(Paulo)*, Jacques Baumer *(The Inspector)*, Rene Bergeron *(Cafe Proprietor)*, Gabrielle Fontan *(Old Woman)*, Arthur Devere *(Mons. Gerbois)*, Georges Douking *(Blind Man)*, Germaine Lix *(Singer)*.

One of the most superb and striking examples of French "poetic realism," and certainly the finest of that country's films of the '30s (it was released in 1939 in Paris, just months before the Occupation). Gabin, in perhaps his finest performance, is a tough, romantic loner who barricades himself in his apartment after murdering, in a crime of passion, the lecherous J. Berry. While the police surround his Normandy dwelling, Gabin slips into three flashbacks involving the two women he loved—Laurent and Arletty—and J. Berry, who wooed both. His first flashback is his meeting with Laurent at the factory where he works. He is soon speaking of marriage, but upon following her one evening to a nightclub, spots her leaving with J. Berry, who performs a delightful poodle act. His assistant, Arletty, is drawn to Gabin. When Berry returns, he makes a play for Arletty, bringing an angry reaction from Gabin. Back in the apartment, Gabin prevents the police from storming his room by placing a large Norman wardrobe in front of the door. His second flashback occurs after he and Arletty have begun their romance, though he is still involved with Laurent. Berry and Gabin meet in a bar, and Berry claims that he is Laurent's father in an attempt to break up the relationship. Laurent denies the claim and professes her love to Gabin, presenting him with a brooch. Later, while trying to end his romance with Arletty, she shows him an identical brooch which she received from Berry, who gives them to all his mistresses. It is nearly daybreak as the neighbors try to coax Gabin out of his room. In the final flashback, J. Berry is nearly thrown from a window after an argument with Gabin over Laurent. The situation relaxes and the pair sit down to talk, but Berry continues to insult Gabin and degrade Laurent. Gabin picks up a pistol and kills Berry. Back in the apartment the leather-jacketed Gabin is stalked by officers armed with tear gas. Without hope, or love, or the will to live, Gabin points the revolver at his heart and fires. As he lies on the floor, clouds of gas rise above him, while from the window daylight streams across the room. While all facets of this film's production are masterful, perhaps the most awe-inspiring is the set design of Alexandre Trauner, whose re-creation of a city street corner decorated with Dubonnet posters is one of the most memorable in film. Due to the political events of the time, the French military censor banned the picture as "demoralizing," though it saw wide international release and in 1952 was named one of the top ten films of all time by the prestigious Sight and Sound poll. (Remade as THE LONG NIGHT.)

d, Marcel Carne; w, Jacques Prevert, Jacques Viot; ph, Curt Courant; m, Maurice Jaubert; ed, Rene le Henaff; set d, Alexandre Trauner; cos, Boris Bilinsky.

Drama (PR:A MPAA:NR)

DAYBREAK** (1948, Brit.) 81m GFD bw

Eric Portman *(Eddie)*, Ann Todd *(Frankie)*, Maxwell Reed *(Olaf)*, Edward Rigby *(Bill Shackle)*, Bill Owen *(Ron)*, Jane Hylton *(Doris)*, Eliot Makeham *(Mr. Bigley)*, Margaret Withers *(Mrs. Bigley)*, John Turnbull *(Superintendent)*, Maurice Denham *(Inspector)*, Milton Rosther *(Governor)*, Lyn Evans *(Waterman)*.

Depressing melodrama starring Portman as a hangman out of work who marries Todd after meeting her in a bar. The couple live on a barge and when Portman returns home unexpectedly to find his wife and a handsome longshoreman, Reed, in a compromising situation, there is a fight and Portman is knocked overboard and disappears. Todd commits suicide and Reed is arrested for the murder and sentenced to death. Little does anyone know that Portman has survived his dip in the drink, and now finds himself the hangman of Reed. At the last moment, Portman reveals that he is alive, saving Reed from having his neck snapped by the state. Rather labored.

p, Sydney Box; d, Compton Bennett; w, Muriel and Sydney Box (based on a play by Monckton Hoffe); ph, Reginald H. Wyer; m, Ben Frankel; ed, Helga Cranston, Peter Price; art d, James Carter; cos, Dorothy Sinclair.

Crime (PR:C-O MPAA:NR)

DAYDREAMER, THE*** (1966) 101m Embassy c

Paul O'Keefe (Hans Christian Andersen), Jack Gilford (Papa Andersen), Ray Bolger (The Pieman), Margaret Hamilton (Mrs. Klopplebobbler), Robert Harter (Big Claus). Voices: Cyril Ritchard (The Sandman), Hayley Mills (The Little Mermaid), Burl Ives (Father Neptune), Tallulah Bankhead (The Sea Witch), Terry-Thomas (1st Tailor: Brigadier), Victor Borge (2nd Tailor: Zebro), Ed Wynn (The Emperor), Patty Duke (Thumbelina), Boris Karloff (The Rat), Sessue Hayakawa (The Mole). Robert Goulet (The Singer).

Live action combined with the Animagic process (stop-motion puppets) created this fantasy which has a young Hans Christian Andersen (O'Keefe) daydream some of his best fables. Nice songs and good voice talents for the animated characters, all presented with style and imagination, make this a rare outing for children. Songs and voices: "The Daydreamer" (Robert Goulet), "Wishes and Teardrops" (Haley Mills), "Luck To Sell" (Paul O'Keefe), "Happy Guy" (Patty Duke), "Who Can Tell" (Ray Bolger), "Simply Wonderful" (Ed Wynn, Chorus of Ministers), "Isn't It Cozy Here" (Sessue Hayakawa).

p, Arthur Rankin, Jr.; d, Jules Bass; w, Rankin (based on the stories "The Little Mermaid," "The Emperor's New Clothes," "Thumbelina," "The Garden of Paradise" by Hans Christian Andersen); ph, Daniel Cavelli, Tad Mochinaga (Animagic, Eastmancolor); m, Maury Laws; art d, Maurice Gordon; m/1, Laws, Bass.

Fantasy (PR:AAA MPAA:NR)

DAYDREAMER, THE** (1975, Fr.) 80m GAU-International-La Gueville-Madeleine/GAU c (LE DISTRAIT, AKA: ABSENT-MINDED)

Pierre Richard (Pierre), Bernard Blier (Guiton), Maria Pacome (Glycia), Pierre Preboist (Klerdene), Maria-Christine Barrault (Lisa), Catherine Samie (Clarisse), Robert Dalban (Mazelin).

Okay French comedy has Richard (best known as THE TALL BLONDE MAN WITH ONE BLACK SHOE) a bumbling idiot at an advertising agency who nevertheless finds success and romance. A number of gags are lifted out of Tati's films, but the film does have its moments.

p&d, Pierre Richard; w, Richard, Andre Ruelan; ph, Daniel Vogel (Eastmancolor); m, Vladimir Cosma; ed, Marie-Josephe Yoyotte; art d, Michel De Broin.

Comedy (PR:A MPAA:NR)

DAYLIGHT ROBBERY** (1964, Brit.) 57m Viewfinder/CFF bw

Trudy Moors (Trudy), Janet Hannington (Janet), Kirk Martin (Kirk), Darryl Read (Darryl), Douglas Robinson (Gangster), John Trenaman (Gangster), Janet Munro, Zena Walker, Patricia Burke, James Villiers, Norman Rossington, Gordon Jackson, Ronald Fraser.

Four children are accidentally locked in a department store over a weekend and they manage to capture a gang of bank robbers. Okay children's film with a surprisingly talented adult cast.

p, John Davis; d, Michael Truman; w, Dermot Quinn (based on a story by Frank Wells).

Children (PR:AA MPAA:NR)

DAYS AND NIGHTS**½ (1946, USSR) 58m Artkino bw (DNI I NOCHI)

Vladimir Soloviev (Capt. Saburov), Dmitri Sagal (Vanin), Yuri Liubimoff (Lt. Maslennikov), Anna Lisyanskaya (Anya Klimenko), Lev Sverdlin (Col. Alexander Protsenko) Mikhail Derjavin (Gen. Matveyev), Vassili Kliucharev (Col. Sergei Remizov), Andrei Alexeyev (Petya).

Russian view of the battle for Stalingrad. Lots of battle footage interrupted by scenes of the soldiers' love for their country shown by their sentimental singing and drinking. Shot in the wartime ruins of Stalingrad, the defense of which broke the back of the Nazis in the East. (In Russian; English subtitles.)

d, Alexander Stolper; w, Konstantine Simonov (based on a novel by Simonov); ph, Yevgeni Andrikanis; m, Nikolai Kryukov; art d, Mauritz Umansky.

War (PR:C MPAA:NR)

DAYS OF BUFFALO BILL** (1946) 56m REP bw

Sunset Carson, Peggy Stewart, Tom London, James Craven, Rex Lease, Edmund Cobb, Eddie Parker, Michael Sloane, Jay Kirby, George Chesebro, Edward Cassidy, Frank O'Connor, Jess Cavan.

Cowboy Carson thinks he has killed a young hothead in a fight, and driven by guilt he goes to the dead man's sister's ranch and helps her out while using an alias. He saves her ranch from rustlers but she discovers that he is the killer of her brother. She wounds him in the shoulder before he disarms her, then she overhears the real killer bragging about his crime and Carson subdues him. Decent series Western.

d, Thomas Carr; w, William Lively, Doris Schroeder; ph, Alfred Keller; ed, Tony Martinelli; md, Richard Cherwin; art d, Fred A. Ritter.

Western (PR:A MPAA:NR)

DAYS OF GLORY**½ (1944) 86m RKO bw

Tamara Toumanova (Nina), Gregory Peck (Vladimir), Alan Reed (Sasha), Maria Palmer (Yelena), Lowell Gilmore (Semyon), Hugo Haas (Fedor), Dena Penn (Olga), Glenn Vernon (Mitya), Igor Dolgoruki (Dimitri), Edward L. Durst (Petrov), Lou Crosby (Johann Staub), William Challee (Ducrenko), Joseph Vitale (Seminov), Erford Gage (Col. Prilenko), Ivan Triesault (German Lieutenant), Maria Bibikov (Vera), Edgar Licho (Anton), Gretl Dupont (Mariya), Peter Helmers (Von Rundhol).

Director Jacques Tourneur's first big-budget picture, which Warner Bros. intended as a showcase for its new, unknown talent (including Peck who had just arrived from Broadway) was a daring and expensive exercise in realism. Plot concerns Peck as the leader of a group of Soviet guerrillas fighting the Nazis during WW II. Romance develops between Peck and Toumanova, and the lovers die together during the big Russian counter-offensive against the Nazis. Casey Robinson's attempt at achieving realism by using actors and actresses never before seen on the screen flopped for just that reason—the absence of marquee names. Toumanova was the former prima ballerina of the Ballet Russe de Monte Carlo and unknown to filmgoers, and she was scolded by reviewers for her bad acting in her first picture. She went on to make four more films before retiring and marrying the producer.

p, Casey Robinson; d, Jacques Tourneur; w, Robinson (based on a story by Melchoir Lengyel); ph, Tony Gu Gaudio; m, Constantin Bakaleinikoff; ed, Joseph Noriega.

War Drama (PR:A MPAA:NR)

DAYS OF HEAVEN***** (1978) 95m PAR c

Richard Gere (Bill), Brooke Adams (Abby), Sam Shepard (The Farmer), Linda Manz (Linda), Robert Wilke (Farm Foreman), Jackie Shultis (Linda's Friend), Stuart Margolin (Mill Foreman), Tim Scott (Harvest Hand), Gene Bell (Dancer), Doug Kershaw (Fiddler), Richard Libertini (Vaudeville Leader), Frenchie Lemond (Vaudeville Wrestler), Sahbra Markus (Vaudeville Dancer), Bob Wilson (Accountant), Muriel Jolliffe (Headmistress), John Wilkinson (Preacher), King Cole (Farm Worker).

Set in the post-industrial revolution America of the early 1900s. DAYS OF HEAVEN chronicles the odyssey of a rootless migrant laborer, Gere, his little sister, Manz, and his girlfriend and soul-mate, Adams, as they flee the industrial blight of the city for the sanctuary and anonymity of the heartland. When the impulsive and hot-tempered Gere kills a steel mill foreman in anger, the three jump and head for the plains of Texas, merging themselves with the endless caravan of homeless immigrants looking for work. Their journey brings them to the land of wealthy, self-made wheat farmer Shepard, who offers them employment during the harvest. Shepard is an enigmatic figure, living alone in a huge Victorian mansion that overlooks his golden empire, who is slowly wasting away from some strange illness. As he watches Adams work in the fields, he grows to love her and sees some private salvation in making her his "queen." Gere learns of the farmer's illness, and reasons that he will be dead soon. He and Adams contrive to masquerade as brother and sister, thus encouraging the farmer to marry Adams and plant the seeds of a future inheritance. For a time after the marriage, the four live together as family in a state of grace and sublime happiness. The scheme goes foul, however, when Adams begins to love Shepard and divorces herself from Gere. Like a spurned Heathcliff, Gere leaves the farm to seek his fortune in the city, returning after a passage of time wealthier and ready to reclaim his woman. When Shepard realizes the lovers' duplicity, the weight of the world falls on him and his rage is that of the Old Testament Jehovah. The death duel between the two suitors precipitates a holocaust that blows apart the fragile paradise that so briefly flourished. Director Malick endows this simple, timeless story with the enormous scope and resonance of myth through a clear vision unclouded by sentimentality and by a deft juxtaposition of image, music, and character. Although this is only his second feature film (BADLANDS, 1973, was his first), he demonstrates an understanding of filmic language that is rare even among "mature" directors. The story is rich with biblical and mythical allegory; there are echoes of Genesis, the Wasteland myth, and Greek tragedy. The vast, uncluttered compositions sometimes render the characters as little more than puppets in the hands of fate, reinforcing the universality of the story. Nestor Almendros' hyper-realistic cinematography is breathtaking; there is none of the soft-focus taint that usually invades "period pictures." In the early days of movies, when directors like Murnau, Lang, and Griffith had to rely exclusively on the power of the image to communicate meaning, it was essential to have a feel for those "pictures" that would trigger a flood of recognition in the viewer. DAYS OF HEAVEN is a film in that tradition. The dialog is sparse and almost incidental, the characters' words insignificant amidst the pervasive whisper of the wheat, the clatter of the threshing machines, and the awful drone of the locust horde that accompanies the final holocaust. The soundtrack alone is a masterwork; Malick is a director who has been known to fix multiple microphones to tree trunks and plants in order to bring the power of nature to suburban movie theaters. Ennio Morricone's haunting, wistful score adds measurably to the sweep and timelessness of the film, with its interplay of ancient sounding melodies. Visual "triggers" are in abundance; the too brilliant red of the thrasher and the motorcycle identify themselves as portents of the characters' impending demise. Ultimately, the characters are powerless against the forces of nature and fate that their actions have unleashed. Their fall from grace echoes the original Fall, and DAYS OF HEAVEN is a film that will echo in the memory for a long time.

p, Bert and Harold Schneider; d&w, Terrence Malick; ph, Nestor Almendros (Metrocolor); m, Ennio Morricone; ed, Billy Weber; art d, Jack Fisk; set d, Robert Gould; cos, Patricia Norris; spec eff, John Thomas, Mel Merrells.

Drama   **Cas.**   **(PR:A   MPAA:PG)**

DAYS OF JESSE JAMES** (1939) 63m REP bw

Roy Rogers (Roy), George "Gabby" Hayes (Gabby), Donald Barry (Jesse James), Pauline Moore (Mary), Harry Woods (Capt. Worthington), Arthur Loft (Sam Wyatt), Wade Boteler (Dr. Samuels), Ethel Wales (Mrs. Samuels), Scotty Beckett (Buster Samuels), Michael Worth (Frank James), Glenn Strange (Cole Younger), Olin Howland (Under-Sheriff), Monte Blue (Fields), Jack Rockwell (McDaniels), Fred Burns (Sheriff), Bud Osborne, Jack Ingram, Carl Sepulveda, Forrest Dillon, Hansel Warner, Lynton Brent, Pasquel Perry, Eddie Acuff, and "Trigger."

Strange oater in which Rogers proves that the James gang, led by Barry as Jesse, didn't rob the Northfield bank as history records. Rogers plays an employee of a national detective agency run by Woods. Rogers suspects that the James boys are innocent and joins the gang incognito to gather evidence to support his hunch. Eventually he discovers that crooked bank officials stole the money and framed the boys from Missouri. This one really stands history on its head.

p&d, Joseph Kane; w, Earle Snell (based on a story by Jack Natteford); ph, Reggie Lanning; ed, Tony Martinelli; md, Cy Feuer.

Western   **(PR:A   MPAA:NR)**

DAYS OF OLD CHEYENNE*½ (1943) 56m REP bw

Don "Red" Barry (Clint Ross), Lynn Merrick (Nancy Carlyle), William Haade (Big Bill Harmon), Emmett "Pappy" Lynn (Tombstone Boggs), Herbert Rawlinson (Gov. Shelby), Charles Miller (John Carlyle), William Ruhl (Steve Brackett), Harry McKim (Bobby), Robert Kortman (Slim Boyd), Nolan Leary (Higgins), Kenne Duncan (Pete), Edwin Parker, Bob Reeves, Art Dillard.

Barry stars as a drifter who is pulled into politics by the scheming Haade, who sets up the cowpoke as governor of the territory so that he can manipulate the ignorant horse-rider into doing his bidding. Barry, of course, catches on quickly and puts a stop to Haade's evil plan.

p, Eddy White; d, Elmer Clifton; w, Norman S. Hall; ph, Reggie Lanning; m, Mort Glickman; ed, Harry Keller; art d, Russell Kimball.

Western   **(PR:A   MPAA:NR)**

DAYS OF 36**** (1972, Gr.) 100m Finos Film c (IMERES TOU 36)

Thanos Grammenos (Convict), George Kyritsis (Deputy).

Grammenos is arrested for the assassination of a Greek politician in 1936. Protesting his innocence, he is visited by Kyritsis. He manages to lock Kyritsis in the cell with him and threatens to kill him if he is not released. The situation drags on for days while the government tries to come to a solution. Finally they hire a sniper to take up a position on a nearby roof and shoot the man in his cell. Excellent political drama based on a true story, superbly photographed and thoughtfully directed. (In Greek; English subtitles.)

p, George Papalios; d&w, Theodor Angelopoulous; ph, Georges Arvanitis.

Drama   **(PR:C   MPAA:NR)**

DAYS OF WINE AND ROSES**** (1962) 117m WB bw

Jack Lemmon (Joe), Lee Remick (Kirsten), Charles Bickford (Arnesen), Jack Klugman (Jim Hungerford), Alan Hewitt (Leland), Tom Palmer (Ballefoy), Debbie Megowan (Debbie), Maxine Stuart (Dottie), Katherine Squire (Mrs. Nolan), Jack Albertson (Trayner), Ken Lynch (Liquor Store Proprietor), Gail Bonney (Gladys), Mary Benoit, Ella Ethridge, Rita Kenaston, J. Pat O'Malley, Robert "Buddy" Shaw, Al Paige (Tenants), Doc Stortt, Rus Bennett, Dick Crockett (Boors), Roger Barrett (Abe), Jack Railey (Waiter), Lisa Guiraut (Belly Dancer), Carl Arnold (Loud Man), Tom Rosqui (Bettor), Barbara Hines, Charlene Holt (Guests).

Every few years Hollywood decides to do a movie about alcohol addiction. Ray Milland in THE LOST WEEKEND was one, Jimmy Cagney in COME FILL THE CUP was another, and Lemmon's portrayal of a boozer must take its place with the aforementioned. He's a young, bright adman who meets and falls in love with attractive, assertive Remick. Her father, Bickford, is not thrilled about their liaison but eventually relents and the kids are married. It's lots of fun until now; a nice relationship, bright dialog, etc. Soon after their marriage, subtle changes begin to occur. Lemmon is under great stress at his office and begins drinking when he comes home from work. He's tired, frustrated, and feels beaten down. Remick adores him and joins in sharing the bottle, more out of love than any alcohol addiction (although she is shown early to be a chocoholic). They drink more and more and become immersed in the liquored life. Lemmon comes out of it long enough to realize that he is killing himself. He joins Alcoholics Anonymous and is aided by Klugman in discovering that life can be fun without hooch. Remick is not able to make the transition to sobriety, and Lemmon, though he adores her more than he can declare, must leave her at home so he can find a new existence. In exiting, he also leaves his young daughter, Megowan, but he knows he'll be back once he is able to stand on his feet without staggering. There are many shattering scenes in the picture and it can get extremely grueling. Lemmon has a mad spell in a greenhouse, then an almost SNAKE PIT siege in a hospital ward. For a man who began as a light comedian, Lemmon shows his incredible versatility and proves he can do just about any role well. The screenplay was based on J. P. Miller's teleplay which starred Cliff Robertson on "Playhouse 90." Robertson was not a star at the time and the decision was made to use Lemmon. The same thing happened to Robertson when he originated "The Hustler" on TV, which went to Paul Newman. Edwards' direction was smooth and neither he nor Miller ever took a stance or moralized or tsk-tsked. They just showed what it was like to be an alcoholic in the 1960s and let the audience draw its own conclusions. Lemmon and Remick were both nominated as Best Actor and Actress but she lost to Anne Bancroft in THE

MIRACLE WORKER and he was edged by Gregory Peck in TO KILL A MOCKINGBIRD. The song by Mancini and Mercer did take the Oscar and, no doubt, helped at the box office.

p, Martin Manulis; d, Blake Edwards; w, J. P. Miller (from his own television play); ph, Phil Lathrop; m, Henry Mancini; ed, Patrick McCormack; art d, Joseph Wright; set d, George James Hopkins; cos, Don Feld; spec eff, Horace L. Hulburd; m/l, "Days of Wine and Roses" (Henry Mancini, Johnny Mercer).

Drama   **Cas.**   **(PR:C   MPAA:NR)**

DAYTONA BEACH WEEKEND Zero (1965) 87m Sixtieth Arts/Dominant c

Del Shannon, Houston & Dorsey, Rayna, Sue Skeen, Don Jackson, The Offbeats.

Low-budget teen exploitation film concerns a bunch of swinging college kids who take their spring vacation in Daytona Beach along with rock'n'roll singer Shannon. Shot on location in 16mm and almost utterly forgettable.

p&d, Robert Welby; (Ansco Color).

Drama   **(PR:A-C   MPAA:NR)**

DAYTON'S DEVILS*** (1968) 103m Madison/CUE c

Rory Calhoun (Mike Page), Leslie Nielsen (Frank Dayton), Lainie Kazan (Leda Martell), Hans Gudegast (Max Eckhart), Barry Sadler (Barney Barry), Pat Renella (Claude Sadi), Georg Stanford Brown (Theon Gibson), Rigg Kennedy (Sonny Merton).

Nielsen leads a group of criminal misfits (Calhoun, Renella, Gudegast, Sadler, and Kazan) in a plot to rob an Air Force base of over a million dollars. The meticulously planned robbery requires weeks of training and the successful impersonation of a top-secret investigative team whose orders come from command headquarters. Competent enough execution of familiar material, helped by a good cast and an entertaining rendition of "Sunny" by Kazan in a nightclub scene.

p, Robert W. Stabler; d, Jack Shea; w, Fred De Gorter; ph, Brick Marquard (Eastmancolor); m, Marlin Skiles; ed, Fred W. Berger; art d, Paul Sylos, Jr.; spec eff, Woodrow Ward.

Crime   **(PR:A   MPAA:NR)**

DE L'AMOUR** (1968, Fr./Ital.) 90m Films de la Pleiade-Cocinor-Les Films Marceau-Cinescolo/Goldstone bw

Anna Karina (Helene), Philippe Avron (Serge), Michel Piccoli (Raoul), Elsa Martinelli (Mathilde), Jean Sorel (Antoine), Joanna Shimkus (Sophie), Bernard Garnier (Werther), Cecil Saint Laurent (Man Who Reads Stendhal), Isabelle Lunghini.

Dentist Piccoli is a habitual philanderer whose current lover (Karina), leaves him only to be picked up and seduced by Avron. Meanwhile, Piccoli waits for a rendezvous with Shimkus, but just as she is about to get in the car, he spots attractive Martinelli in her car and takes off after her. He shows her films of his past lovers, including Karina and Shimkus, and pledges that she is his true love. The next day, he is showing the same films, plus one of Martinelli, to a new woman. Okay romantic comedy based on an 1822 novel by Stendhal.

p, Pierre Braunberger; d, Jean Aurel; w, Cecil Saint Laurent, Aurel (based on the novel De L'amour by Stendhal); ph, Edmond Richard; m, Andre Hodeir; ed, Agnes Guillemot, Genevieve Vaury; art d, Eric Simon.

Comedy   **(PR:C   MPAA:NR)**

DE SADE zero (1969), US/Ger. 113m AIP/CCC/Transcontinental c (AUSSCHWEIFENDE LEBEN DES MARQUIS DE SADE, DAS)

Keir Dullea (Marquis de Sade), Senta Berger (Anne Montreuil), Lilli Palmer (Mme. de Montreuil), Anna Massey (Renee de Montreuil), Sonja Ziemann (La Beauvoisin), Ute Levka (Rose Keller), Herbert Weissbach (Mons. de Montreuil), Christiane Kruger (Marquis's Mistress), Max Kiebach (de Sade as a Boy), John Huston (The Abbe).

Rancid attempt to do a movie biography of the Marquis de Sade falls flat with embarrassing performances from all involved (especially Huston, who didn't mention his participation in this debacle in his autobiography) and lame script credited to Matheson, who claimed his draft of the screenplay was ruined.

p, Samuel Z. Arkoff, James H. Nicholson; d, Cy Endfield; w, Richard Matheson, Peter Berg; ph, Heinz Pehlke (Berkey Pathe Color); m, Billy Strange; cos, Vangie Harrison.

Biography   **(PR:O   MPAA:R)**

DEAD AND BURIED* (1981) 92m Avco Embassy c

James Farentino (Dan), Melody Anderson (Janet), Jack Albertson (Dobbs), Dennis Redfield (Ron), Nancy Locke Hauser (Linda), Lisa Blout (Girl on Beach), Robert Englund (Harry), Bill Quinn (Ernie), Michael Currie (Herman), Christopher Allport (George/Freddie), Joe Medalis (Doctor), Macon McCalman (Ben), Lisa Marie (Hitchhiker), Estelle Omens (Betty), Barry Corbin (Phil), Linda Turley (Waitress), Ed Bakey (Fisherman), Glenn Morshower (Jimmy), Robert Boler (Haskell), Michael Pataki (Sam), Jill Fosse (Nurse), Mark Courtney/Michael Courtney (Jamie), Renee McDonnell (Girl No. 1), Dottie Catching (Lady Car Passenger), Colby Smith (Female Stranger), Judy Ashton (Joyce), Bill Couch, Bill Couch, Jr., Charles Couch, Tony Cecere, Angelo DeMeo.

Stupid and gory horror outing released at the twilight of the "splatter" film cycle. Farentino plays the New England sheriff whose town is plagued with a series of vicious—and graphic—murders of unfortunate tourists who happen to try to pass through his burg. It seems that everyone in town knows what's going on (including Farentino's wife, Anderson) except the sheriff himself. All the clues lead to eccentric coroner/mortician Albertson—he cuts up cadavers while listening to 1940s swing music—who has somehow managed to revive the dead. Most of the plot twists are confusing and haphazardly developed, which makes the movie seem like an excuse to show off Stan Winston's admittedly effective gore effects. This was the veteran comedian and character actor Albertson's last film before his death in the same year.

p, Ronald Shusett, Robert Fentress; d, Gary A. Sherman; w, Shusett, Dan O'Bannon (based on a story by Jeff Millar, Alex Stern); ph, Steve Poster (Technicolor); m, Joe Renzetti; ed, Alan Balsam; art d, Bill Sandel, Joe Aubel; set d, James E. Tocci, Dennis Barton, Claudia; cos, Bill Jobe; spec eff, Stan Winston.

Horror   **Cas.**   **(PR:O MPAA:R)**

DEAD ARE ALIVE, THE*   (1972, Yugo./Ger./Ital.) NGP c

Alex Cord (Jason), Samantha Eggar (Myra), John Marley (Nikos), Nadja Tiller (Leni), Horst Frank (Stephan), Enzo Tarascio (Giuranna), Enzo Cerusico (Alberto), Carlo De Mejo (Igor), Vladan Milasinovic (Otello), Daniela Surina (Irene), Christiane Von Blank (Velia), Mario Maranzana (Vitanza), Pier Luigi D'Orazio (Minelli), Wendy D'Olive (Giselle), Ivan Pavicevac (Policeman).

Cord and Eggar are archaeologists digging in some Etruscan ruins. A series of gruesome murders ensues and all evidence leads to the conclusion that the ancient god Tuchulka is responsible. Dull, muddled horror film is a waste of some talented actors.

p, Mondial Tefi; d, Armando Crispino; w, Lucio Battistrada, Crispino; ph, Enrico Menczer; m, Riz Ortolani; art d, Giantito Burchiellaro; cos, Luca Sabatelli.

Horror   **(PR:O MPAA:R)**

DEAD DON'T DREAM, THE*½   (1948) 62m UA bw

William Boyd (Hopalong Cassidy), Andy Clyde (California Carlson), Rand Brooks (Lucky Jenkins), John Parrish (Jeff Potter), Leonard Penn (Earl Wesson), Mary Tucker (Mary Benton), Francis McDonald (Bert Lansing), Richard Alexander (Duke), Bob Gabriel (Larry Potter), Stanley Andrews (Jesse Williams), Forbes Murray (Sheriff Thompson), Don Haggerty (Deputy).

Boyd solves a murder mystery in which most of the action takes place at night as he chases the killers through misty and dark locations rather than wide-open spaces. Plot sees Boyd trying to find out why three corpses turned up in a frontier hotel. A murky story foretelling the doom of the 66-strong series. The 53-year-old Boyd made one more Hopalong picture before he began reissuing the entire series on TV. (See HOPALONG CASSIDY series, Index.)

p, Lewis J. Rachmil; d, George Archainbaud; w, Francis Rosenwald (based on a character created by Clarence E. Mulford); ph, Mack Stengler; m, Ralph Stanley; ed, Fred W. Berger; art d, Jerome Pycha, Jr.

Western   **(PR:A MPAA:NR)**

DEAD END*****   (1937) 93m UA bw
(AKA: DEAD END; CRADLE OF CRIME)

Sylvia Sidney (Drina), Joel McCrea (Dave), Humphrey Bogart (Baby Face Martin), Wendy Barrie (Kay), Claire Trevor (Francie), Allen Jenkins (Hunk), Marjorie Main (Mrs. Martin), Billy Halop (Tommy), Huntz Hall (Dippy), Bobby Jordan (Angel), Leo Grocey (Spit), Gabriel Dell (T.B.), Bernard Punsley (Milty), Charles Peck (Philip Griswold), Minor Watson (Mr. Griswold), James Burke (Mulligan), Ward Bond (Doorman), Elizabeth Risdon (Mrs. Connell), Esther Dale (Mrs. Fenner), George Humbert (Pascagli), Marcelle Corday (Governess), Jerry Cooper (Milty's Brother), Kath Ann Lujan (Milty's Sister), Bud Geary (Kay's Chauffeur), Gertrude Valerie (Old Lady), Tom Ricketts (Old Man), Esther Howard (Woman with Coarse Voice), Micky Martin, Wesley Girard (Tough Boys), Mona Monet (Nurse), Don Barry (Interne), Earl Askam (Griswold Chauffeur), Frank Shields, Lucile Brown (Well-Dressed Couple), Bob Womans (Cop), Bill Pagwell (Drunk), Charlotte Treadway, Maude Lambert (Women with Poodle), Sidney Kilbrick, Larry Harris, Norman Salling (Boys), Charles Halton (Whitey), Thomas Jackson (Police Lieutenant), Al Bridge, Wade Boteleo (Cops).

Poverty, slums, crime, all the ugly hallmarks of the Great Depression, provide the themes for DEAD END, the sad social evils Hollywood for the most part chose to ignore, gloss over in myriad mindless movie musicals. Sam Goldwyn was an exception among the studio moguls; he felt, after seeing the Sidney Kingsley play (which ran more than 700 performances on Broadway) that realism, not escapism, would do well at the box office, as well as further art which Goldwyn, one time haberdasher, craved and adored. His uncanny instincts again proved him right. DEAD END is a simple and devastating story. After ten years of pursuing a criminal career, from murder to robbery, bad boy Bogart returns to his old New York neighborhood, disguised by heavy plastic surgery, to see his mother (Main), his girl friend of decades earlier (Trevor), and escape a nation-wide dragnet. With him is loyal henchman Jenkins who constantly reminds him that he's "hot" and should "take it on the lam," that there is no room in his harrowing world for sentimental journeys into a past best forgotten. But Bogart will not leave the old slum until he finds Trevor, even after receiving a slap in the face and a lambasting from his mother, Main, who calls him a "dirty dog" for his life of crime. When he does meet Trevor he discovers that she has turned into a lowly, disease-ridden prostitute. In a traumatic scene Bogart first bubbles sweet memories to her. She stops him and tells him: "You're lookin' at me how I used to look." Trevor then steps from the shadows into the sunlight to reveal a ravaged face. Bogart curls his lips in disgust, glares, twitches with realization and spits: "Whyncha get a job?" "They don't grow on trees," she replies. "Why didn't you starve first?" he says. "Why didn't you?" she spits back. He pays her off, sending her out of his life, further insulted when she asks for more money than he offers. Interplaying between the Bogart bad boy story is McCrea, a starving architect with scruples, struggling to get out of the slum. He is in love, he thinks, with Barrie, a rich girl living in a skyscraper apartment building that rear-ends on his street. In love with McCrea is Sidney, that eternal child-woman of the 1930s, a teary-eyed good lady trapped inside the poverty of her generation, struggling to keep her kid brother, Halop, from going wrong. She knows she stands no chance against the fur-wrapped Barrie and encourages McCrea to finish school and better himself, to

forget Barrie's offer to take him to Europe on a paid vacation where he can study the great buildings of the Old Country. Meanwhile, Bogart, to while away the time, begins teaching Halop and the other "Dead End Kids" all the evil tricks he has learned in his misspent life, how to use a knife on an opponent, thieve and lie. McCrea, his boyhood chum, warns him that he will take vengeance upon him unless he stops spreading his rotten influence and departs. The Dead Enders are an hilarious lot with their pranks and primitive conversation as they vex the local cop, Burke, the doorman to the ritzy apartment building, Bond, and a spoiled child, Peck. (They would go on—Halop, Gorcey, Hall, Jordan, Dell and for a while Punsley, to establish a great following through one cheaply produced series after another, notably THE BOWERY BOYS.) Halop gets into a row with Peck's father, Watson, an influential citizen whom he stabs when Watson tries to turn him into police for harassing Peck. Halop escapes and is sought by police; to McCrea he is fast becoming another Bogart and he promises Sidney that he'll find the money to defend the boy in court. Bogart is by then utterly disillusioned with his return to the old neighborhood, spurned by those he once loved and who loved him. He decides to turn a profit from his disastrous homecoming by kidnapping rich kid Peck. When McCrea tries to interfere, he is stabbed by Bogart and tossed into the East River. He survives, however, and before Bogart can carry out the kidnapping, McCrea shoots it out with the gangster in a running gunfight over the rooftops and through the dingy tenements where they once played together as children, mortally wounding Bogart who topples into an alleyway from a fire escape. Police responding to the shooting come down the alleyway to find a dying Bogart, vicious to the end. "Stay away, coppers," he warns them. "I'm going out." They advance guns drawn and he shoots several before the remaining cops empty their pistols into him. McCrea decides that he will not leave with Barrie but stay with Sidney and use the reward money for killing Bogart to defend her brother. At the fadeout the Dead End Kids stroll along the river's edge, pointedly singing a popular song of the era, ending with the words: "If I had the wings of an angel, over these prison walls I would fly." Wyler's flawless direction captures every grimy aspect of slum life in this startling film; his cameras don't shun the garbage-strewn hallways, the filthy street, the rats and roaches which horrify Barrie when she goes in search of McCrea in a world just beyond her posh abode that proves a nightmare. The wonderful set by Richard Day is a duplicate, although enlarged, of that used in the play and Hellman's script changes little of Kingsley's earthy prose, except that Bogart's end is brought about by McCrea in the film where in the play Baby Face Martin is shot down by FBI agents. Goldwyn's favorite director was always Wyler, who had converted stage plays DODSWORTH and THESE THREE to successful films for Goldwyn and would go on to such great triumphs, also for Goldwyn, as THE LITTLE FOXES and THE BEST YEARS OF OUR LIVES. Bogart is captivating as the alienated gangster who proves with his own death Thomas Wolfe's theory of "You Can't Go Home Again," furthering his career greatly upon the success of THE PETRIFIED FOREST a year earlier. He was originally billed beneath Sidney but in re-releases of this film he was given star billing (his role in the Broadway production was enacted by Joseph Downing who later appeared in many Bogie crime movies as a henchman). The film received four Oscar nominations, Best Picture, Best Supporting Actress (Trevor), Best Cinematography, and Best Art Direction. The Dead End Kids, as they would be to future producers, caused no end of annoyance to Goldwyn and Wyler and havoc in their wake from the Broadway hit (which opened at the Belasco Theater on October 28, 1935), even on the train to Hollywood, pulling pranks on porters, playing ball in the aisle and vexing fellow passengers. Once in tinseltown the boys went crazy for cars. Hall and Dell crashed an auto into a telephone pole, Gorcey got four tickets in three weeks and underage Jordan was stopped for driving without a license. They delayed production on the set with their antics and unnerved the film actors by critically comparing them to those who had appeared in the stage production. Their schooling was a disaster, all of them ducking out of classes by claiming they had rehearsals to attend. Imitating Wyler's voice, Dell put through innumerable long distance calls to his mother and those of the other boys. Even the tolerant Goldwyn came under their fire; they refused to show him any respect, calling him "Pop," and giving him the raspberries when he refused to let them go swimming between takes. But the producer held his temper, knowing he was backing a classic. He lavished money on the entire project, reportedly paying $165,000 to Kingsley for the film rights to the play and allowing Day a $50,000 budget in the construction of the marvelous set. Wyler and his genius cameraman Toland practiced their economical style by getting the film in the can in less than two months with approximately 175,000 feet of film. Wyler originally wanted to film the entire movie on-location in the Lower East Side but, as he was later quoted, "Goldwyn wouldn't let me do that. He was afraid I'd get away from him." Wyler doted on every detail of the movie. In one scene Bogart is required to demonstrate his knife-throwing ability by flicking a pen-knife with deadly accuracy into an orange peel several yards away. He practiced this for hours but couldn't get the hang of it until Wyler showed him how to do it. But then Wyler showed them all how to do it, movie after movie.

p, Samuel Goldwyn; d, William Wyler; w, Lillian Hellman (based on the play by Sidney Kingsley); ph, Gregg Toland; m, Alfred Newman; ed, Daniel Mandell; art d, Richard Day; set d, Julie Heron; cos, Omar Kiam; spec eff, James Basevi.

Crime Drama   **(PR:C MPAA:NR)**

DEAD END KIDS ON DRESS PARADE**   (1939) 62m WB bw
(AKA: DEAD END KIDS AT MILITARY SCHOOL)

Billy Halop (Cadet Major Rollins), Leo Gorcey (Slip Duncan), Bobby Jordan (Cadet Ronny Morgan), Huntz Hall (Cadet Johnny Cabot), Gabriel Dell (Cadet Georgie Warren), Bernard Punsley (Dutch), John Litel (Col. Mitchell Reiker), Frankie Thomas (Cadet Lieutenant Murphy), Cecilia "Cissie" Loftus (Mrs. Neely), Selmer Jackson (Capt. Evans Dover), Aldrich Bowker (Father Ryan), Douglas Meins (Hathaway), William Gould (Dr. Lewis), Don Douglas (Col. William Duncan).

Gorcey finds himself at a military school where Litel, who had promised the boy's dying father that he would take care of him, tries to make the "Dead End" kid a man. Halop attempts to help the unruly Gorcey make the transition, but he is thrown out of a two-story window by the thankless brute. Gorcey comes around and proves himself a hero when he saves the life of Dell during a fire in the munitions storeroom. A forced and contrived DEAD END outing, which bends the behavior patterns that had been established for these characters to fit its unlikely premise. Final feature film of THE DEAD END KIDS series. (See BOWERY BOYS series, Index.)

p, Bryan Foy; d, William Clemens, Noel Smith; w, Tom Reed, Charles Belden (based on the story "Dead End Kids in Military School" by Reed); ph, Arthur L. Todd; ed, Douglas Gould.

Comedy/Drama (PR:A MPAA:NR)

DEAD EYES OF LONDON
(SEE: DARK EYES OF LONDON, 1965, Ger.)

DEAD HEAT ON A MERRY-GO-ROUND**½ (1966) 107m COL c
James Coburn (Eli Kotch), Camilla Sparv (Inger Knudson), Aldo Ray (Eddie Hart), Nina Wayne (Frieda Schmid), Robert Webber (Milo Stewart), Rose-Marie (Margaret Kirby), Todd Armstrong (Alfred Morgan), Marian Moses (Dr. Marion Hague), Michael Strong (Paul Feng), Severn Darden (Miles Fisher), James Westerfield (Jack Balter), Phillip E. Pine (George Logan), Simon Scott (William Anderson), Ben Astar (Gen. Mailenkoff), Michael St. Angel (Capt. William Yates), Lawrence D. Mann (Officer Howard), Alex Rodine (Translator), Albert Nalbandian (Willie Manus), Tyler McVey (Lyman Mann), Roy Glenn (Sgt. Elmer K. Coxe), Joey Faye (Taxi Driver), Mary Young (Mrs. Galbrace), George Wallace (Police Chief Yates), Tanya Lemani, Harrison Ford, Stephanie Hill.

Coburn plays a conman who gets himself an early parole from prison by seducing the female psychologist. Once out, he immediately sets into motion a plan to rob the bank at Los Angeles International Airport. He plans the heist to take place during the arrival of the Russian premier, when all the security forces will be concentrated on the visiting dignitary. Good performances help keep this average caper film moving to a surprise denouement, when another woman he has betrayed inherits a fortune of $7 million he knows nothing about.

p, Carter DeHaven III; d&w, Bernard Girard; ph, Lionel Lindon (Eastmancolor); m, Stu Phillips; ed, William Lyon; art d, Walter M. Simonds; set d, Frank Tuttle.

Crime/Comedy (PR:A MPAA:NR)

DEAD KIDS** (1981 Aus./New Zealand) 105m Greater Union/South Street c
(AKA: STRANGE BEHAVIOR)
Michael Murphy (Brady), Louise Fletcher (Barbara Moorhead), Dan Shor (Pete Brady), Fiona Lewis (Gwen Parkinson), Arthur Dignam (LeSange), Scott Brady (Shea), Dey Young (Caroline), Marc McClure (Oliver), Charles Lane (Donovan), Elizabeth Cheshire (Lucy), Beryl Te Wiata (Mrs Haskell).

Australian horror/mystery set in America's midwest (though shot down under) that lives up to its disturbingly grisly title. Murphy stars as the chief of police who tries to solve a series of stabbings of the town's teenagers. The bloody trail leads to the local college where the evil doings are traced to the science department headed up by Lewis.

p, Antony I. Ginnane, John Barnett; d, Michael Laughlin; w, Laughlin, William Condon (based on story "School Days," by Robert Hughes); ph, Louis Horvath (Panavision, Eastmancolor); prod d, Susanna Moore; ed, Petra Von Oellfen; art d, Russell Collins; set d, Moore; cos, Bruce Finlayson; spec eff & makeup, Craig Reardon.

Mystery/Horror (PR:O MPAA:NR)

DEAD LUCKY*½ (1960, Brit.) 64m ACT Films/BL bw
Vincent Ball (Mike Billings), Betty McDowall (Jenny Drew), John le Mesurier (Inspector Corcoran), Alfred Burke (Knocker Parsons), Michael Ripper (Percy Simpson), San Kydd (Harry Winston), Chili Bouchier (Mrs. Winston), John Charlesworth (Hon. Stanley Dewsbury), Brian Worth (Lucky Lewis), Frederick Piper (Harvey Walters), Joan Heal (Barmaid).

Reporter Ball clears girlfriend McDowall of the murder of a gambler who had made advances to her. Routine crime drama.

p, Ralph Bond, Robert Dunbar; d, Montgomery Tully; w, Sidney Nelson, Maurice Harrison.

Crime (PR:C MPAA:NR)

DEAD MAN'S CHEST* (1965, Brit.) 59m Merton Park/AA bw
John Thaw (David Jones), Ann Firbank (Mildred Jones), John Meillon (Johnnie Gordon), John Collin (Inspector Briggs), Peter Bowles (Joe), John Abineri (Arthur), Arthur Brough (Groves), Graham Crowden (Murchie).

Yet another low-budget British crime drama. This one has Thaw a reporter faking the murder of an associate in order to show the weakness of circumstantial evidence. Thoroughly routine.

p, Jack Greenwood; d, Patrick Dromgoole; w, Donal Giltinian.

Crime (PR:A-C MPAA:NR)

DEAD MAN'S EVIDENCE**½ (1962, Brit.) 67m Bayford-RCH/BL bw
Conrad Phillips (David Baxter), Jane Griffiths (Linda Howard), Veronica Hurst (Gay Clifford), Ryck Rydon (Fallon), Alex Mackintosh (Paul Kay), Godfrey Quigley (Inspector O'Brien), Bruce Seton (Col. Somerset), Harry Webster (Andy), Maureen Halligan (Mrs. Mac), Laurie Leigh (Pat), Tommy Duggan (Mr. Casey), Frank Siemon (Barman), Middleton Woods (Kim), Fergus O'Kelly (Night Porter), Gordon Waine (Hotel Waiter), Sonia Fox (Hotel Receptionist), Alan Barry (Airport Clerk), Robert Marshall (Hotel Barman).

Phillips is a British spy sent to investigate a mysterious corpse of a frogman washed up on the Irish coast. At first it is thought the body is that of Rydon, believed to have defected to the communists, but it later turns out that Phillips is the traitor. Slightly above-average spy drama.

p, Francis Searle, Ryck Rydon; d, Searle; w, Arthur la Bern, Gordon Wellesley (based on a story by la Bern); ph, Ken Hodges; m, Ken Thorne; ed, Jim Commock; art d, Duncan Sutherland.

Spy Drama (PR:A-C MPAA:NR)

DEAD MAN'S EYES*½ (1944) 64m UNIV bw
Lon Chaney (Dave Stuart), Jean Parker (Heather Hayden), Paul Kelly (Alan Bittaker), Thomas Gomez (Capt. Drury), Jonathan Hale (Dr. Welles), Edward Fielding (Stanley Hayden), George Meeker (Nick Phillips), Pierre Watkin (Attorney), Eddie Dunn (Policeman), Beatrice Roberts (Nurse), Acquanetta.

Another "Inner Sanctum" mystery starring Chaney as an artist who is blinded when his lovely female model Acquanetta, who is jealous of his fiancee, Parker, throws acid in his face. Chaney must undergo a tricky eye transplant that requires the tissues of another person, dead or alive. The donor is killed and so is Chaney's model. The finger of guilt points at the artist. Uneven pace and a basement budget. (See INNER SANCTUM series, Index.)

p, Will Cowan; d, Reginald LeBorg; w, Dwight Babcock; ph, Paul Ivano; ed, Milton Carruth; md, Paul Sawtell; art d, John B. Goodman, Martin Obzina.

Mystery (PR:A MPAA:NR)

DEAD MAN'S FLOAT** (1980, Aus.) 75m Andromeda/Greg Lynch c
Sally Boyden (Anne), Greg Rowe (Johnny), Jacqui Gordon (Sue), Rick Ireland (Pete), Bill Hunter (Eddie Bell), Sue Jones (Shirley Bell), John Heywood (Capt. Collins), Gus Mercurio (Mr. Dobraski), Brian Hannan (Rex Coates), Marcel Cugola (Mr. Luth), Ernie Sigley (Snarks), Bunney Brooke (Parish), Chris Hayward (Heavy).

Dumb little Australian teenage surfing film starring Boyden and Gordon as two surf beauties who fall for young American stud Ireland. Their beach hideout is on a remote coast of the area, but it is invaded by some drug dealers who have arrived to take delivery on a cache of dope. The kids, with the help of their parents, defeat the dopers and everyone goes back to the surf.

p, Tom Broadbridge; d, Pete Sharp; w, Roger Carr (based on a novel by Carr); ph, David Eggby; ed, Clifford Hayes.

Crime (PR:C MPAA:G)

DEAD MAN'S GOLD** (1948) 60m Western Adventure/Screen Guild bw
Lash LaRue (Lash LaRue), Al "Fuzzy" St. John (Fuzzy Q. Jones), John [Bob] Cason (Matt Conway), Peggy Stewart (June Thornton), Terry Frost (Joe Quirt), Lane Bradford (Ross Evans), Pierce Lyden (Silver), Stephen [Steve] Keyes (Morgan), Cliff Taylor (Miner), Britt Wood (Bartender), Marshall Reed, Bob Woodward.

LaRue and St. John come to Gold Valley to visit an old friend. When they arrive they are greeted with suspicion by Stewart, the man's daughter, who eventually explains that her uncle has been missing for three days. The next day the heroes ride out and find the man's body in a mine. They set a trap and expose Mayor Bradford as the head villain. Enjoyable second-feature Western, LaRue's first after PRC folded in 1948.

p, Ron Ormond; d, Ray Taylor; w, Moree Herring, Gloria Welsch (based on a story by Ormond and Ira Webb); ph, Ernest Miller; m, Walter Greene; ed, Hugh Winn.

Western (PR:A MPAA:NR)

DEAD MAN'S GULCH**½ (1943) 55m REP bw
Don "Red" Barry (Tennessee Colby), Lynn Merrick (Mary Logan), Clancy Cooper (Walt Bledsoe), Emmett "Pappy" Lynn (Fiddlefoot), Malcolm "Bud" McTaggart (Tommy Logan), Jack Rockwell (Bat Matson), John Vosper (Hobart Patterson), Pierce Lyden (Curley Welch), Lee Shumway (Fred Beecher), Rex Lease (Steve Barker), Al Taylor (Buck Lathrop), Robert Frazer, Robert Fiske, Charlie Sullivan, Frank Brownlee.

Interesting Barry oater directed at a break-neck speed by serial veteran English. Plot has Barry battling his one-time pal, McTaggart, who has gone bad and is aiding a gang of mobsters who use strong-arm tactics to maintain their freight line monopoly. One of Barry's best.

p, Eddy White; d, John English; w, Norman S. Hall, Robert Williams (based on a story by Hall); ph, Ernest Miller; m, Mort Glickman; ed, Arthur Roberts; art d, Russell Kimball.

Western (PR:A MPAA:NR)

DEAD MAN'S SHOES** (1939, Brit.) 67m ABF bw
Leslie Banks (Roger de Vetheuil), Joan Marion (Viola de Vetheuil), Geoffrey Atkins (Paul de Vetheuil), Wilfrid Lawson (Lucien Sarrou), Judy Kelly (Michele Allain), Nancy Price (Mme. Pelletier), Walter Hudd (Gaston Alexandri), Peter Bull (Defense Counsel), Henry Oscar (President of the Court), Ludwig Stossel (Dr. Breithaut), Roddy McDowall.

Somewhat contrived, but fairly interesting, tale starring Banks as a wealthy industrialist accused of being the infamous thief Jean Pelletier in the years before the war. He winds up in court and claims he lost his memory when wounded in the war and that his fiancee identified him from a picture in the paper. The former lover of Pelletier takes the stand and swears that Banks is the thief, but the industrialist is saved when a man testifies that he saw Pelletier killed during the war. Banks goes home a free man, only to be cornered by the witness who says he lied and is going to have to blackmail him or tell the cops. Banks, who truly can't remember, begins to wonder whether he really is the criminal or not. Obsessed with finding out, Banks seeks out Pelletier's former mistress, and the thief's mother. These contacts finally convince him that he is indeed the infamous Pelletier, and Banks decides to turn himself in to the authorities. His lawyer, however, talks him out of being so noble and cites the effect it would have on the industrialist's young son. Meanwhile, the mistress learns that the blackmailer is going to tell the cops anyway, so she grabs a gun and kills him.

p, Walter C. Mycroft; d, Thomas Bentley; w, Nina Jarvis (based on the story "Carrefour" by Hans Kafka); ph, Gunther Krampf; ed, Monica Kimmick.

Crime/Mystery   **(PR:A MPAA:NR)**

DEAD MAN'S TRAIL**   (1952) 59m Frontier Pictures/MON bw

Johnny Mack Brown, Jimmy Ellison, Barbara Allen, Lane Bradford, I. Stanford Jolley, Terry Frost, Gregg Barton, Dale Van Sickel, Richard Avonde, Stanley Price.

Tame oater with some good action scenes that are too few as Brown and Ellison save the day for Allen. The bad guys aren't frightening and even the horses seem bored.

p, Vincent M. Fennelly; d, Lewis Collins; w, Joseph Poland, Melville Shyer; ph, Ernest Miller; ed, Sam Fields.

Western   **(PR:A MPAA:NR)**

DEAD MARCH, THE*   (1937) 73m Imperial bw

Solo Doudauz (German Unknown Soldier), Al Rigali (French Unknown Soldier), Al Ritchie (Italian Unknown Soldier), Don Black (British Unknown Soldier), Howard Negley (American Unknown Soldier), Boake Carter (Narrator).

Semi-documentary, anti-war film that uses clips of battle footage from Japan's invasion of Manchukuo, Italy's occupation of Ethiopia, and Bolivia's war with Paraguay to shock viewers into realizing the horror and futility of war. Interspersed with this footage are five "unknown soldiers" representing France, Germany, Italy, England, and the United States who rise from their graves and try to explain the ideologies and beliefs that led them to their unnecessary deaths. Carter narrates the whole thing from a desk. Pretty strange.

p&d, Bud Pollard; w, Samuel Taylor Moore; m, Erno Rapee.

War   **(PR:C MPAA:NR)**

DEAD MELODY* (1938, Ger.) 74m UFA bw (VERKLUNGENE MELODIE)

Brigitte Horney, Willy Birgel, Carl Raddatz, Ver von Langen.

Insipid melodrama has Horney, a good girl, falling in love with Birgel after they survive a plane crash in the Sahara, although he isn't much interested. Horney suffers with her unrequited love, though Birgel's brother, Raddatz, would gladly take her. Of very little interest.

d, V. Tourjanski.

Drama   **(PR:C MPAA:NR)**

DEAD MEN ARE DANGEROUS** (1939, Brit.) 69m Welwyn/Pathe bw

Robert Newton (Aylmer Franklyn), Betty Lynne (Nina), John Warwick (Goddard), Peter Gawthorne (Conroy), Merle Tottenham (Gladys), John Turnbull (Detective), Aubrey Mallalieu (Coroner), P. Kynaston Reeves (Uncle), Googie Withers, Ian Fleming, Charles Mortimer, Winifred Oughton.

Newton, a down-on-his-luck writer, stumbles across a dead body and switches clothes with it. Later he is accused of the murder. Occasionally interesting melodrama.

p, Warwick Ward; d, Harold French; w, Victor Kendall, Harry Hughes, Vernon Clancey (based on the novel Hidden by H.C. Armstrong).

Crime   **(PR:A MPAA:NR)**

DEAD MEN DON'T WEAR PLAID** (1982) 89m UNIV bw

Steve Martin (Rigby Reardon), Rachel Ward (Juliet Forrest), Carl Reiner (Field Marshall Von Kluck), Reni Santoni (Carlos Rodriguez), George Gaynes (Dr. Forrest), Frank McCarthy (Waiter), Adrian Ricard (Mildred), Charles Picerni, Gene Labell, George Sawaya (Hoods), Britt Nilsson (Poppy Secretary), Jean Beaudine (Duty Secretary), John "Easton" Stuart (German Henchman), Ronald Spivey, Bob Hevelone, Dieter Curt, Phil Kearns, Kent Deigaard, Eugene Brezany, Brad Baird.

One of those "cute ideas" for which Martin is known (with increasing dislike) wherein he plays an inept private eye of the 1940s, tracking down killers, and, in the course of his lamely amusing trek, plays opposite old film clips of James Cagney, Edward Arnold, Alan Ladd, Humphrey Bogart, Charles Laughton, Ava Gardner, to name a few. The lifted scenes which are better than the movie itself are taken from such 1940s classics as WHITE HEAT, DOUBLE INDEMNITY, THE KILLERS, THE BIG SLEEP, DECEPTION, THE LOST WEEKEND, DARK PASSAGE, IN A LONELY PLACE, JOHNNY EAGER, THE POSTMAN ALWAYS RINGS TWICE, I WALK ALONE, HUMORESQUE, SUSPICION, and, most notably, THE BRIBE. Naturally the basic film, what there is of it, is shot in black-and-white to merge with the old clips; cinematographer Chapman does a commendable job, specializing in black-and-white photography in an age where color is everything (he worked superbly in bw with RAGING BULL). Ward is alluring as Martin's mysterious paramour but she can't offset the comedian's predictability. Martin is often awful and terribly unfunny in this rip-off gimmick which would have better served as a TV skit which is what it really is, a novelty with unnecessary millions pumped into it to bring it to feature status. This production is typical of many current films employing the "Saturday Nite Live" comics— a single slightly funny idea with no storyline and not enough real talent to sustain any viewer's interest beyond the first reel. Martin, Chase, Aykroyd (Belushi being an exception) and others have exploited these minor ideas as major film offerings when, in truth, they are little more than one-line gags surrounded by enormous and wasteful production budgets. It's the Hollywood badger game: The visitor enters a splendid-looking mansion only to discover that it's a facade with no interior, the front propped up by two-by-fours, an empty lot beyond the door. Dirctor-writer

Reiner has long since ceased to be funny, mechanically restating TV jokes and situations that died with Sid Caesar's "Show of Shows" decades ago.

p, David V. Picker, William E. McEuen; d, Carl Reiner; w, George Gipe, Reiner, Steve Martin; ph, Michael Chapman; m, Miklos Rozsa (from earlier films); ed, Bud Molin; prod d, John DeCuir; cos, Edith Head; spec eff, Glen Robinson.

Comedy   **Cas.**   **(PR:C MPAA:PG)**

DEAD MEN TELL*   (1941) 61m FOX bw

Sidney Toler (Charlie Chan), Sheila Ryan (Kate Ransome), Robert Weldon (Steve Daniels), Sen Yung (Jimmy Chan), Don Douglas (Jed Thomasson), Katharine Aldridge (Laura Thursday), Paul McGrath (Charles Thursday), George Reeves (Bill Lydig), Truman Bradley (Capt. Kane), Ethel Griffies (Patience Nodbury), Lenita Lane (Dr. Anne Bonney), Milton Parsons (Gene La Farge).

Average Chan mystery sees the humble detective investigating the death of eccentric old lady Griffies, who was murdered just before she was to set out on a schooner to find a hidden family treasure. As it turns out, the woman was frightened to death by the killer, who dressed up as the ghost of the lady's dead pirate ancestor. (See CHARLIE CHAN series, Index.)

p, Walter Morosco, Ralph Dietrich; d, Harry Lachman; w, John Larkin (based on the character created by Earl Derr Biggers); ph, Charles Clarke; ed, Harry Reynolds; md, Emil Newman.

Mystery   **(PR:A MPAA:NR)**

DEAD MEN TELL NO TALES** (1939, Brit.) 70m Alliance bw

Emlyn Williams (Dr. Headlam/Friedberg), Sara Seegar (Marjorie), Hugh Williams (Detective Inspector Martin), Marius Goring (Greening), Lesley Brook (Elizabeth Orme), Christine Silver (Miss Haslett), Clive Morton (Frank Fielding), Anne Wilton (Bridget), Jack Vivian (Crump), Marjorie Dale (The Singer), Hal Gordon (Sergeant).

Grim crime tale detailing the murder of a boys' school matron by evil professor Emlyn Williams after she won the French lottery. Emlyn Williams, playing a dual role as both schoolmaster and a suave French loan shark entices her to his rooms, where he kills her and has another woman don the corpse's clothing to collect the winnings. With the law on his trail, and two more murders under his belt, Emlyn Williams commits suicide.

p, John Corfield; d, David MacDonald; w, Walter Summers, Stafford Dickens, Doreen Montgomery, Emlyn Williams (based on the novel The Norwich Victims by Francis Beeding); ph, Bryan Langley; ed, James Corbett.

Crime   **(PR:A MPAA:NR)**

DEAD MEN WALK*   (1943) 63m PRC bw

George Zucco (Dr. Lloyd Clayton/Dr. Elwyn Clayton), Mary Carlisle (Gayle), Nedrick Young (Dr. Bentley), Dwight Frye (Zolarr), Fern Emmett (Kate), Robert Strange (Harper), Hal Price (Sheriff), Sam Flint (Minister).

Zucco plays a dual role in this horror drama concerning twin brothers who are both doctors. One is good, the other evil, and the evil one dabbles in the occult. The nasty brother dies, but with the aid of hunchback assistant Frye he is brought out of his grave and becomes a vampire who murders the locals at night. Witnesses point the accusing finger at the good doctor and he has to do some fancy footwork to avoid being lynched by the standard angry mob.

p, Sigmund Neufeld; d, Sam Newfield; w, Fred Myton; ph, Jack Greenhalgh; ed, Holbrook N. Todd; md, Leo Erdody.

Horror   **Cas.**   **(PR:A MPAA:NR)**

DEAD MOUNTAINEER HOTEL, THE*

(1979, USSR) 90m Tallinnfilm c (OTEL 'U POGIBSHCHEGO ALPINISTA)

Uldis Putsitis, Yuri Yarvet, Lembit Peterson, Mikk Mikiver, K. Sebris, I. Kriauzaite, S. Puik, T. Khyarm.

Fascinating Russian film which combines the detective and science fiction genres and examines and expands upon their narrative forms. A police inspector is summoned to a mysterious hotel situated high in the snowy Ala-Tau mountains of Kazakhstan. Upon his arrival he is surprised to find no crime, but instead a strange group of guests inhabiting the hotel. After a series of strange and inexplicable events, the detective begins to surmise that he is surrounded by a hotel full of beings from another planet. The film becomes a bizarre game wherein the detective must adjust his manner of deductive thinking to a set of beings totally alien to him. He must learn to ignore his normal, human thought patterns and adopt a completely new mode of analytical consciousness. Winner of the Trieste festival of 1980.

d, Grigori Kromarov; w, Boris Strugatsky, Arkady Strugatsky; ph, Yuri Sillart.

Science Fiction   **(PR:C MPAA:NR)**

DEAD OF NIGHT** (1946, Brit.) 104m Rank/Ealing/UNIV bw

Mervyn Johns (Walter Craig), Roland Culver (Eliot Foley), Mary Merrall (Mrs. Foley), Frederick Valk (Dr. Van Straaten), Renee Gadd (Mrs. Craig), Antony Baird (Hugh Grainger), Judy Kelly (Joyce Grainger), Miles Malleson (Hearse Driver), Sally Ann Howes (Sally O'Hara), Michael Allan (Jimmy Watson), Robert Wyndham (Dr. Albury), Googie Withers (Joan Courtland), Ralph Michael (Peter Courtland), Esme Percy (Dealer), Michael Redgrave (Maxwell Frere), Hartley Power (Sylvester Kee), Elizabeth Welch (Beulah), Magda Kun (Mitzi), Garry Marsh (Harry Parker), Basil Radford (George Parratt), Naunton Wayne (Larry Potter), Peggy Bryan (Mary Lee), Johnny Maguire (Dummy), Allan Jeayes (Maurice Olcott).

A truly frightening thriller classic, this film, like TALES OF MANHATTAN and IF I HAD A MILLION, disproves the old Hollywood refrain that episodic films don't work, a tired excuse of uncreative producers fearing the inventive and innovative. Using a "linking story," five supernatural tales are offered, each varying in their subtle terrors, all strung together by the visit of troubled architect Johns who receives a call at the movie's beginning, asking him to come quickly to Pilgrim's Farm, a country house. As he approaches the austere Victorian building in his car, something hauntingly familiar about the house occurs to him. Once inside, Johns meets other guests who find themselves inexplicably present in Culver's home. They begin to relate their worst nightmares, one by one. Johns recognizes everyone present, telling them that they have been part of a recurring nightmare he has but they react with puzzlement. Valk tells Johns that he has never met him before and insists that they are all strangers. His remarks cause Baird to relate the first tale, "The Hearse Driver," one where he, a racetrack driver, purposely misses a bus out of a hunch and the bus crashes. Howes then reports "The Christmas Story," wherein she attends a holiday party and, during a game of hide-and-seek, the teenager finds a crying child in a strange room. She comforts him and later discovers that the child has been long dead, killed by his own sister. Withers, in "The Haunted Mirror," chillingly relates how she is given an antique mirror by her fiance that begins to reflect a Victorian room where a killing once took place. The mirror almost causes her fiance to murder her, but she saves herself at the last minute by smashing it to tiny shards. In "The Golfing Story," the one piece designed for comic relief, Radford and Wayne are two golfers vying for the attentions of one woman; one tricks the other into suicide only to have the deceased return to haunt him as he is about to enjoy his wedding night. The last story, one of the most terrifying ever put on film, is entitled "The Ventriloquist's Dummy" and features Redgrave as a ventriloquist going mad, believing that his dummy is assuming his personality and actual life while he is becoming the manipulated dummy. Placed in a mental institution, Redgrave goes berserk and tears Hugo the dummy limb from limb to prevent the takeover. But when the little wooden body is no more than splinters, Redgrave's personality is Hugo's and his shrill voice is that of Hugo (John Maguire). This single episode is frightening to the marrow as Redgrave sinks into madness with subtle, underplayed gestures until he completely loses his sanity at the last minute like a dam bursting, its contents roaring out until he is sapped, utterly drained, then filled up again with Hugo's maniacal character. The film ends when Johns is back at the roadhouse and finds himself inexplicably strangling Valk the psychiatrist. He flees the house but is stopped by the characters from the other stories and attacked. Johns is suddenly awakened by a shrill phone call which ends his nightmare. But does it? On the phone is Culver who asks the architect to rush out to his place to discuss some business. He does, driving to what turns out to be, once again, Pilgrim's Farm. His nightmare is beginning once more, the terrible tales to repeat, again and again and again in a maddening, looping unceasing nightmare. With typical unconcern for the thread of the story, U.S. distributors thought this excellent British import was too long and cut the golfing sequence and the Christmas ghost tale but this confused audiences who could not understand what Howes, Radford, and Wayne were doing in the linking story. The two takes were later reinstated. Of the four directors helming the various stories, Hamer is a standout with "The Haunted Mirror," and Cavalcanti excels with the two chillers, "The Christmas Story" and "The Ventriloquist's Dummy." The unforgettable Redgrave tale can be seen in a variation of the strange Ben Hecht story, THE GREAT GABBO, an eerie film where ventriloquist Erich Von Stroheim competes with his dummy over the affections of his beautiful assistant, destroying the dummy in a jealous rage at film's end. Of course the theme was blown out of proportion when it filled an entire feature, MAGIC, starring Anthony Hopkins, really a wholesale lift of the Redgrave story. This one is not for children nor adults with frayed nerves, suspicion of psychic abilities, or susceptibility of "the frights."

p, Michael Balcon; d, Alberto Cavalcanti ("The Ventriloquist's Dummy," "The Christmas Story"), Basil Dearden ("The Linking Story," "The Hearse Driver"), Robert Hamer ("The Haunted Mirror"), Charles Crichton ("The Golfing Story"); w, John Baines, Angus MacPhail, T.E.B. Clarke (based on stories by H.G. Wells, E.F. Benson, Baines, MacPhail); ph, Jack Parker, H. Julius; m, Georges Auric; ed, Charles Hasse; md, Ernest Irving; art d, Michael Relph.

Horror **Cas.** **(PR:O MPAA:NR)**

DEAD OF NIGHT, 1972 (SEE: DEATHDREAM, 1972)

DEAD OF SUMMER***
(1970 Ital./Fr.) 105m Titanus c (ONDATA DI CALORE)

Jean Seberg *(Joyce Grasse)*, Luigi Pistilli *(Doctor)*, Lilia Nguyen *(Maid)*, Gianni Belfiore *(Ali)*, Paolo Modugno *(Cherif)*, Franco Acampora *(Bianchi)*.

Seberg turns in an outstanding performance in this obscure foreign psychodrama. Shot in Morocco, the action concerns the efforts of an international team of urban planners to rebuild an area ravaged by an earthquake. Seberg is the lonely wife of an architect working on the project. She spends much of her time holed up in one of the newly built, modern apartments. She begins to have a breakdown due to many factors in her life she feels she cannot control. She cannot communicate in this strange land because she cannot speak the language and there's racial tension between the locals and herself. A vicious sandstorm rages, knocking out the apartment's refrigerator, but the conflict in her life that obsesses her most is her discovery of her husband's penchant for young North African boys. All these tensions lead to her final explosion of rage. Powerful. (Filmed on location in Agadin, Morocco.)

p, Giorgio Venturini; d&w, Nelo Risi (based on a novel by Dana Moseley); ph, Giulio Albonico (Technicolor); m, Pepino De Luca, Carlo Pas; ed, Gian Messeri; art d, Giuseppe Bassan.

Drama **(PR:C-O MPAA:NR)**

DEAD ON COURSE*½
(1952, Brit.) 73m Hammer-Lippert bw (GB: WINGS OF DANGER)

Zachary Scott *(Van)*, Robert Beatty *(Nick Talbot)*, Kay Kendall *(Alexia)*, Colin Tapley *(Maxwell)*, Naomi Chance *(Avril)*, Arthur Lane *(Boyd Spencer)*, Diane Cilento *(Jeannette)*, Harold Lang *(Snell)*, Jack Allen *(Truscott)*, Sheila Raynor *(Nurse)*, Courtney Hope *(Mrs. Clarence-Smith)*, June Ashley *(1st Blonde)*, Natasha Sokolova *(2nd Blonde)*, June Mitchell *(3rd Blonde)*, James Steel *(1st Flying Officer)*, Russ Allen *(2nd Flying Officer)*, Darcy Conyers *(Signals Officer)*.

Mostly boring and largely incomprehensible, this British B movie has Scott an airline pilot saving his pal from the gold smugglers who are blackmailing him into helping them. Another of the variety of exploitation pictures turned out by Hammer Studios before finding their niche with Technicolor remakes of horror classics.

p, Anthony Hinds; d, Terence Fisher; w, John Gilling (based on the novel *Dead On Course* by Elleston Trevor); ph, Walter Harvey; ed, Jim Needs.

Crime **(PR:A-C MPAA:NR)**

DEAD ONE, THE* (1961) 79m Favorite Films c

Monica Davis *(Monica)*, John McKay *(John)*, Linda Ormond *(Linda)*, Clyde Kelly *(Jonas)*, Darlene Myrick *(Bella Bella)*.

Davis stars in this obscure horror outing as a woman afraid she will lose a valuable property inheritance to her cousin and his new wife. To insure her acquisition of the property, she chants a voodoo spell over the corpse of her dead brother and brings him back to life. Then she sends her zombie sibling to persuade her cousin to back off.

p,d&w, Barry Mahon.

Horror **(PR:C MPAA:NR)**

DEAD OR ALIVE** (1944) 56m PRC bw

Dave O'Brien, Tex Ritter, Guy Wilkerson, Rebel Randall, Marjorie Clements, Ray Bennett, Charles King, Budd Buster, Henry Hall, Ted Mapes, Reed Howes, Bud Osborne.

Another entry in the Texas Rangers series has the trio riding into town pretending to be outlaws in order to join the gang that is terrorizing the community. One is exposed by the villains and another is captured by enraged vigilantes, but all manage to escape and join to clean up the town. Typical poverty row Western.

p, Arthur Alexander; d, Elmer P. Clifton; w, Harry Fraser; ph, Robert Cline; ed, Hugh Winn.

Western **Cas.** **(PR:A MPAA:NR)**

DEAD OR ALIVE, 1968
(SEE: MINUTE TO PRAY, A SECOND TO DIE, A, 1968)

DEAD PEOPLE zero (1974) 89m V/M Production/International Cinefilm c
(AKA: MESSIAH OF EVIL; RETURN OF THE LIVING DEAD; REVENGE OF THE SCREAMING DEAD; THE SECOND COMING)

Michael Greer *(Thom)*, Marianna Hill *(Arletty)*, Joy Bang *(Toni)*, Anitra Ford *(Laura)*, Royal Dano *(Joseph Lang)*, Elisha Cook, Jr. *(Charlie)*.

Incoherent horror film about a woman, Hill, searching for her father, a surrealist painter in a small California coastal town that has become overrun with flesh-eating zombies. Katz and Huyck, who enjoyed great success as the writers of George Lucas' AMERICAN GRAFFITI, stooped so low as to attempt to rip off George Romero's low-budget masterpiece NIGHT OF THE LIVING DEAD. When Romero's sequel, DAWN OF THE DEAD, was such a success in 1979, DEAD PEOPLE was re-issued as RETURN OF THE DEAD and the distributors went so far as to steal the advertising copy from Romero's movie which read, "When There's No More Room In Hell The Dead Will Walk The Earth." Romero sued and won.

p, Gloria Katz; d, Willard Huyck; w, Katz, Huyck; ph, Stephen Katz (Techniscope, Technicolor); m, Phillan Bishop; ed, Scott Conrad; art d, Jack Fiske, Joan Mocine.

Horror **(PR:O MPAA:R)**

DEAD PIGEON ON BEETHOVEN STREET***
(1972, Ger.) 102m Bavaria Atelier Gesellschaft c

Glenn Corbett *(Sandy)*, Christa Lang *(Christa)*, Sieghardt Rupp *(Kessin)*, Anton Diffring *(Mensur)*, Alex D'Arcy *(Novka)*, Anthony Ching *(Fong)*, Eric P. Caspar *(Charlie)*.

American director Sam Fuller answered his cult of European fans by making this tongue-in-cheek private-eye movie financed by the Germans. Corbett stars as a detective whose partner is murdered while investigating a gang of drug-dealing extortionists who photograph big-shot international politico-types in compromising situations with the lovely Lang. Corbett goes undercover and joins the gang to get the goods on them. Passable effort (it's always nice to see Fuller's behind-the-camera work), but the usual Fuller intensity is missing.

d&w, Samuel Fuller; ph, Jerzy Lipman (Eastmancolor); ed, Liesgret Schmitt-Klink; art d, Lothar Kirchem.

Mystery **(PR:C MPAA:PG)**

DEAD RECKONING*½** (1947) 100m COL bw

Humphrey Bogart *(Rip Murdock)*, Lizabeth Scott *(Coral Chandler)*, Morris Carnovsky *(Martinelli)*, Charles Cane *(Lt. Kincaid)*, William Prince *(Johnny Drake)*, Marvin Miller *(Krause)*, Wallace Ford *(McGee)*, James Bell *(Father Logan)*, George Chandler *(Louis Ord)*, William Forrest *(Lt. Col. Simpson)*, Ruby Dandridge *(Hyacinth)*, Lillian Wells *(Pretty Girl)*, Charles Jordan *(Mike, Bartender)*, Robert Scott *(Band Leader)*, Lillian Bronson *(Mrs. Putnam)*, Maynard Holmes *(Desk Clerk)*, William Lawrence *(Stewart)*, Dudley Dickerson *(Waiter)*, Syd Saylor *(Morgue Attendant)*, George Eldredge *(Policeman)*, Chester Clute *(Martin)*, Joseph Crehan *(Gen. Steele)*, Gary Owen *(Reporter)*, Alvin Hammer *(Photographer)*, Pat Lane *(General's Aide)*, Frank Wilcox *(Desk Clerk)*, Stymie Beard *(Bellboy)*, Matty Fain *(Ed)*, John Bohn, Sayre Dearing *(Croupiers)*, Harry Denny, Kay Garrett *(Dealers)*, Jack Santoro *(Raker)*, Joe Gilbert *(Croupier)*, Sam Finn *(Raker)*, Dick Gordon *(Dealer)*, Ray Teal *(Motorcycle Policeman)*, Hugh Hooker *(Bellboy)*, Chuck

Hamilton, Robert Ryan (Detectives), Grady Sutton (Maitre d'Hotel), Jesse Graves (Waiter), Byron Foulger (Night Attendant), Tom Dillon (Priest), Isabel Withers (Nurse), Wilton Graff (Surgeon), Paul Bradley (Man), Alyce Goering (Woman).

Bogart and Prince are war heroes going to Washington to receive citations. Prince leaves the train, hopping another to points unknown and Bogart trails him to his home town in the South, finding his body in the morgue, burned to a crisp. When Bogart looks into the hero's past he pieces together a strange conspiracy that has led to Prince's murder. He visits Carnovsky's nightclub to get information from a bartender, Chandler, and meets Scott, one-time singer and Prince's old girl friend. Bogart instantly dislikes the arrogant Carnovsky and, to show him up, takes him for a fortune at the crap table. He and Scott fall in love but his investigation goes haywire. Bartender Chandler, who is about to give him vital information about Prince's killing, is found by Bogart in his hotel room, dead in the next bed. Bogart removes the body just before the police arrive, then digs further, trying to find the person attempting to blackmail him and the one responsible for Prince's death. He confronts the likely suspect, Carnovsky, and is beaten to a pulp by his right-hand thug, Miller (later the voice on TV's "The Millionaire"). He returns to Scott, by then having pieced together his bits of information, all of it adding up to the fact that Scott killed her husband. She admits the slaying but insists that Prince took the blame for her and that Carnovsky has been blackmailing her since he has the murder weapon, a gun kept in his safe at the club. Bogart returns to the club and forces Carnovsky to turn over the gun. He does, only after Bogart sets the place on fire, then flees out a back door where someone hiding in the dark shoots him to death. Bogart knows it was Scott and accuses her, saying he smelled her special perfume, and further states that she thought she was killing him, knowing he went to Carnovsky and that Carnovsky was her secret spouse. As they drive along a lonely road Scott realizes that Bogart now has the whole story and she pulls a gun, shooting Bogie and causing the car to crash. Bogart survives but Scott is mortally injured. He holds her hand as she slips into death. He soothes her fears at the end, instructing her to stand at death's door like a paratrooper, leaping into the darkness, calling out the paratrooper's cry of bravado, "Geronimo!" The ending dramatically shows a parachute opening, then descending into a fadeout. Bogart clears Prince's name at the end, the story told in flashback as Bogart relates his tale to a priest at the film's opening. This tricky film noir entry would have been routine had it not been for Bogart's magic. Carnovsky is much too expansive and intellectual to be believed in his role of a sleazy nightclub owner and the deep-throated Scott, with her conflicting black eyebrows and blonde hair, camps her part so broadly as to be ridiculous. She vamps out a song in the nightclub, "Either It's Love or It Isn't" (Allan Roberts, Doris Fisher), which reportedly made her the rage in Dixie years earlier, a great disservice to Southern taste. Bogart here is not in his usual commanding role, but a man tangled in a thick web of circumstances and intrigue which makes his character all the more appealing and ameliorates the brutality and violence of the film. Miller's sadistic, face-kicking role is wholly repugnant but becomes the epitome of the remorseless modern heavy. DEAD RECKONING is a prime example of post-WW II film noir where the issues are hazy, the hero gropes, and the characters are even more unsavory than the gangsters of the 1930s peddling bootleg hooch, as if they were the debris of the war which had claimed the best of humanity. In this case the innocent victim is Prince, winner of the Congressional Medal of Honor, his country's highest military award, a noble youth murdered in the polluted backwaters of America, ignobly burned to death instead of having his pure heart pierced by an enemy bullet on a foreign shore. Here Hollywood began to look into its own ashcan, studying yesteryear's waste, where nostalgia was mixed with corruption, banging the lid nervously and waiting for the Great Janitor. He arrives not in the form of triumphant justice as in days of old but as a sneering tramp salvaging second-hand lives.

p, Sidney Biddell; d, John Cromwell; w, Oliver H.P. Garrett, Steve Fisher, Allen Rivkin (based on an unpublished story by Gerald Adams and Biddell); ph, Leo Tover; m, Marlin Skiles; ed, Gene Havlick; md, M.W. Stoloff; art d, Stephen Goosson, Rudolph Sternad; set d, Louis Diage; cos, Jean Louis; makeup, Clay Campbell.

Mystery/Crime Drama (PR:C MPAA:NR)

DEAD RINGER** (1964) 115m WB bw (GB: DEAD IMAGE)

Bette Davis (Margaret/Edith), Karl Malden (Sgt. Jim Hobbson), Peter Lawford (Tony Collins), Philip Carey (Sgt. Ben Hoag), Jean Hagen (Dede), George Macready (Paul Harrison), Estelle Winwood (Matriarch), George Chandler (George), Mario Alcalde (Garcia), Cyril Delevanti (Henry), Monika Henreid (Janet), Bert Remsen (Dan), Charles Watts (Apartment Manager), Ken Lynch (Capt. Johnson), Charles Meredith (Defense Lawyer).

Bette Davis did the twins 18 years before in the much better A STOLEN LIFE. This was her followup to WHATEVER HAPPENED TO BABY JANE? and she was into macabre roles not unlike those attempted by Joan Crawford at about the same time in her career. Davis (1) had once loved her brother-in-law and planned to marry him. But she lost him to her sister (2) and the movie begins when the man is being buried. She learns that he only married her sister (2) because he thought she was carrying his child. Davis (1) now runs a small bar while her sister (2) is wealthy. Davis (2) wants to patch up the old tears in the sisterly fabric but (1) rejects her until (1) learns that she is about to lose her tavern and suddenly needs money. She invites (2) to see the squalid apartment in which (1) lives. The two sisters have it out and (2) admits that she did trap the dead husband with a lie about her pregnancy. Davis (1) is enraged, kills (2), changes clothing, writes a suicide note and takes over the identity of her sister. The dead body is found by the boy friend of Davis (1), Malden, who is a Los Angeles detective. He believes that his fiancee is dead. But Davis has no idea what she is stepping into when she climbs into her dead sister's life. It turns out that the sweet lady was having an affair with Peter Lawford, who'd been off in Europe. He returns and spots the difference right away and wants money to keep mum. Davis gives Lawford some of the late woman's baubles. He attempts to pawn them and that's reported to the cops. They search Lawford's apartment and find a load of deadly arsenic. Malden

approaches Davis (thinking she is his dead lover's sister), who admits that Lawford is her lover. Malden now suspects that the dead husband may not have died naturally so he orders the body exhumed and it is found to be filled with arsenic. Davis goes after Lawford, accusing him of murdering the dead man. Lawford tries to kill Davis but he is torn to bits by the late man's Great Dane. Later, Davis is accused of the dead husband's murder. In desperation, she confesses that she is not who she appears to be, but Malden won't believe her. She's convicted and about to be executed when she meets Malden again and tells him that she is Margaret, not Edith (the one he loved and intended to marry). She is lying but believes that will allow him to sleep at night, safe that he hasn't sent the woman he loves to her death. Little touches of THE POSTMAN ALWAYS RINGS TWICE in the ironic twist of being executed for a murder one didn't commit rather than for the murder one did commit. Davis has a chance to let it all hang out in the two roles and she does. Wearing heavy makeup to conceal her 56 years (Malden was 50 and Lawford was 39), Davis is almost grotesque in her performance. At 115 minutes, the picture is usually cut 10 to 12 minutes to accommodate a two-hour TV time slot (with commercials) and the scene that is excised is, perhaps, the most memorable of the picture; it's Davis singing "Shuffle Off to Buffalo." Believe it or not! Bert Remsen (Dan) has appeared in many movies, some of which he may have even cast himself in. Remsen and his wife are among Hollywood's most respected casting directors.

p, William H. Wright; d, Paul Henreid; w, Albert Beich, Oscar Millard (based on the story La Otra by Rian James); ph, Ernest Haller; m, Andre Previn; ed, Folmar Blangsted; art d, Perry Ferguson; set d, William Stevens; cos, Don Feld.

Mystery (PR:A-C MPAA:NR)

DEAD RUN** (1961, Fr./Ital./Ger.) 98m UNIV c

Georges Geret (Carlos), Peter Lawford (Dain), Ira von Furstenberg (Suzanne), Maria Grazia Buccella (Anna), Horst Frank (Manganne), Werner Peters (Bardieff), Jean Tissier (Adelgate), Bernard Tiphaine (Embassy Official), Wolfgang Kieling (Wolfgang), Pierre Cordier (Fence), Eva Pflug (Klaus's Secretary), Wolfgang Preiss, Siegfried Wischnewski, Dean Heyde, Henri Guégan, Alan Collins, Michel Charrel, Roger Treville, Guy Delorme.

Misfired attempt at a wacky espionage comedy (dubbed) sees an international cast chasing after a batch of secret defense papers stolen from a murdered American courier in Berlin by a gang of thugs disguised as ambulance attendants. The papers, in turn, are stolen by an unwitting pickpocket, Geret, who suddenly finds himself being chased across Europe by the gang and the CIA.

p, Peter Hahne; d, Christian-Jaque; w, Michel Levine, Jaque, Pascal Jardin, Dany Tyber (based on the novel by Robert Sheckley); ph, Pierre Petit (Eastmancolor); m, Gerard Calvi; ed, Jacques Desagneau; art d, Jurgen Kiebach.

Spy/Comedy (PR:C MPAA:R)

DEAD TO THE WORLD*½ (1961) 87m National Film Studios/UA bw

Reedy Talton (Barney Cornell), Jana Pearce (Laura), Ford Rainey (Congressman Keach), Casey Peyson (Karen Stone), John McLiam (Goody), John Dorman (Hannigan), Joel Thomas (Paul Evarts), Joseph Julian (Kelly), Leon B. Stevens (Jason Stone), Philip Kenneally (Sam Hand), Len Doyle (DeLuca), Maggie O'Neill (Helga), Michael Gorrin (Milo Crespi), Drew Pearson (Narrator).

Talton works in the State Department and has been accused of funneling top-secret information to a Bulgarian family (a family that had saved his life during WW II). He has also been charged with the murder of Stevens, a political boss. With the help of his girl friend, Pearce, Talton is able to clear his name and unmask the real traitor.

p, F. William Hart; d, Nicholas Webster; w, John Roeburt (based on the novel State Department Murders by Edward Ronns); ph, Bert Spielvogel; m, Charlie Byrd, Eddie Phyfe Jazz Ensemble.

Drama (PR:A MPAA:NR)

DEAD WOMAN'S KISS, A* (1951, Ital.) 81m Casolaro Films bw

Virginia Belmont (Clara Dominici), Gianna Maria Canale (Nara O'Kira), Peter Trent (Conte Guido Severi), Aldo Landi (Enrico Maffei), Vinicio Sofia (Moreno), Paul Muller (Maggiore Hans).

Belmont is a countess whose husband (Trent) and his lover (Canale) plan to poison. The dose doesn't do the job, only throws her into a coma, and when her still-faithful old lover kisses her apparently dead lips, he realizes that she is still alive. She is revived and sees that Trent and Canale get what's coming to them. Depressing melodrama has almost nothing going for it.

d, Guido Brignone; w, Leo Cevenni, Vittorio Martino (based on a story by Francesco Mastriani).

Drama (PR:A MPAA:NR)

DEAD ZONE, THE**½ (1983) 103m PAR c

Christopher Walken (Johnny Smith), Brooke Adams (Sarah Bracknell), Tom Skerrit (Sheriff Bannerman), Herbert Lom (Dr. Sam Welzak), Anthony Zerbe (Roger Stuart), Colleen Dewhurst (Henrietta Dodd), Martin Sheen (Greg Stillson), Nicholas Campbell (Frank Dodd), Sean Sullivan (Herb Smith), Jackie Burroughs (Vera Smith), Geza Kovacs (Sonny Elliman), Simon Craig (Christopher Stuart), Barry Flatman (Walter Bracknell), Raffi Tchalikian, Ken Pogue, Gordon Jocelyn, Bill Copeland, Jack Messinger, Chapelle Jaffe, Cindy Hines, Helen Udy, Ramon Estevez, Joseph Domenchini, Roger Dunn, Wally Bondarenko, Claude Rae, John Koensgen, Les Carlson, Jim Bearden, Hardee Lineham.

The best adaptation of a Stephen King novel (and that's including Kubrick's THE SHINING) directed by an unusually restrained Cronenberg (it's about time) with a great cast and it's still not all that good. Walken stars as a young, shy school teacher who leaves his fiancee Adams one night (despite her invitation for him to spend the night) during a rainstorm and gets into a near-fatal accident with a jackknifed truck trailer. He comes to five years later out of a deep coma, his life forever changed. Adams has married another man, his mother has become a religious fanatic, and he has developed a strange power to see people's futures by touching their hands. After getting a vision that his nurse's child is trapped in a burning house and realizing that it is true (the child is saved in the nick of time), Walken is besieged by media reporters and made famous. He flees into seclusion at his father's house, where he attempts to live a sedentary life. There he is visited by Adams who, though she is happily married, feels that she owes it to him to consummate their relationship after five years. Though Walken still loves her (to him it's been five minutes since he's seen her—not five years—so his feelings of love are still strong) he regretfully cuts off contact with Adams because the sight of her and her child are too much for him to bear (the family he could have had). To distract himself from these thoughts, he agrees to help the local sheriff solve a frustrating murder case that has been plaguing the community. After a long, obvious, bloody, and pointless investigation (this segment bogs down the whole film and does nothing to advance the narrative), the crimes are solved and Walken moves away again to avoid unwanted publicity. In another community he sets up shop as a private tutor and a very rich and powerful man, Zerbe, hires Walken to tutor his son (played by Craig), a shy and lonely boy not unlike Walken himself. Walken and Craig become close friends, and Zerbe is amazed at how quickly the tutor coaxes the boy out of his shell. The relationship ends, however, when Walken sees the boy drown in a hockey accident during one of his visions. He makes a dramatic and violent plea to spare the boy from playing hockey that day, and Zerbe reluctantly agrees, though he forbids Walken from ever seeing the boy again. That afternoon, Zerbe tries to convince the boy to play hockey, but the boy refuses. Zerbe (who is the team organizer) takes the rest of the team out anyway, and two of the boys drown in a horrible accident. Walken's doctor, Lom, is excited by this discovery because it proves that his patient can not only *see* the future, but also *change* it. Once again Walken moves on and is shocked to discover Adams and her husband working for a robust political candidate, Sheen. Walken goes to one of the rallies, but when he shakes hands with the politician he sees that someday this man will be president and he will push the nuclear button, destroying the Earth. Fed up with his life and feeling increasingly ill (he is wracked by painful headaches) Walken decides to assassinate Sheen and change the future. He takes a rifle and hides in the balcony of the small-town auditorium where Sheen is about to give a speech. On stage with the politician are Adams and her husband and child (the cynical Sheen thought they would look good on stage with him). Just as Sheen begins his speech, Walken stands up and fires, the shot misses, and Sheen grabs Adams' baby and uses the crying child for cover. Walken hesitates taking another shot, and is himself shot by Sheen's bodyguard. As he lies dying, Sheen demands to know who he is. Walken grabs the man's hand and sees the cover of a "Newsweek" magazine with a dramatic cover photograph of Sheen shielding himself with Adams' baby. The magazine heralds the end of Sheen's political career. In Walken's vision, Sheen commits suicide. Walken tells Sheen, "It's over," and dies in Adams' arms. Though the film is well acted and directed, once again King's source material bites off more than it can chew, taking a simple story of tragic, unfulfilled love into a psychic horror drama that leads to revelations of world importance, without developing any of the angles particularly well.

p, Debra Hill; d, David Cronenberg; w, Jeffrey Boam (based on the novel by Stephen King); ph, Mark Irwin (Technicolor); m, Michael Kamen; ed, Ronald Saunders; prod d, Carol Spier; art d, Barbara Dunphy; sp eff, Jon Belyou.

Horror **Cas.** **(PR:O MPAA:R)**

DEADFALL*½ (1968, Brit.) 120m FOX c

Michael Caine *(Henry Clarke)*, Giovanna Ralli *(Fe Moreau)*, Eric Portman *(Richard Moreau)*, Nanette Newman *(Girl)*, David Buck *(Salinas)*, Carlos Pierre *(Antonio)*, Leonard Rossiter *(Fillmore)*, Emilio Rodriguez *(Inspector Ballastero)*, Vladek Shaybal *(Dr. Delgado)*, Carmen Dene *(Masseuse)*, Renata Tarrago *(Guitar Soloist)*, John Barry *(Symphony Conductor)*, George Ghent *(Stresemann)*, Geraldine Sherman *(Delgado's Receptionist)*, Antonio Sampere *(Lagranja)*, Reg Howell *(Spanish Chauffeur)*, Santiago Rivero *(Armed Guard)*, Philip Madoc *(Bank Manager)*.

Tedious bore about Caine, who is in an alcoholic recovery sanitarium falling for Ralli, who is married to Portman, a homosexual who is having an affair with Carlos Pierre. They all get together and have Newman join them for a robbery of Buck, a playboy with all sorts of money. Buck is a sadist not unlike Olivier in SLEUTH and enjoys the crooks coming to his home so he can have sport with them. In the end, Caine and Portman both die; Ralli goes to their dual funeral and leaves with the police, and Pierre, the boy friend of Portman, watches it all, shrugs, and exits. Monash had been producing Fox's "Peyton Place" TV series at the time and must have thought he was still in TV. This picture was at least 40 minutes too long and could have used some commercials to break up the incessant talk. When Bryan Forbes is good, he is terrific. But when he has a weak producer who won't tell him that enough is enough, he can get terribly pretentious. Newman is Forbes's wife but don't hold that against her. She is, as always, very professional. There is one 23-minute sequence that was an attempt at emulating the silent scene in TOPKAPI. It doesn't work at all despite Barry's haunting guitar concerto played by Renata Tarrago.

p, Paul Monash; d&w, Bryan Forbes (based on the novel by Desmond Cory); ph, Gerry Turpin (Eastmancolor); m, John Barry; ed, John Jympson; art d, Ray Simm; set d, Simm; cos, Julie Harris; m/l, "My Love Has Two Faces" (John Barry, Jack Lawrence).

Crime Drama **(PR:C MPAA:NR)**

DEADHEAD MILES*** (1982) 93m PAR c

Alan Arkin *(Cooper)*, Paul Benedict *(Tramp)*, Hector Elizondo *(Bad Character)*, Oliver Clark *(Durazno)*, Charles Durning *(Red Ball Rider)*, Larry Wolf *(Pineapple)*, Barnard Hughes *(Old Man)*, William Duell *(Auto Parts Salesman)*, Madison Arnold *(Hostler)*, Loretta Swit *(Woman with Glass Eye)*, Donna Anderson *(Waitress)*, Sue Carol Perry *(Woman Tramp)*, Alan Garfield *(Juicy Brucey)*, Patrick Dennis-Leigh *(Loader)*, Dan Resin *(Foreman)*, Diane Shalet *(Donna James)*, Bruce Bennett *(Johnny Mesquitero)*, Phil Kanneally *(State Trooper)*, John Milius *(2nd State Trooper)*, Bill Littleton *(Chicken Farmer)*, John Steadman *(Old Sam)*, Bill McCutcheon *(Used Car Dealer)*, Tom Waters *(Truck Driver)*, Ida Lupino *(She)*, George Raft *(Himself)*, Avery Schreiber *(The Boss)*.

If you wonder how it is that George Raft looks so good in this 1982 picture when he had died two years before, it's because Paramount sat on this very strange picture for more than a decade before allowing it to emerge into the theaters. Arkin is a former trucker who steals a semi, lets a bum hitchhike with him (Benedict), hauls some black market building materials to pay his way across the country from East to West, and that's about that. It's very episodic with all sorts of cameo performances, an extremely literate script (which probably wasn't understood by the Paramount executives), many metaphors and allusions, and some very funny sequences. Deadhead Miles doesn't refer to anyone's name. To 'Deadhead' is to drop a haul and drive back empty. The major problem with the movie is that it's mile after mile with almost no spine to keep it together. In that, it's as existential as anything Sartre ever wrote. John Milius does a walk-on, and we get a chance to see several actors in some of their first roles. Durning, Swit, and Garfield were all at the beginnings of their excellent careers and Bruce Bennett was ending his before venturing into a successful real estate business. Vernon Zimmerman has not had the kind of success predicted for him by those who saw his earliest films.

p, Vernon Zimmerman, Tony Bill; d, Zimmerman; w, Terence Malick; ph, Ralph Woolsey (uncredited color); m, Tom T. Hall; ed, Bud Smith, cos, Richard Brunno; m/l Dave Dudley.

Comedy **(PR:A-C MPAA:NR)**

DEADLIER THAN THE MALE***
(1957, Fr.) 104m C.I.C.C. (Films Borderie)—S.N. Pathe Cinema-Films G. Agiman/Continental Film bw (LE TEMPS DES ASSASSINS)

Jean Gabin *(Chatelin)*, Daniele Delorme *(Catherine)*, Lucienne Bogaert *(Gabrielle)*, Gerard Blain *(Gerard)*, Germaine Kerjean *(Mme. Chatelin)*, Gabrielle Fontan *(Mme. Jules)*, Robert Manuel *(Bonnacorci)*, Alfred Goulin *(Armand)*, Jean-Paul Roussillon *(Amedee)*, Robert Pizani *(The President)*, Aime Clariond *(Prevot)*, Robert Arnoux *(Bouvier)*, Michel Seldow *(Gentel)*, Liliane Bert *(Bert)*, Gaby Basset *(Waitress)*, Gerard Fallec *(Gaston)*.

Delorme is a young woman who turns up on chef Gabin's doorstep one day and tells him that she is the orphaned daughter of the wife he divorced many years before. He takes her in and eventually marries her, although she is carrying on with Blain, Gabin's best friend. When he finally discovers her affair he begins looking at her with murderous intent, while she begins looking at him and Blain with a similar gaze. Well done drama with an exceptional script and good performances.

d, Julien Duvivier; w, Duvivier, Charles Dorat, P.A. Breal (based on a story by Duvivier, Dorat, Maurice Bessy); ph, Armand Thirard; m, Jean Wiener.

Drama **(PR:C MPAA:NR)**

DEADLIER THAN THE MALE½** (1967, Brit.) 98m UNIV c

Richard Johnson *(Hugh Drummond)*, Elke Sommer *(Irma Eckman)*, Sylva Koscina *(Penelope)*, Nigel Green *(Carl Petersen)*, Suzanna Leigh *(Grace)*, Steve Carlson *(Robert Drummond)*, Virginia North *(Brenda)*, Justine Lord *(Miss Ashenden)*, Zia Mohyeddin *(King Fedra)*, Lee Montague *(Boxer)*, Yasuko Nagazumi *(Mitsouko)*, Laurence Naismith *(Sir John Bledlow)*, George Pastell *(Carloggio)*, Milton Reid *(Chang)*, Leonard Rossiter *(Bridgenorth)*, Didi Sydow *(Anna)*, Dervis Ward *(Keller)*, John Stone *(Wyngarde)*, William Mervyn, Jill Banner *(Pam)*.

Johnson stars as Bulldog Drummond, the modern Robin Hood, who was revived by the British to compete with the successful James Bond series. This film pits Johnson against nefarious industrialist Green who noses into major business deals and then eliminates his partners so he can reap the rewards. His weapons of death include an all-female team of killers led by Sommer. Overlong and silly. (See BULLDOG DRUMMOND series, Index.)

p, Betty Box, Sydney Box, Bruce Newbery; d, Ralph Thomas; w, Jimmy Sangster, David Osborn, Liz Charles-Williams, (based on a story by Sangster and the novels of H. C. "Sapper" McNeile); ph, Ernest Steward (Technicolor); m, Malcolm Lockyer; ed, Alfred Roome; m/1, "Deadlier Than the Male" (John Franz, Scott Engel).

Crime **(PR:C MPAA:NR)**

DEADLIEST SIN, THE½** (1956, Brit.) 90m AA bw (GB: CONFESSION)

Sydney Chaplin *(Mike)*, Audrey Dalton *(Louise)*, John Bentley *(Inspector Kessler)*, Peter Hammond *(Alan)*, John Welsh *(Father Neil)*, Jefferson Clifford *(Pop)*, Patrick Allen *(Corey)*, Pat McGrath *(Williams)*, Robert Raglan *(Beckman)*, Betty Wolfe *(Mrs. Poole)*, Richard Huggett *(Young Priest)*, Eddie Stafford *(Photographer)*, Alan Robinson, Edward Dane, Sheila Allen, Hugh Munroe, Dorinda Stevens, Percy Herbert.

Messy crime drama sees Chaplin, a thief, return home to England after ditching his partner during a holdup and absconding with the proceeds. The angry partner tracks him down, but is killed by Chaplin's future brother-in-law, Hammond, who was only trying to help. Riddled with guilt, Hammond goes to his priest to confess, and Chaplin murders him. Thinking that the priest may have heard too much, he attempts to kill him, too, but the law arrives and corners the crook in the church.

p, Alec Snowden; d, Ken Hughes; w, Hughes (based on a play by Don Martin); ph, Philip Grindrod; m, Richard Taylor; ed, Geoffrey Muller; art d, Harold Watson.

Crime **(PR:A MPAA:NR)**

DEADLINE, THE*½ (1932) 64m COL bw

Buck Jones *(Buck Donlin)*, Loretta Sayers *(Helen Evans)*, Robert Ellis *(Coleman)*, Edwin J. Brady *(Lefty)*, G. Raymond Nye *(Grady)*, Knute Erickson *(Otto)*, George

Ernest *(Jimmy)*, Harry Todd *(Chloride)*, Jack Curtis, Edward LeSaint, James Farley, "Silver."

No, it's not a newspaper picture, it's a Jones western, and there isn't a newspaper to be found. Jones plays a man on parole from a crime he didn't commit. Upon returning home, he discovers that the once friendly townsfolk will have nothing to do with the man they continue to believe killed a detective who was in search of a cattle thief. The only supporters Jones has are a small boy, Ernest, who idolizes him, and his former sweetheart, Sayers. Jones spends the rest of the film tracking down the real killer and brings him to justice.

d&w, Lambert Hillyer; ph, Byron Haskins; ed, Maurice Wright.

Western **(PR:A MPAA:NR)**

DEADLINE*½ (1948) 57m Yucca Pictures/Astor bw

Sunset Carson, Pat Starling, Lee Roberts, Stephen Keyes, Frank Ellis, Forrest Matthews, Al Terry, Pat Gleason, Bob Curtis, Phil Arnold, Joe Hiser, Don Gray, Buck Monroe, Al Wyatt.

Carson is blamed for a crime he didn't commit and spends most of his time in this tepid oater finding the culprit. Not one of Sunset's better efforts.

p, Walt Mattox, Oliver Drake; d&w, Drake; ph, James S. Brown, Jr.; m, Frank Sanucci; ed, Mary Cohn.

Western **(PR:A MPAA:NR)**

DEADLINE AT DAWN½** (1946) 83m RKO bw

Susan Hayward *(June Goff)*, Paul Lukas *(Gus)*, Bill Williams *(Alex Winkley)*, Joseph Calleia *(Bartelli)*, Osa Massen *(Helen Robinson)*, Lola Lane *(Edna Bartelli)*, Jerome Cowan *(Lester Brady)*, Marvin Miller *(Sleepy Parsons)*, Roman Bohnen *(Collarless Man)*, Steven Geray *(Man with Gloves)*, Joe Sawyer *(Babe Dooley)*, Constance Worth *(Mrs. Raymond)*, Joseph Crehan *(Lt. Kane)*, Jason Robards, Sr. *(Policeman)*, Sammy Blum *(Sam, Taxi Driver)*, Emory Parnell *(Capt. Bender)*, Lee Phelps *(Philosophical Policeman)*, Ernie Adams *(Waiter)*, Larry McGrath *(Whispering Man)*, Connie Conrad *(Mrs. Bender)*, Carl Faulkner *(Policeman Drawing Diagram)*, Dorothy Curtis *(Giddy Woman)*, Mike Pat Donovan *(Sweating Trickster)*, Fred Aldrich *(Beefy Guest)*, Pearl Varvalle *(Woman)*, John Ince *(Elderly Sleeper)*, Billy Wayne *(Billy White)*, Jack Kenny *(Headwaiter)*, Edmund Glover, Al Eben *(Taxi Drivers)*, Betty Gillette *(Woman with Dog)*, Annelle Hayes *(Society Woman)*, Larry Wheat *(Derelict)*, Shimen Ruskin *(Sam)*, Myrna Dell *(Hatcheck Girl)*, George Tyne *(Ray)*, Larry Thompson *(Drunk)*, Ed Gargan *(Bouncer)*, Edgar Caldwell *(Dancer)*, Florence Pepper *(Dancing Girl)*, Dorothy Grainger *(Ticket Girl)*, Eddy Chandler, Philip Morris *(Policemen)*, Phil Warren *(Jerry Robinson)*, John Elliott *(Sleepy Man)*, Louis Quince *(Markey)*, Alan Ward *(Yerkes)*, Dick Rush *(Policeman)*, Armand Curly Wright *(Fruit Peddler)*, John Barton *(One-legged Man)*, Dick Elliot *(Chap)*, Earle Hodgins *(Barker)*, Walter Soderling *(Husband)*, Virginia Farmer *(Janitress)*, Al Bridge *(Detective Smiley)*, Ralph Dunn *(Capt. Dill)*, Jack Cheatham, Dick Rush, Frank Meredith, Roger Creed *(Policemen)*, Jerome Franks, Billy Bletcher *(Waiters)*, Tommy Quinn, Peter Breck *(Countermen)*, Jack Daley *(Snoring Man)*, Eddie Hart *(Policeman)*, William Challee *(Ray)*.

Take a hard-edged Cornell Woolrich story about the people who prowl by night, give it a screenplay by Clifford Odets, one of America's most literate authors, add the direction of a Broadway rather than a Hollywood helmer and what do you have? A mish-mash, that's what. Bill Williams is a sailor in NYC from his home base in Norfolk. He winds up playing poker in a rigged game with Calleia at his cafe. Lane, Calleia's sister, slips him some knockout potion. Upon awakening, he discovers that he has well over a thousand bucks in his pocket, but he doesn't know from whence it came. It's two in the morning and he is dizzy and doesn't know what to do so he enlists Hayward, a tired dime-a-dance girl. She is a cynic, hates her work, and wishes this blond sailor would leave her alone, but he is naive and fresh-faced. When she hears that he's carrying all that money that he believes isn't his, she prevails on him to return it. They go to Lane's apartment and find her murdered. Lukas is a cab driver who walks into the apartment when they find the body. He realizes they are innocent and promises to help them. They see Constance Worth sneak into the place to steal some revealing letters Lane had written about an illicit affair between Worth and Cowan. At Cowan's residence, Calleia has heard of his sister's murder and he beats Williams senseless with his gun. Williams is due to return to Norfolk but stays, and when Calleia realizes that he is not the responsible party, the two join forces with Hayward, Lukas, and Cowan to try to learn the identity of the killer. A white carnation had been found at the scene of the murder, and Lane's ex-husband had been known to wear those. He is Marvin Miller, a blind pianist. They interrogate him and he dies of a heart attack, fearing he will be hurt by his former brother-in-law, Calleia. Williams is arrested by the cops and taken to the police station. Suddenly, Lukas, the friendly cab driver, can take it no longer and he confesses to killing Lane. Lane had been seeing his son-in-law, thus making his daughter miserable; when she refused to end the affair, Lukas killed her. The picture concludes with Williams taking Hayward down to Norfolk, Virginia, to meet his mother. If the above sounds complex, confusing, and splayed, you're right on the money. When you add Odets' dialog to it, the feeling is very out-of-place with low-life characters in sleazy areas speaking philosophical cant. Lane, one of three sisters in the movies, born Dorothy Mulligan, retired from the screen after this picture to go into real estate. Among her many husbands were Lew Ayres, director Roland West, and director Alexander Hall. She died in 1981.

p, Adrian Scott; d, Harold Clurman; w, Clifford Odets (based on a novel by William Irish [Cornell Woolrich]); ph, Nicholas Musuraca; m, Hanns Eisler; ed, Roland Gross; md, C. Bakaleinikoff; art d, Albert D'Agostino, Jack Okey; set d, Darrell Silvera; cos, Renie; spec eff, Vernon L. Walker.

Mystery **(PR:A MPAA:NR)**

DEADLINE FOR MURDER½** (1946) 64m FOX bw

Paul Kelly *(Lt. McMullen)*, Kent Taylor *(Millard)*, Sheila Ryan *(Vivian)*, Jerome Cowan *(Lynch)*, Renee Carson *(Zita)*, Joan Blair *(Helen)*, Marian Martin *(Laura)*, Leslie Vincent *(Paul)*, Matt McHugh *(Johnny)*, Jody Gilbert *(Tiny)*, Edward Marr *(Keller)*, Thomas Jackson *(Charles)*, Larry Blake *(Hudson)*, Ray Teal *(Frank)*, Andre Charlot *(Gordon)*, Emory Parnell *(Masseur)*, Lester Dorr *(Stickman)*, Eddie Kane *(Floorman)*, William Newell *(1st Player)*, Jack Mulhall *(2nd Player)*, Bruce Fernald *(3rd Player)*, Joey Ray *(1st Poker Player)*, Ernest Hilliard *(2nd Poker Player)*, Syd Saylor *(Waiter)*, Spec O'Donnell *(Elevator Operator)*, Charles Williams.

Crime drama in which Cowan and Carson fool their old friend and professional gambler, Taylor, into helping them obtain important government documents which they plan to sell to a foreign power. Taylor, realizing he's been duped, works to get the papers back, but a series of killings occurs. Enter detective Kelly, who joins forces with the gambler and together they defeat the crooks, but not before nosy reporter Ryan makes things difficult by complicating the investigation. Good programmer with plenty of action.

p, Sol M. Wurtzel; d, James Tinling; w, Irving Cummings, Jr.; ph, Benjamin Kline; ed, William F. Claxton; art d, Jerome Pycha.

Crime **(PR:A MPAA:NR)**

DEADLINE—U.S.A.*½** (1952) 87m FOX bw (GB: DEADLINE)

Humphrey Bogart *(Ed Hutcheson)*, Ethel Barrymore *(Mrs. Garrison)*, Kim Hunter *(Nora)*, Ed Begley *(Frank Allen)*, Warren Stevens *(Burrows)*, Paul Stewart *(Thompson)*, Martin Gabel *(Rienzi)*, Joseph De Santis *(Schmidt)*, Joyce Mackenzie *(Kitty Garrison Geary)*, Audrey Christie *(Mrs. Willebrandt)*, Fay Baker *(Alice Garrison Courtney)*, Jim Backus *(Cleary)*, Carleton Young *(Crane)*, Selmer Jackson *(Williams)*, Fay Roope *(Judge)*, Parley Baer *(Headwaiter)*, Bette Francine *(Telephone Operator)*, John Doucette *(City News Editor)*, June Eisner *(Bentley)*, Richard Monohan *(Copy Boy)*, Harry Tyler *(Headline Writer)*, Joe Sawyer *(Whitey)*, Florence Shirley *(Barndollar)*, Kasia Orzazewski *(Mrs. Schmidt)*, Raymond Greenleaf *(Mr. White)*, Alex Gerry *(Attorney Prentiss)*, Irene Vernon *(Mrs. Burrows)*, William Forrest *(Mr. Greene)*, Edward Keane *(Mr. Blake)*, Clancy Cooper *(Capt. Finlay)*, Tom Powers *(Wharton)*, Thomas Browne Henry *(Fenway)*, Ashley Cowan *(Lefty)*, Howard Negley *(Police Sergeant)*, Phil Terry *(Lewis Schaefer)*, Joe Mell *(Lugerman)*, Luther Crockett *(National Editor)*, Joseph Crehan *(City Editor)*, Larry Dobkin *(Lawyer Hansen)*, Everett Glass *(Doctor)*, Tudor Owen *(Watchman)*, Ann McCrea *(Sally)*, Willis B. Bouchey *(Henry)*, Paul Dubov *(Mac)*, Harris Brown *(Al Murray)*.

A tough newspaper film has Bogart as the embattled editor of *The Day*, a great paper that is about to be sold and then systematically destroyed by a competing company. Barrymore is the feisty old widow of the paper's altruistic founder who is resisting the efforts of her two daughters, Baker and MacKenzie, to sell off the paper so they can maintain their expensive lifestyles. Coupled to this problem, Bogart is attempting to expose rackets boss Gabel and in so doing is threatened. His staff of expert snoopers—Begley, Stewart, Stevens, Christie, Backus—finally piece together Gabel's corrupt empire and, more important, turn up a murder which they lay at the crime czar's door. To corroborate the killing, Bogart and Stewart track down cowardly, sniveling De Santis who admits that he pimped his sister to Gabel and turned his back when the boss killed her when she threatened to blackmail him. For a hefty sum De Santis begins to dictate his story but he is taken out of the newspaper office by police detectives who turn out to be Gabel henchmen. They kill De Santis by hurling him from a high gangway onto the roaring presses in the printing plant. Bogart, meanwhile, appears before a judge and begs that *The Day* not be sold to the opposition. His impassioned speech about a free press stirs Barrymore to support him and the judge allows a short period of time in which Bogart must prove the newspaper's worth to prevent its sale. He goes after Gabel with a vengeance while trying to patch things up with his estranged wife, Hunter, who has had enough of playing second fiddle to his newspaper. Gabel appears to win out but the dead girl's mother, Orzazewski (the scrubwoman mother of innocent victim Richard Conte in CALL NORTHSIDE 777), suddenly appears at the newspaper office, saying that she has been a loyal reader of *The Day* for decades and has been reading their crusading columns about Gabel and her daughter. She makes a gift to the newspaper of her daughter's diary which will prove Gabel not only a murderer but chief of the crime organization in the city. In the end, the newspaper is sold out from beneath Bogart and Barrymore by the avaricious daughters but the paper runs one last edition in which it prints the showgirl's diary, sealing Gabel's fate. Bogart has lost the newspaper but Hunter returns to him, realizing that he is quite a man, one with whom she wants to share the rest of her life. Bogart is terrific as the no-nonsense, dedicated and relentless editor, and his supporting writers and editors are infected by his idealistic efforts, giving fine cameo performances. Stewart, Stevens, and Begley are outstanding as believable newspaper heroes. Gabel is fascinating, broadly belching out his evil incarnate role. Barrymore is noble and just as tough as Bogart, a fighting lady who refuses to surrender the ethics of her paper. It is implied by her at film's end that she will back Bogart in a new newspaper to continue his brand of upright journalism. DEADLINE—U.S.A. is shot in semi-documentary style by director Brooks, who effectively plays upon the everyday routines of newspaper work, along with the mechanics of the press, the low pay, the rigorous demands. (Brooks and producer Siegel were no strangers to this journalistic drama in that they had both worked in the field at one time.)

p, Sol C. Siegel; d&w, Richard Brooks; ph, Milton Krasner; m, Cyril Mockridge, Sol Kaplan; ed, William B. Murphy; md, Lionel Newman; art d, Lyle Wheeler, George Patrick; set d, Thomas Little, Walter M. Scott; cos, Eloise Jenssen, Charles LeMaire; makeup, Ben Nye; spec eff, Ray Kellogg.

Newspaper Drama **(PR:C MPAA:NR)**

DEADLOCK*½ (1931, Brit.) 85m BUT bw

Stewart Rome (James Whitelaw KC), Marjorie Hume (Mrs. Whitelaw), Warwick Ward (Markham Savage), Annette Benson (Madeleine d'Arblay), Esmond Knight (John Tring), Janice Adair (Joan Whitelaw), Alma Taylor (Mrs. Tring), Cameron Carr (Tony Makepeace), D. Hay Plumb (Publicist), Pauline Peters (Maid), Kyoshi Tekase (Taki), Philip Godfrey (Nifty Weekes), H. Saxon-Snell (Prosecution).

An actor is murdered during the shooting of a scene, and the camera records the killer. Vaguely interesting though technically primitive British second feature.

p&d, George King; w, H. Fowler Mear (based on a story by Charles Bennett, Billie Bristow).

Crime (PR:A MPAA:NR)

DEADLOCK*½ (1943, Brit.) 59m British Foundation/International Film Renters bw

John Slater (Fred/Allan Bamber), Cecile Chevreau (Eileen), Molly Hamley-Clifford (Martha), Hugh Morton (Arkell).

Slater plays twins, one of whom helps the other escape from prison. Routine crime drama produced under wartime strictures.

p&d, Ronald Haines.

Crime (PR:A MPAA:NR)

DEADLOCK, 1961 (SEE: MAN-TRAP, 1961)

DEADLY AFFAIR, THE**** (1967, Brit.) 107m COL c

James Mason (Charles Dobbs), Simone Signoret (Elsa Fennan), Maximilian Schell (Dieter Frey), Harriet Andersson (Ann Dobbs), Harry Andrews (Inspector Mendel), Kenneth Haigh (Bill Appleby), Lynn Redgrave (Virgin), Roy Kinnear (Adam Scarr), Max Adrian (Adviser), Robert Flemyng (Samuel Fennan), Corin Redgrave (Director), Les White (Harek), Kenneth Ives (Stagehand), John Dimech, Julian Sherrier (Waiters), Denis Shaw (Landlord), Sheraton Blount (Eunice Scarr), David Warner (King Edward), Michael Bryant (Gaveston), Stanley Leber (Lancaster), Paul Hardwick (Young Mortimer), Charles Kay (Lightborn), Timothy West (Matrevis), Jonathan Wales (Gurney), William Dysart, Murray Brown, Paul Starr, Peter Harrison, David Quilter, Terence Sewards, Roger Jones (Nobles), Petra Markham (Daughter at Theater), Maria Charles (Blonde), Amanda Walker (Brunette), Janet Hargreaves (Ticket Clerk), Michael Brennan (Barman), Richard Steele, Gertan Klauber (Businessmen), Margaret Lacey (Mrs. Bird), Judy Keirn (Stewardess), June Murphy (1st Witch), Frank Williams (2nd Witch), Rosemary Lord (3rd Witch), Leslie Sands.

By the time they got around to making this first novel by John Le Carré, the spy genre had become so overladen with entries that they were being spoofed unmercifully. THE DEADLY AFFAIR was a serious entry into the market and, had it come out sooner, would have achieved greater box office success, but it was already an old-hat type of film, despite the fact that it was one of the best. Mason is sent to do a security check on Flemyng, a foreign office executive. The man checks out and Mason is quite shocked when he learns that Flemyng has committed suicide. Looking deeper into the matter, he interviews Signoret, the widow, and learns that she is a German Jewess who survived the horrors of the death camps. Mason is an old hand at spying and sniffs that this suicide doesn't seem to be in keeping with the nature of the dead man. When he wants to investigate further, he is called off the case by his superior, Max Adrian. Mason doesn't like anything about the case and resigns, rather than bend to Adrian's wishes. Mason is going to investigate this case on his own time and manages to convince Andrews, a former police officer, and Haigh, an associate at the office, to help him get to the bottom of things. In the course of their nosing around, Mason and Andrews are followed by an auto. They turn the tables and go after the trackers and an attack is made on their lives. All this time, a secondary story is unraveling. Mason is a stoic and unromantic civil servant married to Andersson, a Swedish bombshell, who loves loving and makes no attempt to conceal her sexual liaisons from Mason. He has been willing to put up with her behavior as long as she comes home at night. Now, Andersson makes the decision to go away to Switzerland with Schell, an old pal of Mason's who had been a secret Allied agent during the war under Mason's "control." Mason had been hospitalized due to the earlier attack and had time to do a great deal of thinking. There is no way to avoid what he must do; a complete onslaught on Signoret to find out why Flemyng died. In deciding to do this, Mason gives up his wife, the few remaining shreds of ethics he may have had, and he plunges himself back into the life of a spy. The twists of the plot are secondary to the understated acting on the part of all. Every so often, Lumet falls so in love with technique that he doesn't recall there are actors in the piece. He was guilty of that a few times in THE DEADLY AFFAIR as he strove to keep the picture moving at a fast clip by using jump cuts where short dissolves might have made a better point. It smacks of Hitchcock in the use of the Royal Shakespeare Company playing Marlowe as counterpoint to the action (THE MAN WHO KNEW TOO MUCH), but that's an homage, rather than the ripoff by Colin Higgins in FOUL PLAY.

p&d, Sidney Lumet; w, Paul Dehn (from the novel Call for the Dead by John Le Carre); ph, Frederick Young (Technicolor); m, Quincy Jones; ed, Thelma Connell; art d, John Howell; set d, Pamela Cornell; cos, Cynthia Tingey; song: "Who Needs Forever" sung by Astrud Gilberto.

Spy Drama (PR:A-C MPAA:NR)

DEADLY AS THE FEMALE (SEE: GUN CRAZY, 1949)

DEADLY BEES, THE** (1967, Brit.) 123m Amicus/PAR c

Suzanna Leigh (Vicki Robbins), Frank Finlay (Manfred), Guy Doleman (Hargrove), Catherine Finn (Mrs. Hargrove), John Harvey (Thompson), Michael Ripper (Hawkins), Anthony Bailey (Compere), Tim Barrett (Harcourt), James Cossins (Coroner), Frank Forsyth (Doctor), Katy Wild (Doris Hawkins), Greta Farrer (Sister), Gina Gianelli (Secretary), Michael Gwynn (Dr. Lang), Maurice Good (Vicky's Agent), Alister Williamson (Inspector).

The first killer-bee movie! Unfortunately, it is slow and tedious. Plot concerns pop singer Leigh who is told by her doctors that she is suffering from exhaustion. She travels to a remote British isle to rest and prevent a nervous breakdown. On the quiet island she meets Doleman, who runs the inn. He has a hobby—he's a beekeeper. On her wanderings around the real estate she also discovers the fancy cottage of Finlay, another beekeeper. Things start to look suspicious when a local dog is found stung to death. Things get more serious when Doleman's wife is found dead with a billion bee stings covering her body. The rest of the film boils down to just who (Doleman or Finlay) has developed a strain of killer bees that have been up to no good. The film builds at an excruciatingly slow pace, and at times plays like a high-school biology class due to long explanations about the living habits of the vicious little critters. The special effects are handled well.

p, Max J. Rosenberg, Milton Subotsky; d, Freddie Francis; w, Robert Bloch, Anthony Marriott (based on the novel A Taste of Honey by H. F. Heard); ph, John Wilcox (Techniscope, Technicolor); m, Wilfred Josephs; ed, Oswald Hafenrichter; art d, Bill Constable; set d, Andrew Low; spec eff, Michael Collins.

Horror (PR:C MPAA:NR)

DEADLY BLESSING**½ (1981) 102m Polygram/UA c

Maren Jensen (Martha), Susan Buckner (Vicky), Sharon Stone (Lana), Jeff East (John Schmidt), Lisa Hartman (Faith), Lois Nettleton (Louisa), Ernest Borgnine (Isaiah), Coleen Riley (Melissa), Doug Barr (Jim), Michael Berryman (Gluntz), Kevin Cooney (Sheriff), Bobby Dark (Theater Manager), Kevin Farr (Fat Boy), Neil Fletcher (Gravedigger), Jonathon Gulla (Tom), Chester Kulas, Jr. (Leopold), Lawrence Montaigne (Matthew), Lucky Mosley (Sammy), Dan Shackelford (Medic), Annabelle Weenick (Ruth), Jenna Worthen (Mrs. Gluntz), Percy Rodrigues (Narrator).

Disappointing horror outing from Wes Craven whose previous film, THE HILLS HAVE EYES (1977), stands as a minor masterpiece among the modern wave of horror films. Plot concerns Jensen, who lives alone near a conservative, repressive religious sect (the Hittites) to which her husband once belonged. Her husband had been murdered recently under mysterious circumstances soon after he quit the sect, and two of Jensen's friends from California (Buckner and Stone) arrive to comfort her. Soon the Hittites, led by Borgnine, begin harassing Jensen and her friends to force them to leave. The pressure begins to take its toll, and the girls suffer from nightmares (one of which has a spider dropping into one of their mouths) and actual danger (a snake apppears in the bathwater), which leads to more murders. Craven has built an interesting premise, but the ending is lame and unsatisfying. Outstanding cinematography and a good musical score help the mood of the film greatly. Craven's next outing, SWAMP THING (1982), was another disappointment, but he returned in full force in 1984 with the truly terrifying NIGHTMARE ON ELM ST.

p, Micheline and Max Keller, Pat Herskovic; d, Wes Craven; w, Glenn M. Benest, Matthew Barr, Craven; ph, Robert Jessup (Metrocolor); m, James Horner; ed, Richard Bracken; art d, Jack Marty; cos, Patricia McKiernan.

Horror Cas. (PR:O MPAA:R)

DEADLY CHINA DOLL* (1973, Hong Kong) 94m Panasia Films/MGM c

Angela Mao (Chin Su-hua), Carter Huang (Pai Chien), Yen I-feng (Han Fei), Nan Kung-hsun (Hu Szu), Ke Hsiang-ting (Chin).

Mao is the heroine of this routine Kung Fu exploitation film, taking on a gang of opium smugglers and some hijackers, too. Below average, even for this routinely wretched genre.

p, Andrew G. Vajna; d, Huang Feng; w, Ho Jen; ph, Li Yiu-tang; m, Joseph Koo; ed, Chiang Lung; set d, Tsao Nien-lung; makeup, Siao Hsin-mei.

Martial Arts (PR:O MPAA:R)

DEADLY CIRCLE, THE (SEE: HONEYMOON OF HORROR, 1964)

DEADLY COMPANIONS, THE***

(1961) 90m Carousel/Pathe-American c

Maureen O'Hara (Kit), Brian Keith (Yellowleg), Steve Cochran (Billy), Chill Wills (Turk), Strother Martin (Parson), Will Wright (Doctor), Jim O'Hara (Cal), Peter O'Crotty (Mayor), Billy Vaughan (Mead), Robert Sheldon, John Hamilton, Riley Hill (Gamblers), Hank Gobble (Bartender), Buck Sharpe (Indian), Chuck Hayward (Card Sharp).

First feature film by Sam Peckinpah, who was hired due to his experience directing half-hour episodes of "Have Gun, Will Travel," and "The Westerner." The film, though weak in spots, is an auspicious debut and especially interesting if compared to the director's body of work. The plot, though contrived (Peckinpah was not allowed to change the script—always a bad sign for this director), has enough compelling elements that the viewer is willing to accept the coincidences that force the narrative along. Keith plays a bitter, obsessed gunslinger who accidentally kills dance-hall girl O'Hara's son in a gunfight. Out of guilt, Keith accompanies the woman on a trek into Apache territory to bury the body in a ghost town where the boy's deceased father rests. Along the way, Keith runs into Wills (Peckinpah's first truly psychotic villain), who tried to scalp him during the Civil War (which left Keith with a horrible scar and a lame shooting arm). Wanting revenge but unwilling to lower himself to Wills' gutter level, Keith allows the crazy drifter and his sidekick, a young gunfighter played by Cochran, to join them on their treacherous journey through Apache territory. After a few harrowing (and well directed) run-ins with the Indians, the group reaches the ghost town and Keith gets his revenge. Keith is outstanding and Wills is downright scary as directed by Peckinpah. Though rough going in spots, the film sets an interesting groundwork for the themes and visual images Peckinpah would fine-hone in his later work. It was an omen of things to come when Peckinpah was not allowed final cut on this project and the producers altered his ending. It was a problem that would plague nearly every project in his career, including his final film, THE OSTERMAN WEEKEND (1983). An interesting start for one of modern American cinema's most brilliant and controversial directors.

p, Charles FitzSimons: d, Sam Peckinpah: w, A.S. Fleischman (based on his novel); ph, William Clothier (Panavision, Pathe Color); m, Marlin Skiles; ed, Stanley E. Rabjohn; spec eff, David Koehler; song, "A Dream of Love" (FitzSimons, Skiles); stunts, Chuck Hayward.

Western   **(PR:C   MPAA:NR)**

DEADLY DECISION   (SEE: CANARIS, 1958)

DEADLY DECOYS, THE*   (1962, Fr.) 90m GAU c
(LE GORILLE A MORDU L'ARCHEVEQUE)

Roger Hanin (Le Gorille), Jean Le Poulain (Lehurit), Pierre Dac ("The Old Man"), Roger Dumas (Louis Lehurit), Huguette Hue (Jocelyne), Fernand Fabre (General Secretary), James Campbell (Guemele), Jose Squinquel (Rapus), Robert Puig (Antoine).

Top secret agent Hanin shoots and punches everyone in sight as he tries to save a French Colonial official in Africa from a professional killer. Even action fans will be disappointed.

d, Maurice Labro; w, Antoine Dominique, Antoine Flachot [Roger Hanin], Jacques Pierre, Labro; ph, Robert Lefebvre; m, Michel Magne; ed, Germaine Artus.

Spy Drama/Comedy   **(PR:A-C   MPAA:NR)**

DEADLY DUO*½   (1962) 70m UA bw

Craig Hill (Preston Morgan), Marcia Henderson (Sabena/Dara), Dayton Lummis (Thorne Fletcher), Carlos Romero (Lt. Reyes), David Renard (Manuel), Robert Lowery (Jay Flagg), Irene Tedrow (Leonora), Peter Oliphant (Billy), Manuel Lopez (Policeman), Marco Antonio (Luis).

Cliche suspense outing dealing with twin sisters (played by Henderson) one good, one evil. The evil sister impersonates the good one to receive some money the latter sibling is due. The evil sister even attempts to kill her twin, but the plan goes haywire. Dull, stiff, and boring.

p, Robert E. Kent; d, Reginald LeBorg; w, Owen Harris (based on the novel by Richard Jessup); ph, Gordon Avil; m, Richard LaSalle; ed, Kenneth Crane; set d, Harry Reif; cos, Einar Bourman, Sabine Manela.

Mystery   **(PR:A   MPAA:NR)**

DEADLY EYES**   (1982) 93m Northshore Investments/Golden Communications c (AKA:THE RATS)

Sam Groom (Paul Harris), Sara Batsford (Kelly Leonard), Scatman Crothers (George Fask), Lisa Langlois (Trudy White), Cec Linder (Dr. Luis Spenser), James B. Douglas (Mel Dederick), Lesleh Donaldson (Martha).

A throwback to science fiction drama of the 1950s has a special breed of rats growing to unusually large proportions as they terrorize the city. In between rat attacks, an affair develops between high school science teacher Groom and city health inspector Batsford. Made with a lot of polish for its low budget, with the tension developing at a good pace. One of the more memorable scenes is when the rats take over the local moviehouse, which may send chills up your spine if you ever wonder what could be lurking beneath your seat.

p, Paul Kahnert, Charles Eglee; d, Robert Clouse; w, Eglee (from the novel by James Herbert); ph, Rene Verzier; ed, Ron Wisman; spec eff, Allan Apone.

Horror   **Cas.**   **(PR:O   MPAA:NR)**

DEADLY FEMALES, THE zero   (1976, Brit.) 105m Donwin c

Tracy Reed (Joan), Bernard Holley (Roger), Scott Fredericks (Mark), Heather Chasen (Frances), Brian Jackson (Tony), Roy Purcell (Sir Charles), Jean Harrington (Mary Adams), Olivia Munday (Diana),), Jean Rimmer (Elizabeth), Raymond Young (Michael), Lans Travers (Josie), Angela Jay (Samantha), Gennie Nevison (Vickie), Graham Ashley (Benny), Rula Lenska (Luisa).

Soft-core melodrama features a bevy of beauties who shed their clothes almost as frequently as they perform their duties as female assassins. Blame "auteur" director Donovon Winter who produced, directed, and wrote this trash.

p,d&w, Donovon Winter; ph, Austin Parkinson (Eastmancolor).

Action   **(PR:O   MPAA:NR)**

DEADLY FORCE*   (1983) 95m Embassy c

Wings Hauser (Stoney Cooper), Joyce Ingalls (Eddie Cooper), Paul Shenar (Joshua Adams), Al Ruscio (Sam Goodwin), Arlen Dean Snyder (Ashley Maynard), Lincoln Kilpatrick (Otto Hoxley), Bud Ekins (Harvey), J. Victor Lopez (Diego), Hector Elias (Lopez), Ramon Franco (Jesus), Gina Gallego (Maria).

Vile cop drama from the team who brought viewers the intense, fast-paced, extremely vicious VICE SQUAD (1982). This one stars Hauser (the sleazy lunatic in VICE SQUAD) as a detective handling assignments on both coasts. His Los Angeles case takes up most of his time as he tries to track down a mass murderer while under constant pressure from former colleague Kilpatrick. At the same time, Hauser tries to patch things up with his estranged wife, Ingalls, who happens to be a TV news-reporter covering the murders. The plot twists are telegraphed long before they happen, and Hauser and company just can't generate the magic that made Don Siegel's DIRTY HARRY (1971) or even VICE SQUAD (though to a lesser degree) so effective.

p, Sandy Howard; d, Paul Aaron; w, Ken Barnett, Barry Schneider, Robert Vincent O'Neil; ph, Norman Leigh, David Myers (CFI Color); m, Gary Scott; ed, Roy Watts; prod d, Alan Roderick-Jones; spec-makeup eff, Mark Shostrom.

Crime   **Cas.**   **(PR:O   MPAA:R)**

DEADLY GAME, THE*   (1941) 65m MON bw

Charles Farrell, June Lang, John Miljan, Bernadene Hayes, David Clarke, John Dilson, Dave O'Brien, J. Arthur Young, Tom Herbert, Ottola Nesmith, Fred Gierman, Hans Von Morhart, Walter Bonn, William Vaughn, John Harmon.

Poor programmer has Farrell pulling Lang out of trouble only to enmesh himself in murder. Strong cast can't help this one, a sad entry for Farrell, one-time silent-era superstar (SEVENTH HEAVEN).

p, Dixon R. Harwin; d, Phil Rosen; w, Wellyn Totman; ph, Arthur Martinelli; ed, Martin G. Cohn; art d, Charles Clague.

Mystery   **(PR: MPAA:NR)**

DEADLY GAME, THE**   (1955, Brit.) 70m Hammer/Lippert bw
(GB: THIRD PARTY RISK)

Lloyd Bridges (Philip Graham), Finlay Currie (Mr. Darius), Maureen Swanson (Lolita), Simone Silva (Mitzi), Ferdy Mayne (Maxwell Carey), Peter Dyneley (Tony Roscoe), Roger Delgado (Gonzales), George Woodbridge (Inspector Goldfinch), Russell Waters (Dr. Zeissman), Mary Parker (Mrs. Zeissman), Leslie Wright, Seymour Green, Toots Pound, Patrick Westwood.

Bridges is an American in Spain accused of killing an old war buddy to obtain some microfilm. Bridges, of course, knows nothing about it, but he does manage to clear up the case. Adequate British programmer.

p, Robert Dunbar; d&w, Daniel Birt (based on a novel by Nicolas Bentley); ph, Jimmy Harvey.

Crime   **(PR:A   MPAA:NR)**

DEADLY HERO***   (1976) 99m AE c

Don Murray (Ed Lacy), Diahn Williams (Sally Devereaux), James Earl Jones (Rabbit), Lilia Skala (Mrs. Broderick), George S. Irving (Reilly), Treat Williams (Billings), Charles Siebert (Baker), Hank Garrett (Buckley), Dick A. Williams (D.A. Winston), Mel Berger (Arco), Virginia Sandifur (Ellie), Ronald Weyand (Capt. Stark).

Surprisingly good cop thriller shot entirely in New York City. Williams stars as an innocent young cellist who is attacked by slimy creep Jones. She is saved by cop Murray, who brutalizes the criminal and then kills him. Williams is so shocked at the unnecessary force that she files a complaint about the cop's over-zealousness. This sets Murray off completely (he was a borderline psychotic anyway), and then he begins to terrorize the woman.

p, Thomas J. McGrath; d, Ivan Nagy; w, George Wislocki; ph, Andrzej Bartkowiak (Movielab Color); m, Bard Fiedel, Tommy Mandel; ed, Susan Steinberg; art d, Alan Herman.

Crime   **Cas.**   **(PR:O   MPAA:R)**

DEADLY IS THE FEMALE   (SEE: GUN CRAZY, 1949)

DEADLY MANTIS, THE*½   (1957) 79m UNIV bw
(AKA: THE INCREDIBLE PRAYING MANTIS)

Craig Stevens (Col. Joe Parkman), William Hopper (Dr. Ned Jackson), Alix Talton (Marge Blaine), Donald Randolph (Gen. Mark Ford), Pat Conway (Sgt. Pete Allen), Florenz Ames (Prof. Anton Gunther), Paul Smith (Corporal), Phil Harvey (Lou), Paul Campbell (Lt. Fred Pizar), Jack Mather (Officer), George Lynn (Bus Driver), Skipper McNally (Policeman), Harold Lee (Eskimo Chief), Floyd Simmons, Helen Jay.

Lame rip-off of the sci-fi classic THEM! sees a giant praying mantis thawed out of its icy grave (how a praying mantis ended up in the Arctic is never explained) and flying to America where it chews up most of Washington, D.C., and Manhattan before it is finally killed by poison gas in the Holland Tunnel (of all places). Pretty silly.

p, William Alland; d, Nathan Juran; w, Martin Berkeley (based on a story by Alland); ph, Ellis Carter; m, Joseph Gershenson; ed, Chester Schaeffer; art d, Alexander Golitzen, Robert Clatworthy; spec eff, Fred Knoth.

Science Fiction   **(PR:A   MPAA:NR)**

DEADLY NIGHTSHADE*½   (1953, Brit.) 61m Kenilworth/GFD bw

Emrys Jones (Matthews/Barlow), Zena Marshall (Ann Farrington), John Horsley (Inspector Clements), Joan Hickson (Mrs. Fenton), Hector Ross (Canning), Victor Platt (Sergeant), Roger Maxwell (Col. Smythe), Lesley Deane (Mrs. Smythe), Edward Evans, Alan Gordon, Ian Fleming, Martyn Wyldeck.

Jones, escaping from prison, finds the dead body of a man who looks just like him. He switches identities with the corpse, then discovers that the man was a spy. An idea done much better in Antonioni's THE PASSENGER (1975), but still occasionally entertaining.

p, Robert Baker, Monty Berman; d, John Gilling; w, Lawrence Huntington; ph, Berman.

Crime   **(PR:A   MPAA:NR)**

DEADLY RECORD*½   (1959, Brit.) 58m IA/AA bw

Lee Patterson (Trevor Hamilton), Barbara Shelley (Susan Webb), Jane Hylton (Ann Garfield), Peter Dyneley (Dr. Morrow), Geoffrey Keen (Supt. Ambrose), John Paul (Phil Gamage), Everly Gregg (Mrs. Mac), Edward Cast (Police Constable Ryder), George Pastell (Angelo), Ferdy Mayne (Ramon Casadas), April Olrich (Carmela), Percy Herbert, Geoffrey Tyrrell, Peter Dolphin, Doreen Dawne.

Patterson is a pilot accused of murdering his wife, but he manages to find evidence proving that a jealous receptionist is the real killer. Mediocre second feature.

p, Vivian A. Cox; d, Lawrence Huntington; w, Cox, Huntington (based on a novel by Nina Warner Hooke); ph, Eric Cross.

Mystery   **(PR:A MPAA:NR)**

DEADLY SILENCE   (SEE: TARZAN'S DEADLY SILENCE, 1970)

DEADLY SPAWN, THE zero
(1983) 78m Filmline Communications/21st Century c

Charles George Hildebrandt (Charles), Tom DeFranco (Tom), Richard Lee Porter (Frankie), Jean Tafler (Ellen), Karen Tighe (Kathy), Ethel Michelson (Aunt Millie), John Schmerling (Uncle Herb), James Brewster (Sam), Elissa Neil (Barbara).

Low-low-low budget sci-fi film shot on 16mm by a group of New Jersey sci-fi fanatics who set out to make a feature detailing a meteor shower that lands hundreds of deadly aliens on Earth that attack New Jerseyites in the cheapest and bloodiest manner possible. Yet another inspiration to those out there who think that they, too, can become the next Lucas or Spielberg by buying a movie camera.

p, Ted Bohus; d&w, Douglas McKeown, Tim Sullivan (based on a story by McKeown, Bohus, John Dods) ph, Harvey Birnbaum; m, Michael Perlstein, Ken Walker, Paul Cornell; spec eff, Dods.

Science Fiction   **(PR:O MPAA:R)**

DEADLY STRANGERS**   (1974, Brit.) 93m Rank/Silhouette c

Hayley Mills, Simon Ward, Sterling Hayden, Ken Hutchison, Peter Jeffrey.

Occasionally intriguing tale has Mills and Ward strangers riding in a car together, one of them a mad strangler just escaped from the asylum. Well done, but it seems to bog down in its own cleverness.

d, Sidney Hayers; w, Philip Levene; ph, Graham Edgar (Eastmancolor); m, Ron Goodwin.

Suspense   **Cas.**   **(PR:C MPAA:NR)**

DEADLY TRACKERS*½   (1973) 104m Cine Film/WB c

Richard Harris (Kilpatrick), Rod Taylor (Brand), Al Lettieri (Gutierrez), Neville Brand (Choo Choo), William Smith (Schoolboy), Paul Benjamin (Jacob), Pedro Armendariz, Jr. (Blacksmith), Isela Vega (Maria), Kelly Jean Peters (Katharine), Sean Marshall, Red Morgan, Joan Swift, William Bryant, Ray Moyer, Armando Acosta, Federico Gonzales, John Kennedy.

A senseless, violent, bloody mess that makes Sam Peckinpah look like Walt Disney in comparison. Originally conceived and directed by Sam Fuller, the studio allowed him to shoot over $1 million worth of footage until he was fired because of "artistic" differences with the film's egotistical star, Harris, who simply wouldn't take direction from him. The studio then scrapped all the footage, hired Shear to replace Fuller, and started over. The result is a lame revenge tale wherein Harris, a gentle sheriff, seeks revenge on renegade outlaws, led by Taylor, who had senselessly (and on-screen) slaughtered his family. He spends most of the movie hunting down Taylor and his gang until he finally eliminates them in an extended, bloody climax where everyone is killed (including Harris). Harris is awful as he alternately whispers or shouts his lines while committing gory acts more horrible than the killers he's tracking. By the time it came to score the film, the studio didn't feel like sinking any more cash into the project, so it just borrowed Jerry Fielding's brilliant score for Peckinpah's masterpiece THE WILD BUNCH (1969) and stuck it in during the most inane passages of this fiasco. While the film may be bad, raping Fielding's best work for this trash is a sin.

p, Fouad Said; d, Barry Shear; w, Lukas Heller (based on the story "Riata" by Samuel Fuller); ph, Gabriel Torres (Technicolor); m, Jerry Fielding (uncredited); ed, Michael Economou, Carl Pingitore; art d, Javier T. Torija.

Western   **(PR:O MPAA:PG)**

DEADLY TRAP, THE*½   (1972, Fr./Ital.) 97m
Corona-Pomereu-Oceania/NG c

Faye Dunaway (Jill), Frank Langella (Philip), Barbara Parkins (Cynthia), Karen Blaugueron (Miss Hansen), Raymond Gerome (Commissaire Chenylle), Gerard Buhr (Psychiatrist), Michele Lourie (Cathy), Patrick Vincent (Patrick), Maurice Ronet (Stranger), Louise Chevalier, Tener Eckelberry, Massimo Farinelli.

Langella is a retired industrial spy, an American living in Paris with wife Dunaway and their two children. When Langella's former associates decide to get to him, they kidnap the kids, causing Dunaway to nearly suffer a nervous breakdown. Nice looking but thoroughly confusing melodrama wastes the talents of the leads.

p, Georges Casati, Robert Dorfman; d, Rene Clement; w, Sidney Buchman, Elaine Perry (based on the novel The Children Are Gone by Arthur Cavanaugh); ph, Georges Pastier (Eastmancolor); m, Gilbert Becaud; ed, Francoise Javet; art d, Jean Andre; set d, Robert Andre, George Glon; makeup, Aida Carange Thivat.

Spy Drama   **(PR:C MPAA:PG)**

DEADWOOD PASS*   (1933) 62m Freuler/Monarch bw

Tom Tyler, Alice Dahl, Wally Wales, Buffalo Bill, Jr., Lafe McKee, Bud Osborne, Edmund Cobb, Slim Whitaker, Merrill McCormack, Charlotte [Carlotta] Monti, Duke Lee, Blackie Whiteford, Bill Nestell.

Inept cowboy saga where tight-lipped, bass-voiced Tyler rescues Monti so many times from the baddies that one wonders why he keeps trying. Monti was for years W.C. Fields' paramour, secretary, and clipping service, all at $50 per week. When she asked for a small raise to supplement the meager salary she received from such awful outings as this film, Fields promptly fired her (then rehired her at more money).

p, Burton King; d, J.P. McGowan; w, Oliver Drake (John Wesley Patterson); ph, Edward Kull; ed, Fred Bain.

Western   **(PR:A MPAA:NR)**

DEADWOOD '76 zero   (1965) 100m Fairway-International c

Arch Hall, Jr. (Billy May), Jack Lester (Tennessee Thompson), Melissa Morgan (Poker Kate), William Watters [Arch Hall, Sr.] (Boone May), Robert Dix (Wild Bill Hickok), LaDonna Cottier (Little Bird), Richard S. Cowl (Preacher Smith), David Reed (Fancy Poggin), Rex Marlow (Sam Bass), Gordon Schwenk (Spotted Snake), John Bryant (Hubert), Barbara Moore (Montana), Ray Zachary (Spec Greer), Willard Willingham (Deputy Harding), Harold Bizzy, Read Morgan, John Cardos, Little Jack Little, Bobby Means, Ray Vegas.

Overly plotted independent western written by its star Hall, Jr., who plays a young cowboy who rescues Lester from Indians. Together the duo set out for Deadwood where Hall, Jr., is mistaken for Billy the Kid. Soon the poor sap is captured by Indians, meets up with his father, Hall, Sr., falls in love with squaw Cottier, and eventually faces a showdown with Wild Bill Hickock. Hickock refuses the confrontation when he learns that he's really not the Kid. That's okay because a local gunslinger tries to gun Hall, Jr., down anyway but Hall, Jr., is faster and kills the boy in self defense. The local mob doesn't see it that way and lynches Hall, Jr., mercifully ending the movie. Robert Dix, Hickock in the film, is the son of square-jawed Richard Dix, the strong, silent cowboy star of many western films from the silents to the 1940s.

p, Nicholas Merriwether [Arch Hall, Sr.]; d, James Landis; w, Arch Hall, Jr., William Watters [Arch Hall, Sr.]; ph, William (Vilmos) Zsigmond (Techniscope, Technicolor); m, Manuel Francisco; ed, Anthony M. Lanza; art d, David Reed III; song; "Deadwood," Harper McKay, Arch Hall, Jr.

Western   **(PR:C MPAA:NR)**

DEAF SMITH AND JOHNNY EARS*   (1973, Ital.) 91m MGM c
(AKA: LOS AMIGOS)

Anthony Quinn (Erastus "Deaf" Smith), Franco Nero (Johnny Ears), Pamela Tiffin (Suzie), Franco Graziosi (Gen. Morton), Ira Furstenberg (Hester), Renato Romano (Hoffman), Renzo Moneta (Col. McDonald), Adolfo Lastretti, Antonio Faa Di Bruno, Francesca Benedetti, Cristina Airoldi, Romano Puppo, Franca Sciutto, Enrico Casadei, Lorenzo Fineschi, Mario Carra, Giorgio Dolfin, Luciano Rossi, Margherita Trentini, Tom Felleghy, Fulvio Grimaldi, Paolo Pierani.

They managed to keep the cost of this movie under one and a half million dollars and it still lost money? This was Quinn's first "Spaghetti Western" (western pictures made in Italy to look as though they were made in the states; Clint Eastwood made a bunch, so did Bronson, and Sergio Leone almost raised it to an art form), and it was a bad entry into the field. Quinn plays a deaf mute who had been a hero in the U.S. Civil War. He and Franco Nero are traveling around the West trying to make a living as mercenaries. There's a dictatorship forming in Texas and the two men are hired by some of President (of the Texas Republic) Sam Houston's men to help quash the uprising. Moneta is Quinn's former military boss, and his family has been mass murdered. Quinn investigates and uncovers Franco Graziosi as the villain. Graziosi is being backed by the Germans who want to establish a foothold in the continental U.S. It's Graziosi's plan to attack the capitol and take over. In Austin, Nero has been toying with a local hooker, Pamela Tiffin, and has no time to help his pal. Quinn sneaks into the well-stocked garrison of Graziosi and steals dynamite, then is pursued and caught. Nero thinks he'd better help his pal so he leaves Tiffin's ample body, gets to the fort, and rescues Quinn. The two men set fire to the place and successfully put an end to the heinous plan. Later, both are leaving Texas with Tiffin but that night Quinn realizes there's no room for a menage a trois so he exits, and Nero and Tiffin will presumably roam the West until they wind up in Venice or Parma. There is not enough action to make this intriguing for western fans and not enough comedy to make it a spoof. The picture fails on almost every level except the color photography, which is excellent.

p, Joseph Janni, Luciano Perugia; d, Paolo Cavara; w, Harry Essex, Oscar Saul, Cavara, Lucia Drudi, Augusto Finocchi (based on a story by Essex and Saul); ph, Tonino Delli Colli (Technicolor); m, Daniele Patucchi; ed, Mario Morra; art d, Francesca Calabrese; cos, Pasquale Nigro.

Western   **(PR:C MPAA:PG)**

DEAL OF THE CENTURY*½   (1983) 98m WB c

Chevy Chase (Eddie Muntz), Sigourney Weaver (Mrs. De Voto), Gregory Hines (Ray Kasternak), Vince Edwards (Frank Stryker), William Marquez (Gen. Cordosa), Eduardo Ricard (Col. Salgado), Richard Herd (Lyle), Graham Jarvis (Babers), Wallace Shawn (Harold De Voto), Randi Brooks (Ms. Della Rosa), Ebbe Roe Smith (Bob), Richard Libertini (Masaggi), J. W. Smith (Will), Carmen Moreno (Woman Singer), Charles Levin (Dr. Rechtin), Pepe Serna (Vardis), Maurice Marsac (French-man), Robert Cornthwaite (Huddleston), David Haskell, Alex Colon.

Vastly disappointing black comedy that seemed to have everything going for it; a good director (Friedkin), a good screenwriter (Brickman), and a good cast (Weaver, Chase, Hines). Unfortunately, something went very wrong. The story concerns an arms dealer, Chase, and his partner, Hines, and their wacky adventures selling all manner of death-dealing machines to any country that can rustle up the dough. The whole thing went over like a lead balloon.

p. Bud Yorkin; d, William Friedkin; w, Paul Brickman; ph, Richard H. Kline (Technicolor); m, Arthur B. Rubinstein; ed, Bud Smith, Ned Humphreys, Jere Huggins; prod d, Bill Malley.

Comedy   **Cas.**   **(PR:C MPAA:PG)**

DEALING: OR THE BERKELEY-TO-BOSTON FORTY-BRICK LOST-BAG BLUES*½   (1971) 88m WB c

Barbara Hershey (Susan), Robert F. Lyons (Peter), Charles Durning (Murphy), Joy Bang (Sandra), John Lithgow (John), Ellen Barber (Annie), Gene Borkan (Musty), Ted Williams (Receptionist), Demond Wilson (Rupert), Herbert Kerr (Emir), Paul Williams (Barry), Buzzy Linhart (Buzzy), Anitra Walsh (Townie Girl), Tom Harvey (Capt. Fry).

A word to the wise: any film with a title this long and this lame is trying to hide something. In this case it's a pretty bad film featuring Lithgow (a very important actor in the 1980s, here in an early role) as a snobby Harvard student who goes to Berkeley to purchase a cache of marijuana to transport back to the Ivy League. Hershey plays the hippie with whom he falls in love. Not much to recommend, except to Lithgow fans who may want to see the kind of garbage an outstanding actor has to wade through before he can land decent roles in films like THE WORLD ACCORDING TO GARP (1982) and TERMS OF ENDEARMENT (1983). (Filmed on location in San Francisco and Boston.)

p, Edward R. Pressman; d, Paul Williams; w, Williams, David Odell (based on the novel by Michael and Douglas Crichton); ph, Ed Brown (Panavision, Technicolor); m, Michael Small; ed, Sidney Katz; prod d, Gene Callahan; set d, Brian Beck; makeup, Ken Brooke.

Comedy   **(PR:O   MPAA:R)**

DEAR BRAT★★   (1951) 82m PAR bw

Mona Freeman (Miriam), Billy De Wolfe (Albert), Edward Arnold (Sen. Wilkins), Lyle Bettger (Baxter), Mary Philips (Mrs. Wilkins), Natalie Wood (Pauline), William Reynolds (Robbie), Frank Cady (Mr. Creavy), Lillian Randolph (Dora), Irene Winston (Mrs. Baxter), Patty Lou Arden (Clara).

Third in a series of family comedies based on the play and film DEAR RUTH (1947). This one stars Freeman as the teenage daughter of former judge, now senator, Arnold, who wants to help society as her father does by reforming a criminal. She hires Bettger, a bitter ex-con, to work as the family gardener. Unfortunately, Freeman's father had sentenced Bettger to prison when he was a judge. Most of the action centers around Freeman's efforts to unite the ex-con with his wife, Winston, and his small daughter, Wood, whom he is forbidden to see due to potential parole violations.

p, Mel Epstein; d, William Seiter; w, Devery Freeman; ph, John F. Seitz; m, Van Cleve; ed, Alma Macrorie; art d, Hal Pereira, Harry Bumstead.

Comedy   **(PR:A   MPAA:NR)**

DEAR BRIGETTE★★★½   (1965) 100m FOX c

James Stewart (Prof. Robert Leaf), Fabian (Kenneth), Glynis Johns (Vina Leaf), Cindy Carol (Pandora Leaf), Billy Mumy (Erasmus Leaf), John Williams (Peregrine Upjohn), Jack Kruschen (Dr. Volker), Charles Robinson (George), Howard Freeman (Dean Sawyer), Jane Wald (Terry), Alice Pearce (Unemployment Office Clerk), Jesse White (Argyle), Gene O'Donnell (Lt. Rink), Ed Wynn (The Captain), Brigitte Bardot (Herself), Orville Sherman (Von Schlogg), Maida Severn (School Teacher), Pitt Herbert (Bank Manager), Louise Lane, Adair Jameson (Salesladies), Susan Cramer (Blonde Doll), Harry Fleer (T-Man), Jack Daly (Ticket Seller), William Henry (Cashier), Gloria Clark (Prof. Burns), Robert Fitzpatrick, James Brolin, Clive Clerk, John Stevens (Students), Dick Lane (Sports Announcer), Ted Mapes (Postman), Marcel De la Brosse (Taxi Driver), Bob Biheller.

Charming and off-beat story about an odd family that lives on a houseboat in Sausalito, California. Stewart is a professor at a local college and devoted to the arts. He hates anything to do with science and studiously avoids these subjects. He and his wife, Johns, and children, Mumy and Carol, have a relaxed life that features at-home musicales. Soon enough they learn that Mumy has no musical talent whatsoever, so they attempt to get him into art and discover he is color blind. But the lad does have a talent for numbers, much to the dismay of his computer-hating father. Mumy begins doing Carol's homework for her as well as the work of his boy friend, Fabian. Soon, Fabian and a pal have Mumy doping out the horses at the local track as Carol wants to marry a millionaire and since Fabian isn't one perhaps he can be with Mumy's help. Still with us? John Williams, a con-man, with his pal, Jesse White, a tout, make a proposition to Stewart. If Mumy can make enough money handicapping horses, they'll oversee a foundation devoted to the advancement of the humanities. Meanwhile, through the work of a psychiatrist, Kruschen, we learn that Mumy has but one passion, Brigitte Bardot, and he's been writing letters to her. He wants to make enough money so he can go to France and meet her in the adorable flesh. Mumy won't do any handicapping until he can meet Brigitte, so he and Stewart fly to France and have an audience with the lady. Bardot is quite lovable in her brief scene and gives Mumy a puppy as a remembrance and the two return home. One huge bet is made that Williams intends to use as a stake to abscond. The race is run, the chosen horse wins, and as Williams is getting the cash he is stopped by an Internal Revenue Service agent. Stewart tells the agent that it's all for a nonprofit art organization. He takes the money and life returns to normal aboard the Sausalito residence. Ed Wynn has an in-and-out role as a ferryboat captain in the neighborhood but doesn't get enough to do. Pearce does a standout bit as the clerk at the unemployment office when Stewart quits his job and asks for his unemployment benefits. Bardot was only 30 at the time and was a huge international star. Pity she never was able to learn enough English to play in movies with wider appeal. The screenplay is credited to Hal Kanter (one of the best after-dinner speakers in Hollywood), but the original adaptation was by Nunnally Johnson. When Kanter was brought in by Koster (what the hell, they had the same initials), Johnson asked that his name be removed from the credits rather than submit it to a Writers Guild arbitration which he would have probably won since the arbitrators are notorious for awarding the first-writer credit whenever possible. The habit of bringing in re-writers on screenplays began in silents and continues to this day. Unfortunately, it seldom makes scripts better and just serves to get wavering producers off the hook when the picture is a turkey. DEAR BRIGETTE was a rare exception in that it had charm and joy and Johnson probably should have left his name on the screen, but when you've written such classics as THE GRAPES OF WRATH, TOBACCO ROAD, and THE THREE FACES OF EVE, a little trifle like DEAR BRIGETTE hardly matters.

p&d, Henry Koster; w, Hal Kanter (based on the novel Erasmus With Freckles by John Haase); ph, Lucien Ballard (CinemaScope, DeLuxe Color); m, George Duning; ed, Marjorie Fowler; art d, Jack Martin Smith, Malcolm Brown; set d, Walter M. Scott, Steven Potter; cos, Moss Mabry; spec eff, L. B. Abbott, Emil Kosa, Jr.

Comedy   **(PR:A   MPAA:NR)**

DEAR, DEAD DELILAH zero   (1972) 95m Southern Star/AE TV c

Agnes Moorehead (Delilah), Will Geer (Roy), Michael Ansara (Morgan), Patricia Carmichael (Luddy), Dennis Patrick (Alonzo), Anne Meacham (Grace), Robert Gentry (Richard), Elizabeth Eis (Ellen), Ruth Baker (Buffy), Ann Giggs (Young Luddy), John Marriot (Marshall).

A rabid cult of fans out there extol the virtues of this cheap, bloody attempt at Southern gothic horror, but there is no redeemable quality to be found in it. In fact, if the star rating system could go lower than zero it should go there for a production that embarrasses great actors like Moorehead (it was her last film before she died of lung cancer in 1974) and Geer in their twilight years. Plot concerns Moorehead as a dying, obnoxious, wheelchair-confined matriarch of a mansion where a fortune is buried. The evil relatives race to see who can find the dough first and Geer gets his hand chopped off. Repulsive.

p, Jack Clement; d&w, John Farris; ph, William R. Johnson (Eastmancolor); m, Bill Justis; ed, Ron Dorfman; art d, James Tilton; cos, Nancy Potts; makeup, Vincent Loscalzo.

Horror   **(PR:O   MPAA:R)**

DEAR DETECTIVE★★
                (1978, Fr.) 105m Les Films Ariane-Mondex Films/Cinema 5
                (TENDRE POULET; AKA: DEAR INSPECTOR) c

Annie Girardot (Lise Tanquerelle), Philippe Noiret (Antoine Lemercier), Catherine Alric (Cristine Vallier), Hubert Deschamps (Mr. Charmille), Paulette Dubost Simone (Mother), Roger Dumas (Inspector Dumas), Raymond Gerome (Director of Criminal Division), Guy Marchand (Commissioner Beretti), Simone Renant (Suzanne), Georges Wilson (Alexandre Mignonac), Armelle Pourriche (Catherine Tanquerelle), Czarmiak (Cassard), Maurine Illouz (Picot), Michel Norman (Albert), Georges Riquier (Prof. Pelletier), Alain David (Dean Lavergne).

Noiret, a professor of Greek at the Sorbonne and inveterate womanizer, revives an old affair with Girardot, but is shocked when he discovers that she's a detective working on a murder investigation. The film fizzles more often than it works, and the whole thing is almost disgustingly pleasant. A sequel, JUPITER'S THIGH, was released in 1981, and the film was remade as a Made-for-Television film under the same title with Brenda Vaccaro and Arlen Dean Snyder in the leads. (In French; English subtitles.)

p, Alexandre Mnouchkine; d, Philippe De Broca; w, De Broca, Michel Audiard (based on the novel Le Frelon by Jean-Paul Rouland and Claude Olivier); ph, Jean-Paul Schwartz (Eastmancolor); m, Georges Delerue; ed, Francoise Javet.

Comedy   **Cas.**   **(PR:C   MPAA:NR)**

DEAR HEART★★★   (1964) 114m WB bw

Glenn Ford (Harry Mork), Geraldine Page (Evie Jackson), Michael Anderson, Jr. (Patrick), Barbara Nichols (June), Patricia Barry (Mitchell), Charles Drake (Frank Taylor), Angela Lansbury (Phyllis), Ruth McDevitt (Miss Tait), Neva Patterson (Connie), Alice Pearce (Miss Moore), Richard Deacon (Mr. Cruikshank), Joanna Crawford (Emile Zola Bernkrand), Mary Wickes (Miss Fox), Peter Turgeon (Peterson), Ken Lynch (The Masher), James O'Rear (Marvin), Nelson Olmsted (Herb), Steve Bell.

Pleasant middle-aged romantic comedy stars Page as a postmistress of a small town who travels to New York for a post office convention. There she meets and falls in love with bachelor Ford, who is betrothed to widow Lansbury, mother of a teenage son. Though Ford looks forward to finally having a family, he, too, falls for Page, and the comedy arises from his juggling of the two situations. Good supporting cast with solid direction.

p, Martin Manulis; d, Delbert Mann; w, Tad Mosel (based on his story "The Out-Of-Towners"); ph, Russell Harlan; m, Henry Mancini; ed, Folmar Blangsted; art d, Joseph Wright; set d, Howard Bristol; cos, Don Feld; m/l, "Dear Heart," Henry Mancini, Jay Livingston, Ray Evans.

Comedy   **(PR:A   MPAA:NR)**

DEAR INSPECTOR   (SEE: DEAR DETECTIVE, 1978, Fr.)

DEAR JOHN★★½
                (1966, Swed.) 115m AB Sandrew-Ateljeerna/Sigma III bw (KARE JOHN)

Jarl Kulle (John), Christina Schollin (Anita), Helena Nilsson (Helene), Morgan Anderson (Raymond), Synnove Liljeback (Dagny), Erik Hell (Lindgren), Emy Storm (Mrs. Lindgren), Hakan Serner (Erwin), Hans Wigren (Elon), Erland Norden Falk (Kurt), Bo Wahlstrom (Bosse), Stig Woxter (Taxi Driver).

Pleasant but overrated romantic drama about a young couple who meet and have a brief love affair in the space of a weekend. He is a salty sea captain whose wife has left him, and she is a lonely waitress living with her brother and illegitimate daughter. The film opens as the lovers lie in bed telling each other about their lives and reflecting on the events that brought them there. A charmingly acted and compassionately realized film. DEAR JOHN came to the U.S. almost unheralded, although it had been nominated for an Academy Award for best foreign film (it lost to THE SHOP ON MAIN STREET), and quickly won over the critics and the public. It became the most commercially successful Swedish film ever to play in this country—until I AM CURIOUS YELLOW came along in 1969.

p, Goran Lindgren; d&w, Lars Magnus Lindgren (based on the novel by Olle Lansberg); ph, Rune Ericson; art d, Jan Boleslaw; ed, Lennart Wallen; m, Bengt-Arne Wallin; cos, Gunilla Ponten.

Romance (PR:C MPAA:NR)

DEAR MARTHA (SEE: HONEYMOON KILLERS, THE, 1970)

DEAR MR. PROHACK** (1949, Brit.) 91m
Pinewood Films-Wessex/GFD bw

Cecil Parker (*Arthur Prohack*), Glynis Johns (*Mimi Warburton*), Hermione Baddeley (*Eve Prohack*), Dirk Bogarde (*Charles Prohack*), Sheila Sim (*Mary Prohack*), Heather Thatcher (*Lady Maslam*), Frances Waring (*Nursie*), Charles Goldner (*Manservant*), Campbell Cotts (*Sir Paul Spinner*), Denholm Elliott (*Ozzie Morfrey*), Russell Waters (*Cartwright*), Henry Edwards (*Sir Digby Bunce*), Frederick Valk (*Dr. Viega*), James Hayter (*Carrell Quire*), Bryan Forbes (*Tony*), Jon Pertwee (*Plover*), Ada Reeve (*Mrs. Griggs*), Judith Furse (*Laura Postern*), Lloyd Pearson, Frederick Leister, Jerry Verno, Charles Perry, Janet Burnell, Ian Carmichael.

Parker is an official in the Royal Treasury who, despite his skill in handling the finances of the nation, is unable to manage a fortune he inherits. Mediocre comedy with an excellent cast, including Denholm Elliott in his debut.

p, Ian Dalrymple; d, Thornton Freeland; w, Dalrymple, Donald Bull (based on a play by Edward Knoblock and the novel *Mr. Prohack* by Arnold Bennett); ph, H. E. Fowle, Nigel Huke; m, Temple Abady; ed, Sidney Stone; art d, Fred Pusey; cos, Beatrice Dawson.

Comedy (PR:A MPAA:NR)

DEAR MR. WONDERFUL**½ (1983, Ger.) 100m Lilienthal c

Joe Pesci (*Ruby Dennis*), Karen Ludwig (*Paula*), Evan Handler (*Ray*), Ivy Ray Browning (*Sharon*), Frank Vincent (*Louie*), Paul Herman (*Hesh*), Tony Martin (*Guest*).

Pesci is a bowling alley and nightclub manager in Jersey City with ambitions of making it big in Vegas. Gradually he learns to take what he's got. European films about America are almost always interesting, but almost invariably wrong. This one is no exception, despite a few memorable scenes.

p, Joachim von Vietinghoff; d, Peter Lilienthal; w, Sam Koperwas; ph, Michael Ballhaus; m/l, Joe Pesci, Larry Fallon.

Drama (PR:C MPAA:NR)

DEAR MURDERER** (1947, Brit.) 94m Gainsborough/GFD bw

Eric Portman (*Lee Warren*), Greta Gynt (*Vivien Warren*), Dennis Price (*Richard Fenton*), Jack Warner (*Inspector Pembury*), Maxwell Reed (*Jimmy Martin*), Hazel Court (*Avis Fenton*), Andrew Crawford (*Sgt. Fox*), Jane Hylton (*Rita*), Ernest Butcher (*Porter*), John Blythe (*Ernie*), Charles Rolfe (*Prison Warden*), Judith Carol (*American Secretary*), Valerie Ward (*Warren's Secretary*), Helene Burls (*Charwoman*), Vic Hagan (*American Barman*), John Blythe (*Ernie*), Howard Douglas (*Doctor*), Helen Burke, Vic Hagan, Howard Douglas.

Complex and grim crime drama starring Portman as a British businessman who returns home from an American business trip and suspects his wife is having an affair with a lawyer. He confronts the attorney and tells him that if he (the lawyer) can find a loophole in the perfect murder he has devised, he will let him live. Unfortunately, the lawyer cannot figure a way out, and Portman kills him. He returns home to find his wife with another lover, so he fakes the evidence to make it appear that lover No. 2 killed lover No. 1. As a last laugh, Portman tells his wife that it was he who disposed of both her lovers. Underestimating his wife's cleverness, he falls for *her* trap and is poisoned. A bit far-fetched.

p, Betty Box; d, Arthur Crabtree; w, Muriel and Sydney Box, Peter Rogers (based on the play by St. John Legh Clowes); ph, Stephen Dade; m, Benjamin Frankel; ed, Gordon Hales; md, Muir Mathieson; art d, George Provis, John Elphick; cos, Yvonne Caffin; makeup, Len Garde.

Crime (PR:C MPAA:NR)

DEAR OCTOPUS (SEE: RANDOLPH FAMILY, THE, 1945)

DEAR RUTH*** (1947) 94m PAR bw

Joan Caulfield (*Ruth Wilkins*), William Holden (*Lt. William Seacroft*), Edward Arnold (*Judge Harry Wilkins*), Mary Philips (*Edith Wilkins*), Mona Freeman (*Miriam Wilkins*), Billy De Wolfe (*Albert Kummer*), Virginia Welles (*Martha Seacroft*), Marietta Canty (*Dora, The Maid*), Kenny O'Morrison (*Sgt. Chuck Vincent*), Irving Bacon (*Delivery Man*), Isabel Randolph (*Mrs. Teaker*).

Cute war-time comedy featuring Holden as a soldier on a two-day leave who travels to a small town to meet his pen-pal sweetheart who has been writing him for two years. The girl, Caulfield, knows nothing of the soldier because her younger sister has been sending the letters, using her older sibling's name and picture. Caulfield is engaged to marry the local banker, but not wanting to disappoint the soldier she decides to try and juggle the men for Holden's two-day stay. Of course, Caulfield falls in love with Holden, complicating her life. Good fun with a standout performance by Arnold as the girl's father. Two equally entertaining sequels followed, DEAR WIFE (1949) and DEAR BRAT (1951).

p, Paul Jones; d, William D. Russell; w, Arthur Sheekman (based on the play by Norman Krasna); ph, Ernest Laszlo; m, Robert Emmett Dolan; ed, Archie Marshek; art d, Hans Dreier, Earl Hedrick; set d, Sam Comer.

Comedy (PR:A MPAA:NR)

DEAR WIFE*** (1949) 87m PAR bw

William Holden (*Bill Seacroft*), Joan Caulfield (*Ruth Seacroft*), Billy De Wolfe (*Albert Kummer*), Mona Freeman (*Miriam Wilkins*), Edward Arnold (*Judge Wilkins*),

Arleen Whelan (*Tommy Murphy*), Mary Philips (*Mrs. Wilkins*), Harry Von Zell (*Jeff Cooper*), Raymond Roe (*Ziggy*), Elisabeth Fraser (*Kate Collins*), Bill Murphy (*Dan Collins*), Mary Field (*Mrs. Bixby*), Irving Bacon (*Mike Man*), Gordon Jones (*Taxicab Driver*), Marietta Canty (*Dora*), Don Beddoe (*Metcalfe*), Stanley Stayle (*An Early Riser*), William Cartledge (*Western Union Boy*), Ralph Montgomery (*Control Man*), Franklyn Farnum, Edward Biby, Charles Dayton (*Campaign Men*), Claire DuBrey (*Woman*), Tim Ryan (*Simmons the Cop*), Ida Moore (*Blowsy Woman*), Leon Tyler (*Gawky Boy*), Harry Harvey (*Mr. Channock*), Tom Dugan (*Painter*), Len Hendry (*Bank Teller*), Bess Flowers (*Mrs. Grindle*), Paul E. Burns (*Mr. Grindle*), Harland Tucker (*Mr. Burroughs*), Patty Lou Arden (*Clara*).

It's hard to picture prissy, neurotic Haydn speaking in that nasal voice as the director of this film as well as of the legendary MISS TATLOCK'S MILLIONS, but it's true. He did them both as well as write any number of things under the "nom de cine" of Edward Carp. The entire creative team came from unique backgrounds for this kind of picture. Co-author Sheekman was one of the Marx Brothers' writers; Nash wrote for Broadway (THE RAINMAKER); Producer Maibaum wrote several James Bond movies; and Haydn spent most of his life in roles that Clifton Webb wouldn't play because they were too epicene. In this sequel to 1947's DEAR RUTH, Holden and Caulfield are young marrieds having in-law problems. Father-in-law Arnold is a blustering judge whose word is law around the court and the house. When Holden says that Arnold doesn't know what a good breakfast is (Arnold loves grapefruit in the morning and Holden hates it), the feathers fly. Freeman is the kid sister and now, two years later, she is socially aware and very political and uses her wiles to get Holden into a race for the state senate. That wouldn't be a huge problem except that his opponent is Arnold! Harry Von Zell is a radio announcer who comes to the house to get a breakfast interview with the two men, but neither of them will speak and Von Zell is very funny in his frustration as he attempts to extract some words out of these sphinxes. Whelan arrives and has to stay at the house as there is nowhere else in town to sleep. She has an eye for Holden, and Billy De Wolfe, who was dispensed with in the earlier DEAR RUTH, still has a yen for Caulfield. Both he and Whelan do their best to get Holden and Caulfield to break up so they can move in on the relationship. Everything works out in the house (which still makes it feel like a play, rather than a film), and Freeman eventually gets to make her own movie, DEAR BRAT, a year or so later. Freeman, born Monica Freeman in Baltimore, was in her early twenties when this film was shot, but she is very much like Richard Jaeckel in that she seems to age at a much slower pace than everyone else. In the 1980s, both of them look as though they're in their thirties. She was yet another 'discovery' of Howard Hughes. My, how that man *did* get around. One also wonders if J.D. Salinger might not have been looking at an ad for DEAR RUTH or DEAR WIFE when he saw two names jump out at him...HOLDEN/CAULFIELD. Was that where he found the name for his hero in *Catcher In The Rye*? We'll never know because he'll never grant anyone an interview. But it's interesting to speculate, right?

p, Richard Maibaum; d, Richard Haydn; w, Arthur Sheekman, N. Richard Nash (based on characters created by Norman Krasna for his play "Dear Ruth"); ph, Stuart Thompson; ed, Archie Marshek; art d, Hans Dreier, Earl Hedrick.

Comedy (PR:AA MPAA:NR)

DEATH AT A BROADCAST** (1934, Brit.) 71m Phoenix Films/ABFD bw
(AKA: DEATH AT BROADCASTING HOUSE)

Ian Hunter (*Detective Inspector Gregory*), Austin Trevor (*Leopold Dryden*), Mary Newland (*Joan Dryden*), Henry Kendall (*Rodney Fleming*), Val Gielgud (*Julian Caird*), Peter Haddon (*Guy Bannister*), Betty Davies (*Poppy Levine*), Jack Hawkins (*Herbert Evans*), Donald Wolfit (*Sydney Parsons*), Robert Rendel (*Sir Herbert Farquharson*), Gordon McLeod (*Commissioner of Police*), Bruce Lister (*Peter Ridgwell*), Hannen Swaffer, Vernon Bartlett, Eric Dunstan, Gillie Potter, Eve Becke, Elisabeth Welch, Ivor Barnard, Howard Douglas, Vincent Holman, George de Warfaz, Percy Rhodes, Gershom Parkington Quintet, Percival Mackey and His Band, Ord Hamilton and His Band.

Tedious murder mystery featuring Hunter as a Scotland Yard inspector saddled with solving the murder of a radio actor during a broadcast. Suspicion falls on the other performers, and before Hunter wraps everything up, much is made of the mechanics involved in putting on a radio broadcast.

p, Hugh Percival; d, Reginald Denham; w, Basil Mason (based on a novel by Val Gielgud, Holt Marvell); ph, Gunther Krampf.

Mystery (PR:A MPA:NR)

DEATH BITE (SEE: SPASMS, 1983, Can.)

DEATH BLOW (SEE: TOUCH OF LEATHER, 1968, Brit.)

DEATH COLLECTOR**
(1976) 85m Goldstone Film Enterprise/Epoh c (AKA: FAMILY ENFORCER)

Joseph Cortese, Lou Criscuola, Joseph Pesci, Anne Johns, Keith Davis, Bobby Alto, Frank Vincent, Jack Ramage.

Cortese is a young man in the Jersey City slums who falls in with mobsters. Occasionally interesting melodrama owes much to Scorsese, but lacks his feel for emotions.

p, William N. Panzer; d&w, Ralph DeVito; ph, Bob Bailan.

Crime (PR:O MPAA:R)

DEATH CORDS (SEE: SHOCK WAVES, 1977)

DEATH CROONS THE BLUES*½
(1937, Brit.) 74m St. Margarets/MGM bw
Hugh Wakefield (Jim Martin), Antoinette Cellier (Lady Constance Gaye), George Hayes (Hugo Branker), Gillian Lind, John Turnbull, Hugh Burden (Viscount Brent), Barbara Everest.

Wakefield is a permanently besotted reporter who proves that Cellier's missing brother is innocent of murdering a songstress. Decent cast vaguely distinguishes this programmer.

p, Julius Hagen; d, David MacDonald; w, H. Fowler Mear (based on a novel by James Ronald).

Crime (PR:A MPAA:NR)

DEATH CURSE OF TARTU*
(1967) 87m Falcon International/Thunderbird International c
Fred Pinero (Ed Tison), Babette Sherrill (Julie Tison), Mayra Cristine (Cindy), Sherman Hayes (Johnny), Gary Holtz (Tommy), Maurice Stewart (Joann), Frank Weed (Sam Gunter), Doug Hobart (Tartu), William Marcos (Billy/The Indian).

Okay horror vehicle (vastly superior to director Grefe's rancid foray into the crime genre, THE HOOKED GENERATION) concerning a group of thoughtless archaeology students who accidentally disturb the grave of a Seminole Indian witch doctor named Tartu (Hobart). Tartu comes back to life and goes after the kids, alternately taking the form of a snake, a shark, an alligator, and a zombie, killing off all his victims until he is swallowed up by quicksand, thus fulfilling some obscure native prophecy. The Florida Everglades, the film's location site, provided the quicksand for the chilling finale.

p, Joseph Fink, Juan Hildalgo-Gato; d&w, William Grefe; ph&ed, Julio C. Chavez (Eastmancolor); set d, Thomas Casey; m/l, Al Greene, Al Jacobs.

Horror (PR:C-O MPAA:NR)

DEATH DRIVES THROUGH**
(1935, Brit.) 63m Clifford Taylor/ABF bw
Dorothy "Chili" Bouchier (Kay Lord), Robert Douglas (Kit Woods), Miles Mander (Garry Ames), Percy Walsh (Mr. Lord), Frank Atkinson (Nigger Larson), Lillian Gunns (Binnie).

Douglas is a race car designer who manages to woo Bouchier despite the disapproval of her tycoon father and competition from his rascally business rival. Okay programmer.

p, Clifford Taylor; d, Edward L. Cahn; w, Gordon Wellesley (based on a story by Katherine Strueby and John Huston).

Drama (PR:A MPAA:NR)

DEATH DRUMS ALONG THE RIVER (SEE: SANDERS, 1963, Brit.)

DEATH FLIES EAST**
(1935) 65m COL bw
Conrad Nagel (John Robinson Gordon), Florence Rice (Evelyn Vail), Raymond Walburn (Evans), Geneva Mitchell (Helen Gilbert) Robert Allen (Baker), Oscar Apfel (Burroughs), Mike Morita (Satu), Purnell Pratt (Dr. Landers), Irene Franklin (Mrs. Madison), George Irving (Dr. Moffat), Adrian Rosley (Pastoli), Fred Kelsey (O'Brien), George [Gabby] Hayes (Wotkyns).

Tiresome murder mystery where the action takes place mainly on a transcontinental flight from California to New York. Rice, a nurse who gets paroled from prison after serving time for a poisoning she did not commit, seeks to clear her name. Based on a tip that the real killer is about to be executed (for a different killing) in Sing Sing, Rice flies to New York to extract a confession from the murderer before he fries. On the plane she meets a young college instructor, Nagel, who is transporting top-secret armament formulas to Navy headquarters in Washington, D.C. Suddenly, two passengers wind up poisoned and the papers disappear and suspicion falls on the ex-con nurse. With the help of Nagel, Rice is cleared and the papers recovered. The fact that most of the action takes place on an airplane makes this something of a period piece, featuring the amenities, or lack of them, on a transcontinental flight at practically the dawn of air passenger service.

p, Sid Rogell; d, Phil Rosen; w, Albert Demond, Fred Niblo Jr. (based on a story by Philip Wylie); ph, Al Siegler; ed, John Rawlins.

Mystery (PR:A MPAA:NR)

DEATH FROM A DISTANCE*½
(1936) 73m Invincible/CHES bw
Russell Hopton (Detective Lt. Ted Mallory) Lola Lane (Kay Palmer), George Marion, Sr. (Jim Gray), John St. Polis (Prof. Trowbridge), Lee Kohlmar (Prof. Ernst Einfeld), Lew Kelly (Detective Regan), Wheeler Oakman (Langsdale), Robert Frazer (Morgan), Cornelius Keefe (Gorman), Capt. E. H. Clavert (District Attorney), John Davidson (Ahmad Haidru), John Dilson (City Editor McConnell), Henry Hall (Medical Examiner), Creighton Hale, Jane Keckley, Eric Mayne (Witnesses), Herbert Vigran (Photographer), Charles West (Fingerprint Expert), Lynton Brent, Ralph Brooks, Joel Lyon (Reporters), Frank LaRue (Desk Sgt.), Hal Price (Detective).

Routine murder mystery starring Hopton as the detective and Lane as the reporter trying to solve a murder. The action takes place mainly at a planetarium, with most of the suspects being astronomers. Too long and too weak to sustain even a modicum of interest.

p, Maury M. Cohen; d, Frank Strayer; w, John W. Krafft; ph, M. A. Andersen; ed, Roland Reed; md, Abe Meyer; art d, Edward C. Jewell; spec eff, Jack Cosgrove; prod mgr, Lon Young.

Mystery (PR:A MPAA:NR)

DEATH FROM OUTER SPACE
(SEE: DAY THE SKY EXPLODED, THE, 1961)

DEATH GAME zero
(1977) 89m Levitt-Pickman Film c
Sondra Locke (Jackson), Colleen Camp (Donna), Seymour Cassel (George Manning), Beth Brickell (Karen Manning), Michael Kalmansohn (Delivery Boy), Ruth Warshawsky (Mrs. Grossman).

Almost a total waste of everyone's time, including the audience. The only reason to see this is to sit back and listen to Jimmy Haskell's score, with your eyes closed. Locke and Camp are lesbians who arrive at Cassel's very fancy home in a San Francisco suburb. Cassel has just celebrated his fortieth birthday and those birthdays with zeroes at the end of them can be depressing so Cassel invites the comely wenches into his house. It is pouring and thundering out there and they seek shelter from the storm. Cassel's wife and children are away and he is feeling lonesome. The two playful women seduce Cassel and a menage a trois begins. It would have been swell if it was all fun and games and they left in the morning. But no, these women have a sadistic streak. They tie him up, ruin his gorgeous house, paint their bodies with makeup, drown poor Kalmansohn, who was just a delivery boy minding his own business, and make Cassel's life miserable as they threaten him on and off for what seems like forever. In the end, they are killed when hit by a truck from the anti-cruelty society. Now if that don't beat all! Locke had some success as Eastwood's co-star in several films but she was never as good as he must have thought she was. Cassel, a favorite of Cassavetes, received an Oscar nomination once but he'd be wise to omit this one from his resume.

p, Larry Spiegel, Peter Traynor; d, Traynor; w, Anthony Overman, Michael Ronald Ross; ph, David Worth; m; Jimmie Haskell.

Terror (PR:O MPAA:R)

DEATH GOES NORTH*½
(1939) 64m Warwick bw
Edgar Edwards (Ken Strange), Sheila Bromley (Elsie Barlow), Dorothy Bradshaw (Mrs. Barlow), Jameson Thomas (Mr. Barlow), Walter Byron (Albert Norton), Arthur Kerr (Bart Norton), James McGrath (Puffet), Vivian Combe (Maggie), Reginald Hincks (Freddie), Rin-Tin-Tin, Jr.

Incredibly complicated north woods murder mystery in which two Mounties and Rin-Tin-Tin, Jr., try to sort out the mess. A young lumber heiress, Bromley, is having trouble making her timber payments due to the tampering of a pair of rival lumberjacks who want her land. In desperation, she wires her uncle in England for help, but he has been murdered by his male secretary, who then poses as the uncle and travels to Canada to claim the land for himself and his wife. Somehow, the blame for the killing is laid on the rival lumberjacks, who protest their innocence. Enter a slightly crazed mountain man who claims he owns all the land, which confuses the matter even more. The Mounties and the pooch sort everything out by checking fingerprints (!). Good for laughs.

p, Kenneth Bishop; d, Frank McDonald; w, Edward R. Austin; ph, Harry Forbes; ed, William Austin.

Mystery (PR:A MPAA:NR)

DEATH GOES TO SCHOOL**
(1953, Brit.) 65m IA/Eros bw
Barbara Murray (Miss Shepherd), Gordon Jackson (Inspector Campbell), Pamela Allan (Helen Cooper), Jane Aird (Miss Halstead), Beatrice Varley (Miss Hopkinson), Stanley Rose (Inspector Burgess), Robert Longer (Mr. Lawley), Sam Kydd (Sgt. Harvey), Ann Butchart, Jenine Matto, Imogene Moynihan, Pauline Winter, Enid Stewart, Sandra Whipp, Nina Parry, Julie Stewart.

Murray, the music teacher at a girl's school, proves that a fellow teacher is a strangler. Infrequently effective crime drama.

p, Victor Hanbury; d, Stephen Clarkson; w, Maisie Sharman, Clarkson (based on a novel by Sharman); ph, Eric Cross.

Crime (PR:A MPAA:NR)

DEATH HUNT**½
(1981) 96m FOX c
Charles Bronson (Johnson), Lee Marvin (Millen), Andrew Stevens (Alvin), Carl Weathers (Sundog), Ed Lauter (Hazel), Scott Hylands (Pilot), Angie Dickinson (Vanessa), Henry Beckman (Luce), William Sanderson (Ned Warren), Jon Cedar (Hawkins), James O'Connell (Hurley), Len Lesser (Lewis), Dick Davalos (Beeler), Maury Chaykin (Clarence), August Schellenberg (Deak), Maurice Kowaleski (Charlie Rat), Sean McCann (News Reporter), Steve O.Z. Finkel (W.W. Douglas), Denis Lacroix (Jimmy Tom), Tantoo Martin (Indian Woman), Amy Marie George (Buffalo Woman), Dennis Wallace, James McIntire, Rayford Barnes (Trappers).

What may well have been a minor action masterwork if it had been directed by Robert Aldrich (who was originally slated to do so) turns into a mediocre adventure with an unfortunate waste of talent. Marvin stars as the tough-as-nails Mountie who is sent to track down maverick trapper Bronson, who is accused of murder. Bronson, of course, didn't commit the crime, and he refuses to be brought in. A few moments of good, visual storytelling surface, but it's not enough to save this frustrating disappointment.

p, Murray Shostak; d, Peter Hunt; w, Michael Grais, Mark Victor; ph, James Devis (Panavison, Technicolor); m; Jerrold Immel; ed, Allan Jacobs, John F. Burnett; prod d, Ted Haworth; art d, Tom Doherty; cos, Olga Dimitrov.

Action/Adventure **Cas.** (PR:C MPAA:R)

DEATH IN SMALL DOSES**
(1957) 78m AA bw
Peter Graves (Tom Kayler), Mala Powers (Val Owens), Chuck Connors (Mink Reynolds), Merry Anders (Amy), Roy Engel (Wally), Robert B. Williams (Dunc), Harry Lauter (Hummel), Pete Kooy (Flynt), Robert Christopher (Lennie).

Presumably an important "message" film when released, now a hysterical howl, DEATH IN SMALL DOSES details the efforts of U.S. Food and Drug investigator Graves to stamp out the influx of amphetamines into the trucking industry. It seems that truckers all over the country have been wrecking their rigs in crashes because they are "hopped up" on the "bennies" they have been taking to stay awake on long hauls. Graves poses as a trucker in search of pills to get the goods on the big pushers. He falls for lovely Powers and then discovers that she is one of the biggest pill kingpins in the country. Connors is great as a trucker spaced out on pills. A must-see for low-budget cultists.

p, Richard Heermance; d, Joseph Newman; w, John McGreevey (based on a magazine article by Arthur L. Davis); ph, Carl Guthrie; m, Emil Newman, Robert Wiley Miller; ed, William Austin.

Drama   **(PR:C   MPAA:NR)**

DEATH IN THE GARDEN***   (1977, Fr./Mex.) 97m
Dismage/Teperac/Bauer International c (LA MORT EN CE JARDIN; GINA; LA MUERTE EN ESTA JARDIN; AKA; EVIL EDEN)

Simone Signoret (Djin), Georges Marchal (Chark), Michel Piccoli (Father Lisardi), Michele Girardon (Maria), Charles Vanel (Castin), Tito Junco (Chenko), Luis Aceves Castaneda (Alberto), Jorge Martines de Hoyos (Capt. Ferrero), Raul Ramirez (Alvaro), Alberto Pedret (Lieutenant), Alicia del Lago.

Fleeing a repressive regime, a group of misfits from an Amazonian diamond field make their way through the jungle. Led by Marchal, a prospector who has escaped from jail, the travelers include prostitute Signoret, priest Piccoli, miner Vanel and his deaf-mute daughter, Girardon. As the journey grows more difficult, the travelers begin to shed their individual preoccupations and become better people. The priest stops spouting dogma and tears up his prayer book to light a fire. Then they stumble across a crashed airliner, and while looting the plane for food and money they revert to their old selves. Vanel goes crazy and sees himself as the wrath of God, shooting down the others until he himself is shot and killed by Marchal. Along with Girardon, the only other survivor, Marchal finds a canoe and the pair paddle down the river to safety. One of Bunuel's most accessible films, DEATH IN THE GARDEN is superficially a conventional thriller (one that owes much to THE WAGES OF FEAR), but Bunuel's surrealist world view manages to peek through. In one scene, a large snake Marchal has killed for food begins to move, carried by ants. A fascinating film produced in 1956. (In French; English, subtitles.)

p, David Mage, Oscar Dancigers; d, Luis Bunuel; w, Bunuel, Luis Alcoriza, Raymond Queneau (based on a story by Jose-Andre Lacour); ph, Jorge Stahl, Jr. (Eastmancolor); m, Paul Misraki; ed, Marguerite Renoir; set d, Edward Fitzgerald.

Drama   **(PR:O   MPAA:NR)**

DEATH IN THE SKY*   (1937) 69m Puritan bw (AKA: PILOT X)
Lona Andre (Helen Gage), John Carroll (Jerry Blackwood), Henry Hall (Henry Goering), Leon Ames (Carl Goering), Wheeler Oakman (Lt. Douglas Thompson), Reed Howes (Lt. John Ives), Pat Somerset (Capt. Roland Saunders), Gaston Glass (Lt. Rene La Rue), John S. Peters (Lt. Baron Otto van Guttard), Willard Kent (Inspector Gallagher), John Elliot (Dr. Norris).

A quickly dashed off aviation murder mystery about a crazed ex-WW I pilot (Ames), who kills anyone in the sky. After a lot of deaths and stock plane crashes, Carroll finally shoots the killer down to end the mess. Amateur cinematography and insipid acting keep this low budget fare from ever taking off.

p, Fanchon Royer; d, Elmer Clifton; w, Charles R. Condon, (based on a screen story by Bernard McConville); ph, James Diamond, Art Read; ed, Carl Hinun.

Mystery   **(PR:C   MPAA:NR)**

DEATH IN VENICE****   (1971, Ital./Fr.) 130m WB c
(MORTE A VENEZIA)

Dirk Bogarde (Gustav Von Aschenbach), Bjorn Andresen (Tadzio), Silvana Mangano (Tadzio's Mother), Marisa Berenson (Frau Von Aschenbach), Mark Burns (Alfred), Romolo Valli (Hotel Manager), Nora Ricci (Governess), Carol Andre (Esmeralda), Masha Predit (Singer), Leslie French (Travel Agent), Franco Fabrizi (Barber), Sergio Garafanolo (Polish Youth), Luigi Battaglia (Scapegrace), Ciro Cristofoletti (Hotel Clerk), Dominique Darel.

Overlong but powerful screen adaptation of Thomas Mann's novella by famed Italian director Luchino Visconti. Bogarde plays the aging German composer who visits Venice while on the verge of a physical and mental breakdown. Plagued by fears that he can no longer feel emotion because he has been avoiding it for so long, he continues to remain unfazed by the boorish and obnoxious behavior of those around him. Then suddenly he sees a beautiful, blond boy who is traveling with his mother and sisters, and Bogarde becomes obsessed with him. The boy is the most beautiful thing he has seen in his life and stirs feelings within him he thought he had lost. He seeks out the boy, but refrains from contacting him; he just watches as the boy walks with his family from place to place in the dank, decaying city. Bogarde goes so far as to have a barber make him up as a younger man, but the effect is pathetic and sad. During his stay, Venice is hit with a cholera epidemic, but Bogarde refuses to leave. He prefers to die on the beach, staring at the boy silhouetted against the ocean. Bogarde is superb as the dying composer who has one last rush of beauty and emotion in his life before he decays totally, like the city where the film takes place. Brilliant use of music is made of selections from Mahler's Third and Fifth Symphonies that haunt every frame of the film. The cinematography is beautiful and combined with the art direction it is a powerful evocation of a time and a place past. Not for all tastes, however.

p&d, Luchino Visconti; w, Visconti, Nicola Badalucco (based on the novella by Thomas Mann); ph, Pasquale De Santis (Panavision, Technicolor); m, Gustav Mahler; ed, Ruggero Mastroianni; art d, Ferdinando Scarfiotti; set d, Nedo Azzini; cos, Piero Tosi; makeup, Mario De Silvio, Mauro Gavazzi, Goffredo Rocchetti.

Drama   **Cas.**   **(P:C   MPAA:GP)**

DEATH IS A NUMBER**   (1951, Brit.) 50m Delman/Adelphi bw
Terence Alexander (Alan Robert), Lesley Osmond (John Robert), Denis Webb (John Bridgnorth), Ingeborg Wells (Gipsy), Peter Gawthorne (James Gregson), Isabel George (Nurse).

A race car driver ignores a 300-year old curse and, of course, pays for his foolishness with his life. Okay, if forgotten, melodrama.

p&d, Robert Henryson; w, Charles K. Shaw; ph, Phil Grindrod, Harry Long.

Horror   **(PR:A-C   MPAA:NR)**

DEATH IS A WOMAN   (SEE: LOVE IS A WOMAN, 1967, Brit.)

DEATH IS CALLED ENGELCHEN***   (1963, Czech.) 160 m
Czescoslovensky Film Export bw (FOR WE TOO DO NOT FORGIVE)

Jan Kacer, Eva Polagova, Martin Rusek, Blazena Holisova, Vlado Muller.

Above average, though overlong, film has Kacer a partisan fighter shot in the spine on the last day of the war. As he lies in a hospital bed hovering between life and death, he remembers the fight against the Nazis in a series of episodes. It is finally the thought that Engelchen, the German commander in the area, is still alive and at large that gives Kacer the strength to recover to leave the hospital seeking retribution. Directors Kadar and Klos would make their best known work the following year, THE SHOP ON MAIN STREET.

d, Jan Kadar, Elmar Klos; w, Milos Faber; ph, Rudolf Milic.

War Drama   **(PR:C   MPAA:NR)**

DEATH KISS, THE*   (1933) 74m KBS/World Wide bw/c
David Manners (Franklyn Drew), Adrienne Ames (Marcia Lane), Bela Lugosi (Joseph Steiner), John Wray (Detective Sheehan), Vince Barnett (Officer Gulliver), Alexander Carr (Leon Grossmith), Edward Van Sloan (Tom Avery), Harold Minjir (Howell), Wade Boteler (Hilliker), Al Hill (Assistant Director), Barbara Bedford (Script Clerk), Alan Roscoe (Chalmers), Mona Maris (Mrs. Avery), Edmund Burns (Brent), Jimmy Donlin (Hill), Harold Waldridge (Clerk), Lee Moran (Todd), Wilson Benge (Doorman), Eddy Chandler (Mechanic), Harry Strang (Gaffer), Eddie Boland (Bill), Frank O'Connor (Cop), Forrest Taylor, Paul Porcasi, King Baggott.

Three principal actors from Todd Browning's DRACULA (Lugosi, Manners, and Sloan), star in this muddled mystery about an actor who is murdered during filming on a Hollywood back lot. Confusing plot development, direction that swings from farce to serious mystery, and a poorly thought out script murders this film. (How can an audience care about solving the murder when the characters joke and speak lowly of the victim?) Over and above it being a poorly done mystery, DEATH KISS is another film that offers a fascinating look behind the scenes at a 1930s Hollywood movie studio. The film was shot in Tiffany Studios, located on Sunset Boulevard, which folded because of the Depression. The actual studio projection rooms, dressing rooms, makeup rooms, and street and buildings were used. The film also marked the directorial debut of Edwin L. Marin who, before he died in 1951, was to direct 50 movies, many of them nifty thrillers and bright minor comedies. This picture was one of only a very few talkies which had hand-colored sequences. One, used to good effect, occurs when the film depicting the murder is projected; the story line has the murder film catching fire, and the effect is realized for the audience as the screen reddens with supposed flames.

d, Edwin L. Marin; w, Barry Barringer, Gordon Kahn (based on the novel by Madelon St. Dennis); ph, Norbert Brodine; ed, Rose Loewinger, Martin G. Cohn; md, Val Burton; art d, Ralph M. DeLacey.

Mystery   **Cas.**   **(PR:A   MPAA:NR)**

DEATH MACHINES zero   (1976) 90m Crown International c
Michael Chong, Joshua Johnson, Mari Honjo, Ron Marchini, Chuck Katzaian.

Female crime lord Honjo runs an assassination-for-hire service using a secret serum to create super kung fu killers. Just plain awful.

d, Paul Kyriazi.

Martial Arts   **Cas.**   **(PR:O   MPAA:NR)**

DEATH OF A BUREAUCRAT***   (1979, Cuba) 87m Cuban Film
Institute/Tricontinental Film Distributing bw

Salvador Wood (Nephew), Silvia Planas (Aunt), Manuel Estanillo (Bureaucrat), Gaspar de Santelices (Nephew's Boss), Carlos Ruiz de la Tejera (Psychiatrist), Omar Alfonso (Cojimar), Ricardo Suarez (Tarafa), Luis Romay (El Zorro), Elsa Montero (Sabor).

When the inventor of a machine to produce busts of Cuban hero Jose Martin dies, he is hailed as a model worker and given a lavish funeral. Among the honors, he is buried with his union card, which his widow needs to collect a pension from the state. She asks her nephew to help, and he is soon entangled in a bureaucracy that won't let him obtain an exhumation permit until the body has been buried for two years. Desperate, he steals the body out of its grave, then finds he can't rebury it until he shows his exhumation permit. Full of homages to silent comedians like Laurel and Hardy and Harold Lloyd, the film is both a classic slapstick and a sly satire on the choking bureaucracy of Cuban Communism. Director Alea, whose MEMORIES OF UNDERDEVELOPMENT put him among the first rank of Third World filmmakers, did not go unnoticed in his attack on the government and the film was banned in Cuba after a brief release there in 1966.

d, Tomas Guttierez Alea; w, Alea, Alfredo del Cuelo, Ramon F. Suarez; ph, Suarez; m, Leo Brouwer; ed, Mario Gonzalez.

Comedy   **(PR:A-C   MPAA:NR)**

DEATH OF A CHAMPION   (1939) 67m PAR bw
Lynne Overman (Oliver Quade), Virginia Dale (Patsy Doyle), Joseph Allen, Jr. (Richie Oakes), Donald O'Connor (Small Fry), Susan Paley (Lois Lanyard), Harry

Davenport *(Guy Lanyard)*, Robert Paige *(Alec Temple)*, May Boley *(Ma Sloane)*, Hal Brazeale *(Gerald Lanyard)*, Frank M. Thomas *(Chief Sanders)*, David Clyde *(Angus McTavish)*, Walter Soderling *(Hofnagel)*, Pierre Watkin *(Albert Deacon)*, Bob McKenzie *(Dr. Taylor)*.

An encyclopedia salesman and telepathist, Overman, is forced into playing detective in the case of a murdered show dog. Overman's assistant, a young O'Connor, pulls his boss into sleuthing when his amateurish attempts at discovering the killer get both of them into a variety of predicaments. The suspects range from a friend of the dog owner's daughter, to the owner's nurse. But the dog's killer, as always, is the one no one would suspect. Standard mystery fare, picking up when O'Connor is on the screen, already stealing scenes from older actors although the Chicago-born song-and-dance comedian was only 14 years old and in films only two years.

d, Robert Florey; w, Stuart Palmer, Cortland Fitzsimmons (based on a story by Frank Gruber); ph, Stuart Thompson; ed, Archie Marshek.

Mystery **(PR:A MPAA:NR)**

DEATH OF A CYCLIST (SEE: AGE OF INFIDELITY, 1955)

DEATH OF A GUNFIGHTER½** (1969) 94m UNIV c

Richard Widmark *(Marshal Frank Patch)*, Lena Horne *(Claire Quintana)*, Carroll O'Connor *(Lester Locke)*, David Opatoshu *(Edward Rosenbloom)*, Kent Smith *(Andrew Oxley)*, Jacqueline Scott *(Laurie Mills)*, Morgan Woodward *(Ivan Stanek)*, Larry Gates *(Mayor Chester Sayre)*, Dub Taylor *(Doc Adams)*, John Saxon *(Lou Trinidad)*, Darleen Carr *(Hilda Jorgenson)*, Michael McGreevey *(Dan Joslin)*, Royal Dano *(Arch Brandt)*, James Lydon *(Luke Mills)*, Kathleen Freeman *(Mary Elizabeth)*, Harry Carey, Jr. *(Rev. Rork)*, Amy Thomson *(Angela)*, Mercer Harris *(Will Oxley)*, James O'Hara *(Father Sweeney)*, Walter Sande *(Paul Hammond)*, Victor French *(Phil Miller)*, Robert Sorrells *(Chris Hogg)*, Charles Kuenstle *(Roy Brandt)*, Sara Taft *(Mexican Woman)*.

A strange hybrid of directing styles is the only element in this routine western that holds any interest. Production was begun by director Robert Totten. Halfway through the shoot, Totten was fired when star Widmark refused to continue under his direction. Don Siegel was hired in his place and finished the second half of the film in nine days. The result is a strange mix of Totten's slow and plodding, and Siegel's fast and to-the-point styles, evident in every scene because Totten didn't shoot in sequence (leaving Siegel to fill in the blanks). Widmark plays a gunslinger turned sheriff who is from the old school of justice. The town politicos are courting Eastern investors and fear that the sheriff's uncouth style will scare the investors off, so they band together to oust him. Widmark refuses to be retired (he desperately hangs on to the myth of the "Old West") and the town council sees no other way than to bump him off. Some interesting thematics and deep character studies surface (which Siegel would put to good use later in John Wayne's outstanding final film, THE SHOOTIST, 1976). Horne is wasted as Widmark's mistress (and later, wife), though she does sing "Sweet Apple Wine."

p, Richard E. Lyons; d, Allen Smithee; w, Joseph Calvelli (based on the novel by Lewis B. Patten); ph, Andrew Jackson; m, Oliver Nelson; ed, Robert F. Shugrue; md, Stanley Wilson; art d, Alexander Golitzen, Howard E. Johnson; set d, Sandy Grace, John McCarthy; cos, Helen Colvig; m/l, "Sweet Apple Wine," Oliver Nelson, Carol Hall.

Western **(PR:C MPAA:M)**

DEATH OF A JEW (SEE: SABRA, 1970, Fr./Ital.)

DEATH OF A SALESMAN***** (1952) 115m COL bw

Fredric March *(Willy Loman)*, Mildred Dunnock *(Linda Loman)*, Kevin McCarthy *(Biff)*, Cameron Mitchell *(Happy)*, Howard Smith *(Charley)*, Royal Beal *(Ben)*, Don Keefer *(Bernard)*, Jesse White *(Stanley)*, Claire Carleton *(Miss Francis)*, David Alpert *(Howard Wagner)*, Elizabeth Fraser *(Miss Forsythe)*, Patricia Walker *(Letta)*.

The somber Miller stage play lost none of its classic meaning in the film version with March as the end-of-the-line Willy Loman, one of his greatest performances. March is a man run down at all the edges, incapable of changing a lifestyle and career that has become the past. He is in his early sixties and, after being fired, has nowhere to go, clinging to his petty, mediocre values and looking only backward with soul-wrenching agony. His pride is packed like an old traveling bag; inside of it is a life he chooses to think of as successful. He has a long-suffering wife, Dunnock, and two sons, McCarthy and Mitchell. The older son, Mitchell, is an average business success but he has no spirit, the younger, McCarthy, is completely disillusioned and he, too, loses his job, having no ambition to find another. Further, McCarthy has a long-standing spiritual illness he has never cured; years earlier he found his father with another woman in a hotel room and his ideals were shattered. March tries to get a job but no one wants him. Before the end, a suicide, March realizes that he has instilled in his sons false values and ruthless perspectives. They, like he, have no sense of humanity, no heart for civilization. This film will spare no viewer as March relentlessly trods to his doom, looking for redemption inside empty rooms of the past and babbling cliches to the apparition of his long vanished brother. Dunnock has tolerated March's lifelong excuses for the marginal income he has provided the family and she has struggled to maintain a good life for all, making the final mortgage payment on their house just before March does himself in, almost as a fillip to the tragedy, the grim completion of the American dream of owning one's home. But now no one but this disconsolate woman, abandoned in death, will live in it, waiting for her own end. Lee J. Cobb gave a penetrating performance in the original 1949 stage hit and Dustin Hoffman applied his considerable talent to project the tragic Willy in a 1985 TV presentation (from a stage revival), but he does a caricature such as the whimsical performance rendered in LITTLE BIG MAN, one reaching forward from his own youth to advanced middle age with makeup propping up inner understanding, and legend of the part and his own reputation having to carry the burden of the role. Hoffman has developed the peculiar habit of thrusting his talent into old-age, offbeat or other sex parts (TOOTSIE) rather than dealing with his contemporary self, as if unwilling to risk his far-reaching abilities with any role that is not outlandish or establishment rooted, performances hidden behind disguises, historical or literary characters, or just plain gum arabic. March is still the definitive Willy Loman. He looked, felt and understood the part completely, bringing the character to life and to death as the playwright envisioned him. Kramer's production and Benedek's direction is completely faithful to the film which lost money at the box office as Columbia studio head Harry Cohn said it would. (Cohn hated the film, called it "gloomy and bleak.") Yet it stands as one of the great literary classics on film.

p, Stanley Kramer; d, Laslo Benedek; w, Stanley Roberts (based on the play by Arthur Miller); ph, Frank Planer; m, Alex North; ed, William Lyon, Harry Gerstad; md, Morris Stoloff; prod d, Rudolph Sternadt; art d, Cary Odell; set d, William Kiernan; makeup, Clay Campbell.

Drama **(PR:O MPAA:NR)**

DEATH OF A SCOUNDREL*** (1956) 119m RKO bw

George Sanders *(Clementi Sabourin)*, Yvonne De Carlo *(Bridget Kelly)*, Zsa Zsa Gabor *(Mrs. Ryan)*, Victor Jory *(Leonard Wilson)*, Nancy Gates *(Stephanie North)*, Coleen Gray *(Mrs. Van Renassalear)*, John Hoyt *(Mr. O'Hara)*, Lisa Ferraday *(Zina Monte)*, Tom Conway *(Gerry Monte)*, Celia Lovsky *(Mother Sabourin)*, Werner Klemperer *(Lawyer)*, Justice Watson *(Butler)*, John Sutton *(Actor)*, Curtis Cooksey *(Oswald Van Renassalear)*, Gabriel Curtiz *(Max Freundlich)*, Morris Ankrum *(Captain Lafarge)*, George Brent *(Man with Balloon at Party)*, Robert Morgan, Jewel Lane.

If one looks for a thoroughly rotten human being with no redeeming virtues, not a scintilla of shame, not a sliver of decency, then this is the film to see. Sanders is the scoundrel, corrupt to the marrow, a man who will stop at nothing to get what he wants. His ending, a dead body found in a Park Avenue mansion, begins the film. His personal secretary and business manager, De Carlo, relates his unsavory past, one she shared as a petty thief. Destitute, Sanders, to obtain a reward, informs police where to find his on-the-lam brother Conway who is later executed. (Conway, in real life, was Sanders' brother.) With his thirty pieces of silver Sanders flees to the U.S. He witnesses pickpocket De Carlo lift a wallet from Jory, a Canadian financier and then steals the wallet from her, using the money to glean a fortune from penicillin stock. In his climb to the top Sanders bilks wealthy widow Gabor (Zsa Zsa was then his actual ex-wife), trifling with her as well as Gray, the naive wife of a mail order tycoon (Cooksey) whom he decides to ruin. He promotes the acting career of Gates only with the secret motive of bedding her (he fails). When not skirt chasing and destroying careers, Sanders is busy plotting illegal schemes with his crooked lawyer, Klemperer, and Hoyt, his partner in scams. He deserts De Carlo and it appears as if nothing can stop the ne'er-do-well. Then Conway's widow, Ferraday, arrives from Czechoslovakia to get revenge but she finds that she cannot kill Sanders and, instead, commits suicide. Hoyt, however, the double-crossed partner, does the job for her, shooting Sanders dead as he is about to pull off one more sting. (This produced cheers from audiences when the film was first shown.) DEATH OF A SCOUNDREL was an offbeat film which Sanders enjoyed immensely; some said he was really playing himself in a modern version of "Rake's Progress." The film is actually based on the notorious career of con artist Serge Rubenstein, whose murder in his posh Manhattan apartment on March 26, 1955, was never solved.

p,d&w, Charles Martin; ph, James Wong Howe; m, Max Steiner; ed, Conrad Nervig; art d, Rudi Feld; cos, Waldo.

Crime Drama **(PR:C MPAA:NR)**

DEATH OF AN ANGEL** (1952, Brit.) 64m Hammer-Lesser/Exclusive bw

Jane Baxter *(Mary Welling)*, Patrick Barr *(Robert Welling)*, Julie Somers *(Judy Welling)*, Jean Lodge *(Ann Marlow)*, Raymond Young *(Chris Boswell)*, Russell Waters *(Walter Grannage)*, Russell Napier *(Superintendent Walshaw)*, Katie Johnson *(Sarah Oddy)*, James Mills, Frank Tickle, Robert Brown, John Kelly, Duggie Ascot, Hal Osmond, June Bardsley, David Stoll.

British B movie has Barr as a village doctor whose wife, Baxter, is murdered. Not of much interest.

p, Anthony Hinds, Julian Lesser; d, Charles Saunders; w, Reginald Long (based on the play "This Is Mary's Chair" by Frank King); ph, Walter Harvey.

Crime **(PR:A MPAA:NR)**

DEATH OF HER INNOCENCE (SEE: OUR TIME, 1974)

DEATH OF MARIO RICCI, THE*½ (1983, Ital.) 101m Pegase Films-Television Suisse-Romande-Swanie-FR3-Tele Munchen/Gala c

Gian-Marie Volonte, Magali Noël, Heinz Bennent, Mimsy Farmer, Jean-Michel Dupuis, Michel Robin, Lucas Belevaux, Claudio Caramaschi, Michel Cassagne, Michael Hinz, Marblum Jequier, Jean-Claude Perrin, Andre Schmidt, Bernard Soufflet, Roger Jendly, Bernard Pierre Donnadieu, Claude Inga Barbey, Francois Berthet, Neige Dolsky, Anne Lise Fritsch, Edmee Crozet, Gerard Despierre, Michelle Gleizer.

Pretentious potboiler in the understated European arty manner, where the death of the title character occurs offscreen, forcing the audience to suffer through the machinations of a cynical journalist as he interviews a series of uninteresting people who knew the deceased. It's hard to believe that so many film companies and so many actors and actresses were involved in this sleepy affair.

p, Yves Peyrot, Nobert Saada; d, Claude Goretta; w, Goretta, Georges Haldas; ph, Hans Liechti (Eastmancolor); m, Arie Dzierlatka; ed, Joele Van Effenterre; prod d, Yanko Hodjis.

Drama **(PR:C MPAA:NR)**

DEATH OF MICHAEL TURBIN, THE*
(1954, Brit.) 52m Douglas Fairbanks, Jr./BL bw

Christopher Rhodes, Elizabeth Wallace, Christopher Lee, Martin Benson, Tommy Duggan, June Thorburn, Barbara Mullen, Joseph Tomelty.

Two tedious, sentimental stories in one mercifully brief package. In the first, a political prisoner behind the Iron Curtain escapes a firing squad and is helped across the border to freedom by two friendly border guards. In the second story, an Irishman flees an unhappy love affair and comes to America, where he becomes a despised usurer. A priest teaches him a better way and he is reunited with the long-lost sweetheart. Of little interest and no significance.

p, Tom D. Connachie; d, Bernard Knowles; w, Guy Morgan, Paul Vincent Carroll, Larry Marcus; ph, Jimmy Wilson.

Drama   **(PR:A   MPAA:NR)**

DEATH OF TARZAN, THE**
(1968, Czech) 72m Barrandov Film/Brandon Films Studios bw
(TARZANOVA SMRT)

Rudolf Hrusinsky (Baron Wolfgang von Hoppe/Tarzan), Jana Stepankova (Regina Smith), Martin Rusek (Baron Heinrich von Hoppe), Vlastimil Hasek (Dr. Foreyt), Slavka Budinova (Ring Director), Ilya Racek (Usher), Miroslav Homola (SA Man), Nina Popelikova (Lady with Buckteeth), Elena Halkova (Baroness), Karel Peyer (Boss), Ela Poznerova (Lady), Rudolf Pellar (Scientist), Josef Beyvl (Manager), Zdena Hadrbolcova (German Woman), Josef Hlinomaz (Chimney Sweep), Viktor Maurer (Vicar), Jan Triska (Clown).

An excellent satire with stunning black and white photography. Hrusinsky is a Czech count lost in the jungle in infancy, who is found and brought home to the "civilization" of Nazi-dominated Europe. He goes through a series of hilarious encounters with modern society and its strange rituals, accidentally foils a kidnap plot, and when WW II breaks out over his jungle he rejects everything to become the sideshow "Tarzan" in a traveling circus.

d, Jaroslav Balik; w, Josef Nesvadba, Balik (based on a short story by Nesvadba); ph, Josef Hanus; m, Evzen Illin; ed, Jirina Lukesova; art d, Bohuslav Kulic; cos, Theodor Pistek; m/l, Pavel Kopta.

Comedy   **(PR:C   MPAA:NR)**

DEATH OF THE APEMAN
(SEE: DEATH OF TARZAN, THE, 1968, Czech.)

DEATH OF THE DIAMOND*½   (1934) 69m Metro bw

Robert Young (Larry), Madge Evans (Frances), Nat Pendleton (Hogan), Ted Healy (O'Toole), C. Henry Gordon (Karnes), Paul Kelly (Jimmie), David Landau (Pop Clark), DeWitt Jennings (Patterson), Edward Brophy (Grogan), Willard Robertson (Cato), Mickey Rooney (Mickey), Robert Livingston (Higgins), Joe Sauers [Sawyer] (Spencer), James Ellison (Sherman, the Cincinnati Pitcher), Pat Flaherty (Pat, the Coach), Francis X. Bushman, Jr. (Sam Briscoe, the Pitcher), Franklyn Farnum (Fan), Jack Norton (The Gambler), Harry Semels (Barber Customer), Dennis O'Keefe, Bobby Watson (Radio Announcers), Walter Brennan, Heinie Conklin, Max Wagner (Hot Dog Vendors), Herman Brix [Bruce Bennett], Don Brodie, Sumner Getchell, Jack Raymond (Men on Ticket Line), Sam Flint (Baseball Commissioner), Fred Graham (Cardinal Player), with: Cincinnati Reds, Chicago Cubs, St. Louis Cardinals.

Members of the St. Louis Cardinals baseball team are being murdered and it takes rookie pitcher Young to figure out that the killer is the crazed groundskeeper. He subdues him with a bean ball. A strikeout.

p, Lucien Hubbard; d, Edward Sedgwick; w, Harvey Thew, Joseph Sherman, Ralph Spence (based on a book by Cortland Fitzsimmons); ph, Milton Krasner; ed, Frank Sullivan.

Crime/Mystery   **(PR:A   MPAA:NR)**

DEATH ON THE MOUNTAIN*   (1961, Jap.) 87m Tokyo Eiga/Toho bw
(ARU SONAN)

Hisaya Ito, Takashi Wada, Kiyoshi Kodama, Kyoko Kagawa, Yoshio Tsuchiya.

Three friends go mountain climbing and one of them wanders off a cliff in a fogbank. The next year the dead man's cousin climbs the mountain again with one of the men from the first party. He confronts the man with an accusation that he murdered his cousin. The man readily admits his guilt; he murdered the victim because he was cheating with the man's wife. Then he kills his accuser and starts back down the mountain, only to be buried by an avalanche. Vaguely interesting, mostly for its scenery.

p, Ichiro Nagashima; d, Toshio Sugie; w, Teruo Ishii (based on a story by Seicho Matsumoto); ph, Tokuzo Kuroda; m, Yoshiyuki Kozu.

Drama   **(PR:O   MPAA:NR)**

DEATH ON THE NILE**   (1978, Brit.) 140m EMI/PAR c

Peter Ustinov (Hercule Poirot), Jane Birkin (Louise Bourget), Lois Chiles (Linnet Ridgeway), Bette Davis (Mrs. Van Schuyler), Mia Farrow (Jacqueline de Bellefort), Jon Finch (Mr. Ferguson), Olivia Hussey (Rosalie Otterbourne), I.S. Johar (Manager of the Karnak), George Kennedy (Andrew Pennington), Angela Lansbury (Mrs. Salome Otterbourne), Simon MacCorkindale (Simon Doyle), David Niven (Colonel Rice), Maggie Smith (Miss Bowers), Jack Warden (Dr. Bessner), Harry Andrews (Barnstaple), Sam Wanamaker (Rockford).

This Agatha Christie whodunit takes place on a pleasure boat cruising down the Nile with a cast of wonderful characters on board, not the least of whom is super Belgium sleuth Poirot, masterfully portrayed by Ustinov who employs the picky detective's mannerisms and quirks with remarkable accuracy. When a wealthy, much-hated heiress is murdered, all become suspects and, though the killers go to elaborate extremes and more murders to shroud their identities, Ustinov cleverly discards the red herrings and picks out the rotten fish. Niven is a great pleasure to

behold as Ustinov's cool-headed, aloof traveling companion and aide in the hunt for the killer. Lansbury provides a colorful portrait of a heavy-drinking authoress and wealthy dowager. Davis is her usual commanding self. Everyone excels, including Warden as a German doctor with a thick accent and a dark background, greedy businessman Kennedy and Johar the skipper of the luxury boat. Great entertainment this one, filmed in England and Egypt, with faithful dedication to the novel. The stylish production and superb acting, along with Guillermin's taut, quick-cutting direction, made this follow-up to MURDER ON THE ORIENT EXPRESS superior to the original.

p, John Brabourne, Richard Goodwin; d, John Guillermin; w, Anthony Shaffer (based on the novel by Agatha Christie); ph, Jack Cardiff (Panavision, Technicolor); m, Nino Rota; ed, Malcolm Cooke; prod d, Peter Murton; art d, Brian and Terry Ackland; cos, Anthony Powell.

Mystery   **Cas.**   **(PR:C   MPAA:PG)**

DEATH ON THE SET   (SEE: MURDER ON THE SET, 1936, Brit.)

DEATH OVER MY SHOULDER**   (1958, Brit.) 89m Vicar/Orb bw

Keefe Brasselle (Jack Regan), Bonar Colleano (Joe Longo), Jill Adams (Evelyn Connors), Arlene de Marco (Julie), Charles Farrell (Shiv Maitland), Al Mulock (Brainy Peterson), Sonia Dresdel (Miss Upton), Peter Swanwick.

Detective Brasselle is unable to pay for treatment for his ailing son, so he hires hoodlum Colleano to kill him (Brasselle) so that his son will collect the insurance money. Undistinguished programmer.

p, Frank Bevis; d, Arthur Crabtree; w, Norman Hudis (based on a story by Alyce Canfield); ph, Jimmy Harvey.

Crime   **(PR:A-C   MPAA:NR)**

DEATH PLAY*   (1976) 86m NewLine c

Karen Leslie (Karen), Michael Higgins (Sam), James Keach (Steve), Hy Anzel (Harry), James Catusi (Ernie), Elizabeth Farley (Linda), Don Fellows (Arthur), Jack Hollander (Frank), Robert Jackson (Don), Zina Jasper (Nancy), Virginia Kiser (Laura), James Noble (Norman), Nancy R. Pollock (Esther), Stephen Strimpell (Jerry).

Low-budget tripe concerning a group of cliched characters putting on a Broadway comedy. Higgins is a stage door groupie gone 'round the bend (evidenced by echo chamber effects on his scenes). Produced and performed by New York theatrical people, who should stick to what they know.

p, Norman I. Cohen; d, Arthur Storch; w, Jeff Tamborino; ph, Gerald Cotts; m, Rupert Holmes; ed, Arthur Williams; cos, Francine Tint.

Drama   **(PR:C   MPAA:PG)**

DEATH RACE 2000*   (1975) 78m New World c

David Carradine (Frankenstein), Simone Griffeth (Annie), Sylvester Stallone (Machine Gun Joe Viterbo), Mary Woronov (Calamity Jane), Roberta Collins (Mathilda the Hun), Martin Kove (Nero the Hero), Louisa Moritz (Myra), Don Steele (Junior Bruce).

Violent, hilarious satire has Carradine in a black leather suit and cape as the defending champion in a nationally televised Transcontinental Death Race, where competitors gain points by running over pedestrians. His challengers include Stallone as a gangster type with a machine gun in his car, and Woronov as a western outlaw Amazon. Carradine's navigator (Griffeth) is a revolutionary spy who by the race's end turns Carradine to her side so that, on national TV, Carradine runs over the president and declares an end to violence. Non-stop comic book action, brutally funny. Intended as a ripoff of the big budget ROLLERBALL, it remains a cult favorite, while its bombastic inspiration is forgotten. Producer Roger Corman's ability to exploit promising directors with his New World exploitation production company, formed in 1970 and which attracted bright young film makers eager to break into the Guild-controlled industry, is legendary. As a case in point, the director of the highly profitable DEATH RACE 2000, Paul Bartel, was paid $3,500 for his work on the film.

p, Roger Corman; d, Paul Bartel; w, Robert Thom, Charles Griffith (based on a story by Ib Melchior); ph, Tak Fujimoto (Metrocolor); m, Paul Chihara; ed, Tina Hirsch; art d, Robinson Royce, B. B. Neel; spec eff, Richard MacLean.

Science Fiction/Comedy   **Cas.**   **(PR:O   MPAA:R)**

DEATH RACE*½   (1978, Ital.) 98m S.J. International c

Yul Brynner, Massimo Ranieri, Barbara Bouchet, Martin Balsam, Giancarlo Sbragia.

Brynner is a professional killer hired to rub out a Mafia chieftain in Naples. A waste of talent and celluloid.

p, Umberto Lenzi; d, Anthony Dawson [Antonio Margheretti].

Crime   **Cas.**   **(PR:C-O   MPAA:NR)**

DEATH RIDES A HORSE**   (1969, Ital.) 114m P.E.C./UA c

John Phillip Law (Bill), Lee Van Cleef (Ryan), Luigi Pistilli (Wolcott), Anthony Dawson (Manina), Jose Torres (Pedro), Carla Cassola (Betsy), Archie Savage (Vigro), Mario Brega (One-Eye), Guglielmo Spoletini (Manuel Gugliemo), Giuseppe Castellano (Sheriff), Felicita Fanny, Ignazio Leone, Elena Hall, Carlo Pisacane, Nino Vingelli, Romano Puppo, Giovanni Petrucci, Franco Balducci, Nazareno Natale.

Young Law is hunting for the man who killed his parents. He meets Van Cleef, a master gunfighter who is hunting the bandits who had him imprisoned. Together they find an increasingly civilized American West where the criminals have respectable positions. Law learns that Van Cleef was present at the killing of his parents but doesn't kill him, riding away instead. Routine spaghetti western, a bit more violent than most.

p, Alfonso Sansone, Enrico Chroscicki; d, Giulio Petroni; w, Luciano Vincenzoni, Petroni; ph, Carlo Carlini (Techniscope, Technicolor); m, Ennio Morricone; ed, Eraldo da Roma; art d, Franco Bottari, Rosa Sansone; set d, Rosa Gristina; cos, Enzo Bulgarelli; spec eff, Eros Bacciuchi.

Western　　　　　　　　　　　　　　　**(PR:O　MPAA:M)**

DEATH RIDES THE PLAINS*½　　　　　(1944) 53m PRC bw

Bob Livingston (*Rocky Cameron*), Al "Fuzzy" St. John (*Fuzzy Jones*), Nica Doret (*Virginia*), Ray Bennett (*Ben Gowdey*), I. Stanford Jolley (*Rogan*), George Chesebro (*Trent*), John Elliott (*Marshal*), Kermit Maynard (*Jed*), Slim Whitaker (*Sheriff*), Karl Hackett (*Simms*), Frank Ellis, Ted Mapes, Dan White, Jimmy Aubrey.

Bennett is the villain in this undistinguished oater, inviting prospective buyers to his ranch, then murdering them for the purchase money. Livingston and St. John see that justice is done.

p, Sigmund Neufeld; d, Sam Newfield; w, Joseph O'Donnell (based on a story by Patricia Harper); ph, Robert Cline; ed, Holbrook Todd.

Western　　　　　　**Cas.**　　　　　**(PR:A　MPAA:NR)**

DEATH RIDES THE RANGE*　　　　　(1940) 58m Colony bw

Ken Maynard (*Ken*), Fay McKenzie (*Letty*), Ralph Peters (*Panhandle*), Julian Rivero (*Pancho*), Charles King (*Larkin*), John Elliott (*Crabtree*), William Costello (*Flotow*), Sven Hugo Borg (*Strakoff*), Michael Vallon (*Wahl*), Julian Madison (*Morgan*), Kenneth Rhodes (*Slim*), Murdock McQuarrie, Wally West, "Tarzan," Dick Alexander, Bud Osborne.

Russian spies led by Borg have started a range war as a cover for an operation to pipe helium off the unsuspecting McKenzie's ranch and over the border. Enter Maynard, who seems like an unemployed cowpoke but is really an undercover FBI agent, to put the pieces together and save democracy. Absurdly plotted, murkily shot, and poorly acted.

p, Max and Arthur Alexander; d, Sam Newfield; w, Bill Lively; ph, Art Reed; ed, Holbrook Todd; art d, Fred Preble; m/l, "Get Along, Old Pal," Colin MacDonald.

Western　　　　　　**Cas.**　　　　　**(PR:A　MPAA:NR)**

DEATH SENTENCE*
(1967, Ital.) 90m B.L. Vision c (SENTENZA DI MORTE)

Robin Clarke, Richard Conte, Enrico Maria Salerno, Adolfo Celi, Tomas Milian, Lilli Lembo.

Sub-par Italian oater starring Clarke as a bandit on a vendetta against the four men who killed his brother. The only element that sets this one apart from all the other bad spaghettis is Milian's scenery-chewing performance as an epileptic, albino gunman.

p,d&w, Mario Lanfranchi; ph, Tony Secchi.

Western　　　　　　　　　　　　　**(PR:O　MPAA:NR)**

DEATH SHIP*　　　　　　　　　　(1980, Can.) 91m AE c

George Kennedy (*Ashland*), Richard Crenna (*Trevor Marshall*), Nick Mancuso (*Nick*), Sally Ann Howes (*Margaret Marshall*), Kate Reid (*Sylvia*), Victoria Burgoyne (*Lori*), Jennifer McKinney (*Robin*), Danny Highham (*Ben*), Saul Rubinek (*Jackie*).

A luxury liner collides with a mysterious ship and sinks, leaving nine survivors, including captain Kennedy. Drifting, they spot a strange black ship floating by and climb aboard. Strange things begin to happen as the vessel, which appears to be a Nazi torture ship, tries to kill its passengers and Kennedy becomes possessed by the Nazi evil on board. So ludicrous it's quite funny.

p, Derek Gibson, Harold Greenberg; d, Alvin Rakoff; w, John Robins; ph, Rene Verzier; ed, Mike Campbell; art d, Chris Burke, Michel Prouix; spec eff, Mike Albrechtsen.

Horror　　　　　　　　　　　　　**(PR:O　MPAA:R)**

DEATH TAKES A HOLIDAY****　　　　(1934) 79m PAR bw

Fredric March (*Prince Sirki*), Evelyn Venable (*Grazia*), Sir Guy Standing (*Duke Lambert*), Katherine Alexander (*Alda*), Gail Patrick (*Rhoda*), Helen Westley (*Stephanie*), Kathleen Howard (*Princess Maria*), Kent Taylor (*Corrado*), Henry Travers (*Baron Cesarea*), G.P. Huntley, Jr. (*Eric*), Otto Hoffman (*Fedele*), Edward Van Sloan (*Doctor Valle*), Hector Sarno (*Pietro*), Frank Yaconelli (*Vendor*), Anna De Linsky (*Maid*).

March, as Death, becomes bored with his usual grim-reaping job and is puzzled why humans fear him so. To learn how he is perceived, March takes on human form, pretending to be a handsome young prince and becoming the house guest of Italian nobleman Standing. Several other guests are quickly repelled by the strange, mysterious prince who bluntly talks of their "meeting with Fate" but Venable, a lovely, mystical girl, is drawn to March. While he and she fall in love a strange phenomenon occurs—not a living thing, plant or human, dies while Death dallies, taking a holiday for love. Then March himself has a fear, that Venable will withdraw from him once he reveals his true identity. When he does appear as a shadowy wraith, Venable surprisingly goes to him; he wraps his cloak of Death about her and they leave together. This unusual film stems from Casella's successful European and Broadway play and March is riveting as Death. Standing is also fine as the nervous host who comes to realize who his strange guest is just before Venable departs with him. Audiences had a mixed reaction to DEATH TAKES A HOLIDAY but the theme was not innovative. Death has many times been portrayed as a handsome young man, particularly since this film (THE SANDBOX, DEATH IN VENICE, TEOREMA, THE MILK TRAIN DOESN'T STOP HERE ANYMORE). Paramount suprisingly assigned the directorial chore of this film to an apprentice, Leisen, who had only one previous credit, CRADLE SONG (1932), but his background as a set designer for Cecil B. DeMille stood him well for he presented a magnificent villa in which March frolicked with Venable. He was given a sumptuous budget and made the most of it. Leisen, who would go on to make

HOLD BACK THE DAWN and LADY IN THE DARK, never equalled the splendor of this film. He let March have his head and the actor played out his part with ironic vigor, wearing a monocle, delivering his lines in a Balkan accent and with great arrogance, his spellbinding eyes darting about, studying those who would soon take the final journey with him. He not only represents Death here, as the playwright envisions him, but love, which is as eternal as the Grim Reaper. Of course, March could do no wrong, having won an Oscar only two years earlier for his arresting performance in DR. JEKYLL AND MR. HYDE. (He would win his second for THE BEST YEARS OF OUR LIVES in 1946.) Leisen brought the 21-year-old Venable to the film, her second; she had been Leisen's star in CRADLE SONG. When her first contract was drawn, her father, a stern college professor, insisted that she could not kiss in love scenes, and such a clause was actually inserted.

p, E. Lloyd Sheldon; d, Mitchell Leisen; w, Maxwell Anderson, Gladys Lehman, Walter Ferris (based on the play by Alberto Casella); ph, Charles Lang; art d, Hans Dreier, Ernst Figte.

Fantasy/Romance　　　　　　　　**(PR:C　MPAA:NR)**

DEATH TOOK PLACE LAST NIGHT**½
(1970, Ital./Ger.) 95m Filmes-Lombard-CCC/Titanus
(LA MORTE RISALE A IERI SERA) c

Raf Vallone (*Amanzio Berzagni*), Frank Wolff (*Duca Lamberti*), Gabriele Tinti (*Mascaranti*), Eva Renzi (*Livia*), Gigi Rizzi (*Salvatore*), Gill Bray (*Donatella*), Beryl Cunningham (*Herrern*), Wilma Casagrande (*Concella*).

Wolff and Tinti are a pair of Milan detectives searching for Vallone's simple-minded but beautiful daughter. They learn that she has been abducted by white slavers; their investigations lead them through a seedy underworld of prostitution and perversion. They find her charred body, and the remainder of the film is their search for the killers. Could have been much better but, as is, just another detective story.

d, Duccio Tessari; w, Biaggio Proietti, Tessari (based on a novel by Giorgio Scerbanenco); ph, Lamberto Galm; m, Gianni Farrio; ed, Mario Morra.

Crime　　　　　　　　　　　　　**(PR:O　MPAA:NR)**

DEATH TRAP*½　　　　　　(1962, Brit.) 56m Anglo Guild/Schoenfeld bw

Albert Lieven *Paul Heindrick*), Barbara Shelley (*Jean Anscombe*), John Meillon (*Ross Williams*), Mercy Haystead (*Carol Halston*), Kenneth Cope (*Derek Maitland*), Leslie Sands (*Detective-Inspector Simons*), Barry Linehan (*Detective-Sergeant Rigby*), Richard Bird (*Ted Cupps*), Murray Hayne (*Ramsey*), Barbara Windsor (*Babs Newton*), Gladys Henson (*Housekeeper*).

Routine crime drama starring Haystead as the concerned sister of a suicide victim who investigates the withdrawal of 7,000 pounds from her late sister's bank account right before her death. She queries rich financier Lieven about the suspicious withdrawal, but he pleads ignorance of the situation. Lieven's secretary, however, discovers some incriminating bank slips and attempts to blackmail her boss through her boy friend Meillon. When Meillon winds up dead in a mysterious hit-and-run accident, Scotland Yard becomes involved. It is soon revealed that Lieven has, in fact, murdered Haystead's sister.

p, Jack Greenwood; d, John Moxey; w, John Roddick (based on the novel by Edgar Wallace); ph, Bert Mason; m, Bernard Ebbinghouse; ed, Derek Holding; art d, Peter Mullins.

Crime　　　　　　　　　　　　　**(PR:C　MPAA:NR)**

DEATH TRAP, 1967　　　(SEE: TAKE HER BY SURPRISE, 1967, Can.)

DEATH TRAP, 1976　　　　　　(SEE: EATEN ALIVE, 1976)

DEATH TRAP, 1982　　　　　　(SEE: DEATHTRAP, 1982)

DEATH VALLEY*½　　　　　(1946) 72m Screen Guild/Golden Gate c

Robert Lowery, Nat Pendleton, Helen Gilbert, Sterling Holloway, Barbara Reed, Russell Simpson.

Greed and the scorching sun turn gold prospectors into deadly enemies, and a long chase across the desert follows. The color is nice, but after a while the pursuit grows tiresome.

p, William B. Davis; d, Lew Landers; w, Doris Schroeder; ph, Marcel Le Picard (Cinecolor); m, Carl Hoefle; ed, George McGuire; art d, Harry Reif; set d, Archie Hall.

Western　　　　　　　　　　　　**(PR:A　MPAA:NR)**

DEATH VALLEY*½　　　　　　　　(1982) 87m UNIV c

Paul Le Mat (*Mike*), Catherine Hicks (*Sally*), Stephen McHattie (*Hal*), A. Wilford Brimley (*Sheriff*), Peter Billingsley (*Billy*), Edward Herrmann (*Paul*), Jack O'Leary (*Earl*), Mary Steelsmith (*Baby Sitter*), Gina Christian (*R.V. Girl*), Kirk I. Kiskella (*R.V. Boy No 1*), Frank J. Cimorelli (*R.V. Boy No. 2*), Fred W.S. Newton (*Outlaw*), Arnold C. Waterman (*Onlooker*), J.P.S. Brown (*Western Sheriff*), Roy S. Gunsburg (*Tour Guide*), Glenn McCreedy (*Stu*), Merritt Holloway (*Motel Clerk*), Earl W. Smith, Allan Wood (*Cronies*).

Billingsley is a city boy sent to visit his mother (Hicks) in Arizona. There he discovers a recreational vehicle filled with dead bodies and calls the sheriff, who is soon killed himself. No one else will believe his story and the killer, desert-crazy McHattie, is chasing him with a big knife. Nothing to recommend here.

p, Elliot Kastner, Richard Rothstein, Stanley Beck; w, Rothstein; ph, Stephen H. Burum (Technicolor); m, Dana Kaproff; ed, Joel E. Cox; art d, Allen H. Jones; set d, Leonard A. Mazzola; spec eff, Roy L. Downey, Bill Nicholson.

Crime　　　　　　**Cas.**　　　　　**(PR:O　MPAA:NR)**

DEATH VALLEY GUNFIGHTER** (1949) 60m REP bw

Allan "Rocky" Lane (Himself), Eddy Waller (Nugget Clark), Jim Nolan (Shad Booth), Gail Davis (Trudy Clark), William A. Henry (Sheriff Keith Ames), Harry Harvey (Vinson McKnight), Mauritz Hugo (Tony Richards), George Chesebro (Sam), Forrest Taylor (Lester), George H. Lloyd (George), Lane Bradford (Snake Richards).

Waller's mercury mine is threatened by Nolan, with help from evil banker Harvey and his henchmen. Unable to handle the situation himself, young sheriff Henry calls on Lane to help. Lane takes a job at Waller's mine to draw out the baddies, and soon he has beaten and shot them into submission. Slightly above average for a second-feature oater.

p, Gordon Kay; d, R.G. Springsteen; w, Bob Williams; ph, Ernest Miller; m, Stanley Wilson; ed, Arthur Roberts; art d, Frank Hotaling.

Western **(PR:A MPAA:NR)**

DEATH VALLEY MANHUNT*½ (1943) 55m REP bw

Wild Bill Elliott (Wild Bill), George "Gabby" Hayes (Gabby), Anne Jeffreys (Nicky Hobart), Weldon Heyburn (Richard Quinn), Herbert Heyes (Judge Jim Hobart), Davison Clark (Tex Benson), Pierce Lyden (Clayton), Charlie Murray, Jr. (Danny), Jack Kirk (Ward), Eddie Phillips (Blaine), Bud Geary (Roberts), Al Taylor (Lawson), Marshall Reed, Edward Keane, Curley Dresden.

Independent Indian oil-land owners are being cheated out of their property by a big conglomerate fronted by Heyburn. Lawman Elliott and eternal sidekick Hayes straighten things out with little difficulty. Routine B stuff.

p, Eddy White; d, John English; w, Norman S. Hall, Anthony Coldeway (based on an original story by Fred Myrton, White); ph, Ernest Miller; m, Mort Glickman; ed, Harry Keller; art d, Russell Kimball.

Western **Cas.** **(PR:A MPAA:NR)**

DEATH VALLEY OUTLAWS*½ (1941) 56m REP bw

Don "Red" Barry (Johnny), Lynn Merrick (Carolyn), Milburn Stone (Jeff), Bob McKenzie (Doc Blake), Karl Hackett (Charles W. Gifford), Rex Lease (Jim Collins), Jack Kirk (Johnson), Michael Owen (Bill Weston), Fred S. Toones (Snowflake), Bob Kortman, Curley Dresden, John L. "Bob" Cason, Griff Barnette, Lee Shumway, Wally West, Harry Strang, Reed Howes, George J. Lewis.

Barry swears vengeance on the gang that killed his best friend while posing as vigilantes. He runs up against the town marshal and banker, co-leaders of the gang. In the gunslinging climax he is joined by his long-lost brother, an unwilling member of the outlaws, who pays for his crimes by getting killed before the fadeout. Standard stuff with no comic relief.

p&d, George Sherman; w, Don Ryan, Jack Lait, Jr. (based on a story by Ryan); ph, Edgar Lyons; m, Cy Feuer; ed, Tony Martinelli.

Western **(PR:A MPAA:NR)**

DEATH VALLEY RANGERS**½ (1944) 59m MON bw

Ken Maynard (Ken), Hoot Gibson (Hoot), Bob Steele (Bob), Linda Brent (Lorna), Kenneth Harlan (Kirk), Charles King (Blackie), George Chesebro (Red), John Bridges (Cal), Al Ferguson (Ross), Robert Allen (Ranger), Steve Clark, Wally West, Glenn Strange, Forrest Taylor, Lee Roberts, Weldon Heyburn, Karl Hackett.

Gibson and Maynard are joined by Steele in this Trail Blazers series entry, one of five such low-budget films featuring the three former "top ten western money-makers," two of whom—Maynard and Gibson—emerged from virtual retirement to star in the series. Steele pretends to be an outlaw and joins the gang robbing gold shipments from the Death Valley stage run. Action is almost constant for the picture's 59-minute running time.

p&d, Robert Tansey; w, Frances Kavanaugh, Elizabeth Beecher, Robert Emmett; ph, Edward Kull; ed, Carl Pierson.

Western **(PR:A MPAA:NR)**

DEATH VENGEANCE** (1982) 96m DD/EMI c

Tom Skerritt, Patti LuPone, Michael Sarrazin, Yaphet Kotto, David Rasche, Donna DeVarona, Gina DeAngelis, Jonathan Adam Sherman, Pat Cooper, Jim Lovelett, Joe Ragno, Sal Richards, Frank Sivero, Lewis Van Bergen, Jim Moody.

Another urban vigilante film, but this one struggles with the issues (self-defense or paranoid racism?), which unfortunately muddles the narrative and diffuses any real insight into the characters or situation. Skerritt stars as the fed-up everyman who organizes a vigilante squad to clean up the streets. Kotto is the minority leader who voices concern over an apparent racial backlash that may be created by the situation. Sarrazin is the cop who tries to be the voice of reason. But it is the characterizations of the urban street people that hold the real link to which way the audience's sensibilities will lean, especially in the portrayal of a morally reprehensible and totally unsympathetic pimp whom the viewer will beg to see eliminated.

p, D. Constantine Conte; d, Lewis Teague; w, Tom Hedley, David Z. Goodman; ph, Franco DiGiacomo (Technicolor); m, Piero Piccioni; ed, John J. Fitzstephens; art d, Robert Gundlach.

Crime **(PR:O MPAA:NR)**

DEATH WEEKEND (SEE: HOUSE BY THE LAKE, THE, 1977, Can.)

DEATH WISH** (1974) 93m De Laurentiis/PAR c

Charles Bronson (Paul Kersey), Hope Lange (Joanna Kersey), Vincent Gardenia (Frank Ochoa), Steven Keats (Jack Toby), William Redfield (Sam Kreutzer), Stuart Margolin (Aimes Jainchill), Stephen Elliott (Police Commissioner), Kathleen Tolan (Carol Toby), Jack Wallace (Hank), Fred Scollay (District Attorney), Chris Gampel (Ives), Robert Kya-Hill (Joe Charles), Ed Grover (Lt. Briggs), Jeff Goldblum (Freak 1), Christopher Logan (Freak 2), Gregory Rozakis (Spraycan), Floyd Levine (Desk Sergeant), Helen Martin (Alma Lee Brown), Hank Garrett (Andrew McCabe), Christopher Guest (Patrolman Reilly).

A brutal, traumatizing film, has Bronson as a NYC architect whose wife and married daughter are raped by three drugged-out thugs who force their way into Bronson's apartment. The wife is left dead and the daughter in a permanent coma. Bronson seethes with hate, then takes his revenge by turning vigilante, seeking out and killing would-be muggers and thieves, slaughtering them wholesale until he himself is wounded. Police get on to him and put him under surveillance but he is too smart for them, until his bloody trail is followed up by snooping veteran detective Gardenia. The detective offers Bronson only one option: Get out of town permanently. He does, going to Chicago where it is obvious that he will take up the same crusade there. The stoic Bronson plods through his role murmuring lines hard to discern and Gardenia out-acts him in every scene (which is about as difficult as out-acting a fireplug). Jack Wallace, one of the most brilliant actors today who has not been given proper roles, appears briefly as Gardenia's detective aide. The violence is excessive and the plot predictable, although there is some style to director Winner's approach. To his credit, author Garfield opposed the pell-mell violence and the bloody vigilante philosophy advocated by the film and even pleaded with CBS not to air the film on prime time where immature viewers might readily take up such actions—in vain, of course. When asked by the press if the film was exploiting fear in an irresponsible manner, Bronson arrogantly replied: "We don't make movies for critics since they don't pay to see them anyhow."

p, Hal Landers, Bobby Roberts, Michael Winner; d, Winner; w, Wendell Mayes (based on the novel by Brian Garfield); ph, Arthur J. Ornitz (Technicolor); m, Herbie Hancock; ed, Bernard Gribble; prod d, Robert Gundlach; set d, George De Titta; cos, Joseph G. Aulisi.

Crime **Cas.** **(PR:O MPAA:R)**

DEATH WISH II zero (1982) 93m COL/EMI/WB c

Charles Bronson (Paul Kersey), Jill Ireland (Geri Nichols), Vincent Gardenia (Frank Ochos), J.D. Cannon (New York, D.A.), Anthony Franciosa (L.A. Police Commissioner), Ben Frank (Lt. Mankiewicz), Robin Sherwood (Carol Kersey), Silvana Gillardo (Rosario), Robert F. Lyons (Fred McKenzie), Michael Prince (Elliott Cass), Drew Snyder (Deputy Commissioner Hawkins), Paul Lambert (N.Y. Police Commissioner), Thomas Duffy (Nirvana), Kevyn Major Howard (Stomper), Stuart K. Robinson (Jiver), Laurence Fishburne III (Cutter), E. Lamont Johnson (Punkcut), Frank Campanella, Paul Comi, Hugh Warden, James Begg, Melody Santangelo, Robert Sniveley, Steffen Zacharias, Don Moss, Charles Cyphers, Peter Pan, David Daniels, Don Dubbins, James Galante, Buck Young, Karsen Lee, Leslie Graves, Teresa Baxter, Cindy Daly, Susannah Darrow, Henry Capps, Joshua Gallegos, Paul McCallum, Roberta Collins, Diane Markoff, Cynthia Burr, Michael Tavon, Ezekiel Moss, Ranson Walrod, Gary Boyle, Ava Lazar, Fred Saxon, Henry Youngman, Ginny Cooper, Lesa Weis, Twyla Littleton, Diane Manzo.

The vigilante is at his vendetta again, this time in Los Angeles where he busies himself by bumping off vicious thugs and tracking down the killer drug addicts who raped and murdered his wife and put his daughter in a permanent coma (one which has lasted eight years, since the original DEATH WISH). His Spanish cook is gang-raped and the original attackers of his daughter inexplicably go after her again, raping her once more before throwing her onto an iron-spiked fence where she is impaled to death. Bronson is thus motivated to kill any and all who look the least bit suspicious. The language is filthy, the film moronic, Bronson and his character are as despicable as those he murders and the whole mess should never have been released. DEATH WISH II wades in gore and violence, exploiting hatred, fear and mass murder. Director Winner is a loser here, shamelessly producing garbage for the highly exploitive Golan-Globus organization. Definitely not for children or anyone with an ounce of sensibility or intelligence.

p, Menahem Golan, Yoram Globus; d, Michael Winner; w, David Engelbach (based on characters created by Brian Garfield); ph, Richard H. Kline, Tom Del Ruth; m, Jimmy Page; ed, Arnold Crust, Julian Semilian; prod d, William Hiney; spec eff, Kenneth Pepiot.

Crime **Cas.** **(PR:O MPAA:R)**

DEATHCHEATERS** (1976, Aus.) 96m Roadshow c

John Hargreaves (Steve Hall), Grant Page (Rodney Cann), Margaret Gerard (Julia Hall), Noel Ferrier (Culpepper), Judith Woodroffe (Gloria), Ralph Cotterill (Un-Civil Servant), John Kummel (Anticore Director), Drew Forsythe (Battle Director), Brian Trenchard Smith (Hit and Run Director), Michael Aitkens (Police Driver), Roger Ward (Police Sergeant No. 1), Wallas Eaton (Police Sergeant No. 2), Dale Aspin (Lady Driver), Peter Collingwood (Mr. Langham), Chris Hayward (Butcher), Ann Semler (Lina), Max Aspin, David Bracks (Bank Robbers).

Page and Hargreaves are a pair of Australian commando veterans turned stunt men. They are hired by Ferrier to steal some documents and destroy the base of a Filipino warlord. Plenty of flashbacks to their Vietnam tour spice up the nonstop action. Simple-minded escapist fare.

p&d, Brian Trenchard Smith; w, Michael Cove (based on a story by Smith); ph, John Seale; m, Peter J. Martin; ed, Ron Williams; art d, Darrel Lass; cos, Jenni Campbell; stunts, Grant Page; makeup, Jill Porter.

Adventure **(PR:C MPAA:NR)**

DEATHDREAM** (1972, Can.) 88m Europix c
(AKA: DEATH OF NIGHT; NIGHT WALK; THE VETERAN)

John Marley, Richard Backus, Lynn Carlin Henderson Forsythe, Anya Ormsby.

Scary low-budget horror film from the makers of the equally effective CHILDREN SHOULDN'T PLAY WITH DEAD THINGS and DERANGED. The film opens on Backus and a buddy being killed in battle in Vietnam. Back home, his parents (Marley and Carlin) and his sister (Ormsby) are rocked by the news. Marley grimly accepts the loss of his son, but Carlin refuses to believe it and acts as though her boy is still alive. That night the family dog begins to growl and Carlin suspects burglars. The family is shocked to find Backus standing at the door, in his dress uniform, alive and well. Marley brings some of the neighborhood boys over to entice Backus into playing football (before the war Backus always loved having the children around). Backus ignores the kids (who persistently ask questions regarding the war) but when the family dog begins snarling at him (the dog has acted hostile to Backus since his arrival) he shocks the kids by picking the dog up by the throat and strangling it to death. Marley decides that this is enough and tells his wife that he's taking their son to a doctor. The doctor tries to take Backus' pulse, but can't find it. Backus the doctor and drains some of his blood with a syringe, which he then injects into himself. This revitalizes Backus and he returns home to the protection of his mother. Meanwhile, Backus' sister has arranged a double date between her and her boy friend, and Backus and his old girl friend. The couples go to a drive-in movie and when the girl friend snatches the sun-glasses off Backus' face she is horrified to see that the skin around his eyes has decayed—this "walking dead" is rapidly rotting. Backus kills the girl and his sister's boy friend before taking the car and making a desperate drive for home. Word of the killings gets to his home before he does, and Marley, feeling totally helpless, kills himself. Carlin, however, helps her son escape the police and goes with him to a graveyard, where the now totally decomposed soldier crawls into an open grave and finally comes to rest. DEATHDREAM is a powerful, creepy film which re-works the classic tale, "The Monkey's Paw," and relies on mood and tension to convey the terror. It uses the horror genre quite successfully to explore the difficulty of post-Vietnam war adjustment (stretched to a horrible, exaggerated limit) and the disintegration of the American family in the 1960s. A disturbing film and not for children.

p&d, Bob Clark [Benjamin Clark; Tom Karr]; w, Alan Ormsby; makeup, Clark, Tom Savini.

Horror   **Cas.**   **(PR:O   MPAA:R)**

DEATHLINE*½   (1973, Brit.) 88m AIP c (AKA: RAW MEAT)

Donald Pleasence (Inspector Calhoun), Norman Rossington (Detective Rogers), Christopher Lee (Stratton-Villers), David Ladd (Alex), Sharon Gurney (Patricia), Hugh Armstrong ("The Man"), June Turner ("The Woman"), James Cossins (Manfred), Clive Swift (Inpector Richardson), Heather Stoney (Alice), Hugh Dickson (Dr. Bacon), Jack Woolgar (Inspector), Ron Pember (Lift Operator), Colin McCormack, Gary Winkler (Constables), James Culliford (Publican), Suzanne Winkler (Prostitute), Gerry Crampton, Terry Plummer, Gordon Petrie (Tunnel Workers).

Descendants of an ancient subway disaster have maintained their underground existence by feeding off of London subway riders, posing a problem for Inspector Pleasence, who must try and figure out what's going on. Luckily no one involved in this production took it too seriously.

p, Paul Maslansky; d, Gary Sherman; w, Ceri Jones (based on the story by Sherman); ph, Alex Tomson (Technicolor); m, Jeremy Rose, Wil Mallone; ed, Geoffrey Foot; art d, Dennis Gordon-Orr; spec eff, John Horton.

Horror   **(PR:O   MPAA:NR)**

DEATHMASTER, THE zero   (1972) 88m AIP c

Robert Quarry (Khorda), Bill Ewing (Pico), Brenda Dickson (Rona), John Fiedler (Pop), Betty Anne Rees (Esslin), William Jordan (Monk), LaSesne Hilton (Barbado), John Lasell (Detective), Freda T. Vanterpool (Dancer), Tari Tabakin (Mavis). Kitty Vallacher, Michael Cronin, Charles Hornsby, Olympia Silvers, Bob Woods, Ted Lynn.

COUNT YORGA-inspired horror film starring Quarry as a long-haired vampire whose coffin washes ashore on the Southern California coast. There the creature soon becomes a Charles Manson-like guru to a group of wacky hippies and the grossness soon begins. Songs include "A Man Without a Vision," Ray Conniff, Fred Sadoff, Bob Pickett; "Answers," Bill Mark, Marilynn Lovell.

p, Fred Sadoff; d, Ray Danton; w, R.L. Grove; ph, Wilmer C. Butler (DeLuxe Color); m, Bill Marx; ed, Harold Lime; cos, Fandango, Lynn Bernay; spec eff, makeup, Mark Bussan.

Horror   **(PR:O   MPAA:PG)**

DEATHSHEAD VAMPIRE

(SEE: VAMPIRE BEAST CRAVES BLOOD, THE, (1969), Brit.)

DEATHSPORT**½   (1978) 83m New World c

David Carradine (Kaz Oshay), Claudia Jennings (Deneer), Richard Lynch (Ankar Moor), William Smithers (Doctor Karl), Will Walker (Marcus Karl), David McLean (Lord Zirpola), Jesse Vint (Polna), H.B. Haggerty (Jailer), John Himes (Tritan President), Jim Galante (Tritan Guard), Peter Hooper (Bakkar), Brenda Venus (Adriann), Gene Hartline (Sergeant), Chris Howell (Officer), Valeria Rae Clark (Dancer).

Carradine and Jennings are "Ranger Guides" who ride horses through a post-nuclear desert and fight off motorcycle-riding "Statesmen" who want to capture them for gladiatorial contests, and cannibal mutants who want them for dinner. The film starts in mid-battle and scarcely slows up—a good thing, too, because the few slack spots are heavy-handed mystical interludes without a trace of humor. Jennings, Playboy's Playmate of the Year for 1969, was killed in car crash soon after this film was released.

p, Roger Corman; d, Henry Suso, Allan Arkush; w, Donald Stewart, Suso, (based on a story by Frances Doel); ph, Gary Graver (Metrocolor); m, Andrew Stein; ed, Larry Bock; art d, Sharon Compton; spec eff, Jack Rabin, Philip Huff, Hank Stockert; ch, George Fullwood.

Science Fiction   **Cas.**   **(PR:O   MPAA:R)**

DEATHSTALKER*   (1983, Arg./U.S.) 80m Palo Alto/Aries-New World c
(EL CAZADOR DE LA MUERTE)

Richard Hill, Barbi Benton, Richard Brooker, Lana Clarkson, Victor Bo (Kang), Horace Marussi (Creature Leader), Bernard Erhard, August Larreta, Lilian Ker, Marcos Woinsky, Adrian De Piero, George Sorvic, Boy Olmi.

Swords-and-sorcery nonsense has muscle-bound Hill using the Sword of Justice (which makes him invincible) to defeat the evil Bo. Not the worst of a mercifully short-lived genre, but far from the best.

p, James Sbardellati; d, John Watson; w, Howard Cohen; ph, Leonardo Rodriguez Solis; m, Oscar Cardozo Ocampo; art d, Emilio Basaldua, M.J. Bertotto; spec eff, Michael Bronstein; makeup, John Buechler, William Smith.

Fantasy   **(PR:O   MPAA:NR)**

DEATHTRAP**½   (1982) 115m WB c

Michael Caine (Sidney Bruhl), Christopher Reeve (Clifford Anderson), Dyan Cannon (Myra Bruhl), Irene Worth (Helga ten Dorp), Henry Jones (Porter Milgrim), Joe Silver (Seymour Starger), Tony DiBenedetto (Burt the Bartender), Al LeBreton (Handsome Actor), Rev. Francis B. Creamer, Jr. (Minister), Stewart Klein (Stewart Klein), Jeffrey Lyons (Jeffrey Lyons), Joel Siegel (Joel Siegel), Jenny Lumet (Stage Newsboy), Jayne Heller (Stage Actress), George Peck, Perry Rosen (Stage Actors).

The play was almost universally damned by every critic in New York but then a brief piece in The Times appeared and that saved it. Word of mouth began and it soon was a smash and stayed open for many performances. The secondary rights for local theater will bring in further millions as it is one of those perfect plays for small houses; a tiny cast, one set, lots of laughs and lots of screams. The Allen movie script is a faithful adaptation of the play and there's the rub. The major problem is that Caine doesn't compare to John Wood in acting technique. They must have thought: "He did SLEUTH and that was a mystery play adaptation. This is the same thing, isn't it it?" Well, the answer is no. Whereas SLEUTH was a high-style veddy British piece, DEATHTRAP is quite American, not nearly as biting and often too inventive for its own good. DEATHTRAP appears to be a series of endings piled on each other and by the time we get to the real ending we just don't give a hoot. And yet it's done so well that points must be awarded for the triumph of style over substance. Caine is a playwright who has had several flops in a row. He's married to Cannon and she has all the money in the family and has been supporting him for years. Cannon, by the way, looks terrific but her voice is so shrill and piercing that it's entirely too loud for indoor use. Caine's latest has just flopped when he receives an unsolicited script in the mail. Turns out this young author is a fan of Caine's and heard him speak once. This is the only copy in existence and Caine reckons it can be a huge success. He tells his wife that he plans to kill the author! Cannon is appalled. She has a heart condition and reaches for the nitro immediately. Caine manages to explain that this is the way it must be. The young man, Reeve, arrives and a cat-and-mouse game is played until Cain "strangles" Reeve to death. The body is buried in the garden. Later, Caine and Cannon are celebrating when Reeve, covered in mulch, races in. Cannon drops dead of a heart attack and we learn that Reeve and Caine are lovers and planned this entire plot so they could have each other and Cannon's money. Now the plot begins taking further turns, as a next-door visitor is a Dutch psychic, and she senses what has happened in the room. More turns and twists and such a phony deus ex machina that you just want to throw up. The best line in the play and picture is spoken by Caine when Cannon asks: "Is that play that young man wrote really that good?" Caine, speaking in playwright Ira Levin's voice, sighs and answers to the effect that . . . "Darling, it's so good that it couldn't even be harmed by a gifted director." There is another quote that reviewers enjoyed. The playwright, discussing his failures of recent years, says "Nothing recedes like success." We're not saying it's not possible for two people to have the same idea but that precise quote can be found in the writer's best friend: 20,000 Quips and Quotes by Evan Esar, published in 1968, some years before DEATHTRAP. It worked better on the stage where all the flaws were smaller and could be hidden by lighting, but on a huge screen it is a disappointment. The whole thing is reminiscent of Clouzot's LES DIABOLIQUES (DIABOLIQUE). The original play had as one of its backers Claus Cecil von Bulow, later accused of attempting to murder his wealthy socialite wife Martha "Sunny" Crawford for her money. Ironically, the investors were rewarded when Warner Bros. later purchased the play for $1.5 million, plus a percentage of the gross.

p, Burtt Harris; d, Sidney Lumet; w, Jay Presson Allen (based on the stage play by Iran Levin); ph, Andrzej Bartkowiak (Technicolor); m, Johnny Mandel; ed, John J. Fitzstephens; prod d, cos, Tony Walton; art d, Edward Pisoni; set d, George DeTitta, Sr. spec eff, Bran Ferren.

Mystery   **Cas.**   **(PR: C   MPAA:PG)**

DEATHWATCH***½   (1966) 88m Beverly Pictures bw

Leonard Nimoy (Jules LaFranc), Michael Forest (Greeneyes), Paul Mazursky (Maurice), Gavin McLeod (Emil), Robert Ellenstein (Guard).

Absorbing adaptation of Jean Genet's play has three convicts locked in a cell and battling for status. Forest is the king of the cell because he is a murderer awaiting the guillotine. Nimoy is a pretty thief constantly bickering with Mazursky, a homosexual prisoner. (Mazursky was later a writer-director.) Finally, Nimoy strangles Mazursky in an attempt to gain new stature in the eyes of Forest. Excellent black-and-white photography keeps the single-cell set consistently interesting and fine performances are given by all three actors.

p, Leonard Nimoy, Vic Morrow; d, Morrow; w, Barbara Turner, Morrow (based on a play by Jean Genet); ph, Vilis Lapenieks; m, Gerald Fried; ed, Verna Fields.

Drama   **(PR:O   MPAA:NR)**

DEATHWATCH***½　(1980, Fr./Ger.) 128m Selta Films-Little Bear-Sara-GAU-Antenne 2-SFP-TV 13/Planfilm c
(LA MORTE EN DIRECT; AKA: DEATH IN FULL VIEW)

Romy Schneider (Katherine Mortenhoe), Harvey Keitel (Roddy), Harry Dean Stanton (Vincent Ferriman), Therese Liotard (Tracey), Max Von Sydow (Gerald Mortenhoe) Bernhard Wicki, Caroline Langrise, William Russell.

Film is set in Glasgow in the not-far-off future, where death has been all but conquered by medical science. Schneider is an independent, sensitive, and beautiful woman who has contracted a terminal disease. Stanton, a television producer, finds her imminent death perfect documentary material for a society that can't get enough of death. After he signs her to a contract, though, she disappears to the country to be with her husband, Von Sydow. Stanton, however, foresaw this possibility and dispatches Keitel after her. Keitel has a miniature TV camera in his head that broadcasts everything he sees back to the station for editing and broadcast. Intended as an attack on media invasion of privacy, the film sets up ideas that it doesn't know what to do with, but, all in all, an intelligent adult science fiction film, a rare thing in the age of STAR WARS.

p, Gabriel Boustiani, Janine Rubeiz; d, Bertrand Tavernier; w, David Rayfiel, Tavernier (based on the novel The Continuous Katherine Mortenhoe by David Compton); ph, Pierre-William Glenn (Panavision, Fujicolor); m, Antoine Duhamel; ed, Armand Psenay, Michael Ellis; art d, Tony Pratt.

Science Fiction　　　　**Cas.**　　　　**(PR:O　MPAA:R)**

DEBT OF HONOR**　(1936, Brit.) 83m BN/GFD bw

Leslie Banks (Maj. Jimmy Stanton), Will Fyffe (Fergus McAndrews), Geraldine Fitzgerald (Peggy Mayhew), Niall McGinnis (Lt. Peter Stretton), Reginald Purdell (Pedro Salvas), Garry Marsh (Bill), Stewart Rome (Maj. Purvis), Phyllis Dare (Mrs. Stretton), Joyce Kennedy (Lady Bracebury), William Kendall (Paul Martin), Randle Ayrton (Capt. Turner), Eric Cowley (Richard Denman), David Horne (Col. Mayhew), Kathleen Davis.

At a dusty African outpost, Banks takes the blame for a robbery committed by a friend to help out gambling addict Fitzgerald. Decent story with a distinguished cast.

p, John Corfield; d, Norman Walker; w, Tom Geraghty, Cyril Campion (based on a story by "Sapper" [H.C. McNeile]).

Drama　　　　**(PR:A　MPAA:NR)**

DECAMERON NIGHTS***　(1953, Brit.) 93m Eros/Film Locations c

Main Story: Joan Fontaine (Fiametta), Louis Jourdan (Boccaccio), Binnie Barnes (Contessa), Joan Collins (Pampinea), Mara Lane, Stella Riley, Melissa Stribling (Girls in Villa); Paganino the Pirate: Joan Fontaine (Bartolomea), Louis Jourdan (Paganino), Binnie Barnes (Countess), Godfrey Tearle (Ricciardo), Eliot Makeham (Governor of Majorca); Wager For Virtue: Joan Fontaine (Ginevra), Louis Jourdan (Guilio), Binnie Barnes (Nerina), Godfrey Tearle (Bernabo), Meinhart Maur (Sultan), George and Bert Bernard (Messengers), Van Boolen (Captain), Gordon Bell (Merchant); The Doctor's Daughter: Joan Fontaine (Isabella), Louis Jourdan (Bertrando), Joan Collins (Maria), Binnie Barnes (Old Witch), Noel Purcell (Father Francisco), Hugh Morton (King), Marjorie Rhodes (Signora Bucca).

Boccaccio's lusty, bawdy collection of stories is considerably sanitized here. The main story tells of Jourdan, as Boccaccio, hiding out from a rebel army and wooing Fontaine. Within this frame are hung three stories, each starring Fontaine and Jourdan. In the first, "Paganino the Pirate," a young wife whose aging husband shows more interest in astrology than in her, allows herself to be abducted by a young, virile pirate. When she is rescued, she pretends never to have seen her husband before. The second, "Wager for Virtue," concerns a man tricked into betting on his wife's virtue and then believing circumstantial evidence of his cuckoldry. It ends with the trickster tricked and husband and wife reunited. The third story, "The Doctor's Daughter," concerns a female doctor who saves a king's life and asks to marry one of his courtiers in return. The resentful courtier stands her up at the church and tells her he will only be her husband when she is wearing his ring and bearing his child. How she tricks him into fulfilling these conditions make up the rest of the episode. Despite lush costuming and photography, the film is curiously bland and spiritless, giving proof to the cliche "The book is better."

p, M.J. Frankovich, William Szekely; d, Hugo Fregonese; w, George Oppenheimer (based on a treatment by Geza Herczeg); ph, Guy Greene (Technicolor); m, Anthony Hopkins; ed, Russel Lloyd.

Drama　　　　**Cas.**　　　　**(PR:A　MPAA:NR)**

DECEIVER, THE**　(1931) 66m COL bw

Lloyd Hughes (Tony), Dorothy Sebastian (Ina), Ian Keith (Thorpe), Natalie Moorhead (Mrs. Lawton), Richard Tucker (Mr. Lawton), George Byron (Speedy), Greta Granstedt (Celia), Murray Kinnell (Breckenridge), Dewitt Jennings (Dunn), Allan Garcia (Payne), Harvey Clark (Nat Phillips), Sidney Bracy (Barney), Frank Halliday (Thomas), Colin Campbell (Dr. Schulz), Nick Copeland (Stage Manager).

Ian Keith is a Shakespearian actor who leaves a trail of ruined women and broken marriages in his wake. When he is murdered midway through the film there are a good half-dozen suspects. The second half is largely the questioning of these suspects by the police until it is revealed that the theater prop man, the last one anyone would suspect, did it. Suspenseful, but nothing here to really recommend.

d, Louis King; w, Charles Logue, Jack Cunningham, Joe Swerling (based on the story "Unwanted" by Bella Muni and Abem Finkel); ph, Joseph Walker; ed, Gene Havelick.

Mystery　　　　**(PR:A　MPAA:NR)**

DECEIVERS, THE　　　　(SEE: INTIMACY, 1966)

DECEPTION*　(1933) 65m COL bw

Leo Carrillo (Jim Hurley), Dickie Moore (Dickie Allen), Nat Pendleton (Bucky O'Neill), Thelma Todd (Lola Del Mont), Barbara Weeks (Joan Allen), Frank Sheridan (Leo), Henry Armetta (Nick), Hans Steinke.

Awful film about corruption in professional wrestling stars Pendleton (an actual wrestling champion in the 1922 Olympics) as a football player who goes into professional grappling. He is manipulated by promoter Carrillo through a string of victories until he meets the champ and is soundly thrashed. Pendleton realizes that he's been used and drops out of sight until he's ready to come back and beat the gang at its own game. Pendleton also wrote the story for this waste of celluloid—his attempt at parlaying his Olympic medal into Hollywood stardom. After this he settled into a long and productive career as a character actor of not-too-bright roles.

p, Bryan Foy; d, Lew Seiler; w, Harold Tarshis (based on a story by Nat Pendleton); ph, Chet Lyons; ed, William Austin.

Crime/Sports Drama　　　　**(PR:A　MPAA:NR)**

DECEPTION***　(1946)111m WB bw

Bette Davis (Christine Radcliffe), Paul Henreid (Karel Novak), Claude Rains (Alexander Hollenius), John Abbott (Bertram Gribble), Benson Fong (Manservant), Richard Walsh (Porter), Jane Harker, Suzi Crandall, Dick Erdman, Ross Ford, Russell Arms (Students), Louis Austin (Norma), Alex Pollard (Butler), Jean DeBriac (Andre), Einar Neilsen (Orchestra Conductor), Kenneth Hunter (Manager), Earl Dewey (Jovial Man), Marcelle Corday (Hatcheck Woman), Boyd Irwin (Elderly Gentleman), Cyril Delevanti (Beggar), Philo McCullough, Gertrude Carr, Bess Flowers, Richard Wang, Jean Wong, Ramon Ros (Wedding Guests).

Critics were divided about this remake of 1929's JEALOUSY with Fredric March and Jeanne Eagels. The story could have served Verdi or Wagner as a libretto. Davis is a music teacher who meets Henreid after the war. She'd believed he was dead and when they meet again, she realizes how much she loves this musical genius whose instrument is the cello. Davis brings Henreid back to her plush apartment and he naturally wonders how a music teacher can afford such luxury. She hems and haws and eventually admits that she has been receiving financial aid from Rains, a well-known composer/conductor. Before Henreid can question how close that relationship is, Davis insists they get married. Henreid is delighted and the reception takes place with just a slight hitch; Rains shows up...and he is not happy about the marriage. Davis sees Rains the next day and she pleads with him to keep mum about their once-torrid affair. Rains enjoys being a manipulator, so he offers Henreid a chance to play his new cello concerto at a huge concert. Davis knows that Rains is not all that generous and she observes several disastrous rehearsals as Rains twits Henreid and causes him to explode emotionally. Before the concert is to take place, Davis visits Rains and wonders if he intends to replace Henreid with another soloist. Rains smiles and says he thinks he'll allow Henreid to go on, but not before he will tell the musician that he has been "second cellist" and that Rains was there first! Davis is shocked by Rains's intention, pulls a gun, and shoots Rains dead. With another conductor leading the orchestra, Henreid plays the cello and is a critical success. Later, Davis admits that she killed Rains to keep him from thwarting Henreid's chance to shine. Henreid also worms the truth about her prior situation with Rains. In the end, Henreid will stick by Davis as she faces punishment for the murder. Rains stole the movie as he had the best moments, the most emotions, and the wittiest lines in the script. Director Rapper let Davis pull out all the stops and she overplayed it as blatantly as Korngold's crashing score. Some interesting visual tricks were employed to give the impression of Henreid playing the cello: Two cellists worked in the medium close shots. With Henreid's hands tied behind his back, one cellist stuck his right hand through the actor's right sleeve (in a breakaway coat), as the other worked his left arm through the other sleeve to finger the cello strings. Haller, always an inventive cameraman, shot the performance sequences with a three-quarter view, blocking out the actual cellists so that it appeared that Henreid was actually playing the instrument. Davis never liked the film, quoted as saying in Whitney Stine's Mother Goddam: "DECEPTION was a phony, contrived script from beginning to end. The only worthwhile thing in the finished film was the great performance of Claude Rains." Director Rapper forsook his usual cinematographer for this film, Sol Polito, for Haller, considered a "cosmetic photographer" who made stars look better than they really were. Davis was pregnant at the time and she says she insisted on having Haller to mask her weight.

p, Henry Blanke; d, Irving Rapper; w, John Collier, Joseph Than (based on the play "Jealousy" [AKA: "Monsieur Lamberthier"] by Louis Verneuil); ph, Ernest Haller; m, Erich Wolfgang Korngold; ed, Alan Crosland, Jr.; md, Leo F. Forbstein; cos, Bernard Newman.

Crime/Romance　　　　**(PR:A-C　MPAA:NR)**

DECISION AGAINST TIME**½　(1957, Brit.) 87m EAL/MGM bw
(GB: THE MAN IN THE SKY)

Jack Hawkins (John Mitchell), Elizabeth Sellars (Mary Mitchell), Walter Fitzgerald (Conway), Eddie Byrne (Ashmore), John Stratton (Peter Hook), Victor Maddern (Joe Biggs), Lionel Jeffries (Keith), Donald Pleasence (Crabtree), Catherine Lacey (Mary's Mother), Megs Jenkins (Mrs. Snowden), Ernest Clark (Maine), Raymond Francis (Jenkins), Russell Waters (Sim), Howard Marion-Crawford (Ingrams), Jeremy Bodkin (Nicholas Mitchell), Gerard Lohan (Philip Mitchell), Mary MacKenzie (Betty Harris), Esme Easterbrook (Launderette Assistant).

Hawkins is a test pilot who spends half the film's running time circling an airstrip with a crippled freighter. The owner of the aviation company (Fitzgerald) repeatedly orders him to bail out despite the fact that the loss of the plane will ruin the company. Hawkins, however, manages to bring the plane in safely and save the day. Fairly suspenseful, but not nearly enough to hold real interest.

p, Seth Holt; d, Charles Crichton; w, William Rose, John Eldridge (based on a story by Rose); ph, Douglas Slocombe; m, Gerbrand Schurmann; ed, Peter Tanner; md, Dock Mathieson; art d, Jim Morahan.

Drama (PR:A MPAA:NR)

DECISION AT SUNDOWN***½ (1957) 77m Scott-Brown Productions/COL c

Randolph Scott (Bart Allison), John Carroll (Tate Kimbrough), Karen Steele (Lucy Summerton), Valerie French (Ruby James), Noah Beery (Sam), John Archer (Dr. Storrow), Andrew Duggan (Sheriff Swede Hansen), James Westerfield (Otis), John Litel (Charles Summerton), Ray Teal (Morley Chase), Vaughn Taylor (Barber), Richard Deacon (Zaron), H.M. Wynant (Spanish), Guy Wilkerson (Abe).

Scott gives one of his finest performances as a gunman who rides into town obsessed with killing Carroll, who carried off Scott's wife sometime earlier and whom Scott blames for her subsequent suicide. He finds the whole town, which Carroll runs, against him and learns that his wife had gone with Carroll willingly. When the final showdown comes, French, Carroll's mistress, shoots Carroll in the shoulder so that Scott won't gun him down in a "fair" fight. A superior adult western, thoroughly downbeat, with Scott almost insane in his quest for vengeance.

p, Harry Joe Brown; d, Budd Boetticher; w, Charles Lang, Jr. (based on a story by Vernon L. Fluharty); ph, Burnett Guffey (Technicolor); m, Heinz Roemheld; ed, Al Clark; art d, Robert Peterson.

Western (PR:C MPAA:NR)

DECISION BEFORE DAWN***** (1951) 119m FOX bw

Richard Basehart (Lt. Rennick), Gary Merrill (Col. Devlin), Oskar Werner (Happy), Hildegarde Neff (Hilde), Dominique Blanchar (Monique), O.E. Hasse (Oberst Von Ecker) Wilfried Seyfert (S.S. Man Scholtz), Hans Christian Blech (Tiger), Helene Thimig (Fraulein Schneider), Robert Freytag (Paul), George Tyne (Sgt. Watkins), Adolph Lodel (Kurt), Arno Assmann (Ernst), Loni Heuser (Fritzi), Walter Janssen (Fiedl), Erich Ebert (Freddy), Ruth Brandt (Woman Driver), Liselotte Kirschbaum, Eva Marie Andres (Flak Girls), Aguste Hansen-Kleinmichel (Newspaper Woman), Martin Urtel (Soldier), Otto Friebel (Clerk), Paul Schwed (Wehrmacht Bus Bit), Meta Weber, Henriett Speidel, Ingeborg Luther (Women), Almut Bachmann (Street Car Conductor), Ruth Trumpp (Woman Attendant), Egon Lippert, Gerhard Kittler (Lieutenants), Rainier Geldern (Panzer NCO), Klaus Kinski (Whining Soldier), Von Schmidel (Man), Arnulf Schroder (Old P.W.), Bert Brandt, Erich Jelde, Max Herbst, Klaus Krause, Alex Hohenlohe, Clemens Wildemrod (NCOs), Jasper Gertzen, Ulrich Volkmar, Hans Mohrhard, Kurt Marquardt (P.O.W.s), Jochen Diestelmann, Luitpold Kummer, Heinrich Berg, Dieter Wilsing (Rathskeller Bits), Elfe Gearhart (Bar Maid), Rudolf Heimann (Truck Driver "Leschke"), Werner Fuetterer (von Bülow), Lieselotte Steinweg, Elizabeth Millberg, Ulla Best, Katja Jobs, Eva Maria Hoppe, Maria Landrock, Sonja Kosta (Wehrmacht Girls), Ernst Hoechstaetter (Office Reception Desk), Harald Wolff (Hartmann), Wolfgang Kuhnemann (Clerk in Schleissheim), Walter Ladengast (Sergeant Deserter), Gerhard Steinberg (Sgt. Klinger), Peter Luhr (V. Schirmeck), Maria Wimmer (Woman in the Street), Ursula Voss (Street Car Conductor), Erich Ebert (Freddy).

A superlative espionage thriller, this film realistically shows how an idealistic young medic, Werner, decides to spy on the Nazis to help shorten a war that is destroying his country, Germany. As a prisoner, Werner hears another prisoner criticize Hitler and the Nazis and later overhears his murder. He volunteers to work for the Americans the next day and undergoes training before being parachuted behind German lines. It is his job to locate a powerful German Panzer Corps and this he does, but not before facing countless perils. He is aided by trollop Neff, almost killed by Seyfert, and treated with kindness by Hasse, a colonel with a heart condition whose life Werner saves. Once obtaining the information, Werner joins Basehart, an American officer in charge of the mission, and Blech, another prisoner-turned-spy who is helping the Americans only for what he can get out of it. Blech almost betrays the trio but is killed by Basehart. Werner and Basehart then make it to the Rhine and prepare to swim to American lines but German patrols spot them. Werner runs toward them, surrendering, then breaking away to be shot, an heroic diversion made so that Basehart can escape into the river undetected. Litvak's direction is flawless as he takes his cameras into war-torn Germany, recording Werner's story in semi-documentary style. Other than Basehart, who was then only a new feature player at Fox, Litvak used unknown foreign actors, many of whom came to great attention later, particularly Werner, one of the best actors of his generation, too seldom seen in American films. Neff, the forlorn saloon girl Werner spurns but who still helps him, went on to stardom in foreign films. Blech continued playing German soldiers and appeared in such films as THE LONGEST DAY (it is Blech who first spots the great Allied armada about to invade Normandy). Hasse, one of Germany's best supporting players, appeared in THE BIG LIFT (1950). Planer's photography is realistically grim and creative and Waxman's score is compelling. A standout production from every angle.

p, Anatole Litvak, Frank McCarthy; d, Litvak; w, Peter Viertel (based on the novel Call It Treason by George Howe); ph, Frank Planer; m, Franz Waxman; ed, Dorothy Spencer; art d, Ludwig Reiber.

Spy Drama (PR:A MPAA:NR)

DECISION OF CHRISTOPHER BLAKE, THE* (1948) 73 m WB bw

Alexis Smith (Mrs. Blake), Robert Douglas (Mr. Blake), Cecil Kellaway (Judge Adamson), Ted Donaldson (Christopher Blake), John Hoyt (Mr. Caldwell), Harry Davenport (Courtroom Attendant), Mary Wickes (Clara), Art Baker (Mr. Kurlick), Lois Maxwell (Miss McIntyre), Douglas Kennedy (J. Roger Bascomb), Bert Hanlon (Upton).

Poor little Donaldson is forced to choose between his parents (Smith and Douglas) when they plan to divorce. His decision-making processes (accented by several

awful dream sequences) make for a miserable film, unhelped by performances or direction.

p, Ranald MacDougall; d, Peter Godfrey; w, MacDougall (based on a play by Moss Hart); ph, Karl Freund; m, Max Steiner; ed, Frederick Richards; md, Leo F. Forbstein; art d, John Becleman.

Drama (PR:A MPAA:NR)

DECKS RAN RED, THE**½ (1958) 84m MGM bw

James Mason (Capt. Edwin Rumill), Dorothy Dandridge (Mahia), Broderick Crawford (Henry Scott), Stuart Whitman (Leroy Martin), Katharine Bard (Joan Rumill), Jack Kruschen (Alex Cole), John Gallaudet ("Bull" Pringle), Barney Phillips (Karl Pope), David R. Cross (Mace), Hank Patterson (Mr. Moody), Harry Bartell (Tom Walsh), Joel Fluellen (Pete), Guy Kingsford (Jim Osborne), Jonathan Hole (Mr. Adams), Harlan Warde (Vic), Joel Marston (Russ Henderson), Ed Hinton (Mansard), Marshall Kent (Sammy), Robert Christopher, Art Lewis, Joe Devlin (Seamen).

Andrew and Virginia Stone have made some good, tight little thrillers. This is not one of them. He is a fine director and she is a tasteful editor but neither of them is a dialog writer and the results are often so laughable that they ruin whatever else is good. Mason is miscast as the former first mate of a liner who is flow down under to take over command of a dingy, creaky freighter, the S.S. Berwind, because the captain has just passed away. Once on the ship, Mason is faced by a sullen crew and an overall atmosphere of tension. The presence of Dandridge aboard doesn't help the good humor of the frustrated men. She is married to the Maori cook but not above tossing a come-hither glance around. Crawford and Whitman have other plans for the ship. They intend to murder the captain and the crew, scuttle the vessel to make it look derelict, then bring it in as salvage and collect the insurance money, about a million bucks. There is a huge denouement scene with lots of violence and many of the crew being killed (now you know where the title comes from), with Mason finally vanquishing Crawford and ending the mutiny. The picture made some serious money considering that it didn't cost very much. Nicholson's camerawork was excellent as was the sound recording. The Stones didn't use any music and the sound of the sea and the creaking vessel was accompaniment enough to the suspense. With better dialog, this could have been a corking good picture, but the words sounded like prose rather than the way people speak and therein is the problem.

p, Andrew and Virginia Stone; d&w, Andrew Stone; ph, Meredith M. Nicholson; ed, Virginia Stone.

Crime (PR:A-C MPAA:NR)

DECLINE AND FALL . . . OF A BIRD WATCHER** (1969, Brit.) 113m FOX c (AKA: DECLINE AND FALL)

Robin Phillips (Paul Pennyfeather), Michael Elwyn (Alastair Vane-Trumpington), Norman Scace (Dean), John Glynne Jones (Warden), Donald Sayne-Smith (Bursar), John Cater (Blackall), Kenneth Griffith (Mr. Church), Donald Wolfit (Dr. Fagan), Colin Blakely (Philbrick), Jonathan Collins (Clutterbuck), Robert Harris (Prendergast), Leo McKern (Capt. Grimes), Michael Newport (Lord Tangent), Patience Collier (Flossie Fagan), David McAlister (Peter Beste-Chetwynde), Katy Wild (Giggling Girl), Genevieve Page (Margot Beste-Chetwynde), Michael Nightingale (Col. Clutterbuck), Helen Christie (Mrs. Clutterbuck), Joan Sterndale-Bennett (Lady Circumference), Clifton Jones (Chokey), Ann Lancaster (Mrs. Grimes), Michael Hawkins (Stubbs), Roland Curram (Otto Silenus), Griffith Jones (Sir Humphrey Maltravers), Jeremy Child (Nigel), Anne De Vigier (Nigel's Girl Friend), Joan Haythorne (Miss Hart), Rodney Bewes (Arthur Potts), Sarah Atkinson (Jane), Jill Kerman (Spohie), George Pravda (Harbour Policeman), Marne Maitland (Junior Policeman), Duncan Lamont (Inspector Bruce), Ivor Dean (Old Bailey Policeman), Felix Aylmer (Judge), Victor Maddern, John Trenaman, Kenneth J. Warren, Tom Clegg (Warders), Christopher Banks (Clerk of the Court), Jack Watson (Gallery Warder), Donald Sinden (Prison Governor), Paul Rogers (Chief Warder), Roy Evans (Boney), Patrick Magee (Maniac), Ken Wynne (Drunken Surgeon), Paul Curran (Clergyman).

Labored satire on British society sees Phillips as a naive Oxford student who is subjected to every sort of bizarre humiliation that one can pack into a feature film, and who, by the end of the film, is still amazed at the arrogance and over-indulgence practiced by the upper class. Phillips is hired by the wealthy Page to tutor her unruly son. Soon Phillips falls in love with Page, which leads him on a twisted trail to Tangier and eventually to jail because of this "lady's" criminal activities. After a marriage to a powerful government official, Page is able to get Phillips released from prison with a new identity and life. Definitely hit-and-miss comedy.

p, Ivan Foxwell; d, John Krish; w, Foxwell (additional scenes, Alan Hackney, Hugh Whitemore); (based on the novel by Evelyn Waugh); ph, Desmond Dickinson (Deluxe Color); m, Ron Goodwin; ed, Archie Ludski; art d, Johnathan Barry; cos, Anna Duse, Julie Harris; makeup, Ernest Gasser.

Comedy (PR:C MPAA:NR)

DECOY*** (1946) 70m MON bw

Jean Gillie (Margot Shelby), Edward Norris (Jim Vincent), Robert Armstrong (Frank Olins), Herbert Rudley (Dr. Craig), Sheldon Leonard (Sgt. Joe Portugal), Marjorie Woodworth (Nurse), Phil Van Zandt (Tommy), Carole Donne (Waitress), John Shary (Al), Bert Roach (Bartender), Rosemary Bertrand (Ruth), Bill Self (Station Attendant), Madge Crane (1st Visitor), Betty Lou Head (2nd Visitor), Jody Gilbert (Fat Woman), Louis Mason (Thin Attendant), Ferris Taylor (Fat Attendant), Donald Kerr (Elevator Operator), Bill Ruhl (Guard), Franco Corsaro (Kelsey), Harry Tyler (Counterman), Carol Donne (Waitress), Austin McCoy (Piano Player), Walden Boyle (Chaplain), Dick Elliott (Driver), Pat Flaherty (Policeman), Virginia Farmer

(Maid), Kenneth Patterson *(Joe)*, Ray Teal *(Policeman)*, Don MacCracken *(Prison Guard)*.

Grim *film noir* starring British acress Gillie as one of the most vicious, heartless and cruel women ever seen in an American film. The story opens as a wounded doctor, Rudley, enters the apartment of Gillie, the beautiful but ruthless member of a gang of thieves. Gunshots are heard and soon police sergeant Leonard arrives to find Rudley dead and Gillie dying. Gillie tells her sordid tale to the cop before she dies. In flashback we see that Gillie fell in with gangster Armstrong, who had stolen $400,000 in a robbery in which he had killed a cop. Captured and sentenced to die in the gas chamber, Armstrong tells his gang that he has hidden the dough and with Gillie's help he will return to life after the state has executed him by taking an antidote to the cyanide gas, an antidote developed by Rudley. The plan works like a charm and Armstrong is brought back long enough to give Gillie half the map before he is shot by rival gang member Norris, who kills him a second time after grabbing the other half of the map. Gillie and Norris (obviously in cahoots) force Rudley to help them find the treasure. En route, Gillie fakes a flat tire, and when Norris gets out to fix it, she runs back and forth over him a few times to make sure he is dead. She then makes the doctor dig up the box. When Gillie opens the treasure chest she is consumed with an hysterical madness and cannot stop laughing. She grabs her gun and shoots Rudley. She runs back to her apartment, only to be tracked down by the wounded doctor, who shows up to kill her. At film's end, she reveals to the cop that the box contained only one dollar bill and a note from Armstrong saying that he knew they would double-cross him. With that, Gillie laughs in the cop's face and dies. Gillie is superb. Well worth seeing.

p, Jack Bernhard, Bernard Brandt; d, Bernhard; w, Ned Young (based on an original story by Stanley Rubin); ph, L.W. O'Connell; m, Edward J. Kay; ed, Jason Bernie.

Crime **(PR:C-O MPAA:NR)**

DECOY, 1963 (SEE: MYSTERY SUBMARINE, 1963)

DECOY FOR TERROR zero (1970, Can.) 90m c
(AKA: PLAYGIRL KILLER)

William Kirwin, Jean Christopher, Neil Sedaka, Andree Champagne, Mary Lou Collins.

Kirwin is a deranged artist who, like most deranged artists in schlock horror films, takes to murdering his models, then freezes them in a meat locker. Sedaka sings two songs: "If You Don't Wanna, You Don't Hafta" and "Waterbug." Never released theatrically in this country (for good reason) the film is good for a laugh when it shows up on the late show. Remake of COLOR ME BLOOD RED.

p, Max A. Sendel; d, Enrick Santamaran.

Horror **(PR:O MPAA:NR)**

DEDEE** (1949, Fr.) 95m Vog bw
(DEDEE D'ANVERS; AKA: WOMAN OF ANTWERP)

Bernard Blier *(Rene)*, Simone Signoret *(Dedee)*, Marcel Pagliero *(Francesco)*, Dalio *(Marco)*, Jane Marken *(Germaine)*.

Seedy melodrama starring Signoret as an Antwerp barfly who is very popular with the local male customers. She lives with the brutal bouncer of the bar, Dalio, who treats her badly. Hers is a grim life until the captain of a freighter, Pagliero, offers to take her away with him when he ships out. She accepts, but her dreams are shattered when Dalio kills the skipper. Signoret gets her revenge on her tormenter with the help of bar owner Blier when they finally rid themselves of the brutish Dalio. (In French; English subtitles.)

p, Sacha Gordine; d, Yves Allegret; w, Allegret, Jacques Sigurd (based on a story by Ashelbe); ph, Jean Bourgoin; m, Jacques Besse; set d, George Wakhevitch.

Drama **(PR:C MPAA:NR)**

DEEP, THE** (1977) 124m Casablanca Filmworks/COL c

Robert Shaw *(Romer Treece)*, Jacqueline Bisset *(Gail Berke)*, Nick Nolte *(David Sanders)*, Louis Gossett *(Henri Cloche)*, Eli Wallach *(Adam Coffin)*, Robert Tessier *(Kevin)*, Earl Maynard *(Ronald)*, Dick Anthony Williams *(Slake)*, Bob Minor *(Wiley)*, Teddy Tucker *(Harbor Master)*, Lee McClain *(Johnson)*, Peter Benchley *(Mate)*, Peter Wallach *(Young Adam Coffin)*, Colin Shaw *(Young Romer Treece)*.

Dull undersea adventure that tried to capitalize on the success of the Benchley/Spielberg box-office smash JAWS (1975) by devoting too much screen time to an enormous moray eel as a supposedly equally terrifying watery menace. Plot concerns a young couple, Nolte and Bisset, who discover sunken treasure while skin diving off the coast of Bermuda. Among the relics they find a cache of drugs recently stashed there, and before they know it they are embroiled in a dangerous game of cat-and-mouse with the gangsters who stashed it. Long, confused, and boring, the excellent cast is totally wasted, especially Shaw, who seems cast (in a colorless role) because of his participation in JAWS. There is a disturbing hint of racism in THE DEEP because all the villains are black. The film will mostly be remembered for the wet T-shirt sequences featuring Bisset.

p, Peter Guber; d, Peter Yates, w, Peter Benchley, Tracy Keenan Wynn (based on the novel by Benchley); ph, Christopher Challis (Metrocolor); m, John Barry; ed, Robert Wolfe, David Berlatsky; prod d, Tony Masters; art d, Jack Maxsted; set d, Vernon Dixon; cos, Ron Talsky, Tom Bronson; makeup, Ed Henriques; stunts, Howard Curtis, Bob Minor, Jim Nickerson, Richard Washington; underwater ph, Al Giddings, Stan Waterman.

Crime/Adventure **Cas.** **(PR:O MNAA:PG)**

DEEP BLUE SEA, THE*½** (1955, Brit.) 100m LFP/FOX c

Vivien Leigh *(Hester)*, Kenneth More *(Freddie Page)*, Eric Portman *(Miller)*, Emlyn Williams *(Sir William Collyer)*, Moira Lister *(Dawn Maxwell)*, Alec McCowen *(Ken Thompson)*, Dandy Nichols *(Mrs. Elton)*, Jimmy Hanley *(Dicer Durston)*, Miriam Karlin *(Barmaid)*, Heather Thatcher *(Lady Dawson)*, Bill Shine *(Golfer)*, Brian Oulton *(Drunk)*, Sidney James *(Man in Street)*, Tiec McCowen *(Ken Thompson)*, Gibb McLaughlin *(Collyer's Clerk)*, Arthur Hill *(Jackie Jackson)*.

A first-rate cast in a first-rate story that is marred by the fact that they chose to shoot this rather intimate tale in the wide screen format of CinemaScope. Leigh is the delicate and somewhat nervous wife of solid citizen Williams, a judge of the highest reputation. She has left Williams for the company of RAF pilot More, a happy-go-lucky type who is as responsible as a tomcat. He is a drunk; she is confused. She attempts to kill herself and her life is saved by Portman, a disbarred physician who is now supporting himself as a gambler. Portman lives upstairs and is often in Leigh's apartment both socially and professionally; in the next apartment is Lister who plays a nosy harridan with great aplomb. Williams would take her back in an instant, but Leigh realizes there has to be something out there that is better than the irresponsibility of More and the boredom of Williams. With Portman as her avuncular guide, Leigh grows to understand that she can make a life for herself and does not need a man to be happy. The role was originated on the London stage by now-Dame Peggy Ashcroft, who was bypassed in favor of Leigh for the screen version. More repeats his West End success. The movie was not as large a grosser as they'd wished, perhaps because it was just a trifle too sedentary and intellectual in a year that featured such films as OKLAHOMA, TO CATCH A THIEF, and LOVE IS A MANY-SPLENDORED THING. Dandy Nichols (Mrs. Elton) went on to achieve lasting fame in England as the long-suffering wife to Alf Garnett in the TV series "Till Death Us Do Part" which became the basis for the character of Edith Bunker in "All In The Family."

p, Alexander Korda, Anatole Litvak; d, Litvak; w, Terence Rattigan (based on his play); ph, Jack Hildyard (CinemaScope, DeLuxe Color); m, Malcolm Arnold; ed, A.S. Bates; prod d, Vincent Korda; md, Muir Mathieson; cos, Anna Duse; m/1, "Deep Blue Sea," Francis Chagril, Roy Bradford.

Drama **(PR:C MPAA:NR)**

DEEP DESIRE OF GODS (SEE: KURAGEJIMA—LEGENDS FROM A SOUTHERN ISLAND, 1970, Jap.)

DEEP END*** (1970 Ger./U.S.) 90m Maran Film-COKG-Kettledrum/PAR c

Jane Asher *(Susan)*, John Moulder-Brown *(Mike)*, Karl Michael Vogler *(Swimming Instructor)*, Christopher Sandford *(Fiance)*, Louise Martini *(Prostitute)*, Erica Beer *(Baths Cashier)*, Diana Dors *(Lady Client)*, Anita Lochner *(Kathy)*, Anne-Marie Kuster *(Nightclub Receptionist)*, Karl Ludwig Lindt *(Baths Manager)*, Erika Wackernager *(Mike's Mother)*, Peter Martin Urtel *(Mike's Father)*. Cheryl Hall, Christina Paul *(Hot Dog Girls)*, Dieter Eppler *(Stoker)*, Eduard Linkers *(Cinema Manager)*, Will Danin *(Policeman)*, Gerald Rowland *(Mike's Friend)*, Bert Kwouk *(Hot Dog Stand Man)*, Ursula Mellin *(Lady Client)*.

Moulder-Brown plays a fifteen-year-old boy who is given his first job working in the men's section at a seedy London bathhouse. There he meets a sexy, red-headed twenty-three year old woman, Asher, who teaches him the ropes and gets him to agree to send her his male clients if she will give him her female clients so that they can get better tips. Soon he learns to flirt with the women and let them fantasize about him. Unknown to him, Asher is having an affair with the swimming instructor. Moulder-Brown begins to develop an enormous crush on Asher, but she looks upon him as a boy and rejects his advances by telling him she is engaged. Her constant teasing is driving him wild, and the fact that she continues to see the swimming instructor infuriates him. He attempts to sabotage their date by riding his bike directly into the teacher's car. During his wanderings throughout the seedier sections of London, Moulder-Brown spots a cardboard poster of a topless stripper (who bears a resemblance to Asher) and he is convinced that she is the girl. He steals the poster and confronts her with it. She laughs it off, but her denial is not firm enough. That night he jumps into the swimming pool with the poster, holding it in his arms as if it were Asher herself. The events build to a breaking point when Asher accuses Moulder-Brown of slashing her lover's tires. They fight, and in the scuffle the diamond from her engagement ring comes loose and falls into the snow. The boy helps her find the jewel by bringing bag upon bag of snow into the empty pool, where they sift through it. Asher leaves momentarily to call her fiance, and when she returns she finds the boy lying naked at the bottom of the pool with the diamond in his mouth. As a reward, she decides to let the boy make love to her, and she strips off her clothes and enters the pool. As they begin, a pool employee, unaware of their presence, turns on the water to fill the pool. The water begins to rise, upsetting Asher who tries to leave. Moulder-Brown snaps, his first attempt at love-making a failure, and he tries to stop Asher by swinging a hanging lamp at her as she leaves. The lamp hits her in the head and she falls into the water, dead, with her blood clouding the pool. Moulder-Brown holds her body as he did the poster, as the water turns red. Polish filmmaker Skolimowsky, who wrote the screenplay for Roman Polanski's directorial debut, KNIFE IN THE WATER (1963), made a powerful, disturbing film on the sexual awakening of a young boy in a sleazy environment (the bathhouse). There is an uneasy sense of humor to the film that warns that things are *not* all that funny and that these confused characters may set into motion a series of events that they can no longer control. Well directed, well acted (especially by Asher), and well worth seeing.

p, Helmut Jedele; d, Jerzy Skolimowski; w, Skolimowski, Jerzy Gruza, Boleslaw Sulik; ph, Charly Steinberger (Eastmancolor); m, Cat Stevens and the Can; ed, Barrie Vince, art d, Tony Pratt, Max Ott, Jr.; cos, Ursula Sensburg; makeup, Elke Muller.

Drama **Cas.** **(PR:O MPAA:NR)**

DEEP IN MY HEART**** (1954) 130m MGM c

Jose Ferrer *(Sigmund Romberg)*, Merle Oberon *(Dorothy Donnelly)*, Helen Traubel *(Anna Mueller)*, Doe Avedon *(Lillian Romberg)*, Walter Pidgeon *(J.J. Shubert)*, Paul Henreid *(Florenz Ziegfeld)*, Tamara Toumanova *(Gaby Deslys)*, Paul Stewart *(Bert Towsend)*, Isobel Elsom *(Mrs. Harris)*, David Burns *(Lazar Berrison, Sr.)*, Jim

Backus *(Ben Judson)*, Douglas Fowley *(Harold Butterfield)*, Russ Tamblyn *(Berrison, Jr.)*, Rosemary Clooney, Gene and Fred Kelly, Jane Powell, Vic Damone, Ann Miller, William Olvis, Cyd Charisse, James Mitchell, Howard Keel, Tony Martin, Joan Weldon *(Guest Stars)*, Robert Easton *(Cumberly)*, Suzanne Luckey *(Arabella Bell)*, Ludwig Stossel *(Mr. Novak)*, Else Neft *(Mrs. Novak)*, Norbert Schiller, Torben Meyer *(Card Players)*, Reuben Wendorff, Franz Roehn *(Men)*, Laiola Wendorff *(Woman)*, Henri Letondal *(Francois)*, Lane Nakano *(Japanese Butler)*, John Alvin *(Mr. Mulvaney)*, Jean Vander Pyl *(Miss Zimmerman)*, Mary Alan Hokanson *(Miss Cranbrook)*, Maudie Prickett *(Lady)*, Henry Sylvester *(Judge)*, Bob Carson *(Orchestra Leader)*, Robert Watson *(Florist)*, Marjorie Liszt *(Waitress)*, Gail Bonney, Jean Dante *(Women Guests)*, Dulce Daye, Margaret Bacon, Gloria Moore, Lulumae Bohrman, Tailor Boswell, Richard Beavers *(Bits)*, Gordon Wynne *(Treasurer)*, Mitchell Kowall *(Oscar Hammerstein)*, Joe Roach *(Groom)*, Dee Turnell *(Bride)*.

Making musical biographies of composers' lives are dicey situations. One can do a song-a-thon like WORDS AND MUSIC (about Rodgers and Hart) and forego the story almost entirely, or one can concoct a phoney love tale like NIGHT AND DAY (Cole Porter). There have been many such films and they have usually just served as a stringing together of the composers' hits. This story is somewhat better than that due to Spigelgass's adaptation of Elliot Arnold's intelligent book. Naturally, as is the habit at MGM, they packed the picture full of guest stars and, in one case, provided the audience with a rare glimpse of the Kelly Brothers. Who? Well, it's not known to many people, but Gene Kelly's brother, Fred, was a dancer himself and the two of them teamed for the first and only time on screen in a hysterical number called "I Love To Go Swimmin' With Wimmen!" which was originally written for "Love Birds" in 1921 but dropped. It is mistakenly credited to the 1914 version of "Dancing Around." By this time, you're probably wondering who this film biography is about. It's the protean Sigmund Romberg who was a power in the American musical genre for almost four decades. He wrote more than two thousand songs, did the scores for more than eighty plays, revues, and operettas, and still had time to have a happy life. And that's the major dramatic problem with any biography where the climb is up the ladder with no rungs breaking. Born in Hungary, Romberg came to the USA early, and his rise was steady and steep. Ferrer does well as he essays the young man who got his start in a little café on New York's *outré* Second Avenue. The proprietress, Traubel, encourages his work as does Burns, a Brill Building song pusher. Romberg changes the tempo of one of his tunes into ragtime and has a commercial smash. A series of small-time shows follows until Romberg has such a hit with "Maytime" that one theatre isn't large enough to hold it. For the first, and perhaps only, time in history, *two* companies were playing "Maytime" on Broadway simultaneously. Ferrer has a brief romance with Avedon and they get married almost immediately, so *that* part of his life is out of the way, and the film-makers can concentrate on music and dance. The rest of the picture mixes all the elements necessary to make a successful movie; songs like "One Alone," "The Desert Song," "Lover Come Back To Me," "Softly, As In A Morning Sunrise," "When I Grow Too Old To Dream," "Goodbye Girls," "Mr, and Mrs.," "Fat, Fat Fatima," "Jazza, Jazza, Doo, Do," "Serenade," "Will You Remember," "Miss U.S.A.," "Leg of Mutton," "Stouthearted Men," "Road to Paradise," "One Kiss," "Auf Wiedersehn," "Your Land and My Land," "It"; dances by Ann Miller, Cyd Charisse, and James Mitchell; singing by Vic Damone, Jane Powell, Tony Martin, Rosemary Clooney, and Joan Weldon; and, of course, superior acting by everyone who had a line to speak. Yes, they do take some liberties with history and ascribe some of the songs to the wrong shows, but it's poetic license and even Romberg wouldn't have minded.

p, Roger Edens; d, Stanley Donen; w, Leonard Spigelgass (based on the book by Elliott Arnold); ph, George Folsey (Eastmancolor); m, Sigmund Romberg; ed, Adrienne Fazan; art d, Cedric Gibbons, Edward Carfagno; md, Adolph Deutsch; ch, Eugene Loring; lyrics, Oscar Hammerstein II, Alex Gerber, Otto Harbach, Dorothy Donnelly, Rida Johnson Young, Cyrus Wood, Ballard MacDonald, Herbert Reynolds; choral arr, Robert Tucker; spec eff, Warren Newcombe.

Musical/Biography **(PR:AA MPAA:NR)**

DEEP IN THE HEART** (1983) 101m Thorn/EMI/WB c (AKA: HANDGUN)

Karen Young *(Kathleen Sullivan)*, Clayton Day *(Larry Keeler)*, Suzie Humphreys *(Nancy)*, Helena Humann *(Miss Davis)*, Ben Jones *(Chuck)*.

British director Garnett's American debut is a slightly scathing attack on macho cowboy ideology. Pretty, innocent Boston-bred Young comes to Texas to teach. Day is a lawyer obsessed with guns in violence, eventually driven to attempt rape. Young overcomes her squeamishness and takes pistol in hand, becoming a crack shot and going out for revenge. The second half becomes quite confused, driving away any converts the first half may have made.

p, d&w, Tony Garnett; ph, Charles Stewart; m, Mike Post; ed, William Shapter; prod d, Lilly Kilvert; cos, Janet Lawler.

Drama **(PR:O MPAA:NR)**

DEEP IN THE HEART OF TEXAS** (1942) 62m UNIV bw

Johnny Mack Brown *(Jim Mallory)*, Tex Ritter *(Brent Gordon)*, Fuzzy Knight *("Happy T" Snodgrass)*, Jennifer Holt *(Nan Taylor)*, William Farnum *(Col. Mallory)*, Harry Woods *(Idaho)*, Kenneth Harlan *(Sneed)*, Pat O'Malley *(Jonathan Taylor)*, Roy Brent *(Franklin)*, Edmund Cobb *(Mathews)*, Jimmy Wakely Trio, Earle Hodgins, Budd Buster, Frank Ellis, Tom Smith, Ray Jones, Eddie Polo.

The first of seven teamings of oater stars Brown and Ritter sees Brown returning home to Texas after the Civil War to discover that rascals in his home state have set themselves up as a separate government expressly for the purpose of illegal land-grabbing. The hardest part for Brown to accept is that the leader of the unscrupulous crooks is his father, Farnum. With the help of government agent Ritter, Brown gets Texas back into the union. In addition to the title song by Don Swander and June Hershey, songs include "Song of the Sage," "Johnny Bond," "Sweet Genevieve," "Dixie," and "Cowboy's Lament."

p, Oliver Drake; d, Elmer Clifton; w, Drake, Grace Norton; ph, Harry Newman; md, H.J. Salter, m/1 Johnny Bond, Don Swander, June Hershey.

Western **(PR:A MPAA:NR)**

DEEP RED** (1976, Ital.) 98m Seda Spettacoli Mahler c (PROFUNDO ROSSO; AKA: THE HATCHET MURDERS; DRIPPING DEEP RED; DEEP RED HATCHET MURDERS)

David Hemmings *(Marcus)*, Daria Nicolodi *(Gianna)*, Gabriele Lavia *(Carlo)*, Clara Calamai *(Marta)*, Macha Méril *(Helga)*, Glauco Mauri *(Giordani)*, Eros Pagni *(Calcabrini)*, Giuliana Calandra *(Amanda)*. Nicoletta Elmi *(Olga)*.

Average shocker starring Hemmings as a Britisher in Rome who witnesses the murder of a psychiatrist by a vicious criminal who has committed dozens of killings. Hemmings flees the murderer, but he is drawn helplessly into the case by a series of fascinating clues that pique his interest. Directed with some flair by Argento, whose SUSPIRIA has had something of a cult following.

p, Salvatore Argento; d, Dario Argento; w, Giuseppe Bassan (based on a story by Dario Argento, Bernardo Zapponi); ph, Luigi Kuveiller; m, Giorgio Gaslini and The Goblins; ed, Franco Fratticelli; cos, Elena Mannini; spec eff, Germane Natali, Carlo Rambali.

Suspense **Cas.** **(PR:O MPAA:R)**

DEEP SIX, THE **½ (1958) 105m Jaguar/WB c

Alan Ladd *(Alec Austen)*, Dianne Foster *(Susan Cahill)*, William Bendix *(Frenchy Shapiro)*, Keenan Wynn *(Lt. Cmdr. Edge)*, James Whitmore *(Cmdr. Meredith)*, Efrem Zimbalist, Jr. *(Lt. Blanchard)*, Joey Bishop *(Ski Krakowski)*, Barbara Eiler *(Clair Innes)*, Ross Bagdasarian *(Slobodjian)*, Jeanette Nolan *(Mrs. Austen)*, Walter Reed *(Paul Clemson)*, Peter Hansen *(Lt. Dooley)*, Richard Crane *(Lt. J.G. Swanson)*, Morris Miller *(Collins)*, Perry Lopez *(Al Mendoza)*, Warren Douglas *(Pilot)*, Nestor Paiva *(Pappa Tatos)*, Robert Whitesides *(Eddie Loomis)*, Robert Clarke *(Ens. David Clough)*, Carol Lee Ladd *(Ann)*, Ann Doran *(Elsie)*, Jerry Mathers *(Steve)*, Franz Roehn *(Waiter)*, Officers and Men of the *U.S.S. Stephen Potter*.

What could have been an interesting war movie with a moral dilemma attached to it degenerates into just another sea-and-shells job, due to the weak screenplay. The book the movie is based on was very contemptuous of the navy, and to secure the cooperation of the service and the use of Navy ships, it had to be toned down. Ladd is a Quaker working for an advertising agency as an artist. He's in love with chief art director Foster, and they are about to get married when the Japanese attack Hawaii and he is called to service. He's assigned to the *U.S.S. Poe* as a gunnery officer and immediately becomes friendly with Bendix, playing Frenchy Shapiro, a tough enlisted man with a vulnerability that only his best pals are allowed to see. Wynn is the ass on the ship (there's always one), a hard-bitten patriot who hates the world and secretly is hooked on morphine. Wynn finds out about Ladd's pacifist religion and teases him about it, predicting loudly that when the chips are down, Ladd will fail to come through. A plane comes straight for the ship; Ladd doesn't give the order to fire. Then it's learned that it's a U.S. plane. They would have shot down one of their own but that's not the reason Ladd refused; he just couldn't break his Quaker vows. The crew doesn't trust him at all now but he earns their admiration when he disarms an unexploded bomb. Once they reach port, he further endears himself to the rough-and tumble men by joining them in a battle royal on the waterfront. Yet, there remains the haunting fear that he will not be able to hold his own under fire. He volunteers to participate in a daring attempt to rescue some fliers who are trapped on an island occupied by the Japanese. With Bendix at his side, he swoops in on the dangerous mission. Ladd is able to defend himself only after Bendix is riddled with bullets. Ladd becomes a regular Audie Murphy as he mows down the enemy before fainting from his wounds and being saved by the men he came to rescue. Later, he is reunited with Foster. The film ends with Ladd realizing that certain adjustments had to have been made in his moralistic stance or he wouldn't be there to hold the woman he loves. This is a hell of a theme, worked so well in HIGH NOON (Kelly was a Quaker) and FRIENDLY PERSUASION that one would have wished that sort of coloration could have been offered here. In the book, the captain was a wimp and the doctor was a drunk. For the film, James Whitmore became everybody's uncle and medico Zimbalist was as sweet as William Powell in MR. ROBERTS. Bagdasarian, the sailor with a comely relative in every port, became rich and famous when he invented "The Chipmunks" under his nom de chanson of David Seville. In honor of Liberty Records bosses Al Bennett and Si Waronker, he called the two most famous chipmunks Alvin and Simon. Bagdasarian was a cousin of William Saroyan, who was married to Walter Matthau's wife Carol, and isn't it getting just too confusing for words? Back to the film. . . this might have been a memorable and powerful picture. As it was, it wasn't.

p, Martin Rackin; d, Rudolph Maté; w, John Twist, Harry Brown, Rackin (based on the novel by Martin Dibner); ph, John Seitz (Warner Color); m, David Buttolph; ed, Roland Gross; cos, Howard Shoup.

War Drama **Cas.** **(PR:A MPAA:NR)**

DEEP THRUST—THE HAND OF DEATH* (1973, Hong Kong) 88m Golden-Hong Kong-Harvest/AIP c

Angela Mao, Chang Yi, Pai Ying, June Wu, Anne Liu.

More Kung Fu action as a young man goes after a gang of Japanese gambling bosses. Along the way he must contend with the sister of a girl who committed suicide when he left her. For fans of cartoon violence and bad dubbing only.

p, Raymond Chow; d, Heang Feng.

Martial Arts **(PR:O MPAA:R)**

DEEP VALLEY*½** (1947) 103m WB bw

Ida Lupino *(Libby)*, Dane Clark *(Barry)*, Wayne Morris *(Barker)*, Fay Bainter *(Mrs. Saul)*, Henry Hull *(Mr. Saul)*, Willard Robertson *(Sheriff)*, Rory Mallinson *(Foreman)*, Jack Mower *(Supervisor)*, Harry Strang, Eddie Dunn *(Possemen)*, Ralph Dunn *(Deputy)*, Ray Teal *(Prison Official)*, William Haade, Clancy Cooper *(Guards)*, Bob Lowell, Lennie Bremen, Ross Ford, John Alvin, *(Convicts)*, Ian MacDonald *(Blast Foreman)*.

Lupino stars as a shy young farm girl whose parents (Hull and Bainter) are loveless and repressive. Near their farm a chain-gang works on the new coast highway winding about Big Sur, California. One of the convicts, Clark, escapes during a rainstorm and is discovered by Lupino, who sympathizes with the criminal (he's as locked up as she is) and hides him in her father's barn. The pair are kindred spirits; both awaken to the love to be found in the other. Unfortunately, a posse discovers the hideout; Clark makes a break for the woods. He is gunned down, but dies a peaceful death in Lupino's arms. Lupino's performance is superb, and though the film has been criticized unfavorably as being derivative of HIGH SIERRA (1941), the similarities don't outweigh the refreshing tenderness and compassion of DEEP VALLEY. The film was shot entirely on location in Big Sur and Big Bear because there was a strike at the studio that prevented shooting on the Warner Brothers backlot.

p, Henry Blanke; d, Jean Negulesco; w, Salka Viertel, Stephen Morehouse Avery (based on the novel by Dan Totheroh); ph, Ted McCord; m, Max Steiner; ed, Owen Marks; art d, Max Parker, Frank Durlauf.

Drama (PR:C MPAA:NR)

DEEP WATERS½** (1948) 86 m FOX bw

Dana Andrews *(Hod Stillwell)*, Jean Peters *(Ann Freeman)*, Cesar Romero *(Joe Sanger)*, Dean Stockwell *(Danny Mitchell)*, Anne Revere *(Mary McKay)*, Ed Begley *(Josh Hovey)*, Leona Powers *(Mrs. Freeman)*, Mae Marsh *(Molly Thatcher)*, Will Geer *(Nick Driver)*, Bruno Wick *(Druggist)*, Cliff Clark *(Harris)*, Harry Tyler *(Hopkins)*, Raymond Greenleaf *(Judge Tate)*.

Shot on location in Maine, DEEP WATERS concerns a lobster fisherman, Andrews, whose life is changed when his girl friend, Peters (who works for the state welfare office), forces him to act as a role model for a troubled orphan boy (Stockwell). The boy had been placed in a foster home, but he got into trouble when he was caught stealing. Andrews befriends the boy, and with the help of fellow fisherman Romero, he turns the kid into a responsible citizen. Fairly maudlin premise made somewhat interesting by excellent photography of Maine exteriors.

p, Samuel G. Engel; d, Henry King; w, Richard Murphy (based on the novel *Spoonhandle* by Ruth Moore); ph, Joseph La Shelle; m, Cyril Mockridge; ed, Barbara McLean; md, Lionel Newman; art d, Lyle R. Wheeler, George W. Davis.

Drama (PR:A MPAA:NR)

DEER HUNTER, THE***** (1978) 183m EMI/COL/WB c

Robert DeNiro *(Michael)*, John Cazale *(Stan)*, John Savage *(Steven)*, Christopher Walken *(Nick)*, Meryl Streep *(Linda)*, George Dzundza *(John)*, Chuck Aspegren *(Axel)*, Shirley Stoler *(Steven's Mother)*, Rutanya Alda *(Angela)*, Pierre Segui *(Julien)*, Mady Kaplan *(Axel's Girl)*, Amy Wright *(Bridesmaid)*, Mary Ann Haenel *(Stan's Girl)*, Richard Kuss *(Linda's Father)*, Joe Grifasi *(Bandleader)*, Christopher Colombi, Jr. *(Wedding Man)*, Victoria Karnafel *(Sad Looking Girl)*, Jack Scardino *(Cold Old Man)*, Joe Strand *(Bingo Caller)*, Henen Tomko *(Helen)*, Paul D'Amato *(Sergeant)*, Dennis Watlington, Charlene Darrow, Jane Colette Disko, Michael Wollet, Robert Beard, Joe Dzizmba, Father Stephen Kopestonsky, John F. Buchmelter III, Frank Devore, Tom Becker, Lynn Kongkham, Dale Burroughs, Parris Hicks.

The story of this blockbuster is simple—three close friends, DeNiro, Walken and Savage, are about to undergo a tour of duty in Vietnam, leaving their families and prosaic lives in Clairton, Pennsylvania. The steel workers first attend Savage's wedding to Alda, drinking at their bar hangout and then going on a hunting trip with Aspegren, Cazale and Dzundza. Most of the hunters are amateurs but DeNiro proves his expertise by killing a buck with one shot. With their farewells made, the trio depart for their tour of duty. They are shown skirmishing with Vietcong troops and are surrounded and taken prisoner. The three Americans are taken to a small, crude outpost prison where they are kept beneath a hut on stilts, the prisoners barely keeping their head above water in a cage. Other cages beyond a wooden pier contain prisoners barely able to breathe as water rolls over them. One by one the prisoners are dragged up into the hut, beaten and ordered to play Russian Roulette while their captors make bets on the outcome. DeNiro encourages Savage to play the deadly game, telling him it's the only way to survive, that the Vietcong will kill him anyway. Mad with fear Savage manages to squeeze off a round that grazes his head. He is taken out and tossed into a watery cage. Next Walken is put in front of DeNiro who orders him to play, but he tricks the enemy into putting three bullets into the pistol to make it all the more lethal. In a quick move DeNiro shoots three captors while Walker grabs a rapid fire weapon and destroys the rest. DeNiro, Walken and the wounded Savage then climb upon a tree limb and float downstream until a U.S. helicopter attempts to pick them up. Walken struggles into the craft but Savage falls off one of its runners into the river and DeNiro jumps after him, saving him from drowning and pulling him to shore. He carries Savage inland where he joins a South Vietnamese refugee column, putting his wounded friend on the hood of a jeep then drifting South toward Saigon. Walken is taken to a hospital where he withdraws into himself. When released, he drifts into the red light district of Saigon, playing professional Russian Roulette and miraculously surviving, winning a fortune. Savage by then has been sent back to the States where he loses both legs. DeNiro returns to Clairton, meets Walken's girlfriend Streep and the two become lovers. When DeNiro hears that Savage refuses to leave the California hospital where he is recuperating, DeNiro goes to see him, convincing Savage that he must return to his wife and adjust to civilian life. Savage then shows him a great deal of money he has been receiving from an unknown person in Saigon. DeNiro rightly suspects that the money is from the missing Walken. He returns to the doomed city just before it falls into Vietcong hands and tracks down Walken, finding him playing Russian Roulette; his friend is no more than a robot, his mind unhinged by the experience in the Vietcong prisoner hut. DeNiro begs him to give up his suicidal pursuits and return home with him. He insults him, pleads, uses any means at his command but cannot find a response in his one-time friend. Thinking to jar his memory, DeNiro forces Walken to play opposite him. His memory seems to flicker but before Walken will permit himself the luxury of self-identity and the recognition of a friend, he grabs a pistol and blows out his brains which emotionally destroys DeNiro. Accompanying Walken's body home, DeNiro and friends go to their old hangout where a moody silence dominates. Then, one by one, these unsophisticated young men begin to sing "God Bless America" in one of the most poignant and unforgettable scenes ever put on film. This is only one of many powerful scenes in a dynamic, traumatic and wholly memorable production which portrays in common man terms the corruption and disillusionment of another lost generation. Director Cimino, along with photographer Zsigmond, produced an incredible indictment of war as seen through the eyes of three young citizen soldiers, effectively showing their home lives against the alien world of war they entered with naive patriotism, giving equal time to both experiences and thereby showing the insanity of battle and the precious peace of home town life. The performances of DeNiro and Walken are mesmerizing and Savage, shown to a lesser degree, is superb. Though the Russian Roulette business is blown out of proportion and is not factually representative of Vietcong torture nor South Vietnamese gaming pleasures, the film smacks of authenticity and stands head and shoulders above other so-called Vietnam War films such as APOCALYPSE NOW. All the production credits are well-earned and top notch. This film is a startling view of Armageddon on the realistic plain of those forced into its flaming holocaust. It withholds no brutality and spares no sensibility. It is not for children nor the faint of heart. But for those who want to know the true horrors of war, the masterpiece is an imperative work. (The Vietnam sequences were shot in Thailand.)

p, Barry Spikings, Michael Deeley, Michael Cimino, John Peverall; d, Cimino; w, Deric Washburn. (based on a story by Cimino, Washburn, Louis Garfinkle and Quinn K. Redeker); ph, Vilmos Zsigmond (Panavision, Technicolor); m, Stanley Myers; ed, Peter Zinner; md, John Williams; art d, Ron Hobbs, Kim Swados; set d, Dick Goddard, Alan Hicks, cos, Eric Seelig; spec eff, Fred Cramer; makeup, Del Acevedo, Ed Butterworth.

War Drama Cas. (PR:O MPAA:R)

DEERSLAYER* (1943) 67m REP bw

Bruce Kellogg *(Deerslayer)*, Jean Parker *(Judith)*, Larry Parks *(Jingo-Good)*, Warren Ashe *(Harry March)*, Wanda McKay *(Hetty)*, Yvonne de Carlo *(Wah-Tah)*, Addison Richards *(Mr. Hutter)*, Johnny Michaels *(Bobby Hutter)*, Phil Van Zandt *(Briarthorn)*, Trevor Bardette *(Chief Rivenoak)*, Robert Warwick *(Chief Uncas)*, Many Treaties *(Chief Brave Eagle)*, Clancy Cooper *(Mr. Barlow)*, Princess Whynemah *("Duenna")*, William Edmunds *(A Huron Sub-Chief)*.

An unbelievably inept adaptation of James Fenimore Cooper's classic tale that turns the white boy raised by Mohicans into an Indian-fighting super-hero who gets himself into and out of more jams then the average serial hero did in a month. Kellogg, who is seemingly captured every five minutes, makes innumerable escapes and saves helpless whites from savage redskins to the point of boredom. Truly lame, low-budget stuff from director Landers, who had done much better work in oaters. Remade in 1957.

p, P.S. Harrison, E.B. Derr; d, Lew Landers; w, Harrison, Derr (based on the novel by James Fenimore Cooper, adapted by John W. Krafft); ph, Arthur Martinelli; ed, George McGuire.

Adventure (PR:A MPAA:NR)

DEERSLAYER, THE** (1957) 76m FOX c

Lex Barker *(The Deerslayer)*, Rita Moreno *(Hetty)*, Forrest Tucker *(Harry Marsh)*, Cathy O'Donnell *(Judith)*, Jay C. Flippen *(Old Tom Hutter)*, Carlos Rivas *(Chingachgook)*, John Halloran *(Old Warrior)*, Joseph Vitale *(Huron Chief)*, Rocky Shahan, Phil Schumacker, George Robotham, Carol Henry *(Stunts)*.

A better version (not by much) of James Fenimore Cooper's novel about a white boy raised by Mohicans in pre-colonial times. The now-grown boy, Barker, aids a family of settlers against a tribe of Indians on the warpath. Barker gets involved with old trader Flippen and his two lovely daughters, Moreno and O'Donnell, when he saves them from an attack by the warring Huron tribe. Flippen hates Indians because they scalped his wife years ago; he has been getting his revenge by scalping any redskin he meets. The Indians, in turn, are just trying to retrieve the scalps of their dead so their souls can rest in peace. A pretty loose adaptation, but not as ridiculously incompetent as Lew Landers' 1943 version.

p&d, Kurt Neumann; w, Carroll Young, Neumann (based on the novel by James Fenimore Cooper); ph, Karl Struss (Cinemascope, DeLuxe Color); m, Paul Sawtell, Bert Shefter; ed, Jodie Copelan; art d, Theobold Holsopple.

Adventure (PR:A MPAA:NR)

DEFEAT OF HANNIBAL, THE zero (1937, Ital.) 109m E.N.I.C./Ente Nazionale Industrie Cinematografiche bw
(SCIPIO AFRICANUS; SCIPIONE L'AFRICANO; AKA: SCIPIO, THE AFRICAN)

Annibale Ninchi *(Scipio)*, Camillo Pilotto *(Hannibal)*, Isa Miranda *(Velia)*, Memo Benassi *(Cato)*, Fosco Giachetti *(Massinissa)*, Francesca Braggiotti *(Sofonisba)*, Marcello Giorda *(Siface)*, Lamberto Picasso *(Hasdrubal)*, Franco Coop *(Mezio)*.

A pet project of Benito Mussolini's, this film was alone enough to get Il Duce hung by his heels and spat upon. It simply is one of the few films which deserves to be judged entirely on its intentions, as opposed to the image on the screen. The plot (for the curious) details the life and accomplishments of the young Scipio (played by Ninchi), who talked the senate into letting him invade Africa in 202 B.C. Traveling into the Dark Continent with his troops, Scipio wound up with a remarkable victory over the Carthaginians, returning to his home soil as a hero. Well, it seemed that the big fascismo himself thought this story would greatly inspire troops and troops-to-be into fighting for his cause. Already having one screen credit to his name (THE HUNDRED DAYS, a German picture from 1935, was based on a play of Mussolini's), Il Duce felt it was time for another. His name, however, is not on the credits; instead, he put his son Vittorio in charge of the production. So, what do you get when a film is the brainchild of one of the world's most vile and notorious dictators, and produced by his inexperienced 21-year-old bambino? Toss in the unparalleled talents of director Gallone, who nearly sank the Italian film industry, and you get a big fat nothing. Garbagio. The film reportedly cost twenty times more than the average Italian production, used built-to-scale sets, 12,000 extras who were real troops, 500 camels; 19 real elephants; and 60 papier-mache elephants pushed around by assistants to simulate real animals. On top of it all, the grandiose battle scenes are occasionally blessed with the presence of telephone wires in the background, and wristwatches visible from under the "peasants" robes. As powerful as the Mussolinis were, they couldn't get people to take a liking to their "masterpiece." It had a very short run in New York, but even in its homeland it ran for only a week. Before long, it was being shown to disinterested school children and becoming the butt of many of their jokes. In short, Mussolini knew just about as much about film-making as he did about human rights. Unbelievably, he did make another attempt at the big screen, sending Vittorio to Hollywood in hopes of injecting some American blood into his productions. He proposed a project (which was actually agreed to!) casting Laurel and Hardy in an operetta based on Verdi's "Rigoletto." Thankfully, for Laurel and Hardy's sake, politics interfered.

p, Federic Curiosi; d, Carmine Gallone; w, Camillo Mariani dell' Anguillara, S.A. Luciani, Gallone, Silvio Maurano; ph, Ubaldo Arata, Anchise Brizzi; m, Ildebrando Pizzetti; set d, Gallone.

Biography/Adventure (PR:C MPAA:NR)

DEFECTOR, THE** (1966, Ger./Fr.) 106m WB-Seven Arts c (LAUTLOSE WAFFEN; L'ESPION)
Montgomery Clift (Prof. James Bower), Hardy Kruger (Counselor Peter Heinzman), Roddy McDowall (CIA Agent Adam), Macha Meril (Frieda Hoffman), David Opatoshu (Orlovsky), Christine Delaroche (Ingrid), Hannes Messemer (Dr. Saltzer), Karl Lieffen (The Major), Jean-Luc Godard (Orlovsky's Friend), Uta Levka.

This might have made a fair TV movie if it hadn't been so confused and mushy. The addition of Clift is what took it out of the television market and put it upscale. It didn't help. Clift looked terrible; he died shortly after finishing the movie. He was only forty-five, but the years of drinking, drugs, and who knows what else were all etched on that once-handsome face. He'd been seriously injured in a car accident in 1957, but plastic surgery had brought his features back to near-normal. The pain he was feeling went deeper than skin, and it is there for all to see in THE DEFECTOR. Clift is an American scientist recruited by McDowall to spy for the CIA while on a vacation to East Germany. Clift's job is to contact Messemer, a Jewish Doctor, and bring back a piece of microfilm which has been smuggled out of Russia by a defecting Soviet scientist. Clift is soon uncovered by Kruger, an OGPU (now KGB) agent determined to stop Clift from getting the film across the border. Kruger also wants to "turn" Clift and get him to defect to the East. The microfilm (like many of Hitchcock's McGuffins) is worthless. Clift enlists Messemer's nurse, Meril, to help him return to the West. They hide in the rear of a van, then get aboard bicycles and join a group of workers going across the border. There are several brief scenes where he's almost caught, but he finally makes it across the border in a wild sequence. Kruger, not that easily placated, goes across to get Clift. He poses as a defector; just as he is about to nab Clift to take him back to the East, Kruger is killed by a truck that supposedly has "accidentally" hit him. Anyone watching the film closely will see McDowall's eyebrows rise as he imperceptibly nods recognition to the "innocent" truck driver, so there's no mistaking that the CIA was behind it. Clift's first picture—THE SEARCH—took place in Germany, and so did this, his last. In between, he made 15 other movies and his brief career remains an enigma to those friends and fans who loved his work. The female lead here was, at one time or another, penciled in for Simone Signoret, Leslie Caron, Monica Vitti and Nicole Courcel. In a very small role, look for director Jean-Luc Godard as the pal of Opatoshu.

p&d, Raoul Lévy; w, Robert Guenette, Lewis Gannet, Peter Francke, Lévy (based on the novel The Spy by Paul Thomas); ph, Raoul Coutard (Eastmancolor); m, Serge Gainsbourg; ed, Albert Jürgenson, Roger Dwyre; art d, Pierre Guffrov, Jürgen Kiebach, Ernst Schomer.

Spy Drama (PR:C MPAA:NR)

DEFEND MY LOVE**½ (1956, Ital.) 88m Titanus/HR bw (DIFENDO IL MIO AMORE)
Martine Carol (Elisa), Gabriele Ferzetti (Pietro), Vittorio Gassman (Giovanni), Charles Vanel (Verdisio), Georgia Moll (Angela).

Gassman is a reporter who decides to up circulation by digging into a nice scandal. He targets as his victim Carol, now the wife of banker Ferzetti, but formerly the personal secretary to a nobleman who was murdered by poison. He discovers that she has a daughter with polio apparently born out of wedlock. Carol tells him that she is the daughter of her fiance, a flyer killed in the war. Gassman pursues his journalistic vendetta as the daughter learns through friends at school of the stories in the paper. Ferzetti begins to have his own doubts about his wife. Then, one day, the crippled girl falls and is run over by a truck as she attempts to flee photographers waiting for her. Ferzetti is forgiven his mistrust by his always-faithful wife, and Gassman is fired in disgrace. A fairly good interpretation of a hackneyed plot (probably best done in FIVE STAR FINAL), with an excellent cast.

p, Silvio Clementelli; d, Giulio Macchi; w, Giorgio Prosperi, Jacques Robert.
Drama (PR:A-C MPAA:NR)

DEFENDERS OF THE LAW*½ (1931) 64m Standard/Continental bw
Edmund Breese, Catherine Dale Owen, Joseph Girard, John Holland, Robert Gleckler, Mae Busch, Al Cooke, Kit Guard, Philo McCullough, Paul Panzer, Nick Thompson.

Low-budget gangster opus starring Holland as a police captain ordered to stop an East Coast big-shot gangster from setting up operations in his California town. Holland recognizes the hoodlum as one of his old army buddies, but he proceeds with his mission anyway. It ends up in a lethal shoot-out between the hoodlum and the cops. The gangster loses.

d, Joseph Levering; w, Hampton Del Ruth, Louis Heifetz (based on a story by Del Ruth); ph, James Brown, Jr.; ed, Dwight Caldwell.
Crime (PR:A MPAA:NR)

DEFENSE OF VOLOTCHAYEVSK, THE** (1938, USSR) 108m Lenfilm bw (VOLOCHAYESKIYE DNI; AKA: VOLOCHAYESK DAYS)
Barbara Myasnikova (Masha), Nikolai Dorkhin (Andrei), Boris Blinoff (Bublik), Vladimir Lukin (Egor), Boris Tchirkof (An Old Man), Lev Sverdlin (Colonel Usuzhima), Yuri Lavrof, V. Gushtchinsky (White Guard Officers).

Patriotic Russian drama tells how a brave band of Bolshevik Regulars were joined by gallant Siberian Bolshevik guerrillas to save a strategically vital hill from falling into the hands of Japanese intervention forces and their White Russian lackeys during the Russian Civil War in 1921. Some memorable scenes, especially one where the clever Communists turn the ice and snow of the hill against the yellow hordes charging up it. The film represented a major letdown for the Vasiliev brothers after their triumph of TCHAPAYEF four years earlier. Lev Sverdlin does an impressive job as the Japanese commander and he later wrote that among his preparations for the part, he once sat in a Leningrad restaurant and ate two meals in succession so he could keep watching a Japanese man at a nearby table eating. (In Russian; English subtitles.)

d&w, Sergei and Georgi Vasiliev; ph, Alexander Sigayev, Apollinari Dudko; m, Dmitri Shostakovich; prod d, Y. Rivosh, I. Zablotsky.
War Drama (PR:A MPAA:NR)

DEFENSE RESTS, THE** (1934) 70m COL bw
Jack Holt (Matthew Mitchell), Jean Arthur (Joan Hayes), Nat Pendleton (Rocky), Arthur Hohl (James Randolph), Raymond Walburn (Austin), Harold Huber (Castro), Robert Gleckler (Gentry), Sarah Padden (Mrs. Evans), Shirley Grey (Mabel Wilson), Raymond Hatton (Nick), Vivian Oakland (Mrs. Ballou).

Pretty silly courtroom drama starring Holt as an incredibly successful lawyer who tells his female clients to cross their legs and flirt with the jury to get off. His instructions work so well that his enraged female assistant, Arthur, wants to blow the whistle on his questionable courtroom tactics, but she falls in love with him instead and reforms him. Fast-paced and harmless enough.

d, Lambert Hillyer; w, Jo Swerling; ph, Joseph August; ed, John Rawlins.
Drama (PR:A MPAA:NR)

DEFIANCE*** (1980) 102 m Necta/AI c
Jan Michael Vincent (Tommy), Theresa Saldana (Marsha), Fernando Lopez (Kid), Danny Aiello (Carmine), Art Carney (Abe), Santos Morales (Paolo), Don Blakely (Abbie Jackson), Frank Pesce (Herbie), Rudy Ramos (Angel Cruz), Lee Fraser (Bandana), Randy Herman (Tito), Alberto Vazquez (Slagg), Church Ortiz (Luis), East Carlo (El Bravo), Lenny Montana (Whacko), James Victor (Father Rivera).

Vincent stars as a merchant seaman who moves into a dying neighborhood on New York's lower east side while he awaits new orders to ship out. He soon learns to despise the squalor and gradually becomes the leader of a group of citizens who have refused to be pushed out of their homes by the powerful street gang known as "The Souls." Vincent is pushed to the breaking point as the gang uses desperate (and bloody) methods to run the good tenants out. He becomes a one-man army and rids the neighborhood of the punks once and for all. Vincent turns in a fine performance as the rootless drifter (very similar to the western hero) who enters a community gripped by fear and grows to care enough for the lifestyle he has been denied to become its savior.

p, William S. Gilmore, Jr., Jerry Bruckheimer; d, John Flynn; w, Thomas Michael Donnelly (based on a story by Donnelly and Mark Tulin); ph, Ric Waite (Movielab Color); m, Basil Poledouris; ed, David Finfer; prod d, Bill Malley; set d, Rick T. Gentz; cos, Ellis Cohen; m/l, Gerard McMahon.
Drama **Cas.** (PR:C MPAA:PG)

DEFIANT DAUGHTERS (SEE: SHADOWS GROW LONGER, THE, 1962, Switz./Ger.)

DEFIANT ONES, THE**** (1958) 97m UA bw
Tony Curtis (John "Joker" Jackson), Sidney Poitier (Noah Cullen), Theodore Bikel (Sheriff Max Muller), Charles McGraw (Capt. Frank Gibbons), Lon Chaney (Big Sam), King Donovan (Solly), Claude Akins (Mac), Lawrence Dobkin (Editor), Whit Bissell (Lou Gans), Carl Switzer (Angus), Kevin Coughlin (The Kid), Cara Williams (The Woman).

Always a leader in socially conscious films, director Kramer herewith produces a marvelous movie of racial tension, an oppressive penal system, outlandish humor and grim drama. Curtis and Poitier escape from a southern chain gang while shackled together, a white and black man hating each other but suppressing their ancient prejudices to cooperate in their run for freedom. Dragging and pulling each other, cursing their luck, both jailbirds attempt to break the chain binding them together at the wrists but they fail repeatedly and in frustration lash out at each other, even battling and battering each other with their free hands until, exhausted and realizing they must compromise their feelings, they form a truce and cooperate in their cross-country escape. As bloodhounds chase them through woodlands and swamps, the two jump into a large gravel pit when a truck suddenly appears along the road they are traveling. A heavy rain turns the walls of the deep pit into mud and the hole begins to fill; they barely manage to pull themselves out before drowning. The two are later caught by the angry rednecked townsfolk of a river community and tied back to back in a warehouse while the sheriff is summoned. One of the elders, Lon Chaney, Jr., however, enters the warehouse and sets them free, showing them the scars of chains he himself wore years earlier before he, too, escaped. The pair later take refuge in a farm house where widow Williams welcomes and feeds them, making a play for Curtis, asking him to take her and her son away to the big city. Curtis isn't interested. After he and Poitier finally manage to break their chains he sets out with his companion, now his friend, ultimately refusing Williams who offers him money. Though he is at first tempted, he is later repelled when Williams insists that Poitier be set up as a scapegoat and target of the hunting posse. In the end, with the dogs and deputies closing in, the two convicts try to hop a fast-moving freight that will certainly take them to freedom. Poitier makes it but Curtis cannot catch up, frantically and futilely reaching out to grab Poitier's outstretched hand as he leans from the accelerating train. He can't make it and Poitier reaches out so far that he falls from the freight, tumbling with Curtis down the hill where they are captured by Bikel. It is clear that Poitier has sacrificed his own freedom to stay with his one and only friend Curtis. Both Poitier and Curtis give performances they seldom equalled after this film. In fact it is probably Curtis' finest role as the illiterate red neck who tosses about words like "nigger" as easily as taking a breath, then is genuinely amazed at Poitier when he takes offense. "Well, that's what you are, isn't it?" he asks. He laughs it off, explaining that he's a "honkey," and he doesn't take offense when someone calls him by that name. "It's not the same," Poitier tries to explain but it's as if he's attempting to reeducate generations of ignorant southern whites in a few minutes. (There are lines here reminiscent of Kramer's powerful war film HOME OF THE BRAVE where racism was brilliantly exposed, one of the first films to do so.) Seldom do actors receive such great parts as this film provides and Poitier and Curtis made the most of them. Kramer's direction is superlative. Leavitt's sharp cinematography is consistently striking and maintains Kramer's fluid direction as his subjects run pell-mell for their lives. (Leavitt won an Oscar for his work in this film.) This was the film that established Poitier as a star, the first black to share top billing with a white actor (Paul Robeson's 1930s roles notwithstanding), another measure of Kramer's commercial courage. As expected, the film did not do well in southern states where blatant racism was still in force, but sensible, enlightened America supported and respected this fine film.

p&d, Stanley Kramer; w, Nathan E. Douglas, Harold Jacob Smith; ph, Sam Leavitt; m, Ernest Gold; ed, Frederic Knudtson; prod d, Rudolph Sternad; art d, Fernando Carrere; set d, Joe Kish; cos, Joe King; spec eff, Alex Weldon; makeup, Don Cash.

Prison Drama   Cas.   (PR:C   MPAA:NR)

DEGREE OF MURDER, A***½   (1969, Ger.) 87m UNIV c
(MORD UND TOTSCHLAG)

Anita Pallenberg (Marie), Hans P. Hallwachs (Günther), Manfred Fischbeck (Fritz), Werner Enke (Hans), Angela Hillebrecht, Sonja Karzau, Kurt Bula, Willi Harlander.

Pallenberg accidentally kills her ex-lover during a fight and enlists the aid of a stranger to help her remove the body. He comes to her apartment to do the deed and ends up doing a different, more carnal, deed with her. The stranger calls on a friend to lend a hand and the trio bury the body in a construction site. After leaving with her two helpers, who begin to fight over her, she meets yet another stranger, with whom she plans a trip to Greece. In the meantime, construction has resumed at the work site. An interesting, though weakly cast, film which was one of the earliest (released in Germany in 1967) examples of the New German Cinema. Pallenberg's claim to fame is her association with the Rolling Stones, and as that band's guitarist Keith Richards' common-law wife. One-time Stones guitarist Brian Jones wrote the score not long before his death.

p, Rob Houwer; d, Volker Schlöndorff; w, Schlöndorff, Gregor von Rezzori, Niklas Franz, Arne Boyer; ph, Franz Rath; m, Brian Jones; ed, Claus von Boro; art d, Wolfgang Hundhammer.

Crime Drama   (PR:O   MPAA:R)

DELAVINE AFFAIR, THE**
(1954, Brit.) 64m Croydon-Passmore/Monarch bw

Peter Reynolds (Rex Banner), Honor Blackman (Maxine Banner), Gordon Jackson (Florian), Valerie Vernon (Lola), Michael Balfour (Sammy), Peter Neil (Inspector Johnson), Laurie Main (Summit), Katie Johnson (Mrs. Blissett), Mark Daly (Mr. Blissett), Anna Turner, Mai Bacon, Vernon Kelso, Christie Humphrey.

Jewel thieves kill the stool pigeon who informed on them, then try to frame reporter Reynolds for the crime. Routine crime drama.

p, John Croydon, Henry Passmore; d, Douglas Pierce; w, George Fisher (based on the novel Winter Wears a Shroud by Robert Chapman); ph, Jonah Jones.

Crime   (PR:A   MPAA:NR)

DELAY IN MARIENBORN   (SEE: STOP TRAIN 349, 1963, Ger.)

DELAYED ACTION**   (1954, Brit.) 60m Kenilworth/GFD bw

Robert Ayres (Ned Ellison), Alan Wheatley (Mark Cruden), June Thorburn (Anne Curlew), Michael Kelly (Lob), Bruce Seton (Sellars), Michael Balfour (Honey), Ballard Berkeley (Inspector Crane), John Horsley (Worsley), Dennis Chinnery, Ian

Fleming, Olive Kirby, Charles Lamb, Ryck Rydon, Emrys Leyshon, Myrtle Reed, Derek Prentice, Trevor Reid, Myles Rudge, Donald Vowles, Arthur Hewlett.

Robbers pay suicidal writer Ayres to confess to their crime and kill himself should their scheme fail. An interesting premise in an otherwise dull movie.

p, Robert Baker, Monty Berman; d, John Harlow; w, Geoffrey Orme; ph, Gerald Gibbs.

Crime   (PR:A   MPAA:NR)

DELICATE BALANCE, A**   (1973) 132m American Film Theatre c

Katharine Hepburn (Agnes), Paul Scofield (Tobias), Lee Remick (Julia), Kate Reid (Claire), Joseph Cotten (Harry), Betsy Blair (Edna).

This second in a series of Ely Landau filmed stage plays for a subscription sales system is an unfortunately stiff, dull, and extremely stagy screen adaptation of Edward Albee's Pulitzer Prize-winning play about a collapsing Connecticut family that is pushed to the brink when old friends drop by to visit. Hepburn and Scofield play the couple that must put up with the former's alcoholic sister, Reid, and their 36-year-old, four-time divorcee daughter, Remick. Cotten and Blair play the old friends who arrive at the wrong time. Eventually the intruders leave, and Hepburn restores the family to its "delicate balance".

p, Ely Landau; d, Tony Richardson; w, Edward Albee (based on his play); ph, David Watkin; ed, John Victor Smith; art d, David Brockhurst; cos, Margaret Furse.

Drama   (PR:C   MPAA:PG)

DELICATE DELINQUENT, THE***½   (1957) 100m PAR bw

Jerry Lewis (Sidney Pythias), Darren McGavin (Mike Damon), Martha Hyer (Martha), Robert Ivers (Monk), Horace McMahon (Capt. Riley), Richard Bakalyan (Artie), Joseph Corey (Harry), Mary Webster (Patricia), Milton Frome (Mr. Herman), Jefferson Searles (Mr. Crow), Rocky Marciano (Himself), Emory Parnell (Sgt. Levitch), Emile Meyer (Kelly), Dave Willock (Cadet Goerner), Mike Ross (Police Sergeant), Don Megowan, Irene Winston, Teru Shimada, Kazuo Togo, Don McGuire, Taggart Casey.

Lewis' first feature without Martin is a less-than-successful spoof on the then-current popularity of juvenile delinquent films. Lewis plays a shy and cowardly janitor who lives in terror of the street gangs that infest his neighborhood. One day he accidentally gets stuck in the middle of a gang rumble that is broken up by the police. Lewis is hauled in as one of the young hoodlums. At the station, kindly police captain McMahon turns Lewis over to patrolman McGavin (filling in for Martin for whom the role was written) to be reformed. Eventually, Lewis summons up enough bravery to face the gang. In the end he rescues McGavin and his girl Hyer from the clutches of a tough street gang.

p, Jerry Lewis; d&w, Don McGuire; ph, Haskell Boggs (VistaVision); m, Buddy Bregman; ed, Howard Smith; art d, Hal Pereira, Earl Hedrick; cos, Edith Head; ch, Nick Castle.

Comedy   (PR:A   MPAA:NR)

DELICIOUS**   (1931) 71m FOX bw

Janet Gaynor (Heather Gordon), Charles Farrell (Jerry Beaumont), El Brendel (Jansen), Raul Roulien (Sascha), Lawrence O'Sullivan (O'Flynn), Manya Roberti (Olga), Virginia Cherrill (Diana), Olive Tell (Mrs. Van Bergh), Mischa Auer (Mischa), Marvine Manzel (Tosha), Jeanette Gegna.

Gaynor plays a young Scottish lass on her way to America with her uncle in this overlong and disappointing Ira and George Gershwin musical celebrating immigration. While on board, Gaynor makes friends with a group of Russian musicians who have stowed away. One of them, Roulien, falls in love with her and writes her a song. But Gaynor falls for rich polo-player Farrell who spends most of the rest of the movie dumping his petty and boring fiancee Cherill and seeing the lovely Scottish girl as his true love. Songs include: "Somebody From Somewhere" (sung by Gaynor); "Delishious" (Roulien); "Blah-Blah-Blah" (Brendel); "We're From The Journal, The Wahrheit, The Telegram, The Times"; "Katinkitschka" (Gaynor); and "The New York Rhapsody."

d, Davis Butler; w, Guy Bolton, Sonya Levien (based on an original story by Bolton); ph, Ernest Palmer; m, George Gershwin; ed, Irene Morra; m/l, Ira Gershwin.

Musical   (PR:A   MPAA:NR)

DELIGHTFUL ROGUE*½   (1929) 64m RKO bw

Rod La Rocque, Rita La Roy, Charles Byer, Bert Moorehouse, Ed Brady, Harry Semels, Samuel Blum.

La Rocque plays an infamous pirate who sails to Tapit and there meets an American dance-hall girl (La Roy) and her extremely jealous suitor (Byer). La Rocque takes a liking to the dancer and kidnaps Byer, demanding that La Roy spend a night in his cabin to obtain her beau's release. She does so, falls in love with pirate La Rocque, and bids Byer adieu as he sets sail with the pirate. One mediocre song, "Gay Love," takes its place near the middle of the movie. Silly slop.

p, William LeBaron; d, Leslie Pearce, Lynn Shores; w, Wallace Smith; m/l Oscar Levant, Sidney Clare.

Adventure/Romance   (PR:A   MPAA:NR)

DELIGHTFULLY DANGEROUS**   (1945) 92m UA bw

Jane Powell (Cheryl Williams), Ralph Bellamy (Arthur Hale), Constance Moore (Josephine Williams), Morton Gould and His Orchestra (Themselves), Arthur Treacher (Jeffers), Louise Beavers (Hannah), Ruth Tobey (Molly), Ruth Robinson (Mrs. Jones), Andre Charlot (Professor Bremond), Shirley Hunter Williams (Nadine), Chris Drake.

Powell plays a 15-year-old country girl who travels to the Big Apple to visit her big sister, Moore, who has told the family that she was cast as the lead in a new Broadway musical comedy. To her dismay, Powell discovers her sister doing the bump and grind at a burlesque house. The clever adolescent befriends a producer, Bellamy, in an attempt to get her sister the lead in his new show. As it turns out, Powell herself gets the lead, and her sister gets cast also. Songs include "I'm Only Teasin'," "Through Your Eyes To Your Heart," "In a Shower of Stars," "Mynah Bird," "Delightfully Dangerous," "Once Upon a Song," and a medley of songs by Johann Strauss. A sluggish songfest.

p, Charles R. Rogers; d, Arthur Lubin; w, Walter DeLeon, Arthur Phillips (based on a story by Irving Phillips, Edward Verdier, Frank Tashlin); ph, Milton Krasner; m, Charles Previn; ed, Harvey Manger; md, Previn; art d, Duncan Cramer; m/l, Morton Gould, Edward Heyman, John Jacob Loeb, Redd Evans, Johann Strauss.

Musical (PR:A MPAA:NR)

DELINQUENT DAUGHTERS* (1944) 71m PRC bw

June Carlson *(June Thompson)*, Fifi D'Orsay *(Mimi)*, Teala Loring *(Sally Higgins)*, Mary Bovard *(Betty)*, Marga Dean *(Francine Van Pelt)*, Johnny Duncan *(Rocky Webster)*, Joe Devlin *(Hanahan)*, Jimmy Zaner *(Jerry Sykes)*, Jon Dawson *(Nick Gordon)*, Frank McGlynn, Sr. *(Judge Craig)*, Parker Gee *(Steve Cronin)*, Warren Mills *(Roy Ford)*, John Dobson, John Christian, Frank Stephens, Floyd Criswell, John Valentine, Belle Thomas, Sheila Roberts, Norval Mitchell, Juan de la Cruz, Sheilah Roddick.

Another juvenile delinquent film, this one starring Dawson as an evil cafe owner who talks the kids into committing crimes and then hides them from the law for a share of the loot. Lots of scenes showing drinking, driving, loud music and petty thefts, which lead to the courtroom where the kids and parents are lectured by a judge and learn how to communicate with each other. Very low-budget and ineptly done.

p, Donald C. McKean, Albert Herman; d, Herman; w, Arthur Saint Claire; ph, Ira Morgan; ed, George Merrick; md, Lee Zahler; art d, Paul Palmentola.

Drama Cas. (PR:C MPAA:NR)

DELINQUENT PARENTS* (1938) 62m Progressive/Times bw

Doris Weston *(Carol)*, Maurice Murphy *(Bruce)*, Helen MacKeller *(Judge Ellis)*, Terry Walker *(Betty)*, Richard Tucker *(Mr. Jefferson)*, Morgan Wallace *(Charles Wharton)*, Carlyle Moore, Jr. *(Charles as a Youth)*, Marjorie Reynolds *(Edythe)*, Theodore von Eltz *(Carson)*, Walter Young *(Mr. Caldwell)*, Sybil Harris *(Mrs. Caldwell)*, Janet Young *(Mrs. Miham)*, Byron Foulger *(Mr. Ellis)*, Virginia Brissac *(Mrs. Ellis)*, Harry Hayden *(Mayor Wharton)*, Betty Blythe *(Mrs. Wharton)*.

Overwrought melodrama sees MacKeller, her marriage annulled, take her baby to an orphanage because she can no longer raise her. Years later, MacKeller, having gotten her life in shape, has become a sympathetic judge in juvenile court to ease her frustrated motherhood. But one day, her long-lost daughter is brought before her because she has gotten in trouble with the law. Justice and motherhood triumph.

p, B.N. Judell; d, Nick Grinde; w, Nick Barrows, Robert St. Claire; ph, M.A. Anderson; ed, Roy Luby.

Drama (PR:A MPAA:NR)

DELINQUENTS, THE** (1957) 72m Imperial/UA bw

Tom Laughlin *(Scotty)*, Peter Miller *(Cholly)*, Richard Bakalyan *(Eddy)*, Rosemary Howard *(Janice)*, Helene Hawley *(Mrs. White)*, Leonard Belove *(Mr. White)*, Lotus Corelli *(Mrs. Wilson)*, James Lantz *(Mr. Wilson)*, Christine Altman *(Sissy)*, George Kuhn *(Jay)*, Pat Stedman *(Meg)*, Norman Zands *(Chizzy)*, James Leria *(Steve)*, Jet Pinkston *(Molly)*, Kermit Echols *(Bartender)*, Joe Adleman *(Station Attendant)*.

Robert Altman's first feature film deals with the age-old problem of juvenile delinquency. Laughlin stars as a clean-cut straight-arrow, who is suddenly mixed up with a gang of hoodlums who kidnap his girl (Howard), force him to drink booze, and then frame him for a gas station hold-up they pulled. In the end everyone gets lectured by the cops. Shot in Kansas City using mostly local talent in the casting. The highlight is a rumble scene at a drive-in theater.

p,d&w, Robert Altman; ph, Charles Paddock, Harry Birch; m, Bill Nolan Quintet Minus Two; ed, Helene Turner; art d, Chet Allen; m/l, Nolan, Ronnie Norman.

Drama (PR:C MPAA:NR)

DELIRIUM* (1979) 90m Worldwide/Odyssey c

Debi Chaney *(Susan Norcross)*, Turk Cekovsky *(Paul Dollinger)*, Terry Ten Broeck *(Larry Mead)*, Barron Winchester *(Eric Stern)*, Nick Panouzis *(Charlie Gunther)*, Bob Winters *(Donald Andrews)*, Garrett Bergfeld *(Mark)*, Harry Gorsuch *(Capt. Hearn)*, Chris Chronopolis *(Det. Parker)*, Lloyd Schattyn *(Det. Simms)*, Jack Garvey *(Devlin)*, Mike Kalist *(Specter)*, Myron Kozman *(Wells)*.

A low-budget independent shot on 16mm and blown up to 35mm for distribution. Story concerns members of an underground organization led by successful businessman (and Vietnam veteran) Winchester, who go throughout the country executing criminals whom they feel have gotten away with their crimes due to an ineffectual justice system. Everything goes smoothly for the assassins until one of their agents, Panouzis (another crazed Vietnam veteran), snaps and goes on a killing spree that focuses mainly on pretty women. The rest of the film is one gory scene after another until detectives Cekovsky and Broeck catch the killer and his boss with the help of a victim's roommate, Chaney. Unfortunately the script uses flashbacks to the Vietnam war to explain why the killers were motivated to do what they did, furthering the notion that vets from that war returned as disturbed killers who could explode at any moment.

p, Sunny Vest, Peter Maris; d, Maris; w, Richard Yalem (based on a story by Yalem, Eddie Krell, Jim Loew); m, David Williams; ph, John Huston, Bill Mensch; ed, Dan Perry; spec eff, Bob Shelly.

Crime Cas. (PR:O MPAA:R)

DELIVERANCE*½** (1972) 109m WB c

Jon Voight *(Ed)*, Burt Reynolds *(Lewis)*, Ned Beatty *(Bobby)*, Ronny Cox *(Drew)*, Billy McKinney *(Mountain Man)*, Herbert "Cowboy" Coward *(Toothless Man)*, James Dickey *(Sheriff Bullard)*, Ed Ramey *(Old Man)*, Billy Redden, *(Lonny)*, Seamon Glass *(1st Griner)*, Randall Deal *(2nd Griner)*, Lewis Crone *(1st Deputy)*, Ken Keener *(2nd Deputy)*, Johnny Popwell *(Ambulance Driver)*, John Fowler *(Doctor)*, Kathy Rickman *(Nurse)*, Louise Coldren *(Mrs. Biddiford)*, Pete Ware *(Taxi Driver)*, Hoyt J. Pollard *(Boy at Gas Station)*, Belinha Beatty *(Martha Gentry)*, Charlie Boorman *(Ed's Boy)*.

A morose, depressing and excessively brutal film, DELIVERANCE is still a powerful backwoods saga of how four tenderfeet from Atlanta enter the Appalachian wilds to canoe and fish only to find themselves hunted by cretinous hillbillies bent on sodomy, injury and murder. Voight, Reynolds, Beatty and Cox are the four city men looking for some relaxation. Stopping in the backwoods to leave their car and proceed by canoe, they are observed with contempt by young and old mountain people. Two of these haggard wretches follow them and later force Cox and Beatty to submit to their perverted sexual urges; Beatty is raped by one cretin but before Cox can be abused, Voight and Reynolds appear in their canoe and Reynolds sends an arrow into the sodomist, killing him. The other achondroplastic mountain man, a hideous creature with a toothless sneer, drops his gun and flees into the woods. The four tourists decide to hide the dead man's body, burying it in the woods. They nervously flee down river in their canoes, recklessly running rapids which overturn one canoe. Cox appears to have been shot as he sinks out of sight. The other boat is smashed and Reynolds suffers a terrible compound leg fracture. He is dragged to some rocks next to the river and held there by Beatty as Voight scales a ravine to find another mountain man looking down upon the river. Voight, thinking he is the one who shot and killed Cox, sends an arrow into him. The body is hidden. Then Cox surfaces and the survivors decide to weigh the corpse down with rocks and sink it, to save explanation and cover their disastrous actions. When they emerge from the wilderness a local sheriff (Dickey, the author of the novel upon which the film is based) suspiciously questions them about two missing men but allows them to depart, ruefully saying: "We'll wait and see what comes out of the river." What came out of this film was a repugnant but fascinating portrait of humanity out of its environment, forced to defend itself and becoming as tenacious as those alien elements and humans in opposition. Boorman's direction is gripping and well-constructed and the rapids scenes are electrifying. Cinematographer Zsigmond presents breathtaking scenes that sear the memory. Reynolds was never better before or after this one outing in a serious role as he later admitted: "It's the best film I've ever done. It's a picture that just picks you up and crashes you against the rocks. You feel everything and just crawl out of the theater." One of the most astounding scenes of this film is when the four city men pull up at the shanty asking for someone to drive their car to a point downstream where they will later pick it up. As a moronic type gasses up their car, an emaciated mountain family looks on, one being a boy without teeth and a retarded stare. One of the men sees he has a banjo and he picks up his own, strumming a few notes. The boy answers him. Then the two challenge each other until both go at a frenzied pace banging out a mountain tune. They boy wins hands down but when he stops his moronic grin fades and he resumes his dead-eyed stare. It is at this point where fear begins to emerge slowly until it completely dominates this fascinating film. Certainly not for children nor the genteel. (DELIVERANCE did a whopping $22 million the first time around at the box office. Filmed on the Chattoga River, Georgia.)

p&d, John Boorman; w, James Dickey (based on Dickey's novel); ph, Vilmos Zsigmond (Panavision, Technicolor); m, Eric Weissberg; ed, Tom Priestly; art d, Fred Harpman; spec eff, Marcel Vercoutere; cos, Bucky Rous; makeup, Michael Hancock; song, "Dueling Banjos," Weissberg, Steve Mandel.

Horror Cas. (PR:O MPAA:R)

DELTA FACTOR, THE** (1970) 91m Spillane-Fellows/CD c

Yvette Mimieux *(Kim Stacy)*, Christopher George *(Morgan)*, Diane McBain *(Lisa Gordot)*, Ralph Taeger *(Art Keefer)*, Yvonne De Carlo *(Valerie)*, Sherri Spillane *(Rosa)*, Ted De Corsia *(Ames)*, Rhodes Reason *(Dr. Fredericks)*, Joseph Sirola *(Sal Dekker)*, Richard Ianni, George Ash, Fred Marsell.

Routine actioner based on a Mickey Spillane novel sees George as an international adventurer who is framed for a theft of $40 million. He escapes from prison, but is recaptured and given a choice: either he agrees to assist the CIA in the rescue of an important scientist who is being held captive on a Caribbean island or he goes back to prison. George agrees to the terms and soon finds himself forced to marry Mimieux, a CIA agent, and then pose as a drug dealer to gain access to the Caribbean dictator's fortress where the scientist and other political prisoners are kept. Eventually he frees the scientist, rescues Mimieux (kidnapped by his old war buddy Sirola, the one who had framed him for the $40 million robbery in the first place) and goes off in search of the $40 million in order to finally clear his name.

p,d & w, Tay Garnett (based on the novel by Mickey Spillane); ph, Ted and Vince Saizis; m, Howard Danziger, Raoul Kraushaar; ed, Richard Farrell; art d, Jack Collis, Ben Resella; cos, Soni Karp; stunts, Roger Creed, Jim Climer.

Adventure (PR:C MPAA:R)

DELTA FOX*½ (1979) 92m Sebastian International c

Richard Lynch, Priscilla Barnes, Stuart Whitman, John Ireland, Richard Jaeckel.

Lynch is a drug smuggler being chased across the wide open spaces of America as he tries to make his way to Los Angeles. Strictly for the undiscriminating.

p&d, Beverly and Fred Sebastian.

Crime **Cas.** **(PR:O MPAA:R)**

DELUGE** (1933) 68m RKO bw

Peggy Shannon *(Claire)*, Sidney Blackmer *(Martin)*, Lois Wilson *(Helen)*, Matt Moore *(Tom)*, Fred Kohler *(Jephson)*, Ralf Harolde *(Norwood)*, Edward Van Sloan *(Prof. Carlysle)*, Samuel Hinds *(Chief Forecaster)*, Lane Chandler *(Survivor)*, Philo McCullough, Harry Semels *(Renegades)*.

A very early disaster film which details the demise of New York City after a solar eclipse causes a tidal wave to flood most of the world. Blackmer is the only survivor within the city; he swims upstate and meets Shannon, whom he believes to be the last woman left alive. Presuming his wife and child have perished, Blackmer romances Shannon and fights off a band of vicious scavengers led by Kohler. Eventually Blackmer's wife, Wilson, turns up very much alive. Shannon, seeing the couple reunited, swims off alone to meet her fate. Okay, but low-budget special effects were used from countless Republic Studios serials and features.

p, Samuel Bischoff; d, Felix E. Feist; w, John Goodrich, Warren B. Duff (based on the novel by S. Fowler Wright); m, Edward Kilenyi, Val Burton; ph, Norbert Brodine; ed, Martin G. Cohn, Rose Loewinger; md, Burton; set d, Ralph M. DeLacey; spec eff, Ned Mann, Russell E. Lawson.

Disaster **(PR:A MPAA:NR)**

DELUSIONS OF GRANDEUR*** (1971 Fr.) 105m Gaumont International-Mars Films-Corea/Produzione-Orion Films/GAU c (LA FOLLE DES GRANDEURS)

Yves Montand *(Blaze)*, Louis De Funes *(Salluste)*, Alice Sapritch *(Duenna)*, Karin Schubert *(Queen)*, Alberto De Mendoza *(King)*, Gabriel Tinti *(Cesar)*.

Big-budget French farce loosely based on Victor Hugo's play "Ruy Blas." De Funes plays an ambitious nobleman who has been banished from the court for fathering the illegitimate child of one of the Queen's ladies-in-waiting. Seeking to keep tabs on the happenings of the court, De Funes dresses up his valet, Montand, as his nephew to get him into the court so he can report back what happens. When another nobleman plants a bomb to kill the King and Queen, Montand saves them and is made the tax collector in return. Seeing his opportunity to redistribute the wealth, Montand taxes the rich instead of the poor; he soon feels the wrath of the nobles who try to kill him. He is saved by De Funes, who arranges for Montand to be found in a compromising position with the Queen, thus dishonoring her. The plan goes awry and both Montand and De Funes are sold to Arab slave-traders, though the deposed nobleman plots to return some day. Good mix of fun, swashbuckling adventure, and light slapstick comedy.

d, Gerard Oury; w, Oury, Marcel Julian, Danielle Thompson; ph, Henri Decae (Eastmancolor); m, Michel Poinareff; ed, Albert Jurgenson; art d, Georges Wakhevitch; cos, Jacques Fonteray, Jean Barthet.

Comedy **(PR:C MPAA:NR)**

DEMENTED** (1980) 93m IRC-IWDC-Four Features Partners c

Sallee Elyse *(Linda Rodgers)*, Bruce Gilchrist, Bryan Charles, Chip Matthews, Deborah Alter, Kathryn Clayton, Robert Mendel.

Barely out of the sanitarium after a traumatic gang rape, Elyse takes some boys in monster masks to be her rapists and swings into action against them using guns and knives (and a cleaver). Gets off to a slow start, but once Elyse's mind snaps and she begins seducing these kids, then dispatching them in assorted grisly fashions, the film actually becomes a fairly funny black comedy. Above average for a generally despicable genre.

p, Alex Rebar, Arthur Jeffreys; d, Jeffreys; w, Rebar; ph, Jim Tynes; m, Richard Tufo; spec eff, Robert Burman, Dale Brody.

Horror **Cas.** **(PR:O MPAA:R)**

DEMENTIA*½ (1955) 55m Rizzoli Film/van Wolfe-API bw (AKA: DAUGHTER OF HORROR)

Adrienne Barrett *(The Gamin)*, Bruno Ve Sota *(Rich Man)*, Ben Roseman *(Father—Law Enforcer)*, Richard Barron *(Evil One)*, Ed Hinkle *(Butler)*, Lucille Howland *(Mother)*, Jebbie Ve Sota *(Flower Girl)*, Faith Parker *(Nightclub Girl)*, Gayne Sullivan *(Wino)*, Ed McMahon *(Narrator)*.

Extremely obscure expressionistic horror film starring Barrett, who finds herself propelled through a nightmare evening. She encounters the mysterious dBruno Ve Sota who takes her home to his apartment. She struggles against his advances; Ve Sota falls from his balcony to the street below. Barrett realizes that the dead man has pulled her necklace off in his fall. She runs downstairs to wrest it from his grasp. Unable to pull his fingers open, she uses a knife to saw his hand off. Seized with a maniacal giddiness, she runs into a nearby jazz club, but suddenly awakens in a cheap hotel room. Thinking it was all a dream, she opens the dresser drawer to find a severed hand clutching a necklace. The film was banned by the New York State Board Of Censors in 1955. Believe it or not, it was narrated by Johnny Carson's sidekick, Ed McMahon.

p,d&w, John Parker; ph, William Thompson; m, George Antheil; ed, Joseph Gluck.

Horror **(PR:O MPAA:NR)**

DEMENTIA 13½** (1963) 81m Filmgroup/AIP bw (GB: HAUNTED AND THE HUNTED, THE)

William Campbell *(Richard Haloran)*, Luana Anders *(Louise Haloran)*, Bart Patton *(Billy Haloran)*, Mary Mitchell *(Kane)*, Patrick Magee *(Justin Caleb)*, Eithne Dunne *(Lady Haloran)*, Peter Read *(John Haloran)*, Karl Schanzer *(Simon)*, Ron Perry *(Arthur)*, Derry O'Donovan *(Lillian)*, Barbara Dowling *(Kathleen)*.

This is the first *mainstream* film Francis Ford Coppola directed, and it happens to be a little gem of gothic horror. Stylishly helmed on a shoestring budget (Corman gave Coppola $22,000 and three of the stars of his own THE YOUNG RACERS, which had just wrapped up shooting in Ireland. Coppola served as sound man on that picture and had written the screenplay to DEMENTIA 13 in his spare time). The plot concerns a crazed Irish family being mysteriously killed off by someone who wishes to gain control of a vast inheritance. The film opens with a violent argument between Read and his wife, Anders, over the will of his eccentric mother, Dunne. The argument becomes so heated that Read is stricken with a heart attack and dies. Not wanting to lose her share of the inheritance, Anders sinks her husband's body into a nearby lake and conceals his death from other family members. Meanwhile, more relatives have arrived at the estate (Patton, Campbell, and Campbell's fiancee Mitchell) to attend a memorial ceremony to be held in remembrance of their sister, who had drowned in the lake eight years before. Anders sees her opportunity and decides to drive Dunne completely insane by making her believe that she can communicate with her dead daughter from the great beyond. Before Anders has a chance to enact her scheme, however, she is axed to death. Enter the family doctor, Magee, who is extremely suspicious of the family members. After Dunne is murdered, he orders the lake drained. What they find is a bizarre wax statue of the dead little sister. Patton, brandishing an axe, reveals himself as the crazed killer. Luckily for the other family members, he is killed before he can do any further damage. Patton was a homicidal maniac who had also killed his younger sister eight years ago. Though the plot is rather silly and labored, the film rises above the somewhat confused material through Copolla's budding talent for composition and clever editing, the talent that would make such an impact in both GODFATHER films through APOCALYPSE NOW. As is typical of the Corman low-budget film factory, the film was saddled (some say at Coppola's insistence) with a ridiculous five-minute opening sequence which presented a man supposed to be a psychiatrist, who sat in his office and gave the audience a test to see if they were mentally stable enough to see the movie. The opening was used only in the theatrical release and has never been seen (praise be) on television.

p, Roger Corman, Charles Hannawalt, R. Wright Campbell; d&w, Francis Ford Coppola; ph, Hannawalt; m, Ronald Stein; ed, Stewart O'Brien; art d, Albert Locatelli.

Horror **Cas.** **(PR:C MPAA:NR)**

DEMETRIUS AND THE GLADIATORS*½** (1954) 101m FOX c

Victor Mature *(Demetrius)*, Susan Hayword *(Messalina)*, Michael Rennie *(Peter)*, Debra Paget *(Lucia)*, Anne Bancroft *(Paula)*, Jay Robinson *(Caligula)*, Barry Jones *(Claudius)*, William Marshall *(Glycon)*, Richard Egan *(Dardanius)*, Ernest Borgnine *(Strabo)*, Charles Evans *(Cassius Chaerea)*, Everett Glass *(Kaeso)*, Karl Davis *(Macro)*, Jeff York *(Albus)*, Carmen de Lavallade *(Slave Girl)*, John Cliff *(Varus)*, Barbara James and Willetta Smith *(Specialty Dancers)*, Selmer Jackson *(Senator)*, Douglas Brooks *(Cousin)*, Fred Graham *(Decurion)*, Dayton Lummis *(Magistrate)*, George Eldredge *(Chamberlain)*, Paul Richards *(Prisoner)*, Ray Spiker, Gilbert Perkins, Paul Stader, Jim Winkler, Lyle Fox, Dick Sands, Woody Strode *(Gladiators)*, Paul "Tiny" Newlan *(Potter)*, Allan Kramer *(Clerk)*, Paul Kruger *(Courtier)*, George Bruggeman, William Forrest, Jack Finlay, Peter Mamakos, Shepard Menken, Harry Cording, Richard Burton and Jean Simmons (in film clip from *THE ROBE*).

This sequel to the box office smash THE ROBE finds Mature picking up the story after Burton and Simmons go to the executioner. Before dying, the two converts to Christianity turn over to Mature for safekeeping the robe Christ wore to the Cross. After hiding it, Roman soldiers apprehend him and he is forced into the arena as a gladiator. Though he defeats his opponents, he refuses to kill them. Hayward, as the notorious Messalina, slatternly wife of future Caesar, Claudius (Jones), is attracted to the muscular Mature. She vents her sensuous quirks by insisting that Mature face Marshall, the towering Nubian warrior, Glycon. Marshall tells Mature to try to fake the combat but if the crowd becomes suspicious he will have to kill him. The feeble battle is quickly seen as a farce and Marshall tells Mature to defend himself, that they must fight to the death. Mature, however, deftly downs the giant but refuses to kill him. When Hayward later tries to seduce him, Mature rejects her, incurring her wrath. He is sent back to training. Innocent Paget, a young girl in love with Mature, visits him at the gladiatorial school where Mature is denied her company. Egan and four other gladiators then attempt to seduce her which drives Mature, penned up and witnessing the attack, crazy with anger. Paget collapses and is pronounced dead. Mature renounces God for allowing her death and the next day forces himself into the arena, even though he is not scheduled to fight. He attacks Egan and quickly kills him, then another of Paget's attackers. Marshall drives the remaining three culprits into the arena and Mature takes them all on in an incredible one-man attack, savagely destroying all three men, becoming the greatest gladiator ever seen by Rome. Caligula (Robinson) demands that he renounce the Christian God and swear allegiance only to him. The disillusioned Mature does and is immediately made an officer of the palace guard. Hayward boldly makes a play for Mature and the two become lovers. Then Robinson insists that Mature track down the robe so he can test its miraculous powers. In his search Mature encounters Rennie, Peter the Apostle, who tells him that Paget is not dead but in a strange comatose state, that *she* has the robe, clutching it so fiercely that none have been able to remove it since Egan and the other gladiators attacked her. Mature is moved to agony at the sight of her, begging God's forgiveness for doubting him and imploring him to restore Paget to consciousness. Suddenly she emerges from the deathlike spell, regaining her normal faculties. A grateful Mature takes the robe as a sign of healing to Robinson but the egomaniac wants it only for the godlike powers he believes it will give him. He takes it to a dungeon where a prisoner is being tortured and orders the man stabbed to death. Then Robinson, holding up the robe, commands the dead man to rise. When nothing happens Robinson races back to the palace and throws the robe back to Mature, telling him the robe has no powers, explaining how it failed to bring back to life a man he ordered killed. Mature becomes enraged that Robinson would use the robe for such perverted indulgences and calls the Emperor a lunatic, lunging toward him. Robinson orders Mature back into the arena to fight for his life. When he appears, he refuses to fight. Robinson, against the wishes of the crowd, orders his personal assassin, Davis, to slit Mature's throat. But the Praetorian Guard demands that its hero, Mature, be spared. Robinson goes berserk with rage. "You demand of your god!" he rants. With that a guard sends a spear into Davis before he can murder Mature and another guard sails a spear into Robinson, killing him. Jones is made the new emperor on the spot by the guardsmen. In a conciliatory court scene, Jones pardons Mature and orders the oppression of Christians to stop. Hayward, knowing a liaison with Mature is futile, assumes her role as Jones' wife and empress. Mature leaves the palace with Marshall and Rennie to spread the word of the Lord. Strong on action and spectacle, DEMETRIUS AND THE GLADIATORS minimizes the religious theme. Mature is convincing as the powerful gladiator and all the supporting players are believable in their historic roles. Jones is portrayed as beneficent when Claudius was, in reality, almost as bestial as his nephew Caligula. The latter role is enacted by Robinson as a screaming, hysterical tyrant on the fey side, a preposterous performance that must be seen to be believed. Rennie is appropriately saintly as Peter and Marshall gives a fine performance as the decent Nubian warrior. Paget is rather simpy as the victimized girl and Bancroft as a sleazy courtesan is wasted. Borgnine as the trainer of the gladiators is solid. Egan gives a bravura though brief performance as the merciless and lust-consumed gladiator who earns Mature's special rage. Fast paced and beautifully photographed by Krasner, this film certainly distorts history but it packs a stirring wallop with the gladiatorial scenes and the sequence where Mature kills several tigers bare-handed is overwhelming. The critics didn't like this epic, condemning Hayward's overacting but she had little to work with in a thinly-developed character (who never really repented her promiscuity in real life and was executed for her wild sexual habits). The public loved the spectacle, however, and DEMETRIUS was one of the top drawing films in 1954, re-released with THE ROBE in 1959 to do smashing box office business. Julie Newmar, who later played opposite Hayward in THE MARRIAGE GO-ROUND, appears in DEMETRIUS as a mere dancing girl, using the name Julie Newmeyer.

p, Frank Ross; d, Delmer Daves; w, Philip Dunne (based on characters created by Lloyd C. Douglas in *The Robe*); ph, Milton Krasner (CinemaScope, DeLuxe Color); m, Franz Waxman; ed, Dorothy Spencer, Robert Fritch; md, Alfred Newman; art d, Lyle Wheeler, George W. Davis; cos, Charles LeMaire; spec eff, Ray Kellogg; ch, Stephen Papick.

Religious Epic/Historical Drama   (PR:C MPAA:NR)

DEMI-PARADISE, THE   (SEE: ADVENTURE FOR TWO, 1945)

DEMOBBED**   (1944, Brit.) 96m Mancunian/But bw

Nat Jackley *(Nat)*, Norman Evans *(Norman)*, Dan Young *(Dan)*, Betty Jumel *(Betty)*, Tony Dalton *(Billy Brown)*, Jimmy Plant *(Graham)*, Anne Firth *(Norma Deane)*, Neville Mapp *(John Bentley)*, George Merritt *(James Bentley)*, Fred Kitchen, Jr. *(Black)*, Gus McNaughton *(Capt. Gregson)*, Arthur Hambling, Marianne Lincoln, Kay Lewis, Fred Watts, Sydney Bromley, Edgar Driver, Noel Dainton, Marjorie Gresley, Angela Glynne, Anne Ziegler, Webster Booth, Felix Mendelssohn's Hawaiian Serenaders.

Mustered out of the Army, a group of soldiers prove that the secretary at a factory is a thief. Occasionally okay slapstick comedy.

p&d, John E. Blakeley; w, Roney Parsons, Anthony Toner (based on a story by Julius Cantor, Max Zorlini); ph, Stephen Dade.

Comedy   (PR:A MPAA:NR)

DEMON, THE, 1965   (SEE: ONIBABA, 1965, Jap.)

DEMON, THE**   (1981, S. Africa) 95m Gold Key-Holland c

Jennifer Holmes, Cameron Mitchell, Craig Gardner, Zoli Markey, Mark Tannous.

A mysterious monster from some other dimension is stalking and killing women using his steel claw and some baggies as his weapons. Audiences will swear they've seen this one before.

p,d&w, Percival Rubens; ph, Vincent Cox; m, Nick Labuschagne; makeup, Reggie Wollenschlager.

Horror   Cas.   (PR:O MPAA:NR)

DEMON BARBER OF FLEET STREET, THE*½
          (1939, Brit.) 66m SEL/MGM bw
          (GB: SWEENEY TODD, THE DEMON BARBER OF FLEET STREET)

Tod Slaughter *(Sweeney Todd)*, Eva Lister *(Johanna)*, Bruce Seton *(Mack)*, Davina Craig *(Nan)*, D. J. Williams *(Stephen Oakley)*, Jerry Verno *(Pearley)*, Stello Rho *(Mrs. Lovat)*, Johnny Singer *(The Beadle)*, Billy Holland, Norman Pierce, Ben Sonten.

Early film version of the "Sweeney Todd" story starring "the horror man of Europe," Slaughter. Unfortunately Slaughter's performances were very theatrical, summoning laughs rather than gasps at his histrionics. Story concerns the crazed barber who slits the throats of his wealthier customers and dumps them in his basement via a trap door under his barber chair. There he robs them of their valuables and turns them into meat pies to be sold in the next door bakery. Loosely based on the real-life mass murders committed by Fritz Haarmann and Carl Denke. (Produced in England in 1935.)

p&d, George King; w, Frederick Hayward, H. F. Maltby (based on the play by George Dibdin-Pitt); ph, Ronald Neame.

Horror   (PR:O MPAA:NR)

DEMON FOR TROUBLE, A**   (1934) 58m Supreme/William Steiner bw

Bob Steele, Gloria Shea, Lafe McKee, Walter McGrail, Don Alvarado, Nick Stuart, Carmen LaRoux, Perry Murdock, Blackie Whiteford, Jimmy Aubrey, Buck Morgan.

Outlaws are buying up all the land in the area, then killing the sellers to get their money back. Enter Steele to put a stop to it. Routine oater still good fun for the kids.

p, A.W. Hackel; d, Robert Hill; w, Jack Natteford; ph, William Thompson, ed, William Austin.

Western   (PR:A MPAA:NR)

DEMON FROM DEVIL'S LAKE, THE*   (1964) 81m Phillips-Marker bw

Dave Heath.

Fairly laughable sci-fi film which details the tragic end to "Operation Noah's Ark," a space capsule filled with dozens of animals of all species that crashlands in Lake Texoma. The spacecraft splits apart, exposing the beasts to deadly radiation, which causes them to mutate into one mishmash of a monster.

p, d&w, Russ Marker.

Science Fiction   (PR:A MPAA:NR)

DEMON LOVER, THE zero   (1977) 83m 21st Century c

Christmas Robbins *(Laval Blessing)*, Val Mayerick *(Damian Kaluta)*, Gunnar Hansen *(Professor Peckinpah)*, Tom Hutton *(Tom Frazetta)*, Dave Howard *(Charles Wrightson)*, Susan Bullen *(Susan Ackerman)*, Phil Foreman *(Alex Redondo)*, Linda Conrad *(Elaine Ormsby)*, Ron Hiveley *(Paul Foster)*, Kathy Stewart *(Janis Romero)*, Sonny Bell *(Lester Gould)*, Carol Lasowski *(Sally Jones)*, Michael McGivern *(Garrett Adams)*, Jan Porter *(Jane Corben)*.

They really scraped the bottom of the barrel with this one. A group of lame independent filmmakers churned out this attempt at a satanic cult film which is filled with in-jokes for movie genre and comic-book enthusiasts. All the character names are homages to the filmmakers' favorite horror movie directors and comic book artists. Kaluta, Frazetta, Gould, Jones, Foster, Wrightson, Corben, Adams, and Kirby are all big names in the comic-book field and Romero, Peckinpah, and Ormsby are all directors and writers of violent films. (Ackerman refers to Forest J. Ackerman, publisher of "Famous Monsters" magazine.) Actor Hansen is better known as "Leatherface" in THE TEXAS CHAINSAW MASSACRE and Mayerick is a comic-book artist known for "Howard the Duck."

p,d&w, Donald Jackson, Jerry Younkins.

Horror   Cas.   (PR:O MPAA:R)

DEMON PLANET, THE   (SEE: PLANET OF THE VAMPIRES, 1965, Ital.)

DEMON POND*½**   (1980, Jap.) 88m Kino International-Grange c

Tamasaburo Bando *(Dragon Princess, Wife)*, Hisashi Igawa, Tsutomu Yamasaki, Norihei Miki.

Superb Japanese fantasy about the enchanted inhabitants of a pond and their queen (Bando). Paralleling their story, another, in which Bando plays a wife fearing her husband has left her, is played, and the Dragon Queen is seen sympathizing with her earthly double. Ethereally beautiful photography makes this one a must-see for fans of Japanese film.

d, Masahiro Shinoda; w, (based on a play by K. Izumi); ph, N. Sakamoto.

Fantasy   (PR:C MPAA:NR)

DEMON SEED*   (1977) 94m MGM/UA c

Julie Christie *(Susan Harris)*, Fritz Weaver *(Alex Harris)*, Gerrit Graham *(Walter Gabler)*, Berry Kroeger *(Petrosian)*, Lisa Lu *(Soon Yen)*, Larry J. Blake *(Cameron)*, Dana Laurita *(Amy)*, Robert Vaughn *(Voice of Proteus IV)*, John O'Leary *(Royce)*, Alfred Dennis *(Mokri)*, David Roberts *(Warner)*, E. Hampton Beagle *(Night Operator)*, Michael Glass, Barbara O. Jones *(Technicians)*, Monica MacLean *(Joan Kemp)*, Georgie Paul *(Housekeeper)*, Harold Oblong *(Scientist)*, Michelle Stacy *(Marlene)*, Tiffany Potter, Felix Silla *(Babies)*.

Vastly underrated science-fiction thriller about a super-intelligent computer, Proteus IV, designed by obsessive computer wizard Weaver. His work with the computer destroys his marriage to Christie. The last straw comes when he installs an extension of his brain child into their ultramodern home that controls everthing from the doors and the phones to the television and the stove. Christie throws Weaver out, but the computer stays. It suddenly locks her in and cuts her off from outside contacts. The computer studies her anatomy and behavior because it wants to create a humanoid extension of itself! The computer figures out how to succeed with its plan and in a terrifying (and surprisingly plausible) sequence, it rapes Christie and she conceives its child. The computer holds Christie prisoner until the "baby" is due, to make sure she does not try to harm herself or the child. Weaver eventually figures out a way to break into the house and arrives just in time to witness the startling birth of the machine/child. A good production in every department, the film was unfortunately overshadowed by STAR WARS and CLOSE ENCOUNTERS OF THE THIRD KIND, which were released in the same year.

p, Herb Jaffe; d, Donald Cammell; w, Robert Jaffe, Roger O. Hirson (based on a novel by Dean R. Koontz); ph, Bill Butler (Metrocolor); m, Jerry Fielding; ed, Francisco Mazzola; prod d, Edward C. Carfagno; set d, Barbara Krieger; cos, Sandy Cole, Bucky Ross, Joie Hutchinson; makeup, Lee Harman, Don L. Cash;

spec eff, Tom Fisher; animation visualization & conception, Ron Hays, Bo Gehring, Richard L. Froman, Grant Bassett.

| Science Fiction | Cas. | (PR:O MPAA:R) |

DEMON WITCH CHILD* (1974, Span.) 84m Coliseum c

Julian Mateos, Fernando Sancho, Marian Salgado, Lone Fleming, Angel Del Pozo.

An evil spirit possesses a young girl and after she kills a few people she withers into an old hag. One of the rare Spanish horror films not directed by Jess Franco, this movie lacks his style and is utterly dull.

d, Armondo De Ossorio; ph (Technicolor).

| Horror | (PR:O MPAA:R) |

DEMONIAQUE** (1958, Fr.) 100m Zodiaque/Fernand Rivers S.A. bw
(LES LOUVES; AKA: THE SHE WOLVES)

Francois Perier (Gervais), Micheline Presle (Helene), Jeanne Moreau (Agnes), Madeleine Robinson (Julia), Marc Cassot, (Julia's Fiance, Pierre Mondy), Paul Faivre (The Doctor), Arbessier (Police Commissioner), Simone Angele (The Visitor), Jo Peignot (The Pharmacist), Harari (The Pharmacist's Assistant).

Escaping from a German concentration camp, Perier assumes the identity of a friend who died during the attempt. He travels to the home of his friend's fiancee, a pen pal the dead friend had never seen. She takes him in but soon things start getting a bit strange; her sister is practicing black magic, then the dead man's sister shows up, but she doesn't expose him as an imposter. One of Moreau's earliest screen appearances.

d, Luis Saslavsky; w, Pierre Boileau, Thomas Narcejac, Saslavsky (based on a story by Boileau and Narcejac); ph, Henry Thibault; m, Joseph Kosma.

| Drama | (PR:C-O MPAA:NR) |

DEMONOID*½

(1981) 78m Zach Motion Pictures-Panorama Films S.A./American Panorama c
(AKA: MACABRA)

Samantha Eggar (Jennifer Baines), Stuart Whitman (Father Cunningham), Roy Cameron Jenson (Mark Baines), Narciso Busquets (Dr. Julian Rivkin), Erika Carlsson (Nurse Morgan), Lew Saunders (Sgt. Leo Matson).

Really awful horror item starring Eggar (who appears in far too much of this sort of trash) and husband Jenson who go to Mexcio looking for silver, but instead find the Devil's left hand buried in a silver box. The hand is mobile, of course, and wanders around possessing people who get a sudden urge to remove their left hands. The going gets pretty ridiculous when various of the possessed inflict all manner of pain upon themselves to remove their demonic digits. One man slams his hand in a car door, one puts his wrist on train tracks, and another bursts into a doctor's office brandishing a gun and demands that the surgeon cut off his hand or he'll blow the doctor's head off. Eggar finally calls on a priest, Whitman (who's *really* been in too much trash like this), to exorcise the hand. Whitman outdoes a number of bad performances by demonstrating *both* his Spanish and Irish accents while playing the same character.

p&d, Alfred Zacharias; w, David Lee Fein, Zacharias, E. Amos Powell (based on a story by Zacharias); ph, Alex Phillips, Jr. (CFI Color); m, Richard Gillis; ed, Sandy Nervig; spec eff. Bob Burns.

| Horror | Cas. | (PR:O MPAA:R) |

DEMONS OF LUDLOW, THE** (1983) 94m Titan International/Ram c

Paul Von Hausen, Stephanie Cushna, James Robinson.

Unsuspecting pianists call up evil ghost-demons when they play an old piano. Occasional unsettling moments, but nothing special.

d, Bill Rebane; w, William Arthur.

| Horror | (PR:O (MPAA:NR) |

DEMONS OF THE MIND** (1972, Brit.) 89m Hammer/Cinemation c

Paul Jones (Carl), Patrick Magee (Falkenberg), Yvonne Mitchell (Hilda), Robert Hardy (Friedrich), Gillian Hills (Elizabeth), Michael Hordern (Priest), Kenneth J. Warren (Klaus), Shane Briant (Emil), Virginia Wetherall (Inge).

Psychological drama starring Magee as a doctor who uncovers the real facts behind a 19th-century Baron's act of locking his children (Briant and Hills) up because he suspects they are demonically possessed. Not an insight in sight.

p, Frank Godwin; d, Peter Sykes; w, Christopher Wicking (from a story by Godwin, Wicking); ph, Arthur Grant; m, Harry Robinson.

| Drama | (PR:O MPAA:R) |

DEMONSTRATOR½**

(1971, Aus.) 112m Freeman-Fishburn International/COL c

Joe James (Joe Slater), Irene Inescort (Marion Slater), Gerard Maguire (Steven Slater), Wendy Lingham (Sara Wainwright), Kenneth Tsang (Thao Kimalayo), Michael Long (Hugh Prentiss), Harold Hopkins (Malcolm), Elizabeth Hall (Beth), Kerry Dwyer (Robin), Slim De Grey (Alexander Gurney), John Warwick (Frank Jamieson), Stewart Ginn (Superintendent Ackland), Ken Goodlet (Inspector Graham), Redmond Phillips (Sir David Crawford), Alexander Cann (Henry Hoffman), Alistair Duncan (Ted Packard), Noel Ferrier (Governor General), Paul Karo (Charles East), Doreen Warburton (Australian Lady), Peter Berg (Christian Student), Michael Aitkin (Youth).

Set in the near future, DEMONSTRATOR details the events surrounding a meeting among the Asian nations of the world for ratification of a military alliance to ensure mutual protection. James, the Minister for Defense, leads the discussion, but his well-intentioned efforts are frustrated by his own son, Maguire, who organizes a protest because he opposes militarism in any form. The film separates the characters along generational lines, but never reveals what effect the protests

have on the final outcome of the conference. One of the first well-done Australian films employing almost entirely native actors that had a potential international market. Unfortunately, the film suffers from ill-defined and clichéd characters who have no real life.

p, James Fishburn, David Brice; d, Warwick Freeman; w, Kit Denton (based on a story by Elizabeth and Don Campbell); ph, John McLean (Eastmancolor); m, Bob Young.

| Drama | (PR:O MPAA:NR) |

DEN OF DOOM (SEE: GLASS CAGE, THE, 1964)

DENTIST IN THE CHAIR** (1960, Brit.) 88m REN bw

Bob Monkhouse (David Cookson), Peggy Cummins (Peggy Travers), Kenneth Connor (Sam Field), Eric Barker (The Dean), Ronnie Stevens (Brian Dexter), Vincent Ball (Michaels), Eleanor Summerfield (Ethel), Reginald Beckwith (Mr. Watling), Stuart Saunders (Inspector Richardson), Ian Wallace (Dentist), Peggy Simpson (Miss Brent), Jean St. Clair (Lucy), Charlotte Mitchel (Woman In Surgery), Philip Gilbert (Young Man In Surgery), Jeremy Hawk (Instructor), Harry Hutchinson (Porter), Alfred Dean (Wrestler), Sheree Winton (Jayne), Rosie Lee (Maggie), Michael Fry (Jones), Michael Hawkins (Brown), David Glover (Newman).

Silly comedy starring Monkhouse and Stevens as a pair of wacky dental students who inadvertently get involved with small-time crook Connor, who dumps hundreds of dollars worth of expensive dental equipment in their laps. The rest of the film involves the bumbling students' efforts to get rid of the loot before the cops arrest them as the thieves.

p, Bertram Ostrer; d, Don Chaffey; w, Val Guest, Bob Monkhouse, George Wadmore (based on a novel by Matthew Finch); ph, Reginald Wyer; m, Ken Jones; ed, Bill Lenny; art d, Bill Andrews.

| Comedy | (PR:A MPAA:NR) |

DENTIST ON THE JOB (SEE: GET ON WITH IT, 1963, Brit.)

DENVER AND RIO GRANDE½** (1952) 89m PAR c

Edmond O'Brien (Jim Vesser), Sterling Hayden (McCabe), Dean Jagger (General Palmer), Laura Elliot (Linda Prescott), Lyle Bettger (Johnny Buff), J. Carrol Naish (Harkness), ZaSu Pitts (Jane), Tom Powers (Sloan), Robert Barrat (Haskins), Paul Fix (Engineer Monyhan), Don Haggerty (Bob Nelson), James Burke (Sheriff Masters).

A western railroad saga detailing a battle between two rival freight lines, the Denver and the Rio Grande, and the Canyon City and San Juan, to be the first to cross the Rockies. O'Brien stars as the good-guy chief engineer of the D & RG, and Hayden is the slimy and unscrupulous engineer of the CC & SJ. Action-packed, with gun fights, chases, fist fights and landslides, the climax sees two trains spectacularly crashing head-on. These trains were no Hollywood miniatures; these were actual, *full-size* trains that producer Holt acquired and permitted director Haskin to destroy with obvious relish. The story line gets a bit far-fetched, and the performances a bit overblown, but it's all in good fun.

p, Nat Holt; d, Byron Haskin; w, Frank Gruber; ph, Ray Rennahan (Technicolor); m, Paul Sawtell; ed, Stanley Johnson; art d, Hal Pereira, Franz Bachelin.

| Western | (PR:A MPAA:NR) |

DENVER KID, THE* (1948) 60m REP bw

Allan "Rocky" Lane, Eddy Waller, William Henry, Douglas Fowley, Rory Mallison, George Lloyd, George Meeker, Emmett Vogan, Hank Patterson, Bruce Edwards, Peggy Wynne, Tom Steele, Carole Gallagher, "Black Jack".

Lane, aboard his horse "Black Jack", is a border patrolman who helps catch a killer in this mostly undistinguished saddle opera.

p, Gordon Kay; d, Philip Ford; w, Bob Williams; ph, John MacBurnie; ed, Harold Minter; md, Dale Butts; art d, Frank Arrigo.

| Western | (PR:A MPAA:NR) |

DEPARTMENT STORE* (1935, Brit.) 65m REA bw (AKA: BARGAIN BASEMENT)

Garry Marsh (Timothy Bradbury), Eve Gray (Dolly Flint), Sebastian Shaw (John Goodman Johnson), Geraldine Fitzgerald (Jane Grey), Jack Melford (Bob Goodman), Patric Curwen (James Goodman), Henry Hallet (Mr. Buxton), Hal Walters (Sam Slack).

Dull crime drama involving a dishonest store manager who mistakes an ex-convict for his employer's heir. A poorly written script adds to the confusion.

p, Julius Hagen; d, Leslie Hiscott; w, H. Fowler Mear (based on a story by H. F. Maltby); ph, William Luff.

| Crime | (PR:A MPAA:NR) |

DEPORTED½** (1950) 88m UNIV bw

Marta Toren (Countess Christine), Jeff Chandler (Vic Smith), Claude Dauphin (Vito Bucelli), Marina Barti (Gina Carapia), Richard Rober (Bernardo Gervaso), Silvio Minciotti (Armando Sparducci), Carlo Rizzo (Guido Caruso), Mimi Aguglia (Teresa Sparducci), Adriano Ambrogi (Father Genaro), Michael Tor (Ernesto Pampiglione), Erminio Spalia (Beniamino Barda), Dino Nardi (Donati), Guido Celano (Aldo Brescia), Tito Vuolo (Postal Clerk).

Chandler stars as an Italian-born gangster who is deported back to Italy after serving a five-year jail sentence for stealing $100,000 which was never recovered. Because the feds still want to find the loot, they keep Chandler under surveillance overseas. He becomes a local hero as he lavishes kind deeds upon the villagers. He begins romancing widowed Italian countess Toren, whom he uses as a funnel to bring his loot to the home country. He does this by using Toren's charitable efforts to bring foodstuffs to the poor of Italy, and has his hoodlums in America buy up $100,000 worth of food and ship it to Italy, where he will sell it on the black market and recoup his investment. He aborts the plan, however, when he actually does fall in love with the countess, but it is too late. The cops grab him, though there is an indication that they will be lenient this time. Pretty sappy.

p, Robert Buckner; d, Robert Siodmak; w, Buckner (based on the short story "Paradise Lost, 49" by Lionel Shapiro); ph, William Daniels; m, Walter Scharf; ed, Ralph Dawson; art d, Bernard Herzbrun, Nathan Juran.

Crime   **(PR:A   MPAA:NR)**

DEPRAVED, THE*½   (1957, Brit.) 70m Danziger/UA bw

Anne Heywood (Laura Wilton), Robert Arden (Dave Dillon), Carroll Levis (Maj. Kellaway), Basil Dignam (Tom Wilton), Denis Shaw (Inspector Flynn), Robert Ayres (Colonel), Gary Thorne (Kaufmann), Hal Osmond (Barman), Gilbert Winfield (Sergeant).

Heywood and her lover, U.S. Army officer Arden, murder her alcoholic, abusive husband. The title promises something more lurid than another B murder mystery with an American leading man, but that's all this is.

p, Edward J. and Harry Lee Danziger; d, Paul Dickson; w, Brian Clemens, Edith Dell (based on a story by Dell); ph, Jimmy Wilson.

Crime   **(PR:A-C   MPAA:NR)**

DEPTH CHARGE**   (1960, Brit.) 55m President Pictures/BL bw

Alex McCrindle (Skipper), David Orr (Lt. Forrester), Elliot Playfair (Jamie), J. Mark Roberts (Bob), Alex Allen (Secretary).

A fishing trawler off the Scottish coast accidentally drags up an old depth charge in the nets and it's up to the young coxswain to help the bomb disposal expert defuse the device. Defusing-ticking-bomb movies almost can't help but be suspenseful, but apart from odd moments of anxiety, this one is a dud.

p, James Mellor; d, Jeremy Summers; w, Summers, Kenneth Talbot.

Drama   **(PR:A-C   MPAA:NR)**

DEPUTY DRUMMER, THE*½
                                      (1935, Brit.) 71m St. Georges Pictures/COL bw

Lupino Lane (Adolphus Miggs), Jean Denis (Bubbles O'Hara), Kathleen Kelly (Peggy Sylvester), Wallace Lupino (Robbins), Margaret Yarde (Lady Sylvester), Arthur Rigby (Sir Henry Sylvester), Syd Crossley (Curtis), Reginald Long (Capt. Hindlemarsh), Fred Leslie (Kabitzer), Hal Gordon (Yokel), Harold Brewer, Arthur Clayton, Brutus the Dog.

Lane is an impoverished composer who impersonates an aristocrat in order to crash Yarde's swank party. There, he discovers a gang of jewel thieves at work upstairs. Lane, another member of the celebrated Lupino clan that produced Ida, Stanley, and Wallace, in this movie, did some marvelous work in American silent shorts, but never caught on in talkies, winding up in supporting parts in Ernst Lubitsch musicals and leads in second-rate musicals like this.

p, Ian Sutherland; d, Henry W. George; w, Reginald Long, Arthur Rigby.

Musical   **(PR:A   MPAA:NR)**

DEPUTY MARSHAL**   (1949) 73m Lippert bw

Jon Hall (Ed Garry), Frances Langford (Janet Masters), Dick Foran (Joel Benton), Julie Bishop (Claire Benton), Joe Sawyer (Eli Cressett), Russell Hayden (Bill Masters), Clem Bevans (Doc Vinson), Vince Barnett (Hotel Clerk), Mary Gordon (Mrs. Lance), Kenne Duncan (Kyle Freeling), Stanley Blystone (Leo Hanald), Roy Butler (Weed Toler), Wheaton Chambers (Harley Masters), Forrest Taylor (Sheriff Lance), Tom Greenway (Bartender), Ted Adams (Telegrapher).

Overly talky oater starring Hall as a deputy marshal on the trail of a pair of bank robbers who have gone on the lam to Tumult, Wyoming. There he meets lovely rancher Langford, whose land is being taken by evil trio Foran, Sawyer, and Hayden, who know that the coming railroad will be running right across it. In the end, Hall catches the robbers, stops the landgrabbers, and falls in love with Langford. Average oater that is notable as the first western shot with the Garutso lens, which provided a much greater depth of field than was usual, lending the image an almost three-dimensional look.

p, William Stephens; d&w, William Berke (based on a novel by Charles Heckelmann); ph, Carl Berger; ed, Edward Mann; m/l, "Deadlier than the Male," "Wine and Roses," Irving Bibo, John Stephens.

Western   **(PR:A   MPAA:NR)**

DER FREISCHUTZ**   (1970, Ger.) 127m Polyphon/Polytel c

Tom Krause (Prince Ottokar), Toni Blankenheim (Kuno), Arlene Saunders (Agathe), Edith Mathis (Aennchen), Ernst Kozub (Max), Gottlob Frick (Kaspar), Hans Sotin (Hermit), Franz Grundheber (Kilian), Regina Marheineke (Bridesmaid), Bernard Minetti (Samiel).

A filmed performance of Carl Maria von Weber's opera (libretto by Johann Friedrich Kind) dealing with magic, ghosts, hermits, and the Devil produced for German television and released theatrically in the U.S.

p, Rolf Liebermann; d, Joachim Hess; ph, Hannes Schindler (Eastmancolor); m, Carl Maria von Weber; art d, Herbert Kirchhoff; md, Leopold Ludwig (with the Hamburg State Orchestra, Choir of Hamburg State Orchestra).

Opera   **(PR:A   MPAA:NR)**

DERANGED***   (1974, Can.) 82m AIP c

Roberts Blossom (Ezra Cobb), Cosette Lee (Ma Cobb), Leslie Carlson (Narrator), Robert Warner (Harlan Kootz), Marcia Diamond (Jenny Kootz), Brian Sneagle

---

(Brad Kootz), Robert McHeady (Sheriff), Marion Waldman (Maureen Selby), Jack Mather (Drunk), Micki Moore (Mary Ransom), Pat Orr (Sally Peterson), Arlene Gillen (Miss Johnson).

An accurately recounted horror film inspired by the life of crazed Wisconsin farmer Ed Gein, who actually murdered, skinned and preserved body parts of dozens of women in the late 1950s. PSYCHO (1960) and THE TEXAS CHAINSAW MASSACRE (1974) were also inspired by Gein. Blossom is perfect as the middle-aged psychotic farmer whose domineering mother has warped him into a sick, dangerous killer. He studies the occult, and when mom dies, he preserves her body. As his madness increases, he seeks out younger and more innocent victims to kill and stuff like trophies. A sick little film, but told with a disturbing sense of humor. Writer and co-director Ormsby previously had done a marvelous little low-budget horror outing entitled CHILDREN SHOULDN'T PLAY WITH DEAD THINGS (1972), and went on to write the screenplay for Paul Schrader's version of CAT PEOPLE (1982). The special makeup effects were done by George Romero's—DAWN OF THE DEAD (1979)—favorite actor/effects man Tom Savini. Producer Clark went on to make the stupid but successful PORKY'S (1981) and the outstanding Christmas film A CHRISTMAS STORY (1983).

p, Tom Karr [Bob Clark]; d, Jeff Gillen, Alan Ormsby; w, Ormsby; ph, Jack McGowan (Movielab Color); m, Carl Zittrer; art d, Albert Fisher.

Horror   **(PR:O   MPAA:R)**

DERBY DAY   (SEE: FOUR AGAINST FATE, 1952, Brit.)

DERELICT**   (1930) 73m PAR bw

George Bancroft (Bill Rafferty), Jessie Royce Landis (Helen Lorber), William Boyd (Jed Graves), Donald Stuart (Fin Thomson), James Durkin (Jameson), William Stack (Travis), Wade Boteler (Capt. Gregg), William Walling (Capt. Hogarth), Paul Porcasi (Masoni), Brooks Benedict (McFall).

A fairly realistic (for the time) look at the seafaring life of merchant seamen starring Bancroft and Boyd as a pair of swabbies ready for action. The friendship is strained when Boyd double-crosses Bancroft over the helm of the ship and the love of Landis. The climax sees a vicious storm, during which the best sailor proves his skill.

d, Rowland V. Lee; w, William Slavens McNutt, Grover Jones, Max Marcin; ph, Archie Stout; ed, George Nichols, Jr.

Drama/Adventure   **(PR:A   MPAA:NR)**

DERELICT, THE*   (1937, Brit.) 57m M.V. Gover/IFD bw

Malcolm Morley (Toby Merriman), Jane Griffiths (Mary), Charles Penrose (Toby's Pal), Frank Strickland (Sir Benjamin), Peter Kernohan (Sonny).

Sentimental weepie has poor-but-happy tramp Morley selling his drawings to help widow Griffiths pay for an operation that will allow her crippled son to walk again. People who enjoy being manipulated in the crassest way should relish it.

p, Victor Gover, Joe Rosenthal; d&w, Harold Simpson; w, James Spence.

Drama   **(PR:A   MPAA:NR)**

DERSU UZALA***   (1976, Jap./USSR) 137m Toho-Mosfilm/Sovexport c

Maxim Munzuk (Dersu Uzala), Yuri Solomine (Capt. Vladimir Arseniev).

Solomine, leading a mapping expedition deep into the wilds of 19th-century Siberia, meets an old prospector-trapper (Munzuk) who shows him the ways of nature. The two men become close friends over a number of expeditions with Munzuk acting as guide. Each time Solomine tries to convince the hardy, but aging Siberian to return to the city with him, but each time he refuses. Finally Munzuk does go back to the city, but he can't adapt to streets and buildings instead of paths and trees, so he returns to the forest to die. Filmed in Russia with an all Russian cast, the sole Japanese contribution was the talent of cinematographer Kurosawa, and part of the money. The first half of the film is wonderful, full of reverence for nature and the man who lives among it, but as the film goes on, it becomes increasingly obvious, melodramatic, and sappy, but since second-rate Kurosawa is still much better than the best of most directors, the film is definitely worth seeing. (In Russian; English subtitles).

d, Akira Kurosawa; w, Kurosawa, Yuri Nagibin (based on the journals of Vladimir Arseniev); ph, Asakadru Nakai, Yuri Gantman, Fyodor Dobronavov.

Adventure   **(PR:A   MPAA:NR)**

DESERT ATTACK***
                        (1958, Brit.) 132m ABF-Pathe/FOX (GB: ICE COLD IN ALEX)

John Mills (Capt. Anson), Sylvia Syms (Sister Diane Murdoch), Anthony Quayle (Capt. Van der Poel), Harry Andrews (M.S.M. Pugh), Diane Clare (Sister Denise Norton), Richard Leech (Capt. Crosbie), Liam Redmond (Brigadier), Peter Arne (British Officer), David Lodge (CMP Captain), Allan Cuthbertson (Staff Officer). Michael Nightingale, Basil Hoskins, Walter Gotell, Frederick Jaeger, Richard Marner, Paul Stassino, Vivian Pickles.

Set in North Africa during WW II, this picture has Mills, an alcoholic army officer, on a journey to Alexandria. Traveling in an ambulance, he brings with him a trio of passengers, nurses Syms and Clare and South African officer Quayle. Halfway through the film Clare is killed, the budding romance between Syms and Mills is aborted, and Quayle turns out to be a German spy. There is sufficient tension, however, to keep one's eyes fixed on the screen until the end of the journey.

p, W. A. Whittaker; d, J. Lee-Thompson; w, Christopher Landon, T. J. Morrison (based on Landon's novel); ph, Gilbert Taylor; m, Leighton Lucas; ed, Richard Best.

War Drama   **(PR:A   MPAA:NR)**

DESERT BANDIT*½   (1941) 56m REP bw

Don "Red" Barry (Bob Crandall), Lynn Merrick (Sue Martin), William Haade (Largo), James Gillette (Tim Martin), Dick Wessel (Hawk), Tom Chatterton (Capt. Banning), Tom Ewell (Ordway), Robert Strange (Hatfield), Charles R. Moore (T-Bone), Ernie Stanton (Sheriff Warde); Curley Dresden, Jim Corey, Merrill McCormack, Charles King, Jack Montgomery, Jack O'Shea, Pascale Perry.

Fairly dull Barry oater has the cowboy going undercover and posing as a disgruntled Texas Ranger looking to sell guns along the Mexican border to get the goods on a crooked sheriff and his gang of smugglers. Very little action.

p&d, George Sherman; w, Bennett Cohen, Eliot Gibbons (based on a story by Cohen); ph, William Nobles; m, Cy Feuer; ed, Ray Snyder.

Western   **(PR:A   MPAA:NR)**

DESERT DESPERADOES*½

(1959) 81m Venturini-Express-Nasht/RKO/Franchise bw (AKA: THE SINNER)

Ruth Roman (The Woman), Akim Tamiroff (The Merchant), Othelo Toso (Verrus), Gianni Glori (Fabius), Arnoldo Foa (The Chaldean), Alan Furlan (Rais), Nino Marchetti (Metullus).

Biblical era drama starring Tamiroff as a rich merchant whose caravan discovers mysterious woman Roman stranded in the desert. Tamiroff falls in love with the desert siren, but so does one of the Roman soldiers accompanying the caravan. Shot on a shoe-string budget in Italy and Egypt and dubbed into English.

p, John Nasht; d, Steve Sekely; w, Victor Stolloff, Robert Hill (based on a story by Stolloff and Hill); ph, Massimo Dallamano.

Biblical Drama   **(PR:A   MPAA:NR)**

DESERT FOX, THE****

(1951) 88m FOX bw (GB: ROMMEL—DESERT FOX)

James Mason (Erwin Rommel), Cedric Hardwicke (Dr. Karl Strolin), Jessica Tandy (Frau Rommel), Luther Adler (Hitler), Everett Sloane (Gen. Burgdorf), Leo G. Carroll (Field Marshal Von Rundstedt), George Macready (Gen. Fritz Bayerlein), Richard Boone (Aldinger), Eduard Franz (Col. Von Stauffenberg), Desmond Young (Himself), William Reynolds (Manfred Rommel), Charles Evans (Gen. Schultz), Walter Kingsford (Admiral Ruge), John Hoyt (Keitel), Don De Leo (Gen. Maisel), Richard Elmore (Rommel's Driver in Africa), John Vosper (Maj. Walker), Dan O'Herlihy (Commando Captain), Scott Forbes (Commando Colonel), Victor Wood (British Medic), Lester Matthews (British Officer), Mary Carroll (Maid), Paul Cavanagh (Col. Von Hofaker), Jack Baston (Jodl), Carleton Young (German Major), Freeman Lusk (German Surgeon), Robert Coote (British Medical Officer), Sean McClory (Jock), Lumsden Hare (Doctor), John Goldsworthy (Stulpnagel), Ivan Triesault (German Major), Michael Rennie (Desmond Young's Voice), Trevor Ward, Philip Van Zandt.

This was the first film that attempted to humanize a WW II German military leader, Hitler's greatest field commander, Field Marshal Erwin Rommel, brilliant, brave and, ironically, decent. Mason is magnetic in his portrayal of Rommel, grudgingly respected by his opponents, loyally followed by his men of the Africa Corps. The film opens with British Commandos making a night attack on the headquarters of Rommel in North Africa, a devastating raid where H.Q. buildings are blown to bits and German troops slaughtered. But the commandos, whose sole purpose for the raid is to kill Rommel, fail completely. The wounded leader of the raid, Forbes, looks up at a German officer, Boone, and asks: "Did we get him?" Boone snorts back: "Are you serious, Englishman?" We next see Desmond Young, then a Lieutenant-Colonel in the British Army, being taken prisoner. He is ordered by Triesault to go under a flag of truce to ask his own battery to halt its firing so British troops will not be killed. Young refuses but before Triesault inflicts punishment he is called to a nearby sand dune where an officer in a long black leather coat upbraids him. Triesault returns to Young to tell him that "the Field Marshal says you are right." Young (whose voice is dubbed with that of Michael Rennie for some unexplained reason) recognizes the Field Marshal as Rommel, the elusive and unpredictable German leader whose forces have fought the British to a standstill in North Africa for two years. Young then narrates the career of this enigmatic officer from his African command to his death by suicide in 1944. Mason is shown commanding his troops just before El Alamein, where British soldiers under Montgomery launched an attack which decimated the German armor. (The incredible night barrage of six miles of British guns is a clip from DESERT VICTORY, a notable documentary.) His forces in a shambles, Mason wires Berlin for permission to withdraw his troops. An order signed with Hitler's name instructs Mason to stand firm, it is "victory or death." Macready, as Bayerlein, Rommel's best field commander, objects, telling Mason that Hitler's order is "out of the dark ages." Mason disobeys and orders his troops pulled back. But it is too late. Weeks later the Africa Corps collapses for lack of food, equipment, and petrol. By then, however, Mason is back in Germany, recovering from an illness. He is visited by Hardwicke, a physician and one of the conspirators planning to assassinate Hitler to save Germany from utter destruction. He tries to enlist Mason's help but is put off. Mason is next assigned command of the French coastal defenses. He confers with von Rundstedt, Carroll, to discover that neither of them will direct defenses but that Hitler himself intends to supervise any counterattacks against an Allied invasion. Moreover, Carroll tells him he is being watched. Months later Hardwicke visits Mason once again at home in Germany where Mason all but agrees to help the conspirators. In a later interview with Hitler, Adler, he discovers how mad the German dictator really is, and it is at this time that he joins the conspirators. Mason is wounded, however, during the invasion of Normandy, and is sent home to recuperate from wounds. Meanwhile, Franz plants a bomb at Hitler's remote battle headquarters and just misses killing him. The conspirators are rounded up and executed. Sloane visits Mason and tells him that Berlin knows of his involvement in the conspiracy. He is told that if he demands a public trial his family will be in jeopardy. They will remain safe and his name unsullied, he is told, if he takes the poison Sloane has brought with him. Mason dresses, as if for battle, and leaves with

Hitler's emissaries, going to his death, as his wife Tandy and son, Reynolds, watch the car drive away. The film closes with scenes showing Mason commanding troops in the desert, the place of his greatest victories and fame. British Prime Minister Winston Churchill, who respected Rommel as a gallant foe, is quoted in voiceover: "His ardour and daring inflicted grievous disasters upon us but he deserves the salute which I made him in the House of Commons in January 1942; he also deserves our respect because, although a loyal German soldier, he came to hate Hitler and all his work and took part in the conspiracy to rescue Germany by displacing the maniac and tyrant and for this he paid the forfeit of his life. In the somber wars for modern democracy there is little place for chivalry." Though Mason is properly the whole show in this fragmentary biography done in semi-documentary style, the supporting cast is excellent and Hathaway's direction is as brisk as a panzer attack. Johnson's script is literate and penetrating. Adler gives an unforgettable cameo performance of a lunatic Hitler ranting out his intent to destroy the world. The British critics understandably resented this film but accorded kudos to Mason's performance. The battle scenes were shot at Borrego Springs, in the heart of the California desert. This was the most sympathetic portrait of Rommel. He was profiled as a strutting, cold-hearted Hun by Erich Von Stroheim in FIVE GRAVES TO CAIRO, by Albert Lieven in FOXHOLE IN CAIRO, by Werner Hinz in THE LONGEST DAY, by Gregory Gaye in HITLER, by Christopher Plummer in THE NIGHT OF THE GENERALS, by Wolfgang Preiss in RAID ON ROMMEL, by Karl Michael Vogler in PATTON and, in a reprise role, Mason once more in THE DESERT RATS.

p&w, Nunnally Johnson; d, Henry Hathaway; w, Johnson (based on the biography by Desmond Young); ph, Norbert Brodine; m, Daniele Amfitheatrof; ed, James B. Clark; art d, Lyle Wheeler, Maurice Ransford; set d, Thomas Little, Stuart Reiss; spec eff, Fred Sersen, Ray Kellogg.

War Drama/Biography   **Cas.**   **(PR:A   MPAA:NR)**

DESERT FURY**   (1947) 94m PAR c

John Hodiak (Eddie Bendix), Lizabeth Scott (Paula Haller), Burt Lancaster (Tom Hanson), Wendell Corey (Johnny Ryan), Mary Astor (Fritzie Haller), Kristine Miller (Claire Lindquist), William Harrigan (Judge Berle Lindquist), James Flavin (Pat Johnson), Jane Novak (Mrs. Lindquist), Ana Camargo (Rosa), Milton Kibbee (Mike, the Bartender), Ralph Peters (Pete, the Cafe Owner), John Farrell (Drunk in Jail), Ray Teal (Bus Driver), Harland Tucker (Chuck, the Crap Dealer), Lew Harvey (Doorman), Tom Schamp (Dan, the Sheriff's Deputy), Ed Randolph, Mike Lally (Dealers).

A star-studded cast that regrettably cannot overcome the shortcomings of Robert Rossen's script, which contains vast amounts of explanatory dialog. Story centers on a gambling house in the old west run by Astor who strives to raise her daughter, Scott, so that she will grow up to be a lady instead of a madame.

p, Hal B. Wallis; d, Lewis Allen; w, Robert Rossen (based on a novel by Ramona Stewart); ph, Charles Lang, Edward Cronjager (Technicolor); m, Miklos Rozsa; ed, Warren Low; art d, Perry Ferguson; set d, Sam Comer, Syd Moore; cos, Edith Head; spec eff, Gordon Jennings.

Crime/Western   **(PR:C   MPAA:NR)**

DESERT GOLD*½   (1936) 59m PAR bw

Larry "Buster" Crabbe (Moya), Robert Cummings (Fordyce Mortimer), Marsha Hunt (Jane Belding), Tom Keene (Dick Gale), Glen [Leif] Erikson (Glenn Kasedon), Monte Blue (Chetley Kasedon), Raymond Hatton (Doc Belding), Walter Miller (Ladd), Frank Mayo (Lash), Phillip Morris (Sentry).

Another version of Zane Grey's novel (Paramount did a whole series of superior Grey-based westerns in the very early 1930's with Randolph Scott, directed by Henry Hathaway), this time starring Crabbe as chief of a small tribe of Indians who carefully guard the secrets of rich gold deposits in their territory. Blue and his gang of evil whites try to find a way to make the Indians talk. Meanwhile, Hunt is kidnaped by the gang. Crabbe rescues her and gets her back to her fiance, Keene. Many of the best sequences are actually stock footage from earlier oaters directed by Hathaway.

p, Harold Hurley; d, James Hogan; w, Stuart Anthony, Robert Yost (based on the novel by Zane Grey); ph, George Clemens; ed, Chandler House; art d, Hans Dreier, Dave Garber.

Western   **(PR:A   MPAA:NR)**

DESERT GUNS*   (1936) 70m Beaumont bw

Conway Tearle, Margaret Morris, Charles K. French, Budd Buster, William Gould, Marie Werner, Kate Brinkler, Duke Lee, Roy Rice, Ray Gallagher, Art Felix, Pinky Barnes, Bull Montana, Slim Whitaker.

Dull oater with Tearle battling the bad guys for water rights and land, foiled by Morris whose heart he seeks to win. A cheap programmer.

p, Mitchell Leichter; d, Charles Hutchison; w, Jacques Jaccard.

Western   **Cas.**   **(PR:A   MPAA:NR)**

DESERT HAWK, THE**   (1950) 77m UNIV c

Yvonne De Carlo (Princess Shaharazade), Richard Greene (Omar), Jackie Gleason (Aladdin), George Macready (Prince Murad), Carl Esmond (Kibar), Marc Lawrence (Samad), Lucille Barkley (Undine), Ann Pearce (Yasmin), Lois Andrews (Maznah), Rock Hudson (Capt. Ras), Frank Puglia (Ahmed Bey), Joe Besser (Sinbad), Donald Randolph (Caliph), Ian MacDonald (Yussef), Nestor Paiva (Abdul), Richard Hale (Iman), Mahmud Shaikhaly (Akbar), Buddy Roosevelt (Baku), Virginia Hunter (Slave Girl Dancer), Lester Sharpe (Merchant), Ben Welden (Mokar), Michael Ross (Gorah), Jack Raymond (Sufi), Terry Frost, George Bruggerman (Soldiers), Fred Libby, Michael Ansara (Guards), Jan Arvan, Milton Kibbee (Merchants), Frank Lackteen (One-Eyed Arab), Dale Van Sickel (Kibar Leader), Chet Brandenberg, Vic Romito (Men), Eileen Howe, Hazel Shaw, Norma De Landa, Marian Dennish,

Barbara Kelly, Vonne Lester (Harem Girls), Lane Bradford (Standard Bearer), Shirley Ballard (Naga), Bob Anderson (Judah), Robert Filmer, Bob Wilke (Camel Drivers), Bruce Riley, Louis A. Nicoletti, Wally Walker, Mike Portanova (Sheiks), Wilson Millar, Phil Barnes, Frank Malet (Guards), Wendy Waldron, Shirley Ballard (Slave Girls), Harold Cornsweet (Arab), Lucile Barnes (Girl in Bathtub).

The usual lavish Arabian adventure tale that is great to look at, but hard to sit through due to clichés and predictable scripting. De Carlo is the princess and Greene the blacksmith who throws aside his anvil and picks up a sword to free his oppressed people from the evil despot Macready. Greene uses every trick in the book to defeat the wily prince, and he even manages to marry De Carlo (he tricks her) to further exasperate the ruler. Macready counterattacks and kidnaps the princess in hope that her father, the Caliph, will aid him in quashing the rebellion. Greene rescues De Carlo, who then falls in love with her husband, and all is well in Baghdad. The film is trite and the subject matter has been done better elsewhere, but half the fun of THE DESERT HAWK comes from spotting the bizarre array of supporting players who went on to do other things. Hudson plays an army captain, Besser (one of the replacements for Curly in The Three Stooges) plays Sinbad, and Gleason plays Aladdin! The whole thing was directed by Fred de Cordova who now directs (and has for the last 20 years) Johnny Carson on "The Tonight Show".

p, Leonard Goldstein; d, Frederick de Cordova; w, Aubrey Wisberg, Jack Pollexfen, Gerald Drayson Adams; ph, Russell Metty (Technicolor); m, Frank Skinner; ed, Otto Ludwig, Dan Nathan; art d, Bernard Herzbrun, Emrich Nicholson.

Adventure   (PR:A   MPAA:NR)

DESERT HELL**   (1958) 82m RF/FOX bw
Brian Keith (Capt. Edwards), Barbara Hale (Celie Edwards), Richard Denning (Sgt. Benet), Johnny Desmond (Lt. Forbes), Phillip Pine (Corp. Parini), Richard Shannon (Pvt. Hoffstetter), Duane Grey (Pvt. Arussa), Charles Gray (Pvt. Bandurski), Lud Veigel (Pvt. Knapp), Richard Gilden (Pvt. Kebussyan), Ronald Foster (Pvt. Bergstrom), Patrick O'Moore (Pvt. Corbo), John Verros (Kufra), Bill Hamel (Pvt. Brocklin), Roger Etienne (Pvt. Sirmay), Felix Locher (Marsays), Ben Wright (Col. Remy), Albert Carrier (Sgt. St. Clair), Bhogwan Singh (Holy Marabout), Michael Pate (Ahitagel).

Hokey Foreign Legion melodrama set in the Sahara stars Keith as the commander of a company of soldiers sent out to quell a rebellion by Tuareg tribesmen. Before they leave on their mission, Keith catches his lieutenant, Desmond, in the arms of his (Keith's) wife. The men put aside their differences for the sake of the mission, but tension arises when there is disagreement on how the planning of the attack was handled. It turns out to be a moot point because both men are killed just as they see that the mission was a success.

p, Robert W. Stabler; d, Charles Marquis Warren; w, Endre Bohem (based on a story by Warren); ph, John M. Nicholaus, Jr. (RegalScope); m, Raoul Kraushaar; ed, Fred W. Berger, Al Joseph; art d, James W. Sullivan; set d, Raymond Boltz, Jr.; spec eff, Jack Rabin, Louis DeWitt.

War/Adventure   (PR:A   MPAA:NR)

DESERT HORSEMAN, THE**   (1946) 57M COL bw
Charles Starrett (Capt. Steve Grant/Steve Godfrey/The Durango Kid), Smiley Burnette (Smiley Butterbeam), Adelle Roberts (Mary Ann Jarvis), Richard Bailey (Sam Treadway), John Merton (Rex Young), George Morgan (Pete), Tommy Coates (Buddy), Jack Kirk (Sheriff), Bud Osborne (Walt Jarvis), Riley Hill (Eddie), Walt Shrum and his Colorado Hillbillies.

Another Durango Kid western has Starrett as an Army officer falsely accused of stealing the payroll, court-martialed, and locked up. In the time-honored tradition of falsely accused B western heroes, he breaks out of jail, picks up orderly-sidekick Burnette, and, assuming the disguise of the black-hatted, black-masked Durango Kid, catches up to the real robbers and forces them to confess. Enjoyable if undistinguished programmer.

p, Colbert Clark; d, Ray Nazarro; w, Sherman Lowe; ph, L.W. O'Connell; ed, Paul Borofsky; art d, Charles Clague.

Western   (PR:A   MPAA:NR)

DESERT JUSTICE*½   (1936) 58m Atlantic bw
Jack Perrin, David Sharpe, Warren Hymer, Budd Buster, Dennis Meadows [Moore], Maryan Downing, Roger Williams, William Gould, Fred Toones, Earl Dwire, "Starlight", "Braveheart".

Perrin is a Border patrolman who, accompanied by Starlight the horse and Braveheart the dog, busts up a smuggling ring. Okay, but no more.

p, William Berke; d, Lester Williams [Berke]; w, Gordon Phillips, Lewis Kingdom (based on a story by Allan Hall).

Western   (PR:A   MPAA:NR)

DESERT LEGION**   (1953) 85m UNIV c
Alan Ladd (Paul Lartal), Richard Conte (Crito/Calif), Arlene Dahl (Morjana), Akim Tamiroff (Pvt. Plevko), Oscar Beregi (Khalil), Anthony Caruso (Lt. Messaoud), Leon Askin (Maj. Vasil), George J. Lewis (Lt. Lopez), Sujata and Asoka (Dancers), Henri Letondal (General), Peter Coe (Lt. Doudelet), Ivan Triesault (Cpl. Schmidt), Don Blackman (Kumbaba), Dave Sharpe (Alyoun), Ted Hecht (Tabban), Pat Lane (Villager), Elsa Edsman (Handmaiden).

Little bit of a borrow from Lost Horizon by James Hilton. Ladd is a French Foreign Legionnaire who is the wounded sole survivor of an ambush. He is taken in by Dahl, a gorgeous redheaded princess who is totally out of place in this middle-Eastern mountainous area. She helps him back to health, then prevails on him to aid her but he faints before he can get the details. Next thing he knows, Ladd is toted back to his fort on the rear of a camel and no one believes his wild tale. Later, Ladd gets a message from the Titian vision, Dahl, and he and Akim Tamiroff, a private, go AWOL and trail the message-bearer to the lost city of Madara, hidden

in the mountains. Once there, he meets former Legionnaire Beregi who rules the city but who now fears a coup, led by Conte whose intention is to marry Dahl (Beregi's daughter) and take over the city. Beregi offers his daughter to Ladd—not a bad deal—but Ladd is, first and foremost, a Legionnaire. He has been trailing the scourge of the desert, Omar Ben Calif, who has been attacking lots of innocent people. Then Ladd finds that Conte is both Calif and Crito, so he need look no further. Ladd and Conte fight a duel which Alan wins but just as Conte is being taken away, his men attack and rescue him and take the city. Now Ladd must muster Beregi's remaining soldiers and regain the Shangri-La. Ladd and Beregi's men rescue a troop of Legionnaires who are riding into an ambush; then they go after the city and retake it. Finally, Ladd and Conte have at it mano-a-mano and Ladd emerges victorious. He foregoes Foreign Legion awards and returns to Madara to marry Dahl and rule the paradise in peace. In the 1980s, this movie would have had great nostalgia. In the 1950s, it was just a few years too late. Conte was born in New Jersey and his accent could always be heard throughout his career so this role was totally wrong. Tamiroff provided the comic relief and Dahl couldn't have looked more beautiful. If this action picture were just a tad sillier, it might have been more successful, because it was just a millimeter off being a comedy. In the hands of Lucas or Spielberg, this plot, properly cast, would gross $100 million today.

p, Ted Richmond; d, Joseph Pevney; w, Irving Wallace, Lewis Meltzer (based on the novel The Demon Caravan by George Arthur Surdez); ph, John Seitz (Technicolor); m, Frank Skinner; ed, Frank Gross; art d, Alexander Golitzen, Robert Clatworthy; ch, Asoka.

Adventure   (PR:A   MPAA:NR)

DESERT MESA   (1935) 71m Security bw
Tom Wynn [Wally West], Tonya Beauford, Franklyn Farnum, Bill Patton, Lew Meehan, Denver Dixon [Victor Adamson], William McCall, Allen Greer, Harry Keaton, Delores Booth, Horace B. Carpenter, Tex Miller.

Inept and poorly photographed oater with Wynn winning the west despite all odds. Strictly a poverty row product.

p, Victor Adamson; d, Alan James; w, Van Johnson.

Western   (PR:A   MPAA:NR)

DESERT MICE**½   (1960, Brit.) 83m Welbeck/RANK bw
Alfred Marks (Maj. Poskett), Sidney James (Bert Bennett), Dora Bryan (Gay), Dick Bentley (Gavin O'Toole), Reginald Beckwith (Fred), Irene Handl (Miss Patch), Kenneth Fortescue (Lt. Peter Ribstone), Patricia Bredin (Susan), Liz Fraser (Edie), Joan Benham (Una), Marius Goring (German Major), Anthony Bushell (Plunkett), George Rose (Popados), Alan Tilvern (German Captain), Philo Hauser (Franz), John Le Mesurier (Staff Colonel), Gilbert Davis (General), Nigel Davenport.

Light little comedy starring James, Bryan, Bentley, Benham, Beckwith, Handl, and Fraser as a hopelessly mediocre (at best) troupe of entertainers on the wartime circuit who travel from hot spot to hot spot giving the soldier boys stationed in Africa something to look forward to. Through a series of events the troupe ends up uncovering and capturing a German major posing as a Briton.

p, Basil Dearden; d, Michael Relph; w, David Climie; ph, Kenneth Hodges; m, Philip Green; ed, Reginald Beck.

Comedy   (PR:A   MPAA:NR)

DESERT OF LOST MEN*   (1951) 54m REP bw
Allan "Rocky" Lane (Himself), Irving Bacon (Skeeter Davis), Mary Ellen Kay (Nan Webster), Roy Barcroft (Link Rinter), Ross Elliott (Dr. Jim Haynes), Cliff Clark (Carl Landers), Boyd "Red" Morgan (Frank), Leo Cleary (Dr. Stephens), Kenneth MacDonald (Bill Hackett), Steve Pendleton (Evans), Herman Hack, "Black Jack".

The umpteenth variation on a single plot line sees Lane going undercover and working his way into a gang of thieves so that he can gather enough evidence to convict Clark, the leader of the murdering robbers. Not one of the better Lane oaters.

p&d, Harry Keller; w, M. Coates Webster (based on a story by Webster); ph, John MacBurnie; m, Stanley Wilson; ed, Harold Minter; art d, Frank Arrigo.

Western   (PR:A   MPAA:NR)

DESERT OF THE TARTARS, THE**½
(1976 Fr./Ital./Iranian) 140m Reggane-Fildebroc-FR 3-DeL'Astrophore-Corona-FIDCI/GAU c (LE DESERT DES TARTARES)
Vittorio Gassman (Filimore), Giuliano Gemma (Mattis), Helmut Griem (Simeon), Philippe Noiret (General), Jacques Perrin (Drogo), Francisco Rabal (Tronk), Fernando Rey (Nathanson), Laurent Terzieff (Amerling), Jean-Louis Trintignant (Doctor), Max Von Sydow (Hortiz).

Strange, moody war film that takes place somewhere near the beginning of the 20th century in a large, impressive fort sitting in the desert by the remains of an ancient village. The fort is filled with professional soldiers who sit and wait in tension-filled moments for something to happen. The destroyed village had been overrun by Tartars years ago; the defenders wait for them to return. Perrin plays a young lieutenant who wants out of this boring madness, but is taken ill by the dust emanating from the fort's stone walls. The young soldier is taken to the nearest village, just as the Tartars appear on the horizon, and he is denied the moment of glory for which all the others had been waiting so patiently. This soliloquy on the madness of war loses some power due to its excessive length, but the cast, stunning locations (mainly in Iran) and typically fine musical score by Ennio Morricone help move things along.

d, Valerio Zurlini; w, Andre Brunelin, Jean-Louis Bertucelli (based on the book by Dino Buzzati); ph, Luciano Tavoli (Eastmancolor); m, Ennio Morricone; ed, Raimondo Crocianai.

War/Drama   **Cas.**   (PR:C   MPAA:NR)

DESERT PASSAGE** (1952) 62m RKO bw

Tim Holt *(Tim)*, Joan Dixon *(Emily)*, Walter Reed *(Carver)*, Dorothy Patrick *(Rosa)*, John Dehner *(Bronson)*, Clayton Moore *(Warwick)*, Lane Bradford *(Langdon)*, Michael Mark *(Burley)*, Denver Pyle *(Allen)*, Richard Martin *(Chito Rafferty)*, Francis McDonald.

Holt's last oater for RKO (he did 46 of them) sees the sagebrush star teamed with Martin as owner/operators of a bankrupt stagecoach line who are hired by former bank robber Reed (who has just dug up $100,000 worth of loot) to drive him to Mexico. Not knowing he's a crook, Holt and Martin defend Reed against attacks by disgruntled members of his old gang who want their share of the dough. Holt figures things out, rounds up the bad guys, and returns the money to the daughter of the banker from whom it was stolen. A mediocre end to a series of oaters that occasionally produced a gem. Producer Schlom and director Selander also waved goodbye to RKO with this film.

p, Herman Schlom; d, Lesley Selander; w, Norman Houston; ph, J. Roy Hunt; ed, Paul Weatherwax; md, C. Bakaleinikoff.

Western (PR:A MPAA:NR)

DESERT PATROL* (1938) 56m REP bw

Bob Steele, Rex Lease, Marion Weldon, Ted Adams, Forrest Taylor, Budd Buster, Steve Clark, Jack Ingram, Julian Madison, Tex Palmer.

Steele is a Texas Ranger who tracks down and brings to justice a gang of smugglers who have murdered a fellow ranger. A typical adventure for the diminutive cowpoke.

p, A.W. Hackel; d, Sam Newfield; w, Fred Myton; ph, Robert Cline; ed, Roy Claire.

Western (PR:A MPAA:NR)

DESERT PATROL** (1962, Brit.) 78m Tempean-Rank/UNIV bw (GB: SEA OF SAND)

Richard Attenborough *(Trooper Brody)*, John Gregson *(Capt. Williams)*, Michael Craig *(Capt. Cotton)*, Vincent Ball *(Sgt. Nesbitt)*, Percy Herbert *(Trooper White)*, Barry Foster *(Cpl. Matheson)*, Andrew Faulds *(Sgt. Parker)*, George Murcell *(Cpl. Simms)*, Ray McAnally *(Sgt. Hardy)*, Harold Goodwin *(1st Road Watch)*, Tony Thawnton *(Capt. Giles)*, Dermot Walsh *(Maj. Jeffries)*, Wolf Frees *(German Sergeant)*, George Mikell *(German Officer)*.

Typical war drama starring Gregson as a by-the-book mine expert who arrives in Captain Craig's patrol and is outraged to find a lack of discipline. Of course, as the film progresses and the patrol encounters some heavy action from the Nazis, the two commanders develop a grudging respect for each other which eventually leads to Gregson sacrificing his life to save another British patrol. Well done, but nothing special.

p, Robert S. Baker, Monty Berman; d, Guy Green; w, Robert Westerby (based on a story by Sean Fielding); ph, Wilkie Cooper; m, Clifton Parker; ed, Gordon Pilkington; art d, Maurice Pelling; md, Muir Mathieson; spec eff, Cliff Richardson, Roy Whybrow; makeup, Roy Ashton.

War (PR:C MPAA:NR)

DESERT PHANTOM** (1937) 63m Supreme bw

Johnny Mack Brown *(Billy Donovan)*, Sheila Mannors *(Jean Haloran)*, Ted Adams *(Salizar)*, Karl Hackett *(Tom Jackson)*, Hal Price *(Jim Day)*, Nelson McDowell *(Doc Simpson)*, Charlie King *(Dan)*, Forrest Taylor, Frank Ball.

Typical Brown oater stars Hackett and King as villains who scheme to rob defenseless cowgirl Mannors of her ranch. Defenseless, that is, until stranger Brown rides in to defend her. Directed by former editor S. Roy Luby who remade it from a 1932 Harry Carey western, THE NIGHT RIDER.

p, A.W. Hackel; d, S. Roy Luby; w, Earle Snell (based on a story by E.B. Mann); ph, Bert Longenecker.

Western (PR:A MPAA:NR)

DESERT PURSUIT* (1952) 70m MON bw

Wayne Morris *(Ford Smith)*, Virginia Grey *(Mary Smith)*, George Tobias *(Ghazili)*, Anthony Caruso *(Hassan)*, Emmett Lynn *(Leatherface)*, John Doucette *(Kafan)*; Gloria Talbot, Frank Lackteen, Billy Wilkerson, Robert Bice.

Pretty strange oater featuring Morris and Grey as a mining couple laden with gold and running away across the Death Valley desert from three Arabs (Tobias, Caruso, Doucette) riding camels! Apparently the camels (and the Arabs) were left over from an aborted government program that saw the humpbacks as the solution to desert travel through Death Valley. During the chase, the Arabs are mistaken by various settlers as everything from Indians to the Three Wise Men. Eventually, the couple is helped by real Indians, who get rid of the Arabs. Must be seen to be believed.

p, Lindsley Parsons; d, George Blair; w, W. Scott Darling (based on the novel *Starlight Canyon* by Kenneth Perkins); ph, William Sickner; ed, Leonard Herman; md, Edward J. Kay.

Western (PR:A MPAA:NR)

DESERT RATS, THE***½ (1953) 88m FOX bw

Richard Burton *(Capt. MacRoberts)*, Robert Newton *(Bartlett)*, Robert Douglas *(General)*, Torin Thatcher *(Barney)*, Chips Rafferty *(Smith)*, Charles Tingwell *(Lt. Carstairs)*, James Mason *(Rommel)*, Charles Davis *(Pete)*, Ben Wright *(Mick)*, James Lilburn *(Communications)*, John O'Malley *(Riley)*, Ray Harden *(Hugh)*, John Alderson *(Corp.)*, Richard Peel *(Rusty)*, Michael Pate *(Capt. Currie)*, Frank Pulaski *(Maj. O'Rourke)*, Charles Keane *(Sgt. Donaldson)*, Pat O'Moore *(Jim)*, Trevor Constable *(Ginger)*, Albert Taylor *(Jensen)*, John Wengraf *(German Doctor)*, Arno Frey *(Kramm)*, Alfred Ziesler *(Von Helmholtz)*, Charles Fitzsimons *(Fire Officer)*.

Burton is a tough British officer who takes over command of the 9th Australian Division at Tobruk in 1941 while the desert fortress is surrounded and hard pressed by Rommel's Africa Corps. He feels these troops are inferior fighters to British regulars and he is brusque and unfeeling with his men. Among the garrison is Newton, his old English teacher at college, a lowly volunteer and a raving alcoholic. Newton is the only one who can persuade the relentless Burton to go a bit easy with his men and he soon resumes his hard-bitten ways when finding Newton drunk once too often while on duty. Burton leads a commando raid behind enemy lines and is captured. Wounded, he is taken to a German field hospital tent where he meets Field Marshall Rommel, Mason, and the two converse in civil tones about the fate of Tobruk. Burton later escapes and is ordered to hold a hill outside Tobruk until the arrival of a British relief force. The Australians valiantly hold off one German attack after another. With ammunition almost gone, his forces depleted, and his hope fled, Burton orders his men to surrender. The Aussies, including Newton, refuse to leave their foxholes, insisting upon fighting to the last bayonet. At that moment they hear the bagpipes of the British relief force which hoves into view, its tanks roaring forward as the beleaguered troops cheer, and "Waltzing Matilda" is heard triumphantly. This was a follow-up to the successful THE DESERT FOX, intended to show the other side of the lines, the heroic British troops who fought Rommel over the last grain of sand. Mason appears only briefly and uses a German accent which he later called "rather crummy." Burton is his usual forceful self but Newton steals every scene he's in, playing a floppy, roaring and weepy drunk spouting philosophy and sentiment. He's simply wonderful and spellbinding but when was he not? (In real life Newton was a heavy drinker, a habit which stood him in good stead for this role.) Rafferty, a veteran Australian actor, is superb as the knowing sergeant supporting the testy Burton. Wise's direction is sharp and the technical staff is top drawer.

p, Robert L. Jacks; d, Robert Wise; w, Richard Murphy; ph, Lucien Ballard; m, Leigh Harline; ed, Barbara McLean; art d, Lyle Wheeler, Addison Hehr; spec eff, Ray Kellogg.

War Drama (PR:A MPAA:NR)

DESERT RAVEN, THE*½ (1965) 90m Cal Dunn Studios/AA bw

Rachel Romen *(Raven)*, Rosalind C. Roberts *(Margo)*, Robert Terry *(Bert)*, Robert Ward *(Ed Crane)*, Bea Silvern *(Rena)*, Rance Howard *(Reggie)*, Paul L'Amoreaux *(Deputy)*, Edward Schaaf *(Red Banion)*, Stuart Walsh *(Jim)*, Bill Lloyd *(Al)*, Joe Slattery, Gregg Donovan *(Radio Voices)*.

Terry takes his band of criminals out into the desert after they've robbed and killed a wealthy woman. They hide out with an Indian woman, Silvern, who killed her alcoholic husband after he made advances toward his stepdaughter, Romen. The youngest member of the group of outlaws, Howard, falls in love with Romen and together they plan to go to the police. The police kill Terry; Silvern dies also. Romen gets a reward and plans to wait for Howard to get out of jail.

p, Cal Dunn; d, Alan S. Lee; w, Rachel Romen, Lee; ph, Taylor Byars; m, Richard La Salle; ed, John F. Link; m/l, "The Desert Raven," John Steele (sung by Sondra Steele.)

Crime (PR:A MPAA:NR)

DESERT SANDS**½ (1955) 87m Bel-Air/UA c

Ralph Meeker *(David Malcolm)*, Marla English *(Zara)*, J. Carroll Naish *(Diepel)*, John Smith *(Rex Tyle)*, Ron Randell *(Pete Havers)*, John Carradine *(Jala)*, Keith Larsen *(El Zanal)*, Jarl Victor *(Gina)*, Otto Waldis *(Gabin)*, Peter Mamakos *(Lucia)*, Albert Carrier *(Ducco)*, Mort Mills *(Wolock)*, Philip Tonge *(Sandy)*, Terence deMarney *(Kramer)*, Nico Minardos *(Gerard)*, Lita Milan *(Alita)*, Peter Bourne *(Weems)*, Peter Norman *(Dr. Kleiner)*, Joseph Waring *(Spokesman)*, Aaron Saxon *(Tama)*, Bela Kovacs *(Panton)*.

Average desert opus with a decent cast and well-staged, colorful action scenes stars Meeker as a Foreign Legion captain sent to Fort Valeau to command after the last company of troops was slaughtered by the Arabs, who now hold the fort. After many clever moves by Meeker, including an injection of romance and trickery, the Legionnaires defeat the Arabs, but not until most of their number are killed in battle.

p, Howard W. Koch; d, Lesley Selander; w, George W. George, George F. Slavin, Danny Arnold; ph, Gordon Avil (Superscope/Technicolor); m, Paul Dunlap; ed, John Schreyer; md, Dunlap; art d, Danny Hall; cos, Wes Jefferies.

Adventure (PR:A MPAA:NR)

DESERT SONG, THE**½ (1929) 125m WB bw and partial c

John Boles *(The Red Shadow)*, Carlotta King *(Margot)*, Louise Fazenda *(Susan)*, Johnny Arthur *(Benny Kidd)*, Edward Martindel *(Gen. Bierbeau)*, Jack Pratt *(Pasha)*, Robert E. Guzman *(Sid El Kar)*, Otto Hoffman *(Hasse)*, Marie Wells *(Clementine)*, John Miljan *(Paul Fontaine)*, Del Elliott *(Bebel)*, Myrna Loy *(Azuri)*, Singing chorus of 100.

This was the first of the three versions of the successful stage operetta. Warner Brothers had been the premier studio to debut sound with THE JAZZ SINGER and was determined to keep its position as an innovator, so it acquired the rights to THE DESERT SONG and presented filmdom's first all-talking, all-singing operetta. The curiosity value of the picture, not the plot, was what made it a hit. The story of The Red Shadow and Pierre Birbeau (the same person, played by Boles) was seen often in later years, except it became known as The Scarlet Pimpernel. Boles is a weak wimp while in the guise of Bierbeau, and then becomes the hard-riding leader of The Riffs, who battle the sinister Arabs. The same plot has been used over and over from Zorro to Batman; a double identity with one side being the weakling and the other being the dashing, jut-jawed hero. Most of the screen time is taken up by the Romberg/Hammerstein songs as synch-sung by the actors (this was before it became fashionable to "loop" the voices by better singers). The major musical pieces are "The Riff Song," "One Alone," "Sabre Song," "Then You Will Know," and "The French Marching Song." It looked lots better in the later color versions. Boles was handsome and sang well, Fazenda was very funny, and a very young Myrna Loy was absolutely exquisite. But the film, by today's standards, does not hold up well; they were still without good sound equipment to allow much movement on the part of the actors. It appeared to be little more than a photographed stage play.

d, Roy Del Ruth; w, Harvey Gates (from the operetta by Otto Harbach, Laurence Schwab, Frank Mandel, Oscar Hammerstein II) ph, Bernard McGill (partly in Technicolor); m, Sigmund Romberg; ed, Ralph Dawson.

Musical (PR:A MPAA:NR)

DESERT SONG, THE*** (1943) 90m WB c

Dennis Morgan *(Paul Hudson)*, Irene Manning *(Margot)*, Bruce Cabot *(Col. Fontaine)*, Victor Francen *(Caid Yousseff)*, Lynne Overman *(Johnny Walsh)*, Gene Lockhart *(Pere FanFan)*, Faye Emerson *(Hajy)*, Marcel Dalio *(Tarbouch)*, Felix Basch *(Heinzelman)*, Gerald Mohr *(Haasan)*, Noble Johnson *(Abdel Rahman)*, Curt Bois *(Francois)*, Albert Morin *(Muhammad)*, Jack LaRue *(Lt. Bertin)*, William Edmunds *(Suliman)*, Wallis Clark *(Pajot)*, Sylvia Opert *(Dancer)*, Nestor Paiva, Fritz Leiber, George Renevent, Egon Brecher, Duncan Renaldo.

They updated the plot and added four new tunes and still managed to cut 35 minutes from the 1929 original. It's still the same nonsense, but everyone is so sincere and seems to be having such a good time that it becomes infectious. Morgan is an ex-soldier in the 1939 Spanish Civil War. He's currently tickling the ivories in a Morocco night club and having the start of a fling with Manning, chanteuse at the boite. The Nazis are in control of the area and use Francen to get the local Riffs to work on a railroad they are planning to build across North Africa. The Riffs are under the thumb of the local French. Morgan, playing a dual role as El Khobar—Leader of the Riffs—convinces Cabot, colonel of the French army, that the Riffs are swell guys who deserve their own independence. Cabot agrees when the Riffs help break up the Nazi plans for the railroad. The rest of the movie is cloak-and-dagger juxtaposed with cleavage and dancing. The railroad never gets finished and the Nazis are halted in their conquest of Africa. Considering that this was made at just about the same moment when the Germans were occupying the area, it was remarkably *au courant*. The new songs had music by Romberg, lyrics by Jack Scholl, Serge Walters, and Mario Silva. Good secondary casting with LaRue, Lockhart, Overman, and a beauteous Emerson. Gorgeous color photography and all-around good fun in what is essentially a fairly empty musical other than the Romberg/Hammerstein score.

p, Robert Buckner; d, Robert Florey; w, Buckner (based on the play by Laurence Schwab, Oscar Hammerstein II, Otto Harbach, Frank Mandel, Sigmund Romberg); ph, Bert Glennon (Technicolor); m, Romberg, Heinz Roemheld; ed, Frank Magee; art d, Charles Novi; ch, LeRoy Prinz; m/l, Hammerstein, Scholl, Walters, Silva.

Musical (PR:A MPAA:NR)

DESERT SONG, THE*½ (1953) 110m WB c

Kathryn Grayson *(Margot)*, Gordon MacRae *(Paul Bonnard/El Khobar)*, Steve Cochran *(Capt. Fontaine)*, Raymond Massey *(Yousseff)*, Dick Wesson *(Benjy Kidd)*, Allyn McLerie *(Azuri)*, Ray Collins *(Gen. Birabeau)*, Paul Picerni *(Hassan)*, Frank DeKova *(Mindar)*, William Conrad *(Lachmed)*, Trevor Bardette *(Neri)*, Mark Dana *(Lt. Duvalle)*.

The third and, it is to be hoped, the last version of the creaky old warhorse. First made in 1929 as the opening all-talking, all-singing operetta, then remade in 1943 to incorporate the anti-German sentiment rampant in those wartime days. Let us pray this will put a stop to the use of this very old and, by-now, clichéd story. Gordon MacRae leads the Riffs against dastardly sheik Massey. Grayson is the daughter of general Collins and MacRae wins her love in the guise of El Khobar. Although his name has been changed from Pierre to Paul, the essential character is the same; a weakling who becomes a hero via his Arabian gear. At the end of the film, MacRae kills off his El Khobar character so he and Grayson can marry and MacRae can return to his regular role as an anthropology student, once Massey's in the cold, cold ground. Roland Kibbee, who also co-wrote such winners as THE CRIMSON PIRATE and VERA CRUZ, takes the blame for this screenplay. A very tired story, shot in a very tired fashion, although the singing is above average.

p, Rudi Fehr; d, Bruce Humberstone; w, Roland Kibbee (based on the play by Sigmund Romberg, Laurence Schwab, Oscar Hammerstein II, Frank Mandel, Otto Harbach); ph, Robert Burks (Technicolor); m, Romberg, Max Steiner; ed, William Ziegler; md, Ray Heindorf; art d, Stanley Fleischer; ch, LeRoy Prinz.

Musical (PR:A MPAA:NR)

DESERT TRAIL** (1935) 54m Lone Star/MON bw

John Wayne *(John Scott)*, Mary Kornman *(Anne)*, Paul Fix *(Jim)*, Eddy Chandler *(Kansas Charlie)*, Carmen LaRoux *(Juanita)*, Lafe McKee *(Sheriff Barker)*, Al Ferguson *(Pete)*, Henry Hall *(Banker)*, Frank Ball, Artie Ortego, Lew Meehan, Frank Brownlee, Wally West, Frank Ellis, Dick Dickinson.

Early Wayne vehicle stars the Duke as a star rodeo rider who, along with his best pal and sidekick Chandler, is accused of robbing a bank. The pair take off after the real culprits, Fix and his gang, and bring them to justice. Wayne even finds time to fall in love with Fix's sister, Kornman.

p, Paul Malvern; d, Cullin Lewis; w, Lindsley Parsons; ph, Archie J. Stout; ed, Carl Pierson.

Western **Cas.** (PR:A MPAA:NR)

DESERT VENGEANCE*½ (1931) 62m COL bw

Buck Jones *(Jim Cardew)*, Barbara Bedford *(Anne)*, Douglas Gilmore *(Hugh)*, Al Smith *(McBride)*, Ed Brady *(Beaver)*, Buck Connors, Pee Wee Holmes, Slim Whitaker, Robert Ellis, Bob Fleming, Joe Girard, Barney Bearsley, "Silver."

Jones, not in his customary heroic mold but as leader of an outlaw gang, is bilked by a chiseler while voyaging on a steamship off San Francisco Bay. He traps the swindler's adventuress sister, Bedford, in his mining-town hideout. Jones and Bedford fall in love, of course. A rival gang attacks Jones' stronghold and a lengthy gun battle ensues, leaving only our antihero Jones and his gal alive to ride off to a new life.

p, Sol Lesser; d, Louis King; w, Stuart Anthony (based on a story by Anthony); ph, Ted D. McCord; ed, Ray Snyder.

Western (PR:A MPAA:NR)

DESERT VIGILANTE** (1949) 56m COL bw

Charles Starrett *(Steve Brooks)*, Smiley Burnette *(Himself)*, Peggy Stewart *(Betty Long)*, Tristram Coffin *(Thomas Hadley)*, Mary Newton *(Angel)*, George Chesebro *(Martin)*, Paul Campbell *(Bob Gill)*, Tex Harding *(Jim Gill)*, Jack Ingram *(Sergeant)*, Jimmy Wakely, Ted Mapes, I. Stanford Jolley, The Georgia Crackers.

Starrett, the Durango Kid, stars as a federal agent assigned to stop the illegal flow of silver from Mexico into the U.S. The lawman soon figures out that the local U.S. Attorney, Coffin, is in cahoots with the smugglers. After a few chases and shootouts, Starrett fulfills his mission and rides off. The first film directed by Sears, who would later go on to be one of the most prolific oater directors in the business.

p, Colbert Clark; d, Fred F. Sears; w, Earle Snell (based on a story by Snell); ph, Rex Wimpy; ed, Paul Borosky; art d, Charles Clague; m/l, Burnette, Bob Newman, Jimmy Wakely.

Western (PR:A MPAA:NR)

DESERT WARRIOR*½ (1961 Ital./Span.) 87m Producciones Benito Perojo-Roma Films-Parc/Medallion c (LOS AMANTES DEL DESIERTO; AMANTI DEL DESERTO; AKA: LA FIGLIA DELLO SCEICCO)

Ricardo Montalban *(Prince Said)*, Carmen Sevilla *(Princess Amina)*, Gino Cervi *(Ibrahim)*, Jose Guardiola *(Selim)*, Anna Maria Ferrero, Franca Bettoja, Mariangela Giordano, Manuel Guitian, Domingo Rivas, Manuel Alcon, Arnoldo Foa, Savia Gamal.

Overdone Arabian desert tale starring Montalban as a young prince who flees his kingdom after his father has been assassinated by the evil Guardiola, who installs Cervi as the new sheik. In exile, Montalban organizes a small army with his loyal band of followers and attempts to attain his rightful throne by staging raids on passing caravans to obtain the weapons he needs. Montalban captures Cervi's daughter, Sevilla, in one raid. Eventually, Guardiola kills Cervi and installs himself as sheik, but the populace revolts. Montalban kills Guardiola in a duel, gaining the throne.

p, Benito Perojo; d, Fernando Cerchio, Goffredo Alessandrini, Leon Klimovsky, Gianni Vernuccio, Ricardo Munoz Suay; w, Alfonso Pase, Mariano Ozores (based on a story by Manuel Villegas Lopez); ph, Antonio L. Ballesteros, Mario Damicelli (CinemaScope, Eastmancolor); m, Michel Michelet; ed, Antonio Ramirez; art d, Sigfrido Burman, Francisco R. Asensio, Mario Garbuglia.

Adventure (PR:A MPAA:NR)

DESERTER*** (1934, USSR) 101m Mezhrabpomfilm/Amkino bw

Boris Livanov, *(Karl Renn)*, Tamara Makarova, Vasili Kovrigin, Judith Glizer, A. Chistyakov.

Important Soviet film made by one of the "Big Three" of Russian filmmaking (Eisenstein and Dovzhenko were the other two). It tells the story of a leftist-inspired strike on the docks of Hamburg, Germany, and how Livanov, though devoted to the cause, is sent away to Russia for rest and strengthening of his weak heart. While there, the government grows brutal in its repression of the miners and Livanov, rather than remain safe in the Soviet Union, chooses to go back to Hamburg to fight alongside his comrades. The film is visually rich, with three or four times the number of shots normally found in a film this length, and Pudovkin tried to give the sound the same quality, mincing his soundtrack into almost inaudible chunks in an attempt to bring a visual dialectic (the foundation of the Soviet editing style) to the ears. Audiences then and now are merely confused by the elaborate overlapping and collisions of dialog, crowd noises, and natural sounds. Still worth seeing, though, because subtitles make the dialog clear, and for a few scenes, such as the workers' march through the streets and their clash with police. (In Russian; English subtitles.)

d, Vsevolod Pudovkin; w, Nina Agadzhanova, M. Krasnostavsky, A. Lazaebnikoff; ph, Anatoli Golovnya, Yuli Fogelman; m, Yuri Shaporin; prod d, Sergei Kozlovsky.

Drama (PR:A MPAA:NR)

DESERTER, THE** (1971 Ital./Yugo.) 90m DeLaurentiis/PAR c (LA SPINA DORSALE DEL DIAVOLO)

Bekim Fehmiu *(Capt. Kaleb)*, Richard Crenna *(Major Brown)*, Chuck Connors *(Chaplain)*, Ricardo Montalban *(Natchai)*, Ian Bannen *(Crawford)*, Brandon De Wilde *(Ferguson)*, Slim Pickens *(Tattinger)*, Woody Strode *(Jackson)*, Albert Salmi *(Schmidt)*, Patrick Wayne *(Bill Robinson)*, Fausto Tozzi *(Orozco)*, Mimmo Palmara *(Chief Durango)*, Larry Stewart *(Robinson)*, John Alderson *(O'Toole)*, John Huston *(Gen. Miles)*, Remo D'Angelis *(Mark)*, Gianni Vanicola *(Jeff)*, Lucio Rosato *(Jed)*, Roberto Simmi *(Justin)*, Giancarlo Zampetti *(Indian Prisoner)*, Doc Greaves *(Scott)*.

Cavalry deserter Fehmiu is reinstated to train and lead a "Dirty Dozen" type band of Indian fighters into the heart of Apache territory to remove the savages from their stronghold. As it turns out, the men of the cavalry patrol are the real savages; they wipe out the entire Apache settlement in a lengthy bloodbath. An outstanding cast handles its roles well; they are the only reason to watch this bloody film. Fehmiu is just plain awful. If not, you didn't miss anything. You may remember Fehmiu from THE ADVENTURERS. (English version.)

p, Norman Baer, Ralph Serpe; d, Burt Kennedy; w, Clair Huffaker (based on a story by Stuart J. Byrne, William H. James); ph, Aldo Tonti (Panavision, Technicolor); m, Piero Piccioni; ed, Frank Santillo; prod. d, Mario Chiari; set d, Vincenzo Eusepi; cos, Elio Micheli; makeup, Giuliano Laurenti; spec eff, August Lohman; stunt supervisor, Remo De Angelis.

Western **(PR:O MPAA:GP)**

DESERTER AND THE NOMADS, THE**

(1969, Czech./Ital.) 120m Koliba Film-Ceskoslovensky Film-Ultra Film/Royal c (ZBEHOVIA A PUTNICI; IL DESERTORE E I NOMADI)

Stefan Ladizinsky *(Martin/Russian Captain)*, August Kuban *(Smrt, the Hussar/Death)*, Ferenc Gejza *(Kalman)*, Jana Stehnova *(Bride/Nevesta)*, Helena Grodova *(Lila)*, Alexandra Sekulova *(Mara)*, Vasek Kovarik *(Crippled Christ)*, Frantisek Peto *(Groom)*, Albert Pagac *(Berger)*, Magda Vasaryova *(Peasant)*, Olga Adamcikova, Katarina Tekelova, Olga Vronska, Samuel Adamcik.

Three pacifist tales from Czechoslovakia of varying quality. The first is the best, with Gejza a gypsy who deserts during World War I and returns to his village in time for a wedding. He disguises himself as a woman but is recognized by Hussar Kuban, who chases him down and kills him. Another deserter hiding in the village incites the peasants to revolt, but they are cut down by more Hussars. The massacre is amazing, almost like Peckinpah in its elaborately choreographed carnage, complete with bright red blood spattering on the feathers of white geese while wild gypsy music plays. In the second episode, a band of Russian partisan fighters execute an old man they suspect of being a German spy, then hear that the war is over. Their celebrations are cut short when a German patrol that hasn't heard the news engages them in a bloody skirmish. The last episode has two survivors of nuclear holocaust wandering the bleak terrain looking for other survivors, finding none, then dying. After the terrific start of the first episode, the other two grow increasingly heavy-handed and obvious, but the whole is still worth a look.

p, Moris Ergas; d, Juro Jakubisko; w, Jakubisko, Paolo Rugiero, Karol Sidon, Alberto Liberati, Ladislav Tazky (based on the novel *Zbehove* by Tazky); ph, Jakubisko; m, Stepan Konicek; ed, Maximilian Remen, Alfred Bencic; art d, Ivan Vanicek; cos, Anna Lidakova.

War Drama **(PR:O MPAA:NR)**

DESERTERS*

(1983, Can.) 93m Exile c

Alan Scarfe *(Sgt. Ulysses Hawley)*, Jon Bryden *(Peter)*, Barbara March *(Val)*, Dermot Hennelly *(Noel)*, Ty Haller *(Army Captain)*, Bob Metcalfe, Robin Mossley.

Low-budget drama shot on 16mm and starring Scarfe as a tough-as-nails Army drill instructor who goes after two AWOL trainees who have made a fool of him in front of an officer. He tracks them to the home of a liberal couple (March and Hennelly) who have sheltered the boys and idealized them into antiheroes on the run from the oppressive American government.

p, Tom Braidwood, Jack Darcus; d&w, Darcus; ph, Tony Westman; m, Michael Conway Baker; ed, Darcus; art d, Darcus.

Drama **(PR:C MPAA:NR)**

DESIGN FOR LIVING***

(1933) 90m PAR bw

Fredric March *(Tom Chambers)*, Gary Cooper *(George Curtis)*, Miriam Hopkins *(Gilda Farrell)*, Edward Everett Horton *(Max Plunkett)*, Franklin Pangborn *(Mr. Douglas)*, Isabel Jewell *(Lisping Stenographer)*, Harry Dunkminson *(Mr. Egelbauer)*, Helena Phillips *(Mrs. Egelbauer)*, James Donlin *(Fat Man)*, Vernon Steele, Thomas Braidon *(Managers)*, Jane Darwell *(Housekeeper)*, Armand Kaliz *(Mr. Burton)*, Adrienne D'Ambricourt *(Cafe Proprietress)*, Wyndham Standing *(Max's Butler)*, Nora Cecil *(Tom's Secretary)*, Grace Hayle *(Woman on Staircase)*, Olaf Hytten *(Englishman at Train)*, Mary Gordon *(Theatre Chambermaid)*, Lionel Belmore, Charles K. French *(Theatre Patrons)*, Rolfe Sedan *(Bed Salesman)*, Mathilde Comont *(Heavy Woman)*.

Though this film version of the literate, witty play by Noel Coward is tame by comparison, the "Lubitsch Touch" is very much in evidence. March, an apprentice playwright and Cooper, a young painter, meet commercial artist Hopkins on a Paris-bound train, immediately falling in love with her. When she can't decide which one she loves, she creates a "design for living," one where a *menage a trois* situation takes place. It's all platonic but March and Cooper begin to show jealousies that lead to nasty confrontations. Hopkins finally gets fed up and marries stuffed shirt Horton, going to NYC with him to settle down. But she is bored to tears within a year and welcomes her two friends who show up at one of Horton's insufferable parties. They literally destroy the place and Hopkins, desperate to rejoin the living, goes back to Paris with March and Cooper on either arm. The Hays Office, which had been established to clean up Hollywood morals, considered the Coward play too risque. Director Lubitsch and scriptwriter Hecht were told to tone down the sexual innuendoes and keep the trio's relationship obscure. As a result the film loses much but the performances of the principals is faultless and makes the effort better than average. This had been an Alfred Lunt and Lynn Fontaine vehicle on the stage where Coward himself played the other man. Hecht, the *enfant terrible* of Hollywood, first bristled when he heard the Hays Office decree. Then he shrugged and completely re-wrote Coward's so-called "amoral" dialog, retaining only one line from the original work: "For the good of our immortal souls!" Always the literary elf, Hecht thought it funny to use some of Coward's lines from other plays, "The Vortex" and "Hay Fever," which he worked into the script. Though Coward would appear in the lead of the Hecht-MacArthur film THE SCOUNDREL, Hecht never liked Coward, thought his humor too foreign to the earthy likes of Americans, and that the British playwright was too precious. Some of Hecht's lines tip-toed up to the Hays Office fences and bumped against them: "I haven't got a clean shirt to my name," says Cooper. Replies March: "A clean shirt? What's up? A romance?" Cooper snickers: "I'm not talking pyjamas. Just a clean shirt." Lubitsch worked with Hecht on the script and approved of almost every line, much to the frustration of Hollywood's most successful screenwriter. Hecht later whimsically wrote that "in writing with Mr. Lubitsch on DESIGN FOR LIVING, I was confused by what seemed to be at first glance a sort of manic-depressive psychosis on its upswing. Mr. Lubitsch, when he creates those delicate touches for which he is notorious, has a way of flinging himself around the room like an old-fashioned fancy roller skater. He pirouettes, leaps, claps his ankles together in mid air, screams at the top of his voice, and bursts into tears if contradicted." At one point when Hecht was reading some of his lines to the director, Lubitsch stopped him, asking: "You think that's good?" "Yes, I do," replied Hecht. Said Lubitsch with disgust: "That's the kind of suggestion people send me in the mail."

p&d, Ernst Lubitsch; w, Ben Hecht (based on the play by Noel Coward); ph, Victor Milner; m, Nathaniel Finston; ed, Francis Marsh; art d, Hans Dreier; cos, Travis Banton.

Comedy/Romance **(PR:A MPAA:NR)**

DESIGN FOR LOVING**

(1962, Brit.) 68m Danziger/COL bw

June Thorburn *(Barbara Winters)*, Pete Murray *(Lord Stanford)*, Soraya Rafat *(Irene)*, James Maxwell *(Joe)*, June Cunningham *(Alice)*, Prudence Hyman *(Lady Bayliss)*, Michael Balfour *(Bernie)*, Edward Palmer *(Graves)*, Humphrey Lestocq *(Manager)*, Mary Malcolm *(Commere)*.

Fashion executive Thorburn hires an artistic beatnik to be her chief designer. Expected conflict of values fails to produce much excitement, comic or otherwise.

p, John Ingram; d, Godfrey Grayson; w, Mark Grantham.

Comedy **(PR:A MPAA:NR)**

DESIGN FOR MURDER**

(1940, Brit.) 60m World bw (GB: TRUNK CRIME)

Manning Whiley *(Bentley)*, Barbara Everest *(Ursula)*, Michael Drake *(Grierson)*, Thorley Walters *(Frazier)*, Hay Petrie *(Old Dan)*, Eileen Bennett *(Eve)*, Lewis Stringer *(Hearty)*, Ian Fulton, Tom Gill, Geoffrey Gabriel.

Spooky little suspense film starring Whiley as a young man who has been so tormented to the point of madness his whole life that he finally snaps and plans to murder Drake, a fellow student who has been harassing him. Whiley drugs his victim and puts his body in a trunk. From there, the plan was to take the trunk out to the country and dump it in a deep pit. Unfortunately for Whiley, the plan goes wrong when Drake wakes from the drug too early, causing Whiley's capture and subsequent confession.

p, John Boulting; d, Roy Boulting; w, Francis Miller (based on the play by Edward Percy and Reginald Denham); ph, Wilkie Cooper, Arthur Elvin; ed, Clifton Boote.

Suspense/Crime **(PR:C MPAA:NR)**

DESIGN FOR SCANDAL***

(1941) 82m MGM bw

Rosalind Russell *(Cornelia Porter)*, Walter Pidgeon *(Jeff Sherman)*, Edward Arnold *(Judson M. Blair)*, Vera Vague *(Jane Porter)*, Lee Bowman *(Walter Caldwell)*, Jean Rogers *(Dotty)*, Donald Meek *(Mr. Wade)*, Guy Kibbee *(Judge Graham)*, Mary Beth Hughes *(Adele Blair)*, Bobby Larson *(Freddie)*, Leon Belasco *(Alexander Raoul)*, Charles Coleman *(Wilton)*, Thurston Hall *(Northcott)*, Edgar Dearing *(Joe, the Foreman)*, Eddie Dunn *(Eddie Smith)*, George Magrill, John Butler *(Miners)*, John Dilson *(Court Clerk)*, Dick Bartell, Robert Emmett Keane *(Aides)*, Josephine Whittell *(Woman)*, Anne Revere *(Nettie, the Maid)*, Mitchell Ingraham *(Storekeeper)*, Ed Thomas *(Steward)*, Anne O'Neal *(Travel Bureau Woman)*, Milton Kibbee *(Court Clerk)*, Syd Saylor *(Taxi Driver)*, Dorothy Morris, Marjorie "Babe" Kane, Marjorie Deanne, Ruth Alder *(Telephone Operators)*, Charlotte Wynkers *(Thelma, the Secretary)*, Jessie Arnold *(Miner's Wife)*.

Fun screwball comedy starring Pidgeon as an intrepid reporter who is assigned to smear lady judge Russell after she has handed down a hefty alimony payment to his boss, Arnold. Seeking to the get the goods on her and have her disbarred, Pidgeon (who was given an unlimited expense account) follows the judge to her home in Cape Cod, where he falls in love with her in spite of himself. Russell discovers the plot to discredit her and hauls both Pidgeon and Arnold into court, where the reporter's love for her is revealed during testimony. It's all very silly, but great fun, handled by a skillful cast of players, including Rogers as a flippant manicurist with a wisecracking tongue.

p, John W. Considine, Jr.; d, Norman Taurog; w, Lionel Houser; ph, Leonard Smith, William Daniels; m, Franz Waxman; ed, Elmo Veron; art d, Cedric Gibbons; set d, Edwin B. Willis.

Comedy/Romance **(PR:A MPAA:NR)**

DESIGNING WOMAN***½

(1957) 117m MGM c

Gregory Peck *(Mike Hagen)*, Lauren Bacall *(Marilla Hagen)*, Dolores Gray *(Lori Shannon)*, Sam Levene *(Ned Hammerstein)*, Tom Helmore *(Zachary Wilde)*, Mickey Shaughnessy *(Maxie Stultz)*, Jesse White *(Charlie Arneg)*, Chuck Connors *(Johnnie "O")*, Edward Platt *(Marin J. Daylor)*, Alvy Moore *(Luke Coslow)*, Carol Veazie *(Gwen)*, Jack Cole *(Randy Owen)*.

Vincente Minnelli, George Wells and a heck of a supporting cast have done the impossible; they've made Peck somewhat funny. The great stone face is a sports reporter who has written a hard-hitting series of articles that have exposed the underside of the world of boxing. He's newly married to Bacall, a clothes designer who lives in a chic Upper East Side flat witha view that goes on forever. Peck gives up his messy Village digs (this character was sort of a precursor to Oscar Madison in THE ODD COUPLE: a sloppy sportwriter). Basically a fish-out-of-water story, both Bacall and Peck are uncomfortable with one another's friends. He hangs about with the jock strap set and she's involved with the silk and satin group. They are trying to make this unusual marriage work but it's complicated by the arrival of his former girl friend, Gray, and her former boy friend, Helmore, who is producing the show for which she is designing the clothes. Villains are after Peck for what he's written and Shaughnessy does a bang-up job as a punchy ex-pug who is Peck's bodyguard. Excellent casting of White as a fink, Levene as a sports editor, and Connors as a mobster. The very funny script took the Oscar for best original screenplay in 1957. This was Dore Schary's last film for MGM before getting the Golden Gate from management ("Golden" because he got a huge settlement for resigning). It was a unique movie for him in that it was one of his rare pictures that was pure entertainment with no messages, no points to make, and nothing more than a rollicking 117 minutes of fun. Bacall was excellent and made Peck look good. She was under a great personal strain at the time because Bogart was dying as the film was being made and it must have been hell to go from his side to the set. Bacall, born Betty Joan Perske, took her name from her mother's maiden name, Bacal, which means 'wine glass' in Roumanian, the same as Weinstein (mother's real name) in German.

p, Dore Schary; d, Vincente Minnelli; w, George Wells (based on a suggestion by Helen Rose); ph, John Alton (CinemaScope/Metrocolor); m, Andre Previn; ed, Adrienne Fazan; cos, Helen Rose; ch, Jack Cole.

Comedy   (PR:A MPAA:NR)

DESIGNING WOMEN*½
                (1934, Brit.) 71m Sound City/MGM bw (AKA: HOUSE OF CARDS)
Stewart Rome (Travers), Valerie Taylor (Diana Dent), Tyrell Davis (Hildebrand Way), D.A. Clarke-Smith (Bowsfield), Cyril Gardner (Alan Dent), Kathleen Kelly (Molly), Edgar Driver (Green).

When her wastrel husband dies, Taylor finds happiness and success in the fashion industry. Tiresome drawing room drama for the feminine audience.

p, Norman Loudon; d, Ivar Campbell; w, N.W. Baring-Pemberton (based on a story by George Robinson).

Drama   (PR:A MPAA:NR)

DESIRABLE**½
                                                        (1934) 70m WB bw
Jean Muir (Lois Johnson), George Brent (Stuart McAllister), Verree Teasdale (Helen Walbridge), John Halliday (Austin Stevens), Charles Starrett (Russell Gray), Russell Hopton (Chet), Virginia Hammond (Mrs. Gray), Joan Wheeler (Barbara), Catherine Sheldon (Volunteer Worker), Harry Tyler (Boxoffice Man), Gladys Gale (Large Woman), Edward Keane (Playgoer), Arthur Treacher (Butler), George Humbert (Mario, the Maitre d'), Jim Miller (Elevator Man), Pauline True (Secretary), Jane Darwell, Maude Turner Gordon (Dowagers), Bill Elliot, Dennis O'Keefe (Party Guests), Cornelius Keefe (Eager Young Man), Helene Millard (Blonde), Georgia Cooper (Jennie), Theresa Harris (Maid), Arthur Aylesworth (Eph), Barbara Leonard (Margaret), Doris Atkinson (Girl).

A rivalry between mother and daughter is the subject matter of this drama set in the acting world. Teasdale plays a very vain, selfish, and successful actress who keeps her daughter in a boarding school so she doesn't have to deal with the reality of having a 19-year-old child. Muir is the daughter who has been shunned by her mother since birth, and is now too old and independent to be kept boarded away just so her mother can feel young. She travels to New York to visit her mother and is accidentally confronted by one of Teasdale's greatest admirers, Brent, who, upon seeing the young woman, shifts his attentions to her. Teasdale, mainly from jealousy, tries to prevent her daughter and Brent from starting a romance. It's no use; love wins in the end as Brent weds young, innocent Muir.

p, Edward Chodorov; d, Archie Mayo; w, Mary McCall, Jr. (based on a story by McCall, Jr.); ph, Ernest Haller; ed, Thomas Pratt; art d, John Hughes.

Drama   (PR:A MPAA:NR)

DESIRE****
                                                        (1936) 89m PAR bw
Marlene Dietrich (Madeleine de Beaupre), Gary Cooper (Tom Bradley), John Halliday (Carlos Margoli), William Frawley (Mr. Gibson), Ernest Cossart (Aristide Duval), Akim Tamiroff (Police Official), Alan Mowbray (Dr. Edouard Pauquet), Zeffie Tilbury (Aunt Olga), Enrique Acosta (Pedro), Stanley Andrews (Customs Inspector), Harry Depp (Clerk), Marc Lawrence (Valet), Henry Antrim (Chauffeur), Armand Kaliz (Jewelry Clerk), Gaston Glass (Jewelry Clerk), Albert Pollet (French Policeman), George Davis (Garage Man), Constant Franke (Border Official), Robert O'Connor (Customs Official), Stanley Andrews (Customs Inspector), Rafael Blanco (Haywagon Driver), Alden [Stephen] Chase (Hotel Clerk), Tony Merlo (Waiter), Anna Delinsky (Servant), Alice Feliz (Pepi), George Mac Quarrie (Clerk with Gun), Isabel La Mal (Nurse), Oliver Eckhardt, Blanche Craig (Couple), Rollo Lloyd (Clerk in Mayor's Office), Alfonso Pedrosa (Oxcart Driver).

Superb romance story has Dietrich as a sophisticated jewel thief who subtly tricks gem dealer Cossart out of a priceless string of pearls and flees Paris after implicating stuffy psychiatrist Mowbray. She drives wildly toward the Spanish border and almost runs another car off the road, one driven by Cooper, a young American engineer taking his first vacation in years. At the border Dietrich becomes nervous when she sees guards inspecting a woman's handbag. She spots Cooper waiting in line and drops the necklace into his coat pocket. He is cleared by Spanish customs and drives off, Dietrich in quick pursuit after officials clear her. She passes Cooper's car several times, attempting to flirt with him but the shy American doesn't respond. Several miles ahead of Cooper's car, Dietrich stops her auto and takes a hammer to the engine. Cooper stops to help out, looks at the damage and then takes the lady in distress with him to the resort town of San Sebastian. She later entices him to the country estate of her confederate, "Prince Margoli" (Halliday). By this time Cooper is hopelessly in love with the ravishing Dietrich and he also finds the pearls, knowing what Dietrich and Halliday are after. But what the American doesn't know is that Dietrich has fallen in love with him. Another member of the jewel robbery ring, Tilbury, arrives, telling her to go to Madrid where the pearls will bring a hefty price. Dietrich confesses her love for Cooper but Tilbury tells her that marriage is not for her, that she has a tarnished past that will intrude upon any relationship. Dietrich lies to Cooper, telling him that she's married. To earn his total rejection she admits that she's a thief. But Cooper will

not give her up. When he learns that she's not married, Cooper convinces her to return the pearls. Both go to Paris with the necklace, giving it back to Cossart. Absolved, Dietrich marries Cooper and leaves for Detroit to settle down. DESIRE, though oddly titled (the original title was THE PEARL NECKLACE), was an enormous success with the public and is one of the most stylishly produced films of the 1930s. It is bathed in hot light; the sets, costumes, decor shimmer with white light. Borzage, who helmed the silent classic SEVENTH HEAVEN, carried out the deft production plans of the ever careful Lubitsch who acted as producer for this wonderful film. The decade of the 1930s produced generally female films and this one is no exception. Dietrich dominates the production but, unlike her appearances in earlier Josef von Sternberg films, her posture is not exotic; she is down-to-earth but still sophisticated. This was her first American film without von Sternberg and she blossomed beyond the still-life that that stylist had fashioned. It was her second film with Cooper. Both had appeared in her first American film, MOROCCO, directed by von Sternberg in 1930. After appearing in that film Cooper vowed he would never do another film with Dietrich, not because of the actress but because of von Sternberg who had a stranglehold on her career. But he was only too glad to work with her under the Lubitsch-Borzage helmsmanship. Again, Lubitsch had to sidestep the Production Code of the censoring Hays Office but he was an old hand at getting his films into distribution while implying what could not be said. In BLUEBEARD'S EIGHTH WIFE Lubitsch made sure his leading players were married so their sexual antics were acceptable. In TROUBLE IN PARADISE his leads are jewel thieves who escape with the loot at the end and haven't even gone to the altar but they have triumphed over greater evils to appear just. DESIRE was the film that made Dietrich into an American film star and it remains one of her finest films, one that stands viewing well, again and again. (Dietrich sings one song, "Awake In A Dream.")

p, Ernst Lubitsch; d, Frank Borzage; w, Edwin Justus Mayer, Waldemar Young, Samuel Hoffenstein (based on an original story by Hans Szekeley and R.A. Stemmle); ph, Charles Lang, Victor Milner; m, Frederick Hollander; ed, William Shea; art d, Hans Dreier, Robert Usher; cos, Travis Banton; m/l, Hollander, Leo Robin.

Romance   (PR:A MPAA:NR)

DESIRE IN THE DUST**½
                                                        (1960) 102m FOX bw
Raymond Burr (Col. Ben Marquand), Martha Hyer (Melinda Marquand), Joan Bennett (Mrs. Marquand), Ken Scott (Lonnie Wilson), Brett Halsey (Dr. Ned Thomas), Edward Binns (Luke Connett), Jack Ging (Peter Marquand), Anne Helm (Cass Wilson), Maggie Mahoney (Maude Wilson), Douglas Fowley (Zuba Wilson), Kelly Thordsen (Sheriff Wheaton), Rex Ingram (Burt Crane), Irene Ryan (Nora Finney), Paul Baxley (Thurman Case), Robert Earle (Virgil), Patricia Snow (Nellie), Elemore Morgan (Conductor), Audrey Moore (Frank), Joseph Sidney Felps (Roy), Joe Paul Steiner (Deputy).

After the success of such seamy, Faulkner-based films as THE LONG HOT SUMMER (1958), and THE SOUND AND THE FURY (1959), Fox produced this film which emulates the sex, murder, deceit, and seediness of the earlier films, but has none of the depth of the Faulkner-based material. Scott plays a lowly farmer who returns to his home town after having served a six-year sentence in a chain gang for a crime he didn't commit. He goes to the home of wealthy politician Burr to collect his due. It seems that Scott was having an affair with Burr's daughter Hyer six years ago, and when Hyer accidentally killed her 4-year-old brother, Burr talked Scott into taking the rap for her. He was promised that he would be taken care of, and that Hyer would be waiting for him when he got out. In the meantime, Burr's wife, Bennett, has gone insane since witnessing the accident, and Hyer has married her mother's doctor, Halsey. Scott intends to collect his debt, and he does so for one night, but soon the family leaves him in the lurch and kicks him out. Scott then exposes the whole plot, destroying Burr's political career and leaving father and daughter to themselves. (There are strong suggestions of incest between them.) The drama is labored and overblown, but the performances do lend some credibility to the material. Outstanding black and white cinematography by Lucien Ballard.

p&d, William F. Claxton; w, Charles Lang (based on the novel by Harry Whittington), ph, Lucien Ballard (CinemaScope); m, Paul Dunlap; ed, Richard Farrell; art d, Ernst Fegte, John Mansbridge; makeup, John Sylvester.

Drama   (PR:C MPAA:NR)

DESIRE ME**
                                                        (1947) 90m MGM bw
Greer Garson (Marise Aubert), Robert Mitchum (Paul Aubert), Richard Hart (Jean Renaud), Morris Ankrum (Martin), George Zucco (Father Donnard), Cecil Humphreys (Dr. Andre Leclair), David Hoffman (Postman), Florence Bates (Mrs. Lannie ["Joo-Lou"]), Max Willenz (Dr. Poulin), Clinton Sundberg (Saleman), Tony Carson (Youth), Mitchell Lewis (Old Man), Fernanda Eliscu (Old Woman), Sid D'Albrook (Assistant), David Leonard (Cobbler), Edward Keane (Baker), Belle Mitchell (Baker's Wife), Hans Schumm, Frederic Brunn (German Voices), John Maxwell Hayes (Church Dignitary), Lew Mason (Sailor), Josephine Victor (Woman), Hans Tanzler (German Guard), Maurice Tauzin (Boy), Stanley Andrews (Emile), Harry Woods (Joseph), Earle Hodgins (Barker), Albert Petit (Tinsel Wreath Vendor), Jack and Iris Shafton (Puppet Operators), Tom Plank (Clown), Gil Perkins (Soldier), Pert LeBaron (Bear Trainer), Sam Ash (Master of Ceremonies).

Garson stars as a woman so consumed by guilt that she must visit a psychiatrist to explain why she cannot live with her husband. In flashback we see her husband, Mitchum, go off to war. Garson is deeply in love with him and remains faithful to him, even after official word of his death arrives. Months later, Hart arrives on her doorstep. Hart has been a close friend of Mitchum's in the prison camp in which they both were held, and they had escaped together. Mitchum was gunned down, allowing Hart to make good his getaway. Hart and Garson sense the deep loneliness in each other; she allows him to stay, and they soon fall in love. Things go along smoothly until one day Hart is shocked to find a letter from Mitchum, who is still alive. He intercepts the letter, and encourages Garson to sell her home and business so that they can both leave the area and start a new life. But Mitchum shows up before they leave, and Garson is struck with massive guilt over having betrayed her husband. Mitchum and Hart struggle in a fight near a cliff and Hart is killed when he tumbles over the edge. Mitchum's love for his wife is strong enough for him to forgive her and start anew, but she is so ashamed that she cannot live with him. We return to the present, where a psychiatrist encourages Garson to return to her husband. DESIRE ME was one of the only major MGM releases that didn't carry a directing credit. Remade from a German film, HOMECOMING (1928), DESIRE ME went through many stars (Hart was slated for the lead, then Robert Montgomery, and finally Mitchum) and directors (George Cukor began shooting, Mervyn LeRoy finished, neither wanted credit) before it was released after sitting in the MGM vaults for 18 months. The resulting film is not awful, just muddled with an overly complex structure of flashbacks within flashbacks that tend to confuse the viewer.

p, Arthur Hornblow, Jr.; d, none credited (George Cukor, Mervyn LeRoy); w, Marguerite Roberts, Zoe Akins (based on the novel *Karl and Annath* and the play "Karl and Anna" by Leonhard Frank, adapted by Casey Robinson); ph, Joseph Ruttenberg; m, Herbert Stothart; ed, Joseph Dervin; art d, Cedric Gibbons, Uric McCleary.

Drama (PR:A MPAA:NR)

DESIRE, THE INTERIOR LIFE**

(1980, Ital./Ger.) 105m Cinemaster c (DESIDERIA, LA VITA INTERIORE)

Rosana Marra *(First Desideria)*, Lara Wendel *(Desideria)*, Stefani Sandrelli *(Viola)*, Klaus Lowitsch *(Administrator)*, Vittorio Mezzogiorno *(Eros Occhipinti)*.

Adaptation of Alberto Moravia's *The Inner Life* sees Marra as the fat, ugly-duckling daughter of glamourous, wealthy Sandrelli, who pays no attention whatsoever to her child. Tensions build between the two until, one night, Marra catches her mother in bed with Lowitsch and the maid. Sandrelli is outraged by the intrusion and tells Marra that she was purchased from a prostitute because Sandrelli could not have children of her own. Marra attempts suicide, but ends up hospitalized and returns slim, sexy, and beautiful (now played by Wendel), seeking to destroy her evil mother by using both their sexualities against her. She schemes with a police informant, Mezzogiorno, to kidnap her mother, but the plan backfires and her accomplice is killed. Themes of sick sex (including mother/daughter incest) and vague psychological motivations muddle a pair of fine performances by Marra and Wendel as two versions of the same person.

p, Galliano Juso; d, Gianni Barcelloni; w, Enzo Ungari, Barcelloni (based on a novel by Alberto Moravia); ph, Claudio Cirillo (Eastmancolor); m, Pino Donaggio; ed, Daniele Alabiso; art d, Ferdinando Giovanoni.

Drama (PR:O MPAA:NR)

DESIRE UNDER THE ELMS*   (1958) 111m PAR bw

Sophia Loren *(Anna Cabot)*, Anthony Perkins *(Eben Cabot)*, Burl Ives *(Ephraim Cabot)*, Frank Overton *(Simeon Cabot)*, Pernell Roberts *(Peter Cabot)*, Rebecca Welles *(Lucinda)*, Jean Willes *(Florence)*, Anne Seymour *(Eben's Mother)*, Roy Fant *(Fiddler)*.

O'Neill's sultry classic based on the Greek tragedy "Oedipus," receives a brutal, almost contemptuous approach under the heavy-handed direction of Mann and a turgid script by Irwin Shaw, a much better novelist than a writer of screenplays. Ives is the cold-eyed patriarch of a suppressed New England family, circa 1840, who takes on a new wife, 20-year-old Loren, so red-hot she sizzles the screen. She is a greedy, sluttish immigrant who will do anything to gain property and makes a bargain with Ives. She will sire a son for Ives if he will wed her and will her his farm. He agrees, but it is Perkins, lusting after the harlot, who is the father of the baby Loren produces. Ives, ever the gimlet-eyed braggart, announces his deal with Loren at a celebration for the infant and Perkins, full of rage, departs. Loren, her mind warped, attempts to show her love for him by smothering the child to death. When Ives learns the truth, he disowns his son. Perkins returns, penitent, asking Loren's forgiveness for deserting her. They meekly surrender to the sheriff to await justice. The film is basically a disgrace and a great disservice to O'Neill's complex and arresting play, dwelling as it does on the beauteous, bountiful body of Loren. Mann and Shaw abandon almost completely the intricate interplay between the Perkins and Ives characters, centering attention on Loren in her American film debut which was a disaster. Her command of English is almost non-existent; her accent is so thick that the viewer will understand one word in ten. She has no style, grace or basic acting ability (which was to be the case with most of her films, with the odd exception of TWO WOMEN where she was really enacting incidents from her own life). She was wholly unsuitable for her role which undoubtedly came about through the constant pressure by Italian producer Carlo Ponti, her husband. Perkins renders an acceptable if neurotic performance and Ives is just doing his "Big Daddy" role all over again, but with a New England accent.

p, Don Hartman; d, Delbert Mann; w, Irwin Shaw (based on the play by Eugene O'Neill); ph, Daniel Fapp; m, Elmer Berstein; ed, George Boemler; art d, Hal Pereira, Joseph Macmillan Johnson.

Drama (PR:O MPAA:NR)

DESIREE***   (1954) 110m FOX c

Marlon Brando *(Napoleon Bonaparte)*, Jean Simmons *(Desiree Clary)*, Merle Oberon *(Josephine)*, Michael Rennie *(Bernadotte)*, Cameron Mitchell *(Joseph Bonaparte)*, Elizabeth Sellars *(Julie)*, Charlotte Austin *(Paulette)*, Cathleen Nesbitt *(Mme. Bonaparte)*, Evelyn Varden *(Marie)*, Isobel Elsom *(Madame Clary)*, John Hoyt *(Talleyrand)*, Alan Napier *(Despereaux)*, Nicolas Koster *(Oscar)*, Richard Deacon *(Etienne)*, Edith Evanson *(Queen Hedwig)*, Carolyn Jones *(Mme. Tallien)*, Sam Gilman *(Fouche)*, Larry Craine *(Louis Bonaparte)*, Judy Lester *(Caroline*

Bonaparte), Richard Van Cleemput *(Lucien Bonaparte)*, Florence Dublin *(Eliza Bonaparte)*, Louis Borell *(Baron Morner)*, Peter Bourne *(Count Brahe)*, Dorothy Neumann *(Queen Sofia)*, David Leonard *(Barras)*, Siw Paulsson *(Princess Sofia)*, Lester Mathews *(Caulaincourt)*, Gene Roth *(Von Essen)*, Colin Kenny *(General Becker)*, Leonard George *(Pope Pius VII)*, Richard Garrick *(Count Reynaud)*, Violet Rensing *(Marie Louise)*, Bert Stevens *(Man at Chaumiers)*, George Brand *(Servant)*, Kay Kuter *(Lacky)*, Sven Hugo Borg *(Aide)*, Jac George *(Piano Teacher)*, Jack Mather *(Sergeant)*, J. Ellis *(Swedish Instructor)*, Harry Carter *(Coachman)*, Marina Koshetz *(Singer)*, A. Cameron Grant *(Montel)*.

A lavish but disappointing period piece, DESIREE is a vehicle for Simmons and constitutes an historical soap opera on a grand scale, its most significant contribution being the appearance of Brando in a role he did not want to play. Simmons is the daughter of a wealthy Marseilles merchant who meets an impoverished General Bonaparte, Brando, who later asks for her hand in marriage but is laughed at because he is a man without money or influence, although he claims he will have a sterling future. He is later arrested in the silk store owned by Simmons' father. Before being dragged off, Brando asks Simmons to contact his family. She does, but only Nappy's mother, Nesbitt, seems concerned about him. Brando returns once more to tell Simmons he has been pardoned for alleged crimes against the state and must now hunt down royalists, a task which disgusts him. He is an artillery officer and he vows to return to Paris and convince the revolutionaries to put him in command of the Italian campaign. He doesn't return but his fame reaches Simmons' ears. He is now a great hero, leader of France, and she travels to Paris to see him. Here she sees Oberon, the illustrious Josephine, who is about to marry Brando. In tears, her heart broken, Simmons races to a bridge spanning the Seine, intending to commit suicide. But Rennie, Count Bernadotte, who has witnessed her shock at seeing Brando's new love, goes after her and convinces her not to jump. He asks to see her later but she rebuffs him. Simmons, visiting relatives in Rome, begins recording Brando's military feats as he conquers one country after another. (It is through her diary entries that most of the film's story is conveyed.) She later meets Rennie and becomes his wife, moving to Sweden. Rennie, who has broken with Brando over his dictatorial ways, opposes him after accepting the crown of Sweden. He advises the Russians who defeat the French legions and destroy the Grand Army. Simmons by then is living a reclusive life in Paris, the cold weather and aloof customs of Sweden driving her to warmer climes. Brando, his fortunes reversed, goes to Simmons and asks her to write a letter to her husband Rennie, enlisting his aid for his cause. Rennie refuses and Brando's armies are ultimately defeated and he is driven into exile on Elba. He escapes and raises a new army, marching on Paris. Simmons goes to his headquarters at Malmaison and begs that he give up his drive for power. Brando yields to her persuasion and surrenders his sword, going into permanent exile on St. Helena, never to return to power. DESIREE is, of course, nothing more than an entertaining romance story, its basis in fact nonexistent. No soft-skinned woman ever turned back Bonaparte's lust for power, only the bayonets of British and Belgian troops. Brando took his part reluctantly. He had originally agreed to do THE EGYPTIAN but backed out on the project, later enacted feebly by Edmund Purdom. In short he owed Fox a film and finally met his contractual obligations to the studio. His performance is the only standout in this costume soaper.

p, Julian Blaustein; d, Henry Koster; w, Daniel Taradash (based on the novel by Annemarie Selinko); ph, Milton Krasner (CinemaScope, DeLuxe Color); m, Alex North; ed, William Reynolds; art d, Lyle Wheeler, Leland Fuller; ch, Stephen Papich.

Historical Romance (PR:A MPAA:NR)

DESK SET***   (1957) 103m FOX bw (GB: HIS OTHER WOMAN)

Spencer Tracy *(Richard Sumner)*, Katharine Hepburn *(Bunny Watson)*, Gig Young *(Mike Cutler)*, Joan Blondell *(Peg Costello)*, Dina Merrill *(Sylvia)*, Sue Randall *(Ruthie)*, Neva Patterson *(Miss Warringer)*, Harry Ellerbee *(Smithers)*, Nicholas Joy *(Azae)*, Diane Jergens *(Alice)*, Merry Anders *(Cathy)*, Ida Moore *(Old Lady)*, Rachel Stephens *(Receptionist)*, Sammy Ogg *(Kenny)*, King Mojave, Charles Heard, Harry Evans, Hal Taggart, Jack M. Lee, Bill Duray *(Board Members)*, Dick Gardner *(Fred)*, Renny McEvoy *(Man)*, Jesslyn Fax *(Mrs. Hewitt)*, Shirley Mitchell *(Myra Smithers)*.

An otherwise dull story is turned on its head and made amusing, often hilarious, by the superb talents of Tracy and Hepburn. He is an efficiency expert and she a research expert for a TV network, heading a small, overworked staff. Hepburn has a total recall memory as do her assistants, Blondell, Merrill and others, specializing in certain subjects. Tracy has a machine he has invented which he calls "Emerac" or "Emmy" for short, an electronic brain that can give instant answers on anything and everything. Hepburn and her ladies begin to compete with "Emmy," fearing the machine will put them out of their jobs. Moreover, Tracy's constant contact with Hepburn prompts Young, a reluctant suitor of more than seven years, to propose to Kate. Tracy, however, is too smart for Young. He not only proves that "Emmy" will help the research staff but make their lives easier. In the process he wins Hepburn's heart. DESK SET is a tame little story but the sharp lines of the principals are delivered with polish and vigor. The Tracy-Hepburn combination was unbeatable and their affection for each other permeates the screen. Blondell, as the wise-cracking assistant, is fast and funny with some great lines; at one point she ridicules Hepburn's long-standing courtship with Young, telling her: "You're like an old coat hanging in the closet. Every time he opens the door, there you are."

p, Henry Ephron; d, Walter Lang; w, Phoebe and Henry Ephron (based on the play by William Marchant); ph, Leon Shamroy (CinemaScope, DeLuxe Color); m, Cyril J. Mockridge; ed, Robert Simpson; md, Lionel Newman; art d, Lyle Wheeler, Maurice Randsford; set d, Walter M. Scott, Paul S. Fox; cos, Charles Le Maire; spec eff, Ray Kellogg; makeup, Ben Nye.

Comedy/Romance (PR:A MPAA:NR)

DESPAIR**½

(1978, Ger.) 119m Bavaria Atelier-SFP-Geria/Swan Diffusion c

Dirk Bogarde (Hermann Herman), Andrea Ferreol (Lydia Herman), Volker Spengler (Ardalion), Klaus Lowitsch (Felix Weber), Alexander Allerson (Mayer), Bernhard Wicki (Orlovius), Peter Kern (Muller), Gottfried John (Perebrodov), Roger Fritz (Inspector Braun), Adrian Hoven (Inspector Schelling), Hark Bohm (Doctor), Voli Geiler (Madam), Hans Zander (Muller's Brother), Y Sa Lo (Elsie), Liselotte Eder (Secretary), Armin Meier (Worker in Herman's Factory/Twins in Film-Within-Film), Gitti Djamal (Woman in Pension), Ingrid Caven (Hotel Receptionist), Isolde Barth.

Said the director of this film: "The reason I made DESPAIR comes from the awareness that in everyone's life there comes a point where not only the mind but the body, too, understands that it's over. I want to go on with my life, but there will be no new feelings or experiences for me. At this point people start to rearrange their lives." Set in Berlin in the 1930s, Bogarde plays Hermann Herman, the owner of a chocolate factory, who is unhappy with the sameness of his life. One day he meets a man he is convinced is his double, though he looks nothing like him, and decides to exchange identities. He files an insurance claim for his own death and meets his wife in Switzerland. The authorities catch up with him and, finding him insane, arrest him. This was Fassbinder's 32nd film in only 31 years (and his first in English). A better idea than a film, as with much of Fassbinder's work, it closely resembles his earlier SATAN'S BREW and Antonioni's THE PASSENGER. As usual, it was made with the same "family" of cast and crew as in SATAN'S BREW, the brilliant Bogarde being the exception.

p, Peter Marthesheimer; d, Rainer Werner Fassbinder; w, Tom Stoppard (based on a novel by Vladimir Nabokov); ph, Michael Ballhaus (Eastmancolor); m, Peer Raben; ed, Juliane Lorenz, Franz Walsch; art d, Rolf Zehetbauer.

Drama   Cas.   (PR:O MPAA:NR)

DESPERADO, THE**

(1954) 79m AA bw

Wayne Morris (Sam Garrett), James J. Lydon (Tall Cameron), Beverly Garland (Lauren Bannerman), Rayford Barnes (Ray Novack), Dabbs Greer (Jim Langley), Lee Van Cleef (Buck and Paul Creyton), Nestor Paiva (Capt. Thornton), Roy Barcroft (Martin Novack), John Dierkes (Sgt. Rafferty), Richard Shackleton (Pat Garner), I. Stanford Jolley (Mr. Garner), Charles Garland (Trooper), Florence Lake (Mrs. Cameron).

Lydon and Barnes play a pair of young Texans who flee the carpetbagger rule of the oppressive Paiva. On the trail they meet fugitive gunfighter Morris, who befriends Lydon when he and Barnes have a falling out. Barnes is cornered by Paiva and one of his deputies and he kills them both, and blames the murder on Lydon to get his revenge. Lydon is captured and put on trial, but Morris convinces the arresting marshal, Greer, of the boy's innocence and they get Lydon off the hook and Barnes under the noose. Good performances by the boys, but Morris looks drained.

p, Vincent M. Fennelly; d, Thomas Carr; w, Geoffrey Homes, Clifton Adams (based on the novel by Adams); ph, Joseph M. Novac; ed, Sam Fields.

Western   (PR:A MPAA:NR)

DESPERADO TRAIL, THE**

(1965, Ger./Yugo.) 93m Rialto-Film Philipsen-Jadran/COL bw (WINNETOU III; VINETU III)

Lex Barker (Old Shatterhand), Pierre Brice (Winnetou), Rik Battaglia (Rollins), Ralf Wolter (Sam Hawkins), Carl Lange (Governor), Sophie Hardy (Ann), Veljko Maricic (Vermeulen), Aleksandar Gavric (Kid), Ilija Ivezic (Klark), Miha Baloh (Gomez), Sime Jagarinac, Ivan Novak, Milan Micic, Dragomir Felba, Dusan Vujisic.

Another of the German-Yugoslavian westerns based on the adventure novels of Karl May. This film, the third in the series, sees Barker and Brice trying to thwart Battaglia who is attempting to whip the Apaches into a frenzy to clear some valuable land of settlers. The governor asks Indian chief Brice and his faithful companion Barker to diffuse the situation. When it appears that their intervention will foil his plans, Battaglia frames Brice for the murder of an Apache, which forces rival tribes into a war. Eventually the cavalry arrives to stop the killing, but Brice sacrifices his life to save Barker. Though Brice's character dies in this film, he was quickly resurrected for subsequent installments of the series.

p, Horst Wendlandt; d, Harald Reinl; w, Harald G. Petersson, Joachim Bartsch (based on the novel Winnetou, the Red Gentleman by Karl Friedrich May); ph, Ernst W. Kalinke (Ultrascope, Eastmancolor); m, Martin Bottcher; ed, Jutta Hering; art d, Vladimir Tadej; cos, Irms Pauli.

Western   (PR:A MPAA:NR)

DESPERADOES, THE***

(1943) 85m COL c

Randolph Scott (Steve Upton), Glenn Ford (Cheyenne Rogers), Claire Trevor (Countess Maletta), Evelyn Keyes (Allison MacLeod), Edgar Buchanan (Willie MacLeod), Raymond Walburn (Judge Cameron), Guinn Williams (Nitro Rankin), Porter Hall (Stanley Clanton), Joan Woodbury (Sundown), Bernard Nedell (Jack Lester), Irving Bacon (Dan Walters), Glenn Strange (Lem), Ethan Laidlaw (Cass), Charles Whittaker (Tolliver), Edward Pawley (Blackie), Chester Clute (Rollo), Francis Ford (Hank), Charles King (Outlaw).

Columbia studios' first Technicolor feature stars Scott as the sheriff of a Utah town in the 1860s. Ford, an outlaw and old friend of the sheriff, rides into town to visit and soon the local bank is robbed. Though Ford has been talked into turning over a new leaf by Keyes and has made a good effort to go straight, the finger of guilt points to him, and, though innocent, he is convicted of the crime. Scott helps him escape and together they bring the true culprits to justice. Well-made, fast-paced, with a good cast of performers.

p, Harry Joe Brown; d, Charles Vidor; w, Robert Carson (based on a story by Max Brand); ph, George Meehan, Allen M. Davey (Technicolor); ed, Gene Havlick; md, M. W. Stoloff; art d, Lionel Banks.

Western   (PR:A MPAA:NR)

DESPERADOES ARE IN TOWN, THE**

(1956) 72m FOX bw

Robert Arthur (Lenny Kesh), Kathy Nolan (Alice Rutherford), Rhys Williams (Jud Collins), Rhodes Reason (Frank Banner), Dave O'Brien (Dock Lapman), Kelly Thordsen (Tobe Lapman), Mae Clarke (Jane Kesh), Robert Osterloh (Deputy Sheriff Groome), William Challee (Tom Kesh), Carol Kelly (Hattie), Frank Sully (Branch), Morris Ankrum (Mr. Rutherford), Richard Wessel (Hank), Dorothy Grainger (Woman), Todd Griffin (Ranger), Nancy Evans (Mrs. Rutherford), Ann Stebbins (Girl), Byron Foulger (Jim Day).

Arthur runs away from his parents' poor Southern farm to Texas where he gets involved with outlaws. One outlaw (who would like to go straight) sends Arthur back home, where he works hard and turns the farm into a success. Just as the harvest celebration is about to take place, the outlaw gang shows up and forces Arthur to help them rob the local bank. Rather than help, Arthur kills the leader and his brother, but not before the powerful banker of the community learns of the boy's past criminal activities in Texas. Seeing that Arthur is now a productive member of society, the banker forgives Arthur's past, allowing him to keep the farm and marry his sweetheart, Nolan. Slow going, with no engaging performances to help it along.

p&d, Kurt Neumann; w, Earle Snell, Neumann (based on the story "The Outlaws Are In Town" by Bennett Foster); ph, John Mescall (RegalScope); m, Paul Sawtell, Bert Shefter; ed, Merrill White.

Western   (PR:A MPAA: NR)

DESPERADOES OF DODGE CITY**

(1948) 60m REP bw

Allan "Rocky" Lane (Himself), Black Jack (His Stallion), Eddy Waller (Nugget Clark), Mildred Coles (Gloria Lamoreaux), Roy Barcroft (Homesteader), Tristram Coffin (Ace Durant), William Phipps (Ted Loring), James Craven (Cal Sutton), John Hamilton (Stockton), Edward Cassidy (Jim), House Peters, Jr. (Henry), Dale Van Sickel (Jim), Peggy Wynne (Mary), Ted Mapes (Jake).

Better-than-usual Lane oater has "Rocky" trying to save a band of homesteaders from raids by outlaws. To do this, he obtains a special military order to have the cavalry escort the settlers, but the crooks snatch the paper and Lane must grab the leader of the outlaws and get the orders back.

p, Gordon Kay; d, Philip Ford; w, Bob Williams; ph, John MacBurnie; ed, Harold Minter; md, Morton Scott; art d, Frank Hotaling.

Western   (PR:A MPAA:NR)

DESPERADOES OUTPOST**

(1952) 54m REP bw

Allan "Rocky" Lane (Himself), Black Jack (His Stallion), Eddy Waller (Nugget Clark), Roy Barcroft (Jim Boylan), Myron Healey (Lt. Dan Boylan), Lyle Talbot (Walter Fleming), Claudia Barrett (Kathy), Lane Bradford (Mike), Lee Roberts (Spec Matson), Edward Cassidy (Deputy Marshal), Charles Evans (Maj. Seeley), Zon Murray (Tony), Slim Duncan (Army Sergeant).

Lane plays a federal agent assigned to investigate the destruction of a stagecoach line that has bankrupted the owner, Waller, who was then forced to sell his ranch. The hoods who did the deed buy the property so they can use its running water (the only running water in the area) to siphon off mercury that runs from a nearby mine through the pipes. Lane stops the bandits and saves the valuable mercury for use by the U.S. government.

p, Rudy Ralston; d, Philip Ford; w, Arthur Orloff, Albert DeMond; ph, John MacBurnie; m, Stanley Wilson; ed, Tony Martinelli; art d, Frank Hotaling; set d, John McCarthy, Jr., James Redd.

Western   (PR:A MPAA:NR)

DESPERADOS, THE**

(1969) 90m COL c

Vince Edwards (David Galt), Jack Palance (Parson Josiah Galt), George Maharis (Jacob Galt), Neville Brand (Sheriff Kilpatrick), Sylvia Syms (Laura), Christian Roberts (Adam Galt), Kate O'Mara (Adah), Kenneth Cope (Carlin), John Paul (Lacey), Patrick Holt (Haller), Christopher Malcolm (Gregg), John Clarke (Bandit), Benjamin Edney (Pauly).

Bloody western starring Palance as the crazed head of a family of Confederate guerrillas who continue to plunder, loot, and kill long after the Civil War has ended. One of the sons, Edwards, breaks with the family in revolt against its viciousness. He goes to Texas to make a new life, and six years later the family arrives to continue marauding in his town. The climax is a violent battle between Edwards and his family which sees most of the family killed. Grim, bloody, and given to an overblown performance by Palance, who is almost always rolling his eyes and snarling.

p, Irving Allen; d, Henry Levin; w, Walter Brough (based on a story by Clarke Reynolds); ph, Sam Leavitt (Technicolor); m, David Whitaker; ed, Geoffrey Foot; art d, Jose Alguero; spec eff, Bill Warrington.

Western   (PR:O MPAA:M)

DESPERATE***½

(1947) 73m RKO bw

Steve Brodie (Steve Randall), Audrey Long (Anne Randall), Raymond Burr (Walt Radak), Douglas Fowley (Pete), William Challee (Reynolds), Jason Robards, Sr. (Ferrari), Freddie Steele (Shorty), Lee Frederick (Joe), Paul E. Burns (Uncle Jan), Ilka Gruning (Aunt Klara), Larry Nunn (Al Radak), Robert Bray (Policeman), Carl Kent (Detective), Carol Forman (Mrs. Roberts), Erville Alderson (Simon Pringle), Teddy Infuhr (Richard), Perc Launders (Manny), Ralf Harolde (Doctor with Walt), Kay Christopher (Nurse), Bill Wallace, Carl Saxe (Policemen), Grahame Covert (Man), Jay Norris (Villager), Milt Kibbee (Mac), Dick Elliott (Hat Lewis), Charles

Flynn *(State Trooper)*, Art Miles, Glen Knight *(Truck Drivers)*, Hans Herbert *(Rev. Alex)*, Michael Visaroff, Ernie Adams *(Villagers)*, Elena Warren *(Mrs. Oliver)*, Robert Clarke *(Bus Driver)*, Netta Packer *(Woman on Train)*, George Anderson *(Man on Train)*, Don Kerr *(Vendor on Train)*, Frank O'Connor *(Conductor)*, William Bailey, Marshall Ruth *(Traveling Salesmen)*, Jack Baxley *(Dr. Wilson)*, Joe Recht *(Bellhop)*, Eddie Parks *(Mr. Franks)*, Leza Holland *(Nurse)*.

The first of director Anthony Mann's series of *noir* films (BORDER INCIDENT, HE WALKED BY NIGHT, RAILROADED, RAW DEAL, SIDE STREET, T-MEN) is a disturbing twist on middle-class values, responsibility, and guilt. Brodie is a newlywed truck driver who accidentally becomes involved with a gang that robs a fur warehouse and kills a cop in the process. One of the gang is captured, convicted, and sentenced to die in the electric chair. Burr, the leader of the crooks, plans to frame Brodie into confessing to the murder, and if he balks, the gang will kill his wife. Brodie and his wife flee to the country where they hide out at an isolated farm owned by relatives. The peaceful farm is in direct contrast to the dark, urban world the couple has fled from and they find the setting idyllic. Suddenly the *noir* world invades the country when Burr and his gang find them. Luckily, they are saved moments before Burr can kill them. Mann directs with an assured style and creates a world in which physical violence is very real, intense, and brutal, causing the Brodie character to flee for his life without any regard for trying to bring the rest of the gang to justice. There is a hopelessness to the situation (Brodie cannot go to the police because they think he is the killer) which forces the honest truck driver to disregard social responsibility and flee. Mann creates a grim world where there are few noble choices and all characters are driven to desperation.

p, Michel Kraike; d, Anthony Mann; w, Harry Essex, Martin Rackin (based on a story by Dorothy Atlas and Mann); ph, George E. Diskant; m, Paul Sawtell; ed, Marston Fay; md, Constantin Bakaleinikoff; art d, Albert S. D'Agostino, Walter E. Keller; set d, Darrell Silvera; spec eff, Russell A. Cully.

Crime **(PR:C MPAA:NR)**

DESPERATE ADVENTURE, A** (1938) 63m REP bw

Ramon Novarro *(Andre)*, Marian Marsh *(Ann)*, Margaret Tallichet *(Betty)*, Eric Blore *(Trump)*, Andrew Tombes *(Carrington)*, Tom Rutherford *(Gerald)*, Maurice Cass *(Dornay)*, Erno Verebes *(Marcel)*, Michael Kent *(Maurice)*, Cliff Nazarro *(Tipo)*, Rolfe Sedan *(Prefect of Police)*, Gloria Rich *(Mimi)*, Lois Collier *(Angela)*.

Novarro plays a temperamental French painter who goes wild when he discovers that his friends, in trying to help his career, have made him famous by exhibiting one of his paintings. Unfortunately the painting is that of his dream girl and the artist is embarrassed by having it hanging about Paris. He tries everything to have the painting removed, but then he meets Marsh, who is a perfect match to the dream girl in his work. A decent romantic comedy.

p&d, John H. Auer; w, Barry Trivers (based on a story by Hans Kraly, M. Coates Webster); ph, Jack Marta; ed, Murray Seldeen, Ernest Nims.

Comedy/Romance **(PR:A MPAA:NR)**

DESPERATE CARGO** (1941) 67m PRC bw

Ralph Byrd *(Tony)*, Carol Hughes *(Peggy)*, Julie Duncan *(Ann)*, Jack Mulhall *(Halsey)*, I. Stanford Jolley *(Carter)*, Kenneth Harlan *(MacFarland)*, Richard Clarke *(Ryan)*, Johnstone White *(Madden)*, Paul Bryar *(Dessar)*, Thornton Edwards *(Manuelo)*, Don Forrest *(William)*, Loretta Russell *(Mrs. Pettingill)*.

This fast-paced actioner is directed by William "One Shot" Beaudine (it was rumored that he never did a second take), and stars Hughes and Duncan as two chorus girls stranded in a Latin American town. The women manage to get on board a clipper ship because the purser, Byrd, takes a liking to Duncan. En route home, hoodlums attempt to steal the ship's money cargo and Byrd comes to the rescue, defeating the crooks and their scheme. A typical programmer.

p, John T. Coyle; d, William Beaudine; w, Morgan Cox, Coyle (based on the story "Loot Below" by Eustace L. Adams); ph, Jack Greenhalgh; ed, Whitey Jowett.

Adventure/Romance **(PR:A MPAA:NR)**

DESPERATE CHANCE FOR ELLERY QUEEN, A* (1942) 70m COL bw

William Gargan *(Ellery Queen)*, Margaret Lindsay *(Nikki Porter)*, Charley Grapewin *(Inspector Queen)*, John Litel *(Norman Hadley)*, Lillian Bond *(Adele Belden)*, James Burke *(Sgt. Velie)*, Jack LaRue *(Tommy Gould)*, Morgan Conway *(Ray Stafford)*, Noel Madison *(George Belden)*, Frank Thomas *(Capt. Daley)*, Charlotte Wynters *(Mrs. Norman Hadley)*.

Poor mystery that was the penultimate in an almost entirely lifeless series. Gargan, in his second appearance as the detective, is hired by Wynters to search for her missing banker husband, and along the way he has to contend with burlesque queen Bond and an ever-increasing number of dead bodies.

p, Larry Darmour; d, James Hogan; w, Eric Taylor (based on the radio play "A Good Samaritan" by Ellery Queen [Frederick Dannay, Manfred Bennington Lee]); ph, James S. Brown, Jr.; ed, Dwight Caldwell.

Mystery **(PR:A MPAA:NR)**

DESPERATE CHARACTERS**** (1971) 87m ITC/PAR c

Shirley MacLaine *(Sophie)*, Kenneth Mars *(Otto)*, Gerald O'Loughlin *(Charlie)*, Sada Thompson *(Claire)*, Jack Somack *(Leon)*, Chris Gampel *(Mike)*, Mary Ellen Hokanson *(Flo)*, Robert Bauer *(Young Man)*, Carol Kane *(Young Girl)*, Michael Higgins *(Francis Early)*, Michael McAloney *(Raconteur)*, Wallace Rooney *(Man on Subway)*, Rose Gregorio *(Ruth)*, Elena Karam *(Saleslady)*, Nick Smith *(Caller)*, Robert Delbert *(Hospital Attendant)*, Shanueille Ryder *(Woman Doctor)*, Gonzalee Ford *(Nurse)*, Patrick McVey *(Mr. Haynes)*, L.J. Davis *(Tom)*.

There was nothing desperate about the characters. Rather, it was their very commonness that caused them desperation. MacLaine and Mars are just about flawless in this slice of life (and death) in the big city. It's Friday night. MacLaine and Mars are an upper middle class couple living near once-fashionable Brooklyn Heights in Brooklyn. Violence is all around them and they find themselves becoming inured to it and that is disturbing. Their conversation has deteriorated into the banalities of day-to-day ennui. Mars is an attorney and casually remarks that he is ending his partnership with O'Loughlin, his long-time associate and best friend. When MacLaine wonders how he could do such a thing, Mars explains that O'Loughlin has gone liberal and is spending altogether too much time with causes and not enough with cases. A street cat paws at their door and MacLaine feeds it some milk. The kindness is rewarded by a deep bite on her hand. At a party later that night thrown by psychiatrist Gampel and his wife, Hokanson, the joy of the evening is shattered by a rock that smashes a window. When MacLaine's hand is examined, a suggestion is made that she consult a physician. The fear that the pussy may have been rabid causes MacLaine to turn and toss for hours. In the middle of the night O'Loughlin comes to the door and demands to see Mars. MacLaine shushes him and they take a walk together. O'Loughlin admits that he has fallen out of love with his wife, Gregorio. She is unable to display any feelings toward him or to anyone or anything else and O'Loughlin sees himself as a sensitive human being and wants to live his life as did the character Jarndyce in *Bleak House* by Charles Dickens. Their hair now let down, MacLaine confesses that she's having a brief fling with Higgins, her only fall from fidelity, a handsome man she'd seen earlier that evening at the Gampel house. She calms O'Loughlin down and promises to talk with Mars about the upcoming split. Saturday morning, MacLaine and Mars discover a drunk in front of their brownstone and, in the spirit of the Kitty Genovese generation of people who don't want to get involved, they leave him be. Later, MacLaine meets Gregorio on the subway but is snubbed by the woman. In Manhattan, MacLaine has lunch with Thompson, a woman living an odd existence. Though divorced from her husband, Somack, for twenty years, she allows him to stay at her place because she is terribly lonely. Somack and Thompson have an argument and MacLaine leaves their apartment confused and depressed. She calls Higgins but he doesn't answer the phone as he is quite involved with his latest mistress. That night, MacLaine and Mars go to the local hospital to find out about the hand but they are told they must catch the cat or MacLaine will have to endure a painful series of rabies shots. Later, the cat comes back and they trap it. Mars takes it to the ASPCA to be examined and probably destroyed. The next morning, MacLaine and Mars drive to their country home and find it vandalized and robbed. MacLaine is sobbing and Mars forces her to make love. They had hired local McVey to watch their house and report if anything went wrong. When they suspect that he may have been the person behind the damage, an argument begins. Before it comes to blows, the couple return to the city and walk into their residence to await the phone call from the ASPCA. If the cat is rabid, MacLaine will be put through the pain of the shots. If not, they can celebrate—or can they? Critics were unanimous in their praise of MacLaine and Mars but the public avoided attending the film. It was made on a miniscule budget—under $400,000. Everyone worked on a percentage and minimum salaries and expected to make money over and above their tiny wages. At least one of the stars, Mars, did not make one extra penny. Mars carved a comedy niche for himself with a starring role as the Nazi playwright in THE PRODUCERS and several hysterical parts in various Mel Brooks films. Somack became a successful TV commercials actor and achieved national recognition by complaining about his stomach for Alka-Seltzer. Frank Gilroy won accolades for THE SUBJECT WAS ROSES and many other intelligent pieces. He also wrote and directed ONCE IN PARIS, which was equally interesting as DESPERATE CHARACTERS and was equally quiet at the box office.

p,d&w, Frank D. Gilroy (based on the novel by Paula Fox); ph, Urs Furrer (Eastmancolor); m, Lee Konitz, Jim Hall, Ron Carter; ed, Robert Q. Lovett; art d, Edgar Lansbury; set d, Herbert F. Mulligan; cos, Sally Gifft.

Drama **(PR:A-C MPAA:NR)**

DESPERATE DECISION*½ (1954, Fr.) 95m Hoche/Times Film Corp. bw (LE JEUNE FOLLE)

Daniele Delorme *(Catherine)*, Henri Vidal *(Steve)*, Nicolas Vogel *(Tom)*, Maurice Ronet *(Jim)*, Jean Debucourt *(A Mysterious Man)*, Michele Cordous *(Mary)*, Macqueline Porel *(Mother Superior)*, Marcel Journet *(Chief of Police Donovan)*, Marcel Charvey *(Policeman)*.

An oddity, a French film set in Ireland and dubbed with Brooklyn accents that destroy any verisimilitude the film may have once had. Delorme is a nun who hears of the execution of her brother as an informer by the IRA leader she worships. Gradually she sinks into madness, planning the assassination of her one-time hero. Unrelievedly bleak and not very engrossing, not to mention convincing.

d, Yves Allegret; w, Jacques Sigurd (based on the novel by Catherine Beauchamp).

Drama **(PR:O MPAA:NR)**

DESPERATE HOURS, THE**** (1955) 112m PAR bw

Humphrey Bogart *(Glenn)*, Fredric March *(Dan Hilliard)*, Arthur Kennedy *(Jesse Bard)*, Martha Scott *(Eleanor Hilliard)*, Dewey Martin *(Hal)*, Gig Young *(Chuck)*, Mary Murphy *(Cindy)*, Richard Eyer *(Ralphie)*, Robert Middleton *(Kobish)*, Alan Reed *(Detective)*, Bert Freed *(Winston)*, Ray Collins *(Masters)*, Whit Bissell *(Carson)*, Ray Teal *(Fredericks)*, Michael Moore *(Detective)*, Don Haggerty *(Detective)*, Ric Roman *(Sal)*, Pat Flaherty *(Dutch)*, Beverly Garland *(Miss Swift)*, Louis Lettieri *(Bucky Walling)*, Ann Doran *(Mrs. Walling)*, Walter Baldwin *(Patterson)*.

In one of the last films of his life Bogart goes full circle, enacting a role identical to the part he played almost twenty years earlier in THE PETRIFIED FOREST and he does it with a vengeance. Breaking out of prison with his kid brother, Martin, and a behemoth *non compos mentis*, Middleton, Bogart takes refuge in March's middle-class home. Here he terrorizes the family as he waits for a call from his sweetheart who is supposed to dig up long buried loot and then meet him and his fellow escapees. The woman's call doesn't come and Bogart grows more and more desperate, brutally treating March, his wife, Scott, his attractive daughter, Murphy, and feisty young son, Eyer. Murphy, to allay suspicions, goes out on a brief, nervous date with Young, but her uneasy attitude and tense actions cause Young to be suspicious. When he learns that escaped convicts are in the neighborhood he goes to the police but by then the local cops and the FBI have narrowed the hunt down to March's house. March himself has done everything he can to avoid a confrontation between police and his unwelcome guests to safeguard his family, even using his office as a delivery point for the money Bogart is expecting. When it fails to show up, March withdraws some of his own money from the bank, thus alerting authorities, and gives this to Bogart who instantly realizes what March is doing. Younger brother Martin, who has enough sensitivity to object to Bogart's using March's family, flees on his own. He is approached by a suspicious cop in a diner and, while running away, is killed by a passing truck, calling out his brother's name at the last. Brutish Middleton, who has already murdered a handyman who came to the March home, is tricked by March into sticking his hand through the front door, the one holding a gun. March slams the door with his body, causing Middleton to drop the weapon which March picks up while shoving Middleton outside. The house is surrounded by dozens of lawmen and when Middleton tries to make a break, he is killed. No one is left inside the house now, except March, his little son, Eyer, and Bogart, March having engineered the escape of his wife and daughter. Bogart, not realizing that, in a clever switch, he now has an empty gun, holds the boy in an upstairs bedroom. March's gun is loaded. He confronts the killer and his son. Bogart puts his gun to Eyer's head, telling March: "If you think I won't pull the trigger, you don't know me." March smiles grimly, then stares at his son. He tells the boy to "listen to your father, Ralphie, and do exactly as I say." It is an incredible test of faith, not unlike the test between Abraham and his son Isaac of Biblical yore. Eyer pauses and March tells him to believe in him, that nothing is going to happen to him if he does exactly what he is told. Eyer makes a break for March and Bogart pulls the trigger which registers a hollow click. March sends his son from the house and faces a startled Bogart, marching him down the stairs to the front door, giving him a simple order he knows will mean the death of his tormentor: "Get out of my house!" Bogart goes to the front door, opens it and stares out into dozens of glaring police lights. He steps outside, still clutching the empty gun, placing his hands behind his head as a voice on a bullhorn instructs him to do. Then he runs forward, hurtling the weapon into a floodlight, smashing it, as machine guns open up and cut Bogart to pieces. He crumples dead on the front lawn of March's home. After the cops take away the bodies, close down the lights and disperse, March gathers his family to his side, inviting Young, a playboy whom March has disapproved of up to this time, into his now safe home. The crisis is over and the common man has triumphed. Wyler's direction in this taut, suspenseful film is faultless, and Hayes does a marvelous job in adapting his own novel for the screen. March and Bogart square off in spellbinding performances of good and evil, two old pros who make every article in their lines work hard. Bogie had a few reservations about this film, commenting to Wyler at a sneak preview: "Maybe I'm getting too old to play hoodlums." The story had also been a successful stage play where a much younger Paul Newman had enacted the Bogart role, but the part was purposely "aged" by Hayes to suit Bogie's 55 years, all of which showed on that wonderful craggy face. Young, Murphy, and Eyer are all perfect in their roles and Scott is a standout as March's wife (this was her second film with March, having appeared with him fourteen years earlier in ONE FOOT IN HEAVEN). Garmes' photography is stellar, as always.

p&d, William Wyler; w, Joseph Hayes (based on his novel and play); ph, Lee Garmes (Vistavision); m, Gail Kubik; ed, Robert Swink; art d, Hal Pereira, Joseph Macmillan Johnson; set d, Sam Comer, Grace Gregory; cos, Edith Head; makeup, Wally Westmore; spec eff, John P. Fulton, Farciot Edouart.

Crime Drama (PR:C MPAA:NR)

DESPERATE JOURNEY½** (1942) 107m WB bw

Errol Flynn *(Flight Lt. Terrence Forbes)*, Ronald Reagan *(Flying Officer Johnny Hammond)*, Raymond Massey *(Maj. Otto Baumeister)*, Nancy Coleman *(Kaethe Brahms)*, Alan Hale *(Flight Sgt. Kirk Edwards)*, Arthur Kennedy *(Flying Officer Jed Forrest)*, Sig Rumann *(Preuss)*, Patrick O'Moore *(Squadron Leader Lane-Ferris)*, Ronald Sinclair *(Flight Sgt. Lloyd Hollis)*, Louis Arco *(Feldwebel Gertz)*, Charles Irwin *(Capt. Coswick)*, Richard Fraser *(S/L Clark)*, Lester Matthews *(Wing Commander)*, Robert O. Davis *(Kruse)*, Walter Brooke *(Flight Sgt. Warwick)*, Harry Lewis *(Evans)*, Don Phillips *(Kenton)*, Albert Basserman *(Dr. Mather)*, Felix Basch *(Dr. Herman Brahms)*, Ilka Gruning *(Frau Brahms)*, Elsa Basserman *(Frau Raeder)*, Henry Victor *(Heinrich Schwartzmuller)*, Bruce Lester *(Assistant Plotting Officer)*, Kurt Katch *(Hesse)*, Helmut Dantine *(German Copilot)*, Barry Bernard *(Squadron Commander)*, William Hopper *(Aircraftsman)*, Douglas Walton *(British Officer)*, Harold Daniels *(German Soldier)*, Henry Rowland *(Motorcycle Scout)*; *Walter Bonn (Sentry)*, Frank Alten *(Lieutenant)*, Arno Frey *(Pvt. Trecha)*, Sigfried Tor *(Pvt. Rasek)*, Gene Garrick *(Polish Boy)*, Hans Schumm, Robert Stephenson *(Gestapo Agents)*, Carl Ekberg *(Telephone Repairman)*, Lester Sharpe *(Driver)*, Ludwig Hardt *(Pharmacist)*, Jack Lomas *(Magnus)*, Ferdinand Schumann-Heink *(Sentry)*, Sven Hugo Borg *(Mechanic)*, Roland Varno *(Unteroffizier)*, Otto Reichow *(Pvt. Koenig)*, Rolf Lindau *(Sergeant)*.

If the Germans were as stupid and silly as this film portrayed them, the war would have been over in weeks. But DESPERATE JOURNEY was lensed in 1942 and the home front had to be made to believe that we were on our way to winning, and quickly. It tells the tale of an RAF bomber crew shot down over German-occupied Poland. Eight men are in the plane but only five survive the crash and subsequent travails. Flynn, Reagan, Hale, Kennedy, and Sinclair are going to sneak through the Axis territory and make it back to Jolly Olde. In the course of the picture, they are chased relentlessly by Nazi Massey, they destroy a chemical factory, knock off several Nazis, steal German uniforms, and masquerade as officers by pilfering Goering's car and taking it to an area near Berlin. A bomber is being prepared to attack London's water works and Flynn and Reagan, the remaining members of the crew, steal the plane and fly across the channel. As he's about to land, Flynn says, "Now for Australia and a crack at those Japs!" Coleman has the only female role in the picture as anti-Nazi Basserman's daughter. Flynn rebelled at Reagan being a co-star. He was used to having distaff co-stars and the thought of another man was anathema. Wallis managed to keep Flynn from causing too much trouble and Reagan managed to steal a few scenes and even get some laughs. Reagan was already in the service when the film was released and came out of the war as a captain. Looked at today, the movie is a cinematic comic strip with none of the usual taste for which Wallis was famous. It was just about this time that Wallis was also producing CASABLANCA and the difference is astounding.

p, Hal B. Wallis; d, Raoul Walsh; w, Arthur T. Horman (based on a story, "Forced Landing," by Horman); ph, Bert Glennon; m, Max Steiner; ed, Rudi Fehr; md, Hugo Friedhofer; art d, Carl Jules Weyl; cos, Milo Anderson; spec eff, Edwin DuPar.

War Adventure (PR:A MPAA:NR)

DESPERATE MAN, THE*½ (1959, Brit.) 57m Merton Park/AA bw

Jill Ireland *(Carol Bourne)*, Conrad Phillips *(Curtis)*, William Hartnell *(Smith)*, Charles Gray *(Lawson)*, Peter Swanwick *(Hoad)*, Arthur Gomez *(Landlord)*, John Warwick *(Inspector Cobley)*, Patricia Burke *(Miss Prew)*, Ernest Butcher *(Grocer)*, Doris Yorke, Jean Aubrey, Brian Weske, Marian Collins.

Reporter Phillips and girl friend Ireland get in over their heads while tracking a jewel thief through the Sussex countryside. The crook captures Ireland, and, holding her captive in a castle, forces Phillips to help him. Mostly dull but there is some nice camera work.

p, Jack Greenwood; d, Peter Maxwell; w, James Eastwood (based on the novel *Beginner's Luck* by Paul Somers); ph, Gerald Moss.

Crime (PR:A-C MPAA:NR)

DESPERATE MOMENT*** (1953, Brit.) 88m Fanfare/GED bw

Dirk Bogarde *(Simon van Halder)*, Mai Zetterling *(Anna de Burgh)*, Philip Friend *(Robert Sawyer)*, Albert Lieven *(Paul)*, Frederick Wendhousen *(Grote)*, Carl Jaffe *(Becker)*, Gerard Heinz *(Bones)*, Andre Mikhelson *(Inspector)*, Harold Ayer *(Trevor Wood)*, Simone Silva *(Mink)*, Walter Gotell *(Manservant)*, Friedrich Joloff *(Valentin)*, Ferdy Mayne *(Berlin Detective)*, Walter Rilla *(Col. Bertrand)*, Antonio Gallardo *(Spanish Dancer)*, Paul Hardtmuth *(Ship's Watchman)*; Theodore Bikel *(Anton)*.

Bogarde is a convicted murderer in post-war Germany who escapes on his way to prison. He finds his girl friend, Zetterling, and explains that he has confessed to a murder he hadn't committed when he thought she was dead. Together they evade British troops and German police as they search for the three men who know what happened, one of them being the real killer. Quite suspenseful, with Bogarde turning in an exceptionally fine performance.

p, George H. Brown; d, Compton Bennett; w, Patrick Kirwan, Brown (from the novel by Martha Albrand); ph, C. Pennington Richards; m, Ronald Binge; ed, John Guthridge; art d, Maurice Carter; cos, Julie Harris.

Crime/Drama (PR:A MPAA:NR)

DESPERATE ONES, THE**

(1968 U.S./Span.) 104m David-Pro Artis Iberica/AIP c

Maximilian Schell *(Marek)*, Raf Vallone *(Victor)*, Irene Papas *(Ajmi)*, Theodore Bikel *(Kisielev)*, Maria Perschy *(Marusia)*, Fernando Rey *(Ibram)*, George Voskovec *(Doctor)*, Alberto de Mendoza *(Hamlat)*, Antonio Vico *(Ulug Beg)*, Vincente Sangiovanni *(Shura)*, Robert Palmer *(Ukranian NKVD)*, Danny Stone *(NKVD Guard)*, Mariela Chatlak *(Aka)*, Carmen Carbonell *(Ulug Beg's Wife)*, Fernando Hilbeck, Andres Monreal, Maruchi Fresno, Mark Malicz, Max Slaten, Alexander Ramati, Ricardo Palacios, Cris Huerta, Antonio Duque, Luis Castro, Luis Tejada.

Schell and Vallone play two Polish brothers who escape from a Soviet labor camp and try to join the Polish Army which is in exile across the border in Afghanistan. While they await the arrival of a smuggler who will take them across the border, the brothers rent a room in the home of Rey and his gorgeous wife, Papas. Trouble starts when Schell falls in love with Papas and Vallone falls for Perschy, a waitress. Paranoia sets in under the watchful eye of the Russian secret police and Schell panics when the night-blindness he developed while in prison worsens. The day they are to escape, Vallone is stricken with typhus and needs adrenalin to survive. Unable to travel because of his status, Schell talks Rey into obtaining the drug for his brother. While he is gone, Schell and Papas make love. Consumed with guilt, Papas attempts suicide, but is saved by Schell. Rey returns with the drug and the brothers make a desperate attempt to escape along with Rey, Papas, the smuggler, and his family. As the refugees near the border, a patrol spots them and orders them to halt. Schell runs and draws their fire, sacrificing his life so that the others can make it to safety.

p,d&w, Alexander Ramati (based on his novel *Beyond The Mountains*); ph, Christian Matras (Eastmancolor); m, Cristobal Halffter; ed, Peter Weatherley; art d, Antonio Cortes; ch, Gene Collins; m/l "Ajmi," Jene Freber.

War (PR:C MPAA:NR)

DESPERATE SEARCH½** (1952) 71m MGM bw

Howard Keel *(Vince Heldon)*, Jane Greer *(Julie Heldon)*, Patricia Medina *(Nora Stead)*, Keenan Wynn *("Brandy")*, Robert Burton *(Wayne Langmuir)*, Lee Aaker *(Don)*, Linda Lowell *(Janet)*, Michael Dugan *(Lou)*, Elaine Stewart *(Stewardess)*, Jonathan Cott *(Detective)*, Jeff Richards *(Ed)*, Dick Simmons *(Communicator)*, Robert Whitney, Gil Dennis.

Aaker and Lowell are a brother and sister fighting freezing temperatures and a stalking cougar in the mountains after a plane crash. Searching for the pair is Keel, their father, and Greer and Medina, Keel's wife and ex-wife respectively. Aaker is an appealing performer but little sister Lowell is so insufferable that even Aaker is prompted to wish he were an only child, a wish audiences will share.

p, Matthew Rapf; d, Joseph Lewis; w, Walter Doniger (based on the novel *The Desperate Search* by Arthur Mayse); ph, Harold Lipstein; ed, Joseph Dervin; md, Rudolph G. Kopp; art d, Cedric Gibbons, Eddie Imazu; set d, Edwin B. Willis, Ralph Hurst.

Adventure/Drama　　　　　　　　　　　　　　**(PR:A　MPAA:NR)**

DESPERATE SIEGE　　　　　　　　(SEE: RAWHIDE, 1951)

DESPERATE TRAILS*½　　　　　　(1939) 58m UNIV bw

Johnny Mack Brown *(Steve Hayden)*, Bob Baker *(Clem Waters)*, Fuzzy Knight *(Cousin Willie)*, Bill Cody, Jr. *(Little Bill)*, Francis Robinson *(Judith Longton)*, Russell Simpson *(Big Bill Tanner)*, Clarence H. Wilson *(Mal Culp)*, Charles Stevens *(Ortega)*, Horace Murphy *(Nebraska)*, Ralph Dunn *(Lon)*, Fern Emmett *(Mrs. Plunkett)*, Ed Cassidy *(Marshal Cort)*, Anita Camargo *(Rosita)*, Jack Shannon *(Ab)*, Wilbur McCauley *(Joe)*, Al Haskell, Frank Ellis, Frank McCarroll, Cliff Lyons, Eddie Parker.

Brown plays a government agent who poses as a crook to catch an evil banker and corrupt sheriff who have united to destroy a town. Better than average production values. This was Brown's first series western for Universal.

p&d, Albert Ray; w, Andrew Bennison (based on the story "Christmas Eve at Pilot Butte" by Courtney Riley Cooper); ph, Jerry Ash; ed, Louis Sackin.

Western　　　　　　　　　　　　　　　　**(PR:A　MPAA:NR)**

DESPERATE WOMEN, THE zero　67m Samuel Newman Prods., Inc. bw

Anne Appleton *(Mona)*, Douglas Howard *(Eddie)*, Paul Hahn *(Dr. Martin)*, Ben Daniels *(Capt. Dawson)*, Samuel Newman *(Kovacs)*, Maria Girard *(Flo Brown)*, Virginia Leon *(Miss Parker)*, Karen Moore *(Mary Jane)*, Joseph Allen, Jr. *(Operator)*, Robert Lee *(Publisher)*, Theodore Marcuse *(Doctor)*, Richard Risso *(Jimmy)*, Stanley Glenn *(Mr. Jones)*, Rebecca Young *(Mrs. Calucci)*, Karen Wolfe *(Sadie)*, Raymond Barrett *(Contact Man)*, William Sharpe *(Joe)*, Ross Durfee *(Intern)*, Jean McCampbell *(Mother)*, Richard Learman *(Boy Friend)*, Ragna Kyle *(Operator's Nurse)*, Jo Young *(Room Clerk)*, Joseph Penner *(Barnes)*, Hughes Rudd *(Husband)*, Nilli Carroll *(Wife)*, Virginia Royce *(Nurse)*, Eve Meyer *(Woman)*.

Russ Meyer photographed this trashy warning on the dangers of teenage pregnancy and abortion. Vague plot deals with a reporter tracking down the story, interviewing various case histories along the way. Though not as sensationalized as its publicity would have you believe, it is not interesting or coherent. A bottom-of-the-barrel production.

p, Samuel Newman, Louis B. Appleton, Jr.; d, Appleton, Jr.; w, Newman; ph, Russ Meyer; m, Melvyn Lenard; ed, Albert Shaff.

Drama　　　　　　　　　　　　　　　　**(PR:O　MPAA:NR)**

DESTINATION BIG HOUSE**½　　　(1950) 60m REP bw

Dorothy Patrick *(Janet Brooks)*, Robert Rockwell *(Dr. Walter Phillips)*, James Lydon *(Fred Brooks)*, Robert Armstrong *(Ed Somers)*, Larry J. Blake *(Pete Weiss)*, John Harmon *(Stubby Moore)*, Claire DuBrey *(Celia Brooks)*, Richard Benedict *(Joe Bruno)*, Mickey Knox *(Savonia)*, Danny Morton *(Al Drury)*, Mack Williams *(Dr. Foster)*, Olan E. Soule *(Ralph Newell)*, Peter Prouse *(Ray Olsen)*, Norman Field *(Dr. Evans)*.

Patrick is a school teacher vacationing in a cabin in the woods. She meets Rockwell, a gangster hiding out with $80,000 absconded from his gang. He stashes the money in her cabin but his pursuers catch up with him and kill him. Before he dies he wills the money to Patrick, but without revealing its location. Now everyone believes Patrick has the money, including Rockwell's old gang and another gang. Patrick's brother (Lydon), saddled with gambling debts, finds the cash and the rival gangs converge and shoot it out. Somehow Patrick ends up with the money, which she donates to the local hospital for a polio ward. Routine melodrama, helped by director Blair's rapid pacing.

p, William Lackey; d, George Blair; w, Eric Taylor (based on an unpublished story by Mortimer Braus) ph, John MacBurnie; m, Stanley Wilson; ed, Tony Martinelli; art d, Frank Hotaling.

Crime　　　　　　　　　　　　　　　　**(PR:A　MPAA:NR)**

DESTINATION GOBI***　　　　　　(1953) 89m FOX c

Richard Widmark *(C.P.O. Sam McHale)*, Don Taylor *(Jenkins)*, Casey Adams *(Walter Landers)*, Murvyn Vye *(Kengtu)*, Darryl Hickman *(Wilbur Cohen)*, Martin Milner *(Elwood Halsey)*, Ross Bagdasarian *(Paul Sabatello)*, Judy Dann *(Nura-Satu)*, Rodolfo Acosta *(Tomec)*, Russell Collins *(Comdr. Wyatt)*, Leonard Strong *(Wali-Akham)*, Anthony Earl Numkena *(Son of Kengtu)*, Earl Holliman *(Frank Svenson)*, Edgar Barrier *(Yin Tang)*, Alvy Moore *(Aide)*, Stuart Randall *(Capt. Briggs)*, William Forrest *(Skipper)*, Bert Moorhouse *(Naval Captain)*, Jack Raine *(Admiral)*.

WW II drama based on facts. Widmark is a chief petty officer posted to a weather station in the Gobi Desert. When a Japanese air raid kills the commander, Widmark leads the men 800 miles across the desert to the coast. Along the way they fight off Japanese and try to befriend Mongol nomads headed by Vye. Above average war movie, with excellent action sequences.

p, Stanley Rubin; d, Robert Wise; w, Everett Freeman (based on an unpublished story by Edmund G. Love); ph, Charles G. Clarke (Technicolor); m, Sol Kaplan; ed, Robert Fritch; md, Alfred Newman; art d, Lyle Wheeler, Lewis Creber.

War Drama　　　　　　　　　　　　　**(PR:A　MPAA:NR)**

DESTINATION INNER SPACE*½
　　　　　　(1966) 83m United Pictures/Harold Goldman Associates/Magna c

Scott Brady *(Cmdr. Wayne)*, Sheree North *(Sandra)*, Gary Merrill *(Dr. Le Satier)*, Mike Road *(Hugh)*, Ron Burke *(Monster)*, Wendy Wagner *(Rene)*, John Howard *(Dr. James)*, William Thourlby *(Tex)*, Biff Elliott *(Dr. Wilson)*, Glen Spies *(Mike)*, Richard Niles *(Ellis)*, Roy Barcroft *(Skipper)*, Ken Delo *(Radio Man)*, James Hong *(Ho Lee)*, Ed Charles Sweeny.

Brady and fellow scientists at an underwater laboratory discover a flying saucer at the bottom of the ocean. Inside they find a pod which they take back to the lab. Predictably the pod hatches into a most unterrifying amphibian monster which bears a striking resemblance to The Creature from the Black Lagoon, and the scientists are hard put to stop it. Dull science fiction programmer with Brady going after not only the monster but also North, who wears a nice checkered bathing suit.

p, Earle Lyon; d, Francis D. Lyon; w, Arthur C. Pierce; ph, Brick Marquard (Eastmancolor); m, Paul Dunlap; ed, Robert S. Eisen; art d, Paul Sylos, Jr.; set d, Harry Reif; spec eff, Roger George.

Science Fiction　　　　　　　　　　**(PR:A　MPAA:NR)**

DESTINATION MILAN*　(1954, Brit.) 78m Douglas Fairbanks, Jr./BL bw

Douglas Fairbanks, Jr.; Tommy Duggan, Lorraine Clewes, Christopher Lee, Paul Sheridan, Ann Stephens, Yusef Crandall, Cyril Cusack, John Laurie, Barbara Mullen, Greta Gynt, Peter Reynolds, John Horsley, Mary Merrall.

Trilogy of stories lacks any cohesion either with each other or within themselves. The first has Fairbanks a wealthy American aboard the Orient Express set upon by a clan of sharpers but saved by the intervention of a guard on the train. The daughter of an Irish ne'er-do-well is forbidden to marry the son of a Scottish miser until the skinflint is called up on tax evasion charges and the Irishman helps him out of the difficulty. The last episode has a Norwegian artist murdering his brother, but exposed by his wife, who was the dead man's mistress. Nothing worthwhile.

p. Tom D. Connochie; w, Lawrence Huntington, Leslie Arliss, John Gilling; w, Huntington, Robert Hall, Paul Vincent Carroll, Doreen Montgomery; ph, Jimmy Wilson, Ken Talbot, Brendan J. Stafford.

Drama　　　　　　　　　　　　　　　　**(PR:A　MPAA:NR)**

DESTINATION MOON***　　　　　　(1950) 91m EL c

Warner Anderson *(Dr. Charles Cargraves)*, John Archer *(Jim Barnes)*, Tom Powers *(Gen. Thayer)*, Dick Wesson *(Joe Sweeney)*, Erin O'Brien-Moore *(Emily Cargraves)*, Ted Warde *(Brown)*.

Archer, Anderson, Wesson, and Powers rocket to the moon but find they haven't enough fuel to lift off again. They jettison everything they can but are still too heavy. Wesson decides to sacrifice himself but Archer figures out a way to get along without their heavy pressure suits and so they lift off to safety. Superficially a routine, even dull, science fiction film, this one was actually the most important contribution to the genre of the 1950s. Producer Pal and director Pichel tried to make the film as realistic as possible to distance it from the "Flash Gordon" tradition of the genre. Robert Heinlein coscripted the screenplay, based on his novel, and Walter Lantz contributed a Woody Woodpecker cartoon that explains rocket theory. A major success, both critical and popular, that won an Oscar for special effects. For the most part, the predictions made in the film were remarkably prophetic, down to the realistically conceived moonscape by astronomical painter Chesley Bonestell and designer Ernst Fegte, which took one hundred men more than two months to build. Unfortunately, the production was marred by script quarrels with backers who were afraid the film would flop unless changes were made. Producer Pal fought against them and won, achieving, if a curiously flat film, an important step in the genre's evolution.

p, George Pal; d, Irving Pichel; w, Rip van Ronkel, Robert A. Heinlein, James O'Hanlon (based on the novel *Rocketship Galileo* by Heinlein); ph, Lionel Lindon (Technicolor); m, Leith Stevens; ed, Duke Goldstone; prod d, Ernst Fegte; set d, George Lawley; spec eff, Lee Zavitz; cartoon sequence, Walter Lantz.

Science Fiction　　　　**Cas.**　　　　**(PR:A　MPAA:NR)**

DESTINATION MURDER**½　　　　　(1950) 72m RKO bw

Joyce MacKenzie *(Laura Mansfield)*, Stanley Clements *(Jackie Wales)*, Hurd Hatfield *(Stretch Norton)*, Albert Dekker *(Armitage)*, Myrna Dell *(Alice Wentworth)*, James Flavin *(Lt. Brewster)*, John Dehner *(Frank Niles)*, Richard Emory *(Sgt. Mulcahy)*, Norma Vance *(Inebriated Lady)*, Suzette Harbin *(Harriett, Nightclub Maid)*, Buddy Swan, Bert Wenland *(Messenger Boys)*, Franklyn Farnum *(Mr. Mansfield)*, Steve Gibson's Redcaps.

Thoroughly confusing *film noir* has MacKenzie investigating her father's murder. She dates Clements, whom she suspects is the trigger man, and he introduces her to Hatfield, manager of a night club for Dekker, who likes good music and lives in an exquisitely decorated mansion. Clements is murdered and Hatfield offers to help MacKenzie prove that Dekker, the criminal aesthete, had her father killed. Hatfield kills Dekker and convinces MacKenzie that she did it. After more plot convolutions the police arrive and shoot Hatfield. Slow moving and almost too complicated to follow, but an intriguing contribution to the *noir* cycle.

p, Edward L. Cahn; Maurie M. Suess; d, Cahn; w, Don Martin; ph, Jackson J. Rose; m, Irving Gertz; ed, Phillip Cahn; art d, Boris Leven; set d, Jacque Mapes; cos, Maria P. Donovan, Jerry Bos; m/l, "Let's Go To A Party," James Springs, Steve Gibson; "Palace of Stone," Springs.

Crime　　　　　　　　　　　　　　　　**(PR:C　MPAA:NR)**

DESTINATION 60,000**　　　　　　(1957) 66m AA bw

Preston Foster *(Col. Ed Buckley)*, Pat Conway *(Jeff Connors)*, Jeff Donnell *(Ruth Buckley)*, Coleen Gray *(Mary Ellen)*, Bobby Clark *("Skip" Buckley)*, Denver Pyle *(Mickey Hill)*, Russ Thorson *(Dan Maddox)*, Ann Barton *(Grace Hill)*.

Foster is an aircraft manufacturer testing his new jet. A test pilot story like every other test pilot story, though the aerial sequences (largely stock clips from Douglas Aircraft) are striking.

p, Jack J. Gross, Philip N. Krasne; d&w, George Waggner; ph, Hal McAlpin; m, Al Glasser; ed, Kenneth Crane; art d, Nicolai Remisoff.

Drama　　　　　　　　　　　　　　　**(PR:A MPAA:NR)**

DESTINATION TOKYO****　　　　　　　(1944) 135m WB bw

Cary Grant (Capt. Cassidy), John Garfield (Wolf), Alan Hale (Cookie), John Ridgely (Reserve), Dane Clark (Tin Can), Warner Anderson (Executive), William Prince (Pills), Bob Hutton (Tommy), Tom Tully (Mike), Faye Emerson (Mrs. Cassidy), Peter Whitney (Dakota), Warren Douglas (English Officer), John Forsythe (Sparks), John Alvin (Sound Man), Bill Kennedy (Torpedo Officer), John Whitney (Commanding Officer), William Challee (Quartermaster), Whit Bissell (Yo Yo), George Lloyd (Chief of Boat), Maurice Murphy (Toscanini), Pierre Watkin (Admiral), Stephen Richards (Admiral's Aide), Cliff Clark (Hornet's Admiral), Deborah Daves (Debby Cassidy), Michael Daves (Michael Cassidy), Mark Stevens, Jack Mower (Admiral's Aides), Mary Landa (Tin Can's Girl), Carlyle Blackwell (Man on Phone), Lane Chandler (C.P.O.), Joy Barlowe (Wolf's Girl), Bill Hunter (Market St. Commando), John Hudson (Radio Man), Jimmy Evans, George W. Robotham, Dan Borzage, Bernie Sell, Paul Parry, "Sailor" Vincent, Charles Sherlock, Warren Cross, Wally Walker, William Hudson, Charles Sullivan, Cy Malis, Bob Creasman, John Sylvester, Duke York, Ted Jacques, Harry Bartell, Jay Ward, John Forrest, Alan Wilson (Crew Members), Paul Langton (Barber), Hugh Prosser (Pilot), Frank Tang (Japanese Pilot), Angel Cruz (Japanese Bombardier), Charles Thompson (Rear Admiral), Russ Whiteman (1st Class Yeoman), Tony Hughes (Navy Air Officer), Bob Lowell (Radio Operator), George Anderson (Officer), Eddie Lee, Wing Foo (Japanese at Listening Post), Ya Sing Sung (Japanese on Beach), Benson Fong, James B. Leong (Japanese), Bruce Wong (Japanese Antenna Man), Roland Got (Japanese Officer), Dorothy Schoemer (Saleslady), Kirby Grant (Captain at Briefing), Herbert Gunn (Lieutenant), Warren Ashe (Major), Lou Marcelle (Narrator).

One of the most rousing, action-filled WW II films ever produced with a powerful cast and a terrific story, DESTINATION TOKYO remains a classic war drama to this day. Though there are many cameo stories within the framework of this film, the actual protagonist is the submarine in which the men serve, the U.S.S. Copperfin. Leaving a West Coast port a few days before Christmas, the sub heads out into the Pacific. As the men sing carols on Christmas Eve, Grant, the sub commander, opens his secret orders. The destination is Tokyo, right in the heart of Tokyo Bay, in fact, where, by night, Grant is to put ashore a meteorologist, Ridgely, who will obtain vital data for future air raids over the Japanese metropolis. The boat manages to approach Tokyo Bay but while waiting to slip through the underwater nets, one of the crew members, Hutton, comes down with acute appendicitis and inexperienced pharmacist's mate Prince must perform a delicate operation with crude instruments while reading out of a medical manual. The sailor miraculously survives. When Japanese warships enter the bay, the Copperfin slips inside with them, going directly beneath another ship (this in the days before sonar-detecting devices) to get past the nets. The sub lies inside the underwater mine fields for its own protection and surfaces at night to disembark Ridgely, Garfield and other crew members who go ashore and obtain data. This information is later radioed to the U.S. aircraft carrier Hornet which is carrying Doolittle's bombers which will attack Tokyo for the first time. During the bombing, Grant takes his sub out of the bay amidst the confusion, following enemy ships streaming through the nets to escape destruction. Grant then turns his ship around and sends torpedoes into a Japanese carrier launching fighters to attack American bombers. The underwater attack is detected by the enemy and Japanese destroyers go after the Copperfin. The submarine is relentlessly depth-charged until the boat appears to be coming apart at the seams. With only one destroyer left behind to finish the job, Grant brings his sub up, firing torpedoes. They hit the mark and the destroyer sinks. Grant orders his ship home. The Copperfin sails beneath the Golden Gate Bridge for its berth in San Francisco Bay. A bridge mender looks down and asks a fellow worker if he thinks the sub passing beneath them has seen any action. "Naw," replies the worker, "probably just returning from a routine patrol." As the sub approaches the dock the sailors on deck talk about what they will do on shore leave. Grant and his officers on the control tower look down to see Grant's wife, Emerson, and his children, running to meet the boat. DESTINATION TOKYO, with its excellent cast and sure-handed direction by Daves, was a smash box office hit. Grant was at the peak of his popularity at the time (he had earned $350,000 in 1941) and he gives a steady-as-a-rock performance as the commanding officer, mature, understanding and resolute in his duty. Garfield epitomizes the carefree, wise-cracking, girl-chasing sailor, counter-balanced by old salts Hale and Tully. Prince is outstanding as the sensitive pharmacist's mate and Clark, though he overacts at times in emulating his role model, Garfield, is properly volatile. The intimate feel of submarine life is ever present in this film, from its inherent claustrophobic confinement to its wonderful camaraderie among the shipmates. The suspense is maintained throughout, including one episode where the sub stops in the iceberg bound Aleutians to pick up weather expert Ridgely. Here the helpless sub is bombed and strafed by a Japanese sea-plane bomber which it shoots down. (When good-natured Tully tries to fish the pilot from the water the enemy stabs him to death and Hutton, Tully's protege, jumps on a machine-gun to riddle the pilot.) An unexploded bomb, however, is lodged in the ship and Grant and Hutton defuse it through agonizing minutes before the sub can submerge. Albert Maltz, who scripted this film, later made the so-called "Hollywood Ten" list of unfriendly witnesses before the witch-hunting HUAC inquisitors. Garfield spent a great deal of time with Dane Clark during the shooting of DESTINATION TOKYO. Clark became his alter ego, picking up Garfield's mannerisms and style of speech. It alarmed Garfield a bit so that he gave a restrained performance and in his scenes with Clark (born Bernard Zanville), Garfield (born Julius Garfinkle) appears normal, believable, while Clark is manic and nerve-jangling. Garfield considers this film, along with AIR FORCE and PRIDE OF THE MARINES, one of his best efforts for Warner Brothers.

p, Jerry Wald; d, Delmer Daves; w, Albert Maltz, Daves (based on a story by Steve Fisher); ph, Bert Glennon; m, Franz Waxman; ed, Charles Nyby; md, Leo F.

Forbstein; art d, Leo K. Kuter; set d, Walter Tilford; spec eff, Lawrence Butler, Willard Van Enger; tech adv, Lt. Cdr. Phillip Compton.

War Drama　　　　　　　　　　　　　**(PR:A MPAA:NR)**

DESTINATION UNKNOWN**　　　　　　(1933) 69m UNIV bw

Pat O'Brien (Matt Brennan), Ralph Bellamy (The Stowaway), Alan Hale (Lundstrom), Russell Hopton (Georgie), Tom Brown (Johnny), Betty Compson (Ruby Smith), Noel Madison (Maxie), Stanley Fields (Gattallo), Rollo Lloyd (Dr. Fram), Willard Robertson (Joe Shano), Charles Middleton (Turk), Richard Alexander (Alex), Forrester Harvey (Ring), George Rigas (Tauru).

Strange sea melodrama has a rum-running ship becalmed, out of fresh water, and sinking fast. To top it off, the captain and mate have been swept overboard in a storm, leaving bo'sun Hale in command of a mutinous and desperate crew. Suddenly, stowaway Bellamy emerges and informs the crew that all the casks they thought were full of sherry hold fresh water, foisted on them by a crooked island trader. Using vaguely supernatural powers, he saves the ship and turns its crew of cutthroats into a nice bunch of guys. Then he disappears as mysteriously as he appeared. Hale is magnificent as a big Swede, and the first part of the picture is a tense atmospheric thriller, but soon after Bellamy appears it slips into maudlin sentiment and slapstick comedy. Garnett wrote this film off his resume, later commenting: "In spite of an excellent script and a brilliant cast. . .DESTINATION UNKNOWN should have been titled DESTINATION OBLIVION. It sank without a trace."

d, Tay Garnett; w, Tom Buckingham; ph, Edward Snyder; ed, Milton Carruth.

Drama　　　　　　　　　　　　　　　**(PR:A MPAA:NR)**

DESTINATION UNKNOWN*½　　　　　　(1942) 63m UNIV bw

William Gargan (Briggs Hannon), Irene Hervey (Elena), Sam Levene (Victor), Turhan Bey (Muto), Keye Luke (Secretary), Felix Bash (Karl Renner), Donald Stuart (Wllington), Olaf Hytten (Wing Fu), Edward Colebrook (Lt. Kawabe), Willie Fung (Farmer), Charles Lung (Col. Suyakawa), Herbert Heyes (Daniels), Edward Van Sloan, Hans Schumm.

Forgettable programmer has Flying Tiger Gargan and Hervey chasing one another around pre-Pearl Harbor China for a fortune in jewels that will pay for munitions for Chiang Kai-Shek's beleaguered army. It turns out that they are on the same side all along.

p, Marshall Grant; d, Ray Taylor, w, Lynn Riggs, John Meehan, Jr. (based on a story by Lawrence Hazard and John Kafka); ph, John W. Boyle; md H.J. Salter; ed, Charles Maynard; art d, Jack Otterson.

War　　　　　　　　　　　　　　　**(PR:A MPAA:NR)**

DESTINEES　　　　　(SEE: DAUGHTERS OF DESTINY, 1954, Fr.)

DESTINY**　　　　　　(1938) 74m CineLux bw (IL DESTINO)

Emma Grammatica (Damigella di Bard), Armando Migliri, Mirabella Pardi, Luigi Cimari, Cesare Beltarini.

Grammatica is an aging noblewoman reduced to poverty by the unscrupulous administrator of her estate (Migliri), but content in her memories of youth. In the end, her friends come to the rescue and see her restored to her proper dignity. Beyond a nice performance by Grammatica, not much of interest here.

d, Mario Mattoli.

Drama　　　　　　　　　　　　　　　**(PR:A MPAA:NR)**

DESTINY**½　　　　　　　　　　　　(1944) 65m UNIV bw

Gloria Jean (Jane), Alan Curtis (Cliff), Frank Craven (Clem), Grace McDonald (Betty), Vivian Austin (Phyllis), Frank Fenton (Sam), Minna Gombell (Marie), Selmer Jackson (Warden), Lew Wood (Prison Guard), Perc Launders (Sergeant), Harry Strang (Sgt. Bronson), Lane Chandler (Patrolman), Billy Wayne (Bartender), Bob Homans (Grogan the Watchman), Gayne Whitman (Radio Announcer), Frank Hagney (3rd Motorcycle Cop), Erville Alderson (Man, Cut), Edgar Dearing (4th Motorcycle Cop), Mr. Bones (Dog), Dorothy Vaughn (Maggie, Old Woman), Dale Van Sickel (1st Motorcycle Cop), Bill O'Brien (Waiter), Bob Reeves (Cop), Ken Terrell, Bud Wolfe (Radio Patrolmen), Bill Hall (2nd Motorcycle Cop).

On the run from a crime he didn't commit, Curtis hides out on the isolated farm of Craven and Jean, his blind daughter. At first he plans to rob the pair and run off, but he remains behind and is reformed by the girl. Originally intended as an episode in FLESH AND FANTASY, the film was padded out with an extra 35 minutes of new footage (easily distinguishable). It is surprising to realize when seen today that DESTINY, with its fairy tale-like blending of beauty, mysticism, and horror, had few champions in its day. Nor did Gloria Jean—then a teenage soprano and deemed to be a threat to Universal's reigning songstress, Deanna Durbin—whose career soon after went into a steep decline. Oddly cast in DESTINY was McDonald, the studio's top tap dancer, who not only did not dance in the film but did not even walk, playing her entire role behind the wheel of a car.

p, Howard Benedict, Roy William Neill; d, Reginald Le Borg, Julian Duvivier; ph, George Robinson, Paul Ivano; w, Roy Chanslor, Ernest Pascal; m, Frank Skinner; ed, Paul Landres; art d, John B. Goodman, Abraham Grossman, Richard Riedel.

Drama　　　　　　　　　　　　　　　**(PR:A MPAA:NR)**

DESTINY OF A MAN**　　　　(1961, USSR) 100m Mosfilm/Lopert bw
　　　　　　　　　　　(SUDBA CHELOVEKA; AKA: FATE OF A MAN)

Sergey Bondarchuk (Andrey Sokolov), Pavilk Boriskin (Vanyushka)), Zoya Kiriyenko (Irina), Pavel Volkov (Ivan Timofeyevich), Yuriy Averin (Myuller), K. Alekseyev (German Major), P. Vinnikov, Yevgeniy Teterin, Anatoliy Chemodurov, A. Novikov, L. Borisov, V. Markin, Ye. Kudryashov, A. Kuznetsov, V. Ivanov, Pyotr Savin, Ye. Melnikova, V. Berezko, N. Aparin, N. Pechentsov, A. Puntus, G. Shapovaov, V. Strelnikov.

Bondarchuk tells his life story to a young man as they wait for a ferry. During WW II he was an Army truck driver with a wife and three children. Captured by the

Germans, he witnesses many atrocities inflicted on his fellow soldiers. He escapes once and is captured, then escapes the firing squad by impressing a German officer with his drinking capacity. He becomes a chauffeur and drives the German to the Russian front. After the war he learns that his wife and two daughters were killed in a bombing raid and his son was killed on the last day of the war. He takes a job as a truck driver and adopts an orphan boy to help give him a reason to live. Photography by Monakhov won many awards.

d, Sergey Bondarchuk; w, Yuriy Lukin, Fyodor Shakhamagonov; ph, Vladimir Monakhov; m, Veniamin Basner; ed, Tatyana Likhachyova; art d, I. Novoder-ezhkin, Sergy Voronkov.

Drama **(PR:A MPAA:NR)**

DESTROY ALL MONSTERS**½ (1969, Jap.) 88m Toho/AIP c
(KAIJU SOSHINGEKI)

Akira Kubo (Flight Captain), Jun Tazaki (Dr. Yoshido), Yoshio Tsuchiya (Dr. Otani), Kyoko Ai (Queen of the Kilaaks), Yukiko Kobayashi (Kyoko), Kenji Sahara (Nishikawa), Andrew Hughes (Dr. Stevenson), Nadao Kirino, the Itah Sisters, Susumu Kurobe, Hisaya Ito, Yoshifumi Tajima, Naoya Kusakawa, Ikio Sawamura, Wataru Omura, Kazuo Suzuki, Yutaka Sada.

Female aliens from Kilaak, based on the moon, attach radio controls to the necks of the monsters kept on Ogaswara Island. Godzilla attacks New York, Mothra destroys Peking, Rodan rips up Moscow, Anzilla, Varan, Ebirah, Baragon, Wenda, and Spigas all make contributions to the carnage. Earth regains control over the monsters so the Kilaaks play their last card—they send Ghidrah against it, but the other monsters unite and defeat him in a huge battle at the base of Mount Fuji, saving the world. Toho's twentieth monster movie, for which the studio pulled out all the stops and fielded every monster on the lot. As art, it isn't much. For fans of big monsters smashing model buildings and fighting each other, it is the ultimate.

p, Tomoyuki Tanaka; d, Ishiro Honda; w, Kaoru Mabuchi, Honda; ph, Taiichi Kankura (Tohoscope, Berkley Pathe Color); m, Akira Ifukube; ed. Ryohei Fujii; art d, Takeo Kita; spec eff, Eiji Tsuburaya, Sadamasa Arikawa.

Science Fiction **(PR:A MPAA:G)**

DESTROY, SHE SAID*½ (1969, Fr.) 100m Ancinex-Madelaine/Grove bw
(DETRUITE, DIT-ELLE)

Catherine Sellers (Elizabeth), Nicole Hiss (Alissa), Henri Garcin (Max Thor), Michel Lonsdale (Stein), Daniel Gelin (Bernard Alione).

A college professor, Garcin, and his young wife, Hiss, encounter a young German Jew at a resort in a deep forest. Personalities shift, identities merge, and symbols are tossed about as light as lead. Tediously written and directed by Duras from her novel.

p, Nicole Stephane; d&w, Marguerite Duras (based on a novel by Duras); ph, Jean Penzer; ed, Henri Colpi.

Drama **(PR:O MPAA:NR)**

DESTROYER*** (1943) 99m COL bw

Edward G. Robinson (Steve Boleslavski), Glenn Ford (Mickey Donohue), Marguerite Chapman (Mary Boleslavski), Edgar Buchanan (Kansas Jackson), Leo Gorcey (Sarecky), Regis Toomey (Lt. Cdr. Clark), Ed Brophy (Casey), Warren Ashe (Lt. Morton), Craig Woods (Bigbee), Curt Bois (Yasha), Pierre Watkin (Admiral), Al Hill (Knife Eating Sailor), Bobby Jordan (Sobbing Sailor), Roger Clark (Chief Engineer), Dean Benton (Fireman Moore), David Alison (Fireman Thomas), Paul Perry (Doctor), John Merton (Chief Quartermaster), Don Peters (Helmsman), Virginia Sale (Spinster), Eleanor Counts (Sarecky's Girl), Dale Van Sickel (Sailor), Addison Richards (Gerguson), Lester Dorr (1st Ship Fitter), Bud Geary (2nd Ship Fitter), Eddie Dew (Survivor), Tristram Coffin (Doctor No. 1), Larry Parks (Ens. Johnson), Eddie Chandler (Chief Gunner's Mate), Lloyd Bridges (2nd Fireman), Dennis Moore (Communications Officer), Edmund Cobb (1st Workman), Eddy Waller (Riveter), Charles McGraw (Asst. Chief Engineer).

Robinson is a welder working on a new destroyer, the John Paul Jones, a warship replacing an old vessel on which he had served during WW I. His good-natured ways vanish as he makes a pest of himself, nagging other workers to check every rivet of the ship which he insists must be perfect. When the destroyer is launched Robinson re-enlists and is taken aboard the ship he helped to build by Toomey, the skipper who had once served under Robinson and who credits the old salt with encouraging him to graduate from Annapolis. Ford, a tough, savvy Boatswain's Mate, must take a step down when Robinson comes aboard, yielding to the older man's seniority. What complicates their relationship even further is that Ford is attracted to Robinson's dark-eyed daughter, Chapman. Naturally, the two clash and their feud continues on board ship where Robinson drives the men so hard that dissension undermines the operations of the ship. Toomey is pressured to get rid of Robinson but he sticks by his old friend, lecturing him to "go easy with these kids." Instead, Robinson tries to instill pride in the crew by relating the history of the Jones and the great captain after which the ship was named, vividly recounting the last battle of the Bon Homme Richard. Once in battle Robinson shows his true mettle and becomes a hero, earning the respect of the crew and particularly Ford who comes to admire him as well as winding up with daughter Chapman. DESTROYER is an old-fashioned film, with a thin plot that could have come out of the 1930s, but its worth is Robinson's bravura portrayal of a pugnacious sailor who won't take no for an answer. He snarls, barks and threatens as he did a decade earlier in gangster epics but this time it's for the worthy cause of freedom. Among the youngsters like Ford who ridicule his preposterous behavior Robinson appears out of place and out of step, but that is exactly his role and he plays it to the hilt.

p, Louis F. Edelman; d, William A. Seiter; w, Frank Wead, Lewis Melzer, Borden Chase (based on a story by Wead); ph, Franz F. Planer; m, Anthony Collins; ed, Gene Havlick; md, M.W. Stoloff; art d, Lionel Banks.

War Drama **(PR:A MPAA:NR)**

DESTRUCTION TEST (SEE: CIRCLE OF DECEPTION, 1961, Brit.)

DESTRUCTORS, THE*½ (1968) 97m United Pictures-Harold Goldman Associates/Feature Film Corp. of America c

Richard Egan (Dan Street), Patricia Owens (Charlie), John Ericson (Dutch Holland), Michael Ansara (Count Mario Romano), Joan Blackman (Stassa), David Brian (Hogan), Johnny Seven (Spaniard), Khigh Dhiegh (King Chou Lai), Gregory Morton (Dr. Frazer), John Howard (Bushnell), Eddie Firestone (Barnes), Jayne Massey (Suzie), Michael Dugan (Parkhouse), Jim Adams (Wayne), Olan Soule, Mary Lou Cook, Adele Claire, James Seay, Walter Reed, Douglas Kennedy, Virginia Wood, John Lawrence, Lennie Geer, Robert Riordan, Richard Norris, Linda Kirk, Rick Traeger, King Moody, Cal Currens, Tommy McDonald, Karen Norris, Dodie Warren, Horace Brown, Tex Armstrong, Jim Kline.

Egan is a secret agent after a gang of spies, led by swimsuit manufacturer Ansara, who plan to steal a super laser gun. Inferior ripoff of the James Bond series, complete with high tech hardware.

p, Earle Lyon; d, Francis D. Lyon; w, Arthur C. Pierce, Larry E. Jackson; ph, Alan Stensvold; m, Paul Dunlap; ed, Robert S. Eisen; art d, Paul Sylos; set d, Raymond G. Boltz; spec eff, Roger George.

Spy Drama/Adventure **(PR:C MPAA:NR)**

DESTRUCTORS, THE*½ (1974, Brit.) 89m AIP c
(AKA: THE MARSEILLES CONTRACT)

Michael Caine (Deray), Anthony Quinn (Steve Ventura), James Mason (Brizard), Maureen Kerwin (Lucianne), Marcel Bozzuffi (Calmet), Catherine Rouvel (Brizard's Mistress), Maurice Ronet (Inspector Briac), Andre Oumansky (Marsac), Alexandra Stewart (Rita), Patrick Floersheim (Kovakian), Pierre Salinger (Williams), Hella Petri (Countess), Vernon Dobtcheff (Lazar), Jerry Brouer (Kurt), Georges Lycan (Henri), Jean Bouchaud (Rouget), Georges Beller (Minieri), Robert Rondo (Matthews), Gib Grossac (Fournier), J.L. Fortuit (Fortuit), Pierre Koulak (Wilson), Jonathan Brooks Poole (Kevin), Barbara Sommers (Sally), Martine Kelly (Janet), Dianik Zurakowska (The Girl), Ed Marcus (Detective Fargas), Alan Rosset, Bill Kearns, James Jones, Gene Moskowitz (Poker Players).

Once again Caine has taken a job for what must have been a nice sum of money and he may have failed to read the script. The man is amazing in that he has managed to survive some of the worst films ever made and still retains his charm and ability to make deals for more pictures. Quinn is a tired narcotics officer attached to the U.S. embassy in Paris. He has been attempting to crack a huge drug ring run by Mason, who is heavily protected both physically and politically. Three agents went after Mason and all three turned up dead. To make matters worse, the French government is leaning heavily on Quinn for harassing Mason, a French citizen. Ronet, a Parisian police inspector, unofficially suggests that Quinn might be able to clear things up by arranging for Mason's death by a professional assassin. At first Quinn rebels, then he thinks further about it, weighs the death of his three men against the life of Mason, and agrees. He is amazed to find that the hired killer is Caine, a pal of long standing and a former Algerian war veteran. Caine acquires false papers and insinuates himself inside Mason's Marseilles operation by charming Rouvel, Mason's nubile daughter. He is still not fully accepted until he casually kills an informer by tossing him off a building. Now totally trusted by Mason, Caine is making his plans to kill the man. Meanwhile, Quinn learns that Mason is about to accept a large shipment of narcotics from Turkey and he wants to catch him alive, with the haul, and put him in jail forever. That means that Caine must be contacted and stopped before he carries out the contract on Mason's life. To do that, Quinn has Ronet notify the Marseilles police to go after Caine as a "bank robber." Quinn thinks he can get Caine away from Mason, then have the police release Caine once Quinn calls them off. Mason, whose men are everywhere, finds out that Caine is "wanted" and sends him off on a phony errand far from the gang where his arrest might prove a problem as the narcotics are due and nothing must stop the delivery. Once gone, Mason calls the cops and tells them where Caine is. Caine shoots it out with the police and gets away, returning to Marseilles as a hunted man. Three different factions are now after Caine—Mason, the police, and Quinn, who gets to him first. Mason and his men come after Quinn and Caine. Caine has Mason in his sights, then sees someone aiming at Quinn. He turns to fire at the sniper aiming at Quinn, and Mason uses that split-second to shoot Caine, who dies in Quinn's arms. Quinn is enraged, goes after Mason, and kills him while Mason is dancing at a huge formal ball. He shoots Mason with a silencer and no one knows where the bullets came from. The problem was not the plot. It could have been interesting. But Parrish's direction of Bernard's script compounded banality with dullness and the result was something with little style and less imagination.

p, Judd Bernard; d, Robert Parrish; w, Bernard (based on a story "What Are Friends For?" by Bernard); ph, Douglas Slocombe (Panavision, Movielab Color); m, Roy Budd; ed, Willy Kemplen; art s, Willy Holt.

Drama **Cas.** **(PR:C MPAA:PG)**

DESTRY**½ (1954) 95m UNIV c

Audie Murphy (Tom Destry), Mari Blanchard (Brandy), Lyle Bettger (Decker), Lori Nelson (Martha Phillips), Thomas Mitchell (Rags Barnaby), Edgar Buchanan (Mayor Hiram Sellers), Wallace Ford (Doc Curtis), Mary Wickes (Bessie Mae Curtis), Alan Hale, Jr. (Jack Larson), Lee Aaker (Eli Skinner), Trevor Bardette (Sheriff Joe Bailey), Walter Baldwin (Henry Skinner), George Wallace (Curley), Richard Reeves (Mac), Frank Richards (Dummy), Mitchell Lawrence (Dealer), Ralph Peters (Bartender), John Doucette (Cowhand).

Inferior remake of the thrice-filmed Max Brand novel, directed by George Marshall, who had done the definitive version in 1939. This time Murphy is the gunless lawman bringing order to town, and Blanchard is the wildcat saloon singer whose fight with Wickes provides a much needed high point. In scanty dance hall costumes she also sings some torchy numbers.

p, Stanley Rubin; d, George Marshall; w, Edmund H. North, D.D. Beauchamp (based on a story by Felix Jackson, suggested by the novel Destry Rides Again by

Max Brand); ph, George Robinson (Technicolor); ed, Ted J. Kent; md, Joseph Gershenson; cos, Rosemary Odell; m/l, "Empty Arms," "If You Can Can-Can," "Bang, Bang," Arnold Hughes, Frederick Herbert.

Western **(PR:A MPAA:NR)**

DESTRY RIDES AGAIN** (1932) 53m UNIV bw (AKA: JUSTICE RIDES AGAIN)

Tom Mix *(Thomas J. Destry, Jr.)*, Claudia Dell *(Frenchy)*, ZaSu Pitts *(Temperance Worker)*, Stanley Fields *(Sheriff)*, George Ernest, Andy Devine, Edward Piel, Sr., Francis Ford, Earle Foxe, Frederick Howard, John Ince, Edward J. Le Saint, Charles K. French, Tony the Wonder Horse ["Tony, Jr."] *(Himself)*.

Mix is a stagecoach partner sent to jail by his crooked partner and perjuring witnesses. Now he's out of prison and back for revenge. Mix is showing his 50 years and the film is a dull throwback to the silent horse operas of his prime. The first filmization of Max Brand's novel and the closest to it in plot is also Mix's first talkie. He quit the movies in 1929 to devote himself to his circus, but Universal lured him back with an offer of $10,000 a week, $100,000 budgets for six westerns over which he would have control of script and casting, and the use of Clark, his favorite cameraman.

p, Stanley Bergerman; d, Ben Stoloff; w, Isadore Bernstein, Robert Keith, Richard Schayer (based on the novel by Max Brand); ph, Daniel B. Clark.

Western **(PR:A MPAA:NR)**

DESTRY RIDES AGAIN*½** (1939) 94m UNIV bw

Marlene Dietrich *(Frenchy)*, James Stewart *(Tom Destry)*, Mischa Auer *(Boris Callahan)*, Charles Winninger *("Wash" Dimsdale)*, Brian Donlevy *(Kent)*, Allen Jenkins *(Bugs Watson)*, Warren Hymer *(Gyp Watson)*, Irene Hervey *(Janice Tyndall)*, Una Merkel *(Lily Belle Callahan)*, Tom Fadden *(Lem Claggett)*, Samuel S. Hinds *(Judge Slade)*, Lillian Yarbo *(Clara)*, Edmund MacDonald *(Rockwell)*, Billy Gilbert *(Loupqerou, the Bartender)*, Virginia Brissac *(Sophie Claggett)*, Ann Todd *(Claggett Girl)*, Dickie Jones *(Eli Whitney Claggett)*, Jack Carson *(Jack Tyndall)*, Carmen D'Antonio *(Dancer)*, Joe King *(Sheriff Keogh)*, Harry Cording *(Rowdy)*, Minerva Urecal *(Mrs. DeWitt)*, Bob McKenzie *(Doctor)*, Billy Bletcher *(Pianist)*, Lloyd Ingraham *(Turner, the Express Agent)*, Bill Cody, Jr. *(Small Boy)*, Loren Brown, Harold DeGarro *(Jugglers)*, Harry Tenbrook, Bud McClure *(Stage Drivers)*, Alex Voloshin *(Assistant Bartender)*, Chief John Big Tree *(Indian)*, Bill Steele Gettinger, Dick Alexander *(Cowboys)*.

A hell-for-leather western where Dietrich and Stewart, two of the most unlikely screen lovers, work splendidly together. Stewart is the son of a brave lawman gone to his reward. But he appears to be anything but a two-fisted fighter for justice. He refuses to wear guns and when he steps up to the bar he orders milk. Soft-spoken and mild mannered, Stewart becomes the butt of jokes when he shows up in Bottleneck where Donlevy runs the wildest saloon in town and lords it over the lowly. To disobey an order from Donlevy is to reserve six feet of earth in Boot Hill. His girl friend and star attraction is Dietrich, the famous Frenchy, who belts out tunes while fending off a hundred pawing hands. When newcomer Stewart refuses to fawn over her, Dietrich becomes enraged, and tries to make a fool of him. He has arrived in town as a deputy to Winninger, the town drunk who has been made sheriff by Donlevy as a joke after the gambler killed the regular sheriff. Stewart wears no guns but does put on a display of marksmanship with a borrowed weapon that has the locals double-taking. Merkel, the wife of a man fleeced by Dietrich, arrives spitting mad, taking out her wrath on Dietrich who promptly insults her. Merkel begins to bang Dietrich around and the two get into one of the wildest fights between females ever recorded on film. They punch, wrestle, kick, gouge, bite and roll around on the floor for two minutes of celluloid action (the scene took five days to film). Stewart finally breaks up this incredible donnybrook by dousing both Dietrich and Merkel with a bucket of water. Then Dietrich attacks Stewart who manages to work her off his back. Donlevy and his thugs threaten Stewart who appears to back down which mortifies Winninger who had served with his father and had bragged about how his new deputy would bring law and order to Bottleneck. When he upbraids Stewart later the young man responds with: "You shoot it out with them and for some reason they get to look like heroes. You put 'em behind bars and they look little and cheap." With that Stewart begins cowing lawbreakers with his hands and dragging them to jail. Though Dietrich makes several plays for Stewart he treats her as saloon baggage which further infuriates her; moreover, Stewart seems to have eyes for no one but Hervey, the school marm. All the while Stewart is searching for the dead sheriff's body and finally deceives Jenkins, one of Donlevy's stooges, into digging up the corpse. He arrests Jenkins but after jailing him, Donlevy's goons murder helpless Winninger. This enrages Stewart who puts on his father's guns and heads for Donlevy's saloon, an army of irate ciitzens armed to the teeth following, intending to back him up. A pitched battle ensues. From a balcony, Donlevy takes careful aim with a rifle, his target being Stewart. Seeing what is about to happen, Dietrich races forward to protect the man she loves, taking the bullet intended for Stewart. With one quick flash, Stewart draws and fires, killing Donlevy. Stewart kneels to hold the dying showgirl in his arms. Dietrich looks up at him with sinking eyelids and a wan smile. "Would you mind?" she says softly, and he kisses her. She dies. (The original script had Dietrich's last line as: "Kiss me, good feller.") With the town cleaned up, Stewart is free to pursue happiness with Hervey but the viewer is left with the clear impression that had Dietrich lived his heart would have gone to her. Dietrich's career up to this movie was in fast decline. She had left the protective wing of her directorial mentor Josef von Sternberg in 1935 but most of her movies through the late 1930s were not popular. After appearing in ANGEL, an uncommon failure of Ernst Lubitsch, Dietrich was considered "box office poison" by exhibitors. For three years she made no films of consequence and when Paramount dropped her contract in 1937 she was considered washed up. She went to Paris to appear in THE IMAGE for Julien Duvivier, believing that American film audiences were through with her. Then she got a transatlantic call in the middle of the night from producer Joe Pasternak. He wanted her for a new film he was doing at Universal. (Pasternak did not tell her that Paulette Goddard was the studio's first selection and that he had had to fight desperately with Universal bosses to let him hire Dietrich.) She was thunderstruck when she heard he wanted her for a *western*! And she would only get $75,000 for her performance. One of the most glamorous women in the world who had been associated with either heavy drama or sophisticated roles to play a saloon hussy in a crude oater? But Dietrich took it, accepting the challenge. She was bawdy, tempestuous wicked, but with a heart of gold and she died a heroine's death. Never before had Dietrich been so wonderful in a film and the public responded to her with accolades. Her star shot upward again, higher than before, in this telling turning point of her career. DESTRY RIDES AGAIN is a well-paced western under the firm hand of director Marshall, a veteran of the genre, but it was so raucous in its production that many questionable lines were cut. In one scene, after winning at poker, Dietrich drops some gold coins down her dress. Jenkins howls: "There's gold in them thar hills!" This line never made it past the censors. Dietrich also sang some memorable tunes by Hollander and Loesser: "Little Joe the Wrangler," "You've Got That Look (That Leaves Me Weak)," and "See What The Boys in the Back Room Will Have," the last song becoming umbilical to Dietrich. Stewart's performance was rendered in his usual low key and provided the perfect balance to Dietrich's bold and brassy character. All the great character actors in this film, Donlevy, Auer, Winninger, Jenkins, Hymer were superb and Hinds, normally a kindly grandfather type, turned in a surprising role as a venal judge wearing a top hat, spouting law and pocketing bribes at the same time. DESTRY was filmed three times following the publication of the Max Brand novel in 1930, first as a Tom Mix standard in 1932, again in the 1939 Dietrich-Stewart classic, and in 1954 as a routine western with Audie Murphy.

p, Joe Pasternak; d, George Marshall; w, Felix Jackson, Henry Meyers, Gertrude Purcell (based on the novel by Max Brand); ph, Hal Mohr; m, Frank Skinner; ed, Milton Carruth; md, Charles Previn; art d, Jack Otterson; cos, Vera West; m/l, Frederick Hollander, Frank Loesser.

Western **(PR:A MPAA:NR)**

DETECTIVE, THE*** (1954, Brit.) 91m COL bw (GB: FATHER BROWN)

Alec Guinness *(Father Brown)*, Joan Greenwood *(Lady Warren)*, Peter Finch *(Flambeau)*, Cecil Parker *(the Bishop)*, Bernard Lee *(Inspector Valentine)*, Sidney James *(Parkinson)*, Gerard Oury *(Inspector Dubois)*, Ernest Thesiger *(Vicomte)*, Ernest Clark *(Secretary)*, Austin Trevor *(Herald)*, Noel Howlett *(Auctioneer)*, Marne Maitland *(Maharajah)*, John Salew *(Station Sergeant)*, John Horsley *(Inspector Wilkins)*, Lance Maraschal *(Texan)*, Aubrey Woods *(Charlie)*, Sam Kydd *(Scotland Yard Sergeant)*, Hugh Dempster *(Man in Bowler)*, Jack McNaughton, Eugene Deckers, Betty Baskcomb, Dianne Van Proosdy, Dino Galvani, Hugo Shuster, Guido Lorraine, Jim Gerald, Daniel Clerice, Everley Gregg.

Guinness is an eccentric priest who takes it upon himself to transport a priceless cross from London to Rome. An international jewel thief steals the cross, and Guinness sets out to get it back and save the thief's soul. He travels to Paris, and then to a Burgundy castle, where he finds the cross and other priceless items. He returns to England a hero. An entertaining film with Guinness at his best.

p, Paul Finder Moss, Vivian A. Cox; d, Robert Hamer; w, Thelma Schnee, Hamer (based on "Father Brown" stories by G.K. Chesterton); ph, Harry Waxman; m, Georges Auric; ed, Gordon Hales.

Comedy **(PR:A MPAA:NR)**

DETECTIVE, THE ***½ (1968) 114m FOX c

Frank Sinatra *(Joe Leland)*, Lee Remick *(Karen Leland)*, Ralph Meeker *(Lt. Curran)*, Jack Klugman *(Dave Schoenstein)*, Horace McMahon *(Farrell)*, Lloyd Bochner *(Dr. Roberts)*, William Windom *(Colin MacIver)*, Jacqueline Bisset *(Norma McIver)*, Tony Musante *(Felix)*, Al Freeman, Jr. *(Robbie)*, Robert Duvall *(Nestor)*, Pat Henry *(Mercidis)*, Patrick McVey *(Tanner)*, Dixie Marquis *(Carol Linjack)*, Sugar Ray Robinson *(Kelly)*, Renee Taylor *(Rachael Schoenstein)*, James Inman *(Teddy Leikman)*, Tom Atkins *(Harmon)*, James Dukas *(Medical Examiner)*, Sharon Henesy *(Sharon)*, Earl Montgomery *(Desk Clerk)*, Peg Murray *(Girl at Party)*, Frank Reiter *(Tough Homosexual)*, Peter York *(Decent Boy)*, Mark Dawson *(Desk Sergeant)*, Jose Rodriguez *(Boy in Police Station)*, Tom Gorman *(Prison Priest)*, Lou Nelson *(Procurer)*, Richard Krisher *(Matt Henderson)*, Jilly Rizzo *(Bartender)*, Arnold Soboloff, George Plimpton, Phil Sterling, Don Fellows, Paul Larson, Ted Beniades *(Reporters)*, Jan Farrand *(Karen's Friend at Theater)*, Marion Brash *(Prostitute)*.

Frank Sinatra was heavily into his law and order mood when he made THE DETECTIVE. He made this, TONY ROME, and LADY IN CEMENT within a brief period and obviously enjoyed the experience. This was the most realistic of the three although it wasn't as successful as the others, perhaps because of its hard-core grittiness. All three films were produced by Aaron Rosenberg and directed by Gordon Douglas, with cinematography by Joe Biroc. Once Sinatra assembles a team he enjoys working with, he continues to use them. Sinatra is a New York City detective with a reputation for being excellent. He is investigating the mutilation murder of a homosexual (James Inman) and must visit all the gay haunts in order to crack the case. He arrests Musante and the cops give the guy a hard time but the usual strongarm methods don't work on Musante. Now, Sinatra becomes the "good guy" cop, worms his way into Musante's confidence, causing him to confess to the murder. Musante is tried, convicted, and executed, but it haunts Sinatra, as something doesn't ring true about Musante's confession. Sinatra wins a promotion but he is troubled. Meanwhile, Remick, his wife, has been showing serious signs of nymphomania and its adds to Sinatra's shaky mental condition. Still, he can't bring himself to divorce Remick as he loves her deeply, despite whatever she may have done. Windom commits suicide, or so it seems, but his wife, Bisset, doesn't believe it, so she asks Sinatra to look into the matter. In Windom's private papers, Sinatra finds evidence of a cabal of city officials who pool their money, buy slum buildings, and profit greatly by their inside information. Meeker, a fellow detective, suggests that Sinatra look the other way with this info and some serious cash may change hands. Sinatra responds by decking Meeker. Now Sinatra is almost killed by two pros but he manages to get them first. Next, Bochner, a psychiatrist pal of Bisset's, tries to call Sinatra off the case. Then, Sinatra finds some tapes made by the late

Windom and learns that it was he, not Musante, who killed the homosexual in reel one. Windom had been a late-blooming bisexual, and fallen in love with the victim, had a fight, and murdered him. Sinatra is stunned by the revelation as it means he was instrumental in sending an innocent man, Musante, to his death. That, plus the knowledge that there is so much corruption among his fellow police officers, causes him to go to the newspapers and reveal the whole story (something actually done by SERPICO). Sinatra quits the police after twenty years and hopes he can repair the shards of his life, perhaps with Bisset. . . or without her. Whichever, he knows there's got to be something better than what he has. This was a tough movie and surely more honest than many films made in the middle 1960s. Mann took a few liberties with Thorp's book but it was generally very satisfying. Bochner also appeared in TONY ROME, as a gay drug dealer. Look for Duvall in a small, but telling, role as a "queer-buster." Just as Sinatra used Rocky Graziano in TONY ROME, he does the same with Sugar Ray Robinson here.

p, Aaron Rosenberg; d, Gordon Douglas; w, Abby Mann (based on the novel by Roderick Thorp); ph, Joe Biroc (Panavision, DeLuxe Color); m, Jerry Goldsmith; ed, Robert Simpson; art d, Jack Martin Smith, William Creber; set d, Walter M. Scott, Jerry Wunderlich; cos, Moss Mabry; spec eff, L.B. Abbott, Art Cruickshank.

Police Drama **Cas.** **(PR:C MPAA:NR)**

DETECTIVE BELLI* (1970, Ital.) 103m Fair Film/Plaza Pictures c (UN DETECTIVE)

Franco Nero *(Stefano Belli)*, Florinda Bolkan *(Vera Fontana)*, Adolfo Celi *(Fontana)*, Delia Boccardo *(Sandy Bronson)*, Susanna Martinkova *(Emmanuelle)*, Renzo Palmer *(Baldo)*, Roberto Bisacco *(Claude)*, Maurizio Bonuglia *(Mino Fontana)*.

Bolkan asks corrupt police detective Nero to check out a partner of his son, who owns Embassy Records. Bolkan's wife plans to invest in the company and Bolkan also wants Nero to deport his son's English girl friend, Boccardo. Nero goes to the man's apartment and finds the record company owner murdered. Bolkan's son is killed when he gets into a fight with a photographer and his girl friend is also killed. Nero discovers that Bolkan's wife is the killer and she also eliminates her husband and Nero when they confront her. A tired effort with little suspense.

p, Mario Cecchi Gori; d, Romolo Guerrieri; w, Franco Verucci, Alberto Silvestri, Massimo D'Avack (based on a novel by Ludovico Dentice); ph, Roberto Gerardi; m, Fred Bongusto; ed, Marcello Malvestiti; art d, Giantito Burchiellaro; song: "The World of the Blues."

Crime **(PR:O MPAA:R)**

DETECTIVE KITTY O'DAY** (1944) 61m MON bw

Jean Parker *(Kitty O'Day)*, Peter Cookson *(Johnny Jones)*, Tim Ryan *(Inspector Miles)*, Veda Ann Borg *(Georgia Wentworth)*, Edward Gargan *(Mike Storm)*, Douglas Fowley *(Anton Downs)*, Edward Earle *(Oliver Wentworth)*, Herbert Heyes *(Jeffers)*, Pat Gleason *(Cab Driver)*, Olaf Hytten *(Charles)*.

Parker stars as a screwy amateur detective who drags her boy friend, Cookson, into a mess of situations which eventually sees the couple accused of murder. After a number of bodies have hit the mat the real killer is revealed, clearing the reluctant sleuths. Parker's usual buoyancy lifts the below-average material to an enjoyable level.

p, Lindsley Parsons; d, William Beaudine; w, Tim Ryan, Victor Hammond (based on a story by Hammond); ph, Ira Morgan; ed, Richard Currier; md, Edward Kay; art d, E. R. Hickson.

Mystery/Comedy **(PR:A MPAA:NR)**

DETECTIVE STORY***** (1951) 105m PAR bw

Kirk Douglas *(Jim McLeod)*, Eleanor Parker *(Mary McLeod)*, William Bendix *(Lou Brody)*, Cathy O'Donnell *(Susan Carmichael)*, George Macready *(Karl Schneider)*, Horace McMahon *(Lt. Monahan)*, Gladys George *(Miss Hatch)*, Joseph Wiseman *(Charles Gennini)*, Lee Grant *(Shoplifter)*, Gerald Mohr *(Tami Giacoppetti)*, Frank Faylen *(Gallagher)*, Craig Hill *(Arthur)*, Michael Strong *(Lewis Abbott)*, Luis Van Rooten *(Joe Feinson)*, Bert Freed *(Dakis)*, Warner Anderson *(Endicott Sims)*, Grandon Rhodes *(O'Brien)*, William "Bill" Phillips *(Callahan)*, Russell Evans *(Barnes)*, Howard Joslyn *(Patrolman Keogh)*, James Maloney *(Mr. Pritchett)*, Edmund F. Cobb *(Ed, Detective)*, Burt Mustin *(Janitor)*, Lee Miller *(Policeman)*, Mike Mahoney *(Coleman)*, Catherine Doucet *(Mrs. Farragut)*, Ann Codee *(Frenchwoman)*, Ralph Montgomery *(Finney)*, Pat Flaherty *(Desk Sergeant)*, Jack Shea *(2nd Desk Sergeant)*, Bob Scott *(Mulvey)*, Harper Goff *(Gallantz)*, Charles D. Campbell *(Newspaper Photographer)*, Donald Kerr *(Taxi Driver)*, Kay Wiley *(Hysterical Woman)*.

A tour de force for Wyler and Douglas, DETECTIVE STORY is the granddaddy of all cop dramas and the film is spellbinding from first frame to last. The plotline is thin, filled up with assorted character roles intermingling with Douglas' role of a hardboiled, dedicated by-the-book detective who prides himself on an untarnished record in his one-man war against crime. Douglas is tough on all the lawbreakers he drags in under arrest to detective headquarters, particularly a butchering abortionist, Macready, whom he beats up in a police van before delivering him to the lock-up. McMahon becomes suspicious of Douglas' brutal treatment of the underground physician, and confers with Macready's glib lawyer, Anderson, who threatens an assault and battery suit. McMahon investigates further and it is learned that his ace detective's wife, Parker, had an abortion performed years earlier by Macready, the child being that of Mohr, a racketeer, the very essence of the evil Douglas has been battling. When Douglas finally learns the truth he turns away from Parker, the one person he truly loves in life. So distraught is he that when a psychopathic hoodlum, Wiseman, waiting to be booked, pulls a gun, Douglas jumps in the line of fire and receives a mortal wound. Parker is summoned and Douglas dies in her arms, asking for forgiveness and attempting to murmur the Act of Contrition. Douglas is intense and electrifying as the altruistic but narrow-minded cop who struggles with his wife's indiscretion, finding it impossible to justify her actions but to go on living with the knowledge of her acts and still loving her as he does is also impossible. Wiseman's bullet is a blessing for a man in soul-wrenching torment. Kingsley's modern morality play was deftly handled by pantheon director Wyler who confines the drama to a single set but manages to avoid being stagy. This was accomplished by the lens of that superb cinematographer Garmes, who keeps his cameras fluid and searching, moving from one character to another, the neurotic shoplifter Grant, the lunatic thieves, Wiseman and Strong, the sleazy abortionist Macready, and the detectives who have arrested them, Bendix, the cop with a heart, Freed, the cop annoyed with his paperwork, Faylen, the cop with black humor. The film is so methodical in recording a day's traumatic events in a precinct that it appears documentary, yet the marvelous color and quirks of its characters provide a gasping drama that no viewer will ever forget. Garmes insisted that the floors of the set, though they appeared roughhewn, be smooth as glass. Holes were filled with putty and the wooden floorboards were sandpapered so he could glide his crab dolly quickly across them. Wyler had never used such a device before and when Garmes explained that with the crab dolly he could move his cameras wherever he wanted the director was ecstatic: "Jeez, that will be fantastic!" Dashiell Hammett originally worked on the screenplay for DETECTIVE STORY but he dropped out and the honors went to veteran scripter Yordan and Robert Wyler. Much of the realism of this film is to be found in the stark, hardscrabble set by Pereira and Hedrick, nothing more than floorboards, desks, uncomfortable tables, ancient file cabinets, the grim but realistic view of a police precinct office with no frills, comforts or signs of relief. All of the performances are standouts. Bendix is tough but human and outgoing, his optimism reaching out for the salvation of a young embezzler, Hill, who repents and offers to return the money he has stolen. Bendix even convinces Hill's employer to drop the charges so this first-time offender can begin life anew with his girl friend O'Donnell and then works on Douglas, who made the arrest, to let Hill go. Douglas finds such compassion almost beyond him but, at the last minute, he relents, displaying a sliver of mercy in an otherwise granite personality. Two newcomers to the screen, Grant and Wiseman, made memorable impacts with their small roles. Grant received many movie offers following this film but she preferred to remain on Broadway and was not seen in another film for four years, appearing in STORM FEAR (1956). Wiseman, a most unusual character actor, went on to spotty appearances in films, his most notable being that of the Machiavellian mentor to Marlon Brando in VIVA ZAPATA (1952). Douglas, ever the perfectionist, immersed himself deeply in the role of Detective Jim McLeod, researching his character by going to NYC where he spent days and nights in the 16th Precinct observing the criminal flotsam and jetsam flowing through its doors and studying the reactions of the detectives in charge. Further, Douglas had the play staged at the Sombrero Theater in Phoenix, Arizona and, for weeks, played out the role before enthralled audiences who were actually watching his rehearsals for the film enactment. The painstaking background work and character development is in powerful evidence in the film as Douglas gives one of the best performances in his stellar career.

p&d, William Wyler; w, Philip Yordan, Robert Wyler (based on the play by Sidney Kingsley); ph, Lee Garmes (process ph, Farciot Edouart); ed, Robert Swink; art d, Hal Pereira, Earl Hedrick; set d, Emile Kuri; cos, Edith Head; makeup, Wally Westmore.

Police Drama **(PR:C MPAA:NR)**

DETOUR**** (1945) 67m PRC bw

Tom Neal *(Al Roberts)*, Ann Savage *(Vera)*, Claudia Drake *(Sue)*, Edmund MacDonald *(Charles Haskell, Jr.)*, Tim Ryan *(Diner Proprietor)*, Esther Howard *(Hedy)*, Roger Clark *(Dillon)*, Pat Gleason *(Man)*, Donald Brodie *(Used Car Salesman)*.

Neal is hitchhiking to Los Angeles to join his fiancee. He is picked up by MacDonald, who tells him of a female hitchhiker he had picked up earlier and who had scratched him when he tried to make advances toward her. Later, Neal drives while MacDonald sleeps. When it starts to rain, he tries to awaken MacDonald so they can put the convertible top up, but he finds him dead. Neal panics and dumps the body in the desert after stealing MacDonald's wallet. Later, he stops to pick up hitchhiker Savage, who turns out to be the same woman MacDonald had told him about. She doesn't believe his story and threatens to turn him in unless he does what she says. They arrive in Los Angeles and rent a room while Savage plans to pass Neal off as MacDonald, who has turned out to be a long-lost heir. Neal refuses to go through with the plan and they fight. Savage runs into the other room and shuts the door, threatening to call the police, but she collapses in a drunken stupor with the telephone cord around her neck. From behind the door Neal pulls on the cord and accidentally strangles her. He flees to Reno without seeing his fiancee, where he sits in a diner mulling over the twists of fate that have brought him here. He goes out to the highway to hitch a ride and a police car picks him up. Possibly the bleakest and most nihilistic *film noir*, this is a super low-budget effort shot in just six days and mostly in two locations, the hotel room and the car in front of a rear projection screen. Today it enjoys an outstanding critical reputation for its depiction of a man in the grip of forces beyond his control. Savage is remembered as one of the most despicable vixens in the history of cinema and the scene where she is strangled is the highlight of the film. A very significant, fine motion picture.

p, Leon Fromkess; d, Edgar G. Ulmer; w, Martin Goldsmith; ph, Benjamin H. Kline; m, Leo Erdody; ed, George McGuire; art d, Edward C. Jewell; set d, Glenn P. Thompson, cos, Mona Barry; makeup, Bud Westmore.

Crime Drama **Cas.** **(PR:O MPAA:NR)**

DETOUR, THE½**
(1968, Bulgarian) 78m Bulgarian State Films/Brandon bw (OTKLONENIE)

Nevena Kokanova *(Neda)*, Ivan Andonov *(Boyan)*.

On his way to Sofia to catch a plane to a conference in Vienna, engineer Andonov is forced to make a detour near an archaeological dig. There he sees Kokanova, an old flame, and he gives her a ride. In flashback, they meet as students, have an intense but brief affair, then part, each trying to do something for humanity. Now they are both married to others, but Andonov offers to leave everything if she will come with him. She refuses and leaves the airport, and he boards his plane. Interesting character drama has nice performances by its principals, though it does bog down in talk.

d, Grisha Ostrovski, Todor Stoyanov; w, Blaga Dimitrova; ph, Stoyanov; m, Milcho Leviev.

Drama **(PR:A MPAA:M)**

DETROIT 9000½** (1973) 108m GEN c

Alex Rocco *(Lt. Danny Bassett)*, Hari Rhodes *(Sgt. Jesse Williams)*, Vonetta McGee *(Roby Harris)*, Ella Edwards *(Helen)*, Scatman Crothers *(Rev. Markham)*, Herbert Jefferson, Jr. *(Ferdy)*, Robert Phillips *(Capt. Chalmers)*, Rudy Challenger *(Clayton)*, Ron McIlwain *(Sam)*, Sally Baker *(Ethel)*, George Skaff *(Oscar)*, June Fairchild *(Barbara)*, Dilart Heyson, Davis Roberts, Jason Summers, John Nichols, Richard Bourin, Martha Jean Steinberg, Woody Willis, Bob Charlton, Ernie Winstanley, Council Cargle, Doris Ingraham, Ron Khoury, Jerry Dahlman, Whit Vernon, Don Hayes, Herb Weatherspoon, Michael Tylo.

Violent blaxploitation film stars Rhodes and Rocco as a black and white detective team following the bloody trail of thieves who rip off a political rally. Rocco ends up shot and Rhodes isn't sure at film's end whether he is going to turn in the recovered loot or keep it. DETROIT 9000 is interesting only for an enlightened attitude toward whites rare in blaxploitation films.

p&d, Arthur Marks; w, Orville Hampton (based on a story by Marks, Hampton); ph, Harry May (Panavision, CFI color); m, Luchi DeJesus.

Crime **(PR:O MPAA:R)**

DEVIL, THE½** (1963), Ital.) 103m DD/CD bw
(IL DIAVOLO; AKA: TO BED OR NOT TO BED; AMORE IN STOCKHOLM)

Alberto Sordi *(Amadeo Ferretti)*, Bernhard Tarschys *(Professor Mayer)*, Inger Sjorstrand *(Inger)*, Ulf Palme *(Parson)*, Ulla Smidje *(Parson's Wife)*, Gunoild Gustavson *(Girl On Street)*, Barbo Wastenson *(Eva)*, Gunilla Elm-Tornkvist *(Brigetta)*, Lauritz Falk *(Peer)*, Anne-Charlotte Sjorberg *(Carina)*, Monica Waterson *(Katia)*, Ulla Andersson, Inger Auer, Catherina Norden-Falk.

A delightfully funny romp about a small town Italian, Sordi, who takes a short trip to Sweden, dreaming of all the possible liaisons he could have, now that he is away from his wife for a spell. But his encounters are only with girls who see him as a friendly person, or with women whose energies and adventures are more than Sordi can bear. (Italian, English subtitles)

d, Gian Luigi Polidoro; w, Rodolfo Sonego; ph, Aldo Tonti; m, Piero Piccioni; ed, Tatiana Casini.

Comedy **(PR:A MPAA:NR)**

DEVIL AND DANIEL WEBSTER, THE**** (1941) 107m RKO bw
(AKA: ALL THAT MONEY CAN BUY; HERE IS A MAN; A CERTAIN MR. SCRATCH)

Edward Arnold *(Daniel Webster)*, Walter Huston *(Mr. Scratch)*, Jane Darwell *(Ma Stone)*, Simone Simon *(Belle)*, Gene Lockhart *(Squire Slossum)*, John Qualen *(Miser Stevens)*, Frank Conlan *(Sheriff)*, Lindy Wade *(Daniel Stone)*, Geo Cleveland *(Cy Bibber)*, Anne Shirley *(Mary Stone)*, James Craig *(Jabez Stone)*, H. B. Warner *(Justice Hawthorne)*, Jeff Corey *(Tom Sharp)*, Sonny Bupp *(Martin Van Aldrich)*, Eddie Dew *(Farmer)*, Alec Craig *(Eli Higgins)*, Fern Emmitt *(Wife)*, Robert Emmett Kean *(Husband)*, Carl Stockdale *(Van Brooks)*, Walter Baldwin *(Hank)*, Sarah Edwards *(Lucy Slossum)*, Virginia Williams *(3-Month Old Baby)*, Stewart Richards *(Doctor)*, Patsy Doyle *(Servant)*, Anita Lee *(Infant)*, Harry Hood *(Tailor)*, Harry Humphrey *(Minister)*, Ferris Taylor *(President)*, Robert Dudley *(Lem)*, Frank Austin *(Spectator)*, Jim Toney *(Another Farmer)*, Bob Pittard *(Clerk)*, Charles Herzinger *(Old Farmhand)*, Robert Strange *(Clerk of Court)*, Sherman Sanders *(Caller)*, James Farley *(Studio Gateman)*, William Alland *(Guide)*, Sunny Boyne.

Two fascinating stalwarts, Arnold and Huston, have a go at each other in this marvelous fantasy based on the prize-winning Stephen Vincent Benet short story. Craig is a New England farmer having a difficult time and he casually swears that he would sell his soul for enough money to make life easier. Up pops Huston as Mr. Scratch, the Devil himself, full of evil irony, cute and cunning with sacks of gold which he turns over to Craig after getting his signature on a contract that purchases his soul. In the bargain Craig is to get seven years of grand luck. At first Craig thinks it's all an elaborate joke but when the money comes rolling in and his incredible luck yields countless riches he realizes the sinister reality of his deal. From a simple, good-hearted person, Craig changes to a venal, cold-blooded businessman, taking advantage of his neighbors, hoarding his money. He ignores his wife Shirley and their new-born child, refuses to listen to his mother's (Darwell) cautions and even gives up going to church on Sundays, playing poker with the town's ne'er-do-wells (Lockhart and Conlan) while his wife, child and mother attend services. His phenomenal luck makes the entire farming community suspicious. When droughts and plagues strike the land all suffer but Craig's crops and land go untouched. He loans money but at usurious rates and is hated even more. Moreover, Huston's emissary, Simon, a weird-acting servant girl, goes to live with Craig's family, undermining his affections for his wife and becoming his mistress, guiding him with each evil step. He builds a grand mansion and gives an elegant ball, inviting everyone, including the famous Daniel Webster, Arnold. But everything goes wrong. Strange, crude people arrive and eat savagely at the banquet tables, and an equally strange band plays eerie music to which Simon dances, whirling Qualen wildly about until he collapses. He is dying and begs to be released from *his* contract with Scratch which he has made years earlier. But he goes into Scratch's pocket just the same, a little moth crying vainly for help. The scene terrifies Craig and he flees, following his family whom he has run out of the mansion. He catches up with them on the road and Shirley promises help. She goes to Arnold, begging him to plead her husband's case. The great lawyer agrees to save his fellow New Englander if he can. A trial ensues in Craig's barn but the odds are stacked against Arnold by clever Huston who allows him a trial by jury. The jury, however, is comprised of damned souls from hell, the judge (venerable character actor Warner) being the infamous Justice Hawthorne. Benedict Arnold, Simon Girty and other hellions sit in judgment as Arnold pits his sharp wits and solemn wisdom against Huston's wiles. The courtroom scene is stupendous and is handled with gusto by Arnold and Huston as they wage war over Craig's immortal soul. Arnold deftly appeals to the jury, Americans all, reminding them what priceless treasures they surrendered when turning to the Devil, and that they have the power to not only return Craig to his family but strike a blow against the Evil One who led them astray. In a surprising turnabout, the jury betrays its master Huston and frees Craig. The risks were high; if Arnold had lost he had agreed to forfeit his own soul to Scratch. Once more in the bosom of his family, Craig has won a new lease on life and Arnold has proven that even the Devil was no match for the silver-tongued Daniel Webster. Scratch, however, is seen still full of fight at film's end as Huston consults his black book of prospective souls, his eyes darting greedily about, the camera closing in until his distorted, bewhiskered face fills the screen and his eyes look straight back at the camera, his hand jumping up and finger pointing menacingly at the viewer, as if to chillingly say, "You're next!" Arnold, though appearing only at the end of the film in full force is at his stentorian best and Huston renders a roguish Devil full of snap, crackle and pop. Director Dieterle does a fine job in telling a picturesque story, August's camera work is alive and action-filled and Herrmann's chilling score won a much deserved Oscar. Totheroh's script is both witty and eloquent, faithful to Benet's masterful tale. Though this film was not a box office success, losing $53,000 on its first run, many revivals have made it a minor cult film.

p&d, William Dieterle; w, Dan Totheroh (based on the story "The Devil and Daniel Webster" by Stephen Vincent Benet); ph, Joseph August; m, Bernard Herrmann; ed, Robert Wise; spec eff, Vernon L. Walker.

Fantasy **(PR:A MPAA:NR)**

DEVIL AND MAX DEVLIN, THE½** (1981) 96m BV c

Elliott Gould *(Max Devlin)*, Bill Cosby *(Barney Satin)*, Susan Anspach *(Penny Hart)*, Adam Rich *(Toby Hart)*, Julie Budd *(Stella Summers)*, David Knell *(Nerve Nordlinger)*, Sonny Shroyer *(Big Billy)*, Charles Shamata *(Jerry)*, Deborah Baltzell *(Heidi)*, Ronnie Schell *(Greg)*, Jeannie Wilson *(Laverne)*, Stanley Brock *(Counterman)*, Ted Zeigler *(Billings)*, Vic Dunlop *(Brian)*, Reggie Nalder *(Chairman)*, Lillian Muller *(Veronica)*, Julie Parrish *(Sheila)*, Sally K. Marr *(Mrs. Gormley)*, Madelyn Cates *(Mrs. Trent)*, Stu Gilliam *(Orderly)*, Denise DuBarry *(Secretary)*, Ruth Manning *(Mrs. Davis)*.

Gould is a mean landlord who is run over by a bus full of Hari Krishnas. Flung into Hell, he meets Cosby, the devil, who offers to save him if he can sign up three "unsullied" souls for Hell. Given three months and some magical powers, Gould goes about rounding up three children (Rich, Budd, and Knell). Film starts out well, but degenerates into typical Disney sentimentality and wooden acting.

p, Jerome Courtland; d, Steven Hilliard Stern; w, Mary Rodgers (based on a story by Rodgers and Jimmy Sangster); ph, Howard Schwartz (Technicolor); m, Buddy Baker; ed, Raymond A. de Leuw; art d, John B. Mansbridge, Leon R. Harris; m/l, Marvin Hamlisch, Carole Bayer Sager.

Comedy **Cas.** **(PR:A MPAA:PG)**

DEVIL AND MISS JONES, THE*½** (1941) 92m RKO bw

Jean Arthur *(Mary Jones)*, Robert Cummings *(Joe O'Brien)*, Charles Coburn *(John P. Merrick)*, Edmund Gwenn *(Hooper)*, Spring Byington *(Elizabeth Ellis)*, S.Z. Sakall *(George)*, William Demarest *(1st Detective)*, Walter Kingsford *(Allison)*, Montagu Love *(Harrison)*, Richard Carle *(Oliver)*, Charles Waldron *(Needles)*, Edwin Maxwell *(Withers)*, Edward McNamara *(Police Sergeant)*, Robert Emmett Keane *(Tom Higgins)*, Florence Bates *(Customer)*, Charles Irwin *(2nd Detective)*, Matt McHugh *(Sam)*, Julie Warren *(Dorothy)*, Ilene Brewer *(Sally)*, Regis Toomey *(1st Policeman)*, Pat Moriarty *(2nd Policeman)*.

Coburn, the world's richest man, decides to infiltrate one of his holdings, a department store, to ferret out union organizers who have targeted him as responsible for the miserable conditions his employees work under. He is subjected to many indignities by the management, finally ending up in the shoe department alongside Arthur. She thinks him destitute and takes pity on him, showing him the intricacies of the department. He attends union meetings and carefully notes everybody there, but as the abuse from the store's management becomes more intolerable and as Coburn himself becomes romantically interested in Byington, he has a change of heart, eventually sacking the management and marrying Byington. One of the most sparkling comedies of the decade, directed deftly by comedy veteran Wood and with wonderful performances by the entire cast.

p, Frank Ross, Norman Krasna; d, Sam Wood; w, Krasna; ph, Harry Stradling; m, Roy Webb; ed, Sherman Todd; prod d, William Cameron Menzies: spec eff, Vernon L. Walker.

Comedy **(PR:A MPAA:NR)**

DEVIL AND THE DEEP½** (1932) 72m PAR bw

Tallulah Bankhead *(Pauline Sturm)*, Gary Cooper *(Lt. Sempter)*, Charles Laughton *(Cmdr. Charles Sturm)*, Cary Grant *(Lt. Jaeckel)*, Paul Porcasi *(Hassan)*, Juliette Compton *(Mrs. Planet)*, Henry Kolker *(Hutton)*, Dorothy Christy *(Mrs. Crimp)*, Arthur Hoyt *(Mr. Planet)*, Gordon Westcott *(Lt. Toll)*, Jimmie Dugan *(Condover)*,

Kent Taylor *(A Friend)*, Lucien Littlefield *(Shopkeeper)*, Peter Brocco *(Wireless Operator)*, Wilfred Lucas *(Court Martial Judge)*, Dave O'Brien, Henry Guttman, George Magrill *(Submarine Crewmen)*.

Bankhead is almost inert, Cooper is less than forceful, and Laughton steals the show. Laughton is a submarine commander stationed on the northern coast of Africa. It's peacetime in the British Navy but there is anything but peace in the Laughton household. He's married to Bankhead and a more jealous man could not be found in any climate. As the picture begins, Laughton has transferred one of his aides for "negligence," but it's just a ruse. The true reason is Laughton's gnawing suspicions of his wife's infidelity, none of which are founded. Bankhead and Laughton argue and she goes into the Arabian town where the locals are celebrating a Moslem feast day. She is swept along by the huge crowd and almost panics until a tall young man, Cooper, rescues her and they step into a small shop where he buys her a bottle of inexpensive perfume to placate the jabbering store owner. When the crowd disperses, they drive into the desert. She opens the perfume bottle and spills a bit of it on her dress, then uses his handkerchief to wipe it off. Their relationship deepens quickly and they spend the night together but in the cold light of the following morning she insists that they not see each other again. She returns home and Laughton sniffs the perfume on her dress but keeps his emotions in check as he is happy to have her back. Further, he is buoyed by the knowledge that his new aide (to replace the one he'd sent away) is about to arrive. The new lieutenant walks in and it's . . . you'll never guess . . . Cooper. Laughton, being blessed with a magnificent nose, smells Cooper's handkerchief when the man inadvertently drops it. (Shakespeare used the same sorry device.) Tallulah enters, sees who the new aide is, and almost faints. Laughton goes to the sub and Bankhead follows him there, knowing that he is capable of very strange actions when he is enraged. Laughton traps Bankhead in his cabin, then heads directly for a freighter and hands the controls to Cooper just before they smash into the ship. The vessel sinks and Laughton tells the crew members that Cooper was responsible. The sub sinks to the bottom and, in an emotional scene, Bankhead manages to convince the crew that her husband is mad. The men escape via the hatch as they take orders from Cooper. Laughton takes an axe to his wife's portrait and begins to smash it to bits. The water rushes in and he is drowned in his cabin while all others get away with their lives. The only thing to recommend this movie is Laughton's outstanding performance. Lesser actors would have had a field day chewing up the bulkhead in various "mad" scenes, but Laughton's remarkable restraint made the character all the more plausible. This was his first American film. He was 33 years old and already a giant as an actor, but the best was yet to come.

p, Emmanuel Cohen; d, Marion Gering; w, Benn [Benno] Levy (based on a story by Harry Hervey); ph, Charles Lang; ed, Otho Lovering; art d, Bernard Herzbrun, cos, Travis Banton.

Drama (PR:C MPAA:PR)

DEVIL AND THE TEN COMMANDMENTS, THE**½
(1962, Fr.) 120m Mondex-FS-Procinex-Incei/Cinedia bw (LE DIABLE ET LAS DIX COMMANDEMENTS)

Episode 1: Michel Simon *(Jerome Chambard)*, Lucien Baroux *(Bishop)*, Claude Nollier *(Mother Superior)*; Episode 2: Dany Saval *(Tania)*, Henri Tisot *(Admirer)*; Episode 3: Charles Aznavour *(Denis Mayeux)*, Lino Ventura *(Garigny)*, Maurice Biraud *(Police Inspector)*, Henri Vilbert *(Alexandre)*, Maurice Teynac *(Father Superior)*; Episode 4: Francoise Arnoul *(Francoise Beaufort)*, Micheline Presle *(Micheline)*, Mel Ferrer *(Philip Allan)*, Claude Dauphin *(Georges Beaufort)*; Episode 5: Fernandel *(God)*, Germaine Kerjean *(Grandmother)*, Gaston Modot *(Grandfather)*, Josette Vardier *(Mother)*, Rene Clermont *(Father)*, Claudine Maugey; Episode 6: Alain Delon *(Pierre Messager)*, Danielle Darrieux *(Clarisse Ardant)*, Madeleine Robinson *(Mme. Messager)*, Georges Wilson *(Mons. Messager)*, Roland Armontel *(Mercier)*; Episode 7: Jean-Claude Brialy *(Didier Marin)*, Louis de Funes *(Vaillant)*, Armande Navarre *(Janine)*, Noel Roquevert *(Inspector)*, Denise Gence *(Churchwoman)*, Jean-Paul Moulinot *(Bank Director)*, Jean Carmet *(Tramp)*, Gabriello *(Policeman)*.

Mediocre sketch film on the theme of the Ten Commandments. Episodes include a man who announces he is God, a young man who leaves his adopted home to find his real mother only to have her try to seduce him before she realizes who he is, and a thief who accidentally loses his loot when the bag he carries it in gets confused with a worker's. Stories are well done, all with big name casts, but they rely on trick endings rather than careful writing for effect.

p, Robert Amon, Claude Jaeger; d, Julien Duvivier; w, Rene Barjavel, Pascal Jardin, Henri Jeanson, Michel Audiard, Maurice Bessy, Duvivier; ph, Roger Fellous (Franscope); m, Jacques Brel, Gilbert Becaud, Charles Aznavour, Guy Magenta, Michel Magne, Georges Garvarentz; art d, Francois de Lamothe; ed, Paul Cayatte.

Comedy/Drama (PR:C MPAA:NR)

DEVIL AT FOUR O'CLOCK, THE***½
(1961) 125m COL c

Spencer Tracy *(Fr. Matthew Doonan)*, Frank Sinatra *(Harry)*, Kerwin Matthews *(Fr. Joseph Perreau)*, Jean Pierre Aumont *(Jacques)*, Gregoire Aslan *(Marcel)*, Alexander Scourby *(The Governor)*, Barbara Luna *(Camille)*, Cathy Lewis *(Matron)*, Bernie Hamilton *(Charlie)*, Martin Brandt *(Dr. Wexler)*, Lou Merrill *(Aristide)*, Marcel Dalio *(Gaston)*, Tom Middleton *(Paul)*, Ann Duggan *(Clarisse)*, Louis Mercier *(Corporal)*, Michele Montau *(Margot)*, Nanette Tanaka *(Fleur)*, Tony Maxwell *(Antoine)*, Jean Del Val *(Louis)*, Moki Hana *(Sonia)*, Warren Hsieh *(Napoleon)*, William Keaulani *(Constable)*, "Lucky" Luck *(Capt. Olsen)*, Norman Josef Wright *(Fouquette)*, Robin Shimatsu *(Marianne)*.

Sinatra, Aslan, and Hamilton are three manacled convicts on their way to jail in Tahiti. Their small plane stops for the night on a French South Seas island known as Kalua. The island's volcano is making gurgling sounds and the governor, Scourby, realizes that it may erupt. Also aboard the plane is the young priest, Matthews, who is going to take the place of Tracy, a cleric who has lost his faith in God and found new hope in bottles of hooch. Aumont is the bush pilot who is ferrying the criminals and will take Tracy away with him on the morrow. There's a children's leper hospital up in the mountains and some work has to be completed on the chapel before Tracy departs. He asks for permission to put the three convicts to work and Scourby grants it. Meanwhile, slight earthquakes signal the onset of the volcano's activity. While at work, Sinatra falls in love with a local blind girl played by Luna. They all plan to leave the next day but the volcano erupts. Tracy enlists the convicts to help out when the island is rocked by a huge quake. They must get the children down from the mountain, through the jungle, and down to the sea where a large schooner will wait until the outgoing tide at four o'clock—but not a second longer. The arduous travel takes them through wind, rain, and continuous tremors. Night falls and they huddle in a cave where Tracy marries Sinatra to Luna in a lovely sequence. Early in the morning, Aslan drowns in an accident. Hamilton and Tracy use their strength to hold a swaying bridge as Sinatra leads the kids and Camille across, but the bridge collapses, crushes Hamilton, and leaves Tracy on the wrong side. Sinatra ferries the children to safety, gets them aboard the waiting ship at the harbor, then returns to the jungle to help his compatriots. He finds Hamilton dying while the priest gives the convict the last rites. Sinatra watches, crosses himself, and the volcano explodes at that precise moment. The entire island, now empty except for Tracy, Sinatra, and Hamilton, blows as high as Krakatoa and sinks into the ocean. The ending was downbeat and probably contributed to the lack of huge success at the wickets, despite the presence of such stellar luminaries as Tracy and Sinatra. The title comes from a proverb: "It is hard for man to be brave when he knows he is going to meet the devil at four o'clock." The picture was about 15 minutes too long and one would have wished for a happier conclusion, but it was a sincere attempt at a different kind of picture for both stars.

p, Fred Kohlmar; d, Mervyn LeRoy; w, Liam O'Brien (from the novel by Max Catto); ph, Joseph Biroc (Eastmancolor); m, George Duning; ed, Charles Nelson; art d, John Beckman; set d, Louis Diage; spec eff, Larry Butler, Willis Cook; makeup, Ben Lane.

Adventure/Disaster Cas. (PR:A MPAA:NR)

DEVIL BAT, THE*
(1941) 68m PRC bw (AKA: KILLER BATS)

Bela Lugosi *(Dr. Paul Carruthers)*, Suzanne Kaaren *(Mary Heath)*, Dave O'Brien *(Johnny Layton)*, Guy Usher *(Henry Morton)*, Yolande Mallott *(Maxine)*, Donald Kerr *("One-Shot" Maguire)*, Edward Mortimer *(Martin Heath)*, Gene O'Donnell *(Don Morton)*, Alan Baldwin *(Tommy Heath)*, John Ellis *(Roy Heath)*, Arthur Q. Bryan *(Joe McGinty)*, Hal Price *(Chief Wilkins)*, John Davidson *(Prof. Raines)*, Wally Rairdon *(Walter King)*.

Lugosi is a mad scientist who disposes of his enemies by giving them samples of his shaving lotion and making sure they try it. He says goodbye to them, then returns to his lab to release one of the giant bats he has bred and trained to home in on the scent. A low point for Lugosi, though better than the indignities he was yet to suffer as his career limped painfully along for another 15 years. Five years later, this studio released THE FLYING SERPENT, a virtual re-make.

p, Jack Gallagher; d, Jean Yarbrough; w, John Thomas Neville (based on a story by George Bricker); ph, Arthur Martinelli; ed, Holbrook Todd.

Horror Cas. (PR:A MPAA:NR)

DEVIL BAT'S DAUGHTER, THE*½
(1946) 67m PRC bw

Rosemary La Planche *(Nina)*, John James *(Ted)*, Michael Hale *(Morris)*, Molly Lamont *(Ellen)*, Nolan Leary *(Dr. Elliot)*, Monica Mars *(Myra)*, Ed Cassidy *(Sheriff)*, Eddie Kane *(Apartment House Manager)*, Frank Pharr.

La Planche (Miss America of 1941) is suffering nightmares about her father who is rumored to be a vampire, and goes to psychiatrist Hale. He proceeds to make her even crazier, and murders his wife, convincing La Planche that she had committed the crime. Fortunately, she has met and fallen in love with James, Hale's stepson, and he sees that his hated stepfather is brought to justice. Poverty row melodrama of the mind is merely mediocre, though La Planche turns in a nice performance.

p&d, Frank Wisbar; w, Griffin Jay (based on a story by Wisbar, Leo J. McCarthy, Ernst Jaeger); ph, James S. Brown, Jr.; m, Alexander Steinert; ed, Douglas W. Bagier; art d, Edward G. Jewell; set d, Glenn P. Thompson.

Mystery (PR:A MPAA:NR)

DEVIL BY THE TAIL, THE***
(1969, Fr./Ital.) 93m Fildebroc-Les Productions Artistes Associes-P.E.A./Lopert c (LE DIABLE PAR LA QUEUE; NON TIRATE IL DIAVOLO PER LA CODA)

Yves Montand *(Cesar Maricorne)*, Maria Schell *(Diane)*, Jean Rochefort *(Georges)*, Jean-Pierre Marielle *(Leroy-Martin)*, Claude Pieplu *(Mons. Patin)*, Xavier Gelin *(Charlie)*, Tanya Lopert *(Cookie)*, Marthe Keller *(Amelie)*, Madeleine Renaud *(La Marquise)*, Jacques Balutin *(Balaze)*, Pierre Tornade *(Schwartz)*, Janine Berdin *(Mme. Passereau)*, Eddy Roos *(Mons. Passereau)*, Clotilde Joano *(Jeanne)*.

A wonderfully funny comedy about a poorly run hotel which gets its business by sabotaging passing cars, making it impossible to travel without the drivers' staying overnight. Confusion runs rampant when one guest, Montand, is discovered to be a bank robber. The hotel's employees decide that Montand must go, but his stolen loot must stay. De Broca also directed the comic James Bond spoof THAT MAN FROM RIO.

d, Philippe de Broca; w, Daniel Boulanger, De Broca; ph, Jean Penzer (DeLuxe Color); m, Georges Delerue; ed, Francoise Javet; art d, Dominique Andre.

Crime/Comedy (PR:C MPAA:M)

DEVIL COMMANDS, THE***
(1941) 65m COL bw

Boris Karloff *(Dr. Julian Blair)*, Richard Fiske *(Dr. Richard Sayles)*, Amanda Duff *(Anne Blair)*, Anne Revere *(Mrs. Walters)*, Ralph Penney *(Karl)*, Dorothy Adams

(Mrs. Marcy), Walter Baldwin *(Seth Marcy)*, Kenneth MacDonald *(Sheriff Willis)*, Shirley Warde *(Helen Blair)*.

Karloff is obsessed with the idea of communicating with his late wife, so he rigs up corpses in robot suits connected electrically to a live medium (Revere). When the experiment kills Revere, Karloff straps Duff, his daughter, into the chair. One of Karloff's weirdest films, it is interesting if not entirely successful. Duff's narration in spots throughout the film, explaining the action, is a serious weak point.

p, Wallace MacDonald; d, Edward Dmytryk; w, Robert D. Andrews, Milton Gunzberg (based on the novel *The Edge of Running Water* by William Sloane); ph, Allen G. Siegler; ed, Al Clark.

Horror (PR:C MPAA:NR)

DEVIL DOGS OF THE AIR*** (1935) 90m COS/WB bw

James Cagney *(Tommy O'Toole)*, Pat O'Brien *(Lt. Wm. Brannigan)*, Margaret Lindsay *(Betty Roberts)*, Frank McHugh *(Crash Kelly)*, Helen Lowell *(Ma Roberts)*, John Arledge *(Mac)*, Robert Barrat *(Commandant)*, Russell Hicks *(Captain)*, William B. Davidson *(Adjutant)*, Ward Bond *(Instructor)*, Gordon [Bill] Elliott *(Instructor)*, Samuel S. Hinds *(Fleet Commander)*, Harry Seymour *(Officer)*, Bill Beggs *(2nd Officer)*, Bob Spencer *(Mate)*, Newton House, Ralph Nye *(Officers)*, Selmer Jackson *(Medical Officer)*, Bud Flanagan [Dennis O'Keefe] *(Student)*, Don Turner *(1st Student)*, Dick French *(2nd Student)*, Charles Sherlock *(3rd Student)*, Carlyle Blackwell, Jr. *(Messenger)*, Martha Merrill *(Girl)*, David Newell *(Lt. Brown)*, Olive Jones *(Mrs. Brown)*, Helen Flint *(Mrs. Johnson)*, Joseph Crehan *(Communications Officer)*.

The first Cosmopolitan movie for Warner Bros. after the company moved off the MGM lot in a huff. In case you may wonder who Cosmopolitan was, this was the production arm owned by William Randolph Hearst and Marian Davies. Hearst started the firm to give his beloved Marian a chance to appear in pictures. The movie was as much a paean of praise to the Marines as HERE COMES THE NAVY was to the jolly tars or FLIRTATION WALK was to the West Pointers. Cagney is a wealthy kid from Brooklyn (precious few of those around) who joins the Marine Flying Corps after his buddy, Pat O'Brien, encourages him to become part of the group. Cagney is an ace stunt flyer and shows his mettle immediately. His ability puts him at the top of his class at the academy but his cocksure attitude rankles everyone around him. He is conceited, overconfident, and continuously scoffs at the traditions of Leatherneck life. O'Brien and Cagney both vie for the affections of Lindsay and Cagney finally wins, but not before he learns to respect the traditions of life in the Marines. A service movie, when there is no skirmish to glorify it, can be deadly dull. This was not the case with DEVIL DOGS OF THE AIR. There is some superb stunt flying as well as memorable special effects. The background is as authentic as could be shown and there is plenty of humor from the stars as well as a strong supporting cast, with McHugh as a standout comedy relief.

p, Lou Edelman; d, Lloyd Bacon; w, Malcolm Stuart Boylan, Earl Baldwin (based on the story "Air Devils" by John Monk Saunders); ph, Arthur Edeson; m, Leo F. Forbstein; ed, William Clemens; art d, Arthur J. Kookan; cos, Orry-Kelly.

Service Comedy/Drama (PR:A MPAA:NR)

DEVIL DOLL, THE***½ (1936) 79m MGM bw

Lionel Barrymore *(Paul Lavond)*, Maureen O'Sullivan *(Lorraine Lavond)*, Frank Lawton *(Toto)*, Robert Greig *(Coulvet)*, Lucy Beaumont *(Mme. Lavond)*, Henry B. Walthall *(Marcel)*, Grace Ford *(Lachna)*, Pedro de Cordoba *(Matin)*, Arthur Hohl *(Radin)*, Rafaela Ottiano *(Malita)*, Juanita Quigley *(Marguerite)*, Claire du Brey *(Mme. Coulvet)*, Rollo Lloyd *(Detective)*, E. Allyn Warren *(Commissioner)*, Frank Reicher, Billy Gilbert, Eily Malyon, Egon Brecher. Wilfrid Lucas *(voice only)*.

A strange and offbeat tale by that master of weird films, Tod Browning, THE DEVIL DOLL has the ever-expansive Barrymore as a wrongly convicted prisoner who escapes Devil's Island with mad scientist Walthall. They take refuge in Walthall's old laboratory where he demonstrates his miraculous invention, a serum which reduces all living things to miniature. First animals, dogs and horses, are reduced, before the ailing Walthall perishes, passing on his secret formula to Barrymore. Once in Barrymore's hands, the old man seek vengeance on those who framed him, reducing two of the culprits to tiny dolls which he keeps in his doll store while he masquerades as an old woman. The third evil-doer is so terrified by the fate of the first two, that a confession is made to police and Barrymore's name is cleared which allows his persecuted daughter, O'Sullivan, to find happiness, but not before Barrymore deals with his lunatic assistant Ottiano who is so spellbound by miniaturizing humans that she refuses to stop, at one point hissing: "We'll make the *whole world small!*" Browning is best remembered for the chiller FREAKS and has more cult followers today who admire his offbeat films than those who attended theaters to view his first-run movies. This was Browning's second-to-last film (followed by MIRACLES FOR SALE) and is one of his most arresting. The oversized sets and props are expertly done, with much attention given to detail, and the photography by Leonard Smith is startling and appropriately eerie with its long shadows. The device of using his 12-inch people to sneak into the offices of Barrymore's crooked ex-partners and rob and kill was employed earlier in THE UNHOLY THREE, starring Lon Chaney, Sr., but the miniatures are certainly equal in quality to those presented in THE BRIDE OF FRANKENSTEIN, and superior to the crude special effects used in DR. CYCLOPS. To skirt the strict Production Code at the time, Barrymore's exit into oblivion at the end of THE DEVIL DOLL does not clearly spell out his intended suicide but the strong implication is clear that he will end his own life to pay for his vengeful ways. Von Stroheim's work on the script of this very strange movie is unrecorded but since his career was in sharp decline it is safe to assume that Browning allowed him a stipend to add a few macabre fantasies to a film already packed with bizarre scenes.

p, Edward J. Mannix; d, Tod Browning; w, Garret Fort, Guy Endore, Erich von Stroheim, Browning (based on the novel *Burn Witch Burn* by Abraham Merritt); ph, Leonard Smith; m, Franz Waxman; ed, Frederick Y. Smith; art d, Cedric Gibbons.

Horror/Fantasy (PR:C MPAA:NR)

DEVIL DOLL*** (1964, Brit.) 80m Galaworldfilm-Gordon/Associated Film c

Bryant Halliday *(The Great Vorelli)*, William Sylvester *(Mark English)*, Yvonne Romain *(Marianne)*, Sandra Dorne *(Vorelli's Assistant)*, Karel Stepanek *(Dr. Heller)*, Francis de Wolf *(Dr. Keisling)*, Nora Nicholson *(Aunt Eva)*, Philip Ray *(Uncle Walter)*, Alan Gifford *(Bob Garrett)*, Pamela Law *(Garrett's Girl Friend)*, Heidi Erich *(Grace)*, Antony Baird *(Soldier)*, Trixie Dallas *(Miss Penton)*, Margaret Durnell *(The Countess)*, Ray Landor *(Twist Dancer)*, Ella Tracey *(Louisa)*, Guy Deghy *(Hans)*, David Charlesworth *(Hugo Novik)*, Lorenza Coalville *(Mercedes)*, Jackie Ramsden *(The Nurse)*.

An American reporter in London (Sylvester) attends a performance by Halliday, a ventriloquist and hypnotist. During the act Halliday hypnotizes Romain, Sylvester's girl friend, and afterwards she is struck by a strange malady. Halliday has stolen the girl's soul and transferred it to Hugo, his dummy. But instead of obediently following Halliday's orders, little Hugo gets ideas of his own, like threatening people with a knife. One of the best of the tiny subgenre of ventriloquist's dummy films, with little Hugo thoroughly scary. Taken from the final sequence of the British horror classic, DEAD OF NIGHT.

p, Kenneth Rive, Richard Gordon, Lindsay Shonteff; d, Shonteff; w, George Barclay, Lance Z. Hargreaves (from a story by Frederick E. Smith); ph, Gerald Gibbs; ed, Ernest Bullingham; art d, Stan Shields.

Horror Cas. (PR:C MPAA:NR)

DEVIL GIRL FROM MARS** (1954, Brit.) 77m Danziger/BL bw

Hugh McDermott *(Michael Carter)*, Hazel Court *(Eileen Prestwick)*, Patricia Laffan *(Nyah)*, Peter Reynolds *(Albert)*, Adrienne Corri *(Doris)*, Joseph Tomelty *(Prof. Hennessey)*, Sophie Stewart *(Mrs. Jamieson)*, John Laurie *(Mr. Jamieson)*, Anthony Richmond *(Tommy)*, James Edmond, Stuart Hibberd.

Inferior British retread of THE DAY THE EARTH STOOD STILL that takes place in a small Scottish inn where a stereotypical barmaid (Corri), reporter (McDermott), disillusioned model (Court), scientist (Tomelty), and an escaped murderer (Reynolds) are visited by Laffan, a sexy, leather-clad female Martian accompanied by her silly-looking robot. She announces to the shocked bar patrons that Mars has just had a revolution and women have taken over. She states that she has come to Earth to kidnap healthy men to take back to Mars for breeding purposes. The men refuse, but Reynolds goes along with Laffan in her spaceship and manages to blow it up, sacrificing his life so that poor Earthmen won't have to breed with leather-clad Martian women. This goofy but fun sci-fi opus has gained a cult following in the U.S.

p, Edward J. and Harry Lee Danziger; d, David Macdonald; w, John C. Maher, James Eastwood (based on their play); ph, Jack Cox; m, Edwin Astley; ed, Peter Taylor; spec eff, Jack Whitehead.

Science Fiction Cas. (PR:A MPAA:NR)

DEVIL GODDESS zero (1955) 70m COL bw

Johnny Weissmuller *(Himself)*, Angela Stevens *(Nora Blakely)*, Selmer Jackson *(Prof. Carl Blakely)*, William Tannen *(Nels Comstock)*, Ed Hinton *(Joseph Leopold)*, William M. Griffith *(Ralph Dixon)*, Frank Lackteen *(Nkruma)*, Abel M. Fernandez *(Teinusi)*, Vera M. Francis *(Sarab'na)*, George Berkely *(Bert)*.

Weissmuller plays himself in this silly jungle film. He leads professor Jackson and his daughter Stevens into the interior in search of an associate of Jackson's who has set himself up as a god among the natives. Along the way they clash with villains seeking buried treasure, and watch a tiger fight a hyena. The last of sixteen "Jungle Jim" movies, in the last three of which the "Jim" name was dropped and Weissmuller played himself, and woodenly at that. The one-time Olympic swimmer was now a paunchy 51 years old and after this film he retired from the screen.

p, Sam Katzman; d, Spencer G. Bennet; w, George Plympton (based on a story by Dwight Babcock); ph, Ira H. Morgan; ed, Aaron Stell; md, Mischa Bakaleinikoff; art d, Paul Palmentola.

Adventure (PR:A MPAA:NR)

DEVIL GOT ANGRY, THE (SEE: MAJIN, 1968, Jap.)

DEVIL IN LOVE, THE* (1968, Ital.) 97m Fair Film/WB bw/c

Vittorio Gassman *(Belfagor)*, Mickey Rooney *(Adramalek)*, Claudine Auger *(Magdalena)*, Ettore Manni *(Guard Captain)*, Annabella Incontrera *(Lucretia)*, Liana Orfei *(Innkeeper's Wife)*, Luigi Vannucchi *(Prince)*, Sherill Morgan *(Clarice)*, Giorgia Moll *(Aristocrat's Wife)*, Gabriele Ferzetti *(Lorenzo de Medici)*, Paolo Di Credico *(Cardinal Giovanni)*.

Gassman and Rooney are a pair of emissaries from hell who come to Renaissance Italy to stir up trouble. Gassman falls in love with Auger and loses his unholy powers, and their pairing brings this painful film to a merciful end. Produced in color, the film was exhibited in the U.S. in black and white.

p, Mario Cecchi Gori; d, Ettore Scola; w, Ruggero Maccari, Scola; ph, Aldo Tonti; m, Armando Trovaioli; ed, Marcello Valvestito, Tatiana Casini; art d, Luciano Ricchieri; cos, Maurizio Chiari.

Comedy (PR:C MPAA:NR)

DEVIL IN SILK**½ (1968, Ger.) 102m Fono/United Film Enterprises bw (TEUFEL IN SEIDE)

Lilli Palmer *(Melanie)*, Curt Jurgens *(Thomas Ritter)*, Winnie Markus *(Sabine)*, Adelheid Seeck, Hans Niesen, Wolfgang Buttner, Hilde Korber, Paul Bildt, Helmut Rudolph, Paul Bosiger, Robert Meyn, Otto Graf, Wolfgang Martini.

Struggling composer Jurgens marries Palmer but finds her insanely jealous. Driven into the arms of his secretary (Markus) by his wife's suspicions, he is contemptuous when she fakes a suicide attempt. When she tries again and succeeds he is faced with murder charges and must prove his innocence in court. A good cast is wasted in a routine melodrama. Released in Germany in 1956. (In German; English subtitles.)

d, Rolf Hansen; w, Jochen Ruth (based on the novel *Devil Next Door* by Gina Kaus); ph, Franz Weihmayr; m, Mark Lothar; ed, Anna Hollering; art d, Robert Herlth, Arno Richter, Peter Rohrig.

Drama **(PR:C MPAA:NR)**

DEVIL IN THE CASTLE
(SEE: DAREDEVIL IN THE CASTLE, 1961, Jap.)

DEVIL IN THE FLESH, THE** (1949, Fr.) 110m TRC/UNIV bw
(LE DIABLE AU CORPS)

Micheline Presle *(Marthe Graingier)*, Gerard Philipe *(Francois Jaubert)*, Jean Debucourt *(Mons. Jaubert)*, Denise Grey *(Mme. Grangier)*, Pierre Palau *(Mons. Marin)*, Jean Varas *(Jacques Lacombe)*, Jeanne Perez *(Mme. Marin)*, Germaine Ledoyen *(Mme. Jaubert)*, Maurice Lagrenee *(Doctor)*, Richard Francoeur *(Headwaiter)*, Jacques Tati *(Soldier in Blue)*, Charles Vissieres *(Anselme)*, Andre Bervil *(Reporter)*, Jean Relet, Michel Francois, Edmond Beauchamp, Henri Gautier, Albert Michel, Tristan Severe, Jean Fleury, Rene Garcia.

Long considered a masterpiece of French cinema, this film was also the target of endless criticism, though highly successful in the eyes of the public and many critics. It is the tale of a 17-year-old youth, Philipe, who falls in love with an older woman engaged to a soldier. He cuts classes and sells his stamp collection to be able to spend the day with his love. He learns that her soldier boy friend is in town on an overnight pass and follows the pair to her apartment, where they stay until the following morning. He contemplates suicide, but with the understanding of his father he decides instead to go away. He stays away for six months and when he returns finds that the woman, now married, still cares for him. She explains how indifferent her marriage is, showing him the unloving letters she's received from the soldier. The woman finds that she is pregnant, and the lad makes plans to visit the soldier at camp but lacks the courage to tell him what happened. Instead, the woman makes the trip alone. Her health fails and she is sent by her overbearing mother to a quiet country house where no one can pass judgment on her. Near death, she cries out for the boy, yelling his name. The mother refuses to allow the boy in to see his love, and tells the soldier/husband that the name she is shouting is that of the baby. A number of people who saw the film were furious with the way the soldier—a man risking his life for his country—was deceived. Petitions were sent to the French government urging the film to be banned. Canada agreed to the ban and the New York state censors would show it only after certain cuts were made. The French ambassador to Belgium walked out during a screening at the World Film Fest. Finally, the Legion of Decency condemned the picture for the "sordid and suggestive atmosphere which pervades the film." Autant-Lara (perhaps the most tolerable of the French "Tradition of Quality" filmmakers) and his supporters also insisted that they had remained faithful to the novel the film was based on and had captured its "true spirit." It is surprising, however, for a novel written by an 18-year-old (the author, Raymond Radiguet, was born in 1903 and died 20 years later) to be thoroughly understood by a 44-year-old employee of the French film industry. Autant-Lara called the novel "an anti-war novel," though it is obviously a story of love. THE DEVIL IN THE FLESH was a prime target for the young French critics who made up the New Wave. Because of Francois Truffaut's vicious criticism of this film, Autant-Lara publicly referred to Truffaut as a "hoodlum critic."

p, Paul Graetz; d, Claude Autant-Lara; w, Jean Aurenche, Pierre Bost (based on the novel by Raymond Radiguet); ph, Michel Kelber; m, Rene Cloerec; ed, Madeleine Gug.

Romance **(PR:C MPAA:NR)**

DEVIL IS A SISSY, THE*½** (1936) 92m Metro bw
(AKA: THE DEVIL TAKES THE COUNT)

Freddie Bartholomew *(Claude)*, Jackie Cooper *("Buck" Murphy)*, Mickey Rooney *("Gig" Stevens)*, Ian Hunter *(Jay Pierce)*, Peggy Conklin *(Rose)*, Katharine Alexander *(Hilda Pierce)*, Gene Lockhart *(Mr. Murphy)*, Kathleen Lockhart *(Mrs. Murphy)*, Jonathan Hale *(Judge Holmes)*, Etienne Girardot *(Principal)*, Sherwood Bailey *("Bugs")*, Buster Slavin *("Six-Toes")*, Grant Mitchell *(Paul Krumpp)*, Harold Huber *(Willie)*, Stanley Fields *(Joe)*, Frank Puglia *("Grandma")*, Etta McDaniel *(Molly)*.

MGM teamed its top three juveniles in this pleasant comedy. Bartholomew is an upper-class English kid who winds up in a New York slum fighting for acceptance from Rooney and Cooper, who put him through a series of trials to test his mettle. The script is nothing special, but between Van Dyke's direction and the efforts of the juvenile trinity, quite a winning little film.

p, Frank Davis; d, W. S. Van Dyke; w, John Lee Mahin, Richard Schayer (based on a story by Rowland Brown); ph, Harold Rossen, George Schneidermann; m, Herbert Stothart; ed, Tom Held; art d, Cedric Gibbons; m/l, "Say Ah," Arthur Freed, Nacio Herb Brown.

Comedy **(PR:A MPAA:NR)**

DEVIL IS A WOMAN, THE*** (1935) 85m PAR bw

Marlene Dietrich *(Concha Perez)*, Lionel Atwill *(Don Pasqual)*, Cesar Romero *(Antonio Galvan)*, Edward Everett Horton *(Don Paquito)*, Alison Skipworth *(Senora Perez)*, Don Alvarado *(Morenito)*, Morgan Wallace *(Dr. Mendez)*, Tempe Pigott *(Tuerta)*, Jill Dennett *(Maria)*, Lawrence Grant *(Conductor)*, Charles Sellon *(Letter Writer)*, Luisa Espinal *(Gypsy Dancer)*, Hank Mann *(Foreman, Snowbound Train)*, Edwin Maxwell *(Superintendent, Tobacco Factory)*, Donald Reed *(Miquelito)*, Eddie Borden *(Drunk in Carnival Cafe)*, Henry Roquemore *(Duel Informant)*.

Here Dietrich is a manipulating austere Spanish vamp who makes it her business to destroy men on a wholesale basis without batting one of her famous eyelashes. Young Romero meets Dietrich and is immediately smitten with her exotic charms. Before seeing her again, Romero encounters Atwill, a fellow military officer, and he confides his deep affection for Dietrich. Atwill reacts with alarm, telling his younger friend that this is the same woman who shattered his life. Atwill tells of his experiences with Dietrich and the film goes into flashback, relating how he met the woman on a train five years earlier, becoming utterly captivated by her. He slavishly follows her and assumes the role of her financial guardian, paying her debts, purchasing a wardrobe for her, and providing elegant living quarters, much to the edification of her harridan mother Skipworth. After she has drained him Dietrich insists upon more. Though he has none to give, Atwill, even more excited at her mistreatment of him (a true masochist), goes in search of more riches to give to Dietrich. The vixen rewards his generosity by deserting him. He later finds her dancing in a Cadiz bar. He lavishes money on her but when he is broke she again vanishes. Still later, when Atwill is an inspector of manufactured goods, he spots the mysterious Dietrich rolling cigarettes in a factory. Again his blood boils with passion and again she takes his money and adoration and then departs. At each encounter Atwill depletes his emotions and wealth for Dietrich and receives nothing, which is what the older man stresses to naive Romero toward the end of the film when the story has come full circle. Romero promises his friend to steer clear of the manwrecker but Atwill finds him with Dietrich during the raucous festival abounding with frenetic dancers, thieves, and drunks. Atwill, beside himself with jealousy, challenges Romero to a duel. The two men square off and Romero seriously wounds Atwill. By then the older man thinks Dietrich loves Romero and, to save the younger man for her sake, he fires his shot into the air, then collapses. Dietrich visits the stricken Atwill in the hospital but he tells her he's finished with her and orders her to leave with Romero. She does, apparently without remorse, heading for Paris with Romero. But she has a change of heart at the border and turns around, going back to Atwill in Seville. Whether she is there to be with him out of love and comfort or to go on tormenting him is unclear at the fadeout. Of all the von Sternberg-Dietrich films this is the most unpopular and unsatisfying. The director considered this film the end of his cycle with Dietrich and even undertook the cinematographer's duties to make sure every frame would be as he had envisioned it. It met with critical condemnation and the public stayed away. The Spanish government at the time banned the film and asked the U.S. State Department to approach Paramount in suppressing the film. The State Department complied and Paramount removed most of the prints in circulation. Spain complained that Atwill's role as an officer in the Guardia Civil degraded that organization and that Horton, who appears briefly in the film as a venal Spanish police chief, was a disgrace, particularly when Horton whimsically suggests that arresting lawbreakers is too time-consuming, that it is better to shoot them outright. Scenes showing besotten members of the Guardia Civil staggering through the festival also irked the Spanish government. Whether or not Paramount destroyed the negative of this film is not known, but few prints of this film still survive. Dietrich loaned her own print to the Museum of Modern Art in 1959 for a von Sternberg revival and a few others have been circulating since. Von Sternberg considered this film "a final tribute to the lady [Dietrich] I had seen lean against the winds of a Berlin stage, at the same time planning an affectionate salute to Spain and its traditions." He went on to blame the failure for this film on an inadequate script caused by writer Dos Passos being ill with fever. He hated the title, preferring to call the film CAPRICE ESPAGNOL. Lubitsch, then in charge of production, according to von Sternberg, "set his seal on it by altering the title to THE DEVIL IS A WOMAN. This accent is not mine. Though Mr. Lubitsch's poetic intention to suggest altering the sex of the devil was meant to aid in selling the picture, it did not do so." The film, however, possesses von Sternberg's wonderful compositions. It is frozen art without blood pumping through its heart. The same background was used in Bunuel's THAT OBSCURE OBJECT OF DESIRE.

d, Josef von Sternberg; w, John Dos Passos, S.K. Winston (based on the novel *The Woman and the Puppet* by Pierre Louys); ph, Lucien Ballard, Sternberg; m, Rimski-Korsakov ("Caprice Espagnol"), Ralph Rainger, Adrea Setaro; ed, Sam Winston; art d, Hans Dreier; cos, Travis Banton; m/l, Leo Robin, Ralph Rainger "(If It Isn't Pain) Then It Isn't Love," "Three Sweethearts Have I."

Drama/Romance **(PR:C MPAA:NR)**

DEVIL IS A WOMAN, THE*½ (1975, Brit./Ital.) 105m FOX c

Glenda Jackson *(Sister Geraldine)*, Claudio Cassinelli *(Rodolfo)*, Lisa Harrow *(Emily)*, Adolfo Celi *(Fr. Borelli)*, Arnoldo Foa *(Msgr. Badinsky)*, Rolf Tasna *(Msgr. Meitner)*, Duilio Del Prete *(Msgr. Salvi)*, Gabriele Lavia *(Prince Ottavio)*, Francisco Rabal *(Bishop Marquez)*.

Psychodrama set in a hostel-convent starring Jackson as a maniacal nun who attempts to "cleanse the souls" of the guilty flock that inhabits her domain. A writer, Cassinelli, arrives to do research on one of the residents, a guilt-ridden Polish priest who had collaborated with the Nazis. He meets a beautiful woman, Harrow, whose treachery caused the death of her husband. The reporter and the girl fall in love and Harrow defiantly leaves the convent with her new lover, causing some of the other residents to consider doing the same. In the end Jackson wins when her morally corrupt flock returns for her divine guidance. An indifferently made film that leaves a bad aftertaste.

p, Annis Nohra; d, Damiano Damiani; w, Damiani, Fabrizio Onofri, Audrey Nohra (based on a story by Damiani); ph, Mario Vulpiani; m, Ennio Morricone; ed, Peter Taylor.

Drama **(PR:O MPAA:R)**

DEVIL IS AN EMPRESS, THE½** (1939, Fr.) 70m COL bw
(LE JOUER D'ECHECS; AKA: THE CHECKER PLAYER; THE CHESS PLAYER)

Conrad Veidt *(The Baron)*, Francoise Rosay *(Catherine II of Russia)*, Micheline Francey *(Sonia)*, Edmonde Guy *(Wanda)*, Bernard Lancret *(Prince Serge)*, Paul

Cambo *(Boleslas)*, Gaston Modot *(Maj. Nicolaieff)*, Jacques Gretillat *(Prince Potemkin)*, Temerson *(Prince of Poland)*, Delphin *(Yegor, the Clown)*.

Costumer has Veidt the chief henchman of Rosay's Catherine the Great inventing fiendish mechanical torture devices and keeping Francey and her lover apart. The couple escape Russia by hiding inside one of Veidt's inventions, a mechanical chess player that is beheaded when Rosay learns what has happened. A good cast, and Veidt is always a superb villain.

d, Jean Dreville; w, Dreville (based on the story "The Chess Player of Vilna" by H. Dupuy-Mazuel); ph, Rene and Charles Gaveau; m, Jean Lenoir.

Drama (PR:A MPAA:NR)

DEVIL IS DRIVING, THE*½ (1932) 63m PAR bw

Edmund Lowe *(Gabby Denton)*, Wynne Gibson *(Silver)*, Dickie Moore *(Buddy Evans)*, James Gleason *(Beef Evans)*, Lois Wilson *(Nancy Evans)*, Alan Dinehart *(Jenkins)*, George Rosener *(The Dummy)*, Guinn Williams *(Mac)*, Charlie Williams *(Bill Jones)*, John Kelly *(Dolan)*. Geneva Mitchell *(Nellie)*, Francis McDonald *(Ticker)*, Tom Kennedy *(Fritz)*.

When members of a stolen car ring run over a boy during one of their getaways, the boy's uncle (Lowe) goes after them. Oddly, the ring is headed by a deaf-mute. Routine programmer.

p, Charles P. Rogers; d, Benjamin Stoloff; w, Louis Weitzenkorn, P. J. Wolfson, Allen Rivkin (based on a story by Frank Mitchell Dazey); ph, Henry Sharp.

Drama (PR:A MPAA:NR)

DEVIL IS DRIVING, THE*½ (1937) 69m COL bw

Richard Dix *(Paul Driscoll)*, Joan Perry *(Eve Hammond)*, Nana Bryant *(Mrs. Sanders)*, Frank C. Wilson *(Martin Foster)*, Ian Wolfe *(Sanders)*, Elisha Cook, Jr. *(Tony Stevens)*, Henry Kolker *(Stevens)*, Walter Kingsford *(Wooster)*, Ann Rutherford *(Kitty Wooster)*, Paul Harvey *(Mitchell)*, John Wray *(Peters)*, Charles C. Wilson *(Healy)*.

Dix is a district attorney trying to crack down on drunk driving, but assigned to defend Cook, the son of a friend, on second-degree murder charges stemming from his running over an old lady while he was intoxicated. Dix is the whole show in this disappointing programmer.

d, Harry Lachman; w, Jo Milward, Richard Blake (based on a story by Lee Loeb, Harold Buchman); ph, Allen Siegler; ed, Al Clark; md, Morris Stoloff.

Drama (PR:A MPAA:NR)

DEVIL MADE A WOMAN, THE** (1962, Span.) 87m Medallion c (CARMEN, LA DE RONDA; AKA: A GIRL AGAINST NAPOLEON)

Sarita Montiel *(Carmen)*, George Mistral *(Antonio)*, Maurice Ronet *(Jose)*, Amedeo Nazzari *(Colonel)*, Gerald Cobos *(Lucas)*, Maria Harte *(Micaela)*, Jose Marco Davo, Felix Fernandez, Santiago Rivero.

Ronet, a French sergeant, falls in love with Montiel, a cabaret singer. Both become involved with George Mistral, leader of the Spanish guerrillas who are fighting the Napoleonic forces occupying his country. Their romance in the end brings about their tragic deaths.

p, Benito Perojo; d, Tulio Demicheli; w, Jesus Maria de Arozamena, Antonio Mas Guindal, Demicheli, Jean-Pierre Feydeau (based on the opera "Carmen" by Georges Bizet and the novel by Prosper Merimee); ph, Antonio L. Ballesteros; m, Gregorio Garcia Segura; ed, Antonio Ramirez; set d, Enrique Alarcon.

Drama (PR:A MPAA:NR)

DEVIL MAKES THREE, THE**½ (1952) 89m MGM bw

Gene Kelly *(Capt. Jeff Eliot)*, Pier Angeli *(Wilhelmina Lehrt)*, Richard Rober *(Col. James Terry)*, Richard Egan *(Lt. Parker)*, Claus Clausen *(Heisemann)*, Wilfred Seyferth *(Hansig)*, Margot Rielscher *(Cabaret Singer)*, Annie Rosar *(Mrs. Keigler)*, Harold Benedict *(Sergeant at Airport)*, Otto Gebuhr *(Mr. Nolder)*, Gertrud Wolle *(Mrs. Nolder)*, Heinrich Gretler *(Keigler)*, Charlotte Flemming *(Girl in Phone Booth)*, Charles Gordon Howard *(Lt. Farris)*, Bum Kruger *(Oberlitz)*, Claus Benton Lombard *(Waiter)*, Ivan Petrovich *(Sigmund Neffs)*, Sepp Rist *(Customs Official—German)*, Michael Tellering *(Ernst Haltmann)*.

A nonsinging, nondancing Gene Kelly was never a popular item with the public, despite the fact that he was believable in whatever he did. In this, Kelly is an American Army captain who is returning to Germany to spend Christmas with a family which had saved his life during the war. Once in Munich, he discovers that they died during an American air raid and the only surviving member of the family is Angeli. She's now working as a shill, cadging drinks at a sleazy nightclub. Kelly visits her and discovers a bitter person who hates Americans and is generally cynical about life. Kelly falls in love with the moody young woman and this is noted by several of the peripheral characters who frequent the club. One of them is Clausen who appears to be an epicene singer-comic but is, in reality, a Nazi who is part of a ring that is smuggling gold in order to finance another rise to power. Kelly learns of this and tells Army intelligence. He is ordered to continue his affair with Angeli and to further investigate the plot. His boss is Richard Rober and Richard Egan is assigned to be Kelly's partner. Kelly pretends to be part of the smuggling ring which is, on the surface, just a small group bringing black market items across to Austria. He attempts to find out how the gold is being moved but is having difficulty learning the truth. Angeli is beginning to have affection for Kelly but retains her hatred for Americans in general, if not specifically. She hates Nazis even more, though, and Kelly realizes that she is not part of the plot but is, in fact, a dupe. Kelly finally learns how the Nazis are moving the gold when he finds that the fenders of the car he drives are solid twenty-four karat! Before he can inform the authorities, he and Angeli are captured by the bad guys and sentenced to death. It will take place during a motorcycle jaunt over a frozen lake. The villain is revealed to be Clausen and a chase begins with Kelly after Clausen. The denouement takes place at the Adlerhorst, Hitler's aerie at Berchtesgaden, and Kelly

finally takes Clausen as the rat stands at the picture window of the famed headquarters. The stunts were understandably spectacular because director Marton had come from that second-unit world where he directed such famous events as the battles in THE LONGEST DAY and CLEOPATRA as well as the chariot race in BEN-HUR. The reasons for making this movie went far beneath the script. MGM had frozen funds in Europe that it could not remove but could use to make movies. Kelly received the boon of being able to stay in Europe almost two years and pay no income tax. He agreed to do this film and CREST OF THE WAVE (aka: SEAGULLS OVER SORRENTO) in return for MGM allowing him to make his brilliant INVITATION TO THE DANCE. Pier Angeli, the twin sister to actress Marisa Pavan, died of an overdose of barbiturates at the age of 39 after a troubled marriage to singer Vic Damone and a great difficulty adjusting to the rigors of stardom.

p, Richard Goldstone; d, Andrew Marton; w, Jerry Davis (based on a story by Lawrence Bachmann); ph, Vaclav Vich; m, Rudolph G. Kopp; ed, Ben Lewis; art d, Fritz Maurischat, Paul Markwitz.

Drama (PR:A-C MPAA:NR)

DEVIL MAY CARE**½ (1929) 110m MGM bw/c

Ramon Novarro *(Armand)*, Dorothy Jordan *(Leonie)*, Marion Harris *(Louise)*, John Miljan *(DeGrignon)*, William Humphrey *(Napoleon)*, George Davis *(Groom)*, Clifford Bruce *(Gaston)*.

Novarro's first all-talkie, in which he plays a follower of Napoleon arrested after the emperor's exile. He escapes a firing squad and, while on the run, dashes into Jordan's bedroom and is immediately smitten. It turns out she is a Royalist who turns him in to his pursuers, but he escapes again and after some swordplay he encounters Jordan again and this time she returns his affections. Routine romantic fare with Novarro speaking and singing nicely. One sequence sited in Versailles is in Technicolor. Songs: "Bon Jour," "Louie," "March of the Old Guard," "Why Waste Your Charms," "The Gang Song," "Madame Pompadour," "Charming," "If He Cared" (Herbert Stothart, Clifford Grey).

d, Sidney Franklin; w, Hans Kraly, Zelda Sears, Richard Schrayer (based on the play "La Bataille Des Dames" by A. E. Scribe, E. Legouve); ph, Merritt B. Gerstad; ed, Conrad A. Nervig; cos, Adrian; ch, Albertina Rasch.

Musical/Romance (PR:A MPAA:NR)

DEVIL NEVER SLEEPS, THE (SEE: SATAN NEVER SLEEPS, 1962, U.S./Brit.)

DEVIL ON HORSEBACK, THE** (1936) 71m GN bw/c

Del Campo, Fred Keating, Lili Damita, Tiffany Thayer.

Long-forgotten musical has Campo as a Robin Hood-like gaucho trying to croon Damita's heart away from coffee heir Keating. It was Damita's last film before she retired from the screen when she married Errol Flynn. Songs: "So Divine," "Out of the Hills," "The Love Fiesta," "Oh Bella Mia" (Harry Tobias, Jack Stern).

p, Edward L. Alperson; d&w, Crane Wilbur (based on a story by Wilbur); ed, Joe Lewis; md, Hugo Riesenfeld.

Musical (PR:A MPAA:NR)

DEVIL ON HORSEBACK*** (1954, Brit.) 89m Group 3/BL bw

Googie Withers *(Mrs. Cadell)*, John McCallum *(Charles Roberts)*, Jeremy Spenser *(Moppy Parfitt)*, Meredith Edwards *(Ted Fellowes)*, Liam Redmond *(Scarlett O'Hara)*, Sam Kydd *(Darky)*, Malcolm Knight *(Squib)*, Peter Lindsay *(Len)*, Eric Francis *(Reg Guest)*, Vic Wise *(Fred Cole)*, Peter Swanwick *(Mr. Parfitt)*, Betty Hardy *(Mrs. Parfitt)*, Arthur Lovegrove *(Valet)*, George Rose *(Blacksmith)*, Harry Locke.

Spenser is a young jockey whose head swells after a couple of victories. His arrogance is responsible for a horse's death and ex-jockey Redmond teaches the boy some humility. Good racetrack drama, with excellent performances all around.

p, Isobel Pargiter; d, Cyril Frankel; w, Neil Paterson, Montague Slater, Goeffrey Orme (based on a story by James Curtis); ph, Denny Densham; m, Malcolm Arnold; ed, Sidney Stone.

Drama (PR:A MPAA:NR)

DEVIL ON WHEELS, THE** (1947) 67m PRC bw

James Cardwell, Noreen Nash, Darryl Hickman, Jan Ford, Damian O'Flynn, Lenita Love, Ann Burr, Robert Arthur, Sue England, William Forrest.

Hickman, inspired by his father's reckless driving habits, becomes a hot-rodder who gets involved in a hit and run accident only to find out that his own mother was the victim. Silly melodrama released in PRC's last year of existence.

p, Ben Stoloff; d&w, Crane Wilbur; ph, L. William O'Connell; ed, Al Troffey; md, Irving Friedman.

Drama (PR:A MPAA:NR)

DEVIL PAYS, THE*½ (1932) 60m CHES bw

Jameson Thomas, Florence Britton, Thomas Jackson, Dorothy Christy, Richard Tucker, Lillian Rich, Robert Ellis, Lew Kelly, Carmelita Geraghty, Edmund Burns, Jack Trent, Murdock MacQuarrie.

Thomas is featured as a short story writer who sticks his nose into a murder investigation. Blackmail, stabbings, and mysterious notes circle about a police department that allows the rich to go free while the poor go to jail.

d, Richard Thorpe; w, Arthur Hoerl.

Mystery (PR:A MPAA:NR)

DEVIL PAYS OFF, THE*** (1941) 70m REP bw

J. Edward Bromberg, Oso Massen, William Wright, Margaret Tallichet, Abner Biberman, Martin Kosleck, Charles D. Brown, Ivan Miller, Roland Varno.

Bromberg is a cashiered navy man who redeems his honor by exposing a shipping tycoon's efforts to sell his ships to an enemy government. Above average action drama, with good photography by Alton.

p, Albert J. Cohen; d, John H. Auer; w, Lawrence Kimble, Malcolm Stuart Boylan (based on a story by George W. Yates, Julian Zimet); ph, John Alton; ed, Howard O'Neil; md, Cy Feuer; art d, John Victor Mackay.

Action Drama (PR:A MPAA:NR)

DEVIL PROBABLY, THE*** (1977, FR.) 95m Sunchild-G.M.F./GAU c
(LE DIABLE PROBABLEMENT)

Antoine Monnier (Charles), Tina Irissari (Alberte), Henri De Maublanc (Michel), Laelita Carcano (Edwige), Regis Hanrion (Dr. Mime), Nicolas Deguy (Valentin), Geoffrey Gaussen (Bookseller), Robert Honorat (Commissioner).

Another rigorous—and unusually watchable—exercise in cinematic discipline by Bresson, the master of the minimal. The story, the end of which Bresson reveals immediately, is the drift by young Monnier through politics, religion, and finally to suicide. The actors are all nonprofessionals, who don't so much act as move around and blankly state their lines to the director's intricate commands. The best introduction (along with LANCELOT DU LAC) to the work of one of film's greatest thinkers. (In French; English subtitles.)

p, Stephane Tcholdieff; d&w, Robert Bresson; ph, Pasqualine De Santis (Eastmancolor); m, Philippe Sarde; ed, Germaine Lany.

Drama (PR:C MPAA:NR)

DEVIL RIDES OUT, THE (SEE: DEVIL'S BRIDE, THE, 1968, Brit.)

DEVIL RIDERS*½ (1944) 56m PRC bw

Buster Crabbe (Billy Carson), Al "Fuzzy" St. John (Fuzzy Jones), Patti McCarthy (Sally Farrell), Charles King (Del Stone), John Merton (Jim Higgins), Kermit Maynard (Red), Frank LaRue (Tom Farrell), Jack Ingram (Turner), George Chesebro (Curley), Ed Cassidy (Doc), Al Ferguson, Frank Ellis, Bert Dillard, Bud Osborne, Artie Ortego, Herman Hack, Roy Bucko, Buck Bucko.

Low budget B oater has Crabbe helping defeat a crooked lawyer who wants a land parcel, and then helping get a fledgling stagecoach line off the ground. Undistinguished fare from the Neufeld-Newfield-Cline crew at PRC, Poverty Row's most impoverished studio.

p, Sigmund Neufeld; d, Sam Newfield; w, Joe O'Donnell; ph, Robert Cline; ed, Robert Crandall.

Western (PR:A MPAA:NR)

DEVIL SHIP* (1947) 61m COL bw

Richard Lane (Capt. "Biff" Brown), Louise Campbell (Madge Harris), William Bishop (Sanderson), Damian O'Flynn (Red Mason), Myrna Liles (Jennie), Anthony Caruso (Venetti), Marc Krah (Mike), Anthony Warde (Burke), Denver Pyle (Carl), William Forrest (Evans), Marjorie Wordworth (Dolly), Joseph Kim (Chum), Sam Bernard (Jerry).

Dull programmer about Lane, a tuna boat skipper who augments his income by hauling prisoners out to Alcatraz. The script is thin, and directing fails to pad it out.

p, Martin Mooney; d, Lew Landers; w, Lawrence Edmund Taylor; ph, Allen Siegler; ed, James Sweeney; md, Mischa Bakaleinikoff; art d, Robert Peterson.

Drama (PR:A MPAA:NR)

DEVIL-SHIP PIRATES, THE**½ (1964, Brit.) 89m Hammer/COL c

Christopher Lee (Capt. Robeles), Andrew Keir (Tom), John Cairney (Harry), Duncan Lamont (Bosun), Michael Ripper (Pepe), Ernest Clark (Sir Basil), Barry Warren (Manuel), Suzan Farmer (Angela), Natasha Pyne (Jane), Annette Whiteley (Meg), Charles Houston (Antonio), Philip Latham (Miller), Harry Locke (Bragg), Leonard Fenton (Quintana), Jack Rodney (Mandrake), Barry Linehan (Gustavo), Bruce Beeby (Pedro), Michael Peake (Grande), Johnny Briggs (Pablo), Michael Newport (Smiler), Peter Howell (The Vicar), June Ellis (Mrs. Blake), Joseph O'Conor (Don Jose).

Well-done Hammer swashbuckler that finally saw long-time studio regular Lee get a star billing. Lee plays a ruthless pirate who steers his vessel into criminal activity in 1588 after the Spanish Armada's defeat by Sir Francis Drake. The cutthroats invade a small English coastal town and terrorize the residents until Warren jumps ship and helps organize the villagers to revolt against the pirate's evil rule.

p, Anthony Nelson Keys; d, Don Sharp; w, Jimmy Sangster; ph, Michael Reed (Megascope/Eastmancolor); m, Gary Hughes; ed, James Needs; prod d, Bernard Robinson; art d, Don Mingaye; spec eff, Les Bowie.

Historical Drama (PR:C MPAA:NR)

DEVIL STRIKES AT NIGHT, THE***
(1959, Ger.) 97m Divina/Zenith Int'l bw
(NACHTS, WENN DER TEUFEL KAM;
AKA: NAZI TERROR AT NIGHT; NIGHTS WHEN THE DEVIL CAME)

Claus Holm (Axel Kersten), Mario Adorf (Bruno Ludke), Hannes Messemer (Rossdorf), Annearie Duringer (Helga Hornung), Werner Peters (Willi Keun), Peter Carsten (Mollwitz), Rose Schafer (Anna Hohmann), Monika John (Lucy Hanson), Carl Lange (Maj. Wollenberg), Christa Nielsen (Drunken Guest), Wilmut Borell (SS Officer Henirich), Lucas Amann (Keun's Lawyer).

Fascinating study of criminal justice in the crumbling Nazi empire of 1944. Eighty stranglings have left police and Gestapo mystified. Gestapo chief Messemer calls in an outsider, veteran Holm, to look into the case, and he eventually discovers that the killings were done by one of the Gestapo's own, brutish Adorf. To cover up this incorrect Aryan behavior, a scapegoat is found, tried and executed, while Adorf is sent off to a particularly bad sector of the Russian front. The film marked the return of producer-director Siodmak to his native Germany after the war, and the story is based on a true case discovered in captured Gestapo files. Well worth seeing if only for Adorf's hulking, terrifying killer.

p&d, Robert Siodmak; w, Werner Jork Luddecke; ph, Georg Kraus.

Crime (PR:C MPAA:NR)

DEVIL THUMBS A RIDE, THE** (1947) 63m RKO bw

Lawrence Tierney (Steve), Ted North (Jimmy), Nan Leslie (Carol), Betty Lawford (Agnes), Andrew Tombes (Joe Brayden), Harry Shannon (Owens), Glenn Vernon (Jack), Marian Carr (Diane), William Gould (Capt. Martin), Josephine Whittell (Mother), Phil Warren (Pete), Robert Malcolm (Sheriff).

Drunk conventioneer North is driving home up the California coast when he picks up hitchhiker Tierney, who has just robbed and killed a theater manager. Soon North also picks up two young lady hitchhikers (Leslie and Lawford). Tierney is spotted by a gas station attendant and a police dragnet closes in. They hide out in a beach house where Leslie is killed while trying to flee for help. Finally, the police arrive and Tierney is captured. Standard crime melodrama helped greatly by Tierney's swaggering, menacing performance.

p, Herman Schlom; d&w, Felix Feist (based on the novel by Robert C. DuSoe); ph, J. Roy Hunt; m, Paul Sawtell; ed, Robert Swink; md, Constantin Bakaleinikoff, art d, Alberto D'Agostino, Charles F. Pyke.

Crime (PR:A MPAA:NR)

DEVIL TIGER** (1934) FOX bw

Mary Brewster, Marion Burns, Robert Eller, Kane Richmond, Ramsaye Doyle, Harry Woods, Ah Lee, Remow Satan.

Implausible story of white hunters and a Chinese boy hunting the title beast takes a back seat to Elliott's amazing documentary footage. A crocodile fights a tiger, a boa constrictor fights a buffalo, a lion fights a tiger, another lion fights a python—in fact, almost every big jungle animal is pitted against another in this film.

d, Clyde E. Elliott; w, James O. Spearing, Russell Shields, Lew Lehr; ed, Truman Talley.

Adventure (PR:A MPAA:NR)

DEVIL TIMES FIVE*½ (1974) 90m c
(AKA: PEOPLETOYS;
PEOPLE TOYS; THE HORRIBLE HOUSE ON THE HILL).

Gene Evans, Sorrell Booke, Shelley Morrison, Dawin Lyn, Leif Garrett, Taylor Lacher.

Five juvenile escapees from the state insane asylum take over Evans' mountain retreat and scare the guests. Better than it sounds, but not much.

d, Sean McGregor.

Suspense Cas. (PR:C MPAA:NR)

DEVIL TO PAY, THE*** (1930) 72m UA bw

Ronald Colman (Willie Leeland), Loretta Young (Dorothy Hope), Florence Britton (Susan Leeland), Frederick Kerr (Lord Leeland), David Torrence (Mr. Hope), Mary Forbes (Mrs. Hope), Paul Cavanagh (Grand Duke Paul), Crauford Kent (Arthur Leeland), Myrna Loy (Mary Carlyle).

A charming, airy comedy with Colman being as delightful in 1930 as he was so many years later in CHAMPAGNE FOR CAESAR. Colman is a playboy son of a rich daddy who spends most of his time in the pursuit of pleasure and women. The dialog is breezy as Colman returns to London after having auctioned off the house and furnishings that daddy, Frederick Kerr, provided for him in Africa. Colman used the money to support his high style of living and comes back to England with barely enough left to buy a terrier in a local pet shop. The dog is very funny and mimes his canine advice about which girls Colman should and shouldn't take up with. Once returned, Colman borrows some further poundage from dear old dad, embraces former girl friend Loy, and is immediately rocked back on his heels by the sight of gorgeous Young, a socialite with impeccable credentials and a boy friend, Cavanagh, who is a Grand Duke. Young suspects that Colman is a rakehell and ne'er-do-well and when she offers him some money, he accepts it. She thinks he is a professional gigolo but he has really taken the cash to give to Cavanagh who is all title but no money. Once that's straightened out, Young falls for Colman and the couple unite for a happy ending. Loretta Young was but seventeen when this picture was made and legend has it that she was madly in love with the suave Colman.

p, Samuel Goldwyn; d, George Fitzmaurice; w, Benjamin Glazer, Frederick Lonsdale (based on a play by Lonsdale); ph, George Barnes, Gregg Toland; m, Alfred Newman; ed, Grant Whytock; art d, Capt. Richard Day.

Comedy (PR:A MPAA:NR)

DEVIL WITH HITLER, THE** (1942) 44m UA bw

Alan Mowbray (The Devil), Bobby Watson (Hitler), George E. Stone (Suki Yaki), Joe Devlin (Mussolini), Marjorie Woodworth (Linda), Douglas Fowley (Walter), Herman Bing (Louis), Sig Arno (Julius).

Hal Roach makes his contribution to the war effort with this comedy. The board of directors of hell want to replace Mowbray with Watson (Hitler), so Mowbray comes to Earth to try to make the Fuehrer do a good deed. He succeeds, but when he returns to the underworld he finds Watson there demanding the underworld as well as the world, so he gets the job. Audiences in 1942 were pleased to see Hitler, Mussolini, and Hirohito (here called Suki Yaki) made into buffoons, but today it's harder to laugh at these figures.

p, Hal Roach, Glenn Tryon; d, Gordon Douglas; w, Cortland Fitzsimmons (based on a story by Al Martin), ph, Robert Pittack; ed, Bert Jordan.

Comedy   (PR:A MPAA:NR)

DEVIL WITH WOMEN, A*½   (1930) 63m FOX bw

Victor McLaglen (*Jerry Maxton*), Mona Maris (*Rosita Fernandez*), Humphrey Bogart (*Tom Standish*), Luana Alcaniz (*Dolores*), Michael Vavitch (*Morloff*), Soledad Jiminez (*Jimenez*), Mona Rico (*Alicia*), John St. Polis (*Don Diego*), Robert Edeson (*Gen. Garcia*), Joe De LaCruz.

Muddled story has McLaglen as an adventurer in South America who gets mixed up with bandits, senoritas, gunrunners, and the carefree nephew of the richest man in the country (Bogart). Apparently intended as a kickoff to a McLaglen series, the film was withheld for some time before release. The wait wasn't worth it. It was Bogart's second movie credit.

d, Irving Cummings; w, Dudley Nichols, Henry M. Johnson (based on the novel *Dust and Sun* by Clements Ripley); ph, Arthur Todd, Al Brick; m, Peter Brunelli; ed, Jack Murray; art d, William Darling; m/l, "Amor Mio," James Monaco, Cliff Friend.

Adventure   (PR:A MPAA:NR)

DEVIL WITHIN HER, THE**½   (1976, Brit.) 90m Hammer/AIP c
(AKA: I DON'T WANT TO BE BORN)

Joan Collins (*Lucy*), Eileen Atkins (*Sister Albana*), Donald Pleasence (*Dr. Finch*), Ralph Bates (*Gino*), Caroline Munro (*Mandy*), Hilary Mason (*Mrs. Hyde*), John Steiner (*Tommy*), Janet Key (*Jill*), George Claydon (*Hercules*), Judy Buxton (*Sheila*), Derek Benfield (*Police Inspector*), Stanley Lebor (*Police Sergeant*), John Moore (*Priest*), Phyllis McMahon (*Nun*), Andrew Secombe (*Delivery Boy*), Susan Richards (*Old Lady*).

Collins is cursed by a dwarf when she spurns his advances, and when she gives birth it's to a large, dangerous baby who attacks people and emits unholy howls from his crib. Doctor Pleasence is mangled, Collins is stabbed, Papa Bates is hung, and nun Atkins is left to perform the rites of exorcism. A rip-off of THE EXORCIST and IT'S ALIVE, the film surprises with a few moments of genuine terror. Collins and Pleasence are uncharacteristically excellent.

p, Nato De Angeles; d, Peter Sasdy; w, Stanley Price (based on a story by De Angeles); ph, Kenneth Talbot; m, Ron Grainer; ed, Keith Palmer; art d, Roy Stanard; spec eff, Bert Luxford.

Horror   (PR:O MPAA:R)

DEVIL WOMAN   (SEE: ONIBABA, 1965, Jap.)

DEVIL WOMAN zero   (1976, Phil.) 79m Hallmark c

Rosemarie Gil, Alex Tang Lec, Romy Diax, Robert Chen.

Horror outing about a Gorgon-woman seeking revenge on the local farmers who burned her home and killed her parents. To get back at them she sends lethal cobras out to bite and kill them. An awful movie.

p, Jimmy L. Pasqual; d, Albert Yu, Felix Vilars.

Horror   (PR:O MPAA:R)

DEVIL'S AGENT, THE**½   (1962, Brit.) 77m Emmet Dalton/BL bw

Peter Van Eyck (*George Droste*), Macdonald Carey (*Mr. Smith*), Marianne Koch (*Nora Gulden*), Christopher Lee (*Baron von Staub*), Billie Whitelaw (*Piroska*), David Knight (*Fr. Zombary*), Marius Goring (*Gen. Greenhahn*), Helen Cherry (*Countess Cosimano*), Colin Gordon (*Count Dezsepalvy*), Niall McGinnis (*Paul Vass*), Eric Pohlmann (*Bloch*), Peter Vaughan (*Police Chief*), Michael Brennan (*Horvat*), Jeremy Bulloch (*Johnny Droste*), Walter Gotell (*Dr. Ritter*), John Cowley (*Funnel-Shaped Man*), Peter Lamb (*Muller*), Christopher Casson (*Headmaster*), Bart Bastable (*Cattle Truck Driver*), Charles Byrne (*Vazlan*), Robert Lepler (*Head Waiter*).

Van Eyck, a wine merchant from Vienna, is used as a pawn by Soviet spies, so he offers his services to a U.S. intelligence agency. Occasionally gripping spy drama with a very good cast.

p, Victor Lyndon, Emmet Dalton; d, John Paddy Carstairs; w, Robert Westerby (based on a novel by Hans Habe); ph, Gerald Gibbs; m, Philip Green.

Spy Drama   (PR:C MPAA:NR)

DEVIL'S ANGELS*   (1967) 84m AIP c

John Cassavetes (*Cody*), Beverly Adams (*Lynn*), Mimsy Farmer (*Marianne*), Maurice McEndree (*Joel-the-Mole*), Salli Sachse (*Louise*), Nai Bonet (*Tonya*), Leo Gordon (*Sheriff Henderson*), Russ Bender (*Royce*), Marc Cavell (*Billy-the-Kid*), Buck Taylor (*Gage*), Marianne Kanter (*Rena*), Kip Whitman (*Roy*), Mitzi Hoag (*Karen*), Buck Kartalian (*Funky*), George Sims (*Leroy*), Wally Campo (*Grog*), Dick Anders (*Bruno*), John Craig (*Robot*), Paul Myer (*Mayor*), Lee Wainer (*Cane*), Roy Thiel, Ronnie Dayton (*Deputies*), Henry Kendrick (*Store Owner*).

Cassavetes and his motorcycle gang clash with Sheriff Gordon in this sleazy, ultra-low-budget followup to the popular WILD ANGELS. Everything down to the credits is run-of-the-mill.

p, Burt Topper; d, Daniel Haller; w, Charles Griffith; ph, Richard Moore (Panavision, Pathe Color); m, Mike Curb; ed, Ronald Steiner, Kenneth Crane; m/l "Devil's Angels," Curb, Guy Hemric, Jerry Styner.

Crime   (PR:O MPAA:NR)

DEVIL'S BAIT*   (1959, Brit.) 58m Independent Artists/RFD bw

Geoffrey Keen (*Joe Frisby*), Jane Hylton (*Ellen Frisby*), Gordon Jackson (*Sgt. Malcolm*), Dermot Kelly (*Mr. Love*), Shirley Lawrence (*Shirley*), Eileen Moore (*Barbara*), Molly Urquhart (*Mrs. Tanner*), Rupert Davies (*Landlord*), Gillian

Vaughan, Barbara Archer, Timothy Bateson, Noel Hood, Vivienne Bennett, Jack Stewart.

Baker Keen helps police sergeant Jackson search for a loaf of bread baked in a poisoned container. Strictly routine suspense drama.

p, Arthur Alcott; d, Peter Graham Scott; w, Peter Johnston, Diana Watson; ph, Michael Reed.

Drama   (PR:A MPAA:NR)

DEVIL'S BEDROOM, THE*   (1964) 78m Rebel/Manson bw

John Lupton (*Jim*), Valerie Allen (*Della*), Dick Jones (*Norm*), Alvy Moore, Morgan Woodward, Justice McQueen, Mrs. Arch Pearson, Claude Hall, Bill Buckner, Thomas Commack, Merv Dawson, E.B. Jolly, Lawrence Mooney, W.H. Handley, Ken Ariola, Ralph G. Edwards.

Grim crime drama directed and coproduced by L.Q. Jones (an outstanding character actor—Justice McQueen—who can be seen in many of director and screenwriter Sam Peckinpah's best films) which tells the tale of an evil brother, Dick Jones, who, along with his equally vile sister-in-law, Allen, attempts to drive his sibling Lupton insane, thus gaining access to his land which sits on an untapped oil well. Allen turns the tables on Jones by convincing Lupton that his brother is insane. Lupton has Jones committed, but the brother escapes and makes his way back to the ranch where he is found dead in the barn. Soon after, Allen is found drowned in a well, which sends the angry and suspicious townsfolk into a lynching frenzy. In the end, though the sheriff has determined both deaths to be accidental, Lupton is burned to death by the mob. L.Q. Jones would later go on to direct A BOY AND HIS DOG, an interesting but flawed cult favorite.

p, George Gunter, L.Q. Jones [Justice E. McQueen]; assoc p, Alvy Moore; d, Jones; w, Claude Hall, Morgan Woodward (based on a story by Hall); ph, Gunter, Maitland Stewart; m, William Loose, Emil Cadkin; set d, Judy Masters.

Drama   (PR:O MPAA:NR)

DEVIL'S BRIDE, THE**½ (1968, Brit.) 95m Hammer-Seven Arts/FOX c
(GB: THE DEVIL RIDES OUT)

Christopher Lee (*Duc de Richleau*), Charles Gray (*Mocata*), Nike Arrighi (*Tanith*), Leon Greene (*Rex*), Patrick Mower (*Simon*), Gwen Ffrangcon-Davies (*Countess*), Sarah Lawson (*Marie*), Paul Eddington (*Richard*), Rosalyn Landor (*Peggy*), Russell Waters (*Malin*), Mohan Singh, Keith Pyott, John Brown.

Atmospheric supernatural tale starring Lee as a nobleman who attempts to save the soul of his close friend, Mower, who has become deeply involved in a satanic society run by Gray. Lee's daughter, Landor, is kidnaped by the cult and put up for sacrifice to the Angel of Death, who appears to claim his victim but is driven off by Lee. It all sounds silly, but it is directed with style and flair that creates a creepy mood.

p, Anthony Nelson Keys; d, Terence Fisher; w, Richard Matheson (based on the novel *The Devil Rides Out* by Dennis Wheatley); ph, Arthur Grant (DeLuxe Color); m, James Bernard; ed, James Needs, Spencer Reeve; art d, Bernard Robinson; ch, David Toguri; spec eff, Michael Stainer-Hutchins.

Horror   (PR:O MPAA:NR)

DEVIL'S BRIGADE, THE**   (1968) 131m UA c

William Holden (*Lt. Col. Robert T. Frederick*), Cliff Robertson (*Maj. Alan Crown*), Vince Edwards (*Maj. Cliff Bricker*), Michael Rennie (*Lt. Gen. Mark Clark*), Dana Andrews (*Brig. Gen. Walter Naylor*), Gretchen Wyler (*A Lady of Joy*), Andrew Prine (*Pvt. Theodore Ransom*), Claude Akins (*Rocky Rockman*), Carroll O'Connor (*Maj. Gen. Hunter*), Richard Jaeckel (*Omar Greco*), Jack Watson (*Cpl. Wilfred Peacock*), Paul Hornung (*Lumberjack*), Gene Fullmer (*Bartender*), Jeremy Slate (*Patrick O'Neill*), Don Megowan (*Luke Phelan*), Patric Knowles (*Adm. Lord Louis Mountbatten*), James Craig (*American Officer*), Richard Dawson (*Hugh MacDonald*), Tom Stern (*Capt. Cardwell*), Tom Troupe (*Al Manella*), Luke Askew (*Hubert Hixon*), Bill Fletcher (*Bronc Guthrie*), Jean-Paul Vignon (*Henri Laurent*), Harry Carey, Jr. (*Capt. Rose*), Norman Alden (*M.P. Lieutenant*), David Pritchard (*Cpl. Coker*), Paul Busch (*German Captain*).

THE DEVIL'S BRIGADE is like a trans-continental airplane flight; long stretches of boredom punctuated by moments of terror. It was accused of being a pale imitation of THE DIRTY DOZEN which preceded it by a year but the truth is that THE DIRTY DOZEN was a fiction while this was based on fact. Unfortunately, the script dredged up every cliche we've ever seen and heard in war movies since BIRTH OF A NATION. Holden runs a brigade made up of Americans and Canadians. His seconds-in-command are Robertson (Canada) and Edwards (U.S.A.) and their job is to create a commando force that will attack large groups of Nazis in Scandinavia. They take about twenty minutes to find and form the cadre, and the next 40 minutes in arguing and training and getting to know the characters. The following half hour is further training and some battlefield footage and the final 40 minutes or so is the culmination. The Canadians are portrayed as crack troops while the Americans are just cracked. Holden keeps the two factions together by getting them to compete with one another. This becomes friendship and, finally, respect. The men are now ready for action but their operation is canceled. Holden is disappointed because his men are in fine fettle and raring to go. He appeals to O'Connor and gets a new assignment—nailing the Germans in the Italian Alps. Their task is to scale an impossible mountain and destroy the German emplacements. They move up the side of the mountain and get knocked off one by one. In the end, they manage to overcome the terrain and the Nazis and earn the sobriquet of THE DEVIL'S BRIGADE. The book detailed all of the rigors of the task and it's a shame that this movie strove so hard to fill all the corners of the mural that it became entirely too busy. One trivia note: appearing as the lumberjack was former Notre Dame and Green Bay football star Paul Hornung, and the bartender was one-time boxing champion, Gene Fullmer. O'Connor played this military role several times in his career, most notably a few years later in KELLY'S HEROES, an equally boring movie that covered the same general territory. Dawson, who was born in England and was once married to Diana Dors, had a fairly good career in films before he became a TV game show host and achieved immense popularity by kissing the distaff contestants.

p, David L. Wolper; d, Andrew V. McLaglen; w, William Roberts (based on the book by Robert H. Adleman, Col. George Walton); ph, William H. Clothier (Panavision, DeLuxe Color); m, Alex North; ed, William Cartwright; art d, Alfred Sweeney, Jr.; set d, Morris Hoffman; spec eff, Logan Frazee; stunts, Hal Needham.

War Adventure (PR:C MPAA:NR)

DEVIL'S BROTHER, THE** (1933) 88m MGM bw
(GB: FRA DIAVOLO; BOGUS BANDITS; THE VIRTUOUS TRAMPS)

Stan Laurel (Stanlio), Oliver Hardy (Olio), Dennis King (Fra Diavolo/Marquis de San Marco), Thelma Todd (Lady Pamela), James Finlayson (Lord Rocberg), Lucille Browne (Zerlina), Arthur Pierson (Lorenzo), Henry Armetta (Matteo), Matt McHugh (Francesco), Lane Chandler (Lieutenant), Nena Quartero (Rita), Wilfred Lucas (Alessandro), James C. Morton (1st Woodchopper), Carl Harbaugh (2nd Woodchopper), George Miller (Village Minister), Stanley (Tiny) Sandford (Tremulous Woodchopper), Jack Hill, Dick Gilbert, Arthur Stone (Brigands), John Qualen (Man Who Owned the Bull), Edith Fellows, Jackie Taylor (Village Children), Rolfe Sedan, Kay Deslys, Leo White, Lillian Moore, Walter Shumway, Louise Carver (Tavern Patrons), Harry Bernard (Bandit/Imbiber at the Tavern de Cucu).

This was not one of Laurel and Hardy's major efforts but it still had enough humor to make a pleasant evening at the Bijou at the time and worth watching at home on TV instead of The News. Ollie and Stan are misfit bandits hired as manservants to Dennis King, who is a real bandit. Once again, it is the dual identity story with King acting as a wealthy marquis in order to locate the whereabouts of the treasures worn by the dripping-with-diamonds-damsels. In that, it resembles ZORRO and THE SCARLET PIMPERNEL and any number of other films. Based on the 1830 opera "Fra Diavolo" by Daniel F. Auber, the parts of Beppo and Giacomo in the original were built up for Stan and Ollie. It didn't help. The music was pleasant but got in the way of the Laurel and Hardy humor. Or, if you're more into music than mirth, you might look at it the other way around. Whichever, the movie left much to be desired from both angles. The picture was variously reissued as BOGUS BANDITS and THE VIRTUOUS TRAMPS but the new titles didn't help. Only the "Drinking Scene" stands out for laughter.

p, Hal Roach; d, Charles Rogers, Roach; w, Jeanie Macpherson (based on the comic opera by Daniel F. Auber); ph, Art Lloyd, Hap Depew; m, Auber; ed, Bert Jordan, William Terhune; md, Le Roy Shield.

Comedy Operetta (PR:AAA MPAA:NR)

DEVIL'S CANYON** (1953) 91m RKO c
Virginia Mayo (Abby Nixon), Dale Robertson (Billy Reynolds), Stephen McNally (Jesse Gorman), Arthur Hunnicutt (Frank Taggert), Robert Keith (Steve Morgan), Jay C. Flippen (Capt. Wells), George J. Lewis (Col. Gomez), Whit Bissell (Virgil), Morris Ankrum (Sheriff), James Bell (Dr. Betts), William Phillips (Red), Earl Holliman (Joe), Irving Bacon (Abby's Guard), Jim Hayward (Man in Saloon), Fred Coby (Cole Gorman), John Cliff (Bud Gorman), Glenn Strange (Marshall, the Wagon Driver), Murray Alper (Driver-Guard), Harold "Stubby" Kruger (Prisoner), Paul Fix (Gatling Guard), Gregg Martell (Tower Guard), Larry Blake (Hysterical Prisoner).

Set in a grim Arizona territorial prison at the turn of the century, McNally is a psychotic killer seeking vengeance on Robertson, an ex-lawman serving time. McNally tries to break out, aided by outlaw queen Mayo, but she switches sides at the crucial moment and helps Robertson quell the breakout with a Gatling gun. Depressingly accurate depiction of prison life is the best thing in this undistinguished western shot in 3-D, though Musuraca's somber lighting keeps it from getting too ostentatious.

p, Edmund Grainger; d, Alfred Werker; w, Frederick Hazlitt Brennan, Harry Essex (based on a story by Bennett R. Cohen, Norton S. Parker); ph, Nicholas Musuraca (Natural Vision 3-D, Technicolor); m, Daniele Amfitheatrof; ed, Gene Palmer; art d, Albert D'Agostino, Jack Okey.

Western (PR:A MPAA:NR)

DEVIL'S CARGO, THE*½ (1948) 61m FC bw
John Calvert (Michael Waring/The Falcon), Rochelle Hudson (Margo), Roscoe Karns (Lt. Hardy), Lyle Talbot (Morello), Tom Kennedy (Naga), Paul Regan (Bernie), Theodore Van Eltz (Tom Mallon), Paul Marion (Ramon Delgado).

Marion is accused of killing a racetrack operator so he hires the Falcon, Calvert, to clear him. Later he is poisoned in his cell, and Calvert has to find the culprit, which he does, of course. For the last three films of the Falcon series, Tom Conway was replaced by Calvert and the Falcon name was dropped from the titles. This is the first of Calvert's trio, and the best that can be said is that in spots it approaches the quality of the Conway films. (See FALCON series, Index.)

p, Philip N. Krasne; d, John F. Link; w, Don Martin (based on a story by Robert Tallman, Jason James); ph, Walter Strange; m, Karl Hajos; ed, Asa Boyd Clark.

Detective (PR:A MPAA:NR)

DEVIL'S COMMANDMENT, THE zero (1956, Ital.) 90m RCIP bw
(I VAMPIRI; AKA LUST OF THE VAMPIRES)

Gianna Marie Canale, Antoine Balpetre, Paul Muller, Carlo D'Angelo, Wandisa Guida, Dario Michaelis, Renato Tontini, Charles Fawcett.

Obscure early Italian gothic horror film which tells the story of a doctor who uses human blood to restore the youth of a countess who is aging rapidly. When the film came to the U.S. seeking exhibition, the distributor added a brief bathtub scene and a rape to spice things up for the drive-in crowd.

p, Ermanno Donati, Luigi Carpentieri; d, Riccardo Freda; w, Piero Regnoli, Rik Sjostrom; ph, Mario Bava.

Horror (PR:O MPAA:NR)

DEVIL'S DAFFODIL, THE** (1961, Brit./Ger.) 86m Omnia-Rialto/Goldstone bw
(DAS GEHEIMNIS DER GELDEN NARZIZZEN)

Christopher Lee (Ling Chu), Marius Goring (Oliver Milburgh), Penelope Horner (Anne Rider), Ingrid Van Bergen (Gloria), William Lucas (Jack Tarling), Albert Lieven (Raymond Lyne), Colin Jeavons (Peter Keene), Walter Gotell (Supt. Whiteside), Peter Illing (Jan Putek), Dawn Beret (Katya), Bettine Le Beau (Trudi), Jan Hendriks (Charles), Campbell Singer (Sir Archibald), Lance Percival (French Gendarme), Frederick Bartman (Detective), Grace Denbeigh-Russell (Mrs. Rider), Nancy Nevinson (Sluttish Woman), Martin Lyder (Max), Edwina Carroll (Chinese Girl), Gundel Sargent (Hotel Receptionist), Irene Prador (Maisie).

Lee is a Chinese detective who breaks up a ring smuggling heroin into Britain from Hong Kong in the stems of daffodils. Shot simultaneously in English and German with different supporting casts (Klaus Kinski plays the Jeavons role, a crazed addict who battles Lee in a cemetery, in the German version), the English version is clearly inferior to the German. Lee, who starred in both versions, performed the remarkable acting feat of playing a Chinese detective to a German audience.

p, Steven Pallos, Donald Taylor; d, Akos Rathony; w, Basil Dawson, Donald Taylor (based on the novel The Daffodil Mystery by Edgar Wallace); ph, Desmond Dickinson; m, Keith Papworth; ed, Peter Taylor; art d, William Hutchinson.

Mystery (PR:A MPAA:NR)

DEVIL'S DAUGHTER*** (1949, Fr.) 98m Pathe-Cinema-Safia/International Alliance bw (LA FILLE DU DIABLE)

Pierre Fresnay (Saget), Fernand Ledoux (The Doctor), Andree Clement (Isabelle), Therese Dorny (Aunt Hortense), Albert Remy (Clement), Serge Andreguy (N'A Qu'un Sou), Albert Glado (Little Boy), Francois Patrice (George), Felix Claude (Saint-Jean), Robert Seller (Mayor), Pierre Juvenet (Priest), Paul Frankeur (Bartender), Andre Wasley (Watchman), Amato (Policeman), Henri Charret (Ludovic Mercier).

Fresnay is a bank robber who assumes the identity of a rich man returning to his village after many years. He is recognized by Ledoux, the town doctor, and is blackmailed into donating his loot to various charities. Simultaneously, Fresnay tries to reform town bad girl Clement, who hates him when she thinks he's a millionaire but falls in love when she discovers he's a wanted man. Well done in French "Tradition of Quality" so despised by the New Wave. (In French; English subtitles.)

p, Henri Decoin; d, Maurice Saurel; w, M.G. Sauvajon, Decoin, Alex Joffe (based on a story by Joffe, Jean Le Vltte); ph, Armand Thirard; ed, Bretonneche.

Drama Cas. (PR:A MPAA:NR)

DEVIL'S DISCIPLE, THE*** (1959) 82m Hecht-Hill-Lancaster, Brynaprod/UA bw
Burt Lancaster (Anthony Anderson), Kirk Douglas (Richard Dudgeon), Laurence Olivier (Gen. Burgoyne), Janette Scott (Judith Anderson), Eva Le Gallienne (Mrs. Dudgeon), Harry Andrews (Maj. Swindon), Basil Sydney (Lawyer Hawkins), George Rose (British Sergeant), Neil McCallum (Christopher Dudgeon), Mervyn Johns (Rev. Maindeck Parshotter), David Horne (William), Jenny Jones (Essie), Erik Chitty (Titus).

Irish-born George Bernard Shaw never did like the British and used every opportunity to satirize them. In THE DEVIL'S DISCIPLE the best lines are given to Olivier as Gen. Burgoyne, leader of the Blighty Brigade in the U.S. in 1777, before it was the U.S. Olivier and his men march into a tiny northeastern hamlet on their way down from Canada. The local colonists are not thrilled about being occupied and rebel. To quell the disturbance, Olivier hangs a local luminary which puts a stop to any activity on the part of the frightened townspeople. Lancaster is the local reverend and he returns home to discover his wife, Scott, sitting at the side of Le Gallienne, widow of the slain man. Douglas, son of the dead citizen, arrives. A troublemaker from his buckled shoes to the cleft in his chin, Douglas twits the citizens for rolling over and playing dead. Lancaster worries about Douglas as his wife, Scott, is apparently attracted to him. In another time and in another place, Lancaster and Douglas might have become friends as Lancaster does admire the younger, livelier man. But jealousy begins to rear its head. Olivier wishes he would get his orders to leave so he could return to London in time for the social "season." His aides prevail on him to hang another townsperson, as the villagers are beginning to make rebellious noises once more. The general acquiesces and soldiers are sent to Lancaster's home. Douglas is having tea with Scott and the military men don't know that he is not the pastor. Douglas allows himself to be tried and convicted and sentenced to death and he gallantly never spills the beans. And where, you may well ask, is Lancaster all this time? He is out with the rebels and leading the revolutionary forces on raids. Lancaster intercepts a message sent to Olivier and uses it as a bargaining tool for the life of Douglas, who is standing on the gallows with the noose draped around his neck. Scott now begins to look at her once-dull husband as a hero. She takes him back into her arms and Douglas and Olivier have a spot of tea as the narrator tells the film audience that Burgoyne (Olivier) surrendered just three weeks later. Shaw never really liked this play very much and considered it one of his minor efforts. After the one performance needed to secure copyright, Shaw forbade the play to be produced in England and it wasn't until American actor Richard Masefield staged it in the U.S. that it was seen in full regalia. The funny lines are too many to quote, but Olivier gets most of them. Douglas asks to be shot rather than hanged, but Olivier says hanging would be far less painful because, "Have you any idea of the average marksmanship of the

Army of His Majesty, King George III?'' Excellent supporting players but a generally choppy directorial style are what keep this from being a classic. Lancaster and Douglas both had a hand in the production via their companies but they obviously deferred to Olivier in acting matters, as the visitor from abroad got all the critical nods.

p, Harold Hecht; d, Guy Hamilton; w, Roland Kibbee, John Dighton (based on the play by George Bernard Shaw); ph, Jack Hildyard; m, Richard Rodney Bennett; ed, Alan Osbiston; art d, Terrence Verity, Edward Carrere; cos, Mary Grant.

Historical Drama   **(PR:A MPAA:NR)**

DEVIL'S DOLL   (SEE: DEVIL'S HAND, THE, 1961)

DEVIL'S DOORWAY**½**   (1950) 84m MGM bw

Robert Taylor (*Lance Poole*), Louis Calhern (*Verne Coolan*), Paula Raymond (*Orrie Masters*), Marshall Thompson (*Rod MacDougall*), James Mitchell (*Red Rock*), Edgar Buchanan (*Zeke Carmody*), Rhys Williams (*Scotty MacDougall*), Spring Byington (*Mrs. Masters*), James Millican (*Ike Stapleton*), Bruce Cowling (*Lt. Grimes*), Fritz Leiber (*Mr. Poole*), Harry Antrim (*Dr. C.O. MacQuillan*), Chief John Big Tree (*Thundercloud*).

Interesting off-center casting and a literate script distinguish this from so many ordinary westerns. Taylor, in some heavy makeup, is a Shoshone Indian who won the Congressional Medal of Honor while fighting for the Blues at Gettysburg. He goes home to Wyoming and runs afoul of Calhern, an Indian-hating lawyer who has some whites homestead the Indians' traditional lands. Taylor attempts to assuage matters between the tribe and the settlers by appealing to the authorities for help, but it's a useless gesture. The tribe is trounced in the courts and then on the battlefield and the picture ends with Taylor dying as he averts a massacre of his fellow Indians. This was not a popular movie for many reasons: the hero died, there was little romance (a brief fling with Paula Raymond that one barely notices) and no one much cared for Indian causes at the time, having been brought up on John Wayne's attitudes toward them. Too bad, because this was a good story and Trosper put intelligent words into the mouths of the actors. Although in black and white, Alton's camera manages to capture the light and shade of the Wyoming territory as effectively as an Ansel Adams still of Yosemite.

p, Nicholas Nayfack; d, Anthony Mann; w, Guy Trosper; ph, John Alton; m, Daniele Amfitheatrof; ed, Conrad A. Nervig; art d, Cedric Gibbons, Leonid Vasian.

Western   **(PR:A MPAA:NR)**

DEVIL'S 8, THE**   (1969) 97m AIP c

Christopher George (*Ray Faulkner*), Fabian (*Sonny*), Tom Nardini (*Billy Joe*), Leslie Parrish (*Cissy*), Ross Hagen (*Frank*), Larry Bishop (*Chandler*), Cliff Osmond (*Bubba*), Robert Doqui (*Henry*), Ron Rifkin (*Martin*), Baynes Barron (*Bureau Chief*), Joseph Turkel (*Sam*), Lada Edmund, Jr. (*Inez*), Marjorie Dayne (*Hallie*), Ralph Meeker (*Burl*).

George is a federal agent who helps six men escape from a chain gang, in order to use them in his war on a moonshine ring run by Meeker. Lots of action in the high-speed driver training sequences, during which the men are taught how to hurl lighted bombs at pinpoint targets, after which the six men and George and a second agent are prepared to move against the crooks. A weak screenplay and trite dialog sink this one.

p&d, Burt Topper; w, James Gordon White, John Milius, William Huyck (based on a story by Larry Gordon); ph, Richard C. Glouner (Berkley Pathe Color); m, Mike Curb; ed, Fred Feitshans, Jr.; art d, Paul Sylos; set d, Harry Reif; spec eff, Roger George; m/l, "The Devil's 8," Curb, Guy Hemric; stunts, Chuck Bail.

Crime   **(PR:C MPAA:M)**

DEVIL'S ENVOYS, THE***½**   (1947, Fr.) 118m Superfilm bw
(LES VISITEURS DU SOIR)

Arletty (*Dominique*), Jules Berry (*Devil*), Marie Dea (*Anne*), Fernand Ledoux (*Baron Hugues*), Alain Cuny (*Giles*), Gabriel Gabrio (*La Bourreau*), Marcel Herrand (*Chevalier Renaud*), Pierre Labry (*Le Gros Seignor*).

Produced just after the occupation of France by Germany in WW II, this film by Carne and Prevert attempts to recreate the success of their masterpiece, THE CHILDREN OF PARADISE. This one is based on a French legend of two evil messengers sent from hell to wreak havoc on earth. Satan's thugs are no match for the unconditional love of the tender Arletty, and they refuse to return to the fires of eternal damnation. A lavish spectacle of a very simple love-conquers-all theme.

p, Andre Paulve; d, Marcel Carne; w, Jacques Prevert, Pierre Laroche; ph, Roger Hubert; m, Maurice Thiriet; md, Charles Munch; art d, George Wakhevitch.

Fantasy   **(PR:A MPAA:NR)**

DEVIL'S EXPRESS zero   (1975) 82m Mahler Films c
(AKA: GANG WARS)

Warhawk Tanzania, Larry Fleishman, Sam DeFazio, Wilfredo Roldan, Elsie Roman, Sarah Nyrick.

Unintentionally funny (if this is how you get your kicks) kung-fu/horror outing which sees a young, black, and gifted martial arts student unleash a horrible demon in the New York subway system. A truly bad film done with total technical incompetence.

p, Nick Patton, Steve Madoff; d, Barry Rosen; (Panavision, Technicolor).

Horror   **(PR:O MPAA:R)**

DEVIL'S EYE, THE***   (1960, Swed.) 90m ABSF bw
(DJAVULENS OGA)

Jarl Kulle (*Don Juan*), Bibi Andersson (*Britt-Marie*), Axel Duberg (*Her Fiance*), Nils Poppe (*The Pastor*), Gertrud Fridh (*Pastor's Wife*), Sture Lagerwall (*Pablo*), Stig Jarrel (*Satan*), Gunnar Bjornstrand (*The Actor*), Georg Funkquist (*The Count*), Gunnar Sjoberg (*The Marquis*), Allan Edwall (*The Ear Devil*), Torsten Winge (*Old Man*), Kristina Adolphsson, Ragnar Arvedson, Borje Lundh, Lenn Hjortzberg.

Fanciful comedy by Ingmar Bergman details the efforts of the Devil to stop the swelling in his eye (because, as an old Irish proverb states, "A virgin is a sty in the Devil's eye") by sending Don Juan (Kulle) to seduce the 20-year-old daughter (Andersson) of a kindly country pastor. Accompanied by his servant, Lagerwall, the great seducer arrives to do the Devil's bidding. While Kulle is busy attempting to corrupt the daughter, Lagerwall tries to seduce the pastor's frustrated wife. Kulle momentarily succeeds in causing a rift between Andersson and her fiance, but he is challenged by the girl's indifference to him. Before he knows it, it is he who falls in love. Good performances and cinematography and direction make for an entertaining, albeit minor, Bergman film.

p, Allan Ekelund; d&w, Ingmar Bergman (adapted from the Danish radio play "Don Juan Vender tillbage" by Oluf Bang); ph, Gunner Fischer; m, Domenico Scarlatti; ed, Oscar Rosander; art d, P.A. Lundgren.

Comedy   **Cas.**   **(PR:C MPAA:NR)**

DEVIL'S GENERAL, THE**½**   (1957, Ger.) 124m Real/Distributors
Corp. of America bw (DES TEUFEL'S GENERAL)

Curt Jurgens (*Gen. Harras*), Victor de Kowa (*Schmidt-Lausitz*), Karl John (*Oderbruch*), Eva-Ingeborg Scholz (*Fraulein Mohrungen*), Marrianne Koch (*Dorothea Geiss*), Albert Lieven (*Oberst Eilers*), Erica Balque (*Anne Eilers*), Werner Fuetterer (*Baron Pflungk*), Harry Meyen (*Lt. Hartmann*); Carl-Ludwig Diehl (*Hugo Mohrungen*), Paul Westermeier (*Korrianke*), Camilla Spira (*Olivia Geiss*).

Engrossing drama loosely based on the life of Ernst Udet, the highest ranking German ace to survive the First World War, only to kill himself on the eve of the Second in horror over his role in Nazi rearmament. Jurgens is the Luftwaffe general here, caught in the middle between his loyalty to his country and his comrades and the growing revulsion he feels to the Nazis and the war. In the end, when he crashes a new bomber rather than let it be used to prolong the war, the Nazis proclaim him a hero and martyr to the Reich. The film gets a bit talky at times, but is still worth seeing.

p, Gyula Trebitsch; d, Helmut Kautner; w, Georg Hurdalek, Kautner (based on a play by Carl Zuckmayer); ph, Albert Benitz.

Drama   **(PR:A-C MPAA:NR)**

DEVIL'S GODMOTHER, THE*½**   (1938, Mex.) 74m Varela bw

Jorge Negrete, Maria Fernanda Ibanez, Ramon Pere Diaz.

Negrete is the baritone hero of this Mexican singing caballero film, rescuing Ibanez from the convent where her father (Diaz) has confined her. The singing isn't bad, but its interest is chiefly as a variation on an old Hollywood theme.

d, Ramon Peon.

Western   **(PR:A MPAA:NR)**

DEVIL'S HAIRPIN, THE**½**   (1957) 83m PAR c

Cornel Wilde (*Nick*), Jean Wallace (*Kelly*), Arthur Franz (*Rhinegold*), Mary Astor (*Mrs. Jargin*), Paul Fix (*Doc*), Larry Pennell (*Johnny*), Gerald Milton (*Mike Houston*), Ross Bagdasarian (*Tani*), Jack Kosslyn (*Tony Botari*), Morgan Jones (*Chico Martinez*), Louis Wilde (*The Parrot*), Jack Latham (*Race Announcer*), Mabel Lillian Rea (*Redhead*), Dorene Porter (*Blonde*), Sue England (*Brunette*), John Indrisano (*Gate Guard*), Mike Mahoney (*Starter*), Les Clark (*Bill the Bartender*), Henry Blair (*Newsboy*), Gil Stuart, George Gilbreth, Gordon Mills, John Benson.

Competent but unexciting race car movie cowritten and directed by its star, Wilde. He plays a reckless driver who has retired after having nearly killed his younger brother in a race that left his sibling brain-damaged. Wilde is wooed out of retirement by auto manufacturer Franz and the egostistical racer puts on his helmet and returns to the wheel, much to the dismay of his mother, Astor, and his alcoholic wife, Wallace. The plot motivations and parade of characters that precede the racing footage are slow, dull, and confusing, but the racing itself is well shot.

p&d, Cornel Wilde; w, James Edmiston, Wilde (based on the novel *The Fastest Man on Earth* by Edmiston); ph, Daniel L. Fapp (VistaVision/Technicolor); ed, Floyd Knudtson; art d, Hal Pereira, Hilyard Brown; set d, Sam Comer, Grace Gregory; cos, Edith Head; spec eff, John P. Fulton; m/l, Ross Bagdasarian, Van Cleave.

Action/Drama   **(PR:A MPAA:NR)**

DEVIL'S HAND, THE   (SEE: CARNIVAL OF SINNERS, 1947, FR.)

DEVIL'S HAND, THE*   (1961) 71m Crown International bw
(AKA: DEVIL'S DOLL; THE NAKED GODDESS; LIVE TO LOVE)

Linda Christian (*Bianca*), Robert Alda (*Rick*), Neil Hamilton (*Frank*), Ariadne Welter (*Donna*), Gene Craft, Jeannie Carmen, Julie Scott, Diana Spears.

Supernatural tale starring Alda as a man who finds a curio doll in a small shop that embodies his ideal of a perfect woman. The shop owner informs him that the doll was modeled after a young woman who lives nearby, and the man gives Alda her address. When Alda leaves, the shopkeeper (who is the high priest of a voodoo cult) produces a doll of Alda's girl friend, Welter, and sticks a pin into it. Welter is suddenly stricken and taken to a hospital. Alda meets his "perfect" woman, Christian, who promises him her love if he will join the cult. He goes through with the initiation, but his love for Welter forces him to remove the pin from her doll, freeing her from her malaise. The cult members discover Alda's disloyalty and they kidnap Welter to use as a human sacrifice. Alda comes to his senses, kills the high priest, and the temple is engulfed in flames. The fate of Christian remains unknown and the viewer are left pondering as to whether the evil has really ended. Less than terrifying.

p, Alvis K. Bubis, Rex Carlton; d, William J. Hole, Jr.; w, Jo Heims, Rex Carlton; ph, Meredith M. Nicholson; ed, Howard Epstein; makeup, Jack P. Pierce.

Horror   **(PR:C MPAA:NR)**

DEVIL'S HARBOR**   (1954, Brit.) 70m FOX bw (GB: DEVIL'S POINT)

Richard Arlen (*John*), Greta Gynt (*Peggy*), Donald Houston (*Mallard*), Mary Germaine (*Margaret*), Elspeth Gray (*Mrs. Mallard*), Vincent Ball (*Williams*), Howard Lang (*Marne*), Anthony Vicars (*Inspector Hunt*), Edwin Richfield (*Daller*), Michael Balfour (*Bennett*), Arnold Adrian (*Mark*), Sidney Bromley (*Enson*), Stuart Saunders (*Ryan*), Patricia Salonika (*Pat*), Doreen Holliday (*Susie*), Peter Bernard (*Sam*), Victor Baring, John Dunbar, John Lewis, Stella Andrews, Reginald Hearne, Neil Gibson, Michael Mulcaster.

Uninspired British drama starring Arlen as a riverboat operator who gets involved with illegal drug smugglers one night when he breaks up a gang-fight on the wharf. The hoods leave behind a package and Arlen picks it up. The gang returns to retrieve the stash and Arlen is killed. Thoughtless script and lackluster direction don't help the players, who try their best.

p, Charles Deane; d, Montgomery Tully; w, Deane; ph, Geoffrey Faithful; ed, Peter Seabourne.

Crime   **(PR:C MPAA:NR)**

DEVIL'S HENCHMEN, THE**   (1949) 68m COL bw

Warner Baxter (*Jess Arno*), Mary Beth Hughes (*Silky*), Mike Mazurki (*Rhino*), Peggy Converse (*Connie*), Regis Toomey (*Tip Banning*), Harry Shannon (*Captain*), James Flavin (*Sgt. Briggs*), Julian Rivero (*Organ Grinder*), Ken Christy (*Detective Whalen*), William Forrest (*Anderson*), Alan Bridge (*Elmer Hood*), Paul Marion (*Bill Falls*).

Baxter disguises himself as a down-and-out sailor who goes into the marine junk business to get the goods on illegal smugglers of furs operating on the California waterfront. Soon after he opens for business, gangsters Toomey and Mazurki arrive and a corpse follows. Baxter learns that the deceased is a former gang member, so he joins the smugglers to get evidence on the killers. He discovers that the ringleader of the crooks is Shannon, disguised as a half-wit derelict who hangs around waterfront bars to divert suspicion from his smuggling empire. Baxter pulls a raid on the crooks' warehouse headquarters and justice is served. A decent programmer.

p, Rudolph C. Flothow; d, Seymour Friedman; w, Eric Taylor; ph, Henry Freulich; m, Mischa Bakaleinikoff; ed, Richard Fantl, md, Bakaleinikoff; art d, Harold MacArthur.

Crime   **(PR:A MPAA:NR)**

DEVIL'S HOLIDAY, THE**½   (1930) 80m PAR bw

Nancy Carroll (*Hallie Hobart*), Phillips Holmes (*David Stone*), James Kirkwood (*Mark Stone*), Hobart Bosworth (*Ezra Stone*), Ned Sparks (*Charlie Thorne*), Morgan Farley (*Monkey McConnell*), Jed Prouty (*Kent Carr*), Paul Lukas (*Dr. Reynolds*), ZaSu Pitts (*Ethel*), Morton Downey (*Freddie the Tenor*), Guy Oliver (*Hammond*), Jessie Pringle (*Aunt Betty*), Wade Boteler (*House Detective*), Laura La Varnie (*Mme. Bernstein*).

A scheming manicurist, played superbly by Carroll, plans to marry Holmes, the son of millionaire wheat farmer Bosworth, as her ticket to easy street. Bosworth and Holmes' brother, Kirkwood, violently oppose the union, but the couple marry anyway. Carroll, who was not in love with her new husband, offers to divorce him if Bosworth will pay her $50,000. Dad agrees and Carroll leaves. Her conscience begins to eat at her and she tries to wash away her guilt in parties and alcohol. Meanwhile, Holmes lies seriously ill after a fall he suffered in a fight with his brother over Carroll. Upon hearing this, Carroll realizes that she loves him and returns to his side. DEVIL'S HOLIDAY was the first starring role for contract player Carroll, who landed the role after the original star, Jeanne Eagels, died of a heroin overdose. Collectors of filmic oversights should note the overhead mike shadow cast on the wall of Carroll's room in her scene with Ned Sparks.

d&w, Edmund Goulding; ph, Harry Fischbeck; ed, George Nichols, Jr.; m/l, "You Are a Song," Goulding, Leo Robin.

Drama   **(PR:A MPAA:NR)**

DEVIL'S IMPOSTER, THE   (SEE: POPE JOAN, 1972, Brit.)

DEVIL'S IN LOVE, THE**½   (1933) 70m FOX bw

Victor Jory (*Lt. Andre Morand*), Loretta Young (*Margot*), Vivienne Osborne (*Rena*), David Manners (*Jean*), C. Henry Gordon (*Capt. Radak*), Herbert Mundin (*Bimpy*), Emil Chautard (*Father Carmion*), J. Carrol Naish (*Salazar*), Bela Lugosi (*Military Prosecutor*), Robert Barrat (*Maj. Bertram*), Akim Tamiroff, Dewey Robinson, John Davidson.

Jory stars as an army doctor who joins the French Foreign Legion when he is falsely accused of murder. He falls in love with Young, the niece of the mission priest, until he learns that she is engaged to his best friend. Meanwhile, the police catch up to Jory and he is prosecuted by Lugosi (in a small but key role). In the end he is cleared of all charges and is reunited with Young after her fiance is conveniently killed in battle. Lugosi's role was his last attempt to escape typecasting by appearing in a straight part. But his brief footage in the film went unnoticed by reviewers and producers, and his name is absent from the main credits. The final

straw in this failed attempt to change the course of his career lies in the fact that THE DEVIL'S IN LOVE is not always included in Lugosi's screen listings.

d, Wilhelm Dieterle; w, Howard Estabrook (based on a story by Harry Hervey); ph, Hal Mohr; ed, Ralph Dietrich.

Drama   **(PR:A MPAA:NR)**

DEVIL'S ISLAND***   (1940) 65m WB bw

Boris Karloff (*Dr. Charles Gaudet*), Nedda Harrigan (*Mme. Lucien*), James Stephenson (*Col. Armand*), Adia Kuznetzoff (*Pierre*), Rolla Gourvitch (*Colette*), Will Stanton (*Bobo*), Edward Keane (*Dr. Duval*), Robert Warwick (*Demontre*), Pedro de Cordoba (*Marcal*), Tom Wilson (*Emil*), John Harmon (*Andre*), Richard Bond (*Georges*), Earl Gunn (*Leon*), Sidney Bracey (*Soupy*), George Lloyd (*Dogface*), Charles Richman (*Gov. Beaufort*), Stuart Holmes (*Gustav Le Brun*), Leonard Mudie (*Advocate General*), Egon Brecher (*Debriac*), Frank Reicher (*President of Assize Court*), John Hamilton (*Ship's Captain*), Harry Cording, Al Bridge, Earl Dwire, Dick Rich (*Guards*).

Karloff (in a typically fine performance) plays a famed French brain surgeon who treats an injured escapee from Devil's Island. He is arrested and sentenced to serve ten years on the island. The island is run by a brutal commandant, Stephenson, who treats the inmates worse than animals. Angered by the brutality and corruption he witnesses, Karloff leads the inmates in an attempted revolt, but fails. For his insolence, he and his confederates are sentenced to death. Luckily, they are given a reprieve when the daughter of the commandant is injured in an accident and Stephenson's wife, Harrigan, forces her husband to suspend the death sentences if Karloff will operate on the child. The doctor agrees, and the operation is a success, but Stephenson backs out on his agreement and decides to go on with the executions. Outraged, Harrigan arranges for Karloff and his friends to escape but they are easily recaptured. Seeing no other way to ease her conscience, Harrigan petitions the governor for Karloff's release and succeeds, inadvertently causing the arrest of her husband on corruption charges. Originally released in 1939, DEVIL'S ISLAND was seen as a sensational expose of the brutal conditions of the French penal colony. The French government banned the film and all other Warner Bros. releases. Rather than lose the French market, Warners pulled all its prints of the film, cut some sequences, re-shot and added others, and re-released the picture worldwide in 1940. By this time the controversy had died down and the French were too busy with Hitler to protest.

p, Bryan Foy; d, William Clemens; w, Kenneth Gamet, Don Ryan (based on the story "The Return of Doctor X" by Anthony Coldeway, Raymond Schrock); ph, George Barnes; ed, Frank Magee; art d, Max Parker.

Drama   **(PR:C MPAA:NR)**

DEVIL'S JEST, THE**   (1954, Brit.) 60m Terra Nova/EB bw

Mara Russell-Tavernan (*Lady Irma Enderby*), Ivan Craig (*Maj. Seton*), Valentine Dyall (*Intelligence Director*), Derek Aylwood (*Victor*), Julian Sherrier (*Tony*), Lee Fox (*Maj. Malcolm*), Hamilton Keene (*Col. Lorimer*), Edward Leslie (*Capt. Blynne*).

Aristocratic Russell-Tavernan's former lover, a medical officer in the British army, is revealed to be a Nazi spy. Routine stuff with a no-name cast.

p. Paul King; d, Alfred Goulding; w, Vance Uhden; ph, Hal Young.

Spy Drama   **(PR:A MPAA:NR)**

DEVIL'S LOTTERY*   (1932) 78m FOX bw

Elissa Landi (*Evelyn Beresford*), Victor McLaglen (*Jem Meech*), Alexander Kirkland (*Stephen Alden*), Paul Cavanagh (*Maj. Hugo Beresford*), Ralph Morgan (*Capt. Geoffrey Maitland*), Barbara Weeks (*Joan Mather*), Beryl Mercer (*Mrs. Mary Ann Meech*), Herbert Mundin (*Trowbridge*), Halliwell Hobbes (*Lord Litchfield*), Ruth Warren (*Maid*).

A dull soliloquy on the dangers of greed starring Landi as one of the winners of the Calcutta Sweepstakes, all of whom are invited to spend a holiday on the palatial estate of the winning horse's owner. Soon after their arrival, disasters happen. One guest dies, one is murdered, a recovered war vet is struck with his old paralysis, and a budding romance is shattered, all teaching the characters and the viewer that money isn't everything.

d, Sam Taylor; w, Guy Bolton (based on the novel by Nalbro Bartley); ph, Ernest Palmer; ed, Harold Schuster.

Drama   **(PR:A MPAA:NR)**

DEVIL'S MAN, THE*   (1967, Ital.) 85m GV-SEC/Lion International bw (AKA: DEVILMAN STORY)

Guy Madison, Liz Barrett (*Luisa Baratto*), Aldo Sambrell, Alan Collins (*Luciano Picozzi*), Diana Lorys, Ken Wood (*Giovanni Cianfriglia*).

Italian sci-fi film starring Madison as the hero and Barrett as the distraught daughter of an important scientist who has disappeared. Together the couple traces the father to an abandoned fortress in North Africa, where a crazed "Devilman" has kidnaped the professor and forced him to transplant a superbrain in his head. The incredible climax sees an army of Moors riding to the rescue.

p, Gabrielle Cristani; d, Paul Maxwell (Paolo Binachini), ph, Aldo Greci.

Science Fiction   **(PR:C MPAA:NR)**

DEVIL'S MASK, THE**½   (1946) 66m COL bw

Jim Bannon (*Jack Packard*), Barton Yarborough (*Doc Young*), Anita Louise, Michael Duane, Mona Barrie, Ludwig Donath, Paul E. Burns, Frank Wilcox, Thomas Jackson, Richard Hale, John Elliott, Edward Earle, Frank Mayo.

When a cargo plane crashes, police find five shrunken heads in the wreckage. One head is that of a white man with red hair, and it is immediately assumed that it belonged to an explorer who disappeared in the Amazonian jungle years before.

The explorer's daughter hires Bannon and Yarborough to follow her mother and an associate of her father. The detectives discover that the murder was committed by a taxidermist on the expedition. Enjoyable programmer from the short-lived "I Love a Mystery" movie series.

p, Wallace MacDonald; d, Henry Levin; w, Charles O'Neal, Dwight V. Babcock (based on the radio program "I Love A Mystery" by Carlton E. Morse); ph, Henry Freulich; ed, Jerome Thoms, md, Mischa Bakaleinikoff; art d, Robert Peterson; set d, George Montgomery.

Crime (PR:A MPAA:NR)

DEVIL'S MATE*½ (1933) 65m MON bw

Peggy Shannon (Nancy Weaver), Preston Foster (Inspector O'Brien), Ray Walker (Natural), Hobart Cavanaugh (Parkhurst), Barbara Barondess (Gwen), Paul Porcasi (Nick), Harold Waldridge (Joe), Jason Robards (Clinton), Bryant Washburn (District Attorney), Harry Holman (McGee), George Hayes (Collins), James Durkin (Warden), Gordon DeMaine (Butler), Paul Fix (Maloney), Sam Flint (Prison Doctor), Henry Otho (Witness), Henry Hall (Chaplain).

This murder mystery begins promisingly enough with the victim, a young criminal, murdered as he is being led to his execution in the electric chair. From there on, though, it falls into an obvious pattern with tough lady reporter Shannon trying to solve this strange crime.

p, Ben Verschleiser; d, Phil Rosen; w, Leonard Fields, David Silverstein; ph, Gill Warrenton.

Mystery (PR:A MPAA:NR)

DEVIL'S MAZE, THE*½ (1929, Brit.) 82m GAU bw

Renee Clama (Frances Mildmay), Trilby Clark (Barbara Carlton), Ian Fleming (Derek Riffington), Hayford Hobbs (Hon. James Carlton), Gerald Rawlinson (Robin Masters), Davy Burnaby (Mr. Fry).

After giving birth to a stillborn child, Clama claims she was seduced by an apparently dead explorer, who, of course, then returns. Silly melodrama strictly of historical interest.

p&d, V. Gareth Gundrey; w, Sewell Collins (based on the play "Mostly Fools" by G.R. Malloch); ph, Percy Strong.

Drama (PR:A-C MPAA:NR)

DEVIL'S MEN, THE (SEE: LAND OF THE MINOTAUR, 1976, U.S./Brit.)

DEVIL'S MESSENGER, THE* (1962 U.S./Swed.) 72m Herts-Lion International bw

Lon Chaney, Jr. (The Devil), Karen Kadler (Satanya), Michael Hinn (John Radian), Gunnel Brostrom, Tammy Newmara, John Crawford, Jan Blomberg, Ralph Brown, Ingrid Bedoya, Bertil Johnson, Eve Hossner, Charles Goodlin.

A little known Chaney, Jr., film compiled from three episodes of a Swedish television series called "No. 13 Demon St." Chaney plays the Devil and the film opens as a new arrival, Kadler, enters Hell after committing suicide over a ruined romance. Chaney drafts the beautiful woman to help him seduce new recruits from the surface. The first is a New York photographer who kills one of his models after using a "special" camera given to him by Kadler. The next is an anthropologist who is given a new pickax by the emissary from Hell, which he uses to free a beautiful young woman who was frozen in the ice a million years ago. Desperate to be united with his love he melts the ice that entombed her, and she drowns. The third victim is the man Kadler committed suicide over, and she kills him. Together they descend to Hell and Chaney gives them the formula to the atomic bomb, which they then deliver to the humans. Soon the foolish surface people destroy the Earth with the information, filling Hell to overflowing.

p, Kenneth Herts; d, Herbert L. Strock; w, Leo Guild; ph, William Troiano; m, Alfred Gwyn; art d, Herts.

Horror (PR:C MPAA:NR)

DEVIL'S MISTRESS, THE* (1968) 66m Emerson-WGW/Holiday c

Joan Stapleton (Liah), Robert Gregory (Frank), Forrest Westmoreland (Charlie), Douglas Warren (Joe), Oren Williams (Will), Arthur Resley (Jeroboam).

Strange but ineffective horror-western starring Gregory and Westmoreland (who also produced the film under the pseudonym of "Moreland") as two vicious cowboys on the lam from the law, circa 1870. They decide to pillage and rape their way through Indian territory and begin by killing Resley and raping his Indian wife, Stapleton. Unfortunately for them, Stapleton is a supernatural demon who drives the men to their deaths with her passionate kisses. Upon their deaths, Resley reappears from the woods, and husband and wife are reunited.

p, Wes Moreland [Forrest Westmoreland]; d&w, Orville Wanzer; ph, Teddy Gregory (Eastmancolor); m, Billy Allen, Douglas Warren.

Western/Horror (PR:O MPAA:NR)

DEVIL'S NIGHTMARE, THE zero (1971 Bel./Ital.) 88m Hemisphere c (AKA: VAMPIRE PLAYGIRLS)

Erica Blanc, Jean Servais, Daniel Emilfork, Lucien Raimbourg.

Blanc, a succubus, seduces and kills seven obnoxious tourists who travel to the remote European villa where the female demon who makes love to men in their sleep exists. A quickie Italian effort designed to capitalize on the success of THE EXORCIST, with heavy emphasis on gore.

p, Charles Lecocq; d, Jean Brismee; w, Patrice Rhomm, Lecocq, Andre Hunebelle.

Horror (PR:O MPAA:R)

DEVILS OF DARKNESS, THE*½ (1965, Brit.) 88m Planet Films/FOX c

William Sylvester (Paul Baxter), Hubert Noel (Count Sinistre/Armond du Moliere), Tracy Reed (Karen), Carole Gray (Tania), Diana Decker (Madeline Braun), Rona Anderson (Anne Forest), Peter Illing (Inspector Malin), Gerard Heinz (Bouvier), Victor Brooks (Inspector Hardwick), Avril Angers (Midge), Brian Oulton (The Colonel), Marie Burke (Old Gypsy Woman), Marianne Stone (The Duchess), Rod McLennan (Dave), Geoffrey Kenion (Keith Forest), Burnell Tucker (Derek), Julie Mendez (Snake Dancer), Eddie Byrne.

Sylvester is an Englishman on holiday in Brittany who becomes unwittingly embroiled in a satanic cult led by suave Frenchman Noel, a vampire. The cult requires human sacrifices to survive, and when two of Sylvester's friends are killed and his girl friend Reed is kidnaped, he becomes enraged enough to expose the monster for what he is. In the ensuing confusion, Sylvester escapes with Reed, leaving Noel to wander aimlessly through a cemetery where he trips on a cross and dies.

p, Tom Blakeley; d, Lance Comfort; w, Lyn Fairhurst; ph, Reg Wyer (Eastmancolor); m, Bernie Fenton; ed, John Trumper; art d, John Earl; cos, Muriel Dickson.

Horror (PR:C MPAA:NR)

DEVIL'S OWN, THE** (1967, Brit.) 91m Seven Arts-Hammer Film Prods./FOX c (GB: THE WITCHES)

Joan Fontaine (Gwen Mayfield), Kay Walsh (Stephanie Bax), Alec McCowen (Alan Bax), Ann Bell (Sally), Ingrid Brett (Linda), John Collin (Dowsett), Michele Dotrice (Valerie), Gwen Ffrangcon-Davies (Granny Rigg), Duncan Lamont (Bob Curd), Leonard Rossiter (Dr. Wallis), Martin Stephens (Ronnie Dowsett), Carmel McSharry (Mrs. Dowsett), Viola Keats (Mrs. Curd), Shelagh Fraser (Mrs. Creek), Bryan Marshall (Tom).

Fontaine is a teacher who has a nervous breakdown at her mission school in Africa when a voodoo witch doctor puts a spell on her. She goes back to England and becomes headmistress at a school in a small village. A student, Stephens, is being harassed by a local voodoo cult to keep him away from Brett, who is to be offered as a virgin sacrifice. Fontaine discovers that Walsh, a journalist, has the town in her control through her witchcraft. The teacher foils the cult's sacrifice of the girl and brings about Walsh's death. Fontaine owned the rights to this story and it became her last feature film.

p, Anthony Nelson Keys; d, Cyril Frankel; w, Nigel Kneale (based on the novel by Peter Curtis); ph, Arthur Grant (DeLuxe Color); m, Richard Rodney Bennett; ed, Chris Barnes, James Needs; prod d, Bernard Robinson; md, Philip Martell; art d, Don Mingaye.

Mystery/Witchcraft (PR:C MPAA:NR)

DEVIL'S PARTNER, THE** (1958) 75m Huron/Filmgroup bw

Ed Nelson (Nick/Pete), Jean Allison (Nell), Edgar Buchanan (Doc), Richard Crane (David), Spencer Carlisle (Tom), Byron Foulger (Papers), Claire Carleton (Ida).

Nelson is an old man living in the remote town of Furnace Flats, Texas, who is possessed by the devil. He dies and comes back as his younger self under the name of Nick. The townspeople discover that the younger Nelson performs all the strange rituals that the old man did. When Crane marries Allison he's attacked by his own dog and maimed. This enables Nelson to steal Allison away from Crane. When the sheriff makes a call at Nelson's cabin he is greeted by a large snake. The officer pumps five bullets into the serpent and the snake transforms into the younger Nelson, then the old man, and a priest is called to exorcise the devil from the dying Nelson. Not too hot, even for Scratch himself.

p, Hugh M. Hooker; d, Charles R. Rondeau; w, Stanley Clements, Laura J. Mathews, Dorrell McGowan; ph, Edward Cronjager; m, Ronald Stein; ed, Howard Epstein; art d, Daniel Haller.

Horror (PR:C-O MPAA:NR)

DEVIL'S PARTY, THE** (1938) 62m UNIV bw

Victor McLaglen (Marty Malone), William Gargan (Mike O'Mara), Paul Kelly (Jerry Donovan), Beatrice Roberts (Helen McCoy), Frank Jenks (Sam), John Gallaudet (Joe O'Mara), Samuel S. Hinds (Justice Harrison), Joseph Downing (Frank Diamond), Arthur Hoyt (Webster), David Oliver (Hank Andrews), Ed Gargan (Sgt. Enders), Gordon [Bill] Elliott (James Brewster), Scotty Beckett (Mike O'Mara as a Child), Mickey Rentschler (Marty Malone as a Child), Tommy Bupp (Jerry Donovan as a Child), Juanita Quigley (Helen McCoy as a Child), Dickie Jones (Joe O'Mara as a Child).

Four boys in New York's Hell's Kitchen (who grow up to be McLaglen, Gargan, Kelly, and Gallaudet) make a pact that they will meet once a year for the rest of their lives to renew their friendship. Their plans are altered when the youths accidentally set fire to a warehouse and McLaglen takes the rap and is sent to reform school. Years later, now a professional gambler and owner of a nightclub, he is reunited with his friends, Gargan and Gallaudet (who are now policemen), when they show up in his club to investigate the murder of one of McLaglen's debtors. While investigating the crime, Gallaudet is killed and Kelly, now a priest, sees that justice is served.

p, Edmund Grainger; d, Ray McCarey; w, Roy Chanslor (based on the novel Hells' Kitchen Has a Pantry by Borden Chase); ph, Milton Krasner; ed, Philip Cahn; md, Charles Previn; m/l, Jimmy McHugh, Harold Adamson.

Crime (PR:A MPAA:NR)

DEVIL'S PASS, THE*½ (1957, Brit.) 56m ABP bw

John Slater (Bill Buckle), Christopher Warbey (Jim), Richard George (Ted Trelawney), Joan Newell (Mrs. Trelawney), Archie Duncan (George Jolley), Charles Leno (Headmaster), Ewen Solon, Joy Rodgers.

Warbey stows away on Slater's fishing boat and helps the old man save the boat from unscrupulous wreckers. A rare leading role for Slater, a veteran supporting actor in British films, best remembered for his part in the chucklesome PASSPORT TO PIMLICO.

p, David Henley; d&w, Darcy Conyers; ph, S.D. Onions.

Children   **(PR:AA   MPAA:NR)**

DEVIL'S PIPELINE, THE**   (1940) 65m UNIV bw

Richard Arlen (Dick), Andy Devine (Andy), Jeanne Kelly [Jean Brooks] (Laura), James Flavin (Dowling), Francis McDonald (Gaddi Sang), Mala (Talamu), John Eldredge (Butler), Eddy Waller (Benedict).

Another comedy-adventure starring Arlen and Devine. This time they play petroleum engineers who are sent to the South Seas to investigate disturbing reports from the Company outpost there. They are arrested upon arrival, framed, and sentenced to hard labor. They soon discover that all the convicts are being hired as cheap labor by the local oil magnate, who pockets the salaries sent from the home office. Arlen and Devine lead a successful prisoner revolt against the despot and win their freedom. Implausible fiction, but it is always fun when Devine provides the laughs, as he does in this one.

p, Ben Pivar; d, Christy Cabanne; w, Paul Huston, Clarence Young, Larry Rhine, Ben Chapman (based on the novel Isle of Missing Men by Huston); ph, John Boyle; ed, E. Curtis.

Comedy/Adventure   **(PR:A   MPAA:NR)**

DEVIL'S PITCHFORK   (SEE: ANATAHAN, 1953, Jap.)

DEVIL'S PLAYGROUND**½   (1937) 74m COL bw

Richard Dix (Dorgan), Dolores Del Rio (Carmen), Chester Morris (Mason), George McKay (Red), John Gallaudet (Wounded Soldier), Pierre Watkin (Submarine Commander), Ward Bond (Sidecar Wilson), Don Rowan (Reilly), Francis McDonald (Romano), Stanley Andrews (Salvage Boat Commander), Gene Morgan (Orderly), Garry Owen (Radio Man), Jack Pennick (Gob), William J. Worthington (Vice Admiral), Buddy Roosevelt (Deck Officer), Wesley Hopper (Diver), Sammy Blum (Bartender), Lutra Winslow (Marcia), Edward Hearn (Surgeon), Ann Doran, Alma Chester, Beatrice Curtis (Women).

Average programmer stars Morris as a Navy submarine commander and Dix as his buddy, the U.S. Navy's best deep sea diver. Dix weds the coy Del Rio, a dance hall girl, who makes a sucker of him by falling for Morris when Dix is away on duty. Dix dumps Del Rio and puts his hurt feelings aside when Morris goes down in a sunken submarine. Dix saves Morris and everyone salutes as the fleet sails off. The underwater sequences where Dix rescues Morris and his crew are surprisingly well done. The great Irish short story writer and author of The Informer, Liam O'Flaherty, who worked on DEVIL'S PLAYGROUND with Jerome Chodorov and Dalton Trumbo, must have breezed through this commonplace tale, his first of two ventures in Hollywood and probably as far as he would ever get in spirit and style from his native Aran Islands. Remake of SUBMARINE (1928).

d, Erle C. Kenton: w, Liam O'Flaherty, Jerome Chodorov, Dalton Trumbo (based on a story by Norman Springer); ph, Lucien Ballard; ed, Viola Lawrence; spec eff, Ganahl Carson.

Adventure/Drama   **(PR:A   MPAA:NR)**

DEVIL'S PLAYGROUND, THE*½   (1946) 62m UA bw

William Boyd (Hopalong Cassidy), Andy Clyde (California Carlson), Rand Brooks (Lucky Jenkins), Elaine Riley (Mrs. Evans), Robert Elliott (Judge Morton), Joseph J. Greene (Sheriff), Francis McDonald (Roberts), Ned Young (Curly), Earle Hodgins (Daniel), George Eldredge (U.S. Marshal), Everett Shields (Wolfe), John George (Dwarf).

The 57th Hopalong Cassidy oater sees Boyd now a partner with Carl Leserman and Lou Pennish, who distributed and produced the Cassidy westerns. Plot is the usual fare in which Boyd, Clyde, and Brooks rescue lady-in-trouble Riley from the evil clutches of the corrupt sheriff and his black-hatted gang.

p, Lewis J. Rachmil; d, George Archainbaud; w, Doris Schroeder (based on a story by Ted Wilson, from characters created by Clarence E. Mulford); ph, Mack Stengler; ed, Fred W. Berger; md, David Chudnow; art d, Harvey D. Gillett; set d, George Mitchel.

Western   **(PR:A   MPAA:NR)**

DEVIL'S PLAYGROUND, THE***   (1976, Aus.) 107m Film House c

Arthur Dignam (Brother Francine), Nick Tate (Brother Victor), Simon Burke (Tom Allen), Charles McCallum (Brother Sebastian), John Frawley (Brother Celian), Jonathon Hardy (Brother Arnold), Gerry Duggan (Father Hanrahan), Peter Cox (Brother James), John Diedrich (Fitz), Thomas Keneally (Father Marshall), Sheila Florance (Mrs. Sullivan), Gerda Nicholson (Mrs. Allen), John Proper (Mr. Allen), Anne Phelan, Jillian Archer (Girls in Pub).

Well done film about life at a Catholic boys' school. It contrasts the pangs of puberty experienced in an environment that does not allow the boys to express their urges against the lives of the priests, who have their own problems in the chaste lifestyle they have chosen. Directed by Fred Schepisi who later went on to direct the marvelous western BARBAROSA (1982).

p,d&w, Fred Schepisi; ph, Ian Baker; m, Bruce Smeaton; ed, Brian Kavanaugh.

Drama   **(PR:A   MPAA:NR)**

DEVIL'S PLOT, THE***   (1948, Brit.) 99m BN bw
                                         (GB: COUNTERBLAST)

Robert Beatty (Dr. Rankin), Mervyn Johns (Dr. Bruckner), Nova Pilbeam (Tracy Shaw), Margaretta Scott (Sister Johnson), Sybilla Binder (Martha), Marie Lohr (Mrs.

Coles), Karel Stepanek (Prof. Inman), Alan Wheatley (Kennedy), Gladys Henson (Mrs. Plum), John Salew (Padre), Antony Eustrel (Dr. Forrester), Karl Jaffe (Heinz), Ronald Adam (Col. Ingram), Martin Miller (Seaman), Aubrey Mallalieu (Maj. Walsh), Horace Kenney (Taxi Driver), Archie Duncan, Kynaston Reeves, Jack Melford, Peter Madden, Frederick Schiller, Olive Sloane, Stevins Chambers, John England, Kenneth Keeling, H. G. Guinle.

Johns is a German scientist who escapes from a POW camp, murders an Australian doctor, and assumes his identity. This gives him access to a British laboratory so he can continue bacteriological experiments he started in Germany. The Nazis want to infect the British population with a deadly serum, and Johns plans to see it through. Pilbeam is a lab assistant who becomes his love interest. Beatty, another assistant, grows suspicious and finally exposes Johns. The film wasn't released in the U.S. until 1953 and was thought then to be too violent. Whittingham's script is indeed powerful and shocking.

p, Louis H. Jackson; d, Paul L. Stein; w, Jack Whittingham (based on a story by Guy Morgan); ph, James Wilson.

Thriller   **(PR:C   MPAA:NR)**

DEVIL'S RAIN, THE*   (1975, U.S./Mex.) 85m Bryanston c

Ernest Borgnine (Corbis), Eddie Albert (Dr. Richards), Ida Lupino (Mrs. Preston), William Shatner (Mark Preston), Keenan Wynn (Sheriff Owens), Tom Skerritt (Tom Preston), Joan Prather (Julie Preston), Woodrow Chambliss (John), John Travolta (Danny), Claudio Brooks (Preacher), Lisa Todd (Lilith), George Sawaya (Steve Preston), Erika Carlson (Aaronessa Fyffe), Tony Cortez (1st Captor), Anton La Vey (High Priest), Diane La Vey (Priscilla Corbis), Robert Wallace (Matthew Corbis).

Cheap horror film set in the Southwest but shot in Mexico, and starring an overloaded cast of recognizable faces. Story concerns Skerritt's efforts to locate his family, which has disappeared, and his finding of a cult of satanists led by Borgnine instead. Lupino and Wynn become zombies, Borgnine turns into a goat-headed devil, and Travolta (in a small role) and most of the rest of the cast literally melt during the "Devil's Rain" in the last few minutes of the film. The melting makeup effects (which is the only reason to sit through this trash) were created by Ellis and Tom Burman who helped out on the PLANET OF THE APES series of pictures. The film was re-released when Travolta became a star with his name on top billing even though he is barely on screen.

p, James V. Cullen, Michael S. Glick; d, Robert Fuest; w, Gabe Essoe, James Ashton, Gerald Hopman; ph, Alex Phillips, Jr. (Todd-AO 35); m, Al De Lory; ed, Michael Kahn; prod d, Nikita Knatz; art d, Jose Rodriguez Granada; set d, Carlos Granjean; spec eff, Cliff and Carol Wenger, Thomas Fisher, Frederico Farfan.

Horror   **Cas.**   **(PR:O   MPAA:PG)**

DEVIL'S ROCK*   (1938, Brit.) 54m COL bw

Richard Hayward (Sam Mulhern), Geraldine Mitchell (Geraldine Larmour), Gloria Grainger (Veronica Larmour), Terence Grainger (John Browne), Nancy Cullen (Mrs. Huggins), Charles Fagan (Sgt. Davis), Tom Casement (Dandy Dick), Stendal Todd, Michael Gleason, R.L. O'Mealy, James Close, Lambeg Folk Dance Society, St. Gall's School Choir.

A concert party in Ireland finds itself in dire straits when the box office is held up and all the earnings stolen. Trivial British B with a no-name cast, except for Hayward, who wrote the screenplay and story.

p&d, Germain Gerard Burger; w, Richard Hayward; ph, Burger.

Musical   **(PR:A   MPAA:NR)**

DEVIL'S SADDLE LEGION, THE*½   (1937) 59m WB bw

Dick Foran (Tal Holladay), Anne Nagel (Karan Ordley), Willard Parker (Hub Ordley), Granville Owen (Chris Madden), Carlyle Moore, Jr. (Chip Carter), Gordon Hart (John Ordley), Max Hoffman, Jr. (Butch), Glenn Strange (Peewee), John "Skins" Miller (Spooks), Ernie Stanton (Reggie), Frank Orth (Judge), Jack Mower (Dawson), Milt Kibbee (Spane), George Chesebro (Frayne), Walter Young (John Logan), Charles LeMoyne (Callope), Raphael Bennett (Sheriff Gornman), Dick Botiller (Choctaw), Alan Gregg (Jim Cudlow), Bud Osborne (Boreland), Eddie Acuff, Henry Otho, Raymond Hatton.

Foran returns from riding the range to find his father murdered and his cattle missing. The crooked sheriff of the territory arrests Foran and throws him in jail (yes, the sheriff and his gang are the real culprits). Foran breaks out and forms a band of sagebrush vigilantes who bring the corrupt lawmen to justice. It was directed by Warner Bros. choreographer Connolly, who quickly tapped his way back to musicals after this unsuccessful foray into oaters. Songs: "Ridin' To My Home In Texas," "Dog's Country," "When Moonlight Is Riding" (M.K. Jerome, Jack Scholl).

p, Bryan Foy; d, Bobby Connolly; w, Ed Earl Repp; ph, Ted McCord.

Western   **(PR:A   MPAA:NR)**

DEVIL'S SISTERS, THE*   (1966) 90m Mustang Productions/Thunderbird International bw

Sharon Saxon (Teresa), Fred Pinero (Antonio Sanchez), Velia Martinez (Carmen Alvarado), Anita Crystal (Rita Alvarado), Ramiro Gomez Kemp (Robert Fernandez), William Marcos (Jose Rodriguez), Beryl Taylor (Mrs. Hernandez), Mildred Rodesky (Marta), Babette Sherrill (Ester), Tony Camel (Dolores), Joan Jacobs (Victoria), Nora Alonzo (Emilia), Tammy Simms (First Girl), Michael De Beausset (Englishman), Mark Harris (Henchman).

Abused and humiliated by the man she loves, Saxon answers a help-wanted ad in a Tijuana newspaper and finds herself locked into a windowless room by sisters Martinez and Crystal, who are engaged in a white slavery racket. Beaten and starved into submission, she is forced to work as a prostitute. When her ex-lover, now a policeman, recognizes her, she is shipped out to a barn to be sold to white slavers. When a prospective buyer comes to check out the merchandise, Saxon distracts him while another girl hits him on the head with a bottle. The other girl is murdered and Saxon is stripped, tied with barbed wire, and left to die. The other women revolt and Saxon escapes. The final scene has her telling her story to a sympathetic police captain. Lurid low-budget exploitation set in Mexico but mysteriously filmed in Miami. Should be good fun for folks with low standards.

p, Joseph Fink, Juan Hidalgo-Gato; d, William Grefe, w, John Nicholas, Grefe (based on a story by Nicholas); ph, Julio C. Chavez; m, Al Jacobs; ed, Chavez.

Crime　　　　　　　　　　　　　　　　**(PR:O　MPAA:NR)**

DEVIL'S SLEEP, THE*　　　　　　(1951) 81m Screen Art bw
Lita Grey Chaplin, John Mitchum, William Thomason, Tracy Lynn.

A narcotics ring that preys on teenagers is threatened by the investigation of a crusading woman juvenile judge, Chaplin. The bad guys try to put a stop to her investigation by involving her daughter, Lynn, in their slimy trade.

d, Merle Connell.

Crime　　　　　　　　　　　　　　　　**(PR:A　MPAA:NR)**

DEVIL'S SPAWN, THE　　(SEE: LAST GUNFIGHTER, THE, 1961, Can.)

DEVIL'S SQUADRON**　　　　　　(1936) 80m COL bw
Richard Dix (Paul Redmond), Karen Morley (Martha Dawson), Lloyd Nolan (Dana Kirk), Shirley Ross (Eunice), Henry Mollison (Forrester), Gene Morgan (Barlow), Gordon Jones (Tex), William Stelling (Ritchie), Thurston Hall (Maj. Metcalf), Gertrude Green (Lulu), Boyd Irwin (Col. Dawson), Billy Burrud (Butch), Cora Sue Collins (Mary).

Dix stars as a fearless test pilot of planes designed for use in the U.S. armed services. Morley is the daughter of the airplane manufacturer who dies, leaving his brave girl to carry on. After too many pilots die testing the planes, Morley decides to fold the company and save lives. Dix, of course, will hear none of it and makes the first successful flight of an Army plane prototype. Competent performances help an average script.

d, Erle C. Kenton; w, Howard J. Green, Bruce Manning, Lionel Houser (based on an unpublished story by Richard V. Grace); ph, John Stumar.

Drama　　　　　　　　　　　　　　　　**(PR:A　MPAA:NR)**

DEVIL'S TEMPLE*½　　(1969, Jap.) 76m Daiei Motion Picture Co. c
　　　　　　　　　　　　　　　　　　(ONI NO SUMU YAKATA)
Shintara Katsu (Mumyo Taro), Hideko Takamine (Kaede), Michiyo Aratama (Aizen), Kei Sato (High Priest).

Thief Katsu lives in a ruined temple with domineering Aratama. When the thief's wife finds the pair, she begins to stay there as well, growing entangled in the pair's relationship. A wandering priest comes to the temple and Katsu tries to steal his golden Buddha figure but he is incapacitated by a spell. Aratama recognizes the priest as a man she once knew and goes off with him, promising Katsu to avenge him. Katsu and his wife later see the man bite off his tongue and die rather than come under her influence again. Katsu kills Aratama with his sword, and leaves the temple wearing the priest's clothes. Mediocre Japanese costumer with nothing special to recommend it. (In Japanese; English subtitles).

d, Kenji Misumi; w, Kaneto Shindo (based on a story by Junichiro Tanizaki); ph, Kazuo Miyagawa; m, Akira Ifukube; art d, Akira Naito.

Drama　　　　　　　　　　　　　　　　**(PR:C-O　MPAA:NR)**

DEVIL'S TRAIL, THE*　　　　　　(1942) 61m COL bw
Bill Elliott, Tex Ritter, Eileen O'Hearn, Frank Mitchell, Noah Beery, Sr., Ruth Ford, Joel Friedkin, Joe McGuinn, Edmund Cobb, Tristam Coffin, Paul Newlan, Steve Clark, Sarah Padden, Bud Osborne, Stanley Brown, Buck Moulton.

Even the considerable talents of Elliott and Ritter can't prevent this tepid oater from boring as both battle the bad guys and vie for O'Hearn's favors.

p, Leon Barsha; d, Lambert Hillyer; w, Philip Ketchum (based on the story "The Town In Hell's Backyard" by Robert Lee Johnson).

Western　　　　　　　　　　　　　　　　**(PR:A　MPAA:NR)**

DEVIL'S TRAP, THE**　　　　　　　　(1964, Czech.)
　　　　85m Ceskoslovensky FRlm/Salisbury Film bw (DABLOVA PAST)
Vitezslav Vejrazka (Spaleny), Miroslav Machacek (Prokus), Cestmir Randa (Regent Valecsky Valce), Vlastimil Hasek (Filip), Vit Olmer (Jan), Karla Chadimova (Martina), Frantisek Kovarik (Shepherd), Bedrich Karen (Bishop Dittrichstejn), Josef Hlinomaz (Servant), Zdenek Kutil (Gamekeeper), Jaroslav Moucka (Jakub), Ladislav Kazda (Miller), Jiri Vrstala (Cavalry Officer), Dagmar Kofronova (Miller's Wife), Richard Zahorsky (Parish Clerk), Vikto Ocasek (Writer), Zlatomir Vacek (Vicar), Frantisek Nechyba (Steward), Jirina Bila (Servant).

A miller (Vejrazka) in 16th-century Czechoslovakia finds an underground spring and saves the villagers from drought, only to be accused of witchcraft by the local representative of the Inquisition (Machacek). Ocassionally interesting, but more often heavy-handed and self-conscious. (In Czech; English subtitles).

d, Frantisek Vlacil; w, Frantisek A. Dvorak, Milos V. Kratochvil (based on the novel Mlyn Na Ponorne Rece by Alfred Technik); ph, Rudolf Milic; m, Zdenek Liska; ed. Miroslav Hajek; art d, Karel Skvor.

Drama　　　　　　　　　　　　　　　　**(PR:A-C　MPAA:NR)**

DEVIL'S WANTON, THE**　　　　　　(1962, Swed.)
　　　　72m Terrafilm/Embassy bw (FANGELSE; AKA: PRISON)
Doris Svedlund (Birgitta-Carolina Soderberg), Birger Malmsten (Thomas), Eva Henning (Sofi), Hasse Ekman (Martin Grande), Stig Olin (Peter), Irma Christensson (Linnea), Anders Henrikson (Paul), Marianne Lofgren (Mrs. Bolin), Curt Masreliez

(Alf), Carl-Henrik Fant (Arne), Inger Juel (Greta), Ake Fridell (Magnus), Birgit Lindkvist (Anna), Arne Ragneborn (Anna's Lover).

Somber early Bergman film has Henrikson a former math teacher just discharged from the asylum who goes to his former student, film director Ekman, and suggests a film showing Earth as Hell being run by the Devil. Ekman laughs at him but passes the idea on to writer Malmsten, who is in love with prostitute Svedlund, whose pimp murdered their child. The pimp threatens to ruin Malmsten's life unless Svedlund returns to him. Instead she slashes her wrists. Unrelentingly bleak and for fans of Viking anguish only. Bergman's sixth feature film, released in Sweden in 1949. (In Swedish; English subtitles).

p, Lorens Marmstedt; d&w, Ingmar Bergman; ph, Goran Strindberg; m, Erland von Koch; ed, Lennart Wallen; art d, P.A. Lundgren.

Drama　　　　　　　　　　　　　　　　**(PR:C　MPAA:NR)**

DEVIL'S WEDDING NIGHT, THE zero　(1973, Ital.) 85m Dimension c
Mark Damon (Brothers No. 1 and No. 2), Sarah Bay (Countess), Miriam Barrios, Frances Davis, Stan Papps, Alexander Getty.

An inquisitive archeologist discovers that the infamous Nibelungen Ring, said to have supernatural powers, is being worn by a demon countess, Bay, who bathes in the blood of virgins. He travels to Transylvania to obtain the ring and destroy the countess and her vampire familiars. Gory, inept Italian import loosely based on the notorious Countess Elizabeth Bathory who actually had virgins murdered, their throats slit and bathed in their blood to improve their complexion! (She is credited with murdering 611 persons before Hungarian authorities tried her in 1611, ordering her walled up in her rooms where she died three years later.) This film, like COUNTESS DRACULA, which also draws upon the Bathory nightmare, is shock for its own sake and provides nothing more than filmmaking at its trashcan worst.

p, Ralph Zucker; d, Paul Solvay; w, Zucker, Alan M. Harris.

Horror　　　　　　　**Cas.**　　　　　　　**(PR:O　MPAA:R)**

DEVIL'S WIDOW, THE zero　(1972, Brit.) 107m BIP c (GB: TAMLIN).
Ava Gardner (Michaela), Ian McShane (Tom), Stephanie Beacham (Janet), Cyril Cusack (Vicar), Richard Wattis (Elroy), David Whitman (Oliver), Madeline Smith (Sue), Fabia Drake (Miss Gibbons), Sinead Cusack (Rose), Jennie Hanley (Caroline), Joanne Lumley (Georgia), Pamela Farbrother (Vanna), Bruce Robinson (Alan), Rosemary Blake (Kate), Michael Bills (Michael), Peter Henwood (Guy), Heyward Morse (Andy), Julian Barnes (Terry), Oliver Norman (Peter), Virginia Tingwell (Lottie).

Gardner is an old witch who uses her powers to keep her swinging young friends around her. Boring stuff, with Roddy McDowall directing an aging Gardner in a story that seems to relive a part of the past when, after she left Hollywood in 1957, she surrounded herself with admiring rich playboys and famous matadors in Madrid, until she returned to the screen three years later. Songs composed and sung by The Pentangle, except for "Sun In My Eyes," Salena Jones, William Spier.

p, Alan Ladd, Jr., Stanley Mann; d, Roddy McDowall; w, William Spier; ph, Billy Williams (Panavision, Technicolor); m, Stanley Myers; ed, John Victor Smith; prod d, Don Ashton; art d, John Graysmark; m/l, The Pentangle; cos, Beatrice Dawson, Balmain.

Horror　　　　　　　　　　　　　　　　**(PR:O　MPAA:PG)**

DEVIL'S WOMAN, THE　　　　　　(SEE: EVA, 1964, Fr./Ital.)

DEVONSVILLE TERROR, THE**½　　(1983) 84m MPM/New West c
Suzanna Love (Jenny), Donald Pleasence (Dr. Warley), Deanna Haas (Monica), Mary Walden (Chris), Morrigan Hurt, Leslie Smith, Barbara Cihlar (Witches), Robert Walker, Jr., Paul Willson, Angelica Rebane, Paul Bentzen.

Three hundred years to the day after three witches were burned at the stake in a New England town, a mysterious woman (Love) appears to wreak havoc on the town's patriarchy. When they tie her to the stake and try to send her back where she came from, lightning shoots from her eyes and destroys her persecutors. Quite interesting non-sexist horror film directed by former Fassbinder star Lommel.

p&d, Ulli Lommel; w, Lommel, George T. Lindsey, Suzanna Love; ph, Lommel; m, Ray Colcord, Ed Hill; set d, Priscilla Van Gorder; spec eff, Matthew Mungle, George Rogers, David Hewitt, Donald Flick; makeup, Erica Ueland.

Horror　　　　　　　**Cas.**　　　　　　　**(PR:O　MPAA:PG)**

DEVOTION**½　　　　　　　　　　(1931) 80m RKO bw
Ann Harding (Shirley), Leslie Howard (Trent), Robert Williams (Harrington), O.P. Heggie (Mr. Mortimer), Louise Closser Hale (Mrs. Mortimer), Dudley Digges (Sgt. Coggins), Allison Skipworth (Mrs. Coggins), Olive Tell (Mrs. Trent), Doris Lloyd (Pansie), Ruth Weston (Margaret), Joan Carr (Marjorie), Joyce Coad (Elsie), Douglas Scott (Derek, Trent's Son), Tempe Pigott (Bridget), Forrester Harvey (Gas Inspector), Margaret Daid (Maid), Pat Somerset (Young Man), Claude King (Junior Partner), Donald Stewart (Telegraph Boy), Cyril Delevanti (Reporter).

A veddy British drawing-room drama featuring one of the belles of the era, Harding, as a young miss who is so mad for a London barrister that she disguises herself and takes a job in his home as governess to his son. Harding dons a wig and glasses (it would not fool a blind person) and attempts a slightly different sort of voice so she can be close to dashing Howard. Though taken from a sudsy novel, it should have been a play because it is so hidebound to the one location. Howard is properly gallant and can make even the most banal dialog seem witty. Harding has a lovely face and a mellifluous voice, something that counted for lots of money at the box office during this post-silent period. Howard wins a case for playboy-artist Williams who puts a move on Harding. Of all the roles, Williams' is the most fun, but that isn't saying much in what is essentially a talky and slow-moving film.

p, Charles R. Rogers; d, Robert Milton; w, Graham John, Horace Jackson (based on the novel *A Little Flat In the Temple* by Pamela Wynne); ph, Hal Mohr; ed, Dan Mandell.

Drama (PR:A MPAA:NR)

DEVOTION✶✶ (1946) 108m WB bw

Ida Lupino (*Emily Bronte*), Olivia De Havilland (*Charlotte Bronte*), Nancy Coleman (*Ann Bronte*), Paul Henreid (*Nichols*), Sydney Greenstreet (*Thackeray*), Arthur Kennedy (*Branwell Bronte*), Dame May Whitty (*Lady Thornton*), Victor Francen (*Mons. Heger*), Montagu Love (*Rev. Bronte*), Ethel Griffies (*Aunt Branwell*), Odette Myrtil (*Mme. Heger*), Edmond Breon (*Sir John Thornton*), Marie deBecker (*Tabby*), Donald Stuart (*Butcher*), Forrester Harvey (*Hoggs*), Yorke Sherwood (*Man*), Billy Bevan (*Draper*), John Meredith (*Draper's Assistant*), David Thursby (*Farmer*), David Clyde (*Land Agent*), P.J. Kelly (*Shepherd*), Doris Lloyd (*Mrs. Ingham*), Violet Seton (*Mrs. Crump*), Sylvia Opert, Elyane Lima, Anne Goldthwaite, Irina Semochenko (*French Girl Students*), Howard Davies (*Englishman*), Hartney Arthur (*Man*), Reginald Sheffield (*Dickens*), Brandon Hurst (*Duke of Wellington*), Elspeth Dudgeon (*Elderly Woman*), Hilda Plowright (*Elderly Woman*), Rita Lupino (*Giselle*), Sonia Lefkova (*Marie*), Micheline Cheirel (*Mlle. Blanche*), Edgar Norton, Crauford Kent, Frank Dawson (*Club Members*), Flow Wix (*Englishwoman*).

Warner Bros. advertised this as the story of the Bronte Sisters. It bore as much resemblance to the truth as a press release from Pravda. Thje script took such liberties that scholars everywhere were furious with the omission of details and commission of errors. If one were not aware of the tragic story of the Brontes and their deaths at early ages, this might have made a pleasant fictional diversion. For the record, the film opens with Whitty donating writing paper to the impoverished Bronte sisters who cannot afford to buy their own. Whitty is a peeress of the realm in the town of Haworth in Yorkshire, 1836. The sisters, Lupino, De Havilland, and Coleman, and brother, Kennedy, live with father Montagu Love and aunt Griffies. Kennedy is a drunk but a brilliant artist. He earns what little money he needs for alcohol by sketching patrons in various bars. One day, he brings home Henreid, the new curate of the village. The sisters naturally assume that Henreid is a fellow boozehound but the truth is that he is the person who helped Kennedy home so the poor young man wouldn't wind up face down in the gutter. The sisters take jobs as governesses to raise enough money to send Kennedy to London where he hopes to establish himself as an artist, but he is back very quickly and carps about the philistines in London and how they "don't understand" his work. Meanwhile, Lupino and Henreid are establishing a relationship and she takes him to a dismal moor she calls "Wuthering Heights" and regales him with stories of being beckoned by a rider on a large black horse (a modern analyst might find something vaguely sexual about that). De Havilland doesn't like Henreid and makes that clear to the man, telling him directly that she wishes he would cease seeing her sister. His answer is a kiss on her lips. Henreid doesn't have a great deal of money but he does buy one of Kennedy's paintings to help send Lupino and De Havilland to Belgium where they hope to continue their educations. Lupino is now in love with Henreid but he admits that he doesn't love her in the same way. Once in Brussels, headmaster Francen is very aggressive in his advances (the swine!) and the impressionable De Havilland falls for him. Kennedy becomes ill and the sisters return home to Yorkshire on the eve of the publication of *Wuthering Heights* by Lupino and *Jayne Eyre* by De Havilland. Just prior to his death, Kennedy, who has read both books, tells his sisters that they are in love with the same man (Henreid) a fact revealed by the novels. De Havilland trots off to London to have a good time and Lupino remains in Yorkshire, becoming increasingly frail. In London, De Havilland meets and enjoys the company of Greenstreet (as William Makepeace Thackeray), who squires her all over town. They become close friends and De Havilland finds a confidante in Greenstreet. At one point, she says she's sorry her sister was never able to be passionate in romance and Greenstreet wonders if De Havilland ever read Lupino's book, one of the most passionate of all novels published in the era. De Havilland visits Henreid, who has been reassigned to a London slum. He admits that he loves her but she'll have none of that; they argue and she leaves to return to her home in the North. Lupino dies as she looks out the window and De Havilland realizes that the man on horseback her sister was waiting for was, in fact, Henreid, but that fire burned on only one side of the hearth. Henreid joins De Havilland in the small town and the two bid Lupino a fair trip to heaven. It's all a lot of slush, of course. And the thought that Henreid's cleric character was the inspiration for Rochester and Heathcliff was stretching things just a mite too far. If anyone was the romantic image for those men, it may have been their brother, Branwell, who was just as star-crossed as they were. That these sisters (and brother) were all all so talented proves there is something to genetics. So does the fact that they all died so early in life. In the original plans for the film, De Havilland and sister Joan Fontaine were to have played together on the screen but they were heavily into feuding at the time. Made three years earlier in 1943.

p, Robert Buckner; d, Curtis Bernhardt; w, Keith Winter (based on a story by Theodore Reeves); ph, Ernest Haller; m, Erich Wolfgang Korngold; ed, Rudi Fehr; md, Leo Forbstein; art d, Robert M. Haas; set d, Casey Roberts; spec eff, Jack Holden, Jack Oakie, Rex Wimpy.

Biography (PR:A MPAA:NR)

DEVOTION✶ (1953, Ital.) 78m Cines/I.F.E. Releasing bw

Columba Dominguez (*Annesa*), Roldano Lupi (*Don Paulu*), Juan De Landa (*Uncle Zua*), Gualtiero Tumiati (*Father Virdis*), Franca Marzi (*The Widow*).

Dominguez murders to save her adoptive family and her lover from bankruptcy, only to find they got the money through more legitimate means. Interesting only because it was based on a Nobel Prize-winning novel.

d, Augusto Genina; w, Vitaliano Brancati, Genina (based on the novel *L'Edera* by Grazia Deledda).

Drama (PR:C-O MPAA:NR)

DEVOTION✶½ (1955, USSR) 83m Mosfilm/Artkino bw

S. Ramadanov (*Yegor*), N. Ladynina (*Olga*), L. Gallis (*Andrei*), V. Toporkov (*Ryabchikov*), N. Grebeshkova (*Varya*), A. Mikhailov (*Petya*), S. Chekan (*Vasya*).

Gallis leaves his wife and family for his mistress, but eventually comes back in this tedious, though ideologically "correct" drama. The performances are quite good, and give this film whatever attraction it has, but the direction is unbelievably slack, with some scenes thrown in seemingly just because the director wanted to show a crowd moving through streets. Not as bad as the tractor operas of a few years earlier, but not much better

d, K. Pyryev; w, Pyryev, the Tur brothers.

Drama (PR:A MPAA:NR)

DIABOLICAL DR. MABUSE, THE
(SEE: SECRET OF DR. MABUSE, THE, 1961, Ger.)

DIABOLICAL DR. Z, THE✶½ (1966 Span./Fr.) 83m Hesperia-Speva-Cine-Alliance/U.S. Films bw
(MISS MUETTE; DANS LES GRIFFES DU MANIAQUE)

Mabel Karr (*Irma*), Fernando Montes (*Philip*), Estella Blain (*Nadia*), Antonio J. Escribano (*Dr. Von Zimmer*), Howard Vernon (*Vikass*), Guy Mairesse, Marcelo Arroita, Lucia Prado, Ana Castor, Alberto Dalbes, Jose Maria Prada.

Vernon is Dr. Von Zimmer, who dies of a heart attack after his request to experiment on condemned criminals for his invention to change a person's personality. His daughter, Karr, vows revenge on the medical council he feels killed her father. She uses mind control over Blain, a cabaret dancer, whose long fingernails she wants to use as murder weapons. The first doctor on the council is killed without a hitch, but Karr's control over Blain weakens when she wants her to kill her lover. Karr decides to kill Blain, but the police and Montes show up and Karr is killed instead.

p, Serge Silberman, Michel Safra; d, Jesus Franco; w, Franco, Jean-Claude Carriere (based on a novel by David Kuhne); ph, Alejandro Ulloa; m, Daniel White; ed, Jean Feyte; art d, Antonio Cortes.

Horror (PR:O MPAA:NR)

DIABOLICALLY YOURS✶✶½ (1968, Fr.) 90m Lira/Valoria c
(DIABOLIQUEMENT VOTRE)

Alain Delon (*Pierre*), Senta Berger (*Christiane*), Sergio Fantoni (*Freddie*), Peter Mosbacher (*Kim*).

Delon awakens in a hospital to be told that he and his wife have survived a car crash, but he has lost his memory. His wife, Berger, takes him home to their chateau where the only other residents are a friend of the family, Fantoni, and a Chinese servant, Mosbacher, who lusts after Berger. Delon begins to think things are strange when his wife refuses to sleep with him until he regains his memory. Soon after, he hears voices that tell him to kill himself, and then strange "accidents" begin occurring around the house. He figures things out and discovers that he is not Berger's husband at all, and that the real spouse was murdered by Berger and Fantoni (her lover), who then substituted him (Delon) because he had amnesia. The climax sees the servant kill Fantoni, while he himself is shot and killed by Berger, who then breaks down and confesses the whole plot. An unbelievable plot, at times bordering on camp. This was the last film of veteran French director Julien Duvivier, who died before its release.

d, Julien Duvivier; w, Duvivier, Paul Gegauff (based on the book by Louis Thomas); ph, Henri Decae (Eastmancolor); ed, Paul Cayatte.

Mystery/Crime (PR:C MPAA:NR)

DIABOLIQUE✶✶✶✶ (1955, Fr.) 107m Filmsonor/Vera Films bw
(LES DIABOLIQUES)

Simone Signoret (*Nicole Horner*), Vera Clouzot (*Christina Delasalle*), Paul Meurisse (*Michel Delasalle*), Charles Vanel (*Inspector Fichet*), Jean Brochard (*Plantiveau*), Noel Roquevert (*Herboux*), Therese Dorny (*Mme. Herboux*), Pierre Larquey (*Drain*), Michel Serrault (*Raymond*), Yves-Marc-Maurin (*Moinet*), Georges Poujouly (*Soudieu*), Jean Temerson (*Hotel Valet*), Georges Chamarat (*Dr. Loisy*), Jacques Varennes (*Prof. Bridoux*), Roberto Rodrigo (*Jose*), Jean Pierre Bonnefous (*De Gascuel*), Michel Dumur (*Ritberger*), Henri Humbert (*Patard*).

One of the most suspenseful and creepy films ever made, DIABOLIQUE casts Signoret as a murderer who helps Clouzot kill her husband. Eventually the body is dumped in the pool of a nearby boarding school. When the pool is drained the next day, however, the body is gone. Meurisse, the "dead" man, is then seen for just a moment in the window of the school. One is never quite sure whether Meurisse is breathing or not, and director Clouzot (who scared a decent number of folks with WAGES OF FEAR) keeps you guessing to the final frames. It also includes one of the most effective "eye" scenes in filmmaking, second only to Luis Bunuel and Salvador Dali's UN CHIEN ANDALOU, when the "dead" man rises from the bathtub. This picture went on to receive great critical acclaim, sharing the prestigious New York Film Critics Award for Best Foreign Film with Vittorio de Sica's UMBERTO D. The frightened wife of the dead man, Clouzot is the real-life Mrs. Clouzot. A must for anyone who likes psychological horror, or Hitchcock. (In French; English subtitles.)

p&d, Henri-Georges Clouzot; w, Clouzot, Jerome Geronimi, Frederic Grendel, Rene Masson (from the novel, THE WOMAN WHO WAS NO MORE, by Pierre Boileau, Thomas Narcejac); ph, Armand Thirard; m, Georges Van Parys; ed, Madeleine Gug.

Horror/Suspense Cas. (PR:O MPAA:NR)

DIAGNOSIS: MURDER½   (1974, Brit.) 90m Silhouette c

Jon Finch, Judy Geeson, Christopher Lee, Tony Beckley, Dilys Hamlett, Jane Merrow, Colin Jeavons.

Psychiatrist Finch's wife vanishes and he is accused by the police of murdering her. A good cast lifts this routine story slightly above the swarm of similar movies.

p, Patrick Dromgoole, Peter Miller; d, Sidney Hayers; w, Philip Levene; ph, Bob Edwards (Eastmancolor); m, Laurie Johnson.

Crime   (PR:C MPAA:NR)

DIAL M FOR MURDER**½   (1954) 105m WB c-3D

Ray Milland (Tony Wendice), Grace Kelly (Margot Wendice), Robert Cummings (Mark Halliday), John Williams (Chief Inspector Hubbard), Anthony Dawson (Capt. Lesgate), Leo Britt (Narrator), Patrick Allen (Pearson), George Leigh (William), George Alderson (The Detective), Robin Hughes (Police Sergeant), Alfred Hitchcock (Man in Club Photo), Guy Doleman, Thayer Roberts, Sanders Clark (Detectives), Robert Dobson (Police Photographer), Major Sam Harris (Man in Phone Booth), Jack Cunningham (Bobby).

This successful Frederick Knott play was not quite so successful on the screen, as the movie emphasized the little lies that must be told in a mystery. On a stage, the moves seem so natural that the eye may or may not catch them, but in a film, an "insert" shot must be made so there is no mistaking that a certain weapon is in a certain place at a certain time or whatever the insert shot is for. DIAL M was shot in 3-D but that version is hardly seen by anyone. Knowledgeable viewers will spot those instances when 3-D was put to use, especially the moment when Kelly reaches out to the audience and her hand seems to beg to have something placed in it so she can defend herself. This was one of the rare occasions when 3-D might have harmed the material because the gimmick was superfluous to the story. Cummings and Kelly are having an affair, but she is married to Milland (if you can swallow that trio in that situation, we're half-way home). Milland is a playboy and Kelly has all the money in the family, so he fears her leaving him penniless and in the lurch. The only way to keep Kelly from departing with American writer Cummings is to nip that romance in the bud by putting her to sleep, permanently. To that end, he contacts old chum Dawson, a former pal now operating in the underworld. Milland blackmails Dawson into making a deal to kill Kelly while Milland is conveniently out of town with a watertight alibi. Kelly is home alone and Dawson steps out from behind some drapes to do the deed, but she reaches for a pair of scissors as he's strangling her (see above) and stabs him to death. Milland arrives home and is surprised that his wife lives and his pal doesn't. That doesn't deter him one whit as he suavely shifts the blame to her and convinces Scotland Yard Inspector John Williams that she was being blackmailed by the late Dawson and had every right to kill him. "Naturally, I'll stick by you and we'll get you the best barristers in all of London to clear your name," says Milland...or something like that. Cummings sees right through the slick Milland and he and Williams cook up a final twist that unmasks Milland as perpetrator of the plot. To reveal that in a review would be to do your eyes a disservice. Most of the action takes place in one set, and Hitchcock, who was usually able to handle such confines (ROPE, REAR WINDOW, LIFEBOAT), lets this one get a trifle slow. Perhaps it was the 105-minute length or the fact that Kelly was not yet the electric blonde she became (this was her first picture for Hitch). Cummings was billed as "Robert" as opposed to "Bob," which is what he used for comedies. Cummings did his first movie with Hitchcock in SABOTEUR and Alfred objected to using him because he felt that Bob was too comically oriented to play the serious part of the accused factory worker. Cummings proved him wrong, though, and has done some excellent dramatic work over the years (KINGS ROW, THE LOST MOMENT) which more than made up for the BEACH PARTY films he did for AIP. Despite all of John Williams' credits, it wasn't until he began a series of commercials on late night TV, in which he hawked classical music albums, that he became nationally known.

p&d, Alfred Hitchcock; w, Frederick Knott); (based on the play by Knott); ph, Robert Burks (3-D-Naturalvision, Warner Color); m, Dimitri Tiomkin; ed, Rudi Fehr; art d, Edward Carrere, George James Hopkins; cos, Moss Mabry.

Mystery   Cas.   (PR:A-C MPAA:NR)

DIAL 1119*½   (1950) 74m MGM bw (GB: THE VIOLENT HOUR)

Marshall Thompson (Gunther Wyckoff), Virginia Field (Freddy), Andrea King (Helen), Sam Levene (Dr. John Faron), Leon Ames (Earl), Keefe Brasselle (Skip), Richard Rober (Capt. Henry Keiver), James Bell (Harrison D. Barnes), William Conrad (Chuckles), Dick Simmons (TV Announcer), Hal Fieberling (Lt. "Whitey" Tallman), Ralph Roberts (Boyd).

Grim thriller about an escaped maniac, Thompson (cast against type), who is bent on killing a police psychiatrist, Levene, because he knows too much about his illness. The killer boards a bus, steals the driver's gun and kills him. He then waits in a tavern across the street from Levene's home, where he is recognized by the bartender (Conrad) who sees his face on a television news bulletin. Thompson shoots Conrad as he tries to call the police, and holds the rest of the patrons hostage. Tension builds as the cops try to trick the killer out into the open, but Thompson demands that Levene be sent to him, lest he kill all his captives. Levene bravely enters the bar and is killed by Thompson, who is then jumped by one of his hostages, giving the cops an opportunity to gun him down. A taut and powerful programmer, much was made of the clever use of television newscasts to further the narrative (television then being a fresh and rarely exploited plot device).

p, Richard Goldstone; d, Gerald Mayer; w, John Monks Jr. (based on a story by Hugh King, Don McGuire); ph, Paul C. Vogel; m, Andre Previn; ed, Newell P. Kimlin; art d, Cedric Gibbons, William Ferrari.

Crime   (PR:C MPAA:NR)

DIAL 999, 1937   (SEE: REVENGE OF SCOTLAND YARD, 1937, Brit.)

DIAL 999, 1955   (SEE: WAY OUT, THE, 1955, Brit.)

DIAL RED O*½   (1955) 63m AA bw

Bill Elliott (Lt. Flynn), Keith Larsen (Wyatt), Helene Stanley (Connie), Paul Picerni (Roper), Jack Kruschen (Lavalle), Elaine Riley (Gloria), Robert Bice (Sgt. Colombo), Rick Vallin (Deputy Clark), George Eldredge (Major), John Phillips (Deputy Morgan), Regina Gleason (Mrs. Roper), Rankin Mansfield (Doctor), William J. Tannen (Reporter), Mort Mills (Photographer).

Title refers to how to call the sheriff's office in an emergency. Elliott is a lieutenant in the sheriff's department in charge of tracking down a disturbed ex-GI, Larsen, who has escaped the mental ward and is looking for his wife, who has divorced him. A man-hunt is sent out after him. In reality, he is rational and coherent and just wishes to speak with his former bride. Unfortunately, she is murdered by her married lover who doesn't like the news that she is bearing his child. Larsen is jailed for the murder, but he escapes, having figured out who the real killer is, and goes to get revenge. Luckily, Elliott has also surmised the identity of the murderer and arrives in time to stop Larsen from becoming a killer.

p, Vincent M. Fennelly; d&w, Daniel B. Ullman; ph, Ellsworth Fredricks; m, Marlin Skiles; ed, William Austin.

Crime   (PR:C MPAA:NR)

DIALOGUE*½   (1967, Hung.) 130m Hunnia Filmstudios/Rogosin Films bw
(PARBESZED)

Anita Semjen (Judit Barna), Imre Sinkovits (Laszlo Horvath), Istvan Sztankai (Sandor Kocsis), Mari Torocsik (Eva), Laszlo Csakanyi (Uncle Donci), Sandor Pecsi (Mihaly Safranko), Tibor Molnar (Geza), Katalin Berek (Olga, His Wife), Istvan Avar (Safar), Miklos Gabor (Szalkay), Margit Bara (Szalkayne), Ilona Beres (Jutka), Tibor Bitskey (Actor), Karoly Bicskey (Bela), Elma Bulla (Kocsis' Landlady), Hilda Gobbi (Actress), Florian Kalo (Lukacs), Manyi Kiss (Workwoman), Janos Pasztor (Actor), Maria Majczen (Bori), Gyula Szabo (Jani), Janos Rajz, Erno Szabo, Miklos Szakats, Adam Szirtes, Janos Arva, Jozsef Zsudi, Gyorgy Miklosy, Laszlo Gyorgy, Erzsi Partos, Andor Darday, Bertalan Solti, Gyorgy Gyoffy, Zoltan Maklary, Istvan Nagy, Arpad Gyenge, Janos Hersko.

Liberated from a Nazi concentration camp by Russian tanks, Semjen soon marries idealistic young Sinkovits. After a few months of domestic bliss, he is locked up in a burst of Stalinist oppression. Semjen takes up with her childhood sweetheart, Sztankai, now a proletarian poet. Years pass and Sinkovits is released, but he and Semjen find they have nothing in common anymore. As the social unrest of 1956 climaxes in Russian tanks rolling through Budapest again, she recalls when she was freed from the camp, and is reconciled with Sinkovits. Together they try to build a worker's paradise in their homeland. Dull, overlong melodrama with a heavy-handed political message. (In Hungarian; English subtitles.)

d&w, Janos Hersko; ph, Gyorgy Illes; m, Imre Vincze; ed, Zoltan Kerenyi; art d, Jozsef Romvari; cos, Piroska Katona.

Drama   (PR:A MPAA:NR)

DIAMOND CITY**   (1949, Brit.) 90m Gainsborough/GFD bw

David Farrar (Stafford Parker), Honor Blackman (Mary Hart), Diana Dors (Dora), Niall MacGinnis (Muller), Andrew Crawford (David Raymond), Mervyn Johns (Hart), Phyllis Monkman (Ma Bracken), Hal Osmond (Brandy Bill), Bill Owen (Pinto), Philo Hauser (Piet Quieman), John Blythe (Izzy Cohen), Dennis Vance (Rogers), Reginald Tate (Longden), Ronald Adam (Robert Southey), Norris Smith, John Salew, Tony Quinn, Slim Harris, Julian Somers, Harry Quashie, Arthur Lane, John Warren, Ernest Butcher.

Set in South Africa during the big diamond diggings of the 1870s, DIAMOND CITY details the rivalry between two factions of miners. The good guys, led by Farrar, strive for law-and-order among the miners. The bad guys, led by MacGinnis, care nothing about fairness or law, settling disputes with violence and deceit instead. MacGinnis also makes money on the side by selling liquor to the natives. The law-and-order approach proves more successful.

p, A. Frank Bundy; d, David Macdonald; w, Roger Bray, Roland Pertwee; ph, Reginald Wyer, Bernie Lewis, David Harcourt; m, Clifton Parker; ed, Esmond Seal.

Adventure   (PR:A MPAA:NR)

DIAMOND COUNTRY   (SEE: RUN LIKE A THIEF, 1967, U.S./Span.)

DIAMOND CUT DIAMOND   (SEE: BLAME THE WOMAN, 1932)

DIAMOND EARRINGS
(SEE: EARRINGS OF MADAME DE..., THE, 1954, Fr.)

DIAMOND FRONTIER**   (1940) 73m UNIV bw

Victor McLaglen (Regan), John Loder (Charles Clayton), Anne Nagel (Jean Kreuger), Philip Dorn (Jan de Winter), Cecil Kellaway (Noah), Francis Ford (Derek Bluje), J. Anthony Hughes (Matt Campbell), Ferris Taylor (Paul Willem), Lionel Belmore (Piet Bloem), Hugh Sothern (Travers), Sigfried Arno (Baron La Rocque), Dewey Robinson (Kohler), Dorothy Vaughan, Shirley Mills.

McLaglen stars in this adventure set during the diamond rush in South Africa, but the film is basically a hackneyed western set in a foreign locale. Plot concerns Loder's efforts to maintain some semblance of law and order in the rough, quickly growing mining town run by the ruthless ruler of the diamond country, McLaglen.

p, Marshall Grant; d, Harold Schuster; w, Edmund L. Hartmann, Stanley Rubin (based on the story "Modern Monte Cristo" by Hartmann, Rubin); ph, Milton Krasner.

Adventure   (PR:A MPAA:NR)

DIAMOND HEAD*

(1962) 107m COL c

Charlton Heston (*Richard Howland*), Yvette Mimieux (*Sloan Howland*), George Chakiris (*Dr. Dean Kahana*), France Nuyen (*Mei Chen*), James Darren (*Paul Kahana*), Aline MacMahon (*Kapiolani Kahana*), Elizabeth Allen (*Laura Beckett*), Vaughn Taylor (*Judge James Blanding*), Marc Marno (*Bobbie Chen*), Philip Ahn (*Emekona*), Harold Fong (*Coyama*), Edward Mallory (*Robert Parsons*), Lou Gonsalves (*Mario*), Frank Morris (*Felipe*), Clarence Kim (*Sammy*), Jack Matsumoto (*Photographer*), Yankee Chang (*Newspaperman*), Kam Fong Chun (*Loe Kim Lee*), Leo Ezell (*Pianist*), Alan Lebuse (*Heckler*), R. Ramos (*Nurse*), Seagai Faumunina (*Blue Goose*).

Heston is a vicious, bigoted pineapple baron who goes nuts when his kid sister, Mimieux, announces her engagement to a full-blooded native, Darren (who looks about as Hawaiian as Heston), even though he himself is carrying on an affair with a native girl. Seeking to keep the family blood line pure, Heston "accidentally" kills Darren, but trouble arises when Mimieux takes up with her dead fiance's half-brother Chakiris (another lousy excuse for a real Hawaiian). Things get even stickier (and more ludicrous) when Heston's mistress dies while giving birth to a son, the heir apparent to the pineapple empire. Mimieux and Chakiris run off with the baby before Heston can dispose of it, leaving Heston to brood about his problems with race relations. He decides he's been a real jerk and welcomes everybody back into the family with open arms. Just plain awful.

p, Jerry Bresler; d, Guy Green; w, Marguerite Roberts (based on the novel by Peter Gilman); ph, Sam Leavitt (Panavision/Eastmancolor); m, Johnny Williams; ed, William A. Lyon; prod d, Malcolm Brown; set d, William Kiernan; cos, Pat Barto; title song, Hugo Winterhalter.

Drama **(PR:C MPAA:NR)**

DIAMOND HORSESHOE***

(1945) 104m FOX c
(AKA: BILLY ROSE'S DIAMOND HORSESHOE)

Betty Grable (*Bonnie Collins*), Dick Haymes (*Joe Davis, Jr.*), Phil Silvers (*Blinky Walker*), William Gaxton (*Joe Davis, Sr.*), Beatrice Kay (*Claire Williams*), Margaret Dumont (*Mrs. Standish*), Roy Benson (*Harper*), George Melford (*Pop*), Hal K. Dawson (*Carter*), Kenny Williams (*Dance Director*), Reed Hadley (*Interne*), Eddie Acuff (*Clarinet Player*), Edward Gargan (*Grogan*), Ruth Rickaby (*Wardrobe Woman*), Carmen Cavallaro, Willie Solar (*Specialties*).

Big-budget, musical extravaganza starring Grable, the girl with the "mink coat complex," as the top-draw entertainer in Gaxton's successful nightclub. Trouble starts when Gaxton's son Haymes, a medical student, falls for Grable, who dreams of a stage career, and decides to drop out of school and become a hoofer against his father's wishes. Gaxton blames Grable for his son's career change, but Grable talks Haymes into resuming his studies in medicine, making everyone happy in the end. The picture is a treasure for the glimpse it gives of the nightclubs that are no more—like the Stork Club, The Waldorf, the Copacabana, the Latin Quarter—since it was filmed mostly in one of the best of its time, the Diamond Horseshoe. For that privilege, Fox paid the owner of the club, Billy Rose, $76,000, with the proviso that his name would be used in the picture's title. Producer Buddy De Sylva paid the owner of the Stork Club, Sherman Billingsley, $100,000 for the Stork Club title the same year. Songs include: "I Wish I Knew," "The More I See You," "Welcome to the Diamond Horseshoe," "In Acapulco," "You'll Never Know," "Play Me An Old-Fashioned Melody," "A Nickel's Worth of Jive" (Mack Gordon, Harry Warren); "Carrie Marry Harry" (Junie McCree, Albert von Tilzer); "Let Me Call You Sweetheart" (Beth Slater Whitson, Leo Friedman); "Sleep Baby Sleep" (S.A.Emery), "Shoo Shoo Baby" (Phil Moore); "Aba Daba Honeymoon" (Arthur Fields, Walter Donovan); "I'd Climb the Highest Mountain" (Lew Brown, Sidney Clare); "My Melancholy Baby" (George A. Norton, Ernie Burnett).

p, William Perlberg; d&w, George Seaton (based on a play by John Kenyon Nicholson); ph, Ernest Palmer (Technicolor); ed, Robert Simpson; md, Alfred Newman, Charles Henderson; art d, Lyle Wheeler, Joseph C. Wright; spec eff, Fred Sersen; ch, Hermes Pan.

Musical **(PR:A MPAA:NR)**

DIAMOND HUNTERS (SEE: RUN LIKE A THIEF, 1967, U.S./Span.)

DIAMOND JIM***

(1935) UNIV bw

Edward Arnold (*Diamond Jim Brady*), Jean Arthur (*Jane Matthews/Emma*), Binnie Barnes (*Lillian Russell*), Cesar Romero (*Jerry Richardson*), Eric Blore (*Sampson Fox*), Hugh O'Connell (*Horsley*), George Sidney (*Pawnbroker*), Bill Demarest (*Harry Hill*), Robert McWade (*A.E. Moore*), Bill Hoolahahn (*John L. Sullivan*), Lew Kelley (*Bartender*), Alan Bridge (*Man on Train*), Fred Kelsey (*Secretary*), Otis Harlan (*Drunk*), Charles Sellon (*Station Agent*), Henry Kolker (*Railroad President*), Purnell Pratt (*Physician*), Tully Marshall (*Minister*), Albert Conti, Armand Kaliz, Dorothy Granger, Dot Farley, Barbara Barondess, Arthur Houseman, Matt McHugh, Del Henderson, Maidel Turner, Irving Bacon, Richard Tucker, Mary Wallace, Marina Passerova, John Miltern.

The combination of a great subject and a great character actor should have produced a minor masterpiece but DIAMOND JIM misses the mark. Arnold, a golden-tongued thespian who never gave a bad performance, plays the title role with elan, beginning as a baggage man for the railroads, then a salesman, then a supplier of train equipment to every railroad in the nation. (Actually Diamond Jim made his fortune on the sale of barbed wire first, then railroad equipment.) Only about fifteen minutes is spent on chronicling Diamond Jim's rise when most of the movie should have been given over to this colorful career. The script and director Sutherland, who was always more at home with comedy, introduce several love themes that simply don't work, or, at least, they don't work for Arnold. He proposes early to hometown girl Arthur and she rejects him for another man; in fact, following his humble proposal, Arthur cold-bloodedly replies by asking him if he would like to attend her wedding to another. Arnold goes off to make his fortune and falls in love with Arthur's spitting image, which is logical because it's

Arthur again in another role. Again she is having nothing to do with gracious, kind-hearted, open-pockets Arnold. She's in love with Romero. Arnold then woos Barnes, who plays the famous Lillian Russell, but she doesn't want him either. She's also in love with Romero. And Romero is busy spurning both ladies as he makes his playboy rounds. The rejection is simply too much for Arnold. A man with a bad stomach—his doctors have warned him to lay off the munchies—he decides to commit suicide by eating himself to death (shades of George Arliss in OLD ENGLISH). It is true that Brady embraced gluttony with both hands and the great quantity of rich foods he consumed contributed to his death in 1917 but the manner in which Arnold meets his fate over Barnes is ludicrous at best. Arnold nevertheless gives a bravura performance and he glitters like the walking Christmas Tree that was Diamond Jim Brady, expansive, awarding wonderful gifts, plunging on any kind of crazy bet. The facts might not be straight but the colorful character is wholly captured and it is that enactment by Arnold that saves the film.

p, Edmund Grainger; d, Edward Sutherland; w, Preston Sturges, Harry Clork, Doris Malloy (based on the book *Diamond Jim Brady* by Parker Morell); ph, George Robinson; m, Ferdinand Grofe, Franz Waxman.

Biography **(PR:A MPAA:NR)**

DIAMOND QUEEN, THE**

(1953) 80m Melson/WB c

Fernando Lamas (*Jean Tavernier*), Arlene Dahl (*Maya*), Gilbert Roland (*Baron Paul de Cabannes*), Sheldon Leonard (*Great Mogul*), Jay Novello (*Gujar*), Michael Ansara (*Jumla*), Richard Hale (*Gabriel Tavernier*), Sujata and Asoka (*Dance Specialty*), Evelyn Finley.

A middling 17th-century costumer which casts Lamas and Roland as two adventurous Frenchmen on a journey to India. The object of the trek is a huge diamond worthy of gracing the crown of King Louis XIV. They meet up with voluptuous Dahl, queen of Nepal. Cast as her evil husband in a lackluster performance is Leonard as the Great Mogul, possessor of the blue stone. With the help of a newly developed French hand grenade, the pair are able to snatch the ice. Cortez's photography vividly shows the ornamentation of India's culture.

p, Frank Melford; d, John Brahm; w, Otto Englander (based on a story by Englander); ph, Stanley Cortez (Eastmancolor); m, Paul Sawtell; ed, Francis D. Lyon; prod d, Eugene Lourie.

Romance/Adventure **(PR:A MPAA:NR)**

DIAMOND SAFARI**

(1958) 67m FOX bw

Kevin McCarthy (*Harry Jordan*), Joel Herholdt (*Sgt. van der Cliffe*), Gert van den Bergh (*Compound Manager*), Geoffrey Tsobe (*Stephen Timbu*), Harry Mekels (*Police Boy*), Thomas Buson (*Medicine Man*), Andre Morell (*Williamson*), Joanna Douglas (*Petey*), Betty McDowall (*Louise Saunders*), Patrick Simpson (*Carlton*), John Clifford (*Doc*), Michael McNeile (*Phillips*), Robert Bice (*Reubens*), Frances Driver (*Glass Blower's Wife*).

An unpolished effort that follows American detective McCarthy in Johannesburg, South Africa, as he pushes for a wrongly accused native's freedom. In the process, he crosses paths with McDowall, a girl from the U.S. who leads a diamond smuggling ring. His hunger for justice forces him to turn her in, even though he has fallen for her. Landscape photography is impressive.

p&d, Gerald Mayer; w, Larry Marcus; ph, David Millin, Peter Lang; m, Woolf Phillips; ed, Carl Pierson, Peter Pitt; art d, Gordon Vorster.

Crime **(PR:A MPAA:NR)**

DIAMOND STUD*

(1970) 82m Walnut International/Grads Corp. c

Robert Hall (*Diamond Jim*), John Alderman, Monika Henreid, Victoria Carbe, Michael Greer, Ann Dee, Richard Compton, Jimmie Johnson, Julie Cannons.

Hall is Diamond Jim Brady in this justifiably forgotten film. After making a fortune in railroad car manufacturing, he goes to San Francisco to celebrate. His best friend and his girl friend fall in love, and after learning of their affair, Hall orders a giant meal certain to give him a fatal heart attack. Nothing the least bit entertaining or interesting here.

p, Jay Fineberg; d, Greg Corarito; w, Maurice Smith; ph, Gary Graver (Eastmancolor); ed, Ed Hunt; cos, Sandy Root.

Drama **(PR:C MPAA:NR)**

DIAMOND TRAIL*

(1933) 58m MON bw

Rex Bell, Frances Rich, Bud Osborne, Lloyd Whitlock, Norman Feusier, Jerry Storm, John Webb Dillon, Billy West, Harry LaMont.

A group of East coast jewel smugglers "go West" in pursuit of a go-between. Bell dons some fancy attire as a New York reporter in need of a story. He infiltrates the gang, but is soon found out. Everything in this thin plot is designed to produce the maximum number of fist fights, ignoring any sort of profundity.

p, Trem Carr; d, Harry Fraser; w, Fraser, Sherman Lowe (based on a story by Lowe); ph, Faxon Dean.

Western **(PR:A MPAA:NR)**

DIAMOND WIZARD, THE**

(1954, Brit.) 83m Gibraltar/UA bw
(GB: THE DIAMOND)

Dennis O'Keefe (*Joe Dennison*), Margaret Sheridan (*Marlene Miller*), Philip Friend (*Inspector McClaren*), Alan Wheatley (*Thompson Blake*), Francis de Wolff (*Yeo*), Eric Berry (*Hunzinger*), Michael Balfour (*Hoxie*), Ann Gudrun (*Sgt. Smith*), Paul Hardtmuth (*Dr. Eric Miller*), Cyril Chamberlain (*Castle*), Seymour Green (*Lascelles*), Donald Gray (*Gillies*), Colin Tapley (*Sir Stafford Beach*), Hugh Morton, Gordon McLeod, Paul Whitsun-Jones, Larry Burns, Don Cunningham, Victor Wood, Alastair Hunter.

Cooperation both in law and crime is the framework of this overseas crime drama. Beginning with a major U.S. heist, the film hops to England as O'Keefe tracks the crooks, with the help of Scotland Yard. Their efforts lead them to a pack of U.S. and British thieves. It is also discovered that the Tory crooks are manufacturing artificial diamonds for sale to the Americans. While photographed in 3-D, the script lacks some much-needed dimension. It was released in the U.S. in 2-D.

p, Steven Pallos; d, Montgomery Tully; w, John C. Higgins (based on the novel *Rich Is the Treasure* by Maurice Proctor); ph, Arthur Grahame; m, Matyas Seiber; ed, Helga Cranston.

Crime **(PR:A MPAA:NR)**

DIAMONDS½** (1975, U.S./Israel) 108m AE c

Robert Shaw *(Charles/Earl Hodgson)*, Richard Roundtree *(Archie)*, Barbara Seagull *(Sally)*, Shelley Winters *(Zelda Shapia)*, Shai K. Ophir *(Moshe)*, Gadi Yageel *(Gaby)*, Joseph Shiloah *(Mustafa)*, Jona Elian *(Zippi)*, Yehuda Efroni *(Salzburg)*, Joseph Graber *(Rabinowitz)*, Bomba Zur *(Momo)*, Arie Moscona *(Avram)*, Tali Goldberg *(Policewoman)*, Arik Dichner *(Arik)*, Chen Plotkin *(Danny Rabinowitz)*, Naomi Greenbaum *(Ruth Rabinowitz)*.

Shaw plays twins, one of them a London diamond merchant and the other the designer of the security system for the Tel Aviv diamond exchange. As the Londoner, he allows himself to be robbed, then blackmails the robbers into helping him rob the Tel Aviv exchange as a way of getting back at his brother. Slickly done and fairly entertaining, but superficial.

p&d, Menahem Golan; w, David Paulsen, Golan (based on a story by Golan); ph, Adam Greenberg (Eastmancolor); m, Roy Budd; ed, Dov Hoenig; art d, Kuli Sander; set d, Alfred Gershoni; spec eff, Hanz Kramsky; m/l, "Diamonds," Budd, Jack Fishman (sung by the Three Degrees).

Crime **(PR:C MPAA:PG)**

DIAMONDS AND CRIME (SEE: HI DIDDLE DIDDLE, 1943)

DIAMONDS ARE FOREVER*** (1971, Brit.) 118m Eon-Danjaq/UA c

Sean Connery *(James Bond)*, Jill St. John *(Tiffany Case)*, Charles Gray *(Blofeld)*, Lana Wood *(Plenty O'Toole)*, Jimmy Dean *(Willard Whyte)*, Bruce Cabot *(Saxby)*, Bruce Glover *(Wint)*, Putter Smith *(Kidd)*, Norman Burton *(Felix Leiter)*, Joseph Furst *(Metz)*, Bernard Lee *("M")*, Desmond Llewelyn *("Q")*, Laurence Naismith *(Sir Donald Monger)*, Burt Metcalf *(Maxwell)*, Leonard Barr *(Shady Tree)*, Margaret Lacey *(Mrs. Whistler)*, Lois Maxwell *(Miss Moneypenny)*, Joe Robinson *(Peter Franks)*, Donna Garratt *(Bambi)*, Trina Parks *(Thumper)*, Edward Bishop *(Klaus Hergersheimer)*, Larry Blake *(Barker)*, Henry Rowland *(Dentist)*, Nicky Blair *(Doorman)*, Constantin De Goguel *(Aide to Metz)*, Shane Rimmer *(Tom)*, Clifford Earl *(Immigration Officer)*, David De Keyser *(Doctor)*, Karl Held *(Agent)*, John Abineri *(Airline Representative)*, Max Latimer *(Blofeld's Double)*, Bill Hutchinson *(Moon Crater Controller)*, Frank Mann *(Moon Crater Guard)*, David Bauer *(Slumber)*, Mark Elwes *(Sir Donald's Secretary)*, Frank Olegario *(Man in Fez)*, David Healy *(Vandenburg Launch Director)*, Gordon Ruttan *(Vandenburg Aide)*, Brinsley Forde *(Houseboy)*, Marc Lawrence, Sid Haig, Michael Valente *(Attendants)*, Ed Call *(Maxie)*, Raymond Baker *(Helicopter Pilot)*, Gary Dubin *(Boy)*, Catherine Deeney *(Welfare Worker)*, Jay Sarno *(Sideshow Barker)*, Denise Perrier *(Marie)*, Tom Steele *(Guard)*, George Cooper *(SPECTRE Agent)*, Dick Crockett *(Crane Operator)*, Janos Kurucz *(Aide to Metz)*.

After a one-film hiatus, 007 Sean Connery returns to this thin excuse for more of the same comic-book action. Complete with the most advanced high-tech gadgets, our hero is pitted against the sinister forces of Gray, the third actor to portray the evil Blofeld. Connery and his love interest, St. John, a felon who eventually falls for him, are on the trail of diamond smuggler Gray. A chase ensues through Las Vegas consisting of endless car crashes, karate-kicking girls and heavy gambling, and ends in the uncovering of a plot to send a diamond-powered laser into space. Once in orbit, Gray is going to point it at Washington and demand world disarmament. This picture is an early sign of the technologically oriented future of the Bond series. With all of the gadgetry, the most interesting murder is a strangulation with a bikini top. Lana Wood, sister of the ill-fated Natalie, is cast as a Vegas casino girl who gets tossed from a window. Connery, who had become involved in the political affairs of his native Scotland at the time DIAMONDS ARE FOREVER was being cast, was considered a key selling point for the film, but to lure him to the U.S. to make it was another matter. He had just used his influence to win for Glasgow the European premiere of THE ANDERSON TAPES, the proceeds of which went to Connery's own Scottish International Educational Trust, and he was deep into helping provide educational opportunities which were missing when he was growing up in Edinburgh. Consequently, United Artists made an offer he could not refuse—one and a quarter million dollars, a percentage of the profits on the film, and an agreement to back two films of Connery's choice, in which he could either star or direct. Connery accepted the offer, but was not to be persuaded to do the roll again until NEVER SAY NEVER AGAIN in 1983.

p, Harry Saltzman, Albert R. Broccoli; Guy Hamilton; w, Richard Maibaum, Tom Mankiewcz (based on the novel by Ian Fleming); ph, Ted Moore (Panavision, Technicolor); m, John Barry; ed, Bert Bates; prod d, Ken Adams; art d, Jack Maxsted, Bill Kenney; set d, Peter Lamont, John Austin; cos, Elsa Fennell, Ted Tetrick, Donfeld; spec eff, Leslie Hillman, Albert Whitlock, Wally Veevers, Whitney McMahon; m/l, "Diamonds Are Forever," Barry Don Black (sung by Shirley Bassey); stunts, Bob Simmons, Paul Baxley.

Spy Adventure **Cas.** **(PR:C MPAA:GP)**

DIAMONDS FOR BREAKFAST½** (1968, Brit.) 102m PAR c

Marcello Mastroianni *("Nicky," Grand Duke Nicholas)*, Rita Tushingham *(Bridget)*, Elaine Taylor *(Victoria)*, Maggie Blye *(Honey)*, Francesca Tu *(Jeanne)*, Warren Mitchell *(Popov)*, The Karlins *(Triplets)*, Nora Nicholson *(Anastasia)*, Bryan Pringle *(Police Sergeant)*, Leonard Rossiter *(Inspector)*, Bill Fraser *(Bookseller)*, David Horne *(Duke of Windemere)*, Ann Blake *(Nashka)*, Ian Trigger *(Popov's Assistant)*, Charles Lloyd Pack *(Butler)*.

Mastroianni ventures out of Italy and tackles his first British production. He takes a role as a bumbling boutique owner who is fourth in succession to the Russian throne. His goal is to get back the Imperial Jewels that his father gambled away years before. Together with a comic assortment of playful lovelies, a plan is devised to steal the gems during a fashion show. Modeling ritzy clothes and dazzling diamonds, the fashionable femmes try to sneak out with the rocks they wear. Trouble ensues as things go wrong, alas, and a morass of double-crossing results. Mastroianni may be weak in the role of a crook, but there is no faulting his picking of nubile accomplices. Cardboard script and weak directing by Morahan, making his directorial bow, injure what the film might have been.

p, Selig J. Seligman, Carlo Ponti, Pierre Rouve; d, Christopher Morahan; w, Rouve, N.F. Simpson, Ronald Harwood; ph, Gerry Turpin (Eastmancolor); m, Norman Kaye; ed, Peter Tanner; prod d, Reece Pemberton; cos, Dinah Greet.

Comedy **(PR:C MPAA:M)**

DIAMONDS OF THE NIGHT** (1968, Czech.) 70m Ceskoslovensky Film/Impact bw (DEMANTY NOCI)

Ladislav Jansky *(1st Boy)*, Antonin Kumbera *(2nd Boy)*, Ilse Bischofova *(The Woman)*, Jan Riha, Ivan Asic, August Bischof, Josef Koggel, Oskar Muller, Anton Schich, Rudolf Stolle, Josef Koblizek, Josef Kubat, Rudolf Lukasek, Bohumil Moudry, Karel Navratil, Evzen Pichl, Frantisek Prochazka, Frantisek Vrana.

Two Jewish boys, Jansky and Kumbera, escape a train carrying them to a concentration camp and flee through the woods. After going hungry for two days they spot an old woman carrying food. Stealing it from her, they are unable to eat because their lips are too swollen. They are captured by peasants who get drunk while the mayor decides what to do with them. They are put in front of a mock firing squad, then released to continue their journey. Occasionally pretty good, but more often just tedious as the boys run endlessly through the trees. (In Czech; English subtitles).

d, Jan Nemec; w, Arnost Lustig, Nemec; ph, Jaroslav Kucera; ed, Miroslav Hajek; art d, Oldrich Bosak; cos, Ester Krumbachova.

Drama **(PR:C MPAA:NR)**

DIANE½** (1955) 110m MGM c

Lana Turner *(Diane)*, Pedro Armendariz *(Francis I)*, Roger Moore *(Prince Henri)*, Marisa Pavan *(Catherine de Medici)*, Cedric Hardwicke *(Ruggieri)*, Torin Thatcher *(Count de Breze)*, Taina Elg *(Alys)*, John Lupton *(Regnault)*, Henry Daniell *(Gondi)*, Ronald Green *(The Dauphin)*, Sean McClory *(Count Montgomery)*, Michael Ansara *(Count Ridolfi)*, Paul Cavanagh *(Lord Bonnivet)*, Melville Cooper *(Court Physician)*, Ian Wolfe *(Lord Tremouille)*, Basil Ruysdael *(Chamberlain)*, Christopher Dark *(Gian-Carlo)*, Marc Cavell *(Piero)*, Gene Reynolds *(Montecuculli)*, John O'Malley *(Marechal de Chabannes)*, Peter Gray *(Sardini)*, Mickey Maga *(Charles)*, Ronald Anton *(Francis)*, Geoffrey Toone *(Duke of Savoy)*, Percy Helton *(Court Jester)*, James Drury *(Lieutenant)*, Bob Dix *(Young Officer)*, Stuart Whitman *(Henri's Squire)*, Alicia Ibanez, Ann Brendon, Fay Morley, Barbara Darrow, Ann Staunton, Bunny Cooper *(Ladies-in-Waiting)*.

Pomp and pageantry vie with cleavage and costumes in this 16th-century historical saga about Diane de Poitiers, the French whore who became Henri the Second's mistress and almost pushed Queen Catherine De Medici out of the picture. The film commences as Turner is pleading for the life of her husband, Thatcher, at the court of Armendariz, Francis the First of France. Thatcher has been accused of plotting against the king and Turner makes an impassioned speech on his behalf that touches Armendariz. Thatcher escapes with his life but believes Turner secured his safety by dallying with Armendariz, so he dumps her. Turner is asked by Armendariz if she will teach his son, Moore, all the necessary courtly graces prior to the young man's marriage to De Medici, Pavan. Armendariz likes Turner and despite her being tossed aside by Thatcher, he keeps her at court. Turner teaches Moore lots more than he'd reckoned for and they fall in love. He must marry Pavan but that doesn't deter him from his liaisons with Turner. Armendariz dies in battle and Moore becomes king, but that reign is short-lived as he is quickly dispatched in a jousting tournament because of duplicity on the part of the De Medici family. Pavan orders the Italian cabal executed and is going to use the occasion of Moore's death to rid the world of her rival, Turner. But she has a change of heart and allows Turner to live out her life in interior exile at her country estate. Isherwood took some large license with the script but no one really knew the difference except for a few fuming historians. Moore's character was actually only fourteen years of age when he married Pavan's Catherine De Medici. Further, he was 20 years younger than his mistress, Diane. He died when he was forty and Diane was sixty. This story was originally acquired for Garbo in the 1930s but languished in the MGM story department until someone unearthed it for Turner. It was released at the end of the costume drama cycle and did meager business despite the expense lavished on it. But 1955 was the year when reality-based films had taken the lead; movies like MARTY, THE ROSE TATTOO, EAST OF EDEN, MR. ROBERTS, and PICNIC were all released that year, and DIANE sank in their propwash.

p, Edwin H. Knopf; d, David Miller; w, Christopher Isherwood (based on the novel *Diane de Poitier* by John Erskine); ph, Robert Planck (Cinemascope, Eastmancolor); m, Miklos Rozsa; ed, John McSweeney, Jr.; art d, Cedric Gibbons, Hans Peters; set d, Edwin B. Willis, Henry Grace; cos, Walter Plunkett; spec eff, A. Arnold Gillespie, Warren Newcombe; makeup, William Tuttle.

Historical Drama **(PR:A-C MPAA:NR)**

DIANE'S BODY½** (1969, Fr./Czech.) 90m Rene Productions-Carla Films-Ceskoslovensky Filmexport/Valoria c

Jeanne Moreau *(Diane)*, Charles Denner *(Architect)*, Elisabeth Weiner *(Girl)*, Joelle Latour *(Dancer)*, Henri-Jacques Huet *(Director)*.

Moreau's force and presence is enough to carry this moderate offering about the comedy and psychology of jealousy. Moreau meets her future mate, the unstable Denner, while in Prague. Their fancy becomes a passionate love affair, followed by marriage. After vows are exchanged, they return to France where he becomes increasingly watchful of her ways. Soon he learns that she's been having a time with a girl ballet dancer. As her lies grow, so does his rage, and he tries to kill her. She, however, turns the tables and sends him on his way over the edge of a cliff. Moreau is adequate but doesn't show the sparkle she displays when working with greater directors.

d, Jean-Louis Richard; w, Jean-Francois Hauduroy, Richard Pierre Bourgeade (based on a book by Francoise Sourissier); ph, Miroslav Ondricek (Eastmancolor); m, Antoine Duhamel.

Drama (PR:A MPAA:NR)

DIARY OF A BACHELOR* (1964) 90m AIP bw

William Traylor (Skip O'Hara), Dagne Crane (Joanne), Joe Silver (Charlie Barrett), Denise Lor (Jane Woods), Susan Dean ((Barbara), Eleni Kiamos (Angie Pisano), Jan Crockett (Jennifer Watters), Arlene Golonka (Lois), Joan Holloway (Nancy Feather), Mickey Deems (Barney Washburn), Dom DeLuise (Marvin Rollins), Jackie Kannon (Bob Haney), Leora Thatcher (Mother O'Hara), Bradley Bolke (Bugsy), Jim Alexander (Harley Peterson), Joey Faye (Bartender), Beatrice Pons (Thelma), Joy Claussen (Susan), Chris Noel (Carol), Saliha Tekneci (Belly Dancer), Bonnie Jones (Wanda Smith), Joanne MacCormack (Cynthia Brooks), Ellen Nevdal (Victoria Ampolsk), Paula Stewart (Carlotta Jones), Darlene Enlow, Nai Bonet, Greta Randall, Carolyn Lasater, Len Hammer, Larry Navarro.

If a bachelor's diary held anything of interest it was overlooked in this film adaptation. Traylor is just shy of a walk up the aisle when his bride-to-be, Crane, accidentally stumbles upon one of his diaries. The pages are overflowing with accounts of this modern-day Casanova's affairs. Told in a series of redundant flashbacks, the clumsy hand of producer/director Howard fails to keep interest for long. An unsympathetic character's life told in an uncaptivating style doesn't leave much room for praise.

p&d, Sandy Howard; w, Ken Barnett; ph, Julian Townsend; m, Jack Pleis; ed, Angelo Ross.

Comedy (PR:O MPAA:NR)

DIARY OF A BAD GIRL*½ (1958, Fr.) 87m
Francinex/Films-Around-The-World bw (LE LONG DES TROITTORS)

Anne Vernon (Helene Dupre), Danik Patisson (Christine), Francois Guerin (Dr. Andre Monod), Simone Paris (Sabine), Rene Blancard (Mr. Dupre), Pierre Fromont (Roger), Joelle Bernard, Yves Brainville, Guy Bertil, Sylvaine Humair.

Vernon is a social worker in the worst part of Paris who takes under her wing waif Patisson. She gets her a job working for her fiance, Doctor Guerin, only to have the pair fall in love. Predictable melodrama with Vernon just too good to be real until she explodes in the face of their betrayers. (In French; English subtitles.)

p, Michel Safra; d, Leonide Moguy; w, Raymond Caillava (based on a story by Safra).

Drama (PR:C MPAA:NR)

DIARY OF A CHAMBERMAID***½ (1946) 86m UA bw

Paulette Goddard (Celestine), Burgess Meredith (Capt. Mauger), Hurd Hatfield (Georges), Francis Lederer (Joseph), Judith Anderson (Mme. Lanlaire), Florence Bates (Rose), Irene Ryan (Louise), Almira Sessions (Marianne), Reginald Owen (Capt. Lanlaire).

Goddard is an enterprising young chambermaid who wants nothing more than to wed a rich man. As love would have it, a penniless valet becomes enamored of her. He tries to win her the only way he can—by killing his wealthy employer and taking his riches. A much praised and criticized film. This was a product of Jean Renoir—one of France's greatest directors. Known for his realism—especially deep-focus photography—this picture, done during the director's Hollywood years, reeks of studio artificiality. Upon its release, it brought disillusionment in the studio system, and in Renoir by his French patrons. Perhaps egotistically, but most likely correctly, they insisted that his best work was done in France. Renoir, however, was still Renoir, with or without the studio pressuring him, and his strong humanism and morality breaks through here. A brilliant film which synthesizes the serious and the comic, a direction begun with his classic THE RULES OF THE GAME. Perhaps Renoir's best Hollywood film, it illustrates what Darryl Zanuck once said, "Jean's got a lot of talent, but he's not one of us."

p, Benedict Bogeaus, Burgess Meredith; d, Jean Renoir; w, Meredith (based on the novel A Chambermaid's Diary by Octave Mirbeau and a play by Andre Heuse, Andre de Lorde, Thielly Nores); ph, Lucien Andriot; ed, James Smith; prod d & art d, Eugene Lourie; spec eff, Lee Zavitz.

Drama (PR:A MPAA:NR)

DIARY OF A CHAMBERMAID**** (1964, Fr./Ital.) 97m
Speva-FS-Dear/Cocinor bw (LE JOURNAL D'UNE FEMME DE CHAMBRE; IL DIARIO DI UNA CAMERIERA)

Jeanne Moreau (Celestine), Georges Geret (Joseph), Michel Piccoli (Husband), Francoise Lugagne (Wife), Jean Ozenne (Father), Daniel Ivernel (Capt. Mauger), Jean-Claude Carriere (Cure), Gilberte Geniat (Rose), Bernard Musson (Sacristan), Muni (Marianne), Claude Jaeger (Judge), Jeanne Sauvage-Dandieux (Claire), Madeleine Damien, Geymond Vital, Jean Franval, Marcel Rouze, Jeanne Perez, Andree Tainsy, Francoise Bertin, Pierre Collet, Aline Bertrand, Joelle Bernard, Michel Dacquin, Marcel Le Floch, Marc Eyraud, Gabriel Gobin, Marguerite Bour, Dominique Zardi.

A wonderfully vulgar film from the masterful Spanish director Luis Bunuel which is an adaptation in spirit of Octave Mirbeau's novel and Jean Renoir's 1946 film.

Moreau is the lively chambermaid from the city who turns toward country life to find a rich husband. The typical bourgeois-ribbing style of Bunuel is again evident through foot-fetishists, child molesters, and an interest in sexual corruption and its effects on innocence. An intelligent and wickedly funny satire.

p, Serge Silberman, Michel Safra; d, Luis Bunuel; w, Bunuel, Jean-Claude Carriere (from the novel A Chambermaid's Diary by Octave Mirbeau); ph, Roger Fellous (Franscope); ed, Louisette Hautecoeur-Taverna; art d, set d, & cos, Georges Wakhevitch.

Drama (PR:O MPAA:NR)

DIARY OF A CLOISTERED NUN* (1973, Ital./Fr./Ger.) 97m PAC c
(STORIA DI UNA MONACA DI CLAUSURA)

Catherine Spaak (Elisabeta), Suzy Kendall (Mother Superior), Eleanora Giorgi (Carmela), Umberto Irsini (Don Diego).

Seven years after Jacques Rivette's LA RELIGIEUSE was banned in France, this internationally produced picture covers some of the same ground more graphically and without censorship. Spaak, in Anna Karina's role, plays a nun who is subjected to the corruption of her convent. Set in the 1500s, the film deals with a lesbian mother superior in charge of a nunnery with questionable morals. Lacking Rivette's intellectualism and originality, this dull Paolella opus simply capitalizes on taboo sexuality. An example of how body-revealing films are easier to accept than those that dig into politics and morality.

p, Tonino Cervi; d, Domenico Paolella; w, Cervi, Paolella; ph, Armando Nannuzzi (Technicolor); m, Piero Piccioni; ed, Amadeo Giomini; art d, Pietro Filippone.

Drama (PR:O MPAA:R)

DIARY OF A COUNTRY PRIEST**** (1954, Fr.) 120m UGC bw
(LE JOURNAL D'UN CURE DE CAMPAGNE).

Claude Laydu (Priest of Ambricourt), Jean Riveyre (Count), Andre Guibert (Priest of Torcy), Nicole Maurey (Louise), Nicole Ladmiral (Chantal), Marie-Monique Arkell (Countess), Martine Lemaire (Seraphita), Antoine Balpetre (Dr. Delbende), Jean Danet (Oliver), Gaston Severin (Canon), Jean Etievant (Housekeeper), Bernard Hubrenne (Louis Dufrety).

Laydu is cast as a frail, unnamed priest assigned to his first parish—a small, only somewhat religious town known as Ambricourt. He simply does as saintly priests are known to do—accept the people around them as they are and try to strengthen their faith. He lives a life of poverty, eating only bread and wine, the only food he can eat without falling ill. His major achievement is in bringing a withdrawn countess out of her hatred for God and into a state of peacefulness. She dies during the night and the priest's health worsens and he must put an end to his parish activities when he learns that he has stomach cancer. While the film sounds thoroughly depressing, it is, in fact, quite the opposite. Bresson, returning to the screen after a five-year absence, succeeded in transforming the "spirit" of author George Bernanos' book to a cinematic one. The script went through two unsuccessful versions (one of them an embarrassing misfire on the part of traditional French screenwriter Jean Aurenche, who scripted THE DEVIL IN THE FLESH) before it was finally agreed that Bresson's third interpretation was the most accurate. It has since become a prime example of a brilliant adaptation, remaining faithful to the original without resorting to harmful omissions and additions. Instead of being retold through the words on the page, the film allows the audience to enjoy the identical spiritual experience as the reader of the novel. Bresson, as he usually does, cast an unknown, untrained actor in the lead role. They met every Sunday for a year, discussing the part and visiting monasteries, in order to best understand their subject. Originally 160 minutes long, Bresson was forced by the money-hungry distributors to cut out 40 minutes. The film showed no visible signs of loss. In fact, it received the Grand Prix du Cinema Francais and shared the top prize at the Venice Film Fest with Kurosawa's RASHOMON. It is definitely not a film for everyone's tastes—Bresson's work also has been known for its slow, meditative pace—but a brilliant picture all the same, placing Bresson next to Dreyer (THE PASSION OF JOAN OF ARC, 1928, silent) in terms of cinematic spirituality. (In French; English subtitles.)

p, Leon Carre; d&w, Robert Bresson (based on the novel by George Bernanos); ph, Leonce-Henry Burel; m, Jean-Jacques Grunenwald; ed, Paulette Robert.

Religious Drama (PR:A MPAA:NR)

DIARY OF A HIGH SCHOOL BRIDE* (1959) 72m AIP bw

Anita Sands (Judy), Ronald Foster (Steve), Chris Robinson (Chuck), Wendy Wilde (Gina), Louise Arthur (Mrs. Lewis), Barney Biro (Mr. Lewis), Richard Gering (Richie), Peggy Miller (Patty), Elvira Corona (Dancer), Clark Alan (Guitarist), Joan Connors (Madge), Al Laurie (Tony), Glenn Hughes, Dodie Drake (Beatniks), Lili Rosson (Lydia), Luree Nicholson (Verna), Loretta Nicholson (Jerry), Laura Nicholson (Edie), John Hart, John Garrett, Don Hix (Policemen), Larry Shuttleworth (Truck Driver), Gloria Victor (Truck Driver's Wife).

An attempt to confront the social problems of teen marriages, or so say the opening credits. Seventeen-year-old Sands must justify her wedding to twenty-four-year-old Foster to both her parents and her unbalanced ex-boy friend, Robinson. She agrees to meet Robinson in a deserted sound stage at his father's studio, where he tries to rape her. On a tip-off, Foster bursts in and, in a hair-raising scene on a catwalk, succeeds in electrocuting Robinson. Robinson took his psychotic insights a step further in STANLEY, a 1972 film about a snake-obsessed Vietnam vet, in which Robinson also starred.

p&d, Burt Topper; w, Topper, Mark and Jan Lowell (based on a story by the Lowells); ph, Gil Warrenton; m, Ronald Stein; ed, Edward Sampson; art d, Dan Haller; m/l, "Diary of a High School Bride," "When I Say Bye Bye," Tony Casanova.

Drama (PR:C-O MPAA:NR)

DIARY OF A MAD HOUSEWIFE***½ (1970) 95m UNIV c

Richard Benjamin (Jonathan Balser), Frank Langella (George Prager), Carrie Snodgress (Tina Balser), Lorraine Cullen (Sylvie Balser), Frannie Michel (Liz Balser), Lee Addams (Mrs. Prinz), Peter Dohanos (Samuel Keefer), Katherine Meskill (Charlotte Rady), Leonard Elliott (Mon. Henri), Valma (Margo), Hilda Haynes (Lottie), Don Symington (Pediatrician), Allison Mills (Women's Lib Girl), The Alice Cooper Band (Themselves), Lester Rawlins (Dr. Linstrom), Jeanette Dubois (Vera), William Kiehl (Elliot Asher), Peter Boyle (Man in Group Therapy Session), Cash Baxter, John Tillenger, Lydia Wilen, Beverly Ballard.

Benjamin is one of the great movie twits of our time. He has played this role so often that one wonders if he is that good an actor or is he really a twit playing himself? Here he is a money-mad attorney (is that redundant?) who bullies his wife to the point where she takes a lover, Langella, for matinees and "morners" (which is a "nooner"—only sooner). Soon enough, Snodgress discovers that Langella is every bit the twit Benjamin is, just a different sort of twit. Benjamin's values are out of whack and exaggerated to make them funny, although there must be people who are that overboard—especially in urban locations. Langella is as self-centered as any human can be and will only play with committed women because he is unable to commit himself. Snodgress's children, Cullen and Michel, are brats, just what you'd expect to be spawned from this duo. The plot takes Snodgress into several diverting and episodic incidents and culminates when she divests herself of both husband and lover and seeks balm and solace in group therapy, only to learn that happiness doesn't reside in psychiatry, either. The three leads are excellent and two of them have continued playing those kinds of roles. Benjamin has been seen in many films as the consummate ass: THE MARRIAGE OF A YOUNG STOCKBROKER, THE SUNSHINE BOYS, LOVE AT FIRST BITE, THE STEAGLE and, of course, the ultimate nerd in PORTNOY'S COMPLAINT. Langella played the cad in a few more films and eventually the lead in John Badham's DRACULA. Snodgress was nominated for an Oscar for her role in this film, the only nomination the picture received.

p&d, Frank Perry; w, Eleanor Perry (based on the novel by Sue Kaufman); ph, Gerald Hirschfield (Technicolor); ed, Sidney Katz; prod d, Peter Dohanos; set d, Sam Robert, Robert Drumheller; cos, Ruth Morely, Flo Transfield, James Hagerman.

Comedy/Drama   **Cas.**   **(PR:C-O   MPAA:R)**

DIARY OF A MADMAN** (1963) 96m UA c

Vincent Price (Simon Cordier), Nancy Kovack (Odette), Chris Warfield (Paul), Elaine Devry (Jeanne), Stephen Roberts (Rennedon), Lewis Martin (Priest), Ian Wolfe (Pierre), Edward Colmans (Andre), Mary Adams (Louise), Harvey Stephens (Girot), Nelson Olmstead (Dr. Borman), Joseph Ruskin (The Horla), Dick Wilson, Gloria Clark, George Sawaya, Wayne Collier, Don Brodie, Joseph Del Nostro, Jr.

In self-defense, French magistrate Price strangles a condemned prisoner, only to become possessed by the dead man's evil spirit, or "horla." Price becomes a merciless killer until he discovers that the horla responds unfavorably to fire. To destroy the evil inside him, he must take his own life. He does so by leaping into a blazing inferno. Based on a classic story by Guy de Maupassant, but Price is unable to bring the necessary dimension to the complex role. Of major importance to the literary work, but only hinted at in the film, is the idea that he kills because he is a latent murderer given a license to do so. A subtle and important horror story which is reduced, in a poor adaptation, to a simplistic evil-spirit picture.

p, Robert E. Kent; d, Reginald LeBorg; w, Kent (based on the story "La Horla" by Guy de Maupassant); ph, Ellis W. Carter (Technicolor); m, Richard LaSalle; ed, Grant Whytock; art d, Daniel Haller; set d, Victor Gangelin; cos, Marjorie Corso; spec eff, Norman Breedlove.

Horror   **(PR:C-O   MPAA:NR)**

DIARY OF A NAZI** (1943, USSR) 67m
Soviet Cinema Committee of the USSR/Artkino bw

"District No. 14": Y. Anazhevskaya, M. Bernes, S. Ditlovich, V. Krasnovetsky; "The Beue Cliff": N. Komissarov, L. Kartashova, L. Kmit; "The Signal": N. Bratorsky, V. Bubnov, V. Mironova, B. Runghe.

Three stories of civilian resistance to the Nazis released as part of a series of "Fighting Film Albums." In the first story, the people of Poland try to fight the Nazis but are massacred, only to rise up again. In the second story, an old Czech man forced to drive a truck full of German soldiers over a dangerous mountain road drives over the edge. The third story shows how a group of SS men are captured in a commando-style raid. Mostly meant as propaganda for Russian audiences, the films are still very interesting, the last being the best. (In Russian; English subtitles.)

p, Mikahil Romm; "District No. 14": d, Igor Savchenko; w, Solomon Lazurin; "The Blue Cliff": d, Vladimir Braun; w, L. Smirnova, S. Gergel; "The Signal": d, Mark Donskoy; w, N. Severov.

War   **(PR:C   MPAA:NR)**

DIARY OF A REVOLUTIONIST* (1932, USSR) 81m
Mezhrabpomfilm/Amkino bw

G. V. Mouzalevsky (Fedor Rybakon), F.B. Blazhevitch (Bagour), S.A. Martinson (Col. Belov), Sophie Magaril (Elena, His Wife), M.M. Tarkhanov (Engineer), A. Timotayev (Chauffeur).

Rybakon (Mouzalevsky), looking back on his days fighting against the White Army forces while he is honored with a parade through Red Square. Routine propaganda, less interesting than most Russian films of the period.

d, J.I. Urinov; w, Urinov, J.A. Protozanov; ph, B.A. Kozlov; m, V.A. Oransky.

Drama   **(PR:A   MPAA:NR)**

DIARY OF A SCHIZOPHRENIC GIRL**½ (1970, Ital.) 94m Idi Cinematografica/AA c
(DIARIO DI UNA SCHIZOFRENICA)

Ghislaine d'Orsay (Anna), Umberto Raho (Father), Marija Tocinowsky (Mother), Margarita Lozano (Blanche), Gabriella Mulachie (Nurse), Manlio Busoni, Giuseppe Liuzzi (Doctors), Sara Ridolfi (Housekeeper).

After a failed suicide attempt, 17-year-old d'Orsay is put under the care of psychiatrist Lozano. Lozano learns how the girl was neglected by her parents, who preferred her younger sister. After a long period of treatment, d'Orsay is cured. Apart from some tedious explanations of mental illness by Lozano, the film is quite good, with nicely understated performances and an intelligent script. Based on an actual case history. (In Italian; English subtitles.)

p, Gian Vittorio Baldi; d, Nelo Risi; w, Risi, Fabio Carpi (based on the book Journal d'Une Schizophrene by Renee, with Marguerite Andree Sechehaye); ph, Franco Fornari (Eastmancolor); m, Ivan Vandor.

Drama   **(PR:A   MPAA:GP)**

DIARY OF A SHINJUKU BURGLAR**½ (1969, Jap.) 94m
Sozocha/Shibata c (SHINJUKU DOROBO NIKKI)

Tadanori Yokoo (Birdey), Rie Yokoyama (Umeko), Kei Sato (Man), Kara Juro (Singer).

Caught shoplifting in a Tokyo bookstore, Yokoo is led through a number of political and sexual adventures by shopgirl Yokoyama. A fascinating film, full of symbols and sex, by a major Japanese director. (In Japanese; English subtitles.)

d, Nagisa Oshima; w, Tsutomo Tamura, Mamoru Sasaki, Masao Adachi, Oshima; ph, Yasuhiro Yoshioka, Seizo Sengen (Eastmancolor); ed, Oshima.

Drama   **(PR:O   MPAA:NR)**

DIARY OF AN ITALIAN**½ (1972, Ital.) 99m Faser c (DIARIO DI UN ITALIANO)

Donatello (Valerio), Alida Valli (Olga), Pier Paolo Capponi (Lorenzo), Silvano Tranquilli (Alberto), Mara Venier (Wanda).

A tragic love story set during Mussolini's anti-Semitic reign, officially endorsed with the expulsion of the Jews. Donatello is the military-bound lad in love with Vernier, a girl who won't disclose her religious belief to the authorities. Donatello's suffering begins when his loved one commits suicide by diving into the Arno River. He is then told by his protective mother that his father, an opposition leader, was murdered in prison. Though he is in agony, the boy remains strong and continues in his military direction. Delivered through flashbacks within flashbacks, this complex, yet subtle, love tale unfortunately leans too heavily on its melodramatic crutch.

d&w, Sergio Capogna (based on a short story by Vasco Pratolini); ph, Antonio Piazza (Eastmancolor); m, Giuliano Illiani; art d, Franco Bottari.

War Drama   **(PR:C   MPAA:NR)**

DIARY OF ANNE FRANK, THE**** (1959) 170m FOX bw

Millie Perkins (Anne Frank), Joseph Schildkraut (Otto Frank), Shelley Winters (Mrs. Van Daan), Richard Beymer (Peter Van Daan), Gusti Huber (Edith Frank), Lou Jacobi (Mr. Van Daan), Diane Baker (Margot Frank), Douglas Spencer (Kraer), Dody Heath (Miep), Ed Wynn (Albert Dussell), Charles Wagenheim (Sneak Thief), Frank Tweddell (Night Watchman), Delmar Erickson, Robert Boon (SS Men), Gretchen Goertz (Dutch Girl), William Kirschner (Workman in Shop).

Yes, it's too long and, yes, it's depressing at times, and, yes, some of the performances are not the equivalent of the theme and the script and the direction, but how can we not award high rating to a film that touched so many lives? Is there anyone who doesn't know the story of the young girl who left her book behind when the Nazis extinguished her life? Perkins, in her first movie, is luminescent as the child who observes life in the confines of a single attic where two families hide. Schildkraut is Otto Frank, her father, and stage actress Huber is the mother. George Stevens took great care to cast the picture with the actors he felt were right for the roles rather than be railroaded into miscasting for the sake of marquee value, though there was some question about his selection of Beymer, a Fox contract player whom the studio attempted to make into a star through large parts in many films in which he had no business appearing. For the small role of Peter Van Daan, he is just fine, though, and does not disturb the overall merit of the ensemble acting. The Franks and the Van Daans are forced to take refuge in an attic where they are helped by Spencer and Heath, two Dutch citizens who risk their lives to aid the Jews. This was not uncommon in Holland where the king donned a Jewish star on his arm when all the Jews were forced to wear them for identification. The film is always tense as the fugitives from the Nazis are ever aware that they could be betrayed at any moment, found out, and sent to one of the death camps. For two years, these two very different families must live together. Perkins and Beymer fall in love and attempt to live their lives the way they might on the outside. Winters is perfection as the noisy wife of Jacobi, in a role not unlike so many he's played in other films. Stevens does a magnificent job in keeping his camera flowing within the tight periphery of the small living quarters. And yet, for all the pain and anguish in the film, plus the fact that we know how it will end, there are lovely moments of real comedy that punctuate and please and, although the tears flow freely in the audience, so does the laughter. There were several perplexing choices in the making of THE DIARY OF ANNE FRANK. The idea was to show how tight, how claustrophobic the surroundings and the ability to triumph over that propinquity. Then why did Stevens choose the very wide screen of Cinemascope? Also, perhaps the husband-and-wife team of Goodrich and Hackett might have been better served to excise some of the story for the sake of trimming the almost three hours of length. Yet, picturing the conversations that must have taken place at the studio, everyone had to be frightened of tampering with what has become a must-read for students and a classic in a genre. For all the angst she must have gone through, Anne Frank said (in her book, the play, and the picture): "In spite of everything, I still believe that people are really good at heart." How naive, how sad, how wonderful that she could have felt that way. The inhabitants of the attic were eventually arrested in 1944 and taken away. Anne Frank perished at Auschwitz and only her father, Otto, survived. The movie fades with his voice saying, "She puts me to shame." If there is a dry eye in the house at that moment, it's someone who is totally deaf and can't read lips. Stevens was often criticized for the ratio of his shooting—by ratio, we mean feet of film exposed to feet of film used. He was always guilty of gross overshooting and some say that's the sign of an unsure director. Others say it's the sign of a perfectionist. In Stevens' case, when you consider that he also made GIANT, SHANE, GUNGA DIN, and many more, who can quibble? Stevens was an editor and a cameraman before he became a director and the story goes that he was the infantry camera person who went into several of the Nazi death camps before anyone else and that many of those famous first films were taken by Stevens. If that is the case, it is easier to see why he held the original material of THE DIARY OF ANNE FRANK in such high esteem and held off damaging it. Whatever the reason, Stevens' work on the film remains a high-water mark of large direction in a small location. Winters took an Oscar as Best Supporting Actress and Mellor took one for his cinematography. Nominations went to the picture, Stevens, Wynn, and Alfred Newman. But 1959 was the year that BEN HUR swept across the screen and most of the other pictures released that year were left in the dust of BEN HUR's chariot. Oddly, though Mellor and Cardiff are listed as co-cinematographers, our records show Mellor receiving the Oscar alone.

p&d, George Stevens; w, Frances Goodrich, Albert Hackett (based on their play and the autobiographical *Anne Frank: Diary of A Young Girl*); ph, William C. Mellor, Jack Cardiff; m, Alfred Newman; ed, Robert Swink, William Mace, David Brotherton; md, Edward B. Powell; art d, Lyle R. Wheeler, George W. Davis; spec eff, L.B. Abbott.

Drama   **Cas.**   **(PR:A MPAA:NR)**

DIARY OF FORBIDDEN DREAMS   (SEE: WHAT? 1973, Ital.)

DIARY OF MAJOR THOMPSON, THE
    (SEE: FRENCH, THEY ARE A FUNNY RACE, THE, 1956, Fr.)

DIARY OF OHARU   (SEE: LIFE OF OHARU, THE, 1952, Jap.)

DICK BARTON AT BAY**   (1950, Brit.) 68m Marylebone-Hammer bw

Don Stannard (*Dick Barton*), Tamara Desni (*Anna*), George Ford (*Snowey White*), Meinhart Maur (*Serg Volkoff*), Percy Walsh (*Prof. Mitchell*), Joyce Linden (*Mary Mitchell*), Campbell Singer (*Inspector Cavendish*), John Arnatt (*Jackson*), Richard George (*Inspector Slade*), Beatrice Kane, Patrick MacNee, George Crawford, Fred Owen, Paddy Ryan, Yoshihide Yanai, Ted Butterfield.

The third in the series of Dick Barton films and also the last because Stannard subsequently was killed in an auto accident. Stannard is on the trail of a band of international criminals who plan to destroy England with a death ray. Walsh is the inventor of the ray and he is held captive with his daughter, Desni, until Stannard saves the day. A simple action-adventure that moves at an entertaining pace. (See DICK BARTON series, Index.)

p, Henry Halstead; d, Godfrey Grayson; w, Ambrose Grayson (adapted from a radio serial by Edward J. Mason); ph, Stanley Clinton.

Crime   **(PR:A MPAA:NR)**

DICK BARTON—SPECIAL AGENT*½
    (1948, Brit.) Hammer-Marylebone/Exclusive bw

Don Stannard (*Dick Barton*), George Ford (*Snowey White*), Jack Shaw (*Jock*), Gillian Maude (*Jean Hunter*), Geoffrey Wincott (*Dr. Caspar*), Beatrice Kane (*Miss Horrock*), Ivor Danvers (*Snub*), Colin Douglas, Arthur Bush, Alec Ross, Janice Lowthian, Morris Sweden, Farnham Baxter, Ernest Borrow.

Stannard must stop villain Wincott from dropping germ bombs on England. Poor direction slows the action to a sleeping pace. The Barton character's popularity brought two quick sequels. This was the first production for Hammer Films, a production company that would become famous for horror and science fiction films. (See DICK BARTON series, Index.)

p, Henry Halstead; d, Alfred Goulding; w, Alan Stranks, Alfred Goulding (adapted from a radio serial by Edward J. Mason); ph, Stanley Clinton.

Crime   **(PR:A MPAA:NR)**

DICK BARTON STRIKES BACK**½   (1949, Brit.) 73m Exclusive bw

Don Stannard (*Dick Barton*), Sebastian Cabot (*Fouracada*), Jean Lodge (*Tina*), James Raglan (*Lord Armadale*), Bruce Walker (*Snowey White*), Humphrey Kent (*Col. Gardner*), John Harvey (*Maj. Henderson*), Morris Sweden, Sydney Vivian, Toni Morelli, George Crawford, Laurie Taylor, "Flash" (*The Dog*).

The best of the Dick Barton series, with Stannard taking on Cabot and Raglan who have an atomic device and are bent on destroying what they can aim it at. The film moves at such a pace that the holes in the story blur and are overlooked. The action is tight and entertaining. In the climax, Stannard escapes out of a pit of poisonous snakes and then battles his way to the top of Blackpool Tower, to stop Cabot from aiming the device at the city. (See DICK BARTON series, Index.)

p, Anthony Hinds, Mae Murray; d, Godfrey Grayson; w, Ambrose Grayson (adapted from a radio serial by Edward J. Mason); ph, Cedric Williams.

Crime   **(PR:A MPAA:NR)**

DICK TRACY**½   (1945) 61m RKO bw
    (GB: SPLITFACE; AKA: DICK TRACY, DETECTIVE)

Morgan Conway (*Dick Tracy*), Anne Jeffreys (*Tess Trueheart*), Mike Mazurki (*Splitface*), Jane Greer (*Judith Owens*), Lyle Latell (*Pat Patton*), Joseph Crehan (*Chief Brandon*), Mickey Kuhn (*Tracy, Jr.*), Trevor Bardette (*Prof. Starling*), Morgan Wallace (*Steven Owens*), Milton Parsons (*Deathridge*), William Halligan (*Mayor*), Edythe Elliot (*Mrs. Caraway*), Mary Currier (*Dorothy Stafford*), Ralph Dunn (*Manning*), Edmund Glover (*Radio Announcer*), Bruce Edwards (*Sergeant*), Tanis Chandler (*Miss Stanley*), Jimmy Jordan, Carl Hanson (*Pedestrians*), Franklyn Farnum (*Bystander at Murder*), Jack Gargan, Sam Ash, Carl Faulkner, Frank Meredith, Bob Reeves (*Cops*), Tom Noonan (*Johnny Moko*), Harry Strang, George Magrill (*Detectives*), Robert Douglass (*Busboy*), Alphonse Martell (*Jules, the Waiter*), Gertrude Astor (*Woman*), Jack Chefe (*Headwaiter*), Florence Pepper (*Girl*), Wilbur Mack, Jason Robards, Sr. (*Motorists*).

Chester Gould's comic strip hero comes to life in this full-length picture after taking shorter breaths in Republic's serials. Conway, the square-jawed detective, follows a trail of clues to Mazurki, cast as the sinister Splitface, a mad killer with a disfiguring scar. Mazurki is in pursuit of the jury members who sent him to prison. He kills three before kidnaping Jeffreys, our hero's girl, and Kuhn, his adopted son. Conway sniffs them out, making for the inevitable rescue. A light thriller which never claims to be anything more than a personification of a cartoon. (See DICK TRACY series, Index.)

p, Herman Schlom; d, William Berke; w, Eric Taylor (based on the comic strip by Chester Gould); ph, Frank Redman; m, Roy Webb; ed, Ernie Leadlay; md, Constantin Bakaleinikoff; art d, Albert S. D'Agostino, Ralph Berger; set d, Darrell Silvera, Jean L. Speak.

Crime   **Cas.**   **(PR:A-C MPAA:NR)**

DICK TRACY MEETS GRUESOME**½
    (1947) 65m RKO bw (GB: DICK TRACY'S AMAZING ADVENTURE;
    AKA: DICK TRACY MEETS KARLOFF)

Boris Karloff (*Gruesome*), Ralph Byrd (*Dick Tracy*), Anne Gwynne (*Tess Trueheart*), Edward Ashley (*L.E. Thal*), June Clayworth (*Dr. I.M. Learned*), Lyle Latell (*Pat Patton*), Tony Barrett (*Melody*), Skelton Knaggs (*X-Ray*), Jim Nolan (*Dan Sterne*), Joseph Crehan (*Chief Brandon*), Milton Parsons (*Dr. A. Tomic*), Lex Barker, Lee Phelps, Sean McClory, Harry Harvey, Harry Strang, William Gould.

This final Dick Tracy feature in the series headlines Karloff as the evil ex-con Gruesome. After the fluffy Gwynne witnesses a bank heist in which everyone is temporarily frozen stiff from a mysterious gas wielded by Karloff, she calls in boy friend Byrd. He is soon in hot pursuit of Karloff, and, in the obligatory comic ending, gets his man. Far from serious, this picture is colored with wickedly amusing character tags—L.E. Thal, the inventor of the lethal freeze gas; I.M. Learned, the informative gal doctor; and Dr. A. Tomic, a noted inventor. A fine example of good, clean fun. (See DICK TRACY series, Index.)

p, Herman Schlom; d, John Rawlins; w, Robertson White, Eric Taylor (based on a story by William H. Graffis, Robert E. Kent from the comic strip by Chester Gould); ph, Frank Redman; m, Paul Sawtell; ed, Elmo Williams; md, Constantin Bakaleinikoff; art d, Albert S. D'Agostino, Walter Keller; spec eff, Russell A. Cully.

Crime   **Cas.**   **(PR:A-C MPAA:NR)**

DICK TRACY VS. CUEBALL**   (1946) 62m RKO bw

Morgan Conway (*Dick Tracy*), Anne Jeffreys (*Tess Trueheart*), Lyle Latell (*Pat Patton*), Rita Corday (*Mona Clyde*), Ian Keith (*Vitamin Flintheart*), Dick Wessel (*Cueball*), Douglas Walton (*Priceless*), Esther Howard (*Filthy Flora*), Joseph Crehan (*Chief Brandon*), Byron Foulger (*Little*), Jimmy Crane (*Junior*), Milton Parsons (*Higby*), Skelton Knaggs (*Rudolph*), Ralph Dunn (*Cop*), Harry Cheshire (*Jules Sparkle*), Trevor Bardette (*Lester Abbott*).

The legend lives on as Tracy continues fighting against the forces of evil. Conway, in his second and last performance as Tracy, is after the menacing Cueball, played statuesquely by the bald-wigged Wessel, who is on a rampage, killing fellow gang members who have double-crossed him, strangling them as punishment. Wessel gets his due when his foot gets caught in a train switcher, promptly leading to his obliteration via a speeding train. The admen were able to come up with a catchy tag for this one: "Dick the dauntless dares death to deliver diamonds." Keith's interpretation of Vitamin Flintheart is priceless parody, and Howard as Filthy Flora also is notable. (See DICK TRACY series, Index.)

p, Herman Schlom; d, Gordon M. Douglas; w, Dane Lussier, Robert E. Kent (based on a story by Luci Ward, from the comic strip by Chester Gould); ph, George E. Diskant; m, Constantin Bakaleinikoff, Phil Oman; ed, Philip Martin, Jr.; art d, Albert D'Agostino, Lucius O. Croxton; set d, Darrell Silvera, Shelby Willis.

Crime   **Cas.**   **(PR:C MPAA:NR)**

DICK TRACY'S DILEMMA**
    (1947) 60m RKO bw (GB: MARK OF THE CLAW)

Ralph Byrd (*Dick Tracy*), Kay Christopher (*Tess Trueheart*), Lyle Latell (*Pat Patton*), Jack Lambert (*The Claw*), Ian Keith (*Vitamin Flintheart*), Bernadene Hayes (*Longshot Lillie*), Jimmy Conlin (*Sightless*), William B. Davidson (*Peter Premium*), Tony Barrett (*Sam*), Richard Powers (*Pred*), Harry Strang (*Night Watchman*), Tom London (*Cop in Squad Car*), Jason Robards, Sr. (*Watchman*), Harry Harvey (*Donovan, Cop*), Sean McClory (*Cop*), Al Bridge (*Police Detective*), William Gould (*Police Technician*).

Serial actor Byrd returns to his role as Tracy in this, the third of the cartoon-inspired features. The plot which most resembles the serials, Byrd stalks the Claw, the leader of a gang who stole a shipment of furs and killed the guard. The miscreant, wickedly portrayed by Lambert, is equipped with a steel hook in place of a hand. Justice is served when the Claw accidentally hooks the steel mitt onto a live trolley wire, zapping himself into ashes. Audience members fascinated by the outrageous violence in the Chester Gould comic strip love this finale. (See DICK TRACY series, Index.)

p, Herman Schlom; d, John Rawlins; w, Robert Stephen Brode (based on the comic strip by Chester Gould); ph, Frank Redman; m, Paul Sawtell; ed, Marvin Coll; art d, Albert S. D'Agostino, Lucius O. Croxton.

Crime   **Cas.**   **(PR:C MPAA:NR)**

DICK TURPIN**   (1933, Brit.) 79m Stoll-Stafford/GAU bw

Victor McLaglen (Dick Turpin), Jane Carr (Eleanor Mowbray), Frank Vosper (Tom King), James Finlayson (Jeremy), Cecil Humphreys (Luke Rookwood), Gillian Lind (Nan), Gibb McLaughlin (Governor), Alexander Field (Weazel Jones), Helen Ferrers (Lady Rookwood), Lewis Gilbert (Jem), Roy Findley.

McLaglen plays the role of the famous English highwayman, here riding to York to stop a forced marriage, and losing his beloved mare Black Bess in doing so. The producers took their lumps for selecting McLaglen for the title role, but he turns in a hearty performance in a production where there are occasional slips, unusual considering the British pride in the quality of their work.

p, Clyde Cook; d, John Stafford, Victor Hanbury; w, Victor Kendall (based on the novel Rookwood by W. Harrison Ainsworth); ph, Desmond Dickinson.

DICTATOR, THE**½   (1935, Brit./Ger.) 85m Toeplitz/GAU bw
(AKA: FOR LOVE OF A QUEEN; THE LOVES OF A DICTATOR)

Clive Brook (Struensee), Madeleine Carroll (Queen Caroline), Emlyn Williams (King Charles VIII), Alfred Drayton (Brandt), Nicholas Hannen (Goldberg), Helen Haye (Queen Mother Juliana), Isabel Jeans (Von Eyben), Ruby Miller (Hilda), Frank Cellier (Sir Murray Keith), Heather Thatcher (Lady), Gibb McLaughlin.

A lavish British epic centering on two lovers, Brook and Carroll, in 18th-century Denmark. Brook is a medic who one day attends a drunken king in Hamburg. The king brings the doctor back to Denmark to live a life of royalty. It is here that he meets the Queen, played in a plebian fashion by Carroll, and they fall in love. The vindictive Queen Mother catches Brook in the royal boudoir and has them both imprisoned. Brook arranges for the Queen's escape. She refuses, vowing to stay with him until the end. A spectacle, reportedly costing $500,000, overflowing with elaborate sets and costumes, but with a script so shallow it leaves no room for compassion.

p, Ludovica Toeplitz; d, Victor Saville; w, Benn Levy, Hans Wilhelm, H.G. Lustig, Michael Logan (based on a story by Lustig, Logan); ph, Franz Planer; ed, Paul Weatherwax; m, Carol Rathaus.

Romance   **(PR:A MPAA:NR)**

DID I BETRAY?   (SEE: BLACK ROSES, 1935, Brit.)

DID YOU HEAR THE ONE ABOUT THE TRAVELING
SALESLADY? zero   (1968) 96m UNIV c

Phyllis Diller (Agatha Knabenshu), Bob Denver (Bertram), Joe Flynn (Shelton), Eileen Wesson (Jeanine) Jeanette Nolan (Ma Webb), Paul Reed (Pa Webb), Bob Hastings (Lyle), David Hartman (Constable), George Neise (Ben Milford), Anita Eubank (Young Girl), Kelly Thordson (Enoch Scraggs), Jane Dulo (Clara Buxton), Charles Lane (Mr. Duckworth), Dal McKennon (Old Soldier), Herb Vigran (Baggage Man), Lloyd Kino (Laundry Man), Warde Donovan, Eddie Quillan, Eddie Ness (Salesmen).

As a matter of fact, we have heard this one, in 1956 as THE FIRST TRAVELING SALESLADY. The hard-to-swallow Diller is cast as a 1910 player-piano saleslady in Missouri with Denver and Flynn offering only modest support. The supposedly big payoff is a cow stampede caused by a malfunctioning milking machine. The cast is given the benefit of the doubt for its efforts in this incompetent and childish screenplay. Strictly for Diller devotees.

p, Si Rose; d, Don Weis; w, John Fenton Murray (based on a story by Jim Fritzell, Everett Greenbaum); ph, Bud Thackery (Techniscope/Technicolor); m, Vic Mizzy; ed, Edward Haire, Dale Johnson; art d, Alexander Golitzen, Robert C. MacKichan; set d, John McCarthy, Ralph Sylos; cos, Omar of Omaha.

Comedy   **(PR:A-C MPAA:G)**

DIE, DIE, MY DARLING***   (1965, Brit.) 97m Hammer/COL c
(GB: FANATIC)

Tallulah Bankhead (Mrs. Trefoile), Stefanie Powers (Pat Carroll), Peter Vaughan (Harry), Maurice Kaufmann (Alan Glentower), Yootha Joyce (Anna), Donald Sutherland (Joseph), Gwendolyn Watts (Gloria), Robert Dorning (Ormsby), Philip Gilbert (Oscar), Winifred Dennis (Shopkeeper), Diana King (Woman Shopper).

Bankhead returned from a twelve-year hiatus to make what became her final film. Cast in an eerie role as a religious fanatic, she kidnaps Powers, her dead son's fiancee, who dropped in for a visit. Powers kept locked up in the basement so the psychotic mother-in-law-to-be can cleanse her soul, making her fit to go to heaven with her son. Bankhead is superbly cast and performs far above par in a role which bears striking similarity to Bette Davis's in WHAT EVER HAPPENED TO BABY JANE? Donald Sutherland appears in the dawn of his career as a handyman who reads his Bible upside down.

p, Anthony Hinds; d, Silvio Narizzano; w, Richard Matheson (based on the novel Nightmare by Anne Blaisdell); ph, Arthur Ibbetson (Eastmancolor); m, Wilfred Josephs; ed, James Needs; prod d, Peter Proud.

Horror   **(PR:O MPAA:NR)**

DIE FASTNACHTSBEICHTE**   (1962, Ger.) 101m UFA/Casino Films c

Hans Sohnker (Panezza), Gitty Daruga (Viola), Friedrich Domin (Canon Henrici), Berta Drews (Frau Baumler), Hilde Hildebrandt (Mme. Guttier), Helga Tolle

(Katharina), Rainer Brandt (Ferdinand Baumler), Herbert Tiede (Merzbecher), Grit Bottcher, Ursula Heyer, Helga Schlack, Milena von Eckardt, Albert Bessler, Christian Wolff, Gotz George.

A detective tries to track down the murderer of a man killed in front of a cathedral during the carnival before Ash Wednesday. The suspects include the carnival prince, the man's father, and two women. The real murderer is revealed after a second killing on Ash Wednesday. Dieterle, the director, was famous in the 1930s and 1940s for his bio-pictures, such as JUAREZ and THE LIFE OF EMILE ZOLA.

d, William Dieterle; w, Kurt Heuser (based on a story by Carl Zuckmayer); ph, Heinz Pehlke; m, Siegfried Franz; ed, Carl Otto; art d, Emil Hasler.

Mystery   **(PR:A MPAA:NR)**

DIE FLEDERMAUS**½
(1964, Aust.) 107m Casino/United Film Enterprises c

Peter Alexander (Dr. Gabriel Eisenstein), Marianne Koch (Rosalinde, His Wife), Marika Rokk (Adele, Her Maid), Boy Gobert (Prince Orlofsky), Hans Moser (Frosch), Willy Millowitsch (Frank), Gunther Philipp (Pista von Bundassy), Oskar Sima (Basil Arabayam), Susi Nicoletti (Baroness Martens), Rolf Kutschera (Alfred), Rudolf Carl (Joseph), Carl Gernbach (Gigerl), Ellen Umlauf (Young Lady in Prison), Johannes Roth (Fat Vagabond), Vienna State Ballet, Vienna Volksopera Ballet, Kurt Edelhagen Orchestra.

A classical musical comedy based on the Johann Strauss composition first performed in 1874. Set in turn-of-the-century Vienna, DIE FLEDERMAUS stars Gobert as the Prince who, along with his good friend, Philipp, plans a massive costume ball with which to get even with their friend Alexander. The usual mistaken identity, flirtations, intrigue, comedic subplots, and jealous confrontations ensue, surrounded by a lavish production.

p, Herbert Gruber, Karl Schwetter; d&w, Geza von Cziffra (based on the operetta "Die Fledermaus" by Johann Strauss); ph, Willy Winterstein (Eastmancolor); m, Erich Becht; ed, Arnd Heyne; md, Kurt Feltz; set d, Fritz Juptner-Jonstorff; cos, Paul Seltenhammer, Gudrun Hildebrandt; ch, Willy Dirtl; m/l, Feltz; makeup, Felix Wurzel, Leo Umyssa, Stefan Kulhanek, Frieda Jungwirth.

Musical Comedy   **(PR:A MPAA:NR)**

DIE GANS VON SEDAN**
(1962, Fr/Ger.) 90m UFA-C.A.P.A.C./Casino Films bw
(SANS TAMBOUR NI TROMPETTE)

Hardy Kruger (Fritz), Jean Richard (Leon), Dany Carrel (Marguerite), Francoise Rosay (Grandmother), Theo Lingen (Colonel), Lucien Nat (Captain), Jean Verner, Emile Genevois, Robert Rollis, Fritz Tillmann, Ralf Wolter, Willy Rosner, Georg Gutlich.

Kruger and Richard are opposing soldiers in the Franco-Prussian War of 1870. During a swim they meet and become friends, accidentally exchanging uniforms when they emerge. They go to a farmhouse and are taken in by an old man and his granddaughter. The two men vie for the girl's affections and finally trade back uniforms after another swim. They part friends and return to their respective armies. Predictable comedy with an obvious pacifist message.

d, Helmut Kautner; w, Jean L'Hote, Kautner (based on the novel Un Dimanche Au Champ D'Honneur by L'Hote); ph, Jacques Letellier (Eastmancolor); m, Bernhard Eichhorn; ed, Klaus Dudenhofer; art d, Serge Pimenoff, Jacques Brizzio.

Comedy   **(PR:A MPAA:NR)**

DIE HAMBURGER KRANKHEIT*½
(1979, Ger./Fr.) 113m Hallelujah Film c

Carline Seisser, Helmut Griem, Ulrich Wildgruber, Fernando Arabal, Rainer Langhans, Tilo Prueckner, Rosl Zech, Romy Haag, Leopold Hainisch.

This film owes a lot to Elia Kazan's PANIC IN THE STREETS and, to a lesser extent, George Romero's THE CRAZIES. (Kazan's film dealt with a police search for criminals that unknowingly were infected with highly communicable and deadly disease.) The production is dated and themes are poorly developed. Hamburg has been quarantined because of a strange epidemic that has spread through the city. A group of misfits sneaks out of the city, pursued by authorities before they can spread the disease to too many people.

d, Peter Fleischmann; w, Fleischmann, Otto Jaegersberg, Roland Topor; ph, Colin Mounier.

Thriller   **(PR:C MPAA:NR)**

DIE LAUGHING zero   (1980) 108m Orion/WB c

Robby Benson (Pinsky), Linda Grovenor (Amy), Charles Durning (Arnold), Elsa Lanchester (Sophie), Bud Cort (Mueller), Mary Zagon (Friend), Rita Taggert (Thelma), Larry Hankin (Bock), Sammuel Krachmalnick (Zhukov), Michael David Lee (Einstein), Peter Coyote (Davis), Charles Fleischer (Charlie), Charles Harwood, Melanie Henderson, Carel Struycken, Chuck Dorsett, Morgan Upton, Christopher E. Pray, John Bracci, James Cranna, Joe Bellan, John Tim Burrus, Maurice Argent, Rhoda Gemignani, Nick Outin.

A pitiful black comedy about a kid who is in the wrong place at the wrong time and is blamed for the murder of a top nuclear scientist. Benson is pursued for what seems like an eternity by an obsessed bigot, Cort, and his pal, Durning. An annoying assemblage of the formulated successes of other films, this one randomly tosses in anything that has worked before. An unnerving experience crippled by the box office poison of Benson. Coyote, who later appeared in TIMERIDERS and STRANGER'S KISS, shows some early talents.

p, Mark Canton, Robby Benson; d, Jeff Werner; w, Benson, Jerry Segal, Scott Parker (based on a story by Parker); ph, David Myers (Technicolor); m, Benson,

Segal; ed, Neil Travis; prod d, James H. Spencer; set d, Doug Von Koss; cos, Nancy McArdle.

Comedy   **Cas.**   **(PR:O   MPAA:PG)**

DIE MANNER UM LUCIE**

(1931) 85m Korda/PAR bw (RIVE GAUCHE)

Liane Haid, Walter Rilla, Oskar Karlweis, Trude Hesterberg, Lien Deyers, Ernst Stahl-Nachbaur, Karl Huszar-Puffy, Jaro Furth, Eugen Jensen.

This German-language version of LAUGHTER was Alexander Korda's first assignment in Paris after leaving Hollywood flat broke the year before. At the same time, he directed RIVE GAUCHE, a French-language version of the same story. His technique consisted of a French cast stepping onto the set and reenacting the moves the German cast had made minutes before. His next film would be the classic MARIUS, and from that point his name would be one of the most important in cinema. This, however, represents the end of the trial period before his finest years. It is historically important but not very interesting.

p&d, Alexander Korda; w, Benno Vigny (based on the American film LAUGHTER, taken from a story by Harry D'Abbadie D'Arrast and Douglas Doty); ph, Harry Stradling; m, G. Zoka, Paul Barnaby, Ray Noble, Paul Maye, Jane Bos; ed, Harold Young.

Drama   **(PR:A   MPAA:NR)**

DIE, MONSTER, DIE***

(1965, Brit.) 78m AIP c
(AKA: MONSTER OF TERROR)

Boris Karloff (Nahum Witley), Nick Adams (Stephen Reinhart), Freda Jackson (Letitia Witley), Suzan Farmer (Susan Witley), Terence De Marney (Merwyn), Patrick McGee (Dr. Henderson), Paul Farrell (Jason), George Moon (Cab Driver), Gretchen Franklin (Miss Bailey), Sydney Bromley (Pierce), Billy Milton (Henry), Leslie Dwyer (Potter).

Slow-moving but effective adaptation of H.P. Lovecraft's story, "The Color out of Space," which was the first directing effort by Roger Corman's veteran art director, Daniel Haller. Karloff (in another standout performance) plays a wheelchair-bound scientist who has been trying to control experiments with a radioactive meteorite that can make plants grow to enormous proportions. When Adams, an American, arrives at Karloff's English mansion to visit his fiancee—the scientist's daughter—he notices strange things happening at the house. Karloff does not welcome this intrusion and tries to get the American to leave. Adams is then begged by his fiancee's bed-ridden mother (Jackson) to take her daughter away and leave the house as soon as possible. Adams investigates, but is attacked by the now horribly mutated Jackson, who suddenly collapses into a fiery spray of ashes. Karloff finally realizes he can no longer control the meteor and tries to destroy it, but in the process is mutated himself and attempts to kill his daughter and her fiance. Losing his footing, Karloff falls to the bottom of the staircase and bursts into flames. Soon the house itself is consumed, and the young couple barely escape with their lives. One of the few even marginally successful adaptations of Lovecraft, helped immensely by Karloff. Director Haller tried Lovecraft again in his THE DUNWICH HORROR (1970) with similar results.

p, Pat Green; d, Daniel Haller; w, Jerry Sohl (based on the story "The Color Out Of Space" by H.P. Lovecraft); ph, Paul Beeson (Colorscope, Pathecolor); m, Don Banks; ed, Alfred Cox; md, Philip Martell; art d, Colin Southcott; spec eff, Wally Veevers, Ernest Sullivan.

Horror   **(PR:C   MPAA:NR)**

DIE SCREAMING, MARIANNE**   (1970, Brit.) 104m London Screen c

Susan George (Marianne), Barry Evans (Eli Frome), Christopher Sandford (Sebastian Smith), Judy Huxtable (Hildegarde), Leo Genn (Judge), Kenneth Hendel (Rodriguez), Anthony Sharp (Registrar), Martin Wyldeck (Policeman).

George, a nightclub dancer in Portugal, is the illegitimate daughter of a corrupt judge and she is stalked by a gang of killers who plan to get to her father's money through her, via a blackmailing scheme.

p&d, Pete Walker; w, Murray Smith.

Crime   **Cas.**   **(PR:O   MPAA:NR)**

DIFFERENT SONS*   (1962, Jap.) 95m Toho c (FUTARI NO MUSUKO)

Akira Takarada (Kensuke), Yuzo Kayama (Shoji), Kamatari Fujiwara (Father), Yuko Mochizuki (Mother), Yumi Shirakawa (Kensuke's Wife), Yoko Fujiyama (Daughter), Mie Hama. Chisako Hara, Hiroshi Koizumi, Masami Taura, Yu Fujuki, Takashi Shimura.

Japanese melodrama has Takarada refusing to help his aging and impoverished parents until his brother wrecks his taxi, his sister is run over by a train while fleeing a jealous suitor with a knife, and his father tries to commit suicide. Oriental audiences apparently love this sort of thing. Occidentals are likely to laugh.

p, Sanezumi Fujimoto; d, Yasuki Chiba; w, Zenzo Masuyama; ph, Masao Tamai (Tohoscope, Eastmancolor); m, Akira Ifukube.

Drama   **(PR:O   MPAA:NR)**

DIFFERENT STORY, A**

(1978) 106m AE c

Perry King (Albert), Meg Foster (Stella), Valerie Curtin (Phyllis), Peter Donat (Sills), Richard Bull (Mr. Cooke), Barbara Collentine (Mrs. Cooke), Guerin Barry (Ned), Doug Higgins (Roger), Lisa James (Chris), Eugene Butler (Sam), Linda Carpenter (Chastity), Allan Hunt (Richard I), Burke Byrnes (Richard II), Eddie C. Dyer (Bernie), Richard Altman (Phyllis' neighbor), Richard Seff (Justice of the Peace), George Skaff (Mr. Hashmoni), Sid Conrad (Salesman), Trent Dolan, Dan Mahar (Deputies), Ted Richards III (Justin), Clarke Gordon (Taylor), Gypsi DeYoung (Mrs. Taylor),

Marion Perkins (Receptionist), Florence Di Re (Fitter), Gay Kleimenhapen (Patternmaker), Marie Denn (Coordinator), Kathryn Jackson (Nurse), Hatsuo Uda, Peter Furuta (Businessmen), Jennifer Dumas (Model), Eric Helland (Doorman), Philip Levien (Chicken Man), Stephen Nichols (Man at Bath), Derek Flint (Little Albert 1), Joshua Hansen (Little Albert 2).

Foster, a real estate agent, finds illegal alien King hiding out in an abandoned mansion, where he was dropped by a wealthy lover. She lets him stay at her place, where they both divulge that they are gay. One evening after too much boozing they make love—and like it! To avoid deportation for King, they get married and fall in love. The script slows down when King's suicidal ex-lover returns. Half of a really good film about a relationship between a gay man and woman, which resorts to stereotypes at the midpoint. The film tends to look at homosexuality on a rather blind level, believing that once gays get to know heterosexual life they'll like it and turn straight. Could have been better.

p, Alan Belkin; d, Paul Aaron; w, Henry Olek; ph, Philip Lathrop (CFI Color); m, David Frank; ed, Lynn McCallon; set d, Lee Poll; cos, Robert Demora, Agnes Lyon; m/l, Bob Wahler.

Drama   **Cas.**   **(PR:O   MPAA:R)**

DIFFICULT LOVE, A

(SEE: CLOSELY WATCHED TRAINS, 1967, Czech.)

DIFFICULT YEARS**½

(1950, Ital.) 90m Lopert bw

Umberto Spadaro (Aldo Piscitello), Massimo Girotti (Giovanni), Ave Ninchi (Rosina), Odette Bedogni (Elena), Ernesto Almirante (Grandpa), Di Stefano brothers (The Twins), Milly Vitale (Maria), Enzo Biliotti (Baron), Carletto Sposito (Baron's Son), Loris Gizzi (Fascist Minister), Aldo Silvani (Pharmacist), Turi (American).

A story of a sympathetic government clerk, Spadaro, who is forced by his employer and his wife to join the Fascist party. After Mussolini's dictatorship falls, the Allied Military Government moves in and wrongly accuses Spadaro of being a devout Fascist. The direction is sporadic, but its impact is felt nonetheless. English dialog written by Arthur Miller and spoken by John Garfield, both outspoken anti-fascists, is meant to shed light on the political situation, but instead is cumbersome and distracting. (In Italian; English subtitles.)

p, Fasco Laudati; d, Luigi Zampa; w, Sergio Amedei, Vitaliano Brancati, Franco Evangeliste, Enrico Fulchignoni (based on the novel by Brancati); ph, Carlo Montuori; m, Franco Casavola; English commentary, Arthur Miller; narrator, John Garfield.

War Drama   **(PR:C   MPAA:NR)**

DIG THAT JULIET   (SEE: ROMANOFF AND JULIET, 1961)

DIG THAT URANIUM**

(1956) 61m AA bw

Leo Gorcey (Slip), Huntz Hall (Sach), Bernard Gorcey (Louie), Mary Beth Hughes (Jeanette), Raymond Hatton (Mac), Harry Lauter (Haskell), Myron Healey (Joe Hody), Richard Powers (Frank Loomis), Paul Fierro (Indian), David Condon (Chuck), Bennie Bartlett (Butch), Carl Switzer (Shifty Robertson), Francis McDonald (Chief), Frank Jenks (Olaf), Don Harvey (Tex), David Gorcey (Chuck).

Standard stuff from the Bowery Boys. This time they're in the desert digging for riches in their uranium mine, and a gang of evildoers are on their trail. Highpoint is a dream sequence shootout which pays homage to HIGH NOON. (See BOWERY BOYS series, Index.)

p, Ben Schwalb; d, Edward Bernds; w, Elwood Ullman, Bert Lawrence; ph, Harry Neumann; ed, Lester A. Sansome; William Austin; md, Marlin Skiles; art d, David Milton.

Comedy   **(PR:A   MPAA:NR)**

DIGBY, THE BIGGEST DOG IN THE WORLD*

(1974, Brit.) 88m Cinerama c

Jim Dale (Jeff), Spike Milligan (Dr. Harz), Angela Douglas (Janine), John Bluthal (Jerry), Norman Rossington (Tom), Milo O'Shea (Dr. Jameson), Richard Beaumont (Billy White), Dinsdale Landon (Col. Masters), Garfield Morgan (Rogerson), Victor Spinetti (Prof. Ribart), Harry Towb (Ringmaster), Kenneth J. Warren (Gen. Frank), Bob Todd (The Great Manzini), Margaret Stuart (Assistant), Molly Urquart (Aunt Ina), Victor Maddern (Dog Home Manager), Frank Thornton (Estate Agent), Sandra Caron (General's Aide), Edward Underdown (Grandfather), Ben Aris (Army Captain), Sheila Steafel (Control Operator), Clovissa Newcombe (Bunny Girl), Rob Stewart (Train Driver).

Digby, as the title claims, is a big ol' dog who was a cute little pup before he lapped up a special enlarging chemical meant to produce bigger vegetables. The gargantuan canine makes for the usual sight gags, culminating when Digby licks up a vast lake. Beaumont, the dog's owner, tries to locate a reducing serum before the army blasts his pup into oblivion. Film drags because there are too many times when Digby and owner aren't on the screen, replaced instead with some not-so-comic comics. Producer Shenson also delivered Beatle films HELP! and A HARD DAY'S NIGHT.

p, Walter Shenson; d, Joseph McGrath; w, Michael Pertwee (based on the book by Ted Key); ph, Harry Waxman (Technicolor); m, Edwin T. Astley; ed, Jim Connock; art d, Maurice Fowler; spec eff, Tom come Howard; m/l, Astley, Lily and Leslie Sanderson.

Fantasy/Children   **(PR:AAA   MPAA:G)**

DILLINGER**

(1945) 70m King Bros./MON bw

Edmund Lowe (Specs), Anne Jeffreys (Helen), Lawrence Tierney (Dillinger), Eduardo Ciannelli (Murph), Marc Lawrence (Doc), Elisha Cook, Jr. (Kirk), Ralph

Lewis *(Tony)*, Ludwig Stossel *(Otto)*, Else Jannsen *(Mrs. Otto)*, Hugh Prosser *(Guard)*, Dewey Robinson *(Guard)*, Bob Perry *(Proprietor)*, Kid Chisel *(Watchman)*, Billy Nelson *(Watchman)*, Lee "Lassea" White *(Salesman)*, Lou Lubin *(Walter)*, Constance Worth *(Blonde)*.

This was the film that brought Tierney to fame, even though this had little to do with the real facts of the Dillinger gang or Dillinger himself. Tierney plays the part as a crazed killer who incidentally robs banks, even murdering his mentor, Lowe, by taking an ax to his head while they are "cooling off" in the North Woods of Wisconsin. Jeffreys is the so-called "Lady in Red" who turns Tierney into the FBI. The whole script is fantasy by veteran scripter Yordan who obviously didn't do a bit of research, although J. Edgar Hoover approved of his script. Dillinger as a subject was for years a taboo in Hollywood since studios feared angering Hoover in any kind of interpretation of this desperado since his disappearance in 1934 (contrary to Hoover's insistence, most hard evidence points to the fact that Dillinger was never killed but that another was slain in his place). Giannelli, Lawrence and Cook give good renditions of gangsters in this potboiler, shot on a meager budget and earning a reputation by being banned in its initial release in Chicago and other midwestern cities where Dillinger once dallied.

p, Maurice and Franklin King; d, Max Nosseck; w, Leon Charles, Phil Yordan; ph, Jackson Rose; m, Dimitri Tiomkin; ed, Otto Lovering, Edward Mann; spec eff, Robert Clark.

Crime/Biography **(PR:C-O MPAA:NR)**

DILLINGER zero (1973) 107m AIP c

Warren Oates *(John Dillinger)*, Ben Johnson *(Melvin Purvis)*, Michelle Phillips *(Billie Frechette)*, Cloris Leachman *(Anna Sage)*, Harry Dean Stanton *(Homer Van Meter)*, Geoffrey Lewis *(Harry Pierpont)*, John Ryan *(Charles Mackley)*, Richard Dreyfuss *(Baby Face Nelson)*, Steve Kanaly *(Pretty Boy Floyd)*, John Martino *(Eddie Martin)*, Roy Jenson *(Samuel Cowley)*, Red Morgan *(Big Jim Wollard)*, Frank McRae *(Reed Youngblood)*, Jerry Summers *(Tommy Carroll)*, Terry Leonard *(Theodore "Handsome Jack" Klutas)*, Bob Harris *(Ed Fulton)*.

Although Oates bears some resemblance to Dillinger, this film, like its 1945 predecessor, has little to do with the facts, and, despite its big budget, antique cars and good costuming, is even more laughable than the Tierney programmer. Director Milius is wholly unconcerned with portraying the criminals of the 1930s as they really were, mixing up facts and fiction in a tasteless stew of violence, blood and human gore. He has Homer Van Meter (Stanton) shotgunned to death by farmers when this gangster was shot in a St. Paul, Minnesota, alley by police. He has Charles Arthur "Pretty Boy" Floyd (Kanaly) killed in Wisconsin when he was shot to death in Ohio. Milius' attitude is blatant—that he can offer the viewing public this kind of history and they will accept it as fact, as he did in the ridiculous WIND AND THE LION. His direction is erratic, ungainly, and so boring that the long lulls are only brought to life by machinegun fire. The dialog, also courtesy of the egotistical Mr. Milius, is inane, out of period, and could have been written better by a high school student in Composition One. Oates merely swaggers through a role for which he is entirely miscast, appearing juvenile and amateurish; in fact, Tierney's performance is good by comparison and Lawrence Tierney was an absolute stranger to talent. This is the kind of mess only Milius can make, an awful offal no amount of tissue can wipe away.

p, Buzz Feitshans; d&w, John Milius; ph, Jules Brenner; m, Barry Devorzon; ed, Fred Feitshans, Jr.; art d, Trevor Williams; set d, Charles Pierce; cos, James George, Barbara Siebert; spec eff, A.D.Flowers, Cliff Wenger; m/l, "We're in the Money," Harry Warren, Al Dubin; "Just One More Chance," Arthur Johnston, Sam Coslow; "Honey," Seymour Simons, Harry Gillispie, Richard A. Whiting; "Happy Days Are Here Again," Milton Ager, Jack Yellen; "It's Easy to Remember," Richard Rodgers, Lorenz Hart; "Beyond the Blue Horizon," W. Franke Harling, Whiting, Leo Robin; "Red River Valley," (traditional); stunts, Max Kleven; makeup, Tom Ellingwood.

Crime **Cas.** **(PR:O MPAA:R)**

DILLINGER IS DEAD** (1969, Ital.) 90m Pegaso Film/Italnieggio c

Michel Piccoli *(Glauco)*, Anita Pallenberg *(His Wife)*, Annie Girardot *(Maid)*.

This Italian import has nothing to do with the 1930s bankrobber but deals with Piccoli, an industrial designer who finds an old gun while making himself some dinner. He cleans it up while boiling pasta, then takes it to bed where he suddenly uses it to shoot his wife to death, after bedding the maid. He casually gets into his car, drives to the Coast and then jumps into the ocean, swimming out to a ship sailing for Tahiti. A bizarre fantasy on the dark side that bends a Walter Mitty image into a skull and crossbones.

p, Alfred Levy, Ever Haggiag; d, Marco Ferreri; w, Ferreri, Sergio Bazzini; ph, Mario Vulpiani; m, Tec Usuelli; ed, Mirella Mencio; art d, Nicola Tamburro.

Crime Drama **(PR:O MPAA:NR)**

DIMBOOLA*½** (1979, Aus.) 89m Pram Factory/Greater Union c

Bruce Spence *(Morris McAdam)*, Natalie Bate *(Maureen Delaney)*, Max Gillies *(Vivien Wooster-Jones)*, Bill Garner *(Dangle)*, Kerry Dwyer *(Vivien's Girl)*, Chad Morgan *(Bayonet)*, Tim Robertson *(Father O'Shea)*, Barry Barkla *(Priest)*, Jack Perry *(M.C.)*, Claire Binney *(Stripper)*, John Murphy *(Doctor)*, Max Cullen, Helen Sky, Dick May, Irene Hewitt, Alan Rowe, Esme Melville, Terry McDermott, Paul Hampton, Evelyn Krape, Val Jellay, Sue Ingleton, Laurel Frank, Claire Dobbin, Fay Mokotow, Max Fairchild, Phil Motherwell, Matt Burns, Frankie Raymond, Sandra Evans, Matchbox.

A visually stunning comedy about the inhabitants of Dimboola, a small Australian town, and an English visitor. Gillies, a newsman for the London *Times*, arrives in the town to write a story and finds that his trip coincides with a much-anticipated wedding. In drag, he sneaks into the bride's wedding shower, then later attends the stripper-laden stag party. A delightful assortment of characters are featured, including the groom's mother, who fears that a past affair may also make her the mom of the bride. An introspective look at life down under, which draws parallels to the work of Peter Weir (PICNIC AT HANGING ROCK; THE LAST WAVE). The spindly Spence outshines his supporters and would later appear in ROAD WARRIOR.

p, John Weiley; d, John Duigan; w, Jack Hibberd (based on a play by Hibberd); ph, Tom Cowan (Panavision, Eastmancolor); m, George Dreyfus; ed, Tony Paterson; art d, Larry Eastwood.

Comedy **(PR:O MPAA:NR)**

DIME WITH A HALO½** (1963) 94m MGM bw

Barbara Luna *(Juanita)*, Roger Mobley *(Jose)*, Rafael Lopez *(Chuy Perez)*, Paul Langton *(Mr. Jones)*, Robert Carrcart *(Cashier)*, Manuel Padilla *(Rafael)*, Larry Domasin *(Cesar)*, Tony Maxwell *(Domingo)*, Vito Scotti *(Doorman)*, Jay Adler *(Mr. Lewis)*, Theodore Newton *(Consul Glenson)*, Steven Geray *(Priest)*, Jeno Mate *(Mr. Gonzales)*, Joan Connors *(Stripper)*, Tina Menard *(Mexican Woman)*, Raymond Sanchez *(Newsboy)*.

Padilla, a lovable seven-year old moppet with unrelenting cuteness, steals this Tijuana-based charmer. A quintet of kiddies, who one day "borrow" a dime from the church charity box, place a wager and win big. They have considerable trouble redeeming the blessed ticket, though. The betmaker skips town, and they have to search him out. They eventually find him, but he has a heart attack at the cashier's window, dropping the ticket. In the bustle, it sticks to the bottom of some lucky patron's shoe and is gone forever. A claustrophobic atmosphere which reeks of artificiality, but is brightened by the bright-eyed bunch.

p, Laslo Vadnay, Hans Wilheim; d, Boris Sagal; w, Vadnay, Wilheim; ph, Philip H. Lathrop; m, Ronald Stein; ed, Ralph E. Winters; art d, Charles Myall; set d, Karl Brainard, Bruce MacDonald.

Drama **(PR:A MPAA:NR)**

DIMENSION 5*½
(1966) 88m United Pictures-Harold Goldman/Feature Films c

Jeffrey Hunter *(Justin Power)*, France Nuyen *(Kitty)*, Harold Sakata *(Big Buddha)*, Donald Woods *(Cane)*, Linda Ho *(Nancy Ho)*, Robert Ito *(Sato)*, David Chow *(Stoneface)*, Lee Kolima *(Genghis)*, Jon Lormer, Bill Walker, Virginia Lee, Ken Spalding, Carol Byron, Kam Tong, Tad Horino, Gerald Jann, Maggie Thrett, Kay Michaels, Marianna Case, Deanna Lund, Robert Phillips, Allen Jung, John McKee, Ruth Foster, Tex Armstrong, Ed Parker, Tita Marsell.

Hunter is a secret agent for Espionage, Inc., and he's sent to stop the nuclear bombing of Los Angeles by a Chinese communist organization called the Dragon. With his assistant, Nuyen, and time-travel belts, Hunter is able to save L.A. and put an end to the Dragon organization.

p, Earle Lyon; d, Franklin Adreon; w, Arther C. Pierce; ph, Alan Stensvold (Technicolor); m, Paul Dunlap; ed, Robert S. Eisen; art d, Paul Sylos, Jr.

Science Fiction/Adventure **(PR:A MPAA:NR)**

DIMKA½** (1964, USSR) 77m Gorky Film Studio/Artkino bw
(YA KUPIL PAPU)

Alyosha Zagorskiy *(Dimka)*, Olga Lysenko *(His Mother)*, Vladimir Treschalov *(Andrey)*, S. Ageyeva, M. Gavrilko, V. Klyukin, A. Kasapov, L. Kardonskiy, Lenya Nikitin, Z. Naryshkina, V. Orlova, Vova Semyonov, K. Slavinskiy, A. Strelnikova, V. Taube, G. Frolov, A. Chizova.

Young Zagorskiy decides to skip school one day to look for a father. He has a series of adventures in downtown Moscow before he meets Treschalov, who is charmed by the boy and takes him to an amusement park. When he takes the boy home at the end of the day, Zagorskiy insists he come in and meet his mother. There is an awkward meeting, but as Treschalov leaves Zagorskiy hopes he will return. Absolutely charming film keeps its point of view the child's at all times, and the camera work is superb.

d, Ilya Frez; w, Volf Dolgiy (based on a story by V. Biryukova); ph, Mikahil Kirillov; m, Nikolay Yakolev; ed, V. Mironova; art d, Sergey Serebrenikov; cos, N. Muller.

Comedy/Children **(PR:AA MPAA:NR)**

DIMPLES*** (1936) 78m FOX bw

Shirley Temple *(Sylvia Dolores Appleby [Dimples])*, Frank Morgan *(Prof. Eustace Appleby)*, Helen West *(Mrs. Caroline Drew)*, Robert Kent *(Allen Drew)*, Delma Byron *(Betty Loring)*, Astrid Allwyn *(Cleo Marsh)*, Stepin Fetchit *(Cicero)*, Berton Churchill *(Col. Loring)*, Paul Stanton *(Mr. St. Clair)*, Yulius Tannen *(Hawkins)*, John Carradine *(Richards)*, Herman Bing *(Proprietor)*, Billy McClain *(Rufus)*, The Hall Johnson Choir *(Choir)*, Jack Clifford *(Uncle Tom)*, Betty Jean Hainey *(Topsy)*, Arthur Aylesworth *(Pawnbroker)*, Greta Meyer *(Proprietor's Wife)*, Leonard Kilbrick, Warner, Walter and George Weidler *(Children's Band)*, Jessie Scott, Thurman Black *(The Two Black Dots)*.

An emotional roller-coaster starring curly-top Temple in mid-19th century New York City. The location is the only thing new in this formulated drama. The penniless granddaughter of petty thief Morgan, Temple earns a few cents singing in the streets while grampa empties the pockets of the enthralled onlookers. They get the chance to entertain for high society dame Westley, who, as expected, falls in love with Temple. She offers Morgan $5,000 to adopt her and the little ragamuffin persuades him to take the cash. After later expressing displeasure with her new mom, Shirley is reunited with Morgan, who returns the money. A tearjerker in which Morgan gives the little thespian a challenge in her top-billing. Robinson's dance routines, as one has come to expect, are top notch, allowing Temple's magic toes to effortlessly move her about. Songs include: "Hey, What Did the Bluebird Say?" "He Was a Dandy," "Picture Me Without You," "Oh

Mister Man up in the Moon," "Dixie-Anna," "Get on Board," and "Swing Low Sweet Chariot" (Negro spiritual).

p, Darryl F. Zanuck; d, William A. Seiter; w, Arthur Sheekman, Nar Perrin (based on an idea by Nunnally Johnson); ph, Bert Glennon; ed, Herbert Levy; art d, William Darling; set d, Thomas Little; md, Louis Silvers; ch, Bill Robinson.

Musical/Drama **(PR:AAA MP:NR)**

DINER**** (1982) 110m MGM-UA c

Steve Guttenberg *(Eddie)*, Daniel Stern *(Shrevie)*, Mickey Rourke *(Boogie)*, Kevin Bacon *(Fenwick)*, Timothy Daly *(Billy)*, Ellen Barkin *(Beth)*, Paul Reiser *(Modell)*, Kathryn Dowling *(Barbara)*, Michael Tucker *(Bagel)*, Jessica James *(Mrs. Simmons)*, Colette Blonigan *(Carol Heathrow)*, Kelle Kipp *(Diane)*, John Aquino *(Tank)*, Richard Pierson *(David Frazer)*, Claudia Cron *(Jane Chisholm)*, Tait Ruppert, Tom V.V. Tammi, Pam Gail, Lauren Zaganas, Sharon Ziman, Mark Margolis, Ralph Tabakin, Frank Stoegerer, Nat Benchley, Frank Hennessy, Marvin Hunter, Steve Smith, Lee Case, Clement Fowler.

An auspicious directorial debut for Levinson as he takes us back to the Baltimore of his youth in the late 1950s. On paper or in a conference room, who would have thought that a story about that city at that time would have such appeal? Levinson betrays his writing background as he spends a great deal of time establishing all the characterizations and makes no attempt to dazzle us with cinematic tricks. Five close pals are seen in various crises as they meet at their favorite diner in between problems with women, gambling, and all the attendant woes that go with being twenty-or-so years old. Anyone who has grown up in an urban center knows what it means to have a "gang" (male or female) of friends that one can always rely upon. This gang consists of Guttenberg, who has been engaged for five years and is trying to stay single so he forces his fiancee to pass the world's toughest Baltimore Colts football quiz in order to qualify for marriage; Stern as the married one who would rather spend time with the guys than sit home with a wife who doesn't understand him; Daly has a pregnant girl friend whom he would like to marry, but she is one of the earliest feminists and will get married in her own sweet time, if she chooses to at all; Bacon is rich and usually bombed; and Rourke is the half-rebel, half preppy. He is a hairdresser-law student and spends most of his spare time chasing women. Every one of those boys is recognizable in one way or another and even Reiser (Modell) has a small part as a guy who joins them at the diner but never buys anything, preferring instead to finish everyone else's food. We *all* knew someone like that, right? Even though the music keeps our minds back in the era (Darin, Domino, Elvis, Berry, et al.), the picture is about an era that may be returning; when young people got married, voted Republican, drank cocktails instead of drugs, etc. This picture could have been made in 1959, when it was set, and might have been more successful. As it was, DINER did not turn the turnstiles the way it should have. Perhaps people wanted the escapism of Spielberg and Lucas and not the joyful memories of Levinson. There is not one false note in the picture, either in the script or the performances. Sad to say that Levinson went from this to the disappointing THE NATURAL. There is a character in MY SISTER EILEEN who tells sister Ruth that she ought to write about what she knows rather than attempt things about which she has no knowledge. It's obvious that Levinson knew his subject here but not enough people cared. If you see this in a theater or on a cassette where the free TV censors have not put their shears to it, you will come away glowing with good-natured laughter and memories, even if you didn't live through the period.

p, Jerry Weintraub; d&w, Barry Levinson; ph, Peter Sova (Metrocolor); m, Bruce Brody, Ivan Kral; ed, Stu Linder; art d, Leon Harris; set d, R. Chris Westlund; cos, Gloria Gresham. (Note: Joe Tuley is sometimes credited with music as well.)

Comedy/Drama **Cas.** **(PR:C-O MPAA:R)**

DING DONG WILLIAMS** (1946) 61m RKO bw (GB: MELODY MAKER)

Glenn Vernon *(Ding Dong Williams)*, Marcy McGuire *(Angela)*, Felix Bressart *(Hugo)*, Anne Jeffreys *(Vanessa)*, James Warren *(Steve)*, William Davidson *(Saul)*, Tom Noonan *(Zang)*, Cliff Nazarro *(Zing)*, Ruth Lee *(Laura Cooper)*, Jason Robards *(Kenmore)*, Bob Nolan and the Sons of the Pioneers, Richard Kirbel.

A musical showcase in which music director Bressart hires Vernon, a hot clarinetist, to compose a blues symphony for a new film. Vernon lets on that he can't read or write music—he just plays how he feels. Two musical arrangers, Noonan and Nazarro, are assigned the task of writing what he plays. The obstacle is that when his mood shifts so does his music, so they must concoct a way to stabilize him. Musical selections include a performance by 11-year-old piano virtuoso Korbel of Grieg's Piano Concerto and Chopin's "Fantasie Impromptu." Also included are "I Saw You First," "Candlelight and Wine" (Harold Adamson, Jimmy McHugh), and "Cool Water" (Bob Nolan).

p, Herman Schlom; d, William Berke; w, Brenda Weisberg, M. Coates Webster (based on *Collier's* Magazine stories by Richard English); ph, Frank Redman; ed, Les Millbrook; md, C. Bakaleinikoff; art d, Albert D'Agostino, Lucius Croxton; set d, Darrell Silvers.

Musical Comedy **(PR:A MPAA:NR)**

DINGAKA** (1965, South Africa) 98m Jamie Uys/EM c

Stanley Baker *(Tom Davis)*, Juliet Prowse *(Marion Davis)*, Ken Gampu *(Ntuku Makwena)*, Siegfried Mynhardt *(Judge)*, Bob Courtney *(Prison Chaplain)*, Gordon Hood *(Prosecutor)*, George Moore *(Legal Aid Society Secretary)*, Hugh Rouse *(Bantu Commissioner)*, Simon Swindell *(Doctor)*, Willem Botha *(Court Clerk)*, John Sithebe *(Witch Doctor)*, Paul Makgoba *(Masaba)*, Sophie MqCina *(Choir Soloist)*, Jimmy Sabe *(Lead Singer)*, Daniel Marolen *(Priest)*, Clement Mehlomakulu *(Dancer)*, Cocky Tlhotlhhalemji *(Priest)*, Flora Motaung *(Rurari)*, Fuzi Zazayokwe *(Stick Fighter)*, Thembi *(Oniku)*, Thandi *(Letsea)*.

Gampu, member of a South African tribe, finds one of his twin daughters murdered. He learns that Makgoba killed her for her blood, a potion he must drink to win back his title as stick fighting champion. Gampu murders Makgoba and is arrested. Baker is assigned the case but his wife, Prowse, takes more interest in Gampu's plight. Gampu is sentenced to two years of hard labor and when he gets out he returns to his village and kills the village witch doctor, Sithebe, who prescribed the potion for Makgoba. The village is then free from the power and superstitions of the witch doctor, and Gampu goes to Johannesburg to clear his name with the help of Baker and Prowse. Tribal sequences seem to be a lot of make-believe about a subject that does have dignity of its own.

p,d&w, Jamie Ulys; ph, Manie Botha, Judex C. Vijoen (CinemaScope, Technicolor); m, Bertha Egnos, Eddie Domingo, Basil Gray; ed, John Jympson; art d, Ian MacLeod, Kay Dubinski; cos, Ruth St. Moritz, Anna Richter-Visser; ch, Sheila Wartski.

Drama **(PR:A MPAA:NR)**

DINKY*½ (1935) 65m WB bw

Jackie Cooper *(Dinky)*, Mary Astor *(Mrs. Daniels)*, Roger Pryor *(Tom Marsden)*, Henry Armetta *(The Junkman)*, Bette Jean Haney *(Mary)*, Henry O'Neill *(Mr. Barnes)*, Jimmy Butler *(Cadet Lane)*, George Ernest *(Jojo)*, Edith Fellows *(Sally)*, Sidney Miller *(Sammy)*, Richard Quine *(Jackie Shaw)*, Frank Gernardi *(Mike)*, Clay Clement *(Gerald Standish)*, Florence Fair *(Mrs. Shaw)*, Joseph Crehan *(Supt. Orphanage)*, Addison Richards *(District Attorney)*, James Burke *(Truck Driver)*.

A Cooper who has outgrown the child roles that made him famous stars in this implausible picture about a military cadet and his mom, Astor, who has been jailed for fraud in a frameup. She tries her best to keep her son from learning that she is behind bars, but a classmate broadcasts the news. Cooper enters an orphanage and adapts the same ruse, deception, to keep Mom thinking he is still in the academy. A weak plot makes this one tough to latch on to.

d, D. Ross Lederman, Howard Bretherton; w, Harry Sauber (based on a story by John Fante, Frank Fenton, Samuel Gilson Brown); ph, Arthur Edeson; ed, Thomas Richards; art d, John Hughes.

Drama **(PR:A MPAA:NR)**

DINNER AT EIGHT***** (1933) 113m MGM bw

Marie Dressler *(Carlotta Vance)*, John Barrymore *(Larry Renault)*, Wallace Beery *(Dan Packard)*, Jean Harlow *(Kitty Packard)*, Lionel Barrymore *(Oliver Jordan)*, Lee Tracy *(Max Kane)*, Edmund Lowe *(Dr. Wayne Talbot)*, Billie Burke *(Mrs. Oliver Jordan)*, Madge Evans *(Paula Jordan)*, Jean Hersholt *(Joe Stengel)*, Karen Morley *(Mrs. Wayne Talbot)*, Louise Closser Hale *(Hattie Loomis)*, Phillips Holmes *(Ernest DeGraff)*, May Robson *(Mrs. Wendel)*, Grant Mitchell *(Ed Loomis)*, Phoebe Foster *(Miss Alden)*, Elizabeth Patterson *(Miss Copeland)*, Hilda Vaughn *(Tina, Kitty's Maid)*, Harry Beresford *(Fosdick)*, Edwin Maxwell *(Mr. Fitch, the Hotel Manager)*, John Davidson *(Mr. Hatfield, the Assistant Manager)*, Edward Woods *(Eddie)*, George Baxter *(Gustave, the Butler)*, Herman Bing *(The Waiter)*, Anna Duncan *(Dora, the Maid)*, Herbert Bunston, May Beatty.

Few star-packed vehicles work, being so overloaded with name talent that their roles are cut to short takes and the dazzled viewer is too busy eye-darting from famous face to famous face to follow even the most cursory plot line. Yet DINNER AT EIGHT succeeds with an all-star cast and on a powerful level, telling separate stories that lead to a final conclusion. Flighty, self-centered Burke decides to give a formal dinner party for an aristocratic British couple. She concerns herself only with the details of the fete and maintaining her socialite image, disregarding her exhausted husband Lionel Barrymore, who suffers from a weakening heart and who is about to lose his shipping line. The guest list is short and sweet and all of the invited are as different as land and sea. From the moment the invitations are mailed to the time the guests arrive, the individual tales spin forth, encircling each other. Lionel Barrymore, a kind-hearted self-made man, receives a visit from Dressler in his office. She's an almost forgotten stage star of the 1890s, down to pennies, thin luck. All she has is some stock in Barrymore's firm and she asks him to buy it back, begging him to be discreet. He's an old beau of hers with a warm spot for her. Even though he's next to broke, Barrymore purchases the stock, telling Dressler that he's looking forward to seeing her that night at dinner. Beery, a rough-and-tumble entrepreneur, who immediately buys Dressler's stock, learns from his brassy, social-climbing wife, Harlow, that they have been invited to dine at the very home of the man he is trying to financially ruin. At first Beery adamantly refuses to go but one-time hat-check girl Harlow convinces him that meeting the British couple, the influential Ferncliffes, will further his fortunes. (Her motive is to ingratiate herself to British society.) No sooner does Beery depart than Lowe arrives to see his paramour Harlow. He is a doctor who regrets the affair and is trying to back out. His wife, Morley, later tells him she knows he is seeing Harlow but she is so understanding that Lowe decides to break off the affair and stay with his spouse. Another guest, John Barrymore, a fading matinee idol, will never make it to dinner at eight. He begins his day by secretly seeing Evans, Lionel's daughter, with whom he is trysting and using financially, for his days as a money-making star are over. Next Barrymore insults the one producer, Hersholt, still willing to take a chance on him and loses a vital comeback part. Hersholt explodes at the insult to his generosity, inspecting the ruins of a once-proud actor, snarling: "You sag, Renault, like an old woman...You're a corpse...go get yourself buried!" He does, after his unsympathetic agent, Tracy, mercilessly chastises him for the boozing and wenching that has destroyed his talent. In his cheap flat, Barrymore turns on the gas, then sprawls awkwardly in a chair, inhaling death. Before the last gasp he draws himself up to a noble posture, fixes a light behind his head and reclines so that his great profile is accented, a last little conceit before death. Battling all the way, Harlow and Beery manage to arrive that night at Burke's mansion. Billie has exhausted herself preparing a sumptuous dinner for the Ferncliffes but at the last minute she learns that the British couple will not attend. She drops her Park Avenue pose and shrieks:"Those miserable cockneys!" At this point she sees her ailing husband Lionel and begins to show him some concern. As the guests file toward the elegant dining room Harlow tries to make some witty chit-chat with Dressler, working hard to appear cultured, anything but the product of the streets. "I was reading a book the other day," she remarks. "It's all about civilization or something...Do you know the guy said machinery is going to take the place of every profession." Dressler gives her a long pop-eyed scan, taking in that curvaceous body to which clings a revealing dress. At fade-out Dressler quips back: "That's something you'll never have to worry about!" DINNER AT EIGHT is a masterpiece where the very deliberate Cukor, known for his long takes, carefully pieces together the vignettes of his subjects. All the principals act their roles to perfection. Lionel Barrymore creaks with failing health, Burke bubbles idiotically, Tracy wisecracks ruthlessly, Lowe murmurs a bedside manner as if treating his own soul, and Dressler is magnificent as the theatrical dowager gracefully struggling to preserve her slipping life style and image, as well as that of her era. Her role of Carlotta Vance is almost wholly patterned after the eccentric British actress, Mrs. Patrick Campbell, who had been a stage star at the turn of the century, one who acted in all of George Bernard Shaw's plays and was the playwright's then-favorite actress, as well as his writing pal. Mrs. Campbell went to Hollywood in the early 1930s but her eccentricities prevented her from being accepted in the movie community. She went everywhere with her white Pekingese, Moonbeam, in her arms. Dressler carries about the same kind of dog, utterly devoted to the animal which can do no wrong. When Dressler's dog makes a deposit in the hotel hallway where she resides Marie arches her famous heavy eyebrows and clucks disapproval, but no more. John Barrymore's intense and poignant role, many later said, was patterned after Barrymore himself, a fading movie actor destroying himself with drink, an unflattering role he had no difficulty playing. It is true that by the late 1930s Barrymore became just that, an obnoxious inebriate spouting foul words and urinating in hotel and restaurant lobbies. But in DINNER AT EIGHT this nightmare figure had not yet taken over Barrymore's personality and he worked hard to project the failure he was not at that time. Cukor was later to say of Barrymore: "Jack was a man with no vanity, and enormous knowledge and humor as all the Barrymores had. They were all fascinating creatures. They were really magical people." There was no magic between Harlow and Beery in this film. They insulted each other through all their scenes. At one point Harlow screams at her millionaire husband: "Who do you think you're talkin' to, that first wife of yours out in Montana? That poor mealy-faced thing with her flat chest that didn't have enough nerve to talk up to ya', washin' out your greasy overalls and cookin' and slavin' in some mining shack? No wonder she died. Ya' big windbag!" Big crude Beery lashes back: "Listen, you little piece of scum you...You can go back to that sweet-smelling family of yours, back of the railroad tracks in Passaic! And get this—if that sniveling, money-grubbing, whining old mother of yours comes fooling around my offices anymore, I'm going to give orders to have her thrown down those sixty flights of stairs, so help me!" The on-screen feuding was nothing to the battles Harlow and Beery had offscreen. They simply hated each other. Beery thought Harlow was nothing more than a studio tramp who had slept her way to stardom and he more or less said so to the feisty platinum blonde. She thought him to be rude and crude, a gargantuan, almost bestial person with no sensitivity whatsoever. (Beery would arrive on location in his western films, take some dirt and rub it on his face, then shout at the director: "I'm ready. My makeup is on!") Harlow was later quoted as saying that Beery was "a mean old sonofabitch whose grave I'd love to——on!" He was quoted saying of her: "That woman! If I had to spend the rest of my life on a desert island and I had to choose between the two of them, I'd pick Marie Dressler rather than Harlow." Beery and Dressler were always close friends, having appeared together in such classics as MIN AND BILL and TUGBOAT ANNIE. He had no illusions about himself, and knew that his gnarled, weather-beaten, ugly face was invaluable. "Like my dear old friend, Marie Dressler," he once droned, "my mug has been my fortune." Dressler was, by the early 1930s, making a comeback and she was immensely popular with audiences. She had appeared in films as early as 1914 with TILLIE'S PUNCTURED ROMANCE for Keystone, but had rooted her career in vaudeville and the stage. By the late 1920s her career was exactly like that of the grande dame she played in DINNER AT EIGHT, collapsing. MGM cast her in a number of solid character roles and by 1933 she was billed by that studio as "The World's Greatest Actress." She enjoyed her late-blooming film career only briefly, dying a year after DINNER AT EIGHT, studio mogul Louis B. Mayer personally attending her sickbed to such an extent that she put him off by saying: "You are trying to run my life." Harlow was never a favorite of Mayer's but was the product of MGM executive Paul Bern who later married her, but committed suicide shortly thereafter because of his sexual inadequacies. Her personal life was a disaster and she was a poor actress until doing her MGM films, where she blossomed as a bad girl who destroyed men, but one who had a good heart. To offset the black image of a vamp, Harlow, as in DINNER AT EIGHT, wore nothing but white dresses (always braless, being the first mammary-oriented sex symbol of the films) and her hair was bleached platinum white. Over her bright blue eyes she penciled dark eyebrows in a high arch. Most of the rooms of her Bel Air, California home were painted white, with white furniture. Her coats, negligees, bathing suits were all white. She sends off sparks in her role of the scheming vixen-like wife in DINNER AT EIGHT, a role so arresting that it earned her a *Time* magazine cover story. She, like Dressler, enjoyed a meteoric but brief fame, dying in 1937 after being in movies for only ten years. (The official death report said uremic poisoning, developed because her mother's religion prevented proper medical attention, but a few sources stated that Harlow's death was from an improperly conducted abortion, actor William Powell being the father of the unborn child.) The DINNER AT EIGHT script by Marion and Mankiewicz is faithful to the Kaufman-Ferber play. But the final upbeat remark rendered by Dressler to the ebullient Harlow was tacked on by Donald Ogden Stewart, one of the wittiest wags ever to write for the screen. A man of uncertain modesty, Stewart accepted an Oscar for his screenplay of THE PHILADELPHIA STORY by saying at the ceremonies: "I have no one to thank. I did it all myself." DINNER AT EIGHT, though it employed some of the studio's greatest stars, did not cost anywhere what its expensive look might suggest. Selznick brought it in for under $400,000 and $110,000 of that went to Kaufman and Ferber. Cukor used the big-name stars from two to twelve days, no more. The Breen Office took exception to DINNER AT EIGHT (Joseph I. Breen being the West Coast assistant to Will Hays, who headed the censorship board affixing production codes to films at the time). Selznick was told by Breen that he seemed to have a predilection for suicide in his movies and films such as ANNA KARENINA, WHAT PRICE HOLLYWOOD, and DINNER AT EIGHT were cited. It came as a shock to Selznick that the suicide theme was repeated in so many of his movies. To calm the censors, the scene where John Barrymore actually turns on the gas was cut in DINNER AT EIGHT. Selznick was forever proud of this film, taking particular delight that the chic set decorations of the movie had a considerable "effect upon interior decorating all over the world." In fact, the sets of this film helped to entrench art deco for which the early 1930s became famous. But what irked the producer were the remarks broadly bantered about after Mayer hired him when RKO terminated his contract, putting him in charge of such a stellar production. The most popular quip about Selznick, who had married Mayer's daughter, was that "the son-in-law also rises!" Selznick shrugged it off and went on making masterpieces, never turning back except once to say: "I have learned that nothing matters but the final picture."

p, David O. Selznick; d, George Cukor; w, Frances Marion, Herman J. Mankiewicz, Donald Ogden Stewart (based on the play by George S. Kaufman and Edna Ferber); ph, William Daniels; ed, Ben Lewis; art d, Cedric Gibbons; set d, Hobe Erwin, Fred Hope; cos, Adrian.

Comedy/Drama **(PR:C MPAA:NR)**

DINNER AT THE RITZ** (1937, Brit.) 75m New World/FOX bw

Annabella *(Ranie Racine)*, Paul Lukas *(Baron Philip de Beaufort)*, David Niven *(Paul de Brack)*, Romney Brent *(Jimmy Raine)*, Francis L. Sullivan *(Brogard)*, Stewart Rome *(Racine)*, Nora Swinburne *(Lady Railton)*, Tyrell Davis *(Duval)*, Frederick Leister *(Tarade)*, William Dewhurst *(Devine)*, Vivienne Chatterton *(Marthe)*, Ronald Shiner *(Sydney)*, Raymond Huntley *(Gibout)*, Ralph Truman *(Auctioneer)*, O.B. Clarence *(Messenger)*, Frederick Culley, Patricia Medina.

A confusing film which has Annabella, the daughter of a European financier who is murdered in a conspiracy, trying to find the murderer, with the help of Niven, a government agent. The story limps stodgily along until the end, when the leader of the conspirators, Lukas, an old flame of Annabella's, is exposed during a dinner at the Ritz. Interesting only as an early Niven vehicle, and as the third English-made film for Annabella, the most celebrated young actress in France at the time. She married Tyrone Power in 1939 after coming to the U.S., and divorced him in 1948, after which she returned to Europe.

p, Robert T. Kane; d, Harold D. Schuster; w, Roland Pertwee (based on a story by Pertwee, Romney Brent); ph, Philip Tannura; m, Lee Sims; ed, James B. Clark; cos, Rene Hubert.

Crime **Cas.** **(PR:A MPAA:NR)**

DINNER FOR ADELE
(SEE: ADELE HASN'T HAD HER SUPPER YET, 1978, Czech.)

DINO*** (1957) 93m AA bw

Sal Mineo *(Dino)*, Brian Keith *(Sheridan)*, Susan Kohner *(Shirley)*, Frank Faylen *(Mandel)*, Joe DeSantis *(Mr. Minetta)*, Penny Santon *(Mrs. Minetta)*, Pat DeSimone *(Tony)*, Richard Bakalyan *(Chuck)*, Mollie McCart *(Frances)*, Cindy Robbins *(Sylvia)*, Rafael Campos *(Second Boy)*, Don C. Harvey, Michael Mineo, Ken Miller, Joel Collins, Kip King, Byron Foulger.

A revealing performance which again has Mineo in the role of a juvenile delinquent. Recently released from prison where he was sent for being an accessory to a murder, he returns to his tough turf. Social worker Keith offers guidance to the confused juvenile, who has trouble understanding why, after years of abuse, he is treated with respect. Mineo displays his rebirth when his younger brother, who idolizes him, asks him along on a gang robbery. Instead of participating, he takes the kid to visit Keith, and they both straighten up. A gritty look at a character which, for Mineo, is an extension of his role as Plato in REBEL WITHOUT A CAUSE.

p, Bernice Block; d, Thomas Carr; w, Reginald Rose (based on his teleplay); ph, Wilfrid Cline; m, Gerald Fried; ed, William Austin; art d; David Milton; cos, Bert Henrickson.

Drama **(PR:A MPAA:NR)**

DINOSAURUS** (1960) 85m UNIV c

Ward Ramsey *(Bart Thompson)*, Paul Lukather *(Chuck)*, Kristina Hanson *(Betty Piper)*, Alan Roberts *(Julio)*, Gregg Martell *(Prehistoric Man)*, Fred Engelberg *(Mike Hacker)*, Luci Blain *(Chica)*, Jack Younger *(Jasper)*, Wayne Tredway *(Dumpy)*, Howard Dayton *(Mousey)*, James Logan *(O'Leary)*.

The story of two dinosaurs—a plant eater and a meat eater—and a comical caveman, all of whom are brought to life in modern times. The main thrust is the caveman's struggles to destroy the hungry and threatening carnivore. Slapstick is most fun when the Neanderthal is introduced to new-fangled technology. Definitely for the younger set.

p, Jack H. Harris, Irvin S. Yeaworth, Jr.; d, Yeaworth; w, Jean Yeaworth, Dan E. Weisburd (based on an idea by Harris); ph, Stanley Cortez (Cinemascope, DeLuxe Color); m, Ronald Stein; ed, John A. Bushelman; art d, Jack Senter; set d, Herman Schoebrun; spec eff, Tim Barr, Wah Chang, Gene Warren; makeup, Don Cash.

Fantasy **(PR:AA MPAA:NR)**

DION BROTHERS, THE (SEE: GRAVY TRAIN, THE, 1974)

DIPLOMANIACS½ (1933) 59m RKO bw

Bert Wheeler (Willy Milly), Robert Woolsey (Hercules Glub), Marjorie White (Dolores), Phyllis Barry (Fifi), Louis Calhern (Winklereid), Hugh Herbert (Chinaman), Richard Carle (Captain), William Irving (Schmerzenpuppen), Neely Edwards (Puppenschmerzen), Billy Bletcher (Schmerzenschmerzen), Teddy Hart (Puppenpuppen), Charles Coleman (Butler), Edward Cooper (Chief Adoop), Dewey Robinson (Peter The Hermit).

A likable comedy with Wheeler and Woolsey hired by the Adoop Indians to attend a Geneva peace conference in an attempt to stop the delegates from bickering. Co-penned by Joseph L. Mankiewicz, the script is on target and often ferociously funny. The absurd use of rhyming sing-song dialog is inventive.

d, William A. Seiter; w, Joseph L. Mankiewicz, Henry Myers (based on a story by Mankiewicz); ph, Edward Cronjager; m, Max Steiner; ed, William Hamilton; ch, Larry Ceballos; m/l, "Sing To Me," Harry Akst, Edward Eliscu.

Comedy **Cas.** **(PR:A MPAA:NR)**

DIPLOMATIC CORPSE, THE (1958, Brit.) 65m ACT Films/RFD bw

Robin Bailey (Mike Billings), Susan Shaw (Jenny Drew), Liam Redmond (Inspector Corcoran), Harry Fowler (Knocker Parsons), Maya Koumani (Marian Weaver), Andre Mikhelson (Hamid), Bill Shine (Humphrey Garrad), Charles Farrell (Percy Simpson), Peter Bathurst, Johnny Briggs, Frank Hawkins, George Street, Nicholas Bruce.

Foreign diplomats in London are responsible for killing a diplomat, and reporter Bailey uncovers the conspiracy, saving his girl friend from the bad guys in the bargain. Mediocre spy drama, but with a sense of humor.

p, Francis Searle; d, Montgomery Tully; w, Sidney Nelson, Maurice Harrison; ph, Phil Grindrod.

Spy Drama **(PR:A MPAA:NR)**

DIPLOMATIC COURIER (1952) 97m FOX bw

Tyrone Power (Mike Kells), Patricia Neal (Joan Ross), Stephen McNally (Col. Cagle), Hildegarde Neff (Janine), Karl Malden (Ernie), James Millican (Sam Carew), Stefan Schnabel (Platov), Herbert Berghof (Arnov), Arthur Blake (Max Ralli), Helene Stanley (Stewardess), Michael Ansara (Ivan), Sig Arno (Chef De Train), Alfred Linder (Cherenko), Lee Marvin (M.P. at Trieste), Peter Coe (Zinski), Tyler McVey (Watch Officer), Dabbs Greer (Intelligence Clerk), Carleton Young (Brennan), Charles La Torre (French Ticket Agent), Tom Powers (Cherney), Monique Chantal (French Stewardess), Lumsden Hare (Jacks), Russ Conway (Bill), Stuart Randall (Butrick), Charles Buchinski (Bronson), Mario Siletti (Russian), Hugh Marlowe (Narrator), E.G. Marshall (M.P. at Trieste).

An involved espionage yarn has Power going to Trieste, ostensibly as a diplomatic courier for the U.S. State Department, but in reality as a secret agent for the OSS. Millican, U.S. envoy to Bucharest, is murdered on a continental train by two Russian agents, Siletti and Buchinski (the latter to be known later as Charles Bronson), a vital document detailing the impending Russian invasion of Yugoslavia taken from Millican's body. This is the secret that was to have been passed to Power, who must now work to regain the document, aided by McNally, a U.S. military intelligence officer. In Trieste, Power meets with Neff, the last person to have seen Millican, thought to be a Russian agent. He also runs into an American playgirl, Neal, who seems to be concerned only with having a good time, although Power becomes suspicious when she begins pumping him for information. It turns out that Millican's killers did not get the microfilm after all and Neal, a Russian spy, is trying to obtain it. Neff, in a surprise twist, turns out to be an American spy. Just as Power gets his hands on the microfilm he is almost murdered but McNally's men save him at the last minute and spirit him back to safety, both he and Neff going to Washington. Power is convincing as the courier who finds himself over his head in puzzling intrigue; he often appears to be bumbling into clues and luck. Neal is beautiful and conniving and Neff stunning and sympathetic as a WW II refugee. Hathaway does a good job with a far-fetched script that has several holes in it. Malden is solid as the Army sergeant who pulls Power out of several tight spots. Marshall and Marvin, who were later to become outstanding performers, appear as two U.S. Army MPs in Trieste.

p, Casey Robinson; d, Henry Hathaway; w, Robinson, Liam O'Brien (based on the novel Sinister Errand by Peter Cheyney); ph, Lucien Ballard; m, Sol Kaplan; ed, James B. Clark; md, Lionel Newman; art d, Lyle Wheeler, John DeCuir; set d, Thomas Little, Stuart Reiss; cos, Charles Le Maire, Eloise Janssen; spec eff, Ray Kellogg; makeup, Ben Nye.

Spy Drama **(PR:A MPAA:NR)**

DIPLOMATIC LOVER, THE½ (1934, Brit.) 73m Sound City/FOX bw
(AKA: HOW'S CHANCES)

Harold French (Nottingham), Tamara Desni (Helen), Davy Burnaby (Michelo), Morton Selten (Sir Charles), Reginald Gardiner (Dersingham), Carol Rees (Dolores), Peggy Novak (Olga), Percy Walsh (Castellano), Andrea Malandrinos (Machulla Ahab), Roddy Hughes.

Desni is a Ruritanian ballerina who, to make her friends jealous, pretends to be engaged to a diplomat. Annoying musical frivolity best forgotten. A year after the film came out, Gardiner would delight Broadway audiences with his comic role in "At Home Abroad," and he would go on from there to years of playing polished and urbane supporting roles in Hollywood.

p, Norman Loudon; d, Anthony Kimmins; w, Ivar Campbell, Harry Graham (based on the play "Der Frauendiplomat" by E.B. Leuthege, Kurt Braun).

Musical **(PR:A MPAA:NR)**

DIPLOMATIC PASSPORT (1954, Brit.) 4m Rich & Rich-Princess/Eros bw

Marsha Hunt (Judy Anderson), Paul Carpenter (Roy Anderson), Henry Oscar (Chief), Honor Blackman (Marcelle), Marne Maitland (Philip), John MacLaren (Jack Gordon), John Welsh, David Conville, Henry Longhurst.

Carpenter, an American diplomat in London, is alarmed to discover that his car is being used by smugglers to move jewels in and out. Nothing fresh here except a look at Blackman long before her GOLDFINGER success.

p, Burt Balaban, Gene Martel; d, Martel; w, Paul Tabori; ph, James Wilson.

Crime **(PR:A PAA:NR)**

DIPLOMAT'S MANSION, THE (1961, Jap.) 109m Tokyo Eiga/Toho c
(TOKYO YAWA)

Reiko Dan (Bar Girl), Hiroshi Akutagawa (Diplomat), Tsutomu Yamazaki (His Son), Chikage Awashima (Madam) Nobuko Otowa, Kyoko Kishida, Tetsuro Tamba, Nobuo Nakamura, Chisako Hara, Masao Oda, Frankie Sakai, Ichiro Arishima, Hisaya Morishige.

Akutagawa is an aging diplomat forcibly retired from the Foreign Service and forced to depend on his bartender son, Yamazaki, for support, much to his humiliation. Undistinguished Japanese programmer.

d, Shiro Toyoda.

Drama **(PR:C MPAA:NR)**

DIRIGIBLE (1931) 100m COL bw

Jack Holt (Jack Bradon), Ralph Graves (Frisky Pierce), Fay Wray (Helen), Hobart Bosworth (Rondelle), Roscoe Karns (Sock McGuire), Harold Goodwin (Hansen), Clarence Muse (Clarence), Emmet Corrigan (Adm. Martin), Al Roscoe (Cmdr. Of U.S.S. Lexington), Selmer Jackson (Lt. Rowland).

This was another adventure yarn in a series Columbia produced with the Holt-Graves combination (WAR CORRESPONDENT, FLIGHT, HELL'S ISLAND), but what made it a standout was the direction by imaginative Frank Capra. The story deals with Graves flying over the South Pole a la Admiral Byrd and landing so that the U.S. flag can be planted. The plane cracks up and the occupants are thrown free to begin their freezing trudge back to civilization. It's hopeless, of course, until a U.S. Navy dirigible comes to the rescue under the command of Holt. This film was one of the first big-budget productions approved of by studio mogul Harry Cohn. Capra received a great deal of cooperation from the U.S. Navy and was given the giant lighter-than-air dirigible Los Angeles for many of his scenes. When doing preliminary takes in Lakehurst, New Jersey where the great airship was stored in a huge hangar, Capra's production was shut down by union officials insisting that technicians from New York and New Jersey be hired to double those from California. The two union groups actually fought a pitched battle to see which one would receive the porkbarreling payoff, almost destroying the Navy offices in Lakehurst. (It was at this same docking tower where the dirigible Hindenburg would burn up two years after Capra's film was made.) Cohn allowed Capra to spend thousands of dollars recreating the arctic wastes in the San Gabriel Valley (thousands of tons of cornflakes were used as snowflakes). The entire scene was realistic except that Capra realized that men laboring through the snow would have puffs of steam coming from their mouths. "I've got to see their breaths," he told technicians. Impossible, they told him; the temperature was ninety-five degrees. Someone suggested that little cages be built and inside of these cages pieces of dry ice be placed. These were then inserted into the mouths of the actors to produce the necessary cold-breath effect. But the trouble was that no one could pronounce their words with the contraptions in their mouths. In frustration, Hobart Bosworth took out the cage, removed the dry ice, and shoved it into his mouth. He began to give his speech but then screamed and collapsed. He was taken to a hospital where a dental surgeon worked on him for hours. He lost five teeth, part of his jawbone, and a lot of tissue but he was able to speak again in some months. DIRIGIBLE was a huge success, the first Columbia film to be premiered at Grauman's Chinese Theater where only important films were first seen. Capra was elated to hear, following the film, a standing ovation. He turned about and saw Harry Cohn in the center aisle, taking bows. The mogul had packed the theater with his cronies to make sure of his success. It wasn't necessary. Audiences across the country flocked to see DIRIGIBLE, fascinated by its exaggerated heroics and mostly the wonderful aerial shots captured by Capra's cameras.

p, Harry Cohn; d, Frank Capra; w, Jo Swerling, Dorothy Howell (based on a story by Lt. Comdr. Frank W. Weed); ph, Joe Wilbur, Elmer Dyer; ed, Maurice Wright.

Adventure **(PR:A MPAA:NR)**

DIRT GANG, THE (1972) 89m AIP c

Paul Carr (Monk), Michael Pataki (Snake), Lee DeBroux (Jesse), Jon Shank (Padre), Nancy Harris (Big Beth), T.J. Escott (Biff), Jessica Stuart (Stormy), Tom Anders (Marty), Joe Mosca (Willie), Michael Forest (Zino), Jo Anne Meredith (Dawn), Nanci Beck (Mary), Charles Macaulay (Curt), Hal England (Sidney), Ben Archibek (Jason), William Benedict (Station Attendant).

Sleazy biker film from the exploitation mill at AIP. One of the last examples of a genre that had outlived its time.

p, Joseph E. Bishop, Art Jacobs; d, Jerry Jameson; w, William Mercer, Michael C. Healy.

Crime **(PR:O MPAA:R)**

DIRTY DINGUS MAGEE (1970) 90m MGM c

Frank Sinatra (Dingus Magee), George Kennedy (Hoke), Anne Jackson (Belle), Lois Nettleton (Prudence), Jack Elam (John Wesley Hardin), Michele Carey (Anna), John Dehner (General), Henry Jones (Rev. Green), Harry Carey, Jr. (Stuart), Paul Fix (Chief Crazy Blanket), Donald Barry (Shotgun), Mike Wagner (Driver), Marya Christen (China Poppy), Terry Wilson, David Burk, David Cass, Tom Fadden

(Troopers), Mae Old Coyote, Lillian Hogan, Florence Real Bird, Ina Bad Bear *(Old Crones)*, Willis Bouchey *(Ira Teasdale)*, Mina Martinez, Sheila Foster, Irene Kelly, Diane Sayer, Jean London, Gayle Rogers, Timothy Blake, Lisa Todd, Maray Ayres, Carol Anderson *(Belle's Girls)*.

Reviews ranged from ecstatic to putrid for this western comedy with Sinatra and Kennedy top-lined. We're in the middle. It's sometime in the mid-1880s when Kennedy is traveling near Yerkey's Hole, New Mexico, and Sinatra (Magee) robs him. Kennedy dutifully reports the theft to the mayor of Yerkey's Hole, Anne Jackson, who also runs the town's largest industry, a brothel catering to the local army men at a nearby fort. Jackson deputizes Kennedy who goes out searching for Sinatra and locates him rolling in the bushes with Indian maiden Carey. Sinatra is arrested and tossed in jail. Now Jackson learns that the cavalry is moving out because general John Dehner wants to get to Little Big Horn before that blond upstart Custer. Carey helps Sinatra escape and Jackson tells the general that it was all done by the local Indians who are about to stage an "uprising." The general would be wise to leave his men at Yerkey's Hole or the entire town will be razed and raped. The truth is that the minute the army leaves Jackson's business will fail. Meanwhile, everyone is chasing Magee. He's stolen a strongbox from a stagecoach so Kennedy wants him. The Indians would like to scalp him because he's taken Carey, a valuable squaw. Carey, an early nymphomaniac, is after Sinatra to make "bim bam" but the guy is just getting too old for that kind of dalliance. Sinatra knows that Jackson has lots of money and he aims to get it. In the meantime, he has a fling with Nettleton who is sensational as a sexually repressed schoolmarm who lets it all go the moment Sinatra puts a make on her. The standout role is played by Elam as a muddled gunslinger, John Wesley Hardin. The moment he ambles on screen, it lights up. Would that there were more of Elam and less of many of the others. In the end, Sinatra grabs off the money and Michele and goes off into the sunset. Lots of action and a few funny lines but it is an essentially empty exercise and director Kennedy lets Sinatra and the picture go too far with tawdry double-entendres and many "groaners." The script was by the brothers Waldman (HATARI and others) and Joseph Heller, author of *Catch-22* and *Good As Gold*.

p&d, Burt Kennedy; w, Tom and Frank Waldman, Joseph Heller (based on the novel *The Ballad of Dingus Magee* by David Markson); ph, Harry Stradling, Jr. (Metrocolor); m, Jeff Alexander; ed, William B. Gulick; art d, George Davis, J. McMillan Johnson; set d, Robert R. Benton, Chuck Pierce; cos, Yvonne Wood; spec eff, Marcel Vercoutere; m/l, "The Ballad of Dingus Magee," Mack David, Jeff Alexander.

Western/Comedy (PR:C MPAA:PG)

DIRTY DOZEN, THE***

(1967, Brit.) 149m MGM c

Lee Marvin *(Maj. Reisman)*, Ernest Borgnine *(Gen. Worden)*, Charles Bronson *(Joseph Wladislaw)*, Jim Brown *(Robert Jefferson)*, John Cassavetes *(Victor Franko)*, Richard Jaeckel *(Sgt. Bowren)*, George Kennedy *(Maj. Max Armbruster)*, Trini Lopez *(Pedro Jiminez)*, Ralph Meeker *(Capt. Stuart Kinder)*, Robert Ryan *(Col. Everett Dasher-Breed)*, Telly Savalas *(Archer Maggott)*, Donald Sutherland *(Vernon Pinkley)*, Clint Walker *(Samson Posey)*, Robert Webber *(Gen. Denton)*, Tom Busby *(Milo Vladek)*, Ben Carruthers *(Glenn Gilpin)*, Stuart Cooper *(Roscoe Lever)*, Robert Phillips *(Cpl. Morgan)*, Colin Maitland *(Seth Sawyer)*, Al Mancini *(Tassos Bravos)*, George Roubicek *(Pvt. Arthur James Gardner)*, Thick Wilson *(Worden's Aide)*, Dora Reisser *(German Officer's Girl)*.

Action-packed box office smash that had the same plot as several other films; get a group of unlikely types together and send them on an impossible mission. The difference between this and THE DEVIL'S BRIGADE or any of the others is that Robert Aldrich was a master of mayhem and he had a script by Lukas Heller and the experienced Nunnally Johnson. In most of the other pictures of this ilk, the protagonists are likable types who unite to accomplish some worthwhile GUNS OF NAVARONE task. In THE DIRTY DOZEN, they are exactly that, twelve *really* angry men; felons who have been recruited to achieve a most difficult task: an attack on a Nazi-held chateau that seems impregnable. The script did not shrink from the wartime cliches we've come to recognize in so many 1940s films (i.e. the various ethnic types that make up the squad). Marvin is the no-nonsense major and Jaeckel is his assistant. They go to a prison and cull out the scum of the earth: Cassavetes is a psychotic; Brown is an anti-white brute; Lopez is Brown's buddy; Sutherland is a slightly impaired Dixie-ite; Savalas is a sadistic killer; Walker is an Indian; Bronson is a Pole and....well, you get the idea. Just about the only minority not represented is a gay Hassidic pickpocket. Marvin's superiors are Webber, Borgnine, and Ryan and all three are shown to be more corrupt and certainly much more stupid than the criminals they look down their noses at. So, the plot is divided thusly, get the dozen, train the dozen, send them on their mission, and count the bodies (three return). This is such a violent movie that even violent movie fans were turned off by some of the explicit scenes, as when Savalas murders a German whore just for the pleasure of it. It's a grim picture with just enough leavening humor to keep it from being totally painful. Bronson's performance was such a standout that he began getting larger roles and was a superstar within a few years after this was released. Robert Aldrich specialized in action films, often with so much violence that critics were appalled. In real life, Aldrich was a gentleman who wore a tie loosely tied around his ample neck and he usually had a kind word for everyone on the crew.

p, Kenneth Hyman; d, Robert Aldrich; w, Lukas Heller, Nunnally Johnson (based on the novel by E.M. Nathanson); ph, Edward Scaife (70 mm, Metrocolor); m, Frank DeVol; ed, Michael Luciano; art d, W.E. Hutchinson; spec eff, Cliff Richardson; m/l "The Bramble Bush," DeVol, Mack David; "Einsam," DeVol, Sibylle Siegfried.

War/Adventure Cas. (PR:C-O MPAA:NR)

THE DIRTY GAME**½

(1966, Fr./Ital./Ger.) 91m Franco London Fair-Euro International-Eichberg/AIP bw
(GUERRE SECRET; LA GUERRA SEGRETA: SPIONE UNTER SICH)

Henry Fonda *(Kourlav)*, Robert Ryan *(Gen. Bruce)*, Vittorio Gassman *(Perego)*, Annie Girardot *(Nanette)*, Bourvil *(Laland)*, Robert Hossein *(Dupont)*, Peter Van Eyck *(Berlin CIA Head)*, Maria Grazia Buccela *(Natalia)*, Mario Adorf *(Callagan)*, Jacques Sernas *(Glazou)*, Georges Marchal, Wolfgang Lukschy, Louis Arbessier, Jacky Blanchot, Gabriel Gobin, Helmut Wildt, Violette Marceau, Gabriella Giorgelli, Nino Crisman, Oreste Palella, Renato Terra.

A three-part film about the underside of the espionage world. With three directors, the most notable being Terence Young, who had done some of the James Bond movies. Ryan connects the three stories by relating three spy cases he supervised as he goes to the German East-West border to exchange prisoners. The first story is about an American agent, Gassman, in Rome undercover as a kidnaper in hopes that the enemy will hire him. Russian agents hire him to kidnap an Italian scientist who has invented a new rocket fuel. Gassman prevents the kidnaping and convinces the scientist to give the plans for the fuel to the Americans. The second tale is about U.S. forces stopping an attack on Navy submarines. The third and best segment has Fonda as a foreign agent who escapes from East Germany to wait in a hotel room for enemy agents to catch up with him and terminate him. This is a stark, brutal segment because it is stripped to the emotional bones. Fonda hardly speaks a word but the grim reality of his fate is caught perfectly. The film flopped when it was released in the U.S. and is rarely seen on television, but it would be worth sitting through the first two segments (which are routine spy action) for Fonda's segment. Fonda shot the film after finishing BATTLE OF THE BULGE.

p, Richard Hellman; d, Terence Young, Christian-Jacque, Carlo Lizzani; w, Jo Eisinger (adapted from a screenplay by Jacques Remy, Christian-Jacque, Ennio De Concini, Philippe Bouvard); ph, Pierre Petit, Richard Angst, Enrico Menczer; m, Robert Mellin, Gianfranco Reverberi; ed, Borys Leurn, Alan Osbiston; art d, Robert Gabriti, Heinrich Widemann.

Spy Drama (PR:C MPAA:NR)

DIRTY HANDS***

(1976, Fr/Ital./Ger.) 120m Les Films Boetie-Terra Filmkunst-Juppiter General Cinematografica/New Line c
(LES INNOCENTS AUX MAINS SALES)

Rod Steiger *(Louis)*, Romy Schneider *(Julie)*, Paolo Giusti *(Jeff)*, Jean Rochefort *(Legal)*, Francois Maistre *(Lamy)*, Pierre Santini *(Villon)*, Francois Perrot *(Thorent)*, Hans Christian Blech *(Judge)*.

Schneider plots with lover Giusti to murder her husband, Steiger. All seems to go well until Steiger turns up alive on his widow's doorstep. Interesting, slickly made crime drama with a luscious Schneider sunbathing in the altogether.

d&w, Claude Chabrol (based on the novel *Damned Innocents* by Richard Neely); ph, Jean Rabier (Eastmancolor); m, Pierre Jansen; ed, Jacques Gaillard.

Crime Cas. (PR:O MPAA:NR)

DIRTY HARRY***½

(1971) 102m Malpaso-WB c

Clint Eastwood *(Harry Callahan)*, Reni Santoni *(Chico)*, Harry Guardino *(Bressler)*, Andy Robinson *(Scorpio, Killer)*, John Mitchum *(DeGeorgio)*, John Larch *(Chief)*, John Vernon *(Mayor)*, Mae Mercer *(Mrs. Russell)*, Lyn Edgington *(Norma)*, Ruth Kobart *(Bus Driver)*, Woodrow Parfrey *(Mr. Jaffe)*, Josef Sommer *(Rothko)*, William Paterson *(Bannerman)*, Craig G. Kelly *(Sgt. Reineke)*, James Nolan *(Liquor Store Proprietor)*, Jo DeWinter *(Miss Willis)*, Maurice S. Argent *(Sid Kleinman)*, Melody Thomas *(Ann Mary Deacon, Photographer)*, Albert Popwell, Ernest Robinson *(Robbers)*, Diana Davidson *(Swimmer)*, David Gilliam, Richard Lawson *(Homosexuals)*, George Fargo, Angela Paton *(Homicide Detectives)*, John W. Peebles *(Walkie-Talkie Policeman)*, George R. Burrafato *(Taxi Driver)*, Raymond Johnson, Leslie Fong, John Tracy, Kristoffer Tabori, Frederic D. Ross, Charles A. Murphy, Al Dunlap, Vincent P. Deadrick *(Men)*, Kathleen Harper, Diann Henrichsen, Ann Bowen, Janet Wisely, Laury Monk, Jana D'Amico, Lolita Rios, Ann Noland, Kathleen O'Malley *(Women)*, Charles Dorsett *(Television Watcher)*, Dean Webber, Scott Hale *(Newsmen)*, Joy Carlin *(Communications Secretary)*, Allen Seaman *(Orderly)*, Stuart P. Klitsner, Eddie Garrett *(Policemen)*, Diane Darnell *(Mayor's Secretary)*, Marc Hertsens *(Doctor)*, Lois Foraker *(Hot Mary)*, John F. Vick *(Fired Chief)*, Tony Dario *(Police Sergeant)*, John Garber, Maxwell Gail, Jr., Christopher Pray (Tunnel Hoodlums), Charles C. Washburn *(Intern)*, Mary Ann Neis *(Miss Van Sachs)*, Debbi Scott *(Ann Mary Deacon)*, Denise Dyer, Diane Dyer, Jack Hanson, Derek Jue, Sean Maley, Richard Samuelson, Pamela Tanimura *(Bus Kids)*, Victor Paul *(Car Driver)*, Bob Harris, Joe Finnegan *(Men in Truck)*, Stephen Zacks *(Lake Kid)*, Charles Hicks *(Flower Vendor)*, Wayne Van Horn, Robert J. Miles, Jr., Jerry Maren, Bennie E. Dobbins, Raylene Holliday, Paula Martin, Emory Souza, Carl Rizzo, Billy Curtis, Regina Parton, John Hudkins, Everett Louis Creach, Fred Lerner, Julie Ann Johnson, George C. Sawaya, Larry Duran, Richard Crockett, Boyd "Red" Morgan, Walter Scott, Mark Thomas, Alex A. Brown, Richard A. Washington, Bill Lane, Fred Stromsoe, Alex Sharp, Willie Harris, Eddie Smith, Jane Aull, William T. Couch, Vincent Deadrick *(Stunts and Stunt Doubles)*, Leon Russom, Phil Clark, John Finnegan, James Joyce, Joanne Morre Jordan, Darlene Connelly, Fred Draper, Arnold F. Turner, Michele Tobin, Darren Moloney, Michael Freeman, Wendy Tochi, Jill Riha, Don Haggerty *(Voices)*.

DIRTY HARRY spawned several sequels but this is the best of the bunch and will surely be remembered long after the other DH films as well as the many copies it occasioned. Roughly patterned after the real-life Zodiac Killer in San Francisco, DIRTY HARRY was a script first offered to Frank Sinatra who wanted to call it "Dead Right," with Irv Kershner to direct. He withdrew because of a hand injury. John Wayne was also offered the role but turned it down. Perhaps Harry wasn't right-wing enough, who knows? Robinson, a mild-mannered young man (Edward G. Robinson's son) is in reality a killer who is terrorizing Baghdad By The Bay. Eastwood (Harry Callahan) is called in by his bosses, Guardino and mayor Vernon, to get the killer, who calls himself Scorpio. Robinson wants $100,000, or he will continue his bloody work. The mayor and the others are willing to give in, but Eastwood is against it and knows that it would be the beginning of a bleed by the killer. Eastwood is teamed with young Santoni, against his wishes, but he reluctantly begins to accept the junior partner after a while. Scorpio says he's buried a teenage girl somewhere in the city and will let her die unless the town comes across with $200,000. Harry gets the job of delivering the money (while being backed up by Santoni). He has to take several phone calls and race all over town before he finally gets to Robinson in a park. Once he gets the money, Robinson knocks Harry down and begins kicking him. Santoni races out of the bushes and is shot by Robinson. Eastwood jams a switchblade into Robinson's leg and the man leaps out of the park in terrible pain. A chase begins and Eastwood trails Robinson to Kezar Stadium, a football field, catches him, and tortures him until the killer reveals where the girl is. They find her all right, but she's dead. Robinson tells the authorities that Eastwood tortured him to get the information and, on one of those infuriating twists of legality, Robinson is released by the courts on the technicality of Eastwood searching without a warrant. Now Robinson actually hires a thug to beat him up, then contacts the police and shows them how he's been "beaten" by "Dirty Harry." Eastwood cannot believe that his bosses would take the word of Robinson over his. The killer strikes again, kidnaps a schoolbus (also drawn from a true occurrence in California), and demands ransom as well as an airplane for a getaway. Eastwood can take it no longer. He goes after Robinson on his own. An elaborate scene aboard the bus is followed by an on-foot chase in a factory. Eventually, Robinson puts a gun to the head of a young boy fishing at the bay nearby. He tells Eastwood to toss his .44 magnum down. Eastwood responds by shooting Robinson, but does not kill him. Robinson eyes his gun nearby and is certain that Eastwood is out of bullets. Eastwood, who used this trick in reel one when he captured a bank robber while between shots on a hot dog, gives the man a choice. "I know what you're thinking...Did he fire five shots or six? Ask yourself...do I feel lucky?" Robinson goes for it and Eastwood kills him on the spot! The San Francisco cops arrive and Eastwood disgustedly tosses his badge into the water. No one knew that the picture would gross so much money or they would have kept the badge. This is the film that took Eastwood out of the ordinary ether and put him into superstar stratosphere. It was enormously violent and a precursor to those Bronson vigilante films but, for 1971, it was a departure as the country was coming out of the laid-back mellowness of the 1960s and it hit the movie public like a wet fish in the face. Sequels: MAGNUM FORCE, THE ENFORCER, and SUDDEN IMPACT.

p&d, Don Siegel; w, Harry Julian Fink, Rita M. Fink, Dean Riesner (based on an unpublished story by Fink and Fink); ph, Bruce Surtees (Panavision, Technicolor); m, Lalo Schifrin; ed, Carl Pingitore; art d, Dale Hennesy; set d, Robert DeVestel; cos, Glenn Wright; makeup, Gordon Bau.

Police Drama   **Cas.**   **(PR:O MPAA:R)**

DIRTY HEROES**   (1971, Ital./Fr./Ger.) 105m
Fida Cinematografica-Productions Jacques Roitfeld-Gloria/Golden Eagle c
(DALLE ARDENNE ALL' INFERNO, LA)

Frederick Stafford (Sesamo), Daniela Bianchi (Kristina von Keist), Curt Jurgens (Gen. von Keist), John Ireland (Capt. O'Connor), Adolfo Celi (Rollman), Helmut Schneider (Gen. Hassler), Michael Constantine (Pertowsky), Faida Nicols (Marta/Magda), Howard Ross [Renato Rossini] (Joe), Anthony Dawson (American Colonel), Jacques Monod (Partisan), Tom Felleghi (American NCO), Valentino Macchi.

A group of ex-cons, now U.S. soldiers, and some Dutch partisans set out on a mission near the end of WW II to recover some diamonds (which formerly belonged to the Dutch) from German occupied territory. The plot is good for a succession of explosions and killings which inevitably lead them to their objective. Stafford, in the lead role, can also be seen in Hitchcock's TOPAZ. Fine soundtrack which was co-scored by Morricone.

p, Edmundo Amati; d, Alberto DeMartino; w, Dino Verde, Vincenzo Flamini, Alberto Verucci, DeMartino, Franco Silvestri, Louis Agotay (based on their story); ph, Gianni Bergamini (Technicolor); m, Ennio Morricone, Bruno Nicolai; ed, Otello Colangeli; art d, Nedo Azzini; set d, Pierluigi Basile.

War   **(PR:A MPAA:G)**

DIRTY KNIGHT'S WORK**½
(1976, Brit.) 88m WB-Combat/Gamma III c
(AKA: TRIAL BY COMBAT; CHOICE OF ARMS)

John Mills (Bertie), Donald Pleasence (Sir Giles), Barbara Hershey (Marion), David Birney (Sir John), Margaret Leighton (Ma Gore), Peter Cushing (Sir Edward), Brian Glover, John Savident, John Hallam, Keith Buckley, Neil McCarthy, Thomas Heathcote, Bernard Hill, Alexander John, Diane Langton, Roy Holder, Una Brandon-Jones, Brian Hall, Peter Childs, John Bindon, Brian Coburn, Kevin Lloyd, Max Faulkner, Bill Weston, Mike Horsburgh, Marc Harrison.

Odd little comedy inspired by the popular "The Avengers" TV series of the time. Birney convinces Mills to help him find the killers of his uncle. He turns up a medieval order of knights who have rededicated themselves to fighting crime and righting wrongs, and turn into vigilantes. Occasionally amusing macabre touches, but most of it misses the mark.

p, Fred Weintraub, Paul Heller; d, Kevin Connor; w, Julian Bond, Steven Rossen, Mitchell Smith (based on a story by Weintraub, Heller); ph, Alan Hume (Movielab Color); m, Frank Cordell; ed, Willy Kemplen; prod d, Edward Marshall.

Crime Comedy   **(PR:C MPAA:PG)**

DIRTY LITTLE BILLY**½   (1972) 100m WRG/COL c

Michael J. Pollard (Billy Bonney), Lee Purcell (Berle), Richard Evans (Goldie Evans), Charles Aidman (Ben Antrim), Dran Hamilton (Catherine McCarty), Willard Sage (Henry McCarty), Josip Elic (Jawbone), Mills Watson (Ed), Alex Wilson (Len),

Ronnie Graham (Charlie Niles), Richard Stahl (Earl Lovitt), Gary Busey (Basil Crabtree), Doug Dirken (Orville), Cherie Franklin (Greta Schmidt), Dick Van Patten (Harry), Rosary Nix (Louisiana), Frank Welker (Young Punk), Scott Walker (Stormy), Craig Bovia (Buffalo Hunter), Severn Darden (Big Jim), Henry Proach (Lloyd), Len Lesser (Slits), Ed Lauter (Tyler).

An unromantic portrait of the vile and muddy Old West. It is essentially the genesis of Billy the Kid (Pollard), a mentally deficient psychopath. After learning to fire a six-gun and seduce a woman, little Billy begins his legendary existence as the film comes to a close. Pollard, best remembered for his role as C.W. Moss in BONNIE AND CLYDE, is appropriately dirty in an equally classic performance. Surprisingly slick direction from TV commercial graduate Dragoti, who later helmed the cold LOVE AT FIRST BITE. Gary Busey (THE BUDDY HOLLY STORY) and Dick Van Patten (of TV's Eight Is Enough) are bottom-liners.

p, Jack L. Warner; d, Stan Dragoti; w, Dragoti, Charles Moss; ph, Ralph Woolsey; m, Sascha Burland; ed, Dave Wages; md, Burland; art d, Malcolm Bert; set d, George Hopkins; spec eff, Ralph Ayers, John Coles.

Western   **(PR:C-O MPAA:R)**

DIRTY MARY, CRAZY LARRY*   (1974) 93m FOX c

Peter Fonda (Larry), Susan George (Mary), Adam Roarke (Deke), Vic Morrow (Franklin), Fred Daniels (Hank), Roddy McDowall (Stanton), Lynn Borden (Evelyn), Adrian Herman (Cindy), Janear Hines (Millie), Elizabeth James (Dispatcher), William Campbell (Sur), John Castranova (Steve), Ken Tobey (Donohue).

Fonda and pal Roarke extort $150,000 from store manager McDowall and use it to buy a top-line race car. Laying rubber on highways across California, they are chased by smokeys and bears-in-the-air, picking up the whorish George on the way. A flurry of vehicular choreography which draws praise for the stunt team. There is practically no plot, and even less character development, but the script is somehow based on a novel, most likely a thin one.

p, Norman T. Herman; d, John Hough; w, Leigh Chapman, Antonio Santean (based on the novel The Chase by Richard Unekis); ph, Mark Margulies (DeLuxe Color); m, Jimmy Haskell; ed, Chris Holmes.

Action   **Cas.**   **(PR:O MPAA:PG)**

DIRTY MONEY**   (1977, Fr.) 100m AA c

Alain Delon (Coleman), Catherine Deneuve (Cathy), Richard Crenna (Simon), Riccardo Cucciolla (Paul, Michael Conrad (Costa), Andre Pousse (Albouis), Paul Crauchet (Morand), Simone Valere (Wife), Jean Desailly (Man).

Drug smuggling and murder take place in exotic locations in this crime story, with "tough guy" Delon backdropped by gorgeous scenery and the beautiful Deneuve. Lightweight film noir.

p, Robert Dorfmann; d&w, Jean-Pierre Melville; ph, Walter Wottitz (Eastmancolor); m, Michel Combier; ed, Patricia Renaut; art d, Theo Meurisse; m/l, Charles Aznavour.

Crime   **(PR:C MPAA:PG)**

DIRTY O'NEIL zero   (1974) 89m United Producers/AIP c

Morgan Paull (Jimmy O'Neil), Art Metrano (Lassiter), Pat Anderson (Lisa), Jean Manson (Ruby), Katie Saylor (Vera), Raymond O'Keefe (Lou), Tom Huff (Bennie), Bob Potter (Al), Sam Laws (Clyde), Liv Lindeland (Mrs. Crawford).

Subtitling this as "The Love Life of a Cop" is a real kick to the concept of amore. West coast copper Paull spends more time in bed than on the beat, sacking a different woman every time. An odious offering and boring to boot.

p, John C. Broderick; d, Howard Freen, Lewis Teague; ph, (Movielab Color); w, Freen; m, Raoul Kraushaar.

Drama   **(PR:O MPAA:R)**

DIRTY OUTLAWS, THE**   (1971, Ital.) 103m Daiano-Leone/Transvue c
(EL DESPERADO)

Chip Corman (Steve), Rosemarie Dexter (Katy), Dana Ghia (Lucy), Franco Giornelli (Asher), Piero Lulli (Sam), Aldo Berti (Jonat), Giovanni Petrucci, Andrea Scotti, Pino Polidori, Dino Strano, John Bartha, Giorgio Gruden, Antonio Cantafora, Sandro Serafini, Giuseppe Castellani, Claudio Trionfi, G. Luigi Crescenzi.

Corman is an outlaw in the closing days of the Civil War who stumbles across a dying Confederate officer who tells him about some hidden gold in the home of his blind father. Corman takes the man's uniform and passes himself off to the father and his housekeeper as the son. Before he can find the loot, a gang of outlaws rides into town planning to rob an army payroll wagon. He is forced to help in the robbery and when he tries to take off with the money, he is tortured, shot, and left for dead while the gang shoots the defenseless blind man. Recovering, Corman goes after the gang, killing them off one by one until only the chief (Giornelli) is left. Corman blinds him with mud, sticks a gun in his hand, then shoots him dead. Violent, humorless Spaghetti Western that only devotees of the genre will find entertaining.

p, Ugo Guerra, Franco Rossetti; d, Rossetti; w, Guerra, Rossetti, Vincenzo Cerami; ph, Angelo Filippini (Techniscope, Technicolor); m, Gianni Ferrio; ed, Antonietta Zita; set d, G. Francesco Fantacci.

Western   **(PR:O MPAA:R)**

DIRTY TRICKS*½   (1981, Can.) 91m Filmplan/AE c

Elliott Gould (Colin Chandler), Kate Jackson (Polly Bishop), Arthur Hill (Bert Prosser), Rich Little (Robert Brennan), Nick Campbell (Bill Darcy), Angus McInnes (FBI Jones), Michael Kirby (FBI Wicklow), Michael McNamara (Thorn), Martin McNamara (Ozzie), John Juliani (Roselli), Alberta Watson (Tony), Mavor Moore (Underhill), Cindy Girling (Emily).

Harvard professor Gould is endangered when a student of his is murdered after producing a history-altering letter written by George Washington. Jackson is the investigative reporter who is attracted by the teacher's charms. A comic approach is undermined by realistic scenes of deaths. Fine performances are devalued by a cheap-looking production made under the existing tax shelters in Canada.

p, Claude Heroux; d, Alvin Rakoff; w, William Norton, Sr., Eleanor Elias Norton, Thomas Gifford, Camille Gifford (from a novel by Thomas Gifford); ph, Richard Ciupka; m, Hagood Hardy; ed, Alan Collins.

Comedy   **Cas.**   **(PR:C   MPAA:PG)**

DIRTY WORK**   (1934, Brit.) 78m GAU bw

Ralph Lynn (Jimmy Milligan), Gordon Harker (Nettle), Robertson Hare (Clement Peck), Lillian Bond (Eve Wynne), Basil Sydney (Hugh Stafford), Margaretta Scott (Leonora Stafford), Cecil Parker (Gordon Bray), Gordon James (Toome), Peter Gawthorne (Sgt. Barlow), Louis Bradfield (Charlie Wrench), Leslie Laurier.

Shop assistants in a jewelry store pretend to be crooks in order to trap a gang of thieves. Thin comedy from a mediocre Ben Travers script. Director Walls, a one-time policeman and jockey, turned to acting in 1935 and became a brilliant character presence in British films.

p, Michael Balcon; d, Tom Walls; w, Ben Travers (based on a play by Travers); ph, Philip Tannura.

Comedy   **(PR:A   MPAA:NR)**

DIRTYMOUTH**   (1970) 102m Superior/Howard Mahler c

Bernie Travis (Lenny Bruce), Courtney Sherman (Iris McCabe), Wynn Irwin (Lou Hamilton), Miss Sam Teardrop (Marlene), Harry Spillman (Lewis), Peter Clune (Mr. Murdock), Eleanor Cody Gould (Mrs. McCabe), Bob Allen (Philadelphia Judge), Gene Wood (New York Judge), Chris Gampel (Defense Attorney), John Becher (Harry), Fred Knapp (New York Defense Attorney), Jim Thorne (Assistant District Attorney), Reid Cruickshanks (Brady), Frank Feda (Ed Newton), Court Benson (Johnson), Fuddle Bagley (Comic), Herb Carter (Smith), Phil Carter (Gerber), Horatio Ruller (Tipstaff), Edward Grace (Capote), Michael Zettler, Arthur French (Philadelphia Policemen), Dorothy Claire (Mrs. McHenry), Alice Yourman (Mrs. Amperian), Gladys Lane (Mrs. Gerber), Frankie Mann, Bob Leslie (Themselves).

A well-meaning film about biting social comedian Lenny Bruce which spends more time on Bruce, the phenomenon, than Bruce the person. Travis, as Bruce, is shown passing time in sleazy night spots and federal courtrooms around the country as he opens his mouth to spew out obscenities. Sherman, as his stripper wife, is commendable in a role which gives her nothing to do. The major fault lies in the script. It repeatedly tells what Bruce did to become such a spectacle, but not why. More penetrating and provocative is Bob Fosse's LENNY.

p,d&w, Herbert S. Altman; ph, Bert Spielvogel (Movielab Color); m, Manny Vardi, Lenny Hambro; ed, Edna Paul; m/l, The Free Design.

Drama   **(PR:O   MPAA:NR)**

DISAPPEARANCE, THE**
          (1981, Brit./Can.) 88m Trofar-Tiberius/World Northal c

Donald Sutherland (Jay), Francine Racette (Celandine), Christopher Plummer (Deverell), David Hemmings (Edward), David Warner (Burband), Virginia McKenna (Catherine), John Hurt, Peter Bowles, Michelle Magny.

Hit-man Sutherland returns home one day to find his wife missing. He tries to carry the story along, but a muddled script and self-consciously arty direction drag him down.

p, David Hemmings, Gerry Arbeid; d, Stuart Copper; w, Paul Mayersberg (based on the novel Echoes of Celandine by Derek Marlow); ph, John Alcott (Eastmancolor); m, Robert Farnon; prod d, Anne Pritchard.

Crime   **Cas.**   **(PR:C   MPAA:R)**

DISASTER*   (1948) 60m PAR bw

Richard Denning (Bill Wyatt), Trudy Marshall (Jerry Hansford), Damian O'Flynn (Detective Dearborn), Will Wright (Pop Hansford), James Millican (Sam Payne), Jack Lambert (Frosty Davenport), Jonathan Hale (Police Commissioner).

Fugitive Denning takes a job doing high-rig construction and falls in love with the boss's daughter. He gets a chance to prove his honor by saving dad, who's trapped in a building that's been hit by a plane. Aptly titled.

p, William Pine, William Thomas; d, Pine; w, Thomas Ahearn; ph, Ellis W. Carter; ed, Howard Smith; art d, Lewis H. Creber.

Drama   **(PR:A   MPAA:NR)**

DISBARRED**   (1939) 59m PAR bw

Gail Patrick (Joan Carroll), Robert Preston (Bradley Kent), Otto Kruger (Tyler Cradon), Sidney Toler (G.L. Mardeen), Helen MacKellar (Abbey Tennant), Virginia Dabney (Miss La Rue), Edward Marr (Harp Harrigan), Charles D. Brown (Jackson), Clay Clement (Attorney Roberts), Frank M. Thomas (G.H. Blanchard), Harry Worth, John Hart (Reporters), Virginia Vale (Stewardess), Philip Warren Sheila Darcy (Secretaries), Henry Roquemore (Passenger), Robert Frazer (Brimmer), Jim Pierce (Bailiff), Guy Usher, Edward J. Le Saint (Judges), Stanley Blystone (Schaeffer), Paul Fix (Bomb Thrower), Jack Knoche (Reporter), Pop Byron (Jury Foreman), Wheaton Chambers (Ballistic Expert), Harry Tyler (Cashier), Dick Elliott (Small Town Character).

Disbarred attorney Kruger hooks up with Patrick, a keen girl lawyer from the midwest. He invites her into his practice, which is really a front for his wrongdoings. She's too swift for his game and joins forces with the district attorney to crack Kruger. Adequate performances all around, with Kruger's suave personality standing out.

p, Stuart Walker; d, Robert Florey; w, Lillie Hayword, Robert R. Presnell (based on a story by Harry Sauber); ph, Harry Fischbeck; ed, Arthur Schmidt; md, Boris Morros; art d, Hans Dreier, William Flannery.

Drama   **(PR:A   MPAA:NR)**

DISC JOCKEY**   (1951) 77m AA bw

Ginny Simms (Vickie Peters), Tom Drake (Johnny), Jane Nigh (Marion), Michael O'Shea (Mike Richards), Lenny Kent (Happy), Jerome Cowan (Marley), Tommy Dorsey, George Shearing, Sarah Vaughan, Herb Jeffries, Nick Lucas, The Weavers, Jack Fina, Vito Musso, Red Nichols, Red Norvo, Ben Pollack, Joe Venuti, Foy Willing and The Riders of the Purple Sage, Russ Morgan, Martin Block, Joe Adams, Joe Allison, Bill Anson, Doug Arthur, Don Bell, Paul Brenner, Bob Clayton, Paul Dixon, Ed Gallaher, Dick Gilbert, Bill Gordon, Marty Hart, Bruce Hayes, Eddie Hubbard, Bea Kalmus, Les Malloy, Paul Masterson, Ed McKenzie, Tom Mercein, Gill Newsome, Gene Norman, Art Pallans, Bob Poole, Norman Prescott, Fred Robbins, Ernie Simon, Larry Wilson.

DJ promoter O'Shea makes a claim that he can pick any unknown singer and transform her into a vocal sensation simply with the aid of radio exposure, after one of his pals wants to switch to TV. The chosen warbler is Simms who, with the help of 28 radio jocks across the nation, proves the promoter's point. There can be no argument that the script was written just to showcase the talent. But no excuse is necessary for this collection of musical virtuosity. Songs: "Let's Meander Through The Meadow," "Show Me You Love Me" (S. Steuben, Roz Gordon), "Nobody Wants Me," "After Hours" (Gordon), "Disc Jockey," "In My Heart" (Herb Jeffries, Dick Hazard), "Peaceful Country," "Riders of the Purple Sage" (Foy Willing), "Brain Wave" (George Shearing), "Oh Look at Me Now" (John DeVries, Joe Bushkin), "The Roving Kind" (Jessie Cavanaugh, Arnold Stanton).

p, Maurice Duke; d, Will Jason; w, Clark E. Reynolds (based on his story); ph, Harry Neumann; m, Russ Morgan; ed, Otho Lovering; md, Morgan; art d, David Milton.

Musical   **(PR:A   MPAA:NR)**

DISC JOCKEY JAMBOREE   (SEE: JAMBOREE, 1957)

DISCARDED LOVERS***½   (1932) 55m Tower bw

Natalie Moorhead (Irma Gladden), J. Farrell MacDonald (Chief Sommers), Sharon Lynn (Valerie Christine), Russell Hopton (Bob Adair), Jason Robards (Rex Forsythe), Robert Frazer (Warren Sibley), Fred Kelsey (Sgt. Delaney), Barbara Weeks (Mrs. Sibley), Roy D'Arcy (Andre Leighton), Jack Trent, Allen Dailey.

A familiar mystery that varies with location. Opening on the set of a film, it stars Moorhead as a femme fatale starlet with a couple of husbands and a throng of enemies. After her unmourned death, a list of suspects is placed under surveillence, including an innocent looking secretary. A telephone call tips off police chief MacDonald, who unravels the mystery in the studio's screening room. The clue lies in the projection of the opening scene's rushes, pointing a guilty finger at the writer. MacDonald ends up with the gal Friday, who really was as innocent as she looked. A lot of nice touches in this appealing picture.

d, Fred Newmeyer; w, Edward T. Lowe, Arthur T. Hoyle (based on a story by Lowe); ph, William Hyer; ed, Charles Hunt.

Mystery   **(PR:A   MPAA:NR)**

DISCIPLE OF DEATH*   (1972, Brit.) 90m AE c

Mike Raven, Stephan Bradley, Virginia Wetherall

Raven is one of the living dead who sacrifices virgins to the devil to keep walking the earth. Bradley sets out to stop him with the help of a minister and a Jewish cabalist. Raven starred in CRUCIBLE OF TERROR and was an ex-disc jockey who probably shouldn't have given up radio.

p, Tom Parkinson, Charles Fairman; d, Parkinson; w, Parkinson, Churton Fairman.

Horror   **Cas.**   **(PR:O   MPAA:NR)**

DISCORD**   (1933, Brit.) 80m B&D/PAR British bw

Owen Nares (Peter Stenning), Benita Hume (Phil Stenning), Harold Huth (Lord Quilhampton), Clifford Heatherley (Mr. Moody), Aubrey Fitzgerald (Mr. Bollom), O.B. Clarence (Mr. Hemming), Harold Scott (Harold), Archibald Batty, Esme Hubbard.

Struggling composer Nares saves wife Hume from the amorous clutches of Lord Quilhampton, Huth, who wants to put her in his show. But Nares, as the anonymous author of the musical, has the last word on casting and is able to circumvent the lord's good deed and dark intentions. Nares, born in 1888, who began acting on the stage in 1908, and in the movies in 1914, in his day was known as the longest-lasting matinee idol in the movies, with his last screen credit in 1941.

p, Herbert Wilcox; d, Henry Edwards; w, E. Temple Thurston (based on the play "A Roof and Four Walls" by Thurston).

Drama   **(PR:A   MPAA:NR)**

DISCOVERIES**½   (1939, Brit.) 68m Vogue/GN bw

Carroll Levis (Himself), Afrique (Alfredo), Issy Bonn (Mr. Schwitzer), Julien Vedey (Mr. Spinelli), Bertha Belmore (PCW Duggan), Ronald Shiner (Jim Pike), Doris Hare (Bella Brown), Kathleen Harrison (Maid), Zoe Wynn (Susie), Barbara Everest (Mrs. Venters), Shayle Gardner (Manager), Cyril Levis, Three Ginx, Dump and Tony, George Meaton, Radio Rascals, Pearl Venters, Archie Galbraith, Glyn Davies, Tony Vaughan, David Delmonte, Frank Atkinson, Ken Bonner, May Patterson, Scottish Sextet.

A slender plot about rival manufacturers fighting over sponsorship of a radio program is an excuse for Levis to bring a popular 1930s British radio show and a slew of music hall acts to the screen. Good entertainment.

d, Redd Davis; w, Davis, Cyril Campion, Anatole De Grunwald (based on a radio series by Carroll Levis); ph, Bryan Langley.

Musical (PR:A MPAA:NR)

DISCREET CHARM OF THE BOURGEOISIE, THE**
(1972, Fr.) 100m FOX c
(LE CHARME DISCRET DE LA BOURGEOISIE)

Fernando Rey (*Ambassador*), Delphine Seyrig (*Mme. Simone Thevenot*), Stephane Audran (*Mme. Alice Senechal*), Bulle Ogier (*Florence*), Jean-Pierre Cassel (*Mon. Senechal*), Paul Frankeur (*Mon. Thevenot*), Julien Bertheau (*Bishop Dufour*), Claude Pieplu (*Colonel*), Michel Piccoli (*Home Secretary*), Muni (*Peasant Girl*), Milena Vukotic (*Ines the Maid*), George Douking (*Dying Gardener*), Bernard Musson (*Lt. Hubert de Rochecachin/Youth In Tearoom*), Francois Maistre (*Superintendent of Police*), Maria Gabriella Maione, Pierre Maguelon, Maxence Mailfort, Ellen Bahl, Jacques Rispal, Robert Benoit, Jean Degrave, Pierre Lamy, Le Beal, Diane Vernon.

Luis Bunuel has made a mildly funny and often confounding picture that left viewers mostly confounded. It won an Oscar as Best Foreign Film and was nominated for the best script. Rey is the ambassador from the mythical country of Miranda. His wife is Seyrig. In the course of the picture, they attempt to make love and to have a dinner with some friends and are frustrated by any number of unique interruptions. Part of it is real, part is a dream, and their dinners are stopped by soldiers on maneuvers, then terrorists who come in and kill all the diners (this is a dream). They go to a friend's for dinner and arrive on the wrong day. They try a restaurant and learn it's closed because the owner just died. In between these scenes, they cut to a group walking along a country road...several times. The ambassador is also smuggling drugs in his diplomatic pouch. If you find any of the above funny, then this movie may be for you. It wasn't for us and the fact that it garnered the Oscar for best foreign film is still astounding.

p, Serge Silberman; d, Luis Bunuel; w, Bunuel, Jean-Claude Carriere; ph, Edmond Richard (Eastmancolor); ed, Helene Plemiannikov; art d, Pierre Guffroy.

Comedy/Drama (PR:C MPAA:PG)

DISEMBODIED, THE*
(1957) 65m AA bw

Paul Burke (*Tom*), Allison Hayes (*Tonda*), John E. Wengraf (*Dr. Metz*), Eugenia Paul (*Lara*), Joel Marston (*Norman*), Robert Christopher (*Joe*), Norman Fredric (*Suba*), A.E. Ukonu (*Voodoo Drum Leader*), Paul Thompson (*Gogi*), Otis Greene (*Kabar*).

A doctor's wild wife, Hayes, gives everyone in the jungle voodoo-phobia, an illness which runs rampant when an excess of spells is placed on the community. Hayes succeeds in looking silly as a botanically minded girl who dances suggestively clad only in a loincloth and beads. Jungle gibberish.

p, Ben Schwalb; d, Walter Grauman; w, Jack Townley; ph, Harry Neumann; m, Marlin Skiles; ed, William Austin, Del Harris; art d, David Milton.

Horror (PR:C MPAA:NR)

DISGRACED*
(1933) 63m PAR bw

Helen Twelvetrees (*Gay Holloway*), Bruce Cabot (*Kirk Undwood, Jr.*), Adrienne Ames (*Julia Thorndyke*), William Harrigan (*Capt. Holloway*), Ken Murray (*Jim McGuire*), Charles Middleton (*District Attorney*) Adrienne D'Ambicourt (*Madame*), Ara Haswell (*Miss Peck*), Dorothy Bay (*Flynn*).

A young woman is accused of murder, but her honorable father is really the guilty one, killing the fiance who split before her wedding. A confused film which is on the fence between romance and murder, but not committing to either.

p, Bayard Veiller; d, Erle C. Kenton; w, Alice D.G. Miller, Francis Martin (based on a story by Miller); ph, Karl Struss.

Mystery (PR:A NR)

DISHONOR BRIGHT**
(1936, Brit.) 83m CAP/GFD bw

Tom Walls (*Stephen Champion*), Eugene Pallette (*Busby*), Betty Stockfeld (*Stella*), Diana Churchill (*Ivy Lamb*), Cecil Parker (*Vincent Lamb*), Arthur Wontner (*Judge*), George Sanders (*Lisle*), Henry Oscar (*Blenkinsop*), Hubert Harben (*Lamb*), Mabel Terry-Lewis (*Lady Melbury*), Basil Radford (*Henry Crane*), Charlotte Leigh (*Miss Tapp*) Michael Morel (*Louis*), Denis Val Norton (*Commissionaire*), Jeni le Gon (*Cabaret Dancer*), Bernardi (*Cabaret Singer*), Mervyn Johns.

Defending lawyer Walls marries client Churchill but is really in love with the opposing attorney's wife, blonde beauty Stockfeld. By coincidence, both couples meet in Switzerland where Walls helps Stockfeld out of a romantic predicament. He returns with her to her hotel room, but the relationship stays tame. There are no scandals and everything ends with both marriages preserved. Well-crafted light comedy with Sanders in an early role. Reissued in 1942.

p, Herman Fellner, Max Schach; d, Tom Walls; w, Ben Travers; ph, Philip Tannura.

Comedy (PR:A MPAA:NR)

DISHONORED***
(1931) 91m PAR bw

Marlene Dietrich (*X-27*), Victor McLaglen (*Lt. Kranau, H-14*), Lew Cody (*Col. Kovrin*), Gustav von Seyffertitz (*Secret Service Head*), Warner Oland (*Gen. Von Hindau*), Barry Norton (*Young Lieutenant*), Davison Clark (*Court Officer*), Wilfred Lucas (*Gen. Dymov*), Bill Powell (*Manager*), George Irving (*Contact at Cafe*), Joseph Girard (*Russian Officer*), Ethan Laidlaw (*Russian Corporal*), William B.

Davidson (*Firing Squad Officer*), Buddy Roosevelt (*Russian Officer*), Ruth Mayhew (*Accident Victim*), Alexis Davidoff (*Officer*).

The plot lines for DISHONORED and MATA HARI (1932) were almost the same; both films were melodramatic and impossible. Yet Dietrich's magical cold-ice charm and Garbo's wonderful mystique saved the films. Both films are also based on the infamous and fairly inept spy Mata Hari, shot for espionage by the French in 1917. Where Mata Hari was an exotic dancer, Dietrich is a common streetwalker, encountered in WW I Vienna by Seyffertitz, head of the Austrian Secret Intelligence Service. A policeman threatens her with arrest if she will not move on. Hard as crystal, Dietrich replies: "I'm not afraid of life or death!" Seyffertitz is impressed with her words and begins a conversation. The beautiful young woman asks him to step out of the rain by going to her apartment. There he proposes she make a lot of money by spying on Austria. She immediately calls police and turns him over as a spy. Happily convinced of her loyalty, Seyffertitz enlists her as one of his agents and she is officially designated "X-27." (Mata Hari's code designation in the German spy system was "H.21".) Her first assignment is to obtain evidence against Oland, an Austrian general suspected of passing information to the Russians. Meeting him at a masked ball, Dietrich returns home with him but en route a clown from the ball, a man on crutches, is given a ride by the general. He gives Oland a cigarette which the general pockets. Oland gets a phone call (planned by Seyffertitz) when he arrives home with Dietrich. He takes the call in another room while Dietrich goes through his private papers. A butler enters with champagne and Dietrich asks him for a cigarette. She is told that there are none available since Oland doesn't smoke. Withdrawing the cigarette in Oland's coat pocket, Dietrich finds a secret message from the Russians. When Oland returns she stands triumphantly in front of him, smoking the cigarette. Oland instantly realizes he has been exposed and that Dietrich is an Austrian agent. He courteously excuses himself, goes into the next room, and shoots himself. Dietrich now tracks down the general's contact, the man in the clown suit, McLaglen, a Russian agent masquerading as an Austrian lieutenant, meeting him in a casino where he will be arrested. But McLaglen is too clever for her and escapes. Sneaking into Dietrich's bedroom, McLaglen learns that she is to fly to the Russian-Polish border and, in the disguise of a peasant maid, seduce Cody, a Russian colonel, getting plans from him concerning the next Russian attack. Dietrich does exactly that but McLaglen is waiting for her and has her arrested before she can return to Austria. But McLaglen dallies with her briefly in his quarters where she drugs his wine and then flees with a forged passport. He follows her to Austria where he is arrested but Dietrich by then has fallen in love with McLaglen and she slips him a gun which he uses to escape. For her folly Dietrich herself is arrested, tried, and convicted. She is sentenced to be shot. When asked if she has any last requests, Dietrich says: "Let me die in the uniform in which I served, not my country, but my countrymen." Dressed as a streetwalker, Dietrich faces a firing squad. When the young officer in charge, Norton, can't bring himself to give the order to fire, there is a momentary respite while he is replaced. The camera closes in on Dietrich, a bit bored, as she impassionately applies her lipstick, as if she is about to solicit another customer, this time Death. This is one of the most bizarre scenes in a Dietrich film, and only Von Sternberg, who wrote the script, could have pulled it off with his favorite leading lady, a ghoulish joke over absurd female vanity. The film is probably the least distinguished of the Dietrich-Sternberg productions, but its camp plot and extravagant performance by Dietrich (her second American film after MOROCCO, done at age 30), along with Sternberg's powerful visual approach, make it an offbeat gem. This was the first film when Dietrich stepped out of her glamorous image, but only for the few scenes where she played the peasant girl, her hair tight to her skull in a bun and her makeup scrubbed from a face that still appeared more as a hulking prop than as a leading man. It is a Dietrich opus all the way, almost as unforgettable as THE SCARLET EMPRESS, THE BLUE ANGEL, SHANGHAI EXPRESS, BLONDE VENUS, or her favorite film, THE DEVIL IS A WOMAN, but not quite. Dietrich will always sacrifice for love in her films. But here she dies for it, and her distant image denies that possibility.

d, Josef von Sternberg; w, Daniel N. Rubin, von Sternberg; ph, Lee Garmes; m, Karl Hajos, von Sternberg; art d, Hans Dreier; cos, Travis Banton; musical numbers, "Moonlight Sonata" (Beethoven), "Donauwellen/Danube Waves" (Ion Ivanovici).

Spy Drama (PR:C MPAA:NR)

DISHONORED*½
(1950, Ital.) 103m Roma Films/Casolaro Films bw
(ONORE E SACRIFICIO)

Antonio Vilar (*Pietro Forcella*), Elli Parvo (*Amalia*), Otello Toso (*Alfredo*), Giovanna Scotto (*Barbara*), Nadia Fiorelli (*Maria*), Agostino Salviette (*Gaetano*), Checco Durante (*Checco*).

Vilar and Toso are friends working side by side for the unification of Italy during the upheaval of 1870, but Toso turns out to be a spy for the reactionary forces who murders his friend's father for some information. Some good action scenes and some real suspense can't do much for this unremarkable Italian programmer. (In Italian; English subtitles.)

p, Fortunato Misiano; d, Guido Brignone; w, Leone Ciprelli; ph, Augusto Tiezzi; m, Ezio Carabella.

Drama (PR:A MPAA:NR)

DISHONORED LADY**
(1947) 66m UA bw

Hedy Lamarr (*Madeleine Damien*), Dennis O'Keefe (*Dr. David Cousins*), John Loder (*Felix Courtland*), William Lundigan (*Jack Garet*), Morris Carnovsky (*Dr. Caleb*), Paul Cavanagh (*Victor Kranish*), Natalie Schafer (*Ethel Royce*), Douglas Dumbrille (*District Attorney*), Margaret Hamilton (*Mrs. Geiger*), Nicholas Joy (*Defense Attorney*), James Flavin (*Detective*), Ransom Sherman (*Shirley*), Dewey Robinson (*Jim*), Robert B. Williams (*Plainclothesman*), Ian Wolfe (*E.J. Lutz, Pathologist*).

Lamarr and Loder were husband and wife in real life when this film was made and you could see who the boss was as Hedy was the behind-the-scenes producer and really ran the roost. He was killed off early in the film and they divorced not long afterwards. Lamarr is a magazine editor who is mentally shaky. She tries suicide (shades of LADY IN THE DARK) and is eventually referred to psychiatrist Carnovsky, who tells her she must leave her high-pressure employment and seek calmer pastures elsewhere. She alters her identity (but not that gorgeous face) and moves to Greenwich Village, where she becomes a painter and meets scientist O'Keefe. Love blooms quickly (especially in a movie that's less than 90 minutes long) and they plan to wed. O'Keefe is called out of New York briefly and Lamarr visits a local nightclub where she runs into Loder, a rich jeweler with whom she'd once had a fourteen-karat fling. He takes her home that night and she wants to get away from him as her heart belongs to O'Keefe now, so she slips out the rear door while he is answering the doorbell at the front. The visitor is Lundigan, an employee of Loder's, who once stole some jewels and is coming to plead with Loder not to turn him in to the cops. He promises to make full restitution. Loder won't budge, so Lundigan kills him. But Lamarr was the last person to be seen with Loder and she's arrested for the crime. The trial takes place and O'Keefe, now learning of her past and her relationship with Loder, will not see her. Lamarr becomes so depressed she refuses to defend herself and sits in her chair, totally blank. Carnovsky sees her mental condition and realizes that she must be innocent so he prevails on O'Keefe to come to her side. O'Keefe tells Lamarr how much he loves her and she is shocked out of her stupor and begins to fight for her life. They take her testimony, go through it, return to the victim's house, dust for fingerprints, find those of Lundigan, and confront him with the evidence. He admits having killed Loder, and Lamarr and O'Keefe are happily together at the fadeout. This was a stage play in its original form and quite a bit spicier than what was seen on the screen due to the tight censorship of the era. Lamarr had already become a better actress by this time and more than held her own with her costars. The major problem was that Stevenson's direction was almost non-existent and one got the distinct impression that Lamarr did whatever she pleased and refused to listen to anyone else's comments on her acting. The picture came out well enough despite that but it never excited enough moviegoers to gross much money. Originally played on stage by Katherine Cornell.

p, Jack Chertok; d, Robert Stevenson; w, Edmund H. North (based on the play by Edward Sheldon, Margaret Ayer Barnes); ph, Lucien Andriot; m, Carmen Dragon; ed, John Foley; prod d & art d, Nicolai Remisoff; cos, Elois Jenssen.

Crime   Cas.   (PR:C   MPAA:NR)

DISILLUSION   (1949, Ital.) 90m C&B Films bw

Ruggero Ruggeri (Papa Martin), Bella Starace Sainati (Mama Rosa), Enrico Clori (Charenson), Germana Paolieri (Olympia), Roberto Villa (Armando), Luisella Beghi (Amelia), Nino Crisman (Luciano), Maria Mercader (Margot), Giulio Donadio (Capt. Dubourg).

Villa comes across fine as a gambling youngster who squanders his wealthy dad's cash in the casinos, while telling him he's attending law school. Disillusioned Ruggeri is tough on the boy, but his delivery is stagey. Sometimes exciting entertainment. (In Italian; English subtitles.)

p, Valentino Brosio; d, Mario Bonnard; w, Oreste Biancoli, Bonnard, Akos Tolnay.

Drama   (PR:A   MPAA:NR)

DISOBEDIENT   (1953, Brit.) 86m Adelphi Film bw
                            (AKA: INTIMATE RELATIONS)

Harold Warrender (George), Marian Spencer (Yvonne), Ruth Dunning (Leonie), Russell Enoch (Michael), Elsy Albin (Madeline).

Largely unsatisfying remake of Cocteau's LES PARENTS TERRIBLES in an English setting. Enoch is a young boy who falls in love with father Warrender's mistress. The mother (Spencer) fears she'll lose her son as well as her husband. But Warrender sacrifices his own happiness for his son, while Dunning is the aunt, secretly in love with Warrender, who settles the peace. The film is too talky and constricted by stage motifs. Enoch, and Albin as the mistress, do have a nice chemistry, though.

p, David Dent; d&w, Charles Frank (adapted from Jean Cocteau's play); ph, Wilkie Cooper; m, Rene Cloerec; ed, Peter Bezencenet

Drama   (PR:O   MPAA:NR)

DISORDER*½   (1964, Fr./Ital.) 105m Titanus/Pathe bw
                            (LE DESORDRE; IL DISORDINE)

Louis Jourdan (Tom), Susan Strasberg (Isabella), Curt Jurgens (Tycoon), Alida Valli (Tycoon's Wife), Sami Frey (Carlo), Antonella Lualdi (Mali), Tomas Milian (Bruno), Jean Sorel (Andrea), Georges Wilson (Priest), Renato Salvatori (Mario), Marisa Belli, Emma Baron, Adriana Asti, Lia Angeleri, Luciana Angiolillo, Inger Milton, Jole Mauro.

A laborious piece of junk that takes itself too seriously and becomes preachy. Salvatori is struggling to find a job to help his mother, who is in the hospital. He takes a job as a bartender at a party held by a rich industrialist Jurgens, who can't himself attend the party because he is very sick and is throwing it only out of vanity. Salvatori hopes Jurgens will give him a job, but it doesn't happen. He then meets an old friend who has become wealthy and asks him for a loan for his mother. The friend laughs at him. A priest overhears his plight and offers help. He lets Salvatori stay at his house, which is occupied by many so-called charity cases. Most of these people are whores, criminals, and assorted lowlifes. The next day he receives a large amount of money from an unknown benefactor. He goes to the priest's house and finds that it is being torn down. The priest had sold it to aid Salvatori and his mother. Jourdan, Strasberg, and Jurgens are just passing players in this moralistic mess.

p, Giuseppe Bordogni; d, Franco Brusati; w, Brusati, Francesco Ghedini (French dialog by Felicien Marceau); ph, Leonida Barboni; m, Mario Nascimbene; ed, Ruggero Mastroianni; art d, Mario Garbuglia; cos, Bice Brichetto.

Drama   (PR:A   MPAA:NR)

DISORDER AND EARLY TORMENT*   (1977, Ger.) 85m Jugendfilm c (UNORDNUNG UND FUEHES LEID)

Martin Held (Prof. Abel Cornelius), Ruth Leuwerik (Frau Gerda Cornelius), Sabine von Maydell (Ingrid Cornelius), Frederic Meissner (Bert Cornelius), Sophie Seitz (Lorchen), Markus Sieburg (Beisser), Christian Kohlund (Hergesell), Eva Vaiti (Blau-Anna), Hans Kraus (Xavier Kleinsguetl), Michael Schwarzmaier (Wanda Herzl), Christine Buckegger (Fraulein Kowitl), C.P. Corzilius (Folklore Singer).

Based on a story by Thomas Mann; history professor Held acts and speaks as Mann's alter ego, in a deeply intellectual study of Mann and Germany's 1923 Inflation Year, blessed by beautiful cinematography. Director Seitz is Germany's most authoritative figure in the study of Mann, penning two previous scripts from his works. Bergman's THE SERPENT'S EGG deals with the same historical period.

p,d&w, Franz Seitz (based on a story by Thomas Mann); ph, Wolfgang Treu; m, Hans Pfitzner, Rolf Wilhelm, Friedric Meyer; ed, Adolph Schylssleder; art d, Michael Girschek; cos, Ira Stein.

Drama   (PR:A   MPAA:NR)

DISORDERLY CONDUCT½**   (1932) 82m FOX bw

Sally Eilers (Phyllis Crawford), Spencer Tracy (Dick Fay), El Brendel (Olsen), Ralph Bellamy (Tom Manning), Ralph Morgan (James Crawford), Frank Conroy (Tony Alsotto), Dickie Moore (Jimmy), Alan Dinehart (Fletcher), Clair Maynard (Lunch Room Girl), Cornelius Keefe (Stallings), Nora Lane (Gwen Fiske), Geneva Mitchell (Phoebe Darnton), Charles Grapewin (Limpy), James Todd (Pierce Manners), Sally Blane (Helen Burke).

Tracy is a motorcycle cop who gets demoted when he arrests Eilers for speeding. Her father, Morgan, is a rich and powerful man, thanks mainly to his corruption of city officials. Tracy makes a fool out of his captain, Bellamy, who is seeing Eilers. After his demotion, Tracy becomes a turncoat and warns gangster Conroy that Bellamy is going to raid his place. Bellamy gets wind of the tipoff and has Tracy lead the raid. Eilers is there. Tracy aids in her escape, and then uses this to blackmail her father. When Conroy is released from jail he goes gunning for Tracy but kills Tracy's nephew instead. Tracy decides to go straight. He hunts down and kills the gangster during a shoot-out, returns the blackmail money, and tells Bellamy all. Tracy doesn't pay for his crimes but is promoted back to the motorcycle division.

d, John W. Considine, Jr.; w, William Anthony McGuire (based on a story by McGuire); ph, Ray June; ed, Frank Hull; md, George Lipschultz; art d, Duncan Cramer; cos, Guy S. Duty.

Crime   (PR:A   MPAA:NR)

DISORDERLY ORDERLY, THE*   (1964) 83m PAR c

Jerry Lewis (Jerome Littlefield), Glenda Farrell (Dr. Jean Howard), Everett Sloane (Mr. Tuffington), Karen Sharpe (Julie Blair), Kathleen Freeman (Maggie Higgins), Susan Oliver (Susan Andrews), Del Moore (Dr. Davenport), Alice Pearce (Talkative Patient), Jack E. Leonard (Fat Jack), Barbara Nichols (Actress), Richard Deacon (Mr. Courtney), Danny Costello, Mike Ross (Ambulance Drivers), Herbie Faye (Mrs. Welles), Frank Scannell (Mr. McCaby), Mike Mazurki, Murray Alper, William Wellman, Jr. (Drivers), Benny Rubin, Milton Frome, John Macchia.

Lewis and writer-director Tashlin follow the prescription for success with a nutty hospital orderly who assumes the personalities of his patients. A fine example of the style is a sequence showing Lewis complaining of sympathy pains to a suffering patient. Tashlin, the only person who can adequately capture Lewis's zaniness, is able to produce outrage at a breakneck pace.

p, Paul Jones; exec p, Jerry Lewis; d&w, Frank Tashlin (based on a story by Norm Liebmann, Ed Haas), ph, W. Wallace Kelley (Technicolor), m, Joseph J. Lilley; ed, John Woodcock, Russel Wiles; art d, Hal Pereira, Tambi Larsen; set d, Sam Comer, Ray Moyer; cos, Edith Head; spec eff, John P. Fulton, Paul K. Lerpae, Faricot Edouart.

Comedy   (PR:A   MPAA:NR)

DISPATCH FROM REUTERS, A*   (1940) 89m WB bw
                            (GB: THIS MAN REUTER)

Edward G. Robinson (Julius Reuter), Edna Best (Ida Magnus), Eddie Albert (Max Stargardt), Albert Basserman (Franz Geller), Gene Lockhart (Bauer), Otto Kruger (Dr. Magnus), Nigel Bruce (Sir Randolph Persham), Montagu Love (Delane), James Stephenson (Carew), Walter Kingsford (Napoleon III), David Bruce (Bruce), Dickie Moore (Reuter as Boy), Billy Dawson (Max Stargardt as a Boy), Richard Nichols (Herbert, age 5), Lumsden Hare (Chairman), Alex Craig (Geant), Hugh Sothern (American Ambassador), Frank Jaquet (Reingold), Walter O. Stahl (Von Darnstadt), Paul Irving (Josephat Benfey), Edward McWade (Chemist), Gilbert Emery (Lord Palmerston), Robert Warwick (Opposition Speaker), Ellis Irving (Speaker), Henry Roquemore (Otto), Paul Weigel (Gauss), Joseph Stefani (Assistant), Mary Anderson (Bit Girl), Wolfgang Zilzer (Post Office Clerk), Frederic Mellinger (Man) Stuart Holmes (Attendant), Sunny Boyne (Companion), Ernst Hansman (Heinrich), Grace Stafford (Young Woman), Theodore Von Eltz (Actor), Kenneth Hunter, Holmes Herbert, Leonard Mudie, Lawrence Grant (Members of Parliament), Pat O'Malley (Workman), Cyril Delevanti, Norman Ainsley, Bobby Hale (News Vendors).

Warner Bros. made some of the very best biographies. From DR. EHRLICH'S MAGIC BULLET to YANKEE DOODLE DANDY, the studio and Hal B. Wallis specialized in accurate portrayals of famous, infamous, and sometimes little-known figures in history. Such was the case with Julius Reuter, the press baron who established his European empire for the dissemination of news. It's 1833 and the new telegraph systems are not in total use across Europe, so Reuter (Robinson) establishes his "pigeon post" to transmit news between cities. Soon enough, carrier pigeons become outmoded (and messy) and Reuter switches to telegraph wires. He has a London and a Paris office and sends Louis Napoleon's speech to England, via the wires, and scoops the world. His name is on everyone's lips with this and he soon establishes a worldwide reputation for speed, accuracy, and believability. He is happily married to Edna Best, who is at his side from start to finish and provides him with love as well as moral guidance in his work. Picture ends as Reuter scoops everyone with news of the assassination of Lincoln, even before the American ambassador knows of it. As you can tell from the sparse synopsis, it's not the most exciting film but it is historically accurate and they sacrificed drama for reality. Good work from Lockhart as the parsimonious German banker who is the first "pigeon" subscriber. Bruce is also excellent as Robinson's English financier.

p, Hal B. Wallis; d, William Dieterle; w, Milton Krims (based on the story "Reuter's News Agency" by Valentine Williams and Wolfgang Wilhelm); ph, James Wong Howe; m, Max Steiner; ed, Warren Low; md, Leo F. Forbstein; art d, Anton Grot; spec eff, Byron Haskin, Robert Burke.

Biography **(PR:A MPAA:NR)**

DISPUTED PASSAGE** (1939) 89m PAR bw

Dorothy Lamour *(Audrey Hilton)*, Akim Tamiroff *(Dr. "Tubby" Forster)*, John Howard *(John Wesley Beaven)*, Judith Barrett *(Winifred Bane)*, William Collier, Sr. *(Dr. William Cunningham)*, Victor Varconi *(Dr. La Ferriere)*, Gordon Jones *(Bill Anderson)*, Keye Luke *(Andrew Abbott)*, Elisabeth Risdon *(Mrs. Cunningham)*, Gaylord Pendleton *(Lawrence Carpenter)*, Billy Cook *(Johnny Merkle)*, William Pawley *(Mr. Merkle)*, Renie Riano *(Landlady)*, Z. T. Nyi *(Chinese Ambassador)*, Philip Ahn *(Dr. Fung)*, Lee Ya-Ching *(Aviatrix)*, Philson Ahn *(Kai)*, Dr. E.Y. Chung *(Dr. Ling)*, Roger Gray *(Gibson)*, Jack Chapin *(Terrence Shane)*, Dave Alison *(Intern)*, Mary Skalek *(Dirty Nurse)*, Alma Eidnea *(Scrub Nurse)*, Paul M. MacWilliams *(Doctor)*, Charles Trowbridge *(Dean)*, Dorothy Adams, Jolene King, Henrietta Kaye, Hortense Arbogast, Edith Cagnon, Patsy Mace, Fay McKenzie, Gloria Williams *(Nurses)*, Jimmy F. Hogan *(Messenger Boy)*, Kitty McHugh *(Telephone Operator)*, James B. Carson *(Hotel Clerk)*, Paul England *(Britisher)*, Richard Denning *(Student)*.

Medical student Lamour gets engaged to schoolmate Howard while in the class of well-respected professor Tamiroff, who convinces her to return to her native China and let Howard continue with his studies undistracted. She splits, but Howard follows. Once in the Orient he is injured in a bomb blast in a makeshift hospital, and Tamiroff is called on to perform a chancy operation. An unbelievable plot which is pulled off in an acceptable manner thanks to the fine acting of the three leads.

p, Harlan Thompson; d, Frank Borzage; w, Anthony Veiller, Sheridan Gibney (based on the novel by Lloyd C. Douglas); ph, William C. Mellor; m, Frederick Hollander, John Leopold; ed, James Smith; art d, Hans Dreier, Ronald Anderson.

Drama **(PR:A MPAA:NR)**

DISRAELI*½** (1929) 90m WB bw

George Arliss *(Disraeli)*, Joan Bennett *(Lady Clarissa Pevensey)*, Florence Arliss *(Lady Mary Beaconfield)*, Anthony Bushell *(Charles/Lord Deeford)*, David Torrence *(Sir Michael/Lord Probert)*, Ivan Simpson *(Hugh Meyers)*, Doris Lloyd *(Mrs. Agatha Travers)*, Gwendolyn Logan *(Duchess of Glastonbury)*, Charles E. Evans *(Potter)*, Cosmo Kyrle Bellew *(Mr. Terle)*, Jack Deery *(Bascot)*, Michael Visaroff *(Count Bosrinov)*, Norman Cannon *(Foljambe)*, Henry Carvill *(Duke of Glastonbury)*, Shayle Gardner *(Dr. Williams)*, Powell York *(Flookes)*, Margaret Mann *(Queen Victoria)*, George Atkinson *(Bit)*.

DISRAELI was one of the earliest of the Warner Bros. biographies and set a high standard for the work to come. It marked the film debut of aging Arliss and showed America a style of acting it had not seen much of in the prior silent years as Arliss was stage-trained and able to make the switch from stage to silents to sound with no difficulty. His real-life wife, Florence, played his screen wife and their ability to play off each other was a delight. Rather than attempt a long picture about the Jewish-turned-Christian man who was Queen Victoria's closest ally, they moved in for an extreme close-up and chose to deal only with a brief slice of Dizzy's life. It took some fanciful liberties with the truth and dealt basically with Disraeli's attempt to outwit the Russians in the rush to purchase the Suez Canal. Along the way, we get the opportunity to watch his wit, his amours, his geniality, and, over all, Arliss's stage technique. He had played Disraeli in a 1921 silent film first, but this is the performance that will be recalled. In later years, he specialized in historical figures and did Rothschild, Richelieu, Wellington, Alexander Hamilton, and others. He took great care to cast his own films and in THE MAN WHO PLAYED GOD he chose a young actress with just a bit of stage experience and some tiny roles in routine pictures. Her name was Bette Davis. These days, Arliss's flamboyant style may be scoffed at by the "naturalistic" actors but they would be wise to look hard at his work. He was right for his time and a lot better even today than many of the mush-in-the-mouthers who run rampant across our screens.

d, Alfred E. Green; w, Julien Josephson (based on the play by Louis Napoleon Parker); ph, Lee Garmes; m, Louis Silver; ed, Owen Marks.

Biography **(PR:A MPAA:NR)**

DISTANCE*** (1975) 94m Coe c

Paul Benjamin *(Elwood)*, Eija Pokkinen *(Greta)*, James Woods *(Larry)*, Bibi Besch *(Joanne)*, Hal Miller *(Jesse)*, Polly Holiday *(Mrs. Herman)*, Bruce Kornbluth.

The relationship between a black sergeant, Benjamin, and his white German wife, Pokkinen, is paralleled with a private's affair with an older woman. The sergeant is no longer in love with his wife, but lacks the courage to tell her. After coming on to the private, Woods, at a party, the fraulein kills herself. The normally despicable Woods (ONCE UPON A TIME IN AMERICA, AGAINST ALL ODDS) is brilliant as the philosophical and cold-hearted private.

p, George Coe; d, Anthony Lover; w, Jay Castle; ph&ed, Lover.

Drama **(PR:O MPAA:NR)**

DISTANT DRUMS*½** (1951) 100m United States Pictures/WB c

Gary Cooper *(Capt. Quincy Wyatt)*, Mari Aldon *(Judy Beckett)*, Richard Webb *(Richard Tufts)*, Ray Teal *(Pvt. Mohair)*, Arthur Hunnicutt *(Monk)*, Robert Barrat *(Gen. Zachary Taylor)*, Clancy Cooper *(Sgt. Shane)*, Larry Carper *(Chief Oscala)*, Dan White *(Cpl. Peachtree)*, Mel Archer *(Pvt. Jeremiah Hiff)*, Angelita McCall *(Amelia)*, Lee Roberts *(Pvt. Tibbett)*, Gregg Barton *(Pvt. James Tasher)*, Sheb Wooley *(Pvt. Jessup)*, Warren MacGregor *(Pvt. Sullivan)*, George Scanlan *(Bosun)*, Carl Harbaugh *(M. Duprez)*, Beverly Brandon *(Mme. Duprez)*, Sidney Capo *(Indian Boy)*.

Top-drawer action film has Cooper leading a military expedition against a ring of gunrunners and then being surrounded by hordes of hostile Seminoles who drive him and his men ever deeper into the Everglades, taking love interest Aldon with them. Cooper is stoic and heroic as he leads his men to the supposed safety of his own island. At the end of the trail he has a knife duel with chief Oscala, Carper, just barely winning. His bedraggled soldiers, or what's left of them, are saved at the last moment by U.S. troops who drive off the Indians. Director Walsh provides plenty of quick-paced thrills in this remake of his own WW II film, OBJECTIVE BURMA, which starred Errol Flynn; Steiner's score is as lush as the Everglades that almost swallow up Cooper and company.

p, Milton Sperling; d, Raoul Walsh; w, Niven Busch, Martin Rackin (based on a story by Busch); ph, Sid Hickox (Technicolor); m, Max Steiner; ed, Folmer Blangsted; art d, Douglas Bacon; set d, William Wallace; cos, Marjorie Best; makeup, Gordon Bau.

Adventure **(PR:A MPAA:NR)**

DISTANT JOURNEY***
(1950, Czech.) 78m Czechoslovak State Film Studios/Artkino bw
(DALEKA CESTA)

Blanka Waleska *(Dr. Hannah Kaufman)*, Otomar Krejca *(Dr. Tony Bures)*, Viktor Ocasek *(Mr. Kaufman)*, Zdenka Baldova *(Mrs. Kaufman)*, Jiri Spirit *(Johnny)*, Eduard Kohout *(Professor Reiter)*.

Fascinating, chilling account of one Jewish family's disintegration in the face of the Nazis. Intercut with scenes of the family are newsreel shots, rampaging crowds, and other stylized representations of the horror of the time, all with a pounding, grating soundtrack designed to drive the emotions of fear and helplessness as deep as they can. There is an obligatory joyful liberation by smiling, victorious Red Army troops, but that can't erase the memory of what has gone before. Possibly the best film on the subject and well worth seeing.

d, Alfred Radok; w, Mojmir Drvota, Erik Kolar, Radok.

Drama **(PR:C MPAA:NR)**

DISTANT TRUMPET** (1952, Brit.) 63m Meridian/Apex bw

Derek Bond *(David Anthony)*, Jean Patterson *(Valerie Maitland)*, Derek Elphinstone *(Richard Anthony)*, Anne Brooke *(Beryl Jeffries)*, Grace Gavin *(Mrs. Phillips)*, Keith Pyott *(Sir Rudolph Gettins)*, Jean Webster-Brough *(Mrs. Waterhouse)*, Grace Denbigh-Russell *(Mrs. Hallett)*, Constance Fraser, Alban Blakelock, John Howlett, Peter Fontaine, Gwynne Whitby, Anne Hunter.

When his missionary brother falls ill, Bond abandons his high-society medical practice to change places with him. Competently done drama by a director who was soon to move to horror films.

p, Harold Richmond, Derek Elphinstone; d, Terence Fisher; w, Elphinstone; ph, Gordon Lang.

Drama **(PR:A MPAA:NR)**

DISTANT TRUMPET, A** (1964) 115m WB c

Troy Donahue *(Lt. Matthew Hazard)*, Suzanne Pleshette *(Kitty)*, Diane McBain *(Laura)*, James Gregory *(Gen. Quait)*, William Reynolds *(Lt. Theo Mainwaring)*, Claude Akins *(Seely Jones)*, Kent Smith *(Secretary of War)*, Judson Pratt *(Capt. Cedric Gray)*, Bartlett Robinson *(Maj. Hiram Prescott)*, Bobby Bare *(Cranshaw)*, Larry Ward *(Sgt. Kroger)*, Richard X. Slattery *(Slattery)*, Mary Patton *(Jessica Prescott)*, Russell Johnson *(Capt. Brinker)*, Lane Bradford *(Maj. Miller)*, Guy Eltsosis.

Donahue is a young, enthusiastic lieutenant sent to a desolate Arizona fort in 1883 which soon becomes a powder keg. A battle with the local Indians rages while Donahue is involved with both McBain and Pleshette. The latter is the lucky girl who hitches heart-throb Donahue. This film was, unfortunately, a less-than-glorious exit for the great Raoul Walsh, who simply made a "B" Western on a big budget. Astonishing color lensing of the Red Rocks region and the Painted Desert. Also interesting is the use of the Indians' native language complete with subtitles.

p, William H. Wright; d, Raoul Walsh; w, John Twist (adaptation by Richard Fielder and Albert Beich of a novel by Paul Horgan); ph, William Clothier (Panavision, Technicolor); m, Max Steiner; ed, David Wages; art d, William Campbell; cos, Howard Shoup.

Western (PR:A MPAA:NR)

DITES 33 (SEE: LADY DOCTOR, THE, 1963, Fr./Ital./Span.)

DIVA**** (1982, Fr.) 123m Les Films Galaxie-Greenwich/Palace c

Frederic Andrei (Jules), Wilhelmenia Wiggins Fernandez (Cynthia Hawkins), Richard Bohringer (Gorodish), Thuy An Luu (Alba), Jacques Fabbri (Saporta), Chantal Deruaz (Nadia), Roland Bertin (Weinstadt), Gerard Darmon (L'Antillais), Dominique Pinon (Le Cure), Jean-Jacques Moreau (Krantz), Patrick Floersheim (Zatopek), Raymond Aquilon, Eugene Berthier, Gerard Chaillou, Andree Champeaux, Nathalie Dalian, Laurence Darpy, Michel Debrane, Etienne Draber, Laure Duthilleul, Nane Germon, Gebriel Gobin, Jim Adhi Limas, Louisette Malapert, Dimo Mally, Veneta Mally, Alain Marcel, Isabelle Mergault, Marthe Moudiki-Moreau, Jean-Luc Porraz, Bernard Robin, Yann Roussel, Brigitte Simonin, Jean-Louis Vitrac, Tania Zabaloieff.

A visually astonishing film with a complex plot about a young mail carrier in France (Andrei) and his love for a famous black opera singer (Fernandez). Andrei attends a performance the diva is giving in which she delivers an entrancing aria. He tapes the performance as a Taiwanese man watches him. Andrei then goes backstage to meet Fernandez, and when no one is looking steals her gown. Then a barefoot girl walks through the Paris metro in a daze, followed by two thugs, a punkish bald lad who listens to polkas on his earphones (Pinon) and a tall, gaunt creep (Darmon). Before they can catch the girl, she stumbles over to Andrei's mail-carrier moped and slips a tape into his bag. As the thugs try to toss her in their car, she breaks free and is stopped by an icepick thrown by Pinon. Andrei is warned not to interfere and leaves. He soon meets a chic Vietnamese girl (Luu) and brings her to his loft to listen to the tape. The loft, accessible only via a freight elevator, is an art director's paradise. It is decorated with a smashed Rolls Royce, colorful comic book-like paintings of vintage cars on the walls, and a painting of a nude woman (whose genitalia serve well as a hopscotch board) on the floor. A romance begins. Luu later introduces him to her mentor, a mysterious man into Zen, played wonderfully by Bohringer. He is shocked to hear that Andrei has a copy of the diva's voice, since she has never allowed herself to be recorded. It is soon learned that Andrei is wanted by a Taiwanese pair who have hopes of bootlegging the tape, and by the two thugs who believe he possesses the dead girl's tape which accuses the chief of police (Fabbri) of heading a prostitution ring. Andrei is chased (in one of the best chase scenes ever put on film) through the Metro and his loft is wrecked. He ends up at Fernandez's hotel room to return the stolen gown. She is shocked that he has stolen it but is taken by his devotion to her, and they spend some time together walking through Paris. Andrei learns that she hates bootleggers when the Taiwanese approach her manager with a blackmail proposition. Still unaware that he is carrying the dead girl's tape, he finally discovers it and pops it into a tape deck. The thugs pursue him through a parking garage and a game arcade, firing shots and hitting him twice. He struggles for a phone and calls Bohringer, who comes to his aid. With Luu, they drive to an enchanted lighthouse in an equally enchanting white Citroen. Bohringer arranges for a meeting with the police chief and the Taiwanese (neither of whom is aware that two tapes exist). The police chief arrives and places a bomb in the Citroen. He pays the money that Bohringer asks for and receives the tape. The bootlegging Taiwanese arrive, and, thinking Bohringer has given the cop a tape of the diva, they steal it for their own use. They get away in the Citroen, which is promptly blown up by the police chief. While out on the street, Bohringer opens a garage to reveal yet another, identical, Citroen. The finale has Andrei kidnaped by the thugs who take him back to the loft, via the elevator. They plant another, less incriminating, tape with him, and try to force him to jump down the elevator. A shot rings out and the knife-wielding Pinon falls to his death at the bottom of the shaft, polka music blaring out of his earphones. The police chief comes on the scene and decides to tidy everything up. The prostitution ring is blamed on thug Darmon, who is mercilessly killed by the chief. As Andrei and a detective are about to receive the same fate the lights go out. The police chief heads for the light switch which is dangerously close to the elevator shaft. As he is about to turn it back on, the switch (which hangs from a cord) is moved over the edge of the shaft, he reaches out, and falls to his death. Bohringer is seen just for a moment and quietly disappears, adding even more mystery. Andrei plays the recording for Fernandez, allowing her to hear how beautiful her voice is. The debut film from Jean-Jacques Beineix, DIVA is perhaps the most picturesque film to come out of France in years. Together with art director Hilton McConnico (an American) and cameraman Philippe Rousselot, he has given us awesome shot after awesome shot, so much so that many critics felt the film was too stylish. At times he succeeds in being very "new wave" (as in fashion and music, not the film movement), and at other times, he is intensely impressionistic. These qualities are even further enhanced by his perfect musical score (written by Vladimir Cosma). The criticism of DIVA in France nearly sank the picture, but that was before the public had seen it. Soon word of mouth had spread and it became a hit. In America it was one of the most successful foreign films at the box office, and is still playing art houses in regular runs.

p, Irene Silberman; d, Jean-Jacques Beineix; w, Beineix, Jean Van Hamme (based on a novel by Delacorta); ph, Philippe Rousselot (Eastmancolor); m, Vladimir Cosma; ed, Marie-Josephe Yoyotte, Monique Prim; art d, Hilton McConnico.

Crime/Romance Cas. (PR:C MPAA:NR)

DIVE BOMBER*** (1941) 130m WB-FN bw

Errol Flynn (Lt. Doug Lee), Fred MacMurray (Cmdr. Joe Blake), Ralph Bellamy (Dr. Lance Rogers), Alexis Smith (Linda Fisher), Regis Toomey (Tim Griffin), Robert Armstrong (Art Lyons), Allen Jenkins (Lucky Dice), Craig Stevens (John Thomas Anthony), Herbert Anderson (Chubby), Moroni Olsen, Addison Richards (Senior Flight Surgeons), Louis Jean Heydt (Swede), Dennie Moore (Mrs. James), Cliff Nazarro (Corps Man), Ann Doran (Helen), Russell Hicks, Howard Hickman (Admirals), Dewolfe Hopper, Alan Hale, Jr., Charles Drake, Gig Young, Larry Williams, Sol Gorss, Garland Smith, Tom Skinner, Tom Seidel, Gaylord Pendleton, Lyle Moraine, Garrett Craig, James Anderson, Stanley Smith, David Newell, Don Turner (Pilots), Alexander Lockwood (Squadron Commander), Richard Travis (Commanding Officer), William Forrest, George Meeker (Commanders), Tom Dugan (Corps Man), Owen King (Radio Man), Creighton Hale (Hospital Attendant), Tod Andrews (Telephone Man), Harry Lewis (Flag Man), Wedgewood Nowell (General), Charlotte Wynters (Hostess), Jane Randolph (Singer), Juanita Stark (Cigarette Girl), Alice Talton (Girl at Newsstand), Max Hoffman, Jr. (Squadron C.O.), Walter Sande (Blue Jacket).

DIVE BOMBER was a war movie just before we went to war. Warner Bros. must have had a line into the White House because they lensed this picture and it was released months before the Japanese hit us at Pearl Harbor. It was a propaganda piece for the people and was getting the country in readiness. Flynn is an aviator-doctor (flight surgeon) whose job it is to keep our flyboys fit. MacMurray, Toomey, and Heydt are three flying pals and Flynn is the naval medic assigned to their squadron in Hawaii. Heydt faints during a power dive and crashes but lives long enough to go under Flynn's knife in the operating room. Then he dies. Flynn is stunned. He meets MacMurray and Toomey again in San Diego where he decides to take pilot's training so he can learn more about the problems of flying and why some men "black out" in dives and others don't. Flynn joins with Bellamy and they make some valuable progress in aviation medicine. Toomey is grounded due to flight fatigue. He resigns, joins the RAF and crashes, and we wonder whether the doctors were right in grounding him. MacMurray volunteers to be a guinea pig for Flynn and Bellamy and helps them perfect a high-altitude oxygen suit before he crashes as well. (This is not a film to see if you fear flying.) Lots of wonderful flying sequences, very little romance to speak of (Alexis Smith does a small bit just to provide a minimal romantic interest). Much of the picture was made at San Diego's naval base with extra scenes being done at Pensacola and aboard the aircraft carrier Enterprise. Winton Hoch and Bert Glennon were Oscar-nominated.

p, Hal B. Wallis; d, Michael Curtiz; w, Frank Wead, Robert Buckner (based on the story "Beyond the Blue Sky" by Wead); ph, Bert Glennon, Winton C. Hoch; m, Max Steiner; ed, George Amy; md, Leo F. Forbstein; art d, Robert Haas; spec eff, Byron Haskin, Rex Wimpy; aerial ph, Elmer Dyer, Charles Marshall; chief pilot, Paul Mantz; tech adv, Cmdr. S.H. Warner USN, Marine Capt. J.R. Poppen.

Adventure (PR:A-C MPAA:NR)

DIVIDED HEART, THE*** (1955, Brit.) 89m EAL/REP bw

Cornell Borchers (Inga), Yvonne Mitchell (Sonja), Armin Dahlen (Franz), Alexander Knox (Chief Justice), Geoffrey Keen (Marks), Liam Redmond (1st Justice), Eddie Byrne (2nd Justice), Theodore Bikel (Josip), Ferdy Mayne (Dr. Muller), Andre Mikhelson (Prof. Miran), Pamela Stirling (Mlle. Poncet), Martin Stephens (Hans), Michel Ray, Martin Keller (Toni), Krystyna Rumistrzewicz (Mitzi), Mark Guebhard (Max), Gilgi Hauser, Maria Leontovitsch (Sonja's Daughters), Marianne Walla (Matron), Dorit Welles (Nurse), Hans Kuhn (Foreman), John Schlesinger (Ticket Collector), Philo Hauser, Guy Stephen Deghy, Carl Duering, Dora Lavrencic, Richard Molinas, John Welsh, Nicholas Stuart, Hans Elwenspoek, Frederick Schrecker, Alex McCowen, Orest Orloff, Ilona Ference, Randal Kinkead, Arthur Cortez.

When his father is shot as a partisan by the Germans, and his mother and sisters are sent to concentration camps, a little Yugoslav boy (Ray) is adopted by German parents. The boy grows up happily, but then his mother emerges from Auschwitz and tries to regain custody. Sentimental but worthwhile emotional drama based on a true story from Life magazine.

p, Michael Truman; d, Charles Crichton; w, Jack Whittingham, Richard Hughes; ph, Otto Heller; m, Georges Auric; ed, Peter Bezencenet; md, Dock Mathieson; art d, Edward Carrick.

Drama (PR:A MPAA:NR)

DIVINE EMMA, THE* (1983, Czech.) 105m Filmove Studio Barrandov-Ambassador/UA c

Bozidara Turronovova (Emma Destinn), George Kukura (Victor), Milos Kopecky (Samuel), Jiri Adamire (Colonel), Gabriela Benackova (Singing Voice of Emma), Josef Somr, Cestmir Randa, Josef Kemr, Vaclav Neuzil, Vaclav Lohnisky, Karel Augusta, Vlastimil Bedrna, Jana Smrchova, Frantisek Rehak, Zdenek Dite, Milena Svobodova, Stanislav Zindulka, Milan Karpisek.

A poor film biography of Emma Destinn, a popular soprano early in the century. She was born in what was then Bohemia and often appeared with opera great Enrico Caruso.

p, Jan Syrovy; d, Jiri krejcik; w, Zdenek Mahler, Krejcik; ph, Miroslav Ondricek (Eastmancolor); m, Zdenek Liska, Svatopluk Havelka; ed, Miroslav Hajek; md, Frantisek Belfin, Josef Chaloupka; art d, Jindrich Goetz.

Drama (PR:A MPAA:PG)

DIVINE MR. J., THE zero (1974) 93m c

John Bassberger (Jesus), Bette Midler (The Virgin Mary).

Wretched camp version of the Gospels that had a brief release years after it was made and after Midler had become something of a star. Bad actors camp it up and Midler sings a little. Midler fans stood outside one New York theater where this garbage was showing and handed out statements from Bette disclaiming her role in this movie and admitting the film was "dreadful."

p&d, Peter Alexander.

Comedy (PR:O MPAA:NR)

DIVINE NYMPH, THE** (1979, Ital.) 90m analysis Film Releasing Corp. c
(AKA: DIVINE CREATURE)

Laura Antonelli (*Manoela Roderighi*), Terence Stamp (*Dany di Bagnasco*), Marcello Mastroianni (*Michele Barra*), Michele Placido (*Martino Ghiondelli*), Duilio Del Prete (*Armellini*), Ettore Manni (*Marco Pisani*), Cecilia Polizzi (*Dany's Maid*), Marina Berti (*Manoela's Aunt*), Doris Durnati (*Signora Fones*), Ruth League (*Dany's Friend*), Piero Di Jorio (*Cameriere di Stefano*), Carlo Tamberlani (*Majordomo Pasqualino*).

Another in a long string of Italian soft-core sex movies with Antonelli constantly shucking her period costumes in search of sexual liberation. This time the setting is the 1920s, and Antonelli is a promiscuous young thing (what else?) who drives one lover to suicide and another into joining the Fascist party. Worthless as cinema, it does have the dubious value of the hauntingly beautiful Antonelli. (In Italian; English subtitles).

d, Giuseppe Patroni Griffi; w, Griffi, A. Valdarnini (based on the novel *La Divina Fanciulla* by Luciano Zuccoli); ph, Giuseppe Rotunno; m, Ennio Morricone; prod d, Fiorenzo Senese; cos, Gabriella Pescucci.

Drama **Cas.** **(PR:O MPAA:NR)**

DIVINE SPARK, THE*½ (1935, Brit./Ital.) 81m
Alleanza Cinematografica-Italiana/GAU bw (CASTA DIVA)

Marta Eggerth (*Maddalena Fumaroli*), Phillips Holmes (*Vincenzo Bellini*), Benita Hume (*Giriditta Pasta*), Donald Calthrop (*Judge Fumaroli*), Arthur Margetson (*Ernesto Tosi*), Edmund Breon (*Rossini*), Basil Gill (*Romani*), Hugh Miller (*Paganini*), Edward Chapman (*Mercadanti*), John Clements (*Florimo*), Felix Aylmer (*Butler*), John Deverell (*King*).

Engaged to be married to another, Eggerth rejects her true love—struggling composer Holmes, playing the composer, Vincenzo Bellini—rather than risk his career. He discovers her real feelings after her death, and dedicates the rest of his life and career to her. A dull costume musical made cooperatively between England and Fascist Italy. Filmed simultaneously in English and Italian.

p, Arnold Pressburger; d, Carmine Gallone; w, Emlyn Williams, Richard Benson (based on a story and screenplay by Walter Reisch); ph, Franz Planer.

Musical **(PR:A MPAA:NR)**

DIVING GIRLS' ISLAND, THE
(SEE: VIOLATED PARADISE, 1963, Ital./Jap.)

DIVING GIRLS OF JAPAN
(SEE: VIOLATED PARADISE, 1963, Ital./Jap.)

DIVORCE*½ (1945) 71m T/C MON bw

Kay Francis (*Diane Carter*), Bruce Cabot (*Bob Phillips*), Helen Mack (*Martha Phillips*), Jerome Cowan (*Jim Driscoll*), Craig Reynolds (*Bill Endicott*), Ruth Lee (*Liz Smith*), Jean Fenwick (*June Endicott*), Mary Gordon (*Ellen*), Larry Olsen (*Michael Phillips*), John Calkins (*Robby Phillips*), Jonathan Hale (*Judge Conlon*), Addison Richards (*Plummer*), Leonard Mudie (*Harvey Hicks*), Reid Kilpatrick (*Dr. Andy Cole*), Virginia Wave (*Secretary*), Napoleon Simpson (*Train Porter*), Pierre Watkin (*John B. Carter*).

Habitual divorcee Francis heads for her fifth marriage to her teen sweetheart, the already wed Cabot. His wife sues for divorce and gets custody of the kids. Francis and Cabot set off for Chicago where the sneaky lady sets up a real estate swindle. Cabot wises up to her game and crawls back to his ex. Slow-mover.

p, Jeffrey Bernard, Kay Francis; d, William Nigh; w, Sidney Sutherland, Harvey Gates (based on a story by Sutherland); ph, Harry Neumann; m, Edward J. Kay; ed, Richard Currier, Dave Milton; md, Kay.

Drama **(PR:A MPAA:NR)**

DIVORCE AMERICAN STYLE*** (1967) 109m Tandem-NG/COL c

Dick Van Dyke (*Richard Harmon*), Debbie Reynolds (*Barbara Harmon*), Jason Robards, Jr. (*Nelson Downes*), Jean Simmons (*Nancy Downes*), Van Johnson (*Al Yearling*), Joe Flynn (*Lionel Blandsforth*), Shelley Berman (*David Grieff*), Martin Gabel (*Dr. Zenwinn*), Lee Grant (*Dede Murphy*), Pat Collins (*Herself*), Tom Bosley (*Farley*), Emmaline Henry (*Fern Blandsforth*), Dick Gautier (*Larry Strickland*), Tim Matthieson (*Mark Harmon*), Gary Goetzman (*Jonathan Harmon*), Eileen Brennan (*Eunice*), Shelley Morrison (*Jackie*), Bella Bruck (*Celia*), John J. Anthony (*Judge*).

Van Dyke and Reynolds divorce after fifteen years of marriage, while friends Robards and Simmons create a financial scheme to right it all and real-life hypnotist Pat Collins sees that it works out. A well-honed social commentary on the American way of life. Co-penned by Norman Lear (*All In The Family*), it was an Oscar nominee for Best Screenplay. Dave Grusin's score fits perfectly.

p, Norman Lear; d, Bud Yorkin; w, Lear (based on a story by Robert Kaufman); ph, Conrad Hall (Technicolor), m, David Grusin; ed, Ferris Webster; prod d, Edward Stephenson; set d, Frank Tuttle; cos, Bob Mackie.

Comedy/Satire **Cas.** **(PR:C MPAA:NR)**

DIVORCE AMONG FRIENDS*½ (1931) 65m WB bw

James Hall (*George Morris*), Lew Cody (*Paul Wilcox*), Irene Delroy (*Helen Morris*), Natalie Moorhead (*Joan Whitley*), Edward Martindel (*Tom Chadwick*), Margaret Seddon (*Maid*).

An unfortunate love triangle story which turns into an even more unfortunate love rectangle, eventually splitting into two happy couples. This clumsily scripted early sound picture would have benefited greatly had it been made just a few years previous—in the silent days.

d, Roy Del Ruth; w, Arthur Caesar, Harvey Thew (based on the story "Two Time Marriage" by Jack Townley); ph, Dev Jennings; ed, Owen Marks.

Romance **(PR:C MPAA:NR)**

DIVORCE IN THE FAMILY**½ (1932) 78m MGM bw

Jackie Cooper (*Terry Parker*), Conrad Nagel (*Dr. Shumaker*), Lewis Stone (*John Parker*), Lois Wilson (*Mrs. Shumaker*), Jean Parker (*Lucille*), Maurice Murphy (*Al Parker*), Lawrence Grant (*Kenny*), Richard Wallace (*Snoop*), David Newell (*Intern*), Oscar Rudolph (*Spike*), Louise Beavers (*Rosetta*).

Adorable kid star Cooper changes pace as a divorce-affected youngster who must make a choice between a tough stepdad, Nagel, and his more permissive real one, Stone. Stone tries to get his son back, but Cooper appreciates and understands the necessity of discipline and chooses to stay with tough Nagel. Far removed from his CHAMP role, Cooper proves he is a versatile child thespian.

d, Charles F. Reisner; w, Delmer Daves (based on a story by Daves, Maurice Rapf); ph, Oliver T. Marsh; ed, William Gray.

Drama **(PR:A MPAA:NR)**

DIVORCE, ITALIAN STYLE**** (1962, Ital.) 108m Lux bw
(DIVORZIO ALL'ITALIANA)

Marcello Mastroianni (*Ferdinando*), Daniella Rocca (*Rosalia*), Stefania Sandrelli (*Angela*), Leopoldo Trieste (*Carmelo Patane*), Odoardo Spadaro (*Don Gaetano*), Margherita Girelli (*Sisina*), Angela Cardile (*Agnese*), Bianca Castagnetta (*Donna Matilde*), Lando Buzzanca (*Rosario Mule*), Pietro Tordi (*Attorney DeMarzi*), Laura Tomiselli (*Zia Fifidda*), Ugo Torrente (*Don Calogero*), Antoni Acqua (*The Priest*).

Rocca is a whining sex-crazed Sicilian wife who drives husband Mastroianni to divorce. Unfortunately for Rocca it is easier to murder in Italy than it is to divorce. So that is precisely what is done. The scheming Mastroianni then goes on to marry the proverbial girl next door, after his wife is out of the picture. A brilliant comic performance from Mastroianni which has been compared to the dead-pan style of Keaton. It earned him an Oscar nomination for Best Actor, as well as Best Actor accolades from the Golden Globes and the British Film Academy. An Oscar nomination also went to director Germi, and the screenplay took top honors. Considered by some to be one of the greatest modern comedies.

p, Franco Cristaldi; d, Pietro Germi; w, Ennio DeConcini, Alfredo Giannetti, Germi; ph, Leonida Barboni; m, Carlo Rustichelli; ed, Roberto Cinquini; cos, Dina Di Bari.

Comedy **(PR:A MPAA:NR)**

DIVORCE OF LADY X, THE*** (1938, Brit.) 90m London-Denham/UA c

Merle Oberon (*Leslie Steele*), Laurence Olivier (*Logan*), Binnie Barnes (*Lady Mere*), Ralph Richardson (*Lord Mere*), Morton Selten (*Lord Steele*), J.H. Roberts (*Slade*), Gertrude Musgrove (*Saunders*), Gus McNaughton (*Waiter*), Eileen Peele (*Mrs. Johnson*), Hugh McDermott, H.B. Hallam.

Droll comedy of manners and morals that was based on a play and made as a film once before in 1932 as COUNSEL'S OPINION, directed by Allan Dwan. The four screen writers' literate script of Biro's adaptation of the stage work takes Oberon to a London hotel where she is attending a costume party. The weather turns foul and she must spend the night at the hostelry with several other ladies who were unable to make it home. Olivier is a young lawyer occupying a suite and the manager prevails on him to give up some of the space in his copious quarters, but Olivier is adamant until Oberon uses her wiles on him. The result is that she gets the comfortable bed and Olivier must snooze on the floor in the next room. She leaves in the a.m. before he can find out anything about this fascinating and attractive woman. Her alacrity causes him to wonder if she's married. When he arrives at his office, an old school chum contacts him and wants Olivier to handle his divorce. The man is sure his wife spent the night with another man at the same hotel we've seen earlier. Olivier can't believe this nerd could be married to Oberon. He isn't, of course, and his wife is someone else entirely. But Olivier doesn't know that yet. So it gets down to one of those British drawing room farces where identities are mistaken, accusations are made, absurd situations occur, and Olivier and Oberon are together at the finale. Richardson is very funny as the man who wants a divorce from wife Barnes, who has been married thrice before and has backhanded fidelity on many other occasions. Oberon shows she can play light comedy as well as some of the heavier work she had to do over the years. The Technicolor tinting was supervised by long-time advisor Natalie Kalmus and, although it lent a nice air to the already-airy material, it was totally unnecessary.

p, Alexander Korda; d, Tim Whelan; w, Ian Dalrymple, Arthur Wimperis, Lajos Biro, Robert Sherwood (based on Biro's adaptation of the play "Counsel's Opinion" by Gilbert Wakefield); ph, Harry Stradling (Technicolor); m, Miklos Rosza; ed, William Hornbeck, L.J.W. Stockviss; prod d, Lazare Meerson, P. Sherriff, A. Waugh; md, Muir Mathieson; cos, Irene Hubert; spec eff, Ned Mann.

Comedy **(PR:A NR)**

DIVORCEE, THE***½ (1930) 83m MGM bw

Norma Shearer (*Jerry*), Chester Morris (*Ted*), Conrad Nagel (*Paul*), Robert Montgomery (*Don*), Florence Eldridge (*Helen*), Helene Millard (*Mary*), Robert Elliott (*Bill*), Mary Doran (*Janice*), Tyler Brooke (*Hank*), Zelda Sears (*Hannah*), George Irving (*Dr. Bernard*), Helen Johnson (*Dorothy*).

THE DIVORCEE was hot stuff for 1930 and would still be hot stuff fifty years hence. Based on Ursula Parrott's steamy novel, *Ex-Wife*, it won the Oscar for Norma Shearer as she worked very hard to prove to the Hollywood community that she earned her roles by talent, not because she was sleeping with the studio president. She was also married to the studio boss, Irving Thalberg. The very complex *precis* goes this way: Shearer is having an an affair with Nagel and Irving, her father, wishes she would marry the man. She meets Morris, an Underwood player (read...newspaper man) and becomes affianced. Judith Wood is in love with Nagel and offers him balm in the form of alcohol. The booze fuzzes Nagel's wits and while they drive home, an accident occurs. His arm is broken and Wood's face is horribly scarred. A short while later, Nagel and Wood are married in the hospital while Morris and Shearer get rice thrown at them outside of a church on the same day. Three years pass. Morris and Shearer couldn't be happier. He gets an assignment in the Windy City and is about to leave the residence when a passel of pals arrive, including Mary Doran, a divorcee whom Morris used to tickle pink a few years back. Morris is livid that Doran would come to his house and explains to his beloved Shearer that Doran was only a brief oasis in his life when he was out there looking for water. Morris leaves and Shearer goes to a party with Montgomery, a bit of a wastrel who is Morris' best pal. At the party they meet Doran again and it depresses Shearer. They go home and Shearer invites Montgomery to stay the night! A week later, Morris returns home and Shearer confesses that she's been dating Montgomery. He's stunned. A divorce follows and Shearer begins a sexual hegira that would have had Evita Peron applauding Norma's stamina. She meets Nagel once more and learns that his marriage to Wood is on a shaky precipice. Nagel and Shearer have an exotic two months aboard his yacht and at the end of their exquisite summer, she convinces him to divorce Wood and marry her. Now she learns that Morris is on a drinking binge in Paris where he is working as a tour guide for American visitors. Wood, who had agreed to the divorce, changes her mind and asks Shearer to give up her claim on Nagel. Nagel's response is anger at his wife but Shearer, in a rare selfless moment, sees that the disfigured woman really needs her husband so she bids them farewell and goes to Paris where she tentatively approaches her ex-husband on New Year's Eve. He sees her, opens his arms, and they clinch at the fadeout. Norma Shearer was never one of the screen's great beauties in the way that Garbo or Swanson were. But she did the best with what she had. She trained hard and became a fine actress with an all-too-brief career in talking films. In 1942, she quit show business (Thalberg had died several years before), took up with a ski instructor two decades her junior (he was about 22 and she was 42), and settled into happiness...presumably. THE DIVORCE was also nominated for best picture, best direction, best screenplay, but was trounced by ALL QUIET ON THE WESTERN FRONT.

p&d, Robert Z. Leonard; w, Nick Grinde, Zelda Sears, John Meehan (based on the novel Ex-Wife by Ursula Parrott); ph, Norbert Brodine; ed, Hugh Wynn, Truman K. Wood; art d, Cedric Gibbons; cos, Adrian.

Drama   **(PR:C   MPAA:NR)**

DIXIANA*   (1930) 100m RKO bw & c

Bebe Daniels (Dixiana), Everett Marshall (Carl Van Horn), Bert Wheeler (Pee Wee), Robert Woolsey (Ginger), Joseph Cawthorn (Cornelius Van Horn), Jobyna Howland (Mrs. Van Horn), Dorothy Lee (Poppy), Ralf Harolde (Royal Montague), Edward Chandler (Blondell), George Herman (Contortionist), Raymond Maurel (Cayetano), Bruce Covington (Porter), Bill Robinson (Specialty Dancer), Eugene Jackson (Cupid).

A large waste of talent, time, and money was this box-office bomb about the South. Set in New Orleans at Mardi Gras time, the film uses color in the Fat Tuesday sequence and it helps buck up the proceedings, but not much. Bebe Daniels is a circus performer in 1840s Louisiana. She goes ga-ga for Marshall, a wealthy southerner, but his mother, Jobyna Howland, is not amused and does not approve her prospective daughter-in-law's breeding. She uses her power to keep the couple apart. Also serving to muddle matters is Harolde, playing an oily gambler. He wants Daniels for his own and will stop at nothing to keep her and Marshall apart. Daniels eventually shows up Harolde as a fool and convinces one and all that she is fit to be Marshall's wife. Wheeler and Woolsey are the only humor in the witless screenplay and they stoop to some gags that were old when Andrew Jackson was a boy. Bill Robinson does a dance but it's not enough to save this from sinking. Marshall was a very fine Metropolitan Opera singer and he may have looked good from the balcony in that venerable building on Broadway and 40th but when examined by the unflinching eye of the camera, he fell far short and his career was soon over. There was not one song you could hum in the score. Songs: "Dixiana" (Benny Davis, Harry Tierney), "Here's To The Old Days," "A Tear, a Kiss, a Smile," "My One Ambition Is You," "A Lady Loved a Soldier," Mr. and Mrs. Sippi," "Guiding Star" (Anne Caldwell, Tierney).

p, William LeBaron; d&w, Luther Reed (based on a story by Anne Caldwell); ph, Roy Hunt (Technicolor); m, Harry Tierney; md, Victor Baravalle; orch, Max Steiner; ch, Pearl Eaton.

Musical/Comedy   **(PR:A   MPAA:NR)**

DIXIE*   (1943) 89m Paul Jones/PAR c

Bing Crosby (Dan Emmett), Dorothy Lamour (Millie Cook), Billy de Wolfe (Mr. Bones), Marjorie Reynolds (Jean Mason), Lynne Overman (Mr. Whitlock), Eddie Foy, Jr. (Mr. Felham), Raymond Walburn (Mr. Cook), Grant Mitchell (Mr. Mason), Clara Blandick (Mrs. Mason), Tom Herbert (Homer), Olin Howlin (Mr. Devereau), Robert Warwick (Mr. La Plant), Fortunio Bonanova (Headwaiter), Brandon Hurst (Man in Restaurant), Josephine Whittell (Woman in Restaurant), Paul McVey (Headwaiter in Restaurant), Charles La Torre (Captain of Waiters), Charles R. Moore (News Vendor), Tom Kennedy (Barkeeper), Louis Dardon (Minstrel Dancer), Stanley Andrews (Mr. Masters), Norma Varden (Mrs. La Plant), Hope Landin (Mrs. Masters), James Burke (River Boat Captain), Jimmy Conlin, George Anderson (Publishers), Wilbur Mack (Publisher's Assistant), Henry Roquemore (Man in Audience) Sam Flint (Southern Colonel), Harry Barris (Drummer), Dell Henderson (Stage Manager), Willie Best (Steward), Jack Perrin (Fireman), John "Skins" Miller,

Donald Kerr, Fred Santley, Warren Jackson, Jimmy Ray, Hal Rand, Charles Mayon, Allen Ray, Jerry James, Jimmy Clemons (Minstrel Show), Charles Cane, Edward Emerson, Cyril Ring, Dudley Dickerson, Harry C. Bradley, Bill Halligan, Willie Best.

A fictional account of the life of songwriter and minstrel entertainer Daniel Decatur Emmett. Crosby is the songwriter who leaves his Kentucky home to make it big in New Orleans. On a riverboat he is cheated out of all his money by card shark De Wolfe. In New Orleans, after threatening De Wolfe, they become friends. Crosby meets and plans to marry Lamour, but when he goes back to his home town to tell his fiancee, Reynolds, he finds that she has polio and he ends up marrying her. They go to New York where he sells a few of his songs, but gets little money for his efforts. His song, "Dixie," no one will touch. Crosby returns to New Orleans and starts the first minstrel show. He meets up with Lamour again and Reynolds, realizing that she is just a burden for him, writes a note during one of the shows that she is leaving him. Lamour finds the note and burns it, accidentally setting the theater on fire. Crosby is in the middle of singing "Dixie" and tells the band to pick up the tempo to finish before the fire grows. "Dixie" is propelled from a slow ballad to the South's inspirational theme song because of the speeded-up tempo. A well-crafted production with Crosby and Lamour in top form. This was Crosby's first color film and Mellor's color photography is breathtaking. It is interesting to note that none of the actors used southern accents, which in many ways would have called attention to itself and hampered the performances. Songs: "Sunday, Monday and Always," "If You Please," "She's From Missouri," "Kinda Peculiar Brown," "A Horse That Knows His Way Back Home," "Miss Jemima Walks By" (Jimmy Van Heusen, Johnny Burke), "Dixie" (Daniel Decatur Emmett).

p, Paul Jones; d, A. Edward Sutherland; w, Darrell Ware, Claude Binyon (based on a story by William Rankin); ph, William Mellor (Technicolor); m, Johnny Burke, James Van Heusen; ed, William Shea; md, Robert Emmett Dolan; art d, William Flannery; cos, Raoul Pene Du Bois; spec eff, Gordon Jennings; ch, Seymour Felix.

Musical   **Cas.**   **(PR:A   MPAA:NR)**

DIXIE DUGAN*½   (1943) 63m FOX bw

James Ellison (Roger Hudson), Charlotte Greenwood (Mrs. Dugan), Charlie Ruggles (Pa Dugan), Lois Andrews (Dixie Dugan), Helene Reynolds (Jean Patterson), Raymond Walburn (J.J. Lawson), Ann Todd (Imogene Dugan), Eddie Foy, Jr. (Matt Hogan), Irving Bacon (Mr. Kelly), Sarah Edwards (Mrs. Kelly), George Melford (Mr. Sloan), Mae Marsh (Mrs. Sloan), Morris Ankrum (Editor), Dick French (Phillips), George Lessey (Sen. Patterson), Ruth Warren (Sergeant's Wife), Paul Burns (Sign Painter), Eddie Dunn (Policeman), Milt Kibbee, Billy Wayne (Pressmen), Clarence Hennecke (Postman), Sam Wren (FBI Man), Ray Walker (Burns), Jack Chefe (Artist), Dick Barron (Copy Boy), Byron Foulger (Secretary), John Wald (Announcer), Emmett Vogan (Salesman), Sam McDaniel (Night Porter).

Andrews is Dixie Dugan, a government secretary who wants to be treated on an equal basis, but is instead shoved into conducting a menial survey by the head of her department, Ellison. Tired script and direction are not saved by the antics of Dixie Dugan's wacky parents, Greenwood and Ruggles. Better send this one back to the static newspaper strips; it was never meant to step out into real life.

p, Walter Morosco; d, Otto Brower; w, Lee Loeb, Harold Buchman (based on the comic strip character "Dixie Dugan" created by Joseph P. McEvoy); ph, Peverell Marley; m, Emil Newman, Arthur Lange; ed, J. Watson Webb; art d, Richard Day, Lewis Creber.

Comedy   **(PR:A   MPAA:NR)**

DIXIE DYNAMITE**   (1976) 90m Dimension c

Warren Oates, Christopher George, Jane Anne Johnstone, Kathy McHaley, R.G. Armstrong, Stanley Adams, Wes Bishop, Mark Miller.

When their father is killed by a deputy trying to evict the family off their farm, Johnstone and McHaley try to get even. Routine vengeance stuff for the southern drive-in circuit, though Oates is always worth seeing. Songs performed by classic rockabilly artists Duane Eddy and Dorsey Burnette, in addition to the Mike Curb Congregation.

p, Wes Bishop; d, Lee Frost; w, Frost, Bishop; m/l, Styner & Jordan.

Crime   **Cas.**   **(PR:C   MPAA:PG)**

DIXIE JAMBOREE*½   (1945) 69m PRC bw

Frances Langford (Susan Jackson), Guy Kibbee (Capt. Jackson), Eddie Quillan (Jeff Calhoun), Charles Butterworth (Professor), Fifi D'Orsay (Yvette), Lyle Talbot (Tony Sardell), Frank Jenks (Curly), Almira Sessions (Ellabella Jackson), Joe Devlin (Sergeant), Louise Beavers (Opal), Ben Carter (Sam), Gloria Jetter (Azella), Edward Shattuck (Mr. Doakes), Ethel Shattuck (Mrs. Doakes), Tony Warde (Double), Angel Cruz (Nothing), Ben Carter Choir.

A musical riverboat full of daffy characters rolling down the Mississippi, helmed by captain Kibbee. Doubling as a medicine man, Kibbee is mistaken for a bootlegger by a pair of ex-cons who try to steal elixir-laced whisky. It's hard to tell which covers less ground, the slow-moving boat Ellabella or the script. Songs: "Dixie Showboat," "No, No, No," "If It's a Dream," "You Ain't Right with the Lord," "Big Stuff" (Michael Breen, Sam Neuman).

p, Jack Schwarz; d, Christy Cabanne; w, Sam Neuman (based on a story by Lawrence E. Taylor); ph, Jack Mackenzie; ed, Robert Crandall; art d, Paul Palmentola, Frank Sylos.

Musical/Comedy   **Cas.**   **(PR:A   MPAA:NR)**

DIZZY DAMES***½   (1936) 65m Liberty bw

Marjorie Rambeau (*Lillian Bennett*), Florine McKinney (*Helen*), Lawrence Gray (*Terry*), Inez Courtney (*Arlette*), Berton Churchill (*Dad Hackett*), Fuzzy Knight (*Buzz*), Kitty Kelly (*La Vere*), Lillian Miles (*Gloria*), John Warburton (*Rodney Stokes*), Mary Forbes (*Mrs. Stokes*), Christine Marston (*Rhumba Dancer*).

Rambeau runs a boarding house for stage has-beens and is thrown into a flurry by the unscheduled arrival of her daughter, who is unaware of mom's work. Although the joint is completely respectable, Ma Rambeau has the guests put on their best behavior to impress the girl. Conflict comes when a struggling writer wants to marry the daughter. A harmless piece which includes the musical numbers: "Love Is the Thing" (Harry Tobias, Neil Moret), "I Was Taken by Storm" (Edward Heyman, Louis Alter), Let's Be Frivolous" (Howard Jackson, George Waggner), and "Martinique" (Arthur Swanstrom, Waggner, Alter).

p, M.H. Hoffman; d, William Nigh; w, George Waggner (based on the short story "The Watch Dog" by P.G. Wodehouse); ph, Harry Neumann; m, Howard Jackson.

Musical/Drama   (PR:A   MPAA:NR)

DJANGO**½   (1966 Ital./Span.) 95m B.R.C./TECISA c

Franco Nero, Eduardo Fajardo, Lorendana Nusciak, Jose Bodalo, Angel Alvarez, Rafael Vaquero.

DJANGO would be the first of more than thirty Italian westerns using the Django character. Another violent tale of a man who comes into a town run by rival gangs. This time it's the Ku Klux Klan and Mexican bandits. In superhuman style Nero eliminates opponents from both sides and, in the end, with his hands broken, he gets his revenge by propping his six-shooter on a cross. The DJANGO films, along with Leone's westerns, were the most popular of the spaghetti westerns.

p, Manola Bolognini; d, Sergio Corbucci; w, Sergio and Bruno Corbucci, Franco Rossetti, Jose G. Maesso; ph, Enzo Barboni.

Western   (PR:O   MPAA:NR)

DJANGO KILL**   (1967, Ital./Span.) 120m G.I.A./Hispamer Film c
                                                    (SEI SEI VIVO; SPARA!)

Tomas Milian, Pierro Lulli, Milo Quesada, Roberto Camardiel, Marilu Tolu, Raymond Lovelock.

A violent and surrealistic spaghetti western directed by a man who had worked with Federico Fellini. Milian comes into a town controlled by two gangs. One, a gang of black-leather-outfitted boys who ride white horses, and the other gang run by the storekeeper. Milian, with the help of two Indians, stays alive while everybody is slaughtered around him. A bizarre western.

p&d, Giulio Questi; w, Franco Arcalli; ph, Franco Delli Colli.

Western   (PR:O   MPAA:NR)

DO NOT DISTURB**½   (1965) 102m Arcola-Melcher/FOX c

Doris Day (*Janet Harper*), Rod Taylor (*Mike Harper*), Hermione Baddeley (*Vanessa Courtwright*), Sergio Fantoni (*Paul Bellasi*), Reginald Gardiner (*Simmons*), Maura McGiveny (*Claire Hackett*), Aram Katcher (*Culkos*), Leon Askin (*Langsdorf*), Lisa Pera (*Alicia*), Michael Romanoff (*Delegate*), Albert Carrier (*Reynard*), Barbara Morrison (*Mrs. Ordley*), Dick Winslow (*One-Man Band*), Pierre Salinger (*American Consul*).

Day and Taylor are a twosome in love who wander into extramarital waters, he with his secretary and she with a French antique dealer. They realize their misguided directions before it's too late and return to each others' outstretched arms. Attractive wardrobing and lavish lensing of Paris and London add zest, as does Day's singing of French ditty "Au Revoir Is Goodbye with a Smile."

p, Aaron Rosenberg, Martin Melcher; d, Ralph Levy; w, Milt Rosen, Richard Breen (based on the play "Some Other Love" by William Fairchild); ph, Leon Shamroy (CinemaScope, DeLuxe Color); m, Lionel Newman; ed, Robert Simpson; art d, Jack Martin Smith, Robert Boyle; set d, Walter M. Scott, Jerry Wunderlich; cos, Ray Aghayan; spec eff, L.B. Abbott, Emil Kosa, Jr.; m/l, "Do Not Disturb," Mark Barkan, Ben Raleigh; "Au Revoir Is Goodbye with a Smile," Robert Hilliard, Mort Garson.

Comedy   (PR:A   MPAA:NR)

DO NOT THROW CUSHIONS INTO THE RING**½ (1970) 100m c

Steve Ihnat (*Christopher Belton*), Sally Carter (*The Wife*), Arthur O'Connell (*Business Agent*), Ed Asner (*The Agent*), Carla Borelli, Lolly Oliver, Gaby Michel, Rona Barrett, Sheryl Nowak, Paige Weaver, Brian Hennessey, Louis Teague, Robert Stull, Douglas W. Jackson, Carl Scholze, Cathy Carver, Clifton Archambault, Joseph Archambault, Cathy Andrews.

An actor's diary which lists star Ihnat in most of the picture's production roles. This is actually a collection of the ideas and objectives necessary for becoming an actor. The frustrations Ihnat faces are dealt with through an experimental narrative form. Occasionally poignant. With Ed Asner as the actor's agent.

p,d,w&ed, Steve Ihnat; ph, Louis Teague, Arch Archambault, Basil C. Bradbury (Eastmancolor); m, Nicholas Carras.

Drama   (PR:O   MPAA:NR)

DO YOU KEEP A LION AT HOME?***   (1966, Czech.) 81m
                                      Barrandov Film Studio/Brandon Films c
                                                       (MATE DOMA IVA?)

Ladislav Ocenasek (*Joe/"Pepik"*), Josef Filip (*Johnny/"Honzik"*), Olga Machoninova (*Little Girl*), Milos Preininger (*Father*), Dagmar Kofronova (*Mother*), Frantisek Loring (*Man with Umbrella*), Jan Brychta (*Painter*), Vendelin Sedivy (*Policeman*), Arnost Faltynek (*Museum Doorman*), Jiri Valenta (*Travel Agency Employee*), Evelyna Juhanova (*Fairy*), Mirko Musil (*Water Fairy*), Raoul Schranil (*Devil*),

Gabriela Bartlova (*White Lady*), Karel Vavrik (*Poster Man*), Ela Silarova, Marie Rosulkova (*Ladies*), Karl Krautgartner (*Sorcerer*), Jaroslav Zrotal (*General*), Pavel Hobl (*Man In BMW*), Marcela Sedlackova (*French Lady*), Josef Steigl (*French Man*), Jaroslav Orlicky (*Headless Man*).

Ocenasek and Filip are brothers who go on a wild adventure in Prague when they find their school closed for the day. They roller skate through a museum and then meet a talking dog. The dog takes them to places where animals talk to children. The boys defeat an evil sorcerer, Krautgartner, who has put a spell over a group of musicians. After the two win a car race, they go back to the school where their father is waiting to take them home.

d, Pavel Hobl; w, Sheila Ochova, Bohumil Sobotka, Hobl (based on a story by Ochova); ph, Jiri Vojta; m, Wiliam Bukovy; ed, Miroslav Hajek, Jitka Sulcova; art d, Jan Brychta; set d, Bohumil Pokorny, Jindrich Goetz; cos, Skorepova.

Fantasy   (PR:AA   MPAA:NR)

DO YOU LIKE WOMEN? (SEE: TASTE FOR WOMEN, A, 1964, Fr./Ital.)

DO YOU LOVE ME?***   (1946) 91m FOX c
                                                (AKA: KITTEN ON THE KEYS)

Maureen O'Hara (*Katherine Hilliard*), Dick Haymes (*Jimmy Hale*), Harry James (*Barry Clayton*), Reginald Gardiner (*Herbert Benham*), Richard Gaines (*Ralph Wainwright*), Stanley Prager (*Dilly*), B.S. Pully (*Taxi Driver*), Chick Chandler (*Earl Williams*), Alma Kruger (*Mrs. Crackleton*), Almira Sessions (*Miss Wayburn*), Douglas Wood (*Dr. Dunfee*), Harlan Briggs (*Mr. Higbee*), Julia Dean (*Mrs. Allen*), Harry Hays Morgan (*Prof. Allen*), Harry James Music Makers, Eugene Borden (*Headwaiter*), Lex Barker (*Guest*), Harry Seymour (*Headwaiter*), Sam McDaniel (*Bartender*), William Frambes (*Usher*), Betty Grable (*Clayton's Admirer*), Jesse Graves (*Bartender*), Evelyn Mulhall (*Woman*), Esther Brodelet, Jack Barnett, Lillian Porter, Marjorie Jackson (*Dancers*), Les Clark, Jimmy Cross (*Bellhops*), Maria Shelton (*Miss Fairchild*), Kay Connors (*Secretary*), Philip Morris, Fred Graham (*Doormen*), Eric Freeman (*Painter*), Dale Barringer (*Newsboy*), Charles Aaron (*Sailor*), Albert Morin, Frank Melton, George Sorel, Charles Williams, Ashlye Cowan, Harry Depp, Ernie Adams, William Benedict, Walter O'Connell, Jack Scordi and Diane Ascher [Jack and Dorothy Costello] (*Dance Team*).

The rage has taken hold—in the 1940s it was the time to groove it or lose it. This was the choice given to the docile O'Hara, cast as the dean of a music school. On her way to meet her symphony conductor husband, she meets boppin' big band leader James aboard the train. She's awestruck by the brand new beat that grips her from her head to her feet. Her newfound passion, however, doesn't go over with the rest of her school and she promptly gets canned. In an attempt to prove swing's worth, she and James perform their tunes for the college to hear. Songs: "As If I Didn't Have Enough on My Mind" (Charles Henderson, Lionel Newman, Harry James), "I Didn't Mean a Word I Said" (Harold Adamson, Jimmy McHugh), "Moonlight Propaganda" (Herb Magidson, Matt Malneck), "Do You Love Me?" (Harry Ruby).

p, George Jessel; d, Gregory Ratoff; w, Robert Ellis, Helen Logan, Dorothy Bennett (based on a story by Bert Granet); ph, Edward Cronjager (Technicolor); ed, Robert Simpson; md, Emil Newman, Charles Henderson; art d, Lyle Wheeler, Joseph C. Wright; set d, Thomas Little, Jack Stubbs; spec eff, Fred Sersen; ch, Seymour Felix.

Musical   (PR:A   MPAA:NR)

DOBERMAN GANG, THE**   (1972) 87m Rosamond/Dimension c

Byron Mabe (*Eddie Newton*), Hal Reed (*Barney Greer*), Julie Parrish (*June*), Simmy Bow (*Sammy*), Jojo D'Amore (*Jojo*), John Tull (*Pet Shop Owner*), Jay Paxton (*Bank Manager*), John Strong (*Assistant Manager*), Diane Prior (*Sandy*), Clyde Apperson (*Real Estate Agent*), John Hogan (*Janitor*), Charles Vincent (*Bank Guard*).

An incompetent gang of bank robbers led by Mabe hit on the idea of eliminating human error from their jobs by training a group of dogs to perform for them. They enlist the help of ex-Air Force dog trainer Reed, telling him they are training the dogs for a security service. When Reed figures out what is really going on he tries to leave, but Mabe threatens to kill the dogs, named after famous bank robbers (Dillinger, Pretty Boy Floyd, Ma Barker, Bonnie and Clyde, etc.). The day of the robbery arrives and the canine criminals pull it off without a hitch, though Bonnie is run over by a car as they run for home. When they get back to the gang's headquarters, the dogs refuse to let them get close enough to remove the money bags. The film ends with the dogs running away from the humans who were trying to use them to double-cross the others. A nice idea, with a few genuinely good scenes, but the film shows only too clearly the limitations of its tiny budget. First of three films starring the Dobermans.

p, David Chudnow; d, Byron Chudnow; w, Louis Garfinkle, Frank Ray Perilli; ph, Robert Caramico (Eastmancolor); m, Bradford Craig, Alan Silvestri; ed, Herman Freedman; art d, Budd Costello; animal trainer, Karl Miller.

Crime   (PR:C   MPAA:PG)

DOC**   (1971) 95m UA c

Stacy Keach (*Doc Holliday*), Faye Dunaway (*Kate Elder*), Harris Yulin (*Wyatt Earp*), Mike Witney (*Ike Clanton*), Denver John Collins (*The Kid*), Dan Greenburg (*Editor*), Penelope Allen (*Mattie Earp*), Hedy Sontag (*Alley Earp*), Bruce M. Fischer (*Billy Clanton*), James Greene (*Frank McLowrey*), Richard McKenzie (*Sheriff Beham*), John Scanlon (*Barlett*), Antonia Rey (*Concha*), John Bottoms (*Virgil Earp*), Philip Shafer (*Morgan Earp*), Ferdinand Zogbaum (*James Earp*), Marshall Efron (*Mexican Bartender*), Fred Dennis (*Johnny Ringo*), Mart Hulswit (*Rev. Foster*), Gene Collins (*Hotel Clerk*), Gene Reyes (*Wong*), Luch Tiller, Vivian Allen, Sharon Fruitin (*Whores*), Per Barclay, Dan Van Husen, Henri Bidon (*Clanton Cowboys*).

An anti-western which attempts to deflate the myth of the western gunslingers. Set during the historic gunfight at OK Corral, this picture has no desire to retrace details but instead creates the atmosphere of the times. Keach, in the title role, spends most of his time interested in Dunaway, while down at the jail Yulin energetically portrays the pragmatic Earp. Director Perry, however, is only moderately capable of handling the talents in a film which is either meditative or boring, depending on how it is viewed.

p&d, Frank Perry; w, Pete Hamill; ph, Gerald Hirschfeld (DeLuxe Color); m, Jimmy Webb; ed, Alan Heim; prod d, Gene Callahan; art d, Jose Maria Alarcon; set d, Manolo Mampaso; cos, Sandy Cole.

Western (PR:O MPAA:R)

DOC SAVAGE . . . THE MAN OF BRONZE*½ (1975) 100m WB c

Ron Ely (Doc Savage), Paul Gleason (Long Tom), Bill Lucking (Renny), Michael Miller (Monk), Eldon Quick (Johnny), Darrell Zwerling (Ham), Paul Wexler (Capt. Seas), Janice Heiden (Adrianna), Robyn Hilton (Karen), Pamela Hensley (Mona), Bob Corso (Don Rubio Gorro), Carlos Rivas (Kulkan), Chuy Granco (Cheelok), Alberto Morin (Jose), Victor Millan (Chief Chaac), Jorge Cervera, Jr. (Col. Ramirez), Frederico Roberto (El Presidente), Michael Berryman (Coroner), Robert Tessier (Dutchman), Grace Stafford (Little Lady), Scott Walker (Borden), Dar Robinson (Native).

Childish film based on the pulp hero of the 1930s, Doc Savage, played as a centerfold by Ron Ely. The doc takes a whirl down to Hidalgo and tries to hunt down the lug who killed his father. The guilty one turns out to be Wexler, who is spending time in a jungle gold mine. A negative example of the hot and cold direction of Michael Anderson. Michael Berryman of THE HILLS HAVE EYES has a bit as a coroner.

p, George Pal; d, Michael Anderson; w, Pal, Joe Morhaim (based on the novel by Kenneth Robeson); ph, Fred Koenekamp (Technicolor); m, John Philip Sousa, adapted by Frank De Vol; ed, Thomas McCarthy; art d, Fred Harpman; set d, Marvin March; cos, Patrick Cummings; spec eff, Howard A. Anderson; m/l, De Vol, Don Black; stunts, Toni Eppers.

Action (PR:A MPAA:G)

DOCK BRIEF, THE (SEE: TRIAL AND ERROR, 1962, Brit.)

DOCKS OF NEW ORLEANS* (1948) 67m MON bw

Roland Winters (Charlie Chan), Victor Sen Young (Tommy), Mantan Moreland (Birmingham), John Gallaudet (Capt. McNally), Virginia Dale (Rene), Boyd Irwin (Lafontaine), Carol Forman (Nita Aguire), Howard Negley (Pareaux), Douglas Fowley (Grock), Emmett Vogan (Henri Castanero), Harry Hayden (Swendstrom), Rory Mallinson (Thompson), Stanley Andrews (Von Scherbe), George J. Lewis (Dansiger), Dian Fauntelle (Mrs. Swendstrom), Ferris Taylor (Dr. Doobie), Haywood Jones (Mobile), Eric Wilton (Butler), Forrest Matthews (Detective), Wally Walker (Chauffeur), Larry Steers (Doctor), Paul Conrad (D.A.), Frank Stephens (Sergeant), Fred Miller (Armed Guard).

Less than average Charlie Chan yarn has the Oriental mastermind of criminology tracking a multiple murderer involved in a chemical shipment. A poor entry in the Chan series. (See CHARLIE CHAN series, Index.)

p, James S. Burkett; d, Derwin Abrahams; w, W. Scott Darling (based on characters created by Earl Derr Biggers); ph, William Sickner; m, Edward J. Kay; ed, Ace Herman.

Mystery (PR:A MPAA:NR)

DOCKS OF NEW YORK** (1945) 63m MON bw

Leo Gorcey (Muggs), Huntz Haul (Glimpy), Billy Benedict (Skinny), Bud Gorman (Danny), Mende Koenig (Sam), Gloria Pope (Saundra), Carlyle Blackwell, Jr. (Marty), George Meeker (Naclet), Betty Blythe (Mrs. Darcy), Pierre Watkin (Capt. Jocaba), Joy Reese (Millie), Cyrus Kendall (Compeau), Maurice St. Clair (Patriot), Patsy Moran (Mrs. McGinnis), Bernard Gorcey (Kessel), Leo Borden (Peter), Betty Sinclair (Woman at Pawnshop).

Gorcey and the Bowery gang find a stolen necklace and are wrongly accused of heisting it. The private-eye bug gets the best of them and they set out to finger the real culprit. Standard matinee fare for its time.

p, Sam Katzman, Jack Dietz; d, Wallace Fox; w, Harvey Gates; ph, Ira Morgan; ed, William Austin; md, Edward Kay; art d, David Milton; spec eff, Ray Mercer.

Comedy/Crime (PR:A MPAA:NR)

DOCKS OF SAN FRANCISCO*½ (1932) 54m Action bw

Mary Nolan (Belle), Jason Robards (John Banning), Marjorie Beebe (Rose), John Davidson (Vance), William Haynes (Reggie), Max Davidson (Detective).

Nolan is a girl from the city by the bay who is deeply involved with gangsters, doing scarlet duty as well as holdups on her own. A novelist who understands women of her type helps her quit the rackets, which she succeeds in doing after some bangup action sequences that pack a real wallop. Still a good story of the Barbary Coast of San Francisco. Nolan, a former Ziegfeld Girl whose acting career covered the silents and the early talkies, made two more films in 1932 and retired from the screen.

p, Ralph M. Like; d, George B. Seitz; w, H. H. Van Loan; ph, Jules Cronjager; ed, Byron Robinson, Ralph Dixon.

Crime (PR:A MPAA:NR)

DOCTEUR LAENNEC½** (1949, Fr.) 95m AIC bw

Pierre Blanchar (Dr. Laennec), Saturnin Fabre (Mrs. Laennec), Mireille Perrey (Jacquimine Dargot), Pierre Dux (Prof. Ecamier), Geymond Vital (Dr. Bayle), Jany Holt (Mrs. Bayle), Dynan, Lannier.

Blanchar, as Dr. Laennec the inventor of the stethoscope, is excellent in his portrayal of a man entirely devoted to fighting against the maladies which beset the human condition. An inspiring film which is hampered by a sometimes sterile approach by prize-winning director Cloche. (In French.)

p&d, Maurice Cloche; w, Jean Bernard Duc; ph, Claude Renoir; m, Jean-Jacques Grunenwald; ed, Renee Garey.

Drama (PR:A MPAA:NR)

DOCTEUR POPAUL** (1972, Fr.) 95m Les Films de la Boetie/CIC c
(GB: SCOUNDREL IN WHITE)

Jean-Paul Belmondo (Paul Simay), Mia Farrow (Christine), Laura Antonelli (Martine), Daniel Ivernel (Berthier), Daniel Lacourtois (Dupont), Marlene Appelt (Carole), Michel Peyrelon (Joseph).

Belmondo is an obsessive medic who has an ugly-fetish and falls in love with the homely Farrow. They wed, but before long his vivacious sister Antonelli pays a visit. Belmondo forgets his desire for the blemished and discovers the meaning of beauty. He drugs Farrow each night and ritualistically kills off his sister-in-law's three husbands. Farrow, however, is not blind to his ways and devises a plan which convinces Belmondo that he has become paralyzed. He is driven to kill again, with himself as the victim. A fine black humor comedy from Claude Chabrol, one of the leading directors of the New Wave. In a statement that applies to this film, Chabrol has said that he likes "to lead the audience along, to set them chasing off in one direction, and then turn things inside out."

p, Andre Genoves; d, Claude Chabrol; w, Paul Gegauff (based on a book by Hurbert Monteilhet); ph, Jean Rabier (Eastmancolor); m, Pierre Jansen; ed, Jacques Gaillard; art d, Guy Littaya.

Comedy/Drama (PR:O MPAA:NR)

DOCTOR AND THE GIRL, THE** (1949) 97m MGM bw

Glenn Ford (Dr. Michael Corday), Charles Coburn (Dr. John Corday), Gloria De Haven (Fabienne), Janet Leigh (Evelyn Heldon), Bruce Bennett (Dr. Alfred Norton), Warner Anderson (Dr. George Esmond), Basil Ruysdael (Dr. Francis I. Garard), Nancy Davis (Mariette), Arthur Franz (Dr. Harvey L. Kenmore), Lisa Golm (Hetty), Joanna De Bergh (Child's Mother).

Ford is forced to struggle through a hospital soap opera as the son of a well-to-do physician. When he marries a lower-class patient, dad disowns him. Ford then decides to open shop in a New York slum as a general practitioner. Also included is an anti-abortion message as Ford's sister, De Haven, dies undergoing an abortion, paying the price the production codes in those days demanded.

p, Pandro S. Berman; d, Curtis Bernhardt; w, Theodore Reeves (based on a story by Maxene Van Der Meersch); ph, Robert Planck; ed, Ferris Webster; md, Rudolph G. Kopp; art d, Cedric Gibbons, Preston Ames.

Drama (PR:C MPAA:NR)

DOCTOR AT LARGE½** (1957, Brit.) 104m RANK c

Dirk Bogarde (Simon Sparrow), Muriel Pavlow (Joy), Donald Sinden (Benskin), James Robertson Justice (Sir Lancelot Spratt), Shirley Eaton (Nan), Derek Farr (Dr. Potter-Shine), Michael Medwin (Bingham), Freda Bamford (Eva's Mother), Abe Barker (Dad Ives), Martin Benson (Maharajah), Cyril Chamberlain (P.C.), John Chandos (O'Malley), Edward Chapman (Wilkins), Peggyann Clifford (Large Woman), Campbell Cotts (Butler), George Coulouris (Pascoe), Junia Crawford (Girl on Boat), Judith Furse (Mrs. Digby), Gladys Henson (Mrs. Wilkins), Anne Heywood (Emerald), Ernest Jay (Hopcroft), Lionel Jeffries (Dr. Hatchett), Mervyn Johns (Smith), Geoffrey Keen (2nd Examiner), Dilys Laye (Jasmine), Harry Locke (Porter), Terence Longdon (House Surgeon), A.E. Matthews (Duke of Skye and Lewes), Guy Middleton (Major), Barbara Murray (Kitty), Nicholas Phipps (Mr. Wayland), Frederick Piper (Ernest), George Relph (Dr. Farquarson), Athene Seyler (Lady Hawkins), Ernest Thesiger (1st Examiner), Noel Purcell (Bartender), Donald Pickering, Wensley Pithey, Maureen Pryor, Carol Richmond, Beth Rogan, Barbara Roscoe, Jean St. Clari, Ronnie Stevens, Michael Trubshawe, Molly Urquhart, Charles Lloyd Pack.

Bogarde continues on in his third appearance as MD Simon Sparrow. This time he's making his way through a maze of want ads trying to find a job as a surgeon, and his search takes him to the Riviera, then back to the hospital where he started. Assembly-line film production which works, producing quite a few laughs. Good screen fare. (See DOCTOR series, Index.)

p, Betty E. Box; d, Ralph Thomas; w, Nicholas Phipps, Richard Gordon (based on the novel by Gordon); ph, Ernest Steward (VistaVision, Eastmancolor); m, Bruce Montgomery; ed, Frederick Wilson; art d, Maurice Carter; cos, Yvonne Caffin.

Comedy (PR:A MPAA:NR)

DOCTOR AT SEA½** (1955, Brit.) 93m RANK c

Dirk Bogarde (Simon Sparrow), Brigitte Bardot (Helene Colbert), Brenda De Banzie (Muriel Mallet), James Robertson Justice (Capt. Hogg), Maurice Denham (Easter), Michael Medwin (Trail), Hubert Gregg (Archer), James Kenney (Fellowes), Raymond Huntley (Capt. Beamish), Geoffrey Keen (Hornbeam), George Coulouris (Carpenter), Noel Purcell (Corble), Jill Adams (Jill), Joan Sims (Wendy), Thomas Heathcoate (Wilson), Toke Townley (Jenkins), Cyril Chamberlain (Whimble), Paul Carpenter (Captain), Frederick Piper (Sandyman), Abe Barker, Michael Shepley, Eugene Deckers, Stuart Saunders, Harold Kasket, Martin Benson, Mary Laura Wood, Joan Hickson, Ekali Sokou, Felix Felton.

The second amusing tale by doctor-author Richard Gordon again has Bogarde assuming the role of Sparrow. Now he's a naval doctor on a ship carrying only two women—De Banzie and the nymphish Bardot. The guy-to-gal ratio is the basis for the seafaring humor. A must for fans of "Bebe." In 1955, Bardot, still an unfamiliar figure to American audiences (she then was 21 years old), was introduced in a Variety review of DOCTOR AT SEA as "a looker from Paris," with "an acting talent to match her charm." The New York Times review of the film pointed out that she was "visual proof that the beauties of France are not all geographic." One year later she became an overnight sensation and an international superstar with AND GOD CREATED WOMAN. (See DOCTOR series, Index.)

p, Betty E. Box; d, Ralph Thomas; w, Nicholas Phipps, Richard Gordon, Jack Davies (based on the novel by Gordon); ph, Ernest Steward (VistaVision, Technicolor); m, Bruce Montgomery; ed, Frederick Wilson; md, Muir Mathieson; art d, Carmen Dillon; cos, Joan Ellacott; m/l, Hubert Gregg.

Comedy   Cas.   (PR:A MPAA:NR)

DOCTOR BEWARE*   (1951, Ital.) 71m Bianco/Academy bw
Vittorio De Sica (Dr. Vignali), Anna Magnani (Loletta), Irasema Dillian (Lilly), Adriana Benedetti (Teresa Venerdi).

A clever film which has director and co-writer De Sica playing a doctor who is innocently involved with not one, not two, but three women. While engaged to Magnani he accidentally gets engaged to the daughter of the man buying his house. His medical assistant, Benedetti, is the one who gets him out of the web and ends up keeping him for herself. Amusing.

d, Vittorio De Sica; w, Gherardo Gherhardt, Margherita Magilone, De Sica (based on a story by Gherhardt, Franco Riganti); ph, Vincenzo Seratrice; m, Renzo Rossellini; set d, Ottavio Scotti.

Comedy   (PR:C MPAA:NR)

DR. BLACK AND MR. HYDE½**   (1976) 87m Dimension c
(AKA: THE WATTS MONSTER)
Bernie Casey (Dr. Pride/Hyde), Rosalind Cash (Dr. Billie Worth), Marie O'Henry (Linda), Ji-Tu Cumbuka (Lt. Jackson), Milt Kogan (Lt. O'Connor), Stu Gilliam (Silky).

Entertaining variation on Robert Louis Stevenson's classic. Ex-Los Angeles Rams running back Bernie Casey plays Dr. Pride, a wealthy California physician whose experiments turn him into a murderous white man by night. Climax occurs as he climbs up the Watts Towers, a la a ghetto King Kong. Nothing profound, but a lot of mindless fun from the director of BLACULA. Originally tagged DR. BLACK AND MR. WHITE.

p, Charles Walker; d, William Crain; w, Larry LeBron; ph, Tak Fujimoto (Metrocolor); m, Johnny Pate; ed, Jack Horger.

Horror   Cas.   (PR:O MPAA:R)

DR. BLOOD'S COFFIN   (1961) 92m UA c
Kieron Moore (Dr. Peter Blood), Hazel Court (Linda Parker), Ian Hunter (Dr. Robert Blood), Fred Johnson (Mr. Morton), Kenneth J. Warren (Sgt. Cook), Andy Alston (Beale), Paul Stockman (Steve Parker), John Ronane (Hanson), Gerald C. Lawson (Sweeting), Paul Hardtmuth (Professor).

Disgusting and tasteless, but nevertheless entertaining. The subtly named Dr. Blood, Moore, discovers that he can transplant the heart of a worthless person into the body of someone more valuable. Nurse Court gets mixed up in a love triangle between the doctor and a revived corpse. She knows something isn't right and calls up the police, but it is the hand of the cadaver that delivers the fatal blow to Blood.

p, George Fowler; d, Sidney J. Furie; w, Jerry Juran, James Kelly, Peter Miller; ph, Stephen Dade (Eastmancolor); m, Buxton Orr; ed, Anthony Gibbs; art d, Scott MacGregor; spec eff, Les Bowie, Peter Neilson.

Horror   (PR:O MPAA:NR)

DR. BROADWAY   (1942) 67m PAR bw
Macdonald Carey (Dr. Timothy Kane), Jean Phillips (Connie Madigan), J. Carroll Naish (Jack Venner), Eduardo Ciannelli (Vick Telli), Richard Lane (Patrick Doyle), Joan Woodbury (Margie Dove), Warren Hymer (Maxie, The Goat), Frank Bruno (Marty Weber), Sidney Melton (Louie La Conga), William Haade (Dynamo), Olin Howland (Professor), Abe Dinovitch (Benny), Phil Arnold (Hershel), Mary Gordon (Broadway Carrie), John Kelly (Paul Player), Francis Sayles (Clerk), Arthur Loft (Captain Mahoney).

Carey plays a doctor who's so swell that he saves a chorus girl from leaping off a building in a publicity stunt. He then gets tangled up in the murder of a killer he befriends. The killer asks him to deliver $100,000 to a long-lost daughter, but before the doctor can do so the mob intervenes and kills the killer and steals the key to the killer's safe deposit box. The doctor gets fingered for the murder but proves his worth by helping catch the villains and again saving the same girl performing the same foolish publicity stunt. A poor first film from director Anthony Mann, but it does hint at his later talents.

p, Sol C. Siegel; d, Anthony Mann; w, Art Arthur (based on a story by Borden Chase); ph, Theodore Sparkuhl; ed, Arthur Schmidt; art d, Hans Dreier, Earl Hedrick.

Crime   (PR:C MPAA:NR)

DR. BULL*½   (1933) 75m FOX bw
Will Rogers (Dr. Bull), Vera Allen (Janet Cardmaker), Marian Nixon (May Tripping), Howard Lally (Joe Tripping), Berton Churchill (Herbert Banning), Louise Dresser (Mrs. Banning), Andy Devine (Larry Ward), Rochelle Hudson (Virginia Banning), Ralph Morgan (Dr. Verney), Tempe Pigott (Grandma), Elizabeth Patterson (Aunt Patricia), Nora Cecil (Aunt Emily), Patsy O'Byrne (Susan), Effie Ellsler (Aunt Myra), Veda Buckland (Mary), Helen Freeman (Helen Upjohn), Robert Parrish, Charles Middleton, Francis Ford.

Will Rogers is perfectly cast as a small-town doctor who spends his time mending the community's ills. His spare moments are filled by courting the widowed Allen. Set in Connecticut, director John Ford shows off his acute visual sense which later was applied to the expansive West. An exciting opportunity to see one of the masters in one stage of his development.

d, John Ford; w, Paul Green, Jane Storm (based on the novel The Last Adam by James Gould Cozzens), ph, George Schneiderman; m, Samuel Kaylin.

Drama   (PR:A MPAA:NR)

DR. BUTCHER, M.D.*   (1982, Ital.) 80m Flora/Aquarius c
(AKA: QUEEN OF THE CANNIBALS)
Ian McCulloch (Peter), Alexandra Cole (Lori Ridgway), Sherry Buchanan (Kelly), Peter O'Neal (George), Donald O'Brian (Dr. Abrera).

The M.D. stands for Medical Deviate in this butchered 1979 Italian gore picture. Doctor and anthropologist Cole discovers that an Asiatic tribe is robbing Manhattan of its dead. Scientist McCulloch ventures with Cole to an obscure island where they meet a mad scientist and a slew of cannibals. Cole looks good enough to eat, and is sacrificially prepared, when the natives decide that she's a goddess. Extremely gory dismemberments and cannibal acts splatter the screen in this shocking picture.

p, Terry Levine; d, Frank Martin [Franco Martinelli]; w, Martinelli, Fabrizio de Angelis, Walter Patriarca, Romano Scandariato; ph, F. Zuccoli; m, Walter Sear [Nico Fidenco]; art d, V. Morrozi; spec eff, Maurizio Trani, Rosario Restopino.

Horror   Cas.   (PR:O MPAA:R)

DR. CHRISTIAN MEETS THE WOMEN*   (1940) 65m RKO bw
Jean Hersholt (Dr. Paul Christian), Dorothy Lovett (Judy Price), Edgar Kennedy (George Browning), Rod LaRocque (Prof. Kenneth Parker), Frank Albertson (Bill Ferris), Marilyn Merrick (Kitty Browning), Maude Eburne (Mrs. Hastings), Veda Ann Borg (Carol Compton), Lelah Tyler (Martha Browning), William Gould (Dr. Webster), Heinie Conklin (Ed the Plumber), Bertha Priestly (Alice Mason), Diedra Vale (Gladys Mason), Phyllis Kennedy (Annie).

Hersholt, in the dignified title role, points out the evils of a weight loss program peddled by a fast-talking racketeer. He fights the greed-driven quack and puts an end to his campaign. A weak addition to the DR. CHRISTIAN series, which sinks in its social relevancy. But it is interesting to note that even in 1940 weight loss was a subject that could be expected to draw in the female moviegoers. (See DR. CHRISTIAN series, Index.)

p, William Stephens; d, William McGann; w, Marian Orth; ph, John Alton; m, Constantin Bakaleinikoff; ed, Edward Mann; md, Bakaleinikoff; art d, Earl Wooden; cos, Monroe Friedman.

Drama   PR:A MPAA:NR

DR. COPPELIUS*   (1968, U.S./Span.) 97m Gala c
(EL FANTASTICO MUNDO DEL DR. COPPELIUS)
Walter Slezak (Dr. Coppelius), Claudia Corday (Swanilda/Coppelia), Caj Selling (Franz), Eileen Elliott (Brigitta), Luis Prendes (The Mayor), Milord Moskovitch (Hungarian Dance Champion), Carmen Rojas (Spanish Doll), Veronica Rusmin (Roman Doll), Marcia Bellak, Kathy Jo Brown, Clara Cravey, Kathleen Garrison, Christine Holter, Sharon Kapner (Swanhilda's Friends), Helena Villarroya, Gran Teatro del Liceo Ballet, International Cine Ballet, Aurelio Bogado, Xenia Petrowsky.

Droll doctor Slezak creates a companion for himself—a beautiful dancing robot—with whom the young Selling falls in love. The creator kidnaps Selling and attempts to implant his soul into the doll. It's the youngster's girl friend (Corday, playing a dual role) who bails him out, leaving Slezak alone with his unfeeling doll and wondering whether a village woman wouldn't be a better companion. A child's fable which is heartwarming entertainment for the whole family.

p, Frank J. Hale; d&w, Ted Kneeland (based on the ballet "Coppelia" by Clement Delibes and Charles Nuitter); ph, Cecilio Paniagua (Superpanorama, Technicolor); m, Delibes, Raymond Guy Wilson; ed, Juan Serra; prod d, Florence Lustig; art d, Gill Parrondo; set d, Roberto Carpio; cos, Carpio, Marian Ribas; ch, Jo Anna Kneeland, Richard Dodd.

Children   (PR:AA MPAA:NR)

DOCTOR CRIMEN*   (1953, Mex.) 85m International Cinematogafica bw
(EL MONSTRUO RESUCITADO)
Miroslava, Carlos Navarro, Jose Maria Linares Rivas, Fernando Wagner, Alberto Mariscal, Stefan Berne.

A Mexican horror/science fiction film loosely adapted from the Frankenstein story. Journalist Miroslava is assigned to check on a strange advertisement placed by a doctor, Rivas, a plastic surgeon who is terribly deformed and has become insane. Rivas creates a Frankenstein-like creature, Navarro, to capture Miroslava, with whom he has fallen in love. But the journalist falls in love with Navarro, who kills the man who created him. The director, Urueta, would become well-known in the Mexican cinema for his sex-oriented films.

p, Sergio Kogan; d, Chano Urueta; w, Urueta, Andrino Maiuri; ph, Victor Herrera; spec eff, Jorge Benavides.

Horror/Science Fiction   (PR:C MPAA:NR)

DR. CRIPPEN*   (1963, Brit.) 98m Pathe/WB bw
Donald Pleasence (Dr. Hawley Harvey Crippen), Coral Browne (Belle Crippen), Samantha Eggar (Ethel Le Neve), James Robertson Justice (Capt. Kendall), Geoffrey Toone (Mr. Tobin), Oliver Johnstone (Lord Chief Justice), Edward Ogden (Clerk of the Court), Elspeth March (Mrs. Jackson), Douglas Bradley-Smith (Doctor Pepper), John Arnatt (Chief Inspector Dew), Olga Lindo (Clara Arditti), Betty Baskcombe (Mrs. Stratton), Basil Beale (Sgt. Mitchell), Edward Underdown (Prison Governor), Ted Cast (Warder Harding), Ian Whittaker (Howlett), Donald Wolfit (R.D. Muir), John Lee (Harry).

It's hard for someone to believe a man's claims that he accidentally murdered his wife when the cause of death was an overdose of tranquilizers slipped into her tea—especially when there is a mistress waiting in the wings and she happens to be as tempting as Eggar. That's what this picture expects us to think about this celebrated 1910 murder case. Pleasence, as Dr. Crippen, and Eggar flee to Canada after the wife's death, but the police continue to investigate and find the wife's body in the cellar, where her husband had buried her. Caught and returned to London for trial, he is sentenced to death, still protesting his innocence, while Eggar is acquitted. A lot of implausibilities in this one, calling for a great deal of suspension of belief, but it is historically true.

p, John Clein; d, Robert Lynn; w, Leigh Vance; ph, Nicholas Roeg; m, Kenneth Jones; ed, Lee Doig; md, Jones; art d, Robert Jones; cos, L. and H. Nathan.

Historical Drama/Crime **(PR:C MPAA:NR)**

DR. CYCLOPS½** (1940) 71m PAR c

Albert Dekker *(Dr. Thorkel)*, Janice Logan *(Dr. Mary Mitchell)*, Thomas Coley *(Bill Stockton)*, Charles Halton *(Dr. Bulfinch)*, Victor Kilian *(Steve Baker)*, Frank Yaconelli *(Pedro)*, Bill Wilkerson *(Silent Indian)*, Allen Fox *(Cab Driver)*, Paul Fix *(Dr. Mendoza)*, Frank Reicher *(Prof. Kendall)*.

A fun-filled film from the director of the original KING KONG which casts Dekker as a mad scientist who gets kicks out of shrinking people to one-fifth their normal size. Their plight pits them against an array of obstacles which were once taken for granted as everyday, normal-sized objects. Film has some wonderful special effects, but the subject of tiny folks was dealt with much more interestingly in THE DEVIL DOLL, 1936, and 1957's THE INCREDIBLE SHRINKING MAN. The situation is basically unexplored in this picture, wasting a number of opportunities. Unexplainably absent is the obligatory point-of-view shot from the Lilliputians' height. It all looks so familiar now, but by placing the film in its historical perspective—novel special effects, Technicolor, and the directorial pull of Schoedsack—one can understand its sensational attraction at its time.

p, Dale Van Every; d, Ernest B. Schoedsack; w, Tom Kilpatrick; ph, Henry Sharp, Winton C. Hoch; m, Ernst Toch, Gerard Carbonara, Albert Hay Malotte; ed, Ellsworth Hoagland; art d, Hans Dreier, Earl Hedricks; spec eff, Farciot Edouard, Wallace Kelly.

Horror/Fantasy **(PR:A MPAA:NR)**

DOCTOR DEATH: SEEKER OF SOULS*½ (1973) 87m Cinerama c

John Considine *(Dr. Death)*, Barry Coe *(Fred Saunders)*, Cheryl Miller *(Sandy)*, Stewart Moss *(Greg Vaughn)*, Leon Askin *(Thor)*, Jo Morrow *(Laura Saunders)*, Florence Marly *(Tana)*, Sivi Aberg *(Venus)*, Jim Boles *(Caretaker Franz)*, Athena Lorde *(Spiritualist)*, Moe Howard *(Volunteer)*, Robert E. Ball *(Old Wizard)*, Patrick Dennis Leigh *(Old Man)*, Lin Henson *(TV Watcher)*, Anna Bernard *(Girl in Phone Booth)*, Barbara Boles *(Alice)*, Pierre Gonneau *(Harry)*, Larry Rogers *(Young Man in Park)*, Denise Denise *(Girl with Flat Tire)*, Eric Boles *(Man at Seance)*, Jeffrey Herman *(Man Wanting New Body)*, Leon Williams *(Man to Arrange Seance)*, Larry Vincent *(Strangler)*.

Considine is the title doctor who 1,000 years ago discovered the secret to immortality and now must transfer his soul into a new body every so often. Now he is looking for a soul to transplant into the dead wife of Coe. But the highlight in this one is a scene with seventy-seven-year-old Moe Howard, one-third of the Three Stooges, in his final role.

p&d, Eddie Saeta; w, Sal Ponti; ph, Kent Wakeford, Emil Oster (Movielab Color) m, Richard LaSalle; ed, Tony DiMarco; art d, Ed Graves; cos, Tom Dawson.

Horror **(PR:O MPAA:R)**

DOCTOR DETROIT zero (1983) 91m Rhino-Brillstein Co/UNIV c

Dan Aykroyd *(Clifford Skridlow)*, Howard Hesseman *(Smooth Walker)*, Donna Dixon *(Monica)*, Lydia Lei *(Jasmine)*, T.K. Carter *(Diavolo)*, Lynn Whitfield *(Thelma)*, Franc Drescher *(Karen)*, Kate Murtagh *(Mom)*, George Furth *(Arthur)*, Nan Martin *(Margaret)*, Andrew Duggan *(Harmon)*, Glenne Headly *(Miss Debbylike)*, Robert Cornthwaite *(Prof. Blount)*, Parley Baer *(Judge)*, John A. Moloney *(Commodore)*, Pershing P. Anderson *(Stretch)*, William Munchow *(Prof. Ariel)*, Edward Meekin *(Prof. Durant)*, Hank Salas *(Johnny)*, Rudolf Kovar *(Carson)*, Peter Elbling, Peter Aykroyd, Annabel Armour, Thomas Erhart, Jr., Oliver Clark, Ben Kronen, Linace Kinsey, Lynda Aldon, Carla Barbour, Sue Bowser, Tamara Clarrett, Deidre Cowden, Deborah Koppel, Deanna Joy, Toni Naples, Roni Michelle, Laurie Senit, Robert Swan, Frank G. Rice, Michael Hagerty, Eugene Pressman, Victoria Brown, Ben Frommer, John Kapelos, James Spinks, James Brown, Clyde Barrett, Brad Barrios, Derrick Brice, Patricia Ann Douglas, Sonja Haney, Bruce Heath, Carlton Johnson, Ercelle Johnson, Keny Long, Sioux Marcelli, Ade Small, Dona Davis-Steckling, Blackie Dammett, Vincent J. Isaac, Steven Williams, Cheryl Carter, Diane Robin, Manny Weltman.

There isn't one laugh in this so-called comedy. Aykroyd, who is funny in three-minute skits, simply cannot handle a leading role, because his personality doesn't transfer well to the big screen. In this one he plays a college professor who becomes a pimp, and the following idiotic situations and sophomoric antics make it unwatchable. Friedman's story is also a moronic offering.

p, Robert K. Weiss; d, Michael Pressman; w, Carl Gottlieb, Robert Boris, Bruce Jay Friedman (adapted from Friedman's novel *Detroit Abe*); ph, King Baggot (Technicolor); m, Lalo Schifrin; ed, Christopher Greenbury; prod d, Lawrence G. Paul; cos, Betsy Cox; ch, Carlton Johnson; m/l, Devo.

Comedy **Cas.** **(PR:O MPAA:R)**

DOCTOR DOLITTLE*** (1967) 152m FOX c

Rex Harrison *(Dr. John Dolittle)*, Anthony Newley *(Matthew Mugg)*, Peter Bull *(Gen. Bellowes)*, William Dix *(Tommy Stubbins)*, Portia Nelson *(Sarah Dolittle)*, Samantha Eggar *(Emma Fairfax)*, Richard Attenborough *(Albert Blossom)*, Muriel Landers *(Mrs. Blossom)*, Geoffrey Holder *(Willie Shakespeare)*, Norma Varden *(Lady Petherington)*.

Like CLEOPATRA, another cock-a-doodle-doo for Fox, the machinations behind the scenes of this picture were sometimes more interesting than what went on the screen. Once again, lavish amounts were poured into the production and box office results were less than negligible. What could have happened? Here we have Rex Harrison, as charming a human being on screen as ever lived. Samantha Eggar, beauteous, red-headed, and a good enough actress to have been nominated for an Oscar in THE COLLECTOR. Newley, making his U.S. film debut after enormous stage successes, and a screenplay and score by Leslie Bricusse, Newley's sometime partner. It should have been a smash. Well, for one thing, the whole picture was too long, too dull, and overblown for its material. They thought they had a MARY POPPINS here and spent a fortune on the special effects and all the cute little animals they invented. Doctor Dolittle (a rotund little man in the Hugh Lofting books) is looked upon by his neighbors as a nut and those actions cause him to be arrested. He decides to forego any further intercourse with humans and devote his life to animals. As a man who can speak all the animal tongues (he was taught 498 different languages by his parrot, Polynesia), he is fit to be the link between man and beast. With Newley and Eggar at his side, he sails off to find The Great Pink Sea Snail and The Giant Lunar Moth in the South Seas. Although Eggar, about half Harrison's age, is supposedly his fiancee, there is virtually no contact between them—no doubt for the benefit of the wee ones whom the producers hoped would flock to the theaters. Some excellent cameos abound, notably Attenborough as a circus owner who looks at one of Dolittle's creatures and sings, "I Never Seen Anything Like It in My Life." Attenborough is so good in the role that it is a highlight one remembers long after forgetting much of the rest of the movie. Bricusse took an Oscar for best song with "Talk to the Animals" and he did go on to write for other films such as VICTOR/VICTORIA and GOODBYE, MR. CHIPS (the musical) but his best work and most success came while working with Newley in the 1960s. Fleischer was a strange choice to helm such lighthearted fare. With a directorial history that included such ponderous works as THE DON IS DEAD, MANDINGO, CHE! and other gobblers, why did Fox pick him? We'll never know. Production problems on the film were many, especially due to the use of so many live animals. More than 1,500 beasts took part and the average cost of care and feeding of the featured animals was $750 a week. There are many families who survive on that per month. Alan Jay Lerner was originally set to write the book and lyrics. Lerner attempted to write for over a year but gave up and when he bailed out, Harrison wanted to leave as well. Actually, Rex really didn't want to star in a "children's film" anyhow and it was only the presence of such a prestigious author-lyricist as Lerner that attracted him to the project. With Lerner jettisoned, Harrison began yawning and Plummer was placed in second position. Producer Jacobs still wanted Harrison so he went after Bricusse who worked feverishly until he came up with some of the material eventually heard in the film. Harrison liked the songs and agreed to do the film but now they had to give Plummer several hundred thousand dollars to pay off his contract. This they did so Plummer received a lot of money for not having to appear in a picture that proved very uncomfortable in the making. Harrison complained that, in one sequence, he had to stand in a field of sheep and sing happily while the animals were lifting one leg after another on him and the attendant flies buzzed around his head. In the end, DR. DOLITTLE died. It was too cutesy for even the youngest children and surely much too long for their backsides to endure. Further, it didn't have the wit or the elan that MARY POPPINS or even BEDKNOBS AND BROOMSTICKS demonstrated. Harrison seemed perturbed most of the time, Eggar appeared bewildered, and Newley was undirected. With 30 minutes cut, this could have had a better life at the box office. It plays well on TV with certain snips and the studio might think of re-issuing it at holidays. Songs: "My Friend the Doctor," "The Vegetarian," "Talk to the Animals," "At the Crossroads," "I've Never Seen Anything Like It," "When I Look into Your Eyes," "Like Animals," "After Today," "Fabulous Places," "I Think I Like You," "Doctor Dolittle," "Something in Your Smile" (Leslie Bricusse).

p, Arthur P. Jacobs; d, Richard Fleischer; W. Leslie Bricusse (based on stories by Hugh Lofting); ph, Robert Surtees (Todd-AO, DeLuxeColor); md, Lionel Newman, Alexander Courage; ed, Samuel E. Beetley, Marjorie Fowler; prod d, Mario Chiari; art d, Jack Martin Smith, Ed Graves; set d, Walter M. Scott, Stuart A. Reiss; spec eff, L.B. Abbott, Art Cruickshank, Emil Kosa, Jr., Howard Lydecker; cos, Ray Aghayan; ch, Herbert Ross; makeup, Ben Nye, Marvin Westmore.

Musical/Fantasy **Cas.** **(PR:AAA MPAA:NR)**

DR. EHRLICH'S MAGIC BULLET**** (1940) 103m WB bw
(AKA: THE STORY OF DR. EHRLICH'S MAGIC BULLET)

Edward G. Robinson *(Dr. Paul Ehrlich)*, Ruth Gordon *(Mrs. Ehrlich)*, Otto Kruger *(Dr. Emil von Behring)*, Donald Crisp *(Minister Althoff)*, Maria Ouspenskaya *(Franziska Speyer)*, Montagu Love *(Prof. Hartmann)*, Sig Rumann *(Dr. Hans Wolfert)*, Donald Meek *(Mittlemeyer)*, Henry O'Neill *(Dr. Lentz)*, Albert Basserman *(Dr. Robert Koch)*, Edward Norris *(Dr. Morgenroth)*, Harry Davenport *(Judge)*, Louis Calhern *(Dr. Brockdorf)*, Louis Jean Heydt *(Dr. Kunze)*, Charles Halton *(Sensenbrenner)*, Irving Bacon *(Becker)*, Douglas Wood *(Speidler)*, Theodore von Eltz *(Dr. Kraus)*, Hermine Sterler *(Miss Marquardt)*, John Hamilton *(Hirsch)*, Paul Harvey *(Defense Attorney)*, Frank Reicher *(Old Doctor)*, Torben Meyer *(Kadereit)*, Louis Arco *(Dr. Bertheim)*, Wilfred Hari *(Dr. Hata)*, John Henrick *(Dr. Bucher)*, Ann Todd *(Marianne)*, Polly Stewart *(Steffi)*, Ernst Hausman *(Hans Weisgart)*, Stuart Holmes *(Male Nurse)*, Frank Lackteen *(Arab Man)*, Elaine Renshaw *(Arab Woman)*, Herbert Anderson *(Assistant)*, Egon Brecher *(Martl)*, Robert Strange *(Koerner)*, Cliff Clark *(Haupt)*.

The Warner brothers were determined to educate the American public, whether we liked it or not. This is another of their superb series of biographies of famous and even little-known figures in history. Louis Pasteur, Madame Curie, and Paul Ehrlich might never have been known so far and wide without the efforts of determined filmmakers to bring their stories to light. Robinson is positively electric in a role quite unlike what the public had been accustomed to from him. Here was an actor who'd built his career playing hoodlums and fast talkers but who took a sudden diversion in his career in 1940 to essay Ehrlich and Julius Reuter, two German heroes. Robinson was born Emmanuel Goldenberg in Bucharest but came to the U.S. so young that no accent remained in his speech. In this film, Robinson must age 35 years and he pulls it off quite well, more with his acting ability than tricks with makeup. Robinson is a doctor who is having trouble fitting into the conservative routine of a very unimaginative Berlin hospital. He incurs the wrath of the hospital chiefs by being painfully honest with his patients (a no-no in some medical quarters) and by spending all of his spare time working on experiments that appear far-fetched. Kruger, a medical assistant to Basserman, notes Robinson's experiments and tells Basserman, a very famous and respected physician. Robinson is asked to join Basserman's staff. Once inside the great man's organization, Robinson no longer has to worry about feeding his family. Wife Ruth Gordon is dutifully by his side at all times and minces no words in her feelings about things. Robinson finds that his experiments have caused him to contract TB so he and Gordon go to Egypt for "The Cure." While in the land of the pyramids, he develops the theory for building poison immunity. Back in Berlin, the government gives him a grant to work on various experiments. His research goes on and on and a government committee, eager to see results, cuts off his funds. By this time, his children are grown and he could surely retire on what they have saved, but Gordon takes the bull by the horns and visits Ouspenskaya, a wealthy woman with a penchant for donating money to good causes. At a dinner thrown by Ouspenskaya, Robinson floors the staid guests by talking openly about syphilis. Along the way, Robinson takes a few minutes off to help Kruger develop a shot for diphtheria, then one of childhood's most devastating killers. After many, many attempts, number 606 comes up winners. Assaulted by pleas, Ehrlich releases the compound to the public and millions of lives are saved. But a few are lost as well, and a case is made against Robinson. In court, Kruger comes to Robinson's aid and explains how this works medically and that there will also be some loss of life because people are not created equal and certain patients' bodies cannot take certain medication. Robinson is vindicated and the picture ends with a true depiction of the end of the great man's life. There were virtually no liberties taken with the story as the information for the Oscar-nominated screenplay was provided by the family of Ehrlich and you may be certain they would not have allowed any chicanery for the sake of drama. A gem from one of the great producers, Hal B. Wallis.

p, Jack L. Warner, Hal B. Wallis; d, William Dieterle; w, John Huston, Heinz Herald, Norman Burnside (based on a story by Burnside from letters and notes owned by the Ehrlich family); ph, James Wong Howe; m, Max Steiner; ed, Warren Low; art d, Carl Jules Weyl; spec microscope eff, Robert Burks.

Biography   **(PR:A MPAA:NR)**

DOCTOR FAUSTUS*   (1967, Brit.) 92m COL c

Richard Burton (*Dr. Faustus*), Elizabeth Taylor (*Helen of Troy*), Andreas Teuber (*Mephistopheles*), Ian Marter (*Emperor*), Elizabeth O'Donovan (*Empress*), David McIntosh (*Lucifer*), Jeremy Eccles (*Beelzebub*), Ram Chopra (*Valdes*), Richard Carwardine (*Cornelius*), Richard Heffer, Hugh Williams (*Scholars*), Gwydion Thomas (*Scholar/Lechery*), Richard Durden-Smith (*Knight*), Patrick Barwise (*Wagner*), Adrian Benjamin (*Pope*), Jeremy Chandler (*Attendant*), Angus McIntosh (*Rector Magnificus*), Ambrose Coghill (*Professor/Avarice*), Anthony Kaufman (*Professor/Envy*), Julian Wontner, Richard Harrison, Nevill Coghill (*Professors*), Michael Menaugh (*Good Angel*), John Sandbach (*Boy-Turned-Into-Hind*), Sebastian Walker (*Idiot*), Nicholas Loukes (*Pride/Cardinal*), R. Peverello (*Wrath*), Marie Aitken (*Sloth*), Valerie James (*Idleness*), Bridget Coghill, Petronella Pulsford, Susan Watson (*Gluttony*), Jacqueline Harvey, Sheila Dawson, Carolyn Bennitt (*Dancers*), Jane Wilford (*Nun/Court Lady*).

This is exactly what one may expect from a Burton-Taylor version of the 16th-century Marlowe play. The story of a man who sells his soul to the Devil seems to have been made only for Dick and Liz's entertainment. Directed with an unsure hand by Burton, it was filmed in conjunction with Oxford University, his alma mater, casting students from its drama department. Extremely unskilled cinema from a talented stage actor who should have stayed in the theater.

p, Richard Burton, Richard McWhorter; d, Burton, Nevill Coghill; w, Coghill (based on a play, "The Tragical History of Dr. Faustus," by Christopher Marlowe); ph, Gabor Pogany (Technicolor); m, Mario Nascimbene; ed, John Shirley; prod d, John De Cuir, art d, Boris Juraga; set d, Dario Simoni; cos, Peter Hall; spec eff, Augie Lohman, Peter Harman; ch, Jacqueline Harvey.

Fantasy   **(PR:C MPAA:NR)**

DR. FRANKENSTEIN ON CAMPUS*   (1970, Can.) 83m
                                  Agincourt-Glen Warren/Medford (AKA: FLICK)

Robin Ward (*Viktor Frankenstein*), Kathleen Sawyer (*Susan Harris*), Austin Willis (*Cantwell*), Sean Sullivan (*Prof. Preston*), Ty Haller (*Tony*), Tony Moffat-Lynch (*David*), Stephanie Laird (*Debbie*), Ken Hagan (*Reporter*), Alan Dean, Steffany Lind, Bill Waltho, Janine Sherman, Tony Kleiboer, Liz Rowland, Linda Rennhofer.

Good old Dr. Frankenstein takes a position at a Canadian university. He dallies with one of the co-eds, Sawyer, and, sponsored by Sullivan, who heads the school's computer studies program, starts research in electronic brain control. When some students frame him for selling pot, Frankenstein seeks revenge. He uses his mind-control device on a student who is a karate expert to kill those responsible. When Frankenstein loses his control box, students chase him and he falls to his death. It is then revealed that he was a creation of Sullivan's. (See FRANKENSTEIN series, Index.)

p, Bill Marshall; d, Gilbert W. Taylor; w, Marshall, Taylor, David Cobb; ph, Jackson Samuels; m, Paul Hoffert; ed, Eric Wrate; cos, Roger Palmer, Heather McIntosh.

Horror   **(PR:O MPAA:R)**

DOCTOR FROM SEVEN DIALS, THE
                                  (SEE: CORRIDORS OF BLOOD, 1963, Brit.)

DR. GILLESPIE'S CRIMINAL CASE**   (1943) 89m MGM bw
                                              (GB: CRAZY TO KILL)**

Lionel Barrymore (*Dr. Leonard Gillespie*), Van Johnson (*Dr. Randall Adams*), Donna Reed (*Marcia Bradburn*), Keye Luke (*Dr. Lee Wong How*), John Craven (*Roy Todwell*), Nat Pendleton (*Joe Wayman*), Alma Kruger (*Molly Byrd*), William Lundigan (*Alvin F. Peterson*), Margaret O'Brien (*Margaret*), Walter Kingsford (*Dr. Walter Carew*), Marilyn Maxwell (*Ruth Edly*), Michael Duane (*Sgt. Pat J. Orisin*), Henry O'Neill (*Warden Kenneson*), Marie Blake (*Sally*), Frances Rafferty (*Irene*), Nell Craig (*Nurse Parker*), Arthur Loft (*Dr. Post*), Milton Kibbee (*Briggs*), Grand Withers (*Waddy*), Aileen Pringle (*Chaperon*), John Dilson (*Parole Board Member*), Lee Phelps (*Prison Guard*).

Psychopathic killer Todwell, played by Craven, is the target of crusty old Dr. Gillespie's efforts to right a wrong. He tries to get him transferred to a hospital on the grounds that he is insane, but before he can do so the killer is slain in a prison break. Always interesting in a Dr. Gillespie series picture is what newcomer to films is being displayed, sometimes for the first time in his or her career. In this case, Margaret O'Brien is making one of her earliest appearances on the screen, as is future glamor girl Marilyn Maxwell. (See DR. GILLESPIE series, Index.)

d, Willis Goldbeck; w, Martin Berkeley, Harry Ruskin, Lawrence P. Bachmann (based on characters created by Max Brand); ph, Norbert Brodine; m, Daniele Amfitheatrof; ed, Laurie Vejar; md, Amfitheatrof; art d, Cedric Gibbons.

Drama   **(PR:A MPAA:NR)**

DR. GILLESPIE'S NEW ASSISTANT**   (1942) 87m MGM bw

Lionel Barrymore (*Dr. Gillespie*), Van Johnson (*Dr. Randall Adams*), Susan Peters (*Mrs. Howard Young*), Richard Quine (*Dr. Dennis Lindsey*), Keye Luke (*Dr. Lee Wong How*), Alma Kruger (*Molly Byrd*), Nat Pendleton (*Joe Weyman*), Horace [Stephen] McNally (*Howard Young*), Frank Orth (*Mike Ryan*), Walter Kingsford (*Dr. Walter Carew*), Nell Craig (*Nurse Parker*), Marie Blake (*Sally*), George H. Reed (*Conover*), Ann Richards (*Iris Headley*), Rose Hobart (*Mrs. Black*), Pamela Blake (*Jimmy James*), Paul Fix (*Husband*), Eddie Acuff (*Clifford Genet*).

Doc Barrymore actually gets himself three new assistants—Johnson from Kansas, Luke, an Oriental from Brooklyn, and Quine from Australia—to take the place of departed Dr. Kildare. The path of the series turns to lighter comedy with this varied bunch as they concentrate on amnesia victim Peters. (See DR. GILLESPIE series, Index.)

d, Willis Goldbeck; w, Goldbeck, Harry Ruskin, Lawrence P. Bachmann (based on characters created by Max Brand); m, Daniele Amfitheatrof; ph, George Folsey; ed, Ralph Winters; art d, Cedric Gibbons.

Drama   **(PR:A MPAA:NR)**

DR. GOLDFOOT AND THE BIKINI MACHINE*½ (1965) 88m AIP c

Vincent Price (*Dr. Goldfoot*), Frankie Avalon (*Craig Gamble*), Dwayne Hickman (*Todd Armstrong*), Susan Hart (*Diane*), Jack Mullaney (*Igor*), Fred Clark (*D. J. Pevney*), Alberta Nelson (*Reject No. 12*), Milton Frome (*Motorcycle Cop*), Hal Riddle (*News Vendor*), Kay Elhardt (*Girl in Night Club*), William Baskin (*Guard*), Vincent I. Barnett (*Janitor*), Joe Ploski (*Cook*), Sam and the Ape Man with Diane De Marco (*Themselves*), Patti Chandler, Sally Sachse, Sue Hamilton, Marianne Gaba, Issa Arnal, Pam Rodgers, Sally Frei, Jan Watson, Mary Hughes, Luree Holmes, Laura Nicholson, China Lee, Deanna Lund, Leslie Summers, Kay Michaels, Arlene Charles (*Robots*), Annette Funicello (*Girl in the Stock*), Aron Kincaid (*Sports-Car Driver*), Deborah Walley (*Louise*), Harvey Lembeck (*Man Chained to a Motorcycle*), Carey Loftin.

A film joke which isn't all that funny has mad scientist Price bent on taking over the world. His oddball plot employs beautiful female robots to seduce the wealthy and powerful. Picture includes a cameo by Annette Funicello, a parody of THE PIT AND THE PENDULUM, and a title tune sung by The Supremes. A wide-open finale which leaves room for at least another 90-minute sequel.

p, James H. Nicholson, Samuel Z. Arkoff; d, Norman Taurog; w, Elwood Ullman, Robert Kaufman (based on a story by James Hartford); ph, Sam Leavitt (Panavision, Pathe Color); m, Les Baxter; ed, Ronald Sinclair, Fred Feitshans, Eve Newman; md, Al Simms; art d, Daniel Haller; set d, Clarence Steensen; spec eff, Roger George; ch, Jack Baker; m/l, "The Bikini Machine," Guy Hemric, Jerry Styner (sung by The Supremes), "Wailing," Simms; makeup, Ted Coodley.

Comedy   **(PR:C MPAA:NR)**

DR. GOLDFOOT AND THE GIRL BOMBS*   (1966, Ital.) 85m AIP c

Vincent Price (*Dr. Goldfoot*), Fabian (*Bill Dexter*), Franco Franchi (*Franco*), Ciccio Ingrassia (*Ciccio*), Laura Antonelli (*Rosanna*), Moana Tahi (*Goldfoot's Assistant*), Fracesco Mule.

Price wasn't content with his female robots simply seducing the rich, as in DR. GOLDFOOT AND THE BIKINI MACHINE, so he's made a bit of an alteration. The girls are now programmed to explode. Price is trying to cause a war between the U.S. and the Russians (who isn't?), so he has his robots cuddle up to NATO generals. He places the detonation device in their navels (!) so when a lusty general attempts to make love—kaboom! Entirely different from its predecessor, this sequel is less concerned with humor and more interested in style and eroticism.

p, Louis M. Heyward, Fulvio Luciano; d, Mario Bava; w, Heyward, Castellano Pipolo, Robert Kaufman (based on a story by James Hartford); ph, A. Rinaldi (Technicolor); m, Les Baxter; m/l, "Dr. Goldfoot and the Bikini Bomb," Guy Hemrick, Jerry Styner.

Comedy   **(PR:O MPAA:NR)**

DR. HECKYL AND MR. HYPE½** (1980) 99m Cannon c

Oliver Reed *(Dr. Heckyl/Mr. Hype)*, Sunny Johnson *(Coral Careen)*, Maia Danziger *(Miss Finebum)*, Mel Welles *(Dr. Hinkle)*, Virgil Frye *(Lt. MacDruck "Il Topo")*, Kedrick Wolfe *(Dr. Lew Hoo)*, Jackie Coogan *(Sgt. Fleacollar)*, Corinne Calvet *(Pizelle Puree)*, Sharon Compton *(Mrs. Quivel)*, Denise Hayes *(Liza)*, Charles Howerton, Dick Miller, Jack Warford, Lucretia Love, Ben Frommer, Micky Fox, Catalaine Knell, Jacque Lynn Colton, Lisa Zebro, Stan Ross, Joe Anthony Cox, Duane Thomas, Michael Ciccone, Steve Ciccone, Candi Brough, Randi Brough, Dan Sturkie, Yehuda Efroni, Herta Ware, Samuel Livneh, Dana Feller, Katherine Kirkpatrick, Carin Berger, Cindy Riegel, Merle Ann Taylor, Ed Randolph.

A surprisingly funny exploitation picture which casts Reed as a repulsive-looking podiatrist who tries suicide by drinking a potion. After a couple of gulps he becomes a dashing but violent type. Reed is both wonderfully comic and sinister in his dual role. Scripted "with apologies to Robert Louis Stevenson" by Roger Corman collaborator Griffith, who also penned camp classics such as BUCKET OF BLOOD and THE LITTLE SHOP OF HORRORS. Jackie Coogan is the humorously deranged Sgt. Fleacollar.

p, Menahem Golan, Yoram Globus; d&w, Charles B. Griffith; ph, Robert Carras (Metrocolor); m, Richard Band; ed, Skip Schoolnik; prod d, Maxwell Mendes; art d, Bob Ziembiki; set d, Maria Delia Javier.

Comedy/Horror **Cas.** **(PR:O MPAA:R)**

DOCTOR IN CLOVER (SEE: CARNABY, M.D., 1967, Brit.)

DOCTOR IN DISTRESS** (1963, Brit.) 102m Rank c

Dirk Bogarde *(Simon Sparrow)*, Samantha Eggar *(Delia)*, James Robertson Justice *(Sir Lancelot Spratt)*, Mylene Demongeot *(Sonja)*, Donald Houston *(Maj. French)*, Barbara Murray *(Iris)*, Dennis Price *(Blacker)*, Leo McKern *(Heilbronn)*, Jessie Evans *(Mrs. Parry)*, Ann Lynn *(Mrs. Whittaker)*, Fenella Fielding *(Passenger)*, Jill Adams *(Genevieve)*, Michael Flanders *(Bradby)*, Frank Finlay *(Corsetiere)*, Reginald Beckwith *(Meyer)*, Bill Kerr *(Sailor)*, Ronnie Stevens *(Manager)*, Peter Butterworth *(Driver)*, Madge Ryan *(Mrs. Clapper)*, Amanda Barrie *(Rona)*, Timothy Bateson *(Mr. Holly)*, Rodney Cardiff *(Dr. Stewart)*, Paul Whitsun-Jones *(Grimes)*, Margaret Boyd *(Lady Willoughby)*, Jeanette Landis *(Sailor's Girl Friend)*, Michael Goldie *(P.T. Instructor)*, Joe Robinson *(Sonja's Boy Friend)*, Derek Fowlds, Pauline Jameson, David Weston.

Another in the series of "Doctor" films begun in 1954, based on characters from Richard Gordon's novel. This film sees the return of Bogarde as a more mature Dr. Sparrow. The story concerns pesty surgeon Justice falling in love with physiotherapist Murray. Bogarde, who is in love with Eggar, helps Justice sort out his problems. (See DOCTOR series, Index.)

p, Betty E. Box, Ralph Thomas; d, Thomas; w, Nicholas Phipps, Ronald Scott Thorn (based on characters created by Richard Gordon); ph, Ernest Steward (Eastmancolor); m, Norrie Paramor; ed, Alfred Roome; art d, Alex Vetchinsky; set d, Arthur Taksen; cos, Yvonne Caffin.

Comedy **(PR:A MPAA:NR)**

DOCTOR IN LOVE½** (1960, Brit.) 97m Rank c

Michael Craig *(Dr. Richard Hare)*, James Robertson Justice *(Sir Lancelot Spratt)*, Virginia Maskell *(Nicola Barrington)*, Carole Lesley *(Kitten Strudwick)*, Leslie Phillips *(Tony Burke)*, Reginald Beckwith *(Wildwindes)*, Joan Sims *(Dawn)*, Liz Fraser *(Leonora)*, Nicholas Phipps *(Dr. Clive Cardew)*, Ambrosine Philpotts *(Lady Spratt)*, Irene Handl *(Prof. MacRitchie)*, Fenella Fielding *(Mrs. Tadwich)*, Nicholas Parsons *(Dr. Hinxman)*, Moira Redmond *(Sally Nightingale)*, Ronnie Stevens *(Harold Green)*, Michael Ward *(Dr. Flower)*, John Le Mesurier *(Dr. Mincing)*, Meredith Edwards *(Parker)*, Esma Cannon *(Physiotherapist)*.

A top moneymaker among British films when it came out, this contribution to the popular "Doctor" series finds Craig as a young medic who falls in love with his nurse while a patient at his own hospital. But then when his pal Phillips stands in for him until he breaks his leg and is replaced by a woman doctor, Craig falls for her. Woven into the episodic plot are the usual funny elements which made this a long-running series. (See DOCTOR series, Index.)

p, Betty E. Box, Ralph Thomas; d, Thomas; w, Nicholas Phipps (based on characters created by Richard Gordon); ph, Ernest Steward (Eastmancolor); m, Bruce Montgomery; ed, Alfred Roome; art d, Maurice Carter; set d, Arthur Taksen; cos, Yvonne Caffin; m/l, "Doctor In Love," Ken Hare.

Comedy **(PR:A MPAA:NR)**

DOCTOR IN THE HOUSE*** (1954, Brit.) 92m GFD c

Dirk Bogarde *(Simon)*, Muriel Pavlow *(Joy)*, Kenneth More *(Grimsdyke)*, Donald Sinden *(Benskin)*, Kay Kendall *(Isobel)*, James R. Justice *(Sir Lancelot)*, Donald Houston *(Taffy)*, Suzanne Cloutier *(Stella)*, Geoffrey Keen *(Dean)*, George Coulouris *(Briggs)*, Jean Taylor-Smith *(Sister Virtue)*, Harry Locke *(Jessup)*, Ann Gudrun *(May)*, Joan Sims *(Rigor Mortis)*, Maureen Pryor *(Mrs. Cooper)*, Shirley Eaton *(Milly Groaker)*, Geoffrey Sumner *(Lecturer)*, Nicholas Phipps *(Magistrate)*, Amy Veness *(Grandma)*, Richard Wattis *(Salesman)*, Lisa Gastoni, Shirley Burniston, Joan Hickson, George Benson, Martin Boddey, Cyril Chamberlain, Ernest Clark, Mark Dignam, Felix Felton, Wyndham Goldie, Douglas Ives, Eliot Makeham, Anthony Marlowe, Brian Oulton, Mona Washbourne.

DOCTOR IN THE HOUSE is the original "Doctor" film that spawned all the rest. It is the story of several medical students enduring their five-year training. Bogarde enters the school a raw rookie and is immediately taken over by three student repeaters, all of whom failed their preliminary exams. Clearly in evidence is what made the series so popular—the lighthearted touch, good jokes, and nicely played roles by all the cast. (See DOCTOR series, Index.)

p, Betty E. Box; d, Ralph Thomas; w, Richard Gordon, Ronald Wilkins, Nicholas Phipps (based on the novel by Gordon); ph, Ernest Steward (Technicolor); m, Bruce Montgomery; ed, Gerald Thomas; md, Muir Mathieson; art d, Carmen Dillon; cos, Yvonne Caffin.

Comedy **(PR:A MPAA:NR)**

DOCTOR IN TROUBLE*½ (1970, Brit.) 90m Rank

Leslie Phillips *(Dr. Burke)*, Harry Secombe *(Llewellyn Wendover)*, James Robertson Justice *(Sir Lancelot Spratt)*, Angela Scoular *(Ophelia)*, Irene Handl *(Mrs. Dailey)*, Simon Dee *(Basil Beauchamp)*, Robert Morley *(Capt. George Spratt)*, Freddie Jones *(Master at Arms)*, Joan Sims *(Drobnik Captain)*, John Le Mesurier *(Purser)*, Graham Stark *(Satterjee)*, Janet Mahoney *(Dawn Dailey)*, Graham Chapman *(Roddy)*, Jacki Piper *(Pretty Girl)*, Fred Emney *(Sir Thomas Relph)*, Yuri Borienko *(Enormous Pole)*, Gerald Sim *(1st Doctor)*, Yutte Stensgaard *(Eve)*, Sylvana Henriques *(Audrey)*, Marcia Fox *(Jean)*, Tom Kempinski *(Stedman Green)*, Anthony Sharp *(Chief Surgeon)*, Marianne Stone *(Spinster/Plain Woman)*, John Bluthal *Taxi Driver)*.

Madcap woman-chaser Phillips takes over the lead in this addition to the "Doctor" series. Hell-bent in pursuit of *la femme* (mini-skirted Scoular), Phillips finds himself a stowaway on an ocean liner, where all the the fun and high jinks finally take place, with Phillips, the medico, ending up at work as the captain's steward. Many are the fine jokes in this one, but alas, many also are the poor ones.

p, Betty Box, Ralph Thomas; d, Thomas; w, Jack Davies (based on the novel *Doctor On Toast* by Richard Gordon); ph, Ernest Steward (Eastmancolor); m, Eric Rogers; ed, Peter Boita; art d, Lionel Couch; cos; Courtenay Elliott.

Comedy **(PR:A MPAA:NR)**

DR. JEKYLL AND MR. HYDE**** (1932) 90m PAR bw

Fredric March *(Dr. Henry Jekyll/Mr. Hyde)*, Miriam Hopkins *(Ivy Pearson)*, Rose Hobart *(Muriel Carew)*, Holmes Herbert *(Dr. Lanyon)*, Edgar Norton *(Poole)*, Halliwell Hobbes *(Brig-Gen. Carew)*, Arnold Lucy *(Utterson)*, Tempe Pigott *(Mrs. Hawkins)*, Col. McDonnell *(Hobson)*, Eric Wilton *(Briggs)*, Douglas Walton *(Student)*, John Rogers *(Waiter)*, Murdock MacQuarrie *(Doctor)*, Maj. Sam Harris *(Dance Extra)*.

Of the many versions given this Robert Louis Stevenson horror classic, this is the best, with March providing an incredibly chilling performance of the bedeviled Jekyll and the transformed Hyde. Although heavily made up as a jagged toothed simian, March's body language and fierce posturing, in contrast to the simpering Jekyll, is memory scarring. As Jekyll tampering with nature and chemistry to create the evil side of his nature in living form, March is the essence of gentility, quietly courting the unattainable Hobart, his fiancee, held at a distance by her overprotective father, Hobbes. But as the hideous Hyde, March slums through life with Hopkins, the prostitute excited by his violence and brought to a murderous end by her fascination. Even more grotesque is the final confrontation between March/Hyde and the London police who finally track down the beast, killing him as the animal he has become, only to gasp in shock to see March/Jekyll transformed at death into quiet and innocent repose. In this, his third film, March proved his vast and deep talent, capturing an Oscar for his astounding portrayal (shared with Wallace Beery for THE CHAMP). Director Mamoulian's symbolism and studied pace increase the mystique of this strange story and Struss' outstanding photography (he had worked on the 1920 silent version starring John Barrymore) is a marvel to behold. It is still debated today how Mamoulian and Struss achieved the transformation scenes. Some say with special filters or other techniques, but the secret was never revealed, and it is far superior to the stop-action sequences used to show Lon Chaney Jr.'s transformation in THE WOLF MAN. The brutality is unbridled in this shocker and the accent is more on sex than violence but even usually delicate Hopkins has more than her fair share of violent trysting with March. Hopkins does well in her part, although her image and acting style are difficult to accept unless you are a fan. This film was made two years before the Hays Office came into existence to establish Production Codes, and it therefore takes great liberties by later standards. In fact, when this version was reissued in the late 1930s, ten minutes (mostly of Hyde's advances and pummeling of Hopkins) were cut out and never reinstated in what is considered to be a classic in the genre. Hopkins really didn't want to play the sluttish Ivy, and first bid for the "good girl" role enacted by Hobart. It took Mamoulian quite a bit of convincing to get the dignified Hopkins to play the masochistic streetwalker. When MGM remade the film in 1941, the studio bought all the rights to the story and was able to suppress this version for almost 30 years. It still remains the best of all attempts to film the good-and-evil role Stevenson wrote at hurricane speed while drinking himself into stupors (booze being the real basis in the story as the mysterious chemical formula Jekyll invents to bring out his decidedly ugly other personality). Westmore's makeup appears authentic and helped March considerably to radiate terror.

p&d, Rouben Mamoulian; w, Samuel Hoffenstein, Percy Heath (based on the novel *The Strange Case of Dr. Jekyll and Mr. Hyde* by Robert Louis Stevenson); ph, Karl Struss; ed, William Shea; art d, Hans Dreier; cos, Travis Banton; makeup, Wally Westmore; song, "Champagne Ivy" (sung by Hopkins).

Horror **(PR:O MPAA:NR)**

DR. JEKYLL AND MR. HYDE*** (1941) 127m MGM bw

Spencer Tracy *(Dr. Harry Jekyll/Mr. Hyde)*, Ingrid Bergman *(Ivy Peterson)*, Lana Turner *(Beatrix Emery)*, Donald Crisp *(Sir Charles Emery)*, Ian Hunter *(Dr. John Lanyon)*, Barton MacLane *(Sam Higgins)*, C. Aubrey Smith *(The Bishop)*, Peter Godfrey *(Poole)*, Sara Allgood *(Mrs. Higgins)*, Frederic Worlock *(Dr. Heath)*, William Tannen *(Intern Fenwick)*, Frances Robinson *(Marcia)*, Denis Green *(Freddie)*, Billy Bevan *(Dr. Weller)*, Forrester Harvey *(Old Prouty)*, Lumsden Hare *(Col. Weymouth)*, Lawrence Grant *(Dr. Courtland)*, John Barclay *(Constable)*, Doris Lloyd *(Mrs. Marley)*, Gwen Gaze *(Mrs. French)*, Hillary Brooke *(Mrs. Arnold)*, Mary Field *(Wife)*, Aubrey Mather *(Inspector)*.

In this third version of the Stevenson fright tale, Tracy is the ubiquitous Jekyll/Hyde who uses very little makeup to achieve the personality change. Although his performance was lauded at the time, Tracy's role, wholly unsuited to him, caused the actor to sink into hokum, rolling his eyes like loose marbles, working his jaw to its juttingest. Liberties were taken with the original story. Tracy attempts to help a lunatic at the beginning, begging that his scientific experiments be allowed to aid the man, but the authorities turn him down. Moreover, his fiancee, Turner, is shielded from him by her father, Crisp, who condemns Tracy's experiments as working against God and nature. When Tracy appears to get close to Turner, Crisp whisks her away to the Continent for an extended vacation. Tracy's associates also think him a bit daft but humor him as he talks of his theories at dinner. That night, while returning home, Tracy drives off an assailant attacking Bergman, a beautiful streetwalker. She invites him to her apartment where she tries to seduce him, but Tracy, as the meek-mannered Jekyll, mumbles an escape. Later, he begins his experiments in earnest, drinking a potion which transforms him into his evil self, Hyde. He goes to Bergman and torments her repeatedly, punishment that excites her and brings her masochistic tendencies to the surface. In a rage, as the berserk Hyde, Tracy murders Bergman. His blood lust up, Tracy can no longer control his transformations, more and more being taken over by the Hyde personality until it dominates. In his attempt to seduce Turner, who has returned from abroad, the beast attacks Crisp and kills him. He flees with the police in hot pursuit. They corner him in his lair and he is killed as he struggles with officers. In death, the countenance of the evil one softens back to the innocent face of Jekyll, its tragic creator. Tracy was assigned to this film against his wishes and he did the best he could without a great deal of makeup, using some stop-action techniques to aid in the physical transformation from Jekyll to Hyde. (Robert Donat was originally slated for the role as early as 1940.) Bergman was scheduled to play the sweet fiancee and Turner the slut but director Fleming reversed the roles at Bergman's request, adding some brilliant touches in his approach to the Stevenson classic, more psychological than horrific. At one point Turner's image is seen in a huge frame enlargement inside Hyde's lustful eye. Another sequence depicts two horses, one black and one white, being wildly whipped by Hyde, and their heads are transformed into Bergman and Turner, two gorgeous females in the altogether (medium shoulder and head shots) being driven mercilessly onward. Tracy, when given the part, tried a bit of his own invention, proposing to studio bosses that his lifelong friend and screen partner, Katharine Hepburn, play both the fiancee and the slattern. According to a later interview the great actress stated that "[Tracy] maintained that the good side of Jekyll would see the good girl, and the bad side would see the bad, but that they really were the same." MGM made much hoopla by announcing that Tracy's scenes would be filmed behind sets closed to all but the immediate cast and technicians. No stills showing him in makeup were released, although Life obtained a print and blew up a few frames of the transformation scenes for publication. The most provocative scenes are those where Tracy/Hyde sensually toys with Bergman in her bedroom, roughhousing her, abusing her (by spitting grapeskins in her lovely face!), then making violent love, then murdering her. Though he tried hard, Tracy's portrayal nowhere approaches Fredric March's superb 1932 enactment, nor that of John Barrymore's 1920s silent version. And it is not quite true that Tracy acted behind completely closed sets. One visitor, author Somerset Maugham, watched him closely on the set, noting Tracy's rigorous transformations, then crushingly whispered to director Fleming: "Which one is he now, Jekyll or Hyde?"

p&d, Victor Fleming; w, John Lee Mahin (based on the novel The Strange Case of Dr. Jekyll and Mr. Hyde by Robert Louis Stevenson); ph, Joseph Ruttenberg; m, Franz Waxman; ed, Harold F. Kress; art d, Cedric Gibbons, Daniel B. Cathcart; set d, Edwin B. Willis; cos, Adrian, Gile Steele; makeup, Jack Dawn; spec eff, Warren Newcombe, Peter Ballbusch; ch, Ernst Matray.

Horror (PR:C-O MPAA:NR)

DR. JEKYLL AND SISTER HYDE**½

(1971, Brit.)
97m Hammer/AIP c

Ralph Bates (Dr. Jekyll), Martine Beswick (Sister Hyde), Gerald Sim (Prof. Robertson), Lewis Fiander (Howard), Dorothy Alison (Mrs. Spencer), Neil Wilson (Older Policeman), Ivor Dean (Burke), Paul Whitsun-Jones (Sgt. Danvers), Philip Madoc (Byker), Tony Calvin (Hare), Susan Brodrick (Susan), Dan Meaden (Town Crier), Virginia Wetherell (Betsy), Geoffrey Kenion (1st Policeman), Irene Bradshaw (Yvonne), Anna Brett (Julie), Jackie Poole (Margie), Rosemary Lord (Marie), Petula Portell (Petra), Pat Brackenbury (Helen), Liz Romanoff (Emma), Will Stampe (Mine Host), Roy Evans (Knife Grinder), Derek Steen (1st Sailor), John Lyons (2nd Sailor), Jeanette Wild (Jill), Bobby Parr (Young Apprentice), Julia Wright (Street Singer).

Robert Louis Stevenson's classic 19th-century horror tale goes into a sex change in this sometimes funny, nicely tensioned retelling of the story. Jekyll, played by Bates, is experimenting in ways to prolong life. He murders people and removes their organs, seeking the formula. At one point, he tests the formula on himself and turns into a beautiful woman (Beswick) which pleases and excites him. Now as a male he can chase females, and as a female, he can chase men. The young girl living next door is his first target; the second is her brother, a proper Victorian sort. And this is where Bates makes his mistake. He makes advances on the brother while still in his male form, and the shocked brother tells his sister never to see Bates again.

p, Albert Fennell, Brian Clemens; d, Roy Ward Baker; w, Clemens (based on the novel Dr. Jekyll and Mr. Hyde by Robert Louis Stevenson); ph, Norman Warwick (Technicolor); m, David Whitaker; ed, James Needs; md, Philip Martell; art d, Robert Jones; m/l, "He'll Be There," Clemens; makeup, John Wilcox.

Horror (PR:A MPAA:PG)

DR. JEKYLL AND THE WOLFMAN zero

(1971, Span.) International Cinema Films bw
(DR. JEKYLL Y EL HOMBRE LOBO)

Paul Naschy (Waldemar Daninsky), Shirley Corrigan, Jack Taylor.

Some day they'll use up all the different combinations of monsters and maybe then get to something original and creative. Here, Naschy is the wolfman who goes to the good doctor Taylor to be cured. Taylor cures him, but one of the side effects of his treatment is that Naschy turns into Mr. Hyde who likes to put women on the rack.

p, Jose Frade; d, Leon Klimovsky; w, Jacinto Molina.

Horror (PR:O MPAA:R)

DR. JEKYLL'S DUNGEON OF DEATH zero

(1982) 88m Rochelle/New American c

James Mathers (Dr. Jekyll), John Kearney, Tom Nicholson, Dawn Carver Kelly, Nadine Kalmes.

A poorly made, weird adaptation of Robert Louis Stevenson's classic horror tale. The film is set in 1959 San Francisco and takes place wholly in the basement/dungeon of the title character, played by Mathers, who also wrote this stinker. Mathers is the great grandson of the original Dr. Jekyll, and is experimenting with an aggression serum for mind control which was originally worked on by his great grandfather and later by the Nazis. Mathers injects criminals of both sexes with the serum, then lets them loose to watch their Kung-Fu fights. He also likes to observe torture and various sadistic acts. This absurd film comes to an end in a bloody basement slaughter.

p&d, James Wood; w, James Mathers; ph, Wood; m, Marty Allen; ed, Wood; ch, Rick Alemany.

Horror Cas. (PR:O MPAA:R)

DR. JOSSER KC**

(1931, Brit.) 71m BIP/Pathe bw

Ernie Lotinga (Jimmy Josser), Jack Hobbs (Dick O' Neill), Molly Lamont (Betty O'Neill), Joan Wyndham (Suzette), Binnie Barnes (Rosa Wopp), Harold Wilkinson (Golightly), Arnold Bell (Dick Morris).

Vaudeville comedian Lotinga repeats his role as Josser, an inept criminal who adopts a series of disguises while trying blackmail schemes. Inane slapstick that hasn't aged very well.

p,d&w, Norman Lee (based on a revue sketch "House Full" by Ernest Lotinga, Lee).

Comedy (PR:A MPAA:NR)

DR. KILDARE GOES HOME*½

(1940) 78m MGM bw

Lew Ayres (Dr. James Kildare), Lionel Barrymore (Dr. Leonard Gillespie), Laraine Day (Mary Lamont), Samuel S. Hinds (Dr. Stephen Kildare), Gene Lockhart (George Winslow), John Shelton (Dr. Davidson), Nat Pendleton (Wayman), Emma Dunn (Mrs. Martha Kildare), Alma Kruger (Molly Byrd), Walter Kingsford (Dr. Walter Carew), Nell Craig (Nurse Parker), Cliff Danielson (Dr. Jordan), Henry Wadsworth (Collins), Tom Collins (Joiner), George H. Reed (Conover), Donald Briggs (Mr. Brownlee), Leona Maricle (Mrs. Brownlee), Archie Twitchell (Bates), Marie Blake (Sally), Charles Trowbridge (Atkinson), Arthur O'Connell (Intern).

One of the films in the popular "Dr. Kildare" series. Kildare, Ayres, graduates from his hospital internship and is appointed assistant to the irascible diagnostician, Dr. Gillespie, Barrymore. Quite a bit of the film's action takes place in the small community where Dr. Kildare grew up. While there, he and Barrymore overcome a medical crisis and score a few points for socialized medicine in small communities. (See DOCTOR KILDARE series, Index.)

d, Harold S. Bucquet; w, Harry Ruskin, Willis Goldbeck (based on a story by Max Brand, Goldbeck); ph, Harold Rosson; ed, Howard O'Neill; md, David Snell.

Drama (PR:A MPAA:NR)

DR. KILDARE'S CRISIS**

(1940) 73m MGM bw

Lew Ayres (Dr. James Kildare), Robert Young (Douglas Lamont), Lionel Barrymore (Dr. Leonard Gillespie), Laraine Day (Mary Lamont), Emma Dunn (Mrs. Martha Kildare), Nat Pendleton (Joe Wayman), Bobs Watson (Tommy), Walter Kingsford (Dr. Walter Carew), Alma Kruger (Molly Byrd), Nell Craig (Nurse Parker), Frank Orth (Mike Ryan), Marie Blake (Sally), George Reed (Conover), Horace MacMahon (Foghorn Murphy), Ann Morriss (Betty), Frank Sully (John Root), Byron Foulger (Orderly), Eddie Acuff (Clifford Genet), Lillian Rich (Nurse), Gladys Blake (Maisie), Pierre Watkin (Chandler), Charles Arnt (Stubbins), Ernie Alexander (Ass't. Salesman), Gus Schilling (Orderly).

The brother of Day, the latter now the fiancee of Ayres, arrives from the West to visit his sister. He suffers from a strange affliction which Ayres diagnoses as epilepsy, a hereditary disease that might strike his prospective bride or their children. Grumpy old Barrymore, as Gillespie, discovers that the condition isn't epilepsy but is the result of a head injury the brother once received, and is correctable through a simple operation. The wedding plans continue. (See DR. KILDARE series, Index.)

d, Harold S. Bucquet; w, Harry Ruskin, Willis Goldbeck (based on a story by Max Brand, Goldbeck); ph, John Seitz; m, David Snell; ed, Gene Ruggiero; md, Snell; art d, Cedric Gibbons.

Drama (PR:A MPAA:NR)

DR. KILDARE'S STRANGE CASE**

(1940) 76m MGM bw

Lew Ayres (Dr. James Kildare), Lionel Barrymore (Dr. Leonard Gillespie), Laraine Day (Mary Lamont), Shepperd Strudwick (Dr. Gregory Lane), Samuel S. Hinds (Dr. Stephen Kildare), Emma Dunn (Martha Kildare), Walter Kingsford (Dr. Walter Carew), Alma Kruger (Molly Byrd), John Eldredge (Henry Adams), Nell Craig (Nosey), George H. Reed (Conover), Paul Porcasi (Antonio), Horace MacMahon (Fog Horn), Marie Blake (Sally), Marcia Mae Jones (Florence), Charles Waldron (Dr. Squires), Frank Orth (Mike Ryan), Fay Helm (Mrs. Adams), Nat Pendleton

(Wayman), George Lessey *(Rufus Ingersoll)*, Tom Collins *(Joiner)*, Margaret Seddon *(Mrs. Cray)*.

One of the most successful films in the series has Ayres accepting an offer to head a research institute and then getting the chance to cure a mental patient by such grisly techniques as inducing insulin shock and brain surgery. A couple of brief brain surgery sequences graphically show the exposed gray matter, no doubt adding to the public's titillation in getting a rare look at medical practices and procedures. (See DR. KILDARE series, Index.)

d, Harold S. Bucquet; w, Harry Ruskin, Willis Goldbeck (based on a story by Max Brand, Goldbeck); ph, John Seitz; m, David Snell; ed, Gene Ruggiero; md, Snell; art d, Cedric Gibbons.

Drama   Cas.   (PR:A MPAA:NR)

DR. KILDARE'S VICTORY   (1941) 92m Metro bw

Lew Ayres *(Dr. James Kildare)*, Lionel Barrymore *(Dr. Leonard Gillespie)*, Robert Sterling *(Dr. Roger Winthrop)*, Ann Ayars *(Edith "Cookie" Charles)*, Jean Rogers *(Annabelle Kirke)*, Alma Kruger *(Molly Byrd)*, Walter Kingsford *(Dr. Walter Carew)*, Nell Craig *(Nurse Parker)*, Edward Gargan *(Willie Brooks)*, Marie Blake *(Sally)*, Frank Orth *(Mike Ryan)*, George H. Reed *(Conover)*, Eddie Acuff *(Clifford Genet)*, Barry Nelson *(Sam Z. Cutler)*, Kirby Grant *(Boy)*, William Bakewell *(Mr. Hubbell)*, Charlotte Wynters *(Mrs. Hubbell)*, Gus Schilling, Stuart Crawford.

Ayres' last film as the title character of this series found him with a new director, W.S. Van Dyke II, and a new leading lady, Ayars. Story has a territorial dispute between two rival hospitals that agree not to muscle in on each other's patients. Conflict occurs when an intern, Sterling, brings a glamour girl, Ayars, with a chunk of glass imbedded in her heart, to his hospital. He is fired even though he saves her life, because he found her in the wrong territory. While recovering, Ayars makes a play for Ayres, who is still pining over the loss of his fiancee, Day, who died in DR. KILDARE'S WEDDING DAY. Though many of the faces have changed, this film still retains much of the established style of the series. (See DR. KILDARE series, Index.)

d, W.S. Van Dyke II; w, Harry Ruskin, Willis Goldbeck (based on a story by Joseph Harrington from characters created by Max Brand); ph, William Daniels; ed, Frank E. Hull.

Drama   (PR:A MPAA:NR)

DR. KILDARE'S WEDDING DAY   (1941) 82m Metro bw
                                        (AKA: MARY NAMES THE DAY)

Lew Ayres *(Dr. James Kildare)*, Lionel Barrymore *(Dr. Leonard Gillespie)*, Laraine Day *(Mary Lamont)*, Red Skelton *(Vernon Briggs)*, Fay Holden *(Mrs. Bartlett)*, Walter Kingsford *(Dr. Walter Carew)*, Alma Kruger *(Molly Byrd)*, Samuel S. Hinds *(Dr. Stephen Kildare)*, Emma Dunn *(Mrs. Martha Kildare)*, Nils Asther *(Constanzo Labardi)*, Miles Mander *(Dr. Lockberg)*, Nell Craig *(Nurse Parker)*, Frank Orth *(Mike Ryan)*, Eddie Acuff *(Clifford Genet)*, Ann Doran *(Nurse)*, Connie Gilchrist *(Jennie)*, Ralph Byrd *(Policeman)*, George H. Reed *(Conover)*, Marie Blake *(Sally)*, Margaret Seddon *(Mrs. Bartlett)*.

Audiences waited with bated breath to finally see the wedding of Dr. Kildare, Ayres, and his fiancee nurse, Day. However, the studio heads planned bigger and better parts for Day and wanted her removed from the series, so what is titled DR. KILDARE'S WEDDING DAY, should be called DR. KILDARE'S SADDEST DAY. His wedding preparations and some medical cases that require his attention make up the bulk of the film. Then, on the eve of their wedding, Day is killed when struck by a truck. The blow saps the strength out of Ayres, but Barrymore snaps him out of his self-pity by relating a similar experience that happened in his own life. (See DR. KILDARE series, Index.)

d, Harold S. Bucquet; w, Willis Goldbeck, Harry Ruskin (based on a story by Ormond Ruthven, Lawrence P. Bachmann from characters created by Max Brand); ph, George Folsey; m, Bronislau Kaper; ed, Conrad A. Nervig; art d, Cedric Gibbons.

Drama   (PR:A MPAA:NR)

DR. KNOCK½**   (1936, Fr.) 74m Pathe-Natan/French Motion Pictures bw

Louis Jouvet *(Dr. Knock)*, Palau *(Dr. Parpalaid)*, Le Vigan *(Mousuet)*, Moor *(School Teacher)*, Larquey *(Town Crier)*, Alexandre Rignault *(Halfwit)*, Sorges *(Scipion)*, Zellas *(Raffalons)*, Magdeleine Ozeray *(Maid)*, Germaine Albert *(Mme. Parpalaid)*, Marguerite Ducouret *(Mme. Remy)*.

There are more tricks in Jouvet's bag, as Dr. Knock, then there are pills in this comedic recitation of some of the ills that beset the medical profession. Jouvet buys a practice in a small village from a scheming and lazy old doctor, Palau, who thinks he has put one over on the youngster. Jouvet, though, has other ideas. With his impressive equipment and more impressive jargon, he quickly scares the villager half to death with imagined ills, and soon has a thriving practice. Palau can't believe what has happened. He thinks he can straighten matters out and returns to the village, but before he has spent a night there he, too, is under Jouvet's spell, sick in bed. (In French; English subtitles.)

d, Louis Jouvet, Roger Goupillieres; w, Jules Romains (based on his stage play); m, Jean Weiner.

Comedy   (PR:A MPAA:NR)

DR. MABUSE'S RAYS OF DEATH½**   (1964, Ger./Fr./Ital.) 95m
                        CCC-Film-Franco-Londen-Film/Serena Film bw
                        (DIE TODESSTRAHLEN DES DR. MABUSE)

Peter Van Eyck, O. E. Hasse, Yvonne Furneaux, Wolfgang Preiss, Rika Dialina, Yoko Tani, Charles Fawcett, Gustavo Rojo, Robert Beatty, Leo Genn.

The last in the series of Dr. Mabuse films. Preiss wants to destroy the world with his death ray produced by a giant concave mirror. Van Eyck is the good guy who

foils the doctor's plan. Director Fregonese directed BLOWING WILD (1953) and BLACK TUESDAY (1954). (See DR. MABUSE series, Index.)

p, Artur Brauner; d, Hugo Fregonese; w, Ladislas Fodor; ph, Ricardo Pallottini.

Thriller   (PR:A MPAA:NR)

DR. MINX zero   (1975) 94m Dimension c

Edy Williams, Randy Boone, Harvey Jason, Marlene Schmidt, Alvy Moore, William Smith.

Bad drama has Williams as a doctor who has a string of sleazy affairs. Nothing worthwhile here, and Williams' acting is nothing short of atrocious.

p,d&w, Hikmet Avedis; ph, Masoud Joseph; m, Shorty Rogers; ed, Norman Wallerstein.

Drama   Cas.   (PR:O MPAA:R)

DOCTOR MONICA½**   (1934) 75m WB bw

Kay Francis *(Dr. Monica Braden)*, Warren William *(John Braden)*, Jean Muir *(Mary Hathaway)*, Verree Teasdale *(Anna Littleford)*, Phillip Reed *(Burton)*, Emma Dunn *(Mrs. Monahan)*, Herbert Bunston *(Mr. Pettinghill)*, Ann Shoemaker *(Mrs. Hazlitt)*, Virginia Hammond *(Mrs. Chandor)*, Hale Hamilton *(Dr. Brent)*, Virginia Pine *(Louise)*, Pauline True, Leila McIntyre, Norma Drew *(Maids)*, Edward McWade *(Janitor)*, Harry Seymour *(Taxi Driver)*, Eric Wilton *(Butler)*, Gordon "Bill" Elliott *(Rutherford)*, Reginald Pasch *(Mr. Swiegart)*, Marion Lessing *(Mrs. Swiegart)*, Helen Jerome Eddy *(Miss Gelsey)*, Louise Beavers *(Mary Hathaway's Maid)*.

Kay Francis is the title doctor, an obstetrician who must deliver the baby of the woman her husband has had an affair with. When the woman kills herself, the baby is given to Francis to raise, and her cad of a husband, William, is never allowed to know that the adopted kid is his own.

d, William Keighley; w, Charles Kenyon, Laura Walker Mayer (based on the play by Marja Morozowiez Szczepanowska); ph, Sol Polito; ed, William Clemens; md, Leo F. Forbstein; art d, Anton Grot; cos, Orry-Kelly.

Drama   (PR:A MPAA:NR)

DR. MORELLE—THE CASE OF THE MISSING HEIRESS½**
                                        (1949, Brit.) 73m Exclusive bw

Valentine Dyall *(Dr. Morelle)*, Julia Lang *(Miss Frayle)*, Philip Leaver *(Samuel Kimber)*, Jean Lodge *(Cynthia Mason)*, Peter Drury *(Peter)*, Bruce Walker, James Raglan.

Dyall is a detective called in by his secretary, Lang, to find out why her friend, an heiress, has been incinerated. Strictly second-class crime stuff, but worth checking out to see Dyall, a lean, powerful-voiced actor known to British WW II radio audiences as the "Man In Black."

p, Anthony Hinds; d, Godfrey Grayson; w, Ambrose Grayson, Roy Plomley (based on a radio series by Ernest Dudley and a play by Wilfred Burr); ph, Cedric Williams.

Crime   (PR:A MPAA:NR)

DR. NO**½**   (1962, Brit.) 110m UA c

Sean Connery *(James Bond)*, Jack Lord *(Felix Leiter)*, Joseph Wiseman *(Dr. No)*, Ursula Andress *(Honey)*, Zena Marshall *(Miss Taro)*, Eunice Gayson *(Sylvia)*, Lois Maxwell *(Miss Moneypenny)*, Margaret LeWars *(Photographer)*, John Kitzmiller *(Quarrel)*, Bernard Lee *("M")*, Anthony Dawson *(Prof. Dent)*, Reggie Carter *(Jones)*, Peter Burton *(Maj. Boothroyd)*, William Foster-Davis *(Duff)*, Louis Blaazar *(Playdell-Smith)*, Michele Mok *(Sister Rose)*, Dolores Keator *(Mary)*, Yvonne Shima *(Sister Lily)*, The Byron Lee Band, Tim Moxon *(Strangeways)*, Lester Prendergast *(Puss Feller)*.

The first of a seemingly endless series of spy spoofs starred 32-year-old Connery as 007 (licensed to kill). He continued this well into the 1980s, thereby making James Bond one of the longest-running characters in film. This was a tiny picture by comparison to the later Bond issues. Connery is idly gambling in a London club when he is called by "M" (Lee), his superior in the secret service. One of his compatriots and his secretary have been killed on the island of Jamaica and Connery's job is to discover the whys and wherefores. Once there, he meets up with the U.S.A.'s local CIA rep, Lord, and they discover, with the help of native John Kitzmiller, that a nefarious schemer known as Dr. No (Wiseman) is operating off Crab Key, a remote island/fortress near Jamaica. He has developed a device that can deflect U.S. Cape Canaveral rockets and his plan is to use this to blackmail America. Each of those rockets costs millions and Wiseman thinks the U.S. might have a smart investment in keeping him away from their operations. Along the way, Connery faces the wiles of Gayson and Marshall, a kidnaping at the Jamaican airport, a hairy, yecchy tarantula dropped in his bed, a flame-throwing ersatz dragon that's been made to confuse the local superstitious natives, and the eventual confrontation with Wiseman in an underground laboratory that looks like something Captain Nemo dreamed up. Doctor No seems somewhat simplistic by later Bond standards but it served to kick off the series and the careers of several actors. Andress spends most of her time in a bikini (as well she should) and provides little more than window-dressing as a young woman with her own grudge against Dr. No. Co-author Maibaum worked on many of these movies but was already a successful producer who had provided America with one of the best suspense movies ever, THE BIG CLOCK. He was a wise choice then and continues to be a wise choice 20 years later. Producers Saltzman and Broccoli eventually went their separate ways and Saltzman purchased the venerable theatrical production company, H.M. Tennant Ltd. in London, where he continues well into his seventies. The famous Bond musical theme is by John Barry but Monty Norman is also sometimes credited on this film. Most Bond pictures have the same plot: madman wants to do something fiendish. Bond sent to stop him in various exotic locales with various exotic women. Culmination takes place in a large location where Bond is trapped but he manages to destroy villain, location, and all underlings and winds up with a comely young miss in his arms. Hey, if you've got the winning formula, why mess around with it, right?

p, Harry Saltzman, Albert R. Broccoli; d, Terence Young; w, Richard Maibaum, Johanna Harwood, Berkley Mather (based on the novel by Ian Fleming); ph, Ted Moore (Technicolor); m, John Barry, Monty Norman; ed, Peter Hunt; prod d, Ken Adam; md, Eric Rodgers; art d, Syd Cain; makeup, John O'Gorman; spec eff, Frank George; m/l, "James Bond Theme," Barry; stunts, Bob Simmons.

Spy/Suspense   **Cas.**   **(PR:C MPAA:NR)**

DR. O'DOWD*   (1940, Brit.) 76m WB bw

Shaun Glenville (Marius O'Dowd), Peggy Cummins (Pat O'Dowd), Mary Merrall (Constanta), Liam Gaffney (Stephen O'Dowd), Patricia Roc (Rosemary), James Carney (O'Hara), Walter Hudd (Dr. Crowther), Charles Victor (Dooley), Pat Noonan (Mulvaney), Maire O'Neill (Mrs. Mulvaney), Irene Handl (Sarah), Pamela Wood (Moira), Felix Aylmer (President), Nell Emerald.

A drunken Irish doctor, Glenville, is hounded out of the profession after the death of his daughter-in-law during an operation he performs while tipsy. In true soap opera fashion, a diphtheria outbreak among workers on a dam, on which his now estranged son is an engineer, gives him the chance to prove himself again, and he is reinstated as a doctor at the end.

p, Sam Sax; d, Herbert Mason; w, Derek Twist, Austin Melford (based on the novel by L. A. G. Strong); ph, Basil Emmott.

Drama   **(PR:A MPAA:NR)**

DOCTOR OF DOOM**   (1962, Mex.) 77m
Cinematografic Calderon/Gordon Murray bw
(LAS LUCHADORAS CONTRA EL MEDICO RESINO)

Lorena Velazquez, Roberto Canedo, Armondo Silvestre, Chucho Salinas, Elizabeth Campbell, Jorge Mondragon, Sonia Infante, Martha "Guera" Solis, Irma Rodriguez.

A mad scientist bumbling around with brain transplants hits on the novel idea of transplanting the brain of a gorilla into a man's head, and another in the head of a female wrestler, which eventually kills her. Her sister, who is also a wrestler, enlists the aid of other grapplers and the cops and manages to avenge the sister's death. This was the first in a string of mildly entertaining Mexican female wrestling movies.

p, William Calderon Stell [Guillermo Calderon]; d, Rene Cardona; w, Alfredo Salazar; ph, Enrique Wallace; m, Antonio Diaz Donde; ed, Jorge Bustos; art d, Jose Rodriguez.

Horror   **Cas.**   **(PR:O MPAA:NR)**

DOCTOR OF ST. PAUL, THE*½   (1969, Ger.) 95m
Terra Filmkunst/Constantin c (DER ARZT VON ST. PAULI)

Curt Jurgens (Dr. Jan Diffring), Horst Naumann (Dr. Klaus Diffring), Christiane Ruecker (Margot Rau), Heinz Reincke (Willi Nippes), Marianne Hoffmann (Karin Steffen), Fritz Wepper (Hein Jungermann), Monika Zinnenberg (Gerda Heske), Dieter Borsche (Priest Feddersen), Friedrich Schuetter (Siegfried Gersum), Susanne Roquette (Elisabeth Langhoff).

As a friend to the poor and needy, Dr. Diffring (Jurgens) goes through life good-naturedly helping everybody, a pure idealization of a vanished time in the medical world. His brother, also a doctor, is of another mold—he likes high society and, as a fashionable gynecologist, wallows in a decadent society. A murder case brings the brothers together, and it turns out that brother Naumann is the guilty party. He ends up committing suicide. A fine script with several good supporting performances, make this one still a good "see."

d&w, Rolf Olsen; ph, Franz X. Lederle (Eastmancolor); m, Edwin Halietz; ed, Renate Willeg; set d, Guenter Kob.

Crime   **(PR:C MPAA:NR)**

DOCTOR PHIBES RISES AGAIN***   (1972, Brit.) 88m AIP c

Vincent Price (Dr. Anton Phibes), Robert Quarry (Biederbeck), Valli Kemp (Vulnavia), Hugh Griffith (Ambrose), John Thaw (Shavers), Keith Buckley (Stuart), Lewis Fiander (Baker), Gerald Sim (Hackett), Milton Reid (Cheng, Manservant), Peter Jeffrey (Inspector Trout), John Cater (Supt. Waverley), Peter Cushing (Captain), Beryl Reid (Mrs. Ambrose), Terry-Thomas (Lombardo), Fiona Lewis (Diana), Caroline Munro (Victoria).

This superior sequel to THE ABOMINABLE DR. PHIBES carries on the same tongue-in-cheek tone of horror as its predecessor. Price, as the title doctor, rises from the state of suspended animation in which he has spent three years since the end of the first film. He sets out for Egypt to find the secret elixir of life, so he may resurrect his dead wife. Quarry, a powerful and rich old man, is in search of the same elixir, and tries to stop Price from his quest. This is where the fun comes in as Price is forced to dispatch Quarry's men in ingenious ways. Especially good is a telephone receiver with a spike in it. Chasing both Price and Quarry are Jeffrey and Cater, a pair of inept policemen. The film is directed by Fuest, who was a veteran of "The Avengers" TV series, which had a lot of the same wry attitude in its action.

p, Louis M. Heyward; d, Robert Fuest; w, Fuest, Robert Blees (based on characters created by James Whiton, William Goldstein); ph, Alex Thomson (Movielab Color); m, John Gale; ed, Tristan Cones; art d, Brian Eatwell; cos, Ivy Baker; makeup, Trevor Crole-Rees.

Horror   **(PR:C-O MPAA:PG)**

DR. POPAUL   (SEE: HIGH HEELS, 1972, Fr.)

DR. RENAULT'S SECRET**   (1942) 58m FOX bw

J. Carroll Naish (Mr. Noel), John Shepperd [Shepperd Strudwick] (Dr. Larry Forbes), Lynne Roberts (Madeline Renault), George Zucco (Dr. Renault), Bert Roach (Proprietor), Eugene Borden (Coroner), Jack Norton (Austin), Ray "Crash" Corrigan (The Ape), Charles Wagenheim, Mike Mazurki, Arthur Shields, Jean Del Val.

Dr. Renault's secret is a serum which, along with a little cutting into the brain, turns a jungle ape into a semi-human, Naish. The ape, now regarding himself through a human's eyes, resents what has been done to him and his rage turns murdererous. The first person he vents that rage on is, of course, Zucco, who gave him the sensitivity to pity himself. The director, Lachman, originally was a painter, with works hanging in the Chicago Art Institute as well as in the Prado in Spain. He entered films as a set designer in 1922, and spent the next 20 years as a moviemaker before returning to painting. Art director Juran, who dressed this film up to give it some class, went on as a director of interesting poverty-row science fiction films, including ATTACK OF THE 50-FOOT WOMAN, THE DEADLY MANTIS and 20 MILLION MILES TO EARTH.

p, Sol M. Wurtzel; d, Harry Lachman; w, William Bruckner, Robert F. Metzler; ph, Virgil Miller; m, David Raskin, Emil Newman; ed, Fred Allen; art d, Nathan Juran.

Horror   **(PR:C MPAA:NR)**

DR. RHYTHM**   (1938) 80m PAR bw

Bing Crosby (Dr. Remsen), Mary Carlisle (Judy), Beatrice Lillie (Mrs. Lorelei Dodge-Blodgett), Andy Devine (Patrolman O'Roone), Rufe Davis (Al), Laura Hope Crews (Mr. Twombling), Fred Keating (Chris Le Roy), John Hamilton (Inspector Bryce), Sterling Holloway (Luke), Henry Wadsworth (Otis Eaton), Franklin Pangborn (Mr. Stanchfield), Harold Minjir (Mr. Martingale), William Austin (Mr. Coldwater), Gino Corrado (Cazzetta), Harry Stubbs (Police Captain), Frank Elliott (Crowley), Charles Moore (Chauffeur), Louis Armstrong (Himself), Emory Parnell (Sgt. Olson), Allen Matthews (Henchman), Dolores Casey (Nurse).

Loosely based on an O. Henry story, this tepid musical fails on many levels. It has no songs that anyone will recall, Crosby seems to sleepwalk through it, and the amount of humor in the script could be placed under the toenail of a chicken and still have room left over for a politician's promises made good. Four alumni of Brooklyn's P.S. 43 meet for their yearly reunion at the Central Park Zoo at midnight (why they choose this place at this time is never made clear). Crosby is a wealthy doctor, Devine is a New York City cop, Holloway is an ice cream vendor, and Rufe Davis is the zookeeper. Crosby takes one of Devine's assignments to act as a cop-bodyguard to Mary Carlisle, which results, of course, in his falling in love with her. Bea Lillie is the standout performer and almost saves the movie with her clowning in a burlesque of a Gypsy operetta at the Policeman's Ball. Songs: "My Heart Is Taking Lessons," "This Is My Night To Dream," "On the Sentimental Side," "Doctor Rhythm," "Only a Gypsy Knows," "Trumpet Player's Lament," "P.S. 43" (Johnny Burke, James V. Monaco).

p, Emanuel Cohen; d, Frank Tuttle; w, Jo Swerling, Sr., Richard Connell, Dion Itheradge (based on the story "The Badge of Policeman O'Roone" by O. Henry); ph, Charles Lang; ed, Alexander Troffey; md, George Stoll; ch, Jack Crosby.

Musical/Comedy   **(PR:AA MPAA:NR)**

DR. SIN FANG**   (1937, Brit.) 60m Victory/MGM bw

H. Agar Lyons (Dr. Sin Fang), Anne Grey (Sonia Graham), Robert Hobbs (John Byrne), George Mozart (Bill), Nell Emerald (Mrs. Higgins), Arty Ash (Prof. Graham), Louis Darnley, Ernest Sefton.

Lyons, a Chinese villain of the Fu Manchu school, uses assorted nefarious schemes to lay his hands on Ash's secret formula for curing cancer. Ludicrous, but entertaining nonetheless.

p, Nell Emerald; d, Tony Frenguelli; w, Nigel Byass, Frederick Reynolds (based on a story by Kaye Mason).

Crime   **(PR:A MPAA:NR)**

DR. SOCRATES**   (1935) 74m WB bw

Paul Muni (Dr. Caldwell), Ann Dvorak (Josephine Gray), Barton MacLane (Red Bastian), Raymond Brown (Ben Suggs), Ralph Remley (Bill Payne), Hal K. Dawson (Mel Towne), Grace Stafford (Caroline Suggs), Mayo Methot (Muggsy), Henry O'Neill (Greer), Robert Barrat (Dr. Ginder), Marc Lawrence (Lefty), Helen Lowell (Ma Ganson), John Eldredge (Dr. Burton), Samuel Hinds (Dr. McClintock), Olin Howland (Catlett), Joseph Downing (Cinq Laval), June Travis (Dublin), Gordon [Bill] Elliott (Tom Collins, Greer's Assistant), Sam Wren (Chuck), John Kelly (Al), Ivan Miller (Ed Doolittle), Otis Harlan (Fisher), Carl Stockdale (Abner Cluett), William Wayne (Dave), Maidel Turner, Vangie Beilby (Women), Grady Sutton (Grocery Clerk), James Donlan (Salesman), Ralph Lewis (Proprietor), Emerson Treacy (Young Man), June Martel (Young Woman), Jerry Madden (Boy), Lucille Ward (Stout Woman), Alfred P. James (Farmer), Dick Elliott, Harry Harvey, Jack Gardner, Gene Morgan (Photographers), Ben Hendricks (Sentry), Jack Norton, Harry White (Drunks), Al Hill, Robert Perry, James Dundee, Frank McGlynn, Jr., Larry McGrath (Gangsters), Marie Astaire, Lucille Collins (Molls), Milton Kibbee (Bank Teller), Charlie Sullivan (Henchman), Tom Wilson (Citizen), Hobart Cavanaugh (Floyd Stevens), Adrian Morris (Beanie), Leo White (Tailor), Edward McWade, William Burress.

A rare film in that it is a most minor effort from a most major actor who went on to essay the lives of so many important historical figures, such as JUAREZ, THE LIFE OF EMILE ZOLA, and THE STORY OF LOUIS PASTEUR as well as Al Capone in SCARFACE and Napoleon, Schubert, and Don Juan in SEVEN FACES. This is a comparatively lightweight effort that came at the nadir of the Warner Bros. "gangster" cycle, although it was remade just four years later with

Humphrey Bogart and Kay Francis as KING OF THE UNDERWORLD. Muni is a surgeon who has relocated in a tiny hamlet in an attempt to change his life after the death of his fiancee, a deed he accepts responsibility for but it's only a plot ploy to get him out of the big city and into the tiny burg for the story's sake. MacLane is a bank robber who took several bullets in his last robbery and he and his gang come to Muni so the doc can pull the lead out of MacLane's flesh. Once that's done, the gang members make Muni their official medical advisor, even though he'd rather they just go off somewhere else. Meanwhile, Muni gets warm for Ann Dvorak, a hitchhiker the gang picked up, and the rest of the burghers think that she's part of the criminal contingent, but she isn't. Muni tells the crooks that there is a scarlet fever epidemic and they have all been exposed to it. If not stopped immediately, it can result in a painful death. The men line up for their shots and Muni injects them all with morphine just as they are about to resist a siege at their country hideout. No one explains why the narcotic puts everyone in the gang to sleep except MacLane, who spends the last few minutes taking pot-shots at everyone. But the picture is near the end by that time and licenses were applied for on the part of the screenwriters in order to get the heck out of the plot and put Muni and Dvorak together so viewers could go home. Muni never liked this picture and it's easy to understand why.

p, Robert Lord; d, William Dieterle; w, Lord, Mary C. McCall, Jr. (based on a story by W. R. Burnett); ph, Tony Gaudio; ed, Ralph Dawson; md, Leo F. Forbstein; art d, Anton Grot.

Crime (PR:A-C MPAA:NR)

DR. STRANGELOVE: OR HOW I LEARNED TO STOP WORRYING AND LOVE THE BOMB***½

(1964) 102m COL bw

Peter Sellers (Group Capt. Lionel Mandrake/President Merkin Muffley/Dr. Strangelove), George C. Scott (Gen. "Buck" Turgidson), Sterling Hayden (Gen. Jack D. Ripper), Keenan Wynn (Col. "Bat" Guano), Slim Pickens (Maj. T. J. "King" Kong), Peter Bull (Ambassador de Sadesky), Tracy Reed (Miss Scott), James Earl Jones (Lt. Lothar Zogg), Jack Creley (Mr. Staines), Frank Berry (Lt. H. R. Dietrich), Glenn Beck (Lt. W. D. Kivel), Shane Rimmer (Capt. G. A. "Ace" Owens), Paul Tamarin (Lt. B. Goldberg), Gordon Tanner (Gen. Faceman), Robert O'Neil (Admiral Randolph), Roy Stephens (Frank), Laurence Herder, John McCarthy, Hal Galili (Members of the Defense Team).

Intended as a sort of Grand Guignol comedy, combining anti-establishment theories and an underground indictment of the U.S. government and its policies, DR. STRANGELOVE transcended the campus snicker and art house smugness with caricatures so bold and wild that it became the first significant film of the absurd, one where everyone had a black laugh, no matter the level of perception. Hayden is an Air Force general who goes completely mad, seals off his air base, and sends his bomber wing to attack Russia. The President (Sellers) meets desperately with his advisors, including Scott, a skirt-chasing, immature general, and a crackpot, invalided German scientist, Dr. Strangelove (again Sellers), and a plan to shoot down the American planes by American fighters and missiles is put in motion, with the Russians informed of every move but suspicious enough to set in motion their own dreaded "Doomsday Machine." Meanwhile, a British officer (once more Sellers) and Wynn infiltrate Hayden's post. Sellers busies himself with trying to trick the code from Hayden that will recall his bombers. He is unsuccessful, as the mad general puts him off with explanations about how he has kept his "precious bodily fluids" to himself, "denying women my essence." He then excuses himself, goes into a washroom and blows out his brains. All of his bombers are shot down except one flown by Pickens, a crafty pilot who manages to evade Russian fighters and missiles, as he heads for a Russian target. Even after Sellers figures out the recall code, Pickens and crew believe it to be a trick and keep going. Just as they approach the target trouble arises with the bomb release mechanism. Pickens, ever the enterprising warrior, manually releases it and rides the bomb to earth and destruction like a bronk-busting cowboy. The explosion triggers the Russian "Doomsday Machine." Just before the end of the world, Sellers the President and Sellers the mad German scientist fritter away precious time discussing how the elite of society might survive in underground hideouts. Though there is a higher level of sophistication in DR. STRANGELOVE than in quasi-intellectual black comedies before it, the film is by no means an important philosophical statement. In fact, it is the collegiate-level humor which spawned the cop-out-drop-out trend typifying the political confusion of the 1960s when lemmings reigned. Kubrick showed his masterful talent, however, in making a larger film than what his script encompassed, artfully masking his intercutting news clips and confining his players to a few inexpensive sets. All of it is topped off not by the custard pie fight between the opposing diplomats Kubrick had originally envisioned, but by a sequence showing one A-bomb exploding after another while the sweet voice of Vera Lynn lilts "We'll Meet Again," the last Kubrick sarcasm which ends his film with a bang and a sneer.

p&d, Stanley Kubrick; w, Kubrick, Terry Southern, Peter George (based on the novel Red Alert by Peter George); ph, Melvin Pike; m, Laurie Johnson; ed, Anthony Harvey; prod d, Ken Adams; art d, Peter Murton; cos, Bridget Sellers; spec eff, Wally Veevers; makeup, Stewart Freeborn.

Science Fiction/Comedy Cas. (PR:C MPAA:NR)

DOCTOR SYN**

(1937, Brit.) 81m GAU/GFD bw

George Arliss (Dr. Syn), John Loder (Denis Cobtree), Margaret Lockwood (Imogene), Roy Emerton (Capt. Howard Collyer), Graham Moffatt (Jerry Jerk), Frederick Burtwell (Rash), George Merritt (Mipps), Athole Stewart (Sir Anthony Cobtree), Wally Patch (Bosun), Meinhart Maur (Mulatto), Muriel George (Mrs. Waggetts), Wilson Coleman (Dr. Pepper).

This British period features Arliss in his last role. He is the one-time notorious pirate Clegg who is taken for dead, but has in reality shown up 20 years later as the vicar of Dymchurch and still the head of his pirates who have become

smugglers. While using the cover of a priest, he smuggles at will, and uses the profits to the betterment of the little coastal village over which he presides. The transition from ruthless pirate to pastor is explained by Arliss' education in law school. All of Clegg's plans are thwarted when a revenue agent unmasks Arliss and his band of cutthroats. Film was remade as NIGHT CREATURES in 1962 and then again as DR. SYN, ALIAS THE SCARECROW (1975) produced by Disney.

p, Edward Black, Michael Balcon; d, Roy William Neill; w, Roger Burford, Michael Hogan (based on the novel by Russell Thorndike); ph, Jack Cox, Jack Perry; ed, R.E. Dearing; md, Louis Levy; set d, Alexander Vetchinski.

Adventure Cas. (PR:A MPAA:NR)

DR. SYN, ALIAS THE SCARECROW**

(1975) 84m Disney c

Patrick McGoohan (Dr. Syn), Tony Britton (Bates), George Cole (Mr. Mipps), Michael Hordern (Squire), Geoffrey Keen (Gen. Pugh), Kay Walsh, Patrick Wymark, Alan Dobie, Eric Pohlmann.

Decent Disney telling of the old story of the innocent-looking vicar who doubles as a smuggler. This time it was done for broadcast as a three-part show for American TV in 1962. It was released overseas in 1963. In 1962 Hammer Films made another version of the story released in the U.S. as NIGHT CREATURES, though both are copies of DOCTOR SYN (1937), starring George Arliss.

p, Walt Disney, Bill Anderson; d, James Neilson; w, Robert Westerby (based on the novel Christopher Syn by Russell Thorndike and William Buchanan); ph, Paul Beeson; m, Gerard Schurmann.

Adventure (PR:AA MPAA:G)

DOCTOR TAKES A WIFE**½

(1940) 89m COL bw

Loretta Young (June Cameron), Ray Milland (Dr. Timothy Sterling), Reginald Gardiner (John Pierce), Gail Patrick (Marilyn Thomas), Edmund Gwenn (Dr. Lionel Sterling), Frank Sully (Slapcovitch), Gordon Jones (O'Brien), Georges Metaxa (Jean Rovere), Charles Halton (Dr. Streeter), Joseph Eggenton (Dr. Nielson), Paul McAllister (Dean Lawton), Chester Clute (Johnson), Hal K. Dawson (Charlie), Edward Van Sloan (Burkhardt), John Wray (Farmer), Edgar Dearing (Motor Cop), Irving Bacon (Gas Station Attendant), Spencer Charters (Mr. Quinn), Edward Gargan (Doorman), Don Beddoe, Charles Lane (Reporters), Olin Howland (Hotel Clerk), Frank Darien (Greenwich Editor), Frank Orth (New York Editor), William Austin (Hotel Manager), Ian Maclaren (Professor), Jane Goude (Mrs. Nielson), Erville Alderson (Harrison), Virginia Sale (School Teacher), Helen Ainsworth (Amazon), Myra Marsh (Lydia Johnson), Mary Gordon (Scrubwoman), Edward Earle, Vernon Dent, Sumner Getchell (Men), Gertrude Sutton (Mabel), Edgar Buchanan (Doorman), Ann Lee (Maid), Jane Keckley (Mrs. Quinn), Wesley Giraud (Western Union Boy), Renie Riano (Telegraph Operator), Dorothy Ann Seese, Catherine Courtney, Charlotte Treadway, Helen Davis, Dorothy Appleby (Women).

What happens when a bachelor girl writer, Young, who hates marriage and dominating males, and a medical college instructor, Milland, who yearns to become a professor, meet in the bedroom? THE DOCTOR TAKES A WIFE endeavors to describe the unlikely event, and in doing so dishes up a fast-talking, gibe-poking comedy that is still good for laughs. Young and Milland get involved in publicity linking them to marriage. Young takes advantage of the contretemps to dash off a hot novel, and Milland gets his professorship. Then they must go through with it (pretending), and actually take an apartment, where the bickering and name-calling begins. A wildly contrived ending has them deciding to really get married and set everything straight.

p, William Perlberg; d, Alexander Hall; w, George Seaton, Ken Englund (based on a story by Aleen Leslie); ph, Sid Hickox; ed, Viola Lawrence.

Comedy (PR:AA MPAA:NR)

DR. TARR'S TORTURE DUNGEON**

(1972, Mex.) 88m Group I c

Claude Brook, Ellen Sberman, Martin LaSalle, Robert Dumont, Arthur Hansel.

Weird Mexican horror film based on Poe's "The System of Doctor Tarr and Professor Feather." A reporter visits an asylum taken over by lunatics. Great dollops of sex and violence, but more interesting than the general run of those things.

p, Robert Viskin, J.G. Elster; d, Juan Lopez Moctezuma; w, Charles Illescas (based on the story "The System of Doctor Tarr and Professor Feather" by Edgar Allan Poe).

Horror (PR:O MPAA:R)

DR. TERROR'S GALLERY OF HORRORS zero

(1967) 84m
Dorad Corp.-Borealis Enterprises/American General c
(AKA: BLOOD SUCKERS; RETURN FROM THE PAST)

"Count Alucard": Mitch Evans (Count Alucard), Roger Gentry (Jonathan Harker), Vic McGee (Burgomeister), Gary Daniels (Coachman); "The Witch's Clock": John Carradine (Tristam Halbin), Roger Gentry (Bob Farrell), Karen Joy (Julie Farrell), Vic McGee (Dr. Finchley); "Spark Of Life": Lon Chaney, Jr. (Dr. Mendell) Ron Doyle (Dr. Cushing), Vic McGee (Amos Duncan), Joey Benson (Dr. Sedgewick); "Monster Raid": Rochelle Hudson (Helen Spalding), Ron Doyle (Dr. Spalding), Ron Doyle (Dr. Sewart), Vic McGee (Desmond); "King Vampire": Ron Doyle (Brenner), Ron Brogan (Marsh), Margaret Moore (Mrs. O'Shea), Roger Gentry (Mob Leader).

A five-part horror anthology with some of the lowest production values seen on the screen. The first story is "The Witch's Clock," with Carradine the narrator for this segment about magic. Chaney is a doctor who brings back to life the body of a crazed killer in the segment titled "The Spark Of Life." In "Count Alucard," Dracula fights a werewolf, and "Monster Raid" is about a corpse that comes back to life to have some fun. "King Vampire" has 19th-century London besieged by a blood-loving beast.

p, David L. Hewitt, Ray Dorn; d, Hewitt; w, David Prentiss, Gary R. Heacock, Russ Jones (based on a story by Jones); ph, Austin McKinney (Totalvision, Technicolor); ed, Tim Hinkle; art d, Ray Dorn.

Horror **(PR:O MPAA:NR)**

DR. TERROR'S HOUSE OF HORRORS½** (1965, Brit.) 98m Amicus/RF c

Peter Cushing *(Dr. Schreck)*, Chistopher Lee *(Franklyn Marsh)*, Roy Castle *(Biff Bailey)*, Donald Sutherland *(Bob Carroll)*, Neil McCallum *(Jim Dawson)*, Alan Freeman *(Bill Rogers)*, Max Adrian *(Dr. Blake)*, Edward Underdown *(Tod)*, Ursula Howells *(Deirdre)*, Peter Madden *(Caleb)*, Katy Wild *(Valda)*, Ann Bell *(Ann Rogers)*, Sarah Nicholls *(Carol Rogers)*, Jeremy Kemp *(Drake)*, Kenny Lynch *(Sammy Coin)*, Harold Lang *(Shine)*, Thomas Baptiste *(Dambala)*, Tubby Hayes Quintet *(Bailey's Band)*, Michael Gough *(Eric Landor)*, Isla Blair *(Pretty Girl)*, Jennifer Jayne *(Nicolle)*, Al Mulock *(Detective)*, Bernard Lee *(Hopkins)*, Russ Henderson Steel Band, Christopher Carlos, George Mossman, Russ Henderson, Hedger Wallace, Judy Cornwall, Faith Kent, Brian Hankins, John Martin, Kenneth Kove, Walter Sparrow, Frank Forsyth, Frank Barry, Irene Richmond, Laurie Leigh.

The first and the best of the many Amicus horror anthology films. Five vignettes are loosely held together by a train ride. Five men are traveling on a train and they meet up with bearded Dr. Schreck, played by Cushing. With tarot cards, he proceeds to tell the men how each will die. The first is an architect who, while renovating an old family home for a client, is killed by a female werewolf. Pop musician Castle is done in by the Haitian god Dambala for playing music in a nightclub that he heard at a voodoo ceremony. American doctor Sutherland suspects his wife is a vampire and drives a stake through her heart. He ends up hanging for it. Art critic Lee runs over an artist, and is then haunted by the artist's dismembered hand as it crawls around seeking revenge. The last vignette finds a creeping killer vine growing in a suburban backyard with a distinct grudge against the human race.

p, Milton Subotsky, Max J. Rosenberg; d, Freddie Francis; w, Subotsky; ph, Alan Hume (Techniscope, Technicolor); m, Elisabeth Lutyens; ed, Thelma Connell; md, Philip Martell; art d, William Constable; m/l, "Give Me Love," "Everybody's Got Love," Kenny Lynch, "Voodoo," Tubby Hayes.

Horror **(PR:O MPAA:NR)**

DR. WHO AND THE DALEKS½** (1965, Brit.) 83m Aaru/RF c

Peter Cushing *(Dr. Who)*, Roy Castle *(Ian)*, Jennie Linden *(Barbara)*, Roberta Tovey *(Susan)*, Barrie Ingham *(Alydon)*, Michael Coles *(Ganatus)*, Geoffrey Toone *(Temmosus)*, Mark Peterson *(Elydon)*, John Brown *(Antodus)*, Yvonne Antrobus *(Dyoni)*.

Absent-minded Dr. Who, Cushing, and his two granddaughters, Linden and Tovey, and Tovey's boy friend, Castle, are thrown through time and space when Castle accidentally turns on Cushing's invention, Tardis. They land on a future planet that is being wasted by a neutron bomb. Cushing et al, become involved when they help the Thals, the good people, who are being hunted down by the Daleks in their mobile transporters, which project lethal death rays. Luckily for all the good guys, the Daleks are defeated before they detonate another neutron bomb. The sequel to this film was DALEKS—INVASION EARTH 2150 AD, released in 1966.

p, Milton Subotsky, Max J. Rosenberg; d, Gordon Flemyng; w, Subotsky (based on a BBC television serial by Terry Nation); ph, John Wilcox (Techniscope, Technicolor); m, Malcolm Lockyer, Barry Gray; ed, Oswald Hafenrichter; md, Lockyer; art d, Bill Constable; set d, Scott Slimon; spec eff, Ted Samuels.

Science Fiction **(PR:A MPAA:NR)**

DOCTOR X**** (1932) 77m FN/WB bw/c

Lionel Atwill *(Doctor Xavier, Head of Research Laboratory)*, Lee Tracy *(Lee, a Newspaper Reporter)*, Fay Wray *(Joan, Dr. X's Daughter)*, Preston Foster *(Dr. Wells)*, Arthur Edmund Carewe *(Dr. Rowitz)*, John Wray *(Dr. Haines)*, Harry Beresford *(Dr. Duke)*, George Rosener *(Otto, Dr. X's Brother)*, Leila Bennett *(Mamie, Dr. X's Housekeeper)*, Robert Warwick *(Police Commissioner Stevens)*, Willard Robertson *(O'Halloran, Stevens' Assistant)*, Thomas Jackson *(Editor)*, Harry Holman *(Policeman)*, Tom Dugan *(Sheriff)*, Mae Busch *(The Madame)*.

DOCTOR X in color is one of the most elusive of all the freak classic horror films made in the early 1930s. The film was originally produced in two-color Technicolor, or "Glorious Technicolor" as it was called then, not so much for the aesthetic qualities of color but because Warners had a contractual commitment to the Technicolor company to make a certain number of color films. Color films were to the 1930s what 3-D would be to the 1950s, and were basically used for musicals. However, that genre was in a lull at the time, while horror films were peaking. As a result, DOCTOR X was given the color treatment but the prints were only made for release in major markets, while black and white prints were distributed to lesser markets. DOCTOR X is usually seen in the black and white version, though a color print did surface in 1973. It proved that the use of color in this film wasn't just a gimmick but an imaginative way to add to its creepy atmosphere. The story is set in a spooky old mansion atop the cliffs at Blackstone Shoals, on Long Island. Atwill plays the sinister Dr. Xavier, who runs the research laboratory where most of the action takes place. Foster is his one-armed lab assistant who, having discovered the secret to eternal life, coats his body from head to toe with a synthetic flesh, giving him abnormal powers, and he tends to slip out on full moons and strangle people. Tracy is a newspaper reporter on the trail of the "Moon Murderer" and ultimately comes face-to-face with him. Wray enters the horror film genre as the daughter of Atwill, and proves that she was meant to scream on film. DOCTOR X is one of those rare scare films that provoke true horror. Partial thanks go to Max Factor who designed the makeup for the synthetic flesh. The 1939 film, THE RETURN OF DOCTOR X, is not a sequel to this classic, but just an attempt to cash in on the original's good name.

d, Michael Curtiz; w, Robert Tasker, Earl Baldwin (based on a play by Howard W. Comstock and Allen C. Miller); ph, Ray Rennahan, Richard Tower (Technicolor); ed, George Amy; art d, Anton Grot; makeup Max Factor.

Horror **(PR:A MPAA:NR)**

DOCTOR, YOU'VE GOT TO BE KIDDING** (1967) 93m Trident/MGM c

Sandra Dee *(Heather Halloran)*, George Hamilton *(Harlan Wycliff)*, Celeste Holm *(Louise Halloran)*, Bill Bixby *(Dick Bender)*, Dick Kallman *(Pat Murad)*, Mort Sahl *(Dan Ruskin)*, Dwayne Hickman *(Hank)*, Allen Jenkins *(Joe Bonney)*, Robert Gibbons *(Judge North)*, Med Flory, Scott White, Donald Mitchell *(Policemen)*, Nichelle Nichols *(Jenny Ribbock)*, Charlotte Considine *(Miss Reynolds)*, Allison McKay *(Cigarette Girl)*, Rica Owen Moore *(Folk Singer)*, Wild Affair Trio *(Themselves)*.

Sandra Dee is an unwed, pregnant, would-be-singer. The film starts out with Dee being rushed to the hospital to have her baby. Accompanying her are three men who want to marry her and be the father of her baby. The rest of the film is a flashback, dealing with Dee's rise to stardom as a singer, and the pregnancy which she refuses to believe. Hamilton is Dee's stuffy boss who tries to discourage her from singing, but only pushes her into making a full-time commitment to warbling.

p, Douglas Laurence; d, Peter Tewksbury; w, Phillip Shuken (based on the novel by Patte Wheat Mahan); ph, Fred Koenekamp (Panavision, Metrocolor); m, Kenyon Hopkins; ed, Fredric Steinkamp; art d, George W. Davis, Urie McCleary; set d, Henry Grace, Charles S. Thompson; ch, Earl Barton; m/l, "I Haven't Got Anything Better to Do," "Walk Tall Like a Man," Paul Vance, Lee Pockriss (sung by Sandra Dee), "Talkin' Low," Dale Wasserman, Hopkins, "Little Girl" (both performed by the Wild Affair Trio), "All I Do Is Dream of You," Arthur Freed, Nacio Herb Brown.

Comedy **(PR:A MPAA:NR)**

DOCTOR ZHIVAGO**** (1965) 197m MGM c

Geraldine Chaplin *(Tonya)*, Julie Christie *(Lara)*, Tom Courtenay *(Pasha/Strelnikoff)*, Alec Guinness *(Yevgraf)*, Siobban McKenna *(Anna)*, Ralph Richardson *(Alexander)*, Omar Sharif *(Yuri)*, Rod Steiger *(Komarovsky)*, Rita Tushingham *(The Girl)*, Adrienne Corri *(Amelia)*, Geoffrey Keen *(Prof. Kurt)*, Jeffrey Rockland *(Sasha)*, Lucy Westmore *(Katya)*, Noel Willman *(Razin)*, Gerard Tichy *(Liberius)*, Klaus Kinski *(Kostoyed)*, Jack MacGowran *(Petya)*, Maria Martin *(Gentlewoman)*, Tarek Sharif *(Yuri at 8)*, Mercedes Ruiz *(Tonya at 7)*, Inigo Jackson *(Major)*, Virgilio Texeira *(Captain)*, Bernard Kay *(Bolshevik)*, Eric Chitty *(Old Soldier)*, Jose Nieto *(Priest)*, Mark Eden *(Young Engineer)*, Emilio Carrer *(Mr. Sventytski)*, Gerhard Jersch *(David)*, Wolf Frees *(Comrade Yelkin)*, Gwen Nelson *(Comrade Kaprugina)*, Jose Caffarel *(Militiaman)*, Brigitte Trace *(Streetwalker)*, Luana Alcaniz *(Mrs. Sventytski)*, Lili Murati *(Raddled Woman)*, Catherine Elison *(Raped Woman)*, Maria Vico *(Demented Woman)*, Dodo Assad Bahador *(Dragoon Colonel)*, Peter Madden *(Political Officer)*, Roger Maxwell *(Beef-Faced Colonel)*.

A very good movie but not a masterpiece. Eight Oscar nominations were made and five were awarded (screenplay, music, cinematography, art direction, costumes) but the Academy saw fit to honor THE SOUND OF MUSIC, CAT BALLOU, DARLING, and SHIP OF FOOLS with the bulk of the acting awards. And they were right. Here was an attempt at a Russian version of GONE WITH THE WIND and Lean and Bolt came off their LAWRENCE OF ARABIA hit ready to make this into an all-time winner. But it seemed like such a patent aping of GWTW that it just didn't come together. The book was a heavy tome, replete with all the "clouds of gray that any Russian play could guarantee" (Ira Gershwin's brilliant lyric) and the filmmakers sought to clear that aside and concentrate on the gloss. Sharif is Zhivago, a sensitive doctor married to Chaplin while philandering with Christie. His half-brother is Guinness, a cold-hearted secret police official. Steiger is a sex-crazed politician who will do anything to keep himself successful, and most of his passion is directed toward Christie but that eventually disintegrates and becomes affection and respect. Much of the story is told in flashback as Guinness interrogates Tushingham, whom he believes to be the daughter of Sharif and Christie. He is trying to locate Sharif, now an enemy of the state since the Revolution has taken place. It would be interesting to run DR. ZHIVAGO next to REDS to see how different they are. This film is somewhat old-fashioned and feels about 20 years earlier than REDS in the same era depicted. Basically, it's the story of the Bolshevik takeover through the eyes of Sharif, Christie, Chaplin, Guinness, and the others. The huge novel was pared down to a bit over three hours and it's hard to see how Bolt could have made it any shorter because there was so much to cover, and yet a little less respect for the award-winning novel might have proved more effective. The movie was an enormous success at the box office, due somewhat to the haunting score by Maurice Jarre which became a best seller. Any film about a writer is always on the brink of being boring, as there is nothing duller than watching someone write (ask any author's wife). Zhivago transcends from a semi-ordinary doctor to an extraordinary writer and we don't really note the change in him. That may be the fault of Bolt or Lean or, more likely, Sharif, who was miscast from the beginning, having none of the heroic grandeur in his makeup to cause us to believe he was who he portrayed. The best parts of the film are the visually stunning set pieces filmed mostly in Spain and Finland (to match the terrain of Mother Russia); the exiles transported to Siberia; the Czar's execution of socialists in a Moscow square; racing across the snow in a troika. Lean and Young have created unforgettable imagery in their camera. Lean did it before with LAWRENCE OF ARABIA and THE BRIDGE ON THE RIVER KWAI and later with RYAN'S DAUGHTER and PASSAGE TO INDIA. He is one of the best "spectacle" directors ever but falls short, from time to time, when it comes to the small intimacies that must punctuate every spectacle to make it great. Reviews were mixed, but that most potent of all advertising media, word of mouth, is what made this picture soar over the $100 million mark—and that was before ticket prices had gone into the current ionosphere.

p, Carlo Ponti; d, David Lean; w, Robert Bolt (based on the novel by Boris Pasternak); ph, Freddie Young (Panavision, Metrocolor); m, Maurice Jarre; ed, Norman Savage; prod d, John Box; art d, Terence Marsh; set d, Dario Simoni; cos, Phyllis Dalton; spec eff, Eddie Fowlie; m/l, Jarre.

Drama   **Cas.**   **(PR:A-C MPAA:NR)**

DOCTORS, THE**   (1956, Fr.) 92m Kingsley International bw
                             (LES HOMMES EN BLANC)

Raymond Pellegrin (Dr. Nerac), Jeanne Moreau (Marianne), Jean Chevrier (Dr. Legender), Fernand Ledoux (Dr. Delpuech), Jean Debucourt (Professor Hauberger), Robert Porte (Dr. Ricaud), Mary Marquet (Mme. Ledragon), Bernard Dheran (Clement), Christian Marquant (Phillopon).

Pellegrin plays a young man studying to be a doctor, getting his first chance to practice his trade under the domain of aging country doctor Ledoux. Much of the action is placed upon the changing attitudes of Pellegrin as he starts out as a know-it-all type student ready to take on the world with his knowledge, but learns a great deal about life and the role of a doctor through his association with Ledoux. Charming depiction of French country life.

p, Paul Graetz; d, Ralph Habib; w, Maurice Auberga (based on the novel by Andre Soubiran).

Drama   **(PR:A MPAA:NR)**

DOCTOR'S DIARY, A*   (1937) 77m PAR bw

George Bancroft (Dr. Clem Driscoll), Helen Burgess (Ruth Hanlon), John Trent (Dr. Dan Norris), Ruth Coleman (Catherine Stanwood), Charles Waldron (Dr. Stanwood), Ra Hould (Michael Fielding), Molly Lamont (Mrs. Fielding), Sidney Blackmer (Dr. Ludlow), Charles D. Waldron, Frank Puglia, Milburn Stone, Sue Carol.

Trent is a sometimes militant doctor in a privately owned hospital. Immersed in research on spinal meningitis, he grows impatient with red tape and the eternal committee decisions that seem to hold up progress on every front in modern life. Two patients of one of the doctors die because the staff is unwilling to intrude on his territory. Trent cries malpractice and is sacked from the hospital. A spinal meningitis outbreak then occurs in the hospital and Trent takes back his outburst against his peers in his anxiety to get back to his experiments. Trent's day of reckoning nears, however, in this jerky plot, which suddenly takes a wild side turn. A boy violinist is suing the hospital because an operation done there has cost him control of his bow arm. While on the witness stand, Trent goes back on his word to the boy's mother to support her charges, and the woman pulls a gun from a cop's holster and shoots him. Quite an unethical ending to a picture about unethical practices.

p, B. P. Schulberg; d, Charles Vidor; w, David Boehm (based on a story by Samuel Ornitz, Joseph Anthony); ph, Harry Fischbeck; ed, Richard C. Currier.

Drama   **(PR:A MPAA:NR)**

DOCTOR'S DILEMMA, THE**½   (1958, Brit.) 98m Comet/MGM c

Leslie Caron (Mrs. Dubedat), Dirk Bogarde (Louis Dubedat), Alistair Sim (Cutler Walpole), Robert Morley (Sir Ralph Bloomfield-Bonington), John Robinson (Sir Colenso Ridgeon), Felix Aylmer (Sir Patrick Cullen), Michael Gwynn (Dr. Blenkenson), Maureen Delany (Emmy), Alec McCowen (Redpenny), Colin Gordon (Newspaperman), Gwenda Ewen (Minnie), Terence Alexander (Mr. Lanchester), Derek Prentice (Head Waiter), Peter Sallis (Secretary at Picture Gallery), Clifford Buckton (Butcher).

A good adaptation of George Bernard Shaw's 1903 play, an excellent cast, but much of the impact is lost due to the age of the play and the staleness of many of the issues. It was made due to the enormous success of MY FAIR LADY, which came out a year earlier and made the name Shaw something for moviegoers to contend with. The story concerns Bogarde, an artist and a complete cad who can't resist other women. Caron is his wife, completely blind to his faults because she adores him. Bogarde falls victim to consumption, and here comes the dilemma. Caron pleads with a doctor to treat Bogarde and save his life. The doctor must decide whether to use his limited serum on Bogarde or on a more worthwhile person. He finds a worthier patient and Bogarde dies, remaining a good guy in Caron's eyes.

p, Anatole de Grunwald; d, Anthony Asquith; w, Grunwald (based on the play by George Bernard Shaw); ph, Robert Krasker (Metroscope, Metrocolor); m, Joseph Kosma; ed, Gordon Hales; md, Charles Williams; art d, Paul Sheriff; cos, Cecil Beaton.

Comedy   **(PR:A MPAA:NR)**

DOCTORS DON'T TELL*½   (1941) 65m REP bw

John Beal, Florence Rice, Edward Norris, Ward Bond, Douglas Fowley, Grady Sutton, Bill Shirley, Joseph Crehan, Paul Porcasi, Russell Hicks, Howard Hickman.

TV's "General Hospital," so to speak, a quarter century or so early, with a touch of organized crime, focusing on the affairs of a young doctor, mainly romantic, as he goes after a woman who only has eyes for another. But things start to change once it is revealed that this other doctor is not the most honest of fellows. Don't members of the medical profession ever concern themselves with treating patients?

p, Albert J. Cohen; d, Jacques Tourneur; w, Theodore Reeves, Isabel Reeves (based on the story by Reeves); ph, Ernest Miller; ed, Edward Mann; md, Cy Feuer.

Drama   **(PR:A MPAA:NR)**

DOCTOR'S ORDERS**   (1934, Brit.) 68m BIP/Wardour bw

Leslie Fuller (Bill Blake), John Mills (Ronnie Blake), Marguerite Allan (Gwen Summerfield), Mary Jerrold (Mary Blake), Ronald Shiner (Miggs), Georgie Harris (Duffin), Felix Aylmer (Sir Daniel Summerfield), William Kendall (Jackson), D. J. Williams (Napoleon).

Medical student Mills discovers that his father (Fuller) is a carnival shill. At the same time, a rival for the affections of the girl he loves discovers the same thing, and threatens to expose the old man in front of the girl. It turns out that the shill all along has been aiding a local hospital with his ill-gotten gains. Talented cast help make this deftly amusing.

p, Walter C. Mycroft; d, Norman Lee; w, Clifford Grey, R. P. Weston, Bert Lee (based on a story by Grey, Syd Courtney, Lola Harvey); ph, Bryan Langley.

Comedy   **(PR:A MPAA:NR)**

DOCTOR'S SECRET*   (1929) 61m PAR bw

Ruth Chatterton (Lillian Garson), H. B. Warner (Richard Garson), John Loder (Hugh Paton), Robert Edeson (Dr. Brodie), Wilfred Noy (Mr. Redding), Ethel Wales (Mrs. Redding), Nancy Price (Susie), Frank Finch-Smiles (Wethers).

Early talkie suffers from the problem of being all talk. Story concerns Chatterton as the wife of a rich man who was forced into marriage for money and position. She becomes fed up with her situation and decides to run away with a former suitor to Egypt. Stepping out to call a cab, the suitor is run over and killed by a truck. Edeson, as a doctor, tries to help the man but to no avail. Later, invited to cocktails as a guest of Chatterton's husband, Warner, he relates the story of the woman, whom he doesn't know is Warner's wife, and her ill-fated lover. Warner and the other guests get suspicious of Chatterton, who hasn't shown up yet because she has been removing her goodbye-forever letter from Warner's desk drawer. When she enters the room she plays it cool. Warner accuses her of being the woman in the doctor's tale, but Edeson denies that the two have ever met, keeping her secret.

p,d,&w, William C. DeMille; (based on the play "Half an Hour" by James Barrie); ph, J. Roy Hunt.

Drama   **(PR:A MPAA:NR)**

DOCTORS WEAR SCARLET
                             (SEE: INCENSE FOR THE DAMNED, 1970, Brit.)

DOCTORS' WIVES**   (1931) 79m FOX bw

Warner Baxter (Dr. Judson Penning), Joan Bennett (Nina Wyndram), Victor Varconi (Dr. Kane Ruyter), Helene Millard (Vivian Crosby), Paul Porcasi (Dr. Calucci), Nancy Gardner (Julia Wyndram), John St. Polis (Dr. Mark Wyndram), Cecilia Loftus (Aunt Amelia), George Chandler (Dr. Roberts), Violet Dunn (Lou Roberts), Ruth Warren (Charlotte), Louise MacIntosh (Mrs. Kent), William Maddox (Rudie), Marion Lessing.

A dreary filmic contrivance intending to be a study of the difficult life of a doctor's wife. The plot deals with jealousy fed by mistaken ideas and the lack of communication between Baxter, a doctor, and Bennett, his wife. The trouble starts when a woman calls Baxter out on a house call, planning to seduce him. Bennett follows and spies on the pair, seeing what looks like seduction. For revenge, she goes to her husband's best friend. Baxter finds out and subsequently finds his wife often missing. He is positive she is seeing his friend, which bothers the friend so much he attempts suicide. Baxter must then operate on his friend to save his life and learns that Bennett had been secretly taking nursing classes so she could get a job at the hospital and be closer to him.

d, Frank Borzage; w, Maurice Watkins (based on the novel by Sylva and Henry Lieferant); ph, Arthur Edeson; ed, Jack Dennis.

Drama   **(PR:C MPAA:NR)**

DOCTORS' WIVES*   (1971) 102m COL c

Dyan Cannon (Lorrie Dellman), Richard Crenna (Pete Brennan), Gene Hackman (Dave Randolph), Carroll O'Connor (Joe Gray), Rachel Roberts (Della Randolph), Janice Rule (Amy Brennan), Diana Sands (Helen Straughn), Cara Williams (Maggie Gray), Richard Anderson (D. A. Douglas), Ralph Bellamy (Jake Porter), John Colicos (Mort Dellman), George Gaynes (Paul McGill), Marian McCargo (Elaine McGill), Scott Brady (Sgt. Malloy), Anthony Costello (Mike Traynor), Kristina Holland (Sybil Carter), Mark Jenkins (Lew Saunders), Vincent Van Lynn (Barney Harris), Ernie Barnes (Dr. Penfield), Paul Marin (Dr. Deemster), William Bramley (Dr. Hagstrom), John Lormer (Elderly Doctor).

Dyan Cannon got top billing for her eight-minute romp in this film. She plays the oversexed wife of a doctor, who admits to having slept with most of the doctor friends of her husband. She also claims one of the wives. She is murdered by her husband, Colicos, when he finds her in bed with another man. The rest of the choppy story is about the lives and loves and operations (medical and otherwise) of the surviving characters. Little worth in this shoddy yarn about the over- and under-sexed nouveau riche.

p, M. J. Frankovich; d, George Schaefer; w, Daniel Taradash (based on the novel by Frank G. Slaughter); ph, Charles B. Lang (Eastmancolor); m, Elmer Bernstein; ed, Carl Kress; prod d, Lyle R. Wheeler; set d, Marvin March; cos, Moss Mabry; m/l, "The Costume Ball," Bernstein, Alan and Marilyn Bergman (sung by Mama Cass Elliot); tech adv, Pete Morrow.

Drama   **(PR:O MPAA:R)**

DODESKA-DEN***   (1970, Jap.) 139m Yonkino-Kai-Toho/Toho c
                             (AKA: CLICKETY-CLACK)

Yoshitaka Zushi, Kin Sugai, Toshiyuki Tonomura.

Though void of any straight plot or structured narrative, Kurosawa was able to create a highly emotional depiction of the simple dreams, tragedies, and desires in an impoverished Tokyo slum. The title refers to the sound made by a mentally retarded boy as he impersonates a street car, a role he takes seriously as he struts down the streets looking ridiculous. He is just one of the rather bizarre figures who inhabit this film, also including a man who continually dreams of the palace he intends to build for himself and his son (this actual image being shown to the viewer), while the boy is forced to beg food from restaurants to keep the two alive. All this man's dreams are quickly diminished when the boy dies from eating spoiled food. Another aging craftsman has his home broken into by a thief, to which he humbly responds by making sure the robber is content with his takings and offering him more. The baffled robber responds by going straight. The stunning visuals enhance the atmosphere of these various episodes through an expressionist-like style of bright colors that almost jump out of the screen. The entire effect is one that brings the viewer into the world of these inhabitants of the slums, to look at their world as they do, without searching for the causes of their poverty in some unjust theoretical fashion. Touching, sad, and at the same time a very moving film.

d, Akira Kurosawa; w, Kurosawa, Hideo Oguni, Shinobu Hashimoto (based on the book by Shugoro Yamaoto); ph, Tako Saito, Yasumichi (Eastmancolor); m, Toru Takemitsu; art d, Yoshiro and Shinobu Miraki.

Drama **(PR:C MPAA:NR)**

DODGE CITY**** (1939) 104m WB c

Errol Flynn *(Wade Hatton)*, Olivia de Havilland *(Abbie Irving)*, Ann Sheridan *(Ruby Gilman)*, Bruce Cabot *(Jeff Surrett)*, Frank McHugh *(Joe Clemens)*, Alan Hale *(Rusty Hart)*, John Litel *(Matt Cole)*, Victor Jory *(Yancy)*, Henry Travers *(Dr. Irving)*, Henry O'Neill *(Col. Dodge)*, Guinn "Big Boy" Williams *(Tex Baird)*, Gloria Holden *(Mrs. Cole)*, Douglas Fowley *(Munger)*, William Lundigan *(Lee Irving)*, Georgia Caine *(Mrs. Irving)*, Charles Halton *(Surrett's Lawyer)*, Ward Bond *(Bud Taylor)*, Bobs Watson *(Harry Cole)*, Nat Carr *(Crocker)*, Russell Simpson *(Orth)*, Clem Bevans *(Charlie, the Barber)*, Cora Witherspoon *(Mrs. McCoy)*, Joe Crehan *(Hammond)*, Thurston Hall *(Twitchell)*, Chester Clute *(Coggins)*, Monte Blue *(Barlow, the Indian Agent)*, James Burke *(Cattle Auctioneer)*, Robert Homans *(Mail Clerk)*, George Guhl *(Jason, the Marshall)*, Spencer Charters *(Clergyman)*, Bud Osborne *(Stagecoach Driver/Waiter)*, Pat O'Malley *(Conductor)*, Wilfred Lucas *(Bartender)*, Milton Kibbee *(Printer)*, Vera Lewis *(Woman)*, Ralph Sanford *(Brawler)*, William Merrill McCormick *(Man)*, Fred Graham *(Al)*, Henry Otho *(Conductor)*.

This great action western, Flynn's first, has the intrepid adventurer enter Dodge City, a notorious, wide-open range town, as a cattle buyer. He leads lawmen to villain Cabot and his henchmen, Jory and Fowley, all found guilty of rustling. Later, Flynn and his pals, Hale and Williams, lead a covered wagon train to Dodge City, but, en route, he has trouble with Lundigan, a young hellion who causes a stampede by firing his gun and is crushed by panicking steers. His sister, De Havilland, blames Flynn for Lundigan's death and she refuses to think otherwise when he takes her to relatives in Dodge City. Flynn learns that Cabot and friends now run the town. He backs them down several times and when little Watson is killed in a gun battle Flynn, like Wyatt Earp, upon whom his character is loosely based, takes the sheriff's badge and cleans up the hellhole, even jailing his friend Williams for carrying arms in a restricted district. Sheridan and Flynn have a mild flirtation but his heart belongs to De Havilland who looks upon him now with respect and admiration for his law-and-order stand. Nothing can stop Errol, not stampedes, riots, gun battles, nor treachery. He and his forces for good finally shoot down the vile Cabot and cronies and Dodge City becomes a civilized community with Flynn and De Havilland wedded and moving on to the western frontier. DODGE CITY is top-flight action directed with gusto and invention by Curtiz, the Warner Bros. workhorse. This film was immensely popular with the public, even though it had tough competition in 1939, a year that produced a grand spate of westerns—STAGECOACH, UNION PACIFIC, FRONTIER MARSHALL, THE OKLAHOMA KID, MAN OF CONQUEST, DESTRY RIDES AGAIN, and JESSE JAMES. Shot at the studio ranch in Calabasas and around Modesto, California, and Steiner's score is dynamic, Polito's cameras sweeping and fluid, the color process so rich as to dazzle. (The film was reissued in 1951 with VIRGINIA CITY with black-and-white prints.) The saloon brawl midway in the film is magnificently staged and remains a classic of its kind, used many times over by WB as stock footage. The burning runaway train is also another high moment of excitement in this thoroughly entertaining production. De Havilland disliked her role which had less meat to it than Sheridan's saloon singer hussy part and she mistakenly felt her career was in decline. She later stated that she felt that she was on the verge of a nervous breakdown: "I was in such a depressed state that I could hardly remember the lines." Flynn would make seven more westerns but DODGE CITY remains his best outing in the genre, one of the films that made him one of the 10 top male actors at the box office in 1939. The story line for BLAZING SADDLES was taken from this film.

p, Robert Lord; d, Michael Curtiz; w, Robert Buckner; ph, Sol Polito (Technicolor); m, Max Steiner; ed, George Amy; art d, Ted Smith; cos, Milo Anderson; makeup, Perc Westmore; spec eff, Byron Haskin, Rex Wimpy.

Western **Cas.** **(PR:A MPAA:NR)**

DODGE CITY TRAIL* (1937) 65m COL bw

Charles Starrett *(Steve Braddock)*, Donald Grayson *(Slim Grayson)*, Marion Weldon *(Marian Phillips)*, Russell Hicks *(Kenyon Phillips)*, Si Jenks *(Rawhide)*, Al Bridge *(Dawson)*, Art Mix *(Blackie)*, Ernie Adams *(Dillon)*, Lew Meehan *(Joe)*, Hank Bell *(Red)*, Jack Rockwell, George Chesebro, Blackie Whiteford.

Grayson croons and Starrett rides he-man-like over the dusty trail in this musical interlude to the Starrett series of westerns. The story has Starrett rescuing his prospective bride Weldon from a fake kidnap arranged by her father, Hicks. Starrett proceeds to reform the old man. Then he delivers his cattle and returns to capture Hicks' gang. The reformed Hicks is killed in the process and the gang, in pangs of forgiveness, hide his past so Starrett and Weldon can ride off together with a clean record left behind. Grayson did not appear in any of Starrett's next four films, but joined him in later productions.

d, C. C. Coleman, Jr.; w, Harold Shumate; ph, George Cooper; ed, Dick Fantl; md, Morris Stoloff; m/l, Ned Washington, Sammy Stept.

Western **(PR:A MPAA:NR)**

DODGING THE DOLE** (1936, Brit.) 95m Mancunian bw

Roy Barbour *(The Simplicity of Genius)*, Dan Young *(The Charming Fool)*, Jenny Howard *(The Generator of Electric Radiance)*, Barry K. Barnes *(The Dole Dodger)*, Fred Walmsley *(The Lancashire Favourite)*, Tot Sloan *(The Little Bundle of Fun)*, Bertha Ricardo *(Dainty and Demure)*, Hatton & Manners, Barry Twins, Two Jays, Steffani's Silver Songsters, Archie's Juvenile Band, Bertini and the Tower Blackpool Band.

Decent musical entertainment has a bunch of characters trying to avoid being given jobs by a government agency to get them off the dole. A good example of the English musical before it died in the 1940s.

p&d, John E. Blakeley; w, Arthur Mertz.

Musical **(PR:A MPAA:NR)**

DODSWORTH***** (1936) 90m UA bw

Walter Huston *(Sam Dodsworth)*, Ruth Chatterton *(Fran Dodsworth)*, Paul Lukas *(Arnold Iselin)*, Mary Astor *(Edith Cortright)*, David Niven *(Lockert)*, Gregory Gaye *(Kurt von Obersdorf)*, Maria Ouspenskaya *(Baroness von Obersdorf)*, Odette Myrtil *(Mme. de Penable)*, Kathryn Marlowe *(Emily)*, John Payne *(Harry)*, Spring Byington *(Matey Pearson)*, Harlan Briggs *(Tubby Pearson)*, Beatrice Maude *(Mary the Maid)*, Gino Corrado *(American Express Clerk)*, Ines Palange *(Edith's Housekeeper)*, Charles Halton *(Hazzard)*, Jac George *(Orchestra Leader)*, Fred Malatesta *(Ship's Waiter)*, Dale Van Sickel, John Barclay *(Guests in Ship Salon)*, Wilson Benge *(Steward)*.

The popular stage hit by Sidney Howard adapted from Sinclair Lewis' 1929 novel came to the screen as the kind of tasteful production typifying a Samuel Goldwyn effort. Huston, repeating his 1934 stage role, is the reserved and kindly auto manufacturer who suffers the self-indulgences of wife Chatterton who is obsessed with growing old. She schemes like a court intriguer of old to undermine his business operations until Huston sells off his firm and agrees to travel the world with her. Chatterton seeks excitement, Huston only peace. She finds him dull and begins flirting with assorted gigolos and adventurers, finally informing Huston that she has met a European baron and wants a divorce so she can move into the aristocracy. Lonely, deserted, Huston goes to Italy where he meets Astor once more, having met her with his wife on their voyage to Europe. She is an attractive and understanding widow who captures his heart but he leaves her, then realizes that his life is incomplete without her. He returns to Astor in the movie's final moments for a blissful ending. Wyler's direction is both sensitive and telling as he unravels a tale of marital problems with infinite care and draws from his superb cast, including Niven and Lukas, performances that linger on, lo! these many decades. Huston is magnificent in his portrait of a gentleman, dignified yet compassionate, moralistic yet tolerant. Chatterton is perfect as the greedy-for-life wife, giving one of her best performances, and her last for films. (Her career was sharply declining and even this excellent effort didn't save it.) Astor is a marvel as the other woman, but one so loving and understanding that she appears unreal. This actress, at the time of the movie's release, was undergoing a divorce based on her extra-marital affair with playwright George Kaufman (her intimate and earthy diary revealing her wild sexual activities being turned over by an irate husband to the press which published every sordid detail, except blanked-out obscenities). Astor's off-screen scandal undoubtedly contributed to DODSWORTH's huge success, but the film was a critical and box office triumph in its own right. An Oscar went to art director Day and nominations included Best Picture, Best Director, Best Screenplay, and one to that wonderful character actress, Ouspenskya. Playwright-screenwriter Howard approached Goldwyn as early as 1932 and told him that the story was a natural for film and that the producer could buy the rights for a mere $20,000. Goldwyn did not respond until two years later when the play was a smash hit. He then paid $165,000 for the play. Howard met with him, shaking his head, telling the producer: "I told you I could get it back in 1932 for $20,000." Replied Goldwyn: "I don't care. This way, I buy a successful play, something already in dramatic form. With this, I have more assurance of success and it's worth the extra money I pay." Chatterton replaced Fay Bainter who had solidly established the role of the vain, shallow, and selfish wife. Chatterton was not popular with Wyler who had to repeatedly argue her into performing scenes his way. Goldwyn seldom, if ever, interfered with his talent but he did stray onto the DODSWORTH set, which caused the temperamental Wyler to immediately shut down production, refusing to contine until the producer left. To avoid further hindrance, Wyler had it put into his contract that Goldwyn could never again wander onto his set. Huston performed with effortless ease, and he was so splendid that he received the New York Film Critics award as Best Actor of 1936. Some of his scenes with Chatterton are unforgettable and can be universally applied to every marriage. "You're rushing at old age," Chatterton screams at him in one scene. "I'm not ready for that yet!" When she and two decades of marriage evaporate before his eyes, Huston comes to his adult senses, his predicament summed up in his sage line: "Love has got to stop someplace short of suicide." It does and his love for the sympathetic Astor begins. A great film of common people with uncommon emotions.

p, Samuel Goldwyn; d, William Wyler; w, Sidney Howard (based on his play, adapted from the novel by Sinclair Lewis); ph, Rudolph Mate; m, Alfred Newman; ed, Daniel Mandell; art d, Richard Day; cos, Omar Kiam; spec eff, Ray Binger.

Drama **(PR:A MPAA:NR)**

DOG, A MOUSE AND A SPUTNIK, A (SEE: SPUTNIK, 1958, Fr.)

DOG AND THE DIAMONDS, THE*** (1962, Brit.) 55m
Children's Film Foundation-LIP/Associated British bw

Kathleen Harrison (*Mrs. Fossett*), George Coulouris (*Forbes*), Geoffrey Sumner (*Mr. Gayford*), Brian Oulton (*Mr. Plumpton*), Michael MacGuire (*Jimmy*), Robert Sandford (*Peter*), Robert Scroggins (*Ginger*), Barbara Brown (*Helen*), Molly Osborne (*Linda*), Hal Osmund, Arthur Lane, Dennis Wyndham (*Crooks*).

An enjoyable children's film about a group of kids who build a makeshift zoo because animals are not allowed in their apartment building. The zoo is set up in the garden of an abandoned manor and the children discover that it is the hideout for three jewel thieves. With the animals' help, the kids turn the crooks over to the police. The manor is turned into a youth center and the garden becomes a children's zoo.

p, Peter Rogers; d, Ralph Thomas; w, Patricia Latham (based on a story by Mary Cathcart Borer); ph, Gordon Lang; m, Lambert Williamson; ed, Peter Seabourne; art d, George Provis.

Drama (PR:AA MPAA:NR)

DOG DAY AFTERNOON**** (1975) 130m Artists Entertainment Complex/WB c

Al Pacino (*Sonny*), John Cazale (*Sal*), Charles Durning (*Moretti*), Chris Sarandon (*Leon*), Sully Boyar (*Mulvaney*), Penny Allen (*Sylvia*), James Broderick (*Sheldon*), Carol Kane (*Jenny*), Beulah Garrick (*Margaret*), Sandra Kazan (*Deborah*), Marcia Jean Kurtz (*Miriam*), Amy Levitt (*Maria*), John Marriott (*Howard*), Estelle Omens (*Edna*), Gary Springer (*Bobby*), Lance Henriksen (*Murphy*), Judith Malina (*Vi*), Dominic Chianese (*Vi's Husband*), Marcia Haufrecht (*Vi's Friend*), Susan Peretz (*Angie*), Floyd Levine (*Phone Cop*), Carmine Foresta (*Carmine*), Thomas Murphy (*Policeman with Angie*), William Bogert (*TV Studio Anchorman*), Ron Cummins (*TV Reporter*), Jay Gerber (*Sam*), Philip Charles Mackenzie (*Doctor*), Chu Chu Malave (*Maria's Boy Friend*), Lionel Pina (*Pizza Boy*), Dick Williams (*Limo Driver*).

Bisexual Pacino, to finance a sex-change operation for his transvestite lover, Sarandon, robs the First Savings Bank of Brooklyn with his moronic friend Cazale. Police, headed by Durning, surround the bank and hold the thieves inside who, in turn, hold employees and customers as hostages. Through it all Pacino carries on endless phone conversations with his obese wife (Peretz), his lover, and assorted police and FBI officials. At one point, while releasing a female hostage, Pacino notices the large crowds at the ends of the street, watching from behind barriers as if witnessing a carnival show. To enlist mob sympathy he begins to shout "Attica! Attica!" (The name of the New York prison where authorities inflicted heavy casualties on rioting prisoners.) The crowd picks up the chant, decidedly favoring the bank robbers. As the hours drag on through the long hot afternoon Pacino's situation worsens so that he appears to be in a hopeless position. He threatens to begin shooting the remaining hostages unless he and Cazale are given $1 million and taken to the airport where they will be flown to a distant country. (When Pacino asks dimwit Cazale what country he wants to go to, the *non compos mentis* thief replies: "Wyoming.") An airport bus finally arrives and Pacino, Cazale, and several hostages climb into it. They are driven to a runway where a plane awaits, but Pacino realizes the futility of the situation. The driver is an FBI agent who whirls about and kills Cazale, taking Pacino into custody and freeing the hostages. The language in this film is gratuitously foul, the kind of gutter talk to which Pacino seems addicted (SCARFACE, etc.), but his performance is as jarring as a steel bolt being driven into the iron girder of a new skyscraper. The film is all Pacino and he is both funny and tragic as the uneducated street tough over his head in a lethal situation of his own making, but driven relentlessly to his fate by his oddball love for a snaky, neurotic pervert. Mainstream audiences never identified with these bizarre creatures; like trolls out of some murky German legend, the characters are so strange as to be laughable caricatures, which was the real popularity of this offbeat Lumet production. Pacino had no intention of making this film, vowing that GODFATHER II and SERPICO in 1973 would be his last films in some time, that he intended to work on the Broadway stage. But Lumet lured him back to the screen with a taut script and a story based on a real incident (a gay robbed the Chase Manhattan Bank in Flatbush in the early 1970s for exactly the same reason expressed by Pacino: to fund a sex-change operation for his lover). This outrageous three-ring circus is excessively violent and is heavily laced with objectionable language and should not be watched by young children. But adults with an acquired taste for the absurd will enjoy this expertly produced film with Lumet's no-waste direction making it suspenseful and often fascinating. (A heavy grosser at more than $22 million taken on its initial run.)

p, Martin Bregman, Martin Elfand; d, Sidney Lumet; w, Frank Pierson (based on a magazine article by P. F. Kluge and Thomas Moore); ph, Victor J. Kemper (Technicolor); ed, Dede Allen; prod d, Charles Bailey; art d, Doug Higgins; set d, Robert Drumheller; cos, Anna Hill Johnstone.

Crime Drama Cas. (PR:O MPAA:R)

DOG EAT DOG*½ (1963, U.S./Ger./Ital.) 84m Ernst Neubach-Unione Cinematografica Internazionale-Michael Arthur Films/Ajay bw

(EINER FRISST DEN ANDEREN; LA MORTE VESTITA DI DOLLARI)

Cameron Mitchell (*Lylle Corbett*), Jayne Mansfield (*Darlene*), Elisabeth Flickenschildt (*Xenia*), Isa Miranda (*Sandra*), Dody Heath, Pinkas Braun, Werner Peters, Ivor Salter, Ines Taddio, Aldo Camarda.

Mitchell, Mansfield, and Peters rob a bank of $1 million and hide out on an island in the Adriatic. Peters jumps Mitchell and, thinking he's dead, he and Mansfield take off for another island. Mitchell recovers and tracks them down and takes charge once again. People on the island discover the money the three have and murders start occurring in some original ways. One person is drowned in a goldfish bowl and another is set on fire with gasoline and falls off a cliff. Everybody dies except an old insane woman who watches the $1 million float into the ocean.

p, Carl Szokol; d, Ray Nazarro, Albert Zugsmith; w, Robert Hill, Michael Elkins (based on a novel by Robert Bloomfield); ph, Riccardo Pallottini; m, Carlo Savina; ed, Gene Ruggiero; art d, Wolf Witzemann.

Crime Drama (PR:A MPAA:NR)

DOG OF FLANDERS, A** (1935) 72m RKO bw

Frankie Thomas (*Nello*), Helen Parrish (*Maria*), O.P. Heggie (*Jehan*), Richard Quine (*Pieter*), Christian Rub (*Hans*), Dewitt Jennings (*Cogez*), Ann Shoemaker (*Frau Cogez*), Frank Reicher, Nella Walker, Addison Richards, Joseph Swickard, Sarah Padden, Harry Beresford, Lightning.

A boy and a dog story that didn't exactly click, although the book it was made from was a classic. Belgian boy Thomas finds a sick dog and nurses it back to health. He is also involved with a young girl, and is desperately trying to win an art contest. The triad of factors should have led to a whopping good film, but poor directing and slow timing let it go down as unsuccessful. The first filming of the famous tale by Ouida was made with Jackie Coogan in 1924, and a much better version was made in 1959 with David Ladd.

p, William Sistrom; d, Edward Sloman; w, Ainsworth Morgan, Dorothy Yost (based on the novel by Ouida); ph, J. Roy Hunt; ed, George Crane.

Drama (PR:AAA MPAA:NR)

DOG OF FLANDERS, A***½ (1959) FOX c

David Ladd (*Nello*), Donald Crisp (*Daas*), Theodore Bikel (*Piet*), Max Croiset (*Mr. Cogez*), Monique Ahrens (*Corrie*), Siohban Taylor (*Alois*), Gijsbert Tersteeg, John Soer, Lo van Hernsbergen, Katherine Holland, Patrasche The Wonder Dog.

This is the filmed version of the classic story as it was meant to be. Dutch boy Ladd, who aspires to become a painter but seems to have no chance of ever attaining his dream, lives with his grandfather, Crisp, in Flanders, where they eke out a living by delivering milk from neighboring farms into Antwerp. They find a sickly dog and nurse it back to health, when it becomes their cart-dog. Crisp dies, and boy and dog are thrown on their own. Finally they are adopted by a real-life painter, Bikel, to conclude a charming tale.

p, Robert D. Radnitz; d, James B. Clark; w, Ted Sherdeman (based on the novel by Ouida); ph, Otto Heller (CinemaScope, DeLuxe Color); m, Paul Sawtell, Bert Shefter, performed by the Santa Cecilia Orchestra and Choir of Rome; ed, Benjamin Laird; art d, Nico A.V. Baarle.

Drama (PR:AAA MPAA:NR)

DOGPOUND SHUFFLE** (1975, Can.) 96m Bloom (AKA: SPOT)

Ron Moody, David Soul, Pamela McMyler, Ray Strickland, Raymond Sutton.

A dog comes into the life of two decrepit bums, one a former stage performer and the other a boxer, and brings a spark of enthusiasm and a purpose, though simple, to their meager existences. Complications arise when the dog is whisked off to the pound and the two men must figure out a way to raise the money needed to retrieve their little prize. Slight plot is handled in an effectively cute manner.

d, Jeffrey Bloom.

Drama (PR:A MPAA:NR)

DOGS zero (1976) 90m Mar Vista/La Quinta Film Partners c

David McCallum (*Harlan Thompson*), Sandra McCabe (*Caroline Donoghue*), George Wyner (*Michael Fitzgerald*), Eric Server (*Jimmy Goodman*), Sterling Swanson (*Dr. Martin Koppelman*), Holly Harris (*Mrs. Koppelman*), Fred Hice (*Dick Huber*), Lance Hool (*Robbie Pulaski*), Jim Stathis (*Robert Johnson*), Debbie Davis (*Marilyn Holly*), Barry Greenberg (*Howard Kaplan*), Linda Gray (*Miss Engle*), Dean Santoro (*Prof. Aintry*), Larry Darnell (*Larry Ludecke*), Elizabeth Kerr (*Mrs. McDougal*), Cathy Austin (*Annie Watson*), Mike Davis (*Nichols*), Russ Grieve (*Homer*), Frank Paolasso (*Carl*).

A low-budget nature-revenge film such as was popular in the 1970s. The family dogs in a small town in the Southwest turn on their owners and anybody else they can get their fangs into. McCabe is the lucky person who escapes them with the help of McCallum, the scientist who comes to the rescue. Very little important footage in this one.

p, Allan F. Bodoh, Bruce Cohn; d, Bruce Brinckerhoff; w, O'Brian Tomalin; ph, Bob Steadman; m, Alan Oldfield; ed, John Wright.

Horror (PR:O MPAA:NR)

DOG'S BEST FRIEND, A** (1960) 70m Premium Pictures/UA bw

Bill Williams (*Wes Thurman*), Marcia Henderson (*Millie Thurman*), Roger Mobley (*Pip Wheeler*), Charles Cooper (*Bill Beamer*), Dean Stanton (*Roy Janney*), Roy Engel (*Sheriff Dan Murdock*), Jimmy Baird (*Jimmy Thurman*), Terry Ann Ross (*Amy Thurman*).

A ranching couple, Williams and Henderson, adopt Mobley, a mean-spirited and bitter little boy who immediately dislikes his new parents. The boy finds a wounded German Shepherd, a Marine-trained canine, and begins to spend all of his time with it, in the process finding a gun the dog had taken when it fled from the house where its master had been murdered. Mobley then comes upon the killer and is saved from a like fate by the dog, who attacks the killer and wrests the gun out of his hand.

p, Robert E. Kent; d, Edward L. Cahn; w, Orville H. Hampton; ph, Kenneth Peach; m, Paul Sawtell, Bert Shefter; ed, Michael J. Minth.

Children (PR:AAA MPAA:NR)

DOGS OF WAR, THE** (1980, Brit.) 122m UA c

Christopher Walken (*Shannon*), Tom Berenger (*Drew*), Colin Blakely (*North*), Hugh Millais (*Endean*), Paul Freeman (*Derek*), Jean-Francois Stevenin (*Michel*), JoBeth Williams (*Jessie*), Robert Urquhart (*Capt. Lockhart*), Winston Ntshona (*Dr.*

Okoye), Pedro Armendariz *(Major)*, Harlan Cary Poe *(Richard)*, Ed O'Neill *(Terry)*, Isabel Grandin *(Evelyn)*, Ernest Graves *(Warner)*, Kelvin Thomas *(Black Boy)*, Shane Rimmer *(Dr. Oaks)*, Father Joseph Konrad *(Priest)*, Bruce McLane *(Shop Manager)*, George W. Harris *(Col. Bobi)*, David Schofield *(Endean's Man)*, Terence Rigby *(Hackett)*, Tony Mathews *(Bank Vice President)*, John Quentin *(Party Guest)*, Jean-Pierre Kalfon *(Benny)*, Christopher Malcolm *(Baker)*, Jack Lenoir *(Boucher)*, Andre Penvern, Lawrence Davidson *(Policemen)*, Martin LaSalle, Mario Sanchez *(Customs Officers)*, Maggie Scott *(Gabrielle)*, Hugh Quarshie *(Zangaron Officer)*, Olu Jacobs *(Customs Officer)*, Christopher Asante *(Geoffrey)*, Thomas Baptiste *(Dexter)*, Eddie Tagoe *(Jinja)*, Kenny Ireland, Jim Broadbent *(Film Crew)*, Andre Toffel *(Priest)*, Diana Bracho *(Nun)*, Ilarrio Bisi-Pedro *(Kimba)*, Joanne Flanagan *(Godmother)*, Robert Berger, William B. Cain, Russell T. Carr *(Poker Players)*, Jose Rabelo *(Hotel Clerk)*, Victoria Tennant, Erica Creer, Sheila Ruskin *(Dinner Party Guests)*.

Based on the intense Frederick Forsyth novel, THE DOGS OF WAR is a slickly made film showing the life style of a mercenary. The story centers around Walken, an irresponsible American who becomes a soldier of fortune. After a smash opener, where Walken and some mercenary buddies fight their way out of a war-torn country on the last plane out, the film settles down to show Walken's life. After accepting a job offer to overthrow a small government in Africa made by an American businessman, Millais, Walken makes his plans for the upcoming coup. He visits the country in the guise of a nature photographer, where the suspicious government throws him in jail and tortures him. He meets a dissident political leader in the jail and then is deported from the country. He gathers a group of mercenaries together, and, with some hired Africans provided by Millais, they make an impressive raid (using a large portion of the budget on the special effects) on a military outpost which is also the government headquarters of the African dictator. Surprise ending has Walken double-crossing Millais by appointing his dissident friend from prison as leader of the country instead of the corporation's man. Lots of good action and weaponry, but no character development.

p, Larry DeWaay; d, John Irvin; w, Gary DeVore, George Malko (based on the novel by Frederick Forsyth); ph, Jack Cardiff (Panavision, Technicolor); m, Geoffrey Burgon; ed, Antony Gibbs; prod d, Peter Mullins; art d, John Siddall, Bert Davey; cos, Emma Porteous; spec eff, Larry Cavanaugh, Rudi Liszczak, Steve Lombardi, Mike Collins.

Action/Drama　　　　**Cas.**　　　　**(PR:O　MPAA:R)**

DOING TIME**½　　　(1979, Brit.) 95m Witzend/ITC Film Distributors c
　　　　　　　　　　　　　　(GB: PORRIDGE)

Ronnie Barker *(Fletcher)*, Richard Beckinsale *(Godber)*, Fulton Mackay *(Mackay)*, Brian Wilde *(Barrowclough)*, Peter Vaughan *(Grouty)*, Julian Holloway *(Bainbridge)*, Geoffrey Bayldon *(Governor)*, Christopher Godwin *(Beale)*, Barrie Rutter *(Oakes)*, Daniel Peacock *(Rudge)*.

British farce has Barker playing a long-time inmate at a prison. When a mistake leads to his escaping, Barker goes to extremes to be let back in and avoid any trouble. The use of a real prison location adds a unique flavor to this curious blend of British humor. Barker is very effective in his role.

p, Allan McKeown, Ian La Frenais; d, Dick Clement; w, Clement, La Frenais; ph, Bob Huke; ed, Alan Jones; art d, Tim Gleeson.

Comedy　　　　　　　　　　　　　　**(PR:A　MPAA:NR)**

DOLEMITE*
　　　　　　　(1975) 88m Comedian International/Dimension c
Rudy Ray Moore, D'Urville Martin, Jerry Jones, Lady Reed.

"Jump back, Jack, or your skull is cracked!" threatened Rudy Ray Moore, the star of this obscure black exploitation film. Moore, a raunchy, fat, black comedian, produced a series of actioners in the 1970s, all starring himself. His gimmick was that he spoke all his lines of dialog in rhyme, giving the film a kind of street poetry that makes sitting through some of this trash interesting. In DOLEMITE, Moore plays the title character who is released from prison and is out to settle the scores that went down when he was in the pen. Strictly routine action stuff, badly done, but peppered with Moore's bizarre (and frequently funny) raps.

p, Rudy Ray Moore, T. Toney; d, D'Urville Martin; w, Jerry Jones; ph, Nicholas Josef von Sternberg; m, Arthur Wright; set d, Moore.

Action　　　　　　　　　　　　　　**(PR:O　MPAA:R)**

DOLL, THE**½　·　　　(1962, Fr.) 95m Films Franco-Africains c
　　　　　　　　　　　　　(LA POUPEE; AKA: HE, SHE OR IT)

Zbigniew Cybulski *(Col. Prado Roth/The Rebel)*, Sonne Teal *(Marion/La Poupee)*, Claudio Gora *(Moren, The Banker)*, Catherine Milinaire *(Mirt)*, Jean Aron *(Prof. Palmas)*, Sacha Pitoeff *(Sayas)*, Daniel Emilfork *(Gant de Crin)*, Jacques Dufilho *(The Indian)*, Gabriel Jabbour *(Joachim)*, Michel de Re *(Gervasio)*, Laszlo Szabo *(Pascuel)*, Roger Karl *(Terremoche)*, Jean Galland *(Gonziano)*, Max Montavon *(Scientist)*.

A French science fiction film with strong political overtones, set in a Latin American country that is run by banker Gora and Col. Cybulski. A revolutionary, also played by Cybulski, has set out to overthrow the government and kill the colonel. The colonel is mysteriously assassinated. Gora's wife, Teal, becomes the new figurehead of the revolution. Unknown to all is the fact that she is more or less a robot, thanks to molecular multiplication. Her husband controls the "doll" and has her lead the rebels to their death, and the revolutionary steps into the colonel's place.

p&d, Jacques Baratier; w, Jacques Audiberti; ph, Raoul Coutard; m, Joseph Kosma, Jorge Mischgberg, Bernard Parmeggiani; ed, Leonide Azar; art d, George Koskas.

Science Fiction　　　　　　　　　　**(PR:A　MPAA:NR)**

DOLL, THE**　　　(1964, Swed.) 96m Flora Film/Kanawha Films bw
　　　　　　　　　　　　　　(VAXDOCKAN)

Per Oscarsson *(Night Watchman)*, Gio Petre *(The Doll)*, Tor Isedal *(Barber)*, Elsa Prawitz *(Landlady)*, Bengt Eklund *(Caretaker)*, Malou *(Young Girl)*, Mimi Nelson *(The Mother)*, Rick Axberg *(Young Son)*, Dagmar Olwson *(Charwoman)*, Agneta Prytz *(Cat Woman)*, Olle Gronstedt, Elisabeth Oden *(The Couple)*.

A lonely night watchman (Oscarsson) in a Stockholm department store surprises a couple of burglars while making his rounds through the mannequin storeroom. As the thieves flee, they knock over a dummy, and Oscarsson picks it up and starts talking to it. He takes it home and reports it stolen the next day. In his apartment, he believes the mannequin comes to life and talks to him, demanding nice clothes and the like. He begins to steal things for the dummy, including a diamond bracelet. His brutish neighbor overhears his one-sided conversation with the mannequin and comes over while Oscarsson is out and steals the bracelet. Oscarsson shoots him and then smashes the dummy. Mostly predictable tale of depression and loneliness that only fans of Bergman and his ilk will like. (In Swedish; English subtitles.)

p, Lorens Marmstedt; d, Arne Mattsson; w, Eva Seeberg (based on a story by Lars Forssell); ph, Ake Dahlquist; m, Ulrik Neumann; ed, Ingemar Ejve; art d, Harald Harmland.

Drama　　　　　　　　　　　**(PR:C　MPAA:NR)**

DOLL FACE**½
　　　　　　　(1945) 80m FOX bw (GB: COME BACK TO ME)
Vivian Blaine *(Doll Face)*, Dennis O'Keefe *(Mike Hannegan)*, Perry Como *(Nicky Ricci)*, Carmen Miranda *(Chita)*, Martha Stewart *(Frankie Porter)*, Michael Dunne *(Gerard)*, Reed Hadley *(Flo Hartman)*, Stanley Prager, Charles Tannen *(Aides)*, George E. Stone *(Stage Manager)*, Frank Orth *(Peters)*, Donald McBride *(Lawyer)*, Ciro Rimac *(Dancing Partner)*, Hal K. Dawson *(Hotel Clerk)*, Charles Williams *(Drug Store Clerk)*, Edgar Norton *(Soho)*, Boyd Davis *(Bennett)*, Alvin Hammer *(Harold, Soda Jerk)*, Alex Barker *(Coast Guardsman)*, Philip Morris *(Deputy Sheriff)*.

Film adapted from the play "The Naked Genius," written by [Rose] Louise Hovick, the real name of stripper Gypsy Rose Lee, which makes the subject matter understandable. The story tells of a stripper, Blaine, who wants to make it on Broadway. She undergoes refining when her boy friend/manager, O'Keefe, decides that's what she needs to succeed. They hire a ghostwriter to do an autobiographical book on Blaine's life, which gives her the publicity and respect needed to put her on the Great White Way. However, things get messed up as the writer, Dunne, falls for her. O'Keefe gets jealous and tries to hold up the production of Blaine's show, but things work out in the end. The film is greatly helped by several songs sung by Blaine, Como, and Miranda. Songs: "Dig You Later," "Here Comes Heaven Again," "Chico-Chico," "Somebody's Walkin' In My Dreams," "Red Hot and Beautiful" (Harold Adamson, Jimmy McHugh).

p, Bryan Foy; d, Lewis Seiler; w, Leonard Praskins, Harold Buchman (based on the play "The Naked Genius" by [Rose] Louise Hovick); ph, Joseph La Shelle; ed, Norman Colbert; md, Emil Newman, Charles Henderson; art d, Lyle Wheeler, Boris Leven; set d, Thomas Little, Jack Stubbs; spec eff, Fred Sersen; ch, Kenny Williams.

Musical　　　　**Cas.**　　　　**(PR:A　MPAA:NR)**

DOLL SQUAD, THE zero
　　　　　　　(1973) 101m Geneni c (AKA: HUSTLER SQUAD)
Michael Ansara, Francine York, Anthony Eisley, John Carter, Lisa Todd, Carol Terry, Bert Zeller, Herb Robbins, Lisa Garrett, Lee Christian, Judy McConnell, Tura Santana, William Bagdad, Rafael Campos, Guspave Unger, Bertel Unger.

An all-female team of assassins is hired by the CIA to track down a gang of rocket saboteurs. Director Mikels states that the TV show "Charlie's Angels" was a rip-off of his film. Perhaps he would like to believe that, but THE DOLL SQUAD falls even below "Charlie's Angels." Mikels shot fourteen films in two years, including STRIKE ME DEADLY and BLOOD ORGY OF THE SHE DEVILS. THE DOLL SQUAD was re-released in 1975 by Feature Fare and then again in 1980 by Crown International.

p&d, Ted V. Mikels.

Action　　　　　　　　　　　　　　**(PR:O　MPAA:R)**

DOLL THAT TOOK THE TOWN, THE**
　　　　　　　(1965, Ital.) 81m Peg Produzione/Medallion Pictures bw
　　　　　　　　　　　　　(LA DONNA DEL GIORNO)

Virna Lisi *(Liliana)*, Haya Harareet *(Anna)*, Serge Reggiani *(Mario)*, Franco Fabrizi *(Aldo)*, Elisa Cegani, Vittorio Sanipoli, Antonio Cifariello.

Lisi fakes being assaulted and robbed, and the resulting media attention brings her quick fame. She becomes a model, then wins a beauty contest, and is toasted at all the parties in town. Three men are arrested and charged in the phony crime and the wife of one of them, Harareet, pleads with Lisi to admit the hoax and win freedom for the men. She does at last, and thus ends this frothy little thing from the Mediterranean.

p, Lorenzo Pegoraro, Lucille Emerick; d, Francesco Maselli; w, Cesare Zavattini, Aggeo Sarioli, Maselli, Franco Bemporad (based on a story by Bemporad); ph, Armando Nannuzzi; ed, Mario Serandrei.

Drama　　　　　　　　　　　**PR:A　MPAA:NR)**

DOLLAR**½　　　(1938, Swed.) AB Svenskfilmindustri bw
Georg Rydeberg *(Kurt Balzar)*, Ingrid Bergman *(Julia Balzar)*, Kotti Chave *(Lt. Louis Brenner)*, Tutta Rolf *(Sussi Brenner)*, Hakan Westergren *(Ludwig von Battwyhl)*, Elsa Burnett *(Mary Johnstone)*, Edvin Adolphson *(Dr. Johnson)*, Gosta Cederlund, Eric Rosen, Carl Strom, Alex Hogel, Millan Bolander, David Eriksson, Erland

Colliander, Nils Dahlgren, Gustav Lagerberg, Richard Lindstrom, E. Dethorey, Dickson, Aina Elkman, Hester Harvey, Helge Kihlberg, Allan Linder.

A Swedish comedy with Bergman as the wife of an industrialist. She sells her stock in her husband's company to help pay Chave's gambling debt. This causes a panic on the stock market but a friend of Bergman's husband, Westergren, buys her shares and things get back to normal. Bergman then suspects her husband is having an affair with American Burnett. She invades the ski lodge where she thinks the affair is going on and discovers her suspicions are wrong. Bergman and Rydeberg make up and Burnett falls in love with the lodge's clerk, Adolphson.

d, Gustaf Molander; w, Stina Bergman, Molander (based on the comedy by Hjalmar Bergman); ph, Ake Dahlquist; m, Eric Bengtsson.

Comedy (PR:A MPAA:NR)

$ (DOLLARS)**½ (1971) 119m COL c (GB: THE HEIST)

Warren Beatty (Joe Collins), Goldie Hawn (Dawn Divine), Gert Frobe (Mr. Kessel), Robert Webber (Attorney), Scott Brady (Sarge), Arthur Brauss (Candy Man), Robert Stiles (Major), Wolfgang Kieling (Granich), Robert Herron (Bodyguard), Christiane Maybach (Helga), Hans Hutter (Karl), Monica Stender (Berta), Francoise Blanc (Stripper), Horst Hesslein (Bruno), Wolfgang Kuhlman (Fur Coat), Klaus Tschichan (Knife Man), Tove Platon, Kirsten Lahman (Customs), Darrell Armstrong (Associated Press Reporter), Walter Trott (Stars and Stripes Reporter).

$ (DOLLARS) is a pleasant chase movie with Beatty being as charming as he can be and Hawn showing off as much of her lithe body as the R rating allows. It was sort of a vacation film for all concerned as it was set in Europe, everyone seemed to be having a marvelous time, and the resultant film was enjoyable to watch without taxing anyone's abilities. Richard Brooks wrote and directed the picture and it must have been a welcome change for him as well, as he is one of those filmmakers with some sensibility who had earlier done some very serious cinema (as opposed to movies) like IN COLD BLOOD, THE BROTHERS KARAMAZOV, THE BLACKBOARD JUNGLE, and CAT ON A HOT TIN ROOF. So for Brooks to engage in so flighty a film was news in the Hollywood community. Beatty is a security expert employed in Hamburg. He arranges to steal the innards of several safe deposit boxes which he knows are rented by criminals. His attitude is, "who can they tell?" Beatty's opportunity for the heist occurs when he is engaged to install a new security system. Hawn is a Hamburg whore whom he enlists to help him rob the bank. He arranges to be placed inside the vault (after a bomb scare) and, timing his moves perfectly so the surveillance cameras don't pick him up as they sweep the room, he empties the trio of boxes. Hawn arrives later to empty her safety deposit box (Beatty has put the contents of the other boxes into Hawn's) and exits. Brady is a crooked U.S. Army Sergeant who has stashed all the kickback money he's gotten while running service clubs. Brauss is a drug dealer, and Webber is a Las Vegas courier who has been skimming money from the loot he's supposed to stash in Switzerland. The three join forces and chase Beatty and Hawn in an overlong sequence that winds up on a frozen lake with someone (we won't say who) going through the ice. Basically an exercise in triviality, it nevertheless was entertaining, albeit a bit long at almost two hours, and, other than some gratuitous and somewhat disgusting sexual antics with Hawn, it was harmless. Frobe was outstanding as the bank manager and Quincy Jones' sparse score did the job well. Seems to be a take-off of PERFECT FRIDAY.

p, M.J. "Mike" Frankovich; d&w, Richard Brooks; ph, Petrus Schloemp (Technicolor); m, Quincy Jones; ed, George Grenville; art d, Guy Sheppard, Olaf Ivens; m/l, "Money Is," "Do It," Jones (sung by Little Richard), "When You're Smiling," Mark Fisher, Joe Goodwin, Larry Shay (sung by Roberta Flack).

Crime/Comedy **Cas.** (PR:O MPAA:R)

DOLLARS FOR A FAST GUN*
(1969, Ital./Span.) 97m P.E.A.-Centuro/World Enterprises c
(AKA: 100,000 DOLLARS FOR LASSITER)

Robert Hundar, Pamela Tudor

Hundar, a quick-draw hired by ranch-owning widow Tudor, helps the lady defeat a money-grubbing rancher who won't give up his supply of water. Hundar and his six-gun manage to change the louse's mind.

Western (PR:A MPAA:NR)

DOLLS, THE (SEE: BAMBOLE!, 1965, Ital.)

DOLL'S HOUSE, A*** (1973) 95m PAR c

Claire Bloom (Nora Helmer), Anthony Hopkins (Torvald Helmer), Ralph Richardson (Dr. Rank), Denholm Elliott (Krogstad), Anna Massey (Kristine Linde), Edith Evans (Anne-Marie), Helen Blatch (Helen), Stefanie Summerfield (Emmy), Mark Summerfield (Ivar), Kimberley Hampton (Bob), Daphne Rigg (Old Woman).

A first-rate adaptation of Henrik Ibsen's classic tale of a woman trapped in a man's world. The film is essentially a screen rendering of the successful 1971 Broadway production, a play produced by Elkins, starring his wife, Bloom, and written by Garland and Hampton. All of the above reproduce their effort for the screen. The film, which uses almost all indoor locations, was shot after only two weeks of rehearsals. The story centers on Bloom, the pampered wife of a stuffy bank manager, Hopkins, whose attention to decorum outweighs his love for his wife. Suspense and conflict arise out of Hopkins' illness, which requires him to travel to a warmer climate to recuperate. He has no money on which to travel, so Bloom has an encounter with a disgraced lawyer turned moneylender, Elliot, who comes across with a loan to finance Hopkins' recuperation. The loan is arranged without Hopkins' knowledge and is secured through the forged signature of Bloom's father. When Hopkins later fires Elliot from the bank, grounds for blackmail are laid. Bloom ends up leaving Hopkins and striking out on her own at a time when women were literally the property of men.

p, Hillard Elkins; d, Patrick Garland; w, Christopher Hampton (based on play by Henrik Ibsen); ph, Arthur Ibbetson (Eastmancolor); m, John Barry; ed, John Glen; art d, Elliott Scott; cos, Beatrice Dawson.

Drama **Cas.** (PR:A MPAA:G)

DOLL'S HOUSE, A**
(1973, Brit.) 106m Tomorrow Entertainment/World Film Services c

Jane Fonda (Nora), David Warner (Torvald), Trevor Howard (Dr. Rank), Delphine Seyrig (Kristine Linde), Edward Fox (Krogstad), Anna Wing (Anne-Marie), Pierre Oudrey (Olssen), Frode Lien (Ivar), Tone Floor (Bob), Ingrid Natrud (Dr. Rank's Maid), Freda Krigh (Helmer's Maid), Ellen Holm (Krogstad's Daughter), Dagfinn Hertzberg (Krogstad's Son).

Okay adaptation of Ibsen's classic play features a stunning performance by Howard and talented direction from Losey, but Fonda is not an actress of sufficient talent to carry such a difficult role. A graceful production overall is enriched by some overwhelming shots of Norway, both indoors and out.

p&d, Joseph Losey; w, David Mercer (based on a translation by Michael Meyer of Henrik Ibsen's play); ph, Gerry Fisher; m, Michel Legrand; ed, Reggie Beck; art d, Eileen Diss; cos, John Furniss, Edith Head.

Drama **Cas.** (PR:A MPAA:G)

DOLLY GETS AHEAD*
(1931, Ger.) 87m UFA bw (DOLLY MACHT KARRIERE)

Dolly Haas (Dolly Klaren), Vicky Werckmeister (Orelly), Kurt Gerron (Silbermann), Paul Kemp (Jack), Theo Lingen (Conny Coon), Grete Naizler (Mariette), Herman Blass (O.W. Pietsch), Oscar Karlweiss (Fred Halton), Alfred Abel (Count Eberhard), Gustl Stark-Gstettenbaur (Boy).

A German-made musical done a few years before Hitler came to power and put a halt to the making of "frivolous" films. The movie features Haas as an aspiring actress. Her sweetheart, Karlweiss, wants to be a composer, and the two sing and dance till the end of the film. DOLLY GETS AHEAD was the first film for Haas, who was then twenty years of age, and she won rave reviews for her performance. She later went on to become a much loved German actress in the 1930s and appeared in the Hitchcock film, I CONFESS, in 1953.

d, Anatol Litvak; w, Alfred Halm, Peter Heimann; ph, Fritz Arne Wagner, Robert Heimann; m, Rudolf Nelson, Alfred Strasser, Willy Schmidt-Gentner; md, Gentner; set d, Jack Rotmil, Heinz Fenschel; cos, Prof. Ernest Stern; m/l, Arthur Rebner, I. Cube.

Musical (PR:A MPAA:NR)

DOLLY SISTERS, THE*** (1945) 114m FOX c

Betty Grable (Jenny), John Payne (Harry Fox), June Haver (Rosie), S.Z. Sakall (Uncle Latsie), Reginald Gardiner (Duke), Frank Latimore (Irving Netcher), Gene Sheldon (Prof. Winnup), Sig Ruman (Tsimmis), Trudy Marshall (Leonore), Collette Lyons (Flo Daly), Evan Thomas (Jenny as Child), Donna Jo Gribble (Rosie as Child), Robert Middlemass (Hammerstein), Paul Hurst (Dowling), Lester Allen (Morrie Keno), Frank Orth (Stage Manager). William Nye (Bartender), Herbert Ashley (Fields), Trudy Berliner (German Actress), Eugene Borden (Chauffeur), Claire Richards (Operator), Andre Charlot (Phillipe), Mae Marsh (Flower Lady), Virginia Brissac (Nun), Frank Ferguson (Reporter), Crauford Kent (Man), J. Farrell MacDonald (Doorman), Albert Petit (Croupier), Walter Soderling (Conductor On Train).

Amiable musical about the siblings who took New York by storm in the era around the turn of the century. The Hungarian sisters Jansci and Rozsicka (Jenny and Rosie) were really dark-haired but Fox elected to use Grable and Haver, two of their leading blonde musical lights, to essay the roles as it was almost five decades after the fact and how many people were around to dispute the hair? It's a sort-of biography in that the basic facts are followed but so much data is excised to make room for the many, many songs that it's closer to fiction than fact. Sakall is their adorable uncle who talks Hammerstein (Middlemass) into letting them play a date at his Victoria theater. They become the toasts of New York City and everywhere else in a very short time. Meanwhile, Grable falls in love with composer John Payne (Harry Fox) and Haver goes for Frank Latimore (Irving Netcher). When the picture was made, Mrs. Netcher (Rosie) was still alive and it's presumed that she gave her okay for the screenplay and eventual production. It's almost one musical number after another and the entire movie is little more than an excuse to parade Grable's and Haver's legs and voices and Orry-Kelly's sensational costumes. One of the most pleasant and tuneful musicals Fox ever produced and a joy to watch. "I Can't Begin To Tell You" received an Oscar nomination but lost that year to another Fox film's best song, "It Might As Well Be Spring" from STATE FAIR by Rogers and Hammerstein. Good second banana work by Sakall, Gene Sheldon, Trudy Marshall, Reginald Gardiner, Sig Ruman and Robert Middlemass. A Chopin melody in the film became "I'm Always Chasing Rainbows" with a lyric by Harry Carroll and Joseph McCarthy (no relation to the long-dead senator). Songs: "I Can't Begin To Tell You," (Mack Gordon, James V. Monaco), "I'm Always Chasing Rainbows" (Joseph McCarthy, Harry Carroll—based on a Chopin melody), "Powder, Lipstick and Rouge" (Gordon, Harry Revel), "Give Me the Moonlight" (Lew Brown, Albert von Tilzer), "On the Mississippi" (Ballard MacDonald, Arthur Fields, Carroll), "We Have Been Around" (Gordon, Charles Henderson), "Carolina In the Morning" (Gus Kahn, Walter Donaldson), "Arrah Go On I'm Gonna Go Back To Oregon" (Joe Young, Sam Lewis, Bert Grant), "Darktown Strutters' Ball" (Shelton Brooks), "The Vamp" (Byron Gay), "Hungarian Dance No. 5 in F Sharp Minor" (Brahms), "Smiles" (Will Callahan, Lee S. Roberts), "Oh Frenchie" (Sam Ehrlich, Con Conrad), "Pack Up Your Troubles" (Felix Powell, George Asaf), "Mademoiselle From Armentieres," "The Sidewalks of New York" (James Blake, Charles B. Lawlor).

p, George Jessel; d, Irving Cummings; w, John Larkin, Marian Spitzer; ph, Ernest Palmer (Technicolor); m, Alfred Newman, Charles Henderson, Gene Rose; ed,

Barbara McLean; md, Newman, Henderson; art d, Lyle Wheeler, Leland Fuller; cos, Orry-Kelly; ch, Seymour Felix.
Musical Biography **(PR:AA MPAA:NR)**

DOLORES½** (1949, Span.) 85m Lux bw (LA COPLA DE LA DOLORES)
Imperio Argentina *(Dolores)*, Enrique Diosdade *(Melchior and Flaco)*, Amadeo Novos *(Cirilo)*, Ricardo Canales *(Mariano)*, Manolito Diaz *(Lazaro)*.

After being seduced by a songwriter, Argentina finds her life becoming more and more troubled when this man decides to compose a song based on her, though not presenting her in a very favorable light. In an effort to escape the various rumors resulting from the song, Argentina is forced to flee throughout the countryside, eventually finding a man willing to take her in and marry her. Tends to get lost in overboiling emotional effect, but otherwise an intriguing film. (In Spanish; English subtitles.)

p, Ricardo Nunez; d, Benito Perojo; w, Francesco Madrid (based on the play "The Story of Dolores" by Manuel Acevedo); ph, Antonio Merayo; m, Maestro Breton.
Drama **(PR:A MPAA:NR)**

DOLWYN (SEE: LAST DAYS OF DOLWYN, THE, 1949)

DOMANI A TROPPO TARDI (SEE: TOMORROW IS TOO LATE, 1950, Ital.)

DOMENICA D'AGOSTO (SEE: SUNDAY IN AUGUST, 1950, Ital.)

DOMINANT SEX, THE* (1937, Brit.) 71m ABF bw
Phillips Holmes *(Dick Shale)*, Diana Churchill *(Angela Shale)*, Romney Brent *(Joe Clayton)*, Carol Goodner *(Gwen Clayton)*, Billy Milton *(Alec Winstone)*, Hugh Miller *(Philip Carson)*, Kathleen Kelly *(Mary)*, Olga Edwardes *(Lucy Webster)*, Dora Gregory *(Mrs. Webster)*, Charles Paton *(Mr. Webster)*.

The play of the same name by Michael Egan is the basis for this British-made film. The play ran for two years in London, but bombed in New York. The story concerns a farmer's wife and the struggle she has to keep her own identity after marriage.

p, Walter C. Mycroft; d, Herbert Brenon; w, Vina de Vesci, John Fernald (based on the play by Michael Egan); ph, Walter Harvey.
Comedy **(PR:A MPAA:NR)**

DOMINIQUE** (1978, Brit.) 100m Subotsky c
Jean Simmons *(Dominique Ballard)*, Cliff Robertson *(David Ballard)*, Ron Moody *(Dr. Rogers)*, Jenny Agutter *(Miss Ballard)*, Simon Ward *(Tony Calvert)*, Flora Robson *(Mrs. Davis)*, Michael Jayston *(Arnold Cravan)*, Judy Geeson *(Marjorie Cravan)*, Jack Warner *(Stonemason)*, David Tomlinson *(Lawyer)*, Michael Japher.

Robertson wants the money his wife, Simmons, possesses, so he tries to drive her crazy. She ends up killing herself (or does she?) and haunts her husband. Influenced greatly by the French film DIABOLIQUE.

p, Milton Subotsky, Andrew Donally; d, Michael Anderson; w, Edward and Valerie Abraham.
Thriller **Cas.** **(PR:C MPAA:NR)**

DOMINO KID½** (1957) 74m COL bw
Rory Calhoun *(Domino)*, Kristine Miller *(Barbara Ellison)*, Andrew Duggan *(Wade Harrington)*, Yvette Dugay *(Rosita)*, Peter Whitney *(Lafe Prentiss)*, Eugene Iglesias *(Juan Cortez)*, Robert Burton *(Sheriff Travers)*, Bart Bradley *(Pepe Garcias)*, James Griffith *(Sam Beal)*, Roy Barcroft *(Ed Sandlin)*, Denver Pyle *(Bill Dragger)*, Ray Corrigan *(Buck)*, Wes Christensen *(Dobbs)*, Don Orlando *(Ramon)*.

The first of Calhoun's independent productions is an above-average B western, starring him in the title role. A good revenge story, the film has Calhoun tracking down and killing the five outlaws who killed his father and stole his cattle while he was away fighting for the Confederacy during the Civil War. During the process of Calhoun's tracking and killing he has a romance with Miller and a conflict with Duggan, a money lender who is trying to steal away his ranch.

p, Rory Calhoun, Victor M. Orsatti; d, Ray Nazarro; w, Kenneth Gamet, Hal Biller (based on a story by Calhoun); ph, Irving Lippman; m, Mischa Bakaleinikoff; ed, Gene Havlick; md, Bakaleinikoff; art d, Howard Richmond.
Western **(PR:A MPAA:NR)**

DOMINO PRINCIPLE, THE*½
(1977) 97m ITC-Associated General/AE c (GB: THE DOMINO KILLINGS)
Gene Hackman *(Roy Tucker)*, Candice Bergen *(Ellie Tucker)*, Richard Widmark *(Tagge)*, Mickey Rooney *(Spiventa)*, Edward Albert *(Ross Pine)*, Eli Wallach *(Gen. Tom Reser)*, Ken Swofford *(Ditcher)*, Neva Patterson *(Gaddis)*, Jay Novello *(Capt. Ruiz)*, Claire Brennan *(Ruby)*, Ted Gehring *(Schnaible)*, Joseph Perry *(Bowcamp)*, Majel Barrett *(Mrs. Schnaible)*, Jim Gavin *(Lenny)*, George Fisher *(Henemeyer)*, Denver Mattson *(Murdock)*, Bob Herron *(Brookshire)*, Wayne King *(Nebraska)*, Charles Horvath *(Harley)*, Bear Hudkins *(Truck Driver)*, Farnesio De Bernal *(Bank Official)*, Patricia Luke *(Travel Agency Girl)*, George Sawaya *(Assassination Victim)*.

Stanley Kramer was obviously trying to make a message with this film, but within the intricate plot twists which seem to double back over themselves, it got lost in the shuffle. Hackman is a convict, broken out of prison by a secret organization to kill a public figure. Nothing is explained to Hackman or the audience as to whom or why they want him to kill. The title is derived from the principle of lining up dominos on their ends, about half an inch apart, and knocking down the whole line by knocking over the first one. It is alluded to in the film: Hackman is to set off an international political domino line and, by killing one man, set off a chain reaction leading to bigger things. Hackman spends the entire film stumbling through a crazy maze of events and at the last minute decides he won't do it and escapes from the secret organization. But the end of the film tells us that there is no real escape, as we see Hackman walking along a deserted beach, viewed through the lens of a sniper's scope.

p&d, Stanley Kramer; w, Adam Kennedy (based on his novel); ph, Fred Koenekamp, Ernest Laszlo (Panavision, CFI Color); m, Billy Goldenberg; ed, John Burnett; prod d, Bill Creber; art d, Ron Hobbs; set d, Andy Szolosi, Raphael Bretton; cos, Rita Riggs; spec eff, Phil Cory; m/l, "Some Day Soon," Goldenberg, Harry Shannon; stunts, Bear Hudkins; makeup, Del Armstrong.
Crime/Mystery **Cas.** **(PR:O MPAA:R)**

DON CHICAGO** (1945, Brit.) 80m BN/Anglo bw
Jackie Hunter *(Don Chicago)*, Eddie Gray *(Police Constable Gray)*, Joyce Heron *(Kitty Mannering)*, Claud Allister *(Lord Piccadilly)*, Amy Veness *(Bowie Knife Bella)*, Wylie Watson *(Peabody)*, Don Stannard *(Ken Cressing)*, Charles Farrell *(Don Dooley)*, Finlay Currie *(Bugs Mulligan)*, Cyril Smith *(Flash Kelly)*, Ellen Pollock *(Lady Vanessa)*, Moira Lister *(Telephone Operator)*, Wally Patch *(Sergeant)*, Henry Wolston, Inga Anderson, C. Denier Warren, George Merritt, Charles Doe, Eric Winstone and his Band, the Modernaires.

London bobby Gray thwarts American gangster Hunter's scheme to heist the crown jewels. So-so crime comedy about America's Public Enemy No. 1001 and his antic activities among British high society.

p, Louis H. Jackson; d, Maclean Rogers; w, Austin Melford (based on a novel by C.E. Bechhofer-Roberts); ph, Gerald Gibbs.
Comedy **(PR:A MPAA:NR)**

DON GIOVANNI½** (1955, Brit.) 170m Harmony/Maxwell c
Cesare Siepi *(Don Giovanni)*, Otto Edelmann *(Leporello)*, Elizabeth Grummer *(Donna Anna)*, Lisa della Casa *(Donna Elvira)*, Anton Dermots *(Don Ottavio)*, Erna Berger *(Serlina)*, Walter Berry *(Masetto)*, Dr. Wilhelm Furtwangler *(Conductor)*.

Lavish though overlong filmization of Mozart's opera shot at the 1954 Salzburg Festival on an open-air stage. General audiences will be bored by what definitely is not a filmic experience, though it does make a valuable record of the performance.

p, Paul Czinner, Fred Swann; d, Czinner, Alfred Travers; w, Wolfgang Amadeus Mozart, Lorenzo da Ponte; ph, S.D. Onions (Eastmancolor).
Opera **(PR:A MPAA:NR)**

DON GIOVANNI½** (1979, Fr./Ital./Ger.) 184m GAU c
Ruggero Raimondi *(Don Giovanni)*, John Macurdy *(The Commander)*, Edda Moser *(Donna Anna)*, Kiri Te Kanawa *(Donna Elvira)*, Kenneth Riegel *(Don Ottavio)*, Jose Van Dam *(Leporello)*, Teresa Berganza *(Zerlina)*, Malcolm King *(Masetto)*, Eric Adjani *(Valet in Black)*, Janine Reiss *(Harpsichordist)*.

The idea of taking the elitist art of opera and placing it in a movie theater is a good one. However, this attempt rings up both successes and drawbacks. On the success side is the superb singing performance by the entire cast, the use of real settings in Vicenza, Italy, Gerry Fisher's splendid color cinematography, and the fine costumes of Marthe Mikon. Drawbacks include the three-hour running time and some of the acting of the opera's stars who are used to playing to the top balcony. The opera is Mozart's masterpiece. Based on a literary classic that dates to the Middle Ages, the opera tells the story of the legendary Spanish lover Don Giovanni, portrayed by Raimondi, a gallant libertine whose blasphemous conduct deserves the dramatic punishment he receives. (Italian; English subtitles.)

p, Michael Seydoux; d, Joseph Losey; w, Patricia and Joseph Losey, Frantz Salieri (opera by Wolfgang Amadeus Mozart and Lorenzo Da Ponte); ph, Gerry Fisher (Panavision); ed, Reginald Beck; md, Paul Myers; art d, Alexandre Trauner; cos, Marthe Mikon; opera and chorus of the Paris Opera directed by Lorin Maazel.
Opera **(PR:A MPAA:NR)**

DON IS DEAD, THE**
(1973) 115m UNIV c (AKA: BEAUTIFUL BUT DEADLY)
Anthony Quinn *(Don Angelo)*, Frederic Forrest *(Tony)*, Robert Forster *(Frank)*, Al Lettieri *(Vince)*, Angel Tompkins *(Ruby)*, Charles Cioffi *(Orlando)*, Jo Anne Meredith *(Marie)*, J. Duke Russo *(Don Aggimio Bernardo)*, Louis Zorich *(Mitch)*, Anthony Charnota *(Johnny Tresca)*, Ina Balin *(Nella)*, Joe Santos *(Joe Lucci)*, Frank de Kova *(Giunta)*, Abe Vigoda *(Don Tolusso)*, Victor Argo *(Augie the Horse)*, Val Bisoglio *(Pete Lazatti)*, Robert Carricart *(Mike Spada)*, Frank Christi *(Harold Early)*, Sid Haig *(The Arab)*, Maurice Sherbanee *(Corsican)*, George Skaff *(Vito)*, Vic Tayback *(Ralph Negri)*, Carlos Romero *(Mariano Longobardo)*.

Uninspired attempt to cash in on what they thought would be a new gangster cycle after the success of THE GODFATHER. Marvin H. Albert is a fine novelist whose work has been adapted into several movies, some by him (TONY ROME, etc.), and he's even adapted other novelists' work (TWIST OF SAND) to good advantage, but his own screenplay of his excellent novel falls apart under the heavy hand of Fleischer. Forrest and Forster are accepting delivery of a heroin cache when gunmen burst in, guns blazing. Lettieri has been hidden, just as a precaution, and he gets the drop on the intruders and guns them down. But their presence indicates there has been a leak in their careful security. They return to HQ and Forrest and Lettieri learn that their father, the Don, has expired. Now two dozen of the syndicate's bosses get together in an almost-papal ceremony to choose the new *capo de tutti capi*. All that's missing is the puff of smoke coming out of the enclave where the Cardinals meet. Quinn is chosen to be the boss but Lettieri and Forrest announce that they have no interest in aligning themselves with the Quinn-led forces; they'll go their ways by themselves. Russo is in stir so his accountant, well-played by Cioffi, reps him at the meeting. But Cioffi has a power-mad streak in him and thinks *he* might be able to take over. Forster is engaged to comely Tompkins and Cioffi uses the relationship to get Forster into a rage. He arranges for Tompkins, a singer, to become Quinn's amour while Forster is away on a job. Once Forster learns of this, it's "grab for the machine guns" and war erupts. Forster joins Lettieri and Forrest. Quinn's brother, Zorich, tries to smooth matters over between the families but Quinn cannot conceive that this war is over a woman and nothing more. There must be something else underneath that hatred. The battle continues and Zorich is taken by Forrest and held as hostage. Quinn orders an attack on Fargo's construction business. By this time, Quinn has suffered a heart attack and is recuperating at his Capone-like Florida compound. Zorich is killed and Quinn has a stroke, almost incapacitating him. He watches weakly as Russo and Forrest gleefully cut up the territory after Forster is murdered in Sicily. Cioffi is killed by Russo's men for daring to overstep his bounds and the movie ends with the Cosa Nostra still healthy after all that bloodshed.

p, Hal B. Wallis; d, Richard Fleischer; w, Marvin H. Albert (based on the adaptation by Michael Philip Butler, Christopher Trumbo of Albert's novel); ph, Richard H. Kline (Technicolor); m, Jerry Goldsmith; ed, Edward A. Biery; art d, Preston Ames; set d, Don Sullivan; cos, Edith Head; m/l, Jerry and Carol Goldsmith; stunts, George Sawaya.

Crime   **(PR:O MPAA:R)**

DON JUAN, 1934 (SEE: PRIVATE LIFE OF DON JUAN, THE, 1934, Brit.)

DON JUAN*   (1956, Aust.) 89m Akkrod Film/Times Films c

Actor/Singer: Cesare Danova/Alfred Poell (Don Giovanni), Joseph Meinrad/-Harald Progelhof (Leporello), Evelyne Cormand/Annie Felbermayer (Zerlina), Hans von Borsody/Walter Berry (Masetto), Lotte Tobisch/Hanna Loeser (Donna Elvira), Jean Vinci/Hugo Meyer-Welfing (Don Ottavio), Marianne Schoenauer/Annie Felbermayer (Donna Anna), Fred Hennings/Gottleb Frick (Commendatore), Senta Wengraf (Elvira's Maid).

The film is almost an opera, but not quite. The plot closely follows the story by Lorenzo Da Ponte, librettist of Mozart's Don Giovanni and his other Italianate operas Le Nozze di Figaro and Cosi Fan Tutte. (Da Ponte came to the U.S. in 1805 and became a professor at Columbia University.) The notorious libertine and lecher Danova/Poell, after many conquests of otherwise virtuous ladies and multiple other villainies (assisted by his servant Meinrad/Progelhof), finally gets escorted to Hell by the statue of celebrated Commendatore Hennings/Frick, murdered father of one of his female victims. The dubbed arias—albeit shortened and rendered in German—are all Mozart, but unfortunately, the visuals are superior to the sound quality. The sets and costumes are magnificent, and the action is cinematic, not stagy, as Danova buckles a swash with the best of them (he previously crossed swords with Errol Flynn in the 1954 release aptly titled CROSSED SWORDS). At the time of release, critics were confused by the production, averring that director/adaptor Kolm-Veltee should have made up his mind about whether he wanted to make an opera or a swashbuckling action film. And, for once, let us acknowledge him: English subtitles are by the ubiquitous Herman G. Weinberg. (In German; English subtitles.)

d, H.W. Kolm-Veltee; w, Kolm-Veltee, Alfred Uhl, Ernest Henthaler (based on Lorenzo Da Ponte and Wolfgang Amadeus Mozart's opera "Don Giovanni"; also based on Tursio de Molina's story "El Burlador de Sevilla"); ph, Willy Sohm-Hannes Fuchs (Agfacolor); md, Prof. Birkmeyer; art d, Boris Goldovsky; cos, Hill Reihs-Oromes; ch, Dia Luca; music played by the Vienna Symphony Orchestra; danced by the Ballet Corps of the Vienna State Opera.

Opera/Adventure   **(PR:A MPAA:NR)**

DON JUAN QUILLIGAN*   (1945) 75m FOX bw

William Bendix (Patrick Quilligan), Joan Blondell (Marjorie Mossrock), Phil Silvers (MacDenny), Anne Revere (Mrs. Rostigaff), B.S. Pully (Ed Mossrock), Mary Treen (Lucy), John Russell (Howie Mossrock), Veda Ann Borg (Beattle), Thurston Hall (Judge), Cara Williams (Salesgirl), Richard Gaines (Defense Attorney), Hobart Cavanaugh (Mr. Rostigaff), Renee Carson (Annie Mossrock), George Macready (District Attorney), Helen Freeman (Mrs. Blake), Charles Cane (Artie), Anthony Caruso (One-Eyed Fagen), Eddie Acuff (Customer), Joel Friedkin (Judge), Charles Marsh (Court Clerk), Emmett Vogan (Minister), James Flavin (Police Sergeant), Genevieve Bell (Dowager), Byron Foulger, Frank Johnson (Men), Brick Sullivan (Detective), John Albright (Usher), Charles D. Brown (Police Inspector), Lee Phelps (Police Stenographer), Tom Dugan (Bartender), Carey Harrison (C.P.O.), Jimmy Conlin (Clerk, Marriage Bureau).

William Bendix is the Brooklyn-to-Utica, New York barge captain title character of this film, who suffers from a slight Oedipal complex. Due to the complex, he has overly romantic notions about women, due to the great love he had for his mother, who has been dead for ten years. He becomes engaged to two women simultaneously, one because she laughs like his mother, the other because she cooks like his mother. He marries both of them. To help him escape from this mess, his friend Silvers invents a murder and blames it on Bendix, so the bigamist can pretend to be sent away to prison and escape from both of the women.

p, William Le Baron; d, Frank Tuttle; w, Arthur Kober, Frank Gabrielson (based on a story by Herbert Clyde Lewis); ph, Norbert Brodine; m, David Raskin; ed, Norman Colbert; md, Emil Newman; art d, Lyle Wheeler, Ben Hayne; set d, Thomas Little, Frank E. Hughes; spec eff, Fred Sersen.

Comedy   **(PR:A MPAA:NR)**

DON QUIXOTE****
                            (1935, Fr.) 73m Nelson-Vandor/UA bw

Feodor Chaliapin (Don Quixote), George Robey (Sancho Panza), Sidney Fox (The Niece), Miles Mander (The Duke), Oscar Asche (Police Captain), Dannio (Carrasco), Emily Fitzroy (Sancho's Wife), Frank Stanmore (Priest), Wally Patch (Gypsy King), Lydia Sherwood (Duchess), Renee Valliers (Dulcinea), Genica Anet (Servant at Inn).

Save only the denouement—an allegory added by director Pabst and the French adaptors—this is a fairly faithful rendition of the 300-year-old tale of The Knight of the Mournful Countenance. A 59-year-old Feodor Ivanovich Chaliapin, as famed

for his acting as for his operatic basso, plays El ingenioso hidalgo Don Quixote de la Mancha, the title and cognomen assumed by the age-equivalent protagonist of this remarkable fable. Immersed for years in the library of chivalric romances for the possession of which he has mortgaged his estates, the quiet country gentleman elects to redress the wrongs of the world. Venturing forth on his bony nag Rocinante, Chaliapin enlists the aid of Robey as his squire, promising him great future rewards in return for his faithful service. He pronounces Valliers, a slatternly milkmaid, to be the fair and pure maiden, Dulcinea del Toboso, whose honor he is pledged to protect. Taking windmills for giants and flocks of sheep for armies, he has at them, doing battle with vigor but suffering invariable defeat. Chaliapin's romantic madness is counterpoised against Robey's affectionately tolerant rustic realism, as the latter vainly attempts to keep his "master" safe from serious harm. Chaliapin shuffles wearily to his successive deeds of mad valor with the dignity of utter conviction in Pabst's vision, finally returning home defeated only to see his library of chivalry go up in flames, and with it his self-image, his purpose. His mission gone, Chaliapin forfeits his existence as well, singing his grief as he expires during the lengthy, expressionistic bookburning scene, the beauty of the flames and the slowly transfigured volumes signifying the death of chivalry, the passing of the Quixotic age. Pabst's ending differs completely from Cervantes' original, in which the disillusioned Don Quixote renounces his books of knight-errantry; many viewers saw in this film an allegorical reference to the Nazi bookburnings of the 1930s. Pabst's leftist political orientation had been demonstrated in many of his earlier films, such as KAMERADSCHAFT (1931) and THE THREEPENNY OPERA (1931). However, in 1939, Austrian Pabst unexpectedly moved from France to Hitler's Germany, where he spent WW II and made two motion pictures under the aegis of the Nazis. After WW II, he appeared to shift his allegiance again, making a number of anti-Nazi films.

p, Nelson Vandor; d, G.W. Pabst; w, Paul Morand, Alexandre Arnoux (based on the novel Don Quixote De La Mancha by Miguel de Cervantes); ph, Nicholas Farkas; m, Jacques Ibert; m/l Dargomisjsky.

Drama/Musical   **(PR:A MPAA:NR)**

DON QUIXOTE**** (1961, USSR) 110m Lenfilm/MGM c (DON-KIKHOT)

Actor/English Voice: Nikolai Cherkassov/Arnold Diamond (Don Quixote), Yuri Tolubeyev/Howard Marion Crawford (Sancho Panza), T. Agamirova/Bettina Dickson (Altisidora), V. Freindlich/Peter Elliott (Duke), L. Vertinskaya/Olive Gregg (Duchess), G. Vitsin/Robert Rietty (Carrasco), L. Kasyanova/Nikki Vandersil (Aldonsa), O. Vikland/Marianne Stone (Peasant Girl), Serafima Birman (Housekeeper), A. Beniaminov (Shepherd), S. Grigoryeva (Niece), V. Maksimov (Priest), V. Kolpakov (Barber), G. Volchek (Maritornes), S. Tsomayev (Andres), Vladimir Vasilyev, N. Anisimova, S. Batalova, I. Belskiy, V. Kovel, M. Korolyov, Zh. Letskiy, G. Malyshev, G. Osipenko, V. Osipov, A. Rozanov.

The final Soviet film to reach the U.S. under a joint cultural exchange program halted due to the Cuban crisis and bad relations between the administrations of President Kennedy and Premier Kruschev, this is an excellent and faithful adaptation of the Cervantes novel, barring the epilog, which suggests that the Quixotic ideal will live forever. Cherkassov, the U.S.S.R.'s best-known actor, on screen since 1927 in roles such as ALEXANDER NEVSKY (1938) and the two-part IVAN THE TERRIBLE (1944-46), brings to the comi-tragic knight the same level of demented dignity possessed by Chaliapin in G. W. Pabst's 1935 version. Tolubeyev's Sancho Panza, with his field smarts, is a fine match for Cherkassov's chivalric Don Quixote. Technically adept, in wide screen and color, the film reflects the long-time collaboration of director Kozintsev and cameraman Moskvin, both active in FEX (Factory of Eccentric Actors). The English dubbing is wonderfully handled; the English-language actors' voices are well-cast to suit the roles, which suggests an unusual measure of concern with the responses of the U.S. audiences. Location scenes, resembling the Iberian plain, were shot in the Crimea.

d, Grigoriy Kozintsev; w, Yevgeniy Shvarts (based on Miguel de Cervantes' novel); ph, Andrey Moskvin, Apollinariy Dudko (Sovscope, Sovcolor); m, Kara Karayev; ed, Ye. Makhankova; art d, Yevgenity Yeney.

Drama   **(PR:A MPAA:NR)**

DON QUIXOTE***
                            (1973, Aus.) 107m IA/Walter Reade Organization-CD c

Robert Helpmann (Don Quixote), Ray Powell (Sancho Panza), Rudolf Nureyev (Basilio), Francis Croese (Lorenzo), Lucette Aldous (Kitri), Colin Peasley (Gamache), Marilyn Rowe (Street Dancer), Kelvin Coe (Espada), Gailene Stock, Carolyn Rappel (Kitri's Friends), Alan Alder, Paul Saliba (Gypsy Dancers), Susan Dains (Gypsy Queen), Ronald Bekker (Gypsy King), Julie da Costa, Leigh Rowles (Gypsy Girls), Lucette Aldous (Dulcinea), Marilyn Rowe (Queen of the Dryads), Patricia Cox (Cupid), Janet Vernon, Gary Norman (Fandango Couple), Ronald Bekker, John Meehan, Tex McNeill, Rodney Smith, Joseph Janusaitis, Frederick Wener (Matadors), Dancers of the Australian Ballet.

Not the Cervantes story at all—Don Quixote (Helpmann) and his squire Sancho Panza (Powell) are marginal to the story line in the film—this is a motion picture version of a comic ballet choreographed in 1869 by Marius Petipa, with music by Ludwig Minkus. The plot concerns the romance between a barber, Nureyev, and his sweetheart, Aldous. The latter's father has betrothed her to the well-to-do Peasley. With the help of the mad knight-errant, Helpmann, and his faithful squire Powell, Nureyev wins his lady love. Unlike the usual filmed ballet, DON QUIXOTE melds the traditions of ballet with the scope and verisimilitude of cinema extremely well, probably due to the efforts of co-directors and stars Nureyev and Helpmann. Cinematographer Unsworth employed unusual camera angles and overhead shots to encompass the sweep of the ensemble dancing, eliminating the need to go to extreme distance or wide angles, thus retaining detail. The film jumps between dancing and non-dance continuity sequences, which may prove irritating to balletomanes, but most audiences will find it enjoyable.

p, John Hargreaves; d, Rudolf Nureyev, Robert Helpmann; ph, Geoffrey Unsworth (Eastmancolor); m, Ludwig Minkus; ed, Anthony Buckley; md, John Lanchbery; art d, William Hutchinson; cos, Barry Kay; ch, Nureyev, after Petipa.

Ballet (PR:A MPAA:G)

DON RICARDO RETURNS*
(1946) 63m PRC bw

Fred Colby, Isabelita, Martin Garralagna, Paul Newton, Claire DuBrey, David Leonard, Anthony Warde, Michael Visaroff.

Colby is a Spanish aristocrat who comes to Old California to claim his inheritance. There he finds that his evil cousin has had him declared legally dead. Thus, the cousin can take over the inheritance. Colby goes into hiding, posing as a peasant until he can reassert his claim with the help of friendly priests at the local mission. Lackluster Zorro ripoff from Poverty Row.

p, James S. Burkett; d, Terry O. Morse; w, Jack Dewitt, Renault Duncan (based on a story by Johnston McCully); ph, Vincent Farrar, Ben Kline; m, Alexander Steinert; ed, George McGuire.

Western (PR:A MPAA:NR)

DONA FLOR AND HER TWO HUSBANDS***
(1977, Braz.) 106m GAU-Coline c (DONA FLOR E SEUS DOIS MARIDOS)

Sonia Braga (Dona Flor), Jose Wilker (Vadhino), Mauro Mendonca (Teodoro), Dinorah Brillanti (Rozilda), Nelson Xavier (Mirandao), Arthur Costa Filho (Carlinhos), Rui Rezende (Cazuza).

Wonderfully sexy and funny comedy that was the biggest hit ever in its native Brazil. Braga is a beautiful woman whose gambling, whoring husband drops dead one day following an all night carousel. She decides to marry again and chooses a middle aged, devout and boring pharmacist who rarely wants to make love. As Braga lies in bed one night next to her sleeping husband, the ghost of her first husband appears, nude, in the room. She tries to get rid of him, but he refuses to go. Finally she succumbs to his blandishments and takes the ghost to bed with her, while the second husband continues to sleep. The final scene has the three of them walking arm in arm to the church, the ghost still stark naked, only visible to Braga. Remade in 1982 as KISS ME GOODBYE.

p, Luis Carlos Barreto, Newton Rique, Cia Cerrador; d&w, Bruno Parreto (based on a novel by Jorge Amado); ph, Maurilo Salles (Eastmancolor); m, Chico Buarque; ed, Raimondo Higino.

Comedy Cas. (PR:O MPAA:NR)

DONATELLA**
(1956, Ital.) 101m Sudfilm c

Elsa Martinelli (Donatella), Gabriele Ferzetti (Maurizio), Walter Chiari (Guido), Abbe Lane, Xavier Cugat (Themselves), Aldo Fabrizi (Father).

An odd amalgam, redolent of the mistaken-identity comedies of confusion in the 1930s. Martinelli plays a humble secretary in a well-to-do household who is mistaken as the ultimate legatee of that wealth by a visiting attorney. She thinks it's true love, and becomes miffed when the truth comes out. No matter, romance finds a foothold within the intrigue, so love triumphs after all. One-time model Martinelli was "discovered" by Kirk Douglas, who cast her in THE INDIAN FIGHTER (1955). Demonstrating the actor-mobility which later became commonplace, she immediately returned to Rome to star in two Italian films, DONATELLA and RICE GIRL (AKA: RICE FIELD, 1956), the latter a rip-off of the popular BITTER RICE (1950). Oddly, DONATELLA, an Italian film, features, in speaking parts as well as musical performances, the "Rhumba King" of the 1930s and 1940s, Xavier Cugat, and his third wife, Abbe Lane. The film is a truly cosmopolitan piece of fluff, made with an eye to the box-office potential of its varied parts, a potential which remained unrealized.

p, Roberto Amoroso; d, Mario Monicelli; w, Amoroso, Monicelli, Tellini, Continenza, Maccari; ph, Tonino Delli Colli (CinemaScope, Eastmancolor); m, Xavier Cugat, Gino Filippini.

Comedy (PR:A MPAA:NR)

DONDI**½
(1961) 80m AA bw

David Janssen (Dealey), Patti Page (Liz), Walter Winchell (Himself), Mickey Shaughnessy (Sergeant), Robert Strauss (Sammy Boy), Arnold Stang (Peewee), Louis Quinn (Dimmy), Gale Gordon (Colonel), Dick Patterson (Perky), Susan Kelly (Lt. Calhoun), John Melfi (Jo-Jo), Bonnie Scott (Gladdy), William Wellman, Jr. (Ted), Nola Thorp (Candy), Joan Staley (Sally), David Kory (Dondi).

Every era has its comic-strip orphan, spouting Confucian aphorisms and exuding cuteness and naive good fellowship. The Little Annie Rooney/Little Orphan Annie of the post-WW II years was Dondi, the androgynous little refugee with eyes the size of barrage balloons, whose adventures were distributed by the Chicago Tribune-New York News comic-strip syndicate. To this ageless waif falls the honor of anticipating the trend to big-budget, feature-length films based on comic-strip characters which later blossomed with pictures such as SUPERMAN (the 1978 original and the two sequels, 1980 and 1983) and POPEYE (1980). The film opens with the homeless Italian 5-year-old being befriended by a group of American GI stereotypes on Christmas Eve. When the victorious GIs depart for home, Dondi (Kory) stows away aboard their troop ship, a salami his only luggage. Separated from his GI buddies upon arrival in America, Kory gets lost in New York, having a host of adventures in Macy's department store. Ultimately reunited with his GI buddy Janssen and the latter's singing girl friend, Page, Kory gets a special dispensation with the help of Walter Winchell, is awarded American citizenship by act of Congress, and is adopted by Janssen and his new wife, Page. Despite adverse reaction by critics (" . . . syrupy sweet . . . bomb . . . insipid . . . trite and maudlin . . . saccharinely cute . . . fatuous . . . "), the film did well at the box office, largely as a result of intensive promotional efforts which involved licensed toys and a contest to determine the kid to play the title part. Bug-eyed Kory won on the basis of appearance. The cost of the hype was offset by the

economics of the musical score, which comprised one harmonica, played by composer Morgan. Director, co-producer, co-writer Zugsmith had made a series of sex-and-drug exploitation films prior to making this maudlin tearjerker by way of expiation. Songs sung by Patti Page include the Christmas carol "Jingle Bells," and "Meadow In the Sky," "Dondi" (Earl Shuman, Mort Garson).

p, Albert Zugsmith, Gus Edson; d, Zugsmith; w, Zugsmith, Edson (based on comic strip "Dondi" by Edson, Irwin Hasen); ph, Carl Guthrie; ed, Edward Curtiss; art d, William Glasgow; set d, Rudy Butler; cos, Roger J. Weinberg, Charles Arrico; makeup, Stanley Campbell.

Juvenile (PR:AAA MPAA:NR)

DONKEY SKIN***
(1975, Fr.) 90m Parc Film-Marianne/Janus Films c (PEAU D'ANE)

Catherine Deneuve (Peau d'ane/Blue Queen), Jacques Perrin (Prince), Jean Marais (Blue King), Delphine Seyrig (Fairy Godmother), Fernand Ledoux (Red King), Micheline Presle (Red Queen).

An odd but charming combination of a number of Mother Goose fairy tales, blended with anachronistically modern touches and mixed up with adult themes, which are disguised in the form of mythic euphemisms. Writer-director Demy, whose charming musical tale THE UMBRELLAS OF CHERBOURG (1964) won the Golden Palm at the Cannes Festival, has a knack—much like Jean Cocteau (BEAUTY AND THE BEAST, 1947)—for melding traditional fantasy with contemporary grown-up concerns. Viewers will recognize variations on "The Goose That Laid the Golden Egg," "Cinderella," and "Little Red Riding-Hood," among other classics, all rolled into a contiguous plot line. An incest theme is woven into the plot, but on a most ingenuous level. Marais is king in a strange land which, among other assets, contains a national treasure, a donkey that excretes jewelry and valuable coins. Marais' wife (Deneuve) and daughter (also Deneuve) are the rarest of beauties. On her deathbed, Deneuve the queen forces Marais to promise never to remarry anyone less beautiful than she. At his ministers' urgings that he re-wed, Marais examines pictures of all the local maidens, but none will do: none, that is, save Deneuve the princess, who is thereupon selected to become her father's bride. In an effort to avoid the incestuous liaison, Deneuve calls on her fairy godmother, Seyrig, for assistance the more readily offered because Seyrig is infatuated with Marais. Seyrig has Deneuve make unconscionable demands upon her father-fiance in return for her hand in marriage, including the skin of the treasure-giving donkey. Wrapping herself in the proffered donkey skin, Deneuve runs off to a town where she becomes the mistreated servant of a witch-like woman, retaining her donkey-skin couture save for the odd occasion when, thinking herself unseen, she dresses up in her mistress's gowns. But, of course, she is seen, glimpsed briefly by a handsome young prince, Perrin, who manages to gain possession of her ring, a family heirloom. Entranced, the prince collects all the women in his fiefdom and has them try on the ring. Lo and behold, the dainty finger of the maiden in the repulsive donkey skin is the only one which accepts the ring. At the subsequent nuptials, Marais and Seyrig swoop down in a helicopter to announce their own impending wedding. Curiously, this strange mixture of modified but evocative folk tales has good continuity. Handled with style, grace, and good humor by Demy and a fine cast, it is an enjoyable hour-and-a-half for adults.

p, Mag Bodard; d&w, Jacques Demy (based on "Les Contes de ma mere l'Oye," collected by Charles Perrault); ph, Ghislain Cloquet (Eastmancolor); m, Michel Legrand; ed, Anne-Marie Cotret; art d, Jacques Dugied, Jim Leom.

Fantasy (PR:C-O MPAA:NR)

DONOVAN AFFAIR, THE**½
(1929) 83m COL bw

Jack Holt (Inspector Killian), Dorothy Revier (Jean Rankin), William Collier, Jr. (Cornish), John Roche (Jack Donovan), Fred Kelsey (Carney), Agnes Ayres (Lydia Rankin), Hank Mann (Dr. Lindsey), Wheeler Oakman (Porter), Virginia Brown Faire (Mary Mills), Alphonse Ethier (Capt. Peter Rankin), Edward Hearn (Nelson), Ethel Wales (Mrs. Lindsey), John Wallace (Dobbs).

This early all-dialog talkie was among the first of the many films Frank Capra directed under his contract deal with Harry Cohn, boss of Columbia Pictures, a deal that took Capra from two-reeler Mack Sennett obscurity to total creative freedom—he was the first studio-contract director whose name was permitted to precede the film's title when the credits rolled—and that made Columbia a major studio. In coming years, Capra was to win three Academy Awards for directing within a five-year period (IT HAPPENED ONE NIGHT, 1934; MR. DEEDS GOES TO TOWN, 1936; YOU CAN'T TAKE IT WITH YOU, 1938). THE DONOVAN AFFAIR was Capra's first all-talking picture; a murder mystery, it was an excellent vehicle for the director's penchant for comedy. Loud, self-assured, but bumbling Inspector Holt, assisted by his beefy, stupid aide Kelsey, responds to a darkened-dining-room murder by replicating the circumstances, at which point another murder occurs. Embarrassed, Holt opts for yet a third try; with a little help from the other one-time banqueters, including Collier, Jr., and Revier (the romantic couple) and Wales and Mann (the comic relief), the criminal is tricked and apprehended. Barring a little excessive volume, mostly from the female cast members, the sound recording is surprisingly good in this historically interesting film. To capture a sense of reality Holt took advantage of his star status to insist that the entire cast go without makeup and the affable Capra agreed.

d, Frank Capra; w, Howard Green, Dorothy Howell (based on a play by Owen Davis); ph, Ted Tetzlaff; ed, Arthur Roberts.

Mystery/Comedy (PR:A MPAA:NR)

DONOVAN'S BRAIN***
(1953) 83m UA bw

Lew Ayres (Dr. Patrick J. Cory), Gene Evans (Dr. Frank Schratt), Nancy Davis (Janice Cory), Steve Brodie (Herbie Yocum), Lisa K. Howard (Chloe Donovan), Tom Powers (Advisor), Michael Colgan (Tom Donovan), Kyle James (Ranger Chief Tuttle), Stapleton Kent (W.J. Higgins), Peter Adams (Mr. Webster), Victor Sutherland (Nathaniel Fuller), John Hamilton (Mr. MacNish), Harlan Warde (Mr. Booke),

Paul Hoffman *(Mr. Smith)*, William Cottrell *(Dr. Crane)*, Tony Merrill *(Hotel Desk Clerk)*, Faith Langley *(Receptionist)*, Mark Lowell *(Supply Company Clerk)*, Shimen Ruskin *(Tailor)*.

This second remake of author Siodmak's novel—THE LADY AND THE MONSTER (1944) and VENGEANCE (1963) were also based on the book—is the one which adheres most closely to the story line of the book. Having succeeded in keeping the brain of a dismembered monkey alive *in vitro*, gentle, dedicated scientist Ayres is called upon to assist the victim of an airplane crash, who dies in Ayres' laboratory before he can be hospitalized. Hooking electrodes to the victim's skull, Ayres discovers that the man's brain is still functional. Utilizing his newly discovered techniques, he removes the brain—over the objections of wife Davis and hard-drinking assistant Evans—and keeps it alive in a tank. The brain is that of Donovan, a ruthless, self-made millionaire. The brain gradually takes possession of Ayres' *persona*, a Jekyll-Hyde situation which has Ayres assuming even the physical characteristics and manner of dress of the cruel, vicious businessman. A photographer, Brodie, has gotten into the laboratory and taken a picture of the brain; he blackmails Ayres, who permits him to go into the laboratory for more pictures. The growing brain, ever more powerful, pushes Brodie to suicide. Ayres struggles vainly to free himself from the brain's possession; in his self-contained moments, he records a plan for wife Davis which may result in diminishing the power of the brain. However, the brain again takes over, and decides that Davis and Evans must die. As the possessed Ayres tries to kill Davis, Evans gets into the laboratory and fires a pistol at the brain. The brain, with its growing power, instead forces Evans to shoot himself. When Davis and Ayres reach the laboratory in response to the shots, Ayres forces her to gaze at the brain, which begins to take control of *her* mind, as well. Before it can do so, lightning from a burgeoning storm strikes a lightning rod on the roof which, in accordance with Ayres' plan—recorded for Davis in a lucid, self-contained moment—overloads the brain's support circuits and bakes the brain. Evans recovers from his wound; Ayres is himself again, and reunited with Davis. The film has elements of Mary Shelley's *Frankenstein* story, with its oft-filmed sequelae, and of Robert Louis Stevenson's *Dr. Jekyll and Mr. Hyde*. Ayres handles his transformation sequences well. This actor, whose career was adversely affected by his conscientious-objector status during WW II, experienced a departure from his customary casting, and handled it well. Davis's performance as his long-suffering wife is adequate; audiences may be tempted to draw parallels with her later life-role as First Lady. Perhaps the most interesting thing about the film—and the novel from which it is derived—is that the Mr. Hyde/Monster characterization is not that of a conscienceless hedonist, not that of a warped criminal, but that of a successful *businessman*. Remade in 1965 as THE BRAIN.

p, Tom Gries; d&w, Felix Feist (based on a novel by Curt Siodmak); ph, Joseph Biroc; m, Eddie Dunstedter; ed, Herbert L. Strock; prod d, Boris Leven; spec eff, Harry Redmond, Jr.

Science Fiction **(PR:C MPAA:NR)**

DONOVAN'S REEF*** (1963) 104m PAR c

John Wayne *(Guns Donovan)*, Lee Marvin *(Aloysius "Boats" Gilhooley)*, Elizabeth Allen *(Amelia Dedham)*, Jack Warden *(Dr. Dedham)*, Cesar Romero *(Marquis Andre de Lage)*, Dorothy Lamour *(Fleur)*, Marcel Dalio *(Father Cluzeot)*, Mike Mazurki *(Sgt. Menkowicz)*, Jacqueline Malouf *(Lelani)*, Cherylene Lee *(Sally)*, Tim Stafford *(Luki)*, Edgar Buchanan *(Francis X. O'Brien)*, Jon Fong *(Mr. Eu)*, Yvonne Peattie *(Sister Matthew)*, Ralph Volkie *(James)*, Frank Baker *(Capt. Martin)*, June Y. Kim, Midori *(Servants)*, Ron Nyman *(Naval Officer)*, Carmen Estrabeau *(Sister Gabrielle)*, Pat Wayne *(Aussie Officer)*, Chuck Roberson *(Festus)*, Mae Marsh, Sara Taft, Carl M. Leviness, Fred Jones, Scott Seaton, Maj. Sam Harris *(Members of the Family)*, Duke Green *(Mate)*, King Lockwood *(Lawyer)*, Dick Foran *(Australian Navy Officer)* Charles Seel *(Grand Uncle Sedley Atterbury)*, Cliff Lyon *(Officer)*, Aissa Wayne *(Native Girl)*.

Wayne and Warden, two ex-Navy men, have stayed on in the Pacific islands following WW II, Wayne to operate a saloon called Donovan's Reef, Warden to raise a Polynesian family, despite the fact that he has a mature daughter in Boston. Joining Wayne to celebrate his birthday (December 7) is Marvin, who jumps ship and swims ashore to Haleakaloa. There, he and Wayne renew old friendships by beating each other to pulps, but all in the vein of roughhouse comaraderie. Into this raucous atmosphere comes grownup Allen, in search of her father, Warden. Wayne and Marvin busy themselves with protecting their friend's image by pretending that Warden's three Polynesian children are Wayne's. A comedy of fumbling errors ensues which Warden puts to an end when he finally returns from a trip, confessing to Allen that Stafford, Lee, and Malouf are really his children. Allen, who suspects the fact all along, tolerantly accepts her younger sisters and brother and is united with them in a beautiful Polynesian ceremony at film's end. This is one of Ford's weaker efforts, which he directs as a lark, though there is plenty of gusto in the brawls staged by Wayne and Marvin. Wayne and Marvin stumble about mouthing sentimentalities that Wayne would have punched a man for uttering a decade earlier. Marvin is just plain awful, enacting a part suited to any tongue-tied heavy. Warden is his usual phlegmatic self, but Romero and Dalio, two veteran actors, spice up the film with colorful portrayals. It's as if Ford wanted to film a story about his old drinking and poker-playing parties with as little story as possible. The verdant, lush Hawaiian setting is visually stunning but the slapstick is forced and unbecoming.

p&d, John Ford; w, Frank Nugent, James Edward Grant (based on a story by Edmund Beloin and source material [uncredited] by James Michener); ph, William Clothier (Technicolor); m, Cyril Mockridge; ed, Otho Lovering; art d, Hal Pereira, Eddie Imazu; spec eff, Paul K. Lerpae.

Comedy **Cas.** **(PR:A MPAA:NR)**

DON'S PARTY**** (1976, Aus.) 90m Double Head Productions c

Ray Barrett *(Mal)*, Claire Binney *(Susan)*, Pat Bishop *(Jenny)*, Graeme Blundell *(Simon)*, Jeannie Drynan *(Kath)*, John Gorton *(Himself)*, John Hargreaves *(Don)*, Harold Hopkins *(Cooley)*, Graham Kennedy *(Mack)*, Veronica Lang *(Jody)*, Candy Raymond *(Kerry)*, Kit Taylor *(Evan)*.

Excellent drama from down under concerns a group of friends gathering in the suburbs to watch election results. As the party wears on and everyone is loosened on alcohol, the veneer of camaraderie drops away and the men reveal themselves to be a set of back-biting boors, verbally attacking each other like characters in WHO'S AFRAID OF VIRGINIA WOOLF. Extremely well directed by Beresford (BREAKER MORANT), with terrific performances all around. American audiences may have trouble understanding much of the slang, as well as the thick accents.

p, Philip Adams; d, Bruce Beresford; w, David Williamson (based on his play); ph, Don McAlpine (Panavision, 200 Color); m, Leos Jan; ed, Bill Anderson; art d, set d, Rhoisin Harrison; cos, Anna Senior.

Comedy **Cas.** **(PR:C-O MPAA:NR)**

DON'T ANSWER THE PHONE*

(1980) 94m Scorpion/Crown International Pictures c
(AKA: THE HOLLYWOOD STRANGLER)

James Westmoreland *(Chris)*, Flo Gerrish *(Dr. Gale)*, Ben Frank *(Hatcher)*, Nicholas Worth *(Kirk)*, Stan Haze *(Adkins)*, Gary Allen *(Feldon)*, Pamela Bryant *(Sue)*, Ted Chapman *(Bald Man)*, Denise Galick *(Lisa)*, Dale Kalberg, Deborah Leah Land, Tom Lasswell, Ellen Karston, Mike Levine, Chuck Mitchell, Victor Mohica, Susanna Severeid, Paula Warner, Chris Wallace.

Wretched psycho-killer film has Worth a disturbed Vietnam vet who works through his aggressions by taking a sock with some coins in the end and using it to strangle nubile young women in the Los Angeles area. Loosely based on the Hillside Strangler murders of the 1970s, the plot goes nowhere save toward Worth's inevitable death in the closing frames, an ending one could probably guess before even paying for a ticket. The only reason for watching this is for Worth's performance as the most disturbed of stranglers, overweight and obsessed, into weightlifting, pornography and calling up radio shows and raving on the airwaves.

p&d, Robert Hammer; w, Hammer, Michael Castle; ph, James Carter (Metrocolor); m, Byron Allerd; ed, Joseph Fineman; art d, Kathy Cahill.

Horror **Cas.** **(PR:O MPAA:R)**

DON'T BE A DUMMY* (1932, Brit.) 54m WB-FN/FN bw

William Austin *(Lord Tony Probus)*, Muriel Angelus *(Lady Diana Summers)*, Garry Marsh *(Capt. Fitzgerald)*, Georgie Harris *(Dodds)*, Mike Johnson *(Tramp)*, Sally Stewart *(Florrie)*, Katherine Watts *(Connie Sylvester)*, Charles Castella.

Inane comedy has Austin as a nobleman who has lost his fortune at the gaming tables and is forced to take up a career as a ventriloquist, using a jockey as his dummy. The title serves as a warning to audiences.

p, Irving Asher; d, Frank Richardson; w, Brock Williams.

Comedy **(PR:A MPAA:NR)**

DON'T BET ON BLONDES*½ (1935) 62m WB bw

Warren William *("Odds" Owen)*, Guy Kibbee *(Colonel Jefferson Davis Youngblood)*, Claire Dodd *(Marilyn Young)*, William Gargan *("Numbers")*, Errol Flynn *(David Van Dusen)*, Hobart Cavanaugh *(Philbert O'Slemp)*, Vince Barnett *(Brains)*, Spencer Charters *(Doc)*, Clay Clement *(T. Everett Markham)*, Walter Byron *(Dwight Boardman)*, Eddie Shubert *(Steve)*, Jack Norton *(J. Mortimer Slade)*, Maude Eburne *(Ellen Purdy)*, Mary Treen *(Switchboard Operator)*, Herman Bing *(Professor Friedrich Wilhelm Gruber)*, Joseph Crehan *(Doctor)*, Selmer Jackson, Cyril Ring *(Men)*, Paul Fix *(Youth)*, Ferdinand Schumann-Heink *(Laboratory Assistant)*, Marc Lawrence, Jack Pennick, Ben F. Hendricks, Constantine Romanoff, Frank Moran, Jack Low *(Gangsters)*, Milton Kibbee *(Cashier)*, Pat Somerset *(Usher)*, Buddy Williams *(Black Man)*.

William, a big-time gambler, quits gaming to open an insurance company that will take on anything. Among the policies issued is one for Kentucky Colonel Kibbee against his actress daughter (Dodd) ceasing to become his source of support by getting married. When she starts seeing Flynn (almost invisible in his second American film) William becomes concerned, plotting to step in as her suitor himself. Predictably, he falls in love with her and they are married, though he still has to pay Kibbee a $50,000 settlement on the policy. Obscure comedy remembered today only for the presence of Flynn, whose next film would be CAPTAIN BLOOD.

p, Samuel Bischoff; d, Robert Florey; w, Isabel Dawn, Boyce DeGaw, Arthur Greville Collins; ph, William Rees; ed, Thomas Richards; md, Leo F. Forbstein; art d, Esdras Hartley.

Comedy **(PR:A MPAA:NR)**

DON'T BET ON LOVE** (1933) 62m UNIV bw

Lew Ayres *(Bill McCaffery)*, Ginger Rogers *(Molly Gilbert)*, Charles Grapewin *(Pop McCaffery)*, Shirley Grey *(Goldie)*, Merna Kennedy *(Ruby)*, Tom Dugan *(Scotty)*, Robert Emmett O'Connor *(Sheldon)*, Lucille Webster Gleason *(Mrs. Gilbert)*, Henry Armetta *(Caparillo)*, Brooks Benedict *(Cunningham)*, Clay Clement *(Ross)*, Alfred White *(Rosenbaum)*, Pepe Sinoff *(Mrs. Rosenbaum)*, Charley Lee, Tyler Brooke, Eddie Kane, Craig Reynolds.

Plumber Ayres and manicurist Rogers fall in love and plan to marry, but Rogers calls it off when she learns that Ayres plans to spend their honeymoon at Saratoga betting on the horses. Ayres finds it hard to quit his gambling and return to her because he has picked nothing but winners since she left him. His father, Grapewin, tries to warn him, but Ayres refuses to listen. Only when he loses all his money does he come to his senses and go back to his sweetheart. Vaguely amusing comedy that has been out of circulation for many years.

p, E. M. Asher; d, Murray Roth; w, Roth, Howard Emmett Rogers; ph, Jackson Rose; ed, Robert Carlisle; art d, Charles D. Hall.

Comedy/Romance   **(PR:A MPAA:NR)**

DON'T BET ON WOMEN*½   (1931) 61m FOX bw

Edmund Lowe (Roger Fallon), Jeanette MacDonald (Jeanne Drake), Roland Young (Herbert Drake), Una Merkel (Tallulah Hope), J. M. Kerrigan (Chipley Duff), Helene Millard (Doris Brent), Henry Kolker (Butterfield), Louise Beavers (The Maid), Cyril Ring (A Guest).

Woman-hating Lowe states his suspicions about the sex at a party and is overheard by Young, who bets him $10,000 that the next woman to enter the room will not allow Lowe to kiss her within 48 hours. When MacDonald, Young's wife, turns out to be the next woman in the room, the bet takes on unexpected complications. MacDonald learns of the wager and manipulates the situation to teach both men a needed lesson. Trivial farce based on the French pattern. Una Merkel contributes a nice performance as a philosophical flapper.

p, William Fox; d, William K. Howard; w, Lynn Startling, Leon Gordon (based on the story, "All Women Are Bad," by William Anthony McGuire); ph, Lucien Andriot; ed, Harold Schuster.

Comedy   **(PR:A MPAA:NR)**

DON'T BLAME THE STORK*   (1954, Brit.) 80m Advance-Objective/Adelphi bw

Veronica Hurst (Katie O'Connor), Ian Hunter (Sir George Redway), Reginald Beckwith (Jonathan), Patricia Laffan (Lilian Angel), Brenda de Banzie (Evelyn Steele), Harry Fowler (Harry Fenn), Thora Hird (Agnes O'Connor), Mark Daly (Michael O'Connor), Howard Marion Crawford (Fluffy Faversham), Avril Angers (Renee O'Connor).

When a baby is abandoned on a famous actor's doorstep, actress O'Connor steps forth claiming to be the mother. Dull comedy with little to recommend.

p, David Dent, Victor Katona; d, Akos Rathony; w, Talbot Rothwell, Katona (based on a story by Wolfgang Wilhelm, E. Silas).

Comedy   **(PR:A MPAA:NR)**

DON'T BOTHER TO KNOCK***   (1952) 76m FOX bw

Richard Widmark (Jed Towers), Marilyn Monroe (Nell), Anne Bancroft (Lyn Leslie), Donna Corcoran (Bunny), Jeanne Cagney (Rochelle), Lurene Tuttle (Mrs. Ruth Jones), Elisha Cook, Jr. (Eddie), Jim Backus (Peter Jones), Verna Felton (Mrs. Ballew), Willis B. Bouchey (Bartender), Don Beddoe (Mr. Ballew), Gloria Blondell (Girl Photographer), Grace Hayle (Mrs. McMurdock), Michael Ross (Pat), Eda Reis Merin (Maid), Victor Perrin (Elevator Operator), Dick Cogan (Bell Captain), Robert Foulk (Doorman), Olan Soule (Desk Clerk), Emmett Vogan (Toastmaster).

A taut little chiller, this film has Monroe as a neurotic babysitter who is hired by Backus and Tuttle to mind their child, Corcoran. Monroe arrives at their hotel suite, brought by her uncle, Cook, head bellhop, who nervously warns her to be on her best behavior. Widmark is an airline pilot staying at the hotel so he can see his girl friend, Bancroft, who sings in the lounge. Bancroft breaks it off with Widmark, telling him he is callous. Later Widmark meets Monroe and the two become intimate in the Backus suite, interrupted by Corcoran. Monroe explodes at the little girl, ordering her back into her bedroom. Cook arrives to check on Monroe and Widmark hides in the bathroom, emerging perplexed and accurately believing Monroe has a large hole in her marble bag. Monroe's explosive personality erupts when Cook makes a remark to her and she smashes his head with an ashtray. When Widmark believes Cook is unharmed he leaves, but only after seeing that the little girl is safely in bed. He returns to Bancroft to tell her about the incident and she takes him back after realizing his deep concern for the child. Then Widmark realizes that the child, when he last saw her, was not in her own room. He races back to the suite to find Corcoran tied to the bed and her mother, Tuttle, battling with Monroe, who has a razor. She apparently intended to murder the child for interfering with her tryst with Widmark, whom she wrong-headedly came to believe was her fiance. (Her real fiance had been a pilot killed in WW II.) With Bancroft at his side, Widmark gently takes the razor from Monroe and convinces her that her fiance is really dead. She surrenders meekly to police who take her to an asylum where she had been a former inmate. Bancroft decides that Widmark is indeed a compassionate man and plans to stay with him. DON'T BOTHER TO KNOCK is directed with a quick pace by Baker, the Taradash script is as tight as a sardine can, and all the principals do well with their roles, especially lovely Marilyn Monroe. This was her 15th film and her first real dramatic part, one in which she is a standout as a tormented, nerve-wracked soul battling reality, a condition not unlike the state in which she found herself just before her suicide.

p, Julian Blaustein; d, Roy Baker; w, Daniel Taradash (based on a novel by Charlotte Armstrong); ph, Lucien Ballard; m, Lionel Newman; ed, George A. Gittens; art d, Lyle Wheeler, Richard Irvine; set d, Thomas Little, Paul S. Fox.

Drama   **(PR:O MPAA:NR)**

DON'T BOTHER TO KNOCK, 1964
(SEE: WHY BOTHER TO KNOCK, 1964, Brit.)

DON'T CALL ME A CON MAN**
(1966, Jap.) 109m Toho c (DAIBOKEN)

Hetoshi Ueki (Reporter), Reiko Dan, Fubuki Koshiji, Kei Tani, Hajime Hana.

Adolf Hitler is on the loose again; at least that is what reporter Ueki stumbles upon during a routine investigation of a counterfeiting ring. The old dictator is still harboring dreams of conquering the world, and is busy creating a fleet with which to launch his attack. Absurd premise sparks interest for its novelty, at least.

d, Kengo Furusawa; w, Ryozo Kasahara, Yasuo Tanami; ph, Tadashi Iimura (Tohoscope, Eastmancolor).

Crime/Comedy   **(PR:A MPAA:NR)**

DON'T CRY, IT'S ONLY THUNDER***
(1982) 108m Sanrio Communications c

Dennis Christopher (Brian), Susan Saint James (Katherine), Roger Aaron Brown (Moses), Robert Englund (Tripper), James Whitmore, Jr. (Maj. Flaherty), Lisa Lu (Sister Marie), Thu Thuy (Sister Hoa), Travis Swords (Allen), Mai Thi Lien (Ann), Truong Minh Hal (Duc), Ken Metcalfe (Capt. Morris), Marie Ashton (Peggy), Robert Howland (Bugsy), Paul Hensler (Dr. Goldman), Wynne Dieppe (Immigration Woman), Ronald Sully (Troy), Tom Joyner (Supply Sergeant), Ronald Orso (Michael).

Christopher is a cynical, drug-dealing medic in Vietnam blackmailed by Army doctor Saint James into helping a group of Vietnamese war orphans. Opposing their efforts is the U.S. Government, which eventually pressures Saint James into dropping the matter under threat of ruining her medical career. The best feature of the film is its careful avoidance of easy answers and a refreshingly downbeat finish. One of a small number of movies Christopher appeared in after his fine performance in BREAKING AWAY and before slipping into obscurity again.

p, Walt deFarla; d, Peter Werner; w, Paul Hensler; ph, Don McAlpine (DeLuxe Color); m, Maurice Jarre; ed, Jack Woods, Barbara Pokras; prod d, Robert Checchi.

War/Drama   **Cas.**   **(PR:O MPAA:PG)**

DON'T CRY WITH YOUR MOUTH FULL**½   (1974, Fr.) 116m
Renn Productions-Les Films du Chef-Lieu-O.R.T.F.
(PLEURE PAS LA BOUCHE PLEINE)

Annie Cole (Annie), Jean Carmet (Father), Christina Chamaret (Mother), Helene Dieudonne (Grandmother), Daniel Ceccaldi (Uncle), Claudine Paringaux (Aunt), Friquette (Sister), Barnard Menez (Alexander), Frederic Duru (Frederic).

An innocent film centering on one summer in the life of a 15-year-old girl has Cole as the girl on the threshold of becoming a woman living in an idyllic French village. Apart from the things that go on in her home, which includes an eccentric grandmother who adds a touch of bizarre humor, Cole is just discovering boys in the form of Menez and Duru. The latter is too absorbed in bicycle racing to pay much attention to the budding beauty, leaving the Don Juanish Menez to have the honors of initiating Cole into affairs of the heart. Light, breezy and lacking pretensions, but something that can easily be forgotten about after digestion. (In French; English subtitles.)

d, Pascal Thomas; w, Thomas, Roland Duval, Suzanne Schiffman; ph, Christian Rachman; m, Michael Choquet; ed, Helene Plemianikov.

Drama   **(PR:A MPAA:NR)**

DON'T DRINK THE WATER**   (1969) 98m Joseph E. Levine/AE c

Jackie Gleason (Walter Hollander), Estelle Parsons (Marion Hollander), Ted Bessell (Axel Magee), Joan Delaney (Susan Hollander), Michael Constantine (Krojack), Howard St. John (Ambassador Magee), Danny Meehan (Kilroy), Richard Libertini (Father Drobney), Pierre Olaf (Chef), Avery Schreiber (Sultan), Phil Leeds (Sam), Mark Gordon (Mirik), Dwayne Early (Donald), Joan Murphy (Airline Clerk), Martin Danzig (Mishkin), Rene Constantineau (Organ Grinder), Howard Morris (Getaway Pilot).

Woody Allen wrote the play that this gobbler was based upon and it surely would have had more effect if they'd allowed him to write the screenplay. Filmed in Miami and Quebec, it's the story of Gleason, a New Jersey caterer who with wife Parsons and daughter Delaney, who are kidnaped on a hijacked plane which lands in Vulgaria, a country behind the Iron Curtain. At the Vulgarian airport, Gleason takes some pictures and is immediately suspected of being a spy by secret policeman Constantine, who tries to arrest them. They are given immunity inside the American embassy, which is being run by Ted Bessell, son of ambassador St. John. Inside the embassy they meet Libertini, a wild-eyed priest-patriot who has been living there under asylum for six years. The USA attempts to negotiate for the tourists by offering a captured Vulgarian spy, but he commits suicide before he can be swapped. Gray-haired student agitators storm the embassy (an obvious plant by the authorities) as Gleason, Parsons, and Delaney dress up in the clothing of a visiting Arab potentate and get through the crowd in disguise. They rush to a getaway point and meet an aged pilot who has been waiting for Libertini's escape for six years. There's just enough space for two on the plane, so Gleason and Parsons escape and Delaney marries Bessell and acquires diplomatic immunity. The getaway pilot was played by director Howard Morris, who was funnier in the role than just about anyone else in the movie. Hard to know where to put the blame for this. The play was a mild success, but this looks more like a TV film than a feature. Morris did the best with the screenplay that was handed to him. Bullock and Allen were essentially TV writers, who did many years with Hanna-Barbera, and it's evident. Morris, of course, was one of Sid Caesar's stooges (with Carl Reiner) who made "Your Shows Of Shows" such a smash in the 1950s.

p, Charles H. Joffe; d, Howard Morris; w, R. S. Allen, Harvey Bullock (based on the play by Woody Allen); ph, Harvey Genkins; m, Pat Williams; ed, Ralph Rosenblum; art d, Robert Gundlach; cos, Gene Coffin.

Comedy   **Cas.**   **(PR:A MPAA:G)**

DON'T EVER LEAVE ME*½   (1949, Brit.) 85m J. Arthur Rank-Triton/GFD bw

Jimmy Hanley (Jack Denton), Petula Clark (Sheila Farlane), Hugh Sinclair (Michael Farlane), Linden Travers (Mary Lamont), Edward Rigby (Harry Denton), Anthony Newley (Jimmy Knowles), Barbara Murray (Joan Robbins), Brenda Bruce (Miss Smith), Maurice Denham (Mr. Knowles), Frederick Piper (Max Marshall), Sandra

Dorne (Miss Baines), Anthony Steel (Harris), Patricia Dainton (Girl), Dandy Nichols, John Salew, Cyril Chamberlain, Michael Balfour, James Hayter, Russell Waters, Philip Stainton, Barbara Leake, Arthur Hambling, Ben Williams, Elizabeth Blake, Douglas Herald, Lyn Evans.

Aging criminal Rigby and grandson Hanley kidnap Clark, the daughter of a famous actor. Clark enjoys the experience immensely and foils all attempts at ransoming her back. Easy to take comedy with a decent cast.

p, Betty E. Box; d, Arthur Crabtree; w, Robert Westerby (based on a novel by Anthony Armstrong); ph, Stephan Dade, Dudley Lovell; m, Lambert Williamson; ed, A. Charles Knott.

Crime   **(PR:A MPAA:NR)**

DON'T FENCE ME IN**½

         (1945) 71m REP bw

Roy Rogers (Himself), George "Gabby" Hayes (Gabby Whitaker), Dale Evans (Toni Ames), Robert Livingston (Jack Chandler), Moroni Olsen (Henry Bennett), Marc Lawrence (Cliff Anson), Lucille Gleason (Mrs. Prentiss), Andrew Tombes (Cartwright), Paul Harvey (The Governor), Tom London (The Sheriff), Douglas Fowley (Gordon), Stephen Barclay (Tracy), Edgar Dearing (Chief of Police), Helen Talbot, Bob Nolan and The Sons of the Pioneers, Trigger.

Magazine photographer Evans heads west to research an article about a supposedly long-dead character named Wildcat Kelly. She meets rancher Rogers and sidekick Hayes, who, after some intrigue involving gangsters, turns out to be Kelly. Good example of the contemporary musical western that proved very popular in the 1940s and made Rogers a major box office draw. Songs include "Tumbling Tumbleweeds," "The Last Roundup," and "Don't Fence Me In."

p, Donald H. Brown; d, John English; w, Dorrell and Stuart McGowan, John K. Butler; ph, William Bradford; m, Morton Scott, Dale Butts; ed, Charles Craft; md, Scott; art d, Hilyard Brown; ch, Larry Ceballos; m/l, Cole Porter, Morton Shore, Zeke Manners, Jack Scholl, M. K. Kerome, Billy Hill, Larry Marks, Dick Charles, Eddie DeLange, Freddie Slack, F. Victor, R. Herman, Bob Nolan.

Western/Musical   **(PR:A MPAA:NR)**

DON'T GAMBLE WITH LOVE**

         (1936) 65m COL bw

Ann Sothern (Ann Edwards), Bruce Cabot (Jerry Edwards), Irving Pichel (Rick Collins), Ian Keith (John Crane), Thurston Hall (Martin Gage), George McKay (Dan), Elizabeth Risdon (Grace), Clifford Jones (Bob), Franklin Pangborn (Salesman), Richard Livernoin (Baby).

Cabot is the honest owner of an illegal gambling house. He allows no crooked dice or fixed wheels. Even though he is a virtuous crook, his wife, Sothern, wants him out of the racket so their newborn child can grow up with dignity. Cabot sells the house, only to be swindled when he invests the cash in a supposedly legitimate venture.

d, Dudley Murphy; w, Lee Loeb, Harold Buchman; ph, Henry Freulich; ed, James Sweeney.

Drama   **(PR:A MPAA:NR)**

DON'T GAMBLE WITH STRANGERS*

         (1946) 67m MON bw

Kane Richmond (Mike Sarno), Bernadene Hayes (Fay Benton), Peter Cookson (Bob Randall), Gloria Warren (Ruth Hamilton), Charles Trowbridge (Creighton), Frank Dae (John Randall), Tony Caruso (Pinky Luiz), Phil Van Zandt (Morelli), Harold Goodwin (John Sanders), Leonard Mudie (Robert Elliot), Bill Kennedy (Harry Arnold), Addison Richards (Chief Broderick), Ferris Taylor (Michael Larson), Mary Field (Mrs. Arnold), Edith Evanson (Swedish Maid), Steve Darrell (Tony), Bob Barron (Pete), Sayre Dearing (Dealer).

Richmond and Hayes are a pair of sharpers who combine their talents for a job. Posing as brother and sister, they swindle a town's banker, then take control of the local gambling joint. Richmond starts paying attention to another woman, leading to a fight with Hayes, and shortly thereafter he is found shot to death. Hayes is put on trial for the killing, but ballistics tests prove that a rival gambler did the job. Confusing at times, but fairly entertaining.

p, Jeffrey Bernard; d, William Beaudine; w, Caryl Coleman, Harvey Gates; ph, William Sickner; ed, William Austin; md, Edward J. Kay.

Crime   **(PR:A MPAA:NR)**

DON'T GET ME WRONG**

         (1937, Brit.) 80m WB-FN/FN bw

Max Miller (Wellington Lincoln), George E. Stone (Chuck), Olive Blakeney (Frankie), Glen Alyn (Christine), Clifford Heatherley (Sir George Baffin), Wallace Evennett (Dr. Rudolph Pepper), Alexander Field (Gray).

A mad scientist develops a tablet that can be used as a gasoline substitute and a fairground barker promotes it. Mediocre treatment of an old scam.

p, Irving Asher; d, Arthur Woods, Reginald Purdell; w, Purdell, Brock Williams, Frank Launder; ph, Basil Emmott.

Comedy   **(PR:A MPAA:NR)**

DON'T GET PERSONAL*½

         (1936) 70m UNIV bw

Sally Eilers (Jinxy), James Dunn (Bob), Pinky Tomlin (Arthur), Spencer Charters (Mr. Van Ranesaleer), Doris Lloyd (Mrs. Van Ranesaleer), George Meeker (Fred), George Cleveland (Farmer), Lillian Harmer (Farmer's Wife), Jean Rogers (Blondy), Charles Coleman (Butler), Tom Dugan (Bum In Park), Vera Lewis (Spinster), Alene Carroll (Dizzy Blonde), Elizabeth Heater (Maid), Harry C. Bradley (Foreman), Priscilla Lawson, Lucille Lund, Donna Mae Roberts, June Glory, Lucille & Dorothy McNames (Bridesmaids).

After the success of BAD GIRL in 1931, Eilers and Dunn were teamed up for five more light romantic comedies, none of which approached the moderate standard of the first. In this one, the next to last of the series, Dunn and buddy Tomlin are

booted out of college. To raise money, they hold an auction of their services in Central Park. Eilers submits the winning bid and hires the pair to drive with her in her beat-up jalopy to Ohio. Along the way, Tomlin plays his guitar and sings some songs. Dunn doesn't show much interest in Eilers until the end, when he snatches her from the altar as she is about to wed someone else.

p, David Diamond; d, William Nigh; w, George Waggner, Clarence Marks, Houston Branch (based on a story by William Thiele, Edmund Hartmann); ph, Norbert Brodine; m, Pinky Tomlin; ed, Murray Seldeen.

Comedy/Musical   **(PR:A MPAA:NR)**

DON'T GET PERSONAL*½

         (1941) 60m UNIV bw

Hugh Herbert (Elmer Whippet), Mischa Auer (Charlie), Jane Frazee (Mary Reynolds), Anne Gwynne (Susan Blair), Robert Paige (Paul Stevens), Richard Davies (John Stowe), Ernest Truex (Jules Kinsey), Andrew Tombes (J. M. Snow), Sterling Holloway (Lucky), Ray Walker (Pitchman), Eddy Waller (Slim), Tim Ryan (Traffic Officer).

Inane comedy has Herbert the head of a pickle firm more concerned about the lives of characters in the radio soap—or pickle, in this case—opera he sponsors than in the attempts of a group of shifty executives to take over his company. Some okay songs sung by Frazee help, but not much.

p, Ken Goldsmith; d, Charles Lamont; w, Hugh Wedlock, Jr., Howard Snyder (based on the story "Nobody's Fool" by Bernard Feins); ph, Jerome Ash; m, Charles Previn; m/l, "It Doesn't Make Sense," "Now What Do We Do," (sung by Jane Frazee), "Every Time a Moment Goes By," (sung by Frazee, Robert Paige), Jack Brooks, Norman Berens.

Comedy   **(PR:A MPAA:NR)**

DON'T GIVE UP THE SHIP**

         (1959) 89m PAR bw

Jerry Lewis (John Paul Steckler), Dina Merrill (Ens. Benson), Diana Spencer (Prudence Trabert), Mickey Shaughnessy (Stan Wychinski), Robert Middleton (Adm. Bludde), Gale Gordon (Congressman Mandeville), Mabel Albertson (Mrs. Trabert), Claude Akins (Lt. Comdr. Farber), Hugh Sanders (Adm. Rogers), Richard Shannon (Comdr. Cross), Chuck Wassil (Comdr. Craig).

Lewis is dragged out of bed on his wedding night and brought before a Navy board of inquiry. It seems that a destroyer that Lewis commanded during World War II can't be found, and unless Lewis can prove that he returned it, he'll have to pay for it. In flashback we see Lewis bumbling his way through the war. Finally it is revealed that the ship was accidentally used for target practice and sunk, and when Lewis scuba dives down to the wreck and brings back a piece of it, he is exonerated and allowed to consummate his marriage with Spencer. Below standard even for Lewis.

p, Hal Wallis; d, Norman Taurog; w, Edmund Beloin, Henry Garson, Herbert Baker (based on a story by Ellis Kadison); ph, Haskell Boggs; m, Walter Scharf; ed, Warren Low; art d, Hal Pereira, Walter Tyler; spec eff, John P. Fulton.

Comedy   **(PR:A MPAA:NR)**

DON'T GO IN THE HOUSE zero

         (1980) 82m Film Ventures Intl./Turbine Films c

Dan Grimaldi (Donny), Robert Osth (Bobby), Ruth Dardick (Mrs. Kohler), Charlie Bonet (Ben), Bill Ricci (Vito), Dennis M. Hunter, John Hedberg, Johanna Brushay, Darcy Shean, Mary Ann Chin, Jim Donnegan, Claudia Folts, Denise Woods, Pat Williams, Colin McInness, Ralph D. Bowman, Joey Peschl, Connie Oaks, David McComb, Jean Manning, Ken Kelsch, Tom Brumberger, Nikki Kollins, Kim Roberts, Louise Grimaldi, Gloria Szymkovicz, David Brody, O'Mara Leary, Gail Turner, Eileen Dunn, Christian Isodore.

Worthless horror film stars Grimaldi as a deranged incinerator operator whose mother used to abuse him by burning his arms over the stove. When she dies, he roasts her in his private crematorium, then dresses up the crispy corpse and lets it sit around the house. To keep mom company, Grimaldi cruises discos picking up nubile victims, all of whom end up similarly well-done. In the baffling finale, they all come to life and kill Grimaldi. A film to avoid.

p, Ellen Hammill; d, Joseph Ellison; w, Hammill, Ellison, Joseph Masefield; ph, Oliver Wood (DeLuxe Color); m, Richard Einhorn; ed, Jane Kurson; art d, Sarah Wood; set d, Peter Zsiba; cos, Sharon Lynch.

Horror   **Cas.**   **(PR:O MPAA:R)**

DON'T GO NEAR THE WATER***½

         (1975) 107m MGM c

Glenn Ford (Lt. Max Siegel), Gia Scala (Melora), Earl Holliman (Adam Garrett), Anne Francis (Lt. Alice Tomlen), Keenan Wynn (Gordon Ripwell), Fred Clark (Lt. Cmdr. Clinton Nash), Eva Gabor (Deborah Aldrich), Russ Tamblyn (Ensign Tyson), Jeff Richards (Lt. Ross Pendleton), Mickey Shaughnessy (Farragut Jones), Howard Smith (Adm. Boatwright), Romney Brent (Mr. Alba), Mary Wickes (Janie), Jack Straw (Lt. Cmdr. Gladstone), Robert Nichols (Lt. Cmdr. Hereford), John Alderson (Lt. Cmdr. Diplock), Jack Albertson (Rep. George Jansen), Charles Watts (Rep. Arthur Smithfield).

A very funny satire on the Navy's public relations campaign in the Pacific, notable for one hysterical gag that has foul-mouthed Mickey Shaughnessy as a man unable to speak without using the word that usually separates "PG" from "R" these days but was totally unusable back then. Shaughnessy's every other word is honked on the film's sound track. In some of his speeches it's just one long honk and we wonder what the hell he was saying to merit that kind of censorship. Actually, the sound is that of a boat horn and while some bluenoses felt that it might have been a rotten dirty joke, evil is in the ears of the beholder and it shouldn't disturb your sensibilities one bit. The story is an amiable mishmash of some excellent characters in a hodge-podge of plots, sub-plots and sub-sub-plots, none of which will tax your gray matter and all of which will make you laugh. While Charles Walters did an excellent directorial job, it got out of hand from time to time as super second bananas like Fred Clark, Keenan Wynn, and others kept purloining scenes from Ford, Scala, Francis and Holliman, none of whom is known for comedic talents.

p, Lawrence Weingarten; d, Charles Walters; w, Dorothy Kingsley, George Wells (based on the novel by William Brinkley); ph, Robert Bronner (CinemaScope, Metrocolor); m, Bronislau Kaper; ed, Adrienne Fazan; art d, William A. Horning, Urie McCleary; cos, Helen Rose; m/l, Sammy Cahn.

Comedy   **(PR:A   MPAA:NR)**

DON'T JUST LIE THERE, SAY SOMETHING!*

(1973, Brit.) 91m Comocroft/RANK c

Brian Rix, Leslie Phillips, Joan Sims, Joanna Lumley, Derek Royle, Peter Bland. A politician finds himself in hot water when he winds up sleeping with both his secretary and another woman. Based on a stage play, this one is a sex farce which doesn't do anything but lie there.

d, Bob Kellett; w, Michael Pertwee (based on his play).

Comedy   **(PR:O   MPAA:NR)**

DON'T JUST STAND THERE*½

(1968) 97m UNIV c

Robert Wagner (Lawrence Colby), Mary Tyler Moore (Martine Randall), Glynis Johns (Sabine Manning), Harvey Korman (Merriman Dudley), Barbara Rhoades (Kendall Flanagan), Vincent Beck (Painter), Joseph Perry (Jean-Jacques), Stuart Margolin (Remy), Emile Genest (Henri), David Mauro (Jules), Penny Santon (Renee), Joe Bernard (Police Inspector), Herbert Voland (Moffat), Richard Angarola (Pascal Decaux), Otis Young (Bill Elkins), Willie Koopman (Gabrielle), Bern Hoffman, Gladys Holland.

Occasionally funny story has Wagner an American writer in Europe supporting himself by smuggling watch parts out of Switzerland into France. In return for her help in one of these forays, Wagner agrees to help Moore find her missing friend, sex novelist Johns. Johns is actually on vacation in the Aegean, but the ghost writer hired to finish her novel (Rhoades) has been kidnaped by gangsters, who think she's Johns. Wagner helps her escape and learns she is being sought by the police for the murder of a gangster. Johns eventually turns up and is persuaded to finish her novel. The gangster Rhoades is alleged to have killed conveniently walks in and is quickly subdued, and Wagner and Moore fly off for an Aegean vacation. Fast-moving comedy with little substance, but some decent performances.

p, Stan Margulies; d, Ron Winston; w, Charles Williams (based on his novel The Wrong Venus); ph, Milton Krasner (Techniscope, Technicolor); m, Nick Perito; ed, Richard Bracken; art d, Alexander Golitzen, William DeCinces; set d, John McCarthy, George Milo; makeup, Bud Westmore.

Comedy   **(PR:A   MPAA:NR)**

DON'T KNOCK THE ROCK**½

(1956) 85m Clover/COL bw

Bill Haley (Himself), Alan Dale (Arnie Haines), Alan Freed (Himself), The Treniers (Themselves), Little Richard (Himself), Dave Appell and His Applejacks (Themselves), Patricia Hardy (Francine MacLaine), Fay Baker (Arlene MacLaine), Jana Lund (Sunny Everett), Gail Ganley (Mollie Haines), Pierre Watkin (Mayor George Bagley), George Cisar (Mayor Tom Everett), Dick Elliott (Sheriff Cagle), Jovada and Jimmy Ballard.

Sequel to ROCK AROUND THE CLOCK has Dale a rock'n'roller who comes back to his home town to put on a show, but meets opposition from the strait-laced locals. It's not until he stages a 1920s dance and shows folks how silly they looked doing the Charleston that their resistance vanishes and Dale can be united with Hardy. Along the way, Bill Haley sings "Don't Knock the Rock," "Hot Dog Buddy Buddy," and "Hook, Line and Sinker." The forgotten Treniers and the equally ignored Dave Appell and His Applejacks do a few numbers, but it's Little Richard ripping through "Long Tall Sally" and "Tutti Frutti" who shines, and makes this exploitation film worth catching.

p, Sam Katzman; d, Fred F. Sears; w, Robert E. Kent, James B. Gordon; ph, Benjamin H. Kline; ed, Edwin Bryant, Paul Borofsky; md, Fred Karger, Ross Di Maggio; art d, Paul Palmentola; ch, Earl Barton.

Musical   **(PR:A   MPAA:NR)**

DON'T KNOCK THE TWIST**

(1962) 86m COL bw

Chubby Checker (Himself), Gene Chandler (The Duke of Earl), Vic Dana (Himself), Linda Scott (Herself), The Carroll Brothers (Themselves), The Dovells (Themselves), Lang Jeffries (Ted Haver), Mari Blanchard (Dulcie Corbin), Georgine Darcy (Madge Albright), Stephen Preston (Billy Albright), Barbara Morrison (Mrs. Morrison), Nydia Westman (Dressmaker), James Chandler (Joe Albright), Frank Albertson (Herb Walcott), Elizabeth Harrower (Ruth Emerson), Hortense Petra (Mrs. Kay), Peter Dawson (Frank Emerson), Viola Harris (Fashion Editor), David Landfield (Director), Tim Sullivan (Mr. Fullerton), Ralph Montgomery (Reporter).

Sam Katzman repeats history. In 1956 when he came out with ROCK AROUND THE CLOCK, he quickly followed it up, cashing in with DON'T KNOCK THE ROCK. In 1961 he came out with TWIST AROUND THE CLOCK, and quickly followed it up with this film, DON'T KNOCK THE TWIST. This inevitably titled followup concerns itself with a silly story about preparations for a TV special on the twist and efforts to help a summer camp for orphans; in other words, a way to segue between a dozen musical numbers of varying quality. The best moments are the Dovells doing "The Bristol Stomp," and Gene Chandler soaring through "Duke of Earl." Checker sings a handful of songs and actually turns in a decent performance in a fairly substantial role. Songs include "Don't Knock the Twist," Kal Mann, Dave Appel, sung by Checker; "The Bristol Stomp," "Do the New Continental," Mann, Appell, sung by the Dovells; "Let's Twist a La Paloma," Mann, sung by Checker; "Little Altar Boy," Howlett Smith, sung by Vic Dana; "Yesiree," Linda Scott, sung by Scott, "Duke of Earl;" Eugene Dixon, Bernice

Williams, Earl Edwards, sung by Gene Chandler; "Mash Potato Time," Mann, Bernie Lowe; "Salome Twist," Robert E. Kent, Fred Karger.

p, Sam Katzman; d, Oscar Rudolph; w, James B. Gordon; ph, Gordon Avil; m, Fred Karger; ed, Jerome Thoms; art d, Don Ament; set d, Sidney Clifford; cos, Edna Taylor; ch, Hal Belfer; makeup, Joseph Di Bella.

Musical   **(PR:A   MPAA:NR)**

DON'T LET THE ANGELS FALL**½

(1969, Can.) 97m National Film Board of Canada bw

Arthur Hill (Robert), Sharon Acker (Barbara), Charmion King (Myrna), Jonathon Michaelson (Guy), Michele Magny (Diane), John Kastner (Michael), Monique Mercure (Mrs. Pelletier), Andree Lachapelle (Prostitute), Peter Desbarats (T.V. Host).

Hill is a Canadian insurance agent with a wife and two teenage sons. He falls in love with an American girl while in the States learning to use a computer. When the course is over he leaves her and returns to his family, but is unable to forget his affair. He becomes distant, and the rest of the family can feel him drifting away. The family begins to disintegrate along with Hill's mind, and watching himself avoiding some relevant social questions on television is the final straw. Painfully earnest and very well done, this is the kind of film that often seems such an invasion of privacy that viewers want to turn away in embarrassment.

d, George Kaczender; w, Kaczender, Timothy Findley; ph, Paul Leach; m, The Collectors; ed, Michael McKennirey.

Drama   **(PR:A   MPAA:NR)**

DON'T LOOK IN THE BASEMENT zero

(1973) 89m Hallmark c

Rosie Holotik (Charlotte), Ann McAdams (Dr. Masters), William Bill McGhee (Sam), Gene Ross (Judge Oliver W. Cameron), Jessie Lee Fulton (Jane St. Claire), Camilla Carr (Harriet), Harriet Warren (Jennifer), Hugh Feagin (Sgt. Jaffee), Rhea MacAdams (Mrs. Callingham), Betty Chandler (Allyson), Jessie Kirby (Danny), Robert Dracup (Ray Daniels), Michael Harvey (Dr. Stephens).

A gory piece of trash about Holotik, an inmate in an asylum, who takes the place of the director when he's butchered. People meet their deaths in very bloody and violent ways until there is only one person left, McGhee. Distributed by the same company that handled Wes Craven's LAST HOUSE ON THE LEFT. They used the same slippery ad slogan, "Keep telling yourself it's only a movie." Movie, no; garbage, yes.

p&d, S. F. Brownrigg; w, Tim Pope; art d, Lynda Pendleton; spec eff, Jack Bennett; makeup, Jill Esmond.

Horror   **Cas.**   **(PR:O   MPAA:NR)**

DON'T LOOK NOW**

(1969, Brit./Fr.) 116m Les Films Corona-Lowndes Productions/BV c
(GB: DON'T LOOK NOW...WE'RE BEING SHOT AT; LA GRANDE VADROUILLE)

Terry-Thomas (Reginald), Bourvil (Augustin Bouvet), Louis de Funes (Stanislaus Lefort), Claudio Brook (Peter Cunningham), Marie Dubois (Juliette), Benno Sterzenbach (Col. Achbach), Colette Brosset (Madame Germaine), Andrea Parisy (Sister Marie-Odile), Mike Marshall (Alan MacIntosh), Mary Marquet (Mother Superior), Pierre Bertin (Punch and Judy Operator), Sieghart Rupp, Hans Meyer, Rudy Lenoir, Paul Preboist, Peter Jacob, Daniele Thompson.

Inane, innocuous comedy about a British bomber crew shot down over occupied Paris. They meet a series of difficulties on the way to their escape rendezvous point in a steambath, and are aided by a number of Frenchmen. Their final escape is assured when a cross-eyed German soldier shoots down the German fighter pursuing their freedom-bound gliders. Released in England in 1966.

p, Robert Dorfman; d, Gerard Oury; w, Oury, Georges Tabet, Andre Tabet, Marcel Julian, Daniele Thompson; ph, Claude Renoir (Panavision, Eastmancolor); m, Georges Auric; ed, Albert Jurgenson; art d, Jean Andre; m/l, "Symphonie Fantastique," Hector Berlioz; "Tea for Two," Vincent Youmans, Irving Caesar.

Comedy   **(PR:A   MPAA:G)**

DON'T LOOK NOW***½

(1973, Brit./Ital.) 110m Casey Productions-Eldorado Films-BL/PAR c

Julie Christie (Laura Baxter), Donald Sutherland (John Baxter), Hilary Mason (Heather), Clelia Matania (Wendy), Massimo Serato (Bishop), Renato Scarpa (Inspector Longhi), Giorgio Trestini (Workman), Leopoldo Trieste (Hotel Manager), David Tree (Anthony Babbage), Ann Rye (Mandy Babbage), Nicholas Salter (Johnny Baxter), Sharon Williams (Christine Baxter), Bruno Cattaneo (Detective Sabbione), Adelina Poerio (Dwarf).

Watching any Nicolas Roeg film is like taking a Latin test; it's easy if you know the answers and impossible if you don't. This was the director's third in a long list of infuriating pictures, all distinguished by gorgeous camerawork and obscure story lines. Sutherland, in one of his most restrained performances, is married to Christie. Their daughter was accidentally killed—or was she? They travel to Venice, Italy, in winter where he is to restore a church. Once there, they get involved with two weird sisters, Mason and Matania, one of whom is a blind psychic who says she can get them in touch with their late daughter. Sutherland refuses to believe a word of it, but begins to relent when he sees a small figure darting around Venice dressed in the late daughter's clothes. Once he catches up with the diminutive figure, it turns out to be a maniacal dwarf, who stabs him to death! In DON'T LOOK NOW, nothing is what it seems, and we often wonder if what we're seeing is happening for real or is another "vision." There was lots of talk about the very realistic love scene between Christie and Sutherland and the argument still rages about whether or not they actually "did it"—was it merely superior acting? Visually, the picture is a treat. Roeg began as a cameraman, with credits that include FAHRENHEIT 451, CASINO ROYALE, PETULIA, etc., and his images are exquisite. But, as he's proved in WALKABOUT, ILLUSIONS, THE MAN WHO FELL TO EARTH, and PERFORMANCE (co-directed with Donald Cammell), he is not a master of a story and often sacrifices communicating ideas for his incomparable camera style. Produced by American Boy Wonder Peter Katz, who had several stage hits in London before attempting films, this was expected to be a "breakthrough" movie for Roeg that would achieve the commercial success his others failed to garner. It didn't. Not unlike ROSEMARY'S BABY in the psychological overtones, DON'T LOOK NOW was just too allegorical for most viewers and has now become a cult film that merits midnight showings at tiny theaters in college towns. The love scene has been trimmed somewhat to lose the "X" rating it once had from the British Film Board. Enigmas are all well and good, but one wants answers in the end and DON'T LOOK NOW proved unsatisfying in that department.

p, Peter Katz; d, Nicolas Roeg; w, Allan Scott, Chris Bryant (based on a short story by Daphne du Maurier); ph, Anthony Richmond (Panavision Technicolor); m, Pino Donaggio; ed, Graeme Clifford; art d, Giovanni Soccol.

Mystery   **Cas.**   **(PR:O MPAA:R)**

DON'T LOSE YOUR HEAD*½

(1967, Brit.) 90m RANK c

Sidney James (Sir Rodney Ffing), Kenneth Williams (Citizen Camembert), Jim Dale (Lord Darcy), Charles Hawtrey (Duke de Pommfrit), Joan Sims (Desiree Dubarry), Dany Robin (Jacqueline), Peter Butterworth (Citizen Bidet), Peter Gilmore (Robespierre), Michael Ward (Henri), Leon Greene (Malabonce), Diana Macnamara (Princess Stephanie), Marianne Stone (Landlady), Richard Shaw (Captain of Soldiers).

Another in the interminable "Carry On" series has the usual gang mugging and leering their way through the usual lot of hoary blue jokes and double entendres. This time the setting is the French Revolution, and James is the Scarlet Pimpernel-like Black Fingernail, assuming a bewildering array of disguises (all the more bewildering because none of them even try to hide his face). (See CARRY ON series, Index.)

p, Peter Rogers; d, Gerald Thoms; w, Talbot Rothwell; ph, Alan Hume (Eastmancolor); m, Eric Rogers; ed, Rod Keys.

Comedy   **(PR:C MPAA:NR)**

DON'T MAKE WAVES**

(1967) 100m Filmways-Reynard/MGM

Tony Curtis (Carlo Cofield), Claudia Cardinale (Laura Califatti), Sharon Tate (Malibu), Robert Webber (Rod Prescott), Joanna Barnes (Diane Prescott), David Draper (Harry Hollard), Mort Sahl (Sam Lingonberry), Edgar Bergen (Madame Lavinia), Ann Elder (Millie Gunder), Chester Yorton (Ted Gunder), Marc London (Fred Barker), Douglas Henderson (Henderson), Sarah Selby (Ethyl), Mary Grace Canfield (Seamstress), Dub Taylor (Electrician), Reg Lewis (Monster), Julie Payne (Helen), Hollie Haze (Myrna), Paul Barselow (Pilot), Eduardo Tirella (Decorator), George Tyne, David Fresco, Gilbert Green (Newsmen), Jim Backus, Henny Backus (Themselves).

Okay comedy with Curtis a tourist who meets thrill-seeking Cardinale when she runs his car off the highway. She takes him to her Malibu home and he learns that she is the kept mistress of swimming-pool dealer Webber. Curtis nearly drowns in the ocean and is rescued by skydiver Tate—performing in her third feature film (the wife of Roman Polanski, spectacularly murdered by the Charles Manson "family")—who performs mouth-to-mouth resuscitation. Curtis falls in love with her and decides to stay in the area. He blackmails Webber into giving him a job while he tries to further his romance with Tate. Eventually everyone ends up in a house sliding toward the ocean in a rainstorm, and Curtis discovers that it's Cardinale whom he really loves. Director Mackendrick has done much better work (THE MAN IN THE WHITE SUIT, WHISKY GALORE, THE SWEET SMELL OF SUCCESS) but he does give this film some energy, and Curtis gives a rare competent performance.

p, John Calley, Martin Ransohoff; d, Alexander Mackendrick (skydiving sequences, Leigh Hunt); w, Ira Wallach, George Kirgo, Maurice Richlin (based on the novel Muscle Beach by Wallach); ph, Philip H. Lathrop (skydiving sequences, Bob Buguor) (Panavision, Metrocolor); m, Vic Mizzy; ed, Rita Roland, Thomas Stanford; art d, George W. Davis, Edward Carfagno; set d, Henry Grace, Charles S. Thompson; cos, Donfeld; makeup, William Tuttle; songs performed by The Byrds.

Comedy   **(PR:A MPAA:NR)**

DON'T OPEN THE WINDOW zero

(1974, Ital.) 88m Hallmark c (NON SI SEVE PROFANARE OL SONNE DIE MORTE; AKA: BREAKFAST AT MANCHESTER MORGUE; THE LIVING DEAD AT MANCHESTER MORGUE)

Ray Lovelock (George), Christina Galbo (Edna), Arthur Kennedy (Inspector McCormick), Fernando Hilbeck (Guthrie), Jeanine Mestre (Katie), Jose Ruis Lifante (Martin).

The Italians have a knack for rip-offs and gore and this film is a prime example. Taking the premise of Romero's NIGHT OF THE LIVING DEAD, tossing in gallons of fake blood and animal intestines, DON'T OPEN THE WINDOW should have been titled "Let's See How Sick We Can Get." A gizmo to kill insects causes the dead to become the living dead and, of course, they only dine on human flesh.

p, Edmondo Amati; d, Jorge Grau; w, Grau, Sandro Continenza, Marcello Coscia; spec eff, Gianetto DeRossi.

Horror   **(PR:O MPAA:NR)**

DON'T PANIC CHAPS!*

(1959, Brit.) 85m Hammer-A.C.T. Films/COL bw

Dennis Price (Capt. von Krisling), George Cole (Finch), Thorley Walters (Brown), Harry Fowler (Ackroyd), Nadja Regin (Elsa), Nicholas Phipps (Mortimer), Percy Herbert (Bolter), George Murcell (Meister), Gertan Klauber (Schmidt), Terence Alexander (Babbington), Thomas Foulkes (Voss).

Mindless comedy revolves around two observation teams, German and British, left on a remote Adriatic island, then forgotten. The two sides call a truce and live harmoniously and quite well until beautiful Regin is cast ashore and fighting breaks out anew. Originally the film was to be titled CARRY ON CHAPS, but it was changed in the wake of the success of the "Carry On" series.

p, Teddy Baird, Ralph Bond; d, George Pollock; w, Jack Davies (based on an original radio play by Michael Corston, Ronald Holroyd); ph, Arthur Graham; m, Philip Green; ed, Harry Aldous.

War Comedy   **(PR:A MPAA:NR)**

DON'T PLAY WITH MARTIANS*

(1967, Fr.) 100m Fildebroc-Les Productions Artistes Associes/UA (NE JOUEZ PAS AVEC LES MARTIENS; AKA: COMME MARS EN CAREME)

Jean Rochefort (Rene), Macha Meril (Marie), Andre Vallardy (Job), Haydee Politoff (Maid), Pierre Dac (Doctor), Frederic de Pasquale.

A downright idiotic film about a spacecraft full of Martians landing off the coast of Brittany. Rochefort and Vallardy are journalists who discover the aliens along with Meril, who has psychic powers. The Martians—who are really from an entirely different planet—don't do much through the movie, and the comedy of the two reporters falls flat. When the aliens leave, they take a set of sextuplets with them because one of the "Martians" is the father.

p, Georges Casati; d, Henri Lanoe; w, Lanoe, Johanna Harwood, Philippe de Broca (based on a book by Michel Labry); ph, Rene Mathelin (Eastmancolor); m, Lanoe.

Science Fiction   **(PR:A MPAA:NR)**

DON'T RAISE THE BRIDGE, LOWER THE RIVER*

(1968, Brit.) 99m COL c

Jerry Lewis (George Lester), Terry-Thomas (H. William Homer), Jacqueline Pearce (Pamela Lester), Bernard Cribbins (Fred Davies), Patricia Routledge (Lucille Beatty), Nicholas Parsons (Dudley Heath), Michael Bates (Dr. Spink), Colin Gordon (Mr. Hartford), John Bluthal (Dr. Pinto), Sandra Caron (Pinto's Nurse), Margaret Nolan (Spink's Nurse), Pippa Benedict (Fern Averback), Harold Goodwin (Six-Eyes Wiener), Richard Montez (Arab), Henry Soskin (Bearded Arab), Al Mancini (Portuguese Chauffeur), John Moore (Digby), John Barrard (Zebra Man), Robert Lee (Bruce), Francisca Tu (Chinese Telephonist), Colin Douglas (Barman), Alexandra Dane (Masseuse), Nike Arrighi (Portuguese Waitress), Tatsuo Susuki (Judo Man), Christine Pryor (Manicurist), Molly Peters (Heath's Secretary), Jerry Paris (Baseball Umpire).

Lewis stars—in one of the rare films he didn't also write and produce—as a Walter Mitty-type fantasist who, threatened with divorce by wife Pearce, retreats into daydreams of adventure and excitement. With the aid of confidence trickster Terry-Thomas, Lewis plots to steal the plans for a valuable new invention, a high-speed oil drill, and peddle the plans to oil-rich Arabs. The spoof of spy-thriller yarns continues with the inevitable hidden microfilm, high-speed chases through Lisbon, a sinister double-crossing dentist, and so on. All ends well as dreamer Lewis is reunited with Pearce. TV director Paris takes a small role in this, his second feature-film directorial effort.

p, Walter Shenson; d, Jerry Paris; w, Max Wilk (based on his novel); ph, Otto Heller (Technicolor); m, David Whitaker; ed, Bill Lenny; art d, John Howell; set d, Pamela Cornell; cos, Maxine Leighton; ch, Leo Kharibian; m/l, title song, Hal Shaper (sung by Danny Street).

Comedy   **Cas.**   **(PR:A MPAA:NR)**

DON'T RUSH ME**

(1936, Brit.) 72m PDC bw

Robb Wilton (Samuel Honey), Muriel Aked (Amy Andrews), Haver & Lee (Detectives), Peter Haddon (Adolphe), Bobbie Comber (Louis), Kathleen Kelly (Tilly), Kenneth Love (Bertie Moon), Wallace Douglas (Jack Honey), Dino Galvani (Tony), Hal Walters (Hal), Nor Kiddie (Commissionaire), Wilson Coleman, May Beamish, Elizabeth Kent.

Decent farce centering on the activities of Wilton and Haddon as prominent members of an anti-gambling society, though having a hand in some gambling activities all along. When the two go to London all hell breaks out as they find numerous gambling chances more than they can possibly resist.

p, Fred Karno; d, Norman Lee; w, Con West, Michael Barringer (based on the sketch "When We Are Married" by Karno).

Comedy   **(PR:A MPAA:NR)**

DON'T SAY DIE*½

(1950, Brit.) 61m X Productions/IFD bw (AKA: NEVER SAY DIE)

Desmond Walter-Ellis (Ron Bertie Blarney), Sandra Dorne (Sandra), Charles Heslop (Charles Choosey), Constance Smith (Red Biddy), Tony Quinn (Mike Murphy), Stanley Rose (Gus), Derek Tansley (Potts), Thomas Gallagher (Gorilla), Kenneth Connor (Pat O'Neill), Raymond Rollett, Michael Raghan, Harry Lane, Denis McCarthy.

Walter-Ellis inherits an Irish castle and soon he learns that it is being used as headquarters by smugglers. Not much worthwhile here.

p, Vivian Milroy, Margot Lovell; d, Milroy; w, Dido and Vivian Milroy.

Comedy   **(PR:A MPAA:NR)**

DON'T SCREAM, DORIS MAYS!
(SEE: DAY OF THE NIGHTMARE, 1965)

DON'T TAKE IT TO HEART***   (1944, Brit.) 93m Two Cities/GFD bw
Richard Greene (Peter Hayward), David Horne (Sir Henry Wade, K.C.), Patricia Medina (Lady Mary), Alfred Drayton (Mr. Pike), Joan Hickson (Mrs. Pike), Richard Bird (Ghost Arthur), Wylie Watson (Harry Bucket), Claude Dampier (Loopy), Edward Rigby (Butler), Brefni O'Rourke (Lord Chaunduyt), Patric Curwen (Mr. Smith), Margaret Withers (Mrs. Smith), Moore Marriott (Granfer), Joyce Barbour (Harriet), Ronald Squire (Music Lover), Ernest Thesiger (Magistrate's Clerk), Amy Veness (Cook), George Merritt (Landlord), Esma Cannon (Maid), Harry Fowler, Edie Martin, George Bailey, Ernest Jay, Peter Cotes, John Salew, John Turnbull, Ivor Bernard, Patricia Medina, David Horne.

The British possess an abiding fondness for mocking the traditions of their landed gentry. This fast-paced little gem has to do with an impoverished earl who ekes out a living by functioning as a tour guide on his own country estate. An attorney-sightseer, Greene, fascinated by the estate's old manuscripts—uncovered by a fortuitous German bomb, which also released an ancestral ghost from eons of confinement—takes a room in a nearby village in order to study the documents. Smarmy businessman Drayton, meanwhile, is attempting to snare the estate for his own profiteering purposes. With the assistance of ghost Bird, and of the earl's only daughter, Medina, Greene uncovers the fact that the nominal earl, O'Rourke, has no claim to his title; he is actually a descendant of a long line of local poachers. A Gilbert-and-Sullivan mix-up has occurred: the local poacher is the true earl of the manor. He assumes his rightful estate, and the false lord happily reverts to his ancestral calling, poaching game on the estate he once knew as his own. Lawyer Greene proves to be a titled baron himself. He and Medina wed, assuring her of the lifestyle to which she is accustomed. The talented leads are supported by a fine cast of character actors.

p, Sydney Box; d&w, Jeffrey Dell; ph, Eric Cross; m, Mischa Spoliansky; art d, Alec Vetchinsky.

Comedy   **(PR:A   MPAA:NR)**

DON'T TALK TO STRANGE MEN*   (1962, Brit.) 65m Bryanston bw
Christina Gregg (Jean Painter), Cyril Raymond (Mr. Painter), Gillian Lind (Mrs. Painter), Conrad Phillips (Ron), Janina Faye (Ann Painter), Dandy Nicholls (Molly), Gwen Nelson (Mrs. Mason).

Gregg is a country girl prevented from keeping a date. Good thing, too, because the guy turns out to be a sex maniac. Obscure British exploitation number.

p, Derick Williams; d, Pat Jackson; w, Gwen Cherrell.

Crime   **(PR:C   MPAA:NR)**

DON'T TELL THE WIFE**   (1937) 63m RKO bw
Guy Kibbee (Malcolm Winthrop), Una Merkel (Nancy Dorset), Lynne Overman (Steve Dorset), Thurston Hall (Major Manning), Guinn Williams (Cupid), William Demarest (Larry Tucker), Lucille Ball (Ann Howell), Harry Tyler (Mike Callahan), Charlie West (Joe Hoskins), Alan Curtis (Customer's Man), Donald Kerr (Smith), Bill Jackie (Rooney), Bradley Page (Hagar), Aggie Herring (Charwoman), Barney Furey (Sign Painter), Hattie McDaniel (Nancy's Maid), Si Jenks (Sam Taylor).

During The Great Depression, people were well acquainted with the ephemeral nature of financial investments, and many films of the time reflected public suspicions of stock-and-bond deals. In this one, bucket-shop swindler Hall rejoins his ex-associates after his release from prison, trying for one last big score. He considers this deal a shoo-in, since this time he really has a promotable product: he won the title to a real mine in a card game. He prevails upon retired co-trickster Overman to join him in the swindle, over the trepidations of Overman's wife Merkel—who, as the title suggests, is kept in the dark about the true nature of the deal. Overman advances his savings to establish the company, and simple-minded Kibbee is chosen as figurehead, largely because his surname is the same as that of a prestigious banking family (Winthrop; an obvious Rockefeller euphemism). Kibbee writes his credulous friends to promote the stock, and the Post Office investigates. Kibbee, wising up, visits the mine and discovers that it really does contain extractable high-grade gold ore. He undergoes an immediate transformation into a credible businessman and gets all the innocent folk off the hook, sending Overman and Merkel back to rustic but happy domesticity. The film is notable primarily for the appearance of Lucille Ball in a billed role, a step up from the bit parts she had previously played. Director Cabanne had been D. W. Griffiths' assistant before scoring on his own in both silents and talkies; he directed Douglas Fairbanks, the ultimate swashbuckler, in the latter's first film, THE LAMB (1915).

p, Robert Sisk; d, Christy Cabanne; w, Nat Perrin (based on the play "Once Over Lightly" by George Holland); ph, Harry Wilde; ed, Jack Hively; art d, Van Nest Polglase, Field Gray; cos, Renie; spec eff, Vernon Walker.

Comedy   **(PR:A   MPAA:NR)**

DON'T TEMPT THE DEVIL**   (1964, Fr./Ital.) 106m
Mediterranee-Flora-Mizar/United Motion Picture Organization bw (LES BONNES CAUSES)

Marina Vlady (Catherine Dupre), Bourvil (Magistrate Gaudet), Virna Lisi (Gina Bianchi), Pierre Brasseur (Cassidi), Jose-Luis de Vilallonga (Paul Dupre), Umberto Orsini (Philliet), Mony Dalmes (Madame), Jacques Monod (Judge), Jacques Mauclair (Witness), Robert Vidalin, Francois Darbon, Gilbert Gil.

A standard French programmer which has Vlady betraying her hospital patient and switching his usual medicine for a fatal dosage. The nurse innocently gives him his injection, killing him, and receiving the blame. Vlady's lover, Brasseur, takes the case in Vlady's defense, but is also jilted and ends up arranging her conviction.

p, Georges Cheyko; d, Christian-Jaque; w, Henri Jeanson, Umberto Orsini, Paul Andreota, Christian-Jaque, Jeanson (based on a novel by Jean Laborde); ph,

Armand Thirard (Franscope); m, Georges Garvarentz; ed, Jacques Desagneau; art d, Jean Mandaroux.

Crime Drama   **(PR:A   MPAA:NR)**

DON'T TOUCH MY SISTER   (SEE: GLASS CAGE, THE, 1964)

DON'T TOUCH THE LOOT   (SEE: GRISBI, 1953, Fr.)

DON'T TOUCH WHITE WOMEN!**½
(1974, Fr.) 108m Mara Films-Les Films 66-Laser Productions-P.E.A./CFDC c (TOUCHE PAS A LA FEMME BLANCHE!)

Marcello Mastroianni (Custer), Catherine Deneuve (Marie-Helene), Michel Piccoli (Buffalo Bill), Philippe Noiret (Terry), Ugo Tognazzi (Mitch), Alain Cuny (Sitting Bull), Serge Reggiani (Mad One), Darry Cowl (Archibald), Monique Chaumette (Lucie), Franca Bettoja (Rayon De Lune), Paolo Villagio (CIA Man), Daniele Dublino (Daughter), Franco Fabrizi (Tom), Henri Piccoli (Father).

The French have a romance with anachronism and a passion for paradox, blending old with new, mixing one filmic genre with another. This remarkable melange blends Nixon politics with the genocidal land-grabbing expansionism of the Old West. Mastroianni is George Armstrong Custer, the vain, posturing martinet who led his troops to massacre at the hands, arrows, and scalping knives of the beleaguered Indians of Sitting Bull (here played by Cuny). Deneuve is the archetype modest, reserved frontier belle who, uncharacteristically of her species, literally picks Mastroianni up and tosses him into the sack in order to use him carnally. Piccoli is a pansified Buffalo Bill who, ever the showman, performs at a Parisian nightclub. Tognazzi, an Indian scout, owns a store that sells Indian blankets and trinkets, and which is staffed entirely by overworked, underpaid white women whom he has been warned against touching by the pompous, overbearing Mastroianni. A touch of period reality is found in the merchandising of cigar-store Indians which turn out to be real Indians, murdered, stuffed, and mounted, their extermination by the white settlers made, finally, marketable. This comedic indictment of empire-building, the euphemisms of its nominal period comparable to those of a much later date—pacification; body count—is made almost plausible, and wildly amusing, by a first-rate cast and able direction by transplanted Spaniard Ferreri, "the master of bad taste," whose films such as DILLINGER IS DEAD (1969) and LA GRANDE BOUFFE (1973) demonstrated his mastery of the improbable. To complete the anachronistic cycle, DON'T TOUCH WHITE WOMEN was shot on location in the cleared wreckage of the old Paris marketplace, the non-Western setting where Custer/Mastroianni and his troops come to final grief.

p, Jean-Pierre Rassam, Jean Yanne; d, Marco Ferreri; w, Ferreri, Rafael Azcona; ph, Etienne Becker (Eastmancolor); m, Phillippe Sarde; ed, Ruggero Mastroianni.

Western   **(PR:C   MPAA:NR)**

DON'T TRUST YOUR HUSBAND**
(1948) 90m UA bw (AKA: AN INNOCENT AFFAIR)

Fred MacMurray (Vincent Doane), Madeleine Carroll (Paula Doane), Charles "Buddy" Rogers (Claude Kimball), Rita Johnson (Eve Lawrence), Louise Allbritton (Margot Fraser), Alan Mowbray (Ken St. Clari), "Prince" Mike Romanoff (Maitre D'), Pierre Watkin (T. D. Hendricks), William Tannen (Gaylord), James Seay (Lester Burnley), Matt McHugh (Ted Burke), Marle Blake (Hilda), Susan Miller (Vocalist), Anne Magel (Gladys), Eddie LeBaron (Orchestra Leader), Jane Weeks (Doris).

Hackneyed plot has MacMurray playing an adman trying to get his old girlfriend to buy some advertising space for her company. He keeps her identity a secret, so that wife Carroll won't get jealous. But she knows something is going on and thinks her mate is having an affair. She hires a man to flirt with her in order to turn the tables on her husband. All is resolved in the end, of course. The story is trite and boring, though it has a few laughs. Mowbray gets some of the best moments during a restaurant scene. The maitre d' was played by Romanoff, a real life Beverly Hills restaurant owner. This was Carroll's first film in a long time and she does what she can.

p, James Nasser; d, Lloyd Bacon; w, Lou Breslow and Joseph Hoffman; ph, Edward Cronjager; m, Hans J. Salter; ed, Fred W. Berger; m/l, Walter Kent and Kim Gannon.

Comedy   **(PR:C   MPAA:NR)**

DON'T TURN 'EM LOOSE*   (1936) 68m RKO bw
Lewis Stone (John Webster), James Gleason (Daniels), Bruce Cabot (Bat Roberts), Louise Latimer (Letty), Betty Grable (Mildred), Nella Walker (Mrs. Helen Webster), Grace Bradley (Grace), Frank M. Thomas (Attorney Pierce), Maxine Jennings (Mary), Frank Jenks (Pete), Harry Jans (Vic), John Arledge (Walter), Addison Randall (Al), Fern Emmett (Hattie), Arthur Hoyt (Judge Bass), Frenchy Durelle (Deputy Warden), Phillip Morris (Guard), Tommy Graham (Secretary), Gordon Jones (Joe Graves), John Ince (Parole Board Member), Charles Richman (Governor).

Stone is a high-school principal and respected member of the parole board who finds himself in a position to decide about the parole case of his own son (Cabot), who has turned into a vicious criminal. Cabot threatens to reveal Stone as his father and ruin him unless Stone votes to free him. Stone succumbs to the blackmail, and Cabot goes on a spree with moll Latimer, until shot down by his father. A fast pace goes a long way toward covering holes in the plot. An interesting view of Betty Grable in Cabot's sister, an early billed role for the star who later became the top "pin-up girl" of WW II.

p, Robert F. Sisk; d, Ben Stoloff; w, Ferdinand Reyher, Harry Segall (based on the story "Homecoming" by Thomas Walsh); ph, Jack MacKenzie; ed, William Morgan.

Crime   **(PR:A   MPAA:NR)**

DON'T TURN THE OTHER CHEEK**   (1974, Ital./Ger./Span.) 93m
Hercules Associated-Tritone Filmindustria-Terra Filmkunst-Producciones
Cinematograficas Orduna/International Amusement Corp. c
(VIVA LA MUERTE...TUA)

Eli Wallach, Lynn Redgrave, Franco Nero, Marilu Tolo, Luigi Antonio Guerra,
Horst Yanson, Eduardo Fajardo, Jose Moren, Victor Israel, Gisela Hahn, Jose
Jaspes, Enrique Espinosa, Gunda Hiller, Furio Meniconi, Don Van Husen, Rudy
Gaebell, Carla Mancini, Mirko Ellis.

So-so spaghetti western with Redgrave a radical Irish journalist trying to stir up a
peasant revolt in Mexico. She enlists bandit Wallach's help by saving him from a
death sentence in Utah. They pick up Nero, who claims to be a Russian prince,
and the three cross the border, the two men more interested in gold than revolution. The principals are pretty good, and the script shows some flashes of humor,
but it doesn't have the mythological structure that distinguishes the best European
contributions to the most American of genres.

p, Mickey Knox; d, Duccio Tessari; w, Dino Maiuri, Massimo De Rita, Juan De
Orduna Y Fernandez, Gunter Eber (based on Lewis B. Patten's novel, *The Killer
From Yuma*); ph, Jose F. Aguayo; m, Gianni Ferrio; ed, Enzo Alabiso; set d, Pietro
Filippone; cos, Jurgen Henze.

Western   **(PR:C MPAA:NR)**

DON'T WORRY, WE'LL THINK OF A TITLE*
(1966) 83m Courageous-Kam/UA bw

Morey Amsterdam (*Charlie*), Rose Marie (*Annie*), Richard Deacon (*Police
Chief/Mr. Travis*), Tim Herbert (*Seed/Samu*), Jackie Heller (*Mr. Big*), Joey Adams
(*1st Guy*), Andy Albin (*2nd Guy*), Michael Ford (*Jim Holliston*), January Jones
(*Magda Anders*), Carmen Phillips (*Olga*), Henry Corden (*Lerowski*), Peggy Mondo
(*Fat Lady*), Percy Helton (*Fat Man*), LaRue Farlow (*The Lover*), Moe Howard (*Mr.
Raines*), Yau Shan Tung (*Chinese Girl*), Arline Hunter (*Girl Student*), Annazette
(*2nd Student*), Gregg Amsterdam (*Boy Student*), Darryl Vaughan (*Athlete*), Danny
Thomas, Forrest Tucker, Irene Ryan, Milton Berle, Steve Allen, Carl Reiner,
Slapsy Maxie Rosenbloom, Nick Adams, Cliff Arquette.

Abominable comedy has Amsterdam and Rose Marie (along with Richard Deacon
refugees from "The Dick Van Dyke Show") as a short-order cook and waitress in a
greasy spoon diner. One day their incompetence gets them fired and they go to
help a friend (Jones) run a bookstore she's inherited. A group of Russian spies
mistakes Amsterdam for a defecting cosmonaut and soon spies, counterspies,
federal agents, and local policemen are chasing our inept heroes and each other
up and down the rows of books, not to mention a couple of bank robbers using the
store as a base to tunnel into the vault next door. One of the gags is that the head
spy, "Mr. Big," is a midget. It's all downhill from there.

p, Morey Amsterdam; d, Harmon Jones; w, John Hart, Amsterdam (adaptation
George W. Schenck, William Marks); ph, Brick Marquard; m, Richard De Salle;
ed, Robert C. Jones; cos, Bob Spencer, Marge Makau; spec eff, Frank De Marco;
makeup, Gus Norin.

Comedy   **(PR:A MPAA:NR)**

DON'T YOU CRY   (SEE: MY LOVER, MY SON, 1970, U.S./Brit.)

DONZOKO   (SEE: LOWER DEPTHS, THE, 1962, Jap.)

DOOLINS OF OKLAHOMA, THE***
(1949) 90m COL/bw (AKA: THE GREAT MANHUNT)

Randolph Scott (*Bill Doolin*), George Macready (*Sam Hughes*), Louise Allbritton
(*Rose of Cimarron*), John Ireland (*Bitter Creek*), Virginia Huston (*Elaine Burton*),
Charles Kemper (*Arkansas*), Noah Beery, Jr. (*Little Bill*), Dona Drake (*Cattle
Annie*), Robert H. Barrat (*Heck Thomas*), Lee Patrick (*Melissa Price*), Griff Barnett
(*Deacon Burton*), Frank Fenton (*Red Buck*), James Kirkwood (*Rev. Mears*), Robert
Osterloh (*Wichita*), Virginia Brissac (*Mrs. Burton*), John Sheehan (*Dunn*), Jock
O'Mahoney (*Tulsa Jack*).

An above-average western chronicling one of the last real-life outlaw gangs of the
Southwest, the notorious Doolins, led by Scott, who survives the massacre of the
Dalton Gang in Coffeyville, Kansas, on October 5, 1892. Scott recruits a new
gang, including Ireland, Beery, Fenton, O'Mahoney, and Kemper, and leads raids
against banks and trains. Huston and Scott are in love, but she can't persuade him
to hang up his guns. He is a doomed man and says so, intending to die with his
boots on. One by one the outlaws are cornered and killed by lawmen Macready,
Barrat, and others; Scott is the last to go, wearing his boots and filled with
buckshot. The action is brisk under Douglas' direction and Lawton's
cinematography is a standout, with its sharp black-and-white treatment. Gamet's
screenplay is well-researched and provides considerable black humor in a day
when westerns usually provided humorous relief in a sneeze of Al "Fuzzy" St.
John or a whine from Smiley Burnett. Scott gives a terrific portrayal of a westerner
trapped by the coming of the modern age.

p, Harry Joe Brown; d, Gordon Douglas; w, Kenneth Gamet; ph, Charles Lawton,
Jr.; m, M.W. Stoloff; ed, Charles Nelson; art d, George Brooks

Western   **(PR:A MPAA:NR)**

DOOMED AT SUNDOWN**½   (1937) 55m REP bw

Bob Steele (*Austin*), Lorraine Hayes [Laraine Day] (*Jane*), Warner Richmond
(*Hatfield*), Harold Daniels (*Batch*), David Sharpe (*Williams*), Horace Carpenter
(*Lew*), Earl Dwire, Sherry Tansey, Budd Buster, Jack C. Smith, Jack Kirk, Horace
Murphy, Charles King, Lew Meehan, Jack Ingram.

Above-average Steele vehicle has the diminutive but tough cowpoke as a sheriff's
son prone to playing practical jokes. When his father gets knifed, he straightens his
act out fast and takes off after the killers. He captures them at their hideout on the

border. One curious scene has to do with Steele's initiation into a secret society of
hooded practical jokers.

p, A.W. Hackel; d, Sam Newfield; w, George Plympton (based on a story by Fred
Myton); ph, Bert Longenecker; ed, Roy Clarke.

Western   **Cas.**   **(PR:AA MPAA:NR)**

DOOMED BATTALION, THE**   (1932) 95m UNIV bw

Tala Birell (*Maria Di Mai*), Luis Trenker (*Florian Di Mai*), Victor Varconi (*Artur
Franchini*), Albert Conti (*Captain Kessler*), Gustave Von Seyffertitz (*Austrian
General*), C. Henry Gordon (*Italian General*), Gibson Gowland (*Innerhofer*), Henry
Armetta (*Angelo*), Ferdinand Gottschalk (*Man*).

During WW I, in a snowbound Tyrolean pass, the long stalemate is soon to be
broken when the Italians finish digging a tunnel under an Austrian position, then
blow it sky high. The Austrians know what the Italians are up to, but they have
been ordered not to budge from their position. Trenker is an Austrian who sneaks
over to the Italian lines to discover the exact time of the explosion, hoping to save
the battalion. Varconi, the Italian commander, and Trenker's old friend from
mountain climbing days before the war, is now billeted in Trenker's own house
with the latter's wife (Birell). Good performances somewhat redeem this pointless
attempt to repeat the formula of ALL QUIET ON THE WESTERN FRONT.
Remade in 1940 as SKI PATROL.

d, Cyril Gardner; w, Luis Trenker, Patrick Kearney, Paul Perez, Carl Hartle
(based on a story by Trenker); ph, Charles Stumar, Sepp Allegeler; ed, Clarence
Kolster.

War   **(PR:A MPAA:NR)**

DOOMED CARAVAN***   (1941) 60m PAR bw

William Boyd (*Hopalong Cassidy*), Russell Hayden (*Lucky Jenkins*), Andy Clyde
(*California Jack*), Minna Gombell (*Jane Travers*), Morris Ankrum (*Stephen
Westcott*), Georgia Hawkins (*Diana Westcott*), Trevor Bardette (*Ed Martin*), Pat J.
O'Brien (*Jim Ferber*), Raphael Bennett (*Pete Gregg*), Jose Luis Tortosa (*Don
Pedro*).

Top Hopalong Cassidy oater has black-clad Boyd helping Gombell save her wagon
line from the nefarious schemes of villains Ankrum and Bardette, who plan to use
it to take over all the wagon-train business moving west. Shot on location in the
central California valleys. As usual, Hayden and Clyde are on hand to lend,
respectively, fistic and comic relief. (See HOPALONG CASSIDY series, Index.)

p, Harry Sherman; d, Lesley Selander; w, Johnston McCulley, J. Benton Cheney
(based on characters created by Clarence E. Mulford); ph, Russell Harlan; ed,
Carroll Lewis; art d, Lewis J. Rachmil.

Western   **(PR:A MPAA:NR)**

DOOMED CARGO**
(1936, Brit.) 70m GAU/International Film Renters, Ltd. bw
(GB: SEVEN SINNERS)

Edmund Lowe (*John Harwood*), Constance Cummings (*Caryl Fenton*), Thomy
Bourdelle (*Paul Turbe*), Henry Oscar (*Axel Hoyt*), Felix Aylmer (*Sir Charles Web-
ber*), Joyce Kennedy (*Elizabeth Wentworth*), Allan Jeayes (*Karl Wagner*), O.B.
Clarence (*Registrar*), Mark Lester (*Chief Constable*), Antony Holles (*Receptionist*),
David Horne (*Hotel Manager*), Edwin Laurence (*Guildhall Guide*), James Harcourt
(*Vicar*), Patrick Ludlow, Henry Hallatt, Margaret Davidge.

Lowe is a Yankee detective on the trail of gunrunners who won't stop at wrecking
trains to get their enemies. Cummings is the girl who tags along. Not a bad second
feature, and one that precedes hordes of American detectives, reporters, and
other heroes who infest the British B-Movie.

p, Michael Balcon; d, Albert de Courville; w, Frank Launder, Sidney Gilliat, L.
DuGarde Peach, Austin Melford (based on the play "The Wrecker" by Arnold
Ridley and Bernard Merivale); ph, Mutz Greenbaum; ed, M. Gordon; md, Louis
Levy.

Crime   **(PR:A MPAA:NR)**

DOOMED TO DIE*½   (1940) 68m MON bw

Boris Karloff (*James Lee Wong*), Grant Withers (*Capt. Bill Street*), Marjorie Reyn-
olds (*Bobby Logan*), Melvin Lang (*Wentworth*), Guy Usher (*Fleming*), Catherine
Craig (*Cynthia Wentworth*), William Sterling (*Dick Fleming*), Henry Brandon,
Wilbur Mack.

The last of five "Mr. Wong" films starring Karloff. This time, the oriental sleuth is
investigating the murder of a shipping tycoon in the wake of the sinking of one of
his ships with over $1 million in bonds aboard. Sterling is suspected of the murder,
but a reporter who believes him innocent brings Karloff on the case, and he quickly
sorts through the red herrings to expose the killer. Undistinguished programmer,
but Karloff is always worth seeing, even in bad parts. (See MR. WONG series,
Index.)

p, Paul Malvern; d, William Nigh; w, Ralph G. Bettinson, Michael Jacoby (based on
stories by Hugh Wiley); ph, Harry Neumann; ed, Robert Golden; makeup, Gordon
Bau.

Crime/Mystery   **Cas.**   **(PR:A MPAA:NR)**

DOOMSDAY AT ELEVEN*½   (1963 Brit.) 56m Parroch/GEF bw

Carl Jaffe (*Stefan*), Stanley Morgan (*Wylie*), Alan Heywood (*Peter Godwin*), Derrick de Marney (*Judge Alderbrook*), Jennifer Wright (*Angela Alderbrook*), Delia
Corrie (*Eve Lake*), Alan Edwards (*Wilson*), Geoffrey Dunn (*Jeremiah*).

An injured bomb-disposal expert works with a group of brave volunteers to defuse
a ticking bomb in a maternity home. Will it go off? Do they ever?

p, C. Jack Parsons; d, Theodore Zichy; w, Paul Tabori, Gordon Wellesley.

Drama   **(PR:A-C MPAA:NR)**

DOOMSDAY MACHINE zero (1967) Harvey Rope/First Leisure bw

Grant Williams, Henry Wilcoxon, Ruta Lee, Mala Powers, Bobby Van, Denny Miller, Casey Kasem, Mike Farrell.

The crew of a spaceship heading for Venus watches as Earth is blown to bits by an atomic war. And the rest of the film is devoted to highly stimulating arguments and debates as to whether they should get the human race going again. If the world is going to be repopulated by those in the cast, a second nuclear blast might be in order. Williams, the star in THE INCREDIBLE SHRINKING MAN, is the bad boy of the crew, wanting only to bed down the females. The production is characterized by stock shots from other films and a little inept model work.

p, Harvey Rope; d, Lee Sholem; w, Stuart James Byre.

Science Fiction (PR:A MPAA:NR)

DOOMSDAY VOYAGE* (1972) 88m Futurama International c

Joseph Cotten (Capt. Jason), John Gabriel (Wilson), Ann Randall (Katherine Jason).

A political assassin (Gabriel) flees aboard a New York-bound liner commanded by Cotten. Gabriel takes the captain's daughter (Randall) hostage in her cabin and rapes her. While Cotten paces back and forth in a quandary, Gabriel and Randall have long, pretentious conversations of the sort that only take place in the minds of untalented screenwriters. The tedium is broken only by the gratuitous violence. Release of this film was held up for a long time, and no wonder.

p, Al Adamson; d&w, Vidette; (DeLuxe Color).

Drama (PR:O MPAA:NR)

DOOMWATCH** (1972, Brit.) 92m Tigon c

Ian Bannen, Judy Geeson, John Paul, Simon Oates, George Sanders, Percy Herbert, Geoffrey Keen, George Woolbridge.

Chemicals pollute the water and as a result people become deformed mutants. Sanders is sent by the military to get to the bottom of the mystery and save the world from doom. Pretty standard thriller material based on a BBC television show.

p, Tony Tenser; d, Peter Sasdy; w, Clive Exton; ph, Kenneth Talbot; m, John Scott; ed, Keith Palmer; art d, Colin Grimes.

Science Fiction (PR:C MPAA:NR)

DOOR-TO-DOOR MANIAC (SEE: FIVE MINUTES TO LIVE, 1961)

DOOR WITH SEVEN LOCKS, THE (SEE: CHAMBER OF HORRORS, 1940, Brit.)

DOORWAY TO HELL*½** (1930) 79m WB bw (GB: A HANDFUL OF CLOUDS)

Lewis [Lew] Ayres (Louis Ricarno), Charles Judels (Sam Marconi), Dorothy Mathews (Doris), Leon Janney (Jackie Lamarr), Robert Elliott (Capt. O'Grady), James Cagney (Steve Mileway), Jerry Mandy (Joe), Noel Madison (Rocco), Fred Argus (Machine Gunner), Ruth Hall (Girl), Dwight Frye, Tom Wilson, Al Hill (Gangsters), Bernard "Bunny" Granville, Kenneth Thomson (Captain of Military Academy), Eddie Kane, Richard Purcell, Thomas Jackson.

A hard-hitting gangster film which was one of the first to chronicle the modern-day hoodlum and his quirkish lifestyle. Normally mild-mannered Ayres does a turnabout by playing a ruthless crime overlord who is in power at the film's opening. Ayres settles all disputes about territories and hijackings, gleaning millions. He considers himself a reincarnation of Napoleon Bonaparte and occupies his leisure time by writing his memoirs. At the height of his success, to protect the image of him held by his kid brother who is in military school, Ayres shocks his underlings by quitting the rackets and announcing that he will marry Mathews and retire to Florida. He does, never realizing that Cagney, the lieutenant to whom he turns over his rackets, has been secretly trysting with Mathews. Ayres is lured back to the Manhattan rackets when his brother is kidnaped and killed, run over by a truck while trying to escape the hoodlums holding him. Ayres roars into the Big Town, killing the two men responsible. Cagney is arrested and talks, which causes Ayres to be jailed. His escape is arranged by gangsters who want to kill him. First Ayres meets with Elliott, a kindly police captain who has tried for years to talk him into going straight. Later, in a rural hideout, surrounded by rival gangsters, Ayres nervelessly steps outside to be machine-gunned to death, remembering a line Elliott had often told him: "The best you can get is the worst of it." Somber, grim, and uncompromising, DOORWAY TO HELL was a milestone gangster movie which first showed the use of machine guns in gang wars (and the use of violin cases to carry them), the takeover of the gang, a battle for a warehouse full of booze, and the to-the-death rivalries of Prohibition gangs. At first Warner Bros. declined to give Ayres the crime czar role, executives arguing that his baby face would belie his gangster image. But Ayres overcame the objections and proved convincing. Cagney, of course, in one of his earliest film roles, steals every scene. Mathews became an overnight star at the whim of director Archie Mayo. In preliminary shots of extras, and still needing a leading lady, he literally pulled Mathews from the crowd and told her that she would be the female lead, an act that caused her to swoon. She picked herself up and raced off, looking for a script. Mayo's pace is furious and McGill's camera work is superb as he records underworld mayhem. To avoid censorship, only one man is shown being machine-gunned, other victims being mowed down in takes separating killers and victims. Yet the violence is unavoidable.

d, Archie Mayo; w, George Rosener (based on the play "A Handful of Clouds" by Rowland Brown); ph, Barney "Chick" McGill; m, Leo F. Forbstein; ed, Robert Crandall; makeup, Perc Westmore.

Crime Drama (PR:O MPAA:NR)

DORIAN GRAY*½ (1970, Ital./Brit./Ger./Liechtenstein) 93m Commonwealth United-Towers of London/AIP c (IL DIO CHIAMATO A DORIAN; DAS BILDNESS DES DORIAN GRAY; AKA: THE SECRET OF DORIAN GRAY)

Helmut Berger (Dorian Gray), Richard Todd (Basil Hallward), Herbert Lom (Lord Henry Wotten), Marie Liljedahl (Sybil Vane), Margaret Lee (Gwendolyn Wotten), Maria Rohm (Alice), Beryl Cunningham (Adrienne), Isa Miranda (Mrs. Ruxton), Eleonora Rossi Drago (Esther), Renato Romano (Alan), Stewart Black (James Vane), Francesco Tensi.

Tasteless remake of Oscar Wilde's novel has Berger, fresh from a dubious triumph in THE DAMNED, the thrill seeker who sells his soul to the devil for eternal youth, a portrait of himself aging instead. Wretched and disgusting, with only Lom's performance worthwhile. Producer Towers was arrested in 1980 and charged with running a high-class call-girl service whose clientele included politicians and U.N. diplomats. The 1945 version, PICTURE OF DORIAN GRAY, is far better than this import.

p, Harry Alan Towers; d, Massimo Dallamano; w, Dallamano, Marcello Coscia, Gunter Ebert (based on the novel The Picture of Dorian Gray, by Oscar Wilde); ph, Otello Spila (Movielab Color); m, Peppino DeLuca, Carlo Pes; ed, Nicholas Wentworth; art d, Maria Ambrosino.

Horror Cas. (PR:O MPAA:R)

DORM THAT DRIPPED BLOOD, THE* (1983) 84m New Image-Wescom/Obrow c

Laurine Lapinski, Stephen Sachs, David Snow, Pamela Holland.

A mad killer is stalking the halls of a dormitory knocking off his victims in a variety of clever ways, including an electric drill and a pressure cooker, all so he can be with the woman he loves from afar. When he finally gets next to her, she wants nothing to do with the creep, so he tosses her into the incinerator. Bloody and stupid, strictly for fans of splatter movies.

p, Jeffrey Obrow; d, Obrow, Stephen Carpenter; w, Obrow, Carpenter, Stacey Giachino; ph, Carpenter; m, Chris Young; ed, Obrow.

Horror Cas. (PR:O MPAA:R)

DOS COSMONAUTAS A LA FUERZA* (1967, Span./Ital.) 89m Aggata Films/IMA Films bw

Franco Franchi, Ciccio Ingrassia, Emilio Rodriguez, Monica Randal, Maria Silva, Linda Sini, Chiro Bermejo.

A pair of Soviet cosmonauts heading for the moon appear to be lost in space and so as not to lose face, the government sends up two more space jockeys who look just like the first two. When the second pair, who are to pretend they're the first cosmonauts, locate the first two, the government has some explaining to do. Supposed to be a satire, but that's what really got lost.

d, Lucio Fulci; w, Vittorio Metz, Jose Luis Dibildos, Amedeo Sollazzo; ph, Tino Santoni.

Science Fiction/Comedy (PR:A MPAA:NR)

DOSS HOUSE* (1933, Brit.) 53m Sound City/MGM bw

Frank Cellier (Editor), Arnold Bell (Reporter), Herbert Franklyn (Detective), Mark Daly (Shoeblack), Edgar Driver (Catsmeat Man), J. Hubert Leslie (Murderer), Wilson Coleman (Strangler), Robert MacLachlan (Doctor), Alec Harford, Ray Raymond, James Stadden, Cecil Clayton, Ernest Croxford.

Bell and Franklyn disguise themselves as tramps to search a run-down boarding house for an escaped criminal. An interesting and influential film, one of the first British talkies to deal with the problem of poor social conditions in a realistic, unflinching way. It propelled director Baxter to the ranks of the most important filmmakers in England in the 1930s.

p, Ivar Campbell; d, John Baxter; w, Herbert Ayres.

Crime (PR:A-C MPAA:NR)

DOT AND THE BUNNY½** (1983, Aus.) 80m Yoram Gross Film Studio c

Voices: Drew Forsythe, Barbara Frawley, Ron Haddrick, Anne Haddy, Ross Higgins, Robyn Moore.

The third DOT film which blends live action and animation. Dot is searching for Joey, a kangaroo, and so is the bunny, who wants to be a kangaroo, and is hoping he can take Joey's place. Their search leads them through the back bush of Australia, where they meet all types of creatures. An enjoyable children's film with a moral neatly stuck in. In the U.S., this film has been mostly distributed on cable and home video. Going from live-action sequences of animals that dissolve into the story's animation characters is creatively done.

p&d, Yoram Gross; w, John Palmer (based on a story by Gross); ph, John Shaw, Film Australia (live action), Jenny Ochse, Graham Sharp (animation); m, Bob Young; ed, Christopher Plowright; animation d, Athol Henry.

Animation Cas. (PR:AA MPAA:G)

DOUBLE, THE*½ (1963, Brit) 56m Merton Park Studios bw

Jeannette Sterke (Mary Winston), Alan MacNaughtan (John Cleeve), Robert Brown (Richard Harrison), Jane Griffiths (Jane Winston), Basil Henson (Derreck Alwyn), Anne Lawson (Sally Carter), Diane Clare (Selena Osmonde), Llewellyn Rees (Bradshaw), John Miller (Sir Harry Osmonde), Dorothea Rundle (Martha Bradshaw), Hamilton Dyce (Detective Inspector Ames), Henry McCarthy (Dr. Leighton), Tony Wall (Logan), Patrick Parnell (Cooper), Arlette Dobson (Karen), David Charlesworth (Charles), Thelma Holt (Marie), Brian McGrellis (Delivery Boy), Ron Eagleton (Porter), Derek Sumner (Policeman).

A muddled mystery with Sterke finding MacNaughtan paralyzed from the waist down and suffering from amnesia in Africa. She takes him back to England. MacNaughtan believes that he had killed his partner, Henson, in Africa. It turns out that he's still alive, and Sterke discovers that Henson has assumed MacNaughtan's identity to gain his wealth. When Henson realizes that his scheme has been revealed, he tries to kill MacNaughtan, but is killed himself.

p, Jack Greenwood; d, Lionel Harris; w, Lindsay Galloway, John Roddick (based on the novel by Edgar Wallace); ph, James Wilson; m, Bernard Ebbinghouse; ed, Edward Jarvis; art d, Peter Mullins.

Mystery (PR:A MPAA:NR)

DOUBLE AFFAIR, THE (SEE: SPY WITH MY FACE, THE, 1966)

DOUBLE AGENTS, THE (SEE: NIGHT ENCOUNTER, 1959, Fr.)

DOUBLE ALIBI** (1940) 60m UNIV bw

Wayne Morris (Stephen Wayne), Margaret Lindsay (Sue Carey), William Gargan (Walter Gifford), Roscoe Karns (Jeremiah Jenkins), Robert Emmett Keane (Chick Lester), James Burke (Captain Orr), William Pawley (Dan Kraley), Frank Mitchell (Lennie Nolan), Eddy Chandler (Patrolman Harrigan), Cliff Clark (Inspector Early), Robert Emmett O'Connor (Patrolman Delaney), Wade Boteler (Bartender), Mary Treen (Switchboard Operator).

Morris is accused of killing his estranged wife and his two accomplices from a heist years before. He isn't proven innocent until the final reel, when Police Captain Burke is revealed as the slayer. The story is fairly interesting if not examined too closely, and a number of capable character actors fill out the cast. Good studio B movie.

p, Ben Pivar; d, Philip Rosen; w, Harold Buchman, Roy Chanslor, Charles Grayson (based on the story "The Devil Is Yellow" by Frederick C. Davis); ph, Elwood Bredell; ed, Ted Kent.

Crime/Mystery (PR:A MPAA:NR)

DOUBLE-BARRELLED DETECTIVE STORY, THE**

(1965) 90m Saloon Productions bw

Jeff Siggins (Archie), Greta Thyssen (La Belle), Hurd Hatfield (Father), Jerome Raphel (Sherlock Holmes), Paul Benedict (Wells Fargo Ferguson), Severn Darden (H. S. Stevens), Ray Reinhardt (Judge Parker), Louis Waldon (Shadbelly Higgins), Robert Winston (Sheriff Fairfax), Ernie Austin (Fetlock Jones), Flora Elkins (Amelia), Byrne Piven (Bill Stone), Sudie Bond, George Bartenieff, Ronald Demko, Ned Fay, Marcia Saintz, James Walsh, Alexandra Stone.

Interesting and sometimes funny adaptation of a Mark Twain short story. Hatfield is a carpetbagger who marries the daughter of a prominent plantation owner in order to humiliate him. He mistreats his wife, but she stoically refuses to complain to her father. Finally, he ties her to a tree and lets bloodhounds tear off her clothes. The girl's father dies of embarrassment, and shortly thereafter she gives birth to a son who, judging by his sense of smell, may have a canine paternal progenitor. The son grows up into Siggins, who heads west on a mission to avenge his mother. Finally he sees his father killed by someone else. Good low-budget production, but Mekas has done much better.

p, David Stone; d,w&ed, Adolfas Mekas (based on a story by Mark Twain); ph, Graeme Ferguson, Karl Bissinger; m, Meyer Kupferman; cos, Bathsheba; ch, Leonara Hays; songs, title song sung by Pola Chapelle.

Western/Comedy (PR:A MPAA:NR)

DOUBLE BED, THE* (1965, Fr./Ital.) 120m Cineurop-Metheus/Dicifilm bw
(LE LIT A DEUX PLACES)

Frances Anglade (Wife), Margaret Lee (Carmela), Dominique Boschero (Colette), Sylva Koscina (Giulietta), Michel Serrault (Albert), Jacques Charon (Fiance), Darry Cowl (Visitor), Jean Richard (Father), Carla Calo (Mother).

Episodic comedy revolves around a sale of beds at a furniture store, and the stories of the people who buy them. One story concerns a hotelkeeper renting out his own room to two young men, one of whom is secretly seeing the landlord's daughter. Another episode deals with a frustrated psychiatrist whose wife refuses to go to bed with him; yet another with a couple who get their kicks out of the husband pretending to be dead in bed while the wife lures men up into the room and gets them to pay her before they flee in terror at the sight of the supposed corpse. None of the vignettes is particularly funny, and most of them seem to start and stop almost arbitrarily.

d, Jean Delannoy, Francois Dupont-Midy, Gianni Puccini; w, Alfredo Giannetti, Darry Cowl, Jean-Loup Dabadie (based on fables of Jean de La Fontaine); ph, Robert Lefebvre; ed, Henri Taverna.

Comedy (PR:C MPAA:NR)

DOUBLE BUNK* (1961, Brit.) 92m Bryanston/BL bw

Ian Carmichael (Jack Goddard), Janette Scott (Peggy Deeley), Liz Fraser (Sandra), Sidney James (Sid Randall), Dennis Price (Leonard Watson), Reginald Beckwith (Alfred Harper), Irene Handl (Mrs. Harper), Noel Purcell (O'Malley), Naunton Wayne (1st Conservancy Officer), Bill Shine (2nd Conservancy Officer), Michael Shepley (Granville-Carter), Miles Malleson (Reverend Thomas), Jacques Crey (French Official), Graham Stark (Flower Man), Gladys Henson (Mme. de Sola), Toby Perkins (Pukka Type), Gerald Campion (Charlie), John Harvey (Johnnie), Terry Scott (Policeman), Hedger Wallace (Policeman), Desmond Roberts (Freighter Captain), Peter Swanwick (Freighter Pilot), Tom Gill (Customs Officer), Willoughby Goddard (Possible Buyer), Marianne Stone (Buyer's Wife).

Unengaging comedy with Carmichael and Scott as newlyweds who take up residence in a leaky old houseboat. When Carmichael decides to move the boat to a new location, he makes a mess of river traffic, gets lost in a fog bank, and the next

morning, finds himself washed up on a French beach. The couple borrow some fuel from their landlord, whose yacht happens to be nearby, and he challenges them to a race back to London. On the way, though, the skipper of the yacht gets so drunk that he is unable to keep the boat in a straight line; Carmichael and company win easily. Not especially interesting.

p, George H. Brown; d&w, C.M. Pennington-Richards; ph, Stephen Dade; m, Stanley Black; ed, John D. Guthridge; art d, Maurice Carter; set d, Arthur Taksen; cos, Cynthia Tingey; m/l, Black, Jack Fishman, Michael Pratt.

Comedy (PR:A MPAA:NR)

DOUBLE CON, THE (SEE: TRICK BABY, 1973)

DOUBLE CONFESSION** (1953, Brit.) 80m Stratford/ABF-Pathe bw

Derek Farr (Jim Medway), Joan Hopkins (Ann Corday), Peter Lorre (Paynter), William Hartnell (Charlie Durham), Naunton Wayne (Inspector Tenby), Ronald Howard (Hilary Boscombe), Kathleen Harrison (Kate), Leslie Dwyer (Leonard), Edward Rigby (The Fisherman), George Woodbridge (Sgt. Sawnton), Henry Edwards (Man in the Shelter), Vida Hope (Madam Zilia), Esma Cannon (Madam Cleo), Mona Washbourne (Fussy Mother), Jennifer Cross (Fussy Mother's Child), Andrew Leigh (The Reserved Man), Fred Griffiths (The Spiv), Jane Griffiths (1st Girl), Hal Osmond (Gallery Attendant), Diana Connell (2nd Girl), Norman Astridge (Selby), Roy Plomley (Ticket Collector), Betty Nelson (Girl At Gallery), Sidney Vivian (Stall Attendant), Grace Denbigh Russell (Nosy Woman).

One of Lorre's worst performances was in this mediocre crime melodrama. When the body of his wife and another man are found at the bottom of a seaside cliff, Farr confronts his wife's lover (Hartnell) and tells him that he has killed the pair and that he is going to frame Hartnell for the crime. Hartnell dispatches henchman Lorre to kill Farr, but he fails. Finally it is revealed that the wife committed suicide, but that the other body had been pushed. Lorre tries to confess to the crime, then flees up to the roof. Hartnell goes to try to talk him down, but instead encourages Lorre to jump. This is the evidence of his guilt the police have been waiting for, and they step in to make the arrest. Lorre obviously was not the least bit interested in the film nor his part, and he took the role only for financial reasons.

p, Harry Reynolds; d, Ken Annakin; w, William Templeton, Ralph Keene (based on the novel All On A Summer's Day by John Garden) ph, Geoffrey Unsworth; m, Benjamin Frankel; ed, Carmen Beliaeff; art d, Bernard Robinson.

Crime/Mystery (PR:C MPAA:NR)

DOUBLE CRIME IN THE MAGINOT LINE*½

(1939, Fr.) 83m Tower bw

Victor Francen (Captain Bruchot), Vera Korene (Anna Bruchot), Jacques Baumer (Police Inspector Finois), Fernand Fabre (Commander d'Espinac), Vital (Lt. Le Guen), Henry Guisol (Lt. Capelle), Albert Weiss (Lt. Kuntz), Jacques Berlioz (Cdr. Malatre), Pierre Magnier (Colonel of the 2nd Bureau), Jacques Vitry (Magistrate), Spanelly (Detective Lennard), Maxime Fabert (Gunsmith).

The Maginot Line was an enormous testimonial to just how little France had learned from the carnage of the trenches in WW I. Instead of placing their emphasis on mobility, avoiding the static conditions of that war, the French decided that what was obviously needed was the biggest, deepest trench in the world, a string of interconnected fortifications, pillboxes, machine-gun nests, minefields, and anti-tank obstacles. Faced with this formidable array in 1940, the Germans simply drove their tanks around it, through Belgium, and decisively destroyed the combined French and British armies in less than two weeks. In this relic, the new commander of the Line is murdered by a burst of machine-gun fire, and suspicion falls on three young lieutenants, one of whom is a German spy. Quick-witted counter-intelligence men soon deduce the killer and pursue him to a pillbox less than 200 yards from the German border, but he is trapped and commits suicide rather than be captured. Providing the impressive backdrop for this less-than-impressive spy drama is probably the most useful thing the now-crumbling Maginot Line ever did. (In French; English subtitles.)

p&d, Felix Gandera; w, Gandera, Robert Bibal (based on a novel by Pierre Nord); ph, Nicholas Hayer; m, Jean Lenoir.

Spy Drama (PR:A MPAA:NR)

DOUBLE CROSS** (1941) 64m PRC bw

Kane Richmond (Jim), Pauline Moore (Ellen), Wynne Gibson (Fay), John Miljan (Nick), Richard Beach (Steve), Mary Gordon (Mrs. Murray), Robert Homans (Capt. Murray), William Halligan (Mayor), Frank C. Moran (Cookie), Heinie Conklin (Miggs), Daisy Ford (Nurse), Edward Keane (Police Commissioner), Walter Shumway (Sgt. Tucker), Ted Wray (Sgt. Rand), Jimmie Fox (Camera Shop Proprietor), Harry Harvey (Protective Agency Manager).

Richmond is a second-generation cop who pretends to get kicked off the force in order to infiltrate racketeer Miljan's operation. The action comes to a head when Richmond is assigned to drive a truck full of shotgun-toting hoodlums to a rendezvous where his police chief father is to be ambushed. Richmond manages to warn the cops, and machine-gun bullets shred the would-be assassins. Not a bad B thriller, with more violence than usual.

p, John G. Bachmann; d, Albert Kelley; w, Milton Raison, Ron Ferguson (based on a story by John A. Albert); ph, Arthur Martinelli.

Crime (PR:A MPAA:NR)

DOUBLE CROSS** (1956, Brit.) 71m Beaconsfield/BL bw

Donald Houston (Albert Pascoe), William Hartnell (Whiteway), Fay Compton (Alice Pascoe), Delphi Lawrence (Anna Krassin), Anton Diffring (Dmitri Krassin), Frank Lawton (Chief Constable), John Blythe (Fred Trewin), Allan Cuthbertson (Clifford), Bruce Gordon (Harry Simms), Raymond Francis (Inspector Harris), Ann Stephens

(Rose), Harry Towb, Gene Anderson, Robert Shaw, Bruce Gordon, Helena Pickard, Toby Perkins.

A salmon poacher along the Cornish coast realizes that the passengers who are paying him to ferry them across the English Channel are Soviet spies. He strands them and becomes a hero, but is almost prosecuted for poaching. Lightweight spy stuff.

p, Donald Taylor; d, Anthony Squire; w, Kem Bennett, Squire (based on the novel *The Queer Fish* by Bennett); ph, Kenneth Talbot.

Spy Drama/Thriller **(PR:A-C MPAA:NR)**

DOUBLE CROSS ROADS½** (1930) 59m FOX bw

Robert Ames *(David Harvey)*, Montagu Love *(Gene Dyke)*, Lila Lee *(Mary Carlyle)*, Ned Sparks *(Mappy Max)*, Thomas Jackson *(Deuce Wilson)*, George MacFarlane *(Warden)*, William V. Mong *(Caleb)*, Thomas Jefferson *(Caretaker)*, Charlotte Walker *(Mrs. Tilton)*, Edythe Chapman.

Interesting neglected crime drama has Ames a safecracker trying to go straight while former cellmate Love works on getting him to pull one more job. He arranges for Ames to stay at a remote farm, where he finds peace of mind and love with Lee, but his happiness is shattered when he learns that Lee and her seemingly kindly old grandmother are full-fledged members of the hold-up gang. The standard happy ending has the two reunited and dedicating their lives to going straight. A few slow spots and the lack of any names in the cast are all that keep this above-average melodrama from minor classic status.

d, Alfred Werker, George Middleton; w, George Brooks, Howard Estabrook (based on the novel *Yonder Grow the Daisies* by Willian Lipman); ph, Joseph August, Sol Halperin; ed, Jack Dennis.

Crime **(PR:A MPAA:NR)**

DOUBLE CROSSBONES** (1950) 75m UNIV c

Donald O'Connor *(Dave Crandall)*, Helena Carter *(Lady Sylvia Copeland)*, Will Geer *(Tom Botts)*, John Emery *(Governor Elden)*, Stanley Logan *(Lord Montrose)*, Kathryn Givney *(Lady Montrose)*, Hayden Rorke *(Malcolm Giles)*, Morgan Farley *(Caleb Nicholas)*, Hope Emerson *(Mistress Ann Bonney)*, Charles McGraw *(Capt. Ben Wickett)*, Alan Napier *(Capt. Kidd)*, Robert Barrat *(Henry Morgan)*, Louis Bacigalupi *(Blackbeard)*, Glenn Strange *(Capt. Ben Avery)*, Gregg Martell *(Isaac Wells)*, Jeff Chandler *(Narrator)*.

O'Connor is an apprentice shopkeeper in colonial Charlestown, a notorious pirate hideout. Through a series of accidents and cases of mistaken identity, he finds himself in command of a pirate brigantine and much feared. Most of his attention is taken by his attempts to free Carter, the governor's ward, from an arranged marriage. Decent musical comedy mostly carried by O'Connor's good-naturedness. Songs include: "Percy Had A Heart" and "Song of Adventure."

p, Leonard Goldstein; d, Charles T. Barton; w, Oscar Brodney; ph, Maury Gertsman (Technicolor); m, Frank Skinner; ed, Russell Schoengarth; art d, Bernard Herzbrun, Alexander Golitzen; m/l, Dan Shapiro, Lester Lee.

Musical/Comedy **(PR:AA MPAA:NR)**

DOUBLE DANGER** (1938) 61m RKO bw

Preston Foster *(Robert Crane)*, Whitney Bourne *(Carolyn Morgan)*, Samuel S. Hinds *(David Theron)*, Donald Meek *(Gordon Ainsley)*, Paul Guilfoyle *(Taylor)*, Cecil Kellaway *(Fentriss)*, June Johnson *(Babs Theron)*, Arthur Lake *(Roy West)*, Edythe Elliott *(Edith Theron)*, Harry Hayden *(Dr. Hilliard)*, Vivian Oakland *(Mrs. Cortlandt)*, Alec Craig (Gardener), Richard Bond *(Footman)*, William Corson, Frank Williams, Bill Donnelly.

Foster is another of those gentleman jewel thieves who have infested the screen since silent days. His cover is that of a mystery writer, and his rival for the priceless diamonds is lady jewel thief Bourne, who is at least as interested in making off with Foster as with the gems. Hinds and Meek are the police commissioner and jeweler who team up to catch the crooks. They fail, of course, and Foster and Bourne end up in each others' arms vowing to go straight. Pleasant drawing-room mystery played for laughs.

p, Maury Cohen; d, Lew Landers; w, Arthur T. Horman, J. Robert Bren (based on a story by Horman); ph, Frank Redmond; ed, Desmond Marquette.

Crime/Comedy **(PR:AA MPAA:NR)**

DOUBLE DATE** (1941) 59m UNIV bw

Edmund Lowe *(Roger)*, Una Merkel *(Elsie)*, Peggy Moran *(Penny)*, Rand Brooks *(Jerry)*, Tommy Kelly *(Hodges)*, Hattie Noel *(Lilac)*, Eddy Waller *(Truck Driver)*, William Ruhl *(Motorcycle Cop)*, Sam Flint *(Doctor)*, Pat O'Malley *(Policeman)*, Joey Ray *(Orchestra Leader)*, Charlie Smith *(Bud)*, Nell O'Day *(Mary)*, Elaine Morley *(Girl)*, Andrew Tombes *(Judge Perkins)*, Joe Downing *(Burglar)*, George Chandler *(Attendant)*, Frank Sully *(Hank)*.

Brooks and Moran, returning home from their respective boarding schools, are alarmed to find his father and her aunt (Lowe and Merkel) amorously involved. The two children team up to split the lovers but, after a long chase with some thieves, all four principals wind up in the clink. A kindly judge quickly marries Lowe and Merkel and the children accept the situation. Okay programmer.

p, Joseph G. Sanford; d, Glenn Tryon; w, Scott Darling, Erna Lazarus, Agnes Christine Johnston (based on an original idea by Darling, Lazarus); ph, John Boyle; ed, Otto Ludwig.

Comedy **(PR:AA MPAA:NR)**

DOUBLE DEAL** (1950) 64m Bel-Air Productions/RKO bw

Marie Windsor *(Terry)*, Richard Denning *(Buzz)*, Taylor Holmes *(Corpus)*, Fay Baker *(Lilli)*, James Griffith *(Karns)*, Carleton Young *(Reno)*, Tom Browne Henry *(Sheriff Morelli)*, Jim Hayward *(Mike)*, Richard Reeves *(Webber)*, Paul E. Burns.

Serviceable melodrama has Denning a struggling petroleum engineer who accepts a job from Young to bring in a well. When Young is killed, Windsor inherits the well, despite the opposition of Young's sister, Baker. Denning continues to work on the well and the murderer is eventually revealed as Holmes, thought to be a simple drunk up to that point. Low-budget programmer was made by Bel-Air productions on the condition that RKO buy the picture on completion.

p, James T. Vaughn; d, Abby Berlin; w, Lee Berman, Charles S. Belden (based on a story by Don McGuire), ph, Frank Redman; ed, Robert Swink; md, Constantin Bakaleinikoff; art d, Albert S. D'Agostino, Jack Okey.

Drama **(PR:A MPAA:NR)**

DOUBLE DECEPTION** (1963, Fr.) 101m Speve-Inter Telefilm/United Motion Picture Organization bw

Jacques Riberolles *(Peter)*, Alice Kessler *(Greta)*, Ellen Kessler *(Hildegarde)*, Jean Mercure *(Ludwig)*, Daniel Sorano *(Wladimir)*, Ginette Leclerc *(Odette)*.

Riberolles falls in love with Ellen Kessler, a circus illusionist, without realizing she has an identical twin, Alice Kessler. Their act is immensely popular because of their ability to fool the audience into thinking there is only one sister. To preserve their success, the girls sign a contract that keeps them apart in public. Alice becomes insanely jealous of Ellen's time with Riberolles. Alice is then killed by Riberolles' alcoholic and overly-possessive mother, though the murder is not publicized (again, in keeping with the illusion). Riberolles falls victim to this puzzling atmosphere and, in a blind rage, kills Ellen, the girl he really loves, thinking her to be Alice. An interesting idea which is inherently confusing no matter how skillfully directed.

p, Serge Friedman; w, Francois Boyer, Bernard Revon (based on a story by Pierre Boileau, Thomas Narcejac); ph, Christian Matras; m, George Van Parys; ed, Louisette Hautecoeur; art d, Jean d'Eaubonne.

Drama/Mystery **(PR:A-C MPAA:NR)**

DOUBLE DOOR* (1934) 75m PAR bw

Mary Morris *(Victoria Van Brett)*, Evelyn Venable *(Anne Darrow)*, Kent Taylor *(Rip Van Brett)*, Sir Guy Standing *(Mortimer Neff)*, Anne Revere *(Caroline Van Brett)*, Colin Tapley *(Dr. John Lucas)*, Virginia Howell *(Avery)*, Halliwell Hobbes *(Mr. Chase)*, Frank Dawson *(Telson)*, Helen Shipman *(Louise)*, *Leonard Carey (William)*, Ralph Remley *(Lambert)*, Burr Caruth *(Rev. Dr. Loring)*.

Spinster Morris lives in a Fifth Avenue mansion and doesn't want anyone coming into her family's life. Her brother, Taylor, marries Venable and Morris takes it upon herself to drive her insane. When that doesn't work, she locks the young lady in a vault to die, but her husband rescues her. The spinster accepts defeat and commits suicide. Heavily melodramatic with pretentious and one-dimensional acting.

p, E. Lloyd Shelton; d, Charles Vidor; w, Gladys Lehman, Jack Cunningham, Hermine Klepac (based on the play by Elizabeth McFadden); ph, Harry Fischbeck; ed, James Smith.

Drama **(PR:C-O MPAA:NR)**

DOUBLE DYNAMITE** (1951) 80m RKO bw (AKA: IT'S ONLY MONEY)

Frank Sinatra *(Johnny Dalton)*, Jane Russell *(Mildred "Mibs" Goodhug)*, Groucho Marx *(Emil J. Keck)*, Don McGuire *(Bob Pulsifer, Jr.)*, Howard Freeman *(R.B. Pulsifer, Sr.)*, Harry Hayden *(J.L. McKissack)*, Nestor Paiva *("Hot Horse" Harris)*, Lou Nova *(Max)*, Joe Devlin *(Frankie-Boy)* Frank Orth *(Mr. Kofer)*, William Edmunds *(Baganucci)*, Russ Thorson *(Tailman)*, Charles Coleman *(Santa Claus)*, Ida Moore *(Little Old Lady)*, Hal K. Dawson *(Mr. Hartman)*, George Chandler *(Messenger)*, Jean De Briac *(Maitre D')*, Benny Burt *(Waiter)*, Bill Snyder *(Wire Service Man)*, Bill Erwin, Charles Regan, Dick Gordon, Mike Lally, Jack Jahries, Gil Perkins, Jack Gargan *(Men)*, Claire De Brey *(Hatchet-faced Lady)*, Harry Kingston, Kermit Kegley *(Goons)*, Virgil Johnansen *(Santa Claus)*, William Bailey *(Bank Guard)*, Jack Chefe *(Chef)*, Al Murphy *(Waiter)*, Jim Nolan, Lee Phelps *(Detectives)*, Lillian West *(Hotel Maid)*, Dickie Derrel *(Boy)*, Charles Sullivan *(Sergeant)*, Harold Goodwin *(Lieutenant)*.

A terrific pool of talent got together to make this ho-hum movie and blame must be laid at the feet of Howard Hughes who oversaw the whole thing. Hughes never liked Sinatra and demoted him to third billing in the picture under Marx and Russell. Sinatra responded with a performance that was lackluster at best. Russell and Sinatra are lovers who work side by side in a bank as tellers. They don't have enough money to get married so their friend, Marx, a waiter in a local greasy spoon, suggests that Sinatra rob a bank. He's kidding, of course, but when Sinatra saves the life of Paiva, a bookie who was being beaten, the criminal responds by making a bet in Sinatra's name and the horse pays off $60 grand! He buys a new car and mink for Russell but then the bank finds $75 thousand missing. Sinatra is afraid to share his good fortune news with anyone lest they suspect he's embezzled the money. Meanwhile, Russell is accused because the shortage was found on her adding machine. Later it's learned that her machine is awry and spewing one error after another. So no money has disappeared and it's just a mechanical mistake. Sinatra can now tell everyone what's happened and he and Russell can be married. Other than the quips from Groucho, this had virtually no humor and must rank as one of the dullest movies in which he ever appeared. Sammy Cahn and Jule Styne penned "It's Only Money" and "Kisses and Tears" but the songs were about as exciting as the movie, which meant they weren't. Former boxer Lou Nova was funny in a small bit as Max, and McGuire, the lothario offspring of Freeman, the banker, went on to great success as an author and screenwriter (TOOTSIE and many others).

p, Irving Cummings, Jr.; d, Irving Cummings, Sr.; w, Melville Shavelson; Harry Crane (based on a story by Leo Rosten, and on a character created by Mannie Manheim); ph, Robert de Grasse; m, Leigh Harline; ed, Harry Marker; md,

Constantine Bakaleinikoff; art d, Albert S. D'Agostino, Field M. Gray; set d, Darrell Silvera, Harley Miller; m/l, Sammy Cahn, Jule Styne.

Comedy **(PR:A MPAA:NR)**

DOUBLE EVENT, THE* (1934, Brit.) 68m Triumph/PDC bw

Jane Baxter *(Evelyn Martingale)*, Ruth Taylor *(Aunt Laura)*, O.B. Clarence *(Rev. Martingale)*, Alexander Field *(Charlie Weir)*, Bernard Lee *(Dennison)*, Sebastian Smith *(Uncle James)*.

Baxter, the daughter of a gambling-addicted clergyman and supposedly an art student in London, is actually a bookie and runs the business until her fiance, Lee, also a gambler, breaks her. Depressing comedy with little to recommend it but a couple of decent supporting players.

p, d&w, Leslie Howard Gordon (based on a play by Sidney Blow, Douglas Hoare).

Comedy **(PR:A MPAA:NR)**

DOUBLE EXPOSURE** (1944) 63m PAR bw

Chester Morris *(Larry Burke)*, Nancy Kelly *(Pat Marvin)*, Phillip Terry *(Ben Scribner)*, Jane Farrar *(Dolores Tucker)*, Richard Gaines *(James R. Tarlock)*, Charles Arnt *(Sonny Tucker)*, Claire Rochelle *(Smitty)*, Roma Aldrich *(Mavis)*.

Kelly comes from the Midwest to work on Morris' photo magazine, and he begins to romance her. When Kelly takes some exclusive photos, she becomes a suspect in a murder. Morris finds the real killer and gets his sweetheart out of jail.

p, William H. Pine, William C. Thomas; w, Winston Miller, Maxwell Shane (based on a story by Ralph Graves, Miller); ph, Fred Jackman, Jr.; m, Alex Laszlo; ed, Henry Adams; art d, F. Paul Sylos.

Drama **(PR:A MPAA:NR)**

DOUBLE EXPOSURE*½ (1954, Brit.) 63m Kenilworth-Mid-Century/GFD bw

John Bentley *(Pete Fleming)*, Rona Anderson *(Barbara Leyland)*, Garry Marsh *(Daniel Beaumont)*, Alexander Gauge *(Denis Clayton)*, Ingeborg Wells *(Maxine Goldner)*, John Horsley *(Lamport)*, Rick Rydon *(Trixon)*, Frank Forsyth *(Inspector Grayle)*, Sally Newton, Alan Robinson.

A detective proves that a bookie staged the suicide of a prominent businessman's wife, thus saving the life of a woman photographer who snapped some pictures of the house where the woman was killed. Routine British second feature that has to force a lot of air into the story to make it last 63 minutes.

p, Robert Baker, Monty Berman; d&w, John Gilling (based on a story by John Roddick); ph, Berman.

Crime **(PR:A-C MPAA:NR)**

DOUBLE EXPOSURE zero (1982) 95m Greyhill-Silverstone/Crown c

Michael Callan, Joanna Pettet, James Stacy, Pamela Hensley, Cleavon Little, Seymour Cassel, Misty Rowe, Joey Forman, Terry Moore, R. Tessier.

A hideously empty mystery about a mad killer and a photographer who has violent nightmares. It turns out that the killer is a friend of the photographer's and is compelled to act out the violence. Its all pretty predictable and should probably have never been made at all.

p,d&w, William Byron Hillman; ph, R. M. Stringer; m, Jack Goga; prod d, Ron Talsky; art d, Winston Pruett; makeup, Chris Brice, Sally Childs.

Mystery/Crime **Cas.** **(PR:O MPAA:NR)**

DOUBLE EXPOSURES*½ (1937, Brit.) 67m Triangle/PAR bw (AKA: ALIBI BREAKER)

Julien Mitchell *(Hector Rodman)*, Ruby Miller *(Mrs. Rodman)*, Basil Langton *(Peter Bradfield)*, Mavis Clare *(Jill Rodman)*, Brian Buchel *(Geoffrey Cranswick)*, George Astley *(George Rodman)*, Frank Birch *(Kempton)*, Ivor Barnard *(Mather)*, Fred Withers, Dennis Cowles.

A bumbling reporter, fired from his job, snaps a photo that accidentally proves that a shady lawyer was shot and killed by an industrialist's secretary. Negligible British effort.

p, George King; d, John Paddy Carstairs; w, Gerald Elliott.

Crime **(PR:A MPAA:NR)**

DOUBLE HARNESS*** (1933) 70m RKO bw

Ann Harding *(Joan Colby)*, William Powell *(John Fletcher)*, Henry Stephenson *(Col. Colby)*, Lilian Bond *(Monica Page)*, George Meeker *(Dennis)*, Lucile Browne *(Valerie Colby)*, Reginald Owen *(Butler)*, Kay Hammond *(Eleanor Weston)*, Leigh Allen *(Leonard Weston)*, Hugh Huntley *(Farley Drake)*, Wallis Clark *(Postmaster General)*, Fredric Santley *(Shop Owner)*.

Based on a trivial play that barely had a run in the Big Apple, this stands out as a sophisticated comedy that reflects the period accurately and shows off the stars to best advantage. Harding is mad for Powell, but he's a Casanova with no intentions of uniting for any more than one evening. They are having an affair and she plans on her father catching them *en flagrante delicto* in order to trap Powell into giving up his other amours. In the hands of different creators, this might have become a tawdry story but Cromwell's direction of Murfin's screenplay is such that we are presented with a woman who is not duplicitous. She really does love the wealthy Powell and is eager to keep him from making a fool of himself with various golddiggers. Her approach is totally forthright and her methods are quite modern as she seeks to convince Powell that she is the one person for him. Naturally, it works. Sharp dialog and no-nonsense direction highlight the performances. Powell had never been so urbane and it led the way to many more roles in that vein. Harding, born Dorothy Walton Gatley in 1901, did her first films in 1929 and continued acting through the mid-1950s but never became an enormous superstar, mainly due to the wrong selection of scripts by whomever guided her career. Reginald Owen does his usual excellent job in one of the roles he's almost patented: the Jeevesian butler.

ex p, Merian C. Cooper; d, John Cromwell; w, Jane Murfin (based on the play by Edward Poor Montgomery); ph, J. Roy Hunt; ed. George Nicholls, Jr.; md, Max Steiner; art d, Van Nest Polglase, Charles Kerk.

Comedy **(PR:A-C MPAA:NR)**

DOUBLE INDEMNITY***** (1944) 106m PAR bw

Fred MacMurray *(Walter Neff)*, Barbara Stanwyck *(Phyllis Dietrichson)*, Edward G. Robinson *(Barton Keyes)*, Porter Hall *(Mr. Jackson)*, Jean Heather *(Lola Dietrichson)*, Tom Powers *(Mr. Dietrichson)*, Byron Barr *(Nino Zachette)*, Richard Gaines *(Mr. Norton)*, Fortunio Bonanova *(Sam Gorlopis)*, John Philliber *(Joe Pete)*, Bess Flowers *(Norton's Secretary)*, Kernan Cripps *(Redcap)*, Oscar Smith *(Pullman Porter)*, Betty Farrington *(Nettie, the Maid)*, Edmund Cobb *(Train Conductor)*, Floyd Schackelford, James Adamson *(Pullman Porters)*, Sam McDaniel *(Garage Attendant)*, Judith Gibson *(Pacific All-Risk Telephone Operator)*, Clarence Muse *(Black Man)*, Miriam Franklin *(Keyes' Secretary)*, George Magrill. Not shown in the final release print: William O'Leary *(Chaplain)*, Edward Hearn *(Warden's Secretary)*, Lee Shumway *(Door Guard)*, Boyd Irwin *(First Doctor)*, George Melford *(Second Doctor)*, Alan Bridge *(Execution Chamber Guard)*.

Based on the notorious Snyder-Gray case of 1927, DOUBLE INDEMNITY is a starkly realistic *film noir* that is truly remarkable on all levels—performance, script, direction—a dark masterpiece of murder. The movie opens with a car weaving through dim Los Angeles streets. MacMurray, bleeding from a serious bullet wound, staggers from the car and into his office building. He lets himself into Robinson's office, where he slumps in a chair and begins to dictate the flashback story. He is an insurance salesman seduced by vamp Stanwyck (wearing an atrocious blonde wig for the part), who later convinces MacMurray to fraudulently write a double-indemnity accidental death policy on her husband, Powers. Bit by bit, Stanwyck puts her evil scheme into action, enlisting MacMurray as her accomplice in murdering her husband, making it appear that Powers has accidentally gone to his death, defrauding the insurance firm for which MacMurray works out of enormous funds. Powers has a routine accident, which causes his leg to be put in a cast. The scheming pair then murder the man and drive to a train station where MacMurray, impersonating Powers, cast and all, boards a train. He goes to the rear platform where he momentarily encounters Hall. When Hall leaves the platform, MacMurray jumps off at a prearranged spot. There, Stanwyck is waiting for him with Powers' body, which is placed on the railroad tracks. It's a simple case of accidental death. Powers has fallen from the train and been killed by striking his head. Yet claims adjuster Robinson, a suspicious trouble-shooter for the insurance company, believes Stanwyck has somehow murdered her husband and tells MacMurray so. He stalls settlement while he accumulates evidence against her. MacMurray, viewing the investigation from inside, grows increasingly alarmed. The shrewd Robinson finally pieces it all together, but blames Stanwyck and her young lover, Barr, ostensibly Heather's paramour whom Stanwyck has stolen. Heather, who is Powers' daughter, earlier related to MacMurray how Stanwyck, as a nurse, murdered her ailing mother to marry her father. Before Robinson can place him in the scheme MacMurray goes to Stanwyck to kill her, blaming her death on Barr, the lover. But she is as deceitful and insidious as he. Stanwyck greets her lover with a pistol hidden beneath the pillow of her chair. When MacMurray tells her that it's all over, that she is going to face execution for killing Powers, she shoots him. He comes close to her but she can't shoot again. She's truly in love with him. MacMurray takes the gun from her and shoots her dead, then goes outside where he meets Barr and sends him on his way, telling him to call Heather. As he finishes his tale at the Dictaphone machine, Robinson comes into his office, hearing the confession. MacMurray asks him, for the sake of their friendship, to delay calling the police "until I can make the border." Robinson squints at him: "The border? You won't make the elevator, Walter." MacMurray nevertheless gives it a try and collapses at the entrance. Robinson calls police and kneels next to the dying MacMurray, lighting his cigarette, which he puffs once before dying. (In the original film, MacMurray is shown entering the gas chamber at San Quentin with Robinson witnessing his death, but this was thought to be too grim for audiences and was cut after the premiere showing.) Wilder's typically passionless direction fits beautifully with this sinister story. James M. Cain's tale was further enhanced by being scripted by the great crime writer Raymond Chandler. Everything about this masterpiece of crime is cold as space. Stanwyck, from her blonde wig to her chic ensembles, is an iceberg using men for her own vile purposes. MacMurray is a sharper whose love for her extends just as far as his own safety will afford and he, too, is without empathy. Even the dogged investigator Robinson is dehumanized by his job and is nothing more than a corporate bloodhound. The cold analysis of murder is relentlessly pursued in this astonishing chiller which gives no quarter to the viewer and asks only for the attention it deserves. At first Wilder tried to interest Alan Ladd, then George Raft in the role of the corrupt insurance salesman. As the brilliant director told Raft the story, the actor constantly asked "Where's the lapel?" At the end of the discussion, Raft shrugged and said, "No lapel," refusing the role. Wilder asked Raft what "lapel" meant and Raft explained that "at a certain moment you turn the hero's lapel and it turns out that he's an FBI man or a policeman or someone who works for the government—a good guy really." Then Wilder hit on the idea of using MacMurray, but getting him to play to role was another matter, one where he would have to turn around MacMurray's screen image of a light-hearted good guy to one of evil. "Look," MacMurray told Wilder when he was approached for the role, "I'm a saxophone player. I do little comedies with Carole Lombard." According to Wilder (in an interview with Ivan Moffat), he told MacMurray: "You've got to take this big step." He did, and later looked back on the part as his favorite. Chandler worked on the script with Wilder: this was his first studio chore. He insisted upon his arrival at the studio that he receive a flat $1,000 and was surprised when Wilder told him that he would get $750 *a week*. "Then it only goes two or three weeks?" he asked. "No, fourteen weeks," answered Wilder. Chandler didn't like collaboration with

Wilder, having to sit in a little office on the fourth floor of the Paramount studio and listen to the director's thick German accent while supposedly writing down his bursts of dialog and story line on yellow legal pads. Chandler, a reformed alcoholic, also resented Wilder's drinking, according to Wilder, and the director's many sexual encounters with Paramount starlets. Angered, Chandler finally did not show up at the studio to work on the script, sending executives a letter of complaint about Wilder. Chandler carped that Wilder was rude, drinking, spent a great deal of time on the phone with girls (clocking him at one spell for twelve minutes on the phone), and had once ordered him to pull down the Venetian blinds in the office without saying "Please." Wilder called Chandler into the office and apologized, promising never again to stay on the phone, drink in the office, or chase girls during working hours. Chandler would say to his death that his most miserable writing chore was having to work with Billy Wilder but, according to the director: "However, he said that all he ever knew about pictures was what he had learned from me." The tough, smart dialog peppering the script was not learned from Wilder: the best of it is Chandler's, the hard-boiled cynical style that made Walter and Phyllis unforgettable. Typical is their loveless farewell. With the popular tune "Tangerine" ironically playing in the background, MacMurray tells Stanwyck that he is breaking it off with her, that he has fixed it for her to take the blame for Powers' murder after she is found dead, and that Barr will then take the blame for killing her. She gives him that famous Stanwyck sneer and says: "We're both rotten." MacMurray shoots back: "Yeah, only you're a little more rotten." Chandler also provided the atmospheric background to the seamy side of Los Angeles, the locale he used so effectively in his wonderful Philip Marlowe tales. But technically, Wilder handled all the rest, a masterful production where his direction was almost flawless. One little item, unseen and unnoticed by critics, is in technical error; nothing for the layman, but a man of Wilder's picky ways should have caught it. It occurs in the scene where Robinson is leaving MacMurray's apartment and Stanwyck is outside in the hall. The door is opened outward into the hall, so that, naturally, Stanwyck can jump behind it to hide, the only place technically available. This, of course, was incorrect in that fire regulations (even in 1944, at the time of the film) would have demanded that the door open inward, not to mention the stupidity of having the door hinges on the outside in the hall, which would have made it child's play for any burglar to remove the door and enter at will. Yet the film plays so well and Wilder's direction is so taut that such errors are but flyspecks on a memorable mural of murder and ironic retribution. All of the cast members play their parts to the hilt, Heather replacing Mona Freeman at the last moment. Stanwyck received an Oscar nomination but lost out to Ingrid Bergman for GASLIGHT. Wilder was also nominated for Best Director, as was Seitz's superb cinematography and Rozsa's haunting score. It was the Hays Office that insisted MacMurray's trial and execution, a total of twenty minutes, be cut (the last, Wilder insists, is one of the two greatest scenes he ever directed, seen once and still locked away in Paramount's vaults). The official censor labelled the film "a blueprint for murder," but author Cain loved the production, and it certainly equals his other hard-hitting crime dramas turned to film, MILDRED PIERCE and THE POSTMAN ALWAYS RINGS TWICE. DOUBLE INDEMNITY was remade twice for TV, once in 1954 with Frank Lovejoy as Walter, Laraine Day as Phyllis, and Ray Collins as Keyes, and in 1973 with Samantha Eggar as Phyllis, Richard Crenna as Walter, and Lee J. Cobb as Keyes. Both efforts failed miserably to capture the flavor and talent of the original, just as the remake of THE POSTMAN ALWAYS RINGS TWICE proved to be a repugnant disaster.

p, Joseph Sistrom; d, Billy Wilder; w, Raymond Chandler, Wilder (based on a short story in the book *Three of A Kind* by James M. Cain); ph, John F. Seitz; process photography, Farciot Edouart; m, Miklos Rozsa, with Symphony in D minor by Cesar Franck; ed, Doane Harrison; art d, Hans Dreier, Hal Pereira; set d, Bertram Granger; cos, Edith Head; makeup, Wally Westmore.

Crime Drama (PR:C MPAA:NR)

DOUBLE JEOPARDY* (1955) 70m REP bw

Rod Cameron, Gale Robbins, Allison Hayes, Jack Kelly.

Cameron, a wealthy real estate agent, is accused of killing a blackmailer and devotes his energies to proving his innocence. An ineffectual melodrama which helps wear out one of Hollywood's most over-used plots.

d, R.G. Springsteen; w, Don Martin; ph, John L. Russell, Jr.; ed, Cliff Bell; md, R. Dale Butts; art d, Carroll Clark.

Drama Crime (PR:A MPAA:NR)

DOUBLE LIFE, A***** (1947) 103m Kanin Productions/UNIV bw

Ronald Colman *(Anthony John)*, Signe Hasso *(Brita)*, Edmond O'Brien *(Bill Friend)*, Shelley Winters *(Pat Kroll)*, Ray Collins *(Victor Donlan)*, Phillip Loeb *(Max Lasker)*, Millard Mitchell *(Al Cooley)*, Joe Sawyer *(Pete Bonner)*, Charles LaTorre *(Stellini)*, Whit Bissel *(Dr. Stauffer)*, John Drew Colt *(Stage Manager)*, Peter Thompson *(Assistant Stage Manager)*, Elizabeth Dunne *(Gladys)*, Alan Edmiston *(Rex)*, Art Smith, Sid Tomack *(Wigmakers)*, Wilton Graff *(Dr. Mervin)*, Harlan Briggs *(Oscar Bernard)*, Claire Carleton *(Waitress)*, Betsy Blair, Janet Warren, Marjorie Woodworth *(Girls in Wig Shop)*, Guy Bates Post, Leslie Denison, David Bond, Virginia Patton, Thayer Roberts, Percival Vivian, Boyd Irwin, Fay Kanin, Frederick Worlock, Arthur Gould-Porter *("Othello" Sequence)*, Elliot Reid, Georgia Caine, Mary Young, Percival Vivian *("A Gentleman's Gentleman" Sequence)*, Curt Conway *(Reporter)*, Paddy Chayefsky *(Photographer)*, Nina Gilbert *(Woman)*, John Derek *(Police Stenographer)*, Buddy Roosevelt *(Fingerprint Man)*, Fred Hoose *(Laughing Man)*, Bruce Riley, Wayne Treadway *(Men at Party)*, Pete Sosso *(Tailor)*, Mary Worth *(Woman in Audience)*, Robert E. Keane *(2nd Photographer)*, Kay Lavelle *(Large Woman)*, Sarah Selby *(Anna)*, Alexander Clark *(Barry)*, Harry Bannister *(2nd Actor)*, Joann Dolan *(Ellen)*, Joyce Matthews *(Janet)*, Harry Oldridge, Nick Dennis, Barry Macollum, Frank Richards *(Stagehands)*, Janet Manson, Augusta Roeland *(Girls in Lobby)*, Angela Clarke *(Lucy)*, Russ Conway, Reginald Billado *(Reporters)*, Fernanda Eliscu *(Landlady)*, Joe Bernard *(Husband)*, Charles Jordan *(Bartender)*, Walter McGrail *(Steve)*, Joey Ray *(Boyer)*, Hazel Keener, Ethyl May Halls, Maue Fealy *(Women)*, Jameson Shade, Harry Hays Morgan, Cedric Stevens, George Sherwood *(Guests)*, Don McGill *(Man at Party)*, Carl Milletaire *(Customer)*, Hal Melone *(Head Usher)*, George Manning *(Usher)*, William N. Bailey, Elmo Lincoln *(Detectives)*, Ed Wragge *(Actor)*, Phil MacKenzie *(Police Photographer)*, Howard Mitchell *(Tailor)*, Watson Downs *(Bootmaker)*, Albert Pollet *(Costume Designer)*, Laura Kasley Brooks *(Dowager)*, Countess Elektra Rozanska, Beatrice Gray, Katharine Marlowe, Yvette Reynard, Clare Alden, Doretta Johnson, Diane Lee Stewart, John Morgan, Mike Stokey, Leader De Cordova, George Douglas, James F. Cade, Jerry Salvail *(Audience)*.

A great film from beginning to end, A DOUBLE LIFE depicts the schizoid personality of a gifted stage actor, Colman, whose despair and murderous moods come from the lead role he portrays in "Othello." Colman is a much respected gentleman actor who specializes in classical drama. His courtly manners and winning charm endear him to one and all, even his ex-wife, Hasso, who loves him but fears living with him should his cruel streak once again take over his otherwise even personality. Winters, a buxom, steaming waitress, is attracted to Colman but soon learns that he is capable of violence. He loses all touch with reality, and, believing he is actually the terrible Moor he is portraying on stage, he strangles Winters and returns to his apartment, blanking out the hideous act. O'Brien, an enterprising publicity agent for the play, picks up on the strangulation and tries to link the murder with the play to entice audiences. This blatant sensationalism causes Colman to explode; he attacks O'Brien, who now believes he is mad. O'Brien sets up Colman for the police, arranging for a waitress who is almost Winters' twin to wait on him in a restaurant. Her appearance so alarms the actor that police are convinced he is the killer they seek. Detectives decide to arrest him following the final performance of "Othello." The actor realizes he is exposed; during the play he so becomes his role that he almost strangles Hasso, but manages to pull back to reality to sink a dagger into his own chest, dying in the wings. Colman's performance is riveting, and deservedly won an Oscar, as well as universal applause from critics and public alike. His genteel manners and mellifluous voice all the more readily shocked audiences as they watched him turn into a lethal lunatic, a transformation that is simply amazing to witness. He is a man obsessed, one who can no longer differentiate between his theatrical and everyday personalities. Colman is mesmerizing, brilliant, and even horrific in his role. Kanin and Gordon's script is both literate and packed with suspense, interweaving the dialog of classical theater and that of the street. Cukor's direction is as properly mannered and carefully constructed as is the script, and he draws the complex portrayal out of Colman like the unraveling of a long black bolt of cloth, "from the inside out," as the actor described it. This was Winters' first film break after stage appearances and it established her as a film star. Harry Cohn, head of Columbia Studios, originally bought the script for A DOUBLE LIFE years earlier but later reneged, refusing to pay for it or produce it, calling it "a depressing thing." Kanin was so angry that he vowed never to talk to Cohn again. He would take his vengeance on a literary level, using Cohn as the role model for the brutish Broderick Crawford part in BORN YESTERDAY (which Columbia did produce). Said Colman of his magnificent performance in A DOUBLE LIFE: "It was the most satisfying role I ever had, though there were others I found fulfilling. It tested my total range, and all my resources. And it came at a time in my career when I needed a recharging of my creativity."

p, Michael Kanin; d, George Cukor; w, Ruth Gordon, Garson Kanin (based on the play "Othello" by William Shakespeare); ph, Milton Krasner, special ph, David S. Horsley; m, Miklos Rozsa; ed, Robert Parrish; prod d, Harry Horner; art d, Bernard Herzbrun, Harvey Gillett; set d, Russell A. Gausman, John Austin; cos, Yvonne Wood, Travis Banton; makeup, Bud Westmore; adv on "Othello" sequences, Walter Hampden.

Crime Drama Cas. (PR:C-O MPAA:NR)

DOUBLE MAN, THE** (1967) 105m WB c

Yul Brynner *(Dan Slater/Kalmar)*, Britt Ekland *(Gina)*, Clive Revill *(Frank Wheatly)*, Anton Diffring *(Col. Berthold)*, Moira Lister *(Mrs. Carrington)*, Lloyd Nolan *(Edwards)*, George Mikell *(Max)*, Brandon Brady *(Gregori)*, Julia Arnall *(Anna)*, David Bauer *(Miller)*, Ronald Radd *(General)*, Kenneth J. Warren *(Police Chief)*, David Healy *(Halstead)*, Carl Jaffe *(Police Surgeon)*, Douglas Muir *(Wilfred)*, Frederick Schiller *(Ticket Seller)*, Ernst Walder *(Frischauer)*, Franklin J. Schaffner *(Man at Station)*, Bee Duffell *(Woman on Train)*, John G. Heller *(Bartender)*.

Brynner, a CIA agent, goes to the Austrian Alps to investigate the mysterious death of his son. He's trailed by enemy agents and discovers that he has a double (through plastic surgery) who the Soviets plan to plant in Washington in his place. Only a fair espionage exercise.

p, Hal E. Chester; d, Franklin J. Schaffner; w, Frank Tarloff, Alfred Hayes (based on the novel *Legacy Of A Spy* by Henry S. Maxfield); ph, Denys Coop; (Technicolor); m, Ernie Freeman; ed, Richard Best; art d, Arthur Lawson; set d, David Bill; cos, Christian Dior, Courtney Elliott; makeup, Richard Mills.

Spy Drama (PR:C MPAA:NR)

THE DOUBLE McGUFFIN** (1979) 101m Mulberry Square c

Ernest Borgnine *(Firat)*, George Kennedy *(Chief Talasek)*, Elke Sommer *(Prime Minister Kura)*, Ed "Too Tall" Jones *(Assassin No. 1)*, Lyle Alzado *(Assassin No. 2)*, Rod Browning *(Moras)*, Dion Pride *(Specks)*, Lisa Whelchel *(Jody)*, Jeff Nicholson *(Billy Ray)*, Michael Gerard *(Arthur)*, Greg Hodges *(Homer)*, Vinnie Spano *(Foster)*, Orson Welles *(Narrator)*.

Mulberry Square and Joe Camp produced the Bengi movies, and this was their second non-canine picture. A group of kids in a small southern town realize that Borgnine is planning to kill a Middle East prime minister (Sommer). The police don't believe them, so they save the day themselves, stopping the assassination attempt during a school assembly. Outlandish plot, but the quick-paced action will keep the kids watching.The omniscient voice of Orson Welles starts off the picture explaining the term "McGuffin"—a meaningless word used by Alfred Hitchcock to represent whatever the film's characters were searching for. Hitchcock related the term to a story about a man traveling with a box. A passerby asked what was in the box and was told it contained a "McGuffin." He explained that McGuffins were used to shoot lions in Scotland. The passerby, obviously skeptical, retorted by reminding the man that there were no lions in Scotland. "Then," the man answered pointing to the box, "that is not a McGuffin."

p/d&w, Joe Camp, (based on a story by Camp and Richard Baker); ph, Don Reddy; m, Euel Box; ed, Leon Seith; prod d, Harland Wright; art d, Ed Richardson.

Mystery   **Cas.**   **(PR:A MPAA:PG)**

DOUBLE NEGATIVE*½   (1980, Can.) 96m Quadrant c

Michael Sarrazin (Michael Taylor), Susan Clark (Paula West), Anthony Perkins (Lawrence Miles), Howard Duff (Lester Harlen), Kate Reid (Mrs. Swanscott), Al Waxman (D'Allasandro), Elizabeth Shepherd (Frances), Kenneth Welsh (Dr. Webber), Rawlins (Maury Chaikin).

Finding his wife raped and murdered on his return from the Mideast, when photojournalist Sarrazin was going to ask her for a divorce, Sarrazin winds up in a mental institution from the stress of his assignment and the shock of finding her dead. His present girl friend, Clark, gets him out and he begins a search for the killer. Perkins, his wife's lover, is a prime suspect, and it appears that he killed her at the bidding of Clark, because he is blackmailing her. Actually, Sarrazin killed his wife when he found her in bed with Perkins and has been blocking it from his memory, and Clark is paying off Perkins to keep quiet about it. A muddled film that cannot untie the tangled skein of this thriller.

p, Jerome Simon; d, George Bloomfield; w, Thomas Hedley, Jr., Charles Dennis, Janis Allen (based on the novel The Three Roads by Ross MacDonald); ph, Rene Verzier; m, Paul Hoffert; ed, George Appleby; art d, Mary Kerr.

Mystery/Thriller   **(PR:O MPAA:NR)**

DOUBLE NICKELS*½   (1977) 89m Smokey c

Jack Vacek (Smokey), Ed Abrams (Ed), Patrice Schubert (Jordan), George Cole (George), Heidi Schubert (Tami), Mick Brennan, Michael Cole, Les Taylor.

Vacek and Abrams are highway patrolmen who also work as auto repossessors on the side. They discover that their boss, Cole, is really having them steal cars, and that's when the car chases begin. Plot development is pushed aside so that a couple more cars can crash and burn.

p&d, Jack Vacek; w, Vacek, Patrice Schubert; ph, Tony Syslo, Ron Sawade (Eastmancolor); ed, Vacek, Mick Brennan, Sawade, Syslo.

Action/Drama   **(PR:C MPAA:PG)**

DOUBLE OR NOTHING**   (1937) 90m PAR bw

Bing Crosby (Lefty Boylan), Martha Raye (Liza Lou Lane), Andy Devine (Half-Pint), Mary Carlisle (Vicki Clark), William Frawley (Peterson), Benny Baker (Sailor), Samuel S. Hinds (Jonathan Clark), William Henry (Egbert), Fay Holden (Martha Sewell Clark), Bert Hanlon (Praxitales), Gilbert Emery (Mr. Mitchell), Walter Kingsford (Mr. Lobson), John Gallaudet (Rutherford), Harry Barris (Orchestra Conductor), Jimmy Nataro (Dancing Cop), Olaf Hytten (Eustace), Arthur Housman, Charles Irwin (Drunks), Herbert Ashley (Doorman), Rolfe Sedan (Headwaiter), Jack Pennick (Taxi Driver), Stanley Andrews (Police Lt.), Alphonse Berg, Tex Morrissay, Frances Faye, Ames and Arno, Ed Rickard, Steve and Andre Calgary (Specialties).

The will of an eccentric millionaire calls for four people to receive $5,000 each, and the first one to double that by legitimate means gets $1 million. The dead man wants to prove to his brother that there are honest people in the world. The four lucky souls are Crosby, Raye, Devine, and Frawley, and the dead man's relatives are out to foil all their attempts to get the money. Singer Crosby wins by opening up a nightclub. A lightweight musical comedy with a bare plot and plenty of singing. Songs: "It's On, It's Off" (Al Siegel, Sam Coslow), "Double or Nothing" (Johnny Burke, Victor Young), "Don't Look Now" (Irving Kahal, Johnny Greene), "Listen My Children," "Smarty" (Ralph Freed, Burton Lane), "All You Want to Do Is Dance," "The Moon Got In My Eyes," "It's the Natural Thing to Do" (Burke, Arthur Johnston), "After You" (Siegel, Coslow).

p, Benjamin Glazer; d, Theodore Reed; w, Charles Lederer, Erwin Gelsey, John C. Moffitt, Duke Atterberry (based on a story by M. Coates Webster); ph, Karl Struss; ed, Edward Dmytryk; md, Boris Morros; ch, LeRoy Prinz; m/l, Al Siegel and Sam Coslow, Johnny Burke and Victor Young, Irving Kahal and Johnny Greene, Burke and Arthur Johnston, Ralph Freed and Burton Lane.

Musical/Comedy   **(PR:A MPAA:NR)**

DOUBLE OR QUITS**   (1938, Brit.) 72m WB bw

Patricia Medina (Caroline), Frank Fox (Bill Brooks/Scotty Tucker), Hal Walters (Alf), Ian Fleming (Sir Frederick Beal), Gordon McLeod (School), Jack Raine (Roland), Philip Ray (Hepworth), Charles Paton (Mr. Binks), Mai Bacon (Mrs. Binks), Michael Hogarth, Scott Harold, Sam Blake, W. Edward Hodge.

Fox is a newspaper reporter who is the spitting image of a notorious thief. Both men end up on a transatlantic liner and reporter Fox is accused of thief Fox's misdeeds. Reporter Fox with the help of Medina, captures the crook after a murder and some other shipboard capers. Outdated fluff.

p, Irving Asher; d, Roy William Neill; w, Michael Barringer, ph, Basil Emmott.

Crime Thriller   **(PR:A MPAA:NR)**

DOUBLE STOP**   (1968) 100m World Entertainment c

Jeremiah Sullivan (Mike Westfall), Mimi Torchin (Katherine Westfall), Anthony Walsh (Don Streggor), Billy Kurtz (Pablo Westfall), Barry Gordon (1st Art Student), Gino Arditto (Wilbur), Patti Fairchild (Susan).

A concert musician, Sullivan, pulls his son out of the public school when he finds out the school is in a black neighborhood. Putting the child in a private school causes tension between Sullivan and his liberal-minded wife. His attitudes only change when he finds out that his best friend, who also is a musician, went to the same public school. An independent film shot in Cleveland, one that tries too hard to make its point.

p, Rodger I. Sindell; d, Gerald Seth Sindell; w, R. and G. Sindell; ph, Flemming Olsen (Deluxe Color); m, David Davis; ed, Don Stern; art d, Frank Evans.

Drama   **(PR:C MPAA:NR)**

DOUBLE SUICIDE***   (1970, Jap.) 104m

Hyogensha-Nippon Art Theatre Guild/Toho bw (SHINJU TEN NO AMIJIMA)

Kichiemon Nakamura (Jihei), Shima Iwashita (Koharu/Osan), Hosei Kamatsu (Tahei), Yusuke Takita (Magoemon), Kamatari Fujiwara (Yamatoya Owner), Yoshi Kato (Gosaemon), Shizue Kawarazaki (Osan's Mother), Tokie Hidari (Osugi).

A luxuriously photographed version of an 18th-century puppet play (which is incorporated into the film) with Nakamura, a married shopowner, contracting a suicide bond with his lover Iwashita. He is shocked to overhear that she is hesitant about their pact, and decides to remain faithful to his wife (also played by Iwashita). His wife's father demands that she leave her disgraceful husband, so Nakamura returns to his lover. They make love amongst a cemetery's tombstones and then carry out their pact. A fascinating exploration into the atmosphere of the original puppetwork mixed with modern eroticism, and ultimate violence. Decidedly not for Western tastes or children.

p, Masayuki Nakajima, Masahiro Shinoda; d, Shinoda; w, Taeko Tomioka, Shinoda, Toru Takemitsu (based on a puppet play by Monzaemon Chikamatsu); ph, Toichiro Narushima; m, Takemitsu; art d, Kiyoshi Awazu.

Drama   **(PR:O MPAA:NR)**

DOUBLE TROUBLE**½   (1941) 63m MON bw

Harry Langdon, Charles Rogers, Catherine Lewis, Louis Curry, Benny Rubin, Mira McKinney, Frank Jaquet, Wheeler Oakman, David Cavendish, Dave O'Brien, Edward Kane, Dick Alexander, Ruth Hiatt, Alfred Hall, Guy Kingsford, Fred Santley, Richard Cramer, Art Hamberger.

Langdon and Rogers apply their comic know-how when they get hired to work in a bean factory. In a state of absentmindedness they lose a priceless bracelet in a can of beans, sending them on a wild hunt to get it back. The plot is a familiar one, but it works every time, including here.

p, Dixon R. Harwin; d, William West; w, Jack Natteford; ph, Arthur Martinelli; md, Ross DiMaggio; art d, David Milton.

Comedy   **(PR:A MPAA:NR)**

DOUBLE TROUBLE, 1962   (SEE: SWINGIN' ALONG, 1962)

DOUBLE TROUBLE*   (1967) 91m MGM c

Elvis Presley (Guy Lambert), Annette Day (Jill Conway), John Williams (Gerald Waverly), Yvonne Romain (Claire Dunham), The Wiere Brothers (Themselves), Chips Rafferty (Archie Brown), Norman Rossington (Arthur Babcock), Monty Landis (Georgie), Michael Murphy (Morley), Leon Askin (Inspector De Groote), John Alderson (Iceman), Stanley Adams (Captain Roach), Maurice Marsac (Frenchman), Walter Burke (Mate), Helene Winston (Gerda), Monique LeMaire (Desk Clerk), The G-Men (Themselves).

One of the worst of the Elvis Presley vehicles, with nothing memorable, not even the songs. Elvis is a singer touring Europe with Day chasing after him. Two jewel thieves, Rafferty and Rossington, are following him, too, because they've stashed stolen jewels in his luggage. Songs: "Double Trouble" (Doc Pomus, Mort Shuman), "Baby, If You'll Give Me All of Your Love" (Joy Byers), "Could I Fall In Love?" (Randy Starr), "Long Legged Girl" (J. Leslie McFarland, Winfield Scott), "City by Night" (Bill Giant, Florence Kaye, Bernie Baum), "Old MacDonald Had a Farm" (arranged by Starr), "I Love Only One Girl" (Sid Tepper, Roy C. Bennett), "There's So Much World to See," "It Won't Be Long" (Sid Wayne, Ben Weisman), "Blue River" (Paul Evans, Fred Tobias), "What Now, What Next, Where To?" (Don Robertson, Hal Blair), "Never Ending" (Buddy Kaye, Philip Springer).

p, Judd Bernard, Irwin Winkler; d, Norman Taurog; w, Jo Heims (based on a story by Marc Brandel); ph, Daniel L. Fapp (Panavision, Metrocolor); m, Jeff Alexander; ed, John McSweeney; art d, George W. Davis, Merrill Pye; set d, Henry Grace, Hugh Hunt; cos, Donfeld; spec eff, J. McMillan Johnson, Carroll L. Shepphird; makeup, William Tuttle.

Drama   **(PR:A MPAA:NR)**

DOUBLE WEDDING**½   (1937) 86m MGM bw

William Powell (Charlie Lodge), Myrna Loy (Margit Agnew), Florence Rice (Irene Agnew), John Beal (Waldo Beaver), Jessie Ralph (Mrs. Kensington Bly), Edgar Kennedy (Spike), Sidney Toler (Keough), Mary Gordon (Mrs. Keough), Barnett Parker (Flint), Katharine Alexander (Claire Lodge), Priscilla Lawson (Felice), Donald Meek (The Rev. Dr. Flynn), Henry Taylor (Angelo), Bert Roach (Shrank), Roger Moore (Pianist), Mitchell Lewis (Orator), Jack Dougherty (Chauffeur), G. Pat Collins (Mounted Policeman), Irving Lipschultz (Violinist), Doodles Weaver (Fiddle Player), Charles Coleman (Mrs. Bly's Butler), Billy Dooley (Saxophonist), Oscar O'Shea (Turnkey), Josephine Whittell (Woman Customer), E. Alyn Warren (Al), Jules Cowles (Gus), Jack Baxley (Bartender), Gwen Lee (Woman in Crowd), John "Skins" Miller (Pickpocket), Roger Gray (Mike), George Guhl (Pete).

Another "double" film for Powell (he'd already done DOUBLE HARNESS with Ann Harding). This time, he's teamed with Myrna Loy again (it was their seventh outing as a duo) in another madcap comedy attempt at recapturing the magic they demonstrated in the previous sextet of films. Powell is a wacky painter who lives in a trailer. He doesn't believe in working and feels that life is meant to be lived for the fun of it and nothing more. Loy is a workaholic who runs a chic dress shop and has no time to play. Her younger sister, Rice, rankles under Loy's dominating personality and is especially miffed by the fact that Loy is pushing her toward marriage with Beal, a conservative prig. Rice thinks she's in love with Powell who tells her to shed herself of her encumbrances (namely Beal and Loy) and find true hapiness as an actress. Loy is furious at Powell's intervention and the rest of the film is a fairly standard set of twists culminating in the double wedding of Rice and Beal and Loy and Powell. Jo Swerling's adaptation of Molnar's play is pleasant enough but the farce goes over the top too often and beyond credulity. Every so often, goofiness for the sake of goofiness just doesn't work. It barely makes it here. Toler does a neat job as the butler but the talented Kennedy is wasted as are Meek and Parker. Too much slapstick and not enough wit.

p, Joseph L. Mankiewicz; d, Richard Thorpe; w, Jo Swerling [Waldo Salt, uncredited] (based on the play "Great Love" by Ferenc Molnar); ph, William Daniels; m, Edward Ward; ed, Frank Sullivan; art d, Cedric Gibbons.

Comedy (PR:A MPAA:NR)

DOUBLES** (1978) 90m Doppelganger-Skylight/Cinema World c

Ted D'Arms (Dennis Cooley), Ann Bowden (Linda), Martin LaPlatney (Raymond/Randolph), Dean Meland (Dick), Peggy Nielsen (Sandra), Glen Mazen (Nick), Sally Pritchard (Carol), Niles Brewster (Bob).

A group of friends are brought together by D'Arms to play a fantasy role-playing game. The game gets out of hand and D'Arms finds himself being stalked by a hired killer. A confusing story line where none of the plot elements fits together. The first feature film produced in Seattle.

p, d&w, Bruce Wilson; ph, P. Kip Anderson (Eastmancolor); m, Jim Bredouw, Martin Lund; ed, Art Coburn, Skeets McGrew.

Thriller (PR:C MPAA:NR)

DOUBTING THOMAS*½ (1935) 78m FOX bw

Will Rogers (Thomas Brown), Billie Burke (Paula Brown), Alison Skipworth (Mrs. Pampinelli), Sterling Holloway (Spindler), Andrew Tombes (Hossefrosse), Gail Patrick (Florence McCrickett), Frances Grant (Peggy Burns), Frank Albertson (Jimmy Brown), John Qualen (Von Blitzen), Johnny Arthur (Ralph Twiller), Helen Flint (Nelly Fell), Fred Wallace (Teddy), T. Roy Barnes (LaMaze), Ruth Warren (Jenny), George Cooper (Stage Hand), Helen Freeman (Mrs. Sheppard), William Benedict (Caddie), Lynn Bari (Girl).

A comedy about a blundering amateur theater production. Rogers is the husband of Burke, who has gotten the lead in the local production. He disapproves, but the show must go on. The best laughs come on opening night with scenery falling, actors forgetting their lines, and wardrobe goof-ups. DOUBTING THOMAS was out in the theaters when Rogers was killed in a plane crash in Alaska. (Loose remake of the 1922 silent film THE TORCH BEARERS.)

p, B.G. DeSylva; d, David Butler; w, William Conselman, Bartlett Cormack (based on George Kelly's play "The Torch Bearers"); ph, Joseph Valentine; m, Arthur Lange; art d, Jack Otterson.

Comedy (PR:A MPAA:NR)

DOUCE (SEE: LOVE STORY, 1943, Fr.)

DOUGH BOYS** (1930) 80m MGM bw (GB: FORWARD MARCH)

Buster Keaton (Elmer), Sally Eilers (Mary), Cliff Edwards (Nescopeck), Edward Brophy (Sgt. Brophy), Victor Potel (Svendenburg), Arnold Korff (Gustave), Frank Mayo (Capt. Scott), Pitzy Katz (Abie Cohn), William Steele (Lt. Randolph), Sidney Bracy (Recruiter).

This was Buster Keaton's first talkie, and the best of the sound comedies he would do. Keaton is a wealthy man who accidentally signs up for the army as he searches for a new chauffeur. Coming back from the war, Keaton puts all his buddies on his board of directors and makes their hard-driving sergeant the porter. Keaton said he used his war experiences as a basis for the hilarious film.

d, Edward Sedgwick; w, Al Boasberg, Sidney Lazarus, Richard Schuyer (based on a story by Boasberg, Lazarus); ph, Leonard Smith; ed, William Le Vanway.

Comedy (PR:AAA MPAA:NR)

DOUGHBOYS IN IRELAND½ (1943) 61m COL bw

Kenny Baker (Danny O'Keefe), Jeff Donnell (Molly Callahan), Lynn Merrick (Gloria Gold), Guy Bonham (Chuck Mayers), Red Latham (Corny Smith), Wamp Carlson (Tiny Johnson), Bob Mitchum (Ernie Jones), Buddy Yarus (Jimmy Martin), Harry Shannon (Michael Callahan), Dorothy Vaughan (Mrs. Callahan), Larry Thompson (Captain), Syd Saylor (Sergeant), Herbert Rawlinson (Larry Hunt), Neil Reagan (Medical Capt.), Constance Purdy (Miss Wood), Harry Anderson (Soldier), James Carpenter (Sentry), Craig Woods (Corporal), Muni Seroff (Nick Greco).

A shoddy story that depends on the musical interludes to keep it moving. American soldiers stationed in Northern Ireland in WW II do more singing than fighting and the film was mainly a showcase for Baker's voice. Songs include, "Mother Machree" (Rida Johnson Young, Chauncey Olcott, Ernest R. Ball), "When Irish Eyes Are Smiling" (Ball, Olcott, George Graff, Jr.), "My Wild Irish Rose" (Olcott), "All or Nothing at All" (Jack Lawrence, Arthur Altman), "I Have Faith," "I Knew, Little American Boy," "McNamara's Band" (Shamus O'Connor, John J. Stanford), "There Must Be an Easier Way to Make a Living."

p, Jack Fier; d, Lew Landers; w, Howard J. Green, Monte Brice; ph, L.W. O'Connell; ed, Mel Thorsen; md, M.W. Stoloff; art d, Lionel Banks.

Musical (PR:A MPAA:NR)

DOUGHGIRLS, THE*½ (1944) 102m WB bw

Ann Sheridan (Edna), Alexis Smith (Nan), Jack Carson (Arthur), Jane Wyman (Vivian), Irene Manning (Mrs. Cadman), Charles Ruggles (Slade), Eve Arden (Natalia), John Ridgely (Julian), Alan Mowbray (Breckenridge Drake), John Alexander (Buckley), Craig Stevens (Tom), Barbara Brown (Mrs. Cartwright), Stephen Richards [Mark Stevens] (Lt. Keary), Francis Pierlot (Mr. Jordan), Donald MacBride (Judge Franklin), Regis Toomey (Timothy Walsh), Joe de Rita (The Stranger), John Walsh (Bellhop), Grandon Rhodes, Tom Quinn (Clerks), Fred Kelsey (Man With Suitcase), Dink Trout (Young Husband), John Hamilton (Businessman), Almira Sessions, Minerva Urecal (Hatchet-Faced Women), Earle Dewey (Fat Man), Dolores Conlon, Dorothy Reisner, Helen Gerald, Joan Breslaw, Yolanda Baiano, Julie Arlington (School Girls), Harry Tyler (Angular Man), Marie de Becker, Anita Bolster (Maids), Joan Winfield (Slade's Secretary), Oliver Blake (Porter), Elmer Jerome (Elderly Waiter), Lou Marcelle (Announcer's Voice), Warren Mills, Dick Hirbe, William Frambes (Bellboys), Ralph Sanford (Workman), Jack Mower, John O'Connor (Technicians), Larry Rio (Attendant in Baths), Carlyle Blackwell, Jr., (Messenger), Nick Kobliansky (Father Nicolai), Will Fowler (Lieut.), Walter DePalma (Justice of the Peace).

Based on the Broadway hit, this film version is watered down, thanks to the Hays Office. Wyman, Sheridan, and Smith are hunting for husbands in war-time Washington. Eve Arden outshines everyone as a visiting Russian guerrilla fighter, who keeps her marksmanship up by shooting pigeons, and who keeps pulling the three stars from their messes. Most of the humor of the play got lost somewhere in the transition.

p, Mark Hellinger; d, James V. Kern; w, Kern, Sam Hellman (based on the play by Joseph A. Fields); ph, Ernest Haller, Jack Leicester, William McCann; m, Adolph Deutsch; ed, Folmer Blangsted; art d, Hugh Reticker; spec eff, Haller.

Comedy (PR:A MPAA:NR)

DOUGHNUTS AND SOCIETY (1936) 64m REP bw

Louise Fazenda (Kate Flannagan), Maude Eburne (Belle Dugan), Ann Rutherford (Joan Dugan), Eddie Nugent (Jerry Flannagan), Hedda Hopper (Mrs. Murray Hill), Franklin Pangborn (Benson), Rafael Corio (Ivan Petroff), Harold Minjir (Hoyt), Olaf Hytten (Wellington), Robert Light (Bill), Claudell Kaye (Miss Bradley).

Two waitresses, Fazenda and Eburne, try to break into high society. Pangborn, a social secretary, helps them to meet wealthy Hopper. But she turns out to be a fake. Stale comedy with little thought behind it, which is a shame considering that five writers worked on it.

p, Nat Levine; d, Lewis D. Collins; w, Karen DeWolf, Robert St. Claire, Wallace MacDonald, Gertrude Orr, Matt Brooks; ph, William Nobles; ed, Arthur Brooks.

Comedy Cas. (PR:A MPAA:NR)

DOULOS—THE FINGER MAN (1964, Fr./Ital.) 108m
Rome Paris Films-C.C. Champion/Pathe-Contemporary Films bw

Jean-Paul Belmondo (Silien), Serge Reggiani (Maurice), Jean Desailly (Inspector Clain), Fabienne dali (Fabienne), Michel Piccoli (Nutheccio), Monique Hennessy (Therese), Marcel Cuvelier (1st Inspector), Jack Leonard (2nd Inspector), Aime De March (Jean), Carl Studer (Kern), Jacques De Leon (Armand), Christian Lude (The Doctor), Rene Lefevre (Gilbert), Philippe Nahon (Remy), Paulette Breil (Anita), Charles Bayard (Old Man), Daniel Crohem (Inspector Salignari), Charles Boyillard, Georges Sellier (Barmen), Andres (Maitre d'Hotel).

Reggiani gets out of jail and kills the man who was responsible for his girl friend's death, then hides out with Hennessy. He seeks the aid of Belmondo in a theft, but Hennessy believes Belmondo is a police informer. Belmondo gets Reggiani the tools and help for the crime, then tells the police. When Hennessy finds this out she's killed and Belmondo makes it look as though she died in a car crash. Reggiani is arrested and sent back to prison. Belmondo helps effect Reggiani's early release from prison but not before Reggiani sets Belmondo up for a hit. Reggiani then tries to prevent the hit and is killed by the hired gun who mistakes him for Belmondo. Belmondo arrives and a fierce gun battle between Belmondo and the hired gun leaves both men dead.

p, Carlo Ponti; Georges De Beauregard; d&w, Jean-Pierre Melville (based on the novel Le Doulos by Pierre Lesou); ph, Nicolas Hayer; m, Paul Misraki; ed, Monique Bonnot; art d, Daniel Gueret; set d, Pierre Charron.

Crime (PR:C MPAA:NR)

DOVE, THE* (1974, Brit.) 105m PAR c

Joseph Bottoms (Robin Lee Graham), Deborah Raffin (Patti Ratterree), John McLiam (Lyle Graham), Dabney Coleman (Charles Huntley), John Anderson (Mike Turk), Colby Chester (Tom Barkley), Ivor Barry (Kenniston), Setoki Ceinaturoga (Young Fijian), Rev. Nikula (Minister), Apenisa Naigulevu (Cruise Ship Captain), John Meillon (Tim), Gordon Glenwright (Darwin Harbor Master), Garth Meade (South African Customs Official), Peter Gwynne (Fred C. Pearson), Cecily Polsohn (Mrs. Castaldi), Anthony Fridjohn (License Bureau Clerk), Dale Cutts (Reporter), Jose Augusto de Lima, Sampaio e Silva (Chief Pilot).

A young seaman, Bottoms, sails solo around the world in a small boat, a five-year trek that brings the character to maturity and manhood. On the way he falls in love with Deborah Raffin, who is his constant inspiration. She follows him to Fiji, Australia, South Africa, Panama, and the Galapagos Islands. Stunning location cinematography by Sven Nykvist. Based on a true story.

p, Gregory Peck; d, Charles Jarrott; w, Peter Beagle, Adam Kennedy (based on the book Dove, by Robin Lee Graham with Derek Gill); ph, Sven Nykvist (Panavision, Technicolor); m, John Barry; ed, John Jympson; art d, Peter Lamont.

Drama (PR:AA MPAA: PG)

DOWN AMONG THE SHELTERING PALMS½** (1953) 86m FOX c

William Lundigan *(Capt. Bill Willoby)*, Jane Greer *(Diana Forrester)*, Mitzi Gaynor *(Rozouila)*, David Wayne *(Lt. Carl Schmidt)*, Gloria De Haven *(Angela Toland)*, Gene Lockhart *(Rev. Edgett)*, Jack Paar *(Lt. Mike Sloan)*, Alvin Greenman *(Cpl. Kolta)*, Billy Gilbert *(King Jilouili)*, Henry Kulky *(1st Sergeant)*, Lyle Talbot *(Maj. Curwin)*, Ray Montgomery *(Lt. Everly)*, George Nader *(Lt. Homer Briggs)*, Fay Roope *(Col. Parker)*, David Ahdar *(Witch Doctor)*, Sialofi Jerry Talo *(Toami)*, Clinton Bagwell *(Aide to Colonel)*, Charles Tannen *(Radio Operator)*, Claud Allister *(Woolawei)*, Edith Evanson *(Mrs. Edgett)*, Steve Wayne, Richard Grayson, John Baer *(Officers)*, Jean Charney *(Native Girl)*, Barney Phillips *(Murphy)*, Lee Marvin *(Snively)*, Henry Slate *(Thompson)* Joe Turkel *(Harris)*, David Wolfson, James Ogg, Ray Hyke, Roger McGee, Richard Monohan *(GIs)*.

Lundigan is an Army officer sent to occupy a South Sea island, and his main duty is to keep his men from fraternizing with local women. He tries to set a good example by dating only Greer, the daughter of an American missionary. Problems arise when journalist De Haven arrives on the island and falls for Lundigan. He spurns her, and she writes a story saying that the island king has given his daughter, Gaynor, to Lundigan as a gift. This causes trouble in the ranks, and the Army sends an investigative team to the island. A small musical with songs by Harold Arlen and Ralph Blane. Lundigan and Wayne sing the best number, "I'm a Ruler of a South Sea Island." Scaled-down version of SOUTH PACIFIC. Other songs; "Who Will It Be When the Time Comes?," "What Makes a Difference?," "All of Me," "Down Among the Sheltering Palms," "When You're in Love."

p, Fred Kohlmar; d, Edmund Goulding; w, Claude Binyon, Albert Lewin, Burt Styler (based on a story by Edward Hope); ph, Leon Shamroy (Technicolor); m, Leigh Harline; ed, Louis Loeffler; md, Lionel Newman; art d, Lyle Wheeler, Leland Fuller; spec eff, Fred Sersen; ch, Seymour Felix; m/l, Harold Arlen, Ralph Blane; makeup, Ben Nye.

Musical **(PR:A MPAA:NR)**

DOWN AMONG THE Z MEN**

(1952, Brit.) 71m E.J. Fancey Productions/NR bw

Harry Secombe *(Harry Jones)*, Carole Carr *(Carole Gayley)*, Peter Sellers *(Maj. Bloodnock)*, Michael Bentine *(Prof. Osrick Purehart)*, Spike Milligan *(Pvt. Eccles)*, Television Toppers *(WRACs)*, Robert Cawdron, Graham Stark, Andrew Timothy, Elizabeth Kearns, Miriam Karlin, Eunice Grayson, Jane Morrison, Richard Turner, Judy Horton, Adrienne Scott.

Decent spy comedy has Secombe, a War II "Z" army reservist and sometime detective, drafted into national service while hot on the trail of a professor who has an atomic formula wanted by the enemy. With Carr, he thwarts the crooks who are after the professor and saves the formula for England. Seller's second film.

p, E.J. Fancey; d, Maclean Rogers; w, Jimmy Grafton, Francis Charles; ph, Geoffrey Faithfull.

Comedy **(PR:A MPAA:NR)**

DOWN ARGENTINE WAY*½** (1940) 92m FOX c

Don Ameche *(Ricardo Quintana)*, Betty Grable *(Glenda Crawford)*, Carmen Miranda *(Herself)*, Charlotte Greenwood *(Binnie Crawford)*, J. Carrol Naish *(Casiano)*, Henry Stephenson *(Don Diego Quintana)*, Katharine Aldridge *(Helen Carson)*, Leonid Kinskey *(Tito Acuna)*, Chris-Pin Martin *(Esteban)*, Robert Conway *(Jimmy Blake)*, Gregory Gaye *(Sebastian)*, Bobby Stone *(Panchito)*, Charles Judels *(Ambassador)*, Nicholas Brothers, Thomas and Catherine Dowling, *(Dance Specialties)*, Six Hits and a Miss, Carmen Miranda Band, Edward Fielding *(Willis Crawford)*, Edward Conrad *(Anastasio)*, Fortunio Bonanova, Armand Kaliz *(Hotel Managers)*, Frank Puglia *(Montero)*, Nicholas Brothers, Flores Brothers, Banda Da Lua.

A frothy souffle that never falls flat is this bouncy and colorful picture that introduced the world to the unique Carmen Miranda. Alice Faye was supposed to star in the movie but suffered an emergency appendectomy and Grable was called in from New York to play the lead. She's an American girl vacationing in Argentina where she falls for Don Ameche, a rich horse breeder. Grable is also well-to-do and loves collecting jumping horses. Ameche and Grable are in love and neither knows that their families are like the Hatfields and McCoys and have hated each other since before anyone can recall. Don and Betty convince Don's father, Stephenson, that the feud is a waste of time and all ends well as the young couple get together. Miranda had nothing whatsoever to do with the plot but she scored with audiences and critics alike as she brought her "Souse Amereecahn" magic to the screen. The war was brewing and studios were looking for new markets so they began making movies about South America in the hope that it would buck up the business they lost in Europe. Eight songs included the Oscar-nominated title tune by Harry Warren and Mack Gordon as well as songs by Al Stillman, Jaraca, Vincente Paiva and Gene Rose. Shamroy and Rennahan were also nominated for their photographic efforts. Good comedy from Kinskey and Naish. If you're lucky enough to see a mint print of the picture, the Technicolor will bang out your eyes. A sensational dance number by the Nicholas Brothers highlights the special appearances. Mindless, but fun from "20th Century Fox Presents . . . ." to "The End."

p, Darryl F. Zanuck; d, Irving Cummings; w, Darrell Ware, Karl Tunberg (from a story by Rian James, Ralph Spence); ph, Leon Shamroy, Ray Rennahan (Technicolor); ed, Barbara McLean; md, Emil Newman; art d, Richard Day, Joseph C. Wright; ch, Nick Castle, Geneva Sawyer; m/l, Harry Warren, Mack Gordon.

Musical **(PR: AA MPAA: NR)**

DOWN DAKOTA WAY½** (1949) 67m REP c

Roy Rogers *(Himself)*, Dale Evans *(Ruth Shaw)*, Pat Brady *(Sparrow Biffle)*, Montie Montana *(Sheriff Holbrook)*, Elisabeth Risdon *(Dolly Paxton)*, Byron Barr *(Steve Paxton)*, James Cardwell *(Saunders)*, Roy Barcroft *(H.T. McKenzie)*, Emmett Vogan *(Dr. George Fredericks)*, Foy Willing and the Riders of the Purple Sage.

Rogers comes upon the murder of a local veterinarian and goes hunting for the killer. He discovers that the vet had found that a herd of cattle had hoof-and-mouth disease and he was killed by the owner of the cattle, Barcroft. One of the standouts in the Rogers series. "Candy Kisses," a hit country song of the time, is one of the musical numbers.

p, Edward J. White; d, William Witney; w, John K. Butler, Sloan Nibley; ph, Reggie Lanning (Trucolor); m, Dale Butts; ed, Tony Martinelli; art d, Frank Hotaling; m/l, Nibley, Butts, Sid Robin, Foy Willing, George Morgan.

Western **Cas.** **(PR:A MPAA:NR)**

DOWN IN ARKANSAW* (1938) 65m REP bw

Leon Weaver *(Abner)*, Elviry *(Herself)*, Frank Weaver *(Cicero)*, Ralph Byrd *(John)*, June Storey *(Mary)*, Pinky Tomlin *(Pinky)*, Berton Churchill *(Judge)*, Guinn Williams *(Juble)*, Walter Miller *(Marks)*, Gertrude Green *(Elsie)*, Selmer Jackson *(Edwards)*, Arthur Loft *(Turner)*, John Dilson *(Graves)*, Alan Bridge *(Jake)*, Karl Hackett *(Wilkins)*, Ivan Miller *(Lewis)*.

Vaudeville stars Elviry and the Weaver Brothers headline this weak comedy about the government's attempt to take over some land from a hillbilly town and build a dam. Byrd is the government man trying to sell the town on the plan, and wins approval for it by falling in love with the Weaver's daughter, Storey.

p, Armand Schaefer; d, Nick Grinde; w, Dorrell and Stuart McGowan; ph, Ernest Miller; m, Cy Feuer; ed, William Morgan.

Comedy **(PR:A MPAA:NR)**

DOWN IN SAN DIEGO** (1941) 69m MGM bw

Ray McDonald *(Hank Parker)*, Bonita Granville *(Betty Haines)*, Dan Dailey, Jr. *(Al Haines)*, Leo Gorcey *("Snap" Connors)*, Charles B. Smith *(Crawford Carter)*, Dorothy Morris *(Mildred Burnette)*, Robert O. Davis *(Henry Schrode)*, Joseph Sawyer *(Dutch)*, Anthony Warde *(Tony)*, Stanley Clements *(Louie Schwartz)*, Henry O'Neill *(Col. Halliday)*, William Tannen *(Matt Herman)*, Ludwig Stossel *(Brock)*, Connie Gilchrist *(Proprietress)*, Al Trescony *(Jimmie Collins)*, Frederic Worlock *(Eric Kramer)*, Hobart Cavanaugh *(Telegraph Clerk)*, George Watts *(Sgt. O'Hallihan)*, Veda Ann Borg *(Cashier)*, Ralph Sanford *(Man)*, Ernie Alexander *(Sailor)*, Audrene Brier *(Check Room Girl)*, Ken Christy *(Police Capt. Flarrity)*, Winifred Harris *(Lady)*, Robert Kellard *(Bell Captain)*, Walter Sande *(Sergeant)*, Hans Von Morhart *(Hugo)*, Cliff Danielson, James Millican *(Sentries)*, Fredrik Vogeding *(Operator)*, William Forrest *(Naval Intelligence Officer)*, Paul Newlan *(Tough Waiter)*, Buster Slaven *(Bellhop)*, Frank Mills *(Chauffeur)*, Franco Corsaro *(Barber)*, William Yetter *(Hugo's Assistant)*, Jack Norton *(Drunk)*, James Craven *(Flight Commander)*, Jacques Chapin *(Marine)*.

Few laughs can be found in this war-time comedy about a group of teenagers who thwart a spy ring operating at the San Diego naval base. Directing is languid and "Nancy Drew" Granville seems to be performing in an acting school class. Film originally was entitled YOUNG AMERICANS.

p, Frederick Stephani: d, Robert B. Sinclair; w, Harry Clark, Franz G. Spencer (based on story by Spencer); ph, Paul Vogel; m, David Snell; ed, Ben Lewis; art, Cedric Gibbons, Gabriel Scognamillo; set d, Edwin B. Willis.

Comedy **(PR:A MPAA:NR)**

DOWN LAREDO WAY*½ (1953) 54m REP bw

Rex Allen *(Himself)*, Slim Pickens *(Himself)*, Dona Drake *(Narita)*, Marjorie Lord *(Valerie)*, Roy Barcroft *(Cooper)*, Judy Nugent *(Taffy)*, Percy Helton *(Judge Sully)*, Clayton Moore *(Chip Wells)*, Zon Murray *(Joe)*.

Allen and his partner, Pickens, prevent an eight-year-old girl, Nugent, from being put into an orphanage after her acrobat father, Moore, is killed in a fall. They find that Moore had discovered that his partner, Lord, was part of a diamond smuggling ring and she caused his fall to get rid of him. A plodding story filled with implausible situations.

p, Rudy Ralston; d, William Witney; w, Gerald Geraghty; ph, John MacBurnie; m, Stanley Wilson; ed, Harold Minter; art d, Frank Aprigo.

Western **(PR:A MPAA:NR)**

DOWN MEMORY LANE*** (1949) 70m EL bw

Bing Crosby, W.C. Fields, Donald Novis, Gloria Swanson, Mabel Normand, Ben Turpin, Phyllis Haver, Franklin Pangborn, Charlie Murray, James Finlayson, Mack Swain, Irving Bacon, Frank Nelson, Yvonne Pettie, Steve Allen, Mack Sennett, Keystone Cops.

A compilation of some of the better comedies from the Mack Sennett studios. The best segment is W.C. Fields' THE DENTIST. Allen, playing a TV disc jockey, ties it all together with jokes about the various segments. At the end, Mack Sennett himself makes an appearance, hailing the older productions over the new.

p, Aubrey Schenck; d, Phil Karlson.

Comedy **(PR:A MPAA:NR)**

DOWN MEXICO WAY½** (1941) 77m REP bw

Gene Autry *(Gene)*, Smiley Burnette *(Frog)*, Fay McKenzie *(Maria Elena)*, Harold Huber *(Pancho Grande)*, Sidney Blackmer *(Gibson)*, Joe Sawyer *(Allen)*, Andrew Tombes *(Mayor Tubbs)*, Murray Alper *(Flood)*, Arthur Loft *(Gerard)*, Duncan Renaldo *(Juan)*, Paul Fix *(Davis)*, Julian Rivero *(Don Alvarado)*, Ruth Robinson *(Mercedes)*, Thornton Edwards *(Capt. Rodriguez)*, The Herrara Sisters, Eddie Dean, Esther Estrella, Sam Appel, Helen MacKellar, Elias Gamboa, Rico de Montez, Charles Rivero, Paquita del Rey, Jose Manero, Carmela Cansino, Reed Howes, Hank Bell, Fred Burns, Al Haskell, Jack O'Shea.

Autry and sidekick Burnette chase a band of swindlers who fleeced the people of Sage City, down to Mexico. They catch the crooks and stop them from robbing a rich Mexican rancher. Horses, cars, and motorcycles join in a climactic chase through the badlands at the end of this worthwhile addition to the Autry series.

p, Harry Grey; d, Joseph Santley; w, Olive Cooper and Albert Duffy (based on a story by Dorrell and Stuart McGowan); ph, Jack Marta; ed, Howard O'Neill, md, Raoul Kraushaar.

Western **(PR:A MPAA:NR)**

DOWN MISSOURI WAY**½ (1946) 73m PRC bw

Martha O'Driscoll (Jane Colwell), John Carradine (Thorndyke P. Dunning), Eddie Dean (Mortimer), William Wright (Mike Burton), Roscoe Ates (Pappy), Mabel Todd (Cindy), Renee Godfrey (Gloria Baxter), Eddie Craven (Sam), Chester Clute (Prof. Shaw), Will Wright (Prof. Morris), Paul Scardon (Prof. Lewis), Earle Hodgins, the Tailor Maids, the Notables, Shirley.

Carradine is a flamboyant Hollywood director visiting the Ozarks to find a mule for a hillbilly movie. Complications arise when it is discovered that the mule is being used for experiments at an agricultural school. A routine B-comedy with some smart dialog to help carry it off. The producers flooded Missouri theaters in simultaneous openings for the film, but it turned out to be a major disappointment for PRC.

p&d, Josef Berne; w, Sam Neuman; ph, Vincent J. Farrar; m, Karl Hajos; ed, W. Donn Hayes; m/l, Kim Gannon and Walter Kent; art d, Edward C. Jewell; m/l, "Big Town Gal," "Just Can't Get That Guy," "Never Knew That I Could Sing," Kim Gannon, Walter Kent.

Comedy **(PR:A MPAA:NR)**

DOWN ON THE FARM** (1938) 60m FOX bw

Jed Prouty (John Jones), Spring Byington (Mrs. John Jones), Louise Fazenda (Aunt Ida), Russell Gleason (Herbert Thompson), Ken Howell (Jack Jones), George Ernest (Roger Jones), June Carlson (Lucy Jones), Florence Roberts (Granny Jones), Billy Mahan (Bobby Jones), Eddie Collins (Cyrus Sampson), Dorris Bowdon (Tessie Moody), Roberta Smith (Emma Moody), Marvin Stephens (Tommy McGuire), William Haade (Hefferkamp), John T. Murray (Marvin), William Irving (Coleman).

Another in the Jones Family comedy series, and this time the family is visiting an aunt, Fazenda, down on her farm. The father, Prouty, becomes involved in local politics after winning the cornhusking contest, and finds a lot of crooked things going on. The humor is good in this B comedy, but nothing memorable. (See JONES FAMILY Series, Index.)

p, John Stone; d, Malcolm St. Clair; w, Robert Ellis, Helen Logan (based on stories by Homer Croy, Frank Fenton, Lynn Root, from characters created by Katharine Kavanaugh); ph, Edward Snyder; m, Samuel Kaylin; ed, Harry Reynolds; md, Kaylin; art d, Bernard Herzbrun, Boris Leven.

Comedy **(PR:A MPAA:NR)**

DOWN OUR ALLEY* (1939, Brit.) 56m British Screen Service bw (AKA: GANG SHOW)

Hughie Green (Hughie Dunstable), Wally Patch (Mr. Dunstable), Vivienne Chatterton (Mrs. Dunstable), Sylvia Saetre (Sally), Antony Holles (Tony), Daphne Raglan (Mary), Philip Morant (Eustace), Johnnie Schofield (Waiter), Joe Cunningham, Arnold Sellars, Sadie Corrie, Jean Ray, Danny Norton, Joey Hopkinson, Michael Appleby, Joyce Cannon, Tommy Trainer, Ron Ashen, Lily Summers, Bobby Price, Charlie Wragg, Barry Manning, Queenie Ransley, Anna Smirrell, Ray Pennington, Hughie Green's Gang.

Green is the manager of a music shop and falls for a woman who is engaged. Her fiance is a singer, who also owns a nightclub. Green gets a job as a waiter in the club and with inside help brings in his gang of street singers to perform in the stage show. The gang makes a big hit, and Green wins the girl in the process. Bottom-of-the-scale musical.

p, Germain Burger; d, George A. Cooper; ph, Burger.

Musical **(PR:A MPAA:NR)**

DOWN OUR STREET** (1932, Brit.) 87m PAR bw

Nancy Price (Annie Collins), Elizabeth Allan (Maisie Collins), Morris Harvey (Bill Collins), Hugh Williams (Charlie Stubbs), Alexander Field (Sam), Sydney Fairbrother (Maggie Anning), Binnie Barnes (Tessie Bernstein), Frederick Burtwell (Fred Anning), Merle Tottenham (Rose).

Williams, a slum dweller drifting into a life of crime, reforms out of love for Price and becomes a cab driver. Price's uncle frames him for a smash-and-grab job and he faces jail, except for the good work of Price's mother, who swings to his side and saves the day. Depression-era realism helps make for an effective story.

p, S.E. Fitzgibbon; d&w, Harry Lachman (based on a play by Ernest George).

Drama **(PR:A MPAA:NR)**

DOWN RIO GRANDE WAY**½ (1942) 57m COL bw

Charles Starrett (Steve Martin), Russell Hayden ("Lucky" Haines), Britt Wood (Britt Haines), Rose Anne Stevens (Mary Ann), Norman Willis (Vandall), Davison Clark (Col. Baldridge), Edmund Cobb (Stoner), Budd Buster (Kearney), Joseph Eggenton (Judge Henderson), Paul Newlan (Sam Houston), Betty Roadman (Ma Haines), William Desmond, Jim Corey, Tom Smith, Steve Clark, Forrest Taylor, Edward Piel, Sr., John Cason, Art Mix, Kermit Maynard, Frank McCarroll.

An exciting, action-loaded Starrett western placed at the time when Texas was about to be accepted into the Union. Starrett, a Texas ranger, goes to a violent county to restore order and finds that a tax collector is cheating the ranchers and businessmen. The crook and a local newspaper publisher are also stirring up anti-statehood feelings, but Starrett takes care of matters swiftly.

p, Jack Fier; d, William Berke; w, Paul Franklin; ph, George Meehan; ed, Mel Thorsen.

Western **(PR:A MPAA:NR)**

DOWN RIVER** (1931, Brit.) 73m GAU bw

Charles Laughton (Capt. Grossman), Jane Baxter (Hilary Gordon), Harold Huth (John Durham), Kenneth Kove (Ronnie Gordon), Hartley Power (Lingard), Arthur Goullet (Maxick), Norman Shelley (Blind Rudley), Frederick Leister (Inspector Manning), Cyril McLaglen (Sgt. Proctor), Humberston Wright (Sir Michael Gordon), Hugh E. Wright (Charlie Wong), Helen Howell.

A customs agent proves that the skipper of a Dutch-Chinese tramp steamer is actually the head of a smuggling operation. Laughton's sixth feature, and the last he was to make in England before going to Hollywood.

p, L'Estrange Fawcett; d, Peter Godfrey; w, Ralph Gilbert Bettinson (based on the novel Seamark by Austin Small).

Crime **(PR:A MPAA:NR)**

DOWN TEXAS WAY** (1942) 57m MON bw

Buck Jones (Buck), Tim McCoy (Tim), Raymond Hatton (Sandy), Luana Walters (Mary), Dave O'Brien (Dave), Lois Austin (Stella), Glenn Strange (Sheriff), Harry Woods (Burt), Tom London (Pete), Kansas Moehring (Luke), Jack Daley (John Dodge), "Silver".

Another from Monogram's "Rough Riders" series. Hatton, McCoy, and Jones are the West's Three Musketeers, and when Hatton is accused of murdering his best friend, his two companions search for the real killer. Hatton's friend was a banker who was standing in the way of gangsters who are trying to control the town. The mobsters are stopped, the killer caught, and Hatton is saved from a lynching.

p, Scott R. Dunlap; d, Howard Bretherton; w, Jess Bowers [Adele Buffington]; ph, Harry Neumann; ed, Carl Pierson.

Western **(PR:A MPAA:NR)**

DOWN THE ANCIENT STAIRCASE** (1975, Ital.) 100m FOX c (PER LE ANTICHE SCALE)

Marcello Mastroianni (Doctor), Francoise Fabian (Anna), Marthe Keller (Bianca), Lucia Bose (Fernanda), Adriana Asti (Gianna), Barbara Bouchet (Carla), Charles Fawcett (Director), Pierre Blaise (Tonio).

Mastroianni is the head doctor at an Italian insane asylum in the 1930s. He has a hypothesis that insanity is caused by a virus, and so, caught up in his studies, he hasn't left the hospital grounds in eight years. A young female doctor, Fabian, arrives and finds that the doctor fears for his own sanity but is making life livable by having affairs with the superintendent's wife, Bose, his assistant, Keller, and his colleague's wife, Bouchet. An allegory of the Fascist regime that ran Italy in the 1930s and 1940s, the film falls short of clarity.

p, Fulvio Lucisano; d, Mauro Bolognini; w, Raffaele Andreassi, Mario Arosio, Tullio Pinelli, Bernardion Zapponi (adapted from a novel by Mario Tobino); ph, Ennio Guarnieri (Eastmancolor); m, Ennio Morricane; ed, Nino Baragli.

Drama **(PR:O MPAA:NR)**

DOWN THE STRETCH** (1936) 58m WB bw

Mickey Rooney (Snapper Sinclair), Patricia Ellis (Patricia Barrington), Dennis Moore (Cliff Barrington), William Best (Noah), Gordon Hart (Judge Adams), Gordon Elliott (Robert Bates), Virginia Brissac (Aunt Julia), Charles Wilson (Tex Reardon), Joseph Crehan (Secretary Burch), Mary Treen (Nurse), Edward Keane (Fred Yates), Raymond Brown (Col. Carter), Andre Beranger (Cooper), Bob Tansill (Butch), Frank Faylen (Ben the Bookie), Robert Emmett Keane (Nick), Charles Foy (Arnold Roach), Crauford Kent (Sir Oliver), Jimmy Eagles (Sunny).

A young Mickey Rooney (he was 16 years old at the time) is adopted from a reform school by a rich couple. His new parents have horse stables, and Rooney becomes a jockey like his real father. But his father was a crooked jockey, and Rooney is framed by gamblers using his father's reputation to nail him. Rooney clears himself and wins the English Derby.

p, Bryan Foy; d, William Clemens; w, William Jacobs (based on the story "Blood Lines" by Jacobs); ph, Arthur Todd; ed, Lew Hesse.

Drama **(PR:A MPAA:NR)**

DOWN THE WYOMING TRAIL* (1939) 52m MON bw

Tex Ritter (Tex), Horace Murphy (Missouri), Mary Brodel (Candy), Bobby Lawson (Jerry), Charles King (Red), Bob Terry (Blackie), Jack Ingram (Monte), Earl Douglas (Smith), Frank LaRue (Chattan), Ernie Adams (Limpy), Charles Sargeant (Hand), Ed Coxen (Whiskers), Jean Sothern (Waitress), The Northwesterners, Merle Scobee, A. J. Brier, Wilson D. Rasch, Ray Scobee, Charles Davis.

One in a series of Ritter/Monogram B-oaters with Ritter fighting rustlers in the dead of winter, and still taking time off to sing. Only thing original is that the bad guy, King, kills himself at the end. The murky hue of this picture was caused by a camera malfunction.

p, Edward Finney; d, Al Herman; w, Peter Dixon, Roger Merton; ph, Marcel LePicard; m, Frank Sanucci; ed, Holbrook Todd; md, Sanucci; m/l, Jimmy Davis, Floyd Tillman, Johnny Lange, Lew Porter, Carson Robinson.

Western **(PR:A MPAA:NR)**

DOWN THREE DARK STREETS** (1954) 85m Edward Small/UA bw

Broderick Crawford (Ripley), Ruth Roman (Kate Martel), Martha Hyer (Connie Anderson), Marisa Pavan (Julie Angelino), Casey Adams (Dave Millson), Kenneth Tobey (Zack Stewart), Gene Reynolds (Vince Angelino), William Johnstone (Frank Pace), Harlan Warde (Barker), Jay Adler (Uncle Max), Claude Akins (Matty Pavelich), Suzanne Alexander (Brenda Ralles), Myra Marsh (Mrs. Dones), Joe Bassett

(Joe Walpo), Dede Gainor *(Vicki)*, Alexander Campbell *(Emil Shurk)*, Alan Dexter *(Kuppol)*, Larry Hudson *(Randol)*.

Quick-paced crime yarn has Crawford as an FBI agent solving three serious crimes, hence the title. First Crawford hunts down a bank robber, then captures an interstate auto theft ring, and finally tracks down an extortionist who is victimizing luscious Roman. Solid cast adds to the flavor of this cops-and-robbers yarn, which suffers from three disjointed episodes without a strong interconnecting link. Crawford is unlike any real FBI agent in that he follows few of their known procedures, but rather rough-and-tumbles his way to triumph over miscreants.

p, Arthur Gardner, Jules V. Levy; d, Arthur Laven; w, the Gordon Gordons, Bernard C. Schoenfeld (based on the novel *Case File F.B.I.* by the Gordons); ph, Joseph Biroc; m, Paul Sawtell; ed, Grant Whytock.

Crime **(PR:C MPAA:NR)**

DOWN TO EARTH** (1932) 79m FOX bw

Will Rogers *(Pike Peters)*, Dorothy Jordan *(Julia Pearson)*, Irene Rich *(Idy Peters)*, Matty Kemp *(Ross Peters)*, Clarence Wilson *(Ed Eggers)*, Mary Carlise *(Jackie Harper)*, Theodore Lodi *(Grand Duke Michael)*, Brandon Hurst *(Jeffrey, the Butler)*, Harvey Clark *(Cameron)*, Henry Kolker *(Randolph)*, Luise Mackintosh *(Mrs. Phillips)*.

This is the sequel to THEY HAD TO SEE PARIS. Will Rogers and his family return home from Paris as millionaires. They have a replica of their rented French chateau built for them on their Oklahoma property. A Depression bank failure brings them down from their high society life style and back to normal. A comedy that only works when Rogers is the focus of attention.

d, David Butler; w, Edwin Burke (based on story by Homer Croy); ph, Ernest Palmer.

Comedy **(PR:A MPAA:NR)**

DOWN TO EARTH** (1947) 101m COL c

Rita Hayworth *(Terpsichore/Kitty Pendleton)*, Larry Parks *(Danny Miller)*, Marc Platt *(Eddie Marin)*, Roland Culver *(Mr. Jordan)*, James Gleason *(Max Corkle)*, Edward Everett Horton *(Messenger 7013)*, Adele Jergens *(Georgia Evans)*, George Macready *(Joe Mannion)*, William Frawley *(Police Lieutenant)*, Jean Donahue *(Betty)*, Kathleen O'Malley *(Dolly)*, William Haade *(Spike)*, James Burke *(Kelly)*, Fred Sears *(Orchestra Leader)*, Lynn Merrick, Dusty Anderson, Doris Houck, Shirley Molohon, Peggy Maley, Dorothy Brady, Jo Rattigan, Lucille Casey *(Muses)*, Lucien Littlefield *(Escort 3082)*, Myron Healey *(Sloan)*, Harriette Ann Gray *(Dancer)*, Rudy Cameron *(Stage Manager)*, Arthur Blake *(Mr. Somerset)*, Wilbur Mack *(Messenger)*, Cora Witherspoon *(Woman on Street)*, Kay Vallon *(Rosebud)*, Ernest Hilliard, Fred Howard, Forbes Murray, Cecil Weston, Mary Newton, Ottola Nesmith, Boyd Irwin *(Bits)*, Jean Del Val *(Croupier)*, Billy Bletcher *(Conductor)*, Nicodemus Stewart *(Porter)*, Boyd Irwin *(Man)*, Raoul Freeman, Bob Ryan *(Policemen)*, Matty Fain *(Henchman)*, Frank Darien *(Janitor)*, Jack Norton *(Sleeping Man)*, Tom Hanlon *(Announcer)*, Mary Forbes *(Dowager)*, Grace Hampton, Winifred Harris *(Women)*, Edward Harvey *(Man)*, Count Stefanelli *(Frenchman)*, Eddie Acuff *(Stagehand)*, Alan Bridge *(Police Sergeant)*, Tom Daly *(Reporter)*, Francine Kennedy *(Chorine)*, Virginia Hunter *(Muse)*.

The color is lush and dazzling, the cast impressive, and the story is about as ridiculous as they come. In one of the most idiotic musicals ever conceived, Hayworth is put through her choreography like one might prod a reluctant cow. She is awkward, clumsy, and graceless, attempting to dance to numbers that would baffle the Ritz Brothers. In a takeoff of HERE COMES MR. JORDAN (produced by Columbia in 1941), Hayworth is the Greek goddess Terpsichore who descends to earth to help out an ailing musical on Broadway (the film being infected by the same disease, stupidity), wherein the nine Greek muses are being ridiculed in swingtime jazz, heresy to the gods, of course. She immediately begins to battle producer Parks, trying to convince him to retain the classical Greek dances. She not only fails, but is converted to performing in a modern jazz version of the production, which creates quite a stir in Greek-godland. Culver plays the Mr. Jordan role made famous by Claude Rains but he is simply too British and stuffy to give it the wry interpretation embodied by Rains. Gleason does a reprise as agent Max Corkle and provides the only real entertainment in this otherwise yawning vehicle for Hayworth. The songs are wholly lackluster. (Hayworth's voice when singing is dubbed by Anita Ellis; Kay Starr dubbed the voice of Adele Jergens.) When Hayworth falls in love with Parks, she loses her godliness and becomes human, staying on earth, one might presume, to appear in one preposterous musical after another to torment the gods. DOWN TO EARTH utterly collapsed at the box office, a lead dumpling no one could digest. It soured Columbia's mogul Harry Cohn on doing similar films ever again. Years later George Axelrod proposed doing a fantasy he had written with Columbia but Cohn shuddered at the mere thought of it, snarling: "Fantasies don't make money." Axelrod countered: "But, Harry, you made a brilliant picture right here at your studio, HERE COMES MR. JORDAN. It was a fantasy and it made a lot of money." Cohn answered with the kind of logic peculiar to everyone on earth except Harry Cohn: "Yeah, but think of how much more it would have made if it hadn't been a fantasy!" Remade in 1980 as XANADU.

p, Don Hartman; d, Alexander Hall; w, Edwin Blum, Hartman (based on characters created by Harry Segall in his play "Heaven Can Wait"); ph, Rudolph Mate (Technicolor); m, George Duning, Mario Castelnuovo-Tedesco, Heinz Roemheld; ed, Viola Lawrence; md, Morris W. Stoloff; art d, Stephen Goosson, Rudolph Sternad; set d, William Kiernan; cos, Jean Louis; makeup, Clay Campbell, ch, Jack Cole.

Musical/Comedy/Fantasy **(PR:A MPAA:NR)**

DOWN TO THE SEA* (1936) 69m REP bw (AKA: DOWN UNDER THE SEA)

Russell Hardie *(John Kaminas)*, Ben Lyon *(Steve Londos)*, Ann Rutherford *(Helen Pappas)*, Irving Pichel *(Alex Fotakis)*, Fritz Leiber *(Gregory Pappas)*, Vince Barnett *(Hector)*, Maurice Murphy *(Luis)*, Nigel de Brulier *(Demetrius)*, Paul Porcasi *(Vasilios)*, Vic Potel *(Andy)*, Karl Hackett *(Joe)*, Francisco Maron *(George)*, Frank Yaconelli *(Pete)*, Mike Tellegen *(Cimos)*, John Picorri *(Greek Proprietor)*.

Two Greek brothers, Hardie and Lyon, are sponge trappers in Florida. They both love the same girl, Rutherford, whose father runs most of the sponge trade. Even the location footage and underwater photography can't help this one from sinking.

p, Nat Levine; d, Lewis D. Collins; w, Wellyn Totman, Robert Lee Johnson (based on a story by Eustace Adams, Totman, William A. Ullman, Jr.); ph, Harry Neuman; ed, Charles Craft.

Drama **(PR:A MPAA:NR)**

DOWN TO THE SEA IN SHIPS, 1937
(SEE: LAST ADVENTURERS, THE, 1937, BRIT.)

DOWN TO THE SEA IN SHIPS*** (1949) 120m FOX bw

Richard Widmark *(Dan Lunceford)*, Lionel Barrymore *(Capt. Bering Joy)*, Dean Stockwell *(Jed Joy)*, Cecil Kellaway *(Slush Tubbs)*, Gene Lockhart *(Andrew Bush)*, Berry Kroeger *(Manchester)*, John McIntire *(Thatch)*, Henry Morgan *(Britton)*, Harry Davenport *(Mr. Harris)*, Paul Harvey *(Capt. Briggs)*, Jay C. Flippen *(Luke)*, Fuzzy Knight *(Lem Sykes)*, Arthur Hohl *(Blair)*, Dorothy Adams *(Miss Hopkins)*, Hubert E. Flanagan *(Capt. Rumley)*.

Engrossing sea saga about a whaling vessel in the nineteenth century, with three generations of seafarers represented by Barrymore, Widmark, and Stockwell. Barrymore commands a sea-hardened crew in a long voyage in search of whales, his second-in-command being Widmark, a new breed of sailor who does everything by the book. He has gone to school to learn new nautical methods, which does not endear him to old salt Barrymore. The old captain learns to respect Widmark for his performance on board ship, but must discipline him for leaving the vessel to save the life of his grandson, Stockwell. Later, Barrymore proves his own seamanship by saving the ship after it strikes an iceberg, but he pays for the rescue with his own life. Before dying, he entrusts the care of Stockwell to Widmark. Solid performances by all make this an endearing and poignant tale, with plenty of action.

p, Louis D. Lighton; d, Henry Hathaway; w, John Lee Mahin, Sy Bartlett (based on an original story by Bartlett, from the 1922 version by John L.E. Pell); ph, Joseph MacDonald; m, Alfred Newman; ed, Dorothy Spencer; art d, Lyle Wheeler, Ben Hayne.

Adventure **(PR:AAA MPAA:NR)**

DOWN TO THEIR LAST YACHT* (1934) 64m RKO bw (GB: HAWAIIAN NIGHTS)

Mary Boland *(Queen of Malakamokalu)*, Polly Moran *(Nella Fitzgerald)*, Ned Sparks *(Capt. Dan Roberts)*, Sidney Blackmer *(Michael Forbes)*, Sidney Fox *(Linda Stratton)*, Sterling Holloway *(Freddy Finn)*, Marjorie Gateson *(Mrs. Colt-Stratton)*, Irene Franklin *(Mrs. Gilhooley)*, Charles Coleman *(Sir Guy)*, Ramsey Hill *(Mr. Colt-Stratton)*, Tom Kennedy *(Joe Schultz)*, Gigi Parrish *(Patricia Gilhooley)*, Hazel Forbes, Phil Dunham, Betty Farrington, Martin Cichy, Dot Farley, Helen Collins, Maurice Black, Harry Semels.

A Depression-struck upper-class family charters its yacht to make money. The family ends up shipwrecked on the island of Malakamokalu in this inane musical. Mobster-like natives, a queen who feeds people to her sharks for fun, and amateur hula hula girls bring this bad musical close to a campy level but not close enough. Producer Brock fared better with FLYING DOWN TO RIO and MELODY CRUISE. Songs: "Tiny Little Finger on Your Hand" (Val Burton, Will Jason), "There's Nothing Else to Do in Ma-La-Ka-Mo-Ka-Lu but Love" (Sidney Mitchell, Cliff Friend), "Beach Boy," "Funny Little World," "Queen March," "South Sea Bolero" (Ann Ronnell, Max Steiner).

p, Lou Brock; d, Paul Sloane; w, Marion Dix, Lynn Starling (based on a story by Herbert Fields, Brock); ph, Edward Cronjager, Vernon Walker; ed, Arthur Roberts; md, Max Steiner; ch, Dave Gould; m/l, Ann Ronell, Cliff Friend, Sidney Mitchell, Will Jason, Val Burton, Steiner.

Musical **(PR:A MPAA:NR)**

DOWN UNDER THE SEA (SEE: DOWN TO THE SEA, 1936)

DOWNFALL** (1964, Brit.) 59m Merton Park/AA bw

Maurice Denham *(Sir Harold Crossley)*, Nadja Regin *(Suzanne Crossley)*, T.P. McKenna *(Martin Somers)*, Peter Barkworth *(Tom Cotterell)*, Ellen McIntosh *(Jane Meldrum)*, Iris Russell *(Mrs. Webster)*, Victor Brooks *(Inspector Royd)*, G.H. Mulcaster *(Elderly Man)*.

Lawyer Denham gets a murderer acquitted, hires him as chauffeur, and tries to get him to murder his wife (Regin). The twenty-first of the forty-seven second features based on Edgar Wallace stories produced at Merton Park between 1960 and 1963. An interesting but minor crime drama.

p, Jack Greenwood; d, John Moxey; w, Robert Stewart (based on a story by Edgar Wallace).

Crime **(PR:C MPAA:NR)**

DOWNHILL RACER*½** (1969) 101 Wildwood/PAR c

Robert Redford *(Davis Chappellet)*, Gene Hackman *(Eugene Claire)*, Camilla Sparv *(Carole Stahl)*, Karl Michael Vogler *(Machet)*, Jim McMullan *(Creech)*, Christian Doermer *(Brumm)*, Kathleen Crowley *(American Newspaperwoman)*, Dabney Coleman *(Mayo)*, Kenneth Kirk *(D.K. Bryan)*, Oren Stevens *(Kipsmith)*, Jerry Dexter *(Engel)*, Walter Stroud *(David's Father)*, Carole Carle *(Lena)*, Rip McManus *(Devore)*, Joe Jay Jalbert *(Tommy)*, Tom J. Kirk *(Stiles)*, Robin Hutton-Potts *(Gabriel)*, Heini Schuler *(Meier)*, Peter Rohr *(Boyriven)*, Arnold Alpiger *(Hinsch)*, Eddie Waldburger *(Haas)*, Marco Walli *(Istel)*, Rudi Gertsch *(Selznick)*, James Sandoe *(Spectator)*, Noam Pitlik *(TV Announcer)*, Walter Gnilka *(Austrian Journalist)*, Werner Heyking *(Helgerson)*, Harald Schreiber *(Oliviera)*, Harald Dietl *(Journalist)*, Alexander Stampfer *(Skier No. 16)*, Ulrike von Zerboni *(Jeanine)*, Robert Brendlin *(Announcer)*, Michael Gempart *(Hotel Receptionist)*, Jack Ballard *(Candy Vendor)*.

Almost a docu-drama in style, DOWNHILL RACER marked the entry of Michael Ritchie into features with a strangely dispassionate film about Olympic skiers. Perhaps it was the fact that Redford was so cold as a character that this film was not the success it could have been. One of America's top racers is hurt and coach Hackman sends for two replacements, Redford and Kirk. Redford is a solo act who stays away from the others, bitches about conditions, but still manages some fabulous runs. (Note: Redford did a lot of his own skiing, much to the heart-palpitations of the studio executives. He was photographed by champion Jo Jay Jalbert who followed him down the slopes.) He returns home for summer training and finds himself estranged from his father, Stroud, and coldly dismisses his former girl friend, Carle. He returns to Europe and has an affair with Sparv, assistant to Vogler who is a wealthy manufacturer of ski equipment. On this tour he wins an important race and hones his rivalry with the U.S.A.'s best skier, Jim McMullan. Hackman begins a fund-raising tour for the U.S. team's Olympic funds and truly believes that this may be the year when America takes its place in world competition. Redford and McMullan engage in a very exciting downhill race and McMullan eventually breaks his leg in his final pre-Olympic trial, thus forcing Redford to ski at the Olympics. Redford is at the top of his form and wins a gold medal when the unknown who is going even faster than he takes a fall. The whole attitude of the creators is summed up in a scene between Redford and Stroud. Redford says to his father: "I'll be famous, I'll be a champ." The old man harrumphs back, "World's full of 'em." At the end of the film, after Redford has achieved the glory he's sought so ardently, he is curiously calm, almost disappointed, as this is not the flush he expected. He has no idea what's next in his life and, because of the totally icy way he's treated everyone else, we don't care at all. Redford wanted to make this picture very much and insisted on Ritchie after having seen a TV movie of the young director's. The studio opted for Polanski but Redford was adamant and the teaming turned out critically successful but commercially barren. One assistant director on the film was plucked by Redford for producing chores and that's how Walter Coblenz came to do ALL THE PRESIDENT'S MEN. Lots of actual race footage from Austria was intercut with staged races shot in Colorado, Austria, and Switzerland. If you love skiing, you'll revel in this movie. Much of the dialog was written the night before it was shot and it shows. Not a very literate picture but quite believable.

p, Richard Gregson; d, Michael Ritche; w, James Salter (based on the novel *The Downhill Racers* by Oakley Hall); ph, Brian Probyn (Technicolor); m, Kenyon Hopkins; ed, Nick Archer; art d, Ian Whittaker; cos, Cynthia May; m/l, "You Got Me Climbin' up the Wall," Kenyon Hopkins, "Moon River," Johnny Mercer, Henry Mancini, "That Old Black Magic," Mercer, Harold Arlen, "Olympic Hymn (DisquesErato)," Spiro Samara, Kostia Palarmas.

Drama **Cas.** **(PR:C MPAA:M)**

DOWNSTAIRS*½ (1932) 77m MGM bw

John Gilbert *(Karl)*, Paul Lukas *(Albert)*, Virginia Bruce *(Anna)*, Hedda Hopper *(Countess)*, Reginald Owen *(Baron)*, Olga Baclanova *(Baroness)*, Bodil Rosing *(Sophie)*, Otto Hoffman *(Otto)*, Lucien Littlefield *(Francois)*, Marion Lessing *(Antoinette)*.

John Gilbert's attempt to get his star rising in the sound era just didn't work as is evidenced by this corker that never got off the ground. Having once been a treatment writer himself, Gilbert wrote the scenario for this film about the goings on of a baron's servants. Gilbert is the rogue chauffeur who blackmails the cook to finance his affair with the butler's wife, Bruce. Bruce became Mrs. Gilbert after this production, a marriage that lasted two years.

d, Monta Bell; w, Melville Baker, Lenore Coffee (based on a story by John Gilbert); ph, Harold Rosson; ed, Conrad A. Nervig.

Drama **(PR:A MPAA:NR)**

DOZENS, THE** (1981) 78m First Run-Calliope c

Debra Margolies *(Sally)*, Edward Mason *(Sonny)*, Marian Taylor *(Russel)*, Jessica Hergert *(Jessie)*, Ethel Michelson *(Mother)*, Genevieve Reale *(Debbie)*, Sumru Tekin *(Nivia)*, Catherine DeLeon *(Gypsy)*, Michelle Green *(Michelle)*, Brenda A. Wolley *(Cathy)*, Sharon Brown *(Star)*, Brenda Joyce Wynn *(Tour Guide)*, Debra Kinlaw *(Betsy)*, Jack Sheridan *(Parole Officer)*, Helene Back *(Cottage Officer)*, Mary Jane Williams *(Mrs. Bridewell)*, Dick McGoldrick, Daniel Welch *(Police)*, Jack Borden *(Factory Owner)*, Jackie Brooks, Lanie Zera, George J. Finn, Aida Suris, William J. Sahlein.

An independent feature from Boston based on the true story of a young woman who attempts to put her life back in order after getting out of prison. An admirable effort which never quite feels like anything other than an independent film about a struggling woman.

p&d, Christine Dall, Randall Conrad; w, Dall, Conrad, Marian Taylor; ph, Joe Vitagliano; ed, Dall, Conrad.

Drama **(PR:C MPAA:NR)**

DRACULA**** (1931) 84m UNIV bw

Bela Lugosi *(Count Dracula)*, Helen Chandler *(Mina Seward)*, David Manners *(John Harker)*, Dwight Frye *(Renfield)*, Edward Van Sloan *(Dr. Van Helsing)*, Herbert Bunston *(Dr. Seward)*, Frances Dade *(Lucy Weston)*, Charles Gerrard *(Martin)*, Joan Standing *(Maid)*, Moon Carroll *(Briggs)*, Josephine Velez *(English Nurse)*, Michael Visaroff *(Innkeeper)*, Daisy Belmore *(Coach Passenger)*.

Perhaps the most chilling, genuinely frightening film ever made, DRACULA was the hallmark of Lugosi's strange career, but a role only a little more bizarre than the life story of the Hungarian-born actor. Based on the successful play and Bram Stoker's classic novel, the film is faithful to the original play plot. It opens in Transylvania where Frye, a British real estate salesman, arrives to arrange the sale of a deserted English manor house to a strange nobleman, Count Dracula. By the time he arrives in a small village near Castle Dracula, the sun is setting behind pointed black mountains. The terrain is rugged and hostile to life and the hard-scrabbling villagers are wide-eyed with apprehension. An innkeeper cautions Frye about traveling through the dreaded Borgo Pass to see Dracula but goes no further. Frye manages to hire a nervous cabman to drive his coach to the pass where Dracula's coach is to meet him. He makes the rendezvous while wolves howl and bats flutter through the night winds, unable to see the face of the driver. He is jostled in a mad ride over mountain roads until arriving in the courtyard of the towering, crumbling Castle Dracula. When alighting, he finds there is no driver at the reins. He enters to be greeted affably by a man in a tuxedo, his hair slicked back tight to the skull, his thin lips parted in a smile that has no mirth, only malevolence: It is the 49-year-old Lugosi and he would never be more sinister. He leads Frye up a huge staircase passing through enormous cobwebs without breaking them. Showing Frye to ornately appointed rooms, he invites him to have a late supper before retiring, pouring Frye a goblet of wine. The salesman, whose nerves are by then jangled, asks his host if he will join him. A closeup shows Lugosi's wan smile from which come the words: "I never drink . . . wine." Of course, Frye becomes another victim of the 500-year-old vampire, but he is not drained of his life's blood, only infected with Lugosi's madness, becoming his slave. During the voyage to England Frye releases Lugosi from his coffin and the vampire ravages the ship. When it is found drifting into port the entire crew is dead, the captain lashed to the wheel. All have puncture wounds on their necks and their skin is like alabaster, their blood utterly drained. Only Frye is alive, found as the doors to the cabins below are thrown open; he climbs toward the officials, wild-eyed and laughing madly. Frye is taken to an asylum, judged hopelessly insane, obsessed with eating spiders and assorted insects he can catch to have their blood. (Frye's performance is one of the most eccentric on record, outrageous by all standards; he appears all the more outlandish against the demure personalities of Chandler and Dade and Manners' rather wimpy rendering of Chandler's fiance. Van Sloan is so precise as the vampire hunter that he could be a phonetic teacher giving lessons.) Ensconced in the ruins of an abbey, Lugosi walks the streets of London at night, his first victim being an attractive flower girl. Later, at a theater production, Lugosi meets Chandler and Dade with their families. Since their mansion is near to his lair he visits them in various forms—mist, a wolf, a bat, then his own evil self to drain them of their blood. Dade (Lucy) is lost to the vampire and Chandler's life-blood is almost gone, as is her mind. She insists upon joining Lugosi in the eternal world of the undead, a thought that chills the bones of her father, Bunston, and fiance Manners. Nothing seems to combat the spell until the famous vampire fighter Van Helsing (Van Sloan), appears to aid the family. After he sees Lugosi casts no reflection in a mirror—the acid test for vampires—he knows what evil he's up against and bravely squares off against the monster. The Dutch scientist invites Lugosi into the study where he maneuvers him in front of a mirror. The vampire smashes the mirror, then he steps back to survey a wily opponent, giving him his wicked smile and saying, "For one who has not lived even a single lifetime, you are a wise man, Van Helsing." Before the vampire can attack, Van Sloan holds up a cross, the symbol of goodness, which causes Lugosi to shield himself with his cloak and flee, hissing curses at his antagonist. Van Sloan and Manners find Chandler missing just before dawn and rightly assume that Lugosi has taken her away. They pursue him to his abbey where they see him carrying the spellbound Chandler into the underground vaults where Lugosi has secreted his coffin bearing his native Transylvanian soil, that which preserves his remains during his daytime sleep. Sloan goes to Lugosi's coffin and drives a wooden stake through his heart, killing the monster; Lugosi's body shrivels, becomes a skeleton, then dust. Manners embraces Chandler, who is now free of Lugosi's trance. DRACULA was enormously popular when first released and remains a classic of horror to this day, largely due to the eerie atmosphere created by horror expert Browning and cinematographer Freund, particularly the castle sequences in the Carpathian Mountains at the beginning. But the film is all Lugosi, as it should be; he created the image of the undying vampire on the Broadway stage for three years, beginning in 1927, and despite the many other actors to play the role (John Carradine, Louis Jordan, Francis Lederer, Lon Chaney, Jr., Christopher Lee, Frank Langella), Lugosi remains the definitive Dracula, his name synonymous with the bloodlusting creature, as he wished it. Universal was apprehensive about making the film and feared the public might reject it out of sheer disgust or horror, so its publicity department never mentioned the horror theme, merely advertising the production with the come-on line, "The story of the strangest passion the world has ever known." Lugosi was himself not starred, only grouped with the leading players, for this, his chilling debut. Lon Chaney, Sr., was originally slated for the role of Dracula but he died shortly before Browning went into production so Lugosi was given the part, one which he never left. Studio heads felt that the film would do well abroad so a Spanish language version starring Carlos Villarias in the Dracula role and a completely new all-Spanish cast, directed by George Melford, was produced with the same sets only days after the English version was completed. Universal need not have worried. The film entranced the nation and filled the studio coffers so that another horror film, FRANKENSTEIN, with Boris Karloff, was successfully made the same year, and between these two horror classics Universal was established as the major studio to capture the horror genre. Further enhancing the creepy atmosphere of the film was the lack of music. Used infrequently are snippets from Tchaikovsky's "Swan Lake," but for the most part the sounds of creaking coffin lids, doors opening and slamming, thudding footsteps, the voices of the actors, and the howling of wolves provide the only noise. (To Lugosi/Dracula the wolves baying for blood warm his cold blood; at one point he hears the animal cry in the darkness and coos: "Listen to them—children of the night. What . . . music . . . they make!") There is a somewhat stagy feel to the movie once Lugosi arrives in England, but that's because Browning, at this point, stayed close to the play production. The author of this bizarre work was a somber British professor, Bram (Abraham) Stoker, whose novel appeared in 1897. He had traveled through Transylvania and the Carpathian Mountains and had culled local tales, legends, and folk songs that spoke of the "eternal vampire." His role model was undoubtedly Vlad Tepes (AKA: Vlad the Impaler), a murderous Balkan prince credited with hundreds of murders, a deranged blood drinker. Hamilton Deane, a friend of Stoker's, adapted the novel for the theater, his play opening in 1925 in London. It enjoyed great popularity and ran on and off until 1941. A German production in 1922 rendered a hideous silent film monster with stilts for legs, stiff arms, and claw-like hands, a sunken-faced creature enacted by Max Schreck ("Schreck" meaning "terror" in German, and a pseudonym for the well-known German actor Alfred Abel) and directed by the inventive F.W. Murnau. This film, called NOSFERATU THE VAMPIRE, was really a pirated property. When Murnau failed to obtain the rights to Stoker's novel he went ahead with filming the same story, only changing the name. Stoker's widow sued and won a settlement but received no payment since the production company in Germany had by then declared bankruptcy. Many writers worked on the Universal film, including novelist Louis Bromfield (uncredited), before it went into a costly production. Hall's vast and gloomy sets and Freund's fluid camera, coupled with Browning's unmistakable stamp on every frame, made for a grand netherworld production through which Lugosi glided. The actor created the most awesome and frightening of all monsters for he is in human form, completely without passion, mercy, or human compunction, unlike Karloff in FRANKENSTEIN, who elicits some sympathy since he is somewhat a victim of medical circumstances. Most other monsters are bestial or alien, such as those depicted in THE WOLF MAN or THE THING. Lugosi's monster walks in human form, ostensibly a person of culture, a member of the aristocracy, a *responsible* individual with manners, style, and charm, albeit he is as insidious as a viper. His menace is subtle, his embrace lethal, his vulnerability almost nonexistent. (How do you kill something already dead, or "undead"?) The part of Dracula is umbilical to Lugosi. It was his first major role on Broadway and he knew very little English when he got the role, learning his lines with painful difficulty, speaking phonetically, giving him that peculiar speech where every word is drawn out, clutched by the hooks of his Hungarian tongue. His deliberate, slow-paced actions and words make him all the more frightening. Lugosi's background was shady. He was born either in 1882 or 1884, and made his first stage appearance in "Romeo and Juliet" in 1902 in Budapest after studying at that city's Academy of Theatrical Art. He served in the Hungarian Army as a lieutenant during WW I and was rumored to be involved in the revolution that swept his country in 1921 before migrating to the U.S. where he played romantic leads until being trapped by the role of Dracula. So strongly linked to this part was Lugosi that he was completely typecast thereafter, playing monster after monster, coming to believe that he and Dracula were one in the same. In the mid-1930s Lugosi's mind expanded into his own personal horrors. He became a drug addict, spending his Hollywood fortune over the years on morphine, cocaine, and heroin until, broke and starving, he begged Los Angeles authorities in 1955 to help him take the cure. He quit "cold turkey" but died only three months after being released from an asylum. Throughout his Hollywood heyday, Lugosi went on playing Dracula offscreen as well as on. He attended parties in his white tie and tails and always wore his Dracula cloak, even when strolling down Hollywood Boulevard. His final request that he be buried in this cloak was granted, a last macabre gesture of a bizarre actor. Pieces of the DRACULA set were later used in Universal productions; the frugal ways of the studio left no stone unturned at least five or six times. (Even in the original DRACULA Universal cannibalized some footage from one of its silent sea epics for scenes showing the voyage of the *Vesta* to England.) A few minutes at the tail end of DRACULA were later cut and never restored for arcane reasons. Following the film's end, Sloan comes back on the screen to calm any fear-struck viewers, telling them not to go home with terror in their hearts (nurses were stationed in the lobbies of theaters when DRACULA was first released to attend to any overcome by fright). Before the fadeout, Van Sloan's normally benign countenance suddenly changes to a sinister look as the camera closes in and his tone becomes menacing as he blurts: "Just one word of warning, ladies and gentlemen—there *are* such things as *vampires*!" Sequel: DRACULA'S DAUGHTER.

p, Carl Laemmle, Jr.; d, Tod Browning; w, Garrett Fort (based on the play by Hamilton Deane and John Balderston and the novel by Bram Stoker); ph, Karl Freund; ed, Milton Carruth, Maurice Pivar; art d, Charles D. Hall; music, Petr Illich Tchaikovsky, Richard Wagner.

Horror   **Cas.**   **(PR:C-O MPAA:NR)**

DRACULA, 1958   (SEE: HORROR OF DRACULA, 1958)

DRACULA**   (1979) 109m UNIV c

Frank Langella (*Dracula*), Laurence Olivier (*Van Helsing*), Donald Pleasence (*Seward*), Kate Nelligan (*Lucy*), Trevor Eve (*Harker*), Jan Francis (*Mina*), Janine Duvitski (*Annie*), Tony Haygarth (*Renfield*), Teddy Turner (*Swales*), Kristine Howarth (*Mrs. Galloway*), Joe Belcher (*Tom Hindley*), Ted Carroll (*Scarborough Sailor*), Frank Birch (*Harbormaster*), Gabor Vernon (*Captain of Demeter*), Frank Henson (*Demeter Sailor*), Peter Wallis (*Priest*).

Langella starred in the Broadway version of the play that was distinguished by the black and white sets by Edward Gorey so that when some blood was seen, it popped out at the eye. Langella repeats his performance in this sumptuous screen version, but the magic is somewhat lost in the transference. We all know the

Dracula story and one had hoped that Badham and company might have added some new luster or a different twist. They made the mistake of electing to play it straight and opted for the Vampire's romanticism rather than the fright. LOVE AT FIRST BITE came out around the same time and took the humorous route, thereby garnering the lion's share of the audience and making a fortune in the process. Dracula is slow in starting and by the time any serious fear is introduced, the viewer may have dozed off. Langella is charming but somewhat too epicene to be seriously considered as sensual to any but the most impressionable. The usual ploys are brought into play in attempting to vanquish the Vampire: garlic, crosses, stakes, mirrors, and bullets. Naturally, nothing works. Olivier is Van Helsing, Nelligan is a gorgeous Lucy, and Pleasence does a rare role where he is not a villain. Once again, the moviemakers have committed the sin of remaking a classic and thinking it would draw a crowd. It's not bad and it's not great. It's somewhere in the middle, and that's not the place to be when you are attempting to do a movie based on such a famous trend-setter. Director Badham is a versatile helmsman but there was no way he could save this from being just "okay."

p, Walter Mirisch; d, John Badham; w, W.D. Richter (based on the play by Hamilton Deane and John Balderston, from the novel by Bram Stoker); ph, Gilbert Taylor (Panavision, Technicolor); m, John Williams; ed, John Bloom; prod d, Peter Murton; art d, Brian Ackland-Snow; cos, Julie Harris; spec eff, Roy Arbogast.

Horror   **Cas.**   **(PR:C MPAA:R)**

DRACULA A.D. 1972*   (1972, Brit.) 100m Hammer/WB c
         (AKA: DRACULA TODAY)

Christopher Lee (*Count Dracula*), Peter Cushing (*Prof. Van Helsing/Abraham Van Helsing*), Stephanie Beacham (*Jessica Van Helsing*), Christopher Neame (*Johnny Alucard*), Michael Coles (*Inspector*), William Ellis (*Joe Mitchum*), Marsha Hunt (*Gaynor*), Janet Key (*Anna*), Philip Miller (*Bob*), Michael Kitchen (*Greg*), David Andrews (*Detective Sergeant Pearson*), Caroline Munro (*Laura*), Lally Bowers (*Matron*), Stoneground (*Rock Group*).

Hippies messing around with black magic bring the Count back to life once again. Lee hunts down relatives of the man who put a stake through his heart, and most are beautiful female victims. A modern version of Dracula which is the weakest in the Lee/Hammer series. Sequel: THE SATANIC RITES OF DRACULA.

p, Josephine Douglas; d, Alan Gibson; w, Don Houghton (based on the character created by Bram Stoker); ph, Dick Bush (Eastmancolor); m, Michael Vickers; ed, James Needs; prod d, Don Mingaye; spec eff, Les Bowie; m/l, "Alligator Man," Sal Valentino, "You Better Come Through," Tim Barnes (both songs performed by Stoneground); makeup, Jill Carpenter.

Horror   **(PR:O MPAA:NR)**

DRACULA AND SON**½   (1976, Fr.) 96m GAU c
         (DRACULA PERE ET FILS)

Christopher Lee (*Dracula*), Bernard Mendez (*Son*), Marie-Helene Breillat (*Nicole*), Catherine Breillat (*Wife*), Anna Gael (*Woman*), Jean-Claude Dauphin (*Young Man*).

The first feature from the director of LA CAGE AUX FOLLES is a comedy with Lee playing his familiar role of Dracula. He has a son, Meney, who can't bring himself to bite a person's neck. Father and son are kicked out of the country by the Communists, who use a hammer and sickle "cross" to get rid of them. They get separated, and father ends up in England making horror films and Meney goes to France. They re-unite at a Paris premiere of one of dad's films. They both fall in love with the same woman, who looks like Meney's mother. The American version is butchered with poor dubbing and re-editing.

p, Alain Poire; d, Edouard Molinaro; w, Molinaro, Jean-Marie Poire, Alain Goddard (based on a book by Claude Klotz, from the character created by Bram Stoker); ph, Alain Levent (Eastmancolor); m, Vladimir Cosma; ed, Robert Isnardon.

Comedy   **Cas.**   **(PR:C MPAA:NR)**

DRACULA AND THE SEVEN GOLDEN VAMPIRES*½
         (1978, Brit./Chi.) 110m Shaw-Hammer c

David Chang (*Hsu Tien-an/Hsu Ching*), Peter Cushing (*Prof. Van Helsing*), Shih Szu (*Hsu Meichiao*), Robin Stewart (*Leyland*), Julie Ege (*Vanessa Buren*).

Shaw Bros., known for its kung-fu fare, and Hammer, the English horror production company, team up to bring another off-the-wall variation of the vampire theme. Cushing comes to China to study vampires and it turns out there are seven of them living in a cemetery. Chang and his three brothers (their father was killed by the vampires) use every martial arts trick to exterminate the bloodsuckers and avenge their father's death.

d, Roy Wood Baker; w, Don Houghton (based on the character created by Bram Stoker); ph, John Wilcox, Roy Ford; m, Wang Fu-ling; ed, Chiang Hising-lung, Chris Barnes; art d, Johnson Tsao; spec eff, Les Bowie.

Horror   **(PR:O MPAA:NR)**

DRACULA HAS RISEN FROM HIS GRAVE**½
         (1968, Brit.) Hammer/WB c

Christopher Lee (*Count Dracula*), Rupert Davies (*Monsignor*), Veronica Carlson (*Maria*), Barbara Ewing (*Zena*), Barry Andrews (*Paul*), Ewan Hooper (*Priest*), Michael Ripper (*Max*), George A. Cooper (*Landlord*), Marion Mathie (*Anna*), Norman Bacon (*Boy*), John D. Collins (*Student*), Chris Cunningham (*Farmer*), Carrie Baker (*1st Victim*).

The fourth of nine Dracula films by Hammer, and the violence and eroticism are more out front this time around. Villagers of Keinenburg are terrified when they find a young woman in a church bell, the blood drained out of her. The town's priest, Davies, goes after the Count, and only after the barmaid and the priest's niece become creatures of the night is Lee put back into his grave. Sequel: TASTE THE BLOOD OF DRACULA.

p, Aida Young; d, Freddie Francis; w, John Elder (based on the character created by Bram Stoker); ph, Arthur Grant (Warner Color); m, James Bernard; ed, Spencer Reeve; art d, Bernard Robinson; spec eff, Frank George.

Horror (PR:O MPAA:G)

DRACULA—PRINCE OF DARKNESS**½
(1966, Brit.) 90m Hammer/FOX c

Christopher Lee (Dracula), Barbara Shelley (Helen), Andrew Keir (Father Sandor), Francis Matthews (Charles), Suzan Farmer (Diana), Charles Tingwell (Alan), Thorley Walters (Ludwig), Philip Latham (Klove), Walter Brown (Brother Mark), George Woodbridge (Landlord), Jack Lambert (Brother Peter), Philip Ray (Priest), Joyce Hemson (Mother), John Maxim (Coach Driver).

This is the sequel to Hammer's HORROR OF DRACULA, with Lee again in the title role. Four tourists unfortunately spend the night at the Castle Dracula in the Carpathian Mountains. One of them, Tingwell, is killed and his blood used to raise the vampire. Lee then takes the dead man's wife, Shelley, and turns her into a vampire. Together they go after the remaining couple, who have enlisted the help of a local monk to stop them. A routine scare production from Hammer, and the third in its Dracula series.

p, Anthony Nelson-Keys; d, Terence Fisher; w, John Sansom (adapted from an idea by John Elder, based on characters created by Bram Stoker); ph, Michael Reed (Techniscope, Technicolor); m, James Bernard; ed, Chris Barnes; prod d, Bernard Robinson; art d, Don Mingaye; spec eff, Bowie Films, Ltd.; makeup, Roy Ashton.

Horror (PR:O MPAA:NR)

DRACULA (THE DIRTY OLD MAN)*
(1969) 80m Vega International/Art Films bw

Vince Kelly (Alucard), Ann Hollis (Ann), Bill Whitton (Jackal-man), Libby Caculus (Joan), Joan Puckett (Marge), Sue Allen (Carol), Bob Whitton (Station Attendant), Rebecca Reynolds (Stranded Girl), Adrainne (Susan).

Kelly is a descendant of the Count's and goes to America to feed on naked virgins. Whitton is his servant who tracks down and kidnaps the virgins. He falls in love with one and will not let his master have his way with her. They fight and both are killed.

p,d&w, William Edwards (based on the character created by Bram Stoker); ph, William Troiano; art d, X. O. Vangam.

Horror (PR:O MPAA:NR)

DRACULA TODAY
(SEE: DRACULA A.D. 1972, 1972)

DRACULA VERSUS FRANKENSTEIN zero
(1972, Span.) 84m Fenix c (DRACULA CONTRA FRANKENSTEIN)

Dennis Price, Howard Vernon, Alberto Dalbes, Mary Frances, Genevieve Deloir, Jossiane Gibert, Fernando Bilbao.

This cheap Spanish horror film has Dracula and Dr. Frankenstein running amok through the countryside. Another doctor finally stops the mayhem but the real mayhem is the production itself, which makes little effort to achieve the tone of sincerity of most of the Spanish vampire pictures.

d&w, Jesus Franco; ph, Jose Climent (Techniscope, Eastmancolor).

Horror (PR:O MPAA:NR)

DRACULA'S DAUGHTER**
(1936) 69m UNIV bw

Otto Kruger (Dr. Jeffrey Garth), Gloria Holden (Countess Marya Zaleska), Marguerite Churchill (Janet Blake), Irving Pichel (Sandor), Edward Van Sloan (Dr. Von Helsing), Nan Gray (Lili), Hedda Hopper (Lady Esme Hammond), Gilbert Emery (Sir Basil Humphrey), Claude Allister (Sir Aubrey Vail), E.E. Clive (Sgt. Wilkes), Halliwell Hobbes (Constable Hawkins), Billy Bevan (Albert), Gordon Hart (Host), Douglas Wood (Dr. Townsend), Joseph E. Tozer (Dr. Graham), Eily Malyon (Miss Peabody), Fred Walton (Dr. Bemish), Christian Rub (Coachman), William von Brincken (Policeman), Edgar Norton (Hobbs), Guy Kingsford (Radio Announcer), David Dunbar (Motor Bobby), Paul Weigel (The Innkeeper), George Sorel (Police Officer), Douglas Gordon (Attendant), Eric Wilton (Butler), Agnes Anderson (Bride), William Schramm (Groom), Owen Gorin (Friend), Elsa Janssen, Bert Sprotte (Guests), John Blood (Bobby), Clive Morgan (Desk Sergeant), Hedwig Reicher (Wife), John Power (Police Official).

Unsatisfying sequel to DRACULA (1931), with many of the same people coming back to reprise their roles. Holden, as filmdom's first female Vampire, is the late Count's daughter. Van Sloan has been nailed by Scotland Yard for having done Dracula in. The Yard doesn't believe in the supernatural so Van Sloan is accused of the nefarious crime. Otto Kruger is a psychiatrist (or "alienist" as they used to call them) working on behalf of Van Sloan. He unearths Holden's true identity and is about to be killed by her when Pichel, her servant, kills her. Pichel was almost a parody of the horror-movie servants with his hair slicked down and parted in the middle and wearing what must have been a ton of rice powder makeup on his face. A few shocks, a couple of laughs, and the brief appearance of gossip columnist Hedda Hopper are all that distinguish this film—little enough.

p, E.M. Asher; d, Lambert Hillyer; w, Garrett Fort (story by John Balderston, Oliver Jeffries, from Dracula's Guest by Bram Stoker); ph, George Robinson; m, Heinz Roemheld; ed, Milton Carruth; art d, Albert D'Agostino; spec eff, John P. Fulton.

Horror (PR:O MPAA:NR)

DRACULA'S DOG*
(1978) 90m Crown International c
(GB: ZOLTAN, HOUND OF DRACULA)

Michael Pataki (Michael Drake), Reggie Nalder (Veidt-Smit), Jose Ferrer (Inspector Branco), Jan Shutan (Marla Drake), Libbie Chase (Linda Drake), John Levin (Steve Drake), Simmy Bow (Fisherman), JoJo D'Amore (Fisherman), Arleen Martell (Maj. Hessle), Roger Schumacher (Hiker), Cleo Harrington (Mrs. Parks), Katherine Fitzpatrick.

Stretching the vampire legend to its ludicrous extreme, Zoltan, the Count's dog, has been brought back to life. It then brings Nalder, Dracula's servant back to life also, and together they set off for America to serve the only living relative of the Vampire, Pataki, with Ferrer, a Transylvania inspector, hot on their trail. The two vampires are killed by sunlight as they attack the summer cabin where Pataki and his family are staying. This is all done with a straight face.

p, Albert Band, Frank Ray Perilli; d, Band; w, Perilli (based on characters created by Bram Stoker); ph, Bruce Logan (DeLuxe Color); m, Andrew Belling; ed, Harry Kermidas.

Horror Cas. (PR:O MPAA:R)

DRACULA'S GREAT LOVE*
(1972, Span.) 90m Cinema Shares/
International Amusements c (GRAN AMORE DEL CONDE DRACULA; AKA: COUNT DRACULA'S GREAT LOVE; VAMPIRE PLAYGIRLS)

Paul Naschy (Count Dracula/Wendell), Rossanna Yanni, Haydee Politoff, Mirta Miller, Vic Winner, Ingrid Garbo.

Dracula runs a nursing home where four travelers drop in to spend the night. During the course of their stay, he puts the seal of Dracula on three of them and spares the fourth, a beautiful woman, because he wants her to help him revive his dead daughter. A dismal product from a country that once was a prolific center for vampire films.

p, F. Laura Polop; d, Javier Aguirre; w, Aguirre and Jacinto Molina.

Horror (PR:O MPAA:R)

DRAEGERMAN COURAGE***
(1937) 59m FN-WB bw

Jean Muir (Ellen Haslett), Barton McLane (Andre Beaupre), Henry O'Neill (Dr. Thomas Haslett), Robert Barrat (Martin Crane), Addison Richards (John McNally), Helen MacKellar (Mary Haslett), Gordon Oliver (Pete), Joseph Crehan (Dr. Hunter), Priscilla Lyon (Suzanne), Walter Miller (Maxwell), Herbert Heywood (Steve), Ben Hendricks (Capt. Harper).

A Nova Scotia mine disaster where three men were caught in a cave-in was the basis for this film. A doctor, the mine owner, and a foreman are the ones trapped beneath the ground. McLane is the draegerman in love with the doctor's daughter who leads a group in to save the men. The film builds excitingly to a last-minute rescue in this well-done paean to the draegermen, whose job is to rescue victims of mining accidents.

p, Bryan Foy; d, Louis King; w, Anthony Coldeway (based on the story "Cave In" by Coldeway); ph, Gilbert Warrenton; ed, Jack Killifer.

Drama (PR:A MPAA:NR)

DRAG**
(1929) 118m FN-WB bw

Richard Barthelmess (David Carroll), Lucien Littlefield (Pa Parker), Alice Day (Allie Parker), Katherine Ward (Ma Parker), Tom Dugan (Charlie Parker), Lila Lee (Dot).

Barthelmess is a hard-working newspaper editor in Vermont, and seems content until his wife's parents move in. The title refers to Day's parents and the situations they put Barthelmess in. Dialog is insufferably stiff.

d, Frank Lloyd; w, Bradley King, Gene Towne (based on the novel Drag: A Comedy . . . by William Dudley Pelley); ph, Ernest Haller; ed, Edward Schroeder; art d, John J. Hughes; m/l, "My Song of the Nile," "I'm Too Young to Be Careful," Al Bryan, George W. Meyer.

Comedy (PR:A MPAA:NR)

DRAGNET**½
(1974) 71m Screen Guild bw

Henry Wilcoxon, Mary Brian, Douglas Dumbrille, Virginia Dale, Douglas Blackley, Tom Fadden, Don Harvey, Maxine Semon, Paul Newlan, Ralph Dunn, Bert Conway, Allen Nixon.

Wilcoxon, a Scotland Yard detective, leads a search in New York for a band of jewel thieves. A body found on a beach turns out to be a bogus diplomatic courier who was smuggling the jewels. This clue helps Wilcoxon capture the thieves, but not before he gets his lumps. Plenty of action and suspense.

p, Maurice D. Conn; d, Leslie Goodwins; w, Barbara Worth, Harry Essex (adapted from an original story by Conn); ph, James S. Brown, Jr.; ed, Paul Landres; md, Edward Kate; art d, Frank Sylos.

Mystery (PR:A MPAA:NR)

DRAGNET***
(1954) 89m Mark VII, Ltd./WB c

Jack Webb (Sgt. Joe Friday), Ben Alexander (Officer Frank Smith), Richard Boone (Capt. Hamilton), Ann Robinson (Grace Downey), Stacy Harris (Max Troy), Virginia Gregg (Ethel Marie Starkie), Victor Perrin (Adolph Alexander), Georgia Ellis (Belle Davitt), James Griffith (Jesse Quinn), Dick Cathcart (Roy Cleaver), Malcolm Atterbury (Lee Reinhard), Willard Sage (Chester Davitt), Olan Soule (Ray Pinker), Dennis Weaver (Capt. Lohrman), James Anderson (Fred Kemp), Monte Masters (Fabian Gerard), Herb Vigran (Mr. Archer), Virginia Christine (Mrs. Caldwell), Guy Hamilton (Walker Scott), Ramsey Williams (Wesley Cannon), Harry Bartell (Lt. Stevens), Herb Ellis (Booking Sergeant), Harlan Warde (Interne), Cliff Arquette (Charlie Weaver).

Low-key crime tale, drawn from the immensely successful radio-TV "Dragnet" show, has L.A. cops Webb and Alexander investigating the murder of a former syndicate member. The evidence is slim—four shotgun shell casings and a plaster cast impression of the killer's left foot—but the boys nail the notorious "Red Spot Gang," led by the crafty Harris. Webb is his usual deadpan, cocksure, somewhat intolerable cop, and Alexander his drone-like sidekick (later replaced in a made-for-TV sequel by Harry Morgan in 1959). Police procedure is at the apex of this TV-spinoff feature and there's a lot of grumbling about civil rights getting in the way of the probing cops who use the "third degree" on suspects, urge wiretapping, and carp about the Fifth Amendment. Based on actual L.A. police files, the film nevertheless provides plenty of suspense as Webb and Alexander go through a hard, real world of crime. Boone is terrific as the tough police captain, and Gregg gives a standout performance as a grieving, one-legged widow of the slain crook. The theme beat for the series and this film—"dum-de-dum-dum"—was first used in the film THE KILLERS (1946).

p, Stanley Meyer; d, Jack Webb; w, Richard L. Breen (based on a factual case history of the Los Angeles Police Department); ph, Edward Colman (Warner Color); m, Walter Schumann; ed, Robert L. Leeds; m/l, "Foggy Night in San Francisco" (Herman Saunders, Sidney Miller); tech adv, Capt. James E. Hamilton, L.A.P.D.

Crime Drama				**Cas.**			**(PR:A MPAA:NR)**

DRAGNET NIGHT*				(1931, Fr.) 90m Osso/Leo Brecher bw
												(UN SOIR DE RAFLE)

Albert Prejean (Georget), Annabella (Mariette), Lucien Baroux (The Baron), Edith Mera (Yvonne), Lerner (Fred), Constant Remy (Charly).

A French boxer, Prejean, makes his way up the ladder and gets a shot at the title and wins. He dumps his girl friend, parties, and finally loses the championship to win back the girl. Photography and direction win some plaudits, but otherwise nothing original is to be found here.

d, Carmine Gallone; w, Henri Decoin; ph, L.H. Barel, Toporcoff; m, Phillipe Pares, Van Parys.

Drama								**(PR:A MPAA:NR)**

DRAGNET PATROL*				(1932) 60m Action bw

Vera Reynolds, Glenn Tryon, Marjorie Deebe, Vernon Dent, S. Boulface, Walter Long, George Hayes.

An independent film about a WW I vet who gets entangled with bootleggers. He leaves his wife and eventually gets arrested by prohibition sleuths, but a kindly judge lets him go free because of his war record. A stultifying bit of nonsense and a waste of time.

p, Ralph M. Like; d, Frank Strayer; w, W. Scott Darling; ph, Jules Conjager; ed, Bryon Robinson.

Crime								**(PR:A MPAA:NR)**

DRAGON FLIES, THE
				(SEE: MAN FROM HONG KONG, THE, 1975, Aus./Chin.)

DRAGON INN*½
				(1968, Chi.) 106m Union Film Co. c (LUNG-MEN K'O-CHAN)

Shangkuan Ling-feng (Chu Hui), Shih Cheng (Hsiao Shao-yueh), Pe Ying (Ts'ao Shao-ch'in), Hsu Feng (Yu Ch'ien), Tsao Chien (Innkeeper Wu Ning), Li Chieh (Officer), Kao Ming (Inn Manager), Ko Hsiao-Pao (Inn Servant), Kao Fei (Qun Yu-chang), Hsieh Han (Chu Chi), Han Ying-chieh (Mao Tsung-hsien), Yu Chi-kung (Yu Kuang), Tien Peng (Soldier), Miao Tien (Pi Shao-t'ang), Wan Chung-shan (Tuo La), Chi Wei (Yu Mien), Hsu Yao-kuang and Yun-wen (Chiefs), Lu Chin (Informer).

Chop-socky tale of vengeance in which a former general comes out of his hiding place as innkeeper to band together a small army to battle unscrupulous political powers. Plenty of fast action battles to satisfy a fan of this type of stuff.

p, Sha Yung-fong; d, Hu Chin-chuan; ph, Hua Hui-ying (Uniscope, Eastmancolor); art d, Tsou Jyh-liang.

Adventure							**(PR:C MPAA:NR)**

DRAGON MASTER				(SEE: CANNON FOR CORDOBA, 1970)

DRAGON MURDER CASE, THE*			(1934) 68m WB bw

Warren William (Philo Vance), Margaret Lindsay (Bernice), Lyle Talbot (Leland), Eugene Pallette (Sgt. Heath), Helen Lowell (Mrs. Stamm), Dorothy Tree (Ruby), Robert McWade (Markham), Robert Barrat (Stamm), William B. Davidson (Greef), George Meeker (Montague), George E. Stone (Tatum), Etienne Girardot (Doremus), Charles Wilson (Hennessey), Robert Warwick (Dr. Holliday). Arthur Aylesworth.

Meeker takes a swim in the pool on his estate and doesn't come out. His body is found later with dragon claw marks, and William tries to find the reasons behind the death. A totally implausible story with William fumbling his characterization of the worldly detective Philo Vance. (See PHILO VANCE series, Index.)

p, Henry Blanke; d, H. Bruce Humberstone; w, F. Hugh Herbert, Robert N. Lee, Rian James (based on the novel by S.S. Van Dine); ph, Tony Gaudio; ed, Terry Morse; art d, Jack Okey.

Murder Mystery						**(PR:A MPAA:NR)**

DRAGON OF PENDRAGON CASTLE, THE*
				(1950, Brit.) 52m Elstree Independent/GFD bw

Robin Netscher (Peter Fielding), Hilary Rennie (Judy Fielding), Jane Welsh (Mrs. Fielding), J. Hubert Leslie (Sir William Magnus), Graham Moffatt (Paddy), David Hannaford (Bobby), Leslie Bradley (Mr. Ferber), C. Denier Warren (Mr. Morgan), Lily Lapidus (Mrs. Morgan), David Miller, Anne Blake, Suzanne Gibbs.

Netscher and Rennie, the grandchildren of impoverished peer Leslie, find a sea dragon and use it to heat their drafty castle with the fire and smoke it breathes. Even kids will have a hard time accepting this amateurish offering.

p&d, John Baxter; w, Mary Cathcart Borer (based on a story by Janet M. Smith); ph, Arthur Grant.

Children								**(PR:AA MPAA:NR)**

DRAGON SEED*				(1944) 145m MGM bw

Katharine Hepburn (Jade), Walter Huston (Ling Tan), Aline MacMahon (Mrs. Ling Tan), Akim Tamiroff (Wu Lien), Turhan Bey (Lao Er), Hurd Hatfield (Lao San), Frances Rafferty (Orchid), Agnes Moorehead (3rd Cousin's Wife), Henry Travers (3rd Cousin), Robert Lewis (Capt. Sato), J. Carrol Naish (Japanese Kitchen Overseer), Robert Bice (Lao Ta), Jacqueline de Wit (Mrs. Wu Lien), Clarence Lung (4th Cousin), Paul E. Burns (Neighbor Shen), Anna Demetrio (Wu Soo), Ted Hecht (Maj. Yohagi), Abner Biberman (Capt. Yasuda), Leonard Mudie (Old Peddler), Charles Lung (Japanese Diplomat), Benson Fong (Student), Philip Van Zandt (Japanese Guard), Al Hill (Japanese Officer), J. Alex Havier (Japanese Soldier), Philip Ahn (Leader of City People), Roland Got (Speaker with Movies), Robert Lee (Young Farmer), Frank Puglia (Old Clerk), Claire DuBrey (Hysterical Woman), Lee Tung Foo (Innkeeper), Jay Novello (Japanese Soldier), Leonard Strong (Japanese Official), Lionel Barrymore (Narrator).

A strong cast with their eyelids taped render good performances in this overlong film based on Pearl Buck's best seller. Hepburn is the idealistic wife of Bey who confuses her husband with her practical outlook and aggressive behavior. They live with Bey's wealthy father, Huston, a compassionate farmer with considerable land. He alarms Hepburn when saying that they should not concern themselves with the Japanese invaders approaching their province. Hepburn disagrees with Huston and convinces her husband Bey to go into the mountains to work in the munitions factories as a way of resisting the enemy. En route they stay with Huston's son-in-law Tamiroff, a well-to-do merchant who slavishly collaborates with the Japanese troops in the area. Hepburn learns that Tamiroff is preparing a banquet for Japanese officers and she poisons the food. Tamiroff is accused of killing several high-ranking soldiers and is executed. Hepburn and Bey return to find Huston's attitude toward the Japanese changed drastically. He has been humiliated and his farm looted. He organizes revolt and he and his neighbors put their treasured homes and fields to the torch, leaving nothing but scorched earth before they move into the mountains to join the Chinese fighting the enemy. DRAGON SEED told the plight of China in sensitive, human terms, graphically showing how a peace-loving nation was goaded into battle. Hepburn, Huston, and McMahon are standouts, but the movie drags in spots and could have been edited down by 20 minutes.

p, Pandro S. Berman; d, Jack Conway, Harold S. Bucquet; w, Marguerite Roberts, Jane Murfin (based on the novel by Pearl S. Buck); ph, Sidney Wagner; m, Herbert Stothart; ed, Harold F. Kress; art d, Cedric Gibbons, Lyle R. Wheeler; set d, Edwin B. Willis, Hugh Hunt; cos, Irene Valles; makeup, Jack Dawn; spec eff, Warren Newcombe; tech adv, Wei F. Hsueh.

War Drama							**(PR:A MPAA:NR)**

DRAGON SKY*				(1964, Fr.) 95m Speva Films Cine-Alliance-FS c
												(L'OISEAU DE PARADIS)

Narie Hem (Dara), Sam El (Sok), Nop Nem (Khem), Skarine (Tith), Bopha Devi, Saky Shong.

Camus took to the same format that made his BLACK ORPHEUS such a stunning success, that is, the retelling of an old story, or myth, in an exotic atmosphere filled with bright colors and peopled with extravagant characters. Unfortunately he did not even come close to the earlier success; the visuals are every bit as brilliant, but the story is not integrated well into the backgrounds. The setting this time is the capital city of Cambodia, Phnom Penh, before it was bombed to pieces, with parts also being shot among the ruins of Angkor. Ample atmosphere is provided with which to tell a classic love story about a young man leaving the Buddhist monastery behind to pursue his love for a beautiful dancer. Also onto the charms of the young woman is a sleazy businessman unwilling to allow true love to take its course. This causes the young woman to meet with her death, to be followed by that of the youth; the two are then allowed to continue their love affair in heaven. A musical score by Jarre further heightens the exotic flavor, but the performances are so poor the melodramatics are not effective in the least, making for a beautiful but lifeless film.

p, Michel Safra, Serge Silberman; d, Marcel Camus; w, Jacques Viot, Camus; ph, Raymond Le Moigne (Eastmancolor); m, Maurice Jarre; ed, Andree Feix.

Drama								**(PR:A MPAA:NR)**

DRAGONFLY, THE*				(1955 USSR) 95m Gruslafilm Studio/Artkino c

Lina Abashidze (The Dragonfly), T. Tzutzunava (Efrosine), T. Abashidze (Elpite), L. Asatian (Marinee), A. Omiadze (Georgi), F. Chakhava (Tskriala), R. Chekhikvadze (Shota), D. Abashidze (Bichino), A. Zhorzholiani (Kirile), G. Shavgulidze (Archil), S. Gambashidze (Irakli), A. Toidze (Natto), D. Chichinadze (Tina), T. Tzitzishvill (Shota's Mother), G. Gegechkori (Levan).

A Soviet comedy of mistaken identities with Lina Abashidze, a student, flunking out of school because she loves to sing more than study. She makes it up by raising chickens and becoming Chekhikvadze's wife. Sprightly comedic touches here and there and lively songs give the whole film a touch of levity that is fetching.

d, S. Dolidze; w, M. Baratshvili, L. Hotivari; ph, T. Lobova; m, S. Tzintzadze.

Comedy								**(PR:A MPAA:NR)**

DRAGONFLY, 1976 (SEE: ONE SUMMER LOVE, 1976)

DRAGONFLY SQUADRON*½ (1953) 82m AA bw

John Hodiak (*Maj. Mathew Brady*), Barbara Britton (*Donna Cottrell*), Bruce Bennett (*Dr. Cottrell*), Jess Barker (*Dixon*), Gerald Mohr (*Capt. MacIntyre*), Chuck Connors (*Capt. Warnowski*), Harry Lauter (*Capt. Vedders*), Pamela Duncan (*Anne Taylor*), Adam Williams (*Capt. Wyler*), John Lupton (*Capt. Taylor*), Benson Fong (*Capt. Liehtse*), John Hedloe (*Capt. Wycoff*), Fess Parker (*Texas Lieutenant*), Gene Wesson.

Hodiak, an Air Force major, is in South Korea trying to get the local air force battle-ready. While he pushes the Koreans at a sadistic pace, he finds time to continue his romance with Britton, which had started in Hawaii. Her husband, who she thought was dead, turns up to complicate things. When the North Koreans attack with tanks, the squadron predictably wipes them out. The story line and characters are worn to shreds by previous use.

p, John Champion; d, Lesley Selander; w, Champion; ph, Harry Neumann; ed, Walter Hannemann; md, Paul Dunlap.

War (PR:A MPAA:NR)

DRAGON'S GOLD*½ (1954) 70m UA bw

John Archer (*Mack Rossiter*), Hillary Brooke (*Vivian Crosby*), Noel Cravat (*Gen. Wong Kai Hai*), Dayton Lummis (*Donald McCutcheon*), Merrill Stone (*Conway*), Marvin Press (*Cheng*), Eric Colmer (*Rickshaw Boy*), Frank Yaconelli (*Nico*), Wyatt Ordung (*Chinese Youth*), Reginald Singh (*Sikh Constable*), Roy Engel (*Police Sergeant*), Gilbert Frye (*Police Officer*), Leemei Chu (*Chinese Girl*), Wong Ahtarre (*Lu Sim*), Juney Ellis (*Edna Purleigh*), Bruce Payne (*Rev. Marlowe*), Keith Hitchcock (*Maj. Curzon*), Ernestine Barrier (*Mme. Curzon*), Philip Van Zandt (*Sen*), Anthony Joachim (*Li Tom*), Mauritz Hugo (*Eustace Crosby*), Charles Victor (*Howard Montgomery*), Esther Lee (*Concubine*), Joseph Kim (*Sing Wah*), Harvey Dunn (*Board Member*), Audrey Lau (*2nd Concubine*), David Chow (*Chinese Mercenary*).

Archer is a bonding company investigator in Hong Kong looking for $7 million in missing gold belonging to a man thought dead but who has been reported alive. The report, however, is just a smoke screen set by a cashiered Chinese general who has his sights on the gold. An uneven B-drama that is too talky for its own good.

p,d&w, Aubrey Wisberg, Jack Pollexfen; ph, Stanley Cortez; m, Albert Glasser; ed, Fred Feitshans, Jr.

Drama (PR:A MPAA:NR)

DRAGONSLAYER***½ (1981) 108m Disney/PAR c

Peter MacNicol (*Galen*), Caitlin Clarke (*Valerian*), Ralph Richardson (*Ulrich*), John Hallam (*Tyrian*), Peter Eyre (*Casidorus Rex*), Albert Salmi (*Greil*), Sydney Bromley (*Hodge*), Chloe Salaman (*Princess Elspeth*), Emrys James (*Simon*), Roger Kemp (*Horsrik*), Ian McDiarmid (*Brother Jacopus*), Ken Shorter, Jason White (*Henchmen*), Yolanda Palfrey (*Victim*), Douglas Cooper, Alf Mangon, David Mount, James Payne, Chris Twinn (*Urlanders*).

An Arthurian-type legend is marvelously recreated when MacNicol, a sorcerer's apprentice to Richardson, a great wizard, bungles his way to ridding the kingdom of a monstrous, fire-spitting dragon. Hallam, the king, has made an evil pact wherein he will sacrifice the virgins of his land to the dragon if the giant flying reptile will leave the kingdom in relative peace. When Salaman, his brave daughter, volunteers her own life, Richardson and MacNicol attempt to save her, even though Richardson is dying and his magic fading. MacNichol succeeds in besting the beast but not before some grim fatalities are recorded. Like EXCALIBUR, this film has the same kind of smoky atmosphere, medieval sets, and rugged terrain strange enough to be in the far-away land of myth, and the special effects are positively staggering. The script is literate and wry and Richardson is magnificent and humorous as the unbeatable wizard. Robbins' direction is as quick as a sword slash and the camera work of Vanlint is stunning. There is terror here, and gory violence in spots, not a soft fable for young viewers. The box office aim is imperfect, somewhere between teenagers and adults craving action fantasy, and the expected market did not arrive; the $18 million production lost $12 million even though the giant computerized dragon is worth the whole show.

p, Hal Barwood; d, Matthew Robbins; w, Barwood, Robbins; ph, Derek Vanlint (Panavision, Metrocolor); m, Alex North; ed, Tony Lawson; prod d, Elliot Scott; art d, Alan Cassie; cos, Anthony Mendleson; spec eff, Brian Johnson, Dennis Muren, Industrial Light & Magic, Inc.; ch, Peggy Dixon.

Fantasy **Cas.** (PR:C-O MPAA:PG)

DRAGONWYCK*** (1946) 103m FOX bw

Gene Tierney (*Miranda Wells*), Walter Huston (*Ephraim Wells*), Vincent Price (*Nicholas Van Ryn*), Glenn Langan (*Dr. Jeff Turner*), Anne Revere (*Abigail Wells*), Spring Byington (*Magda*), Connie Marshall (*Katrina Van Ryn*), Henry Morgan (*Bleecker*), Vivienne Osborne (*Johanna Van Ryn*), Jessica Tandy (*Peggy O'Malley*), Trudy Marshall (*Elizabeth Van Borden*), Reinhold Schunzel (*Count De Grenier*), Jane Nigh (*Tabitha*), Ruth Ford (*Cornelia Van Borden*), David Ballard (*Obadiah*), Scott Elliott (*Tom Wells*), Boyd Irwin (*Tompkins*), Maya Van Horn (*Countess De Grenier*), Keith Hitchcock (*Mr. MacNabb*), Francis Pierlot (*Doctor*), Arthur Thompson, Al Winter, Larry Steers, Wallace Dean, Tom Martin (*Servants*), Edwin Davis, Selby Bacon (*Black Boy Dancers on Boat Deck*), Ruth Cherrington, Elizabeth Williams (*Dowagers*), John Chollot (*French Count*), Virginia Lindley (*Helena*), Nanette Vallon (*French Countess*), George Ford, Alexander Sacha, Nestor Eristoff, Ted Jordan, William Carter (*Men*), Mickey Roth (*Nathaniel*), Jamie Dana (*Seth*), Robert Walter Baldwin, Harry Humphrey, Robert Malcolm, Trevor Bardette, Arthur Ayleworth, Tom Fadden, Clancy Cooper, Addison Richards (*Farmers*), Betty Fairfax (*Mrs. Mc Nab*), Douglas Wood (*Mayor*), Steve Olsen (*Vendor*), Gertrude Astor (*Nurse*), Charles Waldron (*Minister*), Grady Sutton (*Hotel Clerk*).

Gothic murder and madness are featured in this intelligent adaptation of Anya Seton's best-seller. The time is the middle 1840s and Vincent Price is a feudal Dutchman who lives on a huge estate in New York's Hudson Valley and takes money from the tenant farmers. He's married to a woman he resents because she's been unable to bear him a son and he must be content with a daughter. Tierney is a distant relative who arrives to take care of the daughter in sort of an *au pair* job. Price falls for Gene, and, unbeknownst to her, kills his wife. Now he proposes to the radiant Tierney, who accepts. She births a son who dies almost immediately. Price takes to the attic, begins using drugs, and becomes psychologically unbalanced (he wasn't that straight beforehand if he was willing to poison his wife). Langan is a local doctor who realizes what's happening. He strives to help Tierney and falls for her. Langan discovers the fact that Price murdered his late wife just as Price is about to get rid of Tierney as well. Price was sensational in the role of the madman although it may have set the tone for many more parts like that in years to come, especially for AIP. Tierney was beautiful but not very convincing. Langan did better in this role than in many subsequent jobs and great things were expected from him but he never did realize his potential and wound up in cheapies like THE AMAZING COLOSSAL MAN and MUTINY IN OUTER SPACE. This was Mankiewicz's first directorial job and established him as a force in the movie business.

p, Darryl F. Zanuck; d&w, Joseph L. Mankiewicz (based on the novel by Anya Seton); ph, Arthur Miller; m, Alfred Newman; ed, Dorothy Spencer; art d, Lyle Wheeler, J. Russell Spencer; set d, Paul S. Fox; cos, Rene Hubert; spec eff, Fred Sersen; ch, Arthur Appel.

Drama (PR:A MPAA:NR)

DRAGON WELLS MASSACRE**½ (1957) 88m AA c

Barry Sullivan (*Link Ferris*), Dennis O'Keefe (*Capt. Matt Riordan*), Mona Freeman (*Ann Bradley*), Katy Jurado (*Mara Fay*), Sebastian Cabot (*Jonah*), Casey Adams (*Phillip Scott*), Jack Elam (*Tioga*), Trevor Bardette (*Marshal Bill Haney*), Jon Shepodd (*Tom*), Hank Worden (*Hopi Charlie*), Warren Douglas (*Jud*), Judy Stranges (*Susan*), Alma Beltran (*Station Agent's Wife*), John War Eagle.

Cavalry captain O'Keefe leads a group of whites trying to escape through Indian territory. The characters on the wagon train range from a killer, Sullivan, who has been recaptured by marshal Bardette, to an entertainer, Jurado, who O'Keefe falls for, much to the disgust of his former girl friend, Freeman. Clothier's location photography is spectacular.

p, Lindsley Parsons; d, Harold Schuster; w, Warren Douglas (based on a story by Oliver Drake); ph, William Clothier (CinemaScope, De Luxe Color); m, Paul Dunlap; ed, Maurice Wright.

Western (PR:A MPAA:NR)

DRAGSTRIP GIRL** (1957) 69m AIP bw

Fay Spain, Steve Terrell, John Ashley, Frank Gorshin, Russ Bender, Tommy Ivo, Gracia Narciso, Tito Vuolo, Dorothy Bruce, Don Shelton, Carla Mercy, Leon Tyler, George Dockstader, Bill Welsh, Edmund Cobb, Woody Lee, Judy Bamber.

Spain is keen for cars and for Terrell, a mechanic and hot-rodder. At the big drag race, Terrell is up against Ashley, a rich punk who just before the race killed a man in a hit-and-run. After the race, which Terrell wins, Ashley is arrested and Terrell goes off with the girl. At the time the film was made, hot-rodding was the thing among teens and the film spoke to many of them.

p, Alex Gordon; d, Edward L. Cahn; w, Lou Rusoff; ph, Frederick E. West; m, Ronald Stein; ed, Ronald Sinclair; art d, Don Ament.

Drama (PR:A MPAA:NR)

DRAGSTRIP RIOT** (1958) 68m AIP bw

Yvonne Lime (*Janet Pearson*), Gary Clarke (*Rick Martin*), Fay Wray (*Mrs. Martin*), Bob Turnbull (*Bart Thorsen*), Connie Stevens (*Marge*), Gabe DeLutri (*Silva*), Marcus Dyrector (*Cliff*), Ted Wedderspoon (*Gramps*), Barry Truex (*Gordie*), Marilyn Carroll (*Rae*), Marla Ryan (*Helen*), Steve Ihnat (*Dutch*), Tony Butula (*Joe*), Carolyn Mitchell (*Betty*), Joan Chandler (*Lisa*), Marc Thompson (*Gary*), Allan Carter (*Mike*).

Another piece of exploitation from American International about juvenile delinquents who come from well-to-do homes and cruise around in Corvettes. Clarke is the leader of the group, who gave his word to his mother, Wray, that he wouldn't fight any more. He's already been in jail once for beating up a fellow teenager. Problems arise when a motorcycle gang begins hassling Clarke and his friends. When one of the cyclists is killed, the police nail Clarke, but everything works out in the end.

p, O. Dale Ireland; d, David Bradley; w, George Hodgins, V.J. Rheims (based on a story by Ireland, Hodgins, Rheims); ph, Gil Warrenton; m, Nicholas Carras; ed, John A. Bushelman.

Drama (PR:C MPAA:NR)

DRAKE CASE, THE** (1929) 74m UNIV bw

Gladys Brockwell (*Lulu Marks*), Forrest Stanley (*District Attorney*), Robert Frazer (*Roger Lane*), James Crane (*Hugo Jepson*), Doris Lloyd (*Georgia*), Barbara Leonard (*Mrs. Drake*), Bill Thorne (*Capt. Condon*), Eddie Hearn (*Edmonds*), Tom Dugan (*Bill*), Byron Douglas (*Judge*).

A courtroom drama about a servant who is accused of murdering her wealthy woman employer. It turns out that the wealthy lady's lover did the deed, and that the servant was the first wife of the wealthy lady's husband. A steady unfolding to the denouement is accomplished mostly from the witness box.

d, Edward Laemmle; w, Charles Logue, J.G. Hawks (based on a story by Logue); ph, Jerome Ash; ed, Ted Kent.

Drama (PR:A MPAA:NR)

DRAKE THE PIRATE*** (1935, Brit.) 96m Wardour bw (GB: DRAKE OF ENGLAND; AKA: ELIZABETH OF ENGLAND)

Matheson Lang *(Francis Drake)*, Athene Seyler *(Queen Elizabeth)*, Jane Baxter *(Elizabeth Sydenham)*, Henry Mollison *(John Doughty)*, Ben Webster *(Lord Burghley)*, Donald Wolfit *(Thomas Doughty)*, George Merritt *(Tom Moone)*, Amy Veness *(Mother Moone)*, Sam Livesey *(Sir George Sydenham)*, Margaret Halstan *(Lady Sydenham)*, Charles Quartermaine *(Parson Fletcher)*, Allan Jeayes *(Don Bernardino)*, Gibb McLaughlin *(Don Enriquez)*, Helen Haye *(Lady Lennox)*, Moore Marriott *(Bright)*.

An enjoyable swashbuckler about Sir Francis Drake, the first English circumnavigator of the globe, and the sinking of the Spanish Armada by his small British fleet in 1588. A romantic subplot deals with the secret marriage of Lang, who plays Drake, and one of Queen Elizabeth's ladies-in-waiting (Baxter).

p, Walter C. Mycroft; d, Arthur Woods; w, Clifford Grey, Akos Toinay, Marjorie Deans, Norman Watson (based on a play by Louis N. Parker); ph, Claude Friese-Greene, Ronald Neame.

Drama **(PR:A MPAA:NR)**

DRAMA OF JEALOUSY, A (SEE: PIZZA TRIANGLE, THE, 1970)

DRAMA OF THE RICH*** (1975, Ital./Fr.) Filmarpa-Lira/PAC c (FATTI DI GENTE PERBENE)

Giancarlo Giannini *(Tullio Murri)*, Catherine Deneuve *(Linda Murri)*, Fernando Rey *(Augusto Murri)*, Marcel Bozzuffi *(Giudice Stanzani)*, Corrado Pani *(Pio Naldi)*, Tina Aumont *(Rosa Bonetti)*, Rina Morelli *(Giannina Murri)*, Laura Betti *(Tisa Borghi)*, Ettore Manni *(Carlo Secchi)*.

A 1900s mystery that is the true story of a woman, Deneuve, her brother, Giannini, her lover, Manni, and Giannini's two aides, Pani and Aumont, who are accused, tried, and convicted of murder. Set against a political turmoil, the case is still recalled in Italy as an example of justice being tempered by politics. All of the evidence was circumstantial and no one is certain if the murder did take place as the courts decreed it did. Fernando Rey is the patriarch of the family and scores as a hypocritical educator who never takes a stance. Deneuve is glorious to look at and does an excellent job in the female lead. Since this was a well-known case, the data is presented as truthfully as possible but there is an undercurrent of commentary by the authors so we are never sure that justice was served. Period costumes and sets are as authentic as tinted daguerreotypes.

d, Maura Bolognini; w, Bolognini, Sergio Bazzini; ph, Ennio Guarnieri (Eastmancolor); m, Ennio Morricone; ed, Nino Baragli; art d, Guido Iosia.

Mystery **(PR:A-C MPAA:NR)**

DRAMATIC SCHOOL½** (1938) 78m MGM bw

Luise Rainer *(Louise)*, Paulette Goddard *(Nana)*, Alan Marshal *(Andre D'Abbencourt)*, Lana Turner *(Mado)*, Anthony Allan [John Hubbard] *(Fleury)*, Henry Stephenson *(Pasquel, Sr.)*, Genevieve Tobin *(Gina Bertier)*, Gale Sondergaard *(Mme. Charlot)*, Melville Cooper *(Boulin)*, Erik Rhodes *(Georges Mounier)*, Virginia Grey *(Simone)*, Ann Rutherford *(Yvonne)*, Hans Conried *(Ramy)*, Rand Brooks *(Pasquel, Jr.)*, Jean Chatburn *(Mimi)*, Marie Blake *(Annette)*, Cecilia C. Callejo *(La Brasiliana)*, Margaret Dumont *(Pantomimic Teacher)*, Frank Puglia *(Alphonse)*, Dorothy Granger *(Fat Girl)*, Maurice Cass *(Verdier, the Composer)*, Marek Windheim *(Greneuil, the Librettist)*, Minerva Urecal *(Rose, Boulin's Secretary)*, Priscilla Totten, Mimi Doyle, Maxine Marx, Barbara Weeks, Beryl Wallace, Ona Munson, Carol Parker, Ocean Claypool, Ruth Alder, Dick Haymes, Rick Vallin, George Travell, Eric Effron, Louis Adlon, Roy Bush, Jack Daniels, Edward Arnold, Jr., John Shelton *(Students)*, Florence Lake *(Factory Worker)*, Esther Dale, *(Forewoman in Factory)*.

Star-studded attempt to get the same audience that attended 1937's STAGE DOOR. This one flops on several levels. The story did not translate well from the original Hungarian play and it seems to splay in several directions as it tries to encompass too many tales. Rainer is a young actress/student in a French acting school in Paris. Her life is dedicated to her work and she is forced to work at night as a factory serf to pay for her schooling. When the other students wonder why she is yawning and dozing, she invents a story about an alleged affair with a nobleman. That lie is soon discovered and her classmates gleefully arrange a meeting between her and the marquis, fully expecting her to be embarrassed once the truth is out. But Marshal is all chivalry and goes along with the gag. Later, he falls for her and puts her in a posh flat, gives her an allowance, and she quickly moves from extreme poverty to a life of ease. Marshal has a short attention span and eventually dumps her in favor of another. Rainer returns to the school, gets the title role in "Joan Of Arc," and throws everyone for a loop with her abilities. Marshal returns but she gives him the air as she realizes that she has no time in her life for men, just the continuing quest for stardom. In reality, this could be the story of several real-life actresses who strove for stardom, achieved it, and woke up at the age of fifty to realize that it was all illusion. Ironically, this is exactly what happened to Rainer; following this film her career went into a fast eclipse. Turner plays a jealous student with relish. She is a witch par excellence. Dumont is a pantomime teacher in one of her rare non-Marx Brothers pictures. But someone must have felt she was nude without a Marx near her, so Maxine Marx, Chico's daughter, was given a small role as one of the fem students. Look for Dick Haymes in a bit part as well as Edward Arnold, Jr., and Ann Rutherford. This was LeRoy's first film for MGM after a string of successes for the brothers Warner, one of whom was his father-in-law (Harry). His son, Warner LeRoy, is the New York restaurateur who established Maxwell's Plum as well as rebirthed the Tavern On The Green.

p, Mervyn LeRoy; d, Robert B. Sinclair; w, Ernst Vadja, Mary C. MCall, Jr. (based on the play "School Of Drama" by Hans Szekely, Zoltan Egyed); ph, William Daniels; m, Franz Waxman; ed, Frederick Y. Smith; art d, Cedric Gibbons, Gabriel Scognamillo; set d, Edwin B. Willis; cos, Adrian.

Drama **(PR:A-C MPAA:NR)**

DRANGO*** (1957) 92m UA bw

Jeff Chandler *(Drango)*, John Lupton *(Marc)*, Joanne Dru *(Kate)*, Morris Ankrum *(Calder)*, Ronald Howard *(Clay)*, Julie London *(Shelby)*, Donald Crisp *(Allen)*, Helen Wallace *(Mrs. Allen)*, Walter Sande *(Dr. Blair)*, Parley Baer *(Randolph)*, Amzie Stickland *(Mrs. Randolph)*, Charles Horvath *(Ragan)*, Barney Phillips *(Cameron)*, David Stollery *(Jeb Bryant)*, Mimi Gibson *(Ellen Bryant)*, Paul Lukather *(Burke)*, Damion O'Flynn *(Blackford)*, Edith Evanson *(Mrs. Blackford)*, Phil Chambers *(Luke)*, David Saber *(Tom Randolph)*, Chuck Webster *(Scott)*, Katherin Warren *(Mrs. Scott)*, Chubby Johnson *(Zeb)*, Milburn Stone *(Col. Bracken)*, Anthony Jochim *(Stryker)*, Maura Murphy *(Young Woman)*.

Chandler is a Union officer assigned to a Georgia town during the Reconstruction period following the Civil War. It isn't easy for him to gain the trust of the community, especially since he was part of Sherman's march to the sea, which left most of Georgia in ruins. Howard tries to rally the townspeole to fight the Union again. Slowly, the town sees that Chandler is sincere in his intentions, and the uprising is stopped when Howard's father, Crisp, kills his son to stop the potential bloodshed. The first film from Chandler's production company, DRANGO merits applause for generally fine acting, and especially the camera work of Howe.

p, Hall Bartlett; d, Bartlett, Jules Bricken; w, Bartlett; ph, James Wong Howe; m, Elmer Bernstein; ed, Leon Seiditz; art d, George Van Marter; cos, Richard Chaney, Neva Bourne; m/l Alan Alch.

Drama **(PR:A MPAA:NR)**

DRAUGHTSMAN'S CONTRACT, THE***
(1983, Brit.) 108m British Film Institute/UA c

Anthony Higgins *(Mr. Neville)*, Janet Suzman *(Mrs. Herbert)*, Anne Louise Lambert *(Mrs. Talmann)*, Hugh Fraser *(Mr. Talmann)*, Neil Cunningham *(Mr. Noyles)*, Dave Hill *(Mr. Herbert)*, David Gant *(Mr. Seymour)*, David Meyer, Tony Meyer *(The Poulencs)*, Nicholas Amer *(Mr. Parkes)*, Suzan Crowley *(Mrs. Pierpont)*, Lynda Marchal *(Mrs. Clement)*, Michael Feast *(The Statue)*, Alastair Cummings *(Philip)*, Steve Ubels *(Mr. Van Hoyton)*, Ben Kirby *(Augustus)*, Sylvia Rotter *(Governess)*, Kate Doherty *(Maid)*, Joss Buckley *(Mr. Porringer)*, Mike Carter *(Mr. Clark)*, Vivienne Chandler *(Laundress)*, Geoffrey Larder *(Mr. Hammond)*, Harry van Engle, George Miller *(Servants)*.

Produced by the British Film Institute, this is a costume comedy of manners during Restoration times. Suzman, an aristocrat's wife, hires Higgins to make twelve drawings of the estate to surprise her husband, Hill, and patch up their shaky marriage. The husband has taken a vacation to enjoy other women. The draughtsman will only do the drawings on the condition that Suzman has sex with him on a daily basis, a condition she accepts. Higgins also fools around with Suzman's married daughter, who desperately wants a child, and he is hounded by the son, who is jealous of the power the artist holds over the household. When Higgins leaves, Hill is found floating in the moat, and Higgins is suspected. The family thinks he left clues to the murder in his drawings, and when the artist comes back, the family kills him and destroys the drawings. Then it becomes apparent that the daughter's husband actually was Hill's murderer in an attempt to grab the land. Striking costumes help make this wordy tale digestible.

p, David Payne; d&w, Peter Greenaway; ph, Curtis Clark; m, Michael Nyman; ed, John Wilson; art d, Bob Ringwood; cos, Sue Blane.

Comedy **(PR:O MPAA:R)**

DREAM COME TRUE, A**
(1963, USSR) 68m Odessa-Feature Studios c (MESHTE NASTRESHU)

Larissa Gordeichik, Otar Koberidze, Boris Borisenko, N. Timofeev, P. Shmakov, A. Genesin, N. Volkov, T. Pockena, L. Chinidzhanei, S. Krupnik.

The people of the planet Centurius become curious about Earth because of a song they are receiving from the planet. They send a team to check things out but it ends up on Mars. A well-designed science fiction film that was a sequel to PLANETA BURG (1962), A DREAM COME TRUE is fascinating for its unusual special visual effects of Earth, Centurius, and Mars.

d, Mikhail Karyukov, Otar Koberidze; w, Karyukov, Alexander Berdink, Ivan Bondin; ph, Aleksei Gerasimov.

Science Fiction **(PR:A MPAA:NR)**

DREAM GIRL½** (1947) 85m PAR bw

Betty Hutton *(Georgina Allerton)*, Macdonald Carey *(Clark Redfield)*, Patric Knowles *(Jim Lucas)*, Virginia Field *(Miriam Allerton Lucas)*, Walter Abel *(George Allerton)*, Peggy Wood *(Lucy Allerton)*, Carolyn Butler *(Claire)*, Lowell Gilmore *(George Hand)*, Zamah Cunningham *(Music Teacher)*, Frank Puglia *(Antonio)*, Selmer Jackson *(Judge "Jed" Allerton)*, Georgia Backus *(Edna)*, Charles Meredith *(Charles)*, Dorothy Christy *(Mollie Hand)*, Antonio Morales *(Lovelita)*, John Dehner *(Radio Announcer)*, Tad Van Brunt *(Dramatic Student)*, Catherine Price *(Aunt)*, Gordon Arnold, George Peters, Robert Rich, John S. Roberts *(Ushers)* Mary MacLaren *(Judge Allerton's Wife)*, Bess Flowers *(Social Secretary)*, Frederic Nay *(Assistant Florist)*, Gino Corrado *(Chef)*, Jerry James *(Best Man)*, Ida Moore *(A Woman)*, John Butler *(Shabby Little Man)*, Al Kikume *(South Sea Island Policeman)*, Noble Johnson *(Bartender)*.

Hutton turns in a wonderful performance as a woman who spends her life in daydreams, many of which are amusing, and some quite moving. Among the best are when she imagines herself the understudy to a Met opera star and manages to save the show, and a heart-broken whore who commits suicide in a cabaret; always when Abel, her father, enters her dream world as the protective papa; and in the musical and dance scenes in her dreams.

p, P. J. Wolfson; d, Mitchell Leisen; w, Arthur Sheekman (based on a play by Elmer Rice); ph, Daniel L. Fapp; m, Victor Young; ed, Alma Macrorie; art d, Hans

Dreier, John Meehan; cos, Edith Head; spec eff, Gordon Jennings; ch, Billy Daniels.

Comedy   **Cas.**   **(PR:A   MPAA:NR)**

DREAM MAKER, THE**

(1963, Brit.) 86m K.N.P.-Magna Films-BL/UNIV c (GB: IT'S ALL HAPPENING)

Tommy Steele (Billy Bowles), Michael Medwin (Max Catlin), Angela Douglas (Julie Singleton), Jean Harvey (Delia), Bernard Bresslaw (Parsons), Walter Hudd (J. B. Madgeburg), John Tate (Julian Singleton), Janet Henfrey (April), Richard Goolden (Lord Sweatstone), Keith Faulkner (Mick), Edward Cast (Hugh), Anthony Dawes (Cyril Bong), Barbara Clegg (Miss Ventnor), Iris Russell (Nellie), Abril Ward (Penny), Michael Thompson (Pete), Geoffrey Chandler (Herbert), Robert Dean (Geoff Munday), Bill Cartwright (Headwaiter), Bruce Beeby (Announcer), Gordon Waine (Stage Manager), Marigold Russell (Pale Girl), Gillian McCutchon (Gushing Girl), Bryan Parker (Archie), Anthony Pelly (Norman Winten), John Barry, The Clyde Valley Stompers, Russ Conway, Johnny De Little, Carol Deene, Shane Fenton and the Fentones, Dick Kallman, Geoff Love, Marion Ryan, Danny Williams, George Mitchell Show, Tony Mercer, John Boulter, Dai Francis (Guest Stars).

A number of England's pop singers and groups of the 1960s are on display in this variety show held together by a slim story line. Steele is a record company talent scout who was raised in an orphanage. He still returns to the orphanage from time to time to sing to the kids, and on one occasion he learns that the home needs money. He stages a music show to help out, and everybody wins. Produced for $430,000, the film was shot and brought into the theaters in a bare six weeks. Songs: "The Dream Maker," "Maximum Plus," "Day Without You," "Summertime" (Philip Green, Norman Newell).

p, Norman Williams; d, Don Sharp; w, Leigh Vance; ph, Ken Hodges (Eastmancolor); m, Philip Green; ed, John Jympson; md, Philip Green; art d, Scott MacGregor; ch, Pamela Davis, Douglas Squires.

Musical   **(PR:A   MPAA:NR)**

DREAM NO MORE*

(1950, Palestine) 72m Palestine Films/Classic Pictures bw

Avraham Doryon (Shlomo Vollums), Chava Alperstein (Leah), Yehuda Ben Moshe (Aaron), Joshua Weiner (Yehoshua), Israel Getler (The Baker), Claire Epstein (The Work Counselor), Chaim Wachgold (The Foreman), Anshel Avraham (The Haganah Officer), Zilla Berkowitz (The Seamstress), Azriel Nekritsch (Azriel), Zvi Liss (The Chairman), Gideon Baratz (The Secretary), Yael Fraenkel (The Receptionist), Zivia Backer (The Nurse).

An oddity produced in Palestine before the British pulled out and the nation was renamed Israel. Doryon handles the lead acting chore admirably as a Jewish refugee who returns to his homeland but is dejected by his lack of laboring skill. He soon takes a regular job and is fully content that he is able to help with the country's expansion—as minor as his contribution may be. Produced without dialog, the film leans on the crutch of English narration. The lack of dialog makes DREAM NO MORE an easy dubbing job for showing the entire world how the Jews have realized their dream of possessing their own country.

p, Joseph Krumgold, Norman Lourie; d&w, Krumgold; ph, Ben Oyserman; m, Lan Adomian; ed, Joseph Elena; narrators, Mason Adams, Ann Shepherd.

Drama   **(PR:A   MPAA:NR)**

DREAM OF A COSSACK** (1982, USSR) 95m Mosfilm/Artkino c
(KAVALER ZOLOTOI ZVEZDY; AKA: CAVALIER OF THE GOLDEN STAR)

Semyon Bondarchuk (Sergei Tutarinov), A. Chemodurov (Semyon Goncharenko), A. Kanayeva (Irina Lyubasheva), Boris Chirkov (Kondratyev), P. Komissarov (Khokhlakov), V. Ratomsky (Ragulin), N. Sevelov (Ostroukhov), N. Gritsenko (Artamashov), I. Pereverzev (Boichenko), P. Kiryutin (Nenashev), T. Noso va (Anfisa), S. Kayukov (Rubstov-Yennitsky).

Incredibly photographed but that's about the only thing to recommend this stagnant tale that quickly fits into the mold of Soviet Realism type of films. Bondarchuk plays the war hero who comes back home to his farm area. It doesn't take long for the stalwart officer to convince the people to cooperate in the building of a canal and dam. Also developed is a love affair between Bondarchuk and a dairy maid that eventually results in marriage, adding a dimension of humanity to a near perfect hero.

d, Yuri Raisman; w, B. Churskov (based on the novel by S. Babyevsky); ph, S. Urusevsky (Magicolor); m, T. Khrennikov.

Drama   **(PR:A   MPAA:NR)**

DREAM OF BUTTERFLY, THE** (1941, Ital.) 96m Grandi Film Storiel/ Esperia bw (IL SOGNO DI BUTTERFLY)

Maria Cebotari (Rosa Belloni), Fosco Giacgetti (Harry Peters), Germanin Paolieri (Mary Peterson), Lucy Englisch (Anna Ranieri), Luigi Almirante (Riccardo Belli), Gioacchino (Little Henry).

Modernistic retelling of the "Madame Butterfly" opera taking place in Italy and centering around the love affair between an opera singer and a composer, the latter making the decision that his career is of the foremost importance, cutting off the affair to meet with success in America. Unknown to the man, his lover is pregnant, but manages to continue with her singing career after the baby is born. The man eventually returns to Italy, but does so accompanied by his American wife and daughter, all three of whom are present when the old lover sings "Madame Butterfly." A bit sappy and long, but a well performed and interesting rendition. (In Italian; English subtitles.)

d, Carmen Gallone; m, Puccini, Chopin, Donzetti, Grieg, Liszt, Schubert, Strauss; md, Luigi Ricci.

Musical   **(PR:A   MPAA:NR)**

DREAM OF KINGS, A*** (1969) 109m NG c

Anthony Quinn (Matsoukas), Irene Papas (Caliope), Inger Stevens (Anna), Sam Levene (Cicero), Radames Pera (Stavros), Tamara Daykarhanova (Mother-in-law), Val Avery (Fatsas), Peter Mamakos (Falconis), Alan Reed, Sr. (Fig King), H. B. Haggerty (Turk), Chris Marks (Teleciles), Alberto Morin (Aristotle), Peter Xantho (Javaras), Zvee Scooler (Zenoitis), George Savalas (Apollo), Ernest Sarracino (Toundas), Tol Avery (Herman), Tony Jochim (Uncle Louie), Effi Columbus (Hope), Sandra Damato (Faith), James Dobson (Young Doctor), James Fortunes (Manulis), Katherine Theodore (Mrs. Cournos), George Michaelides (Doctor in Church), Lisa Pera, Lisa Moore (Nurses), Bill Walker (Kampana), Stasa Damascus (Falconis' Daughter), Theophais Lemonopoulos (Himself), Renati Vanni (Mrs. Falconis), Peter Kogeones (Argelo).

Five years after ZORBA THE GREEK, Quinn was still doing one version of the role or another. In this, Quinn is a Chicago Greek who lives from hand to mouth as he makes a few bucks, then loses them in marathon poker games that last for days. His wife, Papas, is a shrew and he is resigned to life with her for the sake of their son, Pera. Quinn's easy-going attitude is shattered when he discovers that Pera is dying of some unnamed disease. Quinn is convinced that what the boy needs to get well is the sun of Greece. Meanwhile, Quinn is having an affair with Inger Stevens, a local widow who owns a successful bakery. Since her husband died, she's been frosty but Quinn melts that and their liaison flourishes. At church, Pera has an attack of whatever it is he's suffering from and Quinn knows that he must get the boy away from the cold of Chicago and into the warmth of his native land. Sam Levene, Quinn's best friend, offers him the needed money for air fare and they are to meet the next day at the bank where Levene will draw out the necessary cash. But Levene dies of a heart attack before he can do it. Next, Quinn approaches Stevens for the cash but she refuses him. Desperate, Quinn loads some dice and gets into a game of craps. The loaded dice are soon discovered and he allows himself to be beaten brutally by H. B. Haggerty, almost doing Christ-like penance for what he knew all along was the wrong thing to do. Papas steals the money from her mother's life savings and hands a roll of bills to Quinn, urging him to leave immediately. He takes the boy and they depart, but not before he turns to look at Papas for the last time. Whether or not the boy recovers is never realized. Well-directed and acted, A DREAM OF KINGS suffered from the characters never going beneath the surface. Everyone around Quinn revered him but we are never shown why he commanded that much respect. Stevens is excellent as the widow in her final screen appearance before committing suicide. It was her second attempt. The first came after two abortive affairs with well-known stars and it left her sightless for almost a month. After recovering from that 1959 incident, she married musician Ike Jones in 1961 and was thought by all to have finally found peace. It was not to be and she died at 36, still beautiful, still charming, still tortured.

p, Jules Schermer; d, Daniel Mann; w, Harry Mark Petrakis, Ian Hunter (based on the novel by Petrakis); ph, Richard H. Kline (Technicolor); m, Alex North; ed, Ray Daniels, Walter Hannemann; prod d, Boris Leven; art d, Leven; set d, Bill Ford; cos, Eric Seelig.

Drama   **(PR:C   MPAA:R)**

DREAM OF PASSION, A**½

(1978, Gr.) 110m Brenfilm-Melina/SNC-Coline c

Melina Mercouri (Maya/Medea), Ellen Burstyn (Brenda), Andreas Voutsinas (Kostas), Despo Diamantidou (Maria), Dimitris Papamichael (Dimitris/Jason), Yannis Voglis (Edward), Phedon Georgitsis (Ronny), Betty Valassi (Margaret), Andreas Filippides (Stathis), Kostas Arzoglou (Bible Student), Irene Emirza (Diana), Panos Papaioannou (Manos), Manos Katrakis (Kreon), Nilos Galiatsos (Lighting Man), Savvas Axiotis (Soundman), Litsa Vaidou, Olympia Papadouka, Anna Thomaidou, Freddie Germanos, Stefanos Vlachos, Alexis Solomos.

After their enormous comedic success with NEVER ON SUNDAY, husband-wife team of Mercouri and expatriate American Dassin decided to look at the dark side of life with this drama. Mercouri is a well-known actress about to do a production of "Medea" under the helm of director Voutsinas, a man with whom she once had an affair. They learn that Burstyn is living in Greece. She's an American woman who killed her children, just as Medea did, and is now nearby. Voutsinas insists that Mercouri go meet the woman to find out her motivations so a better performance can be presented. The play and the Mercouri-Burstyn interviews are intercut to the conclusion that has Burstyn breaking down while Mercouri, as Medea, kills the children on stage. A curious film that suffers from a lack of directorial path, A DREAM OF PASSION is still worth a look because of the talents of the actresses involved. Dassin can always be counted on to make a left turn where a right one might be indicated. Lots of yelling and screaming as Voutsinas encourages Mercouri to pull out all the stops in her stage performance and go against her intuition to play it restrained. Some goriness but not nearly as much as a director like Brian De Palma, say, might have dictated. To his credit, Dassin does leave something to the imagination and, in doing so, creates even more horror than might have been photographed. (In English and Greek.)

p,d&w, Jules Dassin; ph, George Arvanitis (Eastmancolor); m, Iannis Markopolous; ed, George Klotz, set d&cos, Dionysis Fotopoulos.

Drama   **(PR:C   MPAA:NR)**

DREAM OF SCHONBRUNN** (1933, Aus.) 85m GFD bw
(TRAUM VON SCHONBRUNN)

Martha Eggerth (She), Herman Thimig (He), Hans Junkermann (Prime Minister), Julia Serda (Palace Mistress), Ernst Verebes (Lieutenant), Hilde Koller (Soubrette).

An Austrian musical about a princess, Eggerth, being forced to marry a prince against her will. She falls in love with another man, who just happens to be the prince. Shot in and around the Schonbrunn castle in Vienna. Eggerth, Hungarian by birth and an outstanding German actress in the 1930s, spent the war years in the U.S. and then returned to Germany. (In German.)

p, Schulz, Wuellner; d, Johannes Meyer; w, Walter Wasserman, Walter Schlee; m, Arthur Guttman; ph, Karl Drews.

Musical　　　　　　　　　　　　　　　　**(PR:A　MPAA:NR)**

DREAM OF THE RED CHAMBER, THE**
(1966, Chi.) Hayien Film Studio (HING LOU MENG)
Hsu Yu-lan, Wang Wen-chuan, Lu Jui-ying, Chin Tsai-feng, Chou Pai-kui.

An operatic tale from 18th-century China about the fortunes and failures of a wealthy, prominent family that is stricken with great misfortunes when one of the sons loses the jade piece which had been imbedded in his mouth. The jade piece is eventually returned to the man and luck is revived, but not before the son marries against his will and other tragedies mar the family's cohesiveness and strength.

d, Wang Ping; m/l, Yuehchu Opera Company.

Drama/Opera　　　　　　　　　　　　　　**(PR:A　MPAA:NR)**

DREAM ON*
(1981) 96m Magic Cinema c
Ed Harris, Erin Nico, Steve Hartley, Robin Ginsburg, Bertina Johnson, Charles Boswell, Francine Lembi, Bob Strom, Paul Reubens, Eric Boles, Susan Berlin, Gar Campbell, Gina Banks, Amy Ford, Ian Ford, Phillip Baker Hall.

Harris, before THE RIGHT STUFF and UNDER FIRE, stars in this experimental film about a group of Los Angeles actors who put on a noncommercial, serious play. The players range from a former prostitute, an embarrassed soap opera actor, two confused homosexuals, and a straight couple trying to work things out. A nonexistent script has scenes adding up to nothing.

p, Erin Nico; d,w&ph, Ed Harker (DuArt Color); m, Willie Lee; ed, Dan Borenstein; set d, Mera Cheriyan; cos, Lydia Wilcox.

Experimental Drama　　　　　　　　　　　**(PR:O　MPAA:NR)**

DREAM TOWN*
(1973, Ger.) 124m Independent Film/Maran Film Produktion c (TRAUMSTADT; AKA: CITY OF DREAMS)
Per Oscarsson, Rosemarie Fendel, Eva Maria Meineke, Alexander May, Helen Vita, Herbert Boettcher, Rony Williams, Heinrich Schweiger, Louis Waldon.

A couple go to a small town where people can live out their wildest fantasies. The story runs along the same lines as WESTWORLD, released the same year. The dreams get out of hand and cause the destruction of the town. A boring mess that has well-designed sets and that's about it. Director Schaaf is better known for his film TATOWIERUNG (1967).

p, Heinz Angermeyer; d&w, Johannes Schaff (based on the novel The Other Side by Kubin); ph, Gerard Vanderberg.

Science Fiction　　　　　　　　　　　　　**(PR:C　MPAA:NR)**

DREAM WIFE**½
(1953) 99m MGM bw
Cary Grant (Clemson Reade), Deborah Kerr (Effie), Walter Pidgeon (Walter McBride), Betta St. John (Tarji), Eduard Franz (Khan), Buddy Bear (Vizier), Les Tremayne (Ken Landwell), Donald Randolph (Ali), Bruce Bennett (Charlie Elkwood), Richard Anderson (Henry Malvine), Dan Tobin (Mr. Brown), Movita (Rima), Gloria Holden (Mrs. Landwell), June Clayworth (Mrs. Elkwood), Dean Miller (George), Steve Forrest (Louis), Jonathan Cott (Marine), Patricia Tiernan (Pat), Dan Barton (Sailor), Mary Lawrence (Mrs. Malvine), Faire Binney (Mrs. Parker), Kay Riehl (Woman), Edward Cassidy (Customs Official), Jean Andren (Bit), Perry Sheehan (Evelyn the Receptionist), Harry Stanton, Steve Carruthers, James Farrar (Men), Virginia Mullen (Annie), Marie Brown (Miss Temple), Dick Rich (Delivery Man), Bert Moorhouse (Attlow), Jimmy Moss (Small Boy), Gail Bonney ("Mommy"), Lillian Culver (Woman at Airport), Forbes Murray, Donald Dillaway, Gayne Whitman (Men at Airport), John Alvin, Dorothy Kennedy, William Hamel (Reporters), Allen O'Locklin (Clerk), Andre d'Arcy, William McCormick, Bernie Gozier, Mohamed Ilbagi (Bukistanians), Jim Cronin, Paul F. Smith (Bellhops), Alphonse Martel (Headwaiter), Jack Chefe (Captain), Margie Liszt (Woman Cab Driver), Charles Sullivan (Truck Driver), William Vedder (Old Man), Vernon Rich (McBride's Assistant), Robert E. Nichols (Elevator Boy), Kathleen Freeman (Chambermaid), Aram Katcher (Bukistanian/Messenger), Rudy Rama (Servant), Bob Lugo (Guard), Dabbs Greer (Elevator Boy), Hassan Khyyam (Bukistanian Priest), Gordon Richards (Sir Cecil), Jack George (Clarence), Beryl McCutcheon, Margaret Hedin, Inez Gorman (Secretaries).

Grant and Kerr are at the top of their form but the script and direction aren't. A battle-of-the-sexes romp with a fanciful story and not enough laughs to carry the slim plot. Grant is dating Kerr, an official with the U.S. State Department. He'd like to marry her but wants a woman at home, not in the office. Kerr is loathe to give up her excellent job and, at the moment when Grant asks for her hand, she is in the midst of an oil crisis with the Middle East (30-plus years later, nothing's changed). Grant recalls a gorgeous Arabian princess, Betta St. John, he once met in the mythical country of Bukistan (which sounds like a style of Persian rug) who had spent her life learning how to please a man. He cables her and proposes in a fit of pique. Kerr is sent to Bukistan because of the ticklish problems with the oil cartel and her job is to make certain that Grant does not get out of line in his courtship of St. John. The princess comes to the U.S. and falls under the influence of Kerr, who shows her that women have equal rights to men and there's no need to defer to the male of the species. Once that's established, it's just a matter of a few minutes before Grant and Kerr wind up together at the finale. A stronger hand at the helm might have made this work but Sheldon, now the very popular novelist, lets the actors walk all over him. They must have also taken liberties with the script that he co-authored, because Sheldon, if nothing else, can be a terrific comedy writer, and

Herbert Baker, the second co-author, was acknowledged as one of Hollywood's wits. Baker's special material pieces for the annual Writers Guild dinners are still quoted many years after his death. This was a re-teaming of the successful group who made THE BACHELOR AND THE BOBBY-SOXER five years before, but it just didn't measure up. Walter Pidgeon is co-starred as Kerr's boss but he could have mailed his part in for all the use they made of his considerable abilities. Good work by the featured players, especially Bruce Bennett, Dabbs Greer, Richard Anderson, and Steve Forrest.

p, Dore Schary; d, Sidney Sheldon; w, Sheldon, Herbert Baker, Alfred Lewis Levitt (based on an unpublished story by Levitt); ph, Milton Krasner; m, Conrad Salinger; ed, George White; art d, Cedric Gibbons, Daniel B. Cathcart; set d, Edwin B. Willis, Alfred E. Spencer; spec eff, A. Arnold Gillespie, Warren Newcombe; cos, Helen Rose, Herschel McCoy; m/l, Charles Wolcott, Jamshid Sheibani.

Comedy　　　　　　　　　　　　　　　　**(PR:A　MPAA:NR)**

DREAMBOAT***½
(1952) 83m FOX bw
Clifton Webb (Thornton Sayre), Ginger Rogers (Gloria), Anne Francis (Carol Sayre), Jeffrey Hunter (Bill Ainslee), Elsa Lanchester (Dr. Coffey), Fred Clark (Sam Levitt), Paul Harvey (Harrington), Ray Collins (Timothy Stone), Helene Stanley (Mimi), Richard Garrick (Judge Bowles), George Barrows (Commandant), Jay Adler (Desk Clerk), Marietta Canty (Lavinia), Laura Brooks (Mrs. Gunther), Emory Parnell (Used Car Salesman), Helen Hatch (Mrs. Faust), Harry Cheshire (MacIntosh), Everett Glass (George Bradley), Paul Maxey (Clarence Bornay), Sandor Szabo (Giant Arab), Leo Cleary (Court Clerk), Lee Turnbull (Denham), Helen Brown (Dorothy), Al Herman (Drunk), Howard Banks (Hotel Clerk), Jack Mather (Hotel Detective), Matt Mattox, Frank Radcliffe (Men in Commercial), Gwen Verdon (Girl in Commercial), Bob Easton, Marjorie Halliday (TV Commercial), Donna Lee Hickey (Cigarette Girl), Richard Allan (Student), Clive Morgan (French Captain), Crystal Reeves (Secretary), Vici Raaf, Barbara Woodell (Receptionists), Don Kohler, Robert B. Williams (Photographers), Tony De Mario (Waiter), Joe Recht (Busboy), Steve Carruthers, Warren Mace (Bit Men), Victoria Horne (Waitress), Bob Nichols (Student), Paul Kruger (Doorman), Alphonse Martel (Maitre D'), Fred Graham (Bartender), Jean Corbett (Bit Girl), Mary Treen (Bit Wife), Richard Karlan (Husband), May Wynn (Cigarette Girl).

Charming spoof of television featuring Webb as a highly-regarded professor with a history that no one knows about until a series of old films are shown on TV. It seems that this conservative educator had been a screen star back in the swashbuckling days and the showing of these old films is destroying his credibility as a college instructor of literature. His former co-star, Ginger Rogers, hosts the TV showings and hawks perfume these days, making scads of money in the process. Webb and daughter Francis seek to stop the showing of the films and sue. Webb feels that the movies are being distorted in order to sell the various boutique aromas and that constitutes an invasion of his privacy. He takes it to court and acts as his own attorney when he shows the silly commercials that are being intercut with his original acting work. Webb and Rogers are seen in various takeoffs on movies about WW I, the Foreign Legion, French musketeers, etc. Once involved, Webb is again taken by the old thrill of acting and decides to flee the groves of academe in favor of the movie business. Fine character work from Elsa Lanchester as the university boss who takes another, more passionate stance re Webb when his background is revealed. Hunter as the ad agency man is also good, but the picture belongs to Webb. Very few actors could essay "righteous indignation" as well as Webb and he plays it to the hilt in this role. Note: Donna Lee Hickey changed her name to May Wynn, which was also her character's name in THE CAINE MUTINY.

p, Sol C. Siegel; d&w, Claude Binyon (based on a story by John D. Weaver); ph, Milton Krasner; m, Cyril J. Mockridge; ed, James B. Clark; md, Lionel Newman; art d, Lyle R. Wheeler, Maurice Ransford; set d, Thomas Little, Fred J. Rode; cos, Travilla; spec eff, Ray Kellogg; TV animation, United Productions of America.

Comedy　　　　　　　　　　　　　　　　**(PR:AA　MPAA:NR)**

DREAMER, THE**
(1936, Ger.) 105m Tobis bw (TRAUMULUS)
Emil Jannings (Prof. Niemeyer), Hilde Weissner (Jadwiga, His Wife), Harald Paulsen (Fritz, His Son), Hildegard Barko (Olga), Paul W. Krueger (Pedel Schimke), Hannes Stelzer (Kurt von Zedlitz), Hilde Von Stolz (Lydia Link), Herbert Huebner (Landrat von Kannwurf), Ernst Waldow (Assessor Mollwein), Walter Steinbeck (Maj. Kleinstueber), Hans Brausewetter (Falk).

Oscar winner (1928) Jannings is a school professor whose teaching techniques are outdated. He changes his methods when one of his students takes his reprimand and lecture to heart, and dies before the big school party. (In German.)

p, Carl Froelich; w, Robert Adolf Stemmle, Erich Ebermayer (based on a story by Arno Holz, Oskar Jerschke); Reimar Kuntze.

Drama　　　　　　　　　　　　　　　　**(PR:A　MPAA:NR)**

DREAMER, THE**
(1970, Israel) 86m Toda Films-Cannon c (HA 'TIMHONI)
Tuvia Tavi (Eli), Leora Rivlin (Girl), Berta Litvina (Rachel), Schlomo Bar-Shavit (Manager of Home), Dvora Keidar (Mother), Nathan Kogan (Father), Israel Segal (Waiter), Nathan W. Volfovitz (Mushkin), Bila Rabinovitz (Litvinna), Bronka Zaltzman, Arie Kasbiner, Esther Kadosh, Alina Starnitzka, Issac Mandelbaum, Rodulf Henig, Abraham Markowitz, Adina Fair, Moshe Segal, Harriet Karr, Jacob Timan.

Tavi is a struggling artist who works at an old folks' home in this sensitive portrayal of love and old age. He becomes close friends with Litvina, one of the elderly women at the home. Then he makes love to a young woman whose grandfather has died in the home and at first Litvina is hurt, but she comes to realize that Tavi needs the company of women of his own age, too. But Tavi in the meantime has decided that Litvina and the rest of the people at the home are more important to him than the young woman, Rivlin.

p, Ami Artzi; d&w, Dan Wolman; ph, Paul Glickman; m, Gershon Kingsley; ed, Barry Harte Prince.

Drama   **(PR:O   MPAA:R)**

DREAMER*½   (1979) 79m FOX c

Tim Matheson (Dreamer), Susan Blakely (Karen), Jack Warden (Harry), Richard B. Shull (Taylor), Barbara Stuart (Angie), Owen Bush (The Fan), Marya Small (Elaine), Matt Clark (Spider), John Crawford (Riverboat Captain), Chris Schenkel (Himself), Nelson Burton, Jr. (Color Man), Morgan Farley (Old Timer), Pedro Gonzalez Gonzalez (Too), Speedy Zapata (Juan), Jobe Cerny (Patterson), Azizi Johari (Lady), Dick Weber (Johnny Watkin), Julian Byrd (Red), Rita Ascot Boyd (Grandma), Marie E. Brady (Old Lady), Pat Mullins Brown (Nurse), Richard Cosentino (Official), Beverly Dunn Davis (Betty), Monroe Diestel (Young Dreamer), Wally Engelhardt (Bus Driver), Bert Hinchman, Scott Larson (Policemen), Ray Hoffstetter (Minicam Operator) Richard McGougan (Truck Driver), Stephen A. Bement (Jock), Felix Shuman (Used Car Salesman).

A ROCKY ripoff about a small town bowler, Matheson, who pushes himself into the professional ranks and wins the national championship. Added is the standard crusty old coach, Warden, and a girl friend, Blakely, who wants as much attention from her beau as his bowling ball gets. Bill Conti, who did the ROCKY score, can't help this film to roll a strike.

p, Michael Lobell; d, Noel Nosseck; w, James Proctor, Larry Bishoff; ph, Bruce Surtes (DeLuxe Color); m, Bill Conti; ed, Fred Chulack; art d, Archie Sharp; set d, Bruce Kay; cos, Guy Verhille.

Drama   **Cas.**   **(PR:A   MPAA:PG)**

DREAMING*½   (1944, Brit.) 78m EAL bw

Flanagan & Allen (Bud & Ches), Hazel Court (Wren/Avalah/Miss Grey), Dick Francis (Sir Charles Paddock), Philip Wade (Dr. Goebbels), Gerry Wilmott (U.S. General), Peter Bernard (U.S. Soldier), Ian Maclean (General), Roy Russell (Trainer), Robert Adams (Prince), Teddy Brown Reginald Foort, Gordon Richards, Raymond Glendenning, Bobby Jones, Alfredo Campoli, Band of His Majesty's Coldstream Guards, Donald McCullough, George Street, Sam Blake, Noel Dainton, Maurice Sweden, Kay Kendall.

A soldier on leave is knocked unconscious and dreams of being at the races at Ascot, in Africa, in Germany, and at the Stage Door Canteen. Pleasant but trivial episodic comedy, one of several the popular team of Flanagan & Allen made together.

p&d, John Baxter; w, Bud Flanagan, Reginald Purdell; ph, Stan Pavey.

Comedy   **(PR:A   MPAA:NR)**

DREAMING LIPS*   (1937, Brit.) 94m Trafalgar/UA bw

Elizabeth Bergner (Gaby Lawrence), Raymond Massey (Miguel del Vayo), Romney Brent (Peter Lawrence), Joyce Bland (Christine), Sydney Fairbrother (Mrs. Stanway), Felix Aylmer (Sir Robert Blaker), J. Fisher White (Dr. Wilson), Charles Carson (Impresario), Donald Calthrop (Philosopher), Ronald Shiner (Friend), Cyril Raymond (PC), George Carney (Rescuer), Bruno Barnabe.

Bergner's offbeat child-like personality is perfect for her role of the selfish and neurotic wife of Brent, first violinist for a symphony orchestra. He and Bergner are blissfully happy and Brent dotes on his petite Viennese spouse. Enter her childhood friend and fellow violinist Massey, half-Spanish, all rake. He stays with Bergner and Brent and a love triangle fast ensues with Massey sweeping Bergner into his arms. He is on his way to America for a triumphant tour and asks her to leave her husband and join him there. She promises to do so, but after Massey departs, Brent falls seriously ill. Bergner nurses him day and night, exhausting herself, dreaming distorted love dreams. In one dream she sees herself poisoning her husband and she wakes up hysterically screaming. Massey, not hearing from his beloved, quits his tour and returns to England where he has a brief affair with Bergner. She is so mortified at betraying her husband that she commits suicide by hurling herself into the Thames. Brent reads her last pathetic farewell note, never understanding why she has ended her life. DREAMING LIPS, a version of which Bergner had made years earlier in Germany (DER TRAUMENDE MUND, 1932—THE DREAMING MOUTH), is a lavish production, better than its predecessor with all three principals giving top performances. Massey obviously delights in his role as homewrecker. Garmes, who is credited with co-direction with Czinner, Bergner's husband, was one of the great cinematographers of his day but he oddly left that chore to another in this film. His stamp of fluid camera and roaming shots is nevertheless present.

p, Max Schach, Paul Czinner; d, Czinner, Lee Garmes; w, Margaret Kennedy, Carl Mayer, Lady Cynthia Asquith (based on the play "Melo" by Henri Bernstein); ph, Roy Clark.

Drama   **Cas.**   **(PR:C   MPAA:NR)**

DREAMING LIPS*½   (1958, Ger.) 86m Von Baky/DCA bw
(DER TRAUMENDE MUND)

Maria Schell (Liss), O.W. Fischer (Peter), Peter von Dongen (Michael).

Schell, married to ailing concert violinist Fischer, has an affair with more famous violinist Von Dongen. Then she sees the error of her ways and returns to her husband, who never learns about her transgressions. Competent, though uninspired, film version of Henri Bernstein's play. The 1937 version had the rather Victorian denouement of the straying wife killing herself in shame. (In German.)

d, Josef von Baky; w, Paul Czinner, Johanna Sibelius (based on the play "Melo" by Henri Bernstein); m, Alois Melichar.

Drama   **(PR:C   MPAA:NR)**

DREAMING OUT LOUD**   (1940) 81m RKO bw

Chester Lauck (Lum), Norris Goff (Abner), Frances Langford (Alice), Frank Craven (Dr. Walter Barnes), Bobs Watson (Jimmy), Irving Bacon (Wes Stillman), Clara Blandick (Jessica Spence), Robert Wilcox (Dr. Kenneth Barnes), Donald Briggs (Will Danielson), Robert McKenzie (Caleb Wehunt), Phil Harris (Peter Atkinson), Sheila Sheldon (Effie Lou), Troy Brown, Jr. (Washington).

The legendary (for their time) radio comedians Lum and Abner make their film debut in a career that would continue in a series of B comedies for RKO. The two are store owners in the town of Pine Ridge, Arkansas, and in this episodic story line they act as fundraisers, matchmakers, and detectives hunting a hit-and-run driver.

p, Jack Votion, Sam Coslow; d, Harold Young; w, Howard J. Greene, Barry Trivers, Robert D. Andrews (based on a story by Trivers, Andrews); ph, Philip Tannura; m, Lucien Moraweek; ed, Otto Ludwig; md, Lud Gluskin; art d, Bernard Herzbrun; m/l "Dreaming Out Loud," Coslow.

Comedy   **(PR:A   MPAA:NR)**

DREAMS**   (1960, Swed.) 86m Sandrews Film Studio/Janus bw
(KVINNODROM)

Harriet Andersson (Doris), Eva Dahlbeck (Susanne), Gunnar Bjornstrand (The Consul), Ulf Palme (Henrik Lobelius), Inga Landgre (Marta Lobelius), Sven Lindberg (Palle), Naima Wifstrand (Mrs. Aren), Bengt-Ake Bengtsson (Magnus), Git Gay (Model), Ludde Gentzel (Sundstrom), Kerstin Hedeby (Marianne).

Andersson is the owner of a Stockholm modeling agency and is on vacation. She calls her lover, and the two plan to meet in Oslo, but his wife steps in and ends that plan. She then finds herself on the receiving end of the affections of a wealthy diplomat, but soon sees that he is completely selfish. She returns to Stockholm chastened. Produced in Sweden in 1955, this is a Bergman obscurity. After this film he would produce SMILES OF A SUMMER NIGHT, THE SEVENTH SEAL, and WILD STRAWBERRIES in rapid succession. Although Andersson does a creditable acting job, the film lacks the imaginative touches that would make the director's later work so important.

p,d&w, Ingmar Bergman; ph, Hilding Blahd; ed, Carl-Olav Skeppstedt.

Drama   **(PR:C   MPAA:NR)**

DREAMS COME TRUE*½   (1936, Brit.) 78m Reunion bw

Frances Day (Ilona Ratkay), Nelson Keys (Anton), Hugh Wakefield (Albert von Waldenau), Frederick Bradshaw (Peter), Marie Lohr (Helen von Waldenau), Morris Harvey (Waldemar), Arthur Finn (Manager), Minnie Rayner (Dresser), Ivor Barnard Molly Hamley Clifford, Charles Penrose, Roxy Russell, Arthur Brander, Leo von Pokorny, Netta Lewis, Patrick Susands, David Hawthorne.

A remake of the continental film, LIEBESMELODIE, which adheres closely to the original. Day, in her film debut, is an actress and an opera singer who catches the fancy of a visiting farmer and his son. She runs off with the son, and the father is eventually made to believe that she is his daughter, born out of one of his youthful escapades. Light melodic fun with excellent photography by Heller and Dines.

p, Ilya Salkind, John Gossage; d, Reginald Denham; w, Bruce Sevier, Donald Bull (based on the opera "Clo-Clo" by Franz Lehar); ph, Otto Heller, Gordon Dines; m, Lehar.

Musical   **(PR:A   MPAA:NR)**

DREAMS IN A DRAWER*½   (1957, Fr./Ital.) 105m
Rizzoli-Francinex/Cineriz (I SOGNI NEL CASSETTO)

Lea Massari (Lucia), Enrico Pagani (Mario), Cosetta Greco, Sergio Tofano.

Touching tale of the romance and marriage between Massari and Pagani, two university students who marry under the belief that love conquers everything, despite the realities that stand in their way. Unfortunately, death interferes with their happy existence when the young bride dies in childbirth, leaving her husband with only her memory to guide him further. Not as depressing as the plot would suggest, a lot of humor being included through a depiction of early married life.

d&w, Renato Casstellani; ph, Leonida Barboni; m, Roman Vlad.

Drama   **(PR:A   MPAA:NR)**

DREAMS OF GLASS**   (1969) 83m UNIV c

John Denos (Tom Parsegian), Caroline Barrett (Ann Murakoshi), Joe Lo Presti (Sam Parsegian), Paul Micale (Pucci), Margaret Rich (Hanna Parsegian), Donald Elson (Timothy), Pat Li (Mrs. Murakoshi), The Smokestack Lightnin', Charles Thompson, Tony Benson, Miyoshi Jingu, Danny De Vito, Ken Tilles, Timothy Burns, Robert Strand.

A technically well done if not brilliant independent film, but held back by an underdeveloped story line. Denos is a young man in love with a Japanese girl, Barrett. Neither of their parents like the idea and make no bones about their stand. This naturally sends the young people into each other's arms, and amidst lies and small acts of rebellion the story stumbles to a very weak conclusion.

p,d&w, Robert Clouse; ph, Michael Murphy (Deluxe Color); m, Ian Freebairn-Smith; ed, Stephen L. Lewis; art d, Ann Philip Clouse; m/l, Freebairn-Smith, W. Earl Brown.

Drama   **(PR:C   MPAA:NR)**

DREAMS THAT MONEY CAN BUY*½   (1948) 99m Film Rights c

Jack Bittner, Max Ernst, Julien Levy, Arthur Seymour, Miriam Raeburn, Jo Mitchell.

The only redeeming factor of this low-budget experimental film is that the music of one segment was done by John Cage. DREAMS was shot on 16mm, then blown up to 35 with a total budget of $25,000, and shot mainly in a Manhattan loft. It is broken into segments concerning the dreams of a psychiatrist's patients. Most segments are abstract, and many have their erotic and humorous moments. Everything the film tries was done better in earlier experimental films.

p&d, Hans Richter; w, Richter (based on stories and ideas of Fernand Leger, Max Ernst, Marcel Duchamp, Alexander Calder, and Man Ray); ph, Arnold Eagle (Kodachrome); m, John Cage, John Latouche, Louis Applebaum, Paul Bowles, Darius Milhaud.

Experimental   **(PR:C MPAA:NR)**

DREI VON DER TANKSTELLE
                    (SEE: FROM THE GAS STATION, 1930, Ger.)

DRESSED TO KILL*   (1941) 75m FOX bw

Lloyd Nolan (Michael Shayne), Mary Beth Hughes (Joanne La Marr), Sheila Ryan (Connie Earle), William Demarest (Inspector Pierson), Ben Carter (Rusty), Virginia Brissac (Emily), Erwin Kalser (Otto Kuhn), Henry Daniel (Julian Davis), Dick Rich (Al), Milton Parsons (Max Allaron), Charles Arnt (Hal Brennon), Charles Trowbridge (David Earle), Hamilton MacFadden (Reporter), May Beatty (Phyllis Lathrop), Charles Wilson (Editor), Manton Moreland (Sam).

An above-average entry in the Michael Shayne detective series, Nolan is the tough, wise-cracking sleuth who is about to marry his patient financee Hughes when they hear shots in a nearby theater. Going to investigate, Nolan encounters several murders—all occurring in the theater and adjacent hotel—which are strangely linked to the stage, one production in particular. All the victims are found in the costumes of the drama in which they once appeared and the dogged Nolan finally nails the killer, a disgruntled porter, Kasler, who had been abandoned by his actress-lover. It's a hollow triumph for Nolan. Hughes walks out on him at film's end, disgusted with his penchant for crime, but then she was always doing that, returning to his side in the next film, still hoping for that wedding ring. (See MICHAEL SHAYNE series, Index.)

p, Sol M. Wurtzel; d, Eugene Forde; w, Stanley Rauh, Manning O'Connor (based on a novel by Richard Burke and characters created by Brett Halliday); ph, Glenn MacWilliams; ed, Fred Allen; md, Emil Newman.

Crime Drama   **(PR:A MPAA:NR)**

DRESSED TO KILL**   (1946) 72m UNIV bw

Basil Rathbone (Sherlock Holmes), Nigel Bruce (Dr. Watson), Patricia Morison (Hilda Courtney), Edmond Breon (Gilbert Emery), Frederick Worlock (Col. Cavanaugh), Carl Harbord (Inspector Hopkins), Patricia Cameron (Evelyn Clifford), Tom P. Dillon (Detective Thompson), Harry Cording (Hamid), Topsy Glyn (Kilgour Child), Mary Gordon (Housekeeper), Ian Wolfe (Man), Lillian Bronson (Tourist).

One of the worst of the Rathbone-Bruce whodunits, with a weak script and spotty production values. Three music boxes made by an inmate at the British prison Dartmoor are desperately sought by a bevy of villains for they contain the stolen Bank of England engraving plates. The chief villain is Morison, a female miscreant not unlike Gale Sondergaard in THE WOMAN IN GREEN. Rathbone tracks down the three music boxes containing the elusive plates, Morison's being the last. This is a tepid tale with little excitement, the most amusing moment provided by Bruce when he does an imitation of a duck. This was the twelfth and final Holmes film performed by Rathbone, a series brought to an end through his own decision. At the risk of destroying his friendship with Bruce (it didn't), Rathbone opted for legitimate stage roles. Quite simply, he was fed up with the Great Sleuth. When asked by children seeking his autograph to sign his name "Sherlock Holmes," he turned away, refusing. It was at this juncture that Rathbone felt he had lost his own identity to the ever-deducing creation of Conan Doyle and vowed to regain it by abandoning the character once and for all. He would go on to many stage successes ("The Heiress," "J.B.") but he would be forever linked to the great Sherlock. He had simply performed the part too well and too long to shed the image.

p&d Roy William Neill; w, Leonard Lee, Frank Gruber (based on the story by Sir Arthur Conan Doyle); ph, Maury Gertsman; ed, Saul A. Goodkind; md, Milton Rosen; art d, Jack Otterson, Martin Obzina; m/l, "Ya Never Know Just 'oo Yer Gonna Meet," Jack Brooks (sung by Delos Jewkes).

Mystery   **Cas.**   **(PR:A MPAA:NR)**

DRESSED TO KILL**   (1980) 105m Samuel Z. Arkoff/Filmways c

Michael Caine (Dr. Robert Elliott), Angie Dickinson (Kate Miller), Nancy Allen (Liz Blake), Keith Gordon (Peter Miller), Dennis Franz (Detective Marino), David Margulies (Dr. Levy), Ken Baker (Warren Lockman), Brandon Maggart (Cleveland Sam), Susanna Clemm (Bobbi), Fred Weber (Mike Miller), Sean O'Rinn (Museum Cabbie), Bill Randolph (Chase Cabbie), Robert Lee Rush (Hood No. 1), Mary Davenport (Woman in Coffee Shop).

The much over-rated De Palma, doing his Alfred Hitchcock act with gore and violence, gives us a stylish but predictable thriller. Caine is a suave, but schizoid psychiatrist treating, for the most part, wealthy women with oversexed egos, not the least of whom is sensuous, leggy, doe-eyed Dickinson. Angie fantasizes sexual liaisons that culminate in a steamy encounter at an art museum. The lengthy, wordless hide-and-seek game played by Dickinson and her prey is exciting and is interplayed with the lush paintings surrounding the momentary lovers. She later awakens to discover the devastating fact that she has not only embraced illicit romance but veneral disease. Fleeing her lover's apartment, she remembers leaving her wedding ring and returns only to be trapped in the elevator by a tall razor-wielding psychopathic blonde. De Palma spares us no slashes, no gashes, no blood blisters as the lovely Dickinson meets her ignominious fate. The balance of the film details the investigation into her murder as shown from the perspectives of Gordon, Dickinson's son, and Allen, a blonde prostitute (De Palma's wife), who is also suspected of being the killer. Allen—and this is where the film really gets out

of hand—is told by detective Franz that she must clear herself or he will book her for the murder out of sheer convenience. This leads to several setup shots where Allen attempts to decoy the real killer while Gordon, a computer genius, records her actions in an attempt to identify his mother's murderer. Allen, wearing the sexy wardrobe of her trade, invites disaster in parks, alleys, and, in particular, on the subway where a bevy of would-be black rapists pursue her. The final confrontation is with Caine, who has ostensibly been investigating the killing on his own, trying to track down one of his own disturbed patients. That patient is Caine himself who, in drag, attempts to murder Allen, but is foiled by the police who have been summoned by Gordon. This is a slick, well-produced thriller but the last 30 minutes are telegraphed by too many preceding scenes in which the killer's identity is easily foretold. With less bubbling blood and kinky scenes the film might have approached the level of Hitchcock's mastery. The production crew really carried this work, especially Bode's cinematography. Donaggio's score, and Greenberg's editing. (Angie's sex scenes, and those taken in a shower where De Palma accented abdominal shots, were done by a nameless double with a memorable navel.)

p, George Litto; d&w, Brian De Palma; ph, Ralf Bode (Panavision, Technicolor); m, Pino Donaggio; ed, Jerry Greenberg; md, Natalie Massara; prod d, Gary Weist; set d, Gary Brink; cos, Ann Roth, Gary Jones.

Thriller/Mystery   **Cas.**   **(PR:O MPAA:R)**

DRESSED TO THRILL*   (1935) 68m FOX bw

Tutta Rolf (Colette Dubois/Nadia Petrova), Clive Brook (Bill Trent), Nydia Westman (Anne Trepied), George Hassell (Henri), Mme. Smirnova (Sonya), Leonid Snegoff (Raskolnikoff), G.P. Huntley, Jr. (Charles Penfield). Robert Barrat, Lionel Belmore, Andre Cheron.

A sloppy remake of a well-received French film of the same title. Even the same director can't help this film—about a Russian singer and her look-alike dressmaker—sustain an iota of interest. This was Rolf's American film debut, but her presence and singing "My Heart Is A Violin" and "My One Big Moment" (Lew Pollack, Paul Webster) doesn't make it any easier to sit through.

p, Robert T. Kane; d, Harry Lachman: w, Samson Raphaelson (based on the play "La Couturiere de Luneville" by Alfred Savior); ph, Rudolph Mate; md, Louis DeFrancesco; art d, Jack Otterson, Hans Peters; ch, Jack Donohue.

Musical   **(PR:A MPAA:NR)**

THE DRESSER**   (1983) 118m Goldcrest-World Film/COL c

Albert Finney (Sir), Tom Courtenay (Norman), Edward Fox (Oxenby), Zena Walker (Her Ladyship), Eileen Atkins (Madge), Michael Gough (Frank Carrington), Cathryn Harrison (Irene), Betty Marsden (Violet Manning), Sheila Reid (Lydia Gibson), Lockwood West (Geoffrey Thornton), Donald Eccles (Mr. Godstone), Llewellyn Rees (Horace Brown), Guy Manning (Benton), Anne Mannion (Beryl), Kevin Stoney (C. Rivers Lane), Ann Way (Miss White), John Sharp (Mr. Bottomley), Kathy Staff (Bombazine Woman), Roger Avon (Charles), Christopher Irvin (Evelyn, the Airman), Stuart Richman (Evelyn's Friend), Sandra Gough (Actress on Station), Joe Belcher (Arthur), Johnny Waxfield (Electrician), Paul Luty (Stallkeeper), Lori Well (Barmaid), Alan Starkey (Train Guard).

Finney is the head of a Shakespearean acting troupe touring England during WW II. He's a senile boozer who is looked after by his homosexual dresser, Courtenay. Courtenay's performance borders on camp while Finney's is high caliber, but still something is missing. Finney seems to be parading his acting talents more than revealing a character. As a member of the tawdry company, Fox carries on beautifully against the stiff and mannered directing.

p&d, Peter Yates; w, Ronald Harwood (based on his play); ph, Kelvin Pike; m, James Horner; ed, Ray Lovejoy; prod d, Stephen Grimes; art d, Colin Grimes; cos, Bermans and Nathans.

Drama   **Cas.**   **(PR:C MPAA:PG)**

DREYFUS CASE, THE**   (1931, Brit.) 90m
                        British International/COL bw (GB: DREYFUS)

Cedric Hardwicke (Alfred Dreyfus), Charles Carson (Col. Picquart), George Merritt (Emile Zola), Sam Livesey (Labori), Beatrix Thomson (Lucie Dreyfus), Garry Marsh (Maj. Esterhazy), Randle Ayrton (President, Court-Martial), Henry Caine (Col. Henry), Reginald Dance (President, Zola Trial), George Skillan (Maj. Paty du Clam), Leonard Shepherd (Georges Clemenceau), Arthur Hardy (Gen. Mercier), Alexander Sarner (Matthieu Dreyfus), Frederick Leister (Demange), J. Fisher White (Pellieux), Abraham Sofaer (Dubois), Leslie Frith (Bertillon), George Zucco (Cavaignac), Nigel Barrie (Lauth), Violet Howard (Marguerite).

A very true-to-life rendition of the infamous case that shook France in the late 1800s. Hardwicke (Dreyfus) is the only Jew on the French general staff. When treason is discovered, blame is laid at his feet and he is framed by a forgery and sent to Devil's Island. One of the greatest writers of his time, Emile Zola, felt that Dreyfus had been railroaded. He engages Georges Clemenceau and they succeed in getting the former soldier a new trial. Merritt, as Zola, is nothing short of brilliant, and Shepherd, as Clemenceau, also makes us believe he is the famous Frenchman. With loads of doubt against the case, they still lose and Dreyfus is remanded to Devil's Island once more. It takes several more years until the duplicity is uncovered. Once Dreyfus is vindicated, he returns to his first love, the army. Hardwicke underplays all the way, perhaps a bit too much. Very authentic-looking and not a wasted foot of film.

p, F.W. Kraemer; d, Kraemer, Milton Rosmer; w, Reginald Berkeley, Walter Mycroft (based on the play by Herzog and Rehfisch); ph, W. Winterstein, Walter Harvey, Horace Wheddon; ed, Langford Reed, Betty Spiers.

Historical Drama   **(PR:A MPAA:NR)**

DREYFUS CASE, THE**

(1940, Ger.) International Road Shows bw (AKA: DREYFUS)

Fritz Kortner (Captain Alfred Dreyfus), Grete Moshelm (Lucie Dreyfus), Albert Bassermann (Colonel Picquart), Oscar Homolka (Major Esterhazy), Ferdinand Hart (Major Henry), Heinrich George (Emile Zola), Paul Bildt (Georges Clemenceau).

Originally made in the early 1930s in Germany, just prior to the Nazi coming into full-fledged power. The theme of this film being something that wouldn't set too well with Nazi prejudice, Oswald soon fled to France and Britain before residing permanently in the U.S. Yarn revolves around the trial of a French officer who has been receiving unfair treatment as a result of being Jewish. Though this subject was fitting for the time period, critically the film was not nearly as successful. It suffered from uneven direction and a few slack performances, almost as if rushed through to prepare for the future tragedies.

p,d, Richard Oswald.

Drama (PR:A MPAA:NR)

DRIFT FENCE**½ (1936) 57m PAR bw (AKA: TEXAS DESPERADOES)

Larry "Buster" Crabbe (Slinger Dunn), Katherine DeMille (Molly Dunn), Tom Keene (Jim Travis), Benny Baker (Jim Traft), Glenn Erikson (Curley Prentiss), Stanley Andrews (Clay Jackson), Richard Carle (Sheriff), Irving Bacon (Windy Watkins), Jan Duggan (Carrie Bingham), Walter Long (Bev Wilson), Chester Gan (Clarence), Richard Alexander (Seth Haverly), Bud Fine (Sam Haverly), Jack Pennick.

Superior early oater due more to the high value of the production than for the routine story in which the Texas ranger wanders into cattle, and cattle rustling, territory in search of the man responsible for the murder of his good buddy. More of a vehicle for Keene than for the top-billed Crabbe.

p, Harold Hurley; d, Otto Lovering; w, Stuart Anthony, Robert Yost (based on the story "Nevada" by Zane Grey); ph, Virgil Miller.

Western (PR: A MPAA:NR)

DRIFTER, THE*½ (1932) 60m State Rights bw

William Farnum ("The Drifter"), Noah Beery (John McNary), Phyllis Barrington (Ronnie McNary), Charles Sellon ("Whitey"), Bruce Warren (Paul LaTour), Russell Hopton (Montana), Ann Brody (Marie), Ynez Seabury (Yvonne).

Farnum, a nomad lumberjack, finds himself in the middle of a war between two lumbering powers. A confusing plot line ensues with one lumber boss being Farnum's long-lost brother. The daughter of the other boss is really the daughter of an escaped convict, who kidnaps her without knowing who she is. Farnum is difficult to understand in his use of a French-Canadian accent, and further hampered with the curse of overacting.

p, Willis Kent; d, William O'Connor; w, Oliver Drake; ph, William Nobles; ed, Thomas Persons.

Action/Adventure (PR:A MPAA:NR)

DRIFTER, THE* (1944) 62m PRC bw

Buster Crabbe (Billy Carson/Drifter Davis), Al "Fuzzy" St. John (Fuzzy Jones), Carol Parker (Sally Dawson), Kermit Maynard (Jack), Jack Ingram (Dirk Trent), Roy Brent (Sam), George Chesebro (Blackie), Ray Bennett (Simms), Jimmy Aubrey (Sheriff Perkins), Slim Whitaker (Marshall Hodges).

Buster Crabbe, still looking for a new acting slot after his jungle days as Tarzan, leaves behind his "Billy the Kid" role and takes on the mantle of Billy Carson for this one. Now he is a Robin Hood type doing good for the people of the sage, and he plays a second role as a bank robber trading on the reputation of his other half to cover up his misdeeds. A poor vehicle for somebody looking for a change of pace.

p, Sigmund Neufeld; d, Sam Newfield; w, Patricia Harper; ph, Robert Cline; ed, Holbrook N. Todd.

Western (PR:A MPAA:NR)

DRIFTER, THE** (1966) 85m Surfilms c

John Tracy (Alan), Sadja Marr (Renee), Michael Fair (Mike), Lew Skinner (Musician), Ed Randolph (Club Owner), Paula Feiten (Waitress), Claire Pelly (Girl on Horseback), Michael Onida (Tickettaker).

Tracy, a son alienated from his concert pianist father, moves around the country and from one lonely woman to another, unable to make a commitment to anybody. He meets a woman he once had an affair with, and they take up with each other again. The lady has a son, and it turns out the son is Tracy's. After mooning a while at what might have been, Tracy takes to the road again toward an infinity of vagueness, a sensitive, pathetic victim of rejection.

p, Pierre Lasry; d&w, Alex Matter; ph, Steve Winsten; m, Ken Lauber.

Drama (PR:C MPAA:NR)

DRIFTER*** (1975) 98m Bizarre/European Film Exchange c
(AKA: TWO-WAY DRIFTER)

Joe Adair (Drifter), David Russell (Steve), Joe Caruso (Geno), Dean Shah-Kee (Wagner), Bambi Allen (Klamath), Inga-Maria Pinson (Karen), Ann Collins (Maxine Randall), Gerald Strickland (Dana Howard).

Adair is a male hustler trying to find his place in the separate worlds of gays and straights. Most of the film focuses on his exploratory straight relationships with Pinson and Allen. His affairs with both don't go well but they do help build his self-image. The gays Adair meets are three-dimensional characters, not cardboard cliches, and here lies the film's strongest point. A 16mm production not without its technical problems, but those are easily overlooked because of the strong character development.

---

p,d,ph&ed, Pat Rocco (Technicolor); w, Edward Middletown.

Drama (PR:O MPAA:R)

DRIFTERS, THE (SEE: HALLUCINATION GENERATION, 1966)

DRIFTIN' KID, THE* (1941) 57m MON bw

Tom Keene, Betty Miles, Frank Yaconelli, Slim Andrews, Stanley Price, Gene Alsace [Rocky Camron], Glenn Strange, Steve Clark, Sherry Tansey, Fred Hoose, Wally West, Frank McCarroll, Lou Yaconelli.

Poorly produced oater has Keene battling Yaconelli and henchmen to save Miles and her land from the clutches of the bad guys. Even the sound of the punches are seconds off from the blows. Try another trail.

p&d, Robert Tansey; w, Frances Kavanaugh, Robert Emmett [Tansey]; ph, Marcel LePicard; ed, Fred Bain.

Western (PR:A MPAA:NR)

DRIFTIN' RIVER** (1946) 59m PRC bw

Eddie Dean, Roscoe Ates, Shirley Patterson, Lee Bennett, William Fawcett, Dennis Moore, Bob Callahan, Lottie Harrison, Forrest Taylor, Don Murphy, Lee Roberts, Wyley Grant, Marion Carney, The Sunshine Boys, "Flash" the Horse.

A shipment of horses bound for the Army is hijacked, and soldiers sent to investigate are massacred. Then investigators Dean and Ates take over and after one of them kills the leader of the gang, the others surrender. Routine saddle heroics.

p&d, Robert Emmett Tansey; w, Frances Kavanaugh; ph, Marcel LePicard; ed, Hugh Winn; md, Karl Hajos; art d, Edward C. Jewell; m/l, Eddie Dean, Hal Blair.

Western (PR:A MPAA:NR)

DRIFTING* (1932) 64m Tower/Powers bw

Shirley Grey, Theodore Von Eltz, Raymond Hatton, Edmund Breese.

A wealthy man is framed as a drunk driver who hit a construction worker. To clear his name, he marries a woman he buys for $5,000 (she needs it for an operation to save her father) and claims he was getting married at the time the worker was hit by the car. Hatton, a newspaper reporter, finds a witness to the accident and the wealthy man's alibi holds up. Not worth the bother today.

d, Morris R. Schlank.

Drama (PR:A MPAA:NR)

DRIFTING ALONG**½ (1946) 60m MON bw

Johnny Mack Brown (Steve), Lynne Carver (Pat McBride), Raymond Hatton (Pawnee), Douglas Fowley (Jack Dailey), Smith Ballew (Himself), Milburn Morante (Zeke), Thornton Edwards (Pedro), Steve Clark (Lou Woods), Marshall Reed (Slade), Jack Rockwell (Sheriff Devers), Lynton Brent (Joe), Terry Frost (Gus), Leonard St. Lee (Red), Ted Mapes (Ed), Curt Barrett and the Trailsmen.

Music and song abound in this nugget from Brown's series of westerns, and he himself even croons a number (at least his lips move). The stale plot has Brown coming to the aid of Carver who is trying to fend off cattle rustlers who are out to bankrupt her. The musical idea was dropped from Brown's series after one more attempt to make it work in UNDER NEVADA SKIES. Songs include "Dusty Trails" and "You Can Bet Your Boots and Saddles."

p, Scott R. Dunlap; d, Derwin M. Abrahams; w, Adele Buffington; ph, Harry Neumann; ed, Carrol Lewis; md, Edward Kay.

Western (PR:A MPAA:NR)

DRIFTING WEEDS (SEE: FLOATING WEEDS, 1959, Jap.)

DRIFTING WESTWARD** (1939) 47m MON bw

Jack Randall, Edna Duran, Frank Yaconelli, Julian Rivero, Stanley Blystone, Carmen Bailey, Octavia Giraud, Davie O'Brien, Rose Turich, Dean Spencer, James Sheridan [Sherry Tansey], Rusty the Wonder Horse.

Cowboy Randall helps a Spanish family in Mexico in a fight against bandits led by Blystone, who want a map to a hidden mine. Randall disguises himself as a hired gun of Blystone's and plays both sides until he gets caught in the middle. A quick-paced, enjoyable B-oater.

p, Scott Dunlap; d, Robert Hill; w, Robert Emmett; ph, Bert Longenecker; ed, Howard Dillinger.

Western (PR: A MPAA:NR)

DRIFTWOOD*** (1947) 88m REP bw

Ruth Warrick (Susan), Walter Brennan (Murph), Dean Jagger (Dr. Steve Webster), Charlotte Greenwood (Mathilda), Natalie Wood (Jenny), Jerome Cowan (Mayor Snyder), H.B. Warner (Rev. Hollingsworth), Margaret Hamilton (Essie Keenan), Hobart Cavanaugh (Judge Beckett), Francis Ford (Abner Green), Alan Napier (Dr. Adams), Howland Chamberlin (Hiram Trumbell), James Bell (Sheriff Bolton), Teddy Infuhr (Lester Snyder), James Kirkwood (Rev. MacDougal), Ray Teal (Perkins), Zeke Holland (Blaine).

A young Natalie Wood (she was nine years at the time) plays an orphan adopted by pharmacist Brennan, and she entangles herself in the lives of most of the people in a far West town which has an epidemic of spotted fever on its hands. Jagger plays a doctor trying to fight the fever. The film works well until people start dying, and then it spins off into melodrama. Brennan and Wood give fine performances, and John Alton's cinematography is superb.

d, Allan Dwan; w, Mary Loos, Richard Sale; ph, John Alton; ed, Arthur Roberts; md, Cy Feuer; art d, Frank Arrigo; spec eff, Howard and Theodore Lydecker.

Drama (PR:A MPAA:NR)

DRILLER KILLER*½ (1979) 90m Rochelle Films c

Carolyn Marz, Jimmy Laine, Baybi Day, Bob DeFrank, Peter Yellen, Harry Schultz, Tony Coca Cola and the Roosters, Alan Wynroth.

There's no hack behind the camera in this gory but well-directed art-exploitation film, which has Ferrara attacking New Yorkers with his power drill. Blood spills almost mindlessly as the berserk painter takes out his alienation from society in massacre style. Ferrara went on from here to his vastly superior cult film MS. 45.

p, Rochelle Weisberg; d, Abel Ferrara; w, Nicholas St. John; ph, Ken Kelsch; m, Joseph Delia.

Horror	Cas.	(PR:O MPAA:R)

DRIVE A CROOKED ROAD*** (1954) 83m COL bw

Mickey Rooney (Eddie Shannon), Dianne Foster (Barbara Mathews), Kevin McCarthy (Steve Norris), Jack Kelly (Harold Baker), Harry Landers (Ralph), Jerry Paris (Phil), Paul Picerni (Carl), Dick Crockett (Don), Mort Mills (Garage Foreman), Peggy Maley (Marge), Mike Mahoney, George Paul, John Damler, John Close (Police Officers), Patrick Miller (Teller), Diana Dawson, Irene Bolton, Linda Danson (Women), Mel Roberts (Customer), John Fontaine (Wells), Howard Wright, Jean Engstrom, Richard Cutting (People).

Rooney, a mechanic and race car driver, is chosen by two bank robbers (McCarthy and Kelly) to be their driver for a heist in Palm Springs, California. For bait, they use McCarthy's girl friend, Foster, and she convinces Rooney to do the job because he can handle the mountain back roads. After the robbery is completed, Kelly forces Rooney at gunpoint to drive to a deserted location, but Rooney crashes the car, killing Kelly. Injured, he then returns to McCarthy's hideout and kills him when he finds him beating Foster. The police arrive and arrest them both. A crisply done *film noir* with Rooney taken in by a universal emotional state, a state that was at the root of many *noir* hero's problems, loneliness.

p, Jonie Taps; d, Richard Quine; w, Blake Edwards (based on a story by James Benson Nablo, adapted by Quine); ph, Charles Lawton, Jr.; ed, Jerome Thoms; md, Ross DiMaggio; art d, Walter Holscher; set d, James Crowe.

Crime	(PR:C MPAA:NR)

DRIVE, HE SAID** (1971) 92m BBS/COL c

William Tepper (Hector), Karen Black (Olive), Michael Margotta (Gabriel), Bruce Dern (Coach Bullion), Robert Towne (Richard), Henry Jaglom (Conrad), Mike Warren (Easly), June Fairchild (Sylvie), Don Hammer (Director of Athletics), Lynn Bernay (Dance Instructor), Joey Walsh, Harry Gittes (Announcers), Charles Robinson (Jollop), Bill Sweek (Finnegan), David Stiers (Pro Owner), B.J. Merholz (Pro Lawyer), I.J. Jefferson (Secretary), Kenneth Bayle (President Wallop), Cathy Bradford (Rosemary), Eric Johnson (Pfc. Johnson), Bill Kenney (Phoneman), Lenny Lockabaugh (Policeman), Clyde Crawford (M.P.), Mark Malinsuskee (Psychiatrist), Douglas McKenzie, Robert Page, Oliver O'Ferrall (Doctors), Douglas Ryan (Manager), Cindy Williams (Manager's Girl Friend), Gunnar Malm (Buckholder), Bill Duffy (Trainer).

Most of the sidebar anecdotes about this film are more interesting than the picture itself. Tepper (and whatever happened to him?) stars as a confused basketball star playing in an Ohio college. He can't decide whether he wants to go on to become a pro or spend his spare time rousing rabble with the radicals on campus. His best friend, Margotta, is about to be conscripted and sent off to fight the dirty war in Viet Nam. This unnerves Tepper, but not as much as the affair he's carrying on with Black, who is married to professor Robert Towne. Margotta pretends to be nuts and gets out of his draft commitment but he actually does go crazy due to the overwhelming pressure of attempting to act crazy, so we wonder if he really was crazy or not. Margotta attempts to rape Black but is foiled when Towne returns home with Tepper. Margotta races out and into the science lab where he liberates all of the college's animals and other critters (such as insects). Margotta is eventually taken away in an ambulance, continuing to protest that he is sane. Produced in 1971, DRIVE, HE SAID was at the tail-end of the college antiwar movement and already felt dated when it was released. Prior to making his directorial debut on this film, Nicholson had co-directed THE TERROR (uncredited) in just a few scenes and co-produced THE SHOOTING, and he had written the screenplay and co-produced RIDE THE WHIRLWIND. He also wrote THE TRIP and FLIGHT TO FURY as well as co-writing HEAD. So one might have thought he'd have a stronger hand in this story but it wasn't evident, as confusion reigned supreme. Some of the oddities are that Black later starred for Jaglom (Conrad) when he gave up being an ordinary actor to become a fairly decent director-writer (CAN SHE BAKE A CHERRY PIE?). Towne, of course, went on to write CHINATOWN and many others. Walsh (Announcer) wrote CALIFORNIA SPLIT and Gittes (Announcer) stayed with Nicholson and Towne and it was his name they used for the protagonist in CHINATOWN. (Pro Owner) Stiers enjoyed several years as a TV star as did Williams in "Laverne and Shirley." Warren, former college basketball great, gave up playing for acting and has had an excellent career since. So why was this picture something that might have been served up at Thanksgiving? The blame must be laid at Nicholson's feet for allowing the screenplay to get out of hand. Some heavy sexual scenes are what gives this an "R" rating. Producers Bert Schneider and Blauner come off the "Monkees" TV show and associate producer Fred Roos moved on to produce many of Coppola's best films. Lots of talent here for very little movie.

p, Steve Blauner, Jack Nicholson; d, Nicholson; w, Nicholson, Jeremy Larner (based on the novel by Larner); ph, Bill Butler (Metrocolor); m, David Shire; ed, Pat Somerset, Donn Cambern, Christopher Holmes, Robert I. Wolfe; art d, Harry Gittes; m/l, "I Cried For You," Abe Lyman, Gus Arnheim, Arthur Freed (sung by Billie Holliday), "Spaced," Beaver and Krause, "Classical Gas," Mason Williams, title theme, Louis Hardin [Moondog].

Drama	(PR:O MPAA:R)

DRIVE-IN***½ (1976) 96m COL c

Lisa Lemole (Glowie Hudson), Glenn Morshower (Orville Hennigson), Gary Cavagnaro (Little Bit), Billy Milliken (Enoch), Trey Wilson (Gifford), Gordon Hurst (Will Henry), Louis Zito (Manager), Linda Larimer (Cashier), Kent Perkins (Bill Hill), Ashley Cox (Mary Louise), Lee Newsom, Andy Parks, Reagan Kee (Widow Makers), David Roberts, Phil Ferrell, Joe Flower (Gear Grinders), Bill McGhee (Dr. Demars), Gloria Shaw (Mrs. Demars), Jessie Lee Fulton (Mom), Robert Valgova (Boss), Jack Isbell (Divinity Student), Michelle Franks (Omalee Ledbetter), Dejah Moore (Waitress), Curtis Posey, Billy Vance White (Deputies), Carla Palmer, Carrie Jessup (Glowie's Friends), Barry Gremillion (Diddle Brown).

There are two movies going on here at once, one about the activities of the patrons of a rural Texas drive-in, and the second a movie within a movie at the drive-in. Lemole, the local beauty, is trying to break up with gang leader Milliken to go out with the shy Morshower. Milliken controls all gang activity from a waterbed in his van. He not only watches the movie on the screen, but also Ozzie Nelson reruns on a TV in the van. Morshower's brother wants to watch him and Lemole in action, while Perkins tries to force an engagement ring on his girl friend until he meets the shapely Franks at the concession stand. There are two patrons plotting to rip off the theater, a nervous black couple in a sea of rednecks, and a volunteer vigilante, who turns mom on to pot. The best laughs come from the movie within a movie—a 747 crashes into a burning building of TOWERING INFERNO magnitude, and there is an earthquake and a dam break that cause a tidal wave that capsizes a passenger ship. Hilariously corny dialog and stock footage cleverly satirize disaster films.

p, Alex Rose, Tamara Asseyev; d, Rod Amateau; w, Bob Peete; ph, Robert Jessup (Panavision, Metrocolor); ed, Bernard F. Caputo, Guy Scarpitta; set d, Jack Marty.

Comedy	(PR:O MPAA:PG)

DRIVE-IN MASSACRE** (1976) 78m New American c

Jake Barnes, Adam Lawrence, Douglas Gudbye, Newton Naushaus, Norman Sherlock, Valdesta.

An above-average slasher film about a killer who preys on the patrons of a drive-in theater. Plenty of gore interwoven with police interrogations of a voyeuristic truck driver and a theater manager who despises his customers. The final murder happens in front of the outdoor screen as a western movie plays. The killer escapes with all suspects dead as the drive-in public address system warns that a killer is on the loose, leaving a chilling open end to the film.

p&d, Stuart Segall; w, John Goff, Buck Flower; ph, Kenneth Lloyd Gibb; m, Lonjohn Productions.

Horror	Cas.	(PR:O MPAA:R)

DRIVER, THE**** (1978) 91m FOX c

Ryan O'Neal (The Driver), Bruce Dern (The Detective), Isabelle Adjani (The Player), Ronee Blakley (The Connection), Matt Clark (Red Plainclothesman), Felice Orlandi (Gold Plainclothesman), Joseph Walsh (Glasses), Rudy Ramos (Teeth), Denny Macko (Exchange Man), Frank Bruno (The Kid), Will Walker (Fingers), Sandy Brown Wyeth (Split), Tara King (Frizzy), Richard Carey (Floorman), Fidel Corona (Card Player), Victor Gilmour (Boardman), Nick Dimitri (Blue Mask), Bob Minor (Green Mask), Allen Graf (Uniformed Cop), Angelo Lamonea, Patrick Burns, Karen Kleiman (Patrons), Thomas Myers, Bill McConnell (Passengers), Peter Jason, William Hasley (Commuters).

Walter Hill's second feature is a bare-boned, existential *film noir*. O'Neal is The Driver, a top getaway driver for a gang of crooks, and Dern is The Detective (nobody in the film has a proper name) obsessed with arresting him. It's a sparse story of the struggle of the two men with their obsessions and with each other, and it skillfully develops a mood that is hard to shake after the ending credits. The car chases are breathtaking.

p, Lawrence Gordon; d&w, Walter Hill; ph, Philip Lathrop (Panavision, DeLuxe Color); m, Michael Small; ed, Tina Hirsch, Robert K. Lambert; prod d, Harry Horner; art d, David Haber; set d, Darrell Silvera; spec eff, Charley Spurgeon; stunts, Everett Creach.

Crime	Cas.	(PR:O MPAA:R)

DRIVER'S SEAT, THE* (1975, Ital.) 105m Rizzoli Film/AE c
(AKA: IDENTIKIT)

Elizabeth Taylor (Lise), Ian Bannen (Richard), Guido Mannari (Carlo), Mona Washbourne (Mrs. Fiedke), Maxence Mailfort (Bill), Andy Warhol.

Confusing, elliptical story has Taylor as a woman traveling to Rome and hoping to die. Two men try to pick her up, but she shuns them. Finally she taunts one of them until he kills her. Fans of Taylor may like this, but they would have to be a group with amazingly low standards.

p, Franco Rossellini; d, Giuseppe Patroni Griffi; w, Raffaele La Capria, Griffi (based on the novella by Muriel Sparks); ph, Vittorio Storaro (Technicolor); m, Franco Mannino; art d, Mario Ceroli; cos, Gabriella Pescucci.

Drama	Cas.	(PR:O MPAA:R)

DRIVERS TO HELL (SEE: WILD ONES ON WHEELS, 1967)

DROLE DE DRAME (SEE: BIZARRE, BIZARRE, 1939, Fr.)

DROP DEAD, DARLING (SEE: ARRIVEDERCI, BABY!, 1966, Brit.)

DROP DEAD, MY LOVE**(1968, Italy) 110m Clesi Cinematografica c (IL MARITO E MIO E L'AMAZZO QUANDO MI PARE)

Catherine Spaak (Allegra), Hywel Bennett (Leonardo), Hugh Griffith (Ignazio), Romolo Valli (Butler), Giannco Tedeschi (Embalmer), Francesco Mule (Il Duce—Ostanzo), Paolo Stoppa (Sperenzoni).

A comedy about a young girl (Spaak) who tries to kill her husband (Griffith), a musical genius and 40 years her senior, to free her to marry her beatnik lover (Bennett). Details on how she attempts to do this drain the potential humor and slow the plot flow. Griffith's performance as a man who cherishes life and his young bride is well done, which is quite the opposite for Bennett and Spaak. An Italian production aimed for the larger American market.

p, Silvio Clementelli; d, Pasquale Festa Campanile; w, Luigi Magni, Stefano Strucci, J. Fiastri (based on a story by Aldo De Benedetti); ph, Roberto Gerardi (Eastmancolor); m, Armando Trovaioli; art d, Flavio Mogherini.

Comedy (PR:C MPAA:NR)

DROP THEM OR I'LL SHOOT*½ (1969, Fr./Ger./Span.) 98m Les Films bw Marceau-Neue Emelka/Adelphia c (LE SPECIALSTE)

Johnny Hallyday, Sylvie Fennec, Gaston Moschin, Mario Adorf, Francoise Fabian, Serge Marquand.

An Italian western with hippies? That's what is given in this Corbucci western—a pot-smoking band of outlaw hippies. French singer Hallyday is the man destined to wipe them out. This is a small indication of how surreal (or bizarre) Italian westerns became.

p&d, Sergio Corbucci; w, Corbucci, Sabatine Gruffini; ph, Dario Di Palma.

Western (PR:O MPAA:NR)

DROWNING POOL, THE*** (1975) 108m WB c

Paul Newman (Harper), Joanne Woodward (Iris Devereaux), Tony Franciosa (Detective Broussard), Murray Hamilton (Kilbourne), Gail Strickland (Mavis Kilbourne), Melanie Griffith (Schuyler Devereaux), Linda Haynes (Gretchen), Richard Jaeckel (Detective Franks), Paul Koslo (Candy), Andy Robinson (Pat Reaves), Coral Browne (Olivia Devereaux), Richard Derr (James), Helena Kallianiotes (Elaine Reaves), Leigh French (Redhead), Cecil Elliott (Motel Switchboard Operator), Peter Dassinger (Peter), Yaphet Kotto (Glo).

A slick and stylish sequel to HARPER, this private eye film has Newman reprising the cool gumshoe; he is hired by Woodward, a southern oil baroness, to find out who's behind a blackmailing scheme. Her mother's (Browne) murder further complicates matters until Newman slowly discerns that Hamilton is the culprit behind the blackmailing plot; Hamilton is already worth millions but he's greedy; he merely wants more. The villain entraps Newman and Strickland in a deserted hydrotherapy chamber which is slowly flooded, ergo the title of the film. Newman and the lovely Strickland are in deep hazard as she almost disrobes completely while Newman tries to use her garments and his own to clog the drains, then pulls the plug to save their lives. This and a few other scenes are truly suspenseful but for the most part it's a synthetic, forced story peopled with some interesting characters, not the least of whom is Franciosa as a police detective who was once in love with Woodward. Jaeckel as Franciosa's sadistic police partner, Griffith as Woodward's underage jailbait daughter, and Robinson, the fired family chauffeur originally suspected of having murdered Browne (with no butler available to pin it on), are all standouts, with Hamilton stealing the show as the sleazy oil baron. The direction by Rosenberg is sloppy, unimaginative, and predictable with nothing new added to the craft.

p, Lawrence Turman, David Foster; d, Stuart Rosenberg; w, Tracy Keenan Wynn, Lorenzo Semple, Jr., Walter Hill (based on the novel by Ross MacDonald); ph, Gordon Willis (Panavision, Technicolor); m, Michael Small, Charles Fox; ed, John Howard; prod d, Paul Sylbert; art d, Ed O'Donovan; set d, Phil Abramson; cos, Donald Brooks.

Crime/Mystery Cas. (PR:C MPAA:PG)

DRUM zero (1976) 100m UA c

Warren Oates (Hammond Maxwell), Isela Vega (Marianna), Ken Norton (Drum), Pamela Grier (Regine), Yaphet Kotto (Blaise), John Colicos (DeMarigny), Fiona Lewis (Augusta Chauvet), Paula Kelly (Rachel), Royal Dano (Zeke Montgomery), Lillian Hayman (Lucretia Borgia), Rainbeaux Smith (Sophie Maxwell), Alain Patrick (Lazare), Brenda Sykes (Calinda), Clay Tanner, Lila Finn, Henry Wills, Donna Garrett, Harvey Parry, May Boss.

Unwatchable sequel to the unwatchable MANDINGO. Pure trash about a slave breeder (Oates) and the sex he and his teenage daughter have with their slaves, and the slaves with each other. No redeeming qualities exist in this trash.

p, Ralph Serpe; d, Steve Carver; w, Norman Wexler (based on the novel by Kyle Onstott); ph, Lucien Ballard (Metrocolor); ed, Carl Kress; prod d, Stan Jolley; md, Charlie Smalls; art d, Bill Kenney; set d, John McCarthy.

Drama (PR:O MPAA:R)

DRUM BEAT*** (1954) 111m Jaguar/WB c

Alan Ladd (Johnny MacKay), Audrey Dalton (Nancy Meek), Marisa Pavan (Toby), Robert Keith (Bill Satterwhite), Rodolfo Acosta (Scarface Charlie), Charles Bronson (Capt. Jack), Warner Anderson (Gen. Canby), Elisha Cook, Jr. (Crackel), Anthony Caruso (Manok), Richard Gaines (Dr. Thomas), Edgar Stehli (Jesse Grant), Hayden Rorke (Gen. Grant), Frank De Kova (Modoc Jim), Perry Lopez (Bogus Charlie),

Willis Bouchey (Gen. Gilliam), Peter Hansen (Lt. Goodsall), George Lewis (Capt. Alonzo Clark), Isabel Jewell (Lily White), Frank Ferguson (Mr. Dyar), Peggy Converse (Mrs. Grant), Pat Lawless (O'Brien), Paul Wexler (William Brody), Richard Cutting (Meek), Strother Martin (Scotty).

This was Ladd's first self-owned production under the Jaguar label, in collaboration with veteran western director Daves (BROKEN ARROW) and, since SHANE, it was one of Ladd's best efforts. Ladd, a tough Indian fighter, is presidentially appointed to make peace with the troublesome Medoc Indians of California. But his stagecoach is ambushed by renegade Bronson before his arrival at Fort Klamath and Ladd must resort to gunplay to save his life and those of other passengers, including pretty Dalton. Ladd and Dalton's budding romance angers Pavan, sister of the friendly Medoc chief Caruso; she has been Ladd's sweetheart since childhood. Pavan, despite Ladd's warnings that Bronson is lethal, accompanies the renegade on a mission where she is killed. Ladd explodes and tracks down the bloody killer to his lair where the two go at each other with gun, knife, and bare hands, Ladd finally disposing of the venomous Bronson. DRUM BEAT packs plenty of action and gives generous consideration to the Indian perspective, an attitude generated by director Daves who took pride in his pioneer heritage. This was the first film where Bronson received a major part and he performed it well, if not slipping easily into a mold he made for himself as an unattractive heavy. It was for this film that he discarded his given name of Buchinsky and took Bronson. Based on true incidents occurring in Oregon, circa 1869, DRUM BEAT was filmed on location in Coconino National Forest in Northern Arizona. Ladd, of course, is the whole show and he renders a strong, believable portrayal of a man hard at the edges but understanding at the core.

p, Alan Ladd (uncredited); d&w Delmer Daves; ph, J. Peverell Marley (CinemaScope, Warner Color); m, Victor Young; ed, Clarence Kolster; art d, Leo K. Kuter; set d, Will L. Kuehl; spec eff, H.F. Koenekamp; tech adv, Ben Corbett, George Ross.

Western Cas. (PR:A MPAA:NR)

DRUM TAPS** (1933) 61m KBS/Worldwide bw

Ken Maynard, Dorothy Dix, Junior Coghlan, Charles Stevens, Al Bridge, Harry Semels, Jim Mason, Slim Whitaker, Boy Scout Troop 107 of Los Angeles, Kermit Maynard, Hooper Atchley.

The Boy Scouts are frequently given supporting roles in old B westerns. Usually they seem out of place and are just there to make a pitch for the Scouts. This time they are used inventively, helping Maynard protect his range from land-grabbers by waking other ranchers in true Paul Revere-style, and being mistaken by the bandits for a company of soldiers.

p, Burt Kelly, Sam Bischoff, William Saal; d, J.P. McGowan; w, Alan James (based on a story by McGowan); ph, Jack Young.

Western Cas. (PR:A MPAA:NR)

DRUMMER OF VENGEANCE*½ (1974, Brit.) 89m Times Film c

Ty Hardin, Rossano Brazzi, Craig Hill, Gordon Mitchell, Edda di Benedetta, Rosalda Neri.

Hardin is chasing the six men who murdered his wife and child, and he gets them all in predictable ways. Oddest note is seeing the Italian romantic star Brazzi playing the villain in a western.

p,d&w, Robert Paget; ph, Alvaro Lanzone.

Western (PR:O MPAA:NR)

DRUMS**** (1938, Brit.) 96m LFP-Korda/UA c (GB: THE DRUM)

Sabu (Prince Azim), Raymond Massey (Prince Ghul), Valerie Hobson (Mrs. Carruthers), Roger Livesey (Capt. Carruthers), Desmond Tester (Bill Holder), Martin Walker (Herrick), David Tree (Lt. Escott), Francis L. Sullivan (Governor), Roy Emerton (Wafadar), Edward Lexy (Sgt-Maj. Kernel), Julien Mitchell (Sergeant), Amid Taftazani (Mohammed Khan), Archibald Batty (Maj. Bond), Frederick Culley (Dr. Murphy), Charles Oliver (Rajab), Alf Goodard (Pete Kelly), Michael Martin-Harvey (Mullah), Ronald Adam (Maj. Gregoff), Lawrence Baskcomb (Zarrulah), Miriam Pieris.

Treacherous Massey usurps his brother's kingdom by murdering his sibling and forcing young nephew and heir apparent Sabu into hiding. The boy takes refuge with the British garrison where commander Livesey and wife Hobson treat him with kindness and he learns the regulations of the British Army and how to beat military cadence on a drum which he later uses to warn the garrison that it is about to be slaughtered by Massey and his evil followers. The spectacle is excellent and the direction and cinematography superb. Sabu is fetching as the innocent, wide-eyed, royal youth, and Livesey is a great match for the wily Massey who doesn't have a decent bone in his lanky body.

p, Alexander Korda; d, Zoltan Korda; w, Arthur Wimperis, Patric Kirwan, Hugh Gray (based on Lajos Biro's adaptation of the novel by A.E.W. Mason); ph, Georges Perinal, Osmond Borrodaile, Robert Krasker, Christopher Challis, Geoffrey Unsworth (Technicolor); m, John Greenwood, Miklos Rozsa; ed, William Hornbeck, Henry Cornelius; md, Muir Mathieson; prod d, Vincent Korda; spec eff, Edward Colman [Cohen]; tech adv, Brigadier Hector Campbell, Lt. Col. F.D. Henslowe.

Adventure (PR:A MPAA:NR)

DRUMS ACROSS THE RIVER** (1954) 78m UNIV c

Audie Murphy (Gary Brannon), Lisa Gaye (Jennie Marlowe), Lyle Bettger (Frank Walker), Walter Brennan (Sam Brannon), Mara Corday (Sue), Hugh O'Brian (Morgan), Jay Silverheels (Taos), Regis Toomey (Sheriff Beal), Morris Ankrum (Ouray), James Anderson (Jed Walker), George Wallace (Les Walker), Bob Steele (Billy Costa), Lane Bradford (Ralph Costa), Emile Meyer (Marlowe), Greg Barton (Fallon), Howard McNear (Stilwell), Ken Terrell (Red Knife).

Murphy is set up as the robber of a gold shipment, and with the help of his father, Brennan, he clears his name before they put the rope around his neck. Bettger is the villain who frames Murphy and he also tries to start trouble between the whites and the Ute Indians, so the whites will open the Indian territory. The veteran supporting cast of Steele, Ankrum, Silverheels, and Brennan can't help this cliche-ridden western.

p, Melville Tucker; d, Nathan Juran; w, John K. Butler, Lawrence Roman (based on a story by Butler); ph, Harold Lipstein (Technicolor); ed, Virgil Vogel.

Western (PR:A MPAA:NR)

DRUMS ALONG THE MOHAWK***** (1939) 103m FOX c

Claudette Colbert *(Lana "Magdelana" Martin)*, Henry Fonda *(Gil Martin)*, Edna May Oliver *(Mrs. Sarah McKlennar)*, Eddie Collins *(Christian Reall)*, John Carradine *(Caldwell)*, Dorris Bowdon *(Mary Reall)*, Jessie Ralph *(Mrs. Weaver)*, Arthur Shields *(Rev. Rosenkrantz)*, Robert Lowery *(John Weaver)*, Roger Imhof *(Gen. Nicholas Herkimer)*, Francis Ford *(Joe Boleo)*, Ward Bond *(Adam Helmer)*, Kay Linaker *(Mrs. DeMooth)*, Russell Simpson *(Dr. Petry)*, Spencer Charters *(Landlord)*, Si Jenks *(Jacob Small)*, J. Ronald Pennick *(Amos Hartman)*, Arthur Aylesworth *(George Weaver)*, Chief Big Tree *(Blue Back)*, Charles Tannen *(Dr. Robert Johnson)*, Paul McVey *(Capt. Mark DeMooth)*, Elizabeth "Tiny" Jones *(Mrs. Reall)*, Beulah Hall Jones *(Daisy)*, Edwin Maxwell *(Rev. Daniel Gros)*, Robert Greig *(Mr. Borst)*, Clara Blandick *(Mrs. Borst)*, Tom Tyler *(Capt. Morgan)*, Lionel Pape *(General)*, Noble Johnson *(Indian)*, Clarence H. Wilson *(Paymaster)*, Mae Marsh *(Pioneer Woman)*.

A richly directed and acted colonial epic has Fonda and Colbert as young newlyweds starting out on the frontier of the Mohawk Valley, building a small log cabin home, and clearing the fertile land for crops. Marauding Indians swarm into the area and the couple join other fleeing homesteaders in seeking the safety of the old fort where they beat off the savages, then watch helplessly as their farms are put to the torch. Homeless, Fonda and Colbert go to live with a rich spinster, Oliver, whose large farm and buildings have been left intact. She gives them a small cabin and Fonda works her fields for generous pay. But the British again stir up the Indians as the Revolution continues, and the men march off to do battle. Colbert, an eastern-bred woman of refinement and culture, has a hard time adjusting to the rigors of the wilderness, early on whining like a child for her former creature comforts. But she becomes hardy and bears Fonda a son, then bravely watches him go off with the militia to clear the valley of the plaguing Indians. The men straggle back through a night rainstorm some time later and Colbert searches the clots of stumbling men for Fonda, who is nowhere to be seen. Tyler, the last man of the rear guard, informs Colbert that "There's no one behind me, mam," and Colbert collapses in the road, believing Fonda is dead. She hears his voice weakly calling her, as if in a dream. But he is there, wounded, lying by the side of the road. Fonda is nursed back to health and deep summer begins to yield the rich crops the farmers have so long labored to produce. Again bursting into this tranquil atmosphere are the Indians, led by ruthless British commanders. This time they pour into the Mohawk Valley in great numbers, intent on destroying everything, especially the fort where everyone again takes refuge. A siege ensues and the defenders begin to run low on ammunition as the Indian position strengthens. Fonda volunteers to go for help, insisting that he can reach another outpost and that he "can outrun any Indian alive." At nightfall Fonda slips out of the fort, past the enemy lines, and breaks into the open with several Indians hot on his trail. A terrific long-distance footrace ensues across the plains, through forests, over streams, with Fonda's long legs outdistancing the Indians who drop down exhausted one by one. Toward dawn the Indians overpower the fort's defenders and break inside, but before the wholesale massacre can begin Fonda appears with Continental troops, saving the defenders at the last minute and routing the Indians. The insidious leader Carradine is dispatched by a friendly Indian who signals to the defenders what he has done by donning the renegade's eyepatch. Fonda searches the fort and finds Colbert and his child still alive and the little family, reunited, later witnesses the arrival of regular troops going home. The Revolution is over, the colonials have won, and America is a new-born country. In a stirring finale, the 13-starred Continental flag is hoisted hand-over-hand by the embattled farmers to the top of the church tower inside the fort as one and all gaze upward at their new emblem, the symbol of their struggle and their hard-won freedom. But there is more to do, much more, in the building of a new nation, prosaically summed up by Fonda who tells Colbert: "I reckon we'd better be getting back to work. Gonna be a heap to do from now on." Fonda is superb as the steadfast toiler, and Colbert's transition from a spoiled and pampered young woman to a warm-hearted, radiant wilderness wife is a perfect counterpoint in the pairing up of these fine talents. Oliver steals one scene after another as the feisty and rugged pioneer matriarch who testily refuses to allow invading Indians to burn her bed, compelling them by sheer obstinacy to cart the bed with her in it out of her home before they burn it to the ground. Bond, as the brawny farmer-hunter, and Shields, as the musket-firing parson, are excellent, as is Imhof as crusty old Gen. Herkimer and Chief Big Tree as the friendly Indian chief. Carradine oozes his sinister character without hardly uttering a word. This Fordian chronicle of a far-flung frontier in an earlier time of the Revolution, a period shunned by most studios and directors, is believable in every aspect, encompassing much attention to detail. The Trotti-Levien script is literate, humorous, and in keeping with colonial idiom. Ford's sure grasp of Americana is curled about every frame. The script goes straight to the heart of the wilderness plight and romance of Fonda and Colbert but includes enough cameos from other characters to round out the plot. Fonda's sensitive characterization in YOUNG MR. LINCOLN had proven his ability to handle well historical characters. He was asked by Ford to grow his hair long at a time when such appearances were frowned upon, but he complied. (Fonda would go on complying with Ford over the years, although he developed a deep-seated resentment of the director's heavy-handed ways, a feeling that would later explode when the pair met with disaster in MR. ROBERTS.) One of Ford's biggest problems in making this spectacular film was the unavailability of the necessary props and costumes. Fox had not specialized in costume or historical films, particularly those dealing with the 18th century, and almost everything had to be made from scratch at great cost. The ancient flintlock muskets used in the film by scores of extras were the real weapons of the era, not reproductions. A Fox prop man chased down 100 flintlocks in Ethiopia, where they had actually seen combat in the mid-1930s, used by Ethiopian soldiers trying to repel Mussolini's invading armies. These weapons were shipped to the U.S. and used in the film. This was Ford's first color film and he made the most of it, his cameras recording the lush forests and valleys in northern Utah. Ford took his entire crew and cast, more than 300 people, into high country, about 11,000 feet above sea level, and studio technicians actually had to cut out miles of woods to make roads into this wilderness. According to one report, more than 200,000 feet of lumber had to be transported into the area where the giant fort and several frontier homes were erected for the film. The wonderful Utah weather allowed Ford to capture as many as two dozen scenes a day since most days were cloudless and sun-filled, beginning at 6:00 a.m. when the sky turned pink with dawn and Ford was already shouting "action." So rich and verdant is the color in this film that it later provided stock footage for several Fox productions, chiefly BUFFALO BILL, 1944, and MOHAWK, 1956. Since the entire production was filmed on government land, Ford was obligated to tear down every building erected for the film after completion. This proved next to impossible with the large fort, so well built was it by his expert technicians. Ford solved the problem by writing a few scenes into the script dealing with the final assault on the fort by the Indians and British irregulars, one where they actually blow up most of the fort with gunpowder. Following the shooting, Ford's crew merely picked up the pieces and went home. The censors of the day prohibited explicit showing of the Indian violence, a savagery that included torture, scalping, and the lot. Ford got around this problem by graphically *suggesting* the brutal acts without focusing in on the gore (a much more effective treatment than that used by the gore hounds of today, whose films lack the talent of such a master). As an historical epic and a frontier saga, DRUMS ALONG THE MOHAWK is a peerless classic, directed by one of the world's finest film talents. It is not only great history-telling but great down-to-earth drama.

p, Raymond Griffith; d, John Ford; w, Lamar Trotti, Sonya Levien (based on the novel by Walter D. Edmonds); ph, Bert Glennon, Ray Rennahan (Technicolor); m, Alfred Newman; ed, Robert Simpson; art d, Richard Day, Mark Lee Kirk; set d, Thomas Little; cos, Gwen Wakeling; sound effects ed, Robert Parrish; property master, Joseph C. Behm.

Historical Drama/Adventure (PR:AAA MPAA:NR)

DRUMS IN THE DEEP SOUTH*** (1951) 87m RKO c

James Craig *(Clay)*, Barbara Payton *(Kathy)*, Guy Madison *(Will Denning)*, Barton MacLane *(McCardle)*, Craig Stevens *(Braxton Summers)*, Tom Fadden *(Purdy)*, Robert Osterloh *(Harper)*, Taylor Holmes *(Albert Monroe)*, Robert Easton *(Jerry)*, Lewis Martin *(Gen. Johnston)*, Peter Brocco *(Union Corporal)*, Dan White *(Cpl. Jennings)*, Louis Jean Heydt *(Col. House)*.

This above-average Civil War drama, with unusual twists provided by the talented Menzies, shows Craig, Madison, and Stevens as West Pointers graduating from the same class and meeting in an Atlanta reunion just before the cannons go off. Madison fights for the North and Craig and Stevens for the South, and they meet again three years later when Sherman makes his advance to the sea through bloodied Georgia. The Union troops, Madison being one of their officers, are held up in the shadow of a mountain where Craig and 20 Confederate soldiers have mounted a battery and can pound away at Sherman's trains and supply wagons at will, bombarding the only main road through the plantation wilds. Payton, a buxom blonde, is Craig's wife who resides in a nearby plantation mansion, spying on Madison and his men and delivering information to her husband. Madison regretfully must blow up the top of the mountain to free Sherman's men, and he does so, killing Craig and Payton in the end. Craig gives a sympathetic performance and Madison is rugged and right as the conscience-stricken friend. MacLane, Fadden, and Osterloh all render strong performances as soldiers, but Payton was never any kind of actress as her off-screen escapades proved. This film attracted unusual response from viewers when originally shown following Payton's sordid, highly publicized affairs with Franchot Tone and Tom Neal; the actors got into a fight over her with Neal beating Tone senseless and sending him to a hospital with almost lifelong disabilities. (Neal was later convicted of murdering his third wife and served a long prison term.) Payton's career plummeted following this movie and she was later arrested for prostitution and check forgery. Menzies, who had won an Oscar for art direction in GONE WITH THE WIND, does a commendable job helming DRUMS IN THE DEEP SOUTH, his pace quick and his alert eye fixed well to the story. This was one of the first films to employ Supercinecolor and it's rough in spots, giving grass a blueish hue and, at times, rendering inconsistent coloring. All the technical jobs are performed well, and Tiomkin's score is as lush and sultry as the Georgia landscape.

p, Maurice and Frank King; d, William Cameron Menzies; w, Philip Yordan, Sidney Harmon (based on a story by Hollister Noble); ph, Lionel Linden (Supercinecolor); m, Dimitri Tiomkin; ed, Richard Heermance; art d, Menzies.

War/Historical Drama (PR:A MPAA:NR)

DRUMS O' VOODOO* (1934) 70m International Stageplay Pictures bw (AKA: SHE DEVIL)

Laura Bowman *(Aunt Hagar)*, J. Augustus Smith *(Amos Berry)*, Edna Barr *(Myrtle Simpson)*, Lionel Monogas *(Ebenezer)*, Morris McKenney *(Thomas Catt)*, A.G. Comathieri *(Deacon Dunson)*, Alberta Perkins *(Sister Knight)*, Fred Bonny *(Brother Zero)*, Paul Johnson *(Deacon August)*, Trixie Smith *(Sister Marquerite)*, Carrie Huff *(Sister Zuzan)*. James Davis *(Brother Zumee)*, Ruth Morrison *(Sister Gaghan)*, Harriet Daughtry *(Sister Lauter)*, Bennie Small *(Bou Bouche)*, Pedro Lopez *(Marcon)*, Jennie Day, Gladys Booker, Herminie Sullivan, Lillian Exum, Edith Woodby, Mabel Grant, Marion Hughes, Madeline Smith, Theresa Harris, Dorothy St. Claire, Eleanor Hines, Pauline Freeman, Annabelle Smith, Jacquiline Ghant, Annabelle

Ross, Harriet Scott *(Members of the Flat Rock Washfoot Baptist Church)*, Cherokee Thornton, Arthur McLean, DeWitt Davis, Rudolph Walker, Marvin Everhart, Jimmie Cook, Irene Bagley, Sally Timmons, Beatrice James, Marie Remsen *(Voodoo Dancers)*.

A script adapted from a play that closed after one night on Broadway should indicate the quality of this bottom-of-the-barrel production. The all-black cast, most of limited talent, can't go anywhere with this story of a preacher, Smith, and a voodoo princess, Bowman, who team up to fight a common enemy, Morris. The villain is finally taken care of when he is struck by lightning after he abducts the preacher's daughter from a church. Shoddy production values, from sets to lighting, are evidence of the little time and money put into this film.

p, Louis Weiss; d, Arthur Hoerl; w, J. Augustus Smith (based on Smith's play "Louisiana"); ph, W. Strenge, J. Burgi Conter; ed, Joe Silverstein, art d, Sam Corso.

Drama (PR:A MPAA:NR)

DRUMS OF AFRICA* (1963) 92m MGM c

Frankie Avalon *(Brian Ferrers)*, Mariette Hartley *(Ruth Knight)*, Lloyd Bochner *(David Moore)*, Torin Thatcher *(Jack Cuortemayn)*, Hari Rhodes *(Kasongo)*, George Sawaya *(Arab)*, Michael Pate *(Viledo)*, Ron Whelan *(Ship Captain)*, Peter Mamakos *(Chavera)*.

Stock footage of Africa is used in this low-budget fare, where Hartley and Bochner provide the love interest and Avalon sings. The three are in Equatorial East Africa in 1897, and help do away with slave traders in the area, during the course of which Avalon even sings to the animals, minus his surfboard. Cheap filmmaking and not worth viewing.

p, Al Zimbalist, Philip N. Krasne; d, James B. Clark; w, Robin Estridge (based on a story by Arthur Hoerl, Estridge); ph, Paul C. Vogel (Metrocolor); m, Johnny Mandel; ed, Ben Lewis; art d, George W. Davis, Addison Hehr; set d, Henry Grace, Jack Mills; spec eff, Robert R. Hoag; m/l, "The River Love," Russell Faith, Robert Marcucci (sung by Frankie Avalon).

Action/Adventure (PR:A MPAA:NR)

DRUMS OF DESTINY* (1937) 60m Crescent bw

Tom Keene *(Capt. Jerry Crawford)*, Edna Lawrence *(Rosa Maria Dominguez)*, Budd Buster *(Kentuck)*, Rafael Bennett *(Jenkins)*, Robert Fiske *(Holston)*, Carlos De Valdez *(Don Salvador Dominguez)*, David Sharpe, John Merton, Aurora Navarro, William Hazelitt.

Keene is an American Army captain in Spanish-ruled Florida in 1817. His object is to save his brother from a villainous Spaniard, and he does this by wooing the bad Don's daughter and getting to the brother just before the firing squad does. Lots of mustache twirling by the Don tends to disconcert anybody foolish enough to sit through this one.

p, E.B. Derr; w, Roger Whatley, John Neville (based on a story by Whatley); ph, Arthur Martinelli; ed, Finn Ulback; md, Abe Meyer.

Action/Adventure (PR:A MPAA:NR)

DRUMS OF FU MANCHU** (1943) 68m REP bw

Henry Brandon *(Fu Manchu)*, William Royle *(Sir Nayland Smith)*, Robert Kellard *(Allan Parker)*, Gloria Franklin *(Fah-Lo-Suee)*, Olaf Hytten *(Dr. Petrie)*, Tom Chatterton *(Prof. Randolph)*, Luana Walters *(Mary Randolph)*, Lal Chand Mehra *(Sirdar Prahni)*, George Cleveland *(Prof. Parker)*, John Dilson *(Howard)*, John Merton *(Loki)*, Dwight Frye *(Anderson)*, Wheaton Chambers *(Dr. Humphrey)*, George Pembroke *(Crawford)*, Guy D'Ennery *(Ranah Sang)*.

Brandon plays the evil oriental trying to obtain a scepter that will gain him mind control over wild tribesmen in India, and enable him to conquer Asia. Royle, a British agent, foils the scheme and Brandon is killed. Strictly kids' fare. (See FU MANCHU series, Index.)

p, Hiram S. Brown, Jr.; d, William Witney, John English; w, Franklyn Adreon, Morgan B. Cox, Ronald Davidson, Norman S. Hall, Barney A. Sarecky, Sol Shor (based on a novel by Sax Rohmer); ph, William Nobles; m, Cy Feuer; ed, Edward Todd, William Thompson.

Adventure (PR:A MPAA:NR)

DRUMS OF JEOPARDY* (1931) 65m TIF bw
(AKA: MARK OF TERROR)

Warner Oland *(Boris Karlov)*, June Collyer *(Kitty Conover)*, Lloyd Hughes *(Prince Nicholas Petrov)*, George Fawcett *(Gen. Petrov)*, Ernest Hilliard *(Prince Ivan)*, Wallace MacDonald *(Prince Gregor)*, Hale Hamilton *(Martin Kent)*, Florence Lake *(Anya Karlov)*, Mischa Auer *(Piotr)*, Clara Blandick *(Aunt Abbie)*, Ann Brody *(Tazia)*, Murdoch MacQuarrie *(Stephens)*, Robert Homans *(Detective Brett)*, Ruth Hall *(Girl)*, Harry Semels *(Henchman)*.

Oland plays a villain traveling through Czarist Russia and the U.S. to avenge the death of his daughter. Story line is an exact copy of DR. FU MANCHU, in which Oland also starred, but that doesn't help this dreary production.

d, Geroge B. Seitz; w, Harold MacGrath, Florence Ryerson (based on a story by MacGrath); ph, Arthur Reed; ed, Otto Ludwig; md, Val Burton; art d, Ralph M. DeLacy; cos, Elizabeth Coleman.

Action/Adventure (PR:A MPAA:NR)

DRUMS OF TABU, THE zero (1967, Ital./Span.) 91m Splendor-F.I.S.A.-AS Films/Producers Releasing Organization c (TABU; LA VERGINE DI SAMOA)

James Philbrook *(Bill Harrigan)*, Seyna Seyn *(Anahita)*, Frank Moran [Francisco Moran] *(Yawata)*, Frank Fantasia [Franco Fantasia] *(Padre Lorenzo)*, Beny Deus *(Charlie)*, Chick Cicarelli *(Bruno)*, Carlo Tamberlani *(Inspector Duras)*, John Sutton

(Taaroa), Joseph Han *(Ling)*, Enrique Navarro, Manuel Gallardo, Renato Terra, Fernando Sanchez Polack, Barta Barri.

A gutless South Seas adventure set near Fiji with Philbrook cast as a whiskey-gulping Korean War veteran who befriends Seyn, a native girl on the run from a sadistic nightclub owner. She tells Philbrook that she is "tabu" (she refused a marriage planned by the island's high priest), but Philbrook takes his chances and they both live happily ever after. Produced for a Westinghouse television broadcast, THE DRUMS OF TABU unfortunately found its way into the theaters.

p, Sidney Pink; d, Javier Seto; w, Seto, Santiago Moncada; ph, Modica Antonio (Movielab Color); m, Gregorio Garcia Segura; ed, Antonio Ramirez; art d, Wolfgang Burman; set d, Pablo Gago.

Adventure (PR:A MPAA:NR)

DRUMS OF TAHITI* (1954) 73m COL c

Dennis O'Keefe *(Mike Macklin)*, Patricia Medina *(Wanda Spence)*, Francis L. Sullivan *(Pierre Duvois)*, George Keymas *(Angelo)*, Sylvia Lewis *(Mawaii)*, Cicely Browne *(Gay Knight)*, Raymond Lawrence *(Shoreham)*, Frances Brandt.

A talky 3-D adventure tale set on the titled South Sea island. O'Keefe is a gunrunner supplying arms to the natives so they can rout the French. Medina is his store-bought bride whom he uses as a smokescreen for his smuggling. A French policeman, Sullivan, a hurricane, and an erupting volcano destroy the guns and the revolt. Long-winded dialog with miniscule action makes this sleepy viewing.

p, Sam Katzman; d, William Castle; w, Douglas Heyes, Robert E. Kent; ph, Lester H. White (Technicolor); ed, Jerome Thoms.

Action/Adventure (PR:A MPAA:NR)

DRUMS OF THE CONGO**½ (1942) 59m UNIV bw

Ona Munson *(Dr. Ann Montgomery)*, Stuart Erwin *(Congo Jack)*, Peggy Moran *(Enid)*, Don Terry *(Kirk)*, Richard Lane *(Coutlass)*, Jules Bledsoe *(Kalu)*, Turhan Bey *(Juma)*, Dorothy Dandridge *(Malimi)*, Ernest Whitman *(King Malaba)*, Ed Stanley *(Col. Robinson)*, Jess Lee Brooks *(Chief Madjeduka)*, Napoleon Simpson *(Taroka Leader)*.

Terry, an American intelligence agent, races through the jungle for a material that could help the Allies win the war. Of course, the enemy is looking for it, too. Add to that two warring tribes and wild animals fighting to the death, and the result is an above average B-adventure picture. Cabanne's direction, especially in the native fight scenes, is crisp and well-orchestrated.

p, Henry McRae; d, Christy Cabanne; w, Roy Chanslor, Paul Huston; ph, George Robinson; ed, Maurice Wright; md, H.J. Salter; art d, Jack Otterson; m/l, "Round the Bend," "Hear the Drum Beat Out," "River Man," Everett Carter, Milton Rosen.

Action/Adventure (PR:A MPAA:NR)

DRUMS OF THE DESERT* (1940) 64m MON bw

Ralph Byrd *(Paul Dumont)*, Lorna Gray *(Helene)*, Peter George Lynn *(Raoul)*, William Costello *(Abdullah)*, Manton Moreland *(Sgt. Williams)*, Jean Del-Val *(Col. Fouchet)*, Ann Codee *(Mme. Fouchet)*, Boyd Irwin *(Capt. Andre)*, Neyle Marx *(Ben Ali)*, Albert Morin *(Hassan)*.

Two French Foreign Legion officers, Byrd and Lynn, are in love with the same woman, Gray, and fight over her as they battle hostile natives. A stale script full of cliches, stilted dialog, and typical rendering of black characters for comic relief.

p, Paul Malvern; d, George Waggner; w, Dorothy Reid, Joseph West (based on a story by John T. Neville); ph, Fred Jackman, Jr.; ed, Jack Ogilvie.

Action/Adventure (PR:A MPAA:NR)

DRUNKEN ANGEL**** (1948, Jap.) 102m Toho bw

Toshiro Mifune *(Matsunaga)*, Takashi Shimura *(Dr. Sanada)*, Reizaburo Yamamoto *(Okada)*, Michiyo Kogure *(Nanse)*, Chiefko Nakakita *(Miyo)*, Noriko Sengoku *(Gin)*, Choko Lida *(Old Maid Servant)*.

Kurosawa's DRUNKEN ANGEL captured the mood of post-war Japan in the same way the neo-realist films of Italy captured Italy's. In a war-scarred town controlled by the Yakuza (Japanese gangsters), an alcoholic doctor runs a small clinic. Young Mifune, a gangster, comes to the doctor to have a bullet removed from his hand. Shimura, who detests gangsters, discovers that Mifune has tuberculosis. A love-hate relationship develops between the two, the doctor seeing his lost youth in Mifune. His attempts to save the young man fail when Mifune tries to kill his boss, a pre-war gangster just released from prison. He does this, in part, to save the doctor's nurse (who got caught up with the gangsters), but he is the one who is killed. Mesmerizing performances from Mifune and Shimura (both also starred in Kurosawa's ROSHOMON). This was also Kurosawa's first production where he had total control over the filming. The main theme in this film—one of vindicating oneself for reasons unknown to others—occurs often in Kurosawa's work.

p, Sojiro Motoki; Akira Kurosawa; w, Keinosuke Uegusa, Kurosawa; ph, Takeo Ito; m, Fumio Hayasaka.

Drama **Cas.** (PR:C MPAA:NR)

DRY BIKINI, THE (SEE: HER BIKINI NEVER GOT WET, 1962)

DRY ROT** (1956, Brit.) 87m Romulus-Remus/IF-BL bw

Ronald Shiner *(Alf Tubbs)*, Brian Rix *(Fred Phipps)*, Peggy Mount *(Sgt. Fire)*, Lee Patterson *(Danby)*, Sidney James *(Flash Harry)*, Christian Duvaleix *(Polignac)*, Joan Sims *(Beth)*, Heather Sears *(Susan)*, Michael Shepley *(Col. Wagstaffe)*, Joan Haythorne *(Mrs. Wagstaffe)*, Miles Malleson *(Yokel)*, Raymond Glendenning *(Himself)*, Shirley Ann Field.

Three bookies, Shiner, Rix, and James plot to recover some recent losses by kidnaping the horse favored to win a race and substituting a doped nag in its place. The stage version crossed the finish line long before this inept adaptation. Several cast members went on to long careers in the "Carry On" series. (See CARRY ON series, Index.)

p, Jack Clayton; d, Maurice Elvey; w, John Chapman (based on a play by Chapman); ph, Arthur Grant.

Comedy **(PR:A MPAA:NR)**

DRY SUMMER** (1967, Turkey) 90m Hitit/Manson bw

Ulvi Dogan *(Hassan)*, Erol Tas [Errol Tash] *(Osman)*, Hulya Kocyigit [Julie Kotch] *(Bahar)*, Hakki Haktan, Yavuz Yalinkilic, Zeki Tuney, Alaettin Altiok, Members of Jerusalem Theater Arts Players, Members of Athens Hellenic Theater, Members of Istanbul Theater of Performing Arts.

Tas is the younger brother of the miserly Dogan who refuses to grant the other villagers the use of his water during a drought. One of the townspeople trespasses and is killed by Dogan, but Tas, because he is the younger brother, takes the blame. He is sentenced to a short prison term during which Dogan tells Tas's wife that her husband died. Tas is pardoned, however, and saves his wife from Dogan's lecherous desires and the villagers from a waterless demise.

p, Ulvi Dogan, William Shelton (U.S. version); d, Metin Erksan, David Durston (U.S. version); w, Erksan, Ismet Saydan, Kemal Inci (based on a story by Necati Cumali); ph, Ali Ugur; m, Yamaci, Manos Hadjidakis (performed by Ravi Shankar, The Presidential Philharmonic Orchestra of Turkey); ed, Stuart Gellman; md, Ferit Tuzun.

Drama **(PR:A MPAA:NR)**

DRYLANDERS**½ (1963, Can.) 70m National Film Board of Canada/COL bw

Frances Hyland *(Liza Greer)*, James Douglas *(Dan Greer)*, Lester Nixon *(Bob MacPherson)*, Mary Savage *(Ada MacPherson)*, William Fruete *(Colin)*, Don Francks *(Russel)*, Irena Mayeska *(Thora)*, William Weintraub *(Narrator)*, Jonathon Little.

Canada Film Board's first feature film is a small, but well done, production. Initially written for television, it is the story of Douglas, just back from the Boer war, who finds little that is rewarding in his clerk job and moves his family from the city to the country in 1907. He faces the usual farming problems but in time becomes a successful wheat farmer. Disaster strikes in the way of a drought that destroys most farmers, including Douglas, who dies before the rains come. With new hope, his wife vows to rebuild the farm.

p, Peter Jones; d, Donald Haldane; w, M. Charles Cohen; ph, Reginald Morris (Superscope); m, Eldon Rathburn; ed, John Kemeny, Kirk Jones; art d, Jack McCullagh; cos, Yuki Yoshida; spec eff, Wally Gentleman.

Drama **(PR:A MPAA:NR)**

DU BARRY WAS A LADY** (1943) 96m MGM c

Lucille Ball *(May Daly/Mme. Du Barry)*, Red Skelton *(Louis Blore/King Louis)*, Gene Kelly *(Alec Howe/Black Arrow)*, Douglas Dumbrille *(Willie/Duc De Rigor)*, "Rags" Ragland *(Charlie/Dauphin)*, Donald Meek *(Mr. Jones/Duc De Choiseul)*, George Givot *(Cheezy/De Roquefort)*, Zero Mostel *(Rami the Swami/Cagliostro)*, Tommy Dorsey & His Band *(Themselves)*, Virginia O'Brien *(Ginny)*, Louise Beavers *(Niagara)*, Charles Coleman *(Doorman)*, Dick Haymes *(Dorsey Singer)*, Cecil Cunningham, Harry Hayden *(Couple)*, Clara Blandick *(Old Lady)*, Marie Blake *(Woman)*, Andrew Tombes *(Escort)*, Don Wilson *(Announcer's Voice)*, Dick Alexander, Art Miles, Paul "Tiny" Newlan *(Men)*, Chester Clute *(Doctor)*, Kay Williams, Kay Aldridge, Hazel Brooks *(Girls)*, Lana Turner *(Guest Star)*, Jo Stafford *(Singer)*, Pierre Watkin *(Rich Patron)*, Sig Arno *(Nick)*, Hugh Beaumont *(Footman)*, Georgia Carroll, Inez Cooper, Natalie Draper, Marilyn Maxwell, Eve Whitney *(Showgirls)*, Ernie Alexander *(Delivery Man)*, William Forrest *(Guard Captain)*, Charles Judels *(Innkeeper)*, Michael Bisaroff, William Costello, Dell Henderson, Edward Cooper, Thomas Clarke, Emmett Casey *(Flunkies)*, Christian Frank *(Lackey)*, Emory Parnell *(Gatekeeper)*, Mitchell Lewis *(Renel)*, Maurice Costello *(Passerby)*, Ava Gardner *(Girl)*.

Cole Porter's bawdy, risque, and totally charming musical play was bowdlerized, slashed, and sanitized to satisfy the blue-nosed Hays Office and the result was a pallid imitation of the show that delighted Broadway. Ethel Merman and Bert Lahr starred in New York but were tossed aside in favor of two redheads, Skelton and Ball, whom the studio felt were more important and whose hair would show up better in dazzling Technicolor. The second leads on Broadway were played by Ronald Graham (in the 1970s he was "Mr. Dirt" in gasoline commercials) and Betty Grable. (The Broadway version also had Adele Jergens, Janis Carter, and future movie musical director Charles Walters.) Grable was under contract at Fox and they didn't mind her appearing in New York but they would not give her permission to do an MGM Musical, so she and Graham were replaced by O'Brien and Kelly. The prime example of the timidity of the MGM Moguls was the alteration of Lahr's job as men's room attendant at a New York club (a situation that offered some of the funniest and bluest lines in the play) to coat room clerk, a job that was always handled by a gorgeous woman with important breasts or, at least, a female relative of the owner. Skelton is the hat check boy who is mad for Ball, a sassy showgirl. She won't give him the time of morning until he hits the jackpot on the Irish Sweepstakes for $75,000 (a great steak cost about $2.50 at the time and Beverly Hills mansions went for about $25,000 in 1943, so don't scoff at that figure). Kelly likes Ball as well but the moment Skelton is in the chips, Lucy begins paying attention to Red's advances. Red buys the nightclub and is happy as a lark until his pal, Mostel (a comedy psychic), predicts that the Skelton-Ball wedding will never happen. Red orders a Mickey Finn for Kelly and plans to slip it to him so he won't attend the engagement party. But Red mistakenly drinks the brew himself and the rest of the picture is a dream sequence with Ball as Madame Du Barry, Skelton as the king, and Kelly as the master of derring-do, the piratical Black Arrow. The dream reveals that Du Barry really loves the Black Arrow and pleads with the King to spare his life. Skelton wakes up and realizes what it all means; Ball truly loves Kelly. He cancels the wedding and pushes Kelly and Ball together while he acknowledges the fact that he and O'Brien have been in love all along and he was too dumbstruck by Ball to realize that. Only five of Cole Porter's original songs remain: "Katie Went to Haiti," "Do I Love You, Do I?," "Friendship," "Well, Did You Evah," "Taliostro's Dance," and a host of new material was written that couldn't compare with Porter's work. Mostel and Ragland have the comedy chores and acquit themselves as well as the script will allow them, which is hardly at all. Turner does an unbilled 15-second bit which she shot during a coffee break while making SLIGHTLY DANGEROUS a couple of sound stages down the block. It was her first Technicolor appearance and came in the song "I Love An Esquire Girl" (Ralph Freed, Lew Brown, Roger Edens) in which the lyric sung by Skelton, reads, "and if Lana Turner doesn't set you in a whirl/then you don't love a lovely girl." Lana appears in a photographic trick. She holds Red's elbow, he glances down at her, does a huge double take, and faints. Lana winks at the camera and the scene is over. Look for Dick Haymes and Joe Stafford as Dorsey band singers. Despite all of the errors, you might yet enjoy the picture, if only to see Ball while she still had a voice that didn't sound like she was speaking from the bottom of a mine pit. Other songs: "Du Barry Was a Lady" (Burton Lane, Ralph Freed), "Madame, I Love Your Crepes Suzettes" (Lane, Lew Brown, Freed), "Thinking of You," (Frances Ash, Walter Donaldson), "A Cigarette, Sweet Music and You" (Ringwald), "Sleepy Lagoon" (Coates), "You Are My Sunshine)" (Davis, Mitchell), "I'm Getting Sentimental Over You" (Ned Washington, George Bassman), "Salome," "Ladies of the Bath" (Roger Edens), "King Louis, "Get Me a Taxi," "On to Combat" (Daniele Amfitheatrof), "No Matter How You Slice It, It's Still Salome" (Edens).

p, Arthur Freed; d, Roy Del Ruth; w, Irving Brecher, Nancy Hamilton, Wilkie Mahoney, Albert Mannheimer, Jack McGowan, Charles Sherman, Mary C. McCall, Jr. (based on the play by B.G. De Sylva, Herbert Fields); ph, Karl Freund (Technicolor); ed, Blanche Sewell; md, Georgie Stoll; art d, Cedric Gibbons; set d, Edwin B. Willis, Henry Grace; cos, Irene, Shoup, Gile Steele; ch, Charles Walters.

Musical/Comedy **(PR:A MPAA:R)**

DU BARRY, WOMAN OF PASSION* (1930) 88m UA bw

Norma Talmadge *(Jeanette Vaubernier/Mme. Du Barry)*, William Farnum *(Louis XV)*, Hobart Bosworth *(Corse de Brissac)*, Conrad Nagel *(Duc de Bissac)*, Ullrich Haupt *(Jean Du Barry)*, Allison Skipworth *(La Gourdan)*, E. Alyn Warren *(Denys)*, Edgar Norton *(Renal)*, Edwin Maxwell *(Maupeou)*, Henry Kolker *(L'Aiguillon)*.

Disappointing attempt at making the famous Madame into a sympathetic character. This picture was loaded with melodramatics, lots of hambone acting on the parts of most of the cast, and hardly any wit at all. Talmadge and the rest attempt varying degrees of French accents and none of them work. Talmadge is found in a pond by Nagel, who later becomes her boy friend. She next becomes a hostess in sort of a gambling casino. From there, the next logical step is, of course,a cushy job as the king's mistress, and it ends when she and her lover die. The rest of the picture is a series of scenes attempting to recreate the French royal scene, but most of the shots are mediums and close-ups so there is no sense of grandeur or majesty. Slow-moving and tedious.

p, Joseph M. Schenck; d&w, Sam Taylor (based on the play by David Belasco); ph, Oliver Marsh; ed, Allen McNeil; art d, William Cameron Menzies, Park French.

Historical Drama **(PR:A-C MPAA:NR)**

DUAL ALIBI** (1947, Brit.) 87m Pathe/BN bw

Herbert Lom *(Jules and Georges de Lisle)*, Terence de Marney *(Mike Bergen)*, Phyllis Dixey *(Penny)*, Ronald Frankau *(Vincent Barney)*, Abraham Sofaer *(French Judge)*, Harold Berens *(Ali)*, Clarence Wright *(M. Mangin)*, Marcel Poncin *(French Lawyer)*, Sebastian Cabot *(Official)*, Cromwell Brothers *(Trapeze Act)*, Eugene Deckers *(Ringmaster)*, Ben Williams *(Charlie)*, Margaret Withers *(Blackpool Landlady)*, Gerald Rex *(Call Boy)*, Beryl Measor *(Gwen)*, Wallas Eaton *(Court Official)*.

Lom plays the dual role of twin brothers who are trapeze performers. They have won the French lottery but their public relations man, Marney, steals the ticket with the help of Dixey. One of the brothers murders Marney while the other is performing so neither can be arrested for the crime. They go back to performing in another circus and both brothers encounter very hard luck.

p, Louis H. Jackson; d, Alfred Travers; w, Travers, Stephen Clarkson, Vivienne Ades (based on a story by Renault Capes); ph, James Wilson; m, Hans May; art d, R. Holmes-Paul.

Crime Drama **(PR:A MPAA:NR)**

DUBLIN NIGHTMARE** (1958, Brit.) 64m Penington-Eady/RFD bw

William Sylvester *(John Kevin)*, Marla Landi *(Anna)*, Richard Leech *(Steven Lawlor)*, William Sherwood *(Edward Dillon)*, Harry Hutchinson *(The Vulture)*, Jack Cunningham *(Inspector O'Connor)*, Pat O'Sullivan *(O'Callaghan)*, Helen Lindsay, Paddy Hayes, Richard Curnock, Anne Blake, Dermot Kelly, Paddy Joyce, Gerald C. Lawson.

In Dublin, photographer Sylvester discovers that his apparently murdered friend is a leader in the IRA. Routine crime drama with a plot lifted almost intact from THE THIRD MAN.

p, Jon Penington, David Eady; d, John Pomeroy; w, John Tully; ph, Eric Gross.

Crime **(PR:A-C MPAA:NR)**

DUCHESS AND THE DIRTWATER FOX, THE**

(1976) 104m Fox c

George Segal (Charlie Malloy), Goldie Hawn (Amanda Quaid), Conrad Janis (Gladstone), Thayer David (Widdicombe), Jennifer Lee (Trollop), Roy Jenson (Bloodworth), Pat Ast (Dance Hall Girl), Sid Gould (Rabbi), Bob Hoy, Bennie Dobbins, Walter Scott, Jerry Gatlin (Bloodworth Gang), E.J. Andre, Dick Farnsworth, Clifford Turknett, Harlan Knudson, Jean Fabre, Bill McLaughlin, Richard Jamison, Barbara Ulrich, John Alderson, Jim Frank, Georgine Rozman, Kathy Christopher, Ellen Stern, Pater Rachback, Jerry Taft, Prentis Rowe, Ronald Colizzo, June Constable, Vern Porter.

Hawn is the Duchess, a dance hall girl, and Segal the Fox, an all too lucky gambler in this cornball western. Together they get mixed up with a gang of outlaws and a wagon train of Mormons. The best comic sequence is when Hawn and Segal pose as guests at a Jewish wedding, but most of the time the humor falls flat.

p&d, Melvin Frank; w, Barry Sandler, Jack Rose, Frank (based on a story by Barry Sandler); ph, Joseph Biroc (Panavision, DeLuxe Color); m, Charles Fox, ed, Frank Bracht, William Butler; art d, Trevor Williams, Robert Emmet Smith; set d, Dennis Peeples; m/l, Sammy Cahn, Frank.

Comedy/Western **Cas.** **(PR:C MPAA:PG)**

DUCHESS OF IDAHO, THE**½

(1950) 98m MGM c

Esther Williams (Christine Riverton Duncan), Van Johnson (Dick Layn), John Lund (Douglas J. Morrissen, Jr.), Paula Raymond (Ellen Hallet), Clinton Sundberg (Matson), Connie Haines (Peggy Elliott), Mel Torme (Cyril), Amanda Blake (Linda Kinston), Tommy Farrell (Chuck), Sig Arno (Mons. Le Blanche), Dick Simmons (Alec J. Collins), The Jubalaires (Themselves), Lena Horne, Eleanor Powell, Red Skelton (Guest Stars), Charles Smith (Johnny), John Louis Johnson (Pullman Porter), Roger Moore (Escort), Bunny Waters (Marsha), Dorothy Douglas (Eleanor), Mae Clarke (Betty, the Flower Girl), Johnny Trebach (Waiter), Suzanne Ridgeway (Cleo), Larry Steers, Harold Miller (Men at Table), Allen Ray (Elevator Man).

Typical MGM Musical with lots of singing, dancing, skiing, swimming, and color. Lund is a very rich playboy whom Raymond adores. She's his secretary and her main job appears to be saving Lund from the advances of obvious fortune hunters. Williams would like to help Raymond achieve her goal so she makes a play for Lund, the thinking behind that being that Raymond will again leap into the fray, rescue Lund, and he will begin to realize how valuable she is to him and how much she loves him. Williams and Johnson are in love and Van doesn't quite comprehend Esther's behavior. A few mixups, door slams, and "I'll never ever talk to you agains" and we fade out with everybody in each other's arms. Very predictable but fun. Williams plays a swim star (how else can they justify her natatory scenes?) and Johnson's a bandleader (which allows for lots of music). Horne looks beautiful and Powell came out of retirement to tap her way into our hearts. One remarkable point· with so many songs, anyone but the most fastidious musical film historian would be hard-pressed to remember any of them. In other words, a highly forgettable score. Songs: "Baby Come Out of the Clouds" (Lee Pearl, Henry Nemo), "You Can't Do Wrong Doin' Right," "Let's Choo Choo To Idaho," "Of All Things," "Or Was It Spring," "Warm Hands, Cold Heart" (Al Rinker, Floyd Huddleston), "Singlefoot Serenade" (G.M. Beilenson, M. Beeby), "You Won't Forget Me" (Kermit Goell, Fred Spielman).

p, Joe Pasternak; d, Robert Z. Leonard; w, Dorothy Cooper, Jerry Davis; ph, Charles Schoenbaum (Technicolor); ed, Adreinne Fazan; md, Georgie Stoll; art d, Cedric Gibbons, Malcolm Brown; ch, Jack Donohue.

Musical Comedy **(PR: A MPAA:NR)**

DUCK IN ORANGE SAUCE**

(1976, Ital.) 105m Capital/Cinerix c
(L'ANATRA ALL'ARANCIA)

Monica Vitti (Lisa), Ugo Tognazzi (Ugo), Barbara Bouchet (Patty), John Richardson (Jean Claude).

An Italian sex comedy that initially had George Segal as star and Dino Risi to direct, but that did not pan out. Tognazzi takes Segal's place as an advertiser (he is trying to promote California wine in Italy) whose wife, Vitti, is fooling around at a beach villa with Richardson. Tognazzi's attempts to stop this affair is the catalyst for much of the film's broad humor.

p, Mario Cecchi; d, Luciano Salce; w, Bernardino Zapponi (based on the play by William Douglas Home and Marc Gilbert Saugajon); ph, Franco DiGiacomo (Eastmancolor); m, Armando Trovaioli; ed, Antonio Siciliano; art d, Lorenzo Baraldi.

Comedy **(PR:C MPAA:NR)**

DUCK RINGS AT HALF PAST SEVEN, THE**

(1969, Ger./Ital.) 88m Roxy/Constantin c
(DIE ENTE KLINGELT UM ½ 7)

Heinz Ruehmann (Dr. Alexander), Hertha Feiler (Adela, his Wife), Graziella Granata (Female Lecturer), Charles Regnier (Professor), John van Dreelen (Lawyer), Monica Teuber (Ulrike, House Maid), Inge Marschall (Nurse), Angela Hillebrecht (Mrs. Ilse).

Ruehman, a computer wizard, is thought to be insane when he tells the police that his car was wrecked by an elephant (which it was), and that "the duck is ringing at half past seven" (the duck being his home computer). He is put in a mental institution and finds that the only way out is to act crazy. A cliche premise (a person must be crazy to exist in today's society) with some sharp moments, but not enough of them.

p, Luggi Waldleitner; d, Rolf Thiele; w, Roy Evans, Paul Hengge, Ricardo Ghione; ph, Wolf Wirth (Eastmancolor); m, Martin Boettcher; ed, Ingeborg Taschner; set d, Wolf Englert, Herbert Strabel.

Comedy **(PR:O MPAA:NR)**

DUCK SOUP****

(1933) 70 m PAR bw

Groucho Marx (Rufus T. Firefly), Chico Marx (Chicolini), Harpo Marx (Brownie), Zeppo Marx (Bob Rolland), Raquel Torres (Vera Marcal), Louis Calhern (Ambassador Trentino), Margaret Dumont (Mrs. Teasdale), Verna Hillie (Secretary), Leonid Kinskey (Agitator), Edmund Breese (Zander), Edwin Maxwell (Secretary of War), Edgar Kennedy (Peddler).

DUCK SOUP was not a commercial success when first released. Over the years it has achieved the status of a cult film and has become one of the Marx Brothers' most popular works. Fast-moving, irreverent, almost anarchistic in style, DUCK SOUP marked the last film in which Zeppo appeared. Although there were those who felt he was never necessary at all, there are just as many who enjoyed the respite from the manic scenes when Zeppo did his boy juvenile bit. The story, if one can call it that, concerns Dumont (who did seven of these with the Brothers) as a dowager millionairess who will donate $20 million to the destitute duchy of Freedonia if it will agree to make Groucho (Rufus T. Firefly) the dictator. And such a dictator he is, too. So much so that Mussolini banned the film in Italy, thinking it was a direct insult to him. Naturally, the Marx Brothers were thrilled to hear that. Groucho woos Dumont as he spends his spare time insulting Calhern, ambassador from the neighboring country of Sylvania. Calhern is the villain and hires Torres to vamp Groucho so Calhern can move in on Dumont, marry her, and get control of Freedonia. To help in the chicanery, Calhern hires Chico, a peanut salesman, and Groucho's chauffeur, Harpo. (Note: To director McCarey's credit, neither Harpo nor Chico went near enough to a musical instrument to play it.) Groucho rules Freedonia with an iron hand. When workers complain that they work long hours, he shortens their lunch break. The cabinet is in an uproar so Groucho hires Chico as the war secretary and reckons that Chico will be so annoying that the cabinet will quit in protest. Groucho and his secretary, Zeppo, decide to start a war with Sylvania by insulting Calhern. He interrupts Calhern's proposal of marriage to Dumont, slaps his face with a glove, and declares war between the two countries. Torres is staying with Dumont and her job is to keep an eye on Groucho. Chico and Harpo are sent over to steal the war plans and both dress up as Groucho, thereby beginning one of their most famous bits; the mirror routine. All three brothers look remarkably alike in the costumes and it's hard to know who is who. Groucho looks in the "mirror" and sees his reflection but suspects something is awry when the image is not quite exact. He captures Chico and puts him on trial. The "justice" is as manic as the rest of the movie. In the midst of the proceedings, Dumont tells all that Calhern is on his way to the courthouse in a last attempt to avert war. Groucho agrees to shake hands with the ambassador from Sylvania, but as the moments pass Groucho builds up a "Jack Story" in his mind and thinks what might happen if Calhern refuses to shake hands and make it all nice. Calhern, of course, has every intention of ending the silliness, but when he walks in Groucho immediately slaps his face again rather than suffer the imagined slight of Calhern's refusal. War begins and casualties abound, mostly due to Groucho shooting many of his own men. Harpo and Chico desert Sylvania in favor of Freedonia because they serve better food. Dumont calls Groucho to say that her home is under siege. The Marxes race to her house and capture Calhern. Freedonia has won. Groucho, Chico, Harpo, and Zeppo begin to throw oranges at Calhern until Dumont, in a rush of patriotism, begins to sing the Freedonian National Anthem. It goes without saying that the quartet immediately turn their attentions to Dumont and start throwing oranges at her as the film fades out. This movie may have been inadvertent satire (as some critics thought) but Kalmar, Ruby, Sheekman, and Perrin were men of great insight and wit and must have known what was happening around the world when they wrote this. In the light of history, it plays funnier than it may have originally because we know what kind of dangerous clowns Adolph and Benito were. Perhaps it was that America was not crazy about the government that sent it into a Depression in 1932 or maybe the picture was too hip for the audiences. Whatever, this film didn't maket it then. It sure makes it now.

p, Herman Mankiewicz; d, Leo McCarey; w, Bert Kalmar, Harry Ruby, Arthur Sheekman, Nat Perrin; ph, Henry Sharpe; ed, LeRoy Stone; art d, Hans Dreier, Willard Ihnen; m/l, "Freedonia Hymn," "His Excellency Is Due," "The Country's Going to War," "When the Clock on the Wall Strikes Ten," "The Laws of My Administration," Bert Kalmar, Harry Ruby.

Comedy **Cas.** **(PR:AA MPAA:NR)**

DUCK, YOU SUCKER!***

(1972, Ital.) 139m Rafram-San Marco-Miura/UA c
(GIU LA TESTA; AKA: FISTFUL OF DYNAMITE)

Rod Steiger (Juan Miranda), James Coburn (Sean Mallory), Romolo Valli (Dr. Villega), Maria Monti (Adolita), Rik Battaglia (Santerna), Franco Graziosi (Governor), Antoine Domingo (Guttierrez), Goffredo Pistoni (Nino), Roy Bosier (Landowner), John Frederick (American), Nino Casale (Notary), Jean Rougeul (Priest), Vincenzo Norvese (Pancho), Corrado Solari (Sebastian), Biacio LaRocca (Benito), Renato Pontecchi (Pepe), Franco Collace (Napoleon), Amelio Perlini (Peon), Michael Harvey (Yankee).

Director Leone, who created a new form of western (THE GOOD, THE BAD AND THE UGLY; ONCE UPON A TIME IN THE WEST), focuses on the Mexican revolution. Coburn is a fugitive Irish revolutionary, and Steiger wants to use Coburn's explosives expertise to get into a bank vault. The vault turns out to be full of political prisioners rather than gold, and Steiger becomes a hero for setting them free. Well-plotted action, but, as in most of Leone's films, scenes seem to have been deleted from the American prints.

p, Fulvio Morsella; d, Sergio Leone; w, Luciano Vicenzoni, Sergio Donati, Leone (based on a story by Leone); ph, Giuseppe Ruzzolini (Techniscope, Technicolor); m, Ennio Morricone; ed, Nino Baragli; art d, Andrea Crisanti; set d, Dario Micheli; cos, Franco Carretti; makeup, Amato Garbini.

Western **(PR:C MPAA:PG)**

DUDE BANDIT, THE** (1933) 63m Allied bw

Hoot Gibson, Gloria Shea, "Skeeter Bill" Robbins, Hooper Atchley, Neal Hart, Lafe McKee, Gordon DeMain, Fred Burns, Fred Gilman, Art Mix, George Morrell, Merrill McCormick, Hank Bell, Horace B. Carpenter, Pete Morrison, Charles Whitaker, Blackie Whiteford, Frank Ellis, Charles Brinley, Charles King, Bill Gillis.

Gibson is the mysterious cowpoke who changes colors and becomes a bandit when the situation demands. The fast-paced plot keeps Gibson busy changing his persona as the real villain attempts to swindle ranchers out of their property. Cinematography is exceptional, with the night scenes especially standing out.

d, George Melford; w, Jack Natteford (based on a story by Natteford); ph, Harry Neumann, Tom Galligan; ed, Mildred Johnston.

Western **Cas.** **(PR:A MPAA:NR)**

DUDE COWBOY**½ (1941) 59m RKO bw

Tim Holt (Terry), Marjorie Reynolds (Barbara), Ray Whitley (Smokey), Lee [Lasses] White (Whopper), Louise Currie (Gail Sargent), Helen Holmes (Miss Carter), Eddie Kane (Gordon West), Eddie Drew (French), Byron Foulger (Mr. Adams), Tom London (Sheriff), Lloyd Ingraham (Pop Stebbens), Glenn Strange (Krinkle).

Good Holt western sees the cowboy playing a U.S. Treasury agent out to stop a gang of counterfeiters. The crooks have kidnaped a government engraver and are forcing him to produce phony bills, which they launder at a dude ranch gambling casino. Holt eventually finds the kidnaped government employee hidden in an abandoned mine, and the climax sees a shootout between the agent and the counterfeiters.

p, Bert Gilroy; d, David Howard; w, Morton Grant; ph, Harry Wild; ed, Fredric Knudtson; md, Paul Sawtell; m/l, "Silver Rio," "Dude Cowboy," "End of the Canyon Trail," "Echo Singing in the Wild Wind," Fred Rose, Ray Whitley.

Western **(PR:A MPAA:NR)**

DUDE GOES WEST, THE*** (1948) 87m King Bros./AA bw

Eddie Albert (Daniel Bone), Gale Storm (Liza Crockett), James Gleason (Sam Briggs), Binnie Barnes (Kiki Kelly), Gilbert Roland (Pecos Kid), Barton MacLane (Texas Jack), Douglas Fowley (Beetie), Tom Tyler (Spiggoty), Harry Hayden (Horace Hotchkiss), Chief Yowlachie (Running Wolf), Sarah Padden (Mrs. Hallahan), Catherine Doucet (Grandma Crockett), Edward Gargan (Conductor), Olin Howlin (Finnegan), Francis Pierlot (Mr. Brittle), Tom Fadden (J.J. Jines), Si Jenks (Horse Trader), George Meeker (Gambler), Dick Elliot (Whiskey Drummer), Charles Williams (Harris), Lee [Lasses] White (Baggage Master), Frank Yaconelli, Ben Welden.

Fun western comedy starring Albert as a mild-mannered East Coast gunsmith who decides to pull up stakes and move to Arsenic City, Arizona, because he has heard that everyone there owns a gun and if he relocated his business it would make a fortune. On the trail, every conceivable disaster befalls him. One ray of sunshine breaks through in the person of Storm, with whom he falls in love. Storm is also on her way to Arsenic City to locate the gold mine her father discovered before he was murdered. Together they find the mine and defeat the badmen, with city slicker Albert shooting straighter than any western gunslinger. A good comedy, with an outstanding cast of supporting players.

p, Frank and Maurice King; d, Kurt Neumann; w, Richard Sale, Mary Loos; ph, Karl Struss; m, Dimitri Tiomkin; ed, Richard Heermance.

Comdey/Western **(PR:A MPAA:NR)**

DUDE RANCH** (1931) 60m PAR bw

Jack Oakie (Jennifer), Stuart Erwin (Chester Carr), Eugene Pallette (Judd), Mitzi Green (Alice), June Collyer (Susan Meadows), Charles Sellon (Spruce Meadows), Cecil Weston (Mrs. Merridew), George Webb (Burson), Guy Oliver (Simonson), James Crane (Blaze Denton).

In this comedy with a western flavor, Oakie stars as the leader of a traveling troupe of actors looking for work. The actors come across a dying dude ranch and Oakie strikes a deal with the owner to perform a "Wild West" show in an attempt to keep the few ranch guests from leaving out of boredom. Enter some shady gangsters who plan to rob the local bank and it's up to Oakie to stop them.

d, Frank Tuttle; w, Percy Heath, Grover Jones, Lloyd Corrigan, Herman Mankiewicz (based on a story by Milton Krims); ph, Henry Gerrard.

Comedy **(PR:A MPAA:NR)**

DUDE RANGER, THE**½ (1934) 63m Atherton/FOX bw

George O'Brien (Ernest Selby), Irene Hervey (Anne Hepburn), Leroy Mason (Dale Hyslip), Henry Hall (Sam Hepburn), James Mason (Hawk Selbert), Syd Saylor (Nebraska Kemp), Sid Jordan (Dunk), Alma Chester (Martha), Lloyd Ingraham (Beckett), Earl Dwire, Si Jenks, Lafe McKee, Jack Kirk, Hank Bell.

A surprisingly gentle western starring O'Brien as an easterner who inherits a ranch and moves out west. He soon discovers rustlers working his land and suspects his girl friend's father, Hall, to be the man behind the gang. O'Brien eventually discovers that Mason is the true "brains" and all is forgiven. A detailed view of ranch life, combined with some beautiful scenery and very little gun play.

p, Sol Lesser, John S. Zanft; d, Edward F. Cline; w, Barry Barringer (based on the story by Zane Grey); ph, Frank B. Good; ed, Don Hayes.

Western **Cas.** **(PR:A MPAA:NR)**

DUDE WRANGLER, THE* (1930) 60m Independent/Sono Art-World-Wide bw

Lina Basquette (Helen Dane), George Duryea [Tom Keene] (Wally McCann), Clyde Cook (Pinkey Fripp), Francis X. Bushman (Canby), Margaret Seddon (Aunt Mary), Ethel Wales (Mattie), K. Sojin (Wong), Wilfred North (The "Snorer"), Alice Davenport, Virginia Sale, Julia Swayne Gordon, Louis Payne, Fred Parker, Aileen Carlyle, Jack Richardson (Dude Guests).

Lame early talkie comedy has a filthy rich city boy becoming a dude rancher to impress his girl. Pretty dull, with exceptionally bad dialog.

p, Mrs. Wallace Reid, Cliff Broughton; d, Richard Thorpe; w, Robert Lee [Robert Lee Johnson] (based on the novel The Feminine Touch by Caroline Lockhart).

Comedy **(PR:A MPAA:NR)**

DUDES ARE PRETTY PEOPLE** (1942) 43m UA bw

Jimmy Rogers (Jimmy), Noah Beery, Jr. (Pidge), Marjorie Woodworth (Marcia), Paul Hurst (Two-Gun), Marjorie Gateson (Aunt Elsie), Russell Gleason (Brad), Grady Sutton (George), Jan Duggan (Radio Girl), Sarah Edwards (Miss Priddle), Joe Cunningham (Joe).

Beery and Rogers star as two cowhands whose friendship is strained when Woodworth, an attractive female visitor to their dude ranch, makes a play for Beery. Rogers attempts to break up the budding relationship by scaring the city gal with phony gun play and hints that Beery is already married. Tedious stuff punctuated by a small boy singing "West Wind Whistlin' " by Chet Forrest and Bob Wright.

p, Hal Roach; d, Hal Roach, Jr.; w, Louis S. Kaye (based on a story by Donald Hough); ph, Robert Pittack; m, Edward Ward, Chet Forrest, Bob Wright; ed, Bert Jordan; art d, Charles D. Hall; spec eff, Roy Seawright.

Western/Comedy **(PR:A MPAA:NR)**

DUE SOLDI DI SPERANZA
(SEE: TWO PENNY WORTH OF HOPE, 1952, Brit.)

DUEL, THE**½ (1964, USSR) 93m Mosfilm/Artkino c

Lyudmila Shagalova (Nadezhda Fyodorovna), Oleg Strizhenov (Layeuskiy), Vladimir Druzhnikov (Von Koren), Aleksandr Khvylya (Samoylenko), L. Kadrov (Pobedov), G. Georgiu (Kirilin), Ye. Kuzmina (Marya Konstantinovna), L. Pirogov (Bityugov), Yu. Leonidov (Achmianov), V. Burlakova, P. Vinnik, E. Geller, A. Kuznetsov, V. Kulik, S. Svashenko, P. Sobolevskiy, I Fyodorova, Nina Vilvovskaya, S. Yermilov.

A superbly acted adaptation of a play by Chekhov, THE DUEL tells of the struggles that Strizhenov has with his dull daily routine and the mistress that offers no relief from his boredom. When his mistress' husband dies he is faced with the possibility of marriage—a thought which sends him packing. He tries to borrow money from Druzhnikov but when the lender realizes what the money is for he refuses. Furious Strizhenov challenges him to a duel which ends in neither man hitting his target. Strizhenov is deeply affected by his brush with death and begins life anew.

d, Tatyana Berezantseva, Lev Rudnik; w, Berezantseva (based on a play by Anton Pavlovich Chekhov); ph, Antonina Egina; m, V. Yurovskiy; ed, P. Chechyotkina; art d, V. Kamskiy; cos, V. Nisskaya; makeup, Mikhail Chikiryov; spec eff, B. Gorbachyov.

Drama **(PR:A MPAA:NR)**

DUEL AT APACHE WELLS**½ (1957) 69m REP bw

Anna Maria Alberghetti (Anita Valdez), Ben Cooper (Johnny Shattuck), Jim Davis (Dean Cannary), Harry Shannon (Wayne Shattuck), Francis J. McDonald (Hank), Bob Steele (Joe Dunn), Frank Puglia (Senor Valdez), Argentina Brunetti (Tia Maria), Ian MacDonald (Marcus Wolf), John Dierkes (Bill Sowers), Ric Roman (Frank).

Well-done, low-budget oater starring Cooper as a wayward son who returns home to his father's Arizona ranch after a four-year absence to find that rustler-turned-rancher Davis has siphoned off the only water hole in the area and is slowly killing the father's ranch. Cooper tries to gain access to the water hole through legal methods but his efforts fail and he eventually is pushed to a showdown with Davis.

p&d, Joseph Kane; w, Bob Williams; ph, Jack Marta; m, Gerald Roberts; ed, Richard L. Van Enger; md, Roberts; art d, Frank Arrigo.

Western **(PR:A MPAA:NR)**

DUEL AT DIABLO**½ (1966) 105m UA c

James Garner (Jess Remsberg), Sidney Poitier (Toller), Bibi Andersson (Ellen Grange), Dennis Weaver (Willard Grange), Bill Travers (Lt. McAllister), William Redfield (Sgt. Ferguson), John Hoyt (Chata), John Crawford (Clay Dean), John Hubbard (Maj. Novak), Kevin Coughlin (Norton), Jay Ripley (Tech), Jeff Cooper (Casey), Ralph Bahnsen (Nyles), Bobby Crawford (Swenson), Richard Lapp (Forbes), Armand Alzamora (Ramirez), Alf Elson (Col. Foster), Dawn Little Sky (Chata's Wife), Eddie Little Sky (Alchise), Al Wyatt (Miner), Bill Hart (Cpl. Harrington), J.R. Randall (Crowley), John Daheim (Stableman), Phil Schumacher (Burly Soldier), Richard Farnsworth (1st Wagon Driver), Joe Finnegan (2nd Wagon Driver).

A confused western essay on racism stars Garner as a civilian guide and Travers as an uptight cavalry lieutenant escorting a shipment of ammunition to an isolated fort. Also along on the trail are Poitier, a former Army sergeant now breaking in horses for the military, and Andersson, Travers' wife, who was raped by Apaches and subsequently gave birth to a half-breed child which becomes the subject of racial tension. Garner himself is bent on revenge for the scalping of his Comanche wife. Most of the action is derived from a series of Indian attacks upon the caravan and the film contains a disturbing amount of graphic violence. It suffers greatly from an inappropriate musical score by Neal Hefti. Director Nelson made another, even bloodier western dealing with racism in 1970, SOLDIER BLUE, which also suffers from poor scripting.

p, Fred Engel, Ralph Nelson; d, Nelson; w, Marvin H. Albert, Michael M. Grilikhes (based on the novel Apache Rising by Albert); ph, Charles F. Wheeler (DeLuxe Color); m, Neal Hefti; ed, Fredric Steinkamp; art d, Alfred Ybarra; set d, Victor Gangelin; cos, Yvonne Wood; spec eff, Roscoe Cline, Larry Hampton, George Peckham; head wrangler, Bill Jones.

Western **(PR:A MPAA:NR)**

DUEL AT EZO★★ (1970, Jap.) 131m Tokyo Eiga/Toho c
(EZO YAKATA NO KETTO)

Yuzo Kayama *(Saburota Edo)*, Rentaro Mikuni *(Shimbei Usa)*, Shogo Shimada *(Jirozaemon Ezo)*, Mitsuko Baisho *(Aka Shu)*, Kunie Tanaka *(Kurobei)*, Toru Abe *(Ronin)*, Toshio Kurosawa *(Kyuma)*, Tatsuya Nakadai *(Daizennokami Honjo)*.

Kayama is a shogun warrior who embarks on a mission to save the daughter of a Russian count being held prisoner by Shimada. It turns out that Shimada was actually cheated by the count and is only acting in self-defense. Kayama battles Mikuni, a fellow warrior who is intent on returning a shipment of guns to his Shogunate. The finale has Kayama emerging as the victor in the sword-wielding duel.

d, Kengo Furusawa; w, Ryozo Kasahara (based on a story by Renzaburo Shibata); ph, Hiroshi Murai (Panavision, Eastmancolor); m, Kenjiro Hirose; art d, Motoji Kojima.

Action **(PR:C MPAA:NR)**

DUEL AT SILVER CREEK, THE★★½ (1952) 76m UNIV bw

Audie Murphy *(Silver Kid)*, Faith Domergue *(Opal Lacey)*, Stephan McNally *(Lightning)*, Susan Cabot *(Dusty Fargo)*, Gerald Mohr *(Rod Lacey)*, Eugene Iglesias *(Johnny Sombrero)*, Kyle James *(Rat Face Blake)*, Walter Sande *(Pete Fargo)*, Lee Marvin *(Tinhorn Burgess)*, George Eldredge *(Jim Ryan)*, James Anderson *(Bit)*.

An early film from master action director Don Siegel stars Domergue as the leader of a gang of cutthroats (Mohr, Iglesias, Marvin) who jump gold mine claims and murder anyone who gets in their way. While town marshal McNally is out on the trail searching for the gang, the villains murder an old friend of the sheriff's. On his return, McNally swears vengeance and makes Murphy his deputy after the young man is orphaned by the killers. Domergue, whose identity with the gang has remained a secret, seduces McNally who, despite warnings from Murphy, is blind to her machinations. He wises up and eventually shoots it out with the gang in a big gunfight.

p, Leonard Goldstein; d, Don Siegel; w, Gerald Drayson Adams, Joseph Hoffman (based on a story by Adams); ph, Irving Glassberg (Technicolor); m, Hans J. Salter; ed, Russell Schoengarth; art d, Bernard Herzbrun, Alexander Golitzen; set d, Russell A. Gausman, Joe Kisch.

Western **(PR:A MPAA:NR)**

DUEL IN DURANGO (SEE: GUN DUEL IN DURANGO, 1957)

DUEL IN THE JUNGLE★★½ (1954, Brit.) 105m ABF/WB c

Dana Andrews *(Scott Walters)*, Jeanne Crain *(Marian)*, David Farrar *(Perry and Arthur Henderson)*, Patrick Barr *(Supt. Roberts)*, George Coulouris *(Capt. Malburn)*, Charles Goldner *(Martell)*, Wilfrid Hyde White *(Pitt)*, Mary Merrall *(Mrs. Henderson)*, Heather Thatcher *(Lady on the Nigeria)*, Michael Mataka *(Vincent)*, Paul Carpenter *(Clerk)*, Delphi Lawrence, Mary Mackenzie, Bee Duffell, Alec Finter, Patrick Parnell, John Salew, Walter Gotell, Charles Carson, Bill Fraser, Simone Silva, Irene Handl, Lionel Ngakane, Bill Shine, Robert Sansom.

Andrews stars as an American insurance investigator looking into the mysterious death of diamond broker Farrar, whose life was insured for $1 million. Farrar had reportedly drowned while diving for diamonds off the African coast. Andrews follows the dead man's secretary-fiancee, Crain, through a dangerous safari in the jungle until he discovers Farrar is very much alive. The scheme was conceived by Farrar to raise money to proceed with underwater mining for diamonds. Soon the crook and the agent are off on a canoe chase which ends with the capture of Farrar. Implausible story; weak performances. Shot on location in Rhodesia.

p, Marcel Hellman, Tony Owen; d, George Marshall; w, Sam Marx, T. J. Morrison (based on a story by S. K. Kennedy); ph, Edwin Miller (Technicolor); m, Mischa Spollansky; ed, E.B. Jarvis; m/l, "The Night Belongs To Me," Norman Newell.

Adventure **(PR:A MPAA:NR)**

DUEL IN THE SUN★★★½ (1946) 138m Selznick c

Jennifer Jones *(Pearl Chavez)*, Joseph Cotton *(Jesse McCanles)*, Gregory Peck *(Lewt McCanles)*, Lionel Barrymore *(Sen. McCanles)*, Lillian Gish *(Laura Belle McCanles)*, Walter Huston *(The Sin Killer)*, Herbert Marshall *(Scott Chavez)*, Charles Bickford *(Sam Pierce)*, Joan Tetzel *(Helen Langford)*, Harry Carey *(Lem Smoot)*, Otto Kruger *(Mr. Langford)*, Sidney Blackmer *(The Lover)*, Tilly Losch *(Mrs. Chavez)*, Scott McKay *(Sid)*, Butterfly McQueen *(Vashti)*, Francis McDonald, Victor Kilian *(Gamblers)*, Griff Barnett *(The Jailer)*, Frank Cordell *(Frank)*, Dan White *(Ed)*, Steve Dunhill *(Jake)*, Lane Chandler *(Captain, U.S. Cavalry)*, Lloyd Shaw *(Barbecue Caller)*, Bert Roach *(Eater)*, Si Jenks, Hank Worden, Rose Plummer *(Dancers)*, Guy Wilkerson *(Barfly)*, Lee Phelps *(Engineer)*, Al Taylor *(Man at Barbecue)*, Orson Welles *(Narrator)*, Thomas Dillon *(Engineer)*, Robert McKenzie *(Bartender)*, Charles Dingle *(Sheriff Hardy)*.

Selznick accomplished the impossible here, offering an enormous western jampacked with sex, costumed in a thick melodrama where spurs scar the saloon floorboards, skirts rustle in thick-aired adobe bedrooms, and the thudding beat of a thousand horses tramples the far plains. It's full of grand spectacle, steamy sensualism, and a storyline that could only have snaked out of Hollywood. But, for all its hokum, bully-loves-vixen romance, DUEL IN THE SUN is superlative entertainment. Jones is the half-breed daughter of a gambler, Marshall, who kills his wife, Losch, and her lover, Blackmer, and is hanged. Before mounting the scaffold this cultured gent sends his daughter, Jones, to live with the woman he once really loved, Gish, long the deeply suffering wife of cattle baron Barrymore. When she arrives, Cotten, Barrymore's good son, meets her and takes her to the great ranch where Gish takes her in and the invalided Barrymore, bound to his wheelchair but ever in charge of his endless domain, sneers ridicule at the "Mexican baggage." Peck, Barrymore's evil son—both siblings acting out the part of different natures in the mixed family—lusts after Jones and quickly seduces her

but refuses to take her as his wife. Cotten is kind to Jones, mildly attracted to her, but he, being the educated, refined son, pursues other quarry, chiefly Tetzel, daughter of railroad magnate Kruger. Deserted, except for doting, kindly Gish, Jones befriends the understanding and gentle straw boss, Bickford. He proposes marriage and she accepts. Bickford buys a wedding ring but never lives long enough to slip it on Jones' finger. Evil Peck appears in a bar and tells Bickford that no one shall have his dark-skinned concubine but he. When the unarmed Bickford makes a move for a gun tossed on the bar, Peck shoots him to death, then juts his stubbly jaw at shrinking customers, asking, "Anybody else got ideas about Pearl Chavez?" He is now an outlaw on the run; Barrymore meets secretly with him, giving his spoiled cowboy child funds and telling him to stay away from his cattle empire "until things die down." Meanwhile, the iron horse chugs its way toward Barrymore's sacrosanct lands. When McKay brings the old man word that the railroad is about to cross his lands, Barrymore orders "every man and boy on Spanish Bit" to meet with him and to come armed. The bells in steeples and on ranches resound across the miles of the cattle fiefdom and the ranch hands and cowboys mount up, riding pell-mell for the rendezvous, dozens, then hundreds forming the greatest assemblage of cowboys ever filmed, all thundering after Barrymore, riding in the lead on a white charger, his black cape flying wildly behind him, Cotten reluctantly at his side. The horde descends upon a single fenceline and lines up facing the train belching black smoke that has reached end-of-track just on the other side. Barrymore is met by Carey, lawyer and lawman, and railroad president Kruger. He ignores the legal documents Carey tries to read, telling him that he will "fire on them coolies" if another rail is put down. Cotten tries to talk reason to the old cattleman, but Barrymore ignores him. Cotten joins the railroad men and even prepares to cut the fence. Barrymore warns him that he will order his men to open up if one strand of wire is cut. Before the wirecutters are applied a long troop of cavalry arrives, the soldiers lining up on the other side of the fence, their guns drawn against the cowboys in an historic confrontation between the Old West and the Modern Age. Barrymore stares at the American flag whipping in the breeze and says: "I once fought for that flag . . . I'll not fire on it." He lowers his Stetson-covered head and orders his men back to work, telling Cotten never to set foot on his land again. Now two sons are lost to him. Peck, however, feels that he will strike a blow for his father so he derails a train loaded with dynamite used in railroad construction. It blows up and he rides away, callously singing "I've Been Workin' on the Railroad." Peck returns to find that his brother has taken Jones under his wing following the death of their mother. Challenging his brother to a duel, Peck refuses to wait for Cotten to fill his hand with a weapon, shooting the unarmed Cotten down (as usual). This final despicable act enflames Jones and she rides out after her sadistic lover and they shoot it out in the mountaintops, mortally wounding each other. Jones, in perhaps the most ludicrous moments of this wholly unbelievable romance, crawls for what seems to be miles while spouting blood and shouting love to Peck who is fast sinking with a bullet in the stomach. She manages to reach his lofty lair, crawl into his arms, and they kiss then nod into death. Selznick intended to make this film equal to his epic GONE WITH THE WIND but it falls considerably short, though marvelous performances are rendered by Marshall, Barrymore, Gish, Bickford and, in a few brief scenes, Huston, as a fire-and-brimstone western preacher with six guns strapped to his legs. Cotten is merely a prop to represent decency while Peck and Jones outdo each other in amateur theatrics, although Peck does come close to being just about the most obnoxious cowpoke who ever rode a horse. The accent on sex is heavy-handed and often repugnant, causing jocular critics of the day to dub the film "Lust in the Dust." The budget for this film soared beyond $6 million before it was over and an additional $2 million was used to scandalously promote the sex angle. A storm of protest from Catholic and Protestant leaders alike thunderclapped over Selznick's head. All over America local authorities competed with each other to ban the film. It was censored in Memphis and kicked out of Hartford, Connecticut. Certain scenes had to be edited before DUEL IN THE SUN opened in Philadelphia and other major cities. The publicity was enormous and the public ignored the universal drubbing the film received from critics, flocking to see it and returning $12 million to the Selznick coffers. The film was begun in 1944 and John Wayne was originally set to play the bad cowboy but he veered away from the film after reading the dubious script. Both Teresa Wright and Hedy Lamarr at one time or another were assigned the role of the tempestuous half-breed, but both had to drop out due to pregnancies. Selznick thought this providential in that he wanted his wife Jones to play the role all along, creating a superstar vehicle for her after her triumphs in SINCE YOU WENT AWAY and SONG OF BERNADETTE. The entire production was geared around her sultry, hip-swaying, bronze-tinted persona, one dripping thin grease and gallons of perspiration. The one actor Selznick insisted upon was the stentorian and electrifying Walter Huston, but the actor's agent drove a razor-sharp bargain, demanding and getting $40,000 for his client, plus overtime pay. Shot on location in Arizona, Selznick had miles of track put down for his advancing train and more than 6,500 extras were employed to people the hot, dusty landscape. Hundreds of horses and cattle were imported and the sprawling McCanles ranch was painfully constructed by hundreds of men leveling the land and planting trees. Selznick meddled in this film more than any other, insisting it be perfect for his wife. Veteran director Vidor was hamstrung at every turn, Selznick viewing his rushes and eliminating most of his takes. The mogul brought in a host of other directors to "assist" Vidor, who never required assistance. These included William Cameron Menzies, Josef Von Sternberg, Sydney Franklin, William Dieterle. Sternberg provided creative ideas of using color film and showed his expertise in makeup and costuming, but when he began taking five hours for a simple set-up, Selznick sacked him. Selznick just as easily discarded brilliant cinematographers Lee Garmes and Hal Rosson, letting Renahan finish but only under his immediate supervision. Selznick really wanted every director to quit so he could direct the film himself. Vidor was stubborn and stayed in the production to salvage some of his own work and receive the proper credit. Selznick and Vidor finally had their long-awaited shouting match after 20 months of shooting and the director walked off with two days shooting left. Dieterle was brought in to wrap things up. In the end Selznick sat in a viewing room for weeks scanning almost 1.5 million feet of film, which would approximate 135 two-hour movies, an enormous indulgence of ego and power. A ton was cut, including three complex dances performed by Jones, mostly because they were risque, revealing, and suggestive. The film nevertheless survived its own ponderous, lurching plot and often inane dialog through its sheer spectacle, its breathtaking color photography, and all of it was aided by Tiomkin's bravura and memorable score. The film boomed at the box office but failed to turn Jones into the top sex goddess of the screen as Selznick intended. She simply was not that appealing, crawling about in the dirt, her hair falling in greasy-looking strands, her dark-hued body drenched with sweat, her whispering voice gushing curses and oozing love. There was something prophetic about Welles' narration at the opening of the film as he summarizes Jones' fate: "Pearl, who came from down along the border, and who was like a wildflower sprung from the hard clay, quick to blossom, early to die." He might as well have been talking about the actress' image as a sex goddess.

p, David O. Selznick; d, King Vidor; w, Oliver H. P. Garrett, Selznick (based on the novel by Niven Busch); ph, Lee Garmes, Hal Rosson, Ray Renahan, Charles P. Boyle, Allen Davey (Technicolor); m, Dimitri Tiomkin; ed, Hal C. Kern, William Ziegler, John D. Faure, Charles Freeman; prod d, J. McMillan Johnson; md, Tiomkin; art d, James Basevi, John Ewing; set d, Emil Kuri; cos, Walter Plunkett; spec eff, Clarence Slifer, Jack Cosgrove; ch, Tilly Losch, Lloyd Shaw.

Western **(PR:C-O MPAA:NR)**

DUEL OF CHAMPIONS zero

(1964 Ital./Span.) 93m Lux-Tiberia/Medallion c (ORAZI E CURIAZI)

Alan Ladd (Horatio), Franca Bettoja (Marcia), Franco Fabrizi (Curiazio), Robert Keith (King of Rome), Luciano Marin (Eli), Jacques Sernas (Marcus), Andrea Aureli (King of Alba), Mino Doro (Caio), Osvaldo Ruggeri (Warrior of Alba), Jacqueline Derval (Horatia), Pieor Palmeri (Warrior of Alba), Umberto Raho (Grand Priest), Alfredo Varelli (Sabinus), Alana Ladd (Scilla), Nando Angelini (Official), Franca Pasut (Slave).

What Alan Ladd and director Young (Dr. No) are doing in this cheap Italian costume action film is something both men must have been asking themselves during its production. The company couldn't even come up with the money promised Ladd until another production company jumped in during mid-shoot. The story is based on the Roman legend of the Horatii and Curiatii triplets, sort of Hatfield and McCoy blood feudists. Ladd plays Horatio, a Roman soldier who becomes the only survivor when the triplets finally fight it out to the death. The film is so bad that a U.S. distributor couldn't be found until 1964. It disappeared quickly with the audiences lamenting "Come back, Shane."

p, Angelo Ferrara; d, Terence Young, Ferdinando Baldi; w, Carlo Lizzani, Ennio De Concini, Giuliano Montaldo (based on a story by Luciano Vincenzoni); ph, Amerigo Gengarelli (Totalscope, Eastmancolor); m, Angelo Francesco Lavagnino; ed, Renzo Lucidi; art d, Giulio Bongini; cos, Mario Giorsi.

Drama **(PR:A MPAA:NR)**

DUEL OF THE TITANS**

(1963, Ital.) 91m Titanus-Ajace/PAR c (ROMOLO E REMO)

Steve Reeves (Romulus), Gordon Scott (Remus), Virna Lisi (Julia), Arnelia Vanoni (Tarpia), Jacques Sernas (Curzio), Massimo Girotti (Tazio), Franco Volpi (Amulio), Andrea Bosic (Faustolo), Laura Solari (Rea Silvia), Enzo Cerusico (Numa), Giuliano Dell-Ovo (Publio), Germano Longo (Servio), Franco Balducci (Acilio), Piero Lulli (Sulpicio), Gianni Musy (Celere), Enrico Glori (Priest), Jose Greci (Estria), Inge Nystrom (Sira), Mimmo Poli, Nando Angelini, Inger Milton.

Reeves and Scott flex their big muscles in this film saga of Romulus and Remus, the two babies who were raised by wolves. The boys grow up and fight various battles together, including run-ins with a bear and a volcano, until they both fall in love with Lisi, the daughter of the King of the Sabines. Soon Scott begins to go mad with power. Sensing disaster, Reeves kills his brother and goes on to form the Roman Empire. Directed by Corbucci, who later went on to direct many spaghetti westerns.

p, Alessandro Jacovoni; d, Sergio Corbucci; w, Corbucci, Luciano Martino, Sergio Leone, Sergio Prosperi, Franco Rossetti, Ennio DeConcini, Duccio Tessari; ph, Enzo Barboni, Dario Di Palma (CinemaScope, Eastmancolor); m, Piero Piccioni; ed, Babriele Barriale; art d, Saverio D' Eugenio; set d, Carlo Simi; cos, Pier Luigi Pizzi.

Adventure **(PR:A MPAA:NR)**

DUEL ON THE MISSISSIPPI**

(1955) 72m Clover/COL c

Les Barker (Andre Tulane), Patricia Medina (Lill Scarlet), Warren Stevens (Hugo Marat), Craig Stevens (Rene LaFarge), John Dehner (Jules Tulane), Ian Keith (Jacques Scarlet), Christ Alcaide (Anton), John Mansfield (Louie), Celia Lovsky (Celeste Tulane), Lou Merrill (Georges Gabriel), Mel Welles (Sheriff), Jean Del Val (Bidault), Baynes Barron (Gaspard), Vince M. Townsend, Jr. (Benedict).

Deep South melodrama set in 1820 sees a war on old-time plantations waged by a band of bayou renegades seeking revenge on the southern aristocracy. The ringleader of the gang is Creole girl Medina, who owns a gambling ship and resents the fact that she has not been shown the respect she feels she deserves from the established families. She eventually softens when she falls for Barker, the son of aristocrat Dehner, and allows him to duel it out with her surly lieutenant, Stevens, a fight which Barker wins.

d, William Castle; w, Gerald Drayson Adams (based on a story by Adams); ph, Henry Freulich (Technicolor); ed, Edwin Bryant; md, Mischa Bakaleinikoff; art d, Paul Palmentola.

Adventure **(PR:A MPAA:NR)**

DUEL WITHOUT HONOR*

(1953, Ital.) 105m Manenti/I.F.E. Releasing bw

Annette Bach (Bianca), Constance Dowling (Olga), Massimo Girotti (Carlo), Raldano Lupi (Paolo), Annibale Betrone (Zio Gustavo), Ave Ninchi (Goverante), Renzo Giovampietro (De Lussac).

Bach stars in this underwhelming production about a convent girl who decides against taking her vows and returning to her banker fiance Girotti. She finds him carrying on with Dowling, however, and confronts the woman. Dowling, who has a second lover on the side, is killed by his jealousies, leaving Girotti and Bach with a chance to get together at the finale.

d, Camilio Mastrocinque; w, Mastrocinque, Gaspare Cataldo.

Drama **(PR:A MPAA:NR)**

DUELLISTS, THE***

(1977, Brit.) 95m PAR c

Keith Carradine (D'Hubert), Harvey Keitel (Feraud), Albert Finney (Fouche), Edward Fox (Col. Reynard), Cristina Raines (Adele), Robert Stephens (Gen. Treillard), Tom Conti (Jacquin), John McEnery (2nd Major), Diana Quick (Laura), Alun Armstrong (Lacourbe), Maurice Colbourne (Tall Second), Gay Hamilton (Maid), Meg Wynn Owen (Leonie), Jenny Runacre (Mme. de Lionne), Alan Webb (Chevalier), Matthew Guiness.

Beautifully photographed film that marked the debut of director Scott whose fine talent was realized later in BLADE RUNNER. It's not much more than a series of duels which take place during the Napoleonic era. Keitel and Carradine are odd choices to play French officers but manage to pull it off despite Keitel's Brighton Beach-Coney Island accent that creeps into the dialog every so often. The two men battle each other several times for several reasons over a 16-year period until a truce is called. Adapted from a Conrad story, the main reason to see this is the fascinating attention to detail on the parts of Scott and cameraman Tidy. The film is almost Germanic in its use of honor as a reason to duel. Keitel does his patented role of the near-psychotic who is obsessed, this time with dueling. In the end, Carradine is the victor and lets Keitel live. With so much action, there was hardly any time left in the picture for sympathetic characterization, and the result is that no one really cares who wins or loses. Still, the visual images are so compelling that it's worth a look. Like Kubrick's BARRY LYNDON, it becomes a series of still pictures that are animated. Scott won an award for "Best First Film."

p, David Putnam; d, Ridley Scott; w, Gerald Vaughn-Hughes (based on the story "The Duel" by Joseph Conrad; sometimes called "The Point of Honour"); ph, Frank Tidy; m, Howard Blake; ed, Pamela Powers; art d, Bryan Graves.

Period Drama **Cas.** **(PR:O MPAA:PG)**

DUET FOR CANNIBALS**

(1969, Swed.) 105m Sandrews-Teater/Grove Press bw

Adriana Asti (Francesca Bauer), Lars Ekborg (Artur Bauer), Gosta Ekman, Jr. (Tomas), Agneta Ekmanner (Ingrid), Britta Brunius (Mrs. Grundberg), Stig Engstrom (Lars), Gunnar Lindqvist (Man in Cafeteria).

A perplexing dramatic adventure from writer/film critic/essayist Susan Sontag about a bizarre couple—Asti (previously seen in Bertolucci's BEFORE THE REVOLUTION) and her former left-wing revolutionary leader husband Ekborg. They hire Ekman, a young man who helps Ekborg compile his notebooks for publication. He moves into the house, leaving his fiancee behind, though she too eventually moves in. The plot takes a series of wild twists and turns as all four characters wind up in bed with one another with Ekman getting jealous, Asti apparently trying to poison her husband, Ekborg killing Asti, and then committing suicide. Ekman and his fiancee leave the house as Asti and Ekborg, alive once again (don't ask how or why), watch from their window. It's all pretty strange but Sontag, who's proven her talent in her writings, seems like she knew what she was doing . . . or maybe not.

d&w, Susan Sontag; ph, Lars Swanberg; m, Anton Dvorak, Gustav Mahler, Richard Wagner; ed, Carl-Olov Skeppstedt.

Drama **(PR:O MPAA:NR)**

DUET FOR FOUR*

(1982, Aus.) 97m Burstall c (AKA: PARTNERS)

Mike Preston, Wendy Hughes, Diana Cilento, Michael Pate, Gary Day, Vanessa Leigh, Sigrid Thornton, Rod Mullinar.

Preston is a Melbourne toy manufacturer whose life is one jumbled relationship after another. He first finds that his wife is having an affair, which shouldn't come as too much of a surprise since he has himself a mistress. His lover, however, wants to get married. Life's tough, buddy!

p, Tom Burstall, Tim Burstall; d, Tim Burstall; w, David Williamson; ph, Dan Burstall.

Drama **(PR:C MPAA:NR)**

DUFFY*½

(1968, Brit.) 101m COL c

James Coburn (Duffy), James Mason (Charles Calvert), James Fox (Stefane Calvert), Susannah York (Segolene), John Alderton (Antony Calvert), Guy Deghy (Capt. Schoeller), Carl Duering (Bonivet), Tutte Lemkow (Spaniard), Marne Maitland (Abdul), Andre Maranne (Inspector Garain), Barry Shawzin (Bakirgian), Julie Mendez (Belly Dancer), Steve Plytas, Peter Van Dissel.

Lethargic attempt to cash in on the "hippie" movement has Coburn as an aging flower child living in Tangiers and being approached by Alderton and Fox to help them with a caper. James Mason is a stoical British banker with a cruel bent and a unique talent for making money. Fox and Alderton are his two sons by different mothers and both abhor Mason. Fox is a playboy and Alderton is a mild-mannered serf in his father's employ. They plan to nab several million that Mason is transferring by ship from exotic Tangiers to Marseilles. York is Fox's beloved and she helps recruit Coburn, who is intrigued by a share in the swag as well as closer relations with York. York, Fox, and Coburn get aboard the ship in disguise and steal the money. Coburn and York dive overboard and are picked up by Alderton in a boat equipped with a helicopter as well as a number of fresh corpses. They stuff money into the dead folks' pockets, get aboard the chopper, and then blow up the fishing vessel, leaving behind debris and cadavers with money in their clothing. After reaching their Corsican rendezvous, Alderton returns to France, as York and Coburn remain on the island and await word from Fox, who is busily attempting to find someone to "wash" the money. Coburn soon realizes that it was all a plot set up by Mason, who is York's lover. Mason wanted to have the cash stolen so he could collect insurance on it and keep it as well. Once Coburn is hip to that fact, he contacts the police and tells them that he's found the cash. Mason is thwarted in his plot and must give Coburn a $100,000 reward as the police are now in on it and he can do nothing else. Now much richer, Coburn bids them farewell and goes back to banging his cymbals, or whatever it is aging hippies do. Filmed mostly in Almeria, Spain, the working title was AVEC-AVEC, so it's easy to see why they decided to call it DUFFY. Coburn tries very hard to convince but doesn't. York has little to do but does that adequately. Mason and Fox are wasted and Alderton is the standout performer in an otherwise tedious film.

p, Martin Manulis; d, Robert Parrish; w, Donald Cammell, Harry Joe Brown, Jr. (based on a story by Cammell, Brown, and Pierre de la Salle); ph, Otto Heller (Technicolor); m, Ernie Freeman; ed, Willy Kemplen; art d, Philip Harrison; set d, Patrick McLoughlin; cos, Yvonne Blake; spec eff, John Richardson, David Kay; m/l, "I'm Satisfied," Cynthis Weil, Barry Mann, Ernie Freeman.

Crime/Comedy **(PR:C MPAA:R)**

DUFFY OF SAN QUENTIN** (1954) 76m WB bw
(GB: MEN BEHIND BARS)

Louis Hayward (*Edward Harper*), Joanne Dru (*Anne Halsey*), Paul Kelly (*Warden Clinton T. Duffy*), Maureen O'Sullivan (*Gladys Duffy*), George Macready (*Winant*), Horace McMahon (*Pierson*), Irving Bacon (*Doc*), Joel Fluellen (*Bill*), Joseph Turkel (*Frank*), Jonathan Hale (*Boyd*), Michael McHale (*Pinto*), Peter Brocco (*Nealy*).

Dull tale of prison reform stars Kelly as the new warden of San Quentin who introduces improvements that help rehabilitate the inmates. One such con is Hayward, who is hard and brutal until kindly and patient nurse Dru coaxes some humanity out of him. Contrived and pat, the film was based on a book by the real-life Duffy. Sequel: THE STEEL CAGE.

p, Berman Swarttz, Walter Doniger; d&w, Doniger (story by Doniger, Swarttz, based on the book *The San Quentin Story* by Clinton T. Duffy, Dean Jennings); ph, John Alton; m, Paul Dunlap; ed, Edward Sampson, Jr., Chester Schaeffer.

Crime **(PR:A MPAA:NR)**

DUFFY'S TAVERN*** (1945) 97m PAR bw

Bing Crosby, Betty Hutton, Paulette Goddard, Alan Ladd, Dorothy Lamour, Eddie Bracken, Brian Donlevy, Sonny Tufts, Veronica Lake, Arturo De Cordova, Cass Daley, Diana Lynn, Gary Crosby, Philip Crosby, Dennis Crosby, Lindsay Crosby, William Bendix, Maurice Rocco, James Brown, Joan Caulfield, Gail Russell, Helen Walker, Jean Heather (*Themselves*), Barry Fitzgerald (*Bing Crosby's Father*), Victor Moore (*Michael O'Malley*), Marjorie Reynolds (*Peggy O'Malley*), Barry Sullivan (*Danny Murphy*), Ed Gardner (*Archie*), Charles Canton (*Finnegan*), Eddie Green (*Eddie the Waiter*), Ann Thomas (*Miss Duffy*), Howard da Silva (*Heavy*), Billy De Wolfe (*Doctor*), Walter Abel (*Director*), Charles Quigley (*Ronald*), Olga San Juan (*Gloria*), Robert Watson (*Masseur*), Frank Fayle (*Customer*), Matt McHugh (*Man Following Miss Duffy*), Emmett Vogan (*Makeup Man*), Cyril Ring (*Gaffer*), Jimmie Dundee, Eddie Hall, Jack Lambert, Bill Murphy, Raymond Nash, Billy Jones, Frank Wayne, George Turner, Stephen Wayne, Len Hendry, John Indrisano, Fred Steele, Al Murphy (*Waiters*), Buck Harrington, Phil Dunham, Frank Faylen (*Customers*), Harry Tyler (*Man in Bookie Joint*), Audrey Young, Grace Albertson, Roberta Jonay (*Telephone Operators*), George M. Carleton (*Mr. Richardson*), Addison Richards (*Mr. Smith, C.P.A.*), Charles Cane (*Cop with Smith*), Charles B. Williams (*Mr. Smith's Assistant*), Lester Dorr, Charles Sullivan (*Painters*), Kernan Cripps (*Regan's Assistant*), Davidson Clark (*Guard*), Jack Perrin, James Flavin (*Cops*), Beverly Thompson, Noel Neill, Audrey Korn (*School Kids*), Crane Whitley (*Plainclothesman*), Betty Farrington (*Woman with Baby*), Ray Turner (*Hotel Porter*), Charles Mayon (*Stork*), Barney Dean (*Himself*), Theodore Rand (*Stagehand*), Tony Hughes (*Manager of Green Star Shipping*), George McKay (*Regan*), Jerry Maren (*Midget*), Julie Gibson, Catherine Craig (*Nurses*), Bill Edwards (*Soda Fountain Clerk*), Frances Morris (*Woman Who Screams*), Valmere Barman (*Girl at Soda Fountain*), Albert Ruiz (*Station Master/Soda Clerk*).

A glorious potpourri of almost every star on the Paramount lot is centered about Gardner as the irrepressible Archie of the radio-famed "Duffy's Tavern." He learns that his teetotalling customer Moore is going broke and has to lay off a bunch of ex-servicemen. Gardner goes into action, persuading a truckload of stars to pitch in, perform their bits, and help raise enough money for Moore's record company to go back into business. It's a flimsy excuse for a film but the entertainment is nonstop, with some truly memorable numbers performed by Betty Hutton, who whirlwinds through "Doin' It the Hard Way" (Johnny Burke, Jimmy Van Heusen), and Cass Daley performing an equally frenetic "You Can't Blame a Gal for Trying" (Ben Raleigh, Bernie Wayne). Crosby and Hutton also do an unusual rendition of "Swinging on a Star." Sprinkled throughout are various burlesque bits, gag sequences, and even an oddball radio murder skit performed by Ladd, Lake, and Da Silva, stars of the recent THE BLUE DAHLIA. As the lights go out Da Silva seems to be punching Lake silly, with Ladd daring him to continue. When the lights go on, Ladd gives Lake an arch look and says: "Lady, you'd better get out of here before you get your teeth kicked in!"

p, Danny Dare; d, Hal Walker; w, Melvin Frank, Norman Panama (based on characters created by Ed Gardner); sketches, Frank Panama, Abe S. Burrows, Barney Dean, George White, Eddie Davis, Matt Brooks; ph, Lionel Lindon; process ph, Farciot Edouart; m, Robert Emmett Dolan, Arthur Franklin; ed, Arthur

Schmidt; art d, Hans Dreier, William Flannery; set d, Stephen Seymour; spec eff, Gordon Jennings; ch, Billy Daniel.

Musical/Comedy **(PR:A MPAA:NR)**

DUGAN OF THE BAD LANDS*½ (1931) 56m MON bw

Bill Cody (*Bill Dugan*), Andy Shuford (*Andy*), Blanche Mehaffey (*June Manning*), Ethan Laidlaw (*Dan Kirk*), Earl Dwire (*Lang*), Julian Rivero (*Piedro*), John Elliot (*Sheriff Manning*).

Tired sagebrush saga that sees Cody and Shuford as two saddle tramps running across a sheriff who has been assaulted by a crooked deputy. The two cowboys help the sheriff track down the traitor and earn deputy stars for themselves in the bargain.

p, Trem Carr; d&w, Robert N. Bradbury; ph, Archie Stout; ed, J.S. Harrington.

Western **(PR:A MPAA:NR)**

DUGI BRODOVI (SEE: LONG SHIPS, THE, 1964, Brit./Yugo.)

DUKE COMES BACK, THE*½ (1937) 62m REP bw

Allan Lane (*Duke*), Heather Angel (*Mrs. Foster*), Genevieve Tobin (*Miss Corbin*), Frederick Burton (*Corbin*), Joseph Crehan (*Manager*), Ben Welden (*Second*), John Russell (*Kid*), Selmer Jackson (*Toom*), Art Lasky, George Lynn, Victor Adams, George Cooper, Byron Foulger, Snowflake, Clyde Dilson.

Contrived melodrama starring James as a championship prizefighter who retires from the ring to marry uppercrust, old-money gal Angel. This outrages Angel's father, Burton, but he eventually reconsiders and sets the boxer up with his other daughter who is in the publishing business. Everything is swell until Burton gets in trouble to the tune of $200,000 when he messes with other people's trust funds. Being a good and noble son-in-law, James returns to the ring to win the money to bail out his wife's old man. Another version of this story was made as DUKE OF CHICAGO in 1949.

p, Herman Schlom; d, Irving Pichel; w, Adele Buffington, Edmund Seward (based on a novel by Lucian Cary); ph, Harry Neumann; ed, Ray Snyder, Murray Seldeen.

Drama **(PR:A MPAA:NR)**

DUKE IS THE TOPS, THE** (1938) 72m Million Dollar bw

Ralph Cooper (*Duke Davis*), Lena Horne (*Ethel*), Lawrence Criner (*Doc Dorando*), Monte Hawley (*Marshall*), Vernon McCalla (*Mason*), Edward Thompson (*Fenton*), Neva Peoples (*Ella*), Charles Hawkins (*Sam*), Johnny Taylor (*Dippy*), Everett Brown (*Sheriff*), Arthur Ray (*Druggist*), Ray Martin (*Joe*), Guernsey Morrow (*Lake*), Rubberneck Holmes (*Dancer*), The Cats and the Fiddle (*Instrumental Trio*), Basin Street Boys (*Singing Quartet*).

All-black musical stars Horne and Cooper as a performer-producer team who split when she gets a big break on Broadway. The break turns out to be a bust, but Cooper shows up and together they make it to the top. Poor dialog punctuated with decent musical tunes. "I Know You Remember," sung by Horne, is the standout.

p, Harry M. Popkin; d, William Nolte; w, Phil Dunham; ph, Robert Cline; ch, Lew Crawson; m/l, Harvey Brooks, Ben Ellison.

Musical **Cas.** **(PR:A. MPAA:NR)**

DUKE OF CHICAGO** (1949) 59m REP bw

Tom Brown (*Jimmy Brody*), Audrey Long (*Jane Cunningham*), Grant Withers (*Tony Russo*), Paul Harvey (*Chester Cunningham*), Skeets Gallagher (*Gus Weller*), Lois Hall (*Helen Cunningham*), Matt McHugh (*Terry Shea*), Joseph Crehan (*Tex Harmon*), Harvey Parry (*Bronski*), George Beban (*Speedy*), Keith Richards (*Bryce*), DeForest Kelley (*Ace Martin*), Frankie Van (*Referee*), Dan Tobey (*Fight Announcer*), Dale van Sickel (*Kroner*).

Dull prizefight-crime drama starring Brown as a retired middleweight champ now entrenched in the publishing business. When the company falls into financial trouble, he is forced to come out of retirement to make enough money to save the firm. The match is set up by some shady gamblers who bank on a big loss by the ex-champ, but Brown wins despite a broken hand. This enrages the gamblers who decide to kill him, but cops arrive and stop them.

p, Stephen Auer; d, George Blair; w, Albert DeMond (based on a novel by Lucian Cary); ph, John MacBurnie; m, Stanley Wilson; ed, Cliff Bell; art d, Frank Arrigo.

Drama **(PR:A MPAA:NR)**

DUKE OF THE NAVY*½ (1942) 63m PRC bw

Ralph Byrd ("*Breeze*" *Duke*), Veda Ann Borg (*Maureen*), Stubby Kruger ("*Cookie*"), Herbert Corthell ("*Gen.*" *Courtney*), Margaret Armstrong (*Mrs. John T. Duke*), Val Stanton ("*Sniffy*"), Paul Bryan ("*Bunco*" *Bisbee*), Sammy Cohen ("*Murphy*"), Red Knight ("*Tex*"), Lester Towne ("*Peewee*"), William Beaudine, Jr. ("*Bingo*"), Zack Williams ("*Congo*").

Byrd and Kruger play two sailors on leave who wind up staying in rich woman Armstrong's expensive hotel suite because of the similarities in Byrd and Armstrong's (cast) names. Soon a con man descends on the hapless sailors, thinking Byrd is Armstrong's son, and attempts to bilk the sailor out of the rich lady's fortune. Contrived and silly.

p, John T. Coyle; d, William Beaudine; w, Gerald D. Adams, Beaudine; ph, Mack Stengler; ed, Guy V. Thayer, Jr.

Drama **(PR:A MPAA:NR)**

DUKE OF WEST POINT, THE**½ (1938) 107m UA bw

Louis Hayward (*Steven Early*), Joan Fontaine (*Ann Porter*), Tom Brown (*Sonny Drew*), Richard Carlson (*Jack West*), Alan Curtis (*Cadet Strong*), Donald Barry

(Cadet Grady), Gaylord Pendleton (Cadet Rains), Charles D. Brown (Doc Porter), Jed Prouty (Mr. Drew), Emma Dunn (Mrs. West), George McKay (Varsity Hockey Coach), James Flavin (Plebe Hockey Coach), Nick Lukats (Plebe Football Coach), Kenneth Harlan (Varsity Football Coach), Jonathan Hale (Col. Early), William Bakewell (Honor Committee Captain), Marjorie Gateson (Mrs. Drew), Art Raymond (Country Boy), Anthony Nace (First Capt. of Corps), Mary MacLaren (Nurse), Edward Earle (Surgeon), Alan Connor (Tactical Officer).

Hayward plays a young Cambridge graduate who is sent to West Point to finish his military training and preserve the honor of his family. Fontaine is the girl all the plebes fight over. Good performances, but overlong.

p, Edward Small; d, Alfred E. Green; w, George Bruce; ph, Robert Planck; ed, Grant Whytock.

Drama (PR:A MPAA:NR)

DUKE WORE JEANS, THE** (1958, Brit.) 90m Anglo Amalgamated bw

Tommy Steele (Tony Whitecliffe/Tommy Hudson), June Laverick (Princess Maria), Michael Medwin (Cooper), Eric Pohlmann (Bastini), Alan Wheatley (King of Ritallia), Mary Kerridge (Queen), Ambrosine Phillpotts (Duchess), Clive Morton (Lord Whitecliffe), Noel Hood (Lady Marguerite), Elwyn Brook-Jones (Bartolomeo), Arnold Diamond (M.C.), Philip Leaver (Factory Manager), Susan Travers (Stewardess), Cyril Chamberlain.

British flash-in-the-pan pop star Steele appears in his second film (the first being THE TOMMY STEELE STORY, of course) as the son of a down-on-their-luck aristocratic family pushing their boy into marriage with a Ritallian Princess. Steele balks because he's already secretly married. Luckily he meets a rude young cockney who bears an amazing resemblance to him (also played by Steele) and he grooms the stranger to take his place in Ritallia. Musical numbers include "It's All Happening," "Happy Guitar," and "Thanks a Lot."

p, Nat Cohen, Stuart Levy [Peter Rogers]; d, Gerald Thomas; w, Norman Hudis (based on a story by Lionel Bart, Michael Pratt); ph, Otto Heller; m, Bruce Montgomery, Bart, Pratt; ed, Peter Boita.

Musical (PR:A MPAA:NR)

DULCIMA** (1971, Brit.) 96m EMI/Cinevision c

Carol White (Dulcima Gaskain), John Mills (Mr. Parker), Stuart Wilson (Gamekeeper), Bernard Lee (Mr. Gaskain), Sheila Raynor (Mrs. Gaskain), Dudley Foster (Symes), Cyril Cross (Harris), Neil Wilson (Auctioneer), Peter Reeves (Auctioner's Assistant), George Hilson (Blake), Kristin Hatfield (Dress Shop Assistant), Philip Marsden (Baby Arnold).

White is a runaway girl who seeks salvation from her lousy home life by working on a farm owned by aging widower Mills. As the days go by Mills slowly begins to open up and consider the possibility of marriage again, but his dream is shattered when White runs off with a handsome young gamekeeper, Wilson. Maudlin story that slides along on a sea of sugar glaze.

p, Basil Rayburn; d&w, Frank Nesbitt (based on a story by H.E. Bates); ph, Tony Imi (Cinevision, Technicolor); m, Johnny Douglas; ed, Bill Lewthwaite; art d, Ray Simm; set d, Peter James, makeup, Paul Rabiger.

Drama (PR:A MPAA:PG)

DULCIMER STREET** (1948, Brit.) 112m Individual/GFD bw
(GB: LONDON BELONGS TO ME)

Richard Attenborough (Percy Boon), Alastair Sim (Mr. Squales), Fay Compton (Mrs. Josser), Stephen Murray (Uncle Henry), Wylie Watson (Mr. Josser), Susan Shaw (Doris Josser), Ivy St. Hellier (Connie), Joyce Carey (Mrs. Vizzard), Andrew Crawford (Bill Todds), Eleanor Summerfield (Myrna), Gladys Henson (Mrs. Boon), Hugh Griffith (Headlam Fynne), Maurice Denham (Jack Rufus), Jack McNaughton (Jimmy), Henry Edwards (Supt.), Arthur Howard, Hatton Duprez, Ivor Barnard, Kenneth Downey, Cecil Trouncer, Lionel Grose, Russell Waters, John Salew, Michael Kent, Basil Cunard, Cyril Chamberlain, Edward Evans, Fabia Drake, Myrette Morven, Alexis France, Aubrey Dexter, Henry Hewitt, J. H. Roberts, Wensley Pithey, Standley Rose, John Boxer, Manville Tarrant, George Cross, Owen Reynolds, Sydney Tafler, D. A. Mehan, Susan Buret, Frank Ling, Alan Saynes, Frederick Knight, Ewen Solon, Leonard Morris, Ivy Collins, Joe Clark, Ewan Roberts, Lala Lloyd, Nellie Sheffield, Stanley Beard, Arty Ash, Paula Young, Grace Allardyce, Alexander Field, Elsie Bernard, Arthur Lowe, John Gregson.

A British common people drama focuses on a group of average souls living a life of desperate boredom. Out of this nondescript melange comes a youth, Attenborough, who wants some action, and in acquiring it gets involved in a murder. Inexplicably, the film at this point veers off into a humorous account of a petition drive to save the young man's life, and the pent-up sympathy evoked by his plight scatters like seeds in the wind. Good glimpses of lower-class London help sustain interest, but touches meant to be laugh-getting spoil the show.

p, Frank Launder, Sidney Gilliat; d, Gilliat; w, Gilliat, J.B. Williams (based on a novel by Norman Collins); ph, Wilkie Cooper, Ernie Steward; m, Benjamin Frankel; ed, Thelma Myers; md, Muir Mathieson; art d, Roy Oxley.

Drama (PR:A MPAA:NR)

DULCINEA**½ (1962, Span.) 102m Nivi/Aspa bw

Millie Perkins (Dulcinea/Aldonza), Cameron Mitchell (Priest), Folco Lulli (Sancho), Vittoria Prade (Woman), Walter Santesso (Diego).

A Spanish production starring Perkins as a young barmaid in the sixteenth century who assumes the identity of Don Quixote's fictional beloved, Dulcinea. She does so to ease the troubled thoughts of the noble Don as he lies dying, plagued with doubts about the usefulness of his life. Fueled with a new passion for justice, Perkins goes out to help beggars and other unfortunates to keep Don Quixote's legend of Dulcinea alive. Soon she is arrested and accused of being a witch. After

she refuses to admit that she is masquerading as the fictional Dulcinea, she is burned at the stake. An interesting essay on the nature of myth and legend. (In English.)

d&w, Vicanie Escriva (based on Miguel de Cervantes' Don Quixote); ph, Gofferdo Pacheco; m, C. Basurko.

Drama (PR:C MPAA:NR)

DULCY** (1940) 67m MGM bw

Ann Sothern (Dulcy Ward), Ian Hunter (Gordon Daly), Roland Young (Roger Forbes), Reginald Gardiner (Schuyler Van Dyke), Billie Burke (Eleanor Forbes), Lynne Carver (Angela Forbes), Dan Dailey, Jr. (Bill Ward), Donald Huie ("Sneezy"), Jonathan Hale (Homer Patterson), Guinn "Big Boy" Williams (Henry), Hans Conried (Vincent Leach).

George S. Kaufman and Marc Connelly's dizzy blonde Dulcy gets her third stab at being put on celluloid (she was played by Constance Talmadge in 1923 and Marion Davies in 1929), this time reprised by Sothern. Plot sees the goofy dame spending a hectic weekend at a mountain cabin with her flame, inventor Hunter, who has developed a new carburetor for airplane engines. She schemes for her brother, Dailey, to invite his girl friend and her family up to the cabin for the weekend because the girl friend's father, Young, may be in the market to buy a patent on Hunter's invention. After a series of comic misadventures, Young finally signs an agreement for the new carburetor. Fast-paced and funny.

p, Edgar Selwyn; d, S. Sylvan Simon; w, Albert Mannheimer, Jerome Chodorov, Joseph A. Fields (based on the play by George S. Kaufman, Marc Connelly); ph, Charles Lawton; m, Bronislau Kaper; ed, Frank E. Hull; art d, Cedric Gibbons.

Comedy (PR:A MPAA:NR)

DUMBBELLS IN ERMINE** (1930) 57m WB bw

Robert Armstrong (Jerry Malone), Barbara Kent (Faith Corey), Beryl Mercer (Grandma Corey), James Gleason (Mike), Claude Gillingwater (Uncle Roger), Julia Swayne Gordon (Mrs. Corey), Arthur Hoyt (Siegfried Strong), Mary Foy (Mrs. Strong), Charlotte Merriam (Camilla),

Pleasant little comedy starring Armstrong as a fighter who goes to a small southern town to train for a championship match. There he falls in love with local gal Kent, who returns his affections. Unfortunately, Kent's scheming grandmother, Mercer, wants her granddaughter to marry into a higher station in life and tries everything in her power to force a breakup. Kent rises above Mercer's petty complaints and sticks with her boxer. Along with short subjects and a newsreel, DUMBBELLS made for quite an outing at the movie houses of the time.

d, John G. Adolfi; w, James Gleason, Harvey Thew (based on the comedy play "Weak Sisters" by Lynn Starlings); ph, Dev Jennings;

Comedy (PR:A MPAA:NR)

DUMBO*** (1941) 64m Disney/RKO c

Voices: Edward Brophy (Timothy Mouse), Herman Bing (Ringmaster), Verna Felton (Elephant), Sterling Holloway (Stork), Cliff Edwards (Jim Crow).

One of Disney's finest films, this simple, short tale opens when the stork delivers a baby elephant to Mrs. Jumbo, one of the star attractions of a circus, while the circus winters in the Deep South. At first he is the darling of the animal cages until he sneezes and his enormous ears are exposed, ears that bring cynical remarks and outright condemnation from other lady elephants who sarcastically state that the baby ought to be called "Dumbo," not "Jumbo." After being cruelly treated by some circus-goers, Dumbo is taken out of the cages and Mrs. Jumbo goes wild with grief, causing her to be chained down by keepers thinking her a "mad elephant." Heartbroken, baby Dumbo's sadness is evaporated by a new-found friend, Timothy, a precocious circus mouse. The lonely elephant is next put to work in a clown act, being made the butt of insulting jokes which further embarrass Dumbo. One night the clowns, a crude lot, get drunk, one knocking an open bottle of champagne into a bucket of water from which Dumbo drinks. This produces severe hiccups, then a dizzying drunken state into which Dumbo hallucinates incredible nightmares, the most awesome being a parade of mean, gigantic pink elephants, dancing on top of each other, doubling, then tripling their own sinister forms. By the time the wild images fade, Dumbo and Timothy find themselves high up in a tree, teetering on the branches! Some passing crows are flabbergasted at the sight of the elephant's perch and Timothy is equally perplexed until he reasons that Dumbo must have flown onto the branches. With the happy crows helping, Timothy convinces the little elephant to give it a try and take to the air. He sails downward, apparently toward doom, but at the last minute, with the mouse riding in fright on his head, Dumbo's ears shoot outward and form a perfect set of wings. He sails upward and begins to fly! Returning to the circus that night Dumbo puts on a show that makes the clowns look like the fools they are; he becomes the overnight sensation of the circus, its greatest star. Happiness embraces Dumbo and his friends at movie's end. His mother is given her own private car as the circus train toots northward for its tour, blissful Dumbo flying alongside with his faithful friend Timothy clinging to him. DUMBO is a flawless film, one of the shortest Disney ever made and inexpensive to boot, costing less than $1 million, where films like BAMBI shot well beyond the $2 million mark. Disney, who always oversaw every frame designed by his animators, approved of just about every move they made, uncharacteristically in that he invariably made many many costly changes, as in PINOCCHIO. There is very little dialog and Dumbo never speaks; his mother only speaks to him in the song "Baby Mine," but the visuals are so strong that they carry the story. Humans are shown in shadows and silhouettes, the animals taking stage center. As with all his major feature-length animation films Disney made sure that none of the scenes were flat, that blades of grass rippled in the wind, leaves fluttered in the trees. In the wonderful sequence where the crows encounter the elephant, all of the birds have different forms and mannerisms, one is fat, another lean, another small, another wears glasses and when he doubles up in laughter with his fellow birds, his eyes actually leave his head and roll about inside of his glasses. The song the arrogant, sassy crows sing is a little masterpiece—"When I See an Elephant Fly"—and contains some gem-like puns: "I've seen a peanut stand, I've seen a rubber band." The recent controversy about the crows being stereotyped as blacks is absurd. They are caricatures, wonderfully drawn and individually profiled. It took the Disney geniuses a year and a half to design and execute a film of heart, taste, and overall beauty that will appeal to every child in the world and every adult who can still recall the happy land of childhood fantasies and fables. Songs include "Look Out for Mr. Stork," "Baby of Mine," "All Aboard," "Pink Elephants on Parade," "When I See An Elephant Fly" (Oliver Wallace, Frank Churchill, Ned Washington).

p, Walt Disney; d, Ben Sharpsteen; w, Joe Grant, Dick Huemer (based on a book by Helen Aberson and Harold Pearl); ph (Technicolor); story d, Otto Englander; sequence d, Norman Ferguson, Wilfred Jackson, Bill Roberts, Jack Kinney, Sam Armstrong; animation d, Vladimir Tytla, Fred Moore, Ward Kimball, John Lounsbery, Arthur Babbitt, Wolfgang Reitherman; story devel, Bill Peet, Aurelius Battaglia, Joe Rinaldi, George Stallings, Webb Smith; character designs, John P. Miller, Martin Provensen, John Walbridge, James Bodrero, Maurice Nobel, Elmer Plummer; art d, Herb Ryman, A. Kendall O'Connor, Terrell Stapp, Donald Da Gradi, Al Zinnen, Ernest Nordli, Dick Kelsey, Charles Payzant; animators, Hugh Fraser, Howard Swift, Harvey Toombs, Don Towsley, Milt Neil, Les Clark, Hicks Lokey, Claude Smith, Berny Wolf, Ray Patterson, Jack Campbell, Grant Simmons, Walt Kelly, Joshua Meador, Don Patterson, Bill Shull, Cy Young, Art Palmer; backgrounds, Claude Coats, Albert Dempster, John Hench, Gerald Neivus, Ray Lochrem, Joe Stahley; orchestration, Edward H. Plumb.

Animation/Fantasy/Fable   Cas.   (PR:AAA   MPAA:NR)

DUMMY, THE*   (1929) 70m PAR bw

Ruth Chatterton (Agnes Meredith), Fredric March (Trumbell Meredith), John Cromwell (Walter Babbing), Fred Kohler (Joe Cooper), Mickey Bennett (Barney), Vondell Darr (Peggy Meredith), Jack Oakie (Dopey Hart), ZaSu Pitts (Rose Gleason), Richard Tucker (Blackie Baker), Eugene Pallette (Madison).

A dumb picture that was only distinguished by some strange oddities; Pitts played a kidnaper; it was March's first movie job (he was busily working on stage in "The Royal Family" at night); Ruth Chatterton was top-billed and had even less to do than March who never got one close-up; Oakie, Pallette, and Tucker were hardly noticed. Title comes from the fact that Mickey Bennett, the office boy in John Cromwell's detective agency, pretends to be deaf and dumb in order to nab the kidnapers who took Chatterton and March's child, Vondell Darr. When Bennett mumbles in his sleep, he's found out by the miscreants and eventually saved before they can do any harm to him. All ends well as the parents are reunited with their child and Bennett gets a reward for his bravery. Bad sound synchronization and early sound problems make one yearn for the original silent film of this story which starred Jack Pickford. This was Oakie's fourth film at the age of 26. Oakie was born Lewis Delaney Offield and had several office jobs before making his stage debut at 18 in George M. Cohan's "Little Nellie Kelly" in 1922. Oakie took the old-fashioned "double-take" and added one to make it a "triple-take." No one else has yet been able to top him at it. Mankiewicz's screenplay was far below his usual standards when you consider that he co-wrote CITIZEN KANE, THE PRIDE OF THE YANKEES, THE ENCHANTED COTTAGE, and many more.

p, Hector Turnbull; d, Robert Milton; w, Herman J. Mankiewicz (based on the play by Harvey J. O'Higgins and Harriet Ford and the silent version with titles by Joseph L. Mankiewicz); ph, J. Roy Hunt; ed, George Nichols, Jr.

Crime Drama   (PR:A-C   MPAA:NR)

DUMMY TALKS, THE**   (1943, Brit.) 85m BN/Anglo bw

Jack Warner (Jack), Claude Hulbert (Victor Harbord), Beryl Orde (Beryl), Derna-Hazell (Maya), Ivy Benson (Ivy), Manning Whiley (Russell Warren), Charles Carson (Marvello), G.H. Mulcaster (Piers Harriman), John Carol (Jimmy Royce), Gordon Edwards, Max Earle, Leonard Sharp, Vi Kaley, Harry Herbert, Pamela Hesbitt, Wendy Welling, Arthur Denton, Olive Sloane, Ian Wilson, Barry Morse, Leslie Bradley, Patricia Hayes, Dorothy Gordon, Evelyn Darvell, Ivy Benson's All Ladies Orchestra, Manley and Austin, Sylvester and Nephew, Skating Avalons, Five Lai Founs.

A ventriloquist turns to blackmail and is murdered. A midget pretends to be a dummy as he tries to infiltrate the backstage world of ventriloquism to uncover the killer. A weird but engaging second feature. British character actor Warner's debut.

p, Wallace Orton; d, Oswald Mitchell; w, Michael Barringer (based on a story by Con West, Jack Clifford); ph, Jimmy Wilson.

Crime   (PR:A   MPAA:NR)

DUNGEONS OF HARROW zero
                              (1964) 74m Herts-Lion International Corp. bw
                              (AKA: DUNGEONS OF HORROR)

Russ Harvey, Helen Hogan, Bill McNulty, Maurice Harris, Ron Russell, Lee Morgan, Pat Boyette.

Two people are shipwrecked on an island where a demented count lives. His wife has leprosy and is also mad, and a young slave girl who lives with the couple has had her tongue cut out by pirates. The two survivors of the shipwreck are imprisoned and tortured by the count. They try to escape but have no luck, and soon the wife's leprosy is passed on to everyone. A sad venture to sit and look at, and a positive travesty of the cinematic art form.

d, Pat Boyette; w, Henry Garcia; ph, James Houston; art d, Ron Russell.

Horror   (PR:O   MPAA:NR)

DUNKIRK***   (1958, Brit.)135m EAL/MGM bw

John Mills (Binns), Robert Urquhart (Mike), Ray Jackson (Barlow), Meredith Edwards (Dave Bellman), Anthony Nicholls (Military Spokesman), Bernard Lee (Charles Foreman), Michael Shillo (Jouvet), Richard Attenborough (Holden), Sean Barrett (Frankie), Victor Maddern (Merchant Seaman), Maxine Audley (Diana Foreman), Flanagan and Allen (Themselves), Kenneth Cope (Lt. Lumpkin), Denys Graham (Fraser), Ronald Hines (Miles), Ronald Curram (Harper), Patricia Plunkett (Grace Holden), Rodney Diak (Pannet), Eddie Byrne (Commander), Lionel Jeffries (Colonel), Warwick Ashton (Battery Sgt. Major), Peter Halliday (Battery Major), Cyril Raymond (Viscount Gort), Nicholas Hannen (Vice Adm. Ramsey), Michael Gwynn (Commander), Fred Griffiths (Old Sweet), Christopher Rhodes (Sergeant on Beaches), John Horsley (Padre), Patrick Allen (Sergeant), Lloyd Lamble, John Welsh, Barry Foster, Harry Landis, Dan Gressy, Joss Ambler, Frederick Piper, William Squire, Michael Bates, Bernard Cribbins, Chesney Allen.

A moving British reconstruction of the defeat that turned into a moral victory at Dunkirk. The film follows three separate characters (Mills, Lee, and Attenborough) and sees the events through their eyes. Mills plays a sharp Cockney corporal who, along with a few of his men, get separated from their unit and have to work their way back to safe soil on their own. Lee is a cynical newspaper correspondent who eventually helps out with the evacuation and loses his life. Attenborough plays a complacent civilian who is shaken into a new consciousness by his participation in the event. Well done, with a bit too much of the "stiff upper lip" cheerleading that befalls most films of this type.

p, Michael Balcon; d, Leslie Norman; w, David Divine, W.P. Lipscomb (based on the novel The Big Pick-Up by Elleston Trevor, and on Dunkirk by Lt. Col. Ewan Butler, Maj. J.S. Bradford); ph, Paul Beeson; m, Malcolm Arnold; ed, Gordon Stone; md, Dock Mathieson; art d, Jim Morahan.

War   (PR:A   MPAA:NR)

DUNWICH HORROR, THE½**   (1970) 90m AIP c

Sandra Dee (Nancy Walker), Dean Stockwell (Wilbur Whateley), Ed Begley (Dr. Henry Armitage), Sam Jaffe (Old Whateley), Donna Baccala (Elizabeth Hamilton), Joanna Moore Jordan (Lavinia), Talia Coppola [Shire] (Cora), Barboura Morris (Mrs. Cole), Mike Fox (Dr. Raskin), Jason Wingreen (Police Chief), Michael Haynes (Guard), Lloyd Bochner (Dr. Cory), Beach Dickerson (Mr. Cole), Toby Russ (Librarian), Jack Pierce (Reege).

Fairly successful attempt at adapting H.P. Lovecraft's tale of New England horror to the screen sees Dee as a young college co-ed lured into the mysterious house of Whately by crazed satan worshipper Stockwell. The local community has long suspected that the whole Whately family (the old man, Jaffe, Stockwell, and his mother, who is in an insane asylum) is unholy and soon their suspicions are confirmed. Stockwell intends to use Dee as a human sexual sacrifice to satan. Occult professor Begley (in his last screen appearance) discovers that the family is indeed the offspring of the devil and with the aid of Dee's roommate, Baccala, they kill Stockwell and his demons. Good visual style from director Haller, but a weak script and uneven performances damage the full effect.

p, James H. Nicholson, Samuel Z. Arkoff; d, Daniel Haller; w, Curtis Lee Hanson, Henry Rosenbaum, Ronald Silkosky (based on a story by H.P Lovecraft); ph, Richard C. Glouner (Movielab Color); m, Les Baxter; ed, Fred Feitshans, Jr., Christopher Holmes; art d, Paul Sylos; set d, Ray Boltz; spec eff, Roger George.

Horror   Cas.   (PR:C   MPAA:M)

DURANGO KID, THE½**   (1940) 61m COL bw

Charles Starrett (Bill Lowery/Durango Kid), Luana Walters (Nancy Winslow), Kenneth MacDonald (Mace Ballard), Francis Walker (Steve), Ben Winslow), Melvin Lang (Marshal Trayboe), Bob Nolan (Bob), Bob Brady (Pat), Frank La Rue (Sam Lowry), Jack Rockwell (Evans), John Tyrell (Player), Steve Clark (Bixby), Silvertip Baker (Townsman), Ralph Peters (Taylor), Ben Taggart, Sons of the Pioneers.

First Starrett outing as the Durango Kid, a sort of Robin Hood of the West who helps the lovely Walters (who replaced Starrett's usual love-interest, Iris Meredith), the daughter of a homesteader, defeat the evil MacDonald who has been terrorizing the decent citizens with his gang of rustlers. Starrett would later resurrect the character of the Durango Kid and play him in a series of oaters beginning in 1945. (See DURANGO KID series, Index.)

p, Jack Fier; d, Lambert Hillyer; w, Paul Franklin; ph, John Stumar; ed, Robert Fantl; md, Morris Stoloff; m/l, Bob Nolan, Tim Spencer.

Western   (PR:A   MPAA:NR)

DURANGO VALLEY RAIDERS*   (1938) 56m REP bw

Bob Steele (Keene Cordner), Louise Stanley (Betty McKay), Karl Hackett (John McKay), Ted Adams (Lobo), Forrest Taylor (Sheriff Devlin), Steve Clark (Boone Cordner), Horace Murphy (Matt Tanner), Jack Ingram (Slade), Ernie Adams, Julian Madison, Budd Buster, Frank Ball.

Lame Steele saddle-tramp tale sees the cowboy going undercover as a masked bandit to get the goods on a mysterious desperado known only as "The Shadow." Particularly inept work from top to bottom.

p, A.W. Hackel; d, Sam Newfield; w, George H. Plympton (based on a story by Harry F. Olmsted); ph, Robert Cline; ed, Roy Claire.

Western   Cas.   (PR:A   MPAA:NR)

DURANT AFFAIR, THE**   (1962, Brit.) 73m Danziger/PAR bw

Jane Griffiths (Mary Grant), Conrad Phillips (Julian Armour), Nigel Green (Sir Patrick), Simon Lack (Roland Farley), Katharine Pate (Ethel Durant), Francis de Wolff, Richard Caldicott, Ann Lancaster.

Griffiths plays an unmarried woman born a bastard, who is convinced by solicitor Phillips to contest her mother's will. Some decent performances help a tedious idea made into an equally tedious film.

p, Philip Elton; d, Godfrey Grayson; w, Eldon Howard.

Drama   (PR:A-C MPAA:NR)

DURING ONE NIGHT*   (1962, Brit.) 84m Galaworldfilm/Astor bw

Don Borisenko (David), Susan Hampshire (Jean), Sean Sullivan (Major), Joy Webster (Prostitute), Graydon Gould (Mike), Tom Busby (Sam), Jackie Collins (Girl), Alan Gibson (Harry), Colin Maitland (Gunner), Barbara Ogilivie (Jean's Mother), Michael Golden (Constable), Roy Stephens (Drive), Pamela Barney (Nurse), Barry McClean (Tough), John Bloomfield, Sean McCan (MPs).

Borisenko is an American pilot during WW II who decides to lose his virginity after his buddy is castrated during a mission. He goes AWOL and picks up a hooker but he discovers he's impotent. He meets a young girl and tries to make love to her, but with the same result. MPs catch up with him and he hopes they will shoot him as a deserter. They don't and Borisenko talks to a chaplain who restores his self-importance. He returns to the young girl and finds sexual satisfaction at last.

p, Kenneth Rive, Sidney J. Furie; d&w, Furie; ph, Norman Warwick; m, Bill McGuffie; ed, Antony Gibbs; art d, John Earl.

Drama   (PR:A MPAA:NR)

DUST BE MY DESTINY***   (1939) 88m WB bw

John Garfield (Joe Bell), Priscilla Lane (Mabel), Alan Hale (Mike Leonard), Frank McHugh (Caruthers), Billy Halop (Hank), Bobby Jordan (Jimmy), Charley Grapewin (Pop), Henry Armetta (Nick), Stanley Ridges (Charlie), John Litel (Prosecutor), Moroni Olsen (Slim Jones), Victor Killian (Doc Saunders), Frank Jaquet (Ab Connors), Ferike Boros (Delicatessen Prop.), Marc Lawrence (Veneill), Arthur Aylesworth (Magistrate), William Davidson (Warden), George Irving (Judge).

A well-used theme is overpowered by Garfield's supercharged performance as a slum kid emerging from prison for a crime he did not commit. A product of his evil environment, Garfield is soon picked up for vagrancy and sent to a work farm where he falls in love with the stepdaughter of the straw boss, a mean drunk. The girl, Lane, is the cause of her stepfather's wrath. When he dies, Garfield is labeled the murderer and he flees with Lane. The two are hunted down and Garfield is later tried but found not guilty of the farm boss's death. He is reunited with Lane and they begin a new life together. The story is worn out and so too were the antics of the Dead End Kids, but Garfield's forceful charisma is enough to hold attention. Lane is miscast, but Hale as the truth-seeking editor, Grapewin as a sympathetic brakeman, Armetta as a lunchroom owner, and Olson as the crusading defense attorney, all turn in yeoman performances; these were some of the finest character actors in Hollywood at the time and they carried many a vehicle beyond script limitations. Garfield did not like this role, one of three similar parts Warner Bros. compelled him to enact in 1938 and 1939, and it made him rebel against the studio and later decide to leave it.

p, Lou Edelman (for Hal B. Wallis); d, Lewis Seiler; w, Robert Rossen (based on a novel by Jerome Odlum); ph, James Wong Howe; ed, Warren Low.

Crime Drama   (PR:A MPAA:NR)

DUSTY AND SWEETS McGEE*   (1971) 91m WB c

Clifton Tip Fredell (Tip), Kit Ryder (Male Hustler), Billy Gray (City Life), Bob Graham (Little Boy), Pam (The Girl), Nancy Wheeler (Nancy), Beverly (Dusty), Mitch (Sweets), Russ Knight (Weird Beard), William A. Fraker (The Cellist).

Ill-conceived attempt at dramatizing the dangers of drug abuse that was produced independently for $142,000 and stars a cast of real-time drug addicts with little or no acting experience. The resulting film is an uneven mix of hazy, drug-induced ramblings, with an occasionally insightful comment made on the tragedy of drug abuse. The loose plot concerns the lives of a variety of addicts, whose sordid tales are told to the audience in a confessional manner. A stab at entertainment is made through the music score, which features songs by Blue Images, Nilsson, Van Morrison, and Jake Holmes.

p, Michael S. Laughlin; d&w, Floyd Mutrux; ph, William A. Fraker (Technicolor); m, Rick Nelson; ed, Richard A. Harris; m/l, "Ride Captain Ride," composed and performed by Blues Image; "Don't Leave Me Baby," composed and performed by Harry Nilsson; "Into the Music," composed and performed by Van Morrison; "So Close," composed and performed by Jake Holmes.

Crime   (PR:O MPAA:NR)

DUSTY ERMINE   (SEE: HIDEOUT IN THE ALPS, 1936, Brit.)

DUTCHMAN***   (1966, Brit.) 55m Continental bw

Shirley Knight (Lula), Al Freeman, Jr. (Clay), Frank Lieberman, Robert Calvert, Howard Bennett, Sandy McDonald, Denis Peters, Keith James, Devon Hall (Subway Riders).

Grim film adaptation of Le Roi Jones' off-Broadway play that takes place entirely in a New York subway car. Knight plays a sluttish, racist woman who seduces young middle-class black Freeman and then proceeds to humiliate and taunt him until he finally explodes into a tirade against whites. Enraged, Knight stabs and kills Freeman and then moves on to her next victim. Knight and Freeman are superb.

p, Gene Persson; d, Anthony Harvey; w, Le Roi Jones (dialog from play by Jones); ph, Gerry Turpin; m, John Barry; ed, Harvey; art d, Herbert Smith, Jim Morahan; set d, Ian Whittaker.

Drama   (PR:C MPAA:NR)

DYBBUK, THE***   (1938, Pol.) 122m Foreign Cinema Arts bw

A. Morewski (Wonder Rabbi), R. Samberg (Messenger), M. Libman (Sender), Lili Liliana (Leah), Dina Halpern (Frade), G. Lamberger (Nisson), L. Libgold (Channon), M. Bozyk (Nuta), S. Landau (Zalman), S. Bronecki (Nachman), M. Messinger (Menashe), Z. Katz (Mendel), A. Kurc (Michael), D. Lederman (Meyer).

Eerie filmization of a popular Yiddish play has two children promised to each other in marriage before they are born. Years pass and the young man, never having seen his bride-to-be, comes to her village to study cabalistic lore. He falls in love with her, but her father wants to renege on his promise and have her marry a wealthy man. In despair the young man (Libgold) kills himself and his spirit leaves his body and possesses the body of his beloved (Liliana) during her wedding. She is struck speechless and the wise old rabbi is brought in to perform the esoteric rites of exorcism. One of the few examples of pre-war Polish cinema still in circulation, THE DYBBUK is a fascinating record not only of the height of Eastern European Yiddish theater's accomplishment before its annihilation, but of an almost utterly medieval Jewish way of life where supernatural events are looked upon as common occurrences, a way of life likewise annihilated. (In Yiddish; English subtitles.)

p, Ludvig Previs; d, Machael Waszynski; w, S.A. Kacyzna, Marek Arenstein (based on a play by S. Ansky); m, H. Kon; ed, George Roland; ch, Judita Berg.

Fantasy   (PR:A MPAA:NR)

DYNAMITE***   (1930) 128m MGM bw

Conrad Nagel (Roger Towne), Kay Johnson (Cynthia Crothers), Charles Bickford (Hagon Derk), Julia Faye (Marcia Towne), Muriel McCormac (Katie Derk), Tyler Brooke (Life of the Party), Joel McCrea (Marco the Sheik), Robert T. Haines (The Judge), Douglas Frazer Scott (Bobby), Jane Keckley (Bobby's Mother), Scott Kolk (Radio Announcer), Fred Walton (The Doctor), Leslie Fenton, Barton Hepburn (Young Vultures), Ernest Hilliard, June Nash, Nancy Dover, Neely Edwards, Jerry Zier, Rita LeRoy (Good Mixers), Robert Edeson, William Holden, Henry Stockbridge (Three Wise Fools), Clarence Burton, James Farley (Officers), Blanche Craig, Mary Gordon, Ynez Seabury (Neighbors).

Cecil B. DeMille's first sound epic stars Johnson (in her first motion picture) as a socialite who schemes to marry Bickford, a former miner now on death row, so that she can comply with the requirements that will earn her an inheritance of millions. Counting on the fact that Bickford will be executed soon, which would leave her a rich widow and free to pursue her lover, Nagel, she marries the condemned man on the eve of his execution. At the eleventh hour, Bickford is given a reprieve and Johnson finds herself stuck with a husband she cares nothing about. He soon learns of her scheme, leaves her, and gets a job mining. Because she must be cohabiting with him on a certain date to receive her inheritance, she follows him to the mining camp and persuades him to let her stay a few days. Through a series of complicated events, Bickford, Johnson and her lover become trapped in a mine after a cave-in. Nagel proves himself a hero by exploding a stick of dynamite and sacrificing his life so that Johnson and Bickford can escape. The film is melodramatic, but has the usual grand and exciting DeMille scale that makes the histrionics easier to take.

p&d, Cecil B. DeMille; w, Jeanie Macpherson; John Howard Lawson, Gladys Unger (based on a story by Macpherson); ph, J. Peverell Marley; m, Herbert Stothart; ed, Anne Bachens; m/l, "How Am I to Know?" Dorothy Parker.

Drama   (PR:A MPAA:NR)

DYNAMITE**   (1948) 68m PAR bw

William Gargan (Gunner Peterson), Virginia Welles (Mary), Richard Crane (Johnny Brown), Irving Bacon (Jake), Mary Newton (Nellie Brown), Frank Ferguson (Hard Rock Mason), Douglas Dumbrille (Hank Gibbons).

Action-packed romance stars Gargan and Crane as two dynamite blasters competing for the affections of dynamite contractor Bacon's daughter, Welles. Lots of blasting of land for mines and bridges, punctuated by a few tragic deaths and some heroic deeds.

p, William H. Pine, William Thomas; d, Pine; w, Milton Raison; ph, Ellis W. Carter; ed, Howard Smith; art d, Lewis H. Creber.

Drama   (PR:A MPAA:NR)

DYNAMITE CANYON**   (1941) 58m MON bw

Tom Keene (Tom Evans), Evelyn Finley (Midge Reed), Slim Andrews (Slim), Sugar Dawn (Sugar Grey), Stanley Price (Duke Rand), Kenne Duncan (Rod), Gene Alsace [Rocky Camron] (Capt. Grey), Fred Hoose (Col. Blake), Tom London (John Reed), Rusty the Wonder Horse.

Villain Price murders ranch owner London and Texas ranger Hoose in order to keep secret the location of a lode of copper on London's ranch. Ranger Kenne goes undercover as an outlaw to catch the killer. Price hires him and assigns him to stir up trouble at the ranch now run by Finley, London's daughter. He persuades her to give him a bill of sale to the ranch, then delivers it to Price after alerting the rangers to stand by for action. Price realizes that Kenne is the law and tries to flee, but Kenne and the rangers capture him. Standard six-gun heroics.

p&d, Robert Emmett Tansey; w, Tansey, Frances Kavanaugh; ph, Jack R. Young; ed, Fred Bain; md, Frank Sanucci.

Western   (PR:A MPAA:NR)

DYNAMITE DELANEY*½   (1938) 77m Caravel/Imperial bw

Weldon Heyburn, Eve Farrell, Donald Dillaway, Walter Gilbert, Jane Steele, Jack Squires, Jack Sheehan, Harlan Briggs, Clyde Franklin, Millard Mitchell, Frank Otto, Frank McNellis, Richard Abert.

Heyburn is a cop with the State Highway Patrol of Pennsylvania who has been kicked off the force. Eventually he wins back his post after he captures a group of kidnapers, all the while romancing police barracks waitress Farrell. A cheap production but a fairly good police story.

d, Joseph Rothman; w, Charles Beahan, Rothman; ph, William J. Miller.

Crime   **(PR:A   MPAA:NR)**

DYNAMITE DENNY*   (1932) 52m Like/Mayfair bw

Jay Wilsey, Blanche Mehaffey, William V. Mong, Walter Perry, Matthew Betz, Fern Emmett.

Overblown and contrived railroad drama starring Wilsey as a brave young engineer who breaks the picket line during a strike to keep the trains moving. His union kicks him out but all ends well when he saves the life of railroad owner Mong, who was trapped on a runaway train disguised as an employee to get a clearer idea of what his workers really wanted. For his efforts, Mong awards Wilsey with a new job as yardmaster, and the hand of his daughter, Mehaffey.

d, Frank Strayer; w, W. Scott Darling; ph, Jules Cronjager; ed, Byron Robinson.

Drama   **(PR:A   MPAA:NR)**

DYNAMITE JACK zero   (1961, Fr.) 100m Imperia c

Fernandel (Dynamite Jack/Antoine), Eleonore Vargas (Dolores), Adrienne Corri (Pegeen).

A French spoof on American westerns which turns out to be very unfunny, even with comic Fernandel. He plays a tough gunfighter and a stupid Frenchman who just got off the boat, and the mix is a crock of absurdity.

p, J.P. Bertrand; d, Jean Bastia; w, Jacques Ary, Jean Manse, Jacques Emmanuel, Bastia; ph, Roger Hubert (Eastmancolor); ed, Jacques Desagneaux.

Comedy   **(PR:A   MPAA:NR)**

DYNAMITE JOHNSON zero   (1978, Phil.) 95m Bas Film/Cosmopolis c
(AKA: THE 12 MILLION DOLLAR BOY; THE NEW ADVENTURES OF THE BIONIC BOY)

Johnson Yap, Marie Lee, Ken Metcalfe, Joseph Zucchero, Johnny Wilson, Joe Sison, Alex Pecate, Chito Guerrero, Pete Cooper.

Yap is the Bionic Boy in this sequel to THE BIONIC BOY. With his bionic legs, he snares a former Nazi who still has a grandiose scheme for ruling the world. His idea: focus a laser beam on his targets, then move in. Yap defeats a fire-breathing dragon and thwarts the villain's first move, on Hong Kong, to thankfully bring this mind-paralyzer to an end.

p&d, Bobby A. Suarez; w, Ken Metcalfe, Joseph Zucchero; ph, Baby Cabrales.

Science Fiction   **(PR:A   MPAA:NR)**

DYNAMITE PASS**   (1950) 60m RKO bw

Tim Holt (Ross), Lynne Roberts (Mary), Regis Toomey (Dan), Robert Shayne (Wingate), Don Harvey (Mizzouri), Cleo Moore (Lulu), John Dehner (Thurber), Don

Haggerty (Sheriff), Ross Elliott (Stryker), Denver Pyle (Whip), Richard Martin (Chito Rafferty).

Cowpokes Holt and Martin tire of punching cattle and decide to help Roberts and her husband, Toomey, build a toll-free road from town to the market place so that the citizens will no longer have to suffer under the oppressive tolls charged by the evil road owner Dehner and fellow townsman Shayne. When the two highway robbers balk at the construction of a new roadway and send out their thugs to halt it, Holt and Martin draw their sixshooters and settle the argument.

p, Herman Schlom; d, Lew Landers; w, Norman Houston; ph, Nicholas Musuraca; m, Paul Sawtell; ed, Robert Swink; art d, Albert S. D'Agostino, Walter F. Keller.

Western   **Cas.**   **(PR:A   MPAA:NR)**

DYNAMITE RANCH*½   (1932) 59m KBS/World Wide bw

Ken Maynard, Ruth Hall, Jack Perrin, Arthur Hoyt, Allan Roscoe, Al Smith, John Beck, George Pierce, Lafe McKee, Martha Mattox, Edmund Cobb, Charles LeMoyne, Cliff Lyons, Kermit Maynard (Stuntman and Double), Tarzan the Horse.

Maynard is accused of robbing a train because he's a stranger to the area. He jumps on his horse, finds the real criminals, and falls in love with the heroine. More fast action thrills from one of the great movie cowboys, and one of the best in a series of eight films he made for World Wide studios.

p, Burt Kelly, Sam Bischoff, William Sall; d, Forrest Sheldon; w, Barry Barringer, Sheldon.

Western   **Cas.**   **(PR:A   MPAA:NR)**

DYNAMITERS, THE*   (1956, Brit.) 71m Astor bw

Wayne Morris (Jimmy Baxter), Patrick Holt (Rutherford), Sandra Dorne (Sally Morton), James Kenney (Chapman), Simone Silva (Simone), Eric Pohlmann (Popoulos), Lloyd Lamble (Inspector Felby), Hugh Miller (Crosby), Arthur Young (Scobie), Leigh Crutchley (Hopman), Monti de Lyle (Head Waiter), Bernadette Milnes (Kay), Mark Daly (Carter), Tony Doonan (Jagar), Ossie Waller (Jackson), Bertha Russell (Mrs. Chapman).

Morris stars in this lame British thriller as an American detective hired by an insurance company to catch a gang of dynamiters who have been stealing a fortune from various London locations. Nothing about this raises it above the hackneyed level.

p, Geoffrey Goodhart, Brandon Fleming; d, Terence Fisher, Francis Searle; w, Fleming; ph, Cedric Williams; ed, Douglas Myer; art d, John Elphick; m/l, "Soho Mambo," Gene Crowley.

Crime   **(PR:A   MPAA:NR)**